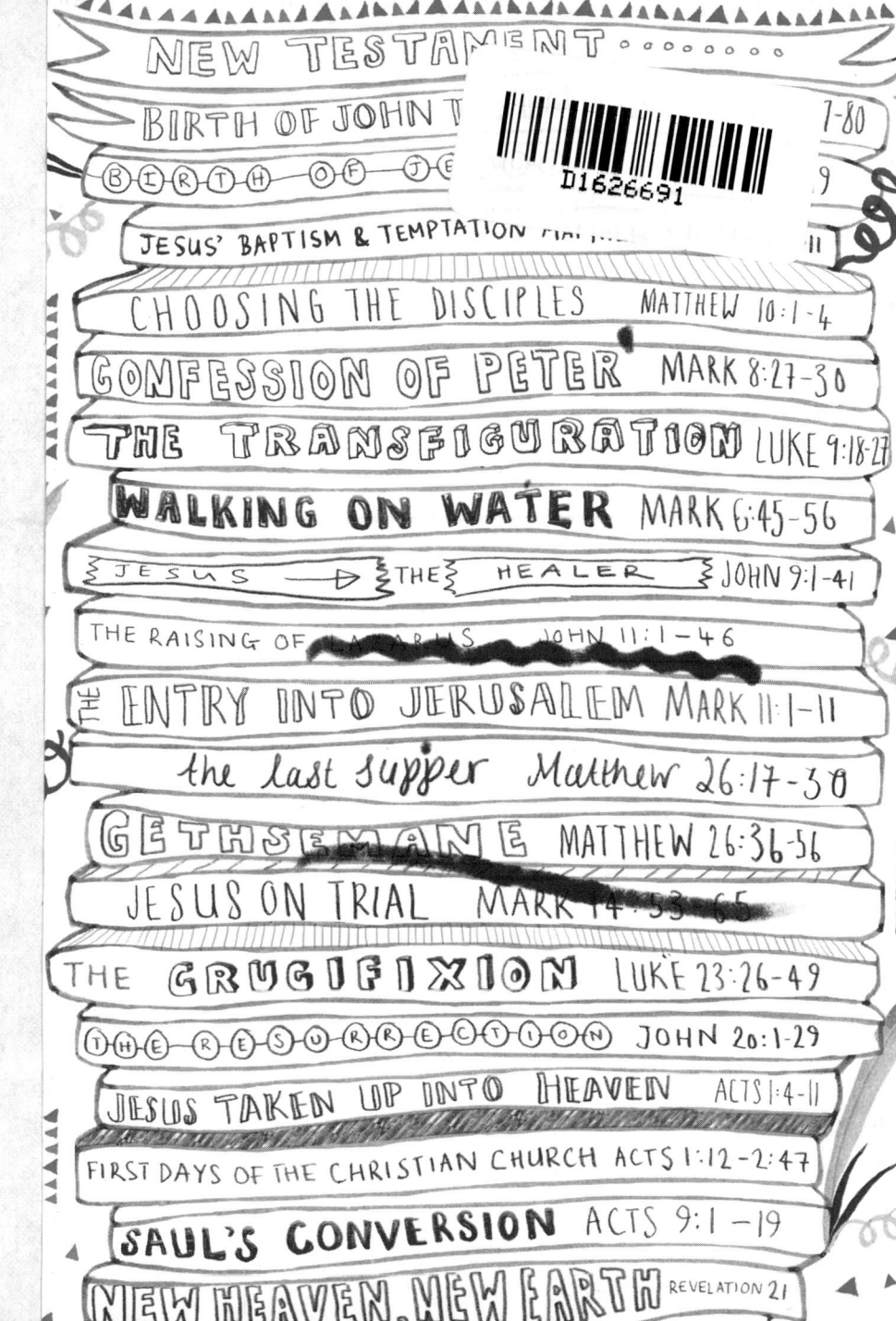

Presented
to
Isobel Nash
July 2013

NEW INTERNATIONAL VERSION

NEW INTERNATIONAL VERSION

HODDER &
STOUGHTON

Welcome letter

Welcome to the Soul Survivor Youth Bible – we're so excited you have this in your hands! We believe the Bible is the most amazing book you will ever read because it has the power to change your life.

We loved reading through the Bible in One Year with so many of you and it spurred us on to put together this Youth Bible, packed full of extra articles and info to help you understand more of God's Word. Whether you have known Jesus for ten days or ten years, we hope that this helps you see more of God's amazing, unchanging love for you, and that God would speak to you and change your life just as he continues to change ours.

We have also loved gathering our friends to share their Bible knowledge on the subjects they're really passionate about, and we have crammed in all sorts of things to help you read and understand the Bible more easily.

There are introductions to every book to help you understand why each book was written, what was happening at the time and what the book's key themes and characters are. You can take a number of 'guided tours' through the Bible using our Storylines, Journeys and Threads.

 Storylines explore the major themes that run throughout the whole Bible, such as where you will find Jesus in all the Scriptures, the importance of sacrifice, and teaching on friendship.

 Journeys are about shaping your heart and will help you go deeper into sections of the Bible. They focus on things like how to pray through the Psalms, and what the book of Ezekiel is all about.

 Threads explore the examples throughout the Bible on key topics, like God's plans for your future, what God has to say about how you handle your money, and understanding God's heart for justice.

   Issues tackle single topics: they might be tricky questions, world issues or life issues.

Lists of all of these are found at the front of the Bible, along with loads of other useful stuff at the back.

You may want to use this Bible to study alone, or with friends. However you choose to use it, remember that although our thoughts will hopefully help you along, there's no substitute for speaking to the author! Let's always open this book praying: *'God, thank you for your Word. Please speak to me today and show me how to live for your glory.'*

Mike

Alphabetical list of books of the Bible

Acts 1319

Amos 1061

1 Chronicles 465

2 Chronicles 505

Colossians 1458

1 Corinthians 1392

2 Corinthians 1416

Daniel 1023

Deuteronomy 211

Ecclesiastes 782

Ephesians 1439

Esther 577

Exodus 72

Ezekiel 962

Ezra 545

Galatians 1429

Genesis 3

Habakkuk 1092

Haggai 1102

Hebrews 1494

Hosea 1042

Isaiah 802

James 1511

Jeremiah 882

Job 586

Joel 1054

1 John 1532

2 John 1540

3 John 1542

John 1275

Jonah 1075

Joshua 253

Jude 1544

Judges 281

1 Kings 393

2 Kings 429

Lamentations 953

Leviticus 125

Luke 1216

Malachi 1116

Mark 1180

Matthew 1123

Micah 1079

Nahum 1088

Nehemiah 558

Numbers 162

Obadiah 1072

1 Peter 1519

2 Peter 1527

Philemon 1492

Philippians 1452

Proverbs 741

Psalms 629

Revelation 1547

Romans 1366

Ruth 311

1 Samuel 319

2 Samuel 358

Song of Songs 794

1 Thessalonians 1467

2 Thessalonians 1472

1 Timothy 1475

2 Timothy 1483

Titus 1489

Zechariah 1105

Zephaniah 1097

Contents

THE OLD TESTAMENT

THE NEW TESTAMENT

The Bible for ABSOLUTE beginners

You have picked up this book for the first time – welcome!

It's pretty easy to be baffled by the method of locating a passage, but it's actually very simple. All the references follow the same pattern. Book, then chapter number, then the verse.

Let's look at an example. Say you want to find the Ten Commandments and someone has told you they can be found at Exodus 20:3–17.

Exodus refers to the book of the Bible the passage is in, and that's the first thing we need to find. (There are sixty-six books in the Bible, by different authors – see page xiv to find out why!) Near the front of the Bible you will find two contents pages. The one on the left is in alphabetical order (very helpful!) and on the right you will find the traditional Bible order. The contents page will refer you to a page number for Exodus. Turn to that page.

The next thing to locate is the chapter. Each book is in sections and there will be a large chapter number usually at the beginning of a paragraph. (For speedy and advanced navigation, you can almost always find it in the header of the page too!) Flick through until you find chapter 20.

Then it's the verse. Each chapter is broken down further into fragments called verses – scroll through until you find a superscript number three like this: [3]. This is the number that tells you that you have reached the start of the section you're looking for. If the reference given has a finishing number, keep reading until the end of the final verse mentioned. So in this example, keep reading until you get to the little number eighteen ([18]).

Sometimes you will come across footnotes marked by letters. These can provide a bit of insight into some of the words or phrases. They are found at the bottom of the page you have been reading.

I'm reading my Bible, but someone else is reading aloud and theirs is slightly different from mine. Why?

Well, the Bible wasn't initially written in English. It has been translated loads of times. The version you have in your hands is the 2011 edition of a popular English language version called the NIV (New International Version). Other people might have different versions. If you're struggling to understand a passage, sometimes looking at the verse in another translation can help. You can find loads of these online at sites like www.biblegateway.com. You can also use this site or a book called a concordance to search for passages – really handy for when your friends ask you tricky questions and you know you have 'read something about that somewhere'!

Now you have got that down, you're free to start exploring all the contents of this book.

How to read the Bible

ANDY CROFT

There are loads of ways to read the Bible. We would suggest you try a few different ones and see which you find the most helpful. Here are a few methods to get you started.

1. Read it like a novel. When you read a good book, you don't stop at every other sentence to ask, 'What does this mean?' You just keep reading. Often those things that aren't clear at the start of the story make more sense as you go on. It's great to do something similar with the Bible. Just choose a book – for example, the Gospel of Mark. Then read it as you would read a novel. Don't worry about pausing at every word, just read it over a week or so. The question you want to be asking God, even as you read, is, 'What does this mean for my life today?' You will be amazed what God will whisper to you as you do this.

2. Study it. This is when you take a smaller portion of the Bible, perhaps a story about King David, or a psalm, and you look at it in a bit more detail.

One thing that can be helpful is to imagine your way into the passage and begin to ask yourself questions. Take David versus Goliath in 1 Samuel 17. Picturing the passage a bit more can help bring it to life: 'What must have been going through David's mind as he saw the size of Goliath?' 'What was the look on David's face as he swung the stone?' Ask God to show you things about passages you missed the first time and don't be afraid to take some time over it.

Another important part of studying is to get some help to understand what the passage meant in its original context. For example, recognising how the Corinthians would have understood Paul's letters in AD 56 helps us understand what they mean today. We need to understand what a passage did mean at the time it was written in order to get what it *does* mean today. The different comments in this book will help you with that, but you might also want to buy a commentary on a particular book of the Bible. Sometimes this feels like hard work, but it's a great way to discover new truths about God.

3. Meditate on it. This is when you just take a single verse of the Bible – perhaps, *'The LORD is my shepherd, I lack nothing'* (Psalm 23:1) – and then chew on it like a piece of gum. Think over the different words of the verse, accept them as truth in your heart. You can think about it on the bus, write it as a note on your phone. Why not live a day just 'chewing' on one verse and see what God says to you?

At times the Bible will seem hard to understand. Stick with it! These words will change you and over time they will become the most incredible source of comfort and strength. Remember that God knows what the Bible means better than any of us, so pray and ask him to help you. And finally, don't go it alone. Get a friend or two and commit to reading together. This might be by meeting up, or it might just be by texting each other verses, but when it comes to reading the Bible, two Christians are always better than one!

Ten top tips

1. The Bible is a collection of sixty-six books. It was developed by many authors, from many places, over centuries. Each book is divided up into chapters and verses.

2. The Bible is translated into English; the original languages and the cultures it's written for can often throw new light onto its meaning. Keep an eye on the footnotes and use a few different Bible translations and commentaries if you want to study a passage in lots of detail.

3. Don't necessarily start at the beginning! The books of the Bible have different purposes and so read them with this in mind. The Walks section at the back of this Bible can help you get started.

4. To begin with, forget about the commentaries and opinions. Don't worry about what other people think (including us!). Read the *Bible* first – it's the greatest (and most popular) book ever written.

5. Read a passage through once to get an idea of the story being told. Read it again, slowly, allow the words to marinate, and think through the finer nuances of what's being communicated.

6. Don't forget to *understand* before you try to *evaluate*. Try to understand the whole story that the writer is trying to communicate (the book introduction may help with this). Next, think about whether they are claiming it as a parable or illustrative story or poem, or if it's written as an actual account of what happened.

7. Use the material we have put together. Choose a theme or topic and enjoy bouncing around the different parts of the Bible. Remember that the boxed articles are not actual Bible text, but we hope they will encourage you to think more deeply about what you're reading.

8. Read it with someone. It's a great way of keeping the momentum as you build up a habit of reading the Bible regularly, and having someone to talk things over with can cement what you have read and help you respond to the challenges you have found.

9. The staggering, wonderful, life-changing thing about this book is that its helpfulness, beauty, challenges, usefulness and goodness come from the fact that it's true. If you don't agree, ask God, and look for truth in these pages. You will find it (Matthew 7:7).

10. Ask God to reveal his Word to you. You have read Scripture, but if you have a relationship with God and his Spirit is in you, you can have a *conversation* with the author! Ask God to reveal the things you might be missing through his Holy Spirit. Also ask God how you might directly apply what you're reading to your own situation.

Why read the Bible?

ANDY CROFT

God speaks through the Bible, more clearly and with more authority than any other place on earth. If you want to hear his voice then this book that you hold in your hand is the place to come.

People who haven't read the Bible can make the mistake of thinking it's just a rulebook full of lists of things we're to stop doing. A much better picture is that the Bible is like a love letter. In it we discover that God is inviting us into a relationship with him. Through his actions in history, the songs about him and ultimately in the person of Jesus we begin to get to know God. Often we can make the Bible all about us and our dreams, but first and foremost it's about God and his plans. As we read we catch a glimpse of the love, the joy, the justice and the power that are at the heart of God. You would never read a love letter to get more information or to learn some facts, or just to find out about yourself – you would read it because you're hungry for relationship with the one who wrote it. It's the same with the Bible: if you're hungry to know God, this is where you will discover him.

Having said that the Bible is a book first and foremost about God, in a strange way it can also act like a mirror. In reading it, we find out more about who we are and what it is to be a human being. From Genesis to Revelation we can read about how humanity has acted and how we should act now. Sometimes the Bible can show us things about ourselves we would rather not see! Through it God points out areas we need to grow in and things we need to learn. Amazingly, though, as we begin to build our lives and our identities on what it teaches us, we find ourselves becoming more fully alive and more secure than ever before. To quote Søren Kierkegaard, 'Now, with God's help, I shall become myself.' The Bible is a mirror that doesn't just reflect us; it transforms us.

The Bible is also the place where we learn how to live. In this respect it functions a bit like a map. Any good map helps you make sense of the landscape around and chart a course that will take you home. The landscape around us, our schools, streets, families and friends, can often be confusing. Most of us will have questions about what we're to do with our lives and how we're to treat people. The Bible helps us to understand the world and it also guides us through it. It's a vital tool for the Christian journey. As you learn how to 'map-read', you will find that the Bible will guide you on a grey Tuesday morning and a dark Monday night. You will find direction for when things are going well and for when things are tough. 2 Timothy 3:16–17 tells us, *'All Scripture is God-breathed and is useful for teaching, rebuking, correcting and training in righteousness, so that the servant of God may be thoroughly equipped for every good work.'* If you want to live as a Christian, this book will equip you thoroughly.

The Bible has changed the lives of millions of people across the world and throughout the ages. Why read it? Put simply, in reading it you will enter into relationship with the Living and the Almighty God.

The Bible in (almost) one page

ANDY CROFT

At first glance the Bible can seem like just a random collection of stories that don't have much in common. In fact, when you step back and take a look you see it tells one magnificent story. It's the story of who God is, why he made us and what life with him looks like. Here's a summary – the whole story of the Bible in (almost) one page.

In the beginning God created everything, from the stars to the insects. The high point of his creation was us, the human race. He made us *'in his own image'* (Genesis 1:27). The first humans were Adam and Eve. Adam and Eve turned away from God, and so did their kids and grandkids. The Bible calls this 'sin'. Eventually God, sick of the human race's selfishness, sent a flood to wash the world clean – but he saved Noah in the hope that humanity would change their ways (Genesis 6).

We didn't.

God then took one part of the human race as his own people and used them to show the rest of the world how amazing relationship with him could be. He started with Abraham (Genesis 12:1–3) and then for hundreds of years stuck close to Abraham's family. They became known as 'the people of Israel'.

Most of the Old Testament is the story of God's relationship with Israel – and it's an epic tale. Years after Abraham, Israel were slaves in Egypt. God used Moses to rescue them (see Exodus). He gave them his laws (see Leviticus, Numbers, Deuteronomy). Joshua led Israel to conquer a new land and then they were ruled by leaders called judges (see Joshua, Judges). Eventually they demanded a king and so God gave them Saul, followed by the great King David and then Solomon. After Solomon the Kingdom of Israel split into two kingdoms and they were ruled by a load of pretty terrible kings (see Kings, Chronicles).

Israel ignored God, even though he had given them everything. He sent prophets to call them back (Isaiah, Jeremiah, Amos and others), but they wouldn't listen. Eventually God allowed a rival kingdom, Babylon, to conquer Israel and they were taken into exile (see 2 Kings 25).

After a while God brought Israel home, hoping to draw them back into a relationship of love. They rebuilt the ruined capital Jerusalem (see Nehemiah and Ezra), but they never truly gave their hearts to God. He sent more prophets (Haggai, Malachi and others), but eventually even they fell silent.

God was quiet for 400 years (the time between the Old and New Testaments). Then he made his greatest move yet: he came himself! Jesus was born. God the Son became one of us. Jesus lived a life of utter kindness, mercy, justice and love (see Matthew, Mark, Luke and John). Then he allowed the human race to put him to death on a cross. Three days later, he rose to life again!

The story of the Bible tells us this happened so that we might be free and forgiven of our sin; so that we might know God as our Father; so that we might come home.

After the accounts of Jesus' life comes the story of the early church. It's full of ordinary people like Paul and Peter, whom God uses to do amazing things (see Acts). We have lots of letters these early Christians wrote to each other (see Romans, Corinthians and others) all about life with God. Revelation, the final book, looks forward to the completion of God's plan, the ending of death and pain and the joy of spending eternity with him.

How the Bible came to be

ANDY CROFT

The Bible is one book, but it also works a bit like a library. It's made up of sixty-six different books, thirty-nine in the Old Testament and twenty-seven in the New Testament. Today it's still by far the number one bestselling book in the world. But who wrote it? And when?

To answer this we need to recognise the following things.

- The different books were written by many different authors. Some of them were kings, prophets and priests, others were historians, some were fishermen and others were shepherds. Quite a mixed bunch!

- They were writing at different times. The Old Testament writings were mainly written between 1400 BC and 530 BC. The New Testament books were written within a hundred years of Jesus' ascension to heaven, between AD 45 and AD 140.

- The books weren't written in English! Most of the Old Testament was originally written in Hebrew (with some parts in Aramaic). The New Testament was written in Greek.

- Many of the authors were writing for different reasons. Some wanted to record the history of God's people, others were writing songs of worship to God, still others were writing letters about God to churches and friends.

So who wrote the Bible? In a nutshell, part of the answer is that it was written by followers of God from all different walks of life over a period of 1,500 years.

The other part of the answer is that the Bible was written by God. This isn't to say that he typed it up and dropped it down from heaven. Rather, as Christians we believe that God was present in the minds and hearts of those who wrote the different books. The words of the Bible aren't just writings from a long time ago; they are words inspired by God himself. It's because it's inspired by God that we believe the Bible has such authority.

Once we're clear who wrote the different books, the other question to ask is how (and when) they came to be collected together into the one Bible. Who decided which books God had inspired and which he hadn't?

When it comes to the Old Testament, there's no set date we can put on this. It happened gradually over time as the different books were written. What we can be certain about is that by the time of Jesus there was a pretty firm consensus among the Jews that the books we now know as the Old Testament were 'inspired'. Jesus himself certainly thought so: he quoted the Old Testament a lot throughout his life (Isaiah seems to have been his favourite book).

The list of New Testament books was agreed upon by Christians at a meeting in AD 393 called the Council of Hippo. In practice, however, from a very early stage the Gospels and many of the letters were seen as having divine authority. They were read aloud in the earliest church meetings and treated on the same level as the Old Testament books.

One person sitting alone in a room did not decide on the books of the Bible: over time the whole Church came to agree on what books should be included. As Christians we believe they didn't do it by themselves, but that God, in his amazing way, was always at work guiding the process. When you look at a huge building you can see the different bricks laid by the builders, but you can also see the 'one mind' of the architect behind the design. In the same way, God used different writers to 'lay the bricks', but when we stand back and look at the Bible from Genesis to Revelation we see the one God behind it all.

What's where

Journeys

Journeys are series that will challenge you about the shape your heart is in. As you go deeper into sections of the Bible, the more we learn about what the Bible has to say about something, the more we find ourselves challenged and changed.

Journeys (continued)

Threads

Threads explore a topic throughout the Bible to help you understand more about the things God is passionate about.

Naturally supernatural

Justice and mercy

Money

Faith in the World

Threads (continued)

Storylines

Storylines explore the major themes that run through the whole Bible. We're looking at the things that crop up throughout the whole of scripture.

The big story

Christ in all the Scriptures

Friendship

Law and grace

Storylines (continued)

Life of Jesus

1. God's greatest promise .... Matthew 1:22–23
2. King of God's people .... Matthew 21:1–11
3. Lord over spiritual powers .... Mark 1:24–28
4. The Lord who saves us from sin .... Luke 7:36–50
5. The ultimate teacher .... Mark 13:31
6. Lord over sickness .... John 4:46–54
7. Lord over nature .... John 6:5–21
8. The one who can be worshipped .... John 20:28
9. Judge of the world .... Acts 10:42
10. Lord of the universe .... Hebrews 1:1–3

People used by God

1. Deborah .... Judges 4
2. Gideon .... Judges 6
3. Ruth .... Ruth 1:17
4. Jonah .... Jonah 1:1
5. Mary Magdalene .... Mark 16:9
6. Elizabeth .... Luke 1
7. Zacchaeus .... Luke 19:1–9
8. Nathanael .... John 1:47
9. John .... John 9:1
10. Paul .... Acts 8:3

Sacrifice

1. Sacrifice 101 .... Genesis 3:21
2. The cost of sin .... Genesis 22:13
3. The Passover .... Exodus 12:27
4. Hannah's sacrifice .... 1 Samuel 1:24–28
5. Worship as sacrifice .... Romans 12:1–2
6. Sacrifice as worship .... Leviticus 9:7
7. Samson's last act .... Judges 16:23–30
8. Saul's lesson in useless sacrifice .... 1 Samuel 15:22
9. David's attitude: offer the best .... 2 Samuel 24:24
10. What's your 'Baal'? .... 1 Kings 18:36

What is Christianity?

1. Doctrine of creation .... Job 38
2. Doctrine of the fall .... Genesis 3
3. Doctrine of God .... Isaiah 55:8–9
4. Doctrine of the Trinity .... Matthew 3:13–17
5. Doctrine of incarnation .... John 1
6. Doctrine of Christ .... Luke 8:22–25
7. Doctrine of salvation .... Romans 5:1–11
8. Doctrine of the church .... 1 Corinthians 12:12–31
9. Doctrine of the Word .... 2 Timothy 3:16
10. Doctrine of the future .... Revelation 22

Issues

In this section we look at single topics, from some of the trickiest questions our friends ask, challenging issues facing the world today, and how the Bible can help us with everyday situations we face.

Tough issues

World issues

Life issues

THE OLD TESTAMENT

GENESIS

DATE

Genesis tells the story of the first few thousand years of human history

AUTHOR

Traditionally attributed to Moses

WHAT'S IT ALL ABOUT?

Genesis is the first of five books which make up the Pentateuch (known to Jewish people as the Law books or Torah). It is a book of beginnings – the beginning of creation, the beginning of humankind and the beginning of the story of God's people. It gives us a detailed family history of the people of Israel and tells many amazing stories, including creation, the fall, Noah and the great flood, and the lives of Abraham, Jacob and Joseph.

WHY SHOULD WE READ IT?

- We discover something of the incredible power of God and his love for the people he created.

- We gain an understanding of relationships (God's relationship with creation, God's relationship with humans, and humans' relationships with one another).

- We can read about some of the heroes of our faith (more than half of the heroes listed in Hebrews 11 have their stories told here in Genesis).

Andy Croft with Liza Hoeksma

The beginning

1 In the beginning God created the heavens and the earth. ²Now the earth was formless and empty, darkness was over the surface of the deep, and the Spirit of God was hovering over the waters.

³And God said, 'Let there be light,' and there was light. ⁴God saw that the light was good, and he separated the light from the darkness. ⁵God called the light 'day', and the darkness he called 'night'. And there was evening, and there was morning – the first day.

⁶And God said, 'Let there be a vault between the waters to separate water from water.' ⁷So God made the vault and separated the water under the vault from the water above it. And it was so. ⁸God called the vault 'sky'. And there was evening, and there was morning – the second day.

⁹And God said, 'Let the water under the sky be gathered to one place, and let dry ground appear.' And it was so. ¹⁰God called the dry ground 'land', and the gathered waters he called 'seas'. And God saw that it was good.

¹¹Then God said, 'Let the land produce vegetation: seed-bearing plants and trees on the land that bear fruit with seed in it, according to their various kinds.' And it was so. ¹²The land produced vegetation: plants bearing seed according to their kinds and trees bearing fruit with seed in it according to their kinds. And God saw that it was good. ¹³And there was evening, and there was morning – the third day.

FAITH IN THE WORLD 1

IF IT'S GOOD IT'S GOD'S

There's a famous story told about the great artist Leonardo da Vinci. He had been working on a painting for months, but not alone – several apprentices were watching him, hoping to pick up the skills of the master. Da Vinci was getting close to finishing the painting, and that was when the shock came for one of the students. The great painter turned to him, offered him his paintbrush and said, 'You finish it.' The student replied. 'I cannot hope to finish such a great work of art!' Da Vinci simply turned to him and said, 'Will not what I have done inspire you to do your best?' It's true, though, isn't it? We're often inspired and motivated to do something by what we see other people doing, whether it's a work of art, building up a business or acting out of compassion. Our response can be, 'I could never do that!' or we can rise to the challenge and say, 'I'll do my best!'

We see God creating the most inspired work of art of all time in Genesis 1 – the universe. God doesn't exactly turn to us and say, 'Finish off my creation for me!' But he does ask us to care for it and for each other. God made us, and he made us good. That means not just that we're amazing works of art, but that we're fit for purpose. Work has a key place in God's universe. It's what we're supposed to be doing most of the time. Work is good. God asks us to help him in the work of looking after his created order. What a wonderful privilege, what an awe-inspiring universe! What God has done should inspire us to work well in our caring for this world and its inhabitants.

Jason Gardner

Genesis 2:15–25

CREATION

2 Timothy 3:16 tells us that *'All scripture is God-breathed and is useful for teaching, rebuking, correcting and training in righteousness'*. So when we come to any text in the Bible we can be assured that it is inspired by God himself and therefore, in the deepest sense of the word, it is absolutely true. But what is God trying to teach us by inspiring the human author to write these words?

Some people read Genesis 1 as literal historical narrative – believing that God took six days of twenty-four hours each, probably around six thousand years ago, to create the earth. Others believe that it describes six periods of time, each possibly lasting thousands or even millions of years. Still others have seen Genesis 1 as a great hymn to the Creator God, which may have been used in worship by the ancient Jews, and do not insist that we read it as a literal historical/scientific document, as this is not its primary function.

So what are we to believe? Certainly God is all-powerful, and therefore is more than capable of creating the universe in six twenty-four-hour days. But what do we say to the claims of science that the universe is billions of years old, and that humans evolved only after the earth had existed for millions of years?

While we need to question the theories of modern science, we should not fear it or see science as the enemy of faith. The author of Genesis is not first and foremost writing a scientific history of the world. Most scholars will agree that the author is writing a majestic tribute to the Creator God, which contains beautiful poetry and reminds the readers that they are not here by accident. The best science attempts to tell us the mechanics of how and when the earth came into being. Genesis primarily teaches us why, and who is behind the magnificent creation project.

The main point of Genesis 1 – 2 is not to affirm a certain scientific theory of origins. It is to proclaim that God is the Creator of all, and that he invites us into relationship with him. This is the stunning, scandalous claim of this passage, and of the whole Bible. The author is not primarily concerned with the technique of creation, but with the intent behind it. It is absolutely true, but allows us to consider a variety of scientific theories when looking at exactly how God created everything.

In these first two chapters of the Bible, we discover the foundational truths that God spoke everything into being, when previously there was nothing (1:1–3); that humankind is the pinnacle of the creation and the bearer of God's image, not an evolutionary accident (1:26–31); and that we are created to be in intimate community with one another (2:18–25). These are the deepest truths of Genesis 1 – 2: the scientific discussion must always be a secondary issue and should not threaten or divide us.

Chris Lane

¹⁴ And God said, 'Let there be lights in the vault of the sky to separate the day from the night, and let them serve as signs to mark sacred times, and days and years, ¹⁵ and let them be lights in the vault of the sky to give light on the earth.' And it was so. ¹⁶ God made two great lights – the greater light to govern the day and the lesser light to govern the night. He also made the stars. ¹⁷ God set them in the vault of the sky to give light on the earth, ¹⁸ to govern the day and the night, and to separate light from darkness. And God saw that it was good. ¹⁹ And there was evening, and there was morning – the fourth day.

²⁰ And God said, 'Let the water teem with living creatures, and let birds fly above the earth across the vault of the sky.' ²¹ So God created the great creatures of the sea and every living thing with which the water teems and that moves about in it, according to their kinds, and every winged bird according to its kind. And God saw that it was good. ²² God blessed them and said, 'Be fruitful and increase in number and fill the water in the seas, and let the birds increase on the earth.' ²³ And there was evening, and there was morning – the fifth day.

²⁴ And God said, 'Let the land produce living creatures according to their kinds: the livestock, the creatures that move along the ground, and the wild animals, each according to its kind.' And it was so. ²⁵ God made the wild animals according to their kinds, the livestock according to their kinds, and all the creatures that move along the ground according to their kinds. And God saw that it was good.

²⁶ Then God said, 'Let us make mankind in our image, in our likeness, so that they may rule over the fish in the sea and the birds in the sky, over the livestock and all the wild animals,ᵃ and over all the creatures that move along the ground.'

²⁷ So God created mankind in his own image,
in the image of God he created them;
male and female he created them.

²⁸ God blessed them and said to them, 'Be fruitful and increase in number; fill the earth and subdue it. Rule over the fish in the sea and the birds in the sky and over every living creature that moves on the ground.' ²⁹ Then God said, 'I give you every seed-bearing plant on the face of the whole earth and every tree that has fruit with seed in it. They will be yours for food. ³⁰ And to all the beasts of the earth and all the birds in the sky and all the creatures that move along the ground – everything that has the breath of life in it – I give every green plant for food.' And it was so.

³¹ God saw all that he had made, and it was very good. And there was evening, and there was morning – the sixth day.

2 Thus the heavens and the earth were completed in all their vast array.

² By the seventh day God had finished the work he had been doing; so on the seventh day he rested from all his work. ³ Then God blessed the seventh day and made it holy, because on it he rested from all the work of creating that he had done.

Adam and Eve

⁴ This is the account of the heavens and the earth when they were created, when the LORD God made the earth and the heavens.

⁵ Now no shrub had yet appeared on the earthᵃ and no plant had yet sprung up, for the LORD God had not sent rain on the earth and there was no one to work the

---

ᵃ 26 Probable reading of the original Hebrew text (see Syriac); Masoretic Text *the earth*

ᵃ 5 Or *land*; also in verse 6

ground, ⁶but streamsᵇ came up from the earth and watered the whole surface of the ground. ⁷Then the LORD God formed a manᶜ from the dust of the ground and breathed into his nostrils the breath of life, and the man became a living being.

ᵇ6 Or mist

ᶜ7 The Hebrew for *man (adam)* sounds like and may be related to the Hebrew for *ground (adamah)*; it is also the name *Adam* (see verse 20).

FAITH IN THE WORLD 2

DID ANYONE ORDER 'ORDER'?

Everybody but everybody loves puzzles. We love solving things! Don't think so? Just look at people on a train or a bus trying to complete a crossword or Sudoku challenge. Then there are all the murder mystery stories on TV: we love trying to work out 'whodunnit'. Also there are the computer games we play, puzzle games on our smartphones, strategy games on our consoles. Even if you're playing an action game, the chances are that you'll have to solve some mystery or complete some task in order to progress. Yes, we love puzzles. Much of our day-to-day study will be about puzzle-solving too. As students we spend time solving equations, completing science experiments or interpreting great works of literature and art.

In Genesis 2 we see Adam given his first puzzle – what to name all the animals. God parades a series of fluffy, furry and bitey things in front of Adam in order to have him name them. Now what is God teaching Adam here? It could be that he's showing Adam the place he has in creation: he stands as the chief of the food chain, lord of the animals, a bit like Tarzan without the strange yodel. But Adam is also doing a work of ordering – puzzle-solving if you like. Did Adam come up with random names, or would he be thinking in terms of species, animal families? God is also showing Adam that if he's going to be a great solution-provider, if he's going to be in charge of 'ordering' planet earth, then he can't do it alone! *'But for Adam no suitable helper was found'* (Genesis 2:20b). Sure, Adam could figure out how to use elephants to carry heavy loads and ox to plough fields, but he needed an equal to help provide order. So along comes Eve, a suitable helper who would also be able to help him produce lots of other little helpers! She would help him organise the world around them and do the key work of taking care of the garden (v. 15). Already we're seeing in Genesis that working is a key part of God's plan for humankind. A chief part of that work is puzzle-solving, finding patterns in God's world and making the most of them in order to *bring* order.In what way is the work that you're doing at school like puzzle-solving? In what way is it about 'bringing order' and finding useful patterns? Isn't a lot of science about recognising patterns in the way the universe behaves and then using it to our advantage? And here's your own puzzle to solve. Why didn't God give us all the answers to how his universe works straightaway? Why, as humankind, do we have to do so much puzzle-solving?

Jason Gardner

 Genesis 1:1–5   Genesis 29:14–30

8 Now the LORD God had planted a garden in the east, in Eden; and there he put the man he had formed. 9 The LORD God made all kinds of trees grow out of the ground – trees that were pleasing to the eye and good for food. In the middle of the garden were the tree of life and the tree of the knowledge of good and evil.

10 A river watering the garden flowed from Eden; from there it was separated into four headwaters. 11 The name of the first is the Pishon; it winds through the entire land of Havilah, where there is gold. 12 (The gold of that land is good; aromatic resin*d* and onyx are also there.) 13 The name of the second river is the Gihon; it winds through the entire land of Cush.*e* 14 The name of the third river is the Tigris; it runs along the east side of Ashur. And the fourth river is the Euphrates.

15 The LORD God took the man and put him in the Garden of Eden to work it and take care of it. 16 And the LORD God commanded the man, 'You are free to eat from any tree in the garden; 17 but you must not eat from the tree of the knowledge of good and evil, for when you eat from it you will certainly die.'

18 The LORD God said, 'It is not good for the man to be alone. I will make a helper suitable for him.'

19 Now the LORD God had formed out of the ground all the wild animals and all the birds in the sky. He brought them to the man to see what he would name them; and whatever the man called each living creature, that was its name. 20 So the man gave names to all the livestock, the birds in the sky and all the wild animals.

But for Adam*f* no suitable helper was found. 21 So the LORD God caused the man to fall into a deep sleep; and while he was sleeping, he took one of the man's ribs*g* and then closed up the place with flesh. 22 Then the LORD God made a woman from the rib*h* he had taken out of the man, and he brought her to the man.

23 The man said,

'This is now bone of my bones
    and flesh of my flesh;
she shall be called "woman",
    for she was taken out of man.'

24 That is why a man leaves his father and mother and is united to his wife, and they become one flesh.

25 Adam and his wife were both naked, and they felt no shame.

The fall

3 Now the snake was more crafty than any of the wild animals the LORD God had made. He said to the woman, 'Did God really say, "You must not eat from any tree in the garden"?'

2 The woman said to the snake, 'We may eat fruit from the trees in the garden, 3 but God did say, "You must not eat fruit from the tree that is in the middle of the garden, and you must not touch it, or you will die."'

4 'You will not certainly die,' the snake said to the woman. 5 'For God knows that when you eat from it your eyes will be opened, and you will be like God, knowing good and evil.'

6 When the woman saw that the fruit of the tree was good for food and pleasing to the eye, and also desirable for gaining wisdom, she took some and ate it. She also gave some to her husband, who was with her, and he ate it. 7 Then the eyes of both of them were opened, and they realised that they were naked; so they sewed fig leaves together and made coverings for themselves.

8 Then the man and his wife heard the sound of the LORD God as he was walking in the garden in the cool of the day, and they hid from the LORD God among the trees of the garden. 9 But the LORD God called to the man, 'Where are you?'

10 He answered, 'I heard you in the garden, and I was afraid because I was naked; so I hid.'

11 And he said, 'Who told you that you were naked? Have you eaten from the tree from which I commanded you not to eat?'

---

d 12 Or *good; pearls*
e 13 Possibly south-east Mesopotamia
f 20 Or *the man*
g 21 Or *took part of the man's side*
h 22 Or *part*

JUSTICE AND MERCY 1

HOW IT ALL BEGAN...

God commands us to seek justice and love mercy as well as walking humbly with him. This thread takes us on a tour of the Bible to unpack why it's an essential part of mission and discipleship to remember the last, the least and the lost – to understand that God is looking for the transformation of society as well as the salvation of individuals, and to see how serving the poor and preaching the gospel fit together.

In the beginning it was all *good*. God – Father, Son and Holy Spirit living in constant and total love – created a perfect universe out of their love for each other. Everything just worked. There was intimacy and security and love; all of creation reflected God's beauty; there was harmony between every part of creation; God walked and talked in intimacy with his people. It is written that Adam and Eve were *'both naked, and they felt no shame'* (Genesis 2:25). This means that they were open, honest, gentle and intimate with each other. There was no agenda, no insecurity. It was very good.

Then it all went wrong. Human beings chose to reject God's love and care instead of embracing it; rather than walking with God, they hid from him; rather than loving each other, they blamed each other. Adam's and Eve's perfect relationship with God was replaced by shame. As a result of their broken relationship with God, within a few chapters creation has fallen into disarray and people are murdering each other, living in fear.

That first broken relationship is the source of all poverty and pain. Nothing would ever be the same again – but God had not given up on his children. He still cared for them: he cared about how they would stay warm and clothed and what they would eat, as well as how they could relate to him. He was involved with, and cared about, every part of their lives. It was the beginning of the fightback against the devastating effects of sin.

It is a fight that carries on to this day. God wants to restore our relationship with him, with each other and with creation. He cares about our spirits, souls and bodies. As his followers, we must share the good news that God is looking to forgive and restore, and we must demonstrate that good news by serving the poor, seeking justice and caring for creation. Just like our Father.

David Westlake

Leviticus 25:8 ▶▶

12 The man said, 'The woman you put here with me – she gave me some fruit from the tree, and I ate it.'

13 Then the LORD God said to the woman, 'What is this you have done?'

The woman said, 'The snake deceived me, and I ate.'

14 So the LORD God said to the snake, 'Because you have done this,

'Cursed are you above all livestock
    and all wild animals!
You will crawl on your belly
    and you will eat dust
    all the days of your life.
15 And I will put enmity
    between you and the woman,
    and between your offspring[a] and
        hers;
he will crush[b] your head,
    and you will strike his heel.'

16 To the woman he said,

'I will make your pains in childbearing
        very severe;
    with painful labour you will give
        birth to children.
Your desire will be for your husband,
    and he will rule over you.'

17 To Adam he said, 'Because you listened to your wife and ate fruit from the tree about which I commanded you, "You must not eat from it,"

'Cursed is the ground because of you;
    through painful toil you will eat
        food from it
    all the days of your life.
18 It will produce thorns and thistles for
        you,
    and you will eat the plants of the field.
19 By the sweat of your brow
    you will eat your food
until you return to the ground,
    since from it you were taken;
for dust you are
    and to dust you will return.'

20 Adam[c] named his wife Eve,[d] because she would become the mother of all the living.

21 The LORD God made garments of skin for Adam and his wife and clothed them. 22 And the LORD God said, 'The man has now become like one of us, knowing good and evil. He must not be allowed to reach out his hand and take also from the tree of life and eat, and live for ever.' 23 So the LORD God banished him from the Garden of Eden to work the ground from which he had been taken. 24 After he drove the man out, he placed on the east side[e] of the Garden of Eden cherubim and a flaming sword flashing back and forth to guard the way to the tree of life.

Cain and Abel

4 Adam[a] made love to his wife Eve, and she became pregnant and gave birth to Cain.[b] She said, 'With the help of the LORD I have brought forth[c] a man.' 2 Later she gave birth to his brother Abel.

Now Abel kept flocks, and Cain worked the soil. 3 In the course of time Cain brought some of the fruits of the soil as an offering to the LORD. 4 But Abel also brought an offering – fat portions from some of the firstborn of his flock. The LORD looked with favour on Abel and his offering, 5 but on Cain and his offering he did not look with favour. So Cain was very angry, and his face was downcast.

6 Then the LORD said to Cain, 'Why are you angry? Why is your face downcast? 7 If you do what is right, will you not be accepted? But if you do not do what is right, sin is crouching at your door; it desires to have you, but you must rule over it.'

8 Now Cain said to his brother Abel, 'Let's go out to the field.'[d] While they were

---

c 20 Or *The man*
d 20 *Eve* probably means *living*.
e 24 Or *placed in front*
a 1 Or *The man*
b 1 *Cain* sounds like the Hebrew for *brought forth* or *acquired*.
c 1 Or *have acquired*
d 8 Samaritan Pentateuch, Septuagint, Vulgate and Syriac; Masoretic Text does not have '*Let's go out to the field.*'

---

a 15 Or *seed*
b 15 Or *strike*

in the field, Cain attacked his brother Abel and killed him.

⁹Then the LORD said to Cain, 'Where is your brother Abel?'

'I don't know,' he replied. 'Am I my brother's keeper?'

¹⁰The LORD said, 'What have you done? Listen! Your brother's blood cries out to me from the ground. ¹¹Now you are under a curse and driven from the ground, which opened its mouth to receive your brother's blood from your hand. ¹²When you work the ground, it will no longer yield its crops for you. You will be a restless wanderer on the earth.'

¹³Cain said to the LORD, 'My punishment

SACRIFICE 1

Sacrifice 101

The very first sacrifice in the Old Testament is easy to miss.

In Genesis 3 Adam and Eve made a terrible decision to follow their own desire for power and knowledge instead of trusting God and doing what he told them. God knew that their decision would have some very hard consequences – which is why he wanted them to listen to him. Nonetheless, Adam and Eve had to learn the hard way, like most of us.

Once Adam and Eve had taken and eaten the fruit from the tree of the knowledge of good and evil, something changed right away. God was walking through the garden and he couldn't find them. This probably wouldn't have been mentioned if it wasn't something new, which leads us to believe that God and Adam and Eve had been in constant connection up to that point. They were great friends, constantly in communication. What a terrible breach of friendship this first sin was for them all. When God finally found them, they told him that they were hiding because they were afraid (the first time they had experienced fear) and they were naked and ashamed (again, the first time they ever felt shame). The consequences of sin are horrible.

We also discover the point of the very first sacrifice: God took the skin of animals and used it to cover Adam's and Eve's nakedness. Those innocent animals had to die in order to cover the sin of the first people (literally the skin of the animal covered the first people). That's when the horrible cycle of sin and sacrifice began. This cycle doesn't end until Jesus offers the final and perfect sacrifice of himself and we are finally free from the curse that Adam and Eve came under. Sacrifice is the giving of one life to cover the sin of another. This sacrifice made in Genesis is the first hint of the ultimate sacrifice coming in Jesus.

Thank God that he made a way for us to escape death through sacrifice!

Danielle Strickland

Genesis 22:13

WHAT IS CHRISTIANITY? 2

Doctrine of the fall, we walk away

We know that the world we live in is full of pain. It's full of broken people, diseases and despair. In moments of honesty, we also know that we ourselves are a long way from perfect. We are nothing like as kind, selfless and loving as we might hope to be. What's going on?

As Christians we believe that the world and the human race exist in a state of 'fallenness'. In other words, we believe that the way things are is not the way that God intended them to be. This story in Genesis 3 describes the event (called 'the fall') that brought this state about.

In Genesis we see that God created the human race for a relationship of love with himself. It's also clear that, starting with Adam and Eve, he gave us free choice. This is one of the amazing things about God. He is all-powerful, but he isn't a dictator. God could have pre-programmed us like robots, but instead he gave us the frightening and dignifying ability to choose whether or not we wanted to know him. Genesis 3 shows us that Adam and Eve walked away from God; eating the fruit wasn't about an apple, it was about choosing independence from God.

What happened with Adam and Eve in the garden set a pattern for what humans have been doing ever since. All of us, in big and small ways, have chosen to live for ourselves instead of for God. The Bible calls this sin. Sin is about what we do, but it's also about the condition of our heart. It's when, in our hearts, we put ourselves above God. As one person put it, 'The heart of the human problem is the problem of the human heart.'

Sin hurts us at every level. Adam's and Eve's relationship with God is damaged (they hide from him and have to leave the garden, Genesis 3:8, 23). Their relationship with each other begins to break down (they start blaming each other, Genesis 3:12). Their relationship to the creation is disrupted and death enters the world (Genesis 3:17–19). They suddenly become self-conscious and insecure (hence the clothes, Genesis 3:7).

The fall explains to us why things are the way they are today. It's not because God created evil, it's because God loves us enough to allow us real choice. Today you and I still have that real choice to follow him.

The rest of the Bible is God's response to the mess we've got ourselves into. He responds to sin with both justice and love. On the cross God takes sin and death on himself to deal with it once and for all. Through Jesus our relationships with God, with one another and with the world and can be healed.

The human race is fallen, but the Bible shows that in an incredible way God ultimately kneels to lift us to our feet again.

Andy Croft

is more than I can bear. **14** Today you are driving me from the land, and I will be hidden from your presence; I will be a restless wanderer on the earth, and whoever finds me will kill me.'

15 But the LORD said to him, 'Not so;*e* anyone who kills Cain will suffer vengeance seven times over.' Then the LORD put a mark on Cain so that no one who found him would kill him. **16** So Cain went out from the LORD's presence and lived in the land of Nod,*f* east of Eden.

17 Cain made love to his wife, and she became pregnant and gave birth to Enoch. Cain was then building a city, and he named it after his son Enoch. **18** To Enoch was born Irad, and Irad was the father of Mehujael, and Mehujael was the father of Methushael, and Methushael was the father of Lamech.

FACT

TWO BROTHERS

According to Genesis, Jabal was the first nomadic herdsman – he lived in tents and kept livestock. His brother, Jubal, was the first musician (Genesis 4:20–21).

19 Lamech married two women, one named Adah and the other Zillah. **20** Adah gave birth to Jabal; he was the father of those who live in tents and raise livestock. **21** His brother's name was Jubal; he was the father of all who play stringed instruments and pipes. **22** Zillah also had a son, Tubal-Cain, who forged all kinds of tools out of*g* bronze and iron. Tubal-Cain's sister was Naamah.

23 Lamech said to his wives,

'Adah and Zillah, listen to me;
 wives of Lamech, hear my words.
I have killed a man for wounding me,
 a young man for injuring me.
24 If Cain is avenged seven times,
 then Lamech seventy-seven times.'

25 Adam made love to his wife again, and she gave birth to a son and named him Seth,*h* saying, 'God has granted me another child in place of Abel, since Cain killed him.' **26** Seth also had a son, and he named him Enosh.

At that time people began to call on*i* the name of the LORD.

From Adam to Noah

5 This is the written account of Adam's family line.

When God created mankind, he made them in the likeness of God. **2** He created them male and female and blessed them. And he named them 'Mankind'*a* when they were created.

3 When Adam had lived 130 years, he had a son in his own likeness, in his own image; and he named him Seth. **4** After Seth was born, Adam lived 800 years and had other sons and daughters. **5** Altogether, Adam lived a total of 930 years, and then he died.

6 When Seth had lived 105 years, he became the father*b* of Enosh. **7** After he became the father of Enosh, Seth lived 807 years and had other sons and daughters. **8** Altogether, Seth lived a total of 912 years, and then he died.

9 When Enosh had lived 90 years, he became the father of Kenan. **10** After he became the father of Kenan, Enosh lived 815 years and had other sons and daughters. **11** Altogether, Enosh lived a total of 905 years, and then he died.

12 When Kenan had lived 70 years, he became the father of Mahalalel. **13** After he became the father of Mahalalel, Kenan lived 840 years and had other sons and

---

e 15 Septuagint, Vulgate and Syriac; Hebrew *Very well*
f 16 *Nod* means *wandering* (see verses 12 and 14).
g 22 Or *who instructed all who work in*

h 25 *Seth* probably means *granted.*
i 26 Or *to proclaim*
a 2 Hebrew *adam*
b 6 *Father* may mean *ancestor;* also in verses 7-26.

daughters. ¹⁴Altogether, Kenan lived a total of 910 years, and then he died.

¹⁵When Mahalalel had lived 65 years, he became the father of Jared. ¹⁶After he became the father of Jared, Mahalalel lived 830 years and had other sons and daughters. ¹⁷Altogether, Mahalalel lived a total of 895 years, and then he died.

ADAM AND EVE

BIRTH:
Genesis 2:7–22
DISOBEDIENCE:
Genesis 3:1–8
EXCUSES:
Genesis 3:9–24
CHILDREN:
Genesis 4:1–19; 5:1–5
CHRIST:
Romans 5:12–21

¹⁸When Jared had lived 162 years, he became the father of Enoch. ¹⁹After he became the father of Enoch, Jared lived 800 years and had other sons and daughters. ²⁰Altogether, Jared lived a total of 962 years, and then he died.

²¹When Enoch had lived 65 years, he became the father of Methuselah. ²²After he became the father of Methuselah, Enoch walked faithfully with God 300 years and had other sons and daughters. ²³Altogether, Enoch lived a total of 365 years. ²⁴Enoch walked faithfully with God; then he was no more, because God took him away.

²⁵When Methuselah had lived 187 years, he became the father of Lamech. ²⁶After he became the father of Lamech, Methuselah lived 782 years and had other sons and daughters. ²⁷Altogether, Methuselah lived a total of 969 years, and then he died.

²⁸When Lamech had lived 182 years, he

had a son. ²⁹He named him Noah^c and said, 'He will comfort us in the labour and painful toil of our hands caused by the ground the LORD has cursed.' ³⁰After Noah was born, Lamech lived 595 years and had other sons and daughters. ³¹Altogether, Lamech lived a total of 777 years, and then he died.

³²After Noah was 500 years old, he became the father of Shem, Ham and Japheth.

Wickedness in the world

6 When human beings began to increase in number on the earth and daughters were born to them, ²the sons of God saw that the daughters of humans were beautiful, and they married any of them they chose. ³Then the LORD said, 'My Spirit will not contend with^a humans for ever, for they are mortal;^b their days will be a hundred and twenty years.'

⁴The Nephilim were on the earth in those days – and also afterwards – when the sons of God went to the daughters of humans and had children by them. They were the heroes of old, men of renown.

⁵The LORD saw how great the wickedness of the human race had become on the earth, and that every inclination of the thoughts of the human heart was only evil all the time. ⁶The LORD regretted that he had made human beings on the earth, and his heart was deeply troubled. ⁷So the LORD said, 'I will wipe from the face of the earth the human race I have created – and with them the animals, the birds and the creatures that move along the ground – for I regret that I have made them.' ⁸But Noah found favour in the eyes of the LORD.

Noah and the flood

⁹This is the account of Noah and his family.

Noah was a righteous man, blameless among the people of his time, and he

---

c 29 Noah sounds like the Hebrew for *comfort.*
a 3 Or My spirit will not remain in
b 3 Or corrupt

walked faithfully with God. [10] Noah had three sons: Shem, Ham and Japheth.

[11] Now the earth was corrupt in God's sight and was full of violence. [12] God saw how corrupt the earth had become, for all the people on earth had corrupted their ways. [13] So God said to Noah, 'I am going to put an end to all people, for the earth is filled with violence because of them. I am surely going to destroy both them and the earth. [14] So make yourself an ark of cypress[c] wood; make rooms in it and coat it with pitch inside and out. [15] This is how you are to build it: the ark is to be three hundred cubits long, fifty cubits wide and thirty cubits high.[d] [16] Make a roof for it, leaving below the roof an opening one cubit[e] high all around.[f] Put a door in the side of the ark and make lower, middle and upper decks. [17] I am going to bring floodwaters on the earth to destroy all life under the heavens, every creature that has the breath of life in it. Everything on earth will perish. [18] But I will establish my covenant with you, and you will enter the ark – you and your sons and your wife and your sons' wives with you. [19] You are to bring into the ark two of all living creatures, male and female, to keep them alive with you. [20] Two of every kind of bird, of every kind of animal and of every kind of creature that moves along the ground will come to you to be kept alive. [21] You are to take every kind of food that is to be eaten and store it away as food for you and for them.'

[22] Noah did everything just as God commanded him.

7 The LORD then said to Noah, 'Go into the ark, you and your whole family, because I have found you righteous in this generation. [2] Take with you seven pairs of every kind of clean animal, a male and its mate, and one pair of every kind of unclean animal, a male and its mate,

[3] and also seven pairs of every kind of bird, male and female, to keep their various kinds alive throughout the earth. [4] Seven days from now I will send rain on the earth for forty days and forty nights, and I will wipe from the face of the earth every living creature I have made.'

[5] And Noah did all that the LORD commanded him.

[6] Noah was six hundred years old when the floodwaters came on the earth. [7] And Noah and his sons and his wife and his sons' wives entered the ark to escape the waters of the flood. [8] Pairs of clean and unclean animals, of birds and of all creatures that move along the ground, [9] male and female, came to Noah and entered the ark, as God had commanded Noah. [10] And after the seven days the floodwaters came on the earth.

[11] In the six hundredth year of Noah's life, on the seventeenth day of the second month – on that day all the springs of the great deep burst forth, and the floodgates of the heavens were opened. [12] And rain fell on the earth for forty days and forty nights.

[13] On that very day Noah and his sons, Shem, Ham and Japheth, together with his wife and the wives of his three sons, entered the ark. [14] They had with them every wild animal according to its kind, all livestock according to their kinds, every creature that moves along the ground according to its kind and every bird according to its kind, everything with wings. [15] Pairs of all creatures that have the breath of life in them came to Noah and entered the ark. [16] The animals going in were male and female of every living thing, as God had commanded Noah. Then the LORD shut him in.

[17] For forty days the flood kept coming on the earth, and as the waters increased they lifted the ark high above the earth. [18] The waters rose and increased greatly on the earth, and the ark floated on the surface of the water. [19] They rose greatly on the earth, and all the high mountains under the entire heavens were covered. [20] The waters rose and covered the mountains to a depth of more than fifteen

---

c 14 The meaning of the Hebrew for this word is uncertain.

d 15 That is, about 135 metres long, 23 metres wide and 14 metres high

e 16 That is, about 45 centimetres

f 16 The meaning of the Hebrew for this clause is uncertain.

cubits.*a,b* 21 Every living thing that moved on land perished – birds, livestock, wild animals, all the creatures that swarm over the earth, and all mankind. 22 Everything on dry land that had the breath of life in its nostrils died. 23 Every living thing on the face of the earth was wiped out; people and animals and the creatures that move along the ground and the birds were wiped from the earth. Only Noah was left, and those with him in the ark.

24 The waters flooded the earth for a hundred and fifty days.

8 But God remembered Noah and all the wild animals and the livestock that were with him in the ark, and he sent a wind over the earth, and the waters receded. 2 Now the springs of the deep and the floodgates of the heavens had been closed, and the rain had stopped falling from the sky. 3 The water receded steadily from the earth. At the end of the hundred and fifty days the water had gone down, 4 and on the seventeenth day of the seventh month the ark came to rest on the mountains of Ararat. 5 The waters continued to recede until the tenth month, and on the first day of the tenth month the tops of the mountains became visible.

6 After forty days Noah opened a window he had made in the ark 7 and sent out a raven, and it kept flying back and forth until the water had dried up from the earth. 8 Then he sent out a dove to see if the water had receded from the surface of the ground. 9 But the dove could find nowhere to perch because there was water over all the surface of the earth; so it returned to Noah in the ark. He reached out his hand and took the dove and brought it back to himself in the ark. 10 He waited seven more days and again sent out the dove from the ark. 11 When the dove returned to him in the evening, there in its beak was a freshly plucked olive leaf! Then Noah knew that the water had receded from the earth. 12 He waited seven more

days and sent the dove out again, but this time it did not return to him.

13 By the first day of the first month of Noah's six hundred and first year, the water had dried up from the earth. Noah then removed the covering from the ark and saw that the surface of the ground was dry. 14 By the twenty-seventh day of the second month the earth was completely dry.

15 Then God said to Noah, 16 'Come out of the ark, you and your wife and your sons and their wives. 17 Bring out every kind of living creature that is with you – the birds, the animals, and all the creatures that move along the ground – so they can multiply on the earth and be fruitful and increase in number on it.'

18 So Noah came out, together with his sons and his wife and his sons' wives. 19 All the animals and all the creatures that move along the ground and all the birds – everything that moves on land – came out of the ark, one kind after another.

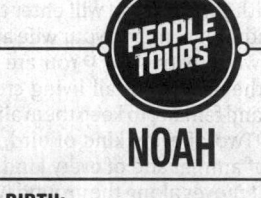

NOAH

BIRTH:
Genesis 5:28–32
WARNING:
Genesis 6:1–22
SEA:
Genesis 7:1–24
LAND:
Genesis 8:1–19
PROMISE:
Genesis 8:20 – 9:17

20 Then Noah built an altar to the LORD and, taking some of all the clean animals and clean birds, he sacrificed burnt offerings on it. 21 The LORD smelled the pleasing aroma and said in his heart: 'Never again will I curse the ground because of humans, even though*a* every inclination

---

a 20 That is, about 6.8 metres
b 20 Or *rose more than fifteen cubits, and the mountains were covered*

a 21 Or *humans, for*

of the human heart is evil from childhood. And never again will I destroy all living creatures, as I have done.

22 'As long as the earth endures,
seedtime and harvest,
cold and heat,
summer and winter,
day and night
will never cease.'

God's covenant with Noah

9 Then God blessed Noah and his sons, saying to them, 'Be fruitful and increase in number and fill the earth. 2 The fear and dread of you will fall on all the beasts of the earth, and on all the birds in the sky, on every creature that moves along the ground, and on all the fish in the sea; they are given into your hands. 3 Everything that lives and moves about will be food for you. Just as I gave you the green plants, I now give you everything.

4 'But you must not eat meat that has its lifeblood still in it. 5 And for your lifeblood I will surely demand an accounting. I will demand an accounting from every animal. And from each human being, too, I will demand an accounting for the life of another human being.

NATURAL DISASTERS

When we see images of cities wrecked by earthquakes and people mourning loved ones; when we see footage of floods that have destroyed whole communities, or tsunamis that have swept fathers away from their children; when we hear of devastating forest fires or violent volcanoes, news of these natural disasters claws at our hearts. At some very deep level we don't believe the world should be such a self-destructive place.

After the flood, God made a covenant with Noah that he would never again flood the world. That's a really important statement right at the start of the Bible's story: natural disasters are not acts of God. But in our day, we have committed violence to the planet and brought floods on ourselves. It's not as if we set out to do it, but simply by the way we have lived in Western society we have over-used the earth's natural resources and pumped too many greenhouse gases into our atmosphere, and it has damaged our environment. These gases act like a blanket over the earth's atmosphere and make it heat up. As the planet gets hotter, the climate changes – often in unpredictable ways. This means more droughts in some places and more flash-floods in others.

But the biggest injustice here is that those of us in rich, oil-guzzling countries are not the worst affected. The people who are most impacted by climate change – who suffer as a result of flooding and droughts and other natural disasters – are the people who have contributed to it the least.

This is one of the greatest injustices of our time.

So what can we do to respond? It's easy to feel guilty about climate change. By just getting on with our normal lives we have played a part in a system that causes other people real suffering. Repentance, though, is about change, not about wallowing in guilt. The challenge of true repentance is for us to live differently. We need to look after this world of ours better.

Matt Valler

6 'Whoever sheds human blood,
    by humans shall their blood be shed;
for in the image of God
    has God made mankind.

7 As for you, be fruitful and increase in number; multiply on the earth and increase upon it.'

8 Then God said to Noah and to his sons with him: 9 'I now establish my covenant with you and with your descendants after you 10 and with every living creature that was with you – the birds, the livestock and all the wild animals, all those that came out of the ark with you – every living creature on earth. 11 I establish my covenant with you: never again will all life be destroyed by the waters of a flood; never again will there be a flood to destroy the earth.'

12 And God said, 'This is the sign of the covenant I am making between me and you and every living creature with you, a

IF WE ARE ALL MADE IN GOD'S IMAGE, WHY ARE SOME PEOPLE BORN WITH DISABILITIES?

It says in Genesis 1:27, *'So God created mankind in his own image, in the image of God he created them; male and female he created them.'* This is before the fall of humanity, when humans were still innocent and perfect. At this time Adam and Eve walked with God and there was no illness, disability or death.

However, in Genesis 3 we read about the fall. Adam and Eve ate the fruit from the tree of the knowledge of good and evil, and they lost their innocence; sin entered the world and with it came things like illness, disability and death. Genesis 3 shows that, although we were created in God's image, because mankind is broken we are not a perfect image of God any more.

Disabilities that people are born with usually happen because of one of two things. The first way disability develops is when someone has a problem with their DNA. DNA is like an instruction manual that tells the body how to make everything and fit it together. Every human has a unique set of DNA. Half comes from a person's mum and half from their dad. Sometimes DNA gets copied badly from their parents, or something might damage their DNA while they are still in the womb.

The second way is if something goes wrong while they are developing in the womb and this causes a disability. One example of this is something called 'foetal alcohol syndrome', where a mother drinks a lot of alcohol while she is pregnant and it causes problems with the development of the baby.

What's important in both of these cases is that something goes wrong with the development of the baby and this causes the disability. If we were still a perfect image of God, such disabilities wouldn't happen; but what's most important is that the baby certainly hasn't done anything to deserve that disability.

Freddie Pimm

covenant for all generations to come: **13** I have set my rainbow in the clouds, and it will be the sign of the covenant between me and the earth. **14** Whenever I bring clouds over the earth and the rainbow appears in the clouds, **15** I will remember my covenant between me and you and all living creatures of every kind. Never again will the waters become a flood to destroy all life. **16** Whenever the rainbow appears in the clouds, I will see it and remember the everlasting covenant between God and all living creatures of every kind on the earth.'

17 So God said to Noah, 'This is the sign of the covenant I have established between me and all life on the earth.'

The sons of Noah

18 The sons of Noah who came out of the ark were Shem, Ham and Japheth. (Ham was the father of Canaan.) **19** These were the three sons of Noah, and from them came the people who were scattered over the whole earth.

20 Noah, a man of the soil, proceeded[a] to plant a vineyard. **21** When he drank some of its wine, he became drunk and lay uncovered inside his tent. **22** Ham, the father of Canaan, saw his father naked and told his two brothers outside. **23** But Shem and Japheth took a garment and laid it across their shoulders; then they walked in backwards and covered their father's naked body. Their faces were turned the other way so that they would not see their father naked.

24 When Noah awoke from his wine and found out what his youngest son had done to him, **25** he said,

'Cursed be Canaan!
The lowest of slaves
will he be to his brothers.'

26 He also said,

'Praise be to the LORD, the God of Shem!
May Canaan be the slave of Shem.

27 May God extend Japheth's[b] territory;
may Japheth live in the tents of Shem,
and may Canaan be the slave of Japheth.'

28 After the flood Noah lived 350 years. **29** Noah lived a total of 950 years, and then he died.

FIRST VINEYARD

According to Genesis, Noah was the first to plant a vineyard. He was also the first person to get drunk (Genesis 9:20–21)!

The table of nations

10 This is the account of Shem, Ham and Japheth, Noah's sons, who themselves had sons after the flood.

The Japhethites

2 The sons[a] of Japheth:
Gomer, Magog, Madai, Javan, Tubal, Meshek and Tiras.
3 The sons of Gomer:
Ashkenaz, Riphath and Togarmah.
4 The sons of Javan:
Elishah, Tarshish, the Kittites and the Rodanites.[b] **5** (From these the maritime peoples spread out into their territories by their clans within their nations, each with its own language.)

The Hamites

6 The sons of Ham:

---

b 27 *Japheth* sounds like the Hebrew for *extend*.
a 2 *Sons* may mean *descendants* or *successors* or *nations*; also in verses 3, 4, 6, 7, 20-23, 29 and 31.
b 4 Some manuscripts of the Masoretic Text and Samaritan Pentateuch (see also Septuagint and 1 Chron. 1:7); most manuscripts of the Masoretic Text *Dodanites*

---

a 20 Or *soil, was the first*

Cush, Egypt, Put and Canaan.
7 The sons of Cush:
Seba, Havilah, Sabtah, Raamah and Sabteka.
The sons of Raamah:
Sheba and Dedan.

8 Cush was the fatherᶜ of Nimrod, who became a mighty warrior on the earth. 9 He was a mighty hunter before the Lᴏʀᴅ; that is why it is said, 'Like Nimrod, a mighty hunter before the Lᴏʀᴅ.' 10 The first centres of his kingdom were Babylon, Uruk, Akkad and Kalneh, inᵈ Shinar.ᵉ 11 From that land he went to Assyria, where he built Nineveh, Rehoboth Ir,ᶠ Calah 12 and Resen, which is between Nineveh and Calah – which is the great city.

13 Egypt was the father of
the Ludites, Anamites, Lehabites, Naphtuhites, 14 Pathrusites, Kasluhites (from whom the Philistines came) and Caphtorites.
15 Canaan was the father of
Sidon his firstborn,ᵍ and of the Hittites, 16 Jebusites, Amorites, Girgashites, 17 Hivites, Arkites, Sinites, 18 Arvadites, Zemarites and Hamathites.

Later the Canaanite clans scattered 19 and the borders of Canaan reached from Sidon towards Gerar as far as Gaza, and then towards Sodom, Gomorrah, Admah and Zeboyim, as far as Lasha.
20 These are the sons of Ham by their clans and languages, in their territories and nations.

The Semites

21 Sons were also born to Shem, whose elder brother wasʰ Japheth; Shem was the ancestor of all the sons of Eber.

22 The sons of Shem:
Elam, Ashur, Arphaxad, Lud and Aram.
23 The sons of Aram:
Uz, Hul, Gether and Meshek.ⁱ
24 Arphaxad was the father ofʲ Shelah, and Shelah the father of Eber.
25 Two sons were born to Eber:
One was named Peleg,ᵏ because in his time the earth was divided; his brother was named Joktan.
26 Joktan was the father of
Almodad, Sheleph, Hazarmaveth, Jerah, 27 Hadoram, Uzal, Diklah, 28 Obal, Abimael, Sheba, 29 Ophir, Havilah and Jobab. All these were sons of Joktan.

30 The region where they lived stretched from Mesha towards Sephar, in the eastern hill country.
31 These are the sons of Shem by their clans and languages, in their territories and nations.

32 These are the clans of Noah's sons, according to their lines of descent, within their nations. From these the nations spread out over the earth after the flood.

The tower of Babel

11 Now the whole world had one language and a common speech. 2 As people moved eastward,ᵃ they found a plain in Shinarᵇ and settled there.
3 They said to each other, 'Come, let's make bricks and bake them thoroughly.' They used brick instead of stone, and bitumen for mortar. 4 Then they said, 'Come, let us build ourselves a city, with a tower that reaches to the heavens, so that we may make a name for ourselves; otherwise we will be scattered over the face of the whole earth.'
5 But the Lᴏʀᴅ came down to see the city and the tower the people were building. 6 The Lᴏʀᴅ said, 'If as one people speaking

---

c 8 *Father* may mean *ancestor* or *predecessor* or *founder*; also in verses 13, 15, 24 and 26.
d 10 Or *Uruk and Akkad – all of them in*
e 10 That is, Babylonia
f 11 Or *Nineveh with its city squares*
g 15 Or *of the Sidonians, the foremost*
h 21 Or *Shem, the elder brother of*

i 23 See Septuagint and 1 Chron. 1:17; Hebrew *Mash*.
j 24 Hebrew; Septuagint *father of Cainan, and Cainan was the father of*
k 25 *Peleg* means *division*.
a 2 Or *from the east; or in the east*
b 2 That is, Babylonia

the same language they have begun to do this, then nothing they plan to do will be impossible for them. 7Come, let us go down and confuse their language so they will not understand each other.'

8So the LORD scattered them from there over all the earth, and they stopped building the city. 9That is why it was called Babelᶜ – because there the LORD confused the language of the whole world. From there the LORD scattered them over the face of the whole earth.

From Shem to Abram

10This is the account of Shem's family line.

Two years after the flood, when Shem was 100 years old, he became the fatherᵈ of Arphaxad. 11And after he became the father of Arphaxad, Shem lived 500 years and had other sons and daughters.

12When Arphaxad had lived 35 years, he became the father of Shelah. 13And after he became the father of Shelah, Arphaxad lived 403 years and had other sons and daughters.ᵉ

14When Shelah had lived 30 years, he became the father of Eber. 15And after he became the father of Eber, Shelah lived 403 years and had other sons and daughters.

16When Eber had lived 34 years, he became the father of Peleg. 17And after he became the father of Peleg, Eber lived 430 years and had other sons and daughters.

18When Peleg had lived 30 years, he became the father of Reu. 19And after he became the father of Reu, Peleg lived 209 years and had other sons and daughters.

20When Reu had lived 32 years, he became the father of Serug. 21And after he became the father of Serug, Reu lived 207 years and had other sons and daughters.

22When Serug had lived 30 years, he became the father of Nahor. 23And after he became the father of Nahor, Serug lived 200 years and had other sons and daughters.

24When Nahor had lived 29 years, he became the father of Terah. 25And after he became the father of Terah, Nahor lived 119 years and had other sons and daughters.

26After Terah had lived 70 years, he became the father of Abram, Nahor and Haran.

Abram's family

27This is the account of Terah's family line.

Terah became the father of Abram, Nahor and Haran. And Haran became the father of Lot. 28While his father Terah was still alive, Haran died in Ur of the Chaldeans, in the land of his birth. 29Abram and Nahor both married. The name of Abram's wife was Sarai, and the name of Nahor's wife was Milkah; she was the daughter of Haran, the father of both Milkah and Iskah. 30Now Sarai was childless because she was not able to conceive.

31Terah took his son Abram, his grandson Lot son of Haran, and his daughter-in-law Sarai, the wife of his son Abram, and together they set out from Ur of the Chaldeans to go to Canaan. But when they came to Harran, they settled there.

32Terah lived 205 years, and he died in Harran.

The call of Abram

12 The LORD had said to Abram, 'Go from your country, your people and your father's household to the land I will show you.

> 2'I will make you into a great nation,
>   and I will bless you;
> I will make your name great,
>   and you will be a blessing.ᵃ
> 3I will bless those who bless you,
>   and whoever curses you I will curse;

ᶜ 9 That is, Babylon; *Babel* sounds like the Hebrew for *confused*.
ᵈ 10 *Father* may mean *ancestor*; also in verses 11-25.
ᵉ 12,13 Hebrew; Septuagint (see also Luke 3:35, 36 and note at Gen. 10:24) *35 years, he became the father of Cainan. 13And after he became the father of Cainan, Arphaxad lived 430 years and had other sons and daughters, and then he died. When Cainan had lived 130 years, he became the father of Shelah. And after he became the father of Shelah, Cainan lived 330 years and had other sons and daughters*

ᵃ 2 Or *be seen as blessed*

THE BIG STORY 4

God starts with one family

When God put into action his plan to save the fallen human race and to restore his broken creation, he started with one man, Abram, soon to be called Abraham, and his family. Abram is called to leave home, not knowing where he's going. He only has a promise that God will lead him to a new homeland and make his descendants a great nation, and that through him all the peoples of the earth will be blessed.

These few verses are among the most important in the whole Bible. They are referred to frequently. Everyone who believes in Jesus, *'the son of Abraham'* (Matthew 1:1), is living proof that these promises came true. Abraham is the model for everyone who wants to have a restored relationship with God. He believed God's promise and obeyed God's command (see Genesis 15:6 and Romans 4:3). He was not perfect, but he demonstrated great faith by trusting God's promises even when it seemed they might not be fulfilled (see Hebrews 11:8–12). Paul saw the promises God made to Abraham as *'the gospel in advance'* (Galatians 3:6–9) and saw all Christians as being *'blessed along with Abraham'*.

The promise about Abraham's descendants being a blessing to all the families, or all the nations, of the earth occurs four further times in Genesis. It is repeated twice to Abraham (18:18; 22:18) and once each to his son Isaac (himself the evidence that God keeps his promises, 26:4) and his grandson Jacob (28:14). Through Abraham God created a people. Through that people he sent his Son, to bring forgiveness and blessing to everyone who believes. The Son then sent his disciples, his church, to make disciples of *'all nations'* (Matthew 28:16–20). Just as Abraham believed the promises about a new home and a future, we are challenged today to believe God's promises through Jesus.

But there is another vital lesson in these verses. When God 'chooses' a person, or a nation, it's always for the sake of others. God chose Abraham so that he could one day offer salvation to everyone. God called Old Testament Israel into existence to show the other nations how to live (*'I will also make you a light for the Gentiles, that my salvation may reach to the ends of the earth'*, Isaiah 49:6), for the sake of all the nations through his Son. God called his church into existence for the sake of those he would bless and save through it. Like Abraham, we are 'chosen', but always because of what God wants to do through us for others. Being chosen, like Abraham, is not about God having favourites. It's about God using us for the sake of others.

Graham Cray

and all peoples on earth
     will be blessed through you.'^b

⁴ So Abram went, as the LORD had told him; and Lot went with him. Abram was seventy-five years old when he set out from Harran. ⁵ He took his wife Sarai, his nephew Lot, all the possessions they had accumulated and the people they had acquired in Harran, and they set out for the land of Canaan, and they arrived there.

⁶ Abram travelled through the land as far as the site of the great tree of Moreh at Shechem. At that time the Canaanites were in the land. ⁷ The LORD appeared to Abram and said, 'To your offspring^c I will give this land.' So he built an altar there to the LORD, who had appeared to him.

⁸ From there he went on towards the hills east of Bethel and pitched his tent, with Bethel on the west and Ai on the east. There he built an altar to the LORD and called on the name of the LORD. ⁹ Then Abram set out and continued towards the Negev.

Abram in Egypt

¹⁰ Now there was a famine in the land, and Abram went down to Egypt to live there for a while because the famine was severe. ¹¹ As he was about to enter Egypt, he said to his wife Sarai, 'I know what a beautiful woman you are. ¹² When the Egyptians see you, they will say, "This is his wife." Then they will kill me but will let you live. ¹³ Say you are my sister, so that I will be treated well for your sake and my life will be spared because of you.'

¹⁴ When Abram came to Egypt, the Egyptians saw that Sarai was a very beautiful woman. ¹⁵ And when Pharaoh's officials saw her, they praised her to Pharaoh, and she was taken into his palace. ¹⁶ He treated Abram well for her sake, and Abram acquired sheep and cattle, male and female donkeys, male and female servants, and camels.

¹⁷ But the LORD inflicted serious diseases on Pharaoh and his household

because of Abram's wife Sarai. ¹⁸ So Pharaoh summoned Abram. 'What have you done to me?' he said. 'Why didn't you tell me she was your wife? ¹⁹ Why did you say, "She is my sister," so that I took her to be my wife? Now then, here is your wife. Take her and go!' ²⁰ Then Pharaoh gave orders about Abram to his men, and they sent him on his way, with his wife and everything he had.

Abram and Lot separate

13 So Abram went up from Egypt to the Negev, with his wife and everything he had, and Lot went with him. ² Abram had become very wealthy in livestock and in silver and gold.

³ From the Negev he went from place to place until he came to Bethel, to the place between Bethel and Ai where his tent had been earlier ⁴ and where he had first built an altar. There Abram called on the name of the LORD.

⁵ Now Lot, who was moving about with Abram, also had flocks and herds and tents. ⁶ But the land could not support them while they stayed together, for their possessions were so great that they were not able to stay together. ⁷ And quarrelling arose between Abram's herdsmen and Lot's. The Canaanites and Perizzites were also living in the land at that time.

⁸ So Abram said to Lot, 'Let's not have any quarrelling between you and me, or between your herdsmen and mine, for we are close relatives. ⁹ Is not the whole land before you? Let's part company. If you go to the left, I'll go to the right; if you go to the right, I'll go to the left.'

¹⁰ Lot looked around and saw that the whole plain of the Jordan towards Zoar was well watered, like the garden of the LORD, like the land of Egypt. (This was before the LORD destroyed Sodom and Gomorrah.) ¹¹ So Lot chose for himself the whole plain of the Jordan and set out towards the east. The two men parted company: ¹² Abram lived in the land of Canaan, while Lot lived among the cities of the plain and pitched his tents near Sodom. ¹³ Now the people of Sodom were wicked and were sinning greatly against the LORD.

---

b 3 Or *earth/will use your name in blessings* (see 48:20)
c 7 Or *seed*

¹⁴The LORD said to Abram after Lot had parted from him, 'Look around from where you are, to the north and south, to the east and west. ¹⁵All the land that you see I will give to you and your offspring*a* for ever. ¹⁶I will make your offspring like the dust of the earth, so that if anyone could count the dust, then your offspring could be counted. ¹⁷Go, walk through the length and breadth of the land, for I am giving it to you.'

¹⁸So Abram went to live near the great trees of Mamre at Hebron, where he pitched his tents. There he built an altar to the LORD.

Abram rescues Lot

14 At the time when Amraphel was king of Shinar,*a* Arioch king of Ellasar, Kedorlaomer king of Elam and Tidal king of Goyim, ²these kings went to war against Bera king of Sodom, Birsha king of Gomorrah, Shinab king of Admah, Shemeber king of Zeboyim, and the king of Bela (that is, Zoar). ³All these latter kings joined forces in the Valley of Siddim (that is, the Dead Sea Valley). ⁴For twelve years they had been subject to Kedorlaomer, but in the thirteenth year they rebelled.

⁵In the fourteenth year, Kedorlaomer and the kings allied with him went out and defeated the Rephaites in Ashteroth Karnaim, the Zuzites in Ham, the Emites in Shaveh Kiriathaim ⁶and the Horites in the hill country of Seir, as far as El Paran near the desert. ⁷Then they turned back and went to En Mishpat (that is, Kadesh), and they conquered the whole territory of the Amalekites, as well as the Amorites who were living in Hazezon Tamar.

⁸Then the king of Sodom, the king of Gomorrah, the king of Admah, the king of Zeboyim and the king of Bela (that is, Zoar) marched out and drew up their battle lines in the Valley of Siddim ⁹against Kedorlaomer king of Elam, Tidal king of Goyim, Amraphel king of Shinar and Arioch king of Ellasar – four kings against five. ¹⁰Now the Valley of Siddim was full of

tar pits, and when the kings of Sodom and Gomorrah fled, some of the men fell into them and the rest fled to the hills. ¹¹The four kings seized all the goods of Sodom and Gomorrah and all their food; then they went away. ¹²They also carried off Abram's nephew Lot and his possessions, since he was living in Sodom.

¹³A man who had escaped came and reported this to Abram the Hebrew. Now Abram was living near the great trees of Mamre the Amorite, a brother*b* of Eshkol and Aner, all of whom were allied with Abram. ¹⁴When Abram heard that his relative had been taken captive, he called out the 318 trained men born in his household and went in pursuit as far as Dan. ¹⁵During the night Abram divided his men to attack them and he routed them, pursuing them as far as Hobah, north of Damascus. ¹⁶He recovered all the goods and brought back his relative Lot and his possessions, together with the women and the other people.

¹⁷After Abram returned from defeating Kedorlaomer and the kings allied with him, the king of Sodom came out to meet him in the Valley of Shaveh (that is, the King's Valley). ¹⁸Then Melchizedek king of Salem brought out bread and wine. He was priest of God Most High, ¹⁹and he blessed Abram, saying,

'Blessed be Abram by God Most High,
    Creator of heaven and earth.
²⁰And praise be to God Most High,
    who delivered your enemies into
        your hand.'

Then Abram gave him a tenth of everything.

²¹The king of Sodom said to Abram, 'Give me the people and keep the goods for yourself.'

²²But Abram said to the king of Sodom, 'With raised hand I have sworn an oath to the LORD, God Most High, Creator of heaven and earth, ²³that I will accept nothing belonging to you, not even a

---

a 15 Or *seed*; also in verse 16
a 1 That is, Babylonia; also in verse 9

b 13 Or *a relative*; or *an ally*

thread or the strap of a sandal, so that you will never be able to say, "I made Abram rich." [24] I will accept nothing but what my men have eaten and the share that belongs to the men who went with me – to Aner, Eshkol and Mamre. Let them have their share.'

The LORD's covenant with Abram

15 After this, the word of the LORD came to Abram in a vision:

'Do not be afraid, Abram.
I am your shield,[a]
your very great reward.'[b]

[2] But Abram said, 'Sovereign LORD, what can you give me since I remain childless and the one who will inherit[c] my estate is Eliezer of Damascus?' [3] And Abram said, 'You have given me no children; so a servant in my household will be my heir.' [4] Then the word of the LORD came to him: 'This man will not be your heir, but a son who is your own flesh and blood will be your heir.' [5] He took him outside and said, 'Look up at the sky and count the stars – if indeed you can count them.' Then he said to him, 'So shall your offspring[d] be.'

[6] Abram believed the LORD, and he credited it to him as righteousness.

[7] He also said to him, 'I am the LORD, who brought you out of Ur of the Chaldeans to give you this land to take possession of it.'

[8] But Abram said, 'Sovereign LORD, how can I know that I shall gain possession of it?'

[9] So the LORD said to him, 'Bring me a heifer, a goat and a ram, each three years old, along with a dove and a young pigeon.'

[10] Abram brought all these to him, cut them in two and arranged the halves opposite each other; the birds, however, he did not cut in half. [11] Then birds of prey came down on the carcasses, but Abram drove them away.

[12] As the sun was setting, Abram fell into a deep sleep, and a thick and dreadful darkness came over him. [13] Then the LORD said to him, 'Know for certain that for four hundred years your descendants will be strangers in a country not their own and that they will be enslaved and ill-treated there. [14] But I will punish the nation they serve as slaves, and afterwards they will come out with great possessions. [15] You, however, will go to your ancestors in peace and be buried at a good old age. [16] In the fourth generation your descendants will come back here, for the sin of the Amorites has not yet reached its full measure.'

[17] When the sun had set and darkness had fallen, a smoking brazier with a blazing torch appeared and passed between the pieces. [18] On that day the LORD made a covenant with Abram and said, 'To your descendants I give this land, from the Wadi[e] of Egypt to the great river, the Euphrates – [19] the land of the Kenites, Kenizzites, Kadmonites, [20] Hittites, Perizzites, Rephaites, [21] Amorites, Canaanites, Girgashites and Jebusites.'

Hagar and Ishmael

16 Now Sarai, Abram's wife, had borne him no children. But she had an Egyptian slave named Hagar; [2] so she said to Abram, 'The LORD has kept me from having children. Go, sleep with my slave; perhaps I can build a family through her.'

Abram agreed to what Sarai said. [3] So after Abram had been living in Canaan ten years, Sarai his wife took her Egyptian slave Hagar and gave her to her husband to be his wife. [4] He slept with Hagar, and she conceived.

When she knew she was pregnant, she began to despise her mistress. [5] Then Sarai said to Abram, 'You are responsible for the wrong I am suffering. I put my slave in your arms, and now that she knows she is

---

a 1 Or *sovereign*
b 1 Or *shield; / your reward will be very great*
c 2 The meaning of the Hebrew for this phrase is uncertain.
d 5 Or *seed*

e 18 Or *river*

pregnant, she despises me. May the LORD judge between you and me.'

⁶'Your slave is in your hands,' Abram said. 'Do with her whatever you think best.' Then Sarai ill-treated Hagar; so she fled from her.

⁷The angel of the LORD found Hagar near a spring in the desert; it was the spring that is beside the road to Shur. ⁸And he said, 'Hagar, slave of Sarai, where have you come from, and where are you going?'

'I'm running away from my mistress Sarai,' she answered.

⁹Then the angel of the LORD told her, 'Go back to your mistress and submit to her.' ¹⁰The angel added, 'I will increase your descendants so much that they will be too numerous to count.'

¹¹The angel of the LORD also said to her:

'You are now pregnant
    and you will give birth to a son.
You shall name him Ishmael,ᵃ
    for the LORD has heard of your
        misery.
¹²He will be a wild donkey of a man;
    his hand will be against everyone
    and everyone's hand against him,
and he will live in hostility
    towardsᵇ all his brothers.'

¹³She gave this name to the LORD who spoke to her: 'You are the God who sees me,' for she said, 'I have now seenᶜ the One who sees me.' ¹⁴That is why the well was called Beer Lahai Roi;ᵈ it is still there, between Kadesh and Bered.

¹⁵So Hagar bore Abram a son, and Abram gave the name Ishmael to the son she had borne. ¹⁶Abram was eighty-six years old when Hagar bore him Ishmael.

The covenant of circumcision

17 When Abram was ninety-nine years old, the LORD appeared to

ABRAHAM

ORIGINS:
Genesis 11:26–31; 12:1–9
EGYPT:
Genesis 12:10 – 13:1
FAMILY:
Genesis 13:2–18
NAME:
Genesis 17:1–27
QUESTIONS:
Genesis 18:16–33
SON:
Genesis 18:1–15; 21:1–8
FAITH:
Genesis 22:1–19

him and said, 'I am God Almighty;ᵃ walk before me faithfully and be blameless. ²Then I will make my covenant between me and you and will greatly increase your numbers.'

³Abram fell face down, and God said to him, ⁴'As for me, this is my covenant with you: you will be the father of many nations. ⁵No longer will you be called Abram;ᵇ your name will be Abraham,ᶜ for I have made you a father of many nations. ⁶I will make you very fruitful; I will make nations of you, and kings will come from you. ⁷I will establish my covenant as an everlasting covenant between me and you and your descendants after you for the generations to come, to be your God and the God of your descendants after you. ⁸The whole land of Canaan, where you now reside as a foreigner, I will give as an everlasting possession to you and your descendants after you; and I will be their God.'

⁹Then God said to Abraham, 'As for you, you must keep my covenant, you and your

---

a 11 *Ishmael* means *God hears.*
b 12 Or *live to the east / of*
c 13 Or *seen the back of*
d 14 *Beer Lahai Roi* means *well of the Living One who sees me.*

a 1 Hebrew *El-Shaddai*
b 5 *Abram* means *exalted father.*
c 5 *Abraham* probably means *father of many.*

descendants after you for the generations to come. 10 This is my covenant with you and your descendants after you, the covenant you are to keep: every male among you shall be circumcised. 11 You are to undergo circumcision, and it will be the sign of the covenant between me and you. 12 For the generations to come every male among you who is eight days old must be circumcised, including those born in your household or bought with money from a foreigner – those who are not your offspring. 13 Whether born in your household or bought with your money, they must be circumcised. My covenant in your flesh is to be an everlasting covenant. 14 Any uncircumcised male, who has not been circumcised in the flesh, will be cut off from his people; he has broken my covenant.'

15 God also said to Abraham, 'As for Sarai your wife, you are no longer to call her Sarai; her name will be Sarah. 16 I will bless her and will surely give you a son by her. I will bless her so that she will be the mother of nations; kings of peoples will come from her.'

17 Abraham fell face down; he laughed and said to himself, 'Will a son be born to a man a hundred years old? Will Sarah bear a child at the age of ninety?' 18 And Abraham said to God, 'If only Ishmael might live under your blessing!'

19 Then God said, 'Yes, but your wife Sarah will bear you a son, and you will call him Isaac.d I will establish my covenant with him as an everlasting covenant for his descendants after him. 20 And as for Ishmael, I have heard you: I will surely bless him; I will make him fruitful and will greatly increase his numbers. He will be the father of twelve rulers, and I will make him into a great nation. 21 But my covenant I will establish with Isaac, whom Sarah will bear to you by this time next year.' 22 When he had finished speaking with Abraham, God went up from him.

23 On that very day Abraham took his son Ishmael and all those born in his household or bought with his money, every male in his household, and circumcised them, as God told him. 24 Abraham was ninety-nine years old when he was circumcised, 25 and his son Ishmael was thirteen; 26 Abraham and his son Ishmael were both circumcised on that very day. 27 And every male in Abraham's household, including those born in his household or bought from a foreigner, was circumcised with him.

The three visitors

18 The LORD appeared to Abraham near the great trees of Mamre while he was sitting at the entrance to his tent in the heat of the day. 2 Abraham looked up and saw three men standing nearby. When he saw them, he hurried from the entrance of his tent to meet them and bowed low to the ground.

3 He said, 'If I have found favour in your eyes, my lord,a do not pass your servant by. 4 Let a little water be brought, and then you may all wash your feet and rest under this tree. 5 Let me get you something to eat, so you can be refreshed and then go on your way – now that you have come to your servant.'

'Very well,' they answered, 'do as you say.'

6 So Abraham hurried into the tent to Sarah. 'Quick,' he said, 'get three seahsb of the finest flour and knead it and bake some bread.'

7 Then he ran to the herd and selected a choice, tender calf and gave it to a servant, who hurried to prepare it. 8 He then brought some curds and milk and the calf that had been prepared, and set these before them. While they ate, he stood near them under a tree.

9 'Where is your wife Sarah?' they asked him.

'There, in the tent,' he said.

10 Then one of them said, 'I will surely return to you about this time next year, and Sarah your wife will have a son.'

Now Sarah was listening at the entrance to the tent, which was behind him. 11 Abraham and Sarah were already very

---

d 19 Isaac means he laughs.

a 3 Or eyes, Lord
b 6 That is, probably about 16 kilograms

old, and Sarah was past the age of child-bearing. ¹²So Sarah laughed to herself as she thought, 'After I am worn out and my lord is old, will I now have this pleasure?'

¹³Then the LORD said to Abraham, 'Why did Sarah laugh and say, "Will I really have a child, now that I am old?" ¹⁴Is anything too hard for the LORD? I will return to you at the appointed time next year, and Sarah will have a son.'

¹⁵Sarah was afraid, so she lied and said, 'I did not laugh.'

But he said, 'Yes, you did laugh.'

Abraham pleads for Sodom

¹⁶When the men got up to leave, they looked down towards Sodom, and Abraham walked along with them to see them on their way. ¹⁷Then the LORD said, 'Shall I hide from Abraham what I am about to do? ¹⁸Abraham will surely become a great and powerful nation, and all nations on earth will be blessed through him.ᶜ ¹⁹For I have chosen him, so that he will direct his children and his household after him to keep the way of the LORD by doing what is right and just, so that the LORD will bring about for Abraham what he has promised him.'

²⁰Then the LORD said, 'The outcry against Sodom and Gomorrah is so great and their sin so grievous ²¹that I will go down and see if what they have done is as bad as the outcry that has reached me. If not, I will know.'

²²The men turned away and went towards Sodom, but Abraham remained standing before the LORD.ᵈ ²³Then Abraham approached him and said: 'Will you sweep away the righteous with the wicked? ²⁴What if there are fifty righteous people in the city? Will you really sweep it away and not spareᵉ the place for the sake of the fifty righteous people in it? ²⁵Far be it from you to do such a thing – to kill the righteous with the wicked, treating the righteous and the wicked alike. Far be

it from you! Will not the Judge of all the earth do right?'

²⁶The LORD said, 'If I find fifty righteous people in the city of Sodom, I will spare the whole place for their sake.'

²⁷Then Abraham spoke up again: 'Now that I have been so bold as to speak to the Lord, though I am nothing but dust and ashes, ²⁸what if the number of the righteous is five less than fifty? Will you destroy the whole city for lack of five people?'

'If I find forty-five there,' he said, 'I will not destroy it.'

²⁹Once again he spoke to him, 'What if only forty are found there?'

He said, 'For the sake of forty, I will not do it.'

³⁰Then he said, 'May the Lord not be angry, but let me speak. What if only thirty can be found there?'

He answered, 'I will not do it if I find thirty there.'

³¹Abraham said, 'Now that I have been so bold as to speak to the Lord, what if only twenty can be found there?'

He said, 'For the sake of twenty, I will not destroy it.'

³²Then he said, 'May the Lord not be angry, but let me speak just once more. What if only ten can be found there?'

He answered, 'For the sake of ten, I will not destroy it.'

³³When the LORD had finished speaking with Abraham, he left, and Abraham returned home.

Sodom and Gomorrah destroyed

19 The two angels arrived at Sodom in the evening, and Lot was sitting in the gateway of the city. When he saw them, he got up to meet them and bowed down with his face to the ground. ²'My lords,' he said, 'please turn aside to your servant's house. You can wash your feet and spend the night and then go on your way early in the morning.'

'No,' they answered, 'we will spend the night in the square.'

³But he insisted so strongly that they did go with him and entered his house. He prepared a meal for them, baking bread

---

ᶜ 18 Or *will use his name in blessings* (see 48:20)
ᵈ 22 Masoretic Text; an ancient Hebrew scribal tradition *but the LORD remained standing before Abraham*
ᵉ 24 Or *forgive*; also in verse 26

without yeast, and they ate. 4Before they had gone to bed, all the men from every part of the city of Sodom – both young and old – surrounded the house. 5They called to Lot, 'Where are the men who came to you tonight? Bring them out to us so that we can have sex with them.'

6Lot went outside to meet them and shut the door behind him 7and said, 'No, my friends. Don't do this wicked thing. 8Look, I have two daughters who have never slept with a man. Let me bring them out to you, and you can do what you like with them. But don't do anything to these men, for they have come under the protection of my roof.'

9'Get out of our way,' they replied. 'This fellow came here as a foreigner, and now he wants to play the judge! We'll treat you worse than them.' They kept bringing pressure on Lot and moved forward to break down the door.

10But the men inside reached out and pulled Lot back into the house and shut the door. 11Then they struck the men who were at the door of the house, young and old, with blindness so that they could not find the door.

12The two men said to Lot, 'Do you have anyone else here – sons-in-law, sons or daughters, or anyone else in the city who belongs to you? Get them out of here, 13because we are going to destroy this place. The outcry to the LORD against its people is so great that he has sent us to destroy it.'

14So Lot went out and spoke to his sons-in-law, who were pledged to marry[a] his daughters. He said, 'Hurry and get out of this place, because the LORD is about to destroy the city!' But his sons-in-law thought he was joking.

15With the coming of dawn, the angels urged Lot, saying, 'Hurry! Take your wife and your two daughters who are here, or you will be swept away when the city is punished.'

16When he hesitated, the men grasped his hand and the hands of his wife and of his two daughters and led them safely out of the city, for the LORD was merciful to them. 17As soon as they had brought them out, one of them said, 'Flee for your lives! Don't look back, and don't stop anywhere in the plain! Flee to the mountains or you will be swept away!'

18But Lot said to them, 'No, my lords,[b] please! 19Your[c] servant has found favour in your[c] eyes, and you[c] have shown great kindness to me in sparing my life. But I can't flee to the mountains; this disaster will overtake me, and I'll die. 20Look, here is a town near enough to run to, and it is small. Let me flee to it – it is very small, isn't it? Then my life will be spared.'

21He said to him, 'Very well, I will grant this request too; I will not overthrow the town you speak of. 22But flee there quickly, because I cannot do anything until you reach it.' (That is why the town was called Zoar.[d])

23By the time Lot reached Zoar, the sun had risen over the land. 24Then the LORD rained down burning sulphur on Sodom and Gomorrah – from the LORD out of the heavens. 25Thus he overthrew those cities and the entire plain, destroying all those living in the cities – and also the vegetation in the land. 26But Lot's wife looked back, and she became a pillar of salt.

27Early the next morning Abraham got up and returned to the place where he had stood before the LORD. 28He looked down towards Sodom and Gomorrah, towards all the land of the plain, and he saw dense smoke rising from the land, like smoke from a furnace.

29So when God destroyed the cities of the plain, he remembered Abraham, and he brought Lot out of the catastrophe that overthrew the cities where Lot had lived.

Lot and his daughters

30Lot and his two daughters left Zoar and settled in the mountains, for he was afraid to stay in Zoar. He and his two daughters lived in a cave. 31One day the elder daughter said to the younger, 'Our

---

a 14 Or were married to

b 18 Or No, Lord; or No, my lord
c 19 The Hebrew is singular.
d 22 Zoar means small.

father is old, and there is no man round here to give us children – as is the custom all over the earth. ³²Let's get our father to drink wine and then sleep with him and preserve our family line through our father.'

³³That night they got their father to drink wine, and the elder daughter went in and slept with him. He was not aware of it when she lay down or when she got up.

³⁴The next day the elder daughter said to the younger, 'Last night I slept with my father. Let's get him to drink wine again tonight, and you go in and sleep with him so we can preserve our family line through our father.' ³⁵So they got their father to drink wine that night also, and the younger daughter went in and slept with him. Again he was not aware of it when she lay down or when she got up.

³⁶So both of Lot's daughters became pregnant by their father. ³⁷The elder daughter had a son, and she named him Moab;ᵉ he is the father of the Moabites of today. ³⁸The younger daughter also had a son, and she named him Ben-Ammi;ᶠ he is the father of the Ammonitesᵍ of today.

Abraham and Abimelek

20 Now Abraham moved on from there into the region of the Negev and lived between Kadesh and Shur. For a while he stayed in Gerar, ²and there Abraham said of his wife Sarah, 'She is my sister.' Then Abimelek king of Gerar sent for Sarah and took her.

³But God came to Abimelek in a dream one night and said to him, 'You are as good as dead because of the woman you have taken; she is a married woman.'

⁴Now Abimelek had not gone near her, so he said, 'Lord, will you destroy an innocent nation? ⁵Did he not say to me, "She is my sister," and didn't she also say, "He is my brother"? I have done this with a clear conscience and clean hands.'

⁶Then God said to him in the dream, 'Yes, I know you did this with a clear

conscience, and so I have kept you from sinning against me. That is why I did not let you touch her. ⁷Now return the man's wife, for he is a prophet, and he will pray for you and you will live. But if you do not return her, you may be sure that you and all who belong to you will die.'

⁸Early the next morning Abimelek summoned all his officials, and when he told them all that had happened, they were very much afraid. ⁹Then Abimelek called Abraham in and said, 'What have you done to us? How have I wronged you that you have brought such great guilt upon me and my kingdom? You have done things to me that should never be done.' ¹⁰And Abimelek asked Abraham, 'What was your reason for doing this?'

¹¹Abraham replied, 'I said to myself, "There is surely no fear of God in this place, and they will kill me because of my wife." ¹²Besides, she really is my sister, the daughter of my father though not of my mother; and she became my wife. ¹³And when God caused me to wander from my father's household, I said to her, "This is how you can show your love to me: everywhere we go, say of me, 'He is my brother.'"'

¹⁴Then Abimelek brought sheep and cattle and male and female slaves and gave them to Abraham, and he returned Sarah his wife to him. ¹⁵And Abimelek said, 'My land is before you; live wherever you like.'

¹⁶To Sarah he said, 'I am giving your brother a thousand shekelsᵃ of silver. This is to cover the offence against you before all who are with you; you are completely vindicated.'

¹⁷Then Abraham prayed to God, and God healed Abimelek, his wife and his female slaves so they could have children again, ¹⁸for the LORD had kept all the women in Abimelek's household from conceiving because of Abraham's wife Sarah.

The birth of Isaac

21 Now the LORD was gracious to Sarah as he had said, and the LORD did for Sarah what he had promised. ²Sarah became pregnant and bore a son to

---

ᵉ 37 *Moab* sounds like the Hebrew for *from father.*
ᶠ 38 *Ben-Ammi* means *son of my father's people.*
ᵍ 38 Hebrew *Bene-Ammon*

ᵃ 16 That is, about 12 kilograms

Abraham in his old age, at the very time God had promised him. ³Abraham gave the name Isaac*a* to the son Sarah bore him. ⁴When his son Isaac was eight days old, Abraham circumcised him, as God commanded him. ⁵Abraham was a hundred years old when his son Isaac was born to him.

⁶Sarah said, 'God has brought me laughter, and everyone who hears about this will laugh with me.' ⁷And she added, 'Who would have said to Abraham that Sarah would nurse children? Yet I have borne him a son in his old age.'

Hagar and Ishmael sent away

⁸The child grew and was weaned, and on the day Isaac was weaned Abraham held a great feast. ⁹But Sarah saw that the son whom Hagar the Egyptian had borne to Abraham was mocking, ¹⁰and she said to Abraham, 'Get rid of that slave woman and her son, for that woman's son will never share in the inheritance with my son Isaac.'

¹¹The matter distressed Abraham greatly because it concerned his son. ¹²But God said to him, 'Do not be so distressed about the boy and your slave woman. Listen to whatever Sarah tells you, because it is through Isaac that your offspring*b* will be reckoned. ¹³I will make the son of the slave into a nation also, because he is your offspring.'

¹⁴Early the next morning Abraham took some food and a skin of water and gave them to Hagar. He set them on her shoulders and then sent her off with the boy. She went on her way and wandered in the Desert of Beersheba.

¹⁵When the water in the skin was gone, she put the boy under one of the bushes. ¹⁶Then she went off and sat down about a bow-shot away, for she thought, 'I cannot watch the boy die.' And as she sat there, she*c* began to sob.

¹⁷God heard the boy crying, and the angel of God called to Hagar from heaven and said to her, 'What is the matter, Hagar? Do not be afraid; God has heard the boy crying as he lies there. ¹⁸Lift the boy up and take him by the hand, for I will make him into a great nation.'

¹⁹Then God opened her eyes and she saw a well of water. So she went and filled the skin with water and gave the boy a drink.

²⁰God was with the boy as he grew up. He lived in the desert and became an archer. ²¹While he was living in the Desert of Paran, his mother got a wife for him from Egypt.

The treaty at Beersheba

²²At that time Abimelek and Phicol the commander of his forces said to Abraham, 'God is with you in everything you do. ²³Now swear to me here before God that you will not deal falsely with me or my children or my descendants. Show to me and the country where you now reside as a foreigner the same kindness that I have shown to you.'

²⁴Abraham said, 'I swear it.'

²⁵Then Abraham complained to Abimelek about a well of water that Abimelek's servants had seized. ²⁶But Abimelek said, 'I don't know who has done this. You did not tell me, and I heard about it only today.'

²⁷So Abraham brought sheep and cattle and gave them to Abimelek, and the two men made a treaty. ²⁸Abraham set apart seven ewe lambs from the flock, ²⁹and Abimelek asked Abraham, 'What is the meaning of these seven ewe lambs you have set apart by themselves?'

³⁰He replied, 'Accept these seven lambs from my hand as a witness that I dug this well.'

³¹So that place was called Beersheba,*d* because the two men swore an oath there.

³²After the treaty had been made at Beersheba, Abimelek and Phicol the commander of his forces returned to the land of the Philistines. ³³Abraham planted a

---

a 3   *Isaac* means *he laughs.*
b 12   Or *seed*

c 16   Hebrew; Septuagint *the child*
d 31   *Beersheba* can mean *well of seven* or *well of the oath.*

tamarisk tree in Beersheba, and there he called on the name of the LORD, the Eternal God. ³⁴And Abraham stayed in the land of the Philistines for a long time.

Abraham tested

22 Some time later God tested Abraham. He said to him, 'Abraham!'
'Here I am,' he replied.
²Then God said, 'Take your son, your only son, whom you love – Isaac – and go to the region of Moriah. Sacrifice him there as a burnt offering on a mountain that I will show you.'
³Early the next morning Abraham got up and loaded his donkey. He took with him two of his servants and his son Isaac. When he had cut enough wood for the burnt offering, he set out for the place God had told him about. ⁴On the third day Abraham looked up and saw the place in the distance. ⁵He said to his servants, 'Stay here with the donkey while I and the boy go over there. We will worship and then we will come back to you.'
⁶Abraham took the wood for the burnt offering and placed it on his son Isaac, and he himself carried the fire and the knife. As the two of them went on together, ⁷Isaac spoke up and said to his father Abraham, 'Father?'
'Yes, my son?' Abraham replied.
'The fire and wood are here,' Isaac said, 'but where is the lamb for the burnt offering?'
⁸Abraham answered, 'God himself will provide the lamb for the burnt offering, my son.' And the two of them went on together.
⁹When they reached the place God had told him about, Abraham built an altar there and arranged the wood on it. He bound his son Isaac and laid him on the altar, on top of the wood. ¹⁰Then he reached out his hand and took the knife to slay his son. ¹¹But the angel of the LORD called out to him from heaven, 'Abraham! Abraham!'
'Here I am,' he replied.
¹²'Do not lay a hand on the boy,' he said. 'Do not do anything to him. Now I know that you fear God, because you have

not withheld from me your son, your only son.'
¹³Abraham looked up and there in a thicket he saw a ramⁿ caught by its horns. He went over and took the ram and sacrificed it as a burnt offering instead of his son. ¹⁴So Abraham called that place The LORD Will Provide. And to this day it is said, 'On the mountain of the LORD it will be provided.'
¹⁵The angel of the LORD called to Abraham from heaven a second time ¹⁶and said, 'I swear by myself, declares the LORD, that because you have done this and have not withheld your son, your only son, ¹⁷I will surely bless you and make your descendants as numerous as the stars in the sky and as the sand on the seashore. Your descendants will take possession of the cities of their enemies, ¹⁸and through your offspringᵇ all nations on earth will be blessed,ᶜ because you have obeyed me.'
¹⁹Then Abraham returned to his servants, and they set off together for Beersheba. And Abraham stayed in Beersheba.

Nahor's sons

²⁰Some time later Abraham was told, 'Milkah is also a mother; she has borne sons to your brother Nahor: ²¹Uz the firstborn, Buz his brother, Kemuel (the father of Aram), ²²Kesed, Hazo, Pildash, Jidlaph and Bethuel.' ²³Bethuel became the father of Rebekah. Milkah bore these eight sons to Abraham's brother Nahor. ²⁴His concubine, whose name was Reumah, also had sons: Tebah, Gaham, Tahash and Maakah.

The death of Sarah

23 Sarah lived to be a hundred and twenty-seven years old. ²She died at Kiriath Arba (that is, Hebron) in the land of Canaan, and Abraham went to mourn for Sarah and to weep over her.

ᵃ 13 Many manuscripts of the Masoretic Text, Samaritan Pentateuch, Septuagint and Syriac; most manuscripts of the Masoretic Text *a ram behind him*
ᵇ 18 Or *seed*
ᶜ 18 Or *and all nations on earth will use the name of your offspring in blessings* (see 48:20)

SACRIFICE 2

The cost of sin

In Genesis 22 God is testing his servant by asking him to take his most precious thing and offer it to God. There was a famous Christian philosopher who suggested that this is the craziest passage in the Bible and in order to even fathom it you have to take a leap of faith. God asked Abraham to sacrifice his son. Now this wasn't just any son – this was his promised son and heir. Isaac was the only hope of Abraham becoming a great nation. This sacrifice was the apparent undoing of *everything* God had done and promised in Abraham's life. Isaac represented Abraham's entire future.

This passage is sometimes hard for us to understand, as today we live under the perfect sacrifice of Jesus, who died once for all of us. We can come to him, say we're sorry and know that we're forgiven. The problem is that sometimes we can get complacent and allow ourselves to think that sin can just be magically wiped out, so that it doesn't really matter what we do. However, we need to be obedient to God both when we understand his reasons and when we don't. Even though we might not understand why God asks something of us, we can't say to him, 'I'll obey you in one area, because I understand how that fits together with your plans – but I won't obey you in this other part of my life, because I don't understand how that fits in.' What if Abraham had said that? The truth is that even now, our disobedience has consequences and somebody pays. Jesus has paid. God may forgive us completely, but we still have to live with the consequences of the decisions we make that go against God's will for us. This passage is about being obedient to God and offering up ourselves and the things we love to worship him, trusting in his greater plan.

Abraham agrees to give up his only son because he understands something central to true sacrifice: nothing really belongs to us. Everything belongs to God. He gives and he takes away. Right at the climax of the story, something happens: another sacrifice miraculously appears so that Abraham can make a sacrifice and Isaac doesn't have to die. God made a way where there was no way. This story is a foreshadowing of an even greater story, the story of the cross. You and I are the son: God spared us by miraculously providing a different sacrifice through Jesus. You and I are also Abraham: invited by God to understand that everything belongs to God. We can trust him with everything, even our future.

Danielle Strickland

 Genesis 3:21

Exodus 12:27

³Then Abraham rose from beside his dead wife and spoke to the Hittites.ᵃ He said, ⁴'I am a foreigner and stranger among you. Sell me some property for a burial site here so that I can bury my dead.'

⁵The Hittites replied to Abraham, ⁶'Sir, listen to us. You are a mighty prince among us. Bury your dead in the choicest of our tombs. None of us will refuse you his tomb for burying your dead.'

⁷Then Abraham rose and bowed down before the people of the land, the Hittites. ⁸He said to them, 'If you are willing to let me bury my dead, then listen to me and intercede with Ephron son of Zohar on my behalf ⁹so that he will sell me the cave of Machpelah, which belongs to him and is at the end of his field. Ask him to sell it to me for the full price as a burial site among you.'

¹⁰Ephron the Hittite was sitting among his people and he replied to Abraham in the hearing of all the Hittites who had come to the gate of his city. ¹¹'No, my lord,' he said. 'Listen to me; I giveᵇ you the field, and I giveᵇ you the cave that is in it. I giveᵇ it to you in the presence of my people. Bury your dead.'

¹²Again Abraham bowed down before the people of the land ¹³and he said to Ephron in their hearing, 'Listen to me, if you will. I will pay the price of the field. Accept it from me so that I can bury my dead there.'

¹⁴Ephron answered Abraham, ¹⁵'Listen to me, my lord; the land is worth four hundred shekelsᶜ of silver, but what is that between you and me? Bury your dead.'

¹⁶Abraham agreed to Ephron's terms and weighed out for him the price he had named in the hearing of the Hittites: four hundred shekels of silver, according to the weight current among the merchants.

¹⁷So Ephron's field in Machpelah near Mamre – both the field and the cave in it, and all the trees within the borders of the field – was legally made over ¹⁸to Abraham as his property in the presence of all the Hittites who had come to the gate of the city. ¹⁹Afterwards Abraham buried his wife Sarah in the cave in the field of Machpelah near Mamre (which is at Hebron) in the land of Canaan. ²⁰So the field and the cave in it were legally made over to Abraham by the Hittites as a burial site.

Isaac and Rebekah

24 Abraham was now very old, and the LORD had blessed him in every way. ²He said to the senior servant in his household, the one in charge of all that he had, 'Put your hand under my thigh. ³I want you to swear by the LORD, the God of heaven and the God of earth, that you will not get a wife for my son from the daughters of the Canaanites, among whom I am living, ⁴but will go to my country and my own relatives and get a wife for my son Isaac.'

⁵The servant asked him, 'What if the woman is unwilling to come back with me to this land? Shall I then take your son back to the country you came from?'

⁶'Make sure that you do not take my son back there,' Abraham said. ⁷'The LORD, the God of heaven, who brought me out of my father's household and my native land and who spoke to me and promised me on oath, saying, "To your offspringᵃ I will give this land" – he will send his angel before you so that you can get a wife for my son from there. ⁸If the woman is unwilling to come back with you, then you will be released from this oath of mine. Only do not take my son back there.' ⁹So the servant put his hand under the thigh of his master Abraham and swore an oath to him concerning this matter.

¹⁰Then the servant left, taking with him ten of his master's camels loaded with all kinds of good things from his master. He set out for Aram Naharaimᵇ and made his way to the town of Nahor. ¹¹He made the camels kneel down near the well outside the town; it was towards evening, the time the women go out to draw water.

ᵃ 3 Or *the descendants of Heth*; also in verses 5, 7, 10, 16, 18 and 20
ᵇ 11 Or *sell*
ᶜ 15 That is, about 4.6 kilograms

ᵃ 7 Or *seed*
ᵇ 10 That is, North-west Mesopotamia

¹²Then he prayed, 'LORD, God of my master Abraham, make me successful today, and show kindness to my master Abraham. ¹³See, I am standing beside this spring, and the daughters of the townspeople are coming out to draw water. ¹⁴May it be that when I say to a young woman, "Please let down your jar that I may have a drink," and she says, "Drink, and I'll water your camels too" – let her be the one you have chosen for your servant Isaac. By this I will know that you have shown kindness to my master.'

¹⁵Before he had finished praying, Rebekah came out with her jar on her shoulder. She was the daughter of Bethuel son of Milkah, who was the wife of Abraham's brother Nahor. ¹⁶The woman was very beautiful, a virgin; no man had ever slept with her. She went down to the spring, filled her jar and came up again.

¹⁷The servant hurried to meet her and said, 'Please give me a little water from your jar.'

¹⁸'Drink, my lord,' she said, and quickly lowered the jar to her hands and gave him a drink.

¹⁹After she had given him a drink, she said, 'I'll draw water for your camels too, until they have had enough to drink.' ²⁰So she quickly emptied her jar into the trough, ran back to the well to draw more water, and drew enough for all his camels. ²¹Without saying a word, the man watched her closely to learn whether or not the LORD had made his journey successful.

²²When the camels had finished drinking, the man took out a gold nose ring weighing a beka*ᶜ* and two gold bracelets weighing ten shekels.*ᵈ* ²³Then he asked, 'Whose daughter are you? Please tell me, is there room in your father's house for us to spend the night?'

²⁴She answered him, 'I am the daughter of Bethuel, the son that Milkah bore to Nahor.' ²⁵And she added, 'We have plenty of straw and fodder, as well as room for you to spend the night.'

²⁶Then the man bowed down and worshipped the LORD, ²⁷saying, 'Praise be to the LORD, the God of my master Abraham, who has not abandoned his kindness and faithfulness to my master. As for me, the LORD has led me on the journey to the house of my master's relatives.'

²⁸The young woman ran and told her mother's household about these things. ²⁹Now Rebekah had a brother named Laban, and he hurried out to the man at the spring. ³⁰As soon as he had seen the nose ring, and the bracelets on his sister's arms, and had heard Rebekah tell what the man said to her, he went out to the man and found him standing by the camels near the spring. ³¹'Come, you who are blessed by the LORD,' he said. 'Why are you standing out here? I have prepared the house and a place for the camels.'

³²So the man went to the house, and the camels were unloaded. Straw and fodder were brought for the camels, and water for him and his men to wash their feet. ³³Then food was set before him, but he said, 'I will not eat until I have told you what I have to say.'

'Then tell us,' Laban said.

³⁴So he said, 'I am Abraham's servant. ³⁵The LORD has blessed my master abundantly, and he has become wealthy. He has given him sheep and cattle, silver and gold, male and female servants, and camels and donkeys. ³⁶My master's wife Sarah has borne him a son in her old age, and he has given him everything he owns. ³⁷And my master made me swear an oath, and said, "You must not get a wife for my son from the daughters of the Canaanites, in whose land I live, ³⁸but go to my father's family and to my own clan, and get a wife for my son."

³⁹'Then I asked my master, "What if the woman will not come back with me?"

⁴⁰'He replied, "The LORD, before whom I have walked faithfully, will send his angel with you and make your journey a success, so that you can get a wife for my son from my own clan and from my father's family. ⁴¹You will be released from my oath if, when you go to my clan, they refuse to give her to you – then you will be released from my oath.'

---

c 22 That is, about 5.7 grams
d 22 That is, about 115 grams

42 'When I came to the spring today, I said, "LORD, God of my master Abraham, if you will, please grant success to the journey on which I have come. 43 See, I am standing beside this spring. If a young woman comes out to draw water and I say to her, 'Please let me drink a little water from your jar,' 44 and if she says to me, 'Drink, and I'll draw water for your camels too,' let her be the one the LORD has chosen for my master's son."

45 'Before I finished praying in my heart, Rebekah came out, with her jar on her shoulder. She went down to the spring and drew water, and I said to her, "Please give me a drink."

46 'She quickly lowered her jar from her shoulder and said, "Drink, and I'll water your camels too." So I drank, and she watered the camels also.

47 'I asked her, "Whose daughter are you?"

'She said, "The daughter of Bethuel son of Nahor, whom Milkah bore to him."

'Then I put the ring in her nose and the bracelets on her arms, 48 and I bowed down and worshipped the LORD. I praised the LORD, the God of my master Abraham, who had led me on the right road to get the granddaughter of my master's brother for his son. 49 Now if you will show kindness and faithfulness to my master, tell me; and if not, tell me, so I may know which way to turn.'

50 Laban and Bethuel answered, 'This is from the LORD; we can say nothing to you one way or the other. 51 Here is Rebekah; take her and go, and let her become the wife of your master's son, as the LORD has directed.'

52 When Abraham's servant heard what they said, he bowed down to the ground before the LORD. 53 Then the servant brought out gold and silver jewellery and articles of clothing and gave them to Rebekah; he also gave costly gifts to her brother and to her mother. 54 Then he and the men who were with him ate and drank and spent the night there.

When they got up the next morning, he said, 'Send me on my way to my master.'

55 But her brother and her mother replied, 'Let the young woman remain with us ten days or so; then you[e] may go.'

56 But he said to them, 'Do not detain me, now that the LORD has granted success to my journey. Send me on my way so I may go to my master.'

57 Then they said, 'Let's call the young woman and ask her about it.' 58 So they called Rebekah and asked her, 'Will you go with this man?'

'I will go,' she said.

59 So they sent their sister Rebekah on her way, along with her nurse and Abraham's servant and his men. 60 And they blessed Rebekah and said to her,

'Our sister, may you increase
    to thousands upon thousands;
may your offspring possess
    the cities of their enemies.'

61 Then Rebekah and her attendants got ready and mounted the camels and went back with the man. So the servant took Rebekah and left.

62 Now Isaac had come from Beer Lahai Roi, for he was living in the Negev. 63 He went out to the field one evening to meditate,[f] and as he looked up, he saw camels approaching. 64 Rebekah also looked up and saw Isaac. She got down from her camel 65 and asked the servant, 'Who is that man in the field coming to meet us?'

'He is my master,' the servant answered. So she took her veil and covered herself.

66 Then the servant told Isaac all he had done. 67 Isaac brought her into the tent of his mother Sarah, and he married Rebekah. So she became his wife, and he loved her; and Isaac was comforted after his mother's death.

The death of Abraham

25 Abraham had taken another wife, whose name was Keturah. 2 She bore him Zimran, Jokshan, Medan, Midian, Ishbak and Shuah. 3 Jokshan was the father of Sheba and Dedan; the

---

e 55 Or *she*
f 63 The meaning of the Hebrew for this word is uncertain.

descendants of Dedan were the Ashurites, the Letushites and the Leummites. ⁴The sons of Midian were Ephah, Epher, Hanok, Abida and Eldaah. All these were descendants of Keturah.

⁵Abraham left everything he owned to Isaac. ⁶But while he was still living, he gave gifts to the sons of his concubines and sent them away from his son Isaac to the land of the east.

⁷Abraham lived a hundred and seventy-five years. ⁸Then Abraham breathed his last and died at a good old age, an old man and full of years; and he was gathered to his people. ⁹His sons Isaac and Ishmael buried him in the cave of Machpelah near Mamre, in the field of Ephron son of Zohar the Hittite, ¹⁰the field Abraham had bought from the Hittites.^a There Abraham was buried with his wife Sarah. ¹¹After Abraham's death, God blessed his son Isaac, who then lived near Beer Lahai Roi.

Ishmael's sons

¹²This is the account of the family line of Abraham's son Ishmael, whom Sarah's slave, Hagar the Egyptian, bore to Abraham.

¹³These are the names of the sons of Ishmael, listed in the order of their birth: Nebaioth the firstborn of Ishmael, Kedar, Adbeel, Mibsam, ¹⁴Mishma, Dumah, Massa, ¹⁵Hadad, Tema, Jetur, Naphish and Kedemah. ¹⁶These were the sons of Ishmael, and these are the names of the twelve tribal rulers according to their settlements and camps. ¹⁷Ishmael lived a hundred and thirty-seven years. He breathed his last and died, and he was gathered to his people. ¹⁸His descendants settled in the area from Havilah to Shur, near the eastern border of Egypt, as you go towards Ashur. And they lived in hostility towards^b all the tribes related to them.

Jacob and Esau

¹⁹This is the account of the family line of Abraham's son Isaac.

Abraham became the father of Isaac, ²⁰and Isaac was forty years old when he married Rebekah daughter of Bethuel the Aramean from Paddan Aram^c and sister of Laban the Aramean.

JACOB

BIRTH:
Genesis 25:19–26
BIRTHRIGHT:
Genesis 25:27–34
BLESSING:
Genesis 27:1–45
LADDER:
Genesis 28:10–22
WRESTLING:
Genesis 32:22–32

²¹Isaac prayed to the LORD on behalf of his wife, because she was childless. The LORD answered his prayer, and his wife Rebekah became pregnant. ²²The babies jostled each other within her, and she said, 'Why is this happening to me?' So she went to enquire of the LORD.

²³The LORD said to her,

'Two nations are in your womb,
   and two peoples from within you
     will be separated;
one people will be stronger than the
     other,
   and the elder will serve the younger.'

²⁴When the time came for her to give birth, there were twin boys in her womb. ²⁵The first to come out was red, and his whole body was like a hairy garment; so they named him Esau.^d ²⁶After this, his brother came out, with his hand grasping Esau's heel; so he was named Jacob.^e Isaac

---

a 10 Or *the descendants of Heth*
b 18 Or *lived to the east of*

c 20 That is, North-west Mesopotamia
d 25 *Esau* may mean *hairy.*
e 26 *Jacob* means *he grasps the heel*, a Hebrew idiom for *he deceives.*

was sixty years old when Rebekah gave birth to them.

²⁷ The boys grew up, and Esau became a skilful hunter, a man of the open country, while Jacob was content to stay at home among the tents. ²⁸ Isaac, who had a taste for wild game, loved Esau, but Rebekah loved Jacob.

²⁹ Once when Jacob was cooking some stew, Esau came in from the open country, famished. ³⁰ He said to Jacob, 'Quick, let me have some of that red stew! I'm famished!' (That is why he was also called Edom.*f*)

³¹ Jacob replied, 'First sell me your birthright.'

³² 'Look, I am about to die,' Esau said. 'What good is the birthright to me?'

³³ But Jacob said, 'Swear to me first.' So he swore an oath to him, selling his birthright to Jacob.

³⁴ Then Jacob gave Esau some bread and some lentil stew. He ate and drank, and then got up and left.

So Esau despised his birthright.

Isaac and Abimelek

26 Now there was a famine in the land – besides the previous famine in Abraham's time – and Isaac went to Abimelek king of the Philistines in Gerar. ² The Lᴏʀᴅ appeared to Isaac and said, 'Do not go down to Egypt; live in the land where I tell you to live. ³ Stay in this land for a while, and I will be with you and will bless you. For to you and your descendants I will give all these lands and will confirm the oath I swore to your father Abraham. ⁴ I will make your descendants as numerous as the stars in the sky and will give them all these lands, and through your offspring*a* all nations on earth will be blessed,*b* ⁵ because Abraham obeyed me and did everything I required of him, keeping my commands, my decrees and my instructions.' ⁶ So Isaac stayed in Gerar.

⁷ When the men of that place asked him about his wife, he said, 'She is my sister,' because he was afraid to say, 'She is my wife.' He thought, 'The men of this place might kill me on account of Rebekah, because she is beautiful.'

⁸ When Isaac had been there a long time, Abimelek king of the Philistines looked down from a window and saw Isaac caressing his wife Rebekah. ⁹ So Abimelek summoned Isaac and said, 'She is really your wife! Why did you say, "She is my sister"?'

Isaac answered him, 'Because I thought I might lose my life on account of her.'

¹⁰ Then Abimelek said, 'What is this you have done to us? One of the men might well have slept with your wife, and you would have brought guilt upon us.'

¹¹ So Abimelek gave orders to all the people: 'Anyone who harms this man or his wife shall surely be put to death.'

¹² Isaac planted crops in that land and the same year reaped a hundredfold, because the Lᴏʀᴅ blessed him. ¹³ The man became rich, and his wealth continued to grow until he became very wealthy. ¹⁴ He had so many flocks and herds and servants that the Philistines envied him. ¹⁵ So all the wells that his father's servants had dug in the time of his father Abraham, the Philistines stopped up, filling them with earth.

¹⁶ Then Abimelek said to Isaac, 'Move away from us; you have become too powerful for us.'

¹⁷ So Isaac moved away from there and camped in the Valley of Gerar, where he settled. ¹⁸ Isaac reopened the wells that had been dug in the time of his father Abraham, which the Philistines had stopped up after Abraham died, and he gave them the same names his father had given them.

¹⁹ Isaac's servants dug in the valley and discovered a well of fresh water there. ²⁰ But the herdsmen of Gerar quarrelled with those of Isaac and said, 'The water is ours!' So he named the well Esek,*c* because they disputed with him. ²¹ Then they

---

f 30 Edom means *red*.
a 4 Or *seed*
b 4 Or *and all nations on earth will use the name of your offspring in blessings* (see 48:20)

c 20 Esek means *dispute*.

dug another well, but they quarrelled over that one also; so he named it Sitnah.*d* ²²He moved on from there and dug another well, and no one quarrelled over it. He named it Rehoboth,*e* saying, 'Now the LORD has given us room and we will flourish in the land.'

²³From there he went up to Beersheba. ²⁴That night the LORD appeared to him and said, 'I am the God of your father Abraham. Do not be afraid, for I am with you; I will bless you and will increase the number of your descendants for the sake of my servant Abraham.'

²⁵Isaac built an altar there and called on the name of the LORD. There he pitched his tent, and there his servants dug a well.

²⁶Meanwhile, Abimelek had come to him from Gerar, with Ahuzzath his personal advisor and Phicol the commander of his forces. ²⁷Isaac asked them, 'Why have you come to me, since you were hostile to me and sent me away?'

²⁸They answered, 'We saw clearly that the LORD was with you; so we said, "There ought to be a sworn agreement between us" – between us and you. Let us make a treaty with you ²⁹that you will do us no harm, just as we did not harm you but always treated you well and sent you away peacefully. And now you are blessed by the LORD.'

³⁰Isaac then made a feast for them, and they ate and drank. ³¹Early the next morning the men swore an oath to each other. Then Isaac sent them on their way, and they went away peacefully.

³²That day Isaac's servants came and told him about the well they had dug. They said, 'We've found water!' ³³He called it Shibah,*f* and to this day the name of the town has been Beersheba.*g*

Jacob takes Esau's blessing

³⁴When Esau was forty years old, he married Judith daughter of Beeri the Hittite, and also Basemath daughter of Elon the Hittite. ³⁵They were a source of grief to Isaac and Rebekah.

27

When Isaac was old and his eyes were so weak that he could no longer see, he called for his elder son Esau and said to him, 'My son.'

'Here I am,' he answered.

²Isaac said, 'I am now an old man and don't know the day of my death. ³Now then, get your equipment – your quiver and bow – and go out to the open country to hunt some wild game for me. ⁴Prepare me the kind of tasty food I like and bring it to me to eat, so that I may give you my blessing before I die.'

⁵Now Rebekah was listening as Isaac spoke to his son Esau. When Esau left for the open country to hunt game and bring it back, ⁶Rebekah said to her son Jacob, 'Look, I overheard your father say to your brother Esau, ⁷"Bring me some game and prepare me some tasty food to eat, so that I may give you my blessing in the presence of the LORD before I die." ⁸Now, my son, listen carefully and do what I tell you: ⁹go out to the flock and bring me two choice young goats, so that I can prepare some tasty food for your father, just the way he likes it. ¹⁰Then take it to your father to eat, so that he may give you his blessing before he dies.'

¹¹Jacob said to Rebekah his mother, 'But my brother Esau is a hairy man while I have smooth skin. ¹²What if my father touches me? I would appear to be tricking him and would bring down a curse on myself rather than a blessing.'

¹³His mother said to him, 'My son, let the curse fall on me. Just do what I say; go and get them for me.'

¹⁴So he went and got them and brought them to his mother, and she prepared some tasty food, just the way his father liked it. ¹⁵Then Rebekah took the best clothes of her elder son Esau, which she had in the house, and put them on her younger son Jacob. ¹⁶She also covered his hands and the smooth part of his neck with the goatskins. ¹⁷Then she handed to her son Jacob the tasty food and the bread she had made.

---

d 21 *Sitnah* means *opposition.*
e 22 *Rehoboth* means *room.*
f 33 *Shibah* can mean *oath* or *seven.*
g 33 *Beersheba* can mean *well of the oath* and *well of seven.*

18 He went to his father and said, 'My father.'

'Yes, my son,' he answered. 'Who is it?'

19 Jacob said to his father, 'I am Esau your firstborn. I have done as you told me. Please sit up and eat some of my game, so that you may give me your blessing.'

20 Isaac asked his son, 'How did you find it so quickly, my son?'

'The LORD your God gave me success,' he replied.

21 Then Isaac said to Jacob, 'Come near so I can touch you, my son, to know whether you really are my son Esau or not.'

22 Jacob went close to his father Isaac, who touched him and said, 'The voice is the voice of Jacob, but the hands are the hands of Esau.' 23 He did not recognise him, for his hands were hairy like those of his brother Esau; so he proceeded to bless him. 24 'Are you really my son Esau?' he asked.

'I am,' he replied.

25 Then he said, 'My son, bring me some of your game to eat, so that I may give you my blessing.'

Jacob brought it to him and he ate; and he brought some wine and he drank. 26 Then his father Isaac said to him, 'Come here, my son, and kiss me.'

27 So he went to him and kissed him. When Isaac caught the smell of his clothes, he blessed him and said,

'Ah, the smell of my son
    is like the smell of a field
    that the LORD has blessed.
28 May God give you heaven's dew
    and earth's richness –
    an abundance of grain and new
        wine.
29 May nations serve you
    and peoples bow down to you.
Be lord over your brothers,
    and may the sons of your mother
        bow down to you.
May those who curse you be cursed
    and those who bless you be
        blessed.'

30 After Isaac finished blessing him, and Jacob had scarcely left his father's presence, his brother Esau came in from hunting. 31 He too prepared some tasty food and brought it to his father. Then he said to him, 'My father, please sit up and eat some of my game, so that you may give me your blessing.'

32 His father Isaac asked him, 'Who are you?'

'I am your son,' he answered, 'your firstborn, Esau.'

33 Isaac trembled violently and said, 'Who was it, then, that hunted game and brought it to me? I ate it just before you came and I blessed him – and indeed he will be blessed!'

34 When Esau heard his father's words, he burst out with a loud and bitter cry and said to his father, 'Bless me – me too, my father!'

35 But he said, 'Your brother came deceitfully and took your blessing.'

36 Esau said, 'Isn't he rightly named Jacob?[a] This is the second time he has taken advantage of me: he took my birthright, and now he's taken my blessing!' Then he asked, 'Haven't you reserved any blessing for me?'

37 Isaac answered Esau, 'I have made him lord over you and have made all his relatives his servants, and I have sustained him with grain and new wine. So what can I possibly do for you, my son?'

38 Esau said to his father, 'Do you have only one blessing, my father? Bless me too, my father!' Then Esau wept aloud.

39 His father Isaac answered him,

'Your dwelling will be
    away from the earth's richness,
    away from the dew of heaven
        above.
40 You will live by the sword
    and you will serve your brother.
But when you grow restless,
    you will throw his yoke
    from off your neck.'

41 Esau held a grudge against Jacob because of the blessing his father had given

---

a 36 Jacob means *he grasps the heel,* a Hebrew idiom for *he takes advantage of* or *he deceives.*

him. He said to himself, 'The days of mourning for my father are near; then I will kill my brother Jacob.'

42 When Rebekah was told what her elder son Esau had said, she sent for her younger son Jacob and said to him, 'Your brother Esau is planning to avenge himself by killing you. 43 Now then, my son, do what I say: flee at once to my brother Laban in Harran. 44 Stay with him for a while until your brother's fury subsides. 45 When your brother is no longer angry with you and forgets what you did to him, I'll send word for you to come back from there. Why should I lose both of you in one day?'

46 Then Rebekah said to Isaac, 'I'm disgusted with living because of these Hittite women. If Jacob takes a wife from among the women of this land, from Hittite women like these, my life will not be worth living.'

28 So Isaac called for Jacob and blessed him. Then he commanded him: 'Do not marry a Canaanite woman. 2 Go at once to Paddan Aram,*a* to the house of your mother's father Bethuel. Take a wife for yourself there, from among the daughters of Laban, your mother's brother. 3 May God Almighty*b* bless you and make you fruitful and increase your numbers until you become a community of peoples. 4 May he give you and your descendants the blessing given to Abraham, so that you may take possession of the land where you now reside as a foreigner, the land God gave to Abraham.' 5 Then Isaac sent Jacob on his way, and he went to Paddan Aram, to Laban son of Bethuel the Aramean, the brother of Rebekah, who was the mother of Jacob and Esau.

6 Now Esau learned that Isaac had blessed Jacob and had sent him to Paddan Aram to take a wife from there, and that when he blessed him he commanded him, 'Do not marry a Canaanite woman,' 7 and that Jacob had obeyed his father and mother and had gone to Paddan Aram.

8 Esau then realised how displeasing the Canaanite women were to his father Isaac; 9 so he went to Ishmael and married Mahalath, the sister of Nebaioth and daughter of Ishmael son of Abraham, in addition to the wives he already had.

Jacob's dream at Bethel

10 Jacob left Beersheba and set out for Harran. 11 When he reached a certain place, he stopped for the night because the sun had set. Taking one of the stones there, he put it under his head and lay down to sleep. 12 He had a dream in which he saw a stairway resting on the earth, with its top reaching to heaven, and the angels of God were ascending and descending on it. 13 There above it*c* stood the LORD, and he said: 'I am the LORD, the God of your father Abraham and the God of Isaac. I will give you and your descendants the land on which you are lying. 14 Your descendants will be like the dust of the earth, and you will spread out to the west and to the east, to the north and to the south. All peoples on earth will be blessed through you and your offspring.*d* 15 I am with you and will watch over you wherever you go, and I will bring you back to this land. I will not leave you until I have done what I have promised you.'

16 When Jacob awoke from his sleep, he thought, 'Surely the LORD is in this place, and I was not aware of it.' 17 He was afraid and said, 'How awesome is this place! This is none other than the house of God; this is the gate of heaven.'

18 Early the next morning Jacob took the stone he had placed under his head and set it up as a pillar and poured oil on top of it. 19 He called that place Bethel,*e* though the city used to be called Luz.

20 Then Jacob made a vow, saying, 'If God will be with me and will watch over me on this journey I am taking and will give me food to eat and clothes to wear 21 so that I return safely to my father's household,

---

a 2 That is, North-west Mesopotamia; also in verses 5, 6 and 7
b 3 Hebrew *El-Shaddai*

c 13 Or *There beside him*
d 14 Or *will use your name and the name of your offspring in blessings* (see 48.20)
e 19 *Bethel* means *house of God*.

then the LORD*f* will be my God 22 and*g* this stone that I have set up as a pillar will be God's house, and of all that you give me I will give you a tenth.'

Jacob arrives in Paddan Aram

29 Then Jacob continued on his journey and came to the land of the eastern peoples. 2 There he saw a well in the open country, with three flocks of sheep lying near it because the flocks were watered from that well. The stone over the mouth of the well was large. 3 When all the flocks were gathered there, the shepherds would roll the stone away from the well's mouth and water the sheep. Then they would return the stone to its place over the mouth of the well.

4 Jacob asked the shepherds, 'My brothers, where are you from?'

'We're from Harran,' they replied.

5 He said to them, 'Do you know Laban, Nahor's grandson?'

'Yes, we know him,' they answered.

6 Then Jacob asked them, 'Is he well?'

'Yes, he is,' they said, 'and here comes his daughter Rachel with the sheep.'

7 'Look,' he said, 'the sun is still high; it is not time for the flocks to be gathered. Water the sheep and take them back to pasture.'

8 'We can't,' they replied, 'until all the flocks are gathered and the stone has been rolled away from the mouth of the well. Then we will water the sheep.'

9 While he was still talking with them, Rachel came with her father's sheep, for she was a shepherd. 10 When Jacob saw Rachel daughter of his uncle Laban, and Laban's sheep, he went over and rolled the stone away from the mouth of the well and watered his uncle's sheep. 11 Then Jacob kissed Rachel and began to weep aloud. 12 He had told Rachel that he was a relative of her father and a son of Rebekah. So she ran and told her father.

13 As soon as Laban heard the news about Jacob, his sister's son, he hurried to meet him. He embraced him and kissed him and brought him to his home, and there Jacob told him all these things. 14 Then Laban said to him, 'You are my own flesh and blood.'

Jacob marries Leah and Rachel

After Jacob had stayed with him for a whole month, 15 Laban said to him, 'Just because you are a relative of mine, should you work for me for nothing? Tell me what your wages should be.'

16 Now Laban had two daughters; the name of the elder one was Leah, and the name of the younger was Rachel. 17 Leah had weak*a* eyes, but Rachel had a lovely figure and was beautiful. 18 Jacob was in love with Rachel and said, 'I'll work for you seven years in return for your younger daughter Rachel.'

19 Laban said, 'It's better that I give her to you than to some other man. Stay here with me.' 20 So Jacob served seven years to get Rachel, but they seemed like only a few days to him because of his love for her.

21 Then Jacob said to Laban, 'Give me my wife. My time is completed, and I want to make love to her.'

22 So Laban brought together all the people of the place and gave a feast. 23 But when evening came, he took his daughter Leah and brought her to Jacob, and Jacob made love to her. 24 And Laban gave his servant Zilpah to his daughter as her attendant.

25 When morning came, there was Leah! So Jacob said to Laban, 'What is this you have done to me? I served you for Rachel, didn't I? Why have you deceived me?'

26 Laban replied, 'It is not our custom here to give the younger daughter in marriage before the elder one. 27 Finish this daughter's bridal week; then we will give you the younger one also, in return for another seven years of work.'

28 And Jacob did so. He finished the week with Leah, and then Laban gave him his daughter Rachel to be his wife. 29 Laban gave his servant Bilhah to his daughter Rachel as her attendant. 30 Jacob made love to Rachel also, and his love for Rachel

---

f 20,21 Or *Since God . . . father's household, the* LORD
g 21,22 Or *household, and the* LORD *will be my God,* 22 *then*

a 17 Or *delicate*

FAITH IN THE WORLD 3

BECAUSE YOU'RE GORGEOUS

A few years ago there was a global competition. Contestants from all over the world entered to win a truly fabulous prize. What was the prize? A big bag of money? A new car? A house? A music recording contract? No. The prize was simply to do 'the best job in the world'. What do you think the best job in the world is? What would it be for you? Professional sports star? Heading up a multinational business empire? Jet plane test pilot? The job was to look after a gorgeous island just off the coast of Australia for half a year. The only mode of transport was a jet-ski and the winner had to scuba dive with a few clownfish and blog about it. The pay? £70,000. The island wanted to promote tourism in the area. Nice work if you can get it!

What kind of reward do we work for? Or is it the prospect of becoming famous? Getting into university? Helping people? Improving life for others? Is it to leave school and earn money so we can do what we want in our leisure time? In Genesis 29 we find Jacob doing a whole lot of work for a particular reward – a gorgeous wife. Jacob has run away from home after a big bust-up with his older brother. He goes and seeks shelter with his Uncle Laban and falls head over heels for his cousin Rachel. In those days, and still in some countries today, you had to pay a dowry – a payment for the bride to her parents. Jacob has to work seven years for Rachel, and then he gets conned on his wedding day: he's given the older sister in marriage first! So then he has to work another seven years as dowry for Rachel. We're told in the text that, for Jacob, working those first seven years only seemed like working a few days. Time flew because of his love for Rachel.

Motivation is key in work and study, and it can help us really thrive. Motivation gurus say that the best kind of work isn't work that rewards us with money or status, but work that we find challenging to ourselves and beneficial to others. We can love being the best, we can love the promotions, we can love recognition for excelling, or the approval of our families and friends, but these only spur us on as short-term rewards. God has designed us to love a good challenge, something that improves us and improves the quality of life for others. Let's not be surprised that a God who loves serving created us to love serving too. Our reward in our studies or our work really should be to know that we're preparing for a future where we will see a smile put on other people's faces by the way we solve problems to help them, using all the gifts and passions that God has given us.

Jason Gardner

 Genesis 2:15–25   Exodus 31:1–11

was greater than his love for Leah. And he worked for Laban another seven years.

Jacob's children

31 When the LORD saw that Leah was not loved, he enabled her to conceive, but Rachel remained childless. 32 Leah became pregnant and gave birth to a son. She named him Reuben,*b* for she said, 'It is because the LORD has seen my misery. Surely my husband will love me now.'

33 She conceived again, and when she gave birth to a son she said, 'Because the LORD heard that I am not loved, he gave me this one too.' So she named him Simeon.*c*

34 Again she conceived, and when she gave birth to a son she said, 'Now at last my husband will become attached to me, because I have borne him three sons.' So he was named Levi.*d*

35 She conceived again, and when she gave birth to a son she said, 'This time I will praise the LORD.' So she named him Judah.*e* Then she stopped having children.

30 When Rachel saw that she was not bearing Jacob any children, she became jealous of her sister. So she said to Jacob, 'Give me children, or I'll die!'

2 Jacob became angry with her and said, 'Am I in the place of God, who has kept you from having children?'

3 Then she said, 'Here is Bilhah, my servant. Sleep with her so that she can bear children for me and I too can build a family through her.'

4 So she gave him her servant Bilhah as a wife. Jacob slept with her, 5 and she became pregnant and bore him a son. 6 Then Rachel said, 'God has vindicated me; he has listened to my plea and given me a son.' Because of this she named him Dan.*a*

7 Rachel's servant Bilhah conceived again and bore Jacob a second son. 8 Then Rachel said, 'I have had a great struggle

with my sister, and I have won.' So she named him Naphtali.*b*

9 When Leah saw that she had stopped having children, she took her servant Zilpah and gave her to Jacob as a wife. 10 Leah's servant Zilpah bore Jacob a son. 11 Then Leah said, 'What good fortune!'*c* So she named him Gad.*d*

12 Leah's servant Zilpah bore Jacob a second son. 13 Then Leah said, 'How happy I am! The women will call me happy.' So she named him Asher.*e*

14 During wheat harvest, Reuben went out into the fields and found some mandrake plants, which he brought to his mother Leah. Rachel said to Leah, 'Please give me some of your son's mandrakes.'

15 But she said to her, 'Wasn't it enough that you took away my husband? Will you take my son's mandrakes too?'

'Very well,' Rachel said, 'he can sleep with you tonight in return for your son's mandrakes.'

16 So when Jacob came in from the fields that evening, Leah went out to meet him. 'You must sleep with me,' she said. 'I have hired you with my son's mandrakes.' So he slept with her that night.

17 God listened to Leah, and she became pregnant and bore Jacob a fifth son. 18 Then Leah said, 'God has rewarded me for giving my servant to my husband.' So she named him Issachar.*f*

19 Leah conceived again and bore Jacob a sixth son. 20 Then Leah said, 'God has presented me with a precious gift. This time my husband will treat me with honour, because I have borne him six sons.' So she named him Zebulun.*g*

21 Some time later she gave birth to a daughter and named her Dinah.

22 Then God remembered Rachel; he listened to her and enabled her to conceive. 23 She became pregnant and gave birth to a son and said, 'God has taken away my

---

b 32 *Reuben* sounds like the Hebrew for *he has seen my misery*; the name means *see, a son*.
c 33 *Simeon* probably means *one who hears*.
d 34 *Levi* sounds like and may be derived from the Hebrew for *attached*.
e 35 *Judah* sounds like and may be derived from the Hebrew for *praise*.
a 6 *Dan* here means *he has vindicated*.

b 8 *Naphtali* means *my struggle*.
c 11 Or 'A troop is coming!'
d 11 *Gad* can mean *good fortune* or *a troop*.
e 13 *Asher* means *happy*.
f 18 *Issachar* sounds like the Hebrew for *reward*.
g 20 *Zebulun* probably means *honour*.

disgrace.' 24She named him Joseph,*h* and said, 'May the LORD add to me another son.'

Jacob's flocks increase

25After Rachel gave birth to Joseph, Jacob said to Laban, 'Send me on my way so that I can go back to my own homeland. 26Give me my wives and children, for whom I have served you, and I will be on my way. You know how much work I've done for you.'

27But Laban said to him, 'If I have found favour in your eyes, please stay. I have learned by divination that the LORD has blessed me because of you.' 28He added, 'Name your wages, and I will pay them.'

29Jacob said to him, 'You know how I have worked for you and how your livestock has fared under my care. 30The little you had before I came has increased greatly, and the LORD has blessed you wherever I have been. But now, when may I do something for my own household?'

31'What shall I give you?' he asked.

'Don't give me anything,' Jacob replied. 'But if you will do this one thing for me, I will go on tending your flocks and watching over them: 32let me go through all your flocks today and remove from them every speckled or spotted sheep, every dark-coloured lamb and every spotted or speckled goat. They will be my wages. 33And my honesty will testify for me in the future, whenever you check on the wages you have paid me. Any goat in my possession that is not speckled or spotted, or any lamb that is not dark-coloured, will be considered stolen.'

34'Agreed,' said Laban. 'Let it be as you have said.' 35That same day he removed all the male goats that were streaked or spotted, and all the speckled or spotted female goats (all that had white on them) and all the dark-coloured lambs, and he placed them in the care of his sons. 36Then he put a three-day journey between himself and Jacob, while Jacob continued to tend the rest of Laban's flocks.

37Jacob, however, took fresh-cut

branches from poplar, almond and plane trees and made white stripes on them by peeling the bark and exposing the white inner wood of the branches. 38Then he placed the peeled branches in all the watering troughs, so that they would be directly in front of the flocks when they came to drink. When the flocks were in heat and came to drink, 39they mated in front of the branches. And they bore young that were streaked or speckled or spotted. 40Jacob set apart the young of the flock by themselves, but made the rest face the streaked and dark-coloured animals that belonged to Laban. Thus he made separate flocks for himself and did not put them with Laban's animals. 41Whenever the stronger females were in heat, Jacob would place the branches in the troughs in front of the animals so that they would mate near the branches, 42but if the animals were weak, he would not place them there. So the weak animals went to Laban and the strong ones to Jacob. 43In this way the man grew exceedingly prosperous and came to own large flocks, and female and male servants, and camels and donkeys.

Jacob flees from Laban

31 Jacob heard that Laban's sons were saying, 'Jacob has taken everything our father owned and has gained all this wealth from what belonged to our father.' 2And Jacob noticed that Laban's attitude towards him was not what it had been.

3Then the LORD said to Jacob, 'Go back to the land of your fathers and to your relatives, and I will be with you.'

4So Jacob sent word to Rachel and Leah to come out to the fields where his flocks were. 5He said to them, 'I see that your father's attitude towards me is not what it was before, but the God of my father has been with me. 6You know that I've worked for your father with all my strength, 7yet your father has cheated me by changing my wages ten times. However, God has not allowed him to harm me. 8If he said, "The speckled ones will be your wages," then all the flocks gave birth to speckled young; and if he said, "The streaked ones will be your wages," then all the flocks

---

h 24 Joseph means may he add.

bore streaked young. 9So God has taken away your father's livestock and has given them to me.

10'In the breeding season I once had a dream in which I looked up and saw that the male goats mating with the flock were streaked, speckled or spotted. 11The angel of God said to me in the dream, "Jacob." I answered, "Here I am." 12And he said, "Look up and see that all the male goats mating with the flock are streaked, speckled or spotted, for I have seen all that Laban has been doing to you. 13I am the God of Bethel, where you anointed a pillar and where you made a vow to me. Now leave this land at once and go back to your native land."'

14Then Rachel and Leah replied, 'Do we still have any share in the inheritance of our father's estate? 15Does he not regard us as foreigners? Not only has he sold us, but he has used up what was paid for us. 16Surely all the wealth that God took away from our father belongs to us and our children. So do whatever God has told you.'

17Then Jacob put his children and his wives on camels, 18and he drove all his livestock ahead of him, along with all the goods he had accumulated in Paddan Aram,a to go to his father Isaac in the land of Canaan.

19When Laban had gone to shear his sheep, Rachel stole her father's household gods. 20Moreover, Jacob deceived Laban the Aramean by not telling him he was running away. 21So he fled with all he had, crossed the River Euphrates, and headed for the hill country of Gilead.

Laban pursues Jacob

22On the third day Laban was told that Jacob had fled. 23Taking his relatives with him, he pursued Jacob for seven days and caught up with him in the hill country of Gilead. 24Then God came to Laban the Aramean in a dream at night and said to him, 'Be careful not to say anything to Jacob, either good or bad.'

25Jacob had pitched his tent in the hill country of Gilead when Laban overtook him, and Laban and his relatives camped there too. 26Then Laban said to Jacob, 'What have you done? You've deceived me, and you've carried off my daughters like captives in war. 27Why did you run off secretly and deceive me? Why didn't you tell me, so that I could send you away with joy and singing to the music of tambourines and harps? 28You didn't even let me kiss my grandchildren and my daughters goodbye. You have done a foolish thing. 29I have the power to harm you; but last night the God of your father said to me, "Be careful not to say anything to Jacob, either good or bad." 30Now you have gone off because you longed to return to your father's household. But why did you steal my gods?'

31Jacob answered Laban, 'I was afraid, because I thought you would take your daughters away from me by force. 32But if you find anyone who has your gods, that person shall not live. In the presence of our relatives, see for yourself whether there is anything of yours here with me; and if so, take it.' Now Jacob did not know that Rachel had stolen the gods.

33So Laban went into Jacob's tent and into Leah's tent and into the tent of the two female servants, but he found nothing. After he came out of Leah's tent, he entered Rachel's tent. 34Now Rachel had taken the household gods and put them inside her camel's saddle and was sitting on them. Laban searched through everything in the tent but found nothing.

35Rachel said to her father, 'Don't be angry, my lord, that I cannot stand up in your presence; I'm having my period.' So he searched but could not find the household gods.

36Jacob was angry and took Laban to task. 'What is my crime?' he asked Laban. 'How have I wronged you that you hunt me down? 37Now that you have searched through all my goods, what have you found that belongs to your household? Put it here in front of your relatives and mine, and let them judge between the two of us.

38'I have been with you for twenty years now. Your sheep and goats have not miscarried, nor have I eaten rams from your flocks. 39I did not bring you animals torn by wild beasts; I bore the loss myself. And you demanded payment from me for whatever was stolen by day or night. **40** This was my situation: the heat consumed me in the daytime and the cold at night, and sleep fled from my eyes. **41** It was like this for the twenty years I was in your household. I worked for you fourteen years for your two daughters and six years for your flocks, and you changed my wages ten times. **42** If the God of my father, the God of Abraham and the Fear of Isaac, had not been with me, you would surely have sent me away empty-handed. But God has seen my hardship and the toil of my hands, and last night he rebuked you.'

43 Laban answered Jacob, 'The women are my daughters, the children are my children, and the flocks are my flocks. All you see is mine. Yet what can I do today about these daughters of mine, or about the children they have borne? **44** Come now, let's make a covenant, you and I, and let it serve as a witness between us.'

45 So Jacob took a stone and set it up as a pillar. **46** He said to his relatives, 'Gather some stones.' So they took stones and piled them in a heap, and they ate there by the heap. **47** Laban called it Jegar Sahadutha, and Jacob called it Galeed.*b*

48 Laban said, 'This heap is a witness between you and me today.' That is why it was called Galeed. **49** It was also called Mizpah,*c* because he said, 'May the LORD keep watch between you and me when we are away from each other. **50** If you ill-treat my daughters or if you take any wives besides my daughters, even though no one is with us, remember that God is a witness between you and me.'

51 Laban also said to Jacob, 'Here is this heap, and here is this pillar I have set up between you and me. **52** This heap is a witness, and this pillar is a witness, that I will not go past this heap to your side to harm you and that you will not go past this heap and pillar to my side to harm me. **53** May the God of Abraham and the God of

Nahor, the God of their father, judge between us.'

So Jacob took an oath in the name of the Fear of his father Isaac. **54** He offered a sacrifice there in the hill country and invited his relatives to a meal. After they had eaten, they spent the night there.

55 Early the next morning Laban kissed his grandchildren and his daughters and blessed them. Then he left and returned home.*d*

Jacob prepares to meet Esau

32^{*a*} Jacob also went on his way, and the angels of God met him. **2** When Jacob saw them, he said, 'This is the camp of God!' So he named that place Mahanaim.*b*

3 Jacob sent messengers ahead of him to his brother Esau in the land of Seir, the country of Edom. **4** He instructed them: 'This is what you are to say to my lord Esau: "Your servant Jacob says, I have been staying with Laban and have remained there till now. **5** I have cattle and donkeys, sheep and goats, male and female servants. Now I am sending this message to my lord, that I may find favour in your eyes." '

6 When the messengers returned to Jacob, they said, 'We went to your brother Esau, and now he is coming to meet you, and four hundred men are with him.'

7 In great fear and distress Jacob divided the people who were with him into two groups,*c* and the flocks and herds and camels as well. **8** He thought, 'If Esau comes and attacks one group,*d* the group*d* that is left may escape.'

9 Then Jacob prayed, 'O God of my father Abraham, God of my father Isaac, LORD, you who said to me, "Go back to your country and your relatives, and I will make you prosper," **10** I am unworthy of all the kindness and faithfulness you have shown your servant. I had only

---

b 47 The Aramaic *Jegar Sahadutha* and the Hebrew *Galeed* both mean *witness heap*.

c 49 *Mizpah* means *watchtower*.

d 55 In Hebrew texts this verse (31:55) is numbered 32:1.

a In Hebrew texts 32:1-32 is numbered 32:2-33.

b 2 *Mahanaim* means *two camps*.

c 7 Or *camps*

d 8 Or *camp*

my staff when I crossed this Jordan, but now I have become two camps. ¹¹Save me, I pray, from the hand of my brother Esau, for I am afraid he will come and attack me, and also the mothers with their children. ¹²But you have said, "I will surely make you prosper and will make your descendants like the sand of the sea, which cannot be counted." '

¹³He spent the night there, and from what he had with him he selected a gift for his brother Esau: ¹⁴two hundred female goats and twenty male goats, two hundred ewes and twenty rams, ¹⁵thirty female camels with their young, forty cows and ten bulls, and twenty female donkeys and ten male donkeys. ¹⁶He put them in the care of his servants, each herd by itself, and said to his servants, 'Go ahead of me, and keep some space between the herds.'

¹⁷He instructed the one in the lead: 'When my brother Esau meets you and asks, "Who do you belong to, and where are you going, and who owns all these animals in front of you?" ¹⁸then you are to say, "They belong to your servant Jacob. They are a gift sent to my lord Esau, and he is coming behind us." '

¹⁹He also instructed the second, the third and all the others who followed the herds: 'You are to say the same thing to Esau when you meet him. ²⁰And be sure to say, "Your servant Jacob is coming behind us." ' For he thought, 'I will pacify him with these gifts I am sending on ahead; later, when I see him, perhaps he will receive me.' ²¹So Jacob's gifts went on ahead of him, but he himself spent the night in the camp.

Jacob wrestles with God

²²That night Jacob got up and took his two wives, his two female servants and his eleven sons and crossed the ford of the Jabbok. ²³After he had sent them across the stream, he sent over all his possessions. ²⁴So Jacob was left alone, and a man wrestled with him till daybreak. ²⁵When the man saw that he could not overpower him, he touched the socket of Jacob's hip so that his hip was wrenched as he wrestled with the man. ²⁶Then the man said, 'Let me go, for it is daybreak.'

But Jacob replied, 'I will not let you go unless you bless me.'

²⁷The man asked him, 'What is your name?'

'Jacob,' he answered.

²⁸Then the man said, 'Your name will no longer be Jacob, but Israel,ᵉ because you have struggled with God and with humans and have overcome.'

²⁹Jacob said, 'Please tell me your name.'

But he replied, 'Why do you ask my name?' Then he blessed him there.

³⁰So Jacob called the place Peniel,ᶠ saying, 'It is because I saw God face to face, and yet my life was spared.'

³¹The sun rose above him as he passed Peniel,ᵍ and he was limping because of his hip. ³²Therefore to this day the Israelites do not eat the tendon attached to the socket of the hip, because the socket of Jacob's hip was touched near the tendon.

Jacob meets Esau

33 Jacob looked up and there was Esau, coming with his four hundred men; so he divided the children among Leah, Rachel and the two female servants. ²He put the female servants and their children in front, Leah and her children next, and Rachel and Joseph in the rear. ³He himself went on ahead and bowed down to the ground seven times as he approached his brother.

⁴But Esau ran to meet Jacob and embraced him; he threw his arms around his neck and kissed him. And they wept. ⁵Then Esau looked up and saw the women and children. 'Who are these with you?' he asked.

Jacob answered, 'They are the children God has graciously given your servant.'

⁶Then the female servants and their children approached and bowed down. ⁷Next, Leah and her children came and bowed down. Last of all came Joseph and Rachel, and they too bowed down.

ᵉ 28 *Israel* probably means *he struggles with God*.
ᶠ 30 *Peniel* means *face of God*.
ᵍ 31 Hebrew *Penuel*, a variant of *Peniel*

8 Esau asked, 'What's the meaning of all these flocks and herds I met?'

'To find favour in your eyes, my lord,' he said.

9 But Esau said, 'I already have plenty, my brother. Keep what you have for yourself.'

10 'No, please!' said Jacob. 'If I have found favour in your eyes, accept this gift from me. For to see your face is like seeing the face of God, now that you have received me favourably. 11 Please accept the present that was brought to you, for God has been gracious to me and I have all I need.' And because Jacob insisted, Esau accepted it.

12 Then Esau said, 'Let us be on our way; I'll accompany you.'

13 But Jacob said to him, 'My lord knows that the children are tender and that I must care for the ewes and cows that are nursing their young. If they are driven hard just one day, all the animals will die. 14 So let my lord go on ahead of his servant, while I move along slowly at the pace of the flocks and herds before me and the pace of the children, until I come to my lord in Seir.'

15 Esau said, 'Then let me leave some of my men with you.'

'But why do that?' Jacob asked. 'Just let me find favour in the eyes of my lord.'

16 So that day Esau started on his way back to Seir. 17 Jacob, however, went to Sukkoth, where he built a place for himself and made shelters for his livestock. That is why the place is called Sukkoth.*a*

18 After Jacob came from Paddan Aram,*b* he arrived safely at the city of Shechem in Canaan and camped within sight of the city. 19 For a hundred pieces of silver,*c* he bought from the sons of Hamor, the father of Shechem, the plot of ground where he pitched his tent. 20 There he set up an altar and called it El Elohe Israel.*d*

Dinah and the Shechemites

34 Now Dinah, the daughter Leah had borne to Jacob, went out to visit the women of the land. 2 When Shechem son of Hamor the Hivite, the ruler of that area, saw her, he took her and raped her. 3 His heart was drawn to Dinah daughter of Jacob; he loved the young woman and spoke tenderly to her. 4 And Shechem said to his father Hamor, 'Get me this girl as my wife.'

FACT

NO ADAM'S APPLE

Adam and Eve ate the fruit of the tree, but the Bible doesn't say what kind (Genesis 2:16–17). It wouldn't have been an apple; they only arrived in the Middle East in Roman times.

5 When Jacob heard that his daughter Dinah had been defiled, his sons were in the fields with his livestock; so he did nothing about it until they came home.

6 Then Shechem's father Hamor went out to talk with Jacob. 7 Meanwhile, Jacob's sons had come in from the fields as soon as they heard what had happened. They were shocked and furious, because Shechem had done an outrageous thing in*a* Israel by sleeping with Jacob's daughter – a thing that should not be done.

8 But Hamor said to them, 'My son Shechem has his heart set on your daughter. Please give her to him as his wife. 9 Intermarry with us; give us your daughters and take our daughters for yourselves. 10 You can settle among us; the land is open to you. Live in it, trade*b* in it, and acquire property in it.'

11 Then Shechem said to Dinah's father

---

a 17 *Sukkoth* means *shelters*.

b 18 That is, North-west Mesopotamia

c 19 Hebrew *hundred kesitahs*; a kesitah was a unit of money of unknown weight and value.

d 20 *El Elohe Israel* can mean *El is the God of Israel* or *mighty is the God of Israel*.

---

a 7 Or *against*

b 10 Or *move about freely*; also in verse 21

and brothers, 'Let me find favour in your eyes, and I will give you whatever you ask. 12 Make the price for the bride and the gift I am to bring as great as you like, and I'll pay whatever you ask me. Only give me the young woman as my wife.'

13 Because their sister Dinah had been defiled, Jacob's sons replied deceitfully as they spoke to Shechem and his father Hamor. 14 They said to them, 'We can't do such a thing; we can't give our sister to a man who is not circumcised. That would be a disgrace to us. 15 We will enter into an agreement with you on one condition only: that you become like us by circumcising all your males. 16 Then we will give you our daughters and take your daughters for ourselves. We'll settle among you and become one people with you. 17 But if you will not agree to be circumcised, we'll take our sister and go.'

18 Their proposal seemed good to Hamor and his son Shechem. 19 The young man, who was the most honoured of all his father's family, lost no time in doing what they said, because he was delighted with Jacob's daughter. 20 So Hamor and his son Shechem went to the gate of their city to speak to the men of their city. 21 'These men are friendly towards us,' they said. 'Let them live in our land and trade in it; the land has plenty of room for them. We can marry their daughters and they can marry ours. 22 But the men will agree to live with us as one people only on the condition that our males be circumcised, as they themselves are. 23 Won't their livestock, their property and all their other animals become ours? So let us agree to their terms, and they will settle among us.'

24 All the men who went out of the city gate agreed with Hamor and his son Shechem, and every male in the city was circumcised.

25 Three days later, while all of them were still in pain, two of Jacob's sons, Simeon and Levi, Dinah's brothers, took their swords and attacked the unsuspecting city, killing every male. 26 They put Hamor and his son Shechem to the sword and took Dinah from Shechem's house and left. 27 The sons of Jacob came upon the dead bodies and looted the city where[c] their sister had been defiled. 28 They seized their flocks and herds and donkeys and everything else of theirs in the city and out in the fields. 29 They carried off all their wealth and all their women and children, taking as plunder everything in the houses.

30 Then Jacob said to Simeon and Levi, 'You have brought trouble on me by making me obnoxious to the Canaanites and Perizzites, the people living in this land. We are few in number, and if they join forces against me and attack me, I and my household will be destroyed.'

31 But they replied, 'Should he have treated our sister like a prostitute?'

Jacob returns to Bethel

35 Then God said to Jacob, 'Go up to Bethel and settle there, and build an altar there to God, who appeared to you when you were fleeing from your brother Esau.'

2 So Jacob said to his household and to all who were with him, 'Get rid of the foreign gods you have with you, and purify yourselves and change your clothes. 3 Then come, let us go up to Bethel, where I will build an altar to God, who answered me in the day of my distress and who has been with me wherever I have gone.' 4 So they gave Jacob all the foreign gods they had and the rings in their ears, and Jacob buried them under the oak at Shechem. 5 Then they set out, and the terror of God fell on the towns all around them so that no one pursued them.

6 Jacob and all the people with him came to Luz (that is, Bethel) in the land of Canaan. 7 There he built an altar, and he called the place El Bethel,[a] because it was there that God revealed himself to him when he was fleeing from his brother.

8 Now Deborah, Rebekah's nurse, died and was buried under the oak outside Bethel. So it was named Allon Bakuth.[b]

9 After Jacob returned from Paddan

---

c 27 Or because

a 7 El Bethel means God of Bethel.

b 8 Allon Bakuth means oak of weeping.

Aram,*c* God appeared to him again and blessed him. [10] God said to him, 'Your name is Jacob,*d* but you will no longer be called Jacob; your name will be Israel.*e*' So he named him Israel.

[11] And God said to him, 'I am God Almighty;*f* be fruitful and increase in number. A nation and a community of nations will come from you, and kings will be among your descendants. [12] The land I gave to Abraham and Isaac I also give to you, and I will give this land to your descendants after you.' [13] Then God went up from him at the place where he had talked with him.

[14] Jacob set up a stone pillar at the place where God had talked with him, and he poured out a drink offering on it; he also poured oil on it. [15] Jacob called the place where God had talked with him Bethel.*g*

The deaths of Rachel and Isaac

[16] Then they moved on from Bethel. While they were still some distance from Ephrath, Rachel began to give birth and had great difficulty. [17] And as she was having great difficulty in childbirth, the midwife said to her, 'Don't despair, for you have another son.' [18] As she breathed her last – for she was dying – she named her son Ben-Oni.*h* But his father named him Benjamin.*i*

[19] So Rachel died and was buried on the way to Ephrath (that is, Bethlehem). [20] Over her tomb Jacob set up a pillar, and to this day that pillar marks Rachel's tomb.

[21] Israel moved on again and pitched his tent beyond Migdal Eder. [22] While Israel was living in that region, Reuben went in and slept with his father's concubine Bilhah, and Israel heard of it.

Jacob had twelve sons:

[23] The sons of Leah:
Reuben the firstborn of Jacob, Simeon, Levi, Judah, Issachar and Zebulun.
[24] The sons of Rachel:
Joseph and Benjamin.
[25] The sons of Rachel's servant Bilhah:
Dan and Naphtali.
[26] The sons of Leah's servant Zilpah:
Gad and Asher.

These were the sons of Jacob, who were born to him in Paddan Aram.

[27] Jacob came home to his father Isaac in Mamre, near Kiriath Arba (that is, Hebron), where Abraham and Isaac had stayed. [28] Isaac lived a hundred and eighty years. [29] Then he breathed his last and died and was gathered to his people, old and full of years. And his sons Esau and Jacob buried him.

Esau's descendants

36 This is the account of the family line of Esau (that is, Edom).

[2] Esau took his wives from the women of Canaan: Adah daughter of Elon the Hittite, and Oholibamah daughter of Anah and granddaughter of Zibeon the Hivite – [3] also Basemath daughter of Ishmael and sister of Nebaioth.

[4] Adah bore Eliphaz to Esau, Basemath bore Reuel, [5] and Oholibamah bore Jeush, Jalam and Korah. These were the sons of Esau, who were born to him in Canaan.

[6] Esau took his wives and sons and daughters and all the members of his household, as well as his livestock and all his other animals and all the goods he had acquired in Canaan, and moved to a land some distance from his brother Jacob. [7] Their possessions were too great for them to remain together; the land where they were staying could not support them both because of their livestock. [8] So Esau (that is, Edom) settled in the hill country of Seir.

---

c 9 That is, North-west Mesopotamia; also in verse 26
d 10 *Jacob* means *he grasps the heel,* a Hebrew idiom for *he deceives.*
e 10 *Israel* probably means *he struggles with God.*
f 11 Hebrew *El-Shaddai*
g 15 *Bethel* means *house of God.*
h 18 *Ben-Oni* means *son of my trouble.*
i 18 *Benjamin* means *son of my right hand.*

⁹This is the account of the family line of Esau the father of the Edomites in the hill country of Seir.

¹⁰These are the names of Esau's sons:
Eliphaz, the son of Esau's wife Adah, and Reuel, the son of Esau's wife Basemath.
¹¹The sons of Eliphaz:
Teman, Omar, Zepho, Gatam and Kenaz.
¹²Esau's son Eliphaz also had a concubine named Timna, who bore him Amalek. These were grandsons of Esau's wife Adah.
¹³The sons of Reuel:
Nahath, Zerah, Shammah and Mizzah. These were grandsons of Esau's wife Basemath.
¹⁴The sons of Esau's wife Oholibamah daughter of Anah and granddaughter of Zibeon, whom she bore to Esau:
Jeush, Jalam and Korah.

¹⁵These were the chiefs among Esau's descendants:
The sons of Eliphaz the firstborn of Esau:
Chiefs Teman, Omar, Zepho, Kenaz, ¹⁶Korah,ᵃ Gatam and Amalek. These were the chiefs descended from Eliphaz in Edom; they were grandsons of Adah.
¹⁷The sons of Esau's son Reuel:
Chiefs Nahath, Zerah, Shammah and Mizzah. These were the chiefs descended from Reuel in Edom; they were grandsons of Esau's wife Basemath.
¹⁸The sons of Esau's wife Oholibamah:
Chiefs Jeush, Jalam and Korah. These were the chiefs descended from Esau's wife Oholibamah daughter of Anah.
¹⁹These were the sons of Esau (that is, Edom), and these were their chiefs.

²⁰These were the sons of Seir the Horite, who were living in the region:
Lotan, Shobal, Zibeon, Anah, ²¹Dishon, Ezer and Dishan. These sons of Seir in Edom were Horite chiefs.
²²The sons of Lotan:
Hori and Homam.ᵇ Timna was Lotan's sister.
²³The sons of Shobal:
Alvan, Manahath, Ebal, Shepho and Onam.
²⁴The sons of Zibeon:
Aiah and Anah. This is the Anah who discovered the hot springsᶜ in the desert while he was grazing the donkeys of his father Zibeon.
²⁵The children of Anah:
Dishon and Oholibamah daughter of Anah.
²⁶The sons of Dishon:ᵈ
Hemdan, Eshban, Ithran and Keran.
²⁷The sons of Ezer:
Bilhan, Zaavan and Akan.
²⁸The sons of Dishan:
Uz and Aran.
²⁹These were the Horite chiefs:
Lotan, Shobal, Zibeon, Anah, ³⁰Dishon, Ezer and Dishan. These were the Horite chiefs, according to their divisions, in the land of Seir.

The rulers of Edom

³¹These were the kings who reigned in Edom before any Israelite king reigned:
³²Bela son of Beor became king of Edom. His city was named Dinhabah.
³³When Bela died, Jobab son of Zerah from Bozrah succeeded him as king.
³⁴When Jobab died, Husham from the land of the Temanites succeeded him as king.
³⁵When Husham died, Hadad son of

ᵃ 16 Masoretic Text; Samaritan Pentateuch (also verse 11 and 1 Chron. 1:36) does not have *Korah*.
ᵇ 22 Hebrew *Hemam*, a variant of *Homam* (see 1 Chron. 1:39)
ᶜ 24 Vulgate; Syriac *discovered water*; the meaning of the Hebrew for this word is uncertain.
ᵈ 26 Hebrew *Dishan*, a variant of *Dishon*

Bedad, who defeated Midian in the country of Moab, succeeded him as king. His city was named Avith.

36 When Hadad died, Samlah from Masrekah succeeded him as king.

37 When Samlah died, Shaul from Rehoboth on the river succeeded him as king.

38 When Shaul died, Baal-Hanan son of Akbor succeeded him as king.

39 When Baal-Hanan son of Akbor died, Hadad*e* succeeded him as king. His city was named Pau, and his wife's name was Mehetabel daughter of Matred, the daughter of Me-Zahab.

40 These were the chiefs descended from Esau, by name, according to their clans and regions:

Timna, Alvah, Jetheth, 41 Oholibamah, Elah, Pinon, 42 Kenaz, Teman, Mibzar, 43 Magdiel and Iram. These were the chiefs of Edom, according to their settlements in the land they occupied.

This is the family line of Esau, the father of the Edomites.

Joseph's dreams

37 Jacob lived in the land where his father had stayed, the land of Canaan.

2 This is the account of Jacob's family line.

Joseph, a young man of seventeen, was tending the flocks with his brothers, the sons of Bilhah and the sons of Zilpah, his father's wives, and he brought their father a bad report about them.

3 Now Israel loved Joseph more than any of his other sons, because he had been born to him in his old age; and he made an

ornate*a* robe for him. 4 When his brothers saw that their father loved him more than any of them, they hated him and could not speak a kind word to him.

5 Joseph had a dream, and when he told it to his brothers, they hated him all the more. 6 He said to them, 'Listen to this dream I had: 7 we were binding sheaves of corn out in the field when suddenly my sheaf rose and stood upright, while your sheaves gathered round mine and bowed down to it.'

8 His brothers said to him, 'Do you intend to reign over us? Will you actually rule us?' And they hated him all the more because of his dream and what he had said.

9 Then he had another dream, and he told it to his brothers. 'Listen,' he said, 'I had another dream, and this time the sun and moon and eleven stars were bowing down to me.'

10 When he told his father as well as his brothers, his father rebuked him and said, 'What is this dream you had? Will your mother and I and your brothers actually come and bow down to the ground before you?' 11 His brothers were jealous of him, but his father kept the matter in mind.

Joseph sold by his brothers

12 Now his brothers had gone to graze their father's flocks near Shechem, 13 and Israel said to Joseph, 'As you know, your brothers are grazing the flocks near Shechem. Come, I am going to send you to them.'

'Very well,' he replied.

14 So he said to him, 'Go and see if all is well with your brothers and with the flocks, and bring word back to me.' Then he sent him off from the Valley of Hebron.

When Joseph arrived at Shechem, 15 a man found him wandering around in the fields and asked him, 'What are you looking for?'

16 He replied, 'I'm looking for my

---

e 39 Many manuscripts of the Masoretic Text, Samaritan Pentateuch and Syriac (see also 1 Chron. 1:50); most manuscripts of the Masoretic Text *Hadar*

a 3 The meaning of the Hebrew for this word is uncertain; also in verses 23 and 32.

brothers. Can you tell me where they are grazing their flocks?'

17 'They have moved on from here,' the man answered. 'I heard them say, "Let's go to Dothan."'

So Joseph went after his brothers and found them near Dothan. 18 But they saw him in the distance, and before he reached them, they plotted to kill him.

19 'Here comes that dreamer!' they said to each other. 20 'Come now, let's kill him and throw him into one of these cisterns and say that a ferocious animal devoured him. Then we'll see what comes of his dreams.'

21 When Reuben heard this, he tried to rescue him from their hands. 'Let's not take his life,' he said. 22 'Don't shed any blood. Throw him into this cistern here in the wilderness, but don't lay a hand on him.' Reuben said this to rescue him from them and take him back to his father.

23 So when Joseph came to his brothers, they stripped him of his robe – the ornate robe he was wearing – 24 and they took him and threw him into the cistern. The cistern was empty; there was no water in it.

25 As they sat down to eat their meal, they looked up and saw a caravan of Ishmaelites coming from Gilead. Their camels were loaded with spices, balm and myrrh, and they were on their way to take them down to Egypt.

26 Judah said to his brothers, 'What will we gain if we kill our brother and cover up his blood? 27 Come, let's sell him to the Ishmaelites and not lay our hands on him; after all, he is our brother, our own flesh and blood.' His brothers agreed.

28 So when the Midianite merchants came by, his brothers pulled Joseph up out of the cistern and sold him for twenty shekels[b] of silver to the Ishmaelites, who took him to Egypt.

29 When Reuben returned to the cistern and saw that Joseph was not there, he tore his clothes. 30 He went back to his brothers and said, 'The boy isn't there! Where can I turn now?'

31 Then they got Joseph's robe, slaughtered a goat and dipped the robe in the blood. 32 They took the ornate robe back to their father and said, 'We found this. Examine it to see whether it is your son's robe.'

33 He recognised it and said, 'It is my son's robe! Some ferocious animal has devoured him. Joseph has surely been torn to pieces.'

34 Then Jacob tore his clothes, put on sackcloth and mourned for his son many days. 35 All his sons and daughters came to comfort him, but he refused to be comforted. 'No,' he said, 'I will continue to mourn until I join my son in the grave.' So his father wept for him.

36 Meanwhile, the Midianites[c] sold Joseph in Egypt to Potiphar, one of Pharaoh's officials, the captain of the guard.

Judah and Tamar

38 At that time, Judah left his brothers and went down to stay with a man of Adullam named Hirah. 2 There Judah met the daughter of a Canaanite man named Shua. He married her and made love to her; 3 she became pregnant and gave birth to a son, who was named Er. 4 She conceived again and gave birth to a son and named him Onan. 5 She gave birth to still another son and named him Shelah. It was at Kezib that she gave birth to him.

6 Judah got a wife for Er, his firstborn, and her name was Tamar. 7 But Er, Judah's firstborn, was wicked in the LORD's sight; so the LORD put him to death.

8 Then Judah said to Onan, 'Sleep with your brother's wife and fulfil your duty to her as a brother-in-law to raise up offspring for your brother.' 9 But Onan knew that the child would not be his; so whenever he slept with his brother's wife, he spilled his semen on the ground to avoid providing offspring for his brother. 10 What he did was wicked in the LORD's sight; so the LORD put him to death also.

11 Judah then said to his daughter-in-law

---

b 28 That is, about 230 grams

c 36 Samaritan Pentateuch, Septuagint, Vulgate and Syriac (see also verse 28); Masoretic Text *Medanites*

Tamar, 'Live as a widow in your father's household until my son Shelah grows up.' For he thought, 'He may die too, just like his brothers.' So Tamar went to live in her father's household.

¹²After a long time Judah's wife, the daughter of Shua, died. When Judah had recovered from his grief, he went up to Timnah, to the men who were shearing his sheep, and his friend Hirah the Adullamite went with him.

¹³When Tamar was told, 'Your father-in-law is on his way to Timnah to shear his sheep,' ¹⁴she took off her widow's clothes, covered herself with a veil to disguise herself, and then sat down at the entrance to Enaim, which is on the road to Timnah. For she saw that, though Shelah had now grown up, she had not been given to him as his wife.

¹⁵When Judah saw her, he thought she was a prostitute, for she had covered her face. ¹⁶Not realising that she was his daughter-in-law, he went over to her by the roadside and said, 'Come now, let me sleep with you.'

'And what will you give me to sleep with you?' she asked.

¹⁷'I'll send you a young goat from my flock,' he said.

'Will you give me something as a pledge until you send it?' she asked.

¹⁸He said, 'What pledge should I give you?'

'Your seal and its cord, and the staff in your hand,' she answered. So he gave them to her and slept with her, and she became pregnant by him. ¹⁹After she left, she took off her veil and put on her widow's clothes again.

²⁰Meanwhile Judah sent the young goat by his friend the Adullamite in order to get his pledge back from the woman, but he did not find her. ²¹He asked the men who lived there, 'Where is the shrine-prostitute who was beside the road at Enaim?'

'There hasn't been any shrine-prostitute here,' they said.

²²So he went back to Judah and said, 'I didn't find her. Besides, the men who lived there said, "There hasn't been any shrine-prostitute here." '

²³Then Judah said, 'Let her keep what she has, or we will become a laughing-stock. After all, I did send her this young goat, but you didn't find her.'

²⁴About three months later Judah was told, 'Your daughter-in-law Tamar is guilty of prostitution, and as a result she is now pregnant.'

Judah said, 'Bring her out and let her be burned to death!'

²⁵As she was being brought out, she sent a message to her father-in-law. 'I am pregnant by the man who owns these,' she said. And she added, 'See if you recognise whose seal and cord and staff these are.'

²⁶Judah recognised them and said, 'She is more righteous than I, since I wouldn't give her to my son Shelah.' And he did not sleep with her again.

²⁷When the time came for her to give birth, there were twin boys in her womb. ²⁸As she was giving birth, one of them put out his hand; so the midwife took a scarlet thread and tied it on his wrist and said, 'This one came out first.' ²⁹But when he drew back his hand, his brother came out, and she said, 'So this is how you have broken out!' And he was named Perez.ᵃ ³⁰Then his brother, who had the scarlet thread on his wrist, came out. And he was named Zerah.ᵇ

Joseph and Potiphar's wife

39 Now Joseph had been taken down to Egypt. Potiphar, an Egyptian who was one of Pharaoh's officials, the captain of the guard, bought him from the Ishmaelites who had taken him there.

²The LORD was with Joseph so that he prospered, and he lived in the house of his Egyptian master. ³When his master saw that the LORD was with him and that the LORD gave him success in everything he did, ⁴Joseph found favour in his eyes and became his attendant. Potiphar put him in charge of his household, and he entrusted to his care everything he owned. ⁵From the time he put him in charge of

---

a 29 Perez means breaking out.
b 30 Zerah can mean scarlet or brightness.

his household and of all that he owned, the LORD blessed the household of the Egyptian because of Joseph. The blessing of the LORD was on everything Potiphar had, both in the house and in the field. 6 So Potiphar left everything he had in Joseph's care; with Joseph in charge, he did not concern himself with anything except the food he ate.

Now Joseph was well-built and handsome, 7 and after a while his master's wife took notice of Joseph and said, 'Come to bed with me!'

8 But he refused. 'With me in charge,' he told her, 'my master does not concern himself with anything in the house; everything he owns he has entrusted to my care. 9 No one is greater in this house than I am. My master has withheld nothing from me except you, because you are his wife. How then could I do such a wicked thing and sin against God?' 10 And though she spoke to Joseph day after day, he refused to go to bed with her or even to be with her.

11 One day he went into the house to attend to his duties, and none of the household servants was inside. 12 She caught him by his cloak and said, 'Come to bed with me!' But he left his cloak in her hand and ran out of the house.

13 When she saw that he had left his cloak in her hand and had run out of the house, 14 she called her household servants. 'Look,' she said to them, 'this Hebrew has been brought to us to make sport of us! He came in here to sleep with me, but I screamed. 15 When he heard me scream for help, he left his cloak beside me and ran out of the house.'

16 She kept his cloak beside her until his master came home. 17 Then she told him this story: 'That Hebrew slave you brought us came to me to make sport of me. 18 But as soon as I screamed for help, he left his cloak beside me and ran out of the house.'

19 When his master heard the story his wife told him, saying, 'This is how your slave treated me,' he burned with anger. 20 Joseph's master took him and put him in prison, the place where the king's prisoners were confined.

But while Joseph was there in the prison, 21 the LORD was with him; he showed him kindness and granted him favour in the eyes of the prison warder. 22 So the warder put Joseph in charge of all those held in the prison, and he was made responsible for all that was done there. 23 The warder paid no attention to anything under Joseph's care, because the LORD was with Joseph and gave him success in whatever he did.

The cupbearer and the baker

40 Some time later, the cupbearer and the baker of the king of Egypt offended their master, the king of Egypt. 2 Pharaoh was angry with his two officials, the chief cupbearer and the chief baker, 3 and put them in custody in the house of the captain of the guard, in the same prison where Joseph was confined. 4 The captain of the guard assigned them to Joseph, and he attended them.

After they had been in custody for some time, 5 each of the two men – the cupbearer and the baker of the king of Egypt, who were being held in prison – had a dream the same night, and each dream had a meaning of its own.

6 When Joseph came to them the next morning, he saw that they were dejected. 7 So he asked Pharaoh's officials who were in custody with him in his master's house, 'Why do you look so sad today?'

8 'We both had dreams,' they answered, 'but there is no one to interpret them.'

Then Joseph said to them, 'Do not interpretations belong to God? Tell me your dreams.'

9 So the chief cupbearer told Joseph his dream. He said to him, 'In my dream I saw a vine in front of me, 10 and on the vine were three branches. As soon as it budded, it blossomed, and its clusters ripened into grapes. 11 Pharaoh's cup was in my hand, and I took the grapes, squeezed them into Pharaoh's cup and put the cup in his hand.'

12 'This is what it means,' Joseph said to him. 'The three branches are three days. 13 Within three days Pharaoh will lift up your head and restore you to your

position, and you will put Pharaoh's cup in his hand, just as you used to do when you were his cupbearer. ¹⁴But when all goes well with you, remember me and show me kindness; mention me to Pharaoh and get me out of this prison. ¹⁵I was forcibly carried off from the land of the Hebrews, and even here I have done nothing to deserve being put in a dungeon.'

¹⁶When the chief baker saw that Joseph had given a favourable interpretation, he said to Joseph, 'I too had a dream: on my head were three baskets of bread.ᵃ ¹⁷In the top basket were all kinds of baked goods for Pharaoh, but the birds were eating them out of the basket on my head.'

¹⁸'This is what it means,' Joseph said. 'The three baskets are three days. ¹⁹Within three days Pharaoh will lift off your head and impale your body on a pole. And the birds will eat away your flesh.'

²⁰Now the third day was Pharaoh's birthday, and he gave a feast for all his officials. He lifted up the heads of the chief cupbearer and the chief baker in the presence of his officials: ²¹he restored the chief cupbearer to his position, so that he once again put the cup into Pharaoh's hand – ²²but he impaled the chief baker, just as Joseph had said to them in his interpretation.

²³The chief cupbearer, however, did not remember Joseph; he forgot him.

Pharaoh's dreams

41 When two full years had passed, Pharaoh had a dream: He was standing by the Nile, ²when out of the river there came up seven cows, sleek and fat, and they grazed among the reeds. ³After them, seven other cows, ugly and gaunt, came up out of the Nile and stood beside those on the river-bank. ⁴And the cows that were ugly and gaunt ate up the seven sleek, fat cows. Then Pharaoh woke up.

⁵He fell asleep again and had a second dream: seven ears of corn, healthy and good, were growing on a single stalk. ⁶After them, seven other ears of corn sprouted – thin and scorched by the east

wind. ⁷The thin ears of corn swallowed up the seven healthy, full ears. Then Pharaoh woke up; it had been a dream.

⁸In the morning his mind was troubled, so he sent for all the magicians and wise men of Egypt. Pharaoh told them his dreams, but no one could interpret them for him.

⁹Then the chief cupbearer said to Pharaoh, 'Today I am reminded of my shortcomings. ¹⁰Pharaoh was once angry with his servants, and he imprisoned me and the chief baker in the house of the captain of the guard. ¹¹Each of us had a dream the same night, and each dream had a meaning of its own. ¹²Now a young Hebrew was there with us, a servant of the captain of the guard. We told him our dreams, and he interpreted them for us, giving each man the interpretation of his dream. ¹³And things turned out exactly as he interpreted them to us: I was restored to my position, and the other man was impaled.'

¹⁴So Pharaoh sent for Joseph, and he was quickly brought from the dungeon. When he had shaved and changed his clothes, he came before Pharaoh.

¹⁵Pharaoh said to Joseph, 'I had a dream, and no one can interpret it. But I have heard it said of you that when you hear a dream you can interpret it.'

¹⁶'I cannot do it,' Joseph replied to Pharaoh, 'but God will give Pharaoh the answer he desires.'

¹⁷Then Pharaoh said to Joseph, 'In my dream I was standing on the bank of the Nile, ¹⁸when out of the river there came up seven cows, fat and sleek, and they grazed among the reeds. ¹⁹After them, seven other cows came up – scrawny and very ugly and lean. I had never seen such ugly cows in all the land of Egypt. ²⁰The lean, ugly cows ate up the seven fat cows that came up first. ²¹But even after they ate them, no one could tell that they had done so; they looked just as ugly as before. Then I woke up.

²²'In my dream I saw seven ears of corn, full and good, growing on a single stalk. ²³After them, seven other ears sprouted – withered and thin and scorched by the east wind. ²⁴The thin ears of corn

---

ᵃ 16 Or three wicker baskets

swallowed up the seven good ears. I told this to the magicians, but none of them could explain it to me.'

25 Then Joseph said to Pharaoh, 'The dreams of Pharaoh are one and the same. God has revealed to Pharaoh what he is about to do. 26 The seven good cows are seven years, and the seven good ears of corn are seven years; it is one and the same dream. 27 The seven lean, ugly cows that came up afterwards are seven years, and so are the seven worthless ears of corn scorched by the east wind: they are seven years of famine.

28 'It is just as I said to Pharaoh: God has shown Pharaoh what he is about to do. 29 Seven years of great abundance are coming throughout the land of Egypt, 30 but seven years of famine will follow them. Then all the abundance in Egypt will be forgotten, and the famine will ravage the land. 31 The abundance in the land will not be remembered, because the famine that follows it will be so severe. 32 The reason the dream was given to Pharaoh in two forms is that the matter has been firmly decided by God, and God will do it soon.

33 'And now let Pharaoh look for a discerning and wise man and put him in charge of the land of Egypt. 34 Let Pharaoh appoint commissioners over the land to take a fifth of the harvest of Egypt during the seven years of abundance. 35 They should collect all the food of these good years that are coming and store up the grain under the authority of Pharaoh, to be kept in the cities for food. 36 This food should be held in reserve for the country, to be used during the seven years of famine that will come upon Egypt, so that the country may not be ruined by the famine.'

37 The plan seemed good to Pharaoh and to all his officials. 38 So Pharaoh asked them, 'Can we find anyone like this man, one in whom is the spirit of God?'*a*

39 Then Pharaoh said to Joseph, 'Since God has made all this known to you, there is no one so discerning and wise as you. 40 You shall be in charge of my palace, and all my people are to submit to your orders.

Only with respect to the throne will I be greater than you.'

Joseph in charge of Egypt

41 So Pharaoh said to Joseph, 'I hereby put you in charge of the whole land of Egypt.' 42 Then Pharaoh took his signet ring from his finger and put it on Joseph's finger. He dressed him in robes of fine linen and put a gold chain round his neck. 43 He made him ride in a chariot as his second-in-command,*b* and people shouted before him, 'Make way*c*!' Thus he put him in charge of the whole land of Egypt.

44 Then Pharaoh said to Joseph, 'I am Pharaoh, but without your word no one will lift hand or foot in all Egypt.' 45 Pharaoh gave Joseph the name Zaphenath-Paneah and gave him Asenath daughter of Potiphera, priest of On,*d* to be his wife. And Joseph went throughout the land of Egypt.

46 Joseph was thirty years old when he entered the service of Pharaoh king of Egypt. And Joseph went out from Pharaoh's presence and travelled throughout Egypt. 47 During the seven years of abundance the land produced plentifully. 48 Joseph collected all the food produced in those seven years of abundance in Egypt and stored it in the cities. In each city he put the food grown in the fields surrounding it. 49 Joseph stored up huge quantities of grain, like the sand of the sea; it was so much that he stopped keeping records because it was beyond measure.

50 Before the years of famine came, two sons were born to Joseph by Asenath daughter of Potiphera, priest of On. 51 Joseph named his firstborn Manasseh*e* and said, 'It is because God has made me forget all my trouble and all my father's household.' 52 The second son he named Ephraim*f* and said, 'It is because God has made me fruitful in the land of my suffering.'

---

a Or *of the gods*

b 43 Or *in the chariot of his second-in-command*; or *in his second chariot*

c 43 Or *Bow down*

d 45 That is, Heliopolis; also in verse 50

e 51 *Manasseh* sounds like and may be derived from the Hebrew for *forget.*

f 52 *Ephraim* sounds like the Hebrew for *twice fruitful.*

MONEY 10

STEWARDSHIP

Being a good steward isn't just about rocking up to Soul Survivor in the summer, wearing a fluorescent yellow jacket and helping people know where to go! It's also a great word which describes good management of what we have – our gifts and talents, our money and resources.

Being a good steward of our money may look different depending on what's going on with life. It may mean saving your money during your gap year for university; or paying off a debt instalment by instalment; or investing your money in something to make even more money; or giving money away to others in need. All these activities could be good stewardship – whether it's saving, spending, investing or giving.

In Genesis 41 we're reading about Pharaoh's dreams and Joseph's interpretation of them. Joseph (of multicoloured coat fame) is revealing the meaning of Pharaoh's odd dreams and explaining that God is planning on sending seven years of famine. However, before this happens, Egypt will have seven years with bumper harvests, so Pharaoh is to save a fifth of the harvest each year to provide for his people during the famine that will follow. Pharaoh needs to be a good steward of his country's provisions in order to be able to care for his people.

Being a good steward involves being smart with what we have. A great way to do this is by creating a budget. Here are four points to consider in your budgeting.

- Choose how much money to give to others (church, individuals, charities, etc.). Scripture talks about giving a tithe (10 per cent) of our money away, so you could chat to God and others about a generous amount to give.

- Work out what you should spend on yourself – including bills, food, fun things (like a holiday or a pair of shoes), paying off debts, etc. Budgeting is a good method to ensure we don't overspend and buy more than we can afford, ending up in debt that we could have avoided.

- Decide if it's a good time to save money and what percentage you can afford to save, whether it's saving for something fun or something essential, big or small – a gap year, a car, university, a pair of trainers, a present for someone.

- Is it appropriate to invest your money in something with the aim that it will increase in value? This often involves taking a risk and may mean losing the money that was invested, so it's worth seeking advice if you think this is something you would like to do.

Creating a budget is a sensible way to look after what we have – so it's time for the flow charts and coloured pens, or the Excel spreadsheets and calculators, to come out and play!

Kiera Singlehurst-Phyo

 Matthew 6:19–24

53 The seven years of abundance in Egypt came to an end, **54** and the seven years of famine began, just as Joseph had said. There was famine in all the other lands, but in the whole land of Egypt there was food. **55** When all Egypt began to feel the famine, the people cried to Pharaoh for food. Then Pharaoh told all the Egyptians, 'Go to Joseph and do what he tells you.'

56 When the famine had spread over the whole country, Joseph opened all the storehouses and sold grain to the Egyptians, for the famine was severe throughout Egypt. **57** And all the world came to Egypt to buy grain from Joseph, because the famine was severe everywhere.

Joseph's brothers go to Egypt

42 When Jacob learned that there was grain in Egypt, he said to his sons, 'Why do you just keep looking at each other?' **2** He continued, 'I have heard that there is grain in Egypt. Go down there and buy some for us, so that we may live and not die.'

3 Then ten of Joseph's brothers went down to buy grain from Egypt. **4** But Jacob did not send Benjamin, Joseph's brother, with the others, because he was afraid that harm might come to him. **5** So Israel's sons were among those who went to buy grain, for there was famine in the land of Canaan also.

6 Now Joseph was the governor of the land, the person who sold grain to all its people. So when Joseph's brothers arrived, they bowed down to him with their faces to the ground. **7** As soon as Joseph saw his brothers, he recognised them, but he pretended to be a stranger and spoke harshly to them. 'Where do you come from?' he asked.

'From the land of Canaan,' they replied, 'to buy food.'

8 Although Joseph recognised his brothers, they did not recognise him. **9** Then he remembered his dreams about them and said to them, 'You are spies! You have come to see where our land is unprotected.'

10 'No, my lord,' they answered. 'Your servants have come to buy food. **11** We are all the sons of one man. Your servants are honest men, not spies.'

12 'No!' he said to them. 'You have come to see where our land is unprotected.'

13 But they replied, 'Your servants were twelve brothers, the sons of one man, who lives in the land of Canaan. The youngest is now with our father, and one is no more.'

14 Joseph said to them, 'It is just as I told you: you are spies! **15** And this is how you will be tested: as surely as Pharaoh lives, you will not leave this place unless your youngest brother comes here. **16** Send one of your number to get your brother; the rest of you will be kept in prison, so that your words may be tested to see if you are telling the truth. If you are not, then as surely as Pharaoh lives, you are spies!' **17** And he put them all in custody for three days.

18 On the third day, Joseph said to them, 'Do this and you will live, for I fear God: **19** if you are honest men, let one of your brothers stay here in prison, while the rest of you go and take grain back for your starving households. **20** But you must bring your youngest brother to me, so that your words may be verified and that you may not die.' This they proceeded to do.

21 They said to one another, 'Surely we are being punished because of our brother. We saw how distressed he was when he pleaded with us for his life, but we would not listen; that's why this distress has come on us.'

22 Reuben replied, 'Didn't I tell you not to sin against the boy? But you wouldn't listen! Now we must give an accounting for his blood.' **23** They did not realise that Joseph could understand them, since he was using an interpreter.

24 He turned away from them and began to weep, but then came back and spoke to them again. He had Simeon taken from them and bound before their eyes.

25 Joseph gave orders to fill their bags with grain, to put each man's silver back in his sack, and to give them provisions for their journey. After this was done for them, **26** they loaded their grain on their donkeys and left.

27 At the place where they stopped for the night one of them opened his sack to get feed for his donkey, and he saw his silver in the mouth of his sack. 28 'My silver has been returned,' he said to his brothers. 'Here it is in my sack.'

Their hearts sank and they turned to each other trembling and said, 'What is this that God has done to us?'

29 When they came to their father Jacob in the land of Canaan, they told him all that had happened to them. They said, 30 'The man who is lord over the land spoke harshly to us and treated us as though we were spying on the land. 31 But we said to him, "We are honest men; we are not spies. 32 We were twelve brothers, sons of one father. One is no more, and the youngest is now with our father in Canaan."

33 'Then the man who is lord over the land said to us, "This is how I will know whether you are honest men: leave one of your brothers here with me, and take food for your starving households and go. 34 But bring your youngest brother to me so I will know that you are not spies but honest men. Then I will give your brother back to you, and you can trade*a* in the land." '

35 As they were emptying their sacks, there in each man's sack was his pouch of silver! When they and their father saw the money pouches, they were frightened. 36 Their father Jacob said to them, 'You have deprived me of my children. Joseph is no more and Simeon is no more, and now you want to take Benjamin. Everything is against me!'

37 Then Reuben said to his father, 'You may put both of my sons to death if I do not bring him back to you. Entrust him to my care, and I will bring him back.'

38 But Jacob said, 'My son will not go down there with you; his brother is dead and he is the only one left. If harm comes to him on the journey you are taking, you will bring my grey head down to the grave in sorrow.'

The second journey to Egypt

43 Now the famine was still severe in the land. 2 So when they had eaten all the grain they had brought from Egypt, their father said to them, 'Go back and buy us a little more food.'

3 But Judah said to him, 'The man warned us solemnly, "You will not see my face again unless your brother is with you." 4 If you will send our brother along with us, we will go down and buy food for you. 5 But if you will not send him, we will not go down, because the man said to us, "You will not see my face again unless your brother is with you." '

6 Israel asked, 'Why did you bring this trouble on me by telling the man you had another brother?'

7 They replied, 'The man questioned us closely about ourselves and our family. "Is your father still living?" he asked us. "Do you have another brother?" We simply answered his questions. How were we to know he would say, "Bring your brother down here"?'

8 Then Judah said to Israel his father, 'Send the boy along with me and we will go at once, so that we and you and our children may live and not die. 9 I myself will guarantee his safety; you can hold me personally responsible for him. If I do not bring him back to you and set him here before you, I will bear the blame before you all my life. 10 As it is, if we had not delayed, we could have gone and returned twice.'

11 Then their father Israel said to them, 'If it must be, then do this: put some of the best products of the land in your bags and take them down to the man as a gift – a little balm and a little honey, some spices and myrrh, some pistachio nuts and almonds. 12 Take double the amount of silver with you, for you must return the silver that was put back into the mouths of your sacks. Perhaps it was a mistake. 13 Take your brother also and go back to the man at once. 14 And may God Almighty*a* grant you mercy before the man so that he

---

a 34 Or *move about freely*

will let your other brother and Benjamin come back with you. As for me, if I am bereaved, I am bereaved.'

¹⁵ So the men took the gifts and double the amount of silver, and Benjamin also. They hurried down to Egypt and presented themselves to Joseph. ¹⁶ When Joseph saw Benjamin with them, he said to the steward of his house, 'Take these men to my house, slaughter an animal and prepare a meal; they are to eat with me at noon.'

¹⁷ The man did as Joseph told him and took the men to Joseph's house. ¹⁸ Now the men were frightened when they were taken to his house. They thought, 'We were brought here because of the silver that was put back into our sacks the first time. He wants to attack us and overpower us and seize us as slaves and take our donkeys.'

¹⁹ So they went up to Joseph's steward and spoke to him at the entrance to the house. ²⁰ 'We beg your pardon, our lord,' they said, 'we came down here the first time to buy food. ²¹ But at the place where we stopped for the night we opened our sacks and each of us found his silver – the exact weight – in the mouth of his sack. So we have brought it back with us. ²² We have also brought additional silver with us to buy food. We don't know who put our silver in our sacks.'

²³ 'It's all right,' he said. 'Don't be afraid. Your God, the God of your father, has given you treasure in your sacks; I received your silver.' Then he brought Simeon out to them.

²⁴ The steward took the men into Joseph's house, gave them water to wash their feet and provided fodder for their donkeys. ²⁵ They prepared their gifts for Joseph's arrival at noon, because they had heard that they were to eat there.

²⁶ When Joseph came home, they presented to him the gifts they had brought into the house, and they bowed down before him to the ground. ²⁷ He asked them how they were, and then he said, 'How is your aged father you told me about? Is he still living?'

²⁸ They replied, 'Your servant our father is still alive and well.' And they bowed

down, prostrating themselves before him.

²⁹ As he looked about and saw his brother Benjamin, his own mother's son, he asked, 'Is this your youngest brother, the one you told me about?' And he said, 'God be gracious to you, my son.' ³⁰ Deeply moved at the sight of his brother, Joseph hurried out and looked for a place to weep. He went into his private room and wept there.

³¹ After he had washed his face, he came out and, controlling himself, said, 'Serve the food.'

³² They served him by himself, the brothers by themselves, and the Egyptians who ate with him by themselves, because Egyptians could not eat with Hebrews, for that is detestable to Egyptians. ³³ The men had been seated before him in the order of their ages, from the firstborn to the youngest; and they looked at each other in astonishment. ³⁴ When portions were served to them from Joseph's table, Benjamin's portion was five times as much as anyone else's. So they feasted and drank freely with him.

A silver cup in a sack

44 Now Joseph gave these instructions to the steward of his house: 'Fill the men's sacks with as much food as they can carry, and put each man's silver in the mouth of his sack. ² Then put my cup, the silver one, in the mouth of the youngest one's sack, along with the silver for his grain.' And he did as Joseph said.

³ As morning dawned, the men were sent on their way with their donkeys. ⁴ They had not gone far from the city when Joseph said to his steward, 'Go after those men at once, and when you catch up with them, say to them, "Why have you repaid good with evil? ⁵ Isn't this the cup my master drinks from and also uses for divination? This is a wicked thing you have done."'

⁶ When he caught up with them, he repeated these words to them. ⁷ But they said to him, 'Why does my lord say such things? Far be it from your servants to do anything like that! ⁸ We even brought

back to you from the land of Canaan the silver we found inside the mouths of our sacks. So why would we steal silver or gold from your master's house? 9 If any of your servants is found to have it, he will die; and the rest of us will become my lord's slaves.'

10 'Very well, then,' he said, 'let it be as you say. Whoever is found to have it will become my slave; the rest of you will be free from blame.'

11 Each of them quickly lowered his sack to the ground and opened it. 12 Then the steward proceeded to search, beginning with the eldest and ending with the youngest. And the cup was found in Benjamin's sack. 13 At this, they tore their clothes. Then they all loaded their donkeys and returned to the city.

14 Joseph was still in the house when Judah and his brothers came in, and they threw themselves to the ground before him. 15 Joseph said to them, 'What is this you have done? Don't you know that a man like me can find things out by divination?'

16 'What can we say to my lord?' Judah replied. 'What can we say? How can we prove our innocence? God has uncovered your servants' guilt. We are now my lord's slaves – we ourselves and the one who was found to have the cup.'

17 But Joseph said, 'Far be it from me to do such a thing! Only the man who was found to have the cup will become my slave. The rest of you, go back to your father in peace.'

18 Then Judah went up to him and said: 'Pardon your servant, my lord, let me speak a word to my lord. Do not be angry with your servant, though you are equal to Pharaoh himself. 19 My lord asked his servants, "Do you have a father or a brother?" 20 And we answered, "We have an aged father, and there is a young son born to him in his old age. His brother is dead, and he is the only one of his mother's sons left, and his father loves him."

21 'Then you said to your servants, "Bring him down to me so I can see him for myself." 22 And we said to my lord, "The boy cannot leave his father; if he leaves him, his father will die." 23 But you told your

servants, "Unless your youngest brother comes down with you, you will not see my face again." 24 When we went back to your servant my father, we told him what my lord had said.

25 'Then our father said, "Go back and buy a little more food." 26 But we said, "We cannot go down. Only if our youngest brother is with us will we go. We cannot see the man's face unless our youngest brother is with us."

27 'Your servant my father said to us, "You know that my wife bore me two sons. 28 One of them went away from me, and I said, 'He has surely been torn to pieces.' And I have not seen him since. 29 If you take this one from me too and harm comes to him, you will bring my grey head down to the grave in misery."

30 'So now, if the boy is not with us when I go back to your servant my father, and if my father, whose life is closely bound up with the boy's life, 31 sees that the boy isn't there, he will die. Your servants will bring the grey head of our father down to the grave in sorrow. 32 Your servant guaranteed the boy's safety to my father. I said, "If I do not bring him back to you, I will bear the blame before you, my father, all my life!"

33 'Now then, please let your servant remain here as my lord's slave in place of the boy, and let the boy return with his brothers. 34 How can I go back to my father if the boy is not with me? No! Do not let me see the misery that would come on my father.'

Joseph makes himself known

45 Then Joseph could no longer control himself before all his attendants, and he cried out, 'Make everyone leave my presence!' So there was no one with Joseph when he made himself known to his brothers. 2 And he wept so loudly that the Egyptians heard him, and Pharaoh's household heard about it.

3 Joseph said to his brothers, 'I am Joseph! Is my father still living?' But his brothers were not able to answer him, because they were terrified at his presence.

4 Then Joseph said to his brothers,

'Come close to me.' When they had done so, he said, 'I am your brother Joseph, the one you sold into Egypt! 5 And now, do not be distressed and do not be angry with yourselves for selling me here, because it was to save lives that God sent me ahead of you. 6 For two years now there has been famine in the land, and for the next five years there will be no ploughing and reaping. 7 But God sent me ahead of you to preserve for you a remnant on earth and to save your lives by a great deliverance. *a*

8 'So then, it was not you who sent

JOSEPH

DREAMS:
Genesis 37:1–36
SLAVE:
Genesis 39:1–23
JAIL:
Genesis 40:1–23
KING:
Genesis 41:1–57
BROTHERS:
Genesis 42:1–38
SURPRISE:
Genesis 45:1–15
DEATH:
Genesis 50:15–26

me here, but God. He made me father to Pharaoh, lord of his entire household and ruler of all Egypt. 9 Now hurry back to my father and say to him, "This is what your son Joseph says: God has made me lord of all Egypt. Come down to me; don't delay. 10 You shall live in the region of Goshen and be near me – you, your children and grandchildren, your flocks and herds, and all you have. 11 I will provide for you there, because five years of famine are still to come. Otherwise you and your household

and all who belong to you will become destitute."

12 'You can see for yourselves, and so can my brother Benjamin, that it is really I who am speaking to you. 13 Tell my father about all the honour accorded me in Egypt and about everything you have seen. And bring my father down here quickly.'

14 Then he threw his arms around his brother Benjamin and wept, and Benjamin embraced him, weeping. 15 And he kissed all his brothers and wept over them. Afterwards his brothers talked with him.

16 When the news reached Pharaoh's palace that Joseph's brothers had come, Pharaoh and all his officials were pleased. 17 Pharaoh said to Joseph, 'Tell your brothers, "Do this: load your animals and return to the land of Canaan, 18 and bring your father and your families back to me. I will give you the best of the land of Egypt and you can enjoy the fat of the land."

19 'You are also instructed to tell them, "Do this: take some carts from Egypt for your children and your wives, and get your father and come. 20 Never mind about your belongings, because the best of all Egypt will be yours."'

21 So the sons of Israel did this. Joseph gave them carts, as Pharaoh had commanded, and he also gave them provisions for their journey. 22 To each of them he gave new clothing, but to Benjamin he gave three hundred shekels*b* of silver and five sets of clothes. 23 And this is what he sent to his father: ten donkeys loaded with the best things of Egypt, and ten female donkeys loaded with grain and bread and other provisions for his journey. 24 Then he sent his brothers away, and as they were leaving he said to them, 'Don't quarrel on the way!'

25 So they went up out of Egypt and came to their father Jacob in the land of Canaan. 26 They told him, 'Joseph is still alive! In fact, he is ruler of all Egypt.' Jacob was stunned; he did not believe them. 27 But when they told him everything Joseph

---

a 7 Or *save you as a great band of survivors*   *b* 22 That is, about 3.5 kilograms had said to them, and when he saw the carts Joseph had sent to carry him back, the spirit of their father Jacob revived. 28 And Israel said, 'I'm convinced! My son Joseph is still alive. I will go and see him before I die.'

Jacob goes to Egypt

46 So Israel set out with all that was his, and when he reached Beersheba, he offered sacrifices to the God of his father Isaac.

2 And God spoke to Israel in a vision at night and said, 'Jacob! Jacob!'

'Here I am,' he replied.

3 'I am God, the God of your father,' he said. 'Do not be afraid to go down to Egypt, for I will make you into a great nation there. 4 I will go down to Egypt with you, and I will surely bring you back again. And Joseph's own hand will close your eyes.'

5 Then Jacob left Beersheba, and Israel's sons took their father Jacob and their children and their wives in the carts that Pharaoh had sent to transport him. 6 So Jacob and all his offspring went to Egypt, taking with them their livestock and the possessions they had acquired in Canaan. 7 Jacob brought with him to Egypt his sons and grandsons and his daughters and granddaughters – all his offspring.

8 These are the names of the sons of Israel (Jacob and his descendants) who went to Egypt:

Reuben the firstborn of Jacob.
9 The sons of Reuben:
    Hanok, Pallu, Hezron and Karmi.
10 The sons of Simeon:
    Jemuel, Jamin, Ohad, Jakin, Zohar and Shaul the son of a Canaanite woman.
11 The sons of Levi:
    Gershon, Kohath and Merari.
12 The sons of Judah:
    Er, Onan, Shelah, Perez and Zerah (but Er and Onan had died in the land of Canaan).
    The sons of Perez:
        Hezron and Hamul.
13 The sons of Issachar:

Tola, Puah,[a] Jashub[b] and Shimron.
14 The sons of Zebulun:
    Sered, Elon and Jahleel.
15 These were the sons Leah bore to Jacob in Paddan Aram,[c] besides his daughter Dinah. These sons and daughters of his were thirty-three in all.

16 The sons of Gad:
    Zephon,[d] Haggi, Shuni, Ezbon, Eri, Arodi and Areli.
17 The sons of Asher:
    Imnah, Ishvah, Ishvi and Beriah.
    Their sister was Serah.
    The sons of Beriah:
        Heber and Malkiel.
18 These were the children born to Jacob by Zilpah, whom Laban had given to his daughter Leah – sixteen in all.

19 The sons of Jacob's wife Rachel:
    Joseph and Benjamin. 20 In Egypt, Manasseh and Ephraim were born to Joseph by Asenath daughter of Potiphera, priest of On.[e]
21 The sons of Benjamin:
    Bela, Beker, Ashbel, Gera, Naaman, Ehi, Rosh, Muppim, Huppim and Ard.
22 These were the sons of Rachel who were born to Jacob – fourteen in all.

23 The son of Dan:
    Hushim.
24 The sons of Naphtali:
    Jahziel, Guni, Jezer and Shillem.
25 These were the sons born to Jacob by Bilhah, whom Laban had given to his daughter Rachel – seven in all.

26 All those who went to Egypt with Jacob – those who were his direct descendants, not counting his sons' wives –

---

a 13 Samaritan Pentateuch and Syriac (see also 1 Chron. 7:1); Masoretic Text *Puvah*
b 13 Samaritan Pentateuch and some Septuagint manuscripts (see also Num. 26:24 and 1 Chron. 7:1); Masoretic Text *Iob*
c 15 That is, North-west Mesopotamia
d 16 Samaritan Pentateuch and Septuagint (see also Num. 26:15); Masoretic Text *Ziphion*
e 20 That is, Heliopolis

numbered sixty-six persons. 27With the two sons*f* who had been born to Joseph in Egypt, the members of Jacob's family, which went to Egypt, were seventy*g* in all.

28Now Jacob sent Judah ahead of him to Joseph to get directions to Goshen. When they arrived in the region of Goshen, 29Joseph had his chariot made ready and went to Goshen to meet his father Israel. As soon as Joseph appeared before him, he threw his arms around his father*h* and wept for a long time.

30Israel said to Joseph, 'Now I am ready to die, since I have seen for myself that you are still alive.'

31Then Joseph said to his brothers and to his father's household, 'I will go up and speak to Pharaoh and will say to him, "My brothers and my father's household, who were living in the land of Canaan, have come to me. 32The men are shepherds; they tend livestock, and they have brought along their flocks and herds and everything they own." 33When Pharaoh calls you in and asks, "What is your occupation?" 34you should answer, "Your servants have tended livestock from our boyhood on, just as our fathers did." Then you will be allowed to settle in the region of Goshen, for all shepherds are detestable to the Egyptians.'

47 Joseph went and told Pharaoh, 'My father and brothers, with their flocks and herds and everything they own, have come from the land of Canaan and are now in Goshen.' 2He chose five of his brothers and presented them before Pharaoh.

3Pharaoh asked the brothers, 'What is your occupation?'

'Your servants are shepherds,' they replied to Pharaoh, 'just as our fathers were.' 4They also said to him, 'We have come to live here for a while, because the famine is severe in Canaan and your servants' flocks

have no pasture. So now, please let your servants settle in Goshen.'

5Pharaoh said to Joseph, 'Your father and your brothers have come to you, 6and the land of Egypt is before you; settle your father and your brothers in the best part of the land. Let them live in Goshen. And if you know of any among them with special ability, put them in charge of my own livestock.'

7Then Joseph brought his father Jacob in and presented him before Pharaoh. After Jacob blessed*a* Pharaoh, 8Pharaoh asked him, 'How old are you?'

9And Jacob said to Pharaoh, 'The years of my pilgrimage are a hundred and thirty. My years have been few and difficult, and they do not equal the years of the pilgrimage of my fathers.' 10Then Jacob blessed*b* Pharaoh and went out from his presence.

11So Joseph settled his father and his brothers in Egypt and gave them property in the best part of the land, the district of Rameses, as Pharaoh directed. 12Joseph also provided his father and his brothers and all his father's household with food, according to the number of their children.

Joseph and the famine

13There was no food, however, in the whole region because the famine was severe; both Egypt and Canaan wasted away because of the famine. 14Joseph collected all the money that was to be found in Egypt and Canaan in payment for the grain they were buying, and he brought it to Pharaoh's palace. 15When the money of the people of Egypt and Canaan was gone, all Egypt came to Joseph and said, 'Give us food. Why should we die before your eyes? Our money is all gone.'

16'Then bring your livestock,' said Joseph. 'I will sell you food in exchange for your livestock, since your money is gone.' 17So they brought their livestock to Joseph, and he gave them food in exchange for their horses, their sheep and goats, their cattle and donkeys. And he brought them through that year with food in exchange for all their livestock.

18When that year was over, they came to

f 27 Hebrew; Septuagint *the nine children*
g 27 Hebrew (see also Exodus 1:5 and note); Septuagint (see also Acts 7:14) *seventy-five*
h 29 Hebrew *around him*
a 7 Or *greeted*
b 10 Or *said farewell to*

him the following year and said, 'We cannot hide from our lord the fact that since our money is gone and our livestock belongs to you, there is nothing left for our lord except our bodies and our land. 19 Why should we perish before your eyes – we and our land as well? Buy us and our land in exchange for food, and we with our land will be in bondage to Pharaoh. Give us seed so that we may live and not die, and that the land may not become desolate.'

20 So Joseph bought all the land in Egypt for Pharaoh. The Egyptians, one and all, sold their fields, because the famine was too severe for them. The land became Pharaoh's, 21 and Joseph reduced the people to servitude, c from one end of Egypt to the other. 22 However, he did not buy the land of the priests, because they received a fixed allowance from Pharaoh and had food enough from the allowance Pharaoh gave them. That is why they did not sell their land.

23 Joseph said to the people, 'Now that I have bought you and your land today for Pharaoh, here is seed for you so you can plant the ground. 24 But when the crop comes in, give a fifth of it to Pharaoh. The other four-fifths you may keep as seed for the fields and as food for yourselves and your households and your children.'

25 'You have saved our lives,' they said. 'May we find favour in the eyes of our lord; we will be in bondage to Pharaoh.'

26 So Joseph established it as a law concerning land in Egypt – still in force today – that a fifth of the produce belongs to Pharaoh. It was only the land of the priests that did not become Pharaoh's.

27 Now the Israelites settled in Egypt in the region of Goshen. They acquired property there and were fruitful and increased greatly in number.

28 Jacob lived in Egypt seventeen years, and the years of his life were a hundred and forty-seven. 29 When the time drew near for Israel to die, he called for his son Joseph and said to him, 'If I have found favour in your eyes, put your hand under my thigh and promise that you will show me kindness and faithfulness. Do not bury me in Egypt, 30 but when I rest with my fathers, carry me out of Egypt and bury me where they are buried.'

'I will do as you say,' he said.

31 'Swear to me,' he said. Then Joseph swore to him, and Israel worshipped as he leaned on the top of his staff. d

Manasseh and Ephraim

48 Some time later Joseph was told, 'Your father is ill.' So he took his two sons Manasseh and Ephraim along with him. 2 When Jacob was told, 'Your son Joseph has come to you,' Israel rallied his strength and sat up on the bed.

3 Jacob said to Joseph, 'God Almighty a appeared to me at Luz in the land of Canaan, and there he blessed me 4 and said to me, "I am going to make you fruitful and increase your numbers. I will make you a community of peoples, and I will give this land as an everlasting possession to your descendants after you."

5 'Now then, your two sons born to you in Egypt before I came to you here will be reckoned as mine; Ephraim and Manasseh will be mine, just as Reuben and Simeon are mine. 6 Any children born to you after them will be yours; in the territory they inherit they will be reckoned under the names of their brothers. 7 As I was returning from Paddan, b to my sorrow Rachel died in the land of Canaan while we were still on the way, a little distance from Ephrath. So I buried her there beside the road to Ephrath' (that is, Bethlehem).

8 When Israel saw the sons of Joseph, he asked, 'Who are these?'

9 'They are the sons God has given me here,' Joseph said to his father.

Then Israel said, 'Bring them to me so that I may bless them.'

10 Now Israel's eyes were failing because of old age, and he could hardly see. So Joseph brought his sons close to him,

---

c 21 Samaritan Pentateuch and Septuagint (see also Vulgate); Masoretic Text *and he moved the people into the cities*

d 31 Or *Israel bowed down at the head of his bed*
a 3 Hebrew *El-Shaddai*
b 7 That is, North-west Mesopotamia

and his father kissed them and embraced them.

¹¹ Israel said to Joseph, 'I never expected to see your face again, and now God has allowed me to see your children too.'

¹² Then Joseph removed them from Israel's knees and bowed down with his face to the ground. ¹³ And Joseph took both of them, Ephraim on his right towards Israel's left hand and Manasseh on his left towards Israel's right hand, and brought them close to him. ¹⁴ But Israel reached out his right hand and put it on Ephraim's head, though he was the younger, and crossing his arms, he put his left hand on Manasseh's head, even though Manasseh was the firstborn.

¹⁵ Then he blessed Joseph and said,

'May the God before whom my fathers
    Abraham and Isaac walked
        faithfully,
the God who has been my shepherd
    all my life to this day,
¹⁶ the Angel who has delivered me from
        all harm
    – may he bless these boys.
May they be called by my name
    and the names of my fathers
        Abraham and Isaac,
and may they increase greatly
        on the earth.'

¹⁷ When Joseph saw his father placing his right hand on Ephraim's head he was displeased; so he took hold of his father's hand to move it from Ephraim's head to Manasseh's head. ¹⁸ Joseph said to him, 'No, my father, this one is the firstborn; put your right hand on his head.'

¹⁹ But his father refused and said, 'I know, my son, I know. He too will become a people, and he too will become great. Nevertheless, his younger brother will be greater than he, and his descendants will become a group of nations.' ²⁰ He blessed them that day and said,

'In yourᶜ name will Israel pronounce
    this blessing:

'May God make you like Ephraim
    and Manasseh."'

So he put Ephraim ahead of Manasseh.

²¹ Then Israel said to Joseph, 'I am about to die, but God will be with youᵈ and take youᵈ back to the land of yourᵈ fathers. ²² And to you I give one more ridge of landᵉ than to your brothers, the ridge I took from the Amorites with my sword and my bow.'

Jacob blesses his sons

49 Then Jacob called for his sons and said: 'Gather round so that I can tell you what will happen to you in days to come.

² 'Assemble and listen, sons of Jacob;
    listen to your father Israel.

³ 'Reuben, you are my firstborn,
    my might, the first sign of my
        strength,
    excelling in honour, excelling in
        power.
⁴ Turbulent as the waters, you will no
        longer excel,
    for you went up onto your father's
        bed,
    onto my couch and defiled it.

⁵ 'Simeon and Levi are brothers –
    their swordsᵃ are weapons of
        violence.
⁶ Let me not enter their council,
    let me not join their assembly,
for they have killed men in their
        anger
    and hamstrung oxen as they
        pleased.
⁷ Cursed be their anger, so fierce,
    and their fury, so cruel!
I will scatter them in Jacob
    and disperse them in Israel.

ᶜ 20 The Hebrew is singular.

ᵈ 21 The Hebrew is plural.

ᵉ 22 The Hebrew for *ridge of land* is identical with the place name Shechem.

ᵃ 5 The meaning of the Hebrew for this word is uncertain.

8 'Judah,*b* your brothers will praise you;
    your hand will be on the neck of
       your enemies;
    your father's sons will bow down to
       you.
9 You are a lion's cub, Judah;
    you return from the prey, my son.
Like a lion he crouches and lies down,
    like a lioness – who dares to rouse
       him?
10 The sceptre will not depart from
       Judah,
    nor the ruler's staff from between
       his feet,*c*
until he to whom it belongs*d* shall
       come
    and the obedience of the nations
       shall be his.
11 He will tether his donkey to a vine,
    his colt to the choicest branch;
he will wash his garments in wine,
    his robes in the blood of grapes.
12 His eyes will be darker than wine,
    his teeth whiter than milk.*e*

13 'Zebulun will live by the seashore
    and become a haven for ships;
    his border will extend towards
       Sidon.

14 'Issachar is a scrawny*f* donkey
    lying down among the sheepfolds.*g*
15 When he sees how good is his resting
       place
    and how pleasant is his land,
he will bend his shoulder to the
       burden
    and submit to forced labour.

16 'Dan*h* will provide justice for his
       people
    as one of the tribes of Israel.
17 Dan will be a snake by the roadside,
    a viper along the path,

that bites the horse's heels
    so that its rider tumbles backwards.

18 'I look for your deliverance, LORD.

19 'Gad*i* will be attacked by a band of
       raiders,
    but he will attack them at their
       heels.

20 'Asher's food will be rich;
    he will provide delicacies fit for a
       king.

21 'Naphtali is a doe set free
    that bears beautiful fawns.*j*

FAVOURITE VERSES

Philippians 4:13

I can do all this through him who gives me strength.

I like this Bible verse because it has helped me a lot recently. I did a lot of stupid things in my past and I turned to doing things I shouldn't have done, but this verse picked me up and I began to realise that God has a plan for my life and that I didn't need to worry about doing that stuff any more. It took me a while to get my head round leaving that stuff behind and living for Jesus, but I'm getting there, and this verse has helped me one heck of a lot!

Maddie, 14

---

b 8 Judah *sounds like and may be derived from the Hebrew for* praise.
c 10 Or *from his descendants*
d 10 Or *to whom tribute belongs*; *the meaning of the Hebrew for this phrase is uncertain.*
e 12 Or *will be dull from wine, / his teeth white from milk*
f 14 Or *strong*
g 14 Or *the campfires*; *or the saddlebags*
h 16 Dan *here means* he provides justice.

i 19 Gad *sounds like the Hebrew for* attack *and also for* band of raiders.
j 21 Or *free*; */ he utters beautiful words*

22 'Joseph is a fruitful vine,
      a fruitful vine near a spring,
      whose branches climb over a wall.*k*
23 With bitterness archers attacked him;
      they shot at him with hostility.
24 But his bow remained steady,
      his strong arms stayed*l* supple,
      because of the hand of the Mighty One
         of Jacob,
      because of the Shepherd, the Rock
         of Israel,
25 because of your father's God, who
         helps you,
      because of the Almighty,*m* who
         blesses you
   with blessings of the skies above,
      blessings of the deep springs below,
      blessings of the breast and womb.
26 Your father's blessings are greater
      than the blessings of the ancient
         mountains,
      than*n* the bounty of the age-old
         hills.
   Let all these rest on the head of Joseph,
      on the brow of the prince among*o*
         his brothers.

27 'Benjamin is a ravenous wolf;
      in the morning he devours the prey,
      in the evening he divides the
         plunder.'

28 All these are the twelve tribes of Israel, and this is what their father said to
them when he blessed them, giving each
the blessing appropriate to him.

The death of Jacob

29 Then he gave them these instructions:
'I am about to be gathered to my people.
Bury me with my fathers in the cave in the
field of Ephron the Hittite, 30 the cave in
the field of Machpelah, near Mamre in Canaan, which Abraham bought along with

the field as a burial place from Ephron
the Hittite. 31 There Abraham and his wife
Sarah were buried, there Isaac and his wife
Rebekah were buried, and there I buried
Leah. 32 The field and the cave in it were
bought from the Hittites.'*p*

33 When Jacob had finished giving instructions to his sons, he drew his feet
up into the bed, breathed his last and was
gathered to his people.

50 Joseph threw himself on his father and wept over him and kissed
him. 2 Then Joseph directed the physicians
in his service to embalm his father Israel.
So the physicians embalmed him, 3 taking
a full forty days, for that was the time required for embalming. And the Egyptians
mourned for him seventy days.

4 When the days of mourning had
passed, Joseph said to Pharaoh's court,
'If I have found favour in your eyes, speak
to Pharaoh for me. Tell him, 5 "My father
made me swear an oath and said, 'I am
about to die; bury me in the tomb I dug
for myself in the land of Canaan.' Now let
me go up and bury my father; then I will
return."'

6 Pharaoh said, 'Go up and bury your father, as he made you swear to do.'

7 So Joseph went up to bury his father. All Pharaoh's officials accompanied
him – the dignitaries of his court and all
the dignitaries of Egypt – 8 besides all the
members of Joseph's household and his
brothers and those belonging to his father's household. Only their children and
their flocks and herds were left in Goshen.
9 Chariots and horsemen*a* also went up
with him. It was a very large company.

10 When they reached the threshing-
floor of Atad, near the Jordan, they la-
mented loudly and bitterly; and there
Joseph observed a seven-day period of
mourning for his father. 11 When the Canaanites who lived there saw the mourning at the threshing-floor of Atad, they
said, 'The Egyptians are holding a solemn ceremony of mourning.' That is why

---

k 22 Or *Joseph is a wild colt, / a wild colt near a spring, / a
wild donkey on a terraced hill*
l 23,24 Or *archers will attack . . . will shoot . . . will
remain . . . will stay*
m 25 Hebrew *Shaddai*
n 26 Or *of my progenitors, / as great as*
o 26 Or *of the one separated from*

p 32 Or *the descendants of Heth*
a 9 Or *charioteers*

that place near the Jordan is called Abel Mizraim.*b*

12 So Jacob's sons did as he had commanded them: 13 they carried him to the land of Canaan and buried him in the cave in the field of Machpelah, near Mamre, which Abraham had bought along with the field as a burial place from Ephron the Hittite. 14 After burying his father, Joseph returned to Egypt, together with his brothers and all the others who had gone with him to bury his father.

Joseph reassures his brothers

15 When Joseph's brothers saw that their father was dead, they said, 'What if Joseph holds a grudge against us and pays us back for all the wrongs we did to him?' 16 So they sent word to Joseph, saying, 'Your father left these instructions before he died: 17 "This is what you are to say to Joseph: I ask you to forgive your brothers the sins and the wrongs they committed in treating you so badly." Now please forgive the sins of the servants of the God of your father.' When their message came to him, Joseph wept.

18 His brothers then came and threw themselves down before him. 'We are your slaves,' they said.

19 But Joseph said to them, 'Don't be afraid. Am I in the place of God? 20 You intended to harm me, but God intended it for good to accomplish what is now being done, the saving of many lives. 21 So then, don't be afraid. I will provide for you and your children.' And he reassured them and spoke kindly to them.

The death of Joseph

22 Joseph stayed in Egypt, along with all his father's family. He lived a hundred and ten years 23 and saw the third generation of Ephraim's children. Also the children of Makir son of Manasseh were placed at birth on Joseph's knees.*c*

24 Then Joseph said to his brothers, 'I am about to die. But God will surely come to your aid and take you up out of this land to the land he promised on oath to Abraham, Isaac and Jacob.' 25 And Joseph made the Israelites swear an oath and said, 'God will surely come to your aid, and then you must carry my bones up from this place.'

26 So Joseph died at the age of a hundred and ten. And after they embalmed him, he was placed in a coffin in Egypt.

---

b 11 *Abel Mizraim* means *mourning of the Egyptians.*

c 23 That is, were counted as his

EXODUS

DATE

It is estimated that the exodus took place around 1446 BC

AUTHOR

Traditionally attributed to Moses

WHAT'S IT ALL ABOUT?

Exodus (which means 'exit') is the second of the five books that make up the Pentateuch. At the end of Genesis we read about the life of Joseph and how God's people became guests in Egypt during a severe famine. Exodus picks up the story many years later, when Joseph is long dead and new rulers are in charge of Egypt, turning the Israelites into their slaves. God has a plan to rescue his people through his servant Moses and the first part of Exodus tells the story of how God freed his people from Egypt's rule, leading them out into the desert. The second part of Exodus tells how God gave Moses the laws for his people to live by and sets out the instructions for using the tabernacle (God's tent) where he was to be worshipped. This was a mobile place of worship for the Israelites as they wandered through the desert. As Moses leads the people, we see what a tough job he had to keep their hearts turned towards God.

WHY SHOULD WE READ IT?

- To hear about the many miracles God performed to free his people from slavery, including the plagues (Exodus 7 – 12) and the parting of the Red Sea (Exodus 14).

- To learn God's plan for the way we should live through reading the Ten Commandments (Exodus 20; also found in Deuteronomy 5).

- To discover Moses' reluctant first steps into leadership (Exodus 4).

Andy Croft with Liza Hoeksma

The Israelites oppressed

1 These are the names of the sons of Israel who went to Egypt with Jacob, each with his family: ² Reuben, Simeon, Levi and Judah; ³ Issachar, Zebulun and Benjamin; ⁴ Dan and Naphtali; Gad and Asher. ⁵ The descendants of Jacob numbered seventy*a* in all; Joseph was already in Egypt.

⁶ Now Joseph and all his brothers and all that generation died, ⁷ but the Israelites were exceedingly fruitful; they multiplied greatly, increased in numbers and became so numerous that the land was filled with them.

⁸ Then a new king, to whom Joseph meant nothing, came to power in Egypt. ⁹ 'Look,' he said to his people, 'the Israelites have become far too numerous for us. ¹⁰ Come, we must deal shrewdly with them or they will become even more numerous and, if war breaks out, will join our enemies, fight against us and leave the country.'

¹¹ So they put slave masters over them to oppress them with forced labour, and they built Pithom and Rameses as store cities for Pharaoh. ¹² But the more they were oppressed, the more they multiplied and spread; so the Egyptians came to dread the Israelites ¹³ and worked them ruthlessly. ¹⁴ They made their lives bitter with harsh labour in brick and mortar and with all kinds of work in the fields; in all their harsh labour, the Egyptians worked them ruthlessly.

a 5 Masoretic Text (see also Gen. 46:27); Dead Sea Scrolls and Septuagint (see also Acts 7:14 and note at Gen. 46:27) *seventy-five*

CHILD MORTALITY

The beginning of the exodus story is brutal. Pharaoh, the powerful leader of a powerful empire, orders the deaths of every male Hebrew child. Huge numbers of innocent children are killed because an oppressive man wants to hold onto power.

Today, like every day, around 21,000 children under the age of five will die. The world has made some real progress in the area of child mortality (the number was 33,000 in 1990). But it's still a heart-breaking, mind-bending number. And it's the result of monumental injustice. A child in Ethiopia is thirty times more likely to die by their fifth birthday than a child born in Western Europe. In sub-Saharan Africa as a whole, around 13 per cent of children die before their fifth birthday. If that were true here, around four of your classmates (in an average class of thirty people) would not even have made it to primary school. Where you're born has a massive impact on whether or not you'll make it to your fifth birthday.

It's hard to believe that we live in a world where an unimaginable number of children die every day from preventable diseases. And the thing is, there may be no Pharaoh giving a direct order, but when children living in poverty die in a world ruled by people with great wealth, they might as well have been given a death order by the empire. High child mortality is not just an injustice in its own right; it is a symptom of a world that is sick and needs healing.

Like Moses, a little baby saved from Pharaoh's murderous plan, will you walk into the heart of the empire of the powerful and demand salvation for the oppressed?

Matt Valler

15 The king of Egypt said to the Hebrew midwives, whose names were Shiphrah and Puah, 16 'When you are helping the Hebrew women during childbirth on the delivery stool, if you see that the baby is a boy, kill him; but if it is a girl, let her live.' 17 The midwives, however, feared God and did not do what the king of Egypt had told them to do; they let the boys live. 18 Then the king of Egypt summoned the midwives and asked them, 'Why have you done this? Why have you let the boys live?'

19 The midwives answered Pharaoh, 'Hebrew women are not like Egyptian women; they are vigorous and give birth before the midwives arrive.'

20 So God was kind to the midwives and the people increased and became even more numerous. 21 And because the midwives feared God, he gave them families of their own.

22 Then Pharaoh gave this order to all his people: 'Every Hebrew boy that is born you must throw into the Nile, but let every girl live.'

The birth of Moses

2 Now a man of the tribe of Levi married a Levite woman, 2 and she became pregnant and gave birth to a son. When she saw that he was a fine child, she hid him for three months. 3 But when she could hide him no longer, she got a papyrus basket[a] for him and coated it with tar and pitch. Then she placed the child in it and put it among the reeds along the bank of the Nile. 4 His sister stood at a distance to see what would happen to him.

5 Then Pharaoh's daughter went down to the Nile to bathe, and her attendants were walking along the river-bank. She saw the basket among the reeds and sent her female slave to get it. 6 She opened it and saw the baby. He was crying, and she felt sorry for him. 'This is one of the Hebrew babies,' she said.

7 Then his sister asked Pharaoh's daughter, 'Shall I go and get one of the Hebrew women to nurse the baby for you?'

8 'Yes, go,' she answered. So the girl went and got the baby's mother. 9 Pharaoh's daughter said to her, 'Take this baby and nurse him for me, and I will pay you.' So the woman took the baby and nursed him. 10 When the child grew older, she took him to Pharaoh's daughter and he became her son. She named him Moses,[b] saying, 'I drew him out of the water.'

Moses flees to Midian

11 One day, after Moses had grown up, he went out to where his own people were and watched them at their hard labour. He saw an Egyptian beating a Hebrew, one of his own people. 12 Looking this way and that and seeing no one, he killed the Egyptian and hid him in the sand. 13 The next day he went out and saw two Hebrews fighting. He asked the one in the wrong, 'Why are you hitting your fellow Hebrew?'

14 The man said, 'Who made you ruler and judge over us? Are you thinking of killing me as you killed the Egyptian?' Then Moses was afraid and thought, 'What I did must have become known.'

15 When Pharaoh heard of this, he tried to kill Moses, but Moses fled from Pharaoh and went to live in Midian, where he sat down by a well. 16 Now a priest of Midian had seven daughters, and they came to draw water and fill the troughs to water their father's flock. 17 Some shepherds came along and drove them away, but Moses got up and came to their rescue and watered their flock.

18 When the girls returned to Reuel their father, he asked them, 'Why have you returned so early today?'

19 They answered, 'An Egyptian rescued us from the shepherds. He even drew water for us and watered the flock.'

20 'And where is he?' Reuel asked his daughters. 'Why did you leave him? Invite him to have something to eat.'

21 Moses agreed to stay with the man, who gave his daughter Zipporah to Moses in marriage. 22 Zipporah gave birth to a

---

a 3 The Hebrew can also mean ark, as in Gen. 6:14.   b 10 Moses sounds like the Hebrew for draw out.

son, and Moses named him Gershom,[c] saying, 'I have become a foreigner in a foreign land.'

²³During that long period, the king of Egypt died. The Israelites groaned in their slavery and cried out, and their cry for help because of their slavery went up to God. ²⁴God heard their groaning and he remembered his covenant with Abraham, with Isaac and with Jacob. ²⁵So God looked on the Israelites and was concerned about them.

Moses and the burning bush

3 Now Moses was tending the flock of Jethro his father-in-law, the priest of Midian, and he led the flock to the far side of the wilderness and came to Horeb, the mountain of God. ²There the angel of the LORD appeared to him in flames of fire from within a bush. Moses saw that though the bush was on fire it did not burn up. ³So Moses thought, 'I will go over and see this strange sight – why the bush does not burn up.'

⁴When the LORD saw that he had gone over to look, God called to him from within the bush, 'Moses! Moses!'

And Moses said, 'Here I am.'

⁵'Do not come any closer,' God said. 'Take off your sandals, for the place where you are standing is holy ground.' ⁶Then he said, 'I am the God of your father,[a] the God of Abraham, the God of Isaac and the God of Jacob.' At this, Moses hid his face, because he was afraid to look at God.

⁷The LORD said, 'I have indeed seen the misery of my people in Egypt. I have heard them crying out because of their slave drivers, and I am concerned about their suffering. ⁸So I have come down to rescue them from the hand of the Egyptians and to bring them up out of that land into a good and spacious land, a land flowing with milk and honey – the home of the Canaanites, Hittites, Amorites, Perizzites, Hivites and Jebusites. ⁹And now the cry of the Israelites has reached me, and I have

seen the way the Egyptians are oppressing them. ¹⁰So now, go. I am sending you to Pharaoh to bring my people the Israelites out of Egypt.'

¹¹But Moses said to God, 'Who am I that I should go to Pharaoh and bring the Israelites out of Egypt?'

¹²And God said, 'I will be with you. And this will be the sign to you that it is I who have sent you: when you have brought the people out of Egypt, you[b] will worship God on this mountain.'

¹³Moses said to God, 'Suppose I go to the Israelites and say to them, "The God of your fathers has sent me to you," and they ask me, "What is his name?" Then what shall I tell them?'

¹⁴God said to Moses, 'I AM WHO I AM.[c] This is what you are to say to the Israelites: "I AM has sent me to you." '

¹⁵God also said to Moses, 'Say to the Israelites, "The LORD,[d] the God of your fathers – the God of Abraham, the God of Isaac and the God of Jacob – has sent me to you."

'This is my name for ever,
    the name you shall call me
    from generation to generation.

¹⁶'Go, assemble the elders of Israel and say to them, "The LORD, the God of your fathers – the God of Abraham, Isaac and Jacob – appeared to me and said: I have watched over you and have seen what has been done to you in Egypt. ¹⁷And I have promised to bring you up out of your misery in Egypt into the land of the Canaanites, Hittites, Amorites, Perizzites, Hivites and Jebusites – a land flowing with milk and honey."

¹⁸'The elders of Israel will listen to you. Then you and the elders are to go to the king of Egypt and say to him, "The LORD, the God of the Hebrews, has met with us. Let us take a three-day journey into the wilderness to offer sacrifices to the LORD our God." ¹⁹But I know that the king of

---

c 22 *Gershom* sounds like the Hebrew for *a foreigner there.*
a 6 Masoretic Text; Samaritan Pentateuch (see Acts 7:32) *fathers*

b 12 The Hebrew is plural.
c 14 Or *I WILL BE WHAT I WILL BE*
d 15 The Hebrew for LORD sounds like and may be related to the Hebrew for *I AM* in verse 14.

Egypt will not let you go unless a mighty hand compels him. 20So I will stretch out my hand and strike the Egyptians with all the wonders that I will perform among them. After that, he will let you go.

21'And I will make the Egyptians favourably disposed towards this people, so that when you leave you will not go empty-handed. 22Every woman is to ask her neighbour and any woman living in her house for articles of silver and gold and for clothing, which you will put on your sons and daughters. And so you will plunder the Egyptians.'

Signs for Moses

4 Moses answered, 'What if they do not believe me or listen to me and say, "The LORD did not appear to you"?'

2Then the LORD said to him, 'What is that in your hand?'

'A staff,' he replied.

3The LORD said, 'Throw it on the ground.'

Moses threw it on the ground and it became a snake, and he ran from it. 4Then the LORD said to him, 'Reach out your hand and take it by the tail.' So Moses reached out and took hold of the snake and it turned back into a staff in his hand. 5'This,' said the LORD, 'is so that they may believe that the LORD, the God of their fathers – the God of Abraham, the God of Isaac and the God of Jacob – has appeared to you.'

6Then the LORD said, 'Put your hand inside your cloak.' So Moses put his hand into his cloak, and when he took it out,

THE NAMES OF GOD 1

God the Almighty (Yahweh)

Yahweh means literally 'to be', 'to exist', 'eternal', 'strong one'.

What's your name?

Moses asks God who he is. God replies mysteriously, *'I AM WHO I AM. This is what you are to say to the Israelites: "I AM has sent me to you"'* (Exodus 3:14). The Hebrew word is *JHWH*, but the name was never uttered for fear of using it blasphemously (Exodus 20:7). Neither was the Hebrew word spelled with any vowels. The name eventually came to be pronounced as 'Jehovah' – the name still seen today in many old hymns. They called God 'Jehovah', using the vowels of *Adonai* ('Lord'). YHWH is the Lord Almighty – the Lord of Hosts (surrounded by myriads of angels).

What did God want to do?

God met Moses in the desert and gave him a message of liberation for his people who were in bondage to the Egyptian Pharaoh. He told Moses to gather the elders of the Israelites together and say to them, *'The LORD, the God of your fathers – the God of Abraham, Isaac and Jacob – appeared to me and said: I have ... seen what has been done to you in Egypt. And I have promised to bring you up out of your misery ... into ... a land flowing with milk and honey'* (Exodus 3:16–17).

David and Mary Pytches

Isaiah 40:29

the skin was leprous[a] – it had become as white as snow.

7 'Now put it back into your cloak,' he said. So Moses put his hand back into his cloak, and when he took it out, it was restored, like the rest of his flesh.

8 Then the LORD said, 'If they do not believe you or pay attention to the first sign, they may believe the second. 9 But if they do not believe these two signs or listen to you, take some water from the Nile and pour it on the dry ground. The water you take from the river will become blood on the ground.'

10 Moses said to the LORD, 'Pardon your servant, Lord. I have never been eloquent, neither in the past nor since you have spoken to your servant. I am slow of speech and tongue.'

11 The LORD said to him, 'Who gave human beings their mouths? Who makes them deaf or mute? Who gives them sight or makes them blind? Is it not I, the LORD? 12 Now go; I will help you speak and will teach you what to say.'

13 But Moses said, 'Pardon your servant, Lord. Please send someone else.'

14 Then the LORD's anger burned against Moses and he said, 'What about your brother, Aaron the Levite? I know he can speak well. He is already on his way to meet you, and he will be glad to see you. 15 You shall speak to him and put words in his mouth; I will help both of you speak and will teach you what to do. 16 He will speak to the people for you, and it will be as if he were your mouth and as if you were God to him. 17 But take this staff in your hand so that you can perform the signs with it.'

Moses returns to Egypt

18 Then Moses went back to Jethro his father-in-law and said to him, 'Let me return to my own people in Egypt to see if any of them are still alive.'

Jethro said, 'Go, and I wish you well.'

19 Now the LORD had said to Moses in Midian, 'Go back to Egypt, for all those who wanted to kill you are dead.' 20 So Moses took his wife and sons, put them on a donkey and started back to Egypt. And he took the staff of God in his hand.

21 The LORD said to Moses, 'When you return to Egypt, see that you perform before Pharaoh all the wonders I have given you the power to do. But I will harden his heart so that he will not let the people go. 22 Then say to Pharaoh, "This is what the LORD says: Israel is my firstborn son, 23 and I told you, 'Let my son go, so that he may worship me.' But you refused to let him go; so I will kill your firstborn son."'

24 At a lodging place on the way, the LORD met Moses[b] and was about to kill him. 25 But Zipporah took a flint knife, cut off her son's foreskin and touched Moses' feet with it.[c] 'Surely you are a bridegroom of blood to me,' she said. 26 So the LORD let him alone. (At that time she said 'bridegroom of blood', referring to circumcision.)

27 The LORD said to Aaron, 'Go into the wilderness to meet Moses.' So he met Moses at the mountain of God and kissed him. 28 Then Moses told Aaron everything the LORD had sent him to say, and also about all the signs he had commanded him to perform.

29 Moses and Aaron brought together all the elders of the Israelites, 30 and Aaron told them everything the LORD had said to Moses. He also performed the signs before the people, 31 and they believed. And when they heard that the LORD was concerned about them and had seen their misery, they bowed down and worshipped.

Bricks without straw

5 Afterwards Moses and Aaron went to Pharaoh and said, 'This is what the LORD, the God of Israel, says: "Let my people go, so that they may hold a festival to me in the wilderness."'

2 Pharaoh said, 'Who is the LORD, that I should obey him and let Israel go? I do

---

a 6 The Hebrew word for *leprous* was used for various diseases affecting the skin.

b 24 Hebrew *him*

c 25 The meaning of the Hebrew for this clause is uncertain.

not know the LORD and I will not let Israel go.'

3 Then they said, 'The God of the Hebrews has met with us. Now let us take a three-day journey into the wilderness to offer sacrifices to the LORD our God, or he may strike us with plagues or with the sword.'

4 But the king of Egypt said, 'Moses and Aaron, why are you taking the people away from their labour? Get back to your work!' 5 Then Pharaoh said, 'Look, the people of the land are now numerous, and you are stopping them from working.'

6 That same day Pharaoh gave this order to the slave drivers and overseers in charge of the people: 7 'You are no longer to supply the people with straw for making bricks; let them go and gather their own straw. 8 But require them to make the same number of bricks as before; don't reduce the quota. They are lazy; that is why they are crying out, "Let us go and sacrifice to our God." 9 Make the work harder for the people so that they keep working and pay no attention to lies.'

10 Then the slave drivers and the overseers went out and said to the people, 'This is what Pharaoh says: "I will not give you any more straw. 11 Go and get your own straw wherever you can find it, but your work will not be reduced at all." ' 12 So the people scattered all over Egypt to gather stubble to use for straw. 13 The slave drivers kept pressing them, saying, 'Complete the work required of you for each day, just as when you had straw.' 14 And Pharaoh's slave drivers beat the Israelite overseers they had appointed, demanding, 'Why haven't you met your quota of bricks yesterday or today, as before?'

15 Then the Israelite overseers went and appealed to Pharaoh: 'Why have you treated your servants this way? 16 Your servants are given no straw, yet we are told, "Make bricks!" Your servants are being beaten, but the fault is with your own people.'

17 Pharaoh said, 'Lazy, that's what you are – lazy! That is why you keep saying, "Let us go and sacrifice to the LORD." 18 Now get to work. You will not be given any straw, yet you must produce your full quota of bricks.'

19 The Israelite overseers realised they were in trouble when they were told, 'You are not to reduce the number of bricks required of you for each day.' 20 When they left Pharaoh, they found Moses and Aaron waiting to meet them, 21 and they said, 'May the LORD look on you and judge you! You have made us obnoxious to Pharaoh and his officials and have put a sword in their hand to kill us.'

God promises deliverance

22 Moses returned to the LORD and said, 'Why, Lord, why have you brought trouble on this people? Is this why you sent me? 23 Ever since I went to Pharaoh to speak in your name, he has brought trouble on this people, and you have not rescued your people at all.'

6 Then the LORD said to Moses, 'Now you will see what I will do to Pharaoh: because of my mighty hand he will let them go; because of my mighty hand he will drive them out of his country.'

2 God also said to Moses, 'I am the LORD. 3 I appeared to Abraham, to Isaac and to Jacob as God Almighty,ᵃ but by my name the LORDᵇ I did not make myself known to them. 4 I also established my covenant with them to give them the land of Canaan, where they resided as foreigners. 5 Moreover, I have heard the groaning of the Israelites, whom the Egyptians are enslaving, and I have remembered my covenant.

6 'Therefore, say to the Israelites: "I am the LORD, and I will bring you out from under the yoke of the Egyptians. I will free you from being slaves to them, and I will redeem you with an outstretched arm and with mighty acts of judgment. 7 I will take you as my own people, and I will be your God. Then you will know that I am the LORD your God, who brought you out from under the yoke of the Egyptians. 8 And I will bring you to the land I swore

---

a 3 Hebrew El-Shaddai
b 3 See note at 3:15.

with uplifted hand to give to Abraham, to Isaac and to Jacob. I will give it to you as a possession. I am the LORD."'

⁹Moses reported this to the Israelites, but they did not listen to him because of their discouragement and harsh labour.

¹⁰Then the LORD said to Moses, ¹¹'Go, tell Pharaoh king of Egypt to let the Israelites go out of his country.'

¹²But Moses said to the LORD, 'If the Israelites will not listen to me, why would Pharaoh listen to me, since I speak with faltering lips?'c

Family record of Moses and Aaron

¹³Now the LORD spoke to Moses and Aaron about the Israelites and Pharaoh king of Egypt, and he commanded them to bring the Israelites out of Egypt.

¹⁴These were the heads of their families:d

The sons of Reuben the firstborn son of Israel were Hanok and Pallu, Hezron and Karmi. These were the clans of Reuben.

¹⁵The sons of Simeon were Jemuel, Jamin, Ohad, Jakin, Zohar and Shaul the son of a Canaanite woman. These were the clans of Simeon.

¹⁶These were the names of the sons of Levi according to their records: Gershon, Kohath and Merari. Levi lived 137 years.

¹⁷The sons of Gershon, by clans, were Libni and Shimei.

¹⁸The sons of Kohath were Amram, Izhar, Hebron and Uzziel. Kohath lived 133 years.

¹⁹The sons of Merari were Mahli and Mushi.

These were the clans of Levi according to their records.

²⁰Amram married his father's sister Jochebed, who bore him Aaron and Moses. Amram lived 137 years.

²¹The sons of Izhar were Korah, Nepheg and Zikri.

²²The sons of Uzziel were Mishael, Elzaphan and Sithri.

²³Aaron married Elisheba, daughter of Amminadab and sister of Nahshon, and she bore him Nadab and Abihu, Eleazar and Ithamar.

²⁴The sons of Korah were Assir, Elkanah and Abiasaph. These were the Korahite clans.

²⁵Eleazar son of Aaron married one of the daughters of Putiel, and she bore him Phinehas.

These were the heads of the Levite families, clan by clan.

²⁶It was this Aaron and Moses to whom the LORD said, 'Bring the Israelites out of Egypt by their divisions.' ²⁷They were the ones who spoke to Pharaoh king of Egypt about bringing the Israelites out of Egypt – this same Moses and Aaron.

Aaron to speak for Moses

²⁸Now when the LORD spoke to Moses in Egypt, ²⁹he said to him, 'I am the LORD. Tell Pharaoh king of Egypt everything I tell you.'

³⁰But Moses said to the LORD, 'Since I speak with faltering lips, why would Pharaoh listen to me?'

7 Then the LORD said to Moses, 'See, I have made you like God to Pharaoh, and your brother Aaron will be your prophet. ²You are to say everything I command you, and your brother Aaron is to tell Pharaoh to let the Israelites go out of his country. ³But I will harden Pharaoh's heart, and though I multiply my signs and wonders in Egypt, ⁴he will not listen to you. Then I will lay my hand on Egypt and with mighty acts of judgment I will bring out my divisions, my people the Israelites. ⁵And the Egyptians will know that I am the LORD when I stretch out my hand against Egypt and bring the Israelites out of it.'

⁶Moses and Aaron did just as the LORD commanded them. ⁷Moses was eighty years old and Aaron eighty-three when they spoke to Pharaoh.

---

c 12 Hebrew *I am uncircumcised of lips*; also in verse 30
d 14 The Hebrew for *families* here and in verse 25 refers to units larger than clans.

Aaron's staff becomes a snake

8 The LORD said to Moses and Aaron, 9 'When Pharaoh says to you, "Perform a miracle," then say to Aaron, "Take your staff and throw it down before Pharaoh," and it will become a snake.'

10 So Moses and Aaron went to Pharaoh and did just as the LORD commanded. Aaron threw his staff down in front of Pharaoh and his officials, and it became a snake. 11 Pharaoh then summoned the wise men and sorcerers, and the Egyptian magicians also did the same things by their secret arts: 12 each one threw down his staff and it became a snake. But Aaron's staff swallowed up their staffs. 13 Yet Pharaoh's heart became hard and he would not listen to them, just as the LORD had said.

The plague of blood

14 Then the LORD said to Moses, 'Pharaoh's heart is unyielding; he refuses to let the people go. 15 Go to Pharaoh in the morning as he goes out to the river. Confront him on the bank of the Nile, and take in your hand the staff that was changed into blood. 16 Then say to him, "The LORD, the God of the Hebrews, has sent me to say to you: Let my people go, so that they may worship me in the wilderness. But until now you have not listened. 17 This is what the LORD says: by this you will know that I am the LORD: with the staff that is in my hand I will strike the water of the Nile, and it will be changed into blood. 18 The fish in the Nile will die, and the river will stink; the Egyptians will not be able to drink its water." '

19 The LORD said to Moses, 'Tell Aaron, "Take your staff and stretch out your hand over the waters of Egypt – over the streams and canals, over the ponds and all the reservoirs – and they will turn to blood." Blood will be everywhere in Egypt, even in vessels*a* of wood and stone.'

20 Moses and Aaron did just as the LORD had commanded. He raised his staff in the presence of Pharaoh and his officials and struck the water of the Nile, and all the water was changed into blood. 21 The fish in the Nile died, and the river smelled so bad that the Egyptians could not drink its water. Blood was everywhere in Egypt.

22 But the Egyptian magicians did the same things by their secret arts, and Pharaoh's heart became hard; he would not listen to Moses and Aaron, just as the LORD had said. 23 Instead, he turned and went into his palace, and did not take even this to heart. 24 And all the Egyptians dug along the Nile to get drinking water, because they could not drink the water of the river.

The plague of frogs

25 Seven days passed after the LORD
8 *a* struck the Nile. 1 Then the LORD said to Moses, 'Go to Pharaoh and say to him, "This is what the LORD says: let my people go, so that they may worship me. 2 If you refuse to let them go, I will send a plague of frogs on your whole country. 3 The Nile will teem with frogs. They will come up into your palace and your bedroom and onto your bed, into the houses of your officials and on your people, and into your ovens and kneading troughs. 4 The frogs will come up on you and your people and all your officials." '

5 Then the LORD said to Moses, 'Tell Aaron, "Stretch out your hand with your staff over the streams and canals and ponds, and make frogs come up on the land of Egypt." '

6 So Aaron stretched out his hand over the waters of Egypt, and the frogs came up and covered the land. 7 But the magicians did the same things by their secret arts; they also made frogs come up on the land of Egypt.

8 Pharaoh summoned Moses and Aaron and said, 'Pray to the LORD to take the frogs away from me and my people, and I will let your people go to offer sacrifices to the LORD.'

9 Moses said to Pharaoh, 'I leave to you the honour of setting the time for me to pray for you and your officials and your

---

a 19 Or *even on their idols*

a In Hebrew texts 8:1-4 is numbered 7:26-29, and 8:5-32 is numbered 8:1-28.

people that you and your houses may be rid of the frogs, except for those that remain in the Nile.'

10 'Tomorrow,' Pharaoh said.

Moses replied, 'It will be as you say, so that you may know there is no one like the LORD our God. 11 The frogs will leave you and your houses, your officials and your people; they will remain only in the Nile.'

12 After Moses and Aaron left Pharaoh, Moses cried out to the LORD about the frogs he had brought on Pharaoh. 13 And the LORD did what Moses asked. The frogs died in the houses, in the courtyards and in the fields. 14 They were piled into heaps, and the land reeked of them. 15 But when Pharaoh saw that there was relief, he hardened his heart and would not listen to Moses and Aaron, just as the LORD had said.

The plague of gnats

16 Then the LORD said to Moses, 'Tell Aaron, "Stretch out your staff and strike the dust of the ground," and throughout the land of Egypt the dust will become gnats.' 17 They did this, and when Aaron stretched out his hand with the staff and struck the dust of the ground, gnats came on people and animals. All the dust throughout the land of Egypt became gnats. 18 But when the magicians tried to produce gnats by their secret arts, they could not.

Since the gnats were on people and animals everywhere, 19 the magicians said to Pharaoh, 'This is the finger of God.' But Pharaoh's heart was hard and he would not listen, just as the LORD had said.

The plague of flies

20 Then the LORD said to Moses, 'Get up early in the morning and confront Pharaoh as he goes to the river and say to him, "This is what the LORD says: let my people go, so that they may worship me. 21 If you do not let my people go, I will send swarms of flies on you and your officials, on your people and into your houses. The houses of the Egyptians will be full of flies; even the ground will be covered with them.

22 ' "But on that day I will deal differently with the land of Goshen, where my people live; no swarms of flies will be there, so that you will know that I, the LORD, am in this land. 23 I will make a distinction[b] between my people and your people. This sign will occur tomorrow." '

24 And the LORD did this. Dense swarms of flies poured into Pharaoh's palace and into the houses of his officials; throughout Egypt the land was ruined by the flies.

25 Then Pharaoh summoned Moses and Aaron and said, 'Go, sacrifice to your God here in the land.'

26 But Moses said, 'That would not be right. The sacrifices we offer the LORD our God would be detestable to the Egyptians. And if we offer sacrifices that are detestable in their eyes, will they not stone us? 27 We must take a three-day journey into the wilderness to offer sacrifices to the LORD our God, as he commands us.'

28 Pharaoh said, 'I will let you go to offer sacrifices to the LORD your God in the wilderness, but you must not go very far. Now pray for me.'

29 Moses answered, 'As soon as I leave you, I will pray to the LORD, and tomorrow the flies will leave Pharaoh and his officials and his people. Only let Pharaoh be sure that he does not act deceitfully again by not letting the people go to offer sacrifices to the LORD.'

30 Then Moses left Pharaoh and prayed to the LORD, 31 and the LORD did what Moses asked. The flies left Pharaoh and his officials and his people; not a fly remained. 32 But this time also Pharaoh hardened his heart and would not let the people go.

The plague on livestock

9 Then the LORD said to Moses, 'Go to Pharaoh and say to him, "This is what the LORD, the God of the Hebrews, says: 'Let my people go, so that they may worship me.' 2 If you refuse to let them go and continue to hold them back, 3 the hand of the LORD will bring a terrible plague on your livestock in the field – on your horses,

---

b 23 Septuagint and Vulgate; Hebrew *will put a deliverance* donkeys and camels and on your cattle, sheep and goats. 4 But the LORD will make a distinction between the livestock of Israel and that of Egypt, so that no animal belonging to the Israelites will die." '

5 The LORD set a time and said, 'Tomorrow the LORD will do this in the land.' 6 And the next day the LORD did it: all the livestock of the Egyptians died, but not one animal belonging to the Israelites died. 7 Pharaoh investigated and found that not even one of the animals of the Israelites had died. Yet his heart was unyielding and he would not let the people go.

The plague of boils

8 Then the LORD said to Moses and Aaron, 'Take handfuls of soot from a furnace and let Moses toss it into the air in the presence of Pharaoh. 9 It will become fine dust over the whole land of Egypt, and festering boils will break out on people and animals throughout the land.'

10 So they took soot from a furnace and stood before Pharaoh. Moses tossed it into the air, and festering boils broke out on people and animals. 11 The magicians could not stand before Moses because of the boils that were on them and on all the Egyptians. 12 But the LORD hardened Pharaoh's heart and he would not listen to Moses and Aaron, just as the LORD had said to Moses.

The plague of hail

13 Then the LORD said to Moses, 'Get up early in the morning, confront Pharaoh and say to him, "This is what the LORD, the God of the Hebrews, says: let my people go, so that they may worship me, 14 or this time I will send the full force of my plagues against you and against your officials and your people, so you may know that there is no one like me in all the earth. 15 For by now I could have stretched out my hand and struck you and your people with a plague that would have wiped you off the earth. 16 But I have raised you up*a* for this very purpose, that I might show you my power and that my name might be proclaimed in all the earth. 17 You still set yourself against my people and will not let them go. 18 Therefore, at this time tomorrow I will send the worst hailstorm that has ever fallen on Egypt, from the day it was founded till now. 19 Give an order now to bring your livestock and everything you have in the field to a place of shelter, because the hail will fall on every person and animal that has not been brought in and is still out in the field, and they will die." '

20 Those officials of Pharaoh who feared the word of the LORD hurried to bring their slaves and their livestock inside. 21 But those who ignored the word of the LORD left their slaves and livestock in the field.

22 Then the LORD said to Moses, 'Stretch out your hand towards the sky so that hail will fall all over Egypt – on people and animals and on everything growing in the fields of Egypt.' 23 When Moses stretched out his staff towards the sky, the LORD sent thunder and hail, and lightning flashed down to the ground. So the LORD rained hail on the land of Egypt; 24 hail fell and lightning flashed back and forth. It was the worst storm in all the land of Egypt since it had become a nation. 25 Throughout Egypt hail struck everything in the fields – both people and animals; it beat down everything growing in the fields and stripped every tree. 26 The only place it did not hail was the land of Goshen, where the Israelites were.

27 Then Pharaoh summoned Moses and Aaron. 'This time I have sinned,' he said to them. 'The LORD is in the right, and I and my people are in the wrong. 28 Pray to the LORD, for we have had enough thunder and hail. I will let you go; you don't have to stay any longer.'

29 Moses replied, 'When I have gone out of the city, I will spread out my hands in prayer to the LORD. The thunder will stop and there will be no more hail, so you may know that the earth is the LORD's. 30 But I know that you and your officials still do not fear the LORD God.'

31 (The flax and barley were destroyed, since the barley was in the ear and the flax was in bloom. 32 The wheat and spelt,

---

a 16 Or *have spared you*

however, were not destroyed, because they ripen later.)

[33] Then Moses left Pharaoh and went out of the city. He spread out his hands towards the LORD; the thunder and hail stopped, and the rain no longer poured down on the land. [34] When Pharaoh saw that the rain and hail and thunder had stopped, he sinned again: he and his officials hardened their hearts. [35] So Pharaoh's heart was hard and he would not let the Israelites go, just as the LORD had said through Moses.

The plague of locusts

10 Then the LORD said to Moses, 'Go to Pharaoh, for I have hardened his heart and the hearts of his officials so that I may perform these signs of mine among them [2] that you may tell your children and grandchildren how I dealt harshly with the Egyptians and how I performed my signs among them, and that you may know that I am the LORD.'

[3] So Moses and Aaron went to Pharaoh and said to him, 'This is what the LORD, the God of the Hebrews, says: "How long will you refuse to humble yourself before me? Let my people go, so that they may worship me. [4] If you refuse to let them go, I will bring locusts into your country tomorrow. [5] They will cover the face of the ground so that it cannot be seen. They will devour what little you have left after the hail, including every tree that is growing in your fields. [6] They will fill your houses and those of all your officials and all the Egyptians – something neither your parents nor your ancestors have ever seen from the day they settled in this land till now." ' Then Moses turned and left Pharaoh.

[7] Pharaoh's officials said to him, 'How long will this man be a snare to us? Let the people go, so that they may worship the LORD their God. Do you not yet realise that Egypt is ruined?'

[8] Then Moses and Aaron were brought back to Pharaoh. 'Go, worship the LORD your God,' he said. 'But tell me who will be going.'

[9] Moses answered, 'We will go with our young and our old, with our sons and our daughters, and with our flocks and herds, because we are to celebrate a festival to the LORD.'

[10] Pharaoh said, 'The LORD be with you – if I let you go, along with your women and children! Clearly you are bent on evil.[a] [11] No! Let only the men go and worship the LORD, since that's what you have been asking for.' Then Moses and Aaron were driven out of Pharaoh's presence.

[12] And the LORD said to Moses, 'Stretch out your hand over Egypt so that locusts swarm over the land and devour everything growing in the fields, everything left by the hail.'

[13] So Moses stretched out his staff over Egypt, and the LORD made an east wind blow across the land all that day and all that night. By morning the wind had brought the locusts; [14] they invaded all Egypt and settled down in every area of the country in great numbers. Never before had there been such a plague of locusts, nor will there ever be again. [15] They covered all the ground until it was black. They devoured all that was left after the hail – everything growing in the fields and the fruit on the trees. Nothing green remained on tree or plant in all the land of Egypt.

[16] Pharaoh quickly summoned Moses and Aaron and said, 'I have sinned against the LORD your God and against you. [17] Now forgive my sin once more and pray to the LORD your God to take this deadly plague away from me.'

[18] Moses then left Pharaoh and prayed to the LORD. [19] And the LORD changed the wind to a very strong west wind, which caught up the locusts and carried them into the Red Sea.[b] Not a locust was left anywhere in Egypt. [20] But the LORD hardened Pharaoh's heart, and he would not let the Israelites go.

The plague of darkness

[21] Then the LORD said to Moses, 'Stretch out your hand towards the sky so that darkness spreads over Egypt – darkness

---

a 10　Or *Be careful, trouble is in store for you!*
b 19　Or *the Sea of Reeds*

that can be felt.' 22 So Moses stretched out his hand towards the sky, and total darkness covered all Egypt for three days. 23 No one could see anyone else or move about for three days. Yet all the Israelites had light in the places where they lived.

24 Then Pharaoh summoned Moses and said, 'Go, worship the LORD. Even your women and children may go with you; only leave your flocks and herds behind.'

25 But Moses said, 'You must allow us to have sacrifices and burnt offerings to present to the LORD our God. 26 Our livestock too must go with us; not a hoof is to be left behind. We have to use some of them in worshipping the LORD our God, and until we get there we will not know what we are to use to worship the LORD.'

27 But the LORD hardened Pharaoh's heart, and he was not willing to let them go. 28 Pharaoh said to Moses, 'Get out of my sight! Make sure you do not appear before me again! The day you see my face you will die.'

29 'Just as you say,' Moses replied. 'I will never appear before you again.'

The plague on the firstborn

11 Now the LORD said to Moses, 'I will bring one more plague on Pharaoh and on Egypt. After that, he will let you go from here, and when he does, he will drive you out completely. 2 Tell the people that men and women alike are to ask their neighbours for articles of silver and gold.' 3 (The LORD made the Egyptians favourably disposed towards the people, and Moses himself was highly regarded in Egypt by Pharaoh's officials and by the people.)

4 So Moses said, 'This is what the LORD says: "About midnight I will go throughout Egypt. 5 Every firstborn son in Egypt will die, from the firstborn son of Pharaoh, who sits on the throne, to the firstborn son of the female slave, who is at her hand mill, and all the firstborn of the cattle as well. 6 There will be loud wailing throughout Egypt – worse than there has ever been or ever will be again. 7 But among the Israelites not a dog will bark at any person or animal." Then you will know that the LORD makes a distinction between Egypt

and Israel. 8 All these officials of yours will come to me, bowing down before me and saying, "Go, you and all the people who follow you!" After that I will leave.' Then Moses, hot with anger, left Pharaoh.

9 The LORD had said to Moses, 'Pharaoh will refuse to listen to you – so that my wonders may be multiplied in Egypt.' 10 Moses and Aaron performed all these wonders before Pharaoh, but the LORD hardened Pharaoh's heart, and he would not let the Israelites go out of his country.

The Passover

12 The LORD said to Moses and Aaron in Egypt, 2 'This month is to be for you the first month, the first month of your year. 3 Tell the whole community of Israel that on the tenth day of this month each man is to take a lamb*a* for his family, one for each household. 4 If any household is too small for a whole lamb, they must share one with their nearest neighbour, having taken into account the number of people there are. You are to determine the amount of lamb needed in accordance with what each person will eat. 5 The animals you choose must be year-old males without defect, and you may take them from the sheep or the goats. 6 Take care of them until the fourteenth day of the month, when all the members of the community of Israel must slaughter them at twilight. 7 Then they are to take some of the blood and put it on the sides and tops of the door-frames of the houses where they eat the lambs. 8 That same night they are to eat the meat roasted over the fire, along with bitter herbs, and bread made without yeast. 9 Do not eat the meat raw or boiled in water, but roast it over a fire – with the head, legs and internal organs. 10 Do not leave any of it till morning; if some is left till morning, you must burn it. 11 This is how you are to eat it: with your cloak tucked into your belt, your sandals on your feet and your staff in your hand. Eat it in haste; it is the LORD's Passover.

12 'On that same night I will pass

---

a 3 The Hebrew word can mean *lamb* or *kid*; also in verse 4.

through Egypt and strike down every first-born of both people and animals, and I will bring judgment on all the gods of Egypt. I am the LORD. 13 The blood will be a sign for you on the houses where you are, and when I see the blood, I will pass over you. No destructive plague will touch you when I strike Egypt.

14 'This is a day you are to commemorate; for the generations to come you shall celebrate it as a festival to the LORD – a lasting ordinance. 15 For seven days you are to eat bread made without yeast. On the first day remove the yeast from your houses, for whoever eats anything with yeast in it from the first day until the seventh must be cut off from Israel. 16 On the first day hold a sacred assembly, and another one on the seventh day. Do no work at all on these days, except to prepare food for everyone to eat; that is all you may do.

17 'Celebrate the Festival of Unleavened Bread, because it was on this very day that I brought your divisions out of Egypt. Celebrate this day as a lasting ordinance for the generations to come. 18 In the first month you are to eat bread made without yeast, from the evening of the fourteenth day until the evening of the twenty-first day. 19 For seven days no yeast is to be found in your houses. And anyone, whether foreigner or native-born, who eats anything with yeast in it must be cut off from the community of Israel. 20 Eat nothing made with yeast. Wherever you live, you must eat unleavened bread.'

21 Then Moses summoned all the elders of Israel and said to them, 'Go at once and select the animals for your families and slaughter the Passover lamb. 22 Take a bunch of hyssop, dip it into the blood in the basin and put some of the blood on the top and on both sides of the door-frame. None of you shall go out of the door of your house until morning. 23 When the LORD goes through the land to strike down the Egyptians, he will see the blood on the top and sides of the door-frame and will pass over that doorway, and he will not permit the destroyer to enter your houses and strike you down.

24 'Obey these instructions as a lasting ordinance for you and your descendants. 25 When you enter the land that the LORD will give you as he promised, observe this ceremony. 26 And when your children ask you, "What does this ceremony mean to you?" 27 then tell them, "It is the Passover sacrifice to the LORD, who passed over the houses of the Israelites in Egypt and spared our homes when he struck down the Egyptians."' Then the people bowed down and worshipped. 28 The Israelites did just what the LORD commanded Moses and Aaron.

29 At midnight the LORD struck down all the firstborn in Egypt, from the firstborn of Pharaoh, who sat on the throne, to the firstborn of the prisoner, who was in the dungeon, and the firstborn of all the livestock as well. 30 Pharaoh and all his officials and all the Egyptians got up during the night, and there was loud wailing in Egypt, for there was not a house without someone dead.

The exodus

31 During the night Pharaoh summoned Moses and Aaron and said, 'Up! Leave my people, you and the Israelites! Go, worship the LORD as you have requested. 32 Take your flocks and herds, as you have said, and go. And also bless me.'

33 The Egyptians urged the people to hurry and leave the country. 'For otherwise,' they said, 'we will all die!' 34 So the people took their dough before the yeast was added, and carried it on their shoulders in kneading troughs wrapped in clothing. 35 The Israelites did as Moses instructed and asked the Egyptians for articles of silver and gold and for clothing. 36 The LORD had made the Egyptians favourably disposed towards the people, and they gave them what they asked for; so they plundered the Egyptians.

37 The Israelites journeyed from Rameses to Sukkoth. There were about six hundred thousand men on foot, besides women and children. 38 Many other people went up with them, and also large droves of livestock, both flocks and herds. 39 With the dough the Israelites had brought from Egypt, they baked loaves of

unleavened bread. The dough was without yeast because they had been driven out of Egypt and did not have time to prepare food for themselves.

⁴⁰ Now the length of time the Israelite people lived in Egypt*ᵇ* was 430 years. ⁴¹ At the end of the 430 years, to the very day,

all the LORD's divisions left Egypt. ⁴² Because the LORD kept vigil that night to bring them out of Egypt, on this night all the Israelites are to keep vigil to honour the LORD for the generations to come.

Passover restrictions

⁴³ The LORD said to Moses and Aaron, 'These are the regulations for the Passover meal:

b 40 Masoretic Text; Samaritan Pentateuch and Septuagint *Egypt and Canaan*

SACRIFICE 3

The Passover

Here is an incredible story of the liberation of an entire race of people: over one million people escaped from slavery in one night! The way it all came about is worth reading (this part of the story starts in Exodus 7), but the last action-packed bit in Exodus 12 is that the Israelites were invited to eat a meal, which became known as 'the Passover'.

All the Israelites were told to sacrifice a lamb for their meal. While they were preparing the meal, they were told to take the blood of the lamb and paint it over the doors of their houses. Egypt had suffered nine different plagues so far, and the last was the worst: God had promised to pass through Egypt and strike down every firstborn son of both people and animals. As God had promised, at midnight death touched every Egyptian household, but didn't touch any home that had the blood of the lamb smeared on the outside.

Pharaoh lost his eldest son and was devastated. All the oppressors were broken-hearted from the plague of death and wanted the Israelites out of their land, and so the Passover was the last meal the Israelites ate in Egypt – the land of their slavery.

The Jews were instructed to practise the Passover every year so that they would not forget the miraculous way in which God rescued them. The Jews still celebrate the Passover each year. The last supper before Jesus was led to the cross was the Passover meal. During this meal, Jesus explained to his disciples that he was going to die. Jesus, the Lamb of God (John 1:29), was sacrificed and his blood covers our 'doors' (heart, life, body) so that we escape death.

We are the slaves until Jesus sets us free. The incredible thing about Jesus' sacrifice is that his death is enough to release us from anything that would hold us captive.

Danielle Strickland

 Genesis 22:13   1 Samuel 1:24–28 ▶

'No foreigner may eat it. 44 Any slave you have bought may eat it after you have circumcised him, 45 but a temporary resident or a hired worker may not eat it.

46 'It must be eaten inside the house; take none of the meat outside the house. Do not break any of the bones. 47 The whole community of Israel must celebrate it.

48 'A foreigner residing among you who wants to celebrate the LORD's Passover must have all the males in his household circumcised; then he may take part like one born in the land. No uncircumcised male may eat it. 49 The same law applies both to the native-born and to the foreigner residing among you.'

50 All the Israelites did just what the LORD had commanded Moses and Aaron. 51 And on that very day the LORD brought the Israelites out of Egypt by their divisions.

Consecration of the firstborn

13 The LORD said to Moses, 2 'Consecrate to me every firstborn male. The first offspring of every womb among the Israelites belongs to me, whether human or animal.'

3 Then Moses said to the people, 'Commemorate this day, the day you came out of Egypt, out of the land of slavery, because the LORD brought you out of it with a mighty hand. Eat nothing containing yeast. 4 Today, in the month of Aviv, you are leaving. 5 When the LORD brings you into the land of the Canaanites, Hittites, Amorites, Hivites and Jebusites – the land he swore to your ancestors to give you, a land flowing with milk and honey – you are to observe this ceremony in this month: 6 for seven days eat bread made without yeast and on the seventh day hold a festival to the LORD. 7 Eat unleavened bread during those seven days; nothing with yeast in it is to be seen among you, nor shall any yeast be seen anywhere within your borders. 8 On that day tell your son, "I do this because of what the LORD did for me when I came out of Egypt." 9 This observance will be for you like a sign on your hand and a reminder on your forehead that this law of the LORD is to be on your lips. For the LORD brought you out of Egypt with his mighty hand. 10 You must keep this ordinance at the appointed time year after year.

11 'After the LORD brings you into the land of the Canaanites and gives it to you, as he promised on oath to you and your ancestors, 12 you are to give over to the LORD the first offspring of every womb. All the firstborn males of your livestock belong to the LORD. 13 Redeem with a lamb every firstborn donkey, but if you do not redeem it, break its neck. Redeem every firstborn among your sons.

14 'In days to come when your son asks you, "What does this mean?" say to him, "With a mighty hand the LORD brought us out of Egypt, out of the land of slavery. 15 When Pharaoh stubbornly refused to let us go, the LORD killed the firstborn of both people and animals in Egypt. This is why I sacrifice to the LORD the first male offspring of every womb and redeem each of my firstborn sons." 16 And it will be like a sign on your hand and a symbol on your forehead that the LORD brought us out of Egypt with his mighty hand.'

Crossing the sea

17 When Pharaoh let the people go, God did not lead them on the road through the Philistine country, though that was shorter. For God said, 'If they face war, they might change their minds and return to Egypt.' 18 So God led the people around by the desert road towards the Red Sea.*a* The Israelites went up out of Egypt ready for battle.

19 Moses took the bones of Joseph with him because Joseph had made the Israelites swear an oath. He had said, 'God will surely come to your aid, and then you must carry my bones up with you from this place.'*b*

20 After leaving Sukkoth they camped at Etham on the edge of the desert. 21 By day the LORD went ahead of them in a pillar of

---

a 18 Or *the Sea of Reeds*
b 19 See Gen. 50:25.

cloud to guide them on their way and by night in a pillar of fire to give them light, so that they could travel by day or night. ²²Neither the pillar of cloud by day nor the pillar of fire by night left its place in front of the people.

14 Then the LORD said to Moses, ²'Tell the Israelites to turn back and camp near Pi Hahiroth, between Migdol and the sea. They are to camp by the sea, directly opposite Baal Zephon. ³Pharaoh will think, "The Israelites are wandering around the land in confusion, hemmed in by the desert." ⁴And I will harden Pharaoh's heart, and he will pursue them. But I will gain glory for myself through Pharaoh and all his army, and the Egyptians will know that I am the LORD.' So the Israelites did this.

⁵When the king of Egypt was told that the people had fled, Pharaoh and his officials changed their minds about them and said, 'What have we done? We have let the Israelites go and have lost their services!' ⁶So he had his chariot made ready and took his army with him. ⁷He took six hundred of the best chariots, along with all the other chariots of Egypt, with officers over all of them. ⁸The LORD hardened the heart of Pharaoh king of Egypt, so that he pursued the Israelites, who were marching out boldly. ⁹The Egyptians – all Pharaoh's horses and chariots, horsemen*ᵃ* and troops – pursued the Israelites and overtook them as they camped by the sea near Pi Hahiroth, opposite Baal Zephon.

¹⁰As Pharaoh approached, the Israelites looked up, and there were the Egyptians, marching after them. They were terrified and cried out to the LORD. ¹¹They said to Moses, 'Was it because there were no graves in Egypt that you brought us to the desert to die? What have you done to us by bringing us out of Egypt? ¹²Didn't we say to you in Egypt, "Leave us alone; let us serve the Egyptians"? It would have been better for us to serve the Egyptians than to die in the desert!'

¹³Moses answered the people, 'Do not be afraid. Stand firm and you will see the deliverance the LORD will bring you today. The Egyptians you see today you will never see again. ¹⁴The LORD will fight for you; you need only to be still.'

¹⁵Then the LORD said to Moses, 'Why are you crying out to me? Tell the Israelites to move on. ¹⁶Raise your staff and stretch out your hand over the sea to divide the water so that the Israelites can go through the sea on dry ground. ¹⁷I will harden the hearts of the Egyptians so that they will go in after them. And I will gain glory through Pharaoh and all his army, through his chariots and his horsemen. ¹⁸The Egyptians will know that I am the LORD when I gain glory through Pharaoh, his chariots and his horsemen.'

¹⁹Then the angel of God, who had been travelling in front of Israel's army, withdrew and went behind them. The pillar of cloud also moved from in front and stood behind them, ²⁰coming between the armies of Egypt and Israel. Throughout the night the cloud brought darkness to the one side and light to the other; so neither went near the other all night long.

²¹Then Moses stretched out his hand over the sea, and all that night the LORD drove the sea back with a strong east wind and turned it into dry land. The waters were divided, ²²and the Israelites went through the sea on dry ground, with a wall of water on their right and on their left.

²³The Egyptians pursued them, and all Pharaoh's horses and chariots and horsemen followed them into the sea. ²⁴During the last watch of the night the LORD looked down from the pillar of fire and cloud at the Egyptian army and threw it into confusion. ²⁵He jammed*ᵇ* the wheels of their chariots so that they had difficulty driving. And the Egyptians said, 'Let's get away from the Israelites! The LORD is fighting for them against Egypt.'

²⁶Then the LORD said to Moses, 'Stretch out your hand over the sea so that the waters may flow back over the Egyptians and their chariots and horsemen.' ²⁷Moses stretched out his hand over the

---

ᵃ9 Or charioteers; also in verses 17, 18, 23, 26 and 28

ᵇ25 See Samaritan Pentateuch, Septuagint and Syriac; Masoretic Text removed sea, and at daybreak the sea went back to its place. The Egyptians were fleeing towards[c] it, and the LORD swept them into the sea. 28 The water flowed back and covered the chariots and horsemen – the entire army of Pharaoh that had followed the Israelites into the sea. Not one of them survived.

29 But the Israelites went through the sea on dry ground, with a wall of water on their right and on their left. 30 That day the LORD saved Israel from the hands of the Egyptians, and Israel saw the Egyptians lying dead on the shore. 31 And when the Israelites saw the mighty hand of the LORD displayed against the Egyptians, the people feared the LORD and put their trust in him and in Moses his servant.

The song of Moses and Miriam

15

Then Moses and the Israelites sang this song to the LORD:

'I will sing to the LORD,
    for he is highly exalted.
Both horse and driver
    he has hurled into the sea.

2 'The LORD is my strength and my
        defence[a];
    he has become my salvation.
He is my God, and I will praise him,
    my father's God, and I will exalt
        him.
3 The LORD is a warrior;
    the LORD is his name.
4 Pharaoh's chariots and his army
    he has hurled into the sea.
The best of Pharaoh's officers
    are drowned in the Red Sea.[b]
5 The deep waters have covered them;
    they sank to the depths like a
        stone.
6 Your right hand, LORD,
    was majestic in power.
Your right hand, LORD,
    shattered the enemy.

7 'In the greatness of your majesty
    you threw down those who
        opposed you.
You unleashed your burning anger;
    it consumed them like stubble.
8 By the blast of your nostrils
    the waters piled up.
The surging waters stood up like a
        wall;
    the deep waters congealed in the
        heart of the sea.
9 The enemy boasted,
    "I will pursue, I will overtake
        them.
I will divide the spoils;
    I will gorge myself on them.
I will draw my sword
    and my hand will destroy them."
10 But you blew with your breath,
    and the sea covered them.
They sank like lead
    in the mighty waters.
11 Who among the gods
    is like you, LORD?
Who is like you –
    majestic in holiness,
awesome in glory,
    working wonders?

12 'You stretch out your right hand,
    and the earth swallows your
        enemies.
13 In your unfailing love you will lead
    the people you have redeemed.
In your strength you will guide them
    to your holy dwelling.
14 The nations will hear and tremble;
    anguish will grip the people of
        Philistia.
15 The chiefs of Edom will be terrified,
    the leaders of Moab will be seized
        with trembling,
the people[c] of Canaan will melt away;
16   terror and dread will fall on them.
By the power of your arm
    they will be as still as a stone –
until your people pass by, LORD,
    until the people you bought[d]
        pass by.

---

c 27 Or *from*
a 2 Or *song*
b 4 Or *the Sea of Reeds*; also in verse 22

c 15 Or *rulers*
d 16 Or *created*

17 You will bring them in and plant
them
   on the mountain of your
   inheritance –
the place, LORD, you made for your
dwelling,
   the sanctuary, Lord, your hands
   established.

18 'The LORD reigns
   for ever and ever.'

19 When Pharaoh's horses, chariots and
horsemen[e] went into the sea, the LORD
brought the waters of the sea back over
them, but the Israelites walked through
the sea on dry ground. 20 Then Miriam
the prophet, Aaron's sister, took a tambourine in her hand, and all the women
followed her, with tambourines and dancing. 21 Miriam sang to them:

   'Sing to the LORD,
      for he is highly exalted.
   Both horse and driver
      he has hurled into the sea.'

The waters of Marah and Elim

22 Then Moses led Israel from the Red
Sea and they went into the Desert of Shur.
For three days they travelled in the desert
without finding water. 23 When they came
to Marah, they could not drink its water
because it was bitter. (That is why the
place is called Marah.[f]) 24 So the people
grumbled against Moses, saying, 'What
are we to drink?'

25 Then Moses cried out to the LORD, and
the LORD showed him a piece of wood. He
threw it into the water, and the water became fit to drink.

There the LORD issued a ruling and instruction for them and put them to the
test. 26 He said, 'If you listen carefully to
the LORD your God and do what is right in
his eyes, if you pay attention to his commands and keep all his decrees, I will not
bring on you any of the diseases I brought

on the Egyptians, for I am the LORD, who
heals you.'

27 Then they came to Elim, where there
were twelve springs and seventy palm
trees, and they camped there near the
water.

Manna and quail

16 The whole Israelite community
set out from Elim and came to the
Desert of Sin, which is between Elim and
Sinai, on the fifteenth day of the second
month after they had come out of Egypt.
2 In the desert the whole community
grumbled against Moses and Aaron. 3 The
Israelites said to them, 'If only we had died
by the LORD's hand in Egypt! There we sat
round pots of meat and ate all the food we
wanted, but you have brought us out into
this desert to starve this entire assembly
to death.'

4 Then the LORD said to Moses, 'I will
rain down bread from heaven for you. The
people are to go out each day and gather
enough for that day. In this way I will test
them and see whether they will follow my
instructions. 5 On the sixth day they are
to prepare what they bring in, and that is
to be twice as much as they gather on the
other days.'

6 So Moses and Aaron said to all the
Israelites, 'In the evening you will know
that it was the LORD who brought you out
of Egypt, 7 and in the morning you will
see the glory of the LORD, because he has
heard your grumbling against him. Who
are we, that you should grumble against
us?' 8 Moses also said, 'You will know that
it was the LORD when he gives you meat
to eat in the evening and all the bread
you want in the morning, because he has
heard your grumbling against him. Who
are we? You are not grumbling against us,
but against the LORD.'

9 Then Moses told Aaron, 'Say to the entire Israelite community, "Come before
the LORD, for he has heard your grumbling." '

10 While Aaron was speaking to the
whole Israelite community, they looked
towards the desert, and there was the
glory of the LORD appearing in the cloud.

---

e 19 Or *charioteers*
f 23 *Marah* means *bitter.*

THE NAMES OF GOD 4

God the Healer (Yahweh Rapha)

It's in God's nature to heal

In the Old Testament God made a covenant promise with his people that he would protect them from plagues and diseases on condition that they kept his commands (Exodus 15:26). With all we know about God, we understand that he loves us, wants good things for us and wants to heal us, and we find evidence of this throughout the Old Testament:

- 'The LORD will keep you free from every disease. He will not inflict on you the horrible diseases you knew in Egypt.' (Deuteronomy 7:15)

- 'I will take away disease from among you.' (Exodus 23:25)

- 'He sent out his word and healed them; he rescued them from the grave.' (Psalm 107:20)

- 'Praise the LORD, my soul, and forget not all his benefits – who forgives all your sins and heals all your diseases.' (Psalm 103:2)

- ' "But I will restore you to health and heal your wounds," declares the LORD.' (Jeremiah 30:17)

Exodus 15:26 also implies that it's our disobedience that causes our sickness. That's not to say that sin is always the direct cause of sickness in an individual (like in John 5:14), but it is sometimes the case.

God's nature to heal was reinforced in the New Testament with the preaching of the kingdom of God. God confirmed Jesus' teaching with healings and miracles. Yet sometimes people's sickness is caused by their own unconfessed sins. Whatever the case, we must avoid being accusing or condemning.

God wants us to be healers

Jesus later commissioned his apostles to preach the gospel, heal the sick and cast out demons. Clearly there were cases in the New Testament where people did not get healed (see the article on this in the Issues section), but the followers of Jesus are still commissioned to heal the sick today. There may be times when the people being prayed for do not appear to get healed, but we keep on praying for them out of obedience to God's will and have to leave the results to him. Our medical practitioners, who get all their talents from God, go on ministering healing, though clearly they do not see everyone getting healed either. If you, the reader, feel the need of prayer for healing, then it would be good to seek out a fellow believer to lay hands on you and pray for your healing. And should you meet up with someone who needs prayer for healing, you might offer to pray for him/her if you feel the prompting of the Holy Spirit to do so.

Since all healing comes from God, we must be sure to keep giving him the glory for each and every healing.

David and Mary Pytches

 1 Kings 17:8   Romans 15:33

¹¹ The LORD said to Moses, ¹² 'I have heard the grumbling of the Israelites. Tell them, "At twilight you will eat meat, and in the morning you will be filled with bread. Then you will know that I am the LORD your God." '

¹³ That evening quail came and covered the camp, and in the morning there was a layer of dew around the camp. ¹⁴ When the dew was gone, thin flakes like frost on the ground appeared on the desert floor. ¹⁵ When the Israelites saw it, they said to each other, 'What is it?' For they did not know what it was.

Moses said to them, 'It is the bread the LORD has given you to eat. ¹⁶ This is what the LORD has commanded: "Everyone is to gather as much as they need. Take an omer*a* for each person you have in your tent." '

¹⁷ The Israelites did as they were told; some gathered much, some little. ¹⁸ And when they measured it by the omer, the one who gathered much did not have too much, and the one who gathered little did not have too little. Everyone had gathered just as much as they needed.

¹⁹ Then Moses said to them, 'No one is to keep any of it until morning.'

²⁰ However, some of them paid no attention to Moses; they kept part of it until morning, but it was full of maggots and began to smell. So Moses was angry with them.

²¹ Each morning everyone gathered as much as they needed, and when the sun grew hot, it melted away. ²² On the sixth day, they gathered twice as much – two omers*b* for each person – and the leaders of the community came and reported this to Moses. ²³ He said to them, 'This is what the LORD commanded: "Tomorrow is to be a day of sabbath rest, a holy sabbath to the LORD. So bake what you want to bake and boil what you want to boil. Save whatever is left and keep it until morning." '

²⁴ So they saved it until morning, as Moses commanded, and it did not stink

or get maggots in it. ²⁵ 'Eat it today,' Moses said, 'because today is a sabbath to the LORD. You will not find any of it on the ground today. ²⁶ Six days you are to gather it, but on the seventh day, the Sabbath, there will not be any.'

²⁷ Nevertheless, some of the people went out on the seventh day to gather it, but they found none. ²⁸ Then the LORD said to Moses, 'How long will you*c* refuse to keep my commands and my instructions? ²⁹ Bear in mind that the LORD has given you the Sabbath; that is why on the sixth day he gives you bread for two days. Everyone is to stay where they are on the seventh day; no one is to go out.' ³⁰ So the people rested on the seventh day.

³¹ The people of Israel called the bread manna.*d* It was white like coriander seed and tasted like wafers made with honey. ³² Moses said, 'This is what the LORD has commanded: "Take an omer of manna and keep it for the generations to come, so they can see the bread I gave you to eat in the wilderness when I brought you out of Egypt." '

³³ So Moses said to Aaron, 'Take a jar and put an omer of manna in it. Then place it before the LORD to be kept for the generations to come.'

³⁴ As the LORD commanded Moses, Aaron put the manna with the tablets of the covenant law, that it might be preserved. ³⁵ The Israelites ate manna for forty years, until they came to a land that was settled; they ate manna until they reached the border of Canaan.

³⁶ (An omer is one tenth of an ephah.)

Water from the rock

17 The whole Israelite community set out from the Desert of Sin, travelling from place to place as the LORD commanded. They camped at Rephidim, but there was no water for the people to drink. ² So they quarrelled with Moses and said, 'Give us water to drink.'

Moses replied, 'Why do you quarrel

---

a 16 That is, possibly about 1.4 kilograms; also in verses 18, 32, 33 and 36
b 22 That is, possibly about 2.8 kilograms
c 28 The Hebrew is plural.
d 31 *Manna* sounds like the Hebrew for *What is it?* (see verse 15).

with me? Why do you put the LORD to the test?'

³But the people were thirsty for water there, and they grumbled against Moses. They said, 'Why did you bring us up out of Egypt to make us and our children and livestock die of thirst?'

⁴Then Moses cried out to the LORD, 'What am I to do with these people? They are almost ready to stone me.'

⁵The LORD answered Moses, 'Go out in front of the people. Take with you some of the elders of Israel and take in your hand the staff with which you struck the Nile, and go. ⁶I will stand there before you by the rock at Horeb. Strike the rock, and water will come out of it for the people to drink.' So Moses did this in the sight of the elders of Israel. ⁷And he called the place Massah*ᵃ* and Meribah*ᵇ* because the Israelites quarrelled and because they tested the LORD saying, 'Is the LORD among us or not?'

The Amalekites defeated

⁸The Amalekites came and attacked the Israelites at Rephidim. ⁹Moses said to Joshua, 'Choose some of our men and go out to fight the Amalekites. Tomorrow I will stand on top of the hill with the staff of God in my hands.'

¹⁰So Joshua fought the Amalekites as Moses had ordered, and Moses, Aaron and Hur went to the top of the hill. ¹¹As long as Moses held up his hands, the Israelites were winning, but whenever he lowered his hands, the Amalekites were winning. ¹²When Moses' hands grew tired, they took a stone and put it under him and he sat on it. Aaron and Hur held his hands up – one on one side, one on the other – so that his hands remained steady till sunset. ¹³So Joshua overcame the Amalekite army with the sword.

¹⁴Then the LORD said to Moses, 'Write this on a scroll as something to be remembered and make sure that Joshua hears it, because I will completely blot out the name of Amalek from under heaven.'

¹⁵Moses built an altar and called it The LORD is my Banner. ¹⁶He said, 'Because hands were lifted up against*ᶜ* the throne of the LORD,*ᵈ* the LORD will be at war against the Amalekites from generation to generation.'

Jethro visits Moses

18 Now Jethro, the priest of Midian and father-in-law of Moses, heard of everything God had done for Moses and for his people Israel, and how the LORD had brought Israel out of Egypt.

²After Moses had sent away his wife Zipporah, his father-in-law Jethro received her ³and her two sons. One son was named Gershom,*ᵃ* for Moses said, 'I have become a foreigner in a foreign land'; ⁴and the other was named Eliezer,*ᵇ* for he said, 'My father's God was my helper; he saved me from the sword of Pharaoh.'

⁵Jethro, Moses' father-in-law, together with Moses' sons and wife, came to him in the wilderness, where he was camped near the mountain of God. ⁶Jethro had sent word to him, 'I, your father-in-law Jethro, am coming to you with your wife and her two sons.'

⁷So Moses went out to meet his father-in-law and bowed down and kissed him. They greeted each other and then went into the tent. ⁸Moses told his father-in-law about everything the LORD had done to Pharaoh and the Egyptians for Israel's sake and about all the hardships they had met along the way and how the LORD had saved them.

⁹Jethro was delighted to hear about all the good things the LORD had done for Israel in rescuing them from the hand of the Egyptians. ¹⁰He said, 'Praise be to the LORD, who rescued you from the hand of the Egyptians and of Pharaoh, and who rescued the people from the hand of the Egyptians. ¹¹Now I know that the LORD is greater than all other gods, for he did

---

a 7 *Massah* means *testing.*
b 7 *Meribah* means *quarrelling.*

c 16 Or *to*
d 16 The meaning of the Hebrew for this clause is uncertain.
a 3 *Gershom* sounds like the Hebrew for *a foreigner there.*
b 4 *Eliezer* means *my God is helper.*

this to those who had treated Israel arrogantly.' 12Then Jethro, Moses' father-in-law, brought a burnt offering and other sacrifices to God, and Aaron came with all the elders of Israel to eat a meal with Moses' father-in-law in the presence of God.

13The next day Moses took his seat to serve as judge for the people, and they stood round him from morning till evening. 14When his father-in-law saw all that Moses was doing for the people, he said, 'What is this you are doing for the people? Why do you alone sit as judge, while all these people stand round you from morning till evening?'

15Moses answered him, 'Because the people come to me to seek God's will.

FRIENDSHIP 1

Moses and Jethro – humility in friendship

Have you ever noticed that it's often so much easier to see the solution for a friend's problem than for our own? God created us that way so that we would rely on each other and not make the mistake of thinking we can do this life alone! Right from the beginning of creation, we're told that we're not meant to do life on our own. God said to Adam that it wasn't good for him to be alone (Genesis 2:18) and so he gave him Eve. But it's not just about being married; it's about living in relationship and community with others. No matter how amazingly talented and gifted one person is, no matter how wise or intelligent, they can't have all the answers.

In Exodus 18 we read about Moses, the great leader, leaning on the advice of Jethro (his father-in-law). Moses was sitting as judge over the people and they would come to him with their disputes and to seek God's will. That would be all well and good, except for the fact that there were so many people and so many disputes and only one Moses, so it was taking a long time. A really long time. Jethro pointed out that Moses would wear himself out trying to handle everything alone; he would never be able to deal with all the people's complaints. Jethro advised Moses to appoint wise, trusted leaders over the people so that the work might be split among them, and Moses gladly followed his advice! Moses had been responding to the need in front of him, but he needed the wisdom of Jethro to help him. Although Moses was the boss, he still listened to his father-in-law, showing his great humility. He didn't insist that the idea was rubbish just because he hadn't thought of it first, and he didn't take offence at Jethro saying he couldn't do it alone. He listened and he acted on Jethro's wisdom. It's a great example to us to be humble, able to listen to others and open to their suggestions. If we're full of our own pride and act as if we don't need anyone else, we'll miss out on so much. We all need each other; it's the way God created us.

Ali Martin

2 Kings 2 ▶▶

¹⁶Whenever they have a dispute, it is brought to me, and I decide between the parties and inform them of God's decrees and instructions.'

¹⁷Moses' father-in-law replied, 'What you are doing is not good. ¹⁸You and these people who come to you will only wear yourselves out. The work is too heavy for you; you cannot handle it alone. ¹⁹Listen now to me and I will give you some advice, and may God be with you. You must be the people's representative before God and bring their disputes to him. ²⁰Teach them his decrees and instructions, and show them the way they are to live and how they are to behave. ²¹But select capable men from all the people – men who fear God, trustworthy men who hate dishonest gain – and appoint them as officials over thousands, hundreds, fifties and tens. ²²Let them serve as judges for the people at all times, but let them bring every difficult case to you; the simple cases they can decide themselves. That will make your load lighter, because they will share it with you. ²³If you do this and God so commands, you will be able to stand the strain, and all these people will go home satisfied.'

²⁴Moses listened to his father-in-law and did everything he said. ²⁵He chose capable men from all Israel and made them leaders of the people, officials over thousands, hundreds, fifties and tens. ²⁶They served as judges for the people at all times. The difficult cases they brought to Moses, but the simple ones they decided themselves.

²⁷Then Moses sent his father-in-law on his way, and Jethro returned to his own country.

At Mount Sinai

19 On the first day of the third month after the Israelites left Egypt – on that very day – they came to the Desert of Sinai. ²After they set out from Rephidim, they entered the Desert of Sinai, and Israel camped there in the desert in front of the mountain.

³Then Moses went up to God, and the LORD called to him from the mountain and said, 'This is what you are to say to the descendants of Jacob and what you are to tell the people of Israel: ⁴"You yourselves have seen what I did to Egypt, and how I carried you on eagles' wings and brought you to myself. ⁵Now if you obey me fully and keep my covenant, then out of all nations you will be my treasured possession. Although the whole earth is mine, ⁶you*ᵃ* will be for me a kingdom of priests and a holy nation." These are the words you are to speak to the Israelites.'

⁷So Moses went back and summoned the elders of the people and set before them all the words the LORD had commanded him to speak. ⁸The people all responded together, 'We will do everything the LORD has said.' So Moses brought their answer back to the LORD.

⁹The LORD said to Moses, 'I am going to come to you in a dense cloud, so that the people will hear me speaking with you and will always put their trust in you.' Then Moses told the LORD what the people had said.

¹⁰And the LORD said to Moses, 'Go to the people and consecrate them today and tomorrow. Make them wash their clothes ¹¹and be ready by the third day, because on that day the LORD will come down on Mount Sinai in the sight of all the people. ¹²Put limits for the people around the mountain and tell them, "Be careful that you do not approach the mountain or touch the foot of it. Whoever touches the mountain is to be put to death. ¹³They are to be stoned or shot with arrows; not a hand is to be laid on them. No person or animal shall be permitted to live." Only when the ram's horn sounds a long blast may they approach the mountain.'

¹⁴After Moses had gone down the mountain to the people, he consecrated them, and they washed their clothes. ¹⁵Then he said to the people, 'Prepare yourselves for the third day. Abstain from sexual relations.'

¹⁶On the morning of the third day there was thunder and lightning, with a thick cloud over the mountain, and a very

_____

a 5,6 Or *possession, for the whole earth is mine.* ⁶*You*

THE BIG STORY 5

Israel – God's people

When God wanted to save the world, he established a nation. They were the next stage of fulfilling his promises to Abraham, and he rescued them from slavery to do it. Through Moses he brought them out of Egypt to Sinai. He set them free and protected them. *'I carried you on eagles' wings and brought you to myself'* (Exodus 19:4). There they worshipped him, and he established a special relationship (*'a covenant'*, v. 5) with them. They would be his *'treasured possession'*, the jewel in his crown.

This was all done unconditionally. It was by God's grace, not something they especially deserved (see Deuteronomy 7:7–9). He made them *'a kingdom of priests'* (v. 6), people with direct access to God in worship, and a people through whom the other nations could come to God (see Zechariah 8:20–22 for a later version of this promise). They would also be *'a holy nation'*, in two senses. First, God had set them apart (the core meaning of 'holy') for his purposes. Their call was not just for their own benefit, but to play a vital part in God's plan for the world. Second, they were to live distinctively, obeying God's commandments (*'obey me fully'*, v. 5), and thus showing how a people flourish when they live according to God's ways. They were to keep God's law out of gratitude for being redeemed from slavery, not so that they could earn God's acceptance. He had already accepted them.

But they did not keep their part of the covenant. Again and again, throughout their history, they worshipped other gods, often worshipping local idols as well as the Lord, rather than instead of him. They were just as often guilty of economic injustice and oppressing the poor, although they themselves had been set free from being poverty-stricken slaves (see Jeremiah 7:1–20). Their unfaithfulness broke God's heart (see Hosea 11:1–9). After a civil war which split the nation in two, between ten northern tribes (Israel) and two southern ones (Judah), Israel was conquered by the Assyrian army and those tribes disappear from the stage of history. Finally Judah was taken into exile in Babylon. They were exiled from the land God had promised Abraham and his descendants! During these years the promise of a Messiah – a Saviour who would set them free and restore God's rule – grew. When Jesus came, in fulfilment of these prophecies and of God's original promises to Abraham, he established a new covenant and re-established *'a chosen people, a royal priesthood, a holy nation, God's special possession, that you may declare the praises of him who called you out of darkness into his wonderful light'* (1 Peter 2:9). Now the church is called to be to the world what Old Testament Israel was intended to be.

Graham Cray

 Genesis 12:1–3   Luke 1:26–48

loud trumpet blast. Everyone in the camp trembled. ¹⁷Then Moses led the people out of the camp to meet with God, and they stood at the foot of the mountain. ¹⁸Mount Sinai was covered with smoke, because the LORD descended on it in fire. The smoke billowed up from it like smoke from a furnace, and the whole mountain^b trembled violently. ¹⁹As the sound of the trumpet grew louder and louder, Moses spoke and the voice of God answered him.^c

²⁰The LORD descended to the top of Mount Sinai and called Moses to the top of the mountain. So Moses went up ²¹and the LORD said to him, 'Go down and warn the people so they do not force their way through to see the LORD and many of them perish. ²²Even the priests, who approach the LORD, must consecrate themselves, or the LORD will break out against them.'

²³Moses said to the LORD, 'The people cannot come up Mount Sinai, because you yourself warned us, "Put limits around the mountain and set it apart as holy."'

²⁴The LORD replied, 'Go down and bring Aaron up with you. But the priests and the people must not force their way through to come up to the LORD, or he will break out against them.'

²⁵So Moses went down to the people and told them.

The Ten Commandments

20 And God spoke all these words:

²'I am the LORD your God, who brought you out of Egypt, out of the land of slavery.

³'You shall have no other gods before^a me.

⁴'You shall not make for yourself an image in the form of anything in heaven above or on the earth beneath or in the waters below. ⁵You shall not bow down to them or worship them; for I, the LORD your God, am a

jealous God, punishing the children for the sin of the parents to the third and fourth generation of those who hate me, ⁶but showing love to a thousand generations of those who love me and keep my commandments.

⁷'You shall not misuse the name of the LORD your God, for the LORD will not hold anyone guiltless who misuses his name.

⁸'Remember the Sabbath day by keeping it holy. ⁹Six days you shall labour and do all your work, ¹⁰but the seventh day is a sabbath to the LORD your God. On it you shall not do any work, neither you, nor your son or daughter, nor your male or female servant, nor your animals, nor any foreigner residing in your towns. ¹¹For in six days the LORD made the heavens and the earth, the sea, and all that is in them, but he rested on the seventh day. Therefore the LORD blessed the Sabbath day and made it holy.

¹²'Honour your father and your mother, so that you may live long in the land the LORD your God is giving you.

¹³'You shall not murder.

¹⁴'You shall not commit adultery.

¹⁵'You shall not steal.

¹⁶'You shall not give false testimony against your neighbour.

¹⁷'You shall not covet your neighbour's house. You shall not covet your neighbour's wife, or his male or female servant, his ox or donkey, or anything that belongs to your neighbour.'

¹⁸When the people saw the thunder and lightning and heard the trumpet and saw the mountain in smoke, they trembled with fear. They stayed at a distance ¹⁹and said to Moses, 'Speak to us yourself and we will listen. But do not let God speak to us or we will die.'

---

b 18 Most Hebrew manuscripts; a few Hebrew manuscripts and Septuagint *and all the people*
c 19 Or *and God answered him with thunder*
a 3 Or *besides*

LAW AND GRACE 2

I am the Law

Have you ever been tempted to do something wrong? Imagine your friends have persuaded you to shoplift a chocolate bar. You head into the shop, the shopkeeper is nowhere to be seen … but then you notice two police officers choosing a paper. You do get a chocolate bar, but you *pay* for it!

The presence of authority – in this case two policemen – caused you to change your mind. In Exodus 20 we see God introducing the most famous laws in existence, the Ten Commandments. To the Israelites God's presence was really scary, and they ask God not to speak to them directly. They're *scared* of God. Isn't that a good thing? Doesn't that mean they'll do what he says and obey the law? A bit like our imaginary shop scenario: you obeyed the law because the authorities were very real to you.

Wouldn't that be the easy thing for God to do? If God really wants people to obey his law, why doesn't he make his authority more visible? Imagine if God used his angels as police, putting one on every street to remind us who is in charge!

It's easy to do right when we fear the consequences. If the policemen hadn't been in the shop, we might have stolen the chocolate bar. The problem wasn't with the law, but with our willingness to disobey it –the decision we made in our heart.

God does want us to recognise his authority, but he doesn't want us to obey him out of fear. He wants us to obey him out of love. Love and the law are close friends: the first law is to *'love the LORD your God with all your heart and with all your soul and with all your strength'* (Deuteronomy 6:5). Love has to be our greatest motivation in keeping God's law.

Grace is God's love in action. God is always ready to forgive. But we must recognise that the law was created out of love. Laws are often put into place to ensure our safety and success. A 30 mph speed limit on a busy street is there to keep everybody safe. Many of the disciplines we follow are laws we give ourselves in order to succeed. 'I'll practise my piano today and not just watch TV, so I can become a better musician.' 'I won't eat doughnuts and burgers all the time, but will eat fresh fruit and veg so my heart stays healthy.' Laws are a good thing and God's laws are the best. We need to respect God's rulings, just as we respect the authority of a doctor who tells us we need to diet or risk heart disease! God has ultimate wisdom and is always just, so his laws are always worth following. The best way to respect and obey God is not to do what's right because we fear, but because we seek to love him above all other things that might tempt us to do wrong.

Jason Gardner

 Psalm 103:6–14   John 8:1–11

20 Moses said to the people, 'Do not be afraid. God has come to test you, so that the fear of God will be with you to keep you from sinning.'

21 The people remained at a distance, while Moses approached the thick darkness where God was.

Idols and altars

22 Then the LORD said to Moses, 'Tell the Israelites this: "You have seen for yourselves that I have spoken to you from heaven: 23 do not make any gods to be alongside me; do not make for yourselves gods of silver or gods of gold.

24 ' "Make an altar of earth for me and sacrifice on it your burnt offerings and fellowship offerings, your sheep and goats and your cattle. Wherever I cause my name to be honoured, I will come to you and bless you. 25 If you make an altar of stones for me, do not build it with dressed stones, for you will defile it if you use a tool on it. 26 And do not go up to my altar on steps, or your private parts may be exposed."

21 'These are the laws you are to set before them:

Hebrew servants

2 'If you buy a Hebrew servant, he is to serve you for six years. But in the seventh year, he shall go free, without paying anything. 3 If he comes alone, he is to go free alone; but if he has a wife when he comes, she is to go with him. 4 If his master gives him a wife and she bears him sons or daughters, the woman and her children shall belong to her master, and only the man shall go free.

5 'But if the servant declares, "I love my master and my wife and children and do not want to go free," 6 then his master must take him before the judges.a He shall take him to the door or the door-post and pierce his ear with an awl. Then he will be his servant for life.

7 'If a man sells his daughter as a servant, she is not to go free as male servants do. 8 If she does not please the master who

has selected her for himself,b he must let her be redeemed. He has no right to sell her to foreigners, because he has broken faith with her. 9 If he selects her for his son, he must grant her the rights of a daughter. 10 If he marries another woman, he must not deprive the first one of her food, clothing and marital rights. 11 If he does not provide her with these three things, she is to go free, without any payment of money.

Personal injuries

12 'Anyone who strikes a person with a fatal blow is to be put to death. 13 However, if it is not done intentionally, but God lets it happen, they are to flee to a place I will designate. 14 But if anyone schemes and kills someone deliberately, that person is to be taken from my altar and put to death.

15 'Anyone who attacksc their father or mother is to be put to death.

16 'Anyone who kidnaps someone is to be put to death, whether the victim has been sold or is still in the kidnapper's possession.

17 'Anyone who curses their father or mother is to be put to death.

18 'If people quarrel and one person hits another with a stone or with their fistd and the victim does not die but is confined to bed, 19 the one who struck the blow will not be held liable if the other can get up and walk around outside with a staff; however, the guilty party must pay the injured person for any loss of time and see that the victim is completely healed.

20 'Anyone who beats their male or female slave with a rod must be punished if the slave dies as a direct result, 21 but they are not to be punished if the slave recovers after a day or two, since the slave is their property.

22 'If people are fighting and hit a pregnant woman and she gives birth prematurelye but there is no serious injury, the offender must be fined whatever the

---

a 6   Or before God

b 8   Or master so that he does not choose her
c 15 Or kills
d 18 Or with a tool
e 22 Or she has a miscarriage

woman's husband demands and the court allows. 23 But if there is serious injury, you are to take life for life, 24 eye for eye, tooth for tooth, hand for hand, foot for foot, 25 burn for burn, wound for wound, bruise for bruise.

26 'An owner who hits a male or female slave in the eye and destroys it must let the slave go free to compensate for the eye. 27 And an owner who knocks out the tooth of a male or female slave must let the slave go free to compensate for the tooth.

28 'If a bull gores a man or woman to death, the bull is to be stoned to death, and its meat must not be eaten. But the owner of the bull will not be held responsible. 29 If, however, the bull has had the habit of goring and the owner has been warned but has not kept it penned up and it kills a man or woman, the bull is to be stoned and its owner also is to be put to death. 30 However, if payment is demanded, the owner may redeem his life by the payment of whatever is demanded. 31 This law also applies if the bull gores a son or a daughter. 32 If the bull gores a male or female slave, the owner must pay thirty shekels*f* of silver to the master of the slave, and the bull is to be stoned to death.

33 'If anyone uncovers a pit or digs one and fails to cover it and an ox or a donkey falls into it, 34 the one who opened the pit must pay the owner for the loss and take the dead animal in exchange.

35 'If anyone's bull injures someone else's bull and it dies, the two parties are to sell the live one and divide both the money and the dead animal equally. 36 However, if it was known that the bull had the habit of goring, yet the owner did not keep it penned up, the owner must pay, animal for animal, and take the dead animal in exchange.

Protection of property

22 *a* 'Whoever steals an ox or a sheep and slaughters it or sells it must pay back five head of cattle for the ox and four sheep for the sheep.

2 'If a thief is caught breaking in at night and is struck a fatal blow, the defender is not guilty of bloodshed; 3 but if it happens after sunrise, the defender is guilty of bloodshed.

'Anyone who steals must certainly make restitution, but if they have nothing, they must be sold to pay for their theft. 4 If the stolen animal is found alive in their possession – whether ox or donkey or sheep – they must pay back double.

5 'If anyone grazes their livestock in a field or vineyard and lets them stray and they graze in someone else's field, the offender must make restitution from the best of their own field or vineyard.

6 'If a fire breaks out and spreads into thorn-bushes so that it burns sheaves of corn or standing corn or the whole field, the one who started the fire must make restitution.

7 'If anyone gives a neighbour silver or goods for safekeeping and they are stolen from the neighbour's house, the thief, if caught, must pay back double. 8 But if the thief is not found, the owner of the house must appear before the judges, and they must*b* determine whether the owner of the house has laid hands on the other person's property. 9 In all cases of illegal possession of an ox, a donkey, a sheep, a garment, or any other lost property about which somebody says, "This is mine," both parties are to bring their cases before the judges.*c* The one whom the judges declare*d* guilty must pay back double to the other.

10 'If anyone gives a donkey, an ox, a sheep or any other animal to their neighbour for safekeeping and it dies or is injured or is taken away while no one is looking, 11 the issue between them will be settled by the taking of an oath before the LORD that the neighbour did not lay hands on the other person's property. The owner is to accept this, and no restitution is required. 12 But if the animal was stolen from the neighbour, restitution

---

f 32 That is, about 345 grams
a In Hebrew texts 22:1 is numbered 21:37, and 22:2-31 is numbered 22:1-30.

b 8 Or *before God, and he will*
c 9 Or *before God*
d 9 Or *whom God declares*

must be made to the owner. ¹³If it was torn to pieces by a wild animal, the neighbour shall bring in the remains as evidence and shall not be required to pay for the torn animal.

¹⁴'If anyone borrows an animal from their neighbour and it is injured or dies while the owner is not present, they must make restitution. ¹⁵But if the owner is with the animal, the borrower will not have to pay. If the animal was hired, the money paid for the hire covers the loss.

Social responsibility

¹⁶'If a man seduces a virgin who is not pledged to be married and sleeps with her, he must pay the bride-price, and she shall be his wife. ¹⁷If her father absolutely refuses to give her to him, he must still pay the bride-price for virgins.

¹⁸'Do not allow a sorceress to live.

¹⁹'Anyone who has sexual relations with an animal is to be put to death.

²⁰'Whoever sacrifices to any god other than the LORD must be destroyed.ᵉ

²¹'Do not ill-treat or oppress a foreigner, for you were foreigners in Egypt.

²²'Do not take advantage of the widow or the fatherless. ²³If you do and they cry out to me, I will certainly hear their cry. ²⁴My anger will be aroused, and I will kill you with the sword; your wives will become widows and your children fatherless.

²⁵'If you lend money to one of my people among you who is needy, do not treat it like a business deal; charge no interest. ²⁶If you take your neighbour's cloak as a pledge, return it by sunset, ²⁷because that cloak is the only covering your neighbour has. What else can they sleep in? When they cry out to me, I will hear, for I am compassionate.

²⁸'Do not blaspheme Godᶠ or curse the ruler of your people.

²⁹'Do not hold back offerings from your granaries or your vats.ᵍ

'You must give me the firstborn of your sons. ³⁰Do the same with your cattle and your sheep. Let them stay with their mothers for seven days, but give them to me on the eighth day.

³¹'You are to be my holy people. So do not eat the meat of an animal torn by wild beasts; throw it to the dogs.

Laws of justice and mercy

23 'Do not spread false reports. Do not help a guilty person by being a malicious witness.

²'Do not follow the crowd in doing wrong. When you give testimony in a lawsuit, do not pervert justice by siding with the crowd, ³and do not show favouritism to a poor person in a lawsuit.

⁴'If you come across your enemy's ox or donkey wandering off, be sure to return it. ⁵If you see the donkey of someone who hates you fallen down under its load, do not leave it there; be sure you help them with it.

⁶'Do not deny justice to your poor people in their lawsuits. ⁷Have nothing to do with a false charge and do not put an innocent or honest person to death, for I will not acquit the guilty.

⁸'Do not accept a bribe, for a bribe blinds those who see and twists the words of the innocent.

⁹'Do not oppress a foreigner; you yourselves know how it feels to be foreigners, because you were foreigners in Egypt.

Sabbath laws

¹⁰'For six years you are to sow your fields and harvest the crops, ¹¹but during the seventh year let the land lie unploughed and unused. Then the poor among your people may get food from it, and the wild animals may eat what is left. Do the same with your vineyard and your olive grove.

¹²'Six days do your work, but on the seventh day do not work, so that your ox

---

ᵉ 20 The Hebrew term refers to the irrevocable giving over of things or persons to the LORD, often by totally destroying them.
ᶠ 28 Or *Do not revile the judges*

ᵍ 29 The meaning of the Hebrew for this phrase is uncertain.

and your donkey may rest, and so that the slave born in your household and the foreigner living among you may be refreshed.

13 'Be careful to do everything I have said to you. Do not invoke the names of other gods; do not let them be heard on your lips.

The three annual festivals

14 'Three times a year you are to celebrate a festival to me.

15 'Celebrate the Festival of Unleavened Bread; for seven days eat bread made without yeast, as I commanded you. Do this at the appointed time in the month of Aviv, for in that month you came out of Egypt.

'No one is to appear before me empty-handed.

16 'Celebrate the Festival of Harvest with the firstfruits of the crops you sow in your field.

'Celebrate the Festival of Ingathering at the end of the year, when you gather in your crops from the field.

17 'Three times a year all the men are to appear before the Sovereign LORD.

18 'Do not offer the blood of a sacrifice to me along with anything containing yeast.

'The fat of my festival offerings must not be kept until morning.

19 'Bring the best of the firstfruits of your soil to the house of the LORD your God.

'Do not cook a young goat in its mother's milk.

God's angel to prepare the way

20 'See, I am sending an angel ahead of you to guard you along the way and to bring you to the place I have prepared. 21 Pay attention to him and listen to what he says. Do not rebel against him; he will not forgive your rebellion, since my Name is in him. 22 If you listen carefully to what he says and do all that I say, I will be an enemy to your enemies and will oppose those who oppose you. 23 My angel will go ahead of you and bring you into the land of the Amorites, Hittites, Perizzites, Canaanites, Hivites and Jebusites, and I will wipe them out. 24 Do not

bow down before their gods or worship them or follow their practices. You must demolish them and break their sacred stones to pieces. 25 Worship the LORD your God, and his blessing will be on your food and water. I will take away disease from among you, 26 and none will miscarry or be barren in your land. I will give you a full life span.

27 'I will send my terror ahead of you and throw into confusion every nation you encounter. I will make all your enemies turn their backs and run. 28 I will send the hornet ahead of you to drive the Hivites, Canaanites and Hittites out of your way. 29 But I will not drive them out in a single year, because the land would become desolate and the wild animals too numerous for you. 30 Little by little I will drive them out before you, until you have increased enough to take possession of the land.

31 'I will establish your borders from the Red Sea[a] to the Mediterranean Sea,[b] and from the desert to the Euphrates River. I will give into your hands the people who live in the land, and you will drive them out before you. 32 Do not make a covenant with them or with their gods. 33 Do not let them live in your land or they will cause you to sin against me, because the worship of their gods will certainly be a snare to you.'

The covenant confirmed

24 Then the LORD said to Moses, 'Come up to the LORD, you and Aaron, Nadab and Abihu, and seventy of the elders of Israel. You are to worship at a distance, 2 but Moses alone is to approach the LORD; the others must not come near. And the people may not come up with him.'

3 When Moses went and told the people all the LORD's words and laws, they responded with one voice, 'Everything the LORD has said we will do.' 4 Moses then wrote down everything the LORD had said.

---

a 31 Or the Sea of Reeds
b 31 Hebrew *to the Sea of the Philistines*

He got up early the next morning and built an altar at the foot of the mountain and set up twelve stone pillars representing the twelve tribes of Israel. ⁵Then he sent young Israelite men, and they offered burnt offerings and sacrificed young bulls as fellowship offerings to the LORD. ⁶Moses took half of the blood and put it in bowls, and the other half he splashed against the altar. ⁷Then he took the Book of the Covenant and read it to the people. They responded, 'We will do everything the LORD has said; we will obey.'

OLDEST MAN

The oldest man in the Bible is Methuselah, who lived to 969 years (Genesis 5:25–27). Moses was eighty when God called him to lead the Israelites.

⁸Moses then took the blood, sprinkled it on the people and said, 'This is the blood of the covenant that the LORD has made with you in accordance with all these words.'

⁹Moses and Aaron, Nadab and Abihu, and the seventy elders of Israel went up ¹⁰and saw the God of Israel. Under his feet was something like a pavement made of lapis lazuli, as bright blue as the sky. ¹¹But God did not raise his hand against these leaders of the Israelites; they saw God, and they ate and drank.

¹²The LORD said to Moses, 'Come up to me on the mountain and stay here, and I will give you the tablets of stone with the law and commandments I have written for their instruction.'

¹³Then Moses set out with Joshua his assistant, and Moses went up on the mountain of God. ¹⁴He said to the elders, 'Wait here for us until we come back to you. Aaron and Hur are with you, and anyone involved in a dispute can go to them.'

¹⁵When Moses went up on the mountain, the cloud covered it, ¹⁶and the glory of the LORD settled on Mount Sinai. For six days the cloud covered the mountain, and on the seventh day the LORD called to Moses from within the cloud. ¹⁷To the Israelites the glory of the LORD looked like a consuming fire on top of the mountain. ¹⁸Then Moses entered the cloud as he went on up the mountain. And he stayed on the mountain forty days and forty nights.

Offerings for the tabernacle

25 The LORD said to Moses, ²'Tell the Israelites to bring me an offering. You are to receive the offering for me from everyone whose heart prompts them to give. ³These are the offerings you are to receive from them: gold, silver and bronze; ⁴blue, purple and scarlet yarn and fine linen; goat hair; ⁵ram skins dyed red and another type of durable leatherᵃ; acacia wood; ⁶olive oil for the light; spices for the anointing oil and for the fragrant incense; ⁷and onyx stones and other gems to be mounted on the ephod and breastpiece.

⁸'Then let them make a sanctuary for me, and I will dwell among them. ⁹Make this tabernacle and all its furnishings exactly like the pattern I will show you.

The ark

¹⁰'Let them make an arkᵇ of acacia wood – two and a half cubits long, a cubit and a half wide, and a cubit and a half high.ᶜ ¹¹Overlay it with pure gold, both inside and out, and make a gold moulding around it. ¹²Cast four gold rings for it and fasten them to its four feet, with two rings on one side and two rings on the other. ¹³Then make poles of acacia wood and overlay them with gold. ¹⁴Insert the poles into the rings on the sides of the ark to carry it. ¹⁵The poles are to remain

---

a 5 Possibly the hides of large aquatic mammals
b 10 That is, a chest
c 10 That is, about 1.1 metres long and 68 centimetres wide and high; similarly in verse 17

in the rings of this ark; they are not to be removed. ¹⁶Then put in the ark the tablets of the covenant law, which I will give you.

¹⁷'Make an atonement cover of pure gold – two and a half cubits long and a cubit and a half wide. ¹⁸And make two cherubim out of hammered gold at the ends of the cover. ¹⁹Make one cherub on one end and the second cherub on the other; make the cherubim of one piece with the cover, at the two ends. ²⁰The cherubim are to have their wings spread upwards, overshadowing the cover with them. The cherubim are to face each other, looking towards the cover. ²¹Place the cover on top of the ark and put in the ark the tablets of the covenant law that I will give you. ²²There, above the cover between the two cherubim that are over the ark of the covenant law, I will meet with you and give you all my commands for the Israelites.

The table

²³'Make a table of acacia wood – two cubits long, a cubit wide and a cubit and a half high.ᵈ ²⁴Overlay it with pure gold and make a gold moulding around it. ²⁵Also make around it a rim a handbreadthᵉ wide and put a gold moulding on the rim. ²⁶Make four gold rings for the table and fasten them to the four corners, where the four legs are. ²⁷The rings are to be close to the rim to hold the poles used in carrying the table. ²⁸Make the poles of acacia wood, overlay them with gold and carry the table with them. ²⁹And make its plates and dishes of pure gold, as well as its pitchers and bowls for the pouring out of offerings. ³⁰Put the bread of the Presence on this table to be before me at all times.

The lampstand

³¹'Make a lampstand of pure gold. Hammer out its base and shaft, and make its flowerlike cups, buds and blossoms of one piece with them. ³²Six branches are to

extend from the sides of the lampstand – three on one side and three on the other. ³³Three cups shaped like almond flowers with buds and blossoms are to be on one branch, three on the next branch, and the same for all six branches extending from the lampstand. ³⁴And on the lampstand there are to be four cups shaped like almond flowers with buds and blossoms. ³⁵One bud shall be under the first pair of branches extending from the lampstand, a second bud under the second pair, and a third bud under the third pair – six branches in all. ³⁶The buds and branches shall all be of one piece with the lampstand, hammered out of pure gold.

³⁷'Then make its seven lamps and set them up on it so that they light the space in front of it. ³⁸Its wick trimmers and trays are to be of pure gold. ³⁹A talentᶠ of pure gold is to be used for the lampstand and all these accessories. ⁴⁰See that you make them according to the pattern shown you on the mountain.

The tabernacle

26 'Make the tabernacle with ten curtains of finely twisted linen and blue, purple and scarlet yarn, with cherubim woven into them by a skilled worker. ²All the curtains are to be the same size – twenty-eight cubits long and four cubits wide.ᵃ ³Join five of the curtains together, and do the same with the other five. ⁴Make loops of blue material along the edge of the end curtain in one set, and do the same with the end curtain in the other set. ⁵Make fifty loops on one curtain and fifty loops on the end curtain of the other set, with the loops opposite each other. ⁶Then make fifty gold clasps and use them to fasten the curtains together so that the tabernacle is a unit.

⁷'Make curtains of goat hair for the tent over the tabernacle – eleven altogether. ⁸All eleven curtains are to be the same size – thirty cubits long and four

---

d 23   That is, about 90 centimetres long, 45 centimetres wide and 68 centimetres high
e 25   That is, about 7.5 centimetres

f 39   That is, about 34 kilograms
a 2   That is, about 13 metres long and 1.8 metres wide

cubits wide.*b* *9*Join five of the curtains together into one set and the other six into another set. Fold the sixth curtain double at the front of the tent. *10*Make fifty loops along the edge of the end curtain in one set and also along the edge of the end curtain in the other set. *11*Then make fifty bronze clasps and put them in the loops to fasten the tent together as a unit. *12*As for the additional length of the tent curtains, the half curtain that is left over is to hang down at the rear of the tabernacle. *13*The tent curtains will be a cubit*c* longer on both sides; what is left will hang over the sides of the tabernacle so as to cover it. *14*Make for the tent a covering of ram skins dyed red, and over that a covering of other durable leather.*d*

15'Make upright frames of acacia wood for the tabernacle. *16*Each frame is to be ten cubits long and a cubit and a half wide,*e* *17*with two projections set parallel to each other. Make all the frames of the tabernacle in this way. *18*Make twenty frames for the south side of the tabernacle *19*and make forty silver bases to go under them – two bases for each frame, one under each projection. *20*For the other side, the north side of the tabernacle, make twenty frames *21*and forty silver bases – two under each frame. *22*Make six frames for the far end, that is, the west end of the tabernacle, *23*and make two frames for the corners at the far end. *24*At these two corners they must be double from the bottom all the way to the top and fitted into a single ring; both shall be like that. *25*So there will be eight frames and sixteen silver bases – two under each frame.

26'Also make crossbars of acacia wood: five for the frames on one side of the tabernacle, *27*five for those on the other side, and five for the frames on the west, at the far end of the tabernacle. *28*The centre crossbar is to extend from end to end at the middle of the frames. *29*Overlay the frames with gold and make gold rings to hold the crossbars. Also overlay the crossbars with gold.

30'Set up the tabernacle according to the plan shown you on the mountain.

31'Make a curtain of blue, purple and scarlet yarn and finely twisted linen, with cherubim woven into it by a skilled worker. *32*Hang it with gold hooks on four posts of acacia wood overlaid with gold and standing on four silver bases. *33*Hang the curtain from the clasps and place the ark of the covenant law behind the curtain. The curtain will separate the Holy Place from the Most Holy Place. *34*Put the atonement cover on the ark of the covenant law in the Most Holy Place. *35*Place the table outside the curtain on the north side of the tabernacle and put the lampstand opposite it on the south side.

36'For the entrance to the tent make a curtain of blue, purple and scarlet yarn and finely twisted linen – the work of an embroiderer. *37*Make gold hooks for this curtain and five posts of acacia wood overlaid with gold. And cast five bronze bases for them.

The altar of burnt offering

27 'Build an altar of acacia wood, three cubits*a* high; it is to be square, five cubits long and five cubits wide.*b* *2*Make a horn at each of the four corners, so that the horns and the altar are of one piece, and overlay the altar with bronze. *3*Make all its utensils of bronze – its pots to remove the ashes, and its shovels, sprinkling bowls, meat forks and firepans. *4*Make a grating for it, a bronze network, and make a bronze ring at each of the four corners of the network. *5*Put it under the ledge of the altar so that it is halfway up the altar. *6*Make poles of acacia wood for the altar and overlay them with bronze. *7*The poles are to be inserted into the rings so they will be on two sides of the altar when it is carried. *8*Make the altar

---

b 8 That is, about 13.5 metres long and 1.8 metres wide

c 13 That is, about 45 centimetres

d 14 Possibly the hides of large aquatic mammals (see 25:5)

e 16 That is, about 4.5 metres long and 68 centimetres wide

---

a 1 That is, about 1.4 metres

b 1 That is, about 2.3 metres long and wide

hollow, out of boards. It is to be made just as you were shown on the mountain.

The courtyard

9 'Make a courtyard for the tabernacle. The south side shall be a hundred cubits^c long and is to have curtains of finely twisted linen, 10 with twenty posts and twenty bronze bases and with silver hooks and bands on the posts. 11 The north side shall also be a hundred cubits long and is to have curtains, with twenty posts and twenty bronze bases and with silver hooks and bands on the posts.

12 'The west end of the courtyard shall be fifty cubits^d wide and have curtains, with ten posts and ten bases. 13 On the east end, towards the sunrise, the courtyard shall also be fifty cubits wide. 14 Curtains fifteen cubits^e long are to be on one side of the entrance, with three posts and three bases, 15 and curtains fifteen cubits long are to be on the other side, with three posts and three bases.

16 'For the entrance to the courtyard, provide a curtain twenty cubits^f long, of blue, purple and scarlet yarn and finely twisted linen – the work of an embroiderer – with four posts and four bases. 17 All the posts around the courtyard are to have silver bands and hooks, and bronze bases. 18 The courtyard shall be a hundred cubits long and fifty cubits wide,^{g} with curtains of finely twisted linen five cubits^h high, and with bronze bases. 19 All the other articles used in the service of the tabernacle, whatever their function, including all the tent pegs for it and those for the courtyard, are to be of bronze.

Oil for the lampstand

20 'Command the Israelites to bring you clear oil of pressed olives for the light so that the lamps may be kept burning. 21 In the tent of meeting, outside the curtain that shields the ark of the covenant law, Aaron and his sons are to keep the lamps burning before the LORD from evening till morning. This is to be a lasting ordinance among the Israelites for the generations to come.

The priestly garments

28 'Let Aaron your brother be brought to you from among the Israelites, with his sons Nadab and Abihu, Eleazar and Ithamar, so that they may serve me as priests. 2 Make sacred garments for your brother Aaron to give him dignity and honour. 3 Tell all the skilled workers to whom I have given wisdom in such matters that they are to make garments for Aaron, for his consecration, so that he may serve me as priest. 4 These are the garments they are to make: a breastpiece, an ephod, a robe, a woven tunic, a turban and a sash. They are to make these sacred garments for your brother Aaron and his sons, so that they may serve me as priests. 5 Make them use gold, and blue, purple and scarlet yarn, and fine linen.

The ephod

6 'Make the ephod of gold, and of blue, purple and scarlet yarn, and of finely twisted linen – the work of skilled hands. 7 It is to have two shoulder pieces attached to two of its corners, so that it can be fastened. 8 Its skilfully woven waistband is to be like it – of one piece with the ephod and made with gold, and with blue, purple and scarlet yarn, and with finely twisted linen.

9 'Take two onyx stones and engrave on them the names of the sons of Israel 10 in the order of their birth – six names on one stone and the remaining six on the other. 11 Engrave the names of the sons of Israel on the two stones the way a gem cutter engraves a seal. Then mount the stones in gold filigree settings 12 and fasten them on the shoulder pieces of the ephod as memorial stones for the sons of Israel. Aaron is to bear the names on his shoulders as a memorial before the LORD. 13 Make gold filigree settings 14 and two braided chains

---

c 9　That is, about 45 metres; also in verse 11
d 12　That is, about 23 metres; also in verse 13
e 14　That is, about 6.8 metres; also in verse 14
f 16　That is, about 9 metres
g 18　That is, about 45 metres long and 23 metres wide
h 18　That is, about 2.3 metres

of pure gold, like a rope, and attach the chains to the settings.

The breastpiece

15 'Fashion a breastpiece for making decisions – the work of skilled hands. Make it like the ephod: of gold, and of blue, purple and scarlet yarn, and of finely twisted linen. 16 It is to be square – a span[a] long and a span wide – and folded double. 17 Then mount four rows of precious stones on it. The first row shall be carnelian, chrysolite and beryl; 18 the second row shall be turquoise, lapis lazuli and emerald; 19 the third row shall be jacinth, agate and amethyst; 20 the fourth row shall be topaz, onyx and jasper.[b] Mount them in gold filigree settings. 21 There are to be twelve stones, one for each of the names of the sons of Israel, each engraved like a seal with the name of one of the twelve tribes.

22 'For the breastpiece make braided chains of pure gold, like a rope. 23 Make two gold rings for it and fasten them to two corners of the breastpiece. 24 Fasten the two gold chains to the rings at the corners of the breastpiece, 25 and the other ends of the chains to the two settings, attaching them to the shoulder pieces of the ephod at the front. 26 Make two gold rings and attach them to the other two corners of the breastpiece on the inside edge next to the ephod. 27 Make two more gold rings and attach them to the bottom of the shoulder pieces on the front of the ephod, close to the seam just above the waistband of the ephod. 28 The rings of the breastpiece are to be tied to the rings of the ephod with blue cord, connecting it to the waistband, so that the breastpiece will not swing out from the ephod.

29 'Whenever Aaron enters the Holy Place, he will bear the names of the sons of Israel over his heart on the breastpiece of decision as a continuing memorial before the LORD. 30 Also put the Urim and the Thummim in the breastpiece, so they may be over Aaron's heart whenever he enters

the presence of the LORD. Thus Aaron will always bear the means of making decisions for the Israelites over his heart before the LORD.

Other priestly garments

31 'Make the robe of the ephod entirely of blue cloth, 32 with an opening for the head in its centre. There shall be a woven edge like a collar[c] around this opening, so that it will not tear. 33 Make pomegranates of blue, purple and scarlet yarn around the hem of the robe, with gold bells between them. 34 The gold bells and the pomegranates are to alternate round the hem of the robe. 35 Aaron must wear it when he ministers. The sound of the bells will be heard when he enters the Holy Place before the LORD and when he comes out, so that he will not die.

36 'Make a plate of pure gold and engrave on it as on a seal: HOLY TO THE LORD. 37 Fasten a blue cord to it to attach it to the turban; it is to be on the front of the turban. 38 It will be on Aaron's forehead, and he will bear the guilt involved in the sacred gifts the Israelites consecrate, whatever their gifts may be. It will be on Aaron's forehead continually so that they will be acceptable to the LORD.

39 'Weave the tunic of fine linen and make the turban of fine linen. The sash is to be the work of an embroiderer. 40 Make tunics, sashes and caps for Aaron's sons to give them dignity and honour. 41 After you put these clothes on your brother Aaron and his sons, anoint and ordain them. Consecrate them so they may serve me as priests.

42 'Make linen undergarments as a covering for the body, reaching from the waist to the thigh. 43 Aaron and his sons must wear them whenever they enter the tent of meeting or approach the altar to minister in the Holy Place, so that they will not incur guilt and die.

'This is to be a lasting ordinance for Aaron and his descendants.

---

a 16 That is, about 23 centimetres
b 20 The precise identification of some of these precious stones is uncertain.

c 32 The meaning of the Hebrew for this word is uncertain.

Consecration of the priests

29 'This is what you are to do to consecrate them, so that they may serve me as priests: take a young bull and two rams without defect. ²And from the finest wheat flour make round loaves without yeast, thick loaves without yeast and with olive oil mixed in, and thin loaves without yeast and brushed with olive oil. ³Put them in a basket and present them in it – along with the bull and the two rams. ⁴Then bring Aaron and his sons to the entrance to the tent of meeting and wash them with water. ⁵Take the garments and dress Aaron with the tunic, the robe of the ephod, the ephod itself and the breastpiece. Fasten the ephod on him by its skilfully woven waistband. ⁶Put the turban on his head and attach the sacred emblem to the turban. ⁷Take the anointing oil and anoint him by pouring it on his head. ⁸Bring his sons and dress them in tunics ⁹and fasten caps on them. Then tie sashes on Aaron and his sons.ᵃ The priesthood is theirs by a lasting ordinance.

FACT

MOUNT SINAI

Some of the most important Bible events took place at Mount Sinai, aka Mount Horeb. But no one is exactly sure where this is. There are at least twelve candidates. The likeliest one is the one called Jebel Musa – Arabic for the 'Mount of Moses'.

'Then you shall ordain Aaron and his sons.

¹⁰'Bring the bull to the front of the tent of meeting, and Aaron and his sons shall lay their hands on its head. ¹¹Slaughter it in the LORD's presence at the entrance to the tent of meeting. ¹²Take some of the bull's blood and put it on the horns of the altar with your finger, and pour out the rest of it at the base of the altar. ¹³Then take all the fat on the internal organs, the covering of the liver, and both kidneys with the fat on them, and burn them on the altar. ¹⁴But burn the bull's flesh and its hide and its intestines outside the camp. It is a sin offering.ᵇ

¹⁵'Take one of the rams, and Aaron and his sons shall lay their hands on its head. ¹⁶Slaughter it and take the blood and splash it against the sides of the altar. ¹⁷Cut the ram into pieces and wash the internal organs and the legs, putting them with the head and the other pieces. ¹⁸Then burn the entire ram on the altar. It is a burnt offering to the LORD, a pleasing aroma, a food offering presented to the LORD.

¹⁹'Take the other ram, and Aaron and his sons shall lay their hands on its head. ²⁰Slaughter it, take some of its blood and put it on the lobes of the right ears of Aaron and his sons, on the thumbs of their right hands, and on the big toes of their right feet. Then splash blood against the sides of the altar. ²¹And take some of the blood on the altar and some of the anointing oil and sprinkle it on Aaron and his garments and on his sons and their garments. Then he and his sons and their garments will be consecrated.

²²'Take from this ram the fat, the fat tail, the fat on the internal organs, the covering of the liver, both kidneys with the fat on them, and the right thigh. (This is the ram for the ordination.) ²³From the basket of bread made without yeast, which is before the LORD, take one round loaf, one thick loaf with olive oil mixed in, and one thin loaf. ²⁴Put all these in the hands of Aaron and his sons and wave them before the LORD as a wave offering. ²⁵Then take them from their hands and burn them on the altar along with the burnt offering for a pleasing aroma to the LORD, a food offering presented to the LORD. ²⁶After you take the breast of the ram for Aaron's ordination, wave it

---

a 9 Hebrew; Septuagint *on them*

b 14 Or *purification offering*; also in verse 36

before the Lord as a wave offering, and it will be your share.

27 'Consecrate those parts of the ordination ram that belong to Aaron and his sons: the breast that was waved and the thigh that was presented. 28 This is always to be the regular share from the Israelites for Aaron and his sons. It is the contribution the Israelites are to make to the Lord from their fellowship offerings.

29 'Aaron's sacred garments will belong to his descendants so that they can be anointed and ordained in them. 30 The son who succeeds him as priest and comes to the tent of meeting to minister in the Holy Place is to wear them seven days.

31 'Take the ram for the ordination and cook the meat in a sacred place. 32 At the entrance to the tent of meeting, Aaron and his sons are to eat the meat of the ram and the bread that is in the basket. 33 They are to eat these offerings by which atonement was made for their ordination and consecration. But no one else may eat them, because they are sacred. 34 And if any of the meat of the ordination ram or any bread is left over till morning, burn it up. It must not be eaten, because it is sacred.

35 'Do for Aaron and his sons everything I have commanded you, taking seven days to ordain them. 36 Sacrifice a bull each day as a sin offering to make atonement. Purify the altar by making atonement for it, and anoint it to consecrate it. 37 For seven days make atonement for the altar and consecrate it. Then the altar will be most holy, and whatever touches it will be holy.

38 'This is what you are to offer on the altar regularly each day: two lambs a year old. 39 Offer one in the morning and the other at twilight. 40 With the first lamb offer a tenth of an ephah c of the finest flour mixed with a quarter of a hin d of oil from pressed olives, and a quarter of a hin of wine as a drink offering. 41 Sacrifice the other lamb at twilight with the same grain offering and its drink offering as in the morning – a pleasing aroma, a food offering presented to the Lord.

42 'For the generations to come this burnt offering is to be made regularly at the entrance to the tent of meeting, before the Lord. There I will meet you and speak to you; 43 there also I will meet with the Israelites, and the place will be consecrated by my glory.

44 'So I will consecrate the tent of meeting and the altar and will consecrate Aaron and his sons to serve me as priests. 45 Then I will dwell among the Israelites and be their God. 46 They will know that I am the Lord their God, who brought them out of Egypt so that I might dwell among them. I am the Lord their God.

The altar of incense

30 'Make an altar of acacia wood for burning incense. 2 It is to be square, a cubit long and a cubit wide, and two cubits high a – its horns of one piece with it. 3 Overlay the top and all the sides and the horns with pure gold, and make a gold moulding around it. 4 Make two gold rings for the altar below the moulding – two on each of the opposite sides – to hold the poles used to carry it. 5 Make the poles of acacia wood and overlay them with gold. 6 Put the altar in front of the curtain that shields the ark of the covenant law – before the atonement cover that is over the tablets of the covenant law – where I will meet with you.

7 'Aaron must burn fragrant incense on the altar every morning when he tends the lamps. 8 He must burn incense again when he lights the lamps at twilight so that incense will burn regularly before the Lord for the generations to come. 9 Do not offer on this altar any other incense or any burnt offering or grain offering, and do not pour a drink offering on it. 10 Once a year Aaron shall make atonement on its horns. This annual atonement must be made with the blood of the atoning sin

---

c 40 That is, probably about 1.6 kilograms
d 40 That is, probably about 1 litre

a 2 That is, about 45 centimetres long and wide and 90 centimetres high offeringᵇ for the generations to come. It is most holy to the Lᴏʀᴅ.'

Atonement money

¹¹ Then the Lᴏʀᴅ said to Moses, ¹² 'When you take a census of the Israelites to count them, each one must pay the Lᴏʀᴅ a ransom for his life at the time he is counted. Then no plague will come on them when you number them. ¹³ Each one who crosses over to those already counted is to give a half shekel,ᶜ according to the sanctuary shekel, which weighs twenty gerahs. This half shekel is an offering to the Lᴏʀᴅ. ¹⁴ All who cross over, those twenty years old or more, are to give an offering to the Lᴏʀᴅ. ¹⁵ The rich are not to give more than a half shekel and the poor are not to give less when you make the offering to the Lᴏʀᴅ to atone for your lives. ¹⁶ Receive the atonement money from the Israelites and use it for the service of the tent of meeting. It will be a memorial for the Israelites before the Lᴏʀᴅ, making atonement for your lives.'

Basin for washing

¹⁷ Then the Lᴏʀᴅ said to Moses, ¹⁸ 'Make a bronze basin, with its bronze stand, for washing. Place it between the tent of meeting and the altar, and put water in it. ¹⁹ Aaron and his sons are to wash their hands and feet with water from it. ²⁰ Whenever they enter the tent of meeting, they shall wash with water so that they will not die. Also, when they approach the altar to minister by presenting a food offering to the Lᴏʀᴅ, ²¹ they shall wash their hands and feet so that they will not die. This is to be a lasting ordinance for Aaron and his descendants for the generations to come.'

Anointing oil

²² Then the Lᴏʀᴅ said to Moses, ²³ 'Take the following fine spices: 500 shekelsᵈ of liquid myrrh, half as much (that is, 250 shekels) of fragrant cinnamon, 250

shekelsᵉ of fragrant calamus, ²⁴ 500 shekels of cassia – all according to the sanctuary shekel – and a hinᶠ of olive oil. ²⁵ Make these into a sacred anointing oil, a fragrant blend, the work of a perfumer. It will be the sacred anointing oil. ²⁶ Then use it to anoint the tent of meeting, the ark of the covenant law, ²⁷ the table and all its articles, the lampstand and its accessories, the altar of incense, ²⁸ the altar of burnt offering and all its utensils, and the basin with its stand. ²⁹ You shall consecrate them so they will be most holy, and whatever touches them will be holy.

³⁰ 'Anoint Aaron and his sons and consecrate them so they may serve me as priests. ³¹ Say to the Israelites, "This is to be my sacred anointing oil for the generations to come. ³² Do not pour it on anyone else's body and do not make any other oil using the same formula. It is sacred, and you are to consider it sacred. ³³ Whoever makes perfume like it and puts it on anyone other than a priest must be cut off from their people."'

Incense

³⁴ Then the Lᴏʀᴅ said to Moses, 'Take fragrant spices – gum resin, onycha and galbanum – and pure frankincense, all in equal amounts, ³⁵ and make a fragrant blend of incense, the work of a perfumer. It is to be salted and pure and sacred. ³⁶ Grind some of it to powder and place it in front of the ark of the covenant law in the tent of meeting, where I will meet with you. It shall be most holy to you. ³⁷ Do not make any incense with this formula for yourselves; consider it holy to the Lᴏʀᴅ. ³⁸ Whoever makes incense like it to enjoy its fragrance must be cut off from their people.'

Bezalel and Oholiab

31 Then the Lᴏʀᴅ said to Moses, ² 'See I have chosen Bezalel son of Uri, the son of Hur, of the tribe of Judah, ³ and I have filled him with the Spirit of God, with wisdom, with understanding,

---

b 10 Or *purification offering*
c 13 That is, about 5.8 grams; also in verse 15
d 23 That is, about 5.8 kilograms; also in verse 24
e 23 That is, about 2.9 kilograms
f 24 That is, probably about 3.8 litres

with knowledge and with all kinds of skills – 4 to make artistic designs for work in gold, silver and bronze, 5 to cut and set stones, to work in wood, and to engage in all kinds of crafts. 6 Moreover, I have appointed Oholiab son of Ahisamak, of the tribe of Dan, to help him. Also I have given ability to all the skilled workers

FAITH IN THE WORLD 4

A SPIRIT-ANOINTED TECHNICIAN?

There's a film called *Limitless* in which the 'hero' of the story is given the chance to take an illegal drug that will improve his brain power by 80 per cent. It does exactly what it says on the can. His brain becomes 'limit-less' – he can now achieve whatever he sets his mind on, be that writing a bestselling book in four days straight, or becoming a stock market genius. Of course, it has majorly bad side effects, but I won't give the game away: you'll have to watch the film.

God won't give us abilities like that overnight, but in Exodus 31 we read of the special skills God gave to Bezalel and Oholiab. Yahweh Elohim, the Lord God, is giving instructions to his people Israel about how his portable place of worship, the tabernacle, is to be built. It's going to take a lot of skill to do this and so we read that God anoints these two for the task: *'I have chosen Bezalel … and I have filled him with the Spirit of God, with wisdom, with understanding, with knowledge and with all kinds of skills – to make artistic designs for work in gold, silver and bronze'* (Exodus 31:2–4). Amazing. So often we can think that God's Spirit is about doing things like miracles or providing people with spiritual gifts – prophecy, speaking in tongues, words of knowledge. But here is the Spirit giving two people the ability to be true craftsmen. Does this mean that the Spirit might help us improve in our work and studies? To be a genius mathematician, plumber or teacher?

The answer is clearly yes, but don't expect the Spirit of God to magically fill in your exam answers for you. The likelihood is that Bezalel and Oholiab were already craftsmen, and the Spirit enhanced their ability. Does that mean that you can be a Spirit-anointed accountant or scientist? Yes! God is interested in all work, not just work that we consider to be 'divinely inspired', like being a church leader. And God didn't create us to work separately from him, but alongside him. That means he wants to play a part in you gaining skills for the workplace *and* to aid you in your work. Can a builder pray for help in planning a house extension? Yes. Can a student pray for help in understanding a subject better? Certainly. Can we pray for motivation to help us revise for exams? Of course! Remember, work is a God-given thing and so it's good. What's your passion? What are you good at? Creative writing? Languages? Software programming? Why don't you try praying to the Holy Spirit to help you be even better at it? Ask the Holy Spirit if it's a gifting you should pursue as a career.

Jason Gardner

 Genesis 29:14–30   Job 38:19–38

to make everything I have commanded you: ⁷the tent of meeting, the ark of the covenant law with the atonement cover on it, and all the other furnishings of the tent – ⁸the table and its articles, the pure gold lampstand and all its accessories, the altar of incense, ⁹the altar of burnt offering and all its utensils, the basin with its stand – ¹⁰and also the woven garments, both the sacred garments for Aaron the priest and the garments for his sons when they serve as priests, ¹¹and the anointing oil and fragrant incense for the Holy Place. They are to make them just as I commanded you.'

The Sabbath

¹²Then the LORD said to Moses, ¹³'Say to the Israelites, "You must observe my Sabbaths. This will be a sign between me and you for the generations to come, so that you may know that I am the LORD, who makes you holy.

¹⁴' "Observe the Sabbath, because it is holy to you. Anyone who desecrates it is to be put to death; those who do any work on that day must be cut off from their people. ¹⁵For six days work is to be done, but the seventh day is a day of sabbath rest, holy to the LORD. Whoever does any work on the Sabbath day is to be put to death. ¹⁶The Israelites are to observe the Sabbath, celebrating it for the generations to come as a lasting covenant. ¹⁷It will be a sign between me and the Israelites for ever, for in six days the LORD made the heavens and the earth, and on the seventh day he rested and was refreshed." '

¹⁸When the LORD finished speaking to Moses on Mount Sinai, he gave him the two tablets of the covenant law, the tablets of stone inscribed by the finger of God.

The golden calf

32 When the people saw that Moses was so long in coming down from the mountain, they gathered round Aaron and said, 'Come, make us gods*ᵃ* who will go before us. As for this fellow Moses who brought us up out of Egypt, we don't know what has happened to him.'

²Aaron answered them, 'Take off the gold earrings that your wives, your sons and your daughters are wearing, and bring them to me.' ³So all the people took off their earrings and brought them to Aaron. ⁴He took what they handed him and made it into an idol cast in the shape of a calf, fashioning it with a tool. Then they said, 'These are your gods,*ᵇ* Israel, who brought you up out of Egypt.'

⁵When Aaron saw this, he built an altar in front of the calf and announced, 'Tomorrow there will be a festival to the LORD.' ⁶So the next day the people rose early and sacrificed burnt offerings and presented fellowship offerings. Afterwards they sat down to eat and drink and got up to indulge in revelry.

⁷Then the LORD said to Moses, 'Go down, because your people, whom you brought up out of Egypt, have become corrupt. ⁸They have been quick to turn away from what I commanded them and have made themselves an idol cast in the shape of a calf. They have bowed down to it and sacrificed to it and have said, "These are your gods, Israel, who brought you up out of Egypt."

⁹'I have seen these people,' the LORD said to Moses, 'and they are a stiff-necked people. ¹⁰Now leave me alone so that my anger may burn against them and that I may destroy them. Then I will make you into a great nation.'

¹¹But Moses sought the favour of the LORD his God. 'LORD,' he said, 'why should your anger burn against your people, whom you brought out of Egypt with great power and a mighty hand? ¹²Why should the Egyptians say, "It was with evil intent that he brought them out, to kill them in the mountains and to wipe them off the face of the earth"? Turn from your fierce anger; relent and do not bring disaster on your people. ¹³Remember your servants Abraham, Isaac and Israel, to whom you swore by your own self: "I will

---

ᵃ 1 Or *a god*; also in verses 23 and 31   *ᵇ* 4 Or *This is your god*; also in verse 8

CHRIST IN ALL THE SCRIPTURES 4

The anticipation of the cross

Exodux 32 is a tragic and yet profoundly moving passage. It shows us the depth of human sin and rebellion and foreshadows God's response in the cross. Moses shows us something of the heart of Jesus.

It was only a few months after the great deliverance from slavery in Egypt. The Israelites had come to Mount Sinai to establish a solemn covenant, a binding agreement, with God. But when Moses was up the mountain longer than they expected, they asked his brother Aaron to make them some gods. Then they thanked the gods Aaron made for bringing them out of Egypt. There is something about the human heart (our will, not just our feelings) which will worship any part of creation rather than the Creator. We end up worshipping things we have made (or bought). We are *'prone to evil'* (v. 22). There in the desert the results could be seen in their behaviour. The day ended tragically and violently.

God's response was clear. His anger burned against them, and initially he said he would destroy them and start a new nation with Moses (v. 10). God's anger is not God losing his temper. It is much scarier than that. His consistent holiness and purity simply cannot ignore wrongdoing. It is who he is, not how he reacts. People who do wrong cannot survive in his presence.

But Moses also reflects God's character, or God would never have listened to his prayer. Moses prays for these corrupt and stiff-necked (vv. 7, 9) people. He asks God to relent (v. 12). He reminds God of his promises to Abraham (v. 13; see Genesis 12:1–3). Most amazingly of all, as he confesses their sin, he asks God to blot *him* out of God's book, rather than the people (v. 32). He seeks to *'make atonement'* for their sin (v. 30). God spares Moses and allows the people to continue towards the Promised Land, although they suffer a plague as punishment.

In this story the cross of Jesus is foreshadowed. God the Holy Trinity is both utter purity and utter love. Father, Son and Holy Spirit can neither ignore sin, nor will they abandon sinners. So the Son became a human being, who lived a life of perfect love, holiness and obedience to the Father, and then went to the cross for us. He was saying to the Father, like Moses does here, 'Blot me out instead of them.' This was not an angry Father punishing a loving Son. This was Father, Son and Spirit bearing the punishment of sin themselves, in their own relationships (see 2 Corinthians 5:19). The Son was separated from the Father on the cross and the Father experienced the loss of his Son – so that our sins could be forgiven. It is beyond understanding, but Moses gave us a picture of it. He showed us Jesus in advance.

Graham Cray

 Numbers 24:4–9   Leviticus 16:1–22

make your descendants as numerous as the stars in the sky and I will give your descendants all this land I promised them, and it will be their inheritance for ever." '
14 Then the LORD relented and did not bring on his people the disaster he had threatened.

15 Moses turned and went down the mountain with the two tablets of the covenant law in his hands. They were inscribed on both sides, front and back. 16 The tablets were the work of God; the writing was the writing of God, engraved on the tablets.

17 When Joshua heard the noise of the people shouting, he said to Moses, 'There is the sound of war in the camp.'
18 Moses replied:

'It is not the sound of victory,
    it is not the sound of defeat;
    it is the sound of singing that I hear.'

19 When Moses approached the camp and saw the calf and the dancing, his anger burned and he threw the tablets out of his hands, breaking them to pieces at the foot of the mountain. 20 And he took the calf the people had made and burned it in the fire; then he ground it to powder, scattered it on the water and made the Israelites drink it.

21 He said to Aaron, 'What did these people do to you, that you led them into such great sin?'
22 'Do not be angry, my lord,' Aaron answered. 'You know how prone these people are to evil. 23 They said to me, "Make us gods who will go before us. As for this fellow Moses who brought us up out of Egypt, we don't know what has happened to him." 24 So I told them, "Whoever has any gold jewellery, take it off." Then they gave me the gold, and I threw it into the fire, and out came this calf!'

25 Moses saw that the people were running wild and that Aaron had let them get out of control and so become a laughing-stock to their enemies. 26 So he stood at the entrance to the camp and said, 'Whoever is for the LORD, come to me.' And all the Levites rallied to him.

27 Then he said to them, 'This is what the LORD, the God of Israel, says: "Each man strap a sword to his side. Go back and forth through the camp from one end to the other, each killing his brother and friend and neighbour." ' 28 The Levites did as Moses commanded, and that day about three thousand of the people died. 29 Then Moses said, 'You have been set apart to the LORD today, for you were against your own sons and brothers, and he has blessed you this day.'

30 The next day Moses said to the people, 'You have committed a great sin. But now I will go up to the LORD; perhaps I can make atonement for your sin.'

31 So Moses went back to the LORD and said, 'Oh, what a great sin these people have committed! They have made themselves gods of gold. 32 But now, please forgive their sin – but if not, then blot me out of the book you have written.'

33 The LORD replied to Moses, 'Whoever has sinned against me I will blot out of my book. 34 Now go, lead the people to the place I spoke of, and my angel will go before you. However, when the time comes for me to punish, I will punish them for their sin.'

35 And the LORD struck the people with a plague because of what they did with the calf Aaron had made.

33 Then the LORD said to Moses, 'Leave this place, you and the people you brought up out of Egypt, and go up to the land I promised on oath to Abraham, Isaac and Jacob, saying, "I will give it to your descendants." 2 I will send an angel before you and drive out the Canaanites, Amorites, Hittites, Perizzites, Hivites and Jebusites. 3 Go up to the land flowing with milk and honey. But I will not go up with you, because you are a stiff-necked people and I might destroy you on the way.'

4 When the people heard these distressing words, they began to mourn and no one put on any ornaments. 5 For the LORD had said to Moses, 'Tell the Israelites, "You are a stiff-necked people. If I were to go with you even for a moment, I might destroy you. Now take off your ornaments and I will decide what to do with you." '

⁶So the Israelites stripped off their ornaments at Mount Horeb.

The tent of meeting

⁷Now Moses used to take a tent and pitch it outside the camp some distance away, calling it the 'tent of meeting'. Anyone enquiring of the LORD would go to the tent of meeting outside the camp. ⁸And whenever Moses went out to the tent, all the people rose and stood at the entrances to their tents, watching Moses until he entered the tent. ⁹As Moses went into the tent, the pillar of cloud would come down and stay at the entrance, while the LORD spoke with Moses. ¹⁰Whenever the people saw the pillar of cloud standing at the entrance to the tent, they all stood and worshipped, each at the entrance to their tent. ¹¹The LORD would speak to Moses face to face, as one speaks to a friend. Then Moses would return to the camp, but his young assistant Joshua son of Nun did not leave the tent.

Moses and the glory of the LORD

¹²Moses said to the LORD, 'You have been telling me, "Lead these people," but you have not let me know whom you will send with me. You have said, "I know you by name and you have found favour with me." ¹³If you are pleased with me, teach me your ways so I may know you and continue to find favour with you. Remember that this nation is your people.'

¹⁴The LORD replied, 'My Presence will go with you, and I will give you rest.'

¹⁵Then Moses said to him, 'If your Presence does not go with us, do not send us up from here. ¹⁶How will anyone know that you are pleased with me and with your people unless you go with us? What else will distinguish me and your people from all the other people on the face of the earth?'

¹⁷And the LORD said to Moses, 'I will do the very thing you have asked, because I am pleased with you and I know you by name.'

¹⁸Then Moses said, 'Now show me your glory.'

¹⁹And the LORD said, 'I will cause all my goodness to pass in front of you, and I will proclaim my name, the LORD, in your presence. I will have mercy on whom I will have mercy, and I will have compassion on whom I will have compassion. ²⁰But,' he said, 'you cannot see my face, for no one may see me and live.'

²¹Then the LORD said, 'There is a place near me where you may stand on a rock. ²²When my glory passes by, I will put you in a cleft in the rock and cover you with my hand until I have passed by. ²³Then I will remove my hand and you will see my back; but my face must not be seen.'

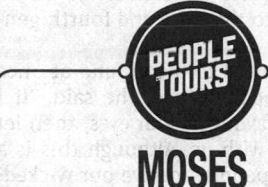

PEOPLE TOURS

MOSES

PRINCE:
Exodus 2:1–25
TREE:
Exodus 3:1–22
PLAGUES:
Exodus 5:1–5; 7:1–25
ESCAPE:
Exodus 11:1 – 12:41
COMMANDMENTS:
Exodus 19:1 – 20:21
CALF:
Exodus 32
DEATH:
Deuteronomy 31:1–13; 34:1–8

The new stone tablets

34 The LORD said to Moses, 'Chisel out two stone tablets like the first ones, and I will write on them the words that were on the first tablets, which you broke. ²Be ready in the morning, and then come up on Mount Sinai. Present yourself to me there on top of the mountain. ³No one is to come with you or be seen anywhere on the mountain; not even the flocks and herds may graze in front of the mountain.'

⁴So Moses chiselled out two stone

tablets like the first ones and went up Mount Sinai early in the morning, as the LORD had commanded him; and he carried the two stone tablets in his hands. ⁵Then the LORD came down in the cloud and stood there with him and proclaimed his name, the LORD. ⁶And he passed in front of Moses, proclaiming, 'The LORD, the LORD, the compassionate and gracious God, slow to anger, abounding in love and faithfulness, ⁷maintaining love to thousands, and forgiving wickedness, rebellion and sin. Yet he does not leave the guilty unpunished; he punishes the children and their children for the sin of the parents to the third and fourth generation.'

⁸Moses bowed to the ground at once and worshipped. ⁹'Lord,' he said, 'if I have found favour in your eyes, then let the Lord go with us. Although this is a stiff-necked people, forgive our wickedness and our sin, and take us as your inheritance.'

¹⁰Then the LORD said: 'I am making a covenant with you. Before all your people I will do wonders never before done in any nation in all the world. The people you live among will see how awesome is the work that I, the LORD, will do for you. ¹¹Obey what I command you today. I will drive out before you the Amorites, Canaanites, Hittites, Perizzites, Hivites and Jebusites. ¹²Be careful not to make a treaty with those who live in the land where you are going, or they will be a snare among you. ¹³Break down their altars, smash their sacred stones and cut down their Asherah poles.ᵃ ¹⁴Do not worship any other god, for the LORD, whose name is Jealous, is a jealous God.

¹⁵'Be careful not to make a treaty with those who live in the land; for when they prostitute themselves to their gods and sacrifice to them, they will invite you and you will eat their sacrifices. ¹⁶And when you choose some of their daughters as wives for your sons and those daughters prostitute themselves to their gods, they will lead your sons to do the same.

¹⁷'Do not make any idols.

¹⁸'Celebrate the Festival of Unleavened Bread. For seven days eat bread made without yeast, as I commanded you. Do this at the appointed time in the month of Aviv, for in that month you came out of Egypt.

¹⁹'The first offspring of every womb belongs to me, including all the firstborn males of your livestock, whether from herd or flock. ²⁰Redeem the firstborn donkey with a lamb, but if you do not redeem it, break its neck. Redeem all your firstborn sons.

'No one is to appear before me empty-handed.

²¹'Six days you shall labour, but on the seventh day you shall rest; even during the ploughing season and harvest you must rest.

²²'Celebrate the Festival of Weeks with the firstfruits of the wheat harvest, and the Festival of Ingathering at the turn of the year.ᵇ ²³Three times a year all your men are to appear before the Sovereign LORD, the God of Israel. ²⁴I will drive out nations before you and enlarge your territory, and no one will covet your land when you go up three times each year to appear before the LORD your God.

²⁵'Do not offer the blood of a sacrifice to me along with anything containing yeast, and do not let any of the sacrifice from the Passover Festival remain until morning.

²⁶'Bring the best of the firstfruits of your soil to the house of the LORD your God.

'Do not cook a young goat in its mother's milk.'

²⁷Then the LORD said to Moses, 'Write down these words, for in accordance with these words I have made a covenant with you and with Israel.' ²⁸Moses was there with the LORD forty days and forty nights without eating bread or drinking water. And he wrote on the tablets the words of the covenant – the Ten Commandments.

ᵃ 13 That is, wooden symbols of the goddess Asherah

ᵇ 22 That is, in the autumn

The radiant face of Moses

29 When Moses came down from Mount Sinai with the two tablets of the covenant law in his hands, he was not aware that his face was radiant because he had spoken with the LORD. 30 When Aaron and all the Israelites saw Moses, his face was radiant, and they were afraid to come near him. 31 But Moses called to them; so Aaron and all the leaders of the community came back to him, and he spoke to them. 32 Afterwards all the Israelites came near him, and he gave them all the commands the LORD had given him on Mount Sinai.

33 When Moses finished speaking to them, he put a veil over his face. 34 But whenever he entered the LORD's presence to speak with him, he removed the veil until he came out. And when he came out and told the Israelites what he had been commanded, 35 they saw that his face was radiant. Then Moses would put the veil back over his face until he went in to speak with the LORD.

Sabbath regulations

35 Moses assembled the whole Israelite community and said to them, 'These are the things the LORD has commanded you to do: 2 for six days, work is to be done, but the seventh day shall be your holy day, a day of sabbath rest to the LORD. Whoever does any work on it is to be put to death. 3 Do not light a fire in any of your dwellings on the Sabbath day.'

Materials for the tabernacle

4 Moses said to the whole Israelite community, 'This is what the LORD has commanded: 5 from what you have, take an offering for the LORD. Everyone who is willing is to bring to the LORD an offering of gold, silver and bronze; 6 blue, purple and scarlet yarn and fine linen; goat hair; 7 ram skins dyed red and another type of durable leather;ᵃ acacia wood; 8 olive oil for the light; spices for the anointing oil and for the fragrant incense; 9 and onyx stones and other gems to be mounted on the ephod and breastpiece.

10 'All who are skilled among you are to come and make everything the LORD has commanded: 11 the tabernacle with its tent and its covering, clasps, frames, crossbars, posts and bases; 12 the ark with its poles and the atonement cover and the curtain that shields it; 13 the table with its poles and all its articles and the bread of the Presence; 14 the lampstand that is for light with its accessories, lamps and oil for the light; 15 the altar of incense with its poles, the anointing oil and the fragrant incense; the curtain for the doorway at the entrance to the tabernacle; 16 the altar of burnt offering with its bronze grating, its poles and all its utensils; the bronze basin with its stand; 17 the curtains of the courtyard with its posts and bases, and the curtain for the entrance to the courtyard; 18 the tent pegs for the tabernacle and for the courtyard, and their ropes; 19 the woven garments worn for ministering in the sanctuary – both the sacred garments for Aaron the priest and the garments for his sons when they serve as priests.'

20 Then the whole Israelite community withdrew from Moses' presence, 21 and everyone who was willing and whose heart moved them came and brought an offering to the LORD for the work on the tent of meeting, for all its service, and for the sacred garments. 22 All who were willing, men and women alike, came and brought gold jewellery of all kinds: brooches, earrings, rings and ornaments. They all presented their gold as a wave offering to the LORD. 23 Everyone who had blue, purple or scarlet yarn or fine linen, or goat hair, ram skins dyed red or other durable leather brought them. 24 Those presenting an offering of silver or bronze brought it as an offering to the LORD, and everyone who had acacia wood for any part of the work brought it. 25 Every skilled woman spun with her hands and brought what she had spun – blue, purple or scarlet yarn or fine linen. 26 And all the women who were willing and had the skill spun the goat hair. 27 The leaders brought onyx stones and other gems to be mounted on

---

ᵃ 7 Possibly the hides of large aquatic mammals; also in verse 23 the ephod and breastpiece. **28**They also brought spices and olive oil for the light and for the anointing oil and for the fragrant incense. **29**All the Israelite men and women who were willing brought to the LORD freewill offerings for all the work the LORD through Moses had commanded them to do.

Bezalel and Oholiab

30Then Moses said to the Israelites, 'See, the LORD has chosen Bezalel son of Uri, the son of Hur, of the tribe of Judah, **31**and he has filled him with the Spirit of God, with wisdom, with understanding, with knowledge and with all kinds of skills – **32**to make artistic designs for work in gold, silver and bronze, **33**to cut and set stones, to work in wood and to engage in all kinds of artistic crafts. **34**And he has given both him and Oholiab son of Ahisamak, of the tribe of Dan, the ability to teach others. **35**He has filled them with skill to do all kinds of work as engravers, designers, embroiderers in blue, purple and scarlet yarn and fine linen, and weavers – all of them skilled workers and **36** designers. **1**So Bezalel, Oholiab and every skilled person to whom the LORD has given skill and ability to know how to carry out all the work of constructing the sanctuary are to do the work just as the LORD has commanded.'

2Then Moses summoned Bezalel and Oholiab and every skilled person to whom the LORD had given ability and who was willing to come and do the work. **3**They received from Moses all the offerings the Israelites had brought to carry out the work of constructing the sanctuary. And the people continued to bring freewill offerings morning after morning. **4**So all the skilled workers who were doing all the work on the sanctuary left what they were doing **5**and said to Moses, 'The people are bringing more than enough for doing the work the LORD commanded to be done.'

6Then Moses gave an order and they sent this word throughout the camp: 'No man or woman is to make anything else as an offering for the sanctuary.' And so

the people were restrained from bringing more, **7**because what they already had was more than enough to do all the work.

THE TABERNACLE

The tabernacle was a portable tent for worship. Its outer covering was some kind of waterproof leather (Exodus 26:14). It's possible that the word used here means the skin of sea mammals, such as porpoises or dolphins. When the Israelites settled in Canaan, they set up the tabernacle at Shiloh (Joshua 18:1).

The tabernacle

8All those who were skilled among the workers made the tabernacle with ten curtains of finely twisted linen and blue, purple and scarlet yarn, with cherubim woven into them by expert hands. **9**All the curtains were the same size – twenty-eight cubits long and four cubits wide.*ᵃ* **10**They joined five of the curtains together and did the same with the other five. **11**Then they made loops of blue material along the edge of the end curtain in one set, and the same was done with the end curtain in the other set. **12**They also made fifty loops on one curtain and fifty loops on the end curtain of the other set, with the loops opposite each other. **13**Then they made fifty gold clasps and used them to fasten the two sets of curtains together so that the tabernacle was a unit.

14They made curtains of goat hair for the tent over the tabernacle – eleven altogether. **15**All eleven curtains were the same size – thirty cubits long and four cubits wide.*ᵇ* **16**They joined five of the

ᵃ 9 That is, about 13 metres long and 1.8 metres wide
ᵇ 15 That is, about 14 metres long and 1.8 metres wide

curtains into one set and the other six into another set. ¹⁷Then they made fifty loops along the edge of the end curtain in one set and also along the edge of the end curtain in the other set. ¹⁸They made fifty bronze clasps to fasten the tent together as a unit. ¹⁹Then they made for the tent a covering of ram skins dyed red, and over that a covering of other durable leather.ᶜ

²⁰They made upright frames of acacia wood for the tabernacle. ²¹Each frame was ten cubits long and a cubit and a half wide,ᵈ ²²with two projections set parallel to each other. They made all the frames of the tabernacle in this way. ²³They made twenty frames for the south side of the tabernacle ²⁴and made forty silver bases to go under them – two bases for each frame, one under each projection. ²⁵For the other side, the north side of the tabernacle, they made twenty frames ²⁶and forty silver bases – two under each frame. ²⁷They made six frames for the far end, that is, the west end of the tabernacle, ²⁸and two frames were made for the corners of the tabernacle at the far end. ²⁹At these two corners the frames were double from the bottom all the way to the top and fitted into a single ring; both were made alike. ³⁰So there were eight frames and sixteen silver bases – two under each frame.

³¹They also made crossbars of acacia wood: five for the frames on one side of the tabernacle, ³²five for those on the other side, and five for the frames on the west, at the far end of the tabernacle. ³³They made the centre crossbar so that it extended from end to end at the middle of the frames. ³⁴They overlaid the frames with gold and made gold rings to hold the crossbars. They also overlaid the crossbars with gold.

³⁵They made the curtain of blue, purple and scarlet yarn and finely twisted linen, with cherubim woven into it by a skilled worker. ³⁶They made four posts of acacia wood for it and overlaid them with gold.

They made gold hooks for them and cast their four silver bases. ³⁷For the entrance to the tent they made a curtain of blue, purple and scarlet yarn and finely twisted linen – the work of an embroiderer; ³⁸and they made five posts with hooks for them. They overlaid the tops of the posts and their bands with gold and made their five bases of bronze.

The ark

37 Bezalel made the ark of acacia wood – two and a half cubits long, a cubit and a half wide, and a cubit and a half high.ᵃ ²He overlaid it with pure gold, both inside and out, and made a gold moulding around it. ³He cast four gold rings for it and fastened them to its four feet, with two rings on one side and two rings on the other. ⁴Then he made poles of acacia wood and overlaid them with gold. ⁵And he inserted the poles into the rings on the sides of the ark to carry it.

⁶He made the atonement cover of pure gold – two and a half cubits long and a cubit and a half wide. ⁷Then he made two cherubim out of hammered gold at the ends of the cover. ⁸He made one cherub on one end and the second cherub on the other; at the two ends he made them of one piece with the cover. ⁹The cherubim had their wings spread upwards, overshadowing the cover with them. The cherubim faced each other, looking towards the cover.

The table

¹⁰Theyᵇ made the table of acacia wood – two cubits long, a cubit wide and a cubit and a half high.ᶜ ¹¹Then they overlaid it with pure gold and made a gold moulding around it. ¹²They also made around it a rim a handbreadthᵈ wide and put a gold moulding on the rim. ¹³They cast four gold rings for the table and fastened them to the four corners, where the four

---

ᶜ 19 Possibly the hides of large aquatic mammals (see 35:7)
ᵈ 21 That is, about 4.5 metres long and 68 centimetres wide

ᵃ 1 That is, about 1.1 metres long and 68 centimetres wide and high; similarly in verse 6
ᵇ 10 Or He; also in verses 11-29
ᶜ 10 That is, about 90 centimetres long, 45 centimetres wide and 68 centimetres high
ᵈ 12 That is, about 7.5 centimetres

legs were. ¹⁴The rings were put close to the rim to hold the poles used in carrying the table. ¹⁵The poles for carrying the table were made of acacia wood and were overlaid with gold. ¹⁶And they made from pure gold the articles for the table – its plates and dishes and bowls and its pitchers for the pouring out of drink offerings.

The lampstand

¹⁷They made the lampstand of pure gold. They hammered out its base and shaft, and made its flowerlike cups, buds and blossoms of one piece with them. ¹⁸Six branches extended from the sides of the lampstand – three on one side and three on the other. ¹⁹Three cups shaped like almond flowers with buds and blossoms were on one branch, three on the next branch and the same for all six branches extending from the lampstand. ²⁰And on the lampstand were four cups shaped like almond flowers with buds and blossoms. ²¹One bud was under the first pair of branches extending from the lampstand, a second bud under the second pair, and a third bud under the third pair – six branches in all. ²²The buds and the branches were all of one piece with the lampstand, hammered out of pure gold.

²³They made its seven lamps, as well as its wick trimmers and trays, of pure gold. ²⁴They made the lampstand and all its accessories from one talent*ᵉ* of pure gold.

The altar of incense

²⁵They made the altar of incense out of acacia wood. It was square, a cubit long and a cubit wide and two cubits high*f* – its horns of one piece with it. ²⁶They overlaid the top and all the sides and the horns with pure gold, and made a gold moulding around it. ²⁷They made two gold rings below the moulding – two on each of the opposite sides – to hold the poles used to carry it. ²⁸They made the poles of acacia wood and overlaid them with gold.

²⁹They also made the sacred anointing oil and the pure, fragrant incense – the work of a perfumer.

The altar of burnt offering

38 They*ᵃ* built the altar of burnt offering of acacia wood, three cubits*ᵇ* high; it was square, five cubits long and five cubits wide.*ᶜ* ²They made a horn at each of the four corners, so that the horns and the altar were of one piece, and they overlaid the altar with bronze. ³They made all its utensils of bronze – its pots, shovels, sprinkling bowls, meat forks and firepans. ⁴They made a grating for the altar, a bronze network, to be under its ledge, halfway up the altar. ⁵They cast bronze rings to hold the poles for the four corners of the bronze grating. ⁶They made the poles of acacia wood and overlaid them with bronze. ⁷They inserted the poles into the rings so they would be on the sides of the altar for carrying it. They made it hollow, out of boards.

The basin for washing

⁸They made the bronze basin and its bronze stand from the mirrors of the women who served at the entrance to the tent of meeting.

The courtyard

⁹Next they made the courtyard. The south side was a hundred cubits*ᵈ* long and had curtains of finely twisted linen, ¹⁰with twenty posts and twenty bronze bases, and with silver hooks and bands on the posts. ¹¹The north side was also a hundred cubits long and had twenty posts and twenty bronze bases, with silver hooks and bands on the posts.

¹²The west end was fifty cubits*ᵉ* wide and had curtains, with ten posts and ten bases, with silver hooks and bands on the posts. ¹³The east end, towards the sunrise, was also fifty cubits wide. ¹⁴Curtains fifteen

---

e 24 That is, about 34 kilograms
f 25 That is, about 45 centimetres long and wide and 90 centimetres high

a 1 Or He; also in verses 2-9
b 1 That is, about 1.4 metres
c 1 That is, about 2.3 metres long and wide
d 9 That is, about 45 metres
e 12 That is, about 23 metres

cubits*f* long were on one side of the entrance, with three posts and three bases, **15** and curtains fifteen cubits long were on the other side of the entrance to the courtyard, with three posts and three bases. **16** All the curtains around the courtyard were of finely twisted linen. **17** The bases for the posts were bronze. The hooks and bands on the posts were silver, and their tops were overlaid with silver; so all the posts of the courtyard had silver bands.

18 The curtain for the entrance to the courtyard was made of blue, purple and scarlet yarn and finely twisted linen – the work of an embroiderer. It was twenty cubits*g* long and, like the curtains of the courtyard, five cubits*h* high, **19** with four posts and four bronze bases. Their hooks and bands were silver, and their tops were overlaid with silver. **20** All the tent pegs of the tabernacle and of the surrounding courtyard were bronze.

The materials used

21 These are the amounts of the materials used for the tabernacle, the tabernacle of the covenant law, which were recorded at Moses' command by the Levites under the direction of Ithamar son of Aaron, the priest. **22** (Bezalel son of Uri, the son of Hur, of the tribe of Judah, made everything the Lord commanded Moses; **23** with him was Oholiab son of Ahisamak, of the tribe of Dan – an engraver and designer, and an embroiderer in blue, purple and scarlet yarn and fine linen.) **24** The total amount of the gold from the wave offering used for all the work on the sanctuary was 29 talents and 730 shekels,*i* according to the sanctuary shekel.

25 The silver obtained from those of the community who were counted in the census was 100 talents*j* and 1,775 shekels,*k* according to the sanctuary shekel – **26** one beka per person, that is, half a shekel,*l*

according to the sanctuary shekel, from everyone who had crossed over to those counted, twenty years old or more, a total of 603,550 men. **27** The 100 talents of silver were used to cast the bases for the sanctuary and for the curtain – 100 bases from the 100 talents, one talent for each base. **28** They used the 1,775 shekels to make the hooks for the posts, to overlay the tops of the posts, and to make their bands.

29 The bronze from the wave offering was 70 talents and 2,400 shekels.*m* **30** They used it to make the bases for the entrance to the tent of meeting, the bronze altar with its bronze grating and all its utensils, **31** the bases for the surrounding courtyard and those for its entrance and all the tent pegs for the tabernacle and those for the surrounding courtyard.

FAVOURITE VERSES

Genesis 1:3

And God said, 'Let there be light,' and there was light.

I like it because it shows God's power. Have you ever spoken light into existence? It's so complex. We struggle to understand light, whereas God commanded it into existence simply by speaking.

Tim, 17

The priestly garments

39 From the blue, purple and scarlet yarn they made woven garments for ministering in the sanctuary. They also made sacred garments for Aaron, as the Lord commanded Moses.

---

f 14 That is, about 6.8 metres
g 18 That is, about 9 metres
h 18 That is, about 2.3 metres
i 24 The weight of the gold was about 1 metric ton.
j 25 That is, about 3.4 metric tons; also in verse 27
k 25 That is, about 20 kilograms; also in verse 28
l 26 That is, about 5.7 grams

---

m 29 The weight of the bronze was about 2.4 metric tons.

The ephod

2 They[a] made the ephod of gold, and of blue, purple and scarlet yarn, and of finely twisted linen. 3 They hammered out thin sheets of gold and cut strands to be worked into the blue, purple and scarlet yarn and fine linen – the work of skilled hands. 4 They made shoulder pieces for the ephod, which were attached to two of its corners, so that it could be fastened. 5 Its skilfully woven waistband was like it – of one piece with the ephod and made with gold, and with blue, purple and scarlet yarn, and with finely twisted linen, as the LORD commanded Moses.

6 They mounted the onyx stones in gold filigree settings and engraved them like a seal with the names of the sons of Israel. 7 Then they fastened them on the shoulder pieces of the ephod as memorial stones for the sons of Israel, as the LORD commanded Moses.

The breastpiece

8 They fashioned the breastpiece – the work of a skilled craftsman. They made it like the ephod: of gold, and of blue, purple and scarlet yarn, and of finely twisted linen. 9 It was square – a span[b] long and a span wide – and folded double. 10 Then they mounted four rows of precious stones on it. The first row was carnelian, chrysolite and beryl; 11 the second row was turquoise, lapis lazuli and emerald; 12 the third row was jacinth, agate and amethyst; 13 the fourth row was topaz, onyx and jasper.[c] They were mounted in gold filigree settings. 14 There were twelve stones, one for each of the names of the sons of Israel, each engraved like a seal with the name of one of the twelve tribes.

15 For the breastpiece they made braided chains of pure gold, like a rope. 16 They made two gold filigree settings and two gold rings, and fastened the rings to two of the corners of the breastpiece. 17 They fastened the two gold chains to the rings at the corners of the breastpiece, 18 and the other ends of the chains to the two settings, attaching them to the shoulder pieces of the ephod at the front. 19 They made two gold rings and attached them to the other two corners of the breastpiece on the inside edge next to the ephod. 20 Then they made two more gold rings and attached them to the bottom of the shoulder pieces on the front of the ephod, close to the seam just above the waistband of the ephod. 21 They tied the rings of the breastpiece to the rings of the ephod with blue cord, connecting it to the waistband so that the breastpiece would not swing out from the ephod – as the LORD commanded Moses.

Other priestly garments

22 They made the robe of the ephod entirely of blue cloth – the work of a weaver – 23 with an opening in the centre of the robe like the opening of a collar,[d] and a band around this opening, so that it would not tear. 24 They made pomegranates of blue, purple and scarlet yarn and finely twisted linen round the hem of the robe. 25 And they made bells of pure gold and attached them around the hem between the pomegranates. 26 The bells and pomegranates alternated round the hem of the robe to be worn for ministering, as the LORD commanded Moses.

27 For Aaron and his sons, they made tunics of fine linen – the work of a weaver – 28 and the turban of fine linen, the linen caps and the undergarments of finely twisted linen. 29 The sash was made of finely twisted linen and blue, purple and scarlet yarn – the work of an embroiderer – as the LORD commanded Moses.

30 They made the plate, the sacred emblem, out of pure gold and engraved on it, like an inscription on a seal: HOLY TO THE LORD. 31 Then they fastened a blue cord to it to attach it to the turban, as the LORD commanded Moses.

---

a 2   Or *He*; also in verses 7, 8 and 22
b 9   That is, about 23 centimetres
c 13   The precise identification of some of these precious stones is uncertain.

d 23   The meaning of the Hebrew for this word is uncertain.

Moses inspects the tabernacle

³²So all the work on the tabernacle, the tent of meeting, was completed. The Israelites did everything just as the Lord commanded Moses. ³³Then they brought the tabernacle to Moses: the tent and all its furnishings, its clasps, frames, cross-bars, posts and bases; ³⁴the covering of ram skins dyed red and the covering of another durable leather*e* and the shielding curtain; ³⁵the ark of the covenant law with its poles and the atonement cover; ³⁶the table with all its articles and the bread of the Presence; ³⁷the pure gold lampstand with its row of lamps and all its accessories, and the olive oil for the light; ³⁸the gold altar, the anointing oil, the fragrant incense, and the curtain for the entrance to the tent; ³⁹the bronze altar with its bronze grating, its poles and all its utensils; the basin with its stand; ⁴⁰the curtains of the courtyard with its posts and bases, and the curtain for the entrance to the courtyard; the ropes and tent pegs for the courtyard; all the furnishings for the tabernacle, the tent of meeting; ⁴¹and the woven garments worn for ministering in the sanctuary, both the sacred garments for Aaron the priest and the garments for his sons when serving as priests.

⁴²The Israelites had done all the work just as the Lord had commanded Moses. ⁴³Moses inspected the work and saw that they had done it just as the Lord had commanded. So Moses blessed them.

Setting up the tabernacle

40 Then the Lord said to Moses: ²'Set up the tabernacle, the tent of meeting, on the first day of the first month. ³Place the ark of the covenant law in it and shield the ark with the curtain. ⁴Bring in the table and set out what belongs on it. Then bring in the lampstand and set up its lamps. ⁵Place the gold altar of incense in front of the ark of the covenant law and put the curtain at the entrance to the tabernacle.

⁶'Place the altar of burnt offering in front of the entrance to the tabernacle,

the tent of meeting; ⁷place the basin between the tent of meeting and the altar and put water in it. ⁸Set up the courtyard around it and put the curtain at the entrance to the courtyard.

⁹'Take the anointing oil and anoint the tabernacle and everything in it; consecrate it and all its furnishings, and it will be holy. ¹⁰Then anoint the altar of burnt offering and all its utensils; consecrate the altar, and it will be most holy. ¹¹Anoint the basin and its stand and consecrate them.

¹²'Bring Aaron and his sons to the entrance to the tent of meeting and wash them with water. ¹³Then dress Aaron in the sacred garments, anoint him and consecrate him so that he may serve me as priest. ¹⁴Bring his sons and dress them in tunics. ¹⁵Anoint them just as you anointed their father, so that they may serve me as priests. Their anointing will be to a priesthood that will continue throughout their generations.' ¹⁶Moses did everything just as the Lord commanded him.

¹⁷So the tabernacle was set up on the first day of the first month in the second year. ¹⁸When Moses set up the tabernacle, he put the bases in place, erected the frames, inserted the crossbars and set up the posts. ¹⁹Then he spread the tent over the tabernacle and put the covering over the tent, as the Lord commanded him.

²⁰He took the tablets of the covenant law and placed them in the ark, attached the poles to the ark and put the atonement cover over it. ²¹Then he brought the ark into the tabernacle and hung the shielding curtain and shielded the ark of the covenant law, as the Lord commanded him.

²²Moses placed the table in the tent of meeting on the north side of the tabernacle outside the curtain ²³and set out the bread on it before the Lord, as the Lord commanded him.

²⁴He placed the lampstand in the tent of meeting opposite the table on the south side of the tabernacle ²⁵and set up the lamps before the Lord, as the Lord commanded him.

²⁶Moses placed the gold altar in the

---

e 34 Possibly the hides of large aquatic mammals

tent of meeting in front of the curtain [27] and burned fragrant incense on it, as the LORD commanded him.

[28] Then he put up the curtain at the entrance to the tabernacle. [29] He set the altar of burnt offering near the entrance to the tabernacle, the tent of meeting, and offered on it burnt offerings and grain offerings, as the LORD commanded him.

[30] He placed the basin between the tent of meeting and the altar and put water in it for washing, [31] and Moses and Aaron and his sons used it to wash their hands and feet. [32] They washed whenever they entered the tent of meeting or approached the altar, as the LORD commanded Moses.

[33] Then Moses set up the courtyard around the tabernacle and altar and put up the curtain at the entrance to the courtyard. And so Moses finished the work.

The glory of the LORD

[34] Then the cloud covered the tent of meeting, and the glory of the LORD filled the tabernacle. [35] Moses could not enter the tent of meeting because the cloud had settled on it, and the glory of the LORD filled the tabernacle.

[36] In all the travels of the Israelites, whenever the cloud lifted from above the tabernacle, they would set out; [37] but if the cloud did not lift, they did not set out – until the day it lifted. [38] So the cloud of the LORD was over the tabernacle by day, and fire was in the cloud by night, in the sight of all the Israelites during all their travels.

LEVITICUS

DATE

The instructions contained in Leviticus were given to Moses during the time the Israelites were in the desert, around 1446–1406 BC

AUTHOR

Traditionally attributed to Moses

WHAT'S IT ALL ABOUT?

Leviticus is the third book of the Pentateuch and has a bit of a bad reputation! It's very detailed in its descriptions of the law, which can make for a tough read, but there is much we can learn as God's followers today. The book lays out instructions for God's people on how to live, including how to offer sacrifices that were acceptable to God, what to eat, how to conduct personal relationships and more. It shows us that for Israel there was no divide between sacred and secular activities as we can sometimes have today. They saw their whole lives as being under God's authority and this book gave them guidance on how to live in a way that would please God. We no longer have to slavishly follow these rules, many of which seem barbaric or at least overly restrictive – but we can learn a lot about letting God be in charge of every aspect of our lives, from what we eat to how we treat people.

WHY SHOULD WE READ IT?

- To understand what worship was like in those times and particularly to see the importance of sacrifice and blood sacrifice, which points us towards the new covenant with Jesus.

- To see the level of detail with which God cares about his people's lives.

- To see how people reacted to the glory of the Lord (Leviticus 9).

- To read about the promised rewards for obedience and punishments for disobedience (Leviticus 26).

Andy Croft with Liza Hoeksma

The burnt offering

1 The LORD called to Moses and spoke to him from the tent of meeting. He said, ²'Speak to the Israelites and say to them: "When anyone among you brings an offering to the LORD, bring as your offering an animal from either the herd or the flock.

³' "If the offering is a burnt offering from the herd, you are to offer a male without defect. You must present it at the entrance to the tent of meeting so that it will be acceptable to the LORD. ⁴You are to lay your hand on the head of the burnt offering, and it will be accepted on your behalf to make atonement for you. ⁵You are to slaughter the young bull before the LORD, and then Aaron's sons the priests shall bring the blood and splash it against the sides of the altar at the entrance to the tent of meeting. ⁶You are to skin the burnt offering and cut it into pieces. ⁷The sons of Aaron the priest are to put fire on the altar and arrange wood on the fire. ⁸Then Aaron's sons the priests shall arrange the pieces, including the head and the fat, on the wood that is burning on the altar. ⁹You are to wash the internal organs and the legs with water, and the priest is to burn all of it on the altar. It is a burnt offering, a food offering, an aroma pleasing to the LORD.

¹⁰' "If the offering is a burnt offering from the flock, from either the sheep or the goats, you are to offer a male without defect. ¹¹You are to slaughter it at the north side of the altar before the LORD, and Aaron's sons the priests shall splash its blood against the sides of the altar. ¹²You are to cut it into pieces, and the priest shall arrange them, including the head and the fat, on the wood that is burning on the altar. ¹³You are to wash the internal organs and the legs with water, and the priest is to bring all of them and burn them on the altar. It is a burnt offering, a food offering, an aroma pleasing to the LORD.

¹⁴' "If the offering to the LORD is a burnt offering of birds, you are to offer a dove or a young pigeon. ¹⁵The priest shall bring it to the altar, wring off the head and burn it on the altar; its blood shall be drained out on the side of the altar. ¹⁶He is to remove the crop and the feathers[a] and throw them down east of the altar where the ashes are. ¹⁷He shall tear it open by the wings, not dividing it completely, and then the priest shall burn it on the wood that is burning on the altar. It is a burnt offering, a food offering, an aroma pleasing to the LORD.

The grain offering

2 ' "When anyone brings a grain offering to the LORD, their offering is to be of the finest flour. They are to pour olive oil on it, put incense on it ²and take it to Aaron's sons the priests. The priest shall take a handful of the flour and oil, together with all the incense, and burn this as a memorial[a] portion on the altar, a food offering, an aroma pleasing to the LORD. ³The rest of the grain offering belongs to Aaron and his sons; it is a most holy part of the food offerings presented to the LORD.

⁴' "If you bring a grain offering baked in an oven, it is to consist of the finest flour: either thick loaves made without yeast and with olive oil mixed in or thin loaves made without yeast and brushed with olive oil. ⁵If your grain offering is prepared on a griddle, it is to be made of the finest flour mixed with oil, and without yeast. ⁶Crumble it and pour oil on it; it is a grain offering. ⁷If your grain offering is cooked in a pan, it is to be made of the finest flour and some olive oil. ⁸Bring the grain offering made of these things to the LORD; present it to the priest, who shall take it to the altar. ⁹He shall take out the memorial portion from the grain offering and burn it on the altar as a food offering, an aroma pleasing to the LORD. ¹⁰The rest of the grain offering belongs to Aaron and his sons; it is a most holy part of the food offerings presented to the LORD.

¹¹' "Every grain offering you bring to the LORD must be made without yeast, for you are not to burn any yeast or honey

---

a 16 Or *crop with its contents*; the meaning of the Hebrew for this word is uncertain.
a 2 Or *representative*; also in verses 9 and 16

in a food offering presented to the LORD. [12] You may bring them to the LORD as an offering of the firstfruits, but they are not to be offered on the altar as a pleasing aroma. [13] Season all your grain offerings with salt. Do not leave the salt of the covenant of your God out of your grain offerings; add salt to all your offerings.

[14] "If you bring a grain offering of firstfruits to the LORD, offer crushed heads of new grain roasted in the fire. [15] Put oil and incense on it; it is a grain offering. [16] The priest shall burn the memorial portion of the crushed grain and the oil, together with all the incense, as a food offering presented to the LORD.

The fellowship offering

3 '"If your offering is a fellowship offering, and you offer an animal from the herd, whether male or female, you are to present before the LORD an animal without defect. [2] You are to lay your hand on the head of your offering and slaughter it at the entrance to the tent of meeting. Then Aaron's sons the priests shall splash the blood against the sides of the altar. [3] From the fellowship offering you are to bring a food offering to the LORD: the internal organs and all the fat that is connected to them, [4] both kidneys with the fat on them near the loins, and the long lobe of the liver, which you will remove with the kidneys. [5] Then Aaron's sons are to burn it on the altar on top of the burnt offering that is lying on the burning wood; it is a food offering, an aroma pleasing to the LORD.

[6] '"If you offer an animal from the flock as a fellowship offering to the LORD, you are to offer a male or female without defect. [7] If you offer a lamb, you are to present it before the LORD, [8] lay your hand on its head and slaughter it in front of the tent of meeting. Then Aaron's sons shall splash its blood against the sides of the altar. [9] From the fellowship offering you are to bring a food offering to the LORD: its fat, the entire fat tail cut off close to the backbone, the internal organs and all the fat that is connected to them, [10] both kidneys with the fat on them near the loins,

and the long lobe of the liver, which you will remove with the kidneys. [11] The priest shall burn them on the altar as a food offering presented to the LORD.

[12] '"If your offering is a goat, you are to present it before the LORD, [13] lay your hand on its head and slaughter it in front of the tent of meeting. Then Aaron's sons shall splash its blood against the sides of the altar. [14] From what you offer you are to present this food offering to the LORD: the internal organs and all the fat that is connected to them, [15] both kidneys with the fat on them near the loins, and the long lobe of the liver, which you will remove with the kidneys. [16] The priest shall burn them on the altar as a food offering, a pleasing aroma. All the fat is the LORD's.

[17] '"This is a lasting ordinance for the generations to come, wherever you live: you must not eat any fat or any blood."'

The sin offering

4 The LORD said to Moses, [2] 'Say to the Israelites: "When anyone sins unintentionally and does what is forbidden in any of the LORD's commands –

[3] '"If the anointed priest sins, bringing guilt on the people, he must bring to the LORD a young bull without defect as a sin offering[a] for the sin he has committed. [4] He is to present the bull at the entrance to the tent of meeting before the LORD. He is to lay his hand on its head and slaughter it there before the LORD. [5] Then the anointed priest shall take some of the bull's blood and carry it into the tent of meeting. [6] He is to dip his finger into the blood and sprinkle some of it seven times before the LORD, in front of the curtain of the sanctuary. [7] The priest shall then put some of the blood on the horns of the altar of fragrant incense that is before the LORD in the tent of meeting. The rest of the bull's blood he shall pour out at the base of the altar of burnt offering at the entrance to the tent of meeting. [8] He shall

---

a 3 Or *purification offering*; here and throughout this chapter remove all the fat from the bull of the sin offering – all the fat that is connected to the internal organs, 9 both kidneys with the fat on them near the loins, and the long lobe of the liver, which he will remove with the kidneys – 10 just as the fat is removed from the ox b sacrificed as a fellowship offering. Then the priest shall burn them on the altar of burnt offering. 11 But the hide of the bull and all its flesh, as well as the head and legs, the internal organs and the intestines – 12 that is, all the rest of the bull – he must take outside the camp to a place ceremonially clean, where the ashes are thrown, and burn it there in a wood fire on the ash heap.

13 ' "If the whole Israelite community sins unintentionally and does what is forbidden in any of the LORD's commands, even though the community is unaware of the matter, when they realise their guilt 14 and the sin they committed becomes known, the assembly must bring a young bull as a sin offering and present it before the tent of meeting. 15 The elders of the community are to lay their hands on the bull's head before the LORD, and the bull shall be slaughtered before the LORD. 16 Then the anointed priest is to take some of the bull's blood into the tent of meeting. 17 He shall dip his finger into the blood and sprinkle it before the LORD seven times in front of the curtain. 18 He is to put some of the blood on the horns of the altar that is before the LORD in the tent of meeting. The rest of the blood he shall pour out at the base of the altar of burnt offering at the entrance to the tent of meeting. 19 He shall remove all the fat from it and burn it on the altar, 20 and do with this bull just as he did with the bull for the sin offering. In this way the priest will make atonement for the community, and they will be forgiven. 21 Then he shall take the bull outside the camp and burn it as he burned the first bull. This is the sin offering for the community.

22 ' "When a leader sins unintentionally and does what is forbidden in any of the commands of the LORD his God, when he realises his guilt 23 and the sin he has committed becomes known, he must bring as his offering a male goat without defect. 24 He is to lay his hand on the goat's head and slaughter it at the place where the burnt offering is slaughtered before the LORD. It is a sin offering. 25 Then the priest shall take some of the blood of the sin offering with his finger and put it on the horns of the altar of burnt offering and pour out the rest of the blood at the base of the altar. 26 He shall burn all the fat on the altar as he burned the fat of the fellowship offering. In this way the priest will make atonement for the leader's sin, and he will be forgiven.

27 ' "If any member of the community sins unintentionally and does what is forbidden in any of the LORD's commands, when they realise their guilt 28 and the sin they have committed becomes known, they must bring as their offering for the sin they committed a female goat without defect. 29 They are to lay their hand on the head of the sin offering and slaughter it at the place of the burnt offering. 30 Then the priest is to take some of the blood with his finger and put it on the horns of the altar of burnt offering and pour out the rest of the blood at the base of the altar. 31 They shall remove all the fat, just as the fat is removed from the fellowship offering, and the priest shall burn it on the altar as an aroma pleasing to the LORD. In this way the priest will make atonement for them, and they will be forgiven.

32 ' "If someone brings a lamb as their sin offering, they are to bring a female without defect. 33 They are to lay their hand on its head and slaughter it for a sin offering at the place where the burnt offering is slaughtered. 34 Then the priest shall take some of the blood of the sin offering with his finger and put it on the horns of the altar of burnt offering and pour out the rest of the blood at the base of the altar. 35 They shall remove all the fat, just as the fat is removed from the lamb

b 10 The Hebrew word can refer to either male or female.

of the fellowship offering, and the priest shall burn it on the altar on top of the food offerings presented to the LORD. In this way the priest will make atonement for them for the sin they have committed, and they will be forgiven.

5 ¹ "If anyone sins because they do not speak up when they hear a public charge to testify regarding something they have seen or learned about, they will be held responsible.

² "If anyone becomes aware that they are guilty – if they unwittingly touch anything ceremonially unclean (whether the carcass of an unclean animal, wild or domestic, or of any unclean creature that moves along the ground) and they are unaware that they have become unclean, but then they come to realise their guilt; ³ or if they touch human uncleanness (anything that would make them unclean) even though they are unaware of it, but then they learn of it and realise their guilt; ⁴ or if anyone thoughtlessly takes an oath to do anything, whether good or evil (in any matter one might carelessly swear about) even though they are unaware of it, but then they learn of it and realise their guilt – ⁵ when anyone becomes aware that they are guilty in any of these matters, they must confess in what way they have sinned. ⁶ As a penalty for the sin they have committed, they must bring to the LORD a female lamb or goat from the flock as a sin offering[a]; and the priest shall make atonement for them for their sin.

⁷ "Anyone who cannot afford a lamb is to bring two doves or two young pigeons to the LORD as a penalty for their sin – one for a sin offering and the other for a burnt offering. ⁸ They are to bring them to the priest, who shall first offer the one for the sin offering. He is to wring its head from its neck, not dividing it completely, ⁹ and is to splash some of the blood of the sin offering against the side of the altar; the rest of the blood must be drained out at the base of the altar. It is a sin offering. ¹⁰ The priest shall then offer the other as a burnt offering in the prescribed way and make atonement for them for the sin they have committed, and they will be forgiven.

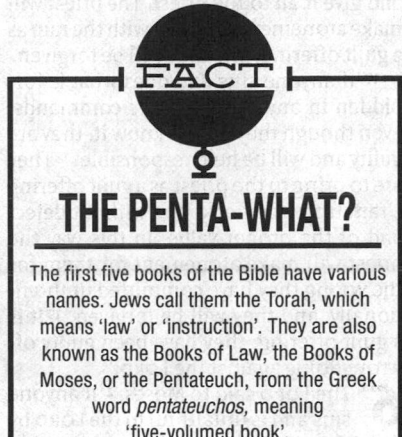

FACT

THE PENTA-WHAT?

The first five books of the Bible have various names. Jews call them the Torah, which means 'law' or 'instruction'. They are also known as the Books of Law, the Books of Moses, or the Pentateuch, from the Greek word *pentateuchos*, meaning 'five-volumed book'.

¹¹ "'If, however, they cannot afford two doves or two young pigeons, they are to bring as an offering for their sin a tenth of an ephah[b] of the finest flour for a sin offering. They must not put olive oil or incense on it, because it is a sin offering. ¹² They are to bring it to the priest, who shall take a handful of it as a memorial[c] portion and burn it on the altar on top of the food offerings presented to the LORD. It is a sin offering. ¹³ In this way the priest will make atonement for them for any of these sins they have committed, and they will be forgiven. The rest of the offering will belong to the priest, as in the case of the grain offering.'"

The guilt offering

¹⁴ The LORD said to Moses: ¹⁵ 'When anyone is unfaithful to the LORD by sinning unintentionally in regard to any of the LORD's holy things, they are to bring to the LORD as a penalty a ram from the flock,

---

a 6 Or *purification offering*; here and throughout this chapter

b 11 That is, probably about 1.6 kilograms

c 12 Or *representative*

one without defect and of the proper value in silver, according to the sanctuary shekel.*d* It is a guilt offering. 16They must make restitution for what they have failed to do in regard to the holy things, pay an additional penalty of a fifth of its value and give it all to the priest. The priest will make atonement for them with the ram as a guilt offering, and they will be forgiven.

17'If anyone sins and does what is forbidden in any of the LORD's commands, even though they do not know it, they are guilty and will be held responsible. 18They are to bring to the priest as a guilt offering a ram from the flock, one without defect and of the proper value. In this way the priest will make atonement for them for the wrong they have committed unintentionally, and they will be forgiven. 19It is a guilt offering; they have been guilty of*e* wrongdoing against the LORD.'

6*a* The LORD said to Moses: 2'If anyone sins and is unfaithful to the LORD by deceiving a neighbour about something entrusted to them or left in their care or about something stolen, or if they cheat their neighbour, 3or if they find lost property and lie about it, or if they swear falsely about any such sin that people may commit – 4when they sin in any of these ways and realise their guilt, they must return what they have stolen or taken by extortion, or what was entrusted to them, or the lost property they found, 5or whatever it was they swore falsely about. They must make restitution in full, add a fifth of the value to it and give it all to the owner on the day they present their guilt offering. 6And as a penalty they must bring to the priest, that is, to the LORD, their guilt offering, a ram from the flock, one without defect and of the proper value. 7In this way the priest will make atonement for them before the LORD, and they will be forgiven for any of the things they did that made them guilty.'

The burnt offering

8The LORD said to Moses: 9'Give Aaron and his sons this command: "These are the regulations for the burnt offering: the burnt offering is to remain on the altar hearth throughout the night, till morning, and the fire must be kept burning on the altar. 10The priest shall then put on his linen clothes, with linen undergarments next to his body, and shall remove the ashes of the burnt offering that the fire has consumed on the altar and place them beside the altar. 11Then he is to take off these clothes and put on others, and carry the ashes outside the camp to a place that is ceremonially clean. 12The fire on the altar must be kept burning; it must not go out. Every morning the priest is to add firewood and arrange the burnt offering on the fire and burn the fat of the fellowship offerings on it. 13The fire must be kept burning on the altar continuously; it must not go out.

The grain offering

14' "These are the regulations for the grain offering: Aaron's sons are to bring it before the LORD, in front of the altar. 15The priest is to take a handful of the finest flour and some olive oil, together with all the incense on the grain offering, and burn the memorial*b* portion on the altar as an aroma pleasing to the LORD. 16Aaron and his sons shall eat the rest of it, but it is to be eaten without yeast in the sanctuary area; they are to eat it in the courtyard of the tent of meeting. 17It must not be baked with yeast; I have given it as their share of the food offerings presented to me. Like the sin offering*c* and the guilt offering, it is most holy. 18Any male descendant of Aaron may eat it. For all generations to come it is his perpetual share of the food offerings presented to the LORD. Whatever touches it will become holy." '*d*

19The LORD also said to Moses, 20'This is

---

d 15 That is, about 12 grams
e 19 Or offering; atonement has been made for their
a In Hebrew texts 6:1-7 is numbered 5:20-26, and 6:8-30 is numbered 6:1-23.

b 15 Or representative
c 17 Or purification offering; also in verses 25 and 30
d 18 Or Whoever touches them must be holy; similarly in verse 27

the offering Aaron and his sons are to bring to the LORD on the day he*e* is anointed: a tenth of an ephah*f* of the finest flour as a regular grain offering, half of it in the morning and half in the evening. 21 It must be prepared with oil on a griddle; bring it well-mixed and present the grain offering broken*g* in pieces as an aroma pleasing to the LORD. 22 The son who is to succeed him as anointed priest shall prepare it. It is the LORD's perpetual share and is to be burned completely. 23 Every grain offering of a priest shall be burned completely; it must not be eaten.'

The sin offering

24 The LORD said to Moses, 25 'Say to Aaron and his sons: "These are the regulations for the sin offering: the sin offering is to be slaughtered before the LORD in the place where the burnt offering is slaughtered; it is most holy. 26 The priest who offers it shall eat it; it is to be eaten in the sanctuary area, in the courtyard of the tent of meeting. 27 Whatever touches any of the flesh will become holy, and if any of the blood is spattered on a garment, you must wash it in the sanctuary area. 28 The clay pot that the meat is cooked in must be broken; but if it is cooked in a bronze pot, the pot is to be scoured and rinsed with water. 29 Any male in a priest's family may eat it; it is most holy. 30 But any sin offering whose blood is brought into the tent of meeting to make atonement in the Holy Place must not be eaten; it must be burned.

The guilt offering

7 ' "These are the regulations for the guilt offering, which is most holy: 2 the guilt offering is to be slaughtered in the place where the burnt offering is slaughtered, and its blood is to be splashed against the sides of the altar. 3 All its fat shall be offered: the fat tail and the fat that covers the internal organs,

4 both kidneys with the fat on them near the loins, and the long lobe of the liver, which is to be removed with the kidneys. 5 The priest shall burn them on the altar as a food offering presented to the LORD. It is a guilt offering. 6 Any male in a priest's family may eat it, but it must be eaten in the sanctuary area; it is most holy.

7 ' "The same law applies to both the sin offering*a* and the guilt offering: they belong to the priest who makes atonement with them. 8 The priest who offers a burnt offering for anyone may keep its hide for himself. 9 Every grain offering baked in an oven or cooked in a pan or on a griddle belongs to the priest who offers it, 10 and every grain offering, whether mixed with olive oil or dry, belongs equally to all the sons of Aaron.

The fellowship offering

11 ' "These are the regulations for the fellowship offering anyone may present to the LORD:

12 ' "If they offer it as an expression of thankfulness, then along with this thank-offering they are to offer thick loaves made without yeast and with olive oil mixed in, thin loaves made without yeast and brushed with oil, and thick loaves of the finest flour well-kneaded and with oil mixed in. 13 Along with their fellowship offering of thanksgiving they are to present an offering with thick loaves of bread made with yeast. 14 They are to bring one of each kind as an offering, a contribution to the LORD; it belongs to the priest who splashes the blood of the fellowship offering against the altar. 15 The meat of their fellowship offering of thanksgiving must be eaten on the day it is offered; they must leave none of it till morning.

16 ' "If, however, their offering is the result of a vow or is a freewill offering, the sacrifice shall be eaten on the day they offer it, but anything left over may be eaten on the next day. 17 Any meat of the sacrifice left over till the third day must be burned. 18 If any meat of the fellowship offering is

---

e 20 Or *each*
f 20 That is, probably about 1.6 kilograms
g 21 The meaning of the Hebrew for this word is uncertain.

---

a 7 Or *purification offering*; also in verse 37

eaten on the third day, the one who offered it will not be accepted. It will not be reckoned to their credit, for it has become impure; the person who eats any of it will be held responsible.

19 ' "Meat that touches anything ceremonially unclean must not be eaten; it must be burned. As for other meat, anyone ceremonially clean may eat it. 20 But if anyone who is unclean eats any meat of the fellowship offering belonging to the LORD, they must be cut off from their people. 21 Anyone who touches something unclean – whether human uncleanness or an unclean animal or any unclean creature that moves along the ground*b* – and then eats any of the meat of the fellowship offering belonging to the LORD must be cut off from their people." '

Eating fat and blood forbidden

22 The LORD said to Moses, 23 'Say to the Israelites: "Do not eat any of the fat of cattle, sheep or goats. 24 The fat of an animal found dead or torn by wild animals may be used for any other purpose, but you must not eat it. 25 Anyone who eats the fat of an animal from which a food offering may be*c* presented to the LORD must be cut off from their people. 26 And wherever you live, you must not eat the blood of any bird or animal. 27 Anyone who eats blood must be cut off from their people." '

The priests' share

28 The LORD said to Moses, 29 'Say to the Israelites: "Anyone who brings a fellowship offering to the LORD is to bring part of it as their sacrifice to the LORD. 30 With their own hands they are to present the food offering to the LORD; they are to bring the fat, together with the breast, and wave the breast before the LORD as a wave offering. 31 The priest shall burn the fat on the altar, but the breast belongs to Aaron and his sons. 32 You are to give the right thigh of your fellowship offerings to the priest as a contribution. 33 The son of Aaron who offers the blood and the fat of the fellowship offering shall have the right thigh as his share. 34 From the fellowship offerings of the Israelites, I have taken the breast that is waved and the thigh that is presented and have given them to Aaron the priest and his sons as their perpetual share from the Israelites." '

35 This is the portion of the food offerings presented to the LORD that were allotted to Aaron and his sons on the day they were presented to serve the LORD as priests. 36 On the day they were anointed, the LORD commanded that the Israelites give this to them as their perpetual share for the generations to come.

37 These, then, are the regulations for the burnt offering, the grain offering, the sin offering, the guilt offering, the ordination offering and the fellowship offering, 38 which the LORD gave Moses at Mount Sinai in the Desert of Sinai on the day he commanded the Israelites to bring their offerings to the LORD.

The ordination of Aaron and his sons

8 The LORD said to Moses, 2 'Bring Aaron and his sons, their garments, the anointing oil, the bull for the sin offering,*a* the two rams and the basket containing bread made without yeast, 3 and gather the entire assembly at the entrance to the tent of meeting.' 4 Moses did as the LORD commanded him, and the assembly gathered at the entrance to the tent of meeting.

5 Moses said to the assembly, 'This is what the LORD has commanded to be done.' 6 Then Moses brought Aaron and his sons forward and washed them with water. 7 He put the tunic on Aaron, tied the sash round him, clothed him with the robe and put the ephod on him. He also fastened the ephod with a decorative waistband, which he tied round him. 8 He placed the breastpiece on him and put the

---

b 21 A few Hebrew manuscripts, Samaritan Pentateuch, Syriac and Targum (see 5:2); most Hebrew manuscripts *any unclean, detestable thing*
c 25 Or *offering is*

a 2 Or *purification offering*; also in verse 14

Urim and Thummim in the breastpiece. ⁹Then he placed the turban on Aaron's head and set the gold plate, the sacred emblem, on the front of it, as the LORD commanded Moses.

¹⁰Then Moses took the anointing oil and anointed the tabernacle and everything in it, and so consecrated them. ¹¹He sprinkled some of the oil on the altar seven times, anointing the altar and all its utensils and the basin with its stand, to consecrate them. ¹²He poured some of the anointing oil on Aaron's head and anointed him to consecrate him. ¹³Then he brought Aaron's sons forward, put tunics on them, tied sashes round them and fastened caps on them, as the LORD commanded Moses.

¹⁴He then presented the bull for the sin offering, and Aaron and his sons laid their hands on its head. ¹⁵Moses slaughtered the bull and took some of the blood, and with his finger he put it on all the horns of the altar to purify the altar. He poured out the rest of the blood at the base of the altar. So he consecrated it to make atonement for it. ¹⁶Moses also took all the fat around the internal organs, the long lobe of the liver, and both kidneys and their fat, and burned it on the altar. ¹⁷But the bull with its hide and its flesh and its intestines he burned outside the camp, as the LORD commanded Moses.

¹⁸He then presented the ram for the burnt offering, and Aaron and his sons laid their hands on its head. ¹⁹Then Moses slaughtered the ram and splashed the blood against the sides of the altar. ²⁰He cut the ram into pieces and burned the head, the pieces and the fat. ²¹He washed the internal organs and the legs with water and burned the whole ram on the altar. It was a burnt offering, a pleasing aroma, a food offering presented to the LORD, as the LORD commanded Moses.

²²He then presented the other ram, the ram for the ordination, and Aaron and his sons laid their hands on its head. ²³Moses slaughtered the ram and took some of its blood and put it on the lobe of Aaron's right ear, on the thumb of his right hand and on the big toe of his right foot. ²⁴Moses also brought Aaron's sons forward and put some of the blood on the lobes of their right ears, on the thumbs of their right hands and on the big toes of their right feet. Then he splashed blood against the sides of the altar. ²⁵After that, he took the fat, the fat tail, all the fat around the internal organs, the long lobe of the liver, both kidneys and their fat and the right thigh. ²⁶And from the basket of bread made without yeast, which was before the LORD, he took one thick loaf, one thick loaf with olive oil mixed in, and one thin loaf, and he put these on the fat portions and on the right thigh. ²⁷He put all these in the hands of Aaron and his sons and they waved them before the LORD as a wave offering. ²⁸Then Moses took them from their hands and burned them on the altar on top of the burnt offering as an ordination offering, a pleasing aroma, a food offering presented to the LORD. ²⁹Moses also took the breast, which was his share of the ordination ram, and waved it before the LORD as a wave offering, as the LORD commanded Moses.

³⁰Then Moses took some of the anointing oil and some of the blood from the altar and sprinkled them on Aaron and his garments and on his sons and their garments. So he consecrated Aaron and his garments and his sons and their garments.

³¹Moses then said to Aaron and his sons, 'Cook the meat at the entrance to the tent of meeting and eat it there with the bread from the basket of ordination offerings, as I was commanded: "Aaron and his sons are to eat it." ³²Then burn the rest of the meat and the bread. ³³Do not leave the entrance to the tent of meeting for seven days, until the days of your ordination are completed, for your ordination will last seven days. ³⁴What has been done today was commanded by the LORD to make atonement for you. ³⁵You must stay at the entrance to the tent of meeting day and night for seven days and do what the LORD requires, so that you will not die; for that is what I have been commanded.'

³⁶So Aaron and his sons did everything the LORD commanded through Moses.

The priests begin their ministry

9 On the eighth day Moses summoned Aaron and his sons and the elders of Israel. ²He said to Aaron, 'Take a bull calf for your sin offering*ᵃ* and a ram for your burnt offering, both without defect, and present them before the LORD. ³Then say to the Israelites: "Take a male goat for a sin offering, a calf and a lamb – both a year old and without defect – for a burnt offering, ⁴and an ox*ᵇ* and a ram for a fellowship offering to sacrifice before the LORD, together with a grain offering mixed with olive oil. For today the LORD will appear to you."'

⁵They took the things Moses

---

a 2 Or *purification offering*; here and throughout this chapter

b 4 The Hebrew word can include both male and female; also in verses 18 and 19.

SACRIFICE 6

Sacrifice as worship

Leviticus is known as one of the most difficult books in the whole Bible to read. We find it tricky because it gives incredibly detailed instructions on how every single thing in the temple of God was meant to work, particularly the details of the worship of sacrifice.

You can read about it all through this book. The book is like an instruction manual for the priests and the people on acceptable sacrifices and how they are to be offered. These can range from quite gruesome (like how to kill the calf and drain its blood) to kind of quirky (like what kinds of birds and spices are acceptable). The whole system is an intricate worship structure intended to get across a very clear point: worship means sacrifice.

The beginning of the process is stated by Moses as being connected with the 'glory' of God (this is what we call the presence of God). When God 'shows up', it's his glory that we are encountering. This is the presence of God that comes through fire, cloud, awe and genuinely incredible supernatural ways. If we want God's presence, then we need to worship – and worship has always been about sacrifice. We bring to God our 'sacrifice', our offering, something that costs us something, as an act of worship. It's a genuine reflection of our understanding that he alone is God and that we worship him.

When we do that, our worship gives us access to his glory. In other words, we get to experience his presence. It's not an exchange. We're not buying God with expensive gifts. Rather, worship that is a sacrifice means we're honouring God with our best. When we do that, he comes near. He knows we're friends. Why not give God your very best as an act of worship – a sacrifice of praise – and spend some time in his presence today?

Danielle Strickland

 Romans 12:1–2   Judges 16:23–30 ▶

commanded to the front of the tent of meeting, and the entire assembly came near and stood before the LORD. 6 Then Moses said, 'This is what the LORD has commanded you to do, so that the glory of the LORD may appear to you.'

7 Moses said to Aaron, 'Come to the altar and sacrifice your sin offering and your burnt offering and make atonement for yourself and the people; sacrifice the offering that is for the people and make atonement for them, as the LORD has commanded.'

8 So Aaron came to the altar and slaughtered the calf as a sin offering for himself. 9 His sons brought the blood to him, and he dipped his finger into the blood and put it on the horns of the altar; the rest of the blood he poured out at the base of the altar. 10 On the altar he burned the fat, the kidneys and the long lobe of the liver from the sin offering, as the LORD commanded Moses; 11 the flesh and the hide he burned outside the camp.

12 Then he slaughtered the burnt offering. His sons handed him the blood,

WORSHIP 1

A response

Worship in the Old Testament looked pretty different from how it does now. Leviticus is full of blood-sprinkling, meat-waving and fat-burning (and not the type of fat-burning that happens at the gym, either). However, strange as these instructions may sound, they were given by God to atone for Israel's sins and to make them 'right' before God. So after Moses, with much anticipation, fulfilled these commands, God appeared to the people as promised, in fire and glory (Leviticus 9:23–24).

Immediately, Israel's response was one of wholehearted, face-down worship.

Could there be a more appropriate reaction than this? Whenever we encounter God and see afresh all that he has done for us, we can't help but fall to our knees. Matt Redman describes worship as 'our all-consuming response to the all-deserving revelation of God'. The Lord reveals himself and we respond.

It's easy to think that by worshipping God, we are the ones making the first move. We certainly have a choice in worship, but anything we bring before God is simply a response. God got in there first. All through the Bible, he is the great initiator of love, from beginning to end. And he has been 'making moves' with us since we were born, pursuing relationship with us and drawing us to himself.

There are many ways in which we respond to God in worship. The Israelites in Leviticus 9 responded by shouting for joy and falling to the ground in awe. Similarly, we can dance, sing, paint or worship in other ways. These expressions will always be a response to who he is and what he has done. We sing because he first sang over us (Zephaniah 3:17), we love because he first loved us (1 John 4:19), and we freely give because we have freely received (Matthew 10:8).

Beth Croft

2 Samuel 24:18–25

and he splashed it against the sides of the altar. 13They handed him the burnt offering piece by piece, including the head, and he burned them on the altar. 14He washed the internal organs and the legs and burned them on top of the burnt offering on the altar.

15Aaron then brought the offering that was for the people. He took the goat for the people's sin offering and slaughtered it and offered it for a sin offering as he did with the first one.

16He brought the burnt offering and offered it in the prescribed way. 17He also brought the grain offering, took a handful of it and burned it on the altar in addition to the morning's burnt offering.

18He slaughtered the ox and the ram as the fellowship offering for the people. His sons handed him the blood, and he splashed it against the sides of the altar. 19But the fat portions of the ox and the ram – the fat tail, the layer of fat, the kidneys and the long lobe of the liver – 20these they laid on the breasts, and then Aaron burned the fat on the altar. 21Aaron waved the breasts and the right thigh before the LORD as a wave offering, as Moses commanded.

22Then Aaron lifted his hands towards the people and blessed them. And having sacrificed the sin offering, the burnt offering and the fellowship offering, he stepped down.

23Moses and Aaron then went into the tent of meeting. When they came out, they blessed the people; and the glory of the LORD appeared to all the people. 24Fire came out from the presence of the LORD and consumed the burnt offering and the fat portions on the altar. And when all the people saw it, they shouted for joy and fell face down.

The death of Nadab and Abihu

10 Aaron's sons Nadab and Abihu took their censers, put fire in them and added incense; and they offered unauthorised fire before the LORD, contrary to his command. 2So fire came out from the presence of the LORD and consumed them, and they died before the LORD.

3Moses then said to Aaron, 'This is what the LORD spoke of when he said:

'"Among those who approach me
   I will be proved holy;
in the sight of all the people
   I will be honoured."'

Aaron remained silent.

4Moses summoned Mishael and Elzaphan, sons of Aaron's uncle Uzziel, and said to them, 'Come here; carry your cousins outside the camp, away from the front of the sanctuary.' 5So they came and carried them, still in their tunics, outside the camp, as Moses ordered.

6Then Moses said to Aaron and his sons Eleazar and Ithamar, 'Do not let your hair become unkempt[a] and do not tear your clothes or you will die and the LORD will be angry with the whole community. But your relatives, all the Israelites, may mourn for those the LORD has destroyed by fire. 7Do not leave the entrance to the tent of meeting or you will die, because the LORD's anointing oil is on you.' So they did as Moses said.

8Then the LORD said to Aaron, 9'You and your sons are not to drink wine or other fermented drink whenever you go into the tent of meeting, or you will die. This is a lasting ordinance for the generations to come, 10so that you can distinguish between the holy and the common, between the unclean and the clean, 11and so you can teach the Israelites all the decrees the LORD has given them through Moses.'

12Moses said to Aaron and his remaining sons, Eleazar and Ithamar, 'Take the grain offering left over from the food offerings prepared without yeast and presented to the LORD and eat it beside the altar, for it is most holy. 13Eat it in the sanctuary area, because it is your share and your sons' share of the food offerings presented to the LORD; for so I have been commanded. 14But you and your sons and your daughters may eat the breast that was waved and the thigh that was presented.

---

a 6 Or *Do not uncover your heads*

Eat them in a ceremonially clean place; they have been given to you and your children as your share of the Israelites' fellowship offerings. ¹⁵The thigh that was presented and the breast that was waved must be brought with the fat portions of the food offerings, to be waved before the Lord as a wave offering. This will be the perpetual share for you and your children, as the Lord has commanded.'

¹⁶When Moses enquired about the goat of the sin offering[b] and found that it had been burned, he was angry with Eleazar and Ithamar, Aaron's remaining sons, and asked, ¹⁷'Why didn't you eat the sin offering in the sanctuary area? It is most holy; it was given to you to take away the guilt of the community by making atonement for them before the Lord. ¹⁸Since its blood was not taken into the Holy Place, you should have eaten the goat in the sanctuary area, as I commanded.'

¹⁹Aaron replied to Moses, 'Today they sacrificed their sin offering and their burnt offering before the Lord, but such things as this have happened to me. Would the Lord have been pleased if I had eaten the sin offering today?' ²⁰When Moses heard this, he was satisfied.

Clean and unclean food

11 The Lord said to Moses and Aaron, ²'Say to the Israelites: "Of all the animals that live on land, these are the ones you may eat: ³you may eat any animal that has a divided hoof and that chews the cud.

⁴'"There are some that only chew the cud or only have a divided hoof, but you must not eat them. The camel, though it chews the cud, does not have a divided hoof; it is ceremonially unclean for you. ⁵The hyrax, though it chews the cud, does not have a divided hoof; it is unclean for you. ⁶The rabbit, though it chews the cud, does not have a divided hoof; it is unclean for you. ⁷And the pig, though it has a divided hoof, does not chew the cud; it is unclean for you. ⁸You must not eat their

meat or touch their carcasses; they are unclean for you.

⁹'"Of all the creatures living in the water of the seas and the streams you may eat any that have fins and scales. ¹⁰But all creatures in the seas or streams that do not have fins and scales – whether among all the swarming things or among all the other living creatures in the water – you are to regard as unclean. ¹¹And since you are to regard them as unclean, you must not eat their meat; you must regard their carcasses as unclean. ¹²Anything living in the water that does not have fins and scales is to be regarded as unclean by you.

¹³'"These are the birds you are to regard as unclean and not eat because they are unclean: the eagle,[a] the vulture, the black vulture, ¹⁴the red kite, any kind of black kite, ¹⁵any kind of raven, ¹⁶the horned owl, the screech owl, the gull, any kind of hawk, ¹⁷the little owl, the cormorant, the great owl, ¹⁸the white owl, the desert owl, the osprey, ¹⁹the stork, any kind of heron, the hoopoe and the bat.

²⁰'"All flying insects that walk on all fours are to be regarded as unclean by you. ²¹There are, however, some flying insects that walk on all fours that you may eat: those that have jointed legs for hopping on the ground. ²²Of these you may eat any kind of locust, cricket, cicada or grasshopper. ²³But all other flying insects that have four legs you are to regard as unclean.

²⁴'"You will make yourselves unclean by these; whoever touches their carcasses will be unclean till evening. ²⁵Whoever picks up one of their carcasses must wash their clothes, and they will be unclean till evening.

²⁶'"Every animal that does not have a divided hoof or that does not chew the cud is unclean for you; whoever touches the carcass of any of them will be unclean. ²⁷Of all the animals that walk on all fours, those that walk on their paws are unclean for you; whoever touches their carcasses will be unclean till evening. ²⁸Anyone who

---

b 16 Or *purification offering*; also in verses 17 and 19

a 13 The precise identification of some of the birds, insects and animals in this chapter is uncertain.

picks up their carcasses must wash their clothes, and they will be unclean till evening. These animals are unclean for you.

29 ' "Of the animals that move along the ground, these are unclean for you: the weasel, the rat, any kind of great lizard, 30 the gecko, the monitor lizard, the wall lizard, the skink and the chameleon. 31 Of all those that move along the ground, these are unclean for you. Whoever touches them when they are dead will be unclean till evening. 32 When one of them dies and falls on something, that article, whatever its use, will be unclean, whether

THE NAMES OF GOD 10

The Holy God (Yahweh Chasid)

What does Leviticus tell us about the character of 'the Holy God'?

God wants his people to know his nature

The book of Leviticus is full of detailed rituals designed to teach the children of Israel that their God is unique. He reveals himself as utterly holy, absolutely pure and truly righteous.

God wants his people to be like him (Leviticus 11:44)

Both the Old and New Testaments remind us of God's desire for us: *'Be holy, because I am holy'*, and *'You ought to live holy and godly lives as you look forward to the day of God and speed its coming'* (2 Peter 3:11). In the same way that God is holy, we should want to be holy. He is our example and we want to be worthy of his presence.

God knows our inmost thoughts and wants to help us (Jeremiah 17:9)

First, he gives us the Holy Spirit to sanctify us (1 Peter 1:2). 'Sanctify' means to set something apart, or declare it to be holy. God does this with us, through his Spirit, to challenge and to change us.

Second, he gives us a new nature (2 Corinthians 5:17) through faith in Jesus Christ. Even though we have this new nature, it doesn't mean that we are always going to get it right. Paul says, *'I find this law at work: although I want to do good, evil is right there with me'* (Romans 7:21). If we get it wrong, we know that it is in God's nature to forgive when we turn back to him.

God wants us to be Christlike (Hebrews 12:14)

Some Christians wear wristbands with the letters WWJD printed on them, to remind them to ask, 'What Would Jesus Do?' It's a good question for whatever situation we find ourselves in. In heaven the angels worship God continually (Revelation 4:8b) and the psalmist told us to *'glory in his holy name'* (Psalm 105:3), so we should aim to do the same, spending each day constantly acknowledging the incredible holiness of God.

David and Mary Pytches

 Romans 8:15

it is made of wood, cloth, hide or sackcloth. Put it in water; it will be unclean till evening, and then it will be clean. ³³ If one of them falls into a clay pot, everything in it will be unclean, and you must break the pot. ³⁴ Any food you are allowed to eat that has come into contact with water from any such pot is unclean, and any liquid that is drunk from such a pot is unclean. ³⁵ Anything that one of their carcasses falls on becomes unclean; an oven or cooking pot must be broken up. They are unclean, and you are to regard them as unclean. ³⁶ A spring, however, or a cistern for collecting water remains clean, but anyone who touches one of these carcasses is unclean. ³⁷ If a carcass falls on any seeds that are to be planted, they remain clean. ³⁸ But if water has been put on the seed and a carcass falls on it, it is unclean for you.

³⁹ ' "If an animal that you are allowed to eat dies, anyone who touches its carcass will be unclean till evening. ⁴⁰ Anyone who eats some of its carcass must wash their clothes, and they will be unclean till evening. Anyone who picks up the carcass must wash their clothes, and they will be unclean till evening.

⁴¹ ' "Every creature that moves along the ground is to be regarded as unclean; it is not to be eaten. ⁴² You are not to eat any creature that moves along the ground, whether it moves on its belly or walks on all fours or on many feet; it is unclean. ⁴³ Do not defile yourselves by any of these creatures. Do not make yourselves unclean by means of them or be made unclean by them. ⁴⁴ I am the LORD your God; consecrate yourselves and be holy, because I am holy. Do not make yourselves unclean by any creature that moves along the ground. ⁴⁵ I am the LORD, who brought you up out of Egypt to be your God; therefore be holy, because I am holy.

⁴⁶ ' "These are the regulations concerning animals, birds, every living thing that moves about in the water and every creature that moves along the ground. ⁴⁷ You must distinguish between the unclean and the clean, between living creatures that may be eaten and those that may not be eaten." '

Purification after childbirth

12 The LORD said to Moses, ² 'Say to the Israelites: "A woman who becomes pregnant and gives birth to a son will be ceremonially unclean for seven days, just as she is unclean during her monthly period. ³ On the eighth day the boy is to be circumcised. ⁴ Then the woman must wait thirty-three days to be purified from her bleeding. She must not touch anything sacred or go to the sanctuary until the days of her purification are over. ⁵ If she gives birth to a daughter, for two weeks the woman will be unclean, as during her period. Then she must wait sixty-six days to be purified from her bleeding.

⁶ ' "When the days of her purification for a son or daughter are over, she is to bring to the priest at the entrance to the tent of meeting a year-old lamb for a burnt offering and a young pigeon or a dove for a sin offering.ᵃ ⁷ He shall offer them before the LORD to make atonement for her, and then she will be ceremonially clean from her flow of blood.

' "These are the regulations for the woman who gives birth to a boy or a girl. ⁸ But if she cannot afford a lamb, she is to bring two doves or two young pigeons, one for a burnt offering and the other for a sin offering. In this way the priest will make atonement for her, and she will be clean." '

Regulations about defiling skin diseases

13 The LORD said to Moses and Aaron, ² 'When anyone has a swelling or a rash or a shiny spot on their skin that may be a defiling skin disease,ᵃ they must be brought to Aaron the priest or to one of his sonsᵇ who is a priest. ³ The priest is to examine the sore on the skin, and if the hair in the sore has turned white and the sore appears to be more than skin deep, it is a defiling skin disease. When the priest

---

a 6 Or *purification offering*; also in verse 8
a 2 The Hebrew word for *defiling skin disease*, traditionally translated 'leprosy', was used for various diseases affecting the skin; here and throughout verses 3-46.
b 2 Or *descendants*

examines that person, he shall pronounce them ceremonially unclean. 4 If the shiny spot on the skin is white but does not appear to be more than skin deep and the hair in it has not turned white, the priest is to isolate the affected person for seven days. 5 On the seventh day the priest is to examine them, and if he sees that the sore is unchanged and has not spread in the skin, he is to isolate them for another seven days. 6 On the seventh day the priest is to examine them again, and if the sore has faded and has not spread in the skin, the priest shall pronounce them clean; it is only a rash. They must wash their clothes, and they will be clean. 7 But if the rash does spread in their skin after they have shown themselves to the priest to be pronounced clean, they must appear before the priest again. 8 The priest is to examine that person, and if the rash has spread in the skin, he shall pronounce them unclean; it is a defiling skin disease.

9 'When anyone has a defiling skin disease, they must be brought to the priest. 10 The priest is to examine them, and if there is a white swelling in the skin that has turned the hair white and if there is raw flesh in the swelling, 11 it is a chronic skin disease and the priest shall pronounce them unclean. He is not to isolate them, because they are already unclean.

12 'If the disease breaks out all over their skin and, so far as the priest can see, it covers all the skin of the affected person from head to foot, 13 the priest is to examine them, and if the disease has covered their whole body, he shall pronounce them clean. Since it has all turned white, they are clean. 14 But whenever raw flesh appears on them, they will be unclean. 15 When the priest sees the raw flesh, he shall pronounce them unclean. The raw flesh is unclean; they have a defiling disease. 16 If the raw flesh changes and turns white, they must go to the priest. 17 The priest is to examine them, and if the sores have turned white, the priest shall pronounce the affected person clean; then they will be clean.

18 'When someone has a boil on their skin and it heals, 19 and in the place where the boil was, a white swelling or reddish-white spot appears, they must present themselves to the priest. 20 The priest is to examine it, and if it appears to be more than skin deep and the hair in it has turned white, the priest shall pronounce that person unclean. It is a defiling skin disease that has broken out where the boil was. 21 But if, when the priest examines it, there is no white hair in it and it is not more than skin deep and has faded, then the priest is to isolate them for seven days. 22 If it is spreading in the skin, the priest shall pronounce them unclean; it is a defiling disease. 23 But if the spot is unchanged and has not spread, it is only a scar from the boil, and the priest shall pronounce them clean.

24 'When someone has a burn on their skin and a reddish-white or white spot appears in the raw flesh of the burn, 25 the priest is to examine the spot, and if the hair in it has turned white, and it appears to be more than skin deep, it is a defiling disease that has broken out in the burn. The priest shall pronounce them unclean; it is a defiling skin disease. 26 But if the priest examines it and there is no white hair in the spot and if it is not more than skin deep and has faded, then the priest is to isolate them for seven days. 27 On the seventh day the priest is to examine that person, and if it is spreading in the skin, the priest shall pronounce them unclean; it is a defiling skin disease. 28 If, however, the spot is unchanged and has not spread in the skin but has faded, it is a swelling from the burn, and the priest shall pronounce them clean; it is only a scar from the burn.

29 'If a man or woman has a sore on their head or chin, 30 the priest is to examine the sore, and if it appears to be more than skin deep and the hair in it is yellow and thin, the priest shall pronounce them unclean; it is a defiling skin disease on the head or chin. 31 But if, when the priest examines the sore, it does not seem to be more than skin deep and there is no black hair in it, then the priest is to isolate the affected person for seven days. 32 On the seventh day the priest is to examine the sore, and

if it has not spread and there is no yellow hair in it and it does not appear to be more than skin deep, [33] then the man or woman must shave themselves, except for the affected area, and the priest is to keep them isolated another seven days. [34] On the seventh day the priest is to examine the sore, and if it has not spread in the skin and appears to be no more than skin deep, the priest shall pronounce them clean. They must wash their clothes, and they will be clean. [35] But if the sore does spread in the skin after they are pronounced clean, [36] the priest is to examine them, and if he finds that the sore has spread in the skin, he does not need to look for yellow hair; they are unclean. [37] If, however, the sore is unchanged so far as the priest can see, and if black hair has grown in it, the affected person is healed. They are clean, and the priest shall pronounce them clean.

[38] 'When a man or woman has white spots on the skin, [39] the priest is to examine them, and if the spots are dull white, it is a harmless rash that has broken out on the skin; they are clean.

[40] 'A man who has lost his hair and is bald is clean. [41] If he has lost his hair from the front of his scalp and has a bald forehead, he is clean. [42] But if he has a reddish-white sore on his bald head or forehead, it is a defiling disease breaking out on his head or forehead. [43] The priest is to examine him, and if the swollen sore on his head or forehead is reddish-white like a defiling skin disease, [44] the man is diseased and is unclean. The priest shall pronounce him unclean because of the sore on his head.

[45] 'Anyone with such a defiling disease must wear torn clothes, let their hair be unkempt,[c] cover the lower part of their face and cry out, "Unclean! Unclean!" [46] As long as they have the disease they remain unclean. They must live alone; they must live outside the camp.

Regulations about defiling moulds

[47] 'As for any fabric that is spoiled with a defiling mould – any woollen or linen clothing, [48] any woven or knitted material of linen or wool, any leather or anything made of leather – [49] if the affected area in the fabric, the leather, the woven or knitted material, or any leather article, is greenish or reddish, it is a defiling mould and must be shown to the priest. [50] The priest is to examine the affected area and isolate the article for seven days. [51] On the seventh day he is to examine it, and if the mould has spread in the fabric, the woven or knitted material, or the leather, whatever its use, it is a persistent defiling mould; the article is unclean. [52] He must burn the fabric, the woven or knitted material of wool or linen, or any leather article that has been spoiled, because the defiling mould is persistent; the article must be burned.

[53] 'But if, when the priest examines it, the mould has not spread in the fabric, the woven or knitted material, or the leather article, [54] he shall order that the spoiled article be washed. Then he is to isolate it for another seven days. [55] After the article has been washed, the priest is to examine it again, and if the mould has not changed its appearance, even though it has not spread, it is unclean. Burn it, no matter which side of the fabric has been spoiled. [56] If, when the priest examines it, the mould has faded after the article has been washed, he is to tear the spoiled part out of the fabric, the leather, or the woven or knitted material. [57] But if it reappears in the fabric, in the woven or knitted material, or in the leather article, it is a spreading mould; whatever has the mould must be burned. [58] Any fabric, woven or knitted material, or any leather article that has been washed and is rid of the mould, must be washed again. Then it will be clean.'

[59] These are the regulations concerning defiling moulds in woollen or linen clothing, woven or knitted material, or any leather article, for pronouncing them clean or unclean.

Cleansing from defiling skin diseases

14 The LORD said to Moses, [2] 'These are the regulations for any diseased person at the time of their ceremonial cleansing, when they are brought

---

c 45 Or clothes, uncover their head

to the priest: ³the priest is to go outside the camp and examine them. If they have been healed of their defiling skin disease,ᵃ ⁴the priest shall order that two live clean birds and some cedar wood, scarlet yarn and hyssop be brought for the person to be cleansed. ⁵Then the priest shall order that one of the birds be killed over fresh water in a clay pot. ⁶He is then to take the live bird and dip it, together with the cedar wood, the scarlet yarn and the hyssop, into the blood of the bird that was killed over the fresh water. ⁷Seven times he shall sprinkle the one to be cleansed of the defiling disease, and then pronounce them clean. After that, he is to release the live bird in the open fields.

⁸'The person to be cleansed must wash their clothes, shave off all their hair and bathe with water; then they will be ceremonially clean. After this they may come into the camp, but they must stay outside their tent for seven days. ⁹On the seventh day they must shave off all their hair; they must shave their head, their beard, their eyebrows and the rest of their hair. They must wash their clothes and bathe themselves with water, and they will be clean.

¹⁰'On the eighth day they must bring two male lambs and one ewe lamb a year old, each without defect, along with three-tenths of an ephahᵇ of the finest flour mixed with olive oil for a grain offering, and one logᶜ of oil. ¹¹The priest who pronounces them clean shall present both the one to be cleansed and their offerings before the Lord at the entrance to the tent of meeting.

¹²'Then the priest is to take one of the male lambs and offer it as a guilt offering, along with the log of oil; he shall wave them before the Lord as a wave offering. ¹³He is to slaughter the lamb in the sanctuary area where the sin offeringᵈ and the

burnt offering are slaughtered. Like the sin offering, the guilt offering belongs to the priest; it is most holy. ¹⁴The priest is to take some of the blood of the guilt offering and put it on the lobe of the right ear of the one to be cleansed, on the thumb of their right hand and on the big toe of their right foot. ¹⁵The priest shall then take some of the log of oil, pour it in the palm of his own left hand, ¹⁶dip his right forefinger into the oil in his palm, and with his finger sprinkle some of it before the Lord seven times. ¹⁷The priest is to put some of the oil remaining in his palm on the lobe of the right ear of the one to be cleansed, on the thumb of their right hand and on the big toe of their right foot, on top of the blood of the guilt offering. ¹⁸The rest of the oil in his palm the priest shall put on the head of the one to be cleansed and make atonement for them before the Lord.

¹⁹'Then the priest is to sacrifice the sin offering and make atonement for the one to be cleansed from their uncleanness. After that, the priest shall slaughter the burnt offering ²⁰and offer it on the altar, together with the grain offering, and make atonement for them, and they will be clean.

²¹'If, however, they are poor and cannot afford these, they must take one male lamb as a guilt offering to be waved to make atonement for them, together with a tenth of an ephahᵉ of the finest flour mixed with olive oil for a grain offering, a log of oil, ²²and two doves or two young pigeons, such as they can afford, one for a sin offering and the other for a burnt offering.

²³'On the eighth day they must bring them for their cleansing to the priest at the entrance to the tent of meeting, before the Lord. ²⁴The priest is to take the lamb for the guilt offering, together with the log of oil, and wave them before the Lord as a wave offering. ²⁵He shall slaughter the lamb for the guilt offering and take some of its blood and put it on the lobe of the right ear of the one to be cleansed,

---

a 3 The Hebrew word for *defiling skin disease*, traditionally translated 'leprosy', was used for various diseases affecting the skin; also in verses 7, 32, 54 and 57.

b 10 That is, probably about 5 kilograms

c 10 That is, about 0.3 litre; also in verses 12, 15, 21 and 24

d 13 Or *purification offering*; also in verses 19, 22 and 31

e 21 That is, probably about 1.6 kilograms

on the thumb of their right hand and on the big toe of their right foot. 26 The priest is to pour some of the oil into the palm of his own left hand, 27 and with his right forefinger sprinkle some of the oil from his palm seven times before the LORD. 28 Some of the oil in his palm he is to put on the same places he put the blood of the guilt offering – on the lobe of the right ear of the one to be cleansed, on the thumb of their right hand and on the big toe of their right foot. 29 The rest of the oil in his palm the priest shall put on the head of the one to be cleansed, to make atonement for them before the LORD. 30 Then he shall sacrifice the doves or the young pigeons, such as the person can afford, 31 one as a sin offering and the other as a burnt offering, together with the grain offering. In this way the priest will make atonement before the LORD on behalf of the one to be cleansed.'

32 These are the regulations for anyone who has a defiling skin disease and who cannot afford the usual offerings for their cleansing.

Cleansing from defiling moulds

33 The LORD said to Moses and Aaron, 34 'When you enter the land of Canaan, which I am giving you as your possession, and I put a spreading mould in a house in that land, 35 the owner of the house must go and tell the priest, "I have seen something that looks like a defiling mould in my house." 36 The priest is to order the house to be emptied before he goes in to examine the mould, so that nothing in the house will be pronounced unclean. After this the priest is to go in and inspect the house. 37 He is to examine the mould on the walls, and if it has greenish or reddish depressions that appear to be deeper than the surface of the wall, 38 the priest shall go out of the doorway of the house and close it up for seven days. 39 On the seventh day the priest shall return to inspect the house. If the mould has spread on the walls, 40 he is to order that the contaminated stones be torn out and thrown into an unclean place outside the town. 41 He must have all the inside walls of the

house scraped and the material that is scraped off dumped into an unclean place outside the town. 42 Then they are to take other stones to replace these and take new clay and plaster the house.

43 'If the defiling mould reappears in the house after the stones have been torn out and the house scraped and plastered, 44 the priest is to go and examine it and, if the mould has spread in the house, it is a persistent defiling mould; the house is unclean. 45 It must be torn down – its stones, timbers and all the plaster – and taken out of the town to an unclean place.

46 'Anyone who goes into the house while it is closed up will be unclean till evening. 47 Anyone who sleeps or eats in the house must wash their clothes.

48 'But if the priest comes to examine it and the mould has not spread after the house has been plastered, he shall pronounce the house clean, because the defiling mould is gone. 49 To purify the house he is to take two birds and some cedar wood, scarlet yarn and hyssop. 50 He shall kill one of the birds over fresh water in a clay pot. 51 Then he is to take the cedar wood, the hyssop, the scarlet yarn and the live bird, dip them in the blood of the dead bird and the fresh water, and sprinkle the house seven times. 52 He shall purify the house with the bird's blood, the fresh water, the live bird, the cedar wood, the hyssop and the scarlet yarn. 53 Then he is to release the live bird in the open fields outside the town. In this way he will make atonement for the house, and it will be clean.'

54 These are the regulations for any defiling skin disease, for a sore, 55 for defiling moulds in fabric or in a house, 56 and for a swelling, a rash or a shiny spot, 57 to determine when something is clean or unclean.

These are the regulations for defiling skin diseases and defiling moulds.

Discharges causing uncleanness

15 The LORD said to Moses and Aaron, 2 'Speak to the Israelites and say to them: "When any man has an unusual bodily discharge, such a discharge is unclean. 3 Whether it continues flowing from his body or is blocked, it will make him unclean. This is how his discharge will bring about uncleanness:

4 "Any bed the man with a discharge lies on will be unclean, and anything he sits on will be unclean. 5 Anyone who touches his bed must wash their clothes and bathe with water, and they will be unclean till evening. 6 Whoever sits on anything that the man with a discharge sat on must wash their clothes and bathe with water, and they will be unclean till evening.

7 "Whoever touches the man who has a discharge must wash their clothes and bathe with water, and they will be unclean till evening.

8 "If the man with the discharge spits on anyone who is clean, they must wash their clothes and bathe with water, and they will be unclean till evening.

9 "Everything the man sits on when riding will be unclean, 10 and whoever touches any of the things that were under him will be unclean till evening; whoever picks up those things must wash their clothes and bathe with water, and they will be unclean till evening.

11 "Anyone the man with a discharge touches without rinsing his hands with water must wash their clothes and bathe with water, and they will be unclean till evening.

12 "A clay pot that the man touches must be broken, and any wooden article is to be rinsed with water.

13 "When a man is cleansed from his discharge, he is to count seven days for his ceremonial cleansing; he must wash his clothes and bathe himself with fresh water, and he will be clean. 14 On the eighth day he must take two doves or two young pigeons and come before the LORD to the entrance to the tent of meeting and give them to the priest. 15 The priest is to sacrifice them, the one for a sin offering*a* and the other for a burnt offering. In this way he will make atonement before the LORD for the man because of his discharge.

16 "When a man has an emission of semen, he must bathe his whole body with water, and he will be unclean till evening. 17 Any clothing or leather that has semen on it must be washed with water, and it will be unclean till evening. 18 When a man has sexual relations with a woman and there is an emission of semen, both of them must bathe with water, and they will be unclean till evening.

19 "When a woman has her regular flow of blood, the impurity of her monthly period will last seven days, and anyone who touches her will be unclean till evening.

20 "Anything she lies on during her period will be unclean, and anything she sits on will be unclean. 21 Anyone who touches her bed will be unclean; they must wash their clothes and bathe with water, and they will be unclean till evening. 22 Anyone who touches anything she sits on will be unclean; they must wash their clothes and bathe with water, and they will be unclean till evening. 23 Whether it is the bed or anything she was sitting on, when anyone touches it, they will be unclean till evening.

24 "If a man has sexual relations with her and her monthly flow touches him, he will be unclean for seven days; any bed he lies on will be unclean.

25 "When a woman has a discharge of blood for many days at a time other than her monthly period or has a discharge that continues beyond her period, she will be unclean as long as she has the discharge, just as in the days of her period. 26 Any bed she lies on while her discharge continues will be unclean, as is her bed during her monthly period, and anything she sits on will be unclean, as during her period. 27 Anyone who touches them will be unclean; they must wash their clothes and bathe with water, and they will be unclean till evening.

28 "When she is cleansed from her discharge, she must count seven days, and after that she will be ceremonially clean. 29 On the eighth day she must take two doves or two young pigeons and bring them to the priest at the entrance to the tent of meeting. 30 The priest is to sacrifice

a 15 Or *purification offering*; also in verse 30

one for a sin offering and the other for a burnt offering. In this way he will make atonement for her before the LORD for the uncleanness of her discharge.

31 ' "You must keep the Israelites separate from things that make them unclean, so they will not die in their uncleanness for defiling my dwelling-place,*b* which is among them." '

32 These are the regulations for a man with a discharge, for anyone made unclean by an emission of semen, 33 for a woman in her monthly period, for a man or a woman with a discharge, and for a man who has sexual relations with a woman who is ceremonially unclean.

The Day of Atonement

16 The LORD spoke to Moses after the death of the two sons of Aaron who died when they approached the LORD. 2 The LORD said to Moses: 'Tell your brother Aaron that he is not to come whenever he chooses into the Most Holy Place behind the curtain in front of the atonement cover on the ark, or else he will die. For I will appear in the cloud over the atonement cover.

3 'This is how Aaron is to enter the Most Holy Place: he must first bring a young bull for a sin offering*a* and a ram for a burnt offering. 4 He is to put on the sacred linen tunic, with linen undergarments next to his body; he is to tie the linen sash round him and put on the linen turban. These are sacred garments; so he must bathe himself with water before he puts them on. 5 From the Israelite community he is to take two male goats for a sin offering and a ram for a burnt offering.

6 'Aaron is to offer the bull for his own sin offering to make atonement for himself and his household. 7 Then he is to take the two goats and present them before the LORD at the entrance to the tent of meeting. 8 He is to cast lots for the two goats — one lot for the LORD and the other for the scapegoat.*b* 9 Aaron shall bring the goat whose lot falls to the LORD and sacrifice it for a sin offering. 10 But the goat chosen by lot as the scapegoat shall be presented alive before the LORD to be used for making atonement by sending it into the wilderness as a scapegoat.

11 'Aaron shall bring the bull for his own sin offering to make atonement for himself and his household, and he is to slaughter the bull for his own sin offering. 12 He is to take a censer full of burning coals from the altar before the LORD and two handfuls of finely ground fragrant incense and take them behind the curtain. 13 He is to put the incense on the fire before the LORD, and the smoke of the incense will conceal the atonement cover above the tablets of the covenant law, so that he will not die. 14 He is to take some of the bull's blood and with his finger sprinkle it on the front of the atonement cover; then he shall sprinkle some of it with his finger seven times before the atonement cover.

15 'He shall then slaughter the goat for the sin offering for the people and take its blood behind the curtain and do with it as he did with the bull's blood: he shall sprinkle it on the atonement cover and in front of it. 16 In this way he will make atonement for the Most Holy Place because of the uncleanness and rebellion of the Israelites, whatever their sins have been. He is to do the same for the tent of meeting, which is among them in the midst of their uncleanness. 17 No one is to be in the tent of meeting from the time Aaron goes in to make atonement in the Most Holy Place until he comes out, having made atonement for himself, his household and the whole community of Israel.

18 'Then he shall come out to the altar that is before the LORD and make atonement for it. He shall take some of the bull's blood and some of the goat's blood and put it on all the horns of the altar. 19 He shall sprinkle some of the blood on it with his finger seven times to cleanse it

b 31 Or *my tabernacle*
a 3 Or *purification offering*; here and throughout this chapter

b 8 The meaning of the Hebrew for this word is uncertain; also in verses 10 and 26.

CHRIST IN ALL THE SCRIPTURES 5

The Day of Atonement

The sacrifices in the Old Testament were ways God provided for his people to atone for their sins: they would confess them, offer up something of value (usually an animal or bird) and receive mercy. The New Testament says these sacrifices are fulfilled in Jesus. God accepted them in advance – because of and as a token of his Son's sacrifice. Many of the different sacrifices are described in this way in the New Testament. The most important are the Passover lamb (Exodus 12), following which Jesus is described as *'the Lamb of God, who takes away the sin of the world'* (John 1:29), and the Day of Atonement (Leviticus 16). (In the New Testament, Hebrews 9 shows how this is an anticipation of the cross.)

In Leviticus the necessity of the cross is illustrated by the layout of the 'tent of meeting' and, later in Israel's history, the temple. At its heart was 'the Most Holy Place' (Leviticus 16:17). This was the place of God's special presence. Only the high priest could go in, and that only once a year. He could only go with a sacrifice for his own sins, and after that with one for the sins of the people, *'to make atonement'* (v. 17). The picture is clear. All humans are sinners. None can survive the presence of God, not even the high priest. Sacrifice was the only remedy for sin.

Jesus fulfilled this in two ways. He was both the high priest and the sacrifice. He offered himself. As we read about this solemn annual ritual, we see Jesus foreshadowed. It's as though we can see him out of the corner of our eye as we focus on Aaron, or the high priests who succeeded him. But there is one vital difference. The high priest had to offer sacrifice for his own sins first (vv. 11–14), *'so that he will not die'* (v. 13). Jesus committed no sin. He had no need to sacrifice for himself. He sacrificed himself for us.

Jesus is the great high priest, because he is the only one who could go into God's presence for us. That is what priests do. They are intermediaries between God and us. Because this ceremony had to be repeated every year, there was always a vital role for the priests to fulfil. But because Jesus did this for us 'once for all', he has opened the way into God's presence for all who have received forgiveness through his sacrifice. So the New Testament never calls Christian leaders 'priests'. (The denominations who still use the term use it of 'pastors').The curtain blocking the way to the Most Holy Place is gone. Jesus was also the great and final sacrifice. The death of animals could never atone for sin. It was a temporary measure, only effective because of the sacrifice he was to make. Every time we read the Old Testament passages about sacrifices for sin, we are to see Jesus out of the corner of our eye.

Graham Cray

 Exodus 32:1–5   Numbers 20:1–13

and consecrate it from the uncleanness of the Israelites.

20 'When Aaron has finished making atonement for the Most Holy Place, the tent of meeting and the altar, he shall bring forward the live goat. 21 He is to lay both hands on the head of the live goat and confess over it all the wickedness and rebellion of the Israelites – all their sins – and put them on the goat's head. He shall send the goat away into the wilderness in the care of someone appointed for the task. 22 The goat will carry on itself all their sins to a remote place; and the man shall release it in the wilderness.

23 'Then Aaron is to go into the tent of meeting and take off the linen garments he put on before he entered the Most Holy Place, and he is to leave them there. 24 He shall bathe himself with water in the sanctuary area and put on his ordinary garments. Then he shall come out and sacrifice the burnt offering for himself and the burnt offering for the people, to make atonement for himself and for the people. 25 He shall also burn the fat of the sin offering on the altar.

26 'The man who releases the goat as a scapegoat must wash his clothes and bathe himself with water; afterwards he may come into the camp. 27 The bull and the goat for the sin offerings, whose blood was brought into the Most Holy Place to make atonement, must be taken outside the camp; their hides, flesh and intestines are to be burned. 28 The man who burns them must wash his clothes and bathe himself with water; afterwards he may come into the camp.

29 'This is to be a lasting ordinance for you: on the tenth day of the seventh month you must deny yourselves[c] and not do any work – whether native-born or a foreigner residing among you – 30 because on this day atonement will be made for you, to cleanse you. Then, before the LORD, you will be clean from all your sins. 31 It is a day of sabbath rest, and you must deny yourselves; it is a lasting ordinance. 32 The priest who is anointed and ordained to

succeed his father as high priest is to make atonement. He is to put on the sacred linen garments 33 and make atonement for the Most Holy Place, for the tent of meeting and the altar, and for the priests and all the members of the community.

34 'This is to be a lasting ordinance for you: atonement is to be made once a year for all the sins of the Israelites.'

And it was done, as the LORD commanded Moses.

Eating blood forbidden

17 The LORD said to Moses, 2 'Speak to Aaron and his sons and to all the Israelites and say to them: "This is what the LORD has commanded: 3 any Israelite who sacrifices an ox,[a] a lamb or a goat in the camp or outside it 4 instead of bringing it to the entrance to the tent of meeting to present it as an offering to the LORD in front of the tabernacle of the LORD – that person shall be considered guilty of bloodshed; they have shed blood and must be cut off from their people. 5 This is so that the Israelites will bring to the LORD the sacrifices they are now making in the open fields. They must bring them to the priest, that is, to the LORD, at the entrance to the tent of meeting and sacrifice them as fellowship offerings. 6 The priest is to splash the blood against the altar of the LORD at the entrance to the tent of meeting and burn the fat as an aroma pleasing to the LORD. 7 They must no longer offer any of their sacrifices to the goat idols[b] to whom they prostitute themselves. This is to be a lasting ordinance for them and for the generations to come."

8 'Say to them: "Any Israelite or any foreigner residing among them who offers a burnt offering or sacrifice 9 and does not bring it to the entrance to the tent of meeting to sacrifice it to the LORD must be cut off from the people of Israel.

10 ' "I will set my face against any Israelite or any foreigner residing among them who eats blood, and I will cut them off

---

c 29 Or *must fast;* also in verse 31

a 3 The Hebrew word can include both male and female.
b 7 Or *the demons*

from the people. ¹¹For the life of a creature is in the blood, and I have given it to you to make atonement for yourselves on the altar; it is the blood that makes atonement for one's life.ᶜ ¹²Therefore I say to the Israelites, 'None of you may eat blood, nor may any foreigner residing among you eat blood.'

¹³'Any Israelite or any foreigner residing among you who hunts any animal or bird that may be eaten must drain out the blood and cover it with earth, ¹⁴because the life of every creature is its blood. That is why I have said to the Israelites, 'You must not eat the blood of any creature, because the life of every creature is its blood; anyone who eats it must be cut off.'

¹⁵'Anyone, whether native-born or foreigner, who eats anything found dead or torn by wild animals must wash their clothes and bathe with water, and they will be ceremonially unclean till evening; then they will be clean. ¹⁶But if they do not wash their clothes and bathe themselves, they will be held responsible.'"

Unlawful sexual relations

18 The LORD said to Moses, ²'Speak to the Israelites and say to them: "I am the LORD your God. ³You must not do as they do in Egypt, where you used to live, and you must not do as they do in the land of Canaan, where I am bringing you. Do not follow their practices. ⁴You must obey my laws and be careful to follow my decrees. I am the LORD your God. ⁵Keep my decrees and laws, for the person who obeys them will live by them. I am the LORD.

⁶'"No one is to approach any close relative to have sexual relations. I am the LORD.

⁷'"Do not dishonour your father by having sexual relations with your mother. She is your mother; do not have relations with her.

⁸'"Do not have sexual relations with your father's wife; that would dishonour your father.

⁹'"Do not have sexual relations with your sister, either your father's daughter or your mother's daughter, whether she was born in the same home or elsewhere.

¹⁰'"Do not have sexual relations with your son's daughter or your daughter's daughter; that would dishonour you.

¹¹'"Do not have sexual relations with the daughter of your father's wife, born to your father; she is your sister.

¹²'"Do not have sexual relations with your father's sister; she is your father's close relative.

¹³'"Do not have sexual relations with your mother's sister, because she is your mother's close relative.

¹⁴'"Do not dishonour your father's brother by approaching his wife to have sexual relations; she is your aunt.

¹⁵'"Do not have sexual relations with your daughter-in-law. She is your son's wife; do not have relations with her.

¹⁶'"Do not have sexual relations with your brother's wife; that would dishonour your brother.

¹⁷'"Do not have sexual relations with both a woman and her daughter. Do not have sexual relations with either her son's daughter or her daughter's daughter; they are her close relatives. That is wickedness.

¹⁸'"Do not take your wife's sister as a rival wife and have sexual relations with her while your wife is living.

¹⁹'"Do not approach a woman to have sexual relations during the uncleanness of her monthly period.

²⁰'"Do not have sexual relations with your neighbour's wife and defile yourself with her.

²¹'"Do not give any of your children to be sacrificed to Molek, for you must not profane the name of your God. I am the LORD.

²²'"Do not have sexual relations with a man as one does with a woman; that is detestable.

²³'"Do not have sexual relations with an animal and defile yourself with it. A woman must not present herself to an animal to have sexual relations with it; that is a perversion.

²⁴'"Do not defile yourselves in any of these ways, because this is how the

---

ᶜ 11 Or *atonement by the life in the blood*

nations that I am going to drive out before you became defiled. 25 Even the land was defiled; so I punished it for its sin, and the land vomited out its inhabitants. 26 But you must keep my decrees and my laws. The native-born and the foreigners residing among you must not do any of these detestable things, 27 for all these things were done by the people who lived in the land before you, and the land became defiled. 28 And if you defile the land, it will vomit you out as it vomited out the nations that were before you.

29 ' "Everyone who does any of these detestable things – such persons must be cut off from their people. 30 Keep my requirements and do not follow any of the detestable customs that were practised before you came and do not defile yourselves with them. I am the LORD your God." '

Various laws

19 The LORD said to Moses, 2 'Speak to the entire assembly of Israel and say to them: "Be holy because I, the LORD your God, am holy.

3 ' "Each of you must respect your mother and father, and you must observe my Sabbaths. I am the LORD your God.

4 ' "Do not turn to idols or make metal gods for yourselves. I am the LORD your God.

5 ' "When you sacrifice a fellowship offering to the LORD, sacrifice it in such a way that it will be accepted on your behalf. 6 It shall be eaten on the day you sacrifice it or on the next day; anything left over until the third day must be burned. 7 If any of it is eaten on the third day, it is impure and will not be accepted. 8 Whoever eats it will be held responsible because they have desecrated what is holy to the LORD; they must be cut off from their people.

9 ' "When you reap the harvest of your land, do not reap to the very edges of your field or gather the gleanings of your harvest. 10 Do not go over your vineyard a second time or pick up the grapes that have fallen. Leave them for the poor and the foreigner. I am the LORD your God.

11 ' "Do not steal.

' "Do not lie.

' "Do not deceive one another.

12 ' "Do not swear falsely by my name and so profane the name of your God. I am the LORD.

13 ' "Do not defraud or rob your neighbour.

' "Do not hold back the wages of a hired worker overnight.

14 ' "Do not curse the deaf or put a stumbling-block in front of the blind, but fear your God. I am the LORD.

15 ' "Do not pervert justice; do not show partiality to the poor or favouritism to the great, but judge your neighbour fairly.

16 ' "Do not go about spreading slander among your people.

' "Do not do anything that endangers your neighbour's life. I am the LORD.

17 ' "Do not hate a fellow Israelite in your heart. Rebuke your neighbour frankly so that you will not share in their guilt.

18 ' "Do not seek revenge or bear a grudge against anyone among your people, but love your neighbour as yourself. I am the LORD.

19 ' "Keep my decrees.

' "Do not mate different kinds of animals.

' "Do not plant your field with two kinds of seed.

' "Do not wear clothing woven of two kinds of material.

20 ' "If a man sleeps with a female slave who is promised to another man but who has not been ransomed or given her freedom, there must be due punishment. *a* Yet they are not to be put to death, because she had not been freed. 21 The man, however, must bring a ram to the entrance to the tent of meeting for a guilt offering to the LORD. 22 With the ram of the guilt offering the priest is to make atonement for him before the LORD for the sin he has committed, and his sin will be forgiven.

23 ' "When you enter the land and plant any kind of fruit tree, regard its fruit as forbidden. *b* For three years you are to consider it forbidden; *b* it must not be eaten. 24 In the fourth year all its fruit will be holy,

---

a 20 Or *be an enquiry*

b 23 Hebrew *uncircumcised*

an offering of praise to the LORD. 25 But in the fifth year you may eat its fruit. In this way your harvest will be increased. I am the LORD your God.

26 ' "Do not eat any meat with the blood still in it.

' "Do not practise divination or seek omens.

27 ' "Do not cut the hair at the sides of your head or clip off the edges of your beard.

28 ' "Do not cut your bodies for the dead or put tattoo marks on yourselves. I am the LORD.

29 ' "Do not degrade your daughter by making her a prostitute, or the land will turn to prostitution and be filled with wickedness.

30 ' "Observe my Sabbaths and have reverence for my sanctuary. I am the LORD.

31 ' "Do not turn to mediums or seek out spiritists, for you will be defiled by them. I am the LORD your God.

32 ' "Stand up in the presence of the aged, show respect for the elderly and revere your God. I am the LORD.

33 ' "When a foreigner resides among you in your land, do not ill-treat them. 34 The foreigner residing among you must be treated as your native-born. Love them as yourself, for you were foreigners in Egypt. I am the LORD your God.

35 ' "Do not use dishonest standards when measuring length, weight or quantity. 36 Use honest scales and honest weights, an honest ephah[c] and an honest hin.[d] I am the LORD your God, who brought you out of Egypt.

37 ' "Keep all my decrees and all my laws and follow them. I am the LORD." '

Punishments for sin

20 The LORD said to Moses, 2 'Say to the Israelites: "Any Israelite or any foreigner residing in Israel who sacrifices any of his children to Molek is to be put to death. The members of the community are to stone him. 3 I myself

---

will set my face against him and will cut him off from his people; for by sacrificing his children to Molek, he has defiled my sanctuary and profaned my holy name. 4 If the members of the community close their eyes when that man sacrifices one of his children to Molek and if they fail to put him to death, 5 I myself will set my face against him and his family and will cut them off from their people together with all who follow him in prostituting themselves to Molek.

FIVE STRANGEST LAWS

NO MIXED FIBRES
Leviticus 19:19
DON'T USE A DONKEY AND AN OX TOGETHER
Deuteronomy 22:10
NEVER EAT FAT
Leviticus 3:17
CAREFUL HOW YOU CUT YOUR HAIR
Leviticus 19:27
DON'T BOIL A KID IN ITS MOTHER'S MILK
Deuteronomy 14:21

6 ' "I will set my face against anyone who turns to mediums and spiritists to prostitute themselves by following them, and I will cut them off from their people.

7 ' "Consecrate yourselves and be holy, because I am the LORD your God. 8 Keep my decrees and follow them. I am the LORD, who makes you holy.

9 ' "Anyone who curses their father or mother is to be put to death. Because they have cursed their father or mother, their blood will be on their own head.

10 ' "If a man commits adultery with another man's wife – with the wife of his

neighbour – both the adulterer and the adulteress are to be put to death.

11 '"If a man has sexual relations with his father's wife, he has dishonoured his father. Both the man and the woman are to be put to death; their blood will be on their own heads.

12 '"If a man has sexual relations with his daughter-in-law, both of them are to be put to death. What they have done is a perversion; their blood will be on their own heads.

13 '"If a man has sexual relations with a man as one does with a woman, both of them have done what is detestable. They are to be put to death; their blood will be on their own heads.

14 '"If a man marries both a woman and her mother, it is wicked. Both he and they must be burned in the fire, so that no wickedness will be among you.

15 '"If a man has sexual relations with an animal, he is to be put to death, and you must kill the animal.

16 '"If a woman approaches an animal to have sexual relations with it, kill both the woman and the animal. They are to be put to death; their blood will be on their own heads.

17 '"If a man marries his sister, the daughter of either his father or his mother, and they have sexual relations, it is a disgrace. They are to be publicly removed from their people. He has dishonoured his sister and will be held responsible.

18 '"If a man has sexual relations with a woman during her monthly period, he has exposed the source of her flow, and she has also uncovered it. Both of them are to be cut off from their people.

19 '"Do not have sexual relations with the sister of either your mother or your father, for that would dishonour a close relative; both of you would be held responsible.

20 '"If a man has sexual relations with his aunt, he has dishonoured his uncle. They will be held responsible; they will die childless.

21 '"If a man marries his brother's wife, it is an act of impurity; he has dishonoured his brother. They will be childless.

22 '"Keep all my decrees and laws and follow them, so that the land where I am bringing you to live may not vomit you out. 23 You must not live according to the customs of the nations I am going to drive out before you. Because they did all these things, I abhorred them. 24 But I said to you, 'You will possess their land; I will give it to you as an inheritance, a land flowing with milk and honey.' I am the LORD your God, who has set you apart from the nations.

25 '"You must therefore make a distinction between clean and unclean animals and between unclean and clean birds. Do not defile yourselves by any animal or bird or anything that moves along the ground – those that I have set apart as unclean for you. 26 You are to be holy to me because I, the LORD, am holy, and I have set you apart from the nations to be my own.

27 '"A man or woman who is a medium or spiritist among you must be put to death. You are to stone them; their blood will be on their own heads."'

Rules for priests

21 The LORD said to Moses, 'Speak to the priests, the sons of Aaron, and say to them: "A priest must not make himself ceremonially unclean for any of his people who die, 2 except for a close relative, such as his mother or father, his son or daughter, his brother, 3 or an unmarried sister who is dependent on him since she has no husband – for her he may make himself unclean. 4 He must not make himself unclean for people related to him by marriage,ᵃ and so defile himself.

5 '"Priests must not shave their heads or shave off the edges of their beards or cut their bodies. 6 They must be holy to their God and must not profane the name of their God. Because they present the food offerings to the LORD, the food of their God, they are to be holy.

7 '"They must not marry women defiled by prostitution or divorced from their husbands, because priests are holy to

---

a 4 Or *unclean as a leader among his people*

their God. ⁸Regard them as holy, because they offer up the food of your God. Consider them holy, because I the LORD am holy – I who make you holy.

⁹ "If a priest's daughter defiles herself by becoming a prostitute, she disgraces her father; she must be burned in the fire.

¹⁰ "The high priest, the one among his brothers who has had the anointing oil poured on his head and who has been ordained to wear the priestly garments, must not let his hair become unkempt*ᵇ* or tear his clothes. ¹¹He must not enter a place where there is a dead body. He must not make himself unclean, even for his father or mother, ¹²nor leave the sanctuary of his God or desecrate it, because he has been dedicated by the anointing oil of his God. I am the LORD.

¹³ "The woman he marries must be a virgin. ¹⁴He must not marry a widow, a divorced woman, or a woman defiled by prostitution, but only a virgin from his own people, ¹⁵so that he will not defile his offspring among his people. I am the LORD, who makes him holy.' "

¹⁶The LORD said to Moses, ¹⁷'Say to Aaron: "For the generations to come none of your descendants who has a defect may come near to offer the food of his God. ¹⁸No man who has any defect may come near: no man who is blind or lame, disfigured or deformed; ¹⁹no man with a crippled foot or hand, ²⁰or who is a hunchback or a dwarf, or who has any eye defect, or who has festering or running sores or damaged testicles. ²¹No descendant of Aaron the priest who has any defect is to come near to present the food offerings to the LORD. He has a defect; he must not come near to offer the food of his God. ²²He may eat the most holy food of his God, as well as the holy food; ²³yet because of his defect, he must not go near the curtain or approach the altar, and so desecrate my sanctuary. I am the LORD, who makes them holy."'

²⁴So Moses told this to Aaron and his sons and to all the Israelites.

22 The LORD said to Moses, ²'Tell Aaron and his sons to treat with respect the sacred offerings the Israelites consecrate to me, so that they will not profane my holy name. I am the LORD.

³'Say to them: "For the generations to come, if any of your descendants is ceremonially unclean and yet comes near the sacred offerings that the Israelites consecrate to the LORD, that person must be cut off from my presence. I am the LORD.

⁴ "If a descendant of Aaron has a defiling skin disease*ᵃ* or a bodily discharge, he may not eat the sacred offerings until he is cleansed. He will also be unclean if he touches something defiled by a corpse or by anyone who has an emission of semen, ⁵or if he touches any crawling thing that makes him unclean, or any person who makes him unclean, whatever the uncleanness may be. ⁶The one who touches any such thing will be unclean till evening. He must not eat any of the sacred offerings unless he has bathed himself with water. ⁷When the sun goes down, he will be clean, and after that he may eat the sacred offerings, for they are his food. ⁸He must not eat anything found dead or torn by wild animals, and so become unclean through it. I am the LORD.

⁹ "The priests are to perform my service in such a way that they do not become guilty and die for treating it with contempt. I am the LORD, who makes them holy.

¹⁰ "No one outside a priest's family may eat the sacred offering, nor may the guest of a priest or his hired worker eat it. ¹¹But if a priest buys a slave with money, or if slaves are born in his household, they may eat his food. ¹²If a priest's daughter marries anyone other than a priest, she may not eat any of the sacred contributions. ¹³But if a priest's daughter becomes a widow or is divorced, yet has no children, and she returns to live in her father's household as in her youth, she may eat

---

ᵇ 10 Or *not uncover his head*

ᵃ 4 The Hebrew word for *defiling skin disease*, traditionally translated 'leprosy', was used for various diseases affecting the skin.

her father's food. No unauthorised person, however, may eat it.

14 ' "Anyone who eats a sacred offering by mistake must make restitution to the priest for the offering and add a fifth of the value to it. 15 The priests must not desecrate the sacred offerings the Israelites present to the Lord 16 by allowing them to eat the sacred offerings and so bring upon them guilt requiring payment. I am the Lord, who makes them holy." '

Unacceptable sacrifices

17 The Lord said to Moses, 18 'Speak to Aaron and his sons and to all the Israelites and say to them: "If any of you – whether an Israelite or a foreigner residing in Israel – presents a gift for a burnt offering to the Lord, either to fulfil a vow or as a freewill offering, 19 you must present a male without defect from the cattle, sheep or goats in order that it may be accepted on your behalf. 20 Do not bring anything with a defect, because it will not be accepted on your behalf. 21 When anyone brings from the herd or flock a fellowship offering to the Lord to fulfil a special vow or as a freewill offering, it must be without defect or blemish to be acceptable. 22 Do not offer to the Lord the blind, the injured or the maimed, or anything with warts or festering or running sores. Do not place any of these on the altar as a food offering presented to the Lord. 23 You may, however, present as a freewill offering an ox *b* or a sheep that is deformed or stunted, but it will not be accepted in fulfilment of a vow. 24 You must not offer to the Lord an animal whose testicles are bruised, crushed, torn or cut. You must not do this in your own land, 25 and you must not accept such animals from the hand of a foreigner and offer them as the food of your God. They will not be accepted on your behalf, because they are deformed and have defects." '

26 The Lord said to Moses, 27 'When a calf, a lamb or a goat is born, it is to remain with its mother for seven days. From

the eighth day on, it will be acceptable as a food offering presented to the Lord. 28 Do not slaughter a cow or a sheep and its young on the same day.

29 'When you sacrifice a thank-offering to the Lord, sacrifice it in such a way that it will be accepted on your behalf. 30 It must be eaten that same day; leave none of it till morning. I am the Lord.

31 'Keep my commands and follow them. I am the Lord. 32 Do not profane my holy name, for I must be acknowledged as holy by the Israelites. I am the Lord, who made you holy 33 and who brought you out of Egypt to be your God. I am the Lord.'

The appointed festivals

23 The Lord said to Moses, 2 'Speak to the Israelites and say to them: "These are my appointed festivals, the appointed festivals of the Lord, which you are to proclaim as sacred assemblies.

The Sabbath

3 ' "There are six days when you may work, but the seventh day is a day of sabbath rest, a day of sacred assembly. You are not to do any work; wherever you live, it is a sabbath to the Lord.

The Passover and Unleavened Bread

4 ' "These are the Lord's appointed festivals, the sacred assemblies you are to proclaim at their appointed times: 5 the Lord's Passover begins at twilight on the fourteenth day of the first month. 6 On the fifteenth day of that month the Lord's Festival of Unleavened Bread begins; for seven days you must eat bread made without yeast. 7 On the first day hold a sacred assembly and do not do any of your ordinary work. 8 For seven days present a food offering to the Lord. And on the seventh day hold a sacred assembly and do not do any of your ordinary work." '

Offering the Firstfruits

9 The Lord said to Moses, 10 'Speak to the Israelites and say to them: "When you enter the land I am going to give you and you reap its harvest, bring to the priest a sheaf of the first grain you harvest. 11 He

---

b 23 The Hebrew word can include both male and female.

is to wave the sheaf before the LORD so it will be accepted on your behalf; the priest is to wave it on the day after the Sabbath. 12 On the day you wave the sheaf, you must sacrifice as a burnt offering to the LORD a lamb a year old without defect, 13 together with its grain offering of one fifth of an ephah*a* of the finest flour mixed with olive oil – a food offering presented to the LORD, a pleasing aroma – and its drink offering of a quarter of a hin*b* of wine. 14 You must not eat any bread, or roasted or new grain, until the very day you bring this offering to your God. This is to be a lasting ordinance for the generations to come, wherever you live.

The Festival of Weeks

15 ' "From the day after the Sabbath, the day you brought the sheaf of the wave offering, count seven full weeks. 16 Count fifty days up to the day after the seventh Sabbath, and then present an offering of new grain to the LORD. 17 From wherever you live, bring two loaves made of one fifth of an ephah of the finest flour, baked with yeast, as a wave offering of firstfruits to the LORD. 18 Present with this bread seven male lambs, each a year old and without defect, one young bull and two rams. They will be a burnt offering to the LORD, together with their grain offerings and drink offerings – a food offering, an aroma pleasing to the LORD. 19 Then sacrifice one male goat for a sin offering*c* and two lambs, each a year old, for a fellowship offering. 20 The priest is to wave the two lambs before the LORD as a wave offering, together with the bread of the firstfruits. They are a sacred offering to the LORD for the priest. 21 On that same day you are to proclaim a sacred assembly and not do any ordinary work. This is to be a lasting ordinance for the generations to come, wherever you live.

22 ' "When you reap the harvest of your land, do not reap to the very edges of your field or gather the gleanings of your

harvest. Leave them for the poor and for the foreigner residing among you. I am the LORD your God." '

The Festival of Trumpets

23 The LORD said to Moses, 24 'Say to the Israelites: "On the first day of the seventh month you are to have a day of sabbath rest, a sacred assembly commemorated with trumpet blasts. 25 Do not do any of your ordinary work, but present a food offering to the LORD." '

The Day of Atonement

26 The LORD said to Moses, 27 'The tenth day of this seventh month is the Day of Atonement. Hold a sacred assembly and deny yourselves,*d* and present a food offering to the LORD. 28 Do not do any work on that day, because it is the Day of Atonement, when atonement is made for you before the LORD your God. 29 Those who do not deny themselves on that day must be cut off from their people. 30 I will destroy from among their people anyone who does any work on that day. 31 You shall do no work at all. This is to be a lasting ordinance for the generations to come, wherever you live. 32 It is a day of sabbath rest for you, and you must deny yourselves. From the evening of the ninth day of the month until the following evening you are to observe your sabbath.'

The Festival of Tabernacles

33 The LORD said to Moses, 34 'Say to the Israelites: "On the fifteenth day of the seventh month the LORD's Festival of Tabernacles begins, and it lasts for seven days. 35 The first day is a sacred assembly; do not do any of your ordinary work. 36 For seven days present food offerings to the LORD, and on the eighth day hold a sacred assembly and present a food offering to the LORD. It is the closing special assembly; do not do any of your ordinary work.

37 (' "These are the LORD's appointed festivals, which you are to proclaim as sacred assemblies for bringing food offerings to the LORD – the burnt offerings

---

a 13 That is, probably about 3.2 kilograms; also in verse 17
b 13 That is, about 1 litre
c 19 Or *purification offering*

d 27 Or *and fast*; similarly in verses 29 and 32

and grain offerings, sacrifices and drink offerings required for each day. **38**These offerings are in addition to those for the LORD's Sabbaths and*e* in addition to your gifts and whatever you have vowed and all the freewill offerings you give to the LORD.)

39 ' "So beginning with the fifteenth day of the seventh month, after you have gathered the crops of the land, celebrate the festival to the LORD for seven days; the first day is a day of sabbath rest, and the eighth day also is a day of sabbath rest. **40**On the first day you are to take branches from luxuriant trees – from palms, willows and other leafy trees – and rejoice before the LORD your God for seven days. **41** Celebrate this as a festival to the LORD for seven days each year. This is to be a lasting ordinance for the generations to come; celebrate it in the seventh month. **42** Live in temporary shelters for seven days: all native-born Israelites are to live in such shelters **43**so that your descendants will know that I made the Israelites live in temporary shelters when I brought them out of Egypt. I am the LORD your God." '

44So Moses announced to the Israelites the appointed festivals of the LORD.

Olive oil and bread set before the LORD

24 The LORD said to Moses, **2** 'Command the Israelites to bring you clear oil of pressed olives for the light so that the lamps may be kept burning continually. **3**Outside the curtain that shields the ark of the covenant law in the tent of meeting, Aaron is to tend the lamps before the LORD from evening till morning, continually. This is to be a lasting ordinance for the generations to come. **4**The lamps on the pure gold lampstand before the LORD must be tended continually.

5 'Take the finest flour and bake twelve loaves of bread, using one fifth of an ephah*a* for each loaf. **6**Arrange them in two piles, six in each pile, on the table of pure gold before the LORD. **7**By each pile put some pure incense as a memorial*b* portion to represent the bread and to be a food offering presented to the LORD. **8**This bread is to be set out before the LORD regularly, Sabbath after Sabbath, on behalf of the Israelites, as a lasting covenant. **9**It belongs to Aaron and his sons, who are to eat it in the sanctuary area, because it is a most holy part of their perpetual share of the food offerings presented to the LORD.'

A blasphemer put to death

10Now the son of an Israelite mother and an Egyptian father went out among the Israelites, and a fight broke out in the camp between him and an Israelite. **11**The son of the Israelite woman used the Name blasphemously with a curse; so they brought him to Moses. (His mother's name was Shelomith, the daughter of Dibri the Danite.) **12**They put him in custody until the will of the LORD should be made clear to them.

13Then the LORD said to Moses: **14**'Take the blasphemer outside the camp. All those who heard him are to lay their hands on his head, and the entire assembly is to stone him. **15**Say to the Israelites: "Anyone who curses their God will be held responsible; **16**anyone who uses the name of the LORD blasphemously is to be put to death. The entire assembly must stone them. Whether foreigner or native-born, when they use the Name blasphemously they are to be put to death.

17 ' "Anyone who takes the life of a human being is to be put to death. **18**Anyone who takes the life of someone's animal must make restitution – life for life. **19**Anyone who injures their neighbour is to be injured in the same manner: **20**fracture for fracture, eye for eye, tooth for tooth. The one who has inflicted the injury must suffer the same injury. **21**Whoever kills an animal must make restitution, but whoever kills a human being is to be put to death. **22**You are to have the same law for

---

e 38 Or *These festivals are in addition to the* LORD's
Sabbaths, and these offerings are
a 5 That is, probably about 3.2 kilograms

b 7 Or *representative*

the foreigner and the native-born. I am the LORD your God.'"

23 Then Moses spoke to the Israelites, and they took the blasphemer outside the camp and stoned him. The Israelites did as the LORD commanded Moses.

The Sabbath Year

25 The LORD said to Moses at Mount Sinai, 2 'Speak to the Israelites and say to them: "When you enter the land I am going to give you, the land itself must observe a sabbath to the LORD. 3 For six years sow your fields, and for six years prune your vineyards and gather their crops. 4 But in the seventh year the land is to have a year of sabbath rest, a sabbath to the LORD. Do not sow your fields or prune your vineyards. 5 Do not reap what grows of itself or harvest the grapes of your untended vines. The land is to have a year of rest. 6 Whatever the land yields during the sabbath year will be food for you – for yourself, your male and female servants, and the hired worker and temporary resident who live among you, 7 as well as for your livestock and the wild animals in your land. Whatever the land produces may be eaten.

The Year of Jubilee

8 ' "Count seven sabbath years – seven times seven years – so that the seven sabbath years amount to a period of forty-nine years. 9 Then sound the trumpet everywhere on the tenth day of the seventh month; on the Day of Atonement sound the trumpet throughout your land. 10 Consecrate the fiftieth year and proclaim liberty throughout the land to all its inhabitants. It shall be a jubilee for you; each of you is to return to your family property and to your own clan. 11 The fiftieth year shall be a jubilee for you; do not sow and do not reap what grows of itself or harvest the untended vines. 12 For it is a jubilee and is to be holy for you; eat only what is taken directly from the fields.

13 ' "In this Year of Jubilee everyone is to return to their own property.

14 ' "If you sell land to any of your own people or buy land from them, do not take advantage of each other. 15 You are to buy from your own people on the basis of the number of years since the Jubilee. And they are to sell to you on the basis of the number of years left for harvesting crops. 16 When the years are many, you are to increase the price, and when the years are few, you are to decrease the price, because what is really being sold to you is the number of crops. 17 Do not take advantage of each other, but fear your God. I am the LORD your God.

18 ' "Follow my decrees and be careful to obey my laws, and you will live safely in the land. 19 Then the land will yield its fruit, and you will eat your fill and live there in safety. 20 You may ask, 'What will we eat in the seventh year if we do not plant or harvest our crops?' 21 I will send you such a blessing in the sixth year that the land will yield enough for three years. 22 While you plant during the eighth year, you will eat from the old crop and will continue to eat from it until the harvest of the ninth year comes in.

23 ' "The land must not be sold permanently, because the land is mine and you reside in my land as foreigners and strangers. 24 Throughout the land that you hold as a possession, you must provide for the redemption of the land.

25 ' "If one of your fellow Israelites becomes poor and sells some of their property, their nearest relative is to come and redeem what they have sold. 26 If, however, there is no one to redeem it for them but later on they prosper and acquire sufficient means to redeem it themselves, 27 they are to determine the value for the years since they sold it and refund the balance to the one to whom they sold it; they can then go back to their own property. 28 But if they do not acquire the means to repay, what was sold will remain in the possession of the buyer until the Year of Jubilee. It will be returned in the Jubilee, and they can then go back to their property.

29 ' "Anyone who sells a house in a walled city retains the right of redemption a full year after its sale. During that time the seller may redeem it. 30 If it is not redeemed before a full year has passed, the house in the walled city shall belong

permanently to the buyer and the buyer's descendants. It is not to be returned in the Jubilee. ³¹ But houses in villages without walls round them are to be considered as belonging to the open country. They can be redeemed, and they are to be returned in the Jubilee.

³² "The Levites always have the right to redeem their houses in the Levitical towns, which they possess. ³³ So the property of the Levites is redeemable – that is, a house sold in any town they hold – and is to be returned in the Jubilee, because the houses in the towns of the Levites are their property among the Israelites. ³⁴ But the pasture-land belonging to their towns must not be sold; it is their permanent possession.

JUSTICE AND MERCY 2

JUBILEE YEARS

The year of jubilee described in Leviticus 25 was one of the things that made God's people different. Every week the Israelites had to take a day off and every seventh year was a whole year off, when they let the earth rest and recover so that they could renew their relationship with God and each other. But then every fifty years there came another year off! It was a once-in-a-lifetime extra year of celebration, when God healed his people and brought about restoration. It was the 'year of the Lord's favour' and was a time when God demonstrated what mattered to him and transformed society.

At the heart of the jubilee year was restoration – restoration of freedom, family, property and wealth. The jubilee year gave everybody a fresh start so that no one would grow up poor and be defined by the wealth of their parents, rather than their own ability, skills and work. If you had become so poor that you had sold yourself into slavery, you were set free; if you had got into debt, your debts were cancelled; if you had become so desperate that you had sold your land, you received it back. God did this so that there would not be a constant cycle of the rich getting richer and the poor getting poorer. He wanted every generation to be free and have a chance to fulfil their destiny. Mary sang about this restoration when she was pregnant with Jesus in Luke 1:51–54, and it was how Jesus described his mission in Luke 4:18–19. If we are to follow Jesus, then we must take action for the last, the least and the lost.

When God led his people into the Promised Land and set up his new society to demonstrate his presence and character to the world, he did not want poverty to exist. If we are his people and if we are seeking to show the promise of God to the world, then we will fight poverty and injustice wherever we find it. Whether it means being friends with the person who is being bullied or supporting poor communities across the world, the work of the kingdom of God always seeks justice and brings good news for the poor. This is the time of God's favour for the last, the least and the lost. Let's be that good news in the world.

David Westlake

 Genesis 3   Proverbs 31:8–9

35 ' "If any of your fellow Israelites become poor and are unable to support themselves among you, help them as you would a foreigner and stranger, so that they can continue to live among you. 36 Do not take interest or any profit from them, but fear your God, so that they may continue to live among you. 37 You must not lend them money at interest or sell them food at a profit. 38 I am the LORD your God, who brought you out of Egypt to give you the land of Canaan and to be your God.

39 ' "If any of your fellow Israelites become poor and sell themselves to you, do not make them work as slaves. 40 They are to be treated as hired workers or temporary residents among you; they are to work for you until the Year of Jubilee. 41 Then they and their children are to be released, and they will go back to their own clans and to the property of their ancestors. 42 Because the Israelites are my servants, whom I brought out of Egypt, they must not be sold as slaves. 43 Do not rule over them ruthlessly, but fear your God.

44 ' "Your male and female slaves are to come from the nations around you; from them you may buy slaves. 45 You may also buy some of the temporary residents living among you and members of their clans born in your country, and they will become your property. 46 You can bequeath them to your children as inherited property and can make them slaves for life, but you must not rule over your fellow Israelites ruthlessly.

47 ' "If a foreigner residing among you becomes rich and any of your fellow Israelites become poor and sell themselves to the foreigner or to a member of the foreigner's clan, 48 they retain the right of redemption after they have sold themselves. One of their relatives may redeem them: 49 an uncle or a cousin or any blood-relative in their clan may redeem them. Or if they prosper, they may redeem themselves. 50 They and their buyer are to count the time from the year they sold themselves up to the Year of Jubilee. The price for their release is to be based on the rate paid to a hired worker for that

number of years. 51 If many years remain, they must pay for their redemption a larger share of the price paid for them. 52 If only a few years remain until the Year of Jubilee, they are to compute that and pay for their redemption accordingly. 53 They are to be treated as workers hired from year to year; you must see to it that those to whom they owe service do not rule over them ruthlessly.

54 ' "Even if someone is not redeemed in any of these ways, they and their children are to be released in the Year of Jubilee, 55 for the Israelites belong to me as servants. They are my servants, whom I brought out of Egypt. I am the LORD your God.

Reward for obedience

26 ' "Do not make idols or set up an image or a sacred stone for yourselves, and do not place a carved stone in your land to bow down before it. I am the LORD your God.

2 ' "Observe my Sabbaths and have reverence for my sanctuary. I am the LORD.

3 ' "If you follow my decrees and are careful to obey my commands, 4 I will send you rain in its season, and the ground will yield its crops and the trees their fruit. 5 Your threshing will continue until grape harvest and the grape harvest will continue until planting, and you will eat all the food you want and live in safety in your land.

6 ' "I will grant peace in the land, and you will lie down and no one will make you afraid. I will remove wild beasts from the land, and the sword will not pass through your country. 7 You will pursue your enemies, and they will fall by the sword before you. 8 Five of you will chase a hundred, and a hundred of you will chase ten thousand, and your enemies will fall by the sword before you.

9 ' "I will look on you with favour and make you fruitful and increase your numbers, and I will keep my covenant with you. 10 You will still be eating last year's harvest when you will have to move it out to make room for the new. 11 I will put my

dwelling-place[a] among you, and I will not abhor you. [12] I will walk among you and be your God, and you will be my people. [13] I am the LORD your God, who brought you out of Egypt so that you would no longer be slaves to the Egyptians; I broke the bars of your yoke and enabled you to walk with heads held high.

Punishment for disobedience

[14] "But if you will not listen to me and carry out all these commands, [15] and if you reject my decrees and abhor my laws and fail to carry out all my commands and so violate my covenant, [16] then I will do this to you: I will bring on you sudden terror, wasting diseases and fever that will destroy your sight and sap your strength. You will plant seed in vain, because your enemies will eat it. [17] I will set my face against you so that you will be defeated by your enemies; those who hate you will rule over you, and you will flee even when no one is pursuing you.

[18] "If after all this you will not listen to me, I will punish you for your sins seven times over. [19] I will break down your stubborn pride and make the sky above you like iron and the ground beneath you like bronze. [20] Your strength will be spent in vain, because your soil will not yield its crops, nor will the trees of your land yield their fruit.

[21] "If you remain hostile towards me and refuse to listen to me, I will multiply your afflictions seven times over, as your sins deserve. [22] I will send wild animals against you, and they will rob you of your children, destroy your cattle and make you so few in number that your roads will be deserted.

[23] "If in spite of these things you do not accept my correction but continue to be hostile towards me, [24] I myself will be hostile towards you and will afflict you for your sins seven times over. [25] And I will bring the sword on you to avenge the breaking of the covenant. When you withdraw into your cities, I will send a plague among you, and you will be given

into enemy hands. [26] When I cut off your supply of bread, ten women will be able to bake your bread in one oven, and they will dole out the bread by weight. You will eat, but you will not be satisfied.

[27] "If in spite of this you still do not listen to me but continue to be hostile towards me, [28] then in my anger I will be hostile towards you, and I myself will punish you for your sins seven times over. [29] You will eat the flesh of your sons and the flesh of your daughters. [30] I will destroy your high places, cut down your incense altars and pile your dead bodies[b] on the lifeless forms of your idols, and I will abhor you. [31] I will turn your cities into ruins and lay waste your sanctuaries, and I will take no delight in the pleasing aroma of your offerings. [32] I myself will lay waste the land, so that your enemies who live there will be appalled. [33] I will scatter you among the nations and will draw out my sword and pursue you. Your land will be laid waste, and your cities will lie in ruins. [34] Then the land will enjoy its sabbath years all the time that it lies desolate and you are in the country of your enemies; then the land will rest and enjoy its sabbaths. [35] All the time that it lies desolate, the land will have the rest it did not have during the sabbaths you lived in it.

[36] "As for those of you who are left, I will make their hearts so fearful in the lands of their enemies that the sound of a wind-blown leaf will put them to flight. They will run as though fleeing from the sword, and they will fall, even though no one is pursuing them. [37] They will stumble over one another as though fleeing from the sword, even though no one is pursuing them. So you will not be able to stand before your enemies. [38] You will perish among the nations; the land of your enemies will devour you. [39] Those of you who are left will waste away in the lands of their enemies because of their sins; also because of their ancestors' sins they will waste away.

[40] "But if they will confess their sins and the sins of their ancestors – their

---

a 11 Or *my tabernacle*   *b* 30 Or *your funeral offerings* unfaithfulness and their hostility towards me, **41** which made me hostile towards them so that I sent them into the land of their enemies – then when their uncircumcised hearts are humbled and they pay for their sin, **42** I will remember my covenant with Jacob and my covenant with Isaac and my covenant with Abraham, and I will remember the land. **43** For the land will be deserted by them and will enjoy its sabbaths while it lies desolate without them. They will pay for their sins because they rejected my laws and abhorred my decrees. **44** Yet in spite of this, when they are in the land of their enemies, I will not reject them or abhor them so as to destroy them completely, breaking my covenant with them. I am the LORD their God. **45** But for their sake I will remember the covenant with their ancestors whom I brought out of Egypt in the sight of the nations to be their God. I am the LORD.' '

46 These are the decrees, the laws and the regulations that the LORD established at Mount Sinai between himself and the Israelites through Moses.

Redeeming what is the LORD's

27 The LORD said to Moses, **2** 'Speak to the Israelites and say to them: "If anyone makes a special vow to dedicate a person to the LORD by giving the equivalent value, **3** set the value of a male between the ages of twenty and sixty at fifty shekels*a* of silver, according to the sanctuary shekel;*b* **4** for a female, set her value at thirty shekels;*c* **5** for a person between the ages of five and twenty, set the value of a male at twenty shekels*d* and of a female at ten shekels;*e* **6** for a person between one month and five years, set the value of a male at five shekels*f* of silver and that of a female at three shekels*g* of silver; **7** for a person sixty years old or more, set

the value of a male at fifteen shekels*h* and of a female at ten shekels. **8** If anyone making the vow is too poor to pay the specified amount, the person being dedicated is to be presented to the priest, who will set the value according to what the one making the vow can afford.

9 ' "If what they vowed is an animal that is acceptable as an offering to the LORD, such an animal given to the LORD becomes holy. **10** They must not exchange it or substitute a good one for a bad one, or a bad one for a good one; if they should substitute one animal for another, both it and the substitute become holy. **11** If what they vowed is a ceremonially unclean animal – one that is not acceptable as an offering to the LORD – the animal must be presented to the priest, **12** who will judge its quality as good or bad. Whatever value the priest then sets, that is what it will be. **13** If the owner wishes to redeem the animal, a fifth must be added to its value.

14 ' "If anyone dedicates their house as something holy to the LORD, the priest will judge its quality as good or bad. Whatever value the priest then sets, so it will remain. **15** If the one who dedicates their house wishes to redeem it, they must add a fifth to its value, and the house will again become theirs.

16 ' "If anyone dedicates to the LORD part of their family land, its value is to be set according to the amount of seed required for it – fifty shekels of silver to a homer*i* of barley seed. **17** If they dedicate a field during the Year of Jubilee, the value that has been set remains. **18** But if they dedicate a field after the Jubilee, the priest will determine the value according to the number of years that remain until the next Year of Jubilee, and its set value will be reduced. **19** If the one who dedicates the field wishes to redeem it, they must add a fifth to its value, and the field will again become theirs. **20** If, however, they do not redeem the field, or if they have sold it to someone else, it can never be redeemed. **21** When the field is released in the Jubilee, it will

---

a 3   That is, about 575 grams; also in verse 16
b 3   That is, about 12 grams; also in verse 25
c 4   That is, about 345 grams
d 5   That is, about 230 grams
e 5   That is, about 115 grams; also in verse 7
f 6   That is, about 58 grams
g 6   That is, about 35 grams

h 7   That is, about 175 grams
i 16   That is, probably about 135 kilograms

become holy, like a field devoted to the LORD; it will become priestly property.

22' "If anyone dedicates to the LORD a field they have bought, which is not part of their family land, 23 the priest will determine its value up to the Year of Jubilee, and the owner must pay its value on that day as something holy to the LORD. 24 In the Year of Jubilee the field will revert to the person from whom it was bought, the one whose land it was. 25 Every value is to be set according to the sanctuary shekel, twenty gerahs to the shekel.

26' "No one, however, may dedicate the firstborn of an animal, since the firstborn already belongs to the LORD; whether an ox*j* or a sheep, it is the LORD's. 27 If it is one of the unclean animals, it may be bought back at its set value, adding a fifth of the value to it. If it is not redeemed, it is to be sold at its set value.

28' "But nothing that a person owns and devotes*k* to the LORD – whether a human being or an animal or family land – may be sold or redeemed; everything so devoted is most holy to the LORD.

29' "No one devoted to destruction*l* may be ransomed; they are to be put to death.

30' "A tithe of everything from the land, whether grain from the soil or fruit from the trees, belongs to the LORD; it is holy to the LORD. 31 Whoever would redeem any of their tithe must add a fifth of the value to it. 32 Every tithe of the herd and flock – every tenth animal that passes under the shepherd's rod – will be holy to the LORD. 33 No one may pick out the good from the bad or make any substitution. If anyone does make a substitution, both the animal and its substitute become holy and cannot be redeemed."'

34These are the commands the LORD gave Moses at Mount Sinai for the Israelites.

---

j 26 The Hebrew word can include both male and female.
k 28 The Hebrew term refers to the irrevocable giving over of things or persons to the LORD.

l 29 The Hebrew term refers to the irrevocable giving over of things or persons to the LORD, often by totally destroying them.

NUMBERS

DATE

The events described in Numbers are estimated to have taken place around 1446–1406 BC

AUTHOR

Traditionally attributed to Moses

WHAT'S IT ALL ABOUT?

This is the fourth of five books that make up the Pentateuch, which means it is largely focused on the law. Its name comes from the census that was taken of Israel (see Numbers 1 and 26), although its Hebrew name, meaning 'In the Desert', also gives us an idea of what the book is about. Numbers continues the story of Israel's journey in the desert, with some similar content to Exodus, Leviticus and Deuteronomy. It tells how God's people rebelled against him and much of the book concerns their complaints about the hardships of the desert. They were unable to trust God and act obediently despite the way in which he had freed them from slavery.

WHY SHOULD WE READ IT?

- To understand the rebellion that led to God keeping the vast majority of the generation that had left Egypt from entering the Promised Land.

- To read about Joshua and Caleb and how their obedience, bravery and faith in God led them to survive the desert and enter the Promised Land.

- To see how God can make meat appear in the desert (Numbers 11), bring water from a rock (Numbers 20) and speak through a donkey (Numbers 22).

Andy Croft with Liza Hoeksma

The census

1 The LORD spoke to Moses in the tent of meeting in the Desert of Sinai on the first day of the second month of the second year after the Israelites came out of Egypt. He said: ² 'Take a census of the whole Israelite community by their clans and families, listing every man by name, one by one. ³ You and Aaron are to count according to their divisions all the men in Israel who are twenty years old or more and able to serve in the army. ⁴ One man from each tribe, each of them the head of his family, is to help you. ⁵ These are the names of the men who are to assist you:

from Reuben, Elizur son of Shedeur;
⁶ from Simeon, Shelumiel son of Zurishaddai;
⁷ from Judah, Nahshon son of Amminadab;
⁸ from Issachar, Nethanel son of Zuar;
⁹ from Zebulun, Eliab son of Helon;
¹⁰ from the sons of Joseph:
from Ephraim, Elishama son of Ammihud;
from Manasseh, Gamaliel son of Pedahzur;
¹¹ from Benjamin, Abidan son of Gideoni;
¹² from Dan, Ahiezer son of Ammishaddai;
¹³ from Asher, Pagiel son of Okran;
¹⁴ from Gad, Eliasaph son of Deuel;
¹⁵ from Naphtali, Ahira son of Enan.'

¹⁶ These were the men appointed from the community, the leaders of their ancestral tribes. They were the heads of the clans of Israel.

¹⁷ Moses and Aaron took these men whose names had been specified, ¹⁸ and they called the whole community together on the first day of the second month. The people registered their ancestry by their clans and families, and the men twenty years old or more were listed by name, one by one, ¹⁹ as the LORD commanded Moses. And so he counted them in the Desert of Sinai:

²⁰ From the descendants of Reuben the firstborn son of Israel:
All the men twenty years old or more who were able to serve in the army were listed by name, one by one, according to the records of their clans and families. ²¹ The number from the tribe of Reuben was 46,500.

²² From the descendants of Simeon:
All the men twenty years old or more who were able to serve in the army were counted and listed by name, one by one, according to the records of their clans and families. ²³ The number from the tribe of Simeon was 59,300.

²⁴ From the descendants of Gad:
All the men twenty years old or more who were able to serve in the army were listed by name, according to the records of their clans and families. ²⁵ The number from the tribe of Gad was 45,650.

²⁶ From the descendants of Judah:
All the men twenty years old or more who were able to serve in the army were listed by name, according to the records of their clans and families. ²⁷ The number from the tribe of Judah was 74,600.

²⁸ From the descendants of Issachar:
All the men twenty years old or more who were able to serve in the army were listed by name, according to the records of their clans and families. ²⁹ The number from the tribe of Issachar was 54,400.

³⁰ From the descendants of Zebulun:
All the men twenty years old or more who were able to serve in the army were listed by name, according to the records of their clans and families. ³¹ The number from the tribe of Zebulun was 57,400.

32 From the sons of Joseph:
From the descendants of Ephraim:
All the men twenty years old or more who were able to serve in the army were listed by name, according to the records of their clans and families. 33 The number from the tribe of Ephraim was 40,500

34 From the descendants of Manasseh:
All the men twenty years old or more who were able to serve in the army were listed by name, according to the records of their clans and families. 35 The number from the tribe of Manasseh was 32,200.

36 From the descendants of Benjamin:
All the men twenty years old or more who were able to serve in the army were listed by name, according to the records of their clans and families. 37 The number from the tribe of Benjamin was 35,400.

38 From the descendants of Dan:
All the men twenty years old or more who were able to serve in the army were listed by name, according to the records of their clans and families. 39 The number from the tribe of Dan was 62,700.

40 From the descendants of Asher:
All the men twenty years old or more who were able to serve in the army were listed by name, according to the records of their clans and families. 41 The number from the tribe of Asher was 41,500.

42 From the descendants of Naphtali:
All the men twenty years old or more who were able to serve in the army were listed by name, according to the records of their clans and families. 43 The number from the tribe of Naphtali was 53,400.

44 These were the men counted by Moses and Aaron and the twelve leaders of Israel, each one representing his family. 45 All the Israelites twenty years old or more who were able to serve in Israel's army were counted according to their families. 46 The total number was 603,550.

47 The ancestral tribe of the Levites, however, was not counted along with the others. 48 The LORD had said to Moses: 49 'You must not count the tribe of Levi or include them in the census of the other Israelites. 50 Instead, appoint the Levites to be in charge of the tabernacle of the covenant law – over all its furnishings and everything belonging to it. They are to carry the tabernacle and all its furnishings; they are to take care of it and camp round it. 51 Whenever the tabernacle is to move, the Levites are to take it down, and whenever the tabernacle is to be set up, the Levites shall do it. Anyone else who approaches it is to be put to death. 52 The Israelites are to set up their tents by divisions, each of them in their own camp under their standard. 53 The Levites, however, are to set up their tents round the tabernacle of the covenant law so that my wrath will not fall on the Israelite community. The Levites are to be responsible for the care of the tabernacle of the covenant law.'

54 The Israelites did all this just as the LORD commanded Moses.

The arrangement of the tribal camps

2 The LORD said to Moses and Aaron: 2 'The Israelites are to camp round the tent of meeting some distance from it, each of them under their standard and holding the banners of their family.'

3 On the east, towards the sunrise, the divisions of the camp of Judah are to camp under their standard. The leader of the people of Judah is Nahshon son of Amminadab. 4 His division numbers 74,600.

5 The tribe of Issachar will camp next to them. The leader of the people of Issachar is Nethanel son of Zuar. 6 His division numbers 54,400.

7 The tribe of Zebulun will be next. The leader of the people of Zebulun is Eliab son of Helon. 8 His division numbers 57,400.

9 All the men assigned to the camp of Judah, according to their divisions, number 186,400. They will set out first.

10 On the south will be the divisions of the camp of Reuben under their standard. The leader of the people of Reuben is Elizur son of Shedeur. 11 His division numbers 46,500.

12 The tribe of Simeon will camp next to them. The leader of the people of Simeon is Shelumiel son of Zurishaddai. 13 His division numbers 59,300.

14 The tribe of Gad will be next. The leader of the people of Gad is Eliasaph son of Deuel.*a* 15 His division numbers 45,650.

16 All the men assigned to the camp of Reuben, according to their divisions, number 151,450. They will set out second.

17 Then the tent of meeting and the camp of the Levites will set out in the middle of the camps. They will set out in the same order as they set up camp, each in their own place under their standard.

18 On the west will be the divisions of the camp of Ephraim under their standard. The leader of the people of Ephraim is Elishama son of Ammihud. 19 His division numbers 40,500.

20 The tribe of Manasseh will be next to them. The leader of the people of Manasseh is Gamaliel son of Pedahzur. 21 His division numbers 32,200.

22 The tribe of Benjamin will be next. The leader of the people of Benjamin is Abidan son of Gideoni. 23 His division numbers 35,400.

24 All the men assigned to the camp of Ephraim, according to their divisions, number 108,100. They will set out third.

25 On the north will be the divisions of the camp of Dan under their standard. The leader of the people of Dan is Ahiezer son of Ammishaddai. 26 His division numbers 62,700.

27 The tribe of Asher will camp next to them. The leader of the people of Asher is Pagiel son of Okran. 28 His division numbers 41,500.

29 The tribe of Naphtali will be next. The leader of the people of Naphtali is Ahira son of Enan. 30 His division numbers 53,400.

31 All the men assigned to the camp of Dan number 157,600. They will set out last, under their standards.

32 These are the Israelites, counted according to their families. All the men in the camps, by their divisions, number 603,550. 33 The Levites, however, were not counted along with the other Israelites, as the LORD commanded Moses.

34 So the Israelites did everything the LORD commanded Moses; that is the way they camped under their standards, and that is the way they set out, each of them with their clan and family.

The Levites

3 This is the account of the family of Aaron and Moses at the time the LORD spoke to Moses at Mount Sinai.

2 The names of the sons of Aaron were Nadab the firstborn and Abihu, Eleazar and Ithamar. 3 Those were the names of Aaron's sons, the anointed priests, who were ordained to serve as priests. 4 Nadab and Abihu, however, died before the LORD when they made an offering with unauthorised fire before him in the Desert of Sinai. They had no sons, so Eleazar and Ithamar served as priests during the lifetime of their father Aaron.

5 The LORD said to Moses, 6 'Bring the tribe of Levi and present them to Aaron the priest to assist him. 7 They are to perform duties for him and for the whole community at the tent of meeting by doing the work of the tabernacle. 8 They are

---

a 14 Many manuscripts of the Masoretic Text, Samaritan Pentateuch and Vulgate (see also 1:14); most manuscripts of the Masoretic Text *Reuel* to take care of all the furnishings of the tent of meeting, fulfilling the obligations of the Israelites by doing the work of the tabernacle. 9 Give the Levites to Aaron and his sons; they are the Israelites who are to be given wholly to him.*a* 10 Appoint Aaron and his sons to serve as priests; anyone else who approaches the sanctuary is to be put to death.'

11 The LORD also said to Moses, 12 'I have taken the Levites from among the Israelites in place of the first male offspring of every Israelite woman. The Levites are mine, 13 for all the firstborn are mine. When I struck down all the firstborn in Egypt, I set apart for myself every firstborn in Israel, whether human or animal. They are to be mine. I am the LORD.'

14 The LORD said to Moses in the Desert of Sinai, 15 'Count the Levites by their families and clans. Count every male a month old or more.' 16 So Moses counted them, as he was commanded by the word of the LORD.

17 These were the names of the sons of Levi:

   Gershon, Kohath and Merari.
18 These were the names of the Gershonite clans:

   Libni and Shimei.
19 The Kohathite clans:

   Amram, Izhar, Hebron and Uzziel.
20 The Merarite clans:

   Mahli and Mushi.

These were the Levite clans, according to their families.

21 To Gershon belonged the clans of the Libnites and Shimeites; these were the Gershonite clans. 22 The number of all the males a month old or more who were counted was 7,500. 23 The Gershonite clans were to camp on the west, behind the tabernacle. 24 The leader of the families of the Gershonites was Eliasaph son of Lael. 25 At the tent of meeting the Gershonites were responsible for the care of the tabernacle and tent, its coverings, the curtain at the entrance to the tent of meeting, 26 the curtains of the courtyard, the curtain at the entrance to the courtyard surrounding the tabernacle and altar, and the ropes – and everything related to their use.

27 To Kohath belonged the clans of the Amramites, Izharites, Hebronites and Uzzielites; these were the Kohathite clans. 28 The number of all the males a month old or more was 8,600.*b* The Kohathites were responsible for the care of the sanctuary. 29 The Kohathite clans were to camp on the south side of the tabernacle. 30 The leader of the families of the Kohathite clans was Elizaphan son of Uzziel. 31 They were responsible for the care of the ark, the table, the lampstand, the altars, the articles of the sanctuary used in ministering, the curtain, and everything related to their use. 32 The chief leader of the Levites was Eleazar son of Aaron, the priest. He was appointed over those who were responsible for the care of the sanctuary.

33 To Merari belonged the clans of the Mahlites and the Mushites; these were the Merarite clans. 34 The number of all the males a month old or more who were counted was 6,200. 35 The leader of the families of the Merarite clans was Zuriel son of Abihail; they were to camp on the north side of the tabernacle. 36 The Merarites were appointed to take care of the frames of the tabernacle, its crossbars, posts, bases, all its equipment, and everything related to their use, 37 as well as the posts of the surrounding courtyard with their bases, tent pegs and ropes.

38 Moses and Aaron and his sons were to camp to the east of the tabernacle, towards the sunrise, in front of the tent of meeting. They were responsible for the care of the sanctuary on behalf of the Israelites. Anyone else who approached the sanctuary was to be put to death.

---

a 9 Most manuscripts of the Masoretic Text; some manuscripts of the Masoretic Text, Samaritan Pentateuch and Septuagint (see also 8:16) *to me*

b 28 Hebrew; some Septuagint manuscripts 8,300

39 The total number of Levites counted at the LORD's command by Moses and Aaron according to their clans, including every male a month old or more, was 22,000.

40 The LORD said to Moses, 'Count all the firstborn Israelite males who are a month old or more and make a list of their names. 41 Take the Levites for me in place of all the firstborn of the Israelites, and the livestock of the Levites in place of all the firstborn of the livestock of the Israelites. I am the LORD.'

42 So Moses counted all the firstborn of the Israelites, as the LORD commanded him. 43 The total number of firstborn males a month old or more, listed by name, was 22,273.

44 The LORD also said to Moses, 45 'Take the Levites in place of all the firstborn of Israel, and the livestock of the Levites in place of their livestock. The Levites are to be mine. I am the LORD. 46 To redeem the 273 firstborn Israelites who exceed the number of the Levites, 47 collect five shekels[c] for each one, according to the sanctuary shekel, which weighs twenty gerahs. 48 Give the money for the redemption of the additional Israelites to Aaron and his sons.'

49 So Moses collected the redemption money from those who exceeded the number redeemed by the Levites. 50 From the firstborn of the Israelites he collected silver weighing 1,365 shekels,[d] according to the sanctuary shekel. 51 Moses gave the redemption money to Aaron and his sons, as he was commanded by the word of the LORD.

The Kohathites

4 The LORD said to Moses and Aaron: 2 'Take a census of the Kohathite branch of the Levites by their clans and families. 3 Count all the men from thirty to fifty years of age who come to serve in the work at the tent of meeting.

4 'This is the work of the Kohathites at the tent of meeting: the care of the most holy things. 5 When the camp is to move, Aaron and his sons are to go in and take down the shielding curtain and put it over the ark of the covenant law. 6 Then they are to cover the curtain with durable leather,[a] spread a cloth of solid blue over that and put the poles in place.

7 'Over the table of the Presence they are to spread a blue cloth and put on it the plates, dishes and bowls, and the jars for drink offerings; the bread that is continually there is to remain on it. 8 They are to spread a scarlet cloth over them, cover that with durable leather and put the poles in place.

9 'They are to take a blue cloth and cover the lampstand that is for light, together with its lamps, its wick trimmers and trays, and all its jars for the oil used to supply it. 10 Then they are to wrap it and all its accessories in a covering of durable leather and put it on a carrying frame.

11 'Over the gold altar they are to spread a blue cloth and cover that with durable leather and put the poles in place.

12 'They are to take all the articles used for ministering in the sanctuary, wrap them in a blue cloth, cover that with durable leather and put them on a carrying frame.

13 'They are to remove the ashes from the bronze altar and spread a purple cloth over it. 14 Then they are to place on it all the utensils used for ministering at the altar, including the firepans, meat forks, shovels and sprinkling bowls. Over it they are to spread a covering of durable leather and put the poles in place.

15 'After Aaron and his sons have finished covering the holy furnishings and all the holy articles, and when the camp is ready to move, only then are the Kohathites to come and do the carrying. But they must not touch the holy things or they will die. The Kohathites are to carry those things that are in the tent of meeting.

---

c 47 That is, about 58 grams
d 50 That is, about 16 kilograms

a 6 Possibly the hides of *large aquatic mammals*; also in verses 8, 10, 11, 12, 14 and 25

16 'Eleazar son of Aaron, the priest, is to have charge of the oil for the light, the fragrant incense, the regular grain offering and the anointing oil. He is to be in charge of the entire tabernacle and everything in it, including its holy furnishings and articles.'

17 The LORD said to Moses and Aaron, 18 'See that the Kohathite tribal clans are not destroyed from among the Levites. 19 So that they may live and not die when they come near the most holy things, do this for them: Aaron and his sons are to go into the sanctuary and assign to each man his work and what he is to carry. 20 But the Kohathites must not go in to look at the holy things, even for a moment, or they will die.'

The Gershonites

21 The LORD said to Moses, 22 'Take a census also of the Gershonites by their families and clans. 23 Count all the men from thirty to fifty years of age who come to serve in the work at the tent of meeting. 24 'This is the service of the Gershonite clans in their carrying and their other work: 25 they are to carry the curtains of the tabernacle, that is, the tent of meeting, its covering and its outer covering of durable leather, the curtains for the entrance to the tent of meeting, 26 the curtains of the courtyard surrounding the tabernacle and altar, the curtain for the entrance to the courtyard, the ropes and all the equipment used in the service of the tent. The Gershonites are to do all that needs to be done with these things. 27 All their service, whether carrying or doing other work, is to be done under the direction of Aaron and his sons. You shall assign to them as their responsibility all they are to carry. 28 This is the service of the Gershonite clans at the tent of meeting. Their duties are to be under the direction of Ithamar son of Aaron, the priest.

The Merarites

29 'Count the Merarites by their clans and families. 30 Count all the men from thirty to fifty years of age who come to serve in the work at the tent of meeting.

31 As part of all their service at the tent, they are to carry the frames of the tabernacle, its crossbars, posts and bases, 32 as well as the posts of the surrounding courtyard with their bases, tent pegs, ropes, all their equipment and everything related to their use. Assign to each man the specific things he is to carry. 33 This is the service of the Merarite clans as they work at the tent of meeting under the direction of Ithamar son of Aaron, the priest.'

The numbering of the Levite clans

34 Moses, Aaron and the leaders of the community counted the Kohathites by their clans and families. 35 All the men from thirty to fifty years of age who came to serve in the work at the tent of meeting, 36 counted by clans, were 2,750. 37 This was the total of all those in the Kohathite clans who served at the tent of meeting. Moses and Aaron counted them according to the LORD's command through Moses.

38 The Gershonites were counted by their clans and families. 39 All the men from thirty to fifty years of age who came to serve in the work at the tent of meeting, 40 counted by their clans and families, were 2,630. 41 This was the total of those in the Gershonite clans who served at the tent of meeting. Moses and Aaron counted them according to the LORD's command.

42 The Merarites were counted by their clans and families. 43 All the men from thirty to fifty years of age who came to serve in the work at the tent of meeting, 44 counted by their clans, were 3,200. 45 This was the total of those in the Merarite clans. Moses and Aaron counted them according to the LORD's command through Moses.

46 So Moses, Aaron and the leaders of Israel counted all the Levites by their clans and families. 47 All the men from thirty to fifty years of age who came to do the work of serving and carrying the tent of meeting 48 numbered 8,580. 49 At the LORD's command through Moses, each was assigned his work and told what to carry.

Thus they were counted, as the LORD commanded Moses.

The purity of the camp

5 The LORD said to Moses, ²'Command the Israelites to send away from the camp anyone who has a defiling skin disease[a] or a discharge of any kind, or who is ceremonially unclean because of a dead body. ³Send away male and female alike; send them outside the camp so that they will not defile their camp, where I dwell among them.' ⁴The Israelites did so; they sent them outside the camp. They did just as the LORD had instructed Moses.

Restitution for wrongs

⁵The LORD said to Moses, ⁶'Say to the Israelites: "Any man or woman who wrongs another in any way[b] and so is unfaithful to the LORD is guilty ⁷and must confess the sin they have committed. They must make full restitution for the wrong they have done, add a fifth of the value to it and give it all to the person they have wronged. ⁸But if that person has no close relative to whom restitution can be made for the wrong, the restitution belongs to the LORD and must be given to the priest, along with the ram with which atonement is made for the wrongdoer. ⁹All the sacred contributions the Israelites bring to a priest will belong to him. ¹⁰Sacred things belong to their owners, but what they give to the priest will belong to the priest."'

The test for an unfaithful wife

¹¹Then the LORD said to Moses, ¹²'Speak to the Israelites and say to them: "If a man's wife goes astray and is unfaithful to him ¹³so that another man has sexual relations with her, and this is hidden from her husband and her impurity is undetected (since there is no witness against her and she has not been caught in the act), ¹⁴and if feelings of jealousy come over her husband and he suspects his wife and she is impure – or if he is jealous and suspects her even though she is not impure – ¹⁵then he is to take his wife to the priest. He must also take an offering of a tenth of an ephah[c] of barley flour on her behalf. He must not pour olive oil on it or put incense on it, because it is a grain offering for jealousy, a reminder-offering to draw attention to wrongdoing.

¹⁶'"The priest shall bring her and make her stand before the LORD. ¹⁷Then he shall take some holy water in a clay jar and put some dust from the tabernacle floor into the water. ¹⁸After the priest has made the woman stand before the LORD, he shall loosen her hair and place in her hands the reminder-offering, the grain offering for jealousy, while he himself holds the bitter water that brings a curse. ¹⁹Then the priest shall put the woman under oath and say to her, 'If no other man has had sexual relations with you and you have not gone astray and become impure while married to your husband, may this bitter water that brings a curse not harm you. ²⁰But if you have gone astray while married to your husband and you have made yourself impure by having sexual relations with a man other than your husband' – ²¹here the priest is to put the woman under this curse – 'may the LORD cause you to become a curse[d] among your people when he makes your womb miscarry and your abdomen swell. ²²May this water that brings a curse enter your body so that your abdomen swells or your womb miscarries.'

'"Then the woman is to say, 'Amen. So be it.'

²³'"The priest is to write these curses on a scroll and then wash them off into the bitter water. ²⁴He shall make the woman drink the bitter water that brings a curse, and this water that brings a curse and causes bitter suffering will enter her. ²⁵The priest is to take from her hands the grain offering for jealousy, wave it before the LORD and bring it to the altar. ²⁶The priest is then to take a handful of the grain offering as a memorial[e] offering and burn

---

a 2 The Hebrew word for *defiling skin disease*, traditionally translated 'leprosy', was used for various diseases affecting the skin.

b 6 Or *woman who commits any wrong common to mankind*

c 15 That is, probably about 1.6 kilograms

d 21 That is, may he cause your name to be used in cursing (see Jer. 29:22); or, may others see that you are cursed; similarly in verse 27.

e 26 Or *representative*

it on the altar; after that, he is to make the woman drink the water. 27 If she has made herself impure and been unfaithful to her husband, this will be the result: when she is made to drink the water that brings a curse and causes bitter suffering, it will enter her, her abdomen will swell and her womb will miscarry, and she will become a curse. 28 If, however, the woman has not made herself impure, but is clean, she will be cleared of guilt and will be able to have children.

29 ' "This, then, is the law of jealousy when a woman goes astray and makes herself impure while married to her husband, 30 or when feelings of jealousy come over a man because he suspects his wife. The priest is to make her stand before the LORD and is to apply this entire law to her. 31 The husband will be innocent of any wrongdoing, but the woman will bear the consequences of her sin." '

FAVOURITE VERSES

John 5:17

In his defence Jesus said to them, 'My Father is always at his work to this very day, and I too am working.'

This my favourite verse because it's part of my testimony. During a really bad week, I was speaking to my Christian friend and he said I should pray and read a bit of the Bible. Anyway, I went away and found this verse and it spoke so much to where I was at and so I just carried on reading!

Toby, 15

The Nazirite

6 The LORD said to Moses, 2 'Speak to the Israelites and say to them: "If a man or woman wants to make a special vow, a vow of dedication to the LORD as a Nazirite,

3 they must abstain from wine and other fermented drink and must not drink vinegar made from wine or other fermented drink. They must not drink grape juice or eat grapes or raisins. 4 As long as they remain under their Nazirite vow, they must not eat anything that comes from the grapevine, not even the seeds or skins.

5 ' "During the entire period of their Nazirite vow, no razor may be used on their head. They must be holy until the period of their dedication to the LORD is over; they must let their hair grow long.

6 ' "Throughout the period of their dedication to the LORD, the Nazirite must not go near a dead body. 7 Even if their own father or mother or brother or sister dies, they must not make themselves ceremonially unclean on account of them, because the symbol of their dedication to God is on their head. 8 Throughout the period of their dedication, they are consecrated to the LORD.

9 ' "If someone dies suddenly in the Nazirite's presence, thus defiling the hair that symbolises their dedication, they must shave their head on the seventh day – the day of their cleansing. 10 Then on the eighth day they must bring two doves or two young pigeons to the priest at the entrance to the tent of meeting. 11 The priest is to offer one as a sin offering*a* and the other as a burnt offering to make atonement for the Nazirite because they sinned by being in the presence of the dead body. That same day they are to consecrate their head again. 12 They must rededicate themselves to the LORD for the same period of dedication and must bring a year-old male lamb as a guilt offering. The previous days do not count, because they became defiled during their period of dedication.

13 ' "Now this is the law of the Nazirite when the period of their dedication is over. They are to be brought to the entrance to the tent of meeting. 14 There they are to present their offerings to the LORD: a year-old male lamb without defect for a burnt offering, a year-old ewe

---

a 11 Or *purification offering*; also in verses 14 and 16

lamb without defect for a sin offering, a ram without defect for a fellowship offering, 15 together with their grain offerings and drink offerings, and a basket of bread made with the finest flour and without yeast – thick loaves with olive oil mixed in, and thin loaves brushed with olive oil.

16 ' "The priest is to present all these before the Lord and make the sin offering and the burnt offering. 17 He is to present the basket of unleavened bread and is to sacrifice the ram as a fellowship offering to the Lord, together with its grain offering and drink offering.

18 ' "Then at the entrance to the tent of meeting, the Nazirite must shave off the hair that symbolises their dedication. They are to take the hair and put it in the fire that is under the sacrifice of the fellowship offering.

19 ' "After the Nazirite has shaved off the hair that symbolises their dedication, the priest is to place in their hands a boiled shoulder of the ram, and one thick loaf and one thin loaf from the basket, both made without yeast. 20 The priest shall then wave these before the Lord as a wave offering; they are holy and belong to the priest, together with the breast that was waved and the thigh that was presented. After that, the Nazirite may drink wine.

21 ' "This is the law of the Nazirite who vows offerings to the Lord in accordance with their dedication, in addition to whatever else they can afford. They must fulfil the vows they have made, according to the law of the Nazirite." '

The priestly blessing

22 The Lord said to Moses, 23 'Tell Aaron and his sons, "This is how you are to bless the Israelites. Say to them:

24 ' " 'The Lord bless you
        and keep you;
25 the Lord make his face shine on you
        and be gracious to you;
26 the Lord turn his face towards you
        and give you peace.' "

27 'So they will put my name on the Israelites, and I will bless them.'

Offerings at the dedication of the tabernacle

7 When Moses finished setting up the tabernacle, he anointed and consecrated it and all its furnishings. He also anointed and consecrated the altar and all its utensils. 2 Then the leaders of Israel, the heads of families who were the tribal leaders in charge of those who were counted, made offerings. 3 They brought as their gifts before the Lord six covered carts and twelve oxen – an ox from each leader and a cart from every two. These they presented before the tabernacle.

4 The Lord said to Moses, 5 'Accept these from them, that they may be used in the work at the tent of meeting. Give them to the Levites as each man's work requires.'

6 So Moses took the carts and oxen and gave them to the Levites. 7 He gave two carts and four oxen to the Gershonites, as their work required, 8 and he gave four carts and eight oxen to the Merarites, as their work required. They were all under the direction of Ithamar son of Aaron, the priest. 9 But Moses did not give any to the Kohathites, because they were to carry on their shoulders the holy things, for which they were responsible.

10 When the altar was anointed, the leaders brought their offerings for its dedication and presented them before the altar. 11 For the Lord had said to Moses, 'Each day one leader is to bring his offering for the dedication of the altar.'

12 The one who brought his offering on the first day was Nahshon son of Amminadab of the tribe of Judah.

13 His offering was one silver plate weighing a hundred and thirty shekels,[a] and one silver sprinkling bowl weighing seventy shekels,[b] both according to the sanctuary shekel, each filled with the finest flour mixed with olive oil as a grain offering;

---

a 13 That is, about 1.5 kilograms; also elsewhere in this chapter
b 13 That is, about 800 grams; also elsewhere in this chapter

14 one gold dish weighing ten shekels, c filled with incense; 15 one young bull, one ram and one male lamb a year old for a burnt offering; 16 one male goat for a sin offering d; 17 and two oxen, five rams, five male goats and five male lambs a year old to be sacrificed as a fellowship offering. This was the offering of Nahshon son of Amminadab.

18 On the second day Nethanel son of Zuar, the leader of Issachar, brought his offering.

19 The offering he brought was one silver plate weighing a hundred and thirty shekels, and one silver sprinkling bowl weighing seventy shekels, both according to the sanctuary shekel, each filled with the finest flour mixed with olive oil as a grain offering; 20 one gold dish weighing ten shekels, filled with incense; 21 one young bull, one ram and one male lamb a year old for a burnt offering; 22 one male goat for a sin offering; 23 and two oxen, five rams, five male goats and five male lambs a year old to be sacrificed as a fellowship offering. This was the offering of Nethanel son of Zuar.

24 On the third day, Eliab son of Helon, the leader of the people of Zebulun, brought his offering.

25 His offering was one silver plate weighing a hundred and thirty shekels, and one silver sprinkling bowl weighing seventy shekels, both according to the sanctuary shekel, each filled with the finest flour mixed with olive oil as a grain offering; 26 one gold dish weighing ten shekels, filled with incense; 27 one young bull, one ram and one male lamb a year old for a burnt offering; 28 one male goat for a sin offering; 29 and two oxen, five

rams, five male goats and five male lambs a year old to be sacrificed as a fellowship offering. This was the offering of Eliab son of Helon.

30 On the fourth day Elizur son of Shedeur, the leader of the people of Reuben, brought his offering.

31 His offering was one silver plate weighing a hundred and thirty shekels, and one silver sprinkling bowl weighing seventy shekels, both according to the sanctuary shekel, each filled with the finest flour mixed with olive oil as a grain offering; 32 one gold dish weighing ten shekels, filled with incense; 33 one young bull, one ram and one male lamb a year old for a burnt offering; 34 one male goat for a sin offering; 35 and two oxen, five rams, five male goats and five male lambs a year old to be sacrificed as a fellowship offering. This was the offering of Elizur son of Shedeur.

36 On the fifth day Shelumiel son of Zurishaddai, the leader of the people of Simeon, brought his offering.

37 His offering was one silver plate weighing a hundred and thirty shekels, and one silver sprinkling bowl weighing seventy shekels, both according to the sanctuary shekel, each filled with the finest flour mixed with olive oil as a grain offering; 38 one gold dish weighing ten shekels, filled with incense; 39 one young bull, one ram and one male lamb a year old for a burnt offering; 40 one male goat for a sin offering; 41 and two oxen, five rams, five male goats and five male lambs a year old to be sacrificed as a fellowship offering. This was the offering of Shelumiel son of Zurishaddai.

42 On the sixth day Eliasaph son of Deuel, the leader of the people of Gad, brought his offering.

43 His offering was one silver plate weighing a hundred and thirty shekels, and one silver sprinkling bowl

---

c 14 That is, about 115 grams; also elsewhere in this chapter

d 16 Or *purification offering*; also elsewhere in this chapter weighing seventy shekels, both according to the sanctuary shekel, each filled with the finest flour mixed with olive oil as a grain offering; 44 one gold dish weighing ten shekels, filled with incense; 45 one young bull, one ram and one male lamb a year old for a burnt offering; 46 one male goat for a sin offering; 47 and two oxen, five rams, five male goats and five male lambs a year old to be sacrificed as a fellowship offering. This was the offering of Eliasaph son of Deuel.

48 On the seventh day Elishama son of Ammihud, the leader of the people of Ephraim, brought his offering.

49 His offering was one silver plate weighing a hundred and thirty shekels, and one silver sprinkling bowl weighing seventy shekels, both according to the sanctuary shekel, each filled with the finest flour mixed with olive oil as a grain offering; 50 one gold dish weighing ten shekels, filled with incense; 51 one young bull, one ram and one male lamb a year old for a burnt offering; 52 one male goat for a sin offering; 53 and two oxen, five rams, five male goats and five male lambs a year old to be sacrificed as a fellowship offering. This was the offering of Elishama son of Ammihud.

54 On the eighth day Gamaliel son of Pedahzur, the leader of the people of Manasseh, brought his offering.

55 His offering was one silver plate weighing a hundred and thirty shekels, and one silver sprinkling bowl weighing seventy shekels, both according to the sanctuary shekel, each filled with the finest flour mixed with olive oil as a grain offering; 56 one gold dish weighing ten shekels, filled with incense; 57 one young bull, one ram and one male lamb a year old for a burnt offering; 58 one male goat for a sin offering; 59 and two oxen, five rams, five male goats and five male lambs a year old to be sacrificed as a

fellowship offering. This was the offering of Gamaliel son of Pedahzur.

60 On the ninth day Abidan son of Gideoni, the leader of the people of Benjamin, brought his offering.

61 His offering was one silver plate weighing a hundred and thirty shekels, and one silver sprinkling bowl weighing seventy shekels, both according to the sanctuary shekel, each filled with the finest flour mixed with olive oil as a grain offering; 62 one gold dish weighing ten shekels, filled with incense; 63 one young bull, one ram and one male lamb a year old for a burnt offering; 64 one male goat for a sin offering; 65 and two oxen, five rams, five male goats and five male lambs a year old to be sacrificed as a fellowship offering. This was the offering of Abidan son of Gideoni.

66 On the tenth day Ahiezer son of Ammishaddai, the leader of the people of Dan, brought his offering.

67 His offering was one silver plate weighing a hundred and thirty shekels, and one silver sprinkling bowl weighing seventy shekels, both according to the sanctuary shekel, each filled with the finest flour mixed with olive oil as a grain offering; 68 one gold dish weighing ten shekels, filled with incense; 69 one young bull, one ram and one male lamb a year old for a burnt offering; 70 one male goat for a sin offering; 71 and two oxen, five rams, five male goats and five male lambs a year old to be sacrificed as a fellowship offering. This was the offering of Ahiezer son of Ammishaddai.

72 On the eleventh day Pagiel son of Okran, the leader of the people of Asher, brought his offering.

73 His offering was one silver plate weighing a hundred and thirty shekels, and one silver sprinkling bowl weighing seventy shekels, both according to the sanctuary shekel, each

filled with the finest flour mixed with olive oil as a grain offering; **74** one gold dish weighing ten shekels, filled with incense; **75** one young bull, one ram and one male lamb a year old for a burnt offering; **76** one male goat for a sin offering; **77** and two oxen, five rams, five male goats and five male lambs a year old to be sacrificed as a fellowship offering. This was the offering of Pagiel son of Okran.

78 On the twelfth day Ahira son of Enan, the leader of the people of Naphtali, brought his offering.

79 His offering was one silver plate weighing a hundred and thirty shekels, and one silver sprinkling bowl weighing seventy shekels, both according to the sanctuary shekel, each filled with the finest flour mixed with olive oil as a grain offering; **80** one gold dish weighing ten shekels, filled with incense; **81** one young bull, one ram and one male lamb a year old for a burnt offering; **82** one male goat for a sin offering; **83** and two oxen, five rams, five male goats and five male lambs a year old to be sacrificed as a fellowship offering. This was the offering of Ahira son of Enan.

84 These were the offerings of the Israelite leaders for the dedication of the altar when it was anointed: twelve silver plates, twelve silver sprinkling bowls and twelve gold dishes. **85** Each silver plate weighed a hundred and thirty shekels, and each sprinkling bowl seventy shekels. Altogether, the silver dishes weighed two thousand four hundred shekels,*e* according to the sanctuary shekel. **86** The twelve gold dishes filled with incense weighed ten shekels each, according to the sanctuary shekel. Altogether, the gold dishes weighed a hundred and twenty shekels.*f* **87** The total number of animals for the burnt offering came to twelve young bulls, twelve rams and twelve male lambs a year

old, together with their grain offering. Twelve male goats were used for the sin offering. **88** The total number of animals for the sacrifice of the fellowship offering came to twenty-four oxen, sixty rams, sixty male goats and sixty male lambs a year old. These were the offerings for the dedication of the altar after it was anointed.

89 When Moses entered the tent of meeting to speak with the LORD, he heard the voice speaking to him from between the two cherubim above the atonement cover on the ark of the covenant law. In this way the LORD spoke to him.

Setting up the lamps

8 The LORD said to Moses, **2** 'Speak to Aaron and say to him, "When you set up the lamps, see that all seven light up the area in front of the lampstand." '

3 Aaron did so; he set up the lamps so that they faced forwards on the lampstand, just as the LORD commanded Moses. **4** This is how the lampstand was made: it was made of hammered gold – from its base to its blossoms. The lampstand was made exactly like the pattern the LORD had shown Moses.

The setting apart of the Levites

5 The LORD said to Moses: **6** 'Take the Levites from among all the Israelites and make them ceremonially clean. **7** To purify them, do this: sprinkle the water of cleansing on them; then make them shave their whole bodies and wash their clothes. And so they will purify themselves. **8** Make them take a young bull with its grain offering of the finest flour mixed with olive oil; then you are to take a second young bull for a sin offering.*a* **9** Bring the Levites to the front of the tent of meeting and assemble the whole Israelite community. **10** You are to bring the Levites before the LORD, and the Israelites are to lay their hands on them. **11** Aaron is to present the Levites before the LORD as a wave offering from the Israelites, so that they may be ready to do the work of the LORD.

---

e 85 That is, about 28 kilograms
f 86 That is, about 1.4 kilograms

a 8 Or *purification offering*; also in verse 12

12 'Then the Levites are to lay their hands on the heads of the bulls, using one for a sin offering to the LORD and the other for a burnt offering, to make atonement for the Levites. 13 Make the Levites stand in front of Aaron and his sons and then present them as a wave offering to the LORD. 14 In this way you are to set the Levites apart from the other Israelites, and the Levites will be mine.

15 'After you have purified the Levites and presented them as a wave offering, they are to come to do their work at the tent of meeting. 16 They are the Israelites who are to be given wholly to me. I have taken them as my own in place of the firstborn, the first male offspring from every Israelite woman. 17 Every firstborn male in Israel, whether human or animal, is mine. When I struck down all the firstborn in Egypt, I set them apart for myself. 18 And I have taken the Levites in place of all the firstborn sons in Israel. 19 From among all the Israelites, I have given the Levites as gifts to Aaron and his sons to do the work at the tent of meeting on behalf of the Israelites and to make atonement for them so that no plague will strike the Israelites when they go near the sanctuary.'

20 Moses, Aaron and the whole Israelite community did with the Levites just as the LORD commanded Moses. 21 The Levites purified themselves and washed their clothes. Then Aaron presented them as a wave offering before the LORD and made atonement for them to purify them. 22 After that, the Levites came to do their work at the tent of meeting under the supervision of Aaron and his sons. They did with the Levites just as the LORD commanded Moses.

23 The LORD said to Moses, 24 'This applies to the Levites: men twenty-five years old or more shall come to take part in the work at the tent of meeting, 25 but at the age of fifty, they must retire from their usual duties and work no longer. 26 They may assist their brothers in performing their duties at the tent of meeting, but they themselves must not do the work. This, then, is how you are to assign the responsibilities of the Levites.'

The Passover

9 The LORD spoke to Moses in the Desert of Sinai in the first month of the second year after they came out of Egypt. He said, 2 'Make the Israelites celebrate the Passover at the appointed time. 3 Celebrate it at the appointed time, at twilight on the fourteenth day of this month, in accordance with all its rules and regulations.'

4 So Moses told the Israelites to celebrate the Passover, 5 and they did so in the Desert of Sinai at twilight on the fourteenth day of the first month. The Israelites did everything just as the LORD commanded Moses.

6 But some of them could not celebrate the Passover on that day because they were ceremonially unclean on account of a dead body. So they came to Moses and Aaron that same day 7 and said to Moses, 'We have become unclean because of a dead body, but why should we be kept from presenting the LORD's offering with the other Israelites at the appointed time?'

8 Moses answered them, 'Wait until I find out what the LORD commands concerning you.'

9 Then the LORD said to Moses, 10 'Tell the Israelites: "When any of you or your descendants are unclean because of a dead body or are away on a journey, they are still to celebrate the LORD's Passover, 11 but they are to do it on the fourteenth day of the second month at twilight. They are to eat the lamb, together with unleavened bread and bitter herbs. 12 They must not leave any of it till morning or break any of its bones. When they celebrate the Passover, they must follow all the regulations. 13 But if anyone who is ceremonially clean and not on a journey fails to celebrate the Passover, they must be cut off from their people for not presenting the LORD's offering at the appointed time. They will bear the consequences of their sin.

14 ' "A foreigner residing among you is also to celebrate the LORD's Passover in accordance with its rules and regulations. You must have the same regulations for both the foreigner and the native-born." '

The cloud above the tabernacle

15 On the day the tabernacle, the tent of the covenant law, was set up, the cloud covered it. From evening till morning the cloud above the tabernacle looked like fire. 16 That is how it continued to be; the cloud covered it, and at night it looked like fire. 17 Whenever the cloud lifted from above the tent, the Israelites set out; wherever the cloud settled, the Israelites set up camp. 18 At the LORD's command the Israelites set out, and at his command they set up camp. As long as the cloud stayed over the tabernacle, they remained in camp. 19 When the cloud remained over the tabernacle a long time, the Israelites obeyed the LORD's order and did not set out. 20 Sometimes the cloud was over the tabernacle for only a few days; at the LORD's command they would set up camp, and then at his command they would set out. 21 Sometimes the cloud stayed only from evening till morning, and when it lifted in the morning, they set out. Whether by day or by night, whenever the cloud lifted, they set out. 22 Whether the cloud stayed over the tabernacle for two days or a month or a year, the Israelites would remain in camp and not set out; but when it lifted, they would set out. 23 At the LORD's command they set up camp, and at the LORD's command they set out. They obeyed the LORD's order, in accordance with his command through Moses.

The silver trumpets

10 The LORD said to Moses: 2 'Make two trumpets of hammered silver, and use them for calling the community together and for the camps to set out. 3 When both are sounded, the whole community is to assemble before you at the entrance to the tent of meeting. 4 If only one is sounded, the leaders – the heads of the clans of Israel – are to assemble before you. 5 When a trumpet blast is sounded, the tribes camping on the east are to set out. 6 At the sounding of a second blast, the camps on the south are to set out. The blast will be the signal for setting out. 7 To gather the assembly, blow the trumpets, but not with the signal for setting out.

8 'The sons of Aaron, the priests, are to blow the trumpets. This is to be a lasting ordinance for you and the generations to come. 9 When you go into battle in your own land against an enemy who is oppressing you, sound a blast on the trumpets. Then you will be remembered by the LORD your God and rescued from your enemies. 10 Also at your times of rejoicing – your appointed festivals and New Moon feasts – you are to sound the trumpets over your burnt offerings and fellowship offerings, and they will be a memorial for you before your God. I am the LORD your God.'

The Israelites leave Sinai

11 On the twentieth day of the second month of the second year, the cloud lifted from above the tabernacle of the covenant law. 12 Then the Israelites set out from the Desert of Sinai and travelled from place to place until the cloud came to rest in the Desert of Paran. 13 They set out, this first time, at the LORD's command through Moses.

14 The divisions of the camp of Judah went first, under their standard. Nahshon son of Amminadab was in command. 15 Nethanel son of Zuar was over the division of the tribe of Issachar, 16 and Eliab son of Helon was over the division of the tribe of Zebulun. 17 Then the tabernacle was taken down, and the Gershonites and Merarites, who carried it, set out.

18 The divisions of the camp of Reuben went next, under their standard. Elizur son of Shedeur was in command. 19 Shelumiel son of Zurishaddai was over the division of the tribe of Simeon, 20 and Eliasaph son of Deuel was over the division of the tribe of Gad. 21 Then the Kohathites set out, carrying the holy things. The tabernacle was to be set up before they arrived.

22 The divisions of the camp of Ephraim went next, under their standard. Elishama son of Ammihud was in command. 23 Gamaliel son of Pedahzur was over the division of the tribe of Manasseh, 24 and Abidan son of Gideoni was over the division of the tribe of Benjamin.

25 Finally, as the rear guard for all the

units, the divisions of the camp of Dan set out under their standard. Ahiezer son of Ammishaddai was in command. 26 Pagiel son of Okran was over the division of the tribe of Asher, 27 and Ahira son of Enan was over the division of the tribe of Naphtali. 28 This was the order of march for the Israelite divisions as they set out.

29 Now Moses said to Hobab son of Reuel the Midianite, Moses' father-in-law, 'We are setting out for the place about which the LORD said, "I will give it to you." Come with us and we will treat you well, for the LORD has promised good things to Israel.'

30 He answered, 'No, I will not go; I am going back to my own land and my own people.'

31 But Moses said, 'Please do not leave us. You know where we should camp in the wilderness, and you can be our eyes. 32 If you come with us, we will share with you whatever good things the LORD gives us.'

33 So they set out from the mountain of the LORD and travelled for three days. The ark of the covenant of the LORD went before them during those three days to find them a place to rest. 34 The cloud of the LORD was over them by day when they set out from the camp.

35 Whenever the ark set out, Moses said,

'Rise up, LORD!
    May your enemies be scattered;
    may your foes flee before you.'

36 Whenever it came to rest, he said,

'Return, LORD,
    to the countless thousands of
        Israel.'

Fire from the LORD

11 Now the people complained about their hardships in the hearing of the LORD, and when he heard them his anger was aroused. Then fire from the LORD burned among them and consumed some of the outskirts of the camp. 2 When the people cried out to Moses, he prayed to the LORD and the fire died down. 3 So

that place was called Taberah, [a] because fire from the LORD had burned among them.

Quail from the LORD

4 The rabble with them began to crave other food, and again the Israelites started wailing and said, 'If only we had meat to eat! 5 We remember the fish we ate in Egypt at no cost – also the cucumbers, melons, leeks, onions and garlic. 6 But now we have lost our appetite; we never see anything but this manna!'

7 The manna was like coriander seed and looked like resin. 8 The people went around gathering it, and then ground it In a hand-mill or crushed it in a mortar. They cooked it in a pot or made it into loaves. And it tasted like something made with olive oil. 9 When the dew settled on the camp at night, the manna also came down.

10 Moses heard the people of every family wailing at the entrance to their tents. The LORD became exceedingly angry, and Moses was troubled. 11 He asked the LORD, 'Why have you brought this trouble on your servant? What have I done to displease you that you put the burden of all these people on me? 12 Did I conceive all these people? Did I give them birth? Why do you tell me to carry them in my arms, as a nurse carries an infant, to the land you promised on oath to their ancestors? 13 Where can I get meat for all these people? They keep wailing to me, "Give us meat to eat!" 14 I cannot carry all these people by myself; the burden is too heavy for me. 15 If this is how you are going to treat me, please go ahead and kill me right now – if I have found favour in your eyes – and do not let me face my own ruin.'

16 The LORD said to Moses: 'Bring me seventy of Israel's elders who are known to you as leaders and officials among the people. Make them come to the tent of meeting, that they may stand there with you. 17 I will come down and speak with you there, and I will take some of the power of the Spirit that is on you and put

_____
a 3 *Taberah* means *burning*.

it on them. They will share the burden of the people with you so that you will not have to carry it alone.

¹⁸'Tell the people: "Consecrate yourselves in preparation for tomorrow, when you will eat meat. The LORD heard you when you wailed, 'If only we had meat to eat! We were better off in Egypt!' Now the LORD will give you meat, and you will eat it. ¹⁹You will not eat it for just one day, or two days, or five, ten or twenty days, ²⁰but for a whole month – until it comes out of your nostrils and you loathe it – because you have rejected the LORD, who is among you, and have wailed before him, saying, 'Why did we ever leave Egypt?'"'

²¹But Moses said, 'Here I am among six hundred thousand men on foot, and you say, "I will give them meat to eat for a whole month!"²²Would they have enough if flocks and herds were slaughtered for them? Would they have enough if all the fish in the sea were caught for them?'

²³The LORD answered Moses, 'Is the LORD's arm too short? Now you will see whether or not what I say will come true for you.'

²⁴So Moses went out and told the people what the LORD had said. He brought together seventy of their elders and made them stand round the tent. ²⁵Then the LORD came down in the cloud and spoke with him, and he took some of the power of the Spirit that was on him and put it on the seventy elders. When the Spirit rested on them, they prophesied – but did not do so again.

²⁶However, two men, whose names were Eldad and Medad, had remained in the camp. They were listed among the elders, but did not go out to the tent. Yet the Spirit also rested on them, and they prophesied in the camp. ²⁷A young man ran and told Moses, 'Eldad and Medad are prophesying in the camp.'

²⁸Joshua son of Nun, who had been Moses' assistant since youth, spoke up and said, 'Moses, my lord, stop them!'

²⁹But Moses replied, 'Are you jealous for my sake? I wish that all the LORD's people were prophets and that the LORD would put his Spirit on them!' ³⁰Then Moses and the elders of Israel returned to the camp.

³¹Now a wind went out from the LORD and drove quail in from the sea. It scattered them up to two cubits[b] deep all around the camp, as far as a day's walk in any direction. ³²All that day and night and all the next day the people went out and gathered quail. No one gathered less than ten homers.[c] Then they spread them out all around the camp. ³³But while the meat was still between their teeth and before it could be consumed, the anger of the LORD burned against the people, and he struck them with a severe plague. ³⁴Therefore the place was named Kibroth Hattaavah,[d] because there they buried the people who had craved other food.

³⁵From Kibroth Hattaavah the people travelled to Hazeroth and stayed there.

Miriam and Aaron oppose Moses

12 Miriam and Aaron began to talk against Moses because of his Cushite wife, for he had married a Cushite. ²'Has the LORD spoken only through Moses?' they asked. 'Hasn't he also spoken through us?' And the LORD heard this.

³(Now Moses was a very humble man, more humble than anyone else on the face of the earth.)

⁴At once the LORD said to Moses, Aaron and Miriam, 'Come out to the tent of meeting, all three of you.' So the three of them went out. ⁵Then the LORD came down in a pillar of cloud; he stood at the entrance to the tent and summoned Aaron and Miriam. When the two of them stepped forward, ⁶he said, 'Listen to my words:

'When there is a prophet among you,
    I, the LORD, reveal myself to them in
        visions,
    I speak to them in dreams.
⁷But this is not true of my servant
        Moses;
    he is faithful in all my house.

---

b 31 That is, about 90 centimetres
c 32 That is, possibly about 1.6 metric tons
d 34 *Kibroth Hattaavah* means *graves of craving*.

8 With him I speak face to face,
   clearly and not in riddles;
   he sees the form of the LORD.
Why then were you not afraid
   to speak against my servant Moses?'

9 The anger of the LORD burned against them, and he left them.

10 When the cloud lifted from above the tent, Miriam's skin was leprous*a* – it became as white as snow. Aaron turned towards her and saw that she had a defiling skin disease, 11 and he said to Moses, 'Please, my lord, I ask you not to hold against us the sin we have so foolishly committed. 12 Do not let her be like a stillborn infant coming from its mother's womb with its flesh half eaten away.'

13 So Moses cried out to the LORD, 'Please, God, heal her!'

14 The LORD replied to Moses, 'If her father had spat in her face, would she not have been in disgrace for seven days? Confine her outside the camp for seven days; after that she can be brought back.' 15 So Miriam was confined outside the camp for seven days, and the people did not move on till she was brought back.

16 After that, the people left Hazeroth and camped in the Desert of Paran.

Exploring Canaan

13 The LORD said to Moses, 2 'Send some men to explore the land of Canaan, which I am giving to the Israelites. From each ancestral tribe send one of its leaders.'

3 So at the LORD's command Moses sent them out from the Desert of Paran. All of them were leaders of the Israelites. 4 These are their names:

  from the tribe of Reuben, Shammua
    son of Zakkur;
5 from the tribe of Simeon, Shaphat
    son of Hori;
6 from the tribe of Judah, Caleb son of
    Jephunneh;

7 from the tribe of Issachar, Igal son of
    Joseph;
8 from the tribe of Ephraim, Hoshea
    son of Nun;
9 from the tribe of Benjamin, Palti son
    of Raphu;
10 from the tribe of Zebulun, Gaddiel
    son of Sodi;
11 from the tribe of Manasseh (a tribe of
    Joseph), Gaddi son of Susi;
12 from the tribe of Dan, Ammiel son of
    Gemalli;
13 from the tribe of Asher, Sethur son of
    Michael;
14 from the tribe of Naphtali, Nahbi son
    of Vophsi;
15 from the tribe of Gad, Geuel son of
    Maki.

16 These are the names of the men Moses sent to explore the land. (Moses gave Hoshea son of Nun the name Joshua.)

PEOPLE TOURS

JOSHUA

SPY:
Numbers 13:1–33
LEADER:
Numbers 27:12–23
PROMISE:
Joshua 1:1–9
JERICHO:
Joshua 5:13 – 6:27
FAREWELL:
Joshua 24:1–31

17 When Moses sent them to explore Canaan, he said, 'Go up through the Negev and on into the hill country. 18 See what the land is like and whether the people who live there are strong or weak, few or many. 19 What kind of land do they live in? Is it good or bad? What kind of towns do they live in? Are they unwalled or fortified? 20 How is the soil? Is it fertile or poor? Are there trees in it or not? Do your

---

a 10 The Hebrew for *leprous* was used for various diseases affecting the skin.

best to bring back some of the fruit of the land.' (It was the season for the first ripe grapes.)

21 So they went up and explored the land from the Desert of Zin as far as Rehob, towards Lebo Hamath. 22 They went up through the Negev and came to Hebron, where Ahiman, Sheshai and Talmai, the descendants of Anak, lived. (Hebron had been built seven years before Zoan in Egypt.) 23 When they reached the Valley of Eshkol,ᵃ they cut off a branch bearing a single cluster of grapes. Two of them carried it on a pole between them, along with some pomegranates and figs. 24 That place was called the Valley of Eshkol because of the cluster of grapes the Israelites cut off there. 25 At the end of forty days they returned from exploring the land.

Report on the exploration

26 They came back to Moses and Aaron and the whole Israelite community at Kadesh in the Desert of Paran. There they reported to them and to the whole assembly and showed them the fruit of the land. 27 They gave Moses this account: 'We went into the land to which you sent us, and it does flow with milk and honey! Here is its fruit. 28 But the people who live there are powerful, and the cities are fortified and very large. We even saw descendants of Anak there. 29 The Amalekites live in the Negev; the Hittites, Jebusites and Amorites live in the hill country; and the Canaanites live near the sea and along the Jordan.'

30 Then Caleb silenced the people before Moses and said, 'We should go up and take possession of the land, for we can certainly do it.'

31 But the men who had gone up with him said, 'We can't attack those people; they are stronger than we are.' 32 And they spread among the Israelites a bad report about the land they had explored. They said, 'The land we explored devours those living in it. All the people we saw there are of great size. 33 We saw the Nephilim there (the descendants of Anak come from the Nephilim). We seemed like grasshoppers in our own eyes, and we looked the same to them.'

The people rebel

14 That night all the members of the community raised their voices and wept aloud. 2 All the Israelites grumbled against Moses and Aaron, and the whole assembly said to them, 'If only we had died in Egypt! Or in this wilderness! 3 Why is the LORD bringing us to this land only to let us fall by the sword? Our wives and children will be taken as plunder. Wouldn't it be better for us to go back to Egypt?' 4 And they said to each other, 'We should choose a leader and go back to Egypt.'

5 Then Moses and Aaron fell face down in front of the whole Israelite assembly gathered there. 6 Joshua son of Nun and Caleb son of Jephunneh, who were among those who had explored the land, tore their clothes 7 and said to the entire Israelite assembly, 'The land we passed through and explored is exceedingly good. 8 If the LORD is pleased with us, he will lead us into that land, a land flowing with milk and honey, and will give it to us. 9 Only do not rebel against the LORD. And do not be afraid of the people of the land, because we will devour them. Their protection is gone, but the LORD is with us. Do not be afraid of them.'

10 But the whole assembly talked about stoning them. Then the glory of the LORD appeared at the tent of meeting to all the Israelites. 11 The LORD said to Moses, 'How long will these people treat me with contempt? How long will they refuse to believe in me, in spite of all the signs I have performed among them? 12 I will strike them down with a plague and destroy them, but I will make you into a nation greater and stronger than they.'

13 Moses said to the LORD, 'Then the Egyptians will hear about it! By your power you brought these people up from among them. 14 And they will tell the inhabitants of this land about it. They have already heard that you, LORD, are with these people and that you, LORD, have been seen face to face, that your cloud stays over

---

a 23 *Eshkol* means *cluster;* also in verse 24.

them, and that you go before them in a pillar of cloud by day and a pillar of fire by night. 15 If you put all these people to death, leaving none alive, the nations who have heard this report about you will say, 16 "The LORD was not able to bring these people into the land he promised them on oath, so he slaughtered them in the wilderness."

17 'Now may the Lord's strength be displayed, just as you have declared: 18 "The LORD is slow to anger, abounding in love and forgiving sin and rebellion. Yet he does not leave the guilty unpunished; he punishes the children for the sin of the parents to the third and fourth generation." 19 In accordance with your great love, forgive the sin of these people, just as you have pardoned them from the time they left Egypt until now.'

20 The LORD replied, 'I have forgiven them, as you asked. 21 Nevertheless, as surely as I live and as surely as the glory of the LORD fills the whole earth, 22 not one of those who saw my glory and the signs I performed in Egypt and in the wilderness but who disobeyed me and tested me ten times – 23 not one of them will ever see the land I promised on oath to their ancestors. No one who has treated me with contempt will ever see it. 24 But because my servant Caleb has a different spirit and follows me wholeheartedly, I will bring him into the land he went to, and his descendants will inherit it. 25 Since the Amalekites and the Canaanites are living in the valleys, turn back tomorrow and set out towards the desert along the route to the Red Sea.' a

26 The LORD said to Moses and Aaron: 27 'How long will this wicked community grumble against me? I have heard the complaints of these grumbling Israelites. 28 So tell them, "As surely as I live, declares the LORD, I will do to you the very thing I heard you say: 29 in this wilderness your bodies will fall – every one of you twenty years old or more who was counted in the census and who has grumbled against

me. 30 Not one of you will enter the land I swore with uplifted hand to make your home, except Caleb son of Jephunneh and Joshua son of Nun. 31 As for your children that you said would be taken as plunder, I will bring them in to enjoy the land you have rejected. 32 But you – your bodies will fall in this wilderness. 33 Your children will be shepherds here for forty years, suffering for your unfaithfulness, until the last of your bodies lies in the wilderness. 34 For forty years – one year for each of the forty days you explored the land – you will suffer for your sins and know what it is like to have me against you." 35 I, the LORD, have spoken, and I will surely do these things to this whole wicked community, which has banded together against me. They will meet their end in this wilderness; here they will die.'

36 So the men Moses had sent to explore the land, who returned and made the whole community grumble against him by spreading a bad report about it – 37 these men who were responsible for spreading the bad report about the land were struck down and died of a plague before the LORD. 38 Of the men who went to explore the land, only Joshua son of Nun and Caleb son of Jephunneh survived.

39 When Moses reported this to all the Israelites, they mourned bitterly. 40 Early the next morning they set out for the highest point in the hill country, saying, 'Now we are ready to go up to the land the LORD promised. Surely we have sinned!'

41 But Moses said, 'Why are you disobeying the LORD's command? This will not succeed! 42 Do not go up, because the LORD is not with you. You will be defeated by your enemies, 43 for the Amalekites and the Canaanites will face you there. Because you have turned away from the LORD, he will not be with you and you will fall by the sword.'

44 Nevertheless, in their presumption they went up towards the highest point in the hill country, though neither Moses nor the ark of the LORD's covenant moved from the camp. 45 Then the Amalekites and the Canaanites who lived in that hill country came down and attacked them

---

a 25 Or the Sea of Reeds

and beat them down all the way to Hormah.

Supplementary offerings

15 The LORD said to Moses, 2 'Speak to the Israelites and say to them: "After you enter the land I am giving you as a home 3 and you present to the LORD food offerings from the herd or the flock, as an aroma pleasing to the LORD – whether burnt offerings or sacrifices, for special vows or freewill offerings or festival offerings – 4 then the person who brings an offering shall present to the LORD a grain offering of a tenth of an ephah*a* of the finest flour mixed with a quarter of a hin*b* of olive oil. 5 With each lamb for the burnt offering or the sacrifice, prepare a quarter of a hin of wine as a drink offering.

6 ' "With a ram prepare a grain offering of one-fifth of an ephah*c* of the finest flour mixed with a third of a hin*d* of olive oil, 7 and a third of a hin of wine as a drink offering. Offer it as an aroma pleasing to the LORD.

8 ' "When you prepare a young bull as a burnt offering or sacrifice, for a special vow or a fellowship offering to the LORD, 9 bring with the bull a grain offering of three-tenths of an ephah*e* of the finest flour mixed with half a hin*f* of olive oil, 10 and also bring half a hin of wine as a drink offering. This will be a food offering, an aroma pleasing to the LORD. 11 Each bull or ram, each lamb or young goat, is to be prepared in this manner. 12 Do this for each one, for as many as you prepare.

13 ' "Everyone who is native-born must do these things in this way when they present a food offering as an aroma pleasing to the LORD. 14 For the generations to come, whenever a foreigner or anyone else living among you presents a food offering as an aroma pleasing to the LORD, they must do exactly as you do. 15 The community is to have the same rules for you

and for the foreigner residing among you; this is a lasting ordinance for the generations to come. You and the foreigner shall be the same before the LORD: 16 the same laws and regulations will apply both to you and to the foreigner residing among you." '

17 The LORD said to Moses, 18 'Speak to the Israelites and say to them: "When you enter the land to which I am taking you 19 and you eat the food of the land, present a portion as an offering to the LORD. 20 Present a loaf from the first of your ground meal and present it as an offering from the threshing-floor. 21 Throughout the generations to come you are to give this offering to the LORD from the first of your ground meal.

Offerings for unintentional sins

22 ' "Now if you as a community unintentionally fail to keep any of these commands the LORD gave Moses – 23 any of the LORD's commands to you through him, from the day the LORD gave them and continuing through the generations to come – 24 and if this is done unintentionally without the community being aware of it, then the whole community is to offer a young bull for a burnt offering as an aroma pleasing to the LORD, along with its prescribed grain offering and drink offering, and a male goat for a sin offering.*g* 25 The priest is to make atonement for the whole Israelite community, and they will be forgiven, for it was not intentional and they have presented to the LORD for their wrong a food offering and a sin offering. 26 The whole Israelite community and the foreigners residing among them will be forgiven, because all the people were involved in the unintentional wrong.

27 ' "But if just one person sins unintentionally, that person must bring a year-old female goat for a sin offering. 28 The priest is to make atonement before the LORD for the one who erred by sinning unintentionally, and when atonement has been made, that person will be forgiven. 29 One and the same law applies to everyone who sins

---

a 4 That is, probably about 1.6 kilograms
b 4 That is, about 1 litre; also in verse 5
c 6 That is, probably about 3.2 kilograms
d 6 That is, about 1.3 litres; also in verse 7
e 9 That is, probably about 5 kilograms
f 9 That is, about 1.9 litres; also in verse 10

---

g 24 Or *purification offering*; also in verses 25 and 27

unintentionally, whether a native-born Israelite or a foreigner residing among you. 30 ' "But anyone who sins defiantly, whether native-born or foreigner, utters blasphemy against the LORD and must be cut off from the people of Israel. 31 Because they have despised the LORD's word and broken his commands, they must surely be cut off; their guilt remains on them." '

The Sabbath-breaker put to death

32 While the Israelites were in the wilderness, a man was found gathering wood on the Sabbath day. 33 Those who found him gathering wood brought him to Moses and Aaron and the whole assembly, 34 and they kept him in custody, because it was not clear what should be done to him. 35 Then the LORD said to Moses, 'The man must die. The whole assembly must stone him outside the camp.' 36 So the assembly took him outside the camp and stoned him to death, as the LORD commanded Moses.

Tassels on garments

37 The LORD said to Moses, 38 'Speak to the Israelites and say to them: "Throughout the generations to come you are to make tassels on the corners of your garments, with a blue cord on each tassel. 39 You will have these tassels to look at and so you will remember all the commands of the LORD, that you may obey them and not prostitute yourselves by chasing after the lusts of your own hearts and eyes. 40 Then you will remember to obey all my commands and will be consecrated to your God. 41 I am the LORD your God, who brought you out of Egypt to be your God. I am the LORD your God." '

Korah, Dathan and Abiram

16 Korah son of Izhar, the son of Kohath, the son of Levi, and certain Reubenites – Dathan and Abiram, sons of Eliab, and On son of Peleth – became insolent*a* 2 and rose up against Moses. With them were 250 Israelite men, well-known

community leaders who had been appointed members of the council. 3 They came as a group to oppose Moses and Aaron and said to them, 'You have gone too far! The whole community is holy, every one of them, and the LORD is with them. Why then do you set yourselves above the LORD's assembly?'

> # FAVOURITE VERSES
>
> *Psalm 37:4*
>
> Take delight in the LORD,
>   and he will give you the desires
>   of your heart.
>
> -
>
> This verse speaks to me about how God wants me close to him and the reward it brings. I also like the fact that he cares about my desires.
>
> **Danai, 20**

4 When Moses heard this, he fell face down. 5 Then he said to Korah and all his followers: 'In the morning the LORD will show who belongs to him and who is holy, and he will make that person come near him. The man he chooses he will cause to come near him. 6 You, Korah, and all your followers are to do this: take censers 7 and tomorrow put burning coals and incense in them before the LORD. The man the LORD chooses will be the one who is holy. You Levites have gone too far!'

8 Moses also said to Korah, 'Now listen, you Levites! 9 Isn't it enough for you that the God of Israel has separated you from the rest of the Israelite community and brought you near himself to do the work at the LORD's tabernacle and to stand before the community and minister to them? 10 He has brought you and all your fellow Levites near himself, but now you are trying to get the priesthood too. 11 It is against the LORD that you and all your

---

a 1 Or Peleth – took men

followers have banded together. Who is Aaron that you should grumble against him?'

¹²Then Moses summoned Dathan and Abiram, the sons of Eliab. But they said, 'We will not come! ¹³Isn't it enough that you have brought us up out of a land flowing with milk and honey to kill us in the wilderness? And now you also want to lord it over us! ¹⁴Moreover, you haven't brought us into a land flowing with milk and honey or given us an inheritance of fields and vineyards. Do you want to treat these men like slavesᵇ? No, we will not come!'

¹⁵Then Moses became very angry and said to the LORD, 'Do not accept their offering. I have not taken so much as a donkey from them, nor have I wronged any of them.'

¹⁶Moses said to Korah, 'You and all your followers are to appear before the LORD tomorrow – you and they and Aaron. ¹⁷Each man is to take his censer and put incense in it – 250 censers in all – and present it before the LORD. You and Aaron are to present your censers also.' ¹⁸So each of them took his censer, put burning coals and incense in it, and stood with Moses and Aaron at the entrance to the tent of meeting. ¹⁹When Korah had gathered all his followers in opposition to them at the entrance to the tent of meeting, the glory of the LORD appeared to the entire assembly. ²⁰The LORD said to Moses and Aaron, ²¹'Separate yourselves from this assembly so that I can put an end to them at once.'

²²But Moses and Aaron fell face down and cried out, 'O God, the God who gives breath to all living things, will you be angry with the entire assembly when only one man sins?'

²³Then the LORD said to Moses, ²⁴'Say to the assembly, "Move away from the tents of Korah, Dathan and Abiram."'

²⁵Moses got up and went to Dathan and Abiram, and the elders of Israel followed him. ²⁶He warned the assembly, 'Move back from the tents of these wicked

men! Do not touch anything belonging to them, or you will be swept away because of all their sins.' ²⁷So they moved away from the tents of Korah, Dathan and Abiram. Dathan and Abiram had come out and were standing with their wives, children and little ones at the entrances to their tents.

²⁸Then Moses said, 'This is how you will know that the LORD has sent me to do all these things and that it was not my idea: ²⁹if these men die a natural death and suffer the fate of all mankind, then the LORD has not sent me. ³⁰But if the LORD brings about something totally new, and the earth opens its mouth and swallows them, with everything that belongs to them, and they go down alive into the realm of the dead, then you will know that these men have treated the LORD with contempt.'

³¹As soon as he finished saying all this, the ground under them split apart ³²and the earth opened its mouth and swallowed them and their households, and all those associated with Korah, together with their possessions. ³³They went down alive into the realm of the dead, with everything they owned; the earth closed over them, and they perished and were gone from the community. ³⁴At their cries, all the Israelites around them fled, shouting, 'The earth is going to swallow us too!'

³⁵And fire came out from the LORD and consumed the 250 men who were offering the incense.

³⁶The LORD said to Moses, ³⁷'Tell Eleazar son of Aaron, the priest, to remove the censers from the charred remains and scatter the coals some distance away, for the censers are holy – ³⁸the censers of the men who sinned at the cost of their lives. Hammer the censers into sheets to overlay the altar, for they were presented before the LORD and have become holy. Let them be a sign to the Israelites.'

³⁹So Eleazar the priest collected the bronze censers brought by those who had been burned to death, and he had them hammered out to overlay the altar, ⁴⁰as the LORD directed him through Moses. This was to remind the Israelites that no one except a descendant of Aaron should come to

b 14 Or *to deceive these men;* Hebrew *Will you gouge out the eyes of these men* burn incense before the LORD, or he would become like Korah and his followers.

⁴¹ The next day the whole Israelite community grumbled against Moses and Aaron. 'You have killed the LORD's people,' they said.

⁴² But when the assembly gathered in opposition to Moses and Aaron and turned towards the tent of meeting, suddenly the cloud covered it and the glory of the LORD appeared. ⁴³ Then Moses and Aaron went to the front of the tent of meeting, ⁴⁴ and the LORD said to Moses, ⁴⁵ 'Get away from this assembly so that I can put an end to them at once.' And they fell face down.

⁴⁶ Then Moses said to Aaron, 'Take your censer and put incense in it, along with burning coals from the altar, and hurry to the assembly to make atonement for them. Wrath has come out from the LORD; the plague has started.' ⁴⁷ So Aaron did as Moses said, and ran into the midst of the assembly. The plague had already started among the people, but Aaron offered the incense and made atonement for them. ⁴⁸ He stood between the living and the dead, and the plague stopped. ⁴⁹ But 14,700 people died from the plague, in addition to those who had died because of Korah. ⁵⁰ Then Aaron returned to Moses at the entrance to the tent of meeting, for the plague had stopped.*c*

The budding of Aaron's staff

17ᵃ The LORD said to Moses, ² 'Speak to the Israelites and get twelve staffs from them, one from the leader of each of their ancestral tribes. Write the name of each man on his staff. ³ On the staff of Levi write Aaron's name, for there must be one staff for the head of each ancestral tribe. ⁴ Place them in the tent of meeting in front of the ark of the covenant law, where I meet with you. ⁵ The staff belonging to the man I choose will sprout, and I will rid myself of this constant grumbling against you by the Israelites.'

⁶ So Moses spoke to the Israelites, and their leaders gave him twelve staffs, one for the leader of each of their ancestral tribes, and Aaron's staff was among them. ⁷ Moses placed the staffs before the LORD in the tent of the covenant law.

⁸ The next day Moses entered the tent and saw that Aaron's staff, which represented the tribe of Levi, had not only sprouted but had budded, blossomed and produced almonds. ⁹ Then Moses brought out all the staffs from the LORD's presence to all the Israelites. They looked at them, and each of the leaders took his own staff.

¹⁰ The LORD said to Moses, 'Put back Aaron's staff in front of the ark of the covenant law, to be kept as a sign to the rebellious. This will put an end to their grumbling against me, so that they will not die.' ¹¹ Moses did just as the LORD commanded him.

¹² The Israelites said to Moses, 'We shall die! We are lost, we are all lost! ¹³ Anyone who even comes near the tabernacle of the LORD will die. Are we all going to die?'

Duties of priests and Levites

18 The LORD said to Aaron, 'You, your sons and your family are to bear the responsibility for offences connected with the sanctuary, and you and your sons alone are to bear the responsibility for offences connected with the priesthood. ² Bring your fellow Levites from your ancestral tribe to join you and assist you when you and your sons minister before the tent of the covenant law. ³ They are to be responsible to you and are to perform all the duties of the tent, but they must not go near the furnishings of the sanctuary or the altar. Otherwise both they and you will die. ⁴ They are to join you and be responsible for the care of the tent of meeting – all the work at the tent – and no one else may come near where you are.

⁵ 'You are to be responsible for the care of the sanctuary and the altar, so that my wrath will not fall on the Israelites again. ⁶ I myself have selected your fellow Levites from among the Israelites as a gift to you, dedicated to the LORD to do the work at the tent of meeting. ⁷ But only you and your sons may serve as priests in

---

c 50 In Hebrew texts 16:36-50 is numbered 17:1-15.
a In Hebrew texts 17:1-13 is numbered 17:16-28.

connection with everything at the altar and inside the curtain. I am giving you the service of the priesthood as a gift. Anyone else who comes near the sanctuary is to be put to death.'

Offerings for priests and Levites

8 Then the LORD said to Aaron, 'I myself have put you in charge of the offerings presented to me; all the holy offerings the Israelites give me I give to you and your sons as your portion, your perpetual share. 9 You are to have the part of the most holy offerings that is kept from the fire. From all the gifts they bring me as most holy offerings, whether grain or sin[a] or guilt offerings, that part belongs to you and your sons. 10 Eat it as something most holy; every male shall eat it. You must regard it as holy.

11 'This also is yours: whatever is set aside from the gifts of all the wave offerings of the Israelites. I give this to you and your sons and daughters as your perpetual share. Everyone in your household who is ceremonially clean may eat it.

12 'I give you all the finest olive oil and all the finest new wine and grain they give to the LORD as the firstfruits of their harvest. 13 All the land's firstfruits that they bring to the LORD will be yours. Everyone in your household who is ceremonially clean may eat it.

14 'Everything in Israel that is devoted[b] to the LORD is yours. 15 The first offspring of every womb, both human and animal, that is offered to the LORD is yours. But you must redeem every firstborn son and every firstborn male of unclean animals. 16 When they are a month old, you must redeem them at the redemption price set at five shekels[c] of silver, according to the sanctuary shekel, which weighs twenty gerahs.

17 'But you must not redeem the firstborn of an ox, a sheep or a goat; they are holy. Splash their blood against the altar and burn their fat as a food offering, an aroma pleasing to the LORD. 18 Their meat

is to be yours, just as the breast of the wave offering and the right thigh are yours. 19 Whatever is set aside from the holy offerings the Israelites present to the LORD I give to you and your sons and daughters as your perpetual share. It is an everlasting covenant of salt before the LORD for both you and your offspring.'

20 The LORD said to Aaron, 'You will have no inheritance in their land, nor will you have any share among them; I am your share and your inheritance among the Israelites.

21 'I give to the Levites all the tithes in Israel as their inheritance in return for the work they do while serving at the tent of meeting. 22 From now on the Israelites must not go near the tent of meeting, or they will bear the consequences of their sin and will die. 23 It is the Levites who are to do the work at the tent of meeting and bear the responsibility for any offences they commit against it. This is a lasting ordinance for the generations to come. They will receive no inheritance among the Israelites. 24 Instead, I give to the Levites as their inheritance the tithes that the Israelites present as an offering to the LORD. That is why I said concerning them: "They will have no inheritance among the Israelites."'

25 The LORD said to Moses, 26 'Speak to the Levites and say to them: "When you receive from the Israelites the tithe I give you as your inheritance, you must present a tenth of that tithe as the LORD's offering. 27 Your offering will be reckoned to you as grain from the threshing-floor or juice from the winepress. 28 In this way you also will present an offering to the LORD from all the tithes you receive from the Israelites. From these tithes you must give the LORD's portion to Aaron the priest. 29 You must present as the LORD's portion the best and holiest part of everything given to you."

30 'Say to the Levites: "When you present the best part, it will be reckoned to you as the product of the threshing-floor or the winepress. 31 You and your households may eat the rest of it anywhere, for it is your wages for your work at the tent of meeting. 32 By presenting the best part of

---

a 9   Or *purification*
b 14   The Hebrew term refers to the irrevocable giving over of things or persons to the LORD.
c 16   That is, about 58 grams

it you will not be guilty in this matter; then you will not defile the holy offerings of the Israelites, and you will not die."'

The water of cleansing

19 The LORD said to Moses and Aaron: 2'This is a requirement of the law that the LORD has commanded: tell the Israelites to bring you a red heifer without defect or blemish and that has never been under a yoke. 3Give it to Eleazar the priest; it is to be taken outside the camp and slaughtered in his presence. 4Then Eleazar the priest is to take some of its blood on his finger and sprinkle it seven times towards the front of the tent of meeting. 5While he watches, the heifer is to be burned – its hide, flesh, blood and intestines. 6The priest is to take some cedar wood, hyssop and scarlet wool and throw them onto the burning heifer. 7After that, the priest must wash his clothes and bathe himself with water. He may then come into the camp, but he will be ceremonially unclean till evening. 8The man who burns it must also wash his clothes and bathe with water, and he too will be unclean till evening.

9'A man who is clean shall gather up the ashes of the heifer and put them in a ceremonially clean place outside the camp. They are to be kept by the Israelite community for use in the water of cleansing; it is for purification from sin. 10The man who gathers up the ashes of the heifer must also wash his clothes, and he too will be unclean till evening. This will be a lasting ordinance both for the Israelites and for the foreigners residing among them.

11'Whoever touches a human corpse will be unclean for seven days. 12They must purify themselves with the water on the third day and on the seventh day; then they will be clean. But if they do not purify themselves on the third and seventh days, they will not be clean. 13If they fail to purify themselves after touching a human corpse, they defile the LORD's tabernacle. They must be cut off from Israel. Because the water of cleansing has not been sprinkled on them, they are unclean; their uncleanness remains on them.

14'This is the law that applies when a person dies in a tent: anyone who enters the tent and anyone who is in it will be unclean for seven days, 15and every open container without a lid fastened on it will be unclean.

16'Anyone out in the open who touches someone who has been killed with a sword or someone who has died a natural death, or anyone who touches a human bone or a grave, will be unclean for seven days.

17'For the unclean person, put some ashes from the burned purification offering into a jar and pour fresh water over them. 18Then a man who is ceremonially clean is to take some hyssop, dip it in the water and sprinkle the tent and all the furnishings and the people who were there. He must also sprinkle anyone who has touched a human bone or a grave or anyone who has been killed or anyone who has died a natural death. 19The man who is clean is to sprinkle those who are unclean on the third and seventh days, and on the seventh day he is to purify them. Those who are being cleansed must wash their clothes and bathe with water, and that evening they will be clean. 20But if those who are unclean do not purify themselves, they must be cut off from the community, because they have defiled the sanctuary of the LORD. The water of cleansing has not been sprinkled on them, and they are unclean. 21This is a lasting ordinance for them.

'The man who sprinkles the water of cleansing must also wash his clothes, and anyone who touches the water of cleansing will be unclean till evening. 22Anything that an unclean person touches becomes unclean, and anyone who touches it becomes unclean till evening.'

Water from the rock

20 In the first month the whole Israelite community arrived at the Desert of Zin, and they stayed at Kadesh. There Miriam died and was buried.

2Now there was no water for the community, and the people gathered in opposition to Moses and Aaron. 3They quarrelled with Moses and said, 'If only we had died when our brothers fell dead before the Lord! 4 Why did you bring the Lord's community into this wilderness, that we and our livestock should die here? 5 Why did you bring us up out of Egypt to this terrible place? It has no corn or figs, grapevines or pomegranates. And there is no water to drink!'

6 Moses and Aaron went from the assembly to the entrance to the tent of meeting and fell face down, and the glory of the Lord appeared to them. 7 The Lord said to Moses, 8 'Take the staff, and you and your brother Aaron gather the assembly together. Speak to that rock before their eyes and it will pour out its water. You will bring water out of the rock for the community so that they and their livestock can drink.'

9 So Moses took the staff from the Lord's presence, just as he commanded him. 10 He and Aaron gathered the assembly together in front of the rock and Moses said to them, 'Listen, you rebels, must we bring you water out of this rock?' 11 Then Moses raised his arm and struck the rock twice with his staff. Water gushed out, and the community and their livestock drank.

12 But the Lord said to Moses and Aaron, 'Because you did not trust in me enough to honour me as holy in the sight of the Israelites, you will not bring this community into the land I give them.'

13 These were the waters of Meribah,*a* where the Israelites quarrelled with the Lord and where he was proved holy among them.

Edom denies Israel passage

14 Moses sent messengers from Kadesh to the king of Edom, saying:

'This is what your brother Israel says: you know about all the hardships that have come on us. 15 Our ancestors went down into Egypt, and we lived there many years. The Egyptians ill-treated us and our ancestors, 16 but when we cried out to the Lord, he heard our cry and sent an angel and brought us out of Egypt.

'Now we are here at Kadesh, a town on the edge of your territory. 17 Please let us pass through your country. We will not go through any field or vineyard, or drink water from any well. We will travel along the King's Highway and not turn to the right or to the left until we have passed through your territory.'

18 But Edom answered:

'You may not pass through here; if you try, we will march out and attack you with the sword.'

19 The Israelites replied:

'We will go along the main road, and if we or our livestock drink any of your water, we will pay for it. We only want to pass through on foot – nothing else.'

20 Again they answered:

'You may not pass through.'

Then Edom came out against them with a large and powerful army. 21 Since Edom refused to let them go through their territory, Israel turned away from them.

The death of Aaron

22 The whole Israelite community set out from Kadesh and came to Mount Hor. 23 At Mount Hor, near the border of Edom, the Lord said to Moses and Aaron, 24 'Aaron will be gathered to his people. He will not enter the land I give the Israelites, because both of you rebelled against my command at the waters of Meribah. 25 Call Aaron and his son Eleazar and take them up Mount Hor. 26 Remove Aaron's garments and put them on his son Eleazar, for Aaron will be gathered to his people; he will die there.'

27 Moses did as the Lord commanded: they went up Mount Hor in the sight of the whole community. 28 Moses removed Aaron's garments and put them on his son Eleazar. And Aaron died there on top

a 13 Meribah means quarrelling.

CHRIST IN ALL THE SCRIPTURES 6

Sustaining God's people

If we are to see Christ in the Old Testament, we need the New Testament as a guide. One of the most remarkable passages is 1 Corinthians 10:1–13, which refers directly to Numbers 20:1–13. The principle we need to understand is that *'These things happened to them as examples and were written down as warnings for us, on whom the culmination of the ages has come'* (1 Corinthians 10:11). These were real historical events, which have been recorded because we can learn from them. They are even more incredible now that the Old Testament promises have been fulfilled in the coming of Jesus. The wonderful, startling New Testament insight about the story of water from the rock is, *'that rock was Christ'* (v. 4). Although there was a physical rock in that desert, 'rock' is also a metaphor for the utter reliability of God if we would only trust him. So these verses do not mean that Moses hit Jesus with his staff! But they do claim that God the Son was there at that very moment: the water was his provision for his people in the wilderness. He provided the food and drink which kept them alive until they reached the Promised Land.

We should not be surprised. They were led through the wilderness by God's visible presence – a pillar of cloud by day and a pillar of fire by night. It was God's presence that saved them and that made them distinctive (Exodus 33:14–16). So why should we be surprised at a presence they were not yet in a position to understand? Christ accompanied them through the wilderness and saw them safe to the Promised Land. In just the same way, he promises to be with us *'to the end of the age'* (Matthew 28:20) even though we cannot physically see him.

There is a more serious application of this story, too. Although they lived in Christ's presence, they still disobeyed God again and again, and even Moses did not trust God as he should. Corinthians continues, *'Nevertheless, God was not pleased with most of them; their bodies were scattered in the wilderness. Now these things occurred as examples to keep us from setting our hearts on evil things as they did'* (1 Corinthians 10:5–6). Jesus promises us his presence and everything we need to serve him faithfully and make it home. He sustains us himself, but we have to choose to trust him and obey him. They did not know that Christ, the Son of God, was there with them, but we do. Sadly, it is still possible to live as though he were absent. He provides what we need, but we still need to honour his presence (v. 12) and live accordingly.

Graham Cray

of the mountain. Then Moses and Eleazar came down from the mountain, [29] and when the whole community learned that Aaron had died, all the Israelites mourned for him thirty days.

Arad destroyed

21 When the Canaanite king of Arad, who lived in the Negev, heard that Israel was coming along the road to Atharim, he attacked the Israelites and captured some of them. [2] Then Israel made this vow to the LORD: 'If you will deliver these people into our hands, we will totally destroy[a] their cities.' [3] The LORD listened to Israel's plea and gave the Canaanites over to them. They completely destroyed them and their towns; so the place was named Hormah.[b]

The bronze snake

[4] They travelled from Mount Hor along the route to the Red Sea,[c] to go round Edom. But the people grew impatient on the way; [5] they spoke against God and against Moses, and said, 'Why have you brought us up out of Egypt to die in the wilderness? There is no bread! There is no water! And we detest this miserable food!'

[6] Then the LORD sent venomous snakes among them; they bit the people and many Israelites died. [7] The people came to Moses and said, 'We sinned when we spoke against the LORD and against you. Pray that the LORD will take the snakes away from us.' So Moses prayed for the people.

[8] The LORD said to Moses, 'Make a snake and put it up on a pole; anyone who is bitten can look at it and live.' [9] So Moses made a bronze snake and put it up on a pole. Then when anyone was bitten by a snake and looked at the bronze snake, they lived.

The journey to Moab

[10] The Israelites moved on and camped at Oboth. [11] Then they set out from Oboth and camped in Iye Abarim, in the wilderness that faces Moab towards the sunrise. [12] From there they moved on and camped in the Zered Valley. [13] They set out from there and camped alongside the Arnon, which is in the wilderness extending into Amorite territory. The Arnon is the border of Moab, between Moab and the Amorites. [14] That is why the Book of the Wars of the LORD says:

'. . . Zahab[d] in Suphah and the ravines,
    the Arnon [15] and[e] the slopes of the
        ravines
that lead to the settlement of Ar
    and lie along the border of Moab.'

[16] From there they continued on to Beer, the well where the LORD said to Moses, 'Gather the people together and I will give them water.'

[17] Then Israel sang this song:

'Spring up, O well!
    Sing about it,
[18] about the well that the princes dug,
    that the nobles of the people sank –
        the nobles with sceptres and staffs.'

Then they went from the wilderness to Mattanah, [19] from Mattanah to Nahaliel, from Nahaliel to Bamoth, [20] and from Bamoth to the valley in Moab where the top of Pisgah overlooks the wasteland.

Defeat of Sihon and Og

[21] Israel sent messengers to say to Sihon king of the Amorites:

[22] 'Let us pass through your country. We will not turn aside into any field or vineyard, or drink water from any well. We will travel along the King's Highway until we have passed through your territory.'

---

a 2 The Hebrew term refers to the irrevocable giving over of things or persons to the LORD, often by totally destroying them; also in verse 3.
b 3 *Hormah* means *destruction*.
c 4 Or *the Sea of Reeds*

d 14 Septuagint; Hebrew *Waheb*
e 14,15 Or *'I have been given from Suphah and the ravines / of the Arnon* [15] *to*

23 But Sihon would not let Israel pass through his territory. He mustered his entire army and marched out into the wilderness against Israel. When he reached Jahaz, he fought with Israel. 24 Israel, however, put him to the sword and took over his land from the Arnon to the Jabbok, but only as far as the Ammonites,

CHRIST IN ALL THE SCRIPTURES 3

The promise of Satan's defeat

When Jesus takes an Old Testament story and applies it to himself, you know you have found him in the Old Testament. Jesus says, *'Just as Moses lifted up the snake in the wilderness, so the Son of Man must be lifted up, that everyone who believes may have eternal life in him'* (John 3:14–15). Later in John's Gospel he talks of being *'lifted up from the earth'*, referring to the way he will die (John 12:31–33). When this happens, *'the prince of this world* [Satan] *will be driven out'*. Jesus' death will free people from the power of evil and the evil one.

These verses in John act like a bookend, placed after the story in Numbers 21:4–9. But there is a bookend before the story as well. It is found in Genesis 3, where Satan, in the guise of a snake, tempts Adam and Eve to disobey God. It is the story of what we call 'the fall'. Men and women need to be forgiven for their sins and delivered from the power of the evil one. In Genesis, God promises that Eve's offspring, her descendant, will crush the snake's head. Her descendant was called Jesus. The story in Numbers anticipates Jesus' victory and hints at how it will happen.

God's people are being rebellious and ungrateful again! They complain and speak against the man who led them out of slavery and, much more serious, against the God who delivered them in such an amazing way. Their sin makes them vulnerable to attack, this time by poisonous snakes. The people repent and Moses prays for them. God tells him to make a metal snake and put it up on a pole. Anyone who has been bitten can look at it and live. Jesus says this is a picture of his death on the cross. Because of his atoning death, anyone who has sinned can come to him, confess their sins, be forgiven and set free from Satan's power.

The Bible is clear that sinners are not only people who do wrong, but people who have been captured by Satan as a result (see Ephesians 2:1–3). Through the cross Jesus not only forgives us, he breaks the power of evil and disarms it (see Colossians 2:13–15). The story of the snake on the pole shows both God's forgiveness and God's deliverance. As you read the story you can almost imagine seeing Jesus there, out of the corner of your eye.

Graham Cray

because their border was fortified. 25 Israel captured all the cities of the Amorites and occupied them, including Heshbon and all its surrounding settlements. 26 Heshbon was the city of Sihon king of the Amorites, who had fought against the former king of Moab and had taken from him all his land as far as the Arnon.

27 That is why the poets say:

'Come to Heshbon and let it be
    rebuilt;
  let Sihon's city be restored.

28 'Fire went out from Heshbon,
    a blaze from the city of Sihon.
  It consumed Ar of Moab,
    the citizens of Arnon's heights.
29 Woe to you, Moab!
  You are destroyed, people of
    Chemosh!
  He has given up his sons as fugitives
    and his daughters as captives
  to Sihon king of the Amorites.

30 'But we have overthrown them;
    Heshbon's dominion has been
      destroyed all the way to Dibon.
  We have demolished them as far as
    Nophah,
  which extends to Medeba.'

31 So Israel settled in the land of the Amorites.

32 After Moses had sent spies to Jazer, the Israelites captured its surrounding settlements and drove out the Amorites who were there. 33 Then they turned and went up along the road towards Bashan, and Og king of Bashan and his whole army marched out to meet them in battle at Edrei.

34 The LORD said to Moses, 'Do not be afraid of him, for I have delivered him into your hands, along with his whole army and his land. Do to him what you did to Sihon king of the Amorites, who reigned in Heshbon.'

35 So they struck him down, together with his sons and his whole army, leaving them no survivors. And they took possession of his land.

Balak summons Balaam

22 Then the Israelites travelled to the plains of Moab and camped along the Jordan opposite Jericho.

2 Now Balak son of Zippor saw all that Israel had done to the Amorites, 3 and Moab was terrified because there were so many people. Indeed, Moab was filled with dread because of the Israelites.

4 The Moabites said to the elders of Midian, 'This horde is going to lick up everything around us, as an ox licks up the grass of the field.'

So Balak son of Zippor, who was king of Moab at that time, 5 sent messengers to summon Balaam son of Beor, who was at Pethor, near the River Euphrates, in his native land. Balak said:

'A people has come out of Egypt; they cover the face of the land and have settled next to me. 6 Now come and put a curse on these people, because they are too powerful for me. Perhaps then I will be able to defeat them and drive them out of the land. For I know that whoever you bless is blessed, and whoever you curse is cursed.'

7 The elders of Moab and Midian left, taking with them the fee for divination. When they came to Balaam, they told him what Balak had said.

8 'Spend the night here,' Balaam said to them, 'and I will report back to you with the answer the LORD gives me.' So the Moabite officials stayed with him.

9 God came to Balaam and asked, 'Who are these men with you?'

10 Balaam said to God, 'Balak son of Zippor, king of Moab, sent me this message: 11 "A people that has come out of Egypt covers the face of the land. Now come and put a curse on them for me. Perhaps then I will be able to fight them and drive them away."'

12 But God said to Balaam, 'Do not go with them. You must not put a curse on those people, because they are blessed.'

13 The next morning Balaam got up and said to Balak's officials, 'Go back to your

own country, for the Lord has refused to let me go with you.'

¹⁴So the Moabite officials returned to Balak and said, 'Balaam refused to come with us.'

¹⁵Then Balak sent other officials, more numerous and more distinguished than the first. ¹⁶They came to Balaam and said:

'This is what Balak son of Zippor says: do not let anything keep you from coming to me, ¹⁷because I will reward you handsomely and do whatever you say. Come and put a curse on these people for me.'

¹⁸But Balaam answered them, 'Even if Balak gave me all the silver and gold in his palace, I could not do anything great or small to go beyond the command of the Lord my God. ¹⁹Now spend the night here so that I can find out what else the Lord will tell me.'

²⁰That night God came to Balaam and said, 'Since these men have come to summon you, go with them, but do only what I tell you.'

Balaam's donkey

²¹Balaam got up in the morning, saddled his donkey and went with the Moabite officials. ²²But God was very angry when he went, and the angel of the Lord stood in the road to oppose him. Balaam was riding on his donkey, and his two servants were with him. ²³When the donkey saw the angel of the Lord standing in the road with a drawn sword in his hand, it turned off the road into a field. Balaam beat it to get it back on the road.

²⁴Then the angel of the Lord stood in a narrow path through the vineyards, with walls on both sides. ²⁵When the donkey saw the angel of the Lord, it pressed close to the wall, crushing Balaam's foot against it. So he beat the donkey again.

²⁶Then the angel of the Lord moved on ahead and stood in a narrow place where there was no room to turn, either to the right or to the left. ²⁷When the donkey saw the angel of the Lord, it lay down under Balaam, and he was angry and beat it

with his staff. ²⁸Then the Lord opened the donkey's mouth, and it said to Balaam, 'What have I done to you to make you beat me these three times?'

²⁹Balaam answered the donkey, 'You have made a fool of me! If only I had a sword in my hand, I would kill you here and now.'

³⁰The donkey said to Balaam, 'Am I not your own donkey, which you have always ridden, to this day? Have I been in the habit of doing this to you?'

'No,' he said.

³¹Then the Lord opened Balaam's eyes, and he saw the angel of the Lord standing in the road with his sword drawn. So he bowed low and fell face down.

³²The angel of the Lord asked him, 'Why have you beaten your donkey these three times? I have come here to oppose you because your path is a reckless one before me.ᵃ ³³The donkey saw me and turned away from me these three times. If it had not turned away, I would certainly have killed you by now, but I would have spared it.'

³⁴Balaam said to the angel of the Lord, 'I have sinned. I did not realise you were standing in the road to oppose me. Now if you are displeased, I will go back.'

³⁵The angel of the Lord said to Balaam, 'Go with the men, but speak only what I tell you.' So Balaam went with Balak's officials.

³⁶When Balak heard that Balaam was coming, he went out to meet him at the Moabite town on the Arnon border, at the edge of his territory. ³⁷Balak said to Balaam, 'Did I not send you an urgent summons? Why didn't you come to me? Am I really not able to reward you?'

³⁸'Well, I have come to you now,' Balaam replied. 'But I can't say whatever I please. I must speak only what God puts in my mouth.'

³⁹Then Balaam went with Balak to Kiriath Huzoth. ⁴⁰Balak sacrificed cattle and sheep, and gave some to Balaam and the

---

a 32 The meaning of the Hebrew for this clause is uncertain.

officials who were with him. 41The next morning Balak took Balaam up to Bamoth Baal, and from there he could see the outskirts of the Israelite camp.

Balaam's first message

23 Balaam said, 'Build me seven altars here, and prepare seven bulls and seven rams for me.' 2Balak did as Balaam said, and the two of them offered a bull and a ram on each altar.

3Then Balaam said to Balak, 'Stay here beside your offering while I go aside. Perhaps the LORD will come to meet with me. Whatever he reveals to me I will tell you.' Then he went off to a barren height.

4God met with him, and Balaam said, 'I have prepared seven altars, and on each altar I have offered a bull and a ram.'

5The LORD put a word in Balaam's mouth and said, 'Go back to Balak and give him this word.'

6So he went back to him and found him standing beside his offering, with all the Moabite officials. 7Then Balaam spoke his message:

'Balak brought me from Aram,
    the king of Moab from the eastern
        mountains.
"Come," he said, "curse Jacob for me;
    come, denounce Israel."
8How can I curse
    those whom God has not cursed?
How can I denounce
    those whom the LORD has not
        denounced?
9From the rocky peaks I see them,
    from the heights I view them.
I see people who live apart
    and do not consider themselves one
        of the nations.
10Who can count the dust of Jacob
    or number even a fourth of
        Israel?
Let me die the death of the righteous,
    and may my final end be like theirs!'

11Balak said to Balaam, 'What have you done to me? I brought you to curse my enemies, but you have done nothing but bless them!'

12He answered, 'Must I not speak what the LORD puts in my mouth?'

Balaam's second message

13Then Balak said to him, 'Come with me to another place where you can see them; you will not see them all but only the outskirts of their camp. And from there, curse them for me.' 14So he took him to the field of Zophim on the top of Pisgah, and there he built seven altars and offered a bull and a ram on each altar.

15Balaam said to Balak, 'Stay here beside your offering while I meet with him over there.'

16The LORD met with Balaam and put a word in his mouth and said, 'Go back to Balak and give him this word.'

17So he went to him and found him standing beside his offering, with the Moabite officials. Balak asked him, 'What did the LORD say?'

18Then he spoke his message:

'Arise, Balak, and listen;
    hear me, son of Zippor.
19God is not human, that he should lie,
    not a human being, that he should
        change his mind.
Does he speak and then not act?
    Does he promise and not fulfil?
20I have received a command to bless;
    he has blessed, and I cannot
        change it.

21'No misfortune is seen in Jacob,
    no misery observed*a* in Israel.
The LORD their God is with them;
    the shout of the King is among
        them.
22God brought them out of Egypt;
    they have the strength of a wild ox.
23There is no divination against*b* Jacob,
    no evil omens against*b* Israel.
It will now be said of Jacob
    and of Israel, "See what God has
        done!"
24The people rise like a lioness;

---

a 21 Or *He has not looked on Jacob's offences / or on the wrongs found*
b 23 Or *in*

they rouse themselves like a lion
that does not rest till it devours its prey
and drinks the blood of its victims.'

25 Then Balak said to Balaam, 'Neither curse them at all nor bless them at all!'

26 Balaam answered, 'Did I not tell you I must do whatever the LORD says?'

Balaam's third message

27 Then Balak said to Balaam, 'Come, let me take you to another place. Perhaps it will please God to let you curse them for me from there.' 28 And Balak took Balaam to the top of Peor, overlooking the wasteland.

29 Balaam said, 'Build me seven altars here, and prepare seven bulls and seven rams for me.' 30 Balak did as Balaam had said, and offered a bull and a ram on each altar.

24 Now when Balaam saw that it pleased the LORD to bless Israel, he did not resort to divination as at other times, but turned his face towards the wilderness. 2 When Balaam looked out and saw Israel encamped tribe by tribe, the Spirit of God came on him 3 and he spoke his message:

'The prophecy of Balaam son of Beor,
    the prophecy of one whose eye sees
    clearly,
4 the prophecy of one who hears the
    words of God,
    who sees a vision from the
    Almighty,ᵃ
    who falls prostrate, and whose eyes
    are opened:

5 'How beautiful are your tents, Jacob,
    your dwelling-places, Israel!

6 'Like valleys they spread out,
    like gardens beside a river,
    like aloes planted by the LORD,
    like cedars beside the waters.
7 Water will flow from their buckets;
    their seed will have abundant
    water.

'Their king will be greater than Agag;
    their kingdom will be exalted.

8 'God brought them out of Egypt;
    they have the strength of a wild ox.
They devour hostile nations
    and break their bones in pieces;
    with their arrows they pierce them.
9 Like a lion they crouch and lie down,
    like a lioness – who dares to rouse
    them?

'May those who bless you be blessed
    and those who curse you be cursed!'

10 Then Balak's anger burned against Balaam. He struck his hands together and said to him, 'I summoned you to curse my enemies, but you have blessed them these three times. 11 Now leave at once and go home! I said I would reward you handsomely, but the LORD has kept you from being rewarded.'

12 Balaam answered Balak, 'Did I not tell the messengers you sent me, 13 "Even if Balak gave me all the silver and gold in his palace, I could not do anything of my own accord, good or bad, to go beyond the command of the LORD – and I must say only what the LORD says"? 14 Now I am going back to my people, but come, let me warn you of what this people will do to your people in days to come.'

Balaam's fourth message

15 Then he spoke his message:

'The prophecy of Balaam son of Beor,
    the prophecy of one whose eye sees
    clearly,
16 the prophecy of one who hears the
    words of God,
    who has knowledge from the Most
    High,
    who sees a vision from the Almighty,
    who falls prostrate, and whose eyes
    are opened:

17 'I see him, but not now;
    I behold him, but not near.
A star will come out of Jacob;
    a sceptre will rise out of Israel.

ᵃ 4 Hebrew *Shaddai*; also in verse 16

He will crush the foreheads of Moab,
   the skulls[b] of[c] all the people of
   Sheth.[d]
[18] Edom will be conquered;
   Seir, his enemy, will be conquered,
   but Israel will grow strong.
[19] A ruler will come out of Jacob
   and destroy the survivors of the
   city.'

Balaam's fifth message

[20] Then Balaam saw Amalek and spoke
his message:

'Amalek was first among the nations,
   but their end will be utter
   destruction.'

Balaam's sixth message

[21] Then he saw the Kenites and spoke
his message:

'Your dwelling-place is secure,
   your nest is set in a rock;
[22] yet you Kenites will be destroyed
   when Ashur takes you captive.'

Balaam's seventh message

[23] Then he spoke his message:

'Alas! Who can live when God does
   this?[e]
[24]   Ships will come from the shores of
   Cyprus;
they will subdue Ashur and Eber,
   but they too will come to ruin.'

[25] Then Balaam got up and returned
home, and Balak went his own way.

Moab seduces Israel

25 While Israel was staying in
Shittim, the men began to indulge in sexual immorality with Moabite

women, [2] who invited them to the sacrifices to their gods. The people ate the
sacrificial meal and bowed down before
these gods. [3] So Israel yoked themselves
to the Baal of Peor. And the Lord's anger
burned against them.

[4] The Lord said to Moses, 'Take all the
leaders of these people, kill them and expose them in broad daylight before the
Lord, so that the Lord's fierce anger may
turn away from Israel.'

[5] So Moses said to Israel's judges, 'Each
of you must put to death those of your
people who have yoked themselves to the
Baal of Peor.'

[6] Then an Israelite man brought into
the camp a Midianite woman right before
the eyes of Moses and the whole assembly
of Israel while they were weeping at the
entrance to the tent of meeting. [7] When
Phinehas son of Eleazar, the son of Aaron,
the priest, saw this, he left the assembly,
took a spear in his hand [8] and followed the
Israelite into the tent. He drove the spear
into both of them, right through the Israelite man and into the woman's stomach. Then the plague against the Israelites
was stopped; [9] but those who died in the
plague numbered 24,000.

[10] The Lord said to Moses, [11] 'Phinehas son of Eleazar, the son of Aaron, the
priest, has turned my anger away from the
Israelites. Since he was as zealous for my
honour among them as I am, I did not put
an end to them in my zeal. [12] Therefore tell
him I am making my covenant of peace
with him. [13] He and his descendants will
have a covenant of a lasting priesthood,
because he was zealous for the honour of
his God and made atonement for the Israelites.'

[14] The name of the Israelite who was
killed with the Midianite woman was
Zimri son of Salu, the leader of a Sime-
onite family. [15] And the name of the Midianite woman who was put to death was
Kozbi daughter of Zur, a tribal chief of a
Midianite family.

[16] The Lord said to Moses, [17] 'Treat the
Midianites as enemies and kill them.
[18] They treated you as enemies when
they deceived you in the Peor incident

---

b 17 Samaritan Pentateuch (see also Jer. 48:45);
the meaning of the word in the Masoretic Text is
uncertain.

c 17 Or possibly *Moab*, / *batter*

d 17 Or *all the noisy boasters*

e 23 Masoretic Text; with a different word division
of the Hebrew *The people from the islands will gather from
the north.*

involving their sister Kozbi, the daughter of a Midianite leader, the woman who was killed when the plague came as a result of that incident.'

The second census

26 After the plague the LORD said to Moses and Eleazar son of Aaron, the priest, ² 'Take a census of the whole Israelite community by families – all those twenty years old or more who are able to serve in the army of Israel.' ³ So on the plains of Moab by the Jordan opposite Jericho, Moses and Eleazar the priest spoke with them and said, ⁴ 'Take a census of men twenty years old or more, as the LORD commanded Moses.'

These were the Israelites who came out of Egypt:

⁵ The descendants of Reuben, the firstborn son of Israel, were:
through Hanok, the Hanokite clan;
through Pallu, the Palluite clan;
⁶ through Hezron, the Hezronite clan;
through Karmi, the Karmite clan.
⁷ These were the clans of Reuben; those numbered were 43,730.
⁸ The son of Pallu was Eliab, ⁹ and the sons of Eliab were Nemuel, Dathan and Abiram. The same Dathan and Abiram were the community officials who rebelled against Moses and Aaron and were among Korah's followers when they rebelled against the LORD. ¹⁰ The earth opened its mouth and swallowed them along with Korah, whose followers died when the fire devoured the 250 men. And they served as a warning sign. ¹¹ The line of Korah, however, did not die out.

¹² The descendants of Simeon by their clans were:
through Nemuel, the Nemuelite clan;
through Jamin, the Jaminite clan;
through Jakin, the Jakinite clan;
¹³ through Zerah, the Zerahite clan;
through Shaul, the Shaulite clan.
¹⁴ These were the clans of Simeon; those numbered were 22,200.

¹⁵ The descendants of Gad by their clans were:
through Zephon, the Zephonite clan;
through Haggi, the Haggite clan;
through Shuni, the Shunite clan;
¹⁶ through Ozni, the Oznite clan;
through Eri, the Erite clan;
¹⁷ through Arodi,ᵃ the Arodite clan;
through Areli, the Arelite clan.
¹⁸ These were the clans of Gad; those numbered were 40,500.

¹⁹ Er and Onan were sons of Judah, but they died in Canaan.
²⁰ The descendants of Judah by their clans were:
through Shelah, the Shelanite clan;
through Perez, the Perezite clan;
through Zerah, the Zerahite clan.
²¹ The descendants of Perez were:
through Hezron, the Hezronite clan;
through Hamul, the Hamulite clan.
²² These were the clans of Judah; those numbered were 76,500.

²³ The descendants of Issachar by their clans were:
through Tola, the Tolaite clan;
through Puah, the Puiteᵇ clan;
²⁴ through Jashub, the Jashubite clan;
through Shimron, the Shimronite clan.
²⁵ These were the clans of Issachar; those numbered were 64,300.

²⁶ The descendants of Zebulun by their clans were:
through Sered, the Seredite clan;
through Elon, the Elonite clan;
through Jahleel, the Jahleelite clan.
²⁷ These were the clans of Zebulun; those numbered were 60,500.

ᵃ 17 Samaritan Pentateuch and Syriac (see also Gen. 46:16); Masoretic Text *Arod*
ᵇ 23 Samaritan Pentateuch, Septuagint, Vulgate and Syriac (see also 1 Chron. 7:1); Masoretic Text *through Puvah, the Punite*

28 The descendants of Joseph by their clans through Manasseh and Ephraim were:

29 The descendants of Manasseh:
     through Makir, the Makirite clan (Makir was the father of Gilead); through Gilead, the Gileadite clan.
30 These were the descendants of Gilead:
     through Iezer, the Iezerite clan; through Helek, the Helekite clan;
31 through Asriel, the Asrielite clan; through Shechem, the Shechemite clan;
32 through Shemida, the Shemidaite clan; through Hepher, the Hepherite clan.
33 (Zelophehad son of Hepher had no sons; he had only daughters, whose names were Mahlah, Noah, Hoglah, Milkah and Tirzah.)
34 These were the clans of Manasseh; those numbered were 52,700.

35 These were the descendants of Ephraim by their clans:
     through Shuthelah, the Shuthelahite clan; through Beker, the Bekerite clan; through Tahan, the Tahanite clan.
36 These were the descendants of Shuthelah:
     through Eran, the Eranite clan.
37 These were the clans of Ephraim; those numbered were 32,500.

These were the descendants of Joseph by their clans.

38 The descendants of Benjamin by their clans were:
     through Bela, the Belaite clan; through Ashbel, the Ashbelite clan; through Ahiram, the Ahiramite clan;
39 through Shupham,*c* the Shuphamite clan;

through Hupham, the Huphamite clan.
40 The descendants of Bela through Ard and Naaman were:
     through Ard,*d* the Ardite clan; through Naaman, the Naamite clan.
41 These were the clans of Benjamin; those numbered were 45,600.

42 These were the descendants of Dan by their clans:
     through Shuham, the Shuhamite clan.
These were the clans of Dan: 43 all of them were Shuhamite clans; and those numbered were 64,400.

44 The descendants of Asher by their clans were:
     through Imnah, the Imnite clan; through Ishvi, the Ishvite clan; through Beriah, the Beriite clan;
45 and through the descendants of Beriah:
     through Heber, the Heberite clan; through Malkiel, the Malkielite clan.
46 (Asher had a daughter named Serah.)
47 These were the clans of Asher; those numbered were 53,400.

48 The descendants of Naphtali by their clans were:
     through Jahzeel, the Jahzeelite clan; through Guni, the Gunite clan;
49 through Jezer, the Jezerite clan; through Shillem, the Shillemite clan.
50 These were the clans of Naphtali; those numbered were 45,400.

51 The total number of the men of Israel was 601,730.

52 The LORD said to Moses, 53 'The land is to be allotted to them as an inheritance based on the number of names. 54 To a larger group give a larger inheritance, and

---

c 39 A few manuscripts of the Masoretic Text, Samaritan Pentateuch, Vulgate and Syriac (see also Septuagint); most manuscripts of the Masoretic Text *Shephupham*

d 40 Samaritan Pentateuch and Vulgate (see also Septuagint); Masoretic Text does not have *through Ard,* to a smaller group a smaller one; each is to receive its inheritance according to the number of those listed. 55 Be sure that the land is distributed by lot. What each group inherits will be according to the names for its ancestral tribe. 56 Each inheritance is to be distributed by lot among the larger and smaller groups.'

57 These were the Levites who were counted by their clans:

through Gershon, the Gershonite clan;

through Kohath, the Kohathite clan;

through Merari, the Merarite clan.

58 These also were Levite clans:

the Libnite clan,

the Hebronite clan,

the Mahlite clan,

the Mushite clan,

the Korahite clan.

(Kohath was the forefather of Amram; 59 the name of Amram's wife was Jochebed, a descendant of Levi, who was born to the Levites[e] in Egypt. To Amram she bore Aaron, Moses and their sister Miriam. 60 Aaron was the father of Nadab and Abihu, Eleazar and Ithamar. 61 But Nadab and Abihu died when they made an offering before the LORD with unauthorised fire.)

62 All the male Levites a month old or more numbered 23,000. They were not counted along with the other Israelites because they received no inheritance among them.

63 These are the ones counted by Moses and Eleazar the priest when they counted the Israelites on the plains of Moab by the Jordan opposite Jericho. 64 Not one of them was among those counted by Moses and Aaron the priest when they counted the Israelites in the Desert of Sinai. 65 For the LORD had told those Israelites they would surely die in the wilderness, and not one of them was left except Caleb son of Jephunneh and Joshua son of Nun.

---

e 59 Or Jochebed, a daughter of Levi, who was born to Levi

Zelophehad's daughters

27 The daughters of Zelophehad son of Hepher, the son of Gilead, the son of Makir, the son of Manasseh, belonged to the clans of Manasseh son of Joseph. The names of the daughters were Mahlah, Noah, Hoglah, Milkah and Tirzah. They came forward 2 and stood before Moses, Eleazar the priest, the leaders and the whole assembly at the entrance to the tent of meeting and said, 3 'Our father died in the wilderness. He was not among Korah's followers, who banded together against the LORD, but he died for his own sin and left no sons. 4 Why should our father's name disappear from his clan because he had no son? Give us property among our father's relatives.'

5 So Moses brought their case before the LORD, 6 and the LORD said to him, 7 'What Zelophehad's daughters are saying is right. You must certainly give them property as an inheritance among their father's relatives and give their father's inheritance to them.

8 'Say to the Israelites, "If a man dies and leaves no son, give his inheritance to his daughter. 9 If he has no daughter, give his inheritance to his brothers. 10 If he has no brothers, give his inheritance to his father's brothers. 11 If his father had no brothers, give his inheritance to the nearest relative in his clan, that he may possess it. This is to have the force of law for the Israelites, as the LORD commanded Moses."'

Joshua to succeed Moses

12 Then the LORD said to Moses, 'Go up this mountain in the Abarim Range and see the land I have given the Israelites. 13 After you have seen it, you too will be gathered to your people, as your brother Aaron was, 14 for when the community rebelled at the waters in the Desert of Zin, both of you disobeyed my command to honour me as holy before their eyes.' (These were the waters of Meribah Kadesh, in the Desert of Zin.)

15 Moses said to the LORD, 16 'May the LORD, the God who gives breath to all living things, appoint someone over this

community [17]to go out and come in before them, one who will lead them out and bring them in, so that the LORD's people will not be like sheep without a shepherd.'

[18]So the LORD said to Moses, 'Take Joshua son of Nun, a man in whom is the spirit of leadership,*a* and lay your hand on him. [19]Make him stand before Eleazar the priest and the entire assembly and commission him in their presence. [20]Give him some of your authority so that the whole Israelite community will obey him. [21]He is to stand before Eleazar the priest, who will obtain decisions for him by enquiring of the Urim before the LORD. At his command he and the entire community of the Israelites will go out, and at his command they will come in.'

[22]Moses did as the LORD commanded him. He took Joshua and made him stand before Eleazar the priest and the whole assembly. [23]Then he laid his hands on him and commissioned him, as the LORD instructed through Moses.

Daily offerings

28 The LORD said to Moses, [2]'Give this command to the Israelites and say to them: "Make sure that you present to me at the appointed time my food offerings, as an aroma pleasing to me." [3]Say to them: "This is the food offering you are to present to the LORD: two lambs a year old without defect, as a regular burnt offering each day. [4]Offer one lamb in the morning and the other at twilight, [5]together with a grain offering of a tenth of an ephah*a* of the finest flour mixed with a quarter of a hin*b* of oil from pressed olives. [6]This is the regular burnt offering instituted at Mount Sinai as a pleasing aroma, a food offering presented to the LORD. [7]The accompanying drink offering is to be a quarter of a hin of fermented drink with each lamb. Pour out the drink offering to the LORD at the sanctuary. [8]Offer the second lamb at twilight, along with the same kind of

grain offering and drink offering that you offer in the morning. This is a food offering, an aroma pleasing to the LORD.

Sabbath offerings

[9]'"On the Sabbath day, make an offering of two lambs a year old without defect, together with its drink offering and a grain offering of one-fifth of an ephah*c* of the finest flour mixed with olive oil. [10]This is the burnt offering for every Sabbath, in addition to the regular burnt offering and its drink offering.

Monthly offerings

[11]'"On the first of every month, present to the LORD a burnt offering of two young bulls, one ram and seven male lambs a year old, all without defect. [12]With each bull there is to be a grain offering of three-tenths of an ephah*d* of the finest flour mixed with oil; with the ram, a grain offering of one-fifth of an ephah of the finest flour mixed with oil; [13]and with each lamb, a grain offering of a tenth of an ephah of the finest flour mixed with oil. This is for a burnt offering, a pleasing aroma, a food offering presented to the LORD. [14]With each bull there is to be a drink offering of half a hin*e* of wine; with the ram, a third of a hin;*f* and with each lamb, a quarter of a hin. This is the monthly burnt offering to be made at each new moon during the year. [15]Besides the regular burnt offering with its drink offering, one male goat is to be presented to the LORD as a sin offering.*g*

The Passover

[16]'"On the fourteenth day of the first month the LORD's Passover is to be held. [17]On the fifteenth day of this month there is to be a festival; for seven days eat bread made without yeast. [18]On the first day hold a sacred assembly and do not do any

---

a 18 Or *the Spirit*

a 5 That is, probably about 1.6 kilograms; also in verses 13, 21 and 29

b 5 That is, about 1 litre; also in verses 7 and 14

c 9 That is, probably about 3.2 kilograms; also in verses 12, 20 and 28

d 12 That is, probably about 5 kilograms; also in verses 20 and 28

e 14 That is, about 1.9 litres

f 14 That is, about 1.3 litres

g 15 Or *purification offering*; also in verse 22

of your ordinary work. ¹⁹ Present to the LORD a food offering consisting of a burnt offering of two young bulls, one ram and seven male lambs a year old, all without defect. ²⁰ With each bull offer a grain offering of three-tenths of an ephah of the finest flour mixed with oil; with the ram, one-fifth; ²¹ and with each of the seven lambs, one-tenth. ²² Include one male goat as a sin offering to make atonement for you. ²³ Offer these in addition to the regular morning burnt offering. ²⁴ In this way present the food offering every day for seven days as an aroma pleasing to the LORD; it is to be offered in addition to the regular burnt offering and its drink offering. ²⁵ On the seventh day hold a sacred assembly and do not do any ordinary work.

The Festival of Weeks

²⁶ ' "On the day of firstfruits, when you present to the LORD an offering of new grain during the Festival of Weeks, hold a sacred assembly and do not do any of your ordinary work. ²⁷ Present a burnt offering of two young bulls, one ram and seven male lambs a year old as an aroma pleasing to the LORD. ²⁸ With each bull there is to be a grain offering of three-tenths of an ephah of the finest flour mixed with oil; with the ram, one-fifth; ²⁹ and with each of the seven lambs, one-tenth. ³⁰ Include one male goat to make atonement for you. ³¹ Offer these together with their drink offerings, in addition to the regular burnt offering and its grain offering. Be sure the animals are without defect.

The Festival of Trumpets

29 ' "On the first day of the seventh month hold a sacred assembly and do not do any of your ordinary work. It is a day for you to sound the trumpets. ² As an aroma pleasing to the LORD, offer a burnt offering of one young bull, one ram and seven male lambs a year old, all without defect. ³ With the bull offer a grain offering of three-tenths of an ephah[a]

of the finest flour mixed with olive oil; with the ram, one-fifth;[b] ⁴ and with each of the seven lambs, one-tenth.[c] ⁵ Include one male goat as a sin offering[d] to make atonement for you. ⁶ These are in addition to the monthly and daily burnt offerings with their grain offerings and drink offerings as specified. They are food offerings presented to the LORD, a pleasing aroma.

FAVOURITE VERSES

Psalm 91:11–12

For he will command his angels
concerning you
to guard you in all your ways;
they will lift you up in their hands,
so that you will not strike your foot
against a stone.

My favourite Bible verse has to be this. It makes me feel so happy to know that God wants to keep me safe.

Jess, 14

The Day of Atonement

⁷ ' "On the tenth day of this seventh month hold a sacred assembly. You must deny yourselves[e] and do no work. ⁸ Present as an aroma pleasing to the LORD a burnt offering of one young bull, one ram and seven male lambs a year old, all without defect. ⁹ With the bull offer a grain offering of three-tenths of an ephah of the finest flour mixed with oil; with the ram,

---

a 3 That is, probably about 5 kilograms; also in verses 9 and 14

b 3 That is, probably about 3.2 kilograms; also in verses 9 and 14
c 4 That is, probably about 1.6 kilograms; also in verses 10 and 15
d 5 Or *purification offering*; also elsewhere in this chapter
e 7 Or *must fast*

one-fifth; [10] and with each of the seven lambs, one-tenth. [11] Include one male goat as a sin offering, in addition to the sin offering for atonement and the regular burnt offering with its grain offering, and their drink offerings.

The Festival of Tabernacles

[12] "On the fifteenth day of the seventh month, hold a sacred assembly and do not do any of your ordinary work. Celebrate a festival to the LORD for seven days. [13] Present as an aroma pleasing to the LORD a food offering consisting of a burnt offering of thirteen young bulls, two rams and fourteen male lambs a year old, all without defect. [14] With each of the thirteen bulls offer a grain offering of three-tenths of an ephah of the finest flour mixed with oil; with each of the two rams, one-fifth; [15] and with each of the fourteen lambs, one-tenth. [16] Include one male goat as a sin offering, in addition to the regular burnt offering with its grain offering and drink offering.

[17] "On the second day offer twelve young bulls, two rams and fourteen male lambs a year old, all without defect. [18] With the bulls, rams and lambs, offer their grain offerings and drink offerings according to the number specified. [19] Include one male goat as a sin offering, in addition to the regular burnt offering with its grain offering, and their drink offerings.

[20] "On the third day offer eleven bulls, two rams and fourteen male lambs a year old, all without defect. [21] With the bulls, rams and lambs, offer their grain offerings and drink offerings according to the number specified. [22] Include one male goat as a sin offering, in addition to the regular burnt offering with its grain offering and drink offering.

[23] "On the fourth day offer ten bulls, two rams and fourteen male lambs a year old, all without defect. [24] With the bulls, rams and lambs, offer their grain offerings and drink offerings according to the number specified. [25] Include one male goat as a sin offering, in addition to the regular burnt offering with its grain offering and drink offering.

[26] "On the fifth day offer nine bulls, two rams and fourteen male lambs a year old, all without defect. [27] With the bulls, rams and lambs, offer their grain offerings and drink offerings according to the number specified. [28] Include one male goat as a sin offering, in addition to the regular burnt offering with its grain offering and drink offering.

[29] "On the sixth day offer eight bulls, two rams and fourteen male lambs a year old, all without defect. [30] With the bulls, rams and lambs, offer their grain offerings and drink offerings according to the number specified. [31] Include one male goat as a sin offering, in addition to the regular burnt offering with its grain offering and drink offering.

[32] "On the seventh day offer seven bulls, two rams and fourteen male lambs a year old, all without defect. [33] With the bulls, rams and lambs, offer their grain offerings and drink offerings according to the number specified. [34] Include one male goat as a sin offering, in addition to the regular burnt offering with its grain offering and drink offering.

[35] "On the eighth day hold a closing special assembly and do not do any of your ordinary work. [36] Present as an aroma pleasing to the LORD a food offering consisting of a burnt offering of one bull, one ram and seven male lambs a year old, all without defect. [37] With the bull, the ram and the lambs, offer their grain offerings and drink offerings according to the number specified. [38] Include one male goat as a sin offering, in addition to the regular burnt offering with its grain offering and drink offering.

[39] "In addition to what you vow and your freewill offerings, offer these to the LORD at your appointed festivals: your burnt offerings, grain offerings, drink offerings and fellowship offerings.'"

[40] Moses told the Israelites all that the LORD commanded him.*f*

---

f 40 In Hebrew texts this verse (29:40) is numbered 30:1.

Vows

30[a] Moses said to the heads of the tribes of Israel: 'This is what the LORD commands: 2 when a man makes a vow to the LORD or takes an oath to bind himself by a pledge, he must not break his word but must do everything he said.

3 'When a young woman still living in her father's household makes a vow to the LORD or binds herself by a pledge 4 and her father hears about her vow or pledge but says nothing to her, then all her vows and every pledge by which she bound herself will stand. 5 But if her father forbids her when he hears about it, none of her vows or the pledges by which she bound herself will stand; the LORD will release her because her father has forbidden her.

6 'If she marries after she makes a vow or after her lips utter a rash promise by which she binds herself 7 and her husband hears about it but says nothing to her, then her vows or the pledges by which she bound herself will stand. 8 But if her husband forbids her when he hears about it, he nullifies the vow that binds her or the rash promise by which she binds herself, and the LORD will release her.

9 'Any vow or obligation taken by a widow or divorced woman will be binding on her.

10 'If a woman living with her husband makes a vow or binds herself by a pledge under oath 11 and her husband hears about it but says nothing to her and does not forbid her, then all her vows or the pledges by which she bound herself will stand. 12 But if her husband nullifies them when he hears about them, then none of the vows or pledges that came from her lips will stand. Her husband has nullified them, and the LORD will release her. 13 Her husband may confirm or nullify any vow she makes or any sworn pledge to deny herself.[b] 14 But if her husband says nothing to her about it from day to day, then he confirms all her vows or the pledges binding on her. He confirms them by saying nothing to her when he hears about

them. 15 If, however, he nullifies them some time after he hears about them, then he must bear the consequences of her wrongdoing.'

16 These are the regulations the LORD gave Moses concerning relationships between a man and his wife, and between a father and his young daughter still living at home.

Vengeance on the Midianites

31 The LORD said to Moses, 2 'Take vengeance on the Midianites for the Israelites. After that, you will be gathered to your people.'

3 So Moses said to the people, 'Arm some of your men to go to war against the Midianites so that they may carry out the LORD's vengeance on them. 4 Send into battle a thousand men from each of the tribes of Israel.' 5 So twelve thousand men armed for battle, a thousand from each tribe, were supplied from the clans of Israel. 6 Moses sent them into battle, a thousand from each tribe, along with Phinehas son of Eleazar, the priest, who took with him articles from the sanctuary and the trumpets for signalling.

7 They fought against Midian, as the LORD commanded Moses, and killed every man. 8 Among their victims were Evi, Rekem, Zur, Hur and Reba – the five kings of Midian. They also killed Balaam son of Beor with the sword. 9 The Israelites captured the Midianite women and children and took all the Midianite herds, flocks and goods as plunder. 10 They burned all the towns where the Midianites had settled, as well as all their camps. 11 They took all the plunder and spoils, including the people and animals, 12 and brought the captives, spoils and plunder to Moses and Eleazar the priest and the Israelite assembly at their camp on the plains of Moab, by the Jordan opposite Jericho.

13 Moses, Eleazar the priest and all the leaders of the community went to meet them outside the camp. 14 Moses was angry with the officers of the army – the commanders of thousands and commanders of hundreds – who returned from the battle.

---

a In Hebrew texts 30:1-16 is numbered 30:2-17.
b 13 Or *to fast*

15 'Have you allowed all the women to live?' he asked them. 16 'They were the ones who followed Balaam's advice and enticed the Israelites to be unfaithful to the Lord in the Peor incident, so that a plague struck the Lord's people. 17 Now kill all the boys. And kill every woman who has slept with a man, 18 but save for yourselves every girl who has never slept with a man.

19 'Anyone who has killed someone or touched someone who was killed must stay outside the camp seven days. On the third and seventh days you must purify yourselves and your captives. 20 Purify every garment as well as everything made of leather, goat hair or wood.'

21 Then Eleazar the priest said to the soldiers who had gone into battle, 'This is what is required by the law that the Lord gave Moses: 22 gold, silver, bronze, iron, tin, lead 23 and anything else that can withstand fire must be put through the fire, and then it will be clean. But it must also be purified with the water of cleansing. And whatever cannot withstand fire must be put through that water. 24 On the seventh day wash your clothes and you will be clean. Then you may come into the camp.'

Dividing the spoils

25 The Lord said to Moses, 26 'You and Eleazar the priest and the family heads of the community are to count all the people and animals that were captured. 27 Divide the spoils equally between the soldiers who took part in the battle and the rest of the community. 28 From the soldiers who fought in the battle, set apart as tribute for the Lord one out of every five hundred, whether people, cattle, donkeys or sheep. 29 Take this tribute from their half share and give it to Eleazar the priest as the Lord's part. 30 From the Israelites' half, select one out of every fifty, whether people, cattle, donkeys, sheep or other animals. Give them to the Levites, who are responsible for the care of the Lord's tabernacle.' 31 So Moses and Eleazar the priest did as the Lord commanded Moses.

32 The plunder remaining from the spoils that the soldiers took was 675,000 sheep, 33 72,000 cattle, 34 61,000 donkeys 35 and 32,000 women who had never slept with a man.

36 The half share of those who fought in the battle was:

337,500 sheep, 37 of which the tribute for the Lord was 675;
38 36,000 cattle, of which the tribute for the Lord was 72;
39 30,500 donkeys, of which the tribute for the Lord was 61;
40 16,000 people, of whom the tribute for the Lord was 32.

41 Moses gave the tribute to Eleazar the priest as the Lord's part, as the Lord commanded Moses.

42 The half belonging to the Israelites, which Moses set apart from that of the fighting men – 43 the community's half – was 337,500 sheep, 44 36,000 cattle, 45 30,500 donkeys 46 and 16,000 people. 47 From the Israelites' half, Moses selected one out of every fifty people and animals, as the Lord commanded him, and gave them to the Levites, who were responsible for the care of the Lord's tabernacle.

48 Then the officers who were over the units of the army – the commanders of thousands and commanders of hundreds – went to Moses 49 and said to him, 'Your servants have counted the soldiers under our command, and not one is missing. 50 So we have brought as an offering to the Lord the gold articles each of us acquired – armlets, bracelets, signet rings, earrings and necklaces – to make atonement for ourselves before the Lord.'

51 Moses and Eleazar the priest accepted from them the gold – all the handcrafted articles. 52 All the gold from the commanders of thousands and commanders of hundreds that Moses and Eleazar presented as a gift to the Lord weighed 16,750 shekels. *a* 53 Each soldier had taken plunder for himself. 54 Moses and Eleazar the priest accepted the gold from the commanders of thousands and commanders

---

a 52 That is, about 190 kilograms

of hundreds and brought it into the tent of meeting as a memorial for the Israelites before the LORD.

The Transjordan tribes

32 The Reubenites and Gadites, who had very large herds and flocks, saw that the lands of Jazer and Gilead were suitable for livestock. 2So they came to Moses and Eleazar the priest and to the leaders of the community, and said, 3'Ataroth, Dibon, Jazer, Nimrah, Heshbon, Elealeh, Sebam, Nebo and Beon – 4the land the LORD subdued before the people of Israel – are suitable for livestock, and your servants have livestock. 5If we have found favour in your eyes,' they said, 'let this land be given to your servants as our possession. Do not make us cross the Jordan.'

6Moses said to the Gadites and Reubenites, 'Should your fellow Israelites go to war while you sit here? 7Why do you discourage the Israelites from crossing over into the land the LORD has given them? 8This is what your fathers did when I sent them from Kadesh Barnea to look over the land. 9After they went up to the Valley of Eshkol and viewed the land, they discouraged the Israelites from entering the land the LORD had given them. 10The LORD's anger was aroused that day and he swore this oath: 11"Because they have not followed me wholeheartedly, not one of those who were twenty years old or more when they came up out of Egypt will see the land I promised on oath to Abraham, Isaac and Jacob – 12not one except Caleb son of Jephunneh the Kenizzite and Joshua son of Nun, for they followed the LORD wholeheartedly." 13The LORD's anger burned against Israel and he made them wander in the wilderness for forty years, until the whole generation of those who had done evil in his sight was gone.

14'And here you are, a brood of sinners, standing in the place of your fathers and making the LORD even more angry with Israel. 15If you turn away from following him, he will again leave all this people in the wilderness, and you will be the cause of their destruction.'

16Then they came up to him and said, 'We would like to build pens here for our livestock and cities for our women and children. 17But we will arm ourselves for battle*a* and go ahead of the Israelites until we have brought them to their place. Meanwhile our women and children will live in fortified cities, for protection from the inhabitants of the land. 18We will not return to our homes until each of the Israelites has received their inheritance. 19We will not receive any inheritance with them on the other side of the Jordan, because our inheritance has come to us on the east side of the Jordan.'

20Then Moses said to them, 'If you will do this – if you will arm yourselves before the LORD for battle 21 and if all of you who are armed cross over the Jordan before the LORD until he has driven his enemies out before him – 22then when the land is subdued before the LORD, you may return and be free from your obligation to the LORD and to Israel. And this land will be your possession before the LORD.

23'But if you fail to do this, you will be sinning against the LORD; and you may be sure that your sin will find you out. 24Build cities for your women and children, and pens for your flocks, but do what you have promised.'

25The Gadites and Reubenites said to Moses, 'We your servants will do as our lord commands. 26Our children and wives, our flocks and herds will remain here in the cities of Gilead. 27But your servants, every man who is armed for battle, will cross over to fight before the LORD, just as our lord says.'

28Then Moses gave orders about them to Eleazar the priest and Joshua son of Nun and to the family heads of the Israelite tribes. 29He said to them, 'If the Gadites and Reubenites, every man armed for battle, cross over the Jordan with you before the LORD, then when the land is subdued before you, you must give them the land of Gilead as their possession. 30But if they do not cross over with you armed,

---

a 17 Septuagint; Hebrew *will be quick to arm ourselves*

they must accept their possession with you in Canaan.'

31 The Gadites and Reubenites answered, 'Your servants will do what the LORD has said. 32 We will cross over before the LORD into Canaan armed, but the property we inherit will be on this side of the Jordan.'

33 Then Moses gave to the Gadites, the Reubenites and the half-tribe of Manasseh son of Joseph the kingdom of Sihon king of the Amorites and the kingdom of Og king of Bashan – the whole land with its cities and the territory around them.

34 The Gadites built up Dibon, Ataroth, Aroer, 35 Atroth Shophan, Jazer, Jogbehah, 36 Beth Nimrah and Beth Haran as fortified cities, and built pens for their flocks. 37 And the Reubenites rebuilt Heshbon, Elealeh and Kiriathaim, 38 as well as Nebo and Baal Meon (these names were changed) and Sibmah. They gave names to the cities they rebuilt.

39 The descendants of Makir son of Manasseh went to Gilead, captured it and drove out the Amorites who were there. 40 So Moses gave Gilead to the Makirites, the descendants of Manasseh, and they settled there. 41 Jair, a descendant of Manasseh, captured their settlements and called them Havvoth Jair.*b* 42 And Nobah captured Kenath and its surrounding settlements and called it Nobah after himself.

Stages in Israel's journey

33 Here are the stages in the journey of the Israelites when they came out of Egypt by divisions under the leadership of Moses and Aaron. 2 At the LORD's command Moses recorded the stages in their journey. This is their journey by stages:

3 The Israelites set out from Rameses on the fifteenth day of the first month, the day after the Passover. They marched out defiantly in full view of all the Egyptians, 4 who were burying all their firstborn, whom the

LORD had struck down among them; for the LORD had brought judgment on their gods.

5 The Israelites left Rameses and camped at Sukkoth.

6 They left Sukkoth and camped at Etham, on the edge of the desert.

7 They left Etham, turned back to Pi Hahiroth, to the east of Baal Zephon, and camped near Migdol.

8 They left Pi Hahiroth*a* and passed through the sea into the desert, and when they had travelled for three days in the Desert of Etham, they camped at Marah.

9 They left Marah and went to Elim, where there were twelve springs and seventy palm trees, and they camped there.

10 They left Elim and camped by the Red Sea.*b*

11 They left the Red Sea and camped in the Desert of Sin.

12 They left the Desert of Sin and camped at Dophkah.

13 They left Dophkah and camped at Alush.

14 They left Alush and camped at Rephidim, where there was no water for the people to drink.

15 They left Rephidim and camped in the Desert of Sinai.

16 They left the Desert of Sinai and camped at Kibroth Hattaavah.

17 They left Kibroth Hattaavah and camped at Hazeroth.

18 They left Hazeroth and camped at Rithmah.

19 They left Rithmah and camped at Rimmon Perez.

20 They left Rimmon Perez and camped at Libnah.

21 They left Libnah and camped at Rissah.

22 They left Rissah and camped at Kehelathah.

---

b 41 Or *them the settlements of Jair*

a 8 Many manuscripts of the Masoretic Text, Samaritan Pentateuch and Vulgate; most manuscripts of the Masoretic Text *left from before Hahiroth*
b 10 Or *the Sea of Reeds*; also in verse 11
a 11 Hebrew *Kinnereth*

23 They left Kehelathah and camped at Mount Shepher.

24 They left Mount Shepher and camped at Haradah.

25 They left Haradah and camped at Makheloth.

26 They left Makheloth and camped at Tahath.

27 They left Tahath and camped at Terah.

28 They left Terah and camped at Mithkah.

29 They left Mithkah and camped at Hashmonah.

30 They left Hashmonah and camped at Moseroth.

31 They left Moseroth and camped at Bene Jaakan.

32 They left Bene Jaakan and camped at Hor Haggidgad.

33 They left Hor Haggidgad and camped at Jotbathah.

34 They left Jotbathah and camped at Abronah.

35 They left Abronah and camped at Ezion Geber.

36 They left Ezion Geber and camped at Kadesh, in the Desert of Zin.

37 They left Kadesh and camped at Mount Hor, on the border of Edom. 38 At the LORD's command Aaron the priest went up Mount Hor, where he died on the first day of the fifth month of the fortieth year after the Israelites came out of Egypt. 39 Aaron was a hundred and twenty-three years old when he died on Mount Hor.

40 The Canaanite king of Arad, who lived in the Negev of Canaan, heard that the Israelites were coming.

41 They left Mount Hor and camped at Zalmonah.

42 They left Zalmonah and camped at Punon.

43 They left Punon and camped at Oboth.

44 They left Oboth and camped at Iye Abarim, on the border of Moab.

45 They left Iye Abarim and camped at Dibon Gad.

46 They left Dibon Gad and camped at Almon Diblathaim.

47 They left Almon Diblathaim and camped in the mountains of Abarim, near Nebo.

48 They left the mountains of Abarim and camped on the plains of Moab by the Jordan opposite Jericho. 49 There on the plains of Moab they camped along the Jordan from Beth Jeshimoth to Abel Shittim.

50 On the plains of Moab by the Jordan opposite Jericho the LORD said to Moses, 51 'Speak to the Israelites and say to them: "When you cross the Jordan into Canaan, 52 drive out all the inhabitants of the land before you. Destroy all their carved images and their cast idols, and demolish all their high places. 53 Take possession of the land and settle in it, for I have given you the land to possess. 54 Distribute the land by lot, according to your clans. To a larger group give a larger inheritance, and to a smaller group a smaller one. Whatever falls to them by lot will be theirs. Distribute it according to your ancestral tribes.

55 ' "But if you do not drive out the inhabitants of the land, those you allow to remain will become barbs in your eyes and thorns in your sides. They will give you trouble in the land where you will live. 56 And then I will do to you what I plan to do to them."'

Boundaries of Canaan

34 The LORD said to Moses, 2 'Command the Israelites and say to them: "When you enter Canaan, the land that will be allotted to you as an inheritance is to have these boundaries:

3 ' "Your southern side will include some of the Desert of Zin along the border of Edom. Your southern boundary will start in the east from the southern end of the Dead Sea, 4 cross south of Scorpion Pass, continue on to Zin and go south of Kadesh Barnea. Then it will go to Hazar Addar and over to Azmon, 5 where it will turn, join the Wadi of Egypt and end at the Mediterranean Sea.

6 ' "Your western boundary will be the coast of the Mediterranean Sea. This will be your boundary on the west.

7 ' "For your northern boundary, run a line from the Mediterranean Sea to Mount Hor 8 and from Mount Hor to Lebo Hamath. Then the boundary will go to Zedad, 9 continue to Ziphron and end at Hazar Enan. This will be your boundary on the north.

FAVOURITE VERSES

2 Corinthians 5:19

...that God was reconciling the world to himself in Christ, not counting people's sins against them. And he has committed to us the message of reconciliation.

If God sees the sin issue as dealt with, then our mission is to show people that there's nothing stopping them being reconciled to God.

Dan Russell

10 ' "For your eastern boundary, run a line from Hazar Enan to Shepham. 11 The boundary will go down from Shepham to Riblah on the east side of Ain and continue along the slopes east of the Sea of Galilee.ᵃ 12 Then the boundary will go down along the Jordan and end at the Dead Sea.

' "This will be your land, with its boundaries on every side." '

13 Moses commanded the Israelites: 'Assign this land by lot as an inheritance. The LORD has ordered that it be given to the nine-and-a-half tribes, 14 because the families of the tribe of Reuben, the tribe of Gad and the half-tribe of Manasseh have received their inheritance. 15 These two-and-a-half tribes have received their inheritance east of the Jordan opposite Jericho, towards the sunrise.'

16 The LORD said to Moses, 17 'These are the names of the men who are to assign the land for you as an inheritance: Eleazar the priest and Joshua son of Nun. 18 And appoint one leader from each tribe to help assign the land. 19 These are their names:

Caleb son of Jephunneh,
from the tribe of Judah;
20 Shemuel son of Ammihud,
from the tribe of Simeon;
21 Elidad son of Kislon,
from the tribe of Benjamin;
22 Bukki son of Jogli,
the leader from the tribe of Dan;
23 Hanniel son of Ephod,
the leader from the tribe of Manasseh son of Joseph;
24 Kemuel son of Shiphtan,
the leader from the tribe of Ephraim son of Joseph;
25 Elizaphan son of Parnak,
the leader from the tribe of Zebulun;
26 Paltiel son of Azzan,
the leader from the tribe of Issachar;
27 Ahihud son of Shelomi,
the leader from the tribe of Asher;
28 Pedahel son of Ammihud,
the leader from the tribe of Naphtali.'

29 These are the men the LORD commanded to assign the inheritance to the Israelites in the land of Canaan.

Towns for the Levites

35 On the plains of Moab by the Jordan opposite Jericho, the LORD said to Moses, 2 'Command the Israelites to give the Levites towns to live in from the inheritance the Israelites will possess. And give them pasture-lands around the towns. 3 Then they will have towns to live in and pasture-lands for the cattle they own and all their other animals.

4 'The pasture-lands around the towns that you give the Levites will extend a thousand cubitsᵃ from the town wall. 5 Outside

_____

ᵃ 4 That is, about 450 metres

the town, measure two thousand cubits[b] on the east side, two thousand on the south side, two thousand on the west and two thousand on the north, with the town in the centre. They will have this area as pasture-land for the towns.

Cities of refuge

6 'Six of the towns you give the Levites will be cities of refuge, to which a person who has killed someone may flee. In addition, give them forty-two other towns. 7 In all you must give the Levites forty-eight towns, together with their pasture-lands. 8 The towns you give the Levites from the land the Israelites possess are to be given in proportion to the inheritance of each tribe: take many towns from a tribe that has many, but few from one that has few.'

9 Then the LORD said to Moses: 10 'Speak to the Israelites and say to them: "When you cross the Jordan into Canaan, 11 select some towns to be your cities of refuge, to which a person who has killed someone accidentally may flee. 12 They will be places of refuge from the avenger, so that anyone accused of murder may not die before they stand trial before the assembly. 13 These six towns you give will be your cities of refuge. 14 Give three on this side of the Jordan and three in Canaan as cities of refuge. 15 These six towns will be a place of refuge for Israelites and for foreigners residing among them, so that anyone who has killed another accidentally can flee there.

16 ' "If anyone strikes someone a fatal blow with an iron object, that person is a murderer; the murderer is to be put to death. 17 Or if anyone is holding a stone and strikes someone a fatal blow with it, that person is a murderer; the murderer is to be put to death. 18 Or if anyone is holding a wooden object and strikes someone a fatal blow with it, that person is a murderer; the murderer is to be put to death. 19 The avenger of blood shall put the murderer to death; when the avenger comes upon the murderer, the avenger shall put the murderer to death. 20 If anyone with malice aforethought pushes another or throws something at them intentionally so that they die 21 or if out of enmity one person hits another with their fist so that the other dies, that person is to be put to death; that person is a murderer. The avenger of blood shall put the murderer to death when they meet.

22 ' "But if without enmity someone suddenly pushes another or throws something at them unintentionally 23 or, without seeing them, drops on them a stone heavy enough to kill them, and they die, then since that other person was not an enemy and no harm was intended, 24 the assembly must judge between the accused and the avenger of blood according to these regulations. 25 The assembly must protect the one accused of murder from the avenger of blood and send the accused back to the city of refuge to which they fled. The accused must stay there until the death of the high priest, who was anointed with holy oil.

26 ' "But if the accused ever goes outside the limits of the city of refuge to which they fled 27 and the avenger of blood finds them outside the city, the avenger of blood may kill the accused without being guilty of murder. 28 The accused must stay in the city of refuge until the death of the high priest; only after the death of the high priest may they return to their own property.

29 ' "This is to have the force of law for you throughout the generations to come, wherever you live.

30 ' "Anyone who kills a person is to be put to death as a murderer only on the testimony of witnesses. But no one is to be put to death on the testimony of only one witness.

31 ' "Do not accept a ransom for the life of a murderer, who deserves to die. They are to be put to death.

32 ' "Do not accept a ransom for anyone who has fled to a city of refuge and so allow them to go back and live on their own land before the death of the high priest.

33 ' "Do not pollute the land where you are. Bloodshed pollutes the land, and atonement cannot be made for the land

---

b 5 That is, about 900 metres

on which blood has been shed, except by the blood of the one who shed it. [34] Do not defile the land where you live and where I dwell, for I, the Lord, dwell among the Israelites.' '

Inheritance of Zelophehad's daughters

36 The family heads of the clan of Gilead son of Makir, the son of Manasseh, who were from the clans of the descendants of Joseph, came and spoke before Moses and the leaders, the heads of the Israelite families. [2] They said, 'When the Lord commanded my lord to give the land as an inheritance to the Israelites by lot, he ordered you to give the inheritance of our brother Zelophehad to his daughters. [3] Now suppose they marry men from other Israelite tribes; then their inheritance will be taken from our ancestral inheritance and added to that of the tribe they marry into. And so part of the inheritance allotted to us will be taken away. [4] When the Year of Jubilee for the Israelites comes, their inheritance will be added to that of the tribe into which they marry, and their property will be taken from the tribal inheritance of our ancestors.'

[5] Then at the Lord's command Moses gave this order to the Israelites: 'What the tribe of the descendants of Joseph is saying is right. [6] This is what the Lord commands for Zelophehad's daughters: they may marry anyone they please as long as they marry within their father's tribal clan. [7] No inheritance in Israel is to pass from one tribe to another, for every Israelite shall keep the tribal inheritance of their ancestors. [8] Every daughter who inherits land in any Israelite tribe must marry someone in her father's tribal clan, so that every Israelite will possess the inheritance of their ancestors. [9] No inheritance may pass from one tribe to another, for each Israelite tribe is to keep the land it inherits.'

[10] So Zelophehad's daughters did as the Lord commanded Moses. [11] Zelophehad's daughters – Mahlah, Tirzah, Hoglah, Milkah and Noah – married their cousins on their father's side. [12] They married within the clans of the descendants of Manasseh son of Joseph, and their inheritance remained in their father's tribe and clan.

[13] These are the commands and regulations the Lord gave through Moses to the Israelites on the plains of Moab by the Jordan opposite Jericho.

DEUTERONOMY

DATE

The teachings of Moses recorded in this book are estimated to have been delivered to the people of Israel in around 1406 BC

AUTHOR

Traditionally attributed to Moses

WHAT'S IT ALL ABOUT?

Deuteronomy is the last of the five books of the Pentateuch and its name means 'Repetition of the Law'. Moses knew he was about to die and this book is his passionate farewell speech to the Israelites who are going to cross over into the Promised Land. He recalled the things he and the Israelites had been through over the last forty years in the desert, reminding the people of the laws God had given them and urging them to obey God so that things might go well for them. He reminded the people of God's great love for them despite all the mistakes they had made.

WHY SHOULD WE READ IT?

- To remember the lessons Israel learned in the desert.
- To be reminded to seek God when things are going well, as well as when things are hard (Deuteronomy 8).
- To read the promises God makes to those who turn to him, and the curses in store for the Israelites who are disobedient (Deuteronomy 28 and 30).
- To read about Moses handing over leadership to Joshua (Deuteronomy 31).
- To read the Ten Commandments (Deuteronomy 5; also found in Exodus 20).

Andy Croft with Liza Hoeksma

The command to leave Horeb

1 These are the words Moses spoke to all Israel in the wilderness east of the Jordan – that is, in the Arabah – opposite Suph, between Paran and Tophel, Laban, Hazeroth and Dizahab. 2(It takes eleven days to go from Horeb to Kadesh Barnea by the Mount Seir road.)

3 In the fortieth year, on the first day of the eleventh month, Moses proclaimed to the Israelites all that the LORD had commanded him concerning them. 4This was after he had defeated Sihon king of the Amorites, who reigned in Heshbon, and at Edrei had defeated Og king of Bashan, who reigned in Ashtaroth.

5 East of the Jordan in the territory of Moab, Moses began to expound this law, saying:

6 The LORD our God said to us at Horeb, 'You have stayed long enough at this mountain. 7 Break camp and advance into the hill country of the Amorites; go to all the neighbouring peoples in the Arabah, in the mountains, in the western foothills, in the Negev and along the coast, to the land of the Canaanites and to Lebanon, as far as the great river, the Euphrates. 8 See, I have given you this land. Go in and take possession of the land that the LORD swore he would give to your fathers – to Abraham, Isaac and Jacob – and to their descendants after them.'

The appointment of leaders

9 At that time I said to you, 'You are too heavy a burden for me to carry alone. 10 The LORD your God has increased your numbers so that today you are as numerous as the stars in the sky. 11 May the LORD, the God of your ancestors, increase you a thousand times and bless you as he has promised! 12 But how can I bear your problems and your burdens and your disputes all by myself? 13 Choose some wise, understanding and respected men from each of your tribes, and I will set them over you.'

14 You answered me, 'What you propose to do is good.'

15 So I took the leading men of your tribes, wise and respected men, and appointed them to have authority over you – as commanders of thousands, of hundreds, of fifties and of tens and as tribal officials. 16 And I charged your judges at that time, 'Hear the disputes between your people and judge fairly, whether the case is between two Israelites or between an Israelite and a foreigner residing among you. 17 Do not show partiality in judging; hear both small and great alike. Do not be afraid of anyone, for judgment belongs to God. Bring me any case too hard for you, and I will hear it.' 18 And at that time I told you everything you were to do.

Spies sent out

19 Then, as the LORD our God commanded us, we set out from Horeb and went towards the hill country of the Amorites through all that vast and dreadful wilderness that you have seen, and so we reached Kadesh Barnea. 20 Then I said to you, 'You have reached the hill country of the Amorites, which the LORD our God is giving us. 21 See, the LORD your God has given you the land. Go up and take possession of it as the LORD, the God of your ancestors, told you. Do not be afraid; do not be discouraged.'

22 Then all of you came to me and said, 'Let us send men ahead to spy out the land for us and bring back a report about the route we are to take and the towns we will come to.'

23 The idea seemed good to me; so I selected twelve of you, one man from each tribe. 24 They left and went up into the hill country, and came to the Valley of Eshkol and explored it. 25 Taking with them some of the fruit of the land, they brought it down to us and reported, 'It is a good land that the LORD our God is giving us.'

Rebellion against the LORD

26 But you were unwilling to go up; you rebelled against the command of the LORD your God. 27 You grumbled in your tents and said, 'The LORD hates us; so he brought us out of Egypt to deliver us into the hands of the Amorites to destroy us.

28 Where can we go? Our brothers have made our hearts melt in fear. They say, "The people are stronger and taller than we are; the cities are large, with walls up to the sky. We even saw the Anakites there."'

29 Then I said to you, 'Do not be terrified; do not be afraid of them. 30 The LORD your God, who is going before you, will fight for you, as he did for you in Egypt, before your very eyes, 31 and in the wilderness. There you saw how the LORD your God carried you, as a father carries his son, all the way you went until you reached this place.'

32 In spite of this, you did not trust in the LORD your God, 33 who went ahead of you on your journey, in fire by night and in a cloud by day, to search out places for you to camp and to show you the way you should go.

34 When the LORD heard what you said, he was angry and solemnly swore: 35 'No one from this evil generation shall see the good land I swore to give your ancestors, 36 except Caleb son of Jephunneh. He will see it, and I will give him and his descendants the land he set his feet on, because he followed the LORD wholeheartedly.'

37 Because of you the LORD became angry with me also and said, 'You shall not enter it, either. 38 But your assistant, Joshua son of Nun, will enter it. Encourage him, because he will lead Israel to inherit it. 39 And the little ones that you said would be taken captive, your children who do not yet know good from bad – they will enter the land. I will give it to them and they will take possession of it. 40 But as for you, turn round and set out towards the desert along the route to the Red Sea.'*a*

41 Then you replied, 'We have sinned against the LORD. We will go up and fight, as the LORD our God commanded us.' So every one of you put on his weapons, thinking it easy to go up into the hill country.

42 But the LORD said to me, 'Tell them, "Do not go up and fight, because I will not be with you. You will be defeated by your enemies."'

43 So I told you, but you would not listen. You rebelled against the LORD's command and in your arrogance you marched up into the hill country. 44 The Amorites who lived in those hills came out against you; they chased you like a swarm of bees and beat you down from Seir all the way to Hormah. 45 You came back and wept before the LORD, but he paid no attention to your weeping and turned a deaf ear to you. 46 And so you stayed in Kadesh many days – all the time you spent there.

Wanderings in the wilderness

2 Then we turned back and set out towards the wilderness along the route to the Red Sea,*a* as the LORD had directed me. For a long time we made our way around the hill country of Seir.

2 Then the LORD said to me, 3 'You have made your way around this hill country long enough; now turn north. 4 Give the people these orders: "You are about to pass through the territory of your relatives the descendants of Esau, who live in Seir. They will be afraid of you, but be very careful. 5 Do not provoke them to war, for I will not give you any of their land, not even enough to put your foot on. I have given Esau the hill country of Seir as his own. 6 You are to pay them in silver for the food you eat and the water you drink."'

7 The LORD your God has blessed you in all the work of your hands. He has watched over your journey through this vast wilderness. These forty years the LORD your God has been with you, and you have not lacked anything.

8 So we went on past our relatives the descendants of Esau, who live in Seir. We turned from the Arabah road, which comes up from Elath and Ezion Geber, and travelled along the desert road of Moab.

9 Then the LORD said to me, 'Do not harass the Moabites or provoke them to war, for I will not give you any part of their land. I have given Ar to the descendants of Lot as a possession.'

10 (The Emites used to live there – a people strong and numerous, and as tall

---

a 40 Or *the Sea of Reeds*

a 1 Or *the Sea of Reeds*

as the Anakites. ¹¹ Like the Anakites, they too were considered Rephaites, but the Moabites called them Emites. ¹² Horites used to live in Seir, but the descendants of Esau drove them out. They destroyed the Horites from before them and settled in their place, just as Israel did in the land the LORD gave them as their possession.)

¹³ And the LORD said, 'Now get up and cross the Zered Valley.' So we crossed the valley.

¹⁴ Thirty-eight years passed from the time we left Kadesh Barnea until we crossed the Zered Valley. By then, that entire generation of fighting men had perished from the camp, as the LORD had sworn to them. ¹⁵ The LORD's hand was against them until he had completely eliminated them from the camp.

¹⁶ Now when the last of these fighting men among the people had died, ¹⁷ the LORD said to me, ¹⁸ 'Today you are to pass by the region of Moab at Ar. ¹⁹ When you come to the Ammonites, do not harass them or provoke them to war, for I will not give you possession of any land belonging to the Ammonites. I have given it as a possession to the descendants of Lot.'

²⁰ (That too was considered a land of the Rephaites, who used to live there; but the Ammonites called them Zamzummites. ²¹ They were a people strong and numerous, and as tall as the Anakites. The LORD destroyed them from before the Ammonites, who drove them out and settled in their place. ²² The LORD had done the same for the descendants of Esau, who lived in Seir, when he destroyed the Horites from before them. They drove them out and have lived in their place to this day. ²³ And as for the Avvites who lived in villages as far as Gaza, the Caphtorites coming out from Caphtor ᵇ destroyed them and settled in their place.)

Defeat of Sihon king of Heshbon

²⁴ 'Set out now and cross the Arnon Gorge. See, I have given into your hand Sihon the Amorite, king of Heshbon, and his country. Begin to take possession of it

and engage him in battle. ²⁵ This very day I will begin to put the terror and fear of you on all the nations under heaven. They will hear reports of you and will tremble and be in anguish because of you.'

²⁶ From the Desert of Kedemoth I sent messengers to Sihon king of Heshbon offering peace and saying, ²⁷ 'Let us pass through your country. We will stay on the main road; we will not turn aside to the right or to the left. ²⁸ Sell us food to eat and water to drink for their price in silver. Only let us pass through on foot – ²⁹ as the descendants of Esau, who live in Seir, and the Moabites, who live in Ar, did for us – until we cross the Jordan into the land the LORD our God is giving us.' ³⁰ But Sihon king of Heshbon refused to let us pass through. For the LORD your God had made his spirit stubborn and his heart obstinate in order to give him into your hands, as he has now done.

³¹ The LORD said to me, 'See, I have begun to deliver Sihon and his country over to you. Now begin to conquer and possess his land.'

³² When Sihon and all his army came out to meet us in battle at Jahaz, ³³ the LORD our God delivered him over to us and we struck him down, together with his sons and his whole army. ³⁴ At that time we took all his towns and completely destroyed ᶜ them – men, women and children. We left no survivors. ³⁵ But the livestock and the plunder from the towns we had captured we carried off for ourselves. ³⁶ From Aroer on the rim of the Arnon Gorge, and from the town in the gorge, even as far as Gilead, not one town was too strong for us. The LORD our God gave us all of them. ³⁷ But in accordance with the command of the LORD our God, you did not encroach on any of the land of the Ammonites, neither the land along the course of the Jabbok nor that around the towns in the hills.

ᶜ 34 The Hebrew term refers to the irrevocable giving over of things or persons to the LORD, often by totally destroying them.

Defeat of Og king of Bashan

3 Next we turned and went up along the road towards Bashan, and Og king of Bashan with his whole army marched out to meet us in battle at Edrei. ²The Lord said to me, 'Do not be afraid of him, for I have delivered him into your hands, along with his whole army and his land. Do to him what you did to Sihon king of the Amorites, who reigned in Heshbon.'

³So the Lord our God also gave into our hands Og king of Bashan and all his army. We struck them down, leaving no survivors. ⁴At that time we took all his cities. There was not one of the sixty cities that we did not take from them – the whole region of Argob, Og's kingdom in Bashan. ⁵All these cities were fortified with high walls and with gates and bars, and there were also a great many unwalled villages. ⁶We completely destroyed*a* them, as we had done with Sihon king of Heshbon, destroying*a* every city – men, women and children. ⁷But all the livestock and the plunder from their cities we carried off for ourselves.

⁸So at that time we took from these two kings of the Amorites the territory east of the Jordan, from the Arnon Gorge as far as Mount Hermon. ⁹(Hermon is called Sirion by the Sidonians; the Amorites call it Senir.) ¹⁰We took all the towns on the plateau, and all Gilead, and all Bashan as far as Salekah and Edrei, towns of Og's kingdom in Bashan. ¹¹(Og king of Bashan was the last of the Rephaites. His bed was decorated with iron and was more than nine cubits long and four cubits wide.*b* It is still in Rabbah of the Ammonites.)

Division of the land

¹²Of the land that we took over at that time, I gave the Reubenites and the Gadites the territory north of Aroer by the Arnon Gorge, including half the hill country of Gilead, together with its towns. ¹³The rest of Gilead and also all of Bashan, the kingdom of Og, I gave to the half-tribe of Manasseh. (The whole region of Argob in Bashan used to be known as a land of the Rephaites. ¹⁴Jair, a descendant of Manasseh, took the whole region of Argob as far as the border of the Geshurites and the Maakathites; it was named after him, so that to this day Bashan is called Havvoth Jair.*c*) ¹⁵And I gave Gilead to Makir. ¹⁶But to the Reubenites and the Gadites I gave the territory extending from Gilead down to the Arnon Gorge (the middle of the gorge being the border) and out to the River Jabbok, which is the border of the Ammonites. ¹⁷Its western border was the Jordan in the Arabah, from Kinnereth to the Sea of the Arabah (that is, the Dead Sea), below the slopes of Pisgah.

FACT

GIANT BED

According to Deuteronomy, King Og of Bashan had a bed over 13 feet (4 metres) long and 6 feet (1.8 metres) wide. Although 'bed' here may mean his coffin. Perhaps he was dead tired (Deuteronomy 3:11).

¹⁸I commanded you at that time: 'The Lord your God has given you this land to take possession of it. But all your able-bodied men, armed for battle, must cross over ahead of the other Israelites. ¹⁹However, your wives, your children and your livestock (I know you have much livestock) may stay in the towns I have given you, ²⁰until the Lord gives rest to your fellow Israelites as he has to you, and they too have taken over the land that the Lord your God is giving them across the Jordan. After that, each of you may go back to the possession I have given you.'

---

a 6 The Hebrew term refers to the irrevocable giving over of things or persons to the Lord, often by totally destroying them.
b 11 That is, about 4 metres long and 1.8 metres wide

c 14 Or *called the settlements of Jair*

Moses forbidden to cross the Jordan

21 At that time I commanded Joshua: 'You have seen with your own eyes all that the LORD your God has done to these two kings. The LORD will do the same to all the kingdoms over there where you are going. 22 Do not be afraid of them; the LORD your God himself will fight for you.'

23 At that time I pleaded with the LORD: 24 'Sovereign LORD, you have begun to show to your servant your greatness and your strong hand. For what god is there in heaven or on earth who can do the deeds and mighty works you do? 25 Let me go over and see the good land beyond the Jordan – that fine hill country and Lebanon.'

26 But because of you the LORD was angry with me and would not listen to me. 'That is enough,' the LORD said. 'Do not speak to me any more about this matter. 27 Go up to the top of Pisgah and look west and north and south and east. Look at the land with your own eyes, since you are not going to cross this Jordan. 28 But commission Joshua, and encourage and strengthen him, for he will lead this people across and will cause them to inherit the land that you will see.' 29 So we stayed in the valley near Beth Peor.

Obedience commanded

4 Now, Israel, hear the decrees and laws I am about to teach you. Follow them so that you may live and may go in and take possession of the land that the LORD, the God of your ancestors, is giving you. 2 Do not add to what I command you and do not subtract from it, but keep the commands of the LORD your God that I give you.

3 You saw with your own eyes what the LORD did at Baal Peor. The LORD your God destroyed from among you everyone who followed the Baal of Peor, 4 but all of you who held fast to the LORD your God are still alive today.

5 See, I have taught you decrees and laws as the LORD my God commanded me, so that you may follow them in the land you are entering to take possession of it. 6 Observe them carefully, for this will show your wisdom and understanding to the nations, who will hear about all these decrees and say, 'Surely this great nation is a wise and understanding people.' 7 What other nation is so great as to have their gods near them the way the LORD our God is near us whenever we pray to him? 8 And what other nation is so great as to have such righteous decrees and laws as this body of laws I am setting before you today?

9 Only be careful, and watch yourselves closely so that you do not forget the things your eyes have seen or let them fade from your heart as long as you live. Teach them to your children and to their children after them. 10 Remember the day you stood before the LORD your God at Horeb, when he said to me, 'Assemble the people before me to hear my words so that they may learn to revere me as long as they live in the land and may teach them to their children.' 11 You came near and stood at the foot of the mountain while it blazed with fire to the very heavens, with black clouds and deep darkness. 12 Then the LORD spoke to you out of the fire. You heard the sound of words but saw no form; there was only a voice. 13 He declared to you his covenant, the Ten Commandments, which he commanded you to follow and then wrote them on two stone tablets. 14 And the LORD directed me at that time to teach you the decrees and laws you are to follow in the land that you are crossing the Jordan to possess.

Idolatry forbidden

15 You saw no form of any kind the day the LORD spoke to you at Horeb out of the fire. Therefore watch yourselves very carefully, 16 so that you do not become corrupt and make for yourselves an idol, an image of any shape, whether formed like a man or a woman, 17 or like any animal on earth or any bird that flies in the air, 18 or like any creature that moves along the ground or any fish in the waters below. 19 And when you look up to the sky and see the sun, the moon and the stars – all the heavenly array – do not be enticed into bowing down to them and worshipping things the LORD your God has apportioned to

all the nations under heaven. 20 But as for you, the LORD took you and brought you out of the iron-smelting furnace, out of Egypt, to be the people of his inheritance, as you now are.

21 The LORD was angry with me because of you, and he solemnly swore that I would not cross the Jordan and enter the good land the LORD your God is giving you as your inheritance. 22 I will die in this land; I will not cross the Jordan; but you are about to cross over and take possession of that good land. 23 Be careful not to forget the covenant of the LORD your God that he made with you; do not make for yourselves an idol in the form of anything the LORD your God has forbidden. 24 For the LORD your God is a consuming fire, a jealous God.

25 After you have had children and grandchildren and have lived in the land a long time – if you then become corrupt and make any kind of idol, doing evil in the eyes of the LORD your God and arousing his anger, 26 I call the heavens and the earth as witnesses against you this day that you will quickly perish from the land that you are crossing the Jordan to possess. You will not live there long but will certainly be destroyed. 27 The LORD will scatter you among the peoples, and only a few of you will survive among the nations to which the LORD will drive you. 28 There you will worship man-made gods of wood and stone, which cannot see or hear or eat or smell. 29 But if from there you seek the LORD your God, you will find him if you seek him with all your heart and with all your soul. 30 When you are in distress and all these things have happened to you, then in later days you will return to the LORD your God and obey him. 31 For the LORD your God is a merciful God; he will not abandon or destroy you or forget the covenant with your ancestors, which he confirmed to them by oath.

The LORD is God

32 Ask now about the former days, long before your time, from the day God created human beings on the earth; ask from one end of the heavens to the other. Has anything so great as this ever happened, or has anything like it ever been heard of? 33 Has any other people heard the voice of God*a* speaking out of fire, as you have, and lived? 34 Has any god ever tried to take for himself one nation out of another nation, by testings, by signs and wonders, by war, by a mighty hand and an outstretched arm, or by great and awesome deeds, like all the things the LORD your God did for you in Egypt before your very eyes?

35 You were shown these things so that you might know that the LORD is God; besides him there is no other. 36 From heaven he made you hear his voice to discipline you. On earth he showed you his great fire, and you heard his words from out of the fire. 37 Because he loved your ancestors and chose their descendants after them, he brought you out of Egypt by his Presence and his great strength, 38 to drive out before you nations greater and stronger than you and to bring you into their land to give it to you for your inheritance, as it is today.

39 Acknowledge and take to heart this day that the LORD is God in heaven above and on the earth below. There is no other. 40 Keep his decrees and commands, which I am giving you today, so that it may go well with you and your children after you and that you may live long in the land the LORD your God gives you for all time.

Cities of refuge

41 Then Moses set aside three cities east of the Jordan, 42 to which anyone who had killed a person could flee if they had unintentionally killed a neighbour without malice aforethought. They could flee into one of these cities and save their life. 43 The cities were these: Bezer in the wilderness plateau, for the Reubenites; Ramoth in Gilead, for the Gadites; and Golan in Bashan, for the Manassites.

Introduction to the law

44 This is the law Moses set before the Israelites. 45 These are the stipulations, decrees and laws Moses gave them when they

---

a 33 Or *of a god*

came out of Egypt [46] and were in the valley near Beth Peor east of the Jordan, in the land of Sihon king of the Amorites, who reigned in Heshbon and was defeated by Moses and the Israelites as they came out of Egypt. [47] They took possession of his land and the land of Og king of Bashan, the two Amorite kings east of the Jordan. [48] This land extended from Aroer on the rim of the Arnon Gorge to Mount Sirion[b] (that is, Hermon), [49] and included all the Arabah east of the Jordan, as far as the Dead Sea,[c] below the slopes of Pisgah.

FAVOURITE VERSES

Deuteronomy 31:8

The LORD himself goes before you and will be with you; he will never leave you nor forsake you. Do not be afraid; do not be discouraged.

These verses really encourage and help me in my life, especially at school where I'm pushed in my faith. They remind me of how God knows what he's doing and tell me that I should listen to him, not to the ones trying to dishearten me.

Molly, 14

The Ten Commandments

5 Moses summoned all Israel and said: Hear, Israel, the decrees and the laws I declare in your hearing today. Learn them and be sure to follow them. [2] The LORD our God made a covenant with us at Horeb. [3] It was not with our ancestors[a] that the LORD made this covenant, but with us, with all of us who are alive here today. [4] The LORD

spoke to you face to face out of the fire on the mountain. [5] (At that time I stood between the LORD and you to declare to you the word of the LORD, because you were afraid of the fire and did not go up the mountain.) And he said:

[6] 'I am the LORD your God, who brought you out of Egypt, out of the land of slavery.

[7] 'You shall have no other gods before[b] me.

[8] 'You shall not make for yourself an image in the form of anything in heaven above or on the earth beneath or in the waters below. [9] You shall not bow down to them or worship them; for I, the LORD your God, am a jealous God, punishing the children for the sin of the parents to the third and fourth generation of those who hate me, [10] but showing love to a thousand generations of those who love me and keep my commandments.

[11] 'You shall not misuse the name of the LORD your God, for the LORD will not hold anyone guiltless who misuses his name.

[12] 'Observe the Sabbath day by keeping it holy, as the LORD your God has commanded you. [13] Six days you shall labour and do all your work, [14] but the seventh day is a sabbath to the LORD your God. On it you shall not do any work, neither you, nor your son or daughter, nor your male or female servant, nor your ox, your donkey or any of your animals, nor any foreigner residing in your towns, so that your male and female servants may rest, as you do. [15] Remember that you were slaves in Egypt and that the LORD your God brought you out of there with a mighty hand and an outstretched arm. Therefore the LORD your God

---

b 48 Syriac (see also 3:9); Hebrew *Siyon*
c 49 Hebrew *the Sea of the Arabah*
a 3 Or *not only with our parents*

b 7 Or *besides*

has commanded you to observe the Sabbath day.

16 'Honour your father and your mother, as the LORD your God has commanded you, so that you may live long and that it may go well with you in the land the LORD your God is giving you.

17 'You shall not murder.

18 'You shall not commit adultery.

19 'You shall not steal.

20 'You shall not give false testimony against your neighbour.

21 'You shall not covet your neighbour's wife. You shall not set your desire on your neighbour's house or land, his male or female servant, his ox or donkey, or anything that belongs to your neighbour.'

22 These are the commandments the LORD proclaimed in a loud voice to your whole assembly there on the mountain from out of the fire, the cloud and the deep darkness; and he added nothing more. Then he wrote them on two stone tablets and gave them to me.

23 When you heard the voice out of the darkness, while the mountain was ablaze with fire, all the leaders of your tribes and your elders came to me. 24 And you said, 'The LORD our God has shown us his glory and his majesty, and we have heard his voice from the fire. Today we have seen that a person can live even if God speaks with them. 25 But now, why should we die? This great fire will consume us, and we will die if we hear the voice of the LORD our God any longer. 26 For what mortal has ever heard the voice of the living God speaking out of fire, as we have, and survived? 27 Go near and listen to all that the LORD our God says. Then tell us whatever the LORD our God tells you. We will listen and obey.'

28 The LORD heard you when you spoke to me, and the LORD said to me, 'I have heard what this people said to you. Everything they said was good. 29 Oh, that their hearts would be inclined to fear me and keep all my commands always, so that it might go well with them and their children for ever!

30 'Go, tell them to return to their tents. 31 But you stay here with me so that I may give you all the commands, decrees and laws that you are to teach them to follow in the land I am giving them to possess.'

32 So be careful to do what the LORD your God has commanded you; do not turn aside to the right or to the left. 33 Walk in obedience to all that the LORD your God has commanded you, so that you may live and prosper and prolong your days in the land that you will possess.

Love the LORD your God

6 These are the commands, decrees and laws the LORD your God directed me to teach you to observe in the land that you are crossing the Jordan to possess, 2 so that you, your children and their children after them may fear the LORD your God as long as you live by keeping all his decrees and commands that I give you, and so that you may enjoy long life. 3 Hear, Israel, and be careful to obey so that it may go well with you and that you may increase greatly in a land flowing with milk and honey, just as the LORD, the God of your ancestors, promised you.

4 Hear, O Israel: the LORD our God, the LORD is one.*a* 5 Love the LORD your God with all your heart and with all your soul and with all your strength. 6 These commandments that I give you today are to be on your hearts. 7 Impress them on your children. Talk about them when you sit at home and when you walk along the road, when you lie down and when you get up. 8 Tie them as symbols on your hands and bind them on your foreheads. 9 Write them on the door-frames of your houses and on your gates.

10 When the LORD your God brings you into the land he swore to your fathers, to Abraham, Isaac and Jacob, to give you – a land with large, flourishing cities you did not build, 11 houses filled with all kinds of

---

a 4 Or *The LORD our God is one LORD*; or *The LORD is our God, the LORD is one*; or *The LORD is our God, the LORD alone* good things you did not provide, wells you did not dig, and vineyards and olive groves you did not plant – then when you eat and are satisfied, 12 be careful that you do not forget the LORD, who brought you out of Egypt, out of the land of slavery.

13 Fear the LORD your God, serve him only and take your oaths in his name. 14 Do not follow other gods, the gods of the peoples around you; 15 for the LORD your God, who is among you, is a jealous God and his anger will burn against you, and he will destroy you from the face of the land. 16 Do not put the LORD your God to the test as you did at Massah. 17 Be sure to keep the commands of the LORD your God and the stipulations and decrees he has given you. 18 Do what is right and good in the LORD's sight, so that it may go well with you and you may go in and take over the good land that the LORD promised on oath to your ancestors, 19 thrusting out all your enemies before you, as the LORD said.

20 In the future, when your son asks you, 'What is the meaning of the stipulations, decrees and laws the LORD our God has commanded you?' 21 tell him: 'We were slaves of Pharaoh in Egypt, but the LORD brought us out of Egypt with a mighty hand. 22 Before our eyes the LORD sent signs and wonders – great and terrible – on Egypt and Pharaoh and his whole household. 23 But he brought us out from there to bring us in and give us the land that he promised on oath to our ancestors. 24 The LORD commanded us to obey all these decrees and to fear the LORD our God, so that we might always prosper and be kept alive, as is the case today. 25 And if we are careful to obey all this law before the LORD our God, as he has commanded us, that will be our righteousness.'

Driving out the nations

7 When the LORD your God brings you into the land you are entering to possess and drives out before you many nations – the Hittites, Girgashites, Amorites, Canaanites, Perizzites, Hivites and Jebusites, seven nations larger and stronger than you – 2 and when the LORD

your God has delivered them over to you and you have defeated them, then you must destroy them totally.*a* Make no treaty with them, and show them no mercy. 3 Do not intermarry with them. Do not give your daughters to their sons or take their daughters for your sons, 4 for they will turn your children away from following me to serve other gods, and the LORD's anger will burn against you and will quickly destroy you. 5 This is what you are to do to them: break down their altars, smash their sacred stones, cut down their Asherah poles*b* and burn their idols in the fire. 6 For you are a people holy to the LORD your God. The LORD your God has chosen you out of all the peoples on the face of the earth to be his people, his treasured possession.

7 The LORD did not set his affection on you and choose you because you were more numerous than other peoples, for you were the fewest of all peoples. 8 But it was because the LORD loved you and kept the oath he swore to your ancestors that he brought you out with a mighty hand and redeemed you from the land of slavery, from the power of Pharaoh king of Egypt. 9 Know therefore that the LORD your God is God; he is the faithful God, keeping his covenant of love to a thousand generations of those who love him and keep his commandments. 10 But

> those who hate him he will repay to
>   their face by destruction;
> he will not be slow to repay to their
>   face those who hate him.

11 Therefore, take care to follow the commands, decrees and laws I give you today.

12 If you pay attention to these laws and are careful to follow them, then the LORD your God will keep his covenant of love with you, as he swore to your ancestors.

---

a 2 The Hebrew term refers to the irrevocable giving over of things or persons to the LORD, often by totally destroying them; also in verse 26.
b 5 That is, wooden symbols of the goddess Asherah; here and elsewhere in Deuteronomy

13 He will love you and bless you and increase your numbers. He will bless the fruit of your womb, the crops of your land – your corn, new wine and oil – the calves of your herds and the lambs of your flocks in the land that he swore to your ancestors to give you. 14 You will be blessed more than any other people; none of your men or women will be childless, nor any of your livestock without young. 15 The LORD will keep you free from every disease. He will not inflict on you the horrible diseases you knew in Egypt, but he will inflict them on all who hate you. 16 You must destroy all the peoples the LORD your God gives over to you. Do not look on them with pity and do not serve their gods, for that will be a snare to you.

17 You may say to yourselves, 'These nations are stronger than we are. How can we drive them out?' 18 But do not be afraid of them; remember well what the LORD your God did to Pharaoh and to all Egypt. 19 You saw with your own eyes the great trials, the signs and wonders, the mighty hand and outstretched arm, with which the LORD your God brought you out. The LORD your God will do the same to all the peoples you now fear. 20 Moreover, the LORD your God will send the hornet among them until even the survivors who hide from you have perished. 21 Do not be terrified by them, for the LORD your God, who is among you, is a great and awesome God. 22 The LORD your God will drive out those nations before you, little by little. You will not be allowed to eliminate them all at once, or the wild animals will multiply around you. 23 But the LORD your God will deliver them over to you, throwing them into great confusion until they are destroyed. 24 He will give their kings into your hand, and you will wipe out their names from under heaven. No one will be able to stand up against you; you will destroy them. 25 The images of their gods you are to burn in the fire. Do not covet the silver and gold on them, and do not take it for yourselves, or you will be ensnared by it, for it is detestable to the LORD your God. 26 Do not bring a detestable thing into your house or you, like it,

will be set apart for destruction. Regard it as vile and utterly detest it, for it is set apart for destruction.

Do not forget the LORD

8 Be careful to follow every command I am giving you today, so that you may live and increase and may enter and possess the land that the LORD promised on oath to your ancestors. 2 Remember how the LORD your God led you all the way in the wilderness these forty years, to humble and test you in order to know what was in your heart, whether or not you would keep his commands. 3 He humbled you, causing you to hunger and then feeding you with manna, which neither you nor your ancestors had known, to teach you that man does not live on bread alone but on every word that comes from the mouth of the LORD. 4 Your clothes did not wear out and your feet did not swell during these forty years. 5 Know then in your heart that as a man disciplines his son, so the LORD your God disciplines you.

6 Observe the commands of the LORD your God, walking in obedience to him and revering him. 7 For the LORD your God is bringing you into a good land – a land with brooks, streams, and deep springs gushing out into the valleys and hills; 8 a land with wheat and barley, vines and fig-trees, pomegranates, olive oil and honey; 9 a land where bread will not be scarce and you will lack nothing; a land where the rocks are iron and you can dig copper out of the hills.

10 When you have eaten and are satisfied, praise the LORD your God for the good land he has given you. 11 Be careful that you do not forget the LORD your God, failing to observe his commands, his laws and his decrees that I am giving you this day. 12 Otherwise, when you eat and are satisfied, when you build fine houses and settle down, 13 and when your herds and flocks grow large and your silver and gold increase and all you have is multiplied, 14 then your heart will become proud and you will forget the LORD your God, who brought you out of Egypt, out of the land of slavery. 15 He led you through the vast

and dreadful wilderness, that thirsty and waterless land, with its venomous snakes and scorpions. He brought you water out of hard rock. 16 He gave you manna to eat in the wilderness, something your ancestors had never known, to humble and test you so that in the end it might go well with you. 17 You may say to yourself, 'My power and the strength of my hands have produced this wealth for me.' 18 But remember the LORD your God, for it is he who gives you the ability to produce wealth, and so confirms his covenant, which he swore to your ancestors, as it is today.

19 If you ever forget the LORD your God and follow other gods and worship and bow down to them, I testify against you today that you will surely be destroyed. 20 Like the nations the LORD destroyed before you, so you will be destroyed for not obeying the LORD your God.

Not because of Israel's righteousness

9 Hear, Israel: you are now about to cross the Jordan to go in and dispossess nations greater and stronger than you, with large cities that have walls up to the sky. 2 The people are strong and tall – Anakites! You know about them and have heard it said: 'Who can stand up against the Anakites?' 3 But be assured today that the LORD your God is the one who goes across ahead of you like a devouring fire. He will destroy them; he will subdue them before you. And you will drive them out and annihilate them quickly, as the LORD has promised you.

4 After the LORD your God has driven them out before you, do not say to yourself, 'The LORD has brought me here to take possession of this land because of my righteousness.' No, it is on account of the wickedness of these nations that the LORD is going to drive them out before you. 5 It is not because of your righteousness or your integrity that you are going in to take possession of their land; but on account of the wickedness of these nations, the LORD your God will drive them out before you, to accomplish what he swore to your fathers, to Abraham, Isaac and Jacob. 6 Understand, then, that it is not because

of your righteousness that the LORD your God is giving you this good land to possess, for you are a stiff-necked people.

The golden calf

7 Remember this and never forget how you aroused the anger of the LORD your God in the wilderness. From the day you left Egypt until you arrived here, you have been rebellious against the LORD. 8 At Horeb you aroused the LORD's wrath so that he was angry enough to destroy you. 9 When I went up on the mountain to receive the tablets of stone, the tablets of the covenant that the LORD had made with you, I stayed on the mountain for forty days and forty nights; I ate no bread and drank no water. 10 The LORD gave me two stone tablets inscribed by the finger of God. On them were all the commandments the LORD proclaimed to you on the mountain out of the fire, on the day of the assembly.

11 At the end of the forty days and forty nights, the LORD gave me the two stone tablets, the tablets of the covenant. 12 Then the LORD told me, 'Go down from here at once, because your people whom you brought out of Egypt have become corrupt. They have turned away quickly from what I commanded them and have made an idol for themselves.'

13 And the LORD said to me, 'I have seen this people, and they are a stiff-necked people indeed! 14 Let me alone, so that I may destroy them and blot out their name from under heaven. And I will make you into a nation stronger and more numerous than they.'

15 So I turned and went down from the mountain while it was ablaze with fire. And the two tablets of the covenant were in my hands. 16 When I looked, I saw that you had sinned against the LORD your God; you had made for yourselves an idol cast in the shape of a calf. You had turned aside quickly from the way that the LORD had commanded you. 17 So I took the two tablets and threw them out of my hands, breaking them to pieces before your eyes.

18 Then once again I fell prostrate before

the LORD for forty days and forty nights; I ate no bread and drank no water, because of all the sin you had committed, doing what was evil in the LORD's sight and so arousing his anger. 19 I feared the anger and wrath of the LORD, for he was angry enough with you to destroy you. But again the LORD listened to me. 20 And the LORD was angry enough with Aaron to destroy him, but at that time I prayed for Aaron too. 21 Also I took that sinful thing of yours, the calf you had made, and burned it in the fire. Then I crushed it and ground it to powder as fine as dust and threw the dust into a stream that flowed down the mountain.

22 You also made the LORD angry at Taberah, at Massah and at Kibroth Hattaavah.

23 And when the LORD sent you out from Kadesh Barnea, he said, 'Go up and take possession of the land I have given you.' But you rebelled against the command of the LORD your God. You did not trust him or obey him. 24 You have been rebellious against the LORD ever since I have known you.

25 I lay prostrate before the LORD those forty days and forty nights because the LORD had said he would destroy you. 26 I prayed to the LORD and said, 'Sovereign LORD, do not destroy your people, your own inheritance that you redeemed by your great power and brought out of Egypt with a mighty hand. 27 Remember your servants Abraham, Isaac and Jacob. Overlook the stubbornness of this people, their wickedness and their sin. 28 Otherwise, the country from which you brought us will say, "Because the LORD was not able to take them into the land he had promised them, and because he hated them, he brought them out to put them to death in the wilderness." 29 But they are your people, your inheritance that you brought out by your great power and your outstretched arm.'

Tablets like the first ones

10 At that time the LORD said to me, 'Chisel out two stone tablets like the first ones and come up to me on the mountain. Also make a wooden ark.*a* 2 I will write on the tablets the words that were on the first tablets, which you broke. Then you are to put them in the ark.'

3 So I made the ark out of acacia wood and chiselled out two stone tablets like the first ones, and I went up on the mountain with the two tablets in my hands. 4 The LORD wrote on these tablets what he had written before, the Ten Commandments he had proclaimed to you on the mountain, out of the fire, on the day of the assembly. And the LORD gave them to me. 5 Then I came back down the mountain and put the tablets in the ark I had made, as the LORD commanded me, and they are there now.

6 (The Israelites travelled from the wells of Bene Jaakan to Moserah. There Aaron died and was buried, and Eleazar his son succeeded him as priest. 7 From there they travelled to Gudgodah and on to Jotbathah, a land with streams of water. 8 At that time the LORD set apart the tribe of Levi to carry the ark of the covenant of the LORD, to stand before the LORD to minister and to pronounce blessings in his name, as they still do today. 9 That is why the Levites have no share or inheritance among their fellow Israelites; the LORD is their inheritance, as the LORD your God told them.)

10 Now I had stayed on the mountain for forty days and forty nights, as I did the first time, and the LORD listened to me at this time also. It was not his will to destroy you. 11 'Go,' the LORD said to me, 'and lead the people on their way, so that they may enter and possess the land that I swore to their ancestors to give them.'

Fear the LORD

12 And now, Israel, what does the LORD your God ask of you but to fear the LORD your God, to walk in obedience to him, to love him, to serve the LORD your God with all your heart and with all your soul, 13 and to observe the LORD's commands and decrees that I am giving you today for your own good?

---

a 1 That is, a chest

14 To the LORD your God belong the heavens, even the highest heavens, the earth and everything in it. 15 Yet the LORD set his affection on your ancestors and loved them, and he chose you, their descendants, above all the nations – as it is today. 16 Circumcise your hearts, therefore, and do not be stiff-necked any longer. 17 For the LORD your God is God of gods and Lord of lords, the great God, mighty and awesome, who shows no partiality and accepts no bribes. 18 He defends the cause of the fatherless and the widow, and loves the foreigner residing among you, giving them food and clothing. 19 And you are to love those who are foreigners, for you yourselves were foreigners in Egypt. 20 Fear the LORD your God and serve him. Hold fast to him and take your oaths in his name. 21 He is your praise; he is your God, who performed for you those great and awesome wonders you saw with your own eyes. 22 Your ancestors who went down into Egypt were seventy in all, and now the LORD your God has made you as numerous as the stars in the sky.

Love and obey the LORD

11 Love the LORD your God and keep his requirements, his decrees, his laws and his commands always. 2 Remember today that your children were not the ones who saw and experienced the discipline of the LORD your God: his majesty, his mighty hand, his outstretched arm; 3 the signs he performed and the things he did in the heart of Egypt, both to Pharaoh king of Egypt and to his whole country; 4 what he did to the Egyptian army, to its horses and chariots, how he overwhelmed them with the waters of the Red Sea*a* as they were pursuing you, and how the LORD brought lasting ruin on them. 5 It was not your children who saw what he did for you in the wilderness until you arrived at this place, 6 and what he did to Dathan and Abiram, sons of Eliab the Reubenite, when the earth opened its mouth right in the middle of all Israel

and swallowed them up with their households, their tents and every living thing that belonged to them. 7 But it was your own eyes that saw all these great things the LORD has done.

8 Observe therefore all the commands I am giving you today, so that you may have the strength to go in and take over the land that you are crossing the Jordan to possess, 9 and so that you may live long in the land that the LORD swore to your ancestors to give to them and their descendants, a land flowing with milk and honey. 10 The land you are entering to take over is not like the land of Egypt, from which you have come, where you planted your seed and irrigated it by foot as in a vegetable garden. 11 But the land you are crossing the Jordan to take possession of is a land of mountains and valleys that drinks rain from heaven. 12 It is a land the LORD your God cares for; the eyes of the LORD your God are continually on it from the beginning of the year to its end.

13 So if you faithfully obey the commands I am giving you today – to love the LORD your God and to serve him with all your heart and with all your soul – 14 then I will send rain on your land in its season, both autumn and spring rains, so that you may gather in your corn, new wine and olive oil. 15 I will provide grass in the fields for your cattle, and you will eat and be satisfied.

16 Be careful, or you will be enticed to turn away and worship other gods and bow down to them. 17 Then the LORD's anger will burn against you, and he will shut the heavens so that it will not rain and the ground will yield no produce, and you will soon perish from the good land the LORD is giving you. 18 Fix these words of mine in your hearts and minds; tie them as symbols on your hands and bind them on your foreheads. 19 Teach them to your children, talking about them when you sit at home and when you walk along the road, when you lie down and when you get up. 20 Write them on the door-frames of your houses and on your gates, 21 so that your days and the days of your children may be many in the land that the LORD swore to give your

---

a 4 Or *the Sea of Reeds*

ancestors, as many as the days that the heavens are above the earth.

22 If you carefully observe all these commands I am giving you to follow – to love the LORD your God, to walk in obedience to him and to hold fast to him – 23 then the LORD will drive out all these nations before you, and you will dispossess nations larger and stronger than you. 24 Every place where you set your foot will be yours: your territory will extend from the desert to Lebanon, and from the River Euphrates to the Mediterranean Sea. 25 No one will be able to stand against you. The LORD your God, as he promised you, will put the terror and fear of you on the whole land, wherever you go.

26 See, I am setting before you today a blessing and a curse – 27 the blessing if you obey the commands of the LORD your God that I am giving you today; 28 the curse if you disobey the commands of the LORD your God and turn from the way that I command you today by following other gods, which you have not known. 29 When the LORD your God has brought you into the land you are entering to possess, you are to proclaim on Mount Gerizim the blessings, and on Mount Ebal the curses. 30 As you know, these mountains are across the Jordan, westward, towards the setting sun, near the great trees of Moreh, in the territory of those Canaanites living in the Arabah in the vicinity of Gilgal. 31 You are about to cross the Jordan to enter and take possession of the land the LORD your God is giving you. When you have taken it over and are living there, 32 be sure that you obey all the decrees and laws I am setting before you today.

The one place of worship

12 These are the decrees and laws you must be careful to follow in the land that the LORD, the God of your ancestors, has given you to possess – as long as you live in the land. 2 Destroy completely all the places on the high mountains, on the hills and under every spreading tree, where the nations you are dispossessing worship their gods. 3 Break down their altars, smash their sacred stones and burn their Asherah poles in the fire; cut down the idols of their gods and wipe out their names from those places.

4 You must not worship the LORD your God in their way. 5 But you are to seek the place the LORD your God will choose from among all your tribes to put his Name there for his dwelling. To that place you must go; 6 there bring your burnt offerings and sacrifices, your tithes and special gifts, what you have vowed to give and your freewill offerings, and the firstborn of your herds and flocks. 7 There, in the presence of the LORD your God, you and your families shall eat and shall rejoice in everything you have put your hand to, because the LORD your God has blessed you.

8 You are not to do as we do here today, everyone doing as they see fit, 9 since you have not yet reached the resting place and the inheritance the LORD your God is giving you. 10 But you will cross the Jordan and settle in the land the LORD your God is giving you as an inheritance, and he will give you rest from all your enemies around you so that you will live in safety. 11 Then to the place the LORD your God will choose as a dwelling for his Name – there you are to bring everything I command you: your burnt offerings and sacrifices, your tithes and special gifts, and all the choice possessions you have vowed to the LORD. 12 And there rejoice before the LORD your God – you, your sons and daughters, your male and female servants, and the Levites from your towns who have no land allotted to them or any inheritance of their own. 13 Be careful not to sacrifice your burnt offerings anywhere you please. 14 Offer them only at the place the LORD will choose in one of your tribes, and there observe everything I command you.

15 Nevertheless, you may slaughter your animals in any of your towns and eat as much of the meat as you want, as if it were gazelle or deer, according to the blessing the LORD your God gives you. Both the ceremonially unclean and the clean may eat it. 16 But you must not eat the blood; pour it out on the ground like water. 17 You must not eat in your own towns the tithe

of your corn and new wine and olive oil, or the firstborn of your herds and flocks, or whatever you have vowed to give, or your freewill offerings or special gifts. 18 Instead, you are to eat them in the presence of the LORD your God at the place the LORD your God will choose – you, your sons and daughters, your male and female servants, and the Levites from your towns – and you are to rejoice before the LORD your God in everything you put your hand to. 19 Be careful not to neglect the Levites as long as you live in your land.

20 When the LORD your God has enlarged your territory as he promised you, and you crave meat and say, 'I would like some meat,' then you may eat as much of it as you want. 21 If the place where the LORD your God chooses to put his Name is too far away from you, you may slaughter animals from the herds and flocks the LORD has given you, as I have commanded you, and in your own towns you may eat as much of them as you want. 22 Eat them as you would gazelle or deer. Both the ceremonially unclean and the clean may eat. 23 But be sure you do not eat the blood, because the blood is the life, and you must not eat the life with the meat. 24 You must not eat the blood; pour it out on the ground like water. 25 Do not eat it, so that it may go well with you and your children after you, because you will be doing what is right in the eyes of the LORD.

26 But take your consecrated things and whatever you have vowed to give, and go to the place the LORD will choose. 27 Present your burnt offerings on the altar of the LORD your God, both the meat and the blood. The blood of your sacrifices must be poured beside the altar of the LORD your God, but you may eat the meat. 28 Be careful to obey all these regulations I am giving you, so that it may always go well with you and your children after you, because you will be doing what is good and right in the eyes of the LORD your God.

29 The LORD your God will cut off before you the nations you are about to invade and dispossess. But when you have driven them out and settled in their land, 30 and after they have been destroyed before

you, be careful not to be ensnared by enquiring about their gods, saying, 'How do these nations serve their gods? We will do the same.' 31 You must not worship the LORD your God in their way, because in worshipping their gods, they do all kinds of detestable things the LORD hates. They even burn their sons and daughters in the fire as sacrifices to their gods.

32 See that you do all I command you; do not add to it or take away from it. a

Worshipping other gods

13 a If a prophet, or one who foretells by dreams, appears among you and announces to you a sign or wonder, 2 and if the sign or wonder spoken of takes place, and the prophet says, 'Let us follow other gods' (gods you have not known) 'and let us worship them,' 3 you must not listen to the words of that prophet or dreamer. The LORD your God is testing you to find out whether you love him with all your heart and with all your soul. 4 It is the LORD your God you must follow, and him you must revere. Keep his commands and obey him; serve him and hold fast to him. 5 That prophet or dreamer must be put to death for inciting rebellion against the LORD your God, who brought you out of Egypt and redeemed you from the land of slavery. That prophet or dreamer tried to turn you from the way the LORD your God commanded you to follow. You must purge the evil from among you.

6 If your very own brother, or your son or daughter, or the wife you love, or your closest friend secretly entices you, saying, 'Let us go and worship other gods' (gods that neither you nor your ancestors have known, 7 gods of the peoples around you, whether near or far, from one end of the land to the other), 8 do not yield to them or listen to them. Show them no pity. Do not spare them or shield them. 9 You must certainly put them to death. Your hand must be the first in putting them to death, and then the hands of all the people. 10 Stone

---

a 32 In Hebrew texts this verse (12:32) is numbered 13:1.
a In Hebrew texts 13:1-18 is numbered 13:2-19.

them to death, because they tried to turn you away from the LORD your God, who brought you out of Egypt, out of the land of slavery. 11 Then all Israel will hear and be afraid, and no one among you will do such an evil thing again.

12 If you hear it said about one of the towns the LORD your God is giving you to live in 13 that troublemakers have arisen among you and have led the people of their town astray, saying, 'Let us go and worship other gods' (gods you have not known), 14 then you must enquire, probe and investigate it thoroughly. And if it is true and it has been proved that this detestable thing has been done among you, 15 you must certainly put to the sword all who live in that town. You must destroy it completely, *b* both its people and its livestock. 16 You are to gather all the plunder of the town into the middle of the public square and completely burn the town and all its plunder as a whole burnt offering to the LORD your God. That town is to remain a ruin for ever, never to be rebuilt, 17 and none of the condemned things *b* are to be found in your hands. Then the LORD will turn from his fierce anger, will show you mercy, and will have compassion on you. He will increase your numbers, as he promised on oath to your ancestors – 18 because you obey the LORD your God by keeping all his commands that I am giving you today and doing what is right in his eyes.

Clean and unclean food

14 You are the children of the LORD your God. Do not cut yourselves or shave the front of your heads for the dead, 2 for you are a people holy to the LORD your God. Out of all the peoples on the face of the earth, the LORD has chosen you to be his treasured possession.

3 Do not eat any detestable thing. 4 These are the animals you may eat: the ox, the sheep, the goat, 5 the deer, the gazelle, the roe deer, the wild goat, the ibex, the antelope and the mountain sheep. *a* 6 You may eat any animal that has a divided hoof and that chews the cud. 7 However, of those that chew the cud or that have a divided hoof you may not eat the camel, the hare or the hyrax. Although they chew the cud, they do not have a divided hoof; they are ceremonially unclean for you. 8 The pig is also unclean; although it has a divided hoof, it does not chew the cud. You are not to eat their meat or touch their carcasses.

9 Of all the creatures living in the water, you may eat any that has fins and scales. 10 But anything that does not have fins and scales you may not eat; for you it is unclean.

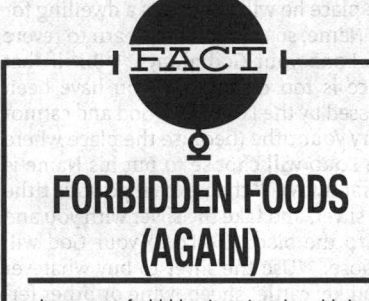

FORBIDDEN FOODS (AGAIN)

Jews were forbidden to eat various birds, including the eagle, the vulture, the red and black kite, any kind of falcon, various owls, the osprey, the cormorant, the stork, any kind of heron, the hoopoe and, confusingly, the bat. Which is not a bird (Deuteronomy 14:11–18).

11 You may eat any clean bird. 12 But these you may not eat: the eagle, the vulture, the black vulture, 13 the red kite, the black kite, any kind of falcon, 14 any kind of raven, 15 the horned owl, the screech owl, the gull, any kind of hawk, 16 the little owl, the great owl, the white owl, 17 the desert owl, the osprey, the cormorant, 18 the stork, any kind of heron, the hoopoe and the bat.

---

b 15,17 The Hebrew term refers to the irrevocable giving over of things or persons to the LORD, often by totally destroying them.

a 5 The precise identification of some of the birds and animals in this chapter is uncertain.

¹⁹All flying insects are unclean to you; do not eat them. ²⁰But any winged creature that is clean you may eat.

²¹Do not eat anything you find already dead. You may give it to the foreigner residing in any of your towns, and they may eat it, or you may sell it to any other foreigner. But you are a people holy to the LORD your God.

Do not cook a young goat in its mother's milk.

Tithes

²²Be sure to set aside a tenth of all that your fields produce each year. ²³Eat the tithe of your corn, new wine and olive oil, and the firstborn of your herds and flocks in the presence of the LORD your God at the place he will choose as a dwelling for his Name, so that you may learn to revere the LORD your God always. ²⁴But if that place is too distant and you have been blessed by the LORD your God and cannot carry your tithe (because the place where the LORD will choose to put his Name is so far away), ²⁵then exchange your tithe for silver, and take the silver with you and go to the place the LORD your God will choose. ²⁶Use the silver to buy whatever you like: cattle, sheep, wine or other fermented drink, or anything you wish. Then you and your household shall eat there in the presence of the LORD your God and rejoice. ²⁷And do not neglect the Levites living in your towns, for they have no land allotted to them or any inheritance of their own.

²⁸At the end of every three years, bring all the tithes of that year's produce and store it in your towns, ²⁹so that the Levites (who have no land allotted to them or any inheritance of their own) and the foreigners, the fatherless and the widows who live in your towns may come and eat and be satisfied, and so that the LORD your God may bless you in all the work of your hands.

The year for cancelling debts

15 At the end of every seven years you must cancel debts. ²This is how it is to be done: every creditor shall cancel any loan they have made to a fellow Israelite. They shall not require payment from anyone among their own people, because the LORD's time for cancelling debts has been proclaimed. ³You may require payment from a foreigner, but you must cancel any debt your fellow Israelite owes you. ⁴However, there need be no poor people among you, for in the land the LORD your God is giving you to possess as your inheritance, he will richly bless you, ⁵if only you fully obey the LORD your God and are careful to follow all these commands I am giving you today. ⁶For the LORD your God will bless you as he has promised, and you will lend to many nations but will borrow from none. You will rule over many nations but none will rule over you.

⁷If anyone is poor among your fellow Israelites in any of the towns of the land that the LORD your God is giving you, do not be hard-hearted or tight-fisted towards them. ⁸Rather, be open-handed and freely lend them whatever they need. ⁹Be careful not to harbour this wicked thought: 'The seventh year, the year for cancelling debts, is near,' so that you do not show ill will towards the needy among your fellow Israelites and give them nothing. They may then appeal to the LORD against you, and you will be found guilty of sin. ¹⁰Give generously to them and do so without a grudging heart; then because of this the LORD your God will bless you in all your work and in everything you put your hand to. ¹¹There will always be poor people in the land. Therefore I command you to be open-handed towards your fellow Israelites who are poor and needy in your land.

Freeing servants

¹²If any of your people – Hebrew men or women – sell themselves to you and serve you for six years, in the seventh year you must let them go free. ¹³And when you release them, do not send them away empty-handed. ¹⁴Supply them liberally from your flock, your threshing-floor and your winepress. Give to them as the LORD your God has blessed you. ¹⁵Remember that you were slaves in Egypt and the LORD

your God redeemed you. That is why I give you this command today.

¹⁶ But if your servant says to you, 'I do not want to leave you,' because he loves you and your family and is well off with you, ¹⁷ then take an awl and push it through his ear lobe into the door, and he will become your servant for life. Do the same for your female servant.

¹⁸ Do not consider it a hardship to set your servant free, because their service to you these six years has been worth twice as much as that of a hired hand. And the LORD your God will bless you in everything you do.

The firstborn animals

¹⁹ Set apart for the LORD your God every firstborn male of your herds and flocks. Do not put the firstborn of your oxen to work, and do not shear the firstborn of your sheep. ²⁰ Each year you and your family are to eat them in the presence of the LORD your God at the place he will choose. ²¹ If an animal has a defect, is lame or blind, or has any serious flaw, you must not sacrifice it to the LORD your God. ²² You are to eat it in your own towns. Both the ceremonially unclean and the clean may eat it, as if it were gazelle or deer. ²³ But you must not eat the blood; pour it out on the ground like water.

The Passover

16 Observe the month of Aviv and celebrate the Passover of the LORD your God, because in the month of Aviv he brought you out of Egypt by night. ² Sacrifice as the Passover to the LORD your God an animal from your flock or herd at the place the LORD will choose as a dwelling for his Name. ³ Do not eat it with bread made with yeast, but for seven days eat unleavened bread, the bread of affliction, because you left Egypt in haste – so that all the days of your life you may remember the time of your departure from Egypt. ⁴ Let no yeast be found in your possession in all your land for seven days. Do not let any of the meat you sacrifice on the evening of the first day remain until morning.

⁵ You must not sacrifice the Passover in any town the LORD your God gives you ⁶ except in the place he will choose as a dwelling for his Name. There you must sacrifice the Passover in the evening, when the sun goes down, on the anniversary*a* of your departure from Egypt. ⁷ Roast it and eat it at the place the LORD your God will choose. Then in the morning return to your tents. ⁸ For six days eat unleavened bread and on the seventh day hold an assembly to the LORD your God and do no work.

FESTIVAL

The three big pilgrimage festivals in the Jewish calendar were Passover, Weeks or Pentecost, and Tabernacles or Booths (Deuteronomy 16:16). These were times when thousands of pilgrims went to Jerusalem. The Hebrew names for these are Pesach (Passover), Shavuot (Pentecost) and Succoth (Booths).

The Festival of Weeks

⁹ Count seven weeks from the time you begin to put the sickle to the standing corn. ¹⁰ Then celebrate the Festival of Weeks to the LORD your God by giving a freewill offering in proportion to the blessings the LORD your God has given you. ¹¹ And rejoice before the LORD your God at the place he will choose as a dwelling for his Name – you, your sons and daughters, your male and female servants, the Levites in your towns, and the foreigners, the fatherless and the widows living among you. ¹² Remember that you were slaves in Egypt, and follow carefully these decrees.

a 6 Or *down, at the time of day*

The Festival of Tabernacles

13 Celebrate the Festival of Tabernacles for seven days after you have gathered the produce of your threshing-floor and your winepress. 14 Be joyful at your festival – you, your sons and daughters, your male and female servants, and the Levites, the foreigners, the fatherless and the widows who live in your towns. 15 For seven days celebrate the festival to the LORD your God at the place the LORD will choose. For the LORD your God will bless you in all your harvest and in all the work of your hands, and your joy will be complete.

16 Three times a year all your men must appear before the LORD your God at the place he will choose: at the Festival of Unleavened Bread, the Festival of Weeks and the Festival of Tabernacles. No one should appear before the LORD empty-handed: 17 each of you must bring a gift in proportion to the way the LORD your God has blessed you.

Judges

18 Appoint judges and officials for each of your tribes in every town the LORD your God is giving you, and they shall judge the people fairly. 19 Do not pervert justice or show partiality. Do not accept a bribe, for a bribe blinds the eyes of the wise and twists the words of the innocent. 20 Follow justice and justice alone, so that you may live and possess the land the LORD your God is giving you.

Worshipping other gods

21 Do not set up any wooden Asherah pole beside the altar you build to the LORD your God, 22 and do not erect a sacred stone, for these the LORD your God hates.

17 Do not sacrifice to the LORD your God an ox or a sheep that has any defect or flaw in it, for that would be detestable to him.

2 If a man or woman living among you in one of the towns the LORD gives you is found doing evil in the eyes of the LORD your God in violation of his covenant, 3 and contrary to my command has worshipped other gods, bowing down to them or to the sun or the moon or the stars in the sky, 4 and this has been brought to your attention, then you must investigate it thoroughly. If it is true and it has been proved that this detestable thing has been done in Israel, 5 take the man or woman who has done this evil deed to your city gate and stone that person to death. 6 On the testimony of two or three witnesses a person is to be put to death, but no one is to be put to death on the testimony of only one witness. 7 The hands of the witnesses must be the first in putting that person to death, and then the hands of all the people. You must purge the evil from among you.

Law courts

8 If cases come before your courts that are too difficult for you to judge – whether bloodshed, lawsuits or assaults – take them to the place the LORD your God will choose. 9 Go to the Levitical priests and to the judge who is in office at that time. Enquire of them and they will give you the verdict. 10 You must act according to the decisions they give you at the place the LORD will choose. Be careful to do everything they instruct you to do. 11 Act according to whatever they teach you and the decisions they give you. Do not turn aside from what they tell you, to the right or to the left. 12 Anyone who shows contempt for the judge or for the priest who stands ministering there to the LORD your God is to be put to death. You must purge the evil from Israel. 13 All the people will hear and be afraid, and will not be contemptuous again.

The king

14 When you enter the land the LORD your God is giving you and have taken possession of it and settled in it, and you say, 'Let us set a king over us like all the nations around us,' 15 be sure to appoint over you a king the LORD your God chooses. He must be from among your fellow Israelites. Do not place a foreigner over you, one who is not an Israelite. 16 The king, moreover, must not acquire great numbers of horses for himself or make the people return to Egypt to get more of them, for the LORD

has told you, 'You are not to go back that way again.' [17] He must not take many wives, or his heart will be led astray. He must not accumulate large amounts of silver and gold.

[18] When he takes the throne of his kingdom, he is to write for himself on a scroll a copy of this law, taken from that of the Levitical priests. [19] It is to be with him, and he is to read it all the days of his life so that he may learn to revere the LORD his God and follow carefully all the words of this law and these decrees [20] and not consider himself better than his fellow Israelites and turn from the law to the right or to the left. Then he and his descendants will reign a long time over his kingdom in Israel.

Offerings for priests and Levites

18 The Levitical priests – indeed, the whole tribe of Levi – are to have no land allotted to them or any inheritance with Israel. They shall live on the food offerings presented to the LORD, for that is their inheritance. [2] They shall have no inheritance among their fellow Israelites; the LORD is their inheritance, as he promised them.

[3] This is the share due to the priests from the people who sacrifice a bull or a sheep: the shoulder, the internal organs and the meat from the head. [4] You are to give them the firstfruits of your corn, new wine and olive oil, and the first wool from the shearing of your sheep, [5] for the LORD your God has chosen them and their descendants out of all your tribes to stand and minister in the LORD's name always.

[6] If a Levite moves from one of your towns anywhere in Israel where he is living, and comes in all earnestness to the place the LORD will choose, [7] he may minister in the name of the LORD his God like all his fellow Levites who serve there in the presence of the LORD. [8] He is to share equally in their benefits even though he has received money from the sale of family possessions.

Occult practices

[9] When you enter the land the LORD your God is giving you, do not learn to imitate the detestable ways of the nations there. [10] Let no one be found among you who sacrifices their son or daughter in the fire, who practises divination or sorcery, interprets omens, engages in witchcraft, [11] or casts spells, or who is a medium or spiritist or who consults the dead. [12] Anyone who does these things is detestable to the LORD; because of these same detestable practices the LORD your God will drive out those nations before you. [13] You must be blameless before the LORD your God.

The prophet

[14] The nations you will dispossess listen to those who practise sorcery or divination. But as for you, the LORD your God has not permitted you to do so. [15] The LORD your God will raise up for you a prophet like me from among you, from your fellow Israelites. You must listen to him. [16] For this is what you asked of the LORD your God at Horeb on the day of the assembly when you said, 'Let us not hear the voice of the LORD our God nor see this great fire any more, or we will die.'

[17] The LORD said to me: 'What they say is good. [18] I will raise up for them a prophet like you from among their fellow Israelites, and I will put my words in his mouth. He will tell them everything I command him. [19] I myself will call to account anyone who does not listen to my words that the prophet speaks in my name. [20] But a prophet who presumes to speak in my name anything I have not commanded, or a prophet who speaks in the name of other gods, is to be put to death.'

[21] You may say to yourselves, 'How can we know when a message has not been spoken by the LORD?' [22] If what a prophet proclaims in the name of the LORD does not take place or come true, that is a message the LORD has not spoken. That prophet has spoken presumptuously, so do not be alarmed.

Cities of refuge

19 When the LORD your God has destroyed the nations whose land he is giving you, and when you have driven them out and settled in their towns and houses, ²then set aside for yourselves three cities in the land the LORD your God is giving you to possess. ³Determine the distances involved and divide into three parts the land the LORD your God is giving you as an inheritance, so that a person who kills someone may flee for refuge to one of these cities.

⁴This is the rule concerning anyone who kills a person and flees there for safety – anyone who kills a neighbour unintentionally, without malice aforethought. ⁵For instance, a man may go into the forest with his neighbour to cut wood, and as he swings his axe to fell a tree, the head may fly off and hit his neighbour and kill him. That man may flee to one of these cities and save his life. ⁶Otherwise, the avenger of blood might pursue him in a rage, overtake him if the distance is too great, and kill him even though he is not deserving of death, since he did it to his neighbour without malice aforethought. ⁷This is why I command you to set aside for yourselves three cities.

⁸If the LORD your God enlarges your territory, as he promised on oath to your ancestors, and gives you the whole land he promised them, ⁹because you carefully follow all these laws I command you today – to love the LORD your God and to walk always in obedience to him – then you are to set aside three more cities. ¹⁰Do this so that innocent blood will not be shed in your land, which the LORD your God is giving you as your inheritance, and so that you will not be guilty of bloodshed.

¹¹But if out of hate someone lies in wait, assaults and kills a neighbour, and then flees to one of these cities, ¹²the killer shall be sent for by the town elders, be brought back from the city, and be handed over to the avenger of blood to die. ¹³Show no pity. You must purge from Israel the guilt of shedding innocent blood, so that it may go well with you.

¹⁴Do not move your neighbour's boundary stone set up by your predecessors in the inheritance you receive in the land the LORD your God is giving you to possess.

Witnesses

¹⁵One witness is not enough to convict anyone accused of any crime or offence they may have committed. A matter must be established by the testimony of two or three witnesses.

¹⁶If a malicious witness takes the stand to accuse someone of a crime, ¹⁷the two people involved in the dispute must stand in the presence of the LORD before the priests and the judges who are in office at the time. ¹⁸The judges must make a thorough investigation, and if the witness proves to be a liar, giving false testimony against a fellow Israelite, ¹⁹then do to the false witness as that witness intended to do to the other party. You must purge the evil from among you. ²⁰The rest of the people will hear of this and be afraid, and never again will such an evil thing be done among you. ²¹Show no pity: life for life, eye for eye, tooth for tooth, hand for hand, foot for foot.

Going to war

20 When you go to war against your enemies and see horses and chariots and an army greater than yours, do not be afraid of them, because the LORD your God, who brought you up out of Egypt, will be with you. ²When you are about to go into battle, the priest shall come forward and address the army. ³He shall say: 'Hear, Israel: today you are going into battle against your enemies. Do not be fainthearted or afraid; do not panic or be terrified by them. ⁴For the LORD your God is the one who goes with you to fight for you against your enemies to give you victory.'

⁵The officers shall say to the army: 'Has anyone built a new house and not yet begun to live in it? Let him go home, or he may die in battle and someone else may begin to live in it. ⁶Has anyone planted a vineyard and not begun to enjoy it? Let him go home, or he may die in battle and

someone else enjoy it. **7**Has anyone become pledged to a woman and not married her? Let him go home, or he may die in battle and someone else marry her.' **8**Then the officers shall add, 'Is anyone afraid or faint-hearted? Let him go home so that his fellow soldiers will not become disheartened too.' **9**When the officers have finished speaking to the army, they shall appoint commanders over it.

10When you march up to attack a city, make its people an offer of peace. **11**If they accept and open their gates, all the people in it shall be subject to forced labour and shall work for you. **12**If they refuse to make peace and they engage you in battle, lay siege to that city. **13**When the LORD your God delivers it into your hand, put to the sword all the men in it. **14**As for the women, the children, the livestock and everything else in the city, you may take these as plunder for yourselves. And you may use the plunder the LORD your God gives you from your enemies. **15**This is how you are to treat all the cities that are at a distance from you and do not belong to the nations nearby.

16However, in the cities of the nations the LORD your God is giving you as an inheritance, do not leave alive anything that breathes. **17**Completely destroy*a* them – the Hittites, Amorites, Canaanites, Perizzites, Hivites and Jebusites – as the LORD your God has commanded you. **18**Otherwise, they will teach you to follow all the detestable things they do in worshipping their gods, and you will sin against the LORD your God.

19When you lay siege to a city for a long time, fighting against it to capture it, do not destroy its trees by putting an axe to them, because you can eat their fruit. Do not cut them down. Are the trees people, that you should besiege them?*b* **20**However, you may cut down trees that you know are not fruit trees and use them to build siege works until the city at war with you falls.

Atonement for an unsolved murder

21 If someone is found slain, lying in a field in the land the LORD your God is giving you to possess, and it is not known who the killer was, **2**your elders and judges shall go out and measure the distance from the body to the neighbouring towns. **3**Then the elders of the town nearest the body shall take a heifer that has never been worked and has never worn a yoke **4**and lead it down to a valley that has not been ploughed or planted and where there is a flowing stream. There in the valley they are to break the heifer's neck. **5**The Levitical priests shall step forward, for the LORD your God has chosen them to minister and to pronounce blessings in the name of the LORD and to decide all cases of dispute and assault. **6**Then all the elders of the town nearest the body shall wash their hands over the heifer whose neck was broken in the valley, **7**and they shall declare: 'Our hands did not shed this blood, nor did our eyes see it done. **8**Accept this atonement for your people Israel, whom you have redeemed, LORD, and do not hold your people guilty of the blood of an innocent person.' Then the bloodshed will be atoned for, **9**and you will have purged from yourselves the guilt of shedding innocent blood, since you have done what is right in the eyes of the LORD.

Marrying a captive woman

10When you go to war against your enemies and the LORD your God delivers them into your hands and you take captives, **11**if you notice among the captives a beautiful woman and are attracted to her, you may take her as your wife. **12**Bring her into your home and make her shave her head, trim her nails **13**and put aside the clothes she was wearing when captured. After she has lived in your house and mourned her father and mother for a full month, then you may go to her and be her husband and she shall be your wife. **14**If you are not pleased with her, let her

---

a 17 The Hebrew term refers to the irrevocable giving over of things or persons to the LORD, often by totally destroying them.
b 19 Or *down to use in the siege, for the fruit trees are for the benefit of people.*

go wherever she wishes. You must not sell her or treat her as a slave, since you have dishonoured her.

The right of the firstborn

15 If a man has two wives, and he loves one but not the other, and both bear him sons but the firstborn is the son of the wife he does not love, 16 when he wills his property to his sons, he must not give the rights of the firstborn to the son of the wife he loves in preference to his actual firstborn, the son of the wife he does not love. 17 He must acknowledge the son of his unloved wife as the firstborn by giving him a double share of all he has. That son is the first sign of his father's strength. The right of the firstborn belongs to him.

A rebellious son

18 If someone has a stubborn and rebellious son who does not obey his father and mother and will not listen to them when they discipline him, 19 his father and mother shall take hold of him and bring him to the elders at the gate of his town. 20 They shall say to the elders, 'This son of ours is stubborn and rebellious. He will not obey us. He is a glutton and a drunkard.' 21 Then all the men of his town are to stone him to death. You must purge the evil from among you. All Israel will hear of it and be afraid.

Various laws

22 If someone guilty of a capital offence is put to death and their body is exposed on a pole, 23 you must not leave the body hanging on the pole overnight. Be sure to bury it that same day, because anyone who is hung on a pole is under God's curse. You must not desecrate the land the LORD your God is giving you as an inheritance.

22 If you see your fellow Israelite's ox or sheep straying, do not ignore it but be sure to take it back to its owner. 2 If they do not live near you or if you do not know who owns it, take it home with you and keep it until they come looking for it. Then give it back. 3 Do the same if you find their donkey or cloak or anything else they have lost. Do not ignore it.

4 If you see your fellow Israelite's donkey or ox fallen on the road, do not ignore it. Help the owner to get it to its feet.

5 A woman must not wear men's clothing, nor a man wear women's clothing, for the LORD your God detests anyone who does this.

6 If you come across a bird's nest beside the road, either in a tree or on the ground, and the mother is sitting on the young or on the eggs, do not take the mother with the young. 7 You may take the young, but be sure to let the mother go, so that it may go well with you and you may have a long life.

8 When you build a new house, make a parapet around your roof so that you may not bring the guilt of bloodshed on your house if someone falls from the roof.

9 Do not plant two kinds of seed in your vineyard; if you do, not only the crops you plant but also the fruit of the vineyard will be defiled. *a*

10 Do not plough with an ox and a donkey yoked together.

11 Do not wear clothes of wool and linen woven together.

12 Make tassels on the four corners of the cloak you wear.

Marriage violations

13 If a man takes a wife and, after sleeping with her, dislikes her 14 and slanders her and gives her a bad name, saying, 'I married this woman, but when I approached her, I did not find proof of her virginity,' 15 then the young woman's father and mother shall bring to the town elders at the gate proof that she was a virgin. 16 Her father will say to the elders, 'I gave my daughter in marriage to this man, but he dislikes her. 17 Now he has slandered her and said, "I did not find your daughter to be a virgin." But here is the proof of my daughter's virginity.' Then her parents shall display the cloth before the elders of the town, 18 and the elders shall take the man and punish him. 19 They shall fine him a hundred shekels*b* of silver and

---

a 9 Or *be forfeited to the sanctuary*
b 19 That is, about 1.2 kilograms

give them to the young woman's father, because this man has given an Israelite virgin a bad name. She shall continue to be his wife; he must not divorce her as long as he lives.

²⁰If, however, the charge is true and no proof of the young woman's virginity can be found, ²¹ she shall be brought to the door of her father's house and there the men of her town shall stone her to death. She has done an outrageous thing in Israel by being promiscuous while still in her father's house. You must purge the evil from among you.

²²If a man is found sleeping with another man's wife, both the man who slept with her and the woman must die. You must purge the evil from Israel.

²³If a man happens to meet in a town a virgin pledged to be married and he sleeps with her, ²⁴you shall take both of them to the gate of that town and stone them to death – the young woman because she was in a town and did not scream for help, and the man because he violated another man's wife. You must purge the evil from among you.

²⁵But if out in the country a man happens to meet a young woman pledged to be married and rapes her, only the man who has done this shall die. ²⁶Do nothing to the woman; she has committed no sin deserving death. This case is like that of someone who attacks and murders a neighbour, ²⁷for the man found the young woman out in the country, and though the betrothed woman screamed, there was no one to rescue her.

²⁸If a man happens to meet a virgin who is not pledged to be married and rapes her and they are discovered, ²⁹he shall pay her father fifty shekels*c* of silver. He must marry the young woman, for he has violated her. He can never divorce her as long as he lives.

³⁰A man is not to marry his father's wife; he must not dishonour his father's bed.*d*

Exclusion from the assembly

23ᵃ No one who has been emasculated by crushing or cutting may enter the assembly of the LORD.

²No one born of a forbidden marriageᵇ nor any of their descendants may enter the assembly of the LORD, not even in the tenth generation.

³No Ammonite or Moabite or any of their descendants may enter the assembly of the LORD, not even in the tenth generation. ⁴For they did not come to meet you with bread and water on your way when you came out of Egypt, and they hired Balaam son of Beor from Pethor in Aram Naharaimᶜ to pronounce a curse on you. ⁵However, the LORD your God would not listen to Balaam but turned the curse into a blessing for you, because the LORD your God loves you. ⁶Do not seek a treaty of friendship with them as long as you live.

⁷Do not despise an Edomite, for the Edomites are related to you. Do not despise an Egyptian, because you resided as foreigners in their country. ⁸The third generation of children born to them may enter the assembly of the LORD.

FACT

TOILET

Deuteronomy has some advice about plumbing! The Israelites were ordered to build their toilet outside the camp. And everyone had to carry a shovel with them (Deuteronomy 23:12–13).

Uncleanness in the camp

⁹When you set up camp against your enemies, keep away from everything

---

c 29 That is, about 575 grams
d 30 In Hebrew texts this verse (22:30) is numbered 23:1.

a In Hebrew texts 23:1-25 is numbered 23:2-26.
b 2 Or *one of illegitimate birth*
c 4 That is, North-west Mesopotamia

impure. ¹⁰If one of your men is unclean because of a nocturnal emission, he is to go outside the camp and stay there. ¹¹But as evening approaches he is to wash himself, and at sunset he may return to the camp.

¹²Designate a place outside the camp where you can go to relieve yourself. ¹³As part of your equipment have something to dig with, and when you relieve yourself, dig a hole and cover up your excrement. ¹⁴For the LORD your God moves about in your camp to protect you and to deliver your enemies to you. Your camp must be holy, so that he will not see among you anything indecent and turn away from you.

Miscellaneous laws

¹⁵If a slave has taken refuge with you, do not hand them over to their master. ¹⁶Let them live among you wherever they like and in whatever town they choose. Do not oppress them.

¹⁷No Israelite man or woman is to become a shrine-prostitute. ¹⁸You must not bring the earnings of a female prostitute or of a male prostitute*d* into the house of the LORD your God to pay any vow, because the LORD your God detests them both.

¹⁹Do not charge a fellow Israelite interest, whether on money or food or anything else that may earn interest. ²⁰You may charge a foreigner interest, but not a fellow Israelite, so that the LORD your God may bless you in everything you put your hand to in the land you are entering to possess.

²¹If you make a vow to the LORD your God, do not be slow to pay it, for the LORD your God will certainly demand it of you and you will be guilty of sin. ²²But if you refrain from making a vow, you will not be guilty. ²³Whatever your lips utter you must be sure to do, because you made your vow freely to the LORD your God with your own mouth.

²⁴If you enter your neighbour's vineyard, you may eat all the grapes you want, but do not put any in your basket. ²⁵If you

enter your neighbour's cornfield, you may pick the ears with your hands, but you must not put a sickle to their standing corn.

24 If a man marries a woman who becomes displeasing to him because he finds something indecent about her, and he writes her a certificate of divorce, gives it to her and sends her from his house, ²and if after she leaves his house she becomes the wife of another man, ³and her second husband dislikes her and writes her a certificate of divorce, gives it to her and sends her from his house, or if he dies, ⁴then her first husband, who divorced her, is not allowed to marry her again after she has been defiled. That would be detestable in the eyes of the LORD. Do not bring sin upon the land the LORD your God is giving you as an inheritance.

⁵If a man has recently married, he must not be sent to war or have any other duty laid on him. For one year he is to be free to stay at home and bring happiness to the wife he has married.

⁶Do not take a pair of millstones – not even the upper one – as security for a debt, because that would be taking a person's livelihood as security.

⁷If someone is caught kidnapping a fellow Israelite and treating or selling them as a slave, the kidnapper must die. You must purge the evil from among you.

⁸In cases of defiling skin diseases,*a* be very careful to do exactly as the Levitical priests instruct you. You must follow carefully what I have commanded them. ⁹Remember what the LORD your God did to Miriam along the way after you came out of Egypt.

¹⁰When you make a loan of any kind to your neighbour, do not go into their house to get what is offered to you as a pledge. ¹¹Stay outside and let the neighbour to whom you are making the loan bring the pledge out to you. ¹²If the neighbour is poor, do not go to sleep with their

---

d 18 Hebrew *of a dog*

a 8 The Hebrew word for *defiling skin diseases*, traditionally translated 'leprosy', was used for various diseases affecting the skin.

pledge in your possession. 13 Return their cloak by sunset so that your neighbour may sleep in it. Then they will thank you, and it will be regarded as a righteous act in the sight of the LORD your God.

14 Do not take advantage of a hired worker who is poor and needy, whether that worker is a fellow Israelite or a foreigner residing in one of your towns. 15 Pay them their wages each day before sunset, because they are poor and are counting on it. Otherwise they may cry to the LORD against you, and you will be guilty of sin.

16 Parents are not to be put to death for their children, nor children put to death for their parents; each will die for their own sin.

17 Do not deprive the foreigner or the fatherless of justice, or take the cloak of the widow as a pledge. 18 Remember that you were slaves in Egypt and the LORD your God redeemed you from there. That is why I command you to do this.

19 When you are harvesting in your field and you overlook a sheaf, do not go back to get it. Leave it for the foreigner, the fatherless and the widow, so that the LORD your God may bless you in all the work of your hands. 20 When you beat the olives from your trees, do not go over the branches a second time. Leave what remains for the foreigner, the fatherless and the widow. 21 When you harvest the grapes in your vineyard, do not go over the vines again. Leave what remains for the foreigner, the fatherless and the widow. 22 Remember that you were slaves in Egypt. That is why I command you to do this.

25 When people have a dispute, they are to take it to court and the judges will decide the case, acquitting the innocent and condemning the guilty. 2 If the guilty person deserves to be beaten, the judge shall make them lie down and have them flogged in his presence with the number of lashes the crime deserves, 3 but the judge must not impose more than forty lashes. If the guilty party is flogged more than that, your fellow Israelite will be degraded in your eyes.

4 Do not muzzle an ox while it is treading out the grain.

5 If brothers are living together and one of them dies without a son, his widow must not marry outside the family. Her husband's brother shall take her and marry her and fulfil the duty of a brother-in-law to her. 6 The first son she bears shall carry on the name of the dead brother so that his name will not be blotted out from Israel.

7 However, if a man does not want to marry his brother's wife, she shall go to the elders at the town gate and say, 'My husband's brother refuses to carry on his brother's name in Israel. He will not fulfil the duty of a brother-in-law to me.' 8 Then the elders of his town shall summon him and talk to him. If he persists in saying, 'I do not want to marry her,' 9 his brother's widow shall go up to him in the presence of the elders, take off one of his sandals, spit in his face and say, 'This is what is done to the man who will not build up his brother's family line.' 10 That man's line shall be known in Israel as The Family of the Unsandalled.

11 If two men are fighting and the wife of one of them comes to rescue her husband from his assailant, and she reaches out and seizes him by his private parts, 12 you shall cut off her hand. Show her no pity.

13 Do not have two differing weights in your bag – one heavy, one light. 14 Do not have two differing measures in your house – one large, one small. 15 You must have accurate and honest weights and measures, so that you may live long in the land the LORD your God is giving you. 16 For the LORD your God detests anyone who does these things, anyone who deals dishonestly.

17 Remember what the Amalekites did to you along the way when you came out of Egypt. 18 When you were weary and worn out, they met you on your journey and attacked all who were lagging behind; they had no fear of God. 19 When the LORD your God gives you rest from all the enemies around you in the land he is giving you to possess as an inheritance, you shall blot out the name of Amalek from under heaven. Do not forget!

MONEY 4

NOT JUST YOUR LEFTOVERS

Do you ever think of yourself as rich? I didn't until recently. I grew up in a family house on a normal street. I went to school, ate three meals a day and had weekly swimming classes after school. What I didn't realise is that in a global perspective, comparing my life to people all over the world, my life is not the norm. In fact, I fall into the rich list; I'm in the richest 10 per cent of the world's population, and the chances are that you are too. We have education, healthcare, running water, a decent toilet, a roof over our heads, a bed to sleep in and food in the cupboards – things I didn't realise made me rich.

Throughout the Bible, Jesus is regularly reminding us, the rich, to remember the poor. As Bono from U2 says, there are over 2,000 verses in the Bible mentioning poverty: 'That's a lot of airtime.' There are many ways in which we can respond to the call to serve those in need – with our time, voices, lifestyle choices and money.

Money is a powerful tool that can be used in brilliant or terrible ways. If we want it to, our money can be a great instrument for good – stored-up power to act. This is when money gets exciting – when we dream about the potential it has.

Dream with me for a moment. Imagine a different world, where people who are sick have medicine; children who can't read receive education; parents who are forced to sell their children to buy food for their other children have fresh vegetables and meat on the table for all their family; the elderly lady on our street can afford to have the central heating on over the winter; the homeless person sleeping on cardboard has a roof over their head and a bed with a big comfy duvet.

That's the world God is dreaming of.

Deuteronomy 24:19 isn't about random leftover olives and grapes. God is laying down principles for a society that remembers those who are living in poverty. The modern-day equivalent of harvesting could be running a business. At the time this scripture was written, they didn't have big brands like we do today, but would have had smaller, local, agricultural, farming businesses. The scripture is instructing 'business owners' to give up some of the profit they could make to provide food and money for those who needed it.

How do we put this principle into practice today?

For some of us, it may shape the future companies we run, where we might decide to forgo profits and allow our employees time to work on charity projects. For others it's what we do with our money, now and in our future, committing to giving 10 per cent away, or even more. This all contributes to God's dream of a different world.

Kiera Singlehurst-Phyo

Firstfruits and tithes

26 When you have entered the land that the LORD your God is giving you as an inheritance and have taken possession of it and settled in it, ²take some of the firstfruits of all that you produce from the soil of the land that the LORD your God is giving you and put them in a basket. Then go to the place that the LORD your God will choose as a dwelling for his Name ³and say to the priest in office at the time, 'I declare today to the LORD your God that I have come to the land the LORD swore to our ancestors to give us.' ⁴The priest shall take the basket from your hands and set it down in front of the altar of the LORD your God. ⁵Then you shall declare before the LORD your God: 'My father was a wandering Aramean, and he went down into Egypt with a few people and lived there and became a great nation, powerful and numerous. ⁶But the Egyptians ill-treated us and made us suffer, subjecting us to harsh labour. ⁷Then we cried out to the LORD, the God of our ancestors, and the LORD heard our voice and saw our misery, toil and oppression. ⁸So the LORD brought us out of Egypt with a mighty hand and an outstretched arm, with great terror and with signs and wonders. ⁹He brought us to this place and gave us this land, a land flowing with milk and honey; ¹⁰and now I bring the firstfruits of the soil that you, LORD, have given me.' Place the basket before the LORD your God and bow down before him. ¹¹Then you and the Levites and the foreigners residing among you shall rejoice in all the good things the LORD your God has given to you and your household.

¹²When you have finished setting aside a tenth of all your produce in the third year, the year of the tithe, you shall give it to the Levite, the foreigner, the fatherless and the widow, so that they may eat in your towns and be satisfied. ¹³Then say to the LORD your God: 'I have removed from my house the sacred portion and have given it to the Levite, the foreigner, the fatherless and the widow, according to all you commanded. I have not turned aside from your commands nor have I

forgotten any of them. ¹⁴I have not eaten any of the sacred portion while I was in mourning, nor have I removed any of it while I was unclean, nor have I offered any of it to the dead. I have obeyed the LORD my God; I have done everything you commanded me. ¹⁵Look down from heaven, your holy dwelling-place, and bless your people Israel and the land you have given us as you promised on oath to our ancestors, a land flowing with milk and honey.'

Follow the LORD's commands

¹⁶The LORD your God commands you this day to follow these decrees and laws; carefully observe them with all your heart and with all your soul. ¹⁷You have declared this day that the LORD is your God and that you will walk in obedience to him, that you will keep his decrees, commands and laws – that you will listen to him. ¹⁸And the LORD has declared this day that you are his people, his treasured possession as he promised, and that you are to keep all his commands. ¹⁹He has declared that he will set you in praise, fame and honour high above all the nations he has made and that you will be a people holy to the LORD your God, as he promised.

The altar on Mount Ebal

27 Moses and the elders of Israel commanded the people: 'Keep all these commands that I give you today. ²When you have crossed the Jordan into the land the LORD your God is giving you, set up some large stones and coat them with plaster. ³Write on them all the words of this law when you have crossed over to enter the land the LORD your God is giving you, a land flowing with milk and honey, just as the LORD, the God of your ancestors, promised you. ⁴And when you have crossed the Jordan, set up these stones on Mount Ebal, as I command you today, and coat them with plaster. ⁵Build there an altar to the LORD your God, an altar of stones. Do not use any iron tool on them. ⁶Build the altar of the LORD your God with stones from the field and offer burnt offerings on it to the LORD your God. 7 Sacrifice fellowship offerings there, eating them and rejoicing in the presence of the LORD your God. 8 And you shall write very clearly all the words of this law on these stones you have set up.'

Curses from Mount Ebal

9 Then Moses and the Levitical priests said to all Israel, 'Be silent, Israel, and listen! You have now become the people of the LORD your God. 10 Obey the LORD your God and follow his commands and decrees that I give you today.'

11 On the same day Moses commanded the people:

12 When you have crossed the Jordan, these tribes shall stand on Mount Gerizim to bless the people: Simeon, Levi, Judah, Issachar, Joseph and Benjamin. 13 And these tribes shall stand on Mount Ebal to pronounce curses: Reuben, Gad, Asher, Zebulun, Dan and Naphtali.

14 The Levites shall recite to all the people of Israel in a loud voice:

15 'Cursed is anyone who makes an idol – a thing detestable to the LORD, the work of skilled hands – and sets it up in secret.'

Then all the people shall say, 'Amen!'

16 'Cursed is anyone who dishonours their father or mother.'

Then all the people shall say, 'Amen!'

17 'Cursed is anyone who moves their neighbour's boundary stone.'

Then all the people shall say, 'Amen!'

18 'Cursed is anyone who leads the blind astray on the road.'

Then all the people shall say, 'Amen!'

19 'Cursed is anyone who withholds justice from the foreigner, the fatherless or the widow.'

Then all the people shall say, 'Amen!'

20 'Cursed is anyone who sleeps with his father's wife, for he dishonours his father's bed.'

Then all the people shall say, 'Amen!'

21 'Cursed is anyone who has sexual relations with any animal.'

Then all the people shall say, 'Amen!'

22 'Cursed is anyone who sleeps with his sister, the daughter of his father or the daughter of his mother.'

Then all the people shall say, 'Amen!'

23 'Cursed is anyone who sleeps with his mother-in-law.'

Then all the people shall say, 'Amen!'

24 'Cursed is anyone who kills their neighbour secretly.'

Then all the people shall say, 'Amen!'

25 'Cursed is anyone who accepts a bribe to kill an innocent person.'

Then all the people shall say, 'Amen!'

26 'Cursed is anyone who does not uphold the words of this law by carrying them out.'

Then all the people shall say, 'Amen!'

Blessings for obedience

28 If you fully obey the LORD your God and carefully follow all his commands that I give you today, the LORD your God will set you high above all the nations on earth. 2 All these blessings will come on you and accompany you if you obey the LORD your God:

3 You will be blessed in the city and blessed in the country.

4 The fruit of your womb will be blessed, and the crops of your land and the young of your livestock – the calves of your herds and the lambs of your flocks.

5 Your basket and your kneading trough will be blessed.

6 You will be blessed when you come in and blessed when you go out.

7 The LORD will grant that the enemies

who rise up against you will be defeated before you. They will come at you from one direction but flee from you in seven.

8 The LORD will send a blessing on your barns and on everything you put your hand to. The LORD your God will bless you in the land he is giving you.

9 The LORD will establish you as his holy people, as he promised you on oath, if you keep the commands of the LORD your God and walk in obedience to him. 10 Then all the peoples on earth will see that you are called by the name of the LORD, and they will fear you. 11 The LORD will grant you abundant prosperity – in the fruit of your womb, the young of your livestock and the crops of your ground – in the land he swore to your ancestors to give you.

12 The LORD will open the heavens, the storehouse of his bounty, to send rain on your land in season and to bless all the work of your hands. You will lend to many nations but will borrow from none. 13 The LORD will make you the head, not the tail. If you pay attention to the commands of the LORD your God that I give you this day and carefully follow them, you will always be at the top, never at the bottom. 14 Do not turn aside from any of the commands I give you today, to the right or to the left, following other gods and serving them.

Curses for disobedience

15 However, if you do not obey the LORD your God and do not carefully follow all his commands and decrees I am giving you today, all these curses will come on you and overtake you:

16 You will be cursed in the city and cursed in the country.

17 Your basket and your kneading trough will be cursed.

18 The fruit of your womb will be cursed, and the crops of your land, and the calves of your herds and the lambs of your flocks.

19 You will be cursed when you come in and cursed when you go out.

20 The LORD will send on you curses, confusion and rebuke in everything you put your hand to, until you are destroyed and come to sudden ruin because of the evil you have done in forsaking him.*a*

21 The LORD will plague you with diseases until he has destroyed you from the land you are entering to possess. 22 The LORD will strike you with wasting disease, with fever and inflammation, with scorching heat and drought, with blight and mildew, which will plague you until you perish. 23 The sky over your head will be bronze, the ground beneath you iron. 24 The LORD will turn the rain of your country into dust and powder; it will come down from the skies until you are destroyed.

25 The LORD will cause you to be defeated before your enemies. You will come at them from one direction but flee from them in seven, and you will become a thing of horror to all the kingdoms on earth. 26 Your carcasses will be food for all the birds and the wild animals, and there will be no one to frighten them away. 27 The LORD will afflict you with the boils of Egypt and with tumours, festering sores and the itch, from which you cannot be cured. 28 The LORD will afflict you with madness, blindness and confusion of mind. 29 At midday you will grope about like a blind person in the dark. You will be unsuccessful in everything you do; day after day you will be oppressed and robbed, with no one to rescue you.

30 You will be pledged to be married to a woman, but another will take her and rape her. You will build a house, but you will not live in it. You will plant a vineyard, but you will not even begin to enjoy its fruit. 31 Your ox will be slaughtered before your eyes, but you will eat none of it. Your donkey will be forcibly taken from you and will not be returned. Your sheep will be given to your enemies, and no one will rescue them. 32 Your sons and daughters will be given to another nation, and you will wear out your eyes watching for them day after day, powerless to lift a hand. 33 A people that you do not know will eat what

---

a 20 Hebrew *me*

your land and labour produce, and you will have nothing but cruel oppression all your days. 34The sights you see will drive you mad. 35The LORD will afflict your knees and legs with painful boils that cannot be cured, spreading from the soles of your feet to the top of your head.

36The LORD will drive you and the king you set over you to a nation unknown to you or your ancestors. There you will worship other gods, gods of wood and stone. 37You will become a thing of horror, a byword and an object of ridicule among all the peoples where the LORD will drive you.

38You will sow much seed in the field but you will harvest little, because locusts will devour it. 39You will plant vineyards and cultivate them but you will not drink the wine or gather the grapes, because worms will eat them. 40You will have olive trees throughout your country but you will not use the oil, because the olives will drop off. 41You will have sons and daughters but you will not keep them, because they will go into captivity. 42Swarms of locusts will take over all your trees and the crops of your land.

43The foreigners who reside among you will rise above you higher and higher, but you will sink lower and lower. 44They will lend to you, but you will not lend to them. They will be the head, but you will be the tail.

45All these curses will come on you. They will pursue you and overtake you until you are destroyed, because you did not obey the LORD your God and observe the commands and decrees he gave you. 46They will be a sign and a wonder to you and your descendants for ever. 47Because you did not serve the LORD your God joyfully and gladly in the time of prosperity, 48therefore in hunger and thirst, in nakedness and dire poverty, you will serve the enemies the LORD sends against you. He will put an iron yoke on your neck until he has destroyed you.

49The LORD will bring a nation against you from far away, from the ends of the earth, like an eagle swooping down, a nation whose language you will not understand, 50a fierce-looking nation without respect for the old or pity for the young. 51They will devour the young of your livestock and the crops of your land until you are destroyed. They will leave you no corn, new wine or olive oil, nor any calves of your herds or lambs of your flocks until you are ruined. 52They will lay siege to all the cities throughout your land until the high fortified walls in which you trust fall down. They will besiege all the cities throughout the land the LORD your God is giving you.

53Because of the suffering your enemy will inflict on you during the siege, you will eat the fruit of the womb, the flesh of the sons and daughters the LORD your God has given you. 54Even the most gentle and sensitive man among you will have no compassion on his own brother or the wife he loves or his surviving children, 55and he will not give to one of them any of the flesh of his children that he is eating. It will be all he has left because of the suffering that your enemy will inflict on you during the siege of all your cities. 56The most gentle and sensitive woman among you – so sensitive and gentle that she would not venture to touch the ground with the sole of her foot – will begrudge the husband she loves and her own son or daughter 57the afterbirth from her womb and the children she bears. For in her dire need she intends to eat them secretly because of the suffering your enemy will inflict on you during the siege of your cities.

58If you do not carefully follow all the words of this law, which are written in this book, and do not revere this glorious and awesome name – the LORD your God – 59the LORD will send fearful plagues on you and your descendants, harsh and prolonged disasters, and severe and lingering illnesses. 60He will bring on you all the diseases of Egypt that you dreaded, and they will cling to you. 61The LORD will also bring on you every kind of sickness and disaster not recorded in this Book of the Law, until you are destroyed. 62You who were as numerous as the stars in the sky will be left but few in number, because you did not obey the LORD your God. 63Just as it pleased the LORD to make you prosper and increase in number, so it will please him to ruin and destroy you. You will be uprooted from the land you are entering to possess.

64 Then the LORD will scatter you among all nations, from one end of the earth to the other. There you will worship other gods – gods of wood and stone, which neither you nor your ancestors have known. 65 Among those nations you will find no repose, no resting place for the sole of your foot. There the LORD will give you an anxious mind, eyes weary with longing, and a despairing heart. 66 You will live in constant suspense, filled with dread both night and day, never sure of your life. 67 In the morning you will say, 'If only it were evening!' and in the evening, 'If only it were morning!' – because of the terror that will fill your hearts and the sights that your eyes will see. 68 The LORD will send you back in ships to Egypt on a journey I said you should never make again. There you will offer yourselves for sale to your enemies as male and female slaves, but no one will buy you.

Renewal of the covenant

29[a] These are the terms of the covenant the LORD commanded Moses to make with the Israelites in Moab, in addition to the covenant he had made with them at Horeb.

2 Moses summoned all the Israelites and said to them:

Your eyes have seen all that the LORD did in Egypt to Pharaoh, to all his officials and to all his land. 3 With your own eyes you saw those great trials, those signs and great wonders. 4 But to this day the LORD has not given you a mind that understands or eyes that see or ears that hear. 5 Yet the LORD says, 'During the forty years that I led you through the wilderness, your clothes did not wear out, nor did the sandals on your feet. 6 You ate no bread and drank no wine or other fermented drink. I did this

so that you might know that I am the LORD your God.'

7 When you reached this place, Sihon king of Heshbon and Og king of Bashan came out to fight against us, but we defeated them. 8 We took their land and gave it as an inheritance to the Reubenites, the Gadites and the half-tribe of Manasseh.

9 Carefully follow the terms of this covenant, so that you may prosper in everything you do. 10 All of you are standing today in the presence of the LORD your God – your leaders and chief men, your elders and officials, and all the other men of Israel, 11 together with your children and your wives, and the foreigners living in your camps who chop your wood and carry your water. 12 You are standing here in order to enter into a covenant with the LORD your God, a covenant the LORD is making with you this day and sealing with an oath, 13 to confirm you this day as his people, that he may be your God as he promised you and as he swore to your fathers, Abraham, Isaac and Jacob. 14 I am making this covenant, with its oath, not only with you 15 who are standing here with us today in the presence of the LORD our God but also with those who are not here today.

16 You yourselves know how we lived in Egypt and how we passed through the countries on the way here. 17 You saw among them their detestable images and idols of wood and stone, of silver and gold. 18 Make sure there is no man or woman, clan or tribe among you today whose heart turns away from the LORD our God to go and worship the gods of those nations; make sure there is no root among you that produces such bitter poison.

19 When such a person hears the words of this oath and they invoke a blessing on themselves, thinking, 'I will be safe, even though I persist in going my own way,' they will bring disaster on the watered land as well as the dry. 20 The LORD will never be willing to forgive them; his wrath and zeal will burn against them. All the curses written in this book will fall on them, and the LORD will blot out their names from under heaven. 21 The LORD will single them out

a In Hebrew texts 29:1 is numbered 28:69, and 29:2-29 is numbered 29:1-28.

from all the tribes of Israel for disaster, according to all the curses of the covenant written in this Book of the Law.

22 Your children who follow you in later generations and foreigners who come from distant lands will see the calamities that have fallen on the land and the diseases with which the Lord has afflicted it. 23 The whole land will be a burning waste of salt and sulphur – nothing planted, nothing sprouting, no vegetation growing on it. It will be like the destruction of Sodom and Gomorrah, Admah and Zeboyim, which the Lord overthrew in fierce anger. 24 All the nations will ask: 'Why has the Lord done this to this land? Why this fierce, burning anger?'

25 And the answer will be: 'It is because this people abandoned the covenant of the Lord, the God of their ancestors, the covenant he made with them when he brought them out of Egypt. 26 They went off and worshipped other gods and bowed down to them, gods they did not know, gods he had not given them. 27 Therefore the Lord's anger burned against this land, so that he brought on it all the curses written in this book. 28 In furious anger and in great wrath the Lord uprooted them from their land and thrust them into another land, as it is now.'

29 The secret things belong to the Lord our God, but the things revealed belong to us and to our children for ever, that we may follow all the words of this law.

Prosperity after turning to the Lord

30 When all these blessings and curses I have set before you come on you and you take them to heart wherever the Lord your God disperses you among the nations, 2 and when you and your children return to the Lord your God and obey him with all your heart and with all your soul according to everything I command you today, 3 then the Lord your God will restore your fortunes[a] and have compassion on you and gather you again from all the nations where he scattered you. 4 Even if you have been banished to the most distant land under the heavens, from there the Lord your God will gather you and bring you back. 5 He will bring you to the land that belonged to your ancestors, and you will take possession of it. He will make you more prosperous and numerous than your ancestors. 6 The Lord your God will circumcise your hearts and the hearts of your descendants, so that you may love him with all your heart and with all your soul, and live. 7 The Lord your God will put all these curses on your enemies who hate and persecute you. 8 You will again obey the Lord and follow all his commands I am giving you today. 9 Then the Lord your God will make you most prosperous in all the work of your hands and in the fruit of your womb, the young of your livestock and the crops of your land. The Lord will again delight in you and make you prosperous, just as he delighted in your ancestors, 10 if you obey the Lord your God and keep his commands and decrees that are written in this Book of the Law and turn to the Lord your God with all your heart and with all your soul.

The offer of life or death

11 Now what I am commanding you today is not too difficult for you or beyond your reach. 12 It is not up in heaven, so that you have to ask, 'Who will ascend into heaven to get it and proclaim it to us so that we may obey it?' 13 Nor is it beyond the sea, so that you have to ask, 'Who will cross the sea to get it and proclaim it to us so that we may obey it?' 14 No, the word is very near you; it is in your mouth and in your heart so that you may obey it.

15 See, I set before you today life and prosperity, death and destruction. 16 For I command you today to love the Lord your God, to walk in obedience to him, and to keep his commands, decrees and laws; then you will live and increase, and the Lord your God will bless you in the land you are entering to possess.

17 But if your heart turns away and you are not obedient, and if you are drawn away to bow down to other gods and worship them, 18 I declare to you this day

---

a 3 Or *will bring you back from captivity*

that you will certainly be destroyed. You will not live long in the land you are crossing the Jordan to enter and possess.

19 This day I call the heavens and the earth as witnesses against you that I have set before you life and death, blessings and curses. Now choose life, so that you and your children may live 20 and that you may love the LORD your God, listen to his voice, and hold fast to him. For the LORD is your life, and he will give you many years in the land he swore to give to your fathers, Abraham, Isaac and Jacob.

Joshua to succeed Moses

31 Then Moses went out and spoke these words to all Israel: 2 'I am now a hundred and twenty years old and I am no longer able to lead you. The LORD has said to me, "You shall not cross the Jordan." 3 The LORD your God himself will cross over ahead of you. He will destroy these nations before you, and you will take possession of their land. Joshua also will cross over ahead of you, as the LORD said. 4 And the LORD will do to them what he did to Sihon and Og, the kings of the Amorites, whom he destroyed along with their land. 5 The LORD will deliver them to you, and you must do to them all that I have commanded you. 6 Be strong and courageous. Do not be afraid or terrified because of them, for the LORD your God goes with you; he will never leave you nor forsake you.'

7 Then Moses summoned Joshua and said to him in the presence of all Israel, 'Be strong and courageous, for you must go with this people into the land that the LORD swore to their ancestors to give them, and you must divide it among them as their inheritance. 8 The LORD himself goes before you and will be with you; he will never leave you nor forsake you. Do not be afraid; do not be discouraged.'

The reading of the law

9 So Moses wrote down this law and gave it to the Levitical priests, who carried the ark of the covenant of the LORD, and to all the elders of Israel. 10 Then Moses commanded them: 'At the end of every seven years, in the year for cancelling debts, during the Festival of Tabernacles, 11 when all Israel comes to appear before the LORD your God at the place he will choose, you shall read this law before them in their hearing. 12 Assemble the people – men, women and children, and the foreigners residing in your towns – so that they can listen and learn to fear the LORD your God and follow carefully all the words of this law. 13 Their children, who do not know this law, must hear it and learn to fear the LORD your God as long as you live in the land you are crossing the Jordan to possess.'

Israel's rebellion predicted

14 The LORD said to Moses, 'Now the day of your death is near. Call Joshua and present yourselves at the tent of meeting, where I will commission him.' So Moses and Joshua came and presented themselves at the tent of meeting.

15 Then the LORD appeared at the tent in a pillar of cloud, and the cloud stood over the entrance to the tent. 16 And the LORD said to Moses: 'You are going to rest with your ancestors, and these people will soon prostitute themselves to the foreign gods of the land they are entering. They will forsake me and break the covenant I made with them. 17 And in that day I will become angry with them and forsake them; I will hide my face from them, and they will be destroyed. Many disasters and calamities will come on them, and in that day they will ask, "Have not these disasters come on us because our God is not with us?" 18 And I will certainly hide my face in that day because of all their wickedness in turning to other gods.

19 'Now write down this song and teach it to the Israelites and make them sing it, so that it may be a witness for me against them. 20 When I have brought them into the land flowing with milk and honey, the land I promised on oath to their ancestors, and when they eat their fill and thrive, they will turn to other gods and worship them, rejecting me and breaking my covenant. 21 And when many disasters and calamities come on them, this song

will testify against them, because it will not be forgotten by their descendants. I know what they are disposed to do, even before I bring them into the land I promised them on oath.' ²²So Moses wrote down this song that day and taught it to the Israelites.

²³The LORD gave this command to Joshua son of Nun: 'Be strong and courageous, for you will bring the Israelites into the land I promised them on oath, and I myself will be with you.'

²⁴After Moses finished writing in a book the words of this law from

DIVORCE

My parents divorced when I was younger and I know from experience that this can be deeply painful and traumatic for many young people. When divorce hits a family, one of the most difficult things is finding that our lives are changed radically and we have little say in what goes on. We can feel helpless, angry, frightened and confused.

In Deuteronomy 31:8 we find the fantastic words that God goes before us, he promises he's with us, he promises never to leave us or forsake us. What amazing words! If we are worried about life, or frightened about having to move house, or we really don't like our parents' new partners, God promises to be with us and never leave us. The verse goes on to say that we don't have to be afraid or discouraged. In the New Testament, we read words of Jesus in John 14:27 when he says, 'Peace I leave with you; my peace I give you... Do not let your hearts be troubled and do not be afraid.' There are dozens of verses that can offer us peace and comfort when our families face divorce. Check out Psalm 46:1 and Isaiah 40:28–31. The Bible is an amazing source of strength. It reminds us that God is with us: we only have to call on him for help.

All kinds of emotions can bubble to the surface and it can be very difficult to know how to handle them. Some people handle these feelings in a wrong way, and they can come out through anger or violence, or just wanting to hit out at someone. It can be really hard if your parents find new partners, or you feel your parents are trying to split you down the middle. One thing is absolutely certain: your parents' divorce is not your fault. Sometimes it can feel as if no one understands us, and there's no one we can tell. I got through my parents' divorce trusting God to help me through prayer and the Bible. In your hands you hold the Bible, and it's packed with advice, encouragement and the fingerprints of God's love for you. There is no single passage in the Bible written specifically to help us when we face divorce, but there are loads of amazing verses that we can draw on.

So as you read the Bible, turn the verses into prayers. Allow the Holy Spirit to speak to you, to show you that you are loved. Ask God to give you all the strength you need, all the grace you need, to face divorce in your family, and know in your heart that he is with you. These are God's promises to you. And God keeps his promises – always.

Mark Russell

beginning to end, 25 he gave this command to the Levites who carried the ark of the covenant of the LORD: 26 'Take this Book of the Law and place it beside the ark of the covenant of the LORD your God. There it will remain as a witness against you. 27 For I know how rebellious and stiff-necked you are. If you have been rebellious against the LORD while I am still alive and with you, how much more will you rebel after I die! 28 Assemble before me all the elders of your tribes and all your officials, so that I can speak these words in their hearing and call the heavens and the earth to testify against them. 29 For I know that after my death you are sure to become utterly corrupt and to turn from the way I have commanded you. In days to come, disaster will fall on you because you will do evil in the sight of the LORD and arouse his anger by what your hands have made.'

The song of Moses

30 And Moses recited the words of this song from beginning to end in the hearing of the whole assembly of Israel:

32

Listen, you heavens, and I will speak;
hear, you earth, the words of my mouth.
2 Let my teaching fall like rain
and my words descend like dew,
like showers on new grass,
like abundant rain on tender plants.

3 I will proclaim the name of the LORD.
Oh, praise the greatness of our God!
4 He is the Rock, his works are perfect,
and all his ways are just.
A faithful God who does no wrong,
upright and just is he.

5 They are corrupt and not his children;
to their shame they are a warped and crooked generation.
6 Is this the way you repay the LORD,

you foolish and unwise people?
Is he not your Father, your Creator,*a*
who made you and formed you?

7 Remember the days of old;
consider the generations long past.
Ask your father and he will tell you,
your elders, and they will explain to you.
8 When the Most High gave the nations their inheritance,
when he divided all mankind,
he set up boundaries for the peoples
according to the number of the sons of Israel.*b*
9 For the LORD's portion is his people,
Jacob his allotted inheritance.

10 In a desert land he found him,
in a barren and howling waste.
He shielded him and cared for him;
he guarded him as the apple of his eye,
11 like an eagle that stirs up its nest
and hovers over its young,
that spreads its wings to catch them
and carries them on its pinions.
12 The LORD alone led him;
no foreign god was with him.

13 He made him ride on the heights of the land
and fed him with the fruit of the fields.
He nourished him with honey from the rock,
and with oil from the flinty crag,
14 with curds and milk from herd and flock
and with fattened lambs and goats,
with choice rams of Bashan
and the finest grains of wheat.
You drank the foaming blood of the grape.

---

a 6 Or *Father, who bought you*
b 8 Masoretic Text; Dead Sea Scrolls (see also Septuagint) *sons of God*

15 Jeshurun^c grew fat and kicked;
  filled with food, they became
    heavy and sleek.
They abandoned the God who made
    them
  and rejected the Rock their
    Saviour.
16 They made him jealous with their
    foreign gods
  and angered him with their
    detestable idols.
17 They sacrificed to false gods, which
    are not God –
  gods they had not known,
  gods that recently appeared,
  gods your ancestors did not fear.
18 You deserted the Rock, who
    fathered you;
  you forgot the God who gave you
    birth.

19 The LORD saw this and rejected
    them
  because he was angered by his
    sons and daughters.
20 'I will hide my face from them,' he
    said,
  'and see what their end will be;
for they are a perverse generation,
  children who are unfaithful.
21 They made me jealous by what is no
    god
  and angered me with their
    worthless idols.
I will make them envious by those
    who are not a people;
  I will make them angry by
    a nation that has no
    understanding.
22 For a fire will be kindled by my wrath,
  one that burns down to the realm
    of the dead below.
It will devour the earth and its
    harvests
  and set on fire the foundations of
    the mountains.

23 'I will heap calamities on them
  and expend my arrows against
    them.

24 I will send wasting famine against
    them,
  consuming pestilence and deadly
    plague;
  I will send against them the fangs of
    wild beasts,
  the venom of vipers that glide in
    the dust.
25 In the street the sword will make
    them childless;
  in their homes terror will reign.
The young men and young women
    will perish,
  the infants and those with grey
    hair.
26 I said I would scatter them
  and erase their name from
    human memory,
27 but I dreaded the taunt of the
    enemy,
  lest the adversary misunderstand
and say, "Our hand has triumphed;
  the LORD has not done all this." '

28 They are a nation without sense,
  there is no discernment in them.
29 If only they were wise and would
    understand this
  and discern what their end will be!
30 How could one man chase a
    thousand,
  or two put ten thousand to flight,
unless their Rock had sold them,
  unless the LORD had given them
    up?
31 For their rock is not like our Rock,
  as even our enemies concede.
32 Their vine comes from the vine of
    Sodom
  and from the fields of Gomorrah.
Their grapes are filled with poison,
  and their clusters with bitterness.
33 Their wine is the venom of serpents,
  the deadly poison of cobras.

34 'Have I not kept this in reserve
  and sealed it in my vaults?
35 It is mine to avenge; I will repay.
  In due time their foot will slip;
their day of disaster is near
  and their doom rushes upon
    them.'

---

c 15 *Jeshurun* means *the upright one*, that is, Israel.

36 The Lord will vindicate his people
and relent concerning his
servants
when he sees their strength is gone
and no one is left, slave or free. *d*
37 He will say: 'Now where are their
gods,
the rock they took refuge in,
38 the gods who ate the fat of their
sacrifices
and drank the wine of their drink
offerings?
Let them rise up to help you!
Let them give you shelter!

39 'See now that I myself am he!
There is no god besides me.
I put to death and I bring to life,
I have wounded and I will heal,
and no one can deliver out of my
hand.
40 I lift my hand to heaven and
solemnly swear:
as surely as I live for ever,
41 when I sharpen my flashing sword
and my hand grasps it in
judgment,
I will take vengeance on my
adversaries
and repay those who hate me.
42 I will make my arrows drunk with
blood,
while my sword devours flesh:
the blood of the slain and the
captives,
the heads of the enemy leaders.'

43 Rejoice, you nations, with his
people, *e,f*
for he will avenge the blood of his
servants;
he will take vengeance on his
enemies
and make atonement for his land
and people.

44 Moses came with Joshua *g* son of Nun
and spoke all the words of this song in the
hearing of the people. 45 When Moses had
finished reciting all these words to all Israel, 46 he said to them, 'Take to heart all
the words I have solemnly declared to you
this day, so that you may command your
children to obey carefully all the words of
this law. 47 They are not just idle words for
you – they are your life. By them you will
live long in the land you are crossing the
Jordan to possess.'

Moses to die on Mount Nebo

48 On that same day the Lord told
Moses, 49 'Go up into the Abarim Range
to Mount Nebo in Moab, opposite Jericho, and view Canaan, the land I am giving the Israelites as their own possession.
50 There on the mountain that you have
climbed you will die and be gathered to
your people, just as your brother Aaron
died on Mount Hor and was gathered to
his people. 51 This is because both of you
broke faith with me in the presence of the
Israelites at the waters of Meribah Kadesh
in the Desert of Zin and because you did
not uphold my holiness among the Israelites. 52 Therefore, you will see the land
only from a distance; you will not enter
the land I am giving to the people of Israel.'

Moses blesses the tribes

33 This is the blessing that Moses the
man of God pronounced on the
Israelites before his death. 2 He said:

'The Lord came from Sinai
and dawned over them from Seir;
he shone forth from Mount
Paran.
He came with *a* myriads of holy ones
from the south, from his
mountain slopes. *b*
3 Surely it is you who love the people;
all the holy ones are in your hand.

---

d 36 Or *and they are without a ruler or leader*
e 43 Or *Make his people rejoice, you nations*
f 43 Masoretic Text; Dead Sea Scrolls (see also
Septuagint) *people, / and let all the angels worship him, /*

g 44 Hebrew *Hoshea,* a variant of *Joshua*
a 2 Or *from*
b 2 The meaning of the Hebrew for this phrase is
uncertain.

At your feet they all bow down,
and from you receive instruction,
4 the law that Moses gave us,
the possession of the assembly of
Jacob.
5 He was king over Jeshurun*c*
when the leaders of the people
assembled,
along with the tribes of Israel.

6 'Let Reuben live and not die,
nor*d* his people be few.'

7 And this he said about Judah:

'Hear, LORD, the cry of Judah;
bring him to his people.
With his own hands he defends his
cause.
Oh, be his help against his foes!'

8 About Levi he said:

'Your Thummim and Urim belong
to your faithful servant.
You tested him at Massah;
you contended with him at the
waters of Meribah.
9 He said of his father and mother,
"I have no regard for them."
He did not recognise his brothers
or acknowledge his own
children,
but he watched over your word
and guarded your covenant.
10 He teaches your precepts to Jacob
and your law to Israel.
He offers incense before you
and whole burnt offerings on
your altar.
11 Bless all his skills, LORD,
and be pleased with the work of
his hands.
Strike down those who rise against
him,
his foes till they rise no more.'

12 About Benjamin he said:

'Let the beloved of the LORD rest
secure in him,
for he shields him all day long,
and the one the LORD loves rests
between his shoulders.'

13 About Joseph he said:

'May the LORD bless his land
with the precious dew from
heaven above
and with the deep waters that lie
below;
14 with the best the sun brings forth
and the finest the moon can
yield;
15 with the choicest gifts of the ancient
mountains
and the fruitfulness of the
everlasting hills;
16 with the best gifts of the earth and
its fullness
and the favour of him who dwelt
in the burning bush.
Let all these rest on the head of
Joseph,
on the brow of the prince among*e*
his brothers.
17 In majesty he is like a firstborn bull;
his horns are the horns of a wild
ox.
With them he will gore the nations,
even those at the ends of the
earth.
Such are the ten thousands of
Ephraim;
such are the thousands of
Manasseh.'

18 About Zebulun he said:

'Rejoice, Zebulun, in your going out,
and you, Issachar, in your tents.
19 They will summon peoples to the
mountain
and there offer the sacrifices of
the righteous;

---

c 5 *Jeshurun* means *the upright one*, that is, Israel; also
in verse 26.
d 6 Or *but let*

e 16 Or *of the one separated from*

they will feast on the abundance of
the seas,
on the treasures hidden in the
sand.'

20 About Gad he said:

'Blessed is he who enlarges Gad's
domain!
Gad lives there like a lion,
tearing at arm or head.
21 He chose the best land for himself;
the leader's portion was kept for
him.
When the heads of the people
assembled,
he carried out the LORD's
righteous will,
and his judgments concerning
Israel.'

22 About Dan he said:

'Dan is a lion's cub,
springing out of Bashan.'

23 About Naphtali he said:

'Naphtali is abounding with the
favour of the LORD
and is full of his blessing;
he will inherit southward to the
lake.'

24 About Asher he said:

'Most blessed of sons is Asher;
let him be favoured by his
brothers,
and let him bathe his feet in oil.
25 The bolts of your gates will be iron
and bronze,
and your strength will equal your
days.

26 'There is no one like the God of
Jeshurun,
who rides across the heavens to
help you
and on the clouds in his
majesty.
27 The eternal God is your refuge,

and underneath are the
everlasting arms.
He will drive out your enemies
before you,
saying, "Destroy them!"
28 So Israel will live in safety;
Jacob will dwell *f* secure
in a land of grain and new wine,
where the heavens drop dew.
29 Blessed are you, Israel!
Who is like you,
a people saved by the LORD?
He is your shield and helper
and your glorious sword.
Your enemies will cower before you,
and you will tread on their
heights.'

The death of Moses

34 Then Moses climbed Mount Nebo
from the plains of Moab to the
top of Pisgah, opposite Jericho. There
the LORD showed him the whole land –
from Gilead to Dan, 2 all of Naphtali, the
territory of Ephraim and Manasseh, all
the land of Judah as far as the Mediterranean Sea, 3 the Negev and the whole region from the Valley of Jericho, the City
of Palms, as far as Zoar. 4 Then the LORD
said to him, 'This is the land I promised on
oath to Abraham, Isaac and Jacob when I
said, "I will give it to your descendants." I
have let you see it with your eyes, but you
will not cross over into it.'

5 And Moses the servant of the LORD
died there in Moab, as the LORD had said.
6 He buried him *a* in Moab, in the valley
opposite Beth Peor, but to this day no one
knows where his grave is. 7 Moses was a
hundred and twenty years old when he
died, yet his eyes were not weak nor his
strength gone. 8 The Israelites grieved for
Moses in the plains of Moab thirty days,
until the time of weeping and mourning
was over.

9 Now Joshua son of Nun was filled with
the spirit *b* of wisdom because Moses had

---

f 28 Septuagint; Hebrew *Jacob's spring is*
a 6 Or *He was buried*
b 9 Or *Spirit*

laid his hands on him. So the Israelites listened to him and did what the LORD had commanded Moses.

¹⁰ Since then, no prophet has risen in Israel like Moses, whom the LORD knew face to face, ¹¹ who did all those signs and wonders the LORD sent him to do in Egypt – to Pharaoh and to all his officials and to his whole land. ¹² For no one has ever shown the mighty power or performed the awesome deeds that Moses did in the sight of all Israel.

JOSHUA

DATE

It is believed that the events of the book of Joshua occurred sometime after 1406 BC

AUTHOR

Unknown, but some think parts of the book were written by Joshua himself

WHAT'S IT ALL ABOUT?

Joshua is the first of the Old Testament's twelve History books and it picks up the story from Deuteronomy after the death of Moses. The Israelites had been wandering in the desert for forty years since they had left Egypt and this book tells how they finally took control of the Promised Land with Joshua as their leader. The first chapters of the book talk about the battles they fought and the victories God gave them so that they might take the land (the most famous is the Battle of Jericho, in Joshua 5 and 6). Once the land had been conquered, the book details how Joshua divided it up between the tribes of Israel and how he urged them to continue to be faithful to God. It concludes with the death of Joshua and his burial in the Promised Land.

WHY SHOULD WE READ IT?

- As a reminder that God always delivers on his promises.

- To remember that as we follow God faithfully we can trust him to win the battle for us.

- To learn from the example of Joshua. He was one of the great leaders of Israel, showing courage, bravery, faith, a great ability in battle and effective leadership skills. During his reign of leadership, Israel was faithful to God.

- To read about the Battle of Jericho (Joshua 6) and how God broke down a whole city wall without anyone touching it.

- To read the story of Rahab, a prostitute who converted to the God of Israel, showed great courage and faith and went on to become an ancestor of Jesus (Joshua 2; also mentioned in the genealogy of Jesus in Matthew 1).

Andy Croft with Liza Hoeksma

Joshua installed as leader

1 After the death of Moses the servant of the Lord, the Lord said to Joshua son of Nun, Moses' assistant: **2** 'Moses my servant is dead. Now then, you and all these people, get ready to cross the River Jordan into the land I am about to give to them – to the Israelites. **3** I will give you every place where you set your foot, as I promised Moses. **4** Your territory will extend from the desert to Lebanon, and from the great river, the Euphrates – all the Hittite country – to the Mediterranean Sea in the west. **5** No one will be able to stand against you all the days of your life. As I was with Moses, so I will be with you; I will never leave you nor forsake you. **6** Be strong and courageous, because you will lead these people to inherit the land I swore to their ancestors to give them.

7 'Be strong and very courageous. Be careful to obey all the law my servant Moses gave you; do not turn from it to the right or to the left, that you may be successful wherever you go. **8** Keep this Book of the Law always on your lips; meditate on it day and night, so that you may be careful to do everything written in it. Then you will be prosperous and successful. **9** Have I not commanded you? Be strong and courageous. Do not be afraid; do not be discouraged, for the Lord your God will be with you wherever you go.'

10 So Joshua ordered the officers of the people: **11** 'Go through the camp and tell the people, "Get your provisions ready. Three days from now you will cross the Jordan here to go in and take possession of the land the Lord your God is giving you for your own."'

12 But to the Reubenites, the Gadites and the half-tribe of Manasseh, Joshua said, **13** 'Remember the command that Moses the servant of the Lord gave you after he said, "The Lord your God will give you rest by giving you this land." **14** Your wives, your children and your livestock may stay in the land that Moses gave you east of the Jordan, but all your fighting men, ready for battle, must cross over ahead of your fellow Israelites. You are to help them **15** until the Lord gives you rest, as he has done

for you, and until they too have taken possession of the land that the Lord your God is giving them. After that, you may go back and occupy your own land, which Moses the servant of the Lord gave you east of the Jordan towards the sunrise.'

16 Then they answered Joshua, 'Whatever you have commanded us we will do, and wherever you send us we will go. **17** Just as we fully obeyed Moses, so we will obey you. Only may the Lord your God be with you as he was with Moses. **18** Whoever rebels against your word and does not obey it, whatever you may command them, will be put to death. Only be strong and courageous!'

Rahab and the spies

2 Then Joshua son of Nun secretly sent two spies from Shittim. 'Go, look over the land,' he said, 'especially Jericho.' So they went and entered the house of a prostitute named Rahab and stayed there.

2 The king of Jericho was told, 'Look, some of the Israelites have come here tonight to spy out the land.' **3** So the king of Jericho sent this message to Rahab: 'Bring out the men who came to you and entered your house, because they have come to spy out the whole land.'

4 But the woman had taken the two men and hidden them. She said, 'Yes, the men came to me, but I did not know where they had come from. **5** At dusk, when it was time to close the city gate, they left. I don't know which way they went. Go after them quickly. You may catch up with them.' **6** (But she had taken them up to the roof and hidden them under the stalks of flax she had laid out on the roof.) **7** So the men set out in pursuit of the spies on the road that leads to the fords of the Jordan, and as soon as the pursuers had gone out, the gate was shut.

8 Before the spies lay down for the night, she went up on the roof **9** and said to them, 'I know that the Lord has given this land to you and that a great fear of you has fallen on us, so that all who live in this country are melting in fear because of you. **10** We have heard how the Lord dried up the water of the Red Sea*a* for you when you came out of Egypt, and what you did to Sihon and Og, the two kings of the Amorites east of the Jordan, whom you completely destroyed.*b* 11 When we heard of it, our hearts sank*c* and everyone's courage failed because of you, for the LORD your God is God in heaven above and on the earth below.

12 'Now then, please swear to me by the LORD that you will show kindness to my family, because I have shown kindness to you. Give me a sure sign 13 that you will spare the lives of my father and mother, my brothers and sisters, and all who belong to them – and that you will save us from death.'

14 'Our lives for your lives!' the men assured her. 'If you don't tell what we are doing, we will treat you kindly and faithfully when the LORD gives us the land.'

15 So she let them down by a rope through the window, for the house she lived in was part of the city wall. 16 She said to them, 'Go to the hills so that the pursuers will not find you. Hide yourselves there for three days until they return, and then go on your way.'

17 Now the men had said to her, 'This oath you made us swear will not be binding on us 18 unless, when we enter the land, you have tied this scarlet cord in the window through which you let us down, and unless you have brought your father and mother, your brothers and all your family into your house. 19 If any of them go outside your house into the street, their blood will be on their own heads; we will not be responsible. As for those who are in the house with you, their blood will be on our head if a hand is laid on them. 20 But if you tell what we are doing, we will be released from the oath you made us swear.'

21 'Agreed,' she replied. 'Let it be as you say.'

So she sent them away, and they departed. And she tied the scarlet cord in the window.

22 When they left, they went into the hills and stayed there three days, until the pursuers had searched all along the road and returned without finding them. 23 Then the two men started back. They went down out of the hills, forded the river and came to Joshua son of Nun and told him everything that had happened to them. 24 They said to Joshua, 'The LORD has surely given the whole land into our hands; all the people are melting in fear because of us.'

Crossing the Jordan

3 Early in the morning Joshua and all the Israelites set out from Shittim and went to the Jordan, where they camped before crossing over. 2 After three days the officers went throughout the camp, 3 giving orders to the people: 'When you see the ark of the covenant of the LORD your God, and the Levitical priests carrying it, you are to move out from your positions and follow it. 4 Then you will know which way to go, since you have never been this way before. But keep a distance of about two thousand cubits*a* between you and the ark; do not go near it.'

5 Joshua told the people, 'Consecrate yourselves, for tomorrow the LORD will do amazing things among you.'

6 Joshua said to the priests, 'Take up the ark of the covenant and pass on ahead of the people.' So they took it up and went ahead of them.

7 And the LORD said to Joshua, 'Today I will begin to exalt you in the eyes of all Israel, so that they may know that I am with you as I was with Moses. 8 Tell the priests who carry the ark of the covenant: "When you reach the edge of the Jordan's waters, go and stand in the river." '

9 Joshua said to the Israelites, 'Come here and listen to the words of the LORD your God. 10 This is how you will know that the living God is among you and that he will certainly drive out before you the Canaanites, Hittites, Hivites, Perizzites,

---

a 10 Or *the Sea of Reeds*

b 10 The Hebrew term refers to the irrevocable giving over of things or persons to the LORD, often by totally destroying them.

c 11 Hebrew *melted in fear.*

---

a 4 That is, about 900 metres

Girgashites, Amorites and Jebusites. ¹¹ See, the ark of the covenant of the Lord of all the earth will go into the Jordan ahead of you. ¹² Now then, choose twelve men from the tribes of Israel, one from each tribe. ¹³ And as soon as the priests who carry the ark of the Lord – the Lord of all the earth – set foot in the Jordan, its waters flowing downstream will be cut off and stand up in a heap.'

¹⁴ So when the people broke camp to cross the Jordan, the priests carrying the ark of the covenant went ahead of them. ¹⁵ Now the Jordan is in flood all during harvest. Yet as soon as the priests who carried the ark reached the Jordan and their feet touched the water's edge, ¹⁶ the water from upstream stopped flowing. It piled up in a heap a great distance away, at a town called Adam in the vicinity of Zarethan, while the water flowing down to the Sea of the Arabah (that is, the Dead Sea) was completely cut off. So the people crossed over opposite Jericho. ¹⁷ The priests who carried the ark of the covenant of the Lord stopped in the middle of the Jordan and stood on dry ground, while all Israel passed by until the whole nation had completed the crossing on dry ground.

4 When the whole nation had finished crossing the Jordan, the Lord said to Joshua, ² 'Choose twelve men from among the people, one from each tribe, ³ and tell them to take up twelve stones from the middle of the Jordan, from right where the priests are standing, and carry them over with you and put them down at the place where you stay tonight.'

⁴ So Joshua called together the twelve men he had appointed from the Israelites, one from each tribe, ⁵ and said to them, 'Go over before the ark of the Lord your God into the middle of the Jordan. Each of you is to take up a stone on his shoulder, according to the number of the tribes of the Israelites, ⁶ to serve as a sign among you. In the future, when your children ask you, "What do these stones mean?" ⁷ tell them that the flow of the Jordan was cut off before the ark of the covenant of the Lord. When it crossed the Jordan, the

waters of the Jordan were cut off. These stones are to be a memorial to the people of Israel for ever.'

⁸ So the Israelites did as Joshua commanded them. They took twelve stones from the middle of the Jordan, according to the number of the tribes of the Israelites, as the Lord had told Joshua; and they carried them over with them to their camp, where they put them down. ⁹ Joshua set up the twelve stones that had been*ᵃ* in the middle of the Jordan at the spot where the priests who carried the ark of the covenant had stood. And they are there to this day.

¹⁰ Now the priests who carried the ark remained standing in the middle of the Jordan until everything the Lord had commanded Joshua was done by the people, just as Moses had directed Joshua. The people hurried over, ¹¹ and as soon as all of them had crossed, the ark of the Lord and the priests came to the other side while the people watched. ¹² The men of Reuben, Gad and the half-tribe of Manasseh crossed over, ready for battle, in front of the Israelites, as Moses had directed them. ¹³ About forty thousand armed for battle crossed over before the Lord to the plains of Jericho for war.

¹⁴ That day the Lord exalted Joshua in the sight of all Israel; and they stood in awe of him all the days of his life, just as they had stood in awe of Moses.

¹⁵ Then the Lord said to Joshua, ¹⁶ 'Command the priests carrying the ark of the covenant law to come up out of the Jordan.'

¹⁷ So Joshua commanded the priests, 'Come up out of the Jordan.'

¹⁸ And the priests came up out of the river carrying the ark of the covenant of the Lord. No sooner had they set their feet on the dry ground than the waters of the Jordan returned to their place and ran in flood as before.

¹⁹ On the tenth day of the first month the people went up from the Jordan and camped at Gilgal on the eastern border of Jericho. ²⁰ And Joshua set up at Gilgal the

_____
a 9 Or *Joshua also set up twelve stones*

twelve stones they had taken out of the Jordan. ²¹He said to the Israelites, 'In the future when your descendants ask their parents, "What do these stones mean?" ²²tell them, "Israel crossed the Jordan on dry ground." ²³For the LORD your God dried up the Jordan before you until you had crossed over. The LORD your God did to the Jordan what he had done to the Red Sea*b* when he dried it up before us until we had crossed over. ²⁴He did this so that all the peoples of the earth might know that the hand of the LORD is powerful and so that you might always fear the LORD your God.'

5 Now when all the Amorite kings west of the Jordan and all the Canaanite kings along the coast heard how the LORD had dried up the Jordan before the Israelites until they*a* had crossed over, their hearts melted in fear and they no longer had the courage to face the Israelites.

Circumcision and passover at Gilgal

²At that time the LORD said to Joshua, 'Make flint knives and circumcise the Israelites again.' ³So Joshua made flint knives and circumcised the Israelites at Gibeath Haaraloth.*b*

⁴Now this is why he did so: all those who came out of Egypt – all the men of military age – died in the wilderness on the way after leaving Egypt. ⁵All the people that came out had been circumcised, but all the people born in the wilderness during the journey from Egypt had not. ⁶The Israelites had moved about in the wilderness for forty years until all the men who were of military age when they left Egypt had died, since they had not obeyed the LORD. For the LORD had sworn to them that they would not see the land that he had solemnly promised their ancestors to give us, a land flowing with milk and honey. ⁷So he raised up their sons in their place, and these were the ones Joshua circumcised. They were still uncircumcised because they had not been circumcised on

the way. ⁸And after the whole nation had been circumcised, they remained where they were in camp until they were healed.

⁹Then the LORD said to Joshua, 'Today I have rolled away the reproach of Egypt from you.' So the place has been called Gilgal*c* to this day.

¹⁰On the evening of the fourteenth day of the month, while camped at Gilgal on the plains of Jericho, the Israelites celebrated the Passover. ¹¹The day after the Passover, that very day, they ate some of the produce of the land: unleavened bread and roasted grain. ¹²The manna stopped the day after*d* they ate this food from the land; there was no longer any manna for the Israelites, but that year they ate the produce of Canaan.

The fall of Jericho

¹³Now when Joshua was near Jericho, he looked up and saw a man standing in front of him with a drawn sword in his hand. Joshua went up to him and asked, 'Are you for us or for our enemies?'

¹⁴'Neither,' he replied, 'but as commander of the army of the LORD I have now come.' Then Joshua fell face down to the ground in reverence, and asked him, 'What message does my Lord*e* have for his servant?'

¹⁵The commander of the LORD's army replied, 'Take off your sandals, for the place where you are standing is holy.' And Joshua did so.

6 Now the gates of Jericho were securely barred because of the Israelites. No one went out and no one came in.

²Then the LORD said to Joshua, 'See, I have delivered Jericho into your hands, along with its king and its fighting men. ³March round the city once with all the armed men. Do this for six days. ⁴Make seven priests carry trumpets of rams' horns in front of the ark. On the seventh day, march round the city seven times, with the priests blowing the trumpets. ⁵When you hear them sound a long blast

---

b 23 Or *the Sea of Reeds*
a 1 Another textual tradition *we*
b 3 *Gibeath Haaraloth* means *the hill of foreskins.*

c 9 *Gilgal* sounds like the Hebrew for *roll.*
d 12 Or *the day*
e 14 Or *lord*

WHY DID GOD KILL ALL THOSE PEOPLE IN THE OLD TESTAMENT?

As we read the exciting stories in Joshua, some difficult questions emerge. Did God really tell the Israelites to wipe out every single person in Jericho? Was there not a better way to do it? How does that fit with Jesus teaching us to love our enemies? These are very important questions, and the answers are sometimes unsatisfactory and need a whole book to deal with them properly! But here are some ideas to give us a framework to start wrestling with this tough subject.

First, God is dealing with a particular people living in a particular culture. This was a violent culture, and the strategy of invading a city and wiping out all its inhabitants (the *herem*) was the common method of warfare at that time, not unique to Israel. God works within this culture but begins to impose restrictions, like not allowing the use of chariots (11:6). He restricts it within strict geographical borders, and in other battles God imposes even more limitations (see Numbers 31). So God is gradually moving the people on, away from such practices. Did God work within the established methods of war even though his ultimate intent was for his people to love their enemies, in a similar way to allowing divorce and slavery although his aim was lifelong marriage and freedom for all?

Second, the talk of wiping out all inhabitants was often a figure of speech referring to total victory: often the reality on the ground was rather different, and the writers of the Bible are quite comfortable with this. In Joshua 10:40 it says there were *'no survivors'*, yet in Judges (whose author would certainly have read Joshua) we are told that lots of the original nations continued to live alongside the Israelites.

We also need to place this story in the big picture of the Bible. The great mission of God given to Abraham and his descendants was always for the blessing of all the nations. The conquest of Canaan is one small part of this, one short time in a long history where the overarching aim is to bring all the nations into the family of God, so that they might worship God in the holy city, where there will be peace and justice. This doesn't mean we should ignore the uncomfortable stories, but it does give us some perspective.

Another important factor is the wickedness of the Canaanites. God told Abraham that their sin had *'not yet reached its full measure'* (Genesis 15:16), but that four generations later, the evil they were committing would have reached such depths that God's judgement would come upon them. They were involved in all kinds of sexual perversions, child sacrifice and oppression, and chose not to repent, and therefore God used the Israelite invasion to punish them.

Finally, there is the story of the Jebusites (Judges 1:21), who should have been destroyed, but were not, and eventually appear to have become attached to the tribe of Benjamin – enemies becoming a part of the people of God. This is the big picture, like the salvation of Rahab, who became an ancestor of Jesus himself.

Chris Lane

on the trumpets, make the whole army give a loud shout; then the wall of the city will collapse and the army will go up, everyone straight in.'

⁶So Joshua son of Nun called the priests and said to them, 'Take up the ark of the covenant of the LORD and make seven priests carry trumpets in front of it.' ⁷And he ordered the army, 'Advance! March round the city, with an armed guard going ahead of the ark of the LORD.'

⁸When Joshua had spoken to the people, the seven priests carrying the seven trumpets before the LORD went forwards, blowing their trumpets, and the ark of the LORD's covenant followed them. ⁹The armed guard marched ahead of the priests who blew the trumpets, and the rear guard followed the ark. All this time the trumpets were sounding. ¹⁰But Joshua had commanded the army, 'Do not give a war cry, do not raise your voices, do not say a word until the day I tell you to shout. Then shout!' ¹¹So he had the ark of the LORD carried round the city, circling it once. Then the army returned to camp and spent the night there.

¹²Joshua got up early the next morning and the priests took up the ark of the LORD. ¹³The seven priests carrying the seven trumpets went forwards, marching before the ark of the LORD and blowing the trumpets. The armed men went ahead of them and the rear guard followed the ark of the LORD, while the trumpets kept sounding. ¹⁴So on the second day they marched round the city once and returned to the camp. They did this for six days.

¹⁵On the seventh day, they got up at daybreak and marched round the city seven times in the same manner, except that on that day they circled the city seven times. ¹⁶The seventh time round, when the priests sounded the trumpet blast, Joshua commanded the army, 'Shout! For the LORD has given you the city! ¹⁷The city and all that is in it are to be devoted*a* to

the LORD. Only Rahab the prostitute and all who are with her in her house shall be spared, because she hid the spies we sent. ¹⁸But keep away from the devoted things, so that you will not bring about your own destruction by taking any of them. Otherwise you will make the camp of Israel liable to destruction and bring trouble on it. ¹⁹All the silver and gold and the articles of bronze and iron are sacred to the LORD and must go into his treasury.'

²⁰When the trumpets sounded, the army shouted, and at the sound of the trumpet, when the men gave a loud shout, the wall collapsed; so everyone charged straight in, and they took the city. ²¹They devoted the city to the LORD and destroyed with the sword every living thing in it – men and women, young and old, cattle, sheep and donkeys.

²²Joshua said to the two men who had spied out the land, 'Go into the prostitute's house and bring her out and all who belong to her, in accordance with your oath to her.' ²³So the young men who had done the spying went in and brought out Rahab, her father and mother, her brothers and sisters and all who belonged to her. They brought out her entire family and put them in a place outside the camp of Israel.

²⁴Then they burned the whole city and everything in it, but they put the silver and gold and the articles of bronze and iron into the treasury of the LORD's house. ²⁵But Joshua spared Rahab the prostitute, with her family and all who belonged to her, because she hid the men Joshua had sent as spies to Jericho – and she lives among the Israelites to this day.

²⁶At that time Joshua pronounced this solemn oath: 'Cursed before the LORD is the one who undertakes to rebuild this city, Jericho:

'At the cost of his firstborn son
   he will lay its foundations;
at the cost of his youngest
   he will set up its gates.'

---

a 17 The Hebrew term refers to the irrevocable giving over of things or persons to the LORD, often by totally destroying them; also in verses 18 and 21.

²⁷So the LORD was with Joshua, and his fame spread throughout the land.

Achan's sin

7 But the Israelites were unfaithful in regard to the devoted things*a*; Achan son of Karmi, the son of Zimri,*b* the son of Zerah, of the tribe of Judah, took some of them. So the LORD's anger burned against Israel.

2 Now Joshua sent men from Jericho to Ai, which is near Beth Aven to the east of Bethel, and told them, 'Go up and spy out the region.' So the men went up and spied out Ai.

3 When they returned to Joshua, they said, 'Not all the army will have to go up against Ai. Send two or three thousand men to take it and do not weary the whole army, for only a few people live there.' 4 So about three thousand went up; but they were routed by the men of Ai, 5 who killed about thirty-six of them. They chased the Israelites from the city gate as far as the stone quarries and struck them down on the slopes. At this the hearts of the people melted in fear and became like water.

6 Then Joshua tore his clothes and fell face down to the ground before the ark of the LORD, remaining there till evening. The elders of Israel did the same, and sprinkled dust on their heads. 7 And Joshua said, 'Alas, Sovereign LORD, why did you ever bring this people across the Jordan to deliver us into the hands of the Amorites to destroy us? If only we had been content to stay on the other side of the Jordan! 8 Pardon your servant, Lord. What can I say, now that Israel has been routed by its enemies? 9 The Canaanites and the other people of the country will hear about this and they will surround us and wipe out our name from the earth. What then will you do for your own great name?'

10 The LORD said to Joshua, 'Stand up! What are you doing down on your face? 11 Israel has sinned; they have violated my covenant, which I commanded them

to keep. They have taken some of the devoted things; they have stolen, they have lied, they have put them with their own possessions. 12 That is why the Israelites cannot stand against their enemies; they turn their backs and run because they have been made liable to destruction. I will not be with you any more unless you destroy whatever among you is devoted to destruction.

13 'Go, consecrate the people. Tell them, "Consecrate yourselves in preparation for tomorrow; for this is what the LORD, the God of Israel, says: there are devoted things among you, Israel. You cannot stand against your enemies until you remove them.

14 '"In the morning, present yourselves tribe by tribe. The tribe that the LORD chooses shall come forward clan by clan; the clan that the LORD chooses shall come forward family by family; and the family that the LORD chooses shall come forward man by man. 15 Whoever is caught with the devoted things shall be destroyed by fire, along with all that belongs to him. He has violated the covenant of the LORD and has done an outrageous thing in Israel!" '

16 Early the next morning Joshua made Israel come forward by tribes, and Judah was chosen. 17 The clans of Judah came forward, and the Zerahites were chosen. He made the clan of the Zerahites come forward by families, and Zimri was chosen. 18 Joshua made his family come forward man by man, and Achan son of Karmi, the son of Zimri, the son of Zerah, of the tribe of Judah, was chosen.

19 Then Joshua said to Achan, 'My son, give glory to the LORD, the God of Israel, and honour him. Tell me what you have done; do not hide it from me.'

20 Achan replied, 'It is true! I have sinned against the LORD, the God of Israel. This is what I have done: 21 when I saw in the plunder a beautiful robe from Babylonia,*c* two hundred shekels*d* of silver and a bar of gold weighing fifty shekels,*e* I coveted

---

a 1 The Hebrew term refers to the irrevocable giving over of things or persons to the LORD, often by totally destroying them; also in verses 11, 12, 13 and 15.
b 1 See Septuagint and 1 Chron. 2:6; Hebrew *Zabdi*; also in verses 17 and 18.
c 21 Hebrew *Shinar*
d 21 That is, about 2.3 kilograms
e 21 That is, about 575 grams

them and took them. They are hidden in the ground inside my tent, with the silver underneath.'

22 So Joshua sent messengers, and they ran to the tent, and there it was, hidden in his tent, with the silver underneath. 23 They took the things from the tent, brought them to Joshua and all the Israelites and spread them out before the LORD.

24 Then Joshua, together with all Israel, took Achan son of Zerah, the silver, the robe, the gold bar, his sons and daughters, his cattle, donkeys and sheep, his tent and all that he had, to the Valley of Achor. 25 Joshua said, 'Why have you brought this trouble on us? The LORD will bring trouble on you today.'

Then all Israel stoned him, and after they had stoned the rest, they burned them. 26 Over Achan they heaped up a large pile of rocks, which remains to this day. Then the LORD turned from his fierce anger. Therefore that place has been called the Valley of Achor f ever since.

Ai destroyed

8 Then the LORD said to Joshua, 'Do not be afraid; do not be discouraged. Take the whole army with you, and go up and attack Ai. For I have delivered into your hands the king of Ai, his people, his city and his land. 2 You shall do to Ai and its king as you did to Jericho and its king, except that you may carry off their plunder and livestock for yourselves. Set an ambush behind the city.'

3 So Joshua and the whole army moved out to attack Ai. He chose thirty thousand of his best fighting men and sent them out at night 4 with these orders: 'Listen carefully. You are to set an ambush behind the city. Don't go very far from it. All of you be on the alert. 5 I and all those with me will advance on the city, and when the men come out against us, as they did before, we will flee from them. 6 They will pursue us until we have lured them away from the city, for they will say, "They are running away from us as they did before."

So when we flee from them, 7 you are to rise up from ambush and take the city. The LORD your God will give it into your hand. 8 When you have taken the city, set it on fire. Do what the LORD has commanded. See to it; you have my orders.'

9 Then Joshua sent them off, and they went to the place of ambush and lay in wait between Bethel and Ai, to the west of Ai – but Joshua spent that night with the people.

10 Early the next morning Joshua mustered his army, and he and the leaders of Israel marched before them to Ai. 11 The entire force that was with him marched up and approached the city and arrived in front of it. They set up camp north of Ai, with the valley between them and the city. 12 Joshua had taken about five thousand men and set them in ambush between Bethel and Ai, to the west of the city. 13 So the soldiers took up their positions – with the main camp to the north of the city and the ambush to the west of it. That night Joshua went into the valley.

14 When the king of Ai saw this, he and all the men of the city hurried out early in the morning to meet Israel in battle at a certain place overlooking the Arabah. But he did not know that an ambush had been set against him behind the city. 15 Joshua and all Israel let themselves be driven back before them, and they fled towards the wilderness. 16 All the men of Ai were called to pursue them, and they pursued Joshua and were lured away from the city. 17 Not a man remained in Ai or Bethel who did not go after Israel. They left the city open and went in pursuit of Israel.

18 Then the LORD said to Joshua, 'Hold out towards Ai the javelin that is in your hand, for into your hand I will deliver the city.' So Joshua held out towards the city the javelin that was in his hand. 19 As soon as he did this, the men in the ambush rose quickly from their position and rushed forward. They entered the city and captured it and quickly set it on fire.

20 The men of Ai looked back and saw the smoke of the city rising up into the sky, but they had no chance to escape in any direction; the Israelites who had been

---

f 26 Achor means trouble.

fleeing towards the wilderness had turned back against their pursuers. ²¹ For when Joshua and all Israel saw that the ambush had taken the city and that smoke was going up from the city, they turned round and attacked the men of Ai. ²² Those in the ambush also came out of the city against them, so that they were caught in the middle, with Israelites on both sides. Israel cut them down, leaving them neither survivors nor fugitives. ²³ But they took the king of Ai alive and brought him to Joshua.

²⁴ When Israel had finished killing all the men of Ai in the fields and in the wilderness where they had chased them, and when every one of them had been put to the sword, all the Israelites returned to Ai and killed those who were in it. ²⁵ Twelve thousand men and women fell that day – all the people of Ai. ²⁶ For Joshua did not draw back the hand that held out his javelin until he had destroyed*ᵃ* all who lived in Ai. ²⁷ But Israel did carry off for themselves the livestock and plunder of this city, as the Lᴏʀᴅ had instructed Joshua.

²⁸ So Joshua burned Ai*ᵇ* and made it a permanent heap of ruins, a desolate place to this day. ²⁹ He impaled the body of the king of Ai on a pole and left it there until evening. At sunset, Joshua ordered them to take the body from the pole and throw it down at the entrance of the city gate. And they raised a large pile of rocks over it, which remains to this day.

The covenant renewed at Mount Ebal

³⁰ Then Joshua built on Mount Ebal an altar to the Lᴏʀᴅ, the God of Israel, ³¹ as Moses the servant of the Lᴏʀᴅ had commanded the Israelites. He built it according to what is written in the Book of the Law of Moses – an altar of uncut stones, on which no iron tool had been used. On it they offered to the Lᴏʀᴅ burnt offerings and sacrificed fellowship offerings. ³² There, in the presence of the Israelites, Joshua wrote on stones a copy of the law

of Moses. ³³ All the Israelites, with their elders, officials and judges, were standing on both sides of the ark of the covenant of the Lᴏʀᴅ, facing the Levitical priests who carried it. Both the foreigners living among them and the native-born were there. Half of the people stood in front of Mount Gerizim and half of them in front of Mount Ebal, as Moses the servant of the Lᴏʀᴅ had formerly commanded when he gave instructions to bless the people of Israel.

³⁴ Afterwards, Joshua read all the words of the law – the blessings and the curses – just as it is written in the Book of the Law. ³⁵ There was not a word of all that Moses had commanded that Joshua did not read to the whole assembly of Israel, including the women and children, and the foreigners who lived among them.

The Gibeonite deception

9 Now when all the kings west of the Jordan heard about these things – the kings in the hill country, in the western foothills, and along the entire coast of the Mediterranean Sea as far as Lebanon (the kings of the Hittites, Amorites, Canaanites, Perizzites, Hivites and Jebusites) – ² they came together to wage war against Joshua and Israel.

³ However, when the people of Gibeon heard what Joshua had done to Jericho and Ai, ⁴ they resorted to a ruse: they went as a delegation whose donkeys were loaded*ᵃ* with worn-out sacks and old wineskins, cracked and mended. ⁵ They put worn and patched sandals on their feet and wore old clothes. All the bread of their food supply was dry and mouldy. ⁶ Then they went to Joshua in the camp at Gilgal and said to him and the Israelites, 'We have come from a distant country; make a treaty with us.'

⁷ The Israelites said to the Hivites, 'But perhaps you live near us, so how can we make a treaty with you?'

---

a 26 The Hebrew term refers to the irrevocable giving over of things or persons to the Lᴏʀᴅ, often by totally destroying them.
b 28 Ai means *the ruin.*

a 4 Most Hebrew manuscripts; some Hebrew manuscripts, Vulgate and Syriac (see also Septuagint) *They prepared provisions and loaded their donkeys*

8 'We are your servants,' they said to Joshua.

But Joshua asked, 'Who are you and where do you come from?'

9 They answered: 'Your servants have come from a very distant country because of the fame of the LORD your God. For we have heard reports of him: all that he did in Egypt, 10 and all that he did to the two kings of the Amorites east of the Jordan – Sihon king of Heshbon, and Og king of Bashan, who reigned in Ashtaroth. 11 And our elders and all those living in our country said to us, "Take provisions for your journey; go and meet them and say to them, 'We are your servants; make a treaty with us.' " 12 This bread of ours was warm when we packed it at home on the day we left to come to you. But now see how dry and mouldy it is. 13 And these wineskins that we filled were new, but see how cracked they are. And our clothes and sandals are worn out by the very long journey.'

14 The Israelites sampled their provisions but did not enquire of the LORD. 15 Then Joshua made a treaty of peace with them to let them live, and the leaders of the assembly ratified it by oath.

16 Three days after they made the treaty with the Gibeonites, the Israelites heard that they were neighbours, living near them. 17 So the Israelites set out and on the third day came to their cities: Gibeon, Kephirah, Beeroth and Kiriath Jearim. 18 But the Israelites did not attack them, because the leaders of the assembly had sworn an oath to them by the LORD, the God of Israel.

The whole assembly grumbled against the leaders, 19 but all the leaders answered, 'We have given them our oath by the LORD, the God of Israel, and we cannot touch them now. 20 This is what we will do to them: we will let them live, so that God's wrath will not fall on us for breaking the oath we swore to them.' 21 They continued, 'Let them live, but let them be woodcutters and water-carriers in the service of the whole assembly.' So the leaders' promise to them was kept.

22 Then Joshua summoned the Gibeonites and said, 'Why did you deceive us by saying, "We live a long way from you," while actually you live near us? 23 You are now under a curse: you will never be released from service as woodcutters and water-carriers for the house of my God.'

24 They answered Joshua, 'Your servants were clearly told how the LORD your God had commanded his servant Moses to give you the whole land and to wipe out all its inhabitants from before you. So we feared for our lives because of you, and that is why we did this. 25 We are now in your hands. Do to us whatever seems good and right to you.'

26 So Joshua saved them from the Israelites, and they did not kill them. 27 That day he made the Gibeonites woodcutters and water-carriers for the assembly, to provide for the needs of the altar of the LORD at the place the LORD would choose. And that is what they are to this day.

The sun stands still

10 Now Adoni-Zedek king of Jerusalem heard that Joshua had taken Ai and totally destroyed[a] it, doing to Ai and its king as he had done to Jericho and its king, and that the people of Gibeon had made a treaty of peace with Israel and had become their allies. 2 He and his people were very much alarmed at this, because Gibeon was an important city, like one of the royal cities; it was larger than Ai, and all its men were good fighters. 3 So Adoni-Zedek king of Jerusalem appealed to Hoham king of Hebron, Piram king of Jarmuth, Japhia king of Lachish and Debir king of Eglon. 4 'Come up and help me attack Gibeon,' he said, 'because it has made peace with Joshua and the Israelites.'

5 Then the five kings of the Amorites – the kings of Jerusalem, Hebron, Jarmuth, Lachish and Eglon – joined forces. They moved up with all their troops and took up positions against Gibeon and attacked it.

6 The Gibeonites then sent word to Joshua in the camp at Gilgal: 'Do not abandon your servants. Come up to us

---

a 1 The Hebrew term refers to the irrevocable giving over of things or persons to the LORD, often by totally destroying them; also in verses 28, 35, 37, 39 and 40.

quickly and save us! Help us, because all the Amorite kings from the hill country have joined forces against us.'

7 So Joshua marched up from Gilgal with his entire army, including all the best fighting men. 8 The LORD said to Joshua, 'Do not be afraid of them; I have given them into your hand. Not one of them will be able to withstand you.'

9 After an all-night march from Gilgal, Joshua took them by surprise. 10 The LORD threw them into confusion before Israel, so Joshua and the Israelites defeated them completely at Gibeon. Israel pursued them along the road going up to Beth Horon and cut them down all the way to Azekah and Makkedah. 11 As they fled before Israel on the road down from Beth Horon to Azekah, the LORD hurled large hailstones down on them, and more of them died from the hail than were killed by the swords of the Israelites.

12 On the day the LORD gave the Amorites over to Israel, Joshua said to the LORD in the presence of Israel:

'Sun, stand still over Gibeon,
    and you, moon, over the Valley of
        Aijalon.'
13 So the sun stood still,
    and the moon stopped,
    till the nation avenged itself on*b* its
        enemies,

as it is written in the Book of Jashar.

The sun stopped in the middle of the sky and delayed going down about a full day. 14 There has never been a day like it before or since, a day when the LORD listened to a human being. Surely the LORD was fighting for Israel!

15 Then Joshua returned with all Israel to the camp at Gilgal.

Five Amorite kings killed

16 Now the five kings had fled and hidden in the cave at Makkedah. 17 When Joshua was told that the five kings had been found hiding in the cave at Makkedah, 18 he said, 'Roll large rocks up to the mouth of the

cave, and post some men there to guard it. 19 But don't stop; pursue your enemies! Attack them from the rear and don't let them reach their cities, for the LORD your God has given them into your hand.'

20 So Joshua and the Israelites defeated them completely, but a few survivors managed to reach their fortified cities. 21 The whole army then returned safely to Joshua in the camp at Makkedah, and no one uttered a word against the Israelites.

22 Joshua said, 'Open the mouth of the cave and bring those five kings out to me.' 23 So they brought the five kings out of the cave – the kings of Jerusalem, Hebron, Jarmuth, Lachish and Eglon. 24 When they had brought these kings to Joshua, he summoned all the men of Israel and said to the army commanders who had come with him, 'Come here and put your feet on the necks of these kings.' So they came forward and placed their feet on their necks.

25 Joshua said to them, 'Do not be afraid; do not be discouraged. Be strong and courageous. This is what the LORD will do to all the enemies you are going to fight.' 26 Then Joshua put the kings to death and exposed their bodies on five poles, and they were left hanging on the poles until evening.

27 At sunset Joshua gave the order and they took them down from the poles and threw them into the cave where they had been hiding. At the mouth of the cave they placed large rocks, which are there to this day.

Southern cities conquered

28 That day Joshua took Makkedah. He put the city and its king to the sword and totally destroyed everyone in it. He left no survivors. And he did to the king of Makkedah as he had done to the king of Jericho.

29 Then Joshua and all Israel with him moved on from Makkedah to Libnah and attacked it. 30 The LORD also gave that city and its king into Israel's hand. The city and everyone in it Joshua put to the sword. He left no survivors there. And he did to its king as he had done to the king of Jericho.

---

b 13 Or *nation triumphed over*

31 Then Joshua and all Israel with him moved on from Libnah to Lachish; he took up positions against it and attacked it. 32 The LORD gave Lachish into Israel's hands, and Joshua took it on the second day. The city and everyone in it he put to the sword, just as he had done to Libnah. 33 Meanwhile, Horam king of Gezer had come up to help Lachish, but Joshua defeated him and his army – until no survivors were left.

34 Then Joshua and all Israel with him moved on from Lachish to Eglon; they took up positions against it and attacked it. 35 They captured it that same day and put it to the sword and totally destroyed everyone in it, just as they had done to Lachish.

36 Then Joshua and all Israel with him went up from Eglon to Hebron and attacked it. 37 They took the city and put it to the sword, together with its king, its villages and everyone in it. They left no survivors. Just as at Eglon, they totally destroyed it and everyone in it.

38 Then Joshua and all Israel with him turned round and attacked Debir. 39 They took the city, its king and its villages, and put them to the sword. Everyone in it they totally destroyed. They left no survivors. They did to Debir and its king as they had done to Libnah and its king and to Hebron.

40 So Joshua subdued the whole region, including the hill country, the Negev, the western foothills and the mountain slopes, together with all their kings. He left no survivors. He totally destroyed all who breathed, just as the LORD, the God of Israel, had commanded. 41 Joshua subdued them from Kadesh Barnea to Gaza and from the whole region of Goshen to Gibeon. 42 All these kings and their lands Joshua conquered in one campaign, because the LORD, the God of Israel, fought for Israel. 43 Then Joshua returned with all Israel to the camp at Gilgal.

Northern kings defeated

11 When Jabin king of Hazor heard of this, he sent word to Jobab king of Madon, to the kings of Shimron and Akshaph, 2 and to the northern kings who were in the mountains, in the Arabah south of Kinnereth, in the western foothills and in Naphoth Dor on the west; 3 to the Canaanites in the east and west; to the Amorites, Hittites, Perizzites and Jebusites in the hill country; and to the Hivites below Hermon in the region of Mizpah. 4 They came out with all their troops and a large number of horses and chariots – a huge army, as numerous as the sand on the seashore. 5 All these kings joined forces and made camp together at the Waters of Merom to fight against Israel.

6 The LORD said to Joshua, 'Do not be afraid of them, because by this time tomorrow I will hand all of them, slain, over to Israel. You are to hamstring their horses and burn their chariots.'

7 So Joshua and his whole army came against them suddenly at the Waters of Merom and attacked them, 8 and the LORD gave them into the hand of Israel. They defeated them and pursued them all the way to Greater Sidon, to Misrephoth Maim, and to the Valley of Mizpah on the east, until no survivors were left. 9 Joshua did to them as the LORD had directed: he hamstrung their horses and burned their chariots.

10 At that time Joshua turned back and captured Hazor and put its king to the sword. (Hazor had been the head of all these kingdoms.) 11 Everyone in it they put to the sword. They totally destroyed a them, not sparing anyone that breathed, and he burned Hazor itself.

12 Joshua took all these royal cities and their kings and put them to the sword. He totally destroyed them, as Moses the servant of the LORD had commanded. 13 Yet Israel did not burn any of the cities built on their mounds – except Hazor, which Joshua burned. 14 The Israelites carried off for themselves all the plunder and livestock of these cities, but all the people they put to the sword until they completely destroyed them, not sparing anyone that breathed. 15 As the LORD

---

a 11 The Hebrew term refers to the irrevocable giving over of things or persons to the LORD, often by totally destroying them; also in verses 12, 20 and 21.

commanded his servant Moses, so Moses commanded Joshua, and Joshua did it; he left nothing undone of all that the LORD commanded Moses.

16 So Joshua took this entire land: the hill country, all the Negev, the whole region of Goshen, the western foothills, the Arabah and the mountains of Israel with their foothills, 17 from Mount Halak, which rises towards Seir, to Baal Gad in the Valley of Lebanon below Mount Hermon. He captured all their kings and put them to death. 18 Joshua waged war against all these kings for a long time. 19 Except for the Hivites living in Gibeon, not one city made a treaty of peace with the Israelites, who took them all in battle. 20 For it was the LORD himself who hardened their hearts to wage war against Israel, so that he might destroy them totally, exterminating them without mercy, as the LORD had commanded Moses.

21 At that time Joshua went and destroyed the Anakites from the hill country: from Hebron, Debir and Anab, from all the hill country of Judah, and from all the hill country of Israel. Joshua totally destroyed them and their towns. 22 No Anakites were left in Israelite territory; only in Gaza, Gath and Ashdod did any survive.

23 So Joshua took the entire land, just as the LORD had directed Moses, and he gave it as an inheritance to Israel according to their tribal divisions. Then the land had rest from war.

List of defeated kings

12 These are the kings of the land whom the Israelites had defeated and whose territory they took over east of the Jordan, from the Arnon Gorge to Mount Hermon, including all the eastern side of the Arabah:

2 Sihon king of the Amorites, who reigned in Heshbon.

He ruled from Aroer on the rim of the Arnon Gorge – from the middle of the gorge – to the River Jabbok, which is the border of the Ammonites. This included half of Gilead. 3 He also ruled over the eastern Arabah from the Sea of Galilee[a] to the Sea of the Arabah (that is, the Dead Sea), to Beth Jeshimoth, and then southward below the slopes of Pisgah.

4 And the territory of Og king of Bashan, one of the last of the Rephaites, who reigned in Ashtaroth and Edrei.

5 He ruled over Mount Hermon, Salekah, all of Bashan to the border of the people of Geshur and Maakah, and half of Gilead to the border of Sihon king of Heshbon.

6 Moses, the servant of the LORD, and the Israelites conquered them. And Moses the servant of the LORD gave their land to the Reubenites, the Gadites and the half-tribe of Manasseh to be their possession.

7 Here is a list of the kings of the land that Joshua and the Israelites conquered on the west side of the Jordan, from Baal Gad in the Valley of Lebanon to Mount Halak, which rises towards Seir. Joshua gave their lands as an inheritance to the tribes of Israel according to their tribal divisions. 8 The lands included the hill country, the western foothills, the Arabah, the mountain slopes, the wilderness and the Negev. These were the lands of the Hittites, Amorites, Canaanites, Perizzites, Hivites and Jebusites. These were the kings:

9 the king of Jericho	one
the king of Ai (near Bethel)	one
10 the king of Jerusalem	one
the king of Hebron	one
11 the king of Jarmuth	one
the king of Lachish	one
12 the king of Eglon	one
the king of Gezer	one
13 the king of Debir	one
the king of Geder	one
14 the king of Hormah	one
the king of Arad	one
15 the king of Libnah	one

---

a 3 Hebrew *Kinnereth*

the king of Adullam	one
16 the king of Makkedah	one
the king of Bethel	one
17 the king of Tappuah	one
the king of Hepher	one
18 the king of Aphek	one
the king of Lasharon	one
19 the king of Madon	one
the king of Hazor	one
20 the king of Shimron Meron	one
the king of Akshaph	one
21 the king of Taanach	one
the king of Megiddo	one
22 the king of Kedesh	one
the king of Jokneam in Carmel	one
23 the king of Dor (in Naphoth Dor)	one
the king of Goyim in Gilgal	one
24 the king of Tirzah	one
	thirty-one kings in all.

Land still to be taken

13 When Joshua had grown old, the LORD said to him, 'You are now very old, and there are still very large areas of land to be taken over.

2 'This is the land that remains: all the regions of the Philistines and Geshurites, 3 from the River Shihor on the east of Egypt to the territory of Ekron on the north, all of it counted as Canaanite though held by the five Philistine rulers in Gaza, Ashdod, Ashkelon, Gath and Ekron; the territory of the Avvites 4 on the south; all the land of the Canaanites, from Arah of the Sidonians as far as Aphek and the border of the Amorites; 5 the area of Byblos; and all Lebanon to the east, from Baal Gad below Mount Hermon to Lebo Hamath.

6 'As for all the inhabitants of the mountain regions from Lebanon to Misrephoth Maim, that is, all the Sidonians, I myself will drive them out before the Israelites. Be sure to allocate this land to Israel for an inheritance, as I have instructed you, 7 and divide it as an inheritance among the nine tribes and half of the tribe of Manasseh.'

Division of the land east of the Jordan

8 The other half of Manasseh,*a* the Reubenites and the Gadites had received the inheritance that Moses had given them east of the Jordan, as he, the servant of the LORD, had assigned it to them.

9 It extended from Aroer on the rim of the Arnon Gorge, and from the town in the middle of the gorge, and included the whole plateau of Medeba as far as Dibon, 10 and all the towns of Sihon king of the Amorites, who ruled in Heshbon, out to the border of the Ammonites. 11 It also included Gilead, the territory of the people of Geshur and Maakah, all of Mount Hermon and all Bashan as far as Salekah – 12 that is, the whole kingdom of Og in Bashan, who had reigned in Ashtaroth and Edrei. (He was the last of the Rephaites.) Moses had defeated them and taken over their land. 13 But the Israelites did not drive out the people of Geshur and Maakah, so they continue to live among the Israelites to this day.

14 But to the tribe of Levi he gave no inheritance, since the food offerings presented to the LORD, the God of Israel, are their inheritance, as he promised them.

15 This is what Moses had given to the tribe of Reuben, according to its clans:

16 The territory from Aroer on the rim of the Arnon Gorge, and from the town in the middle of the gorge, and the whole plateau past Medeba 17 to Heshbon and all its towns on the plateau, including Dibon, Bamoth Baal, Beth Baal Meon, 18 Jahaz, Kedemoth, Mephaath, 19 Kiriathaim, Sibmah, Zereth Shahar on the hill in the valley, 20 Beth Peor, the slopes of Pisgah, and Beth Jeshimoth 21 – all the towns on the plateau and the entire realm of Sihon king of the

a 8 Hebrew With it (that is, with the other half of Manasseh)

Amorites, who ruled at Heshbon. Moses had defeated him and the Midianite chiefs, Evi, Rekem, Zur, Hur and Reba – princes allied with Sihon – who lived in that country. ²²In addition to those slain in battle, the Israelites had put to the sword Balaam son of Beor, who practised divination. ²³The boundary of the Reubenites was the bank of the Jordan. These towns and their villages were the inheritance of the Reubenites, according to their clans.

²⁴This is what Moses had given to the tribe of Gad, according to its clans:

²⁵The territory of Jazer, all the towns of Gilead and half the Ammonite country as far as Aroer, near Rabbah; ²⁶and from Heshbon to Ramath Mizpah and Betonim, and from Mahanaim to the territory of Debir; ²⁷and in the valley, Beth Haram, Beth Nimrah, Sukkoth and Zaphon with the rest of the realm of Sihon king of Heshbon (the east side of the Jordan, the territory up to the end of the Sea of Galilee*b*). ²⁸These towns and their villages were the inheritance of the Gadites, according to their clans.

²⁹This is what Moses had given to the half-tribe of Manasseh, that is, to half the family of the descendants of Manasseh, according to its clans:

³⁰The territory extending from Mahanaim and including all of Bashan, the entire realm of Og king of Bashan – all the settlements of Jair in Bashan, sixty towns, ³¹half of Gilead, and Ashtaroth and Edrei (the royal cities of Og in Bashan). This was for the descendants of Makir son of Manasseh – for half of the sons of Makir, according to their clans.

³²This is the inheritance Moses had given when he was in the plains of Moab

across the Jordan east of Jericho. ³³But to the tribe of Levi, Moses had given no inheritance; the LORD, the God of Israel, is their inheritance, as he promised them.

THE THIRTEEN TRIBES

There are actually thirteen tribes of Israel. The tribes come from Jacob's twelve sons (Genesis 35:23–26), but Joseph was replaced by his sons Ephraim and Manasseh, giving thirteen. These are sometimes called half-tribes, bringing the number back down to twelve (Numbers 1:20–43; Joshua 14:3).

Division of the land west of the Jordan

14 Now these are the areas the Israelites received as an inheritance in the land of Canaan, which Eleazar the priest, Joshua son of Nun and the heads of the tribal clans of Israel allotted to them. ²Their inheritances were assigned by lot to the nine-and-a-half tribes, as the LORD had commanded through Moses. ³Moses had granted the two-and-a-half tribes their inheritance east of the Jordan but had not granted the Levites an inheritance among the rest, ⁴for Joseph's descendants had become two tribes – Manasseh and Ephraim. The Levites received no share of the land but only towns to live in, with pasture-lands for their flocks and herds. ⁵So the Israelites divided the land, just as the LORD had commanded Moses.

Land allotted to Caleb

⁶Now the people of Judah approached Joshua at Gilgal, and Caleb son of Jephunneh the Kenizzite said to him, 'You know

---

b 27 Hebrew *Kinnereth*

what the LORD said to Moses the man of God at Kadesh Barnea about you and me. 7 I was forty years old when Moses the servant of the LORD sent me from Kadesh Barnea to explore the land. And I brought him back a report according to my convictions, 8 but my fellow Israelites who went up with me made the hearts of the people sink.*a* I, however, followed the LORD my God wholeheartedly. 9 So on that day Moses swore to me, "The land on which your feet have walked will be your inheritance and that of your children for ever, because you have followed the LORD my God wholeheartedly."*b*

10 'Now then, just as the LORD promised, he has kept me alive for forty-five years since the time he said this to Moses, while Israel moved about in the wilderness. So here I am today, eighty-five years old! 11 I am still as strong today as the day Moses sent me out; I'm just as vigorous to go out to battle now as I was then. 12 Now give me this hill country that the LORD promised me that day. You yourself heard then that the Anakites were there and their cities were large and fortified, but, the LORD helping me, I will drive them out just as he said.'

13 Then Joshua blessed Caleb son of Jephunneh and gave him Hebron as his inheritance. 14 So Hebron has belonged to Caleb son of Jephunneh the Kenizzite ever since, because he followed the LORD, the God of Israel, wholeheartedly. 15 (Hebron used to be called Kiriath Arba after Arba, who was the greatest man among the Anakites.)

Then the land had rest from war.

Land allotted to Judah

15 The land allotted to the tribe of Judah, according to its clans, extended down to the territory of Edom, to the Desert of Zin in the extreme south.

2 Their southern boundary started from the bay at the southern end of the Dead Sea, 3 crossed south of Scorpion Pass, continued on to Zin and went over to the south of Kadesh Barnea. Then it ran past Hezron up to Addar and curved around to Karka. 4 It then passed along to Azmon and joined the Wadi of Egypt, ending at the Mediterranean Sea. This is their*a* southern boundary.

5 The eastern boundary is the Dead Sea as far as the mouth of the Jordan.

The northern boundary started from the bay of the sea at the mouth of the Jordan, 6 went up to Beth Hoglah and continued north of Beth Arabah to the Stone of Bohan son of Reuben. 7 The boundary then went up to Debir from the Valley of Achor and turned north to Gilgal, which faces the Pass of Adummim south of the gorge. It continued along to the waters of En Shemesh and came out at En Rogel. 8 Then it ran up the Valley of Ben Hinnom along the southern slope of the Jebusite city (that is, Jerusalem). From there it climbed to the top of the hill west of the Hinnom Valley at the northern end of the Valley of Rephaim. 9 From the hilltop the boundary headed towards the spring of the waters of Nephtoah, came out at the towns of Mount Ephron and went down towards Baalah (that is, Kiriath Jearim). 10 Then it curved westward from Baalah to Mount Seir, ran along the northern slope of Mount Jearim (that is, Kesalon), continued down to Beth Shemesh and crossed to Timnah. 11 It went to the northern slope of Ekron, turned toward Shikkeron, passed along to Mount Baalah and reached Jabneel. The boundary ended at the sea.

12 The western boundary is the coastline of the Mediterranean Sea.

These are the boundaries around the people of Judah by their clans.

13 In accordance with the LORD's command to him, Joshua gave to Caleb son

---

a 8 Hebrew *melt*
b 9 Deut. 1:36

a 4 Septuagint; Hebrew *your*

of Jephunneh a portion in Judah – Kiriath Arba, that is, Hebron. (Arba was the forefather of Anak.) [14] From Hebron Caleb drove out the three Anakites – Sheshai, Ahiman and Talmai, the sons of Anak. [15] From there he marched against the people living in Debir (formerly called Kiriath Sepher). [16] And Caleb said, 'I will give my daughter Aksah in marriage to the man who attacks and captures Kiriath Sepher.' [17] Othniel son of Kenaz, Caleb's brother, took it; so Caleb gave his daughter Aksah to him in marriage.

[18] One day when she came to Othniel, she urged him [b] to ask her father for a field. When she got off her donkey, Caleb asked her, 'What can I do for you?'

[19] She replied, 'Do me a special favour. Since you have given me land in the Negev, give me also springs of water.' So Caleb gave her the upper and lower springs.

[20] This is the inheritance of the tribe of Judah, according to its clans:

[21] The southernmost towns of the tribe of Judah in the Negev towards the boundary of Edom were:

Kabzeel, Eder, Jagur, [22] Kinah, Dimonah, Adadah, [23] Kedesh, Hazor, Ithnan, [24] Ziph, Telem, Bealoth, [25] Hazor Hadattah, Kerioth Hezron (that is, Hazor), [26] Amam, Shema, Moladah, [27] Hazar Gaddah, Heshmon, Beth Pelet, [28] Hazar Shual, Beersheba, Biziothiah, [29] Baalah, Iyim, Ezem, [30] Eltolad, Kesil, Hormah, [31] Ziklag, Madmannah, Sansannah, [32] Lebaoth, Shilhim, Ain and Rimmon – a total of twenty-nine towns and their villages.

[33] In the western foothills:

Eshtaol, Zorah, Ashnah, [34] Zanoah, En Gannim, Tappuah, Enam, [35] Jarmuth, Adullam, Sokoh, Azekah, [36] Shaaraim, Adithaim and Gederah

(or Gederothaim) [c] – fourteen towns and their villages.

[37] Zenan, Hadashah, Migdal Gad, [38] Dilean, Mizpah, Joktheel, [39] Lachish, Bozkath, Eglon, [40] Kabbon, Lahmas, Kitlish, [41] Gederoth, Beth Dagon, Naamah and Makkedah – sixteen towns and their villages.

[42] Libnah, Ether, Ashan, [43] Iphtah, Ashnah, Nezib, [44] Keilah, Akzib and Mareshah – nine towns and their villages.

[45] Ekron, with its surrounding settlements and villages; [46] west of Ekron, all that were in the vicinity of Ashdod, together with their villages; [47] Ashdod, its surrounding settlements and villages; and Gaza, its settlements and villages, as far as the Wadi of Egypt and the coastline of the Mediterranean Sea.

[48] In the hill country:

Shamir, Jattir, Sokoh, [49] Dannah, Kiriath Sannah (that is, Debir), [50] Anab, Eshtemoh, Anim, [51] Goshen, Holon and Giloh – eleven towns and their villages.

[52] Arab, Dumah, Eshan, [53] Janim, Beth Tappuah, Aphekah, [54] Humtah, Kiriath Arba (that is, Hebron) and Zior – nine towns and their villages.

[55] Maon, Carmel, Ziph, Juttah, [56] Jezreel, Jokdeam, Zanoah, [57] Kain, Gibeah and Timnah – ten towns and their villages.

[58] Halhul, Beth Zur, Gedor, [59] Maarath, Beth Anoth and Eltekon – six towns and their villages. [d]

[60] Kiriath Baal (that is, Kiriath Jearim) and Rabbah – two towns and their villages.

[61] In the wilderness:

Beth Arabah, Middin, Sekakah, [62] Nibshan, the City of Salt and En Gedi – six towns and their villages.

---

b 18 Hebrew and some Septuagint manuscripts; other Septuagint manuscripts (see also note at Judges 1:14) *Othniel, he urged her*
c 36 Or *Gederah and Gederothaim*

d 59 The Septuagint adds another district of eleven towns, including Tekoa and Ephrathah (Bethlehem).

⁶³Judah could not dislodge the Jebusites, who were living in Jerusalem; to this day the Jebusites live there with the people of Judah.

Land allotted to Ephraim and Manasseh

16 The land allotted to Joseph began at the Jordan, east of the springs of Jericho, and went up from there through the desert into the hill country of Bethel. ²It went on from Bethel (that is, Luz),ᵃ crossed over to the territory of the Arkites in Ataroth, ³descended westward to the territory of the Japhletites as far as the region of Lower Beth Horon and on to Gezer, ending at the Mediterranean Sea.

⁴So Manasseh and Ephraim, the descendants of Joseph, received their inheritance.

⁵This was the territory of Ephraim, according to its clans:

The boundary of their inheritance went from Ataroth Addar in the east to Upper Beth Horon ⁶and continued to the Mediterranean Sea. From Mikmethath on the north it curved eastward to Taanath Shiloh, passing by it to Janoah on the east. ⁷Then it went down from Janoah to Ataroth and Naarah, touched Jericho and came out at the Jordan. ⁸From Tappuah the border went west to the Kanah Ravine and ended at the Mediterranean Sea. This was the inheritance of the tribe of the Ephraimites, according to its clans. ⁹It also included all the towns and their villages that were set aside for the Ephraimites within the inheritance of the Manassites.

¹⁰They did not dislodge the Canaanites living in Gezer; to this day the Canaanites live among the people of Ephraim but are required to do forced labour.

ᵃ 2 Septuagint; Hebrew *Bethel to Luz*

17 This was the land allotted to the tribe of Manasseh as Joseph's firstborn, that is, for Makir, Manasseh's firstborn. Makir was the ancestor of the Gileadites, who had received Gilead and Bashan because the Makirites were great soldiers. ²So this land was allotted to the rest of the people of Manasseh – the clans of Abiezer, Helek, Asriel, Shechem, Hepher and Shemida. These are the other male descendants of Manasseh son of Joseph by their clans.

³Now Zelophehad son of Hepher, the son of Gilead, the son of Makir, the son of Manasseh, had no sons but only daughters, whose names were Mahlah, Noah, Hoglah, Milkah and Tirzah. ⁴They went to Eleazar the priest, Joshua son of Nun, and the leaders and said, 'The LORD commanded Moses to give us an inheritance among our relatives.' So Joshua gave them an inheritance along with the brothers of their father, according to the LORD's command. ⁵Manasseh's share consisted of ten tracts of land besides Gilead and Bashan east of the Jordan, ⁶because the daughters of the tribe of Manasseh received an inheritance among the sons. The land of Gilead belonged to the rest of the descendants of Manasseh.

⁷The territory of Manasseh extended from Asher to Mikmethath east of Shechem. The boundary ran southward from there to include the people living at En Tappuah. ⁸(Manasseh had the land of Tappuah, but Tappuah itself, on the boundary of Manasseh, belonged to the Ephraimites.) ⁹Then the boundary continued south to the Kanah Ravine. There were towns belonging to Ephraim lying among the towns of Manasseh, but the boundary of Manasseh was the northern side of the ravine and ended at the Mediterranean Sea. ¹⁰On the south the land belonged to Ephraim, on the north to Manasseh. The territory of Manasseh reached the Mediterranean Sea and bordered Asher on the north and Issachar on the east.

¹¹Within Issachar and Asher,

Manasseh also had Beth Shan, Ibleam and the people of Dor, Endor, Taanach and Megiddo, together with their surrounding settlements (the third in the list is Naphoth*a*).

12 Yet the Manassites were not able to occupy these towns, for the Canaanites were determined to live in that region. 13 However, when the Israelites grew stronger, they subjected the Canaanites to forced labour but did not drive them out completely.

14 The people of Joseph said to Joshua, 'Why have you allotted us only one portion of land and one share for an inheritance? We are a numerous people, and the LORD has blessed us abundantly.'

15 'If you are so numerous,' Joshua answered, 'and if the hill country of Ephraim is too small for you, go up into the forest and clear land for yourselves there in the land of the Perizzites and Rephaites.'

16 The people of Joseph replied, 'The hill country is not enough for us, and all the Canaanites who live in the plain have chariots fitted with iron, both those in Beth Shan and its settlements and those in the Valley of Jezreel.'

17 But Joshua said to the tribes of Joseph – to Ephraim and Manasseh – 'You are numerous and very powerful. You will have not only one portion of land allotted to you 18 but the forested hill country as well. Clear it, and its farthest limits will be yours; though the Canaanites have chariots fitted with iron and though they are strong, you can drive them out.'

Division of the rest of the land

18 The whole assembly of the Israelites gathered at Shiloh and set up the tent of meeting there. The country was brought under their control, 2 but there were still seven Israelite tribes who had not yet received their inheritance.

3 So Joshua said to the Israelites: 'How long will you wait before you begin to take possession of the land that the LORD,

the God of your ancestors, has given you? 4 Appoint three men from each tribe. I will send them out to make a survey of the land and to write a description of it, according to the inheritance of each. Then they will return to me. 5 You are to divide the land into seven parts. Judah is to remain in its territory on the south and the tribes of Joseph in their territory on the north. 6 After you have written descriptions of the seven parts of the land, bring them here to me and I will cast lots for you in the presence of the LORD our God. 7 The Levites, however, do not get a portion among you, because the priestly service of the LORD is their inheritance. And Gad, Reuben and the half-tribe of Manasseh have already received their inheritance on the east side of the Jordan. Moses the servant of the LORD gave it to them.'

8 As the men started on their way to map out the land, Joshua instructed them, 'Go and make a survey of the land and write a description of it. Then return to me, and I will cast lots for you here at Shiloh in the presence of the LORD.' 9 So the men left and went through the land. They wrote its description on a scroll, town by town, in seven parts, and returned to Joshua in the camp at Shiloh. 10 Joshua then cast lots for them in Shiloh in the presence of the LORD, and there he distributed the land to the Israelites according to their tribal divisions.

Land allotted to Benjamin

11 The first lot came up for the tribe of Benjamin according to its clans. Their allotted territory lay between the tribes of Judah and Joseph:

12 On the north side their boundary began at the Jordan, passed the northern slope of Jericho and headed west into the hill country, coming out at the wilderness of Beth Aven. 13 From there it crossed to the south slope of Luz (that is, Bethel) and went down to Ataroth Addar on the hill south of Lower Beth Horon.

14 From the hill facing Beth Horon on the south the boundary turned south along the western side and

came out at Kiriath Baal (that is, Kiriath Jearim), a town of the people of Judah. This was the western side.

¹⁵The southern side began at the outskirts of Kiriath Jearim on the west, and the boundary came out at the spring of the waters of Nephtoah. ¹⁶The boundary went down to the foot of the hill facing the Valley of Ben Hinnom, north of the Valley of Rephaim. It continued down the Hinnom Valley along the southern slope of the Jebusite city and so to En Rogel. ¹⁷It then curved north, went to En Shemesh, continued to Geliloth, which faces the Pass of Adummim, and ran down to the Stone of Bohan son of Reuben. ¹⁸It continued to the northern slope of Beth Arabahᵃ and on down into the Arabah. ¹⁹It then went to the northern slope of Beth Hoglah and came out at the northern bay of the Dead Sea, at the mouth of the Jordan in the south. This was the southern boundary.

²⁰The Jordan formed the boundary on the eastern side.

These were the boundaries that marked out the inheritance of the clans of Benjamin on all sides.

²¹The tribe of Benjamin, according to its clans, had the following cities:

Jericho, Beth Hoglah, Emek Keziz, ²²Beth Arabah, Zemaraim, Bethel, ²³Avvim, Parah, Ophrah, ²⁴Kephar Ammoni, Ophni and Geba – twelve towns and their villages.

²⁵Gibeon, Ramah, Beeroth, ²⁶Mizpah, Kephirah, Mozah, ²⁷Rekem, Irpeel, Taralah, ²⁸Zelah, Haeleph, the Jebusite city (that is, Jerusalem), Gibeah and Kiriath – fourteen towns and their villages.

This was the inheritance of Benjamin for its clans.

Land allotted to Simeon

19 The second lot came out for the tribe of Simeon according to its clans. Their inheritance lay within the territory of Judah. ²It included:

Beersheba (or Sheba),ᵃ Moladah, ³Hazar Shual, Balah, Ezem, ⁴Eltolad, Bethul, Hormah, ⁵Ziklag, Beth Markaboth, Hazar Susah, ⁶Beth Lebaoth and Sharuhen – thirteen towns and their villages;

⁷Ain, Rimmon, Ether and Ashan – four towns and their villages – ⁸and all the villages around these towns as far as Baalath Beer (Ramah in the Negev).

This was the inheritance of the tribe of the Simeonites, according to its clans. ⁹The inheritance of the Simeonites was taken from the share of Judah, because Judah's portion was more than they needed. So the Simeonites received their inheritance within the territory of Judah.

Land allotted to Zebulun

¹⁰The third lot came up for Zebulun according to its clans:

The boundary of their inheritance went as far as Sarid. ¹¹Going west it ran to Maralah, touched Dabbesheth, and extended to the ravine near Jokneam. ¹²It turned east from Sarid towards the sunrise to the territory of Kisloth Tabor and went on to Daberath and up to Japhia. ¹³Then it continued eastward to Gath Hepher and Eth Kazin; it came out at Rimmon and turned towards Neah. ¹⁴There the boundary went round on the north to Hannathon and ended at the Valley of Iphtah El. ¹⁵Included were Kattath, Nahalal, Shimron, Idalah and Bethlehem. There were twelve towns and their villages.

¹⁶These towns and their villages were the inheritance of Zebulun, according to its clans.

ᵃ 18 Septuagint; Hebrew *slope facing the Arabah*

ᵃ 2 Or *Beersheba, Sheba*; 1 Chron. 4:28 does not have Sheba.

Land allotted to Issachar

¹⁷ The fourth lot came out for Issachar according to its clans. ¹⁸ Their territory included:

Jezreel, Kesulloth, Shunem, ¹⁹ Hapharaim, Shion, Anaharath, ²⁰ Rabbith, Kishion, Ebez, ²¹ Remeth, En Gannim, En Haddah and Beth Pazzez. ²² The boundary touched Tabor, Shahazumah and Beth Shemesh, and ended at the Jordan. There were sixteen towns and their villages.

²³ These towns and their villages were the inheritance of the tribe of Issachar, according to its clans.

Land allotted to Asher

²⁴ The fifth lot came out for the tribe of Asher according to its clans. ²⁵ Their territory included:

Helkath, Hali, Beten, Akshaph, ²⁶ Allammelek, Amad and Mishal. On the west the boundary touched Carmel and Shihor Libnath. ²⁷ It then turned east towards Beth Dagon, touched Zebulun and the Valley of Iphtah El, and went north to Beth Emek and Neiel, passing Kabul on the left. ²⁸ It went to Abdon,^b Rehob, Hammon and Kanah, as far as Greater Sidon. ²⁹ The boundary then turned back towards Ramah and went to the fortified city of Tyre, turned towards Hosah and came out at the Mediterranean Sea in the region of Akzib, ³⁰ Ummah, Aphek and Rehob. There were twenty-two towns and their villages.

³¹ These towns and their villages were the inheritance of the tribe of Asher, according to its clans.

Land allotted to Naphtali

³² The sixth lot came out for Naphtali according to its clans:

³³ Their boundary went from Heleph and the large tree in Zaanannim, passing Adami Nekeb and Jabneel to Lakkum and ending at the Jordan. ³⁴ The boundary ran west through Aznoth Tabor and came out at Hukkok. It touched Zebulun on the south, Asher on the west and the Jordan^c on the east. ³⁵ The fortified cities were Ziddim, Zer, Hammath, Rakkath, Kinnereth, ³⁶ Adamah, Ramah, Hazor, ³⁷ Kedesh, Edrei, En Hazor, ³⁸ Iron, Migdal El, Horem, Beth Anath and Beth Shemesh. There were nineteen towns and their villages.

³⁹ These towns and their villages were the inheritance of the tribe of Naphtali, according to its clans.

Land allotted to Dan

⁴⁰ The seventh lot came out for the tribe of Dan according to its clans. ⁴¹ The territory of their inheritance included:

Zorah, Eshtaol, Ir Shemesh, ⁴² Shaalabbin, Aijalon, Ithlah, ⁴³ Elon, Timnah, Ekron, ⁴⁴ Eltekeh, Gibbethon, Baalath, ⁴⁵ Jehud, Bene Berak, Gath Rimmon, ⁴⁶ Me Jarkon and Rakkon, with the area facing Joppa.

⁴⁷ (When the territory of the Danites was lost to them, they went up and attacked Leshem, took it, put it to the sword and occupied it. They settled in Leshem and named it Dan after their ancestor.)

⁴⁸ These towns and their villages were the inheritance of the tribe of Dan, according to its clans.

Land allotted to Joshua

⁴⁹ When they had finished dividing the land into its allotted portions, the Israelites gave Joshua son of Nun an inheritance among them, ⁵⁰ as the LORD had commanded. They gave him the town he asked for – Timnath Serah^d in the hill country of Ephraim. And he built up the town and settled there.

⁵¹ These are the territories that Eleazar the priest, Joshua son of Nun and the heads of the tribal clans of Israel assigned by lot at Shiloh in the presence of the LORD at the entrance to the tent of

---

b 28 Some Hebrew manuscripts (see also 21:30); most Hebrew manuscripts *Ebron*

c 34 Septuagint; Hebrew *west, and Judah, the Jordan,*

d 50 Also known as *Timnath Heres* (see Judges 2:9)

meeting. And so they finished dividing the land.

Cities of refuge

20 Then the LORD said to Joshua: 2'Tell the Israelites to designate the cities of refuge, as I instructed you through Moses, 3so that anyone who kills a person accidentally and unintentionally may flee there and find protection from the avenger of blood. 4When they flee to one of these cities, they are to stand in the entrance of the city gate and state their case before the elders of that city. Then the elders are to admit the fugitive into their city and provide a place to live among them. 5If the avenger of blood comes in pursuit, the elders must not surrender the fugitive, because the fugitive killed their neighbour unintentionally and without malice aforethought. 6They are to stay in that city until they have stood trial before the assembly and until the death of the high priest who is serving at that time. Then they may go back to their own home in the town from which they fled.'

7So they set apart Kedesh in Galilee in the hill country of Naphtali, Shechem in the hill country of Ephraim, and Kiriath Arba (that is, Hebron) in the hill country of Judah. 8East of the Jordan (on the other side from Jericho) they designated Bezer in the wilderness on the plateau in the tribe of Reuben, Ramoth in Gilead in the tribe of Gad, and Golan in Bashan in the tribe of Manasseh. 9Any of the Israelites or any foreigner residing among them who killed someone accidentally could flee to these designated cities and not be killed by the avenger of blood prior to standing trial before the assembly.

Towns for the Levites

21 Now the family heads of the Levites approached Eleazar the priest, Joshua son of Nun, and the heads of the other tribal families of Israel 2at Shiloh in Canaan and said to them, 'The LORD commanded through Moses that you give us towns to live in, with pasture-lands for our livestock.' 3So, as the LORD had commanded, the Israelites gave the Levites the

following towns and pasture-lands out of their own inheritance:

4The first lot came out for the Kohathites, according to their clans. The Levites who were descendants of Aaron the priest were allotted thirteen towns from the tribes of Judah, Simeon and Benjamin. 5The rest of Kohath's descendants were allotted ten towns from the clans of the tribes of Ephraim, Dan and half of Manasseh.

FAVOURITE VERSES

Jeremiah 17:7–8

*But blessed is the one who trusts
    in the LORD,
    whose confidence is in him.
They will be like a tree planted
    by the water
    that sends out its roots by the
        stream.
It does not fear when heat comes;
    its leaves are always green.
It has no worries in a year of drought
    and never fails to bear fruit.*

- -

This is one of my favourite Bible verses because of the beautiful picture it gives us of life with God. It reminds me that God is my constant provider, and because of him I do not need to fear when things go wrong.

Freddie, 21

6The descendants of Gershon were allotted thirteen towns from the clans of the tribes of Issachar, Asher, Naphtali and the half-tribe of Manasseh in Bashan.

7The descendants of Merari, according to their clans, received twelve towns from the tribes of Reuben, Gad and Zebulun.

8 So the Israelites allotted to the Levites these towns and their pasture-lands, as the LORD had commanded through Moses.

9 From the tribes of Judah and Simeon they allotted the following towns by name 10 (these towns were assigned to the descendants of Aaron who were from the Kohathite clans of the Levites, because the first lot fell to them):
    11 They gave them Kiriath Arba (that is, Hebron), with its surrounding pasture-land, in the hill country of Judah. (Arba was the forefather of Anak.) 12 But the fields and villages around the city they had given to Caleb son of Jephunneh as his possession.
    13 So to the descendants of Aaron the priest they gave Hebron (a city of refuge for one accused of murder), Libnah, 14 Jattir, Eshtemoa, 15 Holon, Debir, 16 Ain, Juttah and Beth Shemesh, together with their pasture-lands – nine towns from these two tribes.
    17 And from the tribe of Benjamin they gave them Gibeon, Geba, 18 Anathoth and Almon, together with their pasture-lands – four towns.
19 The total number of towns for the priests, the descendants of Aaron, came to thirteen, together with their pasture-lands.

20 The rest of the Kohathite clans of the Levites were allotted towns from the tribe of Ephraim:
    21 In the hill country of Ephraim they were given Shechem (a city of refuge for one accused of murder) and Gezer, 22 Kibzaim and Beth Horon, together with their pasture-lands – four towns.
    23 Also from the tribe of Dan they received Eltekeh, Gibbethon, 24 Aijalon and Gath Rimmon, together with their pasture-lands – four towns.
    25 From half the tribe of Manasseh they received Taanach and Gath

Rimmon, together with their pasture-lands – two towns.
26 All these ten towns and their pasture-lands were given to the rest of the Kohathite clans.

27 The Levite clans of the Gershonites were given:
    from the half-tribe of Manasseh,
    Golan in Bashan (a city of refuge for one accused of murder) and Be Eshterah, together with their pasture-lands – two towns;
28 from the tribe of Issachar,
    Kishion, Daberath, 29 Jarmuth and En Gannim, together with their pasture-lands – four towns;
30 from the tribe of Asher,
    Mishal, Abdon, 31 Helkath and Rehob, together with their pasture-lands – four towns;
32 from the tribe of Naphtali,
    Kedesh in Galilee (a city of refuge for one accused of murder), Hammoth Dor and Kartan, together with their pasture-lands – three towns.
33 The total number of towns of the Gershonite clans came to thirteen, together with their pasture-lands.

34 The Merarite clans (the rest of the Levites) were given:
    from the tribe of Zebulun,
    Jokneam, Kartah, 35 Dimnah and Nahalal, together with their pasture-lands – four towns;
36 from the tribe of Reuben,
    Bezer, Jahaz, 37 Kedemoth and Mephaath, together with their pasture-lands – four towns;
38 from the tribe of Gad,
    Ramoth in Gilead (a city of refuge for one accused of murder), Mahanaim, 39 Heshbon and Jazer, together with their pasture-lands – four towns in all.
40 The total number of towns allotted to the Merarite clans, who were the rest of the Levites, came to twelve.
41 The towns of the Levites in the territory held by the Israelites were forty-eight

in all, together with their pasture-lands. **42** Each of these towns had pasture-lands surrounding it; this was true for all these towns.

43 So the LORD gave Israel all the land he had sworn to give their ancestors, and they took possession of it and settled there. **44** The LORD gave them rest on every side, just as he had sworn to their ancestors. Not one of their enemies withstood them; the LORD gave all their enemies into their hands. **45** Not one of all the LORD's good promises to Israel failed; every one was fulfilled.

Eastern tribes return home

22 Then Joshua summoned the Reubenites, the Gadites and the half-tribe of Manasseh **2** and said to them, 'You have done all that Moses the servant of the LORD commanded, and you have obeyed me in everything I commanded. **3** For a long time now – to this very day – you have not deserted your fellow Israelites but have carried out the mission the LORD your God gave you. **4** Now that the LORD your God has given them rest as he promised, return to your homes in the land that Moses the servant of the LORD gave you on the other side of the Jordan. **5** But be very careful to keep the commandment and the law that Moses the servant of the LORD gave you: to love the LORD your God, to walk in obedience to him, to keep his commands, to hold fast to him and to serve him with all your heart and with all your soul.'

6 Then Joshua blessed them and sent them away, and they went to their homes. **7** (To the half-tribe of Manasseh Moses had given land in Bashan, and to the other half of the tribe Joshua gave land on the west side of the Jordan along with their fellow Israelites.) When Joshua sent them home, he blessed them, **8** saying, 'Return to your homes with your great wealth – with large herds of livestock, with silver, gold, bronze and iron, and a great quantity of clothing – and divide the plunder from your enemies with your fellow Israelites.'

9 So the Reubenites, the Gadites and the half-tribe of Manasseh left the Israelites at Shiloh in Canaan to return to Gilead, their own land, which they had acquired in accordance with the command of the LORD through Moses.

10 When they came to Geliloth near the Jordan in the land of Canaan, the Reubenites, the Gadites and the half-tribe of Manasseh built an imposing altar there by the Jordan. **11** And when the Israelites heard that they had built the altar on the border of Canaan at Geliloth near the Jordan on the Israelite side, **12** the whole assembly of Israel gathered at Shiloh to go to war against them.

13 So the Israelites sent Phinehas son of Eleazar, the priest, to the land of Gilead – to Reuben, Gad and the half-tribe of Manasseh. **14** With him they sent ten of the chief men, one from each of the tribes of Israel, each the head of a family division among the Israelite clans.

15 When they went to Gilead – to Reuben, Gad and the half-tribe of Manasseh – they said to them: **16** 'The whole assembly of the LORD says: "How could you break faith with the God of Israel like this? How could you turn away from the LORD and build yourselves an altar in rebellion against him now? **17** Was not the sin of Peor enough for us? Up to this very day we have not cleansed ourselves from that sin, even though a plague fell on the community of the LORD! **18** And are you now turning away from the LORD?

'"If you rebel against the LORD today, tomorrow he will be angry with the whole community of Israel. **19** If the land you possess is defiled, come over to the LORD's land, where the LORD's tabernacle stands, and share the land with us. But do not rebel against the LORD or against us by building an altar for yourselves, other than the altar of the LORD our God. **20** When Achan son of Zerah was unfaithful in regard to the devoted things, *a* did not wrath come on the whole community

---

a 20 The Hebrew term refers to the irrevocable giving over of things or persons to the LORD, often by totally destroying them.

of Israel? He was not the only one who died for his sin." '

21 Then Reuben, Gad and the half-tribe of Manasseh replied to the heads of the clans of Israel: 22 'The Mighty One, God, the LORD! The Mighty One, God, the LORD! He knows! And let Israel know! If this has been in rebellion or disobedience to the LORD, do not spare us this day. 23 If we have built our own altar to turn away from the LORD and to offer burnt offerings and grain offerings, or to sacrifice fellowship offerings on it, may the LORD himself call us to account.

24 'No! We did it for fear that some day your descendants might say to ours, "What do you have to do with the LORD, the God of Israel? 25 The LORD has made the Jordan a boundary between us and you – you Reubenites and Gadites! You have no share in the LORD." So your descendants might cause ours to stop fearing the LORD.

26 'That is why we said, "Let us get ready and build an altar – but not for burnt offerings or sacrifices." 27 On the contrary, it is to be a witness between us and you and the generations that follow, that we will worship the LORD at his sanctuary with our burnt offerings, sacrifices and fellowship offerings. Then in the future your descendants will not be able to say to ours, "You have no share in the LORD."

28 'And we said, "If they ever say this to us, or to our descendants, we will answer: look at the replica of the LORD's altar, which our ancestors built, not for burnt offerings and sacrifices, but as a witness between us and you."

29 'Far be it from us to rebel against the LORD and turn away from him today by building an altar for burnt offerings, grain offerings and sacrifices, other than the altar of the LORD our God that stands before his tabernacle.'

30 When Phinehas the priest and the leaders of the community – the heads of the clans of the Israelites – heard what Reuben, Gad and Manasseh had to say, they were pleased. 31 And Phinehas son of Eleazar, the priest, said to Reuben, Gad and Manasseh, 'Today we know that the LORD is with us, because you have not

been unfaithful to the LORD in this matter. Now you have rescued the Israelites from the LORD's hand.'

32 Then Phinehas son of Eleazar, the priest, and the leaders returned to Canaan from their meeting with the Reubenites and Gadites in Gilead and reported to the Israelites. 33 They were glad to hear the report and praised God. And they talked no more about going to war against them to devastate the country where the Reubenites and the Gadites lived.

34 And the Reubenites and the Gadites gave the altar this name: A Witness Between Us – that the LORD is God.

Joshua's farewell to the leaders

23 After a long time had passed and the LORD had given Israel rest from all their enemies around them, Joshua, by then a very old man, 2 summoned all Israel – their elders, leaders, judges and officials – and said to them: 'I am very old. 3 You yourselves have seen everything the LORD your God has done to all these nations for your sake; it was the LORD your God who fought for you. 4 Remember how I have allotted as an inheritance for your tribes all the land of the nations that remain – the nations I conquered – between the Jordan and the Mediterranean Sea in the west. 5 The LORD your God himself will push them out for your sake. He will drive them out before you, and you will take possession of their land, as the LORD your God promised you.

6 'Be very strong; be careful to obey all that is written in the Book of the Law of Moses, without turning aside to the right or to the left. 7 Do not associate with these nations that remain among you; do not invoke the names of their gods or swear by them. You must not serve them or bow down to them. 8 But you are to hold fast to the LORD your God, as you have until now.

9 'The LORD has driven out before you great and powerful nations; to this day no one has been able to withstand you. 10 One of you routs a thousand, because the LORD your God fights for you, just as he promised. 11 So be very careful to love the LORD your God.

12 'But if you turn away and ally yourselves with the survivors of these nations that remain among you and if you intermarry with them and associate with them, 13 then you may be sure that the LORD your God will no longer drive out these nations before you. Instead, they will become snares and traps for you, whips on your backs and thorns in your eyes, until you perish from this good land, which the LORD your God has given you.

14 'Now I am about to go the way of all the earth. You know with all your heart and soul that not one of all the good promises the LORD your God gave you has failed. Every promise has been fulfilled; not one has failed. 15 But just as all the good things the LORD your God has promised you have come to you, so he will bring on you all the evil things he has threatened, until the LORD your God has destroyed you from this good land he has given you. 16 If you violate the covenant of the LORD your God, which he commanded you, and go and serve other gods and bow down to them, the LORD's anger will burn against you, and you will quickly perish from the good land he has given you.'

The covenant renewed at Shechem

24 Then Joshua assembled all the tribes of Israel at Shechem. He summoned the elders, leaders, judges and officials of Israel, and they presented themselves before God.

2 Joshua said to all the people, 'This is what the LORD, the God of Israel, says: "Long ago your ancestors, including Terah the father of Abraham and Nahor, lived beyond the River Euphrates and worshipped other gods. 3 But I took your father Abraham from the land beyond the Euphrates and led him throughout Canaan and gave him many descendants. I gave him Isaac, 4 and to Isaac I gave Jacob and Esau. I assigned the hill country of Seir to Esau, but Jacob and his family went down to Egypt.

5 ' "Then I sent Moses and Aaron, and I afflicted the Egyptians by what I did there, and I brought you out. 6 When I brought your people out of Egypt, you came to the sea, and the Egyptians pursued them with chariots and horsemen[a] as far as the Red Sea.[b] 7 But they cried to the LORD for help, and he put darkness between you and the Egyptians; he brought the sea over them and covered them. You saw with your own eyes what I did to the Egyptians. Then you lived in the wilderness for a long time.

8 ' "I brought you to the land of the Amorites who lived east of the Jordan. They fought against you, but I gave them into your hands. I destroyed them from before you, and you took possession of their land. 9 When Balak son of Zippor, the king of Moab, prepared to fight against Israel, he sent for Balaam son of Beor to put a curse on you. 10 But I would not listen to Balaam, so he blessed you again and again, and I delivered you out of his hand.

11 ' "Then you crossed the Jordan and came to Jericho. The citizens of Jericho fought against you, as did also the Amorites, Perizzites, Canaanites, Hittites, Girgashites, Hivites and Jebusites, but I gave them into your hands. 12 I sent the hornet ahead of you, which drove them out before you – also the two Amorite kings. You did not do it with your own sword and bow. 13 So I gave you a land on which you did not toil and cities you did not build; and you live in them and eat from vineyards and olive groves that you did not plant."

14 'Now fear the LORD and serve him with all faithfulness. Throw away the gods your ancestors worshipped beyond the River Euphrates and in Egypt, and serve the LORD. 15 But if serving the LORD seems undesirable to you, then choose for yourselves this day whom you will serve, whether the gods your ancestors served beyond the Euphrates, or the gods of the Amorites, in whose land you are living. But as for me and my household, we will serve the LORD.'

16 Then the people answered, 'Far be it from us to forsake the LORD to serve other gods! 17 It was the LORD our God himself who brought us and our parents up out of Egypt, from that land of slavery, and

---

a 6 Or charioteers
b 6 Or the Sea of Reeds

performed those great signs before our eyes. He protected us on our entire journey and among all the nations through which we travelled. 18 And the LORD drove out before us all the nations, including the Amorites, who lived in the land. We too will serve the LORD, because he is our God.'

19 Joshua said to the people, 'You are not able to serve the LORD. He is a holy God; he is a jealous God. He will not forgive your rebellion and your sins. 20 If you forsake the LORD and serve foreign gods, he will turn and bring disaster on you and make an end of you, after he has been good to you.'

21 But the people said to Joshua, 'No! We will serve the LORD.'

22 Then Joshua said, 'You are witnesses against yourselves that you have chosen to serve the LORD.'

'Yes, we are witnesses,' they replied.

23 'Now then,' said Joshua, 'throw away the foreign gods that are among you and yield your hearts to the LORD, the God of Israel.'

24 And the people said to Joshua, 'We will serve the LORD our God and obey him.'

25 On that day Joshua made a covenant for the people, and there at Shechem he reaffirmed for them decrees and laws. 26 And Joshua recorded these things in the Book of the Law of God. Then he took a large stone and set it up there under the oak near the holy place of the LORD.

27 'See!' he said to all the people. 'This stone will be a witness against us. It has heard all the words the LORD has said to us. It will be a witness against you if you are untrue to your God.'

28 Then Joshua dismissed the people, each to their own inheritance.

Buried in the promised land

29 After these things, Joshua son of Nun, the servant of the LORD, died at the age of a hundred and ten. 30 And they buried him in the land of his inheritance, at Timnath Serahc in the hill country of Ephraim, north of Mount Gaash.

31 Israel served the LORD throughout the lifetime of Joshua and of the elders who outlived him and who had experienced everything the LORD had done for Israel.

32 And Joseph's bones, which the Israelites had brought up from Egypt, were buried at Shechem in the tract of land that Jacob bought for a hundred pieces of silverd from the sons of Hamor, the father of Shechem. This became the inheritance of Joseph's descendants.

33 And Eleazar son of Aaron died and was buried at Gibeah, which had been allotted to his son Phinehas in the hill country of Ephraim.

---

c 30 Also known as Timnath Heres (see Judges 2:9)
d 32 Hebrew hundred kesitahs; a kesitah was a unit of money of unknown weight and value.

JUDGES

DATE

Judges covers a time period between about 1220 and 1050 BC

AUTHOR

Traditionally attributed to Samuel, but there were probably several contributors

WHAT'S IT ALL ABOUT?

Judges is the second of the Bible's History books and tells the story of God's people after the death of Joshua, through twelve judges of Israel and up to the start of the monarchy (when Israel was ruled by a king instead of a judge). During this part of their history, the people seemed to go round in circles. They messed up and forgot about God and his commands. Then they were conquered and cried out to God to save them. When he did, they behaved themselves briefly, but before too long they were going their own way again and forgetting God – until they were conquered again and needed his help once more.

WHY SHOULD WE READ IT?

- To hear the stories of some of the famous judges of Israel, including Deborah, Gideon and Samson.

- To see how God used women to lead his people (Judges 4 – 5).

- To see how God uses people who feel weak (Judges 6).

- To read how Gideon tested what the Lord was saying to him by laying out a fleece (Judges 6).

- To see how faithful and patient God is, even when his people are not faithful to him.

Andy Croft with Liza Hoeksma

Israel fights the remaining Canaanites

1 After the death of Joshua, the Israelites asked the LORD, 'Who of us is to go up first to fight against the Canaanites?'

²The LORD answered, 'Judah shall go up; I have given the land into their hands.'

³The men of Judah then said to the Simeonites their fellow Israelites, 'Come up with us into the territory allotted to us, to fight against the Canaanites. We in turn will go with you into yours.' So the Simeonites went with them.

⁴When Judah attacked, the LORD gave the Canaanites and Perizzites into their hands, and they struck down ten thousand men at Bezek. ⁵It was there that they found Adoni-Bezek and fought against him, putting to rout the Canaanites and Perizzites. ⁶Adoni-Bezek fled, but they chased him and caught him, and cut off his thumbs and big toes.

⁷Then Adoni-Bezek said, 'Seventy kings with their thumbs and big toes cut off have picked up scraps under my table. Now God has paid me back for what I did to them.' They brought him to Jerusalem, and he died there.

⁸The men of Judah attacked Jerusalem also and took it. They put the city to the sword and set it on fire.

⁹After that, Judah went down to fight against the Canaanites living in the hill country, the Negev and the western foothills. ¹⁰They advanced against the Canaanites living in Hebron (formerly called Kiriath Arba) and defeated Sheshai, Ahiman and Talmai. ¹¹From there they advanced against the people living in Debir (formerly called Kiriath Sepher).

¹²And Caleb said, 'I will give my daughter Aksah in marriage to the man who attacks and captures Kiriath Sepher.' ¹³Othniel son of Kenaz, Caleb's younger brother, took it; so Caleb gave his daughter Aksah to him in marriage.

¹⁴One day when she came to Othniel, she urged him*a* to ask her father for a field. When she got off her donkey, Caleb asked her, 'What can I do for you?'

¹⁵She replied, 'Do me a special favour. Since you have given me land in the Negev, give me also springs of water.' So Caleb gave her the upper and lower springs.

¹⁶The descendants of Moses' father-in-law, the Kenite, went up from the City of Palms*b* with the people of Judah to live among the inhabitants of the Desert of Judah in the Negev near Arad.

¹⁷Then the men of Judah went with the Simeonites their fellow Israelites and attacked the Canaanites living in Zephath, and they totally destroyed*c* the city. Therefore it was called Hormah.*d* ¹⁸Judah also took*e* Gaza, Ashkelon and Ekron – each city with its territory.

¹⁹The LORD was with the men of Judah. They took possession of the hill country, but they were unable to drive the people from the plains, because they had chariots fitted with iron. ²⁰As Moses had promised, Hebron was given to Caleb, who drove from it the three sons of Anak. ²¹The Benjaminites, however, did not drive out the Jebusites, who were living in Jerusalem; to this day the Jebusites live there with the Benjaminites.

²²Now the tribes of Joseph attacked Bethel, and the LORD was with them. ²³When they sent men to spy out Bethel (formerly called Luz), ²⁴the spies saw a man coming out of the city and they said to him, 'Show us how to get into the city and we will see that you are treated well.' ²⁵So he showed them, and they put the city to the sword but spared the man and his whole family. ²⁶He then went to the land of the Hittites, where he built a city and called it Luz, which is its name to this day.

²⁷But Manasseh did not drive out the people of Beth Shan or Taanach or Dor or Ibleam or Megiddo and their surrounding settlements, for the Canaanites were determined to live in that land. ²⁸When Israel became strong, they pressed the Canaanites into forced labour but never drove them out completely. ²⁹Nor did Ephraim

a 14 Hebrew; Septuagint and Vulgate *Othniel, he urged her*
b 16 That is, Jericho
c 17 The Hebrew term refers to the irrevocable giving over of things or persons to the LORD, often by totally destroying them.
d 17 *Hormah* means *destruction.*
e 18 Hebrew; Septuagint *Judah did not take*

drive out the Canaanites living in Gezer, but the Canaanites continued to live there among them. [30] Neither did Zebulun drive out the Canaanites living in Kitron or Nahalol, so these Canaanites lived among them, but Zebulun did subject them to forced labour. [31] Nor did Asher drive out those living in Akko or Sidon or Ahlab or Akzib or Helbah or Aphek or Rehob. [32] The Asherites lived among the Canaanite inhabitants of the land because they did not drive them out. [33] Neither did Naphtali drive out those living in Beth Shemesh or Beth Anath; but the Naphtalites too lived among the Canaanite inhabitants of the land, and those living in Beth Shemesh and Beth Anath became forced labourers for them. [34] The Amorites confined the Danites to the hill country, not allowing them to come down into the plain. [35] And the Amorites were determined also to hold out in Mount Heres, Aijalon and Shaalbim, but when the power of the tribes of Joseph increased, they too were pressed into forced labour. [36] The boundary of the Amorites was from Scorpion Pass to Sela and beyond.

The angel of the LORD at Bokim

2 The angel of the LORD went up from Gilgal to Bokim and said, 'I brought you up out of Egypt and led you into the land that I swore to give to your ancestors. I said, "I will never break my covenant with you, [2] and you shall not make a covenant with the people of this land, but you shall break down their altars." Yet you have disobeyed me. Why have you done this? [3] And I have also said, "I will not drive them out before you; they will become traps for you, and their gods will become snares to you."'

[4] When the angel of the LORD had spoken these things to all the Israelites, the people wept aloud, [5] and they called that place Bokim.[a] There they offered sacrifices to the LORD.

Disobedience and defeat

[6] After Joshua had dismissed the Israelites, they went to take possession of the land, each to their own inheritance. [7] The people served the LORD throughout the lifetime of Joshua and of the elders who outlived him and who had seen all the great things the LORD had done for Israel.

[8] Joshua son of Nun, the servant of the LORD, died at the age of a hundred and ten. [9] And they buried him in the land of his inheritance, at Timnath Heres[b] in the hill country of Ephraim, north of Mount Gaash.

[10] After that whole generation had been gathered to their ancestors, another generation grew up who knew neither the LORD nor what he had done for Israel. [11] Then the Israelites did evil in the eyes of the LORD and served the Baals. [12] They forsook the LORD, the God of their ancestors, who had brought them out of Egypt. They followed and worshipped various gods of the peoples around them. They aroused the LORD's anger [13] because they forsook him and served Baal and the Ashtoreths. [14] In his anger against Israel the LORD gave them into the hands of raiders who plundered them. He sold them into the hands of their enemies all around, whom they were no longer able to resist. [15] Whenever Israel went out to fight, the hand of the LORD was against them to defeat them, just as he had sworn to them. They were in great distress.

[16] Then the LORD raised up judges,[c] who saved them out of the hands of these raiders. [17] Yet they would not listen to their judges but prostituted themselves to other gods and worshipped them. They quickly turned from the ways of their ancestors, who had been obedient to the LORD's commands. [18] Whenever the LORD raised up a judge for them, he was with the judge and saved them out of the hands of their enemies as long as the judge lived; for the LORD relented because of their groaning under those who oppressed and afflicted them. [19] But when the judge died, the people returned to ways even more corrupt than those of their ancestors, following other gods and serving and worshipping

---

a 5 *Bokim* means *weepers.*

b 9 Also known as *Timnath Serah* (see Joshua 19:50 and 24:30)

c 16 Or *leaders*; similarly in verses 17-19

them. They refused to give up their evil practices and stubborn ways.

20 Therefore the LORD was very angry with Israel and said, 'Because this nation has violated the covenant I ordained for their ancestors and has not listened to me, 21 I will no longer drive out before them any of the nations Joshua left when he died. 22 I will use them to test Israel and see whether they will keep the way of the LORD and walk in it as their ancestors did.' 23 The LORD had allowed those nations to remain; he did not drive them out at once by giving them into the hands of Joshua.

3 These are the nations the LORD left to test all those Israelites who had not experienced any of the wars in Canaan 2 (he did this only to teach warfare to the descendants of the Israelites who had not had previous battle experience): 3 the five rulers of the Philistines, all the Canaanites, the Sidonians, and the Hivites living in the Lebanon mountains from Mount Baal Hermon to Lebo Hamath. 4 They were left to test the Israelites to see whether they would obey the LORD's commands, which he had given their ancestors through Moses.

5 The Israelites lived among the Canaanites, Hittites, Amorites, Perizzites, Hivites and Jebusites. 6 They took their daughters in marriage and gave their own daughters to their sons, and served their gods.

Othniel

7 The Israelites did evil in the eyes of the LORD; they forgot the LORD their God and served the Baals and the Asherahs. 8 The anger of the LORD burned against Israel so that he sold them into the hands of Cushan-Rishathaim king of Aram Naharaim,*a* to whom the Israelites were subject for eight years. 9 But when they cried out to the LORD, he raised up for them a deliverer, Othniel son of Kenaz, Caleb's younger brother, who saved them. 10 The Spirit of the LORD came on him, so that he became Israel's judge*b* and went to war. The LORD gave Cushan-Rishathaim king of Aram

into the hands of Othniel, who overpowered him. 11 So the land had peace for forty years, until Othniel son of Kenaz died.

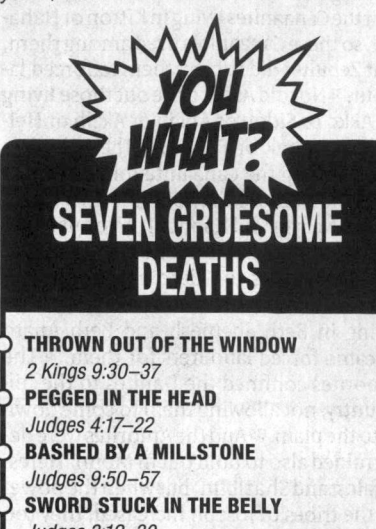

YOU WHAT?

SEVEN GRUESOME DEATHS

○ **THROWN OUT OF THE WINDOW**
2 Kings 9:30–37
○ **PEGGED IN THE HEAD**
Judges 4:17–22
○ **BASHED BY A MILLSTONE**
Judges 9:50–57
○ **SWORD STUCK IN THE BELLY**
Judges 3:12–30
○ **EATEN BY WORMS**
Acts 12:20–23
○ **HEAD CAUGHT IN A TREE**
2 Samuel 18:9–15
○ **DROWNED WITH A CLOTH**
2 Kings 8:7–15

Ehud

12 Again the Israelites did evil in the eyes of the LORD, and because they did this evil the LORD gave Eglon king of Moab power over Israel. 13 Getting the Ammonites and Amalekites to join him, Eglon came and attacked Israel, and they took possession of the City of Palms.*c* 14 The Israelites were subject to Eglon king of Moab for eighteen years.

15 Again the Israelites cried out to the LORD, and he gave them a deliverer – Ehud, a left-handed man, the son of Gera the Benjaminite. The Israelites sent him with tribute to Eglon king of Moab. 16 Now Ehud had made a double-edged sword about a cubit*d* long, which he strapped to his right thigh under his clothing. 17 He presented

---

a 8 That is, North-west Mesopotamia
b 10 Or *leader*

c 13 That is, Jericho
d 16 That is, about 45 centimetres

the tribute to Eglon king of Moab, who was a very fat man. 18 After Ehud had presented the tribute, he sent on their way those who had carried it. 19 But on reaching the stone images near Gilgal he himself went back to Eglon and said, 'Your majesty, I have a secret message for you.'

The king said to his attendants, 'Leave us!' And they all left.

20 Ehud then approached him while he was sitting alone in the upper room of his palace e and said, 'I have a message from God for you.' As the king rose from his seat, 21 Ehud reached with his left hand, drew the sword from his right thigh and plunged it into the king's belly. 22 Even the handle sank in after the blade, and his bowels discharged. Ehud did not pull the sword out, and the fat closed in over it. 23 Then Ehud went out to the porch; f he shut the doors of the upper room behind him and locked them.

24 After he had gone, the servants came and found the doors of the upper room locked. They said, 'He must be relieving himself in the inner room of the palace.' 25 They waited to the point of embarrassment, but when he did not open the doors of the room, they took a key and unlocked them. There they saw their lord fallen to the floor, dead.

26 While they waited, Ehud got away. He passed by the stone images and escaped to Seirah. 27 When he arrived there, he blew a trumpet in the hill country of Ephraim, and the Israelites went down with him from the hills, with him leading them.

28 'Follow me,' he ordered, 'for the LORD has given Moab, your enemy, into your hands.' So they followed him down and took possession of the fords of the Jordan that led to Moab; they allowed no one to cross over. 29 At that time they struck down about ten thousand Moabites, all vigorous and strong; not one escaped. 30 That day Moab was made subject to Israel, and the land had peace for eighty years.

Shamgar

31 After Ehud came Shamgar son of Anath, who struck down six hundred Philistines with an ox-goad. He too saved Israel.

Deborah

4 Again the Israelites did evil in the eyes of the LORD, now that Ehud was dead. 2 So the LORD sold them into the hands of Jabin king of Canaan, who reigned in Hazor. Sisera, the commander of his army, was based in Harosheth Haggoyim. 3 Because he had nine hundred chariots fitted with iron and had cruelly oppressed the Israelites for twenty years, they cried to the LORD for help.

4 Now Deborah, a prophet, the wife of Lappidoth, was leading a Israel at that time. 5 She held court under the Palm of Deborah between Ramah and Bethel in the hill country of Ephraim, and the Israelites went up to her to have their disputes decided. 6 She sent for Barak son of Abinoam from Kedesh in Naphtali and said to him, 'The LORD, the God of Israel, commands you: "Go, take with you ten thousand men of Naphtali and Zebulun and lead them up to Mount Tabor. 7 I will lead Sisera, the commander of Jabin's army, with his chariots and his troops to the River Kishon and give him into your hands." '

8 Barak said to her, 'If you go with me, I will go; but if you don't go with me, I won't go.'

9 'Certainly I will go with you,' said Deborah. 'But because of the course you are taking, the honour will not be yours, for the LORD will deliver Sisera into the hands of a woman.' So Deborah went with Barak to Kedesh. 10 There Barak summoned Zebulun and Naphtali, and ten thousand men went up under his command. Deborah also went up with him.

11 Now Heber the Kenite had left the other Kenites, the descendants of Hobab, Moses' brother-in-law, b and pitched his tent by the great tree in Zaanannim near Kedesh.

---

e 20 The meaning of the Hebrew for this word is uncertain; also in verse 24.
f 23 The meaning of the Hebrew for this word is uncertain.

---

a 4 Traditionally *judging*
b 11 Or *father-in-law*

12 When they told Sisera that Barak son of Abinoam had gone up to Mount Tabor, 13 Sisera summoned from Harosheth Haggoyim to the River Kishon all his men and his nine hundred chariots fitted with iron.

14 Then Deborah said to Barak, 'Go! This is the day the LORD has given Sisera into

PEOPLE USED BY GOD 1

Deborah

Long before Joan of Arc, there was another great woman of strong conviction and courage who stood and fought at the Lord's command.

In Judges 4 we come across Deborah, a woman married to a simple man of no great reputation or wealth. It is thought that she may have begun her service to God with the humble job of caring for the lamps in the tabernacle. Yet Deborah rose to a great position as leader and judge of Israel during their time of captivity with the Canaanites.

How was it possible for a woman, of no particular privilege or position, to rise to such a place of honour? Her husband didn't make it happen; her family or parents weren't the reason; nor was it a job she applied for. She had such great wisdom that the people journeyed to see and listen to her, finding her under the Palm of Deborah, where she would settle their disputes and bring her words from God.

Who she was, the gifts she had and the fruit of her life drew others to her and brought her to this great position. In Isaiah 50:4 it says that the Lord wakes us up each morning to listen so that we will have the words to instruct the tired. It seems as though Deborah was a woman who spent time talking to God, listening to him and asking of him, and then lived her life according to what she heard and requested. Her obedience not only affected her and her family, but also brought an entire nation to freedom from a cruel and oppressive captor. She instructed Barak about the plan of attack, as he was to lead the fight. She never proclaimed herself to be the answer: her heart and intention was to deliver God's message and see his will fulfilled. When Barak received the word from Deborah, he demanded that she accompany him into battle; in fact, he would not go without her! He was afraid; she was courageous. She was a woman who not only spoke God's words, but lived them with heart and soul. Together they went to battle, defeated the enemy and accomplished God's will.

In what great battles does the Lord desire to give you victory? What wisdom and love does he want to show through you? Will you – through prayer, through time spent in the Word, through obedience and growth in a relationship with God – be found in the right place at the right time?

Suzie Brock

Judges 6 ▶▶

your hands. Has not the LORD gone ahead of you?' So Barak went down Mount Tabor, with ten thousand men following him. ¹⁵At Barak's advance, the LORD routed Sisera and all his chariots and army by the sword, and Sisera got down from his chariot and fled on foot.

¹⁶Barak pursued the chariots and army as far as Harosheth Haggoyim, and all Sisera's troops fell by the sword; not a man was left. ¹⁷Sisera, meanwhile, fled on foot to the tent of Jael, the wife of Heber the Kenite, because there was an alliance between Jabin king of Hazor and the family of Heber the Kenite.

¹⁸Jael went out to meet Sisera and said to him, 'Come, my lord, come right in. Don't be afraid.' So he entered her tent, and she covered him with a blanket.

¹⁹'I'm thirsty,' he said. 'Please give me some water.' She opened a skin of milk, gave him a drink, and covered him up.

²⁰'Stand in the doorway of the tent,' he told her. 'If someone comes and asks you, "Is anyone in there?" say "No."'

²¹But Jael, Heber's wife, picked up a tent peg and a hammer and went quietly to him while he lay fast asleep, exhausted. She drove the peg through his temple into the ground, and he died.

²²Just then Barak came by in pursuit of Sisera, and Jael went out to meet him. 'Come,' she said, 'I will show you the man you're looking for.' So he went in with her, and there lay Sisera with the tent peg through his temple – dead.

²³On that day God subdued Jabin king of Canaan before the Israelites. ²⁴And the hand of the Israelites pressed harder and harder against Jabin king of Canaan until they destroyed him.

The song of Deborah

5 On that day Deborah and Barak son of Abinoam sang this song:

² 'When the princes in Israel take the lead,
when the people willingly offer themselves –
praise the LORD!

³ 'Hear this, you kings! Listen, you rulers!
I, even I, will sing toᵃ the LORD;
I will praise the LORD, the God of Israel, in song.

⁴ 'When you, LORD, went out from Seir,
when you marched from the land of Edom,
the earth shook, the heavens poured,
the clouds poured down water.
⁵ The mountains quaked before the LORD, the One of Sinai,
before the LORD, the God of Israel.

⁶ 'In the days of Shamgar son of Anath,
in the days of Jael, the highways were abandoned;
travellers took to winding paths.
⁷ Villagers in Israel would not fight;
they held back until I, Deborah, arose,
until I arose, a mother in Israel.
⁸ God chose new leaders
when war came to the city gates,
but not a shield or spear was seen among forty thousand in Israel.
⁹ My heart is with Israel's princes,
with the willing volunteers among the people.
Praise the LORD!

¹⁰ 'You who ride on white donkeys,
sitting on your saddle blankets,
and you who walk along the road,
consider ¹¹ the voice of the singersᵇ at the watering places.
They recite the victories of the LORD,
the victories of his villagers in Israel.

'Then the people of the LORD went down to the city gates.
¹² "Wake up, wake up, Deborah!
Wake up, wake up, break out in song!
Arise, Barak!
Take captive your captives, son of Abinoam."

ᵃ3 Or of
ᵇ11 The meaning of the Hebrew for this word is uncertain.

13 'The remnant of the nobles came
     down;
    the people of the LORD came down
      to me against the mighty.
14 Some came from Ephraim, whose
     roots were in Amalek;
    Benjamin was with the people who
      followed you.
    From Makir captains came down,
      from Zebulun those who bear a
        commander's^c staff.
15 The princes of Issachar were with
     Deborah;
    yes, Issachar was with Barak,
      sent under his command into the
        valley.
    In the districts of Reuben
      there was much searching of heart.
16 Why did you stay among the
     sheepfolds^d
    to hear the whistling for the flocks?
    In the districts of Reuben
      there was much searching of heart.
17 Gilead stayed beyond the Jordan.
    And Dan, why did he linger by the
      ships?
    Asher remained on the coast
      and stayed in his coves.
18 The people of Zebulun risked their very
      lives;
    so did Naphtali on the terraced
      fields.

19 'Kings came, they fought,
    the kings of Canaan fought.
    At Taanach, by the waters of Megiddo,
      they took no plunder of silver.
20 From the heavens the stars fought,
    from their courses they fought
      against Sisera.
21 The River Kishon swept them away,
    the age-old river, the River Kishon.
    March on, my soul; be strong!
22 Then thundered the horses' hooves –
    galloping, galloping go his mighty
      steeds.
23 "Curse Meroz," said the angel of the
     LORD.

"Curse its people bitterly,
because they did not come to help the
  LORD,
    to help the LORD against the
      mighty."

24 'Most blessed of women be Jael,
    the wife of Heber the Kenite,
    most blessed of tent-dwelling
      women.
25 He asked for water, and she gave him
      milk;
    in a bowl fit for nobles she brought
      him curdled milk.
26 Her hand reached for the tent peg,
    her right hand for the workman's
      hammer.
    She struck Sisera, she crushed his
      head,
    she shattered and pierced his
      temple.
27 At her feet he sank,
    he fell; there he lay.
    At her feet he sank, he fell;
      where he sank, there he fell – dead.

28 'Through the window peered Sisera's
      mother;
    behind the lattice she cried out,
    "Why is his chariot so long in coming?
    Why is the clatter of his chariots
      delayed?"
29 The wisest of her ladies answer her;
    indeed, she keeps saying to herself,
30 "Are they not finding and dividing the
      spoils:
    a woman or two for each man,
    colourful garments as plunder for
      Sisera,
    colourful garments embroidered,
    highly embroidered garments for my
      neck –
    all this as plunder?"

31 'So may all your enemies perish,
    O LORD!
    But may all who love you be like the
      sun
    when it rises in its strength.'

Then the land had peace for forty years.

Gideon

6 The Israelites did evil in the eyes of the Lord, and for seven years he gave them into the hands of the Midianites. ² Because the power of Midian was so oppressive, the Israelites prepared shelters for themselves in mountain clefts, caves and strongholds. ³ Whenever the Israelites planted their crops, the Midianites, Amalekites and other eastern peoples invaded the country. ⁴ They camped on the land and ruined the crops all the way to Gaza and did not spare a living thing for Israel, neither sheep nor cattle nor donkeys. ⁵ They came up with their livestock and their tents like swarms of locusts. It was impossible to count them or their camels; they invaded the land to ravage it. ⁶ Midian so impoverished the Israelites that they cried out to the Lord for help.

⁷ When the Israelites cried out to the Lord because of Midian, ⁸ he sent them a prophet, who said, 'This is what the Lord, the God of Israel, says: I brought you up out of Egypt, out of the land of slavery. ⁹ I rescued you from the hand of the Egyptians. And I delivered you from the hand of all your oppressors; I drove them out before you and gave you their land. ¹⁰ I said to you, "I am the Lord your God; do not worship the gods of the Amorites, in whose land you live." But you have not listened to me.'

¹¹ The angel of the Lord came and sat down under the oak in Ophrah that belonged to Joash the Abiezrite, where his son Gideon was threshing wheat in a winepress to keep it from the Midianites. ¹² When the angel of the Lord appeared to Gideon, he said, 'The Lord is with you, mighty warrior.'

¹³ 'Pardon me, my lord,' Gideon replied, 'but if the Lord is with us, why has all this happened to us? Where are all his wonders that our ancestors told us about when they said, "Did not the Lord bring us up out of Egypt?" But now the Lord has abandoned us and given us into the hand of Midian.'

¹⁴ The Lord turned to him and said, 'Go in the strength you have and save Israel out of Midian's hand. Am I not sending you?'

¹⁵ 'Pardon me, my lord,' Gideon replied, 'but how can I save Israel? My clan is the weakest in Manasseh, and I am the least in my family.'

¹⁶ The Lord answered, 'I will be with you, and you will strike down all the Midianites, leaving none alive.'

¹⁷ Gideon replied, 'If now I have found favour in your eyes, give me a sign that it is really you talking to me. ¹⁸ Please do not go away until I come back and bring my offering and set it before you.'

And the Lord said, 'I will wait until you return.'

¹⁹ Gideon went inside, prepared a young goat, and from an ephah ᵃ of flour he made bread without yeast. Putting the meat in a basket and its broth in a pot, he brought them out and offered them to him under the oak.

²⁰ The angel of God said to him, 'Take the meat and the unleavened bread, place them on this rock, and pour out the broth.' And Gideon did so. ²¹ Then the angel of the Lord touched the meat and the unleavened bread with the tip of the staff that was in his hand. Fire flared from the rock, consuming the meat and the bread. And the angel of the Lord disappeared. ²² When Gideon realised that it was the angel of the Lord, he exclaimed, 'Alas, Sovereign Lord! I have seen the angel of the Lord face to face!'

²³ But the Lord said to him, 'Peace! Do not be afraid. You are not going to die.'

²⁴ So Gideon built an altar to the Lord there and called it The Lord Is Peace. To this day it stands in Ophrah of the Abiezrites.

²⁵ That same night the Lord said to him, 'Take the second bull from your father's herd, the one seven years old.ᵇ Tear down your father's altar to Baal and cut down the Asherah poleᶜ beside it. ²⁶ Then build a proper kind ofᵈ altar to the Lord your God on the top of this height. Using the wood of the Asherah pole that

---

a 19 That is, probably about 16 kilograms
b 25 Or *Take a full-grown, mature bull from your father's herd*
c 25 That is, a wooden symbol of the goddess Asherah; also in verses 26, 28 and 30
d 26 Or *build with layers of stone an*

PEOPLE USED BY GOD 2

Gideon

The life of Gideon encourages us that we are not the only ones to face fears and insecurities when it comes to following God.

We first see him threshing wheat in a winepress where he is hiding from the Midianites oppressing Israel. The angel of the Lord comes and speaks to him: *'The LORD is with you, mighty warrior'* (Judges 6:12). As Gideon looks at the circumstances, he confronts the angel and pretty much says, 'If we're the mighty, then I'd hate to see the weak!'

Israel was under the control of another country and even though they were supposed to be God's chosen people, they were at an all-time low. Gideon couldn't see how God could set the Israelites free, much less how God could use him to do anything about it. The angel speaks again and tells Gideon, *'Go in the strength you have'* (v. 14). When we ask God for help, we are normally looking for something supernatural, but in this situation we see that the Lord's word is, 'Use what I have given you, then I will do the rest.' Our fears and insecurities cause us to withdraw and stop us from moving forward. Gideon felt like this when God called him: 'I'm from one of the weakest clans and my family is the least among them.' But the answer from God was sure: *'I will be with you, and you will strike [them] down'* (v. 16).

When it comes to trusting God, we can really struggle with the thought that God could really use us, or that he would want to use us. When Gideon was told to go and defeat the armies of the Midianites he wanted to know if it was really God speaking or not. Twice God showed him that he was the one speaking and all Gideon needed to do was to obey. This is key in doing God's will. If we would just allow ourselves to obey what we hear the Lord saying in our lives, things really would work out better for us, and for those around us. Maybe we won't have an angel come and visit us, but the voice of God that is recorded in his Word is just as important.

As we keep his commandments and follow all he teaches us, we will find his support to defeat the enemies in our lives. It takes faith and trust to do what is right and not follow the path of least resistance. It's still true that we need help from God, but we also need to do what we can to follow the right path. Just like Gideon, we need to go forward in our strength and allow the Lord to do the rest; and just like Gideon, we will then see the things that hinder us put to flight.

Tom Brock

 Judges 4   Ruth 1:17–18 ⏵

you cut down, offer the second^e bull as a burnt offering.'

²⁷So Gideon took ten of his servants and did as the LORD told him. But because he was afraid of his family and the townspeople, he did it at night rather than in the daytime.

²⁸In the morning when the people of the town got up, there was Baal's altar, demolished, with the Asherah pole beside it cut down and the second bull sacrificed on the newly-built altar!

²⁹They asked each other, 'Who did this?'

When they carefully investigated, they were told, 'Gideon son of Joash did it.'

³⁰The people of the town demanded of Joash, 'Bring out your son. He must die, because he has broken down Baal's altar and cut down the Asherah pole beside it.'

³¹But Joash replied to the hostile crowd around him, 'Are you going to plead Baal's cause? Are you trying to save him? Whoever fights for him shall be put to death by morning! If Baal really is a god, he can defend himself when someone breaks down his altar.' ³²So because Gideon broke down Baal's altar, they gave him the name Jerub-Baal^f that day, saying, 'Let Baal contend with him.'

³³Now all the Midianites, Amalekites and other eastern peoples joined forces and crossed over the Jordan and camped in the Valley of Jezreel. ³⁴Then the Spirit of the LORD came on Gideon, and he blew a trumpet, summoning the Abiezrites to follow him. ³⁵He sent messengers throughout Manasseh, calling them to arms, and also into Asher, Zebulun and Naphtali, so that they too went up to meet them.

³⁶Gideon said to God, 'If you will save Israel by my hand as you have promised – ³⁷look, I will place a wool fleece on the threshing-floor. If there is dew only on the fleece and all the ground is dry, then I will know that you will save Israel by my hand, as you said.' ³⁸And that is what happened. Gideon rose early the next day; he

squeezed the fleece and wrung out the dew – a bowlful of water.

³⁹Then Gideon said to God, 'Do not be angry with me. Let me make just one more request. Allow me one more test with the fleece, but this time make the fleece dry and let the ground be covered with dew.' ⁴⁰That night God did so. Only the fleece was dry; all the ground was covered with dew.

Gideon defeats the Midianites

7 Early in the morning, Jerub-Baal (that is, Gideon) and all his men camped at the spring of Harod. The camp of Midian was north of them in the valley near the hill of Moreh. ²The LORD said to Gideon, 'You have too many men. I cannot deliver Midian into their hands, or Israel would boast against me, "My own strength has saved me." ³Now announce to the army, "Anyone who trembles with fear may turn back and leave Mount Gilead."' So twenty-two thousand men left, while ten thousand remained.

⁴But the LORD said to Gideon, 'There are still too many men. Take them down to the water, and I will thin them out for you there. If I say, "This one shall go with you," he shall go; but if I say, "This one shall not go with you," he shall not go.'

⁵So Gideon took the men down to the water. There the LORD told him, 'Separate those who lap the water with their tongues as a dog laps from those who kneel down to drink.' ⁶Three hundred of them drank from cupped hands, lapping like dogs. All the rest got down on their knees to drink.

⁷The LORD said to Gideon, 'With the three hundred men that lapped I will save you and give the Midianites into your hands. Let all the others go home.' ⁸So Gideon sent the rest of the Israelites home but kept the three hundred, who took over the provisions and trumpets of the others.

Now the camp of Midian lay below him in the valley. ⁹During that night the LORD said to Gideon, 'Get up, go down against the camp, because I am going to give it into your hands. ¹⁰If you are afraid to

e 26 Or *full-grown*; also in verse 28
f 32 *Jerub-Baal* probably means *let Baal contend*.

attack, go down to the camp with your servant Purah ¹¹and listen to what they are saying. Afterwards, you will be encouraged to attack the camp.' So he and Purah his servant went down to the outposts of the camp. ¹²The Midianites, the Amalekites and all the other eastern peoples had settled in the valley, thick as locusts. Their camels could no more be counted than the sand on the seashore.

¹³Gideon arrived just as a man was telling a friend his dream. 'I had a dream,' he was saying. 'A round loaf of barley bread came tumbling into the Midianite camp. It struck the tent with such force that the tent overturned and collapsed.'

¹⁴His friend responded, 'This can be nothing other than the sword of Gideon son of Joash, the Israelite. God has given the Midianites and the whole camp into his hands.'

¹⁵When Gideon heard the dream and its interpretation, he bowed down and worshipped. He returned to the camp of Israel and called out, 'Get up! The LORD has given the Midianite camp into your hands.' ¹⁶Dividing the three hundred men into three companies, he placed trumpets and empty jars in the hands of all of them, with torches inside.

¹⁷'Watch me,' he told them. 'Follow my lead. When I get to the edge of the camp, do exactly as I do. ¹⁸When I and all who are with me blow our trumpets, then from all round the camp blow yours and shout, "For the LORD and for Gideon." '

¹⁹Gideon and the hundred men with him reached the edge of the camp at the beginning of the middle watch, just after they had changed the guard. They blew their trumpets and broke the jars that were in their hands. ²⁰The three companies blew the trumpets and smashed the jars. Grasping the torches in their left hands and holding in their right hands the trumpets they were to blow, they shouted, 'A sword for the LORD and for Gideon!' ²¹While each man held his position round the camp, all the Midianites ran, crying out as they fled.

²²When the three hundred trumpets

sounded, the LORD caused the men throughout the camp to turn on each other with their swords. The army fled to Beth Shittah towards Zererah as far as the border of Abel Meholah near Tabbath. ²³Israelites from Naphtali, Asher and all Manasseh were called out, and they pursued the Midianites. ²⁴Gideon sent messengers throughout the hill country of Ephraim, saying, 'Come down against the Midianites and seize the waters of the Jordan ahead of them as far as Beth Barah.'

So all the men of Ephraim were called out and they seized the waters of the Jordan as far as Beth Barah. ²⁵They also captured two of the Midianite leaders, Oreb and Zeeb. They killed Oreb at the rock of Oreb, and Zeeb at the winepress of Zeeb. They pursued the Midianites and brought the heads of Oreb and Zeeb to Gideon, who was by the Jordan.

Zebah and Zalmunna

8 Now the Ephraimites asked Gideon, 'Why have you treated us like this? Why didn't you call us when you went to fight Midian?' And they challenged him vigorously.

²But he answered them, 'What have I accomplished compared to you? Aren't the gleanings of Ephraim's grapes better than the full grape harvest of Abiezer? ³God gave Oreb and Zeeb, the Midianite leaders, into your hands. What was I able to do compared to you?' At this, their resentment against him subsided.

⁴Gideon and his three hundred men, exhausted yet keeping up the pursuit, came to the Jordan and crossed it. ⁵He said to the men of Sukkoth, 'Give my troops some bread; they are worn out, and I am still pursuing Zebah and Zalmunna, the kings of Midian.'

⁶But the officials of Sukkoth said, 'Do you already have the hands of Zebah and Zalmunna in your possession? Why should we give bread to your troops?'

⁷Then Gideon replied, 'Just for that, when the LORD has given Zebah and Zalmunna into my hand, I will tear your flesh with desert thorns and briers.'

8 From there he went up to Peniel[a] and made the same request of them, but they answered as the men of Sukkoth had. 9 So he said to the men of Peniel, 'When I return in triumph, I will tear down this tower.'

10 Now Zebah and Zalmunna were in Karkor with a force of about fifteen thousand men, all that were left of the armies of the eastern peoples; a hundred and twenty thousand swordsmen had fallen. 11 Gideon went up by the route of the nomads east of Nobah and Jogbehah and attacked the unsuspecting army. 12 Zebah and Zalmunna, the two kings of Midian, fled, but he pursued them and captured them, routing their entire army.

13 Gideon son of Joash then returned from the battle by the Pass of Heres. 14 He caught a young man of Sukkoth and questioned him, and the young man wrote down for him the names of the seventy-seven officials of Sukkoth, the elders of the town. 15 Then Gideon came and said to the men of Sukkoth, 'Here are Zebah and Zalmunna, about whom you taunted me by saying, "Do you already have the hands of Zebah and Zalmunna in your possession? Why should we give bread to your exhausted men?"' 16 He took the elders of the town and taught the men of Sukkoth a lesson by punishing them with desert thorns and briers. 17 He also pulled down the tower of Peniel and killed the men of the town.

18 Then he asked Zebah and Zalmunna, 'What kind of men did you kill at Tabor?'

'Men like you,' they answered, 'each one with the bearing of a prince.'

19 Gideon replied, 'Those were my brothers, the sons of my own mother. As surely as the LORD lives, if you had spared their lives, I would not kill you.' 20 Turning to Jether, his eldest son, he said, 'Kill them!' But Jether did not draw his sword, because he was only a boy and was afraid.

21 Zebah and Zalmunna said, 'Come, do it yourself. "As is the man, so is his strength."' So Gideon stepped forward and killed them, and took the ornaments off their camels' necks.

Gideon's ephod

22 The Israelites said to Gideon, 'Rule over us—you, your son and your grandson—because you have saved us from the hand of Midian.'

23 But Gideon told them, 'I will not rule over you, nor will my son rule over you. The LORD will rule over you.' 24 And he said, 'I do have one request, that each of you give me an earring from your share of the plunder.' (It was the custom of the Ishmaelites to wear gold earrings.)

25 They answered, 'We'll be glad to give them.' So they spread out a garment, and each of them threw a ring from his plunder onto it. 26 The weight of the gold rings he asked for came to seventeen hundred shekels,[b] not counting the ornaments, the pendants and the purple garments worn by the kings of Midian or the chains that were on their camels' necks. 27 Gideon made the gold into an ephod, which he placed in Ophrah, his town. All Israel prostituted themselves by worshipping it there, and it became a snare to Gideon and his family.

Gideon's death

28 Thus Midian was subdued before the Israelites and did not raise its head again. During Gideon's lifetime, the land had peace for forty years.

29 Jerub-Baal son of Joash went back home to live. 30 He had seventy sons of his own, for he had many wives. 31 His concubine, who lived in Shechem, also bore him a son, whom he named Abimelek. 32 Gideon son of Joash died at a good old age and was buried in the tomb of his father Joash in Ophrah of the Abiezrites.

33 No sooner had Gideon died than the Israelites again prostituted themselves to the Baals. They set up Baal-Berith as their god 34 and did not remember the LORD their God, who had rescued them from the hands of all their enemies on every side. 35 They also failed to show any

---

a 8 Hebrew *Penuel*, a variant of *Peniel*; also in verses 9 and 17

b 26 That is, about 20 kilograms

loyalty to the family of Jerub-Baal (that is, Gideon) in spite of all the good things he had done for them.

Abimelek

9 Abimelek son of Jerub-Baal went to his mother's brothers in Shechem and said to them and to all his mother's clan, ² 'Ask all the citizens of Shechem, "Which is better for you: to have all seventy of Jerub-Baal's sons rule over you, or just one man?" Remember, I am your flesh and blood.'

³ When the brothers repeated all this to the citizens of Shechem, they were inclined to follow Abimelek, for they said, 'He is related to us.' ⁴ They gave him seventy shekels*a* of silver from the temple of Baal-Berith, and Abimelek used it to hire reckless scoundrels, who became his followers. ⁵ He went to his father's home in Ophrah and on one stone murdered his seventy brothers, the sons of Jerub-Baal. But Jotham, the youngest son of Jerub-Baal, escaped by hiding. ⁶ Then all the citizens of Shechem and Beth Millo gathered beside the great tree at the pillar in Shechem to crown Abimelek king.

⁷ When Jotham was told about this, he climbed up on the top of Mount Gerizim and shouted to them, 'Listen to me, citizens of Shechem, so that God may listen to you. ⁸ One day the trees went out to anoint a king for themselves. They said to the olive tree, "Be our king."

⁹ 'But the olive tree answered, "Should I give up my oil, by which both gods and humans are honoured, to hold sway over the trees?"

¹⁰ 'Next, the trees said to the fig-tree, "Come and be our king."

¹¹ 'But the fig-tree replied, "Should I give up my fruit, so good and sweet, to hold sway over the trees?"

¹² 'Then the trees said to the vine, "Come and be our king."

¹³ 'But the vine answered, "Should I give up my wine, which cheers both gods and humans, to hold sway over the trees?"

¹⁴ 'Finally all the trees said to the thorn-bush, "Come and be our king."

¹⁵ 'The thorn-bush said to the trees, "If you really want to anoint me king over you, come and take refuge in my shade; but if not, then let fire come out of the thorn-bush and consume the cedars of Lebanon!"

¹⁶ 'Have you acted honourably and in good faith by making Abimelek king? Have you been fair to Jerub-Baal and his family? Have you treated him as he deserves? ¹⁷ Remember that my father fought for you and risked his life to rescue you from the hand of Midian. ¹⁸ But today you have revolted against my father's family. You have murdered his seventy sons on a single stone and have made Abimelek, the son of his female slave, king over the citizens of Shechem because he is related to you. ¹⁹ So have you acted honourably and in good faith towards Jerub-Baal and his family today? If you have, may Abimelek be your joy, and may you be his, too! ²⁰ But if you have not, let fire come out from Abimelek and consume you, the citizens of Shechem and Beth Millo, and let fire come out from you, the citizens of Shechem and Beth Millo, and consume Abimelek!'

²¹ Then Jotham fled, escaping to Beer, and he lived there because he was afraid of his brother Abimelek.

²² After Abimelek had governed Israel for three years, ²³ God stirred up animosity between Abimelek and the citizens of Shechem so that they acted treacherously against Abimelek. ²⁴ God did this in order that the crime against Jerub-Baal's seventy sons, the shedding of their blood, might be avenged on their brother Abimelek and on the citizens of Shechem, who had helped him murder his brothers. ²⁵ In opposition to him these citizens of Shechem set men on the hilltops to ambush and rob everyone who passed by, and this was reported to Abimelek.

²⁶ Now Gaal son of Ebed moved with his clan into Shechem, and its citizens put their confidence in him. ²⁷ After they had gone out into the fields and gathered the grapes and trodden them, they held a festival in the temple of their god.

---

a 4 That is, about 800 grams

While they were eating and drinking, they cursed Abimelek. 28 Then Gaal son of Ebed said, 'Who is Abimelek, and why should we Shechemites be subject to him? Isn't he Jerub-Baal's son, and isn't Zebul his deputy? Serve the family of Hamor, Shechem's father! Why should we serve Abimelek? 29 If only this people were under my command! Then I would get rid of him. I would say to Abimelek, "Call out your whole army!" ' b

30 When Zebul the governor of the city heard what Gaal son of Ebed said, he was very angry. 31 Under cover he sent messengers to Abimelek, saying, 'Gaal son of Ebed and his clan have come to Shechem and are stirring up the city against you. 32 Now then, during the night you and your men should come and lie in wait in the fields. 33 In the morning at sunrise, advance against the city. When Gaal and his men come out against you, seize the opportunity to attack them.'

34 So Abimelek and all his troops set out by night and took up concealed positions near Shechem in four companies. 35 Now Gaal son of Ebed had gone out and was standing at the entrance of the city gate just as Abimelek and his troops came out from their hiding-place.

36 When Gaal saw them, he said to Zebul, 'Look, people are coming down from the tops of the mountains!'

Zebul replied, 'You mistake the shadows of the mountains for men.'

37 But Gaal spoke up again: 'Look, people are coming down from the central hill, c and a company is coming from the direction of the diviners' tree.'

38 Then Zebul said to him, 'Where is your big talk now, you who said, "Who is Abimelek that we should be subject to him?" Aren't these the men you ridiculed? Go out and fight them!'

39 So Gaal led out d the citizens of Shechem and fought Abimelek. 40 Abimelek chased him all the way to the entrance of the gate, and many were killed as they fled. 41 Then Abimelek stayed in Arumah, and Zebul drove Gaal and his clan out of Shechem.

42 The next day the people of Shechem went out to the fields, and this was reported to Abimelek. 43 So he took his men, divided them into three companies and set an ambush in the fields. When he saw the people coming out of the city, he rose to attack them. 44 Abimelek and the companies with him rushed forward to a position at the entrance of the city gate. Then two companies attacked those in the fields and struck them down. 45 All that day Abimelek pressed his attack against the city until he had captured it and killed its people. Then he destroyed the city and scattered salt over it.

46 On hearing this, the citizens in the tower of Shechem went into the stronghold of the temple of El-Berith. 47 When Abimelek heard that they had assembled there, 48 he and all his men went up Mount Zalmon. He took an axe and cut off some branches, which he lifted to his shoulders. He ordered the men with him, 'Quick! Do what you have seen me do!' 49 So all the men cut branches and followed Abimelek. They piled them against the stronghold and set it on fire with the people still inside. So all the people in the tower of Shechem, about a thousand men and women, also died.

50 Next Abimelek went to Thebez and besieged it and captured it. 51 Inside the city, however, was a strong tower, to which all the men and women – all the people of the city – had fled. They had locked themselves in and climbed up on the tower roof. 52 Abimelek went to the tower and attacked it. But as he approached the entrance to the tower to set it on fire, 53 a woman dropped an upper millstone on his head and cracked his skull.

54 Hurriedly he called to his armour-bearer, 'Draw your sword and kill me, so that they can't say, "A woman killed him."' So his servant ran him through, and he died. 55 When the Israelites saw that Abimelek was dead, they went home.

56 Thus God repaid the wickedness that

---

b 29 Septuagint; Hebrew *him. Then he said to Abimelek, 'call out your whole army!'*
c 37 The Hebrew for this phrase means *the navel of the earth.*
d 39 Or *Gaal went out in the sight of*

Abimelek had done to his father by murdering his seventy brothers. 57 God also made the people of Shechem pay for all their wickedness. The curse of Jotham son of Jerub-Baal came on them.

Tola

10 After the time of Abimelek, a man of Issachar named Tola son of Puah, the son of Dodo, rose to save Israel. He lived in Shamir, in the hill country of Ephraim. 2 He led*a* Israel for twenty-three years; then he died, and was buried in Shamir.

Jair

3 He was followed by Jair of Gilead, who led Israel for twenty-two years. 4 He had thirty sons, who rode thirty donkeys. They controlled thirty towns in Gilead, which to this day are called Havvoth Jair.*b* 5 When Jair died, he was buried in Kamon.

Jephthah

6 Again the Israelites did evil in the eyes of the LORD. They served the Baals and the Ashtoreths, and the gods of Aram, the gods of Sidon, the gods of Moab, the gods of the Ammonites and the gods of the Philistines. And because the Israelites forsook the LORD and no longer served him, 7 he became angry with them. He sold them into the hands of the Philistines and the Ammonites, 8 who that year shattered and crushed them. For eighteen years they oppressed all the Israelites on the east side of the Jordan in Gilead, the land of the Amorites. 9 The Ammonites also crossed the Jordan to fight against Judah, Benjamin and Ephraim; Israel was in great distress. 10 Then the Israelites cried out to the LORD, 'We have sinned against you, forsaking our God and serving the Baals.'

11 The LORD replied, 'When the Egyptians, the Amorites, the Ammonites, the Philistines, 12 the Sidonians, the Amalekites and the Maonites*c* oppressed you and you cried to me for help, did I not save

you from their hands? 13 But you have forsaken me and served other gods, so I will no longer save you. 14 Go and cry out to the gods you have chosen. Let them save you when you are in trouble!'

15 But the Israelites said to the LORD, 'We have sinned. Do with us whatever you think best, but please rescue us now.' 16 Then they got rid of the foreign gods among them and served the LORD. And he could bear Israel's misery no longer.

17 When the Ammonites were called to arms and camped in Gilead, the Israelites assembled and camped at Mizpah. 18 The leaders of the people of Gilead said to each other, 'Whoever will take the lead in attacking the Ammonites will be head over all who live in Gilead.'

11 Jephthah the Gileadite was a mighty warrior. His father was Gilead; his mother was a prostitute. 2 Gilead's wife also bore him sons, and when they were grown up, they drove Jephthah away. 'You are not going to get any inheritance in our family,' they said, 'because you are the son of another woman.' 3 So Jephthah fled from his brothers and settled in the land of Tob, where a gang of scoundrels gathered around him and followed him.

4 Some time later, when the Ammonites were fighting against Israel, 5 the elders of Gilead went to get Jephthah from the land of Tob. 6 'Come,' they said, 'be our commander, so we can fight the Ammonites.'

7 Jephthah said to them, 'Didn't you hate me and drive me from my father's house? Why do you come to me now, when you're in trouble?'

8 The elders of Gilead said to him, 'Nevertheless, we are turning to you now; come with us to fight the Ammonites, and you will be head over all of us who live in Gilead.'

9 Jephthah answered, 'Suppose you take me back to fight the Ammonites and the LORD gives them to me – will I really be your head?'

10 The elders of Gilead replied, 'The LORD is our witness; we will certainly do as you say.' 11 So Jephthah went with the elders of Gilead, and the people made him head and commander over them. And he

---

a 2 Traditionally *judged*; also in verse 3
b 4 Or *called the settlements of Jair*
c 12 Hebrew; some Septuagint manuscripts *Midianites*

repeated all his words before the LORD in Mizpah.

12 Then Jephthah sent messengers to the Ammonite king with the question: 'What do you have against me that you have attacked my country?'

13 The king of the Ammonites answered Jephthah's messengers, 'When Israel came up out of Egypt, they took away my land from the Arnon to the Jabbok, all the way to the Jordan. Now give it back peaceably.'

14 Jephthah sent back messengers to the Ammonite king, 15 saying:

'This is what Jephthah says: Israel did not take the land of Moab or the land of the Ammonites. 16 But when they came up out of Egypt, Israel went through the wilderness to the Red Sea*a* and on to Kadesh. 17 Then Israel sent messengers to the king of Edom, saying, "Give us permission to go through your country," but the king of Edom would not listen. They sent also to the king of Moab, and he refused. So Israel stayed at Kadesh.

18 'Next they travelled through the wilderness, skirted the lands of Edom and Moab, passed along the eastern side of the country of Moab, and camped on the other side of the Arnon. They did not enter the territory of Moab, for the Arnon was its border.

19 'Then Israel sent messengers to Sihon king of the Amorites, who ruled in Heshbon, and said to him, "Let us pass through your country to our own place." 20 Sihon, however, did not trust Israel*b* to pass through his territory. He mustered all his troops and encamped at Jahaz and fought with Israel.

21 'Then the LORD, the God of Israel, gave Sihon and his whole army into Israel's hands, and they defeated them. Israel took over all the land of the Amorites who lived in that country, 22 capturing all of it from the Arnon to the Jabbok and from the desert to the Jordan.

23 'Now since the LORD, the God of Israel, has driven the Amorites out before his people Israel, what right have you to take it over? 24 Will you not take what your god Chemosh gives you? Likewise, whatever the LORD our God has given us, we will possess. 25 Are you any better than Balak son of Zippor, king of Moab? Did he ever quarrel with Israel or fight with them? 26 For three hundred years Israel occupied Heshbon, Aroer, the surrounding settlements and all the towns along the Arnon. Why didn't you retake them during that time? 27 I have not wronged you, but you are doing me wrong by waging war against me. Let the LORD, the Judge, decide the dispute this day between the Israelites and the Ammonites.'

28 The king of Ammon, however, paid no attention to the message Jephthah sent him.

29 Then the Spirit of the LORD came on Jephthah. He crossed Gilead and Manasseh, passed through Mizpah of Gilead, and from there he advanced against the Ammonites. 30 And Jephthah made a vow to the LORD: 'If you give the Ammonites into my hands, 31 whatever comes out of the door of my house to meet me when I return in triumph from the Ammonites will be the LORD's, and I will sacrifice it as a burnt offering.'

32 Then Jephthah went over to fight the Ammonites, and the LORD gave them into his hands. 33 He devastated twenty towns from Aroer to the vicinity of Minnith, as far as Abel Keramim. Thus Israel subdued Ammon.

34 When Jephthah returned to his home in Mizpah, who should come out to meet him but his daughter, dancing to the sound of tambourines! She was an only child. Except for her he had neither son nor daughter. 35 When he saw her, he tore his clothes and cried, 'Oh no, my

---

a 16 Or *the Sea of Reeds*
b 20 Or *however, would not make an agreement for Israel*

daughter! You have brought me down and I am devastated. I have made a vow to the LORD that I cannot break.'

36 'My father,' she replied, 'you have given your word to the LORD. Do to me just as you promised, now that the LORD has avenged you of your enemies, the Ammonites. 37 But grant me this one request,' she said. 'Give me two months to roam the hills and weep with my friends, because I will never marry.'

38 'You may go,' he said. And he let her go for two months. She and her friends went into the hills and wept because she would never marry. 39 After the two months, she returned to her father, and he did to her as he had vowed. And she was a virgin. From this comes the Israelite tradition 40 that each year the young women of Israel go out for four days to commemorate the daughter of Jephthah the Gileadite.

Jephthah and Ephraim

12 The Ephraimite forces were called out, and they crossed over to Zaphon. They said to Jephthah, 'Why did you go to fight the Ammonites without calling us to go with you? We're going to burn down your house over your head.'

2 Jephthah answered, 'I and my people were engaged in a great struggle with the Ammonites, and although I called, you didn't save me out of their hands. 3 When I saw that you wouldn't help, I took my life in my hands and crossed over to fight the Ammonites, and the LORD gave me the victory over them. Now why have you come up today to fight me?'

4 Jephthah then called together the men of Gilead and fought against Ephraim. The Gileadites struck them down because the Ephraimites had said, 'You Gileadites are renegades from Ephraim and Manasseh.' 5 The Gileadites captured the fords of the Jordan leading to Ephraim, and whenever a survivor of Ephraim said, 'Let me cross over,' the men of Gilead asked him, 'Are you an Ephraimite?' If he replied, 'No,' 6 they said, 'All right, say "Shibboleth".' If he said, 'Sibboleth', because he could not pronounce the word correctly, they seized him and killed him at the fords of

the Jordan. Forty-two thousand Ephraimites were killed at that time.

7 Jephthah led[a] Israel for six years. Then Jephthah the Gileadite died and was buried in a town in Gilead.

Ibzan, Elon and Abdon

8 After him, Ibzan of Bethlehem led Israel. 9 He had thirty sons and thirty daughters. He gave his daughters away in marriage to those outside his clan, and for his sons he brought in thirty young women as wives from outside his clan. Ibzan led Israel for seven years. 10 Then Ibzan died and was buried in Bethlehem.

11 After him, Elon the Zebulunite led Israel for ten years. 12 Then Elon died and was buried in Aijalon in the land of Zebulun.

13 After him, Abdon son of Hillel, from Pirathon, led Israel. 14 He had forty sons and thirty grandsons, who rode on seventy donkeys. He led Israel for eight years. 15 Then Abdon son of Hillel died and was buried at Pirathon in Ephraim, in the hill country of the Amalekites.

The birth of Samson

13 Again the Israelites did evil in the eyes of the LORD, so the LORD delivered them into the hands of the Philistines for forty years.

2 A certain man of Zorah, named Manoah, from the clan of the Danites, had a wife who was childless, unable to give birth. 3 The angel of the LORD appeared to her and said, 'You are barren and childless, but you are going to become pregnant and give birth to a son. 4 Now see to it that you drink no wine or other fermented drink and that you do not eat anything unclean. 5 You will become pregnant and have a son whose head is never to be touched by a razor because the boy is to be a Nazirite, dedicated to God from the womb. He will take the lead in delivering Israel from the hands of the Philistines.'

6 Then the woman went to her husband and told him, 'A man of God came to me. He looked like an angel of God, very awesome. I didn't ask him where he came

_____

a 7 Traditionally *judged*; also in verses 8-14

from, and he didn't tell me his name. 7 But he said to me, "You will become pregnant and have a son. Now then, drink no wine or other fermented drink and do not eat anything unclean, because the boy will be a Nazirite of God from the womb until the day of his death." '

8 Then Manoah prayed to the LORD: 'Pardon your servant, Lord. I beg you to let the man of God you sent to us come again to teach us how to bring up the boy who is to be born.'

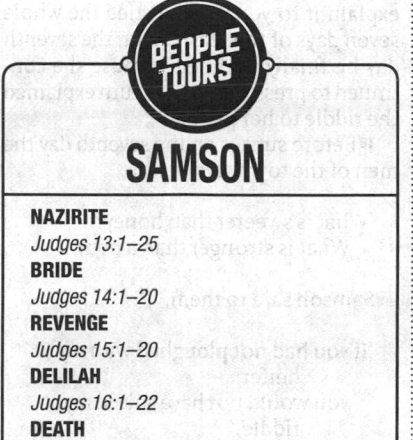

SAMSON

NAZIRITE
Judges 13:1–25
BRIDE
Judges 14:1–20
REVENGE
Judges 15:1–20
DELILAH
Judges 16:1–22
DEATH
Judges 16:23

9 God heard Manoah, and the angel of God came again to the woman while she was out in the field; but her husband Manoah was not with her. 10 The woman hurried to tell her husband, 'He's here! The man who appeared to me the other day!'

11 Manoah got up and followed his wife. When he came to the man, he said, 'Are you the man who talked to my wife?'

'I am,' he said.

12 So Manoah asked him, 'When your words are fulfilled, what is to be the rule that governs the boy's life and work?'

13 The angel of the LORD answered, 'Your wife must do all that I have told her. 14 She must not eat anything that comes from the grapevine, nor drink any wine or other fermented drink nor eat anything

unclean. She must do everything I have commanded her.'

15 Manoah said to the angel of the LORD, 'We would like you to stay until we prepare a young goat for you.'

16 The angel of the LORD replied, 'Even though you detain me, I will not eat any of your food. But if you prepare a burnt offering, offer it to the LORD.' (Manoah did not realise that it was the angel of the LORD.)

17 Then Manoah enquired of the angel of the LORD, 'What is your name, so that we may honour you when your word comes true?'

18 He replied, 'Why do you ask my name? It is beyond understanding.ᵃ' 19 Then Manoah took a young goat, together with the grain offering, and sacrificed it on a rock to the LORD. And the LORD did an amazing thing while Manoah and his wife watched: 20 as the flame blazed up from the altar towards heaven, the angel of the LORD ascended in the flame. Seeing this, Manoah and his wife fell with their faces to the ground. 21 When the angel of the LORD did not show himself again to Manoah and his wife, Manoah realised that it was the angel of the LORD.

22 'We are doomed to die!' he said to his wife. 'We have seen God!'

23 But his wife answered, 'If the LORD had meant to kill us, he would not have accepted a burnt offering and grain offering from our hands, nor shown us all these things or now told us this.'

24 The woman gave birth to a boy and named him Samson. He grew and the LORD blessed him, 25 and the Spirit of the LORD began to stir him while he was in Mahaneh Dan, between Zorah and Eshtaol.

Samson's marriage

14 Samson went down to Timnah and saw there a young Philistine woman. 2 When he returned, he said to his father and mother, 'I have seen a Philistine woman in Timnah; now get her for me as my wife.'

---

a 18 Or is wonderful

³His father and mother replied, 'Isn't there an acceptable woman among your relatives or among all our people? Must you go to the uncircumcised Philistines to get a wife?'

But Samson said to his father, 'Get her for me. She's the right one for me.' ⁴(His parents did not know that this was from the LORD, who was seeking an occasion to confront the Philistines; for at that time they were ruling over Israel.)

⁵Samson went down to Timnah together with his father and mother. As they approached the vineyards of Timnah, suddenly a young lion came roaring towards him. ⁶The Spirit of the LORD came powerfully upon him so that he tore the lion apart with his bare hands as he might have torn a young goat. But he told neither his father nor his mother what he had done. ⁷Then he went down and talked with the woman, and he liked her.

⁸Some time later, when he went back to marry her, he turned aside to look at the lion's carcass, and in it he saw a swarm of bees and some honey. ⁹He scooped out the honey with his hands and ate as he went along. When he rejoined his parents, he gave them some, and they too ate it. But he did not tell them that he had taken the honey from the lion's carcass.

¹⁰Now his father went down to see the woman. And there Samson held a feast, as was customary for young men. ¹¹When the people saw him, they chose thirty men to be his companions.

¹²'Let me tell you a riddle,' Samson said to them. 'If you can give me the answer within the seven days of the feast, I will give you thirty linen garments and thirty sets of clothes. ¹³If you can't tell me the answer, you must give me thirty linen garments and thirty sets of clothes.'

'Tell us your riddle,' they said. 'Let's hear it.'

¹⁴He replied,

'Out of the eater, something to eat;
    out of the strong, something sweet.'

For three days they could not give the answer.

¹⁵On the fourth[a] day, they said to Samson's wife, 'Coax your husband into explaining the riddle for us, or we will burn you and your father's household to death. Did you invite us here to steal our property?'

¹⁶Then Samson's wife threw herself on him, sobbing, 'You hate me! You don't really love me. You've given my people a riddle, but you haven't told me the answer.'

'I haven't even explained it to my father or mother,' he replied, 'so why should I explain it to you?' ¹⁷She cried the whole seven days of the feast. So on the seventh day he finally told her, because she continued to press him. She in turn explained the riddle to her people.

¹⁸Before sunset on the seventh day the men of the town said to him,

'What is sweeter than honey?
    What is stronger than a lion?'

Samson said to them,

'If you had not ploughed with my
        heifer,
    you would not have solved my
        riddle.'

¹⁹Then the Spirit of the LORD came powerfully upon him. He went down to Ashkelon, struck down thirty of their men, stripped them of everything and gave their clothes to those who had explained the riddle. Burning with anger, he returned to his father's home. ²⁰And Samson's wife was given to one of his companions who had attended him at the feast.

Samson's vengeance on the Philistines

15 Later on, at the time of wheat harvest, Samson took a young goat and went to visit his wife. He said, 'I'm going to my wife's room.' But her father would not let him go in.

²'I was so sure you hated her,' he said,

---

a 15 Some Septuagint manuscripts and Syriac; Hebrew *seventh* 'that I gave her to your companion. Isn't her younger sister more attractive? Take her instead.'

3 Samson said to them, 'This time I have a right to get even with the Philistines; I will really harm them.' 4 So he went out and caught three hundred foxes and tied them tail to tail in pairs. He then fastened a torch to every pair of tails, 5 lit the torches and let the foxes loose in the standing corn of the Philistines. He burned up the shocks and standing corn, together with the vineyards and olive groves.

6 When the Philistines asked, 'Who did this?' they were told, 'Samson, the Timnite's son-in-law, because his wife was given to his companion.'

So the Philistines went up and burned her and her father to death. 7 Samson said to them, 'Since you've acted like this, I swear that I won't stop until I get my revenge on you.' 8 He attacked them viciously and slaughtered many of them. Then he went down and stayed in a cave in the rock of Etam.

9 The Philistines went up and camped in Judah, spreading out near Lehi. 10 The people of Judah asked, 'Why have you come to fight us?'

'We have come to take Samson prisoner,' they answered, 'to do to him as he did to us.'

11 Then three thousand men from Judah went down to the cave in the rock of Etam and said to Samson, 'Don't you realise that the Philistines are rulers over us? What have you done to us?'

He answered, 'I merely did to them what they did to me.'

12 They said to him, 'We've come to tie you up and hand you over to the Philistines.'

Samson said, 'Swear to me that you won't kill me yourselves.'

13 'Agreed,' they answered. 'We will only tie you up and hand you over to them. We will not kill you.' So they bound him with two new ropes and led him up from the rock. 14 As he approached Lehi, the Philistines came towards him shouting. The Spirit of the Lord came powerfully upon him. The ropes on his arms became like

charred flax, and the bindings dropped from his hands. 15 Finding a fresh jawbone of a donkey, he grabbed it and struck down a thousand men.

16 Then Samson said,

'With a donkey's jawbone
  I have made donkeys of them.*a*
With a donkey's jawbone
  I have killed a thousand men.'

17 When he finished speaking, he threw away the jawbone; and the place was called Ramath Lehi.*b*

18 Because he was very thirsty, he cried out to the Lord, 'You have given your servant this great victory. Must I now die of thirst and fall into the hands of the uncircumcised?' 19 Then God opened up the hollow place in Lehi, and water came out of it. When Samson drank, his strength returned and he revived. So the spring was called En Hakkore,*c* and it is still there in Lehi.

20 Samson led*d* Israel for twenty years in the days of the Philistines.

Samson and Delilah

16 One day Samson went to Gaza, where he saw a prostitute. He went in to spend the night with her. 2 The people of Gaza were told, 'Samson is here!' So they surrounded the place and lay in wait for him all night at the city gate. They made no move during the night, saying, 'At dawn we'll kill him.'

3 But Samson lay there only until the middle of the night. Then he got up and took hold of the doors of the city gate, together with the two posts, and tore them loose, bar and all. He lifted them to his shoulders and carried them to the top of the hill that faces Hebron.

4 Some time later, he fell in love with a woman in the Valley of Sorek whose name was Delilah. 5 The rulers of the Philistines went to her and said, 'See if you can lure

------

a 16 Or *made a heap or two*; the Hebrew for *donkey* sounds like the Hebrew for *heap*.
b 17 *Ramath Lehi* means *jawbone hill*.
c 19 *En Hakkore* means *caller's spring*.
d 20 Traditionally *judged*

him into showing you the secret of his great strength and how we can overpower him so that we may tie him up and subdue him. Each one of us will give you eleven hundred shekels*a* of silver.'

6 So Delilah said to Samson, 'Tell me the secret of your great strength and how you can be tied up and subdued.'

7 Samson answered her, 'If anyone ties me with seven fresh bow-strings that have not been dried, I'll become as weak as any other man.'

8 Then the rulers of the Philistines brought her seven fresh bow-strings that had not been dried, and she tied him with them. 9 With men hidden in the room, she called to him, 'Samson, the Philistines are upon you!' But he snapped the bow-strings as easily as a piece of string snaps when it comes close to a flame. So the secret of his strength was not discovered.

10 Then Delilah said to Samson, 'You have made a fool of me; you lied to me. Come now, tell me how you can be tied.'

11 He said, 'If anyone ties me securely with new ropes that have never been used, I'll become as weak as any other man.'

12 So Delilah took new ropes and tied him with them. Then, with men hidden in the room, she called to him, 'Samson, the Philistines are upon you!' But he snapped the ropes off his arms as if they were threads.

13 Delilah then said to Samson, 'All this time you have been making a fool of me and lying to me. Tell me how you can be tied.'

He replied, 'If you weave the seven braids of my head into the fabric on the loom and tighten it with the pin, I'll become as weak as any other man.' So while he was sleeping, Delilah took the seven braids of his head, wove them into the fabric 14 and*b* tightened it with the pin.

Again she called to him, 'Samson, the Philistines are upon you!' He awoke from his sleep and pulled up the pin and the loom, with the fabric.

15 Then she said to him, 'How can you say, "I love you," when you won't confide in me? This is the third time you have made a fool of me and haven't told me the secret of your great strength.' 16 With such nagging she prodded him day after day until he was sick to death of it.

17 So he told her everything. 'No razor has ever been used on my head,' he said, 'because I have been a Nazirite dedicated to God from my mother's womb. If my head were shaved, my strength would leave me, and I would become as weak as any other man.'

18 When Delilah saw that he had told her everything, she sent word to the rulers of the Philistines, 'Come back once more; he has told me everything.' So the rulers of the Philistines returned with the silver in their hands. 19 After putting him to sleep on her lap, she called for someone to shave off the seven braids of his hair, and so began to subdue him.*c* And his strength left him.

20 Then she called, 'Samson, the Philistines are upon you!'

He awoke from his sleep and thought, 'I'll go out as before and shake myself free.' But he did not know that the LORD had left him.

21 Then the Philistines seized him, gouged out his eyes and took him down to Gaza. Binding him with bronze shackles, they set him to grinding corn in the prison. 22 But the hair on his head began to grow again after it had been shaved.

The death of Samson

23 Now the rulers of the Philistines assembled to offer a great sacrifice to Dagon their god and to celebrate, saying, 'Our god has delivered Samson, our enemy, into our hands.'

24 When the people saw him, they praised their god, saying,

'Our god has delivered our enemy
　　into our hands,

---

a 5　That is, about 13 kilograms
b 13,14　Some Septuagint manuscripts; Hebrew replied, 'I can if you weave the seven braids of my head into the fabric on the loom.' *14* So she

c 19　Hebrew; some Septuagint manuscripts *and he began to weaken*

the one who laid waste our land
and multiplied our slain.'

25 While they were in high spirits, they shouted, 'Bring out Samson to entertain us.' So they called Samson out of the prison, and he performed for them.
When they stood him among the pillars, 26 Samson said to the servant who held his hand, 'Put me where I can feel the pillars that support the temple, so that I may lean against them.' 27 Now the temple was crowded with men and women; all the rulers of the Philistines were there, and on the roof were about three thousand men and women watching Samson perform. 28 Then Samson prayed to the LORD, 'Sovereign LORD, remember me.

SACRIFICE 7

Samson's last act

The best part of Samson's life was his last act. In fact, in Hebrews it lists Samson and this particular act in Judges 16 as the thing that got Samson into the hall of faith for all time! What did Samson do that was so impressive?

Samson sacrificed his life to destroy the enemy of God's people.

Up until this time, Samson had done a lot to try to destroy the Philistines and keep the Israelites free from their control. Eventually, though, Samson's life became crippled by compromise – particularly the kind that happens with a woman. Samson was soon captured by the enemy, stripped of his supernatural strength and turned into a laughing stock that entertained the Philistines as a party trick. It was embarrassing.

It may be helpful to know that Samson was a Nazirite. This was a particular sect within the Israelites who were super-devout and lived a sacrificial life all the time. This is what gave Samson his power. When he traded in a sacrificial life for comfort and sex, he lost his spiritual impact and it had a deeply horrible effect on his life and on the rest of the Israelites. How sad is that?

After Samson's power was gone, he was tied up and brought out to a Philistine festival so the enemies of God could mock him and rub in their victory. It was here that Samson prayed a powerful prayer – he asked God for power one last time – and then he brought the entire structure of the festival down so that everyone was killed, including himself. Samson finally sacrificed his whole life for the purposes of God and the defeat of the enemy. It was that one act that made Samson a man of faith.

I wonder if God might be calling you to destroy the works of the enemy by living a sacrificial life – by living a life that is wholly devoted to God.

Danielle Strickland

 Leviticus 9:7   1 Samuel 15:22 ▶

Please, God, strengthen me just once more, and let me with one blow get revenge on the Philistines for my two eyes.' ²⁹Then Samson reached towards the two central pillars on which the temple stood. Bracing himself against them, his right hand on the one and his left hand on the other, ³⁰Samson said, 'Let me die with the Philistines!' Then he pushed with all his might, and down came the temple on the rulers and all the people in it. Thus he killed many more when he died than while he lived.

³¹Then his brothers and his father's whole family went down to get him. They brought him back and buried him between Zorah and Eshtaol in the tomb of Manoah his father. He had led*d* Israel for twenty years.

Micah's idols

17 Now a man named Micah from the hill country of Ephraim ²said to his mother, 'The eleven hundred shekels*a* of silver that were taken from you and about which I heard you utter a curse – I have that silver with me; I took it.'

Then his mother said, 'The LORD bless you, my son!'

³When he returned the eleven hundred shekels of silver to his mother, she said, 'I solemnly consecrate my silver to the LORD for my son to make an image overlaid with silver. I will give it back to you.'

⁴So after he returned the silver to his mother, she took two hundred shekels*b* of silver and gave them to a silversmith, who used them to make the idol. And it was put in Micah's house.

⁵Now this man Micah had a shrine, and he made an ephod and some household gods and installed one of his sons as his priest. ⁶In those days Israel had no king; everyone did as they saw fit.

⁷A young Levite from Bethlehem in Judah, who had been living within the clan of Judah, ⁸left that town in search of some other place to stay. On his way*c* he came to Micah's house in the hill country of Ephraim.

⁹Micah asked him, 'Where are you from?'

'I'm a Levite from Bethlehem in Judah,' he said, 'and I'm looking for a place to stay.'

¹⁰Then Micah said to him, 'Live with me and be my father and priest, and I'll give you ten shekels*d* of silver a year, your clothes and your food.' ¹¹So the Levite agreed to live with him, and the young man became like one of his sons to him. ¹²Then Micah installed the Levite, and the young man became his priest and lived in his house. ¹³And Micah said, 'Now I know that the LORD will be good to me, since this Levite has become my priest.'

The Danites settle in Laish

18 In those days Israel had no king. And in those days the tribe of the Danites was seeking a place of their own where they might settle, because they had not yet come into an inheritance among the tribes of Israel. ²So the Danites sent five of their leading men from Zorah and Eshtaol to spy out the land and explore it. These men represented all the Danites. They told them, 'Go, explore the land.'

So they entered the hill country of Ephraim and came to the house of Micah, where they spent the night. ³When they were near Micah's house, they recognised the voice of the young Levite; so they turned in there and asked him, 'Who brought you here? What are you doing in this place? Why are you here?'

⁴He told them what Micah had done for him, and said, 'He has hired me and I am his priest.'

⁵Then they said to him, 'Please enquire of God to learn whether our journey will be successful.'

⁶The priest answered them, 'Go in peace. Your journey has the LORD's approval.'

⁷So the five men left and came to Laish,

---

d 31 Traditionally *judged*
a 2 That is, about 13 kilograms
b 4 That is, about 2.3 kilograms

c 8 Or *To carry on his profession*
d 10 That is, about 115 grams

where they saw that the people were living in safety, like the Sidonians, at peace and secure. And since their land lacked nothing, they were prosperous.*a* Also, they lived a long way from the Sidonians and had no relationship with anyone else.*b*

8When they returned to Zorah and Eshtaol, their fellow Danites asked them, 'How did you find things?'

9They answered, 'Come on, let's attack them! We have seen the land, and it is very good. Aren't you going to do something? Don't hesitate to go there and take it over. 10When you get there, you will find an unsuspecting people and a spacious land that God has put into your hands, a land that lacks nothing whatever.'

11Then six hundred men of the Danites, armed for battle, set out from Zorah and Eshtaol. 12On their way they set up camp near Kiriath Jearim in Judah. This is why the place west of Kiriath Jearim is called Mahaneh Dan*c* to this day. 13From there they went on to the hill country of Ephraim and came to Micah's house.

14Then the five men who had spied out the land of Laish said to their fellow Danites, 'Do you know that one of these houses has an ephod, some household gods and an image overlaid with silver? Now you know what to do.' 15So they turned in there and went to the house of the young Levite at Micah's place and greeted him. 16The six hundred Danites, armed for battle, stood at the entrance of the gate. 17The five men who had spied out the land went inside and took the idol, the ephod and the household gods while the priest and the six hundred armed men stood at the entrance of the gate.

18When the five men went into Micah's house and took the idol, the ephod and the household gods, the priest said to them, 'What are you doing?'

19They answered him, 'Be quiet! Don't say a word. Come with us, and be our

father and priest. Isn't it better that you serve a tribe and clan in Israel as priest rather than just one man's household?' 20The priest was very pleased. He took the ephod, the household gods and the idol and went along with the people. 21Putting their little children, their livestock and their possessions in front of them, they turned away and left.

22When they had gone some distance from Micah's house, the men who lived near Micah were called together and overtook the Danites. 23As they shouted after them, the Danites turned and said to Micah, 'What's the matter with you that you called out your men to fight?'

24He replied, 'You took the gods I made, and my priest, and went away. What else do I have? How can you ask, "What's the matter with you?"'

25The Danites answered, 'Don't argue with us, or some of the men may get angry and attack you, and you and your family will lose your lives.' 26So the Danites went their way, and Micah, seeing that they were too strong for him, turned round and went back home.

27Then they took what Micah had made, and his priest, and went on to Laish, against a people at peace and secure. They attacked them with the sword and burned down their city. 28There was no one to rescue them because they lived a long way from Sidon and had no relationship with anyone else. The city was in a valley near Beth Rehob.

The Danites rebuilt the city and settled there. 29They named it Dan after their ancestor Dan, who was born to Israel – though the city used to be called Laish. 30There the Danites set up for themselves the idol, and Jonathan son of Gershom, the son of Moses,*d* and his sons were priests for the tribe of Dan until the time of the captivity of the land. 31They continued to use the idol Micah had made, all the time the house of God was in Shiloh.

---

*a*7 The meaning of the Hebrew for this clause is uncertain.
*b*7 Hebrew; some Septuagint manuscripts *with the Arameans*
*c*12 *Mahaneh Dan* means *Dan's camp*.

*d*30 An ancient Hebrew scribal tradition, some Septuagint manuscripts and Vulgate; Masoretic Text *Manasseh*

A Levite and his concubine

19 In those days Israel had no king. Now a Levite who lived in a remote area in the hill country of Ephraim took a concubine from Bethlehem in Judah. ²But she was unfaithful to him. She left him and went back to her parents' home in Bethlehem, Judah. After she had been there for four months, ³her husband went to her to persuade her to return. He had with him his servant and two donkeys. She took him into her parents' home, and when her father saw him, he gladly welcomed him. ⁴His father-in-law, the woman's father, prevailed on him to stay; so he remained with him three days, eating and drinking, and sleeping there.

⁵On the fourth day they got up early and he prepared to leave, but the woman's father said to his son-in-law, 'Refresh yourself with something to eat; then you can go.' ⁶So the two of them sat down to eat and drink together. Afterwards the woman's father said, 'Please stay tonight and enjoy yourself.' ⁷And when the man got up to go, his father-in-law persuaded him, so he stayed there that night. ⁸On the morning of the fifth day, when he rose to go, the woman's father said, 'Refresh yourself. Wait till afternoon!' So the two of them ate together.

⁹Then when the man, with his concubine and his servant, got up to leave, his father-in-law, the woman's father, said, 'Now look, it's almost evening. Spend the night here; the day is nearly over. Stay and enjoy yourself. Early tomorrow morning you can get up and be on your way home.' ¹⁰But, unwilling to stay another night, the man left and went towards Jebus (that is, Jerusalem), with his two saddled donkeys and his concubine.

¹¹When they were near Jebus and the day was almost gone, the servant said to his master, 'Come, let's stop at this city of the Jebusites and spend the night.'

¹²His master replied, 'No. We won't go into any city whose people are not Israelites. We will go on to Gibeah.' ¹³He added, 'Come, let's try to reach Gibeah or Ramah and spend the night in one of those places.' ¹⁴So they went on, and the sun set as they neared Gibeah in Benjamin. ¹⁵There they stopped to spend the night. They went and sat in the city square, but no one took them in for the night.

FAVOURITE VERSES

Romans 11:29

For God's gifts and his call are irrevocable.

This is my favourite verse because it truly describes God's plan for our lives! It doesn't matter what we do and what mistakes we make, as long as we keep following him and receiving what he has for us. He always has that amazing, perfect plan for our lives and it will never change.

Rachel, 18

¹⁶That evening an old man from the hill country of Ephraim, who was living in Gibeah (the inhabitants of the place were Benjaminites), came in from his work in the fields. ¹⁷When he looked and saw the traveller in the city square, the old man asked, 'Where are you going? Where did you come from?'

¹⁸He answered, 'We are on our way from Bethlehem in Judah to a remote area in the hill country of Ephraim where I live. I have been to Bethlehem in Judah and now I am going to the house of the LORD.ᵃ No one has taken me in for the night. ¹⁹We have both straw and fodder for our donkeys and bread and wine for ourselves your servants – me, the woman and the young man with us. We don't need anything.'

²⁰'You are welcome at my house,' the old man said. 'Let me supply whatever

---

a 18 Hebrew, Vulgate, Syriac and Targum; Septuagint *going home* you need. Only don't spend the night in the square.' ²¹So he took him into his house and fed his donkeys. After they had washed their feet, they had something to eat and drink.

²²While they were enjoying themselves, some of the wicked men of the city surrounded the house. Pounding on the door, they shouted to the old man who owned the house, 'Bring out the man who came to your house so we can have sex with him.'

²³The owner of the house went outside and said to them, 'No, my friends, don't be so vile. Since this man is my guest, don't do this outrageous thing. ²⁴Look, here is my virgin daughter, and his concubine. I will bring them out to you now, and you can use them and do to them whatever you wish. But as for this man, don't do such an outrageous thing.'

²⁵But the men would not listen to him. So the man took his concubine and sent her outside to them, and they raped her and abused her throughout the night, and at dawn they let her go. ²⁶At daybreak the woman went back to the house where her master was staying, fell down at the door and lay there until daylight.

²⁷When her master got up in the morning and opened the door of the house and stepped out to continue on his way, there lay his concubine, fallen in the doorway of the house, with her hands on the threshold. ²⁸He said to her, 'Get up; let's go.' But there was no answer. Then the man put her on his donkey and set out for home.

²⁹When he reached home, he took a knife and cut up his concubine, limb by limb, into twelve parts and sent them into all the areas of Israel. ³⁰Everyone who saw it was saying to one another, 'Such a thing has never been seen or done, not since the day the Israelites came up out of Egypt. Just imagine! We must do something! So speak up!'

The Israelites punish the Benjaminites

20 Then all Israel from Dan to Beersheba and from the land of Gilead came together as one and assembled before the LORD in Mizpah. ²The leaders of all the people of the tribes of Israel took their places in the assembly of God's people, four hundred thousand men armed with swords. ³(The Benjaminites heard that the Israelites had gone up to Mizpah.) Then the Israelites said, 'Tell us how this awful thing happened.'

⁴So the Levite, the husband of the murdered woman, said, 'I and my concubine came to Gibeah in Benjamin to spend the night. ⁵During the night the men of Gibeah came after me and surrounded the house, intending to kill me. They raped my concubine, and she died. ⁶I took my concubine, cut her into pieces and sent one piece to each region of Israel's inheritance, because they committed this lewd and outrageous act in Israel. ⁷Now, all you Israelites, speak up and tell me what you have decided to do.'

⁸All the men rose up together as one, saying, 'None of us will go home. No, not one of us will return to his house. ⁹But now this is what we'll do to Gibeah: we'll go up against it in the order decided by casting lots. ¹⁰We'll take ten men out of every hundred from all the tribes of Israel, and a hundred from a thousand, and a thousand from ten thousand, to get provisions for the army. Then, when the army arrives at Gibeah*ᵃ* in Benjamin, it can give them what they deserve for this outrageous act done in Israel.' ¹¹So all the Israelites got together and united as one against the city.

¹²The tribes of Israel sent messengers throughout the tribe of Benjamin, saying, 'What about this awful crime that was committed among you? ¹³Now turn those wicked men of Gibeah over to us so that we may put them to death and purge the evil from Israel.'

But the Benjaminites would not listen to their fellow Israelites. ¹⁴From their towns they came together at Gibeah to fight against the Israelites. ¹⁵At once the Benjaminites mobilised twenty-six thousand swordsmen from their towns, in

---

a 10 One Hebrew manuscript; most Hebrew manuscripts *Geba*, a variant of *Gibeah* addition to seven hundred able young men from those living in Gibeah. ¹⁶Among all these soldiers there were seven hundred select troops who were left-handed, each of whom could sling a stone at a hair and not miss.

¹⁷Israel, apart from Benjamin, mustered four hundred thousand swordsmen, all of them fit for battle.

¹⁸The Israelites went up to Bethel[b] and enquired of God. They said, 'Who of us is to go up first to fight against the Benjamites?'

The LORD replied, 'Judah shall go first.'

¹⁹The next morning the Israelites got up and pitched camp near Gibeah. ²⁰The Israelites went out to fight the Benjamites and took up battle positions against them at Gibeah. ²¹The Benjamites came out of Gibeah and cut down twenty-two thousand Israelites on the battlefield that day. ²²But the Israelites encouraged one another and again took up their positions where they had stationed themselves the first day. ²³The Israelites went up and wept before the LORD until evening, and they enquired of the LORD. They said, 'Shall we go up again to fight against the Benjamites, our fellow Israelites?'

The LORD answered, 'Go up against them.'

²⁴Then the Israelites drew near to Benjamin the second day. ²⁵This time, when the Benjamites came out from Gibeah to oppose them, they cut down another eighteen thousand Israelites, all of them armed with swords.

²⁶Then all the Israelites, the whole army, went up to Bethel, and there they sat weeping before the LORD. They fasted that day until evening and presented burnt offerings and fellowship offerings to the LORD. ²⁷And the Israelites enquired of the LORD. (In those days the ark of the covenant of God was there, ²⁸with Phinehas son of Eleazar, the son of Aaron, ministering before it.) They asked, 'Shall we go up again to fight against the Benjamites, our fellow Israelites, or not?'

The LORD responded, 'Go, for tomorrow I will give them into your hands.'

²⁹Then Israel set an ambush around Gibeah. ³⁰They went up against the Benjamites on the third day and took up positions against Gibeah as they had done before. ³¹The Benjamites came out to meet them and were drawn away from the city. They began to inflict casualties on the Israelites as before, so that about thirty men fell in the open field and on the roads – the one leading to Bethel and the other to Gibeah. ³²While the Benjamites were saying, 'We are defeating them as before,' the Israelites were saying, 'Let's retreat and draw them away from the city to the roads.'

³³All the men of Israel moved from their places and took up positions at Baal Tamar, and the Israelite ambush charged out of its place on the west[c] of Gibeah.[d] ³⁴Then ten thousand of Israel's able young men made a frontal attack on Gibeah. The fighting was so heavy that the Benjamites did not realise how near disaster was. ³⁵The LORD defeated Benjamin before Israel, and on that day the Israelites struck down 25,100 Benjamites, all armed with swords. ³⁶Then the Benjamites saw that they were beaten.

Now the men of Israel had given way before Benjamin, because they relied on the ambush they had set near Gibeah. ³⁷Those who had been in ambush made a sudden dash into Gibeah, spread out and put the whole city to the sword. ³⁸The Israelites had arranged with the ambush that they should send up a great cloud of smoke from the city, ³⁹and then the Israelites would counterattack.

The Benjamites had begun to inflict casualties on the Israelites (about thirty), and they said, 'We are defeating them as in the first battle.' ⁴⁰But when the column of smoke began to rise from the city, the Benjamites turned and saw the whole city going up in smoke. ⁴¹Then the Israelites counterattacked, and the Benjamites

c 33 Some Septuagint manuscripts and Vulgate; the meaning of the Hebrew for this word is uncertain.
d 33 Hebrew Geba, a variant of Gibeah

were terrified, because they realised that disaster had come on them. **42** So they fled before the Israelites in the direction of the wilderness, but they could not escape the battle. And the Israelites who came out of the towns cut them down there. **43** They surrounded the Benjaminites, chased them and easily[e] overran them in the vicinity of Gibeah on the east. **44** Eighteen thousand Benjaminites fell, all of them valiant fighters. **45** As they turned and fled towards the wilderness to the rock of Rimmon, the Israelites cut down five thousand men along the roads. They kept pressing after the Benjaminites as far as Gidom and struck down two thousand more.

46 On that day twenty-five thousand Benjaminite swordsmen fell, all of them valiant fighters. **47** But six hundred of them turned and fled into the wilderness to the rock of Rimmon, where they stayed for four months. **48** The men of Israel went back to Benjamin and put all the towns to the sword, including the animals and everything else they found. All the towns they came across they set on fire.

Wives for the Benjaminites

21 The men of Israel had taken an oath at Mizpah: 'Not one of us will give his daughter in marriage to a Benjaminite.'

2 The people went to Bethel,[a] where they sat before God until evening, raising their voices and weeping bitterly. **3** 'LORD, God of Israel,' they cried, 'why has this happened to Israel? Why should one tribe be missing from Israel today?'

4 Early the next day the people built an altar and presented burnt offerings and fellowship offerings.

5 Then the Israelites asked, 'Who from all the tribes of Israel has failed to assemble before the LORD?' For they had taken a solemn oath that anyone who failed to assemble before the LORD at Mizpah was to be put to death.

6 Now the Israelites grieved for the tribe of Benjamin, their fellow Israelites. 'Today one tribe is cut off from Israel,' they said. **7** 'How can we provide wives for those who are left, since we have taken an oath by the LORD not to give them any of our daughters in marriage?' **8** Then they asked, 'Which one of the tribes of Israel failed to assemble before the LORD at Mizpah?' They discovered that no one from Jabesh Gilead had come to the camp for the assembly. **9** For when they counted the people, they found that none of the people of Jabesh Gilead were there.

10 So the assembly sent twelve thousand fighting men with instructions to go to Jabesh Gilead and put to the sword those living there, including the women and children. **11** 'This is what you are to do,' they said. 'Kill every male and every woman who is not a virgin.' **12** They found among the people living in Jabesh Gilead four hundred young women who had never slept with a man, and they took them to the camp at Shiloh in Canaan.

13 Then the whole assembly sent an offer of peace to the Benjaminites at the rock of Rimmon. **14** So the Benjaminites returned at that time and were given the women of Jabesh Gilead who had been spared. But there were not enough for all of them.

15 The people grieved for Benjamin, because the LORD had made a gap in the tribes of Israel. **16** And the elders of the assembly said, 'With the women of Benjamin destroyed, how shall we provide wives for the men who are left? **17** The Benjaminite survivors must have heirs,' they said, 'so that a tribe of Israel will not be wiped out. **18** We can't give them our daughters as wives, since we Israelites have taken this oath: "Cursed be anyone who gives a wife to a Benjaminite." **19** But look, there is the annual festival of the LORD in Shiloh, which lies north of Bethel, east of the road that goes from Bethel to Shechem, and south of Lebonah.'

20 So they instructed the Benjaminites, saying, 'Go and hide in the vineyards **21** and watch. When the young women of Shiloh come out to join in the dancing, rush from the vineyards and each of you seize one of them to be your wife. Then return

---

e 43 The meaning of the Hebrew for this word is uncertain.
a 2 Or *to the house of God*

to the land of Benjamin. ²²When their fathers or brothers complain to us, we will say to them, "Do us the favour of helping them, because we did not get wives for them during the war. You will not be guilty of breaking your oath because you did not give your daughters to them."'

²³So that is what the Benjaminites did. While the young women were dancing, each man caught one and carried her off to be his wife. Then they returned to their inheritance and rebuilt the towns and settled in them.

²⁴At that time the Israelites left that place and went home to their tribes and clans, each to his own inheritance.

²⁵In those days Israel had no king; everyone did as they saw fit.

RUTH

i

DATE

These events were likely to have taken place between about 1220 and 1050 BC

AUTHOR

Unknown

WHAT'S IT ALL ABOUT?

This is a short History book that tells the story of Ruth. She was not a ruler, a judge or anyone who would have been considered historically significant. In fact she was a Moabite who came to know the God of Israel through marriage. However, her story still has much to teach us. The narrative is simple. It tells of how Ruth's husband died, how she refused to leave her mother-in-law, Naomi, and how God provided for them, transforming and redeeming their lives through a kind relative, Boaz. Ruth's faithfulness to God allowed her to become the great-grandmother of David and therefore an ancestor of Jesus.

WHY SHOULD WE READ IT?

- To see what God can teach us through a quiet, 'ordinary' life of someone who is committed to him.

- To see an amazing example of selfless devotion and sacrificial love in the way Ruth committed herself wholeheartedly to Naomi.

- To see how God rewarded Ruth for her faithfulness and looked after her and Naomi.

- To find out about Boaz's generosity and kindness.

Andy Croft with Liza Hoeksma

Naomi loses her husband and sons

1 In the days when the judges ruled,*a* there was a famine in the land. So a man from Bethlehem in Judah, together with his wife and two sons, went to live for a while in the country of Moab. ²The man's name was Elimelek, his wife's name was Naomi, and the names of his two sons were Mahlon and Kilion. They were Ephrathites from Bethlehem, Judah. And they went to Moab and lived there.

---

a 1 Traditionally *judged*

³Now Elimelek, Naomi's husband, died, and she was left with her two sons. ⁴They married Moabite women, one named Orpah and the other Ruth. After they had lived there about ten years, ⁵both Mahlon and Kilion also died, and Naomi was left without her two sons and her husband.

Naomi and Ruth return to Bethlehem

⁶When Naomi heard in Moab that the LORD had come to the aid of his people by providing food for them, she and her daughters-in-law prepared to return home

FRIENDSHIP 3

Ruth and Naomi – sticking together

Every friendship goes through ups and downs. Sometimes you'll love spending time together, at other times it will cost you something to stay committed to a friendship or relationship.

Ruth gives us a powerful example of how we stick with people through thick and thin. When her husband died, Ruth could have followed her mother-in-law's advice and returned to her own family. But she knew Naomi needed her. Both of Naomi's sons had died, as well as her husband, so she was all alone. Ruth refused to leave her, saying that only death would part them. Wow! Ruth wasn't just interested in what would be best for her; she stayed committed to her mother-in-law no matter what.

Ruth is a great example to us if we want to be a good friend to those around us. So what does it mean to be committed to a friendship today? It means you don't give up just because you've had a disagreement. You don't quit the friendship because the evening you had together wasn't that fun. If your friend is having a hard time, you stick by them and are there for them. If they are off school through sickness, you go round and visit even if it's not as much fun to sit by someone's bed as it is to go out with other friends. If others don't like them, you stick up for them. You find a way around your differences and you find a way to stick together no matter what comes.

Friendships need to be treasured and nurtured; they take commitment and perseverance. But they are totally worth it. Friends are one of the most amazing gifts God gives us.

Ali Martin

◀◀ 2 Kings 2   1 Samuel 18:1–3 ▶▶

from there. 7 With her two daughters-in-law she left the place where she had been living and set out on the road that would take them back to the land of Judah.

8 Then Naomi said to her two daughters-in-law, 'Go back, each of you, to your mother's home. May the LORD show you kindness, as you have shown kindness to your dead husbands and to me. 9 May the LORD grant that each of you will find rest in the home of another husband.'

Then she kissed them goodbye and they wept aloud 10 and said to her, 'We will go back with you to your people.'

11 But Naomi said, 'Return home, my daughters. Why would you come with me? Am I going to have any more sons, who could become your husbands? 12 Return home, my daughters; I am too old to have another husband. Even if I thought there was still hope for me – even if I had a husband tonight and then gave birth to sons – 13 would you wait until they grew up? Would you remain unmarried for them? No, my daughters. It is more bitter for me than for you, because the LORD's hand has turned against me!'

14 At this they wept aloud again. Then Orpah kissed her mother-in-law goodbye, but Ruth clung to her.

15 'Look,' said Naomi, 'your sister-in-law is going back to her people and her gods. Go back with her.'

16 But Ruth replied, 'Don't urge me to leave you or to turn back from you. Where you go I will go, and where you stay I will stay. Your people will be my people and your God my God. 17 Where you die I will die, and there I will be buried. May the LORD deal with me, be it ever so severely, if even death separates you and me.' 18 When Naomi realised that Ruth was determined to go with her, she stopped urging her.

19 So the two women went on until they came to Bethlehem. When they arrived in Bethlehem, the whole town was stirred because of them, and the women exclaimed, 'Can this be Naomi?'

20 'Don't call me Naomi,'b she told

them. 'Call me Mara,c because the Almightyd has made my life very bitter. 21 I went away full, but the LORD has brought me back empty. Why call me Naomi? The LORD has afflictede me; the Almighty has brought misfortune upon me.'

22 So Naomi returned from Moab accompanied by Ruth the Moabite, her daughter-in-law, arriving in Bethlehem as the barley harvest was beginning.

Ruth meets Boaz in the cornfield

2 Now Naomi had a relative on her husband's side, a man of standing from the clan of Elimelek, whose name was Boaz.

2 And Ruth the Moabite said to Naomi, 'Let me go to the fields and pick up the leftover grain behind anyone in whose eyes I find favour.'

Naomi said to her, 'Go ahead, my daughter.' 3 So she went out, entered a field and began to glean behind the harvesters. As it turned out, she was working in a field belonging to Boaz, who was from the clan of Elimelek.

4 Just then Boaz arrived from Bethlehem and greeted the harvesters, 'The LORD be with you!'

'The LORD bless you!' they answered.

5 Boaz asked the overseer of his harvesters, 'Who does that young woman belong to?'

6 The overseer replied, 'She is the Moabite who came back from Moab with Naomi. 7 She said, "Please let me glean and gather among the sheaves behind the harvesters." She came into the field and has remained here from morning till now, except for a short rest in the shelter.'

8 So Boaz said to Ruth, 'My daughter, listen to me. Don't go and glean in another field and don't go away from here. Stay here with the women who work for me. 9 Watch the field where the men are harvesting, and follow along after the women. I have told the men not to lay a hand on you. And whenever you are

---

b 20 *Naomi* means *pleasant*.

c 20 *Mara* means *bitter*.

d 20 Hebrew *Shaddai*; also in verse 21

e 21 Or *has testified against*

PEOPLE USED BY GOD 3

Ruth

This is one of the best love stories you will ever find – a story of love and commitment that brought blessings to the whole world.

Ruth was married to Naomi's son, who died while they lived in Moab. Both Naomi's sons and her husband had died and she had made plans to return to her homeland Israel. She had nothing left and nothing waiting for her at home, so she told both her daughters-in-law that they should go and make a new life for themselves. In a famous statement, Ruth says to Naomi, 'I'm not going to leave you. Wherever you go, I will go, and I will choose to stay with you even if we both die' (see Ruth 1:17–18). Naomi had nothing to offer Ruth: she was returning to a life of poverty and she was too old to remarry and have more sons. Ruth looked beyond that and saw that the relationship with Naomi was something of significance, something that meant more than money or position. She decided to stay and care for her.

When Ruth and Naomi returned to Bethlehem, Ruth would go daily to the fields to glean the crops that were left behind. The field belonged to a relative named Boaz. When he saw Ruth, he was attracted to her and began to inquire about her, hearing about her faithfulness to Naomi. Boaz made a deal to become the caregiver (or the 'kinsman redeemer') for Ruth and Naomi, and he and Ruth got married and had children.

What we find here is the fruit of faithfulness. When all was lost and there seemed to be no hope ahead, Ruth decided to follow her heart and remain faithful. Her focus on someone else's needs instead of her own opened a door for her as well as for the person she wanted to care for.

Boaz made a choice too. He wasn't the next in line to help Naomi, but because of his heart for Ruth he made a choice to become that person and brought them both into his household. The amazing thing here is that two people who had nothing were now redeemed and had a life of fullness before them. Ruth became the great-great-grandmother of David, the king of Israel from whom the bloodline of Jesus came. Because Ruth was faithful and true to her heart, both Ruth and Naomi were blessed and Ruth became part of the bloodline that would bring blessing to the nations of the world.

God has a plan for each of us, and as we are true to him and follow him without withdrawing, we will see his plans unfold for us. We can learn from Ruth that faithfulness has its own reward.

Tom Brock

thirsty, go and get a drink from the water jars the men have filled.'

¹⁰ At this, she bowed down with her face to the ground. She asked him, 'Why have I found such favour in your eyes that you notice me – a foreigner?'

¹¹ Boaz replied, 'I've been told all about what you have done for your mother-in-law since the death of your husband – how you left your father and mother and your homeland and came to live with a people you did not know before. ¹² May the LORD repay you for what you have done. May you be richly rewarded by the LORD, the God of Israel, under whose wings you have come to take refuge.'

¹³ 'May I continue to find favour in your eyes, my lord,' she said. 'You have put me at ease by speaking kindly to your servant – though I do not have the standing of one of your servants.'

¹⁴ At mealtime Boaz said to her, 'Come over here. Have some bread and dip it in the wine vinegar.'

When she sat down with the harvesters, he offered her some roasted grain. She ate all she wanted and had some left over. ¹⁵ As she got up to glean, Boaz gave orders to his men, 'Let her gather among the sheaves and don't reprimand her. ¹⁶ Even pull out some stalks for her from the bundles and leave them for her to pick up, and don't rebuke her.'

¹⁷ So Ruth gleaned in the field until evening. Then she threshed the barley she had gathered, and it amounted to about an ephah.ᵃ ¹⁸ She carried it back to town, and her mother-in-law saw how much she had gathered. Ruth also brought out and gave her what she had left over after she had eaten enough.

¹⁹ Her mother-in-law asked her, 'Where did you glean today? Where did you work? Blessed be the man who took notice of you!'

Then Ruth told her mother-in-law about the one at whose place she had been working. 'The name of the man I worked with today is Boaz,' she said.

²⁰ 'The LORD bless him!' Naomi said to her daughter-in-law. 'He has not stopped showing his kindness to the living and the dead.' She added, 'That man is our close relative; he is one of our guardian-redeemers.ᵇ'

²¹ Then Ruth the Moabite said, 'He even said to me, "Stay with my workers until they finish harvesting all my grain."'

²² Naomi said to Ruth her daughter-in-law, 'It will be good for you, my daughter, to go with the women who work for him, because in someone else's field you might be harmed.'

²³ So Ruth stayed close to the women of Boaz to glean until the barley and wheat harvests were finished. And she lived with her mother-in-law.

Ruth and Boaz at the threshing-floor

3 One day Ruth's mother-in-law Naomi said to her, 'My daughter, I must find a homeᵃ for you, where you will be well provided for. ² Now Boaz, with whose women you have worked, is a relative of ours. Tonight he will be winnowing barley on the threshing-floor. ³ Wash, put on perfume, and get dressed in your best clothes. Then go down to the threshing-floor, but don't let him know you are there until he has finished eating and drinking. ⁴ When he lies down, note the place where he is lying. Then go and uncover his feet and lie down. He will tell you what to do.'

⁵ 'I will do whatever you say,' Ruth answered. ⁶ So she went down to the threshing-floor and did everything her mother-in-law told her to do.

⁷ When Boaz had finished eating and drinking and was in good spirits, he went over to lie down at the far end of the grain pile. Ruth approached quietly, uncovered his feet and lay down. ⁸ In the middle of the night something startled the man; he turned – and there was a woman lying at his feet!

⁹ 'Who are you?' he asked.

'I am your servant Ruth,' she said. 'Spread the corner of your garment over

---

b 20 The Hebrew word for *guardian-redeemer* is a legal term for one who has the obligation to redeem a relative in serious difficulty (see Lev. 25:25-55).
a 1 Hebrew *find rest* (see 1:9)

a 17 That is, probably about 13 kilograms

me, since you are a guardian-redeemer[b] of our family.'

¹⁰ 'The LORD bless you, my daughter,' he replied. 'This kindness is greater than that which you showed earlier: you have not run after the younger men, whether rich or poor. ¹¹ And now, my daughter, don't be afraid. I will do for you all you ask. All the people of my town know that you are a woman of noble character. ¹² Although it is true that I am a guardian-redeemer of our family, there is another who is more closely related than I. ¹³ Stay here for the night, and in the morning if he wants to do his duty as your guardian-redeemer, good; let him redeem you. But if he is not willing, as surely as the LORD lives I will do it. Lie here until morning.'

¹⁴ So she lay at his feet until morning, but got up before anyone could be recognised; and he said, 'No one must know that a woman came to the threshing-floor.'

¹⁵ He also said, 'Bring me the shawl you are wearing and hold it out.' When she did so, he poured into it six measures of barley and placed the bundle on her. Then he[c] went back to town.

¹⁶ When Ruth came to her mother-in-law, Naomi asked, 'How did it go, my daughter?'

Then she told her everything Boaz had done for her ¹⁷ and added, 'He gave me these six measures of barley, saying, "Don't go back to your mother-in-law empty-handed."'

¹⁸ Then Naomi said, 'Wait, my daughter, until you find out what happens. For the man will not rest until the matter is settled today.'

Boaz marries Ruth

4 Meanwhile Boaz went up to the town gate and sat down there just as the guardian-redeemer[a] he had mentioned came along. Boaz said, 'Come over here, my friend, and sit down.' So he went over and sat down.

² Boaz took ten of the elders of the town and said, 'Sit here,' and they did so. ³ Then he said to the guardian-redeemer, 'Naomi, who has come back from Moab, is selling the piece of land that belonged to our relative Elimelek. ⁴ I thought I should bring the matter to your attention and suggest that you buy it in the presence of these seated here and in the presence of the elders of my people. If you will redeem it, do so. But if you[b] will not, tell me, so I will know. For no one has the right to do it except you, and I am next in line.'

'I will redeem it,' he said.

⁵ Then Boaz said, 'On the day you buy the land from Naomi, you also acquire Ruth the Moabite, the[c] dead man's widow, in order to maintain the name of the dead with his property.'

⁶ At this, the guardian-redeemer said, 'Then I cannot redeem it because I might endanger my own estate. You redeem it yourself. I cannot do it.'

⁷ (Now in earlier times in Israel, for the redemption and transfer of property to become final, one party took off his sandal and gave it to the other. This was the method of legalising transactions in Israel.)

⁸ So the guardian-redeemer said to Boaz, 'Buy it yourself.' And he removed his sandal.

⁹ Then Boaz announced to the elders and all the people, 'Today you are witnesses that I have bought from Naomi all the property of Elimelek, Kilion and Mahlon. ¹⁰ I have also acquired Ruth the Moabite, Mahlon's widow, as my wife, in order to maintain the name of the dead with his property, so that his name will not

---

b 9 The Hebrew word for *guardian-redeemer* is a legal term for one who has the obligation to redeem a relative in serious difficulty (see Lev. 25:25-55); also in verses 12 and 13.
c 15 Most Hebrew manuscripts; many Hebrew manuscripts, Vulgate and Syriac *she*

a 1 The Hebrew word for *guardian-redeemer* is a legal term for one who has the obligation to redeem a relative in serious difficulty (see Lev. 25:25-55); also in verses 3, 6, 8 and 14.
b 4 Many Hebrew manuscripts, Septuagint, Vulgate and Syriac; most Hebrew manuscripts *he*
c 5 Vulgate and Syriac; Hebrew (see also Septuagint) *Naomi and from Ruth the Moabite, you acquire the*

disappear from among his family or from his home town. Today you are witnesses!'

¹¹ Then the elders and all the people at the gate said, 'We are witnesses. May the LORD make the woman who is coming into your home like Rachel and Leah, who together built up the family of Israel. May you have standing in Ephrathah and be famous in Bethlehem. ¹²Through the offspring the LORD gives you by this young woman, may your family be like that of Perez, whom Tamar bore to Judah.'

FAMILY

As the old saying goes, we can choose our friends, but we can't choose our families!

There is a lot of truth in that, and families come in all shapes and sizes. Sometimes family life is wonderful and sometimes it is a nightmare. The good news is that the Bible has loads to say about families. There is the story of Joseph, Jacob and Esau, David and his brothers, and of course Jesus had a family too.

The thread running through the whole Bible is God's heart for each of us to be part of his family, to know we are his children, to know he loves us. Our challenge is to live out our faith in our own families. Can our families see Jesus in us? Or do we live a different life at home from the one we live in church or youth group?

The book of Ruth is a beautiful story of a family – a family coping with pain and grief, a family that God used to make a difference. Elimelek and his wife Naomi have two sons who each get married. Then disaster strikes and Elimelek dies, and then the two sons die. Poor Naomi is left without her husband and her children. But she has two daughters-in-law, Orpah and Ruth, and she tells them to return to their original families. Orpah leaves. Ruth refuses to go. She promises to stay with Naomi and care for her. Ruth shows total commitment. She is so faithful and loving: *'Where you go I will go, where you stay I will stay'* (1:16).

As the story unfolds, Ruth goes to work in a harvest field and meets a man called Boaz. He knows who she is. News of her faithfulness to Naomi has spread. Everyone is amazed at her love, and Boaz says, 'I've been told all about what you have done for your mother-in-law' (2:11).

Living as a Christian in our families can be hard work, as our families know how to rub us up the wrong way, or maybe our family life is just really painful. But the book of Ruth shows us that if we serve our families sacrificially, God can use us to impact not just our own family, but many more people besides.

The story concludes with Ruth marrying Boaz, and they have a little child called Obed. Chapter 4 shows us how that little baby formed a family line that led to the birth of King David, and ultimately to Jesus himself.

All this came about because Ruth was faithful in loving God and showing God's love to her family. There's a challenge and inspiration for us!

Mark Russell

Naomi gains a son

 13So Boaz took Ruth and she became his wife. When he made love to her, the LORD enabled her to conceive, and she gave birth to a son. **14**The women said to Naomi: 'Praise be to the LORD, who this day has not left you without a guardian-redeemer. May he become famous throughout Israel! **15**He will renew your life and sustain you in your old age. For your daughter-in-law, who loves you and who is better to you than seven sons, has given him birth.'

16Then Naomi took the child in her arms and cared for him. **17**The women living there said, 'Naomi has a son!' And they named him Obed. He was the father of Jesse, the father of David.

The genealogy of David

18This, then, is the family line of Perez:

Perez was the father of Hezron,
19Hezron the father of Ram,
Ram the father of Amminadab,
20Amminadab the father of Nahshon,
Nahshon the father of Salmon,*d*
21Salmon the father of Boaz,
Boaz the father of Obed,
22Obed the father of Jesse,
and Jesse the father of David.

---

d 20 A few Hebrew manuscripts, some Septuagint manuscripts and Vulgate (see also verse 21 and Septuagint of 1 Chron. 2:11); most Hebrew manuscripts *Salma*

1 SAMUEL

DATE

Events in 1 and 2 Samuel are dated at around 1075–975 BC

AUTHOR

Unknown

WHAT'S IT ALL ABOUT?

This History book is given its name after the judge and prophet Samuel. It tells us how discontent started brewing in Israel as God's people lost battles to their enemy, the Philistines, who even managed to capture the sacred ark of the covenant. While Samuel called them to repent of their worship of false gods, and God again gave them victory, they started to think that something was missing: a king who would be visible to other nations. This was a rejection of the Lord as their ruler and although God warned them of the consequences, he gave them what they asked for. Samuel appointed Saul as the first king of Israel, but Saul disobeyed the prophet's instructions and so the Lord rejected him. Samuel anointed David to be Saul's successor. He was brought from the fields, where he was looking after sheep, and was taken to the king's palace to serve him. David won the hearts of the people when he defeated Goliath, and Saul became jealous. He tried to kill his successor and forced him to flee. The book tells us what happened to David while he was on the run and then, in the final chapter, we see that Saul was injured in battle and took his own life, leaving the throne for David.

WHY SHOULD WE READ IT?

- To hear about the awesome power of God (1 Samuel 4 – 6).
- To see the importance of obedience (1 Samuel 15) and the heart (1 Samuel 16).
- To read the famous story of David and Goliath (1 Samuel 17).
- To see how David refused to take the throne from Saul by force, but instead waited on God to secure him victory (1 Samuel 24 and 26).

Andy Croft with Liza Hoeksma

The birth of Samuel

1 There was a certain man from Ramathaim, a Zuphite*a* from the hill country of Ephraim, whose name was Elkanah son of Jeroham, the son of Elihu, the son of Tohu, the son of Zuph, an Ephraimite. ²He had two wives; one was called Hannah and the other Peninnah. Peninnah had children, but Hannah had none.

³Year after year this man went up from his town to worship and sacrifice to the LORD Almighty at Shiloh, where Hophni and Phinehas, the two sons of Eli, were priests of the LORD. ⁴Whenever the day came for Elkanah to sacrifice, he would give portions of the meat to his wife Peninnah and to all her sons and daughters. ⁵But to Hannah he gave a double portion because he loved her, and the LORD had closed her womb. ⁶Because the LORD had closed Hannah's womb, her rival kept provoking her in order to irritate her. ⁷This went on year after year. Whenever Hannah went up to the house of the LORD, her rival provoked her till she wept and would not eat. ⁸Her husband Elkanah would say to her, 'Hannah, why are you weeping? Why don't you eat? Why are you downhearted? Don't I mean more to you than ten sons?'

⁹Once when they had finished eating and drinking in Shiloh, Hannah stood up. Now Eli the priest was sitting on his chair by the doorpost of the LORD's house. ¹⁰In her deep anguish Hannah prayed to the LORD, weeping bitterly. ¹¹And she made a vow, saying, 'LORD Almighty, if you will only look on your servant's misery and remember me, and not forget your servant but give her a son, then I will give him to the LORD for all the days of his life, and no razor will ever be used on his head.'

¹²As she kept on praying to the LORD, Eli observed her mouth. ¹³Hannah was praying in her heart, and her lips were moving but her voice was not heard. Eli thought she was drunk ¹⁴and said to her, 'How long are you going to stay drunk? Put away your wine.'

¹⁵'Not so, my lord,' Hannah replied, 'I am a woman who is deeply troubled. I have not been drinking wine or beer; I was pouring out my soul to the LORD. ¹⁶Do not take your servant for a wicked woman; I have been praying here out of my great anguish and grief.'

¹⁷Eli answered, 'Go in peace, and may the God of Israel grant you what you have asked of him.'

¹⁸She said, 'May your servant find favour in your eyes.' Then she went her way and ate something, and her face was no longer downcast.

¹⁹Early the next morning they arose and worshipped before the LORD and then went back to their home at Ramah. Elkanah made love to his wife Hannah, and the LORD remembered her. ²⁰So in the course of time Hannah became pregnant and gave birth to a son. She named him Samuel,*b* saying, 'Because I asked the LORD for him.'

Hannah dedicates Samuel

²¹When her husband Elkanah went up with all his family to offer the annual sacrifice to the LORD and to fulfil his vow, ²²Hannah did not go. She said to her husband, 'After the boy is weaned, I will take him and present him before the LORD, and he will live there always.'*c*

²³'Do what seems best to you,' her husband Elkanah told her. 'Stay here until you have weaned him; only may the LORD make good his*d* word.' So the woman stayed at home and nursed her son until she had weaned him.

²⁴After he was weaned, she took the boy with her, young as he was, along with a three-year-old bull,*e* an ephah*f* of flour and a skin of wine, and brought him to the house of the LORD at Shiloh. ²⁵When the

---

b 20 *Samuel* sounds like the Hebrew for *heard by God.*
c 22 Masoretic Text; Dead Sea Scrolls *always. I have dedicated him as a Nazirite – all the days of his life.'*
d 23 Masoretic Text; Dead Sea Scrolls, Septuagint and Syriac *your*
e 24 Dead Sea Scrolls, Septuagint and Syriac; Masoretic Text *with three bulls*
f 24 That is, probably about 16 kilograms

---

a 1 See Septuagint and 1 Chron. 6:26-27,33-35; or *from Ramathaim Zuphim.*

bull had been sacrificed, they brought the boy to Eli, **26** and she said to him, 'Pardon me, my lord. As surely as you live, I am the woman who stood here beside you praying to the LORD. **27** I prayed for this child, and the LORD has granted me what I asked of him. **28** So now I give him to the LORD. For his whole life he shall be given over to the LORD.' And he worshipped the LORD there.

Hannah's prayer

2 Then Hannah prayed and said:

'My heart rejoices in the LORD;
  in the LORD my horn*a* is lifted high.
My mouth boasts over my enemies,
  for I delight in your deliverance.

_____

a 1 *Horn* here symbolises strength; also in verse 10.

SACRIFICE 4

Hannah's sacrifice

Hannah is a desperate woman. She is childless. In her day that meant she was worthless, so she said a desperate prayer to God. She asked that God would enable her to have a baby, and if he did, then she would 'sacrifice' or 'dedicate' that baby back to God. God heard her prayer and answered her. She gave birth to a son named Samuel ('God hears'). Hannah made good on her promise and brought Samuel (when he was old enough) to the temple to join the priests and serve the Lord, and Samuel ended up saving the entire tribe of Israel.

Until Samuel came along, no one in Israel could hear God. They were trying to obey him, but lacked the heart-knowledge to do a good job. They were lost. When Samuel's life was given as an offering (or a sacrifice), God responded with his voice and his word, and Samuel could hear God. This is the most important thing in the world (and the thing that the wisest man in the Bible – Solomon – asked for). To hear God and do what he says is the way we please him and navigate our way through this complicated life.

Samuel heard God and loved him and was always faithful to do what he said. This is an example of a sacrificed life. The power of a life fully given to God is that God can use that life to bring his will on the earth. It's a remarkable thing. William Booth, the founder of the Salvation Army, changed the world and caused hundreds of thousands of people to be saved. He once said, 'The greatness of a man or woman's power is the measure of their surrender.'

Danielle Strickland

 Exodus 12:27   Romans 12:1–2

2 'There is no one holy like the LORD;
   there is no one besides you;
   there is no Rock like our God.

3 'Do not keep talking so proudly
   or let your mouth speak such
      arrogance,
for the LORD is a God who knows,
   and by him deeds are weighed.

4 'The bows of the warriors are broken,
   but those who stumbled are armed
      with strength.
5 Those who were full hire themselves
      out for food,
   but those who were hungry are
      hungry no more.
She who was barren has borne seven
      children,
   but she who has had many sons
      pines away.

6 'The LORD brings death and makes
      alive;
   he brings down to the grave and
      raises up.
7 The LORD sends poverty and wealth;
   he humbles and he exalts.
8 He raises the poor from the dust
   and lifts the needy from the ash heap;
he seats them with princes
   and makes them inherit a throne of
      honour.

'For the foundations of the earth are
      the LORD's;
   on them he has set the world.
9 He will guard the feet of his faithful
      servants,
   but the wicked will be silenced in
      the place of darkness.

'It is not by strength that one prevails;
10   those who oppose the LORD will be
      broken.
The Most High will thunder from
      heaven;
   the LORD will judge the ends of the
      earth.

'He will give strength to his king
   and exalt the horn of his anointed.'

11 Then Elkanah went home to Ramah,
but the boy ministered before the LORD
under Eli the priest.

Eli's wicked sons

12 Eli's sons were scoundrels; they had
no regard for the LORD. 13 Now it was the
practice of the priests that, whenever any
of the people offered a sacrifice, the priest's
servant would come with a three-pronged
fork in his hand while the meat was being boiled 14 and would plunge the fork
into the pan or kettle or cauldron or pot.
Whatever the fork brought up the priest
would take for himself. This is how they
treated all the Israelites who came to Shiloh. 15 But even before the fat was burned,
the priest's servant would come and say to
the person who was sacrificing, 'Give the
priest some meat to roast; he won't accept
boiled meat from you, but only raw.'

16 If the person said to him, 'Let the fat
be burned first, and then take whatever
you want,' the servant would answer, 'No,
hand it over now; if you don't, I'll take it
by force.'

17 This sin of the young men was very
great in the LORD's sight, for they[b] were
treating the LORD's offering with contempt.

18 But Samuel was ministering before
the LORD – a boy wearing a linen ephod.
19 Each year his mother made him a little
robe and took it to him when she went
up with her husband to offer the annual
sacrifice. 20 Eli would bless Elkanah and
his wife, saying, 'May the LORD give you
children by this woman to take the place
of the one she prayed for and gave to[c] the
LORD.' Then they would go home. 21 And
the LORD was gracious to Hannah; she
gave birth to three sons and two daughters. Meanwhile, the boy Samuel grew up
in the presence of the LORD.

22 Now Eli, who was very old, heard
about everything his sons were doing to all
Israel and how they slept with the women
who served at the entrance to the tent of

---

b 17 Dead Sea Scrolls and Septuagint; Masoretic
Text *people*
c 20 Dead Sea Scrolls; Masoretic Text *and asked from*

meeting. 23So he said to them, 'Why do you do such things? I hear from all the people about these wicked deeds of yours. 24No, my sons; the report I hear spreading among the LORD's people is not good. 25If one person sins against another, God*d* may mediate for the offender; but if anyone sins against the LORD, who will intercede for them?' His sons, however, did not listen to their father's rebuke, for it was the LORD's will to put them to death.

26And the boy Samuel continued to grow in stature and in favour with the LORD and with people.

Prophecy against the house of Eli

27Now a man of God came to Eli and said to him, 'This is what the LORD says: "Did I not clearly reveal myself to your ancestor's family when they were in Egypt under Pharaoh? 28I chose your ancestor out of all the tribes of Israel to be my priest, to go up to my altar, to burn incense, and to wear an ephod in my presence. I also gave your ancestor's family all the food offerings presented by the Israelites. 29Why do you*e* scorn my sacrifice and offering that I prescribed for my dwelling? Why do you honour your sons more than me by fattening yourselves on the choice parts of every offering made by my people Israel?"

30'Therefore the LORD, the God of Israel, declares: "I promised that members of your family would minister before me for ever." But now the LORD declares: "Far be it from me! Those who honour me I will honour, but those who despise me will be disdained. 31The time is coming when I will cut short your strength and the strength of your priestly house, so that no one in it will reach old age, 32and you will see distress in my dwelling. Although good will be done to Israel, no one in your family line will ever reach old age. 33Every one of you that I do not cut off from serving at my altar I will spare only to destroy your sight and sap your strength, and all your descendants will die in the prime of life.

34'"And what happens to your two sons, Hophni and Phinehas, will be a sign to you – they will both die on the same day. 35I will raise up for myself a faithful priest, who will do according to what is in my heart and mind. I will firmly establish his priestly house, and they will minister before my anointed one always. 36Then everyone left in your family line will come and bow down before him for a piece of silver and a loaf of bread and plead, 'Appoint me to some priestly office so that I can have food to eat.' "'

The LORD calls Samuel

3 The boy Samuel ministered before the LORD under Eli. In those days the word of the LORD was rare; there were not many visions.

2One night Eli, whose eyes were becoming so weak that he could barely see, was lying down in his usual place. 3The lamp of God had not yet gone out, and Samuel was lying down in the house of the LORD, where the ark of God was. 4Then the LORD called Samuel.

Samuel answered, 'Here I am.' 5And he ran to Eli and said, 'Here I am; you called me.'

But Eli said, 'I did not call; go back and lie down.' So he went and lay down.

6Again the LORD called, 'Samuel!' And Samuel got up and went to Eli and said, 'Here I am; you called me.'

'My son,' Eli said, 'I did not call; go back and lie down.'

7Now Samuel did not yet know the LORD: the word of the LORD had not yet been revealed to him.

8A third time the LORD called, 'Samuel!' And Samuel got up and went to Eli and said, 'Here I am; you called me.'

Then Eli realised that the LORD was calling the boy. 9So Eli told Samuel, 'Go and lie down, and if he calls you, say, "Speak, LORD, for your servant is listening." ' So Samuel went and lay down in his place.

10The LORD came and stood there, calling as at the other times, 'Samuel! Samuel!'

Then Samuel said, 'Speak, for your servant is listening.'

---

d 25 Or *the judges*
e 29 The Hebrew is plural.

11 And the LORD said to Samuel: 'See, I am about to do something in Israel that will make the ears of everyone who hears about it tingle. **12** At that time I will carry out against Eli everything I spoke against his family – from beginning to end. **13** For I told him that I would judge his family for ever because of the sin he knew about; his sons uttered blasphemies against God,*a* and he failed to restrain them. **14** Therefore I swore to the house of Eli, "The guilt of Eli's house will never be atoned for by sacrifice or offering." '

15 Samuel lay down until morning and then opened the doors of the house of the LORD. He was afraid to tell Eli the vision, **16** but Eli called him and said, 'Samuel, my son.'

Samuel answered, 'Here I am.'

17 'What was it he said to you?' Eli asked. 'Do not hide it from me. May God deal with you, be it ever so severely, if you hide from me anything he told you.' **18** So Samuel told him everything, hiding nothing from him. Then Eli said, 'He is the LORD; let him do what is good in his eyes.'

19 The LORD was with Samuel as he grew up, and he let none of Samuel's words fall to the ground. **20** And all Israel from Dan to Beersheba recognised that Samuel was attested as a prophet of the LORD. **21** The LORD continued to appear at Shiloh, and there he revealed himself to Samuel through his word.

4 And Samuel's word came to all Israel.

The Philistines capture the ark

Now the Israelites went out to fight against the Philistines. The Israelites camped at Ebenezer, and the Philistines at Aphek. **2** The Philistines deployed their forces to meet Israel, and as the battle spread, Israel was defeated by the Philistines, who killed about four thousand of them on the battlefield. **3** When the soldiers returned to camp, the elders of Israel asked, 'Why did the LORD bring defeat on us today before the Philistines? Let us bring the ark of the LORD's covenant from Shiloh, so that he may go with us and save us from the hand of our enemies.'

4 So the people sent men to Shiloh, and they brought back the ark of the covenant of the LORD Almighty, who is enthroned between the cherubim. And Eli's two sons, Hophni and Phinehas, were there with the ark of the covenant of God.

5 When the ark of the LORD's covenant came into the camp, all Israel raised such a great shout that the ground shook. **6** Hearing the uproar, the Philistines asked, 'What's all this shouting in the Hebrew camp?'

When they learned that the ark of the LORD had come into the camp, **7** the Philistines were afraid. 'A god has*a* come into the camp,' they said. 'Oh no! Nothing like this has happened before. **8** We're doomed! Who will deliver us from the hand of these mighty gods? They are the gods who struck the Egyptians with all kinds of plagues in the wilderness. **9** Be strong, Philistines! Be men, or you will be subject to the Hebrews, as they have been to you. Be men, and fight!'

10 So the Philistines fought, and the Israelites were defeated and every man fled to his tent. The slaughter was very great; Israel lost thirty thousand foot soldiers. **11** The ark of God was captured, and Eli's two sons, Hophni and Phinehas, died.

Death of Eli

12 That same day a Benjaminite ran from the battle line and went to Shiloh with his clothes torn and dust on his head. **13** When he arrived, there was Eli sitting on his chair by the side of the road, watching, because his heart feared for the ark of God. When the man entered the town and told what had happened, the whole town sent up a cry.

14 Eli heard the outcry and asked, 'What is the meaning of this uproar?'

The man hurried over to Eli, **15** who was ninety-eight years old and whose eyes had failed so that he could not see. **16** He told

---

a 13 An ancient Hebrew scribal tradition (see also Septuagint); Masoretic Text *sons made themselves contemptible*

---

a 7 Or '*Gods have* (see Septuagint)

Eli, 'I have just come from the battle line; I fled from it this very day.'

Eli asked, 'What happened, my son?'

17 The man who brought the news replied, 'Israel fled before the Philistines, and the army has suffered heavy losses. Also your two sons, Hophni and Phinehas, are dead, and the ark of God has been captured.'

18 When he mentioned the ark of God, Eli fell backwards off his chair by the side of the gate. His neck was broken and he died, for he was an old man, and he was heavy. He had led[b] Israel for forty years.

19 His daughter-in-law, the wife of Phinehas, was pregnant and near the time of delivery. When she heard the news that the ark of God had been captured and that her father-in-law and her husband were dead, she went into labour and gave birth, but was overcome by her labour pains. 20 As she was dying, the women attending her said, 'Don't despair; you have given birth to a son.' But she did not respond or pay any attention.

21 She named the boy Ichabod,[c] saying, 'The Glory has departed from Israel' – because of the capture of the ark of God and the deaths of her father-in-law and her husband. 22 She said, 'The Glory has departed from Israel, for the ark of God has been captured.'

The ark in Ashdod and Ekron

5 After the Philistines had captured the ark of God, they took it from Ebenezer to Ashdod. 2 Then they carried the ark into Dagon's temple and set it beside Dagon. 3 When the people of Ashdod rose early the next day, there was Dagon, fallen on his face on the ground before the ark of the LORD! They took Dagon and put him back in his place. 4 But the following morning when they rose, there was Dagon, fallen on his face on the ground before the ark of the LORD! His head and hands had been broken off and were lying on the threshold; only his body remained. 5 That is why to this day neither the priests of Dagon

nor any others who enter Dagon's temple at Ashdod step on the threshold.

6 The LORD's hand was heavy on the people of Ashdod and its vicinity; he brought devastation on them and afflicted them with tumours.[a] 7 When the people of Ashdod saw what was happening, they said, 'The ark of the god of Israel must not stay here with us, because his hand is heavy on us and on Dagon our god.' 8 So they called together all the rulers of the Philistines and asked them, 'What shall we do with the ark of the god of Israel?'

They answered, 'Let the ark of the god of Israel be moved to Gath.' So they moved the ark of the God of Israel.

9 But after they had moved it, the LORD's hand was against that city, throwing it into a great panic. He afflicted the people of the city, both young and old, with an outbreak of tumours.[b] 10 So they sent the ark of God to Ekron.

As the ark of God was entering Ekron, the people of Ekron cried out, 'They have brought the ark of the god of Israel round to us to kill us and our people.' 11 So they called together all the rulers of the Philistines and said, 'Send the ark of the god of Israel away; let it go back to its own place, or it[c] will kill us and our people.' For death had filled the city with panic; God's hand was very heavy on it. 12 Those who did not die were afflicted with tumours, and the outcry of the city went up to heaven.

The ark returned to Israel

6 When the ark of the LORD had been in Philistine territory for seven months, 2 the Philistines called for the priests and the diviners and said, 'What shall we do with the ark of the LORD? Tell us how we should send it back to its place.'

3 They answered, 'If you return the ark of the god of Israel, do not send it back to him without a gift; by all means send a guilt offering to him. Then you will be

---

b 18 Traditionally judged

c 21 Ichabod means no glory.

a 6 Hebrew; Septuagint and Vulgate tumours. And rats appeared in their land, and there was death and destruction throughout the city

b 9 Or with tumours in the groin (see Septuagint)

c 11 Or he

healed, and you will know why his hand has not been lifted from you.'

⁴The Philistines asked, 'What guilt offering should we send to him?'

They replied, 'Five gold tumours and five gold rats, according to the number of the Philistine rulers, because the same plague has struck both you and your rulers. ⁵Make models of the tumours and of the rats that are destroying the country, and give glory to Israel's god. Perhaps he will lift his hand from you and your gods and your land. ⁶Why do you harden your hearts as the Egyptians and Pharaoh did? When Israel's god dealt harshly with them, did they not send the Israelites out so that they could go on their way?

⁷'Now then, get a new cart ready, with two cows that have calved and have never been yoked. Hitch the cows to the cart, but take their calves away and pen them up. ⁸Take the ark of the LORD and put it on the cart, and in a chest beside it put the gold objects you are sending back to him as a guilt offering. Send it on its way, ⁹but keep watching it. If it goes up to its own territory, towards Beth Shemesh, then the LORD has brought this great disaster on us. But if it does not, then we shall know that it was not his hand that struck us but that it happened to us by chance.'

¹⁰So they did this. They took two such cows and hitched them to the cart and penned up their calves. ¹¹They placed the ark of the LORD on the cart and along with it the chest containing the gold rats and the models of the tumours. ¹²Then the cows went straight up towards Beth Shemesh, keeping on the road and lowing all the way; they did not turn to the right or to the left. The rulers of the Philistines followed them as far as the border of Beth Shemesh.

¹³Now the people of Beth Shemesh were harvesting their wheat in the valley, and when they looked up and saw the ark, they rejoiced at the sight. ¹⁴The cart came to the field of Joshua of Beth Shemesh, and there it stopped beside a large rock. The people chopped up the wood of the cart and sacrificed the cows as a burnt offering to the LORD. ¹⁵The Levites took down the ark of the LORD, together with

the chest containing the gold objects, and placed them on the large rock. On that day the people of Beth Shemesh offered burnt offerings and made sacrifices to the LORD. ¹⁶The five rulers of the Philistines saw all this and then returned that same day to Ekron.

¹⁷These are the gold tumours the Philistines sent as a guilt offering to the LORD – one each for Ashdod, Gaza, Ashkelon, Gath and Ekron. ¹⁸And the number of the gold rats was according to the number of Philistine towns belonging to the five rulers – the fortified towns with their country villages. The large rock on which the Levites set the ark of the LORD is a witness to this day in the field of Joshua of Beth Shemesh.

¹⁹But God struck down some of the inhabitants of Beth Shemesh, putting seventyᵃ of them to death because they looked into the ark of the LORD. The people mourned because of the heavy blow the LORD had dealt them. ²⁰And the people of Beth Shemesh asked, 'Who can stand in the presence of the LORD, this holy God? To whom will the ark go up from here?'

²¹Then they sent messengers to the people of Kiriath Jearim, saying, 'The Philistines have returned the ark of the LORD. Come down and take it up to your town.'

7 ¹So the men of Kiriath Jearim came and took up the ark of the LORD. They brought it to Abinadab's house on the hill and consecrated Eleazar his son to guard the ark of the LORD. ²The ark remained at Kiriath Jearim a long time – twenty years in all.

Samuel subdues the Philistines at Mizpah

Then all the people of Israel turned back to the LORD. ³So Samuel said to all the Israelites, 'If you are returning to the LORD with all your hearts, then rid yourselves of the foreign gods and the Ashtoreths and commit yourselves to the LORD and serve him only, and he will deliver you out of the hand of the Philistines.' ⁴So the Israelites

---

a 19 A few Hebrew manuscripts; most Hebrew manuscripts and Septuagint 50,070 put away their Baals and Ashtoreths, and served the LORD only.

⁵Then Samuel said, 'Assemble all Israel at Mizpah, and I will intercede with the LORD for you.' ⁶When they had assembled at Mizpah, they drew water and poured it out before the LORD. On that day they fasted and there they confessed, 'We have sinned against the LORD.' Now Samuel was serving as leader*a* of Israel at Mizpah.

PEOPLE TOURS

SAMUEL

DEDICATION
1 Samuel 1:1–28
VOICE
1 Samuel 3:1 – 4:1
SAUL
1 Samuel 10:1–8
DAVID
1 Samuel 16:1–13
DEATH
1 Samuel 25:1; 28:1–25

⁷When the Philistines heard that Israel had assembled at Mizpah, the rulers of the Philistines came up to attack them. When the Israelites heard of it, they were afraid because of the Philistines. ⁸They said to Samuel, 'Do not stop crying out to the LORD our God for us, that he may rescue us from the hand of the Philistines.' ⁹Then Samuel took a suckling lamb and sacrificed it as a whole burnt offering to the LORD. He cried out to the LORD on Israel's behalf, and the LORD answered him.

¹⁰While Samuel was sacrificing the burnt offering, the Philistines drew near to engage Israel in battle. But that day the LORD thundered with loud thunder against the Philistines and threw them into such a panic that they were routed before the Israelites. ¹¹The men of Israel

rushed out of Mizpah and pursued the Philistines, slaughtering them along the way to a point below Beth Kar.

¹²Then Samuel took a stone and set it up between Mizpah and Shen. He named it Ebenezer,*b* saying, 'Thus far the LORD has helped us.'

¹³So the Philistines were subdued and they stopped invading Israel's territory. Throughout Samuel's lifetime, the hand of the LORD was against the Philistines. ¹⁴The towns from Ekron to Gath that the Philistines had captured from Israel were restored to Israel, and Israel delivered the neighbouring territory from the hands of the Philistines. And there was peace between Israel and the Amorites.

¹⁵Samuel continued as Israel's leader all the days of his life. ¹⁶From year to year he went on a circuit from Bethel to Gilgal to Mizpah, judging Israel in all those places. ¹⁷But he always went back to Ramah, where his home was, and there he also held court for Israel. And he built an altar there to the LORD.

Israel asks for a king

8 When Samuel grew old, he appointed his sons as Israel's leaders.*a* ²The name of his firstborn was Joel and the name of his second was Abijah, and they served at Beersheba. ³But his sons did not follow his ways. They turned aside after dishonest gain and accepted bribes and perverted justice.

⁴So all the elders of Israel gathered together and came to Samuel at Ramah. ⁵They said to him, 'You are old, and your sons do not follow your ways; now appoint a king to lead*b* us, such as all the other nations have.'

⁶But when they said, 'Give us a king to lead us,' this displeased Samuel; so he prayed to the LORD. ⁷And the LORD told him: 'Listen to all that the people are saying to you; it is not you they have rejected, but they have rejected me as their king. ⁸As they have done from the day I brought

---

b 12 *Ebenezer* means *stone of help.*
a 1 Traditionally *judges*
b 5 Traditionally *judge*; also in verses 6 and 20

them up out of Egypt until this day, forsaking me and serving other gods, so they are doing to you. ⁹Now listen to them; but warn them solemnly and let them know what the king who will reign over them will claim as his rights.'

¹⁰Samuel told all the words of the LORD to the people who were asking him for a king. ¹¹He said, 'This is what the king who will reign over you will claim as his rights: he will take your sons and make them serve with his chariots and horses, and they will run in front of his chariots. ¹²Some he will assign to be commanders of thousands and commanders of fifties, and others to plough his ground and reap his harvest, and still others to make weapons of war and equipment for his chariots. ¹³He will take your daughters to be perfumers and cooks and bakers. ¹⁴He will take the best of your fields and vineyards and olive groves and give them to his attendants. ¹⁵He will take a tenth of your grain and of your vintage and give it to his officials and attendants. ¹⁶Your male and female servants and the best of your cattleᶜ and donkeys he will take for his own use. ¹⁷He will take a tenth of your flocks, and you yourselves will become his slaves. ¹⁸When that day comes, you will cry out for relief from the king you have chosen, but the LORD will not answer you in that day.'

¹⁹But the people refused to listen to Samuel. 'No!' they said. 'We want a king over us. ²⁰Then we shall be like all the other nations, with a king to lead us and to go out before us and fight our battles.'

²¹When Samuel heard all that the people said, he repeated it before the LORD. ²²The LORD answered, 'Listen to them and give them a king.'

Then Samuel said to the Israelites, 'Everyone go back to your own town.'

Samuel anoints Saul

9 There was a Benjaminite, a man of standing, whose name was Kish son of Abiel, the son of Zeror, the son of Bekorath, the son of Aphiah of Benjamin. ²Kish had a son named Saul, as handsome a young man as could be found anywhere in Israel, and he was a head taller than anyone else.

³Now the donkeys belonging to Saul's father Kish were lost, and Kish said to his son Saul, 'Take one of the servants with you and go and look for the donkeys.' ⁴So he passed through the hill country of Ephraim and through the area around Shalisha, but they did not find them. They went on into the district of Shaalim, but the donkeys were not there. Then he passed through the territory of Benjamin, but they did not find them.

⁵When they reached the district of Zuph, Saul said to the servant who was with him, 'Come, let's go back, or my father will stop thinking about the donkeys and start worrying about us.'

⁶But the servant replied, 'Look, in this town there is a man of God; he is highly respected, and everything he says comes true. Let's go there now. Perhaps he will tell us what way to take.'

⁷Saul said to his servant, 'If we go, what can we give the man? The food in our sacks is gone. We have no gift to take to the man of God. What do we have?'

⁸The servant answered him again. 'Look,' he said, 'I have a quarter of a shekelᵃ of silver. I will give it to the man of God so that he will tell us what way to take.' ⁹(Formerly in Israel, if someone went to enquire of God, they would say, 'Come, let us go to the seer,' because the prophet of today used to be called a seer.)

¹⁰'Good,' Saul said to his servant. 'Come, let's go.' So they set out for the town where the man of God was.

¹¹As they were going up the hill to the town, they met some young women coming out to draw water, and they asked them, 'Is the seer here?'

¹²'He is,' they answered. 'He's ahead of you. Hurry now; he has just come to our town today, for the people have a sacrifice at the high place. ¹³As soon as you enter the town, you will find him before he goes up to the high place to eat. The people will not begin eating until he comes, because

---

c 16 Septuagint; Hebrew *young men*   *a* 8 That is, about 3 grams he must bless the sacrifice; afterwards, those who are invited will eat. Go up now; you should find him about this time.'

14 They went up to the town, and as they were entering it, there was Samuel, coming towards them on his way up to the high place.

15 Now the day before Saul came, the LORD had revealed this to Samuel: 16 'About this time tomorrow I will send you a man from the land of Benjamin. Anoint him ruler over my people Israel; he will deliver them from the hand of the Philistines. I have looked on my people, for their cry has reached me.'

17 When Samuel caught sight of Saul, the LORD said to him, 'This is the man I spoke to you about; he will govern my people.'

18 Saul approached Samuel in the gateway and asked, 'Would you please tell me where the seer's house is?'

19 'I am the seer,' Samuel replied. 'Go up ahead of me to the high place, for today you are to eat with me, and in the morning I will send you on your way and will tell you all that is in your heart. 20 As for the donkeys you lost three days ago, do not worry about them; they have been found. And to whom is all the desire of Israel turned, if not to you and your whole family line?'

21 Saul answered, 'But am I not a Benjamite, from the smallest tribe of Israel, and is not my clan the least of all the clans of the tribe of Benjamin? Why do you say such a thing to me?'

22 Then Samuel brought Saul and his servant into the hall and seated them at the head of those who were invited – about thirty in number. 23 Samuel said to the cook, 'Bring the piece of meat I gave you, the one I told you to lay aside.'

24 So the cook took up the thigh with what was on it and set it in front of Saul. Samuel said, 'Here is what has been kept for you. Eat, because it was set aside for you for this occasion from the time I said, "I have invited guests."' And Saul dined with Samuel that day.

25 After they came down from the high place to the town, Samuel talked with Saul on the roof of his house. 26 They rose about daybreak, and Samuel called to Saul on the roof, 'Get ready, and I will send you on your way.' When Saul got ready, he and Samuel went outside together. 27 As they were going down to the edge of the town, Samuel said to Saul, 'Tell the servant to go on ahead of us' – and the servant did so – 'but you stay here for a while, so that I may give you a message from God.'

10 Then Samuel took a flask of olive oil and poured it on Saul's head and kissed him, saying, 'Has not the LORD anointed you ruler over his inheritance?ᵃ 2 When you leave me today, you will meet two men near Rachel's tomb, at Zelzah on the border of Benjamin. They will say to you, "The donkeys you set out to look for have been found. And now your father has stopped thinking about them and is worried about you. He is asking, 'What shall I do about my son?'"

3 'Then you will go on from there until you reach the great tree of Tabor. Three men going up to worship God at Bethel will meet you there. One will be carrying three young goats, another three loaves of bread, and another a skin of wine. 4 They will greet you and offer you two loaves of bread, which you will accept from them.

5 'After that you will go to Gibeah of God, where there is a Philistine outpost. As you approach the town, you will meet a procession of prophets coming down from the high place with lyres, tambourines, pipes and harps being played before them, and they will be prophesying. 6 The Spirit of the LORD will come powerfully upon you, and you will prophesy with them; and you will be changed into a different person. 7 Once these signs are fulfilled, do whatever your hand finds to do, for God is with you.

8 'Go down ahead of me to Gilgal. I will surely come down to you to sacrifice burnt offerings and fellowship offerings, but you must wait seven days until I come to you and tell you what you are to do.'

---

a 1 Hebrew; Septuagint and Vulgate *over his people Israel? You will reign over the LORD's people and save them from the power of their enemies round about. And this will be a sign to you that the LORD has anointed you ruler over his inheritance:*

Saul made king

9 As Saul turned to leave Samuel, God changed Saul's heart, and all these signs were fulfilled that day. 10 When he and his servant arrived at Gibeah, a procession of prophets met him; the Spirit of God came powerfully upon him, and he joined in their prophesying. 11 When all those who had formerly known him saw him prophesying with the prophets, they asked each other, 'What is this that has happened to the son of Kish? Is Saul also among the prophets?'

12 A man who lived there answered, 'And who is their father?' So it became a saying: 'Is Saul also among the prophets?' 13 After Saul stopped prophesying, he went to the high place.

14 Now Saul's uncle asked him and his servant, 'Where have you been?'

'Looking for the donkeys,' he said. 'But when we saw they were not to be found, we went to Samuel.'

15 Saul's uncle said, 'Tell me what Samuel said to you.'

16 Saul replied, 'He assured us that the donkeys had been found.' But he did not tell his uncle what Samuel had said about the kingship.

17 Samuel summoned the people of Israel to the LORD at Mizpah 18 and said to them, 'This is what the LORD, the God of Israel, says: "I brought Israel up out of Egypt, and I delivered you from the power of Egypt and all the kingdoms that oppressed you." 19 But you have now rejected your God, who saves you out of all your disasters and calamities. And you have said, "No, appoint a king over us." So now present yourselves before the LORD by your tribes and clans.'

20 When Samuel had made all Israel come forward by tribes, the tribe of Benjamin was taken by lot. 21 Then he brought forward the tribe of Benjamin, clan by clan, and Matri's clan was taken. Finally Saul son of Kish was taken. But when they looked for him, he was not to be found. 22 So they enquired further of the LORD, 'Has the man come here yet?'

And the LORD said, 'Yes, he has hidden himself among the supplies.'

23 They ran and brought him out, and as he stood among the people he was a head taller than any of the others. 24 Samuel said to all the people, 'Do you see the man the LORD has chosen? There is no one like him among all the people.'

Then the people shouted, 'Long live the king!'

25 Samuel explained to the people the rights and duties of kingship. He wrote them down on a scroll and deposited it before the LORD. Then Samuel dismissed the people to go to their own homes.

26 Saul also went to his home in Gibeah, accompanied by valiant men whose hearts God had touched. 27 But some scoundrels said, 'How can this fellow save us?' They despised him and brought him no gifts. But Saul kept silent.

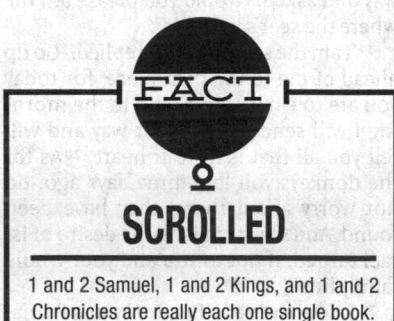

FACT

SCROLLED

1 and 2 Samuel, 1 and 2 Kings, and 1 and 2 Chronicles are really each one single book. They originally got split into two because they were too big to fit on one scroll.

Saul rescues the city of Jabesh

11 Nahash*ᵃ* the Ammonite went up and besieged Jabesh Gilead. And all the men of Jabesh said to him, 'Make a treaty with us, and we will be subject to you.'

2 But Nahash the Ammonite replied, 'I will make a treaty with you only on the condition that I gouge out the right eye of

---

a 1 Masoretic Text; Dead Sea Scrolls *gifts. Now Nahash king of the Ammonites oppressed the Gadites and Reubenites severely. He gouged out all their right eyes and struck terror and dread in Israel. Not a man remained among the Israelites beyond the Jordan whose right eye was not gouged out by Nahash king of the Ammonites, except that seven thousand men fled from the Ammonites and entered Jabesh Gilead. About a month later,* 1 Nahash every one of you and so bring disgrace on all Israel.'

3 The elders of Jabesh said to him, 'Give us seven days so that we can send messengers throughout Israel; if no one comes to rescue us, we will surrender to you.'

4 When the messengers came to Gibeah of Saul and reported these terms to the people, they all wept aloud. 5 Just then Saul was returning from the fields, behind his oxen, and he asked, 'What is wrong with everyone? Why are they weeping?' Then they repeated to him what the men of Jabesh had said.

6 When Saul heard their words, the Spirit of God came powerfully upon him, and he burned with anger. 7 He took a pair of oxen, cut them into pieces, and sent the pieces by messengers throughout Israel, proclaiming, 'This is what will be done to the oxen of anyone who does not follow Saul and Samuel.' Then the terror of the LORD fell on the people, and they came out together as one. 8 When Saul mustered them at Bezek, the men of Israel numbered three hundred thousand and those of Judah thirty thousand.

9 They told the messengers who had come, 'Say to the men of Jabesh Gilead, "By the time the sun is hot tomorrow, you will be rescued."' When the messengers went and reported this to the men of Jabesh, they were elated. 10 They said to the Ammonites, 'Tomorrow we will surrender to you, and you can do to us whatever you like.'

11 The next day Saul separated his men into three divisions; during the last watch of the night they broke into the camp of the Ammonites and slaughtered them until the heat of the day. Those who survived were scattered, so that no two of them were left together.

Saul confirmed as king

12 The people then said to Samuel, 'Who was it that asked, "Shall Saul reign over us?" Turn these men over to us so that we may put them to death.'

13 But Saul said, 'No one will be put to death today, for this day the LORD has rescued Israel.'

14 Then Samuel said to the people, 'Come, let us go to Gilgal and there renew the kingship.' 15 So all the people went to Gilgal and made Saul king in the presence of the LORD. There they sacrificed fellowship offerings before the LORD, and Saul and all the Israelites held a great celebration.

Samuel's farewell speech

12 Samuel said to all Israel, 'I have listened to everything you said to me and have set a king over you. 2 Now you have a king as your leader. As for me, I am old and grey, and my sons are here with you. I have been your leader from my youth until this day. 3 Here I stand. Testify against me in the presence of the LORD and his anointed. Whose ox have I taken? Whose donkey have I taken? Whom have I cheated? Whom have I oppressed? From whose hand have I accepted a bribe to make me shut my eyes? If I have done any of these things, I will make it right.'

4 'You have not cheated or oppressed us,' they replied. 'You have not taken anything from anyone's hand.'

5 Samuel said to them, 'The LORD is witness against you, and also his anointed is witness this day, that you have not found anything in my hand.'

'He is witness,' they said.

6 Then Samuel said to the people, 'It is the LORD who appointed Moses and Aaron and brought your ancestors up out of Egypt. 7 Now then, stand here, because I am going to confront you with evidence before the LORD as to all the righteous acts performed by the LORD for you and your ancestors.

8 'After Jacob entered Egypt, they cried to the LORD for help, and the LORD sent Moses and Aaron, who brought your ancestors out of Egypt and settled them in this place.

9 'But they forgot the LORD their God; so he sold them into the hands of Sisera, the commander of the army of Hazor, and into the hands of the Philistines and the king of Moab, who fought against them. 10 They cried out to the LORD and said, "We have sinned; we have forsaken the

LORD and served the Baals and the Ashtoreths. But now deliver us from the hands of our enemies, and we will serve you." ¹¹ Then the LORD sent Jerub-Baal,*a* Barak,*b* Jephthah and Samuel,*c* and he delivered you from the hands of your enemies all around you, so that you lived in safety.

¹² 'But when you saw that Nahash king of the Ammonites was moving against you, you said to me, "No, we want a king to rule over us" – even though the LORD your God was your king. ¹³ Now here is the king you have chosen, the one you asked for; see, the LORD has set a king over you. ¹⁴ If you fear the LORD and serve and obey him and do not rebel against his commands, and if both you and the king who reigns over you follow the LORD your God – good! ¹⁵ But if you do not obey the LORD, and if you rebel against his commands, his hand will be against you, as it was against your ancestors.

¹⁶ 'Now then, stand still and see this great thing the LORD is about to do before your eyes! ¹⁷ Is it not wheat harvest now? I will call on the LORD to send thunder and rain. And you will realise what an evil thing you did in the eyes of the LORD when you asked for a king.'

¹⁸ Then Samuel called on the LORD, and that same day the LORD sent thunder and rain. So all the people stood in awe of the LORD and of Samuel.

¹⁹ The people all said to Samuel, 'Pray to the LORD your God for your servants so that we will not die, for we have added to all our other sins the evil of asking for a king.'

²⁰ 'Do not be afraid,' Samuel replied. 'You have done all this evil; yet do not turn away from the LORD, but serve the LORD with all your heart. ²¹ Do not turn away after useless idols. They can do you no good, nor can they rescue you, because they are useless. ²² For the sake of his great name the LORD will not reject his people, because the LORD was pleased to make you his own. ²³ As for me, far be it from me

that I should sin against the LORD by failing to pray for you. And I will teach you the way that is good and right. ²⁴ But be sure to fear the LORD and serve him faithfully with all your heart; consider what great things he has done for you. ²⁵ Yet if you persist in doing evil, both you and your king will perish.'

Samuel rebukes Saul

13 Saul was thirty*a* years old when he became king, and he reigned over Israel for forty-*b* two years.

² Saul chose three thousand men from Israel; two thousand were with him at Michmash and in the hill country of Bethel, and a thousand were with Jonathan at Gibeah in Benjamin. The rest of the men he sent back to their homes.

³ Jonathan attacked the Philistine outpost at Geba, and the Philistines heard about it. Then Saul had the trumpet blown throughout the land and said, 'Let the Hebrews hear!' ⁴ So all Israel heard the news: 'Saul has attacked the Philistine outpost, and now Israel has become obnoxious to the Philistines.' And the people were summoned to join Saul at Gilgal.

⁵ The Philistines assembled to fight Israel, with three thousand*c* chariots, six thousand charioteers, and soldiers as numerous as the sand on the seashore. They went up and camped at Michmash, east of Beth Aven. ⁶ When the Israelites saw that their situation was critical and that their army was hard pressed, they hid in caves and thickets, among the rocks, and in pits and cisterns. ⁷ Some Hebrews even crossed the Jordan to the land of Gad and Gilead.

Saul remained at Gilgal, and all the troops with him were quaking with fear. ⁸ He waited for seven days, the time set by Samuel; but Samuel did not come to Gilgal, and Saul's men began to scatter. ⁹ So he said, 'Bring me the burnt offering and

---

a 11 Also called *Gideon*

b 11 Some Septuagint manuscripts and Syriac; Hebrew *Bedan*

c 11 Hebrew; some Septuagint manuscripts and Syriac *Samson*

a 1 A few late manuscripts of the Septuagint; Hebrew does not have *thirty*.

b 1 Probable reading of the original Hebrew text (see Acts 13:21); Masoretic Text does not have *forty-*.

c 5 Some Septuagint manuscripts and Syriac; Hebrew *thirty thousand* the fellowship offerings.' And Saul offered up the burnt offering. [10] Just as he finished making the offering, Samuel arrived, and Saul went out to greet him.

[11] 'What have you done?' asked Samuel.

Saul replied, 'When I saw that the men were scattering, and that you did not come at the set time, and that the Philistines were assembling at Michmash, [12] I thought, "Now the Philistines will come down against me at Gilgal, and I have not sought the LORD's favour." So I felt compelled to offer the burnt offering.'

[13] 'You have done a foolish thing,' Samuel said. 'You have not kept the command the LORD your God gave you; if you had, he would have established your kingdom over Israel for all time. [14] But now your kingdom will not endure; the LORD has sought out a man after his own heart and appointed him ruler of his people, because you have not kept the LORD's command.'

[15] Then Samuel left Gilgal[d] and went up to Gibeah in Benjamin, and Saul counted the men who were with him. They numbered about six hundred.

Israel without weapons

[16] Saul and his son Jonathan and the men with them were staying in Gibeah[e] of Benjamin, while the Philistines camped at Michmash. [17] Raiding parties went out from the Philistine camp in three detachments. One turned towards Ophrah in the vicinity of Shual, [18] another towards Beth Horon, and the third towards the borderland overlooking the Valley of Zeboyim facing the wilderness.

[19] Not a blacksmith could be found in the whole land of Israel, because the Philistines had said, 'Otherwise the Hebrews will make swords or spears!' [20] So all Israel went down to the Philistines to have their ploughshares, mattocks, axes and sickles[f] sharpened. [21] The price was two-thirds of a shekel[g] for sharpening ploughshares and mattocks, and a third of a shekel[h] for sharpening forks and axes and for re-pointing goads.

[22] So on the day of the battle not a soldier with Saul and Jonathan had a sword or spear in his hand; only Saul and his son Jonathan had them.

FAVOURITE VERSES

John 16:33

I have told you these things, so that in me you may have peace. In this world you will have trouble. But take heart! I have overcome the world.

I love this verse because it's such a reminder that being a Christian won't be plain sailing, but God is bigger than any trial, test or sorrow that I will encounter on this earth. It fits my life so well, with things not being plain sailing – but realising that he has never left me, I have just stopped looking.

Joanne, 19

Jonathan attacks the Philistines

[23] Now a detachment of Philistines had gone out to the pass at Michmash.

14

[1] One day Jonathan son of Saul said to his young armour-bearer, 'Come, let's go over to the Philistine outpost on the other side.' But he did not tell his father.

[2] Saul was staying on the outskirts of Gibeah under a pomegranate tree in Migron. With him were about six hundred men, [3] among whom was Ahijah, who was wearing an ephod. He was a son of Ichabod's brother Ahitub son of Phinehas, the

---

d 15 Hebrew; Septuagint *Gilgal and went his way; the rest of the people went after Saul to meet the army, and they went out of Gilgal*

e 16 Two Hebrew manuscripts; most Hebrew manuscripts *Geba*, a variant of *Gibeah*

f 20 Septuagint; Hebrew *ploughshares*

g 21 That is, about 8 grams

h 21 That is, about 4 grams

son of Eli, the LORD's priest in Shiloh. No one was aware that Jonathan had left.

⁴On each side of the pass that Jonathan intended to cross to reach the Philistine outpost was a cliff; one was called Bozez and the other Seneh. ⁵One cliff stood to the north towards Michmash, the other to the south towards Geba.

⁶Jonathan said to his young armour-bearer, 'Come, let's go over to the outpost of those uncircumcised men. Perhaps the LORD will act on our behalf. Nothing can hinder the LORD from saving, whether by many or by few.'

⁷'Do all that you have in mind,' his armour-bearer said. 'Go ahead; I am with you heart and soul.'

⁸Jonathan said, 'Come on, then; we will cross over towards them and let them see us. ⁹If they say to us, "Wait there until we come to you," we will stay where we are and not go up to them. ¹⁰But if they say, "Come up to us," we will climb up, because that will be our sign that the LORD has given them into our hands.'

¹¹So both of them showed themselves to the Philistine outpost. 'Look!' said the Philistines. 'The Hebrews are crawling out of the holes they were hiding in.' ¹²The men of the outpost shouted to Jonathan and his armour-bearer, 'Come up to us and we'll teach you a lesson.'

So Jonathan said to his armour-bearer, 'Climb up after me; the LORD has given them into the hand of Israel.'

¹³Jonathan climbed up, using his hands and feet, with his armour-bearer right behind him. The Philistines fell before Jonathan, and his armour-bearer followed and killed behind him. ¹⁴In that first attack Jonathan and his armour-bearer killed some twenty men in an area of about half an acre.[a]

Israel routs the Philistines

¹⁵Then panic struck the whole army — those in the camp and field, and those in the outposts and raiding parties — and

the ground shook. It was a panic sent by God.[b]

¹⁶Saul's lookouts at Gibeah in Benjamin saw the army melting away in all directions. ¹⁷Then Saul said to the men who were with him, 'Muster the forces and see who has left us.' When they did, it was Jonathan and his armour-bearer who were not there.

¹⁸Saul said to Ahijah, 'Bring the ark of God.' (At that time it was with the Israelites.)[c] ¹⁹While Saul was talking to the priest, the tumult in the Philistine camp increased more and more. So Saul said to the priest, 'Withdraw your hand.'

²⁰Then Saul and all his men assembled and went to the battle. They found the Philistines in total confusion, striking each other with their swords. ²¹Those Hebrews who had previously been with the Philistines and had gone up with them to their camp went over to the Israelites who were with Saul and Jonathan. ²²When all the Israelites who had hidden in the hill country of Ephraim heard that the Philistines were on the run, they joined the battle in hot pursuit. ²³So on that day the LORD saved Israel, and the battle moved on beyond Beth Aven.

Jonathan eats honey

²⁴Now the Israelites were in distress that day, because Saul had bound the people under an oath, saying, 'Cursed be anyone who eats food before evening comes, before I have avenged myself on my enemies!' So none of the troops tasted food.

²⁵The entire army entered the woods, and there was honey on the ground. ²⁶When they went into the woods, they saw the honey oozing out; yet no one put his hand to his mouth, because they feared the oath. ²⁷But Jonathan had not heard that his father had bound the people with the oath, so he reached out the end of the staff that was in his hand and dipped it into the honeycomb. He raised his hand to his mouth, and his eyes brightened.[d]

---

a 14 Or about 2,000 square metres
b 15 Or a terrible panic
c 18 Hebrew; Septuagint 'Bring the ephod.' (At that time he wore the ephod before the Israelites.)
d 27 Or his strength was renewed; similarly in verse 29

²⁸Then one of the soldiers told him, 'Your father bound the army under a strict oath, saying, "Cursed be anyone who eats food today!" That is why the men are faint.'

²⁹Jonathan said, 'My father has made trouble for the country. See how my eyes brightened when I tasted a little of this honey. ³⁰How much better it would have been if the men had eaten today some of the plunder they took from their enemies. Would not the slaughter of the Philistines have been even greater?'

³¹That day, after the Israelites had struck down the Philistines from Michmash to Aijalon, they were exhausted. ³²They pounced on the plunder and, taking sheep, cattle and calves, they butchered them on the ground and ate them, together with the blood. ³³Then someone said to Saul, 'Look, the men are sinning against the LORD by eating meat that has blood in it.'

'You have broken faith,' he said. 'Roll a large stone over here at once.' ³⁴Then he said, 'Go out among the men and tell them, "Each of you bring me your cattle and sheep, and slaughter them here and eat them. Do not sin against the LORD by eating meat with blood still in it."'

So everyone brought his ox that night and slaughtered it there. ³⁵Then Saul built an altar to the LORD; it was the first time he had done this.

³⁶Saul said, 'Let us go down and pursue the Philistines by night and plunder them till dawn, and let us not leave one of them alive.'

'Do whatever seems best to you,' they replied.

But the priest said, 'Let us enquire of God here.'

³⁷So Saul asked God, 'Shall I go down and pursue the Philistines? Will you give them into Israel's hand?' But God did not answer him that day.

³⁸Saul therefore said, 'Come here, all you who are leaders of the army, and let us find out what sin has been committed today. ³⁹As surely as the LORD who rescues Israel lives, even if the guilt lies with my son Jonathan, he must die.' But not one of them said a word.

⁴⁰Saul then said to all the Israelites, 'You stand over there; I and Jonathan my son will stand over here.'

'Do what seems best to you,' they replied.

⁴¹Then Saul prayed to the LORD, the God of Israel, 'Why have you not answered your servant today? If the fault is in me or my son Jonathan, respond with Urim, but if the men of Israel are at fault,ᵉ respond with Thummim.' Jonathan and Saul were taken by lot, and the men were cleared. ⁴²Saul said, 'Cast the lot between me and Jonathan my son.' And Jonathan was taken.

⁴³Then Saul said to Jonathan, 'Tell me what you have done.'

So Jonathan told him, 'I tasted a little honey with the end of my staff. And now I must die!'

⁴⁴Saul said, 'May God deal with me, be it ever so severely, if you do not die, Jonathan.'

⁴⁵But the men said to Saul, 'Should Jonathan die – he who has brought about this great deliverance in Israel? Never! As surely as the LORD lives, not a hair of his head shall fall to the ground, for he did this today with God's help.' So the men rescued Jonathan, and he was not put to death.

⁴⁶Then Saul stopped pursuing the Philistines, and they withdrew to their own land.

⁴⁷After Saul had assumed rule over Israel, he fought against their enemies on every side: Moab, the Ammonites, Edom, the kingsᶠ of Zobah, and the Philistines. Wherever he turned, he inflicted punishment on them.ᵍ ⁴⁸He fought valiantly and defeated the Amalekites, delivering Israel from the hands of those who had plundered them.

Saul's family

⁴⁹Saul's sons were Jonathan, Ishvi and Malki-Shua. The name of his elder

---

ᵉ41 Septuagint; Hebrew does not have 'Why . . . at fault.
ᶠ47 Masoretic Text; Dead Sea Scrolls and Septuagint king
ᵍ47 Hebrew; Septuagint *he was victorious*

daughter was Merab, and that of the younger was Michal. 50 His wife's name was Ahinoam daughter of Ahimaaz. The name of the commander of Saul's army was Abner son of Ner, and Ner was Saul's uncle. 51 Saul's father Kish and Abner's father Ner were sons of Abiel.

52 All the days of Saul there was bitter war with the Philistines, and whenever Saul saw a mighty or brave man, he took him into his service.

The LORD rejects Saul as king

15 Samuel said to Saul, 'I am the one the LORD sent to anoint you king over his people Israel; so listen now to the message from the LORD. 2 This is what the LORD Almighty says: "I will punish the Amalekites for what they did to Israel when they waylaid them as they came up from Egypt. 3 Now go, attack the Amalekites and totally destroy*a* all that belongs to them. Do not spare them; put to death men and women, children and infants, cattle and sheep, camels and donkeys."'

4 So Saul summoned the men and mustered them at Telaim – two hundred thousand foot soldiers and ten thousand from Judah. 5 Saul went to the city of Amalek and set an ambush in the ravine. 6 Then he said to the Kenites, 'Go away, leave the Amalekites so that I do not destroy you along with them; for you showed kindness to all the Israelites when they came up out of Egypt.' So the Kenites moved away from the Amalekites.

7 Then Saul attacked the Amalekites all the way from Havilah to Shur, near the eastern border of Egypt. 8 He took Agag king of the Amalekites alive, and all his people he totally destroyed with the sword. 9 But Saul and the army spared Agag and the best of the sheep and cattle, the fat calves*b* and lambs – everything that was good. These they were unwilling to destroy completely,

but everything that was despised and weak they totally destroyed.

10 Then the word of the LORD came to Samuel: 11 'I regret that I have made Saul king, because he has turned away from me and has not carried out my instructions.' Samuel was angry, and he cried out to the LORD all that night.

12 Early in the morning Samuel got up and went to meet Saul, but he was told, 'Saul has gone to Carmel. There he has set up a monument in his own honour and has turned and gone on down to Gilgal.'

13 When Samuel reached him, Saul said, 'The LORD bless you! I have carried out the LORD's instructions.'

14 But Samuel said, 'What then is this bleating of sheep in my ears? What is this lowing of cattle that I hear?'

15 Saul answered, 'The soldiers brought them from the Amalekites; they spared the best of the sheep and cattle to sacrifice to the LORD your God, but we totally destroyed the rest.'

16 'Enough!' Samuel said to Saul. 'Let me tell you what the LORD said to me last night.'

'Tell me,' Saul replied.

17 Samuel said, 'Although you were once small in your own eyes, did you not become the head of the tribes of Israel? The LORD anointed you king over Israel. 18 And he sent you on a mission, saying, "Go and completely destroy those wicked people, the Amalekites; wage war against them until you have wiped them out." 19 Why did you not obey the LORD? Why did you pounce on the plunder and do evil in the eyes of the LORD?'

20 'But I did obey the LORD,' Saul said. 'I went on the mission the LORD assigned me. I completely destroyed the Amalekites and brought back Agag their king. 21 The soldiers took sheep and cattle from the plunder, the best of what was devoted to God, in order to sacrifice them to the LORD your God at Gilgal.'

22 But Samuel replied:

'Does the LORD delight in burnt
offerings and sacrifices
as much as in obeying the LORD?

---

a 3 The Hebrew term refers to the irrevocable giving over of things or persons to the LORD, often by totally destroying them; also in verses 8, 9, 15, 18, 20 and 21.
b 9 Or *the grown bulls*; the meaning of the Hebrew for this phrase is uncertain.

To obey is better than sacrifice,
  and to heed is better than the fat of
    rams.
23 For rebellion is like the sin of
    divination,
  and arrogance like the evil of
    idolatry.

Because you have rejected the word of
    the LORD,
  he has rejected you as king.'

24Then Saul said to Samuel, 'I have
sinned. I violated the LORD's command
and your instructions. I was afraid of the

SACRIFICE 8

Saul's lesson in useless sacrifice

In a funny way, this whole story in 1 Samuel 15 is about sacrifice.

Saul knows that sacrifice is the way to honour God, but he gets a bit confused because he is not really trying to please God, he is trying to advance his own career. In many ways, what Saul is doing is covering his own actions with some religious activity. When Samuel (the prophet, who should have done the sacrifice) comes, Saul tries to explain that the sacrifice had to be done and so he did it without Samuel. Samuel knows God and knows true sacrifice from false, he senses that something is wrong.

He tells Saul that the Lord requires obedience more than sacrifice. Now, that can be a bit confusing, because we know that sacrifice is essential to our faith. He calls us to sacrifice… so what's the deal?

The thing is that sacrifice is not really about a transaction – it's a relationship. It expresses a heart attitude that works its way out in sacrifice. This is true in any great relationship that's rooted in love. In my role as a wife, I make sacrifices that are based in love. They aren't sacrifices that I have to do, but I do them because I want to put my relationship above other things. As a mother I sacrifice sleep, spare time, clean clothes, a tidy house and other really important things – and I do it not because I have to, but because my relationship with my children is a priority in my life. It's my joy to offer those things. It's not about transaction – it's about relationship.

Saul makes a terrible mistake here because he has a broken relationship with God. He no longer loves God, so he offers a sacrifice that is a transaction instead of a response of love and obedience. This is not what God wants, and Samuel knows it. This is actually the event that signals the end of God's Spirit over Saul as the leader of Israel. It isn't as a punishment for this one particular act, it's the result of a broken relationship. True sacrifice is freely offered and involves our obedience, not because it's the right thing, but because it's our joy – for the sake of relationship.

Danielle Strickland

 Judges 16:23–30   2 Samuel 24:24

men and so I gave in to them. ²⁵Now I beg you, forgive my sin and come back with me, so that I may worship the LORD.'

²⁶But Samuel said to him, 'I will not go back with you. You have rejected the word of the LORD, and the LORD has rejected you as king over Israel!'

²⁷As Samuel turned to leave, Saul caught hold of the hem of his robe, and it tore. ²⁸Samuel said to him, 'The LORD has torn the kingdom of Israel from you today and has given it to one of your neighbours – to one better than you. ²⁹He who is the Glory of Israel does not lie or change his mind; for he is not a human being, that he should change his mind.'

³⁰Saul replied, 'I have sinned. But please honour me before the elders of my people and before Israel; come back with me, so that I may worship the LORD your God.' ³¹So Samuel went back with Saul, and Saul worshipped the LORD.

³²Then Samuel said, 'Bring me Agag king of the Amalekites.'

Agag came to him in chains.ᶜ And he thought, 'Surely the bitterness of death is past.'

³³But Samuel said,

'As your sword has made women childless,
    so will your mother be childless
        among women.'

And Samuel put Agag to death before the LORD at Gilgal.

³⁴Then Samuel left for Ramah, but Saul went up to his home in Gibeah of Saul. ³⁵Until the day Samuel died, he did not go to see Saul again, though Samuel mourned for him. And the LORD regretted that he had made Saul king over Israel.

Samuel anoints David

16 The LORD said to Samuel, 'How long will you mourn for Saul, since I have rejected him as king over Israel? Fill your horn with oil and be on your way; I am sending you to Jesse of Bethlehem. I have chosen one of his sons to be king.'

²But Samuel said, 'How can I go? If Saul hears about it, he will kill me.'

The LORD said, 'Take a heifer with you and say, "I have come to sacrifice to the LORD." ³Invite Jesse to the sacrifice, and I will show you what to do. You are to anoint for me the one I indicate.'

⁴Samuel did what the LORD said. When he arrived at Bethlehem, the elders of the town trembled when they met him. They asked, 'Do you come in peace?'

⁵Samuel replied, 'Yes, in peace; I have come to sacrifice to the LORD. Consecrate yourselves and come to the sacrifice with me.' Then he consecrated Jesse and his sons and invited them to the sacrifice.

⁶When they arrived, Samuel saw Eliab and thought, 'Surely the LORD's anointed stands here before the LORD.'

⁷But the LORD said to Samuel, 'Do not consider his appearance or his height, for I have rejected him. The LORD does not look at the things people look at. People look at the outward appearance, but the LORD looks at the heart.'

⁸Then Jesse called Abinadab and made him pass in front of Samuel. But Samuel said, 'The LORD has not chosen this one either.' ⁹Jesse then made Shammah pass by, but Samuel said, 'Nor has the LORD chosen this one.' ¹⁰Jesse made seven of his sons pass before Samuel, but Samuel said to him, 'The LORD has not chosen these.' ¹¹So he asked Jesse, 'Are these all the sons you have?'

'There is still the youngest,' Jesse answered. 'He is tending the sheep.'

Samuel said, 'Send for him; we will not sit down until he arrives.'

¹²So he sent for him and had him brought in. He was glowing with health and had a fine appearance and handsome features.

Then the LORD said, 'Rise and anoint him; this is the one.'

¹³So Samuel took the horn of oil and anointed him in the presence of his brothers, and from that day on the Spirit of the LORD came powerfully upon David. Samuel then went to Ramah.

ᶜ 32 The meaning of the Hebrew for this phrase is uncertain.

David in Saul's service

¹⁴Now the Spirit of the LORD had departed from Saul, and an evil*ᵃ* spirit from the LORD tormented him.

¹⁵Saul's attendants said to him, 'See, an evil spirit from God is tormenting you. ¹⁶Let our lord command his servants here

───────

a 14 Or *and a harmful*; similarly in verses 15, 16 and 23

to search for someone who can play the lyre. He will play when the evil spirit from God comes on you, and you will feel better.'

¹⁷So Saul said to his attendants, 'Find someone who plays well and bring him to me.'

¹⁸One of the servants answered, 'I have seen a son of Jesse of Bethlehem who

HOW DO I CHOOSE?

In 1 Samuel 16, Samuel is choosing who to anoint as the next king of Israel.

He has previously anointed the Lord's choice of Saul (who turned out to be a bit of a bad egg). This passage reminds me that even the wisest among us can be taken in by the world and make worldly choices. When Samuel looks at Eliab (the eldest son of Jesse), he sees a man who looks like a future king, but God says, 'Don't look at his appearance. I don't. I look at the heart.'

We can be the same when we're choosing our friends, let alone our boyfriends or girlfriends! This is a reminder that although the person could be physically what we're looking for, be from the same type of background, have similar aspirations and have the right interests, they might not be God's best for us.

God asks us to look beyond the physical and to look at the heart.

God is choosing a king to rule over his people, and he doesn't choose an eldest son with fine features, he chooses a ruddy shepherd boy who seems too young to imagine ruling over a country. But as you read the rest of Samuel, you'll discover that David is a great choice: he has patience and a faith in the Lord which makes him (to start with at least) a popular ruler over Israel.

As Samuel is choosing a new king, he is constantly asking God – and we should do the same. We should be asking God what he thinks of a person. Ask your friends and youth leaders to pray too and find out what they think: sometimes godly friends around us can have insight into situations that we don't.

The only problem with asking God what he thinks is that we then need to have the courage to act on what he says! Sometimes God can ask unexpected things of us, so we need to look at the Bible and its teaching, and if it fits in, we need to have the courage to obey.

With all that said, God won't always tell us an answer – he gives us reason and judgement to make decisions too. Just don't forget to ask!

Jane Plackett & Calum Dyke

 1 Corinthians 7:32–34   1 Timothy 5:1–2 ⏩

knows how to play the lyre. He is a brave man and a warrior. He speaks well and is a fine-looking man. And the LORD is with him.'

¹⁹Then Saul sent messengers to Jesse and said, 'Send me your son David, who is with the sheep.' ²⁰So Jesse took a donkey loaded with bread, a skin of wine and a young goat and sent them with his son David to Saul.

²¹David came to Saul and entered his service. Saul liked him very much, and David became one of his armour-bearers. ²²Then Saul sent word to Jesse, saying,

'Allow David to remain in my service, for I am pleased with him.'

²³Whenever the spirit from God came on Saul, David would take up his lyre and play. Then relief would come to Saul; he would feel better, and the evil spirit would leave him.

David and Goliath

17 Now the Philistines gathered their forces for war and assembled at Sokoh in Judah. They pitched camp at Ephes Dammim, between Sokoh and Azekah. ²Saul and the Israelites

WORSHIP 7

Healing

We all know that there's something amazingly powerful about songs.

Most of us have songs that, when they come on the radio, remind us of a particular person or moment. Music has an ability to lift our spirits, set our dreams alight, make us feel we can achieve anything.

If that's what a normal song can do, how much more a song of worship!

When we sing praise to God our Maker, something mysterious and wonderfully good happens. He draws near to us. In 1 Samuel 16:14–23, Saul is troubled by an evil spirit. He gets David to sing, and in that moment finds peace. We are not told exactly what David sang, but given that he wrote many of the psalms in the Bible we can guess it was probably one of these. Perhaps it was one of David's greatest hits, Psalm 23, *'Though I walk through the darkest valley, I will fear no evil, for you [God] are with me'* (Psalm 23:4).

Unlike Saul (v. 14), an evil spirit might not be your problem today; maybe it's loneliness, maybe it's anxiety, maybe it's a painful break-up or another tough relationship with a parent or friend. In our hurt and pain something special happens when we worship God. It's hard to put your finger on exactly what's going on (just as it's hard to put your finger on why you like a particular melody), but in worship we are healed.

This isn't because there's something special about the words or music of worship songs – they are just notes and sounds, after all. It's because in singing them we are engaging with God himself. God is the healer of the broken-hearted and worship is a way of drawing close to him.

Beth Croft

 Mark 14:1–11   Hebrews 12:18–29

assembled and camped in the Valley of Elah and drew up their battle line to meet the Philistines. ³The Philistines occupied one hill and the Israelites another, with the valley between them.

⁴A champion named Goliath, who was from Gath, came out of the Philistine camp. His height was six cubits and a span.ᵃ ⁵He had a bronze helmet on his head and wore a coat of scale armour of bronze weighing five thousand shekels;ᵇ ⁶on his legs he wore bronze greaves, and a bronze javelin was slung on his back. ⁷His spear shaft was like a weaver's rod, and its iron point weighed six hundred shekels.ᶜ His shield-bearer went ahead of him.

⁸Goliath stood and shouted to the ranks of Israel, 'Why do you come out and line up for battle? Am I not a Philistine, and are you not the servants of Saul? Choose a man and let him come down to me. ⁹If he is able to fight and kill me, we will become your subjects; but if I overcome him and kill him, you will become our subjects and serve us.' ¹⁰Then the Philistine said, 'This day I defy the armies of Israel! Give me a man and let us fight each other.' ¹¹On hearing the Philistine's words, Saul and all the Israelites were dismayed and terrified.

¹²Now David was the son of an Ephrathite named Jesse, who was from Bethlehem in Judah. Jesse had eight sons, and in Saul's time he was very old. ¹³Jesse's three eldest sons had followed Saul to the war: the firstborn was Eliab; the second, Abinadab; and the third, Shammah. ¹⁴David was the youngest. The three eldest followed Saul, ¹⁵but David went back and forth from Saul to tend his father's sheep at Bethlehem.

¹⁶For forty days the Philistine came forward every morning and evening and took his stand.

¹⁷Now Jesse said to his son David, 'Take this ephahᵈ of roasted grain and these ten loaves of bread for your brothers and hurry to their camp. ¹⁸Take along these ten cheeses to the commander of their unit. See how your brothers are and bring back some assuranceᵉ from them. ¹⁹They are with Saul and all the men of Israel in the Valley of Elah, fighting against the Philistines.'

²⁰Early in the morning David left the flock in the care of a shepherd, loaded up and set out, as Jesse had directed. He reached the camp as the army was going out to its battle positions, shouting the war cry. ²¹Israel and the Philistines were drawing up their lines facing each other. ²²David left his things with the keeper of supplies, ran to the battle lines and asked his brothers how they were. ²³As he was talking with them, Goliath, the Philistine champion from Gath, stepped out from his lines and shouted his usual defiance, and David heard it. ²⁴Whenever the Israelites saw the man, they all fled from him in great fear.

²⁵Now the Israelites had been saying, 'Do you see how this man keeps coming out? He comes out to defy Israel. The king will give great wealth to the man who kills him. He will also give him his daughter in marriage and will exempt his family from taxes in Israel.'

²⁶David asked the men standing near him, 'What will be done for the man who kills this Philistine and removes this disgrace from Israel? Who is this uncircumcised Philistine that he should defy the armies of the living God?'

²⁷They repeated to him what they had been saying and told him, 'This is what will be done for the man who kills him.'

²⁸When Eliab, David's eldest brother, heard him speaking with the men, he burned with anger at him and asked, 'Why have you come down here? And with whom did you leave those few sheep in the wilderness? I know how conceited you are and how wicked your heart is; you came down only to watch the battle.'

²⁹'Now what have I done?' said David. 'Can't I even speak?' ³⁰He then turned away to someone else and brought up the same matter, and the men answered him

---

ᵃ 4 That is, about 3 metres
ᵇ 5 That is, about 58 kilograms
ᶜ 7 That is, about 6.9 kilograms
ᵈ 17 That is, probably about 16 kilograms

ᵉ 18 Or some token; or some pledge of spoils

as before. **31**What David said was over-heard and reported to Saul, and Saul sent for him.

32David said to Saul, 'Let no one lose heart on account of this Philistine; your servant will go and fight him.'

33Saul replied, 'You are not able to go out against this Philistine and fight him; you are only a young man, and he has been a warrior from his youth.'

34But David said to Saul, 'Your ser-vant has been keeping his father's sheep. When a lion or a bear came and carried off a sheep from the flock, **35**I went after it, struck it and rescued the sheep from its mouth. When it turned on me, I seized it by its hair, struck it and killed it. **36**Your servant has killed both the lion and the bear; this uncircumcised Philistine will be like one of them, because he has defied the armies of the living God. **37**The LORD who rescued me from the paw of the lion and the paw of the bear will rescue me from the hand of this Philistine.'

Saul said to David, 'Go, and the LORD be with you.'

38Then Saul dressed David in his own tunic. He put a coat of armour on him and a bronze helmet on his head. **39**David fastened on his sword over the tunic and tried walking around, because he was not used to them.

'I cannot go in these,' he said to Saul, 'because I am not used to them.' So he took them off. **40**Then he took his staff in his hand, chose five smooth stones from the stream, put them in the pouch of his shepherd's bag and, with his sling in his hand, approached the Philistine.

41Meanwhile, the Philistine, with his shield-bearer in front of him, kept com-ing closer to David. **42**He looked David over and saw that he was little more than a boy, glowing with health and handsome, and he despised him. **43**He said to David, 'Am I a dog, that you come at me with sticks?' And the Philistine cursed David by his gods. **44**'Come here,' he said, 'and I'll give your flesh to the birds and the wild animals!'

45David said to the Philistine, 'You come against me with sword and spear and javelin, but I come against you in the name of the LORD Almighty, the God of the armies of Israel, whom you have de-fied. **46**This day the LORD will deliver you into my hands, and I'll strike you down and cut off your head. This very day I will give the carcasses of the Philistine army to the birds and the wild animals, and the whole world will know that there is a God in Israel. **47**All those gathered here will know that it is not by sword or spear that the LORD saves; for the battle is the LORD's, and he will give all of you into our hands.'

48As the Philistine moved closer to at-tack him, David ran quickly towards the battle line to meet him. **49**Reaching into his bag and taking out a stone, he slung it and struck the Philistine on the forehead. The stone sank into his forehead, and he fell face down on the ground.

50So David triumphed over the Phil-istine with a sling and a stone; without a sword in his hand he struck down the Philistine and killed him.

51David ran and stood over him. He took hold of the Philistine's sword and drew it from the sheath. After he killed him, he cut off his head with the sword.

When the Philistines saw that their hero was dead, they turned and ran. **52**Then the men of Israel and Judah surged forward with a shout and pursued the Philistines to the entrance of Gath*f* and to the gates of Ekron. Their dead were strewn along the Shaaraim road to Gath and Ekron. **53**When the Israelites returned from chasing the Philistines, they plundered their camp.

54David took the Philistine's head and brought it to Jerusalem; he put the Philis-tine's weapons in his own tent.

55As Saul watched David going out to meet the Philistine, he said to Abner, commander of the army, 'Abner, whose son is that young man?'

Abner replied, 'As surely as you live, Your Majesty, I don't know.'

56The king said, 'Find out whose son this young man is.'

57As soon as David returned from kill-ing the Philistine, Abner took him and

---

*f*52 Some Septuagint manuscripts; Hebrew *of a valley*

brought him before Saul, with David still holding the Philistine's head.

⁵⁸'Whose son are you, young man?' Saul asked him.

David said, 'I am the son of your servant Jesse of Bethlehem.'

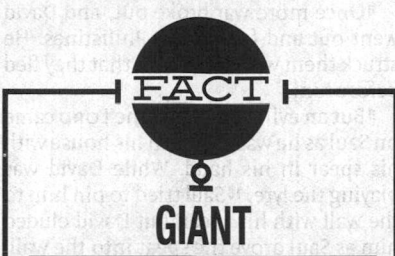

FACT

GIANT

According to 1 Samuel, Goliath's height was six cubits and a span (1 Samuel 17:4). That's about 3 metres, or 9 feet, 9 inches. What's more, he had a brother who was a big man as well (2 Samuel 21:19).

Saul's growing fear of David

18 After David had finished talking with Saul, Jonathan became one in spirit with David, and he loved him as himself. ²From that day Saul kept David with him and did not let him return home to his family. ³And Jonathan made a covenant with David because he loved him as himself. ⁴Jonathan took off the robe he was wearing and gave it to David, along with his tunic, and even his sword, his bow and his belt.

⁵Whatever mission Saul sent him on, David was so successful that Saul gave him a high rank in the army. This pleased all the troops, and Saul's officers as well.

⁶When the men were returning home after David had killed the Philistine, the women came out from all the towns of Israel to meet King Saul with singing and dancing, with joyful songs and with tambourines and lyres. ⁷As they danced, they sang:

'Saul has slain his thousands,
  and David his tens of thousands.'

⁸Saul was very angry; this refrain displeased him greatly. 'They have credited David with tens of thousands,' he thought, 'but me with only thousands. What more can he get but the kingdom?' ⁹And from that time on Saul kept a close eye on David.

¹⁰The next day an evil*a* spirit from God came forcefully on Saul. He was prophesying in his house, while David was playing the lyre, as he usually did. Saul had a spear in his hand ¹¹and he hurled it, saying to himself, 'I'll pin David to the wall.' But David eluded him twice.

¹²Saul was afraid of David, because the LORD was with David but had departed from Saul. ¹³So he sent David away from him and gave him command over a thousand men, and David led the troops in their campaigns. ¹⁴In everything he did he had great success, because the LORD was with him. ¹⁵When Saul saw how successful he was, he was afraid of him. ¹⁶But all Israel and Judah loved David, because he led them in their campaigns.

¹⁷Saul said to David, 'Here is my elder daughter Merab. I will give her to you in marriage; only serve me bravely and fight the battles of the LORD.' For Saul said to himself, 'I will not raise a hand against him. Let the Philistines do that!'

¹⁸But David said to Saul, 'Who am I, and what is my family or my clan in Israel, that I should become the king's son-in-law?' ¹⁹So*b* when the time came for Merab, Saul's daughter, to be given to David, she was given in marriage to Adriel of Meholah.

²⁰Now Saul's daughter Michal was in love with David, and when they told Saul about it, he was pleased. ²¹'I will give her to him,' he thought, 'so that she may be a snare to him and so that the hand of the Philistines may be against him.' So Saul said to David, 'Now you have a second opportunity to become my son-in-law.'

²²Then Saul ordered his attendants: 'Speak to David privately and say, "Look, the king likes you, and his attendants all love you; now become his son-in-law."' ²³They repeated these words to David.

---

a 10 Or *a harmful*
b 19 Or *However,*

But David said, 'Do you think it is a small matter to become the king's son-in-law? I'm only a poor man and little known.'

24 When Saul's servants told him what David had said, 25 Saul replied, 'Say to David, "The king wants no other price for the bride than a hundred Philistine foreskins, to take revenge on his enemies." ' Saul's plan was for David to fall by the hands of the Philistines.

26 When the attendants told David these things, he was pleased to become the king's son-in-law. So before the allotted time elapsed, 27 David took his men with him and went out and killed two hundred Philistines and brought back their foreskins. They counted out the full number to the king so that David might become the king's son-in-law. Then Saul gave him his daughter Michal in marriage.

28 When Saul realised that the LORD was with David and that his daughter Michal loved David, 29 Saul became still more afraid of him, and he remained his enemy for the rest of his days.

30 The Philistine commanders continued to go out to battle, and as often as they did, David met with more success than the rest of Saul's officers, and his name became well known.

Saul tries to kill David

19 Saul told his son Jonathan and all the attendants to kill David. But Jonathan had taken a great liking to David 2 and warned him, 'My father Saul is looking for a chance to kill you. Be on your guard tomorrow morning; go into hiding and stay there. 3 I will go out and stand with my father in the field where you are. I'll speak to him about you and will tell you what I find out.'

4 Jonathan spoke well of David to Saul his father and said to him, 'Let not the king do wrong to his servant David; he has not wronged you, and what he has done has benefited you greatly. 5 He took his life in his hands when he killed the Philistine. The LORD won a great victory for all Israel, and you saw it and were glad. Why then would you do wrong to an innocent man like David by killing him for no reason?'

6 Saul listened to Jonathan and took this oath: 'As surely as the LORD lives, David will not be put to death.'

7 So Jonathan called David and told him the whole conversation. He brought him to Saul, and David was with Saul as before.

8 Once more war broke out, and David went out and fought the Philistines. He struck them with such force that they fled before him.

9 But an evil*a* spirit from the LORD came on Saul as he was sitting in his house with his spear in his hand. While David was playing the lyre, 10 Saul tried to pin him to the wall with his spear, but David eluded him as Saul drove the spear into the wall. That night David made good his escape.

11 Saul sent men to David's house to watch it and to kill him in the morning. But Michal, David's wife, warned him, 'If you don't run for your life tonight, tomorrow you'll be killed.' 12 So Michal let David down through a window, and he fled and escaped. 13 Then Michal took an idol and laid it on the bed, covering it with a garment and putting some goats' hair at the head.

14 When Saul sent the men to capture David, Michal said, 'He is ill.'

15 Then Saul sent the men back to see David and told them, 'Bring him up to me in his bed so that I may kill him.' 16 But when the men entered, there was the idol in the bed, and at the head was some goats' hair.

17 Saul said to Michal, 'Why did you deceive me like this and send my enemy away so that he escaped?'

Michal told him, 'He said to me, "Let me get away. Why should I kill you?" '

18 When David had fled and made his escape, he went to Samuel at Ramah and told him all that Saul had done to him. Then he and Samuel went to Naioth and stayed there. 19 Word came to Saul: 'David is in Naioth at Ramah'; 20 so he sent men to capture him. But when they saw a group of prophets prophesying, with Samuel standing there as their leader, the Spirit

a 9 Or *But a harmful*

of God came on Saul's men, and they also prophesied. 21 Saul was told about it, and he sent more men, and they prophesied too. Saul sent men a third time, and they also prophesied. 22 Finally, he himself left for Ramah and went to the great cistern at Seku. And he asked, 'Where are Samuel and David?'

'Over in Naioth at Ramah,' they said.

23 So Saul went to Naioth at Ramah. But the Spirit of God came even on him,

and he walked along prophesying until he came to Naioth. 24 He stripped off his garments, and he too prophesied in Samuel's presence. He lay naked all that day and all that night. This is why people say, 'Is Saul also among the prophets?'

David and Jonathan

20 Then David fled from Naioth at Ramah and went to Jonathan and asked, 'What have I done? What is my

FRIENDSHIP 4

David and Jonathan – true friendship

The friendship between David and Jonathan is one of the most famous in the Bible.

Jonathan was Saul's son so should have become king when his father died. Instead God had anointed David – and Saul was so jealous of David that he wanted to kill him. Jonathan, on the other hand, didn't see David as a rival but as a treasured friend (1 Samuel 18). We're told that he loved David as much as he loved himself. That's friendship: putting our friend's needs and desires on a level with our own. Jesus took this even further. In John 15 we read that Jesus calls us his friends and he says, *'Greater love has no one than this: to lay down one's life for one's friends'* (v. 13). Jesus is the ultimate best friend. He loves us so much that he went to the cross so that we could have a relationship with God. He sacrificed everything and endured unimaginable pain, all for us!

We won't have to die in the place of our friends, but there are other ways in which we can 'lay down our lives' for each other. Like Jonathan, we can choose not to be jealous of others and their successes, but to love them and support them come what may. That's putting their needs before our own. In the New Testament we read about a group of friends who were desperate to help a friend (Luke 5). Their friend was unable to walk, so they took him on a mat to see Jesus, but they found that the crowd was too big to get near him. They weren't going to be defeated: they took the roof off the house and lowered their friend down so that he was in front of Jesus and could be healed. They could have said, 'We tried, sorry it didn't work out,' but instead they stopped at nothing until they found a way to help their friend. Those are the kind of friends I want to have. That's the kind of friend I want to be.

Ali Martin

crime? How have I wronged your father, that he is trying to kill me?'

² 'Never!' Jonathan replied. 'You are not going to die! Look, my father doesn't do anything, great or small, without letting me know. Why should he hide this from me? It isn't so!'

³ But David took an oath and said, 'Your father knows very well that I have found favour in your eyes, and he has said to himself, "Jonathan must not know this or he will be grieved." Yet as surely as the LORD lives and as you live, there is only a step between me and death.'

⁴ Jonathan said to David, 'Whatever you want me to do, I'll do for you.'

⁵ So David said, 'Look, tomorrow is the New Moon feast, and I am supposed to dine with the king; but let me go and hide in the field until the evening of the day after tomorrow. ⁶ If your father misses me at all, tell him, "David earnestly asked my permission to hurry to Bethlehem, his home town, because an annual sacrifice is being made there for his whole clan." ⁷ If he says, "Very well," then your servant is safe. But if he loses his temper, you can be sure that he is determined to harm me. ⁸ As for you, show kindness to your servant, for you have brought him into a covenant with you before the LORD. If I am guilty, then kill me yourself! Why hand me over to your father?'

⁹ 'Never!' Jonathan said. 'If I had the least inkling that my father was determined to harm you, wouldn't I tell you?'

¹⁰ David asked, 'Who will tell me if your father answers you harshly?'

¹¹ 'Come,' Jonathan said, 'let's go out into the field.' So they went there together.

¹² Then Jonathan said to David, 'I swear by the LORD, the God of Israel, that I will surely sound out my father by this time the day after tomorrow! If he is favourably disposed towards you, will I not send you word and let you know? ¹³ But if my father intends to harm you, may the LORD deal with me, be it ever so severely, if I do not let you know and send you away in peace. May the LORD be with you as he has been with my father. ¹⁴ But show me unfailing

kindness like the LORD's kindness as long as I live, so that I may not be killed, ¹⁵ and do not ever cut off your kindness from my family – not even when the LORD has cut off every one of David's enemies from the face of the earth.'

¹⁶ So Jonathan made a covenant with the house of David, saying, 'May the LORD call David's enemies to account.' ¹⁷ And Jonathan made David reaffirm his oath out of love for him, because he loved him as he loved himself.

¹⁸ Then Jonathan said to David, 'Tomorrow is the New Moon feast. You will be missed, because your seat will be empty. ¹⁹ The day after tomorrow, towards evening, go to the place where you hid when this trouble began, and wait by the stone Ezel. ²⁰ I will shoot three arrows to the side of it, as though I were shooting at a target. ²¹ Then I will send a boy and say, "Go, find the arrows." If I say to him, "Look, the arrows are on this side of you; bring them here," then come, because, as surely as the LORD lives, you are safe; there is no danger. ²² But if I say to the boy, "Look, the arrows are beyond you," then you must go, because the LORD has sent you away. ²³ And about the matter you and I discussed – remember, the LORD is witness between you and me for ever.'

²⁴ So David hid in the field, and when the New Moon feast came, the king sat down to eat. ²⁵ He sat in his customary place by the wall, opposite Jonathan,ᵃ and Abner sat next to Saul, but David's place was empty. ²⁶ Saul said nothing that day, for he thought, 'Something must have happened to David to make him ceremonially unclean – surely he is unclean.' ²⁷ But the next day, the second day of the month, David's place was empty again. Then Saul said to his son Jonathan, 'Why hasn't the son of Jesse come to the meal, either yesterday or today?'

²⁸ Jonathan answered, 'David earnestly asked me for permission to go to Bethlehem. ²⁹ He said, "Let me go, because our family is observing a sacrifice in the town and my brother has ordered me to be

_____

a 25 Septuagint; Hebrew *wall. Jonathan arose*

there. If I have found favour in your eyes, let me go to see my brothers." That is why he has not come to the king's table.'

³⁰Saul's anger flared up at Jonathan and he said to him, 'You son of a perverse and rebellious woman! Don't I know that you have sided with the son of Jesse to your own shame and to the shame of the mother who bore you? ³¹As long as the son of Jesse lives on this earth, neither you nor your kingdom will be established. Now send someone to bring him to me, for he must die!'

³²'Why should he be put to death? What has he done?' Jonathan asked his father. ³³But Saul hurled his spear at him to kill him. Then Jonathan knew that his father intended to kill David.

³⁴Jonathan got up from the table in fierce anger; on that second day of the feast he did not eat, because he was grieved at his father's shameful treatment of David.

³⁵In the morning Jonathan went out to the field for his meeting with David. He had a small boy with him, ³⁶and he said to the boy, 'Run and find the arrows I shoot.' As the boy ran, he shot an arrow beyond him. ³⁷When the boy came to the place where Jonathan's arrow had fallen, Jonathan called out after him, 'Isn't the arrow beyond you?' ³⁸Then he shouted, 'Hurry! Go quickly! Don't stop!' The boy picked up the arrow and returned to his master. ³⁹(The boy knew nothing about all this; only Jonathan and David knew.) ⁴⁰Then Jonathan gave his weapons to the boy and said, 'Go, carry them back to town.'

⁴¹After the boy had gone, David got up from the south side of the stone and bowed down before Jonathan three times, with his face to the ground. Then they kissed each other and wept together – but David wept the most.

⁴²Jonathan said to David, 'Go in peace, for we have sworn friendship with each other in the name of the LORD, saying, "The LORD is witness between you and me, and between your descendants and my descendants for ever."' Then David left, and Jonathan went back to the town.ᵇ

David at Nob

21 ᵃ David went to Nob, to Ahimelek the priest. Ahimelek trembled when he met him, and asked, 'Why are you alone? Why is no one with you?'

²David answered Ahimelek the priest, 'The king sent me on a mission and said to me, "No one is to know anything about the mission I am sending you on." As for my men, I have told them to meet me at a certain place. ³Now then, what have you to hand? Give me five loaves of bread, or whatever you can find.'

⁴But the priest answered David, 'I don't have any ordinary bread to hand; however, there is some consecrated bread here – provided the men have kept themselves from women.'

⁵David replied, 'Indeed women have been kept from us, as usual wheneverᵇ I set out. The men's bodies are holy even on missions that are not holy. How much more so today!' ⁶So the priest gave him the consecrated bread, since there was no bread there except the bread of the Presence that had been removed from before the LORD and replaced by hot bread on the day it was taken away.

⁷Now one of Saul's servants was there that day, detained before the LORD; he was Doeg the Edomite, Saul's chief shepherd.

⁸David asked Ahimelek, 'Don't you have a spear or sword here? I haven't brought my sword or any other weapon, because the king's mission was urgent.'

⁹The priest replied, 'The sword of Goliath the Philistine, whom you killed in the Valley of Elah, is here; it is wrapped in a cloth behind the ephod. If you want it, take it; there is no sword here but that one.'

David said, 'There is none like it; give it to me.'

David at Gath

¹⁰That day David fled from Saul and went to Achish king of Gath. ¹¹But the servants of Achish said to him, 'Isn't this David, the king of the land? Isn't he the one they sing about in their dances:

ᵇ 42 In Hebrew texts this sentence (20:42b) is numbered 21:1.

ᵃ In Hebrew texts 21:1-15 is numbered 21:2-16.
ᵇ 5 Or *from us in the past few days since*

' "Saul has slain his thousands,
    and David his tens of thousands"?'

¹²David took these words to heart and was very much afraid of Achish king of Gath. ¹³So he feigned insanity in their presence; and while he was in their hands he acted like a madman, making marks on the doors of the gate and letting saliva run down his beard.

¹⁴Achish said to his servants, 'Look at the man! He is insane! Why bring him to me? ¹⁵Am I so short of madmen that you have to bring this fellow here to carry on like this in front of me? Must this man come into my house?'

David at Adullam and Mizpah

22 David left Gath and escaped to the cave of Adullam. When his brothers and his father's household heard about it, they went down to him there. ²All those who were in distress or in debt or discontented gathered round him, and he became their commander. About four hundred men were with him.

³From there David went to Mizpah in Moab and said to the king of Moab, 'Would you let my father and mother come and stay with you until I learn what God will do for me?' ⁴So he left them with the king of Moab, and they stayed with him as long as David was in the stronghold.

⁵But the prophet Gad said to David, 'Do not stay in the stronghold. Go into the land of Judah.' So David left and went to the forest of Hereth.

Saul kills the priests of Nob

⁶Now Saul heard that David and his men had been discovered. And Saul was seated, spear in hand, under the tamarisk tree on the hill at Gibeah, with all his officials standing at his side. ⁷He said to them, 'Listen, men of Benjamin! Will the son of Jesse give all of you fields and vineyards? Will he make all of you commanders of thousands and commanders of hundreds? ⁸Is that why you have all conspired against me? No one tells me when my son makes a covenant with the son of Jesse. None of you is concerned about me or tells me that

my son has incited my servant to lie in wait for me, as he does today.'

⁹But Doeg the Edomite, who was standing with Saul's officials, said, 'I saw the son of Jesse come to Ahimelek son of Ahitub at Nob. ¹⁰Ahimelek enquired of the LORD for him; he also gave him provisions and the sword of Goliath the Philistine.'

¹¹Then the king sent for the priest Ahimelek son of Ahitub and all the men of his family, who were the priests at Nob, and they all came to the king. ¹²Saul said, 'Listen now, son of Ahitub.'

'Yes, my lord,' he answered.

¹³Saul said to him, 'Why have you conspired against me, you and the son of Jesse, giving him bread and a sword and enquiring of God for him, so that he has rebelled against me and lies in wait for me, as he does today?'

¹⁴Ahimelek answered the king, 'Who of all your servants is as loyal as David, the king's son-in-law, captain of your bodyguard and highly respected in your household? ¹⁵Was that day the first time I enquired of God for him? Of course not! Let not the king accuse your servant or any of his father's family, for your servant knows nothing at all about this whole affair.'

¹⁶But the king said, 'You shall surely die, Ahimelek, you and your whole family.'

¹⁷Then the king ordered the guards at his side: 'Turn and kill the priests of the LORD, because they too have sided with David. They knew he was fleeing, yet they did not tell me.'

But the king's officials were unwilling to raise a hand to strike the priests of the LORD.

¹⁸The king then ordered Doeg, 'You turn and strike down the priests.' So Doeg the Edomite turned and struck them down. That day he killed eighty-five men who wore the linen ephod. ¹⁹He also put to the sword Nob, the town of the priests, with its men and women, its children and infants, and its cattle, donkeys and sheep.

²⁰But one son of Ahimelek son of Ahitub, named Abiathar, escaped and fled to join David. ²¹He told David that Saul had killed the priests of the LORD. ²²Then

David said to Abiathar, 'That day, when Doeg the Edomite was there, I knew he would be sure to tell Saul. I am responsible for the death of your whole family. 23 Stay with me; don't be afraid. The man who wants to kill you is trying to kill me too. You will be safe with me.'

David saves Keilah

23 When David was told, 'Look, the Philistines are fighting against Keilah and are looting the threshing-floors,' 2 he enquired of the LORD, saying, 'Shall I go and attack these Philistines?'

The LORD answered him, 'Go, attack the Philistines and save Keilah.'

3 But David's men said to him, 'Here in Judah we are afraid. How much more, then, if we go to Keilah against the Philistine forces!'

4 Once again David enquired of the LORD, and the LORD answered him, 'Go down to Keilah, for I am going to give the Philistines into your hand.' 5 So David and his men went to Keilah, fought the Philistines and carried off their livestock. He inflicted heavy losses on the Philistines and saved the people of Keilah. 6 (Now Abiathar son of Ahimelek had brought the ephod down with him when he fled to David at Keilah.)

Saul pursues David

7 Saul was told that David had gone to Keilah, and he said, 'God has delivered him into my hands, for David has imprisoned himself by entering a town with gates and bars.' 8 And Saul called up all his forces for battle, to go down to Keilah to besiege David and his men.

9 When David learned that Saul was plotting against him, he said to Abiathar the priest, 'Bring the ephod.' 10 David said, 'LORD, God of Israel, your servant has heard definitely that Saul plans to come to Keilah and destroy the town on account of me. 11 Will the citizens of Keilah surrender me to him? Will Saul come down, as your servant has heard? LORD, God of Israel, tell your servant.'

And the LORD said, 'He will.'

12 Again David asked, 'Will the citizens of Keilah surrender me and my men to Saul?'

And the LORD said, 'They will.'

13 So David and his men, about six hundred in number, left Keilah and kept moving from place to place. When Saul was told that David had escaped from Keilah, he did not go there.

14 David stayed in the wilderness strongholds and in the hills of the Desert of Ziph. Day after day Saul searched for him, but God did not give David into his hands.

15 While David was at Horesh, in the Desert of Ziph, he learned that[a] Saul had come out to take his life. 16 And Saul's son Jonathan went to David at Horesh and helped him to find strength in God. 17 'Don't be afraid,' he said. 'My father Saul will not lay a hand on you. You shall be king over Israel, and I will be second to you. Even my father Saul knows this.' 18 The two of them made a covenant before the LORD. Then Jonathan went home, but David remained at Horesh.

19 The Ziphites went up to Saul at Gibeah and said, 'Is not David hiding among us in the strongholds at Horesh, on the hill of Hakilah, south of Jeshimon? 20 Now, Your Majesty, come down whenever it pleases you to do so, and we will be responsible for giving him into your hands.'

21 Saul replied, 'The LORD bless you for your concern for me. 22 Go and get more information. Find out where David usually goes and who has seen him there. They tell me he is very crafty. 23 Find out about all the hiding-places he uses and come back to me with definite information. Then I will go with you; if he is in the area, I will track him down among all the clans of Judah.'

24 So they set out and went to Ziph ahead of Saul. Now David and his men were in the Desert of Maon, in the Arabah south of Jeshimon. 25 Saul and his men began the search, and when David was told about it, he went down to the rock and stayed in the Desert of Maon. When Saul heard this, he went into the Desert of Maon in pursuit of David.

---

a 15 Or he was afraid because

²⁶Saul was going along one side of the mountain, and David and his men were on the other side, hurrying to get away from Saul. As Saul and his forces were closing in on David and his men to capture them, ²⁷a messenger came to Saul, saying, 'Come quickly! The Philistines are raiding the land.' ²⁸Then Saul broke off his pursuit of David and went to meet the Philistines. That is why they call this place Sela Hammahlekoth.ᵇ ²⁹And David went up from there and lived in the strongholds of En Gedi.ᶜ

David spares Saul's life

24ᵃ After Saul returned from pursuing the Philistines, he was told, 'David is in the Desert of En Gedi.' ²So Saul took three thousand able young men from all Israel and set out to look for David and his men near the Crags of the Wild Goats.

³He came to the sheepfolds along the way; a cave was there, and Saul went in to relieve himself. David and his men were far back in the cave. ⁴The men said, 'This is the day the LORD spoke of when he saidᵇ to you, "I will give your enemy into your hands for you to deal with as you wish."' Then David crept up unnoticed and cut off a corner of Saul's robe.

⁵Afterwards, David was conscience-stricken for having cut off a corner of his robe. ⁶He said to his men, 'The LORD forbid that I should do such a thing to my master, the LORD's anointed, or lay my hand on him; for he is the anointed of the LORD.' ⁷With these words David sharply rebuked his men and did not allow them to attack Saul. And Saul left the cave and went his way.

⁸Then David went out of the cave and called out to Saul, 'My lord the king!' When Saul looked behind him, David bowed down and prostrated himself with his face to the ground. ⁹He said to Saul, 'Why do you listen when men say, "David

---

b 28 *Sela Hammahlekoth* means *rock of parting.*
c 29 In Hebrew texts this verse (23:29) is numbered 24:1.
a In Hebrew texts 24:1-22 is numbered 24:2-23.
b 4 Or *Today the LORD is saying*

---

is bent on harming you"? ¹⁰This day you have seen with your own eyes how the LORD gave you into my hands in the cave. Some urged me to kill you, but I spared you; I said, "I will not lay my hand on my lord, because he is the LORD's anointed." ¹¹See, my father, look at this piece of your robe in my hand! I cut off the corner of your robe but did not kill you. See that there is nothing in my hand to indicate that I am guilty of wrongdoing or rebellion. I have not wronged you, but you are hunting me down to take my life. ¹²May the LORD judge between you and me. And may the LORD avenge the wrongs you have done to me, but my hand will not touch you. ¹³As the old saying goes, "From evildoers come evil deeds," so my hand will not touch you.

PEOPLE TOURS

DAVID

GOLIATH
1 Samuel 17:1–54

JONATHAN
1 Samuel 20:1–42

ESCAPE
1 Samuel 24:1–22

ARK
2 Samuel 6:1–23

PROMISE
2 Samuel 7:1–29

BATHSHEBA
2 Samuel 11:1 – 12:25

DEATH
1 Kings 1:1–4; 2:1–12

¹⁴'Against whom has the king of Israel come out? Who are you pursuing? A dead dog? A flea? ¹⁵May the LORD be our judge and decide between us. May he consider my cause and uphold it; may he vindicate me by delivering me from your hand.'

¹⁶When David finished saying this, Saul asked, 'Is that your voice, David my son?' And he wept aloud. ¹⁷'You are more

righteous than I,' he said. 'You have treated me well, but I have treated you badly. ¹⁸You have just now told me about the good you did to me; the LORD gave me into your hands, but you did not kill me. ¹⁹When a man finds his enemy, does he let him get away unharmed? May the LORD reward you well for the way you treated me today. ²⁰I know that you will surely be king and that the kingdom of Israel will be established in your hands. ²¹Now swear to me by the LORD that you will not kill off my descendants or wipe out my name from my father's family.'

²²So David gave his oath to Saul. Then Saul returned home, but David and his men went up to the stronghold.

David, Nabal and Abigail

25 Now Samuel died, and all Israel assembled and mourned for him; and they buried him at his home in Ramah. Then David moved down into the Desert of Paran.*ᵃ*

²A certain man in Maon, who had property there at Carmel, was very wealthy. He had a thousand goats and three thousand sheep, which he was shearing in Carmel. ³His name was Nabal and his wife's name was Abigail. She was an intelligent and beautiful woman, but her husband was surly and mean in his dealings – he was a Calebite.

⁴While David was in the wilderness, he heard that Nabal was shearing sheep. ⁵So he sent ten young men and said to them, 'Go up to Nabal at Carmel and greet him in my name. ⁶Say to him: "Long life to you! Good health to you and your household! And good health to all that is yours!

⁷' "Now I hear that it is sheep-shearing time. When your shepherds were with us, we did not ill-treat them, and the whole time they were at Carmel nothing of theirs was missing. ⁸Ask your own servants and they will tell you. Therefore be favourable towards my men, since we come at a festive time. Please give your servants and

your son David whatever you can find for them." '

⁹When David's men arrived, they gave Nabal this message in David's name. Then they waited.

¹⁰Nabal answered David's servants, 'Who is this David? Who is this son of Jesse? Many servants are breaking away from their masters these days. ¹¹Why should I take my bread and water, and the meat I have slaughtered for my shearers, and give it to men coming from who knows where?'

¹²David's men turned round and went back. When they arrived, they reported every word. ¹³David said to his men, 'Each of you strap on your sword!' So they did, and David strapped his on as well. About four hundred men went up with David, while two hundred stayed with the supplies.

¹⁴One of the servants told Abigail, Nabal's wife, 'David sent messengers from the wilderness to give our master his greetings, but he hurled insults at them. ¹⁵Yet these men were very good to us. They did not ill-treat us, and the whole time we were out in the fields near them nothing was missing. ¹⁶Night and day they were a wall around us the whole time we were herding our sheep near them. ¹⁷Now think it over and see what you can do, because disaster is hanging over our master and his whole household. He is such a wicked man that no one can talk to him.'

¹⁸Abigail acted quickly. She took two hundred loaves of bread, two skins of wine, five dressed sheep, five seahs*ᵇ* of roasted grain, a hundred cakes of raisins and two hundred cakes of pressed figs, and loaded them on donkeys. ¹⁹Then she told her servants, 'Go on ahead; I'll follow you.' But she did not tell her husband Nabal.

²⁰As she came riding her donkey into a mountain ravine, there were David and his men descending towards her, and she met them. ²¹David had just said, 'It's been useless – all my watching over this fellow's property in the wilderness so that nothing of his was missing. He has paid me back

---

a 1 Hebrew and some Septuagint manuscripts; other Septuagint manuscripts *Maon*

b 18 That is, probably about 27 kilograms

evil for good. ²²May God deal with David,ᶜ be it ever so severely, if by morning I leave alive one male of all who belong to him!'

²³When Abigail saw David, she quickly got off her donkey and bowed down before David with her face to the ground. ²⁴She fell at his feet and said: 'Pardon your servant, my lord, and let me speak to you; hear what your servant has to say. ²⁵Please pay no attention, my lord, to that wicked man Nabal. He is just like his name – his name means Fool, and folly goes with him. And as for me, your servant, I did not see the men my lord sent. ²⁶And now, my lord, as surely as the LORD your God lives and as you live, since the LORD has kept you from bloodshed and from avenging yourself with your own hands, may your enemies and all who are intent on harming my lord be like Nabal. ²⁷And let this gift, which your servant has brought to my lord, be given to the men who follow you.

²⁸'Please forgive your servant's presumption. The LORD your God will certainly make a lasting dynasty for my lord, because you fight the LORD's battles, and no wrongdoing will be found in you as long as you live. ²⁹Even though someone is pursuing you to take your life, the life of my lord will be bound securely in the bundle of the living by the LORD your God, but the lives of your enemies he will hurl away as from the pocket of a sling. ³⁰When the LORD has fulfilled for my lord every good thing he promised concerning him and has appointed him ruler over Israel, ³¹my lord will not have on his conscience the staggering burden of needless bloodshed or of having avenged himself. And when the LORD your God has brought my lord success, remember your servant.'

³²David said to Abigail, 'Praise be to the LORD, the God of Israel, who has sent you today to meet me. ³³May you be blessed for your good judgment and for keeping me from bloodshed this day and from avenging myself with my own hands. ³⁴Otherwise, as surely as the LORD, the God of Israel, lives, who has kept me from harming you, if you had not come quickly to meet me, not one male belonging to Nabal would have been left alive by daybreak.'

³⁵Then David accepted from her hand what she had brought to him and said, 'Go home in peace. I have heard your words and granted your request.'

³⁶When Abigail went to Nabal, he was in the house holding a banquet like that of a king. He was in high spirits and very drunk. So she told him nothing at all until daybreak. ³⁷Then in the morning, when Nabal was sober, his wife told him all these things, and his heart failed him and he became like a stone. ³⁸About ten days later, the LORD struck Nabal and he died.

³⁹When David heard that Nabal was dead, he said, 'Praise be to the LORD, who has upheld my cause against Nabal for treating me with contempt. He has kept his servant from doing wrong and has brought Nabal's wrongdoing down on his own head.'

Then David sent word to Abigail, asking her to become his wife. ⁴⁰His servants went to Carmel and said to Abigail, 'David has sent us to you to take you to become his wife.'

⁴¹She bowed down with her face to the ground and said, 'I am your servant and am ready to serve you and wash the feet of my lord's servants.' ⁴²Abigail quickly got on a donkey and, attended by her five female servants, went with David's messengers and became his wife. ⁴³David had also married Ahinoam of Jezreel, and they both were his wives. ⁴⁴But Saul had given his daughter Michal, David's wife, to Paltielᵈ son of Laish, who was from Gallim.

David again spares Saul's life

26 The Ziphites went to Saul at Gibeah and said, 'Is not David hiding on the hill of Hakilah, which faces Jeshimon?' ²So Saul went down to the Desert of Ziph, with his three thousand select Israelite troops, to search there for David. ³Saul made his camp beside the road on the hill of Hakilah facing Jeshimon, but David stayed in the wilderness. When he

c 22 Some Septuagint manuscripts; Hebrew *with David's enemies*
d 44 Hebrew *Palti*, a variant of *Paltiel*

saw that Saul had followed him there, **4** he sent out scouts and learned that Saul had definitely arrived.

5 Then David set out and went to the place where Saul had camped. He saw where Saul and Abner son of Ner, the commander of the army, had lain down. Saul was lying inside the camp, with the army camped around him.

6 David then asked Ahimelek the Hittite and Abishai son of Zeruiah, Joab's brother, 'Who will go down into the camp with me to Saul?'

'I'll go with you,' said Abishai.

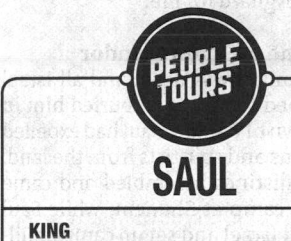

PEOPLE TOURS

SAUL

KING
1 Samuel 9:1 – 10:8
WINNING
1 Samuel 11:1–15
DISOBEDIENCE
1 Samuel 15:1–35
MEDIUM
1 Samuel 28:1–25
DEATH
1 Samuel 31:1–13

7 So David and Abishai went to the army by night, and there was Saul, lying asleep inside the camp with his spear stuck in the ground near his head. Abner and the soldiers were lying round him.

8 Abishai said to David, 'Today God has given your enemy into your hands. Now let me pin him to the ground with one thrust of the spear; I won't strike him twice.'

9 But David said to Abishai, 'Don't destroy him! Who can lay a hand on the LORD's anointed and be guiltless? **10** As surely as the LORD lives,' he said, 'the LORD himself will strike him, or his time will come and he will die, or he will go into battle and perish. **11** But the LORD forbid that I should lay a hand on the LORD's

anointed. Now get the spear and water jug that are near his head, and let's go.'

12 So David took the spear and water jug near Saul's head, and they left. No one saw or knew about it, nor did anyone wake up. They were all sleeping, because the LORD had put them into a deep sleep.

13 Then David crossed over to the other side and stood on top of the hill some distance away; there was a wide space between them. **14** He called out to the army and to Abner son of Ner, 'Aren't you going to answer me, Abner?'

Abner replied, 'Who are you who calls to the king?'

15 David said, 'You're a man, aren't you? And who is like you in Israel? Why didn't you guard your lord the king? Someone came to destroy your lord the king. **16** What you have done is not good. As surely as the LORD lives, you and your men must die, because you did not guard your master, the LORD's anointed. Look around you. Where are the king's spear and water jug that were near his head?'

17 Saul recognised David's voice and said, 'Is that your voice, David my son?'

David replied, 'Yes it is, my lord the king.' **18** And he added, 'Why is my lord pursuing his servant? What have I done, and what wrong am I guilty of? **19** Now let my lord the king listen to his servant's words. If the LORD has incited you against me, then may he accept an offering. If, however, people have done it, may they be cursed before the LORD! They have driven me today from my share in the LORD's inheritance and have said, "Go, serve other gods." **20** Now do not let my blood fall to the ground far from the presence of the LORD. The king of Israel has come out to look for a flea – as one hunts a partridge in the mountains.'

21 Then Saul said, 'I have sinned. Come back, David my son. Because you considered my life precious today, I will not try to harm you again. Surely I have acted like a fool and have been terribly wrong.'

22 'Here is the king's spear,' David answered. 'Let one of your young men come over and get it. **23** The LORD rewards everyone for their righteousness and faithfulness. The LORD gave you into my hands today, but I would not lay a hand on the LORD's anointed. 24 As surely as I valued your life today, so may the LORD value my life and deliver me from all trouble.'

25 Then Saul said to David, 'May you be blessed, David my son; you will do great things and surely triumph.'

So David went on his way, and Saul returned home.

David among the Philistines

27 But David thought to himself, 'One of these days I shall be destroyed by the hand of Saul. The best thing I can do is to escape to the land of the Philistines. Then Saul will give up searching for me anywhere in Israel, and I will slip out of his hand.'

2 So David and the six hundred men with him left and went over to Achish son of Maok king of Gath. 3 David and his men settled in Gath with Achish. Each man had his family with him, and David had his two wives: Ahinoam of Jezreel and Abigail of Carmel, the widow of Nabal. 4 When Saul was told that David had fled to Gath, he no longer searched for him.

5 Then David said to Achish, 'If I have found favour in your eyes, let a place be assigned to me in one of the country towns, that I may live there. Why should your servant live in the royal city with you?'

6 So on that day Achish gave him Ziklag, and it has belonged to the kings of Judah ever since. 7 David lived in Philistine territory for a year and four months.

8 Now David and his men went up and raided the Geshurites, the Girzites and the Amalekites. (From ancient times these peoples had lived in the land extending to Shur and Egypt.) 9 Whenever David attacked an area, he did not leave a man or woman alive, but took sheep and cattle, donkeys and camels, and clothes. Then he returned to Achish.

10 When Achish asked, 'Where did you go raiding today?' David would say, 'Against the Negev of Judah' or 'Against the Negev of Jerahmeel' or 'Against the Negev of the Kenites.' 11 He did not leave a man or woman alive to be brought to Gath, for he thought, 'They might inform on us and

say, "This is what David did."' And such was his practice as long as he lived in Philistine territory. 12 Achish trusted David and said to himself, 'He has become so obnoxious to his people, the Israelites, that he will be my servant for life.'

28 In those days the Philistines gathered their forces to fight against Israel. Achish said to David, 'You must understand that you and your men will accompany me in the army.'

2 David said, 'Then you will see for yourself what your servant can do.'

Achish replied, 'Very well, I will make you my bodyguard for life.'

Saul and the medium at Endor

3 Now Samuel was dead, and all Israel had mourned for him and buried him in his own town of Ramah. Saul had expelled the mediums and spiritists from the land.

4 The Philistines assembled and came and set up camp at Shunem, while Saul gathered all Israel and set up camp at Gilboa. 5 When Saul saw the Philistine army, he was afraid; terror filled his heart. 6 He enquired of the LORD, but the LORD did not answer him by dreams or Urim or prophets. 7 Saul then said to his attendants, 'Find me a woman who is a medium, so that I may go and enquire of her.'

'There is one in Endor,' they said.

8 So Saul disguised himself, putting on other clothes, and at night he and two men went to the woman. 'Consult a spirit for me,' he said, 'and bring up for me the one I name.'

9 But the woman said to him, 'Surely you know what Saul has done. He has cut off the mediums and spiritists from the land. Why have you set a trap for my life to bring about my death?'

10 Saul swore to her by the LORD, 'As surely as the LORD lives, you will not be punished for this.'

11 Then the woman asked, 'Whom shall I bring up for you?'

'Bring up Samuel,' he said.

12 When the woman saw Samuel, she cried out at the top of her voice and said to Saul, 'Why have you deceived me? You are Saul!'

13 The king said to her, 'Don't be afraid. What do you see?'

The woman said, 'I see a ghostly figure[a] coming up out of the earth.'

14 'What does he look like?' he asked.

'An old man wearing a robe is coming up,' she said.

Then Saul knew it was Samuel, and he bowed down and prostrated himself with his face to the ground.

15 Samuel said to Saul, 'Why have you disturbed me by bringing me up?'

'I am in great distress,' Saul said. 'The Philistines are fighting against me, and God has departed from me. He no longer answers me, either by prophets or by dreams. So I have called on you to tell me what to do.'

16 Samuel said, 'Why do you consult me, now that the LORD has departed from you and become your enemy? **17** The LORD has done what he predicted through me. The LORD has torn the kingdom out of your hands and given it to one of your neighbours – to David. **18** Because you did not obey the LORD or carry out his fierce wrath against the Amalekites, the LORD has done this to you today. **19** The LORD will deliver both Israel and you into the hands of the Philistines, and tomorrow you and your sons will be with me. The LORD will also give the army of Israel into the hands of the Philistines.'

20 Immediately Saul fell full length on the ground, filled with fear because of Samuel's words. His strength was gone, for he had eaten nothing all that day and all that night.

21 When the woman came to Saul and saw that he was greatly shaken, she said, 'Look, your servant has obeyed you. I took my life in my hands and did what you told me to do. **22** Now please listen to your servant and let me give you some food so that you may eat and have the strength to go on your way.'

23 He refused and said, 'I will not eat.'

But his men joined the woman in urging him, and he listened to them. He got up from the ground and sat on the couch.

24 The woman had a fattened calf at the house, which she slaughtered at once. She took some flour, kneaded it and baked bread without yeast. **25** Then she set it before Saul and his men, and they ate. That same night they got up and left.

Achish sends David back to Ziklag

29 The Philistines gathered all their forces at Aphek, and Israel camped by the spring in Jezreel. **2** As the Philistine rulers marched with their units of hundreds and thousands, David and his men were marching at the rear with Achish. **3** The commanders of the Philistines asked, 'What about these Hebrews?'

Achish replied, 'Is this not David, who was an officer of Saul king of Israel? He has already been with me for over a year, and from the day he left Saul until now, I have found no fault in him.'

4 But the Philistine commanders were angry with Achish and said, 'Send the man back, that he may return to the place you assigned him. He must not go with us into battle, or he will turn against us during the fighting. How better could he regain his master's favour than by taking the heads of our own men? **5** Isn't this the David they sang about in their dances:

'"Saul has slain his thousands,
    and David his tens of thousands"?'

6 So Achish called David and said to him, 'As surely as the LORD lives, you have been reliable, and I would be pleased for you to serve with me in the army. From the day you came to me until today, I have found no fault in you, but the rulers don't approve of you. **7** Now turn back and go in peace; do nothing to displease the Philistine rulers.'

8 'But what have I done?' asked David. 'What have you found against your servant from the day I came to you until now? Why can't I go and fight against the enemies of my lord the king?'

9 Achish answered, 'I know that you have been as pleasing in my eyes as an angel of God; nevertheless, the Philistine commanders have said, "He must not

---

a 13 Or see spirits; or see gods

go up with us into battle." 10 Now get up early, along with your master's servants who have come with you, and leave in the morning as soon as it is light.'

11 So David and his men got up early in the morning to go back to the land of the Philistines, and the Philistines went up to Jezreel.

FACT

CAMEL EXPERT

Camels were important animals for transport and for military purposes. They were fast: during one battle 400 young men made their escape by camel (1 Samuel 30:17). David had so many camels that he had to appoint an Arab expert – Ofil the Ishmaelite – to look after them (1 Chronicles 27:30).

David destroys the Amalekites

30 David and his men reached Ziklag on the third day. Now the Amalekites had raided the Negev and Ziklag. They had attacked Ziklag and burned it, 2 and had taken captive the women and everyone else in it, both young and old. They killed none of them, but carried them off as they went on their way.

3 When David and his men reached Ziklag, they found it destroyed by fire and their wives and sons and daughters taken captive. 4 So David and his men wept aloud until they had no strength left to weep. 5 David's two wives had been captured – Ahinoam of Jezreel and Abigail, the widow of Nabal of Carmel. 6 David was greatly distressed because the men were talking of stoning him; each one was bitter in spirit because of his sons and daughters. But David found strength in the LORD his God.

7 Then David said to Abiathar the priest, the son of Ahimelek, 'Bring me the ephod.' Abiathar brought it to him, 8 and David

enquired of the LORD, 'Shall I pursue this raiding party? Will I overtake them?'

'Pursue them,' he answered. 'You will certainly overtake them and succeed in the rescue.'

9 David and the six hundred men with him came to the Besor Valley, where some stayed behind. 10 Two hundred of them were too exhausted to cross the valley, but David and the other four hundred continued the pursuit.

11 They found an Egyptian in a field and brought him to David. They gave him water to drink and food to eat – 12 part of a cake of pressed figs and two cakes of raisins. He ate and was revived, for he had not eaten any food or drunk any water for three days and three nights.

13 David asked him, 'Who do you belong to? Where do you come from?'

He said, 'I am an Egyptian, the slave of an Amalekite. My master abandoned me when I became ill three days ago. 14 We raided the Negev of the Kerethites, some territory belonging to Judah and the Negev of Caleb. And we burned Ziklag.'

15 David asked him, 'Can you lead me down to this raiding party?'

He answered, 'Swear to me before God that you will not kill me or hand me over to my master, and I will take you down to them.'

16 He led David down, and there they were, scattered over the countryside, eating, drinking and revelling because of the great amount of plunder they had taken from the land of the Philistines and from Judah. 17 David fought them from dusk until the evening of the next day, and none of them got away, except four hundred young men who rode off on camels and fled. 18 David recovered everything the Amalekites had taken, including his two wives. 19 Nothing was missing: young or old, boy or girl, plunder or anything else they had taken. David brought everything back. 20 He took all the flocks and herds, and his men drove them ahead of the other livestock, saying, 'This is David's plunder.'

21 Then David came to the two hundred men who had been too exhausted

to follow him and who were left behind at the Besor Valley. They came out to meet David and the men with him. As David and his men approached, he asked them how they were. 22 But all the evil men and troublemakers among David's followers said, 'Because they did not go out with us, we will not share with them the plunder we recovered. However, each man may take his wife and children and go.'

23 David replied, 'No, my brothers, you must not do that with what the LORD has given us. He has protected us and delivered into our hands the raiding party that came against us. 24 Who will listen to what you say? The share of the man who stayed with the supplies is to be the same as that of him who went down to the battle. All shall share alike.' 25 David made this a statute and ordinance for Israel from that day to this.

26 When David reached Ziklag, he sent some of the plunder to the elders of Judah, who were his friends, saying, 'Here is a gift for you from the plunder of the LORD's enemies.'

27 David sent it to those who were in Bethel, Ramoth Negev and Jattir; 28 to those in Aroer, Siphmoth, Eshtemoa 29 and Rakal; to those in the towns of the Jerahmeelites and the Kenites; 30 to those in Hormah, Bor Ashan, Athak 31 and Hebron; and to those in all the other places where he and his men had roamed.

Saul takes his life

31 Now the Philistines fought against Israel; the Israelites fled before them, and many fell dead on Mount Gilboa. 2 The Philistines were in hot pursuit of Saul and his sons, and they killed his sons Jonathan, Abinadab and Malki-Shua.

3 The fighting grew fierce around Saul, and when the archers overtook him, they wounded him critically.

4 Saul said to his armour-bearer, 'Draw your sword and run me through, or these uncircumcised fellows will come and run me through and abuse me.'

But the armour-bearer was terrified and would not do it; so Saul took his own sword and fell on it. 5 When the armourbearer saw that Saul was dead, he too fell on his sword and died with him. 6 So Saul and his three sons and his armour-bearer and all his men died together that same day.

7 When the Israelites along the valley and those across the Jordan saw that the Israelite army had fled and that Saul and his sons had died, they abandoned their towns and fled. And the Philistines came and occupied them.

8 The next day, when the Philistines came to strip the dead, they found Saul and his three sons fallen on Mount Gilboa. 9 They cut off his head and stripped off his armour, and they sent messengers throughout the land of the Philistines to proclaim the news in the temple of their idols and among their people. 10 They put his armour in the temple of the Ashtoreths and fastened his body to the wall of Beth Shan.

11 When the people of Jabesh Gilead heard what the Philistines had done to Saul, 12 all their valiant men marched through the night to Beth Shan. They took down the bodies of Saul and his sons from the wall of Beth Shan and went to Jabesh, where they burned them. 13 Then they took their bones and buried them under a tamarisk tree at Jabesh, and they fasted seven days.

2 SAMUEL

DATE

Events in 1 and 2 Samuel are dated at around 1075–975 BC

AUTHOR

Unknown

WHAT'S IT ALL ABOUT?

The second part of the book of Samuel picks up exactly where the first left off and tells of the reign of King David (although all the tribes except Judah contested his authority at first, remaining loyal to the deceased Saul). The book is a fascinating account of a man who was incredibly passionate for God, and yet so flawed that he could not seem to help making mistakes (something, perhaps, to which we can all relate). Under his reign, Israel prospered and defeated their enemies. David even brought back the ark of the covenant, taken by the Philistines in 1 Samuel. In contrast, David also took Bathsheba, another man's wife, to his bed and killed her husband to try to cover up his actions. He was a weak father and his own son, Absalom, rebelled against him and tried to take the throne. Yet throughout the book we see that despite his flaws David was always willing to repent and worship the Lord. He was a strong king and he set the standard by which those who followed him would be judged.

WHY SHOULD WE READ IT?

- To learn about God's promise that David's kingdom will endure for ever, a promise fulfilled when Jesus was born as a descendant of David (2 Samuel 7).

- To see David's incredible example of a man who worships (especially 2 Samuel 6; 12:20 and 22).

- To be encouraged that even when we make mistakes, God still loves us and can still use us.

- To understand what it means to be a true worshipper (especially 2 Samuel 6 and 12).

Andy Croft with Liza Hoeksma

David hears of Saul's death

1 After the death of Saul, David returned from striking down the Amalekites and stayed in Ziklag two days. ²On the third day a man arrived from Saul's camp with his clothes torn and dust on his head. When he came to David, he fell to the ground to pay him honour.

³'Where have you come from?' David asked him.

He answered, 'I have escaped from the Israelite camp.'

⁴'What happened?' David asked. 'Tell me.'

'The men fled from the battle,' he replied. 'Many of them fell and died. And Saul and his son Jonathan are dead.'

⁵Then David said to the young man who brought him the report, 'How do you know that Saul and his son Jonathan are dead?'

⁶'I happened to be on Mount Gilboa,' the young man said, 'and there was Saul, leaning on his spear, with the chariots and their drivers in hot pursuit. ⁷When he turned round and saw me, he called out to me, and I said, "What can I do?"

⁸'He asked me, "Who are you?"

' "An Amalekite," I answered.

⁹'Then he said to me, "Stand here by me and kill me! I'm in the throes of death, but I'm still alive."

¹⁰'So I stood beside him and killed him, because I knew that after he had fallen he could not survive. And I took the crown that was on his head and the band on his arm and have brought them here to my lord.'

¹¹Then David and all the men with him took hold of their clothes and tore them. ¹²They mourned and wept and fasted till evening for Saul and his son Jonathan, and for the army of the LORD and for the nation of Israel, because they had fallen by the sword.

¹³David said to the young man who brought him the report, 'Where are you from?'

'I am the son of a foreigner, an Amalekite,' he answered.

¹⁴David asked him, 'Why weren't you afraid to lift your hand to destroy the LORD's anointed?'

¹⁵Then David called one of his men and said, 'Go, strike him down!' So he struck him down, and he died. ¹⁶For David had said to him, 'Your blood be on your own head. Your own mouth testified against you when you said, "I killed the LORD's anointed." '

David's lament for Saul and Jonathan

¹⁷David took up this lament concerning Saul and his son Jonathan, ¹⁸and he ordered that the people of Judah be taught this lament of the bow (it is written in the Book of Jashar):

¹⁹'A gazelle*a* lies slain on your heights,
　　Israel.
　How the mighty have fallen!

²⁰'Tell it not in Gath,
　　proclaim it not in the streets of
　　　Ashkelon,
　lest the daughters of the Philistines be
　　glad,
　　lest the daughters of the
　　　uncircumcised rejoice.

²¹'Mountains of Gilboa,
　　may you have neither dew nor rain,
　　may no showers fall on your
　　　terraced fields.*b*
　For there the shield of the mighty was
　　despised,
　　the shield of Saul – no longer
　　　rubbed with oil.

²²'From the blood of the slain,
　　from the flesh of the mighty,
　the bow of Jonathan did not turn back,
　　the sword of Saul did not return
　　　unsatisfied.
²³Saul and Jonathan –
　　in life they were loved and admired,
　　and in death they were not parted.
　They were swifter than eagles,
　　they were stronger than lions.

²⁴'Daughters of Israel,
　　weep for Saul,

---

a 19 *Gazelle* here symbolises a human dignitary.
b 21 Or / *nor fields that yield grain for offerings*

who clothed you in scarlet and finery,
who adorned your garments with
ornaments of gold.

25 'How the mighty have fallen in battle!
Jonathan lies slain on your heights.
26 I grieve for you, Jonathan my brother;
you were very dear to me.
Your love for me was wonderful,
more wonderful than that of
women.

27 'How the mighty have fallen!
The weapons of war have perished!'

David anointed king over Judah

2 In the course of time, David enquired
of the LORD. 'Shall I go up to one of
the towns of Judah?' he asked.

The LORD said, 'Go up.'

David asked, 'Where shall I go?'

'To Hebron,' the LORD answered.

2 So David went up there with his two
wives, Ahinoam of Jezreel and Abigail,
the widow of Nabal of Carmel. 3 David also
took the men who were with him, each
with his family, and they settled in Hebron
and its towns. 4 Then the men of Judah
came to Hebron, and there they anointed
David king over the tribe of Judah.

When David was told that it was the
men from Jabesh Gilead who had buried
Saul, 5 he sent messengers to them to say
to them, 'The LORD bless you for showing
this kindness to Saul your master by burying him. 6 May the LORD now show you
kindness and faithfulness, and I too will
show you the same favour because you
have done this. 7 Now then, be strong and
brave, for Saul your master is dead, and
the people of Judah have anointed me
king over them.'

War between the houses of David and Saul

8 Meanwhile, Abner son of Ner, the
commander of Saul's army, had taken Ish-
Bosheth son of Saul and brought him over
to Mahanaim. 9 He made him king
over Gilead, Ashuri and Jezreel, and also
over Ephraim, Benjamin and all Israel.
10 Ish-Bosheth son of Saul was forty

years old when he became king over Israel, and he reigned two years. The tribe of
Judah, however, remained loyal to David.
11 The length of time David was king in
Hebron over Judah was seven years and
six months.

12 Abner son of Ner, together with the
men of Ish-Bosheth son of Saul, left Mahanaim and went to Gibeon. 13 Joab son
of Zeruiah and David's men went out and
met them at the pool of Gibeon. One
group sat down on one side of the pool
and one group on the other side.

14 Then Abner said to Joab, 'Let's have
some of the young men get up and fight
hand to hand in front of us.'

'All right, let them do it,' Joab said.

15 So they stood up and were counted –
twelve men for Benjamin and Ish-Bosheth
son of Saul, and twelve for David. 16 Then
each man grabbed his opponent by the
head and thrust his dagger into his opponent's side, and they fell down together.
So that place in Gibeon was called Helkath
Hazzurim.ᵃ

17 The battle that day was very fierce, and
Abner and the Israelites were defeated by
David's men.

18 The three sons of Zeruiah were there:
Joab, Abishai and Asahel. Now Asahel
was as fleet-footed as a wild gazelle. 19 He
chased Abner, turning neither to the right
nor to the left as he pursued him. 20 Abner looked behind him and asked, 'Is that
you, Asahel?'

'It is,' he answered.

21 Then Abner said to him, 'Turn aside to
the right or to the left; take on one of the
young men and strip him of his weapons.'
But Asahel would not stop chasing him.

22 Again Abner warned Asahel, 'Stop
chasing me! Why should I strike you
down? How could I look your brother Joab
in the face?'

23 But Asahel refused to give up the pursuit; so Abner thrust the butt of his spear
into Asahel's stomach, and the spear came
out through his back. He fell there and
died on the spot. And every man stopped

---

a 16 Helkath Hazzurim means field of daggers or field of hostilities.

when he came to the place where Asahel had fallen and died.

24 But Joab and Abishai pursued Abner, and as the sun was setting, they came to the hill of Ammah, near Giah on the way to the wasteland of Gibeon. 25 Then the men of Benjamin rallied behind Abner. They formed themselves into a group and took their stand on top of a hill.

26 Abner called out to Joab, 'Must the sword devour for ever? Don't you realise that this will end in bitterness? How long before you order your men to stop pursuing their fellow Israelites?'

27 Joab answered, 'As surely as God lives, if you had not spoken, the men would have continued pursuing them until morning.'

28 So Joab blew the trumpet, and all the troops came to a halt; they no longer pursued Israel, nor did they fight any more.

29 All that night Abner and his men marched through the Arabah. They crossed the Jordan, continued through the morning hours[b] and came to Mahanaim.

30 Then Joab stopped pursuing Abner and assembled the whole army. Besides Asahel, nineteen of David's men were found missing. 31 But David's men had killed 360 Benjaminites who were with Abner. 32 They took Asahel and buried him in his father's tomb at Bethlehem. Then Joab and his men marched all night and arrived at Hebron by daybreak.

3 The war between the house of Saul and the house of David lasted a long time. David grew stronger and stronger, while the house of Saul grew weaker and weaker.

2 Sons were born to David in Hebron:

his firstborn was Amnon the son of Ahinoam of Jezreel;

3 his second, Kileab the son of Abigail the widow of Nabal of Carmel;

the third, Absalom the son of Maakah daughter of Talmai king of Geshur;

4 the fourth, Adonijah the son of Haggith;

the fifth, Shephatiah the son of Abital;

5 and the sixth, Ithream the son of David's wife Eglah.

These were born to David in Hebron.

Abner goes over to David

6 During the war between the house of Saul and the house of David, Abner had been strengthening his own position in the house of Saul. 7 Now Saul had had a concubine named Rizpah daughter of Aiah. And Ish-Bosheth said to Abner, 'Why did you sleep with my father's concubine?'

8 Abner was very angry because of what Ish-Bosheth said. So he answered, 'Am I a dog's head – on Judah's side? This very day I am loyal to the house of your father Saul and to his family and friends. I haven't handed you over to David. Yet now you accuse me of an offence involving this woman! 9 May God deal with Abner, be it ever so severely, if I do not do for David what the LORD promised him on oath 10 and transfer the kingdom from the house of Saul and establish David's throne over Israel and Judah from Dan to Beersheba.' 11 Ish-Bosheth did not dare to say another word to Abner, because he was afraid of him.

12 Then Abner sent messengers on his behalf to say to David, 'Whose land is it? Make an agreement with me, and I will help you bring all Israel over to you.'

13 'Good,' said David. 'I will make an agreement with you. But I demand one thing of you: do not come into my presence unless you bring Michal daughter of Saul when you come to see me.' 14 Then David sent messengers to Ish-Bosheth son of Saul, demanding, 'Give me my wife Michal, whom I betrothed to myself for the price of a hundred Philistine foreskins.'

15 So Ish-Bosheth gave orders and had her taken away from her husband Paltiel son of Laish. 16 Her husband, however, went with her, weeping behind her all the way to Bahurim. Then Abner said to him, 'Go back home!' So he went back.

---

b 29 See Septuagint; the meaning of the Hebrew for this phrase is uncertain.

17 Abner conferred with the elders of Israel and said, 'For some time you have wanted to make David your king. **18** Now do it! For the LORD promised David, "By my servant David I will rescue my people Israel from the hand of the Philistines and from the hand of all their enemies."'

19 Abner also spoke to the Benjaminites in person. Then he went to Hebron to tell David everything that Israel and the whole tribe of Benjamin wanted to do. **20** When Abner, who had twenty men with him, came to David at Hebron, David prepared a feast for him and his men. **21** Then Abner said to David, 'Let me go at once and assemble all Israel for my lord the king, so that they may make a covenant with you, and that you may rule over all that your heart desires.' So David sent Abner away, and he went in peace.

Joab murders Abner

22 Just then David's men and Joab returned from a raid and brought with them a great deal of plunder. But Abner was no longer with David in Hebron, because David had sent him away, and he had gone in peace. **23** When Joab and all the soldiers with him arrived, he was told that Abner son of Ner had come to the king and that the king had sent him away and that he had gone in peace.

24 So Joab went to the king and said, 'What have you done? Look, Abner came to you. Why did you let him go? Now he is gone! **25** You know Abner son of Ner; he came to deceive you and observe your movements and find out everything you are doing.'

26 Joab then left David and sent messengers after Abner, and they brought him back from the cistern at Sirah. But David did not know it. **27** Now when Abner returned to Hebron, Joab took him aside into an inner chamber, as if to speak with him privately. And there, to avenge the blood of his brother Asahel, Joab stabbed him in the stomach, and he died.

28 Later, when David heard about this, he said, 'I and my kingdom are for ever innocent before the LORD concerning the blood of Abner son of Ner. **29** May his blood fall on the head of Joab and on his whole family! May Joab's family never be without someone who has a running sore or leprosy*a* or who leans on a crutch or who falls by the sword or who lacks food.'

30 (Joab and his brother Abishai murdered Abner because he had killed their brother Asahel in the battle of Gibeon.)

31 Then David said to Joab and all the people with him, 'Tear your clothes and put on sackcloth and walk in mourning in front of Abner.' King David himself walked behind the bier. **32** They buried Abner in Hebron, and the king wept aloud at Abner's tomb. All the people wept also.

33 The king sang this lament for Abner:

'Should Abner have died as the lawless die?
34   Your hands were not bound,
        your feet were not fettered.
    You fell as one falls before the
        wicked.'

And all the people wept over him again.

35 Then they all came and urged David to eat something while it was still day; but David took an oath, saying, 'May God deal with me, be it ever so severely, if I taste bread or anything else before the sun sets!'

36 All the people took note and were pleased; indeed, everything the king did pleased them. **37** So on that day all the people there and all Israel knew that the king had no part in the murder of Abner son of Ner.

38 Then the king said to his men, 'Do you not realise that a commander and a great man has fallen in Israel this day? **39** And today, though I am the anointed king, I am weak, and these sons of Zeruiah are too strong for me. May the LORD repay the evildoer according to his evil deeds!'

Ish-Bosheth murdered

4 When Ish-Bosheth son of Saul heard that Abner had died in Hebron, he lost courage, and all Israel became alarmed.

---

a 29 The Hebrew for *leprosy* was used for various diseases affecting the skin.

² Now Saul's son had two men who were leaders of raiding bands. One was named Baanah and the other Rekab; they were sons of Rimmon the Beerothite from the tribe of Benjamin – Beeroth is considered part of Benjamin, ³ because the people of Beeroth fled to Gittaim and have resided there as foreigners to this day.

⁴ (Jonathan son of Saul had a son who was lame in both feet. He was five years old when the news about Saul and Jonathan came from Jezreel. His nurse picked him up and fled, but as she hurried to leave, he fell and became disabled. His name was Mephibosheth.)

⁵ Now Rekab and Baanah, the sons of Rimmon the Beerothite, set out for the house of Ish-Bosheth, and they arrived there in the heat of the day while he was taking his noonday rest. ⁶ They went into the inner part of the house as if to get some wheat, and they stabbed him in the stomach. Then Rekab and his brother Baanah slipped away.

⁷ They had gone into the house while he was lying on the bed in his bedroom. After they stabbed and killed him, they cut off his head. Taking it with them, they travelled all night by way of the Arabah. ⁸ They brought the head of Ish-Bosheth to David at Hebron and said to the king, 'Here is the head of Ish-Bosheth son of Saul, your enemy, who tried to kill you. This day the LORD has avenged my lord the king against Saul and his offspring.'

⁹ David answered Rekab and his brother Baanah, the sons of Rimmon the Beerothite, 'As surely as the LORD lives, who has delivered me out of every trouble, ¹⁰ when someone told me, "Saul is dead," and thought he was bringing good news, I seized him and put him to death in Ziklag. That was the reward I gave him for his news! ¹¹ How much more – when wicked men have killed an innocent man in his own house and on his own bed – should I not now demand his blood from your hand and rid the earth of you!'

¹² So David gave an order to his men, and they killed them. They cut off their hands and feet and hung the bodies by the pool in Hebron. But they took the head of Ish-Bosheth and buried it in Abner's tomb at Hebron.

David becomes king over Israel

5 All the tribes of Israel came to David at Hebron and said, 'We are your own flesh and blood. ² In the past, while Saul was king over us, you were the one who led Israel on their military campaigns. And the LORD said to you, "You shall shepherd my people Israel, and you shall become their ruler."'

³ When all the elders of Israel had come to King David at Hebron, the king made a covenant with them at Hebron before the LORD, and they anointed David king over Israel.

⁴ David was thirty years old when he became king, and he reigned for forty years. ⁵ In Hebron he reigned over Judah for seven years and six months, and in Jerusalem he reigned over all Israel and Judah for thirty-three years.

David conquers Jerusalem

⁶ The king and his men marched to Jerusalem to attack the Jebusites, who lived there. The Jebusites said to David, 'You will not get in here; even the blind and the lame can ward you off.' They thought, 'David cannot get in here.' ⁷ Nevertheless, David captured the fortress of Zion – which is the City of David.

⁸ On that day David had said, 'Anyone who conquers the Jebusites will have to use the water shaft to reach those "lame and blind" who are David's enemies.'ᵃ That is why they say, 'The "blind and lame" will not enter the palace.'

⁹ David then took up residence in the fortress and called it the City of David. He built up the area around it, from the terracesᵇ inwards. ¹⁰ And he became more and more powerful, because the LORD God Almighty was with him.

¹¹ Now Hiram king of Tyre sent envoys to David, along with cedar logs and carpenters and stonemasons, and they built a palace for David. ¹² Then David knew that

---

ᵃ 8 Or are hated by David
ᵇ 9 Or the Millo

the LORD had established him as king over Israel and had exalted his kingdom for the sake of his people Israel.

13 After he left Hebron, David took more concubines and wives in Jerusalem, and more sons and daughters were born to him. 14 These are the names of the children born to him there: Shammua, Shobab, Nathan, Solomon, 15 Ibhar, Elishua, Nepheg, Japhia, 16 Elishama, Eliada and Eliphelet.

TWELVE TINY FINGERS, TWELVE TINY TOES

There's a Philistine warrior in the Bible with 24 digits: six fingers on each hand and six toes on each foot. Difficult finding gloves to fit, I should imagine (2 Samuel 21:20).

David defeats the Philistines

17 When the Philistines heard that David had been anointed king over Israel, they went up in full force to search for him, but David heard about it and went down to the stronghold. 18 Now the Philistines had come and spread out in the Valley of Rephaim; 19 so David enquired of the LORD, 'Shall I go and attack the Philistines? Will you deliver them into my hands?'

The LORD answered him, 'Go, for I will surely deliver the Philistines into your hands.'

20 So David went to Baal Perazim, and there he defeated them. He said, 'As waters break out, the LORD has broken out against my enemies before me.' So that place was called Baal Perazim.c 21 The

---

c 20 *Baal Perazim* means *the lord who breaks out.*

Philistines abandoned their idols there, and David and his men carried them off.

22 Once more the Philistines came up and spread out in the Valley of Rephaim; 23 so David enquired of the LORD, and he answered, 'Do not go straight up, but circle round behind them and attack them in front of the poplar trees. 24 As soon as you hear the sound of marching in the tops of the poplar trees, move quickly, because that will mean the LORD has gone out in front of you to strike the Philistine army.' 25 So David did as the LORD commanded him, and he struck down the Philistines all the way from Gibeond to Gezer.

The ark brought to Jerusalem

6 David again brought together all the able young men of Israel – thirty thousand. 2 He and all his men went to Baalaha in Judah to bring up from there the ark of God, which is called by the Name,b the name of the LORD Almighty, who is enthroned between the cherubim on the ark. 3 They set the ark of God on a new cart and brought it from the house of Abinadab, which was on the hill. Uzzah and Ahio, sons of Abinadab, were guiding the new cart 4 with the ark of God on it,c and Ahio was walking in front of it. 5 David and all Israel were celebrating with all their might before the LORD, with castanets,d harps, lyres, tambourines, rattles and cymbals.

6 When they came to the threshing-floor of Nakon, Uzzah reached out and took hold of the ark of God, because the oxen stumbled. 7 The LORD's anger burned against Uzzah because of his irreverent act; therefore God struck him down, and he died there beside the ark of God.

8 Then David was angry because the

---

d 25 Septuagint (see also 1 Chron. 14:16); Hebrew *Geba*
a 2 That is, Kiriath Jearim (see 1 Chron. 13:6)
b 2 Hebrew; Septuagint and Vulgate do not have *the Name.*
c 3,4 Dead Sea Scrolls and some Septuagint manuscripts; Masoretic Text *cart* 4*and they brought it with the ark of God from the house of Abinadab, which was on the hill*
d 5 Masoretic Text; Dead Sea Scrolls and Septuagint (see also 1 Chron. 13:8) *songs*

LORD's wrath had broken out against Uzzah, and to this day that place is called Perez Uzzah.ᵉ

⁹David was afraid of the LORD that day and said, 'How can the ark of the LORD ever come to me?' ¹⁰He was not willing to take the ark of the LORD to be with him in the City of David. Instead, he took it to the house of Obed-Edom the Gittite. ¹¹The ark of the LORD remained in the house of Obed-Edom the Gittite for three months, and the LORD blessed him and his entire household.

¹²Now King David was told, 'The LORD has blessed the household of Obed-Edom and everything he has, because of the ark of God.' So David went to bring up the ark of God from the house of Obed-Edom to the City of David with rejoicing. ¹³When those who were carrying the ark of the LORD had taken six steps, he sacrificed a bull and a fattened calf. ¹⁴Wearing a linen ephod, David was dancing before the LORD with all his might, ¹⁵while he and all Israel were bringing up the ark of the LORD with shouts and the sound of trumpets.

¹⁶As the ark of the LORD was entering the City of David, Michal daughter of Saul watched from a window. And when she saw King David leaping and dancing before the LORD, she despised him in her heart.

¹⁷They brought the ark of the LORD and set it in its place inside the tent that David had pitched for it, and David sacrificed burnt offerings and fellowship offerings before the LORD. ¹⁸After he had finished sacrificing the burnt offerings and fellowship offerings, he blessed the people in the name of the LORD Almighty. ¹⁹Then he gave a loaf of bread, a cake of dates and a cake of raisins to each person in the whole crowd of Israelites, both men and women. And all the people went to their homes.

²⁰When David returned home to bless his household, Michal daughter of Saul came out to meet him and said, 'How the king of Israel has distinguished himself today, going around half-naked in full view of the slave girls of his servants as any vulgar fellow would!'

²¹David said to Michal, 'It was before the LORD, who chose me rather than your father or anyone from his house when he appointed me ruler over the LORD's people Israel – I will celebrate before the LORD. ²²I will become even more undignified than this, and I will be humiliated in my own eyes. But by these slave girls you spoke of, I will be held in honour.'

²³And Michal daughter of Saul had no children to the day of her death.

God's promise to David

7 After the king was settled in his palace and the LORD had given him rest from all his enemies around him, ²he said to Nathan the prophet, 'Here I am, living in a house of cedar, while the ark of God remains in a tent.'

³Nathan replied to the king, 'Whatever you have in mind, go ahead and do it, for the LORD is with you.'

⁴But that night the word of the LORD came to Nathan, saying:

⁵'Go and tell my servant David, "This is what the LORD says: are you the one to build me a house to dwell in? ⁶I have not dwelt in a house from the day I brought the Israelites up out of Egypt to this day. I have been moving from place to place with a tent as my dwelling. ⁷Wherever I have moved with all the Israelites, did I ever say to any of their rulers whom I commanded to shepherd my people Israel, 'Why have you not built me a house of cedar?' "

⁸'Now then, tell my servant David, "This is what the LORD Almighty says: I took you from the pasture, from tending the flock, and appointed you ruler over my people Israel. ⁹I have been with you wherever you have gone, and I have cut off all your enemies from before you. Now I will make your name great, like the names of the greatest men on earth. ¹⁰And I will provide a place for my people Israel and will plant them so

---

ᵉ 8 *Perez Uzzah* means *the outbreak against Uzzah.*

that they can have a home of their own and no longer be disturbed. Wicked people shall not oppress them any more, as they did at the beginning [11] and have done ever since the time I appointed leaders[a] over my people Israel. I will also give you rest from all your enemies.

' "The LORD declares to you that the LORD himself will establish a house for you: [12] when your days are over and you rest with your ancestors, I will raise up your offspring to succeed you, your own flesh and blood, and I will establish his kingdom. [13] He is the one who will build a house for my Name, and I will establish the throne of his kingdom for ever. [14] I will be his father, and he shall be my son. When he does wrong, I will punish him with a rod wielded by men, with floggings inflicted by human hands. [15] But my love will never be taken away from him, as I took it away from Saul, whom I removed from before you. [16] Your house and your kingdom shall endure for ever before me[b]; your throne shall be established for ever." '

[17] Nathan reported to David all the words of this entire revelation.

David's prayer

[18] Then King David went in and sat before the LORD, and he said:

'Who am I, Sovereign LORD, and what is my family, that you have brought me this far? [19] And as if this were not enough in your sight, Sovereign LORD, you have also spoken about the future of the house of your servant – and this decree, Sovereign LORD, is for a mere human![c]

[20] 'What more can David say to you? For you know your servant, Sovereign LORD. [21] For the sake of your word and according to your will, you have done this great thing and made it known to your servant.

[22] 'How great you are, Sovereign LORD! There is no one like you, and there is no God but you, as we have heard with our own ears. [23] And who is like your people Israel – the one nation on earth that God went out to redeem as a people for himself, and to make a name for himself, and to perform great and awesome wonders by driving out nations and their gods from before your people, whom you redeemed from Egypt?[d] [24] You have established your people Israel as your very own for ever, and you, LORD, have become their God.

[25] 'And now, LORD God, keep for ever the promise you have made concerning your servant and his house. Do as you promised, [26] so that your name will be great for ever. Then people will say, "The LORD Almighty is God over Israel!" And the house of your servant David will be established in your sight.

[27] 'LORD Almighty, God of Israel, you have revealed this to your servant, saying, "I will build a house for you." So your servant has found courage to pray this prayer to you. [28] Sovereign LORD, you are God! Your covenant is trustworthy, and you have promised these good things to your servant. [29] Now be pleased to bless the house of your servant, that it may continue for ever in your sight; for you, Sovereign LORD, have spoken, and with your blessing the house of your servant will be blessed for ever.'

David's victories

8 In the course of time, David defeated the Philistines and subdued them, and he took Metheg Ammah from the control of the Philistines.

---

a 11 Traditionally *judges*
b 16 Some Hebrew manuscripts and Septuagint; most Hebrew manuscripts *you*
c 19 Or *for the human race*

d 23 See Septuagint and 1 Chron. 17:21; Hebrew *wonders for your land and before your people, whom you redeemed from Egypt, from the nations and their gods.*

2 David also defeated the Moabites. He made them lie down on the ground and measured them off with a length of cord. Every two lengths of them were put to death, and the third length was allowed to live. So the Moabites became subject to David and brought him tribute.

3 Moreover, David defeated Hadadezer son of Rehob, king of Zobah, when he went to restore his monument at*a* the River Euphrates. 4 David captured a thousand of his chariots, seven thousand charioteers*b* and twenty thousand foot soldiers. He hamstrung all but a hundred of the chariot horses.

5 When the Arameans of Damascus came to help Hadadezer king of Zobah, David struck down twenty-two thousand of them. 6 He put garrisons in the Aramean kingdom of Damascus, and the Arameans became subject to him and brought tribute. The LORD gave David victory wherever he went.

7 David took the gold shields that belonged to the officers of Hadadezer and brought them to Jerusalem. 8 From Tebah*c* and Berothai, towns that belonged to Hadadezer, King David took a great quantity of bronze.

9 When Tou*d* king of Hamath heard that David had defeated the entire army of Hadadezer, 10 he sent his son Joram*e* to King David to greet him and congratulate him on his victory in battle over Hadadezer, who had been at war with Tou. Joram brought with him articles of silver, of gold and of bronze.

11 King David dedicated these articles to the LORD, as he had done with the silver and gold from all the nations he had subdued: 12 Edom*f* and Moab, the Ammonites and the Philistines, and Amalek. He also dedicated the plunder taken from Hadadezer son of Rehob, king of Zobah.

13 And David became famous after he returned from striking down eighteen thousand Edomites*g* in the Valley of Salt.

14 He put garrisons throughout Edom, and all the Edomites became subject to David. The LORD gave David victory wherever he went.

David's officials

15 David reigned over all Israel, doing what was just and right for all his people. 16 Joab son of Zeruiah was over the army; Jehoshaphat son of Ahilud was recorder; 17 Zadok son of Ahitub and Ahimelek son of Abiathar were priests; Seraiah was secretary; 18 Benaiah son of Jehoiada was over the Kerethites and Pelethites; and David's sons were priests.*h*

David and Mephibosheth

9 David asked, 'Is there anyone still left of the house of Saul to whom I can show kindness for Jonathan's sake?'

2 Now there was a servant of Saul's household named Ziba. They summoned him to appear before David, and the king said to him, 'Are you Ziba?'

'At your service,' he replied.

3 The king asked, 'Is there no one still alive from the house of Saul to whom I can show God's kindness?'

Ziba answered the king, 'There is still a son of Jonathan; he is lame in both feet.'

4 'Where is he?' the king asked.

Ziba answered, 'He is at the house of Makir son of Ammiel in Lo Debar.'

5 So King David had him brought from Lo Debar, from the house of Makir son of Ammiel.

6 When Mephibosheth son of Jonathan, the son of Saul, came to David, he bowed down to pay him honour.

David said, 'Mephibosheth!'

'At your service,' he replied.

7 'Don't be afraid,' David said to him,

---

a 3 Or *his control along*

b 4 Septuagint (see also Dead Sea Scrolls and 1 Chron. 18:4); Masoretic Text *captured seventeen hundred of his charioteers*

c 8 See some Septuagint manuscripts (see also 1 Chron. 18:8); Hebrew *Betah.*

d 9 Hebrew *Toi,* a variant of *Tou;* also in verse 10

e 10 A variant of *Hadoram*

f 12 Some Hebrew manuscripts, Septuagint and Syriac (see also 1 Chron. 18:11); most Hebrew manuscripts *Aram*

g 13 A few Hebrew manuscripts, Septuagint and Syriac (see also 1 Chron. 18:12); most Hebrew manuscripts *Aram* (that is, Arameans)

h 18 Or *were chief officials* (see Septuagint and Targum; see also 1 Chron. 18:17) 'for I will surely show you kindness for the sake of your father Jonathan. I will restore to you all the land that belonged to your grandfather Saul, and you will always eat at my table.'

8 Mephibosheth bowed down and said, 'What is your servant, that you should notice a dead dog like me?'

9 Then the king summoned Ziba, Saul's steward, and said to him, 'I have given your master's grandson everything that belonged to Saul and his family. 10 You and your sons and your servants are to farm the land for him and bring in the crops, so that your master's grandson may be provided for. And Mephibosheth, grandson of your master, will always eat at my table.' (Now Ziba had fifteen sons and twenty servants.)

11 Then Ziba said to the king, 'Your servant will do whatever my lord the king commands his servant to do.' So Mephibosheth ate at David's*ᵃ table like one of the king's sons.

12 Mephibosheth had a young son named Mika, and all the members of Ziba's household were servants of Mephibosheth. 13 And Mephibosheth lived in Jerusalem, because he always ate at the king's table; he was lame in both feet.

David defeats the Ammonites

10 In the course of time, the king of the Ammonites died, and his son Hanun succeeded him as king. 2 David thought, 'I will show kindness to Hanun son of Nahash, just as his father showed kindness to me.' So David sent a delegation to express his sympathy to Hanun concerning his father.

When David's men came to the land of the Ammonites, 3 the Ammonite commanders said to Hanun their lord, 'Do you think David is honouring your father by sending envoys to you to express sympathy? Hasn't David sent them to you only to explore the city and spy it out and overthrow it?' 4 So Hanun seized David's envoys, shaved off half of each man's beard, cut off their garments at the buttocks, and sent them away.

5 When David was told about this, he sent messengers to meet the men, for they were greatly humiliated. The king said, 'Stay at Jericho till your beards have grown, and then come back.'

6 When the Ammonites realised that they had become obnoxious to David, they hired twenty thousand Aramean foot soldiers from Beth Rehob and Zobah, as well as the king of Maakah with a thousand men, and also twelve thousand men from Tob.

7 On hearing this, David sent Joab out with the entire army of fighting men. 8 The Ammonites came out and drew up in battle formation at the entrance of their city gate, while the Arameans of Zobah and Rehob and the men of Tob and Maakah were by themselves in the open country.

9 Joab saw that there were battle lines in front of him and behind him; so he selected some of the best troops in Israel and deployed them against the Arameans. 10 He put the rest of the men under the command of Abishai his brother and deployed them against the Ammonites. 11 Joab said, 'If the Arameans are too strong for me, then you are to come to my rescue; but if the Ammonites are too strong for you, then I will come to rescue you. 12 Be strong, and let us fight bravely for our people and the cities of our God. The LORD will do what is good in his sight.'

13 Then Joab and the troops with him advanced to fight the Arameans, and they fled before him. 14 When the Ammonites realised that the Arameans were fleeing, they fled before Abishai and went inside the city. So Joab returned from fighting the Ammonites and came to Jerusalem.

15 After the Arameans saw that they had been routed by Israel, they regrouped. 16 Hadadezer had Arameans brought from beyond the River Euphrates; they went to Helam, with Shobak the commander of Hadadezer's army leading them.

17 When David was told of this, he gathered all Israel, crossed the Jordan and went to Helam. The Arameans formed their battle lines to meet David and fought against him. 18 But they fled before Israel,

a 11 Septuagint; Hebrew *my*

and David killed seven hundred of their charioteers and forty thousand of their foot soldiers.[a] He also struck down Shobak the commander of their army, and he died there. 19 When all the kings who were vassals of Hadadezer saw that they had been routed by Israel, they made peace with the Israelites and became subject to them.

So the Arameans were afraid to help the Ammonites any more.

David and Bathsheba

11 In the spring, at the time when kings go off to war, David sent Joab out with the king's men and the whole Israelite army. They destroyed the Ammonites and besieged Rabbah. But David remained in Jerusalem.

2 One evening David got up from his bed and walked around on the roof of the palace. From the roof he saw a woman washing. The woman was very beautiful, 3 and David sent someone to find out about her. The man said, 'She is Bathsheba, the daughter of Eliam and the wife of Uriah the Hittite.' 4 Then David sent messengers to get her. She came to him, and he slept with her. (Now she was purifying herself from her monthly uncleanness.) Then she went back home. 5 The woman conceived and sent word to David, saying, 'I am pregnant.'

6 So David sent this word to Joab: 'Send me Uriah the Hittite.' And Joab sent him to David. 7 When Uriah came to him, David asked him how Joab was, how the soldiers were and how the war was going. 8 Then David said to Uriah, 'Go down to your house and wash your feet.' So Uriah left the palace, and a gift from the king was sent after him. 9 But Uriah slept at the entrance to the palace with all his master's servants and did not go down to his house.

10 David was told, 'Uriah did not go home.' So he asked Uriah, 'Haven't you just come from a military campaign? Why didn't you go home?'

11 Uriah said to David, 'The ark and Israel

and Judah are staying in tents,[a] and my commander Joab and my lord's men are camped in the open country. How could I go to my house to eat and drink and make love to my wife? As surely as you live, I will not do such a thing!'

12 Then David said to him, 'Stay here one more day, and tomorrow I will send you back.' So Uriah remained in Jerusalem that day and the next. 13 At David's invitation, he ate and drank with him, and David made him drunk. But in the evening Uriah went out to sleep on his mat among his master's servants; he did not go home.

14 In the morning David wrote a letter to Joab and sent it with Uriah. 15 In it he wrote, 'Put Uriah out in front where the fighting is fiercest. Then withdraw from him so that he will be struck down and die.'

16 So while Joab had the city under siege, he put Uriah at a place where he knew the strongest defenders were. 17 When the men of the city came out and fought against Joab, some of the men in David's army fell; moreover, Uriah the Hittite died.

18 Joab sent David a full account of the battle. 19 He instructed the messenger: 'When you have finished giving the king this account of the battle, 20 the king's anger may flare up, and he may ask you, "Why did you get so close to the city to fight? Didn't you know they would shoot arrows from the wall? 21 Who killed Abimelek son of Jerub-Besheth?[b] Didn't a woman drop an upper millstone on him from the wall, so that he died in Thebez? Why did you get so close to the wall?" If he asks you this, then say to him, "Moreover, your servant Uriah the Hittite is dead."'

22 The messenger set out, and when he arrived he told David everything Joab had sent him to say. 23 The messenger said to David, 'The men overpowered us and came out against us in the open, but we drove them back to the entrance of the city gate. 24 Then the archers shot arrows at your servants from the wall, and some

---

a 18 Some Septuagint manuscripts (see also 1 Chron. 19:18); Hebrew horsemen

a 11 Or staying at Sukkoth
b 21 Also known as Jerub-Baal (that is, Gideon)

of the king's men died. Moreover, your servant Uriah the Hittite is dead.'

25 David told the messenger, 'Say this to Joab: "Don't let this upset you; the sword devours one as well as another. Press the attack against the city and destroy it." Say this to encourage Joab.'

26 When Uriah's wife heard that her husband was dead, she mourned for him. 27 After the time of mourning was over, David had her brought to his house, and she became his wife and bore him a son. But the thing David had done displeased the LORD.

Nathan rebukes David

12 The LORD sent Nathan to David. When he came to him, he said, 'There were two men in a certain town, one rich and the other poor. 2 The rich man had a very large number of sheep and cattle, 3 but the poor man had nothing except one little ewe lamb that he had bought. He raised it, and it grew up with him and his children. It shared his food, drank from his cup and even slept in his arms. It was like a daughter to him.

4 'Now a traveller came to the rich man, but the rich man refrained from taking one of his own sheep or cattle to prepare a meal for the traveller who had come to him. Instead, he took the ewe lamb that belonged to the poor man and prepared it for the one who had come to him.'

5 David burned with anger against the man and said to Nathan, 'As surely as the LORD lives, the man who did this must die! 6 He must pay for that lamb four times over, because he did such a thing and had no pity.'

7 Then Nathan said to David, 'You are the man! This is what the LORD, the God of Israel, says: "I anointed you king over Israel, and I delivered you from the hand of Saul. 8 I gave you your master's house to you, and your master's wives into your arms. I gave you all Israel and Judah. And if all this had been too little, I would have given you even more. 9 Why did you despise the word of the LORD by doing what is evil in his eyes? You struck down Uriah the Hittite with the sword and took his wife

to be your own. You killed him with the sword of the Ammonites. 10 Now, therefore, the sword shall never depart from your house, because you despised me and took the wife of Uriah the Hittite to be your own."

11 'This is what the LORD says: "Out of your own household I am going to bring calamity on you. Before your very eyes I will take your wives and give them to one who is close to you, and he will sleep with your wives in broad daylight. 12 You did it in secret, but I will do this thing in broad daylight before all Israel."'

13 Then David said to Nathan, 'I have sinned against the LORD.'

Nathan replied, 'The LORD has taken away your sin. You are not going to die. 14 But because by doing this you have shown utter contempt for*a* the LORD, the son born to you will die.'

15 After Nathan had gone home, the LORD struck the child that Uriah's wife had borne to David, and he became ill. 16 David pleaded with God for the child. He fasted and spent the nights lying in sackcloth*b* on the ground. 17 The elders of his household stood beside him to get him up from the ground, but he refused, and he would not eat any food with them.

18 On the seventh day the child died. David's attendants were afraid to tell him that the child was dead, for they thought, 'While the child was still living, he wouldn't listen to us when we spoke to him. How can we now tell him the child is dead? He may do something desperate.'

19 David noticed that his attendants were whispering among themselves, and he realised that the child was dead. 'Is the child dead?' he asked.

'Yes,' they replied, 'he is dead.'

20 Then David got up from the ground. After he had washed, put on lotions and changed his clothes, he went into the house of the LORD and worshipped. Then he went to his own house, and at his request they served him food, and he ate.

---

a 14 An ancient Hebrew scribal tradition; Masoretic Text *for the enemies of*
b 16 Dead Sea Scrolls and Septuagint; Masoretic Text does not have *in sackcloth*.

SPIRITUAL DISCIPLINES 9

WORSHIP

What is worship? Is it the words we sing, or the way we sing them? Or is it something bigger? Is worship somehow possible in everything we do, every choice we make?

Every decision, big or small, contains within it the opportunity to honour or dishonour God. Every day, every turning point, we either do it right or wrong. The discipline of worship is about choosing the right path, time after time, and in doing so glorifying the God who has changed us.

In its broadest sense, worship is the opposite of sin. Sin describes those things we do, think and say which send us tearing off in the opposite direction from God. Worship is about the (glorious, faltering) steps that we take in our journey back towards him. Worship and sin cannot coexist. We cannot honour God and reject him at the same time. When King David, the great worshipper of the Old Testament, fell from grace with an adulterous affair which cost his mistress's husband his life, his worship fell silent. His passion for God, which had attracted all Israel to follow him as leader, had become compromised. It was left to the prophet Nathan to bring him back to the right path.

In 2 Samuel 12, Nathan delivers some terrible news: as a result of David's sin, his young son will die. David pleads with God that this won't happen. He prays and fasts in the hope that God might change his mind. He doesn't, and the boy dies. What does David do next? He worships God. In spite of the terrible price he has paid, he chooses to turn back to God. He has journeyed from a place of sin to a place of worship.

Worship as a way of life – together and alone

The discipline is most obviously practised through what we call 'acts of worship' – songs, meetings, words of truth that we agree to perform together as a church. But worship is also a lifestyle. God draws us to himself; he is constantly calling us to worship him, and that is what he created us for. That doesn't make him an egomaniac – it just means that he knows what is best for us. So in every moment, God wants us to respond in a way that is right and that brings him glory.

The decision on how we respond, however, rests with us. It is visible in a thousand tiny moments. Do we hold the door open for the woman with the pushchair, or make out that we haven't seen her? Do we give away our last couple of pounds and forsake the milkshake we've been pining for? Do we take the best seat in the cinema row, or leave it for the person shuffling in behind us? Our lives are full of a multitude of opportunities to practise the discipline of worship, the discipline of choice.

Martin Saunders

 1 John 4:7–21 Isaiah 55:11–13

21 His attendants asked him, 'Why are you acting in this way? While the child was alive, you fasted and wept, but now that the child is dead, you get up and eat!'

22 He answered, 'While the child was still alive, I fasted and wept. I thought, "Who knows? The LORD may be gracious to me and let the child live." 23 But now that he is dead, why should I go on fasting? Can I bring him back again? I will go to him, but he will not return to me.'

24 Then David comforted his wife Bathsheba, and he went to her and made love to her. She gave birth to a son, and they named him Solomon. The LORD loved him; 25 and because the LORD loved him, he sent word through Nathan the prophet to name him Jedidiah.*c*

26 Meanwhile Joab fought against Rabbah of the Ammonites and captured the royal citadel. 27 Joab then sent messengers to David, saying, 'I have fought against Rabbah and taken its water supply. 28 Now muster the rest of the troops and besiege the city and capture it. Otherwise I shall take the city, and it will be named after me.'

29 So David mustered the entire army and went to Rabbah, and attacked and captured it. 30 David took the crown from their king's*d* head, and it was placed on his own head. It weighed a talent*e* of gold, and it was set with precious stones. David took a great quantity of plunder from the city 31 and brought out the people who were there, consigning them to labour with saws and with iron picks and axes, and he made them work at brickmaking.*f* David did this to all the Ammonite towns. Then he and his entire army returned to Jerusalem.

Amnon and Tamar

13 In the course of time, Amnon son of David fell in love with Tamar, the beautiful sister of Absalom son of David.

2 Amnon became so obsessed with his sister Tamar that he made himself ill. She was a virgin, and it seemed impossible for him to do anything to her.

3 Now Amnon had an advisor named Jonadab son of Shimeah, David's brother. Jonadab was a very shrewd man. 4 He asked Amnon, 'Why do you, the king's son, look so haggard morning after morning? Won't you tell me?'

Amnon said to him, 'I'm in love with Tamar, my brother Absalom's sister.'

5 'Go to bed and pretend to be ill,' Jonadab said. 'When your father comes to see you, say to him, "I would like my sister Tamar to come and give me something to eat. Let her prepare the food in my sight so that I may watch her and then eat it from her hand." '

6 So Amnon lay down and pretended to be ill. When the king came to see him, Amnon said to him, 'I would like my sister Tamar to come and make some special bread in my sight, so that I may eat from her hand.'

7 David sent word to Tamar at the palace: 'Go to the house of your brother Amnon and prepare some food for him.' 8 So Tamar went to the house of her brother Amnon, who was lying down. She took some dough, kneaded it, made the bread in his sight and baked it. 9 Then she took the pan and served him the bread, but he refused to eat.

'Send everyone out of here,' Amnon said. So everyone left him. 10 Then Amnon said to Tamar, 'Bring the food here into my bedroom so that I may eat from your hand.' And Tamar took the bread she had prepared and brought it to her brother Amnon in his bedroom. 11 But when she took it to him to eat, he grabbed her and said, 'Come to bed with me, my sister.'

12 'No, my brother!' she said to him. 'Don't force me! Such a thing should not be done in Israel! Don't do this wicked thing. 13 What about me? Where could I get rid of my disgrace? And what about you? You would be like one of the wicked fools in Israel. Please speak to the king; he will not keep me from being married to you.' 14 But he refused to listen to her, and since he was stronger than she, he raped her.

---

c 25 Jedidiah means *loved by the LORD.*
d 30 Or *from Milkom's* (that is, Molek's)
e 30 That is, about 34 kilograms
f 31 The meaning of the Hebrew for this clause is uncertain.

¹⁵Then Amnon hated her with intense hatred. In fact, he hated her more than he had loved her. Amnon said to her, 'Get up and get out!'

¹⁶'No!' she said to him. 'Sending me away would be a greater wrong than what you have already done to me.'

But he refused to listen to her. ¹⁷He called his personal servant and said, 'Get this woman out of my sight and bolt the door after her.' ¹⁸So his servant put her out and bolted the door after her. She was wearing an ornate*ᵃ* robe, for this was the kind of garment the virgin daughters of the king wore. ¹⁹Tamar put ashes on her head and tore the ornate robe she was wearing. She put her hands on her head

_____

a 18 The meaning of the Hebrew for this word is uncertain; also in verse 19.

OPPRESSION OF WOMEN

Two women are killed every week in the UK as a result of domestic violence. That counts for about one third of all female homicides. We have to end violence against women.

This story of Tamar's rape by Amnon isn't exactly one that gets talked about often in church. But it is powerful and it opens up some important questions. Who is responsible for the rape of Tamar? It's Amnon, surely! He's the guy who does it. Yet all the characters in the story are complicit in this abuse in different ways. Jonadab puts him up to it. The servants, who must have heard what was going on, kept quiet. Absalom, Tamar's own brother, makes her keep silent, denying her justice. You might think, 'Well, I'd never rape anybody.' That's certainly what I think – but we live in a culture where rape is a hidden problem, and we want to ensure that we're never complicit by our silence.

Most of us will not be exposed to that kind of violence. But if we don't challenge a culture which treats girls as objects, we let the seeds of abuse grow. It might not be anything like as serious as rape – just smutty jokes or put-downs or a bit of 'harmless' physical or sexual manipulation. It can be difficult to speak up, especially if we're scared of the consequences. But silence is a choice we make with consequences of its own.

Speaking out shouldn't be limited to our day-to-day experiences though. When we know that daughters from Cambodia are sold and then trafficked overseas into a lifetime of prostitution, and when we hear about women in Saudi Arabia who aren't permitted to drive, vote or testify in court – what do we do then? It's something so far from our daily experience and it can feel like we're too young and powerless to do anything. It's not true – we have a voice and a tonne of opportunities. We can join campaigns to raise awareness, volunteer our time, email our MPs, write to women unfairly imprisoned, and perhaps go overseas to physically stand alongside charities and organisations committed to supporting those who are oppressed. We can get connected via websites with people all over the world, and when we get together with our youth groups, schools, or the church nationally and internationally, we can have a really big voice.

God created men and women in his image, equal. It is part of his mission to restore relationships between us and to end the oppression of women.

Matt Valler

and went away, weeping aloud as she went.

20 Her brother Absalom said to her, 'Has that Amnon, your brother, been with you? Be quiet for now, my sister; he is your brother. Don't take this thing to heart.' And Tamar lived in her brother Absalom's house, a desolate woman.

21 When King David heard all this, he was furious. 22 And Absalom never said a word to Amnon, either good or bad; he hated Amnon because he had disgraced his sister Tamar.

Absalom kills Amnon

23 Two years later, when Absalom's sheep-shearers were at Baal Hazor near the border of Ephraim, he invited all the king's sons to come there. 24 Absalom went to the king and said, 'Your servant has had shearers come. Will the king and his attendants please join me?'

25 'No, my son,' the king replied. 'All of us should not go; we would only be a burden to you.' Although Absalom urged him, he still refused to go but gave him his blessing.

26 Then Absalom said, 'If not, please let my brother Amnon come with us.'

The king asked him, 'Why should he go with you?' 27 But Absalom urged him, so he sent with him Amnon and the rest of the king's sons.

28 Absalom ordered his men, 'Listen! When Amnon is in high spirits from drinking wine and I say to you, "Strike Amnon down," then kill him. Don't be afraid. Haven't I given you this order? Be strong and brave.' 29 So Absalom's men did to Amnon what Absalom had ordered. Then all the king's sons got up, mounted their mules and fled.

30 While they were on their way, the report came to David: 'Absalom has struck down all the king's sons; not one of them is left.' 31 The king stood up, tore his clothes and lay down on the ground; and all his attendants stood by with their clothes torn.

32 But Jonadab son of Shimeah, David's brother, said, 'My lord should not think that they killed all the princes; only Amnon is dead. This has been Absalom's express intention ever since the day that Amnon raped his sister Tamar. 33 My lord the king should not be concerned about the report that all the king's sons are dead. Only Amnon is dead.'

34 Meanwhile, Absalom had fled.

Now the man standing watch looked up and saw many people on the road west of him, coming down the side of the hill. The watchman went and told the king, 'I see men in the direction of Horonaim, on the side of the hill.' b

35 Jonadab said to the king, 'See, the king's sons have come; it has happened just as your servant said.'

36 As he finished speaking, the king's sons came in, wailing loudly. The king, too, and all his attendants wept very bitterly.

37 Absalom fled and went to Talmai son of Ammihud, the king of Geshur. But King David mourned many days for his son.

38 After Absalom fled and went to Geshur, he stayed there for three years. 39 And King David longed to go to Absalom, for he was consoled concerning Amnon's death.

Absalom returns to Jerusalem

14 Joab son of Zeruiah knew that the king's heart longed for Absalom. 2 So Joab sent someone to Tekoa and had a wise woman brought from there. He said to her, 'Pretend you are in mourning. Dress in mourning clothes, and don't use any cosmetic lotions. Act like a woman who has spent many days grieving for the dead. 3 Then go to the king and speak these words to him.' And Joab put the words in her mouth.

4 When the woman from Tekoa went a to the king, she fell with her face to the ground to pay him honour, and she said, 'Help me, Your Majesty!'

5 The king asked her, 'What is troubling you?'

---

b 34 Septuagint; Hebrew does not have this sentence.
a 4 Many Hebrew manuscripts, Septuagint, Vulgate and Syriac; most Hebrew manuscripts *spoke*

She said, 'I am a widow; my husband is dead. 6 I your servant had two sons. They got into a fight with each other in the field, and no one was there to separate them. One struck the other and killed him. 7 Now the whole clan has risen up against your servant; they say, "Hand over the one who struck his brother down, so that we may put him to death for the life of his brother whom he killed; then we will get rid of the heir as well." They would put out the only burning coal I have left, leaving my husband neither name nor descendant on the face of the earth.'

8 The king said to the woman, 'Go home, and I will issue an order on your behalf.'

9 But the woman from Tekoa said to him, 'Let my lord the king pardon me and my family, and let the king and his throne be without guilt.'

10 The king replied, 'If anyone says anything to you, bring them to me, and they will not bother you again.'

11 She said, 'Then let the king invoke the LORD his God to prevent the avenger of blood from adding to the destruction, so that my son shall not be destroyed.'

'As surely as the LORD lives,' he said, 'not one hair of your son's head will fall to the ground.'

12 Then the woman said, 'Let your servant speak a word to my lord the king.'

'Speak,' he replied.

13 The woman said, 'Why then have you devised a thing like this against the people of God? When the king says this, does he not convict himself, for the king has not brought back his banished son? 14 Like water spilled on the ground, which cannot be recovered, so we must die. But that is not what God desires; rather, he devises ways so that a banished person does not remain banished from him.

15 'And now I have come to say this to my lord the king because the people have made me afraid. Your servant thought, "I will speak to the king; perhaps he will grant his servant's request. 16 Perhaps the king will agree to deliver his servant from the hand of the man who is trying to cut off both me and my son from God's inheritance."

17 'And now your servant says, "May the word of my lord the king secure my inheritance, for my lord the king is like an angel of God in discerning good and evil. May the LORD your God be with you."'

18 Then the king said to the woman, 'Don't keep from me the answer to what I am going to ask you.'

'Let my lord the king speak,' the woman said.

19 The king asked, 'Isn't the hand of Joab with you in all this?'

The woman answered, 'As surely as you live, my lord the king, no one can turn to the right or to the left from anything my lord the king says. Yes, it was your servant Joab who instructed me to do this and who put all these words into the mouth of your servant. 20 Your servant Joab did this to change the present situation. My lord has wisdom like that of an angel of God – he knows everything that happens in the land.'

21 The king said to Joab, 'Very well, I will do it. Go, bring back the young man Absalom.'

22 Joab fell with his face to the ground to pay him honour, and he blessed the king. Joab said, 'Today your servant knows that he has found favour in your eyes, my lord the king, because the king has granted his servant's request.'

23 Then Joab went to Geshur and brought Absalom back to Jerusalem. 24 But the king said, 'He must go to his own house; he must not see my face.' So Absalom went to his own house and did not see the face of the king.

25 In all Israel there was not a man so highly praised for his handsome appearance as Absalom. From the top of his head to the sole of his foot there was no blemish in him. 26 Whenever he cut the hair of his head – he used to cut his hair once a year because it became too heavy for him – he would weigh it, and its weight was two hundred shekels[b] by the royal standard.

27 Three sons and a daughter were born to Absalom. His daughter's name was Tamar, and she became a beautiful woman.

---

b 26 That is, about 2.3 kilograms

²⁸Absalom lived for two years in Jerusalem without seeing the king's face. ²⁹Then Absalom sent for Joab in order to send him to the king, but Joab refused to come to him. So he sent a second time, but he refused to come. ³⁰Then he said to his servants, 'Look, Joab's field is next to mine, and he has barley there. Go and set it on fire.' So Absalom's servants set the field on fire.

³¹Then Joab did go to Absalom's house, and he said to him, 'Why have your servants set my field on fire?'

³²Absalom said to Joab, 'Look, I sent word to you and said, "Come here so that I can send you to the king to ask, 'Why have I come from Geshur? It would be better for me if I were still there!'" Now then, I want to see the king's face, and if I am guilty of anything, let him put me to death.'

³³So Joab went to the king and told him this. Then the king summoned Absalom, and he came in and bowed down with his face to the ground before the king. And the king kissed Absalom.

Absalom's conspiracy

15 In the course of time, Absalom provided himself with a chariot and horses and with fifty men to run ahead of him. ²He would get up early and stand by the side of the road leading to the city gate. Whenever anyone came with a complaint to be placed before the king for a decision, Absalom would call out to him, 'What town are you from?' He would answer, 'Your servant is from one of the tribes of Israel.' ³Then Absalom would say to him, 'Look, your claims are valid and proper, but there is no representative of the king to hear you.' ⁴And Absalom would add, 'If only I were appointed judge in the land! Then everyone who has a complaint or case could come to me and I would see that they receive justice.'

⁵Also, whenever anyone approached him to bow down before him, Absalom would reach out his hand, take hold of him and kiss him. ⁶Absalom behaved in this way towards all the Israelites who came to the king asking for justice, and so he stole the hearts of the people of Israel.

⁷At the end of four*ᵃ* years, Absalom said to the king, 'Let me go to Hebron and fulfil a vow I made to the LORD. ⁸While your servant was living at Geshur in Aram, I made this vow: "If the LORD takes me back to Jerusalem, I will worship the LORD in Hebron."*ᵇ*'

⁹The king said to him, 'Go in peace.' So he went to Hebron.

¹⁰Then Absalom sent secret messengers throughout the tribes of Israel to say, 'As soon as you hear the sound of the trumpets, then say, "Absalom is king in Hebron."' ¹¹Two hundred men from Jerusalem had accompanied Absalom. They had been invited as guests and went quite innocently, knowing nothing about the matter. ¹²While Absalom was offering sacrifices, he also sent for Ahithophel the Gilonite, David's counsellor, to come from Giloh, his home town. And so the conspiracy gained strength, and Absalom's following kept on increasing.

David flees

¹³A messenger came and told David, 'The hearts of the people of Israel are with Absalom.'

¹⁴Then David said to all his officials who were with him in Jerusalem, 'Come! We must flee, or none of us will escape from Absalom. We must leave immediately, or he will move quickly to overtake us and bring ruin on us and put the city to the sword.'

¹⁵The king's officials answered him, 'Your servants are ready to do whatever our lord the king chooses.'

¹⁶The king set out, with his entire household following him; but he left ten concubines to take care of the palace. ¹⁷So the king set out, with all the people following him, and they halted at the edge of the city. ¹⁸All his men marched past him, along with all the Kerethites and Pelethites; and all the six hundred Gittites who had accompanied him from Gath marched before the king.

---

a 7 Some Septuagint manuscripts, Syriac and Josephus; Hebrew *forty*
b 8 Some Septuagint manuscripts; Hebrew does not have *in Hebron.*

¹⁹The king said to Ittai the Gittite, 'Why should you come along with us? Go back and stay with King Absalom. You are a foreigner, an exile from your homeland. ²⁰You came only yesterday. And today shall I make you wander about with us, when I do not know where I am going? Go back, and take your people with you. May the LORD show you kindness and faithfulness.'ᶜ

²¹But Ittai replied to the king, 'As surely as the LORD lives, and as my lord the king lives, wherever my lord the king may be, whether it means life or death, there will your servant be.'

²²David said to Ittai, 'Go ahead, march on.' So Ittai the Gittite marched on with all his men and the families that were with him.

²³The whole countryside wept aloud as all the people passed by. The king also crossed the Kidron Valley, and all the people moved on towards the wilderness.

²⁴Zadok was there, too, and all the Levites who were with him were carrying the ark of the covenant of God. They set down the ark of God, and Abiathar offered sacrifices until all the people had finished leaving the city.

²⁵Then the king said to Zadok, 'Take the ark of God back into the city. If I find favour in the LORD's eyes, he will bring me back and let me see it and his dwelling-place again. ²⁶But if he says, "I am not pleased with you," then I am ready; let him do to me whatever seems good to him.'

²⁷The king also said to Zadok the priest, 'Do you understand? Go back to the city with my blessing. Take your son Ahimaaz with you, and also Abiathar's son Jonathan. You and Abiathar return with your two sons. ²⁸I will wait at the fords in the wilderness until word comes from you to inform me.' ²⁹So Zadok and Abiathar took the ark of God back to Jerusalem and stayed there.

³⁰But David continued up the Mount of Olives, weeping as he went; his head

was covered and he was barefoot. All the people with him covered their heads too and were weeping as they went up. ³¹Now David had been told, 'Ahithophel is among the conspirators with Absalom.' So David prayed, 'LORD, turn Ahithophel's counsel into foolishness.'

³²When David arrived at the summit, where people used to worship God, Hushai the Arkite was there to meet him, his robe torn and dust on his head. ³³David said to him, 'If you go with me, you will be a burden to me. ³⁴But if you return to the city and say to Absalom, "Your Majesty, I will be your servant; I was your father's servant in the past, but now I will be your servant," then you can help me by frustrating Ahithophel's advice. ³⁵Won't the priests Zadok and Abiathar be there with you? Tell them anything you hear in the king's palace. ³⁶Their two sons, Ahimaaz son of Zadok and Jonathan son of Abiathar, are there with them. Send them to me with anything you hear.'

³⁷So Hushai, David's confidant, arrived at Jerusalem as Absalom was entering the city.

David and Ziba

16 When David had gone a short distance beyond the summit, there was Ziba, the steward of Mephibosheth, waiting to meet him. He had a string of donkeys saddled and loaded with two hundred loaves of bread, a hundred cakes of raisins, a hundred cakes of figs and a skin of wine.

²The king asked Ziba, 'Why have you brought these?'

Ziba answered, 'The donkeys are for the king's household to ride on, the bread and fruit are for the men to eat, and the wine is to refresh those who become exhausted in the wilderness.'

³The king then asked, 'Where is your master's grandson?'

Ziba said to him, 'He is staying in Jerusalem, because he thinks, "Today the Israelites will restore to me my grandfather's kingdom."'

⁴Then the king said to Ziba, 'All that belonged to Mephibosheth is now yours.'

'I humbly bow,' Ziba said. 'May I find favour in your eyes, my lord the king.'

Shimei curses David

5 As King David approached Bahurim, a man from the same clan as Saul's family came out from there. His name was Shimei son of Gera, and he cursed as he came out. 6 He pelted David and all the king's officials with stones, though all the troops and the special guard were on David's right and left. 7 As he cursed, Shimei said, 'Get out, get out, you murderer, you scoundrel! 8 The LORD has repaid you for all the blood you shed in the household of Saul, in whose place you have reigned. The LORD has given the kingdom into the hands of your son Absalom. You have come to ruin because you are a murderer!'

FAVOURITE VERSES

1 Corinthians 10:13

No temptation has overtaken you except what is common to mankind. And God is faithful; he will not let you be tempted beyond what you can bear. But when you are tempted, he will also provide a way out so that you can endure it.

I believed God never promised to protect us from what we can't bear. My friend sent me this, and it taught me once again never to give up.

Hayley, 16

---

9 Then Abishai son of Zeruiah said to the king, 'Why should this dead dog curse my lord the king? Let me go over and cut off his head.'

10 But the king said, 'What does this have to do with you, you sons of Zeruiah? If he is cursing because the LORD said to

him, "Curse David," who can ask, "Why do you do this?" '

11 David then said to Abishai and all his officials, 'My son, my own flesh and blood, is trying to kill me. How much more, then, this Benjaminite! Leave him alone; let him curse, for the LORD has told him to. 12 It may be that the LORD will look upon my misery and restore to me his covenant blessing instead of his curse today.'

13 So David and his men continued along the road while Shimei was going along the hillside opposite him, cursing as he went and throwing stones at him and showering him with dirt. 14 The king and all the people with him arrived at their destination exhausted. And there he refreshed himself.

The advice of Hushai and Ahithophel

15 Meanwhile, Absalom and all the men of Israel came to Jerusalem, and Ahithophel was with him. 16 Then Hushai the Arkite, David's confidant, went to Absalom and said to him, 'Long live the king! Long live the king!'

17 Absalom said to Hushai, 'So this is the love you show your friend? If he's your friend, why didn't you go with him?'

18 Hushai said to Absalom, 'No, the one chosen by the LORD, by these people and by all the men of Israel – his I will be, and I will remain with him. 19 Furthermore, whom should I serve? Should I not serve the son? Just as I served your father, so I will serve you.'

20 Absalom said to Ahithophel, 'Give us your advice. What should we do?'

21 Ahithophel answered, 'Sleep with your father's concubines whom he left to take care of the palace. Then all Israel will hear that you have made yourself obnoxious to your father, and the hands of everyone with you will be more resolute.' 22 So they pitched a tent for Absalom on the roof, and he slept with his father's concubines in the sight of all Israel.

23 Now in those days the advice Ahithophel gave was like that of one who enquires of God. That was how both David and Absalom regarded all of Ahithophel's advice.

17 Ahithophel said to Absalom, 'I would*ᵃ* choose twelve thousand men and set out tonight in pursuit of David. ²I would attack him while he is weary and weak. I would strike him with terror, and then all the people with him will flee. I would strike down only the king ³and bring all the people back to you. The death of the man you seek will mean the return of all; all the people will be unharmed.' ⁴This plan seemed good to Absalom and to all the elders of Israel.

⁵But Absalom said, 'Summon also Hushai the Arkite, so that we can hear what he has to say as well.' ⁶When Hushai came to him, Absalom said, 'Ahithophel has given this advice. Should we do what he says? If not, give us your opinion.'

⁷Hushai replied to Absalom, 'The advice Ahithophel has given is not good this time. ⁸You know your father and his men; they are fighters, and as fierce as a wild bear robbed of her cubs. Besides, your father is an experienced fighter; he will not spend the night with the troops. ⁹Even now, he is hidden in a cave or some other place. If he should attack your troops first,*ᵇ* whoever hears about it will say, "There has been a slaughter among the troops who follow Absalom." ¹⁰Then even the bravest soldier, whose heart is like the heart of a lion, will melt with fear, for all Israel knows that your father is a fighter and that those with him are brave.

¹¹'So I advise you: let all Israel, from Dan to Beersheba – as numerous as the sand on the seashore – be gathered to you, with you yourself leading them into battle. ¹²Then we will attack him wherever he may be found, and we will fall on him as dew settles on the ground. Neither he nor any of his men will be left alive. ¹³If he withdraws into a city, then all Israel will bring ropes to that city, and we will drag it down to the valley until not so much as a pebble is left.'

¹⁴Absalom and all the men of Israel said, 'The advice of Hushai the Arkite is better than that of Ahithophel.' For the LORD had determined to frustrate the good advice of Ahithophel in order to bring disaster on Absalom.

¹⁵Hushai told Zadok and Abiathar, the priests, 'Ahithophel has advised Absalom and the elders of Israel to do such and such, but I have advised them to do so and so. ¹⁶Now send a message at once and tell David, "Do not spend the night at the fords in the wilderness; cross over without fail, or the king and all the people with him will be swallowed up."'

¹⁷Jonathan and Ahimaaz were staying at En Rogel. A female servant was to go and inform them, and they were to go and tell King David, for they could not risk being seen entering the city. ¹⁸But a young man saw them and told Absalom. So the two of them left at once and went to the house of a man in Bahurim. He had a well in his courtyard, and they climbed down into it. ¹⁹His wife took a covering and spread it out over the opening of the well and scattered corn over it. No one knew anything about it.

²⁰When Absalom's men came to the woman at the house, they asked, 'Where are Ahimaaz and Jonathan?'

The woman answered them, 'They crossed over the brook.'*ᶜ* The men searched but found no one, so they returned to Jerusalem.

²¹After they had gone, the two climbed out of the well and went to inform King David. They said to him, 'Set out and cross the river at once; Ahithophel has advised such and such against you.' ²²So David and all the people with him set out and crossed the Jordan. By daybreak, no one was left who had not crossed the Jordan.

²³When Ahithophel saw that his advice had not been followed, he saddled his donkey and set out for his house in his home town. He put his house in order and then hanged himself. So he died and was buried in his father's tomb.

Absalom's death

²⁴David went to Mahanaim, and Absalom crossed the Jordan with all the men of

---

a 1 Or Let me
b 9 Or When some of the men fall at the first attack

c 20 Or 'They passed by the sheepfold towards the water.'

Israel. 25 Absalom had appointed Amasa over the army in place of Joab. Amasa was the son of Jether,*d* an Ishmaelite*e* who had married Abigail,*f* the daughter of Nahash and sister of Zeruiah the mother of Joab. 26 The Israelites and Absalom camped in the land of Gilead.

27 When David came to Mahanaim, Shobi son of Nahash from Rabbah of the Ammonites, and Makir son of Ammiel from Lo Debar, and Barzillai the Gileadite from Rogelim 28 brought bedding and bowls and articles of pottery. They also brought wheat and barley, flour and roasted grain, beans and lentils,*g* 29 honey and curds, sheep, and cheese from cows' milk for David and his people to eat. For they said, 'The people have become exhausted and hungry and thirsty in the wilderness.'

18 David mustered the men who were with him and appointed over them commanders of thousands and commanders of hundreds. 2 David sent out his troops, a third under the command of Joab, a third under Joab's brother Abishai son of Zeruiah, and a third under Ittai the Gittite. The king told the troops, 'I myself will surely march out with you.'

3 But the men said, 'You must not go out; if we are forced to flee, they won't care about us. Even if half of us die, they won't care; but you are worth ten thousand of us.*a* It would be better now for you to give us support from the city.'

4 The king answered, 'I will do whatever seems best to you.'

So the king stood beside the gate while all his men marched out in units of hundreds and of thousands. 5 The king commanded Joab, Abishai and Ittai, 'Be gentle with the young man Absalom for my sake.' And all the troops heard the king giving

orders concerning Absalom to each of the commanders.

6 David's army marched out of the city to fight Israel, and the battle took place in the forest of Ephraim. 7 There Israel's troops were routed by David's men, and the casualties that day were great – twenty thousand men. 8 The battle spread out over the whole countryside, and the forest swallowed up more men that day than the sword.

9 Now Absalom happened to meet David's men. He was riding his mule, and as the mule went under the thick branches of a large oak, Absalom's hair got caught in the tree. He was left hanging in mid-air, while the mule he was riding kept on going.

10 When one of the men saw what had happened, he told Joab, 'I have just seen Absalom hanging in an oak tree.'

11 Joab said to the man who had told him this, 'What! You saw him? Why didn't you strike him to the ground right there? Then I would have had to give you ten shekels*b* of silver and a warrior's belt.'

12 But the man replied, 'Even if a thousand shekels*c* were weighed out into my hands, I would not lay a hand on the king's son. In our hearing the king commanded you and Abishai and Ittai, "Protect the young man Absalom for my sake.*d*" 13 And if I had put my life in jeopardy*e* – and nothing is hidden from the king – you would have kept your distance from me.'

14 Joab said, 'I am not going to wait like this for you.' So he took three javelins in his hand and plunged them into Absalom's heart while Absalom was still alive in the oak tree. 15 And ten of Joab's armour-bearers surrounded Absalom, struck him and killed him.

16 Then Joab sounded the trumpet, and the troops stopped pursuing Israel, for Joab halted them. 17 They took Absalom, threw him into a big pit in the forest and

---

d 25 Hebrew *Ithra*, a variant of *Jether*

e 25 Some Septuagint manuscripts (see also 1 Chron. 2:17); Hebrew and other Septuagint manuscripts *Israelite*

f 25 Hebrew *Abigal*, a variant of *Abigail*

g 28 Most Septuagint manuscripts and Syriac; Hebrew *lentils, and roasted grain*

a 3 Two Hebrew manuscripts, some Septuagint manuscripts and Vulgate; most Hebrew manuscripts *care; for now there are ten thousand like us*

b 11 That is, about 115 grams

c 12 That is, about 12 kilograms

d 12 A few Hebrew manuscripts, Septuagint, Vulgate and Syriac; most Hebrew manuscripts may be translated *Absalom, whoever you may be.*

e 13 Or *Otherwise, if I had acted treacherously towards him* piled up a large heap of rocks over him. Meanwhile, all the Israelites fled to their homes.

18 During his life-time Absalom had taken a pillar and erected it in the King's Valley as a monument to himself, for he thought, 'I have no son to carry on the memory of my name.' He named the pillar after himself, and it is called Absalom's Monument to this day.

David mourns

19 Now Ahimaaz son of Zadok said, 'Let me run and take the news to the king that the LORD has vindicated him by delivering him from the hand of his enemies.'

20 'You are not the one to take the news today,' Joab told him. 'You may take the news another time, but you must not do so today, because the king's son is dead.'

21 Then Joab said to a Cushite, 'Go, tell the king what you have seen.' The Cushite bowed down before Joab and ran off.

22 Ahimaaz son of Zadok again said to Joab, 'Come what may, please let me run behind the Cushite.'

But Joab replied, 'My son, why do you want to go? You don't have any news that will bring you a reward.'

23 He said, 'Come what may, I want to run.'

So Joab said, 'Run!' Then Ahimaaz ran by way of the plain*f* and outran the Cushite.

24 While David was sitting between the inner and outer gates, the watchman went up to the roof of the gateway by the wall. As he looked out, he saw a man running alone. 25 The watchman called out to the king and reported it.

The king said, 'If he is alone, he must have good news.' And the runner came closer and closer.

26 Then the watchman saw another runner, and he called down to the gatekeeper, 'Look, another man running alone!'

The king said, 'He must be bringing good news, too.'

27 The watchman said, 'It seems to me that the first one runs like Ahimaaz son of Zadok.'

'He's a good man,' the king said. 'He comes with good news.'

28 Then Ahimaaz called out to the king, 'All is well!' He bowed down before the king with his face to the ground and said, 'Praise be to the LORD your God! He has delivered up those who lifted their hands against my lord the king.'

29 The king asked, 'Is the young man Absalom safe?'

Ahimaaz answered, 'I saw great confusion just as Joab was about to send the king's servant and me, your servant, but I don't know what it was.'

30 The king said, 'Stand aside and wait here.' So he stepped aside and stood there.

31 Then the Cushite arrived and said, 'My lord the king, hear the good news! The LORD has vindicated you today by delivering you from the hand of all who rose up against you.'

32 The king asked the Cushite, 'Is the young man Absalom safe?'

The Cushite replied, 'May the enemies of my lord the king and all who rise up to harm you be like that young man.'

33 The king was shaken. He went up to the room over the gateway and wept. As he went, he said: 'O my son Absalom! My son, my son Absalom! If only I had died instead of you – O Absalom, my son, my son!'*g*

19 *a* Joab was told, 'The king is weeping and mourning for Absalom.' 2 And for the whole army the victory that day was turned into mourning, because on that day the troops heard it said, 'The king is grieving for his son.' 3 The men stole into the city that day as men steal in who are ashamed when they flee from battle. 4 The king covered his face and cried aloud, 'O my son Absalom! O Absalom, my son, my son!'

5 Then Joab went into the house to the king and said, 'Today you have humiliated all your men, who have just saved your life and the lives of your sons and daughters

---

f 23 That is, the plain of the Jordan

g 33 In Hebrew texts this verse (18:33) is numbered 19:1.
a In Hebrew texts 19:1-43 is numbered 19:2-44.

and the lives of your wives and concubines. 6You love those who hate you and hate those who love you. You have made it clear today that the commanders and their men mean nothing to you. I see that you would be pleased if Absalom were alive today and all of us were dead. 7Now go out and encourage your men. I swear by the LORD that if you don't go out, not a man will be left with you by nightfall. This will be worse for you than all the calamities that have come on you from your youth till now.'

8So the king got up and took his seat in the gateway. When the men were told, 'The king is sitting in the gateway,' they all came before him.

Meanwhile, the Israelites had fled to their homes.

David returns to Jerusalem

9Throughout the tribes of Israel, all the people were arguing among themselves, saying, 'The king delivered us from the hand of our enemies; he is the one who rescued us from the hand of the Philistines. But now he has fled the country to escape from Absalom; 10and Absalom, whom we anointed to rule over us, has died in battle. So why do you say nothing about bringing the king back?'

11King David sent this message to Zadok and Abiathar, the priests: 'Ask the elders of Judah, "Why should you be the last to bring the king back to his palace, since what is being said throughout Israel has reached the king at his quarters? 12You are my relatives, my own flesh and blood. So why should you be the last to bring back the king?" 13And say to Amasa, "Are you not my own flesh and blood? May God deal with me, be it ever so severely, if you are not the commander of my army for life in place of Joab."'

14He won over the hearts of the men of Judah so that they were all of one mind. They sent word to the king, 'Return, you and all your men.' 15Then the king returned and went as far as the Jordan.

Now the men of Judah had come to Gilgal to go out and meet the king and bring him across the Jordan. 16Shimei son of Gera, the Benjaminite from Bahurim, hurried down with the men of Judah to meet King David. 17With him were a thousand Benjaminites, along with Ziba, the steward of Saul's household, and his fifteen sons and twenty servants. They rushed to the Jordan, where the king was. 18They crossed at the ford to take the king's household over and to do whatever he wished.

When Shimei son of Gera crossed the Jordan, he fell prostrate before the king 19and said to him, 'May my lord not hold me guilty. Do not remember how your servant did wrong on the day my lord the king left Jerusalem. May the king put it out of his mind. 20For I your servant know that I have sinned, but today I have come here as the first from the tribes of Joseph to come down and meet my lord the king.'

21Then Abishai son of Zeruiah said, 'Shouldn't Shimei be put to death for this? He cursed the LORD's anointed.'

22David replied, 'What does this have to do with you, you sons of Zeruiah? What right do you have to interfere? Should anyone be put to death in Israel today? Don't I know that today I am king over Israel?' 23So the king said to Shimei, 'You shall not die.' And the king promised him on oath.

24Mephibosheth, Saul's grandson, also went down to meet the king. He had not taken care of his feet or trimmed his moustache or washed his clothes from the day the king left until the day he returned safely. 25When he came from Jerusalem to meet the king, the king asked him, 'Why didn't you go with me, Mephibosheth?'

26He said, 'My lord the king, since I your servant am lame, I said, "I will have my donkey saddled and will ride on it, so that I can go with the king." But Ziba my servant betrayed me. 27And he has slandered your servant to my lord the king. My lord the king is like an angel of God; so do whatever you wish. 28All my grandfather's descendants deserved nothing but death from my lord the king, but you gave your servant a place among those who eat at your table. So what right do I have to make any more appeals to the king?'

29 The king said to him, 'Why say more? I order you and Ziba to divide the land.'

30 Mephibosheth said to the king, 'Let him take everything, now that my lord the king has returned home safely.'

31 Barzillai the Gileadite also came down from Rogelim to cross the Jordan with the king and to send him on his way from there. 32 Now Barzillai was very old, eighty years of age. He had provided for the king during his stay in Mahanaim, for he was a very wealthy man. 33 The king said to Barzillai, 'Cross over with me and stay with me in Jerusalem, and I will provide for you.'

34 But Barzillai answered the king, 'How many more years shall I live, that I should go up to Jerusalem with the king? 35 I am now eighty years old. Can I tell the difference between what is enjoyable and what is not? Can your servant taste what he eats and drinks? Can I still hear the voices of male and female singers? Why should your servant be an added burden to my lord the king? 36 Your servant will cross over the Jordan with the king for a short distance, but why should the king reward me in this way? 37 Let your servant return, that I may die in my own town near the tomb of my father and mother. But here is your servant Kimham. Let him cross over with my lord the king. Do for him whatever you wish.'

38 The king said, 'Kimham shall cross over with me, and I will do for him whatever you wish. And anything you desire from me I will do for you.'

39 So all the people crossed the Jordan, and then the king crossed over. The king kissed Barzillai and bade him farewell, and Barzillai returned to his home.

40 When the king crossed over to Gilgal, Kimham crossed with him. All the troops of Judah and half the troops of Israel had taken the king over.

41 Soon all the men of Israel were coming to the king and saying to him, 'Why did our brothers, the men of Judah, steal the king away and bring him and his household across the Jordan, together with all his men?'

42 All the men of Judah answered the men of Israel, 'We did this because the king is closely related to us. Why are you angry about it? Have we eaten any of the king's provisions? Have we taken anything for ourselves?'

43 Then the men of Israel answered the men of Judah, 'We have ten shares in the king; so we have a greater claim on David than you have. Why then do you treat us with contempt? Weren't we the first to speak of bringing back our king?'

But the men of Judah pressed their claims even more forcefully than the men of Israel.

FAVOURITE VERSES

Psalm 33:9

For he spoke, and it came to be;
he commanded, and it stood firm.

I think this verse shows a great sense of authority from God and a sense that he is our God and he is for us. He wants to see us succeed, so if we have a great power over our lives we have a great advantage over our enemies.

Matt, 14

Sheba rebels against David

20 Now a troublemaker named Sheba son of Bikri, a Benjaminite, happened to be there. He sounded the trumpet and shouted,

'We have no share in David,
    no part in Jesse's son!
Every man to his tent, Israel!'

2 So all the men of Israel deserted David to follow Sheba son of Bikri. But the men of Judah stayed by their king all the way from the Jordan to Jerusalem.

3 When David returned to his palace in

Jerusalem, he took the ten concubines he had left to take care of the palace and put them in a house under guard. He provided for them but had no sexual relations with them. They were kept in confinement till the day of their death, living as widows.

⁴Then the king said to Amasa, 'Summon the men of Judah to come to me within three days, and be here yourself.' ⁵But when Amasa went to summon Judah, he took longer than the time the king had set for him.

⁶David said to Abishai, 'Now Sheba son of Bikri will do us more harm than Absalom did. Take your master's men and pursue him, or he will find fortified cities and escape from us.'ᵃ ⁷So Joab's men and the Kerethites and Pelethites and all the mighty warriors went out under the command of Abishai. They marched out from Jerusalem to pursue Sheba son of Bikri.

⁸While they were at the great rock in Gibeon, Amasa came to meet them. Joab was wearing his military tunic, and strapped over it at his waist was a belt with a dagger in its sheath. As he stepped forward, it dropped out of its sheath.

⁹Joab said to Amasa, 'How are you, my brother?' Then Joab took Amasa by the beard with his right hand to kiss him. ¹⁰Amasa was not on his guard against the dagger in Joab's hand, and Joab plunged it into his belly, and his intestines spilled out on the ground. Without being stabbed again, Amasa died. Then Joab and his brother Abishai pursued Sheba son of Bikri.

¹¹One of Joab's men stood beside Amasa and said, 'Whoever favours Joab, and whoever is for David, let him follow Joab!' ¹²Amasa lay wallowing in his blood in the middle of the road, and the man saw that all the troops came to a halt there. When he realised that everyone who came up to Amasa stopped, he dragged him from the road into a field and threw a garment over him. ¹³After Amasa had been removed from the road, everyone went on with Joab to pursue Sheba son of Bikri.

¹⁴Sheba passed through all the tribes of Israel to Abel Beth Maakah and through the entire region of the Bikrites,ᵇ who gathered together and followed him. ¹⁵All the troops with Joab came and besieged Sheba in Abel Beth Maakah. They built a siege ramp up to the city, and it stood against the outer fortifications. While they were battering the wall to bring it down, ¹⁶a wise woman called from the city, 'Listen! Listen! Tell Joab to come here so that I can speak to him.' ¹⁷He went towards her, and she asked, 'Are you Joab?'

'I am,' he answered.

She said, 'Listen to what your servant has to say.'

'I'm listening,' he said.

¹⁸She continued, 'Long ago they used to say, "Get your answer at Abel," and that settled it. ¹⁹We are the peaceful and faithful in Israel. You are trying to destroy a city that is a mother in Israel. Why do you want to swallow up the LORD's inheritance?'

²⁰'Far be it from me!' Joab replied, 'Far be it from me to swallow up or destroy! ²¹That is not the case. A man named Sheba son of Bikri, from the hill country of Ephraim, has lifted up his hand against the king, against David. Hand over this one man, and I'll withdraw from the city.'

The woman said to Joab, 'His head will be thrown to you from the wall.'

²²Then the woman went to all the people with her wise advice, and they cut off the head of Sheba son of Bikri and threw it to Joab. So he sounded the trumpet, and his men dispersed from the city, each returning to his home. And Joab went back to the king in Jerusalem.

David's officials

²³Joab was over Israel's entire army; Benaiah son of Jehoiada was over the Kerethites and Pelethites; ²⁴Adoniramᶜ was in charge of forced labour; Jehoshaphat son of Ahilud was recorder; ²⁵Sheva was secretary; Zadok and Abiathar were priests; ²⁶and Ira the Jairiteᵈ was David's priest.

ᵃ6 Or *and do us serious injury*

ᵇ14 See Septuagint and Vulgate; Hebrew *Berites*.
ᶜ24 Some Septuagint manuscripts (see also 1 Kings 4:6 and 5:14); Hebrew *Adoram*
ᵈ26 Hebrew; some Septuagint manuscripts and Syriac (see also 23:38) *Ithrite*

The Gibeonites avenged

21 During the reign of David, there was a famine for three successive years; so David sought the face of the LORD. The LORD said, 'It is on account of Saul and his blood-stained house; it is because he put the Gibeonites to death.'

²The king summoned the Gibeonites and spoke to them. (Now the Gibeonites were not a part of Israel but were survivors of the Amorites; the Israelites had sworn to spare them, but Saul in his zeal for Israel and Judah had tried to annihilate them.) ³David asked the Gibeonites, 'What shall I do for you? How shall I make atonement so that you will bless the LORD's inheritance?'

⁴The Gibeonites answered him, 'We have no right to demand silver or gold from Saul or his family, nor do we have the right to put anyone in Israel to death.'

'What do you want me to do for you?' David asked.

⁵They answered the king, 'As for the man who destroyed us and plotted against us so that we have been decimated and have no place anywhere in Israel, ⁶let seven of his male descendants be given to us to be killed and their bodies exposed before the LORD at Gibeah of Saul – the LORD's chosen one.'

So the king said, 'I will give them to you.'

⁷The king spared Mephibosheth son of Jonathan, the son of Saul, because of the oath before the LORD between David and Jonathan son of Saul. ⁸But the king took Armoni and Mephibosheth, the two sons of Aiah's daughter Rizpah, whom she had borne to Saul, together with the five sons of Saul's daughter Merab,ᵃ whom she had borne to Adriel son of Barzillai the Meholathite. ⁹He handed them over to the Gibeonites, who killed them and exposed their bodies on a hill before the LORD. All seven of them fell together; they were put to death during the first days of harvest, just as the barley harvest was beginning.

¹⁰Rizpah daughter of Aiah took sackcloth and spread it out for herself on a rock. From the beginning of the harvest till the rain poured down from the heavens on the bodies, she did not let the birds touch them by day or the wild animals by night. ¹¹When David was told what Aiah's daughter Rizpah, Saul's concubine, had done, ¹²he went and took the bones of Saul and his son Jonathan from the citizens of Jabesh Gilead. (They had stolen their bodies from the public square at Beth Shan, where the Philistines had hung them after they struck Saul down on Gilboa.) ¹³David brought the bones of Saul and his son Jonathan from there, and the bones of those who had been killed and exposed were gathered up.

¹⁴They buried the bones of Saul and his son Jonathan in the tomb of Saul's father Kish, at Zela in Benjamin, and did everything the king commanded. After that, God answered prayer on behalf of the land.

Wars against the Philistines

¹⁵Once again there was a battle between the Philistines and Israel. David went down with his men to fight against the Philistines, and he became exhausted. ¹⁶And Ishbi-Benob, one of the descendants of Rapha, whose bronze spearhead weighed three hundred shekelsᵇ and who was armed with a new sword, said he would kill David. ¹⁷But Abishai son of Zeruiah came to David's rescue; he struck the Philistine down and killed him. Then David's men swore to him, saying, 'Never again will you go out with us to battle, so that the lamp of Israel will not be extinguished.'

¹⁸In the course of time, there was another battle with the Philistines, at Gob. At that time Sibbekai the Hushathite killed Saph, one of the descendants of Rapha.

¹⁹In another battle with the Philistines at Gob, Elhanan son of Jairᶜ the Bethlehemite killed the brother ofᵈ Goliath the

---

ᵃ 8 Two Hebrew manuscripts, some Septuagint manuscripts and Syriac (see also 1 Samuel 18:19); most Hebrew and Septuagint manuscripts *Michal*

ᵇ 16 That is, about 3.5 kilograms

ᶜ 19 See 1 Chron. 20:5; Hebrew *Jaare-Oregim*.

ᵈ 19 See 1 Chron. 20:5; Hebrew does not have *the brother of*.

Gittite, who had a spear with a shaft like a weaver's rod.

²⁰ In still another battle, which took place at Gath, there was a huge man with six fingers on each hand and six toes on each foot – twenty-four in all. He also was descended from Rapha. ²¹ When he taunted Israel, Jonathan son of Shimeah, David's brother, killed him.

²² These four were descendants of Rapha in Gath, and they fell at the hands of David and his men.

David's song of praise

22 David sang to the LORD the words of this song when the LORD delivered him from the hand of all his enemies and from the hand of Saul. ² He said:

'The LORD is my rock, my fortress and
    my deliverer;
³   my God is my rock, in whom I take
        refuge,
    my shield^a and the horn^b of my
        salvation.
He is my stronghold, my refuge and
        my saviour –
    from violent people you save me.

⁴ 'I called to the LORD, who is worthy of
        praise,
    and have been saved from my
        enemies.
⁵ The waves of death swirled about me;
    the torrents of destruction
        overwhelmed me.
⁶ The cords of the grave coiled around
        me;
    the snares of death confronted me.

⁷ 'In my distress I called to the LORD;
    I called out to my God.
From his temple he heard my voice;
    my cry came to his ears.
⁸ The earth trembled and quaked,
    the foundations of the heavens^c
        shook;
    they trembled because he was angry.

⁹ Smoke rose from his nostrils;
    consuming fire came from his
        mouth,
    burning coals blazed out of it.
¹⁰ He parted the heavens and came
        down;
    dark clouds were under his feet.
¹¹ He mounted the cherubim and flew;
    he soared^d on the wings of the wind.
¹² He made darkness his canopy around
        him –
    the dark^e rain clouds of the sky.
¹³ Out of the brightness of his presence
    bolts of lightning blazed forth.
¹⁴ The LORD thundered from heaven;
    the voice of the Most High
        resounded.
¹⁵ He shot his arrows and scattered the
        enemy,
    with great bolts of lightning he
        routed them.
¹⁶ The valleys of the sea were exposed
    and the foundations of the earth
        laid bare
at the rebuke of the LORD,
    at the blast of breath from his
        nostrils.

¹⁷ 'He reached down from on high and
        took hold of me;
    he drew me out of deep waters.
¹⁸ He rescued me from my powerful
        enemy,
    from my foes, who were too strong
        for me.
¹⁹ They confronted me in the day of my
        disaster,
    but the LORD was my support.
²⁰ He brought me out into a spacious
        place;
    he rescued me because he delighted
        in me.

²¹ 'The LORD has dealt with me according
        to my righteousness;
    according to the cleanness of my
        hands he has rewarded me.

---

a 3 Or *sovereign*
b 3 *Horn* here symbolises strength.
c 8 Hebrew; Vulgate and Syriac (see also Psalm 18:7) *mountains*

d 11 Many Hebrew manuscripts (see also Psalm 18:10); most Hebrew manuscripts *appeared*
e 12 Septuagint (see also Psalm 18:11); Hebrew *massed*

²² For I have kept the ways of the LORD;
  I am not guilty of turning from my
    God.
²³ All his laws are before me;
  I have not turned away from his
    decrees.
²⁴ I have been blameless before him
  and have kept myself from sin.
²⁵ The LORD has rewarded me according
    to my righteousness,
  according to my cleanness*f* in his
    sight.

²⁶ 'To the faithful you show yourself
    faithful,
  to the blameless you show yourself
    blameless,
²⁷ to the pure you show yourself pure,
  but to the devious you show
    yourself shrewd.
²⁸ You save the humble,
  but your eyes are on the haughty to
    bring them low.
²⁹ You, LORD, are my lamp;
  the LORD turns my darkness into
    light.
³⁰ With your help I can advance against a
    troop*g*;
  with my God I can scale a wall.

³¹ 'As for God, his way is perfect:
  the LORD's word is flawless;
  he shields all who take refuge in him.
³² For who is God besides the LORD?
  And who is the Rock except our God?
³³ It is God who arms me with strength*h*
  and keeps my way secure.
³⁴ He makes my feet like the feet of a
    deer;
  he causes me to stand on the
    heights.
³⁵ He trains my hands for battle;
  my arms can bend a bow of bronze.
³⁶ You make your saving help my shield;
  your help has made*i* me great.

³⁷ You provide a broad path for my feet,
  so that my ankles do not give way.

³⁸ 'I pursued my enemies and crushed
    them;
  I did not turn back till they were
    destroyed.
³⁹ I crushed them completely, and they
    could not rise;
  they fell beneath my feet.
⁴⁰ You armed me with strength for
    battle;
  you humbled my adversaries
    before me.
⁴¹ You made my enemies turn their backs
    in flight,
  and I destroyed my foes.
⁴² They cried for help, but there was no
    one to save them –
  to the LORD, but he did not answer.
⁴³ I beat them as fine as the dust of the
    earth;
  I pounded and trampled them like
    mud in the streets.

⁴⁴ 'You have delivered me from the
    attacks of the peoples;
  you have preserved me as the head
    of nations.
  People I did not know now serve me,
⁴⁵   foreigners cower before me;
  as soon as they hear of me, they
    obey me.
⁴⁶ They all lose heart;
  they come trembling*j* from their
    strongholds.

⁴⁷ 'The LORD lives! Praise be to my Rock!
  Exalted be my God, the Rock, my
    Saviour!
⁴⁸ He is the God who avenges me,
  who puts the nations under me,
⁴⁹   who sets me free from my enemies.
  You exalted me above my foes;
  from a violent man you rescued me.
⁵⁰ Therefore I will praise you, LORD,
    among the nations;
  I will sing the praises of your name.

---

f 25 Hebrew; Septuagint and Vulgate (see also
Psalm 18:24) *to the cleanness of my hands*
g 30 Or *can run through a barricade*
h 33 Dead Sea Scrolls, some Septuagint
manuscripts, Vulgate and Syriac (see also Psalm
18:32); Masoretic Text *who is my strong refuge*
i 36 Dead Sea Scrolls; Masoretic Text *shield; / you stoop
down to make*

j 46 Some Septuagint manuscripts and Vulgate (see
also Psalm 18:45); Masoretic Text *they arm themselves*

51 'He gives his king great victories;
   he shows unfailing kindness to his
      anointed,
   to David and his descendants for
      ever.'

David's last words

23 These are the last words of David:

'The inspired utterance of David son of
    Jesse,
  the utterance of the man exalted by
    the Most High,
the man anointed by the God of
    Jacob,
the hero of Israel's songs:

2 'The Spirit of the LORD spoke
    through me;
  his word was on my tongue.
3 The God of Israel spoke,
  the Rock of Israel said to me:
"When one rules over people in
    righteousness,
  when he rules in the fear of God,
4 he is like the light of morning at
    sunrise
  on a cloudless morning,
like the brightness after rain
  that brings grass from the earth."

5 'If my house were not right with God,
  surely he would not have made
    with me an everlasting
    covenant,
  arranged and secured in every
    part;
surely he would not bring to fruition
    my salvation
and grant me my every desire.
6 But evil men are all to be cast aside
    like thorns,
  which are not gathered with the
    hand.
7 Whoever touches thorns
  uses a tool of iron or the shaft of a
    spear;
  they are burned up where they lie.'

David's mighty warriors

8 These are the names of David's mighty warriors:

Josheb-Basshebeth,ᵃ a Tahkemonite,ᵇ was chief of the Three; he raised his spear against eight hundred men, whom he killedᶜ in one encounter.

9 Next to him was Eleazar son of Dodai the Ahohite. As one of the three mighty warriors, he was with David when they taunted the Philistines gathered at Pas Dammimᵈ for battle. Then the Israelites retreated, 10 but Eleazar stood his ground and struck down the Philistines till his hand grew tired and froze to the sword. The LORD brought about a great victory that day. The troops returned to Eleazar, but only to strip the dead.

11 Next to him was Shammah son of Agee the Hararite. When the Philistines banded together at a place where there was a field full of lentils, Israel's troops fled from them. 12 But Shammah took his stand in the middle of the field. He defended it and struck the Philistines down, and the LORD brought about a great victory.

13 During harvest time, three of the thirty chief warriors came down to David at the cave of Adullam, while a band of Philistines was encamped in the Valley of Rephaim. 14 At that time David was in the stronghold, and the Philistine garrison was at Bethlehem. 15 David longed for water and said, 'Oh, that someone would get me a drink of water from the well near the gate of Bethlehem!' 16 So the three mighty warriors broke through the Philistine lines, drew water from the well near the gate of Bethlehem and carried it back to David. But he refused to drink it; instead, he poured it out before the LORD. 17 'Far be it from me, LORD, to do this!' he said. 'Is it not the blood of men who went at the risk of their lives?' And David would not drink it.

---

a 8 Hebrew; some Septuagint manuscripts suggest *Ish-Bosheth,* that is, *Esh-Baal* (see also 1 Chron. 11:11 *Jashobeam*).
b 8 Probably a variant of *Hakmonite* (see 1 Chron. 11:11)
c 8 Some Septuagint manuscripts (see also 1 Chron. 11:11); Hebrew and other Septuagint manuscripts *Three; it was Adino the Eznite who killed eight hundred men*
d 9 See 1 Chron. 11:13; Hebrew *gathered there.*

Such were the exploits of the three mighty warriors. ¹⁸Abishai the brother of Joab son of Zeruiah was chief of the Three.^e He raised his spear against three hundred men, whom he killed, and so he became as famous as the Three. ¹⁹Was he not held in greater honour than the Three? He became their commander, even though he was not included among them.

²⁰Benaiah son of Jehoiada, a valiant fighter from Kabzeel, performed great exploits. He struck down Moab's two mightiest warriors. He also went down into a pit on a snowy day and killed a lion. ²¹And he struck down a huge Egyptian. Although the Egyptian had a spear in his hand, Benaiah went against him with a club. He snatched the spear from the Egyptian's hand and killed him with his own spear. ²²Such were the exploits of Benaiah son of Jehoiada; he too was as famous as the three mighty warriors. ²³He was held in greater honour than any of the Thirty, but he was not included among the Three. And David put him in charge of his bodyguard.

²⁴Among the Thirty were:
  Asahel the brother of Joab,
  Elhanan son of Dodo from Bethlehem,
  ²⁵Shammah the Harodite,
  Elika the Harodite,
  ²⁶Helez the Paltite,
  Ira son of Ikkesh from Tekoa,
  ²⁷Abiezer from Anathoth,
  Sibbekai^f the Hushathite,
  ²⁸Zalmon the Ahohite,
  Maharai the Netophathite,
  ²⁹Heled^g son of Baanah the Netophathite,
  Ithai son of Ribai from Gibeah in Benjamin,
  ³⁰Benaiah the Pirathonite,

Hiddai^h from the ravines of Gaash,
  ³¹Abi-Albon the Arbathite,
  Azmaveth the Barhumite,
  ³²Eliahba the Shaalbonite,
  the sons of Jashen,
  Jonathan ³³son ofⁱ Shammah the Hararite,
  Ahiam son of Sharar^j the Hararite,
  ³⁴Eliphelet son of Ahasbai the Maakathite,
  Eliam son of Ahithophel the Gilonite,
  ³⁵Hezro the Carmelite,
  Paarai the Arbite,
  ³⁶Igal son of Nathan from Zobah,
  the son of Hagri,^k
  ³⁷Zelek the Ammonite,
  Naharai the Beerothite, the armour-bearer of Joab son of Zeruiah,
  ³⁸Ira the Ithrite,
  Gareb the Ithrite
  ³⁹and Uriah the Hittite.
There were thirty-seven in all.

David enrols the fighting men

24 Again the anger of the LORD burned against Israel, and he incited David against them, saying, 'Go and take a census of Israel and Judah.'

²So the king said to Joab and the army commanders^a with him, 'Go throughout the tribes of Israel from Dan to Beersheba and enrol the fighting men, so that I may know how many there are.'

³But Joab replied to the king, 'May the LORD your God multiply the troops a hundred times over, and may the eyes of my lord the king see it. But why does my lord the king want to do such a thing?'

---

e 18 Most Hebrew manuscripts (see also 1 Chron. 11:20); two Hebrew manuscripts and Syriac *Thirty*
f 27 Some Septuagint manuscripts (see also 21:18; 1 Chron. 11:29); Hebrew *Mebunnai*
g 29 Some Hebrew manuscripts and Vulgate (see also 1 Chron. 11:30); most Hebrew manuscripts *Heleb*

h 30 Hebrew; some Septuagint manuscripts (see also 1 Chron. 11:32) *Hurai*
i 33 Some Septuagint manuscripts (see also 1 Chron. 11:34); Hebrew does not have *son of.*
j 33 Hebrew; some Septuagint manuscripts (see also 1 Chron. 11:35) *Sakar*
k 36 Some Septuagint manuscripts (see also 1 Chron. 11:38); Hebrew *Haggadi*
a 2 Septuagint (see also verse 4 and 1 Chron. 21:2); Hebrew *Joab the army commander*

4 The king's word, however, overruled Joab and the army commanders; so they left the presence of the king to enrol the fighting men of Israel.

5 After crossing the Jordan, they camped near Aroer, south of the town in the gorge, and then went through Gad and on to Jazer. 6 They went to Gilead and the region of Tahtim Hodshi, and on to Dan Jaan and around towards Sidon. 7 Then they went towards the fortress of Tyre and all the towns of the Hivites and Canaanites. Finally, they went on to Beersheba in the Negev of Judah.

8 After they had gone through the entire land, they came back to Jerusalem at the end of nine months and twenty days.

9 Joab reported the number of the fighting men to the king: in Israel there were eight hundred thousand able-bodied

WORSHIP 2

Costly

Can you imagine giving someone a present that you got out of a Christmas cracker?

We all know that presents are meant to cost us something. If there's no sort of cost, it's a pretty poor gift. The best relationships are when people really 'spend themselves' for one another.

Our relationship with God is no different. He invested everything he had into forming relationship with us, paying the highest price by sending his Son Jesus to die so that we could know him. We have received such grace, and in worship we have a chance to respond.

King David understood this when he was building an altar to the Lord in 2 Samuel 24. He was offered some land and materials for free, but he refused to accept the freebies from Araunah, saying, *'I will not sacrifice to the Lord my God burnt offerings that cost me nothing'* (2 Samuel 24:24).

When we come to worship God, it can be so easy to cheapen our acts of praise and present him with an offering that hasn't cost us anything. We can go through the motions – sing the songs, pray the prayers, toss coins into the offering bag – and then find ourselves walking out of church, complaining, 'I didn't get anything out of it today.'

When this happens, we realise that we have become consumers of worship. Consumer worship is the opposite of costly worship! The sole purpose of coming to worship God has always been to bring our praise and adoration to him, not for our personal gain or spiritual satisfaction. If we find ourselves 'not getting anything out of worship', we have missed the point.

Next time you're in a time of worship, choose to praise, choose to glorify, choose to give God your best. He's worth it all.

Beth Croft

 Leviticus 9   Colossians 3:12–17

men who could handle a sword, and in Judah five hundred thousand.

¹⁰ David was conscience-stricken after he had counted the fighting men, and he said to the LORD, 'I have sinned greatly in what I have done. Now, LORD, I beg you, take away the guilt of your servant. I have done a very foolish thing.'

SACRIFICE 9

David's attitude: offer the best

The difference between Saul and David is a big one. They are not only completely different in self-confidence (David is the weakest brother, the runt of the litter). David understands from a very young age that it's not his ability but God's anointing that gives him power.

God says that David is a man after his own heart, and one great way to see David's heart is in 2 Samuel 24:24. David understands that relationships are based in honour and sacrifice. He will not give something to the Lord that costs him nothing. Now, if we are honest with ourselves, we can count a dozen times over the last week when we have offered God something that didn't cost us anything. We give him our time when we have nothing else to do. We give him our money after we have bought whatever it is that we want. We give him our hearts after we have explored other relationships and they don't work out. We give him our energy after we have spent the best of it on the things we enjoy. David turns this all upside down because his relationship with God is rooted in love that expresses itself in true worship through sacrifice. David will not give God anything that isn't worth something. He is not going to give God his leftovers – he is going to give God his best.

How is your relationship with God? Are you offering God your best? Are you giving God costly things or just your leftovers?

The founder of the Seventh Day Adventists was just a young girl when this revelation hit her. Every year her family used to give their old clothes to the poor. When Ellen was going through her clothes to find things she didn't want any more, that suddenly didn't make sense to her. So she went through her things and gave away her best clothes. All the clothes that her parents had just bought for her, that she was waiting to wear to school – she decided that she would give away her best. You can imagine how it went for her after her parents found out! But what happened was that this lesson in her little life began to form a discipleship – a relationship with God that was rooted in the same principle that David had. It was a love that was extravagant, generous. This is the love of people who are devoted to pleasing and loving God and want to give him their best.

Danielle Strickland

 1 Samuel 15:22   1 Kings 18:36

11 Before David got up the next morning, the word of the LORD had come to Gad the prophet, David's seer: 12 'Go and tell David, "This is what the LORD says: I am giving you three options. Choose one of them for me to carry out against you."'

13 So Gad went to David and said to him, 'Shall there come on you three[b] years of famine in your land? Or three months of fleeing from your enemies while they pursue you? Or three days of plague in your land? Now then, think it over and decide how I should answer the one who sent me.'

14 David said to Gad, 'I am in deep distress. Let us fall into the hands of the LORD, for his mercy is great; but do not let me fall into human hands.'

15 So the LORD sent a plague on Israel from that morning until the end of the time designated, and seventy thousand of the people from Dan to Beersheba died. 16 When the angel stretched out his hand to destroy Jerusalem, the LORD relented concerning the disaster and said to the angel who was afflicting the people, 'Enough! Withdraw your hand.' The angel of the LORD was then at the threshing-floor of Araunah the Jebusite.

17 When David saw the angel who was striking down the people, he said to the LORD, 'I have sinned; I, the shepherd,[c] have done wrong. These are but sheep. What have they done? Let your hand fall on me and my family.'

David builds an altar

18 On that day Gad went to David and said to him, 'Go up and build an altar to the LORD on the threshing floor of Araunah the Jebusite.' 19 So David went up, as the LORD had commanded through Gad. 20 When Araunah looked and saw the king and his officials coming towards him, he went out and bowed down before the king with his face to the ground.

21 Araunah said, 'Why has my lord the king come to his servant?'

'To buy your threshing-floor,' David answered, 'so that I can build an altar to the LORD, that the plague on the people may be stopped.'

22 Araunah said to David, 'Let my lord the king take whatever he wishes and offer it up. Here are oxen for the burnt offering, and here are threshing-sledges and ox yokes for the wood. 23 Your Majesty, Araunah[d] gives all this to the king.' Araunah also said to him, 'May the LORD your God accept you.'

24 But the king replied to Araunah, 'No, I insist on paying you for it. I will not sacrifice to the LORD my God burnt offerings that cost me nothing.'

So David bought the threshing-floor and the oxen and paid fifty shekels[e] of silver for them. 25 David built an altar to the LORD there and sacrificed burnt offerings and fellowship offerings. Then the LORD answered his prayer on behalf of the land, and the plague on Israel was stopped.

---

b 13 Septuagint (see also 1 Chron. 21:12); Hebrew *seven*

c 17 Dead Sea Scrolls and Septuagint; Masoretic Text does not have *the shepherd*.

d 23 Some Hebrew manuscripts and Septuagint; most Hebrew manuscripts *King Araunah*

e 24 That is, about 575 grams

1 KINGS

DATE

1 and 2 Kings cover about 400 years of Israel's history, starting around 970 BC

AUTHOR

Unknown

WHAT'S IT ALL ABOUT?

The first book of Kings continues the story from 2 Samuel, telling the history of Israel's monarchy. It begins with King David's last days and details how his son Solomon took over once David died. Solomon is shown to be a wise leader and God's people enjoyed a time of great blessing, with Solomon building the Lord a huge temple. Sadly it did not last. When Solomon became less dependent on God, he started to worship idols and God was so angry that he said he would cause the twelve tribes of Israel to be divided. Sure enough, in 931 BC the tribes split, with Jeroboam leading a rebellion that saw ten tribes become known as the Kingdom of Israel (the Northern tribes that had Samaria as their capital) and the remaining two as the Kingdom of Judah (the Southern tribes, or the 'Jews', who had Jerusalem as their capital). Most of the leaders of the two kingdoms led their people to worship idols and so displeased the Lord. God raised up the prophet Elijah, who tried to turn the people's hearts back to God. He performed many miracles and killed worshippers of Baal, putting his own life at risk.

WHY SHOULD WE READ IT?

- To hear how Solomon's selfless request for wisdom so that he could meet the needs of the people led the Lord to give him wisdom, wealth, health and honour (1 Kings 3).

- To see the consequences of the people's sin (1 Kings 12 onwards).

- To hear about Elijah raising a widow's son from the dead (1 Kings 17).

- To see what happened when Elijah took on the prophets of Baal to show the Lord as the only true God (1 Kings 18).

- To remember how kindly the Lord treats us when we are feeling discouraged (1 Kings 19).

Andy Croft with Liza Hoeksma

Adonijah sets himself up as king

1 When King David was very old, he could not keep warm even when they put covers over him. ²So his attendants said to him, 'Let us look for a young virgin to serve the king and take care of him. She can lie beside him so that our lord the king may keep warm.'

³Then they searched throughout Israel for a beautiful young woman and found Abishag, a Shunammite, and brought her to the king. ⁴The woman was very beautiful; she took care of the king and waited on him, but the king had no sexual relations with her.

⁵Now Adonijah, whose mother was Haggith, put himself forward and said, 'I will be king.' So he got chariots and horses*ᵃ* ready, with fifty men to run ahead of him. ⁶(His father had never rebuked him by asking, 'Why do you behave as you do?' He was also very handsome and was born next after Absalom.)

⁷Adonijah conferred with Joab son of Zeruiah and with Abiathar the priest, and they gave him their support. ⁸But Zadok the priest, Benaiah son of Jehoiada, Nathan the prophet, Shimei and Rei and David's special guard did not join Adonijah.

⁹Adonijah then sacrificed sheep, cattle and fattened calves at the Stone of Zoheleth near En Rogel. He invited all his brothers, the king's sons, and all the royal officials of Judah, ¹⁰but he did not invite Nathan the prophet or Benaiah or the special guard or his brother Solomon.

¹¹Then Nathan asked Bathsheba, Solomon's mother, 'Have you not heard that Adonijah, the son of Haggith, has become king, and our lord David knows nothing about it? ¹²Now then, let me advise you how you can save your own life and the life of your son Solomon. ¹³Go in to King David and say to him, "My lord the king, did you not swear to me your servant: 'Surely Solomon your son shall be king after me, and he will sit on my throne'? Why then has Adonijah become king?" ¹⁴While you are still there talking to the king, I will come in and add my word to what you have said.'

¹⁵So Bathsheba went to see the aged king in his room, where Abishag the Shunammite was attending him. ¹⁶Bathsheba bowed down, prostrating herself before the king.

'What is it you want?' the king asked.

¹⁷She said to him, 'My lord, you yourself swore to me your servant by the LORD your God: "Solomon your son shall become king after me, and he will sit on my throne." ¹⁸But now Adonijah has become king, and you, my lord the king, do not know about it. ¹⁹He has sacrificed great numbers of cattle, fattened calves, and sheep, and has invited all the king's sons, Abiathar the priest and Joab the commander of the army, but he has not invited Solomon your servant. ²⁰My lord the king, the eyes of all Israel are on you, to learn from you who will sit on the throne of my lord the king after him. ²¹Otherwise, as soon as my lord the king is laid to rest with his ancestors, I and my son Solomon will be treated as criminals.'

²²While she was still speaking with the king, Nathan the prophet arrived. ²³And the king was told, 'Nathan the prophet is here.' So he went before the king and bowed with his face to the ground.

²⁴Nathan said, 'Have you, my lord the king, declared that Adonijah shall be king after you, and that he will sit on your throne? ²⁵Today he has gone down and sacrificed great numbers of cattle, fattened calves, and sheep. He has invited all the king's sons, the commanders of the army and Abiathar the priest. At this very moment they are eating and drinking with him and saying, "Long live King Adonijah!" ²⁶But me your servant, and Zadok the priest, and Benaiah son of Jehoiada, and your servant Solomon he did not invite. ²⁷Is this something my lord the king has done without letting his servants know who should sit on the throne of my lord the king after him?'

David makes Solomon king

²⁸Then King David said, 'Call in Bathsheba.' So she came into the king's presence and stood before him. ²⁹The king then took an oath: 'As surely as the LORD lives, who has delivered me

ᵃ 5 Or charioteers

out of every trouble, ³⁰I will surely carry out this very day what I swore to you by the LORD, the God of Israel: Solomon your son shall be king after me, and he will sit on my throne in my place.'

³¹Then Bathsheba bowed down with her face to the ground, prostrating herself before the king, and said, 'May my lord King David live for ever!'

³²King David said, 'Call in Zadok the priest, Nathan the prophet and Benaiah son of Jehoiada.' When they came before the king, ³³he said to them: 'Take your lord's servants with you and put Solomon my son on my own mule and take him down to Gihon. ³⁴There shall Zadok the priest and Nathan the prophet anoint him king over Israel. Blow the trumpet and shout, "Long live King Solomon!" ³⁵Then you are to go up with him, and he is to come and sit on my throne and reign in my place. I have appointed him ruler over Israel and Judah.'

³⁶Benaiah son of Jehoiada answered the king, 'Amen! May the LORD, the God of my lord the king, so declare it. ³⁷As the LORD was with my lord the king, so may he be with Solomon to make his throne even greater than the throne of my lord King David!'

³⁸So Zadok the priest, Nathan the prophet, Benaiah son of Jehoiada, the Kerethites and the Pelethites went down and put Solomon on King David's mule, and they escorted him to Gihon. ³⁹Zadok the priest took the horn of oil from the sacred tent and anointed Solomon. Then they sounded the trumpet and all the people shouted, 'Long live King Solomon!' ⁴⁰And all the people went up after him, playing pipes and rejoicing greatly, so that the ground shook with the sound.

⁴¹Adonijah and all the guests who were with him heard it as they were finishing their feast. On hearing the sound of the trumpet, Joab asked, 'What's the meaning of all the noise in the city?'

⁴²Even as he was speaking, Jonathan son of Abiathar the priest arrived. Adonijah said, 'Come in. A worthy man like you must be bringing good news.'

⁴³'Not at all!' Jonathan answered. 'Our lord King David has made Solomon king. ⁴⁴The king has sent with him Zadok the priest, Nathan the prophet, Benaiah son of Jehoiada, the Kerethites and the Pelethites, and they have put him on the king's mule, ⁴⁵and Zadok the priest and Nathan the prophet have anointed him king at Gihon. From there they have gone up cheering, and the city resounds with it. That's the noise you hear. ⁴⁶Moreover, Solomon has taken his seat on the royal throne. ⁴⁷Also, the royal officials have come to congratulate our lord King David, saying, "May your God make Solomon's name more famous than yours and his throne greater than yours!" And the king bowed in worship on his bed ⁴⁸and said, "Praise be to the LORD, the God of Israel, who has allowed my eyes to see a successor on my throne today." '

⁴⁹At this, all Adonijah's guests rose in alarm and dispersed. ⁵⁰But Adonijah, in fear of Solomon, went and took hold of the horns of the altar. ⁵¹Then Solomon was told, 'Adonijah is afraid of King Solomon and is clinging to the horns of the altar. He says, "Let King Solomon swear to me today that he will not put his servant to death with the sword." '

⁵²Solomon replied, 'If he shows himself to be worthy, not a hair of his head will fall to the ground; but if evil is found in him, he will die.' ⁵³Then King Solomon sent men, and they brought him down from the altar. And Adonijah came and bowed down to King Solomon, and Solomon said, 'Go to your home.'

David's charge to Solomon

2 When the time drew near for David to die, he gave a charge to Solomon his son.

²'I am about to go the way of all the earth,' he said. 'So be strong, act like a man, ³and observe what the LORD your God requires: walk in obedience to him, and keep his decrees and commands, his laws and regulations, as written in the Law of Moses. Do this so that you may prosper in all you do and wherever you go ⁴and that the LORD may keep his promise to me: "If your descendants watch how

they live, and if they walk faithfully before me with all their heart and soul, you will never fail to have a successor on the throne of Israel."

5 'Now you yourself know what Joab son of Zeruiah did to me – what he did to the two commanders of Israel's armies, Abner son of Ner and Amasa son of Jether. He killed them, shedding their blood in peacetime as if in battle, and with that blood he stained the belt round his waist and the sandals on his feet. 6 Deal with him according to your wisdom, but do not let his grey head go down to the grave in peace.

7 'But show kindness to the sons of Barzillai of Gilead and let them be among those who eat at your table. They stood by me when I fled from your brother Absalom.

8 'And remember, you have with you Shimei son of Gera, the Benjaminite from Bahurim, who called down bitter curses on me the day I went to Mahanaim. When he came down to meet me at the Jordan, I swore to him by the LORD: "I will not put you to death by the sword." 9 But now, do not consider him innocent. You are a man of wisdom; you will know what to do to him. Bring his grey head down to the grave in blood.'

10 Then David rested with his ancestors and was buried in the City of David. 11 He had reigned for forty years over Israel – seven years in Hebron and thirty-three in Jerusalem. 12 So Solomon sat on the throne of his father David, and his rule was firmly established.

Solomon's throne established

13 Now Adonijah, the son of Haggith, went to Bathsheba, Solomon's mother. Bathsheba asked him, 'Do you come peacefully?'

He answered, 'Yes, peacefully.' 14 Then he added, 'I have something to say to you.'

'You may say it,' she replied.

15 'As you know,' he said, 'the kingdom was mine. All Israel looked to me as their king. But things changed, and the kingdom has gone to my brother; for it has come to him from the LORD. 16 Now I have one request to make of you. Do not refuse me.'

'You may make it,' she said.

17 So he continued, 'Please ask King Solomon – he will not refuse you – to give me Abishag the Shunammite as my wife.'

18 'Very well,' Bathsheba replied, 'I will speak to the king for you.'

19 When Bathsheba went to King Solomon to speak to him for Adonijah, the king stood up to meet her, bowed down to her and sat down on his throne. He had a throne brought for the king's mother, and she sat down at his right hand.

20 'I have one small request to make of you,' she said. 'Do not refuse me.'

The king replied, 'Make it, my mother; I will not refuse you.'

21 So she said, 'Let Abishag the Shunammite be given in marriage to your brother Adonijah.'

22 King Solomon answered his mother, 'Why do you request Abishag the Shunammite for Adonijah? You might as well request the kingdom for him – after all, he is my older brother – yes, for him and for Abiathar the priest and Joab son of Zeruiah!'

23 Then King Solomon swore by the LORD: 'May God deal with me, be it ever so severely, if Adonijah does not pay with his life for this request! 24 And now, as surely as the LORD lives – he who has established me securely on the throne of my father David and has founded a dynasty for me as he promised – Adonijah shall be put to death today!' 25 So King Solomon gave orders to Benaiah son of Jehoiada, and he struck down Adonijah and he died.

26 To Abiathar the priest the king said, 'Go back to your fields in Anathoth. You deserve to die, but I will not put you to death now, because you carried the ark of the Sovereign LORD before my father David and shared all my father's hardships.' 27 So Solomon removed Abiathar from the priesthood of the LORD, fulfilling the word the LORD had spoken at Shiloh about the house of Eli.

28 When the news reached Joab, who had conspired with Adonijah though not

with Absalom, he fled to the tent of the LORD and took hold of the horns of the altar. ²⁹King Solomon was told that Joab had fled to the tent of the LORD and was beside the altar. Then Solomon ordered Benaiah son of Jehoiada, 'Go, strike him down!'

³⁰So Benaiah entered the tent of the LORD and said to Joab, 'The king says, "Come out!"'

But he answered, 'No, I will die here.'

Benaiah reported to the king, 'This is how Joab answered me.'

³¹Then the king commanded Benaiah, 'Do as he says. Strike him down and bury him, and so clear me and my whole family of the guilt of the innocent blood that Joab shed. ³²The LORD will repay him for the blood he shed, because without my father David knowing it he attacked two men and killed them with the sword. Both of them – Abner son of Ner, commander of Israel's army, and Amasa son of Jether, commander of Judah's army – were better men and more upright than he. ³³May the guilt of their blood rest on the head of Joab and his descendants for ever. But on David and his descendants, his house and his throne, may there be the LORD's peace for ever.'

³⁴So Benaiah son of Jehoiada went up and struck down Joab and killed him, and he was buried at his home out in the country. ³⁵The king put Benaiah son of Jehoiada over the army in Joab's position and replaced Abiathar with Zadok the priest.

³⁶Then the king sent for Shimei and said to him, 'Build yourself a house in Jerusalem and live there, but do not go anywhere else. ³⁷The day you leave and cross the Kidron Valley, you can be sure you will die; your blood will be on your own head.'

³⁸Shimei answered the king, 'What you say is good. Your servant will do as my lord the king has said.' And Shimei stayed in Jerusalem for a long time.

³⁹But three years later, two of Shimei's slaves ran off to Achish son of Maakah, king of Gath, and Shimei was told, 'Your slaves are in Gath.' ⁴⁰At this, he saddled his donkey and went to Achish at Gath in search of his slaves. So Shimei went away and brought the slaves back from Gath.

⁴¹When Solomon was told that Shimei had gone from Jerusalem to Gath and had returned, ⁴²the king summoned Shimei and said to him, 'Did I not make you swear by the LORD and warn you, "On the day you leave to go anywhere else, you can be sure you will die"? At that time you said to me, "What you say is good. I will obey." ⁴³Why then did you not keep your oath to the LORD and obey the command I gave you?'

⁴⁴The king also said to Shimei, 'You know in your heart all the wrong you did to my father David. Now the LORD will repay you for your wrongdoing. ⁴⁵But King Solomon will be blessed, and David's throne will remain secure before the LORD for ever.'

⁴⁶Then the king gave the order to Benaiah son of Jehoiada, and he went out and struck Shimei down and he died.

The kingdom was now established in Solomon's hands.

Solomon asks for wisdom

3 Solomon made an alliance with Pharaoh king of Egypt and married his daughter. He brought her to the City of David until he finished building his palace and the temple of the LORD, and the wall around Jerusalem. ²The people, however, were still sacrificing at the high places, because a temple had not yet been built for the Name of the LORD. ³Solomon showed his love for the LORD by walking according to the instructions given him by his father David, except that he offered sacrifices and burned incense on the high places.

⁴The king went to Gibeon to offer sacrifices, for that was the most important high place, and Solomon offered a thousand burnt offerings on that altar. ⁵At Gibeon the LORD appeared to Solomon during the night in a dream, and God said, 'Ask for whatever you want me to give you.'

⁶Solomon answered, 'You have shown great kindness to your servant, my father David, because he was faithful to you and righteous and upright in heart. You have continued this great kindness to him and

have given him a son to sit on his throne this very day.

7 'Now, LORD my God, you have made your servant king in place of my father David. But I am only a little child and do not know how to carry out my duties. 8 Your servant is here among the people you have chosen, a great people, too numerous to count or number. 9 So give your servant a discerning heart to govern your people and to distinguish between right and wrong. For who is able to govern this great people of yours?'

10 The Lord was pleased that Solomon had asked for this. 11 So God said to him, 'Since you have asked for this and not for long life or wealth for yourself, nor have asked for the death of your enemies but for discernment in administering justice, 12 I will do what you have asked. I will give you a wise and discerning heart, so that there will never have been anyone like you, nor will there ever be. 13 Moreover, I will give you what you have not asked for – both wealth and honour – so that in your lifetime you will have no equal among kings. 14 And if you walk in obedience to me and keep my decrees and commands as David your father did, I will give you a long life.' 15 Then Solomon awoke – and he realised it had been a dream.

He returned to Jerusalem, stood before the ark of the Lord's covenant and sacrificed burnt offerings and fellowship offerings. Then he gave a feast for all his court.

A wise ruling

16 Now two prostitutes came to the king and stood before him. 17 One of them said, 'Pardon me, my lord. This woman and I live in the same house. I had a baby while she was there with me. 18 The third day after my child was born, this woman also had a baby. We were alone; there was no one in the house but the two of us.

19 'During the night this woman's son died because she lay on him. 20 So she got up in the middle of the night and took my son from my side while I your servant was asleep. She put him by her breast and put her dead son by my breast. 21 The next morning, I got up to nurse my son – and

he was dead! But when I looked at him closely in the morning light, I saw that it wasn't the son I had borne.'

22 The other woman said, 'No! The living one is my son; the dead one is yours.'

But the first one insisted, 'No! The dead one is yours; the living one is mine.' And so they argued before the king.

23 The king said, 'This one says, "My son is alive and your son is dead," while that one says, "No! Your son is dead and mine is alive."'

24 Then the king said, 'Bring me a sword.' So they brought a sword for the king. 25 He then gave an order: 'Cut the living child in two and give half to one and half to the other.'

26 The woman whose son was alive was deeply moved out of love for her son and said to the king, 'Please, my lord, give her the living baby! Don't kill him!'

But the other said, 'Neither I nor you shall have him. Cut him in two!'

27 Then the king gave his ruling: 'Give the living baby to the first woman. Do not kill him; she is his mother.'

28 When all Israel heard the verdict the king had given, they held the king in awe, because they saw that he had wisdom from God to administer justice.

Solomon's officials and governors

4 So King Solomon ruled over all Israel. 2 And these were his chief officials:

Azariah son of Zadok – the priest;
3 Elihoreph and Ahijah, sons of Shisha – secretaries;
Jehoshaphat son of Ahilud – recorder;
4 Benaiah son of Jehoiada – commander-in-chief;
Zadok and Abiathar – priests;
5 Azariah son of Nathan – in charge of the district governors;
Zabud son of Nathan – a priest and advisor to the king;
6 Ahishar – palace administrator;
Adoniram son of Abda – in charge of forced labour.

7 Solomon had twelve district governors

over all Israel, who supplied provisions for the king and the royal household. Each one had to provide supplies for one month in the year. 8These are their names:

Ben-Hur – in the hill country of Ephraim;

9Ben-Deker – in Makaz, Shaalbim, Beth Shemesh and Elon Bethha-nan;

10Ben-Hesed – in Arubboth (Sokoh and all the land of Hepher were his);

11Ben-Abinadab – in Naphoth Dor (he was married to Taphath daughter of Solomon);

12Baana son of Ahilud – in Taanach and Megiddo, and in all of Beth Shan next to Zarethan below Jezreel, from Beth Shan to Abel Meholah across to Jokmeam;

13Ben-Geber – in Ramoth Gilead (the settlements of Jair son of Manas-seh in Gilead were his, as well as the region of Argob in Bashan and its sixty large walled cities with bronze gate bars);

14Ahinadab son of Iddo – in Maha-naim;

15Ahimaaz – in Naphtali (he had mar-ried Basemath daughter of Solo-mon);

16Baana son of Hushai – in Asher and in Aloth;

17Jehoshaphat son of Paruah – in Issa-char;

18Shimei son of Ela – in Benjamin;

19Geber son of Uri – in Gilead (the country of Sihon king of the Am-orites and the country of Og king of Bashan). He was the only gover-nor over the district.

Solomon's daily provisions

20The people of Judah and Israel were as numerous as the sand on the seashore; they ate, they drank and they were happy. 21And Solomon ruled over all the king-doms from the River Euphrates to the land of the Philistines, as far as the border of Egypt. These countries brought tribute and were Solomon's subjects all his life.

22Solomon's daily provisions were thirty cors*a* of the finest flour and sixty cors*b* of meal, 23ten head of stall-fed cat-tle, twenty of pasture-fed cattle and a hundred sheep and goats, as well as deer, gazelles, roebucks and choice fowl. 24For he ruled over all the kingdoms west of the River Euphrates, from Tiphsah to Gaza, and had peace on all sides. 25During Sol-omon's lifetime Judah and Israel, from Dan to Beersheba, lived in safety, every-one under their own vine and under their own fig-tree.

26Solomon had four*c* thousand stalls for chariot horses, and twelve thousand horses.*d*

27The district governors, each in his month, supplied provisions for King Solo-mon and all who came to the king's table. They saw to it that nothing was lacking. 28They also brought to the proper place their quotas of barley and straw for the chariot horses and the other horses.

Solomon's wisdom

29God gave Solomon wisdom and very great insight, and a breadth of under-standing as measureless as the sand on the seashore. 30Solomon's wisdom was greater than the wisdom of all the people of the East, and greater than all the wis-dom of Egypt. 31He was wiser than anyone else, including Ethan the Ezrahite – wiser than Heman, Kalkol and Darda, the sons of Mahol. And his fame spread to all the surrounding nations. 32He spoke three thousand proverbs and his songs num-bered a thousand and five. 33He spoke about plant life, from the cedar of Leba-non to the hyssop that grows out of walls. He also spoke about animals and birds, reptiles and fish. 34From all nations peo-ple came to listen to Solomon's wisdom, sent by all the kings of the world, who had heard of his wisdom.*e*

a 22 That is, probably about 5 metric tons
b 22 That is, probably about 10 metric tons
c 26 Some Septuagint manuscripts (see also 2 Chron. 9:25); Hebrew forty
d 26 Or charioteers
e 34 In Hebrew texts 4:21-34 is numbered 5:1-14.

Preparations for building the temple

5 *a* When Hiram king of Tyre heard that Solomon had been anointed king to succeed his father David, he sent his envoys to Solomon, because he had always been on friendly terms with David. ²Solomon sent back this message to Hiram:

³'You know that because of the wars waged against my father David from all sides, he could not build a temple for the Name of the Lord his God until the Lord put his enemies under his feet. ⁴But now the Lord my God has given me rest on every side, and there is no adversary or disaster. ⁵I intend, therefore, to build a temple for the Name of the Lord my God, as the Lord told my father David, when he said, "Your son whom I will put on the throne in your place will build the temple for my Name."

⁶'So give orders that cedars of Lebanon be cut for me. My men will work with yours, and I will pay you for your men whatever wages you set. You know that we have no one so skilled in felling timber as the Sidonians.'

⁷When Hiram heard Solomon's message, he was greatly pleased and said, 'Praise be to the Lord today, for he has given David a wise son to rule over this great nation.'

⁸So Hiram sent word to Solomon:

'I have received the message you sent me and will do all you want in providing the cedar and juniper logs. ⁹My men will haul them down from Lebanon to the Mediterranean Sea, and I will float them as rafts by sea to the place you specify. There I will separate them and you can take them away. And you are to grant my wish by providing food for my royal household.'

¹⁰In this way Hiram kept Solomon supplied with all the cedar and juniper logs he wanted, ¹¹and Solomon gave Hiram twenty thousand cors*b* of wheat as food for his household, in addition to twenty thousand baths*c, d* of pressed olive oil. Solomon continued to do this for Hiram year after year. ¹²The Lord gave Solomon wisdom, just as he had promised him. There were peaceful relations between Hiram and Solomon, and the two of them made a treaty.

¹³King Solomon conscripted labourers from all Israel – thirty thousand men. ¹⁴He sent them off to Lebanon in shifts of ten thousand a month, so that they spent one month in Lebanon and two months at home. Adoniram was in charge of the forced labour. ¹⁵Solomon had seventy thousand carriers and eighty thousand stonecutters in the hills, ¹⁶as well as thirty-three hundred*e* foremen who supervised the project and directed the workers. ¹⁷At the king's command they removed from the quarry large blocks of high-grade stone to provide a foundation of dressed stone for the temple. ¹⁸The craftsmen of Solomon and Hiram and workers from Byblos cut and prepared the timber and stone for the building of the temple.

Solomon builds the temple

6 In the four hundred and eightieth*a* year after the Israelites came out of Egypt, in the fourth year of Solomon's reign over Israel, in the month of Ziv, the second month, he began to build the temple of the Lord.

²The temple that King Solomon built for the Lord was sixty cubits long, twenty wide and thirty high.*b* ³The portico at the front of the main hall of the temple extended the width of the temple, that is

---

b 11 That is, probably about 3,250 metric tons
c 11 Septuagint (see also 2 Chron. 2:10); Hebrew *twenty cors*
d 11 That is, about 440,000 litres
e 16 Hebrew; some Septuagint manuscripts (see also 2 Chron. 2:2,18) *thirty-six hundred*
a 1 Hebrew; Septuagint *four hundred and fortieth*
b 2 That is, about 27 metres long, 9 metres wide and 14 metres high

---

twenty cubits,c and projected ten cubitsd from the front of the temple. 4He made narrow windows high up in the temple walls. 5Against the walls of the main hall and inner sanctuary he built a structure around the building, in which there were side rooms. 6The lowest floor was five cubitse wide, the middle floor six cubitsf and the third floor seven.g He made offset ledges around the outside of the temple so that nothing would be inserted into the temple walls.

7In building the temple, only blocks dressed at the quarry were used, and no hammer, chisel or any other iron tool was heard at the temple site while it was being built.

PEOPLE TOURS

SOLOMON

WISDOM
1 Kings 3:1–28
TEMPLE
1 Kings 6:1–38
SHEBA
1 Kings 10:1–29
STUPIDITY
1 Kings 11:1–43

8The entrance to the lowesth floor was on the south side of the temple; a stairway led up to the middle level and from there to the third. 9So he built the temple and completed it, roofing it with beams and cedar planks. 10And he built the side rooms all along the temple. The height of each was five cubits, and they were attached to the temple by beams of cedar.

11The word of the LORD came to Solomon: 12'As for this temple you are building, if you follow my decrees, observe my laws and keep all my commands and obey them, I will fulfil through you the promise I gave to David your father. 13And I will live among the Israelites and will not abandon my people Israel.'

14So Solomon built the temple and completed it. 15He lined its interior walls with cedar boards, panelling them from the floor of the temple to the ceiling, and covered the floor of the temple with planks of juniper. 16He partitioned off twenty cubits at the rear of the temple with cedar boards from floor to ceiling to form within the temple an inner sanctuary, the Most Holy Place. 17The main hall in front of this room was forty cubitsi long. 18The inside of the temple was cedar, carved with gourds and open flowers. Everything was cedar; no stone was to be seen.

19He prepared the inner sanctuary within the temple to set the ark of the covenant of the LORD there. 20The inner sanctuary was twenty cubits long, twenty wide and twenty high. He overlaid the inside with pure gold, and he also overlaid the altar of cedar. 21Solomon covered the inside of the temple with pure gold, and he extended gold chains across the front of the inner sanctuary, which was overlaid with gold. 22So he overlaid the whole interior with gold. He also overlaid with gold the altar that belonged to the inner sanctuary.

23For the inner sanctuary he made a pair of cherubim out of olive wood, each ten cubits high. 24One wing of the first cherub was five cubits long, and the other wing five cubits – ten cubits from wing tip to wing tip. 25The second cherub also measured ten cubits, for the two cherubim were identical in size and shape. 26The height of each cherub was ten cubits. 27He placed the cherubim inside the innermost room of the temple, with their wings spread out. The wing of one cherub touched one wall, while the wing of the other touched the other wall, and their

---

c 3 That is, about 9 metres; also in verses 16 and 20
d 3 That is, about 4.5 metres; also in verses 23-26
e 6 That is, about 2.3 metres; also in verses 10 and 24
f 6 That is, about 2.7 metres
g 6 That is, about 3.2 metres
h 8 Septuagint; Hebrew *middle*

i 17 That is, about 18 metres

wings touched each other in the middle of the room. 28 He overlaid the cherubim with gold.

29 On the walls all round the temple, in both the inner and outer rooms, he carved cherubim, palm trees and open flowers. 30 He also covered the floors of both the inner and outer rooms of the temple with gold.

31 For the entrance to the inner sanctuary he made doors out of olive wood that were one fifth of the width of the sanctuary. 32 And on the two olive-wood doors he carved cherubim, palm trees and open flowers, and overlaid the cherubim and palm trees with hammered gold. 33 In the same way, for the entrance to the main hall he made doorframes out of olive wood that were one quarter of the width of the hall. 34 He also made two doors out of juniper wood, each having two leaves that turned in sockets. 35 He carved cherubim, palm trees and open flowers on them and overlaid them with gold hammered evenly over the carvings.

36 And he built the inner courtyard of three courses of dressed stone and one course of trimmed cedar beams.

37 The foundation of the temple of the LORD was laid in the fourth year, in the month of Ziv. 38 In the eleventh year in the month of Bul, the eighth month, the temple was finished in all its details according to its specifications. He had spent seven years building it.

Solomon builds his palace

7 It took Solomon thirteen years, however, to complete the construction of his palace. 2 He built the Palace of the Forest of Lebanon a hundred cubits long, fifty wide and thirty high,*a* with four rows of cedar columns supporting trimmed cedar beams. 3 It was roofed with cedar above the beams that rested on the columns – forty-five beams, fifteen to a row. 4 Its windows were placed high in sets of three, facing each other. 5 All the doorways had rectangular frames; they

were in the front part in sets of three, facing each other.*b*

6 He made a colonnade fifty cubits long and thirty wide.*c* In front of it was a portico, and in front of that were pillars and an overhanging roof.

7 He built the throne hall, the Hall of Justice, where he was to judge, and he covered it with cedar from floor to ceiling.*d* 8 And the palace in which he was to live, set farther back, was similar in design. Solomon also made a palace like this hall for Pharaoh's daughter, whom he had married.

9 All these structures, from the outside to the great courtyard and from foundation to eaves, were made of blocks of high-grade stone cut to size and smoothed on their inner and outer faces. 10 The foundations were laid with large stones of good quality, some measuring ten cubits*e* and some eight.*f* 11 Above were high-grade stones, cut to size, and cedar beams. 12 The great courtyard was surrounded by a wall of three courses of dressed stone and one course of trimmed cedar beams, as was the inner courtyard of the temple of the LORD with its portico.

The temple's furnishings

13 King Solomon sent to Tyre and brought Huram,*g* 14 whose mother was a widow from the tribe of Naphtali and whose father was from Tyre and a skilled craftsman in bronze. Huram was filled with wisdom, with understanding and with knowledge to do all kinds of bronze work. He came to King Solomon and did all the work assigned to him.

15 He cast two bronze pillars, each eighteen cubits high and twelve cubits in circumference.*h* 16 He also made two capitals of cast bronze to set on the tops

---

b 5 The meaning of the Hebrew for this verse is uncertain.
c 6 That is, about 23 metres long and 14 metres wide
d 7 Vulgate and Syriac; Hebrew *floor*
e 10 That is, about 4.5 metres; also in verse 23
f 10 That is, about 3.6 metres
g 13 Hebrew *Hiram*, a variant of *Huram*; also in verses 40 and 45
h 15 That is, about 8.1 metres high and 5.4 metres in circumference

---

a 2 That is, about 45 metres long, 23 metres wide and 14 metres high

of the pillars; each capital was five cubits*i*
high. **17**A network of interwoven chains
adorned the capitals on top of the pillars,
seven for each capital. **18**He made pomegranates in two rows*j* encircling each
network to decorate the capitals on top
of the pillars.*k* He did the same for each
capital. **19**The capitals on top of the pillars
in the portico were in the shape of lilies,
four cubits*l* high. **20**On the capitals of both
pillars, above the bowl-shaped part next
to the network, were the two hundred
pomegranates in rows all around. **21**He
erected the pillars at the portico of the
temple. The pillar to the south he named
Jakin*m* and the one to the north Boaz.*n*
22The capitals on top were in the shape of
lilies. And so the work on the pillars was
completed.

23He made the Sea of cast metal, circular in shape, measuring ten cubits from
rim to rim and five cubits high. It took a
line of thirty cubits*o* to measure round it.
24Below the rim, gourds encircled it – ten
to a cubit. The gourds were cast in two
rows in one piece with the Sea.

25The Sea stood on twelve bulls, three
facing north, three facing west, three facing south and three facing east. The Sea
rested on top of them, and their hindquarters were towards the centre. **26**It was
a handbreadth*p* in thickness, and its rim
was like the rim of a cup, like a lily blossom. It held two thousand baths.*q*

27He also made ten movable stands of
bronze; each was four cubits long, four
wide and three high.*r* **28**This is how the
stands were made: they had side panels

attached to uprights. **29**On the panels
between the uprights were lions, bulls
and cherubim – and on the uprights as
well. Above and below the lions and bulls
were wreaths of hammered work. **30**Each
stand had four bronze wheels with bronze
axles, and each had a basin resting on four
supports, cast with wreaths on each side.
31On the inside of the stand there was an
opening that had a circular frame one cubit*s* deep. This opening was round, and
with its basework it measured a cubit and
a half.*t* Around its opening there was engraving. The panels of the stands were
square, not round. **32**The four wheels
were under the panels, and the axles of
the wheels were attached to the stand. The
diameter of each wheel was a cubit and a
half. **33**The wheels were made like chariot
wheels; the axles, rims, spokes and hubs
were all of cast metal.

34Each stand had four handles, one on
each corner, projecting from the stand.
35At the top of the stand there was a circular band half a cubit*u* deep. The supports
and panels were attached to the top of the
stand. **36**He engraved cherubim, lions and
palm trees on the surfaces of the supports
and on the panels, in every available space,
with wreaths all around. **37**This is the way
he made the ten stands. They were all cast
in the same moulds and were identical in
size and shape.

38He then made ten bronze basins,
each holding forty baths*v* and measuring
four cubits across, one basin to go on each
of the ten stands. **39**He placed five of the
stands on the south side of the temple and
five on the north. He placed the Sea on the
south side, at the south-east corner of the
temple. **40**He also made the pots*w* and
shovels and sprinkling bowls.

So Huram finished all the work he had
undertaken for King Solomon in the temple of the LORD:

---

i 16 That is, about 2.3 metres; also in verse 23
j 18 Two Hebrew manuscripts and Septuagint; most
Hebrew manuscripts *made the pillars, and there were
two rows*
k 18 Many Hebrew manuscripts and Syriac; most
Hebrew manuscripts *pomegranates*
l 19 That is, about 1.8 metres; also in verse 38
m 21 *Jakin* probably means *he establishes.*
n 21 *Boaz* probably means *in him is strength.*
o 23 That is, about 14 metres
p 26 That is, about 7.5 centimetres
q 26 That is, about 44,000 litres; the Septuagint
does not have this sentence.
r 27 That is, about 1.8 metres long and wide and 1.4
metres high

s 31 That is, about 45 centimetres
t 31 That is, about 68 centimetres; also in verse 32
u 35 That is, about 23 centimetres
v 38 That is, about 880 litres
w 40 Many Hebrew manuscripts, Septuagint, Syriac
and Vulgate (see also verse 45 and 2 Chron. 4:11);
many other Hebrew manuscripts *basins*

41 the two pillars;

the two bowl-shaped capitals on top of the pillars;

the two sets of network decorating the two bowl-shaped capitals on top of the pillars;

42 the four hundred pomegranates for the two sets of network (two rows of pomegranates for each network decorating the bowl-shaped capitals on top of the pillars);

43 the ten stands with their ten basins;

44 the Sea and the twelve bulls under it;

45 the pots, shovels and sprinkling bowls.

All these objects that Huram made for King Solomon for the temple of the LORD were of burnished bronze. **46** The king had them cast in clay moulds in the plain of the Jordan between Sukkoth and Zarethan. **47** Solomon left all these things unweighed, because there were so many; the weight of the bronze was not determined.

48 Solomon also made all the furnishings that were in the LORD's temple:

the golden altar;

the golden table on which was the bread of the Presence;

49 the lampstands of pure gold (five on the right and five on the left, in front of the inner sanctuary);

the gold floral work and lamps and tongs;

50 the pure gold dishes, wick trimmers, sprinkling bowls, dishes and censers;

and the gold sockets for the doors of the innermost room, the Most Holy Place, and also for the doors of the main hall of the temple.

51 When all the work King Solomon had done for the temple of the LORD was finished, he brought in the things his father David had dedicated – the silver and gold and the furnishings – and he placed them in the treasuries of the LORD's temple.

The ark brought to the temple

8 Then King Solomon summoned into his presence at Jerusalem the elders of Israel, all the heads of the tribes and the chiefs of the Israelite families, to bring up the ark of the LORD's covenant from Zion, the City of David. **2** All the Israelites came together to King Solomon at the time of the festival in the month of Ethanim, the seventh month.

3 When all the elders of Israel had arrived, the priests took up the ark, **4** and they brought up the ark of the LORD and the tent of meeting and all the sacred furnishings in it. The priests and Levites carried them up, **5** and King Solomon and the entire assembly of Israel that had gathered about him were before the ark, sacrificing so many sheep and cattle that they could not be recorded or counted.

6 The priests then brought the ark of the LORD's covenant to its place in the inner sanctuary of the temple, the Most Holy Place, and put it beneath the wings of the cherubim. **7** The cherubim spread their wings over the place of the ark and overshadowed the ark and its carrying poles. **8** These poles were so long that their ends could be seen from the Holy Place in front of the inner sanctuary, but not from outside the Holy Place; and they are still there today. **9** There was nothing in the ark except the two stone tablets that Moses had placed in it at Horeb, where the LORD made a covenant with the Israelites after they came out of Egypt.

10 When the priests withdrew from the Holy Place, the cloud filled the temple of the LORD. **11** And the priests could not perform their service because of the cloud, for the glory of the LORD filled his temple.

12 Then Solomon said, 'The LORD has said that he would dwell in a dark cloud; **13** I have indeed built a magnificent temple for you, a place for you to dwell for ever.'

14 While the whole assembly of Israel was standing there, the king turned round and blessed them. **15** Then he said:

'Praise be to the LORD, the God of Israel, who with his own hand has fulfilled what he promised with his own mouth to my father David. For he said, 16 "Since the day I brought my people Israel out of Egypt, I have not chosen a city in any tribe of Israel to have a temple built so that my Name might be there, but I have chosen David to rule my people Israel."

17 'My father David had it in his heart to build a temple for the Name of the Lord, the God of Israel. 18 But the Lord said to my father David, "You did well to have it in your heart to build a temple for my Name. 19 Nevertheless, you are not the one to build the temple, but your son, your own flesh and blood – he is the one who will build the temple for my Name."

20 'The Lord has kept the promise he made: I have succeeded David my father and now I sit on the throne of Israel, just as the Lord promised, and I have built the temple for the Name of the Lord, the God of Israel. 21 I have provided a place there for the ark, in which is the covenant of the Lord that he made with our ancestors when he brought them out of Egypt.'

Solomon's prayer of dedication

22 Then Solomon stood before the altar of the Lord in front of the whole assembly of Israel, spread out his hands towards heaven 23 and said:

'Lord, the God of Israel, there is no God like you in heaven above or on earth below – you who keep your covenant of love with your servants who continue wholeheartedly in your way. 24 You have kept your promise to your servant David my father; with your mouth you have promised and with your hand you have fulfilled it – as it is today.

25 'Now Lord, the God of Israel, keep for your servant David my father the promises you made to him when you said, "You shall never fail to have a successor to sit before me

on the throne of Israel, if only your descendants are careful in all they do to walk before me faithfully as you have done." 26 And now, God of Israel, let your word that you promised your servant David my father come true.

27 'But will God really dwell on earth? The heavens, even the highest heaven, cannot contain you. How much less this temple I have built! 28 Yet give attention to your servant's prayer and his plea for mercy, Lord my God. Hear the cry and the prayer that your servant is praying in your presence this day. 29 May your eyes be open towards this temple night and day, this place of which you said, "My Name shall be there," so that you will hear the prayer your servant prays towards this place. 30 Hear the supplication of your servant and of your people Israel when they pray towards this place. Hear from heaven, your dwelling place, and when you hear, forgive.

31 'When anyone wrongs their neighbour and is required to take an oath and they come and swear the oath before your altar in this temple, 32 then hear from heaven and act. Judge between your servants, condemning the guilty by bringing down on their heads what they have done, and vindicating the innocent by treating them in accordance with their innocence.

33 'When your people Israel have been defeated by an enemy because they have sinned against you, and when they turn back to you and give praise to your name, praying and making supplication to you in this temple, 34 then hear from heaven and forgive the sin of your people Israel and bring them back to the land you gave to their ancestors.

35 'When the heavens are shut up and there is no rain because your people have sinned against you, and when they pray towards this place and give praise to your name and

turn from their sin because you have afflicted them, 36 then hear from heaven and forgive the sin of your servants, your people Israel. Teach them the right way to live, and send rain on the land you gave your people for an inheritance.

37 'When famine or plague comes to the land, or blight or mildew, locusts or grasshoppers, or when an enemy besieges them in any of their cities, whatever disaster or disease may come, 38 and when a prayer or plea is made by anyone among your people Israel – being aware of the afflictions of their own hearts, and spreading out their hands towards this temple – 39 then hear from heaven, your dwelling-place. Forgive and act; deal with everyone according to all they do, since you know their hearts (for you alone know every human heart), 40 so that they will fear you all the time they live in the land you gave our ancestors.

41 'As for the foreigner who does not belong to your people Israel but has come from a distant land because of your name – 42 for they will hear of your great name and your mighty hand and your outstretched arm – when they come and pray towards this temple, 43 then hear from heaven, your dwelling-place. Do whatever the foreigner asks of you, so that all the peoples of the earth may know your name and fear you, as do your own people Israel, and may know that this house I have built bears your Name.

44 'When your people go to war against their enemies, wherever you send them, and when they pray to the LORD towards the city you have chosen and the temple I have built for your Name, 45 then hear from heaven their prayer and their plea, and uphold their cause.

46 'When they sin against you – for there is no one who does not sin – and you become angry with them and give them over to their enemies, who take them captive to their own lands, far away or near; 47 and if they have a change of heart in the land where they are held captive, and repent and plead with you in the land of their captors and say, "We have sinned, we have done wrong, we have acted wickedly"; 48 and if they turn back to you with all their heart and soul in the land of their enemies who took them captive, and pray to you towards the land you gave their ancestors, towards the city you have chosen and the temple I have built for your Name; 49 then from heaven, your dwelling-place, hear their prayer and their plea, and uphold their cause. 50 And forgive your people, who have sinned against you; forgive all the offences they have committed against you, and cause their captors to show them mercy; 51 for they are your people and your inheritance, whom you brought out of Egypt, out of that iron-smelting furnace.

52 'May your eyes be open to your servant's plea and to the plea of your people Israel, and may you listen to them whenever they cry out to you. 53 For you singled them out from all the nations of the world to be your own inheritance, just as you declared through your servant Moses when you, Sovereign LORD, brought our ancestors out of Egypt.'

54 When Solomon had finished all these prayers and supplications to the LORD, he rose from before the altar of the LORD, where he had been kneeling with his hands spread out towards heaven. 55 He stood and blessed the whole assembly of Israel in a loud voice, saying:

56 'Praise be to the LORD, who has given rest to his people Israel just as he promised. Not one word has failed of all the good promises he gave through his servant Moses. 57 May the LORD our God be with us as he was with our ancestors; may he

never leave us nor forsake us. 58 May he turn our hearts to him, to walk in obedience to him and keep the commands, decrees and laws he gave our ancestors. 59 And may these words of mine, which I have prayed before the LORD, be near to the LORD our God day and night, that he may uphold the cause of his servant and the cause of his people Israel according to each day's need, 60 so that all the peoples of the earth may know that the LORD is God and that there is no other. 61 And may your hearts be fully committed to the LORD our God, to live by his decrees and obey his commands, as at this time.'

The dedication of the temple

62 Then the king and all Israel with him offered sacrifices before the LORD. 63 Solomon offered a sacrifice of fellowship offerings to the LORD: twenty-two thousand cattle and a hundred and twenty thousand sheep and goats. So the king and all the Israelites dedicated the temple of the LORD.

64 On that same day the king consecrated the middle part of the courtyard in front of the temple of the LORD, and there he offered burnt offerings, grain offerings and the fat of the fellowship offerings, because the bronze altar that stood before the LORD was too small to hold the burnt offerings, the grain offerings and the fat of the fellowship offerings.

65 So Solomon observed the festival at that time, and all Israel with him – a vast assembly, people from Lebo Hamath to the Wadi of Egypt. They celebrated it before the LORD our God for seven days and seven days more, fourteen days in all. 66 On the following day he sent the people away. They blessed the king and then went home, joyful and glad in heart for all the good things the LORD had done for his servant David and his people Israel.

The LORD appears to Solomon

9 When Solomon had finished building the temple of the LORD and the royal palace, and had achieved all he had desired to do, 2 the LORD appeared to him a second time, as he had appeared to him at Gibeon. 3 The LORD said to him:

'I have heard the prayer and plea you have made before me; I have consecrated this temple, which you have built, by putting my Name there for ever. My eyes and my heart will always be there.

4 'As for you, if you walk before me faithfully with integrity of heart and uprightness, as David your father did, and do all I command and observe my decrees and laws, 5 I will establish your royal throne over Israel for ever, as I promised David your father when I said, "You shall never fail to have a successor on the throne of Israel."

6 'But if you*a* or your descendants turn away from me and do not observe the commands and decrees I have given you*a* and go off to serve other gods and worship them, 7 then I will cut off Israel from the land I have given them and will reject this temple I have consecrated for my Name. Israel will then become a byword and an object of ridicule among all peoples. 8 This temple will become a heap of rubble. All*b* who pass by will be appalled and will scoff and say, "Why has the LORD done such a thing to this land and to this temple?" 9 People will answer, "Because they have forsaken the LORD their God, who brought their ancestors out of Egypt, and have embraced other gods, worshipping and serving them – that is why the LORD brought all this disaster on them." '

Solomon's other activities

10 At the end of twenty years, during which Solomon built these two buildings – the temple of the LORD and the royal palace – 11 King Solomon gave

---

a 6 The Hebrew is plural.
b 8 See some Septuagint manuscripts, Old Latin, Syriac, Arabic and Targum; Hebrew *And though this temple is now imposing, all*

twenty towns in Galilee to Hiram king of Tyre, because Hiram had supplied him with all the cedar and juniper and gold he wanted. ¹²But when Hiram went from Tyre to see the towns that Solomon had given him, he was not pleased with them. ¹³'What kind of towns are these you have given me, my brother?' he asked. And he called them the Land of Kabul,ᶜ a name they have to this day. ¹⁴Now Hiram had sent to the king 120 talentsᵉ of gold.

¹⁵Here is the account of the forced labour King Solomon conscripted to build the LORD's temple, his own palace, the terraces,ᶠ the wall of Jerusalem, and Hazor, Megiddo and Gezer. ¹⁶(Pharaoh king of Egypt had attacked and captured Gezer. He had set it on fire. He killed its Canaanite inhabitants and then gave it as a wedding gift to his daughter, Solomon's wife. ¹⁷And Solomon rebuilt Gezer.) He built up Lower Beth Horon, ¹⁸Baalath, and Tadmorᵍ in the desert, within his land, ¹⁹as well as all his store cities and the towns for his chariots and for his horsesʰ – whatever he desired to build in Jerusalem, in Lebanon and throughout all the territory he ruled.

²⁰There were still people left from the Amorites, Hittites, Perizzites, Hivites and Jebusites (these peoples were not Israelites). ²¹Solomon conscripted the descendants of all these peoples remaining in the land – whom the Israelites could not exterminateⁱ – to serve as slave labour, as it is to this day. ²²But Solomon did not make slaves of any of the Israelites; they were his fighting men, his government officials, his officers, his captains, and the commanders of his chariots and charioteers. ²³They were also the chief officials in charge of Solomon's projects – 550 officials supervising those who did the work.

²⁴After Pharaoh's daughter had come up from the City of David to the palace Solomon had built for her, he constructed the terraces.

²⁵Three times a year Solomon sacrificed burnt offerings and fellowship offerings on the altar he had built for the LORD, burning incense before the LORD along with them, and so fulfilled the temple obligations.

²⁶King Solomon also built ships at Ezion Geber, which is near Elath in Edom, on the shore of the Red Sea.ʲ ²⁷And Hiram sent his men – sailors who knew the sea – to serve in the fleet with Solomon's men. ²⁸They sailed to Ophir and brought back 420 talentsᵏ of gold, which they delivered to King Solomon.

The queen of Sheba visits Solomon

10 When the queen of Sheba heard about the fame of Solomon and his relationship to the LORD, she came to test Solomon with hard questions. ²Arriving at Jerusalem with a very great caravan – with camels carrying spices, large quantities of gold, and precious stones – she came to Solomon and talked with him about all that she had on her mind. ³Solomon answered all her questions; nothing was too hard for the king to explain to her. ⁴When the queen of Sheba saw all the wisdom of Solomon and the palace he had built, ⁵the food on his table, the seating of his officials, the attending servants in their robes, his cupbearers, and the burnt offerings he made atᵃ the temple of the LORD, she was overwhelmed.

⁶She said to the king, 'The report I heard in my own country about your achievements and your wisdom is true. ⁷But I did not believe these things until I came and saw with my own eyes. Indeed, not even half was told me; in wisdom and wealth you have far exceeded the report I heard. ⁸How happy your people must be! How happy your officials, who continually stand before you and hear your wisdom! ⁹Praise be to the LORD your God, who has

---

c 13 *Kabul* sounds like the Hebrew for *good-for-nothing.*
e 14 That is, about 4 metric tons
f 15 Or *the Millo;* also in verse 24
g 18 The Hebrew may also be read *Tamar.*
h 19 Or *charioteers*
i 21 The Hebrew term refers to the irrevocable giving over of things or persons to the LORD, often by totally destroying them.

j 26 Or *the Sea of Reeds*
k 28 That is, about 14 metric tons
a 5 Or *the ascent by which he went up to*

delighted in you and placed you on the throne of Israel. Because of the LORD's eternal love for Israel, he has made you king to maintain justice and righteousness.'

¹⁰And she gave the king 120 talents[b] of gold, large quantities of spices, and precious stones. Never again were so many spices brought in as those the queen of Sheba gave to King Solomon.

¹¹(Hiram's ships brought gold from Ophir; and from there they brought great cargoes of almug-wood[c] and precious stones. ¹²The king used the almug-wood to make supports[d] for the temple of the LORD and for the royal palace, and to make harps and lyres for the musicians. So much almug-wood has never been imported or seen since that day.)

¹³King Solomon gave the queen of Sheba all she desired and asked for, besides what he had given her out of his royal bounty. Then she left and returned with her retinue to her own country.

Solomon's splendour

¹⁴The weight of the gold that Solomon received yearly was 666 talents,[e] ¹⁵not including the revenues from merchants and traders and from all the Arabian kings and the governors of the territories.

¹⁶King Solomon made two hundred large shields of hammered gold; six hundred shekels[f] of gold went into each shield. ¹⁷He also made three hundred small shields of hammered gold, with three minas[g] of gold in each shield. The king put them in the Palace of the Forest of Lebanon.

¹⁸Then the king made a great throne covered with ivory and overlaid with fine gold. ¹⁹The throne had six steps, and its back had a rounded top. On both sides of the seat were armrests, with a lion standing beside each of them. ²⁰Twelve lions stood on the six steps, one at either end of each step. Nothing like it had ever been made for any other kingdom. ²¹All King Solomon's goblets were gold, and all the household articles in the Palace of the Forest of Lebanon were pure gold. Nothing was made of silver, because silver was considered of little value in Solomon's days. ²²The king had a fleet of trading ships[h] at sea along with the ships of Hiram. Once every three years it returned carrying gold, silver and ivory, and apes and baboons.

²³King Solomon was greater in riches and wisdom than all the other kings of the earth. ²⁴The whole world sought audience with Solomon to hear the wisdom God had put in his heart. ²⁵Year after year, everyone who came brought a gift – articles of silver and gold, robes, weapons and spices, and horses and mules.

²⁶Solomon accumulated chariots and horses; he had fourteen hundred chariots and twelve thousand horses,[i] which he kept in the chariot cities and also with him in Jerusalem. ²⁷The king made silver as common in Jerusalem as stones, and cedar as plentiful as sycamore-fig trees in the foothills. ²⁸Solomon's horses were imported from Egypt and from Kue[j] – the royal merchants purchased them from Kue at the current price. ²⁹They imported a chariot from Egypt for six hundred shekels of silver, and a horse for a hundred and fifty.[k] They also exported them to all the kings of the Hittites and of the Arameans.

Solomon's wives

11 King Solomon, however, loved many foreign women besides Pharaoh's daughter – Moabites, Ammonites, Edomites, Sidonians and Hittites. ²They were from nations about which the LORD had told the Israelites, 'You must not intermarry with them, because they will surely turn your hearts after their gods.' Nevertheless, Solomon held fast to them

---

b 10 That is, about 4 metric tons
c 11 Probably a variant of *algum-wood*; also in verse 12
d 12 The meaning of the Hebrew for this word is uncertain.
e 14 That is, about 23 metric tons
f 16 That is, about 6.9 kilograms; also in verse 29
g 17 That is, about 1.7 kilograms; or perhaps reference is to double minas, that is, about 3.5 kilograms.

h 22 Hebrew *of ships of Tarshish*
i 26 Or *charioteers*
j 28 Probably *Cilicia*
k 29 That is, about 1.7 kilograms

in love. ³He had seven hundred wives of royal birth and three hundred concubines, and his wives led him astray. ⁴As Solomon grew old, his wives turned his heart after other gods, and his heart was not fully devoted to the LORD his God, as the heart of David his father had been. ⁵He followed Ashtoreth the goddess of the Sidonians, and Molek the detestable god of the Ammonites. ⁶So Solomon did evil in the eyes of the LORD; he did not follow the LORD completely, as David his father had done.

⁷On a hill east of Jerusalem, Solomon built a high place for Chemosh the detestable god of Moab, and for Molek the detestable god of the Ammonites. ⁸He did the same for all his foreign wives, who burned incense and offered sacrifices to their gods.

⁹The LORD became angry with Solomon because his heart had turned away from the LORD, the God of Israel, who had appeared to him twice. ¹⁰Although he had forbidden Solomon to follow other gods, Solomon did not keep the LORD's command. ¹¹So the LORD said to Solomon, 'Since this is your attitude and you have not kept my covenant and my decrees, which I commanded you, I will most certainly tear the kingdom away from you and give it to one of your subordinates. ¹²Nevertheless, for the sake of David your father, I will not do it during your lifetime. I will tear it out of the hand of your son. ¹³Yet I will not tear the whole kingdom from him, but will give him one tribe for the sake of David my servant and for the sake of Jerusalem, which I have chosen.'

Solomon's adversaries

¹⁴Then the LORD raised up against Solomon an adversary, Hadad the Edomite, from the royal line of Edom. ¹⁵Earlier when David was fighting with Edom, Joab the commander of the army, who had gone up to bury the dead, had struck down all the men in Edom. ¹⁶Joab and all the Israelites stayed there for six months, until they had destroyed all the men in Edom. ¹⁷But Hadad, still only a boy, fled to Egypt with some Edomite officials who had served his father. ¹⁸They set out from Mid-

ian and went to Paran. Then taking people from Paran with them, they went to Egypt, to Pharaoh king of Egypt, who gave Hadad a house and land and provided him with food.

¹⁹Pharaoh was so pleased with Hadad that he gave him a sister of his own wife, Queen Tahpenes, in marriage. ²⁰The sister of Tahpenes bore him a son named Genubath, whom Tahpenes brought up in the royal palace. There Genubath lived with Pharaoh's own children.

²¹While he was in Egypt, Hadad heard that David rested with his ancestors and that Joab the commander of the army was also dead. Then Hadad said to Pharaoh, 'Let me go, so that I may return to my own country.'

²²'What have you lacked here that you want to go back to your own country?' Pharaoh asked.

'Nothing,' Hadad replied, 'but do let me go!'

²³And God raised up against Solomon another adversary, Rezon son of Eliada, who had fled from his master, Hadadezer king of Zobah. ²⁴When David destroyed Zobah's army, Rezon gathered a band of men around him and became their leader; they went to Damascus, where they settled and took control. ²⁵Rezon was Israel's adversary as long as Solomon lived, adding to the trouble caused by Hadad. So Rezon ruled in Aram and was hostile towards Israel.

Jeroboam rebels against Solomon

²⁶Also, Jeroboam son of Nebat rebelled against the king. He was one of Solomon's officials, an Ephraimite from Zeredah, and his mother was a widow named Zeruah.

²⁷Here is the account of how he rebelled against the king: Solomon had built the terraces*a* and had filled in the gap in the wall of the city of David his father. ²⁸Now Jeroboam was a man of standing, and when Solomon saw how well the young man did his work, he put him in charge of the whole labour force of the tribes of Joseph.

---

a 27 Or the Millo

29 About that time Jeroboam was going out of Jerusalem, and Ahijah the prophet of Shiloh met him on the way, wearing a new cloak. The two of them were alone out in the country, 30 and Ahijah took hold of the new cloak he was wearing and tore it into twelve pieces. 31 Then he said to Jeroboam, 'Take ten pieces for yourself, for this is what the LORD, the God of Israel, says: "See, I am going to tear the kingdom out of Solomon's hand and give you ten tribes. 32 But for the sake of my servant David and the city of Jerusalem, which I have chosen out of all the tribes of Israel, he will have one tribe. 33 I will do this because they have*b* forsaken me and worshipped Ashtoreth the goddess of the Sidonians, Chemosh the god of the Moabites, and Molek the god of the Ammonites, and have not walked in obedience to me, nor done what is right in my eyes, nor kept my decrees and laws as David, Solomon's father, did.

34 ' "But I will not take the whole kingdom out of Solomon's hand; I have made him ruler all the days of his life for the sake of David my servant, whom I chose and who obeyed my commands and decrees. 35 I will take the kingdom from his son's hands and give you ten tribes. 36 I will give one tribe to his son so that David my servant may always have a lamp before me in Jerusalem, the city where I chose to put my Name. 37 However, as for you, I will take you, and you will rule over all that your heart desires; you will be king over Israel. 38 If you do whatever I command you and walk in obedience to me and do what is right in my eyes by obeying my decrees and commands, as David my servant did, I will be with you. I will build you a dynasty as enduring as the one I built for David and will give Israel to you. 39 I will humble David's descendants because of this, but not for ever." '

40 Solomon tried to kill Jeroboam, but Jeroboam fled to Egypt, to Shishak the king, and stayed there until Solomon's death.

Solomon's death

41 As for the other events of Solomon's reign – all he did and the wisdom he displayed – are they not written in the book of the annals of Solomon? 42 Solomon reigned in Jerusalem over all Israel for forty years. 43 Then he rested with his ancestors and was buried in the city of David his father. And Rehoboam his son succeeded him as king.

Israel rebels against Rehoboam

12 Rehoboam went to Shechem, for all Israel had gone there to make him king. 2 When Jeroboam son of Nebat heard this (he was still in Egypt, where he had fled from King Solomon), he returned from*a* Egypt. 3 So they sent for Jeroboam, and he and the whole assembly of Israel went to Rehoboam and said to him: 4 'Your father put a heavy yoke on us, but now lighten the harsh labour and the heavy yoke he put on us, and we will serve you.'

5 Rehoboam answered, 'Go away for three days and then come back to me.' So the people went away.

6 Then King Rehoboam consulted the elders who had served his father Solomon during his lifetime. 'How would you advise me to answer these people?' he asked.

7 They replied, 'If today you will be a servant to these people and serve them and give them a favourable answer, they will always be your servants.'

8 But Rehoboam rejected the advice the elders gave him and consulted the young men who had grown up with him and were serving him. 9 He asked them, 'What is your advice? How should we answer these people who say to me, "Lighten the yoke your father put on us"?'

10 The young men who had grown up with him replied, 'These people have said to you, "Your father put a heavy yoke on us, but make our yoke lighter." Now tell them, "My little finger is thicker than my father's waist. 11 My father laid on you a heavy yoke; I will make it even heavier.

---

b 33 Hebrew; Septuagint, Vulgate and Syriac *because he has*

a 2 Or *he remained in*

My father scourged you with whips; I will scourge you with scorpions."'

12 Three days later Jeroboam and all the people returned to Rehoboam, as the king had said, 'Come back to me in three days.' 13 The king answered the people harshly. Rejecting the advice given him by the elders, 14 he followed the advice of the young men and said, 'My father made your yoke heavy; I will make it even heavier. My father scourged you with whips; I will scourge you with scorpions.' 15 So the king did not listen to the people, for this turn of events was from the LORD, to fulfil the word the LORD had spoken to Jeroboam son of Nebat through Ahijah the Shilonite.

16 When all Israel saw that the king refused to listen to them, they answered the king:

'What share do we have in David,
     what part in Jesse's son?
To your tents, Israel!
Look after your own house, David!'

So the Israelites went home. 17 But as for the Israelites who were living in the towns of Judah, Rehoboam still ruled over them.

18 King Rehoboam sent out Adoniram,*b* who was in charge of forced labour, but all Israel stoned him to death. King Rehoboam, however, managed to get into his chariot and escape to Jerusalem. 19 So Israel has been in rebellion against the house of David to this day.

20 When all the Israelites heard that Jeroboam had returned, they sent and called him to the assembly and made him king over all Israel. Only the tribe of Judah remained loyal to the house of David.

21 When Rehoboam arrived in Jerusalem, he mustered all Judah and the tribe of Benjamin – a hundred and eighty thousand able young men – to go to war against Israel and to regain the kingdom for Rehoboam son of Solomon.

22 But this word of God came to Shemaiah the man of God: 23 'Say to Rehoboam son of Solomon king of Judah, to all Judah and Benjamin, and to the rest of the people, 24 "This is what the LORD says: do not go up to fight against your brothers, the Israelites. Go home, every one of you, for this is my doing."' So they obeyed the word of the LORD and went home again, as the LORD had ordered.

Golden calves at Bethel and Dan

25 Then Jeroboam fortified Shechem in the hill country of Ephraim and lived there. From there he went out and built up Peniel.*c*

26 Jeroboam thought to himself, 'The kingdom is now likely to revert to the house of David. 27 If these people go up to offer sacrifices at the temple of the LORD in Jerusalem, they will again give their allegiance to their lord, Rehoboam king of Judah. They will kill me and return to King Rehoboam.'

28 After seeking advice, the king made two golden calves. He said to the people, 'It is too much for you to go up to Jerusalem. Here are your gods, Israel, who brought you up out of Egypt.' 29 One he set up in Bethel, and the other in Dan. 30 And this thing became a sin; the people came to worship the one at Bethel and went as far as Dan to worship the other.*d*

31 Jeroboam built shrines on high places and appointed priests from all sorts of people, even though they were not Levites. 32 He instituted a festival on the fifteenth day of the eighth month, like the festival held in Judah, and offered sacrifices on the altar. This he did in Bethel, sacrificing to the calves he had made. And at Bethel he also installed priests at the high places he had made. 33 On the fifteenth day of the eighth month, a month of his own choosing, he offered sacrifices on the altar he had built at Bethel. So he instituted the festival for the Israelites and went up to the altar to make offerings.

---

b 18 Some Septuagint manuscripts and Syriac (see also 4:6 and 5:14); Hebrew *Adoram*

c 25 Hebrew *Penuel*, a variant of *Peniel*

d 30 Probable reading of the original Hebrew text; Masoretic Text *people went to the one as far as Dan*

The man of God from Judah

13 By the word of the LORD a man of God came from Judah to Bethel, as Jeroboam was standing by the altar to make an offering. ²By the word of the LORD he cried out against the altar: 'Altar, altar! This is what the LORD says: "A son named Josiah will be born to the house of David. On you he will sacrifice the priests of the high places who make offerings here, and human bones will be burned on you." ' ³That same day the man of God gave a sign: 'This is the sign the LORD has declared: the altar will be split apart and the ashes on it will be poured out.'

⁴When King Jeroboam heard what the man of God cried out against the altar at Bethel, he stretched out his hand from the altar and said, 'Seize him!' But the hand he stretched out towards the man shrivelled up, so that he could not pull it back. ⁵Also, the altar was split apart and its ashes poured out according to the sign given by the man of God by the word of the LORD.

⁶Then the king said to the man of God, 'Intercede with the LORD your God and pray for me that my hand may be restored.' So the man of God interceded with the LORD, and the king's hand was restored and became as it was before.

⁷The king said to the man of God, 'Come home with me for a meal, and I will give you a gift.'

⁸But the man of God answered the king, 'Even if you were to give me half your possessions, I would not go with you, nor would I eat bread or drink water here. ⁹For I was commanded by the word of the LORD: "You must not eat bread or drink water or return by the way you came." ' ¹⁰So he took another road and did not return by the way he had come to Bethel.

¹¹Now there was a certain old prophet living in Bethel, whose sons came and told him all that the man of God had done there that day. They also told their father what he had said to the king. ¹²Their father asked them, 'Which way did he go?' And his sons showed him which road the man of God from Judah had taken. ¹³So he said to his sons, 'Saddle the donkey for me.' And when they had saddled the donkey for him, he mounted it ¹⁴and rode after the man of God. He found him sitting under an oak tree and asked, 'Are you the man of God who came from Judah?'

'I am,' he replied.

¹⁵So the prophet said to him, 'Come home with me and eat.'

¹⁶The man of God said, 'I cannot turn back and go with you, nor can I eat bread or drink water with you in this place. ¹⁷I have been told by the word of the LORD: "You must not eat bread or drink water there or return by the way you came." '

¹⁸The old prophet answered, 'I too am a prophet, as you are. And an angel said to me by the word of the LORD: "Bring him back with you to your house so that he may eat bread and drink water." ' (But he was lying to him.) ¹⁹So the man of God returned with him and ate and drank in his house.

²⁰While they were sitting at the table, the word of the LORD came to the old prophet who had brought him back. ²¹He cried out to the man of God who had come from Judah, 'This is what the LORD says: "You have defied the word of the LORD and have not kept the command the LORD your God gave you. ²²You came back and ate bread and drank water in the place where he told you not to eat or drink. Therefore your body will not be buried in the tomb of your ancestors." '

²³When the man of God had finished eating and drinking, the prophet who had brought him back saddled his donkey for him. ²⁴As he went on his way, a lion met him on the road and killed him, and his body was left lying on the road, with both the donkey and the lion standing beside it. ²⁵Some people who passed by saw the body lying there, with the lion standing beside the body, and they went and reported it in the city where the old prophet lived.

²⁶When the prophet who had brought him back from his journey heard of it, he said, 'It is the man of God who defied the word of the LORD. The LORD has given him over to the lion, which has mauled him and killed him, as the word of the LORD had warned him.'

27The prophet said to his sons, 'Saddle the donkey for me,' and they did so. **28**Then he went out and found the body lying on the road, with the donkey and the lion standing beside it. The lion had neither eaten the body nor mauled the donkey. **29**So the prophet picked up the body of the man of God, laid it on the donkey, and brought it back to his own city to mourn for him and bury him. **30**Then he laid the body in his own tomb, and they mourned over him and said, 'Alas, my brother!'

31After burying him, he said to his sons, 'When I die, bury me in the grave where the man of God is buried; lay my bones beside his bones. **32**For the message he declared by the word of the LORD against the altar in Bethel and against all the shrines on the high places in the towns of Samaria will certainly come true.'

33Even after this, Jeroboam did not change his evil ways, but once more appointed priests for the high places from all sorts of people. Anyone who wanted to become a priest he consecrated for the high places. **34**This was the sin of the house of Jeroboam that led to its downfall and to its destruction from the face of the earth.

Ahijah's prophecy against Jeroboam

14 At that time Abijah son of Jeroboam became ill, **2**and Jeroboam said to his wife, 'Go, disguise yourself, so that you won't be recognised as the wife of Jeroboam. Then go to Shiloh. Ahijah the prophet is there – the one who told me I would be king over this people. **3**Take ten loaves of bread with you, some cakes and a jar of honey, and go to him. He will tell you what will happen to the boy.' **4**So Jeroboam's wife did what he said and went to Ahijah's house in Shiloh.

Now Ahijah could not see; his sight was gone because of his age. **5**But the LORD had told Ahijah, 'Jeroboam's wife is coming to ask you about her son, for he is ill, and you are to give her such and such an answer. When she arrives, she will pretend to be someone else.'

6So when Ahijah heard the sound of her footsteps at the door, he said, 'Come in, wife of Jeroboam. Why this pretence? I have been sent to you with bad news. **7**Go, tell Jeroboam that this is what the LORD, the God of Israel, says: "I raised you up from among the people and appointed you ruler over my people Israel. **8**I tore the kingdom away from the house of David and gave it to you, but you have not been like my servant David, who kept my commands and followed me with all his heart, doing only what was right in my eyes. **9**You have done more evil than all who lived before you. You have made for yourself other gods, idols made of metal; you have aroused my anger and turned your back on me.

10'"Because of this, I am going to bring disaster on the house of Jeroboam. I will cut off from Jeroboam every last male in Israel – slave or free.*a* I will burn up the house of Jeroboam as one burns dung, until it is all gone. **11**Dogs will eat those belonging to Jeroboam who die in the city, and the birds will feed on those who die in the country. The LORD has spoken!"

12'As for you, go back home. When you set foot in your city, the boy will die. **13**All Israel will mourn for him and bury him. He is the only one belonging to Jeroboam who will be buried, because he is the only one in the house of Jeroboam in whom the LORD, the God of Israel, has found anything good.

14'The LORD will raise up for himself a king over Israel who will cut off the family of Jeroboam. Even now this is beginning to happen.*b* **15**And the LORD will strike Israel, so that it will be like a reed swaying in the water. He will uproot Israel from this good land that he gave to their ancestors and scatter them beyond the River Euphrates, because they aroused the LORD's anger by making Asherah poles.*c* **16**And he will give Israel up because of the sins Jeroboam has committed and has caused Israel to commit.'

---

a 10 Or *Israel – every ruler or leader*
b 14 The meaning of the Hebrew for this sentence is uncertain.
c 15 That is, wooden symbols of the goddess Asherah; here and elsewhere in 1 Kings

17 Then Jeroboam's wife got up and left and went to Tirzah. As soon as she stepped over the threshold of the house, the boy died. 18 They buried him, and all Israel mourned for him, as the LORD had said through his servant the prophet Ahijah.

19 The other events of Jeroboam's reign, his wars and how he ruled, are written in the book of the annals of the kings of Israel. 20 He reigned for twenty-two years and then rested with his ancestors. And Nadab his son succeeded him as king.

Rehoboam king of Judah

21 Rehoboam son of Solomon was king in Judah. He was forty-one years old when he became king, and he reigned for seventeen years in Jerusalem, the city the LORD had chosen out of all the tribes of Israel in which to put his Name. His mother's name was Naamah; she was an Ammonite.

22 Judah did evil in the eyes of the LORD. By the sins they committed they stirred up his jealous anger more than those who were before them had done. 23 They also set up for themselves high places, sacred stones and Asherah poles on every high hill and under every spreading tree. 24 There were even male shrine-prostitutes in the land; the people engaged in all the detestable practices of the nations the LORD had driven out before the Israelites.

25 In the fifth year of King Rehoboam, Shishak king of Egypt attacked Jerusalem. 26 He carried off the treasures of the temple of the LORD and the treasures of the royal palace. He took everything, including all the gold shields Solomon had made. 27 So King Rehoboam made bronze shields to replace them and assigned these to the commanders of the guard on duty at the entrance to the royal palace. 28 Whenever the king went to the LORD's temple, the guards bore the shields, and afterwards they returned them to the guardroom.

29 As for the other events of Rehoboam's reign, and all he did, are they not written in the book of the annals of the kings of Judah? 30 There was continual warfare between Rehoboam and Jeroboam. 31 And Rehoboam rested with his ancestors and was buried with them in the City of David.

His mother's name was Naamah; she was an Ammonite. And Abijah*d* his son succeeded him as king.

Abijah king of Judah

15 In the eighteenth year of the reign of Jeroboam son of Nebat, Abijah*a* became king of Judah, 2 and he reigned in Jerusalem for three years. His mother's name was Maakah daughter of Abishalom.*b*

3 He committed all the sins his father had done before him; his heart was not fully devoted to the LORD his God, as the heart of David his forefather had been. 4 Nevertheless, for David's sake the LORD his God gave him a lamp in Jerusalem by raising up a son to succeed him and by making Jerusalem strong. 5 For David had done what was right in the eyes of the LORD and had not failed to keep any of the LORD's commands all the days of his life – except in the case of Uriah the Hittite.

6 There was war between Abijah*c* and Jeroboam throughout Abijah's lifetime. 7 As for the other events of Abijah's reign, and all he did, are they not written in the book of the annals of the kings of Judah? There was war between Abijah and Jeroboam. 8 And Abijah rested with his ancestors and was buried in the City of David. And Asa his son succeeded him as king.

Asa king of Judah

9 In the twentieth year of Jeroboam king of Israel, Asa became king of Judah, 10 and he reigned in Jerusalem for forty-one years. His grandmother's name was Maakah daughter of Abishalom.

11 Asa did what was right in the eyes of the LORD, as his father David had done. 12 He expelled the male shrine-prostitutes from the land and got rid of all the idols

d 31 Some Hebrew manuscripts and Septuagint (see also 2 Chron. 12:16); most Hebrew manuscripts *Abijam*
a 1 Some Hebrew manuscripts and Septuagint (see also 2 Chron. 12:16); most Hebrew manuscripts *Abijam*; also in verses 7 and 8
b 2 A variant of *Absalom*; also in verse 10
c 6 Some Hebrew manuscripts and Syriac *Abijam* (that is, Abijah); most Hebrew manuscripts *Rehoboam*

his ancestors had made. 13 He even deposed his grandmother Maakah from her position as queen mother, because she had made a repulsive image for the worship of Asherah. Asa cut it down and burned it in the Kidron Valley. 14 Although he did not remove the high places, Asa's heart was fully committed to the LORD all his life. 15 He brought into the temple of the LORD the silver and gold and the articles that he and his father had dedicated.

16 There was war between Asa and Baasha king of Israel throughout their reigns. 17 Baasha king of Israel went up against Judah and fortified Ramah to prevent anyone from leaving or entering the territory of Asa king of Judah.

18 Asa then took all the silver and gold that was left in the treasuries of the LORD's temple and of his own palace. He entrusted it to his officials and sent them to Ben-Hadad son of Tabrimmon, the son of Hezion, the king of Aram, who was ruling in Damascus. 19 'Let there be a treaty between me and you,' he said, 'as there was between my father and your father. See, I am sending you a gift of silver and gold. Now break your treaty with Baasha king of Israel so that he will withdraw from me.'

20 Ben-Hadad agreed with King Asa and sent the commanders of his forces against the towns of Israel. He conquered Ijon, Dan, Abel Beth Maakah and all Kinnereth in addition to Naphtali. 21 When Baasha heard this, he stopped building Ramah and withdrew to Tirzah. 22 Then King Asa issued an order to all Judah – no one was exempt – and they carried away from Ramah the stones and timber Baasha had been using there. With them King Asa built up Geba in Benjamin, and also Mizpah.

23 As for all the other events of Asa's reign, all his achievements, all he did and the cities he built, are they not written in the book of the annals of the kings of Judah? In his old age, however, his feet became diseased. 24 Then Asa rested with his ancestors and was buried with them in the city of his father David. And Jehoshaphat his son succeeded him as king.

Nadab king of Israel

25 Nadab son of Jeroboam became king of Israel in the second year of Asa king of Judah, and he reigned over Israel for two years. 26 He did evil in the eyes of the LORD, following the ways of his father and committing the same sin his father had caused Israel to commit.

27 Baasha son of Ahijah from the tribe of Issachar plotted against him, and he struck him down at Gibbethon, a Philistine town, while Nadab and all Israel were besieging it. 28 Baasha killed Nadab in the third year of Asa king of Judah and succeeded him as king.

29 As soon as he began to reign, he killed Jeroboam's whole family. He did not leave Jeroboam anyone that breathed, but destroyed them all, according to the word of the LORD given through his servant Ahijah the Shilonite. 30 This happened because of the sins Jeroboam had committed and had caused Israel to commit, and because he aroused the anger of the LORD, the God of Israel.

31 As for the other events of Nadab's reign, and all he did, are they not written in the book of the annals of the kings of Israel? 32 There was war between Asa and Baasha king of Israel throughout their reigns.

Baasha king of Israel

33 In the third year of Asa king of Judah, Baasha son of Ahijah became king of all Israel in Tirzah, and he reigned for twenty-four years. 34 He did evil in the eyes of the LORD, following the ways of Jeroboam and committing the same sin Jeroboam had caused Israel to commit.

16 Then the word of the LORD came to Jehu son of Hanani concerning Baasha: 2 'I lifted you up from the dust and appointed you ruler over my people Israel, but you followed the ways of Jeroboam and caused my people Israel to sin and to arouse my anger by their sins. 3 So I am about to wipe out Baasha and his house, and I will make your house like that of Jeroboam son of Nebat. 4 Dogs will eat those belonging to Baasha who die in the city, and birds will feed on those who die in the country.'

⁵As for the other events of Baasha's reign, what he did and his achievements, are they not written in the book of the annals of the kings of Israel? ⁶Baasha rested with his ancestors and was buried in Tirzah. And Elah his son succeeded him as king.

⁷Moreover, the word of the LORD came through the prophet Jehu son of Hanani to Baasha and his house, because of all the evil he had done in the eyes of the LORD, arousing his anger by the things he did, becoming like the house of Jeroboam – and also because he destroyed it.

Elah king of Israel

⁸In the twenty-sixth year of Asa king of Judah, Elah son of Baasha became king of Israel, and he reigned in Tirzah for two years.

⁹Zimri, one of his officials, who had command of half his chariots, plotted against him. Elah was in Tirzah at the time, getting drunk in the home of Arza, the palace administrator at Tirzah. ¹⁰Zimri came in, struck him down and killed him in the twenty-seventh year of Asa king of Judah. Then he succeeded him as king.

¹¹As soon as he began to reign and was seated on the throne, he killed off Baasha's whole family. He did not spare a single male, whether relative or friend. ¹²So Zimri destroyed the whole family of Baasha, in accordance with the word of the LORD spoken against Baasha through the prophet Jehu – ¹³because of all the sins Baasha and his son Elah had committed and had caused Israel to commit, so that they aroused the anger of the LORD, the God of Israel, by their worthless idols.

¹⁴As for the other events of Elah's reign, and all he did, are they not written in the book of the annals of the kings of Israel?

Zimri king of Israel

¹⁵In the twenty-seventh year of Asa king of Judah, Zimri reigned in Tirzah for seven days. The army was encamped near Gibbethon, a Philistine town. ¹⁶When the Israelites in the camp heard that Zimri had plotted against the king and murdered him, they proclaimed Omri, the commander of the army, king over Israel that very day there in the camp. ¹⁷Then Omri and all the Israelites with him withdrew from Gibbethon and laid siege to Tirzah. ¹⁸When Zimri saw that the city was taken, he went into the citadel of the royal palace and set the palace on fire around him. So he died, ¹⁹because of the sins he had committed, doing evil in the eyes of the LORD and following the ways of Jeroboam and committing the same sin Jeroboam had caused Israel to commit.

²⁰As for the other events of Zimri's reign, and the rebellion he carried out, are they not written in the book of the annals of the kings of Israel?

Omri king of Israel

²¹Then the people of Israel were split into two factions; half supported Tibni son of Ginath for king, and the other half supported Omri. ²²But Omri's followers proved stronger than those of Tibni son of Ginath. So Tibni died and Omri became king.

²³In the thirty-first year of Asa king of Judah, Omri became king of Israel, and he reigned for twelve years, six of them in Tirzah. ²⁴He bought the hill of Samaria from Shemer for two talents*ᵃ* of silver and built a city on the hill, calling it Samaria, after Shemer, the name of the former owner of the hill.

²⁵But Omri did evil in the eyes of the LORD and sinned more than all those before him. ²⁶He followed completely the ways of Jeroboam son of Nebat, committing the same sin Jeroboam had caused Israel to commit, so that they aroused the anger of the LORD, the God of Israel, by their worthless idols.

²⁷As for the other events of Omri's reign, what he did and the things he achieved, are they not written in the book of the annals of the kings of Israel? ²⁸Omri rested with his ancestors and was buried in Samaria. And Ahab his son succeeded him as king.

---

a 24 That is, about 68 kilograms

Ahab becomes king of Israel

29 In the thirty-eighth year of Asa king of Judah, Ahab son of Omri became king of Israel, and he reigned in Samaria over Israel for twenty-two years. 30 Ahab son of Omri did more evil in the eyes of the LORD than any of those before him. 31 He not only considered it trivial to commit the sins of Jeroboam son of Nebat, but he also married Jezebel daughter of Ethbaal king of the Sidonians, and began to serve Baal and worship him. 32 He set up an altar for Baal in the temple of Baal that he built in Samaria. 33 Ahab also made an Asherah pole and did more to arouse the anger of the LORD, the God of Israel, than did all the kings of Israel before him.

34 In Ahab's time, Hiel of Bethel rebuilt Jericho. He laid its foundations at the cost of his firstborn son Abiram, and he set up its gates at the cost of his youngest son Segub, in accordance with the word of the LORD spoken by Joshua son of Nun.

Elijah announces a great drought

17 Now Elijah the Tishbite, from Tishbe*a* in Gilead, said to Ahab, 'As the LORD, the God of Israel, lives, whom I serve, there will be neither dew nor rain in the next few years except at my word.'

Elijah fed by ravens

2 Then the word of the LORD came to Elijah: 3 'Leave here, turn eastward and hide in the Kerith Ravine, east of the Jordan. 4 You will drink from the brook, and I have instructed the ravens to supply you with food there.'

5 So he did what the LORD had told him. He went to the Kerith Ravine, east

_____

a 1 Or Tishbite, of the settlers

THE NAMES OF GOD 3

God the Provider (Yahweh Jireh)

God provides in many ways.

There are many stories in the Bible about God's provision, often provisions of food (e.g. the case of Elijah in 1 Kings 17:8 and 19:22). Then there's Jesus' miraculous feeding of the 5,000 and 4,000 in Mark 6:30–43 and 8:1–9. There was a story in Chile of a godly widow who prayed aloud in her poor shack of a home, telling God about a friend who was visiting her that day and asking that she might have some food to feed her. A neighbour who mocked her faith got his wife to cook two plates of food which he left at her door. He laughed at her when she found it and began to praise God for it. He told her that it was he who had put it by her door. Hearing this, the widow began to praise God again for causing him to be so kind.

As a young man I was very encouraged by the stories in the Old Testament of the way God provided for his people during the forty years they were in the desert, and greatly challenged by the story of George Müller, who kept several orphanages going in Bristol by God's provision in the nineteenth century. Modern day missionary Heidi Baker is seeing similar miraculous provision in Mozambique today.

Remember, Jesus taught his disciples to pray, 'Give us today our daily bread.'

David and Mary Pytches

 Isaiah 40:29   Exodus 15:26

of the Jordan, and stayed there. 6The ravens brought him bread and meat in the morning and bread and meat in the evening, and he drank from the brook.

Elijah and the widow at Zarephath

7Some time later the brook dried up because there had been no rain in the land. 8Then the word of the LORD came to him: 9'Go at once to Zarephath in the region of Sidon and stay there. I have instructed a widow there to supply you with food.' 10So he went to Zarephath. When he came to the town gate, a widow was there gathering sticks. He called to her and asked, 'Would you bring me a little water in a jar so I may have a drink?' 11As she was going to get it, he called, 'And bring me, please, a piece of bread.'

12'As surely as the LORD your God lives,' she replied, 'I don't have any bread – only a handful of flour in a jar and a little olive oil in a jug. I am gathering a few sticks to take home and make a meal for myself and my son, that we may eat it – and die.'

13Elijah said to her, 'Don't be afraid. Go home and do as you have said. But first make a small loaf of bread for me from what you have and bring it to me, and then make something for yourself and your son. 14For this is what the LORD, the God of Israel, says: "The jar of flour will not be used up and the jug of oil will not run dry until the day the LORD sends rain on the land."'

15She went away and did as Elijah had told her. So there was food every day for Elijah and for the woman and her family. 16For the jar of flour was not used up and the jug of oil did not run dry, in keeping with the word of the LORD spoken by Elijah.

17Some time later the son of the woman who owned the house became ill. He grew worse and worse, and finally stopped breathing. 18She said to Elijah, 'What do you have against me, man of God? Did you come to remind me of my sin and kill my son?'

19'Give me your son,' Elijah replied. He took him from her arms, carried him to the upper room where he was staying, and laid him on his bed. 20Then he cried out to the LORD, 'LORD my God, have you brought tragedy even on this widow I am staying with, by causing her son to die?' 21Then he stretched himself out on the boy three times and cried out to the LORD, 'LORD my God, let this boy's life return to him!'

22The LORD heard Elijah's cry, and the boy's life returned to him, and he lived. 23Elijah picked up the child and carried him down from the room into the house. He gave him to his mother and said, 'Look, your son is alive!'

24Then the woman said to Elijah, 'Now I know that you are a man of God and that the word of the LORD from your mouth is the truth.'

Elijah and Obadiah

18 After a long time, in the third year, the word of the LORD came to Elijah: 'Go and present yourself to Ahab, and I will send rain on the land.' 2So Elijah went to present himself to Ahab.

Now the famine was severe in Samaria, 3and Ahab had summoned Obadiah, his palace administrator. (Obadiah was a devout believer in the LORD. 4While Jezebel was killing off the LORD's prophets, Obadiah had taken a hundred prophets and hidden them in two caves, fifty in each, and had supplied them with food and water.) 5Ahab had said to Obadiah, 'Go through the land to all the springs and valleys. Maybe we can find some grass to keep the horses and mules alive so we will not have to kill any of our animals.' 6So they divided the land they were to cover, Ahab going in one direction and Obadiah in another.

7As Obadiah was walking along, Elijah met him. Obadiah recognised him, bowed down to the ground, and said, 'Is it really you, my lord Elijah?'

8'Yes,' he replied. 'Go tell your master, "Elijah is here."'

9'What have I done wrong,' asked Obadiah, 'that you are handing your servant over to Ahab to be put to death? 10As surely as the LORD your God lives, there is not a nation or kingdom where my master has not sent someone to look for you. And whenever a nation or kingdom claimed you were not there, he made them swear they could not find you. ¹¹ But now you tell me to go to my master and say, "Elijah is here." ¹² I don't know where the Spirit of the LORD may carry you when I leave you. If I go and tell Ahab and he doesn't find you, he will kill me. Yet I your servant have worshipped the LORD since my youth. ¹³ Haven't you heard, my lord, what I did while Jezebel was killing the prophets of the LORD? I hid a hundred of the LORD's prophets in two caves, fifty in each, and supplied them with food and water. ¹⁴ And now you tell me to go to my master and say, "Elijah is here." He will kill me!'

¹⁵ Elijah said, 'As the LORD Almighty lives, whom I serve, I will surely present myself to Ahab today.'

Elijah on Mount Carmel

¹⁶ So Obadiah went to meet Ahab and told him, and Ahab went to meet Elijah. ¹⁷ When he saw Elijah, he said to him, 'Is that you, you troubler of Israel?'

¹⁸ 'I have not made trouble for Israel,' Elijah replied. 'But you and your father's family have. You have abandoned the LORD's commands and have followed the Baals. ¹⁹ Now summon the people from all over Israel to meet me on Mount Carmel. And bring the four hundred and fifty prophets of Baal and the four hundred prophets of Asherah, who eat at Jezebel's table.'

²⁰ So Ahab sent word throughout all Israel and assembled the prophets on Mount Carmel. ²¹ Elijah went before the people and said, 'How long will you waver between two opinions? If the LORD is God, follow him; but if Baal is God, follow him.'

NATURALLY SUPERNATURAL 4

MIRACLES

The Bible is full of miracles. This one in 1 Kings 18 is quite spectacular.

Elijah is so incensed by people worshipping Baal instead of God that he takes them on in a head-to-head challenge. He asks the people to call on Baal and see if he will respond by sending fire from heaven on their offering. When nothing happens he taunts them. And when it comes to his turn he makes the task even harder by pouring water on the offering. Then he prays, asking God to send fire to show that he is the true God. Sure enough, the fire comes and the people are so stunned they fall flat on their faces and cry out to God. Pretty impressive stuff, isn't it?

The Bible tells many stories of miracles – from a whole sea parting so that God's people can walk through on dry land, to Jesus turning water into wine. If we know the things that God has done then we know more about his character and the things he is capable of. That changes the way we view our current problems! The God who raised the dead can heal a headache. The God who rained down manna from heaven to feed his people in the desert can deal with your financial needs. The God who used a virgin to carry his only son as a baby can help you when things seem impossible. Sometimes we just have to step out in faith like Elijah. We go out of our comfort zones and ask God to perform miracles for those around us in need. Be brave, be bold, trust God, and go for it!

Mike Pilavachi

 Ephesians 1:13–14   Matthew 11:1–5

But the people said nothing.

²²Then Elijah said to them, 'I am the only one of the LORD's prophets left, but Baal has four hundred and fifty prophets. ²³Get two bulls for us. Let Baal's prophets choose one for themselves, and let them cut it into pieces and put it on the wood but not set fire to it. I will prepare the other bull and put it on the wood but not set fire to it. ²⁴Then you call on the name of your god, and I will call on the name of the LORD. The god who answers by fire – he is God.'

Then all the people said, 'What you say is good.'

²⁵Elijah said to the prophets of Baal, 'Choose one of the bulls and prepare it first, since there are so many of you. Call on the name of your god, but do not light the fire.' ²⁶So they took the bull that was given to them and prepared it.

Then they called on the name of Baal from morning till noon. 'Baal, answer us!' they shouted. But there was no response; no one answered. And they danced around the altar they had made.

²⁷At noon Elijah began to taunt them. 'Shout louder!' he said. 'Surely he is a god! Perhaps he is deep in thought, or busy, or travelling. Maybe he is sleeping and must be awakened.' ²⁸So they shouted louder and slashed themselves with swords and spears, as was their custom, until their blood flowed. ²⁹Midday passed, and they continued their frantic prophesying until the time for the evening sacrifice. But there was no response, no one answered, no one paid attention.

³⁰Then Elijah said to all the people, 'Come here to me.' They came to him, and he repaired the altar of the LORD, which had been torn down. ³¹Elijah took twelve stones, one for each of the tribes descended from Jacob, to whom the word of the LORD had come, saying, 'Your name shall be Israel.' ³²With the stones he built an altar in the name of the LORD, and he dug a trench round it large enough to hold two seahs*a* of seed. ³³He arranged

the wood, cut the bull into pieces and laid it on the wood. Then he said to them, 'Fill four large jars with water and pour it on the offering and on the wood.'

³⁴'Do it again,' he said, and they did it again.

'Do it a third time,' he ordered, and they did it the third time. ³⁵The water ran down around the altar and even filled the trench.

³⁶At the time of sacrifice, the prophet Elijah stepped forward and prayed: 'LORD, the God of Abraham, Isaac and Israel, let it be known today that you are God in Israel and that I am your servant and have done all these things at your command. ³⁷Answer me, LORD, answer me, so these people will know that you, LORD, are God, and that you are turning their hearts back again.'

³⁸Then the fire of the LORD fell and burned up the sacrifice, the wood, the stones and the soil, and also licked up the water in the trench.

³⁹When all the people saw this, they fell prostrate and cried, 'The LORD – he is God! The LORD – he is God!'

⁴⁰Then Elijah commanded them, 'Seize the prophets of Baal. Don't let anyone get away!' They seized them, and Elijah had them brought down to the Kishon Valley and slaughtered there.

⁴¹And Elijah said to Ahab, 'Go, eat and drink, for there is the sound of a heavy rain.' ⁴²So Ahab went off to eat and drink, but Elijah climbed to the top of Carmel, bent down to the ground and put his face between his knees.

⁴³'Go and look toward the sea,' he told his servant. And he went up and looked.

'There is nothing there,' he said.

Seven times Elijah said, 'Go back.'

⁴⁴The seventh time the servant reported, 'A cloud as small as a man's hand is rising from the sea.'

So Elijah said, 'Go and tell Ahab, "Hitch up your chariot and go down before the rain stops you."'

⁴⁵Meanwhile, the sky grew black with clouds, the wind rose, a heavy rainstorm came on and Ahab rode off to Jezreel. ⁴⁶The power of the LORD came on Elijah

---

a 32 That is, probably about 11 kilograms

and, tucking his cloak into his belt, he ran ahead of Ahab all the way to Jezreel.

Elijah flees to Horeb

19 Now Ahab told Jezebel everything Elijah had done and how he had killed all the prophets with the sword. ²So Jezebel sent a messenger to Elijah to say, 'May the gods deal with me, be it ever so severely, if by this time tomorrow I do not make your life like that of one of them.'

³Elijah was afraid*ᵃ* and ran for his life. When he came to Beersheba in Judah, he left his servant there, ⁴while he himself went a day's journey into the wilderness. He came to a broom bush, sat down under it and prayed that he might die. 'I have had enough, LORD,' he said. 'Take my life; I am no better than my ancestors.' ⁵Then he lay down under the bush and fell asleep.

_____
a 3 Or *Elijah saw*

SACRIFICE 10

What's your 'Baal'?

It's a sacrifice-off in true Old Testament showdown style.

Elijah has gathered all the Baal worshippers in Israel. Baal was a pagan god that Israel was often tempted to worship because all the other nations were doing it. It's important for us to remember that we sacrifice things all the time. Often we make it seem like the only person we sacrifice anything for is God. That isn't true. If we want to excel in sports, we sacrifice time and energy – perhaps we choose to put our sport before our homework. We make sacrifices for relationships that we value. We may choose not to go to a party but to hang out with our best friend instead. This is a sacrifice – but it's a good one.

So, Elijah is tired of Israel making non-stop sacrifices to a god that isn't even real. He challenges the Baal worshippers to a contest. Which god will answer prayer and consume the sacrifice? Now this gets to be pretty funny. Elijah even suggests that perhaps Baal is going to the bathroom and that's why he can't answer! A great example of sarcasm in prophetic ministry. Elijah offers a sacrifice to the living God, Yahweh. And God answers with fire, consuming the sacrifice. Finally, someone showed Israel that sacrificing to gods that aren't real is a waste of everyone's time.

Who do you sacrifice to? Are there any 'idols' in your life that you spend a lot of time and energy on? A friend of mine asked God about this and realised that video games were his Baal. He sacrificed them to the living God and his spiritual life became fresh and exciting. He now looks at the sacrifice as if it was nothing – although at the time it was honest and true and hard. But God accepted it and because God is real, it will make a difference for the rest of my friend's life. How about you? Maybe it's time for your own showdown.

Danielle Strickland

« 2 Samuel 24:24

All at once an angel touched him and said, 'Get up and eat.' 6 He looked around, and there by his head was some bread baked over hot coals, and a jar of water. He ate and drank and then lay down again.

7 The angel of the LORD came back a second time and touched him and said, 'Get up and eat, for the journey is too much for you.' 8 So he got up and ate and drank. Strengthened by that food, he travelled for forty days and forty nights until he reached Horeb, the mountain of God. 9 There he went into a cave and spent the night.

The LORD appears to Elijah

And the word of the LORD came to him: 'What are you doing here, Elijah?'

10 He replied, 'I have been very zealous for the LORD God Almighty. The Israelites have rejected your covenant, torn down your altars, and put your prophets to death with the sword. I am the only one left, and now they are trying to kill me too.'

11 The LORD said, 'Go out and stand on the mountain in the presence of the LORD, for the LORD is about to pass by.'

Then a great and powerful wind tore the mountains apart and shattered the rocks before the LORD, but the LORD was not in the wind. After the wind there was an earthquake, but the LORD was not in the earthquake. 12 After the earthquake came a fire, but the LORD was not in the fire. And after the fire came a gentle whisper. 13 When Elijah heard it, he pulled his cloak over his face and went out and stood at the mouth of the cave.

Then a voice said to him, 'What are you doing here, Elijah?'

14 He replied, 'I have been very zealous for the LORD God Almighty. The Israelites have rejected your covenant, torn down your altars, and put your prophets to death with the sword. I am the only one left, and now they are trying to kill me too.'

15 The LORD said to him, 'Go back the way you came, and go to the Desert of Damascus. When you get there, anoint Hazael king over Aram. 16 Also, anoint Jehu son of Nimshi king over Israel, and anoint Elisha son of Shaphat from Abel Meholah to succeed you as prophet. 17 Jehu will put

to death anyone who escape the sword of Hazael, and Elisha will put to death any who escape the sword of Jehu. 18 Yet I reserve seven thousand in Israel – all whose knees have not bowed down to Baal and whose mouths have not kissed him.'

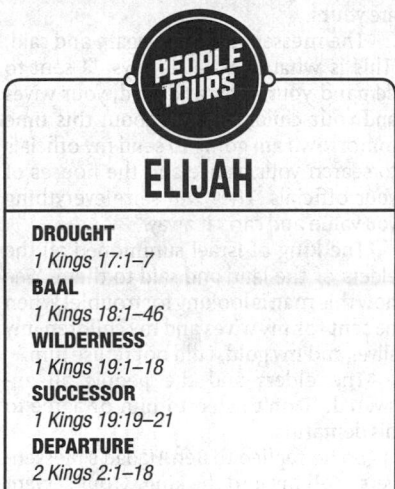

PEOPLE TOURS

ELIJAH

DROUGHT
1 Kings 17:1–7
BAAL
1 Kings 18:1–46
WILDERNESS
1 Kings 19:1–18
SUCCESSOR
1 Kings 19:19–21
DEPARTURE
2 Kings 2:1–18

The call of Elisha

19 So Elijah went from there and found Elisha son of Shaphat. He was ploughing with twelve yoke of oxen, and he himself was driving the twelfth pair. Elijah went up to him and threw his cloak around him. 20 Elisha then left his oxen and ran after Elijah. 'Let me kiss my father and mother goodbye,' he said, 'and then I will come with you.'

'Go back,' Elijah replied. 'What have I done to you?'

21 So Elisha left him and went back. He took his yoke of oxen and slaughtered them. He burned the ploughing equipment to cook the meat and gave it to the people, and they ate. Then he set out to follow Elijah and became his servant.

Ben-Hadad attacks Samaria

20 Now Ben-Hadad king of Aram mustered his entire army. Accompanied by thirty-two kings with their horses and chariots, he went up and besieged Samaria and attacked it. 2 He sent messengers into the city to Ahab king of

Israel, saying, 'This is what Ben-Hadad says: ³ "Your silver and gold are mine, and the best of your wives and children are mine."'

⁴The king of Israel answered, 'Just as you say, my lord the king. I and all I have are yours.'

⁵The messengers came again and said, 'This is what Ben-Hadad says: "I sent to demand your silver and gold, your wives and your children. ⁶But about this time tomorrow I am going to send my officials to search your palace and the houses of your officials. They will seize everything you value and carry it away."'

⁷The king of Israel summoned all the elders of the land and said to them, 'See how this man is looking for trouble! When he sent for my wives and my children, my silver and my gold, I did not refuse him.'

⁸The elders and the people all answered, 'Don't listen to him or agree to his demands.'

⁹So he replied to Ben-Hadad's messengers, 'Tell my lord the king, "Your servant will do all you demanded the first time, but this demand I cannot meet."' They left and took the answer back to Ben-Hadad.

¹⁰Then Ben-Hadad sent another message to Ahab: 'May the gods deal with me, be it ever so severely, if enough dust remains in Samaria to give each of my men a handful.'

¹¹The king of Israel answered, 'Tell him: "One who puts on his armour should not boast like one who takes it off."'

¹²Ben-Hadad heard this message while he and the kings were drinking in their tents,ᵃ and he ordered his men: 'Prepare to attack.' So they prepared to attack the city.

Ahab defeats Ben-Hadad

¹³Meanwhile a prophet came to Ahab king of Israel and announced, 'This is what the LORD says: "Do you see this vast army? I will give it into your hand today, and then you will know that I am the LORD."'

¹⁴'But who will do this?' asked Ahab.

The prophet replied, 'This is what the LORD says: "The junior officers under the provincial commanders will do it."'

'And who will start the battle?' he asked.

The prophet answered, 'You will.'

¹⁵So Ahab summoned the 232 junior officers under the provincial commanders. Then he assembled the rest of the Israelites, 7,000 in all. ¹⁶They set out at noon while Ben-Hadad and the 32 kings allied with him were in their tents getting drunk. ¹⁷The junior officers under the provincial commanders went out first.

Now Ben-Hadad had dispatched scouts, who reported, 'Men are advancing from Samaria.'

¹⁸He said, 'If they have come out for peace, take them alive; if they have come out for war, take them alive.'

¹⁹The junior officers under the provincial commanders marched out of the city with the army behind them ²⁰and each one struck down his opponent. At that, the Arameans fled, with the Israelites in pursuit. But Ben-Hadad king of Aram escaped on horseback with some of his horsemen. ²¹The king of Israel advanced and overpowered the horses and chariots and inflicted heavy losses on the Arameans.

²²Afterwards, the prophet came to the king of Israel and said, 'Strengthen your position and see what must be done, because next spring the king of Aram will attack you again.'

²³Meanwhile, the officials of the king of Aram advised him, 'Their gods are gods of the hills. That is why they were too strong for us. But if we fight them on the plains, surely we will be stronger than they. ²⁴Do this: remove all the kings from their commands and replace them with other officers. ²⁵You must also raise an army like the one you lost – horse for horse and chariot for chariot – so we can fight Israel on the plains. Then surely we will be stronger than they.' He agreed with them and acted accordingly.

²⁶The next spring Ben-Hadad mustered the Arameans and went up to Aphek to fight against Israel. ²⁷When the Israelites were also mustered and given provisions, they marched out to meet them. The

---

ᵃ 12 Or in Sukkoth; also in verse 16

Israelites camped opposite them like two small flocks of goats, while the Arameans covered the countryside.

²⁸The man of God came up and told the king of Israel, 'This is what the LORD says: "Because the Arameans think the LORD is a god of the hills and not a god of the valleys, I will deliver this vast army into your hands, and you will know that I am the LORD."'

²⁹For seven days they camped opposite each other, and on the seventh day the battle was joined. The Israelites inflicted a hundred thousand casualties on the Aramean foot soldiers in one day. ³⁰The rest of them escaped to the city of Aphek, where the wall collapsed on twenty-seven thousand of them. And Ben-Hadad fled to the city and hid in an inner room.

³¹His officials said to him, 'Look, we have heard that the kings of Israel are merciful. Let us go to the king of Israel with sackcloth round our waists and ropes round our heads. Perhaps he will spare your life.'

³²Wearing sackcloth round their waists and ropes round their heads, they went to the king of Israel and said, 'Your servant Ben-Hadad says: "Please let me live."'

The king answered, 'Is he still alive? He is my brother.'

³³The men took this as a good sign and were quick to pick up his word. 'Yes, your brother Ben-Hadad!' they said.

'Go and get him,' the king said. When Ben-Hadad came out, Ahab brought him up into his chariot.

³⁴'I will return the cities my father took from your father,' Ben-Hadad offered. 'You may set up your own market areas in Damascus, as my father did in Samaria.'

Ahab said, 'On the basis of a treaty I will set you free.' So he made a treaty with him, and let him go.

A prophet condemns Ahab

³⁵By the word of the LORD one of the company of the prophets said to his companion, 'Strike me with your weapon,' but he refused.

³⁶So the prophet said, 'Because you have not obeyed the LORD, as soon as you

leave me a lion will kill you.' And after the man went away, a lion found him and killed him.

³⁷The prophet found another man and said, 'Strike me, please.' So the man struck him and wounded him. ³⁸Then the prophet went and stood by the road waiting for the king. He disguised himself with his headband down over his eyes. ³⁹As the king passed by, the prophet called out to him, 'Your servant went into the thick of the battle, and someone came to me with a captive and said, "Guard this man. If he is missing, it will be your life for his life, or you must pay a talent[b] of silver." ⁴⁰While your servant was busy here and there, the man disappeared.'

'That is your sentence,' the king of Israel said. 'You have pronounced it yourself.'

⁴¹Then the prophet quickly removed the headband from his eyes, and the king of Israel recognised him as one of the prophets. ⁴²He said to the king, 'This is what the LORD says: "You have set free a man I had determined should die.[c] Therefore it is your life for his life, your people for his people."' ⁴³Sullen and angry, the king of Israel went to his palace in Samaria.

Naboth's vineyard

21 Some time later there was an incident involving a vineyard belonging to Naboth the Jezreelite. The vineyard was in Jezreel, close to the palace of Ahab king of Samaria. ²Ahab said to Naboth, 'Let me have your vineyard to use for a vegetable garden, since it is close to my palace. In exchange I will give you a better vineyard or, if you prefer, I will pay you whatever it is worth.'

³But Naboth replied, 'The LORD forbid that I should give you the inheritance of my ancestors.'

⁴So Ahab went home, sullen and angry because Naboth the Jezreelite had said, 'I will not give you the inheritance of my ancestors.' He lay on his bed sulking and refused to eat.

---

b 39 That is, about 34 kilograms
c 42 The Hebrew term refers to the irrevocable giving over of things or persons to the LORD, often by totally destroying them.

⁵His wife Jezebel came in and asked him, 'Why are you so sullen? Why won't you eat?'

⁶He answered her, 'Because I said to Naboth the Jezreelite, "Sell me your vineyard; or if you prefer, I will give you another vineyard in its place." But he said, "I will not give you my vineyard." '

⁷Jezebel his wife said, 'Is this how you act as king over Israel? Get up and eat! Cheer up. I'll get you the vineyard of Naboth the Jezreelite.'

⁸So she wrote letters in Ahab's name, placed his seal on them, and sent them to the elders and nobles who lived in Naboth's city with him. ⁹In those letters she wrote:

> 'Proclaim a day of fasting and give Naboth a prominent seat among the people. ¹⁰But put two scoundrels opposite him and get them to bring charges that he has cursed both God and the king. Then take him out and stone him to death.'

¹¹So the elders and nobles who lived in Naboth's city did as Jezebel directed in the letters she had written to them. ¹²They proclaimed a fast and seated Naboth in a prominent place among the people. ¹³Then two scoundrels came and sat opposite him and brought charges against Naboth before the people, saying, 'Naboth has cursed both God and the king.' So they took him outside the city and stoned him to death. ¹⁴Then they sent word to Jezebel: 'Naboth has been stoned to death.'

¹⁵As soon as Jezebel heard that Naboth had been stoned to death, she said to Ahab, 'Get up and take possession of the vineyard of Naboth the Jezreelite that he refused to sell you. He is no longer alive, but dead.' ¹⁶When Ahab heard that Naboth was dead, he got up and went down to take possession of Naboth's vineyard.

¹⁷Then the word of the Lord came to Elijah the Tishbite: ¹⁸'Go down to meet Ahab king of Israel, who rules in Samaria. He is now in Naboth's vineyard, where he has gone to take possession of it. ¹⁹Say to him, "This is what the Lord says: have you not murdered a man and seized his property?" Then say to him, "This is what the Lord says: in the place where dogs licked up Naboth's blood, dogs will lick up your blood – yes, yours!" '

²⁰Ahab said to Elijah, 'So you have found me, my enemy!'

'I have found you,' he answered, 'because you have sold yourself to do evil in the eyes of the Lord. ²¹He says, "I am going to bring disaster on you. I will wipe out your descendants and cut off from Ahab every last male in Israel – slave or free.ᵃ ²²I will make your house like that of Jeroboam son of Nebat and that of Baasha son of Ahijah, because you have aroused my anger and have caused Israel to sin."

²³'And also concerning Jezebel the Lord says: "Dogs will devour Jezebel by the wall ofᵇ Jezreel."

²⁴'Dogs will eat those belonging to Ahab who die in the city, and the birds will feed on those who die in the country.'

²⁵(There was never anyone like Ahab, who sold himself to do evil in the eyes of the Lord, urged on by Jezebel his wife. ²⁶He behaved in the vilest manner by going after idols, like the Amorites the Lord drove out before Israel.)

²⁷When Ahab heard these words, he tore his clothes, put on sackcloth and fasted. He lay in sackcloth and went around meekly.

²⁸Then the word of the Lord came to Elijah the Tishbite: ²⁹'Have you noticed how Ahab has humbled himself before me? Because he has humbled himself, I will not bring this disaster in his day, but I will bring it on his house in the days of his son.'

Micaiah prophesies against Ahab

22 For three years there was no war between Aram and Israel. ²But in the third year Jehoshaphat king of Judah went down to see the king of Israel. ³The king of Israel had said to his officials, 'Don't you know that Ramoth Gilead

---

ᵃ 21 Or Israel – every ruler or leader
ᵇ 23 Most Hebrew manuscripts; a few Hebrew manuscripts, Vulgate and Syriac (see also 2 Kings 9:26) the plot of ground at

belongs to us and yet we are doing nothing to retake it from the king of Aram?' ⁴So he asked Jehoshaphat, 'Will you go with me to fight against Ramoth Gilead?'

Jehoshaphat replied to the king of Israel, 'I am as you are, my people as your people, my horses as your horses.' ⁵But Jehoshaphat also said to the king of Israel, 'First seek the counsel of the LORD.'

⁶So the king of Israel brought together the prophets – about four hundred men – and asked them, 'Shall I go to war against Ramoth Gilead, or shall I refrain?'

'Go,' they answered, 'for the Lord will give it into the king's hand.'

⁷But Jehoshaphat asked, 'Is there no longer a prophet of the LORD here whom we can enquire of?'

⁸The king of Israel answered Jehoshaphat, 'There is still one prophet through whom we can enquire of the LORD, but I hate him because he never prophesies anything good about me, but always bad. He is Micaiah son of Imlah.'

'The king should not say such a thing,' Jehoshaphat replied.

⁹So the king of Israel called one of his officials and said, 'Bring Micaiah son of Imlah at once.'

¹⁰Dressed in their royal robes, the king of Israel and Jehoshaphat king of Judah were sitting on their thrones at the threshing-floor by the entrance of the gate of Samaria, with all the prophets prophesying before them. ¹¹Now Zedekiah son of Kenaanah had made iron horns and he declared, 'This is what the LORD says: "With these you will gore the Arameans until they are destroyed."'

¹²All the other prophets were prophesying the same thing. 'Attack Ramoth Gilead and be victorious,' they said, 'for the LORD will give it into the king's hand.'

¹³The messenger who had gone to summon Micaiah said to him, 'Look, the other prophets without exception are predicting success for the king. Let your word agree with theirs, and speak favourably.'

¹⁴But Micaiah said, 'As surely as the LORD lives, I can tell him only what the LORD tells me.'

¹⁵When he arrived, the king asked him,

'Micaiah, shall we go to war against Ramoth Gilead, or not?'

'Attack and be victorious,' he answered, 'for the LORD will give it into the king's hand.'

¹⁶The king said to him, 'How many times must I make you swear to tell me nothing but the truth in the name of the LORD?'

¹⁷Then Micaiah answered, 'I saw all Israel scattered on the hills like sheep without a shepherd, and the LORD said, "These people have no master. Let each one go home in peace."'

¹⁸The king of Israel said to Jehoshaphat, 'Didn't I tell you that he never prophesies anything good about me, but only bad?'

¹⁹Micaiah continued, 'Therefore hear the word of the LORD: I saw the LORD sitting on his throne with all the multitudes of heaven standing round him on his right and on his left. ²⁰And the LORD said, "Who will entice Ahab into attacking Ramoth Gilead and going to his death there?"

'One suggested this, and another that. ²¹Finally, a spirit came forward, stood before the LORD and said, "I will entice him."

²²'"By what means?" the LORD asked.

'"I will go out and be a deceiving spirit in the mouths of all his prophets," he said.

'"You will succeed in enticing him," said the LORD. "Go and do it."

²³'So now the LORD has put a deceiving spirit in the mouths of all these prophets of yours. The LORD has decreed disaster for you.'

²⁴Then Zedekiah son of Kenaanah went up and slapped Micaiah in the face. 'Which way did the spirit from*a* the LORD go when he went from me to speak to you?' he asked.

²⁵Micaiah replied, 'You will find out on the day you go to hide in an inner room.'

²⁶The king of Israel then ordered, 'Take Micaiah and send him back to Amon the ruler of the city and to Joash the king's son ²⁷and say, "This is what the king says: put this fellow in prison and give him

---

a 24 Or *Spirit of*

nothing but bread and water until I return safely."'

²⁸Micaiah declared, 'If you ever return safely, the LORD has not spoken through me.' Then he added, 'Mark my words, all you people!'

Ahab killed at Ramoth Gilead

²⁹So the king of Israel and Jehoshaphat king of Judah went up to Ramoth Gilead. ³⁰The king of Israel said to Jehoshaphat, 'I will enter the battle in disguise, but you wear your royal robes.' So the king of Israel disguised himself and went into battle.

³¹Now the king of Aram had ordered his thirty-two chariot commanders, 'Do not fight with anyone, small or great, except the king of Israel.' ³²When the chariot commanders saw Jehoshaphat, they thought, 'Surely this is the king of Israel.' So they turned to attack him, but when Jehoshaphat cried out, ³³the chariot commanders saw that he was not the king of Israel and stopped pursuing him.

³⁴But someone drew his bow at random and hit the king of Israel between the sections of his armour. The king told his chariot driver, 'Wheel around and get me out of the fighting. I've been wounded.' ³⁵All day long the battle raged, and the king was propped up in his chariot facing the Arameans. The blood from his wound ran onto the floor of the chariot, and that evening he died. ³⁶As the sun was setting, a cry spread through the army: 'Every man to his town. Every man to his land!'

³⁷So the king died and was brought to Samaria, and they buried him there. ³⁸They washed the chariot at a pool in Samaria (where the prostitutes bathed),ᵇ and the dogs licked up his blood, as the word of the LORD had declared.

³⁹As for the other events of Ahab's reign, including all he did, the palace he built and adorned with ivory, and the cities he fortified, are they not written in the book of the annals of the kings of Israel? ⁴⁰Ahab rested with his ancestors. And Ahaziah his son succeeded him as king.

Jehoshaphat king of Judah

⁴¹Jehoshaphat son of Asa became king of Judah in the fourth year of Ahab king of Israel. ⁴²Jehoshaphat was thirty-five years old when he became king, and he reigned in Jerusalem for twenty-five years. His mother's name was Azubah daughter of Shilhi. ⁴³In everything he followed the ways of his father Asa and did not stray from them; he did what was right in the eyes of the LORD. The high places, however, were not removed, and the people continued to offer sacrifices and burn incense there.ᶜ ⁴⁴Jehoshaphat was also at peace with the king of Israel.

⁴⁵As for the other events of Jehoshaphat's reign, the things he achieved and his military exploits, are they not written in the book of the annals of the kings of Judah? ⁴⁶He rid the land of the rest of the male-shrine prostitutes who remained there even after the reign of his father Asa. ⁴⁷There was then no king in Edom; a provincial governor ruled.

⁴⁸Now Jehoshaphat built a fleet of trading shipsᵈ to go to Ophir for gold, but they never set sail – they were wrecked at Ezion Geber. ⁴⁹At that time Ahaziah son of Ahab said to Jehoshaphat, 'Let my men sail with yours,' but Jehoshaphat refused.

⁵⁰Then Jehoshaphat rested with his ancestors and was buried with them in the city of David his father. And Jehoram his son succeeded him as king.

Ahaziah king of Israel

⁵¹Ahaziah son of Ahab became king of Israel in Samaria in the seventeenth year of Jehoshaphat king of Judah, and he reigned over Israel for two years. ⁵²He did evil in the eyes of the LORD, because he followed the ways of his father and mother and of Jeroboam son of Nebat, who caused Israel to sin. ⁵³He served and worshipped Baal and aroused the anger of the LORD, the God of Israel, just as his father had done.

ᵇ 38 Or *Samaria and cleaned the weapons*

ᶜ 43 In Hebrew texts this sentence (22:43b) is numbered 22:44, and 22:44-53 is numbered 22:45-54.
ᵈ 48 Hebrew *of ships of Tarshish*

2 KINGS

DATE

1 and 2 Kings cover about 400 years of Israel's history, starting around 970 BC

AUTHOR

Unknown

WHAT'S IT ALL ABOUT?

The book of 2 Kings continues telling the history of the Kingdom of Israel and the Kingdom of Judah. It tells of king after king who *'did evil in the eyes of the LORD'*, turning towards false gods and rejecting their true Lord. When the prophet Elijah (whose ministry we mainly read about in 1 Kings) was taken *'up to heaven in a whirlwind'* (2 Kings 2:11), Elisha took on his role, urging God's people to turn back to him. They would not listen and eventually the Kingdom of Israel was conquered by the Assyrians. The Kingdom of Judah hung on a little bit longer, with two kings in particular (Hezekiah and Josiah) who followed the Lord, but eventually Jerusalem was conquered by the Babylonians and God's people were taken into exile.

WHY SHOULD WE READ IT?

- To discover stories of many miracles, including Elijah calling down fire from heaven to prove he was a man of God (2 Kings 1), the parting of the River Jordan, a bottle of oil that would not run dry (2 Kings 4), the raising of a dead man to life (2 Kings 4) and the healing of a person with leprosy (2 Kings 5).

- To hear about the battle where the Lord blinded an entire army but showed Elisha's servant what was happening in the spiritual realm (2 Kings 6).

- To hear why God sent his people into exile (especially 2 Kings 17).

- To see how Hezekiah persuaded God through prayer to change his mind and not to kill him (2 Kings 20).

Andy Croft with Liza Hoeksma

The LORD's judgment on Ahaziah

1 After Ahab's death, Moab rebelled against Israel. ²Now Ahaziah had fallen through the lattice of his upper room in Samaria and injured himself. So he sent messengers, saying to them, 'Go and consult Baal-Zebub, the god of Ekron, to see if I will recover from this injury.'

³But the angel of the LORD said to Elijah the Tishbite, 'Go up and meet the messengers of the king of Samaria and ask them, "Is it because there is no God in Israel that you are going off to consult Baal-Zebub, the god of Ekron?" ⁴Therefore this is what the LORD says: "You will not leave the bed you are lying on. You will certainly die!"' So Elijah went.

⁵When the messengers returned to the king, he asked them, 'Why have you come back?'

⁶'A man came to meet us,' they replied. 'And he said to us, "Go back to the king who sent you and tell him, 'This is what the LORD says: is it because there is no God in Israel that you are sending messengers to consult Baal-Zebub, the god of Ekron? Therefore you will not leave the bed you are lying on. You will certainly die!'"'

⁷The king asked them, 'What kind of man was it who came to meet you and told you this?'

⁸They replied, 'He had a garment of hair*a* and had a leather belt round his waist.'

The king said, 'That was Elijah the Tishbite.'

⁹Then he sent to Elijah a captain with his company of fifty men. The captain went up to Elijah, who was sitting on the top of a hill, and said to him, 'Man of God, the king says, "Come down!"'

¹⁰Elijah answered the captain, 'If I am a man of God, may fire come down from heaven and consume you and your fifty men!' Then the fire fell from heaven and consumed the captain and his men.

¹¹At this the king sent to Elijah another captain with his fifty men. The captain said to him, 'Man of God, this is what the king says, "Come down at once!"'

¹²'If I am a man of God,' Elijah replied, 'may fire come down from heaven and consume you and your fifty men!' Then the fire of God fell from heaven and consumed him and his fifty men.

¹³So the king sent a third captain with his fifty men. This third captain went up and fell on his knees before Elijah. 'Man of God,' he begged, 'please have respect for my life and the lives of these fifty men, your servants! ¹⁴See, fire has fallen from heaven and consumed the first two captains and all their men. But now have respect for my life!'

¹⁵The angel of the LORD said to Elijah, 'Go down with him; do not be afraid of him.' So Elijah got up and went down with him to the king.

¹⁶He told the king, 'This is what the LORD says: is it because there is no God in Israel for you to consult that you have sent messengers to consult Baal-Zebub, the god of Ekron? Because you have done this, you will never leave the bed you are lying on. You will certainly die!' ¹⁷So he died, according to the word of the LORD that Elijah had spoken.

Because Ahaziah had no son, Joram*b* succeeded him as king in the second year of Jehoram son of Jehoshaphat king of Judah. ¹⁸As for all the other events of Ahaziah's reign, and what he did, are they not written in the book of the annals of the kings of Israel?

Elijah taken up to heaven

2 When the LORD was about to take Elijah up to heaven in a whirlwind, Elijah and Elisha were on their way from Gilgal. ²Elijah said to Elisha, 'Stay here; the LORD has sent me to Bethel.'

But Elisha said, 'As surely as the LORD lives and as you live, I will not leave you.' So they went down to Bethel.

³The company of the prophets at Bethel came out to Elisha and asked, 'Do you know that the LORD is going to take your master from you today?'

'Yes, I know,' Elisha replied, 'so be quiet.'

---

a 8 Or *He was a hairy man*   *b* 17 Hebrew *Jehoram,* a variant of *Joram*

⁴Then Elijah said to him, 'Stay here, Elisha; the LORD has sent me to Jericho.'

And he replied, 'As surely as the LORD lives and as you live, I will not leave you.' So they went to Jericho.

⁵The company of the prophets at Jericho went up to Elisha and asked him, 'Do you know that the LORD is going to take your master from you today?'

'Yes, I know,' he replied, 'so be quiet.'

⁶Then Elijah said to him, 'Stay here; the LORD has sent me to the Jordan.'

And he replied, 'As surely as the LORD lives and as you live, I will not leave you.' So the two of them walked on.

⁷Fifty men from the company of the prophets went and stood at a distance, facing the place where Elijah and Elisha had stopped at the Jordan. ⁸Elijah took his cloak, rolled it up and struck the water

FRIENDSHIP 2

Elijah and Elisha – passing on the baton

Elijah was a prophet and before he died God told him to set apart Elisha as his successor.

From the time of that anointing, Elisha was completely committed to Elijah. He left his family and burned his ploughing equipment, completely cutting himself off from his old life to follow Elijah (1 Kings 19:19–21). He would not be parted from Elijah, promising never to leave him (2 Kings 2:4), but here we read about the end of Elijah's life. When Elisha asks for a double portion of Elijah's spirit when he's gone (v. 9), he's not asking to be twice as powerful as Elijah, but is referring to an inheritance law which states that the son who receives a double portion is the rightful heir. Elisha didn't want Elijah's money as an inheritance: he wanted to receive the right to continue his work for the Lord.

Elijah and Elisha shared the same passion and calling and worked closely alongside each other, the younger prophet learning from the older and more experienced one. When you know some of the things God is calling you to do, one of the best ways you can grow in your gift is to find someone who has been doing similar things and ask them to let you learn from them and perhaps let you follow them in their job or passion. If they are willing to be open, ask them about their journey, learn from their mistakes and find out how they think you can develop and grow in the gifts God has given you. Likewise, if there is an area in which you have seen God help you to grow, look out for others who have similar passions and who might appreciate you talking to them about it. Even if you have only been learning for a year longer than they have, they might find it really helpful to spend time together, discussing your shared passions, practising your gifts and growing together. Part of being the body of Christ is to encourage each other, driving one another on in our journeys with God and passing the baton on, just as Elijah did with Elisha.

Ali Martin

 Exodus 18   Ruth 1:8–18 ▶▶

with it. The water divided to the right and to the left, and the two of them crossed over on dry ground.

⁹When they had crossed, Elijah said to Elisha, 'Tell me, what can I do for you before I am taken from you?'

'Let me inherit a double portion of your spirit,' Elisha replied.

¹⁰'You have asked a difficult thing,' Elijah said, 'yet if you see me when I am taken from you, it will be yours – otherwise, it will not.'

¹¹As they were walking along and talking together, suddenly a chariot of fire and horses of fire appeared and separated the two of them, and Elijah went up to heaven in a whirlwind. ¹²Elisha saw this and cried out, 'My father! My father! The chariots and horsemen of Israel!' And Elisha saw him no more. Then he took hold of his garment and tore it in two.

¹³Elisha then picked up Elijah's cloak that had fallen from him and went back and stood on the bank of the Jordan. ¹⁴He took the cloak that had fallen from Elijah and struck the water with it. 'Where now is the LORD, the God of Elijah?' he asked. When he struck the water, it divided to the right and to the left, and he crossed over.

¹⁵The company of the prophets from Jericho, who were watching, said, 'The spirit of Elijah is resting on Elisha.' And they went to meet him and bowed to the ground before him. ¹⁶'Look,' they said, 'we your servants have fifty able men. Let them go and look for your master. Perhaps the Spirit of the LORD has picked him up and set him down on some mountain or in some valley.'

'No,' Elisha replied, 'do not send them.'

¹⁷But they persisted until he was too embarrassed to refuse. So he said, 'Send them.' And they sent fifty men, who searched for three days but did not find him. ¹⁸When they returned to Elisha, who was staying in Jericho, he said to them, 'Didn't I tell you not to go?'

Healing of the water

¹⁹The people of the city said to Elisha, 'Look, our lord, this town is well situated, as you can see, but the water is bad and the land is unproductive.'

²⁰'Bring me a new bowl,' he said, 'and put salt in it.' So they brought it to him. ²¹Then he went out to the spring and threw the salt into it, saying, 'This is what the LORD says: "I have healed this water. Never again will it cause death or make the land unproductive."' ²²And the water has remained pure to this day, according to the word Elisha had spoken.

Elisha is jeered

²³From there Elisha went up to Bethel. As he was walking along the road, some boys came out of the town and jeered at him. 'Get out of here, baldy!' they said. 'Get out of here, baldy!' ²⁴He turned round, looked at them and called down a curse on them in the name of the LORD. Then two bears came out of the woods and mauled forty-two of the boys. ²⁵And he went on to Mount Carmel and from there returned to Samaria.

Moab revolts

3 Joram*ᵃ* son of Ahab became king of Israel in Samaria in the eighteenth year of Jehoshaphat king of Judah, and he reigned for twelve years. ²He did evil in the eyes of the LORD, but not as his father and mother had done. He got rid of the sacred stone of Baal that his father had made. ³Nevertheless he clung to the sins of Jeroboam son of Nebat, which he had caused Israel to commit; he did not turn away from them.

⁴Now Mesha king of Moab raised sheep, and he had to pay the king of Israel a tribute of a hundred thousand lambs and the wool of a hundred thousand rams. ⁵But after Ahab died, the king of Moab rebelled against the king of Israel. ⁶So at that time King Joram set out from Samaria and mobilised all Israel. ⁷He also sent this message to Jehoshaphat king of Judah: 'The king of Moab has rebelled against me. Will you go with me to fight against Moab?'

'I will go with you,' he replied. 'I am as

---

a 1 Hebrew *Jehoram*, a variant of *Joram*; also in verse 6 you are, my people as your people, my horses as your horses.'

8 'By what route shall we attack?' he asked.

'Through the Desert of Edom,' he answered.

9 So the king of Israel set out with the king of Judah and the king of Edom. After a roundabout march of seven days, the army had no more water for themselves or for the animals with them.

10 'What!' exclaimed the king of Israel. 'Has the LORD called us three kings together only to deliver us into the hands of Moab?'

11 But Jehoshaphat asked, 'Is there no prophet of the LORD here, through whom we may enquire of the LORD?'

An officer of the king of Israel answered, 'Elisha son of Shaphat is here. He used to pour water on the hands of Elijah.'[b]

12 Jehoshaphat said, 'The word of the LORD is with him.' So the king of Israel and Jehoshaphat and the king of Edom went down to him.

13 Elisha said to the king of Israel, 'Why do you want to involve me? Go to the prophets of your father and the prophets of your mother.'

'No,' the king of Israel answered, 'because it was the LORD who called us three kings together to deliver us into the hands of Moab.'

14 Elisha said, 'As surely as the LORD Almighty lives, whom I serve, if I did not have respect for the presence of Jehoshaphat king of Judah, I would not pay any attention to you. 15 But now bring me a harpist.'

While the harpist was playing, the hand of the LORD came on Elisha 16 and he said, 'This is what the LORD says: I will fill this valley with pools of water. 17 For this is what the LORD says: you will see neither wind nor rain, yet this valley will be filled with water, and you, your cattle and your other animals will drink. 18 This is an easy thing in the eyes of the LORD; he will also deliver Moab into your hands. 19 You will overthrow every fortified city and every major town. You will cut down every good tree, block up all the springs, and ruin every good field with stones.'

20 The next morning, about the time for offering the sacrifice, there it was – water flowing from the direction of Edom! And the land was filled with water.

21 Now all the Moabites had heard that the kings had come to fight against them; so every man, young and old, who could bear arms was called up and stationed on the border. 22 When they got up early in the morning, the sun was shining on the water. To the Moabites across the way, the water looked red – like blood. 23 'That's blood!' they said. 'Those kings must have fought and slaughtered each other. Now to the plunder, Moab!'

24 But when the Moabites came to the camp of Israel, the Israelites rose up and fought them until they fled. And the Israelites invaded the land and slaughtered the Moabites. 25 They destroyed the towns, and each man threw a stone on every good field until it was covered. They stopped up all the springs and cut down every good tree. Only Kir Hareseth was left with its stones in place, but men armed with slings surrounded it and attacked it.

26 When the king of Moab saw that the battle had gone against him, he took with him seven hundred swordsmen to break through to the king of Edom, but they failed. 27 Then he took his firstborn son, who was to succeed him as king, and offered him as a sacrifice on the city wall. The fury against Israel was great; they withdrew and returned to their own land.

The widow's olive oil

4 The wife of a man from the company of the prophets cried out to Elisha, 'Your servant my husband is dead, and you know that he revered the LORD. But now his creditor is coming to take my two boys as his slaves.'

2 Elisha replied to her, 'How can I help you? Tell me, what do you have in your house?'

'Your servant has nothing there at all,' she said, 'except a small jar of olive oil.'

3 Elisha said, 'Go round and ask all your

---

b 11 That is, he was Elijah's personal servant.

neighbours for empty jars. Don't ask for just a few. ⁴Then go inside and shut the door behind you and your sons. Pour oil into all the jars, and as each is filled, put it to one side.'

⁵She left him and shut the door behind her and her sons. They brought the jars to her and she kept pouring. ⁶When all the jars were full, she said to her son, 'Bring me another one.'

But he replied, 'There is not a jar left.' Then the oil stopped flowing.

⁷She went and told the man of God, and he said, 'Go, sell the oil and pay your debts. You and your sons can live on what is left.'

The Shunammite's son restored to life

⁸One day Elisha went to Shunem. And a well-to-do woman was there, who urged him to stay for a meal. So whenever he passed by, he stopped there to eat. ⁹She said to her husband, 'I know that this man who often comes our way is a holy man of God. ¹⁰Let's make a small room on the roof and put in it a bed and a table, a chair and a lamp for him. Then he can stay there whenever he comes to us.'

¹¹One day when Elisha came, he went up to his room and lay down there. ¹²He said to his servant Gehazi, 'Call the Shunammite.' So he called her, and she stood before him. ¹³Elisha said to him, 'Tell her, "You have gone to all this trouble for us. Now what can be done for you? Can we speak on your behalf to the king or the commander of the army?"'

She replied, 'I have a home among my own people.'

¹⁴'What can be done for her?' Elisha asked.

Gehazi said, 'She has no son, and her husband is old.'

¹⁵Then Elisha said, 'Call her.' So he called her, and she stood in the doorway. ¹⁶'About this time next year,' Elisha said, 'you will hold a son in your arms.'

'No, my lord!' she objected. 'Please, man of God, don't mislead your servant!'

¹⁷But the woman became pregnant, and the next year about that same time

she gave birth to a son, just as Elisha had told her.

¹⁸The child grew, and one day he went out to his father, who was with the reapers. ¹⁹He said to his father, 'My head! My head!'

His father told a servant, 'Carry him to his mother.' ²⁰After the servant had lifted him up and carried him to his mother, the boy sat on her lap until noon, and then he died. ²¹She went up and laid him on the bed of the man of God, then shut the door and went out.

²²She called her husband and said, 'Please send me one of the servants and a donkey so I can go to the man of God quickly and return.'

²³'Why go to him today?' he asked. 'It's not the New Moon or the Sabbath.'

'That's all right,' she said.

²⁴She saddled the donkey and said to her servant, 'Lead on; don't slow down for me unless I tell you.' ²⁵So she set out and came to the man of God at Mount Carmel.

When he saw her in the distance, the man of God said to his servant Gehazi, 'Look! There's the Shunammite! ²⁶Run to meet her and ask her, "Are you all right? Is your husband all right? Is your child all right?"'

'Everything is all right,' she said.

²⁷When she reached the man of God at the mountain, she took hold of his feet. Gehazi came over to push her away, but the man of God said, 'Leave her alone! She is in bitter distress, but the LORD has hidden it from me and has not told me why.'

²⁸'Did I ask you for a son, my lord?' she said. 'Didn't I tell you, "Don't raise my hopes"?'

²⁹Elisha said to Gehazi, 'Tuck your cloak into your belt, take my staff in your hand and run. Don't greet anyone you meet, and if anyone greets you, do not answer. Lay my staff on the boy's face.'

³⁰But the child's mother said, 'As surely as the LORD lives and as you live, I will not leave you.' So he got up and followed her.

³¹Gehazi went on ahead and laid the staff on the boy's face, but there was no sound or response. So Gehazi went back

to meet Elisha and told him, 'The boy has not awakened.'

32 When Elisha reached the house, there was the boy lying dead on his couch. 33 He went in, shut the door on the two of them and prayed to the LORD. 34 Then he got on the bed and lay on the boy, mouth to mouth, eyes to eyes, hands to hands. As he stretched himself out on him, the boy's body grew warm. 35 Elisha turned away and walked back and forth in the room and then got onto the bed and stretched out on him once more. The boy sneezed seven times and opened his eyes.

36 Elisha summoned Gehazi and said, 'Call the Shunammite.' And he did. When she came, he said, 'Take your son.' 37 She came in, fell at his feet and bowed to the ground. Then she took her son and went out.

Death in the pot

38 Elisha returned to Gilgal and there was a famine in that region. While the company of the prophets was meeting with him, he said to his servant, 'Put on the large pot and cook some stew for these prophets.'

39 One of them went out into the fields to gather herbs and found a wild gourd plant and picked as many of its gourds as his garment could hold. When he returned, he cut them up into the pot of stew, though no one knew what they were. 40 The stew was poured out for the men, but as they began to eat it, they cried out, 'Man of God, there is death in the pot!' And they could not eat it.

41 Elisha said, 'Get some flour.' He put it into the pot and said, 'Serve it to the people to eat.' And there was nothing harmful in the pot.

Feeding of a hundred

42 A man came from Baal Shalishah, bringing the man of God twenty loaves of barley bread baked from the first ripe corn, along with some ears of new corn. 'Give it to the people to eat,' Elisha said.

43 'How can I set this before a hundred men?' his servant asked.

But Elisha answered, 'Give it to the people to eat. For this is what the LORD says: "They will eat and have some left over."' 44 Then he set it before them, and they ate and had some left over, according to the word of the LORD.

Naaman healed of leprosy

5 Now Naaman was commander of the army of the king of Aram. He was a great man in the sight of his master and highly regarded, because through him the LORD had given victory to Aram. He was a valiant soldier, but he had leprosy.*a*

2 Now bands of raiders from Aram had gone out and had taken captive a young girl from Israel, and she served Naaman's wife. 3 She said to her mistress, 'If only my master would see the prophet who is in Samaria! He would cure him of his leprosy.'

4 Naaman went to his master and told him what the girl from Israel had said. 5 'By all means, go,' the king of Aram replied. 'I will send a letter to the king of Israel.' So Naaman left, taking with him ten talents*b* of silver, six thousand shekels*c* of gold and ten sets of clothing. 6 The letter that he took to the king of Israel read: 'With this letter I am sending my servant Naaman to you so that you may cure him of his leprosy.'

7 As soon as the king of Israel read the letter, he tore his robes and said, 'Am I God? Can I kill and bring back to life? Why does this fellow send someone to me to be cured of his leprosy? See how he is trying to pick a quarrel with me!'

8 When Elisha the man of God heard that the king of Israel had torn his robes, he sent him this message: 'Why have you torn your robes? Make the man come to me and he will know that there is a prophet in Israel.' 9 So Naaman went with his horses and chariots and stopped at the door of Elisha's house. 10 Elisha sent a messenger to say to him, 'Go, wash yourself seven

---

a 1   The Hebrew for *leprosy* was used for various diseases affecting the skin; also in verses 3, 6, 7, 11 and 27.

b 5   That is, about 340 kilograms

c 5   That is, about 69 kilograms

HEALING & MIRACLES 3

Healing isn't a formula

In the Bible, and today, healing doesn't always happen in the same way every time.

We will never be able to have everything figured out when it comes to ministry. God wants ministry to flow from our relationship with him rather than following a formula of what we have seen in the past.

Naaman was a powerful commander in the army, but with a very painful problem: he had leprosy. At that time, leprosy was a very embarrassing disease to have. God is going to send help for Naaman, but Naaman is going to have to make the choice to listen to God.

God sends a servant girl to give the message of hope to Naaman. This will be his first choice, to humble himself to listen to someone who is just a servant. Many times God will send the most powerful words into our lives through someone we would never have considered. It's never about the messenger, but always about the message.

Sometimes God will ask us to do things that don't really seem to make much sense. But sometimes when we know too much (or think we do), it can keep us from knowing or seeing more of God. Sometimes we have to get past the package God uses to send his message.

God has often asked me to do something that didn't make any sense whatsoever! But we are faced with a choice: will we obey? It's always in obedience – not understanding – that blessing can be released.

When Naaman listened, healing took place. And God didn't just restore Naaman to how he was before; God made his body even better than before.

During the birth of my son John, I broke my tailbone. It was horrible. I had just experienced one of my greatest joys, yet I couldn't do all I wanted to. John's birth was a promise not only to me personally, but also to our family. It was super-frustrating for so many reasons. I remember one night I felt that the Lord wanted me to go to home group. I was not in the mood to go anywhere. I remember sitting there, and instead of worshipping I felt more like complaining. In the midst of my complaining, I felt something click. Then I noticed: all the pain was gone! I was shocked. Here I was complaining about my pain, and still God healed me. It didn't make sense at all that God would do this for me.

Healing will often come through ways and people we may not have planned, but we always face a choice. We can choose to listen when God sends a message. Don't allow yourself to live in a place of not understanding, but rather in a place of trusting.

Christy Wimber

 1 Peter 2:24   Matthew 17:20–21

times in the Jordan, and your flesh will be restored and you will be cleansed.'

¹¹ But Naaman went away angry and said, 'I thought that he would surely come out to me and stand and call on the name of the LORD his God, wave his hand over the spot and cure me of my leprosy. ¹² Are not Abana and Pharpar, the rivers of Damascus, better than all the waters of Israel? Couldn't I wash in them and be cleansed?' So he turned and went off in a rage.

¹³ Naaman's servants went to him and said, 'My father, if the prophet had told you to do some great thing, would you not have done it? How much more, then, when he tells you, "Wash and be cleansed"!' ¹⁴ So he went down and dipped himself in the Jordan seven times, as the man of God had told him, and his flesh was restored and became clean like that of a young boy.

¹⁵ Then Naaman and all his attendants went back to the man of God. He stood before him and said, 'Now I know that there is no God in all the world except in Israel. So please accept a gift from your servant.'

¹⁶ The prophet answered, 'As surely as the LORD lives, whom I serve, I will not accept a thing.' And even though Naaman urged him, he refused.

¹⁷ 'If you will not,' said Naaman, 'please let me, your servant, be given as much earth as a pair of mules can carry, for your servant will never again make burnt offerings and sacrifices to any other god but the LORD. ¹⁸ But may the LORD forgive your servant for this one thing: when my master enters the temple of Rimmon to bow down and he is leaning on my arm and I have to bow there also – when I bow down in the temple of Rimmon, may the LORD forgive your servant for this.'

¹⁹ 'Go in peace,' Elisha said.

After Naaman had travelled some distance, ²⁰ Gehazi, the servant of Elisha the man of God, said to himself, 'My master was too easy on Naaman, this Aramean, by not accepting from him what he brought. As surely as the LORD lives, I will run after him and get something from him.'

²¹ So Gehazi hurried after Naaman. When Naaman saw him running towards him, he got down from the chariot to meet him. 'Is everything all right?' he asked.

²² 'Everything is all right,' Gehazi answered. 'My master sent me to say, "Two young men from the company of the prophets have just come to me from the hill country of Ephraim. Please give them a talent[d] of silver and two sets of clothing."'

²³ 'By all means, take two talents,' said Naaman. He urged Gehazi to accept them, and then tied up the two talents of silver in two bags, with two sets of clothing. He gave them to two of his servants, and they carried them ahead of Gehazi. ²⁴ When Gehazi came to the hill, he took the things from the servants and put them away in the house. He sent the men away and they left.

²⁵ When he went in and stood before his master, Elisha asked him, 'Where have you been, Gehazi?'

'Your servant didn't go anywhere,' Gehazi answered.

²⁶ But Elisha said to him, 'Was not my spirit with you when the man got down from his chariot to meet you? Is this the time to take money or to accept clothes – or olive groves and vineyards, or flocks and herds, or male and female slaves? ²⁷ Naaman's leprosy will cling to you and to your descendants for ever.' Then Gehazi went from Elisha's presence and his skin was leprous – it had become as white as snow.

An axe-head floats

6 The company of the prophets said to Elisha, 'Look, the place where we meet with you is too small for us. ² Let us go to the Jordan, where each of us can get a pole; and let us build a place there for us to meet.'

And he said, 'Go.'

³ Then one of them said, 'Won't you please come with your servants?'

'I will,' Elisha replied. ⁴ And he went with them.

They went to the Jordan and began

---

d 22 That is, about 34 kilograms

to cut down trees. ⁵As one of them was cutting down a tree, the iron axe-head fell into the water. 'Oh no, my lord!' he cried out. 'It was borrowed!'

⁶The man of God asked, 'Where did it fall?' When he showed him the place, Elisha cut a stick and threw it there, and made the iron float. ⁷'Lift it out,' he said. Then the man reached out his hand and took it.

Elisha traps blinded Arameans

⁸Now the king of Aram was at war with Israel. After conferring with his officers, he said, 'I will set up my camp in such and such a place.'

⁹The man of God sent word to the king of Israel: 'Beware of passing that place, because the Arameans are going down there.' ¹⁰So the king of Israel checked on the place indicated by the man of God. Time and again Elisha warned the king, so that he was on his guard in such places.

¹¹This enraged the king of Aram. He summoned his officers and demanded of them, 'Tell me! Which of us is on the side of the king of Israel?'

¹²'None of us, my lord the king,' said one of his officers, 'but Elisha, the prophet who is in Israel, tells the king of Israel the very words you speak in your bedroom.'

¹³'Go, find out where he is,' the king ordered, 'so that I can send men and capture him.' The report came back: 'He is in Dothan.' ¹⁴Then he sent horses and chariots and a strong force there. They went by night and surrounded the city.

¹⁵When the servant of the man of God got up and went out early the next morning, an army with horses and chariots had surrounded the city. 'Oh no, my lord! What shall we do?' the servant asked.

¹⁶'Don't be afraid,' the prophet answered. 'Those who are with us are more than those who are with them.'

¹⁷And Elisha prayed, 'Open his eyes, LORD, so that he may see.' Then the LORD opened the servant's eyes, and he looked and saw the hills full of horses and chariots of fire all round Elisha.

¹⁸As the enemy came down towards him, Elisha prayed to the LORD, 'Strike this army with blindness.' So he struck them with blindness, as Elisha had asked.

¹⁹Elisha told them, 'This is not the road and this is not the city. Follow me, and I will lead you to the man you are looking for.' And he led them to Samaria.

²⁰After they entered the city, Elisha said, 'LORD, open the eyes of these men so that they can see.' Then the LORD opened their eyes and they looked, and there they were, inside Samaria.

²¹When the king of Israel saw them, he asked Elisha, 'Shall I kill them, my father? Shall I kill them?'

²²'Do not kill them,' he answered. 'Would you kill those you have captured with your own sword or bow? Set food and water before them so that they may eat and drink and then go back to their master.' ²³So he prepared a great feast for them, and after they had finished eating and drinking, he sent them away, and they returned to their master. So the bands from Aram stopped raiding Israel's territory.

Famine in besieged Samaria

²⁴Some time later, Ben-Hadad king of Aram mobilised his entire army and marched up and laid siege to Samaria. ²⁵There was a great famine in the city; the siege lasted so long that a donkey's head sold for eighty shekels*a* of silver, and a quarter of a cab*b* of seed pods*c* for five shekels.*d*

²⁶As the king of Israel was passing by on the wall, a woman cried to him, 'Help me, my lord the king!'

²⁷The king replied, 'If the LORD does not help you, where can I get help for you? From the threshing floor? From the winepress?' ²⁸Then he asked her, 'What's the matter?'

She answered, 'This woman said to me, "Give up your son so that we may eat him today, and tomorrow we'll eat my son." ²⁹So we cooked my son and ate him. The next day I said to her, "Give up your son so

---

a 25 That is, about 920 grams
b 25 That is, probably about 100 grams
c 25 Or *of doves' dung*
d 25 That is, about 58 grams

that we may eat him," but she had hidden him.'

³⁰When the king heard the woman's words, he tore his robes. As he went along the wall, the people looked, and they saw that, under his robes, he had sackcloth on his body. ³¹He said, 'May God deal with me, be it ever so severely, if the head of Elisha son of Shaphat remains on his shoulders today!'

³²Now Elisha was sitting in his house, and the elders were sitting with him. The king sent a messenger ahead, but before he arrived, Elisha said to the elders, 'Don't you see how this murderer is sending someone to cut off my head? Look, when the messenger comes, shut the door and hold it shut against him. Is not the sound of his master's footsteps behind him?' ³³While he was still talking to them, the messenger came down to him.

The king said, 'This disaster is from the LORD. Why should I wait for the LORD any longer?'

7 Elisha replied, 'Hear the word of the LORD. This is what the LORD says: about this time tomorrow, a seah*ᵃ* of the finest flour will sell for a shekel*ᵇ* and two seahs*ᶜ* of barley for a shekel at the gate of Samaria.'

²The officer on whose arm the king was leaning said to the man of God, 'Look, even if the LORD should open the floodgates of the heavens, could this happen?'

'You will see it with your own eyes,' answered Elisha, 'but you will not eat any of it!'

The siege lifted

³Now there were four men with leprosy*ᵈ* at the entrance of the city gate. They said to each other, 'Why stay here until we die? ⁴If we say, "We'll go into the city" – the famine is there, and we will die. And if we stay here, we will die. So let's go over

to the camp of the Arameans and surrender. If they spare us, we live; if they kill us, then we die.'

⁵At dusk they got up and went to the camp of the Arameans. When they reached the edge of the camp, no one was there, ⁶for the Lord had caused the Arameans to hear the sound of chariots and horses and a great army, so that they said to one another, 'Look, the king of Israel has hired the Hittite and Egyptian kings to attack us!' ⁷So they got up and fled in the dusk and abandoned their tents and their horses and donkeys. They left the camp as it was and ran for their lives.

⁸The men who had leprosy reached the edge of the camp, entered one of the tents and ate and drank. Then they took silver, gold and clothes, and went off and hid them. They returned and entered another tent and took some things from it and hid them also.

⁹Then they said to each other, 'What we're doing is not right. This is a day of good news and we are keeping it to ourselves. If we wait until daylight, punishment will overtake us. Let's go at once and report this to the royal palace.'

¹⁰So they went and called out to the city gatekeepers and told them, 'We went into the Aramean camp and no one was there – not a sound of anyone – only tethered horses and donkeys, and the tents left just as they were.' ¹¹The gatekeepers shouted the news, and it was reported within the palace.

¹²The king got up in the night and said to his officers, 'I will tell you what the Arameans have done to us. They know we are starving; so they have left the camp to hide in the countryside, thinking, "They will surely come out, and then we will take them alive and get into the city."'

¹³One of his officers answered, 'Make some men take five of the horses that are left in the city. Their plight will be like that of all the Israelites left here – yes, they will only be like all these Israelites who are doomed. So let us send them to find out what happened.'

¹⁴So they selected two chariots with their horses, and the king sent them after

*ᵃ*1 That is, probably about 5.5 kilograms of flour; also in verses 16 and 18
*ᵇ*1 That is, about 12 grams; also in verses 16 and 18
*ᶜ*1 That is, probably about 9 kilograms of barley; also in verses 16 and 18
*ᵈ*3 The Hebrew for *leprosy* was used for various diseases affecting the skin; also in verse 8.

the Aramean army. He commanded the drivers, 'Go and find out what has happened.' ¹⁵They followed them as far as the Jordan, and they found the whole road strewn with the clothing and equipment the Arameans had thrown away in their headlong flight. So the messengers returned and reported to the king. ¹⁶Then the people went out and plundered the camp of the Arameans. So a seah of the finest flour sold for a shekel, and two seahs of barley sold for a shekel, as the LORD had said.

¹⁷Now the king had put the officer on whose arm he leaned in charge of the gate, and the people trampled him in the gateway, and he died, just as the man of God had foretold when the king came down to his house. ¹⁸It happened as the man of God had said to the king: 'About this time tomorrow, a seah of the finest flour will sell for a shekel and two seahs of barley for a shekel at the gate of Samaria.'

¹⁹The officer had said to the man of God, 'Look, even if the LORD should open the floodgates of the heavens, could this happen?' The man of God had replied, 'You will see it with your own eyes, but you will not eat any of it!' ²⁰And that is exactly what happened to him, for the people trampled him in the gateway, and he died.

The Shunammite's land restored

8 Now Elisha had said to the woman whose son he had restored to life, 'Go away with your family and stay for a while wherever you can, because the LORD has decreed a famine in the land that will last seven years.' ²The woman proceeded to do as the man of God said. She and her family went away and stayed in the land of the Philistines for seven years.

³At the end of the seven years she came back from the land of the Philistines and went to appeal to the king for her house and land. ⁴The king was talking to Gehazi, the servant of the man of God, and had said, 'Tell me about all the great things Elisha has done.' ⁵Just as Gehazi was telling the king how Elisha had restored the dead to life, the woman whose son Elisha had

brought back to life came to appeal to the king for her house and land.

Gehazi said, 'This is the woman, my lord the king, and this is her son whom Elisha restored to life.' ⁶The king asked the woman about it, and she told him.

Then he assigned an official to her case and said to him, 'Give back everything that belonged to her, including all the income from her land from the day she left the country until now.'

Hazael murders Ben-Hadad

⁷Elisha went to Damascus, and Ben-Hadad king of Aram was ill. When the king was told, 'The man of God has come all the way up here,' ⁸he said to Hazael, 'Take a gift with you and go to meet the man of God. Consult the LORD through him; ask him, "Will I recover from this illness?" '

⁹Hazael went to meet Elisha, taking with him as a gift forty camel-loads of all the finest wares of Damascus. He went in and stood before him, and said, 'Your son Ben-Hadad king of Aram has sent me to ask, "Will I recover from this illness?" '

¹⁰Elisha answered, 'Go and say to him, "You will certainly recover." Nevertheless,ᵃ the LORD has revealed to me that he will in fact die.' ¹¹He stared at him with a fixed gaze until Hazael was embarrassed. Then the man of God began to weep.

¹²'Why is my lord weeping?' asked Hazael.

'Because I know the harm you will do to the Israelites,' he answered. 'You will set fire to their fortified places, kill their young men with the sword, dash their little children to the ground, and rip open their pregnant women.'

¹³Hazael said, 'How could your servant, a mere dog, accomplish such a feat?'

'The LORD has shown me that you will become king of Aram,' answered Elisha.

¹⁴Then Hazael left Elisha and returned to his master. When Ben-Hadad asked, 'What did Elisha say to you?' Hazael replied, 'He told me that you would certainly recover.' ¹⁵But the next day he took a thick

---

a 10 The Hebrew may also be read *Go and say, 'You will certainly not recover,'* for.

cloth, soaked it in water and spread it over the king's face, so that he died. Then Hazael succeeded him as king.

Jehoram king of Judah

16 In the fifth year of Joram son of Ahab king of Israel, when Jehoshaphat was king of Judah, Jehoram son of Jehoshaphat began his reign as king of Judah. 17 He was thirty-two years old when he became king, and he reigned in Jerusalem for eight years. 18 He followed the ways of the kings of Israel, as the house of Ahab had done, for he married a daughter of Ahab. He did evil in the eyes of the LORD. 19 Nevertheless, for the sake of his servant David, the LORD was not willing to destroy Judah. He had promised to maintain a lamp for David and his descendants for ever.

20 In the time of Jehoram, Edom rebelled against Judah and set up its own king. 21 So Jehoram*b* went to Zair with all his chariots. The Edomites surrounded him and his chariot commanders, but he rose up and broke through by night; his army, however, fled back home. 22 To this day Edom has been in rebellion against Judah. Libnah revolted at the same time.

23 As for the other events of Jehoram's reign, and all he did, are they not written in the book of the annals of the kings of Judah? 24 Jehoram rested with his ancestors and was buried with them in the City of David. And Ahaziah his son succeeded him as king.

Ahaziah king of Judah

25 In the twelfth year of Joram son of Ahab king of Israel, Ahaziah son of Jehoram king of Judah began to reign. 26 Ahaziah was twenty-two years old when he became king, and he reigned in Jerusalem for one year. His mother's name was Athaliah, a granddaughter of Omri king of Israel. 27 He followed the ways of the house of Ahab and did evil in the eyes of the LORD, as the house of Ahab had done, for he was related by marriage to Ahab's family.

28 Ahaziah went with Joram son of Ahab to war against Hazael king of Aram at Ramoth Gilead. The Arameans wounded Joram; 29 so King Joram returned to Jezreel to recover from the wounds the Arameans had inflicted on him at Ramoth*c* in his battle with Hazael king of Aram.

Then Ahaziah son of Jehoram king of Judah went down to Jezreel to see Joram son of Ahab, because he had been wounded.

FAVOURITE VERSES

Acts 4:29

'Now, Lord, consider their threats and enable your servants to speak your word with great boldness. Stretch out your hand to heal and perform signs and wonders through the name of your holy servant Jesus.' After they prayed, the place where they were meeting was shaken. And they were all filled with the Holy Spirit and spoke the word of God boldly.

I love the fact that, even in the face of persecution, they're not asking for it to stop, but for courage to speak God's word. It's a challenging verse.

Cara, 17

Jehu anointed king of Israel

9 The prophet Elisha summoned a man from the company of the prophets and said to him, 'Tuck your cloak into your belt, take this flask of olive oil with you and go to Ramoth Gilead. 2 When you get there, look for Jehu son of Jehoshaphat, the son of Nimshi. Go to him, get him away from his companions and take him

---

b 21 Hebrew *Joram*, a variant of *Jehoram*; also in verses 23 and 24

c 29 Hebrew *Ramah*, a variant of *Ramoth*

into an inner room. ³Then take the flask and pour the oil on his head and declare, "This is what the LORD says: I anoint you king over Israel." Then open the door and run; don't delay!'

⁴So the young prophet went to Ramoth Gilead. ⁵When he arrived, he found the army officers sitting together. 'I have a message for you, commander,' he said.

'For which of us?' asked Jehu.

'For you, commander,' he replied.

⁶Jehu got up and went into the house. Then the prophet poured the oil on Jehu's head and declared, 'This is what the LORD, the God of Israel, says: "I anoint you king over the LORD's people Israel. ⁷You are to destroy the house of Ahab your master, and I will avenge the blood of my servants the prophets and the blood of all the LORD's servants shed by Jezebel. ⁸The whole house of Ahab will perish. I will cut off from Ahab every last male in Israel – slave or free.ᵃ ⁹I will make the house of Ahab like the house of Jeroboam son of Nebat and like the house of Baasha son of Ahijah. ¹⁰As for Jezebel, dogs will devour her on the plot of ground at Jezreel, and no one will bury her."' Then he opened the door and ran.

¹¹When Jehu went out to his fellow officers, one of them asked him, 'Is everything all right? Why did this maniac come to you?'

'You know the man and the sort of things he says,' Jehu replied.

¹²'That's not true!' they said. 'Tell us.'

Jehu said, 'Here is what he told me: "This is what the LORD says: I anoint you king over Israel."'

¹³They quickly took their cloaks and spread them under him on the bare steps. Then they blew the trumpet and shouted, 'Jehu is king!'

Jehu kills Joram and Ahaziah

¹⁴So Jehu son of Jehoshaphat, the son of Nimshi, conspired against Joram. (Now Joram and all Israel had been defending Ramoth Gilead against Hazael king of Aram, ¹⁵but King Joramᵇ had returned to Jezreel to recover from the wounds the Arameans had inflicted on him in the battle with Hazael king of Aram.) Jehu said, 'If you desire to make me king, don't let anyone slip out of the city to go and tell the news in Jezreel.' ¹⁶Then he got into his chariot and rode to Jezreel, because Joram was resting there and Ahaziah king of Judah had gone down to see him.

¹⁷When the lookout standing on the tower in Jezreel saw Jehu's troops approaching, he called out, 'I see some troops coming.'

'Get a horseman,' Joram ordered. 'Send him to meet them and ask, "Do you come in peace?"'

¹⁸The horseman rode off to meet Jehu and said, 'This is what the king says: "Do you come in peace?"'

'What do you have to do with peace?' Jehu replied. 'Fall in behind me.'

The lookout reported, 'The messenger has reached them, but he isn't coming back.'

¹⁹So the king sent out a second horseman. When he came to them he said, 'This is what the king says: "Do you come in peace?"'

Jehu replied, 'What do you have to do with peace? Fall in behind me.'

²⁰The lookout reported, 'He has reached them, but he isn't coming back either. The driving is like that of Jehu son of Nimshi – he drives like a maniac.'

²¹'Hitch up my chariot,' Joram ordered. And when it was hitched up, Joram king of Israel and Ahaziah king of Judah rode out, each in his own chariot, to meet Jehu. They met him at the plot of ground that had belonged to Naboth the Jezreelite. ²²When Joram saw Jehu he asked, 'Have you come in peace, Jehu?'

'How can there be peace,' Jehu replied, 'as long as all the idolatry and witchcraft of your mother Jezebel abound?'

²³Joram turned about and fled, calling out to Ahaziah, 'Treachery, Ahaziah!'

²⁴Then Jehu drew his bow and shot

ᵃ 8 Or *Israel – every ruler or leader*

ᵇ 15 Hebrew *Jehoram*, a variant of *Joram*; also in verses 17 and 21-24

Joram between the shoulders. The arrow pierced his heart and he slumped down in his chariot. 25 Jehu said to Bidkar, his chariot officer, 'Pick him up and throw him on the field that belonged to Naboth the Jezreelite. Remember how you and I were riding together in chariots behind Ahab his father when the LORD spoke this prophecy against him: 26 "Yesterday I saw the blood of Naboth and the blood of his sons, declares the LORD, and I will surely make you pay for it on this plot of ground, declares the LORD." c Now then, pick him up and throw him on that plot, in accordance with the word of the LORD.'

27 When Ahaziah king of Judah saw what had happened, he fled up the road to Beth Haggan. d Jehu chased him, shouting, 'Kill him too!' They wounded him in his chariot on the way up to Gur near Ibleam, but he escaped to Megiddo and died there. 28 His servants took him by chariot to Jerusalem and buried him with his ancestors in his tomb in the City of David. 29 (In the eleventh year of Joram son of Ahab, Ahaziah had become king of Judah.)

Jezebel killed

30 Then Jehu went to Jezreel. When Jezebel heard about it, she put on eye makeup, arranged her hair and looked out of a window. 31 As Jehu entered the gate, she asked, 'Have you come in peace, you Zimri, you murderer of your master?' e

32 He looked up at the window and called out, 'Who is on my side? Who?' Two or three eunuchs looked down at him. 33 'Throw her down!' Jehu said. So they threw her down, and some of her blood spattered the wall and the horses as they trampled her underfoot.

34 Jehu went in and ate and drank. 'Take care of that cursed woman,' he said, 'and bury her, for she was a king's daughter.' 35 But when they went out to bury her, they found nothing except her skull, her feet and her hands. 36 They went back and told Jehu, who said, 'This is the word of the

LORD that he spoke through his servant Elijah the Tishbite: on the plot of ground at Jezreel dogs will devour Jezebel's flesh. f 37 Jezebel's body will be like dung on the ground in the plot at Jezreel, so that no one will be able to say, "This is Jezebel." '

Ahab's family killed

10 Now there were in Samaria seventy sons of the house of Ahab. So Jehu wrote letters and sent them to Samaria: to the officials of Jezreel, a to the elders and to the guardians of Ahab's children. He said, 2 'You have your master's sons with you and you have chariots and horses, a fortified city and weapons. Now as soon as this letter reaches you, 3 choose the best and most worthy of your master's sons and set him on his father's throne. Then fight for your master's house.'

4 But they were terrified and said, 'If two kings could not resist him, how can we?' 5 So the palace administrator, the city governor, the elders and the guardians sent this message to Jehu: 'We are your servants and we will do anything you say. We will not appoint anyone as king; you do whatever you think best.'

6 Then Jehu wrote them a second letter, saying, 'If you are on my side and will obey me, take the heads of your master's sons and come to me in Jezreel by this time tomorrow.'

Now the royal princes, seventy of them, were with the leading men of the city, who were bringing them up. 7 When the letter arrived, these men took the princes and slaughtered all seventy of them. They put their heads in baskets and sent them to Jehu in Jezreel. 8 When the messenger arrived, he told Jehu, 'They have brought the heads of the princes.'

Then Jehu ordered, 'Put them in two piles at the entrance of the city gate until morning.'

9 The next morning Jehu went out. He stood before all the people and said, 'You are innocent. It was I who conspired

---

c 26　See 1 Kings 21:19.
d 27　Or fled by way of the garden house
e 31　Or 'Was there peace for Zimri, who murdered his master?'

f 36　See 1 Kings 21:23.
a 1　Hebrew; some Septuagint manuscripts and Vulgate of the city

against my master and killed him, but who killed all these? ¹⁰Know, then, that not a word the LORD has spoken against the house of Ahab will fail. The LORD has done what he announced through his servant Elijah.' ¹¹So Jehu killed everyone in Jezreel who remained of the house of Ahab, as well as all his chief men, his close friends and his priests, leaving him no survivor.

¹²Jehu then set out and went towards Samaria. At Beth Eked of the Shepherds, ¹³he met some relatives of Ahaziah king of Judah and asked, 'Who are you?'

They said, 'We are relatives of Ahaziah, and we have come down to greet the families of the king and of the queen mother.'

¹⁴'Take them alive!' he ordered. So they took them alive and slaughtered them by the well of Beth Eked – forty-two of them. He left no survivor.

¹⁵After he left there, he came upon Jehonadab son of Rekab, who was on his way to meet him. Jehu greeted him and said, 'Are you in accord with me, as I am with you?'

'I am,' Jehonadab answered.

'If so,' said Jehu, 'give me your hand.' So he did, and Jehu helped him up into the chariot. ¹⁶Jehu said, 'Come with me and see my zeal for the LORD.' Then he made him ride in his chariot.

¹⁷When Jehu came to Samaria, he killed all who were left there of Ahab's family; he destroyed them, according to the word of the LORD spoken to Elijah.

Servants of Baal killed

¹⁸Then Jehu brought all the people together and said to them, 'Ahab served Baal a little; Jehu will serve him much. ¹⁹Now summon all the prophets of Baal, all his servants and all his priests. See that no one is missing, because I am going to hold a great sacrifice for Baal. Anyone who fails to come will no longer live.' But Jehu was acting deceptively in order to destroy the servants of Baal.

²⁰Jehu said, 'Call an assembly in honour of Baal.' So they proclaimed it. ²¹Then he sent word throughout Israel, and all the servants of Baal came; not one stayed away. They crowded into the temple of Baal until it was full from one end to the other. ²²And Jehu said to the keeper of the wardrobe, 'Bring robes for all the servants of Baal.' So he brought out robes for them.

²³Then Jehu and Jehonadab son of Rekab went into the temple of Baal. Jehu said to the servants of Baal, 'Look around and see that no one who serves the LORD is here with you – only servants of Baal.' ²⁴So they went in to make sacrifices and burnt offerings. Now Jehu had posted eighty men outside with this warning: 'If one of you lets any of the men I am placing in your hands escape, it will be your life for his life.'

²⁵As soon as Jehu had finished making the burnt offering, he ordered the guards and officers: 'Go in and kill them; let no one escape.' So they cut them down with the sword. The guards and officers threw the bodies out and then entered the inner shrine of the temple of Baal. ²⁶They brought the sacred stone out of the temple of Baal and burned it. ²⁷They demolished the sacred stone of Baal and tore down the temple of Baal, and people have used it for a latrine to this day.

²⁸So Jehu destroyed Baal worship in Israel. ²⁹However, he did not turn away from the sins of Jeroboam son of Nebat, which he had caused Israel to commit – the worship of the golden calves at Bethel and Dan.

³⁰The LORD said to Jehu, 'Because you have done well in accomplishing what is right in my eyes and have done to the house of Ahab all I had in mind to do, your descendants will sit on the throne of Israel to the fourth generation.' ³¹Yet Jehu was not careful to keep the law of the LORD, the God of Israel, with all his heart. He did not turn away from the sins of Jeroboam, which he had caused Israel to commit.

³²In those days the LORD began to reduce the size of Israel. Hazael overpowered the Israelites throughout their territory ³³east of the Jordan in all the land of Gilead (the region of Gad, Reuben and Manasseh), from Aroer by the Arnon Gorge through Gilead to Bashan.

34 As for the other events of Jehu's reign, all he did, and all his achievements, are they not written in the book of the annals of the kings of Israel? 35 Jehu rested with his ancestors and was buried in Samaria. And Jehoahaz his son succeeded him as king. 36 The time that Jehu reigned over Israel in Samaria was twenty-eight years.

Athaliah and Joash

11 When Athaliah the mother of Ahaziah saw that her son was dead, she proceeded to destroy the whole royal family. 2 But Jehosheba, the daughter of King Jehoram *a* and sister of Ahaziah, took Joash son of Ahaziah and stole him away from among the royal princes, who were about to be murdered. She put him and his nurse in a bedroom to hide him from Athaliah; so he was not killed. 3 He remained hidden with his nurse at the temple of the LORD for six years while Athaliah ruled the land.

4 In the seventh year Jehoiada sent for the commanders of units of a hundred, the Carites and the guards and had them brought to him at the temple of the LORD. He made a covenant with them and put them under oath at the temple of the LORD. Then he showed them the king's son. 5 He commanded them, saying, 'This is what you are to do: you who are in the three companies that are going on duty on the Sabbath – a third of you guarding the royal palace, 6 a third at the Sur Gate, and a third at the gate behind the guard, who take turns guarding the temple – 7 and you who are in the other two companies that normally go off Sabbath duty are all to guard the temple for the king. 8 Station yourselves round the king, each of you with weapon in hand. Anyone who approaches your ranks *b* is to be put to death. Stay close to the king wherever he goes.'

9 The commanders of units of a hundred did just as Jehoiada the priest ordered. Each one took his men – those who were going on duty on the Sabbath and those who were going off duty – and came to Jehoiada the priest. 10 Then he gave the commanders the spears and shields that had belonged to King David and that were in the temple of the LORD. 11 The guards, each with weapon in hand, stationed themselves round the king – near the altar and the temple, from the south side to the north side of the temple.

12 Jehoiada brought out the king's son and put the crown on him; he presented him with a copy of the covenant and proclaimed him king. They anointed him, and the people clapped their hands and shouted, 'Long live the king!'

13 When Athaliah heard the noise made by the guards and the people, she went to the people at the temple of the LORD. 14 She looked and there was the king, standing by the pillar, as the custom was. The officers and the trumpeters were beside the king, and all the people of the land were rejoicing and blowing trumpets. Then Athaliah tore her robes and called out, 'Treason! Treason!'

15 Jehoiada the priest ordered the commanders of units of a hundred, who were in charge of the troops: 'Bring her out between the ranks *c* and put to the sword anyone who follows her.' For the priest had said, 'She must not be put to death in the temple of the LORD.' 16 So they seized her as she reached the place where the horses enter the palace grounds, and there she was put to death.

17 Jehoiada then made a covenant between the LORD and the king and people that they would be the LORD's people. He also made a covenant between the king and the people. 18 All the people of the land went to the temple of Baal and tore it down. They smashed the altars and idols to pieces and killed Mattan the priest of Baal in front of the altars.

Then Jehoiada the priest posted guards at the temple of the LORD. 19 He took with him the commanders of hundreds, the Carites, the guards and all the people of the land, and together they brought the

---

a 2 Hebrew *Joram*, a variant of *Jehoram*
b 8 Or *approaches the precincts*

c 15 Or *out from the precincts*

king down from the temple of the LORD and went into the palace, entering by way of the gate of the guards. The king then took his place on the royal throne. ²⁰All the people of the land rejoiced, and the city was calm, because Athaliah had been slain with the sword at the palace. ²¹Joash*d* was seven years old when he began his reign.*e*

Joash repairs the temple

12ᵃ In the seventh year of Jehu, Joash*b* became king, and he reigned in Jerusalem for forty years. His mother's name was Zibiah; she was from Beersheba. ²Joash did what was right in the eyes of the LORD all the years Jehoiada the priest instructed him. ³The high places, however, were not removed; the people continued to offer sacrifices and burn incense there.

⁴Joash said to the priests, 'Collect all the money that is brought as sacred offerings to the temple of the LORD – the money collected in the census, the money received from personal vows and the money brought voluntarily to the temple. ⁵Let every priest receive the money from one of the treasurers, then use it to repair whatever damage is found in the temple.'

⁶But by the twenty-third year of King Joash the priests still had not repaired the temple. ⁷Therefore King Joash summoned Jehoiada the priest and the other priests and asked them, 'Why aren't you repairing the damage done to the temple? Take no more money from your treasurers, but hand it over for repairing the temple.' ⁸The priests agreed that they would not collect any more money from the people and that they would not repair the temple themselves.

⁹Jehoiada the priest took a chest and bored a hole in its lid. He placed it beside the altar, on the right side as one enters the temple of the LORD. The priests who guarded the entrance put into the chest all the money that was brought to the temple of the LORD. ¹⁰Whenever they saw that there was a large amount of money in the chest, the royal secretary and the high priest came, counted the money that had been brought into the temple of the LORD and put it into bags. ¹¹When the amount had been determined, they gave the money to the men appointed to supervise the work on the temple. With it they paid those who worked on the temple of the LORD – the carpenters and builders, ¹²the masons and stonecutters. They purchased timber and blocks of dressed stone for the repair of the temple of the LORD, and met all the other expenses of restoring the temple.

¹³The money brought into the temple was not spent for making silver basins, wick trimmers, sprinkling bowls, trumpets or any other articles of gold or silver for the temple of the LORD; ¹⁴it was paid to the workers, who used it to repair the temple. ¹⁵They did not require an accounting from those to whom they gave the money to pay the workers, because they acted with complete honesty. ¹⁶The money from the guilt offerings and sin offerings*c* was not brought into the temple of the LORD; it belonged to the priests.

¹⁷About this time Hazael king of Aram went up and attacked Gath and captured it. Then he turned to attack Jerusalem. ¹⁸But Joash king of Judah took all the sacred objects dedicated by his predecessors – Jehoshaphat, Jehoram and Ahaziah, the kings of Judah – and the gifts he himself had dedicated and all the gold found in the treasuries of the temple of the LORD and of the royal palace, and he sent them to Hazael king of Aram, who then withdrew from Jerusalem.

¹⁹As for the other events of the reign of Joash, and all he did, are they not written in the book of the annals of the kings of Judah? ²⁰His officials conspired against him and assassinated him at Beth Millo, on the road down to Silla. ²¹The officials who murdered him were Jozabad son of

---

d 21 Hebrew *Jehoash*, a variant of *Joash*
e 21 In Hebrew texts this verse (11:21) is numbered 12:1.
a In Hebrew texts 12:1-21 is numbered 12:2-22.
b 1 Hebrew *Jehoash*, a variant of *Joash*; also in verses 2, 4, 6, 7 and 18

c 16 Or *purification offerings*

Shimeath and Jehozabad son of Shomer. He died and was buried with his ancestors in the City of David. And Amaziah his son succeeded him as king.

Jehoahaz king of Israel

13 In the twenty-third year of Joash son of Ahaziah king of Judah, Jehoahaz son of Jehu became king of Israel in Samaria, and he reigned for seventeen years. ² He did evil in the eyes of the LORD by following the sins of Jeroboam son of Nebat, which he had caused Israel to commit, and he did not turn away from them. ³ So the LORD's anger burned against Israel, and for a long time he kept them under the power of Hazael king of Aram and Ben-Hadad his son.

⁴ Then Jehoahaz sought the LORD's favour, and the LORD listened to him, for he saw how severely the king of Aram was oppressing Israel. ⁵ The LORD provided a deliverer for Israel, and they escaped from the power of Aram. So the Israelites lived in their own homes as they had before. ⁶ But they did not turn away from the sins of the house of Jeroboam, which he had caused Israel to commit; they continued in them. Also, the Asherah pole*ᵃ* remained standing in Samaria.

⁷ Nothing had been left of the army of Jehoahaz except fifty horsemen, ten chariots and ten thousand foot soldiers, for the king of Aram had destroyed the rest and made them like the dust at threshing time.

⁸ As for the other events of the reign of Jehoahaz, all he did and his achievements, are they not written in the book of the annals of the kings of Israel? ⁹ Jehoahaz rested with his ancestors and was buried in Samaria. And Jehoash*ᵇ* his son succeeded him as king.

Jehoash king of Israel

¹⁰ In the thirty-seventh year of Joash king of Judah, Jehoash son of Jehoahaz became king of Israel in Samaria, and he reigned for sixteen years. ¹¹ He did evil in the eyes of the LORD and did not turn away from any of the sins of Jeroboam son of Nebat, which he had caused Israel to commit; he continued in them.

¹² As for the other events of the reign of Jehoash, all he did and his achievements, including his war against Amaziah king of Judah, are they not written in the book of the annals of the kings of Israel? ¹³ Jehoash rested with his ancestors, and Jeroboam succeeded him on the throne. Jehoash was buried in Samaria with the kings of Israel.

¹⁴ Now Elisha had been suffering from the illness from which he died. Jehoash king of Israel went down to see him and wept over him. 'My father! My father!' he cried. 'The chariots and horsemen of Israel!'

¹⁵ Elisha said, 'Get a bow and some arrows,' and he did so. ¹⁶ 'Take the bow in your hands,' he said to the king of Israel. When he had taken it, Elisha put his hands on the king's hands.

¹⁷ 'Open the east window,' he said, and he opened it. 'Shoot!' Elisha said, and he shot. 'The LORD's arrow of victory, the arrow of victory over Aram!' Elisha declared. 'You will completely destroy the Arameans at Aphek.'

¹⁸ Then he said, 'Take the arrows,' and the king took them. Elisha told him, 'Strike the ground.' He struck it three times and stopped. ¹⁹ The man of God was angry with him and said, 'You should have struck the ground five or six times; then you would have defeated Aram and completely destroyed it. But now you will defeat it only three times.'

²⁰ Elisha died and was buried.

Now Moabite raiders used to enter the country every spring. ²¹ Once while some Israelites were burying a man, suddenly they saw a band of raiders; so they threw the man's body into Elisha's tomb. When the body touched Elisha's bones, the man came to life and stood up on his feet.

²² Hazael king of Aram oppressed Israel throughout the reign of Jehoahaz. ²³ But the LORD was gracious to them and had compassion and showed concern for

a 6 That is, a wooden symbol of the goddess Asherah; here and elsewhere in 2 Kings
b 9 Hebrew *Joash*, a variant of *Jehoash*; also in verses 12-14 and 25

them because of his covenant with Abraham, Isaac and Jacob. To this day he has been unwilling to destroy them or banish them from his presence.

²⁴Hazael king of Aram died, and Ben-Hadad his son succeeded him as king. ²⁵Then Jehoash son of Jehoahaz recaptured from Ben-Hadad son of Hazael the towns he had taken in battle from his father Jehoahaz. Three times Jehoash defeated him, and so he recovered the Israelite towns.

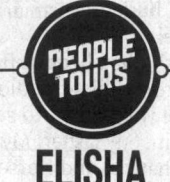

ELISHA

CHOSEN
1 Kings 19:19–21
ELIJAH
2 Kings 2:1–18
NAAMAN
2 Kings 5:1–27
ARMY
2 Kings 6:8–23
DEATH
2 Kings 13:14–21

Amaziah king of Judah

14 In the second year of Jehoash*ᵃ* son of Jehoahaz king of Israel, Amaziah son of Joash king of Judah began to reign. ²He was twenty-five years old when he became king, and he reigned in Jerusalem for twenty-nine years. His mother's name was Jehoaddan; she was from Jerusalem. ³He did what was right in the eyes of the LORD, but not as his father David had done. In everything he followed the example of his father Joash. ⁴The high places, however, were not removed; the people continued to offer sacrifices and burn incense there.

⁵After the kingdom was firmly in his grasp, he executed the officials who had

murdered his father the king. ⁶Yet he did not put the children of the assassins to death, in accordance with what is written in the Book of the Law of Moses where the LORD commanded: 'Parents are not to be put to death for their children, nor children put to death for their parents; each will die for their own sin.'ᵇ

⁷He was the one who defeated ten thousand Edomites in the Valley of Salt and captured Sela in battle, calling it Joktheel, the name it has to this day.

⁸Then Amaziah sent messengers to Jehoash son of Jehoahaz, the son of Jehu, king of Israel, with the challenge: 'Come, let us face each other in battle.'

⁹But Jehoash king of Israel replied to Amaziah king of Judah: 'A thistle in Lebanon sent a message to a cedar in Lebanon, "Give your daughter to my son in marriage." Then a wild beast in Lebanon came along and trampled the thistle underfoot. ¹⁰You have indeed defeated Edom and now you are arrogant. Glory in your victory, but stay at home! Why ask for trouble and cause your own downfall and that of Judah also?'

¹¹Amaziah, however, would not listen, so Jehoash king of Israel attacked. He and Amaziah king of Judah faced each other at Beth Shemesh in Judah. ¹²Judah was routed by Israel, and every man fled to his home. ¹³Jehoash king of Israel captured Amaziah king of Judah, the son of Joash, the son of Ahaziah, at Beth Shemesh. Then Jehoash went to Jerusalem and broke down the wall of Jerusalem from the Ephraim Gate to the Corner Gate – a section about four hundred cubits long.ᶜ ¹⁴He took all the gold and silver and all the articles found in the temple of the LORD and in the treasuries of the royal palace. He also took hostages and returned to Samaria.

¹⁵As for the other events of the reign of Jehoash, what he did and his achievements, including his war against Amaziah king of Judah, are they not written in the book of the annals of the kings of Israel?

---

a 1 Hebrew *Joash*, a variant of *Jehoash*; also in verses 13, 23 and 27

b 6 Deut. 24:16
c 13 That is, about 180 metres

16 Jehoash rested with his ancestors and was buried in Samaria with the kings of Israel. And Jeroboam his son succeeded him as king.

17 Amaziah son of Joash king of Judah lived for fifteen years after the death of Jehoash son of Jehoahaz king of Israel. 18 As for the other events of Amaziah's reign, are they not written in the book of the annals of the kings of Judah?

19 They conspired against him in Jerusalem, and he fled to Lachish, but they sent men after him to Lachish and killed him there. 20 He was brought back by horse and was buried in Jerusalem with his ancestors, in the City of David.

21 Then all the people of Judah took Azariah,d who was sixteen years old, and made him king in place of his father Amaziah. 22 He was the one who rebuilt Elath and restored it to Judah after Amaziah rested with his ancestors.

Jeroboam II king of Israel

23 In the fifteenth year of Amaziah son of Joash king of Judah, Jeroboam son of Jehoash king of Israel became king in Samaria, and he reigned for forty-one years. 24 He did evil in the eyes of the LORD and did not turn away from any of the sins of Jeroboam son of Nebat, which he had caused Israel to commit. 25 He was the one who restored the boundaries of Israel from Lebo Hamath to the Dead Sea,e in accordance with the word of the LORD, the God of Israel, spoken through his servant Jonah son of Amittai, the prophet from Gath Hepher.

26 The LORD had seen how bitterly everyone in Israel, whether slave or free, was suffering;f there was no one to help them. 27 And since the LORD had not said he would blot out the name of Israel from under heaven, he saved them by the hand of Jeroboam son of Jehoash.

28 As for the other events of Jeroboam's reign, all he did, and his military achievements, including how he recovered for Israel both Damascus and Hamath, which had belonged to Judah, are they not written in the book of the annals of the kings of Israel? 29 Jeroboam rested with his ancestors, the kings of Israel. And Zechariah his son succeeded him as king.

Azariah king of Judah

15 In the twenty-seventh year of Jeroboam king of Israel, Azariaha son of Amaziah king of Judah began to reign. 2 He was sixteen years old when he became king, and he reigned in Jerusalem for fifty-two years. His mother's name was Jekoliah; she was from Jerusalem. 3 He did what was right in the eyes of the LORD, just as his father Amaziah had done. 4 The high places, however, were not removed; the people continued to offer sacrifices and burn incense there.

5 The LORD afflicted the king with leprosyb until the day he died, and he lived in a separate house.c Jotham the king's son had charge of the palace and governed the people of the land.

6 As for the other events of Azariah's reign, and all he did, are they not written in the book of the annals of the kings of Judah? 7 Azariah rested with his ancestors and was buried near them in the City of David. And Jotham his son succeeded him as king.

Zechariah king of Israel

8 In the thirty-eighth year of Azariah king of Judah, Zechariah son of Jeroboam became king of Israel in Samaria, and he reigned for six months. 9 He did evil in the eyes of the LORD, as his predecessors had done. He did not turn away from the sins of Jeroboam son of Nebat, which he had caused Israel to commit.

10 Shallum son of Jabesh conspired against Zechariah. He attacked him in front of the people,d assassinated him and succeeded him as king. 11 The other

---

d 21 Also called Uzziah
e 25 Hebrew the Sea of the Arabah
f 26 Or Israel was suffering. They were without a ruler or leader, and

a 1 Also called Uzziah; also in verses 6, 7, 8, 17, 23 and 27
b 5 The Hebrew for leprosy was used for various diseases affecting the skin.
c 5 Or in a house where he was relieved of responsibilities
d 10 Hebrew; some Septuagint manuscripts in Ibleam

events of Zechariah's reign are written in the book of the annals of the kings of Israel. ¹²So the word of the LORD spoken to Jehu was fulfilled: 'Your descendants will sit on the throne of Israel to the fourth generation.'*e*

Shallum king of Israel

¹³Shallum son of Jabesh became king in the thirty-ninth year of Uzziah king of Judah, and he reigned in Samaria for one month. ¹⁴Then Menahem son of Gadi went from Tirzah up to Samaria. He attacked Shallum son of Jabesh in Samaria, assassinated him and succeeded him as king.

¹⁵The other events of Shallum's reign, and the conspiracy he led, are written in the book of the annals of the kings of Israel.

¹⁶At that time Menahem, starting out from Tirzah, attacked Tiphsah and everyone in the city and its vicinity, because they refused to open their gates. He sacked Tiphsah and ripped open all the pregnant women.

Menahem king of Israel

¹⁷In the thirty-ninth year of Azariah king of Judah, Menahem son of Gadi became king of Israel, and he reigned in Samaria for ten years. ¹⁸He did evil in the eyes of the LORD. During his entire reign he did not turn away from the sins of Jeroboam son of Nebat, which he had caused Israel to commit.

¹⁹Then Pul *f* king of Assyria invaded the land, and Menahem gave him a thousand talents*g* of silver to gain his support and strengthen his own hold on the kingdom. ²⁰Menahem exacted this money from Israel. Every wealthy person had to contribute fifty shekels*h* of silver to be given to the king of Assyria. So the king of Assyria withdrew and stayed in the land no longer.

²¹As for the other events of Menahem's reign, and all he did, are they not written in the book of the annals of the kings of Israel? ²²Menahem rested with his ancestors. And Pekahiah his son succeeded him as king.

Pekahiah king of Israel

²³In the fiftieth year of Azariah king of Judah, Pekahiah son of Menahem became king of Israel in Samaria, and he reigned for two years. ²⁴Pekahiah did evil in the eyes of the LORD. He did not turn away from the sins of Jeroboam son of Nebat, which he had caused Israel to commit. ²⁵One of his chief officers, Pekah son of Remaliah, conspired against him. Taking fifty men of Gilead with him, he assassinated Pekahiah, along with Argob and Arieh, in the citadel of the royal palace at Samaria. So Pekah killed Pekahiah and succeeded him as king.

²⁶The other events of Pekahiah's reign, and all he did, are written in the book of the annals of the kings of Israel.

Pekah king of Israel

²⁷In the fifty-second year of Azariah king of Judah, Pekah son of Remaliah became king of Israel in Samaria, and he reigned for twenty years. ²⁸He did evil in the eyes of the LORD. He did not turn away from the sins of Jeroboam son of Nebat, which he had caused Israel to commit.

²⁹In the time of Pekah king of Israel, Tiglath-Pileser king of Assyria came and took Ijon, Abel Beth Maakah, Janoah, Kedesh and Hazor. He took Gilead and Galilee, including all the land of Naphtali, and deported the people to Assyria. ³⁰Then Hoshea son of Elah conspired against Pekah son of Remaliah. He attacked and assassinated him, and then succeeded him as king in the twentieth year of Jotham son of Uzziah.

³¹As for the other events of Pekah's reign, and all he did, are they not written in the book of the annals of the kings of Israel?

Jotham king of Judah

³²In the second year of Pekah son of Remaliah king of Israel, Jotham son of Uzziah king of Judah began to reign. ³³He was twenty-five years old when he became

---

e 12   2 Kings 10:30
f 19   Also called *Tiglath-Pileser*
g 19   That is, about 34 metric tons
h 20   That is, about 575 grams

king, and he reigned in Jerusalem for six-teen years. His mother's name was Jeru-sha daughter of Zadok. ³⁴He did what was right in the eyes of the LORD, just as his fa-ther Uzziah had done. ³⁵The high places, however, were not removed; the people continued to offer sacrifices and burn incense there. Jotham rebuilt the Upper Gate of the temple of the LORD.

³⁶As for the other events of Jotham's reign, and what he did, are they not writ-ten in the book of the annals of the kings of Judah? ³⁷(In those days the LORD be-gan to send Rezin king of Aram and Pekah son of Remaliah against Judah.) ³⁸Jotham rested with his ancestors and was buried with them in the City of David, the city of his father. And Ahaz his son succeeded him as king.

Ahaz king of Judah

16 In the seventeenth year of Pekah son of Remaliah, Ahaz son of Jotham king of Judah began to reign. ²Ahaz was twenty years old when he be-came king, and he reigned in Jerusalem for sixteen years. Unlike David his father, he did not do what was right in the eyes of the LORD his God. ³He followed the ways of the kings of Israel and even sacrificed his son in the fire, engaging in the de-testable practices of the nations the LORD had driven out before the Israelites. ⁴He offered sacrifices and burned incense at the high places, on the hilltops and under every spreading tree.

⁵Then Rezin king of Aram and Pekah son of Remaliah king of Israel marched up to fight against Jerusalem and besieged Ahaz, but they could not overpower him. ⁶At that time, Rezin king of Aram recov-ered Elath for Aram by driving out the peo-ple of Judah. Edomites then moved into Elath and have lived there to this day. ⁷Ahaz sent messengers to say to Tiglath-Pileser king of Assyria, 'I am your servant and vassal. Come up and save me out of the hand of the king of Aram and of the king of Israel, who are attacking me.' ⁸And Ahaz took the silver and gold found in the temple of the LORD and in the treasuries of the royal palace and sent it as a gift to the king of Assyria. ⁹The king of Assyria complied by attacking Damascus and cap-turing it. He deported its inhabitants to Kir and put Rezin to death.

¹⁰Then King Ahaz went to Damascus to meet Tiglath-Pileser king of Assyria. He saw an altar in Damascus and sent to Uriah the priest a sketch of the altar, with detailed plans for its construction. ¹¹So Uriah the priest built an altar in accord-ance with all the plans that King Ahaz had sent from Damascus and finished it before King Ahaz returned. ¹²When the king came back from Damascus and saw the altar, he approached it and presented offerings*ᵃ* on it. ¹³He offered up his burnt offering and grain offering, poured out his drink offering, and splashed the blood of his fellowship offerings against the altar. ¹⁴The bronze altar that stood before the LORD he brought from the front of the temple – from between the new altar and the temple of the LORD – and put it on the north side of the new altar.

¹⁵King Ahaz then gave these orders to Uriah the priest: 'On the large new altar, offer the morning burnt offering and the evening grain offering, the king's burnt offering and his grain offering, and the burnt offering of all the people of the land, and their grain offering and their drink of-fering. Splash against this altar the blood of all the burnt offerings and sacrifices. But I will use the bronze altar for seeking guidance.' ¹⁶And Uriah the priest did just as King Ahaz had ordered.

¹⁷King Ahaz cut off the side panels and removed the basins from the movable stands. He removed the Sea from the bronze bulls that supported it and set it on a stone base. ¹⁸He took away the Sabbath canopy*ᵇ* that had been built at the temple and removed the royal entrance outside the temple of the LORD, in deference to the king of Assyria.

¹⁹As for the other events of the reign of Ahaz, and what he did, are they not written in the book of the annals of the kings of Judah? ²⁰Ahaz rested with his

---

a 12 Or *and went up*
b 18 Or *the dais of his throne* (see Septuagint)

ancestors and was buried with them in the City of David. And Hezekiah his son succeeded him as king.

Hoshea last king of Israel

17 In the twelfth year of Ahaz king of Judah, Hoshea son of Elah became king of Israel in Samaria, and he reigned for nine years. ² He did evil in the eyes of the LORD, but not like the kings of Israel who preceded him.

³ Shalmaneser king of Assyria came up to attack Hoshea, who had been Shalmaneser's vassal and had paid him tribute. ⁴ But the king of Assyria discovered that Hoshea was a traitor, for he had sent envoys to So⁴ king of Egypt, and he no longer paid tribute to the king of Assyria, as he had done year by year. Therefore Shalmaneser seized him and put him in prison. ⁵ The king of Assyria invaded the entire land, marched against Samaria and laid siege to it for three years. ⁶ In the ninth year of Hoshea, the king of Assyria captured Samaria and deported the Israelites to Assyria. He settled them in Halah, in Gozan on the River Habor and in the towns of the Medes.

Israel exiled because of sin

⁷ All this took place because the Israelites had sinned against the LORD their God, who had brought them up out of Egypt from under the power of Pharaoh king of Egypt. They worshipped other gods ⁸ and followed the practices of the nations the LORD had driven out before them, as well as the practices that the kings of Israel had introduced. ⁹ The Israelites secretly did things against the LORD their God that were not right. From watchtower to fortified city they built themselves high places in all their towns. ¹⁰ They set up sacred stones and Asherah poles on every high hill and under every spreading tree. ¹¹ At every high place they burned incense, as the nations whom the LORD had driven out before them had done. They did wicked things that aroused the LORD's anger. ¹² They worshipped idols, though

the LORD had said, 'You shall not do this.'ᵇ ¹³ The LORD warned Israel and Judah through all his prophets and seers: 'Turn from your evil ways. Observe my commands and decrees, in accordance with the entire Law that I commanded your ancestors to obey and that I delivered to you through my servants the prophets.'

¹⁴ But they would not listen and were as stiff-necked as their ancestors, who did not trust in the LORD their God. ¹⁵ They rejected his decrees and the covenant he had made with their ancestors and the statutes he had warned them to keep. They followed worthless idols and themselves became worthless. They imitated the nations around them although the LORD had ordered them, 'Do not do as they do.'

¹⁶ They forsook all the commands of the LORD their God and made for themselves two idols cast in the shape of calves, and an Asherah pole. They bowed down to all the starry hosts, and they worshipped Baal. ¹⁷ They sacrificed their sons and daughters in the fire. They practised divination and sought omens and sold themselves to do evil in the eyes of the LORD, arousing his anger.

¹⁸ So the LORD was very angry with Israel and removed them from his presence. Only the tribe of Judah was left, ¹⁹ and even Judah did not keep the commands of the LORD their God. They followed the practices Israel had introduced. ²⁰ Therefore the LORD rejected all the people of Israel; he afflicted them and gave them into the hands of plunderers, until he thrust them from his presence.

²¹ When he tore Israel away from the house of David, they made Jeroboam son of Nebat their king. Jeroboam enticed Israel away from following the LORD and caused them to commit a great sin. ²² The Israelites persisted in all the sins of Jeroboam and did not turn away from them ²³ until the LORD removed them from his presence, as he had warned through all his servants the prophets. So the people of Israel were taken from their homeland into exile in Assyria, and they are still there.

---

a 4 *So* is probably an abbreviation for *Osorkon*.   *b* 12 Exodus 20:4,5

Samaria resettled

24 The king of Assyria brought people from Babylon, Kuthah, Avva, Hamath and Sepharvaim and settled them in the towns of Samaria to replace the Israelites. They took over Samaria and lived in its towns. 25 When they first lived there, they did not worship the LORD; so he sent lions among them and they killed some of the people. 26 It was reported to the king of Assyria: 'The people you deported and resettled in the towns of Samaria do not know what the god of that country requires. He has sent lions among them, which are killing them off, because the people do not know what he requires.'

27 Then the king of Assyria gave this order: 'Make one of the priests you took captive from Samaria go back to live there and teach the people what the god of the land requires.' 28 So one of the priests who had been exiled from Samaria came to live in Bethel and taught them how to worship the LORD.

29 Nevertheless, each national group made its own gods in the several towns where they settled, and set them up in the shrines a the people of Samaria had made at the high places. 30 The people from Babylon made Sukkoth Benoth, those from Kuthah made Nergal, and those from Hamath made Ashima; 31 the Avvites made Nibhaz and Tartak, and the Sepharvites burned their children in the fire as sacrifices to Adrammelek and Anammelek, the gods of Sepharvaim. 32 They worshipped the LORD, but they also appointed all sorts of their own people to officiate for them as priests in the shrines at the high places. 33 They worshipped the LORD, but they also served their own gods in accordance with the customs of the nations from which they had been brought.

34 To this day they persist in their former practices. They neither worship the LORD nor adhere to the decrees and regulations, the laws and commands that the LORD gave the descendants of Jacob, whom he named Israel. 35 When the LORD made a covenant with the Israelites, he commanded them: 'Do not worship any other gods or bow down to them, serve them

or sacrifice to them. 36 But the LORD, who brought you up out of Egypt with mighty power and outstretched arm, is the one you must worship. To him you shall bow down and to him offer sacrifices. 37 You must always be careful to keep the decrees and regulations, the laws and commands he wrote for you. Do not worship other gods. 38 Do not forget the covenant I have made with you, and do not worship other gods. 39 Rather, worship the LORD your God; it is he who will deliver you from the hand of all your enemies.'

40 They would not listen, however, but persisted in their former practices. 41 Even while these people were worshipping the LORD, they were serving their idols. To this day their children and grandchildren continue to do as their ancestors did.

Hezekiah king of Judah

18 In the third year of Hoshea son of Elah king of Israel, Hezekiah son of Ahaz king of Judah began to reign. 2 He was twenty-five years old when he became king, and he reigned in Jerusalem for twenty-nine years. His mother's name was Abijah a daughter of Zechariah. 3 He did what was right in the eyes of the LORD, just as his father David had done. 4 He removed the high places, smashed the sacred stones and cut down the Asherah poles. He broke into pieces the bronze snake Moses had made, for up to that time the Israelites had been burning incense to it. (It was called Nehushtan. b)

5 Hezekiah trusted in the LORD, the God of Israel. There was no one like him among all the kings of Judah, either before him or after him. 6 He held fast to the LORD and did not stop following him; he kept the commands the LORD had given Moses. 7 And the LORD was with him; he was successful in whatever he undertook. He rebelled against the king of Assyria and did not serve him. 8 From watchtower to fortified city, he defeated the Philistines, as far as Gaza and its territory.

---

a 2 Hebrew *Abi*, a variant of *Abijah*
b 4 *Nehushtan* sounds like the Hebrew for both *bronze* and *snake*.

⁹In King Hezekiah's fourth year, which was the seventh year of Hoshea son of Elah king of Israel, Shalmaneser king of Assyria marched against Samaria and laid siege to it. ¹⁰At the end of three years the Assyrians took it. So Samaria was captured in Hezekiah's sixth year, which was the ninth year of Hoshea king of Israel. ¹¹The king of Assyria deported Israel to Assyria and settled them in Halah, in Gozan on the River Habor and in towns of the Medes. ¹²This happened because they had not obeyed the LORD their God, but had violated his covenant – all that Moses the servant of the LORD commanded. They neither listened to the commands nor carried them out.

¹³In the fourteenth year of King Hezekiah's reign, Sennacherib king of Assyria attacked all the fortified cities of Judah and captured them. ¹⁴So Hezekiah king of Judah sent this message to the king of Assyria at Lachish: 'I have done wrong. Withdraw from me, and I will pay whatever you demand of me.' The king of Assyria exacted from Hezekiah king of Judah three hundred talentsᶜ of silver and thirty talentsᵈ of gold. ¹⁵So Hezekiah gave him all the silver that was found in the temple of the LORD and in the treasuries of the royal palace.

¹⁶At this time Hezekiah king of Judah stripped off the gold with which he had covered the doors and doorposts of the temple of the LORD, and gave it to the king of Assyria.

Sennacherib threatens Jerusalem

¹⁷The king of Assyria sent his supreme commander, his chief officer and his field commander with a large army, from Lachish to King Hezekiah at Jerusalem. They came up to Jerusalem and stopped at the aqueduct of the Upper Pool, on the road to the Washerman's Field. ¹⁸They called for the king; and Eliakim son of Hilkiah the palace administrator, Shebna the secretary, and Joah son of Asaph the recorder went out to them.

¹⁹The field commander said to them, 'Tell Hezekiah:

' "This is what the great king, the king of Assyria, says: on what are you basing this confidence of yours? ²⁰You say you have the counsel and the might for war – but you speak only empty words. On whom are you depending, that you rebel against me? ²¹ Look, I know you are depending on Egypt, that splintered reed of a staff, which pierces the hand of anyone who leans on it! Such is Pharaoh king of Egypt to all who depend on him. ²²But if you say to me, 'We are depending on the LORD our God' – isn't he the one whose high places and altars Hezekiah removed, saying to Judah and Jerusalem, 'You must worship before this altar in Jerusalem'?

²³ ' "Come now, make a bargain with my master, the king of Assyria: I will give you two thousand horses – if you can put riders on them! ²⁴How can you repulse one officer of the least of my master's officials, even though you are depending on Egypt for chariots and horsemenᵉ? ²⁵Furthermore, have I come to attack and destroy this place without word from the LORD? The LORD himself told me to march against this country and destroy it." '

²⁶Then Eliakim son of Hilkiah, and Shebna and Joah said to the field commander, 'Please speak to your servants in Aramaic, since we understand it. Don't speak to us in Hebrew in the hearing of the people on the wall.'

²⁷But the commander replied, 'Was it only to your master and you that my master sent me to say these things, and not to the people sitting on the wall – who, like you, will have to eat their own excrement and drink their own urine?'

²⁸Then the commander stood and

---

c 14 That is, about 10 metric tons
d 14 That is, about one metric ton
e 24 Or charioteers

called out in Hebrew, 'Hear the word of the great king, the king of Assyria! 29This is what the king says: do not let Hezekiah deceive you. He cannot deliver you from my hand. 30Do not let Hezekiah persuade you to trust in the LORD when he says, "The LORD will surely deliver us; this city will not be given into the hand of the king of Assyria."

31'Do not listen to Hezekiah. This is what the king of Assyria says: make peace with me and come out to me. Then each of you will eat fruit from your own vine and fig-tree and drink water from your own cistern, 32until I come and take you to a land like your own – a land of grain and new wine, a land of bread and vineyards, a land of olive trees and honey. Choose life and not death!

'Do not listen to Hezekiah, for he is misleading you when he says, "The LORD will deliver us." 33Has the god of any nation ever delivered his land from the hand of the king of Assyria? 34Where are the gods of Hamath and Arpad? Where are the gods of Sepharvaim, Hena and Ivvah? Have they rescued Samaria from my hand? 35Who of all the gods of these countries has been able to save his land from me? How then can the LORD deliver Jerusalem from my hand?'

36But the people remained silent and said nothing in reply, because the king had commanded, 'Do not answer him.'

37Then Eliakim son of Hilkiah the palace administrator, Shebna the secretary, and Joah son of Asaph the recorder went to Hezekiah, with their clothes torn, and told him what the field commander had said.

Jerusalem's deliverance foretold

19 When King Hezekiah heard this, he tore his clothes and put on sackcloth and went into the temple of the LORD. 2He sent Eliakim the palace administrator, Shebna the secretary and the leading priests, all wearing sackcloth, to the prophet Isaiah son of Amoz. 3They told him, 'This is what Hezekiah says: this day is a day of distress and rebuke and disgrace, as when children come to the moment of birth and there is no strength to deliver them. 4It may be that the LORD your God will hear all the words of the field commander, whom his master, the king of Assyria, has sent to ridicule the living God, and that he will rebuke him for the words the LORD your God has heard. Therefore pray for the remnant that still survives.'

FAVOURITE VERSES

John 11:35

Jesus wept.

It reminds me that Jesus understands and cares about everything we go through, no matter how big or small, and that he went through the same feelings and emotions as we do.

Emily, 16

5When King Hezekiah's officials came to Isaiah, 6Isaiah said to them, 'Tell your master, "This is what the LORD says: do not be afraid of what you have heard – those words with which the underlings of the king of Assyria have blasphemed me. 7Listen! When he hears a certain report, I will make him want to return to his own country, and there I will have him cut down with the sword."'

8When the field commander heard that the king of Assyria had left Lachish, he withdrew and found the king fighting against Libnah.

9Now Sennacherib received a report that Tirhakah, the king of Cush,ª was marching out to fight against him. So he again sent messengers to Hezekiah with this word: 10'Say to Hezekiah king of

_____
a 9 That is, the upper Nile region

Judah: do not let the god you depend on deceive you when he says, "Jerusalem will not be given into the hands of the king of Assyria." ¹¹ Surely you have heard what the kings of Assyria have done to all the countries, destroying them completely. And will you be delivered? ¹²Did the gods of the nations that were destroyed by my predecessors deliver them – the gods of Gozan, Harran, Rezeph and the people of Eden who were in Tel Assar? ¹³Where is the king of Hamath or the king of Arpad? Where are the kings of Lair, Sepharvaim, Hena and Ivvah?'

Hezekiah's prayer

¹⁴Hezekiah received the letter from the messengers and read it. Then he went up to the temple of the LORD and spread it out before the LORD. ¹⁵And Hezekiah prayed to the LORD: 'LORD, the God of Israel, enthroned between the cherubim, you alone are God over all the kingdoms of the earth. You have made heaven and earth. ¹⁶Give ear, LORD, and hear; open your eyes, LORD, and see; listen to the words Sennacherib has sent to ridicule the living God.

¹⁷'It is true, LORD, that the Assyrian kings have laid waste these nations and their lands. ¹⁸They have thrown their gods into the fire and destroyed them, for they were not gods but only wood and stone, fashioned by human hands. ¹⁹Now, LORD our God, deliver us from his hand, so that all the kingdoms of the earth may know that you alone, LORD, are God.'

Isaiah prophesies Sennacherib's fall

²⁰Then Isaiah son of Amoz sent a message to Hezekiah: 'This is what the LORD, the God of Israel, says: I have heard your prayer concerning Sennacherib king of Assyria. ²¹This is the word that the LORD has spoken against him:

' "Virgin Daughter Zion
    despises you and mocks you.
Daughter Jerusalem
    tosses her head as you flee.
²²Who is it you have ridiculed and
    blasphemed?

Against whom have you raised your
    voice
and lifted your eyes in pride?
Against the Holy One of Israel!
²³By your messengers
    you have ridiculed the Lord.
And you have said,
    'With my many chariots
I have ascended the heights of the
    mountains,
    the utmost heights of Lebanon.
I have cut down its tallest cedars,
    the choicest of its junipers.
I have reached its remotest parts,
    the finest of its forests.
²⁴I have dug wells in foreign lands
    and drunk the water there.
With the soles of my feet
I have dried up all the streams of
    Egypt.'

²⁵' "Have you not heard?
    Long ago I ordained it.
In days of old I planned it;
    now I have brought it to pass,
that you have turned fortified cities
    into piles of stone.
²⁶Their people, drained of power,
    are dismayed and put to shame.
They are like plants in the field,
    like tender green shoots,
like grass sprouting on the roof,
    scorched before it grows up.

²⁷' "But I know where you are
    and when you come and go
    and how you rage against me.
²⁸Because you rage against me
    and because your insolence has
        reached my ears,
I will put my hook in your nose
    and my bit in your mouth,
and I will make you return
    by the way you came."

²⁹'This will be the sign for you, Hezekiah:

'This year you will eat what grows by
    itself,
and the second year what springs
    from that.

But in the third year sow and reap,
    plant vineyards and eat their fruit.
³⁰ Once more a remnant of the kingdom
        of Judah
    will take root below and bear fruit
        above.
³¹ For out of Jerusalem will come a
        remnant,
    and out of Mount Zion a band of
        survivors.

'The zeal of the LORD Almighty will accomplish this.

³² 'Therefore this is what the LORD says
concerning the king of Assyria:

' "He will not enter this city
    or shoot an arrow here.
He will not come before it with shield
    or build a siege ramp against it.
³³ By the way that he came he will return;
    he will not enter this city
                declares the LORD.
³⁴ I will defend this city and save it,
    for my sake and for the sake of David
        my servant." '

³⁵ That night the angel of the LORD
went out and put to death a hundred
and eighty-five thousand in the Assyrian
camp. When the people got up the next
morning – there were all the dead bodies!
³⁶ So Sennacherib king of Assyria broke
camp and withdrew. He returned to Nineveh and stayed there.

³⁷ One day, while he was worshipping
in the temple of his god Nisrok, his sons
Adrammelek and Sharezer killed him with
the sword, and they escaped to the land of
Ararat. And Esarhaddon his son succeeded
him as king.

Hezekiah's illness

20 In those days Hezekiah became ill
and was at the point of death. The
prophet Isaiah son of Amoz went to him
and said, 'This is what the LORD says: put
your house in order, because you are going to die; you will not recover.'

² Hezekiah turned his face to the wall
and prayed to the LORD, ³ 'Remember,

LORD, how I have walked before you faithfully and with wholehearted devotion and
have done what is good in your eyes.' And
Hezekiah wept bitterly.

⁴ Before Isaiah had left the middle
court, the word of the LORD came to him:
⁵ 'Go back and tell Hezekiah, the ruler of
my people, "This is what the LORD, the
God of your father David, says: I have
heard your prayer and seen your tears; I
will heal you. On the third day from now
you will go up to the temple of the LORD.
⁶ I will add fifteen years to your life. And
I will deliver you and this city from the
hand of the king of Assyria. I will defend
this city for my sake and for the sake of my
servant David." '

⁷ Then Isaiah said, 'Prepare a poultice of
figs.' They did so and applied it to the boil,
and he recovered.

⁸ Hezekiah had asked Isaiah, 'What will
be the sign that the LORD will heal me and
that I will go up to the temple of the LORD
on the third day from now?'

⁹ Isaiah answered, 'This is the LORD's
sign to you that the LORD will do what
he has promised: shall the shadow go
forward ten steps, or shall it go back ten
steps?'

¹⁰ 'It is a simple matter for the shadow
to go forward ten steps,' said Hezekiah.
'Rather, let it go back ten steps.'

¹¹ Then the prophet Isaiah called on the
LORD, and the LORD made the shadow go
back the ten steps it had gone down on the
stairway of Ahaz.

Envoys from Babylon

¹² At that time Marduk-Baladan son of
Baladan king of Babylon sent Hezekiah
letters and a gift, because he had heard
of Hezekiah's illness. ¹³ Hezekiah received
the envoys and showed them all that was
in his storehouses – the silver, the gold,
the spices and the fine oil – his armoury
and everything found among his treasures. There was nothing in his palace or
in all his kingdom that Hezekiah did not
show them.

¹⁴ Then Isaiah the prophet went to King
Hezekiah and asked, 'What did those men
say, and where did they come from?'

'From a distant land,' Hezekiah replied. 'They came from Babylon.'

15 The prophet asked, 'What did they see in your palace?'

'They saw everything in my palace,' Hezekiah said. 'There is nothing among my treasures that I did not show them.'

16 Then Isaiah said to Hezekiah, 'Hear the word of the LORD: 17 the time will surely come when everything in your palace, and all that your predecessors have stored up until this day, will be carried off to Babylon. Nothing will be left, says the LORD. 18 And some of your descendants, your own flesh and blood who will be born to you, will be taken away, and they will become eunuchs in the palace of the king of Babylon.'

19 'The word of the LORD you have spoken is good,' Hezekiah replied. For he thought, 'Will there not be peace and security in my lifetime?'

20 As for the other events of Hezekiah's reign, all his achievements and how he made the pool and the tunnel by which he brought water into the city, are they not written in the book of the annals of the kings of Judah? 21 Hezekiah rested with his ancestors. And Manasseh his son succeeded him as king.

Manasseh king of Judah

21 Manasseh was twelve years old when he became king, and he reigned in Jerusalem for fifty-five years. His mother's name was Hephzibah. 2 He did evil in the eyes of the LORD, following the detestable practices of the nations the LORD had driven out before the Israelites. 3 He rebuilt the high places his father Hezekiah had destroyed; he also erected altars to Baal and made an Asherah pole, as Ahab king of Israel had done. He bowed down to all the starry hosts and worshipped them. 4 He built altars in the temple of the LORD, of which the LORD had said, 'In Jerusalem I will put my Name.' 5 In the two courts of the temple of the LORD, he built altars to all the starry hosts. 6 He sacrificed his own son in the fire, practised divination, sought omens, and consulted mediums and spiritists.

He did much evil in the eyes of the LORD, arousing his anger.

7 He took the carved Asherah pole he had made and put it in the temple, of which the LORD had said to David and to his son Solomon, 'In this temple and in Jerusalem, which I have chosen out of all the tribes of Israel, I will put my Name for ever. 8 I will not again make the feet of the Israelites wander from the land I gave their ancestors, if only they will be careful to do everything I commanded them and will keep the whole Law that my servant Moses gave them.' 9 But the people did not listen. Manasseh led them astray, so that they did more evil than the nations the LORD had destroyed before the Israelites.

10 The LORD said through his servants the prophets: 11 'Manasseh king of Judah has committed these detestable sins. He has done more evil than the Amorites who preceded him and has led Judah into sin with his idols. 12 Therefore this is what the LORD, the God of Israel, says: I am going to bring such disaster on Jerusalem and Judah that the ears of everyone who hears of it will tingle. 13 I will stretch out over Jerusalem the measuring line used against Samaria and the plumb-line used against the house of Ahab. I will wipe out Jerusalem as one wipes out a dish, wiping it and turning it upside-down. 14 I will forsake the remnant of my inheritance and give them into the hands of enemies. They will be looted and plundered by all their enemies; 15 they have done evil in my eyes and have aroused my anger from the day their ancestors came out of Egypt until this day.'

16 Moreover, Manasseh also shed so much innocent blood that he filled Jerusalem from end to end – besides the sin that he had caused Judah to commit, so that they did evil in the eyes of the LORD.

17 As for the other events of Manasseh's reign, and all he did, including the sin he committed, are they not written in the book of the annals of the kings of Judah? 18 Manasseh rested with his ancestors and was buried in his palace garden, the garden of Uzza. And Amon his son succeeded him as king.

Amon king of Judah

19 Amon was twenty-two years old when he became king, and he reigned in Jerusalem for two years. His mother's name was Meshullemeth daughter of Haruz; she was from Jotbah. 20 He did evil in the eyes of the LORD, as his father Manasseh had done. 21 He followed completely the ways of his father, worshipped the idols his father had worshipped, and bowing down to them. 22 He forsook the LORD, the God of his ancestors, and did not walk in obedience to him.

23 Amon's officials conspired against him and assassinated the king in his palace. 24 Then the people of the land killed all who had plotted against King Amon, and they made Josiah his son king in his place.

25 As for the other events of Amon's reign, and what he did, are they not written in the book of the annals of the kings of Judah? 26 He was buried in his tomb in the garden of Uzza. And Josiah his son succeeded him as king.

The Book of the Law found

22 Josiah was eight years old when he became king, and he reigned in Jerusalem for thirty-one years. His mother's name was Jedidah daughter of Adaiah; she was from Bozkath. 2 He did what was right in the eyes of the LORD and followed completely the ways of his father David, not turning aside to the right or to the left.

3 In the eighteenth year of his reign, King Josiah sent the secretary, Shaphan son of Azaliah, the son of Meshullam, to the temple of the LORD. He said: 4 'Go up to Hilkiah the high priest and make him get ready the money that has been brought into the temple of the LORD, which the doorkeepers have collected from the people. 5 Make them entrust it to the men appointed to supervise the work on the temple. And make these men pay the workers who repair the temple of the LORD – 6 the carpenters, the builders and the masons. Also make them purchase timber and dressed stone to repair the temple. 7 But they need not account for

the money entrusted to them, because they are honest in their dealings.'

8 Hilkiah the high priest said to Shaphan the secretary, 'I have found the Book of the Law in the temple of the LORD.' He gave it to Shaphan, who read it. 9 Then Shaphan the secretary went to the king and reported to him: 'Your officials have paid out the money that was in the temple of the LORD and have entrusted it to the workers and supervisors at the temple.' 10 Then Shaphan the secretary informed the king, 'Hilkiah the priest has given me a book.' And Shaphan read from it in the presence of the king.

11 When the king heard the words of the Book of the Law, he tore his robes. 12 He gave these orders to Hilkiah the priest, Ahikam son of Shaphan, Akbor son of Micaiah, Shaphan the secretary and Asaiah the king's attendant: 13 'Go and enquire of the LORD for me and for the people and for all Judah about what is written in this book that has been found. Great is the LORD's anger that burns against us because those who have gone before us have not obeyed the words of this book; they have not acted in accordance with all that is written there concerning us.'

14 Hilkiah the priest, Ahikam, Akbor, Shaphan and Asaiah went to speak to the prophet Huldah, who was the wife of Shallum son of Tikvah, the son of Harhas, keeper of the wardrobe. She lived in Jerusalem, in the New Quarter.

15 She said to them, 'This is what the LORD, the God of Israel, says: tell the man who sent you to me, 16 "This is what the LORD says: I am going to bring disaster on this place and its people, according to everything written in the book the king of Judah has read. 17 Because they have forsaken me and burned incense to other gods and aroused my anger by all the idols their hands have made,ᵃ my anger will burn against this place and will not be quenched." 18 Tell the king of Judah, who sent you to enquire of the LORD, "This is what the LORD, the God of Israel, says

---

a 17 Or by everything they have done

concerning the words you heard: ¹⁹ because your heart was responsive and you humbled yourself before the LORD when you heard what I have spoken against this place and its people – that they would become a curse^b and be laid waste – and because you tore your robes and wept in my presence, I also have heard you, declares the LORD. ²⁰ Therefore I will gather you to your ancestors, and you will be buried in peace. Your eyes will not see all the disaster I am going to bring on this place.'"

So they took her answer back to the king.

Josiah renews the covenant

23 Then the king called together all the elders of Judah and Jerusalem. ² He went up to the temple of the LORD with the people of Judah, the inhabitants of Jerusalem, the priests and the prophets – all the people from the least to the greatest. He read in their hearing all the words of the Book of the Covenant, which had been found in the temple of the LORD. ³ The king stood by the pillar and renewed the covenant in the presence of the LORD – to follow the LORD and keep his commands, statutes and decrees with all his heart and all his soul, thus confirming the words of the covenant written in this book. Then all the people pledged themselves to the covenant.

⁴ The king ordered Hilkiah the high priest, the priests next in rank and the doorkeepers to remove from the temple of the LORD all the articles made for Baal and Asherah and all the starry hosts. He burned them outside Jerusalem in the fields of the Kidron Valley and took the ashes to Bethel. ⁵ He did away with the idolatrous priests appointed by the kings of Judah to burn incense on the high places of the towns of Judah and on those around Jerusalem – those who burned incense to Baal, to the sun and moon, to the constellations and to all the starry hosts. ⁶ He took the Asherah pole from

the temple of the LORD to the Kidron Valley outside Jerusalem and burned it there. He ground it to powder and scattered the dust over the graves of the common people. ⁷ He also tore down the quarters of the male shrine-prostitutes that were in the

YOU WHAT?

THE 'LOST' BOOKS OF THE BIBLE

○ **THE BOOK OF JASHAR**
2 Samuel 1:18; Joshua 10:12
○ **RECORDS OF NATHAN AND GAD**
1 Chronicles 29:29
○ **THE RECORDS OF SHEMAIAH AND IDDO**
2 Chronicles 12:15
○ **THE RECORDS OF THE PROPHET AHIJAH**
2 Chronicles 9:29
○ **PAUL'S LETTER TO THE LAODICEANS**
Colossians 4:16
○ **THE BOOK OF THE LORD'S BATTLES**
Numbers 21:14
○ **HISTORY OF THE KINGS OF ISRAEL**
1 Kings 14:19
○ **HISTORY OF THE KINGS OF JUDAH**
1 Kings 14:29
○ **THE BOOK OF THE RIGHTS AND DUTIES OF KINGS**
1 Samuel 10:25
○ **THE ANNALS OF SOLOMON**
1 Kings 11:41
○ **THE RECORDS OF JEHU SON OF HANANI**
2 Chronicles 20:34
○ **ISAIAH'S RECORDS OF THE REIGN OF UZZIAH**
2 Chronicles 26:22
○ **PAUL'S LOST LETTER TO CORINTH**
1 Corinthians 5:9

---

b 19 That is, their names would be used in cursing (see Jer. 29:22); or, others would see that they are cursed.

temple of the LORD, the quarters where women did weaving for Asherah.

⁸ Josiah brought all the priests from the towns of Judah and desecrated the high places, from Geba to Beersheba, where the priests had burned incense. He broke down the gateway at the entrance of the Gate of Joshua, the city governor, which was on the left of the city gate. ⁹ Although the priests of the high places did not serve at the altar of the LORD in Jerusalem, they ate unleavened bread with their fellow priests.

¹⁰ He desecrated Topheth, which was in the Valley of Ben Hinnom, so no one could use it to sacrifice their son or daughter in the fire to Molek. ¹¹ He removed from the entrance to the temple of the LORD the horses that the kings of Judah had dedicated to the sun. They were in the courtᵃ near the room of an official named Nathan-Melek. Josiah then burned the chariots dedicated to the sun.

¹² He pulled down the altars the kings of Judah had erected on the roof near the upper room of Ahaz, and the altars Manasseh had built in the two courts of the temple of the LORD. He removed them from there, smashed them to pieces and threw the rubble into the Kidron Valley. ¹³ The king also desecrated the high places that were east of Jerusalem on the south of the Hill of Corruption – the ones Solomon king of Israel had built for Ashtoreth the vile goddess of the Sidonians, for Chemosh the vile god of Moab, and for Molek the detestable god of the people of Ammon. ¹⁴ Josiah smashed the sacred stones and cut down the Asherah poles and covered the sites with human bones.

¹⁵ Even the altar at Bethel, the high place made by Jeroboam son of Nebat, who had caused Israel to sin – even that altar and high place he demolished. He burned the high place and ground it to powder, and burned the Asherah pole also. ¹⁶ Then Josiah looked around, and when he saw the tombs that were there on the hillside, he had the bones removed from them and burned on the altar to defile it, in accordance with the word of the LORD proclaimed by the man of God who foretold these things.

¹⁷ The king asked, 'What is that tombstone I see?'

The people of the city said, 'It marks the tomb of the man of God who came from Judah and pronounced against the altar of Bethel the very things you have done to it.'

¹⁸ 'Leave it alone,' he said. 'Don't let anyone disturb his bones.' So they spared his bones and those of the prophet who had come from Samaria.

¹⁹ Just as he had done at Bethel, Josiah removed all the shrines at the high places that the kings of Israel had built in the towns of Samaria and that had aroused the LORD's anger. ²⁰ Josiah slaughtered all the priests of those high places on the altars and burned human bones on them. Then he went back to Jerusalem.

²¹ The king gave this order to all the people: 'Celebrate the Passover to the LORD your God, as it is written in this Book of the Covenant.' ²² Neither in the days of the judges who led Israel nor in the days of the kings of Israel and the kings of Judah had any such Passover been observed. ²³ But in the eighteenth year of King Josiah, this Passover was celebrated to the LORD in Jerusalem.

²⁴ Furthermore, Josiah got rid of the mediums and spiritists, the household gods, the idols and all the other detestable things seen in Judah and Jerusalem. This he did to fulfil the requirements of the law written in the book that Hilkiah the priest had discovered in the temple of the LORD. ²⁵ Neither before nor after Josiah was there a king like him who turned to the LORD as he did – with all his heart and with all his soul and with all his strength, in accordance with all the Law of Moses.

²⁶ Nevertheless, the LORD did not turn away from the heat of his fierce anger, which burned against Judah because of all that Manasseh had done to arouse his anger. ²⁷ So the LORD said, 'I will remove Judah also from my presence as I removed Israel, and I will reject Jerusalem, the city

---

ᵃ 11 The meaning of the Hebrew for this word is uncertain.

I chose, and this temple, about which I said, "My Name shall be there."*b*

28 As for the other events of Josiah's reign, and all he did, are they not written in the book of the annals of the kings of Judah?

29 While Josiah was king, Pharaoh Necho king of Egypt went up to the River Euphrates to help the king of Assyria. King Josiah marched out to meet him in battle, but Necho faced him and killed him at Megiddo. 30 Josiah's servants brought his body in a chariot from Megiddo to Jerusalem and buried him in his own tomb. And the people of the land took Jehoahaz son of Josiah and anointed him and made him king in place of his father.

Jehoahaz king of Judah

31 Jehoahaz was twenty-three years old when he became king, and he reigned in Jerusalem for three months. His mother's name was Hamutal daughter of Jeremiah; she was from Libnah. 32 He did evil in the eyes of the LORD, just as his predecessors had done. 33 Pharaoh Necho put him in chains at Riblah in the land of Hamath so that he might not reign in Jerusalem, and he imposed on Judah a levy of a hundred talents*c* of silver and a talent*d* of gold. 34 Pharaoh Necho made Eliakim son of Josiah king in place of his father Josiah and changed Eliakim's name to Jehoiakim. But he took Jehoahaz and carried him off to Egypt, and there he died. 35 Jehoiakim paid Pharaoh Necho the silver and gold he demanded. In order to do so, he taxed the land and exacted the silver and gold from the people of the land according to their assessments.

Jehoiakim king of Judah

36 Jehoiakim was twenty-five years old when he became king, and he reigned in Jerusalem for eleven years. His mother's name was Zebidah daughter of Pedaiah; she was from Rumah. 37 And he did evil in

the eyes of the LORD, just as his predecessors had done.

24 During Jehoiakim's reign, Nebuchadnezzar king of Babylon invaded the land, and Jehoiakim became his vassal for three years. But then he turned against Nebuchadnezzar and rebelled. 2 The LORD sent Babylonian,*a* Aramean, Moabite and Ammonite raiders against him to destroy Judah, in accordance with the word of the LORD proclaimed by his servants the prophets. 3 Surely these things happened to Judah according to the LORD's command, in order to remove them from his presence because of the sins of Manasseh and all he had done, 4 including the shedding of innocent blood. For he had filled Jerusalem with innocent blood, and the LORD was not willing to forgive.

5 As for the other events of Jehoiakim's reign, and all he did, are they not written in the book of the annals of the kings of Judah? 6 Jehoiakim rested with his ancestors. And Jehoiachin his son succeeded him as king.

7 The king of Egypt did not march out from his own country again, because the king of Babylon had taken all his territory, from the Wadi of Egypt to the River Euphrates.

Jehoiachin king of Judah

8 Jehoiachin was eighteen years old when he became king, and he reigned in Jerusalem for three months. His mother's name was Nehushta daughter of Elnathan; she was from Jerusalem. 9 He did evil in the eyes of the LORD, just as his father had done.

10 At that time the officers of Nebuchadnezzar king of Babylon advanced on Jerusalem and laid siege to it, 11 and Nebuchadnezzar himself came up to the city while his officers were besieging it. 12 Jehoiachin king of Judah, his mother, his attendants, his nobles and his officials all surrendered to him.

In the eighth year of the reign of the

---

b 27   1 Kings 8:29
c 33   That is, about 3.4 metric tons
d 33   That is, about 34 kilograms

a 2   Or *Chaldean*

king of Babylon, he took Jehoiachin prisoner. ¹³As the LORD had declared, Nebuchadnezzar removed the treasures from the temple of the LORD and from the royal palace, and cut up the gold articles that Solomon king of Israel had made for the temple of the LORD. ¹⁴He carried all Jerusalem into exile: all the officers and fighting men, and all the skilled workers and artisans – a total of ten thousand. Only the poorest people of the land were left. ¹⁵Nebuchadnezzar took Jehoiachin captive to Babylon. He also took from Jerusalem to Babylon the king's mother, his wives, his officials and the prominent people of the land. ¹⁶The king of Babylon also deported to Babylon the entire force of seven thousand fighting men, strong and fit for war, and a thousand skilled workers and artisans. ¹⁷He made Mattaniah, Jehoiachin's uncle, king in his place and changed his name to Zedekiah.

Zedekiah king of Judah

¹⁸Zedekiah was twenty-one years old when he became king, and he reigned in Jerusalem for eleven years. His mother's name was Hamutal daughter of Jeremiah; she was from Libnah. ¹⁹He did evil in the eyes of the LORD, just as Jehoiakim had done. ²⁰It was because of the LORD's anger that all this happened to Jerusalem and Judah, and in the end he thrust them from his presence.

The fall of Jerusalem

Now Zedekiah rebelled against the king of Babylon.

25 So in the ninth year of Zedekiah's reign, on the tenth day of the tenth month, Nebuchadnezzar king of Babylon marched against Jerusalem with his whole army. He camped outside the city and built siege works all around it. ²The city was kept under siege until the eleventh year of King Zedekiah.

³By the ninth day of the fourthª month the famine in the city had become so severe that there was no food for the people to eat. ⁴Then the city wall was broken through, and the whole army fled at night through the gate between the two walls near the king's garden, though the Babyloniansᵇ were surrounding the city. They fled towards the Arabah,ᶜ ⁵but the Babylonianᵈ army pursued the king and overtook him in the plains of Jericho. All his soldiers were separated from him and scattered, ⁶and he was captured.

He was taken to the king of Babylon at Riblah, where sentence was pronounced on him. ⁷They killed the sons of Zedekiah before his eyes. Then they put out his eyes, bound him with bronze shackles and took him to Babylon.

⁸On the seventh day of the fifth month, in the nineteenth year of Nebuchadnezzar king of Babylon, Nebuzaradan commander of the imperial guard, an official of the king of Babylon, came to Jerusalem. ⁹He set fire to the temple of the LORD, the royal palace and all the houses of Jerusalem. Every important building he burned down. ¹⁰The whole Babylonian army under the commander of the imperial guard broke down the walls around Jerusalem. ¹¹Nebuzaradan the commander of the guard carried into exile the people who remained in the city, along with the rest of the populace and those who had deserted to the king of Babylon. ¹²But the commander left behind some of the poorest people of the land to work the vineyards and fields.

¹³The Babylonians broke up the bronze pillars, the movable stands and the bronze Sea that were at the temple of the LORD and they carried the bronze to Babylon. ¹⁴They also took away the pots, shovels, wick trimmers, dishes and all the bronze articles used in the temple service. ¹⁵The commander of the imperial guard took away the censers and sprinkling bowls – all that were made of pure gold or silver.

¹⁶The bronze from the two pillars, the Sea and the movable stands, which Solomon had made for the temple of the

---

ª 3 Probable reading of the original Hebrew text (see Jer. 52:6); Masoretic Text does not have *fourth*.

ᵇ 4 Or *Chaldeans*; also in verses 13, 25 and 26
ᶜ 4 Or *the Jordan Valley*
ᵈ 5 Or *Chaldean*; also in verses 10 and 24

LORD, was more than could be weighed. ¹⁷ Each pillar was eighteen cubits*ᵉ* high. The bronze capital on top of one pillar was three cubits*ᶠ* high and was decorated with a network and pomegranates of bronze all around. The other pillar, with its network, was similar.

¹⁸ The commander of the guard took as prisoners Seraiah the chief priest, Zephaniah the priest next in rank and the three doorkeepers. ¹⁹ Of those still in the city, he took the officer in charge of the fighting men, and five royal advisors. He also took the secretary who was chief officer in charge of conscripting the people of the land and sixty of the conscripts who were found in the city. ²⁰ Nebuzaradan the commander took them all and brought them to the king of Babylon at Riblah. ²¹ There at Riblah, in the land of Hamath, the king had them executed.

So Judah went into captivity, away from her land.

²² Nebuchadnezzar king of Babylon appointed Gedaliah son of Ahikam, the son of Shaphan, to be over the people he had left behind in Judah. ²³ When all the army officers and their men heard that the king of Babylon had appointed Gedaliah as governor, they came to Gedaliah at Mizpah – Ishmael son of Nethaniah, Johanan son of Kareah, Seraiah son of Tanhumeth the Netophathite, Jaazaniah the son of the Maakathite, and their men. ²⁴ Gedaliah took an oath to reassure them and their men. 'Do not be afraid of the Babylonian officials,' he said. 'Settle down in the land and serve the king of Babylon, and it will go well with you.'

²⁵ In the seventh month, however, Ishmael son of Nethaniah, the son of Elishama, who was of royal blood, came with ten men and assassinated Gedaliah and also the men of Judah and the Babylonians who were with him at Mizpah. ²⁶ At this, all the people from the least to the greatest, together with the army officers, fled to Egypt for fear of the Babylonians.

Jehoiachin released

²⁷ In the thirty-seventh year of the exile of Jehoiachin king of Judah, in the year Awel-Marduk became king of Babylon, he released Jehoiachin king of Judah from prison. He did this on the twenty-seventh day of the twelfth month. ²⁸ He spoke kindly to him and gave him a seat of honour higher than those of the other kings who were with him in Babylon. ²⁹ So Jehoiachin put aside his prison clothes and for the rest of his life ate regularly at the king's table. ³⁰ Day by day the king gave Jehoiachin a regular allowance as long as he lived.

---

e 17 That is, about 8.1 metres
f 17 That is, about 1.4 metres

1 CHRONICLES

DATE

1 Chronicles is mainly concerned with events that happened after Saul's death (around 1007 BC) and up to the start of Solomon's reign as king (around 970 BC)

AUTHOR

Unknown (though traditionally attributed to Ezra)

WHAT'S IT ALL ABOUT?

The two books of Chronicles were written for the men returning from exile in Babylon to rebuild Jerusalem and it retells some of the history of God's people. The author wrote long after the events had happened and so he drew on the books of 2 Samuel and Kings and urged the people to learn the lessons from their past and realise that turning away from God leads to judgement and disaster. Chronicles is not intended to be a full history and focuses on the positives (leaving out most of the negative stories about David). It does not even mention the Northern tribes of Israel, instead focusing on the Southern tribes (the Kingdom of Judah). 1 Chronicles begins with a family history, starting at the very beginning of creation with Adam, and ends with the death of David and the start of Solomon's reign. The book served as a reminder to the people about who they were and what God had done for them.

WHY SHOULD WE READ IT?

- To read the highlights of King David's reign, including the return of the ark of the covenant to God's people (1 Chronicles 13).

- To read God's promise to David to establish his kingdom after his death (1 Chronicles 17).

- To see how the Lord reacted when David put his faith in the numbers in his army rather than in the Lord (1 Chronicles 21).

Andy Croft with Liza Hoeksma

Historical records from Adam to Abraham

To Noah's sons

1 Adam, Seth, Enosh, 2 Kenan, Mahalalel, Jared, 3 Enoch, Methuselah, Lamech, Noah.

4 The sons of Noah:a
Shem, Ham and Japheth.

The Japhethites

5 The sonsb of Japheth:
Gomer, Magog, Madai, Javan, Tubal, Meshek and Tiras.
6 The sons of Gomer:
Ashkenaz, Riphathc and Togarmah.
7 The sons of Javan:
Elishah, Tarshish, the Kittites and the Rodanites.

The Hamites

8 The sons of Ham:
Cush, Egypt, Put and Canaan.
9 The sons of Cush:
Seba, Havilah, Sabta, Raamah and Sabteka.
The sons of Raamah:
Sheba and Dedan.
10 Cush was the fatherd of
Nimrod, who became a mighty warrior on earth.
11 Egypt was the father of
the Ludites, Anamites, Lehabites, Naphtuhites, 12 Pathrusites, Kasluhites (from whom the Philistines came) and Caphtorites.
13 Canaan was the father of
Sidon his firstborn,e and of the Hittites, 14 Jebusites, Amorites, Girgashites, 15 Hivites, Arkites, Sinites, 16 Arvadites, Zemarites and Hamathites.

The Semites

17 The sons of Shem:
Elam, Ashur, Arphaxad, Lud and Aram.
The sons of Aram:f
Uz, Hul, Gether and Meshek.
18 Arphaxad was the father of Shelah, and Shelah the father of Eber.
19 Two sons were born to Eber:
one was named Peleg,g because in his time the earth was divided; his brother was named Joktan.
20 Joktan was the father of
Almodad, Sheleph, Hazarmaveth, Jerah, 21 Hadoram, Uzal, Diklah, 22 Obal,h Abimael, Sheba, 23 Ophir, Havilah and Jobab. All these were sons of Joktan.

24 Shem, Arphaxad,i Shelah,
25 Eber, Peleg, Reu,
26 Serug, Nahor, Terah
27 and Abram (that is, Abraham).

The family of Abraham

28 The sons of Abraham:
Isaac and Ishmael.

Descendants of Hagar

29 These were their descendants:
Nebaioth the firstborn of Ishmael, Kedar, Adbeel, Mibsam, 30 Mishma, Dumah, Massa, Hadad, Tema, 31 Jetur, Naphish and Kedemah. These were the sons of Ishmael.

Descendants of Keturah

32 The sons born to Keturah, Abraham's concubine:
Zimran, Jokshan, Medan, Midian, Ishbak and Shuah.
The sons of Jokshan:
Sheba and Dedan.

---

a 4 Septuagint; Hebrew does not have this line.
b 5 Sons may mean descendants or successors or nations; also in verses 6-9, 17 and 23.
c 6 Many Hebrew manuscripts and Vulgate (see also Septuagint and Gen. 10:3); most Hebrew manuscripts Diphath
d 10 Father may mean ancestor or predecessor or founder; also in verses 11, 13, 18 and 20.
e 13 Or of the Sidonians, the foremost

f 17 One Hebrew manuscript and some Septuagint manuscripts (see also Gen. 10:23); most Hebrew manuscripts do not have this line.
g 19 Peleg means division.
h 22 Some Hebrew manuscripts and Syriac (see also Gen. 10:28); most Hebrew manuscripts Ebal
i 24 Hebrew; some Septuagint manuscripts Arphaxad, Cainan (see also note at Gen. 11:10)

33 The sons of Midian:
Ephah, Epher, Hanok, Abida and
Eldaah.
All these were descendants of Ketu-
rah.

Descendants of Sarah

34 Abraham was the father of Isaac.
The sons of Isaac:
Esau and Israel.

Esau's sons

35 The sons of Esau:
Eliphaz, Reuel, Jeush, Jalam and
Korah.
36 The sons of Eliphaz:
Teman, Omar, Zepho,*j* Gatam and
Kenaz;
by Timna: Amalek.*k*
37 The sons of Reuel:
Nahath, Zerah, Shammah and
Mizzah.

The people of Seir in Edom

38 The sons of Seir:
Lotan, Shobal, Zibeon, Anah, Di-
shon, Ezer and Dishan.
39 The sons of Lotan:
Hori and Homam. Timna was Lo-
tan's sister.
40 The sons of Shobal:
Alvan,*l* Manahath, Ebal, Shepho
and Onam.
The sons of Zibeon:
Aiah and Anah.
41 The son of Anah:
Dishon.
The sons of Dishon:
Hemdan,*m* Eshban, Ithran and
Keran.

42 The sons of Ezer:
Bilhan, Zaavan and Akan.*n*
The sons of Dishan:*o*
Uz and Aran.

The rulers of Edom

43 These were the kings who reigned
in Edom before any Israelite king
reigned:
Bela son of Beor, whose city was
named Dinhabah.
44 When Bela died, Jobab son of Zerah
from Bozrah succeeded him as
king.
45 When Jobab died, Husham from the
land of the Temanites succeeded
him as king.
46 When Husham died, Hadad son of
Bedad, who defeated Midian in
the country of Moab, succeeded
him as king. His city was named
Avith.
47 When Hadad died, Samlah from Masrekah succeeded him as king.
48 When Samlah died, Shaul from Rehoboth on the river*p* succeeded
him as king.
49 When Shaul died, Baal-Hanan son of
Akbor succeeded him as king.
50 When Baal-Hanan died, Hadad succeeded him as king. His city was
named Pau,*q* and his wife's name
was Mehetabel daughter of Matred, the daughter of Me-Zahab.
51 Hadad also died.

The chiefs of Edom were:
Timna, Alvah, Jetheth, 52 Oholibamah, Elah, Pinon, 53 Kenaz, Teman, Mibzar, 54 Magdiel and Iram.
These were the chiefs of Edom.

---

j 36 Many Hebrew manuscripts, some Septuagint
manuscripts and Syriac (see also Gen. 36:11); most
Hebrew manuscripts *Zephi*
k 36 Some Septuagint manuscripts (see also Gen.
36:12); Hebrew *Gatam, Kenaz, Timna and Amalek*
l 40 Many Hebrew manuscripts and some
Septuagint manuscripts (see also Gen. 36:23); most
Hebrew manuscripts *Alian*
m 41 Many Hebrew manuscripts and some
Septuagint manuscripts (see also Gen. 36:26); most
Hebrew manuscripts *Hamran*

---

n 42 Many Hebrew and Septuagint manuscripts
(see also Gen. 36:27); most Hebrew manuscripts
Zaavan, Jaakan
o 42 See Gen. 36:28; Hebrew *Dishon,* a variant of
Dishan
p 48 Possibly the Euphrates
q 50 Many Hebrew manuscripts, some Septuagint
manuscripts, Vulgate and Syriac (see also Gen.
36:39); most Hebrew manuscripts *Pai*

Israel's sons

2 These were the sons of Israel: Reuben, Simeon, Levi, Judah, Issachar, Zebulun, ²Dan, Joseph, Benjamin, Naphtali, Gad and Asher.

Judah

To Hezron's sons

³The sons of Judah:
Er, Onan and Shelah. These three were born to him by a Canaanite woman, the daughter of Shua. Er, Judah's firstborn, was wicked in the LORD's sight; so the LORD put him to death. ⁴Judah's daughter-in-law Tamar bore Perez and Zerah to Judah. He had five sons in all.

⁵The sons of Perez:
Hezron and Hamul.

⁶The sons of Zerah:
Zimri, Ethan, Heman, Kalkol and Darda*ᵃ* – five in all.

⁷The son of Karmi:
Achar,*ᵇ* who brought trouble on Israel by violating the ban on taking devoted things.*ᶜ*

⁸The son of Ethan:
Azariah.

⁹The sons born to Hezron were:
Jerahmeel, Ram and Caleb.*ᵈ*

From Ram son of Hezron

¹⁰Ram was the father of Amminadab, and Amminadab the father of Nahshon, the leader of the people of Judah. ¹¹Nahshon was the father of Salmon,*ᵉ* Salmon the father of Boaz, ¹²Boaz the father of Obed and Obed the father of Jesse.

¹³Jesse was the father of Eliab his firstborn; the second son was Abinadab, the third Shimea, ¹⁴the fourth Nethanel, the fifth Raddai, ¹⁵the sixth Ozem and the seventh David. ¹⁶Their sisters were Zeruiah and Abigail. Zeruiah's three sons were Abishai, Joab and Asahel. ¹⁷Abigail was the mother of Amasa, whose father was Jether the Ishmaelite.

Caleb son of Hezron

¹⁸Caleb son of Hezron had children by his wife Azubah (and by Jerioth). These were her sons: Jesher, Shobab and Ardon. ¹⁹When Azubah died, Caleb married Ephrath, who bore him Hur. ²⁰Hur was the father of Uri, and Uri the father of Bezalel.

²¹Later, Hezron, when he was sixty years old, married the daughter of Makir the father of Gilead. He made love to her, and she bore him Segub. ²²Segub was the father of Jair, who controlled twenty-three towns in Gilead. ²³(But Geshur and Aram captured Havvoth Jair,*ᶠ* as well as Kenath with its surrounding settlements – sixty towns.) All these were descendants of Makir the father of Gilead.

²⁴After Hezron died in Caleb Ephrathah, Abijah the wife of Hezron bore him Ashhur the father*ᵍ* of Tekoa.

Jerahmeel son of Hezron

²⁵The sons of Jerahmeel the firstborn of Hezron:
Ram his firstborn, Bunah, Oren, Ozem and*ʰ* Ahijah. ²⁶Jerahmeel had another wife, whose name was Atarah; she was the mother of Onam.

²⁷The sons of Ram the firstborn of Jerahmeel:
Maaz, Jamin and Eker.

---

a 6 Many Hebrew manuscripts, some Septuagint manuscripts and Syriac (see also 1 Kings 4:31); most Hebrew manuscripts *Dara*
b 7 *Achar* means *trouble*; *Achar* is called *Achan* in Joshua.
c 7 The Hebrew term refers to the irrevocable giving over of things or persons to the LORD, often by totally destroying them.
d 9 Hebrew *Kelubai*, a variant of *Caleb*
e 11 Septuagint (see also Ruth 4:21); Hebrew *Salma*
f 23 Or *captured the settlements of Jair*
g 24 *Father* may mean *civic leader* or *military leader*; also in verses 42, 45, 49-52 and possibly elsewhere.
h 25 Or *Oren and Ozem, by*

28 The sons of Onam:
Shammai and Jada.
The sons of Shammai:
Nadab and Abishur.
29 Abishur's wife was named Abihail,
who bore him Ahban and Molid.
30 The sons of Nadab:
Seled and Appaim. Seled died
without children.
31 The son of Appaim:
Ishi, who was the father of Sheshan.
Sheshan was the father of Ahlai.
32 The sons of Jada, Shammai's
brother:
Jether and Jonathan. Jether died
without children.
33 The sons of Jonathan:
Peleth and Zaza.
These were the descendants of Jerahmeel.
34 Sheshan had no sons – only daughters.
He had an Egyptian servant named
Jarha. 35 Sheshan gave his daughter in marriage to his servant
Jarha, and she bore him Attai.
36 Attai was the father of Nathan,
Nathan the father of Zabad,
37 Zabad the father of Ephlal,
Ephlal the father of Obed,
38 Obed the father of Jehu,
Jehu the father of Azariah,
39 Azariah the father of Helez,
Helez the father of Eleasah,
40 Eleasah the father of Sismai,
Sismai the father of Shallum,
41 Shallum the father of Jekamiah,
and Jekamiah the father of Elishama.

The clans of Caleb
42 The sons of Caleb the brother of Jerahmeel:
Mesha his firstborn, who was
the father of Ziph, and his son
Mareshah,*i* who was the father of
Hebron.

43 The sons of Hebron:
Korah, Tappuah, Rekem and
Shema. 44 Shema was the father of
Raham, and Raham the father of
Jorkeam. Rekem was the father
of Shammai. 45 The son of Shammai was Maon, and Maon was the
father of Beth Zur.
46 Caleb's concubine Ephah was the
mother of Haran, Moza and Gazez.
Haran was the father of Gazez.
47 The sons of Jahdai:
Regem, Jotham, Geshan, Pelet,
Ephah and Shaaph.
48 Caleb's concubine Maakah was the
mother of Sheber and Tirhanah.
49 She also gave birth to Shaaph
the father of Madmannah and to
Sheva the father of Makbenah and
Gibea. Caleb's daughter was Aksah. 50 These were the descendants
of Caleb.

The sons of Hur the firstborn of Ephrathah:
Shobal the father of Kiriath Jearim, 51 Salma the father of Bethlehem, and Hareph the father of
Beth Gader.
52 The descendants of Shobal the father
of Kiriath Jearim were:
Haroeh, half the Manahathites,
53 and the clans of Kiriath Jearim:
the Ithrites, Puthites, Shumath-
ites and Mishraites. From these
descended the Zorathites and Eshtaolites.
54 The descendants of Salma:
Bethlehem, the Netophathites,
Atroth Beth Joab, half the Manahathites, the Zorites, 55 and the
clans of scribes*j* who lived at Jabez: the Tirathites, Shimeathites
and Sucathites. These are the Kenites who came from Hammath,
the father of the Rekabites.*k*

---

i 42 The meaning of the Hebrew for this phrase is
uncertain.

j 55 Or *of the Sopherites*
k 55 Or *father of Beth Rekab*

The sons of David

3 These were the sons of David born to him in Hebron:

the firstborn was Amnon the son of Ahinoam of Jezreel;

the second, Daniel the son of Abigail of Carmel;

2 the third, Absalom the son of Maakah daughter of Talmai king of Geshur;

the fourth, Adonijah the son of Haggith;

3 the fifth, Shephatiah the son of Abital;

and the sixth, Ithream, by his wife Eglah.

4 These six were born to David in Hebron, where he reigned seven years and six months.

David reigned in Jerusalem for thirty-three years, 5 and these were the children born to him there:

Shammua,ª Shobab, Nathan and Solomon. These four were by Bathshebaᵇ daughter of Ammiel. 6 There were also Ibhar, Elishua,ᶜ Eliphelet, 7 Nogah, Nepheg, Japhia, 8 Elishama, Eliada and Eliphelet—nine in all. 9 All these were the sons of David, besides his sons by his concubines. And Tamar was their sister.

The kings of Judah

10 Solomon's son was Rehoboam,

Abijah his son,

Asa his son,

Jehoshaphat his son,

11 Jehoramᵈ his son,

Ahaziah his son,

Joash his son,

12 Amaziah his son,

Azariah his son,

Jotham his son,

13 Ahaz his son,

Hezekiah his son,

Manasseh his son,

14 Amon his son,

Josiah his son.

15 The sons of Josiah:

Johanan the firstborn,

Jehoiakim the second son,

Zedekiah the third,

Shallum the fourth.

16 The successors of Jehoiakim:

Jehoiachinᵉ his son,

and Zedekiah.

The royal line after the exile

17 The descendants of Jehoiachin the captive:

Shealtiel his son, 18 Malkiram, Pedaiah, Shenazzar, Jekamiah, Hoshama and Nedabiah.

19 The sons of Pedaiah:

Zerubbabel and Shimei.

The sons of Zerubbabel:

Meshullam and Hananiah.

Shelomith was their sister.

20 There were also five others:

Hashubah, Ohel, Berekiah, Hasadiah and Jushab-Hesed.

21 The descendants of Hananiah:

Pelatiah and Jeshaiah, and the sons of Rephaiah, of Arnan, of Obadiah and of Shekaniah.

22 The descendants of Shekaniah:

Shemaiah and his sons:

Hattush, Igal, Bariah, Neariah and Shaphat – six in all.

23 The sons of Neariah:

Elioenai, Hizkiah and Azrikam – three in all.

24 The sons of Elioenai:

Hodaviah, Eliashib, Pelaiah, Akkub, Johanan, Delaiah and Anani – seven in all.

Other clans of Judah

4 The descendants of Judah:

Perez, Hezron, Karmi, Hur and Shobal.

2 Reaiah son of Shobal was the father of Jahath, and Jahath the father

---

a 5 Hebrew *Shimea*, a variant of *Shammua*
b 5 One Hebrew manuscript and Vulgate (see also Septuagint and 2 Sam. 11:3); most Hebrew manuscripts *Bathshua*
c 6 Two Hebrew manuscripts (see also 2 Samuel 5:15 and 1 Chron. 14:5); most Hebrew manuscripts *Elishama*
d 11 Hebrew *Joram*, a variant of *Jehoram*

e 16 Hebrew *Jeconiah*, a variant of *Jehoiachin*; also in verse 17 of Ahumai and Lahad. These were the clans of the Zorathites.

3 These were the sons[a] of Etam:

Jezreel, Ishma and Idbash. Their sister was named Hazzelelponi. 4 Penuel was the father of Gedor, and Ezer the father of Hushah.

These were the descendants of Hur, the firstborn of Ephrathah and father[b] of Bethlehem.

5 Ashhur the father of Tekoa had two wives, Helah and Naarah.

6 Naarah bore him Ahuzzam, Hepher, Temeni and Haahashtari. These were the descendants of Naarah.

7 The sons of Helah:

Zereth, Zohar, Ethnan, 8 and Koz, who was the father of Anub and Hazzobebah and of the clans of Aharhel son of Harum.

9 Jabez was more honourable than his brothers. His mother had named him Jabez,[c] saying, 'I gave birth to him in pain.' 10 Jabez cried out to the God of Israel, 'Oh, that you would bless me and enlarge my territory! Let your hand be with me, and keep me from harm so that I will be free from pain.' And God granted his request.

11 Kelub, Shuhah's brother, was the father of Mehir, who was the father of Eshton. 12 Eshton was the father of Beth Rapha, Paseah and Tehinnah the father of Ir Nahash.[d] These were the men of Rekah.

13 The sons of Kenaz:

Othniel and Seraiah.

The sons of Othniel:

Hathath and Meonothai.[e] 14 Meonothai was the father of Ophrah.

Seraiah was the father of Joab,

the father of Ge Harashim.[f] It was called this because its people were skilled workers.

15 The sons of Caleb son of Jephunneh:

Iru, Elah and Naam.

The son of Elah:

Kenaz.

16 The sons of Jehallelel:

Ziph, Ziphah, Tiria and Asarel.

17 The sons of Ezrah:

Jether, Mered, Epher and Jalon. One of Mered's wives gave birth to Miriam, Shammai and Ishbah the father of Eshtemoa. 18 (His wife from the tribe of Judah gave birth to Jered the father of Gedor, Heber the father of Soko, and Jekuthiel the father of Zanoah.) These were the children of Pharaoh's daughter Bithiah, whom Mered had married.

19 The sons of Hodiah's wife, the sister of Naham:

the father of Keilah the Garmite, and Eshtemoa the Maakathite.

20 The sons of Shimon:

Amnon, Rinnah, Ben-Hanan and Tilon.

The descendants of Ishi:

Zoheth and Ben-Zoheth.

21 The sons of Shelah son of Judah:

Er the father of Lekah, Laadah the father of Mareshah and the clans of the linen workers at Beth Ashbea, 22 Jokim, the men of Kozeba, and Joash and Saraph, who ruled in Moab and Jashubi Lehem. (These records are from ancient times.) 23 They were the potters who lived at Netaim and Gederah; they stayed there and worked for the king.

Simeon

24 The descendants of Simeon:

Nemuel, Jamin, Jarib, Zerah and Shaul;

25 Shallum was Shaul's son, Mibsam his son and Mishma his son.

26 The descendants of Mishma:

---

a 3 Some Septuagint manuscripts (see also Vulgate); Hebrew *father*

b 4 *Father* may mean *civic leader* or *military leader*; also in verses 12, 14, 17, 18 and possibly elsewhere.

c 9 *Jabez* sounds like the Hebrew for *pain.*

d 12 Or *of the city of Nahash*

e 13 Some Septuagint manuscripts and Vulgate; Hebrew does not have *and Meonothai.*

f 14 *Ge Harashim* means *valley of skilled workers.*

Hammuel his son, Zakkur his son and Shimei his son.

27 Shimei had sixteen sons and six daughters, but his brothers did not have many children; so their entire clan did not become as numerous as the people of Judah. 28 They lived in Beersheba, Moladah, Hazar Shual, 29 Bilhah, Ezem, Tolad, 30 Bethuel, Hormah, Ziklag, 31 Beth Markaboth, Hazar Susim, Beth Biri and Shaaraim. These were their towns until the reign of David. 32 Their surrounding villages were Etam, Ain, Rimmon, Token and Ashan – five towns – 33 and all the villages around these towns as far as Baalath.*g* These were their settlements. And they kept a genealogical record.

34 Meshobab, Jamlech, Joshah son of Amaziah, 35 Joel, Jehu son of Joshibiah, the son of Seraiah, the son of Asiel, 36 also Elioenai, Jaakobah, Jeshohaiah, Asaiah, Adiel, Jesimiel, Benaiah, 37 and Ziza son of Shiphi, the son of Allon, the son of Jedaiah, the son of Shimri, the son of Shemaiah.

38 The men listed above by name were leaders of their clans. Their families increased greatly, 39 and they went to the outskirts of Gedor to the east of the valley in search of pasture for their flocks. 40 They found rich, good pasture, and the land was spacious, peaceful and quiet. Some Hamites had lived there formerly.

41 The men whose names were listed came in the days of Hezekiah king of Judah. They attacked the Hamites in their dwellings and also the Meunites who were there and completely destroyed*h* them, as is evident to this day. Then they settled in their place, because there was pasture for their flocks. 42 And five hundred of these Simeonites, led by Pelatiah, Neariah, Rephaiah and Uzziel, the sons of Ishi, invaded the hill country of Seir. 43 They killed the remaining Amalekites who had escaped, and they have lived there to this day.

Reuben

5 The sons of Reuben the firstborn of Israel (he was the firstborn, but when he defiled his father's marriage bed, his rights as firstborn were given to the sons of Joseph son of Israel; so he could not be listed in the genealogical record in accordance with his birthright, 2 and though Judah was the strongest of his brothers and a ruler came from him, the rights of the firstborn belonged to Joseph) – 3 the sons of Reuben the firstborn of Israel:

Hanok, Pallu, Hezron and Karmi.

4 The descendants of Joel:

Shemaiah his son, Gog his son,
Shimei his son, 5 Micah his son,
Reaiah his son, Baal his son,
6 and Beerah his son, whom Tiglath-Pileser*a* king of Assyria took into exile. Beerah was a leader of the Reubenites.

7 Their relatives by clans, listed according to their genealogical records:

Jeiel the chief, Zechariah, 8 and Bela son of Azaz, the son of Shema, the son of Joel. They settled in the area from Aroer to Nebo and Baal Meon. 9 To the east they occupied the land up to the edge of the desert that extends to the River Euphrates, because their livestock had increased in Gilead.

10 During Saul's reign they waged war against the Hagrites, who were defeated at their hands; they occupied the dwellings of the Hagrites throughout the entire region east of Gilead.

Gad

11 The Gadites lived next to them in Bashan, as far as Salekah:

12 Joel was the chief, Shapham the second, then Janai and Shaphat, in Bashan.

---

g 33 Some Septuagint manuscripts (see also Joshua 19:8); Hebrew *Baal*
h 41 The Hebrew term refers to the irrevocable giving over of things or persons to the LORD, often by totally destroying them.

a 6 Hebrew *Tilgath-Pilneser*, a variant of *Tiglath-Pileser*; also in verse 26

13 Their relatives, by families, were: Michael, Meshullam, Sheba, Jorai, Jakan, Zia and Eber – seven in all. 14 These were the sons of Abihail son of Huri, the son of Jaroah, the son of Gilead, the son of Michael, the son of Jeshishai, the son of Jahdo, the son of Buz.

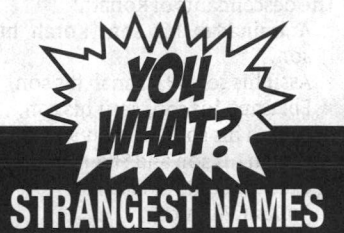

YOU WHAT?
STRANGEST NAMES

NERGAL–SHAREZER OF SAMGAR
Jeremiah 39:3
nuhr'gal-shar-EE-zuhr

MAHER–SHALAL–HASH–BAZ
Isaiah 8:1–3
MAY-huhr-SHAL-al-hash(')-baz

CUSHAN RISHATHAIM
Judges 3:8
koo'shan-rish'uh-THAY-im

MERODACH BALADAN
2 Kings 20:12
MER-oh-dak-BAL-uh-dan

TIGLATH PILESER
1 Chronicles 5:26
tig'lath-pil-EE-zuhr

ZAPHENATH PANEAH
Genesis 41:45
zaf'uh-nath-puh-NEE-uh

SHELUMIEL SON OF ZURISHADDAI
Num 1:6; 2:12; 7:36, 41; 10:19
seh-LOO-mee-ehl

BEREKIAH SON OF MESHILLEMOTH
2 Chronicles 28:12
muh-SHIL-uh-moth

NAHBI SON OF VOPHSI
Numbers 13:14
NAH-bi, VOF-si

SHEAR–JASHUB
Isaiah 7:3
SHEE-uhr-JAY-shuhb

15 Ahi son of Abdiel, the son of Guni, was head of their family. 16 The Gadites lived in Gilead, in Bashan and its outlying villages, and on all the pasture-lands of Sharon as far as they extended. 17 All these were entered in the genealogical records during the reigns of Jotham king of Judah and Jeroboam king of Israel.

18 The Reubenites, the Gadites and the half-tribe of Manasseh had 44,760 men ready for military service – able-bodied men who could handle shield and sword, who could use a bow, and who were trained for battle. 19 They waged war against the Hagrites, Jetur, Naphish and Nodab. 20 They were helped in fighting them, and God delivered the Hagrites and all their allies into their hands, because they cried out to him during the battle. He answered their prayers, because they trusted in him. 21 They seized the livestock of the Hagrites – fifty thousand camels, two hundred and fifty thousand sheep and two thousand donkeys. They also took one hundred thousand people captive, 22 and many others fell slain, because the battle was God's. And they occupied the land until the exile.

The half-tribe of Manasseh

23 The people of the half-tribe of Manasseh were numerous; they settled in the land from Bashan to Baal Hermon, that is, to Senir (Mount Hermon). 24 These were the heads of their families: Epher, Ishi, Eliel, Azriel, Jeremiah, Hodaviah and Jahdiel. They were brave warriors, famous men, and heads of their families. 25 But they were unfaithful to the God of their ancestors and prostituted themselves to the gods of the peoples of the land, whom God had destroyed before them. 26 So the God of Israel stirred up the spirit of Pul king of Assyria (that is, Tiglath-Pileser king of Assyria), who took the Reubenites, the Gadites and the half-tribe of Manasseh into exile. He took them to Halah, Habor, Hara and the river of Gozan, where they are to this day.

Levi

6[a] The sons of Levi:
Gershon, Kohath and Merari.
2 The sons of Kohath:
Amram, Izhar, Hebron and Uzziel.
3 The children of Amram:
Aaron, Moses and Miriam.
The sons of Aaron:
Nadab, Abihu, Eleazar and Ithamar.
4 Eleazar was the father of Phinehas,
Phinehas the father of Abishua,
5 Abishua the father of Bukki,
Bukki the father of Uzzi,
6 Uzzi the father of Zerahiah,
Zerahiah the father of Meraioth,
7 Meraioth the father of Amariah,
Amariah the father of Ahitub,
8 Ahitub the father of Zadok,
Zadok the father of Ahimaaz,
9 Ahimaaz the father of Azariah,
Azariah the father of Johanan,
10 Johanan the father of Azariah (it was he who served as priest in the temple Solomon built in Jerusalem),
11 Azariah the father of Amariah,
Amariah the father of Ahitub,
12 Ahitub the father of Zadok,
Zadok the father of Shallum,
13 Shallum the father of Hilkiah,
Hilkiah the father of Azariah,
14 Azariah the father of Seraiah,
and Seraiah the father of Jozadak.[b]
15 Jozadak was deported when the LORD sent Judah and Jerusalem into exile by the hand of Nebuchadnezzar.

16 The sons of Levi:
Gershon,[c] Kohath and Merari.
17 These are the names of the sons of Gershon:
Libni and Shimei.
18 The sons of Kohath:
Amram, Izhar, Hebron and Uzziel.
19 The sons of Merari:
Mahli and Mushi.
These are the clans of the Levites listed according to their fathers:
20 of Gershon:
Libni his son, Jahath his son,
Zimmah his son, 21 Joah his son,
Iddo his son, Zerah his son
and Jeatherai his son.
22 The descendants of Kohath:
Amminadab his son, Korah his son,
Assir his son, 23 Elkanah his son,
Ebiasaph his son, Assir his son,
24 Tahath his son, Uriel his son,
Uzziah his son and Shaul his son.
25 The descendants of Elkanah:
Amasai, Ahimoth,
26 Elkanah his son,[d] Zophai his son,
Nahath his son, 27 Eliab his son,
Jeroham his son, Elkanah his son
and Samuel his son.[e]
28 The sons of Samuel:
Joel[f] the firstborn
and Abijah the second son.
29 The descendants of Merari:
Mahli, Libni his son,
Shimei his son, Uzzah his son,
30 Shimea his son, Haggiah his son
and Asaiah his son.

The temple musicians

31 These are the men David put in charge of the music in the house of the LORD after the ark came to rest there. 32 They ministered with music before the tabernacle, the tent of meeting, until Solomon built the temple of the LORD in Jerusalem. They performed their duties according to the regulations laid down for them.

33 Here are the men who served, together with their sons:
from the Kohathites:

---

a In Hebrew texts 6:1-15 is numbered 5:27-41, and 6:16-81 is numbered 6:1-66.
b 14 Hebrew *Jehozadak*, a variant of *Jozadak*; also in verse 15
c 16 Hebrew *Gershom*, a variant of *Gershon*; also in verses 17, 20, 43, 62 and 71

d 26 Some Hebrew manuscripts, Septuagint and Syriac; most Hebrew manuscripts *Ahimoth* 26*and Elkanah. The sons of Elkanah:*
e 27 Some Septuagint manuscripts (see also 1 Samuel 1:19,20 and 1 Chron. 6:33,34); Hebrew does not have *and Samuel his son.*
f 28 Some Septuagint manuscripts and Syriac (see also 1 Samuel 8:2 and 1 Chron. 6:33); Hebrew does not have *Joel.*

Heman, the musician,
the son of Joel, the son of Samuel,
34 the son of Elkanah, the son of Jeroham,
the son of Eliel, the son of Toah,
35 the son of Zuph, the son of Elkanah,
the son of Mahath, the son of Amasai,
36 the son of Elkanah, the son of Joel,
the son of Azariah, the son of Zephaniah,
37 the son of Tahath, the son of Assir,
the son of Ebiasaph, the son of Korah,
38 the son of Izhar, the son of Kohath,
the son of Levi, the son of Israel;
39 and Heman's associate Asaph, who served at his right hand:
Asaph son of Berekiah, the son of Shimea,
40 the son of Michael, the son of Baaseiah,g
the son of Malkijah, 41 the son of Ethni,
the son of Zerah, the son of Adaiah,
42 the son of Ethan, the son of Zimmah,
the son of Shimei, 43 the son of Jahath,
the son of Gershon, the son of Levi;
44 and from their associates, the Merarites, at his left hand:
Ethan son of Kishi, the son of Abdi,
the son of Malluk, 45 the son of Hashabiah,
the son of Amaziah, the son of Hilkiah,
46 the son of Amzi, the son of Bani,
the son of Shemer, 47 the son of Mahli,

the son of Mushi, the son of Merari,
the son of Levi.

48 Their fellow Levites were assigned to all the other duties of the tabernacle, the house of God. 49 But Aaron and his descendants were the ones who presented offerings on the altar of burnt offering and on the altar of incense in connection with all that was done in the Most Holy Place, making atonement for Israel, in accordance with all that Moses the servant of God had commanded.

50 These were the descendants of Aaron:
Eleazar his son, Phinehas his son,
Abishua his son, 51 Bukki his son,
Uzzi his son, Zerahiah his son,
52 Meraioth his son, Amariah his son,
Ahitub his son, 53 Zadok his son
and Ahimaaz his son.

54 These were the locations of their settlements allotted as their territory (they were assigned to the descendants of Aaron who were from the Kohathite clan, because the first lot was for them): 55 they were given Hebron in Judah with its surrounding pasture-lands. 56 But the fields and villages around the city were given to Caleb son of Jephunneh.

57 So the descendants of Aaron were given Hebron (a city of refuge), and Libnah,h Jattir, Eshtemoa, 58 Hilen, Debir, 59 Ashan, Juttahi and Beth Shemesh, together with their pasture-lands. 60 And from the tribe of Benjamin they were given Gibeon,j Geba, Alemeth and Anathoth, together with their pasture-lands.

The total number of towns distributed among the Kohathite clans came to thirteen.

---

g 40 Most Hebrew manuscripts; some Hebrew manuscripts, one Septuagint manuscript and Syriac Maaseiah
h 57 See Joshua 21:13; Hebrew given the cities of refuge: Hebron, Libnah.
i 59 Syriac (see also Septuagint and Joshua 21:16); Hebrew does not have Juttah.
j 60 See Joshua 21:17; Hebrew does not have Gibeon.

61 The rest of Kohath's descendants were allotted ten towns from the clans of half the tribe of Manasseh.

62 The descendants of Gershon, clan by clan, were allotted thirteen towns from the tribes of Issachar, Asher and Naphtali, and from the part of the tribe of Manasseh that is in Bashan.

63 The descendants of Merari, clan by clan, were allotted twelve towns from the tribes of Reuben, Gad and Zebulun.

64 So the Israelites gave the Levites these towns and their pasture-lands. 65 From the tribes of Judah, Simeon and Benjamin they allotted the previously named towns.

66 Some of the Kohathite clans were given as their territory towns from the tribe of Ephraim.

67 In the hill country of Ephraim they were given Shechem (a city of refuge), and Gezer,k 68 Jokmeam, Beth Horon, 69 Aijalon and Gath Rimmon, together with their pasture-lands.

70 And from half the tribe of Manasseh the Israelites gave Aner and Bileam, together with their pasture-lands, to the rest of the Kohathite clans.

71 The Gershonites received the following:

from the clan of the half-tribe of Manasseh

they received Golan in Bashan and also Ashtaroth, together with their pasture-lands;

72 from the tribe of Issachar

they received Kedesh, Daberath, 73 Ramoth and Anem, together with their pasture-lands;

74 from the tribe of Asher

they received Mashal, Abdon, 75 Hukok and Rehob, together with their pasture-lands;

76 and from the tribe of Naphtali

they received Kedesh in Galilee,

Hammon and Kiriathaim, together with their pasture-lands.

77 The Merarites (the rest of the Levites) received the following:

from the tribe of Zebulun

they received Jokneam, Kartah,l Rimmono and Tabor, together with their pasture-lands;

78 from the tribe of Reuben across the Jordan east of Jericho

they received Bezer in the wilderness, Jahzah, 79 Kedemoth and Mephaath, together with their pasture-lands;

80 and from the tribe of Gad

they received Ramoth in Gilead, Mahanaim, 81 Heshbon and Jazer, together with their pasture-lands.

Issachar

7 The sons of Issachar:

Tola, Puah, Jashub and Shimron – four in all.

2 The sons of Tola:

Uzzi, Rephaiah, Jeriel, Jahmai, Ibsam and Samuel – heads of their families. During the reign of David, the descendants of Tola listed as fighting men in their genealogy numbered 22,600.

3 The son of Uzzi:

Izrahiah.

The sons of Izrahiah:

Michael, Obadiah, Joel and Ishiah. All five of them were chiefs. 4 According to their family genealogy, they had 36,000 men ready for battle, for they had many wives and children.

5 The relatives who were fighting men belonging to all the clans of Issachar, as listed in their genealogy, were 87,000 in all.

Benjamin

6 Three sons of Benjamin:

Bela, Beker and Jediael.

7 The sons of Bela:

---

k 67 See Joshua 21:21; Hebrew *given the cities of refuge: Shechem, Gezer.*

l 77 See Septuagint and Joshua 21:34; Hebrew does not have *Jokneam, Kartah.*

Ezbon, Uzzi, Uzziel, Jerimoth and Iri, heads of families – five in all. Their genealogical record listed 22,034 fighting men. **8** The sons of Beker:

Zemirah, Joash, Eliezer, Elioenai, Omri, Jeremoth, Abijah, Anathoth and Alemeth. All these were the sons of Beker. **9** Their genealogical record listed the heads of families and 20,200 fighting men. **10** The son of Jediael:

Bilhan.

The sons of Bilhan:

Jeush, Benjamin, Ehud, Kenaa-nah, Zethan, Tarshish and Ahish-ahar. **11** All these sons of Jediael were heads of families. There were 17,200 fighting men ready to go out to war. **12** The Shuppites and Huppites were the descendants of Ir, and the Hu-shites*a* the descendants of Aher.

Naphtali
13 The sons of Naphtali:

Jahziel, Guni, Jezer and Shillem*b* – the descendants of Bilhah.

Manasseh
14 The descendants of Manasseh:

Asriel was his descendant through his Aramean concubine. She gave birth to Makir the father of Gilead. **15** Makir took a wife from among the Huppites and Shuppites. His sister's name was Maakah.

Another descendant was named Zelophehad, who had only daugh-ters.

16 Makir's wife Maakah gave birth to a son and named him Peresh. His brother was named Sheresh, and his sons were Ulam and Rakem. **17** The son of Ulam:

Bedan.

These were the sons of Gilead son of Makir, the son of Manasseh. **18** His sister Hammoleketh gave birth to Ishhod, Abiezer and Mahlah.

19 The sons of Shemida were:

Ahian, Shechem, Likhi and Aniam.

Ephraim
20 The descendants of Ephraim:

Shuthelah, Bered his son, Tahath his son, Eleadah his son, Tahath his son, **21** Zabad his son and Shuthelah his son.

Ezer and Elead were killed by the native-born men of Gath, when they went down to seize their livestock. **22** Their father Ephraim mourned for them many days, and his rela-tives came to comfort him. **23** Then he made love to his wife again, and she became pregnant and gave birth to a son. He named him Beriah,*c* be-cause there had been misfortune in his family. **24** His daughter was Shee-rah, who built Lower and Upper Beth Horon as well as Uzzen Sheerah.

25 Repah was his son, Resheph his son,*d* Telah his son, Tahan his son, **26** Ladan his son, Ammihud his son, Elishama his son, **27** Nun his son and Joshua his son.

28 Their lands and settlements included Bethel and its surrounding villages, Naa-ran to the east, Gezer and its villages to the west, and Shechem and its villages all the way to Ayyah and its villages. **29** Along the borders of Manasseh were Beth Shan, Taanach, Megiddo and Dor, together with their villages. The descendants of Joseph son of Israel lived in these towns.

Asher
30 The sons of Asher:

Imnah, Ishvah, Ishvi and Beriah. Their sister was Serah.

31 The sons of Beriah:

---

a 12 Or Ir. The sons of Dan: Hushim, (see Gen. 46:23); Hebrew does not have The sons of Dan.

b 13 Some Hebrew and Septuagint manuscripts (see also Gen. 46:24 and Num. 26:49); most Hebrew manuscripts Shallum

c 23 Beriah sounds like the Hebrew for misfortune.

d 25 Some Septuagint manuscripts; Hebrew does not have his son.

Heber and Malkiel, who was the father of Birzaith.

32 Heber was the father of Japhlet, Shomer and Hotham and of their sister Shua.

33 The sons of Japhlet:
Pasak, Bimhal and Ashvath. These were Japhlet's sons.

34 The sons of Shomer:
Ahi, Rohgah,*e* Hubbah and Aram.

35 The sons of his brother Helem:
Zophah, Imna, Shelesh and Amal.

36 The sons of Zophah:
Suah, Harnepher, Shual, Beri, Imrah, 37 Bezer, Hod, Shamma, Shilshah, Ithran*f* and Beera.

38 The sons of Jether:
Jephunneh, Pispah and Ara.

39 The sons of Ulla:
Arah, Hanniel and Rizia.

40 All these were descendants of Asher – heads of families, choice men, brave warriors and outstanding leaders. The number of men ready for battle, as listed in their genealogy, was 26,000.

The genealogy of Saul the Benjaminite

8 Benjamin was the father of Bela his firstborn,
Ashbel the second son, Aharah the third,
2 Nohah the fourth and Rapha the fifth.

3 The sons of Bela were:
Addar, Gera, Abihud,*a* 4 Abishua, Naaman, Ahoah, 5 Gera, Shephuphan and Huram.

6 These were the descendants of Ehud, who were heads of families of those living in Geba and were deported to Manahath:

7 Naaman, Ahijah and Gera, who deported them and who was the father of Uzza and Ahihud.

8 Sons were born to Shaharaim in Moab after he had divorced his wives Hushim and Baara. 9 By his

---

e 34 Or of his brother Shomer: Rohgah
f 37 Possibly a variant of Jether
a 3 Or Gera the father of Ehud

---

wife Hodesh he had Jobab, Zibia, Mesha, Malkam, 10 Jeuz, Sakia and Mirmah. These were his sons, heads of families. 11 By Hushim he had Abitub and Elpaal.

FAVOURITE VERSES

Jeremiah 33:3

Call to me and I will answer you and tell you great and unsearchable things you do not know.

I remember when we looked at this verse in a Sunday school session, and it has stayed with me ever since. It reminds me that all I need to do is ask God and he will give me anything to accomplish what I want to achieve, big or small.

Keiran

12 The sons of Elpaal:
Eber, Misham, Shemed (who built Ono and Lod with its surrounding villages), 13 and Beriah and Shema, who were heads of families of those living in Aijalon and who drove out the inhabitants of Gath.

14 Ahio, Shashak, Jeremoth, 15 Zebadiah, Arad, Eder, 16 Michael, Ishpah and Joha were the sons of Beriah.

17 Zebadiah, Meshullam, Hizki, Heber, 18 Ishmerai, Izliah and Jobab were the sons of Elpaal.

19 Jakim, Zikri, Zabdi, 20 Elienai, Zillethai, Eliel, 21 Adaiah, Beraiah and Shimrath were the sons of Shimei.

22 Ishpan, Eber, Eliel, 23 Abdon, Zikri, Hanan, 24 Hananiah, Elam, Anthothijah, 25 Iphdeiah and Penuel were the sons of Shashak.

26 Shamsherai, Shehariah, Athaliah,

²⁷Jaareshiah, Elijah and Zikri were the sons of Jeroham.

²⁸All these were heads of families, chiefs as listed in their genealogy, and they lived in Jerusalem.

²⁹Jeiel^b the father^c of Gibeon lived in Gibeon.

His wife's name was Maakah, ³⁰and his firstborn son was Abdon, followed by Zur, Kish, Baal, Ner,^d Nadab, ³¹Gedor, Ahio, Zeker ³²and Mikloth, who was the father of Shimeah. They too lived near their relatives in Jerusalem.

³³Ner was the father of Kish, Kish the father of Saul, and Saul the father of Jonathan, Malki-Shua, Abinadab and Esh-Baal.^e

³⁴The son of Jonathan:
Merib-Baal,^f who was the father of Micah.

³⁵The sons of Micah:
Pithon, Melek, Tarea and Ahaz.

³⁶Ahaz was the father of Jehoaddah, Jehoaddah was the father of Alemeth, Azmaveth and Zimri, and Zimri was the father of Moza.
³⁷Moza was the father of Binea; Raphah was his son, Eleasah his son and Azel his son.

³⁸Azel had six sons, and these were their names:
Azrikam, Bokeru, Ishmael, Sheariah, Obadiah and Hanan. All these were the sons of Azel.

³⁹The sons of his brother Eshek:
Ulam his firstborn, Jeush the second son and Eliphelet the third. ⁴⁰The sons of Ulam were brave warriors who could handle the bow. They had many sons and grandsons – 150 in all.

All these were the descendants of Benjamin.

9 All Israel was listed in the genealogies in the book of the kings of Israel and Judah. They were taken captive to Babylon because of their unfaithfulness.

The people in Jerusalem

²Now the first to resettle on their own property in their own towns were some Israelites, priests, Levites and temple servants.

³Those from Judah, from Benjamin, and from Ephraim and Manasseh who lived in Jerusalem were:

⁴Uthai son of Ammihud, the son of Omri, the son of Imri, the son of Bani, a descendant of Perez son of Judah.

⁵Of the Shelanites^a:
Asaiah the firstborn and his sons.

⁶Of the Zerahites:
Jeuel.
The people from Judah numbered 690.

⁷Of the Benjaminites:
Sallu son of Meshullam, the son of Hodaviah, the son of Hassenuah;
⁸Ibneiah son of Jeroham; Elah son of Uzzi, the son of Mikri; and Meshullam son of Shephatiah, the son of Reuel, the son of Ibnijah.
⁹The people from Benjamin, as listed in their genealogy, numbered 956. All these men were heads of their families.

¹⁰Of the priests:
Jedaiah; Jehoiarib; Jakin;
¹¹Azariah son of Hilkiah, the son of Meshullam, the son of Zadok, the son of Meraioth, the son of Ahitub, the official in charge of the house of God;
¹²Adaiah son of Jeroham, the son of Pashhur, the son of Malkijah; and Maasai son of Adiel, the son of Jahzerah, the son of Meshullam, the son of Meshillemith, the son of Immer.
¹³The priests, who were heads of families, numbered 1,760. They

---

b 29 Some Septuagint manuscripts (see also 9:35); Hebrew does not have Jeiel.
c 29 Father may mean civic leader or military leader.
d 30 Some Septuagint manuscripts (see also 9:36); Hebrew does not have Ner.
e 33 Also known as Ish-Bosheth
f 34 Also known as Mephibosheth

a 5 See Num. 26:20; Hebrew Shilonites.

were able men, responsible for ministering in the house of God.

14 Of the Levites:
Shemaiah son of Hasshub, the son of Azrikam, the son of Hashabiah, a Merarite; 15 Bakbakkar, Heresh, Galal and Mattaniah son of Mika, the son of Zikri, the son of Asaph; 16 Obadiah son of Shemaiah, the son of Galal, the son of Jeduthun; and Berekiah son of Asa, the son of Elkanah, who lived in the villages of the Netophathites.

17 The gatekeepers:
Shallum, Akkub, Talmon, Ahiman and their fellow Levites, Shallum their chief 18 being stationed at the King's Gate on the east, up to the present time. These were the gatekeepers belonging to the camp of the Levites. 19 Shallum son of Kore, the son of Ebiasaph, the son of Korah, and his fellow gatekeepers from his family (the Korahites) were responsible for guarding the thresholds of the tent just as their ancestors had been responsible for guarding the entrance to the dwelling of the LORD. 20 In earlier times Phinehas son of Eleazar was the official in charge of the gatekeepers, and the LORD was with him. 21 Zechariah son of Meshelemiah was the gatekeeper at the entrance to the tent of meeting.

22 Altogether, those chosen to be gatekeepers at the thresholds numbered 212. They were registered by genealogy in their villages. The gatekeepers had been assigned to their positions of trust by David and Samuel the seer. 23 They and their descendants were in charge of guarding the gates of the house of the LORD – the house called the tent of meeting. 24 The gatekeepers were on the four sides: east, west, north and south. 25 Their fellow Levites in their villages had to come from time to time and share their duties for seven-day periods. 26 But the four principal gatekeepers, who were Levites, were entrusted with the responsibility for the rooms and treasuries in the house of God.

27 They would spend the night stationed round the house of God, because they had to guard it; and they had charge of the key for opening it each morning.

28 Some of them were in charge of the articles used in the temple service; they counted them when they were brought in and when they were taken out. 29 Others were assigned to take care of the furnishings and all the other articles of the sanctuary, as well as the special flour and wine, and the olive oil, incense and spices. 30 But some of the priests took care of mixing the spices. 31 A Levite named Mattithiah, the firstborn son of Shallum the Korahite, was entrusted with the responsibility for baking the offering bread. 32 Some of the Kohathites, their fellow Levites, were in charge of preparing for every Sabbath the bread set out on the table.

33 Those who were musicians, heads of Levite families, stayed in the rooms of the temple and were exempt from other duties because they were responsible for the work day and night.

34 All these were heads of Levite families, chiefs as listed in their genealogy, and they lived in Jerusalem.

The genealogy of Saul

35 Jeiel the father[b] of Gibeon lived in Gibeon.

His wife's name was Maakah, 36 and his firstborn son was Abdon, followed by Zur, Kish, Baal, Ner, Nadab, 37 Gedor, Ahio, Zechariah and Mikloth. 38 Mikloth was the father of Shimeam. They too lived near their relatives in Jerusalem.

39 Ner was the father of Kish, Kish the father of Saul, and Saul the father of Jonathan, Malki-Shua, Abinadab and Esh-Baal.[c]

40 The son of Jonathan:
Merib-Baal,[d] who was the father of Micah.

41 The sons of Micah:

b 35 *Father* may mean *civic leader* or *military leader.*
c 39 Also known as *Ish-Bosheth*
d 40 Also known as *Mephibosheth*

Pithon, Melek, Tahrea and Ahaz.*e*

42 Ahaz was the father of Jadah, Jadah*f* was the father of Alemeth, Azmaveth and Zimri, and Zimri was the father of Moza. 43 Moza was the father of Binea; Rephaiah was his son, Eleasah his son and Azel his son.

44 Azel had six sons, and these were their names:

Azrikam, Bokeru, Ishmael, Sheariah, Obadiah and Hanan. These were the sons of Azel.

Saul takes his life

10 Now the Philistines fought against Israel; the Israelites fled before them, and many fell dead on Mount Gilboa. 2 The Philistines were in hot pursuit of Saul and his sons, and they killed his sons Jonathan, Abinadab and Malki-Shua. 3 The fighting grew fierce around Saul, and when the archers overtook him, they wounded him.

4 Saul said to his armour-bearer, 'Draw your sword and run me through, or these uncircumcised fellows will come and abuse me.'

But his armour-bearer was terrified and would not do it; so Saul took his own sword and fell on it. 5 When the armour-bearer saw that Saul was dead, he too fell on his sword and died. 6 So Saul and his three sons died, and all his house died together.

7 When all the Israelites in the valley saw that the army had fled and that Saul and his sons had died, they abandoned their towns and fled. And the Philistines came and occupied them.

8 The next day, when the Philistines came to strip the dead, they found Saul and his sons fallen on Mount Gilboa. 9 They stripped him and took his head and his armour, and sent messengers throughout the land of the Philistines to proclaim the news among their idols and their people. 10 They put his armour in the temple of their gods and hung up his head in the temple of Dagon.

11 When all the inhabitants of Jabesh Gilead heard what the Philistines had done to Saul, 12 all their valiant men went and took the bodies of Saul and his sons and brought them to Jabesh. Then they buried their bones under the great tree in Jabesh, and they fasted seven days.

13 Saul died because he was unfaithful to the LORD; he did not keep the word of the LORD and even consulted a medium for guidance, 14 and did not enquire of the LORD. So the LORD put him to death and turned the kingdom over to David son of Jesse.

David becomes king over Israel

11 All Israel came together to David at Hebron and said, 'We are your own flesh and blood. 2 In the past, even while Saul was king, you were the one who led Israel on their military campaigns. And the LORD your God said to you, "You will shepherd my people Israel, and you will become their ruler."'

3 When all the elders of Israel had come to King David at Hebron, he made a covenant with them at Hebron before the LORD, and they anointed David king over Israel, as the LORD had promised through Samuel.

David conquers Jerusalem

4 David and all the Israelites marched to Jerusalem (that is, Jebus). The Jebusites who lived there 5 said to David, 'You will not get in here.' Nevertheless, David captured the fortress of Zion – which is the City of David.

6 David had said, 'Whoever leads the attack on the Jebusites will become commander-in-chief.' Joab son of Zeruiah went up first, and so he received the command.

7 David then took up residence in the fortress, and so it was called the City of David. 8 He built up the city around it, from the terraces*a* to the surrounding wall, while Joab restored the rest of the

---

e 41 Vulgate and Syriac (see also Septuagint and 8:35); Hebrew does not have *and Ahaz*.

f 42 Some Hebrew manuscripts and Septuagint (see also 8:36); most Hebrew manuscripts *Jarah, Jarah*

a 8 Or *the Millo*

city. ⁹And David became more and more powerful, because the LORD Almighty was with him.

David's mighty warriors

¹⁰These were the chiefs of David's mighty warriors – they, together with all Israel, gave his kingship strong support to extend it over the whole land, as the LORD had promised – ¹¹this is the list of David's mighty warriors:

Jashobeam,ᵇ a Hakmonite, was chief of the officers;ᶜ he raised his spear against three hundred men, whom he killed in one encounter.

¹²Next to him was Eleazar son of Dodai the Ahohite, one of the three mighty warriors. ¹³He was with David at Pas Dammim when the Philistines gathered there for battle. At a place where there was a field full of barley, the troops fled from the Philistines. ¹⁴But they took their stand in the middle of the field. They defended it and struck the Philistines down, and the LORD brought about a great victory.

¹⁵Three of the thirty chiefs came down to David to the rock at the cave of Adullam, while a band of Philistines was encamped in the Valley of Rephaim. ¹⁶At that time David was in the stronghold, and the Philistine garrison was at Bethlehem. ¹⁷David longed for water and said, 'Oh, that someone would get me a drink of water from the well near the gate of Bethlehem!' ¹⁸So the Three broke through the Philistine lines, drew water from the well near the gate of Bethlehem and carried it back to David. But he refused to drink it; instead, he poured it out to the LORD. ¹⁹'God forbid that I should do this!' he said. 'Should I drink the blood of these men who went at the risk of their lives?' Because they risked their lives to bring it back, David would not drink it.

Such were the exploits of the three mighty warriors.

²⁰Abishai the brother of Joab was chief of the Three. He raised his spear against three hundred men, whom he killed, and so he became as famous as the Three. ²¹He was doubly honoured above the Three and became their commander, even though he was not included among them.

²²Benaiah son of Jehoiada, a valiant fighter from Kabzeel, performed great exploits. He struck down Moab's two mightiest warriors. He also went down into a pit on a snowy day and killed a lion. ²³And he struck down an Egyptian who was five cubitsᵈ tall. Although the Egyptian had a spear like a weaver's rod in his hand, Benaiah went against him with a club. He snatched the spear from the Egyptian's hand and killed him with his own spear. ²⁴Such were the exploits of Benaiah son of Jehoiada; he too was as famous as the three mighty warriors. ²⁵He was held in greater honour than any of the Thirty, but he was not included among the Three. And David put him in charge of his bodyguard.

²⁶The mighty warriors were:
Asahel the brother of Joab,
Elhanan son of Dodo from Bethlehem,
²⁷Shammoth the Harorite,
Helez the Pelonite,
²⁸Ira son of Ikkesh from Tekoa,
Abiezer from Anathoth,
²⁹Sibbekai the Hushathite,
Ilai the Ahohite,
³⁰Maharai the Netophathite,
Heled son of Baanah the Netophathite,
³¹Ithai son of Ribai from Gibeah in Benjamin,
Benaiah the Pirathonite,
³²Hurai from the ravines of Gaash,
Abiel the Arbathite,
³³Azmaveth the Baharumite,
Eliahba the Shaalbonite,
³⁴the sons of Hashem the Gizonite,
Jonathan son of Shagee the Hararite,

ᵇ 11 Possibly a variant of *Jashob-Baal*
ᶜ 11 Or *Thirty*; some Septuagint manuscripts *Three* (see also 2 Samuel 23:8)

ᵈ 23 That is, about 2.3 metres

35 Ahiam son of Sakar the Hararite,
Eliphal son of Ur,
36 Hepher the Mekerathite,
Ahijah the Pelonite,
37 Hezro the Carmelite,
Naarai son of Ezbai,
38 Joel the brother of Nathan,
Mibhar son of Hagri,
39 Zelek the Ammonite,
Naharai the Berothite, the
armour-bearer of Joab son of Zeruiah,
40 Ira the Ithrite,
Gareb the Ithrite,
41 Uriah the Hittite,
Zabad son of Ahlai,
42 Adina son of Shiza the Reubenite,
who was chief of the Reubenites,
and the thirty with him,
43 Hanan son of Maakah,
Joshaphat the Mithnite,
44 Uzzia the Ashterathite,
Shama and Jeiel the sons of Hotham the Aroerite,
45 Jediael son of Shimri,
his brother Joha the Tizite,
46 Eliel the Mahavite,
Jeribai and Joshaviah the sons of
Elnaam,
Ithmah the Moabite,
47 Eliel, Obed and Jaasiel the Mezo-
baite.

Warriors join David

12 These were the men who came to
David at Ziklag, while he was banished from the presence of Saul son of
Kish (they were among the warriors who
helped him in battle; 2 they were armed
with bows and were able to shoot arrows
or to sling stones right-handed or left-
handed; they were relatives of Saul from
the tribe of Benjamin):

3 Ahiezer their chief and Joash the
sons of Shemaah the Gibeathite;
Jeziel and Pelet the sons of Azmaveth; Berakah, Jehu the Anathothite, 4 and Ishmaiah the Gibeonite,
a mighty warrior among the Thirty,
who was a leader of the Thirty; Jeremiah, Jahaziel, Johanan, Jozabad the

Gederathite, a 5 Eluzai, Jerimoth, Bea-
liah, Shemariah and Shephatiah the
Haruphite; 6 Elkanah, Ishiah, Azarel,
Joezer and Jashobeam the Korahites;
7 and Joelah and Zebadiah the sons
of Jeroham from Gedor.

8 Some Gadites defected to David at his
stronghold in the wilderness. They were
brave warriors, ready for battle and able
to handle the shield and spear. Their faces
were the faces of lions, and they were as
swift as gazelles in the mountains.
9 Ezer was the chief,
Obadiah the second in command,
Eliab the third,
10 Mishmannah the fourth, Jeremiah
the fifth,
11 Attai the sixth, Eliel the seventh,
12 Johanan the eighth, Elzabad the
ninth,
13 Jeremiah the tenth and Makbannai
the eleventh.
14 These Gadites were army commanders; the least was a match for a hundred,
and the greatest for a thousand. 15 It was
they who crossed the Jordan in the first
month when it was overflowing all its
banks, and they put to flight everyone living in the valleys, to the east and to the
west.

16 Other Benjaminites and some men
from Judah also came to David in his
stronghold. 17 David went out to meet
them and said to them, 'If you have come
to me in peace to help me, I am ready for
you to join me. But if you have come to
betray me to my enemies when my hands
are free from violence, may the God of our
ancestors see it and judge you.'

18 Then the Spirit came on Amasai, chief
of the Thirty, and he said:

'We are yours, David!
We are with you, son of Jesse!
Success, success to you,
and success to those who help you,
for your God will help you.'

---

a 4 In Hebrew texts the second half of this verse
(*Jeremiah . . . Gederathite*) is numbered 12:5, and 12:5-40
is numbered 12:6-41.

So David received them and made them leaders of his raiding bands.

¹⁹Some of the tribe of Manasseh defected to David when he went with the Philistines to fight against Saul. (He and his men did not help the Philistines because, after consultation, their rulers sent him away. They said, 'It will cost us our heads if he deserts to his master Saul.') ²⁰When David went to Ziklag, these were the men of Manasseh who defected to him: Adnah, Jozabad, Jediael, Michael, Jozabad, Elihu and Zillethai, leaders of units of a thousand in Manasseh. ²¹They helped David against raiding bands, for all of them were brave warriors, and they were commanders in his army. ²²Day after day men came to help David, until he had a great army, like the army of God.*b*

Others join David at Hebron

²³These are the numbers of the men armed for battle who came to David at Hebron to turn Saul's kingdom over to him, as the LORD had said:

²⁴from Judah, carrying shield and spear – 6,800 armed for battle;
²⁵from Simeon, warriors ready for battle – 7,100;
²⁶from Levi – 4,600, ²⁷including Jehoiada, leader of the family of Aaron, with 3,700 men, ²⁸and Zadok, a brave young warrior, with 22 officers from his family;
²⁹from Benjamin, Saul's tribe – 3,000, most of whom had remained loyal to Saul's house until then;
³⁰from Ephraim, brave warriors, famous in their own clans – 20,800;
³¹from half the tribe of Manasseh, designated by name to come and make David king – 18,000;
³²from Issachar, men who understood the times and knew what Israel should do – 200 chiefs, with all their relatives under their command;
³³from Zebulun, experienced soldiers prepared for battle with every type

of weapon, to help David with undivided loyalty – 50,000;
³⁴from Naphtali – 1,000 officers, together with 37,000 men carrying shields and spears;
³⁵from Dan, ready for battle – 28,600;
³⁶from Asher, experienced soldiers prepared for battle – 40,000;
³⁷and from east of the Jordan, from Reuben, Gad and the half-tribe of Manasseh, armed with every type of weapon – 120,000.

³⁸All these were fighting men who volunteered to serve in the ranks. They came to Hebron fully determined to make David king over all Israel. All the rest of the Israelites were also of one mind to make David king. ³⁹The men spent three days there with David, eating and drinking, for their families had supplied provisions for them. ⁴⁰Also, their neighbours from as far away as Issachar, Zebulun and Naphtali came bringing food on donkeys, camels, mules and oxen. There were plentiful supplies of flour, fig cakes, raisin cakes, wine, olive oil, cattle and sheep, for there was joy in Israel.

Bringing back the ark

13 David conferred with each of his officers, the commanders of thousands and commanders of hundreds. ²He then said to the whole assembly of Israel, 'If it seems good to you and if it is the will of the LORD our God, let us send word far and wide to the rest of our people throughout the territories of Israel, and also to the priests and Levites who are with them in their towns and pasture-lands, to come and join us. ³Let us bring the ark of our God back to us, for we did not enquire of*a* it*b* during the reign of Saul.' ⁴The whole assembly agreed to do this, because it seemed right to all the people.

⁵So David assembled all Israel, from the River Shihor in Egypt to Lebo Hamath, to bring the ark of God from Kiriath Jearim. ⁶David and all Israel went to Baalah of Judah (Kiriath Jearim) to bring up from

---

b 22 Or *a great and mighty army*

a 3 Or *we neglected*
b 3 Or *him*

there the ark of God the LORD, who is enthroned between the cherubim – the ark that is called by the Name.

7 They moved the ark of God from Abinadab's house on a new cart, with Uzzah and Ahio guiding it. 8 David and all the Israelites were celebrating with all their might before God, with songs and with harps, lyres, tambourines, cymbals and trumpets.

FAVOURITE VERSES

Psalm 91:4

He will cover you with his feathers,
and under his wings you will find
refuge;
his faithfulness will be your shield
and rampart.

This verse means a lot to me personally as it has helped me stay strong through difficult times. It also reminds me that Jesus has always been and will always be watching over and protecting me.

Rachel, 16

9 When they came to the threshing-floor of Kidon, Uzzah reached out his hand to steady the ark, because the oxen stumbled. 10 The LORD's anger burned against Uzzah, and he struck him down because he had put his hand on the ark. So he died there before God.

11 Then David was angry because the LORD's wrath had broken out against Uzzah, and to this day that place is called Perez Uzzah.c

12 David was afraid of God that day and asked, 'How can I ever bring the ark of God to me?' 13 He did not take the ark to be with him in the City of David. Instead,

he took it to the house of Obed-Edom the Gittite. 14 The ark of God remained with the family of Obed-Edom in his house for three months, and the LORD blessed his household and everything he had.

David's house and family

14 Now Hiram king of Tyre sent messengers to David, along with cedar logs, stonemasons and carpenters to build a palace for him. 2 And David knew that the LORD had established him as king over Israel and that his kingdom had been highly exalted for the sake of his people Israel.

3 In Jerusalem David took more wives and became the father of more sons and daughters. 4 These are the names of the children born to him there: Shammua, Shobab, Nathan, Solomon, 5 Ibhar, Elishua, Elpelet, 6 Nogah, Nepheg, Japhia, 7 Elishama, Beeliadaa and Eliphelet.

David defeats the Philistines

8 When the Philistines heard that David had been anointed king over all Israel, they went up in full force to search for him, but David heard about it and went out to meet them. 9 Now the Philistines had come and raided the Valley of Rephaim; 10 so David enquired of God: 'Shall I go and attack the Philistines? Will you deliver them into my hands?'

The LORD answered him, 'Go, I will deliver them into your hands.'

11 So David and his men went up to Baal Perazim, and there he defeated them. He said, 'As waters break out, God has broken out against my enemies by my hand.' So that place was called Baal Perazim.b 12 The Philistines had abandoned their gods there, and David gave orders to burn them in the fire.

13 Once more the Philistines raided the valley; 14 so David enquired of God again, and God answered him, 'Do not go directly after them, but circle round them and attack them in front of the poplar trees. 15 As soon as you hear the sound of

---

c 11 *Perez Uzzah* means *outbreak against Uzzah.*

a 7 A variant of *Eliada*
b 11 *Baal Perazim* means *the lord who breaks out.*

marching in the tops of the poplar trees, move out to battle, because that will mean God has gone out in front of you to strike the Philistine army.' ¹⁶So David did as God commanded him, and they struck down the Philistine army, all the way from Gibeon to Gezer.

¹⁷So David's fame spread throughout every land, and the LORD made all the nations fear him.

The ark brought to Jerusalem

15 After David had constructed buildings for himself in the City of David, he prepared a place for the ark of God and pitched a tent for it. ²Then David said, 'No one but the Levites may carry the ark of God, because the LORD chose them to carry the ark of the LORD and to minister before him for ever.'

³David assembled all Israel in Jerusalem to bring up the ark of the LORD to the place he had prepared for it. ⁴He called together the descendants of Aaron and the Levites:

⁵from the descendants of Kohath,
   Uriel the leader and 120 relatives;
⁶from the descendants of Merari,
   Asaiah the leader and 220 relatives;
⁷from the descendants of Gershon,ᵃ
   Joel the leader and 130 relatives;
⁸from the descendants of Elizaphan,
   Shemaiah the leader and 200 relatives;
⁹from the descendants of Hebron,
   Eliel the leader and 80 relatives;
¹⁰from the descendants of Uzziel,
   Amminadab the leader and 112 relatives.

¹¹Then David summoned Zadok and Abiathar the priests, and Uriel, Asaiah, Joel, Shemaiah, Eliel and Amminadab the Levites. ¹²He said to them, 'You are the heads of the Levitical families; you and your fellow Levites are to consecrate yourselves and bring up the ark of the LORD, the God of Israel, to the place I have prepared for it. ¹³It was because you, the Levites, did not bring it up the first time that the LORD

our God broke out in anger against us. We did not enquire of him about how to do it in the prescribed way.' ¹⁴So the priests and Levites consecrated themselves in order to bring up the ark of the LORD, the God of Israel. ¹⁵And the Levites carried the ark of God with the poles on their shoulders, as Moses had commanded in accordance with the word of the LORD.

¹⁶David told the leaders of the Levites to appoint their fellow Levites as musicians to make a joyful sound with musical instruments: lyres, harps and cymbals.

¹⁷So the Levites appointed Heman son of Joel; from his relatives, Asaph son of Berekiah; and from their relatives the Merarites, Ethan son of Kushaiah; ¹⁸and with them their relatives next in rank: Zechariah,ᵇ Jaaziel, Shemiramoth, Jehiel, Unni, Eliab, Benaiah, Maaseiah, Mattithiah, Eliphelehu, Mikneiah, Obed-Edom and Jeiel,ᶜ the gatekeepers.

¹⁹The musicians Heman, Asaph and Ethan were to sound the bronze cymbals; ²⁰Zechariah, Jaaziel,ᵈ Shemiramoth, Jehiel, Unni, Eliab, Maaseiah and Benaiah were to play the lyres according to *alamoth*,ᵉ ²¹and Mattithiah, Eliphelehu, Mikneiah, Obed-Edom, Jeiel and Azaziah were to play the harps, directing according to *sheminith*.ᶠ ²²Kenaniah the head Levite was in charge of the singing; that was his responsibility because he was skilful at it.

²³Berekiah and Elkanah were to be doorkeepers for the ark. ²⁴Shebaniah, Joshaphat, Nethanel, Amasai, Zechariah, Benaiah and Eliezer the priests were to blow trumpets before the ark of God. Obed-Edom and Jehiah were also to be doorkeepers for the ark.

²⁵So David and the elders of Israel and the commanders of units of a thousand went to bring up the ark of the covenant of the LORD from the house of Obed-Edom,

---

a 7 Hebrew *Gershom*, a variant of *Gershon*

b 18 Three Hebrew manuscripts and most Septuagint manuscripts (see also verse 20 and 16:5); most Hebrew manuscripts *Zechariah son and* or *Zechariah, Ben and*

c 18 Hebrew; Septuagint (see also verse 21) *Jeiel and Azaziah*

d 20 See verse 18; Hebrew *Aziel*, a variant of *Jaaziel*.

e 20 Probably a musical term

f 21 Probably a musical term

with rejoicing. ²⁶Because God had helped the Levites who were carrying the ark of the covenant of the LORD, seven bulls and seven rams were sacrificed. ²⁷Now David was clothed in a robe of fine linen, as were all the Levites who were carrying the ark, and as were the musicians, and Kenaniah, who was in charge of the singing of the choirs. David also wore a linen ephod. ²⁸So all Israel brought up the ark of the covenant of the LORD with shouts, with the sounding of rams' horns and trumpets, and of cymbals, and the playing of lyres and harps.

²⁹As the ark of the covenant of the LORD was entering the City of David, Michal daughter of Saul watched from a window. And when she saw King David dancing and celebrating, she despised him in her heart.

Ministering before the ark

16 They brought the ark of God and set it inside the tent that David had pitched for it, and they presented burnt offerings and fellowship offerings before God. ²After David had finished sacrificing the burnt offerings and fellowship offerings, he blessed the people in the name of the LORD. ³Then he gave a loaf of bread, a cake of dates and a cake of raisins to each Israelite man and woman.

⁴He appointed some of the Levites to minister before the ark of the LORD, to extol,ᵃ thank, and praise the LORD, the God of Israel: ⁵Asaph was the chief, and next to him in rank were Zechariah, then Jaaziel,ᵇ Shemiramoth, Jehiel, Mattithiah, Eliab, Benaiah, Obed-Edom and Jeiel. They were to play the lyres and harps, Asaph was to sound the cymbals, ⁶and Benaiah and Jahaziel the priests were to blow the trumpets regularly before the ark of the covenant of God.

⁷That day David first appointed Asaph and his associates to give praise to the LORD in this manner:

⁸Give praise to the LORD, proclaim his name;
 make known among the nations what he has done.
⁹Sing to him, sing praise to him;
 tell of all his wonderful acts.
¹⁰Glory in his holy name;
 let the hearts of those who seek the LORD rejoice.
¹¹Look to the LORD and his strength;
 seek his face always.

¹²Remember the wonders he has done,
 his miracles, and the judgments he pronounced,
¹³you his servants, the descendants of Israel,
 his chosen ones, the children of Jacob.
¹⁴He is the LORD our God;
 his judgments are in all the earth.

¹⁵He remembersᶜ his covenant for ever,
 the promise he made, for a thousand generations,
¹⁶the covenant he made with Abraham,
 the oath he swore to Isaac.
¹⁷He confirmed it to Jacob as a decree,
 to Israel as an everlasting covenant:
¹⁸'To you I will give the land of Canaan
 as the portion you will inherit.'

¹⁹When they were but few in number,
 few indeed, and strangers in it,
²⁰theyᵈ wandered from nation to nation,
 from one kingdom to another.
²¹He allowed no one to oppress them;
 for their sake he rebuked kings:
²²'Do not touch my anointed ones;
 do my prophets no harm.'

²³Sing to the LORD, all the earth;
 proclaim his salvation day after day.
²⁴Declare his glory among the nations,
 his marvellous deeds among all peoples.

---

a 4 Or *petition*; or *invoke*

b 5 See 15:18,20; Hebrew *Jeiel*, possibly another name for *Jaaziel*.

c 15 Some Septuagint manuscripts (see also Psalm 105:8); Hebrew *Remember*

d 18-20 One Hebrew manuscript, Septuagint and Vulgate (see also Psalm 105:12); most Hebrew manuscripts *inherit*, /¹⁹*though you are but few in number, / few indeed, and strangers in it.'* /²⁰*They*

25 For great is the LORD and most worthy
    of praise;
  he is to be feared above all gods.
26 For all the gods of the nations are
    idols,
  but the LORD made the heavens.
27 Splendour and majesty are before
    him;
  strength and joy are in his dwelling-
    place.

28 Ascribe to the LORD, all you families of
    nations,
  ascribe to the LORD glory and
    strength.
29 Ascribe to the LORD the glory due to
    his name;
  bring an offering and come before
    him.
  Worship the LORD in the splendour of
    hise holiness.
30   Tremble before him, all the earth!
  The world is firmly established; it
    cannot be moved.

31 Let the heavens rejoice, let the earth be
    glad;
  let them say among the nations,
    'The LORD reigns!'
32 Let the sea resound, and all that is
    in it;
  let the fields be jubilant, and
    everything in them!
33 Let the trees of the forest sing,
  let them sing for joy before the
    LORD,
  for he comes to judge the earth.

34 Give thanks to the LORD, for he is
    good;
  his love endures for ever.
35 Cry out, 'Save us, God our Saviour;
  gather us and deliver us from the
    nations,
  that we may give thanks to your holy
    name,
  and glory in your praise.'
36 Praise be to the LORD, the God of
    Israel,
  from everlasting to everlasting.

---

e 29 Or LORD with the splendour of

Then all the people said 'Amen' and 'Praise
the LORD.'

37 David left Asaph and his associates
before the ark of the covenant of the LORD
to minister there regularly, according to
each day's requirements. 38 He also left
Obed-Edom and his sixty-eight associates
to minister with them. Obed-Edom son
of Jeduthun, and also Hosah, were gatekeepers.

39 David left Zadok the priest and his
fellow priests before the tabernacle of
the LORD at the high place in Gibeon
40 to present burnt offerings to the LORD
on the altar of burnt offering regularly,
morning and evening, in accordance with
everything written in the Law of the LORD,
which he had given Israel. 41 With them
were Heman and Jeduthun and the rest of
those chosen and designated by name to
give thanks to the LORD, 'for his love endures for ever.' 42 Heman and Jeduthun
were responsible for the sounding of the
trumpets and cymbals and for the playing
of the other instruments for sacred song.
The sons of Jeduthun were stationed at
the gate.

43 Then all the people left, each for their
own home, and David returned home to
bless his family.

God's promise to David

17 After David was settled in his palace, he said to Nathan the prophet,
'Here I am, living in a house of cedar,
while the ark of the covenant of the LORD
is under a tent.'

2 Nathan replied to David, 'Whatever
you have in mind, do it, for God is with
you.'

3 But that night the word of God came to
Nathan, saying:

4 'Go and tell my servant David,
"This is what the LORD says: you are
not the one to build me a house
to dwell in. 5 I have not dwelt in a
house from the day I brought Israel
up out of Egypt to this day. I have
moved from one tent site to another,
from one dwelling-place to another.

⁶Wherever I have moved with all the Israelites, did I ever say to any of their leaders*ᵃ* whom I commanded to shepherd my people, 'Why have you not built me a house of cedar?' "

⁷'Now then, tell my servant David, "This is what the LORD Almighty says: I took you from the pasture, from tending the flock, and appointed you ruler over my people Israel. ⁸I have been with you wherever you have gone, and I have cut off all your enemies from before you. Now I will make your name like the names of the greatest men on earth. ⁹And I will provide a place for my people Israel and will plant them so that they can have a home of their own and no longer be disturbed. Wicked people will not oppress them any more, as they did at the beginning ¹⁰and have done ever since the time I appointed leaders over my people Israel. I will also subdue all your enemies.

'"I declare to you that the LORD will build a house for you: ¹¹when your days are over and you go to be with your ancestors, I will raise up your offspring to succeed you, one of your own sons, and I will establish his kingdom. ¹²He is the one who will build a house for me, and I will establish his throne for ever. ¹³I will be his father, and he will be my son. I will never take my love away from him, as I took it away from your predecessor. ¹⁴I will set him over my house and my kingdom for ever; his throne will be established for ever."'

¹⁵Nathan reported to David all the words of this entire revelation.

David's prayer

¹⁶Then King David went in and sat before the LORD, and he said:

'Who am I, LORD God, and what is my family, that you have brought me this far? ¹⁷And as if this were not enough in your sight, my God, you have spoken about the future of the house of your servant. You, LORD God, have looked on me as though I were the most exalted of men.

¹⁸'What more can David say to you for honouring your servant? For you know your servant, ¹⁹LORD. For the sake of your servant and according to your will, you have done this great thing and made known all these great promises.

²⁰'There is no one like you, LORD, and there is no God but you, as we have heard with our own ears. ²¹And who is like your people Israel – the one nation on earth whose God went out to redeem a people for himself, and to make a name for yourself, and to perform great and awesome wonders by driving out nations from before your people, whom you redeemed from Egypt? ²²You made your people Israel your very own for ever, and you, LORD, have become their God.

²³'And now, LORD, let the promise you have made concerning your servant and his house be established for ever. Do as you promised, ²⁴so that it will be established and that your name will be great for ever. Then people will say, "The LORD Almighty, the God over Israel, is Israel's God!" And the house of your servant David will be established before you.

²⁵'You, my God, have revealed to your servant that you will build a house for him. So your servant has found courage to pray to you. ²⁶You, LORD, are God! You have promised these good things to your servant. ²⁷Now you have been pleased to bless the house of your servant, that it may continue for ever in your sight; for you, LORD, have blessed it, and it will be blessed for ever.'

David's victories

18 In the course of time, David defeated the Philistines and subdued them, and he took Gath and its

---

surrounding villages from the control of the Philistines.

2 David also defeated the Moabites, and they became subject to him and brought him tribute.

3 Moreover, David defeated Hadadezer king of Zobah, in the vicinity of Hamath, when he went to set up his monument at*a* the River Euphrates. 4 David captured a thousand of his chariots, seven thousand charioteers and twenty thousand foot soldiers. He hamstrung all but a hundred of the chariot horses.

5 When the Arameans of Damascus came to help Hadadezer king of Zobah, David struck down twenty-two thousand of them. 6 He put garrisons in the Aramean kingdom of Damascus, and the Arameans became subject to him and brought him tribute. The LORD gave David victory wherever he went.

7 David took the gold shields carried by the officers of Hadadezer and brought them to Jerusalem. 8 From Tebah*b* and Kun, towns that belonged to Hadadezer, David took a great quantity of bronze, which Solomon used to make the bronze Sea, the pillars and various bronze articles.

9 When Tou king of Hamath heard that David had defeated the entire army of Hadadezer king of Zobah, 10 he sent his son Hadoram to King David to greet him and congratulate him on his victory in battle over Hadadezer, who had been at war with Tou. Hadoram brought all kinds of articles of gold, of silver and of bronze.

11 King David dedicated these articles to the LORD, as he had done with the silver and gold he had taken from all these nations: Edom and Moab, the Ammonites and the Philistines, and Amalek.

12 Abishai son of Zeruiah struck down eighteen thousand Edomites in the Valley of Salt. 13 He put garrisons in Edom, and all the Edomites became subject to David. The LORD gave David victory wherever he went.

David's officials

14 David reigned over all Israel, doing what was just and right for all his people. 15 Joab son of Zeruiah was over the army; Jehoshaphat son of Ahilud was recorder; 16 Zadok son of Ahitub and Ahimelek*c* son of Abiathar were priests; Shavsha was secretary; 17 Benaiah son of Jehoiada was over the Kerethites and Pelethites; and David's sons were chief officials at the king's side.

David defeats the Ammonites

19 In the course of time, Nahash king of the Ammonites died, and his son succeeded him as king. 2 David thought, 'I will show kindness to Hanun son of Nahash, because his father showed kindness to me.' So David sent a delegation to express his sympathy to Hanun concerning his father.

When David's envoys came to Hanun in the land of the Ammonites to express sympathy to him, 3 the Ammonite commanders said to Hanun, 'Do you think David is honouring your father by sending envoys to you to express sympathy? Haven't his envoys come to you only to explore and spy out the country and overthrow it?' 4 So Hanun seized David's envoys, shaved them, cut off their garments at the buttocks, and sent them away.

5 When someone came and told David about the men, he sent messengers to meet them, for they were greatly humiliated. The king said, 'Stay at Jericho till your beards have grown, and then come back.'

6 When the Ammonites realised that they had become obnoxious to David, Hanun and the Ammonites sent a thousand talents*a* of silver to hire chariots and charioteers from Aram Naharaim,*b* Aram Maakah and Zobah. 7 They hired thirty-two thousand chariots and charioteers, as well as the king of Maakah with his troops, who came and camped near Medeba, while the Ammonites were mustered

---

*a*3 Or *to restore his control over*
*b*8 Hebrew *Tibhath*, a variant of *Tebah*

*c*16 Some Hebrew manuscripts, Vulgate and Syriac (see also 2 Sam. 8:17); most Hebrew manuscripts *Abimelek*
*a*6 That is, about 34 metric tons
*b*6 That is, North-west Mesopotamia

from their towns and moved out for battle.

⁸ On hearing this, David sent Joab out with the entire army of fighting men. ⁹ The Ammonites came out and drew up in battle formation at the entrance to their city, while the kings who had come were by themselves in the open country.

¹⁰ Joab saw that there were battle lines in front of him and behind him; so he selected some of the best troops in Israel and deployed them against the Arameans. ¹¹ He put the rest of the men under the command of Abishai his brother, and they were deployed against the Ammonites. ¹² Joab said, 'If the Arameans are too strong for me, then you are to rescue me; but if the Ammonites are too strong for you, then I will rescue you. ¹³ Be strong, and let us fight bravely for our people and the cities of our God. The LORD will do what is good in his sight.'

¹⁴ Then Joab and the troops with him advanced to fight the Arameans, and they fled before him. ¹⁵ When the Ammonites realised that the Arameans were fleeing, they too fled before his brother Abishai and went inside the city. So Joab went back to Jerusalem.

¹⁶ After the Arameans saw that they had been routed by Israel, they sent messengers and had Arameans brought from beyond the River Euphrates, with Shophak the commander of Hadadezer's army leading them.

¹⁷ When David was told of this, he gathered all Israel and crossed the Jordan; he advanced against them and formed his battle lines opposite them. David formed his lines to meet the Arameans in battle, and they fought against him. ¹⁸ But they fled before Israel, and David killed seven thousand of their charioteers and forty thousand of their foot soldiers. He also killed Shophak the commander of their army.

¹⁹ When the vassals of Hadadezer saw that they had been routed by Israel, they made peace with David and became subject to him.

So the Arameans were not willing to help the Ammonites any more.

The capture of Rabbah

20 In the spring, at the time when kings go off to war, Joab led out the armed forces. He laid waste the land of the Ammonites and went to Rabbah and besieged it, but David remained in Jerusalem. Joab attacked Rabbah and left it in ruins. ² David took the crown from the head of their king*ᵃ* – its weight was found to be a talent*ᵇ* of gold, and it was set with precious stones – and it was placed on David's head. He took a great quantity of plunder from the city ³ and brought out the people who were there, consigning them to labour with saws and with iron picks and axes. David did this to all the Ammonite towns. Then David and his entire army returned to Jerusalem.

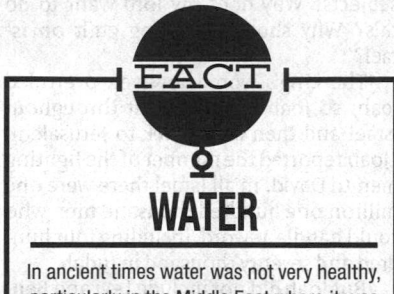

FACT

WATER

In ancient times water was not very healthy, particularly in the Middle East where it was stored in cisterns. Most people mixed wine or vinegar with their water to act as a kind of disinfectant.

War with the Philistines

⁴ In the course of time, war broke out with the Philistines, at Gezer. At that time Sibbekai the Hushathite killed Sippai, one of the descendants of the Rephaites, and the Philistines were subjugated.

⁵ In another battle with the Philistines, Elhanan son of Jair killed Lahmi the brother of Goliath the Gittite, who had a spear with a shaft like a weaver's rod.

⁶ In still another battle, which took place at Gath, there was a huge man with six fingers on each hand and six toes on each foot – twenty-four in all. He also

---

a 2 Or *of Milkom*, that is, Molek
b 2 That is, about 34 kilograms

was descended from Rapha. 7When he taunted Israel, Jonathan son of Shimea, David's brother, killed him.

8These were descendants of Rapha in Gath, and they fell at the hands of David and his men.

David counts the fighting men

21 Satan rose up against Israel and incited David to take a census of Israel. 2So David said to Joab and the commanders of the troops, 'Go and count the Israelites from Beersheba to Dan. Then report back to me so that I may know how many there are.'

3But Joab replied, 'May the LORD multiply his troops a hundred times over. My lord the king, are they not all my lord's subjects? Why does my lord want to do this? Why should he bring guilt on Israel?'

4The king's word, however, overruled Joab; so Joab left and went throughout Israel and then came back to Jerusalem. 5Joab reported the number of the fighting men to David: in all Israel there were one million one hundred thousand men who could handle a sword, including four hundred and seventy thousand in Judah. 6But Joab did not include Levi and Benjamin in the numbering, because the king's command was repulsive to him. 7This command was also evil in the sight of God; so he punished Israel.

8Then David said to God, 'I have sinned greatly by doing this. Now, I beg you, take away the guilt of your servant. I have done a very foolish thing.'

9The LORD said to Gad, David's seer, 10'Go and tell David, "This is what the LORD says: I am giving you three options. Choose one of them for me to carry out against you."'

11So Gad went to David and said to him, 'This is what the LORD says: "Take your choice: 12three years of famine, three months of being swept away*a* before your enemies, with their swords overtaking you, or three days of the sword of the LORD – days of plague in the land, with the angel of the LORD ravaging every part of Israel." Now then, decide how I should answer the one who sent me.'

13David said to Gad, 'I am in deep distress. Let me fall into the hands of the LORD, for his mercy is very great; but do not let me fall into human hands.'

14So the LORD sent a plague on Israel, and seventy thousand men of Israel fell dead. 15And God sent an angel to destroy Jerusalem. But as the angel was doing so, the LORD saw it and relented concerning the disaster and said to the angel who was destroying the people, 'Enough! Withdraw your hand.' The angel of the LORD was then standing at the threshing-floor of Araunah*b* the Jebusite.

16David looked up and saw the angel of the LORD standing between heaven and earth, with a drawn sword in his hand extended over Jerusalem. Then David and the elders, clothed in sackcloth, fell face down.

17David said to God, 'Was it not I who ordered the fighting men to be counted? I, the shepherd,*c* have sinned and done wrong. These are but sheep. What have they done? LORD my God, let your hand fall on me and my family, but do not let this plague remain on your people.'

David builds an altar

18Then the angel of the LORD ordered Gad to tell David to go up and build an altar to the LORD on the threshing-floor of Araunah the Jebusite. 19So David went up in obedience to the word that Gad had spoken in the name of the LORD.

20While Araunah was threshing wheat, he turned and saw the angel; his four sons who were with him hid themselves. 21Then David approached, and when Araunah looked and saw him, he left the threshing-floor and bowed down before David with his face to the ground.

---

a 12 Hebrew; Septuagint and Vulgate (see also 2 Samuel 24:13) *of fleeing*

b 15 Hebrew *Ornan*, a variant of *Araunah*; also in verses 18-28
c 17 Probable reading of the original Hebrew text (see 2 Samuel 24:17 and note); Masoretic Text does not have *the shepherd*.

22 David said to him, 'Let me have the site of your threshing-floor so that I can build an altar to the LORD, that the plague on the people may be stopped. Sell it to me at the full price.'

23 Arauhah said to David, 'Take it! Let my lord the king do whatever pleases him. Look, I will give the oxen for the burnt offerings, the threshing-sledges for the wood, and the wheat for the grain offering. I will give all this.'

24 But King David replied to Araunah, 'No, I insist on paying the full price. I will not take for the LORD what is yours, or sacrifice a burnt offering that costs me nothing.'

25 So David paid Araunah six hundred shekels*d* of gold for the site. 26 David built an altar to the LORD there and sacrificed burnt offerings and fellowship offerings. He called on the LORD, and the LORD answered him with fire from heaven on the altar of burnt offering.

27 Then the LORD spoke to the angel, and he put his sword back into its sheath. 28 At that time, when David saw that the LORD had answered him on the threshing-floor of Araunah the Jebusite, he offered sacrifices there. 29 The tabernacle of the LORD, which Moses had made in the wilderness, and the altar of burnt offering were at that time on the high place at Gibeon. 30 But David could not go before it to enquire of God, because he was afraid of the sword of the angel of the LORD.

22 Then David said, 'The house of the LORD God is to be here, and also the altar of burnt offering for Israel.'

Preparations for the temple

2 So David gave orders to assemble the foreigners residing in Israel, and from among them he appointed stonecutters to prepare dressed stone for building the house of God. 3 He provided a large amount of iron to make nails for the doors of the gateways and for the fittings, and more bronze than could be weighed. 4 He also provided more cedar logs than could be counted, for the Sidonians and Tyrians had brought large numbers of them to David.

5 David said, 'My son Solomon is young and inexperienced, and the house to be built for the LORD should be of great magnificence and fame and splendour in the sight of all the nations. Therefore I will make preparations for it.' So David made extensive preparations before his death.

6 Then he called for his son Solomon and charged him to build a house for the LORD, the God of Israel. 7 David said to Solomon: 'My son, I had it in my heart to build a house for the Name of the LORD my God. 8 But this word of the LORD came to me: "You have shed much blood and have fought many wars. You are not to build a house for my Name, because you have shed much blood on the earth in my sight. 9 But you will have a son who will be a man of peace and rest, and I will give him rest from all his enemies on every side. His name will be Solomon,*a* and I will grant Israel peace and quiet during his reign. 10 He is the one who will build a house for my Name. He will be my son, and I will be his father. And I will establish the throne of his kingdom over Israel for ever."

11 'Now, my son, the LORD be with you, and may you have success and build the house of the LORD your God, as he said you would. 12 May the LORD give you discretion and understanding when he puts you in command over Israel, so that you may keep the law of the LORD your God. 13 Then you will have success if you are careful to observe the decrees and laws that the LORD gave to Moses for Israel. Be strong and courageous. Do not be afraid or discouraged.

14 'I have taken great pains to provide for the temple of the LORD a hundred thousand talents*b* of gold, a million talents*c* of silver, quantities of bronze and iron too great to be weighed, and wood and stone. And you may add to them. 15 You have many workers: stonecutters,

---

d 25 That is, about 6.9 kilograms

a 9 *Solomon* sounds like and may be derived from the Hebrew for *peace*.
b 14 That is, about 3,400 metric tons
c 14 That is, about 34,000 metric tons

masons and carpenters, as well as those skilled in every kind of work ¹⁶in gold and silver, bronze and iron – craftsmen beyond number. Now begin the work, and the LORD be with you.'

¹⁷Then David ordered all the leaders of Israel to help his son Solomon. ¹⁸He said to them, 'Is not the LORD your God with you? And has he not granted you rest on every side? For he has given the inhabitants of the land into my hands, and the land is subject to the LORD and to his people. ¹⁹Now devote your heart and soul to seeking the LORD your God. Begin to build the sanctuary of the LORD God, so that you may bring the ark of the covenant of the LORD and the sacred articles belonging to God into the temple that will be built for the Name of the LORD.'

The Levites

23 When David was old and full of years, he made his son Solomon king over Israel.

²He also gathered together all the leaders of Israel, as well as the priests and Levites. ³The Levites thirty years old or more were counted, and the total number of men was thirty-eight thousand. ⁴David said, 'Of these, twenty-four thousand are to be in charge of the work of the temple of the LORD and six thousand are to be officials and judges. ⁵Four thousand are to be gatekeepers and four thousand are to praise the LORD with the musical instruments I have provided for that purpose.'

⁶David separated the Levites into divisions corresponding to the sons of Levi: Gershon, Kohath and Merari.

Gershonites

⁷Belonging to the Gershonites:
Ladan and Shimei.

⁸The sons of Ladan:
Jehiel the first, Zetham and Joel – three in all.

⁹The sons of Shimei:
Shelomoth, Haziel and Haran – three in all.
These were the heads of the families of Ladan.

¹⁰And the sons of Shimei:

Jahath, Ziza,ᵃ Jeush and Beriah. These were the sons of Shimei – four in all.

¹¹Jahath was the first and Ziza the second, but Jeush and Beriah did not have many sons; so they were counted as one family with one assignment.

Kohathites

¹²The sons of Kohath:
Amram, Izhar, Hebron and Uzziel – four in all.

¹³The sons of Amram:
Aaron and Moses.
Aaron was set apart, he and his descendants for ever, to consecrate the most holy things, to offer sacrifices before the LORD, to minister before him and to pronounce blessings in his name for ever. ¹⁴The sons of Moses the man of God were counted as part of the tribe of Levi.

¹⁵The sons of Moses:
Gershom and Eliezer.

¹⁶The descendants of Gershom:
Shubael was the first.

¹⁷The descendants of Eliezer:
Rehabiah was the first.
Eliezer had no other sons, but the sons of Rehabiah were very numerous.

¹⁸The sons of Izhar:
Shelomith was the first.

¹⁹The sons of Hebron:
Jeriah the first, Amariah the second, Jahaziel the third and Jekameam the fourth.

²⁰The sons of Uzziel:
Micah the first and Ishiah the second.

Merarites

²¹The sons of Merari:
Mahli and Mushi.
The sons of Mahli:
Eleazar and Kish.

ᵃ 10 One Hebrew manuscript, Septuagint and Vulgate (see also verse 11); most Hebrew manuscripts *Zina*

22 Eleazar died without having sons: he had only daughters. Their cousins, the sons of Kish, married them.
23 The sons of Mushi:
Mahli, Eder and Jerimoth – three in all.

24 These were the descendants of Levi by their families – the heads of families as they were registered under their names and counted individually, that is, the workers twenty years old or more who served in the temple of the LORD. 25 For David had said, 'Since the LORD, the God of Israel, has granted rest to his people and has come to dwell in Jerusalem for ever, 26 the Levites no longer need to carry the tabernacle or any of the articles used in its service.' 27 According to the last instructions of David, the Levites were counted from those twenty years old or more.
28 The duty of the Levites was to help Aaron's descendants in the service of the temple of the LORD: to be in charge of the courtyards, the side rooms, the purification of all sacred things and the performance of other duties at the house of God. 29 They were in charge of the bread set out on the table, the special flour for the grain offerings, the thin loaves made without yeast, the baking and the mixing, and all measurements of quantity and size. 30 They were also to stand every morning to thank and praise the LORD. They were to do the same in the evening 31 and whenever burnt offerings were presented to the LORD on the Sabbaths, at the New Moon feasts and at the appointed festivals. They were to serve before the LORD regularly in the proper number and in the way prescribed for them.
32 And so the Levites carried out their responsibilities for the tent of meeting, for the Holy Place and, under their relatives the descendants of Aaron, for the service of the temple of the LORD.

The divisions of priests

24 These were the divisions of the descendants of Aaron:
The sons of Aaron were Nadab, Abihu, Eleazar and Ithamar. 2 But Nadab and Abihu died before their father did, and they had no sons; so Eleazar and Ithamar served as the priests. 3 With the help of Zadok a descendant of Eleazar and Ahimelek a descendant of Ithamar, David separated them into divisions for their appointed order of ministering. 4 A larger number of leaders were found among Eleazar's descendants than among Ithamar's, and they were divided accordingly: sixteen heads of families from Eleazar's descendants and eight heads of families from Ithamar's descendants. 5 They divided them impartially by casting lots, for there were officials of the sanctuary and officials of God among the descendants of both Eleazar and Ithamar.
6 The scribe Shemaiah son of Nethanel, a Levite, recorded their names in the presence of the king and of the officials: Zadok the priest, Ahimelek son of Abiathar and the heads of families of the priests and of the Levites – one family being taken from Eleazar and then one from Ithamar.

7 The first lot fell to Jehoiarib,
the second to Jedaiah,
8 the third to Harim,
the fourth to Seorim,
9 the fifth to Malkijah,
the sixth to Mijamin,
10 the seventh to Hakkoz,
the eighth to Abijah,
11 the ninth to Jeshua,
the tenth to Shekaniah,
12 the eleventh to Eliashib,
the twelfth to Jakim,
13 the thirteenth to Huppah,
the fourteenth to Jeshebeab,
14 the fifteenth to Bilgah,
the sixteenth to Immer,
15 the seventeenth to Hezir,
the eighteenth to Happizzez,
16 the nineteenth to Pethahiah,
the twentieth to Jehezkel,
17 the twenty-first to Jakin,
the twenty-second to Gamul,
18 the twenty-third to Delaiah
and the twenty-fourth to Maaziah.

19 This was their appointed order of ministering when they entered the

temple of the LORD, according to the regulations prescribed for them by their ancestor Aaron, as the LORD, the God of Israel, had commanded him.

The rest of the Levites

20 As for the rest of the descendants of Levi:

from the sons of Amram: Shubael;
from the sons of Shubael: Jehdeiah.
21 As for Rehabiah, from his sons:
Ishiah was the first.
22 From the Izharites: Shelomoth;
from the sons of Shelomoth: Jahath.
23 The sons of Hebron: Jeriah the first,*a*
Amariah the second, Jahaziel the third and Jekameam the fourth.
24 The son of Uzziel: Micah;
from the sons of Micah: Shamir.
25 The brother of Micah: Ishiah;
from the sons of Ishiah: Zechariah.
26 The sons of Merari: Mahli and Mushi.
The son of Jaaziah: Beno.
27 The sons of Merari:
from Jaaziah: Beno, Shoham, Zakkur and Ibri.
28 From Mahli: Eleazar, who had no sons.
29 From Kish: the son of Kish:
Jerahmeel.
30 And the sons of Mushi: Mahli, Eder and Jerimoth.

These were the Levites, according to their families. 31 They also cast lots, just as their relatives the descendants of Aaron did, in the presence of King David and of Zadok, Ahimelek, and the heads of families of the priests and of the Levites. The families of the eldest brother were treated the same as those of the youngest.

The musicians

25 David, together with the commanders of the army, set apart some of the sons of Asaph, Heman and Jeduthun for the ministry of prophesying, accompanied by harps, lyres and cymbals. Here is the list of the men who performed this service:

2 from the sons of Asaph:
Zakkur, Joseph, Nethaniah and Asarelah. The sons of Asaph were under the supervision of Asaph, who prophesied under the king's supervision.
3 As for Jeduthun, from his sons:
Gedaliah, Zeri, Jeshaiah, Shimei,*a* Hashabiah and Mattithiah, six in all, under the supervision of their father Jeduthun, who prophesied, using the harp in thanking and praising the LORD.
4 As for Heman, from his sons:
Bukkiah, Mattaniah, Uzziel, Shubael and Jerimoth; Hananiah, Hanani, Eliathah, Giddalti and Romamti-Ezer; Joshbekashah, Mallothi, Hothir and Mahazioth. 5 (All these were sons of Heman the king's seer. They were given to him through the promises of God to exalt him. God gave Heman fourteen sons and three daughters.)

6 All these men were under the supervision of their father for the music of the temple of the LORD, with cymbals, lyres and harps, for the ministry at the house of God.

Asaph, Jeduthun and Heman were under the supervision of the king. 7 Along with their relatives – all of them trained and skilled in music for the LORD – they numbered 288. 8 Young and old alike, teacher as well as student, cast lots for their duties.

9 The first lot, which was for Asaph, fell to Joseph,

---

a 23 Two Hebrew manuscripts and some Septuagint manuscripts (see also 23:19); most Hebrew manuscripts *The sons of Jeriah:*

a 3 One Hebrew manuscript and some Septuagint manuscripts (see also verse 17); most Hebrew manuscripts do not have *Shimei.*

his sons and relatives[b]   12[c]
the second to Gedaliah,
    him and his relatives and
    sons   12
10 the third to Zakkur,
    his sons and relatives   12
11 the fourth to Izri,[d]
    his sons and relatives   12
12 the fifth to Nethaniah,
    his sons and relatives   12
13 the sixth to Bukkiah,
    his sons and relatives   12
14 the seventh to Jesarelah,[e]
    his sons and relatives   12
15 the eighth to Jeshaiah,
    his sons and relatives   12
16 the ninth to Mattaniah,
    his sons and relatives   12
17 the tenth to Shimei,
    his sons and relatives   12
18 the eleventh to Azarel,[f]
    his sons and relatives   12
19 the twelfth to Hashabiah,
    his sons and relatives   12
20 the thirteenth to Shubael,
    his sons and relatives   12
21 the fourteenth to Mattithiah,
    his sons and relatives   12
22 the fifteenth to Jerimoth,
    his sons and relatives   12
23 the sixteenth to Hananiah,
    his sons and relatives   12
24 the seventeenth to Joshbekashah,
    his sons and relatives   12
25 the eighteenth to Hanani,
    his sons and relatives   12
26 the nineteenth to Mallothi,
    his sons and relatives   12
27 the twentieth to Eliathah,
    his sons and relatives   12
28 the twenty-first to Hothir,
    his sons and relatives   12
29 the twenty-second to Giddalti,
    his sons and relatives   12
30 the twenty-third to Mahazioth,

---

b 9 See Septuagint; Hebrew does not have *his sons and relatives*.
c 9 See the total in verse 7; Hebrew does not have *twelve*.
d 11 A variant of *Zeri*
e 14 A variant of *Asarelah*
f 18 A variant of *Uzziel*

his sons and relatives   12
31 the twenty-fourth to Romamti-
    Ezer,
    his sons and relatives.   12

FAVOURITE VERSES

Philippians 4:4

Rejoice in the Lord always. I will say it again: rejoice!

I love this. I think we all forget to do this sometimes, in our stressful and pressured day-to-day lives. I think sometimes being a Christian, especially for young people, can feel more constraining than releasing. We get angry with God because we think he's stopping us from having a good time. But actually the Bible is commanding us to be joyful with God and about God! If we're not being joyful and happy in the Lord, we're not being obedient to him. And it's all the time: even when we're grey and weary, we are still to be joyful and worship the Lord. What a wonderful attitude to have.

Katie, 19

The gatekeepers

26 The divisions of the gate-keepers:

from the Korahites: Meshelemiah son of Kore, one of the sons of Asaph.

2 Meshelemiah had sons:
    Zechariah the firstborn,
    Jediael the second,
    Zebadiah the third,
    Jathniel the fourth,
   3 Elam the fifth,
    Jehohanan the sixth
    and Eliehoenai the seventh.

4 Obed-Edom also had sons:
Shemaiah the firstborn,
Jehozabad the second,
Joah the third,
Sakar the fourth,
Nethanel the fifth,
5 Ammiel the sixth,
Issachar the seventh
and Peullethai the eighth.
(For God had blessed Obed-Edom.)

6 Obed-Edom's son Shemaiah also had sons, who were leaders in their father's family because they were very capable men. 7 The sons of Shemaiah: Othni, Rephael, Obed and Elzabad; his relatives Elihu and Semakiah were also able men. 8 All these were descendants of Obed-Edom; they and their sons and their relatives were capable men with the strength to do the work – descendants of Obed-Edom, 62 in all. 9 Meshelemiah had sons and relatives, who were able men – 18 in all.

10 Hosah the Merarite had sons: Shimri the first (although he was not the firstborn, his father had appointed him the first), 11 Hilkiah the second, Tabaliah the third and Zechariah the fourth. The sons and relatives of Hosah were 13 in all.

12 These divisions of the gatekeepers, through their leaders, had duties for ministering in the temple of the LORD, just as their relatives had. 13 Lots were cast for each gate, according to their families, young and old alike.
14 The lot for the East Gate fell to Shelemiah.ᵃ Then lots were cast for his son Zechariah, a wise counsellor, and the lot for the North Gate fell to him. 15 The lot for the South Gate fell to Obed-Edom, and the lot for the storehouse fell to his sons. 16 The lots for the West Gate and the Shalleketh Gate on the upper road fell to Shuppim and Hosah.

Guard was alongside guard: 17 there were six Levites a day on the east, four a day on the north, four a day on the south and two at a time at the storehouse. 18 As for the courtᵇ to the west, there were four at the road and two at the courtᶜ itself.
19 These were the divisions of the gatekeepers who were descendants of Korah and Merari.

The treasurers and other officials

20 Their fellow Levites wereᵈ in charge of the treasuries of the house of God and the treasuries for the dedicated things.
21 The descendants of Ladan, who were Gershonites through Ladan and who were heads of families belonging to Ladan the Gershonite, were Jehieli, 22 the sons of Jehieli, Zetham and his brother Joel. They were in charge of the treasuries of the temple of the LORD.
23 From the Amramites, the Izharites, the Hebronites and the Uzzielites:

24 Shubael, a descendant of Gershom son of Moses, was the official in charge of the treasuries. 25 His relatives through Eliezer: Rehabiah his son, Jeshaiah his son, Joram his son, Zikri his son and Shelomith his son. 26 Shelomith and his relatives were in charge of all the treasuries for the things dedicated by King David, by the heads of families who were the commanders of thousands and commanders of hundreds, and by the other army commanders. 27 Some of the plunder taken in battle they dedicated for the repair of the temple of the LORD. 28 And everything dedicated by Samuel the seer and by Saul son of Kish, Abner son of Ner and Joab son of Zeruiah, and all the other dedicated things were in the care of Shelomith and his relatives.
29 From the Izharites: Kenaniah and his

ᵃ 14 A variant of *Meshelemiah*

ᵇ 18 The meaning of the Hebrew for this word is uncertain.
ᶜ 18 The meaning of the Hebrew for this word is uncertain.
ᵈ 20 Septuagint; Hebrew *As for the Levites, Ahijah was*

sons were assigned duties away from the temple, as officials and judges over Israel. ³⁰ From the Hebronites: Hashabiah and his relatives – seventeen hundred able men – were responsible in Israel west of the Jordan for all the work of the LORD and for the king's service. ³¹ As for the Hebronites, Jeriah was their chief according to the genealogical records of their families. In the fortieth year of David's reign a search was made in the records, and capable men among the Hebronites were found at Jazer in Gilead. ³² Jeriah had two thousand seven hundred relatives, who were able men and heads of families, and King David put them in charge of the Reubenites, the Gadites and the half-tribe of Manasseh for every matter pertaining to God and for the affairs of the king.

Army divisions

27 This is the list of the Israelites – heads of families, commanders of thousands and commanders of hundreds, and their officers, who served the king in all that concerned the army divisions that were on duty month by month throughout the year. Each division consisted of 24,000 men.

² In charge of the first division, for the first month, was Jashobeam son of Zabdiel. There were 24,000 men in his division. ³ He was a descendant of Perez and chief of all the army officers for the first month.

⁴ In charge of the division for the second month was Dodai the Ahohite; Mikloth was the leader of his division. There were 24,000 men in his division. ⁵ The third army commander, for the third month, was Benaiah son of Jehoiada the priest. He was chief and there were 24,000 men in his division. ⁶ This was the Benaiah who was a mighty warrior among the Thirty and was over the Thirty. His son

Ammizabad was in charge of his division.

⁷ The fourth, for the fourth month, was Asahel the brother of Joab; his son Zebadiah was his successor. There were 24,000 men in his division. ⁸ The fifth, for the fifth month, was the commander Shamhuth the Izrahite. There were 24,000 men in his division. ⁹ The sixth, for the sixth month, was Ira the son of Ikkesh the Tekoite. There were 24,000 men in his division. ¹⁰ The seventh, for the seventh month, was Helez the Pelonite, an Ephraimite. There were 24,000 men in his division. ¹¹ The eighth, for the eighth month, was Sibbekai the Hushathite, a Zerahite. There were 24,000 men in his division. ¹² The ninth, for the ninth month, was Abiezer the Anathothite, a Benjaminite. There were 24,000 men in his division. ¹³ The tenth, for the tenth month, was Maharai the Netophathite, a Zerahite. There were 24,000 men in his division. ¹⁴ The eleventh, for the eleventh month, was Benaiah the Pirathonite, an Ephraimite. There were 24,000 men in his division. ¹⁵ The twelfth, for the twelfth month, was Heldai the Netophathite, from the family of Othniel. There were 24,000 men in his division.

Leaders of the tribes

¹⁶ The leaders of the tribes of Israel:

over the Reubenites: Eliezer son of Zikri;
over the Simeonites: Shephatiah son of Maakah;
¹⁷ over Levi: Hashabiah son of Kemuel;
over Aaron: Zadok;
¹⁸ over Judah: Elihu, a brother of David;
over Issachar: Omri son of Michael;
¹⁹ over Zebulun: Ishmaiah son of Obadiah;

over Naphtali: Jerimoth son of Azriel;
20 over the Ephraimites: Hoshea son of Azaziah;
over half the tribe of Manasseh: Joel son of Pedaiah;
21 over the half-tribe of Manasseh in Gilead: Iddo son of Zechariah;
over Benjamin: Jaasiel son of Abner;
22 over Dan: Azarel son of Jeroham.
These were the leaders of the tribes of Israel.

23 David did not take the number of the men twenty years old or less, because the Lord had promised to make Israel as numerous as the stars in the sky. 24 Joab son of Zeruiah began to count the men but did not finish. God's wrath came on Israel on account of this numbering, and the number was not entered in the book*a* of the annals of King David.

The king's overseers
25 Azmaveth son of Adiel was in charge of the royal storehouses.

Jonathan son of Uzziah was in charge of the storehouses in the outlying districts, in the towns, the villages and the watchtowers.
26 Ezri son of Kelub was in charge of the workers who farmed the land.
27 Shimei the Ramathite was in charge of the vineyards.

Zabdi the Shiphmite was in charge of the produce of the vineyards for the wine vats.
28 Baal-Hanan the Gederite was in charge of the olive and sycamore-fig trees in the western foothills.

Joash was in charge of the supplies of olive oil.
29 Shitrai the Sharonite was in charge of the herds grazing in Sharon.

Shaphat son of Adlai was in charge of the herds in the valleys.
30 Obil the Ishmaelite was in charge of the camels.

Jehdeiah the Meronothite was in charge of the donkeys.

_____
a 24 Septuagint; Hebrew *number*

31 Jaziz the Hagrite was in charge of the flocks.

All these were the officials in charge of King David's property.

32 Jonathan, David's uncle, was a counsellor, a man of insight and a scribe. Jehiel son of Hakmoni took care of the king's sons.
33 Ahithophel was the king's counsellor.

Hushai the Arkite was the king's confidant. 34 Ahithophel was succeeded by Jehoiada son of Benaiah and by Abiathar.

Joab was the commander of the royal army.

David's plans for the temple
28 David summoned all the officials of Israel to assemble at Jerusalem: the officers over the tribes, the commanders of the divisions in the service of the king, the commanders of thousands and commanders of hundreds, and the officials in charge of all the property and livestock belonging to the king and his sons, together with the palace officials, the warriors and all the brave fighting men.

2 King David rose to his feet and said: 'Listen to me, my fellow Israelites, my people. I had it in my heart to build a house as a place of rest for the ark of the covenant of the Lord, for the footstool of our God, and I made plans to build it. 3 But God said to me, "You are not to build a house for my Name, because you are a warrior and have shed blood."

4 'Yet the Lord, the God of Israel, chose me from my whole family to be king over Israel for ever. He chose Judah as leader, and from the tribe of Judah he chose my family, and from my father's sons he was pleased to make me king over all Israel. 5 Of all my sons – and the Lord has given me many – he has chosen my son Solomon to sit on the throne of the kingdom of the Lord over Israel. 6 He said to me, "Solomon your son is the one who will build my house and my courts, for I have chosen him to be my son, and I will be his father. 7 I will establish his kingdom for ever if he is unswerving in carrying out my

commands and laws, as is being done at this time."

⁸'So now I charge you in the sight of all Israel and of the assembly of the LORD, and in the hearing of our God: be careful to follow all the commands of the LORD your God, that you may possess this good land and pass it on as an inheritance to your descendants for ever.

⁹'And you, my son Solomon, acknowledge the God of your father, and serve him with wholehearted devotion and with a willing mind, for the LORD searches every heart and understands every desire and every thought. If you seek him, he will be found by you; but if you forsake him, he will reject you for ever. ¹⁰Consider now, for the LORD has chosen you to build a house as the sanctuary. Be strong and do the work.'

¹¹Then David gave his son Solomon the plans for the portico of the temple, its buildings, its storerooms, its upper parts, its inner rooms and the place of atonement. ¹²He gave him the plans of all that the Spirit had put in his mind for the courts of the temple of the LORD and all the surrounding rooms, for the treasuries of the temple of God and for the treasuries for the dedicated things. ¹³He gave him instructions for the divisions of the priests and Levites, and for all the work of serving in the temple of the LORD, as well as for all the articles to be used in its service. ¹⁴He designated the weight of gold for all the gold articles to be used in various kinds of service, and the weight of silver for all the silver articles to be used in various kinds of service: ¹⁵the weight of gold for the gold lampstands and their lamps, with the weight for each lampstand and its lamps; and the weight of silver for each silver lampstand and its lamps, according to the use of each lampstand; ¹⁶the weight of gold for each table for consecrated bread; the weight of silver for the silver tables; ¹⁷the weight of pure gold for the forks, sprinkling bowls and pitchers; the weight of gold for each gold dish; the weight of silver for each silver dish; ¹⁸and the weight of the refined gold for the altar of incense. He also gave him the plan for the chariot, that is, the cherubim of gold that spread their wings and overshadow the ark of the covenant of the LORD.

¹⁹'All this,' David said, 'I have in writing as a result of the LORD's hand on me, and he enabled me to understand all the details of the plan.'

²⁰David also said to Solomon his son, 'Be strong and courageous, and do the work. Do not be afraid or discouraged, for the LORD God, my God, is with you. He will not fail you or forsake you until all the work for the service of the temple of the LORD is finished. ²¹The divisions of the priests and Levites are ready for all the work on the temple of God, and every willing person skilled in any craft will help you in all the work. The officials and all the people will obey your every command.'

Gifts for building the temple

29 Then King David said to the whole assembly: 'My son Solomon, the one whom God has chosen, is young and inexperienced. The task is great, because this palatial structure is not for man but for the LORD God. ²With all my resources I have provided for the temple of my God – gold for the gold work, silver for the silver, bronze for the bronze, iron for the iron and wood for the wood, as well as onyx for the settings, turquoise,ᵃ stones of various colours, and all kinds of fine stone and marble – all of these in large quantities. ³Besides, in my devotion to the temple of my God I now give my personal treasures of gold and silver for the temple of my God, over and above everything I have provided for this holy temple: ⁴three thousand talentsᵇ of gold (gold of Ophir) and seven thousand talentsᶜ of refined silver, for the overlaying of the walls of the buildings, ⁵for the gold work and the silver work, and for all the work to be done by the craftsmen. Now, who is willing to consecrate themselves to the LORD today?'

⁶Then the leaders of families, the

ᵃ 2 The meaning of the Hebrew for this word is uncertain.
ᵇ 4 That is, about 100 metric tons
ᶜ 4 That is, about 235 metric tons

MONEY 1

MY MONEY IS NOT MINE

One summer holiday I worked as a waitress in a pizza restaurant and for the first time had my own decent income. It was great. I had earned this money, worked hard for this money, I deserved this money, it was my money.

1 Chronicles 29:14 tells us that everything belongs to the Lord.

Does it? Really? If you're anything like me, that may feel a bit annoying. You may ask, 'Why have I woken up so early in the morning or worked so late in the evening to earn this, if it's not even mine?'

When we choose to follow Jesus, we are saying that everything in our life is surrendered to him, including our finances. This principle challenges our idea of ownership. It dares to dispute the belief that there are certain things in life that are owned solely by me. It says, with a big gentle voice, that when it comes to following Jesus, there is no 'me, myself and I' but instead 'we, us, together'.

If we think of our money as belonging to the Lord, does that change our perspective on how we use it? Yes it does. It doesn't mean we're not allowed to buy that jumper we really like, but it does mean the way we think about money may be different from the way our culture and mates think about money.

I enjoyed being able to buy things when I earned money – decent shampoo, a meal out with family, a present for a friend. This is OK. The God we follow does not have a spirit of poverty. God is up for us living life and celebrating it, not taking things for granted but instead appreciating and being thankful for the things we have and can afford.

Earning money also meant I could be responsible – pay my bills, contribute to rent and pay off any debt I owed. These are really important things to do with our money, and values driven by Scripture. As Jesus says, 'Pay to Caesar what is his.' When our money belongs to God, we pay our tax!

To have money is no bad thing. It can be really good. But we need to live out of Jesus' principles. This includes celebrating life and being responsible with our finances, and loving others with our money – being generous, being sacrificial and remembering people living in poverty.

The Bible has a lot to say about money. It doesn't tell us what God would go shopping for or how much Jesus would spend on a holiday, but it does warn us of the temptations of money. It urges us to keep Jesus as our number one love, and talks about creating wealth and sharing wealth.

As we read through the money thread, let's remember this principle: when we follow Jesus we give God everything. Our money belongs to him, whether we're spending it on ourselves, paying our bills, or giving in deep sacrifice.

Kiera Singlehurst-Phyo

Luke 14:12–14

officers of the tribes of Israel, the commanders of thousands and commanders
of hundreds, and the officials in charge
of the king's work gave willingly. 7 They
gave towards the work on the temple of
God five thousand talents*d* and ten thousand darics*e* of gold, ten thousand talents*f*
of silver, eighteen thousand talents*g* of
bronze and a hundred thousand talents*h*
of iron. 8 Anyone who had precious stones
gave them to the treasury of the temple
of the LORD in the custody of Jehiel the
Gershonite. 9 The people rejoiced at the
willing response of their leaders, for they
had given freely and wholeheartedly to
the LORD. David the king also rejoiced
greatly.

David's prayer

10 David praised the LORD in the presence of the whole assembly, saying,

'Praise be to you, LORD,
    the God of our father Israel,
    from everlasting to everlasting.
11 Yours, LORD, is the greatness and the
      power
    and the glory and the majesty and
      the splendour,
    for everything in heaven and earth is
      yours.
Yours, LORD, is the kingdom;
    you are exalted as head over all.
12 Wealth and honour come from you;
    you are the ruler of all things.
In your hands are strength and
      power
    to exalt and give strength to all.
13 Now, our God, we give you thanks,
    and praise your glorious name.

14 'But who am I, and who are my people, that we should be able to give as generously as this? Everything comes from
you, and we have given you only what
comes from your hand. 15 We are foreigners and strangers in your sight, as were all

---

d 7 That is, about 170 metric tons
e 7 That is, about 84 kilograms
f 7 That is, about 340 metric tons
g 7 That is, about 610 metric tons
h 7 That is, about 3,400 metric tons

our ancestors. Our days on earth are like a
shadow, without hope. 16 LORD our God,
all this abundance that we have provided
for building you a temple for your Holy
Name comes from your hand, and all of it
belongs to you. 17 I know, my God, that you
test the heart and are pleased with integrity. All these things I have given willingly
and with honest intent. And now I have
seen with joy how willingly your people
who are here have given to you. 18 LORD,
the God of our fathers Abraham, Isaac and
Israel, keep these desires and thoughts in
the hearts of your people for ever, and
keep their hearts loyal to you. 19 And give
my son Solomon the wholehearted devotion to keep your commands, statutes
and decrees and to do everything to build
the palatial structure for which I have provided.'

20 Then David said to the whole assembly, 'Praise the LORD your God.' So they all
praised the LORD, the God of their fathers;
they bowed down, prostrating themselves
before the LORD and the king.

Solomon acknowledged as king

21 The next day they made sacrifices to
the LORD and presented burnt offerings
to him: a thousand bulls, a thousand rams
and a thousand male lambs, together with
their drink offerings, and other sacrifices
in abundance for all Israel. 22 They ate and
drank with great joy in the presence of the
LORD that day.

Then they acknowledged Solomon son
of David as king a second time, anointing
him before the LORD to be ruler and Zadok to be priest. 23 So Solomon sat on the
throne of the LORD as king in place of his
father David. He prospered and all Israel
obeyed him. 24 All the officers and warriors,
as well as all of King David's sons, pledged
their submission to King Solomon.

25 The LORD highly exalted Solomon in
the sight of all Israel and bestowed on him
royal splendour such as no king over Israel
ever had before.

The death of David

26 David son of Jesse was king over all
Israel. 27 He ruled over Israel for forty

years – seven in Hebron and thirty-three in Jerusalem. 28 He died at a good old age, having enjoyed long life, wealth and honour. His son Solomon succeeded him as king.

29 As for the events of King David's reign, from beginning to end, they are written in the records of Samuel the seer, the records of Nathan the prophet and the records of Gad the seer, 30 together with the details of his reign and power, and the circumstances that surrounded him and Israel and the kingdoms of all the other lands.

2 CHRONICLES

DATE

2 Chronicles details events from around 970 BC to about 587 BC

AUTHOR

Unknown (though traditionally attributed to Ezra)

WHAT'S IT ALL ABOUT?

This second book of Chronicles, like the first, was written for the men returning from exile in Babylon to rebuild Jerusalem, and was written many years after the events it describes. It begins with the start of Solomon's reign and follows the history of God's people (via the Kingdom of Judah) through to the fall of Jerusalem. The writer does not acknowledge the kings of Israel and he also leaves out the negative history of Solomon (that can be read in 1 Kings). The book ends with the fall of Jerusalem, but the writer finds a note of hope that God's people could return to the city and rebuild God's temple.

WHY SHOULD WE READ IT?

- To hear about Solomon's gift of wisdom (2 Chronicles 1 and 9).
- To read about the glory of the Lord filling the temple (2 Chronicles 6 and 7).
- To read the history of the kings of Judah (2 Chronicles 10 onwards).
- To see how the Lord fought battles for his people (2 Chronicles 20).

Andy Croft with Liza Hoeksma

Solomon asks for wisdom

1 Solomon son of David established himself firmly over his kingdom, for the LORD his God was with him and made him exceedingly great.

2 Then Solomon spoke to all Israel – to the commanders of thousands and commanders of hundreds, to the judges and to all the leaders in Israel, the heads of families – 3 and Solomon and the whole assembly went to the high place at Gibeon, for God's tent of meeting was there, which Moses the LORD's servant had made in the wilderness. 4 Now David had brought up the ark of God from Kiriath Jearim to the place he had prepared for it, because he had pitched a tent for it in Jerusalem. 5 But the bronze altar that Bezalel son of Uri, the son of Hur, had made was in Gibeon in front of the tabernacle of the LORD; so Solomon and the assembly enquired of him there. 6 Solomon went up to the bronze altar before the LORD in the tent of meeting and offered a thousand burnt offerings on it.

7 That night God appeared to Solomon and said to him, 'Ask for whatever you want me to give you.'

8 Solomon answered God, 'You have shown great kindness to David my father and have made me king in his place. 9 Now, LORD God, let your promise to my father David be confirmed, for you have made me king over a people who are as numerous as the dust of the earth. 10 Give me wisdom and knowledge, that I may lead this people, for who is able to govern this great people of yours?'

11 God said to Solomon, 'Since this is your heart's desire and you have not asked for wealth, possessions or honour, nor for the death of your enemies, and since you have not asked for a long life but for wisdom and knowledge to govern my people over whom I have made you king, 12 therefore wisdom and knowledge will be given you. And I will also give you wealth, possessions and honour, such as no king who was before you ever had and none after you will have.'

13 Then Solomon went to Jerusalem from the high place at Gibeon, from before the tent of meeting. And he reigned over Israel.

14 Solomon accumulated chariots and horses; he had fourteen hundred chariots and twelve thousand horses,*a* which he kept in the chariot cities and also with him in Jerusalem. 15 The king made silver and gold as common in Jerusalem as stones, and cedar as plentiful as sycamore-fig trees in the foothills. 16 Solomon's horses were imported from Egypt and from Kue*b* – the royal merchants purchased them from Kue at the current price. 17 They imported a chariot from Egypt for six hundred shekels*c* of silver, and a horse for a hundred and fifty.*d* They also exported them to all the kings of the Hittites and of the Arameans.

Preparations for building the temple

2*a* Solomon gave orders to build a temple for the Name of the LORD and a royal palace for himself. 2 He conscripted 70,000 men as carriers and 80,000 as stonecutters in the hills and 3,600 as foremen over them.

3 Solomon sent this message to Hiram*b* king of Tyre:

'Send me cedar logs as you did for my father David when you sent him cedar to build a palace to live in. 4 Now I am about to build a temple for the Name of the LORD my God and to dedicate it to him for burning fragrant incense before him, for setting out the consecrated bread regularly, and for making burnt offerings every morning and evening and on the Sabbaths, at the New Moons and at the appointed festivals of the LORD our God. This is a lasting ordinance for Israel.

5 'The temple I am going to build will be great, because our God is

---

a 14 Or *charioteers*
b 16 Probably Cilicia
c 17 That is, about 6.9 kilograms
d 17 That is, about 1.7 kilograms
a In Hebrew texts 2:1 is numbered 1:18, and 2:2-18 is numbered 2:1-17.
b 3 Hebrew *Huram*, a variant of *Hiram*; also in verses 11 and 12

greater than all other gods. 6But who is able to build a temple for him, since the heavens, even the highest heavens, cannot contain him? Who then am I to build a temple for him, except as a place to burn sacrifices before him?

7'Send me, therefore, a man skilled to work in gold and silver, bronze and iron, and in purple, crimson and blue yarn, and experienced in the art of engraving, to work in Judah and Jerusalem with my skilled workers, whom my father David provided.

8'Send me also cedar, juniper and algumᶜ logs from Lebanon, for I know that your servants are skilled in cutting timber there. My servants shall work with yours 9to provide me with plenty of timber, because the temple I build must be large and magnificent. 10I will give your servants, the woodsmen who cut the timber, twenty thousand corsᵈ of ground wheat, twenty thousand bathsᵉ of barley, twenty thousand bathsᶠ of wine and twenty thousand baths of olive oil.'

11 Hiram king of Tyre replied by letter to Solomon:

'Because the LORD loves his people, he has made you their king.'

12And Hiram added:

'Praise be to the LORD, the God of Israel, who made heaven and earth! He has given King David a wise son, endowed with intelligence and discernment, who will build a temple for the LORD and a palace for himself.

13'I am sending you Huram-Abi, a man of great skill, 14whose mother was from Dan and whose father was from Tyre. He is trained to work in gold and silver, bronze and iron, stone and wood, and with purple and blue and crimson yarn and fine linen. He is experienced in all kinds of engraving and can execute any design given to him. He will work with your skilled workers and with those of my lord, David your father.

15'Now let my lord send his servants the wheat and barley and the olive oil and wine he promised, 16and we will cut all the logs from Lebanon that you need and will float them as rafts by sea down to Joppa. You can then take them up to Jerusalem.'

17Solomon took a census of all the foreigners residing in Israel, after the census his father David had taken; and they were found to be 153,600. 18He assigned 70,000 of them to be carriers and 80,000 to be stonecutters in the hills, with 3,600 foremen over them to keep the people working.

Solomon builds the temple

3 Then Solomon began to build the temple of the LORD in Jerusalem on Mount Moriah, where the LORD had appeared to his father David. It was on the threshing-floor of Araunahᵃ the Jebusite, the place provided by David. 2He began building on the second day of the second month in the fourth year of his reign.

3The foundation Solomon laid for building the temple of God was sixty cubits long and twenty cubits wideᵇ (using the cubit of the old standard). 4The portico at the front of the temple was twenty cubitsᶜ long across the width of the building and twentyᵈ cubits high.

He overlaid the inside with pure gold. 5He panelled the main hall with juniper

---

c 8 Probably a variant of *almug*

d 10 That is, probably about 3,200 metric tons of wheat

e 10 That is, probably about 2,700 metric tons of barley

f 10 That is, about 440,000 litres

---

a 1 Hebrew *Ornan*, a variant of *Araunah*

b 3 That is, about 27 metres long and 9 metres wide

c 4 That is, about 9 metres; also in verses 8, 11 and 13

d 4 Some Septuagint and Syriac manuscripts; Hebrew *and a hundred and twenty* and covered it with fine gold and decorated it with palm tree and chain designs. 6 He adorned the temple with precious stones. And the gold he used was gold of Parvaim. 7 He overlaid the ceiling beams, door-frames, walls and doors of the temple with gold, and he carved cherubim on the walls.

8 He built the Most Holy Place, its length corresponding to the width of the temple – twenty cubits long and twenty cubits wide. He overlaid the inside with six hundred talents*e* of fine gold. 9 The gold nails weighed fifty shekels.*f* He also overlaid the upper parts with gold.

10 For the Most Holy Place he made a pair of sculptured cherubim and overlaid them with gold. 11 The total wing-span of the cherubim was twenty cubits. One wing of the first cherub was five cubits*g* long and touched the temple wall, while its other wing, also five cubits long, touched the wing of the other cherub. 12 Similarly one wing of the second cherub was five cubits long and touched the other temple wall, and its other wing, also five cubits long, touched the wing of the first cherub. 13 The wings of these cherubim extended twenty cubits. They stood on their feet, facing the main hall.*h*

14 He made the curtain of blue, purple and crimson yarn and fine linen, with cherubim worked into it.

15 For the front of the temple he made two pillars, which together were thirty-five cubits*i* long, each with a capital five cubits high. 16 He made interwoven chains*j* and put them on top of the pillars. He also made a hundred pomegranates and attached them to the chains. 17 He erected the pillars in the front of the temple, one to the south and one to the north. The one to the south he named Jakin*k* and the one to the north Boaz.*l*

The temple's furnishings

4 He made a bronze altar twenty cubits long, twenty cubits wide and ten cubits high.*a* 2 He made the Sea of cast metal, circular in shape, measuring ten cubits from rim to rim and five cubits*b* high. It took a line of thirty cubits*c* to measure round it. 3 Below the rim, figures of bulls encircled it – ten to a cubit.*d* The bulls were cast in two rows in one piece with the Sea.

4 The Sea stood on twelve bulls, three facing north, three facing west, three facing south and three facing east. The Sea rested on top of them, and their hindquarters were towards the centre. 5 It was a handbreadth*e* in thickness, and its rim was like the rim of a cup, like a lily blossom. It held three thousand baths.*f*

6 He then made ten basins for washing and placed five on the south side and five on the north. In them the things to be used for the burnt offerings were rinsed, but the Sea was to be used by the priests for washing.

7 He made ten gold lampstands according to the specifications for them and placed them in the temple, five on the south side and five on the north.

8 He made ten tables and placed them in the temple, five on the south side and five on the north. He also made a hundred gold sprinkling bowls.

9 He made the courtyard of the priests, and the large court and the doors for the court, and overlaid the doors with bronze. 10 He placed the Sea on the south side, at the south-east corner.

11 And Huram also made the pots and shovels and sprinkling bowls.

So Huram finished the work he had undertaken for King Solomon in the temple of God:

---

e 8 That is, about 21 metric tons
f 9 That is, about 575 grams
g 11 That is, about 2.3 metres; also in verse 15
h 13 Or *facing inwards*
i 15 That is, about 16 metres
j 16 Or possibly *made chains in the inner sanctuary*; the meaning of the Hebrew for this phrase is uncertain.
k 17 *Jakin* probably means *he establishes.*
l 17 *Boaz* probably means *in him is strength.*

a 1 That is, about 9 metres long and wide and 4.5 metres high
b 2 That is, about 2.3 metres
c 2 That is, about 14 metres
d 3 That is, about 45 centimetres
e 5 That is, about 7.5 centimetres
f 5 That is, about 66,000 litres

12 the two pillars;
   the two bowl-shaped capitals on top
     of the pillars;
   the two sets of network decorating
     the two bowl-shaped capitals on
     top of the pillars;
13 the four hundred pomegranates for
     the two sets of network (two rows
     of pomegranates for each net-
     work, decorating the bowl-shaped
     capitals on top of the pillars);
14 the stands with their basins;
15 the Sea and the twelve bulls un-
     der it;
16 the pots, shovels, meat forks and all
     related articles.

All the objects that Huram-Abi made
for King Solomon for the temple of the
LORD were of polished bronze. 17 The king
had them cast in clay moulds in the plain
of the Jordan between Sukkoth and Zarethan.*g* 18 All these things that Solomon
made amounted to so much that the
weight of the bronze could not be calculated.

19 Solomon also made all the furnishings that were in God's temple:

   the golden altar;
   the tables on which was the bread of
     the Presence;
20 the lampstands of pure gold with
     their lamps, to burn in front of the
     inner sanctuary as prescribed;
21 the gold floral work and lamps and
     tongs (they were solid gold);
22 the pure gold wick trimmers, sprink-
     ling bowls, dishes and censers;
     and the gold doors of the temple:
     the inner doors to the Most Holy
     Place and the doors of the main
     hall.

5 When all the work Solomon had done
   for the temple of the LORD was finished, he brought in the things his father

David had dedicated – the silver and gold
and all the furnishings – and he placed
them in the treasuries of God's temple.

The ark brought to the temple

2 Then Solomon summoned to Jerusalem the elders of Israel, all the heads
of the tribes and the chiefs of the Israelite
families, to bring up the ark of the LORD's
covenant from Zion, the City of David.
3 And all the Israelites came together to
the king at the time of the festival in the
seventh month.

4 When all the elders of Israel had arrived, the Levites took up the ark, 5 and
they brought up the ark and the tent of
meeting and all the sacred furnishings in
it. The Levitical priests carried them up;
6 and King Solomon and the entire assembly of Israel that had gathered about him
were before the ark, sacrificing so many
sheep and cattle that they could not be recorded or counted.

7 The priests then brought the ark of the
LORD's covenant to its place in the inner
sanctuary of the temple, the Most Holy
Place, and put it beneath the wings of the
cherubim. 8 The cherubim spread their
wings over the place of the ark and covered the ark and its carrying poles. 9 These
poles were so long that their ends, extending from the ark, could be seen from
in front of the inner sanctuary, but not
from outside the Holy Place; and they are
still there today. 10 There was nothing in
the ark except the two tablets that Moses
had placed in it at Horeb, where the LORD
made a covenant with the Israelites after
they came out of Egypt.

11 The priests then withdrew from the
Holy Place. All the priests who were there
had consecrated themselves, regardless of
their divisions. 12 All the Levites who were
musicians – Asaph, Heman, Jeduthun and
their sons and relatives – stood on the east
side of the altar, dressed in fine linen and
playing cymbals, harps and lyres. They
were accompanied by 120 priests sounding trumpets. 13 The trumpeters and musicians joined in unison to give praise
and thanks to the LORD. Accompanied by
trumpets, cymbals and other instruments,

---

g 17 Hebrew *Zeredatha*, a variant of *Zarethan*

the singers raised their voices in praise to the LORD and sang:

'He is good;
his love endures for ever.'

Then the temple of the LORD was filled with the cloud, **14** and the priests could not perform their service because of the cloud, for the glory of the LORD filled the temple of God.

6 Then Solomon said, 'The LORD has said that he would dwell in a dark cloud; **2** I have built a magnificent temple for you, a place for you to dwell for ever.'

3 While the whole assembly of Israel was standing there, the king turned round and blessed them. **4** Then he said:

'Praise be to the LORD, the God of Israel, who with his hands has fulfilled what he promised with his mouth to my father David. For he said, **5** "Since the day I brought my people out of Egypt, I have not chosen a city in any tribe of Israel to have a temple built so that my Name might be there, nor have I chosen anyone to be ruler over my people Israel. **6** But now I have chosen Jerusalem for my Name to be there, and I have chosen David to rule my people Israel."

7 'My father David had it in his heart to build a temple for the Name of the LORD, the God of Israel. **8** But the LORD said to my father David, "You did well to have it in your heart to build a temple for my Name. **9** Nevertheless, you are not the one to build the temple, but your son, your own flesh and blood – he is the one who will build the temple for my Name."

10 'The LORD has kept the promise he made. I have succeeded David my father and now I sit on the throne of Israel, just as the LORD promised, and I have built the temple for the Name of the LORD, the God of Israel. **11** There I have placed the ark, in which is the covenant of the LORD that he made with the people of Israel.'

Solomon's prayer of dedication

12 Then Solomon stood before the altar of the LORD in front of the whole assembly of Israel and spread out his hands. **13** Now he had made a bronze platform, five cubits long, five cubits wide and three cubits high,*a* and had placed it in the centre of the outer court. He stood on the platform and then knelt down before the whole assembly of Israel and spread out his hands towards heaven. **14** He said:

'LORD, the God of Israel, there is no God like you in heaven or on earth – you who keep your covenant of love with your servants who continue wholeheartedly in your way. **15** You have kept your promise to your servant David my father; with your mouth you have promised and with your hand you have fulfilled it – as it is today.

16 'Now, LORD, the God of Israel, keep for your servant David my father the promises you made to him when you said, "You shall never fail to have a successor to sit before me on the throne of Israel, if only your descendants are careful in all they do to walk before me according to my law, as you have done." **17** And now, LORD, the God of Israel, let your word that you promised your servant David come true.

18 'But will God really dwell on earth with humans? The heavens, even the highest heavens, cannot contain you. How much less this temple that I have built! **19** Yet, LORD my God, give attention to your servant's prayer and his plea for mercy. Hear the cry and the prayer that your servant is praying in your presence. **20** May your eyes be open towards this temple day and night, this place of which you said you would put your Name there. May you hear the prayer your servant prays towards this place. **21** Hear the supplications of your servant and of

---

a 13 That is, about 2.3 metres long and wide and 1.4 metres high your people Israel when they pray towards this place. Hear from heaven, your dwelling-place; and when you hear, forgive.

22 'When anyone wrongs their neighbour and is required to take an oath and they come and swear the oath before your altar in this temple, 23 then hear from heaven and act. Judge between your servants, condemning the guilty and bringing down on their heads what they have done, and vindicating the innocent by treating them in accordance with their innocence.

24 'When your people Israel have been defeated by an enemy because they have sinned against you and when they turn back and give praise to your name, praying and making supplication before you in this temple, 25 then hear from heaven and forgive the sin of your people Israel and bring them back to the land you gave to them and their ancestors.

26 'When the heavens are shut up and there is no rain because your people have sinned against you, and when they pray towards this place and give praise to your name and turn from their sin because you have afflicted them, 27 then hear from heaven and forgive the sin of your servants, your people Israel. Teach them the right way to live, and send rain on the land that you gave your people for an inheritance.

28 'When famine or plague comes to the land, or blight or mildew, locusts or grasshoppers, or when enemies besiege them in any of their cities, whatever disaster or disease may come, 29 and when a prayer or plea is made by anyone among your people Israel – being aware of their afflictions and pains, and spreading out their hands towards this temple – 30 then hear from heaven, your dwelling-place. Forgive, and deal with everyone according to all they do, since you know their hearts (for you alone know the human heart),

31 so that they will fear you and walk in obedience to you all the time they live in the land that you gave our ancestors.

32 'As for the foreigner who does not belong to your people Israel but has come from a distant land because of your great name and your mighty hand and your outstretched arm – when they come and pray towards this temple, 33 then hear from heaven, your dwelling-place. Do whatever the foreigner asks of you, so that all the peoples of the earth may know your name and fear you, as do your own people Israel, and may know that this house that I have built bears your Name.

34 'When your people go to war against their enemies, wherever you send them, and when they pray to you towards this city you have chosen and the temple I have built for your Name, 35 then hear from heaven their prayer and their plea, and uphold their cause.

36 'When they sin against you – for there is no one who does not sin – and you become angry with them and give them over to the enemy, who takes them captive to a land far away or near; 37 and if they have a change of heart in the land where they are held captive, and repent and plead with you in the land of their captivity and say, "We have sinned, we have done wrong and acted wickedly"; 38 and if they turn back to you with all their heart and soul in the land of their captivity where they were taken, and pray towards the land that you gave their ancestors, towards the city you have chosen and towards the temple that I have built for your Name; 39 then from heaven, your dwelling-place, hear their prayer and their pleas, and uphold their cause. And forgive your people, who have sinned against you.

40 'Now, my God, may your eyes be open and your ears attentive to the prayers offered in this place.

41 'Now arise, LORD God, and come
     to your resting place,
     you and the ark of your might.
 May your priests, LORD God, be
     clothed with salvation,
 may your faithful people
     rejoice in your goodness.
42 LORD God, do not reject your
     anointed one.
 Remember the great love
     promised to David your
     servant.'

The dedication of the temple

7 When Solomon finished praying, fire
came down from heaven and consumed the burnt offering and the sacrifices, and the glory of the LORD filled the
temple. 2 The priests could not enter the
temple of the LORD because the glory of
the LORD filled it. 3 When all the Israelites
saw the fire coming down and the glory
of the LORD above the temple, they knelt
on the pavement with their faces to the
ground, and they worshipped and gave
thanks to the LORD, saying,

 'He is good;
     his love endures for ever.'

4 Then the king and all the people offered
sacrifices before the LORD. 5 And King Solomon offered a sacrifice of twenty-two
thousand head of cattle and a hundred
and twenty thousand sheep and goats.
So the king and all the people dedicated
the temple of God. 6 The priests took up
their positions, as did the Levites with the
LORD's musical instruments, which King
David had made for praising the LORD and
which were used when he gave thanks, saying, 'His love endures for ever.' Opposite
the Levites, the priests blew their trumpets, and all the Israelites were standing.

7 Solomon consecrated the middle part
of the courtyard in front of the temple of
the LORD, and there he offered burnt offerings and the fat of the fellowship offerings, because the bronze altar he had
made could not hold the burnt offerings,
the grain offerings and the fat portions.
8 So Solomon observed the festival at

that time for seven days, and all Israel with
him – a vast assembly, people from Lebo
Hamath to the Wadi of Egypt. 9 On the
eighth day they held an assembly, for they
had celebrated the dedication of the altar
for seven days and the festival for seven
days more. 10 On the twenty-third day of
the seventh month he sent the people to
their homes, joyful and glad in heart for
the good things the LORD had done for
David and Solomon and for his people
Israel.

The LORD appears to Solomon

11 When Solomon had finished the temple of the LORD and the royal palace, and
had succeeded in carrying out all he had in
mind to do in the temple of the LORD and
in his own palace, 12 the LORD appeared to
him at night and said:

 'I have heard your prayer and have
 chosen this place for myself as a temple for sacrifices.

13 'When I shut up the heavens
so that there is no rain, or command locusts to devour the land or
send a plague among my people,
14 if my people, who are called by
my name, will humble themselves
and pray and seek my face and turn
from their wicked ways, then I will
hear from heaven, and I will forgive
their sin and will heal their land.
15 Now my eyes will be open and my
ears attentive to the prayers offered
in this place. 16 I have chosen and
consecrated this temple so that my
Name may be there for ever. My eyes
and my heart will always be there.

17 'As for you, if you walk before
me faithfully as David your father
did, and do all I command, and observe my decrees and laws, 18 I will
establish your royal throne, as I covenanted with David your father when
I said, "You shall never fail to have a
successor to rule over Israel."

19 'But if you*a* turn away and forsake
the decrees and commands I have

---

a 19 The Hebrew is plural.

given you[b] and go off to serve other gods and worship them, [20] then I will uproot Israel from my land, which I have given them, and will reject this temple which I have consecrated for my Name. I will make it a byword and an object of ridicule among all peoples. [21] This temple will become a heap of rubble. All[c] who pass by will be appalled and say, "Why has the LORD done such a thing to this land and to this temple?" [22] People will answer, "Because they have forsaken the LORD, the God of their ancestors, who brought them out of Egypt, and have embraced other gods, worshipping and serving them – that is why he brought all this disaster on them."'

---

b 19 The Hebrew is plural.
c 21 See some Septuagint manuscripts, Old Latin, Syriac, Arabic and Targum; Hebrew *And though this temple is now so imposing, all*

Solomon's other activities

8 At the end of twenty years, during which Solomon built the temple of the LORD and his own palace, [2] Solomon

---

EVANGELISM 8

In prayer

2 Chronicles 7:14 is often quoted but actually, it's not an easy scripture to take on board. Often we like to focus on the last bit – the hearing from heaven and healing the land bit. But the part before is also really important!

I am aware that I am flawed and that I really need God. He is gracious with me, but that does not mean I can ignore the sin. If there are things God has put his finger on for you to face, know that he loves you, but that you do need to face them. Take a few moments with God, to see if there is anything he wants to show you.

As I said at the beginning of these studies, if we don't do this evangelism thing with God, we can't do it! Let's remind ourselves again that it's all about God and about what he is doing. Sometimes I think I know exactly what needs to happen in a situation and find myself praying that God will make it happen. As you begin to pray for your friends, ask God what he is doing in their lives and if there is anything that he wants to show you. That way you can pray in line with God and his heart for your friends.

Sometimes we see prayer as a last resort. I would challenge you to make it the first and the last resort, and all the resorts in the middle! I once heard prayer described as a huge magnifying glass. When you use a magnifying glass in the sun, it captures all the energy and power and concentrates it in one place. I love to think of prayer in that way. It captures all the energy and power of God and focuses it on one person. Why would we not start there?

Seek God today and pray for those people you are journeying with.

Mark Ritchie

 1 Peter 3:15

Luke 2:16–18

rebuilt the villages that Hiram*ᵃ* had given him, and settled Israelites in them. ³ Solomon then went to Hamath Zobah and captured it. ⁴ He also built up Tadmor in the desert and all the store cities he had built in Hamath. ⁵ He rebuilt Upper Beth Horon and Lower Beth Horon as fortified cities, with walls and with gates and bars, ⁶ as well as Baalath and all his store cities, and all the cities for his chariots and for his horses*ᵇ* – whatever he desired to build in Jerusalem, in Lebanon and throughout all the territory that he ruled.

⁷ There were still people left from the Hittites, Amorites, Perizzites, Hivites and Jebusites (these people were not Israelites). ⁸ Solomon conscripted the descendants of all these people remaining in the land – whom the Israelites had not destroyed – to serve as slave labour, as it is to this day. ⁹ But Solomon did not make slaves of the Israelites for his work; they were his fighting men, commanders of his captains, and commanders of his chariots and charioteers. ¹⁰ They were also King Solomon's chief officials – two hundred and fifty officials supervising the men.

¹¹ Solomon brought Pharaoh's daughter up from the City of David to the palace he had built for her, for he said, 'My wife must not live in the palace of David king of Israel, because the places the ark of the Lord has entered are holy.'

¹² On the altar of the Lord that he had built in front of the portico, Solomon sacrificed burnt offerings to the Lord, ¹³ according to the daily requirement for offerings commanded by Moses for the Sabbaths, the New Moons and the three annual festivals – the Festival of Unleavened Bread, the Festival of Weeks and the Festival of Tabernacles. ¹⁴ In keeping with the ordinance of his father David, he appointed the divisions of the priests for their duties and the Levites to lead the praise and to assist the priests according to each day's requirement. He also appointed the gatekeepers by divisions for the various gates, because this was what David the man of God had ordered. ¹⁵ They did not deviate from the king's commands to the priests or to the Levites in any matter, including that of the treasuries.

¹⁶ All Solomon's work was carried out, from the day the foundation of the temple of the Lord was laid until its completion. So the temple of the Lord was finished.

¹⁷ Then Solomon went to Ezion Geber and Elath on the coast of Edom. ¹⁸ And Hiram sent him ships commanded by his own men, sailors who knew the sea. These, with Solomon's men, sailed to Ophir and brought back four hundred and fifty talents*ᶜ* of gold, which they delivered to King Solomon.

The queen of Sheba visits Solomon

9 When the queen of Sheba heard of Solomon's fame, she came to Jerusalem to test him with hard questions. Arriving with a very great caravan – with camels carrying spices, large quantities of gold, and precious stones – she came to Solomon and talked with him about all she had on her mind. ² Solomon answered all her questions; nothing was too hard for him to explain to her. ³ When the queen of Sheba saw the wisdom of Solomon, as well as the palace he had built, ⁴ the food on his table, the seating of his officials, the attending servants in their robes, the cupbearers in their robes and the burnt offerings he made at*ᵃ* the temple of the Lord, she was overwhelmed.

⁵ She said to the king, 'The report I heard in my own country about your achievements and your wisdom is true. ⁶ But I did not believe what they said until I came and saw with my own eyes. Indeed, not even half the greatness of your wisdom was told me; you have far exceeded the report I heard. ⁷ How happy your people must be! How happy your officials, who continually stand before you and hear your wisdom! ⁸ Praise be to the Lord your God, who has delighted in you and placed you on his throne as king to rule for the Lord your God. Because of the love of your God

for Israel and his desire to uphold them for ever, he has made you king over them, to maintain justice and righteousness.'

⁹Then she gave the king 120 talentsᵇ of gold, large quantities of spices, and precious stones. There had never been such spices as those the queen of Sheba gave to King Solomon.

¹⁰(The servants of Hiram and the servants of Solomon brought gold from Ophir; they also brought algum-woodᶜ and precious stones. ¹¹The king used the algum-wood to make steps for the temple of the LORD and for the royal palace, and to make harps and lyres for the musicians. Nothing like them had ever been seen in Judah.)

¹²King Solomon gave the queen of Sheba all she desired and asked for; he gave her more than she had brought to him. Then she left and returned with her retinue to her own country.

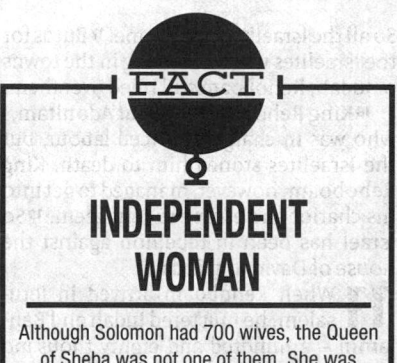

FACT
INDEPENDENT WOMAN

Although Solomon had 700 wives, the Queen of Sheba was not one of them. She was just a visitor. Sheba, or Saba, corresponds roughly to modern Yemen
(2 Chronicles 9:1–12).

Solomon's splendour

¹³The weight of the gold that Solomon received yearly was 666 talents,ᵈ ¹⁴not including the revenues brought in by merchants and traders. Also all the kings of Arabia and the governors of the territories brought gold and silver to Solomon.

¹⁵King Solomon made two hundred large shields of hammered gold; six hundred shekelsᵉ of hammered gold went into each shield. ¹⁶He also made three hundred small shields of hammered gold, with three hundred shekelsᶠ of gold in each shield. The king put them in the Palace of the Forest of Lebanon.

¹⁷Then the king made a great throne covered with ivory and overlaid with pure gold. ¹⁸The throne had six steps, and a footstool of gold was attached to it. On both sides of the seat were armrests, with a lion standing beside each of them. ¹⁹Twelve lions stood on the six steps, one at either end of each step. Nothing like it had ever been made for any other kingdom. ²⁰All King Solomon's goblets were gold, and all the household articles in the Palace of the Forest of Lebanon were pure gold. Nothing was made of silver, because silver was considered of little value in Solomon's day. ²¹The king had a fleet of trading shipsᵍ manned by Hiram'sʰ servants. Once every three years it returned, carrying gold, silver and ivory, and apes and baboons.

²²King Solomon was greater in riches and wisdom than all the other kings of the earth. ²³All the kings of the earth sought audience with Solomon to hear the wisdom God had put in his heart. ²⁴Year after year, everyone who came brought a gift – articles of silver and gold, and robes, weapons and spices, and horses and mules.

²⁵Solomon had four thousand stalls for horses and chariots, and twelve thousand horses,ᶦ which he kept in the chariot cities and also with him in Jerusalem. ²⁶He ruled over all the kings from the River Euphrates to the land of the Philistines, as far as the border of Egypt. ²⁷The king made silver as common in Jerusalem as stones, and cedar as plentiful as sycamore-fig trees in the foothills. ²⁸Solomon's horses were imported from Egypt and from all other countries.

---

b 9 That is, about 4 metric tons
c 10 Probably a variant of *almug-wood*
d 13 That is, about 23 metric tons

e 15 That is, about 6.9 kilograms
f 16 That is, about 3.5 kilograms
g 21 Hebrew *of ships that could go to Tarshish*
h 21 Hebrew *Huram*, a variant of *Hiram*
i 25 Or *charioteers*

Solomon's death

²⁹As for the other events of Solomon's reign, from beginning to end, are they not written in the records of Nathan the prophet, in the prophecy of Ahijah the Shilonite and in the visions of Iddo the seer concerning Jeroboam son of Nebat? ³⁰Solomon reigned in Jerusalem over all Israel for forty years. ³¹Then he rested with his ancestors and was buried in the city of David his father. And Rehoboam his son succeeded him as king.

Israel rebels against Rehoboam

10 Rehoboam went to Shechem, for all Israel had gone there to make him king. ²When Jeroboam son of Nebat heard this (he was in Egypt, where he had fled from King Solomon), he returned from Egypt. ³So they sent for Jeroboam, and he and all Israel went to Rehoboam and said to him: ⁴'Your father put a heavy yoke on us, but now lighten the harsh labour and the heavy yoke he put on us, and we will serve you.'

⁵Rehoboam answered, 'Come back to me in three days.' So the people went away.

⁶Then King Rehoboam consulted the elders who had served his father Solomon during his lifetime. 'How would you advise me to answer these people?' he asked.

⁷They replied, 'If you will be kind to these people and please them and give them a favourable answer, they will always be your servants.'

⁸But Rehoboam rejected the advice the elders gave him and consulted the young men who had grown up with him and were serving him. ⁹He asked them, 'What is your advice? How should we answer these people who say to me, "Lighten the yoke your father put on us"?'

¹⁰The young men who had grown up with him replied, 'The people have said to you, "Your father put a heavy yoke on us, but make our yoke lighter." Now tell them, "My little finger is thicker than my father's waist. ¹¹My father laid on you a heavy yoke; I will make it even heavier. My father scourged you with whips; I will scourge you with scorpions."'

¹²Three days later Jeroboam and all the people returned to Rehoboam, as the king had said, 'Come back to me in three days.' ¹³The king answered them harshly. Rejecting the advice of the elders, ¹⁴he followed the advice of the young men and said, 'My father made your yoke heavy; I will make it even heavier. My father scourged you with whips; I will scourge you with scorpions.' ¹⁵So the king did not listen to the people, for this turn of events was from God, to fulfil the word that the LORD had spoken to Jeroboam son of Nebat through Ahijah the Shilonite.

¹⁶When all Israel saw that the king refused to listen to them, they answered the king:

'What share do we have in David,
    what part in Jesse's son?
To your tents, Israel!
    Look after your own house, David!'

So all the Israelites went home. ¹⁷But as for the Israelites who were living in the towns of Judah, Rehoboam still ruled over them.

¹⁸King Rehoboam sent out Adoniram,ᵃ who was in charge of forced labour, but the Israelites stoned him to death. King Rehoboam, however, managed to get into his chariot and escape to Jerusalem. ¹⁹So Israel has been in rebellion against the house of David to this day.

11 When Rehoboam arrived in Jerusalem, he mustered Judah and Benjamin – a hundred and eighty thousand able young men – to go to war against Israel and to regain the kingdom for Rehoboam.

²But this word of the LORD came to Shemaiah the man of God: ³'Say to Rehoboam son of Solomon king of Judah and to all Israel in Judah and Benjamin, ⁴"This is what the LORD says: do not go up to fight against your fellow Israelites. Go home, every one of you, for this is my doing."' So they obeyed the words of the LORD and turned back from marching against Jeroboam.

ᵃ 18 Hebrew *Hadoram*, a variant of *Adoniram*

Rehoboam fortifies Judah

5 Rehoboam lived in Jerusalem and built up towns for defence in Judah: 6 Bethlehem, Etam, Tekoa, 7 Beth Zur, Soko, Adullam, 8 Gath, Mareshah, Ziph, 9 Adoraim, Lachish, Azekah, 10 Zorah, Aijalon and Hebron. These were fortified cities in Judah and Benjamin. 11 He strengthened their defences and put commanders in them, with supplies of food, olive oil and wine. 12 He put shields and spears in all the cities, and made them very strong. So Judah and Benjamin were his.

13 The priests and Levites from all their districts throughout Israel sided with him. 14 The Levites even abandoned their pasture-lands and property and came to Judah and Jerusalem, because Jeroboam and his sons had rejected them as priests of the LORD 15 when he appointed his own priests for the high places and for the goat and calf idols he had made. 16 Those from every tribe of Israel who set their hearts on seeking the LORD, the God of Israel, followed the Levites to Jerusalem to offer sacrifices to the LORD, the God of their ancestors. 17 They strengthened the kingdom of Judah and supported Rehoboam son of Solomon for three years, following the ways of David and Solomon during this time.

Rehoboam's family

18 Rehoboam married Mahalath, who was the daughter of David's son Jerimoth and of Abihail, the daughter of Jesse's son Eliab. 19 She bore him sons: Jeush, Shemariah and Zaham. 20 Then he married Maakah daughter of Absalom, who bore him Abijah, Attai, Ziza and Shelomith. 21 Rehoboam loved Maakah daughter of Absalom more than any of his other wives and concubines. In all, he had eighteen wives and sixty concubines, twenty-eight sons and sixty daughters.

22 Rehoboam appointed Abijah son of Maakah as crown prince among his brothers, in order to make him king. 23 He acted wisely, dispersing some of his sons throughout the districts of Judah and Benjamin, and to all the fortified cities.

He gave them abundant provisions and took many wives for them.

Shishak attacks Jerusalem

12 After Rehoboam's position as king was established and he had become strong, he and all Israel*a* with him abandoned the law of the LORD. 2 Because they had been unfaithful to the LORD, Shishak king of Egypt attacked Jerusalem in the fifth year of King Rehoboam. 3 With twelve hundred chariots and sixty thousand horsemen and the innumerable troops of Libyans, Sukkites and Cushites*b* that came with him from Egypt, 4 he captured the fortified cities of Judah and came as far as Jerusalem.

5 Then the prophet Shemaiah came to Rehoboam and to the leaders of Judah who had assembled in Jerusalem for fear of Shishak, and he said to them, 'This is what the LORD says: "You have abandoned me; therefore, I now abandon you to Shishak."'

6 The leaders of Israel and the king humbled themselves and said, 'The LORD is just.'

7 When the LORD saw that they humbled themselves, this word of the LORD came to Shemaiah: 'Since they have humbled themselves, I will not destroy them but will soon give them deliverance. My wrath will not be poured out on Jerusalem through Shishak. 8 They will, however, become subject to him, so that they may learn the difference between serving me and serving the kings of other lands.'

9 When Shishak king of Egypt attacked Jerusalem, he carried off the treasures of the temple of the LORD and the treasures of the royal palace. He took everything, including the gold shields that Solomon had made. 10 So King Rehoboam made bronze shields to replace them and assigned these to the commanders of the guard on duty at the entrance to the royal palace. 11 Whenever the king went to the

---

a 1 That is, Judah, as frequently in 2 Chronicles
b 3 That is, people from the upper Nile region

LORD's temple, the guards went with him, bearing the shields, and afterwards they returned them to the guardroom.

¹²Because Rehoboam humbled himself, the LORD's anger turned from him, and he was not totally destroyed. Indeed, there was some good in Judah.

¹³King Rehoboam established himself firmly in Jerusalem and continued as king. He was forty-one years old when he became king, and he reigned for seventeen years in Jerusalem, the city the LORD had chosen out of all the tribes of Israel in which to put his Name. His mother's name was Naamah; she was an Ammonite. ¹⁴He did evil because he had not set his heart on seeking the LORD.

¹⁵As for the events of Rehoboam's reign, from beginning to end, are they not written in the records of Shemaiah the prophet and of Iddo the seer that deal with genealogies? There was continual warfare between Rehoboam and Jeroboam. ¹⁶Rehoboam rested with his ancestors and was buried in the City of David. And Abijah his son succeeded him as king.

FACT

BIG FAMILY

King Rehoboam had 88 children: 28 sons and 60 daughters (2 Chronicles 11:21). Birthday parties must have been a nightmare.

Abijah king of Judah

13 In the eighteenth year of the reign of Jeroboam, Abijah became king of Judah, ²and he reigned in Jerusalem for three years. His mother's name was Maakah,ᵃ a daughterᵇ of Uriel of Gibeah.

There was war between Abijah and Jeroboam. ³Abijah went into battle with an army of four hundred thousand able fighting men, and Jeroboam drew up a battle line against him with eight hundred thousand able troops.

⁴Abijah stood on Mount Zemaraim, in the hill country of Ephraim, and said, 'Jeroboam and all Israel, listen to me! ⁵Don't you know that the LORD, the God of Israel, has given the kingship of Israel to David and his descendants for ever by a covenant of salt? ⁶Yet Jeroboam son of Nebat, an official of Solomon son of David, rebelled against his master. ⁷Some worthless scoundrels gathered around him and opposed Rehoboam son of Solomon when he was young and indecisive and not strong enough to resist them.

⁸'And now you plan to resist the kingdom of the LORD, which is in the hands of David's descendants. You are indeed a vast army and have with you the golden calves that Jeroboam made to be your gods. ⁹But didn't you drive out the priests of the LORD, the sons of Aaron, and the Levites, and make priests of your own as the peoples of other lands do? Whoever comes to consecrate himself with a young bull and seven rams may become a priest of what are not gods.

¹⁰'As for us, the LORD is our God, and we have not forsaken him. The priests who serve the LORD are sons of Aaron, and the Levites assist them. ¹¹Every morning and evening they present burnt offerings and fragrant incense to the LORD. They set out the bread on the ceremonially clean table and light the lamps on the gold lampstand every evening. We are observing the requirements of the LORD our God. But you have forsaken him. ¹²God is with us; he is our leader. His priests with their trumpets will sound the battle cry against you. People of Israel, do not fight against the LORD, the God of your ancestors, for you will not succeed.'

¹³Now Jeroboam had sent troops round to the rear, so that while he was in front of Judah the ambush was behind them. ¹⁴Judah turned and saw that they were being attacked at both front and rear. Then they

---

a 2 Most Septuagint manuscripts and Syriac (see also 11:20 and 1 Kings 15:2); Hebrew *Micaiah*
b 2 Or *granddaughter*

cried out to the LORD. The priests blew their trumpets ¹⁵and the men of Judah raised the battle cry. At the sound of their battle cry, God routed Jeroboam and all Israel before Abijah and Judah. ¹⁶The Israelites fled before Judah, and God delivered them into their hands. ¹⁷Abijah and his troops inflicted heavy losses on them, so that there were five hundred thousand casualties among Israel's able men. ¹⁸The Israelites were subdued on that occasion, and the people of Judah were victorious because they relied on the LORD, the God of their ancestors.

¹⁹Abijah pursued Jeroboam and took from him the towns of Bethel, Jeshanah and Ephron, with their surrounding villages. ²⁰Jeroboam did not regain power during the time of Abijah. And the LORD struck him down and he died.

²¹But Abijah grew in strength. He married fourteen wives and had twenty-two sons and sixteen daughters.

²²The other events of Abijah's reign, what he did and what he said, are written in the annotations of the prophet Iddo.

14 ᵃ And Abijah rested with his ancestors and was buried in the City of David. Asa his son succeeded him as king, and in his days the country was at peace for ten years.

Asa king of Judah

²Asa did what was good and right in the eyes of the LORD his God. ³He removed the foreign altars and the high places, smashed the sacred stones and cut down the Asherah poles.ᵇ ⁴He commanded Judah to seek the LORD, the God of their ancestors, and to obey his laws and commands. ⁵He removed the high places and incense altars in every town in Judah, and the kingdom was at peace under him. ⁶He built up the fortified cities of Judah, since the land was at peace. No one was at war with him during those years, for the LORD gave him rest.

⁷'Let us build up these towns,' he said

to Judah, 'and put walls round them, with towers, gates and bars. The land is still ours, because we have sought the LORD our God; we sought him and he has given us rest on every side.' So they built and prospered.

⁸Asa had an army of three hundred thousand men from Judah, equipped with large shields and with spears, and two hundred and eighty thousand from Benjamin, armed with small shields and with bows. All these were brave fighting men.

⁹Zerah the Cushite marched out against them with an army of thousands upon thousands and three hundred chariots, and came as far as Mareshah. ¹⁰Asa went out to meet him, and they took up battle positions in the Valley of Zephathah near Mareshah.

¹¹Then Asa called to the LORD his God and said, 'LORD, there is no one like you to help the powerless against the mighty. Help us, LORD our God, for we rely on you, and in your name we have come against this vast army. LORD, you are our God; do not let mere mortals prevail against you.'

¹²The LORD struck down the Cushites before Asa and Judah. The Cushites fled, ¹³and Asa and his army pursued them as far as Gerar. Such a great number of Cushites fell that they could not recover; they were crushed before the LORD and his forces. The men of Judah carried off a large amount of plunder. ¹⁴They destroyed all the villages around Gerar, for the terror of the LORD had fallen on them. They looted all these villages, since there was much plunder there. ¹⁵They also attacked the camps of the herdsmen and carried off droves of sheep and goats and camels. Then they returned to Jerusalem.

Asa's reform

15 The Spirit of God came on Azariah son of Oded. ²He went out to meet Asa and said to him, 'Listen to me, Asa and all Judah and Benjamin. The LORD is with you when you are with him. If you seek him, he will be found by you, but if you forsake him, he will forsake you. ³For a long time Israel was without the true God, without a

---

ᵃ In Hebrew texts 14:1 is numbered 13:23, and 14:2-15 is numbered 14:1-14.
ᵇ 3 That is, wooden symbols of the goddess Asherah; here and elsewhere in 2 Chronicles

priest to teach and without the law. 4 But in their distress they turned to the LORD, the God of Israel, and sought him, and he was found by them. 5 In those days it was not safe to travel about, for all the inhabitants of the lands were in great turmoil. 6 One nation was being crushed by another and one city by another, because God was troubling them with every kind of distress. 7 But as for you, be strong and do not give up, for your work will be rewarded.'

8 When Asa heard these words and the prophecy of Azariah son of*a* Oded the prophet, he took courage. He removed the detestable idols from the whole land of Judah and Benjamin and from the towns he had captured in the hills of Ephraim. He repaired the altar of the LORD that was in front of the portico of the LORD's temple.

9 Then he assembled all Judah and Benjamin and the people from Ephraim, Manasseh and Simeon who had settled among them, for large numbers had come over to him from Israel when they saw that the LORD his God was with him.

10 They assembled at Jerusalem in the third month of the fifteenth year of Asa's reign. 11 At that time they sacrificed to the LORD seven hundred head of cattle and seven thousand sheep and goats from the plunder they had brought back. 12 They entered into a covenant to seek the LORD, the God of their ancestors, with all their heart and soul. 13 All who would not seek the LORD, the God of Israel, were to be put to death, whether small or great, man or woman. 14 They took an oath to the LORD with loud acclamation, with shouting and with trumpets and horns. 15 All Judah rejoiced about the oath because they had sworn it wholeheartedly. They sought God eagerly, and he was found by them. So the LORD gave them rest on every side.

16 King Asa also deposed his grandmother Maakah from her position as queen mother, because she had made a repulsive image for the worship of Asherah. Asa cut it down, broke it up and burned it in the Kidron Valley. 17 Although he did not remove the high places from Israel, Asa's heart was fully committed to the LORD all his life. 18 He brought into the temple of God the silver and gold and the articles that he and his father had dedicated.

19 There was no more war until the thirty-fifth year of Asa's reign.

Asa's last years

16 In the thirty-sixth year of Asa's reign Baasha king of Israel went up against Judah and fortified Ramah to prevent anyone from leaving or entering the territory of Asa king of Judah.

2 Asa then took the silver and gold out of the treasuries of the LORD's temple and of his own palace and sent it to Ben-Hadad king of Aram, who was ruling in Damascus. 3 'Let there be a treaty between me and you,' he said, 'as there was between my father and your father. See, I am sending you silver and gold. Now break your treaty with Baasha king of Israel so that he will withdraw from me.'

4 Ben-Hadad agreed with King Asa and sent the commanders of his forces against the towns of Israel. They conquered Ijon, Dan, Abel Maim*a* and all the store cities of Naphtali. 5 When Baasha heard this, he stopped building Ramah and abandoned his work. 6 Then King Asa brought all the men of Judah, and they carried away from Ramah the stones and timber Baasha had been using. With them he built up Geba and Mizpah.

7 At that time Hanani the seer came to Asa king of Judah and said to him: 'Because you relied on the king of Aram and not on the LORD your God, the army of the king of Aram has escaped from your hand. 8 Were not the Cushites*b* and Libyans a mighty army with great numbers of chariots and horsemen*c*? Yet when you relied on the LORD, he delivered them into

---

a 8 Vulgate and Syriac (see also Septuagint and verse 1); Hebrew does not have *Azariah son of*.

a 4 Also known as *Abel Beth Maakah*
b 8 That is, people from the upper Nile region
c 8 Or *charioteers*

your hand. 9 For the eyes of the LORD range throughout the earth to strengthen those whose hearts are fully committed to him. You have done a foolish thing, and from now on you will be at war.'

10 Asa was angry with the seer because of this; he was so enraged that he put him in prison. At the same time Asa brutally oppressed some of the people.

11 The events of Asa's reign, from beginning to end, are written in the book of the kings of Judah and Israel. 12 In the thirty-ninth year of his reign Asa was afflicted with a disease in his feet. Though his disease was severe, even in his illness he did not seek help from the LORD, but only from the doctors. 13 Then in the forty-first year of his reign Asa died and rested with his ancestors. 14 They buried him in the tomb that he had cut out for himself in the City of David. They laid him on a bier covered with spices and various blended perfumes, and they made a huge fire in his honour.

Jehoshaphat king of Judah

17 Jehoshaphat his son succeeded him as king and strengthened himself against Israel. 2 He stationed troops in all the fortified cities of Judah and put garrisons in Judah and in the towns of Ephraim that his father Asa had captured.

3 The LORD was with Jehoshaphat because he followed the ways of his father David before him. He did not consult the Baals 4 but sought the God of his father and followed his commands rather than the practices of Israel. 5 The LORD established the kingdom under his control; and all Judah brought gifts to Jehoshaphat, so that he had great wealth and honour. 6 His heart was devoted to the ways of the LORD; furthermore, he removed the high places and the Asherah poles from Judah.

7 In the third year of his reign he sent his officials Ben-Hail, Obadiah, Zechariah, Nethanel and Micaiah to teach in the towns of Judah. 8 With them were certain Levites – Shemaiah, Nethaniah, Zebadiah, Asahel, Shemiramoth, Jehonathan, Adonijah, Tobijah and Tob-Adonijah – and the priests Elishama and Jehoram. 9 They

taught throughout Judah, taking with them the Book of the Law of the LORD; they went round to all the towns of Judah and taught the people.

10 The fear of the LORD fell on all the kingdoms of the lands surrounding Judah, so that they did not go to war against Jehoshaphat. 11 Some Philistines brought Jehoshaphat gifts and silver as tribute, and the Arabs brought him flocks: seven thousand seven hundred rams and seven thousand seven hundred goats.

12 Jehoshaphat became more and more powerful; he built forts and store cities in Judah 13 and had large supplies in the towns of Judah. He also kept experienced fighting men in Jerusalem. 14 Their enrolment by families was as follows:

from Judah, commanders of units of 1,000:
Adnah the commander, with 300,000 fighting men;
15 next, Jehohanan the commander, with 280,000;
16 next, Amasiah son of Zikri, who volunteered himself for the service of the LORD, with 200,000.
17 From Benjamin:
Eliada, a valiant soldier, with 200,000 men armed with bows and shields;
18 next, Jehozabad, with 180,000 men armed for battle.

19 These were the men who served the king, besides those he stationed in fortified cities throughout Judah.

Micaiah prophesies against Ahab

18 Now Jehoshaphat had great wealth and honour, and he allied himself with Ahab by marriage. 2 Some years later he went down to see Ahab in Samaria. Ahab slaughtered many sheep and cattle for him and the people with him and urged him to attack Ramoth Gilead. 3 Ahab king of Israel asked Jehoshaphat king of Judah, 'Will you go with me against Ramoth Gilead?'

Jehoshaphat replied, 'I am as you are, and my people as your people; we will join you in the war.' 4 But Jehoshaphat also said to the king of Israel, 'First seek the counsel of the LORD.'

5 So the king of Israel brought together the prophets – four hundred men – and asked them, 'Shall we go to war against Ramoth Gilead, or shall I not?'

'Go,' they answered, 'for God will give it into the king's hand.'

6 But Jehoshaphat asked, 'Is there no longer a prophet of the LORD here whom we can enquire of?'

7 The king of Israel answered Jehoshaphat, 'There is still one prophet through whom we can enquire of the LORD, but I hate him because he never prophesies anything good about me, but always bad. He is Micaiah son of Imlah.'

'The king should not say such a thing,' Jehoshaphat replied.

8 So the king of Israel called one of his officials and said, 'Bring Micaiah son of Imlah at once.'

9 Dressed in their royal robes, the king of Israel and Jehoshaphat king of Judah were sitting on their thrones at the threshing-floor by the entrance of the gate of Samaria, with all the prophets prophesying before them. 10 Now Zedekiah son of Kenaanah had made iron horns, and he declared, 'This is what the LORD says: "With these you will gore the Arameans until they are destroyed."'

11 All the other prophets were prophesying the same thing. 'Attack Ramoth Gilead and be victorious,' they said, 'for the LORD will give it into the king's hand.'

12 The messenger who had gone to summon Micaiah said to him, 'Look, the other prophets without exception are predicting success for the king. Let your word agree with theirs, and speak favourably.'

13 But Micaiah said, 'As surely as the LORD lives, I can tell him only what my God says.'

14 When he arrived, the king asked him, 'Micaiah, shall we go to war against Ramoth Gilead, or shall I not?'

'Attack and be victorious,' he answered, 'for they will be given into your hand.'

15 The king said to him, 'How many times must I make you swear to tell me nothing but the truth in the name of the LORD?'

16 Then Micaiah answered, 'I saw all Israel scattered on the hills like sheep without a shepherd, and the LORD said, "These people have no master. Let each one go home in peace."'

17 The king of Israel said to Jehoshaphat, 'Didn't I tell you that he never prophesies anything good about me, but only bad?'

18 Micaiah continued, 'Therefore hear the word of the LORD: I saw the LORD sitting on his throne with all the multitudes of heaven standing on his right and on his left. 19 And the LORD said, "Who will entice Ahab king of Israel into attacking Ramoth Gilead and going to his death there?"

'One suggested this, and another that. 20 Finally, a spirit came forward, stood before the LORD and said, "I will entice him."

'"By what means?" the LORD asked.

21 '"I will go and be a deceiving spirit in the mouths of all his prophets," he said.

'"You will succeed in enticing him," said the LORD. "Go and do it."

22 'So now the LORD has put a deceiving spirit in the mouths of these prophets of yours. The LORD has decreed disaster for you.'

23 Then Zedekiah son of Kenaanah went up and slapped Micaiah in the face. 'Which way did the spirit from*a* the LORD go when he went from me to speak to you?' he asked.

24 Micaiah replied, 'You will find out on the day you go to hide in an inner room.'

25 The king of Israel then ordered, 'Take Micaiah and send him back to Amon the ruler of the city and to Joash the king's son, 26 and say, "This is what the king says: put this fellow in prison and give him nothing but bread and water until I return safely."'

27 Micaiah declared, 'If you ever return safely, the LORD has not spoken through me.' Then he added, 'Mark my words, all you people!'

_____

a 23 Or *Spirit of*

Ahab killed at Ramoth Gilead

28 So the king of Israel and Jehoshaphat king of Judah went up to Ramoth Gilead. 29 The king of Israel said to Jehoshaphat, 'I will enter the battle in disguise, but you wear your royal robes.' So the king of Israel disguised himself and went into battle.

30 Now the king of Aram had ordered his chariot commanders, 'Do not fight with anyone, small or great, except the king of Israel.' 31 When the chariot commanders saw Jehoshaphat, they thought, 'This is the king of Israel.' So they turned to attack him, but Jehoshaphat cried out, and the LORD helped him. God drew them away from him, 32 for when the chariot commanders saw that he was not the king of Israel, they stopped pursuing him.

33 But someone drew his bow at random and hit the king of Israel between the breastplate and the scale armour. The king told the chariot driver, 'Wheel round and get me out of the fighting. I've been wounded.' 34 All day long the battle raged, and the king of Israel propped himself up in his chariot facing the Arameans until evening. Then at sunset he died.

19 When Jehoshaphat king of Judah returned safely to his palace in Jerusalem, 2 Jehu the seer, the son of Hanani, went out to meet him and said to the king, 'Should you help the wicked and love*a* those who hate the LORD? Because of this, the wrath of the LORD is on you. 3 There is, however, some good in you, for you have rid the land of the Asherah poles and have set your heart on seeking God.'

Jehoshaphat appoints judges

4 Jehoshaphat lived in Jerusalem, and he went out again among the people from Beersheba to the hill country of Ephraim and turned them back to the LORD, the God of their ancestors. 5 He appointed judges in the land, in each of the fortified cities of Judah. 6 He told them, 'Consider carefully what you do, because you are not judging for mere mortals but for the LORD, who is with you whenever you give a verdict. 7 Now let the fear of the LORD be

on you. Judge carefully, for with the LORD our God there is no injustice or partiality or bribery.'

8 In Jerusalem also, Jehoshaphat appointed some of the Levites, priests and heads of Israelite families to administer the law of the LORD and to settle disputes. And they lived in Jerusalem. 9 He gave them these orders: 'You must serve faithfully and wholeheartedly in the fear of the LORD. 10 In every case that comes before you from your people who live in the cities – whether bloodshed or other concerns of the law, commands, decrees or regulations – you are to warn them not to sin against the LORD; otherwise his wrath will come on you and your people. Do this, and you will not sin.

11 'Amariah the chief priest will be over you in any matter concerning the LORD, and Zebadiah son of Ishmael, the leader of the tribe of Judah, will be over you in any matter concerning the king, and the Levites will serve as officials before you. Act with courage, and may the LORD be with those who do well.'

Jehoshaphat defeats Moab and Ammon

20 After this, the Moabites and Ammonites with some of the Meunites*a* came to wage war against Jehoshaphat.

2 Some people came and told Jehoshaphat, 'A vast army is coming against you from Edom,*b* from the other side of the Dead Sea. It is already in Hazezon Tamar' (that is, En Gedi). 3 Alarmed, Jehoshaphat resolved to enquire of the LORD, and he proclaimed a fast for all Judah. 4 The people of Judah came together to seek help from the LORD; indeed, they came from every town in Judah to seek him.

5 Then Jehoshaphat stood up in the assembly of Judah and Jerusalem at the temple of the LORD in the front of the new courtyard 6 and said:

---

a 2 Or *and make alliances with*

a 1 Some Septuagint manuscripts; Hebrew *Ammonites*

b 2 One Hebrew manuscript; most Hebrew manuscripts, Septuagint and Vulgate *Aram*

'LORD, the God of our ancestors, are you not the God who is in heaven? You rule over all the kingdoms of the nations. Power and might are in your hand, and no one can withstand you. ⁷Our God, did you not drive out the inhabitants of this land before your people Israel and give it for ever to the descendants of Abraham your friend? ⁸They have lived in it and have built in it a sanctuary for your Name, saying, ⁹"If calamity comes upon us, whether the sword of judgment, or plague or famine, we will stand in your presence before this temple that bears your Name and will cry out to you in our distress, and you will hear us and save us."

¹⁰'But now here are men from Ammon, Moab and Mount Seir, whose territory you would not allow Israel to invade when they came from Egypt; so they turned away from them and did not destroy them. ¹¹See how they are repaying us by coming to drive us out of the possession you gave us as an inheritance. ¹²Our God, will you not judge them? For we have no power to face this vast army that is attacking us. We do not know what to do, but our eyes are on you.'

¹³All the men of Judah, with their wives and children and little ones, stood there before the LORD.

¹⁴Then the Spirit of the LORD came on Jahaziel son of Zechariah, the son of Benaiah, the son of Jeiel, the son of Mattaniah, a Levite and descendant of Asaph, as he stood in the assembly.

¹⁵He said: 'Listen, King Jehoshaphat and all who live in Judah and Jerusalem! This is what the LORD says to you: "Do not be afraid or discouraged because of this vast army. For the battle is not yours, but God's. ¹⁶Tomorrow march down against them. They will be climbing up by the Pass of Ziz, and you will find them at the end of the gorge in the Desert of Jeruel. ¹⁷You will not have to fight this battle. Take up your positions; stand firm and see the deliverance the LORD will give you, Judah

and Jerusalem. Do not be afraid; do not be discouraged. Go out to face them tomorrow, and the LORD will be with you."'

¹⁸Jehoshaphat bowed down with his face to the ground, and all the people of Judah and Jerusalem fell down in worship before the LORD. ¹⁹Then some Levites from the Kohathites and Korahites stood up and praised the LORD, the God of Israel, with a very loud voice.

FAVOURITE VERSES

1 Peter 5:6

Humble yourselves, therefore, under God's mighty hand, that he may lift you up in due time.

In a family where religion is treated with no respect and mocked, I knew deciding to live for the Lord would be challenging. People told me, 'Look to the Lord for strength and guidance.' I would ask myself the same question over and over: 'Why would the Lord care about me? There are so many other people out there.' To all the people beginning their journey with the Lord: do not deny your importance in his presence. He is with you always, watching you, listening to you. Remember, anything is possible through the Lord. I am now preparing to get baptised with my family's approval. God is great.

Blaine, 18

²⁰Early in the morning they left for the Desert of Tekoa. As they set out, Jehoshaphat stood and said, 'Listen to me, Judah and people of Jerusalem! Have faith in the LORD your God and you will be upheld;

have faith in his prophets and you will be successful.' ²¹ After consulting the people, Jehoshaphat appointed men to sing to the LORD and to praise him for the splendour of his^c holiness as they went out at the head of the army, saying:

'Give thanks to the LORD,
     for his love endures for ever.'

²² As they began to sing and praise, the LORD set ambushes against the men of Ammon and Moab and Mount Seir who were invading Judah, and they were defeated. ²³ The Ammonites and Moabites rose up against the men from Mount Seir to destroy and annihilate them. After they finished slaughtering the men from Seir, they helped to destroy one another.

²⁴ When the men of Judah came to the place that overlooks the desert and looked towards the vast army, they saw only dead bodies lying on the ground; no one had escaped. ²⁵ So Jehoshaphat and his men went to carry off their plunder, and they found among them a great amount of equipment and clothing^d and also articles of value – more than they could take away. There was so much plunder that it took three days to collect it. ²⁶ On the fourth day they assembled in the Valley of Berakah, where they praised the LORD. This is why it is called the Valley of Berakah^e to this day.

²⁷ Then, led by Jehoshaphat, all the men of Judah and Jerusalem returned joyfully to Jerusalem, for the LORD had given them cause to rejoice over their enemies. ²⁸ They entered Jerusalem and went to the temple of the LORD with harps and lyres and trumpets.

²⁹ The fear of God came on all the surrounding kingdoms when they heard how the LORD had fought against the enemies of Israel. ³⁰ And the kingdom of Jehoshaphat was at peace, for his God had given him rest on every side.

The end of Jehoshaphat's reign

³¹ So Jehoshaphat reigned over Judah. He was thirty-five years old when he became king of Judah, and he reigned in Jerusalem for twenty-five years. His mother's name was Azubah daughter of Shilhi. ³² He followed the ways of his father Asa and did not stray from them; he did what was right in the eyes of the LORD. ³³ The high places, however, were not removed, and the people still had not set their hearts on the God of their ancestors.

³⁴ The other events of Jehoshaphat's reign, from beginning to end, are written in the annals of Jehu son of Hanani, which are recorded in the book of the kings of Israel.

³⁵ Later, Jehoshaphat king of Judah made an alliance with Ahaziah king of Israel, whose ways were wicked. ³⁶ He agreed with him to construct a fleet of trading ships.^f After these were built at Ezion Geber, ³⁷ Eliezer son of Dodavahu of Mareshah prophesied against Jehoshaphat, saying, 'Because you have made an alliance with Ahaziah, the LORD will destroy what you have made.' The ships were wrecked and were not able to set sail to trade.^g

21 Then Jehoshaphat rested with his ancestors and was buried with them in the City of David. And Jehoram his son succeeded him as king. ² Jehoram's brothers, the sons of Jehoshaphat, were Azariah, Jehiel, Zechariah, Azariahu, Michael and Shephatiah. All these were sons of Jehoshaphat king of Israel.^a ³ Their father had given them many gifts of silver and gold and articles of value, as well as fortified cities in Judah, but he had given the kingdom to Jehoram because he was his firstborn son.

Jehoram king of Judah

⁴ When Jehoram established himself firmly over his father's kingdom, he put all his brothers to the sword along with some of the officials of Israel. ⁵ Jehoram

---

c 21 Or *him with the splendour of*
d 25 Some Hebrew manuscripts and Vulgate; most Hebrew manuscripts *corpses*
e 26 *Berakah* means *praise.*

f 36 Hebrew *of ships that could go to Tarshish*
g 37 Hebrew *sail for Tarshish*
a 2 That is, Judah, as frequently in 2 Chronicles

was thirty-two years old when he became king, and he reigned in Jerusalem for eight years. 6 He followed the ways of the kings of Israel, as the house of Ahab had done, for he married a daughter of Ahab. He did evil in the eyes of the LORD. 7 Nevertheless, because of the covenant the LORD had made with David, the LORD was not willing to destroy the house of David. He had promised to maintain a lamp for him and his descendants for ever.

8 In the time of Jehoram, Edom rebelled against Judah and set up its own king. 9 So Jehoram went there with his officers and all his chariots. The Edomites surrounded him and his chariot commanders, but he rose up and broke through by night. 10 To this day Edom has been in rebellion against Judah.

Libnah revolted at the same time, because Jehoram had forsaken the LORD, the God of his ancestors. 11 He had also built high places on the hills of Judah and had caused the people of Jerusalem to prostitute themselves and had led Judah astray.

12 Jehoram received a letter from Elijah the prophet, which said:

'This is what the LORD, the God of your father David, says: "You have not followed the ways of your father Jehoshaphat or of Asa king of Judah. 13 But you have followed the ways of the kings of Israel, and you have led Judah and the people of Jerusalem to prostitute themselves, just as the house of Ahab did. You have also murdered your own brothers, members of your own family, men who were better than you. 14 So now the LORD is about to strike your people, your sons, your wives and everything that is yours, with a heavy blow. 15 You yourself will be very ill with a lingering disease of the bowels, until the disease causes your bowels to come out." '

16 The LORD aroused against Jehoram the hostility of the Philistines and of the Arabs who lived near the Cushites. 17 They attacked Judah, invaded it and carried off all the goods found in the king's palace, together with his sons and wives. Not a son was left to him except Ahaziah,b the youngest.

18 After all this, the LORD afflicted Jehoram with an incurable disease of the bowels. 19 In the course of time, at the end of the second year, his bowels came out because of the disease, and he died in great pain. His people made no funeral fire in his honour, as they had for his predecessors.

20 Jehoram was thirty-two years old when he became king, and he reigned in Jerusalem for eight years. He passed away, to no one's regret, and was buried in the City of David, but not in the tombs of the kings.

Ahaziah king of Judah

22 The people of Jerusalem made Ahaziah, Jehoram's youngest son, king in his place, since the raiders, who came with the Arabs into the camp, had killed all the older sons. So Ahaziah son of Jehoram king of Judah began to reign.

2 Ahaziah was twenty-twoa years old when he became king, and he reigned in Jerusalem for one year. His mother's name was Athaliah, a granddaughter of Omri.

3 He too followed the ways of the house of Ahab, for his mother encouraged him to act wickedly. 4 He did evil in the eyes of the LORD, as the house of Ahab had done, for after his father's death they became his advisors, to his undoing. 5 He also followed their counsel when he went with Joramb son of Ahab king of Israel to wage war against Hazael king of Aram at Ramoth Gilead. The Arameans wounded Joram; 6 so he returned to Jezreel to recover from the wounds they had inflicted on him at Ramothc in his battle with Hazael king of Aram.

---

b 17 Hebrew *Jehoahaz*, a variant of *Ahaziah*
a 2 Some Septuagint manuscripts and Syriac (see also 2 Kings 8:26); Hebrew *forty-two*
b 5 Hebrew *Jehoram*, a variant of *Joram*; also in verses 6 and 7
c 6 Hebrew *Ramah*, a variant of *Ramoth*

Then Ahaziah[d] son of Jehoram king of Judah went down to Jezreel to see Joram son of Ahab because he had been wounded.

[7] Through Ahaziah's visit to Joram, God brought about Ahaziah's downfall. When Ahaziah arrived, he went out with Joram to meet Jehu son of Nimshi, whom the Lord had anointed to destroy the house of Ahab. [8] While Jehu was executing judgment on the house of Ahab, he found the officials of Judah and the sons of Ahaziah's relatives, who had been attending Ahaziah, and he killed them. [9] He then went in search of Ahaziah, and his men captured him while he was hiding in Samaria. He was brought to Jehu and put to death. They buried him, for they said, 'He was a son of Jehoshaphat, who sought the Lord with all his heart.' So there was no one in the house of Ahaziah powerful enough to retain the kingdom.

Athaliah and Joash

[10] When Athaliah the mother of Ahaziah saw that her son was dead, she proceeded to destroy the whole royal family of the house of Judah. [11] But Jehosheba,[e] the daughter of King Jehoram, took Joash son of Ahaziah and stole him away from among the royal princes who were about to be murdered and put him and his nurse in a bedroom. Because Jehosheba,[f] the daughter of King Jehoram and wife of the priest Jehoiada, was Ahaziah's sister, she hid the child from Athaliah so that she could not kill him. [12] He remained hidden with them at the temple of God for six years while Athaliah ruled the land.

23 In the seventh year Jehoiada showed his strength. He made a covenant with the commanders of units of a hundred: Azariah son of Jeroham, Ishmael son of Jehohanan, Azariah son of Obed, Maaseiah son of Adaiah, and Elishaphat son of Zikri. [2] They went throughout Judah and gathered the Levites and the

heads of Israelite families from all the towns. When they came to Jerusalem, [3] the whole assembly made a covenant with the king at the temple of God.

FAVOURITE VERSES
Galatians 6:14

May I never boast except in the cross of our Lord Jesus Christ, through which the world has been crucified to me, and I to the world.

This is my favourite verse because I think it says a lot to us about how a Christian should behave. I also think it's a good reminder that we should tell our friends about Jesus and what he has done for us.

Hywel, 18

Jehoiada said to them, 'The king's son shall reign, as the Lord promised concerning the descendants of David. [4] Now this is what you are to do: a third of you priests and Levites who are going on duty on the Sabbath are to keep watch at the doors, [5] a third of you at the royal palace and a third at the Foundation Gate, and all the others are to be in the courtyards of the temple of the Lord. [6] No one is to enter the temple of the Lord except the priests and Levites on duty; they may enter because they are consecrated, but all the others are to observe the Lord's command not to enter.[a] [7] The Levites are to station themselves round the king, each with weapon in hand. Anyone who enters the temple is to be put to death. Stay close to the king wherever he goes.'

[8] The Levites and all the men of Judah did just as Jehoiada the priest ordered.

---

d 6 Some Hebrew manuscripts, Septuagint, Vulgate and Syriac (see also 2 Kings 8:29); most Hebrew manuscripts *Azariah*

e 11 Hebrew *Jehoshabeath*, a variant of *Jehosheba*

f 11 Hebrew *Jehoshabeath*, a variant of *Jehosheba*

a 6 Or *are to stand guard where the Lord has assigned them*

Each one took his men – those who were going on duty on the Sabbath and those who were going off duty – for Jehoiada the priest had not released any of the divisions. ⁹Then he gave the commanders of units of a hundred the spears and the large and small shields that had belonged to King David and that were in the temple of God. ¹⁰He stationed all the men, each with his weapon in his hand, round the king – near the altar and the temple, from the south side to the north side of the temple.

¹¹Jehoiada and his sons brought out the king's son and put the crown on him; they presented him with a copy of the covenant and proclaimed him king. They anointed him and shouted, 'Long live the king!'

¹²When Athaliah heard the noise of the people running and cheering the king, she went to them at the temple of the LORD. ¹³She looked, and there was the king, standing by his pillar at the entrance. The officers and the trumpeters were beside the king, and all the people of the land were rejoicing and blowing trumpets, and musicians with their instruments were leading the praises. Then Athaliah tore her robes and shouted, 'Treason! Treason!'

¹⁴Jehoiada the priest sent out the commanders of units of a hundred, who were in charge of the troops, and said to them: 'Bring her out between the ranks*b* and put to the sword anyone who follows her.' For the priest had said, 'Do not put her to death at the temple of the LORD.' ¹⁵So they seized her as she reached the entrance of the Horse Gate on the palace grounds, and there they put her to death.

¹⁶Jehoiada then made a covenant that he, the people and the king*c* would be the LORD's people. ¹⁷All the people went to the temple of Baal and tore it down. They smashed the altars and idols and killed Mattan the priest of Baal in front of the altars.

¹⁸Then Jehoiada placed the oversight of the temple of the LORD in the hands of the Levitical priests, to whom David had made assignments in the temple, to present the burnt offerings of the LORD as written in the Law of Moses, with rejoicing and singing, as David had ordered. ¹⁹He also stationed gatekeepers at the gates of the LORD's temple so that no one who was in any way unclean might enter.

²⁰He took with him the commanders of hundreds, the nobles, the rulers of the people and all the people of the land and brought the king down from the temple of the LORD. They went into the palace through the Upper Gate and seated the king on the royal throne. ²¹All the people of the land rejoiced, and the city was calm, because Athaliah had been slain with the sword.

Joash repairs the temple

24 Joash was seven years old when he became king, and he reigned in Jerusalem for forty years. His mother's name was Zibiah; she was from Beersheba. ²Joash did what was right in the eyes of the LORD all the years of Jehoiada the priest. ³Jehoiada chose two wives for him, and he had sons and daughters.

⁴Some time later Joash decided to restore the temple of the LORD. ⁵He called together the priests and Levites and said to them, 'Go to the towns of Judah and collect the money due annually from all Israel, to repair the temple of your God. Do it now.' But the Levites did not act at once.

⁶Therefore the king summoned Jehoiada the chief priest and said to him, 'Why haven't you required the Levites to bring in from Judah and Jerusalem the tax imposed by Moses the servant of the LORD and by the assembly of Israel for the tent of the covenant law?'

⁷Now the sons of that wicked woman Athaliah had broken into the temple of God and had used even its sacred objects for the Baals.

⁸At the king's command, a chest was made and placed outside, at the gate of the temple of the LORD. ⁹A proclamation was then issued in Judah and Jerusalem that

---

b 14　Or *out from the precincts*
c 16　Or *covenant between the LORD and the people and the king that they* (see 2 Kings 11:17)

they should bring to the LORD the tax that Moses the servant of God had required of Israel in the wilderness. ¹⁰All the officials and all the people brought their contributions gladly, dropping them into the chest until it was full. ¹¹Whenever the chest was brought in by the Levites to the king's officials and they saw that there was a large amount of money, the royal secretary and the officer of the chief priest would come and empty the chest and carry it back to its place. They did this regularly and collected a great amount of money. ¹²The king and Jehoiada gave it to those who carried out the work required for the temple of the LORD. They hired masons and carpenters to restore the LORD's temple, and also workers in iron and bronze to repair the temple.

¹³The men in charge of the work were diligent, and the repairs progressed under them. They rebuilt the temple of God according to its original design and reinforced it. ¹⁴When they had finished, they brought the rest of the money to the king and Jehoiada, and with it were made articles for the LORD's temple: articles for the service and for the burnt offerings, and also dishes and other objects of gold and silver. As long as Jehoiada lived, burnt offerings were presented continually in the temple of the LORD.

¹⁵Now Jehoiada was old and full of years, and he died at the age of a hundred and thirty. ¹⁶He was buried with the kings in the City of David, because of the good he had done in Israel for God and his temple.

The wickedness of Joash

¹⁷After the death of Jehoiada, the officials of Judah came and paid homage to the king, and he listened to them. ¹⁸They abandoned the temple of the LORD, the God of their ancestors, and worshipped Asherah poles and idols. Because of their guilt, God's anger came on Judah and Jerusalem. ¹⁹Although the LORD sent prophets to the people to bring them back to him, and though they testified against them, they would not listen.

²⁰Then the Spirit of God came on Zechariah son of Jehoiada the priest. He stood before the people and said, 'This is what God says: "Why do you disobey the LORD's commands? You will not prosper. Because you have forsaken the LORD, he has forsaken you."'

²¹But they plotted against him, and by order of the king they stoned him to death in the courtyard of the LORD's temple. ²²King Joash did not remember the kindness Zechariah's father Jehoiada had shown him but killed his son, who said as he lay dying, 'May the LORD see this and call you to account.'

²³At the turn of the year,ᵃ the army of Aram marched against Joash; it invaded Judah and Jerusalem and killed all the leaders of the people. They sent all the plunder to their king in Damascus. ²⁴Although the Aramean army had come with only a few men, the LORD delivered into their hands a much larger army. Because Judah had forsaken the LORD, the God of their ancestors, judgment was executed on Joash. ²⁵When the Arameans withdrew, they left Joash severely wounded. His officials conspired against him for murdering the son of Jehoiada the priest, and they killed him in his bed. So he died and was buried in the City of David, but not in the tombs of the kings. ²⁶Those who conspired against him were Zabad,ᵇ son of Shimeath an Ammonite woman, and Jehozabad, son of Shimrithᶜ a Moabite woman. ²⁷The account of his sons, the many prophecies about him, and the record of the restoration of the temple of God are written in the annotations on the book of the kings. And Amaziah his son succeeded him as king.

Amaziah king of Judah

25 Amaziah was twenty-five years old when he became king, and he reigned in Jerusalem for twenty-nine years. His mother's name was Jehoaddan; she was from Jerusalem. ²He did what was right in the eyes of the LORD, but not

---

a 23 Probably in the spring
b 26 A variant of *Jozabad*
c 26 A variant of *Shomer*

wholeheartedly. ³After the kingdom was firmly in his control, he executed the officials who had murdered his father the king. ⁴Yet he did not put their children to death, but acted in accordance with what is written in the Law, in the Book of Moses, where the LORD commanded: 'Parents shall not be put to death for their children, nor children be put to death for their parents; each will die for their own sin.'ᵃ

⁵Amaziah called the people of Judah together and assigned them according to their families to commanders of thousands and commanders of hundreds for all Judah and Benjamin. He then mustered those twenty years old or more and found that there were three hundred thousand men fit for military service, able to handle the spear and shield. ⁶He also hired a hundred thousand fighting men from Israel for a hundred talentsᵇ of silver.

⁷But a man of God came to him and said, 'Your Majesty, these troops from Israel must not march with you, for the LORD is not with Israel – not with any of the people of Ephraim. ⁸Even if you go and fight courageously in battle, God will overthrow you before the enemy, for God has the power to help or to overthrow.'

⁹Amaziah asked the man of God, 'But what about the hundred talents I paid for these Israelite troops?'

The man of God replied, 'The LORD can give you much more than that.'

¹⁰So Amaziah dismissed the troops who had come to him from Ephraim and sent them home. They were furious with Judah and left for home in a great rage.

¹¹Amaziah then marshalled his strength and led his army to the Valley of Salt, where he killed ten thousand men of Seir. ¹²The army of Judah also captured ten thousand men alive, took them to the top of a cliff and threw them down so that all were dashed to pieces.

¹³Meanwhile the troops that Amaziah had sent back and had not allowed to take part in the war raided towns belonging to Judah from Samaria to Beth Horon. They killed three thousand people and carried off great quantities of plunder.

¹⁴When Amaziah returned from slaughtering the Edomites, he brought back the gods of the people of Seir. He set them up as his own gods, bowed down to them and burned sacrifices to them. ¹⁵The anger of the LORD burned against Amaziah, and he sent a prophet to him, who said, 'Why do you consult this people's gods, which could not save their own people from your hand?'

¹⁶While he was still speaking, the king said to him, 'Have we appointed you an advisor to the king? Stop! Why be struck down?'

So the prophet stopped but said, 'I know that God has determined to destroy you, because you have done this and have not listened to my counsel.'

¹⁷After Amaziah king of Judah consulted his advisors, he sent this challenge to Jehoashᶜ son of Jehoahaz, the son of Jehu, king of Israel: 'Come, let us face each other in battle.'

¹⁸But Jehoash king of Israel replied to Amaziah king of Judah, 'A thistle in Lebanon sent a message to a cedar in Lebanon, "Give your daughter to my son in marriage." Then a wild beast in Lebanon came along and trampled the thistle underfoot. ¹⁹You say to yourself that you have defeated Edom, and now you are arrogant and proud. But stay at home! Why ask for trouble and cause your own downfall and that of Judah also?'

²⁰Amaziah, however, would not listen, for God so worked that he might deliver them into the hands of Jehoash, because they sought the gods of Edom. ²¹So Jehoash king of Israel attacked. He and Amaziah king of Judah faced each other at Beth Shemesh in Judah. ²²Judah was routed by Israel, and every man fled to his home. ²³Jehoash king of Israel captured Amaziah king of Judah, the son of Joash, the son of Ahaziah,ᵈ at Beth Shemesh. Then

---

a 4 Deut. 24:16
b 6 That is, about 3.4 metric tons; also in verse 9

c 17 Hebrew *Joash*, a variant of *Jehoash*; also in verses 18, 21, 23 and 25
d 23 Hebrew *Jehoahaz*, a variant of *Ahaziah*

Jehoash brought him to Jerusalem and broke down the wall of Jerusalem from the Ephraim Gate to the Corner Gate – a section about four hundred cubits[e] long. [24] He took all the gold and silver and all the articles found in the temple of God that had been in the care of Obed-Edom, together with the palace treasures and the hostages, and returned to Samaria.

[25] Amaziah son of Joash king of Judah lived for fifteen years after the death of Jehoash son of Jehoahaz king of Israel. [26] As for the other events of Amaziah's reign, from beginning to end, are they not written in the book of the kings of Judah and Israel? [27] From the time that Amaziah turned away from following the LORD, they conspired against him in Jerusalem and he fled to Lachish, but they sent men after him to Lachish and killed him there. [28] He was brought back by horse and was buried with his ancestors in the City of Judah.[f]

Uzziah king of Judah

26 Then all the people of Judah took Uzziah,[a] who was sixteen years old, and made him king in place of his father Amaziah. [2] He was the one who rebuilt Elath and restored it to Judah after Amaziah rested with his ancestors.

[3] Uzziah was sixteen years old when he became king, and he reigned in Jerusalem for fifty-two years. His mother's name was Jekoliah; she was from Jerusalem. [4] He did what was right in the eyes of the LORD, just as his father Amaziah had done. [5] He sought God during the days of Zechariah, who instructed him in the fear[b] of God. As long as he sought the LORD, God gave him success.

[6] He went to war against the Philistines and broke down the walls of Gath, Jabneh and Ashdod. He then rebuilt towns near Ashdod and elsewhere among the

Philistines. [7] God helped him against the Philistines and against the Arabs who lived in Gur Baal and against the Meunites. [8] The Ammonites brought tribute to Uzziah, and his fame spread as far as the border of Egypt, because he had become very powerful.

[9] Uzziah built towers in Jerusalem at the Corner Gate, at the Valley Gate and at the angle of the wall, and he fortified them. [10] He also built towers in the wilderness and dug many cisterns, because he had much livestock in the foothills and in the plain. He had people working his fields and vineyards in the hills and in the fertile lands, for he loved the soil.

DISUNITED KINGDOM

The 'United Kingdom' of Israel only lasted for about 120 years, under Saul, David and Solomon. After that the kingdom split into two: Israel in the north and Judah in the south.

[11] Uzziah had a well-trained army, ready to go out by divisions according to their numbers as mustered by Jeiel the secretary and Maaseiah the officer under the direction of Hananiah, one of the royal officials. [12] The total number of family leaders over the fighting men was 2,600. [13] Under their command was an army of 307,500 men trained for war, a powerful force to support the king against his enemies. [14] Uzziah provided shields, spears, helmets, coats of armour, bows and slingstones for the entire army. [15] In Jerusalem he made devices invented for use on the towers and on the corner defences so that soldiers could shoot arrows and hurl large stones from the walls. His fame spread far and wide, for he was greatly helped until he became powerful.

e 23   That is, about 180 metres
f 28   Most Hebrew manuscripts; some Hebrew manuscripts, Septuagint, Vulgate and Syriac (see also 2 Kings 14:20) *David*
a 1   Also called *Azariah*
b 5   Many Hebrew manuscripts, Septuagint and Syriac; other Hebrew manuscripts *vision*

16 But after Uzziah became powerful, his pride led to his downfall. He was unfaithful to the LORD his God, and entered the temple of the LORD to burn incense on the altar of incense. 17 Azariah the priest with eighty other courageous priests of the LORD followed him in. 18 They confronted King Uzziah and said, 'It is not right for you, Uzziah, to burn incense to the LORD. That is for the priests, the descendants of Aaron, who have been consecrated to burn incense. Leave the sanctuary, for you have been unfaithful; and you will not be honoured by the LORD God.'

19 Uzziah, who had a censer in his hand ready to burn incense, became angry. While he was raging at the priests in their presence before the incense altar in the LORD's temple, leprosy^c broke out on his forehead. 20 When Azariah the chief priest and all the other priests looked at him, they saw that he had leprosy on his forehead, so they hurried him out. Indeed, he himself was eager to leave, because the LORD had afflicted him.

21 King Uzziah had leprosy until the day he died. He lived in a separate house^d – leprous, and excluded from the temple of the LORD. Jotham his son had charge of the palace and governed the people of the land.

22 The other events of Uzziah's reign, from beginning to end, are recorded by the prophet Isaiah son of Amoz. 23 Uzziah rested with his ancestors and was buried near them in a cemetery that belonged to the kings, for people said, 'He had leprosy.' And Jotham his son succeeded him as king.

Jotham king of Judah

27 Jotham was twenty-five years old when he became king, and he reigned in Jerusalem for sixteen years. His mother's name was Jerusha daughter of Zadok. 2 He did what was right in the eyes of the LORD, just as his father Uzziah had done, but unlike him he did not enter the

temple of the LORD. The people, however, continued their corrupt practices. 3 Jotham rebuilt the Upper Gate of the temple of the LORD and did extensive work on the wall at the hill of Ophel. 4 He built towns in the hill country of Judah and forts and towers in the wooded areas.

5 Jotham waged war against the king of the Ammonites and conquered them. That year the Ammonites paid him a hundred talents^a of silver, ten thousand cors^b of wheat and ten thousand cors^c of barley. The Ammonites brought him the same amount also in the second and third years.

6 Jotham grew powerful because he walked steadfastly before the LORD his God.

7 The other events in Jotham's reign, including all his wars and the other things he did, are written in the book of the kings of Israel and Judah. 8 He was twenty-five years old when he became king, and he reigned in Jerusalem for sixteen years. 9 Jotham rested with his ancestors and was buried in the City of David. And Ahaz his son succeeded him as king.

Ahaz king of Judah

28 Ahaz was twenty years old when he became king, and he reigned in Jerusalem for sixteen years. Unlike David his father, he did not do what was right in the eyes of the LORD. 2 He followed the ways of the kings of Israel and also made idols for worshipping the Baals. 3 He burned sacrifices in the Valley of Ben Hinnom and sacrificed his children in the fire, engaging in the detestable practices of the nations that the LORD had driven out before the Israelites. 4 He offered sacrifices and burned incense at the high places, on the hilltops and under every spreading tree.

5 Therefore the LORD his God delivered him into the hands of the king of Aram. The Arameans defeated him and

---

c 19 The Hebrew for *leprosy* was used for various diseases affecting the skin; also in verses 20, 21 and 23.
d 21 Or *in a house where he was relieved of responsibilities*

a 5 That is, about 3.4 metric tons
b 5 That is, probably about 1,600 metric tons of wheat
c 5 That is, probably about 1,350 metric tons of barley

took many of his people as prisoners and brought them to Damascus.

He was also given into the hands of the king of Israel, who inflicted heavy casualties on him. ⁶In one day Pekah son of Remaliah killed a hundred and twenty thousand soldiers in Judah – because Judah had forsaken the Lord, the God of their ancestors. ⁷Zikri, an Ephraimite warrior, killed Maaseiah the king's son, Azrikam the officer in charge of the palace, and Elkanah, second to the king. ⁸The men of Israel took captive from their fellow Israelites who were from Judah two hundred thousand wives, sons and daughters. They also took a great deal of plunder, which they carried back to Samaria.

⁹But a prophet of the Lord named Oded was there, and he went out to meet the army when it returned to Samaria. He said to them, 'Because the Lord, the God of your ancestors, was angry with Judah, he gave them into your hand. But you have slaughtered them in a rage that reaches to heaven. ¹⁰And now you intend to make the men and women of Judah and Jerusalem your slaves. But aren't you also guilty of sins against the Lord your God? ¹¹Now listen to me! Send back your fellow Israelites that you have taken as prisoners, for the Lord's fierce anger rests on you.'

¹²Then some of the leaders in Ephraim – Azariah son of Jehohanan, Berekiah son of Meshillemoth, Jehizkiah son of Shallum, and Amasa son of Hadlai – confronted those who were arriving from the war. ¹³'You must not bring those prisoners here,' they said, 'or we will be guilty before the Lord. Do you intend to add to our sin and guilt? For our guilt is already great, and his fierce anger rests on Israel.'

¹⁴So the soldiers gave up the prisoners and plunder in the presence of the officials and all the assembly. ¹⁵The men designated by name took the prisoners, and from the plunder they clothed all who were naked. They provided them with clothes and sandals, food and drink, and healing balm. All those who were weak they put on donkeys. So they took them back to their fellow Israelites at Jericho, the City of Palms, and returned to Samaria.

¹⁶At that time King Ahaz sent to the kingsᵃ of Assyria for help. ¹⁷The Edomites had again come and attacked Judah and carried away prisoners, ¹⁸while the Philistines had raided towns in the foothills and in the Negev of Judah. They captured and occupied Beth Shemesh, Aijalon and Gederoth, as well as Soko, Timnah and Gimzo, with their surrounding villages. ¹⁹The Lord had humbled Judah because of Ahaz king of Israel,ᵇ for he had promoted wickedness in Judah and had been most unfaithful to the Lord. ²⁰Tiglath-Pileserᶜ king of Assyria came to him, but gave him trouble instead of help. ²¹Ahaz took some of the things from the temple of the Lord and from the royal palace and from the officials and presented them to the king of Assyria, but that did not help him.

²²In his time of trouble King Ahaz became even more unfaithful to the Lord. ²³He offered sacrifices to the gods of Damascus, who had defeated him; for he thought, 'Since the gods of the kings of Aram have helped them, I will sacrifice to them so that they will help me.' But they were his downfall and the downfall of all Israel.

²⁴Ahaz gathered together the furnishings from the temple of God and cut them in pieces. He shut the doors of the Lord's temple and set up altars at every street corner in Jerusalem. ²⁵In every town in Judah he built high places to burn sacrifices to other gods and aroused the anger of the Lord, the God of his ancestors.

²⁶The other events of his reign and all his ways, from beginning to end, are written in the book of the kings of Judah and Israel. ²⁷Ahaz rested with his ancestors and was buried in the city of Jerusalem, but he was not placed in the tombs of the kings of Israel. And Hezekiah his son succeeded him as king.

ᵃ 16 Most Hebrew manuscripts; one Hebrew manuscript, Septuagint and Vulgate (see also 2 Kings 16:7) *king*
ᵇ 19 That is, Judah, as frequently in 2 Chronicles
ᶜ 20 Hebrew *Tilgath-Pilneser*, a variant of *Tiglath-Pileser*

Hezekiah purifies the temple

29 Hezekiah was twenty-five years old when he became king, and he reigned in Jerusalem for twenty-nine years. His mother's name was Abijah daughter of Zechariah. ² He did what was right in the eyes of the LORD, just as his father David had done.

³ In the first month of the first year of his reign, he opened the doors of the temple of the LORD and repaired them. ⁴ He brought in the priests and the Levites, assembled them in the square on the east side ⁵ and said, 'Listen to me, Levites! Consecrate yourselves now and consecrate the temple of the LORD, the God of your ancestors. Remove all defilement from the sanctuary. ⁶ Our parents were unfaithful; they did evil in the eyes of the LORD our God and forsook him. They turned their faces away from the LORD's dwelling-place and turned their backs on him. ⁷ They also shut the doors of the portico and put out the lamps. They did not burn incense or present any burnt offerings at the sanctuary to the God of Israel. ⁸ Therefore, the anger of the LORD has fallen on Judah and Jerusalem; he has made them an object of dread and horror and scorn, as you can see with your own eyes. ⁹ This is why our fathers have fallen by the sword and why our sons and daughters and our wives are in captivity. ¹⁰ Now I intend to make a covenant with the LORD, the God of Israel, so that his fierce anger will turn away from us. ¹¹ My sons, do not be negligent now, for the LORD has chosen you to stand before him and serve him, to minister before him and to burn incense.'

¹² Then these Levites set to work:

from the Kohathites,
    Mahath son of Amasai and Joel son of Azariah;
from the Merarites,
    Kish son of Abdi and Azariah son of Jehallelel;
from the Gershonites,
    Joah son of Zimmah and Eden son of Joah;
¹³ from the descendants of Elizaphan,
    Shimri and Jeiel;
from the descendants of Asaph,

    Zechariah and Mattaniah;
¹⁴ from the descendants of Heman,
    Jehiel and Shimei;
from the descendants of Jeduthun,
    Shemaiah and Uzziel.

¹⁵ When they had assembled their fellow Levites and consecrated themselves, they went in to purify the temple of the LORD, as the king had ordered, following the word of the LORD. ¹⁶ The priests went into the sanctuary of the LORD to purify it. They brought out to the courtyard of the LORD's temple everything unclean that they found in the temple of the LORD. The Levites took it and carried it out to the Kidron Valley. ¹⁷ They began the consecration on the first day of the first month, and by the eighth day of the month they reached the portico of the LORD. For eight more days they consecrated the temple of the LORD itself, finishing on the sixteenth day of the first month.

¹⁸ Then they went in to King Hezekiah and reported: 'We have purified the entire temple of the LORD, the altar of burnt offering with all its utensils, and the table for setting out the consecrated bread, with all its articles. ¹⁹ We have prepared and consecrated all the articles that King Ahaz removed in his unfaithfulness while he was king. They are now in front of the LORD's altar.'

²⁰ Early the next morning King Hezekiah gathered the city officials together and went up to the temple of the LORD. ²¹ They brought seven bulls, seven rams, seven male lambs and seven male goats as a sin offering*ᵃ* for the kingdom, for the sanctuary and for Judah. The king commanded the priests, the descendants of Aaron, to offer these on the altar of the LORD. ²² So they slaughtered the bulls, and the priests took the blood and splashed it against the altar; next they slaughtered the rams and splashed their blood against the altar; then they slaughtered the lambs and splashed their blood against the altar. ²³ The goats for the sin offering were brought before the king and the assembly, and they laid their hands on them. ²⁴ The

---

a 21 Or *purification offering; also in verses 23 and 24*

priests then slaughtered the goats and presented their blood on the altar for a sin offering to atone for all Israel, because the king had ordered the burnt offering and the sin offering for all Israel.

25 He stationed the Levites in the temple of the LORD with cymbals, harps and lyres in the way prescribed by David and Gad the king's seer and Nathan the prophet; this was commanded by the LORD through his prophets. 26 So the Levites stood ready with David's instruments, and the priests with their trumpets.

27 Hezekiah gave the order to sacrifice the burnt offering on the altar. As the offering began, singing to the LORD began also, accompanied by trumpets and the instruments of David king of Israel. 28 The whole assembly bowed in worship, while the musicians played and the trumpets sounded. All this continued until the sacrifice of the burnt offering was completed.

29 When the offerings were finished, the king and everyone present with him knelt down and worshipped. 30 King Hezekiah and his officials ordered the Levites to praise the LORD with the words of David and of Asaph the seer. So they sang praises with gladness and bowed down and worshipped.

31 Then Hezekiah said, 'You have now dedicated yourselves to the LORD. Come and bring sacrifices and thank-offerings to the temple of the LORD.' So the assembly brought sacrifices and thank-offerings, and all whose hearts were willing brought burnt offerings.

32 The number of burnt offerings the assembly brought was seventy bulls, a hundred rams and two hundred male lambs – all of them for burnt offerings to the LORD. 33 The animals consecrated as sacrifices amounted to six hundred bulls and three thousand sheep and goats. 34 The priests, however, were too few to skin all the burnt offerings; so their relatives the Levites helped them until the task was finished and until other priests had been consecrated, for the Levites had been more conscientious in consecrating themselves than the priests had been. 35 There were burnt offerings in abundance, together with the fat of the fellowship offerings and the drink offerings that accompanied the burnt offerings.

So the service of the temple of the LORD was re-established. 36 Hezekiah and all the people rejoiced at what God had brought about for his people, because it was done so quickly.

FAVOURITE VERSES

Joshua 1:9

Have I not commanded you? Be strong and courageous. Do not be afraid; do not be discouraged, for the LORD your God will be with you wherever you go.

I had decided I wanted to be baptised, but was freaking out over having a full immersion in water. While I was making my decision, I looked at the pen I was writing my testimony with – and this verse was written on it. My decision was made. I had nothing to fear.

Fiona, 16

Hezekiah celebrates the Passover

30 Hezekiah sent word to all Israel and Judah and also wrote letters to Ephraim and Manasseh, inviting them to come to the temple of the LORD in Jerusalem and celebrate the Passover to the LORD, the God of Israel. 2 The king and his officials and the whole assembly in Jerusalem decided to celebrate the Passover in the second month. 3 They had not been able to celebrate it at the regular time because not enough priests had consecrated themselves and the people had not assembled in Jerusalem. 4 The plan seemed right both to the king and to the whole assembly. 5 They decided to send a proclamation throughout Israel, from Beersheba to Dan, calling the people to come to Jerusalem and celebrate the Passover to the LORD, the God of Israel. It had not been celebrated in large numbers according to what was written.

⁶At the king's command, couriers went throughout Israel and Judah with letters from the king and from his officials, which read:

'People of Israel, return to the LORD, the God of Abraham, Isaac and Israel, that he may return to you who are left, who have escaped from the hand of the kings of Assyria. ⁷Do not be like your parents and your fellow Israelites, who were unfaithful to the LORD, the God of their ancestors, so that he made them an object of horror, as you see. ⁸Do not be stiff-necked, as your ancestors were; submit to the LORD. Come to his sanctuary, which he has consecrated for ever. Serve the LORD your God, so that his fierce anger will turn away from you. ⁹If you return to the LORD, then your fellow Israelites and your children will be shown compassion by their captors and will return to this land, for the LORD your God is gracious and compassionate. He will not turn his face from you if you return to him.'

¹⁰The couriers went from town to town in Ephraim and Manasseh, as far as Zebulun, but people scorned and ridiculed them. ¹¹Nevertheless, some from Asher, Manasseh and Zebulun humbled themselves and went to Jerusalem. ¹²Also in Judah the hand of God was on the people to give them unity of mind to carry out what the king and his officials had ordered, following the word of the LORD.

¹³A very large crowd of people assembled in Jerusalem to celebrate the Festival of Unleavened Bread in the second month. ¹⁴They removed the altars in Jerusalem and cleared away the incense altars and threw them into the Kidron Valley. ¹⁵They slaughtered the Passover lamb

on the fourteenth day of the second month. The priests and the Levites were ashamed and consecrated themselves and brought burnt offerings to the temple of the LORD. ¹⁶Then they took up their usual positions as prescribed in the Law of Moses the man of God. The priests splashed against the altar the blood handed to them by the Levites. ¹⁷Since many in the crowd had not consecrated themselves, the Levites had to kill the Passover lambs for all those who were not ceremonially clean and could not consecrate their lambsᵃ to the LORD. ¹⁸Although most of the many people who came from Ephraim, Manasseh, Issachar and Zebulun had not purified themselves, yet they ate the Passover, contrary to what was written. But Hezekiah prayed for them, saying, 'May the LORD, who is good, pardon everyone ¹⁹who sets their heart on seeking God – the LORD, the God of their ancestors – even if they are not clean according to the rules of the sanctuary.' ²⁰And the LORD heard Hezekiah and healed the people.

²¹The Israelites who were present in Jerusalem celebrated the Festival of Unleavened Bread for seven days with great rejoicing, while the Levites and priests praised the LORD every day with resounding instruments dedicated to the LORD.ᵇ

²²Hezekiah spoke encouragingly to all the Levites, who showed good understanding of the service of the LORD. For the seven days they ate their assigned portion and offered fellowship offerings and praisedᶜ the LORD, the God of their ancestors.

²³The whole assembly then agreed to celebrate the festival seven more days; so for another seven days they celebrated joyfully. ²⁴Hezekiah king of Judah provided a thousand bulls and seven thousand sheep and goats for the assembly, and the officials provided them with a thousand bulls and ten thousand sheep and goats. A great number of priests consecrated

---

ᵃ 17 Or *consecrate themselves*
ᵇ 21 Or *priests sang to the LORD every day, accompanied by the LORD's instruments of praise*
ᶜ 22 Or *and confessed their sins to*

The History Books		537		2 CHRONICLES 31:19

themselves. 25 The entire assembly of Judah rejoiced, along with the priests and Levites and all who had assembled from Israel, including the foreigners who had come from Israel and also those who resided in Judah. 26 There was great joy in Jerusalem, for since the days of Solomon son of David king of Israel there had been nothing like this in Jerusalem. 27 The priests and the Levites stood to bless the people, and God heard them, for their prayer reached heaven, his holy dwelling-place.

31 When all this had ended, the Israelites who were there went out to the towns of Judah, smashed the sacred stones and cut down the Asherah poles. They destroyed the high places and the altars throughout Judah and Benjamin and in Ephraim and Manasseh. After they had destroyed all of them, the Israelites returned to their own towns and to their own property.

Contributions for worship

2 Hezekiah assigned the priests and Levites to divisions – each of them according to their duties as priests or Levites – to offer burnt offerings and fellowship offerings, to minister, to give thanks and to sing praises at the gates of the LORD's dwelling. 3 The king contributed from his own possessions for the morning and evening burnt offerings and for the burnt offerings on the Sabbaths, at the New Moons and at the appointed festivals as written in the Law of the LORD. 4 He ordered the people living in Jerusalem to give the portion due to the priests and Levites so that they could devote themselves to the Law of the LORD. 5 As soon as the order went out, the Israelites generously gave the firstfruits of their grain, new wine, olive oil and honey and all that the fields produced. They brought a great amount, a tithe of everything. 6 The people of Israel and Judah who lived in the towns of Judah also brought a tithe of their herds and flocks and a tithe of the holy things dedicated to the LORD their God, and they piled them in heaps. 7 They began doing this in the third month and finished in the seventh

month. 8 When Hezekiah and his officials came and saw the heaps, they praised the LORD and blessed his people Israel.

9 Hezekiah asked the priests and Levites about the heaps; 10 and Azariah the chief priest, from the family of Zadok, answered, 'Since the people began to bring their contributions to the temple of the LORD, we have had enough to eat and plenty to spare, because the LORD has blessed his people, and this great amount is left over.'

11 Hezekiah gave orders to prepare storerooms in the temple of the LORD, and this was done. 12 Then they faithfully brought in the contributions, tithes and dedicated gifts. Konaniah, a Levite, was the overseer in charge of these things, and his brother Shimei was next in rank. 13 Jehiel, Azaziah, Nahath, Asahel, Jerimoth, Jozabad, Eliel, Ismakiah, Mahath and Benaiah were assistants of Konaniah and Shimei his brother. All these served by appointment of King Hezekiah and Azariah the official in charge of the temple of God.

14 Kore son of Imnah the Levite, keeper of the East Gate, was in charge of the freewill offerings given to God, distributing the contributions made to the LORD and also the consecrated gifts. 15 Eden, Miniamin, Jeshua, Shemaiah, Amariah and Shekaniah assisted him faithfully in the towns of the priests, distributing to their fellow priests according to their divisions, old and young alike.

16 In addition, they distributed to the males three years old or more whose names were in the genealogical records – all who would enter the temple of the LORD to perform the daily duties of their various tasks, according to their responsibilities and their divisions. 17 And they distributed to the priests enrolled by their families in the genealogical records and likewise to the Levites twenty years old or more, according to their responsibilities and their divisions. 18 They included all the little ones, the wives, and the sons and daughters of the whole community listed in these genealogical records. For they were faithful in consecrating themselves. 19 As for the priests, the descendants

of Aaron, who lived on the farmlands around their towns or in any other towns, men were designated by name to distribute portions to every male among them and to all who were recorded in the genealogies of the Levites.

²⁰This is what Hezekiah did throughout Judah, doing what was good and right and faithful before the LORD his God. ²¹In everything that he undertook in the service of God's temple and in obedience to the law and the commands, he sought his God and worked wholeheartedly. And so he prospered.

Sennacherib threatens Jerusalem

32 After all that Hezekiah had so faithfully done, Sennacherib king of Assyria came and invaded Judah. He laid siege to the fortified cities, thinking to conquer them for himself. ²When Hezekiah saw that Sennacherib had come and that he intended to wage war against Jerusalem, ³he consulted with his officials and military staff about blocking off the water from the springs outside the city, and they helped him. ⁴They gathered a large group of people who blocked all the springs and the stream that flowed through the land. 'Why should the kings*a* of Assyria come and find plenty of water?' they said. ⁵Then he worked hard repairing all the broken sections of the wall and building towers on it. He built another wall outside that one and reinforced the terraces*b* of the City of David. He also made large numbers of weapons and shields.

⁶He appointed military officers over the people and assembled them before him in the square at the city gate and encouraged them with these words: ⁷'Be strong and courageous. Do not be afraid or discouraged because of the king of Assyria and the vast army with him, for there is a greater power with us than with him. ⁸With him is only the arm of flesh, but with us is the LORD our God to help us and to fight our battles.' And the people

gained confidence from what Hezekiah the king of Judah said.

⁹Later, when Sennacherib king of Assyria and all his forces were laying siege to Lachish, he sent his officers to Jerusalem with this message for Hezekiah king of Judah and for all the people of Judah who were there:

¹⁰'This is what Sennacherib king of Assyria says: on what are you basing your confidence, that you remain in Jerusalem under siege? ¹¹When Hezekiah says, "The LORD our God will save us from the hand of the king of Assyria," he is misleading you, to let you die of hunger and thirst. ¹²Did not Hezekiah himself remove this god's high places and altars, saying to Judah and Jerusalem, "You must worship before one altar and burn sacrifices on it"?

¹³'Do you not know what I and my predecessors have done to all the peoples of the other lands? Were the gods of those nations ever able to deliver their land from my hand? ¹⁴Who of all the gods of these nations that my predecessors destroyed has been able to save his people from me? How then can your god deliver you from my hand? ¹⁵Now do not let Hezekiah deceive you and mislead you like this. Do not believe him, for no god of any nation or kingdom has been able to deliver his people from my hand or the hand of my predecessors. How much less will your god deliver you from my hand!'

¹⁶Sennacherib's officers spoke further against the LORD God and against his servant Hezekiah. ¹⁷The king also wrote letters ridiculing the LORD, the God of Israel, and saying this against him: 'Just as the gods of the peoples of the other lands did not rescue their people from my hand, so the god of Hezekiah will not rescue his people from my hand.' ¹⁸Then they called out in Hebrew to the people of Jerusalem who were on the wall, to terrify them and

---

a 4 Hebrew; Septuagint and Syriac *king*
b 5 Or *the Millo*

make them afraid in order to capture the city. ¹⁹They spoke about the God of Jerusalem as they did about the gods of the other peoples of the world – the work of human hands.

²⁰King Hezekiah and the prophet Isaiah son of Amoz cried out in prayer to heaven about this. ²¹And the LORD sent an angel, who annihilated all the fighting men and the commanders and officers in the camp of the Assyrian king. So he withdrew to his own land in disgrace. And when he went into the temple of his god, some of his sons, his own flesh and blood, cut him down with the sword.

²²So the LORD saved Hezekiah and the people of Jerusalem from the hand of Sennacherib king of Assyria and from the hand of all others. He took care of them^c on every side. ²³Many brought offerings to Jerusalem for the LORD and valuable gifts for Hezekiah king of Judah. From then on he was highly regarded by all the nations.

Hezekiah's pride, success and death

²⁴In those days Hezekiah became ill and was at the point of death. He prayed to the LORD, who answered him and gave him a miraculous sign. ²⁵But Hezekiah's heart was proud and he did not respond to the kindness shown him; therefore the LORD's wrath was on him and on Judah and Jerusalem. ²⁶Then Hezekiah repented of the pride of his heart, as did the people of Jerusalem; therefore the LORD's wrath did not come on them during the days of Hezekiah.

²⁷Hezekiah had very great wealth and honour, and he made treasuries for his silver and gold and for his precious stones, spices, shields and all kinds of valuables. ²⁸He also made buildings to store the harvest of grain, new wine and olive oil; and he made stalls for various kinds of cattle, and pens for the flocks. ²⁹He built villages and acquired great numbers of flocks and herds, for God had given him very great riches.

³⁰It was Hezekiah who blocked the upper outlet of the Gihon spring and channelled the water down to the west side of the City of David. He succeeded in everything he undertook. ³¹But when envoys were sent by the rulers of Babylon to ask him about the miraculous sign that had occurred in the land, God left him to test him and to know everything that was in his heart.

³²The other events of Hezekiah's reign and his acts of devotion are written in the vision of the prophet Isaiah son of Amoz in the book of the kings of Judah and Israel. ³³Hezekiah rested with his ancestors and was buried on the hill where the tombs of David's descendants are. All Judah and the people of Jerusalem honoured him when he died. And Manasseh his son succeeded him as king.

Manasseh king of Judah

33 Manasseh was twelve years old when he became king, and he reigned in Jerusalem for fifty-five years. ²He did evil in the eyes of the LORD, following the detestable practices of the nations the LORD had driven out before the Israelites. ³He rebuilt the high places his father Hezekiah had demolished; he also erected altars to the Baals and made Asherah poles. He bowed down to all the starry hosts and worshipped them. ⁴He built altars in the temple of the LORD, of which the LORD had said, 'My Name will remain in Jerusalem for ever.' ⁵In both courts of the temple of the LORD, he built altars to all the starry hosts. ⁶He sacrificed his children in the fire in the Valley of Ben Hinnom, practised divination and witchcraft, sought omens, and consulted mediums and spiritists. He did much evil in the eyes of the LORD, arousing his anger.

⁷He took the image he had made and put it in God's temple, of which God had said to David and to his son Solomon, 'In this temple and in Jerusalem, which I have chosen out of all the tribes of Israel, I will put my Name for ever. ⁸I will not again make the feet of the Israelites leave the land I assigned to your ancestors, if only they will be careful to do everything

---

c 22 Hebrew; Septuagint and Vulgate *He gave them rest*

that I commanded them concerning all the laws, decrees and regulations given through Moses.' ⁹But Manasseh led Judah and the people of Jerusalem astray, so that they did more evil than the nations the LORD had destroyed before the Israelites. ¹⁰The LORD spoke to Manasseh and his people, but they paid no attention. ¹¹So the LORD brought against them the army commanders of the king of Assyria, who took Manasseh prisoner, put a hook in his nose, bound him with bronze shackles and took him to Babylon. ¹²In his distress he sought the favour of the LORD his God and humbled himself greatly before the God of his ancestors. ¹³And when he prayed to him, the LORD was moved by his entreaty and listened to his plea; so he brought him back to Jerusalem and to his kingdom. Then Manasseh knew that the LORD is God.

¹⁴Afterwards he rebuilt the outer wall of the City of David, west of the Gihon spring in the valley, as far as the entrance of the Fish Gate and encircling the hill of Ophel; he also made it much higher. He stationed military commanders in all the fortified cities in Judah.

¹⁵He got rid of the foreign gods and removed the image from the temple of the LORD, as well as all the altars he had built on the temple hill and in Jerusalem; and he threw them out of the city. ¹⁶Then he restored the altar of the LORD and sacrificed fellowship offerings and thank-offerings on it, and told Judah to serve the LORD, the God of Israel. ¹⁷The people, however, continued to sacrifice at the high places, but only to the LORD their God.

¹⁸The other events of Manasseh's reign, including his prayer to his God and the words the seers spoke to him in the name of the LORD, the God of Israel, are written in the annals of the kings of Israel. *a* ¹⁹His prayer and how God was moved by his entreaty, as well as all his sins and unfaithfulness, and the sites where he built high places and set up Asherah poles and idols before he humbled himself – all these are

written in the records of the seers. *b* ²⁰Manasseh rested with his ancestors and was buried in his palace. And Amon his son succeeded him as king.

Amon king of Judah

²¹Amon was twenty-two years old when he became king, and he reigned in Jerusalem for two years. ²²He did evil in the eyes of the LORD, as his father Manasseh had done. Amon worshipped and offered sacrifices to all the idols Manasseh had made. ²³But unlike his father Manasseh, he did not humble himself before the LORD; Amon increased his guilt.

²⁴Amon's officials conspired against him and assassinated him in his palace. ²⁵Then the people of the land killed all who had plotted against King Amon, and they made Josiah his son king in his place.

Josiah's reforms

34 Josiah was eight years old when he became king, and he reigned in Jerusalem for thirty-one years. ²He did what was right in the eyes of the LORD and followed the ways of his father David, not turning aside to the right or to the left.

³In the eighth year of his reign, while he was still young, he began to seek the God of his father David. In his twelfth year he began to purge Judah and Jerusalem of high places, Asherah poles and idols. ⁴Under his direction the altars of the Baals were torn down; he cut to pieces the incense altars that were above them, and smashed the Asherah poles and the idols. These he broke to pieces and scattered over the graves of those who had sacrificed to them. ⁵He burned the bones of the priests on their altars, and so he purged Judah and Jerusalem. ⁶In the towns of Manasseh, Ephraim and Simeon, as far as Naphtali, and in the ruins around them, ⁷he tore down the altars and the Asherah poles and crushed the idols to powder and cut to pieces all the

---

a 18 That is, Judah, as frequently in 2 Chronicles

b 19 One Hebrew manuscript and Septuagint; most Hebrew manuscripts *of Hozai* incense altars throughout Israel. Then he went back to Jerusalem.

8 In the eighteenth year of Josiah's reign, to purify the land and the temple, he sent Shaphan son of Azaliah and Maaseiah the ruler of the city, with Joah son of Joahaz, the recorder, to repair the temple of the LORD his God.

9 They went to Hilkiah the high priest and gave him the money that had been brought into the temple of God, which the Levites who were the gatekeepers had collected from the people of Manasseh, Ephraim and the entire remnant of Israel and from all the people of Judah and Benjamin and the inhabitants of Jerusalem. 10 Then they entrusted it to the men appointed to supervise the work on the LORD's temple. These men paid the workers who repaired and restored the temple. 11 They also gave money to the carpenters and builders to purchase dressed stone, and timber for joists and beams for the buildings that the kings of Judah had allowed to fall into ruin.

12 The workers laboured faithfully. Over them to direct them were Jahath and Obadiah, Levites descended from Merari, and Zechariah and Meshullam, descended from Kohath. The Levites – all who were skilled in playing musical instruments – 13 had charge of the labourers and supervised all the workers from job to job. Some of the Levites were secretaries, scribes and gatekeepers.

The Book of the Law found

14 While they were bringing out the money that had been taken into the temple of the LORD, Hilkiah the priest found the Book of the Law of the LORD that had been given through Moses. 15 Hilkiah said to Shaphan the secretary, 'I have found the Book of the Law in the temple of the LORD.' He gave it to Shaphan.

16 Then Shaphan took the book to the king and reported to him: 'Your officials are doing everything that has been committed to them. 17 They have paid out the money that was in the temple of the LORD and have entrusted it to the supervisors and workers.' 18 Then Shaphan the

secretary informed the king, 'Hilkiah the priest has given me a book.' And Shaphan read from it in the presence of the king.

19 When the king heard the words of the Law, he tore his robes. 20 He gave these orders to Hilkiah, Ahikam son of Shaphan, Abdon son of Micah,*a* Shaphan the secretary and Asaiah the king's attendant: 21 'Go and enquire of the LORD for me and for the remnant in Israel and Judah about what is written in this book that has been found. Great is the LORD's anger that is poured out on us because those who have gone before us have not kept the word of the LORD; they have not acted in accordance with all that is written in this book.'

22 Hilkiah and those the king had sent with him*b* went to speak to the prophet Huldah, who was the wife of Shallum son of Tokhath,*c* the son of Hasrah,*d* keeper of the wardrobe. She lived in Jerusalem, in the New Quarter.

23 She said to them, 'This is what the LORD, the God of Israel, says: tell the man who sent you to me, 24 "This is what the LORD says: I am going to bring disaster on this place and its people – all the curses written in the book that has been read in the presence of the king of Judah. 25 Because they have forsaken me and burned incense to other gods and aroused my anger by all that their hands have made,*e* my anger will be poured out on this place and will not be quenched." 26 Tell the king of Judah, who sent you to enquire of the LORD, "This is what the LORD, the God of Israel, says concerning the words you heard: 27 because your heart was responsive and you humbled yourself before God when you heard what he spoke against this place and its people, and because you humbled yourself before me and tore your robes and wept in my presence, I have heard you, declares the LORD. 28 Now I will gather you to your ancestors, and you will

---

a 20 Also called *Akbor son of Micaiah*
b 22 One Hebrew manuscript, Vulgate and Syriac; most Hebrew manuscripts do not have *had sent with him.*
c 22 Also called *Tikvah*
d 22 Also called *Harhas*
e 25 Or *by everything they have done*

be buried in peace. Your eyes will not see all the disaster I am going to bring on this place and on those who live here."'

So they took her answer back to the king.

29 Then the king called together all the elders of Judah and Jerusalem. 30 He went up to the temple of the LORD with the people of Judah, the inhabitants of Jerusalem, the priests and the Levites – all the people from the least to the greatest. He read in their hearing all the words of the Book of the Covenant, which had been found in the temple of the LORD. 31 The king stood by his pillar and renewed the covenant in the presence of the LORD – to follow the LORD and keep his commands, statutes and decrees with all his heart and all his soul, and to obey the words of the covenant written in this book.

32 Then he made everyone in Jerusalem and Benjamin pledge themselves to it; the people of Jerusalem did this in accordance with the covenant of God, the God of their ancestors.

33 Josiah removed all the detestable idols from all the territory belonging to the Israelites, and he made all who were present in Israel serve the LORD their God. As long as he lived, they did not fail to follow the LORD, the God of their ancestors.

Josiah celebrates the Passover

35 Josiah celebrated the Passover to the LORD in Jerusalem, and the Passover lamb was slaughtered on the fourteenth day of the first month. 2 He appointed the priests to their duties and encouraged them in the service of the LORD's temple. 3 He said to the Levites, who instructed all Israel and who had been consecrated to the LORD: 'Put the sacred ark in the temple that Solomon son of David king of Israel built. It is not to be carried about on your shoulders. Now serve the LORD your God and his people Israel. 4 Prepare yourselves by families in your divisions, according to the instructions written by David king of Israel and by his son Solomon.

5 'Stand in the holy place with a group of Levites for each sub-division of the families of your fellow Israelites, the lay people. 6 Slaughter the Passover lambs, consecrate yourselves and prepare the lambs for your fellow Israelites, doing what the LORD commanded through Moses.'

7 Josiah provided for all the lay people who were there a total of thirty thousand lambs and goats for the Passover offerings, and also three thousand cattle – all from the king's own possessions.

8 His officials also contributed voluntarily to the people and the priests and Levites. Hilkiah, Zechariah and Jehiel, the officials in charge of God's temple, gave the priests two thousand six hundred Passover offerings and three hundred cattle. 9 Also Konaniah along with Shemaiah and Nethanel, his brothers, and Hashabiah, Jeiel and Jozabad, the leaders of the Levites, provided five thousand Passover offerings and five hundred head of cattle for the Levites.

10 The service was arranged and the priests stood in their places with the Levites in their divisions as the king had ordered. 11 The Passover lambs were slaughtered, and the priests splashed against the altar the blood handed to them, while the Levites skinned the animals. 12 They set aside the burnt offerings to give them to the sub-divisions of the families of the people to offer to the LORD, as it is written in the Book of Moses. They did the same with the cattle. 13 They roasted the Passover animals over the fire as prescribed, and boiled the holy offerings in pots, cauldrons and pans and served them quickly to all the people. 14 After this, they made preparations for themselves and for the priests, because the priests, the descendants of Aaron, were sacrificing the burnt offerings and the fat portions until nightfall. So the Levites made preparations for themselves and for the Aaronic priests.

15 The musicians, the descendants of Asaph, were in the places prescribed by David, Asaph, Heman and Jeduthun the king's seer. The gatekeepers at each gate did not need to leave their posts, because their fellow Levites made the preparations for them.

16 So at that time the entire service of

the LORD was carried out for the celebration of the Passover and the offering of burnt offerings on the altar of the LORD, as King Josiah had ordered. ¹⁷The Israelites who were present celebrated the Passover at that time and observed the Festival of Unleavened Bread for seven days. ¹⁸The Passover had not been observed like this in Israel since the days of the prophet Samuel; and none of the kings of Israel had ever celebrated such a Passover as did Josiah, with the priests, the Levites and all Judah and Israel who were there with the people of Jerusalem. ¹⁹This Passover was celebrated in the eighteenth year of Josiah's reign.

The death of Josiah

²⁰After all this, when Josiah had set the temple in order, Necho king of Egypt went up to fight at Carchemish on the Euphrates, and Josiah marched out to meet him in battle. ²¹But Necho sent messengers to him saying, 'What quarrel is there, king of Judah, between you and me? It is not you I am attacking at this time, but the house with which I am at war. God has told me to hurry; so stop opposing God, who is with me, or he will destroy you.'

²²Josiah, however, would not turn away from him, but disguised himself to engage him in battle. He would not listen to what Necho had said at God's command but went to fight him on the plain of Megiddo.

²³Archers shot King Josiah, and he told his officers, 'Take me away; I am badly wounded.' ²⁴So they took him out of his chariot, put him in his other chariot and brought him to Jerusalem, where he died. He was buried in the tombs of his ancestors, and all Judah and Jerusalem mourned for him.

²⁵Jeremiah composed laments for Josiah, and to this day all the male and female singers commemorate Josiah in the laments. These became a tradition in Israel and are written in the Laments.

²⁶The other events of Josiah's reign and his acts of devotion in accordance with what is written in the Law of the LORD – ²⁷all the events, from beginning to end, are written in the book of the kings of

36
Israel and Judah. ¹And the people of the land took Jehoahaz son of Josiah and made him king in Jerusalem in place of his father.

Jehoahaz king of Judah

²Jehoahaz*ᵃ* was twenty-three years old when he became king, and he reigned in Jerusalem for three months. ³The king of Egypt dethroned him in Jerusalem and imposed on Judah a levy of a hundred talentsᵇ of silver and a talentᶜ of gold. ⁴The king of Egypt made Eliakim, a brother of Jehoahaz, king over Judah and Jerusalem and changed Eliakim's name to Jehoiakim. But Necho took Eliakim's brother Jehoahaz and carried him off to Egypt.

Jehoiakim king of Judah

⁵Jehoiakim was twenty-five years old when he became king, and he reigned in Jerusalem for eleven years. He did evil in the eyes of the LORD his God. ⁶Nebuchadnezzar king of Babylon attacked him and bound him with bronze shackles to take him to Babylon. ⁷Nebuchadnezzar also took to Babylon articles from the temple of the LORD and put them in his templeᵈ there.

⁸The other events of Jehoiakim's reign, the detestable things he did and all that was found against him, are written in the book of the kings of Israel and Judah. And Jehoiachin his son succeeded him as king.

Jehoiachin king of Judah

⁹Jehoiachin was eighteenᵉ years old when he became king, and he reigned in Jerusalem for three months and ten days. He did evil in the eyes of the LORD. ¹⁰In the spring, King Nebuchadnezzar sent for him and brought him to Babylon, together with articles of value from the

---

a 2 Hebrew *Joahaz*, a variant of *Jehoahaz*; also in verse 4
b 3 That is, about 3.4 metric tons
c 3 That is, about 34 kilograms
d 7 Or *palace*
e 9 One Hebrew manuscript, some Septuagint manuscripts and Syriac (see also 2 Kings 24:8); most Hebrew manuscripts *eight*

temple of the Lord, and he made Jehoiachin's uncle,*f* Zedekiah, king over Judah and Jerusalem.

Zedekiah king of Judah

¹¹ Zedekiah was twenty-one years old when he became king, and he reigned in Jerusalem for eleven years. ¹² He did evil in the eyes of the Lord his God and did not humble himself before Jeremiah the prophet, who spoke the word of the Lord. ¹³ He also rebelled against King Nebuchadnezzar, who had made him take an oath in God's name. He became stiff-necked and hardened his heart and would not turn to the Lord, the God of Israel. ¹⁴ Furthermore, all the leaders of the priests and the people became more and more unfaithful, following all the detestable practices of the nations and defiling the temple of the Lord, which he had consecrated in Jerusalem.

The fall of Jerusalem

¹⁵ The Lord, the God of their ancestors, sent word to them through his messengers again and again, because he had pity on his people and on his dwelling-place. ¹⁶ But they mocked God's messengers, despised his words and scoffed at his prophets until the wrath of the Lord was aroused against his people and there was no remedy. ¹⁷ He brought up against them the king of the Babylonians,*g* who killed

their young men with the sword in the sanctuary, and did not spare young men or young women, the elderly or the infirm. God gave them all into the hands of Nebuchadnezzar. ¹⁸ He carried to Babylon all the articles from the temple of God, both large and small, and the treasures of the Lord's temple and the treasures of the king and his officials. ¹⁹ They set fire to God's temple and broke down the wall of Jerusalem; they burned all the palaces and destroyed everything of value there.

²⁰ He carried into exile to Babylon the remnant, who escaped from the sword, and they became servants to him and his successors until the kingdom of Persia came to power. ²¹ The land enjoyed its sabbath rests; all the time of its desolation it rested, until the seventy years were completed in fulfilment of the word of the Lord spoken by Jeremiah.

²² In the first year of Cyrus king of Persia, in order to fulfil the word of the Lord spoken by Jeremiah, the Lord moved the heart of Cyrus king of Persia to make a proclamation throughout his realm and also to put it in writing:

²³ 'This is what Cyrus king of Persia says:

   ' "The Lord, the God of heaven, has given me all the kingdoms of the earth and he has appointed me to build a temple for him at Jerusalem in Judah. Any of his people among you may go up, and may the Lord their God be with them." '

---

f 10 Hebrew *brother*, that is, relative (see 2 Kings 24:17)
g 17 Or *Chaldeans*

EZRA

DATE

Events in Ezra, Nehemiah and Esther cover almost 100 years, between 538 and 433 BC

AUTHOR

Traditionally attributed to Ezra

WHAT'S IT ALL ABOUT?

Ezra tells the story of the Jews' return from exile and overlaps by a few verses with the end of 2 Chronicles. The Persians, having conquered the Babylonians, decided to let the people who had been exiled for seventy years return to Jerusalem. This was a hugely significant time for God's people and a reason for great celebration, but they found their beloved city in ruins. The temple had been destroyed and the people made it their first priority to rebuild it, despite the opposition they faced. There is likely to have been a sixty-year gap between the dedication of the temple at the end of chapter 6 and the return of Ezra to Jerusalem in chapter 7 (during which time the events of the book of Esther took place). Ezra was a priest and teacher who tried to keep the people focused on worshipping God. They seemed not to have learned the hard lessons from their exile, though, and were still marrying other races which led to worship of other gods. The final chapter shows Ezra leading the people through a confession of their sin and recommitting themselves to God.

WHY SHOULD WE READ IT?

- Originally the books of Ezra and Nehemiah were one, so it is worth reading them both together.

- To see the emotional reaction of God's people as the first foundations of the new temple were laid (Ezra 3).

- To hear how Ezra refused to ask the king of Persia for protection on his journey back to Jerusalem, but prayed and fasted so that the Lord might protect them (Ezra 8).

- To see Ezra's style of leadership. Rather than telling the people off for their sins, Ezra wept over their disobedience and cried out to God for them (Ezra 9).

Andy Croft with Liza Hoeksma

Cyrus helps the exiles to return

1 In the first year of Cyrus king of Persia, in order to fulfil the word of the LORD spoken by Jeremiah, the LORD moved the heart of Cyrus king of Persia to make a proclamation throughout his realm and also to put it in writing:

² 'This is what Cyrus king of Persia says:

' "The LORD, the God of heaven, has given me all the kingdoms of the earth and he has appointed me to build a temple for him at Jerusalem in Judah. ³ Any of his people among you may go up to Jerusalem in Judah and build the temple of the LORD, the God of Israel, the God who is in Jerusalem, and may their God be with them. ⁴ And in any locality where survivors may now be living, the people are to provide them with silver and gold, with goods and livestock, and with freewill offerings for the temple of God in Jerusalem." '

⁵ Then the family heads of Judah and Benjamin, and the priests and Levites — everyone whose heart God had moved — prepared to go up and build the house of the LORD in Jerusalem. ⁶ All their neighbours assisted them with articles of silver and gold, with goods and livestock, and with valuable gifts, in addition to all the freewill offerings.

⁷ Moreover, King Cyrus brought out the articles belonging to the temple of the LORD, which Nebuchadnezzar had carried away from Jerusalem and had placed in the temple of his god.ᵃ ⁸ Cyrus king of Persia had them brought by Mithredath the treasurer, who counted them out to Sheshbazzar the prince of Judah.

⁹ This was the inventory:

gold dishes	30
silver dishes	1,000
silver pansᵇ	29
¹⁰ gold bowls	30
matching silver bowls	410
other articles	1,000

¹¹ In all, there were 5,400 articles of gold and of silver. Sheshbazzar brought all these along with the exiles when they came up from Babylon to Jerusalem.

The list of the exiles who returned

2 Now these are the people of the province who came up from the captivity of the exiles, whom Nebuchadnezzar king of Babylon had taken captive to Babylon (they returned to Jerusalem and Judah, each to their own town, ² in company with Zerubbabel, Joshua, Nehemiah, Seraiah, Reelaiah, Mordecai, Bilshan, Mispar, Bigvai, Rehum and Baanah):

The list of the men of the people of Israel:

³ the descendants of Parosh	2,172
⁴ of Shephatiah	372
⁵ of Arah	775
⁶ of Pahath-Moab (through the line of Jeshua and Joab)	2,812
⁷ of Elam	1,254
⁸ of Zattu	945
⁹ of Zakkai	760
¹⁰ of Bani	642
¹¹ of Bebai	623
¹² of Azgad	1,222
¹³ of Adonikam	666
¹⁴ of Bigvai	2,056
¹⁵ of Adin	454
¹⁶ of Ater (through Hezekiah)	98
¹⁷ of Bezai	323
¹⁸ of Jorah	112
¹⁹ of Hashum	223
²⁰ of Gibbar	95
²¹ the men of Bethlehem	123
²² of Netophah	56
²³ of Anathoth	128
²⁴ of Azmaveth	42

ᵃ 7 Or *gods*

ᵇ 9 The meaning of the Hebrew for this word is uncertain.

25 of Kiriath Jearim,*a* Kephirah
 and Beeroth   743
26 of Ramah and Geba 621
27 of Mikmash 122
28 of Bethel and Ai 223
29 of Nebo 52
30 of Magbish 156
31 of the other Elam 1,254
32 of Harim 320
33 of Lod, Hadid and Ono 725
34 of Jericho 345
35 of Senaah 3,630

36 The priests:

the descendants of Jedaiah
 (through the family of
 Jeshua) 973
37 of Immer 1,052
38 of Pashhur 1,247
39 of Harim 1,017

40 The Levites:

the descendants of Jeshua
 and Kadmiel (of the line of
 Hodaviah) 74

41 The musicians:

the descendants of Asaph 128

42 The gatekeepers of the temple:

the descendants of
 Shallum, Ater, Talmon,
 Akkub, Hatita and Shobai 139

43 The temple servants:

the descendants of
 Ziha, Hasupha, Tabbaoth,
44 Keros, Siaha, Padon,
45 Lebanah, Hagabah, Akkub,
46 Hagab, Shalmai, Hanan,
47 Giddel, Gahar, Reaiah,
48 Rezin, Nekoda, Gazzam,
49 Uzza, Paseah, Besai,
50 Asnah, Meunim, Nephussim,

51 Bakbuk, Hakupha, Harhur,
52 Bazluth, Mehida, Harsha,
53 Barkos, Sisera, Temah,
54 Neziah and Hatipha

55 The descendants of the servants of
Solomon:

the descendants of
 Sotai, Hassophereth, Peruda,
56 Jaala, Darkon, Giddel,
57 Shephatiah, Hattil,
 Pokereth-Hazzebaim and
 Ami

58 The temple servants and the
 descendants of the servants
 of Solomon 392

59 The following came up from
the towns of Tel Melah, Tel Harsha,
Kerub, Addon and Immer, but they
could not show that their families
were descended from Israel:

60 The descendants of
 Delaiah, Tobiah and
 Nekoda 652

61 And from among the priests:

The descendants of
 Hobaiah, Hakkoz and Barzillai
 (a man who had married
 a daughter of Barzillai the
 Gileadite and was called by
 that name).

62 These searched for their family records, but they could not find
them and so were excluded from the
priesthood as unclean. 63 The governor ordered them not to eat any of
the most sacred food until there was
a priest ministering with the Urim
and Thummim.

64 The whole company numbered
42,360, 65 besides their 7,337 male
and female slaves; and they also had
200 male and female singers. 66 They
had 736 horses, 245 mules, 67 435
camels and 6,720 donkeys.

---

a 25 See Septuagint (see also Neh. 7:29); Hebrew
Kiriath Arim.

68 When they arrived at the house of the LORD in Jerusalem, some of the heads of the families gave freewill offerings towards the rebuilding of the house of God on its site. 69 According to their ability they gave to the treasury for this work 61,000 daricsᵇ of gold, 5,000 minasᶜ of silver and 100 priestly garments.

70 The priests, the Levites, the musicians, the gatekeepers and the temple servants settled in their own towns, along with some of the other people, and the rest of the Israelites settled in their towns.

Rebuilding the altar

3 When the seventh month came and the Israelites had settled in their towns, the people assembled together as one in Jerusalem. 2 Then Joshua son of Jozadak and his fellow priests and Zerubbabel son of Shealtiel and his associates began to build the altar of the God of Israel to sacrifice burnt offerings on it, in accordance with what is written in the Law of Moses the man of God. 3 Despite their fear of the peoples around them, they built the altar on its foundation and sacrificed burnt offerings on it to the LORD, both the morning and evening sacrifices. 4 Then in accordance with what is written, they celebrated the Festival of Tabernacles with the required number of burnt offerings prescribed for each day. 5 After that, they presented the regular burnt offerings, the New Moon sacrifices and the sacrifices for all the appointed sacred festivals of the LORD, as well as those brought as freewill offerings to the LORD. 6 On the first day of the seventh month they began to offer burnt offerings to the LORD, though the foundation of the LORD's temple had not yet been laid.

Rebuilding the temple

7 Then they gave money to the masons and carpenters, and gave food and drink and olive oil to the people of Sidon and Tyre, so that they would bring cedar logs

by sea from Lebanon to Joppa, as authorised by Cyrus king of Persia.

8 In the second month of the second year after their arrival at the house of God in Jerusalem, Zerubbabel son of Shealtiel, Joshua son of Jozadak and the rest of the people (the priests and the Levites and all who had returned from the captivity to Jerusalem) began the work. They appointed Levites twenty years old and older to supervise the building of the house of the LORD. 9 Joshua and his sons and brothers and Kadmiel and his sons (descendants of Hodaviahᵃ) and the sons of Henadad and their sons and brothers – all Levites – joined together in supervising those working on the house of God.

10 When the builders laid the foundation of the temple of the LORD, the priests in their vestments and with trumpets, and the Levites (the sons of Asaph) with cymbals, took their places to praise the LORD, as prescribed by David king of Israel. 11 With praise and thanksgiving they sang to the LORD:

'He is good;
    his love towards Israel endures for
      ever.'

And all the people gave a great shout of praise to the LORD, because the foundation of the house of the LORD was laid. 12 But many of the older priests and Levites and family heads, who had seen the former temple, wept aloud when they saw the foundation of this temple being laid, while many others shouted for joy. 13 No one could distinguish the sound of the shouts of joy from the sound of weeping, because the people made so much noise. And the sound was heard far away.

Opposition to the rebuilding

4 When the enemies of Judah and Benjamin heard that the exiles were building a temple for the LORD, the God of Israel, 2 they came to Zerubbabel and to

---

b 69 That is, about 500 kilograms
c 69 That is, about 2.8 metric tons

a 9 Hebrew *Yehudah*, probably a variant of *Hodaviah*

the heads of the families and said, 'Let us help you build because, like you, we seek your God and have been sacrificing to him since the time of Esarhaddon king of Assyria, who brought us here.'

³ But Zerubbabel, Joshua and the rest of the heads of the families of Israel answered, 'You have no part with us in building a temple to our God. We alone will build it for the LORD, the God of Israel, as King Cyrus, the king of Persia, commanded us.'

⁴ Then the peoples around them set out to discourage the people of Judah and make them afraid to go on building.*a* ⁵ They bribed officials to work against them and frustrate their plans during the entire reign of Cyrus king of Persia and down to the reign of Darius king of Persia.

Later opposition under Xerxes and Artaxerxes

⁶ At the beginning of the reign of Xerxes,*b* they lodged an accusation against the people of Judah and Jerusalem.

⁷ And in the days of Artaxerxes king of Persia, Bishlam, Mithredath, Tabeel and the rest of his associates wrote a letter to Artaxerxes. The letter was written in Aramaic script and in the Aramaic language.*c,d*

⁸ Rehum the commanding officer and Shimshai the secretary wrote a letter against Jerusalem to Artaxerxes the king as follows:

⁹ Rehum the commanding officer and Shimshai the secretary, together with the rest of their associates – the judges, officials and administrators over the people from Persia, Uruk and Babylon, the Elamites of Susa, ¹⁰ and the other people whom the great and honourable Ashurbanipal deported and settled in the city of Samaria and elsewhere in Trans-Euphrates.

¹¹ (This is a copy of the letter they sent him.)

To King Artaxerxes,

From your servants, the men of Trans-Euphrates:

¹² The king should know that the people who came up to us from you have gone to Jerusalem and are rebuilding that rebellious and wicked city. They are restoring the walls and repairing the foundations.

¹³ Furthermore, the king should know that if this city is built and its walls are restored, no more taxes, tribute or duty will be paid, and eventually the royal revenues will suffer.*e* ¹⁴ Now since we are under obligation to the palace and it is not proper for us to see the king dishonoured, we are sending this message to inform the king, ¹⁵ so that a search may be made in the archives of your predecessors. In these records you will find that this city is a rebellious city, troublesome to kings and provinces, a place with a long history of sedition. That is why this city was destroyed. ¹⁶ We inform the king that if this city is built and its walls are restored, you will be left with nothing in Trans-Euphrates.

¹⁷ The king sent this reply:

To Rehum the commanding officer, Shimshai the secretary and the rest of their associates living in Samaria and elsewhere in Trans-Euphrates:

Greetings.

¹⁸ The letter you sent us has been read and translated in my presence. ¹⁹ I issued an order and a search was made, and it was found that this city has a long history of revolt against

---

a 4 Or *and troubled them as they built*
b 6 Hebrew *Ahasuerus*
c 7 Or *written in Aramaic and translated*
d 7 The text of 4:8 – 6:18 is in Aramaic.

e 13 The meaning of the Aramaic for this clause is uncertain.

kings and has been a place of rebellion and sedition. ²⁰Jerusalem has had powerful kings ruling over the whole of Trans-Euphrates, and taxes, tribute and duty were paid to them. ²¹Now issue an order to these men to stop work, so that this city will not be rebuilt until I so order. ²²Be careful not to neglect this matter. Why let this threat grow, to the detriment of the royal interests?

²³As soon as the copy of the letter of King Artaxerxes was read to Rehum and Shimshai the secretary and their associates, they went immediately to the Jews in Jerusalem and compelled them by force to stop.

²⁴Thus the work on the house of God in Jerusalem came to a standstill until the second year of the reign of Darius king of Persia.

Tattenai's letter to Darius

5 Now Haggai the prophet and Zechariah the prophet, a descendant of Iddo, prophesied to the Jews in Judah and Jerusalem in the name of the God of Israel, who was over them. ²Then Zerubbabel son of Shealtiel and Joshua son of Jozadak set to work to rebuild the house of God in Jerusalem. And the prophets of God were with them, supporting them.

³At that time Tattenai, governor of Trans-Euphrates, and Shethar-Bozenai and their associates went to them and asked, 'Who authorised you to rebuild this temple and to finish it?' ⁴They*ᵃ* also asked, 'What are the names of those who are constructing this building?' ⁵But the eye of their God was watching over the elders of the Jews, and they were not stopped until a report could go to Darius and his written reply be received.

⁶This is a copy of the letter that Tattenai, governor of Trans-Euphrates, and Shethar-Bozenai and their associates, the officials of Trans-Euphrates, sent to King Darius. ⁷The report they sent him read as follows:

To King Darius:

Cordial greetings.

⁸The king should know that we went to the district of Judah, to the temple of the great God. The people are building it with large stones and placing the timbers in the walls. The work is being carried on with diligence and is making rapid progress under their direction.

⁹We questioned the elders and asked them, 'Who authorised you to rebuild this temple and to finish it?' ¹⁰We also asked them their names, so that we could write down the names of their leaders for your information.

¹¹This is the answer they gave us:

'We are the servants of the God of heaven and earth, and we are rebuilding the temple that was built many years ago, one that a great king of Israel built and finished. ¹²But because our ancestors angered the God of heaven, he gave them into the hands of Nebuchadnezzar the Chaldean, king of Babylon, who destroyed this temple and deported the people to Babylon.

¹³'However, in the first year of Cyrus king of Babylon, King Cyrus issued a decree to rebuild this house of God. ¹⁴He even removed from the temple*ᵇ* of Babylon the gold and silver articles of the house of God, which Nebuchadnezzar had taken from the temple in Jerusalem and brought to the temple*ᵇ* in Babylon. Then King Cyrus gave them to a man named Sheshbazzar, whom he had appointed governor, ¹⁵and he told him, "Take these articles and go and deposit them in the temple in Jerusalem. And rebuild the house of God on its site."

---

a 4 See Septuagint; Aramaic *We*.   *b* 14 Or *palace*

16 'So this Sheshbazzar came and laid the foundations of the house of God in Jerusalem. From that day to the present it has been under construction but is not yet finished.'

17 Now if it pleases the king, let a search be made in the royal archives of Babylon to see if King Cyrus did in fact issue a decree to rebuild this house of God in Jerusalem. Then let the king send us his decision in this matter.

The decree of Darius

6 King Darius then issued an order, and they searched in the archives stored in the treasury at Babylon. 2 A scroll was found in the citadel of Ecbatana in the province of Media, and this was written on it:

Memorandum:

3 In the first year of King Cyrus, the king issued a decree concerning the temple of God in Jerusalem:

Let the temple be rebuilt as a place to present sacrifices, and let its foundations be laid. It is to be sixty cubits[a] high and sixty cubits wide, 4 with three courses of large stones and one of timber. The costs are to be paid by the royal treasury. 5 Also, the gold and silver articles of the house of God, which Nebuchadnezzar took from the temple in Jerusalem and brought to Babylon, are to be returned to their places in the temple in Jerusalem; they are to be deposited in the house of God.

6 Now then, Tattenai, governor of Trans-Euphrates, and Shethar-Bozenai and you other officials of that province, stay away from there. 7 Do not interfere with the work on this temple of God. Let the governor

of the Jews and the Jewish elders rebuild this house of God on its site.

8 Moreover, I hereby decree what you are to do for these elders of the Jews in the construction of this house of God:

Their expenses are to be fully paid out of the royal treasury, from the revenues of Trans-Euphrates, so that the work will not stop. 9 Whatever is needed – young bulls, rams, male lambs for burnt offerings to the God of heaven, and wheat, salt, wine and olive oil, as requested by the priests in Jerusalem – must be given them daily without fail, 10 so that they may offer sacrifices pleasing to the God of heaven and pray for the well-being of the king and his sons.

11 Furthermore, I decree that if anyone defies this edict, a beam is to be pulled from their house and they are to be impaled on it. And for this crime their house is to be made a pile of rubble. 12 May God, who has caused his Name to dwell there, overthrow any king or people who lifts a hand to change this decree or to destroy this temple in Jerusalem.

I Darius have decreed it. Let it be carried out with diligence.

Completion and dedication of the temple

13 Then, because of the decree King Darius had sent, Tattenai, governor of Trans-Euphrates, and Shethar-Bozenai and their associates carried it out with diligence. 14 So the elders of the Jews continued to build and prosper under the preaching of Haggai the prophet and Zechariah, a descendant of Iddo. They finished building the temple according to the command of the God of Israel and the decrees of Cyrus, Darius and Artaxerxes, kings of Persia. 15 The temple was completed on the third day of the month Adar, in the sixth year of the reign of King Darius.

16 Then the people of Israel – the priests, the Levites and the rest of the exiles – celebrated the dedication of the house of God with joy. 17 For the dedication of this

---

a 3 That is, about 27 metres

house of God they offered a hundred bulls, two hundred rams, four hundred male lambs and, as a sin offering*b* for all Israel, twelve male goats, one for each of the tribes of Israel. ¹⁸And they installed the priests in their divisions and the Levites in their groups for the service of God at Jerusalem, according to what is written in the Book of Moses.

The Passover

¹⁹On the fourteenth day of the first month, the exiles celebrated the Passover. ²⁰The priests and Levites had purified themselves and were all ceremonially clean. The Levites slaughtered the Passover lamb for all the exiles, for their relatives the priests and for themselves. ²¹So the Israelites who had returned from the exile ate it, together with all who had separated themselves from the unclean practices of their Gentile neighbours in order to seek the LORD, the God of Israel. ²²For seven days they celebrated with joy the Festival of Unleavened Bread, because the LORD had filled them with joy by changing the attitude of the king of Assyria so that he assisted them in the work on the house of God, the God of Israel.

Ezra comes to Jerusalem

7 After these things, during the reign of Artaxerxes king of Persia, Ezra son of Seraiah, the son of Azariah, the son of Hilkiah, ²the son of Shallum, the son of Zadok, the son of Ahitub, ³the son of Amariah, the son of Azariah, the son of Meraioth, ⁴the son of Zerahiah, the son of Uzzi, the son of Bukki, ⁵the son of Abishua, the son of Phinehas, the son of Eleazar, the son of Aaron the chief priest – ⁶this Ezra came up from Babylon. He was a teacher well versed in the Law of Moses, which the LORD, the God of Israel, had given. The king had granted him everything he asked, for the hand of the LORD his God was on him. ⁷Some of the Israelites, including priests, Levites, musicians, gatekeepers and temple servants, also

came up to Jerusalem in the seventh year of King Artaxerxes.

⁸Ezra arrived in Jerusalem in the fifth month of the seventh year of the king. ⁹He had begun his journey from Babylon on the first day of the first month, and he arrived in Jerusalem on the first day of the fifth month, for the gracious hand of his God was on him. ¹⁰For Ezra had devoted himself to the study and observance of the Law of the LORD, and to teaching its decrees and laws in Israel.

PEOPLE TOURS

EZRA

SCRIBE
Ezra 7:1–28
PRAYER
Ezra 8:15–23
JERUSALEM
Ezra 8:31–36
MARRIAGES
Ezra 9:1–15
LAW
Nehemiah 8:1–12

King Artaxerxes' letter to Ezra

¹¹This is a copy of the letter King Artaxerxes had given to Ezra the priest, a teacher of the Law, a man learned in matters concerning the commands and decrees of the LORD for Israel:

¹²Artaxerxes, king of kings,

To Ezra the priest, teacher of the Law of the God of heaven:

Greetings.

¹³Now I decree that any of the Israelites in my kingdom, including priests and Levites, who volunteer to go to Jerusalem with you, may go. ¹⁴You are sent by the king and his seven advisors to enquire about

Judah and Jerusalem with regard to the Law of your God, which is in your hand. ¹⁵ Moreover, you are to take with you the silver and gold that the king and his advisors have freely given to the God of Israel, whose dwelling is in Jerusalem, ¹⁶ together with all the silver and gold you may obtain from the province of Babylon, as well as the freewill offerings of the people and priests for the temple of their God in Jerusalem. ¹⁷ With this money be sure to buy bulls, rams and male lambs, together with their grain offerings and drink offerings, and sacrifice them on the altar of the temple of your God in Jerusalem.

¹⁸ You and your fellow Israelites may then do whatever seems best with the rest of the silver and gold, in accordance with the will of your God. ¹⁹ Deliver to the God of Jerusalem all the articles entrusted to you for worship in the temple of your God. ²⁰ And anything else needed for the temple of your God that you are responsible to supply, you may provide from the royal treasury.

²¹ Now I, King Artaxerxes, decree that all the treasurers of Trans-Euphrates are to provide with diligence whatever Ezra the priest, the teacher of the Law of the God of heaven, may ask of you – ²² up to a hundred talents*a* of silver, a hundred cors*b* of wheat, a hundred baths*c* of wine, a hundred baths*c* of olive oil, and salt without limit. ²³ Whatever the God of heaven has prescribed, let it be done with diligence for the temple of the God of heaven. Why should his wrath fall on the realm of the king and of his sons? ²⁴ You are also to know that you have no authority to impose taxes, tribute or duty on any of the priests, Levites, musicians, gatekeepers, temple servants or other workers at this house of God.

²⁵ And you, Ezra, in accordance with the wisdom of your God, which you possess, appoint magistrates and judges to administer justice to all the people of Trans-Euphrates – all who know the laws of your God. And you are to teach any who do not know them. ²⁶ Whoever does not obey the law of your God and the law of the king must surely be punished by death, banishment, confiscation of property, or imprisonment.*d*

²⁷ Praise be to the Lᴏʀᴅ, the God of our ancestors, who has put it into the king's heart to bring honour to the house of the Lᴏʀᴅ in Jerusalem in this way ²⁸ and who has extended his good favour to me before the king and his advisors and all the king's powerful officials. Because the hand of the Lᴏʀᴅ my God was on me, I took courage and gathered leaders from Israel to go up with me.

List of the family heads returning with Ezra

8 These are the family heads and those registered with them who came up with me from Babylon during the reign of King Artaxerxes:

² of the descendants of Phinehas, Gershom;
of the descendants of Ithamar, Daniel;
of the descendants of David, Hattush ³ of the descendants of Shekaniah;

of the descendants of Parosh, Zechariah, and with him were registered 150 men;
⁴ of the descendants of Pahath-Moab, Eliehoenai son of Zerahiah, and with him 200 men;
⁵ of the descendants of Zattu,*a* Shekaniah son of Jahaziel, and with him 300 men;

---

a 22 That is, about 3.4 metric tons
b 22 That is, probably about 16 metric tons
c 22 That is, about 2,200 litres

d 26 The text of 7:12-26 is in Aramaic.
a 5 Some Septuagint manuscripts (also 1 Esdras 8:32); Hebrew does not have *Zattu*.

6 of the descendants of Adin, Ebed son of Jonathan, and with him 50 men;

7 of the descendants of Elam, Jeshaiah son of Athaliah, and with him 70 men;

8 of the descendants of Shephatiah, Zebadiah son of Michael, and with him 80 men;

9 of the descendants of Joab, Obadiah son of Jehiel, and with him 218 men;

10 of the descendants of Bani,*b* Shelomith son of Josiphiah, and with him 160 men;

11 of the descendants of Bebai, Zechariah son of Bebai, and with him 28 men;

12 of the descendants of Azgad, Johanan son of Hakkatan, and with him 110 men;

13 of the descendants of Adonikam, the last ones, whose names were Eliphelet, Jeuel and Shemaiah, and with them 60 men;

14 of the descendants of Bigvai, Uthai and Zakkur, and with them 70 men.

The return to Jerusalem

15 I assembled them at the canal that flows towards Ahava, and we camped there three days. When I checked among the people and the priests, I found no Levites there. **16** So I summoned Eliezer, Ariel, Shemaiah, Elnathan, Jarib, Elnathan, Nathan, Zechariah and Meshullam, who were leaders, and Joiarib and Elnathan, who were men of learning, **17** and I ordered them to go to Iddo, the leader in Kasiphia. I told them what to say to Iddo and his fellow Levites, the temple servants in Kasiphia, so that they might bring attendants to us for the house of our God. **18** Because the gracious hand of our God was on us, they brought us Sherebiah, a capable man, from the descendants of Mahli son of Levi, the son of Israel, and Sherebiah's sons and brothers, 18 in all;

19 and Hashabiah, together with Jeshaiah from the descendants of Merari, and his brothers and nephews, 20 men in all. **20** They also brought 220 of the temple servants – a body that David and the officials had established to assist the Levites. All were registered by name.

21 There, by the Ahava Canal, I proclaimed a fast, so that we might humble ourselves before our God and ask him for a safe journey for us and our children, with all our possessions. **22** I was ashamed to ask the king for soldiers and horsemen to protect us from enemies on the road, because we had told the king, 'The gracious hand of our God is on everyone who looks to him, but his great anger is against all who forsake him.' **23** So we fasted and petitioned our God about this, and he answered our prayer.

24 Then I set apart twelve of the leading priests, namely, Sherebiah, Hashabiah and ten of their brothers, **25** and I weighed out to them the offering of silver and gold and the articles that the king, his advisors, his officials and all Israel present there had donated for the house of our God. **26** I weighed out to them 650 talents*c* of silver, silver articles weighing 100 talents,*d* 100 talents*d* of gold, **27** 20 bowls of gold valued at 1,000 darics,*e* and two fine articles of polished bronze, as precious as gold.

28 I said to them, 'You as well as these articles are consecrated to the LORD. The silver and gold are a freewill offering to the LORD, the God of your ancestors. **29** Guard them carefully until you weigh them out in the chambers of the house of the LORD in Jerusalem before the leading priests and the Levites and the family heads of Israel.' **30** Then the priests and Levites received the silver and gold and sacred articles that had been weighed out to be taken to the house of our God in Jerusalem.

31 On the twelfth day of the first month we set out from the Ahava Canal to go to Jerusalem. The hand of our God was on us, and he protected us from enemies and

---

b 10 Some Septuagint manuscripts (also 1 Esdras 8:36); Hebrew does not have *Bani*.

c 26 That is, about 22 metric tons
d 26 That is, about 3.4 metric tons
e 27 That is, about 8.4 kilograms

bandits along the way. 32So we arrived in Jerusalem, where we rested three days.

33On the fourth day, in the house of our God, we weighed out the silver and gold and the sacred articles into the hands of Meremoth son of Uriah, the priest. Eleazar son of Phinehas was with him, and so were the Levites Jozabad son of Jeshua and Noadiah son of Binnui. 34Everything was accounted for by number and weight, and the entire weight was recorded at that time.

35Then the exiles who had returned from captivity sacrificed burnt offerings to the God of Israel: twelve bulls for all Israel, ninety-six rams, seventy-seven male lambs and, as a sin offering,f twelve male goats. All this was a burnt offering to the LORD. 36They also delivered the king's orders to the royal satraps and to the governors of Trans-Euphrates, who then gave assistance to the people and to the house of God.

Ezra's prayer about intermarriage

9 After these things had been done, the leaders came to me and said, 'The people of Israel, including the priests and the Levites, have not kept themselves separate from the neighbouring peoples with their detestable practices, like those of the Canaanites, Hittites, Perizzites, Jebusites, Ammonites, Moabites, Egyptians and Amorites. 2They have taken some of their daughters as wives for themselves and their sons, and have mingled the holy race with the peoples around them. And the leaders and officials have led the way in this unfaithfulness.'

3When I heard this, I tore my tunic and cloak, pulled hair from my head and beard and sat down appalled. 4Then everyone who trembled at the words of the God of Israel gathered round me because of this unfaithfulness of the exiles. And I sat there appalled until the evening sacrifice.

5Then, at the evening sacrifice, I rose from my self-abasement, with my tunic and cloak torn, and fell on my knees with my hands spread out to the LORD my God 6and prayed:

'I am too ashamed and disgraced, my God, to lift up my face to you, because our sins are higher than our heads and our guilt has reached to the heavens. 7From the days of our ancestors until now, our guilt has been great. Because of our sins, we and our kings and our priests have been subjected to the sword and captivity, to pillage and humiliation at the hand of foreign kings, as it is today.

8'But now, for a brief moment, the LORD our God has been gracious in leaving us a remnant and giving us a firm placea in his sanctuary, and so our God gives light to our eyes and a little relief in our bondage. 9Though we are slaves, our God has not forsaken us in our bondage. He has shown us kindness in the sight of the kings of Persia: he has granted us new life to rebuild the house of our God and repair its ruins, and he has given us a wall of protection in Judah and Jerusalem.

10'But now, our God, what can we say after this? For we have forsaken the commands 11you gave through your servants the prophets when you said: "The land you are entering to possess is a land polluted by the corruption of its peoples. By their detestable practices they have filled it with their impurity from one end to the other. 12Therefore, do not give your daughters in marriage to their sons or take their daughters for your sons. Do not seek a treaty of friendship with them at any time, that you may be strong and eat the good things of the land and leave it to your children as an everlasting inheritance."

13'What has happened to us is a result of our evil deeds and our great

---

f 35 Or purification offering   a 8 Or a foothold

guilt, and yet, our God, you have punished us less than our sins have deserved and have given us a remnant like this. ¹⁴Shall we then break your commands again and intermarry with the peoples who commit such detestable practices? Would you not be angry enough with us to destroy us, leaving us no remnant or survivor? ¹⁵LORD, the God of Israel, you are righteous! We are left this day as a remnant. Here we are before you in our guilt, though because of it not one of us can stand in your presence.'

The people's confession of sin

10 While Ezra was praying and confessing, weeping and throwing himself down before the house of God, a large crowd of Israelites – men, women and children – gathered round him. They too wept bitterly. ²Then Shekaniah son of Jehiel, one of the descendants of Elam, said to Ezra, 'We have been unfaithful to our God by marrying foreign women from the peoples around us. But in spite of this, there is still hope for Israel. ³Now let us make a covenant before our God to send away all these women and their children, in accordance with the counsel of my lord and of those who fear the commands of our God. Let it be done according to the Law. ⁴Rise up; this matter is in your hands. We will support you, so take courage and do it.'

⁵So Ezra rose up and put the leading priests and Levites and all Israel under oath to do what had been suggested. And they took the oath. ⁶Then Ezra withdrew from before the house of God and went to the room of Jehohanan son of Eliashib. While he was there, he ate no food and drank no water, because he continued to mourn over the unfaithfulness of the exiles.

⁷A proclamation was then issued throughout Judah and Jerusalem for all the exiles to assemble in Jerusalem. ⁸Anyone who failed to appear within three days would forfeit all his property, in accordance with the decision of the officials

and elders, and would himself be expelled from the assembly of the exiles.

⁹Within the three days, all the men of Judah and Benjamin had gathered in Jerusalem. And on the twentieth day of the ninth month, all the people were sitting in the square before the house of God, greatly distressed by the occasion and because of the rain. ¹⁰Then Ezra the priest stood up and said to them, 'You have been unfaithful; you have married foreign women, adding to Israel's guilt. ¹¹Now honour*ᵃ* the LORD, the God of your ancestors, and do his will. Separate yourselves from the peoples around you and from your foreign wives.'

¹²The whole assembly responded with a loud voice: 'You are right! We must do as you say. ¹³But there are many people here and it is the rainy season; so we cannot stand outside. Besides, this matter cannot be taken care of in a day or two, because we have sinned greatly in this thing. ¹⁴Let our officials act for the whole assembly. Then let everyone in our towns who has married a foreign woman come at a set time, along with the elders and judges of each town, until the fierce anger of our God in this matter is turned away from us.' ¹⁵Only Jonathan son of Asahel and Jahzeiah son of Tikvah, supported by Meshullam and Shabbethai the Levite, opposed this.

¹⁶So the exiles did as was proposed. Ezra the priest selected men who were family heads, one from each family division, and all of them designated by name. On the first day of the tenth month they sat down to investigate the cases, ¹⁷and by the first day of the first month they finished dealing with all the men who had married foreign women.

Those guilty of intermarriage

¹⁸Among the descendants of the priests, the following had married foreign women:

From the descendants of Joshua son of Jozadak, and his brothers

---
ᵃ 11 Or Now make confession to

Maaseiah, Eliezer, Jarib and Gedaliah. 19(They all gave their hands in pledge to put away their wives, and for their guilt they each presented a ram from the flock as a guilt offering.)
20 From the descendants of Immer:
Hanani and Zebadiah.
21 From the descendants of Harim:
Maaseiah, Elijah, Shemaiah, Jehiel and Uzziah.
22 From the descendants of Pashhur:
Elioenai, Maaseiah, Ishmael, Nethanel, Jozabad and Elasah.

23 Among the Levites:

Jozabad, Shimei, Kelaiah (that is Kelita), Pethahiah, Judah and Eliezer.
24 From the musicians:
Eliashib.
From the gatekeepers:
Shallum, Telem and Uri.

25 And among the other Israelites:

From the descendants of Parosh:
Ramiah, Izziah, Malkijah, Mijamin, Eleazar, Malkijah and Benaiah.
26 From the descendants of Elam:
Mattaniah, Zechariah, Jehiel, Abdi, Jeremoth and Elijah.
27 From the descendants of Zattu:
Elioenai, Eliashib, Mattaniah, Jeremoth, Zabad and Aziza.
28 From the descendants of Bebai:
Jehohanan, Hananiah, Zabbai and Athlai.

29 From the descendants of Bani:
Meshullam, Malluk, Adaiah, Jashub, Sheal and Jeremoth.
30 From the descendants of Pahath-Moab:
Adna, Kelal, Benaiah, Maaseiah, Mattaniah, Bezalel, Binnui and Manasseh.
31 From the descendants of Harim:
Eliezer, Ishijah, Malkijah, Shemaiah, Shimeon, 32 Benjamin, Malluk and Shemariah.
33 From the descendants of Hashum:
Mattenai, Mattattah, Zabad, Eliphelet, Jeremai, Manasseh and Shimei.
34 From the descendants of Bani:
Maadai, Amram, Uel, 35 Benaiah, Bedeiah, Keluhi, 36 Vaniah, Meremoth, Eliashib, 37 Mattaniah, Mattenai and Jaasu.
38 From the descendants of Binnui:b
Shimei, 39 Shelemiah, Nathan, Adaiah, 40 Maknadebai, Shashai, Sharai, 41 Azarel, Shelemiah, Shemariah, 42 Shallum, Amariah and Joseph.
43 From the descendants of Nebo:
Jeiel, Mattithiah, Zabad, Zebina, Jaddai, Joel and Benaiah.

44 All these had married foreign women, and some of them had children by these wives.c

---

b 37,38 See Septuagint (also 1 Esdras 9:34); Hebrew Jaasu 38and Bani and Binnui,
c 44 Or and they sent them away with their children

NEHEMIAH

DATE

Events in Ezra, Nehemiah and Esther cover almost 100 years, between 538 and 433 BC

AUTHOR

Unknown

WHAT'S IT ALL ABOUT?

Nehemiah worked for the government of Persia, but his heart was still with his people who had returned to Jerusalem. Greatly distressed to hear that they had found their city in ruins, he fasted and prayed, calling out to God before asking his boss, the king, if he could return to his people. When he returned to Jerusalem he began rebuilding the walls around the city. This gave Jerusalem protection from anyone who might try to attack and Nehemiah got everyone involved in the work. Upon its completion the people gathered and asked to hear the law of God, and so Ezra read to them. Although they began to weep at first, Ezra called them to rejoice in the sacred day. The nation was led to repentance for its mistakes, they confessed the faithfulness of God to his people and committed themselves to following his ways. But before the book ends we see that they had already slipped back into some of their old habits.

WHY SHOULD WE READ IT?

- Originally the books of Ezra and Nehemiah were one document, so it is worth reading them both together.

- It demonstrates the importance of prayer and action together (especially Nehemiah 1).

- To see that Nehemiah was a leader who was not interested in his position within the king's court, but whose passion was God and the continuation of his people.

- To see how everyone played their part in the rebuilding of the wall, both men and women of different professions, from perfume-makers to goldsmiths (Nehemiah 3).

- To hear about Nehemiah's stand against injustice (Nehemiah 5).

- To remember how God was faithful even though the people had sinned again and again (Nehemiah 9).

Andy Croft with Liza Hoeksma

Nehemiah's prayer

1 The words of Nehemiah son of Hakaliah:

In the month of Kislev in the twentieth year, while I was in the citadel of Susa, ²Hanani, one of my brothers, came from Judah with some other men, and I questioned them about the Jewish remnant that had survived the exile, and also about Jerusalem.

³They said to me, 'Those who survived the exile and are back in the province are in great trouble and disgrace. The wall of Jerusalem is broken down, and its gates have been burned with fire.'

⁴When I heard these things, I sat down and wept. For some days I mourned and fasted and prayed before the God of heaven. ⁵Then I said:

'LORD, the God of heaven, the great and awesome God, who keeps his covenant of love with those who love him and keep his commandments, ⁶let your ear be attentive and your eyes open to hear the prayer your servant is praying before you day and night for your servants, the people of Israel. I confess the sins we Israelites, including myself and my father's family, have committed against you. ⁷We have acted very wickedly towards you. We have not obeyed the commands, decrees and laws you gave your servant Moses.

⁸'Remember the instruction you gave your servant Moses, saying, "If you are unfaithful, I will scatter you among the nations, ⁹but if you return to me and obey my commands, then even if your exiled people are at the farthest horizon, I will gather them from there and bring them to the place I have chosen as a dwelling for my Name."

¹⁰'They are your servants and your people, whom you redeemed by your great strength and your mighty hand. ¹¹Lord, let your ear be attentive to the prayer of this your servant and to the prayer of your servants who delight in revering your name. Give your servant success today by granting him favour in the presence of this man.'

I was cupbearer to the king.

Artaxerxes sends Nehemiah to Jerusalem

2 In the month of Nisan in the twentieth year of King Artaxerxes, when wine was brought for him, I took the wine and gave it to the king. I had not been sad in his presence before, ²so the king asked me, 'Why does your face look so sad when you are not ill? This can be nothing but sadness of heart.'

I was very much afraid, ³but I said to the king, 'May the king live for ever! Why should my face not look sad when the city where my ancestors are buried lies in ruins, and its gates have been destroyed by fire?'

⁴The king said to me, 'What is it you want?'

Then I prayed to the God of heaven, ⁵and I answered the king, 'If it pleases the king and if your servant has found favour in his sight, let him send me to the city in Judah where my ancestors are buried so that I can rebuild it.'

⁶Then the king, with the queen sitting beside him, asked me, 'How long will your journey take, and when will you get back?' It pleased the king to send me; so I set a time.

⁷I also said to him, 'If it pleases the king, may I have letters to the governors of Trans-Euphrates, so that they will provide me safe-conduct until I arrive in Judah? ⁸And may I have a letter to Asaph, keeper of the royal park, so he will give me timber to make beams for the gates of the citadel by the temple and for the city wall and for the residence I will occupy?' And because the gracious hand of my God was on me, the king granted my requests. ⁹So I went to the governors of Trans-Euphrates and gave them the king's letters. The king had also sent army officers and cavalry with me.

¹⁰When Sanballat the Horonite and

Tobiah the Ammonite official heard about this, they were very much disturbed that someone had come to promote the welfare of the Israelites.

Nehemiah inspects Jerusalem's walls

11 I went to Jerusalem, and after staying there three days 12 I set out during the night with a few others. I had not told anyone what my God had put in my heart to

do for Jerusalem. There were no mounts with me except the one I was riding on.

13 By night I went out through the Valley Gate towards the Jackal*a* Well and the Dung Gate, examining the walls of Jerusalem, which had been broken down, and its gates, which had been destroyed by fire. 14 Then I moved on towards the

_____

a 13 Or *Serpent* or *Fig*

PRAYER 4

PRAYING THE NEWS

When you watch the news on TV, or listen to it on the radio, or read it on the web, does it make you smile? Or does it make you furious? Does it make you pray?

Nehemiah received a terrible, shocking report about the state of the city of Jerusalem and the people of God there (1:3). He immediately turned to the Lord in prayer. And what a prayer! He cried for days and even fasted (1:4) to show God how serious he was.

There are three big themes in Nehemiah's prayer. First he says *sorry* – sorry for all that we, your people, have done wrong. Then he asks the Lord to *remember* – remember your promises that when people get praying you will restore them. Finally he pleads, saying *please listen* – 'Let your ear be attentive' to these prayers (1:11).

The thing I like about Nehemiah is that he's praying about major issues relating to international affairs, yet he still expects his prayers to make a difference in his life, *today* (1:11). He is so confident that God is on the case that he makes plans to talk to the king. Nehemiah serves the king as a cupbearer – a very important role which involves spending time with the king every day. Speaking to the king is an extremely dangerous thing for a mere cupbearer to do, however, so Nehemiah is *'very much afraid'* (2:2). Kings have their own agenda and expect servants to do their jobs and not interrupt with political opinions or requests for a holiday to sort out things at home (2:5).

So what about you? What's on the news feed today? What has grabbed your mind or your heart? How is it going to make you pray? What are you going to do about the situation, and what do you need the Lord to do? What do you expect will happen? Does it make you afraid, or has the time of prayer you have had left you feeling that the Lord will come through for you?

Hugo Anson

 Acts 12:1–19   Matthew 18:18–20 ▶

Fountain Gate and the King's Pool, but there was not enough room for my mount to get through; [15] so I went up the valley by night, examining the wall. Finally, I turned back and re-entered through the Valley Gate. [16] The officials did not know where I had gone or what I was doing, because as yet I had said nothing to the Jews or the priests or nobles or officials or any others who would be doing the work.

[17] Then I said to them, 'You see the trouble we are in: Jerusalem lies in ruins, and its gates have been burned with fire. Come, let us rebuild the wall of Jerusalem, and we will no longer be in disgrace.' [18] I also told them about the gracious hand of my God on me and what the king had said to me.

They replied, 'Let us start rebuilding.' So they began this good work.

[19] But when Sanballat the Horonite, Tobiah the Ammonite official and Geshem the Arab heard about it, they mocked and ridiculed us. 'What is this you are doing?' they asked. 'Are you rebelling against the king?'

[20] I answered them by saying, 'The God of heaven will give us success. We his servants will start rebuilding, but as for you, you have no share in Jerusalem or any claim or historic right to it.'

Builders of the wall

3 Eliashib the high priest and his fellow priests went to work and rebuilt the Sheep Gate. They dedicated it and set its doors in place, building as far as the Tower of the Hundred, which they dedicated, and as far as the Tower of Hananel. [2] The men of Jericho built the adjoining section, and Zakkur son of Imri built next to them.

[3] The Fish Gate was rebuilt by the sons of Hassenaah. They laid its beams and put its doors and bolts and bars in place. [4] Meremoth son of Uriah, the son of Hakkoz, repaired the next section. Next to him Meshullam son of Berekiah, the son of Meshezabel, made repairs, and next to him Zadok son of Baana also made repairs. [5] The next section was repaired by the men of Tekoa, but their nobles would not put their shoulders to the work under their supervisors. [a]

[6] The Jeshanah[b] Gate was repaired by Joiada son of Paseah and Meshullam son of Besodeiah. They laid its beams and put its doors with their bolts and bars in place. [7] Next to them, repairs were made by men from Gibeon and Mizpah – Melatiah of Gibeon and Jadon of Meronoth – places under the authority of the governor of Trans-Euphrates. [8] Uzziel son of Harhaiah, one of the goldsmiths, repaired the next section; and Hananiah, one of the perfume-makers, made repairs next to that. They restored Jerusalem as far as the Broad Wall. [9] Rephaiah son of Hur, ruler of a half-district of Jerusalem, repaired the next section. [10] Adjoining this, Jedaiah son of Harumaph made repairs opposite his house, and Hattush son of Hashabneiah made repairs next to him. [11] Malkijah son of Harim and Hasshub son of Pahath-Moab repaired another section and the Tower of the Ovens. [12] Shallum son of Hallohesh, ruler of a half-district of Jerusalem, repaired the next section with the help of his daughters.

[13] The Valley Gate was repaired by Hanun and the residents of Zanoah. They rebuilt it and put its doors with their bolts and bars in place. They also repaired a thousand cubits[c] of the wall as far as the Dung Gate.

[14] The Dung Gate was repaired by Malkijah son of Rekab, ruler of the district of Beth Hakkerem. He rebuilt it and put its doors with their bolts and bars in place.

[15] The Fountain Gate was repaired by Shallun son of Kol-Hozeh, ruler of the district of Mizpah. He rebuilt it, roofing it over and putting its doors and bolts and bars in place. He also repaired the wall of

---

a 5 Or *their Lord* or *the governor*
b 6 Or *Old*
c 13 That is, about 450 metres

the Pool of Siloam,ᵈ by the King's Garden, as far as the steps going down from the City of David. ¹⁶Beyond him, Nehemiah son of Azbuk, ruler of a half-district of Beth Zur, made repairs up to a point opposite the tombsᵉ of David, as far as the artificial pool and the House of the Heroes.

¹⁷Next to him, the repairs were made by the Levites under Rehum son of Bani. Beside him, Hashabiah, ruler of half the district of Keilah, carried out repairs for his district. ¹⁸Next to him, the repairs were made by their fellow Levites under Binnuiʄson of Henadad, ruler of the other half-district of Keilah. ¹⁹Next to him, Ezer son of Jeshua, ruler of Mizpah, repaired another section, from a point facing the ascent to the armoury as far as the angle of the wall. ²⁰Next to him, Baruch son of Zabbai zealously repaired another section, from the angle to the entrance of the house of Eliashib the high priest. ²¹Next to him, Meremoth son of Uriah, the son of Hakkoz, repaired another section, from the entrance of Eliashib's house to the end of it.

²²The repairs next to him were made by the priests from the surrounding region. ²³Beyond them, Benjamin and Hasshub made repairs in front of their house; and next to them, Azariah son of Maaseiah, the son of Ananiah, made repairs beside his house. ²⁴Next to him, Binnui son of Henadad repaired another section, from Azariah's house to the angle and the corner, ²⁵and Palal son of Uzai worked opposite the angle and the tower projecting from the upper palace near the court of the guard. Next to him, Pedaiah son of Parosh ²⁶and the temple servants living on the hill of Ophel made repairs up to a point opposite the Water Gate towards the east and the projecting tower. ²⁷Next to them, the men of Tekoa repaired another section, from the great projecting tower to the wall of Ophel.

²⁸Above the Horse Gate, the priests made repairs, each in front of his own house. ²⁹Next to them, Zadok son of Immer made repairs opposite his house. Next to him, Shemaiah son of Shekaniah, the guard at the East Gate, made repairs. ³⁰Next to him, Hananiah son of Shelemiah, and Hanun, the sixth son of Zalaph, repaired another section. Next to them, Meshullam son of Berekiah made repairs opposite his living quarters. ³¹Next to him, Malkijah, one of the goldsmiths, made repairs as far as the house of the temple servants and the merchants, opposite the Inspection Gate, and as far as the room above the corner; ³²and between the room above the corner and the Sheep Gate the goldsmiths and merchants made repairs.

Opposition to the rebuilding

4ᵃ When Sanballat heard that we were rebuilding the wall, he became angry and was greatly incensed. He ridiculed the Jews, ²and in the presence of his associates and the army of Samaria, he said, 'What are those feeble Jews doing? Will they restore their wall? Will they offer sacrifices? Will they finish in a day? Can they bring the stones back to life from those heaps of rubble – burned as they are?'

³Tobiah the Ammonite, who was at his side, said, 'What they are building – even a fox climbing up on it would break down their wall of stones!'

⁴Hear us, our God, for we are despised. Turn their insults back on their own heads. Give them over as plunder in a land of captivity. ⁵Do not cover up their guilt or blot out their sins from your sight, for they have thrown insults in the face ofᵇ the builders.

ᵈ 15 Hebrew *Shelah*, a variant of *Shiloah*, that is, Siloam
ᵉ 16 Hebrew; Septuagint, some Vulgate manuscripts and Syriac *tomb*
ʄ 18 Two Hebrew manuscripts and Syriac (see also Septuagint and verse 24); most Hebrew manuscripts *Bavvai*

ᵃ In Hebrew texts 4:1-6 is numbered 3:33-38, and 4:7-23 is numbered 4:1-17.
ᵇ 5 Or *have aroused your anger before*

6 So we rebuilt the wall till all of it reached half its height, for the people worked with all their heart.

7 But when Sanballat, Tobiah, the Arabs, the Ammonites and the people of Ashdod heard that the repairs to Jerusalem's walls had gone ahead and that the gaps were being closed, they were very angry. 8 They all plotted together to come and fight against Jerusalem and stir up trouble against it. 9 But we prayed to our God and posted a guard day and night to meet this threat.

10 Meanwhile, the people in Judah said, 'The strength of the labourers is giving out, and there is so much rubble that we cannot rebuild the wall.'

11 Also our enemies said, 'Before they know it or see us, we will be right there among them and will kill them and put an end to the work.'

12 Then the Jews who lived near them came and told us ten times over, 'Wherever you turn, they will attack us.'

13 Therefore I stationed some of the people behind the lowest points of the wall at the exposed places, posting them by families, with their swords, spears and bows. 14 After I looked things over, I stood up and said to the nobles, the officials and the rest of the people, 'Don't be afraid of them. Remember the Lord, who is great and awesome, and fight for your families, your sons and your daughters, your wives and your homes.'

15 When our enemies heard that we were aware of their plot and that God had frustrated it, we all returned to the wall, each to our work.

16 From that day on, half of my men did the work, while the other half were equipped with spears, shields, bows and armour. The officers posted themselves behind all the people of Judah 17 who were building the wall. Those who carried materials did their work with one hand and held a weapon in the other, 18 and each of the builders wore his sword at his side as he worked. But the man who sounded the trumpet stayed with me.

19 Then I said to the nobles, the officials and the rest of the people, 'The work is extensive and spread out, and we are widely separated from each other along the wall. 20 Wherever you hear the sound of the trumpet, join us there. Our God will fight for us!'

21 So we continued the work with half the men holding spears, from the first light of dawn till the stars came out. 22 At that time I also said to the people, 'Let every man and his helper stay inside Jerusalem at night, so that they can serve us as guards by night and as workers by day.' 23 Neither I nor my brothers nor my men nor the guards with me took off our clothes; each had his weapon, even when he went for water.c

Nehemiah helps the poor

5 Now the men and their wives raised a great outcry against their fellow Jews. 2 Some were saying, 'We and our sons and daughters are numerous; in order for us to eat and stay alive, we must get grain.'

3 Others were saying, 'We are mortgaging our fields, our vineyards and our homes to get grain during the famine.'

4 Still others were saying, 'We have had to borrow money to pay the king's tax on our fields and vineyards. 5 Although we are of the same flesh and blood as our fellow Jews and though our children are as good as theirs, yet we have to subject our sons and daughters to slavery. Some of our daughters have already been enslaved, but we are powerless, because our fields and our vineyards belong to others.'

6 When I heard their outcry and these charges, I was very angry. 7 I pondered them in my mind and then accused the nobles and officials. I told them, 'You are charging your own people interest!' So I called together a large meeting to deal with them 8 and said: 'As far as possible, we have bought back our fellow Jews who were sold to the Gentiles. Now you are selling your own people, only for them to be sold back to us!' They kept quiet, because they could find nothing to say.

9 So I continued, 'What you are doing is not right. Shouldn't you walk in the fear of

---

c 23 The meaning of the Hebrew for this clause is uncertain.

our God to avoid the reproach of our Gentile enemies? ¹⁰ I and my brothers and my men are also lending the people money and grain. But let us stop charging interest! ¹¹ Give back to them immediately their fields, vineyards, olive groves and houses, and also the interest you are charging them – one per cent of the money, grain, new wine and olive oil.'

¹² 'We will give it back,' they said. 'And we will not demand anything more from them. We will do as you say.'

Then I summoned the priests and made the nobles and officials take an oath to do what they had promised. ¹³ I also shook out the folds of my robe and said, 'In this way may God shake out of their house and possessions anyone who does not keep this promise. So may such a person be shaken out and emptied!'

At this the whole assembly said, 'Amen,' and praised the LORD. And the people did as they had promised.

¹⁴ Moreover, from the twentieth year of King Artaxerxes, when I was appointed to be their governor in the land of Judah, until his thirty-second year – twelve years – neither I nor my brothers ate the food allotted to the governor. ¹⁵ But the earlier governors – those preceding me – placed a heavy burden on the people and took forty shekels^a of silver from them in addition to food and wine. Their assistants also lorded it over the people. But out of reverence for God I did not act like that. ¹⁶ Instead, I devoted myself to the work on this wall. All my men were assembled there for the work; we^b did not acquire any land.

¹⁷ Furthermore, a hundred and fifty Jews and officials ate at my table, as well as those who came to us from the surrounding nations. ¹⁸ Each day one ox, six choice sheep and some poultry were prepared for me, and every ten days an abundant supply of wine of all kinds. In spite of all this, I never demanded the food allotted

to the governor, because the demands were heavy on these people.

¹⁹ Remember me with favour, my God, for all I have done for these people.

Further opposition to the rebuilding

6 When word came to Sanballat, Tobiah, Geshem the Arab and the rest of our enemies that I had rebuilt the wall and not a gap was left in it – though up to that time I had not set the doors in the gates – ² Sanballat and Geshem sent me this message: 'Come, let us meet together in one of the villages^a on the plain of Ono.'

But they were scheming to harm me; ³ so I sent messengers to them with this reply: 'I am carrying on a great project and cannot go down. Why should the work stop while I leave it and go down to you?' ⁴ Four times they sent me the same message, and each time I gave them the same answer.

⁵ Then, the fifth time, Sanballat sent his assistant to me with the same message, and in his hand was an unsealed letter ⁶ in which was written:

'It is reported among the nations – and Geshem^b says it is true – that you and the Jews are plotting to revolt, and therefore you are building the wall. Moreover, according to these reports you are about to become their king ⁷ and have even appointed prophets to make this proclamation about you in Jerusalem: "There is a king in Judah!" Now this report will get back to the king; so come, let us meet together.'

⁸ I sent him this reply: 'Nothing like what you are saying is happening; you are just making it up out of your head.'

⁹ They were all trying to frighten us, thinking, 'Their hands will get too weak for the work, and it will not be completed.'

But I prayed, 'Now strengthen my hands.'

---

a 15 That is, about 460 grams
b 16 Most Hebrew manuscripts; some Hebrew manuscripts, Septuagint, Vulgate and Syriac I

a 2 Or *in Kephirim*
b 6 Hebrew *Gashmu*, a variant of *Geshem*

10 One day I went to the house of Shemaiah son of Delaiah, the son of Mehetabel, who was shut in at his home. He said, 'Let us meet in the house of God, inside the temple, and let us close the temple doors, because men are coming to kill you – by night they are coming to kill you.' 11 But I said, 'Should a man like me run away? Or should someone like me go into the temple to save his life? I will not go!' 12 I realised that God had not sent him, but that he had prophesied against me because Tobiah and Sanballat had hired him. 13 He had been hired to intimidate me so that I would commit a sin by doing this, and then they would give me a bad name to discredit me.

14 Remember Tobiah and Sanballat, my God, because of what they have done; remember also the prophet Noadiah and how she and the rest of the prophets have been trying to intimidate me. 15 So the wall was completed on the twenty-fifth of Elul, in fifty-two days.

Opposition to the completed wall

16 When all our enemies heard about this, all the surrounding nations were afraid and lost their self-confidence, because they realised that this work had been done with the help of our God. 17 Also, in those days the nobles of Judah were sending many letters to Tobiah, and replies from Tobiah kept coming to them. 18 For many in Judah were under oath to him, since he was son-in-law to Shekaniah son of Arah, and his son Jehohanan had married the daughter of Meshullam son of Berekiah. 19 Moreover, they kept reporting to me his good deeds and then telling him what I said. And Tobiah sent letters to intimidate me.

7 After the wall had been rebuilt and I had set the doors in place, the gatekeepers, the musicians and the Levites were appointed. 2 I put in charge of Jerusalem my brother Hanani, along with Hananiah the commander of the citadel, because he was a man of integrity and feared God more than most people do. 3 I said to them, 'The gates of Jerusalem

are not to be opened until the sun is hot. While the gatekeepers are still on duty, make them shut the doors and bar them. Also appoint residents of Jerusalem as guards, some at their posts and some near their own houses.'

The list of the exiles who returned

4 Now the city was large and spacious, but there were few people in it, and the houses had not yet been rebuilt. 5 So my God put it into my heart to assemble the nobles, the officials and the common people for registration by families. I found the genealogical record of those who had been the first to return. This is what I found written there:

6 These are the people of the province who came up from the captivity of the exiles whom Nebuchadnezzar king of Babylon had taken captive (they returned to Jerusalem and Judah, each to his own town, 7 in company with Zerubbabel, Joshua, Nehemiah, Azariah, Raamiah, Nahamani, Mordecai, Bilshan, Mispereth, Bigvai, Nehum and Baanah):

The list of the men of Israel:

8 the descendants of Parosh	2,172
9 of Shephatiah	372
10 of Arah	652
11 of Pahath-Moab (through the line of Joshua and Joab)	2,818
12 of Elam	1,254
13 of Zattu	845
14 of Zakkai	760
15 of Binnui	648
16 of Bebai	628
17 of Azgad	2,322
18 of Adonikam	667
19 of Bigvai	2,067
20 of Adin	655
21 of Ater (through Hezekiah)	98
22 of Hashum	328
23 of Bezai	324
24 of Hariph	112
25 of Gibeon	95

26 the men of Bethlehem and
    Netophah   188
27 of Anathoth   128
28 of Beth Azmaveth   42
29 of Kiriath Jearim, Kephirah
    and Beeroth   743
30 of Ramah and Geba   621
31 of Mikmash   122
32 of Bethel and Ai   123
33 of the other Nebo   52
34 of the other Elam   1,254
35 of Harim   320
36 of Jericho   345
37 of Lod, Hadid and Ono   721
38 of Senaah   3,930

39 The priests:

    the descendants of Jedaiah
    (through the family of
    Jeshua)   973
40 of Immer   1,052
41 of Pashhur   1,247
42 of Harim   1,017

43 The Levites:

    the descendants of Jeshua
    (through Kadmiel through
    the line of Hodaviah)   74

44 The musicians:

    the descendants of Asaph   148

45 The gatekeepers:

    the descendants of
    Shallum, Ater, Talmon,
    Akkub, Hatita and Shobai   138

46 The temple servants:

    the descendants of
    Ziha, Hasupha, Tabbaoth,
47 Keros, Sia, Padon,
48 Lebana, Hagaba, Shalmai,
49 Hanan, Giddel, Gahar,
50 Reaiah, Rezin, Nekoda,
51 Gazzam, Uzza, Paseah,
52 Besai, Meunim, Nephussim,
53 Bakbuk, Hakupha, Harhur,

54 Bazluth, Mehida, Harsha,
55 Barkos, Sisera, Temah,
56 Neziah and Hatipha

YOU WHAT?
THE STRANGEST PEOPLE NAMES

○ **NETOPHATHITES**
1 Chronicles 2:54; 9:16; Nehemiah 12:28
ne-tof'-a-thites
○ **JERAHMEELITES**
1 Samuel 30:29
je-ra'-me-al-ites
○ **KERETHITES**
2 Samuel 15:18
ke-re-thites
○ **ZORATHITES AND ESHTAOLITES**
1 Chronicles 2:52–53
zo'-rath-ites, eshta-u'-lites
○ **UZZIELITES**
Numbers 3:27
uz-EE-al-ites

57 The descendants of the servants of
Solomon:

    the descendants of
    Sotai, Sophereth, Perida,
58 Jaala, Darkon, Giddel,
59 Shephatiah, Hattil,
    Pokereth-Hazzebaim and Amon

60 The temple servants and the
    descendants of the servants of
    Solomon   392

61 The following came up from
the towns of Tel Melah, Tel Harsha,
Kerub, Addon and Immer, but they
could not show that their families
were descended from Israel:

62 the descendants of
Delaiah, Tobiah and
Nekoda   642

63 And from among the priests:

the descendants of
Hobaiah, Hakkoz and Barzillai
(a man who had married
a daughter of Barzillai the
Gileadite and was called by that
name).
64 These searched for their family records, but they could not find
them and so were excluded from the
priesthood as unclean. 65 The governor, therefore, ordered them not to
eat any of the most sacred food until
there should be a priest ministering
with the Urim and Thummim.

66 The whole company numbered
42,360, 67 besides their 7,337 male
and female slaves; and they also had
245 male and female singers. 68 There
were 736 horses, 245 mules,a 69 435
camels and 6,720 donkeys.

70 Some of the heads of the families contributed to the work. The
governor gave to the treasury 1,000
daricsb of gold, 50 bowls and 530
garments for priests. 71 Some of the
heads of the families gave to the
treasury for the work 20,000 daricsc
of gold and 2,200 minasd of silver.
72 The total given by the rest of the
people was 20,000 darics of gold,
2,000 minase of silver and 67 garments for priests.
73 The priests, the Levites, the gatekeepers, the musicians and the temple servants, along with certain of
the people and the rest of the Israelites, settled in their own towns.

Ezra reads the Law

When the seventh month came and the
8 Israelites had settled in their towns,
1 all the people came together as one
in the square before the Water Gate. They
told Ezra the teacher of the Law to bring
out the Book of the Law of Moses, which
the LORD had commanded for Israel.
2 So on the first day of the seventh
month Ezra the priest brought the Law
before the assembly, which was made up
of men and women and all who were able
to understand. 3 He read it aloud from
daybreak till noon as he faced the square
before the Water Gate in the presence of
the men, women and others who could
understand. And all the people listened
attentively to the Book of the Law.
4 Ezra the teacher of the Law stood on a
high wooden platform built for the occasion. Beside him on his right stood Mattithiah, Shema, Anaiah, Uriah, Hilkiah and
Maaseiah; and on his left were Pedaiah,
Mishael, Malkijah, Hashum, Hashbadda-
nah, Zechariah and Meshullam.
5 Ezra opened the book. All the people could see him because he was standing above them; and as he opened it, the
people all stood up. 6 Ezra praised the
LORD, the great God; and all the people
lifted their hands and responded, 'Amen!
Amen!' Then they bowed down and worshipped the LORD with their faces to the
ground.
7 The Levites – Jeshua, Bani, Sherebiah,
Jamin, Akkub, Shabbethai, Hodiah, Maaseiah, Kelita, Azariah, Jozabad, Hanan
and Pelaiah – instructed the people in
the Law while the people were standing
there. 8 They read from the Book of the
Law of God, making it cleara and giving
the meaning so that the people understood what was being read.
9 Then Nehemiah the governor, Ezra the
priest and teacher of the Law, and the Levites who were instructing the people said
to them all, 'This day is holy to the LORD
your God. Do not mourn or weep.' For all
the people had been weeping as they listened to the words of the Law.

---

a 68 Some Hebrew manuscripts (see also Ezra 2:66);
most Hebrew manuscripts do not have this verse.
b 70 That is, about 8.4 kilograms
c 71 That is, about 170 kilograms; also in verse 72
d 71 That is, about 1.2 metric tons
e 72 That is, about 1.1 metric tons

---

a 8 Or God, translating it

¹⁰Nehemiah said, 'Go and enjoy choice food and sweet drinks, and send some to those who have nothing prepared. This day is holy to our Lord. Do not grieve, for the joy of the LORD is your strength.'

¹¹The Levites calmed all the people, saying, 'Be still, for this is a holy day. Do not grieve.'

¹²Then all the people went away to eat and drink, to send portions of food and to celebrate with great joy, because they now understood the words that had been made known to them.

¹³On the second day of the month, the heads of all the families, along with the priests and the Levites, gathered round Ezra the teacher of the Law to give attention to the words of the Law. ¹⁴They found written in the Law, which the LORD had commanded through Moses, that the Israelites were to live in temporary shelters during the festival of the seventh month ¹⁵and that they should proclaim this word and spread it throughout their towns and in Jerusalem: 'Go out into the hill country and bring back branches from olive and wild olive trees, and from myrtles, palms and other leafy trees, to make temporary shelters' – as it is written.*ᵇ*

¹⁶So the people went out and brought back branches and built themselves temporary shelters on their own roofs, in their courtyards, in the courts of the house of God and in the square by the Water Gate and the one by the Gate of Ephraim. ¹⁷The whole company that had returned from exile built temporary shelters and lived in them. From the days of Joshua son of Nun until that day, the Israelites had not celebrated it like this. And their joy was very great.

¹⁸Day after day, from the first day to the last, Ezra read from the Book of the Law of God. They celebrated the festival for seven days, and on the eighth day, in accordance with the regulation, there was an assembly.

The Israelites confess their sins

9 On the twenty-fourth day of the same month, the Israelites gathered together, fasting and wearing sackcloth and putting dust on their heads. ²Those of Israelite descent had separated themselves from all foreigners. They stood in their places and confessed their sins and the sins of their ancestors. ³They stood where they were and read from the Book of the Law of the LORD their God for a quarter of the day, and spent another quarter in confession and in worshipping the LORD their God. ⁴Standing on the stairs of the Levites were Jeshua, Bani, Kadmiel, Shebaniah, Bunni, Sherebiah, Bani and Kenani. They cried out with loud voices to the LORD their God. ⁵And the Levites – Jeshua, Kadmiel, Bani, Hashabneiah, Sherebiah, Hodiah, Shebaniah and Pethahiah – said: 'Stand up and praise the LORD your God, who is from everlasting to everlasting.*ᵃ*'

'Blessed be your glorious name, and may it be exalted above all blessing and praise. ⁶You alone are the LORD. You made the heavens, even the highest heavens, and all their starry host, the earth and all that is on it, the seas and all that is in them. You give life to everything, and the multitudes of heaven worship you.

⁷'You are the LORD God, who chose Abram and brought him out of Ur of the Chaldeans and named him Abraham. ⁸You found his heart faithful to you, and you made a covenant with him to give to his descendants the land of the Canaanites, Hittites, Amorites, Perizzites, Jebusites and Girgashites. You have kept your promise because you are righteous.

⁹'You saw the suffering of our ancestors in Egypt; you heard their cry at the Red Sea.*ᵇ* ¹⁰You sent signs and wonders against Pharaoh, against all his officials and all the people of his land, for you knew how arrogantly

---

ᵇ 15 See Lev. 23:37-40.

ᵃ 5 Or God for ever and ever
ᵇ 9 Or the Sea of Reeds

the Egyptians treated them. You made a name for yourself, which remains to this day. [11] You divided the sea before them, so that they passed through it on dry ground, but you hurled their pursuers into the depths, like a stone into mighty waters. [12] By day you led them with a pillar of cloud, and by night with a pillar of fire to give them light on the way they were to take.

[13] 'You came down on Mount Sinai; you spoke to them from heaven. You gave them regulations and laws that are just and right, and decrees and commands that are good. [14] You made known to them your holy Sabbath and gave them commands, decrees and laws through your servant Moses. [15] In their hunger you gave them bread from heaven and in their thirst you brought them water from the rock; you told them to go in and take possession of the land you had sworn with uplifted hand to give them.

[16] 'But they, our ancestors, became arrogant and stiff-necked, and they did not obey your commands. [17] They refused to listen and failed to remember the miracles you performed among them. They became stiff-necked and in their rebellion appointed a leader in order to return to their slavery. But you are a forgiving God, gracious and compassionate, slow to anger and abounding in love. Therefore you did not desert them, [18] even when they cast for themselves an image of a calf and said, "This is your god, who brought you up out of Egypt," or when they committed awful blasphemies.

[19] 'Because of your great compassion you did not abandon them in the wilderness. By day the pillar of cloud did not fail to guide them on their path, nor the pillar of fire by night to shine on the way they were to take. [20] You gave your good Spirit to instruct them. You did not withhold your manna from their mouths, and

you gave them water for their thirst. [21] For forty years you sustained them in the wilderness; they lacked nothing, their clothes did not wear out nor did their feet become swollen.

[22] 'You gave them kingdoms and nations, allotting to them even the remotest frontiers. They took over the country of Sihon[c] king of Heshbon and the country of Og king of Bashan. [23] You made their children as numerous as the stars in the sky, and you brought them into the land that you told their parents to enter and possess. [24] Their children went in and took possession of the land. You subdued before them the Canaanites, who lived in the land; you gave the Canaanites into their hands, along with their kings and the peoples of the land, to deal with them as they pleased. [25] They captured fortified cities and fertile land; they took possession of houses filled with all kinds of good things, wells already dug, vineyards, olive groves and fruit trees in abundance. They ate to the full and were well-nourished; they revelled in your great goodness.

[26] 'But they were disobedient and rebelled against you; they turned their backs on your law. They killed your prophets, who had warned them in order to turn them back to you; they committed awful blasphemies. [27] So you delivered them into the hands of their enemies, who oppressed them. But when they were oppressed they cried out to you. From heaven you heard them, and in your great compassion you gave them deliverers, who rescued them from the hand of their enemies.

[28] 'But as soon as they were at rest, they again did what was evil in your sight. Then you abandoned them to the hand of their enemies so that they ruled over them. And when they

---

c 22 One Hebrew manuscript and Septuagint; most Hebrew manuscripts *Sihon, that is, the country of the* cried out to you again, you heard from heaven, and in your compassion you delivered them time after time.

29 'You warned them in order to turn them back to your law, but they became arrogant and disobeyed your commands. They sinned against your ordinances, of which you said, "The person who obeys them will live by them." Stubbornly they turned their backs on you, became stiff-necked and refused to listen. 30 For many years you were patient with them. By your Spirit you warned them through your prophets. Yet they paid no attention, so you gave them into the hands of the neighbouring peoples. 31 But in your great mercy you did not put an end to them or abandon them, for you are a gracious and merciful God.

32 'Now therefore, our God, the great God, mighty and awesome, who keeps his covenant of love, do not let all this hardship seem trifling in your eyes – the hardship that has come on us, on our kings and leaders, on our priests and prophets, on our ancestors and all your people, from the days of the kings of Assyria until today. 33 In all that has happened to us, you have remained righteous; you have acted faithfully, while we acted wickedly. 34 Our kings, our leaders, our priests and our ancestors did not follow your law; they did not pay attention to your commands or the statutes you warned them to keep. 35 Even while they were in their kingdom, enjoying your great goodness to them in the spacious and fertile land you gave them, they did not serve you or turn from their evil ways.

36 'But see, we are slaves today, slaves in the land you gave our ancestors so that they could eat its fruit and the other good things it produces. 37 Because of our sins, its abundant harvest goes to the kings you have placed over us. They rule over our bodies and our cattle as they please. We are in great distress.

The agreement of the people

38 'In view of all this, we are making a binding agreement, putting it in writing, and our leaders, our Levites and our priests are affixing their seals to it.'*d*

10 *a* Those who sealed it were:

Nehemiah the governor, the son of Hakaliah.

Zedekiah, 2 Seraiah, Azariah, Jeremiah,
3 Pashhur, Amariah, Malkijah,
4 Hattush, Shebaniah, Malluk,
5 Harim, Meremoth, Obadiah,
6 Daniel, Ginnethon, Baruch,
7 Meshullam, Abijah, Mijamin,
8 Maaziah, Bilgai and Shemaiah.
These were the priests.

9 The Levites:

Jeshua son of Azaniah, Binnui of the sons of Henadad, Kadmiel,
10 and their associates: Shebaniah, Hodiah, Kelita, Pelaiah, Hanan,
11 Mika, Rehob, Hashabiah,
12 Zakkur, Sherebiah, Shebaniah,
13 Hodiah, Bani and Beninu.

14 The leaders of the people:

Parosh, Pahath-Moab, Elam, Zattu, Bani,
15 Bunni, Azgad, Bebai,
16 Adonijah, Bigvai, Adin,
17 Ater, Hezekiah, Azzur,
18 Hodiah, Hashum, Bezai,
19 Hariph, Anathoth, Nebai,
20 Magpiash, Meshullam, Hezir,
21 Meshezabel, Zadok, Jaddua,
22 Pelatiah, Hanan, Anaiah,
23 Hoshea, Hananiah, Hasshub,

---

d 38 In Hebrew texts this verse (9:38) is numbered 10:1.
a In Hebrew texts 10:1-39 is numbered 10:2-40.

24 Hallohesh, Pilha, Shobek,
25 Rehum, Hashabnah, Maaseiah,
26 Ahiah, Hanan, Anan,
27 Malluk, Harim and Baanah.

28 'The rest of the people – priests, Levites, gatekeepers, musicians, temple servants and all who separated themselves from the neighbouring peoples for the sake of the Law of God, together with their wives and all their sons and daughters who are able to understand – 29 all these now join their fellow Israelites the nobles, and bind themselves with a curse and an oath to follow the Law of God given through Moses the servant of God and to obey carefully all the commands, regulations and decrees of the LORD our Lord.

30 'We promise not to give our daughters in marriage to the peoples around us or take their daughters for our sons.

31 'When the neighbouring peoples bring merchandise or grain to sell on the Sabbath, we will not buy from them on the Sabbath or on any holy day. Every seventh year we will forgo working the land and will cancel all debts.

32 'We assume the responsibility for carrying out the commands to give a third of a shekel[b] each year for the service of the house of our God: 33 for the bread set out on the table; for the regular grain offerings and burnt offerings; for the offerings on the Sabbaths, at the New Moon feasts and at the appointed festivals; for the holy offerings; for sin offerings[c] to make atonement for Israel; and for all the duties of the house of our God.

34 'We – the priests, the Levites and the people – have cast lots to determine when each of our families is to bring to the house of our God at set times each year a contribution of wood to burn on the altar of the LORD our God, as it is written in the Law.

35 'We also assume responsibility for bringing to the house of the LORD each year the firstfruits of our crops and of every fruit tree.

36 'As it is also written in the Law, we will bring the firstborn of our sons and of our cattle, of our herds and of our flocks to the house of our God, to the priests ministering there.

37 'Moreover, we will bring to the storerooms of the house of our God, to the priests, the first of our ground meal, of our grain offerings, of the fruit of all our trees and of our new wine and olive oil. And we will bring a tithe of our crops to the Levites, for it is the Levites who collect the tithes in all the towns where we work. 38 A priest descended from Aaron is to accompany the Levites when they receive the tithes, and the Levites are to bring a tenth of the tithes up to the house of our God, to the storerooms of the treasury. 39 The people of Israel, including the Levites, are to bring their contributions of grain, new wine and olive oil to the storerooms, where the articles for the sanctuary and for the ministering priests, the gatekeepers and the musicians are also kept.

'We will not neglect the house of our God.'

The new residents of Jerusalem

11 Now the leaders of the people settled in Jerusalem. The rest of the people cast lots to bring one out of every ten of them to live in Jerusalem, the holy city, while the remaining nine were to stay in their own towns. 2 The people commended all who volunteered to live in Jerusalem.

3 These are the provincial leaders who settled in Jerusalem (now some Israelites, priests, Levites, temple servants and descendants of Solomon's servants lived in the towns of Judah, each on their own property in the various towns, 4 while

---

b 32 That is, about 4 grams
c 33 Or *purification offerings*

other people from both Judah and Benjamin lived in Jerusalem):

From the descendants of Judah:

Athaiah son of Uzziah, the son of Zechariah, the son of Amariah, the son of Shephatiah, the son of Mahalalel, a descendant of Perez; **5**and Maaseiah son of Baruch, the son of Kol-Hozeh, the son of Hazaiah, the son of Adaiah, the son of Joiarib, the son of Zechariah, a descendant of Shelah. **6**The descendants of Perez who lived in Jerusalem totalled 468 men of standing.

FAVOURITE VERSES

Ephesians 2:6

And God raised us up with Christ and seated us with him in the heavenly realms in Christ Jesus.

- -

This, to me, is an amazing verse that speaks of the grace of God to unite us with Jesus in everything he did through his death and resurrection. We have the privilege of giving our lives to something that's bigger than we could ever know. The fact that we are currently seated with Christ in heavenly realms gives us his perspective. We need never wonder what God is thinking or be unsure of what to do: we are seated in the control room of creation, the heavenly realms!

Michael McGlynn

7From the descendants of Benjamin:

Sallu son of Meshullam, the son of Joed, the son of Pedaiah, the son of

Kolaiah, the son of Maaseiah, the son of Ithiel, the son of Jeshaiah, **8**and his followers, Gabbai and Sallai – 928 men. **9**Joel son of Zikri was their chief officer, and Judah son of Hassenuah was over the New Quarter of the city.

10From the priests:

Jedaiah; the son of Joiarib; Jakin; **11**Seraiah son of Hilkiah, the son of Meshullam, the son of Zadok, the son of Meraioth, the son of Ahitub, the official in charge of the house of God, **12**and their associates, who carried on work for the temple – 822 men; Adaiah son of Jeroham, the son of Pelaliah, the son of Amzi, the son of Zechariah, the son of Pashhur, the son of Malkijah, **13**and his associates, who were heads of families – 242 men; Amashsai son of Azarel, the son of Ahzai, the son of Meshillemoth, the son of Immer, **14**and his*ᵃ* associates, who were men of standing – 128. Their chief officer was Zabdiel son of Haggedolim.

15From the Levites:

Shemaiah son of Hasshub, the son of Azrikam, the son of Hashabiah, the son of Bunni; **16**Shabbethai and Jozabad, two of the heads of the Levites, who had charge of the outside work of the house of God; **17**Mattaniah son of Mika, the son of Zabdi, the son of Asaph, the director who led in thanksgiving and prayer; Bakbukiah, second among his associates; and Abda son of Shammua, the son of Galal, the son of Jeduthun. **18**The Levites in the holy city totalled 284.

19The gatekeepers:

Akkub, Talmon and their associates, who kept watch at the gates – 172 men.

---

a 14 Most Septuagint manuscripts; Hebrew *their*

20 The rest of the Israelites, with the priests and Levites, were in all the towns of Judah, each on their ancestral property.

21 The temple servants lived on the hill of Ophel, and Ziha and Gishpa were in charge of them.

22 The chief officer of the Levites in Jerusalem was Uzzi son of Bani, the son of Hashabiah, the son of Mattaniah, the son of Mika. Uzzi was one of Asaph's descendants, who were the musicians responsible for the service of the house of God. 23 The musicians were under the king's orders, which regulated their daily activity.

24 Pethahiah son of Meshezabel, one of the descendants of Zerah son of Judah, was the king's agent in all affairs relating to the people.

25 As for the villages with their fields, some of the people of Judah lived in Kiriath Arba and its surrounding settlements, in Dibon and its settlements, in Jekabzeel and its villages, 26 in Jeshua, in Moladah, in Beth Pelet, 27 in Hazar Shual, in Beersheba and its settlements, 28 in Ziklag, in Mekonah and its settlements, 29 in En Rimmon, in Zorah, in Jarmuth, 30 Zanoah, Adullam and their villages, in Lachish and its fields, and in Azekah and its settlements. So they were living all the way from Beersheba to the Valley of Hinnom.

31 The descendants of the Benjaminites from Geba lived in Mikmash, Aija, Bethel and its settlements, 32 in Anathoth, Nob and Ananiah, 33 in Hazor, Ramah and Gittaim, 34 in Hadid, Zeboim and Neballat, 35 in Lod and Ono, and in Ge Harashim.

36 Some of the divisions of the Levites of Judah settled in Benjamin.

Priests and Levites

12 These were the priests and Levites who returned with Zerubbabel son of Shealtiel and with Joshua:
Seraiah, Jeremiah, Ezra,
2 Amariah, Malluk, Hattush,
3 Shekaniah, Rehum, Meremoth,
4 Iddo, Ginnethon,[a] Abijah,
5 Mijamin,[b] Moadiah, Bilgah,
6 Shemaiah, Joiarib, Jedaiah,
7 Sallu, Amok, Hilkiah and Jedaiah.
These were the leaders of the priests and their associates in the days of Joshua.

8 The Levites were Jeshua, Binnui, Kadmiel, Sherebiah, Judah, and also Mattaniah, who, together with his associates, was in charge of the songs of thanksgiving. 9 Bakbukiah and Unni, their associates, stood opposite them in the services.

10 Joshua was the father of Joiakim, Joiakim the father of Eliashib, Eliashib the father of Joiada, 11 Joiada the father of Jonathan, and Jonathan the father of Jaddua.

12 In the days of Joiakim, these were the heads of the priestly families:
of Seraiah's family, Meraiah;
of Jeremiah's, Hananiah;
13 of Ezra's, Meshullam;
of Amariah's, Jehohanan;
14 of Malluk's, Jonathan;
of Shekaniah's,[c] Joseph;
15 of Harim's, Adna;
of Meremoth's,[d] Helkai;
16 of Iddo's, Zechariah;
of Ginnethon's, Meshullam;
17 of Abijah's, Zikri;
of Miniamin's and of Moadiah's, Piltai;
18 of Bilgah's, Shammua;
of Shemaiah's, Jehonathan;
19 of Joiarib's, Mattenai;
of Jedaiah's, Uzzi;
20 of Sallu's, Kallai;
of Amok's, Eber;
21 of Hilkiah's, Hashabiah;
of Jedaiah's, Nethanel.

22 The family heads of the Levites in the days of Eliashib, Joiada, Johanan and Jaddua, as well as those of the priests, were recorded in the reign of Darius the Persian. 23 The family heads among the descendants of Levi up to the time of Johanan son of Eliashib were recorded in the book of the annals. 24 And the leaders of

---

b 5 A variant of Miniamin
c 14 Very many Hebrew manuscripts, some Septuagint manuscripts and Syriac (see also verse 3); most Hebrew manuscripts Shebaniah's
d 15 Some Septuagint manuscripts (see also verse 3); Hebrew Meraioth's

the Levites were Hashabiah, Sherebiah, Jeshua son of Kadmiel, and their associates, who stood opposite them to give praise and thanksgiving, one section responding to the other, as prescribed by David the man of God.

25 Mattaniah, Bakbukiah, Obadiah, Meshullam, Talmon and Akkub were gatekeepers who guarded the storerooms at the gates. 26 They served in the days of Joiakim son of Joshua, the son of Jozadak, and in the days of Nehemiah the governor and of Ezra the priest, the teacher of the Law.

Dedication of the wall of Jerusalem

27 At the dedication of the wall of Jerusalem, the Levites were sought out from where they lived and were brought to Jerusalem to celebrate joyfully the dedication with songs of thanksgiving and with the music of cymbals, harps and lyres. 28 The musicians also were brought together from the region around Jerusalem – from the villages of the Netophathites, 29 from Beth Gilgal, and from the area of Geba and Azmaveth, for the musicians had built villages for themselves around Jerusalem. 30 When the priests and Levites had purified themselves ceremonially, they purified the people, the gates and the wall.

31 I had the leaders of Judah go up on top of e the wall. I also assigned two large choirs to give thanks. One was to proceed on top off the wall to the right, towards the Dung Gate. 32 Hoshaiah and half the leaders of Judah followed them, 33 along with Azariah, Ezra, Meshullam, 34 Judah, Benjamin, Shemaiah, Jeremiah, 35 as well as some priests with trumpets, and also Zechariah son of Jonathan, the son of Shemaiah, the son of Mattaniah, the son of Micaiah, the son of Zakkur, the son of Asaph, 36 and his associates – Shemaiah, Azarel, Milalai, Gilalai, Maai, Nethanel, Judah and Hanani – with musical instruments prescribed by David the man of God. Ezra the teacher of the Law led the procession. 37 At the Fountain Gate they continued directly up the steps of the City

of David on the ascent to the wall and passed above the site of David's palace to the Water Gate on the east.

38 The second choir proceeded in the opposite direction. I followed them on top of g the wall, together with half the people – past the Tower of the Ovens to the Broad Wall, 39 over the Gate of Ephraim, the Jeshanah h Gate, the Fish Gate, the Tower of Hananel and the Tower of the Hundred, as far as the Sheep Gate. At the Gate of the Guard they stopped.

40 The two choirs that gave thanks then took their places in the house of God; so did I, together with half the officials, 41 as well as the priests – Eliakim, Maaseiah, Miniamin, Micaiah, Elioenai, Zechariah and Hananiah with their trumpets – 42 and also Maaseiah, Shemaiah, Eleazar, Uzzi, Jehohanan, Malkijah, Elam and Ezer. The choirs sang under the direction of Jezrahiah. 43 And on that day they offered great sacrifices, rejoicing because God had given them great joy. The women and children also rejoiced. The sound of rejoicing in Jerusalem could be heard far away.

44 At that time men were appointed to be in charge of the storerooms for the contributions, firstfruits and tithes. From the fields around the towns they were to bring into the storerooms the portions required by the Law for the priests and the Levites, for Judah was pleased with the ministering priests and Levites. 45 They performed the service of their God and the service of purification, as did also the musicians and gatekeepers, according to the commands of David and his son Solomon. 46 For long ago, in the days of David and Asaph, there had been directors for the musicians and for the songs of praise and thanksgiving to God. 47 So in the days of Zerubbabel and of Nehemiah, all Israel contributed the daily portions for the musicians and the gatekeepers. They also set aside the portion for the other Levites, and the Levites set aside the portion for the descendants of Aaron.

---

e 31 Or go alongside
f 31 Or proceed alongside

g 38 Or them alongside
h 39 Or Old

Nehemiah's final reforms

13 On that day the Book of Moses was read aloud in the hearing of the people and there it was found written that no Ammonite or Moabite should ever be admitted into the assembly of God, ²because they had not met the Israelites with food and water but had hired Balaam to call a curse down on them. (Our God, however, turned the curse into a blessing.) ³When the people heard this law, they excluded from Israel all who were of foreign descent.

⁴Before this, Eliashib the priest had been put in charge of the storerooms of the house of our God. He was closely associated with Tobiah, ⁵and he had provided him with a large room formerly used to store the grain offerings and incense and temple articles, and also the tithes of grain, new wine and olive oil prescribed for the Levites, musicians and gatekeepers, as well as the contributions for the priests.

⁶But while all this was going on, I was not in Jerusalem, for in the thirty-second year of Artaxerxes king of Babylon I had returned to the king. Some time later I asked his permission ⁷and came back to Jerusalem. Here I learned about the evil thing Eliashib had done in providing Tobiah a room in the courts of the house of God. ⁸I was greatly displeased and threw all Tobiah's household goods out of the room. ⁹I gave orders to purify the rooms, and then I put back into them the equipment of the house of God, with the grain offerings and the incense.

¹⁰I also learned that the portions assigned to the Levites had not been given to them, and that all the Levites and musicians responsible for the service had gone back to their own fields. ¹¹So I rebuked the officials and asked them, 'Why is the house of God neglected?' Then I called them together and stationed them at their posts.

¹²All Judah brought the tithes of grain, new wine and olive oil into the storerooms. ¹³I put Shelemiah the priest, Zadok the scribe, and a Levite named Pedaiah in charge of the storerooms and made Hanan son of Zakkur, the son of Mattaniah, their assistant, because they were considered trustworthy. They were made responsible for distributing the supplies to their fellow Levites.

¹⁴Remember me for this, my God, and do not blot out what I have so faithfully done for the house of my God and its services.

¹⁵In those days I saw people in Judah treading winepresses on the Sabbath and bringing in grain and loading it on donkeys, together with wine, grapes, figs and all other kinds of loads. And they were bringing all this into Jerusalem on the Sabbath. Therefore I warned them against selling food on that day. ¹⁶People from Tyre who lived in Jerusalem were bringing in fish and all kinds of merchandise and selling them in Jerusalem on the Sabbath to the people of Judah. ¹⁷I rebuked the nobles of Judah and said to them, 'What is this wicked thing you are doing – desecrating the Sabbath day? ¹⁸Didn't your ancestors do the same things, so that our God brought all this calamity on us and on this city? Now you are stirring up more wrath against Israel by desecrating the Sabbath.'

¹⁹When evening shadows fell on the gates of Jerusalem before the Sabbath, I ordered the doors to be shut and not opened until the Sabbath was over. I stationed some of my own men at the gates so that no load could be brought in on the Sabbath day. ²⁰Once or twice the merchants and sellers of all kinds of goods spent the night outside Jerusalem. ²¹But I warned them and said, 'Why do you spend the night by the wall? If you do this again, I will arrest you.' From that time on they no longer came on the Sabbath. ²²Then I commanded the Levites to purify themselves and go and guard the gates in order to keep the Sabbath day holy.

Remember me for this also, my God, and show mercy to me according to your great love.

23 Moreover, in those days I saw men of Judah who had married women from Ashdod, Ammon and Moab. 24 Half of their children spoke the language of Ashdod or the language of one of the other peoples, and did not know how to speak the language of Judah. 25 I rebuked them and called curses down on them. I beat some of the men and pulled out their hair. I made them take an oath in God's name and said: 'You are not to give your daughters in marriage to their sons, nor are you to take their daughters in marriage for your sons or for yourselves. 26 Was it not because of marriages like these that Solomon king of Israel sinned? Among the many nations there was no king like him. He was loved by his God, and God made him king over all Israel, but even he was led into sin by foreign women. 27 Must we hear now that you too are doing all this terrible wickedness and are being unfaithful to our God by marrying foreign women?'

28 One of the sons of Joiada son of Eliashib the high priest was son-in-law to Sanballat the Horonite. And I drove him away from me.

29 Remember them, my God, because they defiled the priestly office and the covenant of the priesthood and of the Levites.

30 So I purified the priests and the Levites of everything foreign, and assigned them duties, each to his own task. 31 I also made provision for contributions of wood at designated times, and for the firstfruits.

Remember me with favour, my God.

ESTHER

DATE

The events in Esther happened sometime between 538 and 433 BC

AUTHOR

Unknown

WHAT'S IT ALL ABOUT?

While some of the Jews returned home to Jerusalem to rebuild the temple (see the book of Ezra), many remained in the provinces of the Persian Empire and Esther tells the story of how one man plotted to have these Jews killed. When King Xerxes's wife disobeyed him, he had her thrown out of court and looked for a replacement. After a search was made, a young and beautiful Jewish girl, Esther, was brought to him and made queen. Esther's uncle Mordecai advised her to keep her identity as a Jew secret, but when Mordecai uncovered a plot to kill all the Jewish people, he told Esther she must plead with the king for her people. The man intent on destroying the Jews was Haman, one of the king's men, who was angry that Mordecai wouldn't bow down to him. Esther risked her life to save her people, but she was successful – and although God's name isn't mentioned, it's clear that he hadn't abandoned his people, but had placed Esther in the right place at the right time to rescue his people.

WHY SHOULD WE READ IT?

- To see Esther's example of bravery in the way she risked her life to save the Jewish people (Esther 4).

- Because it's the only book of the Bible that doesn't mention God by name. Its story reminds us that even if we don't see God's hand in explicit ways, we can still see his fingerprints all over our lives, giving us hope and a purpose.

- To read how God brought justice for his people. Mordecai honoured God and although Haman plotted against him, Haman was hung on the very gallows he had prepared for his enemy (Esther 7).

Andy Croft with Liza Hoeksma

Queen Vashti deposed

1 This is what happened during the time of Xerxes,[a] the Xerxes who ruled over 127 provinces stretching from India to Cush[b]: ² at that time King Xerxes reigned from his royal throne in the citadel of Susa, ³ and in the third year of his reign he gave a banquet for all his nobles and officials. The military leaders of Persia and Media, the princes, and the nobles of the provinces were present.

⁴ For a full 180 days he displayed the vast wealth of his kingdom and the splendour and glory of his majesty. ⁵ When these days were over, the king gave a banquet, lasting seven days, in the enclosed garden of the king's palace, for all the people from the least to the greatest who were in the citadel of Susa. ⁶ The garden had hangings of white and blue linen, fastened with cords of white linen and purple material to silver rings on marble pillars. There were couches of gold and silver on a mosaic pavement of porphyry, marble, mother-of-pearl and other costly stones. ⁷ Wine was served in goblets of gold, each one different from the other, and the royal wine was abundant, in keeping with the king's liberality. ⁸ By the king's command each guest was allowed to drink without restriction, for the king instructed all the wine stewards to serve each man what he wished.

⁹ Queen Vashti also gave a banquet for the women in the royal palace of King Xerxes.

¹⁰ On the seventh day, when King Xerxes was in high spirits from wine, he commanded the seven eunuchs who served him – Mehuman, Biztha, Harbona, Bigtha, Abagtha, Zethar and Karkas – ¹¹ to bring before him Queen Vashti, wearing her royal crown, in order to display her beauty to the people and nobles, for she was lovely to look at. ¹² But when the attendants delivered the king's command, Queen Vashti refused to come. Then the king became furious and burned with anger.

¹³ Since it was customary for the king to consult experts in matters of law and justice, he spoke with the wise men who understood the times ¹⁴ and were closest to the king – Karshena, Shethar, Admatha, Tarshish, Meres, Marsena and Memukan, the seven nobles of Persia and Media who had special access to the king and were highest in the kingdom.

¹⁵ 'According to law, what must be done to Queen Vashti?' he asked. 'She has not obeyed the command of King Xerxes that the eunuchs have taken to her.'

¹⁶ Then Memukan replied in the presence of the king and the nobles, 'Queen Vashti has done wrong, not only against the king but also against all the nobles and the peoples of all the provinces of King Xerxes. ¹⁷ For the queen's conduct will become known to all the women, and so they will despise their husbands and say, "King Xerxes commanded Queen Vashti to be brought before him, but she would not come." ¹⁸ This very day the Persian and Median women of the nobility who have heard about the queen's conduct will respond to all the king's nobles in the same way. There will be no end of disrespect and discord.

¹⁹ 'Therefore, if it pleases the king, let him issue a royal decree and let it be written in the laws of Persia and Media, which cannot be repealed, that Vashti is never again to enter the presence of King Xerxes. Also let the king give her royal position to someone else who is better than she. ²⁰ Then when the king's edict is proclaimed throughout all his vast realm, all the women will respect their husbands, from the least to the greatest.'

²¹ The king and his nobles were pleased with this advice, so the king did as Memukan proposed. ²² He sent dispatches to all parts of the kingdom, to each province in its own script and to each people in their own language, proclaiming that every man should be ruler over his own household, using his native tongue.

Esther made queen

2 Later when King Xerxes' fury had subsided, he remembered Vashti and what she had done and what he had

---

a 1 Hebrew *Ahasuerus*; here and throughout Esther
b 1 That is, the upper Nile region

decreed about her. ²Then the king's personal attendants proposed, 'Let a search be made for beautiful young virgins for the king. ³Let the king appoint commissioners in every province of his realm to bring all these beautiful young women into the harem at the citadel of Susa. Let them be placed under the care of Hegai, the king's eunuch, who is in charge of the women; and let beauty treatments be given to them. ⁴Then let the young woman who pleases the king be queen instead of Vashti.' This advice appealed to the king, and he followed it.

⁵Now there was in the citadel of Susa a Jew of the tribe of Benjamin, named Mordecai son of Jair, the son of Shimei, the son of Kish, ⁶who had been carried into exile from Jerusalem by Nebuchadnezzar king of Babylon, among those taken captive with Jehoiachin*a* king of Judah. ⁷Mordecai had a cousin named Hadassah, whom he had brought up because she had neither father nor mother. This young woman, who was also known as Esther, had a lovely figure and was beautiful. Mordecai had taken her as his own daughter when her father and mother died.

⁸When the king's order and edict had been proclaimed, many young women were brought to the citadel of Susa and put under the care of Hegai. Esther also was taken to the king's palace and entrusted to Hegai, who had charge of the harem. ⁹She pleased him and won his favour. Immediately he provided her with her beauty treatments and special food. He assigned to her seven female attendants selected from the king's palace and moved her and her attendants into the best place in the harem.

¹⁰Esther had not revealed her nationality and family background, because Mordecai had forbidden her to do so. ¹¹Every day he walked to and fro near the courtyard of the harem to find out how Esther was and what was happening to her.

¹²Before a young woman's turn came to go in to King Xerxes, she had to complete twelve months of beauty treatments

prescribed for the women, six months with oil of myrrh and six with perfumes and cosmetics. ¹³And this is how she would go to the king: anything she wanted was given to her to take with her from the harem to the king's palace. ¹⁴In the evening she would go there and in the morning return to another part of the harem to the care of Shaashgaz, the king's eunuch who was in charge of the concubines. She would not return to the king unless he was pleased with her and summoned her by name.

¹⁵When the turn came for Esther (the young woman Mordecai had adopted, the daughter of his uncle Abihail) to go to the king, she asked for nothing other than what Hegai, the king's eunuch who was in charge of the harem, suggested. And Esther won the favour of everyone who saw her. ¹⁶She was taken to King Xerxes in the royal residence in the tenth month, the month of Tebeth, in the seventh year of his reign.

¹⁷Now the king was attracted to Esther more than to any of the other women, and she won his favour and approval more than any of the other virgins. So he set a royal crown on her head and made her queen instead of Vashti. ¹⁸And the king gave a great banquet, Esther's banquet, for all his nobles and officials. He proclaimed a holiday throughout the provinces and distributed gifts with royal liberality.

Mordecai uncovers a conspiracy

¹⁹When the virgins were assembled a second time, Mordecai was sitting at the king's gate. ²⁰But Esther had kept secret her family background and nationality just as Mordecai had told her to do, for she continued to follow Mordecai's instructions as she had done when he was bringing her up.

²¹During the time Mordecai was sitting at the king's gate, Bigthana*b* and Teresh, two of the king's officers who guarded the doorway, became angry and conspired to assassinate King Xerxes. ²²But Mordecai found out about the plot and told Queen

---

a 6 Hebrew *Jeconiah*, a variant of *Jehoiachin*   *b* 21 Hebrew *Bigthan*, a variant of *Bigthana*

Esther, who in turn reported it to the king, giving credit to Mordecai. 23 And when the report was investigated and found to be true, the two officials were impaled on poles. All this was recorded in the book of the annals in the presence of the king.

Haman's plot to destroy the Jews

3 After these events, King Xerxes honoured Haman son of Hammedatha, the Agagite, elevating him and giving him a seat of honour higher than that of all the other nobles. 2 All the royal officials at the king's gate knelt down and paid honour to Haman, for the king had commanded this concerning him. But Mordecai would not kneel down or pay him honour.

3 Then the royal officials at the king's gate asked Mordecai, 'Why do you disobey the king's command?' 4 Day after day they spoke to him but he refused to comply. Therefore they told Haman about it to see whether Mordecai's behaviour would be tolerated, for he had told them he was a Jew.

5 When Haman saw that Mordecai would not kneel down or pay him honour, he was enraged. 6 Yet having learned who Mordecai's people were, he scorned the idea of killing only Mordecai. Instead Haman looked for a way to destroy all Mordecai's people, the Jews, throughout the whole kingdom of Xerxes.

7 In the twelfth year of King Xerxes, in the first month, the month of Nisan, the *pur* (that is, the lot) was cast in the presence of Haman to select a day and month. And the lot fell on*a* the twelfth month, the month of Adar.

8 Then Haman said to King Xerxes, 'There is a certain people dispersed among the peoples in all the provinces of your kingdom who keep themselves separate. Their customs are different from those of all other people, and they do not obey the king's laws; it is not in the king's best interest to tolerate them. 9 If it pleases the king, let a decree be issued to destroy them, and I will give ten thousand

talents*b* of silver to the king's administrators for the royal treasury.'

10 So the king took his signet ring from his finger and gave it to Haman son of Hammedatha, the Agagite, the enemy of the Jews. 11 'Keep the money,' the king said to Haman, 'and do with the people as you please.'

12 Then on the thirteenth day of the first month the royal secretaries were summoned. They wrote out in the script of each province and in the language of each people all Haman's orders to the king's satraps, the governors of the various provinces and the nobles of the various peoples. These were written in the name of King Xerxes himself and sealed with his own ring. 13 Dispatches were sent by couriers to all the king's provinces with the order to destroy, kill and annihilate all the Jews – young and old, women and children – on a single day, the thirteenth day of the twelfth month, the month of Adar, and to plunder their goods. 14 A copy of the text of the edict was to be issued as law in every province and made known to the people of every nationality so that they would be ready for that day.

15 The couriers went out, spurred on by the king's command, and the edict was issued in the citadel of Susa. The king and Haman sat down to drink, but the city of Susa was bewildered.

Mordecai persuades Esther to help

4 When Mordecai learned of all that had been done, he tore his clothes, put on sackcloth and ashes, and went out into the city, wailing loudly and bitterly. 2 But he went only as far as the king's gate, because no one clothed in sackcloth was allowed to enter it. 3 In every province to which the edict and order of the king came, there was great mourning among the Jews, with fasting, weeping and wailing. Many lay in sackcloth and ashes.

4 When Esther's eunuchs and female attendants came and told her about Mordecai, she was in great distress. She sent

---

a 7 Septuagint; Hebrew does not have *And the lot fell on.*

b 9 That is, about 340 metric tons

clothes for him to put on instead of his sackcloth, but he would not accept them. ⁵Then Esther summoned Hathak, one of the king's eunuchs assigned to attend her, and ordered him to find out what was troubling Mordecai and why.

⁶So Hathak went out to Mordecai in the open square of the city in front of the king's gate. ⁷Mordecai told him everything that had happened to him, including the exact amount of money Haman had promised to pay into the royal treasury for the destruction of the Jews. ⁸He also gave him a copy of the text of the edict for their annihilation, which had been published in Susa, to show to Esther and explain it to her, and he told him to instruct her to go into the king's presence to beg for mercy and plead with him for her people.

⁹Hathak went back and reported to Esther what Mordecai had said. ¹⁰Then she instructed him to say to Mordecai, ¹¹'All the king's officials and the people of the royal provinces know that for any man or woman who approaches the king in the inner court without being summoned the king has but one law: that they be put to death unless the king extends the gold sceptre to them and spares their lives. But thirty days have passed since I was called to go to the king.'

¹²When Esther's words were reported to Mordecai, ¹³he sent back this answer: 'Do not think that because you are in the king's house you alone of all the Jews will escape. ¹⁴For if you remain silent at this time, relief and deliverance for the Jews will arise from another place, but you and your father's family will perish. And who knows but that you have come to your royal position for such a time as this?'

¹⁵Then Esther sent this reply to Mordecai: ¹⁶'Go, gather together all the Jews who are in Susa, and fast for me. Do not eat or drink for three days, night or day. I and my attendants will fast as you do. When this is done, I will go to the king, even though it is against the law. And if I perish, I perish.'

¹⁷So Mordecai went away and carried out all of Esther's instructions.

Esther's request to the king

5 On the third day Esther put on her royal robes and stood in the inner court of the palace, in front of the king's hall. The king was sitting on his royal throne in the hall, facing the entrance. ²When he saw Queen Esther standing in the court, he was pleased with her and held out to her the gold sceptre that was in his hand. So Esther approached and touched the tip of the sceptre.

³Then the king asked, 'What is it, Queen Esther? What is your request? Even up to half the kingdom, it will be given you.'

⁴'If it pleases the king,' replied Esther, 'let the king, together with Haman, come today to a banquet I have prepared for him.'

⁵'Bring Haman at once,' the king said, 'so that we may do what Esther asks.'

So the king and Haman went to the banquet Esther had prepared. ⁶As they were drinking wine, the king again asked Esther, 'Now what is your petition? It will be given you. And what is your request? Even up to half the kingdom, it will be granted.'

⁷Esther replied, 'My petition and my request is this: ⁸If the king regards me with favour and if it pleases the king to grant my petition and fulfil my request, let the king and Haman come tomorrow to the banquet I will prepare for them. Then I will answer the king's question.'

Haman's rage against Mordecai

⁹Haman went out that day happy and in high spirits. But when he saw Mordecai at the king's gate and observed that he neither rose nor showed fear in his presence, he was filled with rage against Mordecai. ¹⁰Nevertheless, Haman restrained himself and went home.

Calling together his friends and Zeresh, his wife, ¹¹Haman boasted to them about his vast wealth, his many sons, and all the ways the king had honoured him and how he had elevated him above the other nobles and officials. ¹²'And that's not all,' Haman added. 'I'm the only person Queen Esther invited to accompany the king to the banquet she gave. And she has invited me along with the king tomorrow. ¹³ But all this gives me no satisfaction as long as I see that Jew Mordecai sitting at the king's gate.'

¹⁴ His wife Zeresh and all his friends said to him, 'Have a pole set up, reaching to a height of fifty cubits,ᵃ and ask the king in the morning to have Mordecai impaled on it. Then go with the king to the banquet and enjoy yourself.' This suggestion delighted Haman, and he had the pole set up.

Mordecai honoured

6 That night the king could not sleep; so he ordered the book of the chronicles, the record of his reign, to be brought in and read to him. ² It was found recorded there that Mordecai had exposed Bigthana and Teresh, two of the king's officers who guarded the doorway, who had conspired to assassinate King Xerxes.

³ 'What honour and recognition has Mordecai received for this?' the king asked.

'Nothing has been done for him,' his attendants answered.

⁴ The king said, 'Who is in the court?' Now Haman had just entered the outer court of the palace to speak to the king about impaling Mordecai on the pole he had set up for him.

⁵ His attendants answered, 'Haman is standing in the court.'

'Bring him in,' the king ordered.

⁶ When Haman entered, the king asked him, 'What should be done for the man the king delights to honour?'

Now Haman thought to himself, 'Who is there that the king would rather honour than me?' ⁷ So he answered the king, 'For the man the king delights to honour, ⁸ let them bring a royal robe the king has worn and a horse the king has ridden, one with a royal crest placed on its head. ⁹ Then let the robe and horse be entrusted to one of the king's most noble princes. Let them robe the man the king delights to honour, and lead him on the horse through the city streets, proclaiming before him,

"This is what is done for the man the king delights to honour!" '

¹⁰ 'Go at once,' the king commanded Haman. 'Get the robe and the horse and do just as you have suggested for Mordecai the Jew, who sits at the king's gate. Do not neglect anything you have recommended.'

¹¹ So Haman got the robe and the horse. He robed Mordecai, and led him on horseback through the city streets, proclaiming before him, 'This is what is done for the man the king delights to honour!'

¹² Afterwards Mordecai returned to the king's gate. But Haman rushed home, with his head covered in grief, ¹³ and told Zeresh his wife and all his friends everything that had happened to him.

His advisors and his wife Zeresh said to him, 'Since Mordecai, before whom your downfall has started, is of Jewish origin, you cannot stand against him – you will surely come to ruin!' ¹⁴ While they were still talking with him, the king's eunuchs arrived and hurried Haman away to the banquet Esther had prepared.

Haman impaled

7 So the king and Haman went to Queen Esther's banquet, ² and as they were drinking wine on the second day, the king again asked, 'Queen Esther, what is your petition? It will be given you. What is your request? Even up to half the kingdom, it will be granted.'

³ Then Queen Esther answered, 'If I have found favour with you, Your Majesty, and if it pleases you, grant me my life – this is my petition. And spare my people – this is my request. ⁴ For I and my people have been sold to be destroyed, killed and annihilated. If we had merely been sold as male and female slaves, I would have kept quiet, because no such distress would justify disturbing the king.ᵃ'

⁵ King Xerxes asked Queen Esther, 'Who is he? Where is he – the man who has dared to do such a thing?'

ᵃ 14 That is, about 23 metres

ᵃ 4 Or quiet, but the compensation our adversary offers cannot be compared with the loss the king would suffer

6 Esther said, 'An adversary and enemy! This vile Haman!'

Then Haman was terrified before the king and queen. 7 The king got up in a rage, left his wine and went out into the palace garden. But Haman, realising that the king had already decided his fate, stayed behind to beg Queen Esther for his life.

8 Just as the king returned from the palace garden to the banqueting hall, Haman was falling on the couch where Esther was reclining.

The king exclaimed, 'Will he even molest the queen while she is with me in the house?'

As soon as the word left the king's mouth, they covered Haman's face. 9 Then Harbona, one of the eunuchs attending the king, said, 'A pole reaching to a height of fifty cubits[b] stands by Haman's house. He had it set up for Mordecai, who spoke up to help the king.'

The king said, 'Impale him on it!' 10 So they impaled Haman on the pole he had set up for Mordecai. Then the king's fury subsided.

The king's edict on behalf of the Jews

8 That same day King Xerxes gave Queen Esther the estate of Haman, the enemy of the Jews. And Mordecai came into the presence of the king, for Esther had told how he was related to her. 2 The king took off his signet ring, which he had reclaimed from Haman, and presented it to Mordecai. And Esther appointed him over Haman's estate.

3 Esther again pleaded with the king, falling at his feet and weeping. She begged him to put an end to the evil plan of Haman the Agagite, which he had devised against the Jews. 4 Then the king extended the gold sceptre to Esther and she arose and stood before him.

5 'If it pleases the king,' she said, 'and if he regards me with favour and thinks it the right thing to do, and if he is pleased with me, let an order be written overruling the dispatches that Haman son of Hammedatha, the Agagite, devised and wrote to destroy the Jews in all the king's provinces. 6 For how can I bear to see disaster fall on my people? How can I bear to see the destruction of my family?'

7 King Xerxes replied to Queen Esther and to Mordecai the Jew, 'Because Haman attacked the Jews, I have given his estate to Esther, and they have impaled him on the pole he set up. 8 Now write another decree in the king's name on behalf of the Jews as seems best to you, and seal it with the king's signet ring – for no document written in the king's name and sealed with his ring can be revoked.'

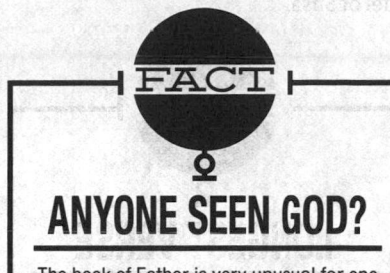

ANYONE SEEN GOD?

The book of Esther is very unusual for one particular reason: it's the only book of the Bible which doesn't mention God.

9 At once the royal secretaries were summoned – on the twenty-third day of the third month, the month of Sivan. They wrote out all Mordecai's orders to the Jews, and to the satraps, governors and nobles of the 127 provinces stretching from India to Cush.[a] These orders were written in the script of each province and the language of each people and also to the Jews in their own script and language. 10 Mordecai wrote in the name of King Xerxes, sealed the dispatches with the king's signet ring, and sent them by mounted couriers, who rode fast horses especially bred for the king.

11 The king's edict granted the Jews in every city the right to assemble and protect themselves; to destroy, kill and annihilate the armed men of any nationality or province who might attack them and

_____

b 9 That is, about 23 metres   **a** 9 That is, the upper Nile region their women and children,ᵇ and to plunder the property of their enemies. ¹²The day appointed for the Jews to do this in all the provinces of King Xerxes was the thirteenth day of the twelfth month, the month of Adar. ¹³A copy of the text of the edict was to be issued as law in every province and made known to the people of every nationality so that the Jews would be ready on that day to avenge themselves on their enemies.

¹⁴The couriers, riding the royal horses, went out, spurred on by the king's command, and the edict was issued in the citadel of Susa.

FACT

LONGEST VERSE

The longest single verse in the Bible is Esther 8:9, which runs to a whopping 72 words in the NIV (although it's only 43 words in the Hebrew).

The triumph of the Jews

¹⁵When Mordecai left the king's presence, he was wearing royal garments of blue and white, a large crown of gold and a purple robe of fine linen. And the city of Susa held a joyous celebration. ¹⁶For the Jews it was a time of happiness and joy, gladness and honour. ¹⁷In every province and in every city to which the edict of the king came, there was joy and gladness among the Jews, with feasting and celebrating. And many people of other nationalities became Jews because fear of the Jews had seized them.

9 On the thirteenth day of the twelfth month, the month of Adar, the edict commanded by the king was to be carried out. On this day the enemies of the

Jews had hoped to overpower them, but now the tables were turned and the Jews got the upper hand over those who hated them. ²The Jews assembled in their cities in all the provinces of King Xerxes to attack those determined to destroy them. No one could stand against them, because the people of all the other nationalities were afraid of them. ³And all the nobles of the provinces, the satraps, the governors and the king's administrators helped the Jews, because fear of Mordecai had seized them. ⁴Mordecai was prominent in the palace; his reputation spread throughout the provinces, and he became more and more powerful.

⁵The Jews struck down all their enemies with the sword, killing and destroying them, and they did what they pleased to those who hated them. ⁶In the citadel of Susa, the Jews killed and destroyed five hundred men. ⁷They also killed Parshandatha, Dalphon, Aspatha, ⁸Poratha, Adalia, Aridatha, ⁹Parmashta, Arisai, Aridai and Vaizatha, ¹⁰the ten sons of Haman son of Hammedatha, the enemy of the Jews. But they did not lay their hands on the plunder.

¹¹The number of those killed in the citadel of Susa was reported to the king that same day. ¹²The king said to Queen Esther, 'The Jews have killed and destroyed five hundred men and the ten sons of Haman in the citadel of Susa. What have they done in the rest of the king's provinces? Now what is your petition? It will be given you. What is your request? It will also be granted.'

¹³'If it pleases the king,' Esther answered, 'give the Jews in Susa permission to carry out this day's edict tomorrow also, and let Haman's ten sons be impaled on poles.'

¹⁴So the king commanded that this be done. An edict was issued in Susa, and they impaled the ten sons of Haman. ¹⁵The Jews in Susa came together on the fourteenth day of the month of Adar, and they put to death in Susa three hundred men, but they did not lay their hands on the plunder.

¹⁶Meanwhile, the remainder of the

---

b 11 Or *province, together with their women and children, who might attack them;*

Jews who were in the king's provinces also assembled to protect themselves and get relief from their enemies. They killed seventy-five thousand of them but did not lay their hands on the plunder. 17 This happened on the thirteenth day of the month of Adar, and on the fourteenth they rested and made it a day of feasting and joy.

18 The Jews in Susa, however, had assembled on the thirteenth and fourteenth, and then on the fifteenth they rested and made it a day of feasting and joy. 19 That is why rural Jews – those living in villages – observe the fourteenth of the month of Adar as a day of joy and feasting, a day for giving presents to each other.

Purim established

20 Mordecai recorded these events, and he sent letters to all the Jews throughout the provinces of King Xerxes, near and far, 21 that they should celebrate annually the fourteenth and fifteenth days of the month of Adar 22 as the time when the Jews got relief from their enemies, and as the month when their sorrow was turned into joy and their mourning into a day of celebration. He wrote to them to observe the days as days of feasting and joy and giving presents of food to one another and gifts to the poor.

23 So the Jews agreed to continue the celebration they had begun, doing what Mordecai had written to them. 24 For Haman son of Hammedatha, the Agagite, the enemy of all the Jews, had plotted against the Jews to destroy them and had cast the *pur* (that is, the lot) for their ruin and destruction. 25 But when the plot came to the king's attention,*a* he issued written orders that the evil scheme Haman had devised against the Jews should come back on to his own head, and that he and his sons should be impaled on

poles. 26 (Therefore these days were called Purim, from the word *pur*.) Because of everything written in this letter and because of what they had seen and what had happened to them, 27 the Jews took it on themselves to establish the custom that they and their descendants and all who join them should without fail observe these two days every year, in the way prescribed and at the time appointed. 28 These days should be remembered and observed in every generation by every family, and in every province and in every city. And these days of Purim should never fail to be celebrated by the Jews – nor should the memory of these days die out among their descendants.

29 So Queen Esther, daughter of Abihail, along with Mordecai the Jew, wrote with full authority to confirm this second letter concerning Purim. 30 And Mordecai sent letters to all the Jews in the 127 provinces of Xerxes's kingdom – words of goodwill and assurance – 31 to establish these days of Purim at their designated times, as Mordecai the Jew and Queen Esther had decreed for them, and as they had established for themselves and their descendants in regard to their times of fasting and lamentation. 32 Esther's decree confirmed these regulations about Purim, and it was written down in the records.

The greatness of Mordecai

10 King Xerxes imposed tribute throughout the empire, to its distant shores. 2 And all his acts of power and might, together with a full account of the greatness of Mordecai, whom the king had promoted, are they not written in the book of the annals of the kings of Media and Persia? 3 Mordecai the Jew was second in rank to King Xerxes, preeminent among the Jews, and held in high esteem by his many fellow Jews, because he worked for the good of his people and spoke up for the welfare of all the Jews.

---

a 25 Or *when Esther came before the king*

JOB

DATE

Unknown, but probably between 2000–1500 BC

AUTHOR

Unknown

WHAT'S IT ALL ABOUT?

Job is a book about one of life's key struggles: suffering. Job was a righteous man who worshipped God, but Satan believed he only loved God because of all that God had given him. So in one day Job lost almost everything. His cattle (a mark of his wealth and the means of his income) were wiped out and then all his children were killed in an accident. The book follows what happened in the wake of these tragedies as Job and his friends debated why such suffering came into Job's life. While his friends insisted that Job must have sinned (a commonly held belief of the day regarding pain), Job maintained that he had done nothing wrong. As readers, we have a unique perspective in that we see the conversation between God and Satan that Job and his mates knew nothing about. Job refused to turn his back on God and instead cried out to him, asking God to tell him why he had to suffer so much. Towards the end of the book we read God's response. His voice thundered from a storm as he told Job of his majesty and might. He may not have answered Job's questions directly (and as far as we know he never told him about the conversation with Satan), but Job was humbled and satisfied with the response; he knew that God had not abandoned him and he knew that God was good.

WHY SHOULD WE READ IT?

- To remember that we can't always see the full picture of what God is doing in our lives.

- To see Job's amazing response of worship to the disaster that came into his life (Job 1).

- To understand that it's OK to question God when we're going through hard times we don't understand.

- To read God's amazing response to Job's questions (Job 38 – 41).

Andy Croft with Liza Hoeksma

Prologue

1 In the land of Uz there lived a man whose name was Job. This man was blameless and upright; he feared God and shunned evil. ² He had seven sons and three daughters, ³ and he owned seven thousand sheep, three thousand camels, five hundred yoke of oxen and five hundred donkeys, and had a large number of servants. He was the greatest man among all the people of the East.

⁴ His sons used to hold feasts in their homes on their birthdays, and they would invite their three sisters to eat and drink with them. ⁵ When a period of feasting had run its course, Job would make arrangements for them to be purified. Early in the morning he would sacrifice a burnt offering for each of them, thinking, 'Perhaps my children have sinned and cursed God in their hearts.' This was Job's regular custom.

WORSHIP 9

A choice

What a mess. What an absolute, awful mess. There's really nothing else to say. It's just a mess. Job has lost everything.

Everything dear to him – it has all gone. His camels, his donkeys, all his servants. It has all gone. He has lost his family, his sons, his daughters. Job's whole life, his whole livelihood, all he holds dear, has been completely stripped from him in an instant.

Any kind of unanswered question is frustrating. Whether it's not knowing your plans for the weekend or simply not knowing what the time is – if you ask a question you feel is important, you want to know the answer. But when really messed-up stuff happens, knowing what the time is suddenly becomes the furthest thing from your mind and frustration doesn't even begin to describe how you feel. There are far bigger, more important questions that you need answering. 'Why did this happen to me?' 'Where's God in all this?' 'Doesn't he care?' But in the midst of all these questions, what does Job do? *'He fell to the ground in worship'* (Job 1:20).

In the midst of questions like these, worshipping God can be the hardest thing to do. When everything around you is crumbling, it's a hardcore choice to believe that God is with you and that he knows what he's doing. But this is worship. Worship is choosing to believe and declare that God is who he says he is. Worship is choosing to give your heart to him even when everyone else is telling you he's someone different.

When we're wrestling with some loaded questions, worship can really feel like a choice. Anyone can praise God when things are going great, but the real challenge is to worship when it feels as if we've lost everything. Let's bring God the most valuable kind of worship: songs of choice.

Beth Croft

 Hebrews 12:18–29   Amos 5:21–24

⁶One day the angels*ᵃ* came to present themselves before the LORD, and Satan*ᵇ* also came with them. ⁷The LORD said to Satan, 'Where have you come from?'

Satan answered the LORD, 'From roaming throughout the earth, going to and fro on it.'

⁸Then the LORD said to Satan, 'Have you considered my servant Job? There is no one on earth like him; he is blameless and upright, a man who fears God and shuns evil.'

⁹'Does Job fear God for nothing?' Satan replied. ¹⁰'Have you not put a hedge around him and his household and everything he has? You have blessed the work of his hands, so that his flocks and herds are spread throughout the land. ¹¹But now stretch out your hand and strike everything he has, and he will surely curse you to your face.'

¹²The LORD said to Satan, 'Very well, then, everything he has is in your power, but on the man himself do not lay a finger.'

Then Satan went out from the presence of the LORD.

¹³One day when Job's sons and daughters were feasting and drinking wine at the eldest brother's house, ¹⁴a messenger came to Job and said, 'The oxen were ploughing and the donkeys were grazing nearby, ¹⁵and the Sabeans attacked and made off with them. They put the servants to the sword, and I am the only one who has escaped to tell you!'

¹⁶While he was still speaking, another messenger came and said, 'The fire of God fell from the heavens and burned up the sheep and the servants, and I am the only one who has escaped to tell you!'

¹⁷While he was still speaking, another messenger came and said, 'The Chaldeans formed three raiding parties and swept down on your camels and made off with them. They put the servants to the sword, and I am the only one who has escaped to tell you!'

¹⁸While he was still speaking, yet another messenger came and said, 'Your sons and daughters were feasting and drinking wine at the eldest brother's house, ¹⁹when suddenly a mighty wind swept in from the desert and struck the four corners of the house. It collapsed on them and they are dead, and I am the only one who has escaped to tell you!'

²⁰At this, Job got up and tore his robe and shaved his head. Then he fell to the ground in worship ²¹and said:

'Naked I came from my mother's womb,
   and naked I shall depart.*ᶜ*
The LORD gave and the LORD has taken
   away;
   may the name of the LORD be
      praised.'

²²In all this, Job did not sin by charging God with wrongdoing.

2 On another day the angels*ᵃ* came to present themselves before the LORD, and Satan also came with them to present himself before him. ²And the LORD said to Satan, 'Where have you come from?'

Satan answered the LORD, 'From roaming throughout the earth, going to and fro on it.'

³Then the LORD said to Satan, 'Have you considered my servant Job? There is no one on earth like him; he is blameless and upright, a man who fears God and shuns evil. And he still maintains his integrity, though you incited me against him to ruin him without any reason.'

⁴'Skin for skin!' Satan replied. 'A man will give all he has for his own life. ⁵But now stretch out your hand and strike his flesh and bones, and he will surely curse you to your face.'

⁶The LORD said to Satan, 'Very well, then, he is in your hands; but you must spare his life.'

⁷So Satan went out from the presence of the LORD and afflicted Job with painful

a 6 Hebrew *the sons of God*
b 6 Hebrew *satan* means *adversary*.

c 21 Or *shall return there*
a 1 Hebrew *the sons of God*

sores from the soles of his feet to the crown of his head. **8**Then Job took a piece of broken pottery and scraped himself with it as he sat among the ashes.

9His wife said to him, 'Are you still maintaining your integrity? Curse God and die!'

10He replied, 'You are talking like a foolish*b* woman. Shall we accept good from God, and not trouble?'

In all this, Job did not sin in what he said.

b 10 The Hebrew word rendered *foolish* denotes moral deficiency.

PAIN AND SUFFERING 8

MORE GOING ON THAN WE KNOW ABOUT

As far as bad days go, Job is having the worst. First, three separate incidents wipe out all of his flock (and therefore his livelihood). Then a house collapses on his seven sons and three daughters and they are all killed. Things don't get any better. Job breaks out in painful and festering sores over his entire body.

Ouch. Why does all this happen to Job? Does God hate him? Has he done something wrong to deserve a punishment? No. Quite the opposite. We can see behind the scenes and read about a conversation between God and Satan, and we hear that God has nothing but praise for Job. God's really pleased with Job and says he's done absolutely nothing wrong. But the devil has a question: does Job love God because his life is good, or would he love God anyway?

Good question. It's one we should take a minute to answer for ourselves. Do we love God for the things he gives us? Do we love him when it's easy and we feel good? Do we love him when we're on a spiritual high? When life is going our way? When the worship band is playing our favourite song? Or will we love him even if life is difficult? If things don't turn out as planned, we don't get the grades we want, the college place we want, the job we want, the boyfriend or girlfriend we want – will we still love him then? Can we love God in the midst of our suffering and pain? Can we hold on to the truth that God is worthy of our love and praise no matter what?

There may be things happening in your life that are utterly confusing right now. It may be that over time you will see what was going on and how God was working. Or it may remain a mystery until you meet with God in heaven. Job never gets the perspective on his story that we get. He doesn't get to hear the conversation in heaven. God doesn't explain it to him and Job doesn't have the advantage of reading the Bible. But throughout the book of Job we see him refusing to turn away from God. So he proves God right: Job was able to love God for who he is and not just for the good things he gave Job. When difficult times come our way, will we be proved as faithful?

Mike Pilavachi

11 When Job's three friends, Eliphaz the Temanite, Bildad the Shuhite and Zophar the Naamathite, heard about all the troubles that had come upon him, they set out from their homes and met together by agreement to go and sympathise with him and comfort him. 12 When they saw him from a distance, they could hardly recognise him; they began to weep aloud, and they tore their robes and sprinkled dust on their heads. 13 Then they sat on the ground with him for seven days and seven nights. No one said a word to him, because they saw how great his suffering was.

Job speaks

3 After this, Job opened his mouth and cursed the day of his birth. 2 He said:

3 'May the day of my birth perish,
    and the night that said, "A boy is
        conceived!"
4 That day – may it turn to darkness;
    may God above not care about it;
    may no light shine on it.
5 May gloom and utter darkness claim it
        once more;
    may a cloud settle over it;
    may blackness overwhelm it.
6 That night – may thick darkness seize it;

FRIENDSHIP 8

Sticking with friends in tough times

When life gets tough, we find out who our true friends are. In Job 2:11–13, Job's friends come to him when he has lost all his children and his livestock in one day. Can you imagine the kind of pain he was in? Where would you find the words to comfort someone going through such awful suffering?

We can sometimes be tempted to avoid people who are having a tough time because we can't find the right words to say how sorry we are. The truth is, there are some situations where words just aren't adequate. We'll never find the right ones to say. Sometimes you don't actually have to say anything at all. There's a time and a place for trying to cheer someone up, distract them from their problems and tell them things will get better. There's also a place for doing what Job's friends did. They went to him and sat with him in his misery, saying nothing because they knew no words that would bring him comfort. They stuck with him and didn't leave him alone in his time of need.

Sadly, through the rest of the book of Job we see that they didn't live up to this early potential of being great friends. They started trying to find theories as to why Job was going through the things he was, and they actually made things worse for Job. But they still set us an amazing example in the early days of Job's grief. They stuck by their friend when his whole life was falling apart. He knew that no matter how painful things were, he wasn't on his own and that always brings comfort, even on our darkest night.

Ali Martin

◀◀ 2 Timothy 1   Matthew 26:69–75 ▶▶

may it not be included among the
days of the year
nor be entered in any of the months.
⁷ May that night be barren;
may no shout of joy be heard in it.
⁸ May those who curse days*a* curse that
day,
those who are ready to rouse
Leviathan.
⁹ May its morning stars become dark;
may it wait for daylight in vain
and not see the first rays of dawn,
¹⁰ for it did not shut the doors of the
womb on me
to hide trouble from my eyes.

¹¹ 'Why did I not perish at birth,
and die as I came from the womb?
¹² Why were there knees to receive me
and breasts that I might be nursed?
¹³ For now I would be lying down in peace;
I would be asleep and at rest
¹⁴ with kings and rulers of the earth,
who built for themselves places now
lying in ruins,
¹⁵ with princes who had gold,
who filled their houses with silver.
¹⁶ Or why was I not hidden away in the
ground like a stillborn child,
like an infant who never saw the light
of day?
¹⁷ There the wicked cease from turmoil,
and there the weary are at rest.
¹⁸ Captives also enjoy their ease;
they no longer hear the slave driver's
shout.
¹⁹ The small and the great are there,
and the slaves are freed from their
owners.

²⁰ 'Why is light given to those in misery,
and life to the bitter of soul,
²¹ to those who long for death that does
not come,
who search for it more than for
hidden treasure,
²² who are filled with gladness
and rejoice when they reach the
grave?
²³ Why is life given to a man

whose way is hidden,
whom God has hedged in?
²⁴ For sighing has become my daily food;
my groans pour out like water.
²⁵ What I feared has come upon me;
what I dreaded has happened to me.
²⁶ I have no peace, no quietness;
I have no rest, but only turmoil.'

Eliphaz

4 Then Eliphaz the Temanite replied:

² 'If someone ventures a word with you,
will you be impatient?
But who can keep from speaking?
³ Think how you have instructed many,
how you have strengthened feeble
hands.
⁴ Your words have supported those who
stumbled;
you have strengthened faltering
knees.
⁵ But now trouble comes to you, and you
are discouraged;
it strikes you, and you are dismayed.
⁶ Should not your piety be your
confidence
and your blameless ways your hope?

⁷ 'Consider now: who, being innocent,
has ever perished?
Where were the upright ever
destroyed?
⁸ As I have observed, those who plough
evil
and those who sow trouble reap it.
⁹ At the breath of God they perish;
at the blast of his anger they are no
more.
¹⁰ The lions may roar and growl,
yet the teeth of the great lions are
broken.
¹¹ The lion perishes for lack of prey,
and the cubs of the lioness are
scattered.

¹² 'A word was secretly brought to me,
my ears caught a whisper of it.
¹³ Amid disquieting dreams in the night,
when deep sleep falls on people,
¹⁴ fear and trembling seized me
and made all my bones shake.

---

a 8 Or *curse the sea*

15 A spirit glided past my face,
    and the hair on my body stood on
      end.
16 It stopped,
    but I could not tell what it was.
A form stood before my eyes,
    and I heard a hushed voice:
17 "Can a mortal be more righteous than
      God?
    Can even a strong man be more pure
      than his Maker?
18 If God places no trust in his servants,
    if he charges his angels with error,
19 how much more those who live in
      houses of clay,
    whose foundations are in the dust,
    who are crushed more readily than a
      moth!
20 Between dawn and dusk they are broken
      to pieces;
    unnoticed, they perish for ever.
21 Are not the cords of their tent pulled up,
    so that they die without wisdom?"

5 'Call if you will, but who will answer
    you?
    To which of the holy ones will you
      turn?
2 Resentment kills a fool,
    and envy slays the simple.
3 I myself have seen a fool taking root,
    but suddenly his house was cursed.
4 His children are far from safety,
    crushed in court without a defender.
5 The hungry consume his harvest,
    taking it even from among thorns,
    and the thirsty pant after his wealth.
6 For hardship does not spring from the
      soil,
    nor does trouble sprout from the
      ground.
7 Yet man is born to trouble
    as surely as sparks fly upwards.

8 'But if I were you, I would appeal to God;
    I would lay my cause before him.
9 He performs wonders that cannot be
      fathomed,
    miracles that cannot be counted.
10 He provides rain for the earth;
    he sends water on the countryside.
11 The lowly he sets on high,

and those who mourn are lifted to
      safety.
12 He thwarts the plans of the crafty,
    so that their hands achieve no
      success.
13 He catches the wise in their craftiness,
    and the schemes of the wily are swept
      away.
14 Darkness comes upon them in the
      daytime;
    at noon they grope as in the night.
15 He saves the needy from the sword in
      their mouth;
    he saves them from the clutches of
      the powerful.
16 So the poor have hope,
    and injustice shuts its mouth.

17 'Blessed is the one whom God corrects;
    so do not despise the discipline of the
      Almighty.*a*
18 For he wounds, but he also binds up;
    he injures, but his hands also heal.
19 From six calamities he will rescue you;
    in seven no harm will touch you.
20 In famine he will deliver you from
      death,
    and in battle from the stroke of the
      sword.
21 You will be protected from the lash of
      the tongue,
    and need not fear when destruction
      comes.
22 You will laugh at destruction and
      famine,
    and need not fear the wild animals.
23 For you will have a covenant with the
      stones of the field,
    and the wild animals will be at peace
      with you.
24 You will know that your tent is secure;
    you will take stock of your property
      and find nothing missing.
25 You will know that your children will be
      many,
    and your descendants like the grass of
      the earth.
26 You will come to the grave in full vigour,
    like sheaves gathered in season.

_____

a 17 Hebrew *Shaddai*; here and throughout Job

27 'We have examined this, and it is true.
So hear it and apply it to yourself.'

Job

6 Then Job replied:

2 'If only my anguish could be weighed
and all my misery be placed on the
scales!
3 It would surely outweigh the sand of the
seas –
no wonder my words have been
impetuous.
4 The arrows of the Almighty are in me,
my spirit drinks in their poison;
God's terrors are marshalled against
me.
5 Does a wild donkey bray when it has
grass,
or an ox bellow when it has fodder?
6 Is tasteless food eaten without salt,
or is there flavour in the sap of the
mallow*a*?
7 I refuse to touch it;
such food makes me ill.

8 'Oh, that I might have my request,
that God would grant what I hope for,
9 that God would be willing to crush me,
to let loose his hand and cut off my
life!
10 Then I would still have this consolation –
my joy in unrelenting pain –
that I had not denied the words of the
Holy One.

11 'What strength do I have, that I should
still hope?
What prospects, that I should be
patient?
12 Do I have the strength of stone?
Is my flesh bronze?
13 Do I have any power to help myself,
now that success has been driven
from me?

14 'Anyone who withholds kindness from a
friend
forsakes the fear of the Almighty.

15 But my brothers are as undependable as
intermittent streams,
as the streams that overflow
16 when darkened by thawing ice
and swollen with melting snow,
17 but that stop flowing in the dry season,
and in the heat vanish from their
channels.
18 Caravans turn aside from their routes;
they go off into the wasteland and
perish.
19 The caravans of Tema look for water,
the travelling merchants of Sheba
look in hope.
20 They are distressed, because they had
been confident;
they arrive there, only to be
disappointed.
21 Now you too have proved to be of no
help;
you see something dreadful and are
afraid.
22 Have I ever said, "Give something on my
behalf,
pay a ransom for me from your
wealth,
23 deliver me from the hand of the enemy,
rescue me from the clutches of the
ruthless"?

24 'Teach me, and I will be quiet;
show me where I have been wrong.
25 How painful are honest words!
But what do your arguments prove?
26 Do you mean to correct what I say,
and treat my desperate words as
wind?
27 You would even cast lots for the
fatherless
and barter away your friend.

28 'But now be so kind as to look at me.
Would I lie to your face?
29 Relent, do not be unjust;
reconsider, for my integrity is at
stake.*b*
30 Is there any wickedness on my lips?
Can my mouth not discern malice?

---

a 6 The meaning of the Hebrew for this phrase is
uncertain.

b 29 Or *my righteousness still stands*

WHY DOES GOD ALLOW SUFFERING?

Job is not the only Bible character to complain to God about his suffering. Habakkuk brought several complaints to God, as did the psalmists and other prophets. Why does God not just intervene and sort everything out?

To answer this question we need to go back to the beginning of the Bible. God made the world, and it was good. Then, when he made humans, he saw that it was very good. All was well in the world at this time and there was an incredible intimacy between God and humanity. Heaven and earth were one. But God gave Adam and Eve free choice, and they chose to rebel against his one prohibition and eat the fruit of the forbidden tree. This began a downward spiral of events which show us what it looks like when humans rebel against God. There is murder, incest, the great flood, revenge and the Tower of Babel rebellion. It's a bleak picture.

Humankind is fallen, lost in sin, responsible for the suffering of the world. So in Genesis 12, the great rescue plan begins. God calls Abram and his descendants to show the world how to live and to be a blessing to all the families of the earth. God always carries out his plans in relationship with people, giving us the choice to obey. When we refuse to obey, we carry on the great rebellion that has defiled God's good creation. The story of Abraham's descendants shows us this: again and again they rebel and cause more suffering.

So God acts decisively, and in the line of Abraham, Jesus comes, God incarnate, to show us how to live. He dies on the cross, but rises again and defeats the power of death and sin for ever. Jesus and his followers, filled with the Spirit, proclaim that God's future kingdom is already here, and prove it by healing the sick, raising the dead, serving the poor and casting out demons. But even the apostles don't see everyone get healed (2 Timothy 4:20), and all of them die eventually. So they realise they are living in a crossover time. The kingdom of God is here, but not yet fully. One day there will be no more crying, death and pain, but for now we get glimpses of that future when we see the sick healed and relationships restored.

So we live in the gap between Jesus' resurrection and the great resurrection, when all the dead will rise and God will complete the task of putting the world to rights. We will see some people healed, but not all. We may even see people raised from the dead – but eventually those people will die again. It is only when Jesus returns that we will say, 'Death, where is your victory?'

We must remember that we live in a fallen world where humans are primarily responsible for each other's suffering; that God is good, and despite our circumstances one day our suffering will be over.

Chris Lane

7

'Do not mortals have hard service on earth?
  Are not their days like those of hired labourers?
2 Like a slave longing for the evening shadows,
  or a hired labourer waiting to be paid,
3 so I have been allotted months of futility,
  and nights of misery have been assigned to me.
4 When I lie down I think, "How long before I get up?"
  The night drags on, and I toss and turn until dawn.
5 My body is clothed with worms and scabs,
  my skin is broken and festering.

6 'My days are swifter than a weaver's shuttle,
  and they come to an end without hope.
7 Remember, O God, that my life is but a breath;
  my eyes will never see happiness again.
8 The eye that now sees me will see me no longer;
  you will look for me, but I will be no more.
9 As a cloud vanishes and is gone,
  so one who goes down to the grave does not return.
10 He will never come to his house again;
  his place will know him no more.

11 'Therefore I will not keep silent;
  I will speak out in the anguish of my spirit,
  I will complain in the bitterness of my soul.
12 Am I the sea, or the monster of the deep,
  that you put me under guard?
13 When I think my bed will comfort me
  and my couch will ease my complaint,
14 even then you frighten me with dreams
  and terrify me with visions,
15 so that I prefer strangling and death,
  rather than this body of mine.

16 I despise my life; I would not live for ever.
  Let me alone; my days have no meaning.

17 'What is mankind that you make so much of them,
  that you give them so much attention,
18 that you examine them every morning
  and test them every moment?
19 Will you never look away from me,
  or let me alone even for an instant?
20 If I have sinned, what have I done to you,
  you who see everything we do?
  Why have you made me your target?
  Have I become a burden to you?[a]
21 Why do you not pardon my offences
  and forgive my sins?
  For I shall soon lie down in the dust;
  you will search for me, but I shall be no more.'

Bildad

8

Then Bildad the Shuhite replied:

2 'How long will you say such things?
  Your words are a blustering wind.
3 Does God pervert justice?
  Does the Almighty pervert what is right?
4 When your children sinned against him,
  he gave them over to the penalty of their sin.
5 But if you will seek God earnestly
  and plead with the Almighty,
6 If you are pure and upright,
  even now he will rouse himself on your behalf
  and restore you to your prosperous state.
7 Your beginnings will seem humble,
  so prosperous will your future be.

8 'Ask the former generations
  and find out what their ancestors learned,

---

a 20 A few manuscripts of the Masoretic Text, an ancient Hebrew scribal tradition and Septuagint; most manuscripts of the Masoretic Text *I have become a burden to myself.*

⁹ for we were born only yesterday and
        know nothing,
    and our days on earth are but a
        shadow.
¹⁰ Will they not instruct you and tell you?
    Will they not bring forth words from
        their understanding?
¹¹ Can papyrus grow tall where there is no
        marsh?
    Can reeds thrive without water?
¹² While still growing and uncut,
    they wither more quickly than grass.
¹³ Such is the destiny of all who forget
        God;
    so perishes the hope of the godless.
¹⁴ What they trust in is fragile*a*;
    what they rely on is a spider's web.
¹⁵ They lean on the web, but it gives way;
    they cling to it, but it does not hold.
¹⁶ They are like a well-watered plant in the
        sunshine,
    spreading its shoots over the garden;
¹⁷ it entwines its roots round a pile of
        rocks
    and looks for a place among the
        stones.
¹⁸ But when it is torn from its spot,
    that place disowns it and says, "I
        never saw you."
¹⁹ Surely its life withers away,
    and*b* from the soil other plants grow.

²⁰ 'Surely God does not reject one who is
        blameless
    or strengthen the hands of evildoers.
²¹ He will yet fill your mouth with
        laughter
    and your lips with shouts of joy.
²² Your enemies will be clothed in shame,
    and the tents of the wicked will be no
        more.'

Job

9 Then Job replied:

² 'Indeed, I know that this is true.
    But how can mere mortals prove their
        innocence before God?

³ Though they wished to dispute with
        him,
    they could not answer him once in a
        thousand times.
⁴ His wisdom is profound, his power is
        vast.
    Who has resisted him and come out
        unscathed?
⁵ He moves mountains without their
        knowing it
    and overturns them in his anger.
⁶ He shakes the earth from its place
    and makes its pillars tremble.
⁷ He speaks to the sun and it does not
        shine;
    he seals off the light of the stars.
⁸ He alone stretches out the heavens
    and treads on the waves of the sea.
⁹ He is the Maker of the Bear*a* and Orion,
    the Pleiades and the constellations of
        the south.
¹⁰ He performs wonders that cannot be
        fathomed,
    miracles that cannot be counted.
¹¹ When he passes me, I cannot see him;
    when he goes by, I cannot perceive
        him.
¹² If he snatches away, who can stop him?
    Who can say to him, "What are you
        doing?"
¹³ God does not restrain his anger;
    even the cohorts of Rahab cowered at
        his feet.

¹⁴ 'How then can I dispute with him?
    How can I find words to argue with
        him?
¹⁵ Though I were innocent, I could not
        answer him;
    I could only plead with my Judge for
        mercy.
¹⁶ Even if I summoned him and he
        responded,
    I do not believe he would give me a
        hearing.
¹⁷ He would crush me with a storm
    and multiply my wounds for no
        reason.
¹⁸ He would not let me catch my breath

---

a 14   The meaning of the Hebrew for this word is
uncertain.
b 19   Or *Surely all the joy it has / is that*

a 9   Or *of Leo*

but would overwhelm me with
misery.
19 If it is a matter of strength, he is mighty!
And if it is a matter of justice, who can
challenge him[b]?
20 Even if I were innocent, my mouth
would condemn me;
if I were blameless, it would
pronounce me guilty.

21 'Although I am blameless,
I have no concern for myself;
I despise my own life.
22 It is all the same; that is why I say,
"He destroys both the blameless and
the wicked."
23 When a scourge brings sudden death,
he mocks the despair of the innocent.
24 When a land falls into the hands of the
wicked,
he blindfolds its judges.
If it is not he, then who is it?

25 'My days are swifter than a runner;
they fly away without a glimpse of joy.
26 They skim past like boats of papyrus,
like eagles swooping down on their
prey.
27 If I say, "I will forget my complaint,
I will change my expression, and
smile,"
28 I still dread all my sufferings,
for I know you will not hold me
innocent.
29 Since I am already found guilty,
why should I struggle in vain?
30 Even if I washed myself with soap
and my hands with cleansing powder,
31 you would plunge me into a slime pit
so that even my clothes would detest
me.

32 'He is not a mere mortal like me that I
might answer him,
that we might confront each other in
court.
33 If only there were someone to mediate
between us,
someone to bring us together,
34 someone to remove God's rod from me,

so that his terror would frighten me
no more.
35 Then I would speak up without fear of
him,
but as it now stands with me, I
cannot.

10 'I loathe my very life;
therefore I will give free rein to my
complaint
and speak out in the bitterness of my
soul.
2 I say to God: do not declare me guilty,
but tell me what charges you have
against me.
3 Does it please you to oppress me,
to spurn the work of your hands,
while you smile on the plans of the
wicked?
4 Do you have eyes of flesh?
Do you see as a mortal sees?
5 Are your days like those of a mortal
or your years like those of a strong
man,
6 that you must search out my faults
and probe after my sin –
7 though you know that I am not guilty
and that no one can rescue me from
your hand?

8 'Your hands shaped me and made me.
Will you now turn and destroy me?
9 Remember that you moulded me like
clay.
Will you now turn me to dust again?
10 Did you not pour me out like milk
and curdle me like cheese,
11 clothe me with skin and flesh
and knit me together with bones and
sinews?
12 You gave me life and showed me
kindness,
and in your providence watched over
my spirit.

13 'But this is what you concealed in your
heart,
and I know that this was in your
mind:
14 if I sinned, you would be watching me
and would not let my offence go
unpunished.

---

b 19 See Septuagint; Hebrew *me*.

¹⁵ If I am guilty – woe to me!
Even if I am innocent, I cannot lift my
head,
for I am full of shame
and drowned in^a my affliction.
¹⁶ If I hold my head high, you stalk me like
a lion
and again display your awesome
power against me.
¹⁷ You bring new witnesses against me
and increase your anger towards me;
your forces come against me wave
upon wave.

¹⁸ 'Why then did you bring me out of the
womb?
I wish I had died before any eye saw
me.
¹⁹ If only I had never come into being,
or had been carried straight from the
womb to the grave!
²⁰ Are not my few days almost over?
Turn away from me so that I can have
a moment's joy
²¹ before I go to the place of no return,
to the land of gloom and utter
darkness,
²² to the land of deepest night,
of utter darkness and disorder,
where even the light is like
darkness.'

Zophar

11 Then Zophar the Naamathite replied:

² 'Are all these words to go unanswered?
Is this talker to be vindicated?
³ Will your idle talk reduce others to
silence?
Will no one rebuke you when you
mock?
⁴ You say to God, "My beliefs are flawless
and I am pure in your sight."
⁵ Oh, how I wish that God would speak,
that he would open his lips against
you
⁶ and disclose to you the secrets of
wisdom,
for true wisdom has two sides.

Know this: God has even forgotten
some of your sin.

⁷ 'Can you fathom the mysteries of God?
Can you probe the limits of the
Almighty?
⁸ They are higher than the heavens
above – what can you do?
They are deeper than the depths
below – what can you know?
⁹ Their measure is longer than the earth
and wider than the sea.

¹⁰ 'If he comes along and confines you in
prison
and convenes a court, who can
oppose him?
¹¹ Surely he recognises deceivers;
and when he sees evil, does he not
take note?
¹² But the witless can no more become
wise
than a wild donkey's colt can be born
human.^a

¹³ 'Yet if you devote your heart to him
and stretch out your hands to him,
¹⁴ if you put away the sin that is in your
hand
and allow no evil to dwell in your
tent,
¹⁵ then, free of fault, you will lift up your
face;
you will stand firm and without fear.
¹⁶ You will surely forget your trouble,
recalling it only as waters gone by.
¹⁷ Life will be brighter than noonday,
and darkness will become like
morning.
¹⁸ You will be secure, because there is
hope;
you will look about you and take your
rest in safety.
¹⁹ You will lie down, with no one to make
you afraid,
and many will court your favour.
²⁰ But the eyes of the wicked will fail,
and escape will elude them;
their hope will become a dying gasp.'

---

a 15 Or *and aware of*

a 12 Or *wild donkey can be born tame*

Job

12
Then Job replied:

2 'Doubtless you are the only people who
matter,
and wisdom will die with you!
3 But I have a mind as well as you;
I am not inferior to you.
Who does not know all these things?

4 'I have become a laughing-stock to my
friends,
though I called on God and he
answered –
a mere laughing-stock, though
righteous and blameless!
5 Those who are at ease have contempt
for misfortune
as the fate of those whose feet are
slipping.
6 The tents of marauders are undisturbed,
and those who provoke God are
secure –
those whom God has in his hand.*a*

7 'But ask the animals, and they will teach
you,
or the birds in the sky, and they will
tell you;
8 or speak to the earth, and it will teach
you,
or let the fish in the sea inform you.
9 Which of all these does not know
that the hand of the LORD has done
this?
10 In his hand is the life of every creature
and the breath of all mankind.
11 Does not the ear test words
as the tongue tastes food?
12 Is not wisdom found among the aged?
Does not long life bring
understanding?

13 'To God belong wisdom and power;
counsel and understanding are his.
14 What he tears down cannot be rebuilt;
those he imprisons cannot be
released.
15 If he holds back the waters, there is
drought;

if he lets them loose, they devastate
the land.
16 To him belong strength and insight;
both deceived and deceiver are his.
17 He leads rulers away stripped
and makes fools of judges.
18 He takes off the shackles put on by kings
and ties a loincloth*b* round their
waist.
19 He leads priests away stripped
and overthrows officials long
established.
20 He silences the lips of trusted advisors
and takes away the discernment of
elders.
21 He pours contempt on nobles
and disarms the mighty.
22 He reveals the deep things of darkness
and brings utter darkness into the
light.
23 He makes nations great, and destroys
them;
he enlarges nations, and disperses
them.
24 He deprives the leaders of the earth of
their reason;
he makes them wander in a trackless
waste.
25 They grope in darkness with no light;
he makes them stagger like
drunkards.

13
'My eyes have seen all this,
my ears have heard and understood
it.
2 What you know, I also know;
I am not inferior to you.
3 But I desire to speak to the Almighty
and to argue my case with God.
4 You, however, smear me with lies;
you are worthless physicians, all of
you!
5 If only you would be altogether silent!
For you, that would be wisdom.
6 Hear now my argument;
listen to the pleas of my lips.
7 Will you speak wickedly on God's
behalf?
Will you speak deceitfully for him?
8 Will you show him partiality?

---

a 6 Or *those whose god is in their own hand*   *b* 18 Or *shackles of kings / and ties a belt*

Will you argue the case for God?
9 Would it turn out well if he examined
    you?
  Could you deceive him as you might
    deceive a mortal?
10 He would surely call you to account
    if you secretly showed partiality.
11 Would not his splendour terrify you?
  Would not the dread of him fall on
    you?
12 Your maxims are proverbs of ashes;
  your defences are defences of clay.

13 'Keep silent and let me speak;
  then let come to me what may.
14 Why do I put myself in jeopardy
  and take my life in my hands?
15 Though he slay me, yet will I hope in
    him;
  I will surely*a* defend my ways to his
    face.
16 Indeed, this will turn out for my
    deliverance,
  for no godless person would dare
    come before him!
17 Listen carefully to what I say;
  let my words ring in your ears.
18 Now that I have prepared my case,
  I know I will be vindicated.
19 Can anyone bring charges against me?
  If so, I will be silent and die.

20 'Only grant me these two things, God,
  and then I will not hide from you:
21 withdraw your hand far from me,
  and stop frightening me with your
    terrors.
22 Then summon me and I will answer,
  or let me speak, and you reply to me.
23 How many wrongs and sins have I
    committed?
  Show me my offence and my sin.
24 Why do you hide your face
  and consider me your enemy?
25 Will you torment a wind-blown leaf?
  Will you chase after dry chaff?
26 For you write down bitter things against
    me
  and make me reap the sins of my
    youth.

27 You fasten my feet in shackles;
  you keep close watch on all my paths
    by putting marks on the soles of my
    feet.

28 'So man wastes away like something
    rotten,
  like a garment eaten by moths.

14
'Mortals, born of woman,
  are of few days and full of trouble.
2 They spring up like flowers and wither
    away;
  like fleeting shadows, they do not
    endure.
3 Do you fix your eye on them?
  Will you bring them*a* before you for
    judgment?
4 Who can bring what is pure from the
    impure?
  No one!
5 A person's days are determined;
  you have decreed the number of his
    months
  and have set limits he cannot exceed.
6 So look away from him and let him
    alone,
  till he has put in his time like a hired
    labourer.

7 'At least there is hope for a tree:
  if it is cut down, it will sprout again,
  and its new shoots will not fail.
8 Its roots may grow old in the ground
  and its stump die in the soil,
9 yet at the scent of water it will bud
  and put forth shoots like a plant.
10 But a man dies and is laid low;
  he breathes his last and is no more.
11 As the water of a lake dries up
  or a river bed becomes parched and
    dry,
12 so he lies down and does not rise;
  till the heavens are no more, people
    will not awake
  or be roused from their sleep.

13 'If only you would hide me in the grave
  and conceal me till your anger has
    passed!

---

a 15 Or *He will surely slay me; I have no hope — / yet I will*   *a* 3 Septuagint, Vulgate and Syriac; Hebrew *me*

If only you would set me a time
   and then remember me!
14 If someone dies, will they live again?
   All the days of my hard service
     I will wait for my renewal[b] to come.
15 You will call and I will answer you;
   you will long for the creature your
     hands have made.
16 Surely then you will count my steps
   but not keep track of my sin.
17 My offences will be sealed up in a bag;
   you will cover over my sin.

18 'But as a mountain erodes and
     crumbles
   and as a rock is moved from its
     place,
19 as water wears away stones
   and torrents wash away the soil,
   so you destroy a person's hope.
20 You overpower them once for all, and
     they are gone;
   you change their countenance and
     send them away.
21 If their children are honoured, they do
     not know it;
   if their children are brought low, they
     do not see it.
22 They feel but the pain of their own
     bodies
   and mourn only for themselves.'

Eliphaz

15 Then Eliphaz the Temanite replied:

2 'Would a wise person answer with
     empty notions
   or fill their belly with the hot east
     wind?
3 Would they argue with useless words,
   with speeches that have no value?
4 But you even undermine piety
   and hinder devotion to God.
5 Your sin prompts your mouth;
   you adopt the tongue of the crafty.
6 Your own mouth condemns you, not
     mine;
   your own lips testify against you.

7 'Are you the first man ever born?
   Were you brought forth before the
     hills?
8 Do you listen in on God's council?
   Do you have a monopoly on wisdom?
9 What do you know that we do not
     know?
   What insights do you have that we do
     not have?
10 The grey-haired and the aged are on our
     side,
   men even older than your father.
11 Are God's consolations not enough for
     you,
   words spoken gently to you?
12 Why has your heart carried you away,
   and why do your eyes flash,
13 so that you vent your rage against God
   and pour out such words from your
     mouth?

14 'What are mortals, that they could be
     pure,
   or those born of woman, that they
     could be righteous?
15 If God places no trust in his holy ones,
   if even the heavens are not pure in his
     eyes,
16 how much less mortals, who are vile
     and corrupt,
   who drink up evil like water!

17 'Listen to me and I will explain to you;
   let me tell you what I have seen,
18 what the wise have declared,
   hiding nothing received from their
     ancestors
19 (to whom alone the land was given
   when no foreigners moved among
     them):
20 all his days the wicked man suffers
     torment,
   the ruthless man through all the
     years stored up for him.
21 Terrifying sounds fill his ears;
   when all seems well, marauders
     attack him.
22 He despairs of escaping the realm of
     darkness;
   he is marked for the sword.
23 He wanders about for food like a
     vulture;

---

b 14 Or *release*

he knows the day of darkness is at
      hand.
24 Distress and anguish fill him with
      terror;
   troubles overwhelm him, like a king
      poised to attack,
25 because he shakes his fist at God
   and vaunts himself against the
      Almighty,
26 defiantly charging against him
   with a thick, strong shield.

27 'Though his face is covered with fat
   and his waist bulges with flesh,
28 he will inhabit ruined towns
   and houses where no one lives,
   houses crumbling to rubble.
29 He will no longer be rich and his wealth
      will not endure,
   nor will his possessions spread over
      the land.
30 He will not escape the darkness;
   a flame will wither his shoots,
   and the breath of God's mouth will
      carry him away.
31 Let him not deceive himself by trusting
      what is worthless,
   for he will get nothing in return.
32 Before his time he will wither,
   and his branches will not flourish.
33 He will be like a vine stripped of its
      unripe grapes,
   like an olive tree shedding its
      blossoms.
34 For the company of the godless will be
      barren,
   and fire will consume the tents of
      those who love bribes.
35 They conceive trouble and give birth to
      evil;
   their womb fashions deceit.'

Job

16 Then Job replied:

2 'I have heard many things like these;
   you are miserable comforters, all of
      you!
3 Will your long-winded speeches never
      end?
   What ails you that you keep on
      arguing?

4 I also could speak like you,
   if you were in my place;
   I could make fine speeches against you
   and shake my head at you.
5 But my mouth would encourage you;
   comfort from my lips would bring
      you relief.

6 'Yet if I speak, my pain is not relieved;
   and if I refrain, it does not go away.
7 Surely, God, you have worn me out;
   you have devastated my entire
      household.
8 You have shrivelled me up – and it has
      become a witness;
   my gauntness rises up and testifies
      against me.
9 God assails me and tears me in his anger
   and gnashes his teeth at me;
   my opponent fastens on me his
      piercing eyes.
10 People open their mouths to jeer at me;
   they strike my cheek in scorn
   and unite together against me.
11 God has turned me over to the ungodly
   and thrown me into the clutches of
      the wicked.
12 All was well with me, but he shattered
      me;
   he seized me by the neck and crushed
      me.
   He has made me his target;
13   his archers surround me.
   Without pity, he pierces my kidneys
   and spills my gall on the ground.
14 Again and again he bursts upon me;
   he rushes at me like a warrior.

15 'I have sewed sackcloth over my skin
   and buried my brow in the dust.
16 My face is red with weeping,
   dark shadows ring my eyes;
17 yet my hands have been free of violence
   and my prayer is pure.

18 'Earth, do not cover my blood;
   may my cry never be laid to rest!
19 Even now my witness is in heaven;
   my advocate is on high.
20 My intercessor is my friend*a*

_____
a 20 Or *My friends treat me with scorn*

as my eyes pour out tears to God;
²¹ on behalf of a man he pleads with God
as one pleads for a friend.

²² 'Only a few years will pass
before I take the path of no return.

17 ¹ My spirit is broken,
my days are cut short,
the grave awaits me.
² Surely mockers surround me;
my eyes must dwell on their
hostility.

POVERTY

Poverty robs people of many things in life: employment, education, even basic necessities like clean water and food. Worst of all, though, poverty crushes hope.

Richard was a just another young guy. But he lived in Ogongora, Uganda, where life is difficult and opportunities seem few. Richard turned to drink and often got into fights. He got married, but would beat his wife. Once children came along, he would get drunk rather than provide food for them. Hopelessness kills, and Richard was on the way out.

But the local church in Richard's community did not give up hope. They helped him see the potential in his life and the responsibility he had to his family. They also helped him and his wife expand their farming so that they could bring in a better income and provide food for their children. For Richard, hope came in both practical and spiritual ways: faith came in through one door, and poverty began to ebb out through the other. This is one of the things that churches do best!

Really tackling poverty for the long term has to start with hope. Tearfund is working with churches in some of the poorest places of the world to help bring hope to their local communities. Because the church cares about people's spiritual well-being as well as their physical needs, Christians are helping communities get under the skin of their material needs to work out how, together, they can transform their situation. It's having profound effects as communities work themselves out of poverty and regain hope.

This is something we can all be involved in, whatever church we are part of. Every community needs hope! Here's a way to engage with bringing hope to the poorest places of the world.

Action

Use these words based on Job 17 to reflect on the power of hope. Pray for those who are low on hope, that God would give them eyes to see possibilities.

I'm broken / Knocked down / For you just to laugh at / I'm beaten / Right down / For you to despise me / Got nothing left / Can't do nothing right / Look to me, look to me / See how I'm crumbling. / But my heart will beat / A different tune / Though my hope is weak / The darkness is fading / The light it is coming / The night it is trembling / Where is hope? Not out here. / But in here. / Will it stay? Will it fall away? / Will I fall away?

Matt Valler

3 'Give me, O God, the pledge you
      demand.
   Who else will put up security for me?
4 You have closed their minds to
      understanding;
   therefore you will not let them
      triumph.
5 If anyone denounces their friends for
      reward,
   the eyes of their children will fail.

6 'God has made me a byword to
      everyone,
   a man in whose face people spit.
7 My eyes have grown dim with grief;
   my whole frame is but a shadow.
8 The upright are appalled at this;
   the innocent are aroused against the
      ungodly.
9 Nevertheless, the righteous will hold to
      their ways,
   and those with clean hands will grow
      stronger.

10 'But come on, all of you, try again!
   I will not find a wise man among you.
11 My days have passed, my plans are
      shattered.
   Yet the desires of my heart
12 turn night into day;
   in the face of the darkness light is
      near.
13 If the only home I hope for is the grave,
   if I spread out my bed in the realm of
      darkness,
14 if I say to corruption, "You are my
      father,"
   and to the worm, "My mother" or
      "My sister",
15 where then is my hope –
   who can see any hope for me?
16 Will it go down to the gates of death?
   Will we descend together into the
      dust?'

Bildad

18
Then Bildad the Shuhite replied:

2 'When will you end these speeches?
   Be sensible, and then we can talk.
3 Why are we regarded as cattle
   and considered stupid in your sight?

4 You who tear yourself to pieces in your
      anger,
   is the earth to be abandoned for your
      sake?
   Or must the rocks be moved from
      their place?

5 'The lamp of a wicked man is snuffed
      out;
   the flame of his fire stops burning.
6 The light in his tent becomes dark;
   the lamp beside him goes out.
7 The vigour of his step is weakened;
   his own schemes throw him down.
8 His feet thrust him into a net;
   he wanders into its mesh.
9 A trap seizes him by the heel;
   a snare holds him fast.
10 A noose is hidden for him on the
      ground;
   a trap lies in his path.
11 Terrors startle him on every side
   and dog his every step.
12 Calamity is hungry for him;
   disaster is ready for him when he
      falls.
13 It eats away parts of his skin;
   death's firstborn devours his limbs.
14 He is torn from the security of his tent
   and marched off to the king of
      terrors.
15 Fire resides*a* in his tent;
   burning sulphur is scattered over his
      dwelling.
16 His roots dry up below
   and his branches wither above.
17 The memory of him perishes from the
      earth;
   he has no name in the land.
18 He is driven from light into the realm of
      darkness
   and is banished from the world.
19 He has no offspring or descendants
      among his people,
   no survivor where once he lived.
20 People of the west are appalled at his
      fate;
   those of the east are seized with
      horror.

_____
a 15 Or *Nothing he had remains*

21 Surely such is the dwelling of an evil
man;
such is the place of one who does not
know God.'

Job

19

Then Job replied:

2 'How long will you torment me
and crush me with words?
3 Ten times now you have reproached me;
shamelessly you attack me.
4 If it is true that I have gone astray,
my error remains my concern alone.
5 If indeed you would exalt yourselves
above me
and use my humiliation against me,
6 then know that God has wronged me
and drawn his net around me.

7 'Though I cry, "Violence!" I get no
response;
though I call for help, there is no
justice.
8 He has blocked my way so that I cannot
pass;
he has shrouded my paths in
darkness.
9 He has stripped me of my honour
and removed the crown from my
head.
10 He tears me down on every side till I am
gone;
he uproots my hope like a tree.
11 His anger burns against me;
he counts me among his enemies.
12 His troops advance in force;
they build a siege ramp against me
and encamp around my tent.

13 'He has alienated my family from me;
my acquaintances are completely
estranged from me.
14 My relatives have gone away;
my closest friends have forgotten me.
15 My guests and my female servants count
me a foreigner;
they look upon me as a stranger.
16 I summon my servant, but he does not
answer,
though I beg him with my own
mouth.

17 My breath is offensive to my wife;
I am loathsome to my own family.
18 Even the little boys scorn me;
when I appear, they ridicule me.
19 All my intimate friends detest me;
those I love have turned against me.
20 I am nothing but skin and bones;
I have escaped only by the skin of my
teeth.*a*

21 'Have pity on me, my friends, have pity,
for the hand of God has struck me.
22 Why do you pursue me as God does?
Will you never get enough of my
flesh?

23 'Oh, that my words were recorded,
that they were written on a scroll,
24 that they were inscribed with an iron
tool on*b* lead,
or engraved in rock for ever!
25 I know that my redeemer*c* lives,
and that in the end he will stand on
the earth.*d*
26 And after my skin has been destroyed,
yet*e* in*f* my flesh I will see God;
27 I myself will see him
with my own eyes – I, and not
another.
How my heart yearns within me!

28 'If you say, "How we will hound him,
since the root of the trouble lies in
him,*g*"
29 you should fear the sword yourselves;
for wrath will bring punishment by
the sword,
and then you will know that there is
judgment.*h*'

Zophar

20

Then Zophar the Naamathite replied:

---

a 20 Or *only by my gums*
b 24 Or *and*
c 25 Or *vindicator*
d 25 Or *on my grave*
e 26 Or *And after I awake, / though this body has been
destroyed, / then*
f 26 Or *destroyed, / apart from*
g 28 Many Hebrew manuscripts, Septuagint and
Vulgate; most Hebrew manuscripts *me*
h 29 Or *sword, / that you may come to know the Almighty*

2 'My troubled thoughts prompt me to
    answer
    because I am greatly disturbed.
3 I hear a rebuke that dishonours me,
    and my understanding inspires me to
    reply.

4 'Surely you know how it has been from
    of old,
    ever since mankind*a* was placed on
    the earth,
5 that the mirth of the wicked is brief,
    the joy of the godless lasts but a
    moment.
6 Though the pride of the godless person
    reaches to the heavens
    and his head touches the clouds,
7 he will perish for ever, like his own
    dung;
    those who have seen him will say,
    "Where is he?"
8 Like a dream he flies away, no more to
    be found,
    banished like a vision of the night.
9 The eye that saw him will not see him
    again;
    his place will look on him no more.
10 His children must make amends to the
    poor;
    his own hands must give back his
    wealth.
11 The youthful vigour that fills his bones
    will lie with him in the dust.

12 'Though evil is sweet in his mouth
    and he hides it under his tongue,
13 though he cannot bear to let it go
    and lets it linger in his mouth,
14 yet his food will turn sour in his
    stomach;
    it will become the venom of serpents
    within him.
15 He will spit out the riches he swallowed;
    God will make his stomach vomit
    them up.
16 He will suck the poison of serpents;
    the fangs of an adder will kill him.
17 He will not enjoy the streams,
    the rivers flowing with honey and
    cream.

18 What he toiled for he must give back
    uneaten;
    he will not enjoy the profit from his
    trading.
19 For he has oppressed the poor and left
    them destitute;
    he has seized houses he did not
    build.

20 'Surely he will have no respite from his
    craving;
    he cannot save himself by his
    treasure.
21 Nothing is left for him to devour;
    his prosperity will not endure.
22 In the midst of his plenty, distress will
    overtake him;
    the full force of misery will come
    upon him.
23 When he has filled his belly,
    God will vent his burning anger
    against him
    and rain down his blows on him.
24 Though he flees from an iron weapon,
    a bronze-tipped arrow pierces him.
25 He pulls it out of his back,
    the gleaming point out of his liver.
    Terrors will come over him;
26   total darkness lies in wait for his
    treasures.
    A fire unfanned will consume him
    and devour what is left in his tent.
27 The heavens will expose his guilt;
    the earth will rise up against him.
28 A flood will carry off his house,
    rushing waters*b* on the day of God's
    wrath.
29 Such is the fate God allots the wicked,
    the heritage appointed for them by
    God.'

Job

21 Then Job replied:

2 'Listen carefully to my words;
    let this be the consolation you give
    me.
3 Bear with me while I speak,
    and after I have spoken, mock on.

---

a 4 Or *Adam*

b 28 Or *The possessions in his house will be carried off, /
washed away*

4 'Is my complaint directed to a human
     being?
   Why should I not be impatient?
5 Look at me and be appalled;
   clap your hand over your mouth.
6 When I think about this, I am terrified;
   trembling seizes my body.
7 Why do the wicked live on,
   growing old and increasing in power?
8 They see their children established
     around them,
   their offspring before their eyes.
9 Their homes are safe and free from fear;
   the rod of God is not on them.
10 Their bulls never fail to breed;
   their cows calve and do not miscarry.
11 They send forth their children as a flock;
   their little ones dance about.
12 They sing to the music of tambourine
     and lyre;
   they make merry to the sound of the
     pipe.
13 They spend their years in prosperity
   and go down to the grave in peace.*a*
14 Yet they say to God, "Leave us alone!
   We have no desire to know your ways.
15 Who is the Almighty, that we should
     serve him?
   What would we gain by praying to
     him?"
16 But their prosperity is not in their own
     hands,
   so I stand aloof from the plans of the
     wicked.

17 'Yet how often is the lamp of the wicked
     snuffed out?
   How often does calamity come upon
     them,
   the fate God allots in his anger?
18 How often are they like straw before the
     wind,
   like chaff swept away by a gale?
19 It is said, "God stores up the
     punishment of the wicked for
     their children."
   Let him repay the wicked, so that they
     themselves will experience it!
20 Let their own eyes see their destruction;

   let them drink the cup of the wrath of
     the Almighty.
21 For what do they care about the families
     they leave behind
   when their allotted months come to
     an end?

22 'Can anyone teach knowledge to God,
   since he judges even the highest?
23 One person dies in full vigour,
   completely secure and at ease,
24 well nourished in body,*b*
   bones rich with marrow.
25 Another dies in bitterness of soul,
   never having enjoyed anything good.
26 Side by side they lie in the dust,
   and worms cover them both.

27 'I know full well what you are thinking,
   the schemes by which you would
     wrong me.
28 You say, "Where now is the house of the
     great,
   the tents where the wicked lived?"
29 Have you never questioned those who
     travel?
   Have you paid no regard to their
     accounts –
30 that the wicked are spared from the day
     of calamity,
   that they are delivered from*c* the day
     of wrath?
31 Who denounces their conduct to their
     face?
   Who repays them for what they have
     done?
32 They are carried to the grave,
   and watch is kept over their tombs.
33 The soil in the valley is sweet to them;
   everyone follows after them,
   and a countless throng goes*d* before
     them.

34 'So how can you console me with your
     nonsense?
   Nothing is left of your answers but
     falsehood!'

---

b 24 The meaning of the Hebrew for this word is
uncertain.
c 30 Or *wicked are reserved for the day of calamity, / that
they are brought forth to*
d 33 Or *them, / as a countless throng went*

---

a 13 Or *in an instant*

Eliphaz

22 Then Eliphaz the Temanite replied:

2 'Can a man be of benefit to God?
    Can even a wise person benefit him?
3 What pleasure would it give the
        Almighty if you were righteous?
    What would he gain if your ways were
        blameless?

4 'Is it for your piety that he rebukes you
    and brings charges against you?
5 Is not your wickedness great?
    Are not your sins endless?
6 You demanded security from your
        relatives for no reason;
    you stripped people of their clothing,
        leaving them naked.
7 You gave no water to the weary
    and you withheld food from the
        hungry,
8 though you were a powerful man,
        owning land –
    an honoured man, living on it.
9 And you sent widows away
        empty-handed
    and broke the strength of the
        fatherless.
10 That is why snares are all around you,
    why sudden peril terrifies you,
11 why it is so dark that you cannot see,
    and why a flood of water covers you.

12 'Is not God in the heights of heaven?
    And see how lofty are the highest
        stars!
13 Yet you say, "What does God know?
    Does he judge through such
        darkness?
14 Thick clouds veil him, so he does not
        see us
    as he goes about in the vaulted
        heavens."
15 Will you keep to the old path
    that the wicked have trod?
16 They were carried off before their
        time,
    their foundations washed away by a
        flood.
17 They said to God, "Leave us alone!
    What can the Almighty do to us?"

18 Yet it was he who filled their houses
        with good things,
    so I stand aloof from the plans of the
        wicked.
19 The righteous see their ruin and
        rejoice;
    the innocent mock them, saying,
20 "Surely our foes are destroyed,
    and fire devours their wealth."

21 'Submit to God and be at peace with
        him;
    in this way prosperity will come to
        you.
22 Accept instruction from his mouth
    and lay up his words in your heart.
23 If you return to the Almighty, you will be
        restored:
    if you remove wickedness far from
        your tent
24 and assign your nuggets to the dust,
    your gold of Ophir to the rocks in the
        ravines,
25 then the Almighty will be your gold,
    the choicest silver for you.
26 Surely then you will find delight in the
        Almighty
    and will lift up your face to God.
27 You will pray to him, and he will hear
        you,
    and you will fulfil your vows.
28 What you decide on will be done,
    and light will shine on your ways.
29 When people are brought low and you
        say, "Lift them up!"
    then he will save the downcast.
30 He will deliver even one who is not
        innocent,
    who will be delivered through the
        cleanness of your hands.'

Job

23 Then Job replied:

2 'Even today my complaint is bitter;
    his hand*a* is heavy in spite of*b* my
        groaning.
3 If only I knew where to find him;
    if only I could go to his dwelling!

---

a 2 Septuagint and Syriac; Hebrew / *the hand on me*
b 2 Or *heavy on me in*

4 I would state my case before him
    and fill my mouth with arguments.
5 I would find out what he would answer
    me,
    and consider what he would say
    to me.
6 Would he vigorously oppose me with
    great power?
    No, he would not press charges
    against me.
7 There the upright can establish their
    innocence before him,
    and there I would be delivered for
    ever from my judge.

8 'But if I go to the east, he is not there;
    if I go to the west, I do not find him.
9 When he is at work in the north, I do not
    see him;
    when he turns to the south, I catch no
    glimpse of him.
10 But he knows the way that I take;
    when he has tested me, I shall come
    forth as gold.
11 My feet have closely followed his
    steps;
    I have kept to his way without turning
    aside.
12 I have not departed from the commands
    of his lips;
    I have treasured the words of his
    mouth more than my daily
    bread.

13 'But he stands alone, and who can
    oppose him?
    He does whatever he pleases.
14 He carries out his decree against me,
    and many such plans he still has in
    store.
15 That is why I am terrified before him;
    when I think of all this, I fear him.
16 God has made my heart faint;
    the Almighty has terrified me.
17 Yet I am not silenced by the darkness,
    by the thick darkness that covers my
    face.

24 'Why does the Almighty not set
       times for judgment?
    Why must those who know him look
    in vain for such days?

2 There are those who move boundary
    stones;
    they pasture flocks they have stolen.
3 They drive away the orphan's donkey
    and take the widow's ox in pledge.
4 They thrust the needy from the path
    and force all the poor of the land into
    hiding.
5 Like wild donkeys in the desert,
    the poor go about their labour of
    foraging food;
    the wasteland provides food for their
    children.
6 They gather fodder in the fields
    and glean in the vineyards of the
    wicked.
7 Lacking clothes, they spend the night
    naked;
    they have nothing to cover
    themselves in the cold.
8 They are drenched by mountain rains
    and hug the rocks for lack of shelter.
9 The fatherless child is snatched from the
    breast;
    the infant of the poor is seized for a
    debt.
10 Lacking clothes, they go about naked;
    they carry the sheaves, but still go
    hungry.
11 They crush olives among the terraces[a];
    they tread the winepresses, yet suffer
    thirst.
12 The groans of the dying rise from the
    city,
    and the souls of the wounded cry out
    for help.
    But God charges no one with
    wrongdoing.

13 'There are those who rebel against the
    light,
    who do not know its ways
    or stay in its paths.
14 When daylight is gone, the murderer
    rises up,
    kills the poor and needy,
    and in the night steals forth like a
    thief.

---

a 11 The meaning of the Hebrew for this word is
uncertain.

15 The eye of the adulterer watches for
        dusk;
    he thinks, "No eye will see me,"
    and he keeps his face concealed.
16 In the dark, thieves break into houses,
    but by day they shut themselves in;
    they want nothing to do with the
        light.
17 For all of them, midnight is their
        morning;
    they make friends with the terrors of
        darkness.

18 'Yet they are foam on the surface of the
        water;
    their portion of the land is cursed,
    so that no one goes to the vineyards.
19 As heat and drought snatch away the
        melted snow,
    so the grave snatches away those who
        have sinned.
20 The womb forgets them,
    the worm feasts on them;
    the wicked are no longer remembered
    but are broken like a tree.
21 They prey on the barren and childless
        woman,
    and to the widow they show no
        kindness.
22 But God drags away the mighty by his
        power;
    though they become established,
    they have no assurance of life.
23 He may let them rest in a feeling of
        security,
    but his eyes are on their ways.
24 For a little while they are exalted, and
        then they are gone;
    they are brought low and gathered up
        like all others;
    they are cut off like ears of corn.

25 'If this is not so, who can prove me false
    and reduce my words to nothing?'

Bildad

25
Then Bildad the Shuhite replied:

2 'Dominion and awe belong to God;
    he establishes order in the heights of
        heaven.
3 Can his forces be numbered?

On whom does his light not rise?
4 How then can a mortal be righteous
        before God?
    How can one born of woman be pure?
5 If even the moon is not bright
    and the stars are not pure in his eyes,
6 how much less a mortal, who is but a
        maggot –
    a human being, who is only a worm!'

Job

26
Then Job replied:

2 'How you have helped the powerless!
    How you have saved the arm that is
        feeble!
3 What advice you have offered to one
        without wisdom!
    And what great insight you have
        displayed!
4 Who has helped you utter these words?
    And whose spirit spoke from your
        mouth?

5 'The dead are in deep anguish,
    those beneath the waters and all that
        live in them.
6 The realm of the dead is naked before
        God;
    Destruction*a* lies uncovered.
7 He spreads out the northern skies over
        empty space;
    he suspends the earth over nothing.
8 He wraps up the waters in his clouds,
    yet the clouds do not burst under
        their weight.
9 He covers the face of the full moon,
    spreading his clouds over it.
10 He marks out the horizon on the face of
        the waters
    for a boundary between light and
        darkness.
11 The pillars of the heavens quake,
    aghast at his rebuke.
12 By his power he churned up the sea;
    by his wisdom he cut Rahab to pieces.
13 By his breath the skies became fair;
    his hand pierced the gliding serpent.
14 And these are but the outer fringe of his
        works;

---

a 6 Hebrew *Abaddon*

how faint the whisper we hear of him!
Who then can understand the
thunder of his power?'

Job's final word to his friends

27 And Job continued his discourse:

2 'As surely as God lives, who has denied
me justice,
the Almighty, who has made my life
bitter,
3 as long as I have life within me,
the breath of God in my nostrils,
4 my lips will not say anything wicked,
and my tongue will not utter lies.
5 I will never admit you are in the right;
till I die, I will not deny my integrity.
6 I will maintain my innocence and never
let go of it;
my conscience will not reproach me
as long as I live.

7 'May my enemy be like the wicked,
my adversary like the unjust!
8 For what hope have the godless when
they are cut off,
when God takes away their life?
9 Does God listen to their cry
when distress comes upon them?
10 Will they find delight in the Almighty?
Will they call on God at all times?

11 'I will teach you about the power of God;
the ways of the Almighty I will not
conceal.
12 You have all seen this yourselves.
Why then this meaningless talk?

13 'Here is the fate God allots to the
wicked,
the heritage a ruthless man receives
from the Almighty:
14 However many his children, their fate is
the sword;
his offspring will never have enough
to eat.
15 The plague will bury those who survive
him,
and their widows will not weep for
them.
16 Though he heaps up silver like dust
and clothes like piles of clay,

17 what he lays up the righteous will wear,
and the innocent will divide his silver.
18 The house he builds is like a moth's
cocoon,
like a hut made by a watchman.
19 He lies down wealthy, but will do so no
more;
when he opens his eyes, all is gone.
20 Terrors overtake him like a flood;
a tempest snatches him away in the
night.
21 The east wind carries him off, and he is
gone;
it sweeps him out of his place.
22 It hurls itself against him without mercy
as he flees headlong from its power.
23 It claps its hands in derision
and hisses him out of his place.'

YOU WHAT?
CRAZY ANIMALS

A TALKING DONKEY
Numbers 22:22–35
**VEGETARIAN LIONS AND
PACIFIST WOLVES**
Isaiah 11:1–9
ASSASSIN BEARS
2 Kings 2:23–25
A LION STANDING GUARD
1 Kings 13:20–32
A MAN-EATING FISH
Jonah 1:1–17
FOOD-DELIVERING RAVENS
1 Kings 17:4–6

Interlude: where wisdom is found

28 There is a mine for silver
and a place where gold is refined.
2 Iron is taken from the earth,
and copper is smelted from ore.
3 Mortals put an end to the darkness;
they search out the farthest recesses
for ore in the blackest darkness.

⁴ Far from human dwellings they cut a
    shaft,
  in places untouched by human feet;
  far from other people they dangle
    and sway.
⁵ The earth, from which food comes,
  is transformed below as by fire;
⁶ lapis lazuli comes from its rocks,
  and its dust contains nuggets of gold.
⁷ No bird of prey knows that hidden path,
  no falcon's eye has seen it.
⁸ Proud beasts do not set foot on it,
  and no lion prowls there.
⁹ People assault the flinty rock with their
    hands
  and lay bare the roots of the
    mountains.
¹⁰ They tunnel through the rock;
  their eyes see all its treasures.
¹¹ They search*a* the sources of the rivers
  and bring hidden things to light.

¹² But where can wisdom be found?
  Where does understanding dwell?
¹³ No mortal comprehends its worth;
  it cannot be found in the land of the
    living.
¹⁴ The deep says, 'It is not in me';
  the sea says, 'It is not with me.'
¹⁵ It cannot be bought with the finest gold,
  nor can its price be weighed out in
    silver.
¹⁶ It cannot be bought with the gold of
    Ophir,
  with precious onyx or lapis lazuli.
¹⁷ Neither gold nor crystal can compare
    with it,
  nor can it be had for jewels of gold.
¹⁸ Coral and jasper are not worthy of
    mention;
  the price of wisdom is beyond rubies.
¹⁹ The topaz of Cush cannot compare
    with it;
  it cannot be bought with pure gold.

²⁰ Where then does wisdom come from?
  Where does understanding dwell?
²¹ It is hidden from the eyes of every living
    thing,

concealed even from the birds in the
    sky.
²² Destruction*b* and Death say,
  'Only a rumour of it has reached our
    ears.'
²³ God understands the way to it
  and he alone knows where it dwells,
²⁴ for he views the ends of the earth
  and sees everything under the
    heavens.
²⁵ When he established the force of the
    wind
  and measured out the waters,
²⁶ when he made a decree for the rain
  and a path for the thunderstorm,
²⁷ then he looked at wisdom and
    appraised it;
  he confirmed it and tested it.
²⁸ And he said to the human race,
  'The fear of the Lord – that is
    wisdom,
  and to shun evil is understanding.'

Job's final defence

29
Job continued his discourse:

² 'How I long for the months gone by,
  for the days when God watched over
    me,
³ when his lamp shone on my head
  and by his light I walked through
    darkness!
⁴ Oh, for the days when I was in my prime,
  when God's intimate friendship
    blessed my house,
⁵ when the Almighty was still with me
  and my children were around me,
⁶ when my path was drenched with cream
  and the rock poured out for me
    streams of olive oil.

⁷ 'When I went to the gate of the city
  and took my seat in the public square,
⁸ the young men saw me and stepped
    aside
  and the old men rose to their feet;
⁹ the chief men refrained from speaking
  and covered their mouths with their
    hands;
¹⁰ the voices of the nobles were hushed,

---

a 11 Septuagint, Aquila and Vulgate; Hebrew *They
dam up*

b 22 Hebrew *Abaddon*

and their tongues stuck to the roof of
their mouths.

11 Whoever heard me spoke well of me,
and those who saw me commended
me,

12 because I rescued the poor who cried for
help,
and the fatherless who had none to
assist them.

13 The one who was dying blessed me;
I made the widow's heart sing.

14 I put on righteousness as my clothing;
justice was my robe and my turban.

15 I was eyes to the blind
and feet to the lame.

16 I was a father to the needy;
I took up the case of the stranger.

17 I broke the fangs of the wicked
and snatched the victims from their
teeth.

18 'I thought, "I shall die in my own house,
my days as numerous as the grains of
sand.

19 My roots will reach to the water,
and the dew will lie all night on my
branches.

20 My glory will not fade;
the bow will be ever new in my hand."

21 'People listened to me expectantly,
waiting in silence for my counsel.

22 After I had spoken, they spoke no more;
my words fell gently on their ears.

23 They waited for me as for showers
and drank in my words as the spring
rain.

24 When I smiled at them, they scarcely
believed it;
the light of my face was precious to
them.[a]

25 I chose the way for them and sat as their
chief;
I dwelt as a king among his troops;
I was like one who comforts
mourners.

30 'But now they mock me,
men younger than I,

whose fathers I would have disdained
to put with my sheep dogs.

2 Of what use was the strength of their
hands to me,
since their vigour had gone from
them?

3 Haggard from want and hunger,
they roamed[a] the parched land
in desolate wastelands at night.

4 In the brush they gathered salt herbs,
and their food[b] was the root of the
broom bush.

5 They were banished from human
society,
shouted at as if they were thieves.

6 They were forced to live in the dry
stream beds,
among the rocks and in holes in the
ground.

7 They brayed among the bushes
and huddled in the undergrowth.

8 A base and nameless brood,
they were driven out of the land.

9 'And now those young men mock me in
song;
I have become a byword among
them.

10 They detest me and keep their distance;
they do not hesitate to spit in my face.

11 Now that God has unstrung my bow and
afflicted me,
they throw off restraint in my
presence.

12 On my right the tribe[c] attacks;
they lay snares for my feet,
they build their siege ramps against
me.

13 They break up my road;
they succeed in destroying me.
"No one can help him," they say.

14 They advance as through a gaping
breach;
amid the ruins they come rolling in.

15 Terrors overwhelm me;
my dignity is driven away as by the
wind,
my safety vanishes like a cloud.

---

a 24 The meaning of the Hebrew for this clause is
uncertain.

a 3 Or gnawed
b 4 Or fuel
c 12 The meaning of the Hebrew for this word is
uncertain.

16 'And now my life ebbs away;
      days of suffering grip me.
17 Night pierces my bones;
      my gnawing pains never rest.
18 In his great power God becomes like
         clothing to me*d*;
      he binds me like the neck of my
         garment.
19 He throws me into the mud,
      and I am reduced to dust and ashes.

20 'I cry out to you, God, but you do not
         answer;
      I stand up, but you merely look at me.
21 You turn on me ruthlessly;
      with the might of your hand you
         attack me.
22 You snatch me up and drive me before
         the wind;
      you toss me about in the storm.
23 I know you will bring me down to death,
      to the place appointed for all the
         living.

24 'Surely no one lays a hand on a broken
         man
      when he cries for help in his distress.
25 Have I not wept for those in trouble?
      Has not my soul grieved for the poor?
26 Yet when I hoped for good, evil came;
      when I looked for light, then came
         darkness.
27 The churning inside me never stops;
      days of suffering confront me.
28 I go about blackened, but not by the sun;
      I stand up in the assembly and cry for
         help.
29 I have become a brother of jackals,
      a companion of owls.
30 My skin grows black and peels;
      my body burns with fever.
31 My lyre is tuned to mourning,
      and my pipe to the sound of wailing.

31 'I made a covenant with my eyes
         not to look lustfully at a young
         woman.
2 For what is our lot from God above,
      our heritage from the Almighty on
         high?

3 Is it not ruin for the wicked,
      disaster for those who do wrong?
4 Does he not see my ways
      and count my every step?

5 'If I have walked with falsehood
      or my foot has hurried after deceit –
6 let God weigh me in honest scales
      and he will know that I am
         blameless –
7 if my steps have turned from the path,
      if my heart has been led by my eyes,
      or if my hands have been defiled,
8 then may others eat what I have sown,
      and may my crops be uprooted.

9 'If my heart has been enticed by a
         woman,
      or if I have lurked at my neighbour's
         door,
10 then may my wife grind another man's
         grain,
      and may other men sleep with her.
11 For that would have been wicked,
      a sin to be judged.
12 It is a fire that burns to Destruction;*a*
      it would have uprooted my harvest.

13 'If I have denied justice to any of my
         servants,
      whether male or female,
      when they had a grievance against
         me,
14 what will I do when God confronts me?
      What will I answer when called to
         account?
15 Did not he who made me in the womb
         make them?
      Did not the same one form us both
         within our mothers?

16 'If I have denied the desires of the poor
      or let the eyes of the widow grow
         weary,
17 if I have kept my bread to myself,
      not sharing it with the fatherless –
18 but from my youth I reared them as a
         father would,
      and from my birth I guided the
         widow –

d 18 Hebrew; Septuagint *power he grasps my clothing*   *a* 12 Hebrew *Abaddon*

19 if I have seen anyone perishing for lack
of clothing,
or the needy without garments,
20 and their hearts did not bless me
for warming them with the fleece
from my sheep,
21 if I have raised my hand against the
fatherless,
knowing that I had influence in court,
22 then let my arm fall from the shoulder,
let it be broken off at the joint.
23 For I dreaded destruction from God,
and for fear of his splendour I could
not do such things.

24 'If I have put my trust in gold
or said to pure gold, "You are my
security,"
25 if I have rejoiced over my great wealth,
the fortune my hands had gained,
26 if I have regarded the sun in its radiance
or the moon moving in splendour,
27 so that my heart was secretly enticed
and my hand offered them a kiss of
homage,
28 then these also would be sins to be
judged,
for I would have been unfaithful to
God on high.

29 'If I have rejoiced at my enemy's
misfortune
or gloated over the trouble that came
to him –
30 I have not allowed my mouth to sin
by invoking a curse against their
life –
31 if those of my household have never
said,
"Who has not been filled with Job's
meat?" –
32 but no stranger had to spend the night
in the street,
for my door was always open to the
traveller –
33 if I have concealed my sin as people do,*b*
by hiding my guilt in my heart
34 because I so feared the crowd
and so dreaded the contempt of the
clans

that I kept silent and would not go
outside –

35 ('Oh, that I had someone to hear me!
I sign now my defence – let the
Almighty answer me;
let my accuser put his indictment in
writing.
36 Surely I would wear it on my shoulder,
I would put it on like a crown.
37 I would give him an account of my every
step;
I would present it to him as to a
ruler.') –

38 'if my land cries out against me
and all its furrows are wet with tears,
39 if I have devoured its yield without
payment
or broken the spirit of its tenants,
40 then let briers come up instead of wheat
and stinkweed instead of barley.'

The words of Job are ended.

Elihu

32 So these three men stopped answering Job, because he was righteous in his own eyes. 2 But Elihu son of Barakel the Buzite, of the family of Ram, became very angry with Job for justifying himself rather than God. 3 He was also angry with the three friends, because they had found no way to refute Job, and yet had condemned him.*a* 4 Now Elihu had waited before speaking to Job because they were older than he. 5 But when he saw that the three men had nothing more to say, his anger was aroused.

6 So Elihu son of Barakel the Buzite said:

'I am young in years,
and you are old;
that is why I was fearful,
not daring to tell you what I know.
7 I thought, "Age should speak;
advanced years should teach
wisdom."

---

b 33 Or *as Adam did*

a 3 Masoretic Text; an ancient Hebrew scribal tradition *Job, and so had condemned God*

8 But it is the spirit[b] in a person,
   the breath of the Almighty, that gives
     them understanding.
9 It is not only the old[c] who are wise,
   not only the aged who understand
     what is right.

10 'Therefore I say: listen to me;
   I too will tell you what I know.
11 I waited while you spoke,
   I listened to your reasoning;
   while you were searching for words,
12   I gave you my full attention.
   But not one of you has proved Job
     wrong;
   none of you has answered his
     arguments.
13 Do not say, "We have found wisdom;
   let God, not a man, refute him."
14 But Job has not marshalled his words
     against me,
   and I will not answer him with your
     arguments.

FACT

FIRST PRINTED BOOK

The first book ever printed using modern printing techniques was a Bible. In the fifteenth century Johannes Gutenberg invented the printing press, and in 1454 his first product was a copy of the Bible.

15 'They are dismayed and have no more to
     say;
   words have failed them.
16 Must I wait, now that they are silent,
   now that they stand there with no
     reply?
17 I too will have my say;
   I too will tell what I know.

18 For I am full of words,
   and the spirit within me compels me;
19 inside I am like bottled-up wine,
   like new wineskins ready to burst.
20 I must speak and find relief;
   I must open my lips and reply.
21 I will show no partiality,
   nor will I flatter anyone;
22 for if I were skilled in flattery,
   my Maker would soon take me away.

33 'But now, Job, listen to my words;
     pay attention to everything I say.
2 I am about to open my mouth;
   my words are on the tip of my
     tongue.
3 My words come from an upright heart;
   my lips sincerely speak what I know.
4 The Spirit of God has made me;
   the breath of the Almighty gives me
     life.
5 Answer me then, if you can;
   stand up and argue your case before
     me.
6 I am the same as you; in God's sight;
   I too am a piece of clay.
7 No fear of me should alarm you,
   nor should my hand be heavy on you.

8 'But you have said in my hearing –
   I heard the very words –
9 "I am pure, I have done no wrong;
   I am clean and free from sin.
10 Yet God has found fault with me;
   he considers me his enemy.
11 He fastens my feet in shackles;
   he keeps close watch on all my
     paths."

12 'But I tell you, in this you are not right,
   for God is greater than any mortal.
13 Why do you complain to him
   that he responds to no one's words[a]?
14 For God does speak – now one way, now
     another –
   though no one perceives it.
15 In a dream, in a vision of the night,
   when deep sleep falls on people
   as they slumber in their beds,

---

b 8 Or *Spirit*; also in verse 18
c 9 Or *many*; or *great*

a 13 Or *that he does not answer for any of his actions*

16 he may speak in their ears
and terrify them with warnings,
17 to turn them from wrongdoing
and keep them from pride,
18 to preserve them from the pit,
their lives from perishing by the
sword.*b*

19 'Or someone may be chastened on a bed
of pain
with constant distress in their bones,
20 so that their body finds food repulsive
and their soul loathes the choicest
meal.
21 Their flesh wastes away to nothing,
and their bones, once hidden, now
stick out.
22 They draw near to the pit,
and their life to the messengers of
death.*c*
23 Yet if there is an angel at their side,
a messenger, one out of a thousand,
sent to tell them how to be upright,
24 and he is gracious to that person and
says to God,
"Spare them from going down to the
pit;
I have found a ransom for them –
25 let their flesh be renewed like a child's;
let them be restored as in the days of
their youth" –
26 then that person can pray to God and
find favour with him,
they will see God's face and shout for
joy;
he will restore them to full well-
being.
27 And they will go to others and say,
"I have sinned, and I have perverted
what is right,
but I did not get what I deserved.
28 God has delivered me from going down
to the pit,
and I shall live to enjoy the light of
life."

29 'God does all these things to a person –
twice, even three times –

30 to turn them back from the pit,
that the light of life may shine on
them.

31 'Pay attention, Job, and listen to me;
be silent, and I will speak.
32 If you have anything to say, answer me;
speak up, for I want to vindicate you.
33 But if not, then listen to me;
be silent, and I will teach you
wisdom.'

34 Then Elihu said:

2 'Hear my words, you wise men;
listen to me, you men of learning.
3 For the ear tests words
as the tongue tastes food.
4 Let us discern for ourselves what is
right;
let us learn together what is good.

5 'Job says, "I am innocent,
but God denies me justice.
6 Although I am right,
I am considered a liar;
although I am guiltless,
his arrow inflicts an incurable
wound."
7 Is there anyone like Job,
who drinks scorn like water?
8 He keeps company with evildoers;
he associates with the wicked.
9 For he says, "There is no profit
in trying to please God."

10 'So listen to me, you men of
understanding.
Far be it from God to do evil,
from the Almighty to do wrong.
11 He repays everyone for what they have
done;
he brings on them what their conduct
deserves.
12 It is unthinkable that God would do
wrong,
that the Almighty would pervert
justice.
13 Who appointed him over the earth?
Who put him in charge of the whole
world?
14 If it were his intention

---

b 18 Or *from crossing the river*
c 22 Or *to the place of the dead*

and he withdrew his spirit[a] and
    breath,
15 all humanity would perish together
    and mankind would return to the
    dust.

16 'If you have understanding, hear this;
    listen to what I say.
17 Can someone who hates justice govern?
    Will you condemn the just and
    mighty One?
18 Is he not the One who says to kings,
    "You are worthless,"
    and to nobles, "You are wicked,"
19 who shows no partiality to princes
    and does not favour the rich over the
    poor,
    for they are all the work of his hands?
20 They die in an instant, in the middle of
    the night;
    the people are shaken and they pass
    away;
    the mighty are removed without
    human hand.

21 'His eyes are on the ways of mortals;
    he sees their every step.
22 There is no deep shadow, no utter
    darkness,
    where evildoers can hide.
23 God has no need to examine men
    further,
    that they should come before him for
    judgment.
24 Without enquiry he shatters the mighty
    and sets up others in their place.
25 Because he takes note of their deeds,
    he overthrows them in the night and
    they are crushed.
26 He punishes them for their wickedness
    where everyone can see them,
27 because they turned from following
    him
    and had no regard for any of his ways.
28 They caused the cry of the poor to come
    before him,
    so that he heard the cry of the needy.
29 But if he remains silent, who can
    condemn him?
    If he hides his face, who can see him?

Yet he is over individual and nation
    alike,
30 to keep the godless from ruling,
    from laying snares for the people.

31 'Suppose someone says to God,
    "I am guilty but will offend no more.
32 Teach me what I cannot see;
    if I have done wrong, I will not do so
    again."
33 Should God then reward you on your
    terms,
    when you refuse to repent?
    You must decide, not I;
    so tell me what you know.

34 'Men of understanding declare,
    wise men who hear me say to me,
35 "Job speaks without knowledge;
    his words lack insight."
36 Oh, that Job might be tested to the
    utmost
    for answering like a wicked man!
37 To his sin he adds rebellion;
    scornfully he claps his hands among
    us
    and multiplies his words against
    God.'

35 Then Elihu said:

2 'Do you think this is just?
    You say, "I am in the right, not God."
3 Yet you ask him, "What profit is it to
    me,[a]
    and what do I gain by not sinning?"

4 'I would like to reply to you
    and to your friends with you.
5 Look up at the heavens and see;
    gaze at the clouds so high above you.
6 If you sin, how does that affect him?
    If your sins are many, what does that
    do to him?
7 If you are righteous, what do you give to
    him,
    or what does he receive from your
    hand?
8 Your wickedness only affects humans
    like yourself,

---

a 14 Or *Spirit*   *a* 3 Or *you*

and your righteousness only other
people.

9 'People cry out under a load of
oppression;
they plead for relief from the arm of
the powerful.
10 But no one says, "Where is God my
Maker,
who gives songs in the night,
11 who teaches us more than he teaches[b]
the beasts of the earth
and makes us wiser than[c] the birds in
the sky?"
12 He does not answer when people cry
out
because of the arrogance of the
wicked.
13 Indeed, God does not listen to their
empty plea;
the Almighty pays no attention to it.
14 How much less, then, will he listen
when you say that you do not see
him,
that your case is before him
and you must wait for him,
15 and further, that his anger never
punishes
and he does not take the least notice
of wickedness.[d]
16 So Job opens his mouth with empty
talk;
without knowledge he multiplies
words.'

36 Elihu continued:

2 'Bear with me a little longer and I will
show you
that there is more to be said on God's
behalf.
3 I get my knowledge from afar;
I will ascribe justice to my Maker.
4 Be assured that my words are not false;
one who has perfect knowledge is
with you.

5 'God is mighty, but despises no one;
he is mighty, and firm in his purpose.
6 He does not keep the wicked alive
but gives the afflicted their rights.
7 He does not take his eyes off the
righteous;
he enthrones them with kings
and exalts them for ever.
8 But if people are bound in chains,
held fast by cords of affliction,
9 he tells them what they have done –
that they have sinned arrogantly.
10 He makes them listen to correction
and commands them to repent of
their evil.

FAVOURITE VERSES
Job 38:4

*Where were you when I laid the
earth's foundation?
Tell me, if you understand.*

This verse and the following
chapters are my favourite because
they give me a glimpse of how
amazing God is and let me know
that no problem is too big for him.

Benedicta, 18

11 If they obey and serve him,
they will spend the rest of their days
in prosperity
and their years in contentment.
12 But if they do not listen,
they will perish by the sword[a]
and die without knowledge.

13 'The godless in heart harbour
resentment;
even when he fetters them, they do
not cry for help.
14 They die in their youth,

---

b 10,11 Or night, / 11who teaches us by
c 11 Or us wise by
d 15 Symmachus, Theodotion and Vulgate; the
meaning of the Hebrew for this word is uncertain.

a 12 Or will cross the river

among male prostitutes of the
shrines.

15 But those who suffer he delivers in their
suffering;
he speaks to them in their affliction.

16 'He is wooing you from the jaws of
distress
to a spacious place free from
restriction,
to the comfort of your table laden
with choice food.

17 But now you are laden with the
judgment due to the wicked;
judgment and justice have taken hold
of you.

18 Be careful that no one entices you by
riches;
do not let a large bribe turn you aside.

19 Would your wealth or even all your
mighty efforts
sustain you so you would not be in
distress?

20 Do not long for the night,
to drag people away from their
homes.*b*

21 Beware of turning to evil,
which you seem to prefer to
affliction.

22 'God is exalted in his power.
Who is a teacher like him?

23 Who has prescribed his ways for him,
or said to him, "You have done
wrong"?

24 Remember to extol his work,
which people have praised in song.

25 All humanity has seen it;
mortals gaze on it from afar.

26 How great is God – beyond our
understanding!
The number of his years is past
finding out.

27 'He draws up the drops of water,
which distil as rain to the streams*c*;

28 the clouds pour down their moisture

and abundant showers fall on
mankind.

29 Who can understand how he spreads
out the clouds,
how he thunders from his pavilion?

30 See how he scatters his lightning about
him,
bathing the depths of the sea.

31 This is the way he governs*d* the nations
and provides food in abundance.

32 He fills his hands with lightning
and commands it to strike its mark.

33 His thunder announces the coming
storm;
even the cattle make known its
approach.*e*

37 'At this my heart pounds
and leaps from its place.

2 Listen! Listen to the roar of his voice,
to the rumbling that comes from his
mouth.

3 He unleashes his lightning beneath the
whole heaven
and sends it to the ends of the earth.

4 After that comes the sound of his roar;
he thunders with his majestic voice.
When his voice resounds,
he holds nothing back.

5 God's voice thunders in marvellous
ways;
he does great things beyond our
understanding.

6 He says to the snow, "Fall on the
earth,"
and to the rain shower, "Be a mighty
downpour."

7 So that everyone he has made may know
his work,
he stops all people from their
labour.*a*

8 The animals take cover;
they remain in their dens.

9 The tempest comes out from its
chamber,
the cold from the driving winds.

10 The breath of God produces ice,

---

b 20 The meaning of the Hebrew for verses 18-20
is uncertain.
c 27 Or *distil from the mist as rain*

d 31 Or *nourishes*
e 33 Or *announces his coming – / the One zealous against evil*
a 7 Or *work, / he fills all people with fear by his power*

and the broad waters become
frozen.

11 He loads the clouds with moisture;
he scatters his lightning through
them.

12 At his direction they swirl around
over the face of the whole earth
to do whatever he commands them.

13 He brings the clouds to punish people,
or to water his earth and show his
love.

14 'Listen to this, Job;
stop and consider God's wonders.

15 Do you know how God controls the
clouds
and makes his lightning flash?

16 Do you know how the clouds hang
poised,
those wonders of him who is perfect
in knowledge?

17 You who swelter in your clothes
when the land lies hushed under the
south wind,

18 can you join him in spreading out the
skies,
hard as a mirror of cast bronze?

19 'Tell us what we should say to him;
we cannot draw up our case because
of our darkness.

20 Should he be told that I want to speak?
Would anyone ask to be swallowed
up?

21 Now no one can look at the sun,
bright as it is in the skies
after the wind has swept them
clean.

22 Out of the north he comes in golden
splendour;
God comes in awesome majesty.

23 The Almighty is beyond our reach and
exalted in power;
in his justice and great righteousness,
he does not oppress.

24 Therefore, people revere him,
for does he not have regard for all the
wise in heart?*b*'

The LORD speaks

38 Then the LORD spoke to Job out of
the storm. He said:

2 'Who is this that obscures my plans
with words without knowledge?

3 Brace yourself like a man;
I will question you,
and you shall answer me.

4 'Where were you when I laid the earth's
foundation?
Tell me, if you understand.

5 Who marked off its dimensions? Surely
you know!
Who stretched a measuring line
across it?

6 On what were its footings set,
or who laid its cornerstone –

7 while the morning stars sang together
and all the angels*a* shouted for joy?

8 'Who shut up the sea behind doors
when it burst forth from the womb,

9 when I made the clouds its garment
and wrapped it in thick darkness,

10 when I fixed limits for it
and set its doors and bars in place,

11 when I said, "This far you may come and
no farther;
here is where your proud waves halt"?

12 'Have you ever given orders to the
morning,
or shown the dawn its place,

13 that it might take the earth by the edges
and shake the wicked out of it?

14 The earth takes shape like clay under a
seal;
its features stand out like those of a
garment.

15 The wicked are denied their light,
and their uplifted arm is broken.

16 'Have you journeyed to the springs of
the sea
or walked in the recesses of the deep?

17 Have the gates of death been shown to
you?

---

b 24 Or *for he does not have regard for any who think they
are wise.*

a 7 Hebrew *the sons of God*

WHAT IS CHRISTIANITY? 1

Doctrine of creation: what a wonderful world

Up until this point in Job, God has not said much. Job and his mates have been debating what has caused his suffering. They have been asking question after question, and now God interrupts. He decides it's his turn to ask a few questions...

Job 38 – 39 make up some of the most wonderful descriptions of creation in the whole Bible (for other creation sections you might want to check out Genesis 1 and Psalm 8). Here we read about everything from constellations of stars to tiny drops of dew. People today have many different understandings of how the world came to be. What do we believe as Christians about what creation is and where it came from?

Job shows us that there is a person behind creation. It didn't just spring up by accident. It was designed by God. We can all make things, so long as we have the raw materials – paint, a couple of loo rolls and some glue. But God created everything we see around us from absolutely nothing. Wow!

This tells us two things. First, God is totally different from creation. He's the only Maker in (and outside) the universe. He is totally other and unique.

Second, everything in creation depends on God. You and I don't just need oxygen, water and food. Whether we're aware of it or not, every second we live is a result of God's will. God is the only truly independent being to exist.

Creation doesn't just depend on God for its existence. It depends on God for its meaning. Without a Maker, the world would just be an accident. It would be empty of purpose. As Christians, because we believe there is a person behind creation, we know there is a purpose to creation. Not only do our individual lives have meaning – the whole world does!

Job 38 gives us a glimpse of the ultimate purpose of creation. It displays God's glory. In the vastness and variety of creation, in the expanse and detail, we see the power, imagination and sheer energy and zest for life that exist in our God. What's more, when God made creation to display his glory, it was not as if he was making a car to get him from A to B. God is like an artist who paints for the joy of creating beauty itself. Have you ever wondered how many stunning sunsets he made that no human being ever saw?

Sometimes we can miss the goodness of creation. God made a world full of pleasures – warm fires, soft beds, ice-cold drinks, soaring mountain peaks. He made it for us to care for, but also for us to enjoy. Creation is not God, but it is good. It's rational and ordered (which is why science experiments are worth doing), but it's also full of surprises and new things to discover. The more we discover of God's creation, the more we discover of the God it glorifies.

Andy Croft

Genesis 3 ⏩

Have you seen the gates of the
  deepest darkness?
18 Have you comprehended the vast
  expanses of the earth?
  Tell me, if you know all this.

19 'What is the way to the abode of light?
  And where does darkness reside?
20 Can you take them to their places?
  Do you know the paths to their
    dwellings?
21 Surely you know, for you were already
    born!
  You have lived so many years!

22 'Have you entered the storehouses of
    the snow
  or seen the storehouses of the hail,
23 which I reserve for times of trouble,
  for days of war and battle?
24 What is the way to the place where the
    lightning is dispersed,
  or the place where the east winds are
    scattered over the earth?
25 Who cuts a channel for the torrents of
    rain,
  and a path for the thunderstorm,
26 to water a land where no one lives,
  an uninhabited desert,
27 to satisfy a desolate wasteland
  and make it sprout with grass?
28 Does the rain have a father?
  Who fathers the drops of dew?
29 From whose womb comes the ice?
  Who gives birth to the frost from the
    heavens
30 when the waters become hard as stone,
  when the surface of the deep is
    frozen?

31 'Can you bind the chains*b* of the
    Pleiades?
  Can you loosen Orion's belt?
32 Can you bring forth the constellations
    in their seasons*c*
  or lead out the Bear*d* with its cubs?
33 Do you know the laws of the heavens?

Can you set up God's*e* dominion over
  the earth?

34 'Can you raise your voice to the clouds
  and cover yourself with a flood of
    water?
35 Do you send the lightning bolts on their
    way?
  Do they report to you, "Here we are"?
36 Who gives the ibis wisdom*f*
  or gives the cockerel understanding?*g*
37 Who has the wisdom to count the
    clouds?
  Who can tip over the water jars of the
    heavens
38 when the dust becomes hard
  and the clods of earth stick together?

39 'Do you hunt the prey for the lioness
  and satisfy the hunger of the lions
40 when they crouch in their dens
  or lie in wait in a thicket?
41 Who provides food for the raven
  when its young cry out to God
  and wander about for lack of food?

39 'Do you know when the mountain
  goats give birth?
  Do you watch when the doe bears her
    fawn?
2 Do you count the months till they bear?
  Do you know the time they give
    birth?
3 They crouch down and bring forth their
    young;
  their labour pains are ended.
4 Their young thrive and grow strong in
    the wilds;
  they leave and do not return.

5 'Who let the wild donkey go free?
  Who untied its ropes?
6 I gave it the wasteland as its home,
  the salt flats as its habitat.
7 It laughs at the commotion in the
    town;
  it does not hear a driver's shout.

---

b 31 Septuagint; Hebrew *beauty*
c 32 Or *the morning star in its season*
d 32 Or *out Leo*

e 33 Or *their*
f 36 That is, wisdom about the flooding of the Nile
g 36 That is, understanding of when to crow; the
  meaning of the Hebrew for this verse is uncertain.

⁸ It ranges the hills for its pasture
  and searches for any green thing.

⁹ 'Will the wild ox consent to serve you?
  Will it stay by your manger at night?
¹⁰ Can you hold it to the furrow with a
  harness?
  Will it till the valleys behind you?

¹¹ Will you rely on it for its great
  strength?
  Will you leave your heavy work to it?
¹² Can you trust it to haul in your grain
  and bring it to your threshing-floor?

¹³ 'The wings of the ostrich flap joyfully,
  though they cannot compare

FAITH IN THE WORLD 5

GOD GETS HIS HANDS DIRTY

Has anybody ever stopped you to ask directions to somewhere? Chances are that you find it really disappointing if you can't help. If you can, though, it gives you a real sense of satisfaction. That's the way God created us: we love helping people out – we love meeting a need.

The book of Job is about a man who suffers horribly but still holds on to his faith in God. He asks big questions about why he has had to go through so much pain. When he (finally) answers, God paints a bigger picture for him: *'Who cuts a channel for the torrents of rain, and a path for the thunderstorm, to water a land where no one lives?'* (Job 38:25–26). God is reassuring Job that no matter what happens, he is in charge of creation: Job should trust his wisdom. Job is concerned with his own suffering as an individual; God cares about the bigger picture – the well-being of the whole world, as well as each individual. So we see a God who cares deeply for his creation, who meets its needs and loves doing so. God 'satisfies' the desolate wasteland with rain.

We also see that God loves getting his hands dirty. We can often think that God is all about distancing himself from dirt, refusing to take part in the action. Nothing could be further from the truth. In Job we meet a God who digs channels in the desert, wrestles creatures of the deep and sends lightning bolts on their way! God loves work. God loves meeting the needs of his creation.

In fact, pretty much all work is about meeting a variety of needs. From doing a newspaper round to forecasting the weather, our work is about helping other people to do their work, or to live their life. We might not always love the work we do, but we should ask: is it meeting a need? Not just our own needs: getting an education means we can provide food and shelter for ourselves later in life. Are we preparing to help out with the needs of the wider world? If we do work that genuinely helps people out, we'll find it richly rewarding.

Looking for a career doesn't mean you have to wait for sign-writing in the sky from God saying, 'Be an orthopaedic surgeon!' You can simply ask: is it something I'm passionate about doing, and does it meet a real need in the world?

Jason Gardner

 Exodus 31:1–11   Isaiah 28:23–29

with the wings and feathers of the
stork.

14 She lays her eggs on the ground
and lets them warm in the sand,
15 unmindful that a foot may crush them,
that some wild animal may trample
them.
16 She treats her young harshly, as if they
were not hers;
she cares not that her labour was in
vain,
17 for God did not endow her with
wisdom
or give her a share of good sense.
18 Yet when she spreads her feathers to
run,
she laughs at horse and rider.

19 'Do you give the horse its strength
or clothe its neck with a flowing
mane?
20 Do you make it leap like a locust,
striking terror with its proud
snorting?
21 It paws fiercely, rejoicing in its strength,
and charges into the fray.
22 It laughs at fear, afraid of nothing;
it does not shy away from the sword.
23 The quiver rattles against its side,
along with the flashing spear and
lance.
24 In frenzied excitement it eats up the
ground;
it cannot stand still when the trumpet
sounds.
25 At the blast of the trumpet it snorts,
"Aha!"
It catches the scent of battle from
afar,
the shout of commanders and the
battle cry.

26 'Does the hawk take flight by your
wisdom
and spread its wings towards the
south?
27 Does the eagle soar at your command
and build its nest on high?
28 It dwells on a cliff and stays there at
night;
a rocky crag is its stronghold.
29 From there it looks for food;

its eyes detect it from afar.
30 Its young ones feast on blood,
and where the slain are, there it is.'

40 The LORD said to Job:

2 'Will the one who contends with the
Almighty correct him?
Let him who accuses God answer
him!'

3 Then Job answered the LORD:

4 'I am unworthy – how can I reply to you?
I put my hand over my mouth.
5 I spoke once, but I have no answer –
twice, but I will say no more.'

6 Then the LORD spoke to Job out of the
storm:

7 'Brace yourself like a man;
I will question you,
and you shall answer me.

8 'Would you discredit my justice?
Would you condemn me to justify
yourself?
9 Do you have an arm like God's,
and can your voice thunder like his?
10 Then adorn yourself with glory and
splendour,
and clothe yourself in honour and
majesty.
11 Unleash the fury of your wrath,
look at all who are proud and bring
them low,
12 look at all who are proud and humble
them,
crush the wicked where they stand.
13 Bury them all in the dust together;
shroud their faces in the grave.
14 Then I myself will admit to you
that your own right hand can save
you.

15 'Look at Behemoth,
which I made along with you
and which feeds on grass like an ox.
16 What strength it has in its loins,
what power in the muscles of its
belly!

¹⁷ Its tail sways like a cedar;
    the sinews of its thighs are close-knit.
¹⁸ Its bones are tubes of bronze,
    its limbs like rods of iron.
¹⁹ It ranks first among the works of God,

    yet its Maker can approach it with his
    sword.
²⁰ The hills bring it their produce,
    and all the wild animals play nearby.
²¹ Under the lotus plant it lies,

PAIN AND SUFFERING 9

NOT 'WHY' BUT WHO HE IS

When life is painful, there's one question we're all tempted to ask. Why? Why me? Why do I have to go through this? We can look at other people and get annoyed when we perceive that their lives are more straightforward and easier than our own. So we ask, 'Why, God, why?'

In terms of the 'why' in Job's life, we read in Job 1 that there was a conversation going on between God and Satan that Job knew nothing about. Ever since then, we have heard Job's friends' theories about what's going on and we have heard Job questioning everything. But none of them has been even close to working out what's really happening.

Then, in chapters 38 – 41, God answers back. This is what Job has been crying out for, but if he thinks it's going to be easy, he's got another think coming. God speaks, but he doesn't say, 'There, there, Job. Really sorry I had to put you through that, but this is what was going on … we won, you proved my point, and I've sent Satan packing. Well done, Job. You did it!' In fact, God doesn't answer the 'why' at all. Instead he tells Job a couple of facts about himself. You can only imagine his voice thundering from heaven and Job trembling on the ground as he gets a response he never expected. The Lord reminds Job that he is God, and catalogues one or two important details about the position. He reminds Job that he is in control of everything. He created the entire universe and he can do whatever he wants with it. He tells of his incredible power and questions Job about whether he knows how the world works.

Thankfully Job doesn't make an idiot of himself by trying to bluster a reply. He holds his hands up and admits that God is all-powerful and that he himself has been talking about things he doesn't really understand (42:3).

While God seems completely happy with us questioning him, we have to keep in mind that he doesn't have to answer to us. We're not his boss. He is God and we're not. God doesn't always answer our 'why' questions. I don't think we would understand most of the answers even if he did. But in our times of pain and suffering he will always remind us of who he is. He tells us that he is powerful, loving and kind. He reminds us that no matter what we are suffering, he is always good and he is always with us. When we grasp that fact, we will, like Job, loosen our grip on our need for a reason why.

Mike Pilavachi

 Job 2   Hebrews 12:1–3 ▶

hidden among the reeds in the marsh.

²² The lotuses conceal it in their shadow;
the poplars by the stream surround it.

²³ A raging river does not alarm it;
it is secure, though the Jordan should surge against its mouth.

²⁴ Can anyone capture it by the eyes,
or trap it and pierce its nose?

41 ᵃ 'Can you pull in Leviathan with a fishhook

or tie down its tongue with a rope?

² Can you put a cord through its nose
or pierce its jaw with a hook?

³ Will it keep begging you for mercy?
Will it speak to you with gentle words?

⁴ Will it make an agreement with you
for you to take it as your slave for life?

⁵ Can you make a pet of it like a bird
or put it on a leash for the young women in your house?

⁶ Will traders barter for it?
Will they divide it up among the merchants?

⁷ Can you fill its hide with harpoons
or its head with fishing spears?

⁸ If you lay a hand on it,
you will remember the struggle and never do it again!

⁹ Any hope of subduing it is false;
the mere sight of it is overpowering.

¹⁰ No one is fierce enough to rouse it.
Who then is able to stand against me?

¹¹ Who has a claim against me that I must pay?
Everything under heaven belongs to me.

¹² 'I will not fail to speak of Leviathan's limbs,
its strength and its graceful form.

¹³ Who can strip off its outer coat?
Who can penetrate its double coat of armourᵇ?

¹⁴ Who dares open the doors of its mouth,
ringed about with its fearsome teeth?

¹⁵ Its back hasᶜ rows of shields
tightly sealed together;

¹⁶ each is so close to the next
that no air can pass between.

¹⁷ They are joined fast to one another;
they cling together and cannot be parted.

¹⁸ Its snorting throws out flashes of light;
its eyes are like the rays of dawn.

¹⁹ Flames stream from its mouth;
sparks of fire shoot out.

²⁰ Smoke pours from its nostrils
as from a boiling pot over burning reeds.

²¹ Its breath sets coals ablaze,
and flames dart from its mouth.

²² Strength resides in its neck;
dismay goes before it.

²³ The folds of its flesh are tightly joined;
they are firm and immovable.

²⁴ Its chest is hard as rock,
hard as a lower millstone.

²⁵ When it rises up, the mighty are terrified;
they retreat before its thrashing.

²⁶ The sword that reaches it has no effect,
nor does the spear or the dart or the javelin.

²⁷ Iron it treats like straw
and bronze like rotten wood.

²⁸ Arrows do not make it flee;
slingstones are like chaff to it.

²⁹ A club seems to it but a piece of straw;
it laughs at the rattling of the lance.

³⁰ Its undersides are jagged potsherds,
leaving a trail in the mud like a threshing-sledge.

³¹ It makes the depths churn like a boiling cauldron
and stirs up the sea like a pot of ointment.

³² It leaves a glistening wake behind it;
one would think the deep had white hair.

³³ Nothing on earth is its equal –
a creature without fear.

³⁴ It looks down on all that are haughty;
it is king over all that are proud.'

ᵃ In Hebrew texts 41:1-8 is numbered 40:25-32, and 41:9-34 is numbered 41:1-26.
ᵇ 13 Septuagint; Hebrew *double bridle*

ᶜ 15 Or *Its pride is its*

Job

42
Then Job replied to the LORD:

2 'I know that you can do all things;
　no purpose of yours can be thwarted.
3 You asked, "Who is this that obscures
　　my plans without knowledge?"
　Surely I spoke of things I did not
　　understand,
　things too wonderful for me to
　　know.

4 'You said, "Listen now, and I will speak;
　I will question you,
　and you shall answer me."
5 My ears had heard of you
　but now my eyes have seen you.
6 Therefore I despise myself
　and repent in dust and ashes.'

Epilogue

7 After the LORD had said these things to Job, he said to Eliphaz the Temanite, 'I am angry with you and your two friends, because you have not spoken the truth about me, as my servant Job has. 8 So now take seven bulls and seven rams and go to my servant Job and sacrifice a burnt offering for yourselves. My servant Job will pray for you, and I will accept his prayer and not deal with you according to your folly. You have not spoken the truth about me, as my servant Job has.' 9 So Eliphaz the Temanite, Bildad the Shuhite and Zophar the Naamathite did what the LORD told them; and the LORD accepted Job's prayer.

10 After Job had prayed for his friends, the LORD restored his fortunes and gave him twice as much as he had before. 11 All his brothers and sisters and everyone who had known him before came and ate with him in his house. They comforted and consoled him over all the trouble the LORD had brought on him, and each one gave him a piece of silver^a and a gold ring.

12 The LORD blessed the latter part of Job's life more than the former part. He had fourteen thousand sheep, six thousand camels, a thousand yoke of oxen and a thousand donkeys. 13 And he also had seven sons and three daughters. 14 The first daughter he named Jemimah, the second Keziah and the third Keren-Happuch. 15 Nowhere in all the land were there found women as beautiful as Job's daughters, and their father granted them an inheritance along with their brothers.

16 After this, Job lived a hundred and forty years; he saw his children and their children to the fourth generation. 17 And so Job died, an old man and full of years.

a 11 Hebrew *him a kesitah*; a kesitah was a unit of money of unknown weight and value.

PSALMS

DATE

The Psalms were written over a long period of time before being gathered together in one book. It is thought that around two thirds were written before the exile to Babylon and the last third afterwards.

AUTHOR

There were a number of writers, including King David

WHAT'S IT ALL ABOUT?

The Psalms were a hymn book for God's people; they were the original songs of worship. They cover the full range of human emotion, from bursting joy at God's goodness to the depths of despair at the agony the people were dealing with. There are five different types of psalm: hymns that tell of God's character and actions, laments (songs of grief) for national disasters, laments for personal crises, royal psalms that tell of a special occasion in the life of a king, and psalms of thanksgiving. The psalms of lament are the largest group and remind us that God is big enough to handle all of our questions. The writers were completely honest about how they were feeling, but always came back to a key fact: God is good and worthy of praise, no matter what.

WHY SHOULD WE READ IT?

- Much of the Bible tells us the history of God's people or what God was saying to his people through his prophets. The Psalms tell us what the people were saying to God.

- When we are stuck for words, the Psalms give us amazing words to use as prayer and praise.

- The Psalms help us remember that it's OK to cry out to God when we are in pain, and it's OK to be completely honest with him.

Andy Croft with Liza Hoeksma

Book I
Psalms 1 – 41

Psalm 1

1 Blessed is the one
    who does not walk in step with the
        wicked
  or stand in the way that sinners take
  or sit in the company of mockers,
2 but whose delight is in the law of the
        LORD,
    and who meditates on his law day and
        night.
3 That person is like a tree planted by
        streams of water,
    which yields its fruit in season
  and whose leaf does not wither –
    whatever they do prospers.

4 Not so the wicked!
    They are like chaff
    that the wind blows away.
5 Therefore the wicked will not stand in
        the judgment,
    nor sinners in the assembly of the
        righteous.

6 For the LORD watches over the way of
        the righteous,
    but the way of the wicked leads to
        destruction.

Psalm 2

1 Why do the nations conspire*a*
    and the peoples plot in vain?
2 The kings of the earth rise up
    and the rulers band together
    against the LORD and against his
        anointed, saying,
3 'Let us break their chains
    and throw off their shackles.'

4 The One enthroned in heaven laughs;
    the Lord scoffs at them.
5 He rebukes them in his anger
    and terrifies them in his wrath,
        saying,

6 'I have installed my king
    on Zion, my holy mountain.'

7 I will proclaim the LORD's decree:

He said to me, 'You are my son;
    today I have become your father.
8 Ask me,
    and I will make the nations your
        inheritance,
    the ends of the earth your
        possession.
9 You will break them with a rod of iron*b*;
    you will dash them to pieces like
        pottery.'

10 Therefore, you kings, be wise;
    be warned, you rulers of the earth.
11 Serve the LORD with fear
    and celebrate his rule with trembling.
12 Kiss his son, or he will be angry
    and your way will lead to your
        destruction,
  for his wrath can flare up in a moment.
  Blessed are all who take refuge in
        him.

Psalm 3*a*
A psalm of David. When he fled from his son Absalom.

1 LORD, how many are my foes!
    How many rise up against me!
2 Many are saying of me,
    'God will not deliver him.'*b*

3 But you, LORD, are a shield around me,
    my glory, the One who lifts my head
        high.
4 I call out to the LORD,
    and he answers me from his holy
        mountain.

5 I lie down and sleep;
    I wake again, because the LORD
        sustains me.
6 I will not fear though tens of thousands
    assail me on every side.

b 9 Or *will rule them with an iron sceptre* (see Septuagint
and Syriac)
a In Hebrew texts 3:1-8 is numbered 3:2-9.
b 2 The Hebrew has *Selah* (a word of uncertain
meaning) here and at the end of verses 4 and 8.

a 1 Hebrew; Septuagint *rage*

CHRIST IN ALL THE SCRIPTURES 8

The Son of God

When we find a verse from a psalm which the Father pronounces over his Son when his Son is baptised, we need to take careful notice.

'You are my Son,' says the voice from heaven (Mark 1:11), quoting Psalm 2:7. The psalm is a celebration of Israel's king. It is one of the Old Testament passages most quoted in the New Testament. (As well as Matthew, Mark and Luke, v. 7 is quoted in Acts 13 and Hebrews 1 and 5). It is a psalm about the Messiah (Christ), as it imagines God's rule being extended to all nations.

From the early days, God spoke of the king as his 'son'. *'I will be his father, and he shall be my son'* (2 Samuel 7:14). The king was to be God's regent, his representative, ruling the nation according to God's law, ministering God's justice and mercy and demonstrating what Israel's God was like. (Psalm 72 spells this out in detail.) This was the ideal, but very few Old Testament kings came near to it. So increasingly Israel looked for the anointed king whom God would send – the Messiah. This psalm would have been familiar to Jesus from childhood. It would have been a regular part of his prayers. He probably knew it by heart. So imagine the moment when the Father spoke it directly to him as the Holy Spirit fell on him! It was not just an assurance of the Father's love; it was a commission to be the King who would bring God's rule to all the nations and to the ends of the earth.

To people at that time, the title 'Son of God' did not imply that the person called that was divine. But as Jesus began to exercise his ministry, his followers started to realise that this was the Creator come to earth – that the 'son of God', God's appointed king and Messiah, was in fact 'God the Son'. It took several more centuries of thinking for the Church to work this out fully, but the deity of Jesus is clearly taught in the New Testament (e.g. John 1:1–4; 20:28). By the end of the Gospel accounts they are worshipping him (Matthew 28:16). Every time we read of a king of Israel in the Old Testament we should think of Jesus. He is what they were meant to be. He is there, in the wings, as each story is acted out, waiting for his moment to step onto the stage of history.

But what sort of King would he be? This psalm uses quite violent imagery. The people of Israel expected their Messiah to defeat all their pagan enemies. Instead, he became King by dying for them, as we shall see when we look at the theme of God's servant.

Graham Cray

7 Arise, Lord!
  Deliver me, my God!
  Strike all my enemies on the jaw;
  break the teeth of the wicked.

8 From the Lord comes deliverance.
  May your blessing be on your
    people.

Psalm 4[a]

For the director of music. With stringed instruments.
A psalm of David.

1 Answer me when I call to you,
  my righteous God.
  Give me relief from my distress;
  have mercy on me and hear my
    prayer.

2 How long will you people turn my glory
    into shame?
  How long will you love delusions and
    seek false gods?[b,c]
3 Know that the Lord has set apart his
    faithful servant for himself;
  the Lord hears when I call to him.

4 Tremble and[d] do not sin;
  when you are on your beds,
  search your hearts and be silent.
5 Offer the sacrifices of the righteous
  and trust in the Lord.

6 Many, Lord, are asking, 'Who will bring
    us prosperity?'
  Let the light of your face shine
    on us.
7 Fill my heart with joy
  when their grain and new wine
    abound.

8 In peace I will lie down and sleep,
  for you alone, Lord,
  make me dwell in safety.

Psalm 5[a]

For the director of music. For pipes. A psalm of David.

1 Listen to my words, Lord,
  consider my lament.
2 Hear my cry for help,
  my King and my God,
  for to you I pray.

3 In the morning, Lord, you hear my
    voice;
  in the morning I lay my requests
    before you
  and wait expectantly.
4 For you are not a God who is pleased
    with wickedness;
  with you, evil people are not
    welcome.
5 The arrogant cannot stand
  in your presence.
  You hate all who do wrong;
6   you destroy those who tell lies.
  The bloodthirsty and deceitful
  you, Lord, detest.
7 But I, by your great love,
  can come into your house;
  in reverence I bow down
    towards your holy temple.

8 Lead me, Lord, in your righteousness
  because of my enemies –
  make your way straight before me.
9 Not a word from their mouth can be
    trusted;
  their heart is filled with malice.
  Their throat is an open grave;
  with their tongues they tell lies.
10 Declare them guilty, O God!
  Let their intrigues be their downfall.
  Banish them for their many sins,
  for they have rebelled against you.
11 But let all who take refuge in you be glad;
  let them ever sing for joy.
  Spread your protection over them,
  that those who love your name may
    rejoice in you.

12 Surely, Lord, you bless the righteous;
  you surround them with your favour
  as with a shield.

---

a In Hebrew texts 4:1-8 is numbered 4:2-9.
b 2 Or *seek lies*
c 2 The Hebrew has *Selah* (a word of uncertain meaning) here and at the end of verse 4.
d 4 Or *In your anger* (see Septuagint)

a In Hebrew texts 5:1-12 is numbered 5:2-13.

Psalm 6[a]

For the director of music. With stringed instruments.
According to sheminith.[b] *A psalm of David.*

1 LORD, do not rebuke me in your anger
　　or discipline me in your wrath.
2 Have mercy on me, LORD, for I am faint;
　　heal me, LORD, for my bones are in
　　　agony.
3 My soul is in deep anguish.
　　How long, LORD, how long?

4 Turn, LORD, and deliver me;
　　save me because of your unfailing
　　　love.
5 Among the dead no one proclaims your
　　name.
　　Who praises you from his grave?

6 I am worn out from my groaning.

All night long I flood my bed with
　　weeping
and drench my couch with tears.
7 My eyes grow weak with sorrow;
　　they fail because of all my foes.

8 Away from me, all you who do evil,
　　for the LORD has heard my weeping.
9 The LORD has heard my cry for mercy;
　　the LORD accepts my prayer.
10 All my enemies will be overwhelmed
　　　with shame and anguish;
　　they will turn back and suddenly be
　　　put to shame.

Psalm 7[a]

A shiggaion[b] *of David, which he sang to the* LORD
concerning Cush, a Benjaminite.

1 LORD my God, I take refuge in you;
　　save and deliver me from all who
　　　pursue me,
2 or they will tear me apart like a lion
　　and rip me to pieces with no one to
　　　rescue me.

3 LORD my God, if I have done this
　　and there is guilt on my hands —
4 if I have repaid my ally with evil
　　or without cause have robbed my
　　　foe —
5 then let my enemy pursue and overtake
　　me;
　　let him trample my life to the ground
　　and make me sleep in the dust.[c]

6 Arise, LORD, in your anger;
　　rise up against the rage of my
　　　enemies.
　　Awake, my God; decree justice.
7 Let the assembled peoples gather round
　　you,
　　while you sit enthroned over them on
　　　high.
8 　Let the LORD judge the peoples.
　　Vindicate me, LORD, according to my
　　　righteousness,
　　according to my integrity, O Most
　　　High.
9 Bring to an end the violence of the
　　wicked
　　and make the righteous secure —
you, the righteous God
　　who probes minds and hearts.

10 My shield[d] is God Most High,
　　who saves the upright in heart.
11 God is a righteous judge,
　　a God who displays his wrath every
　　　day.
12 If he does not relent,
　　he[e] will sharpen his sword;
　　he will bend and string his bow.
13 He has prepared his deadly weapons;
　　he makes ready his flaming arrows.

14 Whoever is pregnant with evil
　　conceives trouble and gives birth to
　　　disillusionment.
15 Whoever digs a hole and scoops it out
　　falls into the pit they have made.
16 The trouble they cause recoils on them;
　　their violence comes down on their
　　　own heads.

---

a In Hebrew texts 6:1-10 is numbered 6:2-11.
b Title: Probably a musical term
a In Hebrew texts 7:1-17 is numbered 7:2-18.
b Title: Probably a literary or musical term

c 5　The Hebrew has Selah (a word of uncertain
　　meaning) here.
d 10　Or *sovereign*
e 12　Or *If anyone does not repent, / God*

17 I will give thanks to the LORD because of
his righteousness;
I will sing the praises of the name of
the LORD Most High.

Psalm 8[a]
*For the director of music. According to gittith.[b]
A psalm of David.*

1 LORD, our Lord,
how majestic is your name in all the
earth!

You have set your glory
in the heavens.
2 Through the praise of children and
infants
you have established a stronghold
against your enemies,
to silence the foe and the avenger.
3 When I consider your heavens,
the work of your fingers,
the moon and the stars,
which you have set in place,
4 what is mankind that you are mindful of
them,
human beings that you care for
them?[c]

5 You have made them[d] a little lower than
the angels[e]
and crowned them[f] with glory and
honour.
6 You made them rulers over the works of
your hands;
you put everything under their[g] feet:
7 all flocks and herds,
and the animals of the wild,
8 the birds in the sky,
and the fish in the sea,
all that swim the paths of the seas.

9 LORD, our Lord,
how majestic is your name in all the
earth!

Psalm 9[a,b]
*For the director of music. To the tune of 'The Death of the
Son'. A psalm of David.*

1 I will give thanks to you, LORD, with all
my heart;
I will tell of all your wonderful deeds.
2 I will be glad and rejoice in you;
I will sing the praises of your name,
O Most High.

3 My enemies turn back;
they stumble and perish before you.
4 For you have upheld my right and my
cause,
sitting enthroned as the righteous
judge.
5 You have rebuked the nations and
destroyed the wicked;
you have blotted out their name for
ever and ever.
6 Endless ruin has overtaken my
enemies,
you have uprooted their cities;
even the memory of them has
perished.

7 The LORD reigns for ever;
he has established his throne for
judgment.
8 He rules the world in righteousness
and judges the peoples with equity.
9 The LORD is a refuge for the oppressed,
a stronghold in times of trouble.
10 Those who know your name trust in
you,
for you, LORD, have never forsaken
those who seek you.

11 Sing the praises of the LORD, enthroned
in Zion;
proclaim among the nations what he
has done.
12 For he who avenges blood remembers;
he does not ignore the cries of the
afflicted.

---

a In Hebrew texts 8:1-9 is numbered 8:2-10.
b Title: Probably a musical term
c 4 Or *what is a human being that you are mindful of him, / a
son of man that you care for him?*
d 5 Or *him*
e 5 Or *than God*
f 5 Or *him*
g 6 Or *made him ruler . . . ; / . . . his*

---

a Psalms 9 and 10 may originally have been a single
acrostic poem in which alternating lines began with
the successive letters of the Hebrew alphabet. In the
Septuagint they constitute one psalm.
b In Hebrew texts 9:1-20 is numbered 9:2-21.

¹³ LORD, see how my enemies persecute
me!
     Have mercy and lift me up from the
gates of death,
¹⁴ that I may declare your praises

in the gates of Daughter Zion,
     and there rejoice in your salvation.

¹⁵ The nations have fallen into the pit they
have dug;

CHRIST IN ALL THE SCRIPTURES 2

Creation

The New Testament teaches that the universe was created through Christ (see John 1:3; Colossians 1:16; Hebrews 1:2). When we read the Old Testament accounts of creation (Genesis 1 – 2; Psalm 104; Job 38 – 39) we can be sure that he is there. Psalm 8 is one of many which address God as Creator and praise him for the creation, but it brings together Christ and creation in a highly distinctive way.

The writer sees God's majesty in his creation. He is awed by the night sky and the vastness of the universe. It makes him wonder how God could ever be bothered with little humans. But he acknowledges that God has made little humans the rulers over creation, over the animals, birds and fish. In this psalm little people are exalted by a majestic God. But when the psalm is quoted in the New Testament, the person whom God has *'crowned … with glory and honour and put everything under [his] feet'* is Jesus (Hebrews 2:6–8). Jesus is there in Psalm 8. How can the two be held together?

In the psalm God has given the human race responsibility for the earth. We still have that responsibility, but as a fallen race we exercise it very badly. We use the earth for ourselves, rather than see it as the arena where God's majesty is displayed. By making human beings in his own image, God had *'crowned them with glory and honour',* but we have dishonoured the God who honoured us. So the one through whom God created the whole world, including the human race, became human, became one of us, became part of the world. We are *'lower than the angels'.* He became *'lower than the angels'* who, in heaven, continually worship him. So that, through him, the human race could be restored to its original dignity and responsibility.

The incarnation of Jesus, his becoming human, gives the human race extraordinary dignity. He considered it worth becoming one of us! At the moment of creation God looked at his human creatures and declared them *'very good'* (Genesis 1:31). Despite our sin, God still values us in this way. It seems that 'nothing we can do could make him love us less' (Philip Yancey). By becoming human, God gave an unmistakable signal that he has not changed his mind, and he will not do so. He thinks we're worth it!

Graham Cray

their feet are caught in the net they
   have hidden.
16 The LORD is known by his acts of justice;
   the wicked are ensnared by the work
      of their hands.c
17 The wicked go down to the realm of the
      dead,
   all the nations that forget God.
18 But God will never forget the needy;
   the hope of the afflicted will never
      perish.

19 Arise, LORD, do not let mortals
      triumph;
   let the nations be judged in your
      presence.
20 Strike them with terror, LORD;
   let the nations know they are only
      mortal.

Psalm 10a

1 Why, LORD, do you stand far off?
   Why do you hide yourself in times of
      trouble?

2 In his arrogance the wicked man hunts
      down the weak,
   who are caught in the schemes he
      devises.
3 He boasts about the cravings of his
      heart;
   he blesses the greedy and reviles the
      LORD.
4 In his pride the wicked man does not
      seek him;
   in all his thoughts there is no room
      for God.
5 His ways are always prosperous;
   your laws are rejected byb him;
   he sneers at all his enemies.
6 He says to himself, 'Nothing will ever
      shake me.'

He swears, 'No one will ever do me
      harm.'

7 His mouth is full of lies and threats;
   trouble and evil are under his tongue.
8 He lies in wait near the villages;
   from ambush he murders the
      innocent.
   His eyes watch in secret for his victims;
9   like a lion in cover he lies in wait.
   He lies in wait to catch the helpless;
   he catches the helpless and drags
      them off in his net.
10 His victims are crushed, they collapse;
   they fall under his strength.
11 He says to himself, 'God will never
      notice;
   he covers his face and never sees.'

12 Arise, LORD! Lift up your hand, O God.
   Do not forget the helpless.
13 Why does the wicked man revile God?
   Why does he say to himself,
   'He won't call me to account'?
14 But you, God, see the trouble of the
      afflicted;
   you consider their grief and take it in
      hand.
   The victims commit themselves to you;
   you are the helper of the fatherless.
15 Break the arm of the wicked man;
   call the evildoer to account for his
      wickedness
   that would not otherwise be found
      out.

16 The LORD is King for ever and ever;
   the nations will perish from his land.
17 You, LORD, hear the desire of the
      afflicted;
   you encourage them, and you listen
      to their cry,
18 defending the fatherless and the
      oppressed,
   so that mere earthly mortals
   will never again strike terror.

Psalm 11
For the director of music. Of David.

1 In the LORD I take refuge.
   How then can you say to me:

---

c 16 The Hebrew has *Higgaion* and *Selah* (words of
uncertain meaning) here; *Selah* occurs also at the
end of verse 20.
a Psalms 9 and 10 may originally have been a single
acrostic poem in which alternating lines began with
the successive letters of the Hebrew alphabet. In the
Septuagint they constitute one psalm.
b 5 See Septuagint; Hebrew / *they are haughty, and your
laws are far from*

'Flee like a bird to your mountain.
2 For look, the wicked bend their bows;
    they set their arrows against the
        strings
to shoot from the shadows
    at the upright in heart.
3 When the foundations are being
        destroyed,
    what can the righteous do?'

4 The LORD is in his holy temple;
    the LORD is on his heavenly
        throne.

He observes everyone on earth;
    his eyes examine them.
5 The LORD examines the righteous,
    but the wicked, those who love
        violence,
    he hates with a passion.
6 On the wicked he will rain
    fiery coals and burning sulphur;
    a scorching wind will be their lot.

7 For the LORD is righteous,
    he loves justice;
    the upright will see his face.

PRAYING THE PSALMS 1

Wanting to run away

Want to run away?

'It's all going wrong. The foundations are being destroyed. Run! Run away and hide. There's no point in being good and expecting things to go your way. The dishonest always win. If you're determined to be honest, then escape into the mountains and hide. You'll be safe there. There's no other hope for you!'

'Rubbish!' says the song writer. 'The Lord is still on his heavenly throne!' (Psalm 11:4).

Are you an optimist or a pessimist? Are you used to things 'always going right' or 'always going wrong'? Which of these you are will affect the way you see the two voices in Psalm 11. You may agree with the 'it's all going wrong' type. After all, the world is unjust. Often the strong but evil succeed where the kind and good get crushed. Face it, the world is not fair!

But we know there is a God. We know that God is fair. We know that he will eventually turn the world the right side up. Beyond the injustice of this world there is a God who has intervened and will intervene again. He loves justice. Evil will get its comeuppance! Those who have acted justly, loved mercy and walked humbly with the Lord will soon inherit the earth (Matthew 5:5; Micah 6:8). We trust that the Lord will come through for us – in the end.

It's good that this psalm allows us to express that tension, because in this life such tension is often there.

Whether you are positive by nature or find it easier to see what's going wrong, let this psalm help you hear the other voice's point of view. Feel the tension. Live with it. Don't run away. Tell the Lord that you trust him – even if you don't always understand what he is up to.

Hugo Anson

Psalm 22

Psalm 12[a]

For the director of music. According to sheminith.[b]
A psalm of David.

¹ Help, Lord, for no one is faithful any
    more;
    those who are loyal have vanished
    from the human race.
² Everyone lies to their neighbour;
    they flatter with their lips
    but harbour deception in their hearts.

³ May the Lord silence all flattering lips
    and every boastful tongue –
⁴ those who say,
    'By our tongues we will prevail;
    our own lips will defend us – who is
    lord over us?'

⁵ 'Because the poor are plundered and the
    needy groan,
    I will now arise,' says the Lord.
    'I will protect them from those who
    malign them.'
⁶ And the words of the Lord are flawless,
    like silver purified in a crucible,
    like gold[c] refined seven times.

⁷ You, Lord, will keep the needy safe
    and will protect us for ever from the
    wicked,
⁸ who freely strut about
    when what is vile is honoured by the
    human race.

Psalm 13[a]

For the director of music. A psalm of David.

¹ How long, Lord? Will you forget me for
    ever?
    How long will you hide your face
    from me?
² How long must I wrestle with my
    thoughts
    and day after day have sorrow in my
    heart?

How long will my enemy triumph
    over me?

³ Look on me and answer, Lord my God.
    Give light to my eyes, or I will sleep in
    death,
⁴ and my enemy will say, 'I have overcome
    him,'
    and my foes will rejoice when I fall.

⁵ But I trust in your unfailing love;
    my heart rejoices in your salvation.
⁶ I will sing the Lord's praise,
    for he has been good to me.

Psalm 14

For the director of music. Of David.

¹ The fool[a] says in his heart,
    'There is no God.'
    They are corrupt, their deeds are vile;
    there is no one who does good.

² The Lord looks down from heaven
    on all mankind
    to see if there are any who understand,
    any who seek God.
³ All have turned away, all have become
    corrupt;
    there is no one who does good,
    not even one.

⁴ Do all these evildoers know nothing?

    They devour my people as though
    eating bread;
    they never call on the Lord.
⁵ But there they are, overwhelmed with
    dread,
    for God is present in the company of
    the righteous.
⁶ You evildoers frustrate the plans of the
    poor,
    but the Lord is their refuge.

⁷ Oh, that salvation for Israel would come
    out of Zion!
    When the Lord restores his people,
    let Jacob rejoice and Israel be glad!

---

a In Hebrew texts 12:1-8 is numbered 12:2-9.
b Title: Probably a musical term
c 6 Probable reading of the original Hebrew text;
Masoretic Text *earth*
a In Hebrew texts 13:1-6 is numbered 13:2-6.

a 1 The Hebrew words rendered *fool* in Psalms
denote one who is morally deficient.

Psalm 15
A psalm of David.

¹ LORD, who may dwell in your sacred
tent?
Who may live on your holy
mountain?

² The one whose way of life is blameless,
who does what is righteous,
who speaks the truth from their
heart;
³ whose tongue utters no slander,
who does no wrong to a neighbour,
and casts no slur on others;
⁴ who despises a vile person
but honours those who fear the
LORD;
who keeps an oath even when it hurts,
and does not change their mind;

PAIN AND SUFFERING 3

IT'S OK TO QUESTION GOD

Life hurts, doesn't it? Friends and family hurt us and let us down. We get sick. Exams don't go our way. People break our hearts. We lose people we love. We see those we love suffering.

It can feel in these times as if God has walked away and forgotten us. We can't hear his voice, we don't know what he's saying, we're confused and our prayers seem to bounce around the room, never getting anywhere near God's ears.

The psalmists seem to know how we feel. They cry out again and again, 'God, where are you?' 'Why aren't you helping us?' 'What's going on?' They don't hold anything back or try to make it sound as though everything is OK. They are completely honest with God about how they are feeling. God could have left these questions and feelings out of the Bible, but he included them for a reason. He's telling us it's OK to ask questions when we're in pain. He's big enough to deal with it. He doesn't want us to pretend we're happy when life is miserable or fake a smile in his presence when we're in pain. God wants us to be honest with him, no matter what we're feeling. He's not worried by our questions (I think he'd be more concerned if we made it through life without asking any). These questions in the Psalms remind us that it's not disrespectful to ask what's going on when we're confused.

We need to take another lesson from the psalmists too. Here in Psalm 13, as in many psalms, the writer doesn't end with his questions. He doesn't wallow in self-indulgent pity. He lets out his frustration, confusion and pain – but then he says that despite what's going on, he will trust in God's *'unfailing love'* (v. 5) and he will still rejoice and worship God in song (v. 6). What an important lesson for us! God is still worthy of our love, adoration and praise even when life isn't going our way. He is always good. His love never fails, even if we don't feel it in that exact moment. He knows what he is doing even if we can't make any sense of our circumstances. We never need to deny our pain, but let's make sure that we hold on to the truth of who God is at the same time.

Mike Pilavachi

 2 Corinthians 1:8–11   Habakkuk 3:17

⁵ who lends money to the poor without interest;
who does not accept a bribe against the innocent.

Whoever does these things will never be shaken.

Psalm 16
A miktam[a] of David.

¹ Keep me safe, my God,
for in you I take refuge.

² I say to the LORD, 'You are my Lord;
apart from you I have no good thing.'
³ I say of the holy people who are in the land,
'They are the noble ones in whom is all my delight.'
⁴ Those who run after other gods will suffer more and more.
I will not pour out libations of blood to such gods
or take up their names on my lips.

⁵ LORD, you alone are my portion and my cup;
you make my lot secure.
⁶ The boundary lines have fallen for me in pleasant places;
surely I have a delightful inheritance.
⁷ I will praise the LORD, who counsels me;
even at night my heart instructs me.
⁸ I keep my eyes always on the LORD.
With him at my right hand, I shall not be shaken.

⁹ Therefore my heart is glad and my tongue rejoices;
my body also will rest secure,
¹⁰ because you will not abandon me to the realm of the dead,
nor will you let your faithful[b] one see decay.
¹¹ You make known to me the path of life;
you will fill me with joy in your presence,

with eternal pleasures at your right hand.

Psalm 17
A prayer of David.

¹ Hear me, LORD, my plea is just;
listen to my cry.
Hear my prayer –
it does not rise from deceitful lips.
² Let my vindication come from you;
may your eyes see what is right.

³ Though you probe my heart,
though you examine me at night and test me,
you will find that I have planned no evil;
my mouth has not transgressed.
⁴ Though people tried to bribe me,
I have kept myself from the ways of the violent
through what your lips have commanded.
⁵ My steps have held to your paths;
my feet have not stumbled.

⁶ I call on you, my God, for you will answer me;
turn your ear to me and hear my prayer.
⁷ Show me the wonders of your great love,
you who save by your right hand
those who take refuge in you from their foes.
⁸ Keep me as the apple of your eye;
hide me in the shadow of your wings
⁹ from the wicked who are out to destroy me,
from my mortal enemies who surround me.

¹⁰ They close up their callous hearts,
and their mouths speak with arrogance.
¹¹ They have tracked me down, they now surround me,
with eyes alert, to throw me to the ground.
¹² They are like a lion hungry for prey,
like a fierce lion crouching in cover.

---

a Title: Probably a literary or musical term
b 10 Or *holy*

¹³ Rise up, Lᴏʀᴅ, confront them, bring
         them down;
   with your sword rescue me from the
         wicked.
¹⁴ By your hand save me from such people,
         Lᴏʀᴅ,
   from those of this world whose
         reward is in this life.
May what you have stored up for the
         wicked fill their bellies;
   may their children gorge themselves
         on it,
   and may there be leftovers for their
         little ones.

¹⁵ As for me, I shall be vindicated and shall
         see your face;
   when I awake, I shall be satisfied with
         seeing your likeness.

Psalm 18ᵃ

For the director of music. Of David the servant of the
Lᴏʀᴅ. He sang to the Lᴏʀᴅ the words of this song when
the Lᴏʀᴅ delivered him from the hand of all his enemies
and from the hand of Saul. He said:

¹ I love you, Lᴏʀᴅ, my strength.

² The Lᴏʀᴅ is my rock, my fortress and my
         deliverer;
   my God is my rock, in whom I take
         refuge,
   my shieldᵇ and the hornᶜ of my
         salvation, my stronghold.

³ I called to the Lᴏʀᴅ, who is worthy of
         praise,
   and I have been saved from my
         enemies.
⁴ The cords of death entangled me;
   the torrents of destruction
         overwhelmed me.
⁵ The cords of the grave coiled around
         me;
   the snares of death confronted me.

⁶ In my distress I called to the Lᴏʀᴅ;
   I cried to my God for help.

From his temple he heard my voice;
   my cry came before him, into his
         ears.
⁷ The earth trembled and quaked,
   and the foundations of the
         mountains shook;
   they trembled because he was angry.
⁸ Smoke rose from his nostrils;
   consuming fire came from his
         mouth,
   burning coals blazed out of it.

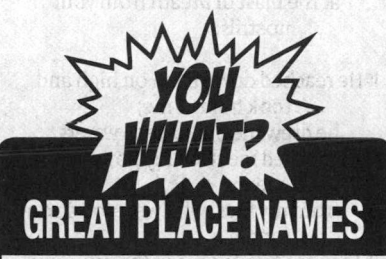

YOU WHAT?
GREAT PLACE NAMES

○ **JEGAR SAHADUTHA**
Genesis 31:45–53
JEE-guhr-say-huh-DOO-thuh
○ **MISREPHOTH MAIM**
Joshua 11:6–8
○ **THE LAND OF NOD**
Genesis 4:16
○ **THE DESERT OF ZIN AND THE**
SCORPION PASS
Numbers 34:3–5
○ **MIKMASH AND THE VALLEY OF**
ZEBOYIM
1 Samuel 13:16–18
zuh-BOH-im
○ **THE GREAT TREES OF MAMRE**
Genesis 13:18; 14:13
MAM-ree

⁹ He parted the heavens and came down;
   dark clouds were under his feet.
¹⁰ He mounted the cherubim and flew;
   he soared on the wings of the wind.
¹¹ He made darkness his covering, his
         canopy around him –
   the dark rain clouds of the sky.
¹² Out of the brightness of his presence
         clouds advanced,
   with hailstones and bolts of
         lightning.

---

a In Hebrew texts 18:1-50 is numbered 18:2-51.
b 2 Or *sovereign*
c 2 *Horn* here symbolises strength.

13 The LORD thundered from heaven;
  the voice of the Most High
    resounded.*d*
14 He shot his arrows and scattered the
    enemy,
  with great bolts of lightning he
    routed them.
15 The valleys of the sea were exposed
    and the foundations of the earth laid
    bare
  at your rebuke, LORD,
    at the blast of breath from your
    nostrils.

16 He reached down from on high and
    took hold of me;
  he drew me out of deep waters.
17 He rescued me from my powerful
    enemy,
  from my foes, who were too strong
    for me.
18 They confronted me in the day of my
    disaster,
  but the LORD was my support.
19 He brought me out into a spacious
    place;
  he rescued me because he delighted
    in me.

20 The LORD has dealt with me according to
    my righteousness;
  according to the cleanness of my
    hands he has rewarded me.
21 For I have kept the ways of the LORD;
  I am not guilty of turning from my
    God.
22 All his laws are before me;
  I have not turned away from his
    decrees.
23 I have been blameless before him
  and have kept myself from sin.
24 The LORD has rewarded me according to
    my righteousness,
  according to the cleanness of my
    hands in his sight.

25 To the faithful you show yourself
    faithful,

to the blameless you show yourself
  blameless,
26 to the pure you show yourself pure,
  but to the devious you show yourself
    shrewd.
27 You save the humble
  but bring low those whose eyes are
    haughty.
28 You, LORD, keep my lamp burning;
  my God turns my darkness into light.
29 With your help I can advance against a
    troop;*e*
  with my God I can scale a wall.

30 As for God, his way is perfect:
  the LORD's word is flawless;
  he shields all who take refuge in him.
31 For who is God besides the LORD?
  And who is the Rock except our God?
32 It is God who arms me with strength
  and keeps my way secure.
33 He makes my feet like the feet of a deer;
  he causes me to stand on the heights.
34 He trains my hands for battle;
  my arms can bend a bow of bronze.
35 You make your saving help my shield,
  and your right hand sustains me;
  your help has made me great.
36 You provide a broad path for my feet,
  so that my ankles do not give way.

37 I pursued my enemies and overtook
    them;
  I did not turn back till they were
    destroyed.
38 I crushed them so that they could not
    rise;
  they fell beneath my feet.
39 You armed me with strength for battle;
  you humbled my adversaries before
    me.
40 You made my enemies turn their backs
    in flight,
  and I destroyed my foes.
41 They cried for help, but there was no
    one to save them —
  to the LORD, but he did not answer.
42 I beat them as fine as windblown dust;

---

d 13 Some Hebrew manuscripts and Septuagint (see
also 2 Samuel 22:14); most Hebrew manuscripts
resounded, / amid hailstones and bolts of lightning

---

e 29 Or *can run through a barricade*

I trampled them*f* like mud in the
   streets.
43 You have delivered me from the attacks
      of the people;
   you have made me the head of
      nations.
   People I did not know now serve me,
44   foreigners cower before me;
   as soon as they hear of me, they obey
      me.
45 They all lose heart;
   they come trembling from their
      strongholds.

46 The LORD lives! Praise be to my Rock!
   Exalted be God my Saviour!
47 He is the God who avenges me,
   who subdues nations under me,
48   who saves me from my enemies.
   You exalted me above my foes;
   from a violent man you rescued me.
49 Therefore I will praise you, LORD,
      among the nations;
   I will sing the praises of your name.

50 He gives his king great victories;
   he shows unfailing love to his
      anointed,
   to David and to his descendants for
      ever.

Psalm 19*a*

For the director of music. A psalm of David.

1 The heavens declare the glory of God;
   the skies proclaim the work of his
      hands.
2 Day after day they pour forth speech;
   night after night they reveal
      knowledge.
3 They have no speech, they use no words;
   no sound is heard from them.
4 Yet their voice*b* goes out into all the
      earth,
   their words to the ends of the world.

In the heavens God has pitched a tent
   for the sun.
5 It is like a bridegroom coming out of
      his chamber,
   like a champion rejoicing to run his
      course.
6 It rises at one end of the heavens
   and makes its circuit to the other;
   nothing is deprived of its warmth.

7 The law of the LORD is perfect,
   refreshing the soul.
The statutes of the LORD are
      trustworthy,
   making wise the simple.
8 The precepts of the LORD are right,
   giving joy to the heart.
The commands of the LORD are radiant,
   giving light to the eyes.
9 The fear of the LORD is pure,
   enduring for ever.
The decrees of the LORD are firm,
   and all of them are righteous.

10 They are more precious than gold,
   than much pure gold;
they are sweeter than honey,
   than honey from the honeycomb.
11 By them your servant is warned;
   in keeping them there is great
      reward.
12 But who can discern their own errors?
   Forgive my hidden faults.
13 Keep your servant also from wilful sins;
   may they not rule over me.
Then I will be blameless,
   innocent of great transgression.

14 May these words of my mouth and this
      meditation of my heart
   be pleasing in your sight,
   LORD, my Rock and my Redeemer.

Psalm 20*a*

For the director of music. A psalm of David.

1 May the LORD answer you when you are
      in distress;
   may the name of the God of Jacob
      protect you.

2 May he send you help from the
    sanctuary
  and grant you support from Zion.
3 May he remember all your sacrifices
  and accept your burnt offerings.*b*
4 May he give you the desire of your heart
  and make all your plans succeed.
5 May we shout for joy over your victory
  and lift up our banners in the name
    of our God.

May the LORD grant all your requests.

---

b 3 The Hebrew has *Selah* (a word of uncertain
meaning) here.

6 Now this I know:
  the LORD gives victory to his
    anointed.
He answers him from his heavenly
    sanctuary
  with the victorious power of his right
    hand.
7 Some trust in chariots and some in
    horses,
  but we trust in the name of the LORD
    our God.
8 They are brought to their knees and fall,
  but we rise up and stand firm.
9 LORD, give victory to the king!
  Answer us when we call!

PRAYING THE PSALMS 2

Creation worships God

I love a starry night. I used to live in the city – where the streetlights were so bright it was rare to see the whole Milky Way in its full glory. Recently we moved to the country and on crisp, cloudless nights the stars are spectacular.

As this song writer says, *'The heavens declare the glory of God'* (Psalm 19:1). If I look long enough, it's almost as if the sky fills with a celestial choir singing that its Maker is enormous, wonderful, amazing and glorious!

If we don't praise God, the stones will cry out (Luke 19:40). In fact, creation already does! Even with no speech, no words and no sound, *'their voice goes out into all the earth'* (v. 4). God made a wonderful universe. It now tells of God's eternal power and divine nature, revealing it to the whole earth (Romans 1:20). Each thing God made speaks out, telling us that God is there and describing what he's like. The description can be heard in the grandeur of majestic mountains and it can be seen in the simple, profound truth that *'unless a grain of wheat falls to the ground and dies, it remains only a single seed. But if it dies, it produces many seeds'* (John 12:24). The massive power, and the sacrificial love. Creation tells us the whole story.

With such a wonderful worship leader, doesn't it make you want to join in? Go for a walk and drink in the revelation of God in the countryside, thanking him for seasons, colours, smells. Watch a wildlife documentary and see again the detail and intricacy. Admire the trickling rivers that giggle God's delight in it all. Open the windows as the sun peeks over the horizon and sing along with the dawn chorus!

Hugo Anson

 Psalm 11   Psalm 22

Psalm 21 [a]

For the director of music. A psalm of David.

[1] The king rejoices in your strength, Lord.
How great is his joy in the victories
you give!

[2] You have granted him his heart's desire
and have not withheld the request of
his lips.[b]
[3] You came to greet him with rich
blessings
and placed a crown of pure gold on
his head.
[4] He asked you for life, and you gave it to
him —
length of days, for ever and ever.
[5] Through the victories you gave, his glory
is great;
you have bestowed on him splendour
and majesty.
[6] Surely you have granted him unending
blessings
and made him glad with the joy of
your presence.
[7] For the king trusts in the Lord;
through the unfailing love of the
Most High
he will not be shaken.

[8] Your hand will lay hold on all your
enemies;
your right hand will seize your foes.
[9] When you appear for battle,
you will burn them up as in a blazing
furnace.
The Lord will swallow them up in his
wrath,
and his fire will consume them.
[10] You will destroy their descendants from
the earth,
their posterity from mankind.
[11] Though they plot evil against you
and devise wicked schemes, they
cannot succeed.
[12] You will make them turn their backs
when you aim at them with drawn
bow.

[13] Be exalted in your strength, Lord;
we will sing and praise your might.

Psalm 22 [a]

*For the director of music. To the tune of 'The Doe of the
Morning'. A psalm of David.*

[1] My God, my God, why have you forsaken
me?
Why are you so far from saving me,
so far from my cries of anguish?
[2] My God, I cry out by day, but you do not
answer,
by night, but I find no rest.[b]

[3] Yet you are enthroned as the Holy One;
you are the one Israel praises.[c]
[4] In you our ancestors put their trust;
they trusted and you delivered them.
[5] To you they cried out and were saved;
in you they trusted and were not put
to shame.

[6] But I am a worm and not a man,
scorned by everyone, despised by the
people.
[7] All who see me mock me;
they hurl insults, shaking their
heads.
[8] 'He trusts in the Lord,' they say,
'let the Lord rescue him.
Let him deliver him,
since he delights in him.'

[9] Yet you brought me out of the womb;
you made me trust in you, even at my
mother's breast.
[10] From birth I was cast on you;
from my mother's womb you have
been my God.

[11] Do not be far from me,
for trouble is near
and there is no one to help.

[12] Many bulls surround me;
strong bulls of Bashan encircle me.
[13] Roaring lions that tear their prey

---

a In Hebrew texts 21:1-13 is numbered 21:2-14.
b 2 The Hebrew has *Selah* (a word of uncertain
meaning) here.

a In Hebrew texts 22:1-31 is numbered 22:2-32.
b 2 Or *night, and am not silent*
c 3 Or *Yet you are holy, / enthroned on the praises of Israel*

open their mouths wide against me.
14 I am poured out like water,
    and all my bones are out of joint.
My heart has turned to wax;
    it has melted within me.
15 My mouth*d* is dried up like a potsherd,
    and my tongue sticks to the roof of
        my mouth;
    you lay me in the dust of death.

16 Dogs surround me,
    a pack of villains encircles me;

---

d 15 Probable reading of the original Hebrew text;
Masoretic Text *strength*

they pierce*e* my hands and my feet.
17 All my bones are on display;
    people stare and gloat over me.
18 They divide my clothes among them
    and cast lots for my garment.

19 But you, LORD, do not be far from me.
    You are my strength; come quickly to
        help me.
20 Deliver me from the sword,

---

e 16 Dead Sea Scrolls and some manuscripts of
the Masoretic Text, Septuagint and Syriac; most
manuscripts of the Masoretic Text *me,* / *like a lion*

PRAYING THE PSALMS 3

My God, My God, why?

The beginning of Psalm 22 sounds disorientated and lost – but the end is victorious!

Jesus quoted the first line of this psalm in the anguish and pain of dying on the cross (Matthew 27:46). Was he just confused about what God the Father was doing? Or was he telling us, even in the middle of his agony, that he could already see the certainty of resurrection and the spread of the gospel to the 'ends of the earth'?

The total eclipse of the Son. That's what is being described in the opening lines. The man whom God had become was taking the blame for the human race. God was making *'him who had no sin to be sin for us, so that in him we might become the righteousness of God'* (2 Corinthians 5:21). God the Father could not look at the Son while all our sin was on him. The Father turned away. Jesus experienced the absence of God. As he did, his mind searched the Scriptures for a description of what he was feeling. *'My God, my God, why have you forsaken me?'* (v. 1). Those were the right words. His mind continued to move forward through the psalm. *'I am a worm'* (v. 6), squirming on a cross desperately trying to find a way to breathe. *'All who see me mock me'* (v. 7). That is happening too. Keep going. What does it say at the end?

God *'has not despised or scorned the suffering of the afflicted one; he has not hidden his face from him but has listened to his cry for help'* (v. 24). *'All the families of the nations will bow down before him'* (v. 27).

Right now, it really hurts. But it is going to be OK!

If that's how you feel today, Jesus understands. He has been there.

Hugo Anson

 Psalm 19

Psalm 24

CHRIST IN ALL THE SCRIPTURES 7

Psalms – the prayer book of Jesus

The Psalms are unique in the Bible. They form the only book entirely made up of words inspired by the Holy Spirit which people say to God, rather than words from God to us. They are also a wonderful evidence of God's grace.

It is marvellous how many different feelings and experiences can be expressed to God with his blessing. The Psalms free us to be real in the presence of God. Most are songs as well as prayers. They were the hymn book of the temple in Jesus' day. Many were used in the great worship festivals. But they were also personal prayers which Jesus, and many devout Jews, used for themselves. He knew many of these by heart and they will have formed a central part of his prayer life. Try reading them as the prayers of Jesus, who knew that he himself was the fulfilment of the longings which they expressed and the climax of the history they celebrate. You will not so much be identifying Jesus in the Old Testament as praying the Old Testament from Jesus' perspective.

This is what makes Psalm 22 so remarkable. Jesus prayed the opening words from the cross (Matthew 27:46). Often when the New Testament quotes an Old Testament passage, it quotes the opening words to direct us to the whole text. It may be that Jesus sustained himself during his time of agony on the cross by praying this psalm. It is a psalm which graphically describes features of crucifixion, long before crucifixion was known in that part of the world. But the psalm is only indirectly a prophecy. It is a prayer. It expresses the horror of the loss of the Father's presence (vv. 1–2). It cries to God about the scorn, humiliation and insults. He prays that his bones are being pulled out of joint and that he is desperately thirsty (vv. 14–15). As he hangs naked, he sees the soldiers casting lots for his clothes (v. 18). And from the cross, knowing that the cross is necessary, he trusts God for vindication. The psalm changes from verse 22. God has listened (v. 24). Beyond the cross is resurrection and the proclamation of the gospel. *'All the ends of the earth will remember and turn to the LORD'* (v. 27) and bow down before him (see Philippians 2:9–11). And this will reach to us, for *'future generations will be told about the Lord'* (v. 30) and we will pass the message on: *'They will proclaim his righteousness … to a people yet unborn'* (v. 31).

Here is Christ in the Scriptures, fulfilling the Scriptures and praying the Scriptures, for us. Read the Psalms as the prayer book of Jesus.

See also the series called 'Praying the Psalms'.

Graham Cray

my precious life from the power of
the dogs.
21 Rescue me from the mouth of the
lions;
save me from the horns of the wild
oxen.

22 I will declare your name to my people;
in the assembly I will praise you.
23 You who fear the LORD, praise him!
All you descendants of Jacob, honour
him!
Revere him, all you descendants of
Israel!
24 For he has not despised or scorned
the suffering of the afflicted one;
he has not hidden his face from him
but has listened to his cry for help.

25 From you comes the theme of my praise
in the great assembly;
before those who fear you *f* I will fulfil
my vows.
26 The poor will eat and be satisfied;
those who seek the LORD will praise
him –
may your hearts live for ever!

27 All the ends of the earth
will remember and turn to the LORD,
and all the families of the nations
will bow down before him,
28 for dominion belongs to the LORD
and he rules over the nations.

29 All the rich of the earth will feast and
worship;
all who go down to the dust will kneel
before him –
those who cannot keep themselves
alive.
30 Posterity will serve him;
future generations will be told about
the Lord.
31 They will proclaim his righteousness,
declaring to a people yet unborn:
He has done it!

Psalm 23
A psalm of David.

1 The LORD is my shepherd, I lack
nothing.
2 He makes me lie down in green
pastures,
he leads me beside quiet waters,
3 he refreshes my soul.
He guides me along the right paths
for his name's sake.
4 Even though I walk
through the darkest valley, *a*
I will fear no evil,
for you are with me;
your rod and your staff,
they comfort me.

5 You prepare a table before me
in the presence of my enemies.
You anoint my head with oil;
my cup overflows.
6 Surely your goodness and love will
follow me
all the days of my life,
and I will dwell in the house of the
LORD
for ever.

Psalm 24
Of David. A psalm.

1 The earth is the LORD's, and everything
in it,
the world, and all who live in it;
2 for he founded it on the seas
and established it on the waters.

3 Who may ascend the mountain of the
LORD?
Who may stand in his holy place?
4 The one who has clean hands and a pure
heart,
who does not trust in an idol
or swear by a false god. *a*

5 They will receive blessing from the
LORD

---

f 25 Hebrew *him*

a 4 Or *the valley of the shadow of death*
a 4 Or *swear falsely*

and vindication from God their
    Saviour.
6 Such is the generation of those who
    seek him,
who seek your face, God of Jacob.*b,c*

7 Lift up your heads, you gates;
    be lifted up, you ancient doors,
    that the King of glory may come in.
8 Who is this King of glory?
    The LORD strong and mighty,
    the LORD mighty in battle.

b 6 Two Hebrew manuscripts and Syriac (see also
Septuagint); most Hebrew manuscripts *face, Jacob*
c 6 The Hebrew has *Selah* (a word of uncertain
meaning) here and at the end of verse 10.

9 Lift up your heads, you gates;
    lift them up, you ancient doors,
    that the King of glory may come in.
10 Who is he, this King of glory?
    The LORD Almighty –
    he is the King of glory.

Psalm 25*a*

Of David.

1 In you, LORD my God,
    I put my trust.

a This psalm is an acrostic poem, the verses of
which begin with the successive letters of the
Hebrew alphabet.

THE NAMES OF GOD 6

God the Good Shepherd (Yaweh Rohi)

*'The LORD is my shepherd, I lack nothing. He makes me lie down in green
pastures, he leads me beside quiet waters…'*

Psalm 23, written by King David, is probably the best-known passage of Scripture
in the whole Bible, and one of the most comforting as it describes a God who
cares.

Farming methods have changed radically since the time when David was a young
shepherd boy looking after his father's sheep in the hills of Israel. Back then wild
animals roamed the countryside looking for prey, and David's job would have been
to protect his sheep from the constant dangers lurking around them. He would
also have had the responsibility of finding the best grazing pastures during the day
and making sure they were safely penned up at night – and he would have been
required to lay himself across the entrance to the pen as a guard.

Like any good shepherd, God has committed himself to his people. He has
promised never to forsake us or leave us. He has made it his responsibility to
guard us, to feed us and to comfort us. In the midst of difficulties and problems
we can experience God's goodness and love.

Our response to all this has to be to learn to know the Good Shepherd's voice,
to obey it and follow him wherever he might lead us. When the sheep wandered
off on their own, away from the flock and from the shepherd, they usually found
themselves in trouble. The safest place for them was to stay close to their
shepherd. The safest place for us is close to Jesus.

David and Mary Pytches

 Romans 15:33

Hebrews 13:5

2 I trust in you;
    do not let me be put to shame,
    nor let my enemies triumph
       over me.
3 No one who hopes in you
    will ever be put to shame,
but shame will come on those
    who are treacherous without cause.

4 Show me your ways, Lord,
    teach me your paths.
5 Guide me in your truth and teach me,
    for you are God my Saviour,
    and my hope is in you all day long.
6 Remember, Lord, your great mercy and
       love,
    for they are from of old.

PRAYING THE PSALMS 4

Who may ascend?

Psalms are songs – songs to help us praise God, worship God or pour out our hearts to God. The words are full of meaning, but they are also full of structure so that everyone has parts to sing and can join in. So, in an ancient worship event, Psalm 24 might have started like this:

Group 1: *'The earth is the Lord's!'*   Group 2: *'And everything in it.'*

Group 1: *'The world...'*   Group 2: *'...and all who live in it!'*

Imagine the great temple with these groups advancing up the steps.

Group 1: *'Who may ascend the mountain of the Lord? Who may stand in his holy place?'*   Group 2: *'The one who has clean hands and a pure heart...'*

Well, do you? As you come to worship the Lord today – whether by yourself or together with a big crowd of worshippers – do you have *'clean hands and a pure heart'*? That's what you are meant to question as you reach this point in the song. If the answer is 'No! I have unclean hands', then go and sort that out. Ask God to forgive your sins and cleanse you. Then come back and try again.

The crowd reaches the enormous doors, starts to walk through into the temple courts and moves into the chorus. The multitude sing to those who have control over the gates, *'Lift up your heads, you gates; be lifted up, you ancient doors, that the King of glory may come in.'*

So the doorkeepers question, *'Who is this King of glory?'*

With a loud voice the crowd thunders back, *'The Lord strong and mighty...'*

Don't you wish you could have been there? And isn't it great when we're in a big crowd worshipping the Lord in similar ways today?

See also Graham Cray's entry on Psalm 22 for how the Psalms reveal Christ in all the Scriptures.

Hugo Anson

 Psalm 22   Psalm 25

7 Do not remember the sins of my youth
    and my rebellious ways;
according to your love remember me,
    for you, LORD, are good.

8 Good and upright is the LORD;
    therefore he instructs sinners in his
    ways.
9 He guides the humble in what is right
    and teaches them his way.

10 All the ways of the LORD are loving and
    faithful
    toward those who keep the demands
    of his covenant.
11 For the sake of your name, LORD,
    forgive my iniquity, though it is
    great.

12 Who, then, are those who fear the
    LORD?

PRAYING THE PSALMS 5

Show me your ways

Have you ever woken up in a cold sweat remembering some horrible thing you once did that you'd forgotten about? Ever lie awake while every silly mistake you've made runs through your mind?

David knows he's made some big mistakes and he's worried (Psalm 25:7, 11). There are plenty of people around who want to make themselves look good while bringing David down.

It's so much worse to remember a mistake you've made when you know other people remember it too. How often do we see people ridiculed in the media for one mistake? Does it make you look down on them, or feel angry, or afraid to trip up and be treated the same?

David wrote this song to tell the Lord how he felt about his situation. He doesn't want to be shamed and made to look a fool. He knows that is a real possibility, but he also knows the one who decides who looks good will not be the media, but God! So he prays.

David pleads with God, *'Show me your ways, LORD. Do not remember the sin of my youth.'* A good prayer! He has turned away from his past behaviour and he's looking to learn God's way instead.

Next time your stomach churns with the fear of making a mistake, or you wake up thinking of that thing you wish you hadn't done, try praying like David does in this psalm: *'My eyes are ever on the Lord, for only he will release me from the snare'* (v. 15). Instead of dwelling in guilt, tell God that you're sorry and you want to turn away from your mistakes. Talk with him about your fear and remember: when he forgives, it's already forgotten where it really counts, and you have new hope in him.

Hugo Anson

 Psalm 24

Psalm 91

He will instruct them in the ways they
should choose.*b*

13 They will spend their days in prosperity,
and their descendants will inherit the
land.

14 The LORD confides in those who fear
him;
he makes his covenant known to
them.

15 My eyes are ever on the LORD,
for only he will release my feet from
the snare.

16 Turn to me and be gracious to me,
for I am lonely and afflicted.

17 Relieve the troubles of my heart
and free me from my anguish.

18 Look on my affliction and my distress
and take away all my sins.

19 See how numerous are my enemies
and how fiercely they hate me!

20 Guard my life and rescue me;
do not let me be put to shame,
for I take refuge in you.

21 May integrity and uprightness protect
me,
because my hope, LORD,*c* is in you.

22 Deliver Israel, O God,
from all their troubles!

Psalm 26

Of David.

1 Vindicate me, LORD,
for I have led a blameless life;
I have trusted in the LORD
and have not faltered.

2 Test me, LORD, and try me,
examine my heart and my mind;

3 for I have always been mindful of your
unfailing love
and have lived in reliance on your
faithfulness.

4 I do not sit with the deceitful,
nor do I associate with hypocrites.

5 I abhor the assembly of evildoers
and refuse to sit with the wicked.

6 I wash my hands in innocence,
and go about your altar, LORD,

7 proclaiming aloud your praise
and telling of all your wonderful
deeds.

8 LORD, I love the house where you live,
the place where your glory dwells.

9 Do not take away my soul along with
sinners,
my life with those who are
bloodthirsty,

10 in whose hands are wicked schemes,
whose right hands are full of bribes.

11 I lead a blameless life;
deliver me and be merciful to me.

12 My feet stand on level ground;
in the great congregation I will praise
the LORD.

Psalm 27

Of David.

1 The LORD is my light and my salvation –
whom shall I fear?
The LORD is the stronghold of my life –
of whom shall I be afraid?

2 When the wicked advance against me
to devour*a* me,
it is my enemies and my foes
who will stumble and fall.

3 Though an army besiege me,
my heart will not fear;
though war break out against me,
even then I will be confident.

4 One thing I ask from the LORD,
this only do I seek:
that I may dwell in the house of the
LORD
all the days of my life,
to gaze on the beauty of the LORD
and to seek him in his temple.

5 For in the day of trouble
he will keep me safe in his dwelling;

---

b 12 Or *ways he chooses*
c 21 Septuagint; Hebrew does not have LORD.

a 2 Or *slander*

he will hide me in the shelter of his
sacred tent
and set me high upon a rock.

6 Then my head will be exalted
above the enemies who surround
me;
at his sacred tent I will sacrifice with
shouts of joy;
I will sing and make music to the
LORD.

7 Hear my voice when I call, LORD;
be merciful to me and answer me.
8 My heart says of you, 'Seek his face!'
Your face, LORD, I will seek.
9 Do not hide your face from me,
do not turn your servant away in
anger;
you have been my helper.
Do not reject me or forsake me,
God my Saviour.
10 Though my father and mother forsake
me,
the LORD will receive me.
11 Teach me your way, LORD;
lead me in a straight path
because of my oppressors.
12 Do not hand me over to the desire of my
foes,
for false witnesses rise up against me,
spouting malicious accusations.

13 I remain confident of this:
I will see the goodness of the LORD
in the land of the living.
14 Wait for the LORD;
be strong and take heart
and wait for the LORD.

Psalm 28

Of David.

1 To you, LORD, I call;
you are my Rock,
do not turn a deaf ear to me.
For if you remain silent,
I shall be like those who go down to
the pit.
2 Hear my cry for mercy
as I call to you for help,
as I lift up my hands

towards your Most Holy Place.

3 Do not drag me away with the wicked,
with those who do evil,
who speak cordially with their
neighbours
but harbour malice in their hearts.
4 Repay them for their deeds
and for their evil work;
repay them for what their hands have
done
and bring back on them what they
deserve.

5 Because they have no regard for the
deeds of the LORD
and what his hands have done,
he will tear them down
and never build them up again.

6 Praise be to the LORD,
for he has heard my cry for mercy.
7 The LORD is my strength and my shield;
my heart trusts in him, and he helps
me.
My heart leaps for joy,
and with my song I praise him.

8 The LORD is the strength of his people,
a fortress of salvation for his anointed
one.
9 Save your people and bless your
inheritance;
be their shepherd and carry them for
ever.

Psalm 29

A psalm of David.

1 Ascribe to the LORD, you heavenly
beings,
ascribe to the LORD glory and
strength.
2 Ascribe to the LORD the glory due to his
name;
worship the LORD in the splendour of
his*a* holiness.

3 The voice of the LORD is over the
waters;

---

a 2 Or LORD *with the splendour of*

the God of glory thunders,
　the LORD thunders over the mighty
　　waters.
4 The voice of the LORD is powerful;
　the voice of the LORD is majestic.
5 The voice of the LORD breaks the cedars;
　the LORD breaks in pieces the cedars
　　of Lebanon.
6 He makes Lebanon leap like a calf,
　Sirion[b] like a young wild ox.
7 The voice of the LORD strikes
　with flashes of lightning.
8 The voice of the LORD shakes the desert;
　the LORD shakes the Desert of
　　Kadesh.
9 The voice of the LORD twists the oaks[c]
　and strips the forests bare.
And in his temple all cry, 'Glory!'

10 The LORD sits enthroned over the flood;
　the LORD is enthroned as King for
　　ever.
11 The LORD gives strength to his people;
　the LORD blesses his people with
　　peace.

Psalm 30[a]

*A psalm. A song. For the dedication of the temple.[b]
Of David.*

1 I will exalt you, LORD,
　for you lifted me out of the depths
　and did not let my enemies gloat
　　over me.
2 LORD my God, I called to you for help,
　and you healed me.
3 You, LORD, brought me up from the
　　realm of the dead;
　you spared me from going down to
　　the pit.

4 Sing the praises of the LORD, you his
　　faithful people;
　praise his holy name.
5 For his anger lasts only a moment,
　but his favour lasts a lifetime;
　weeping may stay for the night,
　but rejoicing comes in the morning.

6 When I felt secure, I said,
　'I shall never be shaken.'
7 LORD, when you favoured me,
　you made my royal mountain[c] stand
　　firm;
but when you hid your face,
　I was dismayed.

8 To you, LORD, I called;
　to the Lord I cried for mercy:
9 'What is gained if I am silenced,
　if I go down to the pit?
Will the dust praise you?
　Will it proclaim your faithfulness?
10 Hear, LORD, and be merciful to me;
　LORD, be my help.'

11 You turned my wailing into dancing;
　you removed my sackcloth and
　　clothed me with joy,
12 that my heart may sing your praises and
　　not be silent.
　LORD my God, I will praise you for
　　ever.

Psalm 31[a]

For the director of music. A psalm of David.

1 In you, LORD, I have taken refuge;
　let me never be put to shame;
　deliver me in your righteousness.
2 Turn your ear to me,
　come quickly to my rescue;
　be my rock of refuge,
　a strong fortress to save me.
3 Since you are my rock and my fortress,
　for the sake of your name lead and
　　guide me.
4 Keep me free from the trap that is set for
　　me,
　for you are my refuge.
5 Into your hands I commit my spirit;
　deliver me, LORD, my faithful God.

6 I hate those who cling to worthless idols;
　as for me, I trust in the LORD.
7 I will be glad and rejoice in your love,
　for you saw my affliction
　and knew the anguish of my soul.

---

b 6　That is, Mount Hermon
c 9　Or *LORD makes the deer give birth*
a In Hebrew texts 30:1-12 is numbered 30:2-13.
b Title: Or *palace*

---

c 7　That is, Mount Zion
a In Hebrew texts 31:1-24 is numbered 31:2-25.

8 You have not given me into the hands of
    the enemy
    but have set my feet in a spacious
    place.

9 Be merciful to me, LORD, for I am in
    distress;
    my eyes grow weak with sorrow,
    my soul and body with grief.
10 My life is consumed by anguish
    and my years by groaning;
    my strength fails because of my
    affliction,*b*
    and my bones grow weak.

b 10 Or *guilt*

11 Because of all my enemies,
    I am the utter contempt of my
    neighbours
    and an object of dread to my closest
    friends –
    those who see me on the street flee
    from me.
12 I am forgotten as though I were dead;
    I have become like broken pottery.
13 For I hear many whispering,
    'Terror on every side!'
    They conspire against me
    and plot to take my life.

14 But I trust in you, LORD;
    I say, 'You are my God.'

WORSHIP 5

Honesty

Have you ever had an encounter with someone you have just met, when out of pure politeness you ask them how they are? Then suddenly, out of nowhere, they bare their soul to you and tell you what's going on in the deepest chasms of their hearts. Some of us feel overwhelmed. Some of us feel freaked out. Some of us feel as if we want to run a million miles in the opposite direction to this weirdo... But not God.

In Psalm 31 we see in verses 9–14 that David does exactly that. He simply bares his soul to God, saying, *'My life is consumed by anguish and my years by groaning.'* Heavy stuff! Here we see David being totally honest and real with God.

Worship is first and foremost for God. It's a place where we glorify him and sometimes it's right to choose to do that, even when we don't feel like it. At the same time worship is never about faking anything. The truth is, we are all broken, life is hard and we have all been hurt. Worship is where we offer the brutal honesty of our broken state to the God who is longing to be the strength that we so lack.

When we offer our weakness, in that moment we are taking action that says we believe that God can be our Rock. He is the one to whom you can completely bare your soul. There's no need to fear rejection, ridicule or any blame. This decision, this action, says more about God than any words could ever say or any song could ever express. We are saying to him that we understand who he is and his heart for us. When we make the choice to be brutally honest with God, we are choosing to say, *'I trust in you, LORD; I say, "You are my God."'*

Beth Croft

 Matthew 22:34–40   Mark 14:1–11

15 My times are in your hands;
  deliver me from the hands of my
    enemies,
  from those who pursue me.
16 Let your face shine on your servant;
  save me in your unfailing love.
17 Let me not be put to shame, LORD,
  for I have cried out to you;
  but let the wicked be put to shame
  and be silent in the realm of the dead.
18 Let their lying lips be silenced,
  for with pride and contempt
  they speak arrogantly against the
    righteous.

19 How abundant are the good things
  that you have stored up for those who
    fear you,
  that you bestow in the sight of all,
  on those who take refuge in you.
20 In the shelter of your presence you hide
    them
  from all human intrigues;
  you keep them safe in your dwelling
  from accusing tongues.

21 Praise be to the LORD,
  for he showed me the wonders of his
    love
  when I was in a city under siege.
22 In my alarm I said,
  'I am cut off from your sight!'
  Yet you heard my cry for mercy
  when I called to you for help.

23 Love the LORD, all his faithful people!
  The LORD preserves those who are
    true to him,
  but the proud he pays back in full.
24 Be strong and take heart,
  all you who hope in the LORD.

Psalm 32

Of David. A maskil. ^a

1 Blessed is the one
  whose transgressions are forgiven,
  whose sins are covered.
2 Blessed is the one

whose sin the LORD does not count
    against them
  and in whose spirit is no deceit.

3 When I kept silent,
  my bones wasted away
  through my groaning all day long.
4 For day and night
  your hand was heavy on me;
  my strength was sapped
  as in the heat of summer.^b

5 Then I acknowledged my sin to you
  and did not cover up my iniquity.
  I said, 'I will confess
  my transgressions to the LORD.'
  And you forgave
  the guilt of my sin.

6 Therefore let all the faithful pray to you
  while you may be found;
  surely the rising of the mighty waters
  will not reach them.
7 You are my hiding-place;
  you will protect me from trouble
  and surround me with songs of
    deliverance.

8 I will instruct you and teach you in the
    way you should go;
  I will counsel you with my loving eye
    on you.
9 Do not be like the horse or the mule,
  which have no understanding
  but must be controlled by bit and bridle
  or they will not come to you.
10 Many are the woes of the wicked,
  but the LORD's unfailing love
  surrounds the one who trusts in him.

11 Rejoice in the LORD and be glad, you
    righteous;
  sing, all you who are upright in heart!

Psalm 33

1 Sing joyfully to the LORD, you righteous;
  it is fitting for the upright to praise
    him.

---

a Title: Probably a literary or musical term

b 4 The Hebrew has *Selah* (a word of uncertain meaning) here and at the end of verses 5 and 7.

2 Praise the LORD with the harp;
    make music to him on the ten-
        stringed lyre.
3 Sing to him a new song;
    play skilfully, and shout for joy.

4 For the word of the LORD is right and
        true;
    he is faithful in all he does.
5 The LORD loves righteousness and
        justice;
    the earth is full of his unfailing love.

6 By the word of the LORD the heavens
        were made,
    their starry host by the breath of his
        mouth.
7 He gathers the waters of the sea into
        jars;[a]
    he puts the deep into storehouses.
8 Let all the earth fear the LORD;
    let all the people of the world revere
        him.
9 For he spoke, and it came to be;
    he commanded, and it stood firm.

10 The LORD foils the plans of the nations;
    he thwarts the purposes of the
        peoples.
11 But the plans of the LORD stand firm for
        ever,
    the purposes of his heart through all
        generations.

12 Blessed is the nation whose God is the
        LORD,
    the people he chose for his
        inheritance.
13 From heaven the LORD looks down
    and sees all mankind;
14 from his dwelling-place he watches
    all who live on earth –
15 he who forms the hearts of all,
    who considers everything they do.

16 No king is saved by the size of his army;
    no warrior escapes by his great
        strength.
17 A horse is a vain hope for deliverance;
    despite all its great strength it cannot
        save.
18 But the eyes of the LORD are on those
        who fear him,
    on those whose hope is in his
        unfailing love,
19 to deliver them from death
    and keep them alive in famine.

20 We wait in hope for the LORD;
    he is our help and our shield.
21 In him our hearts rejoice,
    for we trust in his holy name.
22 May your unfailing love be with us,
        LORD,
    even as we put our hope in you.

Psalm 34[a,b]

*Of David. When he pretended to be insane before
Abimelek, who drove him away, and he left.*

1 I will extol the LORD at all times;
    his praise will always be on my lips.
2 I will glory in the LORD;
    let the afflicted hear and rejoice.
3 Glorify the LORD with me:
    let us exalt his name together.

4 I sought the LORD, and he answered
        me;
    he delivered me from all my fears.
5 Those who look to him are radiant;
    their faces are never covered with
        shame.
6 This poor man called, and the LORD
        heard him;
    he saved him out of all his troubles.
7 The angel of the LORD encamps around
        those who fear him,
    and he delivers them.

8 Taste and see that the LORD is good;
    blessed is the one who takes refuge in
        him.
9 Fear the LORD, you his holy people,
    for those who fear him lack nothing.
10 The lions may grow weak and hungry,

---

a 7 Or *sea as into a heap*

a This psalm is an acrostic poem, the verses of
which begin with the successive letters of the
Hebrew alphabet.
b In Hebrew texts 34:1-22 is numbered 34:2-23.

but those who seek the LORD lack no
    good thing.
11 Come, my children, listen to me;
    I will teach you the fear of the LORD.
12 Whoever of you loves life
    and desires to see many good days,
13 keep your tongue from evil
    and your lips from telling lies.
14 Turn from evil and do good;
    seek peace and pursue it.

FAVOURITE VERSES

Psalm 34:14

*Turn from evil and do good;
    seek peace and pursue it.*

- -

This is my favourite Bible verse
because it's straight to the point and
can be used in many circumstances.
It helped me through my first year
of being a Christian and made me
closer to God.

Yasmine, 16

15 The eyes of the LORD are on the
    righteous,
    and his ears are attentive to their
    cry;
16 but the face of the LORD is against those
    who do evil,
    to blot out their name from the
    earth.

17 The righteous cry out, and the LORD
    hears them;
    he delivers them from all their
    troubles.
18 The LORD is close to the broken-hearted
    and saves those who are crushed in
    spirit.

19 The righteous person may have many
    troubles,

but the LORD delivers him from them
    all;
20 he protects all his bones,
    not one of them will be broken.

21 Evil will slay the wicked;
    the foes of the righteous will be
    condemned.
22 The LORD will rescue his servants;
    no one who takes refuge in him will
    be condemned.

Psalm 35

Of David.

1 Contend, LORD, with those who
    contend with me;
    fight against those who fight against
    me.
2 Take up shield and armour;
    arise and come to my aid.
3 Brandish spear and javelin*a*
    against those who pursue me.
Say to me,
    'I am your salvation.'

4 May those who seek my life
    be disgraced and put to shame;
    may those who plot my ruin
    be turned back in dismay.
5 May they be like chaff before the wind,
    with the angel of the LORD driving
    them away;
6 may their path be dark and slippery,
    with the angel of the LORD pursuing
    them.

7 Since they hid their net for me without
    cause
    and without cause dug a pit for me,
8 may ruin overtake them by surprise –
    may the net they hid entangle them,
    may they fall into the pit, to their ruin.
9 Then my soul will rejoice in the LORD
    and delight in his salvation.
10 My whole being will exclaim,
    'Who is like you, LORD?
You rescue the poor from those too
    strong for them,

---

a 3 Or *and block the way*

the poor and needy from those who
rob them.'

11 Ruthless witnesses come forward;
they question me on things I know
nothing about.
12 They repay me evil for good
and leave me like one bereaved.
13 Yet when they were ill, I put on
sackcloth
and humbled myself with fasting.
When my prayers returned to me
unanswered,
14 I went about mourning
as though for my friend or brother.
I bowed my head in grief
as though weeping for my mother.
15 But when I stumbled, they gathered in
glee;
assailants gathered against me
without my knowledge.
They slandered me without ceasing.
16 Like the ungodly they maliciously
mocked;*b*
they gnashed their teeth at me.

17 How long, Lord, will you look on?
Rescue me from their ravages,
my precious life from these lions.
18 I will give you thanks in the great
assembly;
among the throngs I will praise you.
19 Do not let those gloat over me
who are my enemies without cause;
do not let those who hate me without
reason
maliciously wink the eye.
20 They do not speak peaceably,
but devise false accusations
against those who live quietly in the
land.
21 They sneer at me and say, 'Aha! Aha!
With our own eyes we have seen it.'

22 Lord, you have seen this; do not be
silent.
Do not be far from me, Lord.
23 Awake, and rise to my defence!
Contend for me, my God and Lord.

24 Vindicate me in your righteousness,
Lord my God;
do not let them gloat over me.
25 Do not let them think, 'Aha, just what
we wanted!'
or say, 'We have swallowed him up.'

26 May all who gloat over my distress
be put to shame and confusion;
may all who exalt themselves over me
be clothed with shame and disgrace.
27 May those who delight in my
vindication
shout for joy and gladness;
may they always say, 'The Lord be
exalted,
who delights in the well-being of his
servant.'

28 My tongue will proclaim your
righteousness,
your praises all day long.

Psalm 36*a*

*For the director of music. Of David the servant
of the Lord.*

1 I have a message from God in my heart
concerning the sinfulness of the
wicked:*b*
There is no fear of God
before their eyes.

2 In their own eyes they flatter themselves
too much to detect or hate their sin.
3 The words of their mouths are wicked
and deceitful;
they fail to act wisely or do good.
4 Even on their beds they plot evil;
they commit themselves to a sinful
course
and do not reject what is wrong.

5 Your love, Lord, reaches to the heavens,
your faithfulness to the skies.
6 Your righteousness is like the highest
mountains,
your justice like the great deep.

---

b 16 Septuagint; Hebrew may mean *ungodly circle of
mockers.*

a In Hebrew texts 36:1-12 is numbered 36:2-13.
b 1 Or *A message from God: The transgression of the wicked /
resides in their hearts.*

You, LORD, preserve both people and
    animals.
7 How priceless is your unfailing love,
    O God!
  People take refuge in the shadow of
    your wings.
8 They feast in the abundance of your
    house;
  you give them drink from your river
    of delights.
9 For with you is the fountain of life;
    in your light we see light.

10 Continue your love to those who know
    you,
  your righteousness to the upright in
    heart.
11 May the foot of the proud not come
    against me,
  nor the hand of the wicked drive me
    away.
12 See how the evildoers lie fallen –
    thrown down, not able to rise!

Psalm 37[a]
Of David.

1 Do not fret because of those who are
    evil
  or be envious of those who do wrong;
2 for like the grass they will soon wither,
  like green plants they will soon die
    away.

3 Trust in the LORD and do good;
    dwell in the land and enjoy safe
    pasture.
4 Take delight in the LORD,
  and he will give you the desires of
    your heart.

5 Commit your way to the LORD;
    trust in him and he will do this:
6 he will make your righteous reward
    shine like the dawn,
  your vindication like the noonday
    sun.

7 Be still before the LORD
    and wait patiently for him;
  do not fret when people succeed in their
    ways,
  when they carry out their wicked
    schemes.

8 Refrain from anger and turn from
    wrath;
  do not fret – it leads only to evil.
9 For those who are evil will be destroyed,
  but those who hope in the LORD will
    inherit the land.

10 A little while, and the wicked will be no
    more;
  though you look for them, they will
    not be found.
11 But the meek will inherit the land
  and enjoy peace and prosperity.

12 The wicked plot against the righteous
  and gnash their teeth at them;
13 but the Lord laughs at the wicked,
  for he knows their day is coming.

14 The wicked draw the sword
  and bend the bow
  to bring down the poor and needy,
  to slay those whose ways are upright.
15 But their swords will pierce their own
    hearts,
  and their bows will be broken.

16 Better the little that the righteous have
  than the wealth of many wicked;
17 for the power of the wicked will be
    broken,
  but the LORD upholds the righteous.

18 The blameless spend their days under
    the LORD's care,
  and their inheritance will endure for
    ever.
19 In times of disaster they will not
    wither;
  in days of famine they will enjoy
    plenty.

20 But the wicked will perish:
  though the LORD's enemies are like
    the flowers of the field,

---

a This psalm is an acrostic poem, the stanzas of
which begin with the successive letters of the
Hebrew alphabet.

they will be consumed, they will go
up in smoke.

²¹ The wicked borrow and do not repay,
but the righteous give generously;
²² those the LORD blesses will inherit the
land,
but those he curses will be
destroyed.

²³ The LORD makes firm the steps
of the one who delights in him;
²⁴ though he may stumble, he will not
fall,
for the LORD upholds him with his
hand.

²⁵ I was young and now I am old,
yet I have never seen the righteous
forsaken
or their children begging bread.
²⁶ They are always generous and lend
freely;
their children will be a blessing.*b*

²⁷ Turn from evil and do good;
then you will dwell in the land for
ever.
²⁸ For the LORD loves the just
and will not forsake his faithful
ones.

Wrongdoers will be completely
destroyed*c*;
the offspring of the wicked will
perish.
²⁹ The righteous will inherit the land
and dwell in it for ever.

³⁰ The mouths of the righteous utter
wisdom,
and their tongues speak what is just.
³¹ The law of their God is in their hearts;
their feet do not slip.

³² The wicked lie in wait for the righteous,
intent on putting them to death;

³³ but the LORD will not leave them in the
power of the wicked
or let them be condemned when
brought to trial.

³⁴ Hope in the LORD
and keep his way.
He will exalt you to inherit the land;
when the wicked are destroyed, you
will see it.

³⁵ I have seen a wicked and ruthless man
flourishing like a luxuriant native
tree,
³⁶ but he soon passed away and was no
more;
though I looked for him, he could
not be found.

³⁷ Consider the blameless, observe the
upright;
a future awaits those who seek
peace.*d*
³⁸ But all sinners will be destroyed;
there will be no future*e* for the
wicked.

³⁹ The salvation of the righteous comes
from the LORD;
he is their stronghold in time of
trouble.
⁴⁰ The LORD helps them and delivers them;
he delivers them from the wicked and
saves them,
because they take refuge in him.

Psalm 38*a*

A psalm of David. A petition.

¹ LORD, do not rebuke me in your anger
or discipline me in your wrath.
² Your arrows have pierced me,
and your hand has come down on
me.
³ Because of your wrath there is no health
in my body;
there is no soundness in my bones
because of my sin.

---

b 26 Or *freely; / the names of their children will be used in
blessings* (see Gen. 48:20); or *freely; / others will see that
their children are blessed*
c 28 See Septuagint; Hebrew *They will be protected
for ever*

d 37 Or *upright; / those who seek peace will have posterity*
e 38 Or *posterity*
a In Hebrew texts 38:1-22 is numbered 38:2-23.

⁴ My guilt has overwhelmed me
   like a burden too heavy to bear.

⁵ My wounds fester and are loathsome
   because of my sinful folly.
⁶ I am bowed down and brought very low;
   all day long I go about mourning.
⁷ My back is filled with searing pain;
   there is no health in my body.
⁸ I am feeble and utterly crushed;
   I groan in anguish of heart.

⁹ All my longings lie open before you,
      Lord:
   my sighing is not hidden from you.
¹⁰ My heart pounds, my strength fails me;
   even the light has gone from my eyes.
¹¹ My friends and companions avoid me
      because of my wounds;
   my neighbours stay far away.
¹² Those who want to kill me set their
      traps,
   those who would harm me talk of my
      ruin;
   all day long they scheme and lie.

¹³ I am like the deaf, who cannot hear,
   like the mute, who cannot speak;
¹⁴ I have become like one who does not
      hear,
   whose mouth can offer no reply.
¹⁵ Lord, I wait for you;
   you will answer, Lord my God.
¹⁶ For I said, 'Do not let them gloat
   or exalt themselves over me when my
      feet slip.'

¹⁷ For I am about to fall,
   and my pain is ever with me.
¹⁸ I confess my iniquity;
   I am troubled by my sin.
¹⁹ Many have become my enemies without
      cause[b];
   those who hate me without reason
      are numerous.
²⁰ Those who repay my good with evil
   lodge accusations against me,
   though I seek only to do what is good.

²¹ Lord, do not forsake me;
   do not be far from me, my God.
²² Come quickly to help me,
   my Lord and my Saviour.

Psalm 39[a]

*For the director of music. For Jeduthun. A psalm
of David.*

¹ I said, 'I will watch my ways
   and keep my tongue from sin;
   I will put a muzzle on my mouth
   while in the presence of the wicked.'
² So I remained utterly silent,
   not even saying anything good.
   But my anguish increased;
³   my heart grew hot within me.
   While I meditated, the fire burned;
   then I spoke with my tongue:

⁴ 'Show me, Lord, my life's end
   and the number of my days;
   let me know how fleeting my life is.
⁵ You have made my days a mere
      handbreadth;
   the span of my years is as nothing
      before you.
   Everyone is but a breath,
   even those who seem secure.[b]

⁶ 'Surely everyone goes around like a
      mere phantom;
   in vain they rush about, heaping up
      wealth
   without knowing whose it will
      finally be.

⁷ 'But now, Lord, what do I look for?
   My hope is in you.
⁸ Save me from all my transgressions;
   do not make me the scorn of fools.
⁹ I was silent; I would not open my
      mouth,
   for you are the one who has done
      this.
¹⁰ Remove your scourge from me;
   I am overcome by the blow of your
      hand.

---

b 19 One Dead Sea Scrolls manuscript; Masoretic
Text *my vigorous enemies*

a In Hebrew texts 39:1-13 is numbered 39:2-14.
b 5 The Hebrew has *Selah* (a word of uncertain
meaning) here and at the end of verse 11.

11 When you rebuke and discipline anyone
    for their sin,
  you consume their wealth like a
    moth –
  surely everyone is but a breath.

12 'Hear my prayer, LORD,
  listen to my cry for help;
  do not be deaf to my weeping.
I dwell with you as a foreigner,
  a stranger, as all my ancestors were.
13 Look away from me, that I may enjoy life
    again
  before I depart and am no more.'

Psalm 40[a]

For the director of music. Of David. A psalm.

1 I waited patiently for the LORD;
  he turned to me and heard my cry.
2 He lifted me out of the slimy pit,
  out of the mud and mire;
he set my feet on a rock
  and gave me a firm place to stand.
3 He put a new song in my mouth,
  a hymn of praise to our God.
Many will see and fear the LORD
  and put their trust in him.

4 Blessed is the one
  who trusts in the LORD,
who does not look to the proud,
  to those who turn aside to false
    gods.[b]
5 Many, LORD my God,
  are the wonders you have done,
  the things you planned for us.
None can compare with you;
  were I to speak and tell of your deeds,
  they would be too many to declare.

6 Sacrifice and offering you did not
    desire –
  but my ears you have opened;[c] –
  burnt offerings and sin offerings[d] you
    did not require.

7 Then I said, 'Here I am, I have come –
  it is written about me in the scroll.[e]
8 I desire to do your will, my God;
  your law is within my heart.'

9 I proclaim your saving acts in the great
    assembly;
  I do not seal my lips, LORD,
  as you know.
10 I do not hide your righteousness in my
    heart;
  I speak of your faithfulness and your
    saving help.
I do not conceal your love and your
    faithfulness
  from the great assembly.

11 Do not withhold your mercy from me,
    LORD;
  may your love and faithfulness always
    protect me.
12 For troubles without number surround
    me;
  my sins have overtaken me, and I
    cannot see.
They are more than the hairs of my
    head,
  and my heart fails within me.
13 Be pleased to save me, LORD;
  come quickly, LORD, to help me.

14 May all who want to take my life
  be put to shame and confusion;
may all who desire my ruin
  be turned back in disgrace.
15 May those who say to me, 'Aha! Aha!'
  be appalled at their own shame.
16 But may all who seek you
  rejoice and be glad in you;
may those who long for your saving
    help always say,
  'The LORD is great!'

17 But as for me, I am poor and needy;
  may the Lord think of me.
You are my help and my deliverer;
  you are my God, do not delay.

---

a In Hebrew texts 40:1-17 is numbered 40:2-18.
b 4 Or *to lies*
c 6 Hebrew; some Septuagint manuscripts *but a body you have prepared for me*
d 6 Or *purification offerings*

---

e 7 Or *come / with the scroll written for me*

Psalm 41[a]

For the director of music. A psalm of David.

1 Blessed are those who have regard for
   the weak;
   the LORD delivers them in times of
   trouble.
2 The LORD protects and preserves them –
   they are counted among the blessed
      in the land –
   he does not give them over to the
      desire of their foes.
3 The LORD sustains them on their
      sick-bed
   and restores them from their bed of
      illness.

4 I said, 'Have mercy on me, LORD;
   heal me, for I have sinned against
      you.'
5 My enemies say of me in malice,
   'When will he die and his name
      perish?'
6 When one of them comes to see me,
   he speaks falsely, while his heart
      gathers slander;
   then he goes out and spreads it
      around.

7 All my enemies whisper together
      against me;
   they imagine the worst for me,
      saying,
8 'A vile disease has afflicted him;
   he will never get up from the place
      where he lies.'
9 Even my close friend,
   someone I trusted,
   one who shared my bread,
   has turned[b] against me.

10 But may you have mercy on me, LORD;
   raise me up, that I may repay them.
11 I know that you are pleased with me,
   for my enemy does not triumph
      over me.
12 Because of my integrity you uphold me
   and set me in your presence for ever.

13 Praise be to the LORD, the God of Israel,
   from everlasting to everlasting.
   Amen and Amen.

Book II
Psalms 42 – 72

Psalm 42[a,b]

*For the director of music. A maskil[c] of the Sons
of Korah.*

1 As the deer pants for streams of water,
   so my soul pants for you, my God.
2 My soul thirsts for God, for the living
      God.
   When can I go and meet with God?
3 My tears have been my food
   day and night,
   while people say to me all day long,
   'Where is your God?'
4 These things I remember
   as I pour out my soul:
   how I used to go to the house of God
      under the protection of the Mighty
      One[d]
   with shouts of joy and praise
      among the festive throng.

5 Why, my soul, are you downcast?
   Why so disturbed within me?
   Put your hope in God,
   for I will yet praise him,
   my Saviour and my God.

6 My soul is downcast within me;
   therefore I will remember you
   from the land of the Jordan,
      the heights of Hermon – from Mount
      Mizar.
7 Deep calls to deep
   in the roar of your waterfalls;
   all your waves and breakers
   have swept over me.

---

a In Hebrew texts 41:1-13 is numbered 41:2-14.
b 9 Hebrew *has lifted up his heel*

a In many Hebrew manuscripts Psalms 42 and 43
constitute one psalm.
b In Hebrew texts 42:1-11 is numbered 42:2-12.
c Title: Probably a literary or musical term
d 4 See Septuagint and Syriac; the meaning of the
Hebrew for this line is uncertain.

8 By day the LORD directs his love,
   at night his song is with me –
   a prayer to the God of my life.

9 I say to God my Rock,
   'Why have you forgotten me?
Why must I go about mourning,
   oppressed by the enemy?'
10 My bones suffer mortal agony
   as my foes taunt me,
saying to me all day long,
   'Where is your God?'

11 Why, my soul, are you downcast?
   Why so disturbed within me?
Put your hope in God,
   for I will yet praise him,
   my Saviour and my God.

FACT

ANIMALS

The most mentioned animal in the Bible is
the sheep. There are 410 mentions of sheep,
lambs or rams. The next highest is the goat
(169), followed closely by the horse (166),
then the donkey (153).

Psalm 43[a]

1 Vindicate me, my God,
   and plead my cause
   against an unfaithful nation.
Rescue me from those who are
   deceitful and wicked.
2 You are God my stronghold.
   Why have you rejected me?
Why must I go about mourning,
   oppressed by the enemy?
3 Send me your light and your faithful
   care,
   let them lead me;

let them bring me to your holy
   mountain,
   to the place where you dwell.
4 Then I will go to the altar of God,
   to God, my joy and my delight.
I will praise you with the lyre,
   O God, my God.

5 Why, my soul, are you downcast?
   Why so disturbed within me?
Put your hope in God,
   for I will yet praise him,
   my Saviour and my God.

Psalm 44[a]

For the director of music. Of the Sons of Korah.
A maskil.[b]

1 We have heard it with our ears, O God;
   our ancestors have told us
what you did in their days,
   in days long ago.
2 With your hand you drove out the
   nations
   and planted our ancestors;
you crushed the peoples
   and made our ancestors flourish.
3 It was not by their sword that they won
   the land,
   nor did their arm bring them victory;
it was your right hand, your arm,
   and the light of your face, for you
   loved them.

4 You are my King and my God,
   who decrees[c] victories for Jacob.
5 Through you we push back our enemies;
   through your name we trample our
   foes.
6 I put no trust in my bow,
   my sword does not bring me victory;
7 but you give us victory over our enemies,
   you put our adversaries to shame.
8 In God we make our boast all day long,
   and we will praise your name for
   ever.[d]

---

a In many Hebrew manuscripts Psalms 42 and 43
constitute one psalm.

a In Hebrew texts 44:1-26 is numbered 44:2-27.
b Title: Probably a literary or musical term
c 4 Septuagint, Aquila and Syriac; Hebrew *King,*
O God; / command
d 8 The Hebrew has *Selah* (a word of uncertain
meaning) here.

9 But now you have rejected and humbled
us;
   you no longer go out with our armies.
10 You made us retreat before the enemy,
   and our adversaries have plundered
   us.
11 You gave us up to be devoured like sheep
   and have scattered us among the
   nations.
12 You sold your people for a pittance,
   gaining nothing from their sale.

13 You have made us a reproach to our
   neighbours,
   the scorn and derision of those
   around us.
14 You have made us a byword among the
   nations;
   the peoples shake their heads at us.
15 I live in disgrace all day long,
   and my face is covered with shame
16 at the taunts of those who reproach and
   revile me,
   because of the enemy, who is bent on
   revenge.

17 All this came upon us,
   though we had not forgotten you;
   we had not been false to your
   covenant.
18 Our hearts had not turned back;
   our feet had not strayed from your
   path.
19 But you crushed us and made us a haunt
   for jackals;
   you covered us over with deep
   darkness.

20 If we had forgotten the name of our God
   or spread out our hands to a foreign
   god,
21 would not God have discovered it,
   since he knows the secrets of the
   heart?
22 Yet for your sake we face death all day
   long;
   we are considered as sheep to be
   slaughtered.

23 Awake, Lord! Why do you sleep?
   Rouse yourself! Do not reject us for
   ever.

24 Why do you hide your face
   and forget our misery and
   oppression?

25 We are brought down to the dust;
   our bodies cling to the ground.
26 Rise up and help us;
   rescue us because of your unfailing
   love.

Psalm 45*a*

*For the director of music. To the tune of 'Lilies'. Of the
Sons of Korah. A maskil. b A wedding song.*

1 My heart is stirred by a noble theme
   as I recite my verses for the king;
   my tongue is the pen of a skilful
   writer.

2 You are the most excellent of men
   and your lips have been anointed
   with grace,
   since God has blessed you for ever.

3 Gird your sword on your side, you
   mighty one;
   clothe yourself with splendour and
   majesty.
4 In your majesty ride forth victoriously
   in the cause of truth, humility and
   justice;
   let your right hand achieve awesome
   deeds.
5 Let your sharp arrows pierce the hearts
   of the king's enemies;
   let the nations fall beneath your feet.
6 Your throne, O God,c will last for ever
   and ever;
   a sceptre of justice will be the sceptre
   of your kingdom.
7 You love righteousness and hate
   wickedness;
   therefore God, your God, has set you
   above your companions
   by anointing you with the oil of joy.
8 All your robes are fragrant with myrrh
   and aloes and cassia;
   from palaces adorned with ivory

---

a In Hebrew texts 45:1-17 is numbered 45:2-18.
b Title: Probably a literary or musical term
c 6 Here the king is addressed as God's
representative.

the music of the strings makes you
glad.
⁹ Daughters of kings are among your
honoured women;
at your right hand is the royal bride in
gold of Ophir.

¹⁰ Listen, daughter, and pay careful
attention:
Forget your people and your father's
house.
¹¹ Let the king be enthralled by your
beauty;
honour him, for he is your lord.
¹² The city of Tyre will come with a gift,ᵈ
people of wealth will seek your
favour.
¹³ All glorious is the princess within her
chamber;
her gown is interwoven with gold.
¹⁴ In embroidered garments she is led to
the king;
her virgin companions follow her –
those brought to be with her.
¹⁵ Led in with joy and gladness,
they enter the palace of the king.

¹⁶ Your sons will take the place of your
fathers;
you will make them princes
throughout the land.

¹⁷ I will perpetuate your memory through
all generations;
therefore the nations will praise you
for ever and ever.

Psalm 46ᵃ

For the director of music. Of the Sons of Korah.
According to alamoth.ᵇ A song.

¹ God is our refuge and strength,
an ever-present help in trouble.
² Therefore we will not fear, though the
earth give way
and the mountains fall into the heart
of the sea,

³ though its waters roar and foam
and the mountains quake with their
surging.ᶜ

⁴ There is a river whose streams make
glad the city of God,
the holy place where the Most High
dwells.
⁵ God is within her, she will not fall;
God will help her at break of day.
⁶ Nations are in uproar, kingdoms fall;
he lifts his voice, the earth melts.

⁷ The LORD Almighty is with us;
the God of Jacob is our fortress.

⁸ Come and see what the LORD has done,
the desolations he has brought on
the earth.
⁹ He makes wars cease
to the ends of the earth.
He breaks the bow and shatters the
spear;
he burns the shieldsᵈ with fire.
¹⁰ He says, 'Be still, and know that I am
God;
I will be exalted among the nations,
I will be exalted in the earth.'

¹¹ The LORD Almighty is with us;
the God of Jacob is our fortress.

Psalm 47ᵃ

For the director of music. Of the Sons of Korah.
A psalm.

¹ Clap your hands, all you nations;
shout to God with cries of joy.

² For the LORD Most High is awesome,
the great King over all the earth.
³ He subdued nations under us,
peoples under our feet.
⁴ He chose our inheritance for us,
the pride of Jacob, whom he loved.ᵇ

ᵈ 12 Or *A Tyrian robe is among the gifts*
ᵃ In Hebrew texts 46:1-11 is numbered 46:2-12.
ᵇ Title: Probably a musical term

ᶜ 3 The Hebrew has *Selah* (a word of uncertain meaning) here and at the end of verses 7 and 11.
ᵈ 9 Or *chariots*
ᵃ In Hebrew texts 47:1-9 is numbered 47:2-10.
ᵇ 4 The Hebrew has *Selah* (a word of uncertain meaning) here.

SPIRITUAL DISCIPLINES 2

MEDITATION

'Be still, and know that I am God,' **writes the psalmist in Psalm 46. In a culture that moves and changes at a thousand miles an hour, that's easier said than done.**

We never stop moving; we never stop doing. One of the new waves of technology is the 'companion device' – a smartphone, tablet or other web-enabled micro-computer which allows you to get involved with a second activity at the same time as a first. So now we don't just watch television, we also send messages to our friends, add to blogs, vote and more while we're watching. We're now in the age of 'second screens' – an indication that our attention spans have become so short and so frenzied that our default setting is to do more than one thing at a time. It's getting harder and harder, more and more alien to our culture, to 'be still'.

The spiritual discipline of meditation helps us to do exactly that. Simply put, Christian meditation is the art of thinking and listening reflectively. When we meditate, we don't clear our minds to connect with the universe (as in some other kinds of meditation); rather, we allow our minds to be filled by the God who made the universe. It's a simple and straightforward activity on one level, yet because the person we're thinking about and listening to is the most complex, interesting, rewarding voice in the universe, it's also just about the richest and most profound experience a person can have.

There's no magic formula. To try it, simply pick one of the three 'directions' listed below, find a quiet space where you won't be distracted, *turn off your phone,* and be still.

- **Towards God.** As we slow ourselves right down, we reflect solely on his character. We remember his promises to us; we bring to mind the things that we know about him. The cross is perhaps the most natural focus for our meditation; equally we can bring to mind the reality of his resurrection and all that this means for us as his followers.

- **Inwards.** This gives us space to put our own lives under the microscope. This isn't self-obsessed navel-gazing; it's a chance to look at how God lives within us, to see where he has already impacted and changed us, and where he is still at work, refining our characters. Inward meditation is the process of reflecting on our own ongoing transformation through the power of God.

- **Towards the Bible.** This is not the act of rigorously interrogating the text (the discipline of study), but the practice of allowing God to speak to us through his Word. Bible meditation taps into the fact that the Word of God is a living book, because the Holy Spirit interprets and clarifies the enduring message of the Bible to us.

Martin Saunders

 Luke 4:1–15   Psalm 119:9–16 ▶▶

5 God has ascended amid shouts of joy,
  the LORD amid the sounding of
    trumpets.
6 Sing praises to God, sing praises;
  sing praises to our King, sing praises.
7 For God is the King of all the earth;
  sing to him a psalm of praise.

8 God reigns over the nations;
  God is seated on his holy throne.
9 The nobles of the nations assemble
  as the people of the God of Abraham,
for the kings^c of the earth belong to
    God;
  he is greatly exalted.

Psalm 48^a

A song. A psalm of the Sons of Korah.

1 Great is the LORD, and most worthy of
    praise,
  in the city of our God, his holy
    mountain.

2 Beautiful in its loftiness,
  the joy of the whole earth,
like the heights of Zaphon^b is Mount
    Zion,
  the city of the Great King.
3 God is in her citadels;
  he has shown himself to be her
    fortress.

4 When the kings joined forces,
  when they advanced together,
5 they saw her and were astounded;
  they fled in terror.
6 Trembling seized them there,
  pain like that of a woman in labour.
7 You destroyed them like ships of
    Tarshish
  shattered by an east wind.

8 As we have heard,
  so we have seen
in the city of the LORD Almighty,
  in the city of our God:

God makes her secure
  for ever.^c

9 Within your temple, O God,
  we meditate on your unfailing love.
10 Like your name, O God,
  your praise reaches to the ends of the
    earth;
  your right hand is filled with
    righteousness.
11 Mount Zion rejoices,
  the villages of Judah are glad
because of your judgments.

12 Walk about Zion, go round her,
  count her towers,
13 consider well her ramparts,
  view her citadels,
that you may tell of them
  to the next generation.

14 For this God is our God for ever and ever;
  he will be our guide even to the end.

Psalm 49^a

For the director of music. Of the Sons of Korah. A psalm.

1 Hear this, all you peoples;
  listen, all who live in this world,
2 both low and high,
  rich and poor alike:
3 My mouth will speak words of wisdom;
  the meditation of my heart will give
    you understanding.
4 I will turn my ear to a proverb;
  with the harp I will expound my
    riddle:

5 Why should I fear when evil days come,
  when wicked deceivers surround
    me —
6 those who trust in their wealth
  and boast of their great riches?
7 No one can redeem the life of another
  or give to God a ransom for them —
8 the ransom for a life is costly,
  no payment is ever enough —
9 so that they should live on for ever

---

c 9 Or *shields*
a In Hebrew texts 48:1-14 is numbered 48:2-15.
b 2 *Zaphon* was the most sacred mountain of the
Canaanites.

c 8 The Hebrew has *Selah* (a word of uncertain
meaning) here.
a In Hebrew texts 49:1-20 is numbered 49:2-21.

and not see decay.

¹⁰ For all can see that the wise die,
   that the foolish and the senseless
      also perish,
   leaving their wealth to others.
¹¹ Their tombs will remain their houses[b]
      for ever,
   their dwellings for endless
      generations,
   though they had[c] named lands after
      themselves.

¹² People, despite their wealth, do not
      endure;
   they are like the beasts that perish.

¹³ This is the fate of those who trust in
      themselves,
   and of their followers, who approve
      their sayings.[d]
¹⁴ They are like sheep and are destined to
      die;
   death will be their shepherd
   (but the upright will prevail over
      them in the morning).
   Their forms will decay in the grave,
   far from their princely mansions.
¹⁵ But God will redeem me from the realm
      of the dead;
   he will surely take me to himself.
¹⁶ Do not be overawed when others grow
      rich,
   when the splendour of their houses
      increases;
¹⁷ for they will take nothing with them
      when they die,
   their splendour will not descend with
      them.
¹⁸ Though while they live they count
      themselves blessed –
   and people praise you when you
      prosper –
¹⁹ they will join those who have gone
      before them,
   who will never again see the light of
      life.

²⁰ People who have wealth but lack
      understanding
   are like the beasts that perish.

Psalm 50

A psalm of Asaph.

¹ The Mighty One, God, the LORD,
   speaks and summons the earth
   from the rising of the sun to where it
      sets.
² From Zion, perfect in beauty,
   God shines forth.
³ Our God comes
   and will not be silent;
   a fire devours before him,
   and around him a tempest rages.
⁴ He summons the heavens above,
   and the earth, that he may judge his
      people:
⁵ 'Gather to me this consecrated people,
   who made a covenant with me by
      sacrifice.'
⁶ And the heavens proclaim his
      righteousness,
   for he is a God of justice.[a,b]

⁷ 'Listen, my people, and I will speak;
   I will testify against you, Israel:
   I am God, your God.
⁸ I bring no charges against you
      concerning your sacrifices
   or concerning your burnt offerings,
   which are ever before me.
⁹ I have no need of a bull from your stall
   or of goats from your pens,
¹⁰ for every animal of the forest is mine,
   and the cattle on a thousand hills.
¹¹ I know every bird in the mountains,
   and the insects in the fields are mine.
¹² If I were hungry I would not tell you,
   for the world is mine, and all that is in
      it.
¹³ Do I eat the flesh of bulls
   or drink the blood of goats?

¹⁴ 'Sacrifice thank-offerings to God,
   fulfil your vows to the Most High,

---

b 11 Septuagint and Syriac; Hebrew *In their thoughts their houses will remain*
c 11 Or *generations, / for they have*
d 13 The Hebrew has *Selah* (a word of uncertain meaning) here and at the end of verse 15.

---

a 6 With a different word division of the Hebrew; Masoretic Text *for God himself is judge*
b 6 The Hebrew has *Selah* (a word of uncertain meaning) here.

15 and call on me in the day of trouble;
   I will deliver you, and you will honour
   me.'

16 But to the wicked person, God says:

'What right have you to recite my laws
   or take my covenant on your lips?
17 You hate my instruction
   and cast my words behind you.
18 When you see a thief, you join with him;
   you throw in your lot with adulterers.
19 You use your mouth for evil
   and harness your tongue to deceit.
20 You sit and testify against your brother
   and slander your own mother's son.
21 When you did these things and I kept
   silent,
   you thought I was exactlyc like you.
   But I now arraign you
   and set my accusations before you.

22 'Consider this, you who forget God,
   or I will tear you to pieces, with no
   one to rescue you:
23 those who sacrifice thank-offerings
   honour me,
   and to the blamelessd I will show my
   salvation.'

Psalm 51 a

*For the director of music. A psalm of David. When the
prophet Nathan came to him after David had committed
adultery with Bathsheba.*

1 Have mercy on me, O God,
   according to your unfailing love;
   according to your great compassion
   blot out my transgressions.
2 Wash away all my iniquity
   and cleanse me from my sin.

3 For I know my transgressions,
   and my sin is always before me.
4 Against you, you only, have I sinned
   and done what is evil in your sight;
   so you are right in your verdict

and justified when you judge.
5 Surely I was sinful at birth,
   sinful from the time my mother
   conceived me.
6 Yet you desired faithfulness even in the
   womb;
   you taught me wisdom in that secret
   place.

7 Cleanse me with hyssop, and I shall be
   clean;
   wash me, and I shall be whiter than
   snow.
8 Let me hear joy and gladness;
   let the bones you have crushed
   rejoice.
9 Hide your face from my sins
   and blot out all my iniquity.

10 Create in me a pure heart, O God,
   and renew a steadfast spirit within
   me.
11 Do not cast me from your presence
   or take your Holy Spirit from me.
12 Restore to me the joy of your salvation
   and grant me a willing spirit, to
   sustain me.

13 Then I will teach transgressors your
   ways,
   so that sinners will turn back to you.
14 Deliver me from the guilt of bloodshed,
   O God,
   you who are God my Saviour,
   and my tongue will sing of your
   righteousness.
15 Open my lips, Lord,
   and my mouth will declare your
   praise.
16 You do not delight in sacrifice, or I
   would bring it;
   you do not take pleasure in burnt
   offerings.
17 My sacrifice, O God, isb a broken spirit;
   a broken and contrite heart
   you, God, will not despise.

18 May it please you to prosper Zion,
   to build up the walls of Jerusalem.

---

c 21 Or *thought the "I AM" was*
d 23 Probable reading of the original Hebrew text;
the meaning of the Masoretic Text for this phrase
is uncertain.
a In Hebrew texts 51:1-19 is numbered 51:3-21.

b 17 Or *The sacrifices of God are*

19 Then you will delight in the sacrifices of
    the righteous,
  in burnt offerings offered whole;
  then bulls will be offered on your
    altar.

Psalm 52 [a]

*For the director of music. A maskil [b] of David. When
Doeg the Edomite had gone to Saul and told him: 'David
has gone to the house of Ahimelek.'*

1 Why do you boast of evil, you mighty
    hero?
  Why do you boast all day long,
  you who are a disgrace in the eyes of
    God?
2 You who practise deceit,
  your tongue plots destruction;
  it is like a sharpened razor.
3 You love evil rather than good,
  falsehood rather than speaking the
    truth. [c]
4 You love every harmful word,
  you deceitful tongue!

5 Surely God will bring you down to
    everlasting ruin:
  he will snatch you up and pluck you
    from your tent;
  he will uproot you from the land of
    the living.
6 The righteous will see and fear;
  they will laugh at you, saying,
7 'Here now is the man
  who did not make God his
    stronghold
  but trusted in his great wealth
  and grew strong by destroying
    others!'

8 But I am like an olive tree
    flourishing in the house of God;
  I trust in God's unfailing love
    for ever and ever.
9 For what you have done I will always
    praise you
  in the presence of your faithful
    people.

And I will hope in your name,
  for your name is good.

Psalm 53 [a]

For the director of music. According to mahalath. [b]
A maskil [c] *of David.*

1 The fool says in his heart,
  'There is no God.'
  They are corrupt, and their ways are vile;
  there is no one who does good.

2 God looks down from heaven
  on all mankind
  to see if there are any who understand,
  any who seek God.
3 Everyone has turned away, all have
    become corrupt;
  there is no one who does good,
  not even one.

4 Do all these evildoers know nothing?

  They devour my people as though eating
    bread;
  they never call on God.
5 But there they are, overwhelmed with
    dread,
  where there was nothing to dread.
  God scattered the bones of those who
    attacked you;
  you put them to shame, for God
    despised them.

6 Oh, that salvation for Israel would come
    out of Zion!
  When God restores his people,
  let Jacob rejoice and Israel be glad!

Psalm 54 [a]

*For the director of music. With stringed instruments.
A* maskil [b] *of David. When the Ziphites had gone to
Saul and said, 'Is not David hiding among us?'*

1 Save me, O God, by your name;
  vindicate me by your might.
2 Hear my prayer, O God;

---

a In Hebrew texts 52:1-9 is numbered 52:3-11.
b Title: Probably a literary or musical term
c 3 The Hebrew has *Selah* (a word of uncertain
meaning) here and at the end of verse 5.

a In Hebrew texts 53:1-6 is numbered 53:2-7.
b Title: Probably a musical term
c Title: Probably a literary or musical term
a In Hebrew texts 54:1-7 is numbered 54:3-9.
b Title: Probably a literary or musical term

listen to the words of my mouth.

3 Arrogant foes are attacking me;
  ruthless people are trying to kill me –
  people without regard for God.[c]

4 Surely God is my help;
  the Lord is the one who sustains me.

5 Let evil recoil on those who slander me;
  in your faithfulness destroy them.

6 I will sacrifice a freewill offering to you;
  I will praise your name, LORD, for it is
  good.
7 You have delivered me from all my
  troubles,
  and my eyes have looked in triumph
  on my foes.

Psalm 55[a]

*For the director of music. With stringed instruments.
A maskil[b] of David.*

1 Listen to my prayer, O God,
  do not ignore my plea;
2   hear me and answer me.
  My thoughts trouble me and I am
  distraught
3   because of what my enemy is saying,
  because of the threats of the wicked;
  for they bring down suffering on me
  and assail me in their anger.

4 My heart is in anguish within me;
  the terrors of death have fallen on me.
5 Fear and trembling have beset me;
  horror has overwhelmed me.
6 I said, 'Oh, that I had the wings of a
  dove!
  I would fly away and be at rest.
7 I would flee far away
  and stay in the desert[c];
8 I would hurry to my place of shelter,
  far from the tempest and storm.'

9 Lord, confuse the wicked, confound
  their words,
  for I see violence and strife in the city.
10 Day and night they prowl about on its
  walls;
  malice and abuse are within it.
11 Destructive forces are at work in the city;
  threats and lies never leave its streets.

FAVOURITE VERSES

Ephesians 6:11

*Put on the full armour of God, so
that you can take your stand against
the devil's schemes.*

While preparing for baptism, I went
under spiritual attack and this verse
has kept me strong through the
troubles the devil throws at me.

Grace, 18

12 If an enemy were insulting me,
  I could endure it;
  if a foe were rising against me,
  I could hide.
13 But it is you, a man like myself,
  my companion, my close friend,
14 with whom I once enjoyed sweet
  fellowship
  at the house of God,
  as we walked about
  among the worshippers.

15 Let death take my enemies by surprise;
  let them go down alive to the realm
  of the dead,
  for evil finds lodging among them.

16 As for me, I call to God,
  and the LORD saves me.
17 Evening, morning and noon
  I cry out in distress,

c 3 The Hebrew has *Selah* (a word of uncertain meaning) here.
a In Hebrew texts 55:1-23 is numbered 55:2-24.
b Title: Probably a literary or musical term
c 7 The Hebrew has *Selah* (a word of uncertain meaning) here and in the middle of verse 19.

and he hears my voice.
¹⁸ He rescues me unharmed
from the battle waged against me,
even though many oppose me.
¹⁹ God, who is enthroned from of old,
who does not change –
he will hear them and humble them,
because they have no fear of God.

²⁰ My companion attacks his friends;
he violates his covenant.
²¹ His talk is smooth as butter,
yet war is in his heart;
his words are more soothing than oil,
yet they are drawn swords.

²² Cast your cares on the LORD
and he will sustain you;
he will never let
the righteous be shaken.
²³ But you, God, will bring down the
wicked
into the pit of decay;
the bloodthirsty and deceitful
will not live out half their days.

But as for me, I trust in you.

Psalm 56 ᵃ

*For the director of music. To the tune of 'A Dove on
Distant Oaks'. Of David. A miktam. ᵇ When the
Philistines had seized him in Gath.*

¹ Be merciful to me, my God,
for my enemies are in hot pursuit;
all day long they press their attack.
² My adversaries pursue me all day long;
in their pride many are attacking me.

³ When I am afraid, I put my trust in you.
⁴ In God, whose word I praise –
in God I trust and am not afraid.
What can mere mortals do to me?

⁵ All day long they twist my words;
all their schemes are for my ruin.
⁶ They conspire, they lurk,
they watch my steps,
hoping to take my life.

⁷ Because of their wickedness do notᶜ let
them escape;
in your anger, God, bring the nations
down.

⁸ Record my misery;
list my tears on your scrollᵈ –
are they not in your record?
⁹ Then my enemies will turn back
when I call for help.
By this I will know that God is for me.

¹⁰ In God, whose word I praise,
in the LORD, whose word I praise –
¹¹ in God I trust and am not afraid.
What can man do to me?

¹² I am under vows to you, my God;
I will present my thank-offerings to
you.
¹³ For you have delivered me from death
and my feet from stumbling,
that I may walk before God
in the light of life.

Psalm 57 ᵃ

*For the director of music. To the tune of 'Do Not Destroy'.
Of David. A miktam. ᵇ When he had fled from Saul
into the cave.*

¹ Have mercy on me, my God, have mercy
on me,
for in you I take refuge.
I will take refuge in the shadow of your
wings
until the disaster has passed.

² I cry out to God Most High,
to God, who vindicates me.
³ He sends from heaven and saves me,
rebuking those who hotly pursue
me – ᶜ
God sends forth his love and his
faithfulness.

ᵃ In Hebrew texts 56:1-13 is numbered 56:2-14.
ᵇ Title: Probably a literary or musical term

ᶜ 7 Probable reading of the original Hebrew text;
Masoretic Text does not have *do not*.
ᵈ 8 Or *misery; / put my tears in your wineskin*
ᵃ In Hebrew texts 57:1-11 is numbered 57:2-12.
ᵇ Title: Probably a literary or musical term
ᶜ 3 The Hebrew has *Selah* (a word of uncertain
meaning) here and at the end of verse 6.

4 I am in the midst of lions;
   I am forced to dwell among ravenous
      beasts –
men whose teeth are spears and
      arrows,
   whose tongues are sharp swords.

5 Be exalted, O God, above the heavens;
   let your glory be over all the earth.

6 They spread a net for my feet –
   I was bowed down in distress.
They dug a pit in my path –
   but they have fallen into it
      themselves.

7 My heart, O God, is steadfast,
   my heart is steadfast;
   I will sing and make music.
8 Awake, my soul!
   Awake, harp and lyre!
   I will awaken the dawn.

9 I will praise you, Lord, among the
      nations;
   I will sing of you among the peoples.
10 For great is your love, reaching to the
      heavens;
   your faithfulness reaches to the skies.

11 Be exalted, O God, above the heavens;
   let your glory be over all the earth.

Psalm 58[a]

For the director of music. To the tune of 'Do Not Destroy'.
Of David. A miktam.[b]

1 Do you rulers indeed speak justly?
   Do you judge people with equity?
2 No, in your heart you devise injustice,
   and your hands mete out violence on
      the earth.

3 Even from birth the wicked go astray;
   from the womb they are wayward,
      spreading lies.
4 Their venom is like the venom of a
      snake,

like that of a cobra that has stopped
   its ears,
5 that will not heed the tune of the
      charmer,
   however skilful the enchanter
      may be.

6 Break the teeth in their mouths, O God;
   LORD, tear out the fangs of those
      lions!
7 Let them vanish like water that flows
      away;
   when they draw the bow, let their
      arrows fall short.
8 May they be like a slug that melts away as
      it moves along,
   like a stillborn child that never sees
      the sun.

9 Before your pots can feel the heat of the
      thorns –
   whether they be green or dry – the
      wicked will be swept away.[c]
10 The righteous will be glad when they are
      avenged,
   when they dip their feet in the blood
      of the wicked.
11 Then people will say,
   'Surely the righteous still are
      rewarded;
   surely there is a God who judges the
      earth.'

Psalm 59[a]

For the director of music. To the tune of 'Do Not Destroy'.
Of David. A miktam.[b] When Saul had sent men to
watch David's house in order to kill him.

1 Deliver me from my enemies, O God;
   be my fortress against those who are
      attacking me.
2 Deliver me from evildoers
   and save me from those who are after
      my blood.

3 See how they lie in wait for me!
   Fierce men conspire against me
   for no offence or sin of mine, LORD.

---

c 9 The meaning of the Hebrew for this verse is
uncertain.
a In Hebrew texts 59:1-17 is numbered 59:2-18.
b Title: Probably a literary or musical term

---

a In Hebrew texts 58:1-11 is numbered 58:2-12.
b Title: Probably a literary or musical term

4 I have done no wrong, yet they are ready
   to attack me.
   Arise to help me; look on my plight!
5 You, LORD God Almighty,
   you who are the God of Israel,
   rouse yourself to punish all the nations;
   show no mercy to wicked traitors.*c*

6 They return at evening,
   snarling like dogs,
   and prowl about the city.
7 See what they spew from their mouths –
   the words from their lips are sharp as
    swords,
   and they think, 'Who can hear us?'
8 But you laugh at them, LORD;
   you scoff at all those nations.

9 You are my strength, I watch for you;
   you, God, are my fortress,
10   my God on whom I can rely.

   God will go before me
   and will let me gloat over those who
    slander me.
11 But do not kill them, Lord our shield,*d*
   or my people will forget.
   In your might uproot them
   and bring them down.
12 For the sins of their mouths,
   for the words of their lips,
   let them be caught in their pride.
   For the curses and lies they utter,
13   consume them in your wrath,
   consume them till they are no more.
   Then it will be known to the ends of the
    earth
   that God rules over Jacob.

14 They return at evening,
   snarling like dogs,
   and prowl about the city.
15 They wander about for food
   and howl if not satisfied.
16 But I will sing of your strength,
   in the morning I will sing of your love;
   for you are my fortress,
   my refuge in times of trouble.

17 You are my strength, I sing praise to you;
   you, God, are my fortress,
   my God on whom I can rely.

Psalm 60*a*

For the director of music. To the tune of 'The Lily of the
*Covenant'. A miktam*b *of David. For teaching. When*
*he fought Aram Naharaim*c *and Aram Zobah,*d *and*
when Joab returned and struck down twelve thousand
Edomites in the Valley of Salt.

1 You have rejected us, God, and burst
   upon us;
   you have been angry – now restore
   us!
2 You have shaken the land and torn it
   open;
   mend its fractures, for it is quaking.
3 You have shown your people desperate
   times;
   you have given us wine that makes us
   stagger.
4 But for those who fear you, you have
   raised a banner
   to be unfurled against the bow.*e*

5 Save us and help us with your right
   hand,
   that those you love may be delivered.
6 God has spoken from his sanctuary:
   'In triumph I will parcel out Shechem
   and measure off the Valley of
   Sukkoth.
7 Gilead is mine, and Manasseh is mine;
   Ephraim is my helmet,
   Judah is my sceptre.
8 Moab is my washbasin,
   on Edom I toss my sandal;
   over Philistia I shout in triumph.'

9 Who will bring me to the fortified city?
   Who will lead me to Edom?
10 Is it not you, God, you who have now
   rejected us

---

*c*5 The Hebrew has *Selah* (a word of uncertain
meaning) here and at the end of verse 13.
*d*11 Or *sovereign*

a In Hebrew texts 60:1-12 is numbered 60:3-14.
b Title: Probably a literary or musical term
c Title: That is, Arameans of North-west
Mesopotamia
d Title: That is, Arameans of central Syria
*e*4 The Hebrew has *Selah* (a word of uncertain
meaning) here.

and no longer go out with our
armies?
11 Give us aid against the enemy,
for human help is worthless.
12 With God we shall gain the victory,
and he will trample down our
enemies.

Psalm 61 *a*

*For the director of music. With stringed instruments.
Of David.*

1 Hear my cry, O God;
listen to my prayer.

2 From the ends of the earth I call to you,
I call as my heart grows faint;
lead me to the rock that is higher
than I.
3 For you have been my refuge,
a strong tower against the foe.

4 I long to dwell in your tent for ever
and take refuge in the shelter of your
wings. *b*
5 For you, God, have heard my vows;
you have given me the heritage of
those who fear your name.

6 Increase the days of the king's life,
his years for many generations.
7 May he be enthroned in God's presence
for ever;
appoint your love and faithfulness to
protect him.

8 Then I will ever sing in praise of your
name
and fulfil my vows day after day.

Psalm 62 *a*

*For the director of music. For Jeduthun. A psalm
of David.*

1 Truly my soul finds rest in God;
my salvation comes from him.
2 Truly he is my rock and my salvation;

he is my fortress, I shall never be
shaken.

3 How long will you assault me?
Would all of you throw me down –
this leaning wall, this tottering fence?
4 Surely they intend to topple me
from my lofty place;
they take delight in lies.
With their mouths they bless,
but in their hearts they curse. *b*

5 Yes, my soul, find rest in God;
my hope comes from him.
6 Truly he is my rock and my salvation;
he is my fortress, I shall not be
shaken.
7 My salvation and my honour depend on
God *c*;
he is my mighty rock, my refuge.
8 Trust in him at all times, you people;
pour out your hearts to him,
for God is our refuge.

9 Surely the lowborn are but a breath,
the highborn are but a lie.
If weighed on a balance, they are
nothing;
together they are only a breath.
10 Do not trust in extortion
or put vain hope in stolen goods;
though your riches increase,
do not set your heart on them.

11 One thing God has spoken,
two things I have heard:
'Power belongs to you, God,
12   and with you, Lord, is unfailing love';
and, 'You reward everyone
according to what they have done.'

Psalm 63 *a*

A psalm of David. When he was in the Desert of Judah.

1 You, God, are my God,
earnestly I seek you;
I thirst for you,
my whole being longs for you,

a In Hebrew texts 61:1-8 is numbered 61:2-9.
b 4 The Hebrew has *Selah* (a word of uncertain
meaning) here.
a In Hebrew texts 62:1-12 is numbered 62:2-13.

b 4 The Hebrew has *Selah* (a word of uncertain
meaning) here and at the end of verse 8.
c 7 Or / *God Most High is my salvation and my honour*
a In Hebrew texts 63:1-11 is numbered 63:2-12.

in a dry and parched land
   where there is no water.

2 I have seen you in the sanctuary
   and beheld your power and your
      glory.
3 Because your love is better than life,
   my lips will glorify you.
4 I will praise you as long as I live,
   and in your name I will lift up my
      hands.
5 I will be satisfied as with the richest of
      foods;
   with singing lips my mouth will
      praise you.

6 On my bed I remember you;
   I think of you through the watches of
      the night.
7 Because you are my help,
   I sing in the shadow of your wings.
8 I cling to you;
   your right hand upholds me.

9 Those who want to kill me will be
      destroyed;
   they will go down to the depths of the
      earth.
10 They will be given over to the sword
   and become food for jackals.

11 But the king will rejoice in God;
   all who swear by God will glory in him,
   while the mouths of liars will be
      silenced.

Psalm 64*a*

For the director of music. A psalm of David.

1 Hear me, my God, as I voice my
      complaint;
   protect my life from the threat of the
      enemy.

2 Hide me from the conspiracy of the
      wicked,
   from the plots of evildoers.
3 They sharpen their tongues like swords
   and aim cruel words like deadly
      arrows.

4 They shoot from ambush at the
      innocent;
   they shoot suddenly, without fear.

5 They encourage each other in evil plans,
   they talk about hiding their snares;
   they say, 'Who will see it?'*b*
6 They plot injustice and say,
   'We have devised a perfect plan!'
   Surely the human mind and heart are
      cunning.

7 But God will shoot them with his
      arrows;
   they will suddenly be struck down.
8 He will turn their own tongues against
      them
   and bring them to ruin;
   all who see them will shake their
      heads in scorn.
9 All people will fear;
   they will proclaim the works of God
   and ponder what he has done.

10 The righteous will rejoice in the LORD
   and take refuge in him;
   all the upright in heart will glory in
      him!

Psalm 65*a*

For the director of music. A psalm of David. A song.

1 Praise awaits*b* you, our God, in Zion;
   to you our vows will be fulfilled.
2 You who answer prayer,
   to you all people will come.
3 When we were overwhelmed by sins,
   you forgave*c* our transgressions.
4 Blessed are those you choose
   and bring near to live in your courts!
   We are filled with the good things of
      your house,
   of your holy temple.

5 You answer us with awesome and
      righteous deeds,
   God our Saviour,

---

a In Hebrew texts 64:1-10 is numbered 64:2-11.

b 5 Or *us*
a In Hebrew texts 65:1-13 is numbered 65:2-14.
b 1 Or *befits*; the meaning of the Hebrew for this
word is uncertain.
c 3 Or *made atonement for*

the hope of all the ends of the earth
and of the farthest seas,
6 who formed the mountains by your
power,
having armed yourself with strength,
7 who stilled the roaring of the seas,
the roaring of their waves,
and the turmoil of the nations.
8 The whole earth is filled with awe at
your wonders;
where morning dawns, where
evening fades,
you call forth songs of joy.

9 You care for the land and water it;
you enrich it abundantly.
The streams of God are filled with water
to provide the people with corn,
for so you have ordained it.*d*
10 You drench its furrows and level its
ridges;
you soften it with showers and bless
its crops.
11 You crown the year with your bounty,
and your carts overflow with
abundance.
12 The grasslands of the wilderness
overflow;
the hills are clothed with gladness.
13 The meadows are covered with flocks
and the valleys are mantled with
corn;
they shout for joy and sing.

Psalm 66

For the director of music. A song. A psalm.

1 Shout for joy to God, all the earth!
2   Sing the glory of his name;
make his praise glorious.
3 Say to God, 'How awesome are your
deeds!
So great is your power
that your enemies cringe before you.
4 All the earth bows down to you;
they sing praise to you,
they sing the praises of your name.'*a*

5 Come and see what God has done,

his awesome deeds for mankind!
6 He turned the sea into dry land,
they passed through the waters on
foot –
come, let us rejoice in him.
7 He rules for ever by his power,
his eyes watch the nations –
let not the rebellious rise up against
him.

FACT

LONGEST BOOK

The longest book of the Bible is the Psalms,
which contains 150 chapters. The shortest
book is 3 John, which only contains one
chapter of 323 words.

8 Praise our God, all peoples,
let the sound of his praise be heard;
9 he has preserved our lives
and kept our feet from slipping.
10 For you, God, tested us;
you refined us like silver.
11 You brought us into prison
and laid burdens on our backs.
12 You let people ride over our heads;
we went through fire and water,
but you brought us to a place of
abundance.

13 I will come to your temple with burnt
offerings
and fulfil my vows to you –
14 vows my lips promised and my mouth
spoke
when I was in trouble.
15 I will sacrifice fat animals to you
and an offering of rams;
I will offer bulls and goats.

16 Come and hear, all you who fear God;
let me tell you what he has done for
me.

d 9   Or *for that is how you prepare the land*
a 4   The Hebrew has *Selah* (a word of uncertain
meaning) here and at the end of verses 7 and 15.

17 I cried out to him with my mouth;
  his praise was on my tongue.
18 If I had cherished sin in my heart,
  the Lord would not have listened;
19 but God has surely listened
  and has heard my prayer.
20 Praise be to God,
  who has not rejected my prayer
  or withheld his love from me!

Psalm 67 *a*

For the director of music. With stringed instruments.
A psalm. A song.

1 May God be gracious to us and bless us
  and make his face shine on us – *b*
2 so that your ways may be known on
    earth,
  your salvation among all nations.

3 May the peoples praise you, God;
  may all the peoples praise you.
4 May the nations be glad and sing for
    joy,
  for you rule the peoples with equity
  and guide the nations of the earth.
5 May the peoples praise you, God;
  may all the peoples praise you.

6 The land yields its harvest;
  God, our God, blesses us.
7 May God bless us still,
  so that all the ends of the earth will
    fear him.

Psalm 68 *a*

For the director of music. Of David. A psalm. A song.

1 May God arise, may his enemies be
    scattered;
  may his foes flee before him.
2 May you blow them away like smoke –
  as wax melts before the fire,
  may the wicked perish before God.
3 But may the righteous be glad
  and rejoice before God;
  may they be happy and joyful.

4 Sing to God, sing in praise of his name,
  extol him who rides on the clouds *b*;
  rejoice before him – his name is the
    LORD.
5 A father to the fatherless, a defender of
    widows,
  is God in his holy dwelling.
6 God sets the lonely in families, *c*
  he leads out the prisoners with
    singing;
  but the rebellious live in a sun-
    scorched land.

7 When you, God, went out before your
    people,
  when you marched through the
    wilderness, *d*
8 the earth shook, the heavens poured
    down rain,
  before God, the One of Sinai,
  before God, the God of Israel.
9 You gave abundant showers, O God;
  you refreshed your weary inheritance.
10 Your people settled in it,
  and from your bounty, God, you
    provided for the poor.

11 The Lord announces the word,
  and the women who proclaim it are a
    mighty throng:
12 'Kings and armies flee in haste;
  the women at home divide the
    plunder.
13 Even while you sleep among the
    sheepfolds, *e*
  the wings of my dove are sheathed
    with silver,
  its feathers with shining gold.'
14 When the Almighty *f* scattered the kings
    in the land,
  it was like snow fallen on Mount
    Zalmon.

15 Mount Bashan, majestic mountain,
  Mount Bashan, rugged mountain,

---

b 4 Or *name, / prepare the way for him who rides through
the deserts*
c 6 Or *the desolate in a homeland*
d 7 The Hebrew has *Selah* (a word of uncertain
meaning) here and at the end of verses 19 and 32.
e 13 Or *the campfires; or the saddlebags*
f 14 Hebrew *Shaddai*

---

a In Hebrew texts 67:1-7 is numbered 67:2-8.
b 1 The Hebrew has *Selah* (a word of uncertain
meaning) here and at the end of verse 4.
a In Hebrew texts 68:1-35 is numbered 68:2-36.

16 why gaze in envy, you rugged mountain,
at the mountain where God chooses
to reign,
where the Lord himself will dwell for
ever?
17 The chariots of God are tens of
thousands
and thousands of thousands;
the Lord has come from Sinai into his
sanctuary.*g*
18 When you ascended on high,
you took many captives;
you received gifts from people,
even from*h* the rebellious –
that you,*i* Lord God, might dwell
there.

19 Praise be to the Lord, to God our
Saviour,
who daily bears our burdens.
20 Our God is a God who saves;
from the Sovereign Lord comes
escape from death.
21 Surely God will crush the heads of his
enemies,
the hairy crowns of those who go on
in their sins.
22 The Lord says, 'I will bring them from
Bashan;
I will bring them from the depths of
the sea,
23 that your feet may wade in the blood of
your foes,
while the tongues of your dogs have
their share.'

24 Your procession, God, has come into
view,
the procession of my God and King
into the sanctuary.
25 In front are the singers, after them the
musicians;
with them are the young women
playing the tambourines.
26 Praise God in the great congregation;
praise the Lord in the assembly of
Israel.

27 There is the little tribe of Benjamin,
leading them,
there the great throng of Judah's
princes,
and there the princes of Zebulun and
of Naphtali.

28 Summon your power, God;*j*
show us your strength, our God, as
you have done before.
29 Because of your temple at Jerusalem
kings will bring you gifts.
30 Rebuke the beast among the reeds,
the herd of bulls among the calves of
the nations.
Humbled, may the beast bring bars of
silver.
Scatter the nations who delight in
war.
31 Envoys will come from Egypt;
Cush*k* will submit herself to God.

32 Sing to God, you kingdoms of the earth,
sing praise to the Lord,
33 to him who rides across the highest
heavens, the ancient heavens,
who thunders with mighty voice.
34 Proclaim the power of God,
whose majesty is over Israel,
whose power is in the heavens.
35 You, God, are awesome in your
sanctuary;
the God of Israel gives power and
strength to his people.

Praise be to God!

Psalm 69*a*

For the director of music. To the tune of 'Lilies'.
Of David.

1 Save me, O God,
for the waters have come up to my
neck.
2 I sink in the miry depths,
where there is no foothold.
I have come into the deep waters;

g 17 Probable reading of the original Hebrew text;
Masoretic Text *Lord is among them at Sinai in holiness*
h 18 Or *gifts for people, / even*
i 18 Or *they*
j 28 Many Hebrew manuscripts, Septuagint and
Syriac; most Hebrew manuscripts *Your God has
summoned power for you*
k 31 That is, the upper Nile region
a In Hebrew texts 69:1-36 is numbered 69:2-37.

the floods engulf me.
3 I am worn out calling for help;
    my throat is parched.
My eyes fail,
    looking for my God.
4 Those who hate me without reason
    outnumber the hairs of my head;
many are my enemies without cause,
    those who seek to destroy me.
I am forced to restore
    what I did not steal.

5 You, God, know my folly;
    my guilt is not hidden from you.

6 Lord, the LORD Almighty,
    may those who hope in you
    not be disgraced because of me;
God of Israel,
    may those who seek you
    not be put to shame because of me.
7 For I endure scorn for your sake,
    and shame covers my face.
8 I am a foreigner to my own family,
    a stranger to my own mother's
        children;
9 for zeal for your house consumes me,
    and the insults of those who insult
        you fall on me.
10 When I weep and fast,
    I must endure scorn;
11 when I put on sackcloth,
    people make sport of me.
12 Those who sit at the gate mock me,
    and I am the song of the drunkards.

13 But I pray to you, LORD,
    in the time of your favour;
in your great love, O God,
    answer me with your sure salvation.
14 Rescue me from the mire,
    do not let me sink;
deliver me from those who hate me,
    from the deep waters.
15 Do not let the floodwaters engulf me
    or the depths swallow me up
    or the pit close its mouth over me.

16 Answer me, LORD, out of the goodness
        of your love;
    in your great mercy turn to me.
17 Do not hide your face from your servant;

answer me quickly, for I am in trouble.
18 Come near and rescue me;
    deliver me because of my foes.

19 You know how I am scorned, disgraced
        and shamed;
    all my enemies are before you.
20 Scorn has broken my heart
    and has left me helpless;
I looked for sympathy, but there was
        none,
    for comforters, but I found none.
21 They put gall in my food
    and gave me vinegar for my thirst.

22 May the table set before them become a
        snare;
    may it become retribution and*b* a
        trap.
23 May their eyes be darkened so that they
        cannot see,
    and their backs be bent for ever.
24 Pour out your wrath on them;
    let your fierce anger overtake them.
25 May their place be deserted;
    let there be no one to dwell in their
        tents.
26 For they persecute those you wound
    and talk about the pain of those you
        hurt.
27 Charge them with crime upon crime;
    do not let them share in your
        salvation.
28 May they be blotted out of the book of
        life
    and not be listed with the righteous.

29 But as for me, afflicted and in pain –
    may your salvation, God, protect me.

30 I will praise God's name in song
    and glorify him with thanksgiving.
31 This will please the LORD more than
        an ox,
    more than a bull with its horns and
        hooves.
32 The poor will see and be glad –
    you who seek God, may your hearts
        live!
33 The LORD hears the needy

---

b 22 Or *snare / and their fellowship become*

and does not despise his captive
people.

³⁴ Let heaven and earth praise him,
the seas and all that move in them,
³⁵ for God will save Zion
and rebuild the cities of Judah.
Then people will settle there and
possess it;
³⁶ the children of his servants will
inherit it,
and those who love his name will
dwell there.

Psalm 70*a*

For the director of music. Of David. A petition.

¹ Hasten, O God, to save me;
come quickly, Lord, to help me.

² May those who want to take my life
be put to shame and confusion;
may all who desire my ruin
be turned back in disgrace.
³ May those who say to me, 'Aha! Aha!'
turn back because of their shame.
⁴ But may all who seek you
rejoice and be glad in you;
may those who long for your saving
help always say,
'The Lord is great!'

⁵ But as for me, I am poor and needy;
come quickly to me, O God.
You are my help and my deliverer;
Lord, do not delay.

Psalm 71

¹ In you, Lord, I have taken refuge;
let me never be put to shame.
² In your righteousness, rescue me and
deliver me;
turn your ear to me and save me.
³ Be my rock of refuge,
to which I can always go;
give the command to save me,
for you are my rock and my fortress.
⁴ Deliver me, my God, from the hand of
the wicked,

from the grasp of those who are evil
and cruel.

⁵ For you have been my hope, Sovereign
Lord,
my confidence since my youth.
⁶ From my birth I have relied on you;
you brought me forth from my
mother's womb.
I will ever praise you.
⁷ I have become a sign to many;
you are my strong refuge.
⁸ My mouth is filled with your praise,
declaring your splendour all day long.

⁹ Do not cast me away when I am old;
do not forsake me when my strength
is gone.
¹⁰ For my enemies speak against me;
those who wait to kill me conspire
together.
¹¹ They say, 'God has forsaken him;
pursue him and seize him,
for no one will rescue him.'
¹² Do not be far from me, my God;
come quickly, God, to help me.
¹³ May my accusers perish in shame;
may those who want to harm me
be covered with scorn and disgrace.

¹⁴ As for me, I shall always have hope;
I will praise you more and more.

¹⁵ My mouth will tell of your righteous
deeds,
of your saving acts all day long –
though I know not how to relate
them all.
¹⁶ I will come and proclaim your mighty
acts, Sovereign Lord;
I will proclaim your righteous deeds,
yours alone.
¹⁷ Since my youth, God, you have taught
me,
and to this day I declare your
marvellous deeds.
¹⁸ Even when I am old and grey,
do not forsake me, my God,
till I declare your power to the next
generation,
your mighty acts to all who are to
come.

---

a In Hebrew texts 70:1-5 is numbered 70:2-6.

19 Your righteousness, God, reaches to the
heavens,
you who have done great things.
Who is like you, God?
20 Though you have made me see troubles,
many and bitter,
you will restore my life again;
from the depths of the earth
you will again bring me up.
21 You will increase my honour
and comfort me once more.

22 I will praise you with the harp
for your faithfulness, my God;
I will sing praise to you with the lyre,
Holy One of Israel.
23 My lips will shout for joy
when I sing praise to you –
I whom you have delivered.
24 My tongue will tell of your righteous
acts
all day long,
for those who wanted to harm me
have been put to shame and
confusion.

Psalm 72
Of Solomon.

1 Endow the king with your justice,
O God,
the royal son with your
righteousness.
2 May he judge your people in
righteousness,
your afflicted ones with justice.

3 May the mountains bring prosperity to
the people,
the hills the fruit of righteousness.
4 May he defend the afflicted among the
people
and save the children of the needy;
may he crush the oppressor.
5 May he endure*a* as long as the sun,
as long as the moon, through all
generations.
6 May he be like rain falling on a mown
field,
like showers watering the earth.

7 In his days may the righteous flourish
and prosperity abound till the moon
is no more.

8 May he rule from sea to sea
and from the River*b* to the ends of the
earth.
9 May the desert tribes bow before him
and his enemies lick the dust.
10 May the kings of Tarshish and of distant
shores
bring tribute to him.
May the kings of Sheba and Seba
present him with gifts.
11 May all kings bow down to him
and all nations serve him.

12 For he will deliver the needy who cry
out,
the afflicted who have no one to help.
13 He will take pity on the weak and the
needy
and save the needy from death.
14 He will rescue them from oppression
and violence,
for precious is their blood in his
sight.

15 Long may he live!
May gold from Sheba be given to
him.
May people ever pray for him
and bless him all day long.
16 May corn abound throughout the land;
on the tops of the hills may it sway.
May the crops flourish like Lebanon
and thrive*c* like the grass of the field.
17 May his name endure for ever;
may it continue as long as the sun.

Then all nations will be blessed through
him,*d*
and they will call him blessed.

18 Praise be to the LORD God, the God of
Israel,
who alone does marvellous deeds.
19 Praise be to his glorious name for ever;

a 5 Septuagint; Hebrew *You will be feared*

b 8 That is, the Euphrates
c 16 Probable reading of the original Hebrew text;
Masoretic Text *Lebanon, / from the city*
d 17 Or *will use his name in blessings* (see Gen. 48:20)

may the whole earth be filled with his
glory.
Amen and Amen.

20 This concludes the prayers of David son
of Jesse.

Book III
Psalms 73 – 89

Psalm 73
A psalm of Asaph.

1 Surely God is good to Israel,
to those who are pure in heart.

2 But as for me, my feet had almost
slipped;
I had nearly lost my foothold.
3 For I envied the arrogant
when I saw the prosperity of the
wicked.

4 They have no struggles;
their bodies are healthy and strong.*a*
5 They are free from common human
burdens;
they are not plagued by human ills.
6 Therefore pride is their necklace;
they clothe themselves with violence.
7 From their callous hearts comes
iniquity;*b*
their evil imaginations have no
limits.
8 They scoff, and speak with malice;
with arrogance they threaten
oppression.
9 Their mouths lay claim to heaven,
and their tongues take possession of
the earth.
10 Therefore their people turn to them
and drink up waters in abundance.*c*
11 They say, 'How would God know?
Does the Most High know anything?'

12 This is what the wicked are like –
always free of care, they go on
amassing wealth.

13 Surely in vain I have kept my heart pure
and have washed my hands in
innocence.
14 All day long I have been afflicted,
and every morning brings new
punishments.

15 If I had spoken out like that,
I would have betrayed your children.
16 When I tried to understand all this,
it troubled me deeply
17 till I entered the sanctuary of God;
then I understood their final destiny.

FAVOURITE VERSES

Philippians 4:13

*I can do all this through him who
gives me strength.*

This was once prophesied over me
and it spoke directly to my life, as I
used to feel weak, but now I know
that I can do anything with God's
strength.

Issy, 16

18 Surely you place them on slippery
ground;
you cast them down to ruin.
19 How suddenly are they destroyed,
completely swept away by terrors!
20 They are like a dream when one awakes;
when you arise, Lord,
you will despise them as fantasies.

21 When my heart was grieved
and my spirit embittered,
22 I was senseless and ignorant;
I was a brute beast before you.

---

a 4 With a different word division of the Hebrew;
Masoretic Text *struggles at their death; / their bodies are
healthy*
b 7 Syriac (see also Septuagint); Hebrew *Their eyes
bulge with fat*
c 10 The meaning of the Hebrew for this verse is
uncertain.

23 Yet I am always with you;
   you hold me by my right hand.
24 You guide me with your counsel,
   and afterwards you will take me into
      glory.
25 Whom have I in heaven but you?
   And earth has nothing I desire
      besides you.
26 My flesh and my heart may fail,
   but God is the strength of my heart
   and my portion for ever.

27 Those who are far from you will perish;
   you destroy all who are unfaithful to
      you.
28 But as for me, it is good to be near God.
   I have made the Sovereign LORD my
      refuge;
   I will tell of all your deeds.

Psalm 74

A maskil[a] of Asaph.

1 O God, why have you rejected us for
      ever?
   Why does your anger smoulder
      against the sheep of your
      pasture?
2 Remember the nation you purchased
      long ago,
   the people of your inheritance,
      whom you redeemed –
   Mount Zion, where you dwelt.
3 Turn your steps towards these
      everlasting ruins,
   all this destruction the enemy has
      brought on the sanctuary.

4 Your foes roared in the place where you
      met with us;
   they set up their standards as signs.
5 They behaved like men wielding axes
   to cut through a thicket of trees.
6 They smashed all the carved panelling
   with their axes and hatchets.
7 They burned your sanctuary to the
      ground;
   they defiled the dwelling-place of
      your Name.

8 They said in their hearts, 'We will crush
      them completely!'
   They burned every place where God
      was worshipped in the land.

9 We are given no signs from God;
   no prophets are left,
   and none of us knows how long this
      will be.
10 How long will the enemy mock you,
      God?
   Will the foe revile your name
      for ever?
11 Why do you hold back your hand, your
      right hand?
   Take it from the folds of your garment
      and destroy them!

12 But God is my King from long ago;
   he brings salvation on the earth.

13 It was you who split open the sea by your
      power;
   you broke the heads of the monster
      in the waters.
14 It was you who crushed the heads of
      Leviathan
   and gave it as food to the creatures of
      the desert.
15 It was you who opened up springs and
      streams;
   you dried up the ever-flowing rivers.
16 The day is yours, and yours also the
      night;
   you established the sun and moon.
17 It was you who set all the boundaries of
      the earth;
   you made both summer and winter.

18 Remember how the enemy has mocked
      you, LORD,
   how foolish people have reviled your
      name.
19 Do not hand over the life of your dove to
      wild beasts;
   do not forget the lives of your
      afflicted people for ever.
20 Have regard for your covenant,
   because haunts of violence fill the
      dark places of the land.
21 Do not let the oppressed retreat in
      disgrace;

---

a Title: Probably a literary or musical term

may the poor and needy praise your
name.
22 Rise up, O God, and defend your cause;
remember how fools mock you all
day long.
23 Do not ignore the clamour of your
adversaries,
the uproar of your enemies, which
rises continually.

Psalm 75[a]
For the director of music. To the tune of 'Do Not Destroy'.
A psalm of Asaph. A song.

1 We praise you, God,
we praise you, for your Name is near;
people tell of your wonderful deeds.

2 You say, 'I choose the appointed time;
it is I who judge with equity.
3 When the earth and all its people quake,
it is I who hold its pillars firm.[b]
4 To the arrogant I say, "Boast no more,"
and to the wicked, "Do not lift up
your horns.[c]
5 Do not lift your horns against heaven;
do not speak so defiantly."'

6 No one from the east or the west
or from the desert can exalt
themselves.
7 It is God who judges:
he brings one down, he exalts
another.
8 In the hand of the LORD is a cup
full of foaming wine mixed with
spices;
he pours it out, and all the wicked of the
earth
drink it down to its very dregs.

9 As for me, I will declare this for ever;
I will sing praise to the God of Jacob,
10 who says, 'I will cut off the horns of all
the wicked,

but the horns of the righteous shall
be lifted up.'

Psalm 76[a]
For the director of music. With stringed instruments.
A psalm of Asaph. A song.

1 God is renowned in Judah;
in Israel his name is great.
2 His tent is in Salem,
his dwelling-place in Zion.
3 There he broke the flashing arrows,
the shields and the swords, the
weapons of war.[b]

4 You are radiant with light,
more majestic than mountains rich
with game.
5 The valiant lie plundered,
they sleep their last sleep;
not one of the warriors
can lift his hands.
6 At your rebuke, God of Jacob,
both horse and chariot lie still.

7 It is you alone who are to be feared.
Who can stand before you when you
are angry?
8 From heaven you pronounced
judgment,
and the land feared and was
quiet –
9 when you, God, rose up to judge,
to save all the afflicted of the land.
10 Surely your wrath against mankind
brings you praise,
and the survivors of your wrath are
restrained.[c]

11 Make vows to the LORD your God and
fulfil them;
let all the neighbouring lands
bring gifts to the One to be feared.
12 He breaks the spirit of rulers;
he is feared by the kings of the
earth.

---

a In Hebrew texts 75:1-10 is numbered 75:2-11.
b 3 The Hebrew has *Selah* (a word of uncertain meaning) here.
c 4 *Horns* here symbolise strength; also in verses 5 and 10.

a In Hebrew texts 76:1-12 is numbered 76:2-13.
b 3 The Hebrew has *Selah* (a word of uncertain meaning) here and at the end of verse 9.
c 10 Or *Surely the wrath of mankind brings you praise, / and with the remainder of wrath you arm yourself*

Psalm 77[a]

For the director of music. For Jeduthun. Of Asaph.
A psalm.

1 I cried out to God for help;
    I cried out to God to hear me.
2 When I was in distress, I sought the
        Lord;
    at night I stretched out untiring
        hands,
    and I would not be comforted.

3 I remembered you, God, and I groaned;
    I meditated, and my spirit grew faint.[b]
4 You kept my eyes from closing;
    I was too troubled to speak.
5 I thought about the former days,
    the years of long ago;
6 I remembered my songs in the night.
    My heart meditated and my spirit
        asked:

7 'Will the Lord reject for ever?
    Will he never show his favour again?
8 Has his unfailing love vanished for ever?
    Has his promise failed for all time?
9 Has God forgotten to be merciful?
    Has he in anger withheld his
        compassion?'

10 Then I thought, 'To this I will appeal:
    the years when the Most High
        stretched out his right hand.
11 I will remember the deeds of the LORD;
    yes, I will remember your miracles of
        long ago.
12 I will consider all your works
    and meditate on all your mighty
        deeds.'

13 Your ways, God, are holy.
    What god is as great as our God?
14 You are the God who performs miracles;
    you display your power among the
        peoples.
15 With your mighty arm you redeemed
        your people,
    the descendants of Jacob and Joseph.

16 The waters saw you, God,
    the waters saw you and writhed;
    the very depths were convulsed.
17 The clouds poured down water,
    the heavens resounded with thunder;
    your arrows flashed back and forth.
18 Your thunder was heard in the
        whirlwind,
    your lightning lit up the world;
    the earth trembled and quaked.
19 Your path led through the sea,
    your way through the mighty waters,
    though your footprints were not
        seen.

20 You led your people like a flock
    by the hand of Moses and Aaron.

Psalm 78

A maskil[a] of Asaph.

1 My people, hear my teaching;
    listen to the words of my mouth.
2 I will open my mouth with a parable;
    I will utter hidden things, things from
        of old –
3 things we have heard and known,
    things our ancestors have told us.
4 We will not hide them from their
        descendants;
    we will tell the next generation
    the praiseworthy deeds of the LORD,
    his power, and the wonders he has
        done.
5 He decreed statutes for Jacob
    and established the law in Israel,
    which he commanded our ancestors
    to teach their children,
6 so that the next generation would know
        them,
    even the children yet to be born,
    and they in turn would tell their
        children.
7 Then they would put their trust in God
    and would not forget his deeds
    but would keep his commands.
8 They would not be like their ancestors –
    a stubborn and rebellious
        generation,
    whose hearts were not loyal to God,

---

a In Hebrew texts 77:1-20 is numbered 77:2-21.
b 3 The Hebrew has *Selah* (a word of uncertain
meaning) here and at the end of verses 9 and 15.

a Title: Probably a literary or musical term

whose spirits were not faithful to
    him.

9 The men of Ephraim, though armed
        with bows,
    turned back on the day of battle;
10 they did not keep God's covenant
    and refused to live by his law.
11 They forgot what he had done,
    the wonders he had shown them.
12 He did miracles in the sight of their
        ancestors
    in the land of Egypt, in the region of
        Zoan.
13 He divided the sea and led them
        through;
    he made the water stand up like a
        wall.
14 He guided them with the cloud by day
    and with light from the fire all night.
15 He split the rocks in the wilderness
    and gave them water as abundant as
        the seas;
16 he brought streams out of a rocky crag
    and made water flow down like rivers.

17 But they continued to sin against him,
    rebelling in the wilderness against
        the Most High.
18 They wilfully put God to the test
    by demanding the food they craved.
19 They spoke against God;
    they said, 'Can God really
    spread a table in the wilderness?
20 True, he struck the rock,
    and water gushed out,
    streams flowed abundantly,
    but can he also give us bread?
    Can he supply meat for his people?'
21 When the LORD heard them, he was
        furious;
    his fire broke out against Jacob,
    and his wrath rose against Israel,
22 for they did not believe in God
    or trust in his deliverance.
23 Yet he gave a command to the skies
        above
    and opened the doors of the heavens;
24 he rained down manna for the people
        to eat,
    he gave them the grain of heaven.
25 Human beings ate the bread of angels;

he sent them all the food they could
        eat.
26 He let loose the east wind from the
        heavens
    and by his power made the south
        wind blow.
27 He rained meat down on them like dust,
    birds like sand on the seashore.
28 He made them come down inside their
        camp,
    all around their tents.
29 They ate till they were gorged –
    he had given them what they craved.
30 But before they turned from what they
        craved,
    even while the food was still in their
        mouths,
31 God's anger rose against them;
    he put to death the sturdiest among
        them,
    cutting down the young men of
        Israel.

32 In spite of all this, they kept on sinning;
    in spite of his wonders, they did not
        believe.
33 So he ended their days in futility
    and their years in terror.
34 Whenever God slew them, they would
        seek him;
    they eagerly turned to him again.
35 They remembered that God was their
        Rock,
    that God Most High was their
        Redeemer.
36 But then they would flatter him with
        their mouths,
    lying to him with their tongues;
37 their hearts were not loyal to him,
    they were not faithful to his covenant.
38 Yet he was merciful;
    he forgave their iniquities
    and did not destroy them.
    Time after time he restrained his anger
    and did not stir up his full wrath.
39 He remembered that they were but
        flesh,
    a passing breeze that does not return.

40 How often they rebelled against him in
        the wilderness
    and grieved him in the wasteland!

41 Again and again they put God to the test;
   they vexed the Holy One of Israel.
42 They did not remember his power –
   the day he redeemed them from the
      oppressor,
43 the day he displayed his signs in Egypt,
   his wonders in the region of Zoan.
44 He turned their river into blood;
   they could not drink from their
      streams.
45 He sent swarms of flies that devoured
      them,
   and frogs that devastated them.
46 He gave their crops to the grasshopper,
   their produce to the locust.
47 He destroyed their vines with hail
   and their sycamore-figs with sleet.
48 He gave over their cattle to the hail,
   their livestock to bolts of lightning.
49 He unleashed against them his hot
      anger,
   his wrath, indignation and hostility –
   a band of destroying angels.
50 He prepared a path for his anger;
   he did not spare them from death
   but gave them over to the plague.
51 He struck down all the firstborn of Egypt,
   the firstfruits of manhood in the
      tents of Ham.
52 But he brought his people out like a
      flock;
   he led them like sheep through the
      wilderness.
53 He guided them safely, so they were
      unafraid;
   but the sea engulfed their enemies.
54 And so he brought them to the border
   of his holy land,
   to the hill country his right hand had
      taken.
55 He drove out nations before them
   and allotted their lands to them as an
      inheritance;
   he settled the tribes of Israel in their
      homes.

56 But they put God to the test
   and rebelled against the Most High;
   they did not keep his statutes.
57 Like their ancestors they were disloyal
      and faithless,
   as unreliable as a faulty bow.

58 They angered him with their high
      places;
   they aroused his jealousy with their
      idols.
59 When God heard them, he was furious;
   he rejected Israel completely.
60 He abandoned the tabernacle of Shiloh,
   the tent he had set up among
      humans.
61 He sent the ark of his might into
      captivity,
   his splendour into the hands of the
      enemy.
62 He gave his people over to the sword;
   he was furious with his inheritance.
63 Fire consumed their young men,
   and their young women had no
      wedding songs;
64 their priests were put to the sword,
   and their widows could not weep.

65 Then the Lord awoke as from sleep,
   as a warrior wakes from the stupor of
      wine.
66 He beat back his enemies;
   he put them to everlasting shame.
67 Then he rejected the tents of Joseph,
   he did not choose the tribe of
      Ephraim;
68 but he chose the tribe of Judah,
   Mount Zion, which he loved.
69 He built his sanctuary like the heights,
   like the earth that he established for
      ever.
70 He chose David his servant
   and took him from the sheepfolds;
71 from tending the sheep he brought him
   to be the shepherd of his people
      Jacob,
   of Israel his inheritance.
72 And David shepherded them with
      integrity of heart;
   with skilful hands he led them.

Psalm 79

A psalm of Asaph.

1 O God, the nations have invaded your
      inheritance;
   they have defiled your holy temple,
   they have reduced Jerusalem to
      rubble.

2 They have left the dead bodies of your
   servants
      as food for the birds of the sky,
      the flesh of your own people for the
      animals of the wild.
3 They have poured out blood like water
   all around Jerusalem,
      and there is no one to bury the
      dead.
4 We are objects of contempt to our
   neighbours,
      of scorn and derision to those
      around us.

5 How long, LORD? Will you be angry for
   ever?
      How long will your jealousy burn like
      fire?
6 Pour out your wrath on the nations
   that do not acknowledge you,
   on the kingdoms
      that do not call on your name;
7 for they have devoured Jacob
      and devastated his homeland.

8 Do not hold against us the sins of past
   generations;
      may your mercy come quickly to
      meet us,
      for we are in desperate need.
9 Help us, God our Saviour,
      for the glory of your name;
   deliver us and forgive our sins
      for your name's sake.
10 Why should the nations say,
   'Where is their God?'

   Before our eyes, make known among
      the nations
      that you avenge the outpoured blood
      of your servants.
11 May the groans of the prisoners come
      before you;
      with your strong arm preserve those
      condemned to die.
12 Pay back into the laps of our neighbours
      seven times
      the contempt they have hurled at you,
      Lord.
13 Then we your people, the sheep of your
      pasture,
      will praise you for ever;

from generation to generation
   we will proclaim your praise.

Psalm 80 *a*

For the director of music. To the tune of 'The Lilies of the
Covenant'. Of Asaph. A psalm.

1 Hear us, Shepherd of Israel,
      you who lead Joseph like a flock.
   You who sit enthroned between the
      cherubim,
      shine forth 2 before Ephraim,
      Benjamin and Manasseh.
   Awaken your might;
      come and save us.

3 Restore us, O God;
      make your face shine on us,
      that we may be saved.

4 How long, LORD God Almighty,
      will your anger smoulder
      against the prayers of your people?
5 You have fed them with the bread of
      tears;
      you have made them drink tears by
      the bowlful.
6 You have made us an object of derision *b*
      to our neighbours,
      and our enemies mock us.

7 Restore us, God Almighty;
      make your face shine on us,
      that we may be saved.

8 You transplanted a vine from Egypt;
      you drove out the nations and
      planted it.
9 You cleared the ground for it,
      and it took root and filled the land.
10 The mountains were covered with its
      shade,
      the mighty cedars with its branches.
11 Its branches reached as far as the Sea, *c*
      its shoots as far as the River. *d*

---

a In Hebrew texts 80:1-19 is numbered 80:2-20.
b 6 Probable reading of the original Hebrew text;
Masoretic Text *contention*
c 11 Probably the Mediterranean
d 11 That is, the Euphrates

¹² Why have you broken down its walls
     so that all who pass by pick its grapes?
¹³ Boars from the forest ravage it,
     and insects from the fields feed on it.
¹⁴ Return to us, God Almighty!
     Look down from heaven and see!
     Watch over this vine,
¹⁵   the root your right hand has planted,
     the son*ᵉ* you have raised up for
     yourself.

¹⁶ Your vine is cut down, it is burned with
     fire;
     at your rebuke your people perish.
¹⁷ Let your hand rest on the man at your
     right hand,
     the son of man you have raised up for
     yourself.
¹⁸ Then we will not turn away from you;
     revive us, and we will call on your
     name.

¹⁹ Restore us, LORD God Almighty;
     make your face shine on us,
     that we may be saved.

Psalm 81*ᵃ*

For the director of music. According to gittith.*ᵇ*
Of Asaph.

¹ Sing for joy to God our strength;
     shout aloud to the God of Jacob!
² Begin the music, strike the tambourine,
     play the melodious harp and lyre.

³ Sound the ram's horn at the New Moon,
     and when the moon is full, on the day
     of our Feast;
⁴ this is a decree for Israel,
     an ordinance of the God of Jacob.
⁵ When God went out against Egypt,
     he established it as a statute for
     Joseph.

I heard an unknown voice say:

⁶ 'I removed the burden from their
     shoulders;

     their hands were set free from the
     basket.
⁷ In your distress you called and I rescued
     you,
     I answered you out of a
     thundercloud;
     I tested you at the waters of Meribah.*ᶜ*
⁸ Hear me, my people, and I will warn
     you –
     if you would only listen to me, Israel!
⁹ You shall have no foreign god among
     you;
     you shall not worship any god other
     than me.
¹⁰ I am the LORD your God,
     who brought you up out of Egypt.
     Open wide your mouth and I will fill it.

READ IT OUT!

Apparently, the entire Bible can be read
aloud in 70 hours.
Of course, it all depends on how fast
you read it!

¹¹ 'But my people would not listen to me;
     Israel would not submit to me.
¹² So I gave them over to their stubborn
     hearts
     to follow their own devices.

¹³ 'If my people would only listen to me,
     if Israel would only follow my ways,
¹⁴ how quickly I would subdue their
     enemies
     and turn my hand against their foes!
¹⁵ Those who hate the LORD would cringe
     before him,
     and their punishment would last for
     ever.

---

e 15 Or *branch*
a In Hebrew texts 81:1-16 is numbered 81:2-17.
b Title: Probably a musical term

c 7 The Hebrew has *Selah* (a word of uncertain
meaning) here.

16 But you would be fed with the finest of
wheat;
  with honey from the rock I would
  satisfy you.'

Psalm 82
A psalm of Asaph.

1 God presides in the great assembly;
  he renders judgment among the
  'gods':

2 'How long will you*a* defend the unjust
  and show partiality to the wicked?*b*
3 Defend the weak and the fatherless;
  uphold the cause of the poor and the
  oppressed.
4 Rescue the weak and the needy;
  deliver them from the hand of the
  wicked.

5 'The "gods" know nothing, they
  understand nothing.
  They walk about in darkness;
  all the foundations of the earth are
  shaken.

6 'I said, "You are 'gods';
  you are all sons of the Most High."
7 But you will die like mere mortals;
  you will fall like every other ruler.'

8 Rise up, O God, judge the earth,
  for all the nations are your
  inheritance.

Psalm 83*a*
A song. A psalm of Asaph.

1 O God, do not remain silent;
  do not turn a deaf ear,
  do not stand aloof, O God.
2 See how your enemies growl,
  how your foes rear their heads.
3 With cunning they conspire against your
  people;
  they plot against those you cherish.

4 'Come,' they say, 'let us destroy them as
  a nation,
  so that Israel's name is remembered
  no more.'

5 With one mind they plot together;
  they form an alliance against you –
6 the tents of Edom and the Ishmaelites,
  of Moab and the Hagrites,
7 Byblos, Ammon and Amalek,
  Philistia, with the people of Tyre.
8 Even Assyria has joined them
  to reinforce Lot's descendants.*b*

9 Do to them as you did to Midian,
  as you did to Sisera and Jabin at the
  River Kishon,
10 who perished at Endor
  and became like dung on the ground.
11 Make their nobles like Oreb and Zeeb,
  all their princes like Zebah and
  Zalmunna,
12 who said, 'Let us take possession
  of the pasture-lands of God.'

13 Make them like tumble-weed, my God,
  like chaff before the wind.
14 As fire consumes the forest
  or a flame sets the mountains ablaze,
15 so pursue them with your tempest
  and terrify them with your storm.
16 Cover their faces with shame, LORD,
  so that they will seek your name.

17 May they ever be ashamed and dismayed;
  may they perish in disgrace.
18 Let them know that you, whose name is
  the LORD –
  that you alone are the Most High over
  all the earth.

Psalm 84*a*
For the director of music. According to gittith. *b*
Of the Sons of Korah. A psalm.

1 How lovely is your dwelling-place,
  LORD Almighty!
2 My soul yearns, even faints,

---

a 2 The Hebrew is plural.
b 2 The Hebrew has *Selah* (a word of uncertain
meaning) here.
a In Hebrew texts 83:1-18 is numbered 83:2-19.

b 8 The Hebrew has *Selah* (a word of uncertain
meaning) here.
a In Hebrew texts 84:1-12 is numbered 84:2-13.
b Title: Probably a musical term

for the courts of the LORD;
my heart and my flesh cry out
for the living God.
3 Even the sparrow has found a home,
and the swallow a nest for herself,
where she may have her young –
a place near your altar,
LORD Almighty, my King and my God.
4 Blessed are those who dwell in your
house;
they are ever praising you.*c*

5 Blessed are those whose strength is in
you,
whose hearts are set on pilgrimage.
6 As they pass through the Valley of Baka,
they make it a place of springs;
the autumn rains also cover it with
pools.*d*
7 They go from strength to strength,
till each appears before God in Zion.

8 Hear my prayer, LORD God Almighty;
listen to me, God of Jacob.
9 Look on our shield,*e* O God;
look with favour on your anointed
one.

10 Better is one day in your courts
than a thousand elsewhere;
I would rather be a doorkeeper in the
house of my God
than dwell in the tents of the wicked.
11 For the LORD God is a sun and shield;
the LORD bestows favour and honour;
no good thing does he withhold
from those whose way of life is
blameless.

12 LORD Almighty,
blessed is the one who trusts in you.

Psalm 85*a*

For the director of music. Of the Sons of Korah. A psalm.

1 You, LORD, showed favour to your land;
you restored the fortunes of Jacob.

2 You forgave the iniquity of your
people
and covered all their sins.*b*
3 You set aside all your wrath
and turned from your fierce anger.

4 Restore us again, God our Saviour,
and put away your displeasure
towards us.
5 Will you be angry with us for ever?
Will you prolong your anger through
all generations?
6 Will you not revive us again,
that your people may rejoice in you?
7 Show us your unfailing love, LORD,
and grant us your salvation.

8 I will listen to what God the LORD says;
he promises peace to his people, his
faithful servants –
but let them not turn to folly.
9 Surely his salvation is near those who
fear him,
that his glory may dwell in our land.

10 Love and faithfulness meet together;
righteousness and peace kiss each
other.
11 Faithfulness springs forth from the
earth,
and righteousness looks down from
heaven.
12 The LORD will indeed give what is
good,
and our land will yield its harvest.
13 Righteousness goes before him
and prepares the way for his steps.

Psalm 86

A prayer of David.

1 Hear me, LORD, and answer me,
for I am poor and needy.
2 Guard my life, for I am faithful to you;
save your servant who trusts in you.
You are my God; 3 have mercy on me,
Lord,
for I call to you all day long.

c 4 The Hebrew has *Selah* (a word of uncertain
meaning) here and at the end of verse 8.
d 6 Or *blessings*
e 9 Or *sovereign*
a In Hebrew texts 85:1-13 is numbered 85:2-14.

b 2 The Hebrew has *Selah* (a word of uncertain
meaning) here.

⁴ Bring joy to your servant, Lord,
    for I put my trust in you.

⁵ You, Lord, are forgiving and good,
    abounding in love to all who call to
        you.
⁶ Hear my prayer, LORD;
    listen to my cry for mercy.
⁷ When I am in distress, I call to you,
    because you answer me.

⁸ Among the gods there is none like you,
        Lord;
    no deeds can compare with yours.
⁹ All the nations you have made
    will come and worship before you,
        Lord;
    they will bring glory to your name.
¹⁰ For you are great and do marvellous
        deeds;
    you alone are God.

¹¹ Teach me your way, LORD,
    that I may rely on your faithfulness;
    give me an undivided heart,
    that I may fear your name.
¹² I will praise you, Lord my God, with all
        my heart;
    I will glorify your name for ever.
¹³ For great is your love towards me;
    you have delivered me from the
        depths,
    from the realm of the dead.

¹⁴ Arrogant foes are attacking me, O God;
    ruthless people are trying to
        kill me –
    they have no regard for you.
¹⁵ But you, Lord, are a compassionate and
        gracious God,
    slow to anger, abounding in love and
        faithfulness.
¹⁶ Turn to me and have mercy on me;
    show your strength on behalf of your
        servant;
    save me, because I serve you
    just as my mother did.
¹⁷ Give me a sign of your goodness,
    that my enemies may see it and be
        put to shame,
    for you, LORD, have helped me and
        comforted me.

Psalm 87
Of the Sons of Korah. A psalm. A song.

¹ He has founded his city on the holy
        mountain.
² The LORD loves the gates of Zion
    more than all the other dwellings of
        Jacob.

³ Glorious things are said of you,
    city of God:[a]
⁴ 'I will record Rahab[b] and Babylon
    among those who acknowledge me –
    Philistia too, and Tyre, along with Cush[c] –
    and will say, "This one was born in
        Zion." '[d]
⁵ Indeed, of Zion it will be said,
    'This one and that one were born in
        her,
    and the Most High himself will
        establish her.'
⁶ The LORD will write in the register of the
        peoples:
    'This one was born in Zion.'

⁷ As they make music they will sing,
    'All my fountains are in you.'

Psalm 88[a]
*A song. A psalm of the Sons of Korah. For the director
of music. According to* mahalath leannoth.[b]
A maskil[c] of Heman the Ezrahite.

¹ LORD, you are the God who saves me;
    day and night I cry out to you.
² May my prayer come before you;
    turn your ear to my cry.

³ I am overwhelmed with troubles
    and my life draws near to death.
⁴ I am counted among those who go
        down to the pit;
    I am like one without strength.

---

a 3 The Hebrew has *Selah* (a word of uncertain
meaning) here and at the end of verse 6.
b 4 A poetic name for Egypt
c 4 That is, the upper Nile region
d 4 Or *'I will record concerning those who acknowledge me:* /
*"This one was born in Zion." / Hear this, Rahab and Babylon, /
and you too, Philistia, Tyre and Cush.'*
a In Hebrew texts 88:1-18 is numbered 88:2-19.
b Title: Possibly a tune, 'The Suffering of Affliction'
c Title: Probably a literary or musical term

5 I am set apart with the dead,
    like the slain who lie in the grave,
whom you remember no more,
    who are cut off from your care.

6 You have put me in the lowest pit,
    in the darkest depths.
7 Your wrath lies heavily on me;
    you have overwhelmed me with all
        your waves.*d*
8 You have taken from me my closest
        friends
    and have made me repulsive to them.
I am confined and cannot escape;
9   my eyes are dim with grief.

I call to you, LORD, every day;
    I spread out my hands to you.
10 Do you show your wonders to the
        dead?
    Do their spirits rise up and praise
        you?
11 Is your love declared in the grave,
    your faithfulness in Destruction?*e*
12 Are your wonders known in the place of
        darkness,
    or your righteous deeds in the land of
        oblivion?

13 But I cry to you for help, LORD;
    in the morning my prayer comes
        before you.
14 Why, LORD, do you reject me
    and hide your face from me?

15 From my youth I have suffered and been
        close to death;
    I have borne your terrors and am in
        despair.
16 Your wrath has swept over me;
    your terrors have destroyed me.
17 All day long they surround me like a
        flood;
    they have completely engulfed me.
18 You have taken from me friend and
        neighbour –
    darkness is my closest friend.

Psalm 89*a*

*A maskil*b *of Ethan the Ezrahite.*

1 I will sing of the LORD's great love for
        ever;
    with my mouth I will make your
        faithfulness known
    through all generations.
2 I will declare that your love stands firm
        for ever,
    that you have established your
        faithfulness in heaven itself.
3 You said, 'I have made a covenant with
        my chosen one,
    I have sworn to David my servant,
4 "I will establish your line for ever
    and make your throne firm through
        all generations." '*c*

5 The heavens praise your wonders, LORD,
    your faithfulness too, in the assembly
        of the holy ones.
6 For who in the skies above can compare
        with the LORD?
    Who is like the LORD among the
        heavenly beings?
7 In the council of the holy ones God is
        greatly feared;
    he is more awesome than all who
        surround him.
8 Who is like you, LORD God Almighty?
    You, LORD, are mighty, and your
        faithfulness surrounds you.

9 You rule over the surging sea;
    when its waves mount up, you still
        them.
10 You crushed Rahab like one of the
        slain;
    with your strong arm you scattered
        your enemies.
11 The heavens are yours, and yours also
        the earth;
    you founded the world and all that is
        in it.
12 You created the north and the south;

---

d 7 The Hebrew has *Selah* (a word of uncertain
meaning) here and at the end of verse 10.
e 11 Hebrew *Abaddon*

a In Hebrew texts 89:1-52 is numbered 89:2-53.
b Title: Probably a literary or musical term
c 4 The Hebrew has *Selah* (a word of uncertain
meaning) here and at the end of verses 37, 45
and 48.

Tabor and Hermon sing for joy at
your name.
13 Your arm is endowed with power;
your hand is strong, your right hand
exalted.

14 Righteousness and justice are the
foundation of your throne;
love and faithfulness go before you.
15 Blessed are those who have learned to
acclaim you,
who walk in the light of your
presence, LORD.
16 They rejoice in your name all day long;
they celebrate your righteousness.
17 For you are their glory and strength,
and by your favour you exalt our
horn.*d*
18 Indeed, our shield*e* belongs to the LORD,
our king to the Holy One of Israel.

19 Once you spoke in a vision,
to your faithful people you said:
'I have bestowed strength on a warrior;
I have raised up a young man from
among the people.
20 I have found David my servant;
with my sacred oil I have anointed
him.
21 My hand will sustain him;
surely my arm will strengthen him.
22 The enemy will not get the better of
him;
the wicked will not oppress him.
23 I will crush his foes before him
and strike down his adversaries.
24 My faithful love will be with him,
and through my name his horn*f* will
be exalted.
25 I will set his hand over the sea,
his right hand over the rivers.
26 He will call out to me, "You are my
Father,
my God, the Rock my Saviour."
27 And I will appoint him to be my
firstborn,
the most exalted of the kings of the
earth.

28 I will maintain my love to him for ever,
and my covenant with him will never
fail.
29 I will establish his line for ever,
his throne as long as the heavens
endure.

30 'If his sons forsake my law
and do not follow my statutes,
31 if they violate my decrees
and fail to keep my commands,
32 I will punish their sin with the rod,
their iniquity with flogging;
33 but I will not take my love from him,
nor will I ever betray my faithfulness.
34 I will not violate my covenant
or alter what my lips have uttered.
35 Once for all, I have sworn by my
holiness –
and I will not lie to David –
36 that his line will continue for ever
and his throne endure before me like
the sun;
37 it will be established for ever like the
moon,
the faithful witness in the sky.'

38 But you have rejected, you have
spurned,
you have been very angry with your
anointed one.
39 You have renounced the covenant with
your servant
and have defiled his crown in the
dust.
40 You have broken through all his walls
and reduced his strongholds to
ruins.
41 All who pass by have plundered him;
he has become the scorn of his
neighbours.
42 You have exalted the right hand of his
foes;
you have made all his enemies
rejoice.
43 Indeed, you have turned back the edge
of his sword
and have not supported him in
battle.
44 You have put an end to his splendour
and cast his throne to the ground.
45 You have cut short the days of his youth;

---

d 17 *Horn here symbolises strong one.*
e 18 *Or sovereign*
f 24 *Horn here symbolises strength.*

you have covered him with a mantle
of shame.

46 How long, LORD? Will you hide yourself
for ever?
How long will your wrath burn like
fire?
47 Remember how fleeting is my life.
For what futility you have created all
humanity!
48 Who can live and not see death,
or who can escape the power of the
grave?
49 Lord, where is your former great love,
which in your faithfulness you swore
to David?
50 Remember, Lord, how your servant has*g*
been mocked,
how I bear in my heart the taunts of
all the nations,
51 the taunts with which your enemies,
LORD, have mocked,
with which they have mocked every
step of your anointed one.

52 Praise be to the LORD for ever!
Amen and Amen.

Book IV

Psalms 90 – 106

Psalm 90

A prayer of Moses the man of God.

1 Lord, you have been our dwelling-place
throughout all generations.
2 Before the mountains were born
or you brought forth the whole world,
from everlasting to everlasting you
are God.

3 You turn people back to dust,
saying, 'Return to dust, you mortals.'
4 A thousand years in your sight
are like a day that has just gone by,
or like a watch in the night.
5 Yet you sweep people away in the sleep
of death –
they are like the new grass of the
morning:

6 In the morning it springs up new,
but by evening it is dry and withered.

7 We are consumed by your anger
and terrified by your indignation.
8 You have set our iniquities before you,
our secret sins in the light of your
presence.
9 All our days pass away under your
wrath;
we finish our years with a moan.
10 Our days may come to seventy years,
or eighty, if our strength endures;
yet the best of them are but trouble and
sorrow,
for they quickly pass, and we fly away.
11 If only we knew the power of your anger!
Your wrath is as great as the fear that
is your due.
12 Teach us to number our days,
that we may gain a heart of wisdom.

13 Relent, LORD! How long will it be?
Have compassion on your servants.
14 Satisfy us in the morning with your
unfailing love,
that we may sing for joy and be glad
all our days.
15 Make us glad for as many days as you
have afflicted us,
for as many years as we have seen
trouble.
16 May your deeds be shown to your
servants,
your splendour to their children.

17 May the favour*a* of the Lord our God rest
on us;
establish the work of our hands for
us –
yes, establish the work of our hands.

Psalm 91

1 Whoever dwells in the shelter of the
Most High
will rest in the shadow of the
Almighty.*a*

---

g 50 Or *your servants have*

a 17 Or *beauty*
a 1 Hebrew *Shaddai*

2 I will say of the LORD, 'He is my refuge
 and my fortress,
 my God, in whom I trust.'

3 Surely he will save you
 from the fowler's snare
 and from the deadly pestilence.

4 He will cover you with his feathers,
 and under his wings you will find
 refuge;
 his faithfulness will be your shield
 and rampart.

5 You will not fear the terror of night,
 nor the arrow that flies by day,

6 nor the pestilence that stalks in the
 darkness,

nor the plague that destroys at
 midday.

7 A thousand may fall at your side,
 ten thousand at your right hand,
 but it will not come near you.

8 You will only observe with your eyes
 and see the punishment of the
 wicked.

9 If you say, 'The LORD is my refuge,'
 and you make the Most High your
 dwelling,

10 no harm will overtake you,
 no disaster will come near your tent.

11 For he will command his angels
 concerning you

PRAYING THE PSALMS 6

A thousand may fall

At face value Psalm 91 seems to be a series of promises about how the Lord will protect us from harm and danger, but there is a hidden message.

Think about it! If you need rescuing, you must already be in serious trouble. It says, *'A thousand may fall at your side … but it will not come near you'* (v. 7). What poetic irony! If a thousand people fall at your side, it has already come near you! This song of praise and faith is written for those who are living in the context of fear and threat.

I first began to really understand this psalm when our son was very sick with a flu-like lung infection called RSV bronchiolitis. He was in children's intensive care for over six weeks and it was often touch and go whether or not he would survive. All around him children died – often of RSV or other equally scary things, like meningitis. During that time, I did fear! I feared the terror of the night. I feared the deadly pestilence that stalks in darkness. I feared the plague that destroys at midday (v. 6), but I still enjoyed having this psalm in the Bible. I could read it through gritted teeth. I could pull its heavenly stuff into our earthly mess. It made me reach out for God and hope for the best.

Jesus understood this. The devil quoted verse 12 at him, telling him to throw himself off a high tower and trust that he wouldn't even stub his toe (Matthew 4:5–7). Jesus knew this song was not a series of disembodied promises that nothing will ever go wrong, even if you do something really stupid! No. But God is there. He loves us and is up for rescuing us – whatever the trouble we are in (v. 15).

Hugo Anson

 Psalm 25

Psalm 110 ▶▶

to guard you in all your ways;
12 they will lift you up in their hands,
so that you will not strike your foot
against a stone.
13 You will tread on the lion and the cobra;
you will trample the great lion and
the serpent.

14 'Because he[b] loves me,' says the LORD, 'I
will rescue him;
I will protect him, for he
acknowledges my name.
15 He will call on me, and I will answer
him;
I will be with him in trouble,
I will deliver him and honour him.
16 With long life I will satisfy him
and show him my salvation.'

Psalm 92[a]

A psalm. A song. For the Sabbath day.

1 It is good to praise the LORD
and make music to your name,
O Most High,
2 proclaiming your love in the morning
and your faithfulness at night,
3 to the music of the ten-stringed lyre
and the melody of the harp.

4 For you make me glad by your deeds,
LORD;
I sing for joy at what your hands have
done.
5 How great are your works, LORD,
how profound your thoughts!
6 Senseless people do not know,
fools do not understand,
7 that though the wicked spring up like
grass
and all evildoers flourish,
they will be destroyed for ever.

8 But you, LORD, are for ever exalted.

9 For surely your enemies, LORD,
surely your enemies will perish;
all evildoers will be scattered.

10 You have exalted my horn[b] like that of a
wild ox;
fine oils have been poured on me.
11 My eyes have seen the defeat of my
adversaries;
my ears have heard the rout of my
wicked foes.

12 The righteous will flourish like a palm
tree,
they will grow like a cedar of
Lebanon;
13 planted in the house of the LORD,
they will flourish in the courts of our
God.
14 They will still bear fruit in old age,
they will stay fresh and green,
15 proclaiming, 'The LORD is upright;
he is my Rock, and there is no
wickedness in him.'

Psalm 93

1 The LORD reigns, he is robed in majesty;
the LORD is robed in majesty and
armed with strength;
indeed, the world is established, firm
and secure.
2 Your throne was established long ago;
you are from all eternity.

3 The seas have lifted up, LORD,
the seas have lifted up their voice;
the seas have lifted up their pounding
waves.
4 Mightier than the thunder of the great
waters,
mightier than the breakers of the
sea —
the LORD on high is mighty.

5 Your statutes, LORD, stand firm;
holiness adorns your house
for endless days.

Psalm 94

1 The LORD is a God who avenges.
O God who avenges, shine forth.

---

b 14 That is, probably the king
a In Hebrew texts 92:1-15 is numbered 92:2-16.

---

b 10 *Horn* here symbolises strength.

2 Rise up, Judge of the earth;
    pay back to the proud what they
        deserve.
3 How long, LORD, will the wicked,
    how long will the wicked be jubilant?

4 They pour out arrogant words;
    all the evildoers are full of boasting.
5 They crush your people, LORD;
    they oppress your inheritance.
6 They slay the widow and the foreigner;
    they murder the fatherless.
7 They say, 'The LORD does not see;
    the God of Jacob takes no notice.'

8 Take notice, you senseless ones among
        the people;
    you fools, when will you become
        wise?
9 Does he who fashioned the ear not
        hear?
    Does he who formed the eye not
        see?
10 Does he who disciplines nations not
        punish?
    Does he who teaches mankind lack
        knowledge?
11 The LORD knows all human plans;
    he knows that they are futile.

12 Blessed is the one you discipline, LORD,
    the one you teach from your law;
13 you grant them relief from days of
        trouble,
    till a pit is dug for the wicked.
14 For the LORD will not reject his people;
    he will never forsake his inheritance.
15 Judgment will again be founded on
        righteousness,
    and all the upright in heart will
        follow it.

16 Who will rise up for me against the
        wicked?
    Who will take a stand for me against
        evildoers?
17 Unless the LORD had given me help,
    I would soon have dwelt in the silence
        of death.
18 When I said, 'My foot is slipping,'
    your unfailing love, LORD, supported
        me.

19 When anxiety was great within me,
    your consolation brought me joy.

20 Can a corrupt throne be allied with
        you –
    a throne that brings on misery by its
        decrees?
21 The wicked band together against the
        righteous
    and condemn the innocent to death.
22 But the LORD has become my fortress,
    and my God the rock in whom I take
        refuge.
23 He will repay them for their sins
    and destroy them for their
        wickedness;
    the LORD our God will destroy them.

Psalm 95

1 Come, let us sing for joy to the LORD;
    let us shout aloud to the Rock of our
        salvation.
2 Let us come before him with
        thanksgiving
    and extol him with music and song.

3 For the LORD is the great God,
    the great King above all gods.
4 In his hand are the depths of the earth,
    and the mountain peaks belong to
        him.
5 The sea is his, for he made it,
    and his hands formed the dry land.

6 Come, let us bow down in worship,
    let us kneel before the LORD our
        Maker;
7 for he is our God
    and we are the people of his pasture,
    the flock under his care.

Today, if only you would hear his
        voice,
8 'Do not harden your hearts as you did at
        Meribah,*a*
    as you did that day at Massah*b* in the
        wilderness,
9 where your ancestors tested me;

---

a 8 Meribah means *quarrelling.*
b 8 Massah means *testing.*

they tried me, though they had seen
what I did.

10 For forty years I was angry with that
generation;
I said, "They are a people whose
hearts go astray,
and they have not known my ways."

11 So I declared on oath in my anger,
"They shall never enter my rest." '

Psalm 96

1 Sing to the LORD a new song;
sing to the LORD, all the earth.

2 Sing to the LORD, praise his name;
proclaim his salvation day after day.

3 Declare his glory among the nations,
his marvellous deeds among all
peoples.

4 For great is the LORD and most worthy
of praise;
he is to be feared above all gods.

5 For all the gods of the nations are
idols,
but the LORD made the heavens.

6 Splendour and majesty are before him;
strength and glory are in his
sanctuary.

7 Ascribe to the LORD, all you families of
nations,
ascribe to the LORD glory and
strength.

8 Ascribe to the LORD the glory due to his
name;
bring an offering and come into his
courts.

9 Worship the LORD in the splendour of
his*a* holiness;
tremble before him, all the earth.

10 Say among the nations, 'The LORD
reigns.'
The world is firmly established, it
cannot be moved;
he will judge the peoples with equity.

11 Let the heavens rejoice, let the earth be
glad;
let the sea resound, and all that is in it.

12 Let the fields be jubilant, and everything
in them;
let all the trees of the forest sing for
joy.

13 Let all creation rejoice before the LORD,
for he comes,
he comes to judge the earth.
He will judge the world in righteousness
and the peoples in his faithfulness.

Psalm 97

1 The LORD reigns, let the earth be glad;
let the distant shores rejoice.

2 Clouds and thick darkness surround
him;
righteousness and justice are the
foundation of his throne.

3 Fire goes before him
and consumes his foes on every side.

4 His lightning lights up the world;
the earth sees and trembles.

5 The mountains melt like wax before the
LORD,
before the Lord of all the earth.

6 The heavens proclaim his
righteousness,
and all peoples see his glory.

7 All who worship images are put to
shame,
those who boast in idols –
worship him, all you gods!

8 Zion hears and rejoices
and the villages of Judah are glad
because of your judgments, LORD.

9 For you, LORD, are the Most High over
all the earth;
you are exalted far above all gods.

10 Let those who love the LORD hate evil,
for he guards the lives of his faithful
ones
and delivers them from the hand of
the wicked.

11 Light shines*a* on the righteous
and joy on the upright in heart.

---

a 9 Or LORD *with the splendour of*

a 11 One Hebrew manuscript and ancient versions
(see also 112:4); most Hebrew manuscripts *Light is
sown*

12 Rejoice in the LORD, you who are
righteous,
and praise his holy name.

Psalm 98

A psalm.

1 Sing to the LORD a new song,
for he has done marvellous things;
his right hand and his holy arm
have worked salvation for him.
2 The LORD has made his salvation known
and revealed his righteousness to the
nations.
3 He has remembered his love
and his faithfulness to Israel;
all the ends of the earth have seen
the salvation of our God.

4 Shout for joy to the LORD, all the earth,
burst into jubilant song with music;
5 make music to the LORD with the harp,
with the harp and the sound of
singing,
6 with trumpets and the blast of the ram's
horn—
shout for joy before the LORD, the
King.

7 Let the sea resound, and everything in it,
the world, and all who live in it.
8 Let the rivers clap their hands,
let the mountains sing together for
joy;
9 let them sing before the LORD,
for he comes to judge the earth.
He will judge the world in
righteousness
and the peoples with equity.

Psalm 99

1 The LORD reigns,
let the nations tremble;
he sits enthroned between the
cherubim,
let the earth shake.
2 Great is the LORD in Zion;
he is exalted over all the nations.
3 Let them praise your great and awesome
name—
he is holy.

4 The King is mighty, he loves justice—
you have established equity;
in Jacob you have done
what is just and right.
5 Exalt the LORD our God
and worship at his footstool;
he is holy.

6 Moses and Aaron were among his
priests,
Samuel was among those who called
on his name;
they called on the LORD
and he answered them.
7 He spoke to them from the pillar of
cloud;
they kept his statutes and the decrees
he gave them.

8 LORD our God,
you answered them;
you were to Israel a forgiving God,
though you punished their
misdeeds.*a*
9 Exalt the LORD our God
and worship at his holy mountain,
for the LORD our God is holy.

Psalm 100

A psalm. For giving grateful praise.

1 Shout for joy to the LORD, all the earth.
2   Worship the LORD with gladness;
come before him with joyful songs.
3 Know that the LORD is God.
It is he who made us, and we are
his;*a*
we are his people, the sheep of his
pasture.

4 Enter his gates with thanksgiving
and his courts with praise;
give thanks to him and praise his
name.
5 For the LORD is good and his love
endures for ever;
his faithfulness continues through
all generations.

---

a 8 Or *God, / an avenger of the wrongs done to them*
a 3 Or *and not we ourselves*

Psalm 101
Of David. A psalm.

1 I will sing of your love and justice;
to you, Lᴏʀᴅ, I will sing praise.
2 I will be careful to lead a blameless
life –
when will you come to me?

I will conduct the affairs of my house
with a blameless heart.
3 I will not look with approval
on anything that is vile.

ACROSTIC

There are lots of acrostics in the Bible.
An acrostic is a poem where the lines or
sections start in an order (like starting the
first line with 'a', the next with 'b', then
'c', and so on). Acrostics can be found in
Psalms 111 and 112, Proverbs 31:10–31 and
Lamentations 1, 2 and 4.

I hate what faithless people do;
I will have no part in it.
4 The perverse of heart shall be far from
me;
I will have nothing to do with what is
evil.

5 Whoever slanders their neighbour in
secret,
I will put to silence;
whoever has haughty eyes and a proud
heart,
I will not tolerate.

6 My eyes will be on the faithful in the
land,
that they may dwell with me;
the one whose way of life is blameless
will minister to me.

7 No one who practises deceit
will dwell in my house;
no one who speaks falsely
will stand in my presence.

8 Every morning I will put to silence
all the wicked in the land;
I will cut off every evildoer
from the city of the Lᴏʀᴅ.

Psalm 102 *a*
*A prayer of an afflicted person who has grown weak
and pours out a lament before the Lᴏʀᴅ.*

1 Hear my prayer, Lᴏʀᴅ;
let my cry for help come to you.
2 Do not hide your face from me
when I am in distress.
Turn your ear to me;
when I call, answer me quickly.

3 For my days vanish like smoke;
my bones burn like glowing embers.
4 My heart is blighted and withered like
grass;
I forget to eat my food.
5 In my distress I groan aloud
and am reduced to skin and bones.
6 I am like a desert owl,
like an owl among the ruins.
7 I lie awake; I have become
like a bird alone on a roof.
8 All day long my enemies taunt me;
those who rail against me use my
name as a curse.
9 For I eat ashes as my food
and mingle my drink with tears
10 because of your great wrath,
for you have taken me up and thrown
me aside.
11 My days are like the evening shadow;
I wither away like grass.

12 But you, Lᴏʀᴅ, sit enthroned for ever;
your renown endures through all
generations.
13 You will arise and have compassion on
Zion,

---

a In Hebrew texts 102:1-28 is numbered 102:2-29.

for it is time to show favour to her;
    the appointed time has come.
14 For her stones are dear to your
        servants;
    her very dust moves them to pity.
15 The nations will fear the name of the
        LORD,
    all the kings of the earth will revere
        your glory.
16 For the LORD will rebuild Zion
    and appear in his glory.
17 He will respond to the prayer of the
        destitute;
    he will not despise their plea.

18 Let this be written for a future
        generation,
    that a people not yet created may
        praise the LORD:
19 'The LORD looked down from his
        sanctuary on high,
    from heaven he viewed the earth,
20 to hear the groans of the prisoners
    and release those condemned to
        death.'
21 So the name of the LORD will be
        declared in Zion
    and his praise in Jerusalem
22 when the peoples and the kingdoms
    assemble to worship the LORD.

23 In the course of my life[b] he broke my
        strength;
    he cut short my days.
24 So I said:
'Do not take me away, my God, in the
    midst of my days;
    your years go on through all
        generations.
25 In the beginning you laid the
        foundations of the earth,
    and the heavens are the work of your
        hands.
26 They will perish, but you remain;
    they will all wear out like a garment.
Like clothing you will change them
    and they will be discarded.
27 But you remain the same,
    and your years will never end.

---

b 23 Or By his power

28 The children of your servants will live in
        your presence;
    their descendants will be established
        before you.'

Psalm 103

Of David.

1 Praise the LORD, my soul;
    all my inmost being, praise his holy
        name.
2 Praise the LORD, my soul,
    and forget not all his benefits –
3 who forgives all your sins
    and heals all your diseases,
4 who redeems your life from the pit
    and crowns you with love and
        compassion,
5 who satisfies your desires with good
        things
    so that your youth is renewed like the
        eagle's.

6 The LORD works righteousness
    and justice for all the oppressed.

7 He made known his ways to Moses,
    his deeds to the people of Israel:
8 the LORD is compassionate and
        gracious,
    slow to anger, abounding in love.
9 He will not always accuse,
    nor will he harbour his anger for
        ever;
10 he does not treat us as our sins deserve
    or repay us according to our
        iniquities.
11 For as high as the heavens are above the
        earth,
    so great is his love for those who fear
        him;
12 as far as the east is from the west,
    so far has he removed our
        transgressions from us.

13 As a father has compassion on his
        children,
    so the LORD has compassion on
        those who fear him;
14 for he knows how we are formed,
    he remembers that we are dust.
15 The life of mortals is like grass,

they flourish like a flower of the field;
16 the wind blows over it and it is gone,
    and its place remembers it no more.
17 But from everlasting to everlasting
    the LORD's love is with those who fear
        him,
    and his righteousness with their
        children's children –
18 with those who keep his covenant
    and remember to obey his precepts.

19 The LORD has established his throne in
    heaven,
    and his kingdom rules over all.

20 Praise the LORD, you his angels,
    you mighty ones who do his
        bidding,
    who obey his word.
21 Praise the LORD, all his heavenly hosts,
    you his servants who do his will.

LAW AND GRACE 1

Grace walks with us

Have you ever done something where you were only given one chance to get it right? Every year thousands of people apply to the talent shows on TV to get one chance to prove that they are good enough – or *ridiculously* bad enough – to be worth showing on TV. One chance. That's it. That's harsh.

Very few of us get it right the first time, and most of us would love a second chance. Now imagine that you had auditioned and hadn't met the standard, but that there was a judge on the panel who said, 'Don't worry, I'll come alongside you and dedicate myself to making sure you pass.' This illustration helps us think about law and grace.

God has a standard for very good reasons. No one, not even a criminal, wants to live in a country where there are no standards, no laws. Law is not just a good thing, but a great thing. When it comes to right and wrong, God sets a very high standard – one that we have all failed to meet (apart from Jesus – but more on that later). One of the reasons God sets a high standard is that he knows things go badly wrong when we reject his law. We only have to look at the news headlines to know that. But God says, 'Don't worry, I'll come alongside you to make sure you do get it right!' With God there's always a first, second and even a seven-hundredth chance. God is infinitely caring. More than that, he wants us to reach our potential and we can only do that under his guidance. That's grace. Law sets the standard. Grace helps us achieve it.

The writer of Psalm 103 knew that God loves to forgive us when we turn to him and apologise, and then to work with us so that we can begin to obey his law. God's love is amazing. God is judge, but also coach… He wants to do all he can to help us reach his standards. That's grace in action. Time and again God makes the first move when we fail. He always wants to see us back on our feet again.

Jason Gardner

Exodus 20:1–17

22 Praise the LORD, all his works
    everywhere in his dominion.

Praise the LORD, my soul.

Psalm 104

1 Praise the LORD, my soul.

LORD my God, you are very great;
    you are clothed with splendour and
       majesty.

2 The LORD wraps himself in light as with
       a garment;
    he stretches out the heavens like a
       tent
3   and lays the beams of his upper
       chambers on their waters.
He makes the clouds his chariot
    and rides on the wings of the wind.
4 He makes winds his messengers,[a]
    flames of fire his servants.

5 He set the earth on its foundations;
    it can never be moved.
6 You covered it with the watery depths as
       with a garment;
    the waters stood above the
       mountains.
7 But at your rebuke the waters fled,
    at the sound of your thunder they
       took to flight;
8 they flowed over the mountains,
    they went down into the valleys,
    to the place you assigned for them.
9 You set a boundary they cannot cross;
    never again will they cover the earth.

10 He makes springs pour water into the
       ravines;
    it flows between the mountains.
11 They give water to all the beasts of the
       field;
    the wild donkeys quench their thirst.
12 The birds of the sky nest by the waters;
    they sing among the branches.
13 He waters the mountains from his
       upper chambers;

the land is satisfied by the fruit of his
       work.
14 He makes grass grow for the cattle,
    and plants for people to cultivate –
    bringing forth food from the earth:
15 wine that gladdens human hearts,
    oil to make their faces shine,
    and bread that sustains their hearts.
16 The trees of the LORD are well watered,
    the cedars of Lebanon that he
       planted.
17 There the birds make their nests;
    the stork has its home in the junipers.
18 The high mountains belong to the wild
       goats;
    the crags are a refuge for the hyrax.

19 He made the moon to mark the
       seasons,
    and the sun knows when to go down.
20 You bring darkness, it becomes night,
    and all the beasts of the forest prowl.
21 The lions roar for their prey
    and seek their food from God.
22 The sun rises, and they steal away;
    they return and lie down in their
       dens.
23 Then people go out to their work,
    to their labour until evening.

24 How many are your works, LORD!
    In wisdom you made them all;
    the earth is full of your creatures.
25 There is the sea, vast and spacious,
    teeming with creatures beyond
       number –
    living things both large and small.
26 There the ships go to and fro,
    and Leviathan, which you formed to
       frolic there.

27 All creatures look to you
    to give them their food at the proper
       time.
28 When you give it to them,
    they gather it up;
when you open your hand,
    they are satisfied with good things.
29 When you hide your face,
    they are terrified;
when you take away their breath,
    they die and return to the dust.

_____
a 4 Or angels

30 When you send your Spirit,
    they are created,
    and you renew the face of the ground.

31 May the glory of the LORD endure for
    ever;
    may the LORD rejoice in his
    works —

32 he who looks at the earth, and it
    trembles,
    who touches the mountains, and
    they smoke.

33 I will sing to the LORD all my life;
    I will sing praise to my God as long as
    I live.

THE BIG STORY 1

Creation

Life is God's gift. The first great truth revealed in the Bible is that God, who has always existed and will always exist, chose, out of love, to create the universe.

He continues to sustain it, and everything in it, including us. Psalm 104 is a praise song, celebrating the wonder and creativity of God's work. Creation is continuous. God did not wind up creation like an old-fashioned clock and leave it to run by itself. He actively upholds his creation still, and will continue to do so. God is involved in his world. We exist in each moment only because he wishes it! His Holy Spirit continually renews the earth (vv. 27–30).

Humans have two vital roles within this extraordinarily rich environment. One is to work to cultivate the land responsibly (v. 23), and also to enjoy the fruits of our work (vv. 14–15), to travel and to trade (v. 26). The other is to praise. *'I will sing praise to my God as long as I live'* (vv. 1, 33–35). Worship lies right at the heart of being human. If the earth and everything in it are God's gifts, how could we not praise? Perhaps the most important thing to notice is that humans are not the centre of attention here. The psalm is all about God! The creation displays the greatness, splendour and majesty of God (v. 1). It demonstrates his wisdom (v. 24). He does it all (vv. 10–18) and it is for him to enjoy (v. 31). Although we know that God has given humans special responsibility within his creation (Genesis 1:26–31), humans are also just one part of the diverse community of creation, which exists for God's pleasure. We are not the centre of the universe. We matter to God, but we are not the only creatures who matter to him on the earth. What is unique about us is our capacity for praise. We can express praise on behalf of the whole creation. We can put this sense of wonder into words and songs like the Psalms.

Sadly, something casts a shadow over this spectacular hymn of creation. Not all humans live as they should. They are rebels against God (*'sinners'*) and live *'wicked'* lives rather than lives full of gratitude, wonder and praise (v. 35).

Graham Cray

Romans 5:12–14 ⏩

34 May my meditation be pleasing to him,
  as I rejoice in the LORD.'
35 But may sinners vanish from the earth
  and the wicked be no more.

Praise the LORD, my soul.

Praise the LORD.[b]

Psalm 105

1 Give praise to the LORD, proclaim his
    name;
  make known among the nations
    what he has done.
2 Sing to him, sing praise to him;
  tell of all his wonderful acts.
3 Glory in his holy name;
  let the hearts of those who seek the
    LORD rejoice.
4 Look to the LORD and his strength;
  seek his face always.

5 Remember the wonders he has done,
  his miracles, and the judgments he
    pronounced,
6 you his servants, the descendants of
    Abraham,
  his chosen ones, the children of
    Jacob.
7 He is the LORD our God;
  his judgments are in all the earth.

8 He remembers his covenant for ever,
  the promise he made, for a thousand
    generations,
9 the covenant he made with Abraham,
  the oath he swore to Isaac.
10 He confirmed it to Jacob as a decree,
  to Israel as an everlasting covenant:
11 'To you I will give the land of Canaan
  as the portion you will inherit.'

12 When they were but few in number,
  few indeed, and strangers in it,
13 they wandered from nation to nation,
  from one kingdom to another.
14 He allowed no one to oppress them;
  for their sake he rebuked kings:

15 'Do not touch my anointed ones;
  do my prophets no harm.'

16 He called down famine on the land
  and destroyed all their supplies of
    food;
17 and he sent a man before them –
  Joseph, sold as a slave.
18 They bruised his feet with shackles,
  his neck was put in irons,
19 till what he foretold came to pass,
  till the word of the LORD proved him
    true.
20 The king sent and released him,
  the ruler of peoples set him free.
21 He made him master of his household,
  ruler over all he possessed,
22 to instruct his princes as he pleased
  and teach his elders wisdom.

23 Then Israel entered Egypt;
  Jacob resided as a foreigner in the
    land of Ham.
24 The LORD made his people very fruitful;
  he made them too numerous for
    their foes,
25 whose hearts he turned to hate his
    people,
  to conspire against his servants.
26 He sent Moses his servant,
  and Aaron, whom he had chosen.
27 They performed his signs among
    them,
  his wonders in the land of Ham.
28 He sent darkness and made the land
    dark –
  for had they not rebelled against his
    words?
29 He turned their waters into blood,
  causing their fish to die.
30 Their land teemed with frogs,
  which went up into the bedrooms of
    their rulers.
31 He spoke, and there came swarms of
    flies,
  and gnats throughout their country.
32 He turned their rain into hail,
  with lightning throughout their
    land;
33 he struck down their vines and fig-trees
  and shattered the trees of their
    country.

_____

b 35 Hebrew *Hallelu Yah*; in the Septuagint this line
stands at the beginning of Psalm 105.

34 He spoke, and the locusts came,
  grasshoppers without number;
35 they ate up every green thing in their
  land,
  ate up the produce of their soil.
36 Then he struck down all the firstborn in
  their land,
  the firstfruits of all their manhood.
37 He brought out Israel, laden with silver
  and gold,
  and from among their tribes no one
  faltered.
38 Egypt was glad when they left,
  because dread of Israel had fallen on
  them.

39 He spread out a cloud as a covering,
  and a fire to give light at night.
40 They asked, and he brought them
  quail;
  he fed them well with the bread of
  heaven.
41 He opened the rock, and water gushed
  out;
  it flowed like a river in the desert.

42 For he remembered his holy promise
  given to his servant Abraham.
43 He brought out his people with
  rejoicing,
  his chosen ones with shouts of joy;
44 he gave them the lands of the nations,
  and they fell heir to what others had
  toiled for –
45 that they might keep his precepts
  and observe his laws.

  Praise the LORD.*a*

Psalm 106

1 Praise the LORD.*a*

  Give thanks to the LORD, for he is good;
  his love endures for ever.

2 Who can proclaim the mighty acts of the
  LORD
  or fully declare his praise?

3 Blessed are those who act justly,
  who always do what is right.

4 Remember me, LORD, when you show
  favour to your people,
  come to my aid when you save them,
5 that I may enjoy the prosperity of your
  chosen ones,
  that I may share in the joy of your
  nation
  and join your inheritance in giving
  praise.

6 We have sinned, even as our ancestors
  did;
  we have done wrong and acted
  wickedly.
7 When our ancestors were in Egypt,
  they gave no thought to your miracles;
  they did not remember your many
  kindnesses,
  and they rebelled by the sea, the Red
  Sea.*b*
8 Yet he saved them for his name's sake,
  to make his mighty power known.
9 He rebuked the Red Sea, and it dried up;
  he led them through the depths as
  through a desert.
10 He saved them from the hand of the foe;
  from the hand of the enemy he
  redeemed them.
11 The waters covered their adversaries;
  not one of them survived.
12 Then they believed his promises
  and sang his praise.

13 But they soon forgot what he had done
  and did not wait for his plan to
  unfold.
14 In the desert they gave in to their
  craving;
  in the wilderness they put God to the
  test.
15 So he gave them what they asked for,
  but sent a wasting disease among
  them.
16 In the camp they grew envious of Moses
  and of Aaron, who was consecrated
  to the LORD.

---

a 45 Hebrew *Hallelu Yah*
a 1 Hebrew *Hallelu Yah*; also in verse 48

---

b 7 Or *the Sea of Reeds*; also in verses 9 and 22

17 The earth opened up and swallowed
      Dathan;
   it buried the company of Abiram.
18 Fire blazed among their followers;
      a flame consumed the wicked.
19 At Horeb they made a calf
      and worshipped an idol cast from
         metal.
20 They exchanged their glorious God
      for an image of a bull, which eats
         grass.
21 They forgot the God who saved them,
      who had done great things in Egypt,
22 miracles in the land of Ham
      and awesome deeds by the Red Sea.
23 So he said he would destroy them –
      had not Moses, his chosen one,
   stood in the breach before him
      to keep his wrath from destroying
         them.

24 Then they despised the pleasant land;
      they did not believe his promise.
25 They grumbled in their tents
      and did not obey the LORD.
26 So he swore to them with uplifted
         hand
      that he would make them fall in the
         wilderness,
27 make their descendants fall among the
         nations
      and scatter them throughout the
         lands.

28 They yoked themselves to the Baal of
         Peor
      and ate sacrifices offered to lifeless
         gods;
29 they aroused the LORD's anger by their
         wicked deeds,
      and a plague broke out among them.
30 But Phinehas stood up and intervened,
      and the plague was checked.
31 This was credited to him as
         righteousness
      for endless generations to come.
32 By the waters of Meribah they angered
         the LORD,
      and trouble came to Moses because
         of them;
33 for they rebelled against the Spirit of
         God,

   and rash words came from Moses'
      lips.c

34 They did not destroy the peoples
      as the LORD had commanded them,
35 but they mingled with the nations
      and adopted their customs.
36 They worshipped their idols,
      which became a snare to them.
37 They sacrificed their sons
      and their daughters to false gods.
38 They shed innocent blood,
      the blood of their sons and
         daughters,
   whom they sacrificed to the idols of
         Canaan,
      and the land was desecrated by their
         blood.
39 They defiled themselves by what they
         did;
      by their deeds they prostituted
         themselves.

40 Therefore the LORD was angry with his
         people
      and abhorred his inheritance.
41 He gave them into the hands of the
         nations,
      and their foes ruled over them.
42 Their enemies oppressed them
      and subjected them to their power.
43 Many times he delivered them,
      but they were bent on rebellion
      and they wasted away in their sin.
44 Yet he took note of their distress
      when he heard their cry;
45 for their sake he remembered his
         covenant
      and out of his great love he
         relented.
46 He caused all who held them captive
      to show them mercy.

47 Save us, LORD our God,
      and gather us from the nations,
   that we may give thanks to your holy
         name
      and glory in your praise.

_____
c 33 Or *against his spirit,* / *and rash words came from his lips*

48 Praise be to the LORD, the God of Israel,
　　from everlasting to everlasting.

Let all the people say, 'Amen!'

Praise the LORD.

Book V
Psalms 107 – 150

Psalm 107

1 Give thanks to the LORD, for he is good;
　　his love endures for ever.

2 Let the redeemed of the LORD tell their
　　　story –
　　those he redeemed from the hand of
　　　the foe,
3 those he gathered from the lands,
　　from east and west, from north and
　　　south.*a*

4 Some wandered in desert wastelands,
　　finding no way to a city where they
　　　could settle.
5 They were hungry and thirsty,
　　and their lives ebbed away.
6 Then they cried out to the LORD in their
　　　trouble,
　　and he delivered them from their
　　　distress.
7 He led them by a straight way
　　to a city where they could settle.
8 Let them give thanks to the LORD for his
　　　unfailing love
　　and his wonderful deeds for
　　　mankind,
9 for he satisfies the thirsty
　　and fills the hungry with good things.

10 Some sat in darkness, in utter darkness,
　　prisoners suffering in iron chains,
11 because they rebelled against God's
　　　commands
　　and despised the plans of the Most
　　　High.
12 So he subjected them to bitter labour;
　　they stumbled, and there was no one
　　　to help.

a 3 Hebrew *north and the sea*

13 Then they cried to the LORD in their
　　　trouble,
　　and he saved them from their
　　　distress.
14 He brought them out of darkness, the
　　　utter darkness,
　　and broke away their chains.
15 Let them give thanks to the LORD for his
　　　unfailing love
　　and his wonderful deeds for
　　　mankind,
16 for he breaks down gates of bronze
　　and cuts through bars of iron.

17 Some became fools through their
　　　rebellious ways
　　and suffered affliction because of
　　　their iniquities.
18 They loathed all food
　　and drew near the gates of death.
19 Then they cried to the LORD in their
　　　trouble,
　　and he saved them from their
　　　distress.
20 He sent out his word and healed them;
　　he rescued them from the grave.
21 Let them give thanks to the LORD for his
　　　unfailing love
　　and his wonderful deeds for
　　　mankind.
22 Let them sacrifice thank-offerings
　　and tell of his works with songs of joy.

23 Some went out on the sea in ships;
　　they were merchants on the mighty
　　　waters.
24 They saw the works of the LORD,
　　his wonderful deeds in the deep.
25 For he spoke and stirred up a tempest
　　that lifted high the waves.
26 They mounted up to the heavens and
　　　went down to the depths;
　　in their peril their courage melted
　　　away.
27 They reeled and staggered like
　　　drunkards;
　　they were at their wits' end.
28 Then they cried out to the LORD in their
　　　trouble,
　　and he brought them out of their
　　　distress.
29 He stilled the storm to a whisper;

the waves of the sea[b] were hushed.
30 They were glad when it grew calm,
    and he guided them to their desired
    haven.
31 Let them give thanks to the LORD for his
    unfailing love
    and his wonderful deeds for
    mankind.
32 Let them exalt him in the assembly of
    the people
    and praise him in the council of the
    elders.

33 He turned rivers into a desert,
    flowing springs into thirsty ground,
34 and fruitful land into a salt waste,
    because of the wickedness of those
    who lived there.
35 He turned the desert into pools of water
    and the parched ground into flowing
    springs;
36 there he brought the hungry to live,
    and they founded a city where they
    could settle.
37 They sowed fields and planted
    vineyards
    that yielded a fruitful harvest;
38 he blessed them, and their numbers
    greatly increased,
    and he did not let their herds
    diminish.

39 Then their numbers decreased, and they
    were humbled
    by oppression, calamity and sorrow;
40 he who pours contempt on nobles
    made them wander in a trackless
    waste.
41 But he lifted the needy out of their
    affliction
    and increased their families like
    flocks.
42 The upright see and rejoice,
    but all the wicked shut their mouths.

43 Let the one who is wise heed these
    things
    and ponder the loving deeds of the
    LORD.

Psalm 108[a]
A song. A psalm of David.

1 My heart, O God, is steadfast;
    I will sing and make music with all my
    soul.
2 Awake, harp and lyre!
    I will awaken the dawn.
3 I will praise you, LORD, among the
    nations;
    I will sing of you among the peoples.
4 For great is your love, higher than the
    heavens;
    your faithfulness reaches to the skies.
5 Be exalted, O God, above the heavens;
    let your glory be over all the earth.

6 Save us and help us with your right
    hand,
    that those you love may be delivered.
7 God has spoken from his sanctuary:
    'In triumph I will parcel out Shechem
    and measure off the Valley of
    Sukkoth.
8 Gilead is mine, Manasseh is mine;
    Ephraim is my helmet,
    Judah is my sceptre.
9 Moab is my washbasin,
    on Edom I toss my sandal;
    over Philistia I shout in triumph.'

10 Who will bring me to the fortified city?
    Who will lead me to Edom?
11 Is it not you, God, you who have
    rejected us
    and no longer go out with our
    armies?
12 Give us aid against the enemy,
    for human help is worthless.
13 With God we shall gain the victory,
    and he will trample down our
    enemies.

Psalm 109
For the director of music. Of David. A psalm.

1 My God, whom I praise,
    do not remain silent,
2 for people who are wicked and
    deceitful

---

b 29 Dead Sea Scrolls; Masoretic Text / *their waves*   a In Hebrew texts 108:1-13 is numbered 108:2-14.

have opened their mouths against
  me;
they have spoken against me with
  lying tongues.
3 With words of hatred they surround me;
  they attack me without cause.
4 In return for my friendship they accuse
  me,
  but I am a man of prayer.
5 They repay me evil for good,
  and hatred for my friendship.

6 Appoint someone evil to oppose my
  enemy;
  let an accuser stand at his right hand.
7 When he is tried, let him be found
  guilty,
  and may his prayers condemn him.
8 May his days be few;
  may another take his place of
  leadership.
9 May his children be fatherless
  and his wife a widow.
10 May his children be wandering beggars;
  may they be driven[a] from their ruined
  homes.
11 May a creditor seize all he has;
  may strangers plunder the fruits of
  his labour.
12 May no one extend kindness to him
  or take pity on his fatherless children.
13 May his descendants be cut off,
  their names blotted out from the
  next generation.
14 May the iniquity of his fathers be
  remembered before the LORD;
  may the sin of his mother never be
  blotted out.
15 May their sins always remain before the
  LORD,
  that he may blot out their name from
  the earth.

16 For he never thought of doing a
  kindness,
  but hounded to death the poor
  and the needy and the
  broken-hearted.

17 He loved to pronounce a curse –
  may it come back on him.
  He found no pleasure in blessing –
  may it be far from him.
18 He wore cursing as his garment;
  it entered into his body like water,
  into his bones like oil.
19 May it be like a cloak wrapped about
  him,
  like a belt tied for ever round him.
20 May this be the LORD's payment to my
  accusers,
  to those who speak evil of me.

21 But you, Sovereign LORD,
  help me for your name's sake;
  out of the goodness of your love,
  deliver me.
22 For I am poor and needy,
  and my heart is wounded
  within me.
23 I fade away like an evening shadow;
  I am shaken off like a locust.
24 My knees give way from fasting;
  my body is thin and gaunt.
25 I am an object of scorn to my
  accusers;
  when they see me, they shake their
  heads.

26 Help me, LORD my God;
  save me according to your unfailing
  love.
27 Let them know that it is your hand,
  that you, LORD, have done it.
28 While they curse, may you bless;
  may those who attack me be put to
  shame,
  but may your servant rejoice.
29 May my accusers be clothed with
  disgrace
  and wrapped in shame as in a
  cloak.

30 With my mouth I will greatly extol the
  LORD;
  in the great throng of worshippers I
  will praise him.
31 For he stands at the right hand of the
  needy,
  to save their lives from those who
  would condemn them.

---

a 10 Septuagint; Hebrew *sought*

Psalm 110
Of David. A psalm.

1 The LORD says to my lord:*a*

'Sit at my right hand
  until I make your enemies
  a footstool for your feet.'

2 The LORD will extend your mighty
      sceptre from Zion, saying,
    'Rule in the midst of your enemies!'

3 Your troops will be willing
    on your day of battle.
  Arrayed in holy splendour,
    your young men will come to you
    like dew from the morning's womb.*b*

4 The LORD has sworn
    and will not change his mind:
  'You are a priest for ever,
    in the order of Melchizedek.'

---

a 1 Or Lord

b 3 The meaning of the Hebrew for this sentence
is uncertain.

PRAYING THE PSALMS 7

Jesus

The song in Psalm 110 is all about the Lord Jesus. Twice in the book of Hebrews it is quoted to tell us who Jesus is and what he is doing now (Hebrews 1:13; 5:6–10).

The scholars debate the exact meaning, but one interpretation is that it describes what happened after Jesus walked on earth, was crucified, rose from the dead and ascended to the Father. The Father then said to him, *'Sit at my right hand until I make your enemies a footstool for your feet.'* He couldn't put his feet up yet (he would need a footstool for that!), but he could sit down. He had done the hard work. So he rested, waiting for the Father to bring things to completion – joining in every now and then (Acts 9:5), but mostly staying there to 'intercede' for us (Romans 5:34).

Then the LORD (capital letters means the original was 'JAHWEH', which some say means 'Father God') says, *'Rule in the midst of your enemies!'* Some think that explains the way Jesus rules today. The enemies of evil and suffering still roam the earth, but in the middle of all that, Jesus' kingdom advances. The battle is a spiritual one (Ephesians 6:12). Jesus wins a bit more every time people worship God and live for his kingdom.

The original Christian worship is to break bread and share wine as a way of remembering and proclaiming Jesus (1 Corinthians 11:23–26). The first time that simple act of worship happened, a man called Melchizedek provided it – around 2,000 years before Jesus (Genesis 14:18). Today Jesus is the 'priest' who provides us with bread and wine in the midst of the battle (Hebrews 5:6–10). One day the struggle will be over and we will meet him face to face!

Hugo Anson

 Psalm 91   Psalm 119:97–112

5 The Lord is at your right hand*c*;
    he will crush kings on the day of his
        wrath.
6 He will judge nations, heaping up the
        dead
    and crushing the rulers of the whole
        earth.
7 He will drink from a brook along the
        way;*d*
    and so he will lift his head high.

Psalm 111*a*

1 Praise the Lord.*b*

I will extol the Lord with all my heart
    in the council of the upright and in
        the assembly.

2 Great are the works of the Lord;
    they are pondered by all who delight
        in them.
3 Glorious and majestic are his deeds,
    and his righteousness endures for
        ever.
4 He has caused his wonders to be
        remembered;
    the Lord is gracious and
        compassionate.
5 He provides food for those who fear
        him;
    he remembers his covenant for ever.

6 He has shown his people the power of
        his works,
    giving them the lands of other
        nations.
7 The works of his hands are faithful and
        just;
    all his precepts are trustworthy.
8 They are established for ever and ever,
    enacted in faithfulness and
        uprightness.
9 He provided redemption for his
        people;

he ordained his covenant for ever –
    holy and awesome is his name.

10 The fear of the Lord is the beginning of
        wisdom;
    all who follow his precepts have
        good understanding.
    To him belongs eternal praise.

Psalm 112*a*

1 Praise the Lord.*b*

Blessed are those who fear the Lord,
    who find great delight in his
        commands.

2 Their children will be mighty in the
        land;
    the generation of the upright will be
        blessed.
3 Wealth and riches are in their houses,
    and their righteousness endures for
        ever.
4 Even in darkness light dawns for the
        upright,
    for those who are gracious and
        compassionate and righteous.
5 Good will come to those who are
        generous and lend freely,
    who conduct their affairs with justice.

6 Surely the righteous will never be
        shaken;
    they will be remembered for ever.
7 They will have no fear of bad news;
    their hearts are steadfast, trusting in
        the Lord.
8 Their hearts are secure, they will have no
        fear;
    in the end they will look in triumph
        on their foes.
9 They have freely scattered their gifts to
        the poor,
    their righteousness endures for ever;
    their horn*c* will be lifted high in
        honour.

---

c 5 Or *My lord is at your right hand, Lord*
d 7 The meaning of the Hebrew for this clause is
uncertain.
a This psalm is an acrostic poem, the lines of which
begin with the successive letters of the Hebrew
alphabet.
b 1 Hebrew *Hallelu Yah*

---

a This psalm is an acrostic poem, the lines of which
begin with the successive letters of the Hebrew
alphabet.
b 1 Hebrew *Hallelu Yah*
c 9 *Horn* here symbolises dignity.

10 The wicked will see and be vexed,
they will gnash their teeth and waste
away;
the longings of the wicked will come
to nothing.

Psalm 113

1 Praise the LORD.*a*

Praise the LORD, you his servants;
praise the name of the LORD.
2 Let the name of the LORD be praised,
both now and for evermore.
3 From the rising of the sun to the place
where it sets,
the name of the LORD is to be praised.

4 The LORD is exalted over all the nations,
his glory above the heavens.
5 Who is like the LORD our God,
the One who sits enthroned on high,
6 who stoops down to look
on the heavens and the earth?

7 He raises the poor from the dust
and lifts the needy from the ash heap;
8 he seats them with princes,
with the princes of his people.
9 He settles the childless woman in her
home
as a happy mother of children.

Praise the LORD.

Psalm 114

1 When Israel came out of Egypt,
Jacob from a people of foreign
tongue,
2 Judah became God's sanctuary,
Israel his dominion.

3 The sea looked and fled,
the Jordan turned back;
4 the mountains leaped like rams,
the hills like lambs.

5 Why was it, sea, that you fled?
Why, Jordan, did you turn back?

6 Why, mountains, did you leap like rams,
you hills, like lambs?

7 Tremble, earth, at the presence of the
Lord,
at the presence of the God of Jacob,
8 who turned the rock into a pool,
the hard rock into springs of water.

Psalm 115

1 Not to us, LORD, not to us
but to your name be the glory,
because of your love and
faithfulness.

2 Why do the nations say,
'Where is their God?'
3 Our God is in heaven;
he does whatever pleases him.
4 But their idols are silver and gold,
made by human hands.
5 They have mouths, but cannot speak,
eyes, but cannot see.
6 They have ears, but cannot hear,
noses, but cannot smell.
7 They have hands, but cannot feel,
feet, but cannot walk,
nor can they utter a sound with their
throats.
8 Those who make them will be like
them,
and so will all who trust in them.

9 All you Israelites, trust in the LORD –
he is their help and shield.
10 House of Aaron, trust in the LORD –
he is their help and shield.
11 You who fear him, trust in the LORD –
he is their help and shield.

12 The LORD remembers us and will bless
us:
he will bless his people Israel,
he will bless the house of Aaron,
13 he will bless those who fear the LORD –
small and great alike.

14 May the LORD cause you to flourish,
both you and your children.
15 May you be blessed by the LORD,
the Maker of heaven and earth.

---

a 1 Hebrew *Hallelu Yah*; also in verse 9

16 The highest heavens belong to the
Lord,
but the earth he has given to the
human race.
17 It is not the dead who praise the Lord,
those who go down to the place of
silence;
18 it is we who extol the Lord,
both now and for evermore.

Praise the Lord.*a*

Psalm 116

1 I love the Lord, for he heard my voice;
he heard my cry for mercy.
2 Because he turned his ear to me,
I will call on him as long as I live.

3 The cords of death entangled me,
the anguish of the grave came over
me;
I was overcome by distress and
sorrow.
4 Then I called on the name of the Lord:
'Lord, save me!'

5 The Lord is gracious and righteous;
our God is full of compassion.
6 The Lord protects the unwary;
when I was brought low, he saved me.

7 Return to your rest, my soul,
for the Lord has been good to you.

8 For you, Lord, have delivered me from
death,
my eyes from tears,
my feet from stumbling,
9 that I may walk before the Lord
in the land of the living.

10 I trusted in the Lord when I said,
'I am greatly afflicted';
11 in my alarm I said,
'Everyone is a liar.'

12 What shall I return to the Lord
for all his goodness to me?

13 I will lift up the cup of salvation
and call on the name of the Lord.
14 I will fulfil my vows to the Lord
in the presence of all his people.

15 Precious in the sight of the Lord
is the death of his faithful servants.
16 Truly I am your servant, Lord;
I serve you just as my mother did;
you have freed me from my chains.

17 I will sacrifice a thank-offering to you
and call on the name of the Lord.
18 I will fulfil my vows to the Lord
in the presence of all his people,
19 in the courts of the house of the Lord –
in your midst, Jerusalem.

Praise the Lord.*a*

Psalm 117

1 Praise the Lord, all you nations;
extol him, all you peoples.
2 For great is his love towards us,
and the faithfulness of the Lord
endures for ever.

Praise the Lord.*a*

Psalm 118

1 Give thanks to the Lord, for he is good;
his love endures for ever.

2 Let Israel say:
'His love endures for ever.'
3 Let the house of Aaron say:
'His love endures for ever.'
4 Let those who fear the Lord say:
'His love endures for ever.'

5 When hard pressed, I cried to the Lord;
he brought me into a spacious place.
6 The Lord is with me; I will not be
afraid.
What can mere mortals do to me?
7 The Lord is with me; he is my helper.
I look in triumph on my enemies.

⁸ It is better to take refuge in the Lord
than to trust in humans.
⁹ It is better to take refuge in the Lord
than to trust in princes.
¹⁰ All the nations surrounded me,
but in the name of the Lord I cut
them down.
¹¹ They surrounded me on every side,
but in the name of the Lord I cut
them down.
¹² They swarmed around me like bees,
but they were consumed as quickly as
burning thorns;
in the name of the Lord I cut them
down.
¹³ I was pushed back and about to fall,
but the Lord helped me.
¹⁴ The Lord is my strength and my
defence*ᵃ*;
he has become my salvation.

SHORTEST CHAPTER

The book of Psalms contains both the
shortest and the longest chapters of the
Bible. The shortest chapter is Psalm 117,
with only 29 words. The longest is Psalm
119, with 2,322 words.

¹⁵ Shouts of joy and victory
resound in the tents of the righteous:
'The Lord's right hand has done mighty
things!
¹⁶ The Lord's right hand is lifted high;
the Lord's right hand has done
mighty things!'
¹⁷ I will not die but live,
and will proclaim what the Lord has
done.
¹⁸ The Lord has chastened me severely,
but he has not given me over to death.
¹⁹ Open for me the gates of the righteous;

I will enter and give thanks to the
Lord.
²⁰ This is the gate of the Lord
through which the righteous may
enter.
²¹ I will give you thanks, for you answered
me;
you have become my salvation.

²² The stone the builders rejected
has become the cornerstone;
²³ the Lord has done this,
and it is marvellous in our eyes.
²⁴ The Lord has done it this very day;
let us rejoice today and be glad.

²⁵ Lord, save us!
Lord, grant us success!

²⁶ Blessed is he who comes in the name of
the Lord.
From the house of the Lord we bless
you.*ᵇ*
²⁷ The Lord is God,
and he has made his light shine on
us.
With boughs in hand, join in the festal
procession
up*ᶜ* to the horns of the altar.

²⁸ You are my God, and I will praise you;
you are my God, and I will exalt you.

²⁹ Give thanks to the Lord, for he is good;
his love endures for ever.

Psalm 119*ᵃ*

א Aleph

¹ Blessed are those whose ways are
blameless,
who walk according to the law of the
Lord.
² Blessed are those who keep his statutes
and seek him with all their heart –
³ they do no wrong

---

b 26 The Hebrew is plural.
c 27 Or *Bind the festal sacrifice with ropes / and take it*
a This psalm is an acrostic poem, the stanzas of
which begin with successive letters of the Hebrew
alphabet; moreover, the verses of each stanza begin
with the same letter of the Hebrew alphabet.

---

a 14 Or *song*

SPIRITUAL DISCIPLINES 3

STUDY

Is God in the subjects we study at school (or university)? He's pretty involved in RE, obviously, but what about Maths, Geography, Science and Art? God's never mentioned in them, after all. The spiritual discipline of study is a way to discover God's hand in every aspect of creation, every element of human creativity.

Studying is a four-step process, through which we look at a subject in depth and detail. That might be something manmade – a film, a lecture, a book; or it might be something created directly by God – a beautiful view, an animal, a person.

So when we talk about study, we are not just talking about the Bible – although this is perhaps the most important thing a Christian can choose to study – 'hiding the word in our hearts' as Psalm 119 suggests (see v. 11).

The Christian discipline of study involves four activities, as outlined by the amazing Richard Foster in his book *Celebration of Discipline*.

- **Repetition.** It's not so popular today, but until relatively recently many youth groups were asked to learn Bible verses by rote: repeating the words over and again until they become etched on the brain. As we look at something over and again, it becomes more and more familiar to us. This is the first step of the discipline.

- **Concentration.** Now we move from repeatedly returning to our subject, to giving our full attention to it. To concentrate is counter-cultural, because we live in an age of distraction. However, if we are able to concentrate our minds, fully and at length, on one subject to the exclusion of others, then we open ourselves up to far greater learning and deeper understanding.

- **Comprehension.** Next we try to understand our subject. Jesus himself says in John 8:32 that it's the knowledge of the truth that sets us free. Comprehension is about gaining insight into the knowledge of the truth. Sometimes we have an almost immediate grasp of a Bible passage or subject; at other times we understand only through investing time and thought.

- **Reflection.** Having better understood the subject or passage we're studying, we now take a step back and ask: what is the significance of this? What does it mean for my life and – most importantly of all – what does this tell me about God? He's absolutely everywhere; his fingerprints are smeared all over creation. When we spot them, it allows us to know him just a little better.

Through this process, we can examine anything in order to better understand both that subject and our God who is its Creator. Don't let the association with school put you off. The discipline of study can help us make greater sense of the world and our place in it, and might even breathe new life and meaning into some of your least favourite subjects!

Martin Saunders

 Psalm 46　　　　　　　　　　　　　　　　Mark 9:30–35

but follow his ways.

⁴ You have laid down precepts
  that are to be fully obeyed.
⁵ Oh, that my ways were steadfast
  in obeying your decrees!
⁶ Then I would not be put to shame
  when I consider all your commands.
⁷ I will praise you with an upright heart
  as I learn your righteous laws.
⁸ I will obey your decrees;
  do not utterly forsake me.

ב Beth

⁹ How can a young person stay on the
    path of purity?
  By living according to your word.
¹⁰ I seek you with all my heart;
  do not let me stray from your
    commands.
¹¹ I have hidden your word in my heart
  that I might not sin against you.
¹² Praise be to you, Lord;
  teach me your decrees.
¹³ With my lips I recount
  all the laws that come from your
    mouth.
¹⁴ I rejoice in following your statutes
  as one rejoices in great riches.
¹⁵ I meditate on your precepts
  and consider your ways.
¹⁶ I delight in your decrees;
  I will not neglect your word.

ג Gimel

¹⁷ Be good to your servant while I live,
  that I may obey your word.
¹⁸ Open my eyes that I may see
  wonderful things in your law.
¹⁹ I am a stranger on earth;
  do not hide your commands from me.
²⁰ My soul is consumed with longing
  for your laws at all times.
²¹ You rebuke the arrogant, who are
    accursed,
  those who stray from your
    commands.
²² Remove from me scorn and contempt,
  for I keep your statutes.
²³ Though rulers sit together and slander
    me,
  your servant will meditate on your
    decrees.

²⁴ Your statutes are my delight;
  they are my counsellors.

ד Daleth

²⁵ I am laid low in the dust;
  preserve my life according to your
    word.
²⁶ I gave an account of my ways and you
    answered me;
  teach me your decrees.
²⁷ Cause me to understand the way of your
    precepts,
  that I may meditate on your
    wonderful deeds.
²⁸ My soul is weary with sorrow;
  strengthen me according to your
    word.
²⁹ Keep me from deceitful ways;
  be gracious to me and teach me your
    law.
³⁰ I have chosen the way of faithfulness;
  I have set my heart on your laws.
³¹ I hold fast to your statutes, Lord;
  do not let me be put to shame.
³² I run in the path of your commands,
  for you have broadened my
    understanding.

ה He

³³ Teach me, Lord, the way of your
    decrees,
  that I may follow it to the end.*b*
³⁴ Give me understanding, so that I may
    keep your law
  and obey it with all my heart.
³⁵ Direct me in the path of your
    commands,
  for there I find delight.
³⁶ Turn my heart towards your statutes
  and not towards selfish gain.
³⁷ Turn my eyes away from worthless
    things;
  preserve my life according to your
    word.*c*
³⁸ Fulfil your promise to your servant,
  so that you may be feared.
³⁹ Take away the disgrace I dread,
  for your laws are good.

---

b 33 Or *follow it for its reward*
c 37 Two manuscripts of the Masoretic Text and
Dead Sea Scrolls; most manuscripts of the Masoretic
Text *life in your way*

40 How I long for your precepts!
  In your righteousness preserve my
    life.

ו Waw

41 May your unfailing love come to me,
    LORD,
  your salvation, according to your
    promise;
42 then I can answer anyone who taunts
    me,
  for I trust in your word.
43 Never take your word of truth from my
    mouth,
  for I have put my hope in your laws.
44 I will always obey your law,
  for ever and ever.
45 I will walk about in freedom,
  for I have sought out your precepts.
46 I will speak of your statutes before kings
  and will not be put to shame,
47 for I delight in your commands
  because I love them.
48 I reach out for your commands, which I
    love,
  that I may meditate on your decrees.

ז Zayin

49 Remember your word to your servant,
  for you have given me hope.
50 My comfort in my suffering is this:
  your promise preserves my life.
51 The arrogant mock me unmercifully,
  but I do not turn from your law.
52 I remember, LORD, your ancient laws,
  and I find comfort in them.
53 Indignation grips me because of the
    wicked,
  who have forsaken your law.
54 Your decrees are the theme of my song
  wherever I lodge.
55 In the night, LORD, I remember your
    name,
  that I may keep your law.
56 This has been my practice:
  I obey your precepts.

ח Heth

57 You are my portion, LORD;
  I have promised to obey your words.
58 I have sought your face with all my
    heart;

be gracious to me according to your
    promise.
59 I have considered my ways
  and have turned my steps to your
    statutes.
60 I will hasten and not delay
  to obey your commands.
61 Though the wicked bind me with ropes,
  I will not forget your law.
62 At midnight I rise to give you thanks
  for your righteous laws.
63 I am a friend to all who fear you,
  to all who follow your precepts.
64 The earth is filled with your love, LORD;
  teach me your decrees.

ט Teth

65 Do good to your servant
  according to your word, LORD.
66 Teach me knowledge and good
    judgment,
  for I trust your commands.
67 Before I was afflicted I went astray,
  but now I obey your word.
68 You are good, and what you do is good;
  teach me your decrees.
69 Though the arrogant have smeared me
    with lies,
  I keep your precepts with all my heart.
70 Their hearts are callous and unfeeling,
  but I delight in your law.
71 It was good for me to be afflicted
  so that I might learn your decrees.
72 The law from your mouth is more
    precious to me
  than thousands of pieces of silver and
    gold.

י Yodh

73 Your hands made me and formed me;
  give me understanding to learn your
    commands.
74 May those who fear you rejoice when
    they see me,
  for I have put my hope in your word.
75 I know, LORD, that your laws are
    righteous,
  and that in faithfulness you have
    afflicted me.
76 May your unfailing love be my comfort,
  according to your promise to your
    servant.

77 Let your compassion come to me that I
    may live,
  for your law is my delight.
78 May the arrogant be put to shame for
    wronging me without cause;
  but I will meditate on your precepts.
79 May those who fear you turn to me,
    those who understand your statutes.
80 May I wholeheartedly follow your
    decrees,
  that I may not be put to shame.

כ Kaph

81 My soul faints with longing for your
    salvation,
  but I have put my hope in your word.
82 My eyes fail, looking for your promise;
  I say, 'When will you comfort me?'
83 Though I am like a wineskin in the
    smoke,
  I do not forget your decrees.
84 How long must your servant wait?
  When will you punish my
    persecutors?
85 The arrogant dig pits to trap me,
  contrary to your law.
86 All your commands are trustworthy;
  help me, for I am being persecuted
    without cause.
87 They almost wiped me from the earth,
  but I have not forsaken your precepts.
88 In your unfailing love preserve my life,
  that I may obey the statutes of your
    mouth.

ל Lamedh

89 Your word, LORD, is eternal;
  it stands firm in the heavens.
90 Your faithfulness continues through all
    generations;
  you established the earth, and it
    endures.
91 Your laws endure to this day,
  for all things serve you.
92 If your law had not been my delight,
  I would have perished in my
    affliction.
93 I will never forget your precepts,
  for by them you have preserved my
    life.
94 Save me, for I am yours;
  I have sought out your precepts.

95 The wicked are waiting to destroy me,
  but I will ponder your statutes.
96 To all perfection I see a limit,
  but your commands are boundless.

מ Mem

97 Oh, how I love your law!
  I meditate on it all day long.
98 Your commands are always with me
    and make me wiser than my
      enemies.
99 I have more insight than all my
    teachers,
  for I meditate on your statutes.
100 I have more understanding than the
    elders,
  for I obey your precepts.
101 I have kept my feet from every evil path
  so that I might obey your word.
102 I have not departed from your laws,
  for you yourself have taught me.
103 How sweet are your words to my taste,
  sweeter than honey to my mouth!
104 I gain understanding from your
    precepts;
  therefore I hate every wrong path.

נ Nun

105 Your word is a lamp for my feet,
  a light on my path.
106 I have taken an oath and confirmed it,
  that I will follow your righteous laws.
107 I have suffered much;
  preserve my life, LORD, according to
    your word.
108 Accept, LORD, the willing praise of my
    mouth,
  and teach me your laws.
109 Though I constantly take my life in my
    hands,
  I will not forget your law.
110 The wicked have set a snare for me,
  but I have not strayed from your
    precepts.
111 Your statutes are my heritage for ever;
  they are the joy of my heart.
112 My heart is set on keeping your decrees
  to the very end. *d*

_____
d 112 Or *decrees / for their enduring reward*

ס Samekh

113 I hate double-minded people,
　　but I love your law.
114 You are my refuge and my shield;
　　I have put my hope in your word.
115 Away from me, you evildoers,
　　　that I may keep the commands of my
　　　God!
116 Sustain me, my God, according to your
　　　promise, and I shall live;
　　do not let my hopes be dashed.
117 Uphold me, and I shall be delivered;
　　I shall always have regard for your
　　　decrees.
118 You reject all who stray from your
　　　decrees,

for their delusions come to nothing.
119 All the wicked of the earth you discard
　　　like dross;
　　therefore I love your statutes.
120 My flesh trembles in fear of you;
　　I stand in awe of your laws.

ע Ayin

121 I have done what is righteous and just;
　　do not leave me to my oppressors.
122 Ensure your servant's well-being;
　　do not let the arrogant oppress me.
123 My eyes fail, looking for your salvation,
　　looking for your righteous promise.
124 Deal with your servant according to
　　your love

PRAYING THE PSALMS 8

Light for the way

Thank you for the Bible Lord. Psalm 119 tells me its words are *'a lamp for my feet, a light on my path'* (v. 105).

They show me where to put my feet next. They also shine light on the way ahead. The Holy Spirit speaks through the words and teaches me what to do (v. 102). It's as if I'm walking through the woods and come upon an empty beehive and find a fresh honeycomb (v. 103). So sweet. So surprisingly joyful.

But don't let me get puffed up or arrogant. This psalmist seems to have received your grace by reading the law, and is now gloating over the elders and his teachers (vv. 99–100). He says, 'I'm wiser than you lot!' Keep me free of that kind of pride, please, Lord.

I love the Bible. It helps me to know you, God. To know what you want for me and for us. But I don't want to hate people (v. 113). Surely even the 'double-minded' cannot be made better by being hated. Help me to love even difficult people. In the context of the rest of the Bible – especially everything I know about Jesus – I know there is a higher way. A better way! A bigger way! A kinder way!

I know people have these feelings of anger and pride, but why is it OK to express them in a psalm that will be included in the Bible? Maybe it's because you would prefer us to talk to you, even when our hearts are twisted, rather than insist on us being perfect before we can enter your presence.

Hugo Anson

 Psalm 110　　　　　　　　　　　Psalm 121 ▶▶

and teach me your decrees.

125 I am your servant; give me discernment
that I may understand your statutes.

126 It is time for you to act, LORD;
your law is being broken.

127 Because I love your commands
more than gold, more than pure gold,

128 and because I consider all your precepts
right,
I hate every wrong path.

ꝑ Pe

129 Your statutes are wonderful;
therefore I obey them.

130 The unfolding of your words gives light;
it gives understanding to the simple.

131 I open my mouth and pant,
longing for your commands.

132 Turn to me and have mercy on me,
as you always do to those who love
your name.

133 Direct my footsteps according to your
word;
let no sin rule over me.

134 Redeem me from human oppression,
that I may obey your precepts.

135 Make your face shine on your servant
and teach me your decrees.

136 Streams of tears flow from my eyes,
for your law is not obeyed.

צ Tsadhe

137 You are righteous, LORD,
and your laws are right.

138 The statutes you have laid down are
righteous;
they are fully trustworthy.

139 My zeal wears me out,
for my enemies ignore your words.

140 Your promises have been thoroughly
tested,
and your servant loves them.

141 Though I am lowly and despised,
I do not forget your precepts.

142 Your righteousness is everlasting
and your law is true.

143 Trouble and distress have come
upon me,
but your commands give me delight.

144 Your statutes are always righteous;
give me understanding that I may
live.

ק Qoph

145 I call with all my heart; answer me,
LORD,
and I will obey your decrees.

146 I call out to you; save me
and I will keep your statutes.

147 I rise before dawn and cry for help;
I have put my hope in your word.

148 My eyes stay open through the watches
of the night,
that I may meditate on your
promises.

149 Hear my voice in accordance with your
love;
preserve my life, LORD, according to
your laws.

150 Those who devise wicked schemes are
near,
but they are far from your law.

151 Yet you are near, LORD,
and all your commands are true.

152 Long ago I learned from your statutes
that you established them to last for
ever.

ר Resh

153 Look on my suffering and deliver me,
for I have not forgotten your law.

154 Defend my cause and redeem me;
preserve my life according to your
promise.

155 Salvation is far from the wicked,
for they do not seek out your decrees.

156 Your compassion, LORD, is great;
preserve my life according to your
laws.

157 Many are the foes who persecute me,
but I have not turned from your
statutes.

158 I look on the faithless with loathing,
for they do not obey your word.

159 See how I love your precepts;
preserve my life, LORD, in accordance
with your love.

160 All your words are true;
all your righteous laws are eternal.

שׂ Sin and Shin

161 Rulers persecute me without cause,
but my heart trembles at your word.

162 I rejoice in your promise
like one who finds great spoil.

163 I hate and detest falsehood
    but I love your law.
164 Seven times a day I praise you
    for your righteous laws.
165 Great peace have those who love your
      law,
    and nothing can make them stumble.
166 I wait for your salvation, LORD,
    and I follow your commands.
167 I obey your statutes,
    for I love them greatly.
168 I obey your precepts and your statutes,
    for all my ways are known to you.

ת Taw

169 May my cry come before you, LORD;
    give me understanding according to
      your word.
170 May my supplication come before you;
    deliver me according to your
      promise.
171 May my lips overflow with praise,
    for you teach me your decrees.
172 May my tongue sing of your word,
    for all your commands are righteous.
173 May your hand be ready to help me,
    for I have chosen your precepts.
174 I long for your salvation, LORD,
    and your law gives me delight.
175 Let me live that I may praise you,
    and may your laws sustain me.
176 I have strayed like a lost sheep.
    Seek your servant,
    for I have not forgotten your
      commands.

Psalm 120

A song of ascents.

1 I call on the LORD in my distress,
    and he answers me.
2 Save me, LORD,
    from lying lips
    and from deceitful tongues.

3 What will he do to you,
    and what more besides,
    you deceitful tongue?
4 He will punish you with a warrior's
      sharp arrows,
    with burning coals of the broom
      bush.

5 Woe to me that I dwell in Meshek,
    that I live among the tents of Kedar!
6 Too long have I lived
    among those who hate peace.
7 I am for peace;
    but when I speak, they are for war.

Psalm 121

A song of ascents.

1 I lift up my eyes to the mountains –
    where does my help come from?
2 My help comes from the LORD,
    the Maker of heaven and earth.

3 He will not let your foot slip –
    he who watches over you will not
      slumber;
4 indeed, he who watches over Israel
    will neither slumber nor sleep.

5 The LORD watches over you –
    the LORD is your shade at your right
      hand;
6 the sun will not harm you by day,
    nor the moon by night.

7 The LORD will keep you from all
      harm –
    he will watch over your life;
8 the LORD will watch over your coming
      and going
    both now and for evermore.

Psalm 122

A song of ascents. Of David.

1 I rejoiced with those who said to me,
    'Let us go to the house of the LORD.'
2 Our feet are standing
    in your gates, Jerusalem.

3 Jerusalem is built like a city
    that is closely compacted together.
4 That is where the tribes go up –
    the tribes of the LORD –
    to praise the name of the LORD
    according to the statute given to
      Israel.
5 There stand the thrones for
      judgment,
    the thrones of the house of David.

6 Pray for the peace of Jerusalem:
  'May those who love you be
      secure.
7 May there be peace within your walls
    and security within your citadels.'
8 For the sake of my family and
      friends,
  I will say, 'Peace be within you.'
9 For the sake of the house of the LORD
      our God,
  I will seek your prosperity.

Psalm 123
A song of ascents.

1 I lift up my eyes to you,
    to you who sit enthroned in heaven.
2 As the eyes of slaves look to the hand of
      their master,
  as the eyes of a female slave look to
      the hand of her mistress,
  so our eyes look to the LORD our God,
      till he shows us his mercy.

PRAYING THE PSALMS 9

Lift up your eyes to the mountains

**The people of Israel had various festivals in the year when they all went up
to Jerusalem. They normally walked together in big groups. The journey
was often dangerous, as bandits could attack them along the way.**

Those who loved the Lord would also be upset because when they looked up to
the hilltops surrounding the road, they would see shrines to various false gods. As
they travelled they would sing Psalm 121 together.

'I lift up my eyes to the mountains' – where bandits hide and I can see the places
where people worship idols. *'Where does my help come from?'* The reply is
simple. *'My help comes from the LORD, the Maker of heaven and earth'* – including
these hills!

Imagine yourself travelling down a road through one of our large cities. What
do you see around you? The various shrines of consumerism – normally known
as malls or shopping centres. A darkened street corner where the graffiti feels
menacing and scary. A large billboard advertising a sleazy late-night programme
on a new TV channel. Or another telling us that real life is found in downing a
particular soft drink or running with trainers that have a particular label.

These sights could make us feel afraid or upset that people are worshipping
things that are not the true living God. So let's use this psalm as a framework to
pray as we travel.

Something like this:

'I look at the adverts and dark graffiti and wonder, "If people are worshipping
these things, who can help us?" I know who can help us: the Lord, who made the
earth beneath my feet. And I am not afraid! Because I know that this God is alive
and awake, protecting me as I travel.'

Hugo Anson

 Psalm 119:97–112   Psalm 133

3 Have mercy on us, Lord, have mercy
  on us,
  for we have endured no end of
    contempt.
4 We have endured no end
  of ridicule from the arrogant,
  of contempt from the proud.

Psalm 124
A song of ascents. Of David.

1 If the Lord had not been on our side –
  let Israel say –
2 if the Lord had not been on our side
  when people attacked us,
3 they would have swallowed us alive
  when their anger flared against us;
4 the flood would have engulfed us,
  the torrent would have swept over us,
5 the raging waters
  would have swept us away.

6 Praise be to the Lord,
  who has not let us be torn by their
    teeth.
7 We have escaped like a bird
  from the fowler's snare;
  the snare has been broken,
  and we have escaped.
8 Our help is in the name of the Lord,
  the Maker of heaven and earth.

Psalm 125
A song of ascents.

1 Those who trust in the Lord are like
  Mount Zion,
  which cannot be shaken but endures
    for ever.
2 As the mountains surround Jerusalem,
  so the Lord surrounds his people
  both now and for evermore.

3 The sceptre of the wicked will not
    remain
  over the land allotted to the
    righteous,
  for then the righteous might use
  their hands to do evil.

4 Lord, do good to those who are good,
  to those who are upright in heart.

5 But those who turn to crooked ways
  the Lord will banish with the
    evildoers.

Peace be on Israel.

Psalm 126
A song of ascents.

1 When the Lord restored the fortunes
  of[a] Zion,
  we were like those who dreamed.[b]
2 Our mouths were filled with laughter,
  our tongues with songs of joy.
  Then it was said among the nations,
  'The Lord has done great things for
    them.'
3 The Lord has done great things for us,
  and we are filled with joy.

4 Restore our fortunes,[c] Lord,
  like streams in the Negev.
5 Those who sow with tears
  will reap with songs of joy.
6 Those who go out weeping,
  carrying seed to sow,
  will return with songs of joy,
  carrying sheaves with them.

Psalm 127
A song of ascents. Of Solomon.

1 Unless the Lord builds the house,
  the builders labour in vain.
  Unless the Lord watches over the city,
  the guards stand watch in vain.
2 In vain you rise early
  and stay up late,
  toiling for food to eat –
  for he grants sleep to[a] those he loves.

3 Children are a heritage from the Lord,
  offspring a reward from him.
4 Like arrows in the hands of a warrior
  are children born in one's youth.
5 Blessed is the man
  whose quiver is full of them.
  They will not be put to shame

---

a 1 Or Lord *brought back the captives to*
b 1 Or *those restored to health*
c 4 Or *Bring back our captives*
a 2 Or eat – / *for while they sleep he provides for*

when they contend with their
opponents in court.

Psalm 128
A song of ascents.

1 Blessed are all who fear the LORD,
who walk in obedience to him.
2 You will eat the fruit of your labour;
blessings and prosperity will be
yours.
3 Your wife will be like a fruitful vine
within your house;
your children will be like olive shoots
round your table.
4 Yes, this will be the blessing
for the man who fears the LORD.

5 May the LORD bless you from Zion;
may you see the prosperity of
Jerusalem
all the days of your life.
6 May you live to see your children's
children –
peace be on Israel.

Psalm 129
A song of ascents.

1 'They have greatly oppressed me from
my youth,'
let Israel say;
2 'they have greatly oppressed me from
my youth,
but they have not gained the victory
over me.
3 Ploughmen have ploughed my back
and made their furrows long.
4 But the LORD is righteous;
he has cut me free from the cords of
the wicked.'

5 May all who hate Zion
be turned back in shame.
6 May they be like grass on the roof,
which withers before it can grow;
7 a reaper cannot fill his hands with it,
nor one who gathers fill his arms.
8 May those who pass by not say to them,
'The blessing of the LORD be on you;
we bless you in the name of the
LORD.'

Psalm 130
A song of ascents.

1 Out of the depths I cry to you, LORD;
2 Lord, hear my voice.
Let your ears be attentive
to my cry for mercy.

3 If you, LORD, kept a record of sins,
Lord, who could stand?
4 But with you there is forgiveness,
so that we can, with reverence, serve
you.

5 I wait for the LORD, my whole being
waits,
and in his word I put my hope.
6 I wait for the Lord
more than watchmen wait for the
morning,
more than watchmen wait for the
morning.

7 Israel, put your hope in the LORD,
for with the LORD is unfailing love
and with him is full redemption.
8 He himself will redeem Israel
from all their sins.

Psalm 131
A song of ascents. Of David.

1 My heart is not proud, LORD,
my eyes are not haughty;
I do not concern myself with great
matters
or things too wonderful for me.
2 But I have calmed and quietened
myself,
I am like a weaned child with its
mother;
like a weaned child I am
content.

3 Israel, put your hope in the LORD
both now and for evermore.

Psalm 132
A song of ascents.

1 LORD, remember David
and all his self-denial.

2 He swore an oath to the LORD,
he made a vow to the Mighty One of
Jacob:
3 'I will not enter my house
or go to my bed,
4 I will allow no sleep to my eyes
or slumber to my eyelids,
5 till I find a place for the LORD,
a dwelling for the Mighty One of
Jacob.'

6 We heard it in Ephrathah,
we came upon it in the fields of Jaar:*a*
7 'Let us go to his dwelling-place,
let us worship at his footstool,
saying,
8 "Arise, LORD, and come to your resting
place,
you and the ark of your might.
9 May your priests be clothed with your
righteousness;
may your faithful people sing for
joy."'

10 For the sake of your servant David,
do not reject your anointed one.

11 The LORD swore an oath to David,
a sure oath he will not revoke:
'One of your own descendants
I will place on your throne.
12 If your sons keep my covenant
and the statutes I teach them,
then their sons shall sit
on your throne for ever and ever.'

13 For the LORD has chosen Zion,
he has desired it for his dwelling,
saying,
14 'This is my resting place for ever and
ever;
here I will sit enthroned, for I have
desired it.
15 I will bless her with abundant
provisions;
her poor I will satisfy with food.
16 I will clothe her priests with salvation,

and her faithful people shall ever
sing for joy.

17 'Here I will make a horn*b* grow for
David
and set up a lamp for my anointed
one.
18 I will clothe his enemies with shame,
but his head shall be adorned with a
radiant crown.'

Psalm 133
A song of ascents. Of David.

1 How good and pleasant it is
when God's people live together in
unity!

2 It is like precious oil poured on the
head,
running down on the beard,
running down on Aaron's beard,
down on the collar of his robe.
3 It is as if the dew of Hermon
were falling on Mount Zion.
For there the LORD bestows his blessing,
even life for evermore.

Psalm 134
A song of ascents.

1 Praise the LORD, all you servants of the
LORD
who minister by night in the house of
the LORD.
2 Lift up your hands in the sanctuary
and praise the LORD.

3 May the LORD bless you from Zion,
he who is the Maker of heaven and
earth.

Psalm 135

1 Praise the LORD.*a*

Praise the name of the LORD;
praise him, you servants of the LORD,

---

a 6 Or *heard of it in Ephrathah, / we found it in the fields of Jearim.* (See 1 Chron. 13:5,6) (and no quotation marks around verses 7-9)

b 17 *Horn* here symbolises strong one, that is, king.
a 1 Hebrew *Hallelu Yah*; also in verses 3 and 21

2 you who minister in the house of the
LORD,
in the courts of the house of our God.

3 Praise the LORD, for the LORD is good;
sing praise to his name, for that is
pleasant.
4 For the LORD has chosen Jacob to be his
own,
Israel to be his treasured possession.

5 I know that the LORD is great,
that our Lord is greater than all gods.
6 The LORD does whatever pleases him,
in the heavens and on the earth,
in the seas and all their depths.

7 He makes clouds rise from the ends of
the earth;
he sends lightning with the rain
and brings out the wind from his
storehouses.

8 He struck down the firstborn of Egypt,
the firstborn of people and animals.
9 He sent his signs and wonders into your
midst, Egypt,
against Pharaoh and all his servants.
10 He struck down many nations
and killed mighty kings –
11 Sihon king of the Amorites,
Og king of Bashan,
and all the kings of Canaan –

PRAYING THE PSALMS 10

Unity

We know from Genesis 2:18 that God intended us to live in unity with others.

Imagine an ancient high priest. He has wonderful robes, with colourful jewels encrusted in the breastpiece. He has a full head of hair and a long bushy beard. Now imagine another priest coming over with a golden bowl full of warm spiced olive oil. The high priest stands still as the other priest lifts the vessel and boldly pours it over his hair. It pours down in every direction, catching the candlelight and releasing the strong smell of incense. All those around smile and begin to hum a song. A truly wonderful feeling fills every heart. They look up at the high priest with his shining hair and radiant smile. They thank God for the moment, the togetherness they are sharing in this simple act of worship.

I long for moments like this one in Psalm 133 when I meet with other Christians. Maybe we don't have a physical high priest in our midst, but Jesus is with us. If we love one another, enjoy spending time with one another and serve together in unity, it can almost feel as if we have taken a bowl of incense and poured it over Jesus' head. It feels great and it makes me want to worship.

So let's ask God to work in and through us so that more of those moments can happen. Pray for the church groups you know to love one another deeply, enjoy each other's company and agree with each person about all they are trying to do. Pray that, as a result of that unity, the Lord will 'bestow a blessing' on all of them – just as he has promised (see v. 3).

Hugo Anson

 Psalm 121

12 and he gave their land as an inheritance,
　　an inheritance to his people Israel.

13 Your name, LORD, endures for ever,
　　your renown, LORD, through all
　　　generations.
14 For the LORD will vindicate his people
　　and have compassion on his
　　　servants.

15 The idols of the nations are silver and
　　　gold,
　　made by human hands.
16 They have mouths, but cannot speak,
　　eyes, but cannot see.
17 They have ears, but cannot hear,
　　nor is there breath in their mouths.
18 Those who make them will be like them,
　　and so will all who trust in them.

19 All you Israelites, praise the LORD;
　　house of Aaron, praise the LORD;
20 house of Levi, praise the LORD;
　　you who fear him, praise the LORD.
21 Praise be to the LORD from Zion,
　　to him who dwells in Jerusalem.

Praise the LORD.

Psalm 136

1 Give thanks to the LORD, for he is good.
　　His love endures for ever.
2 Give thanks to the God of gods.
　　His love endures for ever.
3 Give thanks to the Lord of lords:
　　His love endures for ever.

4 to him who alone does great wonders,
　　His love endures for ever.
5 who by his understanding made the
　　　heavens,
　　His love endures for ever.
6 who spread out the earth upon the
　　　waters,
　　His love endures for ever.
7 who made the great lights –
　　His love endures for ever.
8 the sun to govern the day,
　　His love endures for ever.
9 the moon and stars to govern the night;
　　His love endures for ever.

10 to him who struck down the firstborn of
　　　Egypt
　　His love endures for ever.
11 and brought Israel out from among
　　　them
　　His love endures for ever.
12 with a mighty hand and outstretched
　　　arm;
　　His love endures for ever.

13 to him who divided the Red Sea*a*
　　　asunder
　　His love endures for ever.
14 and brought Israel through the midst
　　　of it,
　　His love endures for ever.
15 but swept Pharaoh and his army into
　　　the Red Sea;
　　His love endures for ever.

16 to him who led his people through the
　　　wilderness;
　　His love endures for ever.

17 to him who struck down great kings,
　　His love endures for ever.
18 and killed mighty kings –
　　His love endures for ever.
19 Sihon king of the Amorites
　　His love endures for ever.
20 and Og king of Bashan –
　　His love endures for ever.
21 and gave their land as an inheritance,
　　His love endures for ever.
22 an inheritance to his servant Israel.
　　His love endures for ever.

23 He remembered us in our low estate
　　His love endures for ever.
24 and freed us from our enemies.
　　His love endures for ever.
25 He gives food to every creature.
　　His love endures for ever.

26 Give thanks to the God of heaven.
　　His love endures for ever.

---

a 13 Or *the Sea of Reeds*; also in verse 15

Psalm 137

1 By the rivers of Babylon we sat and wept
  when we remembered Zion.
2 There on the poplars
  we hung our harps,
3 for there our captors asked us for songs,
  our tormentors demanded songs of
    joy;
  they said, 'Sing us one of the songs of
    Zion!'

4 How can we sing the songs of the LORD
  while in a foreign land?
5 If I forget you, Jerusalem,
  may my right hand forget its skill.
6 May my tongue cling to the roof of my
    mouth
  if I do not remember you,
if I do not consider Jerusalem
  my highest joy.

7 Remember, LORD, what the Edomites
    did
  on the day Jerusalem fell.
'Tear it down,' they cried,
  'tear it down to its foundations!'
8 Daughter Babylon, doomed to
    destruction,
  happy is the one who repays you
according to what you have done
    to us.
9 Happy is the one who seizes your infants
  and dashes them against the rocks.

Psalm 138

Of David.

1 I will praise you, LORD, with all my
    heart;
  before the 'gods' I will sing your
    praise.
2 I will bow down towards your holy
    temple
  and will praise your name
for your unfailing love and your
    faithfulness,
for you have so exalted your solemn
    decree
  that it surpasses your fame.
3 When I called, you answered me;
  you greatly emboldened me.

4 May all the kings of the earth praise you,
    LORD,
  when they hear what you have
    decreed.
5 May they sing of the ways of the LORD,
  for the glory of the LORD is great.

6 Though the LORD is exalted, he looks
    kindly on the lowly;
  though lofty, he sees them from afar.
7 Though I walk in the midst of trouble,
  you preserve my life.
You stretch out your hand against the
    anger of my foes;
  with your right hand you save me.
8 The LORD will vindicate me;
  your love, LORD, endures for ever –
do not abandon the works of your
    hands.

Psalm 139

For the director of music. Of David. A psalm.

1 You have searched me, LORD,
  and you know me.
2 You know when I sit and when I rise;
  you perceive my thoughts from afar.
3 You discern my going out and my lying
    down;
  you are familiar with all my ways.
4 Before a word is on my tongue
  you, LORD, know it completely.
5 You hem me in behind and before,
  and you lay your hand upon me.
6 Such knowledge is too wonderful for
    me,
  too lofty for me to attain.

7 Where can I go from your Spirit?
  Where can I flee from your presence?
8 If I go up to the heavens, you are there;
  if I make my bed in the depths, you
    are there.
9 If I rise on the wings of the dawn,
  if I settle on the far side of the sea,
10 even there your hand will guide me,
  your right hand will hold me fast.
11 If I say, 'Surely the darkness will hide me
  and the light become night around
    me,'
12 even the darkness will not be dark to
    you;

the night will shine like the day,
for darkness is as light to you.

¹³ For you created my inmost being;
you knit me together in my mother's
womb.
¹⁴ I praise you because I am fearfully and
wonderfully made;
your works are wonderful,
I know that full well.
¹⁵ My frame was not hidden from you
when I was made in the secret place,
when I was woven together in the
depths of the earth.
¹⁶ Your eyes saw my unformed body;
all the days ordained for me were
written in your book
before one of them came to be.
¹⁷ How precious to me are your thoughts,ᵃ
God!
How vast is the sum of them!
¹⁸ Were I to count them,
they would outnumber the grains of
sand –
when I awake, I am still with you.

¹⁹ If only you, God, would slay the wicked!
Away from me, you who are
bloodthirsty!
²⁰ They speak of you with evil intent;
your adversaries misuse your name.
²¹ Do I not hate those who hate you,
LORD,
and abhor those who are in rebellion
against you?
²² I have nothing but hatred for them;
I count them my enemies.
²³ Search me, God, and know my heart;
test me and know my anxious
thoughts.
²⁴ See if there is any offensive way in me,
and lead me in the way everlasting.

Psalm 140ᵃ
For the director of music. A psalm of David.

¹ Rescue me, LORD, from evildoers;
protect me from the violent,
² who devise evil plans in their hearts

and stir up war every day.
³ They make their tongues as sharp as a
serpent's;
the poison of vipers is on their lips.ᵇ

⁴ Keep me safe, LORD, from the hands of
the wicked;
protect me from the violent,
who devise ways to trip my feet.
⁵ The arrogant have hidden a snare for
me;
they have spread out the cords of
their net
and have set traps for me along my
path.

⁶ I say to the LORD, 'You are my God.'
Hear, LORD, my cry for mercy.
⁷ Sovereign LORD, my strong deliverer,
you shield my head in the day of
battle.
⁸ Do not grant the wicked their desires,
LORD;
do not let their plans succeed.

⁹ Those who surround me proudly rear
their heads;
may the mischief of their lips engulf
them.
¹⁰ May burning coals fall on them;
may they be thrown into the fire,
into miry pits, never to rise.
¹¹ May slanderers not be established in the
land;
may disaster hunt down the violent.

¹² I know that the LORD secures justice for
the poor
and upholds the cause of the needy.
¹³ Surely the righteous will praise your
name,
and the upright will live in your
presence.

Psalm 141
A psalm of David.

¹ I call to you, LORD, come quickly to me;
hear me when I call to you.

ᵃ 17 Or *How amazing are your thoughts concerning me*
ᵃ In Hebrew texts 140:1-13 is numbered 140:2-14.

ᵇ 3 The Hebrew has *Selah* (a word of uncertain
meaning) here and at the end of verses 5 and 8.

2 May my prayer be set before you like
    incense;
  may the lifting up of my hands be like
    the evening sacrifice.

3 Set a guard over my mouth, LORD;
  keep watch over the door of my lips.
4 Do not let my heart be drawn to what is
    evil
  so that I take part in wicked deeds
along with those who are evildoers;
  do not let me eat their delicacies.

5 Let a righteous man strike me – that is a
    kindness;
  let him rebuke me – that is oil on my
    head.
My head will not refuse it,
  for my prayer will still be against the
    deeds of evildoers.

6 Their rulers will be thrown down from
    the cliffs,
  and the wicked will learn that my
    words were well spoken.
7 They will say, 'As one ploughs and
    breaks up the earth,
  so our bones have been scattered at
    the mouth of the grave.'

8 But my eyes are fixed on you, Sovereign
    LORD;
  in you I take refuge – do not give me
    over to death.
9 Keep me safe from the traps set by
    evildoers,
  from the snares they have laid for me.
10 Let the wicked fall into their own nets,
  while I pass by in safety.

Psalm 142[a]

*A maskil[b] of David. When he was in the cave.
A prayer.*

1 I cry aloud to the LORD;
  I lift up my voice to the LORD for
    mercy.
2 I pour out before him my complaint;
  before him I tell my trouble.

3 When my spirit grows faint within me,
  it is you who watch over my way.
In the path where I walk
  people have hidden a snare for me.
4 Look and see, there is no one at my
    right hand;
  no one is concerned for me.
I have no refuge;
  no one cares for my life.

5 I cry to you, LORD;
  I say, 'You are my refuge,
  my portion in the land of the living.'

6 Listen to my cry,
  for I am in desperate need;
rescue me from those who pursue me,
  for they are too strong for me.
7 Set me free from my prison,
  that I may praise your name.
Then the righteous will gather about me
  because of your goodness to me.

Psalm 143

A psalm of David.

1 LORD, hear my prayer,
  listen to my cry for mercy;
in your faithfulness and righteousness
  come to my relief.
2 Do not bring your servant into
    judgment,
  for no one living is righteous before
    you.
3 The enemy pursues me,
  he crushes me to the ground;
he makes me dwell in the darkness
  like those long dead.
4 So my spirit grows faint within me;
  my heart within me is dismayed.
5 I remember the days of long ago;
  I meditate on all your works
  and consider what your hands have
    done.
6 I spread out my hands to you;
  I thirst for you like a parched land.[a]

7 Answer me quickly, LORD;
  my spirit fails.

---

a In Hebrew texts 142:1-7 is numbered 142:2-8.
b Title: Probably a literary or musical term

a 6 The Hebrew has *Selah* (a word of uncertain
meaning) here.

Do not hide your face from me
        or I will be like those who go down to
        the pit.
8 Let the morning bring me word of your
        unfailing love,
        for I have put my trust in you.
    Show me the way I should go,
        for to you I entrust my life.
9 Rescue me from my enemies, LORD,
        for I hide myself in you.
10 Teach me to do your will,
        for you are my God;
    may your good Spirit
        lead me on level ground.

11 For your name's sake, LORD, preserve
        my life;
        in your righteousness, bring me out
        of trouble.
12 In your unfailing love, silence my
        enemies;
        destroy all my foes,
        for I am your servant.

Psalm 144
Of David.

1 Praise be to the LORD my Rock,
        who trains my hands for war,
        my fingers for battle.
2 He is my loving God and my fortress,
        my stronghold and my deliverer,
    my shield, in whom I take refuge,
        who subdues peoples*a* under me.

3 LORD, what are human beings that you
        care for them,
        mere mortals that you think of
        them?
4 They are like a breath;
        their days are like a fleeting shadow.

5 Part your heavens, LORD, and come
        down;
        touch the mountains, so that they
        smoke.
6 Send forth lightning and scatter the
        enemy;

shoot your arrows and rout them.
7 Reach down your hand from on high;
        deliver me and rescue me
    from the mighty waters,
        from the hands of foreigners
8 whose mouths are full of lies,
        whose right hands are deceitful.

9 I will sing a new song to you, my God;
        on the ten-stringed lyre I will make
        music to you,
10 to the One who gives victory to kings,
        who delivers his servant David.

From the deadly sword 11 deliver me;
    rescue me from the hands of
        foreigners
whose mouths are full of lies,
        whose right hands are deceitful.

12 Then our sons in their youth
        will be like well-nurtured plants,
    and our daughters will be like pillars
        carved to adorn a palace.
13 Our barns will be filled
        with every kind of provision.
    Our sheep will increase by thousands,
        by tens of thousands in our
        fields;
14   our oxen will draw heavy loads.*b*
    There will be no breaching of walls,
        no going into captivity,
        no cry of distress in our streets.
15 Blessed is the people of whom this is
        true;
        blessed is the people whose God is
        the LORD.

Psalm 145*a*
A psalm of praise. Of David.

1 I will exalt you, my God the King;
        I will praise your name for ever and
        ever.
2 Every day I will praise you
        and extol your name for ever and
        ever.

---

a 2 Many manuscripts of the Masoretic Text,
Dead Sea Scrolls, Aquila, Jerome and Syriac; most
manuscripts of the Masoretic Text *subdues my people*

b 14 Or *our chieftains will be firmly established*
a This psalm is an acrostic poem, the verses
of which (including verse 13b) begin with the
successive letters of the Hebrew alphabet.

3 Great is the LORD and most worthy of
  praise;
  his greatness no one can fathom.
4 One generation commends your works
  to another;
  they tell of your mighty acts.
5 They speak of the glorious splendour of
  your majesty –
  and I will meditate on your wonderful
  works.*b*
6 They tell of the power of your awesome
  works –
  and I will proclaim your great deeds.
7 They celebrate your abundant goodness
  and joyfully sing of your
  righteousness.

8 The LORD is gracious and
  compassionate,
  slow to anger and rich in love.

9 The LORD is good to all;
  he has compassion on all he has
  made.
10 All your works praise you, LORD;
  your faithful people extol you.
11 They tell of the glory of your kingdom
  and speak of your might,
12 so that all people may know of your
  mighty acts
  and the glorious splendour of your
  kingdom.
13 Your kingdom is an everlasting
  kingdom,
  and your dominion endures through
  all generations.

The LORD is trustworthy in all he
  promises
  and faithful in all he does.*c*
14 The LORD upholds all who fall
  and lifts up all who are bowed down.
15 The eyes of all look to you,
  and you give them their food at the
  proper time.

16 You open your hand
  and satisfy the desires of every living
  thing.

17 The LORD is righteous in all his ways
  and faithful in all he does.
18 The LORD is near to all who call on him,
  to all who call on him in truth.
19 He fulfils the desires of those who fear
  him;
  he hears their cry and saves them.
20 The LORD watches over all who love
  him,
  but all the wicked he will destroy.

21 My mouth will speak in praise of the
  LORD.
  Let every creature praise his holy
  name
  for ever and ever.

Psalm 146

1 Praise the LORD.*a*

  Praise the LORD, my soul.

2 I will praise the LORD all my life;
  I will sing praise to my God as long as
  I live.
3 Do not put your trust in princes,
  in human beings, who cannot save.
4 When their spirit departs, they return to
  the ground;
  on that very day their plans come to
  nothing.
5 Blessed are those whose help is the God
  of Jacob,
  whose hope is in the LORD their God.

6 He is the Maker of heaven and earth,
  the sea, and everything in them –
  he remains faithful for ever.
7 He upholds the cause of the oppressed
  and gives food to the hungry.
  The LORD sets prisoners free,
8   the LORD gives sight to the blind,
  the LORD lifts up those who are bowed
  down,
  the LORD loves the righteous.

---

b 5 Dead Sea Scrolls and Syriac (see also
Septuagint): Masoretic Text *On the glorious splendour of
your majesty / and on your wonderful works I will meditate*
c 13 One manuscript of the Masoretic Text, Dead
Sea Scrolls and Syriac (see also Septuagint); most
manuscripts of the Masoretic Text do not have the
last two lines of verse 13.

---

a 1 Hebrew *Hallelu Yah*; also in verse 10

9 The LORD watches over the foreigner
   and sustains the fatherless and the
   widow,
      but he frustrates the ways of the
      wicked.

10 The LORD reigns for ever,
   your God, O Zion, for all
   generations.

   Praise the LORD.

Psalm 147

1 Praise the LORD.[a]

How good it is to sing praises to our
   God,
   how pleasant and fitting to praise
   him!

2 The LORD builds up Jerusalem;
   he gathers the exiles of Israel.
3 He heals the broken-hearted
   and binds up their wounds.
4 He determines the number of the stars
   and calls them each by name.
5 Great is our Lord and mighty in power;
   his understanding has no limit.
6 The LORD sustains the humble
   but casts the wicked to the ground.

7 Sing to the LORD with grateful praise;
   make music to our God on the harp.

8 He covers the sky with clouds;
   he supplies the earth with rain
   and makes grass grow on the hills.
9 He provides food for the cattle
   and for the young ravens when they
   call.

10 His pleasure is not in the strength of the
   horse,
   nor his delight in the legs of the
   warrior;
11 the LORD delights in those who fear
   him,
   who put their hope in his unfailing
   love.

12 Extol the LORD, Jerusalem;
   praise your God, Zion.

13 He strengthens the bars of your gates
   and blesses your people within you.
14 He grants peace to your borders
   and satisfies you with the finest of
   wheat.

15 He sends his command to the earth;
   his word runs swiftly.
16 He spreads the snow like wool
   and scatters the frost like ashes.
17 He hurls down hail like pebbles.
   Who can withstand his icy blast?
18 He sends his word and melts them;
   he stirs up his breezes, and the waters
   flow.

19 He has revealed his word to Jacob,
   his laws and decrees to Israel.
20 He has done this for no other nation;
   they do not know his laws.[b]

   Praise the LORD.

Psalm 148

1 Praise the LORD.[a]

Praise the LORD from the heavens;
   praise him in the heights above.
2 Praise him, all his angels;
   praise him, all his heavenly hosts.
3 Praise him, sun and moon;
   praise him, all you shining stars.
4 Praise him, you highest heavens
   and you waters above the skies.

5 Let them praise the name of the LORD,
   for at his command they were
   created,
6 and he established them for ever and
   ever –
   he issued a decree that will never
   pass away.

---

b 20 Masoretic Text; Dead Sea Scrolls and
Septuagint *nation; / he has not made his laws known to
them*
a 1 Hebrew *Hallelu Yah*; also in verse 14

---

a 1 Hebrew *Hallelu Yah*; also in verse 20

7 Praise the LORD from the earth,
  you great sea creatures and all ocean
    depths,
8 lightning and hail, snow and clouds,
  stormy winds that do his bidding,
9 you mountains and all hills,
  fruit trees and all cedars,
10 wild animals and all cattle,
  small creatures and flying birds,
11 kings of the earth and all nations,
  you princes and all rulers on earth,
12 young men and women,
  old men and children.

YOU WHAT?

SONG AND DANCE

MOSES SINGS A SONG
Deuteronomy 31:30 – 32:43
DEBORAH DUETS WITH BARAK
Judges 5:1–31
DAVID DANCES BEFORE THE ARK
2 Samuel 6:16–23
THE BOOGIEING PRIESTS OF BAAL
1 Kings 18:25–38
HEMAN AND HIS WORSHIP BAND
1 Chronicles 6:31–47
THE CHOIR AT THE DUNG GATE
Nehemiah 12:27–36
AMOS HATES THE MUSIC
Amos 5:21–24

13 Let them praise the name of the LORD,
  for his name alone is exalted;
    his splendour is above the earth and
      the heavens.
14 And he has raised up for his people a
    horn,*b*
  the praise of all his faithful servants,
  of Israel, the people close to his
    heart.

Praise the LORD.

---

b 14 *Horn* here symbolises strength.

Psalm 149

1 Praise the LORD.*a*

Sing to the LORD a new song,
  his praise in the assembly of his
    faithful people.

2 Let Israel rejoice in their Maker;
  let the people of Zion be glad in their
    King.
3 Let them praise his name with dancing
  and make music to him with
    tambourine and harp.
4 For the LORD takes delight in his
    people;
  he crowns the humble with
    victory.
5 Let his faithful people rejoice in this
    honour
  and sing for joy on their beds.

6 May the praise of God be in their
    mouths
  and a double-edged sword in their
    hands,
7 to inflict vengeance on the nations
  and punishment on the peoples,
8 to bind their kings with fetters,
  their nobles with shackles of iron,
9 to carry out the sentence written
    against them –
  this is the glory of all his faithful
    people.

Praise the LORD.

Psalm 150

1 Praise the LORD.*a*

Praise God in his sanctuary;
  praise him in his mighty heavens.
2 Praise him for his acts of power;
  praise him for his surpassing
    greatness.

---

a 1 Hebrew *Hallelu Yah*; also in verse 9
a 1 Hebrew *Hallelu Yah*; also in verse 6

³ Praise him with the sounding of the
    trumpet,
  praise him with the harp and lyre,
⁴ praise him with tambourine and
    dancing,
  praise him with the strings and
    pipe,

⁵ praise him with the clash of cymbals,
  praise him with resounding cymbals.

⁶ Let everything that has breath praise the
  LORD.

Praise the LORD.

PROVERBS

DATE

This book was probably written around 1000 BC

AUTHOR

Much of the book was written by King Solomon (whose life we read about in 1 Kings and 2 Chronicles)

WHAT'S IT ALL ABOUT?

The book of Proverbs is about wisdom. It's not God-given law, but the author's reflections on the way the world works and the patterns he has observed, trying to point the reader towards a godly life. The book uses a lot of figurative language and even personifies wisdom as a woman. It gives many warnings about being foolish and commends the benefits of wisdom, stating that fearing God is the beginning of all knowledge (1:7). It's split into three main sections, the first being a general introduction to wisdom (chapters 1 – 9), the second a collection of wise sayings (chapters 10 – 31:9) and the last a poem about the perfect wife (31:10–31).

WHY SHOULD WE READ IT?

- Proverbs is packed full of wisdom on how to live. Its subjects are wide and varied, including warnings against adultery and seduction, the importance of love, the value of taming the tongue, the need for discipline and advice on how to pick friends.

- To understand the value of wisdom (Proverbs 8).

- To read the description of a perfect wife (Proverbs 31)!

Andy Croft with Liza Hoeksma

Purpose and theme

1 The proverbs of Solomon son of David, king of Israel:

2 for gaining wisdom and instruction;
  for understanding words of insight;
3 for receiving instruction in prudent
    behaviour,
  doing what is right and just and fair;
4 for giving prudence to those who are
    simple,*a*
  knowledge and discretion to the
    young –
5 let the wise listen and add to their
    learning,
  and let the discerning get guidance –
6 for understanding proverbs and
    parables,
  the sayings and riddles of the wise.*b*

7 The fear of the Lord is the beginning of
    knowledge,
  but fools*c* despise wisdom and
    instruction.

Prologue: exhortations to embrace wisdom

Warning against the invitation of sinful men

8 Listen, my son, to your father's
    instruction
  and do not forsake your mother's
    teaching.
9 They are a garland to grace your head
  and a chain to adorn your neck.

10 My son, if sinful men entice you,
  do not give in to them.
11 If they say, 'Come along with us;
  let's lie in wait for innocent blood,
  let's ambush some harmless soul;
12 let's swallow them alive, like the grave,

and whole, like those who go down
    to the pit;
13 we will get all sorts of valuable things
  and fill our houses with plunder;
14 cast lots with us;
  we will all share the loot' –
15 my son, do not go along with them,
  do not set foot on their paths;
16 for their feet rush into evil,
  they are swift to shed blood.
17 How useless to spread a net
  where every bird can see it!
18 These men lie in wait for their own
    blood;
  they ambush only themselves!
19 Such are the paths of all who go after
    ill-gotten gain;
  it takes away the life of those who
    get it.

Wisdom's rebuke

20 Out in the open wisdom calls aloud,
  she raises her voice in the public
    square;
21 on top of the wall*d* she cries out,
  at the city gate she makes her speech:

22 'How long will you who are simple love
    your simple ways?
  How long will mockers delight in
    mockery
  and fools hate knowledge?
23 Repent at my rebuke!
  Then I will pour out my thoughts to
    you,
  I will make known to you my
    teachings.
24 But since you refuse to listen when I call
  and no one pays attention when I
    stretch out my hand,
25 since you disregard all my advice
  and do not accept my rebuke,
26 I in turn will laugh when disaster strikes
    you;
  I will mock when calamity overtakes
    you –
27 when calamity overtakes you like a
    storm,
  when disaster sweeps over you like a
    whirlwind,

---

a 4 The Hebrew word rendered *simple* in Proverbs
denotes a person who is gullible, without moral
direction and inclined to evil.
b 6 Or *understanding a proverb, namely, a parable, / and the
sayings of the wise, their riddles*
c 7 The Hebrew words rendered *fool* in Proverbs,
and often elsewhere in the Old Testament, denote a
person who is morally deficient.

---

d 21 Septuagint; Hebrew / *at noisy street corners*

when distress and trouble overwhelm
you.

28 'Then they will call to me but I will not
answer;
they will look for me but will not
find me,
29 since they hated knowledge
and did not choose to fear the LORD.
30 Since they would not accept my advice
and spurned my rebuke,
31 they will eat the fruit of their ways
and be filled with the fruit of their
schemes.
32 For the waywardness of the simple will
kill them,
and the complacency of fools will
destroy them;
33 but whoever listens to me will live in
safety
and be at ease, without fear of harm.'

Moral benefits of wisdom

2 My son, if you accept my words
and store up my commands within
you,
2 turning your ear to wisdom
and applying your heart to
understanding –
3 indeed, if you call out for insight
and cry aloud for understanding,
4 and if you look for it as for silver
and search for it as for hidden
treasure,
5 then you will understand the fear of the
LORD
and find the knowledge of God.
6 For the LORD gives wisdom;
from his mouth come knowledge
and understanding.
7 He holds success in store for the
upright,
he is a shield to those whose way of
life is blameless,
8 for he guards the course of the just
and protects the way of his faithful
ones.

9 Then you will understand what is right
and just
and fair – every good path.
10 For wisdom will enter your heart,

and knowledge will be pleasant to
your soul.
11 Discretion will protect you,
and understanding will guard you.

12 Wisdom will save you from the ways of
wicked men,
from men whose words are perverse,
13 who have left the straight paths
to walk in dark ways,
14 who delight in doing wrong
and rejoice in the perverseness of
evil,
15 whose paths are crooked
and who are devious in their ways.

16 Wisdom will save you also from the
adulterous woman,
from the wayward woman with her
seductive words,
17 who has left the partner of her youth
and ignored the covenant she made
before God.*a*
18 Surely her house leads down to death
and her paths to the spirits of the
dead.
19 None who go to her return
or attain the paths of life.

20 Thus you will walk in the ways of the
good
and keep to the paths of the
righteous.
21 For the upright will live in the land,
and the blameless will remain in it;
22 but the wicked will be cut off from the
land,
and the unfaithful will be torn from it.

Wisdom bestows well-being

3 My son, do not forget my teaching,
but keep my commands in your heart,
2 for they will prolong your life many
years
and bring you peace and prosperity.

3 Let love and faithfulness never leave
you;
bind them round your neck,
write them on the tablet of your heart.

---

a 17 Or *covenant of her God*

⁴ Then you will win favour and a good
  name
    in the sight of God and man.

⁵ Trust in the LORD with all your heart
    and lean not on your own
      understanding;
⁶ in all your ways submit to him,
    and he will make your paths straight.ᵃ

⁷ Do not be wise in your own eyes;
    fear the LORD and shun evil.
⁸ This will bring health to your body
    and nourishment to your bones.

⁹ Honour the LORD with your wealth,
    with the firstfruits of all your crops;
¹⁰ then your barns will be filled to
    overflowing,
    and your vats will brim over with new
      wine.

¹¹ My son, do not despise the LORD's
    discipline,
    and do not resent his rebuke,
¹² because the LORD disciplines those he
    loves,
    as a father the son he delights in.ᵇ

¹³ Blessed are those who find wisdom,
    those who gain understanding,
¹⁴ for she is more profitable than silver
    and yields better returns than gold.
¹⁵ She is more precious than rubies;
    nothing you desire can compare with
      her.
¹⁶ Long life is in her right hand;
    in her left hand are riches and
      honour.
¹⁷ Her ways are pleasant ways,
    and all her paths are peace.
¹⁸ She is a tree of life to those who take
    hold of her;
    those who hold her fast will be
      blessed.

¹⁹ By wisdom the LORD laid the earth's
    foundations,

by understanding he set the heavens
  in place;
²⁰ by his knowledge the watery depths
    were divided,
    and the clouds let drop the dew.

²¹ My son, do not let wisdom and
    understanding out of your
      sight,
    preserve sound judgment and
      discretion;
²² they will be life for you,
    an ornament to grace your neck.
²³ Then you will go on your way in safety,
    and your foot will not stumble.
²⁴ When you lie down, you will not be
    afraid;
    when you lie down, your sleep will be
      sweet.
²⁵ Have no fear of sudden disaster
    or of the ruin that overtakes the
      wicked,
²⁶ for the LORD will be at your side
    and will keep your foot from being
      snared.

²⁷ Do not withhold good from those to
    whom it is due,
    when it is in your power to act.
²⁸ Do not say to your neighbour,
    'Come back tomorrow and I'll give it
      to you' –
    when you already have it with you.
²⁹ Do not plot harm against your
    neighbour,
    who lives trustfully near you.
³⁰ Do not accuse anyone for no reason –
    when they have done you no harm.

³¹ Do not envy the violent
    or choose any of their ways.

³² For the LORD detests the perverse
    but takes the upright into his
      confidence.
³³ The LORD's curse is on the house of the
    wicked,
    but he blesses the home of the
      righteous.
³⁴ He mocks proud mockers
    but shows favour to the humble and
      oppressed.

ᵃ 6 Or *will direct your paths*
ᵇ 12 Hebrew; Septuagint *loves, / and he chastens
everyone he accepts as his child*

35 The wise inherit honour,
   but fools get only shame.

Get wisdom at any cost

4 Listen, my sons, to a father's
   instruction;
      pay attention and gain
         understanding.
2 I give you sound learning,
   so do not forsake my teaching.
3 For I too was a son to my father,
   still tender, and cherished by my
      mother.
4 Then he taught me, and he said to me,
   'Take hold of my words with all your
      heart;
   keep my commands, and you will
      live.
5 Get wisdom, get understanding;
   do not forget my words or turn away
      from them.
6 Do not forsake wisdom, and she will
      protect you;
   love her, and she will watch over you.
7 The beginning of wisdom is this: get[a]
      wisdom.
   Though it cost all you have,[b] get
      understanding.
8 Cherish her, and she will exalt you;
   embrace her, and she will honour
      you.
9 She will give you a garland to grace your
      head
   and present you with a glorious
      crown.'

10 Listen, my son, accept what I say,
   and the years of your life will be
      many.
11 I instruct you in the way of wisdom
   and lead you along straight paths.
12 When you walk, your steps will not be
      hampered;
   when you run, you will not stumble.
13 Hold on to instruction, do not let it go;
   guard it well, for it is your life.
14 Do not set foot on the path of the
      wicked
   or walk in the way of evildoers.

15 Avoid it, do not travel on it;
   turn from it and go on your way.
16 For they cannot rest until they do evil;
   they are robbed of sleep till they
      make someone stumble.
17 They eat the bread of wickedness
   and drink the wine of violence.
18 The path of the righteous is like the
      morning sun,
   shining ever brighter till the full light
      of day.
19 But the way of the wicked is like deep
      darkness;
   they do not know what makes them
      stumble.

20 My son, pay attention to what I say;
   turn your ear to my words.
21 Do not let them out of your sight,
   keep them within your heart;
22 for they are life to those who find them
   and health to one's whole body.
23 Above all else, guard your heart,
   for everything you do flows from it.
24 Keep your mouth free of perversity;
   keep corrupt talk far from your lips.
25 Let your eyes look straight ahead;
   fix your gaze directly before you.
26 Give careful thought to the[c] paths for
      your feet
   and be steadfast in all your ways.
27 Do not turn to the right or the left;
   keep your foot from evil.

Warning against adultery

5 My son, pay attention to my wisdom,
   turn your ear to my words of insight,
2 that you may maintain discretion
   and your lips may preserve
      knowledge.
3 For the lips of the adulterous woman
      drip honey,
   and her speech is smoother than oil;
4 but in the end she is bitter as gall,
   sharp as a double-edged sword.
5 Her feet go down to death;
   her steps lead straight to the grave.
6 She gives no thought to the way of life;

---

a 7 Or *Wisdom is supreme; therefore get*
b 7 Or *wisdom. / Whatever else you get*

c 26 Or *Make level*

her paths wander aimlessly, but she
   does not know it.

7 Now then, my sons, listen to me;
   do not turn aside from what I say.
8 Keep to a path far from her,
   do not go near the door of her
     house,
9 lest you lose your honour to others
   and your dignity*a* to one who is
     cruel,
10 lest strangers feast on your wealth
   and your toil enrich the house of
     another.
11 At the end of your life you will groan,
   when your flesh and body are spent.
12 You will say, 'How I hated discipline!
   How my heart spurned correction!
13 I would not obey my teachers
   or turn my ear to my instructors.
14 And I was soon in serious trouble
   in the assembly of God's people.'

15 Drink water from your own cistern,
   running water from your own well.
16 Should your springs overflow in the
    streets,
   your streams of water in the public
    squares?
17 Let them be yours alone,
   never to be shared with strangers.
18 May your fountain be blessed,
   and may you rejoice in the wife of
    your youth.
19 A loving doe, a graceful deer –
   may her breasts satisfy you always,
   may you ever be intoxicated with her
    love.
20 Why, my son, be intoxicated with
    another man's wife?
   Why embrace the bosom of a
    wayward woman?

21 For your ways are in full view of the
    Lord,
   and he examines all your paths.
22 The evil deeds of the wicked ensnare
    them;
   the cords of their sins hold them fast.

23 For lack of discipline they will die,
   led astray by their own great folly.

Warnings against folly

6 My son, if you have put up security for
   your neighbour,
   if you have shaken hands in pledge
    for a stranger,
2 you have been trapped by what you said,
   ensnared by the words of your
    mouth.
3 So do this, my son, to free yourself,
   since you have fallen into your
    neighbour's hands:
   go – to the point of exhaustion – *a*
    and give your neighbour no rest!
4 Allow no sleep to your eyes,
   no slumber to your eyelids.
5 Free yourself, like a gazelle from the
    hand of the hunter,
   like a bird from the snare of the
    fowler.

6 Go to the ant, you sluggard;
   consider its ways and be wise!
7 It has no commander,
   no overseer or ruler,
8 yet it stores its provisions in summer
   and gathers its food at harvest.

9 How long will you lie there, you
    sluggard?
   When will you get up from your
    sleep?
10 A little sleep, a little slumber,
   a little folding of the hands to rest –
11 and poverty will come on you like a thief
   and scarcity like an armed man.

12 A troublemaker and a villain,
   who goes about with a corrupt
    mouth,
13   who winks maliciously with his eye,
   signals with his feet
   and motions with his fingers,
14   who plots evil with deceit in his
    heart –
   he always stirs up conflict.
15 Therefore disaster will overtake him in
    an instant;

---

a 9 Or *years*

a 3 Or *Go and humble yourself,*

he will suddenly be destroyed –
without remedy.

16 There are six things the LORD hates,
seven that are detestable to him:
17   haughty eyes,
    a lying tongue,
    hands that shed innocent blood,
18   a heart that devises wicked
       schemes,
    feet that are quick to rush into evil,
19   a false witness who pours out lies
    and a person who stirs up conflict
       in the community.

Warning against adultery

20 My son, keep your father's command
    and do not forsake your mother's
       teaching.
21 Bind them always on your heart;
    fasten them round your neck.
22 When you walk, they will guide you;
    when you sleep, they will watch over
       you;
    when you awake, they will speak to
       you.
23 For this command is a lamp,
    this teaching is a light,
    and correction and instruction
       are the way to life,
24 keeping you from your neighbour's
       wife,
    from the smooth talk of a wayward
       woman.

25 Do not lust in your heart after her
       beauty
    or let her captivate you with her
       eyes.

26 For a prostitute can be had for a loaf of
       bread,
    but another man's wife preys on your
       very life.
27 Can a man scoop fire into his lap
    without his clothes being burned?
28 Can a man walk on hot coals
    without his feet being scorched?
29 So is he who sleeps with another man's
       wife;
    no one who touches her will go
       unpunished.

30 People do not despise a thief if he
       steals
    to satisfy his hunger when he is
       starving.
31 Yet if he is caught, he must pay
       sevenfold,
    though it costs him all the wealth of
       his house.
32 But a man who commits adultery has no
       sense;
    whoever does so destroys himself.
33 Blows and disgrace are his lot,
    and his shame will never be wiped
       away.

34 For jealousy arouses a husband's
       fury,
    and he will show no mercy when he
       takes revenge.
35 He will not accept any compensation;
    he will refuse a bribe, however great
       it is.

Warning against the adulterous woman

7 My son, keep my words
and store up my commands within
you.
2 Keep my commands and you will live;
    guard my teachings as the apple of
       your eye.
3 Bind them on your fingers;
    write them on the tablet of your
       heart.
4 Say to wisdom, 'You are my sister,'
    and to insight, 'You are my relative.'
5 They will keep you from the adulterous
       woman,
    from the wayward woman with her
       seductive words.

6 At the window of my house
    I looked down through the lattice.
7 I saw among the simple,
    I noticed among the young men,
    a youth who had no sense.
8 He was going down the street near her
       corner,
    walking along in the direction of her
       house
9 at twilight, as the day was fading,
    as the dark of night set in.

10 Then out came a woman to meet him,
　　dressed like a prostitute and with
　　crafty intent.
11 (She is unruly and defiant,
　　her feet never stay at home;
12 now in the street, now in the squares,
　　at every corner she lurks.)
13 She took hold of him and kissed him
　　and with a brazen face she said:

14 'Today I fulfilled my vows,
　　and I have food from my fellowship
　　　offering at home.
15 So I came out to meet you;
　　I looked for you and have found you!
16 I have covered my bed
　　with coloured linens from Egypt.
17 I have perfumed my bed
　　with myrrh, aloes and cinnamon.
18 Come, let's drink deeply of love till
　　　morning;
　　let's enjoy ourselves with love!
19 My husband is not at home;
　　he has gone on a long journey.
20 He took his purse filled with money
　　and will not be home till full moon.'

21 With persuasive words she led him
　　　astray;
　　she seduced him with her smooth
　　　talk.
22 All at once he followed her
　　like an ox going to the slaughter,
　　like a deer*a* stepping into a noose*b*
23　till an arrow pierces his liver,
　　like a bird darting into a snare,
　　　little knowing it will cost him his
　　　life.

24 Now then, my sons, listen to me;
　　pay attention to what I say.
25 Do not let your heart turn to her ways
　　or stray into her paths.
26 Many are the victims she has brought
　　　down;
　　her slain are a mighty throng.
27 Her house is a highway to the grave,

leading down to the chambers of
　　death.

Wisdom's call

8 Does not wisdom call out?
　　Does not understanding raise her
　　voice?
2 At the highest point along the way,
　　where the paths meet, she takes her
　　　stand;
3 beside the gate leading into the city,
　　at the entrance, she cries aloud:
4 'To you, O people, I call out;
　　I raise my voice to all humanity.
5 You who are simple, gain prudence;
　　you who are foolish, set your hearts
　　　on it.*a*
6 Listen, for I have trustworthy things to
　　　say;
　　I open my lips to speak what is right.
7 My mouth speaks what is true,
　　for my lips detest wickedness.
8 All the words of my mouth are just;
　　none of them is crooked or perverse.
9 To the discerning all of them are right;
　　they are upright to those who have
　　　found knowledge.
10 Choose my instruction instead of silver,
　　knowledge rather than choice gold,
11 for wisdom is more precious than
　　　rubies,
　　and nothing you desire can compare
　　　with her.

12 'I, wisdom, dwell together with
　　　prudence;
　　I possess knowledge and discretion.
13 To fear the LORD is to hate evil;
　　I hate pride and arrogance,
　　evil behaviour and perverse speech.
14 Counsel and sound judgment are
　　　mine;
　　I have insight, I have power.
15 By me kings reign
　　and rulers issue decrees that are just;
16 by me princes govern,
　　and nobles – all who rule on earth.*b*
17 I love those who love me,

---

a 22 Syriac (see also Septuagint); Hebrew *fool*
b 22 The meaning of the Hebrew for this line is
uncertain.

a 5 Septuagint; Hebrew *foolish, instruct your minds*
b 16 Some Hebrew manuscripts and Septuagint;
other Hebrew manuscripts *all righteous rulers*

and those who seek me find me.
¹⁸ With me are riches and honour,
   enduring wealth and prosperity.
¹⁹ My fruit is better than fine gold;
   what I yield surpasses choice silver.
²⁰ I walk in the way of righteousness,
   along the paths of justice,
²¹ bestowing a rich inheritance on those
      who love me
   and making their treasuries full.

²² 'The LORD brought me forth as the first
      of his works,[c,d]
   before his deeds of old;
²³ I was formed long ages ago,
   at the very beginning, when the world
      came to be.
²⁴ When there were no watery depths, I
      was given birth,
   when there were no springs
      overflowing with water;
²⁵ before the mountains were settled in
      place,
   before the hills, I was given birth,
²⁶ before he made the world or its fields
   or any of the dust of the earth.
²⁷ I was there when he set the heavens in
      place,
   when he marked out the horizon on
      the face of the deep,
²⁸ when he established the clouds above
   and fixed securely the fountains of
      the deep,
²⁹ when he gave the sea its boundary
   so that the waters would not overstep
      his command,
   and when he marked out the
      foundations of the earth.
³⁰   Then I was constantly[e] at his side.
   I was filled with delight day after day,
      rejoicing always in his presence,
³¹ rejoicing in his whole world
   and delighting in the human race.

³² 'Now then, my children, listen to me;
   blessed are those who keep my ways.
³³ Listen to my instruction and be wise;
   do not disregard it.

³⁴ Blessed are those who listen to me,
   watching daily at my doors,
   waiting at my doorway.
³⁵ For those who find me find life
   and receive favour from the LORD.
³⁶ But those who fail to find me harm
      themselves;
   all who hate me love death.'

Invitations of wisdom and folly

9 Wisdom has built her house;
   she has set up[a] its seven pillars.
² She has prepared her meat and mixed
      her wine;
   she has also set her table.
³ She has sent out her servants, and she
      calls
   from the highest point of the city,
⁴   'Let all who are simple come to my
      house!'
   To those who have no sense she says,
⁵   'Come, eat my food
   and drink the wine I have mixed.
⁶ Leave your simple ways and you will
      live;
   walk in the way of insight.'

⁷ Whoever corrects a mocker invites
      insults;
   whoever rebukes the wicked incurs
      abuse.
⁸ Do not rebuke mockers or they will hate
      you;
   rebuke the wise and they will love you.
⁹ Instruct the wise and they will be wiser
      still;
   teach the righteous and they will add
      to their learning.

¹⁰ The fear of the LORD is the beginning of
      wisdom,
   and knowledge of the Holy One is
      understanding.
¹¹ For through wisdom[b] your days will be
      many,
   and years will be added to your life.
¹² If you are wise, your wisdom will reward
      you;

---

c 22 Or *way*; or *dominion*
d 22 Or *The LORD possessed me at the beginning of his work*;
or *The LORD brought me forth at the beginning of his work*
e 30 Or *was the master worker*; or *was a little child*

a 1 Septuagint, Syriac and Targum; Hebrew *has
hewn out*
b 11 Septuagint, Syriac and Targum; Hebrew *me*

if you are a mocker, you alone will
    suffer.

13 Folly is an unruly woman;
    she is simple and knows nothing.

14 She sits at the door of her house,
    on a seat at the highest point of the
      city,
15 calling out to those who pass by,
    who go straight on their way,

DINOSAURS

**Dinosaurs are great! Do you have a six-year-old in your life who loves
to dazzle you with their knowledge of dinosaur names: Tyrannosaurus,
Brachiosaurus, Velociraptor?**

Proverbs 8 tells us about wisdom and the role that wisdom plays in God's
creation. The writer of Proverbs depicts wisdom as a person sitting at God's side
being delighted with everything God creates, rather like our excited six-year-
olds. (In fact, some Bible scholars think the word 'craftsman' would be better
translated as 'little child'.) It's not surprising that, as people made in God's image,
we love to find out about the world and how things work. It's amazing, and it
leads us to worship. Think about things in nature that make you say 'Wow!'
and thank God for them. You could use Psalm 148 as inspiration. If you get the
chance, try shouting it from a mountaintop!

But dinosaurs can be confusing. Why are they not in the Bible? Scientists say
dinosaur fossils are millions of years old, while the Bible says the world was
made in six days. Are the scientists wrong? Is God tricking or testing us by
putting dinosaur fossils in the ground?

The question 'Did God create in millions of years or thousands?' is one of those
issues on which Christians have different opinions. Some Christians read Genesis
1 – 3 very much as they would a science textbook. On the other hand, many
evangelical theologians and biblical scholars say that taking things at face value
is not wise: Genesis is a true story, but it's not meant to be a scientific textbook
and needs to interpreted very carefully in its historical and cultural context. So
some Christians think the world was made in six 24-hour days a few thousand
years ago and the 'millions of years' are a mistake; some think that God gave
things the appearance of age (which raises questions about how God tells us the
truth); and others think God created slowly using evolution. It's good to remember
that 'taking a passage literally' means finding out what the author intended to say!

Despite the difficult questions this topic raises, all Christians believe that the
Bible is true, that God created everything we see, that he loves us, that the
world is broken and that we need Jesus. It's worth taking time to think about
this for yourself (as Proverbs says, seek wisdom!), but don't let the debates put
you off studying the world God made using the tools of science. Praise God
for his amazing creation, go to a science museum and enjoy finding out about
the incredible creatures we call dinosaurs. Maybe some of you will be the next
generation of palaeontologists (fossil-hunters) who will amaze us all with your
discoveries.

Ruth Bancewicz

16 'Let all who are simple come to my
     house!'
To those who have no sense she
     says,
17 'Stolen water is sweet;
     food eaten in secret is delicious!'
18 But little do they know that the dead
     are there,
     that her guests are deep in the realm
     of the dead.

Proverbs of Solomon

10 The proverbs of Solomon:

A wise son brings joy to his father,
     but a foolish son brings grief to his
     mother.

2 Ill-gotten treasures have no lasting
     value,
     but righteousness delivers from
     death.

3 The LORD does not let the righteous go
     hungry,
     but he thwarts the craving of the
     wicked.

4 Lazy hands make for poverty,
     but diligent hands bring wealth.

5 He who gathers crops in summer is a
     prudent son,
     but he who sleeps during harvest is a
     disgraceful son.

6 Blessings crown the head of the
     righteous,
     but violence overwhelms the mouth
     of the wicked.*a*

7 The name of the righteous is used in
     blessings,*b*
     but the name of the wicked will rot.

8 The wise in heart accept commands,
     but a chattering fool comes to ruin.

9 Whoever walks in integrity walks
     securely,
     but whoever takes crooked paths will
     be found out.

10 Whoever winks maliciously causes
     grief,
     and a chattering fool comes to ruin.

11 The mouth of the righteous is a fountain
     of life,
     but the mouth of the wicked conceals
     violence.

12 Hatred stirs up conflict,
     but love covers over all wrongs.

13 Wisdom is found on the lips of the
     discerning,
     but a rod is for the back of one who
     has no sense.

14 The wise store up knowledge,
     but the mouth of a fool invites ruin.

15 The wealth of the rich is their fortified
     city,
     but poverty is the ruin of the poor.

16 The wages of the righteous is life,
     but the earnings of the wicked are sin
     and death.

17 Whoever heeds discipline shows the
     way to life,
     but whoever ignores correction leads
     others astray.

18 Whoever conceals hatred with lying lips
     and spreads slander is a fool.

19 Sin is not ended by multiplying words,
     but the prudent hold their tongues.

20 The tongue of the righteous is choice
     silver,
     but the heart of the wicked is of little
     value.

21 The lips of the righteous nourish
     many,
     but fools die for lack of sense.

a 6 Or *righteous, / but the mouth of the wicked conceals
violence*
b 7 See Gen. 48:20.

22 The blessing of the LORD brings wealth,
  without painful toil for it.

23 A fool finds pleasure in wicked
    schemes,
  but a person of understanding
    delights in wisdom.

24 What the wicked dread will overtake
    them;
  what the righteous desire will be
    granted.

25 When the storm has swept by, the
    wicked are gone,
  but the righteous stand firm for ever.

26 As vinegar to the teeth and smoke to the
    eyes,
  so are sluggards to those who send
    them.

27 The fear of the LORD adds length to life,
  but the years of the wicked are cut
    short.

28 The prospect of the righteous is joy,
  but the hopes of the wicked come to
    nothing.

29 The way of the LORD is a refuge for the
    blameless,
  but it is the ruin of those who do
    evil.

30 The righteous will never be uprooted,
  but the wicked will not remain in the
    land.

31 From the mouth of the righteous comes
    the fruit of wisdom,
  but a perverse tongue will be
    silenced.

32 The lips of the righteous know what
    finds favour,
  but the mouth of the wicked only
    what is perverse.

11 The LORD detests dishonest scales,
  but accurate weights find favour
  with him.

2 When pride comes, then comes
    disgrace,
  but with humility comes wisdom.

3 The integrity of the upright guides
    them,
  but the unfaithful are destroyed by
    their duplicity.

4 Wealth is worthless in the day of wrath,
  but righteousness delivers from
    death.

5 The righteousness of the blameless
    makes their paths straight,
  but the wicked are brought down by
    their own wickedness.

6 The righteousness of the upright
    delivers them,
  but the unfaithful are trapped by evil
    desires.

7 Hopes placed in mortals die with them;
  all the promise of[a] their power comes
    to nothing.

8 The righteous person is rescued from
    trouble,
  and it falls on the wicked instead.

9 With their mouths the godless destroy
    their neighbours,
  but through knowledge the righteous
    escape.

10 When the righteous prosper, the city
    rejoices;
  when the wicked perish, there are
    shouts of joy.

11 Through the blessing of the upright a
    city is exalted,
  but by the mouth of the wicked it is
    destroyed.

12 Whoever derides their neighbour has no
    sense,

---

*a 7 Two Hebrew manuscripts; most Hebrew
manuscripts, Vulgate, Syriac and Targum When the
wicked die, their hope perishes; / all they expected from*

but the one who has understanding
   holds their tongue.

13 A gossip betrays a confidence,
   but a trustworthy person keeps a
     secret.

14 For lack of guidance a nation falls,
   but victory is won through many
     advisors.

15 Whoever puts up security for a stranger
     will surely suffer,
   but whoever refuses to shake hands
     in pledge is safe.

16 A kind-hearted woman gains honour,
   but ruthless men gain only wealth.

17 Those who are kind benefit themselves,
   but the cruel bring ruin on
     themselves.

18 A wicked person earns deceptive wages,
   but the one who sows righteousness
     reaps a sure reward.

19 Truly the righteous attain life,
   but whoever pursues evil finds
     death.

20 The LORD detests those whose hearts are
     perverse,
   but he delights in those whose ways
     are blameless.

21 Be sure of this: the wicked will not go
     unpunished,
   but those who are righteous will go
     free.

22 Like a gold ring in a pig's snout
   is a beautiful woman who shows no
     discretion.

23 The desire of the righteous ends only in
     good,
   but the hope of the wicked only in
     wrath.

24 One person gives freely, yet gains even
     more;

another withholds unduly, but comes
   to poverty.

25 A generous person will prosper;
   whoever refreshes others will be
     refreshed.

26 People curse the one who hoards grain,
   but they pray God's blessing on the
     one who is willing to sell.

27 Whoever seeks good finds favour,
   but evil comes to one who searches
     for it.

28 Those who trust in their riches will fall,
   but the righteous will thrive like a
     green leaf.

29 Whoever brings ruin on their family will
     inherit only wind,
   and the fool will be servant to the
     wise.

30 The fruit of the righteous is a tree of
     life,
   and the one who is wise saves lives.

31 If the righteous receive their due on
     earth,
   how much more the ungodly and the
     sinner!

12 Whoever loves discipline loves
     knowledge,
   but whoever hates correction is
     stupid.

2 Good people obtain favour from the
     LORD,
   but he condemns those who devise
     wicked schemes.

3 No one can be established through
     wickedness,
   but the righteous cannot be
     uprooted.

4 A wife of noble character is her
     husband's crown,
   but a disgraceful wife is like decay in
     his bones.

5 The plans of the righteous are just,
   but the advice of the wicked is
      deceitful.

6 The words of the wicked lie in wait for
      blood,
   but the speech of the upright rescues
      them.

7 The wicked are overthrown and are no
      more,
   but the house of the righteous stands
      firm.

8 A person is praised according to their
      prudence,
   and one with a warped mind is
      despised.

9 Better to be a nobody and yet have a
      servant
   than pretend to be somebody and
      have no food.

10 The righteous care for the needs of their
      animals,
   but the kindest acts of the wicked are
      cruel.

11 Those who work their land will have
      abundant food,
   but those who chase fantasies have
      no sense.

12 The wicked desire the stronghold of
      evildoers,
   but the root of the righteous endures.

13 Evildoers are trapped by their sinful
      talk,
   and so the innocent escape trouble.

14 From the fruit of their lips people are
      filled with good things,
   and the work of their hands brings
      them reward.

15 The way of fools seems right to them,
   but the wise listen to advice.

16 Fools show their annoyance at once,
   but the prudent overlook an insult.

17 An honest witness tells the truth,
   but a false witness tells lies.

18 The words of the reckless pierce like
      swords,
   but the tongue of the wise brings
      healing.

19 Truthful lips endure for ever,
   but a lying tongue lasts only a
      moment.

20 Deceit is in the hearts of those who plot
      evil,
   but those who promote peace have
      joy.

21 No harm overtakes the righteous,
   but the wicked have their fill of
      trouble.

22 The Lord detests lying lips,
   but he delights in people who are
      trustworthy.

23 The prudent keep their knowledge to
      themselves,
   but a fool's heart blurts out folly.

24 Diligent hands will rule,
   but laziness ends in forced
      labour.

25 Anxiety weighs down the heart,
   but a kind word cheers it up.

26 The righteous choose their friends
      carefully,
   but the way of the wicked leads them
      astray.

27 The lazy do not roast*a* any game,
   but the diligent feed on the riches of
      the hunt.

28 In the way of righteousness there is life;
   along that path is immortality.

---

a 27 The meaning of the Hebrew for this word is
uncertain.

HEALING & MIRACLES 9

Healing in our words

The tongue: one of the smallest parts of our body, yet it can carry the greatest power (Proverbs 12:18).

In fact, it carries the power of life and death (Proverbs 18:21). It's easy to miss or misunderstand the importance of this knowledge because of the simplicity of the message, but our words can change the direction of people's choices and therefore change their lives. We find many verses in Proverbs that spotlight the power of the tongue, and although we don't often think of healing being brought by what we say, everything we say carries power.

How many things do we say without thinking? Our lives spill out through our words all the time. Life hits me with unexpected events and whatever is inside me comes pouring out each time I take a hit. As sharing our hearts is part of life, we don't have to worry too much about that, but we do have to worry about what is spilling. It's quite difficult to filter out the negative things that pop into our minds and only say the good things. So, if I'm worried about what will spill out of my mouth, I really need to worry about what I'm filled with and what my heart looks like (Luke 6:45). Whatever we think about is what affects our heart, but whatever is in our heart is what will spill from our mouths. If I'm feeding myself the importance of learning to love and what it means to be like Jesus, eventually this thinking will affect everything I say.

Sometimes it takes real wisdom to wait and see what God has placed on people's lives, instead of the behaviour they may be acting out in the present. But wisdom says, 'Instead of saying the obvious, I choose to be silent until I can see what's really inside this person.' When we're able to catch God's heart for people, wisdom can be released through our words. This is when healing can change everything.

There's wisdom in knowing when to speak and when to be silent. My parents used to say, 'If you can't say anything nice, just don't say anything at all.' Well, that meant silence for me on many occasions! Think before speaking, think about what you say, and if its intent is not to be encouraging, then don't say anything. Don't allow yourself to say anything unless it's wrapped in kindness. When you speak words of healing, you will notice how healing begins to take place – and not only will it bring healing to whoever you're speaking to, it will also empower you in ministering.

I've seen how words have the power to change someone's life. For the most part, people know what's wrong with them, but to have someone point out their potential can bring healing to someone who has never believed before that they could change. Instead of confirming the death someone already feels, it speaks to the life that can be.

Christy Wimber

 Mark 5:25–34   Galatians 5:1–15

13

A wise son heeds his father's instruction,
but a mocker does not respond to rebukes.

2 From the fruit of their lips people enjoy good things,
but the unfaithful have an appetite for violence.

3 Those who guard their lips preserve their lives,
but those who speak rashly will come to ruin.

4 A sluggard's appetite is never filled,
but the desires of the diligent are fully satisfied.

5 The righteous hate what is false,
but the wicked make themselves obnoxious
and bring shame on themselves.

6 Righteousness guards the person of integrity,
but wickedness overthrows the sinner.

7 One person pretends to be rich, yet has nothing;
another pretends to be poor, yet has great wealth.

8 A person's riches may ransom their life,
but the poor cannot respond to threatening rebukes.

9 The light of the righteous shines brightly,
but the lamp of the wicked is snuffed out.

10 Where there is strife, there is pride,
but wisdom is found in those who take advice.

11 Dishonest money dwindles away,
but whoever gathers money little by little makes it grow.

12 Hope deferred makes the heart sick,
but a longing fulfilled is a tree of life.

13 Whoever scorns instruction will pay for it,
but whoever respects a command is rewarded.

14 The teaching of the wise is a fountain of life,
turning a person from the snares of death.

15 Good judgment wins favour,
but the way of the unfaithful leads to their destruction.*a*

16 All who are prudent act with*b* knowledge,
but fools expose their folly.

17 A wicked messenger falls into trouble,
but a trustworthy envoy brings healing.

18 Whoever disregards discipline comes to poverty and shame,
but whoever heeds correction is honoured.

19 A longing fulfilled is sweet to the soul,
but fools detest turning from evil.

20 Walk with the wise and become wise,
for a companion of fools suffers harm.

21 Trouble pursues the sinner,
but the righteous are rewarded with good things.

22 A good person leaves an inheritance for their children's children,
but a sinner's wealth is stored up for the righteous.

23 An unploughed field produces food for the poor,
but injustice sweeps it away.

---

a 15 Septuagint and Syriac; the meaning of the Hebrew for this phrase is uncertain.
b 16 Or *prudent protect themselves through*

24 Whoever spares the rod hates their children,
> but the one who loves their children is careful to discipline them.

25 The righteous eat to their hearts' content,
> but the stomach of the wicked goes hungry.

14 The wise woman builds her house, but with her own hands the foolish one tears hers down.

2 Whoever fears the LORD walks uprightly,
> but those who despise him are devious in their ways.

3 A fool's mouth lashes out with pride,
> but the lips of the wise protect them.

FRIENDSHIP 10

Choose wisely

The Bible can be really practical and shows us that God is interested in all areas of our lives, including our friendships. The book of Proverbs gives us lots of wisdom on all sorts of subjects and it mentions friendship a number of times.

In Proverbs 13 we are told to choose our friends wisely, because we become like the people we spend time with. You have probably noticed it before: you hang out with someone for long enough and you take on their mannerisms and start finding you have the same opinions and characteristics as each other. With that in mind, think for a minute about the type of person you want to be. What are the qualities you would most like to possess (like kindness, wisdom, purity or compassion)? Who do you know who has those qualities you admire? Those are the people you should be trying to spend time with and have amongst your group of friends, because, as the writer of Proverbs says, if you want to be wise, spend time with a wise person.

This doesn't mean you can't have friends who are different from you. It especially doesn't mean you shouldn't have friendships outside church, or with people who are struggling in various ways. Friends from all walks of life and in all types of circumstances may have many qualities we can admire and learn from. What it does mean is that we should make sure that among our closest friends and the people we see most often are people we want to be like. People we admire, people who will help us go where we want to be in our lives and relationship with Jesus. In Proverbs 27:17 we're told, *'As iron sharpens iron, so one person sharpens another.'* Our friendships shape us, so let's be intentional in choosing the people we spend time with.

Ali Martin

 Matthew 26:69–75

4 Where there are no oxen, the manger is
empty,
but from the strength of an ox come
abundant harvests.

5 An honest witness does not deceive,
but a false witness pours out lies.

6 The mocker seeks wisdom and finds
none,
but knowledge comes easily to the
discerning.

7 Stay away from a fool,
for you will not find knowledge on
their lips.

8 The wisdom of the prudent is to give
thought to their ways,
but the folly of fools is deception.

9 Fools mock at making amends for
sin,
but goodwill is found among the
upright.

10 Each heart knows its own bitterness,
and no one else can share its joy.

11 The house of the wicked will be
destroyed,
but the tent of the upright will
flourish.

12 There is a way that appears to be
right,
but in the end it leads to death.

13 Even in laughter the heart may ache,
and rejoicing may end in grief.

14 The faithless will be fully repaid for
their ways,
and the good rewarded for theirs.

15 The simple believe anything,
but the prudent give thought to their
steps.

16 The wise fear the LORD and shun evil,
but a fool is hotheaded and yet feels
secure.

17 A quick-tempered person does foolish
things,
and the one who devises evil
schemes is hated.

18 The simple inherit folly,
but the prudent are crowned with
knowledge.

19 Evildoers will bow down in the presence
of the good,
and the wicked at the gates of the
righteous.

20 The poor are shunned even by their
neighbours,
but the rich have many friends.

21 It is a sin to despise one's neighbour,
but blessed is the one who is kind to
the needy.

22 Do not those who plot evil go astray?
But those who plan what is good
find*a* love and faithfulness.

23 All hard work brings a profit,
but mere talk leads only to poverty.

24 The wealth of the wise is their crown,
but the folly of fools yields folly.

25 A truthful witness saves lives,
but a false witness is deceitful.

26 Whoever fears the LORD has a secure
fortress,
and for their children it will be a
refuge.

27 The fear of the LORD is a fountain of life,
turning a person from the snares of
death.

28 A large population is a king's glory,
but without subjects a prince is
ruined.

29 Whoever is patient has great
understanding,

_____
a 22 Or *show*

but one who is quick-tempered
displays folly.

30 A heart at peace gives life to the body,
but envy rots the bones.

31 Whoever oppresses the poor shows
contempt for their Maker,
but whoever is kind to the needy
honours God.

32 When calamity comes, the wicked are
brought down,
but even in death the righteous seek
refuge in God.

33 Wisdom reposes in the heart of the
discerning
and even among fools she lets herself
be known.*b*

34 Righteousness exalts a nation,
but sin condemns any people.

35 A king delights in a wise servant,
but a shameful servant arouses his
fury.

15 A gentle answer turns away wrath,
but a harsh word stirs up
anger.

2 The tongue of the wise adorns
knowledge,
but the mouth of the fool gushes
folly.

3 The eyes of the LORD are everywhere,
keeping watch on the wicked and the
good.

4 The soothing tongue is a tree of life,
but a perverse tongue crushes the
spirit.

5 A fool spurns a parent's discipline,
but whoever heeds correction shows
prudence.

6 The house of the righteous contains
great treasure,
but the income of the wicked brings
ruin.

7 The lips of the wise spread
knowledge,
but the hearts of fools are not
upright.

8 The LORD detests the sacrifice of the
wicked,
but the prayer of the upright pleases
him.

9 The LORD detests the way of the
wicked,
but he loves those who pursue
righteousness.

10 Stern discipline awaits anyone who
leaves the path;
the one who hates correction will
die.

11 Death and Destruction*a* lie open before
the LORD –
how much more do human hearts!

12 Mockers resent correction,
so they avoid the wise.

13 A happy heart makes the face cheerful,
but heartache crushes the spirit.

14 The discerning heart seeks knowledge,
but the mouth of a fool feeds on
folly.

15 All the days of the oppressed are
wretched,
but the cheerful heart has a continual
feast.

16 Better a little with the fear of the LORD
than great wealth with turmoil.

17 Better a dish of vegetables with love
than a fattened calf with hatred.

b 33 Hebrew; Septuagint and Syriac *discerning / but in the heart of fools she is not known*

a 11 Hebrew *Abaddon*

18 A hot-tempered person stirs up conflict,
 but the one who is patient calms a
  quarrel.

19 The way of the sluggard is blocked with
  thorns,
 but the path of the upright is a
  highway.

20 A wise son brings joy to his father,
 but a foolish man despises his
  mother.

21 Folly brings joy to one who has no
  sense,
 but whoever has understanding
  keeps a straight course.

22 Plans fail for lack of counsel,
 but with many advisors they succeed.

23 A person finds joy in giving an apt
  reply —
 and how good is a timely word!

24 The path of life leads upward for the
  prudent
 to keep them from going down to the
  realm of the dead.

25 The Lord tears down the house of the
  proud,
 but he sets the widow's boundary
  stones in place.

26 The Lord detests the thoughts of the
  wicked,
 but gracious words are pure in his
  sight.

27 The greedy bring ruin to their
  households,
 but the one who hates bribes will live.

28 The heart of the righteous weighs its
  answers,
 but the mouth of the wicked gushes
  evil.

29 The Lord is far from the wicked,
 but he hears the prayer of the
  righteous.

30 Light in a messenger's eyes brings joy to
  the heart,
 and good news gives health to the
  bones.

31 Whoever heeds life-giving correction
 will be at home among the wise.

32 Those who disregard discipline despise
  themselves,
 but the one who heeds correction
  gains understanding.

33 Wisdom's instruction is to fear the
  Lord,
 and humility comes before honour.

16 To humans belong the plans of the
  heart,
 but from the Lord comes the proper
  answer of the tongue.

2 All a person's ways seem pure to them,
 but motives are weighed by the Lord.

3 Commit to the Lord whatever you do,
 and he will establish your plans.

4 The Lord works out everything to its
  proper end —
 even the wicked for a day of disaster.

5 The Lord detests all the proud of heart.
 Be sure of this: they will not go
  unpunished.

6 Through love and faithfulness sin is
  atoned for;
 through the fear of the Lord evil is
  avoided.

7 When the Lord takes pleasure in
  anyone's way,
 he causes their enemies to make
  peace with them.

8 Better a little with righteousness
 than much gain with injustice.

9 In their hearts humans plan their
  course,
 but the Lord establishes their steps.

10 The lips of a king speak as an oracle,
and his mouth does not betray
justice.

11 Honest scales and balances belong to
the LORD;
all the weights in the bag are of his
making.

12 Kings detest wrongdoing,
for a throne is established through
righteousness.

13 Kings take pleasure in honest lips;
they value the one who speaks what is
right.

14 A king's wrath is a messenger of death,
but the wise will appease it.

15 When a king's face brightens, it means
life;
his favour is like a rain cloud in
spring.

16 How much better to get wisdom than
gold,
to get insight rather than silver!

17 The highway of the upright avoids evil;
those who guard their ways preserve
their lives.

18 Pride goes before destruction,
a haughty spirit before a fall.

19 Better to be lowly in spirit along with
the oppressed
than to share plunder with the proud.

20 Whoever gives heed to instruction
prospers,*a*
and blessed is the one who trusts in
the LORD.

21 The wise in heart are called discerning,
and gracious words promote
instruction.*b*

22 Prudence is a fountain of life to the
prudent,
but folly brings punishment to fools.

23 The hearts of the wise make their
mouths prudent,
and their lips promote instruction.*c*

24 Gracious words are a honeycomb,
sweet to the soul and healing to the
bones.

25 There is a way that appears to be right,
but in the end it leads to death.

26 The appetite of labourers works for
them;
their hunger drives them on.

27 A scoundrel plots evil,
and on their lips it is like a scorching
fire.

28 A perverse person stirs up conflict,
and a gossip separates close friends.

29 A violent person entices their neighbour
and leads them down a path that is
not good.

30 Whoever winks with their eye is plotting
perversity;
whoever purses their lips is bent on
evil.

31 Grey hair is a crown of splendour;
it is attained in the way of
righteousness.

32 Better a patient person than a warrior,
one with self-control than one who
takes a city.

33 The lot is cast into the lap,
but its every decision is from the
LORD.

17 Better a dry crust with peace and
quiet

---

a 20 Or *whoever speaks prudently finds what is good*
b 21 Or *words make a person persuasive*

c 23 Or *prudent / and make their lips persuasive*

than a house full of feasting, with
strife.

² A prudent servant will rule over a
disgraceful son,
and will share the inheritance as one
of the family.

³ The crucible for silver and the furnace
for gold,
but the LORD tests the heart.

⁴ A wicked person listens to deceitful lips;
a liar pays attention to a destructive
tongue.

⁵ Whoever mocks the poor shows
contempt for their Maker;
whoever gloats over disaster will not
go unpunished.

⁶ Children's children are a crown to the
aged,
and parents are the pride of their
children.

⁷ Eloquent lips are unsuited to a godless
fool –
how much worse lying lips to a ruler!

⁸ A bribe is seen as a charm by the one
who gives it;
they think success will come at every
turn.

⁹ Whoever would foster love covers over
an offence,
but whoever repeats the matter
separates close friends.

¹⁰ A rebuke impresses a discerning person
more than a hundred lashes a fool.

¹¹ Evildoers foster rebellion against God;
the messenger of death will be sent
against them.

¹² Better to meet a bear robbed of her cubs
than a fool bent on folly.

¹³ Evil will never leave the house
of one who pays back evil for good.

¹⁴ Starting a quarrel is like breaching a dam;
so drop the matter before a dispute
breaks out.

¹⁵ Acquitting the guilty and condemning
the innocent –
the LORD detests them both.

¹⁶ Why should fools have money in hand
to buy wisdom,
when they are not able to understand
it?

¹⁷ A friend loves at all times,
and a brother is born for a time of
adversity.

¹⁸ One who has no sense shakes hands in
pledge
and puts up security for a neighbour.

¹⁹ Whoever loves a quarrel loves sin;
whoever builds a high gate invites
destruction.

²⁰ One whose heart is corrupt does not
prosper;
one whose tongue is perverse falls
into trouble.

²¹ To have a fool for a child brings grief;
there is no joy for the parent of a
godless fool.

²² A cheerful heart is good medicine,
but a crushed spirit dries up the
bones.

²³ The wicked accept bribes in secret
to pervert the course of justice.

²⁴ A discerning person keeps wisdom in
view,
but a fool's eyes wander to the ends of
the earth.

²⁵ A foolish son brings grief to his father
and bitterness to the mother who
bore him.

²⁶ If imposing a fine on the innocent is not
good,

surely to flog honest officials is not
  right.

27 The one who has knowledge uses words
  with restraint,
    and whoever has understanding is
      even-tempered.

28 Even fools are thought wise if they keep
  silent,
    and discerning if they hold their
      tongues.

18 An unfriendly person pursues
      selfish ends
    and against all sound judgment starts
      quarrels.

2 Fools find no pleasure in understanding
    but delight in airing their own
      opinions.

3 When wickedness comes, so does
      contempt,
    and with shame comes reproach.

4 The words of the mouth are deep
      waters,
    but the fountain of wisdom is a
      rushing stream.

5 It is not good to be partial to the wicked
    and so deprive the innocent of
      justice.

6 The lips of fools bring them strife,
    and their mouths invite a beating.

7 The mouths of fools are their undoing,
    and their lips are a snare to their very
      lives.

8 The words of a gossip are like choice
      morsels;
    they go down to the inmost parts.

9 One who is slack in his work
    is brother to one who destroys.

10 The name of the Lord is a fortified
      tower;
    the righteous run to it and are safe.

11 The wealth of the rich is their fortified
      city;
    they imagine it a wall too high to
      scale.

12 Before a downfall the heart is haughty,
    but humility comes before
      honour.

13 To answer before listening –
    that is folly and shame.

14 The human spirit can endure in times of
      illness,
    but a crushed spirit who can bear?

15 The heart of the discerning acquires
      knowledge,
    for the ears of the wise seek it out.

16 A gift opens the way
    and ushers the giver into the
      presence of the great.

17 In a lawsuit the first to speak seems
      right,
    until someone comes forward and
      cross-examines.

18 Casting the lot settles disputes
    and keeps strong opponents apart.

19 A brother wronged is more unyielding
      than a fortified city;
    disputes are like the barred gates of a
      citadel.

20 From the fruit of their mouth a person's
      stomach is filled;
    with the harvest of their lips they are
      satisfied.

21 The tongue has the power of life and
      death,
    and those who love it will eat its
      fruit.

22 He who finds a wife finds what is good
    and receives favour from the Lord.

23 The poor plead for mercy,
    but the rich answer harshly.

24 One who has unreliable friends soon
    comes to ruin,
    but there is a friend who sticks closer
    than a brother.

19 Better the poor whose way of life is
    blameless
    than a fool whose lips are perverse.

2 Desire without knowledge is not good –
    how much more will hasty feet miss
    the way!

3 A person's own folly leads to their ruin,
    yet their heart rages against the LORD.

4 Wealth attracts many friends,
    but even the closest friend of the
    poor person deserts them.

5 A false witness will not go unpunished,
    and whoever pours out lies will not
    go free.

6 Many curry favour with a ruler,
    and everyone is the friend of one who
    gives gifts.

7 The poor are shunned by all their
    relatives –
    how much more do their friends
    avoid them!
Though the poor pursue them with
    pleading,
    they are nowhere to be found.*a*

8 The one who gets wisdom loves life;
    the one who cherishes understanding
    will soon prosper.

9 A false witness will not go unpunished,
    and whoever pours out lies will
    perish.

10 It is not fitting for a fool to live in
    luxury –
    how much worse for a slave to rule
    over princes!

11 A person's wisdom yields patience;
    it is to one's glory to overlook an
    offence.

12 A king's rage is like the roar of a lion,
    but his favour is like dew on the grass.

13 A foolish child is a father's ruin,
    and a quarrelsome wife is like
    the constant dripping of a leaky roof.

14 Houses and wealth are inherited from
    parents,
    but a prudent wife is from the LORD.

15 Laziness brings on deep sleep,
    and the shiftless go hungry.

16 Whoever keeps commandments keeps
    their life,
    but whoever shows contempt for
    their ways will die.

17 Whoever is kind to the poor lends to the
    LORD,
    and he will reward them for what they
    have done.

18 Discipline your children, for in that
    there is hope;
    do not be a willing party to their
    death.

19 A hot-tempered person must pay the
    penalty;
    rescue them, and you will have to do
    it again.

20 Listen to advice and accept discipline,
    and at the end you will be counted
    among the wise.

21 Many are the plans in a person's heart,
    but it is the LORD's purpose that
    prevails.

22 What a person desires is unfailing
    love;*b*
    better to be poor than a liar.

---

a 7 The meaning of the Hebrew for this sentence
is uncertain.

b 22 Or *Greed is a person's shame*

23 The fear of the LORD leads to life;
   then one rests content, untouched by
      trouble.

24 A sluggard buries his hand in the
      dish;
   he will not even bring it back to his
      mouth!

25 Flog a mocker, and the simple will learn
      prudence;
   rebuke the discerning, and they will
      gain knowledge.

26 Whoever robs their father and drives
      out their mother
   is a child who brings shame and
      disgrace.

27 Stop listening to instruction, my son,
   and you will stray from the words of
      knowledge.

28 A corrupt witness mocks at justice,
   and the mouth of the wicked gulps
      down evil.

29 Penalties are prepared for mockers,
   and beatings for the backs of
      fools.

20 Wine is a mocker and beer a
      brawler;
   whoever is led astray by them is not
      wise.

2 A king's wrath strikes terror like the roar
      of a lion;
   those who anger him forfeit their
      lives.

3 It is to one's honour to avoid strife,
   but every fool is quick to quarrel.

4 Sluggards do not plough in season;
   so at harvest time they look but find
      nothing.

5 The purposes of a person's heart are
      deep waters,
   but one who has insight draws them
      out.

6 Many claim to have unfailing love,
   but a faithful person who can find?

7 The righteous lead blameless lives;
   blessed are their children after
      them.

8 When a king sits on his throne to
      judge,
   he winnows out all evil with his
      eyes.

9 Who can say, 'I have kept my heart pure;
   I am clean and without sin'?

10 Differing weights and differing
      measures –
   the LORD detests them both.

11 Even small children are known by their
      actions,
   so is their conduct really pure and
      upright?

12 Ears that hear and eyes that see –
   the LORD has made them both.

13 Do not love sleep or you will grow
      poor;
   stay awake and you will have food to
      spare.

14 'It's no good, it's no good!' says the
      buyer –
   then goes off and boasts about the
      purchase.

15 Gold there is, and rubies in abundance,
   but lips that speak knowledge are a
      rare jewel.

16 Take the garment of one who puts up
      security for a stranger;
   hold it in pledge if it is done for an
      outsider.

17 Food gained by fraud tastes sweet,
   but one ends up with a mouth full of
      gravel.

18 Plans are established by seeking advice;
   so if you wage war, obtain guidance.

¹⁹ A gossip betrays a confidence;
>> so avoid anyone who talks too much.

²⁰ If someone curses their father or
>> mother,
>> their lamp will be snuffed out in pitch
>> darkness.

²¹ An inheritance claimed too soon
>> will not be blessed at the end.

²² Do not say, 'I'll pay you back for this
>> wrong!'
>> Wait for the LORD, and he will avenge
>> you.

²³ The LORD detests differing weights,
>> and dishonest scales do not please
>> him.

²⁴ A person's steps are directed by the
>> LORD.
>> How then can anyone understand
>> their own way?

²⁵ It is a trap to dedicate something rashly
>> and only later to consider one's vows.

²⁶ A wise king winnows out the wicked;
>> he drives the threshing wheel over
>> them.

²⁷ The human spirit is^a the lamp of the
>> LORD
>> that sheds light on one's inmost
>> being.

²⁸ Love and faithfulness keep a king safe;
>> through love his throne is made
>> secure.

²⁹ The glory of young men is their
>> strength,
>> grey hair the splendour of the old.

³⁰ Blows and wounds scrub away evil,
>> and beatings purge the inmost being.

21 In the LORD's hand the king's heart
>> is a stream of water

that he channels towards all who
>> please him.

² A person may think their own ways are
>> right,
>> but the LORD weighs the heart.

³ To do what is right and just
>> is more acceptable to the LORD than
>> sacrifice.

⁴ Haughty eyes and a proud heart –
>> the unploughed field of the wicked –
>> produce sin.

⁵ The plans of the diligent lead to profit
>> as surely as haste leads to poverty.

⁶ A fortune made by a lying tongue
>> is a fleeting vapour and a deadly
>> snare.^a

FACT

NUMBERS

There are 66 books in the Bible: 39 in the
Old Testament and 27 in the New. These
books are split up into 1,189 chapters and
then into 31,101 verses.

⁷ The violence of the wicked will drag
>> them away,
>> for they refuse to do what is right.

⁸ The way of the guilty is devious,
>> but the conduct of the innocent is
>> upright.

⁹ Better to live on a corner of the roof
>> than share a house with a
>> quarrelsome wife.

a 27 Or *A person's words are*

a 6 Some Hebrew manuscripts, Septuagint and
Vulgate; most Hebrew manuscripts *vapour for those
who seek death*

10 The wicked crave evil;
   their neighbours get no mercy from
      them.

11 When a mocker is punished, the simple
      gain wisdom;
   by paying attention to the wise they
      get knowledge.

12 The Righteous One[b] takes note of the
      house of the wicked
   and brings the wicked to ruin.

13 Whoever shuts their ears to the cry of
      the poor
   will also cry out and not be answered.

14 A gift given in secret soothes anger,
   and a bribe concealed in the cloak
      pacifies great wrath.

15 When justice is done, it brings joy to the
      righteous
   but terror to evildoers.

16 Whoever strays from the path of
      prudence
   comes to rest in the company of the
      dead.

17 Whoever loves pleasure will become
      poor;
   whoever loves wine and olive oil will
      never be rich.

18 The wicked become a ransom for the
      righteous,
   and the unfaithful for the upright.

19 Better to live in a desert
   than with a quarrelsome and nagging
      wife.

20 The wise store up choice food and olive
      oil,
   but fools gulp theirs down.

21 Whoever pursues righteousness and love
   finds life, prosperity[c] and honour.

22 One who is wise can go up against the
      city of the mighty
   and pull down the stronghold in
      which they trust.

23 Those who guard their mouths and their
      tongues
   keep themselves from calamity.

24 The proud and arrogant person –
      'Mocker' is his name –
   behaves with insolent fury.

25 The craving of a sluggard will be the
      death of him,
   because his hands refuse to work.
26 All day long he craves for more,
   but the righteous give without
      sparing.

27 The sacrifice of the wicked is
      detestable –
   how much more so when brought
      with evil intent!

28 A false witness will perish,
   but a careful listener will testify
      successfully.

29 The wicked put up a bold front,
   but the upright give thought to their
      ways.

30 There is no wisdom, no insight, no plan
   that can succeed against the LORD.

31 The horse is made ready for the day of
      battle,
   but victory rests with the LORD.

22 A good name is more desirable
      than great riches;
   to be esteemed is better than silver or
      gold.

2 Rich and poor have this in common:
   The LORD is the Maker of them all.

3 The prudent see danger and take
      refuge,
   but the simple keep going and pay
      the penalty.

b 12 Or *The righteous person*
c 21 Or *righteousness*

4 Humility is the fear of the LORD;
    its wages are riches and honour and
    life.

5 In the paths of the wicked are snares and
    pitfalls,
    but those who would preserve their
    life stay far from them.

6 Start children off on the way they should
    go,
    and even when they are old they will
    not turn from it.

7 The rich rule over the poor,
    and the borrower is slave to the
    lender.

8 Whoever sows injustice reaps calamity,
    and the rod they wield in fury will be
    broken.

9 The generous will themselves be
    blessed,
    for they share their food with the
    poor.

10 Drive out the mocker, and out goes
    strife;
    quarrels and insults are ended.

11 One who loves a pure heart and who
    speaks with grace
    will have the king for a friend.

12 The eyes of the LORD keep watch over
    knowledge,
    but he frustrates the words of the
    unfaithful.

13 The sluggard says, 'There's a lion
    outside!
    I'll be killed in the public square!'

14 The mouth of an adulterous woman is a
    deep pit;
    a man who is under the LORD's wrath
    falls into it.

15 Folly is bound up in the heart of a child,
    but the rod of discipline will drive it
    far away.

16 One who oppresses the poor to increase
    his wealth
    and one who gives gifts to the rich –
    both come to poverty.

Thirty sayings of the wise

Saying 1

17 Pay attention and turn your ear to the
    sayings of the wise;
    apply your heart to what I teach,
18 for it is pleasing when you keep them in
    your heart
    and have all of them ready on your
    lips.
19 So that your trust may be in the LORD,
    I teach you today, even you.
20 Have I not written thirty sayings for
    you,
    sayings of counsel and knowledge,
21 teaching you to be honest and to speak
    the truth,
    so that you bring back truthful
    reports
    to those you serve?

Saying 2

22 Do not exploit the poor because they
    are poor
    and do not crush the needy in court,
23 for the LORD will take up their case
    and will exact life for life.

Saying 3

24 Do not make friends with a
    hot-tempered person,
    do not associate with one easily
    angered,
25 or you may learn their ways
    and get yourself ensnared.

Saying 4

26 Do not be one who shakes hands in
    pledge
    or puts up security for debts;
27 if you lack the means to pay,
    your very bed will be snatched from
    under you.

Saying 5

28 Do not move an ancient boundary
    stone
    set up by your ancestors.

Saying 6

²⁹ Do you see someone skilled in their
    work?
    They will serve before kings;
    they will not serve before officials of
    low rank.

Saying 7

23 When you sit to dine with a ruler,
    note well what*ᵃ* is before you,
² and put a knife to your throat
    if you are given to gluttony.
³ Do not crave his delicacies,
    for that food is deceptive.

Saying 8

⁴ Do not wear yourself out to get rich;
    do not trust your own cleverness.
⁵ Cast but a glance at riches, and they are
    gone,
    for they will surely sprout wings
    and fly off to the sky like an eagle.

Saying 9

⁶ Do not eat the food of a stingy host,
    do not crave his delicacies;
⁷ for he is the kind of person
    who is always thinking about the
    cost.*ᵇ*
    'Eat and drink,' he says to you,
    but his heart is not with you.
⁸ You will vomit up the little you have
    eaten
    and will have wasted your
    compliments.

Saying 10

⁹ Do not speak to fools,
    for they will scorn your prudent
    words.

Saying 11

¹⁰ Do not move an ancient boundary
    stone
    or encroach on the fields of the
    fatherless,
¹¹ for their Defender is strong;
    he will take up their case against you.

Saying 12

¹² Apply your heart to instruction
    and your ears to words of knowledge.

Saying 13

¹³ Do not withhold discipline from a child;
    if you punish them with the rod, they
    will not die.
¹⁴ Punish them with the rod
    and save them from death.

Saying 14

¹⁵ My son, if your heart is wise,
    then my heart will be glad indeed;
¹⁶ my inmost being will rejoice
    when your lips speak what is right.

Saying 15

¹⁷ Do not let your heart envy sinners,
    but always be zealous for the fear of
    the LORD.
¹⁸ There is surely a future hope for you,
    and your hope will not be cut off.

Saying 16

¹⁹ Listen, my son, and be wise,
    and set your heart on the right path:
²⁰ do not join those who drink too much
    wine
    or gorge themselves on meat,
²¹ for drunkards and gluttons become
    poor,
    and drowsiness clothes them in rags.

Saying 17

²² Listen to your father, who gave you life,
    and do not despise your mother
    when she is old.
²³ Buy the truth and do not sell it —
    wisdom, instruction and insight as
    well.
²⁴ The father of a righteous child has great
    joy;
    a man who fathers a wise son rejoices
    in him.
²⁵ May your father and mother rejoice;
    may she who gave you birth be joyful!

Saying 18

²⁶ My son, give me your heart
    and let your eyes delight in my ways,
²⁷ for an adulterous woman is a deep pit,

---

a 1 Or *who*
b 7 Or *for as he thinks within himself, / so he is*; or *for as he
puts on a feast, / so he is*

and a wayward wife is a narrow well.
28 Like a bandit she lies in wait
and multiplies the unfaithful among
men.

Saying 19

29 Who has woe? Who has sorrow?
Who has strife? Who has
complaints?
Who has needless bruises? Who has
bloodshot eyes?
30 Those who linger over wine,
who go to sample bowls of mixed
wine.
31 Do not gaze at wine when it is red,
when it sparkles in the cup,
when it goes down smoothly!
32 In the end it bites like a snake
and poisons like a viper.
33 Your eyes will see strange sights,
and your mind will imagine
confusing things.
34 You will be like one sleeping on the
high seas,
lying on top of the rigging.
35 'They hit me,' you will say, 'but I'm not
hurt!
They beat me, but I don't feel it!
When will I wake up
so I can find another drink?'

Saying 20

24 Do not envy the wicked,
do not desire their company;
2 for their hearts plot violence,
and their lips talk about making
trouble.

Saying 21

3 By wisdom a house is built,
and through understanding it is
established;
4 through knowledge its rooms are filled
with rare and beautiful treasures.

Saying 22

5 The wise prevail through great power,
and those who have knowledge
muster their strength.
6 Surely you need guidance to wage war,
and victory is won through many
advisors.

Saying 23

7 Wisdom is too high for fools;
in the assembly at the gate they must
not open their mouths.

Saying 24

8 Whoever plots evil
will be known as a schemer.
9 The schemes of folly are sin,
and people detest a mocker.

Saying 25

10 If you falter in a time of trouble,
how small is your strength!
11 Rescue those being led away to death;
hold back those staggering towards
slaughter.
12 If you say, 'But we knew nothing about
this,'
does not he who weighs the heart
perceive it?
Does not he who guards your life know
it?
Will he not repay everyone according
to what they have done?

Saying 26

13 Eat honey, my son, for it is good;
honey from the comb is sweet to your
taste.
14 Know also that wisdom is like honey for
you:
if you find it, there is a future hope for
you,
and your hope will not be cut off.

Saying 27

15 Do not lurk like a thief near the house
of the righteous,
do not plunder their
dwelling-place;
16 for though the righteous fall seven
times, they rise again,
but the wicked stumble when
calamity strikes.

Saying 28

17 Do not gloat when your enemy falls;
when they stumble, do not let your
heart rejoice,
18 or the LORD will see and disapprove
and turn his wrath away from them.

Saying 29

19 Do not fret because of evildoers
    or be envious of the wicked,
20 for the evildoer has no future hope,
    and the lamp of the wicked will be
        snuffed out.

Saying 30

21 Fear the LORD and the king, my son,
    and do not join with rebellious
        officials,
22 for those two will send sudden
        destruction on them,
    and who knows what calamities they
        can bring?

Further sayings of the wise

23 These also are sayings of the wise:

To show partiality in judging is not
    good:
24 whoever says to the guilty, 'You are
        innocent,'
    will be cursed by peoples and
        denounced by nations.
25 But it will go well with those who
        convict the guilty,
    and rich blessing will come on them.

26 An honest answer
    is like a kiss on the lips.

27 Put your outdoor work in order
    and get your fields ready;
    after that, build your house.

28 Do not testify against your neighbour
        without cause –
    would you use your lips to mislead?
29 Do not say, 'I'll do to them as they have
        done to me;
    I'll pay them back for what they did.'

30 I went past the field of a sluggard,
    past the vineyard of someone who
        has no sense;
31 thorns had come up everywhere,
    the ground was covered with weeds,
    and the stone wall was in ruins.
32 I applied my heart to what I observed
    and learned a lesson from what I saw:
33 a little sleep, a little slumber,

a little folding of the hands to rest –
34 and poverty will come on you like a thief
    and scarcity like an armed man.

More proverbs of Solomon

25 These are more proverbs of Solomon, compiled by the men of
Hezekiah king of Judah:

2 It is the glory of God to conceal a matter;
    to search out a matter is the glory of
        kings.
3 As the heavens are high and the earth is
        deep,
    so the hearts of kings are
        unsearchable.

4 Remove the dross from the silver,
    and a silversmith can produce a
        vessel;
5 remove wicked officials from the king's
        presence,
    and his throne will be established
        through righteousness.

6 Do not exalt yourself in the king's
        presence,
    and do not claim a place among his
        great men;
7 it is better for him to say to you, 'Come
        up here,'
    than for him to humiliate you before
        his nobles.

What you have seen with your eyes
8   do not bring*a* hastily to court,
    for what will you do in the end
        if your neighbour puts you to shame?

9 If you take your neighbour to court,
    do not betray another's confidence,
10 or the one who hears it may shame you
    and the charge against you will
        stand.

11 Like apples*b* of gold in settings of silver
    is a ruling rightly given.
12 Like an earring of gold or an ornament
        of fine gold

---

a 7,8 Or *nobles / on whom you had set your eyes.* / *8Do not go*
b 11 Or possibly *apricots*

is the rebuke of a wise judge to a
　　listening ear.

13 Like a snow-cooled drink at harvest time
　　is a trustworthy messenger to the one
　　　who sends him;
　　he refreshes the spirit of his master.
14 Like clouds and wind without rain
　　is one who boasts of gifts never given.

15 Through patience a ruler can be
　　　persuaded,
　　and a gentle tongue can break a bone.

16 If you find honey, eat just enough –
　　too much of it, and you will vomit.
17 Seldom set foot in your neighbour's
　　　house –
　　too much of you, and they will hate
　　　you.

18 Like a club or a sword or a sharp arrow
　　is one who gives false testimony
　　　against a neighbour.
19 Like a broken tooth or a lame foot
　　is reliance on the unfaithful in a time
　　　of trouble.
20 Like one who takes away a garment on a
　　　cold day,
　　or like vinegar poured on a wound,
　　is one who sings songs to a heavy
　　　heart.

21 If your enemy is hungry, give him food
　　　to eat;
　　if he is thirsty, give him water to
　　　drink.
22 In doing this, you will heap burning
　　　coals on his head,
　　and the LORD will reward you.

23 Like a north wind that brings
　　　unexpected rain
　　is a sly tongue – which provokes a
　　　horrified look.

24 Better to live on a corner of the roof
　　than share a house with a
　　　quarrelsome wife.

25 Like cold water to a weary soul
　　is good news from a distant land.

26 Like a muddied spring or a polluted well
　　are the righteous who give way to the
　　　wicked.

27 It is not good to eat too much honey,
　　nor is it honourable to search out
　　　matters that are too deep.

28 Like a city whose walls are broken
　　　through
　　is a person who lacks self-control.

26 Like snow in summer or rain in
　　harvest,
　　honour is not fitting for a fool.
2 Like a fluttering sparrow or a darting
　　　swallow,
　　an undeserved curse does not come
　　　to rest.
3 A whip for the horse, a bridle for the
　　　donkey,
　　and a rod for the backs of fools!
4 Do not answer a fool according to his
　　　folly,
　　or you yourself will be just like him.
5 Answer a fool according to his folly,
　　or he will be wise in his own eyes.
6 Sending a message by the hands of a
　　　fool
　　is like cutting off one's feet or
　　　drinking poison.
7 Like the useless legs of one who is lame
　　is a proverb in the mouth of a fool.
8 Like tying a stone in a sling
　　is the giving of honour to a fool.
9 Like a thorn-bush in a drunkard's hand
　　is a proverb in the mouth of a fool.
10 Like an archer who wounds at random
　　is one who hires a fool or any
　　　passer-by.
11 As a dog returns to its vomit,
　　so fools repeat their folly.
12 Do you see a person wise in their own
　　　eyes?
　　There is more hope for a fool than for
　　　them.

13 A sluggard says, 'There's a lion in the
　　　road,
　　a fierce lion roaming the streets!'
14 As a door turns on its hinges,
　　so a sluggard turns on his bed.
15 A sluggard buries his hand in the dish;

he is too lazy to bring it back to his
mouth.
16 A sluggard is wiser in his own eyes
than seven people who answer
discreetly.

17 Like one who grabs a stray dog by the
ears
is someone who rushes into a quarrel
not their own.

18 Like a maniac shooting
flaming arrows of death
19 is one who deceives their neighbour
and says, 'I was only joking!'

20 Without wood a fire goes out;
without a gossip a quarrel dies down.
21 As charcoal to embers and as wood to
fire,
so is a quarrelsome person for
kindling strife.
22 The words of a gossip are like choice
morsels;
they go down to the inmost parts.

23 Like a coating of silver dross on
earthenware
are fervent*a* lips with an evil heart.
24 Enemies disguise themselves with their
lips,
but in their hearts they harbour
deceit.
25 Though their speech is charming, do
not believe them,
for seven abominations fill their
hearts.
26 Their malice may be concealed by
deception,
but their wickedness will be exposed
in the assembly.
27 Whoever digs a pit will fall into it;
if someone rolls a stone, it will roll
back on them.
28 A lying tongue hates those it hurts,
and a flattering mouth works ruin.

27 Do not boast about tomorrow,
for you do not know what a day
may bring.

---
a 23 Hebrew; Septuagint *smooth*

2 Let someone else praise you, and not
your own mouth;
an outsider, and not your own lips.

3 Stone is heavy and sand a burden,
but a fool's provocation is heavier
than both.

4 Anger is cruel and fury overwhelming,
but who can stand before jealousy?

5 Better is open rebuke
than hidden love.

6 Wounds from a friend can be trusted,
but an enemy multiplies kisses.

7 One who is full loathes honey from the
comb,
but to the hungry even what is bitter
tastes sweet.

8 Like a bird that flees its nest
is anyone who flees from home.

9 Perfume and incense bring joy to the
heart,
and the pleasantness of a friend
springs from their heartfelt advice.

10 Do not forsake your friend or a friend of
your family,
and do not go to your relative's
house when disaster strikes
you –
better a neighbour nearby than a
relative far away.

11 Be wise, my son, and bring joy to my
heart;
then I can answer anyone who treats
me with contempt.

12 The prudent see danger and take
refuge,
but the simple keep going and pay
the penalty.

13 Take the garment of one who puts up
security for a stranger;
hold it in pledge if it is done for an
outsider.

RELATIONSHIPS 4

TO CORRECT AND REBUKE

If you're anything like either of us, when you're sitting in a room with someone you know is about to challenge your behaviour, there's that toe-curling moment of awkwardness as you prepare for what's about to be said.

Similarly, if you're the person giving your opinion on someone's behaviour, then that can be just as difficult. It's easy to work yourself up into a complete state, every time you have to challenge anyone on any aspect of their life, work or play.

At a first read of Proverbs 27:5–6, *'hidden love'* and *'open rebuke'* don't seem easy to compare. The first thing to notice is that when it talks about hidden love, it doesn't mean an illicit relationship you don't tell anyone about. In this instance it means that love speaks out when it's difficult. Openly telling our friends when they hurt and disappoint us is not only better than secret anger or disdain, it's better than secret love which, through staying silent, allows people to continue hurting others or themselves.

Practically, though, there are good ways to correct people, and there are terrible ways! First, look at yourself. A wise friend told me that before correcting another, you should take a look at your own heart. If you feel nauseous at the thought of having this conversation, if you worry about it at night and it feels like a real burden, then you're probably OK to go ahead. It should be a reassurance that we find it difficult to say things that may be hurtful to our friends, even if it's for their best. If any part of you is excited, however slightly, about telling them off, then perhaps you should carefully consider your motivation. Second, give thought to where and when you should say it: it's probably best not late at night and not in front of others. If you're not sure whether to say anything at all, consider this acronym. Is it: **T**rue, **H**elpful, **I**nspiring, **N**ecessary and **K**ind (THINK)?

Correction is a two-way street. In this passage it talks about giving correction, but the other part is about receiving it. Our closest friends and particularly those we're dating will probably see the greater extremes of us at our best and our worst. We should trust our friends to speak honestly into our lives and we should carefully weigh up the advice or observations they offer.

Practical tips

- Choose friends who will be honest, rather than tell you what you want to hear.
- Don't be afraid to challenge your friends when you don't think they're right.
- Don't jump straight into an argument after either giving or receiving correction. Pray about it, and wait until you can discuss it calmly.
- The nursery rhyme 'Sticks and stones' is absolute nonsense! Bruises can fade from the body, but words don't fade from the memory. Words are irretrievable and can be hurtful, so use them wisely (James 3).

Jane Plackett and Calum Dyke

 1 Corinthians 7:32–34   1 Corinthians 13

14 If anyone loudly blesses their neighbour
    early in the morning,
    it will be taken as a curse.

15 A quarrelsome wife is like the dripping
    of a leaky roof in a rainstorm;
16 restraining her is like restraining the
    wind
    or grasping oil with the hand.

17 As iron sharpens iron,
    so one person sharpens another.

18 The one who guards a fig-tree will eat its
    fruit,
    and whoever protects their master
    will be honoured.

19 As water reflects the face,
    so one's life reflects the heart.*a*

20 Death and Destruction*b* are never
    satisfied,
    and neither are human eyes.

21 The crucible for silver and the furnace
    for gold,
    but people are tested by their praise.

22 Though you grind a fool in a mortar,
    grinding them like grain with a
    pestle,
    you will not remove their folly from
    them.

23 Be sure you know the condition of your
    flocks,
    give careful attention to your herds;
24 for riches do not endure for ever,
    and a crown is not secure for all
    generations.
25 When the hay is removed and new
    growth appears
    and the grass from the hills is
    gathered in,
26 the lambs will provide you with
    clothing,
    and the goats with the price of a
    field.

27 You will have plenty of goats' milk to
    feed your family
    and to nourish your female servants.

28 The wicked flee though no one
    pursues,
    but the righteous are as bold as a lion.

2 When a country is rebellious, it has
    many rulers,
    but a ruler with discernment and
    knowledge maintains order.

3 A ruler*a* who oppresses the poor
    is like driving rain that leaves no
    crops.

4 Those who forsake instruction praise
    the wicked,
    but those who heed it resist them.

5 Evildoers do not understand what is
    right,
    but those who seek the LORD
    understand it fully.

6 Better the poor whose way of life is
    blameless
    than the rich whose ways are
    perverse.

7 A discerning son heeds instruction,
    but a companion of gluttons
    disgraces his father.

8 Whoever increases wealth by taking
    interest or profit from the poor
    amasses it for another, who will be
    kind to the poor.

9 If anyone turns a deaf ear to my
    instruction,
    even their prayers are detestable.

10 Whoever leads the upright along an evil
    path
    will fall into their own trap,
    but the blameless will receive a good
    inheritance.

---

a 19 Or *so others reflect your heart back to you*
b 20 Hebrew *Abaddon*

a 3 Or *A poor person*

11 The rich are wise in their own eyes;
   one who is poor and discerning sees
   how deluded they are.

12 When the righteous triumph, there is
    great elation;
   but when the wicked rise to power,
    people go into hiding.

13 Whoever conceals their sins does not
    prosper,
   but the one who confesses and
    renounces them finds mercy.

14 Blessed is the one who always trembles
    before God,
   but whoever hardens their heart falls
    into trouble.

15 Like a roaring lion or a charging bear
   is a wicked ruler over a helpless
    people.

16 A tyrannical ruler practises extortion,
   but one who hates ill-gotten gain will
    enjoy a long reign.

17 Anyone tormented by the guilt of
    murder
   will seek refuge in the grave;
   let no one hold them back.

18 The one whose way of life is blameless is
    kept safe,
   but the one whose ways are perverse
    will fall into the pit.*b*

19 Those who work their land will have
    abundant food,
   but those who chase fantasies will
    have their fill of poverty.

20 A faithful person will be richly blessed,
   but one eager to get rich will not go
    unpunished.

21 To show partiality is not good –
   yet a person will do wrong for a piece
    of bread.

22 The stingy are eager to get rich
   and are unaware that poverty awaits
    them.

23 Whoever rebukes a person will in the
    end gain favour
   rather than one who has a flattering
    tongue.

24 Whoever robs their father or mother
   and says, 'It's not wrong,'
   is partner to one who destroys.

25 The greedy stir up conflict,
   but those who trust in the LORD will
    prosper.

26 Those who trust in themselves are fools,
   but those who walk in wisdom are
    kept safe.

27 Those who give to the poor will lack
    nothing,
   but those who close their eyes to
    them receive many curses.

28 When the wicked rise to power, people
    go into hiding;
   but when the wicked perish, the
    righteous thrive.

29 Whoever remains stiff-necked
    after many rebukes
   will suddenly be destroyed – without
    remedy.

2 When the righteous thrive, the people
    rejoice;
   when the wicked rule, the people
    groan.

3 A man who loves wisdom brings joy to
    his father,
   but a companion of prostitutes
    squanders his wealth.

4 By justice a king gives a country stability,
   but those who are greedy for*a* bribes
    tear it down.

---

b 18 Syriac (see Septuagint); Hebrew *into one*   *a* 4 Or *who give*

5 Those who flatter their neighbours
   are spreading nets for their feet.

6 Evildoers are snared by their own sin,
   but the righteous shout for joy and
     are glad.

7 The righteous care about justice for the
     poor,
   but the wicked have no such concern.

8 Mockers stir up a city,
   but the wise turn away anger.

9 If a wise person goes to court with a
     fool,
   the fool rages and scoffs, and there is
     no peace.

10 The bloodthirsty hate a person of
     integrity
   and seek to kill the upright.

11 Fools give full vent to their rage,
   but the wise bring calm in the end.

12 If a ruler listens to lies,
   all his officials become wicked.

13 The poor and the oppressor have this in
     common:
   the Lord gives sight to the eyes of
     both.

14 If a king judges the poor with fairness,
   his throne will be established for ever.

15 A rod and a reprimand impart wisdom,
   but a child left undisciplined
     disgraces its mother.

16 When the wicked thrive, so does sin,
   but the righteous will see their
     downfall.

17 Discipline your children, and they will
     give you peace;
   they will bring you the delights you
     desire.

18 Where there is no revelation, people
     cast off restraint;

but blessed is the one who heeds
   wisdom's instruction.

19 Servants cannot be corrected by mere
     words;
   though they understand, they will
     not respond.

20 Do you see someone who speaks in
     haste?
   There is more hope for a fool than for
     them.

21 A servant pampered from youth
   will turn out to be insolent.

22 An angry person stirs up conflict,
   and a hot-tempered person commits
     many sins.

23 Pride brings a person low,
   but the lowly in spirit gain honour.

24 The accomplices of thieves are their own
     enemies;
   they are put under oath and dare not
     testify.

25 Fear of man will prove to be a snare,
   but whoever trusts in the Lord is kept
     safe.

26 Many seek an audience with a ruler,
   but it is from the Lord that one gets
     justice.

27 The righteous detest the dishonest;
   the wicked detest the upright.

Sayings of Agur

30 The sayings of Agur son of Jakeh –
   an inspired utterance.

This man's utterance to Ithiel:

'I am weary, God,
   but I can prevail.*a*
2 Surely I am only a brute, not a man;
   I do not have human understanding.

---

a 1 With a different word division of the Hebrew;
Masoretic Text *utterance to Ithiel, / to Ithiel and Ukal:*

³ I have not learned wisdom,
   nor have I attained to the knowledge
      of the Holy One.
⁴ Who has gone up to heaven and come
      down?
   Whose hands have gathered up the
      wind?
   Who has wrapped up the waters in a
      cloak?
   Who has established all the ends of
      the earth?
   What is his name, and what is the name
      of his son?
   Surely you know!

⁵ 'Every word of God is flawless;
   he is a shield to those who take
      refuge in him.
⁶ Do not add to his words,
   or he will rebuke you and prove you a
      liar.

⁷ 'Two things I ask of you, LORD;
   do not refuse me before I die:
⁸ keep falsehood and lies far from me;
   give me neither poverty nor riches,
   but give me only my daily bread.
⁹ Otherwise, I may have too much and
      disown you
   and say, "Who is the LORD?"
   Or I may become poor and steal,
   and so dishonour the name of my
      God.

¹⁰ 'Do not slander a servant to their
      master,
   or they will curse you, and you will
      pay for it.

¹¹ 'There are those who curse their
      fathers
   and do not bless their mothers;
¹² those who are pure in their own eyes
   and yet are not cleansed of their
      filth;
¹³ those whose eyes are ever so haughty,
   whose glances are so disdainful;
¹⁴ those whose teeth are swords
   and whose jaws are set with knives
   to devour the poor from the earth
   and the needy from among the
      human race.

¹⁵ 'The leech has two daughters.
   "Give! Give!" they cry.

   'There are three things that are never
      satisfied,
   four that never say, "Enough!":
¹⁶ the grave, the barren womb,
   land, which is never satisfied with
      water,
   and fire, which never says, "Enough!"

¹⁷ 'The eye that mocks a father,
   that scorns an aged mother,
   will be pecked out by the ravens of the
      valley,
   will be eaten by the vultures.

¹⁸ 'There are three things that are too
      amazing for me,
   four that I do not understand:
¹⁹ the way of an eagle in the sky,
   the way of a snake on a rock,
   the way of a ship on the high seas,
   and the way of a man with a young
      woman.

²⁰ 'This is the way of an adulterous
      woman:
   she eats and wipes her mouth
   and says, "I've done nothing wrong."

²¹ 'Under three things the earth trembles,
   under four it cannot bear up:
²² a servant who becomes king,
   a godless fool who gets plenty to eat,
²³ a contemptible woman who gets
      married,
   and a servant who displaces her
      mistress.

²⁴ 'Four things on earth are small,
   yet they are extremely wise:
²⁵ ants are creatures of little strength,
   yet they store up their food in the
      summer;
²⁶ hyraxes are creatures of little power,
   yet they make their home in the
      crags;
²⁷ locusts have no king,
   yet they advance together in ranks;
²⁸ a lizard can be caught with the hand,
   yet it is found in kings' palaces.

²⁹ 'There are three things that are stately in
   their stride,
   four that move with stately bearing:
³⁰ a lion, mighty among beasts,
   who retreats before nothing;
³¹ a strutting cock, a he-goat,
   and a king secure against revolt.^b

³² 'If you play the fool and exalt yourself,
   or if you plan evil,

---

^b 31 The meaning of the Hebrew for this phrase is
uncertain.

clap your hand over your mouth!
³³ For as churning cream produces butter,
   and as twisting the nose produces
   blood,
   so stirring up anger produces strife.'

Sayings of King Lemuel

31 The sayings of King Lemuel – an inspired utterance his mother taught
him.

² Listen, my son! Listen, son of my
   womb!

JUSTICE AND MERCY 3

A LITTLE ACTION...

Oppressed people don't have the opportunity to speak up for themselves; often their voice has been taken away by their oppressors. This means that they are left completely alone in their injustice unless someone else is willing to get involved, stand with them and help them find their voice.

Who are we talking about? Women and children sold into prostitution; farmers who aren't given a living wage for their crops; people who work in appalling and dangerous conditions in order to make cheap clothes for us; Christians who are imprisoned for their faith; citizens persecuted for criticising their government.

Situations like these are heartbreaking, but the amazing thing is that today there are so many ways in which we can speak up for the voiceless. Through the internet we can participate in brilliant campaigns that challenge those in power to serve the last, the least and the lost. Every time you sign a petition, like a Facebook campaign page, or email a politician or business leader, you are using your voice to call out for justice.

There are other ways you can make your voice heard as well, like buying fair-trade clothes and food. Every time you buy a fair-trade bar of chocolate or T-shirt, you are saying that it is not OK to rip people off, but that every person who does a day's work deserves a day's pay.

The amazing thing is that when all of us take these small actions, they add up to a huge amount of noise. We may never meet those for whom we are speaking, but we can be sure that God sees. He sees our every action and inaction, just as he sees every tear cried by those who are suffering injustice. He says, *'Whoever oppresses the poor shows contempt for their Maker, but whoever is kind to the needy honours God'* (Proverbs 14:31).

David Westlake

 Leviticus 25:8   Isaiah 58

Listen, my son, the answer to my
prayers!
³ Do not spend your strength*a* on women,
your vigour on those who ruin kings.

⁴ It is not for kings, Lemuel –
it is not for kings to drink wine,

_____

a 3 Or *wealth*

not for rulers to crave beer,
⁵ lest they drink and forget what has been
decreed,
and deprive all the oppressed of their
rights.
⁶ Let beer be for those who are perishing,
wine for those who are in anguish!
⁷ Let them drink and forget their poverty
and remember their misery no more.

MONEY 7

MAKING MONEY

The Pope recently said it was our moral duty to create wealth. Controversial.

We read stories in the Bible about the rich young ruler and how entering heaven as a rich man is as difficult as a camel passing through the eye of a needle. Is the Pope wrong? Should we be poor? Would that make it easier to enter heaven? What is our perception of having wealth? Is it something we all secretly want, but won't admit, because we think it's not holy?

If we follow Jesus' principles in how we create wealth, so that we're making money in an ethical way, and if we use our money as Scripture guides us, we can debunk the idea that creating wealth is bad.

I love Proverbs 31, which describes a mother working hard and creating wealth. She has all sorts of money-making projects – buying land, growing vineyards, trading her garments – the equivalent of a businesswoman. With her wealth she provides for her family, buys her children good-quality clothes to keep them warm, pays her staff and is generous to those in need. This creation of wealth isn't just 'not bad'. It's good.

Wealth used appropriately contributes to life and society in amazing ways. It allows us to pay for what we need, to celebrate life together. It alleviates poverty and enables people to give to others. If someone lived in poverty and didn't have a job, it would be great if they started earning money and creating wealth – this would be something we would celebrate.

There is a difference between the love of money and striving for riches, and creating wealth. As with every area of life, we need to be aware of our motives and self-first attitudes, but we don't need to think of making money as something to be ashamed of, or awkward about, or fearful of. In fact, if we make and spend our money in a way that is honouring to God, we can encourage and be thankful for the creation of wealth.

Kiera Singlehurst-Phyo

◀◀ Acts 2   James 5:4 ▶▶

8 Speak up for those who cannot speak
    for themselves,
    for the rights of all who are destitute.
9 Speak up and judge fairly;
    defend the rights of the poor and
    needy.

Epilogue: the wife of noble character

10 *b* A wife of noble character who can find?
    She is worth far more than rubies.
11 Her husband has full confidence in her
    and lacks nothing of value.
12 She brings him good, not harm,
    all the days of her life.
13 She selects wool and flax
    and works with eager hands.
14 She is like the merchant ships,
    bringing her food from afar.
15 She gets up while it is still night;
    she provides food for her family
    and portions for her female servants.
16 She considers a field and buys it;
    out of her earnings she plants a
    vineyard.
17 She sets about her work vigorously;
    her arms are strong for her tasks.
18 She sees that her trading is profitable,
    and her lamp does not go out at
    night.
19 In her hand she holds the distaff
    and grasps the spindle with her
    fingers.

20 She opens her arms to the poor
    and extends her hands to the needy.
21 When it snows, she has no fear for her
    household;
    for all of them are clothed in scarlet.
22 She makes coverings for her bed;
    she is clothed in fine linen and
    purple.
23 Her husband is respected at the city
    gate,
    where he takes his seat among the
    elders of the land.
24 She makes linen garments and sells
    them,
    and supplies the merchants with
    sashes.
25 She is clothed with strength and dignity;
    she can laugh at the days to come.
26 She speaks with wisdom,
    and faithful instruction is on her
    tongue.
27 She watches over the affairs of her
    household
    and does not eat the bread of
    idleness.
28 Her children arise and call her blessed;
    her husband also, and he praises her:
29 'Many women do noble things,
    but you surpass them all.'
30 Charm is deceptive, and beauty is
    fleeting;
    but a woman who fears the LORD is to
    be praised.
31 Honour her for all that her hands have
    done,
    and let her works bring her praise at
    the city gate.

---

b 10 Verses 10-31 are an acrostic poem, the verses
of which begin with the successive letters of the
Hebrew alphabet.

ECCLESIASTES

DATE AND AUTHOR

Unknown. Sometimes Ecclesiastes is attributed to King Solomon (who we read about in 1 Kings and 2 Chronicles), which would date the book to around 1000 BC.

WHAT'S IT ALL ABOUT?

Ecclesiastes is one of the Wisdom books and at first glance it can seem a bit melancholy, if not downright depressing. The writer is an old man looking back over his life and reflecting on how futile and pointless much of it has been. He seems to have been a wise man, who has known great pleasures and riches, but they failed to satisfy him. He struggled with one of the world's great mysteries: what is the meaning of life? His conclusion is that without God there can be no satisfactory answer to that question. He urges the reader, *'Fear God and keep his commandments, for this is the duty of all mankind'* (Ecclesiastes 12:12).

WHY SHOULD WE READ IT?

- To see how God brings meaning and purpose to an otherwise confusing existence.

- As a reminder to enjoy all that we can of life.

- To read the well-known passage which declares, *'There is a time for everything…'* (Ecclesiastes 3).

- To learn about the importance of friendship (Ecclesiastes 4).

- To read wise teaching regarding the love of money (Ecclesiastes 5:10).

- To see why we should trust and obey God (Ecclesiastes 12).

Andy Croft with Liza Hoeksma

Everything is meaningless

1 The words of the Teacher,*a* son of David, king of Jerusalem:

2 'Meaningless! Meaningless!'
    says the Teacher.
  'Utterly meaningless!
    Everything is meaningless.'

3 What do people gain from all their
      labours
    at which they toil under the sun?
4 Generations come and generations go,
    but the earth remains for ever.
5 The sun rises and the sun sets,
    and hurries back to where it rises.
6 The wind blows to the south
    and turns to the north;
  round and round it goes,
    ever returning on its course.
7 All streams flow into the sea,
    yet the sea is never full.
  To the place the streams come from,
    there they return again.
8 All things are wearisome,
    more than one can say.
  The eye never has enough of seeing,
    nor the ear its fill of hearing.
9 What has been will be again,
    what has been done will be done
      again;
    there is nothing new under the sun.
10 Is there anything of which one can say,
    'Look! This is something new'?
  It was here already, long ago;
    it was here before our time.
11 No one remembers the former
      generations,
    and even those yet to come
  will not be remembered
    by those who follow them.

Wisdom is meaningless

12 I, the Teacher, was king over Israel in Jerusalem. 13 I applied my mind to study and to explore by wisdom all that is done under the heavens. What a heavy burden God has laid on mankind! 14 I have seen all the things that are done under the sun; all of them are meaningless, a chasing after the wind.

15 What is crooked cannot be
      straightened;
    what is lacking cannot be counted.

16 I said to myself, 'Look, I have increased in wisdom more than anyone who has ruled over Jerusalem before me; I have experienced much of wisdom and knowledge.' 17 Then I applied myself to the understanding of wisdom, and also of madness and folly, but I learned that this, too, is a chasing after the wind.

18 For with much wisdom comes much
      sorrow;
    the more knowledge, the more grief.

Pleasures are meaningless

2 I said to myself, 'Come now, I will test you with pleasure to find out what is good.' But that also proved to be meaningless. 2 'Laughter,' I said, 'is madness. And what does pleasure accomplish?' 3 I tried cheering myself with wine, and embracing folly – my mind still guiding me with wisdom. I wanted to see what was good for people to do under the heavens during the few days of their lives.

4 I undertook great projects: I built houses for myself and planted vineyards. 5 I made gardens and parks and planted all kinds of fruit trees in them. 6 I made reservoirs to water groves of flourishing trees. 7 I bought male and female slaves and had other slaves who were born in my house. I also owned more herds and flocks than anyone in Jerusalem before me. 8 I amassed silver and gold for myself, and the treasure of kings and provinces. I acquired male and female singers, and a harem*a* as well – the delights of a man's heart. 9 I became greater by far than anyone in Jerusalem before me. In all this my wisdom stayed with me.

---

a 1 Or *the leader of the assembly;* also in verses 2 and 12

a 8 The meaning of the Hebrew for this phrase is uncertain.

10 I denied myself nothing my eyes
    desired;
I refused my heart no pleasure.
My heart took delight in all my labour,
    and this was the reward for all my
    toil.
11 Yet when I surveyed all that my hands
    had done
    and what I had toiled to achieve,
everything was meaningless, a chasing
    after the wind;
    nothing was gained under the sun.

Wisdom and folly are meaningless

12 Then I turned my thoughts to consider
    wisdom,
    and also madness and folly.
What more can the king's successor do
    than what has already been done?
13 I saw that wisdom is better than folly,
    just as light is better than darkness.
14 The wise have eyes in their heads,
    while the fool walks in the darkness;
but I came to realise
    that the same fate overtakes them
    both.

15 Then I said to myself,

'The fate of the fool will overtake me
    also.
What then do I gain by being wise?'
I said to myself,
'This too is meaningless.'
16 For the wise, like the fool, will not be
    long remembered;
the days have already come when
    both have been forgotten.
Like the fool, the wise too must die!

Toil is meaningless

17 So I hated life, because the work that
is done under the sun was grievous to me.
All of it is meaningless, a chasing after the
wind. **18** I hated all the things I had toiled for
under the sun, because I must leave them
to the one who comes after me. **19** And who
knows whether that person will be wise or
foolish? Yet they will have control over all
the fruit of my toil into which I have poured
my effort and skill under the sun. This too
is meaningless. **20** So my heart began to
despair over all my toilsome labour under
the sun. **21** For a person may labour with
wisdom, knowledge and skill, and then
they must leave all they own to another
who has not toiled for it. This too is meaningless and a great misfortune. **22** What do
people get for all the toil and anxious striving with which they labour under the sun?
23 All their days their work is grief and pain;
even at night their minds do not rest. This
too is meaningless.

24 A person can do nothing better than
to eat and drink and find satisfaction
in their own toil. This too, I see, is from
the hand of God, **25** for without him, who
can eat or find enjoyment? **26** To the person who pleases him, God gives wisdom,
knowledge and happiness, but to the sinner he gives the task of gathering and stor-
ing up wealth to hand it over to the one
who pleases God. This too is meaningless,
a chasing after the wind.

A time for everything

3 There is a time for everything,
and a season for every activity under
the heavens:

2 a time to be born and a time to die,
    a time to plant and a time to uproot,
3 a time to kill and a time to heal,
    a time to tear down and a time to
    build,
4 a time to weep and a time to laugh,
    a time to mourn and a time to dance,
5 a time to scatter stones and a time to
    gather them,
a time to embrace and a time to
    refrain from embracing,
6 a time to search and a time to give up,
    a time to keep and a time to throw
    away,
7 a time to tear and a time to mend,
    a time to be silent and a time to
    speak,
8 a time to love and a time to hate,
    a time for war and a time for peace.

9 What do workers gain from their toil?
10 I have seen the burden God has laid on
the human race. **11** He has made everything beautiful in its time. He has also set

eternity in the human heart; yet*a* no one can fathom what God has done from beginning to end. ¹²I know that there is nothing better for people than to be happy and to do good while they live. ¹³That each of them may eat and drink, and find satisfaction in all their toil – this is the gift of God. ¹⁴I know that everything God does will endure for ever; nothing can be added to it and nothing taken from it. God does it so that people will fear him.

¹⁵Whatever is has already been,
    and what will be has been before;
    and God will call the past to account.*b*

¹⁶And I saw something else under the sun:

in the place of judgment – wickedness
    was there,
in the place of justice – wickedness
    was there.

¹⁷I said to myself,

'God will bring into judgment
    both the righteous and the wicked,
for there will be a time for every activity,
    a time to judge every deed.'

¹⁸I also said to myself, 'As for humans, God tests them so that they may see that they are like the animals. ¹⁹Surely the fate of human beings is like that of the animals; the same fate awaits them both: as one dies, so dies the other. All have the same breath*c*; humans have no advantage over animals. Everything is meaningless. ²⁰All go to the same place; all come from dust, and to dust all return. ²¹Who knows if the human spirit rises upward and if the spirit of the animal goes down into the earth?'

²²So I saw that there is nothing better for a person than to enjoy their work, because that is their lot. For who can bring them to see what will happen after them?

Oppression, toil, friendlessness

4 Again I looked and saw all the oppression that was taking place under the sun:

I saw the tears of the oppressed –
    and they have no comforter;
power was on the side of their
    oppressors –
    and they have no comforter.
²And I declared that the dead,
    who had already died,
are happier than the living,
    who are still alive.
³But better than both
    is the one who has never been born,
who has not seen the evil
    that is done under the sun.

⁴And I saw that all toil and all achievement spring from one person's envy of another. This too is meaningless, a chasing after the wind.

⁵Fools fold their hands
    and ruin themselves.
⁶Better one handful with tranquillity
    than two handfuls with toil
    and chasing after the wind.

⁷Again I saw something meaningless under the sun:

⁸there was a man all alone;
    he had neither son nor brother.
There was no end to his toil,
    yet his eyes were not content with his
    wealth.
'For whom am I toiling,' he asked,
    'and why am I depriving myself of
    enjoyment?'
This too is meaningless –
    a miserable business!

⁹Two are better than one,
    because they have a good return for
    their labour:
¹⁰if either of them falls down,
    one can help the other up.

---

a 11 Or *also placed ignorance in the human heart, so that*
b 15 Or *God calls back the past*
c 19 Or *spirit*

RELATIONSHIPS 2

TO FULFIL HIS PURPOSES

If I'm left to work on my own, it's a nightmare! I'm so easily distracted. So when I read that *'Two are better than one, because they have a good return for their labour'* (Ecclesiastes 4:9), it's something I really relate to.

I love working as part of a team. It's quicker, because lots of people are working with the same aim. It's more efficient, as we share ideas – and it's a whole lot more fun! Also, when things are difficult, there are people around to encourage us (v. 12). Relationships are about teamwork.

Are you more effective together than apart (v. 9)?

An important part of a relationship is having compatible goals. That doesn't mean doing the same job, or the same stuff at church, but do you have similar passions? Will your relationship help you fulfil what God has put on your heart to do? That's not to say our entire motivation for having relationships should be so we can be better at doing God's work, but when God asks you to do something, that ought to fit with what your boyfriend or girlfriend thinks God has asked them to do. If your relationship takes you away from the things God has asked of you, perhaps it's time to consider if it's really right.

Are you the best of friends (v. 10)?

Friends pick each other up when things are difficult. It is essential to a great relationship that they have the potential to become your very best friend. Be really careful that it's not just having someone special that you love – this simply leads to two selfish people staying together to meet each other's needs. That's nothing like God's best for your relationship, and God doesn't expect us to settle for less than that. Ali Martin has written a brilliant series on friendship which you should read too.

Is your relationship inclusive (v. 12)?

It's important to spend time with your boyfriend or girlfriend, but it's also important to see other friends! We all know that relationships are strengthened when we share memories from trips we've been on or things we've done, or go through difficult situations together. The problem is that the experiences that include some people on one level often exclude them on another. Work hard at keeping friends in your life. Your relationships should model God's relationship with us: God makes a covenant relationship with us, but not merely on a one-on-one basis. His relationship with us is between him and the whole Christian community. We should be actively loving our entire communities, as a reflection of God's love for us.

Jane Plackett

 1 John 5:6   1 Corinthians 7:32–34 ▶

But pity anyone who falls
and has no one to help them up.
11 Also, if two lie down together, they will
keep warm.
But how can one keep warm alone?
12 Though one may be overpowered,
two can defend themselves.
A cord of three strands is not quickly
broken.

Advancement is meaningless

13 Better a poor but wise youth than an old but foolish king who no longer knows how to heed a warning. 14 The youth may have come from prison to the kingship, or he may have been born in poverty within his kingdom. 15 I saw that all who lived and walked under the sun followed the youth, the king's successor. 16 There was no end to all the people who were before them. But those who came later were not pleased with the successor. This too is meaningless, a chasing after the wind.

Fulfil your vow to God

5 *a* Guard your steps when you go to the house of God. Go near to listen rather than to offer the sacrifice of fools, who do not know that they do wrong.

2 Do not be quick with your mouth,
do not be hasty in your heart
to utter anything before God.
God is in heaven
and you are on earth,
so let your words be few.
3 A dream comes when there are many
cares,
and many words mark the speech of a
fool.

4 When you make a vow to God, do not delay to fulfil it. He has no pleasure in fools; fulfil your vow. 5 It is better not to make a vow than to make one and not fulfil it. 6 Do not let your mouth lead you into sin. And do not protest to the temple messenger, 'My vow was a mistake.' Why should God be angry at what you say and

destroy the work of your hands? 7 Much dreaming and many words are meaningless. Therefore fear God.

Riches are meaningless

8 If you see the poor oppressed in a district, and justice and rights denied, do not be surprised at such things; for one official is eyed by a higher one, and over them both are others higher still. 9 The increase from the land is taken by all; the king himself profits from the fields.

10 Whoever loves money never has
enough;
whoever loves wealth is never
satisfied with their income.
This too is meaningless.

11 As goods increase,
so do those who consume them.
And what benefit are they to the
owners
except to feast their eyes on them?

12 The sleep of a labourer is sweet,
whether they eat little or much,
but as for the rich, their abundance
permits them no sleep.

13 I have seen a grievous evil under the sun:

wealth hoarded to the harm of its
owners,
14 or wealth lost through some
misfortune,
so that when they have children
there is nothing left for them to
inherit.
15 Everyone comes naked from their
mother's womb,
and as everyone comes, so they
depart.
They take nothing from their toil
that they can carry in their hands.

16 This too is a grievous evil:

as everyone comes, so they depart,
and what do they gain,
since they toil for the wind?

---

a In Hebrew texts 5:1 is numbered 4:17, and 5:2-20 is numbered 5:1-19.

17 All their days they eat in darkness,
  with great frustration, affliction and
    anger.

18 This is what I have observed to be
good: that it is appropriate for a person
to eat, to drink and to find satisfaction
in their toilsome labour under the sun
during the few days of life God has given
them – for this is their lot. **19** Moreover,
when God gives someone wealth and possessions, and the ability to enjoy them,
to accept their lot and be happy in their
toil – this is a gift of God. **20** They seldom
reflect on the days of their life, because
God keeps them occupied with gladness
of heart.

6 I have seen another evil under the
sun, and it weighs heavily on mankind: **2** God gives some people wealth,
possessions and honour, so that they lack
nothing their hearts desire, but God does
not grant them the ability to enjoy them,
and strangers enjoy them instead. This is
meaningless, a grievous evil.

3 A man may have a hundred children
and live many years; yet no matter how
long he lives, if he cannot enjoy his prosperity and does not receive proper burial,
I say that a stillborn child is better off than
he. **4** It comes without meaning, it departs
in darkness, and in darkness its name is
shrouded. **5** Though it never saw the sun or
knew anything, it has more rest than does
that man – **6** even if he lives a thousand
years twice over but fails to enjoy his prosperity. Do not all go to the same place?

7 Everyone's toil is for their mouth,
  yet their appetite is never satisfied.
8 What advantage have the wise over
    fools?
What do the poor gain
  by knowing how to conduct
    themselves before others?
9 Better what the eye sees
  than the roving of the appetite.
This too is meaningless,
  a chasing after the wind.

10 Whatever exists has already been
    named,

and what humanity is has been
    known;
no one can contend
  with someone who is stronger.
11 The more the words,
  the less the meaning,
  and how does that profit anyone?

12 For who knows what is good for a person in life, during the few and meaningless days they pass through like a shadow?
Who can tell them what will happen under the sun after they are gone?

Wisdom

7 A good name is better than fine
  perfume,
  and the day of death better than the
    day of birth.
2 It is better to go to a house of
    mourning
  than to go to a house of feasting,
for death is the destiny of everyone;
  the living should take this to heart.
3 Frustration is better than laughter,
  because a sad face is good for the
    heart.
4 The heart of the wise is in the house of
    mourning,
  but the heart of fools is in the house
    of pleasure.
5 It is better to heed the rebuke of a wise
    person
  than to listen to the song of fools.
6 Like the crackling of thorns under the
    pot,
  so is the laughter of fools.
  This too is meaningless.

7 Extortion turns a wise person into a
    fool,
  and a bribe corrupts the heart.
8 The end of a matter is better than its
    beginning,
  and patience is better than pride.
9 Do not be quickly provoked in your
    spirit,
  for anger resides in the lap of fools.

10 Do not say, 'Why were the old days
    better than these?'

For it is not wise to ask such
    questions.

11 Wisdom, like an inheritance, is a good
    thing
    and benefits those who see the sun.
12 Wisdom is a shelter
    as money is a shelter,
but the advantage of knowledge is this:
    wisdom preserves those who have it.

13 Consider what God has done:

who can straighten
    what he has made crooked?
14 When times are good, be happy;
    but when times are bad, consider
    this:
God has made the one
    as well as the other.
Therefore, no one can discover
    anything about their future.

15 In this meaningless life of mine I have
seen both of these:

the righteous perishing in their
    righteousness,
    and the wicked living long in their
    wickedness.
16 Do not be over-righteous,
    neither be overwise –
    why destroy yourself?
17 Do not be overwicked,
    and do not be a fool –
    why die before your time?
18 It is good to grasp the one
    and not let go of the other.
    Whoever fears God will avoid all
    extremes.*a*

19 Wisdom makes one wise person more
    powerful
    than ten rulers in a city.

20 Indeed, there is no one on earth who is
    righteous,
    no one who does what is right and
    never sins.

21 Do not pay attention to every word
    people say,
    or you may hear your servant cursing
    you –
22 for you know in your heart
    that many times you yourself have
    cursed others.

23 All this I tested by wisdom and I said,

'I am determined to be wise' –
    but this was beyond me.
24 Whatever exists is far off and most
    profound –
    who can discover it?
25 So I turned my mind to understand,
    to investigate and to search out
        wisdom and the scheme of
        things
and to understand the stupidity of
    wickedness
    and the madness of folly.

26 I find more bitter than death
    the woman who is a snare,
whose heart is a trap
    and whose hands are chains.
The man who pleases God will escape
    her,
    but the sinner she will ensnare.

27 'Look,' says the Teacher,*b* 'this is what
I have discovered:

'Adding one thing to another to discover
    the scheme of things –
28   while I was still searching
    but not finding –
I found one upright man among a
    thousand,
    but not one upright woman among
    them all.
29 This only have I found:
    God created mankind upright,
    but they have gone in search of many
    schemes.'

8 Who is like the wise?
    Who knows the explanation of
    things?

---

a 18 Or *will follow them both*   *b* 27 Or *the leader of the assembly*

A person's wisdom brightens their face and changes its hard appearance.

Obey the king

2 Obey the king's command, I say, because you took an oath before God. 3 Do not be in a hurry to leave the king's presence. Do not stand up for a bad cause, for he will do whatever he pleases. 4 Since a king's word is supreme, who can say to him, 'What are you doing?'

5 Whoever obeys his command will come
  to no harm,
  and the wise heart will know the
    proper time and procedure.
6 For there is a proper time and procedure
    for every matter,
  though a person may be weighed
    down by misery.

7 Since no one knows the future,
  who can tell someone else what is to
    come?
8 As no one has power over the wind to
    contain it,
  so[a] no one has power over the time
    of their death.
  As no one is discharged in time of war,
  so wickedness will not release those
    who practise it.

9 All this I saw, as I applied my mind to everything done under the sun. There is a time when a man lords it over others to his own[b] hurt. 10 Then too, I saw the wicked buried – those who used to come and go from the holy place and receive praise[c] in the city where they did this. This too is meaningless.

11 When the sentence for a crime is not quickly carried out, people's hearts are filled with schemes to do wrong. 12 Although a wicked person who commits a hundred crimes may live a long time, I know that it will go better with those who fear God, who are reverent before him. 13 Yet because the wicked do not fear God,

it will not go well with them, and their days will not lengthen like a shadow.

14 There is something else meaningless that occurs on earth: the righteous who get what the wicked deserve, and the wicked who get what the righteous deserve. This too, I say, is meaningless. 15 So I commend the enjoyment of life, because there is nothing better for a person under the sun than to eat and drink and be glad. Then joy will accompany them in their toil all the days of the life God has given them under the sun.

16 When I applied my mind to know wisdom and to observe the labour that is done on earth – people getting no sleep day or night – 17 then I saw all that God has done. No one can comprehend what goes on under the sun. Despite all their efforts to search it out, no one can discover its meaning. Even if the wise claim they know, they cannot really comprehend it.

A common destiny for all

9 So I reflected on all this and concluded that the righteous and the wise and what they do are in God's hands, but no one knows whether love or hate awaits them. 2 All share a common destiny – the righteous and the wicked, the good and the bad,[a] the clean and the unclean, those who offer sacrifices and those who do not.

As it is with the good,
  so with the sinful;
as it is with those who take oaths,
  so with those who are afraid to take
    them.

3 This is the evil in everything that happens under the sun: The same destiny overtakes all. The hearts of people, moreover, are full of evil and there is madness in their hearts while they live, and afterwards they join the dead. 4 Anyone who is among the living has hope[b] – even a live dog is better off than a dead lion!

a 8 Or *over the human spirit to retain it,* / *and so*
b 9 Or *to their*
c 10 Some Hebrew manuscripts and Septuagint (Aquila); most Hebrew manuscripts *and are forgotten*

a 2 Septuagint (Aquila), Vulgate and Syriac; Hebrew does not have *and the bad.*
b 4 Or *What then is to be chosen? With all who live, there is hope*

⁵ For the living know that they will die,
but the dead know nothing;
they have no further reward,
and even their name is forgotten.
⁶ Their love, their hate
and their jealousy have long since
vanished;
never again will they have a part
in anything that happens under the
sun.

⁷ Go, eat your food with gladness, and drink your wine with a joyful heart, for God has already approved what you do. ⁸ Always be clothed in white, and always anoint your head with oil. ⁹ Enjoy life with your wife, whom you love, all the days of this meaningless life that God has given you under the sun – all your meaningless days. For this is your lot in life and in your toilsome labour under the sun. ¹⁰ Whatever your hand finds to do, do it with all your might, for in the realm of the dead, where you are going, there is neither working nor planning nor knowledge nor wisdom.

¹¹ I have seen something else under the sun:

The race is not to the swift
or the battle to the strong,
nor does food come to the wise
or wealth to the brilliant
or favour to the learned;
but time and chance happen to
them all.

¹² Moreover, no one knows when their hour will come:

As fish are caught in a cruel net,
or birds are taken in a snare,
so people are trapped by evil times
that fall unexpectedly upon them.

Wisdom better than folly

¹³ I also saw under the sun this example of wisdom that greatly impressed me: ¹⁴ there was once a small city with only a few people in it. And a powerful king came against it, surrounded it and built huge

siege works against it. ¹⁵ Now there lived in that city a man poor but wise, and he saved the city by his wisdom. But nobody remembered that poor man. ¹⁶ So I said, 'Wisdom is better than strength.' But the poor man's wisdom is despised, and his words are no longer heeded.

¹⁷ The quiet words of the wise are more to
be heeded
than the shouts of a ruler of fools.
¹⁸ Wisdom is better than weapons of
war,
but one sinner destroys much good.

10 As dead flies give perfume a bad
smell,
so a little folly outweighs wisdom and
honour.
² The heart of the wise inclines to the
right,
but the heart of the fool to the left.
³ Even as fools walk along the road,
they lack sense
and show everyone how stupid they
are.
⁴ If a ruler's anger rises against you,
do not leave your post;
calmness can lay great offences to
rest.

⁵ There is an evil I have seen under the
sun,
the sort of error that arises from a
ruler:
⁶ fools are put in many high positions,
while the rich occupy the low ones.
⁷ I have seen slaves on horseback,
while princes go on foot like slaves.

⁸ Whoever digs a pit may fall into it;
whoever breaks through a wall may
be bitten by a snake.
⁹ Whoever quarries stones may be injured
by them;
whoever splits logs may be
endangered by them.

¹⁰ If the axe is dull
and its edge unsharpened,
more strength is needed,
but skill will bring success.

11 If a snake bites before it is charmed,
  the charmer receives no fee.

12 Words from the mouth of the wise are
    gracious,
  but fools are consumed by their own
    lips.
13 At the beginning their words are folly;
  at the end they are wicked madness –
14 and fools multiply words.

No one knows what is coming –
  who can tell someone else what will
    happen after them?

15 The toil of fools wearies them;
  they do not know the way to town.

16 Woe to the land whose king was a
    servant[a]
  and whose princes feast in the
    morning.
17 Blessed is the land whose king is of
    noble birth
  and whose princes eat at a proper
    time –
  for strength and not for
    drunkenness.

18 Through laziness, the rafters sag;
  because of idle hands, the house
    leaks.

19 A feast is made for laughter,
  wine makes life merry,
  and money is the answer for
    everything.

20 Do not revile the king even in your
    thoughts,
  or curse the rich in your bedroom,
  because a bird in the sky may carry your
    words,
  and a bird on the wing may report
    what you say.

Invest in many ventures

11 Ship your grain across the sea;
  after many days you may receive a
    return.

2 Invest in seven ventures, yes, in eight;
  you do not know what disaster may
    come upon the land.

3 If clouds are full of water,
  they pour rain on the earth.
 Whether a tree falls to the south or to
    the north,
  in the place where it falls, there it will
    lie.
4 Whoever watches the wind will not
    plant;
  whoever looks at the clouds will not
    reap.

5 As you do not know the path of the
    wind,
  or how the body is formed[a] in a
    mother's womb,
 so you cannot understand the work of
    God,
  the Maker of all things.

6 Sow your seed in the morning,
  and at evening let your hands not be
    idle,
 for you do not know which will succeed,
  whether this or that,
  or whether both will do equally well.

Remember your Creator while young

7 Light is sweet,
  and it pleases the eyes to see the sun.
8 However many years anyone may live,
  let them enjoy them all.
 But let them remember the days of
    darkness,
  for there will be many.
  Everything to come is meaningless.

9 You who are young, be happy while you
    are young,
  and let your heart give you joy in the
    days of your youth.
 Follow the ways of your heart
  and whatever your eyes see,
 but know that for all these things
  God will bring you into judgment.
10 So then, banish anxiety from your heart

---

a 16 Or *king is a child*

a 5 Or *know how life (or the spirit) / enters the body being
formed*

and cast off the troubles of your
     body,
for youth and vigour are
     meaningless.

12 Remember your Creator
     in the days of your youth,
before the days of trouble come
     and the years approach when you will
          say,
     'I find no pleasure in them' –
2 before the sun and the light
     and the moon and the stars grow
          dark,
     and the clouds return after the rain;
3 when the keepers of the house tremble,
     and the strong men stoop,
when the grinders cease because they
     are few,
     and those looking through the
          windows grow dim;
4 when the doors to the street are closed
     and the sound of grinding fades;
when people rise up at the sound of
     birds,
     but all their songs grow faint;
5 when people are afraid of heights
     and of dangers in the streets;
when the almond tree blossoms
     and the grasshopper drags itself
          along
     and desire no longer is stirred.
Then people go to their eternal home
     and mourners go about the streets.

6 Remember him – before the silver cord
     is severed,
     and the golden bowl is broken;

before the pitcher is shattered at the
     spring,
     and the wheel broken at the well,
7 and the dust returns to the ground it
     came from,
     and the spirit returns to God who
          gave it.

8 'Meaningless! Meaningless!' says the
     Teacher.*a*
     'Everything is meaningless!'

The conclusion of the matter

9 Not only was the Teacher wise, but
also he imparted knowledge to the people. He pondered and searched out and
set in order many proverbs. 10 The Teacher
searched to find just the right words, and
what he wrote was upright and true.
    11 The words of the wise are like goads,
their collected sayings like firmly embed-
ded nails – given by one shepherd.*b* 12 Be
warned, my son, of anything in addition
to them.
    Of making many books there is no end,
and much study wearies the body.

13 Now all has been heard;
     here is the conclusion of the matter:
     fear God and keep his commandments,
          for this is the duty of all mankind.
14 For God will bring every deed into
          judgment,
     including every hidden thing,
          whether it is good or evil.

---

a 8   Or *the leader of the assembly*; also in verses 9 and 10
b 11 Or *Shepherd*

SONG OF SONGS

DATE

Unknown

AUTHOR

Although traditionally attributed to Solomon (the book is sometimes called The Song of Solomon) the question of whether he actually wrote it remains unanswered.

WHAT'S IT ALL ABOUT?

As its title suggests, this book is a song. In fact, its title claims it to be the greatest song of all the songs ever written about love – quite a feat, given how popular the subject has been for songwriters over the centuries! The book follows the story of a courtship between a man and a young woman which leads to their wedding celebrations, their wedding night and their maturing love over the years. Their physical attraction to each other and their desire to be intimate shows us that God does not consider sex something to be hidden away; the book is honest about the importance of the sexual expression of love. Some have suggested that, rather than being about the love between man and woman, this book paints a picture of God's love for his people. This may have been due to people's embarrassment and confusion about something considered so erotic appearing in the holy Word of God. It is more likely to be a love song that highlights God's designs and desires for human marriages.

WHY SHOULD WE READ IT?

- To see God's intention for marriage.

- To understand that God isn't ashamed of sex. He doesn't see it as something dirty that should be hidden, but in the context of a marriage it should be celebrated and enjoyed.

- To read about the strength and power of love (Song of Songs 8:6–8).

Andy Croft with Liza Hoeksma

1
Solomon's Song of Songs.

She[a]

2 Let him kiss me with the kisses of his
   mouth –
   for your love is more delightful than
   wine.
3 Pleasing is the fragrance of your
   perfumes;
   your name is like perfume poured
   out.
   No wonder the young women love
   you!
4 Take me away with you – let us hurry!
   Let the king bring me into his
   chambers.

Friends

   We rejoice and delight in you;[b]
   we will praise your love more than
   wine.

She

   How right they are to adore you!

5 Dark am I, yet lovely,
   daughters of Jerusalem,
   dark like the tents of Kedar,
   like the tent curtains of Solomon.[c]
6 Do not stare at me because I am dark,
   because I am darkened by the sun.
   My mother's sons were angry with me
   and made me take care of the
   vineyards;
   my own vineyard I had to neglect.
7 Tell me, you whom I love,
   where you graze your flock
   and where you rest your sheep at
   midday.
   Why should I be like a veiled woman
   beside the flocks of your friends?

Friends

8 If you do not know, most beautiful of
   women,
   follow the tracks of the sheep
   and graze your young goats
   by the tents of the shepherds.

He

9 I liken you, my darling, to a mare
   among Pharaoh's chariot horses.
10 Your cheeks are beautiful with earrings,
   your neck with strings of jewels.
11 We will make you earrings of gold,
   studded with silver.

She

12 While the king was at his table,
   my perfume spread its fragrance.
13 My beloved is to me a sachet of myrrh
   resting between my breasts.
14 My beloved is to me a cluster of henna
   blossoms
   from the vineyards of En Gedi.

He

15 How beautiful you are, my darling!
   Oh, how beautiful!
   Your eyes are doves.

She

16 How handsome you are, my beloved!
   Oh, how charming!
   And our bed is verdant.

He

17 The beams of our house are cedars;
   our rafters are firs.

She[a]

2
I am a rose[b] of Sharon,
   a lily of the valleys.

He

2 Like a lily among thorns
   is my darling among the young
   women.

---

a 1 The main male and female speakers (identified primarily on the basis of the gender of the relevant Hebrew forms) are indicated by the captions *He* and *She* respectively. The words of others are marked *Friends*. In some instances the divisions and their captions are debatable.
b 4 The Hebrew is masculine singular.
c 5 Or *Salma*

---

a 1 Or *He*
b 1 Probably a member of the crocus family

She
³ Like an apple[c] tree among the trees of
　　the forest
　is my beloved among the young men.
I delight to sit in his shade,
　and his fruit is sweet to my taste.
⁴ Let him lead me to the banquet hall,

---

c 3 Or possibly *apricot*; also in 8:5

and let his banner over me be love.
⁵ Strengthen me with raisins,
　refresh me with apples,
　for I am faint with love.
⁶ His left arm is under my head,
　and his right arm embraces me.
⁷ Daughters of Jerusalem, I charge you
　by the gazelles and by the does of the
　field:

RELATIONSHIPS 8

KEEPING RELATIONSHIPS PURE (PART 2)

What does it mean, *'Do not arouse or awaken love until it so desires'* (Song of Songs 2:7)?

We shouldn't read this as when we desire love, but when it desires us. We need to be wise about when we enter into a relationship. Sometimes we desperately want one, but only God knows when we're actually ready for it. If we try to rush into it, or turn ourselves into someone we're not in order to attract a person by dressing or behaving differently, we'll attract the wrong person, in the wrong timing. It's so easy to take the chance to pick the one we want and pray for the best, rather than wait for the one God has in store for us.

We're designed by God, and God designed sex only for marriage. He is our Creator and our Law-maker, and his rules allow us to be the best that we can be. If we break his laws, we end up hurting ourselves because we're going against his design for us.

While we should go all-out to have relationships that have integrity, are good for us, are good for the other person, and are God-centred, it's almost inevitable that we'll fall short at some point. God forgives, restores and heals us (Isaiah 1:18) and brings us back into right relationship with him.

Some practical advice:

- Find yourself an accountability partner/mentor.

- Talk about physical boundaries in your relationships, and talk about it early, before it's an issue. If you leave it until the moment, it's too late!

- Relationships should be with someone who is, or has the potential to be, your best friend. You need to be able talk about difficult stuff together and draw conclusions.

- Set clear boundaries and discuss them with your mentor, so they can hold you to account and advise you.

Jane Plackett & Calum Dyke

 1 Timothy 5:1–2　　　　　　　　　　　Galatians 5:13

Do not arouse or awaken love
    until it so desires.

8 Listen! My beloved!
    Look! Here he comes,
leaping across the mountains,
    bounding over the hills.
9 My beloved is like a gazelle or a young
    stag.
Look! There he stands behind our
    wall,
gazing through the windows,
    peering through the lattice.
10 My beloved spoke and said to me,
    'Arise, my darling,
    my beautiful one, come with me.
11 See! The winter is past;
    the rains are over and gone.
12 Flowers appear on the earth;
    the season of singing has come,
the cooing of doves
    is heard in our land.
13 The fig-tree forms its early fruit;
    the blossoming vines spread their
      fragrance.
Arise, come, my darling;
    my beautiful one, come with me.'

He
14 My dove in the clefts of the rock,
    in the hiding-places on the
      mountainside,
show me your face,
    let me hear your voice;
for your voice is sweet,
    and your face is lovely.
15 Catch for us the foxes,
    the little foxes
that ruin the vineyards,
    our vineyards that are in bloom.

She
16 My beloved is mine and I am his;
    he browses among the lilies.
17 Until the day breaks
    and the shadows flee,
turn, my beloved,
    and be like a gazelle
or like a young stag
    on the rugged hills. *d*

3 All night long on my bed
    I looked for the one my heart loves;
    I looked for him but did not find him.
2 I will get up now and go about the city,
    through its streets and squares;
I will search for the one my heart loves.
    So I looked for him but did not find
      him.
3 The watchmen found me
    as they made their rounds in the city.
'Have you seen the one my heart
      loves?'
4 Scarcely had I passed them
    when I found the one my heart loves.
I held him and would not let him go
    till I had brought him to my mother's
      house,
to the room of the one who
      conceived me.
5 Daughters of Jerusalem, I charge you
    by the gazelles and by the does of the
      field:
do not arouse or awaken love
    until it so desires.

6 Who is this coming up from the
      wilderness
    like a column of smoke,
perfumed with myrrh and incense
    made from all the spices of the
      merchant?
7 Look! It is Solomon's carriage,
    escorted by sixty warriors,
    the noblest of Israel,
8 all of them wearing the sword,
    all experienced in battle,
each with his sword at his side,
    prepared for the terrors of the night.
9 King Solomon made for himself the
      carriage;
    he made it of wood from Lebanon.
10 Its posts he made of silver,
    its base of gold.
Its seat was upholstered with purple,
    its interior inlaid with love.
Daughters of Jerusalem, 11 come out,
    and look, you daughters of Zion.
Look*a* on King Solomon wearing a
      crown,

---

d 17 Or *the hills of Bether*

a 10,11 Or *interior lovingly inlaid / by the daughters of Jerusalem. / *11 *Come out, you daughters of Zion, / and look*

the crown with which his mother
  crowned him
on the day of his wedding,
  the day his heart rejoiced.

He

4 How beautiful you are, my darling!
  Oh, how beautiful!
  Your eyes behind your veil are doves.
Your hair is like a flock of goats
  descending from the hills of Gilead.
2 Your teeth are like a flock of sheep just
  shorn,
  coming up from the washing.
Each has its twin;
  not one of them is alone.
3 Your lips are like a scarlet ribbon;
  your mouth is lovely.
Your temples behind your veil
  are like the halves of a pomegranate.
4 Your neck is like the tower of David,
  built with courses of stone;*a*
on it hang a thousand shields,
  all of them shields of warriors.
5 Your breasts are like two fawns,
  like twin fawns of a gazelle
  that browse among the lilies.
6 Until the day breaks
  and the shadows flee,
I will go to the mountain of myrrh
  and to the hill of incense.
7 You are altogether beautiful, my darling;
  there is no flaw in you.

8 Come with me from Lebanon, my bride,
  come with me from Lebanon.
Descend from the crest of Amana,
  from the top of Senir, the summit of
  Hermon,
from the lions' dens
  and the mountain haunts of
  leopards.
9 You have stolen my heart, my sister, my
  bride;
  you have stolen my heart
with one glance of your eyes,
  with one jewel of your necklace.
10 How delightful is your love, my sister,
  my bride!

How much more pleasing is your love
  than wine,
and the fragrance of your perfume
  more than any spice!
11 Your lips drop sweetness as the
  honeycomb, my bride;
  milk and honey are under your
  tongue.
The fragrance of your garments
  is like the fragrance of Lebanon.
12 You are a garden locked up, my sister,
  my bride;
  you are a spring enclosed, a sealed
  fountain.
13 Your plants are an orchard of
  pomegranates
  with choice fruits,
  with henna and nard,
14   nard and saffron,
  calamus and cinnamon,
  with every kind of incense tree,
  with myrrh and aloes
  and all the finest spices.
15 You are*b* a garden fountain,
  a well of flowing water
  streaming down from Lebanon.

She

16 Awake, north wind,
  and come, south wind!
Blow on my garden,
  that its fragrance may spread
  everywhere.
Let my beloved come into his garden
  and taste its choice fruits.

He

5 I have come into my garden, my sister,
  my bride;
  I have gathered my myrrh with my
  spice.
I have eaten my honeycomb and my
  honey;
  I have drunk my wine and my milk.

Friends

Eat, friends, and drink;
  drink your fill of love.

---

a 4 The meaning of the Hebrew for this phrase is
uncertain.

b 15 Or *I am* (spoken by *She*)

She

2 I slept but my heart was awake.
   Listen! My beloved is knocking:
'Open to me, my sister, my darling,
   my dove, my flawless one.
My head is drenched with dew,
   my hair with the dampness of the
      night.'
3 I have taken off my robe –
   must I put it on again?
I have washed my feet –
   must I soil them again?
4 My beloved thrust his hand through the
      latch-opening;
   my heart began to pound for him.
5 I arose to open for my beloved,
   and my hands dripped with myrrh,
my fingers with flowing myrrh,
   on the handles of the bolt.
6 I opened for my beloved,
   but my beloved had left; he was
      gone.
My heart sank at his departure.*a*
I looked for him but did not find him.
   I called him but he did not answer.
7 The watchmen found me
   as they made their rounds in the city.
They beat me, they bruised me;
   they took away my cloak,
   those watchmen of the walls!
8 Daughters of Jerusalem, I charge you –
   if you find my beloved,
what will you tell him?
   Tell him I am faint with love.

Friends

9 How is your beloved better than others,
   most beautiful of women?
How is your beloved better than others,
   that you so charge us?

She

10 My beloved is radiant and ruddy,
   outstanding among ten thousand.
11 His head is purest gold;
   his hair is wavy
   and black as a raven.
12 His eyes are like doves
   by the water streams,
   washed in milk,

   mounted like jewels.
13 His cheeks are like beds of spice
   yielding perfume.
His lips are like lilies
   dripping with myrrh.
14 His arms are rods of gold
   set with topaz.
His body is like polished ivory
   decorated with lapis lazuli.
15 His legs are pillars of marble
   set on bases of pure gold.
His appearance is like Lebanon,
   choice as its cedars.
16 His mouth is sweetness itself;
   he is altogether lovely.
This is my beloved, this is my friend,
   daughters of Jerusalem.

Friends

6 Where has your beloved gone,
   most beautiful of women?
Which way did your beloved turn,
   that we may look for him with you?

She

2 My beloved has gone down to his
      garden,
   to the beds of spices,
to browse in the gardens
   and to gather lilies.
3 I am my beloved's and my beloved is
      mine;
   he browses among the lilies.

He

4 You are as beautiful as Tirzah, my
      darling,
   as lovely as Jerusalem,
   as majestic as troops with banners.
5 Turn your eyes from me;
   they overwhelm me.
Your hair is like a flock of goats
   descending from Gilead.
6 Your teeth are like a flock of sheep
   coming up from the washing.
Each has its twin,
   not one of them is missing.
7 Your temples behind your veil
   are like the halves of a pomegranate.
8 Sixty queens there may be,
   and eighty concubines,
   and virgins beyond number;

---

a 6 Or *heart had gone out to him when he spoke*

9 but my dove, my perfect one, is unique,
　　the only daughter of her mother,
　　the favourite of the one who bore her.
The young women saw her and called
　　her blessed;
　　the queens and concubines praised
　　her.

Friends

10 Who is this that appears like the dawn,
　　fair as the moon, bright as the sun,
　　majestic as the stars in procession?

He

11 I went down to the grove of nut trees
　　to look at the new growth in the
　　valley,
　　to see if the vines had budded
　　or the pomegranates were in bloom.
12 Before I realised it,
　　my desire set me among the royal
　　chariots of my people.*a*

Friends

13 Come back, come back, O Shulammite;
　　come back, come back, that we may
　　gaze on you!

He

Why would you gaze on the Shulammite
　　as on the dance of Mahanaim?*b*

7 *a* How beautiful your sandalled feet,
　　O prince's daughter!
Your graceful legs are like jewels,
　　the work of an artist's hands.
2 Your navel is a rounded goblet
　　that never lacks blended wine.
Your waist is a mound of wheat
　　encircled by lilies.
3 Your breasts are like two fawns,
　　like twin fawns of a gazelle.
4 Your neck is like an ivory tower.
Your eyes are the pools of Heshbon
　　by the gate of Bath Rabbim.
Your nose is like the tower of Lebanon
　　looking towards Damascus.

5 Your head crowns you like Mount
　　Carmel.
Your hair is like royal tapestry;
　　the king is held captive by its tresses.
6 How beautiful you are and how
　　pleasing,
　　my love, with your delights!
7 Your stature is like that of the palm,
　　and your breasts like clusters of fruit.
8 I said, 'I will climb the palm tree;
　　I will take hold of its fruit.'
May your breasts be like clusters of
　　grapes on the vine,
　　the fragrance of your breath like
　　apples,
9 and your mouth like the best wine.

She

May the wine go straight to my beloved,
　　flowing gently over lips and teeth.*b*
10 I belong to my beloved,
　　and his desire is for me.
11 Come, my beloved, let us go to the
　　countryside,
　　let us spend the night in the villages.*c*
12 Let us go early to the vineyards
　　to see if the vines have budded,
　　if their blossoms have opened,
　　and if the pomegranates are in
　　bloom –
　　there I will give you my love.
13 The mandrakes send out their fragrance,
　　and at our door is every delicacy,
　　both new and old,
　　that I have stored up for you, my
　　beloved.

8 If only you were to me like a brother,
　　who was nursed at my mother's
　　breasts!
Then, if I found you outside,
　　I would kiss you,
　　and no one would despise me.
2 I would lead you
　　and bring you to my mother's
　　house –
　　she who has taught me.
I would give you spiced wine to drink,

---

a 12　Or *among the chariots of Amminadab; or among the
chariots of the people of the prince*
b 13　In Hebrew texts this verse 6:13 is numbered 7:1.
a In Hebrew texts 7:1-13 is numbered 7:2-14.

b 9　Septuagint, Aquila, Vulgate and Syriac; Hebrew
lips of sleepers
c 11　Or *the henna bushes*

the nectar of my pomegranates.
3 His left arm is under my head
    and his right arm embraces me.
4 Daughters of Jerusalem, I charge you:
    do not arouse or awaken love
    until it so desires.

Friends

5 Who is this coming up from the
        wilderness
    leaning on her beloved?

She

Under the apple tree I roused you;
    there your mother conceived you,
    there she who was in labour gave you
        birth.
6 Place me like a seal over your heart,
    like a seal on your arm;
for love is as strong as death,
    its jealousy*a* unyielding as the grave.
It burns like blazing fire,
    like a mighty flame.*b*
7 Many waters cannot quench love;
    rivers cannot sweep it away.
If one were to give
    all the wealth of one's house for love,
    it*c* would be utterly scorned.

Friends

8 We have a little sister,
    and her breasts are not yet grown.

---

a 6 Or *ardour*
b 6 Or *fire, / like the very flame of the* LORD
c 7 Or *he*

What shall we do for our sister
    on the day she is spoken for?
9 If she is a wall,
    we will build towers of silver on her.
If she is a door,
    we will enclose her with panels of
        cedar.

She

10 I am a wall,
    and my breasts are like towers.
Thus I have become in his eyes
    like one bringing contentment.
11 Solomon had a vineyard in Baal Hamon;
    he let out his vineyard to tenants.
Each was to bring for its fruit
    a thousand shekels*d* of silver.
12 But my own vineyard is mine to give;
    the thousand shekels are for you,
        Solomon,
    and two hundred*e* are for those who
        tend its fruit.

He

13 You who dwell in the gardens
    with friends in attendance,
    let me hear your voice!

She

14 Come away, my beloved,
    and be like a gazelle
or like a young stag
    on the spice-laden mountains.

---

d 11 That is, about 12 kilograms; also in verse 12
e 12 That is, about 2.3 kilograms

ISAIAH

DATE

Isaiah was called by God to be a prophet around 740 BC and he prophesied for over 40 years

AUTHOR

Traditionally credited to Isaiah

WHAT'S IT ALL ABOUT?

Isaiah is the first book of the Prophets and it deals with the themes of both God's judgement and his salvation. Isaiah saw a vision of the Lord's glory and he dedicated himself to God's service in response. God sent him to tell the Jewish people that they would be judged for their sin, but he also brought them the reassurance that God loved them and was longing to forgive them. The book is split into two main parts. Chapters 1 – 39 are likely to have been written before the exile, and they mainly deal with God's judgement of his people. Chapters 40 – 66 were written during the exile, and focus on God's love and compassion for his worn-down people, promising that he will save them. The book of Isaiah also contains many prophecies regarding Jesus as the bringer of ultimate salvation for God's people, and it talks of the time when God will create new heavens and a new earth.

WHY SHOULD WE READ IT?

- To see God's promise to bring strength to the weary (Isaiah 40).

- To hear the prophecies about Jesus (especially Isaiah 42, 52 – 53).

- To see how God longed to forgive Israel even though they had sinned against him (Isaiah 43).

- To understand that God isn't interested in people going through the motions of religion; he wants his followers to act with love and integrity in all areas of their lives (Isaiah 58).

- To hear about the promised glory for God's people.

- To read the words Jesus would go on to quote, saying he fulfilled their promise (Isaiah 61).

Andy Croft with Liza Hoeksma

1

The vision concerning Judah and Jerusalem that Isaiah son of Amoz saw during the reigns of Uzziah, Jotham, Ahaz and Hezekiah, kings of Judah.

A rebellious nation

2 Hear me, you heavens! Listen, earth!
   For the LORD has spoken:
'I reared children and brought
      them up,
   but they have rebelled against me.
3 The ox knows its master,
   the donkey its owner's manger,
but Israel does not know,
   my people do not understand.'

4 Woe to the sinful nation,
   a people whose guilt is great,
a brood of evildoers,
   children given to corruption!
They have forsaken the LORD;
   they have spurned the Holy One of
      Israel
   and turned their backs on him.

5 Why should you be beaten any more?
   Why do you persist in rebellion?
Your whole head is injured,
   your whole heart afflicted.
6 From the sole of your foot to the top of
      your head
   there is no soundness –
only wounds and bruises
   and open sores,
not cleansed or bandaged
   or soothed with oil.

7 Your country is desolate,
   your cities burned with fire;
your fields are being stripped by
      foreigners
   right before you,
   laid waste as when overthrown by
      strangers.
8 Daughter Zion is left
   like a shelter in a vineyard,
like a hut in a cucumber field,
   like a city under siege.
9 Unless the LORD Almighty
   had left us some survivors,
we would have become like Sodom,
   we would have been like Gomorrah.

10 Hear the word of the LORD,
   you rulers of Sodom;
listen to the instruction of our God,
   you people of Gomorrah!
11 'The multitude of your sacrifices –
   what are they to me?' says the LORD.
'I have more than enough of burnt
      offerings,
   of rams and the fat of fattened
      animals;
I have no pleasure
   in the blood of bulls and lambs and
      goats.
12 When you come to appear before me,
   who has asked this of you,
   this trampling of my courts?
13 Stop bringing meaningless offerings!
   Your incense is detestable to me.
New Moons, Sabbaths and
      convocations –
   I cannot bear your worthless
      assemblies.
14 Your New Moon feasts and your
      appointed festivals
I hate with all my being.
   They have become a burden to me;
   I am weary of bearing them.
15 When you spread out your hands in
      prayer,
   I hide my eyes from you;
even when you offer many prayers,
   I am not listening.

Your hands are full of blood!

16 Wash and make yourselves clean.
   Take your evil deeds out of my sight;
   stop doing wrong.
17 Learn to do right; seek justice.
   Defend the oppressed.*a*
Take up the cause of the fatherless;
   plead the case of the widow.

18 'Come now, let us settle the matter,'
   says the LORD.
'Though your sins are like scarlet,
   they shall be as white as snow;
though they are red as crimson,
   they shall be like wool.
19 If you are willing and obedient,

---

a 17 Or *justice. / Correct the oppressor*

you will eat the good things of the
    land;
²⁰ but if you resist and rebel,
    you will be devoured by the sword.'
            For the mouth of the LORD
                    has spoken.

²¹ See how the faithful city
    has become a prostitute!
    She once was full of justice;
        righteousness used to dwell in her —
        but now murderers!
²² Your silver has become dross,
    your choice wine is diluted with
        water.
²³ Your rulers are rebels,
    partners with thieves;
    they all love bribes
        and chase after gifts.
    They do not defend the cause of the
        fatherless;
        the widow's case does not come
            before them.

²⁴ Therefore the Lord, the LORD
    Almighty,
    the Mighty One of Israel, declares:
    'Ah! I will vent my wrath on my foes
        and avenge myself on my enemies.
²⁵ I will turn my hand against you;*b*
    I will thoroughly purge away your
        dross
        and remove all your impurities.
²⁶ I will restore your leaders as in days of
        old,
    your rulers as at the beginning.
    Afterwards you will be called
        the City of Righteousness,
        the Faithful City.'

²⁷ Zion will be delivered with justice,
    her penitent ones with righteousness.
²⁸ But rebels and sinners will both be
        broken,
    and those who forsake the LORD will
        perish.

²⁹ 'You will be ashamed because of the
        sacred oaks
    in which you have delighted;

you will be disgraced because of the
    gardens
    that you have chosen.
³⁰ You will be like an oak with fading
    leaves,
    like a garden without water.
³¹ The mighty man will become tinder
    and his work a spark;
    both will burn together,
        with no one to quench the fire.'

The mountain of the LORD

2 This is what Isaiah son of Amoz saw
    concerning Judah and Jerusalem:

² In the last days

the mountain of the LORD's temple will
        be established
    as the highest of the mountains;
    it will be exalted above the hills,
        and all nations will stream to it.

³ Many peoples will come and say,

'Come, let us go up to the mountain of
        the LORD,
    to the temple of the God of Jacob.
    He will teach us his ways,
        so that we may walk in his paths.'
    The law will go out from Zion,
        the word of the LORD from
            Jerusalem.
⁴ He will judge between the nations
    and will settle disputes for many
        peoples.
    They will beat their swords into
        ploughshares
    and their spears into pruning hooks.
    Nation will not take up sword against
        nation,
        nor will they train for war any more.

⁵ Come, descendants of Jacob,
    let us walk in the light of the LORD.

The day of the LORD

⁶ You, LORD, have abandoned your
        people,
    the descendants of Jacob.
    They are full of superstitions from the
        East;

---

b 25 That is, against Jerusalem

they practise divination like the
     Philistines
and embrace pagan customs.
7 Their land is full of silver and gold;
     there is no end to their treasures.
Their land is full of horses;
     there is no end to the chariots.
8 Their land is full of idols;
     they bow down to the work of their
          hands,
     to what their fingers have made.
9 So people will be brought low
     and everyone humbled –
     do not forgive them.*a*

10 Go into the rocks, hide in the ground
     from the fearful presence of the
          LORD
     and the splendour of his majesty!
11 The eyes of the arrogant will be humbled
     and human pride brought low;
     the LORD alone will be exalted in that
          day.

12 The LORD Almighty has a day in store
     for all the proud and lofty,
     for all that is exalted
          (and they will be humbled),
13 for all the cedars of Lebanon, tall and
          lofty,
     and all the oaks of Bashan,
14 for all the towering mountains
     and all the high hills,
15 for every lofty tower
     and every fortified wall,
16 for every trading ship*b*
     and every stately vessel.
17 The arrogance of man will be brought
          low
     and human pride humbled;
     the LORD alone will be exalted in that
          day,
18 and the idols will totally disappear.

19 People will flee to caves in the rocks
     and to holes in the ground
     from the fearful presence of the LORD
     and the splendour of his majesty,
     when he rises to shake the earth.

20 In that day people will throw away
     to the moles and bats
     their idols of silver and idols of gold,
     which they made to worship.
21 They will flee to caverns in the rocks
     and to the overhanging crags
     from the fearful presence of the LORD
     and the splendour of his majesty,
     when he rises to shake the earth.

22 Stop trusting in mere humans,
     who have but a breath in their
          nostrils.
     Why hold them in esteem?

Judgment on Jerusalem and Judah

3 See now, the Lord,
     the LORD Almighty,
     is about to take from Jerusalem and
          Judah
     both supply and support:
     all supplies of food and all supplies of
          water,
2   the hero and the warrior,
     the judge and the prophet,
     the diviner and the elder,
3 the captain of fifty and the man of
          rank,
     the counsellor, skilled craftsman and
          clever enchanter.

4 'I will make mere youths their officials;
     children will rule over them.'

5 People will oppress each other –
     man against man, neighbour against
          neighbour.
The young will rise up against the old,
     the nobody against the honoured.

6 A man will seize one of his brothers
     in his father's house, and say,
'You have a cloak, you be our leader;
     take charge of this heap of ruins!'
7 But in that day he will cry out,
     'I have no remedy.
I have no food or clothing in my house;
     do not make me the leader of the
          people.'

8 Jerusalem staggers,
     Judah is falling;

---

a 9   Or *not raise them up*
b 16   Hebrew *every ship of Tarshish*

their words and deeds are against the
LORD,
defying his glorious presence.
9 The look on their faces testifies against
them;
they parade their sin like Sodom;
they do not hide it.
Woe to them!
They have brought disaster upon
themselves.

10 Tell the righteous it will be well with
them,
for they will enjoy the fruit of their
deeds.
11 Woe to the wicked!
Disaster is upon them!
They will be paid back
for what their hands have done.

12 Youths oppress my people,
women rule over them.
My people, your guides lead you
astray;
they turn you from the path.

13 The LORD takes his place in court;
he rises to judge the people.
14 The LORD enters into judgment
against the elders and leaders of his
people:
'It is you who have ruined my vineyard;
the plunder from the poor is in your
houses.
15 What do you mean by crushing my
people
and grinding the faces of the poor?'
declares the Lord,
the LORD Almighty.

16 The LORD says,
'The women of Zion are haughty,
walking along with outstretched
necks,
flirting with their eyes,
strutting along with swaying hips,
with ornaments jingling on their
ankles.
17 Therefore the Lord will bring sores
on the heads of the women of
Zion;
the LORD will make their scalps bald.'

18 In that day the Lord will snatch away
their finery: the bangles and headbands
and crescent necklaces, 19 the earrings and
bracelets and veils, 20 the head-dresses and
anklets and sashes, the perfume bottles
and charms, 21 the signet rings and nose
rings, 22 the fine robes and the capes and
cloaks, the purses 23 and mirrors, and the
linen garments and tiaras and shawls.

24 Instead of fragrance there will be a
stench;
instead of a sash, a rope;
instead of well-dressed hair, baldness;
instead of fine clothing, sackcloth;
instead of beauty, branding.
25 Your men will fall by the sword,
your warriors in battle.
26 The gates of Zion will lament and
mourn;
destitute, she will sit on the ground.

4 1 In that day seven women
will take hold of one man
and say, 'We will eat our own food
and provide our own clothes;
only let us be called by your name.
Take away our disgrace!'

The Branch of the LORD

2 In that day the Branch of the LORD will
be beautiful and glorious, and the fruit
of the land will be the pride and glory of
the survivors in Israel. 3 Those who are
left in Zion, who remain in Jerusalem,
will be called holy, all who are recorded
among the living in Jerusalem. 4 The Lord
will wash away the filth of the women of
Zion; he will cleanse the bloodstains from
Jerusalem by a spirit*a* of judgment and a
spirit*a* of fire. 5 Then the LORD will create
over all of Mount Zion and over those who
assemble there a cloud of smoke by day
and a glow of flaming fire by night; over
everything the glory*b* will be a canopy. 6 It
will be a shelter and shade from the heat
of the day, and a refuge and hiding-place
from the storm and rain.

---

a 4 Or *the Spirit*
b 5 Or *over all the glory there*

The song of the vineyard

5 I will sing for the one I love
a song about his vineyard:
my loved one had a vineyard
on a fertile hillside.
2 He dug it up and cleared it of stones
and planted it with the choicest
vines.
He built a watchtower in it
and cut out a winepress as well.
Then he looked for a crop of good
grapes,
but it yielded only bad fruit.

3 'Now you dwellers in Jerusalem and
people of Judah,
judge between me and my vineyard.
4 What more could have been done for
my vineyard
than I have done for it?
When I looked for good grapes,
why did it yield only bad?
5 Now I will tell you
what I am going to do to my
vineyard:
I will take away its hedge,
and it will be destroyed;
I will break down its wall,
and it will be trampled.
6 I will make it a wasteland,
neither pruned nor cultivated,
and briers and thorns will grow there.
I will command the clouds
not to rain on it.'

7 The vineyard of the LORD Almighty
is the nation of Israel,
and the people of Judah
are the vines he delighted in.
And he looked for justice, but saw
bloodshed;
for righteousness, but heard cries of
distress.

Woes and judgments

8 Woe to you who add house to house
and join field to field
till no space is left
and you live alone in the land.

9 The LORD Almighty has declared in my
hearing:

'Surely the great houses will become
desolate,
the fine mansions left without
occupants.
10 A ten-acre*a* vineyard will produce only a
bath*b* of wine;
a homer*c* of seed will yield only an
ephah*d* of grain.'

11 Woe to those who rise early in the
morning
to run after their drinks,
who stay up late at night
till they are inflamed with wine.
12 They have harps and lyres at their
banquets,
pipes and tambourines and wine,
but they have no regard for the deeds of
the LORD,
no respect for the work of his hands.
13 Therefore my people will go into exile
for lack of understanding;
those of high rank will die of hunger
and the common people will be
parched with thirst.
14 Therefore Death expands its jaws,
opening wide its mouth;
into it will descend their nobles and
masses
with all their brawlers and revellers.
15 So people will be brought low
and everyone humbled,
the eyes of the arrogant humbled.
16 But the LORD Almighty will be exalted
by his justice,
and the holy God will be proved holy
by his righteous acts.
17 Then sheep will graze as in their own
pasture;
lambs will feed*e* among the ruins of
the rich.

18 Woe to those who draw sin along with
cords of deceit,
and wickedness as with cart ropes,
19 to those who say, 'Let God hurry;
let him hasten his work

---

a 10 Or *a vineyard of four hectares*
b 10 That is, about 22 litres
c 10 That is, probably about 160 kilograms
d 10 That is, probably about 16 kilograms
e 17 Septuagint; Hebrew / *strangers will eat*

so that we may see it.
The plan of the Holy One of Israel –
    let it approach, let it come into view,
    so that we may know it.'

20 Woe to those who call evil good
    and good evil,
who put darkness for light
    and light for darkness,
who put bitter for sweet
    and sweet for bitter.

21 Woe to those who are wise in their own
        eyes
    and clever in their own sight.

22 Woe to those who are heroes at
        drinking wine
    and champions at mixing drinks,
23 who acquit the guilty for a bribe,
    but deny justice to the innocent.
24 Therefore, as tongues of fire lick up
        straw
    and as dry grass sinks down in the
        flames,
so their roots will decay
    and their flowers blow away like dust;
for they have rejected the law of the
    LORD Almighty
and spurned the word of the Holy
    One of Israel.
25 Therefore the LORD's anger burns
        against his people;
    his hand is raised and he strikes
        them down.
The mountains shake,
    and the dead bodies are like refuse in
        the streets.

Yet for all this, his anger is not turned
        away,
    his hand is still upraised.

26 He lifts up a banner for the distant
        nations,
    he whistles for those at the ends of
        the earth.
Here they come,
    swiftly and speedily!
27 Not one of them grows tired or
        stumbles,
    not one slumbers or sleeps;

not a belt is loosened at the waist,
    not a sandal strap is broken.
28 Their arrows are sharp,
    all their bows are strung;
their horses' hooves seem like flint,
    their chariot wheels like a whirlwind.
29 Their roar is like that of the lion,
    they roar like young lions;
they growl as they seize their prey
    and carry it off with no one to rescue.
30 In that day they will roar over it
    like the roaring of the sea.
And if one looks at the land,
    there is only darkness and distress;
    even the sun will be darkened by
        clouds.

Isaiah's commission

6 In the year that King Uzziah died, I
saw the Lord, high and exalted, seated
on a throne; and the train of his robe filled
the temple. 2 Above him were seraphim,
each with six wings: with two wings they
covered their faces, with two they covered
their feet, and with two they were flying.
3 And they were calling to one another:

'Holy, holy, holy is the LORD Almighty;
    the whole earth is full of his glory.'

4 At the sound of their voices the doorposts and thresholds shook and the temple was filled with smoke.

5 'Woe to me!' I cried. 'I am ruined! For I
am a man of unclean lips, and I live among
a people of unclean lips, and my eyes have
seen the King, the LORD Almighty.'

6 Then one of the seraphim flew to me
with a live coal in his hand, which he had
taken with tongs from the altar. 7 With it
he touched my mouth and said, 'See, this
has touched your lips; your guilt is taken
away and your sin atoned for.'

8 Then I heard the voice of the Lord saying, 'Whom shall I send? And who will go
for us?'

And I said, 'Here am I. Send me!'
9 He said, 'Go and tell this people:

' "Be ever hearing, but never
        understanding;
    be ever seeing, but never perceiving."

[10] Make the heart of this people calloused;
   make their ears dull
   and close their eyes.[a]
Otherwise they might see with their
   eyes,
   hear with their ears,
   understand with their hearts,
   and turn and be healed.'

[11] Then I said, 'For how long, Lord?'
And he answered:

'Until the cities lie ruined
   and without inhabitant,
until the houses are left deserted
   and the fields ruined and ravaged,
[12] until the LORD has sent everyone far
   away
   and the land is utterly forsaken.
[13] And though a tenth remains in the land,
   it will again be laid waste.
But as the terebinth and oak
   leave stumps when they are cut
   down,
   so the holy seed will be the stump in
   the land.'

The sign of Immanuel

7 When Ahaz son of Jotham, the son of
Uzziah, was king of Judah, King Rezin
of Aram and Pekah son of Remaliah king
of Israel marched up to fight against Jerusalem, but they could not overpower it.

[2] Now the house of David was told,
'Aram has allied itself with[a] Ephraim'; so
the hearts of Ahaz and his people were
shaken, as the trees of the forest are
shaken by the wind.

[3] Then the LORD said to Isaiah, 'Go out,
you and your son Shear-Jashub,[b] to meet
Ahaz at the end of the aqueduct of the
Upper Pool, on the road to the Launderer's
Field. [4] Say to him, "Be careful, keep calm
and don't be afraid. Do not lose heart because of these two smouldering stubs of
firewood – because of the fierce anger of

Rezin and Aram and of the son of Remaliah. [5] Aram, Ephraim and Remaliah's son
have plotted your ruin, saying, [6] 'Let us invade Judah; let us tear it apart and divide
it among ourselves, and make the son of
Tabeel king over it.' [7] Yet this is what the
Sovereign LORD says:

'"It will not take place,
   it will not happen,
[8] for the head of Aram is Damascus,
   and the head of Damascus is only
   Rezin.
Within sixty-five years
   Ephraim will be too shattered to be a
   people.
[9] The head of Ephraim is Samaria,
   and the head of Samaria is only
   Remaliah's son.
If you do not stand firm in your faith,
   you will not stand at all."'

[10] Again the LORD spoke to Ahaz, [11] 'Ask
the LORD your God for a sign, whether
in the deepest depths or in the highest
heights.'

[12] But Ahaz said, 'I will not ask; I will not
put the LORD to the test.'

[13] Then Isaiah said, 'Hear now, you
house of David! Is it not enough to try
the patience of humans? Will you try the
patience of my God also? [14] Therefore the
Lord himself will give you[c] a sign: the virgin[d] will conceive and give birth to a son,
and[e] will call him Immanuel.[f] [15] He will be
eating curds and honey when he knows
enough to reject the wrong and choose
the right, [16] for before the boy knows
enough to reject the wrong and choose
the right, the land of the two kings you
dread will be laid waste. [17] The LORD will
bring on you and on your people and on
the house of your father a time unlike any
since Ephraim broke away from Judah –
he will bring the king of Assyria.'

---

a 9,10 Hebrew; Septuagint ' "You will be ever hearing,
but never understanding; / you will be ever seeing, but never
perceiving." / [10] This people's heart has become calloused; / they
hardly hear with their ears, / and they have closed their eyes
a 2 Or has set up camp in
b 3 Shear-Jashub means a remnant will return.

---

c 14 The Hebrew is plural.
d 14 Or young woman
e 14 Masoretic Text; Dead Sea Scrolls son, and he or
son, and they
f 14 Immanuel means God with us.

Assyria, the Lord's instrument

18 In that day the Lord will whistle for flies from the Nile delta in Egypt and for bees from the land of Assyria. **19** They will all come and settle in the steep ravines and in the crevices in the rocks, on all the thornbushes and at all the water holes. **20** In that day the Lord will use a razor hired from beyond the River Euphrates – the king of Assyria – to shave your heads and private parts, and to cut off your beards also. **21** In that day, a person will keep alive a young cow and two goats. **22** And because of the abundance of the milk they give, there will be curds to eat. All who remain in the land will eat curds and honey. **23** In that day, in every place where there were a thousand vines worth a thousand silver shekels,*g* there will be only briers and thorns. **24** Hunters will go there with bow and arrow, for the land will be covered with briers and thorns. **25** As for all the hills once cultivated by the hoe, you will no longer go there for fear of the briers and thorns; they will become places where cattle are turned loose and where sheep run.

⊢ FACT ⊢

LONGEST NAME

The longest personal name in the Bible is Maher-shalal-hash-baz (Isaiah 8:1–4). This is a prediction. It means 'quick to the plunder, swift to the spoil', and refers to the danger from the Assyrians.

Isaiah and his children as signs

8 The Lord said to me, 'Take a large scroll and write on it with an ordinary pen: Maher-Shalal-Hash-Baz.'*a* **2** So I called in Uriah the priest and Zechariah

son of Jeberekiah as reliable witnesses for me. **3** Then I made love to the prophetess, and she conceived and gave birth to a son. And the Lord said to me, 'Name him Maher-Shalal-Hash-Baz. **4** For before the boy knows how to say "My father" or "My mother", the wealth of Damascus and the plunder of Samaria will be carried off by the king of Assyria.'

5 The Lord spoke to me again:

6 'Because this people has rejected
   the gently flowing waters of Shiloah
and rejoices over Rezin
   and the son of Remaliah,
7 therefore the Lord is about to bring
      against them
   the mighty floodwaters of the
      Euphrates –
   the king of Assyria with all his pomp.
It will overflow all its channels,
   run over all its banks
8 and sweep on into Judah, swirling
      over it,
   passing through it and reaching up
      to the neck.
Its outspread wings will cover the
      breadth of your land,
   Immanuel!'*b*

9 Raise the war cry,*c* you nations, and be
      shattered!
   Listen, all you distant lands.
Prepare for battle, and be shattered!
   Prepare for battle, and be shattered!
10 Devise your strategy, but it will be
      thwarted;
   propose your plan, but it will not
      stand,
   for God is with us.*d*

11 This is what the Lord says to me with his strong hand upon me, warning me not to follow the way of this people:

12 'Do not call conspiracy
      everything this people calls a
      conspiracy;

---

g 23 That is, about 12 kilograms
a 1 *Maher-Shalal-Hash-Baz* means *quick to the plunder, swift to the spoil*; also in verse 3.

b 8 *Immanuel* means *God with us*.
c 9 Or *Do your worst*
d 10 Hebrew *Immanuel*

do not fear what they fear,
and do not dread it.
13 The LORD Almighty is the one you are to
regard as holy,
he is the one you are to fear,
he is the one you are to dread.
14 He will be a holy place;
for both Israel and Judah he will be
a stone that causes people to stumble
and a rock that makes them fall.
And for the people of Jerusalem he
will be
a trap and a snare.
15 Many of them will stumble;
they will fall and be broken,
they will be snared and captured.'

16 Bind up this testimony of warning
and seal up God's instruction among
my disciples.
17 I will wait for the LORD,
who is hiding his face from the
descendants of Jacob.
I will put my trust in him.

18 Here am I, and the children the LORD
has given me. We are signs and symbols
in Israel from the LORD Almighty, who
dwells on Mount Zion.

The darkness turns to light

19 When someone tells you to consult
mediums and spiritists, who whisper and
mutter, should not a people enquire of
their God? Why consult the dead on behalf
of the living? 20 Consult God's instruction
and the testimony of warning. If anyone
does not speak according to this word,
they have no light of dawn. 21 Distressed
and hungry, they will roam through the
land; when they are famished, they will
become enraged and, looking upwards,
will curse their king and their God. 22 Then
they will look towards the earth and see
only distress and darkness and fearful
gloom, and they will be thrust into utter
darkness.

9 *a* Nevertheless, there will be no
more gloom for those who were in
distress. In the past he humbled the land
of Zebulun and the land of Naphtali, but
in the future he will honour Galilee of the
nations, by the Way of the Sea, beyond the
Jordan –

2 The people walking in darkness
have seen a great light;
on those living in the land of deep
darkness
a light has dawned.
3 You have enlarged the nation
and increased their joy;
they rejoice before you
as people rejoice at the harvest,
as warriors rejoice
when dividing the plunder.
4 For as in the day of Midian's defeat,
you have shattered
the yoke that burdens them,
the bar across their shoulders,
the rod of their oppressor.
5 Every warrior's boot used in battle
and every garment rolled in blood
will be destined for burning,
will be fuel for the fire.
6 For to us a child is born,
to us a son is given,
and the government will be on his
shoulders.
And he will be called
Wonderful Counsellor, Mighty God,
Everlasting Father, Prince of Peace.
7 Of the greatness of his government and
peace
there will be no end.
He will reign on David's throne
and over his kingdom,
establishing and upholding it
with justice and righteousness
from that time on and for ever.
The zeal of the LORD Almighty
will accomplish this.

The LORD's anger against Israel

8 The Lord has sent a message against
Jacob;
it will fall on Israel.
9 All the people will know it –
Ephraim and the inhabitants of
Samaria –
who say with pride

---

a In Hebrew texts 9:1 is numbered 8:23, and 9:2-21 is
numbered 9:1-20.

and arrogance of heart,
10 'The bricks have fallen down,
    but we will rebuild with dressed
      stone;
the fig trees have been felled,
    but we will replace them with
      cedars.'
11 But the LORD has strengthened Rezin's
      foes against them
    and has spurred their enemies on.
12 Arameans from the east and Philistines
      from the west
    have devoured Israel with open
      mouth.

Yet for all this, his anger is not turned
    away,
    his hand is still upraised.

13 But the people have not returned to
      him who struck them,
    nor have they sought the LORD
      Almighty.
14 So the LORD will cut off from Israel both
      head and tail,
    both palm branch and reed in a
      single day;
15 the elders and dignitaries are the head,
    the prophets who teach lies are the
      tail.
16 Those who guide this people mislead
      them,
    and those who are guided are led
      astray.
17 Therefore the Lord will take no pleasure
      in the young men,
    nor will he pity the fatherless and
      widows,
for everyone is ungodly and wicked,
    every mouth speaks folly.

Yet for all this, his anger is not turned
    away,
    his hand is still upraised.

18 Surely wickedness burns like a fire;
    it consumes briers and thorns,
it sets the forest thickets ablaze,
    so that it rolls upwards in a column
      of smoke.
19 By the wrath of the LORD Almighty
    the land will be scorched

and the people will be fuel for the fire;
    they will not spare one another.
20 On the right they will devour,
    but still be hungry;
on the left they will eat,
    but not be satisfied.
Each will feed on the flesh of their own
    offspring:*b*
21   Manasseh will feed on Ephraim, and
      Ephraim on Manasseh;
    together they will turn against
      Judah.

Yet for all this, his anger is not turned
    away,
    his hand is still upraised.

10 Woe to those who make unjust
    laws,
    to those who issue oppressive
      decrees,
2 to deprive the poor of their rights
    and withhold justice from the
      oppressed of my people,
making widows their prey
    and robbing the fatherless.
3 What will you do on the day of
      reckoning,
    when disaster comes from afar?
To whom will you run for help?
    Where will you leave your riches?
4 Nothing will remain but to cringe
      among the captives
    or fall among the slain.

Yet for all this, his anger is not turned
    away,
    his hand is still upraised.

God's judgment on Assyria

5 'Woe to the Assyrian, the rod of my
      anger,
    in whose hand is the club of my
      wrath!
6 I send him against a godless nation,
    I dispatch him against a people who
      anger me,
to seize loot and snatch plunder,
    and to trample them down like mud
      in the streets.

---

b 20 Or *arm*

7 But this is not what he intends,
>   this is not what he has in mind;
> his purpose is to destroy,
>   to put an end to many nations.
8 "Are not my commanders all kings?" he
>   says.
9   "Has not Kalno fared like
>   Carchemish?
> Is not Hamath like Arpad,
>   and Samaria like Damascus?
10 As my hand seized the kingdoms of the
>   idols,
>   kingdoms whose images excelled
>   those of Jerusalem and
>   Samaria –
11 shall I not deal with Jerusalem and her
>   images
>   as I dealt with Samaria and her
>   idols?" '

12 When the Lord has finished all his work against Mount Zion and Jerusalem, he will say, 'I will punish the king of Assyria for the wilful pride of his heart and the haughty look in his eyes. 13 For he says:

> ' "By the strength of my hand I have
>   done this,
>   and by my wisdom, because I have
>   understanding.
> I removed the boundaries of nations,
>   I plundered their treasures;
>   like a mighty one I subdued[a] their
>   kings.
14 As one reaches into a nest,
>   so my hand reached for the wealth of
>   the nations;
> as people gather abandoned eggs,
>   so I gathered all the countries;
> not one flapped a wing,
>   or opened its mouth to chirp." '

15 Does the axe raise itself above the
>   person who swings it,
>   or the saw boast against the one who
>   uses it?
> As if a rod were to wield the person who
>   lifts it up,
>   or a club brandish the one who is not
>   wood!

16 Therefore, the Lord, the LORD Almighty,
>   will send a wasting disease upon his
>   sturdy warriors;
> under his pomp a fire will be kindled
>   like a blazing flame.
17 The Light of Israel will become a fire,
>   their Holy One a flame;
> in a single day it will burn and consume
>   his thorns and his briers.
18 The splendour of his forests and fertile
>   fields
>   it will completely destroy,
>   as when one who is ill wastes away.
19 And the remaining trees of his forests
>   will be so few
>   that a child could write them down.

The remnant of Israel

20 In that day the remnant of Israel,
>   the survivors of Jacob,
> will no longer rely on him
>   who struck them down
> but will truly rely on the LORD,
>   the Holy One of Israel.
21 A remnant will return,[b] a remnant of
>   Jacob
>   will return to the Mighty God.
22 Though your people be like the sand by
>   the sea, Israel,
>   only a remnant will return.
> Destruction has been decreed,
>   overwhelming and righteous.
23 The Lord, the LORD Almighty, will carry
>   out
>   the destruction decreed upon the
>   whole land.

24 Therefore this is what the Lord, the LORD Almighty, says:

> 'My people who live in Zion,
>   do not be afraid of the Assyrians,
> who beat you with a rod
>   and lift up a club against you, as
>   Egypt did.
25 Very soon my anger against you will
>   end
>   and my wrath will be directed to their
>   destruction.'

---

a 13 Or *treasures; / I subdued the mighty,*

b 21 Hebrew *shear-jashub* (see 7:3 and note); also in verse 22

26 The LORD Almighty will lash them with
        a whip,
    as when he struck down Midian at
        the rock of Oreb;
    and he will raise his staff over the
        waters,
        as he did in Egypt.
27 In that day their burden will be lifted
        from your shoulders,
    their yoke from your neck;
    the yoke will be broken
        because you have grown so fat.c

28 They enter Aiath;
    they pass through Migron;
    they store supplies at Michmash.
29 They go over the pass, and say,
    'We will camp overnight at Geba.'
    Ramah trembles;
    Gibeah of Saul flees.
30 Cry out, Daughter Gallim!
    Listen, Laishah!
    Poor Anathoth!
31 Madmenah is in flight;
    the people of Gebim take cover.
32 This day they will halt at Nob;
    they will shake their fist
    at the mount of Daughter Zion,
    at the hill of Jerusalem.

33 See, the Lord, the LORD Almighty,
    will lop off the boughs with great
        power.
    The lofty trees will be felled,
        the tall ones will be brought low.
34 He will cut down the forest thickets
        with an axe;
    Lebanon will fall before the Mighty
        One.

The branch from Jesse

11 A shoot will come up from the
        stump of Jesse;
    from his roots a Branch will bear fruit.
2 The Spirit of the LORD will rest on him —
    the Spirit of wisdom and of
        understanding,
    the Spirit of counsel and of might,
    the Spirit of the knowledge and fear
        of the LORD —

3 and he will delight in the fear of the
        LORD.

He will not judge by what he sees with
        his eyes,
    or decide by what he hears with his
        ears;
4 but with righteousness he will judge
        the needy,
    with justice he will give decisions for
        the poor of the earth.
He will strike the earth with the rod of
        his mouth;
    with the breath of his lips he will slay
        the wicked.
5 Righteousness will be his belt
    and faithfulness the sash round his
        waist.

6 The wolf will live with the lamb,
    the leopard will lie down with the
        goat,
    the calf and the lion and the yearlinga
        together;
    and a little child will lead them.
7 The cow will feed with the bear,
    their young will lie down together,
    and the lion will eat straw like the ox.
8 The infant will play near the cobra's
        den,
    and the young child will put its hand
        into the viper's nest.
9 They will neither harm nor destroy
    on all my holy mountain,
    for the earth will be filled with the
        knowledge of the LORD
    as the waters cover the sea.

10 In that day the Root of Jesse will stand
as a banner for the peoples; the nations
will rally to him, and his resting place will
be glorious. 11 In that day the Lord will
reach out his hand a second time to re-
claim the surviving remnant of his people from Assyria, from Lower Egypt, from
Upper Egypt, from Cush,b from Elam, from
Babylonia,c from Hamath and from the
islands of the Mediterranean.

---

c 27 Hebrew; Septuagint *broken / from your shoulders*

a 6 Hebrew; Septuagint *lion will feed*
b 11 That is, the upper Nile region
c 11 Hebrew *Shinar*

12 He will raise a banner for the nations
      and gather the exiles of Israel;
he will assemble the scattered people
      of Judah
      from the four quarters of the
         earth.
13 Ephraim's jealousy will vanish,
      and Judah's enemies*d* will be
         destroyed;
Ephraim will not be jealous of Judah,
      nor Judah hostile towards
         Ephraim.
14 They will swoop down on the slopes of
      Philistia to the west;
      together they will plunder the people
      to the east.
They will subdue Edom and Moab,
      and the Ammonites will be subject to
      them.
15 The LORD will dry up
      the gulf of the Egyptian sea;
with a scorching wind he will sweep his
      hand
      over the River Euphrates.
He will break it up into seven streams
      so that anyone can cross over in
      sandals.
16 There will be a highway for the remnant
      of his people
      that is left from Assyria,
as there was for Israel
      when they came up from Egypt.

Songs of praise

12 In that day you will say:

'I will praise you, LORD.
      Although you were angry with me,
your anger has turned away
      and you have comforted me.
2 Surely God is my salvation;
      I will trust and not be afraid.
The LORD, the LORD himself, is my
      strength and my defence*a*;
he has become my salvation.'
3 With joy you will draw water
      from the wells of salvation.

4 In that day you will say:

'Give praise to the LORD, proclaim his
      name;
      make known among the nations
         what he has done,
      and proclaim that his name is exalted.
5 Sing to the LORD, for he has done
      glorious things;
      let this be known to all the world.
6 Shout aloud and sing for joy, people of
      Zion,
      for great is the Holy One of Israel
         among you.'

A prophecy against Babylon

13 A prophecy against Babylon that
Isaiah son of Amoz saw:

2 Raise a banner on a bare hilltop,
      shout to them;
beckon to them
      to enter the gates of the nobles.
3 I have commanded those I prepared for
      battle;
      I have summoned my warriors to
         carry out my wrath –
      those who rejoice in my triumph.

4 Listen, a noise on the mountains,
      like that of a great multitude!
Listen, an uproar among the kingdoms,
      like nations massing together!
The LORD Almighty is mustering
      an army for war.
5 They come from faraway lands,
      from the ends of the heavens –
the LORD and the weapons of his
      wrath –
      to destroy the whole country.

6 Wail, for the day of the LORD is near;
      it will come like destruction from the
      Almighty.*a*
7 Because of this, all hands will go limp,
      every heart will melt with fear.
8 Terror will seize them,
      pain and anguish will grip them;
      they will writhe like a woman in
      labour.

---

d 13 Or *hostility*
a 2 Or *song*

a 6 Hebrew *Shaddai*

They will look aghast at each other,
  their faces aflame.

⁹ See, the day of the LORD is coming
  – a cruel day, with wrath and fierce
    anger –
to make the land desolate
  and destroy the sinners within it.
¹⁰ The stars of heaven and their
    constellations
  will not show their light.
The rising sun will be darkened
  and the moon will not give its light.
¹¹ I will punish the world for its evil,
  the wicked for their sins.
I will put an end to the arrogance of the
    haughty
  and will humble the pride of the
    ruthless.
¹² I will make people scarcer than pure
    gold,
  more rare than the gold of Ophir.
¹³ Therefore I will make the heavens
    tremble;
  and the earth will shake from its
    place
at the wrath of the LORD Almighty,
  in the day of his burning anger.

¹⁴ Like a hunted gazelle,
  like sheep without a shepherd,
they will all return to their own people,
  they will flee to their native land.
¹⁵ Whoever is captured will be thrust
    through;
  all who are caught will fall by the
    sword.
¹⁶ Their infants will be dashed to pieces
    before their eyes;
  their houses will be looted and their
    wives violated.

¹⁷ See, I will stir up against them the
    Medes,
  who do not care for silver
  and have no delight in gold.
¹⁸ Their bows will strike down the young
    men;
  they will have no mercy on infants
  nor will they look with compassion
    on children.
¹⁹ Babylon, the jewel of kingdoms,

the pride and glory of the
    Babylonians,ᵇ
will be overthrown by God
  like Sodom and Gomorrah.
²⁰ She will never be inhabited
  or lived in through all generations;
there no nomads will pitch their tents,
  there no shepherds will rest their
    flocks.
²¹ But desert creatures will lie there,
  jackals will fill her houses;
there the owls will dwell,
  and there the wild goats will leap
    about.
²² Hyenas will inhabit her strongholds,
  jackals her luxurious palaces.
Her time is at hand,
  and her days will not be prolonged.

14 The LORD will have compassion on
    Jacob;
  once again he will choose Israel
  and will settle them in their own
    land.
Foreigners will join them
  and unite with the descendants of
    Jacob.
² Nations will take them
  and bring them to their own place.
And Israel will take possession of the
    nations
  and make them male and female
    servants in the LORD's land.
They will make captives of their captors
  and rule over their oppressors.

³ On the day the LORD gives you relief
from your suffering and turmoil and from
the harsh labour forced on you, ⁴ you will
take up this taunt against the king of Babylon:

How the oppressor has come to an end!
  How his furyᵃ has ended!
⁵ The LORD has broken the rod of the
    wicked,
  the sceptre of the rulers,
⁶ which in anger struck down peoples

ᵇ 19 Or *Chaldeans*
ᵃ 4 Dead Sea Scrolls, Septuagint and Syriac; the
meaning of the word in the Masoretic Text is
uncertain.

with unceasing blows,
and in fury subdued nations
with relentless aggression.
7 All the lands are at rest and at peace;
they break into singing.
8 Even the junipers and the cedars of
Lebanon
gloat over you and say,
'Now that you have been laid low,
no one comes to cut us down.'

9 The realm of the dead below is all astir
to meet you at your coming;
it rouses the spirits of the departed to
greet you –
all those who were leaders in the
world;
it makes them rise from their thrones –
all those who were kings over the
nations.
10 They will all respond,
they will say to you,
'You also have become weak, as we are;
you have become like us.'
11 All your pomp has been brought down
to the grave,
along with the noise of your harps;
maggots are spread out beneath you
and worms cover you.

12 How you have fallen from heaven,
morning star, son of the dawn!
You have been cast down to the earth,
you who once laid low the nations!
13 You said in your heart,
'I will ascend to the heavens;
I will raise my throne
above the stars of God;
I will sit enthroned on the mount of
assembly,
on the utmost heights of Mount
Zaphon.b
14 I will ascend above the tops of the
clouds;
I will make myself like the Most
High.'
15 But you are brought down to the realm
of the dead,
to the depths of the pit.

16 Those who see you stare at you,
they ponder your fate:
'Is this the man who shook the earth
and made kingdoms tremble,
17 the man who made the world a
wilderness,
who overthrew its cities
and would not let his captives go
home?'

18 All the kings of the nations lie in state,
each in his own tomb.
19 But you are cast out of your tomb
like a rejected branch;
you are covered with the slain,
with those pierced by the sword,
those who descend to the stones of
the pit.
Like a corpse trampled underfoot,
20 you will not join them in burial,
for you have destroyed your land
and killed your people.

Let the offspring of the wicked
never be mentioned again.
21 Prepare a place to slaughter his
children
for the sins of their ancestors;
they are not to rise to inherit the land
and cover the earth with their cities.

22 'I will rise up against them,'
declares the LORD Almighty.
'I will wipe out Babylon's name and
survivors,
her offspring and descendants,'
declares the LORD.
23 'I will turn her into a place for owls
and into swampland;
I will sweep her with the broom of
destruction,'
declares the LORD Almighty.

24 The LORD Almighty has sworn,

'Surely, as I have planned, so it will be,
and as I have purposed, so it will
happen.
25 I will crush the Assyrian in my land;
on my mountains I will trample him
down.
His yoke will be taken from my people,

---

b 13 Or of the north; Zaphon was the most sacred
mountain of the Canaanites.

and his burden removed from their
shoulders.'

26 This is the plan determined for the
whole world;
this is the hand stretched out over all
nations.
27 For the Lord Almighty has purposed,
and who can thwart him?
His hand is stretched out, and who
can turn it back?

A prophecy against the Philistines

28 This prophecy came in the year King
Ahaz died:

29 Do not rejoice, all you Philistines,
that the rod that struck you is broken;
from the root of that snake will spring
up a viper,
its fruit will be a darting, venomous
serpent.
30 The poorest of the poor will find
pasture,
and the needy will lie down in safety.
But your root I will destroy by famine;
it will slay your survivors.

31 Wail, you gate! Howl, you city!
Melt away, all you Philistines!
A cloud of smoke comes from the north,
and there is not a straggler in its
ranks.
32 What answer shall be given
to the envoys of that nation?
'The Lord has established Zion,
and in her his afflicted people will
find refuge.'

A prophecy against Moab

15 A prophecy against Moab:

Ar in Moab is ruined,
destroyed in a night!
Kir in Moab is ruined,
destroyed in a night!
2 Dibon goes up to its temple,
to its high places to weep;
Moab wails over Nebo and Medeba.
Every head is shaved
and every beard cut off.
3 In the streets they wear sackcloth;

on the roofs and in the public
squares
they all wail,
prostrate with weeping.
4 Heshbon and Elealeh cry out,
their voices are heard all the way to
Jahaz.
Therefore the armed men of Moab cry
out,
and their hearts are faint.

5 My heart cries out over Moab;
her fugitives flee as far as Zoar,
as far as Eglath Shelishiyah.
They go up the hill to Luhith,
weeping as they go;
on the road to Horonaim
they lament their destruction.
6 The waters of Nimrim are dried up
and the grass is withered;
the vegetation is gone
and nothing green is left.
7 So the wealth they have acquired and
stored up
they carry away over the Ravine of the
Poplars.
8 Their outcry echoes along the border of
Moab;
their wailing reaches as far as Eglaim,
their lamentation as far as Beer Elim.
9 The waters of Dimon*a* are full of blood,
but I will bring still more upon
Dimon*a* –
a lion upon the fugitives of Moab
and upon those who remain in the
land.

16 Send lambs as tribute
to the ruler of the land,
from Sela, across the desert,
to the mount of Daughter Zion.
2 Like fluttering birds
pushed from the nest,
so are the women of Moab
at the fords of the Arnon.

3 'Make up your mind,' Moab says.
'Render a decision.
Make your shadow like night –

---

a 9 *Dimon*, a wordplay on *Dibon* (see verse 2) sounds
like the Hebrew for *blood*.

at high noon.
Hide the fugitives,
  do not betray the refugees.
⁴ Let the Moabite fugitives stay with you;
  be their shelter from the destroyer.'

The oppressor will come to an end,
  and destruction will cease;
  the aggressor will vanish from the
    land.
⁵ In love a throne will be established;
  in faithfulness a man will sit on it –
  one from the house*a* of David –
one who in judging seeks justice
  and speeds the cause of
    righteousness.

⁶ We have heard of Moab's pride –
  how great is her arrogance! –
of her conceit, her pride and her
    insolence;
  but her boasts are empty.
⁷ Therefore the Moabites wail,
  they wail together for Moab.
Lament and grieve
  for the raisin cakes of Kir Hareseth.
⁸ The fields of Heshbon wither,
  the vines of Sibmah also.
The rulers of the nations
  have trampled down the choicest
    vines,
which once reached Jazer
  and spread towards the desert.
Their shoots spread out
  and went as far as the sea.*b*
⁹ So I weep, as Jazer weeps,
  for the vines of Sibmah.
Heshbon and Elealeh,
  I drench you with tears!
The shouts of joy over your ripened fruit
  and over your harvests have been
    stilled.
¹⁰ Joy and gladness are taken away from
    the orchards;
  no one sings or shouts in the
    vineyards;
no one treads out wine at the presses,
  for I have put an end to the shouting.
¹¹ My heart laments for Moab like a harp,

a 5 Hebrew *tent*
b 8 Probably the Dead Sea

my inmost being for Kir Hareseth.
¹² When Moab appears at her high place,
  she only wears herself out;
when she goes to her shrine to pray,
  it is to no avail.

¹³ This is the word the LORD has already
spoken concerning Moab. ¹⁴ But now the
LORD says: 'Within three years, as a servant
bound by contract would count them,
Moab's splendour and all her many people will be despised, and her survivors will
be very few and feeble.'

A prophecy against Damascus

17 A prophecy against Damascus:

'See, Damascus will no longer be a city
  but will become a heap of ruins.
² The cities of Aroer will be deserted
  and left to flocks, which will lie
    down,
  with no one to make them afraid.
³ The fortified city will disappear from
    Ephraim,
  and royal power from Damascus;
the remnant of Aram will be
  like the glory of the Israelites,'
            declares the LORD Almighty.

⁴ 'In that day the glory of Jacob will
    fade;
  the fat of his body will waste away.
⁵ It will be as when reapers harvest the
    standing corn,
  gathering the corn in their arms –
as when someone gleans ears of corn
  in the Valley of Rephaim.
⁶ Yet some gleanings will remain,
  as when an olive tree is beaten,
leaving two or three olives on the
    topmost branches,
  four or five on the fruitful boughs,'
            declares the LORD,
              the God of Israel.

⁷ In that day people will look to their
    Maker
  and turn their eyes to the Holy One of
    Israel.
⁸ They will not look to the altars,
  the work of their hands,

and they will have no regard for the
        Asherah poles*a*
    and the incense altars their fingers
        have made.

⁹In that day their strong cities, which
they left because of the Israelites, will be
like places abandoned to thickets and
undergrowth. And all will be desolation.

¹⁰You have forgotten God your Saviour;
        you have not remembered the Rock,
            your fortress.
    Therefore, though you set out the finest
            plants
        and plant imported vines,
¹¹though on the day you set them out,
            you make them grow,
        and on the morning when you plant
            them, you bring them to bud,
    yet the harvest will be as nothing
        in the day of disease and incurable
            pain.

¹²Woe to the many nations that rage –
        they rage like the raging sea!
    Woe to the peoples who roar –
        they roar like the roaring of great
            waters!
¹³Although the peoples roar like the roar
            of surging waters,
        when he rebukes them they flee far
            away,
    driven before the wind like chaff on the
            hills,
        like tumble-weed before a gale.
¹⁴In the evening, sudden terror!
    Before the morning, they are gone!
    This is the portion of those who
            loot us,
        the lot of those who plunder us.

A prophecy against Cush

18 Woe to the land of whirring wings*a*
        along the rivers of Cush,*b*
    ²which sends envoys by sea
        in papyrus boats over the water.

Go, swift messengers,
    to a people tall and smooth-skinned,
    to a people feared far and wide,
    an aggressive nation of strange speech,
        whose land is divided by rivers.

FAVOURITE
VERSES
Matthew 7:7–8

*Ask and it will be given to you; seek
and you will find; knock and the door
will be opened to you. For everyone
who asks receives; the one who
seeks finds; and to the one who
knocks, the door will be opened.*

I like this verse because it reminds
me that when the going gets tough
God is always with me, whether it's
family, friend or work related.

Beth, 15

³All you people of the world,
        you who live on the earth,
    when a banner is raised on the
            mountains,
        you will see it,
    and when a trumpet sounds,
        you will hear it.
⁴This is what the LORD says to me:
    'I will remain quiet and will look on
            from my dwelling-place,
    like shimmering heat in the sunshine,
        like a cloud of dew in the heat of
            harvest.'
⁵For, before the harvest, when the
            blossom is gone
        and the flower becomes a ripening
            grape,
    he will cut off the shoots with pruning
            knives,
        and cut down and take away the
            spreading branches.

---

a 8 That is, wooden symbols of the goddess
Asherah
a 1 Or *of locusts*
b 1 That is, the upper Nile region

6 They will all be left to the mountain
    birds of prey
    and to the wild animals;
    the birds will feed on them all summer,
    the wild animals all winter.

7 At that time gifts will be brought to the
    LORD Almighty

from a people tall and smooth-skinned,
    from a people feared far and wide,
an aggressive nation of strange speech,
    whose land is divided by rivers —

the gifts will be brought to Mount Zion, the
place of the Name of the LORD Almighty.

A prophecy against Egypt

19 A prophecy against Egypt:

See, the LORD rides on a swift cloud
    and is coming to Egypt.
The idols of Egypt tremble before him,
    and the hearts of the Egyptians melt
      with fear.

2 'I will stir up Egyptian against
      Egyptian —
    brother will fight against brother,
    neighbour against neighbour,
    city against city,
    kingdom against kingdom.
3 The Egyptians will lose heart,
    and I will bring their plans to
      nothing;
    they will consult the idols and the
      spirits of the dead,
    the mediums and the spiritists.
4 I will hand the Egyptians over
    to the power of a cruel master,
and a fierce king will rule over them,'
    declares the Lord, the LORD
      Almighty.

5 The waters of the river will dry up,
    and the river bed will be parched and
      dry.
6 The canals will stink;
    the streams of Egypt will dwindle and
      dry up.
The reeds and rushes will wither,
7   also the plants along the Nile,

at the mouth of the river.
Every sown field along the Nile
    will become parched, will blow away
    and be no more.
8 The fishermen will groan and lament,
    all who cast hooks into the Nile;
those who throw nets on the water
    will pine away.
9 Those who work with combed flax will
      despair,
    the weavers of fine linen will lose
      hope.
10 The workers in cloth will be dejected,
    and all the wage earners will be sick
      at heart.

11 The officials of Zoan are nothing but
      fools;
    the wise counsellors of Pharaoh give
      senseless advice.
How can you say to Pharaoh,
    'I am one of the wise men,
    a disciple of the ancient kings'?

12 Where are your wise men now?
    Let them show you and make known
    what the LORD Almighty
    has planned against Egypt.
13 The officials of Zoan have become
      fools,
    the leaders of Memphis are deceived;
the cornerstones of her peoples
    have led Egypt astray.
14 The LORD has poured into them
    a spirit of dizziness;
they make Egypt stagger in all that she
      does,
    as a drunkard staggers around in his
      vomit.
15 There is nothing Egypt can do —
    head or tail, palm branch or reed.

16 In that day the Egyptians will become
weaklings. They will shudder with fear at
the uplifted hand that the LORD Almighty
raises against them. **17** And the land of
Judah will bring terror to the Egyptians;
everyone to whom Judah is mentioned
will be terrified, because of what the LORD
Almighty is planning against them.
18 In that day five cities in Egypt will
speak the language of Canaan and swear

allegiance to the LORD Almighty. One of them will be called the City of the Sun.*ᵃ*

¹⁹ In that day there will be an altar to the LORD in the heart of Egypt, and a monument to the LORD at its border. ²⁰ It will be a sign and witness to the LORD Almighty in the land of Egypt. When they cry out to the LORD because of their oppressors, he will send them a saviour and defender, and he will rescue them. ²¹ So the LORD will make himself known to the Egyptians, and in that day they will acknowledge the LORD. They will worship with sacrifices and grain offerings; they will make vows to the LORD and keep them. ²² The LORD will strike Egypt with a plague; he will strike them and heal them. They will turn to the LORD, and he will respond to their pleas and heal them.

²³ In that day there will be a highway from Egypt to Assyria. The Assyrians will go to Egypt and the Egyptians to Assyria. The Egyptians and Assyrians will worship together. ²⁴ In that day Israel will be the third, along with Egypt and Assyria, a blessing*ᵇ* on the earth. ²⁵ The LORD Almighty will bless them, saying, 'Blessed be Egypt my people, Assyria my handiwork, and Israel my inheritance.'

A prophecy against Egypt and Cush

20 In the year that the supreme commander, sent by Sargon king of Assyria, came to Ashdod and attacked and captured it – ² at that time the LORD spoke through Isaiah son of Amoz. He said to him, 'Take off the sackcloth from your body and the sandals from your feet.' And he did so, going around stripped and barefoot.

³ Then the LORD said, 'Just as my servant Isaiah has gone stripped and barefoot for three years, as a sign and portent against Egypt and Cush,*ᵃ* ⁴ so the king of Assyria will lead away stripped and barefoot the

Egyptian captives and Cushite exiles, young and old, with buttocks bared – to Egypt's shame. ⁵ Those who trusted in Cush and boasted in Egypt will be dismayed and put to shame. ⁶ In that day the people who live on this coast will say, "See what has happened to those we relied on, those we fled to for help and deliverance from the king of Assyria! How then can we escape?" '

A prophecy against Babylon

21 A prophecy against the Desert by the Sea:

Like whirlwinds sweeping through the
     southland,
     an invader comes from the desert,
     from a land of terror.

² A dire vision has been shown to me:
     the traitor betrays, the looter takes
         loot.
Elam, attack! Media, lay siege!
     I will bring to an end all the groaning
         she caused.

³ At this my body is racked with pain,
     pangs seize me, like those of a
         woman in labour;
I am staggered by what I hear,
     I am bewildered by what I see.
⁴ My heart falters,
     fear makes me tremble;
the twilight I longed for
     has become a horror to me.

⁵ They set the tables,
     they spread the rugs,
     they eat, they drink!
Get up, you officers,
     oil the shields!

⁶ This is what the Lord says to me:

'Go, post a lookout
     and let him report what he sees.
⁷ When he sees chariots
     with teams of horses,
riders on donkeys
     or riders on camels,
let him be alert,
     fully alert.'

ᵃ 18   Some manuscripts of the Masoretic Text, Dead Sea Scrolls, Symmachus and Vulgate; most manuscripts of the Masoretic Text *City of Destruction*
ᵇ 24   Or *Assyria, whose names will be used in blessings* (see Gen. 48:20); or *Assyria, who will be seen by others as blessed*
ᵃ 3   That is, the upper Nile region; also in verse 5

8 And the lookout[a] shouted,

'Day after day, my lord, I stand on the
    watchtower;
    every night I stay at my post.
9 Look, here comes a man in a chariot
    with a team of horses.
And he gives back the answer:
    "Babylon has fallen, has fallen!
All the images of its gods
    lie shattered on the ground!" '

10 My people who are crushed on the
    threshing-floor,
    I tell you what I have heard
from the LORD Almighty,
    from the God of Israel.

A prophecy against Edom

11 A prophecy against Dumah:[b]

Someone calls to me from Seir,
    'Watchman, what is left of the night?
    Watchman, what is left of the night?'
12 The watchman replies,
    'Morning is coming, but also the
      night.
If you would ask, then ask;
    and come back yet again.'

A prophecy against Arabia

13 A prophecy against Arabia:

You caravans of Dedanites,
    who camp in the thickets of Arabia,
14 bring water for the thirsty;
you who live in Tema,
    bring food for the fugitives.
15 They flee from the sword,
    from the drawn sword,
from the bent bow
    and from the heat of battle.

16 This is what the Lord says to me:
'Within one year, as a servant bound by
contract would count it, all the splendour
of Kedar will come to an end. 17 The survivors of the archers, the warriors of Kedar,

will be few.' The LORD, the God of Israel,
has spoken.

A prophecy about Jerusalem

22 A prophecy against the Valley of
Vision:

What troubles you now,
    that you have all gone up on the roofs,
2 you town so full of commotion,
    you city of tumult and revelry?
Your slain were not killed by the sword,
    nor did they die in battle.
3 All your leaders have fled together;
    they have been captured without
      using the bow.
All you who were caught were taken
      prisoner together,
    having fled while the enemy was still
      far away.
4 Therefore I said, 'Turn away from me;
    let me weep bitterly.
Do not try to console me
    over the destruction of my people.'

5 The Lord, the LORD Almighty, has a day
    of tumult and trampling and terror
    in the Valley of Vision,
a day of battering down walls
    and of crying out to the mountains.
6 Elam takes up the quiver,
    with her charioteers and horses;
    Kir uncovers the shield.
7 Your choicest valleys are full of chariots,
    and horsemen are posted at the city
      gates.

8 The Lord stripped away the defences of
    Judah,
    and you looked in that day
    to the weapons in the Palace of the
      Forest.
9 You saw that the walls of the City of
    David
    were broken through in many places;
you stored up water
    in the Lower Pool.
10 You counted the buildings in Jerusalem
    and tore down houses to strengthen
      the wall.
11 You built a reservoir between the two
    walls

---

a 8   Dead Sea Scrolls and Syriac; Masoretic Text *A lion*
b 11   *Dumah*, a word play on *Edom*, means *silence* or
stillness.

for the water of the Old Pool,
but you did not look to the One who
made it,
or have regard for the One who
planned it long ago.

12 The Lord, the LORD Almighty,
called you on that day
to weep and to wail,
to tear out your hair and put on
sackcloth.
13 But see, there is joy and revelry,
slaughtering of cattle and killing of
sheep,
eating of meat and drinking of wine!
'Let us eat and drink,' you say,
'for tomorrow we die!'

14 The LORD Almighty has revealed this
in my hearing: 'Till your dying day this sin
will not be atoned for,' says the Lord, the
LORD Almighty.

15 This is what the Lord, the LORD
Almighty, says:

'Go, say to this steward,
to Shebna the palace administrator:
16 what are you doing here and who gave
you permission
to cut out a grave for yourself here,
hewing your grave on the height
and chiselling your resting place in
the rock?

17 'Beware, the LORD is about to take firm
hold of you
and hurl you away, you mighty man.
18 He will roll you up tightly like a ball
and throw you into a large country.
There you will die
and there the chariots you were so
proud of
will become a disgrace to your
master's house.
19 I will depose you from your office,
and you will be ousted from your
position.

20 'In that day I will summon my servant, Eliakim son of Hilkiah. 21 I will clothe
him with your robe and fasten your sash

around him and hand your authority over
to him. He will be a father to those who
live in Jerusalem and to the people of Judah. 22 I will place on his shoulder the key
to the house of David; what he opens no
one can shut, and what he shuts no one
can open. 23 I will drive him like a peg into
a firm place; he will become a seat*a* of
honour for the house of his father. 24 All
the glory of his family will hang on him:
its offspring and offshoots – all its lesser
vessels, from the bowls to all the jars.

25 'In that day,' declares the LORD
Almighty, 'the peg driven into the firm
place will give way; it will be sheared off
and will fall, and the load hanging on it
will be cut down.' The LORD has spoken.

A prophecy against Tyre

23

A prophecy against Tyre:

Wail, you ships of Tarshish!
For Tyre is destroyed
and left without house or harbour.
From the land of Cyprus
word has come to them.

2 Be silent, you people of the island
and you merchants of Sidon,
whom the seafarers have enriched.
3 On the great waters
came the grain of the Shihor;
the harvest of the Nile*a* was the revenue
of Tyre,
and she became the market-place of
the nations.

4 Be ashamed, Sidon, and you fortress of
the sea,
for the sea has spoken:
'I have neither been in labour nor given
birth;
I have neither reared sons nor
brought up daughters.'
5 When word comes to Egypt,
they will be in anguish at the report
from Tyre.

---

a 23 Or *throne*
a 2,3 Masoretic Text; Dead Sea Scrolls *Sidon, / who
cross over the sea; / your envoys* 3 *are on the great waters. / The
grain of the Shihor, / the harvest of the Nile,*

6 Cross over to Tarshish;
  wail, you people of the island.
7 Is this your city of revelry,
  the old, old city,
  whose feet have taken her
  to settle in far-off lands?
8 Who planned this against Tyre,
  the bestower of crowns,
  whose merchants are princes,
  whose traders are renowned in the
    earth?
9 The LORD Almighty planned it,
  to bring down her pride in all her
    splendour
  and to humble all who are renowned
    on the earth.

10 Till[b] your land as they do along the Nile,
  Daughter Tarshish,
  for you no longer have a harbour.
11 The LORD has stretched out his hand
    over the sea
  and made its kingdoms tremble.
He has given an order concerning
    Phoenicia
  that her fortresses be destroyed.
12 He said, 'No more of your revelling,
  Virgin Daughter Sidon, now crushed!

  'Up, cross over to Cyprus;
  even there you will find no rest.'
13 Look at the land of the Babylonians,[c]
  this people that is now of no
    account!
The Assyrians have made it
  a place for desert creatures;
  they raised up their siege towers,
  they stripped its fortresses bare
  and turned it into a ruin.

14 Wail, you ships of Tarshish;
  your fortress is destroyed!

15 At that time Tyre will be forgotten for
seventy years, the span of a king's life. But
at the end of these seventy years, it will
happen to Tyre as in the song of the prostitute:

16 'Take up a harp, walk through the city,
  you forgotten prostitute;
  play the harp well, sing many a song,
  so that you will be remembered.'

17 At the end of seventy years, the LORD
will deal with Tyre. She will return to her
lucrative prostitution and will ply her
trade with all the kingdoms on the face of
the earth. **18** Yet her profit and her earnings
will be set apart for the LORD; they will not
be stored up or hoarded. Her profits will
go to those who live before the LORD, for
abundant food and fine clothes.

The LORD's devastation of the earth

24 See, the LORD is going to lay waste
  the earth
  and devastate it;
  he will ruin its face
  and scatter its inhabitants –
2 it will be the same
  for priest as for people,
  for the master as for his servant,
  for the mistress as for her servant,
  for seller as for buyer,
  for borrower as for lender,
  for debtor as for creditor.
3 The earth will be completely laid waste
  and totally plundered.
          The LORD has spoken
                  this word.

4 The earth dries up and withers,
  the world languishes and withers,
  the heavens languish with the earth.
5 The earth is defiled by its people;
  they have disobeyed the laws,
violated the statutes
  and broken the everlasting covenant.
6 Therefore a curse consumes the earth;
  its people must bear their guilt.
Therefore earth's inhabitants are
    burned up,
  and very few are left.
7 The new wine dries up and the vine
    withers;
  all the merrymakers groan.
8 The joyful tambourines are stilled,
  the noise of the revellers has
    stopped,
  the joyful harp is silent.

---

b 10 Dead Sea Scrolls and some Septuagint
manuscripts; Masoretic Text *Go through*
c 13 Or *Chaldeans*

9 No longer do they drink wine with a
    song;
  the beer is bitter to its drinkers.
10 The ruined city lies desolate;
  the entrance to every house is
    barred.
11 In the streets they cry out for wine;
  all joy turns to gloom,
  all joyful sounds are banished from
    the earth.
12 The city is left in ruins,
  its gate is battered to pieces.
13 So will it be on the earth
  and among the nations,
  as when an olive tree is beaten,
  or as when gleanings are left after
    the grape harvest.

14 They raise their voices, they shout for
    joy;
  from the west they acclaim the
    LORD's majesty.
15 Therefore in the east give glory to the
    LORD;
  exalt the name of the LORD, the God
    of Israel,
  in the islands of the sea.
16 From the ends of the earth we hear
    singing:
  'Glory to the Righteous One.'

But I said, 'I waste away, I waste away!
    Woe to me!
  The treacherous betray!
    With treachery the treacherous
      betray!'
17 Terror and pit and snare await you,
  people of the earth.
18 Whoever flees at the sound of terror
  will fall into a pit;
  whoever climbs out of the pit
  will be caught in a snare.

The floodgates of the heavens are
    opened,
  the foundations of the earth
    shake.
19 The earth is broken up,
  the earth is split asunder,
  the earth is violently shaken.
20 The earth reels like a drunkard,
  it sways like a hut in the wind;

so heavy upon it is the guilt of its
    rebellion
  that it falls – never to rise again.

21 In that day the LORD will punish
  the powers in the heavens above
  and the kings on the earth below.
22 They will be herded together
  like prisoners bound in a dungeon;
  they will be shut up in prison
  and be punished*a* after many days.
23 The moon will be dismayed,
  the sun ashamed;
  for the LORD Almighty will reign
  on Mount Zion and in Jerusalem,
  and before its elders – with great
    glory.

Praise to the LORD

25 LORD, you are my God;
  I will exalt you and praise your
    name,
  for in perfect faithfulness
  you have done wonderful things,
  things planned long ago.
2 You have made the city a heap of
    rubble,
  the fortified town a ruin,
  the foreigners' stronghold a city no
    more;
  it will never be rebuilt.
3 Therefore strong peoples will honour
    you;
  cities of ruthless nations will revere
    you.
4 You have been a refuge for the poor,
  a refuge for the needy in their
    distress,
  a shelter from the storm
  and a shade from the heat.
For the breath of the ruthless
  is like a storm driving against a wall
5   and like the heat of the desert.
You silence the uproar of foreigners;
  as heat is reduced by the shadow of a
    cloud,
  so the song of the ruthless is stilled.

6 On this mountain the LORD Almighty
  will prepare

_____
a 22 Or *released*

a feast of rich food for all peoples,
a banquet of aged wine –
   the best of meats and the finest of
     wines.
7 On this mountain he will destroy
   the shroud that enfolds all peoples,
the sheet that covers all nations;
8   he will swallow up death for ever.
The Sovereign LORD will wipe away the
   tears
   from all faces;
he will remove his people's disgrace
   from all the earth.
               The LORD has spoken.

9 In that day they will say,

'Surely this is our God;
   we trusted in him, and he saved us.
This is the LORD, we trusted in him;
   let us rejoice and be glad in his
     salvation.'

10 The hand of the LORD will rest on this
     mountain;
   but Moab will be trampled in their
     land
   as straw is trampled down in the
     manure.
11 They will stretch out their hands in it,
   as swimmers stretch out their hands
     to swim.
God will bring down their pride
   despite the cleverness*a* of their
     hands.
12 He will bring down your high fortified
     walls
   and lay them low;
he will bring them down to the ground,
   to the very dust.

A song of praise

26 In that day this song will be sung
in the land of Judah:

We have a strong city;
   God makes salvation
   its walls and ramparts.
2 Open the gates

---
*a 11 The meaning of the Hebrew for this word is
uncertain.*

that the righteous nation may enter,
   the nation that keeps faith.
3 You will keep in perfect peace
   those whose minds are steadfast,
   because they trust in you.
4 Trust in the LORD for ever,
   for the LORD, the LORD himself, is the
     Rock eternal.
5 He humbles those who dwell on high,
   he lays the lofty city low;
  he levels it to the ground
   and casts it down to the dust.
6 Feet trample it down –
   the feet of the oppressed,
   the footsteps of the poor.

FAVOURITE VERSES

Psalm 91:11–12

*For he will command his angels
   concerning you
  to guard you in all your ways;
they will lift you up in their hands,
  so that you will not strike your foot
   against a stone.*

These verses gave me hope in
fighting cancer. Life has tough
times – look at Paul the apostle. But
God promises that we'll be carried
through those tough times by
angels. Mindblowing!

Adina, 30

7 The path of the righteous is level;
   you, the Upright One, make the way
     of the righteous smooth.
8 Yes, LORD, walking in the way of your
     laws,*a*
   we wait for you;
your name and renown
   are the desire of our hearts.

---
a 8 Or judgments

9 My soul yearns for you in the night;
in the morning my spirit longs for
you.
When your judgments come upon the
earth,
the people of the world learn
righteousness.
10 But when grace is shown to the wicked,
they do not learn righteousness;
even in a land of uprightness they go on
doing evil
and do not regard the majesty of the
LORD.
11 LORD, your hand is lifted high,
but they do not see it.
Let them see your zeal for your people
and be put to shame;
let the fire reserved for your enemies
consume them.

12 LORD, you establish peace for us;
all that we have accomplished you
have done for us.
13 LORD our God, other lords besides you
have ruled over us,
but your name alone do we honour.
14 They are now dead, they live no more;
their spirits do not rise.
You punished them and brought them
to ruin;
you wiped out all memory of them.
15 You have enlarged the nation, LORD;
you have enlarged the nation.
You have gained glory for yourself;
you have extended all the borders of
the land.

16 LORD, they came to you in their distress;
when you disciplined them,
they could barely whisper a prayer.*b*
17 As a pregnant woman about to give
birth
writhes and cries out in her pain,
so were we in your presence, LORD.
18 We were with child, we writhed in
labour,
but we gave birth to wind.
We have not brought salvation to the
earth,

and the people of the world have not
come to life.

19 But your dead will live, LORD;
their bodies will rise –
let those who dwell in the dust
wake up and shout for joy –
your dew is like the dew of the
morning;
the earth will give birth to her dead.

20 Go, my people, enter your rooms
and shut the doors behind you;
hide yourselves for a little while
until his wrath has passed by.
21 See, the LORD is coming out of his
dwelling
to punish the people of the earth for
their sins.
The earth will disclose the blood shed
on it;
the earth will conceal its slain no
longer.

Deliverance of Israel

27 In that day,

the LORD will punish with his sword –
his fierce, great and powerful sword –
Leviathan the gliding serpent,
Leviathan the coiling serpent;
he will slay the monster of the sea.

2 In that day –

'Sing about a fruitful vineyard:
3 I, the LORD, watch over it;
I water it continually.
I guard it day and night
so that no one may harm it.
4 I am not angry.
If only there were briers and thorns
confronting me!
I would march against them in battle;
I would set them all on fire.
5 Or else let them come to me for refuge;
let them make peace with me,
yes, let them make peace with me.'

6 In days to come Jacob will take root,
Israel will bud and blossom
and fill all the world with fruit.

---

b 16 The meaning of the Hebrew for this clause is
uncertain.

⁷ Has the LORD struck her
    as he struck down those who struck
        her?
Has she been killed
    as those were killed who killed her?
⁸ By warfare*a* and exile you contend with
    her –
    with his fierce blast he drives her out,
    as on a day the east wind blows.
⁹ By this, then, will Jacob's guilt be
    atoned for,
    and this will be the full fruit of the
        removal of his sin:
when he makes all the altar stones
    to be like limestone crushed to
        pieces,
no Asherah poles*b* or incense altars
    will be left standing.
¹⁰ The fortified city stands desolate,
    an abandoned settlement, forsaken
        like the wilderness;
there the calves graze,
    there they lie down;
    they strip its branches bare.
¹¹ When its twigs are dry, they are broken
    off
    and women come and make fires
        with them.
For this is a people without
    understanding;
    so their Maker has no compassion
        on them,
    and their Creator shows them no
        favour.

¹² In that day the LORD will thresh from the flowing Euphrates to the Wadi of Egypt, and you, Israel, will be gathered up one by one. ¹³ And in that day a great trumpet will sound. Those who were perishing in Assyria and those who were exiled in Egypt will come and worship the LORD on the holy mountain in Jerusalem.

Woe to the leaders of Ephraim and Judah

28 Woe to that wreath, the pride of
    Ephraim's drunkards,

to the fading flower, his glorious
    beauty,
set on the head of a fertile valley –
    to that city, the pride of those laid
        low by wine!
² See, the Lord has one who is powerful
    and strong.
Like a hailstorm and a destructive
    wind,
like a driving rain and a flooding
    downpour,
    he will throw it forcefully to the
        ground.
³ That wreath, the pride of Ephraim's
    drunkards,
    will be trampled underfoot.
⁴ That fading flower, his glorious
    beauty,
    set on the head of a fertile valley,
will be like figs ripe before harvest –
    as soon as people see them and take
        them in hand,
    they swallow them.

⁵ In that day the LORD Almighty
    will be a glorious crown,
a beautiful wreath
    for the remnant of his people.
⁶ He will be a spirit of justice
    to the one who sits in judgment,
a source of strength
    to those who turn back the battle at
        the gate.

⁷ And these also stagger from wine
    and reel from beer:
priests and prophets stagger from beer
    and are befuddled with wine;
they reel from beer,
    they stagger when seeing visions,
    they stumble when rendering
        decisions.
⁸ All the tables are covered with vomit
    and there is not a spot without filth.

⁹ 'Who is it he is trying to teach?
    To whom is he explaining his
        message?
To children weaned from their milk,
    to those just taken from the breast?
¹⁰ For it is:
    do this, do that,

---

a 8 See Septuagint; the meaning of the Hebrew for this word is uncertain.

b 9 That is, wooden symbols of the goddess Asherah

a rule for this, a rule for that;[a]
a little here, a little there.'

11 Very well then, with foreign lips and
     strange tongues
    God will speak to this people,
12 to whom he said,
    'This is the resting-place, let the
      weary rest';
and, 'This is the place of repose' –
    but they would not listen.
13 So then, the word of the LORD to them
     will become:
do this, do that,
a rule for this, a rule for that;
a little here, a little there –
so that as they go they will fall
    backwards;
    they will be injured and snared and
      captured.

14 Therefore hear the word of the LORD,
    you scoffers
    who rule this people in Jerusalem.
15 You boast, 'We have entered into a
     covenant with death,
    with the realm of the dead we have
      made an agreement.
When an overwhelming scourge
    sweeps by,
    it cannot touch us,
for we have made a lie our refuge
    and falsehood[b] our hiding-place.'

16 So this is what the Sovereign LORD
says:

    'See, I lay a stone in Zion, a tested stone,
    a precious cornerstone for a sure
      foundation;
    the one who relies on it
    will never be stricken with panic.
17 I will make justice the measuring line
    and righteousness the plumb-line;
hail will sweep away your refuge, the
    lie,
and water will overflow your hiding-
    place.

18 Your covenant with death will be
    annulled;
    your agreement with the realm of the
      dead will not stand.
When the overwhelming scourge
    sweeps by,
    you will be beaten down by it.
19 As often as it comes it will carry you
    away;
    morning after morning, by day and
      by night,
    it will sweep through.'

The understanding of this message
    will bring sheer terror.
20 The bed is too short to stretch out on,
    the blanket too narrow to wrap
      around you.
21 The LORD will rise up as he did at Mount
    Perazim,
    he will rouse himself as in the Valley
      of Gibeon –
to do his work, his strange work,
    and perform his task, his alien task.
22 Now stop your mocking,
    or your chains will become heavier;
the Lord, the LORD Almighty, has told
    me
    of the destruction decreed against
      the whole land.

23 Listen and hear my voice;
    pay attention and hear what I say.
24 When a farmer ploughs for planting,
    does he plough continually?
    Does he keep on breaking up and
      working the soil?
25 When he has levelled the surface,
    does he not sow caraway and scatter
      cummin?
Does he not plant wheat in its place,[c]
    barley in its plot,[c]
    and spelt in its field?
26 His God instructs him
    and teaches him the right way.

27 Caraway is not threshed with a sledge,
    nor is the cartwheel rolled over
      cummin;

---

a 10 Hebrew / *sav lasav sav lasav* / *kav lakav kav lakav*
(probably meaningless sounds mimicking the
prophet's words); also in verse 13
b 15 Or *false gods*

c 25 The meaning of the Hebrew for this word is
uncertain.

FAITH IN THE WORLD 6

WISDOM FOR WORK

It's amazing what modern science is teaching us about how the human brain works. For instance, did you know that when you do a repetitive task your brain can remember how to do it without you directly thinking about it? It forms 'neural pathways' – Google it if you're interested, but for now all you need to know is that your brain is really good at remembering how to do stuff!

Take, for instance, playing a scale on a guitar or a piano. At first, learning the scale takes time. You need to really focus to place your fingers in the right position on the fretboard or keys. After practice, though, you can play the scale without thinking where to place your fingers. Amazing! That's your genius brain at work.

God designed us to get better and better at a whole host of tasks. That's why the saying 'practice makes perfect' has a whole lot of truth in it. In Isaiah 28:23–29 God speaks of a farmer who is really good at his job. He knows not just when but where to plant the right seed so that it thrives. And the farmer knows exactly how he should harvest his crop, and which tools to use so that it can be turned into food to eat. God is using this example to refer to his relationship with Israel. God knows exactly what to do with his people in order to bring about the best for them. We should trust his wisdom. In the middle of this, though, God makes a wonderful comment about how he partners with us in work: *'Does he not plant wheat in its place, barley in its plot, and spelt in its field? His God instructs him and teaches him the right way.'*

As we have said before in thinking about work and the Bible (see Exodus 31), God can give us wisdom for a particular task. But most of God's equipping us for work has already been done by giving us the miracle that is the human brain. It's incredible what we can 'learn' to do. And our brain is hungry for information so we can improve. That's partly why some scientists think we're so hooked to the internet: lots and lots of lovely new facts and lessons for us to absorb. Yet we have to 'use it or lose it'. Your brain loves a good challenge, so remember to work it well. Don't just feed it TV, computer games and celebrity gossip! You'll be surprised how satisfying you find overcoming challenges, and how you improve with practice. 'Brain training' is something we should all be involved in, in order to improve ourselves and our world. Remember that God made us to look after and take care of the created order, so don't be surprised that he gave us a fantastic tool for the job. What will you and your amazing brain accomplish?

Jason Gardner

⏪ Job 38:19–38   Mark 6:1–6 ⏩

caraway is beaten out with a rod,
and cummin with a stick.
28 Grain must be ground to make bread;
so one does not go on threshing it
for ever.
The wheels of a threshing-cart may be
rolled over it,
but one does not use horses to grind
grain.
29 All this also comes from the LORD
Almighty,
whose plan is wonderful,
whose wisdom is magnificent.

Woe to David's city

29 Woe to you, Ariel, Ariel,
the city where David settled!
Add year to year
and let your cycle of festivals go on.
2 Yet I will besiege Ariel;
she will mourn and lament,
she will be to me like an altar
hearth.*a*
3 I will encamp against you on all sides;
I will encircle you with towers
and set up my siege works against
you.
4 Brought low, you will speak from the
ground;
your speech will mumble out of the
dust.
Your voice will come ghostlike from the
earth;
out of the dust your speech will
whisper.

5 But your many enemies will become
like fine dust,
the ruthless hordes like blown
chaff.
Suddenly, in an instant,
6   the LORD Almighty will come
with thunder and earthquake and great
noise,
with whirlwind and tempest and
flames of a devouring fire.
7 Then the hordes of all the nations that
fight against Ariel,

that attack her and her fortress and
besiege her,
will be as it is with a dream,
with a vision in the night –
8 as when a hungry person dreams of
eating,
but awakens hungry still;
as when a thirsty person dreams of
drinking,
but awakens faint and thirsty still.
So will it be with the hordes of all the
nations
that fight against Mount Zion.

9 Be stunned and amazed,
blind yourselves and be sightless;
be drunk, but not from wine,
stagger, but not from beer.
10 The LORD has brought over you a deep
sleep:
he has sealed your eyes (the
prophets);
he has covered your heads (the seers).

11 For you this whole vision is nothing
but words sealed in a scroll. And if you give
the scroll to someone who can read, and
say, 'Read this, please,' they will answer,
'I can't; it is sealed.' 12 Or if you give the
scroll to someone who cannot read, and
say, 'Read this, please,' they will answer, 'I
don't know how to read.'

13 The Lord says:

'These people come near to me with
their mouth
and honour me with their lips,
but their hearts are far from me.
Their worship of me
is based on merely human rules they
have been taught.*b*
14 Therefore once more I will astound
these people
with wonder upon wonder;
the wisdom of the wise will perish,
the intelligence of the intelligent will
vanish.'

---

a 2 The Hebrew for *altar hearth* sounds like the
Hebrew for *Ariel.*

b 13 Hebrew; Septuagint *They worship me in vain; / their
teachings are merely human rules*

¹⁵ Woe to those who go to great depths
to hide their plans from the Lord,
who do their work in darkness and
think,
'Who sees us? Who will know?'
¹⁶ You turn things upside down,
as if the potter were thought to be
like the clay!
Shall what is formed say to the one who
formed it,
'You did not make me'?
Can the pot say to the potter,
'You know nothing'?

¹⁷ In a very short time, will not Lebanon
be turned into a fertile field
and the fertile field seem like a
forest?
¹⁸ In that day the deaf will hear the words
of the scroll,
and out of gloom and darkness
the eyes of the blind will see.
¹⁹ Once more the humble will rejoice in
the Lord;
the needy will rejoice in the Holy One
of Israel.
²⁰ The ruthless will vanish,
the mockers will disappear,
and all who have an eye for evil will
be cut down —
²¹ those who with a word make someone
out to be guilty,
who ensnare the defender in court
and with false testimony deprive the
innocent of justice.

²² Therefore this is what the Lord,
who redeemed Abraham, says to the descendants of Jacob:

'No longer will Jacob be ashamed;
no longer will their faces grow pale.
²³ When they see among them their
children,
the work of my hands,
they will keep my name holy;
they will acknowledge the holiness
of the Holy One of Jacob,
and will stand in awe of the God of
Israel.
²⁴ Those who are wayward in spirit will
gain understanding;

those who complain will accept
instruction.'

Woe to the obstinate nation

30 'Woe to the obstinate children,'
declares the Lord,
'to those who carry out plans that are
not mine,
forming an alliance, but not by my
Spirit,
heaping sin upon sin;
² who go down to Egypt
without consulting me;
who look for help to Pharaoh's
protection,
to Egypt's shade for refuge.
³ But Pharaoh's protection will be to your
shame,
Egypt's shade will bring you disgrace.
⁴ Though they have officials in Zoan
and their envoys have arrived in
Hanes,
⁵ everyone will be put to shame
because of a people useless to them,
who bring neither help nor advantage,
but only shame and disgrace.'

⁶ A prophecy concerning the animals of
the Negev:

Through a land of hardship and
distress,
of lions and lionesses,
of adders and darting snakes,
the envoys carry their riches on
donkeys' backs,
their treasures on the humps of
camels,
to that unprofitable nation,
⁷ to Egypt, whose help is utterly
useless.
Therefore I call her
Rahab the Do-Nothing.

⁸ Go now, write it on a tablet for them,
inscribe it on a scroll,
that for the days to come
it may be an everlasting witness.
⁹ For these are rebellious people,
deceitful children,
children unwilling to listen to the
Lord's instruction.

10 They say to the seers,
   'See no more visions!'
and to the prophets,
   'Give us no more visions of what is
      right!
Tell us pleasant things,
   prophesy illusions.
11 Leave this way,
   get off this path,
and stop confronting us
   with the Holy One of Israel!'

12 Therefore this is what the Holy One of
Israel says:

'Because you have rejected this
      message,
   relied on oppression
   and depended on deceit,
13 this sin will become for you
   like a high wall, cracked and bulging,
   that collapses suddenly, in an instant.
14 It will break in pieces like pottery,
   shattered so mercilessly
   that among its pieces not a fragment
      will be found
   for taking coals from a hearth
   or scooping water out of a cistern.'

15 This is what the Sovereign LORD, the
Holy One of Israel, says:

'In repentance and rest is your salvation,
   in quietness and trust is your
      strength,
   but you would have none of it.
16 You said, "No, we will flee on horses."
   Therefore you will flee!
You said, "We will ride off on swift
      horses."
   Therefore your pursuers will be swift!
17 A thousand will flee
   at the threat of one;
at the threat of five
   you will all flee away,
till you are left
   like a flagstaff on a mountaintop,
   like a banner on a hill.'
18 Yet the LORD longs to be gracious to you;
   therefore he will rise up to show you
      compassion.

For the LORD is a God of justice.
   Blessed are all who wait for him!

19 People of Zion, who live in Jerusalem,
you will weep no more. How gracious he
will be when you cry for help! As soon as
he hears, he will answer you. 20 Although
the Lord gives you the bread of adversity
and the water of affliction, your teachers
will be hidden no more; with your own
eyes you will see them. 21 Whether you
turn to the right or to the left, your ears
will hear a voice behind you, saying, 'This
is the way; walk in it.' 22 Then you will desecrate your idols overlaid with silver and
your images covered with gold; you will
throw them away like a menstrual cloth
and say to them, 'Away with you!'

23 He will also send you rain for the
seed you sow in the ground, and the food
that comes from the land will be rich and
plentiful. In that day your cattle will graze
in broad meadows. 24 The oxen and donkeys that work the soil will eat fodder and
mash, spread out with fork and shovel.
25 In the day of great slaughter, when the
towers fall, streams of water will flow on
every high mountain and every lofty hill.
26 The moon will shine like the sun, and
the sunlight will be seven times brighter,
like the light of seven full days, when the
LORD binds up the bruises of his people
and heals the wounds he inflicted.

27 See, the Name of the LORD comes from
      afar,
   with burning anger and dense clouds
      of smoke;
his lips are full of wrath,
   and his tongue is a consuming fire.
28 His breath is like a rushing torrent,
   rising up to the neck.
He shakes the nations in the sieve of
      destruction;
   he places in the jaws of the peoples
   a bit that leads them astray.
29 And you will sing
   as on the night you celebrate a holy
      festival;
your hearts will rejoice
   as when people playing pipes go up

to the mountain of the LORD,
to the Rock of Israel.
³⁰ The LORD will cause people to hear his
majestic voice
and will make them see his arm
coming down
with raging anger and consuming fire,
with cloudburst, thunderstorm and
hail.
³¹ The voice of the LORD will shatter
Assyria;
with his rod he will strike them
down.
³² Every stroke the LORD lays on them
with his punishing club
will be to the music of tambourines and
harps,
as he fights them in battle with the
blows of his arm.
³³ Topheth has long been prepared;
it has been made ready for the king.
Its fire pit has been made deep and
wide,
with an abundance of fire and wood;
the breath of the LORD,
like a stream of burning sulphur,
sets it ablaze.

Woe to those who rely on Egypt

31 Woe to those who go down to Egypt
for help,
who rely on horses,
who trust in the multitude of their
chariots
and in the great strength of their
horsemen,
but do not look to the Holy One of
Israel,
or seek help from the LORD.
² Yet he too is wise and can bring
disaster;
he does not take back his words.
He will rise up against that wicked
nation,
against those who help evildoers.
³ But the Egyptians are mere mortals and
not God;
their horses are flesh and not spirit.
When the LORD stretches out his hand,
those who help will stumble,
those who are helped will fall;
all will perish together.

⁴ This is what the LORD says to me:

'As a lion growls,
a great lion over its prey –
and though a whole band of
shepherds
is called together against it,
it is not frightened by their shouts
or disturbed by their clamour –
so the LORD Almighty will come down
to do battle on Mount Zion and on
its heights.
⁵ Like birds hovering overhead,
the LORD Almighty will shield
Jerusalem;
he will shield it and deliver it,
he will "pass over" it and will
rescue it.'

⁶ Return, you Israelites, to the One you
have so greatly revolted against. ⁷ For in
that day every one of you will reject the
idols of silver and gold your sinful hands
have made.

⁸ 'Assyria will fall by no human sword;
a sword, not of mortals, will devour
them.
They will flee before the sword
and their young men will be put to
forced labour.
⁹ Their stronghold will fall because of
terror;
at the sight of the battle standard
their commanders will panic,'
declares the LORD,
whose fire is in Zion,
whose furnace is in Jerusalem.

The kingdom of righteousness

32 See, a king will reign in
righteousness
and rulers will rule with justice.
² Each one will be like a shelter from the
wind
and a refuge from the storm,
like streams of water in the desert
and the shadow of a great rock in a
thirsty land.

³ Then the eyes of those who see will no
longer be closed,

and the ears of those who hear will
   listen.
⁴The fearful heart will know and
   understand,
and the stammering tongue will be
   fluent and clear.
⁵No longer will the fool be called noble
   nor the scoundrel be highly
   respected.
⁶For fools speak folly,
   their hearts are bent on evil:
they practise ungodliness
   and spread error concerning the
   Lord;
the hungry they leave empty
   and from the thirsty they withhold
   water.
⁷Scoundrels use wicked methods,
   they make up evil schemes
to destroy the poor with lies,
   even when the plea of the needy is
   just.
⁸But the noble make noble plans,
   and by noble deeds they stand.

The women of Jerusalem
⁹You women who are so complacent,
   rise up and listen to me;
you daughters who feel secure,
   hear what I have to say!
¹⁰In little more than a year
   you who feel secure will tremble;
the grape harvest will fail,
   and the harvest of fruit will not come.
¹¹Tremble, you complacent women;
   shudder, you daughters who feel
   secure!
Strip off your fine clothes
   and wrap yourselves in rags.
¹²Beat your breasts for the pleasant fields,
   for the fruitful vines
¹³and for the land of my people,
   a land overgrown with thorns and
   briers –
yes, mourn for all houses of merriment
   and for this city of revelry.
¹⁴The fortress will be abandoned,
   the noisy city deserted;
citadel and watchtower will become a
   wasteland for ever,
   the delight of donkeys, a pasture for
   flocks,

¹⁵till the Spirit is poured on us from on
   high,
and the desert becomes a fertile
   field,
and the fertile field seems like a
   forest.
¹⁶The Lord's justice will dwell in the
   desert,
his righteousness live in the fertile
   field.
¹⁷The fruit of that righteousness will be
   peace;
its effect will be quietness and
   confidence for ever.

YOU WHAT?
SPORTING STORIES

JACOB'S WRESTLING MATCH
Genesis 32:22–32
JOSHUA HOLDS THE JAVELIN
Joshua 8:18–23
SAMSON GOES WEIGHTLIFTING
Judges 16:1–3
JONATHAN'S ARCHERY PRACTICE
1 Samuel 20:18–29
JEREMIAH TALKS HORSE-RACING
Jeremiah 12:5–6
PAUL FINISHES THE RACE
2 Timothy 4:6–8
THE BEST DON'T ALWAYS WIN
Ecclesiastes 9:11–12

¹⁸My people will live in peaceful
   dwelling-places,
in secure homes,
   in undisturbed places of rest.
¹⁹Though hail flattens the forest
   and the city is levelled completely,
²⁰how blessed you will be,
   sowing your seed by every stream,
   and letting your cattle and donkeys
   range free.

Distress and help

33 Woe to you, destroyer,
you who have not been destroyed!
Woe to you, betrayer,
   you who have not been betrayed!
When you stop destroying,
   you will be destroyed;
when you stop betraying,
   you will be betrayed.

2 LORD, be gracious to us;
   we long for you.
Be our strength every morning,
   our salvation in time of distress.
3 At the uproar of your army, the peoples
   flee;
   when you rise up, the nations
   scatter.
4 Your plunder, O nations, is harvested as
   by young locusts;
   like a swarm of locusts people
   pounce on it.

5 The LORD is exalted, for he dwells on
   high;
   he will fill Zion with his justice and
   righteousness.
6 He will be the sure foundation for your
   times,
   a rich store of salvation and wisdom
   and knowledge;
   the fear of the LORD is the key to this
   treasure.*a*

7 Look, their brave men cry aloud in the
   streets;
   the envoys of peace weep bitterly.
8 The highways are deserted,
   no travellers are on the roads.
The treaty is broken,
   its witnesses*b* are despised,
   no one is respected.
9 The land dries up and wastes away,
   Lebanon is ashamed and withers;
Sharon is like the Arabah,
   and Bashan and Carmel drop their
   leaves.

10 'Now will I arise,' says the LORD.
'Now will I be exalted;
   now will I be lifted up.
11 You conceive chaff,
   you give birth to straw;
   your breath is a fire that consumes
   you.
12 The peoples will be burned to ashes;
   like cut thorn-bushes they will be set
   ablaze.'

13 You who are far away, hear what I have
   done;
   you who are near, acknowledge my
   power!
14 The sinners in Zion are terrified;
   trembling grips the godless:
'Who of us can dwell with the
   consuming fire?
Who of us can dwell with everlasting
   burning?'
15 Those who walk righteously
   and speak what is right,
who reject gain from extortion
   and keep their hands from accepting
   bribes,
who stop their ears against plots of
   murder
   and shut their eyes against
   contemplating evil –
16 they are the ones who will dwell on the
   heights,
   whose refuge will be the mountain
   fortress.
Their bread will be supplied,
   and water will not fail them.

17 Your eyes will see the king in his
   beauty
   and view a land that stretches afar.
18 In your thoughts you will ponder the
   former terror:
'Where is that chief officer?
Where is the one who took the
   revenue?
   Where is the officer in charge of the
   towers?'
19 You will see those arrogant people no
   more,
   people whose speech is obscure,
   whose language is strange and
   incomprehensible.

a 6 Or *is a treasure from him*
b 8 Dead Sea Scrolls; Masoretic Text / *the cities*

20 Look on Zion, the city of our festivals;
    your eyes will see Jerusalem,
    a peaceful abode, a tent that will not
        be moved;
    its stakes will never be pulled up,
        nor any of its ropes broken.
21 There the LORD will be our Mighty One.
    It will be like a place of broad rivers
        and streams.
    No galley with oars will ride them,
        no mighty ship will sail them.
22 For the LORD is our judge,
    the LORD is our lawgiver,
    the LORD is our king;
    it is he who will save us.

23 Your rigging hangs loose:
    the mast is not held secure,
    the sail is not spread.
    Then an abundance of spoils will be
        divided
    and even the lame will carry off
        plunder.
24 No one living in Zion will say, 'I am ill';
    and the sins of those who dwell there
        will be forgiven.

Judgment against the nations

34 Come near, you nations, and
    listen;
    pay attention, you peoples!
    Let the earth hear, and all that is in it,
        the world, and all that comes out of it!
2 The LORD is angry with all nations;
    his wrath is on all their armies.
    He will totally destroy*a* them,
    he will give them over to slaughter.
3 Their slain will be thrown out,
    their dead bodies will stink;
    the mountains will be soaked with
        their blood.
4 All the stars in the sky will be dissolved
    and the heavens rolled up like a
        scroll;
    all the starry host will fall
    like withered leaves from the vine,
    like shrivelled figs from the fig-tree.

5 My sword has drunk its fill in the
        heavens;
    see, it descends in judgment on
        Edom,
    the people I have totally destroyed.
6 The sword of the LORD is bathed in
        blood,
    it is covered with fat –
    the blood of lambs and goats,
    fat from the kidneys of rams.
    For the LORD has a sacrifice in Bozrah
    and a great slaughter in the land of
        Edom.
7 And the wild oxen will fall with them,
    the bull calves and the great bulls.
    Their land will be drenched with blood,
    and the dust will be soaked with fat.

8 For the LORD has a day of vengeance,
    a year of retribution, to uphold
        Zion's cause.
9 Edom's streams will be turned into
        pitch,
    her dust into burning sulphur;
    her land will become blazing pitch!
10 It will not be quenched night or day;
    its smoke will rise for ever.
    From generation to generation it will
        lie desolate;
    no one will ever pass through it
        again.
11 The desert owl*b* and screech owl*b* will
        possess it;
    the great owl*b* and the raven will nest
        there.
    God will stretch out over Edom
    the measuring line of chaos
    and the plumb-line of desolation.
12 Her nobles will have nothing there to
        be called a kingdom,
    all her princes will vanish away.
13 Thorns will overrun her citadels,
    nettles and brambles her
        strongholds.
    She will become a haunt for jackals,
    a home for owls.
14 Desert creatures will meet with hyenas,
    and wild goats will bleat to each
        other;

---

a 2   The Hebrew term refers to the irrevocable giving
over of things or persons to the LORD, often by
totally destroying them; also in verse 5.

b 11   The precise identification of these birds is
uncertain.

there the night creatures will also lie
down
and find for themselves places of rest.
15 The owl will nest there and lay eggs,
she will hatch them, and care for her
young
under the shadow of her wings;
there also the falcons will gather,
each with its mate.

16 Look in the scroll of the Lord and
read:

None of these will be missing,
not one will lack her mate.
For it is his mouth that has given the
order,
and his Spirit will gather them
together.
17 He allots their portions;
his hand distributes them by
measure.
They will possess it for ever
and dwell there from generation to
generation.

Joy of the redeemed

35 The desert and the parched land
will be glad;
the wilderness will rejoice and
blossom.
Like the crocus, 2 it will burst into
bloom;
it will rejoice greatly and shout for
joy.
The glory of Lebanon will be given to it,
the splendour of Carmel and
Sharon;
they will see the glory of the Lord,
the splendour of our God.

3 Strengthen the feeble hands,
steady the knees that give way;
4 say to those with fearful hearts,
'Be strong, do not fear;
your God will come,
he will come with vengeance;
with divine retribution
he will come to save you.'

5 Then will the eyes of the blind be
opened

and the ears of the deaf unstopped.
6 Then will the lame leap like a deer,
and the mute tongue shout for joy.
Water will gush forth in the wilderness
and streams in the desert.
7 The burning sand will become a pool,
the thirsty ground bubbling springs.
In the haunts where jackals once lay,
grass and reeds and papyrus will
grow.

8 And a highway will be there;
it will be called the Way of Holiness;
it will be for those who walk on that
Way.
The unclean will not journey on it;
wicked fools will not go about on it.
9 No lion will be there,
nor any ravenous beast;
they will not be found there.
But only the redeemed will walk there,
10 and those the Lord has rescued will
return.
They will enter Zion with singing;
everlasting joy will crown their heads.
Gladness and joy will overtake them,
and sorrow and sighing will flee
away.

Sennacherib threatens Jerusalem

36 In the fourteenth year of King Hezekiah's reign, Sennacherib king
of Assyria attacked all the fortified cities
of Judah and captured them. 2 Then the
king of Assyria sent his field commander
with a large army from Lachish to King
Hezekiah at Jerusalem. When the commander stopped at the aqueduct of the
Upper Pool, on the road to the Launderer's
Field, 3 Eliakim son of Hilkiah the palace
administrator, Shebna the secretary, and
Joah son of Asaph the recorder went out
to him.
4 The field commander said to them,
'Tell Hezekiah:

' "This is what the great king, the
king of Assyria, says: on what are
you basing this confidence of yours?
5 You say you have counsel and might
for war – but you speak only empty
words. On whom are you depending,

that you rebel against me? 6 Look, I know you are depending on Egypt, that splintered reed of a staff, which pierces the hand of anyone who leans on it! Such is Pharaoh king of Egypt to all who depend on him. 7 But if you say to me, 'We are depending on the LORD our God' – isn't he the one whose high places and altars Hezekiah removed, saying to Judah and Jerusalem, 'You must worship before this altar'?

8 ' "Come now, make a bargain with my master, the king of Assyria: I will give you two thousand horses – if you can put riders on them! 9 How then can you repulse one officer of the least of my master's officials, even though you are depending on Egypt for chariots and horsemen*a*? 10 Furthermore, have I come to attack and destroy this land without the LORD? The LORD himself told me to march against this country and destroy it." '

11 Then Eliakim, Shebna and Joah said to the field commander, 'Please speak to your servants in Aramaic, since we understand it. Don't speak to us in Hebrew in the hearing of the people on the wall.'

12 But the commander replied, 'Was it only to your master and you that my master sent me to say these things, and not to the people sitting on the wall – who, like you, will have to eat their own excrement and drink their own urine?'

13 Then the commander stood and called out in Hebrew, 'Hear the words of the great king, the king of Assyria! 14 This is what the king says: do not let Hezekiah deceive you. He cannot deliver you! 15 Do not let Hezekiah persuade you to trust in the LORD when he says, "The LORD will surely deliver us; this city will not be given into the hand of the king of Assyria."

16 'Do not listen to Hezekiah. This is what the king of Assyria says: make peace with me and come out to me. Then each of you will eat fruit from your own vine and fig-tree and drink water from your

own cistern, 17 until I come and take you to a land like your own – a land of corn and new wine, a land of bread and vineyards.

18 'Do not let Hezekiah mislead you when he says, "The LORD will deliver us." Have the gods of any nations ever delivered their lands from the hand of the king of Assyria? 19 Where are the gods of Hamath and Arpad? Where are the gods of Sepharvaim? Have they rescued Samaria from my hand? 20 Who of all the gods of these countries have been able to save their lands from me? How then can the LORD deliver Jerusalem from my hand?'

21 But the people remained silent and said nothing in reply, because the king had commanded, 'Do not answer him.'

22 Then Eliakim son of Hilkiah the palace administrator, Shebna the secretary and Joah son of Asaph the recorder went to Hezekiah, with their clothes torn, and told him what the field commander had said.

Jerusalem's deliverance foretold

37 When King Hezekiah heard this, he tore his clothes and put on sackcloth and went into the temple of the LORD. 2 He sent Eliakim the palace administrator, Shebna the secretary, and the leading priests, all wearing sackcloth, to the prophet Isaiah son of Amoz. 3 They told him, 'This is what Hezekiah says: this day is a day of distress and rebuke and disgrace, as when children come to the moment of birth and there is no strength to deliver them. 4 It may be that the LORD your God will hear the words of the field commander, whom his master, the king of Assyria, has sent to ridicule the living God, and that he will rebuke him for the words the LORD your God has heard. Therefore pray for the remnant that still survives.'

5 When King Hezekiah's officials came to Isaiah, 6 Isaiah said to them, 'Tell your master, "This is what the LORD says: do not be afraid of what you have heard – those words with which the underlings of the king of Assyria have blasphemed me. 7 Listen! When he hears a certain report, I will make him want to return to his

a 9 Or charioteers

own country, and there I will have him cut down with the sword." '

8 When the field commander heard that the king of Assyria had left Lachish, he withdrew and found the king fighting against Libnah.

9 Now Sennacherib received a report that Tirhakah, the king of Cush,*a* was marching out to fight against him. When he heard it, he sent messengers to Hezekiah with this word: 10 'Say to Hezekiah king of Judah: do not let the god you depend on deceive you when he says, "Jerusalem will not be given into the hands of the king of Assyria." 11 Surely you have heard what the kings of Assyria have done to all the countries, destroying them completely. And will you be delivered? 12 Did the gods of the nations that were destroyed by my predecessors deliver them – the gods of Gozan, Harran, Rezeph and the people of Eden who were in Tel Assar? 13 Where is the king of Hamath or the king of Arpad? Where are the kings of Lair, Sepharvaim, Hena and Ivvah?'

Hezekiah's prayer

14 Hezekiah received the letter from the messengers and read it. Then he went up to the temple of the Lord and spread it out before the Lord. 15 And Hezekiah prayed to the Lord: 16 'Lord Almighty, the God of Israel, enthroned between the cherubim, you alone are God over all the kingdoms of the earth. You have made heaven and earth. 17 Give ear, Lord, and hear; open your eyes, Lord, and see; listen to all the words Sennacherib has sent to ridicule the living God.

18 'It is true, Lord, that the Assyrian kings have laid waste all these peoples and their lands. 19 They have thrown their gods into the fire and destroyed them, for they were not gods but only wood and stone, fashioned by human hands. 20 Now, Lord our God, deliver us from his hand, so that all the kingdoms of the earth may know that you, Lord, are the only God.*b*'

Sennacherib's fall

21 Then Isaiah son of Amoz sent a message to Hezekiah: 'This is what the Lord, the God of Israel, says: because you have prayed to me concerning Sennacherib king of Assyria, 22 this is the word the Lord has spoken against him:

'Virgin Daughter Zion
    despises and mocks you.
Daughter Jerusalem
    tosses her head as you flee.
23 Who is it you have ridiculed and
    blasphemed?
    Against whom have you raised your
      voice
and lifted your eyes in pride?
    Against the Holy One of Israel!
24 By your messengers
    you have ridiculed the Lord.
And you have said,
    "With my many chariots
I have ascended the heights of the
      mountains,
    the utmost heights of Lebanon.
I have cut down its tallest cedars,
    the choicest of its junipers.
I have reached its remotest heights,
    the finest of its forests.
25 I have dug wells in foreign lands*c*
    and drunk the water there.
With the soles of my feet
    I have dried up all the streams of
      Egypt."

26 'Have you not heard?
    Long ago I ordained it.
In days of old I planned it;
    now I have brought it to pass,
that you have turned fortified cities
    into piles of stone.
27 Their people, drained of power,
    are dismayed and put to shame.
They are like plants in the field,
    like tender green shoots,

---

a 9 That is, the upper Nile region
b 20 Dead Sea Scrolls (see also 2 Kings 19:19);
Masoretic Text *you alone are the Lord*

c 25 Dead Sea Scrolls (see also 2 Kings 19:24);
Masoretic Text does not have *in foreign lands.*

like grass sprouting on the roof,
　scorched[d] before it grows up.

28 'But I know where you are
　and when you come and go
　and how you rage against me.
29 Because you rage against me
　and because your insolence has
　　reached my ears,
I will put my hook in your nose
　and my bit in your mouth,
and I will make you return
　by the way you came.

30 'This will be the sign for you, Hezekiah:

'This year you will eat what grows by
　itself,
and the second year what springs
　from that.
But in the third year sow and reap,
　plant vineyards and eat their fruit.
31 Once more a remnant of the kingdom
　of Judah
will take root below and bear fruit
　above.
32 For out of Jerusalem will come a
　remnant,
and out of Mount Zion a band of
　survivors.
The zeal of the LORD Almighty
　will accomplish this.

33 'Therefore this is what the LORD says
concerning the king of Assyria:

'He will not enter this city
　or shoot an arrow here.
He will not come before it with shield
　or build a siege ramp against it.
34 By the way that he came he will return;
　he will not enter this city,'
　　　　　　　　　declares the LORD.
35 'I will defend this city and save it,
　for my sake and for the sake of David
　my servant!'

---

36 Then the angel of the LORD went out and put to death a hundred and eighty-five thousand in the Assyrian camp. When the people got up the next morning – there were all the dead bodies! 37 So Sennacherib king of Assyria broke camp and withdrew. He returned to Nineveh and stayed there.

38 One day, while he was worshipping in the temple of his god Nisrok, his sons Adrammelek and Sharezer killed him with the sword, and they escaped to the land of Ararat. And Esarhaddon his son succeeded him as king.

Hezekiah's illness

38 In those days Hezekiah became ill and was at the point of death. The prophet Isaiah son of Amoz went to him and said, 'This is what the LORD says: put your house in order, because you are going to die; you will not recover.'

2 Hezekiah turned his face to the wall and prayed to the LORD, 3 'Remember, LORD, how I have walked before you faithfully and with wholehearted devotion and have done what is good in your eyes.' And Hezekiah wept bitterly.

4 Then the word of the LORD came to Isaiah: 5 'Go and tell Hezekiah, "This is what the LORD, the God of your father David, says: I have heard your prayer and seen your tears; I will add fifteen years to your life. 6 And I will deliver you and this city from the hand of the king of Assyria. I will defend this city.

7 '"This is the LORD's sign to you that the LORD will do what he has promised: 8 I will make the shadow cast by the sun go back the ten steps it has gone down on the stairway of Ahaz."' So the sunlight went back the ten steps it had gone down.

9 A writing of Hezekiah king of Judah after his illness and recovery:

10 I said, 'In the prime of my life
　must I go through the gates of death
　and be robbed of the rest of my
　　years?'
11 I said, 'I will not again see the LORD
　himself

in the land of the living;
no longer will I look on my fellow man,
or be with those who now dwell in
this world.
¹² Like a shepherd's tent my house
has been pulled down and taken
from me.
Like a weaver I have rolled up my life,
and he has cut me off from the loom;
day and night you made an end
of me.
¹³ I waited patiently till dawn,
but like a lion he broke all my
bones;
day and night you made an end
of me.
¹⁴ I cried like a swift or thrush,
I moaned like a mourning dove.
My eyes grew weak as I looked to the
heavens.
I am being threatened; Lord, come to
my aid!'

¹⁵ But what can I say?
He has spoken to me, and he himself
has done this.
I will walk humbly all my years
because of this anguish of my soul.
¹⁶ Lord, by such things people live;
and my spirit finds life in them too.
You restored me to health
and let me live.
¹⁷ Surely it was for my benefit
that I suffered such anguish.
In your love you kept me
from the pit of destruction;
you have put all my sins
behind your back.
¹⁸ For the grave cannot praise you,
death cannot sing your praise;
those who go down to the pit
cannot hope for your faithfulness.
¹⁹ The living, the living – they praise you,
as I am doing today;
parents tell their children
about your faithfulness.

²⁰ The LORD will save me,
and we will sing with stringed
instruments
all the days of our lives
in the temple of the LORD.

²¹ Isaiah had said, 'Prepare a poultice of figs and apply it to the boil, and he will recover.'

²² Hezekiah had asked, 'What will be the sign that I will go up to the temple of the LORD?'

Envoys from Babylon

39 At that time Marduk-Baladan son of Baladan king of Babylon sent Hezekiah letters and a gift, because he had heard of his illness and recovery. ² Hezekiah received the envoys gladly and showed them what was in his storehouses – the silver, the gold, the spices, the fine olive oil – his entire armoury and everything found among his treasures. There was nothing in his palace or in all his kingdom that Hezekiah did not show them.

³ Then Isaiah the prophet went to King Hezekiah and asked, 'What did those men say, and where did they come from?'

'From a distant land,' Hezekiah replied. 'They came to me from Babylon.'

⁴ The prophet asked, 'What did they see in your palace?'

'They saw everything in my palace,' Hezekiah said. 'There is nothing among my treasures that I did not show them.'

⁵ Then Isaiah said to Hezekiah, 'Hear the word of the LORD Almighty: ⁶ the time will surely come when everything in your palace, and all that your predecessors have stored up until this day, will be carried off to Babylon. Nothing will be left, says the LORD. ⁷ And some of your descendants, your own flesh and blood who will be born to you, will be taken away, and they will become eunuchs in the palace of the king of Babylon.'

⁸ 'The word of the LORD you have spoken is good,' Hezekiah replied. For he thought, 'There will be peace and security in my lifetime.'

Comfort for God's people

40 Comfort, comfort my people, says your God.
² Speak tenderly to Jerusalem,
and proclaim to her
that her hard service has been
completed,

that her sin has been paid for,
that she has received from the LORD's
hand
    double for all her sins.

3 A voice of one calling:
'In the wilderness prepare
    the way for the LORD;*a*
make straight in the desert
    a highway for our God.*b*
4 Every valley shall be raised up,
    every mountain and hill made low;
the rough ground shall become level,
    the rugged places a plain.
5 And the glory of the LORD will be
    revealed,
    and all people will see it together.
            For the mouth of the LORD
                has spoken.'

6 A voice says, 'Cry out.'
    And I said, 'What shall I cry?'

'All people are like grass,
    and all their faithfulness is like the
        flowers of the field.
7 The grass withers and the flowers fall,
    because the breath of the LORD
        blows on them.
    Surely the people are grass.
8 The grass withers and the flowers fall,
    but the word of our God endures for
        ever.'

9 You who bring good news to Zion,
    go up on a high mountain.
You who bring good news to Jerusalem,*c*
    lift up your voice with a shout,
lift it up, do not be afraid;
    say to the towns of Judah,
    'Here is your God!'
10 See, the Sovereign LORD comes with
    power,
    and he rules with a mighty arm.
See, his reward is with him,

and his recompense accompanies
    him.
11 He tends his flock like a shepherd:
    he gathers the lambs in his arms
and carries them close to his heart;
    he gently leads those that have
        young.

12 Who has measured the waters in the
    hollow of his hand,
    or with the breadth of his hand
        marked off the heavens?
Who has held the dust of the earth in a
    basket,
    or weighed the mountains on the
        scales
    and the hills in a balance?
13 Who can fathom the Spirit*d* of the
    LORD,
    or instruct the LORD as his
        counsellor?
14 Whom did the LORD consult to
    enlighten him,
    and who taught him the right way?
Who was it that taught him knowledge,
    or showed him the path of
        understanding?

15 Surely the nations are like a drop in a
    bucket;
    they are regarded as dust on the
        scales;
    he weighs the islands as though they
        were fine dust.
16 Lebanon is not sufficient for altar fires,
    nor its animals enough for burnt
        offerings.
17 Before him all the nations are as
    nothing;
    they are regarded by him as
        worthless
    and less than nothing.

18 With whom, then, will you compare
    God?
    To what image will you liken him?
19 As for an idol, a metalworker casts it,
    and a goldsmith overlays it with gold
    and fashions silver chains for it.

---

a 3 Or *A voice of one calling in the wilderness: / 'Prepare the way for the LORD*
b 3 Hebrew; Septuagint *make straight the paths of our God*
c 9 Or *Zion, bringer of good news, / go up on a high mountain. / Jerusalem, bringer of good news*

d 13 Or *mind*

20 A person too poor to present such an
    offering
    selects wood that will not rot;
  they look for a skilled worker
    to set up an idol that will not topple.

21 Do you not know?
    Have you not heard?
  Has it not been told you from the
    beginning?
  Have you not understood since the
    earth was founded?
22 He sits enthroned above the circle of
    the earth,
  and its people are like grasshoppers.
  He stretches out the heavens like a
    canopy,
    and spreads them out like a tent to
    live in.
23 He brings princes to naught
    and reduces the rulers of this world
    to nothing.
24 No sooner are they planted,
    no sooner are they sown,
    no sooner do they take root in the
    ground,
  than he blows on them and they wither,
    and a whirlwind sweeps them away
    like chaff.

25 'To whom will you compare me?
    Or who is my equal?' says the Holy
    One.
26 Lift up your eyes and look to the
    heavens:
    who created all these?
  He who brings out the starry host one
    by one
    and calls forth each of them by
    name.
  Because of his great power and mighty
    strength,
    not one of them is missing.

27 Why do you complain, Jacob?
    Why do you say, Israel,
  'My way is hidden from the LORD;
    my cause is disregarded by my God'?
28 Do you not know?
    Have you not heard?
  The LORD is the everlasting God,
    the Creator of the ends of the earth.

  He will not grow tired or weary,
    and his understanding no one can
    fathom.
29 He gives strength to the weary
    and increases the power of the weak.
30 Even youths grow tired and weary,
    and young men stumble and fall;
31 but those who hope in the LORD
    will renew their strength.
  They will soar on wings like eagles;
    they will run and not grow weary,
    they will walk and not be faint.

The helper of Israel

41 'Be silent before me, you islands!
    Let the nations renew their
    strength!
  Let them come forward and speak;
    let us meet together at the place of
    judgment.

2 'Who has stirred up one from the east,
    calling him in righteousness to his
    service?[a]
  He hands nations over to him
    and subdues kings before him.
  He turns them to dust with his sword,
    to wind-blown chaff with his bow.
3 He pursues them and moves on
    unscathed,
    by a path his feet have not travelled
    before.
4 Who has done this and carried it
    through,
    calling forth the generations from
    the beginning?
  I, the LORD – with the first of them
    and with the last – I am he.'

5 The islands have seen it and fear;
    the ends of the earth tremble.
  They approach and come forward;
6   they help each other
    and say to their companions, 'Be
    strong!'
7 The metalworker encourages the
    goldsmith,
    and the one who smooths with the
    hammer

---

a 2 Or *east, / whom victory meets at every step*

spurs on the one who strikes the anvil.
One says of the welding, 'It is good.'
  The other nails down the idol so that it will not topple.

8 'But you, Israel, my servant,
  Jacob, whom I have chosen,
  you descendants of Abraham my friend,
9 I took you from the ends of the earth,
  from its farthest corners I called you.
I said, "You are my servant";
  I have chosen you and have not rejected you.
10 So do not fear, for I am with you;
  do not be dismayed, for I am your God.
I will strengthen you and help you;

I will uphold you with my righteous right hand.

11 'All who rage against you
  will surely be ashamed and disgraced;
those who oppose you
  will be as nothing and perish.
12 Though you search for your enemies,
  you will not find them.
Those who wage war against you
  will be as nothing at all.
13 For I am the LORD your God
  who takes hold of your right hand
and says to you, Do not fear;
  I will help you.
14 Do not be afraid, you worm Jacob,
  little Israel, do not fear,

THE NAMES OF GOD 2

God the Creator (Yahweh Bara)

'Do you not know? Have you not heard? The LORD is the everlasting God, the Creator of the ends of the earth.' (Isaiah 40:28)

God created us

The universe did not come into being by chance. Whatever theories of evolution we may hold, there has to have been a *first cause* behind the 'big bang' or whatever, and Christians believe that the *first cause* was God.

He reveals himself to us

God created us in his image to have a special relationship with him. This has been made possible to sinful humans through Jesus. He both reconciled us to God and revealed himself to us: *'Anyone who has seen me has seen the Father'* (John 14:9). The Bible opens with the book of Genesis, where God is introduced to the reader as *El* or *Elohim*, and he is frequently referred to as Lord (*Adonai*).

He commissions us

'The LORD God took the man and put him in the Garden of Eden to work it and take care of it' (Genesis 2:15). He made this earth and peopled it, but he also charged mankind to care for it responsibly. It's all too easy to take God's creation for granted and to forget that he wants us all to look after it.

David and Mary Pytches

 Exodus 3:14   1 Kings 17:8; 19:24

for I myself will help you,' declares the
   LORD,
      your Redeemer, the Holy One of
         Israel.
15 'See, I will make you into a
      threshing-sledge,
      new and sharp, with many teeth.
   You will thresh the mountains and
      crush them,
      and reduce the hills to chaff.
16 You will winnow them, the wind will
      pick them up,
      and a gale will blow them away.
   But you will rejoice in the LORD
      and glory in the Holy One of Israel.

17 'The poor and needy search for water,
      but there is none;
      their tongues are parched with thirst.
   But I the LORD will answer them;
      I, the God of Israel, will not forsake
         them.
18 I will make rivers flow on barren
      heights,
      and springs within the valleys.
   I will turn the desert into pools of
      water,
      and the parched ground into springs.
19 I will put in the desert
      the cedar and the acacia, the myrtle
         and the olive.
   I will set junipers in the wasteland,
      the fir and the cypress together,
20 so that people may see and know,
      may consider and understand,
   that the hand of the LORD has done
      this,
      that the Holy One of Israel has
         created it.

21 'Present your case,' says the LORD.
      'Set forth your arguments,' says
         Jacob's King.
22 'Tell us, you idols,
      what is going to happen.
   Tell us what the former things were,
      so that we may consider them
      and know their final outcome.
   Or declare to us the things to come,
23   tell us what the future holds,
      so that we may know you are gods.
   Do something, whether good or bad,

so that we will be dismayed and filled
   with fear.
24 But you are less than nothing
      and your works are utterly
         worthless;
      whoever chooses you is detestable.

25 'I have stirred up one from the north,
      and he comes –
      one from the rising sun who calls on
         my name.
   He treads on rulers as if they were
      mortar,
      as if he were a potter treading the
         clay.
26 Who told of this from the beginning, so
      that we could know,
      or beforehand, so that we could say,
         "He was right"?
   No one told of this,
      no one foretold it,
      no one heard any words from you.
27 I was the first to tell Zion, "Look, here
      they are!"
      I gave to Jerusalem a messenger of
         good news.
28 I look but there is no one –
      no one among the gods to give
         counsel,
      no one to give answer when I ask
         them.
29 See, they are all false!
      Their deeds amount to nothing;
      their images are but wind and
         confusion.

The servant of the LORD

42 'Here is my servant, whom I
      uphold,
      my chosen one in whom I delight;
   I will put my Spirit on him,
      and he will bring justice to the
         nations.
2 He will not shout or cry out,
      or raise his voice in the streets.
3 A bruised reed he will not break,
      and a smouldering wick he will not
         snuff out.
   In faithfulness he will bring forth
      justice;
4   he will not falter or be discouraged
      till he establishes justice on earth.

In his teaching the islands will put
their hope.'

5 This is what God the LORD says –
the Creator of the heavens, who
stretches them out,
who spreads out the earth with all
that springs from it,
who gives breath to its people,
and life to those who walk on it:
6 'I, the LORD, have called you in
righteousness;
I will take hold of your hand.
I will keep you and will make you
to be a covenant for the people
and a light for the Gentiles,
7 to open eyes that are blind,
to free captives from prison
and to release from the dungeon
those who sit in darkness.

8 'I am the LORD; that is my name!
I will not yield my glory to another
or my praise to idols.
9 See, the former things have taken
place,
and new things I declare;
before they spring into being
I announce them to you.'

Song of praise to the LORD

10 Sing to the LORD a new song,
his praise from the ends of the earth,
you who go down to the sea, and all
that is in it,
you islands, and all who live in
them.
11 Let the wilderness and its towns raise
their voices;
let the settlements where Kedar lives
rejoice.
Let the people of Sela sing for joy;
let them shout from the
mountaintops.
12 Let them give glory to the LORD
and proclaim his praise in the
islands.
13 The LORD will march out like a
champion,
like a warrior he will stir up his zeal;
with a shout he will raise the battle cry
and will triumph over his enemies.

14 'For a long time I have kept silent,
I have been quiet and held myself
back.
But now, like a woman in childbirth,
I cry out, I gasp and pant.
15 I will lay waste the mountains and hills
and dry up all their vegetation;
I will turn rivers into islands
and dry up the pools.
16 I will lead the blind by ways they have
not known,
along unfamiliar paths I will guide
them;
I will turn the darkness into light before
them
and make the rough places smooth.
These are the things I will do;
I will not forsake them.
17 But those who trust in idols,
who say to images, "You are our
gods,"
will be turned back in utter shame.

Israel blind and deaf

18 'Hear, you deaf;
look, you blind, and see!
19 Who is blind but my servant,
and deaf like the messenger I send?
Who is blind like the one in covenant
with me,
blind like the servant of the LORD?
20 You have seen many things, but you pay
no attention;
your ears are open, but you do not
listen.'
21 It pleased the LORD
for the sake of his righteousness
to make his law great and glorious.
22 But this is a people plundered and
looted,
all of them trapped in pits
or hidden away in prisons.
They have become plunder,
with no one to rescue them;
they have been made loot,
with no one to say, 'Send them back.'

23 Which of you will listen to this
or pay close attention in time to
come?
24 Who handed Jacob over to become
loot,

and Israel to the plunderers?
Was it not the LORD,
    against whom we have sinned?
For they would not follow his ways;
    they did not obey his law.
25 So he poured out on them his burning
        anger,
    the violence of war.
It enveloped them in flames, yet they
        did not understand;
    it consumed them, but they did not
        take it to heart.

Israel's only Saviour

43 But now, this is what the LORD
    says –
    he who created you, Jacob,
    he who formed you, Israel:
'Do not fear, for I have redeemed you;
    I have summoned you by name; you
        are mine.
2 When you pass through the waters,
    I will be with you;
and when you pass through the rivers,
    they will not sweep over you.
When you walk through the fire,
    you will not be burned;
    the flames will not set you ablaze.
3 For I am the LORD your God,
    the Holy One of Israel, your Saviour;
I give Egypt for your ransom,
    Cush*a* and Seba in your stead.
4 Since you are precious and honoured in
        my sight,
    and because I love you,
I will give people in exchange for you,
    nations in exchange for your life.
5 Do not be afraid, for I am with you;
    I will bring your children from the
        east
    and gather you from the west.
6 I will say to the north, "Give them up!"
    and to the south, "Do not hold them
        back."
Bring my sons from afar
    and my daughters from the ends of
        the earth –
7 everyone who is called by my name,
    whom I created for my glory,
    whom I formed and made.'

8 Lead out those who have eyes but are
        blind,
    who have ears but are deaf.
9 All the nations gather together
    and the peoples assemble.
Which of their gods foretold this
    and proclaimed to us the former
        things?
Let them bring in their witnesses to
        prove they were right,
    so that others may hear and say, 'It is
        true.'
10 'You are my witnesses,' declares the
        LORD,
    'and my servant whom I have chosen,
so that you may know and believe me
    and understand that I am he.
Before me no god was formed,
    nor will there be one after me.
11 I, even I, am the LORD,
    and apart from me there is no
        saviour.
12 I have revealed and saved and
        proclaimed –
    I, and not some foreign god among
        you.
You are my witnesses,' declares the
    LORD, 'that I am God.
13   Yes, and from ancient days I am he.
No one can deliver out of my hand.
    When I act, who can reverse it?'

God's mercy and Israel's unfaithfulness

14 This is what the LORD says –
    your Redeemer, the Holy One of
        Israel:
'For your sake I will send to Babylon
    and bring down as fugitives all the
        Babylonians,*b*
    in the ships in which they took pride.
15 I am the LORD, your Holy One,
    Israel's Creator, your King.'

16 This is what the LORD says –
    he who made a way through the sea,
    a path through the mighty waters,
17 who drew out the chariots and horses,
    the army and reinforcements
        together,

---

a 3 That is, the upper Nile region   *b* 14 Or *Chaldeans*

and they lay there, never to rise again,
   extinguished, snuffed out like a wick:
18 'Forget the former things;
   do not dwell on the past.
19 See, I am doing a new thing!
   Now it springs up; do you not
      perceive it?
I am making a way in the wilderness
   and streams in the wasteland.
20 The wild animals honour me,
   the jackals and the owls,
because I provide water in the
      wilderness
   and streams in the wasteland,
to give drink to my people, my chosen,
21   the people I formed for myself
   that they may proclaim my praise.

22 'Yet you have not called on me, Jacob,
   you have not wearied yourselves for
      me, Israel.
23 You have not brought me sheep for
      burnt offerings,
   nor honoured me with your
      sacrifices.
I have not burdened you with grain
      offerings
   nor wearied you with demands for
      incense.
24 You have not bought any fragrant
      calamus for me,
   or lavished on me the fat of your
      sacrifices.
_____
c 22 Or Jacob; / surely you have grown weary of

THE NAMES OF GOD 8

God Who Saves (Yaweh Yasha)

'For I am the LORD your God, the Holy One of Israel, your Saviour...' (Isaiah 43:3)

The angel who visited Joseph instructed him to give his son the name Jesus, *'because he will save his people from their sins'* (Matthew 1:21). The name Jesus comes from the name Yasha or Joshua, which means 'the Lord saves'.

Whatever our age, our conscience tells us that we are not perfect. We can turn over a new leaf every year, but sadly we soon break our vows to do better. We seem incapable of living even up to our own standards, let alone God's. Sometimes we can make amends for our mistakes and bad behaviour and for a while that might ease our conscience, but if we are honest, we soon realise that we need more than another person's forgiveness, even if we are fortunate enough to receive it.

God knows what we need, and he has provided us with a Saviour, Jesus. It's a bit like having a swap-shop at our disposal. We hand over our sins to Jesus by telling him about them absolutely truthfully, holding nothing back, and then we receive in return his forgiveness. It might seem a bit too easy and we may think we should, at least, make some payment. But forgiveness is a free gift. What is required of us, from now on, is to walk humbly with God, aware of our weakness, grateful for the amazing gift we have received, and calling out for his strength to walk in his ways for the rest of our lives.

David and Mary Pytches

 Hebrews 13:5   Romans 8:15

But you have burdened me with your
    sins
    and wearied me with your offences.

25 'I, even I, am he who blots out
    your transgressions, for my own sake,
    and remembers your sins no more.
26 Review the past for me,
    let us argue the matter together;
    state the case for your innocence.
27 Your first father sinned;
    those I sent to teach you rebelled
      against me.
28 So I disgraced the dignitaries of your
      temple;
    I consigned Jacob to destruction*d*
    and Israel to scorn.

Israel the chosen

44 'But now listen, Jacob, my servant,
    Israel, whom I have chosen.
2 This is what the LORD says –
    he who made you, who formed you
      in the womb,
    and who will help you:
    do not be afraid, Jacob, my servant,
    Jeshurun,*a* whom I have chosen.
3 For I will pour water on the thirsty land,
    and streams on the dry ground;
    I will pour out my Spirit on your
      offspring,
    and my blessing on your descendants.
4 They will spring up like grass in a
      meadow,
    like poplar trees by flowing streams.
5 Some will say, "I belong to the LORD";
    others will call themselves by the
      name of Jacob;
    still others will write on their hand,
      "The LORD's,"
    and will take the name Israel.

The LORD, not idols

6 'This is what the LORD says –
    Israel's King and Redeemer, the LORD
      Almighty:
    I am the first and I am the last;
    apart from me there is no God.

7 Who then is like me? Let him
      proclaim it.
    Let him declare and lay out
      before me
    what has happened since I established
      my ancient people,
    and what is yet to come –
    yes, let them foretell what will come.
8 Do not tremble, do not be afraid.
    Did I not proclaim this and foretell it
      long ago?
    You are my witnesses. Is there any God
      besides me?
    No, there is no other Rock; I know
      not one.'

9 All who make idols are nothing,
    and the things they treasure are
      worthless.
    Those who would speak up for them are
      blind;
    they are ignorant, to their own
      shame.
10 Who shapes a god and casts an idol,
    which can profit nothing?
11 People who do that will be put to
      shame;
    such craftsmen are only human
      beings.
    Let them all come together and take
      their stand;
    they will be brought down to terror
      and shame.

12 The blacksmith takes a tool
    and works with it in the coals;
    he shapes an idol with hammers,
    he forges it with the might of his
      arm.
    He gets hungry and loses his strength;
    he drinks no water and grows faint.
13 The carpenter measures with a line
    and makes an outline with a marker;
    he roughs it out with chisels
    and marks it with compasses.
    He shapes it in human form,
    human form in all its glory,
    that it may dwell in a shrine.
14 He cut down cedars,
    or perhaps took a cypress or oak.
    He let it grow among the trees of the
      forest,

---

d 28 The Hebrew term refers to the irrevocable
giving over of things or persons to the LORD, often
by totally destroying them.
a 2 *Jeshurun* means *the upright one*, that is, Israel.

or planted a pine, and the rain made
    it grow.
15 It is used as fuel for burning;
    some of it he takes and warms
        himself,
    he kindles a fire and bakes bread.
    But he also fashions a god and
        worships it;
    he makes an idol and bows down
        to it.
16 Half of the wood he burns in the fire;
    over it he prepares his meal,
    he roasts his meat and eats his fill.
    He also warms himself and says,
    'Ah! I am warm; I see the fire.'
17 From the rest he makes a god, his idol;
    he bows down to it and worships.
    He prays to it and says,
    'Save me! You are my god!'
18 They know nothing, they understand
        nothing;
    their eyes are plastered over so that
        they cannot see,
    and their minds closed so that they
        cannot understand.
19 No one stops to think,
    no one has the knowledge or
        understanding to say,
    'Half of it I used for fuel;
    I even baked bread over its coals,
    I roasted meat and I ate.
    Shall I make a detestable thing from
        what is left?
    Shall I bow down to a block of wood?'
20 Such a person feeds on ashes; a deluded
        heart misleads him;
    he cannot save himself, or say,
    'Is not this thing in my right hand a
        lie?'

21 'Remember these things, Jacob,
    for you, Israel, are my servant.
    I have made you, you are my servant;
    Israel, I will not forget you.
22 I have swept away your offences like a
        cloud,
    your sins like the morning mist.
    Return to me,
    for I have redeemed you.'

23 Sing for joy, you heavens, for the LORD
    has done this;

shout aloud, you earth beneath.
    Burst into song, you mountains,
    you forests and all your trees,
    for the LORD has redeemed Jacob,
    he displays his glory in Israel.

Jerusalem to be inhabited

24 'This is what the LORD says –
    your Redeemer, who formed you in
        the womb:

I am the LORD,
    the Maker of all things,
    who stretches out the heavens,
    who spreads out the earth by myself,
25 who foils the signs of false prophets
    and makes fools of diviners,
    who overthrows the learning of the wise
    and turns it into nonsense,
26 who carries out the words of his servants
    and fulfils the predictions of his
        messengers,

who says of Jerusalem, "It shall be
        inhabited,"
    of the towns of Judah, "They shall be
        rebuilt,"
    and of their ruins, "I will restore
        them,"
27 who says to the watery deep, "Be dry,
    and I will dry up your streams,"
28 who says of Cyrus, "He is my shepherd
    and will accomplish all that I please;
    he will say of Jerusalem, 'Let it be
        rebuilt,'
    and of the temple, 'Let its
        foundations be laid.' "

45 'This is what the LORD says to his
    anointed,
    to Cyrus, whose right hand I take
        hold of
    to subdue nations before him
    and to strip kings of their armour,
    to open doors before him
    so that gates will not be shut:
2 I will go before you
    and will level the mountains;*a*
    I will break down gates of bronze

---

a 2 Dead Sea Scrolls and Septuagint; the meaning
of the word in the Masoretic Text is uncertain.

and cut through bars of iron.
3 I will give you hidden treasures,
    riches stored in secret places,
so that you may know that I am the
    LORD,
    the God of Israel, who summons you
    by name.
4 For the sake of Jacob my servant,
    of Israel my chosen,
I summon you by name
    and bestow on you a title of honour,
    though you do not acknowledge me.
5 I am the LORD, and there is no other;
    apart from me there is no God.
I will strengthen you,
    though you have not acknowledged
    me,
6 so that from the rising of the sun
    to the place of its setting
people may know there is none besides
    me.
    I am the LORD, and there is no other.
7 I form the light and create darkness,
    I bring prosperity and create disaster;
    I, the LORD, do all these things.

8 'You heavens above, rain down my
    righteousness;
    let the clouds shower it down.
Let the earth open wide,
    let salvation spring up,
let righteousness flourish with it;
    I, the LORD, have created it.

9 'Woe to those who quarrel with their
    Maker,
    those who are nothing but potsherds
    among the potsherds on the ground.
Does the clay say to the potter,
    "What are you making?"
Does your work say,
    "The potter has no hands"?
10 Woe to the one who says to a father,
    "What have you begotten?"
    or to a mother,
    "What have you brought to birth?"

11 'This is what the LORD says –
    the Holy One of Israel, and its Maker:
concerning things to come,
    do you question me about my
    children,

or give me orders about the work of
    my hands?
12 It is I who made the earth
    and created mankind on it.
My own hands stretched out the
    heavens;
    I marshalled their starry hosts.
13 I will raise up Cyrus[b] in my
    righteousness:
    I will make all his ways straight.
He will rebuild my city
    and set my exiles free,
but not for a price or reward,
    says the LORD Almighty.'

14 This is what the LORD says:

'The products of Egypt and the
        merchandise of Cush,[c]
    and those tall Sabeans –
they will come over to you
    and will be yours;
they will trudge behind you,
    coming over to you in chains.
They will bow down before you
    and plead with you, saying,
"Surely God is with you, and there is no
    other;
    there is no other god."'

15 Truly you are a God who has been
        hiding himself,
    the God and Saviour of Israel.
16 All the makers of idols will be put to
        shame and disgraced;
    they will go off into disgrace
    together.
17 But Israel will be saved by the LORD
    with an everlasting salvation;
you will never be put to shame or
        disgraced,
    to ages everlasting.

18 For this is what the LORD says –
    he who created the heavens,
        he is God;
    he who fashioned and made the earth,
        he founded it;
    he did not create it to be empty,

---

b 13 Hebrew *him*
c 14 That is, the upper Nile region

but formed it to be inhabited –
he says:
'I am the LORD,
and there is no other.
19 I have not spoken in secret,
from somewhere in a land of
darkness;
I have not said to Jacob's descendants,
"Seek me in vain."
I, the LORD, speak the truth;
I declare what is right.

20 'Gather together and come;
assemble, you fugitives from the
nations.
Ignorant are those who carry about
idols of wood,
who pray to gods that cannot save.
21 Declare what is to be, present it –
let them take counsel together.
Who foretold this long ago,
who declared it from the distant
past?
Was it not I, the LORD?
And there is no God apart from me,
a righteous God and a Saviour;
there is none but me.

22 'Turn to me and be saved,
all you ends of the earth;
for I am God, and there is no other.
23 By myself I have sworn,
my mouth has uttered in all integrity
a word that will not be revoked:
before me every knee will bow;
by me every tongue will swear.
24 They will say of me, "In the LORD alone
are deliverance and strength." '
All who have raged against him
will come to him and be put to
shame.
25 But all the descendants of Israel
will find deliverance in the LORD
and will make their boast in him.

Gods of Babylon

46 Bel bows down, Nebo stoops low;
their idols are borne by beasts of
burden.*a*

---

a 1 Or *are but beasts and cattle*

The images that are carried about are
burdensome,
a burden for the weary.
2 They stoop and bow down together;
unable to rescue the burden,
they themselves go off into captivity.

3 'Listen to me, you descendants of Jacob,
all the remnant of the people of
Israel,
you whom I have upheld since your
birth,
and have carried since you were born.
4 Even to your old age and grey hairs
I am he, I am he who will sustain you.
I have made you and I will carry you;
I will sustain you and I will rescue
you.

5 'With whom will you compare me or
count me equal?
To whom will you liken me that we
may be compared?
6 Some pour out gold from their bags
and weigh out silver on the scales;
they hire a goldsmith to make it into a
god,
and they bow down and worship it.
7 They lift it to their shoulders and carry it;
they set it up in its place, and there it
stands.
From that spot it cannot move.
Even though someone cries out to it, it
cannot answer;
it cannot save them from their
troubles.

8 'Remember this, keep it in mind,
take it to heart, you rebels.
9 Remember the former things, those of
long ago;
I am God, and there is no other;
I am God, and there is none like me.
10 I make known the end from the
beginning,
from ancient times, what is still to
come.
I say, "My purpose will stand,
and I will do all that I please."
11 From the east I summon a bird of prey;
from a far-off land, a man to fulfil my
purpose.

What I have said, that I will bring about;
   what I have planned, that I will do.
12 Listen to me, you stubborn-hearted,
   you who are now far from my
      righteousness.
13 I am bringing my righteousness near,
   it is not far away;
   and my salvation will not be delayed.
I will grant salvation to Zion,
   my splendour to Israel.

The fall of Babylon

47 'Go down, sit in the dust,
   Virgin Daughter Babylon;
sit on the ground without a throne,
   queen city of the Babylonians.*a*
No more will you be called
   tender or delicate.
2 Take millstones and grind flour;
   take off your veil.
Lift up your skirts, bare your legs,
   and wade through the streams.
3 Your nakedness will be exposed
   and your shame uncovered.
I will take vengeance;
   I will spare no one.'

4 Our Redeemer – the LORD Almighty is
      his name –
is the Holy One of Israel.

5 'Sit in silence, go into darkness,
   queen city of the Babylonians;
no more will you be called
   queen of kingdoms.
6 I was angry with my people
   and desecrated my inheritance;
I gave them into your hand,
   and you showed them no mercy.
Even on the aged
   you laid a very heavy yoke.
7 You said, "I am for ever –
   the eternal queen!"
But you did not consider these things
   or reflect on what might happen.

8 'Now then, listen, you lover of pleasure,
   lounging in your security
and saying to yourself,
   "I am, and there is none besides me.

I will never be a widow
   or suffer the loss of children."
9 Both of these will overtake you
   in a moment, on a single day:
   loss of children and widowhood.
They will come upon you in full
      measure,
   in spite of your many sorceries
   and all your potent spells.

FAVOURITE VERSES

2 Timothy 1:7

For the Spirit God gave us does not make us timid, but gives us power, love and self-discipline.

This verse was given to me by a missionary when my husband Ian was called out of stock-brokering to be a church minister. Within four days, God powerfully called us. Ian should have been working in New York when the 9/11 attacks happened, but he left his job there two weeks before: God had other plans for our lives. This verse has been my strength when confronting others with the gospel and my role as a minister's wife!

Andrea, 39

10 You have trusted in your wickedness
   and have said, "No one sees me."
Your wisdom and knowledge mislead
      you
   when you say to yourself,
   "I am, and there is none besides me."
11 Disaster will come upon you,
   and you will not know how to
      conjure it away.
A calamity will fall upon you
   that you cannot ward off with a
      ransom;

------

a 1 Or *Chaldeans*; also in verse 5

a catastrophe you cannot foresee
will suddenly come upon you.

12 'Keep on, then, with your magic spells
and with your many sorceries,
which you have laboured at since
childhood.
Perhaps you will succeed,
perhaps you will cause terror.
13 All the counsel you have received has
only worn you out!
Let your astrologers come forward,
those stargazers who make predictions
month by month,
let them save you from what is
coming upon you.
14 Surely they are like stubble;
the fire will burn them up.
They cannot even save themselves
from the power of the flame.
These are not coals for warmth;
this is not a fire to sit by.
15 That is all they are to you –
these you have dealt with
and laboured with since
childhood.
All of them go on in their error;
there is not one that can save you.

Stubborn Israel

48 'Listen to this, you descendants
of Jacob,
you who are called by the name of
Israel
and come from the line of Judah,
you who take oaths in the name of the
LORD
and invoke the God of Israel –
but not in truth or righteousness –
2 you who call yourselves citizens of the
holy city
and claim to rely on the God of
Israel –
the LORD Almighty is his name:
3 I foretold the former things long ago,
my mouth announced them and I
made them known;
then suddenly I acted, and they came
to pass.
4 For I knew how stubborn you were;
your neck muscles were iron,
your forehead was bronze.

5 Therefore I told you these things long
ago;
before they happened I announced
them to you
so that you could not say,
"My images brought them about;
my wooden image and metal god
ordained them."
6 You have heard these things; look at
them all.
Will you not admit them?

'From now on I will tell you of new
things,
of hidden things unknown to you.
7 They are created now, and not long ago;
you have not heard of them before
today.
So you cannot say,
"Yes, I knew of them."
8 You have neither heard nor
understood;
from of old your ears have not been
open.
Well do I know how treacherous you
are;
you were called a rebel from birth.
9 For my own name's sake I delay my
wrath;
for the sake of my praise I hold it
back from you,
so as not to destroy you completely.
10 See, I have refined you, though not as
silver;
I have tested you in the furnace of
affliction.
11 For my own sake, for my own sake, I do
this.
How can I let myself be defamed?
I will not yield my glory to another.

Israel freed

12 'Listen to me, Jacob,
Israel, whom I have called:
I am he;
I am the first and I am the last.
13 My own hand laid the foundations of
the earth,
and my right hand spread out the
heavens;
when I summon them,
they all stand up together.

14 'Come together, all of you, and listen:
     which of the idols has foretold these
     things?
The LORD's chosen ally
     will carry out his purpose against
     Babylon;
     his arm will be against the
     Babylonians.*a*
15 I, even I, have spoken;
     yes, I have called him.
I will bring him,
     and he will succeed in his mission.

16 'Come near me and listen to this:

'From the first announcement I have
     not spoken in secret;
     at the time it happens, I am there.'

And now the Sovereign LORD has sent
     me,
     endowed with his Spirit.

17 This is what the LORD says –
     your Redeemer, the Holy One of
     Israel:
'I am the LORD your God,
     who teaches you what is best for you,
     who directs you in the way you
     should go.
18 If only you had paid attention to my
     commands,
     your peace would have been like a
     river,
     your well-being like the waves of the
     sea.
19 Your descendants would have been like
     the sand,
     your children like its numberless
     grains;
     their name would never be blotted out
     nor destroyed from before me.'

20 Leave Babylon,
     flee from the Babylonians!
Announce this with shouts of joy
     and proclaim it.
Send it out to the ends of the earth;
     say, 'The LORD has redeemed his
     servant Jacob.'

21 They did not thirst when he led them
     through the deserts;
     he made water flow for them from
     the rock;
he split the rock
     and water gushed out.

22 'There is no peace,' says the LORD, 'for
     the wicked.'

The servant of the LORD

49 Listen to me, you islands;
     hear this, you distant nations:
before I was born the LORD called me;
     from my mother's womb he has
     spoken my name.
2 He made my mouth like a sharpened
     sword,
     in the shadow of his hand he hid me;
he made me into a polished arrow
     and concealed me in his quiver.
3 He said to me, 'You are my servant,
     Israel, in whom I will display my
     splendour.'
4 But I said, 'I have laboured in vain;
     I have spent my strength for nothing
     at all.
Yet what is due to me is in the LORD's
     hand,
     and my reward is with my God.'

5 And now the LORD says –
     he who formed me in the womb to
     be his servant
to bring Jacob back to him
     and gather Israel to himself,
for I am*a* honoured in the eyes of the
     LORD
     and my God has been my strength –
6 he says:
'It is too small a thing for you to be my
     servant
     to restore the tribes of Jacob
     and bring back those of Israel I have
     kept.
I will also make you a light for the
     Gentiles,
     that my salvation may reach to the
     ends of the earth.'

---

a 14 Or *Chaldeans*; also in verse 20

a 5 Or *him, / but Israel would not be gathered; / yet I will be*

7 This is what the LORD says –
the Redeemer and Holy One of
Israel –
to him who was despised and abhorred
by the nation,
to the servant of rulers:
'Kings will see you and stand up,
princes will see and bow down,
because of the LORD, who is faithful,
the Holy One of Israel, who has
chosen you.'

YOU WHAT?
SEVEN UNUSUAL GIFTS AND OFFERINGS

BALM, HONEY, SPICES, MYRRH, PISTACHIOS AND ALMONDS
Genesis 43:11–15

FIVE GOLD TUMOURS AND FIVE GOLD RATS
1 Samuel 6:1–12

THE LEVITES
Numbers 8:14–19

THE CITY OF GEZER AS A WEDDING GIFT
1 Kings 9:16

THE HEAD OF ISH-BAAL
2 Samuel 4:5–12

FORTY CAMEL-LOADS OF ALL THE FINEST WARES OF DAMASCUS
2 Kings 8:7–15

GOLD, FRANKINCENSE AND MYRRH
Matthew 2:11

Restoration of Israel

8 This is what the LORD says:

'In the time of my favour I will answer
you,
and in the day of salvation I will help
you;
I will keep you and will make you
to be a covenant for the people,
to restore the land
and to reassign its desolate
inheritances,
9 to say to the captives, "Come out,"
and to those in darkness, "Be free!"

'They will feed beside the roads
and find pasture on every barren hill.
10 They will neither hunger nor thirst,
nor will the desert heat or the sun
beat down on them.
He who has compassion on them will
guide them
and lead them beside springs of
water.
11 I will turn all my mountains into roads,
and my highways will be raised up.
12 See, they will come from afar –
some from the north, some from the
west,
some from the region of Aswan.'[b]

13 Shout for joy, you heavens;
rejoice, you earth;
burst into song, you mountains!
For the LORD comforts his people
and will have compassion on his
afflicted ones.

14 But Zion said, 'The LORD has forsaken
me,
the Lord has forgotten me.'

15 'Can a mother forget the baby at her
breast
and have no compassion on the child
she has borne?
Though she may forget,
I will not forget you!
16 See, I have engraved you on the palms
of my hands;
your walls are ever before me.
17 Your children hasten back,
and those who laid you waste depart
from you.
18 Lift up your eyes and look around;
all your children gather and come to
you.

---

b 12 Dead Sea Scrolls; Masoretic Text *Sinim*

As surely as I live,' declares the LORD,
  'you will wear them all as
    ornaments;
  you will put them on, like a bride.

19 'Though you were ruined and made
    desolate
  and your land laid waste,
now you will be too small for your
    people,
  and those who devoured you will be
    far away.
20 The children born during your
    bereavement
  will yet say in your hearing,
"This place is too small for us;
  give us more space to live in."
21 Then you will say in your heart,
  "Who bore me these?
I was bereaved and barren;
  I was exiled and rejected.
Who brought these up?
I was left all alone,
  but these – where have they come
    from?"'

22 This is what the Sovereign LORD says:

'See, I will beckon to the nations,
  I will lift up my banner to the
    peoples;
they will bring your sons in their arms
  and carry your daughters on their
    hips.
23 Kings will be your foster fathers,
  and their queens your nursing
    mothers.
They will bow down before you with
    their faces to the ground;
  they will lick the dust at your feet.
Then you will know that I am the
    LORD;
  those who hope in me will not be
    disappointed.'

24 Can plunder be taken from warriors,
  or captives be rescued from the
    fierce?[c]

25 But this is what the LORD says:

'Yes, captives will be taken from
    warriors,
  and plunder retrieved from the
    fierce;
I will contend with those who contend
    with you,
  and your children I will save.
26 I will make your oppressors eat their
    own flesh;
  they will be drunk on their own
    blood, as with wine.
Then all mankind will know
  that I, the LORD, am your Saviour,
  your Redeemer, the Mighty One of
    Jacob.'

Israel's sin and the servant's obedience

50
This is what the LORD says:

'Where is your mother's certificate of
    divorce
  with which I sent her away?
Or to which of my creditors
  did I sell you?
Because of your sins you were sold;
  because of your transgressions your
    mother was sent away.
2 When I came, why was there no one?
  When I called, why was there no one
    to answer?
Was my arm too short to deliver you?
  Do I lack the strength to rescue you?
By a mere rebuke I dry up the sea,
  I turn rivers into a desert;
their fish rot for lack of water
  and die of thirst.
3 I clothe the heavens with darkness
  and make sackcloth its covering.'

4 The Sovereign LORD has given me a
    well-instructed tongue,
  to know the word that sustains the
    weary.
He wakens me morning by morning,
  wakens my ear to listen like one
    being instructed.
5 The Sovereign LORD has opened my
    ears;
  I have not been rebellious,

---

c 24 Dead Sea Scrolls, Vulgate and Syriac (see also
Septuagint and verse 25); Masoretic Text *righteous*

I have not turned away.
6 I offered my back to those who beat me,
     my cheeks to those who pulled out
         my beard;
I did not hide my face
     from mocking and spitting.
7 Because the Sovereign LORD helps me,
     I will not be disgraced.
Therefore have I set my face like flint,
     and I know I will not be put to
         shame.
8 He who vindicates me is near.
     Who then will bring charges against
         me?
     Let us face each other!
Who is my accuser?
     Let him confront me!
9 It is the Sovereign LORD who helps me.
     Who will condemn me?
They will all wear out like a garment;
     the moths will eat them up.

10 Who among you fears the LORD
     and obeys the word of his servant?
Let the one who walks in the dark,
     who has no light,
trust in the name of the LORD
     and rely on their God.
11 But now, all you who light fires
     and provide yourselves with flaming
         torches,
go, walk in the light of your fires
     and of the torches you have set
         ablaze.
This is what you shall receive from my
         hand:
     you will lie down in torment.

Everlasting salvation for Zion

51 'Listen to me, you who pursue
     righteousness
     and who seek the LORD:
look to the rock from which you were
         cut
     and to the quarry from which you
         were hewn;
2 look to Abraham, your father,
     and to Sarah, who gave you birth.
When I called him he was only one man,
     and I blessed him and made him
         many.
3 The LORD will surely comfort Zion

and will look with compassion on all
     her ruins;
he will make her deserts like Eden,
     her wastelands like the garden of the
         LORD.
Joy and gladness will be found in her,
     thanksgiving and the sound of
         singing.

4 'Listen to me, my people;
     hear me, my nation:
instruction will go out from me;
     my justice will become a light to the
         nations.
5 My righteousness draws near speedily,
     my salvation is on the way,
and my arm will bring justice to the
         nations.
The islands will look to me
     and wait in hope for my arm.
6 Lift up your eyes to the heavens,
     look at the earth beneath;
the heavens will vanish like smoke,
     the earth will wear out like a garment
     and its inhabitants die like flies.
But my salvation will last for ever,
     my righteousness will never fail.

7 'Hear me, you who know what is right,
     you people who have taken my
         instruction to heart:
do not fear the reproach of mere
         mortals
     or be terrified by their insults.
8 For the moth will eat them up like a
         garment;
     the worm will devour them like
         wool.
But my righteousness will last for ever,
     my salvation through all
         generations.'

9 Awake, awake, arm of the LORD,
     clothe yourself with strength!
Awake, as in days gone by,
     as in generations of old.
Was it not you who cut Rahab to pieces,
     who pierced that monster through?
10 Was it not you who dried up the sea,
     the waters of the great deep,
who made a road in the depths of the
         sea

so that the redeemed might cross
    over?
11 Those the LORD has rescued will return.
    They will enter Zion with singing;
    everlasting joy will crown their heads.
    Gladness and joy will overtake them,
    and sorrow and sighing will flee
    away.

12 'I, even I, am he who comforts you.
    Who are you that you fear mere
      mortals,
    human beings who are but grass,
13 that you forget the LORD your Maker,
    who stretches out the heavens
    and who lays the foundations of the
      earth,
    that you live in constant terror every
      day
    because of the wrath of the
      oppressor,
    who is bent on destruction?
    For where is the wrath of the
      oppressor?
14   The cowering prisoners will soon be
      set free;
    they will not die in their dungeon,
    nor will they lack bread.
15 For I am the LORD your God,
    who stirs up the sea so that its waves
      roar –
    the LORD Almighty is his name.
16 I have put my words in your mouth
    and covered you with the shadow of
      my hand –
    I who set the heavens in place,
    who laid the foundations of the
      earth,
    and who say to Zion, "You are my
      people." '

The cup of the LORD's wrath

17 Awake, awake!
    Rise up, Jerusalem,
    you who have drunk from the hand of
      the LORD
    the cup of his wrath,
    you who have drained to its dregs
      the goblet that makes people stagger.
18 Among all the children she bore
    there was none to guide her;
    among all the children she brought up

there was none to take her by the
    hand.
19 These double calamities have come
      upon you –
    who can comfort you? –
    ruin and destruction, famine and
      sword –
    who can*a* console you?
20 Your children have fainted;
    they lie at every street corner,
    like antelope caught in a net.
    They are filled with the wrath of the
      LORD,
    with the rebuke of your God.

21 Therefore hear this, you afflicted one,
    made drunk, but not with wine.
22 This is what your Sovereign LORD says,
    your God, who defends his people:
    'See, I have taken out of your hand
      the cup that made you stagger;
    from that cup, the goblet of my wrath,
      you will never drink again.
23 I will put it into the hands of your
      tormentors,
    who said to you,
    "Fall prostrate that we may walk on
      you."
    And you made your back like the
      ground,
    like a street to be walked on.'

52 Awake, awake, Zion,
    clothe yourself with strength!
    Put on your garments of splendour,
    Jerusalem, the holy city.
    The uncircumcised and defiled
    will not enter you again.
2 Shake off your dust;
    rise up, sit enthroned, Jerusalem.
    Free yourself from the chains on your
      neck,
    Daughter Zion, now a captive.

3 For this is what the LORD says:

    'You were sold for nothing,
    and without money you will be
      redeemed.'

---

a 19 Dead Sea Scrolls, Septuagint, Vulgate and
Syriac; Masoretic Text / *how can I*

CHRIST IN ALL THE SCRIPTURES 9

The Servant of God

While it's true that Christ can be found in the Old Testament Scriptures, it's equally true that the Old Testament Scriptures shaped Christ. Jesus knew these writings intimately. They told the stories which shaped his understanding. They were the prayers he prayed. They were the promises he was called to fulfil.

One group of passages which profoundly shaped his understanding are the 'Servant Songs' from Isaiah (Isaiah 42:1–9; 49:1–13; 50:4–9; 52:13 – 53:12). These 'songs' focus on a figure who at times seems to be the nation of Israel, but more often is an individual called to serve Israel and God's purposes through Israel, through suffering. When Jesus was baptised, the Father spoke to him and quoted not just Psalm 2:7, but Isaiah 42:1 as well. The Father spoke to his Son in the words of the first verse of the first Servant Song. Later, when the Gospel of Matthew describes Jesus' healing ministry, it says he fulfilled Isaiah 42:1–4 (Matthew 12:15–21). From the beginning, Jesus knew he would exercise his ministry as God's anointed King through service and suffering.

The best-known Servant Song (Isaiah 52:13 – 53:12) anticipates Jesus' crucifixion and resurrection. He predicted his death on the cross long before it took place (Mark 8:31; 9:31; 10:34), and said, *'Whoever wants to be my disciple must deny themselves and take up their cross and follow me'* (Mark 8:34). How did he know? In part, he knew because his understanding was shaped by reading Isaiah 53, after hearing the Father's words. He knew what his calling would cost. He had to be the Servant of the Lord, serving us by dying for us. He was to be *'despised and rejected by mankind'* (Isaiah 53:3a), so he never let the early adulation of the crowds mislead him. He was to be *'familiar with pain'* (v. 3b). It would look as though God was punishing him, that he was *'stricken'* by God (v. 4). But *'he was pierced for our transgressions, he was crushed for our iniquities; the punishment that brought us peace was on him, and by his wounds we are healed. We all, like sheep, have gone astray, each of us has turned to our own way; and the LORD has laid on him the iniquity of us all'* (v. 5–6). The words are chillingly precise. *'He was assigned a grave with the wicked'* (v. 9), executed as a criminal. He was *'with the rich in his death'* (v. 9), as he was laid in a rich man's tomb. But the song does not end there. *'After he has suffered, he will see the light of life and be satisfied; by his knowledge my righteous servant will justify many, and he will bear their iniquities. Therefore I will give him a portion among the great'* (v. 11–12). Confident in this promise, Jesus also predicted his resurrection. Passages like this are not merely prophecies which Jesus fulfilled. They are passages which shaped his identity and showed him his calling.

Graham Cray

 Psalm 2   Daniel 7:9–14 ▶

4 For this is what the Sovereign LORD says:

'At first my people went down to Egypt
  to live;
  lately, Assyria has oppressed them.

5 'And now what do I have here?' declares the LORD.

'For my people have been taken away
  for nothing,
  and those who rule them mock,'ᵃ
          declares the LORD.
'And all day long
  my name is constantly blasphemed.
6 Therefore my people will know my
  name;
  therefore in that day they will know
  that it is I who foretold it.
  Yes, it is I.'

7 How beautiful on the mountains
  are the feet of those who bring good
    news,
who proclaim peace,
  who bring good tidings,
  who proclaim salvation,
who say to Zion,
  'Your God reigns!'
8 Listen! Your watchmen lift up their
    voices;
  together they shout for joy.
When the LORD returns to Zion,
  they will see it with their own eyes.
9 Burst into songs of joy together,
  you ruins of Jerusalem,
for the LORD has comforted his people,
  he has redeemed Jerusalem.
10 The LORD will lay bare his holy arm
  in the sight of all the nations,
and all the ends of the earth will see
  the salvation of our God.

11 Depart, depart, go out from there!
  Touch no unclean thing!
Come out from it and be pure,
  you who carry the articles of the
    LORD's house.
12 But you will not leave in haste

or go in flight;
for the LORD will go before you,
  the God of Israel will be your rear
    guard.

The suffering and glory of the servant
13 See, my servant will act wisely;ᵇ
  he will be raised and lifted up and
    highly exalted.
14 Just as there were many who were
    appalled at himᶜ –
  his appearance was so disfigured
    beyond that of any human
    being
  and his form marred beyond human
    likeness –
15 so he will sprinkle many nations,ᵈ
  and kings will shut their mouths
    because of him.
For what they were not told, they will
    see,
  and what they have not heard, they
    will understand.

53 Who has believed our message
  and to whom has the arm of the
  LORD been revealed?
2 He grew up before him like a tender
    shoot,
  and like a root out of dry ground.
He had no beauty or majesty to attract
    us to him,
  nothing in his appearance that we
    should desire him.
3 He was despised and rejected by
    mankind,
  a man of suffering, and familiar with
    pain.
Like one from whom people hide their
    faces
  he was despised, and we held him in
    low esteem.

4 Surely he took up our pain
  and bore our suffering,
yet we considered him punished by
    God,
  stricken by him, and afflicted.

ᵃ 5 Dead Sea Scrolls and Vulgate; Masoretic Text wail
ᵇ 13 Or will prosper
ᶜ 14 Hebrew you
ᵈ 15 Or so will many nations be amazed at him (see also Septuagint)

⁵ But he was pierced for our
    transgressions,
    he was crushed for our iniquities;
the punishment that brought us peace
    was on him,
    and by his wounds we are healed.
⁶ We all, like sheep, have gone astray,
    each of us has turned to our own
    way;
and the LORD has laid on him
    the iniquity of us all.

⁷ He was oppressed and afflicted,
    yet he did not open his mouth;
he was led like a lamb to the slaughter,
    and as a sheep before its shearers is
    silent,
    so he did not open his mouth.
⁸ By oppression*a* and judgment he was
    taken away.
    Yet who of his generation
    protested?
For he was cut off from the land of the
    living;
    for the transgression of my people
    he was punished.*b*
⁹ He was assigned a grave with the
    wicked,
    and with the rich in his death,
though he had done no violence,
    nor was any deceit in his mouth.

¹⁰ Yet it was the LORD's will to crush him
    and cause him to suffer,
    and though the LORD makes*c* his life
    an offering for sin,
he will see his offspring and prolong
    his days,
    and the will of the LORD will prosper
    in his hand.
¹¹ After he has suffered,
    he will see the light of life*d* and be
    satisfied;*e*

by his knowledge *f* my righteous servant
    will justify many,
    and he will bear their iniquities.
¹² Therefore I will give him a portion
    among the great,*g*
    and he will divide the spoils with the
    strong,*h*
because he poured out his life unto
    death,
    and was numbered with the
    transgressors.
For he bore the sin of many,
    and made intercession for the
    transgressors.

The future glory of Zion

54 'Sing, barren woman,
    you who never bore a child;
burst into song, shout for joy,
    you who were never in labour;
because more are the children of the
    desolate woman
    than of her who has a husband,'
                 says the LORD.
² 'Enlarge the place of your tent,
    stretch your tent curtains wide,
    do not hold back;
lengthen your cords,
    strengthen your stakes.
³ For you will spread out to the right and
    to the left;
    your descendants will dispossess
    nations
    and settle in their desolate cities.

⁴ 'Do not be afraid; you will not be put to
    shame.
    Do not fear disgrace; you will not be
    humiliated.
You will forget the shame of your youth
    and remember no more the reproach
    of your widowhood.
⁵ For your Maker is your husband –
    the LORD Almighty is his name –
    the Holy One of Israel is your Redeemer;
    he is called the God of all the earth.
⁶ The LORD will call you back

---

a 8 Or *From arrest*
b 8 Or *generation considered / that he was cut off from the
land of the living, / that he was punished for the transgression
of my people?*
c 10 Hebrew *though you make*
d 11 Dead Sea Scrolls (see also Septuagint);
Masoretic Text does not have *the light of life*.
e 11 Or (with Masoretic Text) ¹¹*He will see the fruit of his
suffering / and will be satisfied*

---

f 11 Or *by knowledge of him*
g 12 Or *many*
h 12 Or *numerous*

as if you were a wife deserted and
 distressed in spirit –
a wife who married young,
 only to be rejected,' says your God.
7 'For a brief moment I abandoned you,
 but with deep compassion I will
 bring you back.
8 In a surge of anger
 I hid my face from you for a moment,
but with everlasting kindness
 I will have compassion on you,'
says the LORD your Redeemer.

9 'To me this is like the days of Noah,
 when I swore that the waters of Noah
 would never again cover the
 earth.
So now I have sworn not to be angry
 with you,
 never to rebuke you again.
10 Though the mountains be shaken
 and the hills be removed,
yet my unfailing love for you will not be
 shaken
 nor my covenant of peace be
 removed,'
 says the LORD, who has compassion
 on you.

11 'Afflicted city, lashed by storms and not
 comforted,
 I will rebuild you with stones of
 turquoise,*a*
 your foundations with lapis lazuli.
12 I will make your battlements of rubies,
 your gates of sparkling jewels,
 and all your walls of precious stones.
13 All your children will be taught by the
 LORD,
 and great will be their peace.
14 In righteousness you will be
 established:
 tyranny will be far from you;
 you will have nothing to fear.
Terror will be far removed;
 it will not come near you.
15 If anyone does attack you, it will not be
 my doing;

whoever attacks you will surrender to
 you.
16 'See, it is I who created the blacksmith
 who fans the coals into flame
 and forges a weapon fit for its work.
And it is I who have created the
 destroyer to wreak havoc;
17 no weapon forged against you will
 prevail,
 and you will refute every tongue that
 accuses you.
This is the heritage of the servants of
 the LORD,
 and this is their vindication from me,'
 declares the LORD.

Invitation to the thirsty

55 'Come, all you who are thirsty,
 come to the waters;
and you who have no money,
 come, buy and eat!
Come, buy wine and milk
 without money and without cost.
2 Why spend money on what is not
 bread,
 and your labour on what does not
 satisfy?
Listen, listen to me, and eat what is
 good,
 and you will delight in the richest of
 fare.
3 Give ear and come to me;
 listen, that you may live.
I will make an everlasting covenant with
 you,
 my faithful love promised to David.
4 See, I have made him a witness to the
 peoples,
 a ruler and commander of the
 peoples.
5 Surely you will summon nations you
 know not,
 and nations you do not know will
 come running to you,
because of the LORD your God,
 the Holy One of Israel,
 for he has endowed you with
 splendour.'

6 Seek the LORD while he may be found;
 call on him while he is near.

---

a 11 The meaning of the Hebrew for this word is
uncertain.

7 Let the wicked forsake their ways
and the unrighteous their thoughts.
Let them turn to the LORD, and he will
have mercy on them,
and to our God, for he will freely
pardon.

8 'For my thoughts are not your thoughts,
neither are your ways my ways,'
declares the LORD.
9 'As the heavens are higher than the
earth,
so are my ways higher than your ways
and my thoughts than your
thoughts.
10 As the rain and the snow
come down from heaven,
and do not return to it
without watering the earth
and making it bud and flourish,
so that it yields seed for the sower
and bread for the eater,
11 so is my word that goes out from my
mouth:
it will not return to me empty,
but will accomplish what I desire
and achieve the purpose for which I
sent it.
12 You will go out in joy
and be led forth in peace;
the mountains and hills
will burst into song before you,
and all the trees of the field
will clap their hands.
13 Instead of the thorn-bush will grow the
juniper,
and instead of briers the myrtle will
grow.
This will be for the LORD's renown,
for an everlasting sign,
that will endure for ever.'

Salvation for others

56

This is what the LORD says:

'Maintain justice
and do what is right,
for my salvation is close at hand
and my righteousness will soon be
revealed.
2 Blessed is the one who does this –
the person who holds it fast,

who keeps the Sabbath without
desecrating it,
and keeps their hands from doing
any evil.'

3 Let no foreigner who is bound to the
LORD say,
'The LORD will surely exclude me
from his people.'
And let no eunuch complain,
'I am only a dry tree.'

4 For this is what the LORD says:

'To the eunuchs who keep my Sabbaths,
who choose what pleases me
and hold fast to my covenant –
5 to them I will give within my temple
and its walls
a memorial and a name
better than sons and daughters;
I will give them an everlasting name
that will endure for ever.
6 And foreigners who bind themselves to
the LORD
to minister to him,
to love the name of the LORD,
and to be his servants,
all who keep the Sabbath without
desecrating it
and who hold fast to my covenant –
7 these I will bring to my holy mountain
and give them joy in my house of
prayer.
Their burnt offerings and sacrifices
will be accepted on my altar;
for my house will be called
a house of prayer for all nations.'
8 The Sovereign LORD declares –
he who gathers the exiles of Israel:
'I will gather still others to them
besides those already gathered.'

God's accusation against the wicked

9 Come, all you beasts of the field,
come and devour, all you beasts of
the forest!
10 Israel's watchmen are blind,
they all lack knowledge;
they are all mute dogs,
they cannot bark;
they lie around and dream,

SPIRITUAL DISCIPLINES 10

CELEBRATION

What are Christians known for today? Are we known for standing up for the poor and oppressed? Perhaps. Are we known for opposing some of society's worst 'sins'? Definitely. Yet there's one central aspect of our faith for which we are not well known and which is not heavily reported: Christians are people who *celebrate*.

We are a people who truly know *joy*. That doesn't mean we're always feeling on top of the world; instead, it means we have discovered the purpose of life, and we have learned that it's *good news*.

Jesus did not only die, he was resurrected! When that happened, the universe was turned upside down; the path between us and God was cleared, and eternity beckoned. This is the most sensational news in the history of the world: we can know God and live for ever with him. What's the most natural reaction to news like that? To party, of course!

If we're not careful, we can start to take this incredible news for granted. Like a spoilt child who tosses aside her opened Christmas presents in a ravenous search for more, we can miss the glorious implications of what's sitting right in front of us. Jesus' resurrection is an unquenchable fountain of joy … so why is it that we're not known for that response?

The gospel we communicate with our lives is so much more powerful than the one we speak out from our lips. Listen to these life-giving words from Isaiah: *'You will go out in joy and be led forth in peace; the mountains and hills will burst into song before you, and all the trees of the field will clap their hands'* (Isaiah 55:12). Don't read it as a nice sentiment – read it as an order! 'Going out in' or practising joy should be as central to our Christian lives as praying or reading the Bible.

It's not just about singing loudly in church, though. Practising celebration means we look for every opportunity to enjoy ourselves in God. It means relishing the gifts, talents and interests he has given us. It means squeezing every last drop of enjoyment from the football pitch, the gig, the novel we're reading. It means looking for positives in every situation; it means investing ourselves in friendship and love. It's a discipline just like any other – even though it might seem like too much fun – and we have to make deliberate decisions each day to celebrate what's good, to uncover joy wherever it might be hiding.

To neglect the discipline of celebration is to empty the Christian faith of one of its greatest truths: that we win. What difference might it make to your town, to your nation even, if Christians were known once again not for what they stand against, but for what they stand for? The world will only change if each of us makes that distinction. If we want to see that happen, then it's time to rediscover joy.

Martin Saunders

 2 Samuel 12:1–20

WHAT IS CHRISTIANITY? 3

Doctrine of God: God beyond

If someone asked you the question 'What is God like?', what would you say?

When it comes to 'getting to know' any part of our planet, or even our universe, we human beings have become pretty good at it. We can put things in test tubes, or observe them through telescopes, and come up with a description of what they are like. God is different. He's not contained by the physical world. As a result Christians believe the only way we can know God is if he chooses to make himself known. The Bible calls this 'revelation'.

The amazing thing is that God has shown himself to us!

All the way through the Bible, God reveals what he is like. In some cases we see that God is similar to us (like a parent might be similar to their kids). This is because we are made *'in the image of God'* (Genesis 1:26). So God is a relational God (he is Father, Son and Holy Spirit), and we are relational creatures. God is a God of love, justice and compassion; at our best, we humans can show these qualities. God is intelligent and rational; we also have reason and the ability to figure things out.

Many of us, however, just dwell on these similarities between God and ourselves. The real revelation comes when we start to dwell on the differences!

The quality of God's love is different. We may love sometimes, but God's love is pure, selfless and consistent in a way that is beyond any human relationship we will ever know. 'God is love' (1 John 4:8).

The extent of God's knowledge is incomprehensibly beyond ours. God tells us through Isaiah, *'As the heavens are higher than the earth, so are my ways higher than your ways and my thoughts than your thoughts'* (Isaiah 55:8–9). After many hours, we might have mastered GCSE Maths, but God's *'understanding has no limit'* (Psalm 147:5).

As human beings, we're dependent on the world we live in to survive. But God is the Creator. *'I know every bird in the mountains, and the insects in the fields are mine. If I were hungry I would not tell you, for the world is mine, and all that is in it'* (Psalm 50:11–12).

Think about how different God is from you. He is outside time, he isn't constrained by space, he has no beginning or end, and he is unchanging. What's more, God is infinite. One of the wonderful things this means is that there will always be more of God to discover. You can spend a lifetime living with someone on this earth and get to know them pretty well. But when, one day, we see God Almighty face to face, we'll realise that a lifetime following him was only just the beginning.

Every now and then we think we've got God in our pocket. The doctrine of God reminds us that we always walk along the palm of his hand.

Andy Croft

 Genesis 3   Matthew 3:13–17

they love to sleep.
11 They are dogs with mighty appetites;
    they never have enough.
They are shepherds who lack
    understanding;
they all turn to their own way,
    they seek their own gain.
12 'Come,' each one cries, 'let me get wine!
    Let us drink our fill of beer!
And tomorrow will be like today,
    or even far better.'

57

The righteous perish,
    and no one takes it to heart;
the devout are taken away,
    and no one understands
that the righteous are taken away
    to be spared from evil.
2 Those who walk uprightly
    enter into peace;
they find rest as they lie in death.

3 'But you – come here, you children of a
    sorceress,
you offspring of adulterers and
    prostitutes!
4 Who are you mocking?
    At whom do you sneer
and stick out your tongue?
Are you not a brood of rebels,
    the offspring of liars?
5 You burn with lust among the oaks
    and under every spreading tree;
you sacrifice your children in the
    ravines
and under the overhanging crags.
6 The idols among the smooth stones of
    the ravines are your portion;
indeed, they are your lot.
Yes, to them you have poured out drink
    offerings
and offered grain offerings.
In view of all this, should I relent?
7 You have made your bed on a high and
    lofty hill;
there you went up to offer your
    sacrifices.
8 Behind your doors and your doorposts
    you have put your pagan symbols.
Forsaking me, you uncovered your bed,
    you climbed into it and opened it
    wide;

you made a pact with those whose beds
    you love,
and you looked with lust on their
    naked bodies.
9 You went to Molek[a] with olive oil
    and increased your perfumes.
You sent your ambassadors[b] far away;
    you descended to the very realm of
    the dead!
10 You wearied yourself by such going
    about,
    but you would not say, "It is
    hopeless."
You found renewal of your strength,
    and so you did not faint.

11 'Whom have you so dreaded and feared
    that you have not been true to me,
and have neither remembered me
    nor taken this to heart?
Is it not because I have long been silent
    that you do not fear me?
12 I will expose your righteousness and
    your works,
    and they will not benefit you.
13 When you cry out for help,
    let your collection of idols save you!
The wind will carry all of them off,
    a mere breath will blow them away.
But whoever takes refuge in me
    will inherit the land
    and possess my holy mountain.'

Comfort for the contrite
14 And it will be said:

'Build up, build up, prepare the road!
    Remove the obstacles out of the way
    of my people.'
15 For this is what the high and exalted
    One says –
he who lives for ever, whose name is
    holy:
'I live in a high and holy place,
    but also with the one who is contrite
    and lowly in spirit,
to revive the spirit of the lowly
    and to revive the heart of the
    contrite.

---

a 9 Or to the king
b 9 Or idols

16 I will not accuse them for ever,
   nor will I always be angry,
for then they would faint away because
   of me –
   the very people I have created.
17 I was enraged by their sinful greed;
   I punished them, and hid my face in
   anger,
   yet they kept on in their wilful ways.
18 I have seen their ways, but I will heal
   them;
   I will guide them and restore comfort
   to Israel's mourners,
19   creating praise on their lips.
Peace, peace, to those far and near,'
   says the LORD. 'And I will heal them.'
20 But the wicked are like the tossing sea,
   which cannot rest,
   whose waves cast up mire and mud.
21 'There is no peace,' says my God, 'for
   the wicked.'

True fasting

58 'Shout it aloud, do not hold back.
      Raise your voice like a trumpet.
Declare to my people their rebellion
   and to the descendants of Jacob their
   sins.
2 For day after day they seek me out;
   they seem eager to know my ways,
as if they were a nation that does what
   is right
   and has not forsaken the commands
   of its God.
They ask me for just decisions
   and seem eager for God to come near
   them.
3 "Why have we fasted," they say,
   "and you have not seen it?
Why have we humbled ourselves,
   and you have not noticed?"

'Yet on the day of your fasting, you do as
   you please
   and exploit all your workers.
4 Your fasting ends in quarrelling and
   strife,
   and in striking each other with
   wicked fists.
You cannot fast as you do today
   and expect your voice to be heard on
   high.

5 Is this the kind of fast I have chosen,
   only a day for people to humble
   themselves?
Is it only for bowing one's head like a
   reed
   and for lying in sackcloth and ashes?
Is that what you call a fast,
   a day acceptable to the LORD?

6 'Is not this the kind of fasting I have
   chosen:
to loose the chains of injustice
   and untie the cords of the yoke,
to set the oppressed free
   and break every yoke?
7 Is it not to share your food with the
   hungry
   and to provide the poor wanderer
   with shelter –
when you see the naked, to clothe
   them,
   and not to turn away from your own
   flesh and blood?
8 Then your light will break forth like the
   dawn,
   and your healing will quickly appear;
then your righteousness*a* will go before
   you,
   and the glory of the LORD will be your
   rear guard.
9 Then you will call, and the LORD will
   answer;
   you will cry for help, and he will say:
   here am I.

'If you do away with the yoke of
   oppression,
   with the pointing finger and
   malicious talk,
10 and if you spend yourselves on behalf of
   the hungry
   and satisfy the needs of the
   oppressed,
then your light will rise in the darkness,
   and your night will become like the
   noonday.
11 The LORD will guide you always;
   he will satisfy your needs in a sun-
   scorched land
   and will strengthen your frame.

---

a 8 Or *your righteous One*

You will be like a well-watered garden,
    like a spring whose waters never fail.
12 Your people will rebuild the ancient
        ruins
    and will raise up the age-old
        foundations;
    you will be called Repairer of Broken
        Walls,
        Restorer of Streets with Dwellings.

13 'If you keep your feet from breaking the
        Sabbath
    and from doing as you please on my
        holy day,

if you call the Sabbath a delight
    and the LORD's holy day honourable,
and if you honour it by not going your
        own way
    and not doing as you please or
        speaking idle words,
14 then you will find your joy in the LORD,
    and I will cause you to ride in
        triumph on the heights of the
        land
    and to feast on the inheritance of
        your father Jacob.'
        For the mouth of the LORD
            has spoken.

JUSTICE AND MERCY 4

MORE THAN SONGS

God doesn't leave us in the dark trying to guess what he wants from us. All through the Bible he tells us plainly that we can't pay lip service to being his followers; we have to really live it out. In Isaiah 58 we meet some people who are keen followers of God. They pray and worship and go to the meetings. They even fast. But these people are not just devout, they are angry with God. They are angry because, in spite of all their praying and worshipping and devotion, God is still not answering their prayers. He seems far away from them. Their complaint to God is that they are doing all the stuff they were meant to do, and God is still distant. Does that sound familiar?

Unfortunately for them, God is actually unhappy with them as well. He is unhappy because, while they are singing worship songs, they are also mistreating their workers, gossiping, and leaving the hungry and naked unfed and unclothed. Their attitude to the poor and their lack of justice drowned out all their worship songs.

God is looking for more than the outward appearance of people who follow him. He wants our hearts to be like his. And his heart breaks when he sees injustice.

Amazingly, the chapter ends with wonderful promises that God will heal these people, answer their prayers and be close to them. God never condemns – he challenges and shows a way out of the mess. The way out of the mess is for these people to seek justice as well as singing worship songs; to care for the vulnerable as well as praying for their own needs. If they do these things, then the promise is not only that their needs will be satisfied (58:11), but that God will use them to be good news in a broken world (v. 12) and they will find great joy (v. 14).

David Westlake

 Proverbs 31:8–9   Micah 6:8

Sin, confession and redemption

59 Surely the arm of the LORD is not
too short to save,
nor his ear too dull to hear.
2 But your iniquities have separated
you from your God;
your sins have hidden his face from you,
so that he will not hear.
3 For your hands are stained with blood,
your fingers with guilt.
Your lips have spoken falsely,
and your tongue mutters wicked
things.
4 No one calls for justice;
no one pleads a case with integrity.
They rely on empty arguments, they
utter lies;
they conceive trouble and give birth
to evil.
5 They hatch the eggs of vipers
and spin a spider's web.
Whoever eats their eggs will die,
and when one is broken, an adder is
hatched.
6 Their cobwebs are useless for clothing;
they cannot cover themselves with
what they make.
Their deeds are evil deeds,
and acts of violence are in their
hands.
7 Their feet rush into sin;
they are swift to shed innocent
blood.
They pursue evil schemes;
acts of violence mark their ways.
8 The way of peace they do not know;
there is no justice in their paths.
They have turned them into crooked
roads;
no one who walks along them will
know peace.

9 So justice is far from us,
and righteousness does not reach us.
We look for light, but all is darkness;
for brightness, but we walk in deep
shadows.
10 Like the blind we grope along the wall,
feeling our way like people without
eyes.
At midday we stumble as if it were
twilight;

among the strong, we are like the
dead.
11 We all growl like bears;
we moan mournfully like doves.
We look for justice, but find none;
for deliverance, but it is far away.

12 For our offences are many in your sight,
and our sins testify against us.
Our offences are ever with us,
and we acknowledge our iniquities:
13 rebellion and treachery against the
LORD,
turning our backs on our God,
inciting revolt and oppression,
uttering lies our hearts have
conceived.
14 So justice is driven back,
and righteousness stands at a
distance;
truth has stumbled in the streets,
honesty cannot enter.
15 Truth is nowhere to be found,
and whoever shuns evil becomes a
prey.

The LORD looked and was displeased
that there was no justice.
16 He saw that there was no one,
he was appalled that there was no
one to intervene;
so his own arm achieved salvation for
him,
and his own righteousness sustained
him.
17 He put on righteousness as his
breastplate,
and the helmet of salvation on his
head;
he put on the garments of vengeance
and wrapped himself in zeal as in a
cloak.
18 According to what they have done,
so will he repay
wrath to his enemies
and retribution to his foes;
he will repay the islands their due.
19 From the west, people will fear the
name of the LORD,
and from the rising of the sun, they
will revere his glory.
For he will come like a pent-up flood

that the breath of the LORD drives
along.*a*

20 'The Redeemer will come to Zion,
    to those in Jacob who repent of their
        sins,'
            declares the LORD.

21 'As for me, this is my covenant with
them,' says the LORD. 'My Spirit, who is
on you, will not depart from you, and my
words that I have put in your mouth will
always be on your lips, on the lips of your
children and on the lips of their descendants – from this time on and for ever,' says
the LORD.

The glory of Zion

60 'Arise, shine, for your light has
come,
    and the glory of the LORD rises upon
        you.
2 See, darkness covers the earth
    and thick darkness is over the
        peoples,
but the LORD rises upon you
    and his glory appears over you.
3 Nations will come to your light,
    and kings to the brightness of your
        dawn.

4 'Lift up your eyes and look about you:
    all assemble and come to you;
your sons come from afar,
    and your daughters are carried on the
        hip.
5 Then you will look and be radiant,
    your heart will throb and swell with
        joy;
the wealth on the seas will be brought
        to you,
    to you the riches of the nations will
        come.
6 Herds of camels will cover your land,
    young camels of Midian and Ephah.
And all from Sheba will come,
    bearing gold and incense
    and proclaiming the praise of the
        LORD.

7 All Kedar's flocks will be gathered to
        you,
    the rams of Nebaioth will serve you;
they will be accepted as offerings on my
        altar,
    and I will adorn my glorious temple.

8 'Who are these that fly along like
        clouds,
    like doves to their nests?
9 Surely the islands look to me;
    in the lead are the ships of Tarshish,*a*
bringing your children from afar,
    with their silver and gold,
to the honour of the LORD your God,
    the Holy One of Israel,
    for he has endowed you with
        splendour.

10 'Foreigners will rebuild your walls,
    and their kings will serve you.
Though in anger I struck you,
    in favour I will show you compassion.
11 Your gates will always stand open,
    they will never be shut, day or night,
so that people may bring you the wealth
        of the nations –
    their kings led in triumphal
        procession.
12 For the nation or kingdom that will not
        serve you will perish;
    it will be utterly ruined.

13 'The glory of Lebanon will come to you,
    the juniper, the fir and the cypress
        together,
to adorn my sanctuary;
    and I will glorify the place for my
        feet.
14 The children of your oppressors will
        come bowing before you;
    all who despise you will bow down at
        your feet
and will call you the City of the LORD,
    Zion of the Holy One of Israel.

15 'Although you have been forsaken and
        hated,
    with no one travelling through,
    I will make you the everlasting pride

---

a 19 Or *When enemies come in like a flood, / the Spirit of the*
LORD will put them to flight   *a* 9 Or *the trading ships*

and the joy of all generations.

¹⁶ You will drink the milk of nations
   and be nursed at royal breasts.
Then you will know that I, the LORD, am
      your Saviour,
   your Redeemer, the Mighty One of
      Jacob.
¹⁷ Instead of bronze I will bring you gold,
   and silver in place of iron.
Instead of wood I will bring you
      bronze,
   and iron in place of stones.
I will make peace your governor
   and well-being your ruler.
¹⁸ No longer will violence be heard in your
      land,
   nor ruin or destruction within your
      borders,
but you will call your walls Salvation
   and your gates Praise.
¹⁹ The sun will no more be your light by
      day,
   nor will the brightness of the moon
      shine on you,
for the LORD will be your everlasting
      light,
   and your God will be your glory.
²⁰ Your sun will never set again,
   and your moon will wane no more;
the LORD will be your everlasting light,
   and your days of sorrow will end.
²¹ Then all your people will be righteous
   and they will possess the land for
      ever.
They are the shoot I have planted,
   the work of my hands,
   for the display of my splendour.
²² The least of you will become a
      thousand,
   the smallest a mighty nation.
I am the LORD;
   in its time I will do this swiftly.'

The year of the LORD's favour

61 The Spirit of the Sovereign LORD is
on me,
   because the LORD has anointed me
   to proclaim good news to the poor.
He has sent me to bind up the
      broken-hearted,
   to proclaim freedom for the
      captives

and release from darkness for the
      prisoners,ᵃ
² to proclaim the year of the LORD's favour
   and the day of vengeance of our God,
to comfort all who mourn,
³   and provide for those who grieve in
      Zion –
to bestow on them a crown of beauty
   instead of ashes,
the oil of joy
   instead of mourning,
and a garment of praise
   instead of a spirit of despair.
They will be called oaks of
      righteousness,
   a planting of the LORD
   for the display of his splendour.

⁴ They will rebuild the ancient ruins
   and restore the places long
      devastated;
they will renew the ruined cities
   that have been devastated for
      generations.
⁵ Strangers will shepherd your flocks;
   foreigners will work your fields and
      vineyards.
⁶ And you will be called priests of the
      LORD,
   you will be named ministers of our
      God.
You will feed on the wealth of nations,
   and in their riches you will boast.

⁷ Instead of your shame
   you will receive a double portion,
and instead of disgrace
   you will rejoice in your inheritance.
And so you will inherit a double portion
   in your land,
   and everlasting joy will be yours.

⁸ 'For I, the LORD, love justice;
   I hate robbery and wrongdoing.
In my faithfulness I will reward my
      people
   and make an everlasting covenant
      with them.
⁹ Their descendants will be known
   among the nations

_____
a 1 Hebrew; Septuagint *the blind*

SLAVERY

God is heartbroken that there are 27 million people, whom he created, living as slaves today. He abhors the fact that a child is sold every two minutes. He hates human trafficking, an industry worth $31.6 billion a year – the second biggest form of organised crime.

In Isaiah 61, Isaiah tells us that God doesn't just like the idea of freedom and justice: he loves it – it's actually part of who he is. His plan is for us to have both freedom from sin through the death and resurrection of Jesus, and freedom from slavery. What's more, he has given us the gift of the Holy Spirit – to help us get involved in his plan and bring good news to the poor, comfort the broken-hearted, release captives and bring freedom to prisoners.

In 1787 a group of twelve evangelical Christians and Quakers teamed up to oppose the slave trade within the British Empire. They began an influential movement, led by William Wilberforce, that brought in a new law abolishing slavery across the Empire.

Today, though, there are more slaves around the world than at the very height of the slave trade. Isaiah 61 shows us that bringing freedom to the captives and good news to the poor is part of our worship, an act of thanksgiving for the righteousness we have received in Jesus. What if we made the same stand as those brave individuals back in the eighteenth century? We could see the end of modern-day slavery!

Sometimes it seems impossible to know where to start with such a huge problem. But there are many ways you can get involved.

Campaign – there are many organisations pressing world leaders to end slavery – why not get involved; or write to your local MP to ask what they are doing to stop slavery?

Pray – for those people enslaved in the UK and around the world, and for those with the power to end this injustice to have the courage to act justly.

Shop ethically – we can use our power as consumers to make a difference. Have you thought about who made your clothes, or your phone, or grew the food you eat? Why not make sure those involved were treated fairly whenever you shop?

Look locally – slavery isn't just a problem in poor countries, it happens right on our doorstep. Why don't you work out how your church could help?

The 27 million slaves in our world today are all created in God's image – they should not be bought and sold. Let's live out this message from Isaiah and stand up and fight for them as our own brothers and sisters!

Sarah Palmer-Felgate

and their offspring among the
peoples.
All who see them will acknowledge
that they are a people the LORD has
blessed.'

10 I delight greatly in the LORD;
my soul rejoices in my God.
For he has clothed me with garments of
salvation
and arrayed me in a robe of his
righteousness,
as a bridegroom adorns his head like a
priest,
and as a bride adorns herself with her
jewels.
11 For as the soil makes the young plant
come up
and a garden causes seeds to grow,
so the Sovereign LORD will make
righteousness
and praise spring up before all
nations.

Zion's new name

62 For Zion's sake I will not keep
silent,
for Jerusalem's sake I will not remain
quiet,
till her vindication shines out like the
dawn,
her salvation like a blazing torch.
2 The nations will see your vindication,
and all kings your glory;
you will be called by a new name
that the mouth of the LORD will
bestow.
3 You will be a crown of splendour in the
LORD's hand,
a royal diadem in the hand of your
God.
4 No longer will they call you Deserted,
or name your land Desolate.
But you will be called Hephzibah,*a*
and your land Beulah;*b*
for the LORD will take delight in you,
and your land will be married.
5 As a young man marries a young
woman,

so will your Builder marry you;
as a bridegroom rejoices over his bride,
so will your God rejoice over you.

6 I have posted watchmen on your walls,
Jerusalem;
they will never be silent day or night.
You who call on the LORD,
give yourselves no rest,
7 and give him no rest till he establishes
Jerusalem
and makes her the praise of the earth.

8 The LORD has sworn by his right hand
and by his mighty arm:
'Never again will I give your grain
as food for your enemies,
and never again will foreigners drink
the new wine
for which you have toiled;
9 but those who harvest it will eat it
and praise the LORD,
and those who gather the grapes will
drink it
in the courts of my sanctuary.'

10 Pass through, pass through the gates!
Prepare the way for the people.
Build up, build up the highway!
Remove the stones.
Raise a banner for the nations.

11 The LORD has made proclamation
to the ends of the earth:
'Say to Daughter Zion,
"See, your Saviour comes!
See, his reward is with him,
and his recompense accompanies
him."'
12 They will be called the Holy People,
the Redeemed of the LORD;
and you will be called Sought After,
the City No Longer Deserted.

God's day of vengeance and redemption

63 Who is this coming from Edom,
from Bozrah, with his garments
stained crimson?
Who is this, robed in splendour,
striding forward in the greatness of
his strength?

---

a 4 *Hephzibah* means *my delight is in her.*
b 4 *Beulah* means *married.*

'It is I, proclaiming victory,
    mighty to save.'

2 Why are your garments red,
    like those of one treading the
        winepress?

3 'I have trodden the winepress alone;
    from the nations no one was with
        me.
I trampled them in my anger
    and trod them down in my wrath;
their blood spattered my garments,
    and I stained all my clothing.
4 It was for me the day of vengeance;
    the year for me to redeem had come.
5 I looked, but there was no one to help,
    I was appalled that no one gave
        support;
so my own arm achieved salvation for
        me,
    and my own wrath sustained me.
6 I trampled the nations in my anger;
    in my wrath I made them drunk
    and poured their blood on the
        ground.'

Praise and prayer

7 I will tell of the kindnesses of the LORD,
    the deeds for which he is to be
        praised,
    according to all the LORD has done
        for us –
yes, the many good things
    he has done for Israel,
    according to his compassion and
        many kindnesses.
8 He said, 'Surely they are my people,
    children who will be true to me';
    and so he became their Saviour.
9 In all their distress he too was
        distressed,
    and the angel of his presence saved
        them.*a*
In his love and mercy he redeemed
        them;
    he lifted them up and carried them
        all the days of old.
10 Yet they rebelled

and grieved his Holy Spirit.
So he turned and became their enemy
    and he himself fought against them.

11 Then his people recalled*b* the days of
        old,
    the days of Moses and his people –
where is he who brought them through
        the sea,
    with the shepherd of his flock?
Where is he who set
    his Holy Spirit among them,
12 who sent his glorious arm of power
    to be at Moses' right hand,
who divided the waters before them,
    to gain for himself everlasting
        renown,
13 who led them through the depths?
Like a horse in open country,
    they did not stumble;
14 like cattle that go down to the plain,
    they were given rest by the Spirit of
        the LORD.
This is how you guided your people
    to make for yourself a glorious
        name.

15 Look down from heaven and see,
    from your lofty throne, holy and
        glorious.
Where are your zeal and your might?
    Your tenderness and compassion are
        withheld from us.
16 But you are our Father,
    though Abraham does not know us
    or Israel acknowledge us;
you, LORD, are our Father,
    our Redeemer from of old is your
        name.
17 Why, LORD, do you make us wander
        from your ways
    and harden our hearts so we do not
        revere you?
Return for the sake of your servants,
    the tribes that are your inheritance.
18 For a little while your people possessed
        your holy place,
    but now our enemies have trampled
        down your sanctuary.
19 We are yours from of old;

---

a 9 Or Saviour *9 in their distress. / It was no envoy or angel / but his own presence that saved them*

b 11 Or *But may he recall*

but you have not ruled over them,
    they have not been called[c] by your
    name.

64 [a] Oh, that you would rend the heavens and come down,
    that the mountains would tremble
    before you!
2 As when fire sets twigs ablaze
    and causes water to boil,
come down to make your name known
    to your enemies
    and cause the nations to quake
    before you!
3 For when you did awesome things that
    we did not expect,
    you came down, and the mountains
    trembled before you.
4 Since ancient times no one has heard,
    no ear has perceived,
no eye has seen any God besides you,
    who acts on behalf of those who wait
    for him.
5 You come to the help of those who
    gladly do right,
    who remember your ways.
But when we continued to sin against
    them,
    you were angry.
    How then can we be saved?
6 All of us have become like one who is
    unclean,
    and all our righteous acts are like
    filthy rags;
we all shrivel up like a leaf,
    and like the wind our sins sweep us
    away.
7 No one calls on your name
    or strives to lay hold of you;
for you have hidden your face from us
    and have given us over to[b] our sins.

8 Yet you, LORD, are our Father.
    We are the clay, you are the potter;
    we are all the work of your hand.

---

c 19 Or *We are like those you have never ruled, / like those
never called*
a In Hebrew texts 64:1 is numbered 63:19b, and
64:2-12 is numbered 64:1-11.
b 7 Septuagint, Syriac and Targum; Hebrew *have
made us melt because of*

9 Do not be angry beyond measure,
    LORD;
    do not remember our sins for ever.
Oh, look upon us we pray,
    for we are all your people.
10 Your sacred cities have become a
    wasteland;
    even Zion is a wasteland, Jerusalem a
    desolation.
11 Our holy and glorious temple, where
    our ancestors praised you,
    has been burned with fire,
    and all that we treasured lies in
    ruins.
12 After all this, LORD, will you hold
    yourself back?
    Will you keep silent and punish us
    beyond measure?

Judgment and salvation

65 'I revealed myself to those who did not ask for me;
    I was found by those who did not
    seek me.
To a nation that did not call on my
    name,
    I said, "Here am I, here am I."
2 All day long I have held out my hands
    to an obstinate people,
who walk in ways not good,
    pursuing their own imaginations —
3 a people who continually provoke me
    to my very face,
offering sacrifices in gardens
    and burning incense on altars of
    brick;
4 who sit among the graves
    and spend their nights keeping
    secret vigil;
who eat the flesh of pigs,
    and whose pots hold broth of
    impure meat;
5 who say, "Keep away; don't come near
    me,
    for I am too sacred for you!"
Such people are smoke in my nostrils,
    a fire that keeps burning all day.

6 'See, it stands written before me;
    I will not keep silent but will pay back
    in full;
    I will pay it back into their laps —

7 both your sins and the sins of your
   ancestors,'
   says the LORD.
'Because they burned sacrifices on the
   mountains
   and defied me on the hills,
I will measure into their laps
   the full payment for their former
   deeds.'

8 This is what the LORD says:

'As when juice is still found in a cluster
   of grapes
   and people say, "Don't destroy it,
   there is still a blessing in it,"
so will I do on behalf of my servants;
   I will not destroy them all.
9 I will bring forth descendants from
   Jacob,
   and from Judah those who will
   possess my mountains;
my chosen people will inherit them,
   and there will my servants live.
10 Sharon will become a pasture for
   flocks,
   and the Valley of Achor a resting
   place for herds,
   for my people who seek me.

11 'But as for you who forsake the LORD
   and forget my holy mountain,
who spread a table for Fortune
   and fill bowls of mixed wine for
   Destiny,
12 I will destine you for the sword,
   and all of you will fall in the
   slaughter;
for I called but you did not answer,
   I spoke but you did not listen.
You did evil in my sight
   and chose what displeases me.'

13 Therefore this is what the Sovereign
LORD says:

'My servants will eat,
   but you will go hungry;
my servants will drink,
   but you will go thirsty;
my servants will rejoice,
   but you will be put to shame.

14 My servants will sing
   out of the joy of their hearts,
but you will cry out
   from anguish of heart
   and wail in brokenness of spirit.
15 You will leave your name
   for my chosen ones to use in their
   curses;
the Sovereign LORD will put you to
   death,
   but to his servants he will give
   another name.
16 Whoever invokes a blessing in the land
   will do so by the one true God;
whoever takes an oath in the land
   will swear by the one true God.
For the past troubles will be forgotten
   and hidden from my eyes.

New heavens and a new earth
17 'See, I will create
   new heavens and a new earth.
The former things will not be
   remembered,
   nor will they come to mind.
18 But be glad and rejoice for ever
   in what I will create,
for I will create Jerusalem to be a delight
   and its people a joy.
19 I will rejoice over Jerusalem
   and take delight in my people;
the sound of weeping and of crying
   will be heard in it no more.

20 'Never again will there be in it
   an infant who lives but a few days,
   or an old man who does not live out
   his years;
the one who dies at a hundred
   will be thought a mere child;
the one who fails to reach[a] a hundred
   will be considered accursed.
21 They will build houses and dwell in
   them;
   they will plant vineyards and eat their
   fruit.
22 No longer will they build houses and
   others live in them,
   or plant and others eat.

---

a 20 Or the sinner who reaches

For as the days of a tree,
  so will be the days of my people;
my chosen ones will long enjoy
  the work of their hands.
23 They will not labour in vain,
    nor will they bear children doomed
      to misfortune;
  for they will be a people blessed by the
    LORD,
    they and their descendants with
      them.
24 Before they call I will answer;
    while they are still speaking I will
      hear.
25 The wolf and the lamb will feed
      together,
    and the lion will eat straw like
      the ox,
    and dust will be the serpent's food.
  They will neither harm nor destroy
    on all my holy mountain,'
                    says the LORD.

Judgment and hope

66 This is what the LORD says:

'Heaven is my throne,
  and the earth is my footstool.
Where is the house you will build for
    me?
  Where will my resting place be?
2 Has not my hand made all these
      things,
  and so they came into being?'
                    declares the LORD.

'These are the ones I look on with
    favour:
  those who are humble and contrite
      in spirit,
  and who tremble at my word.
3 But whoever sacrifices a bull
  is like one who kills a person,
and whoever offers a lamb
  is like one who breaks a dog's neck;
whoever makes a grain offering
  is like one who presents pig's blood,
and whoever burns memorial incense
  is like one who worships an idol.
They have chosen their own ways,
  and they delight in their
    abominations;

4 so I also will choose harsh treatment
      for them
  and will bring on them what they
      dread.
For when I called, no one answered,
  when I spoke, no one listened.
They did evil in my sight
  and chose what displeases me.'

5 Hear the word of the LORD,
  you who tremble at his word;
'Your own people who hate you,
  and exclude you because of my
    name, have said,
"Let the LORD be glorified,
  that we may see your joy!"
  Yet they will be put to shame.
6 Hear that uproar from the city,
  hear that noise from the
    temple!
It is the sound of the LORD
  repaying his enemies all they
    deserve.

7 'Before she goes into labour,
  she gives birth;
before the pains come upon her,
  she delivers a son.
8 Who has ever heard of such things?
  Who has ever seen things like
    this?
Can a country be born in a day
  or a nation be brought forth in a
    moment?
Yet no sooner is Zion in labour
  than she gives birth to her children.
9 Do I bring to the moment of birth
  and not give delivery?' says the
    LORD.
'Do I close up the womb
  when I bring to delivery?' says your
    God.
10 'Rejoice with Jerusalem and be glad for
      her,
  all you who love her;
rejoice greatly with her,
  all you who mourn over her.
11 For you will feed and be satisfied
    at her comforting breasts;
you will drink deeply
  and delight in her overflowing
    abundance.'

¹²For this is what the LORD says:

'I will extend peace to her like a river,
    and the wealth of nations like a
        flooding stream;
you will feed and be carried on her arm
    and dandled on her knees.
¹³As a mother comforts her child,
    so will I comfort you;
    and you will be comforted over
        Jerusalem.'

¹⁴When you see this, your heart will
        rejoice
    and you will flourish like grass;
the hand of the LORD will be made
        known to his servants,
    but his fury will be shown to his foes.
¹⁵See, the LORD is coming with fire,
    and his chariots are like a whirlwind;
he will bring down his anger with fury,
    and his rebuke with flames of fire.
¹⁶For with fire and with his sword
    the LORD will execute judgment on
        all people,
    and many will be those slain by the
        LORD.

¹⁷'Those who consecrate and purify
themselves to go into the gardens, following one who is among those who eat
the flesh of pigs, rats and other unclean
things – they will meet their end together
with the one they follow,' declares the
LORD.

¹⁸'And I, because of what they have
planned and done, am about to comeᵃ

and gather the people of all nations and
languages, and they will come and see my
glory.

¹⁹'I will set a sign among them, and I
will send some of those who survive to
the nations – to Tarshish, to the Libyansᵇ
and Lydians (famous as archers), to Tubal
and Greece, and to the distant islands that
have not heard of my fame or seen my
glory. They will proclaim my glory among
the nations. ²⁰And they will bring all your
people, from all the nations, to my holy
mountain in Jerusalem as an offering
to the LORD – on horses, in chariots and
wagons, and on mules and camels,' says
the LORD. 'They will bring them, as the
Israelites bring their grain offerings, to
the temple of the LORD in ceremonially
clean vessels. ²¹And I will select some of
them also to be priests and Levites,' says
the LORD.

²²'As the new heavens and the new
earth that I make will endure before me,'
declares the LORD, 'so will your name and
descendants endure. ²³From one New
Moon to another and from one Sabbath
to another, all mankind will come and
bow down before me,' says the LORD.
²⁴'And they will go out and look on the
dead bodies of those who rebelled against
me; the worms that eat them will not
die, the fire that burns them will not be
quenched, and they will be loathsome to
all mankind.'

---

a 18 The meaning of the Hebrew for this clause is
uncertain.

b 19 Some Septuagint manuscripts *Put* (Libyans);
Hebrew *Pul*

JEREMIAH

DATE

Jeremiah prophesied from around 627 BC for about 40 years

AUTHOR

Jeremiah

WHAT'S IT ALL ABOUT?

Jeremiah was a prophet who lived about 100 years after Isaiah and at about the same time as the prophets Habakkuk, Zephaniah, Daniel and Ezekiel. He raged at the people about their idolatry, warning them to turn from their sin. He prophesied that if they didn't, God would bring judgement on his people, using the might of the Babylonian army to punish them. This wasn't a popular message and Jeremiah found himself imprisoned and then thrown down a well to starve to death. Yet despite his frustration, Jeremiah couldn't seem to keep himself from loving the people and praying for them. Although the Kingdom of Judah was conquered as Jeremiah had prophesied, he maintained a sense of hope that God wouldn't abandon his people, but would be faithful to the covenant he had sworn to their ancestors and would redeem them because he loved them.

WHY SHOULD WE READ IT?

- To understand why God was so angry with his people.

- To see how the Lord longed to forgive Judah and how he longed to have a real relationship with them once more.

- To put into context a well-known verse, '"For I know the plans I have for you," declares the LORD, "plans to prosper you and not to harm you, plans to give you hope and a future"' (Jeremiah 29:11).

- To see the opposition Jeremiah faced and how he continued to speak the word of the Lord regardless (Jeremiah 37 – 38).

Andy Croft with Liza Hoeksma

1

The words of Jeremiah son of Hilkiah, one of the priests at Anathoth in the territory of Benjamin. ²The word of the LORD came to him in the thirteenth year of the reign of Josiah son of Amon king of Judah, ³and through the reign of Jehoiakim son of Josiah king of Judah, down to the fifth month of the eleventh year of Zedekiah son of Josiah king of Judah, when the people of Jerusalem went into exile.

The call of Jeremiah

⁴The word of the LORD came to me, saying,

⁵'Before I formed you in the womb I
    knew*ᵃ* you,
    before you were born I set you apart;
    I appointed you as a prophet to the
      nations.'

⁶'Alas, Sovereign LORD,' I said, 'I do not know how to speak; I am too young.'

⁷But the LORD said to me, 'Do not say, "I am too young." You must go to everyone I send you to and say whatever I command you. ⁸Do not be afraid of them, for I am with you and will rescue you,' declares the LORD.

⁹Then the LORD reached out his hand and touched my mouth and said to me, 'I have put my words in your mouth. ¹⁰See, today I appoint you over nations and kingdoms to uproot and tear down, to destroy and overthrow, to build and to plant.'

¹¹The word of the LORD came to me: 'What do you see, Jeremiah?'

'I see the branch of an almond tree,' I replied.

¹²The LORD said to me, 'You have seen correctly, for I am watching*ᵇ* to see that my word is fulfilled.'

¹³The word of the LORD came to me again: 'What do you see?'

'I see a pot that is boiling,' I answered. 'It is tilting towards us from the north.'

¹⁴The LORD said to me, 'From the north disaster will be poured out on all who live in the land. ¹⁵I am about to summon all the peoples of the northern kingdoms,' declares the LORD.

'Their kings will come and set up their
    thrones
    in the entrance of the gates of
      Jerusalem;
they will come against all her
    surrounding walls
    and against all the towns of Judah.
¹⁶I will pronounce my judgments on my
    people
    because of their wickedness in
      forsaking me,
in burning incense to other gods
    and in worshipping what their hands
      have made.

¹⁷'Get yourself ready! Stand up and say to them whatever I command you. Do not be terrified by them, or I will terrify you before them. ¹⁸Today I have made you a fortified city, an iron pillar and a bronze wall to stand against the whole land – against the kings of Judah, its officials, its priests and the people of the land. ¹⁹They will fight against you but will not overcome you, for I am with you and will rescue you,' declares the LORD.

Israel forsakes God

2

The word of the LORD came to me: ²'Go and proclaim in the hearing of Jerusalem:

'This is what the LORD says:

'"I remember the devotion of your
      youth,
    how as a bride you loved me
and followed me through the
      wilderness,
    through a land not sown.
³Israel was holy to the LORD,
    the firstfruits of his harvest;
all who devoured her were held
      guilty,
    and disaster overtook them," '
               declares the LORD.

---

a 5 Or *chose*
b 12 The Hebrew for *watching* sounds like the Hebrew for *almond tree.*

4 Hear the word of the Lord, you
        descendants of Jacob,
    all you clans of Israel.

5 This is what the Lord says:

'What fault did your ancestors find in
        me,
    that they strayed so far from me?
They followed worthless idols
    and became worthless themselves.
6 They did not ask, "Where is the Lord,
    who brought us up out of Egypt
and led us through the barren
        wilderness,
    through a land of deserts and
        ravines,
    a land of drought and utter darkness,
    a land where no one travels and no
        one lives?"
7 I brought you into a fertile land
    to eat its fruit and rich produce.
But you came and defiled my land
    and made my inheritance detestable.
8 The priests did not ask,
    "Where is the Lord?"
Those who deal with the law did not
        know me;
    the leaders rebelled against me.
The prophets prophesied by Baal,
    following worthless idols.

9 'Therefore I bring charges against you
        again,'
                    declares the Lord.
    'And I will bring charges against your
        children's children.
10 Cross over to the coasts of Cyprus and
        look,
    send to Kedar*a* and observe closely;
    see if there has ever been anything
        like this:
11 has a nation ever changed its gods?
    (Yet they are not gods at all.)
But my people have exchanged their
        glorious God
    for worthless idols.
12 Be appalled at this, you heavens,
    and shudder with great horror,'
                    declares the Lord.

13 'My people have committed two sins:
They have forsaken me,
    the spring of living water,
and have dug their own cisterns,
    broken cisterns that cannot hold
        water.
14 Is Israel a servant, a slave by birth?
    Why then has he become plunder?
15 Lions have roared;
    they have growled at him.
They have laid waste his land;
    his towns are burned and deserted.
16 Also, the men of Memphis and
        Tahpanhes
    have cracked your skull.
17 Have you not brought this on
        yourselves
    by forsaking the Lord your God
    when he led you in the way?
18 Now why go to Egypt
    to drink water from the Nile?*b*
And why go to Assyria
    to drink water from the Euphrates?
19 Your wickedness will punish you;
    your backsliding will rebuke you.
Consider then and realise
    how evil and bitter it is for you
when you forsake the Lord your God
    and have no awe of me,'
                    declares the Lord,
                    the Lord Almighty.

20 'Long ago you broke off your yoke
    and tore off your bonds;
    you said, "I will not serve you!"
Indeed, on every high hill
    and under every spreading tree
    you lay down as a prostitute.
21 I had planted you like a choice vine
    of sound and reliable stock.
How then did you turn against me
    into a corrupt, wild vine?
22 Although you wash yourself with soap
    and use an abundance of cleansing
        powder,
    the stain of your guilt is still before
        me,'
                    declares the Sovereign Lord.
23 'How can you say, "I am not defiled;
    I have not run after the Baals"?

---

a 10 In the Syro-Arabian desert   *b* 18 Hebrew *Shihor*; that is, a branch of the Nile

885

See how you behaved in the valley;
  consider what you have done.
You are a swift she-camel
  running here and there,
24 a wild donkey accustomed to the
    desert,
    sniffing the wind in her craving –
  in her heat who can restrain her?
Any males that pursue her need not tire
    themselves;
  at mating time they will find her.
25 Do not run until your feet are bare
  and your throat is dry.
But you said, "It's no use!
  I love foreign gods,
  and I must go after them."

26 'As a thief is disgraced when he is
    caught,
  so the people of Israel are disgraced –
they, their kings and their officials,
  their priests and their prophets.
27 They say to wood, "You are my father,"
  and to stone, "You gave me birth."
They have turned their backs to me
  and not their faces;
yet when they are in trouble, they say,
  "Come and save us!"
28 Where then are the gods you made for
    yourselves?
  Let them come if they can save you
  when you are in trouble!
For you, Judah, have as many gods
  as you have towns.

29 'Why do you bring charges against me?
  You have all rebelled against me,'
            declares the LORD.
30 'In vain I punished your people;
  they did not respond to correction.
Your sword has devoured your
    prophets
  like a ravenous lion.

31 'You of this generation, consider the
word of the LORD:

'Have I been a desert to Israel
  or a land of great darkness?
Why do my people say, "We are free to
    roam;
  we will come to you no more"?

32 Does a young woman forget her
    jewellery,
  a bride her wedding ornaments?
Yet my people have forgotten me,
  days without number.
33 How skilled you are at pursuing love!
  Even the worst of women can learn
    from your ways.
34 On your clothes is found
  the lifeblood of the innocent poor,
  though you did not catch them
    breaking in.
Yet in spite of all this
35   you say, "I am innocent;
  he is not angry with me."
But I will pass judgment on you
  because you say, "I have not sinned."
36 Why do you go about so much,
  changing your ways?
You will be disappointed by Egypt
  as you were by Assyria.
37 You will also leave that place
  with your hands on your head,
for the LORD has rejected those you trust;
  you will not be helped by them.

3 'If a man divorces his wife
  and she leaves him and marries
    another man,
should he return to her again?
  Would not the land be completely
    defiled?
But you have lived as a prostitute with
    many lovers –
  would you now return to me?'
            declares the LORD.
2 'Look up to the barren heights and see.
  Is there any place where you have not
    been ravished?
By the roadside you sat waiting for
    lovers,
  sat like a nomad in the desert.
You have defiled the land
  with your prostitution and
    wickedness.
3 Therefore the showers have been
    withheld,
  and no spring rains have fallen.
Yet you have the brazen look of a
    prostitute;
  you refuse to blush with shame.
4 Have you not just called to me:

"My Father, my friend from my youth,
5 will you always be angry?
    Will your wrath continue for ever?"
This is how you talk,
    but you do all the evil you can.'

Unfaithful Israel

6 During the reign of King Josiah, the LORD said to me, 'Have you seen what faithless Israel has done? She has gone up on every high hill and under every spreading tree and has committed adultery there. 7 I thought that after she had done all this she would return to me but she did not, and her unfaithful sister Judah saw it. 8 I gave faithless Israel her certificate of divorce and sent her away because of all her adulteries. Yet I saw that her unfaithful sister Judah had no fear; she also went out and committed adultery. 9 Because Israel's immorality mattered so little to her, she defiled the land and committed adultery with stone and wood. 10 In spite of all this, her unfaithful sister Judah did not return to me with all her heart, but only in pretence,' declares the LORD.

11 The LORD said to me, 'Faithless Israel is more righteous than unfaithful Judah. 12 Go, proclaim this message towards the north:

  '"Return, faithless Israel," declares the
    LORD,
  "I will frown on you no longer,
for I am faithful," declares the LORD,
  "I will not be angry for ever.
13 Only acknowledge your guilt –
  you have rebelled against the LORD
    your God,
you have scattered your favours to
    foreign gods
  under every spreading tree,
  and have not obeyed me,"'
                declares the LORD.

14 'Return, faithless people,' declares the LORD, 'for I am your husband. I will choose you – one from a town and two from a clan – and bring you to Zion. 15 Then I will give you shepherds after my own heart, who will lead you with knowledge and understanding. 16 In those days, when your numbers have increased greatly in the land,' declares the LORD, 'people will no longer say, "The ark of the covenant of the LORD." It will never enter their minds or be remembered; it will not be missed, nor will another one be made. 17 At that time they will call Jerusalem The Throne of the LORD, and all nations will gather in Jerusalem to honour the name of the LORD. No longer will they follow the stubbornness of their evil hearts. 18 In those days the people of Judah will join the people of Israel, and together they will come from a northern land to the land I gave your ancestors as an inheritance.

19 'I myself said,

  '"How gladly would I treat you like my
    children
  and give you a pleasant land,
    the most beautiful inheritance of any
      nation."
I thought you would call me "Father"
  and not turn away from
    following me.
20 But like a woman unfaithful to her
    husband,
  so you, Israel, have been unfaithful
    to me,'
                declares the LORD.

21 A cry is heard on the barren heights,
  the weeping and pleading of the
    people of Israel,
because they have perverted their ways
  and have forgotten the LORD their
    God.

22 'Return, faithless people;
  I will cure you of backsliding.'

'Yes, we will come to you,
  for you are the LORD our God.
23 Surely the idolatrous commotion on
    the hills
  and mountains is a deception;
surely in the LORD our God
  is the salvation of Israel.
24 From our youth shameful gods have
    consumed
  the fruits of our ancestors' labour –
    their flocks and herds,

their sons and daughters.
25 Let us lie down in our shame,
  and let our disgrace cover us.
We have sinned against the LORD our
    God,
  both we and our ancestors;
from our youth till this day
  we have not obeyed the LORD our
      God.'

4 'If you, Israel, will return,
    then return to me,'
                      declares the LORD.
'If you put your detestable idols out of
    my sight
  and no longer go astray,
2 and if in a truthful, just and righteous
    way
  you swear, "As surely as the LORD
      lives,"
then the nations will invoke blessings
    by him
  and in him they will boast.'

3 This is what the LORD says to the people of Judah and to Jerusalem:

'Break up your unploughed ground
  and do not sow among thorns.
4 Circumcise yourselves to the LORD,
  circumcise your hearts,
    you people of Judah and inhabitants
        of Jerusalem,
or my wrath will flare up and burn like
    fire
  because of the evil you have
      done –
burn with no one to quench it.

Disaster from the North
5 'Announce in Judah and proclaim in
      Jerusalem and say:
  "Sound the trumpet throughout the
      land!"
Cry aloud and say:
  "Gather together!
Let us flee to the fortified cities!"
6 Raise the signal to go to Zion!
  Flee for safety without delay!
For I am bringing disaster from the
    north,
  even terrible destruction.'

7 A lion has come out of his lair;
  a destroyer of nations has set out.
He has left his place
  to lay waste your land.
Your towns will lie in ruins
  without inhabitant.
8 So put on sackcloth,
  lament and wail,
for the fierce anger of the LORD
  has not turned away from us.

9 'In that day,' declares the LORD,
  'the king and the officials will lose
      heart,
the priests will be horrified,
  and the prophets will be appalled.'

10 Then I said, 'Alas, Sovereign LORD!
How completely you have deceived this
people and Jerusalem by saying, "You
will have peace," when the sword is at our
throats!'

11 At that time this people and Jerusalem will be told, 'A scorching wind from
the barren heights in the desert blows
towards my people, but not to winnow
or cleanse; 12 a wind too strong for that
comes from me. Now I pronounce my
judgments against them.'

13 Look! He advances like the clouds,
  his chariots come like a whirlwind,
his horses are swifter than eagles.
  Woe to us! We are ruined!
14 Jerusalem, wash the evil from your
      heart and be saved.
  How long will you harbour wicked
      thoughts?
15 A voice is announcing from Dan,
  proclaiming disaster from the hills of
      Ephraim.
16 'Tell this to the nations,
  proclaim concerning Jerusalem:
"A besieging army is coming from a
    distant land,
  raising a war cry against the cities of
      Judah.
17 They surround her like men guarding a
      field,
  because she has rebelled against me,"'
                      declares the LORD.
18 'Your own conduct and actions

have brought this on you.
This is your punishment.
How bitter it is!
How it pierces to the heart!'

19 Oh, my anguish, my anguish!
I writhe in pain.
Oh, the agony of my heart!
My heart pounds within me,
I cannot keep silent.
For I have heard the sound of the
trumpet;
I have heard the battle cry.
20 Disaster follows disaster;
the whole land lies in ruins.
In an instant my tents are destroyed,
my shelter in a moment.
21 How long must I see the battle standard
and hear the sound of the trumpet?

22 'My people are fools;
they do not know me.
They are senseless children;
they have no understanding.
They are skilled in doing evil;
they know not how to do good.'

23 I looked at the earth,
and it was formless and empty;
and at the heavens,
and their light was gone.
24 I looked at the mountains,
and they were quaking;
all the hills were swaying.
25 I looked, and there were no people;
every bird in the sky had flown away.
26 I looked, and the fruitful land was a
desert;
all its towns lay in ruins
before the LORD, before his fierce
anger.

27 This is what the LORD says:

'The whole land will be ruined,
though I will not destroy it
completely.
28 Therefore the earth will mourn
and the heavens above grow dark,
because I have spoken and will not
relent,
I have decided and will not turn back.'

29 At the sound of horsemen and archers
every town takes to flight.
Some go into the thickets;
some climb up among the rocks.
All the towns are deserted;
no one lives in them.

30 What are you doing, you devastated
one?
Why dress yourself in scarlet
and put on jewels of gold?
Why highlight your eyes with makeup?
You adorn yourself in vain.
Your lovers despise you;
they want to kill you.

31 I hear a cry as of a woman in labour,
a groan as of one bearing her first
child –
the cry of Daughter Zion gasping for
breath,
stretching out her hands and saying,
'Alas! I am fainting;
my life is given over to murderers.'

Not one is upright

5 'Go up and down the streets of
Jerusalem,
look around and consider,
search through her squares.
If you can find but one person
who deals honestly and seeks the
truth,
I will forgive this city.
2 Although they say, "As surely as the
LORD lives,"
still they are swearing falsely.'

3 LORD, do not your eyes look for truth?
You struck them, but they felt no
pain;
you crushed them but they refused
correction.
They made their faces harder than stone
and refused to repent.
4 I thought, 'These are only the poor;
they are foolish,
for they do not know the way of the
LORD,
the requirements of their God.
5 So I will go to the leaders
and speak to them;

surely they know the way of the LORD,
the requirements of their God.'
But with one accord they too had
broken off the yoke
and torn off the bonds.
6 Therefore a lion from the forest will
attack them,
a wolf from the desert will ravage
them,
a leopard will lie in wait near their
towns
to tear to pieces any who venture
out,
for their rebellion is great
and their backslidings many.

YOU WHAT?

FIVE PROPHECIES INVOLVING DONKEYS

○ **JUDAH WILL TETHER HIS DONKEY TO A VINE**
Genesis 49:8–12

○ **ISSACHAR IS A SCRAWNY DONKEY**
Genesis 49:14–15

○ **THE DONKEYS WILL EAT WELL**
Isaiah 30:23–26

○ **THE KING WILL BE BURIED LIKE A DONKEY**
Jeremiah 22:13–19

○ **THE KING WILL ARRIVE ON A DONKEY**
Zechariah 9:9–10; John 12:14

7 'Why should I forgive you?
Your children have forsaken me
and sworn by gods that are not gods.
I supplied all their needs,
yet they committed adultery
and thronged to the houses of
prostitutes.
8 They are well-fed, lusty stallions,
each neighing for another man's
wife.

9 Should I not punish them for this?'
declares the LORD.
'Should I not avenge myself
on such a nation as this?

10 'Go through her vineyards and ravage
them,
but do not destroy them completely.
Strip off her branches,
for these people do not belong to the
LORD.
11 The people of Israel and the people of
Judah
have been utterly unfaithful to me,'
declares the LORD.

12 They have lied about the LORD;
they said, 'He will do nothing!
No harm will come to us;
we will never see sword or famine.
13 The prophets are but wind
and the word is not in them;
so let what they say be done to
them.'

14 Therefore this is what the LORD God
Almighty says:

'Because the people have spoken these
words,
I will make my words in your mouth
a fire
and these people the wood it
consumes.
15 People of Israel,' declares the LORD,
'I am bringing a distant nation
against you –
an ancient and enduring nation,
a people whose language you do not
know,
whose speech you do not
understand.
16 Their quivers are like an open grave;
all of them are mighty warriors.
17 They will devour your harvests and
food,
devour your sons and daughters;
they will devour your flocks and herds,
devour your vines and fig trees.
With the sword they will destroy
the fortified cities in which you
trust.

18 'Yet even in those days,' declares the LORD, 'I will not destroy you completely. 19 And when the people ask, "Why has the LORD our God done all this to us?" you will tell them, "As you have forsaken me and served foreign gods in your own land, so now you will serve foreigners in a land not your own."

20 'Announce this to the descendants of Jacob
    and proclaim it in Judah:
21 Hear this, you foolish and senseless people,
    who have eyes but do not see,
    who have ears but do not hear:
22 Should you not fear me?' declares the LORD.
    'Should you not tremble in my presence?
I made the sand a boundary for the sea,
    an everlasting barrier it cannot cross.
The waves may roll, but they cannot prevail;
    they may roar, but they cannot cross it.
23 But these people have stubborn and rebellious hearts;
    they have turned aside and gone away.
24 They do not say to themselves,
    "Let us fear the LORD our God,
who gives autumn and spring rains in season,
    who assures us of the regular weeks of harvest."
25 Your wrongdoings have kept these away;
    your sins have deprived you of good.

26 'Among my people are the wicked
    who lie in wait like men who snare birds
    and like those who set traps to catch people.
27 Like cages full of birds,
    their houses are full of deceit;
they have become rich and powerful
28   and have grown fat and sleek.
    Their evil deeds have no limit;
    they do not seek justice.

They do not promote the case of the fatherless;
    they do not defend the just cause of the poor.
29 Should I not punish them for this?' declares the LORD.
    'Should I not avenge myself on such a nation as this?

30 'A horrible and shocking thing has happened in the land:
31 the prophets prophesy lies,
    the priests rule by their own authority,
and my people love it this way.
    But what will you do in the end?

Jerusalem under siege

6 'Flee for safety, people of Benjamin!
    Flee from Jerusalem!
Sound the trumpet in Tekoa!
    Raise the signal over Beth Hakkerem!
For disaster looms out of the north,
    even terrible destruction.
2 I will destroy Daughter Zion,
    so beautiful and delicate.
3 Shepherds with their flocks will come against her;
    they will pitch their tents round her,
    each tending his own portion.'

4 'Prepare for battle against her!
    Arise, let us attack at noon!
But, alas, the daylight is fading,
    and the shadows of evening grow long.
5 So arise, let us attack at night
    and destroy her fortresses!'

6 This is what the LORD Almighty says:

'Cut down the trees
    and build siege ramps against Jerusalem.
This city must be punished;
    it is filled with oppression.
7 As a well pours out its water,
    so she pours out her wickedness.
Violence and destruction resound in her;
    her sickness and wounds are ever before me.

⁸Take warning, Jerusalem,
    or I will turn away from you
and make your land desolate
    so that no one can live in it.'

⁹This is what the LORD Almighty says:

'Let them glean the remnant of Israel
    as thoroughly as a vine;
pass your hand over the branches again,
    like one gathering grapes.'

¹⁰To whom can I speak and give warning?
    Who will listen to me?
Their ears are closed*a*
    so that they cannot hear.
The word of the LORD is offensive to
    them;
    they find no pleasure in it.
¹¹But I am full of the wrath of the LORD,
    and I cannot hold it in.

'Pour it out on the children in the street
    and on the young men gathered
    together;
both husband and wife will be caught
    in it,
    and the old, those weighed down
    with years.
¹²Their houses will be turned over to
    others,
    together with their fields and their
    wives,
when I stretch out my hand
    against those who live in the land,'
    declares the LORD.
¹³'From the least to the greatest,
    all are greedy for gain;
prophets and priests alike,
    all practise deceit.
¹⁴They dress the wound of my people
    as though it were not serious.
"Peace, peace," they say,
    when there is no peace.
¹⁵Are they ashamed of their detestable
    conduct?
No, they have no shame at all;
    they do not even know how to blush.
So they will fall among the fallen;

they will be brought down when I
    punish them,'
        says the LORD.

¹⁶This is what the LORD says:

'Stand at the crossroads and look;
    ask for the ancient paths,
ask where the good way is, and walk
    in it,
    and you will find rest for your souls.
    But you said, "We will not walk in it."
¹⁷I appointed watchmen over you and
    said,
    "Listen to the sound of the trumpet!"
    But you said, "We will not listen."
¹⁸Therefore hear, you nations;
    you who are witnesses,
    observe what will happen to them.
¹⁹Hear, you earth:
    I am bringing disaster on this people,
    the fruit of their schemes,
because they have not listened to my
    words
    and have rejected my law.
²⁰What do I care about incense from
    Sheba
    or sweet calamus from a distant
    land?
Your burnt offerings are not
    acceptable;
    your sacrifices do not please me.'

²¹Therefore this is what the LORD says:

'I will put obstacles before this people.
    Parents and children alike will
    stumble over them;
    neighbours and friends will perish.'

²²This is what the LORD says:

'Look, an army is coming
    from the land of the north;
a great nation is being stirred up
    from the ends of the earth.
²³They are armed with bow and spear;
    they are cruel and show no mercy.
They sound like the roaring sea
    as they ride on their horses;
they come like men in battle formation
    to attack you, Daughter Zion.'

---

a 10 Hebrew *uncircumcised*

24 We have heard reports about them,
    and our hands hang limp.
Anguish has gripped us,
    pain like that of a woman in labour.
25 Do not go out to the fields
    or walk on the roads,
for the enemy has a sword,
    and there is terror on every side.
26 Put on sackcloth, my people,
    and roll in ashes;
mourn with bitter wailing
    as for an only son,
for suddenly the destroyer
    will come upon us.

27 'I have made you a tester of metals
    and my people the ore,
that you may observe
    and test their ways.
28 They are all hardened rebels,
    going about to slander.
They are bronze and iron;
    they all act corruptly.
29 The bellows blow fiercely
    to burn away the lead with fire,
but the refining goes on in vain;
    the wicked are not purged out.
30 They are called rejected silver,
    because the LORD has rejected them.'

False religion worthless

7 This is the word that came to Jeremiah
from the LORD: 2 'Stand at the gate of
the LORD's house and there proclaim this
message:
'"Hear the word of the LORD, all you
people of Judah who come through these
gates to worship the LORD. 3 This is what
the LORD Almighty, the God of Israel,
says: reform your ways and your actions,
and I will let you live in this place. 4 Do
not trust in deceptive words and say, 'This
is the temple of the LORD, the temple of
the LORD, the temple of the LORD!' 5 If you
really change your ways and your actions
and deal with each other justly, 6 if you do
not oppress the foreigner, the fatherless
or the widow and do not shed innocent
blood in this place, and if you do not follow other gods to your own harm, 7 then
I will let you live in this place, in the land
I gave to your ancestors for ever and ever.

8 But look, you are trusting in deceptive
words that are worthless.
9 '"Will you steal and murder, commit adultery and perjury,ª burn incense
to Baal and follow other gods you have
not known, 10 and then come and stand
before me in this house, which bears my
Name, and say, 'We are safe' – safe to do all
these detestable things? 11 Has this house,
which bears my Name, become a den of
robbers to you? But I have been watching!
declares the LORD.
12 '"Go now to the place in Shiloh where
I first made a dwelling for my Name, and
see what I did to it because of the wickedness of my people Israel. 13 While you were
doing all these things, declares the LORD, I
spoke to you again and again, but you did
not listen; I called you, but you did not
answer. 14 Therefore, what I did to Shiloh
I will now do to the house that bears my
Name, the temple you trust in, the place
I gave to you and your ancestors. 15 I will
thrust you from my presence, just as I did
all your fellow Israelites, the people of
Ephraim."
16 'So do not pray for this people nor offer any plea or petition for them; do not
plead with me, for I will not listen to you.
17 Do you not see what they are doing in
the towns of Judah and in the streets of
Jerusalem? 18 The children gather wood,
the fathers light the fire, and the women
knead the dough and make cakes to offer
to the Queen of Heaven. They pour out
drink offerings to other gods to arouse
my anger. 19 But am I the one they are provoking? declares the LORD. Are they not
rather harming themselves, to their own
shame?
20 '"Therefore this is what the Sovereign LORD says: my anger and my wrath
will be poured out on this place – on man
and beast, on the trees of the field and on
the crops of your land – and it will burn
and not be quenched.
21 '"This is what the LORD Almighty, the
God of Israel, says: go ahead, add your
burnt offerings to your other sacrifices
and eat the meat yourselves! 22 For when

___
ª 9 Or and swear by false gods

I brought your ancestors out of Egypt and spoke to them, I did not just give them commands about burnt offerings and sacrifices, 23 but I gave them this command: obey me, and I will be your God and you will be my people. Walk in obedience to all I command you, that it may go well with you. 24 But they did not listen or pay attention; instead, they followed the stubborn inclinations of their evil hearts. They went backwards and not forwards. 25 From the time your ancestors left Egypt until now, day after day, again and again I sent you my servants the prophets. 26 But they did not listen to me or pay attention. They were stiff-necked and did more evil than their ancestors."

27 'When you tell them all this, they will not listen to you; when you call to them, they will not answer. 28 Therefore say to them, "This is the nation that has not obeyed the LORD its God or responded to correction. Truth has perished; it has vanished from their lips.

29 ' "Cut off your hair and throw it away; take up a lament on the barren heights, for the LORD has rejected and abandoned this generation that is under his wrath.

The valley of slaughter

30 ' "The people of Judah have done evil in my eyes, declares the LORD. They have set up their detestable idols in the house that bears my Name and have defiled it. 31 They have built the high places of Topheth in the Valley of Ben Hinnom to burn their sons and daughters in the fire — something I did not command, nor did it enter my mind. 32 So beware, the days are coming, declares the LORD, when people will no longer call it Topheth or the Valley of Ben Hinnom, but the Valley of Slaughter, for they will bury the dead in Topheth until there is no more room. 33 Then the carcasses of this people will become food for the birds and the wild animals, and there will be no one to frighten them away. 34 I will bring an end to the sounds of joy and gladness and to the voices of bride and bridegroom in the towns of Judah and the streets of Jerusalem, for the land will become desolate.

8 ' "At that time, declares the LORD, the bones of the kings and officials of Judah, the bones of the priests and prophets, and the bones of the people of Jerusalem will be removed from their graves. 2 They will be exposed to the sun and the moon and all the stars of the heavens, which they have loved and served and which they have followed and consulted and worshipped. They will not be gathered up or buried, but will be like dung lying on the ground. 3 Wherever I banish them, all the survivors of this evil nation will prefer death to life, declares the LORD Almighty."

Sin and punishment

4 'Say to them, "This is what the LORD says:

' "When people fall down, do they not
      get up?
  When someone turns away, do they
      not return?
5 Why then have these people turned
      away?
  Why does Jerusalem always turn
      away?
  They cling to deceit;
      they refuse to return.
6 I have listened attentively,
      but they do not say what is right.
  None of them repent of their
      wickedness,
      saying, 'What have I done?'
  Each pursues their own course
      like a horse charging into battle.
7 Even the stork in the sky
      knows her appointed seasons,
  and the dove, the swift and the thrush
      observe the time of their
         migration.
  But my people do not know
      the requirements of the LORD.

8 ' "How can you say, 'We are wise,
      for we have the law of the LORD,'
  when actually the lying pen of the
         scribes
      has handled it falsely?
9 The wise will be put to shame;
      they will be dismayed and trapped.

Since they have rejected the word of the
LORD,
　　what kind of wisdom do they have?
10 Therefore I will give their wives to other
　　men
　　and their fields to new owners.
From the least to the greatest,
　　all are greedy for gain;
prophets and priests alike,
　　all practise deceit.
11 They dress the wound of my people
　　as though it were not serious.
'Peace, peace,' they say,
　　when there is no peace.
12 Are they ashamed of their detestable
　　conduct?
　　No, they have no shame at all;
they do not even know how to
　　blush.
So they will fall among the fallen;
　　they will be brought down when
　　they are punished,
　　　　　　　　　　　　says the LORD.

13 ' "I will take away their harvest,
　　　　　　　　　　declares the LORD.
There will be no grapes on the vine.
There will be no figs on the tree,
　　and their leaves will wither.
What I have given them
　　will be taken from them." ' *a*

14 Why are we sitting here?
　　Gather together!
Let us flee to the fortified cities
　　and perish there!
For the LORD our God has doomed us to
　　perish
　　and given us poisoned water to drink,
　　because we have sinned against him.
15 We hoped for peace
　　but no good has come,
for a time of healing
　　but there is only terror.
16 The snorting of the enemy's horses
　　is heard from Dan;
at the neighing of their stallions
　　the whole land trembles.
They have come to devour

the land and everything in it,
　　the city and all who live there.

17 'See, I will send venomous snakes
　　　　among you,
vipers that cannot be charmed,
　　and they will bite you,'
　　　　　　　　declares the LORD.

18 You who are my Comforter*b* in sorrow,
　　my heart is faint within me.
19 Listen to the cry of my people
　　from a land far away:
'Is the LORD not in Zion?
　　Is her King no longer there?'

'Why have they aroused my anger with
　　their images,
with their worthless foreign idols?'

20 'The harvest is past,
　　the summer has ended,
　　and we are not saved.'

21 Since my people are crushed, I am
　　crushed;
I mourn, and horror grips me.
22 Is there no balm in Gilead?
　　Is there no physician there?
Why then is there no healing
　　for the wound of my people?

9*a* 1 Oh, that my head were a spring of
　　water
and my eyes a fountain of tears!
I would weep day and night
　　for the slain of my people.
2 Oh, that I had in the desert
　　a lodging place for travellers,
so that I might leave my people
　　and go away from them;
for they are all adulterers,
　　a crowd of unfaithful people.

3 'They make ready their tongue
　　like a bow, to shoot lies;
it is not by truth
　　that they triumph*b* in the land.

---

b 18 The meaning of the Hebrew for this word is
uncertain.
a In Hebrew texts 9:1 is numbered 8:23, and 9:2-26 is
numbered 9:1-25.
b 3 Or *lies; / they are not valiant for truth*

---

a 13 The meaning of the Hebrew for this sentence
is uncertain.

They go from one sin to another;
    they do not acknowledge me,'
          declares the LORD.
4 'Beware of your friends;
    do not trust anyone in your clan.
For every one of them is a deceiver,c
    and every friend a slanderer.
5 Friend deceives friend,
    and no one speaks the truth.
They have taught their tongues to lie;
    they weary themselves with sinning.
6 Youd live in the midst of deception;
    in their deceit they refuse to
        acknowledge me,'
          declares the LORD.

7 Therefore this is what the LORD Almighty says:

'See, I will refine and test them,
    for what else can I do
    because of the sin of my people?
8 Their tongue is a deadly arrow;
    it speaks deceitfully.
With their mouths they all speak
        cordially to their neighbours,
but in their hearts they set traps for
    them.
9 Should I not punish them for this?'
    declares the LORD.
'Should I not avenge myself
    on such a nation as this?'

10 I will weep and wail for the mountains
    and take up a lament concerning the
        wilderness grasslands.
They are desolate and untravelled,
    and the lowing of cattle is not heard.
The birds have all fled
    and the animals are gone.

11 'I will make Jerusalem a heap of ruins,
    a haunt of jackals;
and I will lay waste the towns of Judah
    so that no one can live there.'

12 Who is wise enough to understand this? Who has been instructed by the LORD and can explain it? Why has the land been

ruined and laid waste like a desert that no one can cross?

13 The LORD said, 'It is because they have forsaken my law, which I set before them; they have not obeyed me or followed my law. 14 Instead, they have followed the stubbornness of their hearts; they have followed the Baals, as their ancestors taught them.' 15 Therefore this is what the LORD Almighty, the God of Israel, says: 'See, I will make this people eat bitter food and drink poisoned water. 16 I will scatter them among nations that neither they nor their ancestors have known, and I will pursue them with the sword until I have made an end of them.'

17 This is what the LORD Almighty says:

'Consider now! Call for the wailing
      women to come;
    send for the most skilful of them.
18 Let them come quickly
    and wail over us
till our eyes overflow with tears
    and water streams from our eyelids.
19 The sound of wailing is heard from Zion:
    "How ruined we are!
    How great is our shame!
We must leave our land
    because our houses are in ruins." '

20 Now, you women, hear the word of the
    LORD;
    open your ears to the words of his
        mouth.
Teach your daughters how to wail;
    teach one another a lament.
21 Death has climbed in through our
        windows
    and has entered our fortresses;
it has removed the children from the
        streets
    and the young men from the public
        squares.

22 Say, 'This is what the LORD declares:

' "Dead bodies will lie
    like dung on the open field,
like cut corn behind the reaper,
    with no one to gather them." '

---

c 4 Or a deceiving Jacob
d 6 That is, Jeremiah (the Hebrew is singular)

23 This is what the LORD says:

'Let not the wise boast of their wisdom
   or the strong boast of their strength
   or the rich boast of their riches,
24 but let the one who boasts boast about
   this:
   that they have the understanding to
     know me,
   that I am the LORD, who exercises
     kindness,
   justice and righteousness on earth,
   for in these I delight,'
                 declares the LORD.

25 'The days are coming,' declares the LORD, 'when I will punish all who are circumcised only in the flesh – **26** Egypt, Judah, Edom, Ammon, Moab and all who live in the wilderness in distant places.*e* For all these nations are really uncircumcised, and even the whole house of Israel is uncircumcised in heart.'

God and idols

10 Hear what the LORD says to you, people of Israel. **2** This is what the LORD says:

'Do not learn the ways of the nations
   or be terrified by signs in the
     heavens,
   though the nations are terrified by
     them.
3 For the practices of the peoples are
   worthless;
   they cut a tree out of the forest,
   and a craftsman shapes it with his
     chisel.
4 They adorn it with silver and gold;
   they fasten it with hammer and
     nails
   so that it will not totter.
5 Like a scarecrow in a cucumber field,
   their idols cannot speak;
   they must be carried
     because they cannot walk.
Do not fear them;
   they can do no harm
   nor can they do any good.'

6 No one is like you, LORD;
   you are great,
   and your name is mighty in power.
7 Who should not fear you,
   King of the nations?
   This is your due.
Among all the wise leaders of the
     nations
   and in all their kingdoms,
   there is no one like you.

8 They are all senseless and foolish;
   they are taught by worthless wooden
     idols.
9 Hammered silver is brought from
     Tarshish
   and gold from Uphaz.
What the craftsman and goldsmith have
     made
   is then dressed in blue and purple –
   all made by skilled workers.
10 But the LORD is the true God;
   he is the living God, the eternal King.
When he is angry, the earth trembles;
   the nations cannot endure his wrath.

BIBLICAL LANGUAGE

The Bible is written in two main languages: Hebrew and Greek. However, some parts of the Old Testament are also in Aramaic, while the New Testament contains the odd Aramaic and Latin word.

11 'Tell them this: "These gods, who did not make the heavens and the earth, will perish from the earth and from under the heavens." '*a*

12 But God made the earth by his power;
   he founded the world by his wisdom

---

e 26 Or *wilderness and who clip the hair by their foreheads*   *a* 11 The text of this verse is in Aramaic.

and stretched out the heavens by his understanding.

¹³ When he thunders, the waters in the heavens roar;
he makes clouds rise from the ends of the earth.
He sends lightning with the rain
and brings out the wind from his storehouses.

¹⁴ Everyone is senseless and without knowledge;
every goldsmith is shamed by his idols.
The images he makes are a fraud;
they have no breath in them.

¹⁵ They are worthless, the objects of mockery;
when their judgment comes, they will perish.

¹⁶ He who is the Portion of Jacob is not like these,
for he is the Maker of all things,
including Israel, the people of his inheritance –
the LORD Almighty is his name.

Coming destruction

¹⁷ Gather up your belongings to leave the land,
you who live under siege.

¹⁸ For this is what the LORD says:
'At this time I will hurl out those who live in this land;
I will bring distress on them so that they may be captured.'

¹⁹ Woe to me because of my injury!
My wound is incurable!
Yet I said to myself,
'This is my sickness, and I must endure it.'

²⁰ My tent is destroyed;
all its ropes are snapped.
My children are gone from me and are no more;
no one is left now to pitch my tent or to set up my shelter.

²¹ The shepherds are senseless
and do not enquire of the LORD;
so they do not prosper
and all their flock is scattered.

²² Listen! The report is coming –
a great commotion from the land of the north!
It will make the towns of Judah desolate,
a haunt of jackals.

Jeremiah's prayer

²³ LORD, I know that people's lives are not their own;
it is not for them to direct their steps.

²⁴ Discipline me, LORD, but only in due measure –
not in your anger,
or you will reduce me to nothing.

²⁵ Pour out your wrath on the nations that do not acknowledge you,
on the peoples who do not call on your name.
For they have devoured Jacob;
they have devoured him completely and destroyed his homeland.

The covenant is broken

11 This is the word that came to Jeremiah from the LORD: ² 'Listen to the terms of this covenant and tell them to the people of Judah and to those who live in Jerusalem. ³ Tell them that this is what the LORD, the God of Israel, says: "Cursed is the one who does not obey the terms of this covenant – ⁴ the terms I commanded your ancestors when I brought them out of Egypt, out of the iron-smelting furnace." I said, "Obey me and do everything I command you, and you will be my people, and I will be your God. ⁵ Then I will fulfil the oath I swore to your ancestors, to give them a land flowing with milk and honey" – the land you possess today.'

I answered, 'Amen, LORD.'

⁶ The LORD said to me, 'Proclaim all these words in the towns of Judah and in the streets of Jerusalem: "Listen to the terms of this covenant and follow them. ⁷ From the time I brought your ancestors up from Egypt until today, I warned them again and again, saying, 'Obey me.' ⁸ But they did not listen or pay attention; instead, they followed the stubbornness of their evil hearts. So I brought on them all the curses

of the covenant I had commanded them to follow but that they did not keep." '

⁹ Then the LORD said to me, 'There is a conspiracy among the people of Judah and those who live in Jerusalem. ¹⁰ They have returned to the sins of their ancestors, who refused to listen to my words. They have followed other gods to serve them. Both Israel and Judah have broken the covenant I made with their ancestors. ¹¹ Therefore this is what the LORD says: "I will bring on them a disaster they cannot escape. Although they cry out to me, I will not listen to them. ¹² The towns of Judah and the people of Jerusalem will go and cry out to the gods to whom they burn incense, but they will not help them at all when disaster strikes. ¹³ You, Judah, have as many gods as you have towns; and the altars you have set up to burn incense to that shameful god Baal are as many as the streets of Jerusalem."

¹⁴ 'Do not pray for this people or offer any plea or petition for them, because I will not listen when they call to me in the time of their distress.

¹⁵ 'What is my beloved doing in my
       temple
    as she, with many others, works out
       her evil schemes?
    Can consecrated meat avert your
       punishment?
    When you engage in your wickedness,
       then you rejoice.'ᵃ

¹⁶ The LORD called you a thriving olive tree
    with fruit beautiful in form.
    But with the roar of a mighty storm
    he will set it on fire,
    and its branches will be broken.

¹⁷ The LORD Almighty, who planted you, has decreed disaster for you, because the people of both Israel and Judah have done evil and aroused my anger by burning incense to Baal.

Plot against Jeremiah

¹⁸ Because the LORD revealed their plot to me, I knew it, for at that time he showed me what they were doing. ¹⁹ I had been like a gentle lamb led to the slaughter; I did not realise that they had plotted against me, saying,

'Let us destroy the tree and its fruit;
    let us cut him off from the land of the
       living,
    that his name be remembered no
       more.'
²⁰ But you, LORD Almighty, who judge
       righteously
    and test the heart and mind,
    let me see your vengeance on
       them,
    for to you I have committed my
       cause.

²¹ 'Therefore this is what the LORD says about the people of Anathoth who are threatening to kill you, saying, "Do not prophesy in the name of the LORD or you will die by our hands" – ²² therefore this is what the LORD Almighty says: "I will punish them. Their young men will die by the sword, their sons and daughters by famine. ²³ Not even a remnant will be left to them, because I will bring disaster on the people of Anathoth in the year of their punishment."'

Jeremiah's complaint

12 You are always righteous, LORD,
    when I bring a case before you.
    Yet I would speak with you about your
       justice:
    why does the way of the wicked
       prosper?
    Why do all the faithless live at ease?
² You have planted them, and they have
       taken root;
    they grow and bear fruit.
    You are always on their lips
    but far from their hearts.
³ Yet you know me, LORD;
    you see me and test my thoughts
       about you.
    Drag them off like sheep to be
       butchered!

ᵃ 15 Or *Could consecrated meat avert your punishment? / Then you would rejoice*

Set them apart for the day of
slaughter!
4 How long will the land lie parched
and the grass in every field be
withered?
Because those who live in it are wicked,
the animals and birds have
perished.
Moreover, the people are saying,
'He will not see what happens to us.'

God's answer

5 'If you have raced with men on foot
and they have worn you out,
how can you compete with horses?
If you stumble*a* in safe country,
how will you manage in the thickets
by*b* the Jordan?
6 Your relatives, members of your own
family –
even they have betrayed you;
they have raised a loud cry against
you.
Do not trust them,
though they speak well of you.

7 'I will forsake my house,
abandon my inheritance;
I will give the one I love
into the hands of her enemies.
8 My inheritance has become to me
like a lion in the forest.
She roars at me;
therefore I hate her.
9 Has not my inheritance become to me
like a speckled bird of prey
that other birds of prey surround and
attack?
Go and gather all the wild beasts;
bring them to devour.
10 Many shepherds will ruin my vineyard
and trample down my field;
they will turn my pleasant field
into a desolate wasteland.
11 It will be made a wasteland,
parched and desolate before me;
the whole land will be laid waste
because there is no one who cares.
12 Over all the barren heights in the desert

destroyers will swarm,
for the sword of the LORD will devour
from one end of the land to the
other;
no one will be safe.
13 They will sow wheat but reap thorns;
they will wear themselves out but
gain nothing.
They will bear the shame of their
harvest
because of the LORD's fierce anger.'

14 This is what the LORD says: 'As for all my wicked neighbours who seize the inheritance I gave to my people Israel, I will uproot them from their lands and I will uproot the people of Judah from among them. 15 But after I uproot them, I will again have compassion and will bring each of them back to their own inheritance and their own country. 16 And if they learn well the ways of my people and swear by my name, saying, "As surely as the LORD lives" – even as they once taught my people to swear by Baal – then they will be established among my people. 17 But if any nation does not listen, I will completely uproot and destroy it,' declares the LORD.

A linen belt

13 This is what the LORD said to me: 'Go and buy a linen belt and put it round your waist, but do not let it touch water.' 2 So I bought a belt, as the LORD directed, and put it round my waist.

3 Then the word of the LORD came to me a second time: 4 'Take the belt you bought and are wearing round your waist, and go now to Perath*a* and hide it there in a crevice in the rocks.' 5 So I went and hid it at Perath, as the LORD told me.

6 Many days later the LORD said to me, 'Go now to Perath and get the belt I told you to hide there.' 7 So I went to Perath and dug up the belt and took it from the place where I had hidden it, but now it was ruined and completely useless.

8 Then the word of the LORD came to me: 9 'This is what the LORD says: "In the

---

a 5 Or *you feel secure only*
b 5 Or *the flooding of*

a 4 Or possibly *to the Euphrates*; similarly in verses 5-7 same way I will ruin the pride of Judah and the great pride of Jerusalem. ¹⁰These wicked people, who refuse to listen to my words, who follow the stubbornness of their hearts and go after other gods to serve and worship them, will be like this belt – completely useless! ¹¹For as a belt is bound round the waist, so I bound all the people of Israel and all the people of Judah to me," declares the LORD, "to be my people for my renown and praise and honour. But they have not listened."

Wineskins

¹²'Say to them: "This is what the LORD, the God of Israel, says: every wineskin should be filled with wine." And if they say to you, "Don't we know that every wineskin should be filled with wine?" ¹³then tell them, "This is what the LORD says: I am going to fill with drunkenness all who live in this land, including the kings who sit on David's throne, the priests, the prophets and all those living in Jerusalem. ¹⁴I will smash them one against the other, parents and children alike, declares the LORD. I will allow no pity or mercy or compassion to keep me from destroying them."'

Threat of captivity

¹⁵Hear and pay attention,
do not be arrogant,
for the LORD has spoken.
¹⁶Give glory to the LORD your God
before he brings the darkness,
before your feet stumble
on the darkening hills.
You hope for light,
but he will turn it to utter darkness
and change it to deep gloom.
¹⁷If you do not listen,
I will weep in secret
because of your pride;
my eyes will weep bitterly,
overflowing with tears,
because the LORD's flock will be
taken captive.

¹⁸Say to the king and to the queen
mother,
'Come down from your thrones,
for your glorious crowns

will fall from your heads.'
¹⁹The cities in the Negev will be shut up,
and there will be no one to open
them.
All Judah will be carried into exile,
carried completely away.

²⁰Look up and see
those who are coming from the
north.
Where is the flock that was entrusted to
you,
the sheep of which you boasted?
²¹What will you say when the LORD sets
over you
those you cultivated as your special
allies?
Will not pain grip you
like that of a woman in labour?
²²And if you ask yourself,
'Why has this happened to me?' –
it is because of your many sins
that your skirts have been torn off
and your body ill-treated.
²³Can an Ethiopian[b] change his skin
or a leopard its spots?
Neither can you do good
who are accustomed to doing evil.

²⁴'I will scatter you like chaff
driven by the desert wind.
²⁵This is your lot,
the portion I have decreed for you,'
declares the LORD,
'because you have forgotten me
and trusted in false gods.
²⁶I will pull up your skirts over your face
that your shame may be seen –
²⁷your adulteries and lustful neighings,
your shameless prostitution!
I have seen your detestable acts
on the hills and in the fields.
Woe to you, Jerusalem!
How long will you be unclean?'

Drought, famine, sword

14 This is the word of the LORD that came to Jeremiah concerning the drought:

---

b 23 Hebrew *Cushite* (probably a person from the upper Nile region)

2 'Judah mourns,
    her cities languish;
they wail for the land,
    and a cry goes up from Jerusalem.
3 The nobles send their servants for
       water;
    they go to the cisterns
    but find no water.
They return with their jars unfilled;
    dismayed and despairing,
    they cover their heads.
4 The ground is cracked
    because there is no rain in the land;
the farmers are dismayed
    and cover their heads.
5 Even the doe in the field
    deserts her newborn fawn
    because there is no grass.
6 Wild donkeys stand on the barren
       heights
    and pant like jackals;
their eyes fail
    for lack of food.'

7 Although our sins testify against us,
    do something, LORD, for the sake of
       your name.
For we have often rebelled;
    we have sinned against you.
8 You who are the hope of Israel,
    its Saviour in times of distress,
why are you like a stranger in the land,
    like a traveller who stays only a night?
9 Why are you like a man taken by
       surprise,
    like a warrior powerless to save?
You are among us, LORD,
    and we bear your name;
    do not forsake us!

10 This is what the LORD says about this
people:

'They greatly love to wander;
    they do not restrain their feet.
So the LORD does not accept them;
    he will now remember their
       wickedness
    and punish them for their sins.'

11 Then the LORD said to me, 'Do not
pray for the well-being of this people.

12 Although they fast, I will not listen to
their cry; though they offer burnt offerings and grain offerings, I will not accept
them. Instead, I will destroy them with
the sword, famine and plague.'
13 But I said, 'Alas, Sovereign LORD! The
prophets keep telling them, "You will not
see the sword or suffer famine. Indeed, I
will give you lasting peace in this place."'
14 Then the LORD said to me, 'The prophets are prophesying lies in my name. I
have not sent them or appointed them or
spoken to them. They are prophesying to
you false visions, divinations, idolatries[a]
and the delusions of their own minds.
15 Therefore this is what the LORD says
about the prophets who are prophesying
in my name: I did not send them, yet they
are saying, "No sword or famine will touch
this land." Those same prophets will perish by sword and famine. 16 And the people they are prophesying to will be thrown
out into the streets of Jerusalem because
of the famine and sword. There will be no
one to bury them, their wives, their sons
and their daughters. I will pour out on
them the calamity they deserve.

17 'Speak this word to them:

' "Let my eyes overflow with tears
    night and day without ceasing;
for the Virgin Daughter, my people,
    has suffered a grievous wound,
    a crushing blow.
18 If I go into the country,
    I see those slain by the sword;
if I go into the city,
    I see the ravages of famine.
Both prophet and priest
    have gone to a land they know not." '

19 Have you rejected Judah completely?
    Do you despise Zion?
Why have you afflicted us
    so that we cannot be healed?
We hoped for peace
    but no good has come,
for a time of healing
    but there is only terror.

---

a 14 Or *visions, worthless divinations*

20 We acknowledge our wickedness, Lord,
  and the guilt of our ancestors;
  we have indeed sinned against you.
21 For the sake of your name do not
    despise us;
  do not dishonour your glorious
    throne.
  Remember your covenant with us
  and do not break it.
22 Do any of the worthless idols of the
    nations bring rain?
  Do the skies themselves send down
    showers?
  No, it is you, Lord our God.
  Therefore our hope is in you,
  for you are the one who does all this.

15 Then the Lord said to me: 'Even if Moses and Samuel were to stand before me, my heart would not go out to this people. Send them away from my presence! Let them go! 2 And if they ask you, "Where shall we go?" tell them, "This is what the Lord says:

  ' "Those destined for death, to death;
  those for the sword, to the sword;
  those for starvation, to starvation;
  those for captivity, to captivity." "

3 'I will send four kinds of destroyers against them,' declares the Lord, 'the sword to kill and the dogs to drag away and the birds and the wild animals to devour and destroy. 4 I will make them abhorrent to all the kingdoms of the earth because of what Manasseh son of Hezekiah king of Judah did in Jerusalem.

5 'Who will have pity on you, Jerusalem?
  Who will mourn for you?
  Who will stop to ask how you are?
6 You have rejected me,' declares the
    Lord.
  'You keep on backsliding.
  So I will reach out and destroy you;
  I am tired of holding back.
7 I will winnow them with a winnowing
    fork
  at the city gates of the land.
  I will bring bereavement and
    destruction on my people,
  for they have not changed their ways.
8 I will make their widows more
    numerous
  than the sand of the sea.
  At midday I will bring a destroyer
  against the mothers of their young
    men;
  suddenly I will bring down on them
    anguish and terror.
9 The mother of seven will grow faint
    and breathe her last.
  Her sun will set while it is still day;
  she will be disgraced and humiliated.
  I will put the survivors to the sword
  before their enemies,'
                      declares the Lord.

10 Alas, my mother, that you gave me birth,
  a man with whom the whole land
    strives and contends!
  I have neither lent nor borrowed,
  yet everyone curses me.

11 The Lord said,

  'Surely I will deliver you for a good
    purpose;
  surely I will make your enemies plead
    with you
  in times of disaster and times of
    distress.

12 'Can a man break iron –
  iron from the north – or bronze?

13 'Your wealth and your treasures
  I will give as plunder, without
    charge,
  because of all your sins
  throughout your country.
14 I will enslave you to your enemies
  in *a* a land you do not know,
  for my anger will kindle a fire
  that will burn against you.'

15 Lord, you understand;
  remember me and care for me.
  Avenge me on my persecutors.

---

a 14 Some Hebrew manuscripts, Septuagint and Syriac (see also 17:4); most Hebrew manuscripts *I will cause your enemies to bring you / into*

You are long-suffering – do not take me
      away;
   think of how I suffer reproach for
      your sake.
16 When your words came, I ate them;
      they were my joy and my heart's
         delight,
   for I bear your name,
      LORD God Almighty.
17 I never sat in the company of revellers,
      never made merry with them;
   I sat alone because your hand was on me
      and you had filled me with
         indignation.
18 Why is my pain unending
      and my wound grievous and
         incurable?
   You are to me like a deceptive brook,
      like a spring that fails.

19 Therefore this is what the LORD says:

   'If you repent, I will restore you
      that you may serve me;
   if you utter worthy, not worthless,
         words,
      you will be my spokesman.
   Let this people turn to you,
      but you must not turn to them.
20 I will make you a wall to this people,
      a fortified wall of bronze;
   they will fight against you
      but will not overcome you,
   for I am with you
      to rescue and save you,'
                  declares the LORD.
21 'I will save you from the hands of the
         wicked
      and deliver you from the grasp of the
         cruel.'

Day of disaster

16 Then the word of the LORD came
to me: 2 'You must not marry and
have sons or daughters in this place.' 3 For
this is what the LORD says about the sons
and daughters born in this land and about
the women who are their mothers and the
men who are their fathers: 4 'They will die of
deadly diseases. They will not be mourned
or buried but will be like dung lying on
the ground. They will perish by sword and
famine, and their dead bodies will become
food for the birds and the wild animals.'

5 For this is what the LORD says: 'Do
not enter a house where there is a funeral meal; do not go to mourn or show
sympathy, because I have withdrawn my
blessing, my love and my pity from this
people,' declares the LORD. 6 'Both high
and low will die in this land. They will not
be buried or mourned, and no one will
cut themselves or shave their head for the
dead. 7 No one will offer food to comfort
those who mourn for the dead – not even
for a father or a mother – nor will anyone
give them a drink to console them.

8 'And do not enter a house where there
is feasting and sit down to eat and drink.
9 For this is what the LORD Almighty, the
God of Israel, says: Before your eyes and in
your days I will bring an end to the sounds
of joy and gladness and to the voices of
bride and bridegroom in this place.

10 'When you tell these people all this
and they ask you, "Why has the LORD decreed such a great disaster against us?
What wrong have we done? What sin have
we committed against the LORD our God?"
11 then say to them, "It is because your ancestors forsook me," declares the LORD,
"and followed other gods and served and
worshipped them. They forsook me and
did not keep my law. 12 But you have behaved more wickedly than your ancestors.
See how all of you are following the stubbornness of your evil hearts instead of
obeying me. 13 So I will throw you out of
this land into a land neither you nor your
ancestors have known, and there you will
serve other gods day and night, for I will
show you no favour."

14 'However, the days are coming,' declares the LORD, 'when it will no longer
be said, "As surely as the LORD lives, who
brought the Israelites up out of Egypt,"
15 but it will be said, "As surely as the LORD
lives, who brought the Israelites up out
of the land of the north and out of all the
countries where he had banished them."
For I will restore them to the land I gave to
their ancestors.

16 'But now I will send for many fishermen,' declares the LORD, 'and they will

catch them. After that I will send for many hunters, and they will hunt them down on every mountain and hill and from the crevices of the rocks. [17] My eyes are on all their ways; they are not hidden from me, nor is their sin concealed from my eyes. [18] I will repay them double for their wickedness and their sin, because they have defiled my land with the lifeless forms of their vile images and have filled my inheritance with their detestable idols.'

[19] LORD, my strength and my fortress,
　　my refuge in time of distress,
to you the nations will come
　　from the ends of the earth and say,
'Our ancestors possessed nothing but
　　　　false gods,
　　worthless idols that did them no
　　　　good.
[20] Do people make their own gods?
　　Yes, but they are not gods!'

[21] 'Therefore I will teach them –
　　this time I will teach them
　　my power and might.
Then they will know
　　that my name is the LORD.

17

'Judah's sin is engraved with an
　　iron tool,
　　inscribed with a flint point,
on the tablets of their hearts
　　and on the horns of their altars.
[2] Even their children remember
　　　their altars and Asherah poles[a]
beside the spreading trees
　　and on the high hills.
[3] My mountain in the land
　　and your[b] wealth and all your
　　　　treasures
I will give away as plunder,
　　together with your high places,
　　because of sin throughout your
　　　　country.
[4] Through your own fault you will lose
　　the inheritance I gave you.
I will enslave you to your enemies
　　in a land you do not know,

for you have kindled my anger,
　　and it will burn for ever.'

[5] This is what the LORD says:

'Cursed is the one who trusts in man,
　　who draws strength from mere flesh
　　and whose heart turns away from the
　　　　LORD.
[6] That person will be like a bush in the
　　　　wastelands;
　　they will not see prosperity when it
　　　　comes.
They will dwell in the parched places of
　　　　the desert,
　　in a salt land where no one lives.

[7] 'But blessed is the one who trusts in the
　　　　LORD,
　　whose confidence is in him.
[8] They will be like a tree planted by the
　　　　water
　　that sends out its roots by the
　　　　stream.
It does not fear when heat comes;
　　its leaves are always green.
It has no worries in a year of drought
　　and never fails to bear fruit.'

[9] The heart is deceitful above all things
　　and beyond cure.
　　Who can understand it?

[10] 'I the LORD search the heart
　　and examine the mind,
to reward each person according to
　　　　their conduct,
　　according to what their deeds
　　　　deserve.'

[11] Like a partridge that hatches eggs it did
　　　　not lay
　　are those who gain riches by unjust
　　　　means.
When their lives are half gone, their
　　　　riches will desert them,
　　and in the end they will prove to be
　　　　fools.

[12] A glorious throne, exalted from the
　　　　beginning,
　　is the place of our sanctuary.

---

[a] 2 That is, wooden symbols of the goddess Asherah
[b] 2,3 Or hills / [3] and the mountains of the land. / Your

13 LORD, you are the hope of Israel;
   all who forsake you will be put to
      shame.
Those who turn away from you will be
      written in the dust
   because they have forsaken the
      LORD,
   the spring of living water.

14 Heal me, LORD, and I shall be healed;
   save me and I shall be saved,
      for you are the one I praise.
15 They keep saying to me,
   'Where is the word of the LORD?
   Let it now be fulfilled!'
16 I have not run away from being your
      shepherd;
   you know I have not desired the day
      of despair.
   What passes my lips is open before
      you.
17 Do not be a terror to me;
   you are my refuge in the day of
      disaster.
18 Let my persecutors be put to shame,
   but keep me from shame;
   let them be terrified,
   but keep me from terror.
Bring on them the day of disaster;
   destroy them with double
      destruction.

Keeping the Sabbath holy

19 This is what the LORD said to me: 'Go and stand at the Gate of the People,c through which the kings of Judah go in and out; stand also at all the other gates of Jerusalem. 20 Say to them, "Hear the word of the LORD, you kings of Judah and all people of Judah and everyone living in Jerusalem who come through these gates. 21 This is what the LORD says: be careful not to carry a load on the Sabbath day or bring it through the gates of Jerusalem. 22 Do not bring a load out of your houses or do any work on the Sabbath, but keep the Sabbath day holy, as I commanded your ancestors. 23 Yet they did not listen or pay attention; they were stiff-necked and would not listen or respond to discipline.

24 But if you are careful to obey me, declares the LORD, and bring no load through the gates of this city on the Sabbath, but keep the Sabbath day holy by not doing any work on it, 25 then kings who sit on David's throne will come through the gates of this city with their officials. They and their officials will come riding in chariots and on horses, accompanied by the men of Judah and those living in Jerusalem, and this city will be inhabited for ever. 26 People will come from the towns of Judah and the villages around Jerusalem, from the territory of Benjamin and the western foothills, from the hill country and the Negev, bringing burnt offerings and sacrifices, grain offerings and incense, and bringing thank-offerings to the house of the LORD. 27 But if you do not obey me to keep the Sabbath day holy by not carrying any load as you come through the gates of Jerusalem on the Sabbath day, then I will kindle an unquenchable fire in the gates of Jerusalem that will consume her fortresses." '

At the potter's house

18 This is the word that came to Jeremiah from the LORD: 2 'Go down to the potter's house, and there I will give you my message.' 3 So I went down to the potter's house, and I saw him working at the wheel. 4 But the pot he was shaping from the clay was marred in his hands; so the potter formed it into another pot, shaping it as seemed best to him.

5 Then the word of the LORD came to me. 6 He said, 'Can I not do with you, Israel, as this potter does?' declares the LORD. 'Like clay in the hand of the potter, so are you in my hand, Israel. 7 If at any time I announce that a nation or kingdom is to be uprooted, torn down and destroyed, 8 and if that nation I warned repents of its evil, then I will relent and not inflict on it the disaster I had planned. 9 And if at another time I announce that a nation or kingdom is to be built up and planted, 10 and if it does evil in my sight and does not obey me, then I will reconsider the good I had intended to do for it.

11 'Now therefore say to the people of

Judah and those living in Jerusalem, "This is what the LORD says: look! I am preparing a disaster for you and devising a plan against you. So turn from your evil ways, each one of you, and reform your ways and your actions." 12 But they will reply, "It's no use. We will continue with our own plans; we will all follow the stubbornness of our evil hearts."'

13 Therefore this is what the LORD says:

'Enquire among the nations:
    who has ever heard anything like
        this?
A most horrible thing has been done
    by Virgin Israel.
14 Does the snow of Lebanon
    ever vanish from its rocky slopes?
Do its cool waters from distant sources
    ever stop flowing?*a*
15 Yet my people have forgotten me;
    they burn incense to worthless idols,
which made them stumble in their
        ways,
    in the ancient paths.
They made them walk in byways,
    on roads not built up.
16 Their land will be an object of horror
    and of lasting scorn;
all who pass by will be appalled
    and will shake their heads.
17 Like a wind from the east,
    I will scatter them before their
        enemies;
I will show them my back and not my
        face
    in the day of their disaster.'

18 They said, 'Come, let's make plans against Jeremiah; for the teaching of the law by the priest will not cease, nor will counsel from the wise, nor the word from the prophets. So come, let's attack him with our tongues and pay no attention to anything he says.'

19 Listen to me, LORD;
    hear what my accusers are saying!

a 14 The meaning of the Hebrew for this sentence is uncertain.

20 Should good be repaid with evil?
    Yet they have dug a pit for me.
Remember that I stood before you
    and spoke on their behalf
    to turn your wrath away from them.

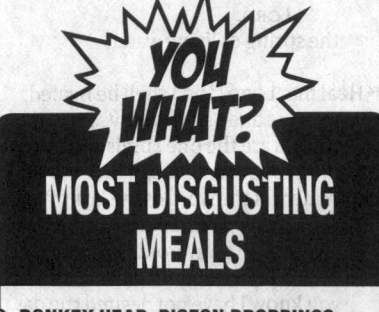

YOU WHAT?

MOST DISGUSTING MEALS

○ **DONKEY HEAD, PIGEON DROPPINGS, AND WORSE**
2 Kings 6:24–32
○ **YOUR OWN BODILY WASTE**
Isaiah 36:11–12
○ **GRAVEL**
Lamentations 3:16–18
○ **A SCROLL**
Ezekiel 3:1–3
○ **YOUR OWN PARENTS**
Ezekiel 5:9–12
○ **GRASS**
Daniel 4:28–33

21 So give their children over to famine;
    hand them over to the power of the
        sword.
Let their wives be made childless and
        widows;
    let their men be put to death,
    their young men slain by the sword
        in battle.
22 Let a cry be heard from their houses
    when you suddenly bring invaders
        against them,
for they have dug a pit to capture me
    and have hidden snares for my feet.
23 But you, LORD, know
    all their plots to kill me.
Do not forgive their crimes
    or blot out their sins from your sight.
Let them be overthrown before you;
    deal with them in the time of your
        anger.

19 This is what the LORD says: 'Go and buy a clay jar from a potter. Take along some of the elders of the people and of the priests 2 and go out to the Valley of Ben Hinnom, near the entrance of the Potsherd Gate. There proclaim the words I tell you, 3 and say, "Hear the word of the LORD, you kings of Judah and people of Jerusalem. This is what the LORD Almighty, the God of Israel, says: listen! I am going to bring a disaster on this place that will make the ears of everyone who hears of it tingle. 4 For they have forsaken me and made this a place of foreign gods; they have burned incense in it to gods that neither they nor their ancestors nor the kings of Judah ever knew, and they have filled this place with the blood of the innocent. 5 They have built the high places of Baal to burn their children in the fire as offerings to Baal – something I did not command or mention, nor did it enter my mind. 6 So beware, the days are coming, declares the LORD, when people will no longer call this place Topheth or the Valley of Ben Hinnom, but the Valley of Slaughter.

7 ' "In this place I will ruin*a* the plans of Judah and Jerusalem. I will make them fall by the sword before their enemies, at the hands of those who want to kill them, and I will give their carcasses as food to the birds and the wild animals. 8 I will devastate this city and make it an object of horror and scorn; all who pass by will be appalled and will scoff because of all its wounds. 9 I will make them eat the flesh of their sons and daughters, and they will eat one another's flesh because their enemies will press the siege so hard against them to destroy them."

10 'Then break the jar while those who go with you are watching, 11 and say to them, "This is what the LORD Almighty says: I will smash this nation and this city just as this potter's jar is smashed and cannot be repaired. They will bury the dead in Topheth until there is no more room. 12 This is what I will do to this place and to those who live here, declares the

LORD. I will make this city like Topheth. 13 The houses in Jerusalem and those of the kings of Judah will be defiled like this place, Topheth – all the houses where they burned incense on the roofs to all the starry hosts and poured out drink offerings to other gods." '

14 Jeremiah then returned from Topheth, where the LORD had sent him to prophesy, and stood in the court of the LORD's temple and said to all the people, 15 'This is what the LORD Almighty, the God of Israel, says: "Listen! I am going to bring on this city and on all the villages around it every disaster I pronounced against them, because they were stiff-necked and would not listen to my words." '

Jeremiah and Pashhur

20 When the priest Pashhur son of Immer, the official in charge of the temple of the LORD, heard Jeremiah prophesying these things, 2 he had Jeremiah the prophet beaten and put in the stocks at the Upper Gate of Benjamin at the LORD's temple. 3 The next day, when Pashhur released him from the stocks, Jeremiah said to him, 'The LORD's name for you is not Pashhur, but Terror on Every Side. 4 For this is what the LORD says: "I will make you a terror to yourself and to all your friends; with your own eyes you will see them fall by the sword of their enemies. I will give all Judah into the hands of the king of Babylon, who will carry them away to Babylon or put them to the sword. 5 I will deliver all the wealth of this city into the hands of their enemies – all its products, all its valuables and all the treasures of the kings of Judah. They will take it away as plunder and carry it off to Babylon. 6 And you, Pashhur, and all who live in your house will go into exile to Babylon. There you will die and be buried, you and all your friends to whom you have prophesied lies." '

Jeremiah's complaint

7 You deceived*a* me, LORD, and I was deceived;*a*

---

a 7 The Hebrew for *ruin* sounds like the Hebrew for *jar* (see verses 1 and 10).

a 7 Or *persuaded*

you overpowered me and prevailed.
I am ridiculed all day long;
    everyone mocks me.
⁸ Whenever I speak, I cry out
    proclaiming violence and
        destruction.
So the word of the LORD has brought me
    insult and reproach all day long.
⁹ But if I say, 'I will not mention his word
    or speak any more in his name,'
his word is in my heart like a fire,
    a fire shut up in my bones.
I am weary of holding it in;
    indeed, I cannot.
¹⁰ I hear many whispering,
    'Terror on every side!
    Denounce him! Let's denounce him!'
All my friends
    are waiting for me to slip, saying,
    'Perhaps he will be deceived;
    then we will prevail over him
    and take our revenge on him.'

¹¹ But the LORD is with me like a mighty
        warrior;
    so my persecutors will stumble and
        not prevail.
They will fail and be thoroughly
        disgraced;
    their dishonour will never be
        forgotten.
¹² LORD Almighty, you who examine the
        righteous
    and probe the heart and mind,
let me see your vengeance on them,
    for to you I have committed my
        cause.

¹³ Sing to the LORD!
    Give praise to the LORD!
He rescues the life of the needy
    from the hands of the wicked.

¹⁴ Cursed be the day I was born!
    May the day my mother bore me not
        be blessed!
¹⁵ Cursed be the man who brought my
        father the news,
    who made him very glad, saying,
    'A child is born to you – a son!'
¹⁶ May that man be like the towns
    the LORD overthrew without pity.

May he hear wailing in the morning,
    a battle cry at noon.
¹⁷ For he did not kill me in the womb,
    with my mother as my grave,
    her womb enlarged for ever.
¹⁸ Why did I ever come out of the womb
    to see trouble and sorrow
    and to end my days in shame?

God rejects Zedekiah's request

21 The word came to Jeremiah from the LORD when King Zedekiah sent to him Pashhur son of Malkijah and the priest Zephaniah son of Maaseiah. They said: ² 'Enquire now of the LORD for us because Nebuchadnezzar*ᵃ* king of Babylon is attacking us. Perhaps the LORD will perform wonders for us as in times past so that he will withdraw from us.'

³ But Jeremiah answered them, 'Tell Zedekiah, ⁴ "This is what the LORD, the God of Israel, says: I am about to turn against you the weapons of war that are in your hands, which you are using to fight the king of Babylon and the Babylonians*ᵇ* who are outside the wall besieging you. And I will gather them inside this city. ⁵ I myself will fight against you with an outstretched hand and a mighty arm in furious anger and in great wrath. ⁶ I will strike down those who live in this city – both man and beast – and they will die of a terrible plague. ⁷ After that, declares the LORD, I will give Zedekiah king of Judah, his officials and the people in this city who survive the plague, sword and famine, into the hands of Nebuchadnezzar king of Babylon and to their enemies who want to kill them. He will put them to the sword; he will show them no mercy or pity or compassion."

⁸ 'Furthermore, tell the people, "This is what the LORD says: see, I am setting before you the way of life and the way of death. ⁹ Whoever stays in this city will die by the sword, famine or plague. But whoever goes out and surrenders to the Babylonians who are besieging you will live;

---

a 2 Hebrew *Nebuchadrezzar*, of which *Nebuchadnezzar* is a variant; here and often in Jeremiah and Ezekiel
b 4 Or *Chaldeans*; also in verse 9

they will escape with their lives. ¹⁰I have determined to do this city harm and not good, declares the Lord. It will be given into the hands of the king of Babylon, and he will destroy it with fire."

¹¹'Moreover, say to the royal house of Judah, "Hear the word of the Lord. ¹²This is what the Lord says to you, house of David:

'"Administer justice every morning;
   rescue from the hand of the
      oppressor
   the one who has been robbed,
or my wrath will break out and burn
   like fire
   because of the evil you have done –
   burn with no one to quench it.
¹³ I am against you, Jerusalem,
   you who live above this valley
   on the rocky plateau, declares the
      Lord –
you who say, 'Who can come
   against us?
Who can enter our refuge?'
¹⁴ I will punish you as your deeds deserve,
   declares the Lord.
I will kindle a fire in your forests
   that will consume everything around
      you."'

Judgment against wicked kings

22 This is what the Lord says: 'Go down to the palace of the king of Judah and proclaim this message there: ²"Hear the word of the Lord to you, king of Judah, you who sit on David's throne – you, your officials and your people who come through these gates. ³This is what the Lord says: do what is just and right. Rescue from the hand of the oppressor the one who has been robbed. Do no wrong or violence to the foreigner, the fatherless or the widow, and do not shed innocent blood in this place. ⁴For if you are careful to carry out these commands, then kings who sit on David's throne will come through the gates of this palace, riding in chariots and on horses, accompanied by their officials and their people. ⁵But if you do not obey these commands, declares the Lord, I swear by myself that this palace will become a ruin."'

⁶For this is what the Lord says about the palace of the king of Judah:

'Though you are like Gilead to me,
   like the summit of Lebanon,
I will surely make you like a wasteland,
   like towns not inhabited.
⁷I will send destroyers against you,
   each man with his weapons,
and they will cut up your fine cedar
      beams
   and throw them into the fire.

⁸'People from many nations will pass by this city and will ask one another, "Why has the Lord done such a thing to this great city?" ⁹And the answer will be: "Because they have forsaken the covenant of the Lord their God and have worshipped and served other gods."'

¹⁰Do not weep for the dead king or
   mourn his loss;
rather, weep bitterly for him who is
   exiled,
because he will never return
   nor see his native land again.

¹¹For this is what the Lord says about Shallum[a] son of Josiah, who succeeded his father as king of Judah but has gone from this place: 'He will never return. ¹²He will die in the place where they have led him captive; he will not see this land again.'

¹³'Woe to him who builds his palace by
   unrighteousness,
   his upper rooms by injustice,
making his own people work for
   nothing,
   not paying them for their labour.
¹⁴He says, "I will build myself a great
   palace
   with spacious upper rooms."
So he makes large windows in it,
   panels it with cedar
   and decorates it in red.

¹⁵'Does it make you a king
   to have more and more cedar?

---

a 11 Also called *Jehoahaz*

Did not your father have food and drink?
    He did what was right and just,
    so all went well with him.
16 He defended the cause of the poor and
        needy,
    and so all went well.
    Is that not what it means to know me?'
        declares the LORD.
17 'But your eyes and your heart
    are set only on dishonest gain,
    on shedding innocent blood
    and on oppression and extortion.'

18 Therefore this is what the LORD says
about Jehoiakim son of Josiah king of Judah:

    'They will not mourn for him:
        "Alas, my brother! Alas, my sister!"
    They will not mourn for him:
        "Alas, my master! Alas, his
            splendour!"
19 He will have the burial of a donkey –
    dragged away and thrown
    outside the gates of Jerusalem.'

20 'Go up to Lebanon and cry out,
    let your voice be heard in Bashan,
    cry out from Abarim,
    for all your allies are crushed.
21 I warned you when you felt secure,
    but you said, "I will not listen!"
    This has been your way from your youth;
    you have not obeyed me.
22 The wind will drive all your shepherds
        away,
    and your allies will go into exile.
    Then you will be ashamed and disgraced
    because of all your wickedness.
23 You who live in "Lebanon,*b*"
    who are nestled in cedar buildings,
    how you will groan when pangs come
        upon you,
    pain like that of a woman in labour!

24 'As surely as I live,' declares the LORD,
'even if you, Jehoiachin*c* son of Jehoiakim
king of Judah, were a signet ring on my
right hand, I would still pull you off. 25 I will

deliver you into the hands of those who
want to kill you, those you fear – Nebuchadnezzar king of Babylon and the Babylonians.*d* 26 I will hurl you and the mother
who gave you birth into another country,
where neither of you was born, and there
you both will die. 27 You will never come
back to the land you long to return to.'

28 Is this man Jehoiachin a despised,
        broken pot,
    an object no one wants?
    Why will he and his children be hurled
        out,
    cast into a land they do not know?
29 O land, land, land,
    hear the word of the LORD!
30 This is what the LORD says:
    'Record this man as if childless,
    a man who will not prosper in his
        lifetime,
    for none of his offspring will prosper,
    none will sit on the throne of David
    or rule any more in Judah.'

The righteous branch

23 'Woe to the shepherds who are destroying and scattering the
sheep of my pasture!' declares the LORD.
2 Therefore this is what the LORD, the God
of Israel, says to the shepherds who tend
my people: 'Because you have scattered
my flock and driven them away and have
not bestowed care on them, I will bestow
punishment on you for the evil you have
done,' declares the LORD. 3 'I myself will
gather the remnant of my flock out of all
the countries where I have driven them
and will bring them back to their pasture,
where they will be fruitful and increase
in number. 4 I will place shepherds over
them who will tend them, and they will
no longer be afraid or terrified, nor will
any be missing,' declares the LORD.

5 'The days are coming,' declares the
        LORD,
    'when I will raise up for David*a* a
        righteous Branch,

---

b 23 That is, the palace in Jerusalem (see 1 Kings 7:2)
c 24 Hebrew *Koniah*, a variant of *Jehoiachin*; also in
verse 28

d 25 Or *Chaldeans*
a 5 Or *up from David's line*

a King who will reign wisely
  and do what is just and right in the
    land.
6 In his days Judah will be saved
  and Israel will live in safety.
This is the name by which he will be
    called:
  The LORD Our Righteous Saviour.

7 'So then, the days are coming,' declares
the LORD, 'when people will no longer say,
"As surely as the LORD lives, who brought
the Israelites up out of Egypt," **8** but they
will say, "As surely as the LORD lives, who
brought the descendants of Israel up out
of the land of the north and out of all the
countries where he had banished them."
Then they will live in their own land.'

Lying prophets

9 Concerning the prophets:

My heart is broken within me;
  all my bones tremble.
I am like a drunken man,
  like a strong man overcome by wine,
because of the LORD
  and his holy words.
10 The land is full of adulterers;
  because of the curse[b] the land lies
    parched
  and the pastures in the wilderness
    are withered.
The prophets follow an evil course
  and use their power unjustly.

11 'Both prophet and priest are godless;
  even in my temple I find their
    wickedness,'
                    declares the LORD.
12 'Therefore their path will become
    slippery;
  they will be banished to darkness
    and there they will fall.
I will bring disaster on them
  in the year they are punished,'
                    declares the LORD.
13 'Among the prophets of Samaria
  I saw this repulsive thing:

they prophesied by Baal
  and led my people Israel astray.
14 And among the prophets of Jerusalem
  I have seen something horrible:
  they commit adultery and live a lie.
They strengthen the hands of evildoers,
  so that not one of them turns from
    their wickedness.
They are all like Sodom to me;
  the people of Jerusalem are like
    Gomorrah.'

15 Therefore this is what the LORD
Almighty says concerning the prophets:

'I will make them eat bitter food
  and drink poisoned water,
because from the prophets of
    Jerusalem
  ungodliness has spread throughout
    the land.'

16 This is what the LORD Almighty says:

'Do not listen to what the prophets are
    prophesying to you;
  they fill you with false hopes.
They speak visions from their own
    minds,
  not from the mouth of the LORD.
17 They keep saying to those who despise
    me,
  "The LORD says: you will have peace."
And to all who follow the stubbornness
    of their hearts
  they say, "No harm will come to you."
18 But which of them has stood in the
    council of the LORD
  to see or to hear his word?
Who has listened and heard his
    word?
19 See, the storm of the LORD
  will burst out in wrath,
a whirlwind swirling down
  on the heads of the wicked.
20 The anger of the LORD will not turn
    back
  until he fully accomplishes
  the purposes of his heart.
In days to come
  you will understand it clearly.
21 I did not send these prophets,

---

b 10 Or *because of these things*

yet they have run with their message;
I did not speak to them,
    yet they have prophesied.
22 But if they had stood in my council,
    they would have proclaimed my
        words to my people
and would have turned them from their
        evil ways
    and from their evil deeds.

23 'Am I only a God nearby,'
                declares the LORD,
    'and not a God far away?
24 Who can hide in secret places
    so that I cannot see them?'
                declares the LORD.
'Do not I fill heaven and earth?'
                declares the LORD.

25 'I have heard what the prophets say who prophesy lies in my name. They say, "I had a dream! I had a dream!" 26 How long will this continue in the hearts of these lying prophets, who prophesy the delusions of their own minds? 27 They think the dreams they tell one another will make my people forget my name, just as their ancestors forgot my name through Baal worship. 28 Let the prophet who has a dream recount the dream, but let the one who has my word speak it faithfully. For what has straw to do with grain?' declares the LORD. 29 'Is not my word like fire,' declares the LORD, 'and like a hammer that breaks a rock in pieces?

30 'Therefore,' declares the LORD, 'I am against the prophets who steal from one another words supposedly from me. 31 Yes,' declares the LORD, 'I am against the prophets who wag their own tongues and yet declare, "The LORD declares." 32 Indeed, I am against those who prophesy false dreams,' declares the LORD. 'They tell them and lead my people astray with their reckless lies, yet I did not send or appoint them. They do not benefit these people in the least,' declares the LORD.

False prophecy

33 'When these people, or a prophet or a priest, ask you, "What is the message from the LORD?" say to them, "What message? I

will forsake you, declares the LORD." 34 If a prophet or a priest or anyone else claims, "This is a message from the LORD," I will punish them and their household. 35 This is what each of you keeps saying to your friends and other Israelites: "What is the LORD's answer?" or "What has the LORD spoken?" 36 But you must not mention "a message from the LORD" again, because each one's word becomes their own message. So you distort the words of the living God, the LORD Almighty, our God. 37 This is what you keep saying to a prophet: "What is the LORD's answer to you?" or "What has the LORD spoken?" 38 Although you claim, "This is a message from the LORD," this is what the LORD says: you used the words, "This is a message from the LORD," even though I told you that you must not claim, "This is a message from the LORD." 39 Therefore, I will surely forget you and cast you out of my presence along with the city I gave to you and your ancestors. 40 I will bring on you everlasting disgrace – everlasting shame that will not be forgotten.'

Two baskets of figs

24 After Jehoiachin[a] son of Jehoiakim king of Judah and the officials, the skilled workers and the craftsmen of Judah were carried into exile from Jerusalem to Babylon by Nebuchadnezzar king of Babylon, the LORD showed me two baskets of figs placed in front of the temple of the LORD. 2 One basket had very good figs, like those that ripen early; the other basket had very bad figs, so bad that they could not be eaten.

3 Then the LORD asked me, 'What do you see, Jeremiah?'

'Figs,' I answered. 'The good ones are very good, but the bad ones are so bad that they cannot be eaten.'

4 Then the word of the LORD came to me: 5 'This is what the LORD, the God of Israel, says: "Like these good figs, I regard as good the exiles from Judah, whom I sent away from this place to the land of the

---

a 1 Hebrew *Jeconiah*, a variant of *Jehoiachin*

Babylonians.[b] [6]My eyes will watch over them for their good, and I will bring them back to this land. I will build them up and not tear them down; I will plant them and not uproot them. [7]I will give them a heart to know me, that I am the LORD. They will be my people, and I will be their God, for they will return to me with all their heart.

[8]'"But like the bad figs, which are so bad that they cannot be eaten," says the LORD, "so will I deal with Zedekiah king of Judah, his officials and the survivors from Jerusalem, whether they remain in this land or live in Egypt. [9]I will make them abhorrent and an offence to all the kingdoms of the earth, a reproach and a byword, a curse[c] and an object of ridicule, wherever I banish them. [10]I will send the sword, famine and plague against them until they are destroyed from the land I gave to them and their ancestors."'

Seventy years of captivity

25 The word came to Jeremiah concerning all the people of Judah in the fourth year of Jehoiakim son of Josiah king of Judah, which was the first year of Nebuchadnezzar king of Babylon. [2]So Jeremiah the prophet said to all the people of Judah and to all those living in Jerusalem: [3]For twenty-three years – from the thirteenth year of Josiah son of Amon king of Judah until this very day – the word of the LORD has come to me and I have spoken to you again and again, but you have not listened.

[4]And though the LORD has sent all his servants the prophets to you again and again, you have not listened or paid any attention. [5]They said, 'Turn now, each of you, from your evil ways and your evil practices, and you can stay in the land the LORD gave to you and your ancestors for ever and ever. [6]Do not follow other gods to serve and worship them; do not arouse my anger with what your hands have made. Then I will not harm you.'

[7]'But you did not listen to me,' declares

the LORD, 'and you have aroused my anger with what your hands have made, and you have brought harm to yourselves.'

[8]Therefore the LORD Almighty says this: 'Because you have not listened to my words, [9]I will summon all the peoples of the north and my servant Nebuchadnezzar king of Babylon,' declares the LORD, 'and I will bring them against this land and its inhabitants and against all the surrounding nations. I will completely destroy[a] them and make them an object of horror and scorn, and an everlasting ruin. [10]I will banish from them the sounds of joy and gladness, the voices of bride and bridegroom, the sound of millstones and the light of the lamp. [11]This whole country will become a desolate wasteland, and these nations will serve the king of Babylon for seventy years.

[12]'But when the seventy years are fulfilled, I will punish the king of Babylon and his nation, the land of the Babylonians,[b] for their guilt,' declares the LORD, 'and will make it desolate for ever. [13]I will bring on that land all the things I have spoken against it, all that are written in this book and prophesied by Jeremiah against all the nations. [14]They themselves will be enslaved by many nations and great kings; I will repay them according to their deeds and the work of their hands.'

The cup of God's wrath

[15]This is what the LORD, the God of Israel, said to me: 'Take from my hand this cup filled with the wine of my wrath and make all the nations to whom I send you drink it. [16]When they drink it, they will stagger and go mad because of the sword I will send among them.'

[17]So I took the cup from the LORD's hand and made all the nations to whom he sent me drink it: [18]Jerusalem and the towns of Judah, its kings and officials, to make them a ruin and an object of

---

b 5 Or *Chaldeans*
c 9 That is, their names will be used in cursing (see 29:22); or, others will see that they are cursed.

a 9 The Hebrew term refers to the irrevocable giving over of things or persons to the LORD, often by totally destroying them.
b 12 Or *Chaldeans*

horror and scorn, a curse^c – as they are today; ¹⁹Pharaoh king of Egypt, his attendants, his officials and all his people, ²⁰and all the foreign people there; all the kings of Uz; all the kings of the Philistines (those of Ashkelon, Gaza, Ekron, and the people left at Ashdod); ²¹Edom, Moab and Ammon; ²²all the kings of Tyre and Sidon; the kings of the coastlands across the sea; ²³Dedan, Tema, Buz and all who are in distant places^d; ²⁴all the kings of Arabia and all the kings of the foreign people who live in the wilderness; ²⁵all the kings of Zimri, Elam and Media; ²⁶and all the kings of the north, near and far, one after the other – all the kingdoms on the face of the earth. And after all of them, the king of Sheshak^e will drink it too.

²⁷'Then tell them, "This is what the LORD Almighty, the God of Israel, says: drink, get drunk and vomit, and fall to rise no more because of the sword I will send among you." ²⁸But if they refuse to take the cup from your hand and drink, tell them, "This is what the LORD Almighty says: You must drink it! ²⁹See, I am beginning to bring disaster on the city that bears my Name, and will you indeed go unpunished? You will not go unpunished, for I am calling down a sword on all who live on the earth, declares the LORD Almighty."

³⁰'Now prophesy all these words against them and say to them:

'"The LORD will roar from on high;
    he will thunder from his holy
        dwelling
    and roar mightily against his land.
He will shout like those who tread the
        grapes,
    shout against all who live on the
        earth.
³¹The tumult will resound to the ends of
        the earth,
    for the LORD will bring charges
        against the nations;
    he will bring judgment on all mankind

and put the wicked to the sword,"'
                        declares the LORD.

³²This is what the LORD Almighty says:

'Look! Disaster is spreading
    from nation to nation;
a mighty storm is rising
    from the ends of the earth.'

³³At that time those slain by the LORD will be everywhere – from one end of the earth to the other. They will not be mourned or gathered up or buried, but will be like dung lying on the ground.

³⁴Weep and wail, you shepherds;
    roll in the dust, you leaders of the
        flock.
For your time to be slaughtered has
        come;
    you will fall like the best of the rams.^f
³⁵The shepherds will have nowhere to
        flee,
    the leaders of the flock no place to
        escape.
³⁶Hear the cry of the shepherds,
    the wailing of the leaders of the
        flock,
    for the LORD is destroying their
        pasture.
³⁷The peaceful meadows will be laid
        waste
    because of the fierce anger of the
        LORD.
³⁸Like a lion he will leave his lair,
    and their land will become desolate
    because of the sword^g of the oppressor
    and because of the LORD's fierce
        anger.

Jeremiah threatened with death

26 Early in the reign of Jehoiakim son of Josiah king of Judah, this word came from the LORD: ²'This is what the LORD says: Stand in the courtyard of the LORD's house and speak to all the

---

^c18 That is, their names to be used in cursing (see 29:22); or, to be seen by others as cursed
^d23 Or *who clip the hair by their foreheads*
^e26 *Sheshak* is a cryptogram for Babylon.

^f34 Septuagint; Hebrew *fall and be shattered like fine pottery*
^g38 Some Hebrew manuscripts and Septuagint (see also 46:16 and 50:16); most Hebrew manuscripts *anger*

people of the towns of Judah who come to worship in the house of the LORD. Tell them everything I command you; do not omit a word. ³Perhaps they will listen and each will turn from their evil ways. Then I will relent and not inflict on them the disaster I was planning because of the evil they have done. ⁴Say to them, "This is what the LORD says: if you do not listen to me and follow my law, which I have set before you, ⁵and if you do not listen to the words of my servants the prophets, whom I have sent to you again and again (though you have not listened), ⁶then I will make this house like Shiloh and this city a curse*ᵃ* among all the nations of the earth."'

⁷The priests, the prophets and all the people heard Jeremiah speak these words in the house of the LORD. ⁸But as soon as Jeremiah finished telling all the people everything the LORD had commanded him to say, the priests, the prophets and all the people seized him and said, 'You must die! ⁹Why do you prophesy in the LORD's name that this house will be like Shiloh and this city will be desolate and deserted?' And all the people crowded around Jeremiah in the house of the LORD.

¹⁰When the officials of Judah heard about these things, they went up from the royal palace to the house of the LORD and took their places at the entrance of the New Gate of the LORD's house. ¹¹Then the priests and the prophets said to the officials and all the people, 'This man should be sentenced to death because he has prophesied against this city. You have heard it with your own ears!'

¹²Then Jeremiah said to all the officials and all the people: 'The LORD sent me to prophesy against this house and this city all the things you have heard. ¹³Now reform your ways and your actions and obey the LORD your God. Then the LORD will relent and not bring the disaster he has pronounced against you. ¹⁴As for me, I am in your hands; do with me whatever you think is good and right. ¹⁵Be assured, however, that if you put me to death, you will bring the guilt of innocent blood on yourselves and on this city and on those who live in it, for in truth the LORD has sent me to you to speak all these words in your hearing.'

¹⁶Then the officials and all the people said to the priests and the prophets, 'This man should not be sentenced to death! He has spoken to us in the name of the LORD our God.'

¹⁷Some of the elders of the land stepped forward and said to the entire assembly of people, ¹⁸'Micah of Moresheth prophesied in the days of Hezekiah king of Judah. He told all the people of Judah, "This is what the LORD Almighty says:

'"Zion will be ploughed like a field,
    Jerusalem will become a heap of
        rubble,
    the temple hill a mound overgrown
        with thickets."ᵇ

¹⁹'Did Hezekiah king of Judah or anyone else in Judah put him to death? Did not Hezekiah fear the LORD and seek his favour? And did not the LORD relent, so that he did not bring the disaster he pronounced against them? We are about to bring a terrible disaster on ourselves!'

²⁰(Now Uriah son of Shemaiah from Kiriath Jearim was another man who prophesied in the name of the LORD; he prophesied the same things against this city and this land as Jeremiah did. ²¹When King Jehoiakim and all his officers and officials heard his words, the king was determined to put him to death. But Uriah heard of it and fled in fear to Egypt. ²²King Jehoiakim, however, sent Elnathan son of Akbor to Egypt, along with some other men. ²³They brought Uriah out of Egypt and took him to King Jehoiakim, who had him struck down with a sword and his body thrown into the burial place of the common people.)

²⁴Furthermore, Ahikam son of Shaphan supported Jeremiah, and so he was not handed over to the people to be put to death.

---

a 6 That is, its name will be used in cursing (see 29:22); or, others will see that it is cursed.   *b* 18 Micah 3:12

Judah to serve Nebuchadnezzar

27 Early in the reign of Zedekiah*a* son of Josiah king of Judah, this word came to Jeremiah from the LORD: ²this is what the LORD said to me: 'Make a yoke out of straps and crossbars and put it on your neck. ³Then send word to the kings of Edom, Moab, Ammon, Tyre and Sidon through the envoys who have come to Jerusalem to Zedekiah king of Judah. ⁴Give them a message for their masters and say, "This is what the LORD Almighty, the God of Israel, says: 'Tell this to your masters: ⁵with my great power and outstretched arm I made the earth and its people and the animals that are on it, and I give it to anyone I please. ⁶Now I will give all your countries into the hands of my servant Nebuchadnezzar king of Babylon; I will make even the wild animals subject to him. ⁷All nations will serve him and his son and his grandson until the time for his land comes; then many nations and great kings will subjugate him.

⁸ " 'If, however, any nation or kingdom will not serve Nebuchadnezzar king of Babylon or bow its neck under his yoke, I will punish that nation with the sword, famine and plague, declares the LORD, until I destroy it by his hand. ⁹So do not listen to your prophets, your diviners, your interpreters of dreams, your mediums or your sorcerers who tell you, "You will not serve the king of Babylon." ¹⁰They prophesy lies to you that will only serve to remove you far from your lands; I will banish you and you will perish. ¹¹But if any nation will bow its neck under the yoke of the king of Babylon and serve him, I will let that nation remain in its own land to till it and to live there, declares the LORD.' " '

¹²I gave the same message to Zedekiah king of Judah. I said, 'Bow your neck under the yoke of the king of Babylon; serve him and his people, and you will live. ¹³Why will you and your people die by the sword, famine and plague with which the LORD has threatened any nation that will

not serve the king of Babylon? ¹⁴Do not listen to the words of the prophets who say to you, "You will not serve the king of Babylon," for they are prophesying lies to you. ¹⁵"I have not sent them," declares the LORD. "They are prophesying lies in my name. Therefore, I will banish you and you will perish, both you and the prophets who prophesy to you." '

¹⁶Then I said to the priests and all these people, 'This is what the LORD says: do not listen to the prophets who say, "Very soon now the articles from the LORD's house will be brought back from Babylon." They are prophesying lies to you. ¹⁷Do not listen to them. Serve the king of Babylon, and you will live. Why should this city become a ruin? ¹⁸If they are prophets and have the word of the LORD, let them plead with the LORD Almighty that the articles which remain in the house of the LORD and in the palace of the king of Judah and in Jerusalem will not be taken to Babylon. ¹⁹For this is what the LORD Almighty says about the pillars, the bronze Sea, the movable stands and the other articles that are left in this city, ²⁰which Nebuchadnezzar king of Babylon did not take away when he carried Jehoiachin*b* son of Jehoiakim king of Judah into exile from Jerusalem to Babylon, along with all the nobles of Judah and Jerusalem – ²¹yes, this is what the LORD Almighty, the God of Israel, says about the things that are left in the house of the LORD and in the palace of the king of Judah and in Jerusalem: ²²"They will be taken to Babylon and there they will remain until the day I come for them," declares the LORD. "Then I will bring them back and restore them to this place." '

The false prophet Hananiah

28 In the fifth month of that same year, the fourth year, early in the reign of Zedekiah king of Judah, the prophet Hananiah son of Azzur, who was from Gibeon, said to me in the house of the LORD in the presence of the priests and all the people: ²'This is what the

---

a 1 A few Hebrew manuscripts and Syriac (see also 27:3,12 and 28:1); most Hebrew manuscripts *Jehoiakim* (most Septuagint manuscripts do not have this verse.)

b 20 Hebrew *Jeconiah*, a variant of *Jehoiachin*; also in 28:4 and 29:2

LORD Almighty, the God of Israel, says: "I will break the yoke of the king of Babylon. ³Within two years I will bring back to this place all the articles of the LORD's house that Nebuchadnezzar king of Babylon removed from here and took to Babylon. ⁴I will also bring back to this place Jehoiachin son of Jehoiakim king of Judah and all the other exiles from Judah who went to Babylon", declares the LORD, "for I will break the yoke of the king of Babylon."'

⁵Then the prophet Jeremiah replied to the prophet Hananiah before the priests and all the people who were standing in the house of the LORD. ⁶He said, 'Amen! May the LORD do so! May the LORD fulfil the words you have prophesied by bringing the articles of the LORD's house and all the exiles back to this place from Babylon. ⁷Nevertheless, listen to what I have to say in your hearing and in the hearing of all the people: ⁸from early times the prophets who preceded you and me have prophesied war, disaster and plague against many countries and great kingdoms. ⁹But the prophet who prophesies peace will be recognised as one truly sent by the LORD only if his prediction comes true.'

¹⁰Then the prophet Hananiah took the yoke off the neck of the prophet Jeremiah and broke it, ¹¹and he said before all the people, 'This is what the LORD says: "In the same way I will break the yoke of Nebuchadnezzar king of Babylon off the neck of all the nations within two years."' At this, the prophet Jeremiah went on his way.

¹²After the prophet Hananiah had broken the yoke off the neck of the prophet Jeremiah, the word of the LORD came to Jeremiah: ¹³'Go and tell Hananiah, "This is what the LORD says: you have broken a wooden yoke, but in its place you will get a yoke of iron. ¹⁴This is what the LORD Almighty, the God of Israel, says: I will put an iron yoke on the necks of all these nations to make them serve Nebuchadnezzar king of Babylon, and they will serve him. I will even give him control over the wild animals."'

¹⁵Then the prophet Jeremiah said to Hananiah the prophet, 'Listen, Hananiah! The LORD has not sent you, yet you have persuaded this nation to trust in lies. ¹⁶Therefore this is what the LORD says: "I am about to remove you from the face of the earth. This very year you are going to die, because you have preached rebellion against the LORD."'

¹⁷In the seventh month of that same year, Hananiah the prophet died.

FIRST MODERN ENGLISH TRANSLATION

The first printed English New Testament was published in 1525 by William Tyndale. He produced it in Germany, as the English authorities forbade the translation. Many of these Tyndale Testaments were smuggled into England, hidden in barrels, rolls of cloth and bundles of wood.

A letter to the exiles

29 This is the text of the letter that the prophet Jeremiah sent from Jerusalem to the surviving elders among the exiles and to the priests, the prophets and all the other people Nebuchadnezzar had carried into exile from Jerusalem to Babylon. ²(This was after King Jehoiachin and the queen mother, the court officials and the leaders of Judah and Jerusalem, the skilled workers and the craftsmen had gone into exile from Jerusalem.) ³He entrusted the letter to Elasah son of Shaphan and to Gemariah son of Hilkiah, whom Zedekiah king of Judah sent to King Nebuchadnezzar in Babylon. It said:

⁴This is what the LORD Almighty, the God of Israel, says to all those I carried into exile from Jerusalem to Babylon: ⁵'Build houses and settle down;

plant gardens and eat what they produce. 6 Marry and have sons and daughters; find wives for your sons and give your daughters in marriage, so that they too may have sons and daughters. Increase in number there; do not decrease. 7 Also, seek the peace and prosperity of the city to which I have carried you into exile. Pray to the LORD for it, because if it prospers, you too will prosper.' 8 Yes, this is what the LORD Almighty, the God of Israel, says: 'Do not let the prophets and diviners among you deceive you. Do not listen to the dreams you encourage them to have. 9 They are prophesying lies to you in my name. I have not sent them,' declares the LORD.

10 This is what the LORD says: 'When seventy years are completed for Babylon, I will come to you and fulfil my good promise to bring you back to this place. 11 For I know the plans I have for you,' declares the LORD, 'plans to prosper you and not to harm you, plans to give you hope and a future. 12 Then you will call on me and come and pray to me, and I will listen to you. 13 You will seek me and find me when you seek me with all your heart. 14 I will be found by you,' declares the LORD, 'and will bring you back from captivity.ª I will gather you from all the nations and places where I have banished you,' declares the LORD, 'and will bring you back to the place from which I carried you into exile.'

15 You may say, 'The LORD has raised up prophets for us in Babylon,' 16 but this is what the LORD says about the king who sits on David's throne and all the people who remain in this city, your fellow citizens who did not go with you into exile – 17 yes, this is what the LORD Almighty says: 'I will send the sword, famine and plague against them and I will make them like figs that are so bad they cannot be eaten. 18 I will pursue them with the sword, famine and plague and will make them abhorrent to all the kingdoms of the earth, a curseᵇ and an object of horror, of scorn and reproach, among all the nations where I drive them. 19 For they have not listened to my words,' declares the LORD, 'words that I sent to them again and again by my servants the prophets. And you exiles have not listened either,' declares the LORD.

20 Therefore, hear the word of the LORD, all you exiles whom I have sent away from Jerusalem to Babylon. 21 This is what the LORD Almighty, the God of Israel, says about Ahab son of Kolaiah and Zedekiah son of Maaseiah, who are prophesying lies to you in my name: 'I will deliver them into the hands of Nebuchadnezzar king of Babylon, and he will put them to death before your very eyes. 22 Because of them, all the exiles from Judah who are in Babylon will use this curse: "May the LORD treat you like Zedekiah and Ahab, whom the king of Babylon burned in the fire." 23 For they have done outrageous things in Israel; they have committed adultery with their neighbours' wives, and in my name they have uttered lies – which I did not authorise. I know it and am a witness to it,' declares the LORD.

Message to Shemaiah

24 Tell Shemaiah the Nehelamite, 25 'This is what the LORD Almighty, the God of Israel, says: you sent letters in your own name to all the people in Jerusalem, to the priest Zephaniah son of Maaseiah, and to all the other priests. You said to Zephaniah, 26 "The LORD has appointed you priest in place of Jehoiada to be in charge of the house of the LORD; you should put any maniac who acts like a prophet into the stocks and neck-irons. 27 So why have you not reprimanded Jeremiah from Anathoth, who poses as a prophet among

---

a 14 Or *will restore your fortunes*

b 18 That is, their names will be used in cursing (see verse 22); or, others will see that they are cursed.

you? 28 He has sent this message to us in Babylon: it will be a long time. Therefore build houses and settle down; plant gardens and eat what they produce." '

29 Zephaniah the priest, however, read the letter to Jeremiah the prophet. 30 Then the word of the LORD came to Jeremiah: 31 'Send this message to all the exiles: "This is what the LORD says about Shemaiah the Nehelamite: because Shemaiah has prophesied to you, even though I did not send him, and has persuaded you to trust in lies, 32 this is what the LORD says: I will surely punish Shemaiah the Nehelamite and his descendants. He will have no one left among this people, nor will he see the good things I will do for my people, declares the LORD, because he has preached rebellion against me." '

Restoration of Israel

30 This is the word that came to Jeremiah from the LORD: 2 'This is what the LORD, the God of Israel, says: "Write in a book all the words I have spoken to you. 3 The days are coming," declares the LORD, "when I will bring my people Israel and Judah back from captivity[a] and restore them to the land I gave to their ancestors to possess," says the LORD.'

4 These are the words the LORD spoke concerning Israel and Judah: 5 'This is what the LORD says:

' "Cries of fear are heard –
    terror, not peace.
6 Ask and see:
    can a man bear children?
Then why do I see every strong man
    with his hands on his stomach like a
        woman in labour,
    every face turned deathly pale?
7 How awful that day will be!
    No other will be like it.
It will be a time of trouble for Jacob,
    but he will be saved out of it.

8 ' "In that day," declares the LORD Almighty,
    "I will break the yoke off their necks

and will tear off their bonds;
    no longer will foreigners enslave
        them.
9 Instead, they will serve the LORD their
        God
    and David their king,
    whom I will raise up for them.

FAVOURITE VERSES
Jeremiah 29:11

'For I know the plans I have for you,' declares the LORD, 'plans to prosper you and not to harm you, plans to give you hope and a future.'

- -

When I was baptised, this verse was read out. At the time I was worried about my future, as I felt I didn't have a goal, when many people around me seemed to. This verse helped me massively. Whenever I look back at it, I'm assured that God has big plans for everyone!

Chloe, 16

10 ' "So do not be afraid, Jacob my servant;
    do not be dismayed, Israel,"
        declares the LORD.
"I will surely save you out of a distant
        place,
    your descendants from the land of
        their exile.
Jacob will again have peace and
        security,
    and no one will make him afraid.
11 I am with you and will save you,"
    declares the LORD.
"Though I completely destroy all the
        nations
    among which I scatter you,
    I will not completely destroy you.
I will discipline you but only in due
        measure;

---

a 3 Or *will restore the fortunes of my people Israel and Judah*

I will not let you go entirely
unpunished."

12 'This is what the LORD says:

' "Your wound is incurable,
your injury beyond healing.
13 There is no one to plead your cause,
no remedy for your sore,
no healing for you.
14 All your allies have forgotten you;
they care nothing for you.
I have struck you as an enemy would
and punished you as would the cruel,
because your guilt is so great
and your sins so many.
15 Why do you cry out over your wound,
your pain that has no cure?
Because of your great guilt and many
sins
I have done these things to you.

16 ' "But all who devour you will be
devoured;
all your enemies will go into exile.
Those who plunder you will be
plundered;
all who make spoil of you I will
despoil.
17 But I will restore you to health
and heal your wounds,"
declares the LORD,
"because you are called an outcast,
Zion for whom no one cares."

18 'This is what the LORD says:

' "I will restore the fortunes of Jacob's
tents
and have compassion on his
dwellings;
the city will be rebuilt on her ruins,
and the palace will stand in its proper
place.
19 From them will come songs of
thanksgiving
and the sound of rejoicing.
I will add to their numbers,
and they will not be decreased;
I will bring them honour,
and they will not be disdained.
20 Their children will be as in days of old,

and their community will be
established before me;
I will punish all who oppress them.
21 Their leader will be one of their own;
their ruler will arise from among
them.
I will bring him near and he will come
close to me –
for who is he who will devote himself
to be close to me?"
declares the LORD.
22 ' "So you will be my people,
and I will be your God." '

23 See, the storm of the LORD
will burst out in wrath,
a driving wind swirling down
on the heads of the wicked.
24 The fierce anger of the LORD will not
turn back
until he fully accomplishes
the purposes of his heart.
In days to come
you will understand this.

31

'At that time,' declares the LORD, 'I
will be the God of all the families of
Israel, and they will be my people.'
2 This is what the LORD says:

'The people who survive the sword
will find favour in the wilderness;
I will come to give rest to Israel.'

3 The LORD appeared to us in the past,[a]
saying:

'I have loved you with an everlasting
love;
I have drawn you with unfailing
kindness.
4 I will build you up again,
and you, Virgin Israel, will be rebuilt.
Again you will take up your tambourines
and go out to dance with the joyful.
5 Again you will plant vineyards
on the hills of Samaria;
the farmers will plant them
and enjoy their fruit.

---

a 3 Or LORD has appeared to us from afar

⁶There will be a day when watchmen cry
  out
    on the hills of Ephraim,
  "Come, let us go up to Zion,
    to the LORD our God."'

⁷This is what the LORD says:

'Sing with joy for Jacob;
  shout for the foremost of the
    nations.
Make your praises heard, and say,
  "LORD, save your people,
    the remnant of Israel."
⁸See, I will bring them from the land of
    the north
  and gather them from the ends of
    the earth.
Among them will be the blind and the
    lame,
  expectant mothers and women in
    labour;
  a great throng will return.
⁹They will come with weeping;
  they will pray as I bring them back.
I will lead them beside streams of water
  on a level path where they will not
    stumble,
because I am Israel's father,
  and Ephraim is my firstborn son.

¹⁰'Hear the word of the LORD, you
    nations;
  proclaim it in distant coastlands:
  "He who scattered Israel will gather
    them
  and will watch over his flock like a
    shepherd."
¹¹For the LORD will deliver Jacob
  and redeem them from the hand of
    those stronger than they.
¹²They will come and shout for joy on the
    heights of Zion;
  they will rejoice in the bounty of the
    LORD –
the grain, the new wine and the olive
    oil,
  the young of the flocks and herds.
They will be like a well-watered garden,
  and they will sorrow no more.
¹³Then young women will dance and be
    glad,

young men and old as well.
I will turn their mourning into
    gladness;
  I will give them comfort and joy
    instead of sorrow.
¹⁴I will satisfy the priests with abundance,
  and my people will be filled with my
    bounty,'
              declares the LORD.

¹⁵This is what the LORD says:

'A voice is heard in Ramah,
  mourning and great weeping,
Rachel weeping for her children
  and refusing to be comforted,
  because they are no more.'

¹⁶This is what the LORD says:

'Restrain your voice from weeping
  and your eyes from tears,
for your work will be rewarded,'
              declares the LORD.
'They will return from the land of the
    enemy.
¹⁷So there is hope for your descendants,'
              declares the LORD.
'Your children will return to their
    own land.

¹⁸'I have surely heard Ephraim's
    moaning:
  "You disciplined me like an unruly
    calf,
  and I have been disciplined.
Restore me, and I will return,
  because you are the LORD my God.
¹⁹After I strayed,
  I repented;
after I came to understand,
  I beat my breast.
I was ashamed and humiliated
  because I bore the disgrace of my
    youth."
²⁰Is not Ephraim my dear son,
  the child in whom I delight?
Though I often speak against him,
  I still remember him.
Therefore my heart yearns for him;
  I have great compassion for him,'
              declares the LORD.

21 'Set up road signs;
    put up guideposts.
Take note of the highway,
    the road that you take.
Return, Virgin Israel,
    return to your towns.
22 How long will you wander,
    unfaithful Daughter Israel?
The LORD will create a new thing on
        earth –
    the woman will return to[b] the man.'

23 This is what the LORD Almighty, the
God of Israel, says: 'When I bring them
back from captivity,[c] the people in the land
of Judah and in its towns will once again
use these words: "The LORD bless you, you
prosperous city, you sacred mountain."
24 People will live together in Judah and all
its towns – farmers and those who move
about with their flocks. 25 I will refresh the
weary and satisfy the faint.'
26 At this I awoke and looked around.
My sleep had been pleasant to me.
27 'The days are coming,' declares the
LORD, 'when I will plant the kingdoms
of Israel and Judah with the offspring of
people and of animals. 28 Just as I watched
over them to uproot and tear down, and
to overthrow, destroy and bring disaster,
so I will watch over them to build and to
plant,' declares the LORD. 29 'In those days
people will no longer say,

    "The parents have eaten sour grapes,
        and the children's teeth are set on
            edge."

30 Instead, everyone will die for their own
sin; whoever eats sour grapes – their own
teeth will be set on edge.

31 'The days are coming,' declares the
        LORD,
    'when I will make a new covenant
with the people of Israel
    and with the people of Judah.
32 It will not be like the covenant
    I made with their ancestors

when I took them by the hand
    to lead them out of Egypt,
because they broke my covenant,
    though I was a husband to[d] them,'[e]
                declares the LORD.
33 'This is the covenant that I will make
        with the people of Israel
    after that time,' declares the LORD.
'I will put my law in their minds
    and write it on their hearts.
I will be their God,
    and they will be my people.
34 No longer will they teach their
        neighbour,
    or say to one another, "Know the
        LORD,"
because they will all know me,
    from the least of them to the
        greatest,'
                declares the LORD.
'For I will forgive their wickedness
    and will remember their sins no
        more.'

35 This is what the LORD says,

he who appoints the sun
    to shine by day,
who decrees the moon and stars
    to shine by night,
who stirs up the sea
    so that its waves roar –
    the LORD Almighty is his name:
36 'Only if these decrees vanish from my
        sight,'
    declares the LORD,
'will Israel ever cease
    being a nation before me.'

37 This is what the LORD says:

'Only if the heavens above can be
        measured
    and the foundations of the earth
        below be searched out
will I reject all the descendants of Israel
    because of all they have done,'
                declares the LORD.

---

b 22 Or will protect
c 23 Or I restore their fortunes

d 32 Hebrew; Septuagint and Syriac covenant, / and I
turned away from
e 32 Or was their master

38 'The days are coming,' declares the LORD, 'when this city will be rebuilt for me from the Tower of Hananel to the Corner Gate. 39 The measuring line will stretch from there straight to the hill of Gareb and then turn to Goah. 40 The whole valley where dead bodies and ashes are thrown, and all the terraces out to the Kidron Valley on the east as far as the corner of the Horse Gate, will be holy to the LORD. The city will never again be uprooted or demolished.'

Jeremiah buys a field

32 This is the word that came to Jeremiah from the LORD in the tenth year of Zedekiah king of Judah, which was the eighteenth year of Nebuchadnezzar. 2 The army of the king of Babylon was then besieging Jerusalem, and Jeremiah the prophet was confined in the courtyard of the guard in the royal palace of Judah.

3 Now Zedekiah king of Judah had imprisoned him there, saying, 'Why do you prophesy as you do? You say, "This is what the LORD says: I am about to give this city into the hands of the king of Babylon, and he will capture it. 4 Zedekiah king of Judah will not escape the Babylonians[a] but will certainly be given into the hands of the king of Babylon, and will speak with him face to face and see him with his own eyes. 5 He will take Zedekiah to Babylon, where he will remain until I deal with him, declares the LORD. If you fight against the Babylonians, you will not succeed." '

6 Jeremiah said, 'The word of the LORD came to me: 7 Hanamel son of Shallum your uncle is going to come to you and say, "Buy my field at Anathoth, because as nearest relative it is your right and duty to buy it."

8 'Then, just as the LORD had said, my cousin Hanamel came to me in the courtyard of the guard and said, "Buy my field at Anathoth in the territory of Benjamin. Since it is your right to redeem it and possess it, buy it for yourself."

'I knew that this was the word of the LORD; 9 so I bought the field at Anathoth from my cousin Hanamel and weighed out for him seventeen shekels[b] of silver. 10 I signed and sealed the deed, had it witnessed, and weighed out the silver on the scales. 11 I took the deed of purchase – the sealed copy containing the terms and conditions, as well as the unsealed copy – 12 and I gave this deed to Baruch son of Neriah, the son of Mahseiah, in the presence of my cousin Hanamel and of the witnesses who had signed the deed and of all the Jews sitting in the courtyard of the guard.

13 'In their presence I gave Baruch these instructions: 14 "This is what the LORD Almighty, the God of Israel, says: take these documents, both the sealed and unsealed copies of the deed of purchase, and put them in a clay jar so that they will last a long time. 15 For this is what the LORD Almighty, the God of Israel, says: houses, fields and vineyards will again be bought in this land."

16 'After I had given the deed of purchase to Baruch son of Neriah, I prayed to the LORD:

17 'Ah, Sovereign LORD, you have made the heavens and the earth by your great power and outstretched arm. Nothing is too hard for you. 18 You show love to thousands but bring the punishment for the parents' sins into the laps of their children after them. Great and mighty God, whose name is the LORD Almighty, 19 great are your purposes and mighty are your deeds. Your eyes are open to the ways of all mankind; you reward each person according to their conduct and as their deeds deserve. 20 You performed signs and wonders in Egypt and have continued them to this day, in Israel and among all mankind, and have gained the renown that is still yours. 21 You brought your people Israel out of Egypt with signs and wonders, by a mighty hand and an outstretched arm and with great terror. 22 You gave them this land you

---

a 4 Or *Chaldeans*; also in verses 5, 24, 25, 28, 29 and 43

b 9 That is, about 200 grams

had sworn to give to their ancestors, a land flowing with milk and honey. 23 They came in and took possession of it, but they did not obey you or follow your law; they did not do what you commanded them to do. So you brought all this disaster on them.

24 'See how the siege ramps are built up to take the city. Because of the sword, famine and plague, the city will be given into the hands of the Babylonians who are attacking it. What you said has happened, as you now see. 25 And though the city will be given into the hands of the Babylonians, you, Sovereign LORD, say to me, "Buy the field with silver and have the transaction witnessed." '

26 Then the word of the LORD came to Jeremiah: 27 'I am the LORD, the God of all mankind. Is anything too hard for me? 28 Therefore this is what the LORD says: I am about to give this city into the hands of the Babylonians and to Nebuchadnezzar king of Babylon, who will capture it. 29 The Babylonians who are attacking this city will come in and set it on fire; they will burn it down, along with the houses where the people aroused my anger by burning incense on the roofs to Baal and by pouring out drink offerings to other gods.

30 'The people of Israel and Judah have done nothing but evil in my sight from their youth; indeed, the people of Israel have done nothing but arouse my anger with what their hands have made, declares the LORD. 31 From the day it was built until now, this city has so aroused my anger and wrath that I must remove it from my sight. 32 The people of Israel and Judah have provoked me by all the evil they have done – they, their kings and officials, their priests and prophets, the people of Judah and those living in Jerusalem. 33 They turned their backs to me and not their faces; though I taught them again and again, they would not listen or respond to discipline. 34 They set up their vile images in the house that bears my Name and defiled it. 35 They built high places for Baal in the Valley of Ben Hinnom to sacrifice their

sons and daughters to Molek, though I never commanded – nor did it enter my mind – that they should do such a detestable thing and so make Judah sin.

36 'You are saying about this city, "By the sword, famine and plague it will be given into the hands of the king of Babylon"; but this is what the LORD, the God of Israel, says: 37 I will surely gather them from all the lands where I banish them in my furious anger and great wrath; I will bring them back to this place and let them live in safety. 38 They will be my people, and I will be their God. 39 I will give them singleness of heart and action, so that they will always fear me and that all will then go well for them and for their children after them. 40 I will make an everlasting covenant with them: I will never stop doing good to them, and I will inspire them to fear me, so that they will never turn away from me. 41 I will rejoice in doing them good and will assuredly plant them in this land with all my heart and soul.

42 'This is what the LORD says: as I have brought all this great calamity on this people, so I will give them all the prosperity I have promised them. 43 Once more fields will be bought in this land of which you say, "It is a desolate waste, without people or animals, for it has been given into the hands of the Babylonians." 44 Fields will be bought for silver, and deeds will be signed, sealed and witnessed in the territory of Benjamin, in the villages around Jerusalem, in the towns of Judah and in the towns of the hill country, of the western foothills and of the Negev, because I will restore their fortunes,c declares the LORD.'

Promise of restoration

33 While Jeremiah was still confined in the courtyard of the guard, the word of the LORD came to him a second time: 2 'This is what the LORD says, he who made the earth, the LORD who formed it and established it – the LORD is his name: 3 "Call to me and I will answer you and tell you great and unsearchable things you do not know." 4 For this is what the LORD,

---

c 44 Or *will bring them back from captivity*

the God of Israel, says about the houses in this city and the royal palaces of Judah that have been torn down to be used against the siege ramps and the sword [5] in the fight with the Babylonians[a]: "They will be filled with the dead bodies of the people I will slay in my anger and wrath. I will hide my face from this city because of all its wickedness.

[6] "Nevertheless, I will bring health and healing to it; I will heal my people and will let them enjoy abundant peace and security. [7] I will bring Judah and Israel back from captivity[b] and will rebuild them as they were before. [8] I will cleanse them from all the sin they have committed against me and will forgive all their sins of rebellion against me. [9] Then this city will bring me renown, joy, praise and honour before all nations on earth that hear of all the good things I do for it; and they will be in awe and will tremble at the abundant prosperity and peace I provide for it."

[10] 'This is what the LORD says: "You say about this place, 'It is a desolate waste, without people or animals.' Yet in the towns of Judah and the streets of Jerusalem that are deserted, inhabited by neither people nor animals, there will be heard once more [11] the sounds of joy and gladness, the voices of bride and bridegroom, and the voices of those who bring thank offerings to the house of the LORD, saying,

'Give thanks to the LORD Almighty,
     for the LORD is good;
     his love endures for ever.'

For I will restore the fortunes of the land as they were before," says the LORD.

[12] 'This is what the LORD Almighty says: "In this place, desolate and without people or animals – in all its towns there will again be pastures for shepherds to rest their flocks. [13] In the towns of the hill country, of the western foothills and of the Negev, in the territory of Benjamin, in the villages around Jerusalem and in the towns of Judah, flocks will again pass under the hand of the one who counts them," says the LORD.

[14] ' "The days are coming," declares the LORD, "when I will fulfil the good promise I made to the people of Israel and Judah.

[15] ' "In those days and at that time
     I will make a righteous Branch sprout
         from David's line;
     he will do what is just and right in the
         land.
[16] In those days Judah will be saved
     and Jerusalem will live in safety.
This is the name by which it[c] will be
     called:
     The LORD Our Righteous Saviour."

FAVOURITE VERSES

John 1:1

In the beginning was the Word, and the Word was with God, and the Word was God.

It's my favourite verse because it shows that God was around before time began, he's around in time now, and he'll be around after time has run out. He's in everything all the time.

Mim, 12

[17] For this is what the LORD says: "David will never fail to have a man to sit on the throne of Israel, [18] nor will the Levitical priests ever fail to have a man to stand before me continually to offer burnt offerings, to burn grain offerings and to present sacrifices."'

[19] The word of the LORD came to Jeremiah: [20] 'This is what the LORD says: "If

---

a 5 Or *Chaldeans*
b 7 Or *will restore the fortunes of Judah and Israel*
c 16 Or *he*

you can break my covenant with the day and my covenant with the night, so that day and night no longer come at their appointed time, **21** then my covenant with David my servant – and my covenant with the Levites who are priests ministering before me – can be broken and David will no longer have a descendant to reign on his throne. **22** I will make the descendants of David my servant and the Levites who minister before me as countless as the stars in the sky and as measureless as the sand on the seashore." '

23 The word of the LORD came to Jeremiah: **24** 'Have you not noticed that these people are saying, "The LORD has rejected the two kingdoms*d* he chose"? So they despise my people and no longer regard them as a nation. **25** This is what the LORD says: "If I have not made my covenant with day and night and established the laws of heaven and earth, **26** then I will reject the descendants of Jacob and David my servant and will not choose one of his sons to rule over the descendants of Abraham, Isaac and Jacob. For I will restore their fortunes*e* and have compassion on them." '

Warning to Zedekiah

34 While Nebuchadnezzar king of Babylon and all his army and all the kingdoms and peoples in the empire he ruled were fighting against Jerusalem and all its surrounding towns, this word came to Jeremiah from the LORD: **2** 'This is what the LORD, the God of Israel, says: go to Zedekiah king of Judah and tell him, "This is what the LORD says: I am about to give this city into the hands of the king of Babylon, and he will burn it down. **3** You will not escape from his grasp but will surely be captured and given into his hands. You will see the king of Babylon with your own eyes, and he will speak with you face to face. And you will go to Babylon.

4 ' "Yet hear the LORD's promise to you, Zedekiah king of Judah. This is what the LORD says concerning you: you will not die by the sword; **5** you will die peacefully.

As people made a funeral fire in honour of your predecessors, the kings who ruled before you, so they will make a fire in your honour and lament, 'Alas, master!' I myself make this promise, declares the LORD." '

6 Then Jeremiah the prophet told all this to Zedekiah king of Judah, in Jerusalem, **7** while the army of the king of Babylon was fighting against Jerusalem and the other cities of Judah that were still holding out – Lachish and Azekah. These were the only fortified cities left in Judah.

Freedom for slaves

8 The word came to Jeremiah from the LORD after King Zedekiah had made a covenant with all the people in Jerusalem to proclaim freedom for the slaves. **9** Everyone was to free their Hebrew slaves, both male and female; no one was to hold a fellow Hebrew in bondage. **10** So all the officials and people who entered into this covenant agreed that they would free their male and female slaves and no longer hold them in bondage. They agreed, and set them free. **11** But afterwards they changed their minds and took back the slaves they had freed and enslaved them again.

12 Then the word of the LORD came to Jeremiah: **13** 'This is what the LORD, the God of Israel, says: I made a covenant with your ancestors when I brought them out of Egypt, out of the land of slavery. I said, **14** "Every seventh year each of you must free any fellow Hebrews who have sold themselves to you. After they have served you for six years, you must let them go free."*a* Your ancestors, however, did not listen to me or pay attention to me. **15** Recently you repented and did what is right in my sight: each of you proclaimed freedom to your own people. You even made a covenant before me in the house that bears my Name. **16** But now you have turned round and profaned my name; each of you has taken back the male and female slaves you had set free to go where they wished. You

---

d 24 Or *families*
e 26 Or *will bring them back from captivity*

a 14 Deut. 15:12

have forced them to become your slaves again.

17 'Therefore this is what the LORD says: you have not obeyed me; you have not proclaimed freedom to your own people. So I now proclaim "freedom" for you, declares the LORD – "freedom" to fall by the sword, plague and famine. I will make you abhorrent to all the kingdoms of the earth. 18 Those who have violated my covenant and have not fulfilled the terms of the covenant they made before me, I will treat like the calf they cut in two and then walked between its pieces. 19 The leaders of Judah and Jerusalem, the court officials, the priests and all the people of the land who walked between the pieces of the calf, 20 I will deliver into the hands of their enemies who want to kill them. Their dead bodies will become food for the birds and the wild animals.

21 'I will deliver Zedekiah king of Judah and his officials into the hands of their enemies who want to kill them, to the army of the king of Babylon, which has withdrawn from you. 22 I am going to give the order, declares the LORD, and I will bring them back to this city. They will fight against it, take it and burn it down. And I will lay waste the towns of Judah so that no one can live there.'

The Rekabites

35 This is the word that came to Jeremiah from the LORD during the reign of Jehoiakim son of Josiah king of Judah: 2 'Go to the Rekabite family and invite them to come to one of the side rooms of the house of the LORD and give them wine to drink.'

3 So I went to get Jaazaniah son of Jeremiah, the son of Habazziniah, and his brothers and all his sons – the whole family of the Rekabites. 4 I brought them into the house of the LORD, into the room of the sons of Hanan son of Igdaliah the man of God. It was next to the room of the officials, which was over that of Maaseiah son of Shallum the door-keeper. 5 Then I set bowls full of wine and some cups before the Rekabites and said to them, 'Drink some wine.'

6 But they replied, 'We do not drink wine, because our forefather Jehonadab[a] son of Rekab gave us this command: "Neither you nor your descendants must ever drink wine. 7 Also you must never build houses, sow seed or plant vineyards; you must never have any of these things, but must always live in tents. Then you will live a long time in the land where you are nomads." 8 We have obeyed everything our forefather Jehonadab son of Rekab commanded us. Neither we nor our wives nor our sons and daughters have ever drunk wine 9 or built houses to live in or had vineyards, fields or crops. 10 We have lived in tents and have fully obeyed everything our forefather Jehonadab commanded us. 11 But when Nebuchadnezzar king of Babylon invaded this land, we said, "Come, we must go to Jerusalem to escape the Babylonian[b] and Aramean armies." So we have remained in Jerusalem.'

12 Then the word of the LORD came to Jeremiah, saying: 13 'This is what the LORD Almighty, the God of Israel, says: go and tell the people of Judah and those living in Jerusalem, "Will you not learn a lesson and obey my words?" declares the LORD. 14 "Jehonadab son of Rekab ordered his descendants not to drink wine and this command has been kept. To this day they do not drink wine, because they obey their forefather's command. But I have spoken to you again and again, yet you have not obeyed me. 15 Again and again I sent all my servants the prophets to you. They said, 'Each of you must turn from your wicked ways and reform your actions; do not follow other gods to serve them. Then you shall live in the land I have given to you and your ancestors.' But you have not paid attention or listened to me. 16 The descendants of Jehonadab son of Rekab have carried out the command their forefather gave them, but these people have not obeyed me."

17 'Therefore this is what the LORD God Almighty, the God of Israel, says: "Listen! I am going to bring on Judah and on

a 6 Hebrew *Jonadab*, a variant of *Jehonadab*; here and often in this chapter
b 11 Or *Chaldean*

everyone living in Jerusalem every disaster I pronounced against them. I spoke to them, but they did not listen; I called to them, but they did not answer.'"

18 Then Jeremiah said to the family of the Rekabites, 'This is what the LORD Almighty, the God of Israel, says: "You have obeyed the command of your forefather Jehonadab and have followed all his instructions and have done everything he ordered." 19 Therefore this is what the LORD Almighty, the God of Israel, says: "Jehonadab son of Rekab shall never fail to have a descendant to serve me."'

Jehoiakim burns Jeremiah's scroll

36 In the fourth year of Jehoiakim son of Josiah king of Judah, this word came to Jeremiah from the LORD: 2 'Take a scroll and write on it all the words I have spoken to you concerning Israel, Judah and all the other nations from the time I began speaking to you in the reign of Josiah till now. 3 Perhaps when the people of Judah hear about every disaster I plan to inflict on them, they will each turn from their wicked ways; then I will forgive their wickedness and their sin.'

4 So Jeremiah called Baruch son of Neriah, and while Jeremiah dictated all the words the LORD had spoken to him, Baruch wrote them on the scroll. 5 Then Jeremiah told Baruch, 'I am restricted; I am not allowed to go to the LORD's temple. 6 So you go to the house of the LORD on a day of fasting and read to the people from the scroll the words of the LORD that you wrote as I dictated. Read them to all the people of Judah who come in from their towns. 7 Perhaps they will bring their petition before the LORD and will each turn from their wicked ways, for the anger and wrath pronounced against this people by the LORD are great.'

8 Baruch son of Neriah did everything Jeremiah the prophet told him to do; at the LORD's temple he read the words of the LORD from the scroll. 9 In the ninth month of the fifth year of Jehoiakim son of Josiah king of Judah, a time of fasting before the LORD was proclaimed for all the people in Jerusalem and those who had come from the towns of Judah. 10 From the room of Gemariah son of Shaphan the secretary, which was in the upper courtyard at the entrance of the New Gate of the temple, Baruch read to all the people at the LORD's temple the words of Jeremiah from the scroll.

11 When Micaiah son of Gemariah, the son of Shaphan, heard all the words of the LORD from the scroll, 12 he went down to the secretary's room in the royal palace, where all the officials were sitting: Elishama the secretary, Delaiah son of Shemaiah, Elnathan son of Akbor, Gemariah son of Shaphan, Zedekiah son of Hananiah, and all the other officials. 13 After Micaiah told them everything he had heard Baruch read to the people from the scroll, 14 all the officials sent Jehudi son of Nethaniah, the son of Shelemiah, the son of Cushi, to say to Baruch, 'Bring the scroll from which you have read to the people and come.' So Baruch son of Neriah went to them with the scroll in his hand. 15 They said to him, 'Sit down, please, and read it to us.'

So Baruch read it to them. 16 When they heard all these words, they looked at each other in fear and said to Baruch, 'We must report all these words to the king.' 17 Then they asked Baruch, 'Tell us, how did you come to write all this? Did Jeremiah dictate it?'

18 'Yes,' Baruch replied, 'he dictated all these words to me, and I wrote them in ink on the scroll.'

19 Then the officials said to Baruch, 'You and Jeremiah, go and hide. Don't let anyone know where you are.'

20 After they put the scroll in the room of Elishama the secretary, they went to the king in the courtyard and reported everything to him. 21 The king sent Jehudi to get the scroll, and Jehudi brought it from the room of Elishama the secretary and read it to the king and all the officials standing beside him. 22 It was the ninth month and the king was sitting in the winter apartment, with a fire burning in the brazier in front of him. 23 Whenever Jehudi had read three or four columns of the scroll, the king cut them off with a scribe's knife and threw them into the brazier, until the

entire scroll was burned in the fire. 24 The king and all his attendants who heard all these words showed no fear, nor did they tear their clothes. 25 Even though Elnathan, Delaiah and Gemariah urged the king not to burn the scroll, he would not listen to them. 26 Instead, the king commanded Jerahmeel, a son of the king, Seraiah son of Azriel and Shelemiah son of Abdeel to arrest Baruch the scribe and Jeremiah the prophet. But the LORD had hidden them.

27 After the king burned the scroll containing the words that Baruch had written at Jeremiah's dictation, the word of the LORD came to Jeremiah: 28 'Take another scroll and write on it all the words that were on the first scroll, which Jehoiakim king of Judah burned up. 29 Also tell Jehoiakim king of Judah, "This is what the LORD says: you burned that scroll and said, 'Why did you write on it that the king of Babylon would certainly come and destroy this land and wipe from it both man and beast?' 30 Therefore this is what the LORD says about Jehoiakim king of Judah: he will have no one to sit on the throne of David; his body will be thrown out and exposed to the heat by day and the frost by night. 31 I will punish him and his children and his attendants for their wickedness; I will bring on them and those living in Jerusalem and the people of Judah every disaster I pronounced against them, because they have not listened." '

32 So Jeremiah took another scroll and gave it to the scribe Baruch son of Neriah, and as Jeremiah dictated, Baruch wrote on it all the words of the scroll that Jehoiakim king of Judah had burned in the fire. And many similar words were added to them.

Jeremiah in prison

37 Zedekiah son of Josiah was made king of Judah by Nebuchadnezzar king of Babylon; he reigned in place of Jehoiachin[a] son of Jehoiakim. 2 Neither he nor his attendants nor the people of the land paid any attention to the words

the LORD had spoken through Jeremiah the prophet.

3 King Zedekiah, however, sent Jehukal son of Shelemiah with the priest Zephaniah son of Maaseiah to Jeremiah the prophet with this message: 'Please pray to the LORD our God for us.'

4 Now Jeremiah was free to come and go among the people, for he had not yet been put in prison. 5 Pharaoh's army had marched out of Egypt, and when the Babylonians[b] who were besieging Jerusalem heard the report about them, they withdrew from Jerusalem.

6 Then the word of the LORD came to Jeremiah the prophet: 7 'This is what the LORD, the God of Israel, says: tell the king of Judah, who sent you to enquire of me, "Pharaoh's army, which has marched out to support you, will go back to its own land, to Egypt. 8 Then the Babylonians will return and attack this city; they will capture it and burn it down."

9 'This is what the LORD says: do not deceive yourselves, thinking, "The Babylonians will surely leave us." They will not! 10 Even if you were to defeat the entire Babylonian[c] army that is attacking you and only wounded men were left in their tents, they would come out and burn this city down.'

11 After the Babylonian army had withdrawn from Jerusalem because of Pharaoh's army, 12 Jeremiah started to leave the city to go to the territory of Benjamin to get his share of the property among the people there. 13 But when he reached the Benjamin Gate, the captain of the guard, whose name was Irijah son of Shelemiah, the son of Hananiah, arrested him and said, 'You are deserting to the Babylonians!'

14 'That's not true!' Jeremiah said. 'I am not deserting to the Babylonians.' But Irijah would not listen to him; instead, he arrested Jeremiah and brought him to the officials. 15 They were angry with Jeremiah and had him beaten and imprisoned in the house of Jonathan the secretary, which they had made into a prison.

16 Jeremiah was put into a vaulted cell

in a dungeon, where he remained a long time. ¹⁷Then King Zedekiah sent for him and had him brought to the palace, where he asked him privately, 'Is there any word from the LORD?'

'Yes,' Jeremiah replied, 'you will be delivered into the hands of the king of Babylon.'

¹⁸Then Jeremiah said to King Zedekiah, 'What crime have I committed against you or your attendants or this people, that you have put me in prison? ¹⁹Where are your prophets who prophesied to you, "The king of Babylon will not attack you or this land"? ²⁰But now, my lord the king, please listen. Let me bring my petition before you: do not send me back to the house of Jonathan the secretary, or I shall die there.'

²¹King Zedekiah then gave orders for Jeremiah to be placed in the courtyard of the guard and given a loaf of bread from the street of the bakers each day until all the bread in the city was gone. So Jeremiah remained in the courtyard of the guard.

Jeremiah thrown into a cistern

38 Shephatiah son of Mattan, Gedaliah son of Pashhur, Jehukal[a] son of Shelemiah, and Pashhur son of Malkijah heard what Jeremiah was telling all the people when he said, ²'This is what the LORD says: "Whoever stays in this city will die by the sword, famine or plague, but whoever goes over to the Babylonians[b] will live. They will escape with their lives; they will live." ³And this is what the LORD says: "This city will certainly be given into the hands of the army of the king of Babylon, who will capture it."'

⁴Then the officials said to the king, 'This man should be put to death. He is discouraging the soldiers who are left in this city, as well as all the people, by the things he is saying to them. This man is not seeking the good of these people but their ruin.'

⁵'He is in your hands,' King Zedekiah answered. 'The king can do nothing to oppose you.'

⁶So they took Jeremiah and put him into the cistern of Malkijah, the king's son, which was in the courtyard of the guard. They lowered Jeremiah by ropes into the cistern; it had no water in it, only mud, and Jeremiah sank down into the mud.

⁷But Ebed-Melek, a Cushite,[c] an official[d] in the royal palace, heard that they had put Jeremiah into the cistern. While the king was sitting in the Benjamin Gate, ⁸Ebed-Melek went out of the palace and said to him, ⁹'My lord the king, these men have acted wickedly in all they have done to Jeremiah the prophet. They have thrown him into a cistern, where he will starve to death when there is no longer any bread in the city.'

¹⁰Then the king commanded Ebed-Melek the Cushite, 'Take thirty men from here with you and lift Jeremiah the prophet out of the cistern before he dies.'

¹¹So Ebed-Melek took the men with him and went to a room under the treasury in the palace. He took some old rags and worn-out clothes from there and let them down with ropes to Jeremiah in the cistern. ¹²Ebed-Melek the Cushite said to Jeremiah, 'Put these old rags and worn-out clothes under your arms to pad the ropes.' Jeremiah did so, ¹³and they pulled him up with the ropes and lifted him out of the cistern. And Jeremiah remained in the courtyard of the guard.

Zedekiah questions Jeremiah again

¹⁴Then King Zedekiah sent for Jeremiah the prophet and had him brought to the third entrance to the temple of the LORD. 'I am going to ask you something,' the king said to Jeremiah. 'Do not hide anything from me.'

¹⁵Jeremiah said to Zedekiah, 'If I give you an answer, will you not kill me? Even if I did give you counsel, you would not listen to me.'

¹⁶But King Zedekiah swore this oath secretly to Jeremiah: 'As surely as the LORD lives, who has given us breath, I will neither kill you nor hand you over to those who want to kill you.'

---

a 1 Hebrew *Jukal*, a variant of *Jehukal*
b 2 Or *Chaldeans*; also in verses 18, 19 and 23

c 7 Probably from the upper Nile region
d 7 Or *a eunuch*

17 Then Jeremiah said to Zedekiah, 'This is what the LORD God Almighty, the God of Israel, says: "If you surrender to the officers of the king of Babylon, your life will be spared and this city will not be burned down; you and your family will live. **18** But if you will not surrender to the officers of the king of Babylon, this city will be given into the hands of the Babylonians and they will burn it down; you yourself will not escape from them." '

19 King Zedekiah said to Jeremiah, 'I am afraid of the Jews who have gone over to the Babylonians, for the Babylonians may hand me over to them and they will ill-treat me.'

20 'They will not hand you over,' Jeremiah replied. 'Obey the LORD by doing what I tell you. Then it will go well with you, and your life will be spared. **21** But if you refuse to surrender, this is what the LORD has revealed to me: **22** all the women left in the palace of the king of Judah will be brought out to the officials of the king of Babylon. Those women will say to you:

' "They misled you and overcame you –
those trusted friends of yours.
Your feet are sunk in the mud;
your friends have deserted you."

23 'All your wives and children will be brought out to the Babylonians. You yourself will not escape from their hands but will be captured by the king of Babylon; and this city will*e* be burned down.'

24 Then Zedekiah said to Jeremiah, 'Do not let anyone know about this conversation, or you may die. **25** If the officials hear that I talked with you, and they come to you and say, "Tell us what you said to the king and what the king said to you; do not hide it from us or we will kill you," **26** then tell them, "I was pleading with the king not to send me back to Jonathan's house to die there." '

27 All the officials did come to Jeremiah and question him, and he told them everything the king had ordered him to say. So

they said no more to him, for no one had heard his conversation with the king.

28 And Jeremiah remained in the courtyard of the guard until the day Jerusalem was captured.

The fall of Jerusalem

39 This is how Jerusalem was taken: **1** In the ninth year of Zedekiah king of Judah, in the tenth month, Nebuchadnezzar king of Babylon marched against Jerusalem with his whole army and laid siege to it. **2** And on the ninth day of the fourth month of Zedekiah's eleventh year, the city wall was broken through. **3** Then all the officials of the king of Babylon came and took seats in the Middle Gate: Nergal-Sharezer of Samgar, Nebo-Sarsekim a chief officer, Nergal-Sharezer a high official and all the other officials of the king of Babylon. **4** When Zedekiah king of Judah and all the soldiers saw them, they fled; they left the city at night by way of the king's garden, through the gate between the two walls, and headed towards the Arabah.*a*

5 But the Babylonian*b* army pursued them and overtook Zedekiah in the plains of Jericho. They captured him and took him to Nebuchadnezzar king of Babylon at Riblah in the land of Hamath, where he pronounced sentence on him. **6** There at Riblah the king of Babylon slaughtered the sons of Zedekiah before his eyes and also killed all the nobles of Judah. **7** Then he put out Zedekiah's eyes and bound him with bronze shackles to take him to Babylon.

8 The Babylonians*c* set fire to the royal palace and the houses of the people and broke down the walls of Jerusalem. **9** Nebuzaradan commander of the imperial guard carried into exile to Babylon the people who remained in the city, along with those who had gone over to him, and the rest of the people. **10** But Nebuzaradan the commander of the guard left behind in the land of Judah some of the poor people, who owned nothing; and at that time he gave them vineyards and fields.

e 23 Or *and you will cause this city to*
a 4 Or *the Jordan Valley*
b 5 Or *Chaldean*
c 8 Or *Chaldeans*

11 Now Nebuchadnezzar king of Babylon had given these orders about Jeremiah through Nebuzaradan commander of the imperial guard: 12 'Take him and look after him; don't harm him but do for him whatever he asks.' 13 So Nebuzaradan the commander of the guard, Nebushazban a chief officer, Nergal-Sharezer a high official and all the other officers of the king of Babylon 14 sent and had Jeremiah taken out of the courtyard of the guard. They handed him over to Gedaliah son of Ahikam, the son of Shaphan, to take him back to his home. So he remained among his own people.

YOU WHAT?
WEIRDEST CREATURES IN THE BIBLE

○ **EZEKIEL'S WINGED CREATURES**
Ezekiel 1:4–14
○ **LEVIATHAN, THE SEA MONSTER**
Isaiah 27:1
○ **FOUR BEASTS IN DANIEL**
Daniel 7:3–10
○ **HORSE-SIZED LOCUSTS … WITH HAIR**
Revelation 9:7–10
○ **SEVEN-HEADED BEAST WITH TEN HORNS**
Revelation 13:1–3

15 While Jeremiah had been confined in the courtyard of the guard, the word of the LORD came to him: 16 'Go and tell Ebed-Melek the Cushite, "This is what the LORD Almighty, the God of Israel, says: I am about to fulfil my words against this city – words concerning disaster, not prosperity. At that time they will be fulfilled before your eyes. 17 But I will rescue you on that day, declares the LORD; you will not be given into the hands of those you fear. 18 I

will save you; you will not fall by the sword but will escape with your life, because you trust in me, declares the LORD."'

Jeremiah freed

40 The word came to Jeremiah from the LORD after Nebuzaradan commander of the imperial guard had released him at Ramah. He had found Jeremiah bound in chains among all the captives from Jerusalem and Judah who were being carried into exile to Babylon. 2 When the commander of the guard found Jeremiah, he said to him, 'The LORD your God decreed this disaster for this place. 3 And now the LORD has brought it about; he has done just as he said he would. All this happened because you people sinned against the LORD and did not obey him. 4 But today I am freeing you from the chains on your wrists. Come with me to Babylon, if you like, and I will look after you; but if you do not want to, then don't come. Look, the whole country lies before you; go wherever you please.' 5 However, before Jeremiah turned to go,*a* Nebuzaradan added, 'Go back to Gedaliah son of Ahikam, the son of Shaphan, whom the king of Babylon has appointed over the towns of Judah, and live with him among the people, or go anywhere else you please.'

Then the commander gave him provisions and a present and let him go. 6 So Jeremiah went to Gedaliah son of Ahikam at Mizpah and stayed with him among the people who were left behind in the land.

Gedaliah assassinated

7 When all the army officers and their men who were still in the open country heard that the king of Babylon had appointed Gedaliah son of Ahikam as governor over the land and had put him in charge of the men, women and children who were the poorest in the land and who had not been carried into exile to Babylon, 8 they came to Gedaliah at Mizpah – Ishmael son of Nethaniah, Johanan and Jonathan the sons of Kareah, Seraiah son of Tanhumeth, the sons of Ephai the Netophathite, and

---

a 5 Or Jeremiah answered

Jaazaniah[b] the son of the Maakathite, and their men. 9 Gedaliah son of Ahikam, the son of Shaphan, took an oath to reassure them and their men. 'Do not be afraid to serve the Babylonians,'[c] he said. 'Settle down in the land and serve the king of Babylon, and it will go well with you. 10 I myself will stay in Mizpah to represent you before the Babylonians who come to us, but you are to harvest the wine, summer fruit and olive oil, and put them in your storage jars, and live in the towns you have taken over.'

11 When all the Jews in Moab, Ammon, Edom and all the other countries heard that the king of Babylon had left a remnant in Judah and had appointed Gedaliah son of Ahikam, the son of Shaphan, as governor over them, 12 they all came back to the land of Judah, to Gedaliah at Mizpah, from all the countries where they had been scattered. And they harvested an abundance of wine and summer fruit.

13 Johanan son of Kareah and all the army officers still in the open country came to Gedaliah at Mizpah 14 and said to him, 'Don't you know that Baalis king of the Ammonites has sent Ishmael son of Nethaniah to take your life?' But Gedaliah son of Ahikam did not believe them.

15 Then Johanan son of Kareah said privately to Gedaliah in Mizpah, 'Let me go and kill Ishmael son of Nethaniah, and no one will know it. Why should he take your life and cause all the Jews who are gathered around you to be scattered and the remnant of Judah to perish?'

16 But Gedaliah son of Ahikam said to Johanan son of Kareah, 'Don't do such a thing! What you are saying about Ishmael is not true.'

41 In the seventh month Ishmael son of Nethaniah, the son of Elishama, who was of royal blood and had been one of the king's officers, came with ten men to Gedaliah son of Ahikam at Mizpah. While they were eating together there, 2 Ishmael son of Nethaniah and the ten men who were with him got up and struck down Gedaliah son of Ahikam, the son of

Shaphan, with the sword, killing the one whom the king of Babylon had appointed as governor over the land. 3 Ishmael also killed all the men of Judah who were with Gedaliah at Mizpah, as well as the Babylonian[a] soldiers who were there.

4 The day after Gedaliah's assassination, before anyone knew about it, 5 eighty men who had shaved off their beards, torn their clothes and cut themselves came from Shechem, Shiloh and Samaria, bringing grain offerings and incense with them to the house of the LORD. 6 Ishmael son of Nethaniah went out from Mizpah to meet them, weeping as he went. When he met them, he said, 'Come to Gedaliah son of Ahikam.' 7 When they went into the city, Ishmael son of Nethaniah and the men who were with him slaughtered them and threw them into a cistern. 8 But ten of them said to Ishmael, 'Don't kill us! We have wheat and barley, olive oil and honey, hidden in a field.' So he let them alone and did not kill them with the others. 9 Now the cistern where he threw all the bodies of the men he had killed along with Gedaliah was the one King Asa had made as part of his defence against Baasha king of Israel. Ishmael son of Nethaniah filled it with the dead.

10 Ishmael made captives of all the rest of the people who were in Mizpah – the king's daughters along with all the others who were left there, over whom Nebuzaradan commander of the imperial guard had appointed Gedaliah son of Ahikam. Ishmael son of Nethaniah took them captive and set out to cross over to the Ammonites.

11 When Johanan son of Kareah and all the army officers who were with him heard about all the crimes Ishmael son of Nethaniah had committed, 12 they took all their men and went to fight Ishmael son of Nethaniah. They caught up with him near the great pool in Gibeon. 13 When all the people Ishmael had with him saw Johanan son of Kareah and the army officers who were with him, they were glad. 14 All the people Ishmael had taken captive at

---

b 8 Hebrew *Jezaniah*, a variant of *Jaazaniah*
c 9 Or *Chaldeans*; also in verse 10

a 3 Or *Chaldean*

Mizpah turned and went over to Johanan son of Kareah. ¹⁵But Ishmael son of Nethaniah and eight of his men escaped from Johanan and fled to the Ammonites.

Flight to Egypt

¹⁶Then Johanan son of Kareah and all the army officers who were with him led away all the people of Mizpah who had survived, whom Johanan had recovered from Ishmael son of Nethaniah after Ishmael had assassinated Gedaliah son of Ahikam – the soldiers, women, children and court officials he had recovered from Gibeon. ¹⁷And they went on, stopping at Geruth Kimham near Bethlehem on their way to Egypt ¹⁸to escape the Babylonians.ᵇ They were afraid of them because Ishmael son of Nethaniah had killed Gedaliah son of Ahikam, whom the king of Babylon had appointed as governor over the land.

42 Then all the army officers, including Johanan son of Kareah and Jezaniahᵃ son of Hoshaiah, and all the people from the least to the greatest approached ²Jeremiah the prophet and said to him, 'Please hear our petition and pray to the LORD your God for this entire remnant. For as you now see, though we were once many, now only a few are left. ³Pray that the LORD your God will tell us where we should go and what we should do.'

⁴'I have heard you,' replied Jeremiah the prophet. 'I will certainly pray to the LORD your God as you have requested; I will tell you everything the LORD says and will keep nothing back from you.'

⁵Then they said to Jeremiah, 'May the LORD be a true and faithful witness against us if we do not act in accordance with everything the LORD your God sends you to tell us. ⁶Whether it is favourable or unfavourable, we will obey the LORD our God, to whom we are sending you, so that it will go well with us, for we will obey the LORD our God.'

⁷Ten days later the word of the LORD came to Jeremiah. ⁸So he called together Johanan son of Kareah and all the army officers who were with him and all the people from the least to the greatest. ⁹He said to them, 'This is what the LORD, the God of Israel, to whom you sent me to present your petition, says: ¹⁰"If you stay in this land, I will build you up and not tear you down; I will plant you and not uproot you, for I have relented concerning the disaster I have inflicted on you. ¹¹Do not be afraid of the king of Babylon, whom you now fear. Do not be afraid of him, declares the LORD, for I am with you and will save you and deliver you from his hands. ¹²I will show you compassion so that he will have compassion on you and restore you to your land."

¹³'However, if you say, "We will not stay in this land," and so disobey the LORD your God, ¹⁴and if you say, "No, we will go and live in Egypt, where we will not see war or hear the trumpet or be hungry for bread," ¹⁵then hear the word of the LORD, you remnant of Judah. This is what the LORD Almighty, the God of Israel, says: "If you are determined to go to Egypt and you do go to settle there, ¹⁶then the sword you fear will overtake you there, and the famine you dread will follow you into Egypt, and there you will die. ¹⁷Indeed, all who are determined to go to Egypt to settle there will die by the sword, famine and plague; not one of them will survive or escape the disaster I will bring on them." ¹⁸This is what the LORD Almighty, the God of Israel, says: "As my anger and wrath have been poured out on those who lived in Jerusalem, so will my wrath be poured out on you when you go to Egypt. You will be a curseᵇ and an object of horror, a curseᵇ and an object of reproach; you will never see this place again."

¹⁹'Remnant of Judah, the LORD has told you, "Do not go to Egypt." Be sure of this: I warn you today ²⁰that you made a fatal mistake when you sent me to the LORD your God and said, "Pray to the LORD our God for us; tell us everything he says and we will do it." ²¹I have told you today, but

---

ᵇ 18 Or *Chaldeans*
ᵃ 1 Hebrew; Septuagint (see also 43:2) *Azariah*

ᵇ 18 That is, your name will be used in cursing (see 29:22); or, others will see that you are cursed.

you still have not obeyed the LORD your God in all he sent me to tell you. 22 So now, be sure of this: you will die by the sword, famine and plague in the place where you want to go to settle.'

43 When Jeremiah had finished telling the people all the words of the LORD their God – everything the LORD had sent him to tell them – 2 Azariah son of Hoshaiah and Johanan son of Kareah and all the arrogant men said to Jeremiah, 'You are lying! The LORD our God has not sent you to say, "You must not go to Egypt to settle there." 3 But Baruch son of Neriah is inciting you against us to hand us over to the Babylonians, *a* so that they may kill us or carry us into exile to Babylon.'

4 So Johanan son of Kareah and all the army officers and all the people disobeyed the LORD's command to stay in the land of Judah. 5 Instead, Johanan son of Kareah and all the army officers led away all the remnant of Judah who had come back to live in the land of Judah from all the nations where they had been scattered. 6 They also led away all those whom Nebuzaradan commander of the imperial guard had left with Gedaliah son of Ahikam, the son of Shaphan – the men, the women, the children and the king's daughters. And they took Jeremiah the prophet and Baruch son of Neriah along with them. 7 So they entered Egypt in disobedience to the LORD and went as far as Tahpanhes.

8 In Tahpanhes the word of the LORD came to Jeremiah: 9 'While the Jews are watching, take some large stones with you and bury them in clay in the brick pavement at the entrance to Pharaoh's palace in Tahpanhes. 10 Then say to them, "This is what the LORD Almighty, the God of Israel, says: I will send for my servant Nebuchadnezzar king of Babylon, and I will set his throne over these stones I have buried here; he will spread his royal canopy above them. 11 He will come and attack Egypt, bringing death to those destined for death, captivity to those destined for captivity, and the sword to those destined for the

sword. 12 He will set fire to the temples of the gods of Egypt; he will burn their temples and take their gods captive. As a shepherd picks his garment clean of lice, so he will pick Egypt clean and depart. 13 There in the temple of the sun *b* in Egypt he will demolish the sacred pillars and will burn down the temples of the gods of Egypt." '

Disaster because of idolatry

44 This word came to Jeremiah concerning all the Jews living in Lower Egypt – in Migdol, Tahpanhes and Memphis – and in Upper Egypt: 2 'This is what the LORD Almighty, the God of Israel, says: you saw the great disaster I brought on Jerusalem and on all the towns of Judah. Today they lie deserted and in ruins 3 because of the evil they have done. They aroused my anger by burning incense to and worshipping other gods that neither they nor you nor your ancestors ever knew. 4 Again and again I sent my servants the prophets, who said, "Do not do this detestable thing that I hate!" 5 But they did not listen or pay attention; they did not turn from their wickedness or stop burning incense to other gods. 6 Therefore, my fierce anger was poured out; it raged against the towns of Judah and the streets of Jerusalem and made them the desolate ruins they are today.

7 'Now this is what the LORD God Almighty, the God of Israel, says: why bring such great disaster on yourselves by cutting off from Judah the men and women, the children and infants, and so leave yourselves without a remnant? 8 Why arouse my anger with what your hands have made, burning incense to other gods in Egypt, where you have come to live? You will destroy yourselves and make yourselves a curse *a* and an object of reproach among all the nations on earth. 9 Have you forgotten the wickedness committed by your ancestors and by the kings and queens of Judah and the wickedness

---

b 13 Or in Heliopolis
a 8 That is, your name will be used in cursing (see 29:22); or, others will see that you are cursed; also in verse 12; similarly in verse 22.

a 3 Or Chaldeans

committed by you and your wives in the land of Judah and the streets of Jerusalem? ¹⁰To this day they have not humbled themselves or shown reverence, nor have they followed my law and the decrees I set before you and your ancestors.

¹¹'Therefore this is what the LORD Almighty, the God of Israel, says: I am determined to bring disaster on you and to destroy all Judah. ¹²I will take away the remnant of Judah who were determined to go to Egypt to settle there. They will all perish in Egypt; they will fall by the sword or die from famine. From the least to the greatest, they will die by sword or famine. They will become a curse and an object of horror, a curse and an object of reproach. ¹³I will punish those who live in Egypt with the sword, famine and plague, as I punished Jerusalem. ¹⁴None of the remnant of Judah who have gone to live in Egypt will escape or survive to return to the land of Judah, to which they long to return and live; none will return except a few fugitives.'

¹⁵Then all the men who knew that their wives were burning incense to other gods, along with all the women who were present – a large assembly – and all the people living in Lower and Upper Egypt, said to Jeremiah, ¹⁶'We will not listen to the message you have spoken to us in the name of the LORD! ¹⁷We will certainly do everything we said we would: we will burn incense to the Queen of Heaven and will pour out drink offerings to her just as we and our ancestors, our kings and our officials did in the towns of Judah and in the streets of Jerusalem. At that time we had plenty of food and were well off and suffered no harm. ¹⁸But ever since we stopped burning incense to the Queen of Heaven and pouring out drink offerings to her, we have had nothing and have been perishing by sword and famine.'

¹⁹The women added, 'When we burned incense to the Queen of Heaven and poured out drink offerings to her, did not our husbands know that we were making cakes impressed with her image and pouring out drink offerings to her?'

²⁰Then Jeremiah said to all the people, both men and women, who were answering him, ²¹'Did not the LORD remember and call to mind the incense burned in the towns of Judah and the streets of Jerusalem by you and your ancestors, your kings and your officials and the people of the land? ²²When the LORD could no longer endure your wicked actions and the detestable things you did, your land became a curse and a desolate waste without inhabitants, as it is today. ²³Because you have burned incense and have sinned against the LORD and have not obeyed him or followed his law or his decrees or his stipulations, this disaster has come upon you, as you now see.'

²⁴Then Jeremiah said to all the people, including the women, 'Hear the word of the LORD, all you people of Judah in Egypt. ²⁵This is what the LORD Almighty, the God of Israel, says: you and your wives have done what you said you would do when you promised, "We will certainly carry out the vows we made to burn incense and pour out drink offerings to the Queen of Heaven."

'Go ahead then, do what you promised! Keep your vows! ²⁶But hear the word of the LORD, all you Jews living in Egypt: "I swear by my great name," says the LORD, "that no one from Judah living anywhere in Egypt shall ever again invoke my name or swear, 'As surely as the Sovereign LORD lives.' ²⁷For I am watching over them for harm, not for good; the Jews in Egypt will perish by sword and famine until they are all destroyed. ²⁸Those who escape the sword and return to the land of Judah from Egypt will be very few. Then the whole remnant of Judah who came to live in Egypt will know whose word will stand – mine or theirs.

²⁹'"This will be the sign to you that I will punish you in this place," declares the LORD, "so that you will know that my threats of harm against you will surely stand." ³⁰This is what the LORD says: "I am going to deliver Pharaoh Hophra king of Egypt into the hands of his enemies who want to kill him, just as I gave Zedekiah king of Judah into the hands of Nebuchadnezzar king of Babylon, the enemy who wanted to kill him."'

A message to Baruch

45 When Baruch son of Neriah wrote on a scroll the words Jeremiah the prophet dictated in the fourth year of Jehoiakim son of Josiah king of Judah, Jeremiah said this to Baruch: ²'This is what the LORD, the God of Israel, says to you, Baruch: ³You said, "Woe to me! The LORD has added sorrow to my pain; I am worn out with groaning and find no rest." ⁴But the LORD has told me to say to you, "This is what the LORD says: I will overthrow what I have built and uproot what I have planted, throughout the earth. ⁵Should you then seek great things for yourself? Do not seek them. For I will bring disaster on all people, declares the LORD, but wherever you go I will let you escape with your life."'

A message about Egypt

46 This is the word of the LORD that came to Jeremiah the prophet concerning the nations:

²Concerning Egypt:

This is the message against the army of Pharaoh Necho king of Egypt, which was defeated at Carchemish on the River Euphrates by Nebuchadnezzar king of Babylon in the fourth year of Jehoiakim son of Josiah king of Judah:

³'Prepare your shields, both large and small,
    and march out for battle!
⁴Harness the horses,
    mount the steeds!
Take your positions
    with helmets on!
Polish your spears,
    put on your armour!
⁵What do I see?
    They are terrified,
    they are retreating,
    their warriors are defeated.
They flee in haste
    without looking back,
    and there is terror on every side,'
        declares the LORD.
⁶'The swift cannot flee
    nor the strong escape.

In the north by the River Euphrates
    they stumble and fall.

⁷'Who is this that rises like the Nile,
    like rivers of surging waters?
⁸Egypt rises like the Nile,
    like rivers of surging waters.
She says, "I will rise and cover the earth;
    I will destroy cities and their people."
⁹Charge, you horses!
    Drive furiously, you charioteers!
March on, you warriors – men of Cush*a*
    and Put who carry shields,
    men of Lydia who draw the bow.
¹⁰But that day belongs to the Lord, the
    LORD Almighty –
    a day of vengeance, for vengeance on
    his foes.
The sword will devour till it is satisfied,
    till it has quenched its thirst with
    blood.
For the Lord, the LORD Almighty, will
    offer sacrifice
    in the land of the north by the River
    Euphrates.

¹¹'Go up to Gilead and get balm,
    Virgin Daughter Egypt.
But you try many medicines in vain;
    there is no healing for you.
¹²The nations will hear of your shame;
    your cries will fill the earth.
One warrior will stumble over another;
    both will fall down together.'

¹³This is the message the LORD spoke to Jeremiah the prophet about the coming of Nebuchadnezzar king of Babylon to attack Egypt:

¹⁴'Announce this in Egypt, and proclaim
    it in Migdol;
    proclaim it also in Memphis and
    Tahpanhes:
"Take your positions and get ready,
    for the sword devours those around
    you."
¹⁵Why will your warriors be laid low?
    They cannot stand, for the LORD will
    push them down.

---

a 9 That is, the upper Nile region

16 They will stumble repeatedly;
  they will fall over each other.
They will say, "Get up, let us go back
  to our own people and our native
    lands,
  away from the sword of the
    oppressor."
17 There they will exclaim,
  "Pharaoh king of Egypt is only a loud
    noise;
  he has missed his opportunity."

18 'As surely as I live,' declares the King,
  whose name is the LORD Almighty,
  'one will come who is like Tabor among
    the mountains,
  like Carmel by the sea.
19 Pack your belongings for exile,
  you who live in Egypt,
for Memphis will be laid waste
  and lie in ruins without inhabitant.

20 'Egypt is a beautiful heifer,
  but a gadfly is coming
    against her from the north.
21 The mercenaries in her ranks
  are like fattened calves.
They too will turn and flee together,
  they will not stand their ground,
for the day of disaster is coming upon
    them,
  the time for them to be punished.
22 Egypt will hiss like a fleeing serpent
  as the enemy advances in force;
they will come against her with axes,
  like men who cut down trees.
23 They will chop down her forest,'
                declares the LORD,
  'dense though it be.
They are more numerous than locusts,
  they cannot be counted.
24 Daughter Egypt will be put to shame,
  given into the hands of the people of
    the north.'

25 The LORD Almighty, the God of Israel,
says: 'I am about to bring punishment
on Amon god of Thebes, on Pharaoh, on
Egypt and her gods and her kings, and on
those who rely on Pharaoh. 26 I will give
them into the hands of those who want
to kill them – Nebuchadnezzar king of
Babylon and his officers. Later, however,
Egypt will be inhabited as in times past,'
declares the LORD.

27 'Do not be afraid, Jacob my servant;
  do not be dismayed, Israel.
I will surely save you out of a distant
    place,
  your descendants from the land of
    their exile.
Jacob will again have peace and security,
  and no one will make him afraid.
28 Do not be afraid, Jacob my servant,
  for I am with you,' declares the LORD.
'Though I completely destroy all the
    nations
  among which I scatter you,
  I will not completely destroy you.
I will discipline you but only in due
    measure;
  I will not let you go entirely
    unpunished.'

A message about the Philistines

47 This is the word of the LORD that
came to Jeremiah the prophet
concerning the Philistines before Pharaoh attacked Gaza:

2 This is what the LORD says:

'See how the waters are rising in the
    north;
  they will become an overflowing
    torrent.
They will overflow the land and
    everything in it,
  the towns and those who live in
    them.
The people will cry out;
  all who dwell in the land will wail
3 at the sound of the hooves of galloping
    steeds,
  at the noise of enemy chariots
  and the rumble of their wheels.
Parents will not turn to help their
    children;
  their hands will hang limp.
4 For the day has come
  to destroy all the Philistines
and to remove all survivors
  who could help Tyre and Sidon.

The LORD is about to destroy the
    Philistines,
  the remnant from the coasts of
    Caphtor.*a*
5 Gaza will shave her head in mourning;
  Ashkelon will be silenced.
You remnant on the plain,
  how long will you cut yourselves?

6 ' "Alas, sword of the LORD,
  how long till you rest?
Return to your sheath;
  cease and be still."
7 But how can it rest
  when the LORD has commanded it,
when he has ordered it
  to attack Ashkelon and the coast?'

A message about Moab

48 Concerning Moab:

This is what the LORD Almighty, the God
of Israel, says:

'Woe to Nebo, for it will be ruined.
  Kiriathaim will be disgraced and
    captured;
  the stronghold*a* will be disgraced and
    shattered.
2 Moab will be praised no more;
  in Heshbon*b* people will plot her
    downfall:
  "Come, let us put an end to that
    nation."
You, the people of Madmen,*c* will also
    be silenced;
  the sword will pursue you.
3 Cries of anguish arise from Horonaim,
  cries of great havoc and destruction.
4 Moab will be broken;
  her little ones will cry out.*d*
5 They go up the hill to Luhith,
  weeping bitterly as they go;
on the road down to Horonaim

anguished cries over the destruction
  are heard.
6 Flee! Run for your lives;
  become like a bush*e* in the desert.
7 Since you trust in your deeds and riches,
  you too will be taken captive,
and Chemosh will go into exile,
  together with his priests and
    officials.
8 The destroyer will come against every
    town,
  and not a town will escape.
The valley will be ruined
  and the plateau destroyed,
because the LORD has spoken.
9 Put salt on Moab,
  for she will be laid waste;*f*
her towns will become desolate,
  with no one to live in them.

10 'A curse on anyone who is lax in doing
    the LORD's work!
  A curse on anyone who keeps their
    sword from bloodshed!

11 'Moab has been at rest from youth,
  like wine left on its dregs,
not poured from one jar to another –
  she has not gone into exile.
So she tastes as she did,
  and her aroma is unchanged.
12 But days are coming,'
  declares the LORD,
'when I will send men who pour from
    pitchers,
  and they will pour her out;
they will empty her pitchers
  and smash her jars.
13 Then Moab will be ashamed of
    Chemosh,
  as Israel was ashamed
when they trusted in Bethel.

14 'How can you say, "We are warriors,
    men valiant in battle"?
15 Moab will be destroyed and her towns
    invaded;
  her finest young men will go down in
    the slaughter,'

---

a 4 That is, Crete
a 1 Or *captured;* / *Misgab*
b 2 The Hebrew for *Heshbon* sounds like the Hebrew
for *plot.*
c 2 The name of the Moabite town Madmen sounds
like the Hebrew for *be silenced.*
d 4 Hebrew; Septuagint / *proclaim it to Zoar*

e 6 Or *like Aroer*
f 9 Or *Give wings to Moab,* / *for she will fly away*

declares the King, whose name is the
LORD Almighty.
16 'The fall of Moab is at hand;
   her calamity will come quickly.
17 Mourn for her, all who live around her,
   all who know her fame;
   say, "How broken is the mighty sceptre,
   how broken the glorious staff!"

18 'Come down from your glory
   and sit on the parched ground,
   you inhabitants of Daughter Dibon,
for the one who destroys Moab
   will come up against you
   and ruin your fortified cities.
19 Stand by the road and watch,
   you who live in Aroer.
Ask the man fleeing and the woman
   escaping,
   ask them, "What has happened?"
20 Moab is disgraced, for she is shattered.
   Wail and cry out!
Announce by the Arnon
   that Moab is destroyed.
21 Judgment has come to the plateau –
   to Holon, Jahzah and Mephaath,
22   to Dibon, Nebo and Beth
      Diblathaim,
23   to Kiriathaim, Beth Gamul and Beth
      Meon,
24   to Kerioth and Bozrah –
   to all the towns of Moab, far and near.
25 Moab's horn*g* is cut off;
   her arm is broken,'
                declares the LORD.

26 'Make her drunk,
   for she has defied the LORD.
Let Moab wallow in her vomit;
   let her be an object of ridicule.
27 Was not Israel the object of your
      ridicule?
Was she caught among thieves,
   that you shake your head in scorn
   whenever you speak of her?
28 Abandon your towns and dwell among
      the rocks,
   you who live in Moab.
Be like a dove that makes its nest
   at the mouth of a cave.

29 'We have heard of Moab's pride –
   how great is her arrogance! –
of her insolence, her pride, her conceit
   and the haughtiness of her heart.
30 I know her insolence but it is futile,'
                declares the LORD,
   'and her boasts accomplish nothing.
31 Therefore I wail over Moab,
   for all Moab I cry out,
   I moan for the people of Kir
      Hareseth.
32 I weep for you, as Jazer weeps,
   you vines of Sibmah.
Your branches spread as far as the sea*h*;
   they reached as far as*i* Jazer.
The destroyer has fallen
   on your ripened fruit and grapes.
33 Joy and gladness are gone
   from the orchards and fields of
      Moab.
I have stopped the flow of wine from
      the presses;
   no one treads them with shouts of
      joy.
Although there are shouts,
   they are not shouts of joy.

34 'The sound of their cry rises
   from Heshbon to Elealeh and Jahaz,
from Zoar as far as Horonaim and
      Eglath Shelishiyah,
   for even the waters of Nimrim are
      dried up.
35 In Moab I will put an end
   to those who make offerings on the
      high places
   and burn incense to their gods,'
                declares the LORD.
36 'So my heart laments for Moab like the
      music of a pipe;
   it laments like a pipe for the people
      of Kir Hareseth.
The wealth they acquired is gone.
37 Every head is shaved
   and every beard cut off;
   every hand is slashed
      and every waist is covered with
      sackcloth.

---

g 25 Horn here symbolises strength.

h 32 Probably the Dead Sea
i 32 Two Hebrew manuscripts and Septuagint; most
Hebrew manuscripts as far as the Sea of

38 On all the roofs in Moab
     and in the public squares
  there is nothing but mourning,
     for I have broken Moab
  like a jar that no one wants,'
               declares the LORD.
39 'How shattered she is! How they wail!
     How Moab turns her back in shame!
  Moab has become an object of ridicule,
     an object of horror to all those
       around her.'

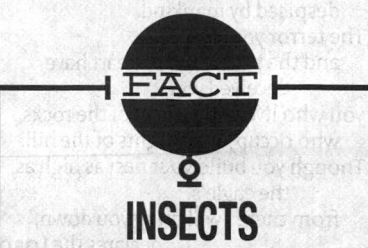

INSECTS

Old Testament law forbids the eating of
insects, with one exception: any insect
with jointed legs. That means that for a
Jew it was OK to eat locusts, crickets or
grasshoppers. It's possible this was allowed
because locusts caused famine by eating all
the crops. So poor Jews would have nothing
to eat *but* locusts. Yum.

40 This is what the LORD says:

  'Look! An eagle is swooping down,
     spreading its wings over Moab.
41 Kerioth *j* will be captured
     and the strongholds taken.
  In that day the hearts of Moab's
     warriors
       will be like the heart of a woman in
         labour.
42 Moab will be destroyed as a nation
     because she defied the LORD.
43 Terror and pit and snare await you,
     you people of Moab,'
               declares the LORD.
44 'Whoever flees from the terror
     will fall into a pit,
  whoever climbs out of the pit

will be caught in a snare;
  for I will bring on Moab
     the year of her punishment,'
               declares the LORD.

45 'In the shadow of Heshbon
     the fugitives stand helpless,
  for a fire has gone out from Heshbon,
     a blaze from the midst of Sihon;
  it burns the foreheads of Moab,
     the skulls of the noisy boasters.
46 Woe to you, Moab!
     The people of Chemosh are
       destroyed;
  your sons are taken into exile
     and your daughters into captivity.

47 'Yet I will restore the fortunes of Moab
     in days to come,'
               declares the LORD.

Here ends the judgment on Moab.

A message about Ammon

49 Concerning the Ammonites:

  This is what the LORD says:

  'Has Israel no sons?
     Has Israel no heir?
  Why then has Molek *a* taken possession
     of Gad?
  Why do his people live in its towns?
2 But the days are coming,'
     declares the LORD,
  'when I will sound the battle cry
     against Rabbah of the Ammonites;
  it will become a mound of ruins,
     and its surrounding villages will be
       set on fire.
  Then Israel will drive out
     those who drove her out,'
               says the LORD.
3 'Wail, Heshbon, for Ai is destroyed!
     Cry out, you inhabitants of Rabbah!
  Put on sackcloth and mourn;
     rush here and there inside the walls,
  for Molek will go into exile,
     together with his priests and
       officials.

⁴ Why do you boast of your valleys,
  boast of your valleys so fruitful?
Unfaithful Daughter Ammon,
  you trust in your riches and say,
  "Who will attack me?"
⁵ I will bring terror on you
  from all those around you,'
              declares the Lord,
              the LORD Almighty.
'Every one of you will be driven away,
  and no one will gather the
    fugitives.

⁶ 'Yet afterwards, I will restore the
    fortunes of the Ammonites,'
              declares the LORD.

A message about Edom

⁷ Concerning Edom:

This is what the LORD Almighty says:

'Is there no longer wisdom in Teman?
  Has counsel perished from the
    prudent?
  Has their wisdom decayed?
⁸ Turn and flee, hide in deep caves,
  you who live in Dedan,
for I will bring disaster on Esau
  at the time when I punish him.
⁹ If grape-pickers came to you,
  would they not leave a few grapes?
If thieves came during the night,
  would they not steal only as much as
    they wanted?
¹⁰ But I will strip Esau bare;
  I will uncover his hiding-places,
  so that he cannot conceal himself.
His armed men are destroyed,
  also his allies and neighbours,
  so there is no one to say,
¹¹ "Leave your fatherless children; I will
    keep them alive.
  Your widows too can depend on
    me."'

¹² This is what the LORD says: 'If those
who do not deserve to drink the cup must
drink it, why should you go unpunished?
You will not go unpunished, but must
drink it. ¹³ I swear by myself,' declares the
LORD, 'that Bozrah will become a ruin and

a curse,ᵇ an object of horror and reproach;
and all its towns will be in ruins for ever.'

¹⁴ I have heard a message from the LORD;
  an envoy was sent to the nations to
    say,
  'Assemble yourselves to attack it!
  Rise up for battle!'

¹⁵ 'Now I will make you small among the
    nations,
  despised by mankind.
¹⁶ The terror you inspire
  and the pride of your heart have
    deceived you,
you who live in the clefts of the rocks,
  who occupy the heights of the hill.
Though you build your nest as high as
    the eagle's,
  from there I will bring you down,'
              declares the LORD.
¹⁷ 'Edom will become an object of horror;
  all who pass by will be appalled and
    will scoff
  because of all its wounds.
¹⁸ As Sodom and Gomorrah were
    overthrown,
  along with their neighbouring
    towns,'
              says the LORD,
'so no one will live there;
  no people will dwell in it.

¹⁹ 'Like a lion coming up from Jordan's
    thickets
  to a rich pasture-land,
I will chase Edom from its land in an
    instant.
  Who is the chosen one I will appoint
    for this?
Who is like me and who can challenge
    me?
  And what shepherd can stand against
    me?'

²⁰ Therefore, hear what the LORD has
    planned against Edom,
  what he has purposed against those
    who live in Teman:

ᵇ 13 That is, its name will be used in cursing (see
29:22); or, others will see that it is cursed.

the young of the flock will be dragged
        away;
    their pasture will be appalled at their
        fate.
²¹ At the sound of their fall the earth will
        tremble;
    their cry will resound to the Red Sea.^c
²² Look! An eagle will soar and swoop
        down,
    spreading its wings over Bozrah.
In that day the hearts of Edom's
        warriors
    will be like the heart of a woman in
        labour.

A message about Damascus

²³ Concerning Damascus:

'Hamath and Arpad are dismayed,
    for they have heard bad news.
They are disheartened,
    troubled like^d the restless sea.
²⁴ Damascus has become feeble,
    she has turned to flee
    and panic has gripped her;
anguish and pain have seized her,
    pain like that of a woman in labour.
²⁵ Why has the city of renown not been
        abandoned,
    the town in which I delight?
²⁶ Surely, her young men will fall in the
        streets;
    all her soldiers will be silenced in
        that day,'
            declares the LORD Almighty.
²⁷ 'I will set fire to the walls of Damascus;
    it will consume the fortresses of
        Ben-Hadad.'

A message about Kedar and Hazor

²⁸ Concerning Kedar and the kingdoms
of Hazor, which Nebuchadnezzar king of
Babylon attacked:

This is what the LORD says:

'Arise, and attack Kedar
    and destroy the people of the East.
²⁹ Their tents and their flocks will be taken;

their shelters will be carried off
    with all their goods and camels.
People will shout to them,
    "Terror on every side!"

³⁰ 'Flee quickly away!
    Stay in deep caves, you who live in
        Hazor,'
            declares the LORD.
'Nebuchadnezzar king of Babylon has
        plotted against you;
    he has devised a plan against you.

³¹ 'Arise and attack a nation at ease,
    which lives in confidence,'
            declares the LORD,
'a nation that has neither gates nor
        bars;
    its people live far from danger.
³² Their camels will become plunder,
    and their large herds will be spoils of
        war.
I will scatter to the winds those who are
        in distant places^e
    and will bring disaster on them from
        every side,'
            declares the LORD.
³³ 'Hazor will become a haunt of jackals,
    a desolate place for ever.
No one will live there;
    no people will dwell in it.'

A message about Elam

³⁴ This is the word of the LORD that
came to Jeremiah the prophet concerning Elam, early in the reign of Zedekiah
king of Judah:

³⁵ This is what the LORD Almighty says:

'See, I will break the bow of Elam,
    the mainstay of their might.
³⁶ I will bring against Elam the four winds
    from the four quarters of heaven;
I will scatter them to the four winds,
    and there will not be a nation
    where Elam's exiles do not go.
³⁷ I will shatter Elam before their foes,
    before those who want to kill them;
I will bring disaster on them,

---

c 21 Or the Sea of Reeds
d 23 Hebrew on or by

e 32 Or who clip the hair by their foreheads

even my fierce anger,'
> declares the LORD.
'I will pursue them with the sword
until I have made an end of them.
38 I will set my throne in Elam
and destroy her king and officials,'
> declares the LORD.

39 'Yet I will restore the fortunes of Elam
in days to come,'
> declares the LORD.

A message about Babylon

50 This is the word the LORD spoke through Jeremiah the prophet concerning Babylon and the land of the Babylonians:*a*

2 'Announce and proclaim among the
nations,
lift up a banner and proclaim it;
keep nothing back, but say,
"Babylon will be captured;
Bel will be put to shame,
Marduk filled with terror.
Her images will be put to shame
and her idols filled with terror."
3 A nation from the north will attack her
and lay waste her land.
No one will live in it;
both people and animals will flee
away.

4 'In those days, at that time,'
> declares the LORD,
'the people of Israel and the people of
Judah together
will go in tears to seek the LORD their
God.
5 They will ask the way to Zion
and turn their faces towards it.
They will come and bind themselves to
the LORD
in an everlasting covenant
that will not be forgotten.

6 'My people have been lost sheep;
their shepherds have led them astray
and caused them to roam on the
mountains.

---

a 1 Or *Chaldeans*; also in verses 8, 25, 35 and 45

They wandered over mountain and hill
and forgot their own resting place.
7 Whoever found them devoured them;
their enemies said, "We are not guilty,
for they sinned against the LORD, their
verdant pasture,
the LORD, the hope of their
ancestors."

FAVOURITE VERSES

Ephesians 3:17–20

So that Christ may dwell in your hearts through faith. And I pray that you, being rooted and established in love, may have power, together with all the Lord's holy people, to grasp how wide and long and high and deep is the love of Christ, and to know this love that surpasses knowledge – that you may be filled to the measure of all the fullness of God. Now to him who is able to do immeasurably more than all we ask or imagine, according to his power that is at work within us…

- -

In a world that can sometimes
feel full of hate, these verses are a
glimmer of hope. We can know that
through it all, God loves us so much.

Emily, 17

8 'Flee out of Babylon;
leave the land of the Babylonians,
and be like the goats that lead the
flock.
9 For I will stir up and bring against
Babylon
an alliance of great nations from the
land of the north.
They will take up their positions against
her,

and from the north she will be
captured.
Their arrows will be like skilled warriors
who do not return empty-handed.
10 So Babylonia[b] will be plundered;
all who plunder her will have their
fill,'
declares the LORD.

11 'Because you rejoice and are glad,
you who pillage my inheritance,
because you frolic like a heifer
threshing corn
and neigh like stallions,
12 your mother will be greatly ashamed;
she who gave you birth will be
disgraced.
She will be the least of the nations –
a wilderness, a dry land, a desert.
13 Because of the LORD's anger she will not
be inhabited
but will be completely desolate.
All who pass Babylon will be appalled;
they will scoff because of all her
wounds.

14 'Take up your positions round Babylon,
all you who draw the bow.
Shoot at her! Spare no arrows,
for she has sinned against the LORD.
15 Shout against her on every side!
She surrenders, her towers fall,
her walls are torn down.
Since this is the vengeance of the LORD,
take vengeance on her;
do to her as she has done to others.
16 Cut off from Babylon the sower,
and the reaper with his sickle at
harvest.
Because of the sword of the oppressor
let everyone return to their own
people,
let everyone flee to their own land.

17 'Israel is a scattered flock
that lions have chased away.
The first to devour them
was the king of Assyria;
the last to crush their bones

was Nebuchadnezzar king of
Babylon.'

18 Therefore this is what the LORD
Almighty, the God of Israel, says:

'I will punish the king of Babylon and
his land
as I punished the king of Assyria.
19 But I will bring Israel back to their own
pasture,
and they will graze on Carmel and
Bashan;
their appetite will be satisfied
on the hills of Ephraim and Gilead.
20 In those days, at that time,'
declares the LORD,
'search will be made for Israel's guilt,
but there will be none,
and for the sins of Judah,
but none will be found,
for I will forgive the remnant I spare.

21 'Attack the land of Merathaim
and those who live in Pekod.
Pursue, kill and completely destroy[c]
them,'
declares the LORD.
'Do everything I have commanded
you.
22 The noise of battle is in the land,
the noise of great destruction!
23 How broken and shattered
is the hammer of the whole earth!
How desolate is Babylon
among the nations!
24 I set a trap for you, Babylon,
and you were caught before you
knew it;
you were found and captured
because you opposed the LORD.
25 The LORD has opened his arsenal
and brought out the weapons of his
wrath,
for the Sovereign LORD Almighty has
work to do
in the land of the Babylonians.
26 Come against her from afar.

---

b 10 Or Chaldea

c 21 The Hebrew term refers to the irrevocable
giving over of things or persons to the LORD, often
by totally destroying them; also in verse 26.

Break open her granaries;
    pile her up like heaps of grain.
Completely destroy her
    and leave her no remnant.
27 Kill all her young bulls;
    let them go down to the slaughter!
Woe to them! For their day has come,
    the time for them to be punished.
28 Listen to the fugitives and refugees
    from Babylon
declaring in Zion
how the LORD our God has taken
    vengeance,
    vengeance for his temple.

29 'Summon archers against Babylon,
    all those who draw the bow.
Encamp all round her;
    let no one escape.
Repay her for her deeds;
    do to her as she has done.
For she defied the LORD,
    the Holy One of Israel.
30 Therefore, her young men will fall in
    the streets;
all her soldiers will be silenced in
    that day,'
                   declares the LORD.
31 'See, I am against you, you arrogant
    one,'
    declares the Lord, the LORD Almighty,
'for your day has come,
    the time for you to be punished.
32 The arrogant one will stumble and fall
    and no one will help her up;
I will kindle a fire in her towns
    that will consume all who are around
    her.'

33 This is what the LORD Almighty says:

'The people of Israel are oppressed,
    and the people of Judah as well.
All their captors hold them fast,
    refusing to let them go.
34 Yet their Redeemer is strong;
    the LORD Almighty is his name.
He will vigorously defend their cause
    so that he may bring rest to their
    land,
but unrest to those who live in
    Babylon.

35 'A sword against the Babylonians!'
    declares the LORD –
'against those who live in Babylon
    and against her officials and wise
    men!
36 A sword against her false prophets!
    They will become fools.
A sword against her warriors!
    They will be filled with terror.
37 A sword against her horses and chariots
    and all the foreigners in her ranks!
    They will become weaklings.
A sword against her treasures!
    They will be plundered.
38 A drought on*d* her waters!
    They will dry up.
For it is a land of idols,
    idols that will go mad with terror.

39 'So desert creatures and hyenas will live
    there,
    and there the owl will dwell.
It will never again be inhabited
    or lived in from generation to
    generation.
40 As I overthrew Sodom and Gomorrah
    along with their neighbouring
    towns,'
                  declares the LORD,
'so no one will live there;
    no people will dwell in it.

41 'Look! An army is coming from the
    north;
a great nation and many kings
    are being stirred up from the ends of
    the earth.
42 They are armed with bows and spears;
    they are cruel and without mercy.
They sound like the roaring sea
    as they ride on their horses;
they come like men in battle formation
    to attack you, Daughter Babylon.
43 The king of Babylon has heard reports
    about them,
    and his hands hang limp.
Anguish has gripped him,
    pain like that of a woman in labour.
44 Like a lion coming up from Jordan's
    thickets

---

d 38 Or *A sword against*

to a rich pasture-land,
I will chase Babylon from its land in an
instant.
Who is the chosen one I will appoint
for this?
Who is like me and who can challenge
me?
And what shepherd can stand against
me?'

45 Therefore, hear what the LORD has
planned against Babylon,
what he has purposed against the
land of the Babylonians:
the young of the flock will be dragged
away;
their pasture will be appalled at their
fate.
46 At the sound of Babylon's capture the
earth will tremble;
its cry will resound among the
nations.

51

This is what the LORD says:

'See, I will stir up the spirit of a
destroyer
against Babylon and the people of
Leb Kamai.*a*
2 I will send foreigners to Babylon
to winnow her and to devastate her
land;
they will oppose her on every side
in the day of her disaster.
3 Let not the archer string his bow,
nor let him put on his armour.
Do not spare her young men;
completely destroy*b* her army.
4 They will fall down slain in Babylon,*c*
fatally wounded in her streets.
5 For Israel and Judah have not been
forsaken
by their God, the LORD Almighty,
though their land*d* is full of guilt
before the Holy One of Israel.

6 'Flee from Babylon!
Run for your lives!
Do not be destroyed because of her
sins.
It is time for the LORD's vengeance;
he will repay her what she deserves.
7 Babylon was a gold cup in the LORD's
hand;
she made the whole earth drunk.
The nations drank her wine;
therefore they have now gone mad.
8 Babylon will suddenly fall and be
broken.
Wail over her!
Get balm for her pain;
perhaps she can be healed.

9 ' "We would have healed Babylon,
but she cannot be healed;
let us leave her and each go to our own
land,
for her judgment reaches to the skies,
it rises as high as the heavens."

10 ' "The LORD has vindicated us;
come, let us tell in Zion
what the LORD our God has done."

11 'Sharpen the arrows,
take up the shields!
The LORD has stirred up the kings of the
Medes,
because his purpose is to destroy
Babylon.
The LORD will take vengeance,
vengeance for his temple.
12 Lift up a banner against the walls of
Babylon!
Reinforce the guard,
station the watchmen,
prepare an ambush!
The LORD will carry out his purpose,
his decree against the people of
Babylon.
13 You who live by many waters
and are rich in treasures,
your end has come,
the time for you to be destroyed.
14 The LORD Almighty has sworn by
himself:
I will surely fill you with troops, as
with a swarm of locusts,

---

a 1 *Leb Kamai* is a cryptogram for Chaldea, that is,
Babylonia.
b 3 The Hebrew term refers to the irrevocable giving
over of things or persons to the LORD, often by
totally destroying them.
c 4 Or *Chaldea*
d 5 Or *Almighty, / and the land of the Babylonians*

and they will shout in triumph over
　　you.

15 'He made the earth by his power;
　　he founded the world by his wisdom
　　and stretched out the heavens by his
　　　understanding.
16 When he thunders, the waters in the
　　　heavens roar;
　　he makes clouds rise from the ends
　　　of the earth.
He sends lightning with the rain
　　and brings out the wind from his
　　　storehouses.

17 'Everyone is senseless and without
　　　knowledge;
　　every goldsmith is shamed by his
　　　idols.
The images he makes are a fraud;
　　they have no breath in them.
18 They are worthless, the objects of
　　　mockery;
　　when their judgment comes, they
　　　will perish.
19 He who is the Portion of Jacob is not
　　　like these,
　　for he is the Maker of all things,
　　including the people of his
　　　inheritance –
　　the LORD Almighty is his name.

20 'You are my war club,
　　my weapon for battle –
　　with you I shatter nations,
　　with you I destroy kingdoms,
21 with you I shatter horse and rider,
　　with you I shatter chariot and driver,
22 with you I shatter man and woman,
　　with you I shatter old man and
　　　youth,
　　with you I shatter young man and
　　　young woman,
23 with you I shatter shepherd and flock,
　　with you I shatter farmer and oxen,
　　with you I shatter governors and
　　　officials.

24 'Before your eyes I will repay Babylon
and all who live in Babylonia[e] for all the

wrong they have done in Zion,' declares
the LORD.

25 'I am against you, you destroying
　　　mountain,
　　you who destroy the whole earth,'
　　　　declares the LORD.
'I will stretch out my hand against you,
　　roll you off the cliffs,
　　and make you a burnt-out
　　　mountain.
26 No rock will be taken from you for a
　　　cornerstone,
　　nor any stone for a foundation,
　　for you will be desolate for ever,'
　　　　declares the LORD.

27 'Lift up a banner in the land!
　　Blow the trumpet among the
　　　nations!
Prepare the nations for battle against
　　　her;
　　summon against her these
　　　kingdoms:
　　Ararat, Minni and Ashkenaz.
Appoint a commander against her;
　　send up horses like a swarm of
　　　locusts.
28 Prepare the nations for battle against
　　　her –
　　the kings of the Medes,
　　their governors and all their officials,
　　and all the countries they rule.
29 The land trembles and writhes,
　　for the LORD's purposes against
　　　Babylon stand –
　　to lay waste the land of Babylon
　　so that no one will live there.
30 Babylon's warriors have stopped
　　　fighting;
　　they remain in their strongholds.
Their strength is exhausted;
　　they have become weaklings.
Her dwellings are set on fire;
　　the bars of her gates are broken.
31 One courier follows another
　　and messenger follows messenger
　　to announce to the king of Babylon
　　that his entire city is captured,
32 the river crossings seized,
　　the marshes set on fire,
　　and the soldiers terrified.'

_____
e 24 Or *Chaldea*; also in verse 35

³³This is what the LORD Almighty, the God of Israel, says:

'Daughter Babylon is like a
    threshing-floor
    at the time it is trampled;
    the time to harvest her will soon
        come.'

³⁴'Nebuchadnezzar king of Babylon has
        devoured us,
    he has thrown us into confusion,
    he has made us an empty jar.
Like a serpent he has swallowed us
    and filled his stomach with our
        delicacies,
    and then has spewed us out.
³⁵May the violence done to our flesh*f* be
        on Babylon,'
    say the inhabitants of Zion.
'May our blood be on those who live in
        Babylonia,'
    says Jerusalem.

³⁶Therefore this is what the LORD says:

'See, I will defend your cause
    and avenge you;
I will dry up her sea
    and make her springs dry.
³⁷Babylon will be a heap of ruins,
    a haunt of jackals,
    an object of horror and scorn,
    a place where no one lives.
³⁸Her people all roar like young lions,
    they growl like lion cubs.
³⁹But while they are aroused,
    I will set out a feast for them
    and make them drunk,
so that they shout with laughter –
    then sleep for ever and not awake,'
        declares the LORD.
⁴⁰'I will bring them down
    like lambs to the slaughter,
    like rams and goats.

⁴¹'How Sheshak*g* will be captured,
    the boast of the whole earth seized!
How desolate Babylon will be

among the nations!
⁴²The sea will rise over Babylon;
    its roaring waves will cover her.
⁴³Her towns will be desolate,
    a dry and desert land,
    a land where no one lives,
    through which no one travels.
⁴⁴I will punish Bel in Babylon
    and make him spew out what he has
        swallowed.
The nations will no longer stream to
        him.
    And the wall of Babylon will fall.

⁴⁵'Come out of her, my people!
    Run for your lives!
    Run from the fierce anger of the
        LORD.
⁴⁶Do not lose heart or be afraid
    when rumours are heard in the
        land;
one rumour comes this year, another
        the next,
    rumours of violence in the land
    and of ruler against ruler.
⁴⁷For the time will surely come
    when I will punish the idols of
        Babylon;
her whole land will be disgraced
    and her slain will all lie fallen within
        her.
⁴⁸Then heaven and earth and all that is in
        them
    will shout for joy over Babylon,
for out of the north
    destroyers will attack her,'
        declares the LORD.

⁴⁹'Babylon must fall because of Israel's
        slain,
    just as the slain in all the earth
    have fallen because of Babylon.
⁵⁰You who have escaped the sword,
    leave and do not linger!
Remember the LORD in a distant land,
    and call to mind Jerusalem.'

⁵¹'We are disgraced,
    for we have been insulted
    and shame covers our faces,
because foreigners have entered
    the holy places of the LORD's house.'

---

f 35   Or *done to us and to our children*
g 41   *Sheshak* is a cryptogram for Babylon.

⁵²'But days are coming,' declares the
      LORD,
   'when I will punish her idols,
   and throughout her land
      the wounded will groan.
⁵³ Even if Babylon ascends to the heavens
      and fortifies her lofty stronghold,
   I will send destroyers against her,'
                        declares the LORD.

⁵⁴ 'The sound of a cry comes from
      Babylon,
   the sound of great destruction
      from the land of the Babylonians.ʰ
⁵⁵ The LORD will destroy Babylon;
      he will silence her noisy din.
   Waves of enemies will rage like great
      waters;
   the roar of their voices will
      resound.
⁵⁶ A destroyer will come against Babylon;
      her warriors will be captured,
   and their bows will be broken.
   For the LORD is a God of retribution;
      he will repay in full.
⁵⁷ I will make her officials and wise men
      drunk,
   her governors, officers and warriors
      as well;
   they will sleep for ever and not awake,'
      declares the King, whose name is the
      LORD Almighty.

⁵⁸ This is what the LORD Almighty says:

'Babylon's thick wall will be levelled
      and her high gates set on fire;
   the peoples exhaust themselves for
      nothing,
   the nations' labour is only fuel for
      the flames.'

⁵⁹ This is the message Jeremiah the
prophet gave to the staff officer Seraiah
son of Neriah, the son of Mahseiah, when
he went to Babylon with Zedekiah king
of Judah in the fourth year of his reign.
⁶⁰ Jeremiah had written on a scroll about
all the disasters that would come upon
Babylon – all that had been recorded

concerning Babylon. ⁶¹ He said to Seraiah,
'When you get to Babylon, see that you
read all these words aloud. ⁶² Then say,
"LORD, you have said you will destroy this
place, so that neither people nor animals
will live in it; it will be desolate for ever."
⁶³ When you finish reading this scroll, tie
a stone to it and throw it into the Euphrates. ⁶⁴ Then say, "So will Babylon sink to
rise no more because of the disaster I will
bring on her. And her people will fall."'

The words of Jeremiah end here.

The fall of Jerusalem

52 Zedekiah was twenty-one years
old when he became king, and
he reigned in Jerusalem for eleven years.
His mother's name was Hamutal daughter of Jeremiah; she was from Libnah.
² He did evil in the eyes of the LORD, just
as Jehoiakim had done. ³ It was because
of the LORD's anger that all this happened
to Jerusalem and Judah, and in the end he
thrust them from his presence.

Now Zedekiah rebelled against the king
of Babylon.

⁴ So in the ninth year of Zedekiah's
reign, on the tenth day of the tenth
month, Nebuchadnezzar king of Babylon
marched against Jerusalem with his whole
army. They encamped outside the city and
built siege works all around it. ⁵ The city
was kept under siege until the eleventh
year of King Zedekiah.

⁶ By the ninth day of the fourth month
the famine in the city had become so severe that there was no food for the people to eat. ⁷ Then the city wall was broken
through, and the whole army fled. They
left the city at night through the gate
between the two walls near the king's
garden, though the Babyloniansᵃ were
surrounding the city. They fled towards
the Arabah,ᵇ ⁸ but the Babylonianᶜ army
pursued King Zedekiah and overtook him
in the plains of Jericho. All his soldiers

ʰ 54 Or *Chaldeans*

ᵃ 7 Or *Chaldeans*; also in verse 17
ᵇ 7 Or *the Jordan Valley*
ᶜ 8 Or *Chaldean*; also in verse 14

were separated from him and scattered, ⁹and he was captured.

He was taken to the king of Babylon at Riblah in the land of Hamath, where he pronounced sentence on him. ¹⁰There at Riblah the king of Babylon killed the sons of Zedekiah before his eyes; he also killed all the officials of Judah. ¹¹Then he put out Zedekiah's eyes, bound him with bronze shackles and took him to Babylon, where he put him in prison till the day of his death.

¹²On the tenth day of the fifth month, in the nineteenth year of Nebuchadnezzar king of Babylon, Nebuzaradan commander of the imperial guard, who served the king of Babylon, came to Jerusalem. ¹³He set fire to the temple of the LORD, the royal palace and all the houses of Jerusalem. Every important building he burned down. ¹⁴The whole Babylonian army, under the commander of the imperial guard, broke down all the walls around Jerusalem. ¹⁵Nebuzaradan the commander of the guard carried into exile some of the poorest people and those who remained in the city, along with the rest of the craftsmen^d and those who had deserted to the king of Babylon. ¹⁶But Nebuzaradan left behind the rest of the poorest people of the land to work the vineyards and fields.

¹⁷The Babylonians broke up the bronze pillars, the movable stands and the bronze Sea that were at the temple of the LORD and they carried all the bronze to Babylon. ¹⁸They also took away the pots, shovels, wick trimmers, sprinkling bowls, dishes and all the bronze articles used in the temple service. ¹⁹The commander of the imperial guard took away the basins, censers, sprinkling bowls, pots, lampstands, dishes and bowls used for drink offerings – all that were made of pure gold or silver.

²⁰The bronze from the two pillars, the Sea and the twelve bronze bulls under it, and the movable stands, which King Solomon had made for the temple of the LORD, was more than could be weighed.

²¹Each pillar was eighteen cubits high and twelve cubits in circumference^e; each was four fingers thick, and hollow. ²²The bronze capital on the top of one pillar was five cubits^f high and was decorated with a network and pomegranates of bronze all around. The other pillar, with its pomegranates, was similar. ²³There were ninety-six pomegranates on the sides; the total number of pomegranates above the surrounding network was a hundred.

²⁴The commander of the guard took as prisoners Seraiah the chief priest,

---

e 21 That is, about 8.1 metres high and 5.4 metres in circumference
f 22 That is, about 2.3 metres

Zephaniah the priest next in rank and the three doorkeepers. ²⁵ Of those still in the city, he took the officer in charge of the fighting men, and seven royal advisers. He also took the secretary who was chief officer in charge of conscripting the people of the land, sixty of whom were found in the city. ²⁶ Nebuzaradan the commander took them all and brought them to the king of Babylon at Riblah. ²⁷ There at Riblah, in the land of Hamath, the king had them executed.

So Judah went into captivity, away from her land. ²⁸ This is the number of the people Nebuchadnezzar carried into exile:

in the seventh year, 3,023 Jews;
²⁹ in Nebuchadnezzar's eighteenth year, 832 people from Jerusalem;
³⁰ in his twenty-third year,

745 Jews taken into exile by Nebuzaradan the commander of the imperial guard.
There were 4,600 people in all.

Jehoiachin released

³¹ In the thirty-seventh year of the exile of Jehoiachin king of Judah, in the year Awel-Marduk became king of Babylon, on the twenty-fifth day of the twelfth month, he released Jehoiachin king of Judah and freed him from prison. ³² He spoke kindly to him and gave him a seat of honour higher than those of the other kings who were with him in Babylon. ³³ So Jehoiachin put aside his prison clothes and for the rest of his life ate regularly at the king's table. ³⁴ Day by day the king of Babylon gave Jehoiachin a regular allowance as long as he lived, till the day of his death.

LAMENTATIONS

DATE

Lamentations was written about Jerusalem being conquered by the Babylonians in around 586 BC

AUTHOR

Unknown – sometimes credited to the prophet Jeremiah

WHAT'S IT ALL ABOUT?

To lament means to express sadness or grief and so the title gives us a pretty big clue about the nature of the book. The writer had witnessed the fall of the city of Jerusalem (when Judah was conquered by the Babylonians and taken into exile) and he details his grief at the events. Things were certainly grim: the once great city was in ruins, the remaining people were starving to death, their enemies had taken the treasures from the temple and, worse, the pagans had entered God's holy sanctuary. Although the destruction came at the hands of the Babylonians, the people knew it was orchestrated by God as punishment because they had constantly turned away from him. But it's not all doom and gloom; there is a ray of light. Despite all he had seen, the author still found reason to hope in God. He recalled the truth of who God is, his compassion and mercy, and proclaimed God's goodness even in the midst of his grief.

Lamentations is made up of five poems (each with its own chapter) and in the original Hebrew the first four were acrostics (where each line started with a different letter of the Hebrew alphabet).

WHY SHOULD WE READ IT?

- To remember that there is always hope in God, no matter how bad things seem.

- To see how desperate God's people felt when they thought God had abandoned them.

- To understand the impact that the fall of Jerusalem had on the people.

- To read how the punishment brought the people to repentance for their sin.

Andy Croft with Liza Hoeksma

1 ^a How deserted lies the city,
    once so full of people!
How like a widow is she,
    who once was great among the
        nations!
She who was queen among the
        provinces
    has now become a slave.

2 Bitterly she weeps at night,
    tears are on her cheeks.
Among all her lovers
    there is no one to comfort her.
All her friends have betrayed her;
    they have become her enemies.

3 After affliction and harsh labour,
    Judah has gone into exile.
She dwells among the nations;
    she finds no resting place.
All who pursue her have overtaken
        her
    in the midst of her distress.

4 The roads to Zion mourn,
    for no one comes to her appointed
        festivals.
All her gateways are desolate,
    her priests groan,
her young women grieve,
    and she is in bitter anguish.

5 Her foes have become her masters;
    her enemies are at ease.
The LORD has brought her grief
    because of her many sins.
Her children have gone into exile,
    captive before the foe.

6 All the splendour has departed
    from Daughter Zion.
Her princes are like deer
    that find no pasture;
in weakness they have fled
    before the pursuer.

7 In the days of her affliction and
        wandering

Jerusalem remembers all the
        treasures
    that were hers in days of old.
When her people fell into enemy
        hands,
    there was no one to help her.
Her enemies looked at her
    and laughed at her destruction.

8 Jerusalem has sinned greatly
    and so has become unclean.
All who honoured her despise her,
    for they have all seen her naked;
she herself groans
    and turns away.

9 Her filthiness clung to her skirts;
    she did not consider her future.
Her fall was astounding;
    there was none to comfort her.
'Look, LORD, on my affliction,
    for the enemy has triumphed.'

10 The enemy laid hands
    on all her treasures;
she saw pagan nations
    enter her sanctuary –
those you had forbidden
    to enter your assembly.

11 All her people groan
    as they search for bread;
they barter their treasures for
        food
    to keep themselves alive.
'Look, LORD, and consider,
    for I am despised.'

12 'Is it nothing to you, all you who
        pass by?
Look around and see.
Is any suffering like my suffering
    that was inflicted on me,
that the LORD brought on me
    in the day of his fierce anger?

13 'From on high he sent fire,
    sent it down into my bones.
He spread a net for my feet
    and turned me back.
He made me desolate,
    faint all the day long.

---

a This chapter is an acrostic poem, the verses of
which begin with the successive letters of the
Hebrew alphabet.

14 'My sins have been bound into a yoke[b];
   by his hands they were woven
      together.
They have been hung on my neck,
   and the Lord has sapped my
      strength.
He has given me into the hands
   of those I cannot withstand.

15 'The Lord has rejected
   all the warriors in my midst;
he has summoned an army against me
   to[c] crush my young men.
In his winepress the Lord has trampled
   Virgin Daughter Judah.

16 'This is why I weep
   and my eyes overflow with tears.
No one is near to comfort me,
   no one to restore my spirit.
My children are destitute
   because the enemy has prevailed.'

17 Zion stretches out her hands,
   but there is no one to comfort her.
The LORD has decreed for Jacob
   that his neighbours become his foes;
Jerusalem has become
   an unclean thing among them.

18 'The LORD is righteous,
   yet I rebelled against his command.
Listen, all you peoples;
   look on my suffering.
My young men and young women
   have gone into exile.

19 'I called to my allies
   but they betrayed me.
My priests and my elders
   perished in the city
while they searched for food
   to keep themselves alive.

20 'See, LORD, how distressed I am!
   I am in torment within,
and in my heart I am disturbed,
   for I have been most rebellious.

Outside, the sword bereaves;
   inside, there is only death.

21 'People have heard my groaning,
   but there is no one to comfort me.
All my enemies have heard of my
      distress;
   they rejoice at what you have done.
May you bring the day you have
      announced
   so that they may become like me.

22 'Let all their wickedness come before
      you;
   deal with them
as you have dealt with me
   because of all my sins.
My groans are many
   and my heart is faint.'

2[a] How the Lord has covered Daughter
      Zion
   with the cloud of his anger![b]
He has hurled down the splendour of
      Israel
   from heaven to earth;
he has not remembered his footstool
   in the day of his anger.

2 Without pity the Lord has swallowed
      up
   all the dwellings of Jacob;
in his wrath he has torn down
   the strongholds of Daughter Judah.
He has brought her kingdom and its
      princes
   down to the ground in dishonour.

3 In fierce anger he has cut off
   every horn[c,d] of Israel.
He has withdrawn his right hand
   at the approach of the enemy.
He has burned in Jacob like a flaming
      fire
   that consumes everything around it.

---

b 14 Most Hebrew manuscripts; many Hebrew
manuscripts and Septuagint *He kept watch over my sins*
c 15 Or *has set a time for me / when he will*

a This chapter is an acrostic poem, the verses of
which begin with the successive letters of the
Hebrew alphabet.
b 1 Or *How the Lord in his anger / has treated Daughter Zion
with contempt!*
c 3 Or *off / all the strength*; or *every king*
d 3 *Horn* here symbolises strength.

4 Like an enemy he has strung his
    bow;
  his right hand is ready.
Like a foe he has slain
  all who were pleasing to the eye;
he has poured out his wrath like fire
  on the tent of Daughter Zion.

5 The Lord is like an enemy;
  he has swallowed up Israel.
He has swallowed up all her
    palaces
  and destroyed her strongholds.
He has multiplied mourning and
    lamentation
  for Daughter Judah.

6 He has laid waste his dwelling like a
    garden;
  he has destroyed his place of
    meeting.
The LORD has made Zion forget
  her appointed festivals and her
    Sabbaths;
in his fierce anger he has spurned
  both king and priest.

7 The Lord has rejected his altar
  and abandoned his sanctuary.
He has given the walls of her palaces
  into the hands of the enemy;
they have raised a shout in the house of
    the LORD
  as on the day of an appointed
    festival.

8 The LORD determined to tear down
  the wall around Daughter Zion.
He stretched out a measuring line
  and did not withhold his hand from
    destroying.
He made ramparts and walls lament;
  together they wasted away.

9 Her gates have sunk into the ground;
  their bars he has broken and
    destroyed.
Her king and her princes are exiled
    among the nations,
  the law is no more,
and her prophets no longer find
  visions from the LORD.

10 The elders of Daughter Zion
  sit on the ground in silence;
they have sprinkled dust on their heads
  and put on sackcloth.
The young women of Jerusalem
  have bowed their heads to the
    ground.

11 My eyes fail from weeping,
  I am in torment within;
my heart is poured out on the ground
  because my people are destroyed,
because children and infants faint
  in the streets of the city.

12 They say to their mothers,
  'Where is bread and wine?'
as they faint like the wounded
  in the streets of the city,
as their lives ebb away
  in their mothers' arms.

13 What can I say for you?
  With what can I compare you,
    Daughter Jerusalem?
To what can I liken you,
  that I may comfort you,
    Virgin Daughter Zion?
Your wound is as deep as the sea.
  Who can heal you?

14 The visions of your prophets
  were false and worthless;
they did not expose your sin
  to ward off your captivity.
The prophecies they gave you
  were false and misleading.

15 All who pass your way
  clap their hands at you;
they scoff and shake their heads
  at Daughter Jerusalem:
'Is this the city that was called
  the perfection of beauty,
  the joy of the whole earth?'

16 All your enemies open their mouths
  wide against you;
they scoff and gnash their teeth
  and say, 'We have swallowed her up.
This is the day we have waited for;
  we have lived to see it.'

17 The Lord has done what he planned;
he has fulfilled his word,
which he decreed long ago.
He has overthrown you without pity,
he has let the enemy gloat over you,
he has exalted the horn[e] of your
foes.

18 The hearts of the people
cry out to the Lord.
You walls of Daughter Zion,
let your tears flow like a river
day and night;
give yourself no relief,
your eyes no rest.

19 Arise, cry out in the night,
as the watches of the night begin;
pour out your heart like water
in the presence of the Lord.
Lift up your hands to him
for the lives of your children,
who faint from hunger
at every street corner.

20 'Look, Lord, and consider:
whom have you ever treated like
this?
Should women eat their offspring,
the children they have cared for?
Should priest and prophet be killed
in the sanctuary of the Lord?

21 'Young and old lie together
in the dust of the streets;
my young men and young women
have fallen by the sword.
You have slain them in the day of your
anger;
you have slaughtered them without
pity.

22 'As you summon to a feast day,
so you summoned against me terrors
on every side.
In the day of the Lord's anger
no one escaped or survived;
those I cared for and reared
my enemy has destroyed.'

3[a] I am the man who has seen affliction
by the rod of the Lord's wrath.
2 He has driven me away and made me
walk
in darkness rather than light;
3 indeed, he has turned his hand against
me
again and again, all day long.

4 He has made my skin and my flesh grow
old
and has broken my bones.
5 He has besieged me and surrounded me
with bitterness and hardship.
6 He has made me dwell in darkness
like those long dead.

7 He has walled me in so that I cannot
escape;
he has weighed me down with
chains.
8 Even when I call out or cry for help,
he shuts out my prayer.
9 He has barred my way with blocks of
stone;
he has made my paths crooked.

10 Like a bear lying in wait,
like a lion in hiding,
11 he dragged me from the path and
mangled me
and left me without help.
12 He drew his bow
and made me the target for his
arrows.

13 He pierced my heart
with arrows from his quiver.
14 I became the laughing-stock of all my
people;
they mock me in song all day long.
15 He has filled me with bitter herbs
and given me gall to drink.

16 He has broken my teeth with gravel;
he has trampled me in the dust.
17 I have been deprived of peace;
I have forgotten what prosperity is.

---

e 17 *Horn* here symbolises strength.

a This chapter is an acrostic poem; the verses of
each stanza begin with the successive letters of the
Hebrew alphabet, and the verses within each stanza
begin with the same letter.

PAIN AND SUFFERING 1

HOPE IN THE MIDST OF PAIN

You can tell from its name that Lamentations isn't a happy book. The writer is overwhelmed with misery and sorrow as he pours out his heart, grieving over what has happened to God's people. He has seen the great city of Jerusalem destroyed. Many have been killed and those who survived are starving and desperate. There has been devastation, destruction and slaughter. Why? God's people have defied him and are now dealing with the consequences.

Amazingly, God doesn't punish us for our sin today because Jesus took that punishment on himself, but many of us still know what it's like to feel overwhelmed with sadness and grief. Although Lamentations can seem like one of the most depressing books of the Bible, it still contains some nuggets of wisdom. Halfway through chapter 3, the writer finds a reason to hope (3:21). Up until that point he has poured out his pain over the things he has seen, but here he refocuses his gaze and calls to mind some truths. God is loving! God's compassion never fails us! So he decides to wait on God. He remembers that God is good to those who hope in him. He recalls the ways in which God has helped him when he has felt desperate in the past (vv. 55–58). He reminds himself that even though he feels as if God won't listen to him (v. 8), God in fact sees what is happening (v. 59).

This hope is vital for the writer and for us. We can endure so much when we have hope; without it we feel as if we might as well give up. We need to know that no matter what is going on in our lives, we can have hope, because with God there is always hope. Like the writer here, we can call to mind God's characteristics – the Bible is full of them! God will always love us and he will always work things for our good (Romans 8:28); he will never leave us (Deuteronomy 31:6); and he will sustain us (Psalm 55:22). These are all reasons to rejoice, even on our darkest day. We also know that God can take any situation, no matter how bleak it looks, and turn it around into something amazing. Joseph was sold into slavery by his brothers and sent to prison for something he didn't do, but ultimately God used it for good and saved his people from starvation during a drought. When Jesus was hung on a cross, many thought that was the end – the so-called Messiah had been defeated. But we know what happened! God was doing something far greater than anyone could ever have imagined. Sometimes it looks as if everything is at an end and is going completely wrong, when actually God is doing something amazing. Let's hold on to hope even in the tough times. Hope will help us persevere, trusting that God has everything in hand and knowing that he never fails us.

Mike Pilavachi

2 Corinthians 1:8–11 ▶

18 So I say, 'My splendour is gone
  and all that I had hoped from the
  LORD.'

19 I remember my affliction and my
  wandering,
  the bitterness and the gall.
20 I well remember them,
  and my soul is downcast within me.
21 Yet this I call to mind
  and therefore I have hope:

22 Because of the LORD's great love we are
  not consumed,
  for his compassions never fail.
23 They are new every morning;
  great is your faithfulness.
24 I say to myself, 'The LORD is my
  portion;
  therefore I will wait for him.'

25 The LORD is good to those whose hope
  is in him,
  to the one who seeks him;
26 it is good to wait quietly
  for the salvation of the LORD.
27 It is good for a man to bear the yoke
  while he is young.

28 Let him sit alone in silence,
  for the LORD has laid it on him.
29 Let him bury his face in the dust –
  there may yet be hope.
30 Let him offer his cheek to one who
  would strike him,
  and let him be filled with disgrace.

31 For no one is cast off
  by the Lord for ever.
32 Though he brings grief, he will show
  compassion,
  so great is his unfailing love.
33 For he does not willingly bring
  affliction
  or grief to anyone.

34 To crush underfoot
  all prisoners in the land,
35 to deny people their rights
  before the Most High,
36 to deprive them of justice –
  would not the Lord see such things?

37 Who can speak and have it happen
  if the Lord has not decreed it?
38 Is it not from the mouth of the Most
  High
  that both calamities and good things
  come?
39 Why should the living complain
  when punished for their sins?

40 Let us examine our ways and test them,
  and let us return to the LORD.
41 Let us lift up our hearts and our hands
  to God in heaven, and say:
42 'We have sinned and rebelled
  and you have not forgiven.

43 'You have covered yourself with anger
  and pursued us;
  you have slain without pity.
44 You have covered yourself with a cloud
  so that no prayer can get through.
45 You have made us scum and refuse
  among the nations.

46 'All our enemies have opened their
  mouths
  wide against us.
47 We have suffered terror and pitfalls,
  ruin and destruction.'
48 Streams of tears flow from my eyes
  because my people are destroyed.

49 My eyes will flow unceasingly,
  without relief,
50 until the LORD looks down
  from heaven and sees.
51 What I see brings grief to my soul
  because of all the women of my city.

52 Those who were my enemies without
  cause
  hunted me like a bird.
53 They tried to end my life in a pit
  and threw stones at me;
54 the waters closed over my head,
  and I thought I was about to perish.

55 I called on your name, LORD,
  from the depths of the pit.
56 You heard my plea: 'Do not close your
  ears
  to my cry for relief.'

57 You came near when I called you,
    and you said, 'Do not fear.'

58 You, Lord, took up my case;
    you redeemed my life.
59 LORD, you have seen the wrong done
      to me.
    Uphold my cause!
60 You have seen the depth of their
      vengeance,
    all their plots against me.

61 LORD, you have heard their insults,
    all their plots against me –
62 what my enemies whisper and mutter
    against me all day long.
63 Look at them! Sitting or standing,
    they mock me in their songs.

64 Pay them back what they deserve, LORD,
    for what their hands have done.
65 Put a veil over their hearts,
    and may your curse be on them!
66 Pursue them in anger and destroy them
    from under the heavens of the LORD.

4 *a* How the gold has lost its lustre,
      the fine gold become dull!
    The sacred gems are scattered
      at every street corner.

2 How the precious children of Zion,
    once worth their weight in gold,
  are now considered as pots of clay,
    the work of a potter's hands!

3 Even jackals offer their breasts
    to nurse their young,
  but my people have become heartless
    like ostriches in the desert.

4 Because of thirst the infant's tongue
    sticks to the roof of its mouth;
  the children beg for bread,
    but no one gives it to them.

5 Those who once ate delicacies
    are destitute in the streets.

Those brought up in royal purple
    now lie on ash heaps.

6 The punishment of my people
    is greater than that of Sodom,
  which was overthrown in a moment
    without a hand turned to help her.

7 Their princes were brighter than snow
    and whiter than milk,
  their bodies more ruddy than rubies,
    their appearance like lapis lazuli.

8 But now they are blacker than soot;
    they are not recognised in the
      streets.
  Their skin has shrivelled on their bones;
    it has become as dry as a stick.

9 Those killed by the sword are better off
    than those who die of famine;
  racked with hunger, they waste away
    for lack of food from the field.

10 With their own hands compassionate
      women
    have cooked their own children,
  who became their food
    when my people were destroyed.

11 The LORD has given full vent to his wrath;
    he has poured out his fierce anger.
  He kindled a fire in Zion
    that consumed her foundations.

12 The kings of the earth did not believe,
    nor did any of the peoples of the
      world,
  that enemies and foes could enter
    the gates of Jerusalem.

13 But it happened because of the sins of
      her prophets
    and the iniquities of her priests,
  who shed within her
    the blood of the righteous.

14 Now they grope through the streets
    as if they were blind.
  They are so defiled with blood
    that no one dares to touch their
      garments.

---

a This chapter is an acrostic poem, the verses of
which begin with the successive letters of the
Hebrew alphabet.

15 'Go away! You are unclean!' people cry
to them.
'Away! Away! Don't touch us!'
When they flee and wander about,
people among the nations say,
'They can stay here no longer.'

16 The LORD himself has scattered them;
he no longer watches over them.
The priests are shown no honour,
the elders no favour.

17 Moreover, our eyes failed,
looking in vain for help;
from our towers we watched
for a nation that could not save us.

18 People stalked us at every step,
so we could not walk in our streets.
Our end was near, our days were
numbered,
for our end had come.

19 Our pursuers were swifter
than eagles in the sky;
they chased us over the mountains
and lay in wait for us in the desert.

20 The LORD's anointed, our very life
breath,
was caught in their traps.
We thought that under his shadow
we would live among the nations.

21 Rejoice and be glad, Daughter Edom,
you who live in the land of Uz.
But to you also the cup will be passed;
you will be drunk and stripped
naked.

22 Your punishment will end, Daughter
Zion;
he will not prolong your exile.
But he will punish your sin, Daughter
Edom,
and expose your wickedness.

5

Remember, LORD, what has
happened to us;
look, and see our disgrace.
2 Our inheritance has been turned over
to strangers,
our homes to foreigners.
3 We have become fatherless,
our mothers are widows.
4 We must buy the water we drink;
our wood can be had only at a
price.
5 Those who pursue us are at our heels;
we are weary and find no rest.
6 We submitted to Egypt and Assyria
to get enough bread.
7 Our ancestors sinned and are no
more,
and we bear their punishment.
8 Slaves rule over us,
and there is no one to free us from
their hands.
9 We get our bread at the risk of our lives
because of the sword in the desert.
10 Our skin is hot as an oven,
feverish from hunger.
11 Women have been violated in Zion,
and virgins in the towns of Judah.
12 Princes have been hung up by their
hands;
elders are shown no respect.
13 Young men toil at the millstones;
boys stagger under loads of wood.
14 The elders are gone from the city gate;
the young men have stopped their
music.
15 Joy is gone from our hearts;
our dancing has turned to
mourning.
16 The crown has fallen from our head.
Woe to us, for we have sinned!
17 Because of this our hearts are faint;
because of these things our eyes
grow dim
18 for Mount Zion, which lies desolate,
with jackals prowling over it.

19 You, LORD, reign for ever;
your throne endures from
generation to generation.
20 Why do you always forget us?
Why do you forsake us so long?
21 Restore us to yourself, LORD, that we
may return;
renew our days as of old
22 unless you have utterly rejected us
and are angry with us beyond
measure.

EZEKIEL

DATE

It's thought that Ezekiel received his call to be a prophet in 593 BC (after the Jews had been exiled to Babylon in 597 BC) and prophesied for 22 years

AUTHOR

Ezekiel

WHAT'S IT ALL ABOUT?

The prophet Ezekiel wrote this book after he was taken into exile when the Babylonians attacked Jerusalem. He saw an incredible vision of God and received God's command for him to prophesy to the people, telling them of God's judgement on them for their long history of rebellion. They had ignored warnings from other prophets such as Isaiah and so God had punished them by letting them be taken into exile. Ezekiel warned that further punishment was about to happen: the Babylonians would destroy God's temple. This would have been devastating to the people, as God's holy place symbolised his presence with them. God spoke to Ezekiel through symbols and visions and asked him to perform prophetic actions that can sound utterly crazy to us – like asking him to lie on his side for 430 days (Ezekiel 4); to pack his belongings and dig through a wall (Ezekiel 12); and not to cry when his wife died (Ezekiel 24). About thirteen years after he lost his wife, Ezekiel prophesied again, but this time there was hope in his voice. He began speaking of a time when God's people would return to Jerusalem and see the restoration of the temple. Although the prophet died before he saw these things himself, his prophecies came to pass.

WHY SHOULD WE READ IT?

- To hear Ezekiel's amazing vision which led him to serve God as a prophet (Ezekiel 1 – 3).

- To see Ezekiel's obedience to God, whether he was asked to lie on his side for 430 days as a prophetic act (Ezekiel 4) or to shave his head and beard and set fire to the hair (Ezekiel 5).

- To read the famous story of the valley of dry bones (Ezekiel 37).

- As a reminder of how seriously God takes sin and therefore how amazing the forgiveness we receive through Jesus is.

Andy Croft with Liza Hoeksma

Ezekiel's inaugural vision

1 In my thirtieth year, in the fourth month on the fifth day, while I was among the exiles by the River Kebar, the heavens were opened and I saw visions of God.

2 On the fifth of the month – it was the fifth year of the exile of King Jehoiachin – 3 the word of the LORD came to Ezekiel the priest, the son of Buzi, by the River Kebar in the land of the Babylonians.*a* There the hand of the LORD was on him.

4 I looked, and I saw a violent storm coming out of the north – an immense cloud with flashing lightning and surrounded by brilliant light. The centre of the fire looked like glowing metal, 5 and in the fire was what looked like four living creatures. In appearance their form was human, 6 but each of them had four faces and four wings. 7 Their legs were straight; their feet were like those of a calf and gleamed like burnished bronze. 8 Under their wings on their four sides they had human hands. All four of them had faces and wings, 9 and the wings of one touched the wings of another. Each one went straight ahead; they did not turn as they moved.

10 Their faces looked like this: each of the four had the face of a human being, and on the right side each had the face of a lion, and on the left the face of an ox; each also had the face of an eagle. 11 Such were their faces. They each had two wings spreading out upwards, each wing touching that of the creature on either side; and each had two other wings covering its body. 12 Each one went straight ahead. Wherever the spirit would go, they would go, without turning as they went. 13 The appearance of the living creatures was like burning coals of fire or like torches. Fire moved back and forth among the creatures; it was bright, and lightning flashed out of it. 14 The creatures sped back and forth like flashes of lightning.

15 As I looked at the living creatures, I saw a wheel on the ground beside each creature with its four faces. 16 This was the appearance and structure of the wheels: they sparkled like topaz, and all four looked alike. Each appeared to be made like a wheel intersecting a wheel. 17 As they moved, they would go in any one of the four directions the creatures faced; the wheels did not change direction as the creatures went. 18 Their rims were high and awesome, and all four rims were full of eyes all around.

19 When the living creatures moved, the wheels beside them moved; and when the living creatures rose from the ground, the wheels also rose. 20 Wherever the spirit would go, they would go, and the wheels would rise along with them, because the spirit of the living creatures was in the wheels. 21 When the creatures moved, they also moved; when the creatures stood still, they also stood still; and when the creatures rose from the ground, the wheels rose along with them, because the spirit of the living creatures was in the wheels.

22 Spread out above the heads of the living creatures was what looked something like a vault, sparkling like crystal, and awesome. 23 Under the vault their wings were stretched out one towards the other, and each had two wings covering its body. 24 When the creatures moved, I heard the sound of their wings, like the roar of rushing waters, like the voice of the Almighty,*b* like the tumult of an army. When they stood still, they lowered their wings.

25 Then there came a voice from above the vault over their heads as they stood with lowered wings. 26 Above the vault over their heads was what looked like a throne of lapis lazuli, and high above on the throne was a figure like that of a man. 27 I saw that from what appeared to be his waist up he looked like glowing metal, as if full of fire, and that from there down he looked like fire; and brilliant light surrounded him. 28 Like the appearance of a rainbow in the clouds on a rainy day, so was the radiance around him.

This was the appearance of the likeness of the glory of the LORD. When I saw it, I

---

a 3 Or *Chaldeans*   *b* 24 Hebrew *Shaddai*

THROUGH EZEKIEL 1

A history lesson...

Ezekiel is one of my biblical heroes, and it's his book that has most challenged, equipped and inspired me for the last six years.

To see why, let's start with a bit of historical background. Ezekiel was twenty-five when he was among the thousands of Judeans deported to Babylon after King Jehoiachin finally surrendered to King Nebuchadnezzar: he was a refugee. Almost all the people forced from their city assumed that their move from Jerusalem was a temporary blip – after all, they had this amazing history as God's chosen people! A false prophet called Hananiah had been around to reassure them with his so-called 'prophecies' too (you can read about him in Jeremiah 28). Jeremiah, however, had told them that a short exile was not God's plan – they were to be in exile for seventy years (Jeremiah 29:1–23). Everyone thought that their relationship with God was completely tied into God's presence resting in the temple in Jerusalem, so they couldn't believe that their city could be taken. Also,125 years earlier (see 2 Kings 17 – 19) Jerusalem had been miraculously saved after the fall of Samaria, so it's no wonder people thought that this time would be no different! God had been sending prophets like Jeremiah to warn them that they had broken their covenant with him, and because of this they would forfeit their land, but they didn't listen.

The book of Ezekiel is probably most famous for chapters 3 and 33 – describing the roles and responsibilities of a watchman – but the whole book shows us an example of incredible obedience, and a man willing to put aside his respectability, status and pride for God and his people. I would recommend reading the whole of Ezekiel and not just jumping through to the next bit of commentary, so that you can see his story in full.

It's not often that people get a call as dramatic as Ezekiel's, but I love the fact that his reaction is like so many of ours – shell-shocked. Ezekiel doesn't respond by shouting, 'Yes, God! You've chosen me for this task and I'm so delighted – let's go and get on with it immediately!' Instead he spends seven days simply being overwhelmed and sitting beside the river (Ezekiel 3:15). I don't know if God has ever asked you to do anything difficult or odd, or if he has revealed himself in a strange way, but there have been times when I have felt a bit stunned and have just needed to pull myself together before getting on with whatever God has asked me to do. What reassures me is that God waits patiently for the seven days it takes Ezekiel to get his head together before he talks to Ezekiel more about what the calling is going to involve.

Jane Plackett

Ezekiel 3

fell face down, and I heard the voice of one speaking.

Ezekiel's call to be a prophet

2 He said to me, 'Son of man, *a* stand up on your feet and I will speak to you.' ²As he spoke, the Spirit came into me and raised me to my feet, and I heard him speaking to me.

³He said: 'Son of man, I am sending you to the Israelites, to a rebellious nation that has rebelled against me; they and their ancestors have been in revolt against me to this very day. ⁴The people to whom I am sending you are obstinate and stubborn. Say to them, "This is what the Sovereign LORD says." ⁵And whether they listen or fail to listen – for they are a rebellious people – they will know that a prophet has been among them. ⁶And you, son of man, do not be afraid of them or their words. Do not be afraid, though briers and thorns are all around you and you live among scorpions. Do not be afraid of what they say or be terrified by them, though they are a rebellious people. ⁷You must speak my words to them, whether they listen or fail to listen, for they are rebellious. ⁸But you, son of man, listen to what I say to you. Do not rebel like that rebellious people; open your mouth and eat what I give you.'

⁹Then I looked, and I saw a hand stretched out to me. In it was a scroll, ¹⁰which he unrolled before me. On both sides of it were written words of lament and mourning and woe.

3 And he said to me, 'Son of man, eat what is before you, eat this scroll; then go and speak to the people of Israel.' ²So I opened my mouth, and he gave me the scroll to eat.

³Then he said to me, 'Son of man, eat this scroll I am giving you and fill your stomach with it.' So I ate it, and it tasted as sweet as honey in my mouth.

⁴He then said to me: 'Son of man, go now to the people of Israel and speak my words to them. ⁵You are not being sent to a people of obscure speech and strange language, but to the people of Israel – ⁶not to many peoples of obscure speech and strange language, whose words you cannot understand. Surely if I had sent you to them, they would have listened to you. ⁷But the people of Israel are not willing to listen to you because they are not willing to listen to me, for all the Israelites are hardened and obstinate. ⁸But I will make you as unyielding and hardened as they are. ⁹I will make your forehead like the hardest stone, harder than flint. Do not be afraid of them or terrified by them, though they are a rebellious people.'

¹⁰And he said to me, 'Son of man, listen carefully and take to heart all the words I speak to you. ¹¹Go now to your people in exile and speak to them. Say to them, "This is what the Sovereign LORD says," whether they listen or fail to listen.'

¹²Then the Spirit lifted me up, and I heard behind me a loud rumbling sound as the glory of the LORD rose from the place where it was standing.*a* ¹³It was the sound of the wings of the living creatures brushing against each other and the sound of the wheels beside them, a loud rumbling sound. ¹⁴The Spirit then lifted me up and took me away, and I went in bitterness and in the anger of my spirit, with the strong hand of the LORD on me. ¹⁵I came to the exiles who lived at Tel Aviv near the River Kebar. And there, where they were living, I sat among them for seven days – deeply distressed.

Ezekiel's task as watchman

¹⁶At the end of seven days the word of the LORD came to me: ¹⁷'Son of man, I have made you a watchman for the people of Israel; so hear the word I speak and give them warning from me. ¹⁸When I say to a wicked person, "You will surely die," and you do not warn them or speak out to dissuade them from their evil ways in order to save their life, that wicked person

u 1 The Hebrew phrase *ben adam* means *human being*. The phrase *son of man* is retained as a form of address here and throughout Ezekiel because of its possible association with 'Son of Man' in the New Testament.

a 12 Probable reading of the original Hebrew text; Masoretic Text *sound – may the glory of the LORD be praised from his place* will die for[b] their sin, and I will hold you accountable for their blood. 19 But if you do warn the wicked person and they do not turn from their wickedness or from their evil ways, they will die for their sin; but you will have saved yourself.

20 'Again, when a righteous person turns from their righteousness and does evil, and I put a stumbling-block before them, they will die. Since you did not

warn them, they will die for their sin. The righteous things that person did will not be remembered, and I will hold you accountable for their blood. 21 But if you do warn the righteous person not to sin and they do not sin, they will surely live because they took warning, and you will have saved yourself.'

22 The hand of the LORD was on me there, and he said to me, 'Get up and go out to the plain, and there I will speak

b 18 Or *in*; also in verses 19 and 20

THROUGH EZEKIEL 2

Being a watchman

It's probably just as well that God leaves Ezekiel for seven days to come to terms with what's being asked of him (Ezekiel 3:1–15). When we read what comes next (3:16–27), we realise the huge responsibility involved in being a person called by God.

Your calling may not be as huge as Ezekiel's, and it might not be your lifetime vocation, but God calls us to be obedient not just in the calling for our lives, but also in the everyday. When I read this passage I realised for the first time the potential costs of ignoring the prompting of God in my life. What if God asks us to talk to someone and we don't? What if that person never changes their behaviour and something terrible happens? Aren't we a bit responsible?

Our heavenly Father doesn't call us to fulfil each of our individual needs (though ultimately it's living in his will that fulfils us more than anything else we can do), but he calls us so that we can look after the people he cares about – every single person on the earth. We're called to feed the hungry, love the lonely and look after widows and prisoners (Matthew 25:40). Those around us are people he loved so deeply that he sent his Son to die for them. This passage is a really powerful reminder that there are consequences not only for the things we do, but also for the things we don't do. Is it possible that there may be people who aren't in heaven with us solely as a result of our own disobedience? Is it possible that we can be held to account for their absence? I'm not sure, but reading this passage in Ezekiel makes me want to do my utmost to ensure that the question doesn't arise.

St Teresa of Avila once said, 'Christ has no body on earth but yours, no hands but yours, no feet but yours. Yours are the eyes through which Christ's compassion for the world is to look out; yours are the feet with which he is to go about doing good; and yours are the hands with which he is to bless us now.'

Jane Plackett

 Ezekiel 3:15   Ezekiel 4

to you.' 23 So I got up and went out to the plain. And the glory of the LORD was standing there, like the glory I had seen by the River Kebar, and I fell face down.

24 Then the Spirit came into me and raised me to my feet. He spoke to me and said: 'Go, shut yourself inside your house. 25 And you, son of man, they will tie with ropes; you will be bound so that you cannot go out among the people. 26 I will make your tongue stick to the roof of your mouth so that you will be silent and unable to rebuke them, for they are a rebellious people. 27 But when I speak to you, I will open your mouth and you shall say to them, "This is what the Sovereign LORD says." Whoever will listen let them listen, and whoever will refuse let them refuse; for they are a rebellious people.

Siege of Jerusalem symbolised

4 'Now, son of man, take a block of clay, put it in front of you and draw the city of Jerusalem on it. 2 Then lay siege to it: erect siege works against it, build a ramp up to it, set up camps against it and put battering-rams around it. 3 Then take an iron pan, place it as an iron wall between you and the city and turn your face towards it. It will be under siege, and you shall besiege it. This will be a sign to the people of Israel.

4 'Then lie on your left side and put the sin of the people of Israel upon yourself.*a* You are to bear their sin for the number of days you lie on your side. 5 I have assigned you the same number of days as the years of their sin. So for 390 days you will bear the sin of the people of Israel.

6 'After you have finished this, lie down again, this time on your right side, and bear the sin of the people of Judah. I have assigned you 40 days, a day for each year. 7 Turn your face towards the siege of Jerusalem and with bared arm prophesy against her. 8 I will tie you up with ropes so that you cannot turn from one side to the other until you have finished the days of your siege.

9 'Take wheat and barley, beans and lentils, millet and spelt; put them in a storage jar and use them to make bread for yourself. You are to eat it during the 390 days you lie on your side. 10 Weigh out twenty shekels*b* of food to eat each day and eat it at set times. 11 Also measure out a sixth of a hin*c* of water and drink it at set times. 12 Eat the food as you would a loaf of barley bread; bake it in the sight of the people, using human excrement for fuel.' 13 The LORD said, 'In this way the people of Israel will eat defiled food among the nations where I will drive them.'

14 Then I said, 'Not so, Sovereign LORD! I have never defiled myself. From my youth until now I have never eaten anything found dead or torn by wild animals. No impure meat has ever entered my mouth.'

15 'Very well,' he said, 'I will let you bake your bread over cow dung instead of human excrement.'

16 He then said to me: 'Son of man, I am about to cut off the food supply in Jerusalem. The people will eat rationed food in anxiety and drink rationed water in despair, 17 for food and water will be scarce. They will be appalled at the sight of each other and will waste away because of*d* their sin.

God's razor of judgment

5 'Now, son of man, take a sharp sword and use it as a barber's razor to shave your head and your beard. Then take a set of scales and divide up the hair. 2 When the days of your siege come to an end, burn a third of the hair inside the city. Take a third and strike it with the sword all around the city. And scatter a third to the wind. For I will pursue them with drawn sword. 3 But take a few hairs and tuck them away in the folds of your garment. 4 Again, take a few of these and throw them into the fire and burn them up. A fire will spread from there to all Israel.

5 'This is what the Sovereign LORD says: this is Jerusalem, which I have set in the centre of the nations, with countries all

---

a 4 Or *upon your side*

b 10 That is, about 230 grams
c 11 That is, about 0.6 litre
d 17 Or *away in*

THROUGH EZEKIEL 3
Ezekiel's first prophecy

Ezekiel has now understood the consequences of what God is asking of him, and so God begins to reveal his first prophecy (Ezekiel 4). It's a strange but amazing one. (Incidentally, all the other prophets have a particular style, but Ezekiel is the only one presented as a narrative.) Read Ezekiel 4 again and think about what it really says.

How would that have looked? Ezekiel is asked to draw a picture of Jerusalem on a clay tablet, then to construct a model camp around it and lay siege to the city, and finally to set battering rams around it. Pretty strange, but it gets stranger…

Next he is asked to place an iron pan between himself and the city and turn his face towards it. The city is under siege, and Ezekiel represents God to the people, keeping it under siege. Some people think the pan represents the unbreakable strength of the siege, but I wonder if the pan represents the people's sin – which stops God intervening in the siege, and stops Ezekiel's prophecies getting through to the people.

He is then asked to eat a strange diet which he has to cook in public, and to lie on his side for a number of days to represent each year of the people's sin. Only after he has done this is he allowed to prophesy to the people. Why?

People don't leave themselves open to public ridicule without a purpose; people don't lie on their side in front of a model they have created, cooking their bread over cow manure, without a reason. Ezekiel doesn't lie on his side, thinking each day about the sin of Israel for more than a year, without good motivation. His actions not only arouse curiosity, they give his words integrity.

Finally, when he goes to prophesy with bared arm, they should realise that his words are valid. How? Because when you lie on your side for more than a year, and then turn over and lie for over a month on the other side, you're not going to be left physically unmarked. There will be muscle wastage, and you'll get cramp. Imagine going to speak to a group of people and the pain of raising your hand as you make a point: it's going to be excruciating, but the message is worth the pain.

God doesn't always ask us to do things that are palatable to everyone, and while that's not often going to involve what Ezekiel had to do here, this is a reminder that the people God created don't always want to hear what he has to say, and sometimes he'll ask us to go to great lengths to engage people's attention. When God asks us to share a word of knowledge, run an assembly in our school, take our friends to church or give someone a Bible, what will we do? How much are we prepared to trust God and look daft in the process to give our words integrity?

Jane Plackett

 Ezekiel 3   Ezekiel 34 ▶▶

around her. 6Yet in her wickedness she has rebelled against my laws and decrees more than the nations and countries around her. She has rejected my laws and has not followed my decrees.

7'Therefore this is what the Sovereign Lord says: you have been more unruly than the nations around you and have not followed my decrees or kept my laws. You have not evena conformed to the standards of the nations around you.

8'Therefore this is what the Sovereign Lord says: I myself am against you, Jerusalem, and I will inflict punishment on you in the sight of the nations. 9Because of all your detestable idols, I will do to you what I have never done before and will never do again. 10Therefore in your midst parents will eat their children, and children will eat their parents. I will inflict punishment on you and will scatter all your survivors to the winds. 11Therefore as surely as I live, declares the Sovereign Lord, because you have defiled my sanctuary with all your vile images and detestable practices, I myself will shave you; I will not look on you with pity or spare you. 12A third of your people will die of the plague or perish by famine inside you; a third will fall by the sword outside your walls; and a third I will scatter to the winds and pursue with drawn sword.

13'Then my anger will cease and my wrath against them will subside, and I will be avenged. And when I have spent my wrath on them, they will know that I the Lord have spoken in my zeal.

14'I will make you a ruin and a reproach among the nations around you, in the sight of all who pass by. 15You will be a reproach and a taunt, a warning and an object of horror to the nations around you when I inflict punishment on you in anger and in wrath and with stinging rebuke. I the Lord have spoken. 16When I shoot at you with my deadly and destructive arrows of famine, I will shoot to destroy you. I will bring more and more famine upon you and cut off your supply of food. 17I will send famine and wild beasts against

you, and they will leave you childless. Plague and bloodshed will sweep through you, and I will bring the sword against you. I the Lord have spoken.'

Doom for the mountains of Israel

6 The word of the Lord came to me: 2'Son of man, set your face against the mountains of Israel; prophesy against them 3and say: "You mountains of Israel, hear the word of the Sovereign Lord. This is what the Sovereign Lord says to the mountains and hills, to the ravines and valleys: I am about to bring a sword against you, and I will destroy your high places. 4Your altars will be demolished and your incense altars will be smashed; and I will slay your people in front of your idols. 5I will lay the dead bodies of the Israelites in front of their idols, and I will scatter your bones around your altars. 6Wherever you live, the towns will be laid waste and the high places demolished, so that your altars will be laid waste and devastated, your idols smashed and ruined, your incense altars broken down, and what you have made wiped out. 7Your people will fall slain among you, and you will know that I am the Lord.

8'"But I will spare some, for some of you will escape the sword when you are scattered among the lands and nations. 9Then in the nations where they have been carried captive, those who escape will remember me – how I have been grieved by their adulterous hearts, which have turned away from me, and by their eyes, which have lusted after their idols. They will loathe themselves for the evil they have done and for all their detestable practices. 10And they will know that I am the Lord; I did not threaten in vain to bring this calamity on them.

11'"This is what the Sovereign Lord says: strike your hands together and stamp your feet and cry out 'Alas!' because of all the wicked and detestable practices of the people of Israel, for they will fall by the sword, famine and plague. 12One who is far away will die of the plague, and one who is near will fall by the sword, and any one who survives and is spared will die of

---

a 7 Most Hebrew manuscripts; some Hebrew manuscripts and Syriac *You have* famine. So will I pour out my wrath on them. ¹³And they will know that I am the LORD, when their people lie slain among their idols around their altars, on every high hill and on all the mountaintops, under every spreading tree and every leafy oak – places where they offered fragrant incense to all their idols. ¹⁴And I will stretch out my hand against them and make the land a desolate waste from the desert to Diblah[a] – wherever they live. Then they will know that I am the LORD." '

The end has come

7 The word of the LORD came to me: ²'Son of man, this is what the Sovereign LORD says to the land of Israel:

' "The end! The end has come
upon the four corners of the land!
³The end is now upon you,
and I will unleash my anger against you.
I will judge you according to your conduct
and repay you for all your detestable practices.
⁴I will not look on you with pity;
I will not spare you.
I will surely repay you for your conduct
and for the detestable practices among you.

' "Then you will know that I am the LORD."

⁵'This is what the Sovereign LORD says:

' "Disaster! Unheard-of[a] disaster!
See, it comes!
⁶The end has come!
The end has come!
It has roused itself against you.
See, it comes!
⁷Doom has come upon you,
upon you who dwell in the land.
The time has come! The day is near!
There is panic, not joy, on the mountains.

⁸I am about to pour out my wrath on you
and spend my anger against you.
I will judge you according to your conduct
and repay you for all your detestable practices.
⁹I will not look on you with pity;
I will not spare you.
I will repay you for your conduct
and for the detestable practices among you.

' "Then you will know that it is I the LORD who strikes you.

¹⁰' "See, the day!
See, it comes!
Doom has burst forth,
the rod has budded,
arrogance has blossomed!
¹¹Violence has arisen,[b]
a rod to punish the wicked.
None of the people will be left,
none of that crowd –
none of their wealth,
nothing of value.
¹²The time has come!
The day has arrived!
Let not the buyer rejoice
nor the seller grieve,
for my wrath is on the whole crowd.
¹³The seller will not recover
the property that was sold –
as long as both buyer and seller live.
For the vision concerning the whole crowd
will not be reversed.
Because of their sins, not one of them
will preserve their life.

¹⁴' "They have blown the trumpet,
they have made all things ready,
but no one will go into battle,
for my wrath is on the whole crowd.
¹⁵Outside is the sword;
inside are plague and famine.
Those in the country
will die by the sword;
those in the city

---

a 14 Most Hebrew manuscripts; a few Hebrew manuscripts *Riblah*
a 5 Most Hebrew manuscripts; some Hebrew manuscripts and Syriac *Disaster after*

b 11 Or *The violent one has become*

will be devoured by famine and
plague.
16 The fugitives who escape
will flee to the mountains.
Like doves of the valleys,
they will all moan,
each for their own sins.
17 Every hand will go limp;
every leg will be wet with urine.
18 They will put on sackcloth
and be clothed with terror.
Every face will be covered with shame,
and every head will be shaved.

19 ' "They will throw their silver into the
streets,
and their gold will be treated as a
thing unclean.
Their silver and gold
will not be able to deliver them
in the day of the LORD's wrath.
It will not satisfy their hunger
or fill their stomachs,
for it has caused them to stumble
into sin.
20 They took pride in their beautiful
jewellery
and used it to make their detestable
idols.
They made it into vile images;
therefore I will make it a thing
unclean for them.
21 I will give their wealth as plunder to
foreigners
and as loot to the wicked of the
earth,
who will defile it.
22 I will turn my face away from the
people,
and robbers will desecrate the place I
treasure.
They will enter it
and will defile it.

23 ' "Prepare chains!
For the land is full of bloodshed,
and the city is full of violence.
24 I will bring the most wicked of
nations
to take possession of their houses.
I will put an end to the pride of the
mighty,

and their sanctuaries will be
desecrated.
25 When terror comes,
they will seek peace in vain.
26 Calamity upon calamity will come,
and rumour upon rumour.
They will go searching for a vision from
the prophet,
priestly instruction in the law will
cease,
the counsel of the elders will come to
an end.
27 The king will mourn,
the prince will be clothed with
despair,
and the hands of the people of the
land will tremble.
I will deal with them according to their
conduct,
and by their own standards I will
judge them.

' "Then they will know that I am the
LORD." '

Idolatry in the temple

8 In the sixth year, in the sixth month
on the fifth day, while I was sitting in
my house and the elders of Judah were sitting before me, the hand of the Sovereign
LORD came on me there. 2 I looked, and I
saw a figure like that of a man.*a* From what
appeared to be his waist down he was like
fire, and from there up his appearance was
as bright as glowing metal. 3 He stretched
out what looked like a hand and took me
by the hair of my head. The Spirit lifted
me up between earth and heaven and in
visions of God he took me to Jerusalem,
to the entrance of the north gate of the
inner court, where the idol that provokes
to jealousy stood. 4 And there before me
was the glory of the God of Israel, as in the
vision I had seen in the plain.

5 Then he said to me, 'Son of man, look
towards the north.' So I looked, and in
the entrance north of the gate of the altar
I saw this idol of jealousy.

a 2 Or saw a fiery figure

6And he said to me, 'Son of man, do you see what they are doing – the utterly detestable things the Israelites are doing here, things that will drive me far from my sanctuary? But you will see things that are even more detestable.'

7Then he brought me to the entrance to the court. I looked, and I saw a hole in the wall. 8He said to me, 'Son of man, now dig into the wall.' So I dug into the wall and saw a doorway there.

9And he said to me, 'Go in and see the wicked and detestable things they are doing here.' 10So I went in and looked, and I saw portrayed all over the walls all kinds of crawling things and unclean animals and all the idols of Israel. 11In front of them stood seventy elders of Israel, and Jaazaniah son of Shaphan was standing among them. Each had a censer in his hand, and a fragrant cloud of incense was rising.

12He said to me, 'Son of man, have you seen what the elders of Israel are doing in the darkness, each at the shrine of his own idol? They say, "The LORD does not see us; the LORD has forsaken the land."'
13Again, he said, 'You will see them doing things that are even more detestable.'

14Then he brought me to the entrance of the north gate of the house of the LORD, and I saw women sitting there, mourning the god Tammuz. 15He said to me, 'Do you see this, son of man? You will see things that are even more detestable than this.'

16He then brought me into the inner court of the house of the LORD, and there at the entrance to the temple, between the portico and the altar, were about twenty-five men. With their backs towards the temple of the LORD and their faces towards the east, they were bowing down to the sun in the east.

17He said to me, 'Have you seen this, son of man? Is it a trivial matter for the people of Judah to do the detestable things they are doing here? Must they also fill the land with violence and continually arouse my anger? Look at them putting the branch to their nose! 18Therefore I will deal with them in anger; I will not look on them with pity or spare them. Although they shout in my ears, I will not listen to them.'

Judgment on the idolaters

9 Then I heard him call out in a loud voice, 'Bring near those who are appointed to execute judgment on the city, each with a weapon in his hand.' 2And I saw six men coming from the direction of the upper gate, which faces north, each with a deadly weapon in his hand. With them was a man clothed in linen who had a writing kit at his side. They came in and stood beside the bronze altar.

3Now the glory of the God of Israel went up from above the cherubim, where it had been, and moved to the threshold of the temple. Then the LORD called to the man clothed in linen who had the writing kit at his side 4and said to him, 'Go throughout the city of Jerusalem and put a mark on the foreheads of those who grieve and lament over all the detestable things that are done in it.'

5As I listened, he said to the others, 'Follow him through the city and kill, without showing pity or compassion. 6Slaughter the old men, the young men and women, the mothers and children, but do not touch anyone who has the mark. Begin at my sanctuary.' So they began with the old men who were in front of the temple.

7Then he said to them, 'Defile the temple and fill the courts with the slain. Go!' So they went out and began killing throughout the city. 8While they were killing and I was left alone, I fell face down, crying out, 'Alas, Sovereign LORD! Are you going to destroy the entire remnant of Israel in this outpouring of your wrath on Jerusalem?'

9He answered me, 'The sin of the people of Israel and Judah is exceedingly great; the land is full of bloodshed and the city is full of injustice. They say, "The LORD has forsaken the land; the LORD does not see." 10So I will not look on them with pity or spare them, but I will bring down on their own heads what they have done.'

11Then the man in linen with the writing kit at his side brought back word, saying, 'I have done as you commanded.'

God's glory departs from the temple

10 I looked, and I saw the likeness of a throne of lapis lazuli above the vault that was over the heads of the cherubim. ² The LORD said to the man clothed in linen, 'Go in among the wheels beneath the cherubim. Fill your hands with burning coals from among the cherubim and scatter them over the city.' And as I watched, he went in.

³ Now the cherubim were standing on the south side of the temple when the man went in, and a cloud filled the inner court. ⁴ Then the glory of the LORD rose from above the cherubim and moved to the threshold of the temple. The cloud filled the temple, and the court was full of the radiance of the glory of the LORD. ⁵ The sound of the wings of the cherubim could be heard as far away as the outer court, like the voice of God Almighty*a* when he speaks.

⁶ When the LORD commanded the man in linen, 'Take fire from among the wheels, from among the cherubim,' the man went in and stood beside a wheel. ⁷ Then one of the cherubim reached out his hand to the fire that was among them. He took up some of it and put it into the hands of the man in linen, who took it and went out. ⁸ (Under the wings of the cherubim could be seen what looked like human hands.)

⁹ I looked, and I saw beside the cherubim four wheels, one beside each of the cherubim; the wheels sparkled like topaz. ¹⁰ As for their appearance, the four of them looked alike; each was like a wheel intersecting a wheel. ¹¹ As they moved, they would go in any one of the four directions the cherubim faced; the wheels did not turn about*b* as the cherubim went. The cherubim went in whatever direction the head faced, without turning as they went. ¹² Their entire bodies, including their backs, their hands and their wings, were completely full of eyes, as were their four wheels. ¹³ I heard the wheels being called 'the whirling wheels'. ¹⁴ Each of the

cherubim had four faces: one face was that of a cherub, the second the face of a human being, the third the face of a lion, and the fourth the face of an eagle.

¹⁵ Then the cherubim rose upward. These were the living creatures I had seen by the River Kebar. ¹⁶ When the cherubim moved, the wheels beside them moved; and when the cherubim spread their wings to rise from the ground, the wheels did not leave their side. ¹⁷ When the cherubim stood still, they also stood still; and when the cherubim rose, they rose with them, because the spirit of the living creatures was in them.

¹⁸ Then the glory of the LORD departed from over the threshold of the temple and stopped above the cherubim. ¹⁹ While I watched, the cherubim spread their wings and rose from the ground, and as they went, the wheels went with them. They stopped at the entrance of the east gate of the LORD's house, and the glory of the God of Israel was above them.

²⁰ These were the living creatures I had seen beneath the God of Israel by the River Kebar, and I realised that they were cherubim. ²¹ Each had four faces and four wings, and under their wings was what looked like human hands. ²² Their faces had the same appearance as those I had seen by the River Kebar. Each one went straight ahead.

God's sure judgment on Jerusalem

11 Then the Spirit lifted me up and brought me to the gate of the house of the LORD that faces east. There at the entrance of the gate were twenty-five men, and I saw among them Jaazaniah son of Azzur and Pelatiah son of Benaiah, leaders of the people. ² The LORD said to me, 'Son of man, these are the men who are plotting evil and giving wicked advice in this city. ³ They say, "Haven't our houses been recently rebuilt? This city is a pot, and we are the meat in it." ⁴ Therefore prophesy against them; prophesy, son of man.'

⁵ Then the Spirit of the LORD came on me, and he told me to say: 'This is what the LORD says: that is what you are saying, you leaders in Israel, but I know what

a 5 Hebrew *El-Shaddai*
b 11 Or *aside*

is going through your mind. 6 You have killed many people in this city and filled its streets with the dead.

7 'Therefore this is what the Sovereign LORD says: the bodies you have thrown there are the meat and this city is the pot, but I will drive you out of it. 8 You fear the sword, and the sword is what I will bring against you, declares the Sovereign LORD. 9 I will drive you out of the city and deliver you into the hands of foreigners and inflict punishment on you. 10 You will fall by the sword, and I will execute judgment on you at the borders of Israel. Then you will know that I am the LORD. 11 This city will not be a pot for you, nor will you be the meat in it; I will execute judgment on you at the borders of Israel. 12 And you will know that I am the LORD, for you have not followed my decrees or kept my laws but have conformed to the standards of the nations around you.'

13 Now as I was prophesying, Pelatiah son of Benaiah died. Then I fell face down and cried out in a loud voice, 'Alas, Sovereign LORD! Will you completely destroy the remnant of Israel?'

The promise of Israel's return

14 The word of the LORD came to me: 15 'Son of man, the people of Jerusalem have said of your fellow exiles and all the other Israelites, "They are far away from the LORD; this land was given to us as our possession."

16 'Therefore say: "This is what the Sovereign LORD says: although I sent them far away among the nations and scattered them among the countries, yet for a little while I have been a sanctuary for them in the countries where they have gone."

17 'Therefore say: "This is what the Sovereign LORD says: I will gather you from the nations and bring you back from the countries where you have been scattered, and I will give you back the land of Israel again."

18 'They will return to it and remove all its vile images and detestable idols. 19 I will give them an undivided heart and put a new spirit in them; I will remove from them their heart of stone and give them a heart of flesh. 20 Then they will follow my

decrees and be careful to keep my laws. They will be my people, and I will be their God. 21 But as for those whose hearts are devoted to their vile images and detestable idols, I will bring down on their own heads what they have done, declares the Sovereign LORD.'

22 Then the cherubim, with the wheels beside them, spread their wings, and the glory of the God of Israel was above them. 23 The glory of the LORD went up from within the city and stopped above the mountain east of it. 24 The Spirit lifted me up and brought me to the exiles in Babylonia*a* in the vision given by the Spirit of God.

Then the vision I had seen went up from me, 25 and I told the exiles everything the LORD had shown me.

The exile symbolised

12 The word of the LORD came to me: 2 'Son of man, you are living among a rebellious people. They have eyes to see but do not see and ears to hear but do not hear, for they are a rebellious people.

3 'Therefore, son of man, pack your belongings for exile and in the daytime, as they watch, set out and go from where you are to another place. Perhaps they will understand, though they are a rebellious people. 4 During the daytime, while they watch, bring out your belongings packed for exile. Then in the evening, while they are watching, go out like those who go into exile. 5 While they watch, dig through the wall and take your belongings out through it. 6 Put them on your shoulder as they are watching and carry them out at dusk. Cover your face so that you cannot see the land, for I have made you a sign to the Israelites.'

7 So I did as I was commanded. During the day I brought out my things packed for exile. Then in the evening I dug through the wall with my hands. I took my belongings out at dusk, carrying them on my shoulders while they watched.

8 In the morning the word of the LORD came to me: 9 'Son of man, did not the

_____
a 24 Or *Chaldea*

Israelites, that rebellious people, ask you, "What are you doing?"

¹⁰ 'Say to them, "This is what the Sovereign LORD says: this prophecy concerns the prince in Jerusalem and all the Israelites who are there." ¹¹ Say to them, "I am a sign to you."

'As I have done, so it will be done to them. They will go into exile as captives.

¹² 'The prince among them will put his things on his shoulder at dusk and leave, and a hole will be dug in the wall for him to go through. He will cover his face so that he cannot see the land. ¹³ I will spread my net for him, and he will be caught in my snare; I will bring him to Babylonia, the land of the Chaldeans, but he will not see it, and there he will die. ¹⁴ I will scatter to the winds all those around him – his staff and all his troops – and I will pursue them with drawn sword.

¹⁵ 'They will know that I am the LORD, when I disperse them among the nations and scatter them through the countries. ¹⁶ But I will spare a few of them from the sword, famine and plague, so that in the nations where they go they may acknowledge all their detestable practices. Then they will know that I am the LORD.'

¹⁷ The word of the LORD came to me: ¹⁸ 'Son of man, tremble as you eat your food, and shudder in fear as you drink your water. ¹⁹ Say to the people of the land: "This is what the Sovereign LORD says about those living in Jerusalem and in the land of Israel: they will eat their food in anxiety and drink their water in despair, for their land will be stripped of everything in it because of the violence of all who live there. ²⁰ The inhabited towns will be laid waste and the land will be desolate. Then you will know that I am the LORD." '

There will be no delay

²¹ The word of the LORD came to me: ²² 'Son of man, what is this proverb you have in the land of Israel: "The days go by and every vision comes to nothing"? ²³ Say to them, "This is what the Sovereign LORD says: I am going to put an end to this proverb, and they will no longer quote it

in Israel." Say to them, "The days are near when every vision will be fulfilled. ²⁴ For there will be no more false visions or flattering divinations among the people of Israel. ²⁵ But I the LORD will speak what I will, and it shall be fulfilled without delay. For in your days, you rebellious people, I will fulfil whatever I say, declares the Sovereign LORD." '

²⁶ The word of the LORD came to me: ²⁷ 'Son of man, the Israelites are saying, "The vision he sees is for many years from now, and he prophesies about the distant future."

²⁸ 'Therefore say to them, "This is what the Sovereign LORD says: none of my words will be delayed any longer; whatever I say will be fulfilled, declares the Sovereign LORD." '

False prophets condemned

13 The word of the LORD came to me: ² 'Son of man, prophesy against the prophets of Israel who are now prophesying. Say to those who prophesy out of their own imagination: "Hear the word of the LORD! ³ This is what the Sovereign LORD says: woe to the foolish*a* prophets who follow their own spirit and have seen nothing! ⁴ Your prophets, Israel, are like jackals among ruins. ⁵ You have not gone up to the breaches in the wall to repair it for the people of Israel so that it will stand firm in the battle on the day of the LORD. ⁶ Their visions are false and their divinations a lie. Even though the LORD has not sent them, they say, 'The LORD declares', and expect him to fulfil their words. ⁷ Have you not seen false visions and uttered lying divinations when you say, 'The LORD declares', though I have not spoken?

⁸ ' "Therefore this is what the Sovereign LORD says: because of your false words and lying visions, I am against you, declares the Sovereign LORD. ⁹ My hand will be against the prophets who see false visions and utter lying divinations. They will not belong to the council of my people or be listed in the records of Israel, nor

---

a 3 Or wicked

will they enter the land of Israel. Then you will know that I am the Sovereign LORD.

10 ' "Because they lead my people astray, saying, 'Peace', when there is no peace, and because, when a flimsy wall is built, they cover it with whitewash, 11 therefore tell those who cover it with whitewash that it is going to fall. Rain will come in torrents, and I will send hailstones hurtling down, and violent winds will burst forth. 12 When the wall collapses, will people not ask you, 'Where is the whitewash you covered it with?'

13 ' "Therefore this is what the Sovereign LORD says: in my wrath I will unleash a violent wind, and in my anger hailstones and torrents of rain will fall with destructive fury. 14 I will tear down the wall you have covered with whitewash and will level it to the ground so that its foundation will be laid bare. When it*b* falls, you will be destroyed in it; and you will know that I am the LORD. 15 So I will pour out my wrath against the wall and against those who covered it with whitewash. I will say to you, 'The wall is gone and so are those who whitewashed it, 16 those prophets of Israel who prophesied to Jerusalem and saw visions of peace for her when there was no peace, declares the Sovereign LORD.' "

17 'Now, son of man, set your face against the daughters of your people who prophesy out of their own imagination. Prophesy against them 18 and say, "This is what the Sovereign LORD says: woe to the women who sew magic charms on all their wrists and make veils of various lengths for their heads in order to ensnare people. Will you ensnare the lives of my people but preserve your own? 19 You have profaned me among my people for a few handfuls of barley and scraps of bread. By lying to my people, who listen to lies, you have killed those who should not have died and have spared those who should not live.

20 ' "Therefore this is what the Sovereign LORD says: I am against your magic charms with which you ensnare people

like birds and I will tear them from your arms; I will set free the people that you ensnare like birds. 21 I will tear off your veils and save my people from your hands, and they will no longer fall prey to your power. Then you will know that I am the LORD. 22 Because you disheartened the righteous with your lies, when I had brought them no grief, and because you encouraged the wicked not to turn from their evil ways and so save their lives, 23 therefore you will no longer see false visions or practise divination. I will save my people from your hands. And then you will know that I am the LORD." '

Idolaters condemned

14 Some of the elders of Israel came to me and sat down in front of me. 2 Then the word of the LORD came to me: 3 'Son of man, these men have set up idols in their hearts and put wicked stumbling-blocks before their faces. Should I let them enquire of me at all? 4 Therefore speak to them and tell them, "This is what the Sovereign LORD says: when any of the Israelites set up idols in their hearts and put a wicked stumbling-block before their faces and then go to a prophet, I the LORD will answer them myself in keeping with their great idolatry. 5 I will do this to recapture the hearts of the people of Israel, who have all deserted me for their idols."

6 'Therefore say to the people of Israel, "This is what the Sovereign LORD says: repent! Turn from your idols and renounce all your detestable practices!

7 ' "When any of the Israelites or any foreigner residing in Israel separate themselves from me and set up idols in their hearts and put a wicked stumbling-block before their faces and then go to a prophet to enquire of me, I the LORD will answer them myself. 8 I will set my face against them and make them an example and a by-word. I will remove them from my people. Then you will know that I am the LORD.

9 ' "And if the prophet is enticed to utter a prophecy, I the LORD have enticed that prophet, and I will stretch out my hand against him and destroy him from among my people Israel. 10 They will bear their

---

b 14 Or *the city*

guilt – the prophet will be as guilty as the one who consults him. ¹¹Then the people of Israel will no longer stray from me, nor will they defile themselves any more with all their sins. They will be my people, and I will be their God, declares the Sovereign LORD.''

Jerusalem's judgment inescapable

¹²The word of the LORD came to me: ¹³'Son of man, if a country sins against me by being unfaithful and I stretch out my hand against it to cut off its food supply and send famine upon it and kill its people and their animals, ¹⁴even if these three men – Noah, Daniel*a* and Job – were in it, they could save only themselves by their righteousness, declares the Sovereign LORD.

¹⁵'Or if I send wild beasts through that country and they leave it childless and it becomes desolate so that no one can pass through it because of the beasts, ¹⁶as surely as I live, declares the Sovereign LORD, even if these three men were in it, they could not save their own sons or daughters. They alone would be saved, but the land would be desolate.

¹⁷'Or if I bring a sword against that country and say, "Let the sword pass throughout the land," and I kill its people and their animals, ¹⁸as surely as I live, declares the Sovereign LORD, even if these three men were in it, they could not save their own sons or daughters. They alone would be saved.

¹⁹'Or if I send a plague into that land and pour out my wrath on it through bloodshed, killing its people and their animals, ²⁰as surely as I live, declares the Sovereign LORD, even if Noah, Daniel and Job were in it, they could save neither son nor daughter. They would save only themselves by their righteousness.

²¹'For this is what the Sovereign LORD says: how much worse will it be when I send against Jerusalem my four dreadful judgments – sword and famine and wild beasts and plague – to kill its men and

their animals! ²²Yet there will be some survivors – sons and daughters who will be brought out of it. They will come to you, and when you see their conduct and their actions, you will be consoled regarding the disaster I have brought on Jerusalem – every disaster I have brought on it. ²³You will be consoled when you see their conduct and their actions, for you will know that I have done nothing in it without cause, declares the Sovereign LORD.'

FAVOURITE VERSES

Psalm 73:26

*My flesh and my heart may fail,
but God is the strength of my heart
and my portion forever.*

When it feels as if every person in the world (including myself!) has let me down, this reminds me that Jesus really is all that I'll ever need, and that his love never fails.

Tessa, 18

Jerusalem as a useless vine

15 The word of the LORD came to me: ²'Son of man, how is the wood of a vine different from that of a branch from any of the trees in the forest? ³Is wood ever taken from it to make anything useful? Do they make pegs from it to hang things on? ⁴And after it is thrown on the fire as fuel and the fire burns both ends and chars the middle, is it then useful for anything? ⁵If it was not useful for anything when it was whole, how much less can it be made into something useful when the fire has burned it and it is charred?

⁶'Therefore this is what the Sovereign LORD says: as I have given the wood of the vine among the trees of the forest as fuel for the fire, so will I treat the people

---

a 14 Or *Danel*, a man of renown in ancient literature; also in verse 20 living in Jerusalem. ⁷I will set my face against them. Although they have come out of the fire, the fire will yet consume them. And when I set my face against them, you will know that I am the LORD. ⁸I will make the land desolate because they have been unfaithful, declares the Sovereign LORD.'

Jerusalem as an adulterous wife

16 The word of the LORD came to me: ²'Son of man, confront Jerusalem with her detestable practices ³and say, "This is what the Sovereign LORD says to Jerusalem: your ancestry and birth were in the land of the Canaanites; your father was an Amorite and your mother a Hittite. ⁴On the day you were born your cord was not cut, nor were you washed with water to make you clean, nor were you rubbed with salt or wrapped in cloths. ⁵No one looked on you with pity or had compassion enough to do any of these things for you. Rather, you were thrown out into the open field, for on the day you were born you were despised.

⁶' "Then I passed by and saw you kicking about in your blood, and as you lay there in your blood I said to you, 'Live!'ᵃ ⁷I made you grow like a plant of the field. You grew and developed and entered puberty. Your breasts had formed and your hair had grown, yet you were stark naked.

⁸' "Later I passed by, and when I looked at you and saw that you were old enough for love, I spread the corner of my garment over you and covered your naked body. I gave you my solemn oath and entered into a covenant with you, declares the Sovereign LORD, and you became mine.

⁹' "I bathed you with water and washed the blood from you and put ointments on you. ¹⁰I clothed you with an embroidered dress and put sandals of fine leather on you. I dressed you in fine linen and covered you with costly garments. ¹¹I adorned you with jewellery: I put bracelets on your arms and a necklace round your neck,

¹²and I put a ring on your nose, earrings on your ears and a beautiful crown on your head. ¹³So you were adorned with gold and silver; your clothes were of fine linen and costly fabric and embroidered cloth. Your food was honey, olive oil and the finest flour. You became very beautiful and rose to be a queen. ¹⁴And your fame spread among the nations on account of your beauty, because the splendour I had given you made your beauty perfect, declares the Sovereign LORD.

¹⁵' "But you trusted in your beauty and used your fame to become a prostitute. You lavished your favours on anyone who passed by and your beauty became his. ¹⁶You took some of your garments to make gaudy high places, where you carried on your prostitution. You went to him, and he possessed your beauty.ᵇ ¹⁷You also took the fine jewellery I gave you, the jewellery made of my gold and silver, and you made for yourself male idols and engaged in prostitution with them. ¹⁸And you took your embroidered clothes to put on them, and you offered my oil and incense before them. ¹⁹Also the food I provided for you – the flour, olive oil and honey I gave you to eat – you offered as fragrant incense before them. That is what happened, declares the Sovereign LORD.

²⁰' "And you took your sons and daughters whom you bore to me and sacrificed them as food to the idols. Was your prostitution not enough? ²¹You slaughtered my children and sacrificed them to the idols. ²²In all your detestable practices and your prostitution you did not remember the days of your youth, when you were naked and bare, kicking about in your blood.

²³' "Woe! Woe to you, declares the Sovereign LORD. In addition to all your other wickedness, ²⁴you built a mound for yourself and made a lofty shrine in every public square. ²⁵At every street corner you built your lofty shrines and degraded your beauty, spreading your legs with increasing promiscuity to anyone who passed by. ²⁶You engaged in prostitution with

---

ᵃ 6 A few Hebrew manuscripts, Septuagint and Syriac; most Hebrew manuscripts repeat *and as you lay there in your blood I said to you, 'Live!'*

ᵇ 16 The meaning of the Hebrew for this sentence is uncertain.

the Egyptians, your neighbours with large genitals, and aroused my anger with your increasing promiscuity. ²⁷So I stretched out my hand against you and reduced your territory; I gave you over to the greed of your enemies, the daughters of the Philistines, who were shocked by your lewd conduct. ²⁸You engaged in prostitution with the Assyrians too, because you were insatiable; and even after that, you still were not satisfied. ²⁹Then you increased your promiscuity to include Babylonia,ᶜ a land of merchants, but even with this you were not satisfied.

³⁰'"I am filled with fury against you,ᵈ declares the Sovereign Lᴏʀᴅ, when you do all these things, acting like a brazen prostitute! ³¹When you built your mounds at every street corner and made your lofty shrines in every public square, you were unlike a prostitute, because you scorned payment.

³²'"You adulterous wife! You prefer strangers to your own husband! ³³All prostitutes receive gifts, but you give gifts to all your lovers, bribing them to come to you from everywhere for your illicit favours. ³⁴So in your prostitution you are the opposite of others; no one runs after you for your favours. You are the very opposite, for you give payment and none is given to you.

³⁵'"Therefore, you prostitute, hear the word of the Lᴏʀᴅ! ³⁶This is what the Sovereign Lᴏʀᴅ says: because you poured out your lust and exposed your naked body in your promiscuity with your lovers, and because of all your detestable idols, and because you gave them your children's blood, ³⁷therefore I am going to gather all your lovers, with whom you found pleasure, those you loved as well as those you hated. I will gather them against you from all around and will strip you in front of them, and they will see you stark naked. ³⁸I will sentence you to the punishment of women who commit adultery and who shed blood; I will bring on you the blood vengeance of my wrath and jealous anger. ³⁹Then I will deliver you into the hands of

your lovers, and they will tear down your mounds and destroy your lofty shrines. They will strip you of your clothes and take your fine jewellery and leave you stark naked. ⁴⁰They will bring a mob against you, who will stone you and hack you to pieces with their swords. ⁴¹They will burn down your houses and inflict punishment on you in the sight of many women. I will put a stop to your prostitution, and you will no longer pay your lovers. ⁴²Then my wrath against you will subside and my jealous anger will turn away from you; I will be calm and no longer angry.

⁴³'"Because you did not remember the days of your youth but enraged me with all these things, I will surely bring down on your head what you have done, declares the Sovereign Lᴏʀᴅ. Did you not add lewdness to all your other detestable practices?

⁴⁴'"Everyone who quotes proverbs will quote this proverb about you: 'Like mother, like daughter.' ⁴⁵You are a true daughter of your mother, who despised her husband and her children; and you are a true sister of your sisters, who despised their husbands and their children. Your mother was a Hittite and your father an Amorite. ⁴⁶Your elder sister was Samaria, who lived to the north of you with her daughters; and your younger sister, who lived to the south of you with her daughters, was Sodom. ⁴⁷You not only followed their ways and copied their detestable practices, but in all your ways you soon became more depraved than they. ⁴⁸As surely as I live, declares the Sovereign Lᴏʀᴅ, your sister Sodom and her daughters never did what you and your daughters have done.

⁴⁹'"Now this was the sin of your sister Sodom: she and her daughters were arrogant, overfed and unconcerned; they did not help the poor and needy. ⁵⁰They were haughty and did detestable things before me. Therefore I did away with them as you have seen. ⁵¹Samaria did not commit half the sins you did. You have done more detestable things than they, and have made your sisters seem righteous by all these things you have done. ⁵²Bear your disgrace, for you have furnished some justification for your sisters. Because your

---

ᶜ29 Or *Chaldea*
ᵈ30 Or *How feverish is your heart,*

sins were more vile than theirs, they appear more righteous than you. So then, be ashamed and bear your disgrace, for you have made your sisters appear righteous.

⁵³ ' "However, I will restore the fortunes of Sodom and her daughters and of Samaria and her daughters, and your fortunes along with them, ⁵⁴ so that you may bear your disgrace and be ashamed of all you have done in giving them comfort. ⁵⁵ And your sisters, Sodom with her daughters and Samaria with her daughters, will return to what they were before; and you and your daughters will return to what you were before. ⁵⁶ You would not even mention your sister Sodom in the day of your pride, ⁵⁷ before your wickedness was uncovered. Even so, you are now scorned by the daughters of Edomᵉ and all her neighbours and the daughters of the Philistines – all those around you who despise you. ⁵⁸ You will bear the consequences of your lewdness and your detestable practices, declares the LORD.

⁵⁹ ' "This is what the Sovereign LORD says: I will deal with you as you deserve, because you have despised my oath by breaking the covenant. ⁶⁰ Yet I will remember the covenant I made with you in the days of your youth, and I will establish an everlasting covenant with you. ⁶¹ Then you will remember your ways and be ashamed when you receive your sisters, both those who are older than you and those who are younger. I will give them to you as daughters, but not on the basis of my covenant with you. ⁶² So I will establish my covenant with you, and you will know that I am the LORD. ⁶³ Then, when I make atonement for you for all you have done, you will remember and be ashamed and never again open your mouth because of your humiliation, declares the Sovereign LORD." '

Two eagles and a vine

17 The word of the LORD came to me: ² 'Son of man, set forth an allegory and tell it to the Israelites as a parable. ³ Say to them, "This is what the Sovereign

LORD says: a great eagle with powerful wings, long feathers and full plumage of varied colours came to Lebanon. Taking hold of the top of a cedar, ⁴ he broke off its topmost shoot and carried it away to a land of merchants, where he planted it in a city of traders.

⁵ ' "He took one of the seedlings of the land and put it in fertile soil. He planted it like a willow by abundant water, ⁶ and it sprouted and became a low, spreading vine. Its branches turned towards him, but its roots remained under it. So it became a vine and produced branches and put out leafy boughs.

⁷ ' "But there was another great eagle with powerful wings and full plumage. The vine now sent out its roots towards him from the plot where it was planted and stretched out its branches to him for water. ⁸ It had been planted in good soil by abundant water so that it would produce branches, bear fruit and become a splendid vine."

⁹ 'Say to them, "This is what the Sovereign LORD says: will it thrive? Will it not be uprooted and stripped of its fruit so that it withers? All its new growth will wither. It will not take a strong arm or many people to pull it up by the roots. ¹⁰ It has been planted, but will it thrive? Will it not wither completely when the east wind strikes it – wither away in the plot where it grew?" '

¹¹ Then the word of the LORD came to me: ¹² 'Say to this rebellious people, "Do you not know what these things mean?" Say to them: "The king of Babylon went to Jerusalem and carried off her king and her nobles, bringing them back with him to Babylon. ¹³ Then he took a member of the royal family and made a treaty with him, putting him under oath. He also carried away the leading men of the land, ¹⁴ so that the kingdom would be brought low, unable to rise again, surviving only by keeping his treaty. ¹⁵ But the king rebelled against him by sending his envoys to Egypt to get horses and a large army. Will he succeed? Will he who does such things escape? Will he break the treaty and yet escape?

¹⁶ ' "As surely as I live, declares the

Sovereign LORD, he shall die in Babylon, in the land of the king who put him on the throne, whose oath he despised and whose treaty he broke. ¹⁷ Pharaoh with his mighty army and great horde will be of no help to him in war, when ramps are built and siege works erected to destroy many lives. ¹⁸ He despised the oath by breaking the covenant. Because he had given his hand in pledge and yet did all these things, he shall not escape.

¹⁹ ' "Therefore this is what the Sovereign LORD says: as surely as I live, I will repay him for despising my oath and breaking my covenant. ²⁰ I will spread my net for him, and he will be caught in my snare. I will bring him to Babylon and execute judgment on him there because he was unfaithful to me. ²¹ All his choice troops will fall by the sword, and the survivors will be scattered to the winds. Then you will know that I the LORD have spoken.

²² ' "This is what the Sovereign LORD says: I myself will take a shoot from the very top of a cedar and plant it; I will break off a tender sprig from its topmost shoots and plant it on a high and lofty mountain. ²³ On the mountain heights of Israel I will plant it; it will produce branches and bear fruit and become a splendid cedar. Birds of every kind will nest in it; they will find shelter in the shade of its branches. ²⁴ All the trees of the forest will know that I the LORD bring down the tall tree and make the low tree grow tall. I dry up the green tree and make the dry tree flourish.

' "I the LORD have spoken, and I will do it." '

The one who sins will die

18 The word of the LORD came to me: ² 'What do you people mean by quoting this proverb about the land of Israel:

' "The parents eat sour grapes,
    and the children's teeth are set on
       edge"?

³ 'As surely as I live, declares the Sovereign LORD, you will no longer quote this proverb in Israel. ⁴ For everyone belongs

to me, the parent as well as the child – both alike belong to me. The one who sins is the one who will die.

⁵ 'Suppose there is a righteous man
    who does what is just and right.
⁶ He does not eat at the mountain
    shrines
    or look to the idols of Israel.
He does not defile his neighbour's wife
    or have sexual relations with a
       woman during her period.
⁷ He does not oppress anyone,
    but returns what he took in pledge
       for a loan.
He does not commit robbery,
    but gives his food to the hungry
    and provides clothing for the naked.
⁸ He does not lend to them at interest
    or take a profit from them.
He withholds his hand from doing
       wrong
    and judges fairly between two
       parties.
⁹ He follows my decrees
    and faithfully keeps my laws.
That man is righteous;
    he will surely live,
       declares the Sovereign LORD.

¹⁰ 'Suppose he has a violent son, who sheds blood or does any of these other things^a ¹¹ (though the father has done none of them):

'He eats at the mountain shrines.
He defiles his neighbour's wife.
¹² He oppresses the poor and needy.
He commits robbery.
He does not return what he took in
       pledge.
He looks to the idols.
He does detestable things.
¹³ He lends at interest and takes a profit.

Will such a man live? He will not! Because he has done all these detestable things, he is to be put to death; his blood will be on his own head.

¹⁴ 'But suppose this son has a son who

---

^a 10 Or *things to a brother*

sees all the sins his father commits, and though he sees them, he does not do such things:

15 'He does not eat at the mountain
        shrines
    or look to the idols of Israel.
    He does not defile his neighbour's wife.
16 He does not oppress anyone
    or require a pledge for a loan.
    He does not commit robbery,
        but gives his food to the hungry
        and provides clothing for the naked.
17 He withholds his hand from ill-treating
        the poor
    and takes no interest or profit from
        them.
    He keeps my laws and follows my
        decrees.

He will not die for his father's sin; he will surely live. 18 But his father will die for his own sin, because he practised extortion, robbed his brother and did what was wrong among his people.

19 'Yet you ask, "Why does the son not share the guilt of his father?" Since the son has done what is just and right and has been careful to keep all my decrees, he will surely live. 20 The one who sins is the one who will die. The child will not share the guilt of the parent, nor will the parent share the guilt of the child. The righteousness of the righteous will be credited to them, and the wickedness of the wicked will be charged against them.

21 'But if a wicked person turns away from all the sins they have committed and keeps all my decrees and does what is just and right, that person will surely live; they will not die. 22 None of the offences they have committed will be remembered against them. Because of the righteous things they have done, they will live. 23 Do I take any pleasure in the death of the wicked? declares the Sovereign LORD. Rather, am I not pleased when they turn from their ways and live?

24 'But if a righteous person turns from their righteousness and commits sin and does the same detestable things the wicked person does, will they live? None of the righteous things that person has done will be remembered. Because of the unfaithfulness they are guilty of and because of the sins they have committed, they will die.

25 'Yet you say, "The way of the Lord is not just." Hear, you Israelites: is my way unjust? Is it not your ways that are unjust? 26 If a righteous person turns from their righteousness and commits sin, they will die for it; because of the sin they have committed they will die. 27 But if a wicked person turns away from the wickedness they have committed and does what is just and right, they will save their life. 28 Because they consider all the offences they have committed and turn away from them, that person will surely live; they will not die. 29 Yet the Israelites say, "The way of the Lord is not just." Are my ways unjust, people of Israel? Is it not your ways that are unjust?

30 'Therefore, you Israelites, I will judge each of you according to your own ways, declares the Sovereign LORD. Repent! Turn away from all your offences; then sin will not be your downfall. 31 Rid yourselves of all the offences you have committed, and get a new heart and a new spirit. Why will you die, people of Israel? 32 For I take no pleasure in the death of anyone, declares the Sovereign LORD. Repent and live!

A lament over Israel's princes

19 'Take up a lament concerning the princes of Israel 2 and say:

' "What a lioness was your mother
        among the lions!
    She lay down among them
        and reared her cubs.
3 She brought up one of her cubs,
        and he became a strong lion.
    He learned to tear the prey
        and he became a man-eater.
4 The nations heard about him,
        and he was trapped in their pit.
    They led him with hooks
        to the land of Egypt.

5 ' "When she saw her hope unfulfilled,
        her expectation gone,
    she took another of her cubs

and made him a strong lion.
⁶He prowled among the lions,
    for he was now a strong lion.
He learned to tear the prey
    and he became a man-eater.
⁷He broke down*a* their strongholds
    and devastated their towns.
The land and all who were in it
    were terrified by his roaring.
⁸Then the nations came against him,
    those from regions round about.
They spread their net for him,
    and he was trapped in their pit.
⁹With hooks they pulled him into a cage
    and brought him to the king of
        Babylon.
They put him in prison,
    so his roar was heard no longer
        on the mountains of Israel.

¹⁰'"Your mother was like a vine in your
        vineyard*b*
    planted by the water;
it was fruitful and full of branches
    because of abundant water.
¹¹Its branches were strong,
    fit for a ruler's sceptre.
It towered high
    above the thick foliage,
conspicuous for its height
    and for its many branches.
¹²But it was uprooted in fury
    and thrown to the ground.
The east wind made it shrivel,
    it was stripped of its fruit;
its strong branches withered
    and fire consumed them.
¹³Now it is planted in the desert,
    in a dry and thirsty land.
¹⁴Fire spread from one of its main*c*
        branches
    and consumed its fruit.
No strong branch is left on it
    fit for a ruler's sceptre.'

'This is a lament and is to be used as a lament.'

a 7 Targum (see Septuagint); Hebrew *He knew*
b 10 Two Hebrew manuscripts; most Hebrew manuscripts *your blood*
c 14 Or *from under its*

Rebellious Israel purged

20 In the seventh year, in the fifth month on the tenth day, some of the elders of Israel came to enquire of the LORD, and they sat down in front of me.

²Then the word of the LORD came to me: ³'Son of man, speak to the elders of Israel and say to them, "This is what the Sovereign LORD says: have you come to enquire of me? As surely as I live, I will not let you enquire of me, declares the Sovereign LORD."

⁴'Will you judge them? Will you judge them, son of man? Then confront them with the detestable practices of their ancestors ⁵and say to them: "This is what the Sovereign LORD says: on the day I chose Israel, I swore with uplifted hand to the descendants of Jacob and revealed myself to them in Egypt. With uplifted hand I said to them, 'I am the LORD your God.' ⁶On that day I swore to them that I would bring them out of Egypt into a land I had searched out for them, a land flowing with milk and honey, the most beautiful of all lands. ⁷And I said to them, 'Each of you, get rid of the vile images you have set your eyes on, and do not defile yourselves with the idols of Egypt. I am the LORD your God.'

⁸'"But they rebelled against me and would not listen to me; they did not get rid of the vile images they had set their eyes on, nor did they forsake the idols of Egypt. So I said I would pour out my wrath on them and spend my anger against them in Egypt. ⁹But for the sake of my name, I brought them out of Egypt. I did it to keep my name from being profaned in the eyes of the nations among whom they lived and in whose sight I had revealed myself to the Israelites. ¹⁰Therefore I led them out of Egypt and brought them into the wilderness. ¹¹I gave them my decrees and made known to them my laws, by which the person who obeys them will live. ¹²Also I gave them my Sabbaths as a sign between us, so they would know that I the LORD made them holy.

¹³'"Yet the people of Israel rebelled against me in the wilderness. They did not follow my decrees but rejected my laws –

by which the person who obeys them will live – and they utterly desecrated my Sabbaths. So I said I would pour out my wrath on them and destroy them in the wilderness. ¹⁴ But for the sake of my name I did what would keep it from being profaned in the eyes of the nations in whose sight I had brought them out. ¹⁵ Also with uplifted hand I swore to them in the wilderness that I would not bring them into the land I had given them – a land flowing with milk and honey, the most beautiful of all lands – ¹⁶ because they rejected my laws and did not follow my decrees and desecrated my Sabbaths. For their hearts were devoted to their idols. ¹⁷ Yet I looked on them with pity and did not destroy them or put an end to them in the wilderness. ¹⁸ I said to their children in the wilderness, 'Do not follow the statutes of your parents or keep their laws or defile yourselves with their idols. ¹⁹ I am the LORD your God; follow my decrees and be careful to keep my laws. ²⁰ Keep my Sabbaths holy, that they may be a sign between us. Then you will know that I am the LORD your God.'

²¹ ' "But the children rebelled against me: they did not follow my decrees, they were not careful to keep my laws, of which I said, 'The person who obeys them will live by them,' and they desecrated my Sabbaths. So I said I would pour out my wrath on them and spend my anger against them in the wilderness. ²² But I withheld my hand, and for the sake of my name I did what would keep it from being profaned in the eyes of the nations in whose sight I had brought them out. ²³ Also with uplifted hand I swore to them in the wilderness that I would disperse them among the nations and scatter them through the countries, ²⁴ because they had not obeyed my laws but had rejected my decrees and desecrated my Sabbaths, and their eyes lusted after their parents' idols. ²⁵ So I gave them other statutes that were not good and laws through which they could not live; ²⁶ I defiled them through their gifts – the sacrifice of every firstborn – that I might fill them with horror so that they would know that I am the LORD."

²⁷ 'Therefore, son of man, speak to the people of Israel and say to them, "This is what the Sovereign LORD says: in this also your ancestors blasphemed me by being unfaithful to me: ²⁸ when I brought them into the land I had sworn to give them and they saw any high hill or any leafy tree, there they offered their sacrifices, made offerings that aroused my anger, presented their fragrant incense and poured out their drink offerings. ²⁹ Then I said to them: what is this high place you go to?" ' (It is called Bamah*a* to this day.)

Rebellious Israel renewed

³⁰ 'Therefore say to the Israelites: "This is what the Sovereign LORD says: will you defile yourselves the way your ancestors did and lust after their vile images? ³¹ When you offer your gifts – the sacrifice of your children in the fire – you continue to defile yourselves with all your idols to this day. Am I to let you enquire of me, you Israelites? As surely as I live, declares the Sovereign LORD, I will not let you enquire of me.

³² ' "You say, 'We want to be like the nations, like the peoples of the world, who serve wood and stone.' But what you have in mind will never happen. ³³ As surely as I live, declares the Sovereign LORD, I will reign over you with a mighty hand and an outstretched arm and with outpoured wrath. ³⁴ I will bring you from the nations and gather you from the countries where you have been scattered – with a mighty hand and an outstretched arm and with outpoured wrath. ³⁵ I will bring you into the wilderness of the nations and there, face to face, I will execute judgment upon you. ³⁶ As I judged your ancestors in the wilderness of the land of Egypt, so I will judge you, declares the Sovereign LORD. ³⁷ I will take note of you as you pass under my rod, and I will bring you into the bond of the covenant. ³⁸ I will purge you of those who revolt and rebel against me. Although I will bring them out of the land where they are living, yet they will not enter the land of Israel. Then you will know that I am the LORD.

---

a 29 *Bamah* means *high place*.

39 ' "As for you, people of Israel, this is what the Sovereign LORD says: go and serve your idols, every one of you! But afterwards you will surely listen to me and no longer profane my holy name with your gifts and idols. **40** For on my holy mountain, the high mountain of Israel, declares the Sovereign LORD, there in the land all the people of Israel will serve me, and there I will accept them. There I will require your offerings and your choice gifts, *b* along with all your holy sacrifices. **41** I will accept you as fragrant incense when I bring you out from the nations and gather you from the countries where you have been scattered, and I will be proved holy through you in the sight of the nations. **42** Then you will know that I am the LORD, when I bring you into the land of Israel, the land I had sworn with uplifted hand to give to your ancestors. **43** There you will remember your conduct and all the actions by which you have defiled yourselves, and you will loathe yourselves for all the evil you have done. **44** You will know that I am the LORD, when I deal with you for my name's sake and not according to your evil ways and your corrupt practices, you people of Israel, declares the Sovereign LORD." '

Prophecy against the south

45 The word of the LORD came to me: **46** 'Son of man, set your face towards the south; preach against the south and prophesy against the forest of the southland. **47** Say to the southern forest: "Hear the word of the LORD. This is what the Sovereign LORD says: I am about to set fire to you, and it will consume all your trees, both green and dry. The blazing flame will not be quenched, and every face from south to north will be scorched by it. **48** Everyone will see that I the LORD have kindled it; it will not be quenched." '

49 Then I said, 'Sovereign LORD, they are saying of me, "Isn't he just telling parables?" ' *c*

Babylon as God's sword of judgment

21 *a* The word of the LORD came to me: **2** 'Son of man, set your face against Jerusalem and preach against the sanctuary. Prophesy against the land of Israel **3** and say to her: "This is what the LORD says: I am against you. I will draw my sword from its sheath and cut off from you both the righteous and the wicked. **4** Because I am going to cut off the righteous and the wicked, my sword will be unsheathed against everyone from south to north. **5** Then all people will know that I the LORD have drawn my sword from its sheath; it will not return again."

6 'Therefore groan, son of man! Groan before them with broken heart and bitter grief. **7** And when they ask you, "Why are you groaning?" you shall say, "Because of the news that is coming. Every heart will melt with fear and every hand go limp; every spirit will become faint and every leg will be wet with urine." It is coming! It will surely take place, declares the Sovereign LORD.'

8 The word of the LORD came to me: **9** 'Son of man, prophesy and say, "This is what the Lord says:

' "A sword, a sword,
    sharpened and polished –
10 sharpened for the slaughter,
    polished to flash like lightning!

' "Shall we rejoice in the sceptre of my royal son? The sword despises every such stick.

11 ' "The sword is appointed to be polished,
    to be grasped with the hand;
it is sharpened and polished,
    made ready for the hand of the slayer.
12 Cry out and wail, son of man,
    for it is against my people;
it is against all the princes of Israel.
They are thrown to the sword
    along with my people.
Therefore beat your breast.

---

b 40 Or *and the gifts of your firstfruits*
c 49 In Hebrew texts 20:45-49 is numbered 21:1-5.

a In Hebrew texts 21:1-32 is numbered 21:6-37.

¹³'"Testing will surely come. And what if even the sceptre, which the sword despises, does not continue? declares the Sovereign LORD."

¹⁴'So then, son of man, prophesy
    and strike your hands together.
Let the sword strike twice,
    even three times.
It is a sword for slaughter —
    a sword for great slaughter,
    closing in on them from every side.
¹⁵So that hearts may melt with fear
    and the fallen be many,
I have stationed the sword for
        slaughter[b]
    at all their gates.
Look! It is forged to strike like lightning,
    it is grasped for slaughter.
¹⁶Slash to the right, you sword,
    then to the left,
    wherever your blade is turned.
¹⁷I too will strike my hands together,
    and my wrath will subside.
I the LORD have spoken.'

¹⁸The word of the LORD came to me: ¹⁹'Son of man, mark out two roads for the sword of the king of Babylon to take, both starting from the same country. Make a signpost where the road branches off to the city. ²⁰Mark out one road for the sword to come against Rabbah of the Ammonites and another against Judah and fortified Jerusalem. ²¹For the king of Babylon will stop at the fork in the road, at the junction of the two roads, to seek an omen: he will cast lots with arrows, he will consult his idols, he will examine the liver. ²²Into his right hand will come the lot for Jerusalem, where he is to set up battering-rams, to give the command to slaughter, to sound the battle cry, to set battering-rams against the gates, to build a ramp and to erect siege works. ²³It will seem like a false omen to those who have sworn allegiance to him, but he will remind them of their guilt and take them captive.

²⁴'Therefore this is what the Sovereign LORD says: "Because you people have brought to mind your guilt by your open rebellion, revealing your sins in all that you do – because you have done this, you will be taken captive.

²⁵'"You profane and wicked prince of Israel, whose day has come, whose time of punishment has reached its climax, ²⁶this is what the Sovereign LORD says: take off the turban, remove the crown. It will not be as it was: The lowly will be exalted and the exalted will be brought low. ²⁷A ruin! A ruin! I will make it a ruin! The crown will not be restored until he to whom it rightfully belongs shall come; to him I will give it."

²⁸'And you, son of man, prophesy and say, "This is what the Sovereign LORD says about the Ammonites and their insults:

'"A sword, a sword,
    drawn for the slaughter,
    polished to consume
    and to flash like lightning!
²⁹Despite false visions concerning you
    and lying divinations about you,
it will be laid on the necks
    of the wicked who are to be slain,
    whose day has come,
    whose time of punishment has
        reached its climax.

³⁰'"Let the sword return to its sheath.
    In the place where you were
        created,
    in the land of your ancestry,
    I will judge you.
³¹I will pour out my wrath on you
    and breathe out my fiery anger
        against you;
I will deliver you into the hands of
    brutal men,
    men skilled in destruction.
³²You will be fuel for the fire,
    your blood will be shed in your land,
    you will be remembered no more;
    for I the LORD have spoken."'

Judgment on Jerusalem's sins

22 The word of the LORD came to me:

---

b 15 Septuagint; the meaning of the Hebrew for this word is uncertain.

2 'Son of man, will you judge her? Will you judge this city of bloodshed? Then confront her with all her detestable practices 3 and say: "This is what the Sovereign LORD says: you city that brings on herself doom by shedding blood in her midst and defiles herself by making idols, 4 you have become guilty because of the blood you have shed and have become defiled by the idols you have made. You have brought your days to a close, and the end of your years has come. Therefore I will make you an object of scorn to the nations and a laughing-stock to all the countries. 5 Those who are near and those who are far away will mock you, you infamous city, full of turmoil.

6 ' "See how each of the princes of Israel who are in you uses his power to shed blood. 7 In you they have treated father and mother with contempt; in you they have oppressed the foreigner and ill-treated the fatherless and the widow. 8 You have despised my holy things and desecrated my Sabbaths. 9 In you are slanderers who are bent on shedding blood; in you are those who eat at the mountain shrines and commit lewd acts. 10 In you are those who dishonour their father's bed; in you are those who violate women during their period, when they are ceremonially unclean. 11 In you one man commits a detestable offence with his neighbour's wife, another shamefully defiles his daughter-in-law, and another violates his sister, his own father's daughter. 12 In you are people who accept bribes to shed blood; you take interest and make a profit from the poor. You extort unjust gain from your neighbours. And you have forgotten me, declares the Sovereign LORD.

13 ' "I will surely strike my hands together at the unjust gain you have made and at the blood you have shed in your midst. 14 Will your courage endure or your hands be strong in the day I deal with you? I the LORD have spoken, and I will do it. 15 I will disperse you among the nations and scatter you through the countries; and I will put an end to your uncleanness. 16 When you have been defiled a in the eyes of the nations, you will know that I am the LORD." '

17 Then the word of the LORD came to me: 18 'Son of man, the people of Israel have become dross to me; all of them are the copper, tin, iron and lead left inside a furnace. They are but the dross of silver. 19 Therefore this is what the Sovereign LORD says: "Because you have all become dross, I will gather you into Jerusalem. 20 As silver, copper, iron, lead and tin are gathered into a furnace to be melted with a fiery blast, so will I gather you in my anger and my wrath and put you inside the city and melt you. 21 I will gather you and I will blow on you with my fiery wrath, and you will be melted inside her. 22 As silver is melted in a furnace, so you will be melted inside her, and you will know that I the LORD have poured out my wrath on you." '

23 Again the word of the LORD came to me: 24 'Son of man, say to the land, "You are a land that has not been cleansed or rained on in the day of wrath." 25 There is a conspiracy of her princes b within her like a roaring lion tearing its prey; they devour people, take treasures and precious things and make many widows within her. 26 Her priests do violence to my law and profane my holy things; they do not distinguish between the holy and the common; they teach that there is no difference between the unclean and the clean; and they shut their eyes to the keeping of my Sabbaths, so that I am profaned among them. 27 Her officials within her are like wolves tearing their prey; they shed blood and kill people to make unjust gain. 28 Her prophets whitewash these deeds for them by false visions and lying divinations. They say, "This is what the Sovereign LORD says" – when the LORD has not spoken. 29 The people of the land practise extortion and commit robbery; they oppress the poor and needy and ill-treat the foreigner, denying them justice.

30 'I looked for someone among them who would build up the wall and stand before me in the gap on behalf of the land so that I would not have to destroy it, but

---

a 16 Or When I have allotted you your inheritance   b 25 Septuagint; Hebrew prophets

I found no one. ³¹ So I will pour out my wrath on them and consume them with my fiery anger, bringing down on their own heads all they have done, declares the Sovereign LORD.'

Two adulterous sisters

23 The word of the LORD came to me: ² 'Son of man, there were two women, daughters of the same mother. ³ They became prostitutes in Egypt, engaging in prostitution from their youth. In that land their breasts were fondled and their virgin bosoms caressed. ⁴ The elder one was named Oholah, and her sister was Oholibah. They were mine and gave birth to sons and daughters. Oholah is Samaria, and Oholibah is Jerusalem.

⁵ 'Oholah engaged in prostitution while she was still mine; and she lusted after her lovers, the Assyrians – warriors ⁶ clothed in blue, governors and commanders, all of them handsome young men, and mounted horsemen. ⁷ She gave herself as a prostitute to all the elite of the Assyrians and defiled herself with all the idols of everyone she lusted after. ⁸ She did not give up the prostitution she began in Egypt, when during her youth men slept with her, caressed her virgin bosom and poured out their lust on her.

⁹ 'Therefore I delivered her into the hands of her lovers, the Assyrians, for whom she lusted. ¹⁰ They stripped her naked, took away her sons and daughters and killed her with the sword. She became a byword among women, and punishment was inflicted on her.

¹¹ 'Her sister Oholibah saw this, yet in her lust and prostitution she was more depraved than her sister. ¹² She too lusted after the Assyrians – governors and commanders, warriors in full dress, mounted horsemen, all handsome young men. ¹³ I saw that she too defiled herself; both of them went the same way.

¹⁴ 'But she carried her prostitution still further. She saw men portrayed on a wall, figures of Chaldeans*a* portrayed in red, ¹⁵ with belts round their waists and flowing turbans on their heads; all of them looked like Babylonian chariot officers, natives of Chaldea.*b* ¹⁶ As soon as she saw them, she lusted after them and sent messengers to them in Chaldea. ¹⁷ Then the Babylonians came to her, to the bed of love, and in their lust they defiled her. After she had been defiled by them, she turned away from them in disgust. ¹⁸ When she carried on her prostitution openly and exposed her naked body, I turned away from her in disgust, just as I had turned away from her sister. ¹⁹ Yet she became more and more promiscuous as she recalled the days of her youth, when she was a prostitute in Egypt. ²⁰ There she lusted after her lovers, whose genitals were like those of donkeys and whose emission was like that of horses. ²¹ So you longed for the lewdness of your youth, when in Egypt your bosom was caressed and your young breasts fondled.*c*

²² 'Therefore, Oholibah, this is what the Sovereign LORD says: I will stir up your lovers against you, those you turned away from in disgust, and I will bring them against you from every side – ²³ the Babylonians and all the Chaldeans, the men of Pekod and Shoa and Koa, and all the Assyrians with them, handsome young men, all of them governors and commanders, chariot officers and men of high rank, all mounted on horses. ²⁴ They will come against you with weapons,*d* chariots and wagons and with a throng of people; they will take up positions against you on every side with large and small shields and with helmets. I will turn you over to them for punishment, and they will punish you according to their standards. ²⁵ I will direct my jealous anger against you, and they will deal with you in fury. They will cut off your noses and your ears, and those of you who are left will fall by the sword. They will take away your sons and daughters, and those of you who are left will be consumed by fire. ²⁶ They will also strip you of

---

a 14 Or *Babylonians*

b 15 Or *Babylonia*; also in verse 16

c 21 Syriac (see also verse 3); Hebrew *caressed because of your young breasts*

d 24 The meaning of the Hebrew for this word is uncertain.

your clothes and take your fine jewellery. **27**So I will put a stop to the lewdness and prostitution you began in Egypt. You will not look on these things with longing or remember Egypt any more.

28'For this is what the Sovereign LORD says: I am about to deliver you into the hands of those you hate, to those you turned away from in disgust. **29**They will deal with you in hatred and take away everything you have worked for. They will leave you stark naked, and the shame of your prostitution will be exposed. Your lewdness and promiscuity **30**have brought this on you, because you lusted after the nations and defiled yourself with their idols. **31**You have gone the way of your sister; so I will put her cup into your hand.

32'This is what the Sovereign LORD says:

'You will drink your sister's cup,
   a cup large and deep;
it will bring scorn and derision,
   for it holds so much.
33You will be filled with drunkenness and
   sorrow,
   the cup of ruin and desolation,
   the cup of your sister Samaria.
34You will drink it and drain it dry
   and chew on its pieces –
   and you will tear your breasts.

I have spoken, declares the Sovereign LORD.

35'Therefore this is what the Sovereign LORD says: since you have forgotten me and turned your back on me, you must bear the consequences of your lewdness and prostitution.'

36The LORD said to me: 'Son of man, will you judge Oholah and Oholibah? Then confront them with their detestable practices, **37**for they have committed adultery and blood is on their hands. They committed adultery with their idols; they even sacrificed their children, whom they bore to me, as food for them. **38**They have also done this to me: at that same time they defiled my sanctuary and desecrated my Sabbaths. **39**On the very day they sacrificed their children to their idols,

they entered my sanctuary and desecrated it. That is what they did in my house.

40'They even sent messengers for men who came from far away, and when they arrived you bathed yourself for them, applied eye makeup and put on your jewellery. **41**You sat on an elegant couch, with a table spread before it on which you had placed the incense and olive oil that belonged to me.

42'The noise of a carefree crowd was around her; drunkards were brought from the desert along with men from the rabble, and they put bracelets on the wrists of the woman and her sister and beautiful crowns on their heads. **43**Then I said about the one worn out by adultery, "Now let them use her as a prostitute, for that is all she is." **44**And they slept with her. As men sleep with a prostitute, so they slept with those lewd women, Oholah and Oholibah. **45**But righteous judges will sentence them to the punishment of women who commit adultery and shed blood, because they are adulterous and blood is on their hands.

46'This is what the Sovereign LORD says: bring a mob against them and give them over to terror and plunder. **47**The mob will stone them and cut them down with their swords; they will kill their sons and daughters and burn down their houses.

48'So I will put an end to lewdness in the land, that all women may take warning and not imitate you. **49**You will suffer the penalty for your lewdness and bear the consequences of your sins of idolatry. Then you will know that I am the Sovereign LORD.'

Jerusalem as a cooking pot

24 In the ninth year, in the tenth month on the tenth day, the word of the LORD came to me: **2**'Son of man, record this date, this very date, because the king of Babylon has laid siege to Jerusalem this very day. **3**Tell this rebellious people a parable and say to them: "This is what the Sovereign LORD says:

'"Put on the cooking pot; put it on
   and pour water into it.

4 Put into it the pieces of meat,
  all the choice pieces – the leg and the
    shoulder.
Fill it with the best of these bones;
5   take the pick of the flock.
Pile wood beneath it for the bones;
  bring it to the boil
  and cook the bones in it.

6 ' "For this is what the Sovereign LORD
says:

  ' "Woe to the city of bloodshed,
    to the pot now encrusted,
    whose deposit will not go away!
  Take the meat out piece by piece
    in whatever order it comes.

7 ' "For the blood she shed is in her
    midst:
  she poured it on the bare rock;
  she did not pour it on the ground,
    where the dust would cover it.
8 To stir up wrath and take revenge
  I put her blood on the bare rock,
    so that it would not be covered.

9 ' "Therefore this is what the Sovereign
LORD says:

  ' "Woe to the city of bloodshed!
  I, too, will pile the wood high.
10 So heap on the wood
    and kindle the fire.
  Cook the meat well,
    mixing in the spices;
    and let the bones be charred.
11 Then set the empty pot on the coals
    till it becomes hot and its copper
      glows,
  so that its impurities may be melted
    and its deposit burned away.
12 It has frustrated all efforts;
    its heavy deposit has not been
      removed,
    not even by fire.

13 ' "Now your impurity is lewdness. Because I tried to cleanse you but you would
not be cleansed from your impurity, you
will not be clean again until my wrath
against you has subsided.

14 ' "I the LORD have spoken. The time
has come for me to act. I will not hold
back; I will not have pity, nor will I relent.
You will be judged according to your conduct and your actions, declares the Sovereign LORD." '

Ezekiel's wife dies

15 The word of the LORD came to me:
16 'Son of man, with one blow I am about
to take away from you the delight of your
eyes. Yet do not lament or weep or shed
any tears. 17 Groan quietly; do not mourn
for the dead. Keep your turban fastened
and your sandals on your feet; do not
cover your moustache and beard or eat
the customary food of mourners.'

18 So I spoke to the people in the morning, and in the evening my wife died. The
next morning I did as I had been commanded.

19 Then the people asked me, 'Won't
you tell us what these things have to do
with us? Why are you acting like this?'

20 So I said to them, 'The word of the
LORD came to me: 21 say to the people of Israel, "This is what the Sovereign LORD says:
I am about to desecrate my sanctuary – the
stronghold in which you take pride, the
delight of your eyes, the object of your affection. The sons and daughters you left
behind will fall by the sword. 22 And you will
do as I have done. You will not cover your
moustache and beard or eat the customary
food of mourners. 23 You will keep your
turbans on your heads and your sandals on
your feet. You will not mourn or weep but
will waste away because of*a* your sins and
groan among yourselves. 24 Ezekiel will
be a sign to you; you will do just as he has
done. When this happens, you will know
that I am the Sovereign LORD."

25 'And you, son of man, on the day
I take away their stronghold, their joy
and glory, the delight of their eyes, their
heart's desire, and their sons and daughters as well – 26 on that day a fugitive will
come to tell you the news. 27 At that time
your mouth will be opened; you will speak
with him and will no longer be silent. So

_____
a 23 Or *away in*

you will be a sign to them, and they will know that I am the Lord.'

A prophecy against Ammon

25 The word of the Lord came to me: 2 'Son of man, set your face against the Ammonites and prophesy against them. 3 Say to them, "Hear the word of the Sovereign Lord. This is what the Sovereign Lord says: because you said 'Aha!' over my sanctuary when it was desecrated and over the land of Israel when it was laid waste and over the people of Judah when they went into exile, 4 therefore I am going to give you to the people of the East as a possession. They will set up their camps and pitch their tents among you; they will eat your fruit and drink your milk. 5 I will turn Rabbah into a pasture for camels and Ammon into a resting place for sheep. Then you will know that I am the Lord. 6 For this is what the Sovereign Lord says: because you have clapped your hands and stamped your feet, rejoicing with all the malice of your heart against the land of Israel, 7 therefore I will stretch out my hand against you and give you as plunder to the nations. I will wipe you out from among the nations and exterminate you from the countries. I will destroy you, and you will know that I am the Lord."'

A prophecy against Moab

8 'This is what the Sovereign Lord says: "Because Moab and Seir said, 'Look, Judah has become like all the other nations,' 9 therefore I will expose the flank of Moab, beginning at its frontier towns – Beth Jeshimoth, Baal Meon and Kiriathaim – the glory of that land. 10 I will give Moab along with the Ammonites to the people of the East as a possession, so that the Ammonites will not be remembered among the nations; 11 and I will inflict punishment on Moab. Then they will know that I am the Lord."'

A prophecy against Edom

12 'This is what the Sovereign Lord says: "Because Edom took revenge on Judah and became very guilty by doing so, 13 therefore this is what the Sovereign Lord says: I will

stretch out my hand against Edom and kill both man and beast. I will lay it waste, and from Teman to Dedan they will fall by the sword. 14 I will take vengeance on Edom by the hand of my people Israel, and they will deal with Edom in accordance with my anger and my wrath; they will know my vengeance, declares the Sovereign Lord."'

A prophecy against Philistia

15 'This is what the Sovereign Lord says: "Because the Philistines acted in vengeance and took revenge with malice in their hearts, and with ancient hostility sought to destroy Judah, 16 therefore this is what the Sovereign Lord says: I am about to stretch out my hand against the Philistines, and I will wipe out the Kerethites and destroy those remaining along the coast. 17 I will carry out great vengeance on them and punish them in my wrath. Then they will know that I am the Lord, when I take vengeance on them."'

A prophecy against Tyre

26 In the eleventh month of the twelfth[a] year, on the first day of the month, the word of the Lord came to me: 2 'Son of man, because Tyre has said of Jerusalem, "Aha! The gate to the nations is broken, and its doors have swung open to me; now that she lies in ruins I will prosper," 3 therefore this is what the Sovereign Lord says: I am against you, Tyre, and I will bring many nations against you, like the sea casting up its waves. 4 They will destroy the walls of Tyre and pull down her towers; I will scrape away her rubble and make her a bare rock. 5 Out in the sea she will become a place to spread fishing nets, for I have spoken, declares the Sovereign Lord. She will become plunder for the nations, 6 and her settlements on the mainland will be ravaged by the sword. Then they will know that I am the Lord.

7 'For this is what the Sovereign Lord says: from the north I am going to bring against Tyre Nebuchadnezzar[b] king of

---

a 1 Probable reading of the original Hebrew text; Masoretic Text does not have *month of the twelfth*.
b 7 Hebrew *Nebuchadrezzar*, of which *Nebuchadnezzar* is a variant; here and often in Ezekiel and Jeremiah

Babylon, king of kings, with horses and chariots, with horsemen and a great army. [8] He will ravage your settlements on the mainland with the sword; he will set up siege works against you, build a ramp up to your walls and raise his shields against you. [9] He will direct the blows of his battering-rams against your walls and demolish your towers with his weapons. [10] His horses will be so many that they will cover you with dust. Your walls will tremble at the noise of the war horses, wagons and chariots when he enters your gates as men enter a city whose walls have been broken through. [11] The hooves of his horses will trample all your streets; he will kill your people with the sword, and your strong pillars will fall to the ground. [12] They will plunder your wealth and loot your merchandise; they will break down your walls and demolish your fine houses and throw your stones, timber and rubble into the sea. [13] I will put an end to your noisy songs, and the music of your harps will be heard no more. [14] I will make you a bare rock, and you will become a place to spread fishing nets. You will never be rebuilt, for I the LORD have spoken, declares the Sovereign LORD.

[15] 'This is what the Sovereign LORD says to Tyre: will not the coastlands tremble at the sound of your fall, when the wounded groan and the slaughter takes place in you? [16] Then all the princes of the coast will step down from their thrones and lay aside their robes and take off their embroidered garments. Clothed with terror, they will sit on the ground, trembling every moment, appalled at you. [17] Then they will take up a lament concerning you and say to you:

' "How you are destroyed, city of
      renown,
   peopled by men of the sea!
   You were a power on the seas,
      you and your citizens;
   you put your terror
      on all who lived there.
[18] Now the coastlands tremble
      on the day of your fall;
   the islands in the sea
      are terrified at your collapse."

[19] 'This is what the Sovereign LORD says: when I make you a desolate city, like cities no longer inhabited, and when I bring the ocean depths over you and its vast waters cover you, [20] then I will bring you down with those who go down to the pit, to the people of long ago. I will make you dwell in the earth below, as in ancient ruins, with those who go down to the pit, and you will not return or take your place[c] in the land of the living. [21] I will bring you to a horrible end and you will be no more. You will be sought, but you will never again be found, declares the Sovereign LORD.'

A lament over Tyre

27 The word of the LORD came to me: [2] 'Son of man, take up a lament concerning Tyre. [3] Say to Tyre, situated at the gateway to the sea, merchant of peoples on many coasts, "This is what the Sovereign LORD says:

' "You say, Tyre,
   'I am perfect in beauty.'
[4] Your domain was on the high seas;
   your builders brought your beauty to
      perfection.
[5] They made all your timbers
   of juniper from Senir;[a]
they took a cedar from Lebanon
   to make a mast for you.
[6] Of oaks from Bashan
   they made your oars;
of cypress wood[b] from the coasts of
      Cyprus
   they made your deck, adorned with
      ivory.
[7] Fine embroidered linen from Egypt was
      your sail
   and served as your banner;
your awnings were of blue and purple
   from the coasts of Elishah.
[8] Men of Sidon and Arvad were your
      oarsmen;
   your skilled men, Tyre, were aboard
      as your sailors.

---

c 20 Septuagint; Hebrew *return, and I will give glory*
a 5 That is, Mount Hermon
b 6 Targum; the Masoretic Text has a different division of the consonants.

9 Veteran craftsmen of Byblos were on board
    as shipwrights to caulk your seams.
All the ships of the sea and their sailors
    came alongside to trade for your
    wares.

10 '"Men of Persia, Lydia and Put
    served as soldiers in your army.
They hung their shields and helmets on
    your walls,
    bringing you splendour.
11 Men of Arvad and Helek
    guarded your walls on every side;
men of Gammad
    were in your towers.
They hung their shields around your
    walls;
    they brought your beauty to
    perfection.

12 '"Tarshish did business with you because of your great wealth of goods; they
exchanged silver, iron, tin and lead for
your merchandise.
13 '"Greece, Tubal and Meshek did business with you; they traded human beings
and articles of bronze for your wares.
14 '"Men of Beth Togarmah exchanged
chariot horses, cavalry horses and mules
for your merchandise.
15 '"The men of Rhodesᶜ traded with
you, and many coastlands were your customers; they paid you with ivory tusks and
ebony.
16 '"Aramᵈ did business with you because of your many products; they
exchanged turquoise, purple fabric, embroidered work, fine linen, coral and
rubies for your merchandise.
17 '"Judah and Israel traded with you;
they exchanged wheat from Minnith and
confections,ᵉ honey, olive oil and balm
for your wares.
18 '"Damascus did business with you
because of your many products and great
wealth of goods. They offered wine from

Helbon, wool from Zahar 19 and casks of
wine from Izal in exchange for your wares:
wrought iron, cassia and calamus.
20 '"Dedan traded in saddle blankets
with you.
21 '"Arabia and all the princes of Kedar
were your customers; they did business
with you in lambs, rams and goats.
22 '"The merchants of Sheba and Raamah traded with you; for your merchandise they exchanged the finest of all kinds
of spices and precious stones, and gold.
23 '"Harran, Kanneh and Eden and merchants of Sheba, Ashur and Kilmad traded
with you. 24 In your market-place they
traded with you beautiful garments, blue
fabric, embroidered work and multicoloured rugs with cords twisted and tightly
knotted.

25 '"The ships of Tarshish serve
    as carriers for your wares.
You are filled with heavy cargo
    as you sail the sea.
26 Your oarsmen take you
    out to the high seas.
But the east wind will break you to
    pieces
    far out at sea.
27 Your wealth, merchandise and wares,
    your mariners, sailors and
    shipwrights,
    your merchants and all your soldiers,
    and everyone else on board
will sink into the heart of the sea
    on the day of your shipwreck.
28 The shorelands will quake
    when your sailors cry out.
29 All who handle the oars
    will abandon their ships;
the mariners and all the sailors
    will stand on the shore.
30 They will raise their voice
    and cry bitterly over you;
they will sprinkle dust on their heads
    and roll in ashes.
31 They will shave their heads because of
    you
    and will put on sackcloth.
They will weep over you with anguish of
    soul
    and with bitter mourning.

ᶜ 15 Septuagint; Hebrew *Dedan*
ᵈ 16 Most Hebrew manuscripts; some Hebrew
manuscripts and Syriac *Edom*
ᵉ 17 The meaning of the Hebrew for this word is
uncertain.

32 As they wail and mourn over you,
  they will take up a lament concerning
    you:
'Who was ever silenced like Tyre,
  surrounded by the sea?'
33 When your merchandise went out on
    the seas,
  you satisfied many nations;
with your great wealth and your wares
  you enriched the kings of the earth.
34 Now you are shattered by the sea
  in the depths of the waters;
your wares and all your company
  have gone down with you.
35 All who live in the coastlands
  are appalled at you;
their kings shudder with horror
  and their faces are distorted with
    fear.
36 The merchants among the nations scoff
    at you;
  you have come to a horrible end
    and will be no more."'

A prophecy against the king of Tyre

28 The word of the LORD came to
me: 2 'Son of man, say to the ruler
of Tyre, "This is what the Sovereign LORD
says:

'"In the pride of your heart
  you say, 'I am a god;
I sit on the throne of a god
  in the heart of the seas.'
But you are a mere mortal and not a god,
  though you think you are as wise as a
    god.
3 Are you wiser than Daniel?[a]
  Is no secret hidden from you?
4 By your wisdom and understanding
  you have gained wealth for yourself
and amassed gold and silver
  in your treasuries.
5 By your great skill in trading
  you have increased your wealth,
and because of your wealth
  your heart has grown proud.

6 ' "Therefore this is what the Sovereign
LORD says:

'"Because you think you are wise,
  as wise as a god,
7 I am going to bring foreigners against
    you,
  the most ruthless of nations;
they will draw their swords against your
    beauty and wisdom
  and pierce your shining splendour.
8 They will bring you down to the pit,
  and you will die a violent death
  in the heart of the seas.
9 Will you then say, 'I am a god,'
  in the presence of those who kill you?
You will be but a mortal, not a god,
  in the hands of those who slay you.
10 You will die the death of the
    uncircumcised
  at the hands of foreigners.

I have spoken, declares the Sovereign
LORD."'

11 The word of the LORD came to me:
12 'Son of man, take up a lament concerning the king of Tyre and say to him: "This
is what the Sovereign LORD says:

'"You were the seal of perfection,
  full of wisdom and perfect in beauty.
13 You were in Eden,
  the garden of God;
every precious stone adorned you:
  carnelian, chrysolite and emerald,
  topaz, onyx and jasper,
  lapis lazuli, turquoise and beryl.[b]
Your settings and mountings[c] were
    made of gold;
  on the day you were created they
    were prepared.
14 You were anointed as a guardian
    cherub,
  for so I ordained you.
You were on the holy mount of God;
  you walked among the fiery stones.
15 You were blameless in your ways
  from the day you were created
  till wickedness was found in you.
16 Through your widespread trade

---

a 3 Or *Danel*, a man of renown in ancient literature

b 13 The precise identification of some of these
precious stones is uncertain.
c 13 The meaning of the Hebrew for this phrase is
uncertain.

you were filled with violence,
and you sinned.
So I drove you in disgrace from the
mount of God,
and I expelled you, guardian cherub,
from among the fiery stones.
17 Your heart became proud
on account of your beauty,
and you corrupted your wisdom
because of your splendour.
So I threw you to the earth;
I made a spectacle of you before kings.
18 By your many sins and dishonest trade
you have desecrated your
sanctuaries.
So I made a fire come out from you,
and it consumed you,
and I reduced you to ashes on the
ground
in the sight of all who were watching.
19 All the nations who knew you
are appalled at you;
you have come to a horrible end
and will be no more." '

A prophecy against Sidon

20 The word of the LORD came to me:
21 'Son of man, set your face against Sidon;
prophesy against her 22 and say: "This is
what the Sovereign LORD says:

' "I am against you, Sidon,
and among you I will display my
glory.
You will know that I am the LORD,
when I inflict punishment on you
and within you am proved to be holy.
23 I will send a plague upon you
and make blood flow in your streets.
The slain will fall within you,
with the sword against you on every
side.
Then you will know that I am the LORD.

24 ' "No longer will the people of Israel
have malicious neighbours who are painful briers and sharp thorns. Then they will
know that I am the Sovereign LORD.
25 ' "This is what the Sovereign LORD
says: when I gather the people of Israel
from the nations where they have been
scattered, I will be proved holy through

them in the sight of the nations. Then they
will live in their own land, which I gave to
my servant Jacob. 26 They will live there
in safety and will build houses and plant
vineyards; they will live in safety when I inflict punishment on all their neighbours
who maligned them. Then they will know
that I am the LORD their God." '

A prophecy against Egypt
Judgment on Pharaoh

29 In the tenth year, in the tenth
month on the twelfth day, the
word of the LORD came to me: 2 'Son of
man, set your face against Pharaoh king
of Egypt and prophesy against him and
against all Egypt. 3 Speak to him and say:
"This is what the Sovereign LORD says:

' "I am against you, Pharaoh king of
Egypt,
you great monster lying among your
streams.
You say, 'The Nile belongs to me;
I made it for myself.'
4 But I will put hooks in your jaws
and make the fish of your streams
stick to your scales.
I will pull you out from among your
streams,
with all the fish sticking to your
scales.
5 I will leave you in the desert,
you and all the fish of your streams.
You will fall on the open field
and not be gathered or picked up.
I will give you as food
to the beasts of the earth and the
birds of the sky.

6 Then all who live in Egypt will know that
I am the LORD.

' "You have been a staff of reed for the
people of Israel. 7 When they grasped you
with their hands, you splintered and you
tore open their shoulders; when they
leaned on you, you broke and their backs
were wrenched. a

---

a 7 Syriac (see also Septuagint and Vulgate); Hebrew
and you caused their backs to stand

8 ' "Therefore this is what the Sovereign LORD says: I will bring a sword against you and kill both man and beast. 9 Egypt will become a desolate wasteland. Then they will know that I am the LORD.

' "Because you said, 'The Nile is mine; I made it,' 10 therefore I am against you and against your streams, and I will make the land of Egypt a ruin and a desolate waste from Migdol to Aswan, as far as the border of Cush.*b* 11 The foot of neither man nor beast will pass through it; no one will live there for forty years. 12 I will make the land of Egypt desolate among devastated lands, and her cities will lie desolate for forty years among ruined cities. And I will disperse the Egyptians among the nations and scatter them through the countries.

13 ' "Yet this is what the Sovereign LORD says: at the end of forty years I will gather the Egyptians from the nations where they were scattered. 14 I will bring them back from captivity and return them to Upper Egypt, the land of their ancestry. There they will be a lowly kingdom. 15 It will be the lowliest of kingdoms and will never again exalt itself above the other nations. I will make it so weak that it will never again rule over the nations. 16 Egypt will no longer be a source of confidence for the people of Israel but will be a reminder of their sin in turning to her for help. Then they will know that I am the Sovereign LORD." '

Nebuchadnezzar's reward

17 In the twenty-seventh year, in the first month on the first day, the word of the LORD came to me: 18 'Son of man, Nebuchadnezzar king of Babylon drove his army in a hard campaign against Tyre; every head was rubbed bare and every shoulder made raw. Yet he and his army got no reward from the campaign he led against Tyre. 19 Therefore this is what the Sovereign LORD says: I am going to give Egypt to Nebuchadnezzar king of Babylon, and he will carry off its wealth. He will loot and plunder the land as pay for his army.

20 I have given him Egypt as a reward for his efforts because he and his army did it for me, declares the Sovereign LORD. 21 'On that day I will make a horn*c* grow for the Israelites, and I will open your mouth among them. Then they will know that I am the LORD.'

A lament over Egypt

30

The word of the LORD came to me: 2 'Son of man, prophesy and say: "This is what the Sovereign LORD says:

' "Wail and say,
    'Alas for that day!'
3 For the day is near,
    the day of the LORD is near –
a day of clouds,
    a time of doom for the nations.
4 A sword will come against Egypt,
    and anguish will come upon Cush.*a*
When the slain fall in Egypt,
    her wealth will be carried away
    and her foundations torn down.

5 Cush and Libya, Lydia and all Arabia, Kub and the people of the covenant land will fall by the sword along with Egypt.

6 ' "This is what the LORD says:

' "The allies of Egypt will fall
    and her proud strength will fail.
From Migdol to Aswan
    they will fall by the sword within her,
        declares the Sovereign LORD.
7 ' "They will be desolate
    among desolate lands,
and their cities will lie
    among ruined cities.
8 Then they will know that I am the LORD,
    when I set fire to Egypt
    and all her helpers are crushed.

9 ' "On that day messengers will go out from me in ships to frighten Cush out of her complacency. Anguish will take hold of them on the day of Egypt's doom, for it is sure to come.

---

b 10 That is, the upper Nile region

c 21 *Horn* here symbolises strength.

a 4 That is, the upper Nile region; also in verses 5 and 9

10 ' "This is what the Sovereign LORD says:

'"I will put an end to the hordes of
    Egypt
  by the hand of Nebuchadnezzar king
    of Babylon.
11 He and his army – the most ruthless of
    nations –
  will be brought in to destroy the
    land.
They will draw their swords against
    Egypt
  and fill the land with the slain.
12 I will dry up the waters of the Nile
  and sell the land to an evil nation;
by the hand of foreigners
  I will lay waste the land and
    everything in it.

I the LORD have spoken.

13 ' "This is what the Sovereign LORD says:

'"I will destroy the idols
  and put an end to the images in
    Memphis.
No longer will there be a prince in Egypt,
  and I will spread fear throughout the
    land.
14 I will lay waste Upper Egypt,
  set fire to Zoan
  and inflict punishment on Thebes.
15 I will pour out my wrath on Pelusium,
  the stronghold of Egypt,
  and wipe out the hordes of Thebes.
16 I will set fire to Egypt;
  Pelusium will writhe in agony.
Thebes will be taken by storm;
  Memphis will be in constant distress.
17 The young men of Heliopolis and
    Bubastis
  will fall by the sword,
  and the cities themselves will go into
    captivity.
18 Dark will be the day at Tahpanhes
  when I break the yoke of Egypt;
  there her proud strength will come
    to an end.
She will be covered with clouds,
  and her villages will go into captivity.

19 So I will inflict punishment on Egypt,
  and they will know that I am the
    LORD." '

Pharaoh's arms are broken

20 In the eleventh year, in the first month on the seventh day, the word of the LORD came to me: 21 'Son of man, I have broken the arm of Pharaoh king of Egypt. It has not been bound up to be healed or put in a splint so that it may become strong enough to hold a sword. 22 Therefore this is what the Sovereign LORD says: I am against Pharaoh king of Egypt. I will break both his arms, the good arm as well as the broken one, and make the sword fall from his hand. 23 I will disperse the Egyptians among the nations and scatter them through the countries. 24 I will strengthen the arms of the king of Babylon and put my sword in his hand, but I will break the arms of Pharaoh, and he will groan before him like a mortally wounded man. 25 I will strengthen the arms of the king of Babylon, but the arms of Pharaoh will fall limp. Then they will know that I am the LORD, when I put my sword into the hand of the king of Babylon and he brandishes it against Egypt. 26 I will disperse the Egyptians among the nations and scatter them through the countries. Then they will know that I am the LORD.'

Pharaoh as a felled cedar of Lebanon

31 In the eleventh year, in the third month on the first day, the word of the LORD came to me: 2 'Son of man, say to Pharaoh king of Egypt and to his hordes:

'"Who can be compared with you in
    majesty?
3 Consider Assyria, once a cedar in
    Lebanon,
  with beautiful branches
    overshadowing the forest;
it towered on high,
  its top above the thick foliage.
4 The waters nourished it,
  deep springs made it grow tall;
their streams flowed
  all around its base
and sent their channels

to all the trees of the field.
5 So it towered higher
    than all the trees of the field;
  its boughs increased
    and its branches grew long,
  spreading because of abundant
    waters.
6 All the birds of the sky
    nested in its boughs,
  all the wild animals
    gave birth under its branches;
  all the great nations
    lived in its shade.
7 It was majestic in beauty,
    with its spreading boughs,
  for its roots went down
    to abundant waters.
8 The cedars in the garden of God
    could not rival it,
  nor could the junipers
    equal its boughs,
  nor could the plane trees
    compare with its branches –
  no tree in the garden of God
    could match its beauty.
9 I made it beautiful
    with abundant branches,
  the envy of all the trees of Eden
    in the garden of God.

10 ' "Therefore this is what the Sovereign LORD says: because the great cedar towered over the thick foliage, and because it was proud of its height, 11 I gave it into the hands of the ruler of the nations, for him to deal with according to its wickedness. I cast it aside, 12 and the most ruthless of foreign nations cut it down and left it. Its boughs fell on the mountains and in all the valleys; its branches lay broken in all the ravines of the land. All the nations of the earth came out from under its shade and left it. 13 All the birds settled on the fallen tree, and all the wild animals lived among its branches. 14 Therefore no other trees by the waters are ever to tower proudly on high, lifting their tops above the thick foliage. No other trees so well-watered are ever to reach such a height; they are all destined for death, for the earth below, among mortals who go down to the realm of the dead.

15 ' "This is what the Sovereign LORD says: on the day it was brought down to the realm of the dead I covered the deep springs with mourning for it; I held back its streams, and its abundant waters were restrained. Because of it I clothed Lebanon with gloom, and all the trees of the field withered away. 16 I made the nations tremble at the sound of its fall when I brought it down to the realm of the dead to be with those who go down to the pit. Then all the trees of Eden, the choicest and best of Lebanon, the well-watered trees, were consoled in the earth below. 17 They too, like the great cedar, had gone down to the realm of the dead, to those killed by the sword, along with the armed men who lived in its shade among the nations.

18 ' "Which of the trees of Eden can be compared with you in splendour and majesty? Yet you, too, will be brought down with the trees of Eden to the earth below; you will lie among the uncircumcised, with those killed by the sword.

' "This is Pharaoh and all his hordes, declares the Sovereign LORD." '

A lament over Pharaoh

32 In the twelfth year, in the twelfth month on the first day, the word of the LORD came to me: 2 'Son of man, take up a lament concerning Pharaoh king of Egypt and say to him:

' "You are like a lion among the nations;
    you are like a monster in the seas
  thrashing about in your streams,
    churning the water with your feet
    and muddying the streams.

3 ' "This is what the Sovereign LORD says:

' "With a great throng of people
    I will cast my net over you,
    and they will haul you up in my net.
4 I will throw you on the land
    and hurl you on the open field.
  I will let all the birds of the sky settle on
    you
    and all the wild animals gorge
    themselves on you.

⁵ I will spread your flesh on the
 mountains
 and fill the valleys with your remains.
⁶ I will drench the land with your flowing
 blood
 all the way to the mountains,
 and the ravines will be filled with
 your flesh.
⁷ When I snuff you out, I will cover the
 heavens
 and darken their stars;
 I will cover the sun with a cloud,
 and the moon will not give its light.
⁸ All the shining lights in the heavens
 I will darken over you;
 I will bring darkness over your land,
 declares the Sovereign LORD.
⁹ I will trouble the hearts of many
 peoples
 when I bring about your destruction
 among the nations,
 among*a* lands you have not known.
¹⁰ I will cause many peoples to be appalled
 at you,
 and their kings will shudder with
 horror because of you
 when I brandish my sword before
 them.
 On the day of your downfall
 each of them will tremble
 every moment for his life.

¹¹ ' "For this is what the Sovereign LORD
says:

' "The sword of the king of Babylon
 will come against you.
¹² I will cause your hordes to fall
 by the swords of mighty men –
 the most ruthless of all nations.
 They will shatter the pride of Egypt,
 and all her hordes will be
 overthrown.
¹³ I will destroy all her cattle
 from beside abundant waters
 no longer to be stirred by the foot of
 man
 or muddied by the hooves of cattle.
¹⁴ Then I will let her waters settle

---

a 9 Hebrew; Septuagint *bring you into captivity among
the nations, / to*

and make her streams flow like oil,
 declares the Sovereign LORD.
¹⁵ When I make Egypt desolate
 and strip the land of everything in it,
 when I strike down all who live there,
 then they will know that I am the
 LORD."

¹⁶ 'This is the lament they will chant for her. The daughters of the nations will chant it; for Egypt and all her hordes they will chant it, declares the Sovereign LORD.'

Egypt's descent into the realm of the dead

¹⁷ In the twelfth year, on the fifteenth day of the month, the word of the LORD came to me: ¹⁸ 'Son of man, wail for the hordes of Egypt and consign to the earth below both her and the daughters of mighty nations, along with those who go down to the pit. ¹⁹ Say to them, "Are you more favoured than others? Go down and be laid among the uncircumcised." ²⁰ They will fall among those killed by the sword. The sword is drawn; let her be dragged off with all her hordes. ²¹ From within the realm of the dead the mighty leaders will say of Egypt and her allies, "They have come down and they lie with the uncircumcised, with those killed by the sword."

²² 'Assyria is there with her whole army; she is surrounded by the graves of all her slain, all who have fallen by the sword. ²³ Their graves are in the depths of the pit and her army lies around her grave. All who had spread terror in the land of the living are slain, fallen by the sword.

²⁴ 'Elam is there, with all her hordes around her grave. All of them are slain, fallen by the sword. All who had spread terror in the land of the living went down uncircumcised to the earth below. They bear their shame with those who go down to the pit. ²⁵ A bed is made for her among the slain, with all her hordes around her grave. All of them are uncircumcised, killed by the sword. Because their terror had spread in the land of the living, they bear their shame with those who go down to the pit; they are laid among the slain.

26 'Meshek and Tubal are there, with all their hordes around their graves. All of them are uncircumcised, killed by the sword because they spread their terror in the land of the living. 27 But they do not lie with the fallen warriors of old,[b] who went down to the realm of the dead with their weapons of war – their swords placed under their heads and their shields[c] resting on their bones – though these warriors also had terrorised the land of the living.

28 'You too, Pharaoh, will be broken and will lie among the uncircumcised, with those killed by the sword.

29 'Edom is there, her kings and all her princes; despite their power, they are laid with those killed by the sword. They lie with the uncircumcised, with those who go down to the pit.

30 'All the princes of the north and all the Sidonians are there; they went down with the slain in disgrace despite the terror caused by their power. They lie uncircumcised with those killed by the sword and bear their shame with those who go down to the pit.

31 'Pharaoh – he and all his army – will see them and he will be consoled for all his hordes that were killed by the sword, declares the Sovereign LORD. 32 Although I allowed him to spread terror in the land of the living, Pharaoh and all his hordes will be laid among the uncircumcised, with those killed by the sword, declares the Sovereign LORD.'

Renewal of Ezekiel's call as watchman

33 The word of the LORD came to me: 2 'Son of man, speak to your people and say to them: "When I bring the sword against a land, and the people of the land choose one of their men and make him their watchman, 3 and he sees the sword coming against the land and blows the trumpet to warn the people, 4 then if anyone hears the trumpet but does not heed the warning and the sword comes and takes their life, their blood will be on their own head. 5 Since they heard the sound of the trumpet but did not heed the warning, their blood will be on their own head. If they had heeded the warning, they would have saved themselves.

6 But if the watchman sees the sword coming and does not blow the trumpet to warn the people and the sword comes and takes someone's life, that person's life will be taken because of their sin, but I will hold the watchman accountable for their blood."

7 'Son of man, I have made you a watchman for the people of Israel; so hear the word I speak and give them warning from me. 8 When I say to the wicked, "You wicked person, you will surely die," and you do not speak out to dissuade them from their ways, that wicked person will die for[a] their sin, and I will hold you accountable for their blood. 9 But if you do warn the wicked person to turn from their ways and they do not do so, they will die for their sin, though you yourself will be saved.

10 'Son of man, say to the Israelites, "This is what you are saying: 'Our offences and sins weigh us down, and we are wasting away because of[b] them. How then can we live?' " 11 Say to them, "As surely as I live, declares the Sovereign LORD, I take no pleasure in the death of the wicked, but rather that they turn from their ways and live. Turn! Turn from your evil ways! Why will you die, people of Israel?"

12 'Therefore, son of man, say to your people, "If someone who is righteous disobeys, that person's former righteousness will count for nothing. And if someone who is wicked repents, that person's former wickedness will not bring condemnation. The righteous person who sins will not be allowed to live even though they were formerly righteous." 13 If I tell a righteous person that they will surely live, but then they trust in their righteousness and do evil, none of the righteous things that person has done will be remembered; they will die for the evil they have done.

---

b 27 Septuagint; Hebrew *warriors who were uncircumcised*

c 27 Probable reading of the original Hebrew text; Masoretic Text *punishment*

a 8 Or *in*; also in verse 9

b 10 Or *away in*

14 And if I say to a wicked person, "You will surely die," but they then turn away from their sin and do what is just and right – 15 if they give back what they took in pledge for a loan, return what they have stolen, follow the decrees that give life, and do no evil – that person will surely live; they will not die. 16 None of the sins that person has committed will be remembered against them. They have done what is just and right; they will surely live.

17 'Yet your people say, "The way of the Lord is not just." But it is their way that is not just. 18 If a righteous person turns from their righteousness and does evil, they will die for it. 19 And if a wicked person turns away from their wickedness and does what is just and right, they will live by doing so. 20 Yet you Israelites say, "The way of the Lord is not just." But I will judge each of you according to your own ways.'

Jerusalem's fall explained

21 In the twelfth year of our exile, in the tenth month on the fifth day, a man who had escaped from Jerusalem came to me and said, 'The city has fallen!' 22 Now the evening before the man arrived, the hand of the Lord was on me, and he opened my mouth before the man came to me in the morning. So my mouth was opened and I was no longer silent.

23 Then the word of the Lord came to me: 24 'Son of man, the people living in those ruins in the land of Israel are saying, "Abraham was only one man, yet he possessed the land. But we are many; surely the land has been given to us as our possession." 25 Therefore say to them, "This is what the Sovereign Lord says: since you eat meat with the blood still in it and look to your idols and shed blood, should you then possess the land? 26 You rely on your sword, you do detestable things, and each of you defiles his neighbour's wife. Should you then possess the land?"

27 'Say this to them: "This is what the Sovereign Lord says: as surely as I live, those who are left in the ruins will fall by the sword, those out in the country I will give to the wild animals to be devoured, and those in strongholds and caves will

die of a plague. 28 I will make the land a desolate waste, and her proud strength will come to an end, and the mountains of Israel will become desolate so that no one will cross them. 29 Then they will know that I am the Lord, when I have made the land a desolate waste because of all the detestable things they have done."

30 'As for you, son of man, your people are talking together about you by the walls and at the doors of the houses, saying to each other, "Come and hear the message that has come from the Lord." 31 My people come to you, as they usually do, and sit before you to hear your words, but they do not put them into practice. Their mouths speak of love, but their hearts are greedy for unjust gain. 32 Indeed, to them you are nothing more than one who sings love songs with a beautiful voice and plays an instrument well, for they hear your words but do not put them into practice.

33 'When all this comes true – and it surely will – then they will know that a prophet has been among them.'

The Lord will be Israel's shepherd

34 The word of the Lord came to me: 2 'Son of man, prophesy against the shepherds of Israel; prophesy and say to them: "This is what the Sovereign Lord says: woe to you shepherds of Israel who only take care of yourselves! Should not shepherds take care of the flock? 3 You eat the curds, clothe yourselves with the wool and slaughter the choice animals, but you do not take care of the flock. 4 You have not strengthened the weak or healed those who are ill or bound up the injured. You have not brought back the strays or searched for the lost. You have ruled them harshly and brutally. 5 So they were scattered because there was no shepherd, and when they were scattered they became food for all the wild animals. 6 My sheep wandered over all the mountains and on every high hill. They were scattered over the whole earth, and no one searched or looked for them.

7 ' "Therefore, you shepherds, hear the word of the Lord: 8 as surely as I live, declares the Sovereign Lord, because my

flock lacks a shepherd and so has been plundered and has become food for all the wild animals, and because my shepherds did not search for my flock but cared for themselves rather than for my flock, 9 therefore, you shepherds, hear the word of the Lord: 10 this is what the Sovereign Lord says: I am against the shepherds and will hold them accountable for my flock. I will remove them from tending the flock so that the shepherds can no longer feed themselves. I will rescue my flock from their mouths, and it will no longer be food for them.

11 ' "For this is what the Sovereign Lord says: I myself will search for my sheep and look after them. 12 As a shepherd looks after his scattered flock when he is with them, so will I look after my sheep. I will rescue them from all the places where they were scattered on a day of clouds and darkness. 13 I will bring them out from the nations and gather them from the countries, and I will bring them into their own land. I will pasture them on the mountains of Israel, in the ravines and in all the settlements in the land. 14 I will tend them in a good pasture, and the mountain heights of Israel will be their grazing land. There they will lie down in good grazing land, and there they will feed in a rich pasture on the mountains of Israel. 15 I myself will tend my sheep and make them lie down, declares the Sovereign Lord. 16 I will search for the lost and bring back the strays. I will bind up the injured and strengthen the weak, but the sleek and the strong I will destroy. I will shepherd the flock with justice.

17 ' "As for you, my flock, this is what the Sovereign Lord says: I will judge between one sheep and another, and between rams and goats. 18 Is it not enough for you to feed on the good pasture? Must you also trample the rest of your pasture with your feet? Is it not enough for you to drink clear water? Must you also muddy the rest with your feet? 19 Must my flock feed on what you have trampled and drink what you have muddied with your feet?

20 ' "Therefore this is what the Sovereign Lord says to them: see, I myself will judge between the fat sheep and the lean sheep. 21 Because you shove with flank and shoulder, butting all the weak sheep with your horns until you have driven them away, 22 I will save my flock, and they will no longer be plundered. I will judge between one sheep and another. 23 I will place over them one shepherd, my servant David, and he will tend them; he will tend them and be their shepherd. 24 I the Lord will be their God, and my servant David will be prince among them. I the Lord have spoken.

25 ' "I will make a covenant of peace with them and rid the land of savage beasts so that they may live in the wilderness and sleep in the forests in safety. 26 I will make them and the places surrounding my hill a blessing.a I will send down showers in season; there will be showers of blessing. 27 The trees will yield their fruit and the ground will yield its crops; the people will be secure in their land. They will know that I am the Lord, when I break the bars of their yoke and rescue them from the hands of those who enslaved them. 28 They will no longer be plundered by the nations, nor will wild animals devour them. They will live in safety, and no one will make them afraid. 29 I will provide for them a land renowned for its crops, and they will no longer be victims of famine in the land or bear the scorn of the nations. 30 Then they will know that I, the Lord their God, am with them and that they, the Israelites, are my people, declares the Sovereign Lord. 31 You are my sheep, the sheep of my pasture, and I am your God, declares the Sovereign Lord." '

A prophecy against Edom

35 The word of the Lord came to me: 2 'Son of man, set your face against Mount Seir; prophesy against it 3 and say: "This is what the Sovereign Lord says: I am against you, Mount Seir, and I will stretch out my hand against you and make you a desolate waste. 4 I will turn your towns

---

a 26 Or I will cause them and the places surrounding my hill to be named in blessings (see Gen. 48:20); or I will cause them and the places surrounding my hill to be seen as blessed into ruins and you will be desolate. Then you will know that I am the LORD.

5 ' "Because you harboured an ancient hostility and delivered the Israelites over to the sword at the time of their calamity, the time their punishment reached its climax, 6 therefore as surely as I live, declares the Sovereign LORD, I will give you over to bloodshed and it will pursue you. Since you did not hate bloodshed, bloodshed will pursue you. 7 I will make Mount Seir a desolate waste and cut off from it all who come and go. 8 I will fill your mountains with the slain; those killed by the sword will fall on your hills and in your valleys

and in all your ravines. 9 I will make you desolate for ever; your towns will not be inhabited. Then you will know that I am the LORD.

10 ' "Because you have said, 'These two nations and countries will be ours and we will take possession of them,' even though I the LORD was there, 11 therefore as surely as I live, declares the Sovereign LORD, I will treat you in accordance with the anger and jealousy you showed in your hatred of them and I will make myself known among them when I judge you. 12 Then you will know that I the LORD have heard all the contemptible things you have said

THROUGH EZEKIEL 4

The cost of sharing God's heart

You will have found out that Ezekiel 33 repeats so much of what we read in Ezekiel 3, and so we have a real sense of a new beginning after some really hard times for the prophet. For years he has been able to speak only the words of God (3:26), so other than when he has been prophesying, he has been completely silent (33:22). Now, however, Jerusalem has fallen at the end of its siege, and his words have been proved true, so he can finally speak again.

Now God is going to give his people words of hope for the future. He says he will search for the people who love him (34:11–12) and he will provide for them. He will create a new covenant of peace with them (34:26) and place them under the rule of David (34:23).

David was a shepherd, an unlikely candidate chosen to be king, but he knew from his days guarding the sheep that big sacrifices were sometimes required to look after things you love. God looked at his heart and knew that he would be an excellent ruler over Israel. In the early years of David's reign, Israel flourished.

God then promised not only to create a new covenant and provide for his people, but to break them free from their harnesses and rescue them from the people who enslaved them. Does that sound familiar? It's not only a promise made to the Israelites in the Old Testament and partially fulfilled in David, but it's wholly fulfilled (see Galatians 5:1) in the death and resurrection of Jesus (who is in David's bloodline, see Ezekiel 34:23; Matthew 1:6–16).

Jane Plackett

 Ezekiel 4   Ezekiel 37

against the mountains of Israel. You said, 'They have been laid waste and have been given over to us to devour.' 13 You boasted against me and spoke against me without restraint, and I heard it. 14 This is what the Sovereign LORD says: while the whole earth rejoices, I will make you desolate. 15 Because you rejoiced when the inheritance of Israel became desolate, that is how I will treat you. You will be desolate, Mount Seir, you and all of Edom. Then they will know that I am the LORD."'

Hope for the mountains of Israel

36 'Son of man, prophesy to the mountains of Israel and say, "Mountains of Israel, hear the word of the LORD. 2 This is what the Sovereign LORD says: the enemy said of you, 'Aha! The ancient heights have become our possession.' " 3 Therefore prophesy and say, "This is what the Sovereign LORD says: because they ravaged and crushed you from every side so that you became the possession of the rest of the nations and the object of people's malicious talk and slander, 4 therefore, mountains of Israel, hear the word of the Sovereign LORD: this is what the Sovereign LORD says to the mountains and hills, to the ravines and valleys, to the desolate ruins and the deserted towns that have been plundered and ridiculed by the rest of the nations around you – 5 this is what the Sovereign LORD says: in my burning zeal I have spoken against the rest of the nations, and against Edom, for with glee and with malice in their hearts they made my land their own possession so that they might plunder its pastureland." 6 Therefore prophesy concerning the land of Israel and say to the mountains and hills, to the ravines and valleys: "This is what the Sovereign LORD says: I speak in my jealous wrath because you have suffered the scorn of the nations. 7 Therefore this is what the Sovereign LORD says: I swear with uplifted hand that the nations around you will also suffer scorn.

8 ' "But you, mountains of Israel, will produce branches and fruit for my people Israel, for they will soon come home. 9 I am concerned for you and will look on

you with favour; you will be ploughed and sown, 10 and I will cause many people to live on you – yes, all of Israel. The towns will be inhabited and the ruins rebuilt. 11 I will increase the number of people and animals living on you, and they will be fruitful and become numerous. I will settle people on you as in the past and will make you prosper more than before. Then you will know that I am the LORD. 12 I will cause people, my people Israel, to live on you. They will possess you, and you will be their inheritance; you will never again deprive them of their children.

13 ' "This is what the Sovereign LORD says: because some say to you, 'You devour people and deprive your nation of its children,' 14 therefore you will no longer devour people or make your nation childless, declares the Sovereign LORD. 15 No longer will I make you hear the taunts of the nations, and no longer will you suffer the scorn of the peoples or cause your nation to fall, declares the Sovereign LORD."'

Israel's restoration assured

16 Again the word of the LORD came to me: 17 'Son of man, when the people of Israel were living in their own land, they defiled it by their conduct and their actions. Their conduct was like a woman's monthly uncleanness in my sight. 18 So I poured out my wrath on them because they had shed blood in the land and because they had defiled it with their idols. 19 I dispersed them among the nations, and they were scattered through the countries; I judged them according to their conduct and their actions. 20 And wherever they went among the nations they profaned my holy name, for it was said of them, "These are the LORD's people, and yet they had to leave his land." 21 I had concern for my holy name, which the people of Israel profaned among the nations where they had gone.

22 'Therefore say to the Israelites, "This is what the Sovereign LORD says: it is not for your sake, people of Israel, that I am going to do these things, but for the sake of my holy name, which you have

profaned among the nations where you have gone. ²³ I will show the holiness of my great name, which has been profaned among the nations, the name you have profaned among them. Then the nations will know that I am the LORD, declares the Sovereign LORD, when I am proved holy through you before their eyes.

²⁴ ' "For I will take you out of the nations; I will gather you from all the countries and bring you back into your own land. ²⁵ I will sprinkle clean water on you, and you will be clean; I will cleanse you from all your impurities and from all your idols. ²⁶ I will give you a new heart and put a new spirit in you; I will remove from you your heart of stone and give you a heart of flesh. ²⁷ And I will put my Spirit in you and move you to follow my decrees and be careful to keep my laws. ²⁸ Then you will live in the land I gave your ancestors; you will be my people, and I will be your God. ²⁹ I will save you from all your uncleanness. I will call for the corn and make it plentiful and will not bring famine upon you. ³⁰ I will increase the fruit of the trees and the crops of the field, so that you will no longer suffer disgrace among the nations because of famine. ³¹ Then you will remember your evil ways and wicked deeds, and you will loathe yourselves for your sins and detestable practices. ³² I want you to know that I am not doing this for your sake, declares the Sovereign LORD. Be ashamed and disgraced for your conduct, people of Israel!

³³ ' "This is what the Sovereign LORD says: on the day I cleanse you from all your sins, I will resettle your towns, and the ruins will be rebuilt. ³⁴ The desolate land will be cultivated instead of lying desolate in the sight of all who pass through it. ³⁵ They will say, 'This land that was laid waste has become like the garden of Eden; the cities that were lying in ruins, desolate and destroyed, are now fortified and inhabited.' ³⁶ Then the nations around you that remain will know that I the LORD have rebuilt what was destroyed and have replanted what was desolate. I the LORD have spoken, and I will do it."

³⁷ 'This is what the Sovereign LORD says: once again I will yield to Israel's plea and

do this for them: I will make their people as numerous as sheep, ³⁸ as numerous as the flocks for offerings at Jerusalem during her appointed festivals. So will the ruined cities be filled with flocks of people. Then they will know that I am the LORD.'

The valley of dry bones

37 The hand of the LORD was on me, and he brought me out by the Spirit of the LORD and set me in the middle of a valley; it was full of bones. ² He led me to and fro among them, and I saw a great many bones on the floor of the valley, bones that were very dry. ³ He asked me, 'Son of man, can these bones live?'

I said, 'Sovereign LORD, you alone know.'

⁴ Then he said to me, 'Prophesy to these bones and say to them, "Dry bones, hear the word of the LORD! ⁵ This is what the Sovereign LORD says to these bones: I will make breath*ᵃ* enter you, and you will come to life. ⁶ I will attach tendons to you and make flesh come upon you and cover you with skin; I will put breath in you, and you will come to life. Then you will know that I am the LORD."'

⁷ So I prophesied as I was commanded. And as I was prophesying, there was a noise, a rattling sound, and the bones came together, bone to bone. ⁸ I looked, and tendons and flesh appeared on them and skin covered them, but there was no breath in them.

⁹ Then he said to me, 'Prophesy to the breath; prophesy, son of man, and say to it, "This is what the Sovereign LORD says: come, breath, from the four winds and breathe into these slain, that they may live."' ¹⁰ So I prophesied as he commanded me, and breath entered them; they came to life and stood up on their feet – a vast army.

¹¹ Then he said to me: 'Son of man, these bones are the people of Israel. They say, "Our bones are dried up and our hope is gone; we are cut off." ¹² Therefore prophesy and say to them: "This is what

---

ᵃ 5 The Hebrew for this word can also mean *wind* or *spirit* (see verses 6-14).

the Sovereign Lord says: my people, I am going to open your graves and bring you up from them; I will bring you back to the land of Israel. 13 Then you, my people, will know that I am the Lord, when I open your graves and bring you up from them. 14 I will put my Spirit in you and you will live, and I will settle you in your own land. Then you will know that I the Lord have spoken, and I have done it, declares the Lord." '

One nation under one king

15 The word of the Lord came to me: 16 'Son of man, take a stick of wood and write on it, "Belonging to Judah and the Israelites associated with him." Then take another stick of wood, and write on it, "Belonging to Joseph (that is, to Ephraim) and all the Israelites associated with him." 17 Join them together into one stick so that they will become one in your hand.

18 'When your people ask you, "Won't you tell us what you mean by this?" 19 say to them, "This is what the Sovereign Lord says: I am going to take the stick of Joseph – which is in Ephraim's hand – and of the Israelite tribes associated with him, and join it to Judah's stick. I will make them into a single stick of wood, and they will become one in my hand." 20 Hold before their eyes the sticks you have written on 21 and say to them, "This is what the Sovereign Lord says: I will take the Israelites out of the nations where they have gone. I will gather them from all around and bring them back into their own land. 22 I will make them one nation in the land, on the mountains of Israel. There will be one king over all of them and they will never again be two nations or be divided into two kingdoms. 23 They will no longer defile themselves with their idols and vile images or with any of their offences, for I will save them from all their sinful backsliding,*b* and I will cleanse them. They will be my people, and I will be their God. 24 ' "My servant David will be king over

them, and they will all have one shepherd. They will follow my laws and be careful to keep my decrees. 25 They will live in the land I gave to my servant Jacob, the land where your ancestors lived. They and their children and their children's children will live there for ever, and David my servant will be their prince for ever. 26 I will make a covenant of peace with them; it will be an everlasting covenant. I will establish them and increase their numbers, and I will put my sanctuary among them for ever. 27 My dwelling-place will be with them; I will be their God, and they will be my people. 28 Then the nations will know that I the Lord make Israel holy, when my sanctuary is among them for ever." '

The Lord's great victory over the nations

38 The word of the Lord came to me: 2 'Son of man, set your face against Gog, of the land of Magog, the chief prince of*a* Meshek and Tubal; prophesy against him 3 and say: "This is what the Sovereign Lord says: I am against you, Gog, chief prince of*b* Meshek and Tubal. 4 I will turn you around, put hooks in your jaws and bring you out with your whole army – your horses, your horsemen fully armed, and a great horde with large and small shields, all of them brandishing their swords. 5 Persia, Cush*c* and Put will be with them, all with shields and helmets, 6 also Gomer with all its troops, and Beth Togarmah from the far north with all its troops – the many nations with you.

7 ' "Get ready; be prepared, you and all the hordes gathered about you, and take command of them. 8 After many days you will be called to arms. In future years you will invade a land that has recovered from war, whose people were gathered from many nations to the mountains of Israel, which had long been desolate. They had been brought out from the nations, and now all of them live in safety. 9 You and all your troops and the many nations with

---

b 23 Many Hebrew manuscripts (see also Septuagint); most Hebrew manuscripts *all their dwelling-places where they sinned*

a 2 Or *the prince of Rosh,*
b 3 Or *Gog, prince of Rosh,*
c 5 That is, the upper Nile region

THROUGH EZEKIEL 5
Resurrection and restoration

This is it. Ezekiel 37. My favourite chapter in the Bible.

I realise it's an unorthodox choice – it's not a nice summary of the gospel, it doesn't directly tell me God loves me and will never forsake me, it doesn't explicitly tell me of my sin and my need for salvation, and it's not John 3:16!

I don't think it would be many people's first choice, and I'm not sure this piece of Scripture would speak to everybody in the same way God has used it to speak to me, but if I had to choose one chapter to read, over and over again for the rest of my life, this would be it. I'm going to explain how God has spoken to me through this, and I hope I might challenge you to read Scripture differently. This is unlikely to be your chapter too, but I hope it helps you to see how God speaks through Scripture today.

This is the passage that made me know God was calling me to become a vicar. When I read this, I don't see dry bones in a valley, and if I rewrote Ezekiel 37 as the Holy Spirit reveals Scripture to me, it would go something like this:

Then the Spirit came on me and took me into the poorest parts of the nation and I saw desperate families, children from broken homes, not achieving their potential in school, disadvantaged by their parents' poverty. I saw the lonely, the drug addicts, the self-harmers and the suicidal – people completely broken and dry, people without hope. God said to me, 'Jane, can these people have a life like yours?' I said, 'Lord, I don't know, it all seems so desperate.'

Then God said, 'Sort this mess out.' And I said, 'But how do I start?' God replied, 'Provide for them. Organise parenting classes, homework clubs, financial advice clinics, life skills classes. Go into schools and teach young people about their value, have AA meetings in your home and in the church, build community, network Christian councillors, be a friend and an ear, get taken advantage of and delight in it, for your time and money doesn't really belong to you.' I heard a rattling sound, as I saw people's lives slowly come back together.

Then he said to me, 'Jane, tell these people what really changes their lives, tell them to ask me to breathe life into their hearts.' So I did. I saw people whose practical needs had been solved by the church go from death into life as they came to know Jesus. I saw people leave their old ways behind, I saw people full of the Holy Spirit, and both they and I knew that only God could have done it.

And God said, 'My dwelling place will be with them for ever. I will be their God, and they will be my people.'

God's Word speaks today, the imagery is still as poignant, and the challenges are still as powerful. Ask the Holy Spirit to reveal it to you as you read.

Jane Plackett

you will go up, advancing like a storm; you will be like a cloud covering the land.

10 ' "This is what the Sovereign LORD says: on that day thoughts will come into your mind and you will devise an evil scheme. 11 You will say, 'I will invade a land of unwalled villages; I will attack a peaceful and unsuspecting people – all of them living without walls and without gates and bars. 12 I will plunder and loot and turn my hand against the resettled ruins and the people gathered from the nations, rich in livestock and goods, living at the centre of the land.*d'* 13 Sheba and Dedan and the merchants of Tarshish and all her villages*e* will say to you, 'Have you come to plunder? Have you gathered your hordes to loot, to carry off silver and gold, to take away livestock and goods and to seize much plunder?' "

14 'Therefore, son of man, prophesy and say to Gog: "This is what the Sovereign LORD says: in that day, when my people Israel are living in safety, will you not take notice of it? 15 You will come from your place in the far north, you and many nations with you, all of them riding on horses, a great horde, a mighty army. 16 You will advance against my people Israel like a cloud that covers the land. In days to come, Gog, I will bring you against my land, so that the nations may know me when I am proved holy through you before their eyes.

17 ' "This is what the Sovereign LORD says: you are the one I spoke of in former days by my servants the prophets of Israel. At that time they prophesied for years that I would bring you against them. 18 This is what will happen in that day: when Gog attacks the land of Israel, my hot anger will be aroused, declares the Sovereign LORD. 19 In my zeal and fiery wrath I declare that at that time there shall be a great earthquake in the land of Israel. 20 The fish in the sea, the birds in the sky, the beasts of the field, every creature that moves along the ground, and all the people on the face of the earth will tremble at my presence. The mountains will be overturned, the cliffs will crumble and every wall will fall to the ground. 21 I will summon a sword against Gog on all my mountains, declares the Sovereign LORD. Every man's sword will be against his brother. 22 I will execute judgment on him with plague and bloodshed; I will pour down torrents of rain, hailstones and burning sulphur on him and on his troops and on the many nations with him. 23 And so I will show my greatness and my holiness, and I will make myself known in the sight of many nations. Then they will know that I am the LORD."

39 'Son of man, prophesy against Gog and say: "This is what the Sovereign LORD says: I am against you, Gog, chief prince of*a* Meshek and Tubal. 2 I will turn you around and drag you along. I will bring you from the far north and send you against the mountains of Israel. 3 Then I will strike your bow from your left hand and make your arrows drop from your right hand. 4 On the mountains of Israel you will fall, you and all your troops and the nations with you. I will give you as food to all kinds of carrion birds and to the wild animals. 5 You will fall in the open field, for I have spoken, declares the Sovereign LORD. 6 I will send fire on Magog and on those who live in safety in the coastlands, and they will know that I am the LORD.

7 ' "I will make known my holy name among my people Israel. I will no longer let my holy name be profaned, and the nations will know that I the LORD am the Holy One in Israel. 8 It is coming! It will surely take place, declares the Sovereign LORD. This is the day I have spoken of.

9 ' "Then those who live in the towns of Israel will go out and use the weapons for fuel and burn them up – the small and large shields, the bows and arrows, the war clubs and spears. For seven years they will use them for fuel. 10 They will not need to gather wood from the fields or cut it from the forests, because they will use the weapons for fuel. And they will

---

d 12 The Hebrew for this phrase means *the navel of the earth.*

e 13 Or *her strong lions*

a 1 Or *Gog, prince of Rosh,*

plunder those who plundered them and loot those who looted them, declares the Sovereign LORD.

11 ' "On that day I will give Gog a burial place in Israel, in the valley of those who travel east of the Sea. It will block the way of travellers, because Gog and all his hordes will be buried there. So it will be called the Valley of Hamon Gog.b

12 ' "For seven months the Israelites will be burying them in order to cleanse the land. 13 All the people of the land will bury them, and the day I display my glory will be a memorable day for them, declares the Sovereign LORD. 14 People will be continually employed in cleansing the land. They will spread out across the land and, along with others, they will bury any bodies that are lying on the ground.

' "After the seven months they will carry out a more detailed search. 15 As they go through the land, anyone who sees a human bone will leave a marker beside it until the gravediggers bury it in the Valley of Hamon Gog, 16 near a town called Hamonah.c And so they will cleanse the land."

17 'Son of man, this is what the Sovereign LORD says: call out to every kind of bird and all the wild animals: "Assemble and come together from all around to the sacrifice I am preparing for you, the great sacrifice on the mountains of Israel. There you will eat flesh and drink blood. 18 You will eat the flesh of mighty men and drink the blood of the princes of the earth as if they were rams and lambs, goats and bulls – all of them fattened animals from Bashan. 19 At the sacrifice I am preparing for you, you will eat fat till you are glutted and drink blood till you are drunk. 20 At my table you will eat your fill of horses and riders, mighty men and soldiers of every kind," declares the Sovereign LORD.

21 'I will display my glory among the nations, and all the nations will see the punishment I inflict and the hand I lay on them. 22 From that day forward the people of Israel will know that I am the LORD their God. 23 And the nations will know that the people of Israel went into exile for their sin, because they were unfaithful to me. So I hid my face from them and handed them over to their enemies, and they all fell by the sword. 24 I dealt with them according to their uncleanness and their offences, and I hid my face from them.

25 'Therefore this is what the Sovereign LORD says: I will now restore the fortunes of Jacobd and will have compassion on all the people of Israel, and I will be zealous for my holy name. 26 They will forget their shame and all the unfaithfulness they showed towards me when they lived in safety in their land with no one to make them afraid. 27 When I have brought them back from the nations and have gathered them from the countries of their enemies, I will be proved holy through them in the sight of many nations. 28 Then they will know that I am the LORD their God, for though I sent them into exile among the nations, I will gather them to their own land, not leaving any behind. 29 I will no longer hide my face from them, for I will pour out my Spirit on the people of Israel, declares the Sovereign LORD.'

The temple area restored

40 In the twenty-fifth year of our exile, at the beginning of the year, on the tenth of the month, in the fourteenth year after the fall of the city – on that very day the hand of the LORD was on me and he took me there. 2 In visions of God he took me to the land of Israel and set me on a very high mountain, on whose south side were some buildings that looked like a city. 3 He took me there, and I saw a man whose appearance was like bronze; he was standing in the gateway with a linen cord and a measuring rod in his hand. 4 The man said to me, 'Son of man, look carefully and listen closely and pay attention to everything I am going to show you, for that is why you have been brought here. Tell the people of Israel everything you see.'

---

b 11 *Hamon Gog* means *hordes of Gog.*
c 16 *Hamonah* means *horde.*

d 25 Or *now bring Jacob back from captivity*

The east gate to the outer court

5 I saw a wall completely surrounding the temple area. The length of the measuring rod in the man's hand was six long cubits,*a* each of which was a cubit and a handbreadth. He measured the wall; it was one measuring rod thick and one rod high.

6 Then he went to the east gate. He climbed its steps and measured the threshold of the gate; it was one rod deep. 7 The alcoves for the guards were one rod long and one rod wide, and the projecting walls between the alcoves were five cubits*b* thick. And the threshold of the gate next to the portico facing the temple was one rod deep.

8 Then he measured the portico of the gateway; 9 it*c* was eight cubits*d* deep and its jambs were two cubits*e* thick. The portico of the gateway faced the temple.

10 Inside the east gate were three alcoves on each side; the three had the same measurements, and the faces of the projecting walls on each side had the same measurements. 11 Then he measured the width of the entrance of the gateway; it was ten cubits and its length was thirteen cubits.*f* 12 In front of each alcove was a wall one cubit high, and the alcoves were six cubits square. 13 Then he measured the gateway from the top of the rear wall of one alcove to the top of the opposite one; the distance was twenty-five cubits*g* from one parapet opening to the opposite one. 14 He measured along the faces of the projecting walls all around the inside of the gateway – sixty cubits.*h* The measurement

was up to the portico*i* facing the courtyard.*j* 15 The distance from the entrance of the gateway to the far end of its portico was fifty cubits.*k* 16 The alcoves and the projecting walls inside the gateway were surmounted by narrow parapet openings all round, as was the portico; the openings all round faced inward. The faces of the projecting walls were decorated with palm trees.

The outer court

17 Then he brought me into the outer court. There I saw some rooms and a pavement that had been constructed all round the court; there were thirty rooms along the pavement. 18 It abutted the sides of the gateways and was as wide as they were long; this was the lower pavement. 19 Then he measured the distance from the inside of the lower gateway to the outside of the inner court; it was a hundred cubits*l* on the east side as well as on the north.

The north gate

20 Then he measured the length and width of the north gate, leading into the outer court. 21 Its alcoves – three on each side – its projecting walls and its portico had the same measurements as those of the first gateway. It was fifty cubits long and twenty-five cubits wide. 22 Its openings, its portico and its palm tree decorations had the same measurements as those of the gate facing east. Seven steps led up to it, with its portico opposite them. 23 There was a gate to the inner court facing the north gate, just as there was on the east. He measured from one gate to the opposite one; it was a hundred cubits.

The south gate

24 Then he led me to the south side and I saw the south gate. He measured its jambs

---

a 5 That is, about 3.2 metres; also in verse 12. The long cubit of about 53 centimetres is the basic unit of measurement of length throughout chapters 40–48.

b 7 That is, about 2.7 metres; also in verse 48

c 8,9 Many Hebrew manuscripts, Septuagint, Vulgate and Syriac; most Hebrew manuscripts *gateway facing the temple; it was one rod deep. 9 Then he measured the portico of the gateway; it*

d 9 That is, about 4.2 metres

e 9 That is, about about 1 metre

f 11 That is, about 5.3 metres wide and 6.9 metres long

g 13 That is, about 13 metres; also in verses 21, 25, 29, 30, 33 and 36

h 14 That is, about 32 metres

i 14 Septuagint; Hebrew *projecting wall*

j 14 The meaning of the Hebrew for this verse is uncertain.

k 15 That is, about 27 metres; also in verses 21, 25, 29, 33 and 36

l 19 That is, about 53 metres; also in verses 23, 27 and 47 and its portico, and they had the same measurements as the others. 25 The gateway and its portico had narrow openings all round, like the openings of the others. It was fifty cubits long and twenty-five cubits wide. 26 Seven steps led up to it, with its portico opposite them; it had palm tree decorations on the faces of the projecting walls on each side. 27 The inner court also had a gate facing south, and he measured from this gate to the outer gate on the south side; it was a hundred cubits.

The gates to the inner court

28 Then he brought me into the inner court through the south gate, and he measured the south gate; it had the same measurements as the others. 29 Its alcoves, its projecting walls and its portico had the same measurements as the others. The gateway and its portico had openings all round. It was fifty cubits long and twenty-five cubits wide. 30 (The porticoes of the gateways around the inner court were twenty-five cubits wide and five cubits deep.) 31 Its portico faced the outer court; palm trees decorated its jambs, and eight steps led up to it.

32 Then he brought me to the inner court on the east side, and he measured the gateway; it had the same measurements as the others. 33 Its alcoves, its projecting walls and its portico had the same measurements as the others. The gateway and its portico had openings all round. It was fifty cubits long and twenty-five cubits wide. 34 Its portico faced the outer court; palm trees decorated the jambs on either side, and eight steps led up to it.

35 Then he brought me to the north gate and measured it. It had the same measurements as the others, 36 as did its alcoves, its projecting walls and its portico, and it had openings all round. It was fifty cubits long and twenty-five cubits wide. 37 Its portico[m] faced the outer court; palm trees decorated the jambs on either side, and eight steps led up to it.

The rooms for preparing sacrifices

38 A room with a doorway was by the portico in each of the inner gateways, where the burnt offerings were washed. 39 In the portico of the gateway were two tables on each side, on which the burnt offerings, sin offerings[n] and guilt offerings were slaughtered. 40 By the outside wall of the portico of the gateway, near the steps at the entrance of the north gateway were two tables, and on the other side of the steps were two tables. 41 So there were four tables on one side of the gateway and four on the other – eight tables in all – on which the sacrifices were slaughtered. 42 There were also four tables of dressed stone for the burnt offerings, each a cubit and a half long, a cubit and a half wide and a cubit high.[o] On them were placed the utensils for slaughtering the burnt offerings and the other sacrifices. 43 And double-pronged hooks, each a handbreadth[p] long, were attached to the wall all round. The tables were for the flesh of the offerings.

The rooms for the priests

44 Outside the inner gate, within the inner court, were two rooms, one[q] at the side of the north gate and facing south, and another at the side of the south[r] gate and facing north. 45 He said to me, 'The room facing south is for the priests who guard the temple, 46 and the room facing north is for the priests who guard the altar. These are the sons of Zadok, who are the only Levites who may draw near to the LORD to minister before him.'

47 Then he measured the court: it was square – a hundred cubits long and a hundred cubits wide. And the altar was in front of the temple.

The new temple

48 He brought me to the portico of the temple and measured the jambs of the

---

m 37 Septuagint (see also verses 31 and 34); Hebrew jambs

n 39 Or purification offerings
o 42 That is, about 80 centimetres long and wide and 53 centimetres high
p 43 That is, about 9 centimetres
q 44 Septuagint; Hebrew were rooms for singers, which were
r 44 Septuagint; Hebrew east

portico; they were five cubits wide on either side. The width of the entrance was fourteen cubits[s] and its projecting walls were[t] three cubits[u] wide on either side. [49] The portico was twenty cubits[v] wide, and twelve[w] cubits[x] from front to back. It was reached by a flight of stairs,[y] and there were pillars on each side of the jambs.

41 Then the man brought me to the main hall and measured the jambs; the width of the jambs was six cubits[a] on each side.[b] [2] The entrance was ten cubits[c] wide, and the projecting walls on each side of it were five cubits[d] wide. He also measured the main hall; it was forty cubits long and twenty cubits wide.[e]

[3] Then he went into the inner sanctuary and measured the jambs of the entrance; each was two cubits[f] wide. The entrance was six cubits wide, and the projecting walls on each side of it were seven cubits[g] wide. [4] And he measured the length of the inner sanctuary; it was twenty cubits, and its width was twenty cubits across the end of the main hall. He said to me, 'This is the Most Holy Place.'

[5] Then he measured the wall of the temple; it was six cubits thick, and each side room round the temple was four cubits[h] wide. [6] The side rooms were on three levels, one above another, thirty on each level. There were ledges all round the wall of the temple to serve as supports for the side rooms, so that the supports were not inserted into the wall of the temple. [7] The side rooms all round the temple were wider at each successive level. The structure surrounding the temple was built in ascending stages, so that the rooms widened as one went upwards. A stairway went up from the lowest floor to the top floor through the middle floor.

[8] I saw that the temple had a raised base all round it, forming the foundation of the side rooms. It was the length of the rod, six long cubits. [9] The outer wall of the side rooms was five cubits thick. The open area between the side rooms of the temple [10] and the priests' rooms was twenty cubits wide all round the temple. [11] There were entrances to the side rooms from the open area, one on the north and another on the south; and the base adjoining the open area was five cubits wide all round.

[12] The building facing the temple courtyard on the west side was seventy cubits[i] wide. The wall of the building was five cubits thick all round, and its length was ninety cubits.[j]

[13] Then he measured the temple; it was a hundred cubits[k] long, and the temple courtyard and the building with its walls were also a hundred cubits long. [14] The width of the temple courtyard on the east, including the front of the temple, was a hundred cubits.

[15] Then he measured the length of the building facing the courtyard at the rear of the temple, including its galleries on each side; it was a hundred cubits.

The main hall, the inner sanctuary and the portico facing the court, [16] as well as the thresholds and the narrow windows and galleries round the three of them – everything beyond and including the threshold was covered with wood. The floor, the wall up to the windows, and the windows were covered. [17] In the space above the outside of the entrance to the inner sanctuary and on the walls at regular intervals all round the inner and outer sanctuary [18] were carved cherubim and palm trees. Palm trees alternated with cherubim. Each cherub had two faces: [19] the face of a human being towards the

---

s 48 That is, about 7.4 metres
t 48 Septuagint; Hebrew *entrance was*
u 48 That is, about 1.6 metres
v 49 That is, about 11 metres
w 49 Septuagint; Hebrew *eleven*
x 49 That is, about 6.4 metres
y 49 Hebrew; Septuagint *Ten steps led up to it*
a 1 That is, about 3.2 metres; also in verses 3, 5 and 8
b 1 One Hebrew manuscript and Septuagint; most Hebrew manuscripts *side, the width of the tent*
c 2 That is, about 5.3 metres
d 2 That is, about 2.7 metres; also in verses 9, 11 and 12
e 2 That is, about 21 metres long and 11 metres wide
f 3 That is, about 1.1 metres; also in verse 22
g 3 That is, about 3.7 metres
h 5 That is, about 2.1 metres

i 12 That is, about 37 metres
j 12 That is, about 48 metres
k 13 That is, about 53 metres; also in verses 14 and 15

palm tree on one side and the face of a lion towards the palm tree on the other. They were carved all round the whole temple. 20 From the floor to the area above the entrance, cherubim and palm trees were carved on the wall of the main hall.

21 The main hall had a rectangular door-frame, and the one at the front of the Most Holy Place was similar. 22 There was a wooden altar three cubits*l* high and two cubits square;*m* its corners, its base*n* and its sides were of wood. The man said to me, 'This is the table that is before the LORD.' 23 Both the main hall and the Most Holy Place had double doors. 24 Each door had two leaves – two hinged leaves for each door. 25 And on the doors of the main hall were carved cherubim and palm trees like those carved on the walls, and there was a wooden overhang on the front of the portico. 26 On the side walls of the portico were narrow windows with palm trees carved on each side. The side rooms of the temple also had overhangs.

The rooms for the priests

42 Then the man led me northward into the outer court and brought me to the rooms opposite the temple courtyard and opposite the outer wall on the north side. 2 The building whose door faced north was a hundred cubits long and fifty cubits wide.*a* 3 Both in the section twenty cubits*b* from the inner court and in the section opposite the pavement of the outer court, gallery faced gallery at the three levels. 4 In front of the rooms was an inner passageway ten cubits wide and a hundred cubits*c* long*d*. Their doors were on the north. 5 Now the upper rooms were narrower, for the galleries took more space from them than from the rooms on the lower and middle floors of the building. 6 The rooms on the top floor had no

pillars, as the courts had; so they were smaller in floor space than those on the lower and middle floors. 7 There was an outer wall parallel to the rooms and the outer court; it extended in front of the rooms for fifty cubits. 8 While the row of rooms on the side next to the outer court was fifty cubits long, the row on the side nearest the sanctuary was a hundred cubits long. 9 The lower rooms had an entrance on the east side as one enters them from the outer court.

10 On the south side*e* along the length of the wall of the outer court, adjoining the temple courtyard and opposite the outer wall, were rooms 11 with a passageway in front of them. These were like the rooms on the north; they had the same length and width, with similar exits and dimensions. Similar to the doorways on the north 12 were the doorways of the rooms on the south. There was a doorway at the beginning of the passageway that was parallel to the corresponding wall extending eastward, by which one enters the rooms.

13 Then he said to me, 'The north and south rooms facing the temple courtyard are the priests' rooms, where the priests who approach the LORD will eat the most holy offerings. There they will put the most holy offerings – the grain offerings, the sin offerings*f* and the guilt offerings – for the place is holy. 14 Once the priests enter the holy precincts, they are not to go into the outer court until they leave behind the garments in which they minister, for these are holy. They are to put on other clothes before they go near the places that are for the people.'

15 When he had finished measuring what was inside the temple area, he led me out by the east gate and measured the area all around: 16 he measured the east side with the measuring rod; it was five hundred cubits.*g,h* 17 He measured the north

l 22 That is, about 1.5 metres
m 22 Septuagint; Hebrew *long*
n 22 Septuagint; Hebrew *length*
a 2 That is, about 53 metres long and 27 metres wide
b 3 That is, about 11 metres
c 4 Septuagint and Syriac; Hebrew *and one cubit*
d 4 That is, about 5.3 metres wide and 53 metres long

e 10 Septuagint; Hebrew *Eastward*
f 13 Or *purification offerings*
g 16 See Septuagint of verse 17; Hebrew *rods*; also in verses 18 and 19.
h 16 Five hundred cubits equal about 265 metres; also in verses 17, 18 and 19.

side; it was five hundred cubits[i] by the measuring rod. 18 He measured the south side; it was five hundred cubits by the measuring rod. 19 Then he turned to the west side and measured; it was five hundred cubits by the measuring rod. 20 So he measured the area on all four sides. It had a wall round it, five hundred cubits long and five hundred cubits wide, to separate the holy from the common.

God's glory returns to the temple

43 Then the man brought me to the gate facing east, 2 and I saw the glory of the God of Israel coming from the east. His voice was like the roar of rushing waters, and the land was radiant with his glory. 3 The vision I saw was like the vision I had seen when he[a] came to destroy the city and like the visions I had seen by the River Kebar, and I fell face down. 4 The glory of the LORD entered the temple through the gate facing east. 5 Then the Spirit lifted me up and brought me into the inner court, and the glory of the LORD filled the temple.

6 While the man was standing beside me, I heard someone speaking to me from inside the temple. 7 He said: 'Son of man, this is the place of my throne and the place for the soles of my feet. This is where I will live among the Israelites for ever. The people of Israel will never again defile my holy name – neither they nor their kings – by their prostitution and the funeral offerings[b] for their kings at their death.[c] 8 When they placed their threshold next to my threshold and their doorposts beside my doorposts, with only a wall between me and them, they defiled my holy name by their detestable practices. So I destroyed them in my anger. 9 Now let them put away from me their prostitution and the funeral offerings for their kings, and I will live among them for ever.

10 'Son of man, describe the temple to the people of Israel, that they may be ashamed of their sins. Let them consider its perfection, 11 and if they are ashamed of all they have done, make known to them the design of the temple – its arrangement, its exits and entrances – its whole design and all its regulations[d] and laws. Write these down before them so that they may be faithful to its design and follow all its regulations.

12 'This is the law of the temple: all the surrounding area on top of the mountain will be most holy. Such is the law of the temple.

The great altar restored

13 'These are the measurements of the altar in long cubits,[e] that cubit being a cubit and a handbreadth: its gutter is a cubit deep and a cubit wide, with a kerb of one span[f] around the edge. And this is the height of the altar: 14 from the gutter on the ground up to the lower ledge that goes round the altar it is two cubits high, and the ledge is a cubit wide.[g] From this lower ledge to the upper ledge that goes round the altar it is four cubits high, and that ledge is also a cubit wide.[h] 15 Above that, the altar hearth is four cubits high, and four horns project upwards from the hearth. 16 The altar hearth is square, twelve cubits[i] long and twelve cubits wide. 17 The upper ledge also is square, fourteen cubits[j] long and fourteen cubits wide. All round the altar is a gutter of one cubit with a kerb of half a cubit.[k] The steps of the altar face east.'

18 Then he said to me, 'Son of man, this is what the Sovereign LORD says: these will be the regulations for sacrificing burnt offerings and splashing blood against the

---

i 17 Septuagint; Hebrew *rods*

a 3 Some Hebrew manuscripts and Vulgate; most Hebrew manuscripts *I*

b 7 Or *the memorial monuments*; also in verse 9

c 7 Or *their high places*

d 11 Some Hebrew manuscripts and Septuagint; most Hebrew manuscripts *regulations and its whole design*

e 13 That is, about 53 centimetres; also in verses 14 and 17. The long cubit is the basic unit for linear measurement throughout chapters 40–48.

f 13 That is, about 27 centimetres

g 14 That is, about 105 centimetres high and 53 centimetres wide

h 14 That is, about 2.1 metres high and 53 centimetres wide

i 16 That is, about 6.4 metres

j 17 That is, about 7.4 metres

k 17 That is, about 27 centimetres

altar when it is built: 19 you are to give a young bull as a sin offering[l] to the Levitical priests of the family of Zadok, who come near to minister before me, declares the Sovereign LORD. 20 You are to take some of its blood and put it on the four horns of the altar and on the four corners of the upper ledge and all round the rim, and so purify the altar and make atonement for it. 21 You are to take the bull for the sin offering and burn it in the designated part of the temple area outside the sanctuary.

22 'On the second day you are to offer a male goat without defect for a sin offering, and the altar is to be purified as it was purified with the bull. 23 When you have finished purifying it, you are to offer a young bull and a ram from the flock, both without defect. 24 You are to offer them before the LORD, and the priests are to sprinkle salt on them and sacrifice them as a burnt offering to the LORD.

25 'For seven days you are to provide a male goat daily for a sin offering; you are also to provide a young bull and a ram from the flock, both without defect. 26 For seven days they are to make atonement for the altar and cleanse it; thus they will dedicate it. 27 At the end of these days, from the eighth day on, the priests are to present your burnt offerings and fellowship offerings on the altar. Then I will accept you, declares the Sovereign LORD.'

The priesthood restored

44 Then the man brought me back to the outer gate of the sanctuary, the one facing east, and it was shut. 2 The LORD said to me, 'This gate is to remain shut. It must not be opened; no one may enter through it. It is to remain shut because the LORD, the God of Israel, has entered through it. 3 The prince himself is the only one who may sit inside the gateway to eat in the presence of the LORD. He is to enter by way of the portico of the gateway and go out the same way.'

4 Then the man brought me by way of the north gate to the front of the temple. I looked and saw the glory of the LORD

filling the temple of the LORD, and I fell face down.

5 The LORD said to me, 'Son of man, look carefully, listen closely and give attention to everything I tell you concerning all the regulations and instructions regarding the temple of the LORD. Give attention to the entrance to the temple and all the exits of the sanctuary. 6 Say to rebellious Israel, "This is what the Sovereign LORD says: enough of your detestable practices, people of Israel! 7 In addition to all your other detestable practices, you brought foreigners uncircumcised in heart and flesh into my sanctuary, desecrating my temple while you offered me food, fat and blood, and you broke my covenant. 8 Instead of carrying out your duty in regard to my holy things, you put others in charge of my sanctuary. 9 This is what the Sovereign LORD says: no foreigner uncircumcised in heart and flesh is to enter my sanctuary, not even the foreigners who live among the Israelites.

10 ' "The Levites who went far from me when Israel went astray and who wandered from me after their idols must bear the consequences of their sin. 11 They may serve in my sanctuary, having charge of the gates of the temple and serving in it; they may slaughter the burnt offerings and sacrifices for the people and stand before the people and serve them. 12 But because they served them in the presence of their idols and made the people of Israel fall into sin, therefore I have sworn with uplifted hand that they must bear the consequences of their sin, declares the Sovereign LORD. 13 They are not to come near to serve me as priests or come near any of my holy things or my most holy offerings; they must bear the shame of their detestable practices. 14 And I will appoint them to guard the temple for all the work that is to be done in it.

15 ' "But the Levitical priests, who are descendants of Zadok and who guarded my sanctuary when the Israelites went astray from me, are to come near to minister before me; they are to stand before me to offer sacrifices of fat and blood, declares the Sovereign LORD. 16 They alone are

---

l 19 Or *purification offering*; also in verse 21, 22 and 25 to enter my sanctuary; they alone are to come near my table to minister before me and serve me as guards.

17 ' "When they enter the gates of the inner court, they are to wear linen clothes; they must not wear any woollen garment while ministering at the gates of the inner court or inside the temple. 18 They are to wear linen turbans on their heads and linen undergarments round their waists. They must not wear anything that makes them perspire. 19 When they go out into the outer court where the people are, they are to take off the clothes they have been ministering in and leave them in the sacred rooms, and put on other clothes,

THROUGH EZEKIEL 6

The last word

All the prophets spend time teaching us about God's sovereignty over everything on the earth, and Ezekiel, more than any other, has an almost palpable sense of desperation that people should see God and acknowledge him. *'That they will know I am the LORD'* is a phrase used sixty-five times!

God used Ezekiel's actions to back up or symbolise his spoken prophecies, more than for any other prophet. To see Ezekiel's obedience even when it cost him greatly is inspiring. You see, God is a jealous God, and his holiness needs to be protected. As his people worshipped other gods, he could no longer be in relationship with them.

What pictures of hope we find in the last eight chapters, though! They're full of amazing imagery that gives us some idea of what the restored temple will be like. There's a lot of information about its dimensions. It's big – in fact it's enormous, as a reminder to us all of the importance of worship. Don't miss the central point, however: in the middle of Ezekiel's very detailed description of the temple he talks about the return of Yahweh (43:1–9) and his restored relationship with his people. Also, I hope you didn't miss the mention of the river flowing from the temple (47:1–12).

You see, ultimately this book isn't about condemnation, it's about redemption. It's about the way God is going to save the world and bring his people back into relationship with him. It tells us how God will bring his people back from death to life (Ezekiel 37); how he'll create a new covenant with them (34:25); how he'll send his Holy Spirit to be the 'water of life' (Ezekiel 47); how he'll be his people's shepherd and look after them with compassion (Ezekiel 34); how he'll restore them through the hand of David (Ezekiel 37); how he'll dwell among them again (Ezekiel 43). Does this sound familiar? The message of Ezekiel prepares us for the New Testament and for Jesus, as well as being about what are believed to be the final events of the world's history (which you may hear called 'eschatology').

An incredible book, don't you think?

Jane Plackett

 Ezekiel 37

so that the people are not consecrated through contact with their garments.

20 ' "They must not shave their heads or let their hair grow long, but they are to keep the hair of their heads trimmed. 21 No priest is to drink wine when he enters the inner court. 22 They must not marry widows or divorced women; they may marry only virgins of Israelite descent or widows of priests. 23 They are to teach my people the difference between the holy and the common and show them how to distinguish between the unclean and the clean.

24 ' "In any dispute, the priests are to serve as judges and decide it according to my ordinances. They are to keep my laws and my decrees for all my appointed festivals, and they are to keep my Sabbaths holy.

25 ' "A priest must not defile himself by going near a dead person; however, if the dead person was his father or mother, son or daughter, brother or unmarried sister, then he may defile himself. 26 After he is cleansed, he must wait seven days. 27 On the day he goes into the inner court of the sanctuary to minister in the sanctuary, he is to offer a sin offering*a* for himself, declares the Sovereign LORD.

28 ' "I am to be the only inheritance the priests have. You are to give them no possession in Israel; I will be their possession. 29 They will eat the grain offerings, the sin offerings and the guilt offerings; and everything in Israel devoted*b* to the LORD will belong to them. 30 The best of all the firstfruits and of all your special gifts will belong to the priests. You are to give them the first portion of your ground meal so that a blessing may rest on your household. 31 The priests must not eat anything, whether bird or animal, found dead or torn by wild animals.

Israel fully restored

45 ' "When you allot the land as an inheritance, you are to present to the LORD a portion of the land as a sacred district, 25,000 cubits*a* long and 20,000*b* cubits*c* wide; the entire area will be holy. 2 Of this, a section 500 cubits*d* square is to be for the sanctuary, with 50 cubits*e* around it for open land. 3 In the sacred district, measure off a section 25,000 cubits long and 10,000 cubits*f* wide. In it will be the sanctuary, the Most Holy Place. 4 It will be the sacred portion of the land for the priests, who minister in the sanctuary and who draw near to minister before the LORD. It will be a place for their houses as well as a holy place for the sanctuary. 5 An area 25,000 cubits long and 10,000 cubits wide will belong to the Levites, who serve in the temple, as their possession for towns to live in.*g*

6 ' "You are to give the city as its property an area 5,000 cubits*h* wide and 25,000 cubits long, adjoining the sacred portion; it will belong to all Israel.

7 ' "The prince will have the land bordering each side of the area formed by the sacred district and the property of the city. It will extend westward from the west side and eastward from the east side, running lengthwise from the western to the eastern border parallel to one of the tribal portions. 8 This land will be his possession in Israel. And my princes will no longer oppress my people but will allow the people of Israel to possess the land according to their tribes.

9 ' "This is what the Sovereign LORD says: you have gone far enough, princes of Israel! Give up your violence and oppression and do what is just and right. Stop dispossessing my people, declares Sovereign LORD. 10 You are to use accurate

---

a 27 Or *purification offering*; also in verse 29
b 29 The Hebrew term refers to the irrevocable giving over of things or persons to the LORD.

a 1 That is, about 8 miles or about 13 kilometres; also in verses 3, 5 and 6
b 1 Septuagint (see also verses 3 and 5 and 48:9); Hebrew 10,000
c 1 That is, about 6 1/2 miles or about 11 kilometres
d 2 That is, about 265 metres
e 2 That is, about 27 metres
f 3 That is, about 3 1/3 miles or about 5.3 kilometres; also in verse 5
g 5 Septuagint; Hebrew *temple; they will have as their possession* 20 rooms
h 6 That is, about 1 2/3 miles or about 2.7 kilometres

scales, an accurate ephah[i] and an accurate bath.[j] 11 The ephah and the bath are to be the same size, the bath containing a tenth of a homer and the ephah a tenth of a homer; the homer is to be the standard measure for both. 12 The shekel[k] is to consist of twenty gerahs. Twenty shekels plus twenty-five shekels plus fifteen shekels equal one mina.[l]

13 " "This is the special gift you are to offer: a sixth of an ephah[m] from each homer of wheat and a sixth of an ephah[n] from each homer of barley. 14 The prescribed portion of olive oil, measured by the bath, is a tenth of a bath[o] from each cor (which consists of ten baths or one homer, for ten baths are equivalent to a homer). 15 Also one sheep is to be taken from every flock of two hundred from the well-watered pastures of Israel. These will be used for the grain offerings, burnt offerings and fellowship offerings to make atonement for the people, declares the Sovereign LORD. 16 All the people of the land will be required to give this special offering to the prince in Israel. 17 It will be the duty of the prince to provide the burnt offerings, grain offerings and drink offerings at the festivals, the New Moons and the Sabbaths – at all the appointed festivals of Israel. He will provide the sin offerings,[p] grain offerings, burnt offerings and fellowship offerings to make atonement for the Israelites.

18 " "This is what the Sovereign LORD says: in the first month on the first day you are to take a young bull without defect and purify the sanctuary. 19 The priest is to take some of the blood of the sin offering and put it on the doorposts of the temple, on the four corners of the upper ledge of the altar and on the gateposts of the inner court. 20 You are to do the same on the seventh day of the month for anyone who sins unintentionally or through ignorance; so you are to make atonement for the temple.

21 " "In the first month on the fourteenth day you are to observe the Passover, a festival lasting seven days, during which you shall eat bread made without yeast. 22 On that day the prince is to provide a bull as a sin offering for himself and for all the people of the land. 23 Every day during the seven days of the Festival he is to provide seven bulls and seven rams without defect as a burnt offering to the LORD, and a male goat for a sin offering. 24 He is to provide as a grain offering an ephah for each bull and an ephah for each ram, along with a hin[q] of olive oil for each ephah.

25 " "During the seven days of the Festival, which begins in the seventh month on the fifteenth day, he is to make the same provision for sin offerings, burnt offerings, grain offerings and oil.

46

" "This is what the Sovereign LORD says: the gate of the inner court facing east is to be shut on the six working days, but on the Sabbath day and on the day of the New Moon it is to be opened. 2 The prince is to enter from the outside through the portico of the gateway and stand by the gatepost. The priests are to sacrifice his burnt offering and his fellowship offerings. He is to bow down in worship at the threshold of the gateway and then go out, but the gate will not be shut until evening. 3 On the Sabbaths and New Moons the people of the land are to worship in the presence of the LORD at the entrance of that gateway. 4 The burnt offering the prince brings to the LORD on the Sabbath day is to be six male lambs and a ram, all without defect. 5 The grain offering given with the ram is to be an ephah,[a] and the grain offering with the lambs is to be as much as he pleases, along with a hin[b] of olive oil for each ephah. 6 On the day of the New Moon he is to offer a young

---

i 10 An ephah was a dry measure of capacity of about 22 litres.
j 10 A bath was a liquid measure of capacity of about 22 litres.
k 12 A shekel weighed about 12 grams.
l 12 That is, 60 shekels; the common mina was 50 shekels. Sixty shekels were about 690 grams.
m 13 That is, probably about 2.7 kilograms
n 13 That is, probably about 2.25 kilograms
o 14 That is, about 2.2 litres
p 17 Or *purification offerings*; also in verses 19, 22, 23 and 25

q 24 That is, about 3.8 litres
a 5 That is, probably about 16 kilograms; also in verses 7 and 11
b 5 That is, about 3.8 litres; also in verses 7 and 11

bull, six lambs and a ram, all without defect. [7] He is to provide as a grain offering one ephah with the bull, one ephah with the ram, and with the lambs as much as he wants to give, along with a hin of oil for each ephah. [8] When the prince enters, he is to go in through the portico of the gateway, and he is to come out the same way.

[9] ' "When the people of the land come before the Lord at the appointed festivals, whoever enters by the north gate to worship is to go out by the south gate; and whoever enters by the south gate is to go out by the north gate. No one is to return through the gate by which they entered, but each is to go out by the opposite gate. [10] The prince is to be among them, going in when they go in and going out when they go out. [11] At the feasts and the appointed festivals, the grain offering is to be an ephah with a bull, an ephah with a ram, and with the lambs as much as he pleases, along with a hin of oil for each ephah.

[12] ' "When the prince provides a freewill offering to the Lord – whether a burnt offering or fellowship offerings – the gate facing east is to be opened for him. He shall offer his burnt offering or his fellowship offerings as he does on the Sabbath day. Then he shall go out, and after he has gone out, the gate will be shut.

[13] ' "Every day you are to provide a year-old lamb without defect for a burnt offering to the Lord; morning by morning you shall provide it. [14] You are also to provide with it morning by morning a grain offering, consisting of a sixth of an ephah[c] with a third of a hin[d] of oil to moisten the flour. The presenting of this grain offering to the Lord is a lasting ordinance. [15] So the lamb and the grain offering and the oil shall be provided morning by morning for a regular burnt offering.

[16] ' "This is what the Sovereign Lord says: if the prince makes a gift from his inheritance to one of his sons, it will also belong to his descendants; it is to be their property by inheritance. [17] If, however, he makes a gift from his inheritance to one of his servants, the servant may keep it until the year of freedom; then it will revert to the prince. His inheritance belongs to his sons only; it is theirs. [18] The prince must not take any of the inheritance of the people, driving them off their property. He is to give his sons their inheritance out of his own property, so that not one of my people will be separated from their property." '

[19] Then the man brought me through the entrance at the side of the gate to the sacred rooms facing north, which belonged to the priests, and showed me a place at the western end. [20] He said to me, 'This is the place where the priests are to cook the guilt offering and the sin offering[e] and bake the grain offering, to avoid bringing them into the outer court and consecrating the people.'

[21] He then brought me to the outer court and led me round to its four corners, and I saw in each corner another court. [22] In the four corners of the outer court were enclosed[f] courts, forty cubits long and thirty cubits wide;[g] each of the courts in the four corners was the same size. [23] Around the inside of each of the four courts was a ledge of stone, with places for fire built all round under the ledge. [24] He said to me, 'These are the kitchens where those who minister at the temple are to cook the sacrifices of the people.'

The river from the temple

47 The man brought me back to the entrance to the temple, and I saw water coming out from under the threshold of the temple towards the east (for the temple faced east). The water was coming down from under the south side of the temple, south of the altar. [2] He then brought me out through the north gate and led me round the outside to the outer gate facing east, and the water was trickling from the south side.

---

c 14 That is, probably about 2.7 kilograms
d 14 That is, about 1.3 litres

e 20 Or purification offering
f 22 The meaning of the Hebrew for this word is uncertain.
g 22 That is, about 21 metres long and 16 metres wide

³As the man went eastward with a measuring line in his hand, he measured off a thousand cubits*a* and then led me through water that was ankle-deep. ⁴He measured off another thousand cubits and led me through water that was knee-deep. He measured off another thousand and led me through water that was up to the waist. ⁵He measured off another thousand, but now it was a river that I could not cross, because the water had risen and was deep enough to swim in – a river that no one could cross. ⁶He asked me, 'Son of man, do you see this?'

Then he led me back to the bank of the river. ⁷When I arrived there, I saw a great number of trees on each side of the river. ⁸He said to me, 'This water flows towards the eastern region and goes down into the Arabah,*b* where it enters the Dead Sea. When it empties into the sea, the salty water there becomes fresh. ⁹Swarms of living creatures will live wherever the river flows. There will be large numbers of fish, because this water flows there and makes the salt water fresh; so where the river flows everything will live. ¹⁰Fishermen will stand along the shore; from En Gedi to En Eglaim there will be places for spreading nets. The fish will be of many kinds – like the fish of the Mediterranean Sea. ¹¹But the swamps and marshes will not become fresh; they will be left for salt. ¹²Fruit trees of all kinds will grow on both banks of the river. Their leaves will not wither, nor will their fruit fail. Every month they will bear fruit, because the water from the sanctuary flows to them. Their fruit will serve for food and their leaves for healing.'

The boundaries of the land

¹³This is what the Sovereign LORD says: 'These are the boundaries of the land that you will divide among the twelve tribes of Israel as their inheritance, with two portions for Joseph. ¹⁴You are to divide it equally among them. Because I swore with uplifted hand to give it to your ancestors, this land will become your inheritance.

¹⁵'This is to be the boundary of the land:

'On the north side it will run from the Mediterranean Sea by the Hethlon road past Lebo Hamath to Zedad, ¹⁶Berothah*c* and Sibraim (which lies on the border between Damascus and Hamath), as far as Hazer Hatti-kon, which is on the border of Hauran. ¹⁷The boundary will extend from the sea to Hazar Enan,*d* along the northern border of Damascus, with the border of Hamath to the north. This will be the northern boundary. ¹⁸'On the east side the boundary will run between Hauran and Damascus, along the Jordan between Gilead and the land of Israel, to the Dead Sea and as far as Tamar.*e* This will be the eastern boundary. ¹⁹'On the south side it will run from Tamar as far as the waters of Meribah Kadesh, then along the Wadi of Egypt to the Mediterranean Sea. This will be the southern boundary. ²⁰'On the west side, the Mediterranean Sea will be the boundary to a point opposite Lebo Hamath. This will be the western boundary.

²¹'You are to distribute this land among yourselves according to the tribes of Israel. ²²You are to allot it as an inheritance for yourselves and for the foreigners residing among you and who have children. You are to consider them as native-born Israelites; along with you they are to be allotted an inheritance among the tribes of Israel. ²³In whatever tribe a foreigner resides, there you are to give them their inheritance,' declares the Sovereign LORD.

The division of the land

48 'These are the tribes, listed by name: at the northern frontier, Dan will have one portion; it will follow

---

a 3 That is, about 530 metres
b 8 Or *the Jordan Valley*

c 15,16 See Septuagint and 48:1; Hebrew *road to go into Zedad,* ¹⁶*Hamath, Berothah*.
d 17 Hebrew *Enon,* a variant of *Enan*
e 18 See Syriac; Hebrew *Israel. You will measure to the Dead Sea.*

the Hethlon road to Lebo Hamath; Hazar Enan and the northern border of Damascus next to Hamath will be part of its border from the east side to the west side.

2 'Asher will have one portion; it will border the territory of Dan from east to west.

3 'Naphtali will have one portion; it will border the territory of Asher from east to west.

4 'Manasseh will have one portion; it will border the territory of Naphtali from east to west.

5 'Ephraim will have one portion; it will border the territory of Manasseh from east to west.

6 'Reuben will have one portion; it will border the territory of Ephraim from east to west.

7 'Judah will have one portion; it will border the territory of Reuben from east to west.

8 'Bordering the territory of Judah from east to west will be the portion you are to present as a special gift. It will be 25,000 cubits*a* wide, and its length from east to west will equal one of the tribal portions; the sanctuary will be in the centre of it.

9 'The special portion you are to offer to the LORD will be 25,000 cubits long and 10,000 cubits*b* wide. 10 This will be the sacred portion for the priests. It will be 25,000 cubits long on the north side, 10,000 cubits wide on the west side, 10,000 cubits wide on the east side and 25,000 cubits long on the south side. In the centre of it will be the sanctuary of the LORD. 11 This will be for the consecrated priests, the Zadokites, who were faithful in serving me and did not go astray as the Levites did when the Israelites went astray. 12 It will be a special gift to them from the sacred portion of the land, a most holy portion, bordering the territory of the Levites.

13 'Alongside the territory of the priests, the Levites will be allotted a portion of land 25,000 cubits long and 10,000

cubits wide. Its total length will be 25,000 cubits and its width 10,000 cubits. 14 They must not sell or exchange any of it. This is the best of the land and must not pass into other hands, because it is holy to the LORD.

FAVOURITE VERSES

1 Peter 2:1

Therefore, rid yourselves of all malice and all deceit, hypocrisy, envy, and slander of every kind.

I love this verse because it gives me strength when I falter: God made me holy – and he has already overcome my sin!

James, 19

15 'The remaining area, 5,000 cubits*c* wide and 25,000 cubits long, will be for the common use of the city, for houses and for pasture-land. The city will be in the centre of it 16 and will have these measurements: the north side 4,500 cubits,*d* the south side 4,500 cubits, the east side 4,500 cubits, and the west side 4,500 cubits. 17 The pasture-land for the city will be 250 cubits*e* on the north, 250 cubits on the south, 250 cubits on the east, and 250 cubits on the west. 18 What remains of the area, bordering on the sacred portion and running the length of it, will be 10,000 cubits on the east side and 10,000 cubits on the west side. Its produce will supply food for the workers of the city. 19 The workers from the city who farm it will come from all the tribes of Israel. 20 The entire portion will be a square, 25,000 cubits

---

a 8 That is, about 8 miles or about 13 kilometres; also in verses 9, 10, 13, 15, 20 and 21

b 9 That is, about 3 1/3 miles or about 5.3 kilometres; also in verses 10, 13 and 18

c 15 That is, about 1 2/3 miles or about 2.7 kilometres

d 16 That is, about 1 1/2 miles or about 2.4 kilometres; also in verses 30, 32, 33 and 34

e 17 That is, about 135 metres

on each side. As a special gift you will set aside the sacred portion, along with the property of the city.

21 'What remains on both sides of the area formed by the sacred portion and the property of the city will belong to the prince. It will extend eastward from the 25,000 cubits of the sacred portion to the eastern border, and westward from the 25,000 cubits to the western border. Both these areas running the length of the tribal portions will belong to the prince, and the sacred portion with the temple sanctuary will be in the centre of them. 22 So the property of the Levites and the property of the city will lie in the centre of the area that belongs to the prince. The area belonging to the prince will lie between the border of Judah and the border of Benjamin.

23 'As for the rest of the tribes: Benjamin will have one portion; it will extend from the east side to the west side.

24 'Simeon will have one portion; it will border the territory of Benjamin from east to west.

25 'Issachar will have one portion; it will border the territory of Simeon from east to west.

26 'Zebulun will have one portion; it will border the territory of Issachar from east to west.

27 'Gad will have one portion; it will border the territory of Zebulun from east to west.

28 'The southern boundary of Gad will run south from Tamar to the waters of Meribah Kadesh, then along the Wadi of Egypt to the Mediterranean Sea.

29 'This is the land you are to allot as an inheritance to the tribes of Israel, and these will be their portions,' declares the Sovereign LORD.

The gates of the new city

30 'These will be the exits of the city: beginning on the north side, which is 4,500 cubits long, 31 the gates of the city will be named after the tribes of Israel. The three gates on the north side will be the gate of Reuben, the gate of Judah and the gate of Levi.

32 'On the east side, which is 4,500 cubits long, will be three gates: the gate of Joseph, the gate of Benjamin and the gate of Dan.

33 'On the south side, which measures 4,500 cubits, will be three gates: the gate of Simeon, the gate of Issachar and the gate of Zebulun.

34 'On the west side, which is 4,500 cubits long, will be three gates: the gate of Gad, the gate of Asher and the gate of Naphtali.

35 'The distance all around will be 18,000 cubits.*f*

'And the name of the city from that time on will be:

THE LORD IS THERE.'

f35 That is, about 6 miles or about 9.5 kilometres

DANIEL

DATE

Events in this book begin when Daniel and his friends were taken into exile, probably around 605 BC

AUTHOR

Possibly Daniel

WHAT'S IT ALL ABOUT?

The first half of the book of Daniel tells how its author was taken from Jerusalem to Babylon (as part of the exile) and gained a position in King Nebuchadnezzar's palace because he was intelligent. He and his friends served there, but they refused to conform to the customs of their new surroundings and were determined to be faithful to God. Although Nebuchadnezzar occasionally acknowledged that they worshipped the true God, he eventually demanded that Daniel and his friends bow down to an idol or face death. Assured of the greatness of God, the men refused, and were faced with being thrown into a fire and then into a den of hungry lions. They survived without a scratch and the king again acknowledged the goodness of the true God.

The second half of the book is filled with Daniel's spectacular visions, which are very hard for even great biblical scholars to decipher. They contain many symbols which could have several interpretations and are referred to as 'apocalyptic' writing, as they seem to predict disaster. The overarching message of the entire book of Daniel is easier to access: God is in control of history.

WHY SHOULD WE READ IT?

- To read about the inspiring example set by Daniel and his friends. They trusted in God and bravely refused to bow down to any idol, no matter what it cost them.

- To see the context of the famous stories of Daniel in the lion's den and the fiery furnace, and be reminded of the miraculous ways in which God saved his servants.

- To understand that there may be spiritual reasons why answers to our prayers seem delayed (Daniel 9).

- To see that God speaks through dreams and visions.

Andy Croft with Liza Hoeksma

Daniel's training in Babylon

1 In the third year of the reign of Jehoiakim king of Judah, Nebuchadnezzar king of Babylon came to Jerusalem and besieged it. ²And the Lord delivered Jehoiakim king of Judah into his hand, along with some of the articles from the temple of God. These he carried off to the temple of his god in Babylonia*a* and put in the treasure-house of his god.

³Then the king ordered Ashpenaz, chief of his court officials, to bring into the king's service some of the Israelites from the royal family and the nobility – ⁴young men without any physical defect, handsome, showing aptitude for every kind of learning, well informed, quick to understand, and qualified to serve in the king's palace. He was to teach them the language and literature of the Babylonians.*b* ⁵The king assigned them a daily amount of food and wine from the king's table. They were to be trained for three years, and after that they were to enter the king's service.

⁶Among those who were chosen were some from Judah: Daniel, Hananiah, Mishael and Azariah. ⁷The chief official gave them new names: to Daniel, the name Belteshazzar; to Hananiah, Shadrach; to Mishael, Meshach; and to Azariah, Abednego.

⁸But Daniel resolved not to defile himself with the royal food and wine, and he asked the chief official for permission not to defile himself in this way. ⁹Now God had caused the official to show favour and compassion to Daniel, ¹⁰but the official told Daniel, 'I am afraid of my lord the king, who has assigned your*c* food and drink. Why should he see you looking worse than the other young men of your age? The king would then have my head because of you.'

¹¹Daniel then said to the guard whom the chief official had appointed over Daniel, Hananiah, Mishael and Azariah, ¹²'Please test your servants for ten days: give us nothing but vegetables to eat and water to drink. ¹³Then compare our appearance with that of the young men who eat the royal food, and treat your servants in accordance with what you see.' ¹⁴So he agreed to this and tested them for ten days.

¹⁵At the end of the ten days they looked healthier and better nourished than any of the young men who ate the royal food. ¹⁶So the guard took away their choice food and the wine they were to drink and gave them vegetables instead.

¹⁷To these four young men God gave knowledge and understanding of all kinds of literature and learning. And Daniel could understand visions and dreams of all kinds.

¹⁸At the end of the time set by the king to bring them into his service, the chief official presented them to Nebuchadnezzar. ¹⁹The king talked with them, and he found none equal to Daniel, Hananiah, Mishael and Azariah; so they entered the king's service. ²⁰In every matter of wisdom and understanding about which the king questioned them, he found them ten times better than all the magicians and enchanters in his whole kingdom.

²¹And Daniel remained there until the first year of King Cyrus.

Nebuchadnezzar's dream

2 In the second year of his reign, Nebuchadnezzar had dreams; his mind was troubled and he could not sleep. ²So the king summoned the magicians, enchanters, sorcerers and astrologers*a* to tell him what he had dreamed. When they came in and stood before the king, ³he said to them, 'I have had a dream that troubles me and I want to know what it means.'*b*

⁴Then the astrologers answered the king,*c* 'May the king live for ever! Tell your servants the dream, and we will interpret it.'

⁵The king replied to the astrologers, 'This is what I have firmly decided: if you

---

*a*2 Hebrew *Shinar*
*b*4 Or *Chaldeans*
*c*10 The Hebrew for *your* and *you* in this verse is plural.

*a*2 Or *Chaldeans*; also in verses 4, 5 and 10
*b*3 Or *was*
*c*4 At this point the Hebrew text has *in Aramaic*, indicating that the text from here to the end of chapter 7 is in Aramaic.

do not tell me what my dream was and interpret it, I will have you cut into pieces and your houses turned into piles of rubble. 6 But if you tell me the dream and explain it, you will receive from me gifts and rewards and great honour. So tell me the dream and interpret it for me.'

7 Once more they replied, 'Let the king tell his servants the dream, and we will interpret it.'

8 Then the king answered, 'I am certain that you are trying to gain time, because you realise that this is what I have firmly decided: 9 if you do not tell me the dream, there is only one penalty for you. You have conspired to tell me misleading and wicked things, hoping the situation will change. So then, tell me the dream, and I will know that you can interpret it for me.'

10 The astrologers answered the king, 'There is no one on earth who can do what the king asks! No king, however great and mighty, has ever asked such a thing of any magician or enchanter or astrologer. 11 What the king asks is too difficult. No one can reveal it to the king except the gods, and they do not live among humans.'

12 This made the king so angry and furious that he ordered the execution of all the wise men of Babylon. 13 So the decree was issued to put the wise men to death, and men were sent to look for Daniel and his friends to put them to death.

14 When Arioch, the commander of the king's guard, had gone out to put to death the wise men of Babylon, Daniel spoke to him with wisdom and tact. 15 He asked the king's officer, 'Why did the king issue such a harsh decree?' Arioch then explained the matter to Daniel. 16 At this, Daniel went in to the king and asked for time, so that he might interpret the dream for him.

17 Then Daniel returned to his house and explained the matter to his friends Hananiah, Mishael and Azariah. 18 He urged them to plead for mercy from the God of heaven concerning this mystery, so that he and his friends might not be executed with the rest of the wise men of Babylon. 19 During the night the mystery was revealed to

Daniel in a vision. Then Daniel praised the God of heaven 20 and said:

'Praise be to the name of God for ever and ever;
    wisdom and power are his.
21 He changes times and seasons;
    he deposes kings and raises up others.
He gives wisdom to the wise
    and knowledge to the discerning.
22 He reveals deep and hidden things;
    he knows what lies in darkness,
    and light dwells with him.
23 I thank and praise you, God of my ancestors:
    you have given me wisdom and power,
you have made known to me what we asked of you,
    you have made known to us the dream of the king.'

Daniel interprets the dream

24 Then Daniel went to Arioch, whom the king had appointed to execute the wise men of Babylon, and said to him, 'Do not execute the wise men of Babylon. Take me to the king, and I will interpret his dream for him.'

25 Arioch took Daniel to the king at once and said, 'I have found a man among the exiles from Judah who can tell the king what his dream means.'

26 The king asked Daniel (also called Belteshazzar), 'Are you able to tell me what I saw in my dream and interpret it?'

27 Daniel replied, 'No wise man, enchanter, magician or diviner can explain to the king the mystery he has asked about, 28 but there is a God in heaven who reveals mysteries. He has shown King Nebuchadnezzar what will happen in days to come. Your dream and the visions that passed through your mind as you were lying in bed are these:

29 'As Your Majesty was lying there, your mind turned to things to come, and the revealer of mysteries showed you what is going to happen. 30 As for me, this mystery has been revealed to me, not because I have greater wisdom than anyone else

alive, but so that Your Majesty may know the interpretation and that you may understand what went through your mind.

31 'Your Majesty looked, and there before you stood a large statue – an enormous, dazzling statue, awesome in appearance. 32 The head of the statue was made of pure gold, its chest and arms of silver, its belly and thighs of bronze, 33 its legs of iron, its feet partly of iron and partly of baked clay. 34 While you were watching, a rock was cut out, but not by human hands. It struck the statue on its feet of iron and clay and smashed them. 35 Then the iron, the clay, the bronze, the silver and the gold were all broken to pieces and became like chaff on a threshing-floor in the summer. The wind swept them away without leaving a trace. But the rock that struck the statue became a huge mountain and filled the whole earth.

36 'This was the dream, and now we will interpret it to the king. 37 Your Majesty, you are the king of kings. The God of heaven has given you dominion and power and might and glory; 38 in your hands he has placed all mankind and the beasts of the field and the birds in the sky. Wherever they live, he has made you ruler over them all. You are that head of gold.

39 'After you, another kingdom will arise, inferior to yours. Next, a third kingdom, one of bronze, will rule over the whole earth. 40 Finally, there will be a fourth kingdom, strong as iron – for iron breaks and smashes everything – and as iron breaks things to pieces, so it will crush and break all the others. 41 Just as you saw that the feet and toes were partly of baked clay and partly of iron, so this will be a divided kingdom; yet it will have some of the strength of iron in it, even as you saw iron mixed with clay. 42 As the toes were partly iron and partly clay, so this kingdom will be partly strong and partly brittle. 43 And just as you saw the iron mixed with baked clay, so the people will be a mixture and will not remain united, any more than iron mixes with clay.

44 'In the time of those kings, the God of heaven will set up a kingdom that will never be destroyed, nor will it be left to

another people. It will crush all those kingdoms and bring them to an end, but it will itself endure for ever. 45 This is the meaning of the vision of the rock cut out of a mountain, but not by human hands – a rock that broke the iron, the bronze, the clay, the silver and the gold to pieces.

'The great God has shown the king what will take place in the future. The dream is true and its interpretation is trustworthy.'

46 Then King Nebuchadnezzar fell prostrate before Daniel and paid him honour and ordered that an offering and incense be presented to him. 47 The king said to Daniel, 'Surely your God is the God of gods and the Lord of kings and a revealer of mysteries, for you were able to reveal this mystery.'

48 Then the king placed Daniel in a high position and lavished many gifts on him. He made him ruler over the entire province of Babylon and placed him in charge of all its wise men. 49 Moreover, at Daniel's request the king appointed Shadrach, Meshach and Abednego chief ministers over the province of Babylon, while Daniel himself remained at the royal court.

The image of gold and the blazing furnace

3 King Nebuchadnezzar made an image of gold, sixty cubits high and six cubits wide,*a* and set it up on the plain of Dura in the province of Babylon. 2 He then summoned the satraps, prefects, governors, advisors, treasurers, judges, magistrates and all the other provincial officials to come to the dedication of the image he had set up. 3 So the satraps, prefects, governors, advisors, treasurers, judges, magistrates and all the other provincial officials assembled for the dedication of the image that King Nebuchadnezzar had set up, and they stood before it.

4 Then the herald loudly proclaimed, 'Nations and peoples of every language, this is what you are commanded to do: 5 as soon as you hear the sound of the horn,

---

a 1 That is, about 27 metres high and 2.7 metres wide

flute, zither, lyre, harp, pipe and all kinds of music, you must fall down and worship the image of gold that King Nebuchadnezzar has set up. 6Whoever does not fall down and worship will immediately be thrown into a blazing furnace.'

7Therefore, as soon as they heard the sound of the horn, flute, zither, lyre, harp and all kinds of music, all the nations and peoples of every language fell down and worshipped the image of gold that King Nebuchadnezzar had set up.

8At this time some astrologersb came forward and denounced the Jews. 9They said to King Nebuchadnezzar, 'May the king live for ever! 10Your Majesty has issued a decree that everyone who hears the sound of the horn, flute, zither, lyre, harp, pipe and all kinds of music must fall down and worship the image of gold, 11and that whoever does not fall down and worship will be thrown into a blazing furnace. 12But there are some Jews whom you have set over the affairs of the province of Babylon – Shadrach, Meshach and Abednego – who pay no attention to you, Your Majesty. They neither serve your gods nor worship the image of gold you have set up.'

13Furious with rage, Nebuchadnezzar summoned Shadrach, Meshach and Abednego. So these men were brought before the king, 14and Nebuchadnezzar said to them, 'Is it true, Shadrach, Meshach and Abednego, that you do not serve my gods or worship the image of gold I have set up? 15Now when you hear the sound of the horn, flute, zither, lyre, harp, pipe and all kinds of music, if you are ready to fall down and worship the image I made, very good. But if you do not worship it, you will be thrown immediately into a blazing furnace. Then what god will be able to rescue you from my hand?'

16Shadrach, Meshach and Abednego replied to him, 'King Nebuchadnezzar, we do not need to defend ourselves before you in this matter. 17If we are thrown into the blazing furnace, the God we serve is able to deliver us from it, and he will deliver usc from Your Majesty's hand. 18But even if he does not, we want you to know, Your Majesty, that we will not serve your gods or worship the image of gold you have set up.'

19Then Nebuchadnezzar was furious with Shadrach, Meshach and Abednego, and his attitude towards them changed. He ordered the furnace to be heated seven times hotter than usual 20and commanded some of the strongest soldiers in his army to tie up Shadrach, Meshach and Abednego and throw them into the blazing furnace. 21So these men, wearing their robes, trousers, turbans and other clothes, were bound and thrown into the blazing furnace. 22The king's command was so urgent and the furnace so hot that the flames of the fire killed the soldiers who took up Shadrach, Meshach and Abednego, 23and these three men, firmly tied, fell into the blazing furnace.

24Then King Nebuchadnezzar leaped to his feet in amazement and asked his advisors, 'Weren't there three men that we tied up and threw into the fire?'

They replied, 'Certainly, Your Majesty.'

25He said, 'Look! I see four men walking around in the fire, unbound and unharmed, and the fourth looks like a son of the gods.'

26Nebuchadnezzar then approached the opening of the blazing furnace and shouted, 'Shadrach, Meshach and Abednego, servants of the Most High God, come out! Come here!'

So Shadrach, Meshach and Abednego came out of the fire, 27and the satraps, prefects, governors and royal advisors crowded around them. They saw that the fire had not harmed their bodies, nor was a hair of their heads singed; their robes were not scorched, and there was no smell of fire on them.

28Then Nebuchadnezzar said, 'Praise be to the God of Shadrach, Meshach and Abednego, who has sent his angel and rescued his servants! They trusted in him and defied the king's command and were

---

b 8 Or Chaldeans

c 17 Or If the God we serve is able to deliver us, then he will deliver us from the blazing furnace and willing to give up their lives rather than serve or worship any god except their own God. ²⁹ Therefore I decree that the people of any nation or language who say anything against the God of Shadrach, Meshach and Abednego be cut into pieces and their houses be turned into piles of rubble, for no other god can save in this way.'

³⁰ Then the king promoted Shadrach, Meshach and Abednego in the province of Babylon.

Nebuchadnezzar's dream of a tree

4 *ª* King Nebuchadnezzar,

To the nations and peoples of every language, who live in all the earth:

May you prosper greatly!

² It is my pleasure to tell you about the miraculous signs and wonders that the Most High God has performed for me.

³ How great are his signs,
    how mighty his wonders!
His kingdom is an eternal
        kingdom;
    his dominion endures from
        generation to generation.

⁴ I, Nebuchadnezzar, was at home in my palace, contented and prosperous. ⁵ I had a dream that made me afraid. As I was lying in bed, the images and visions that passed through my mind terrified me. ⁶ So I commanded that all the wise men of Babylon be brought before me to interpret the dream for me. ⁷ When the magicians, enchanters, astrologers*ᵇ* and diviners came, I told them the dream, but they could not interpret it for me. ⁸ Finally, Daniel came into my presence and I told him the

dream. (He is called Belteshazzar, after the name of my god, and the spirit of the holy gods is in him.)

⁹ I said, 'Belteshazzar, chief of the magicians, I know that the spirit of the holy gods is in you, and no mystery is too difficult for you. Here is my dream; interpret it for me. ¹⁰ These are the visions I saw while lying in bed: I looked, and there before me stood a tree in the middle of the land. Its height was enormous. ¹¹ The tree grew large and strong and its top touched the sky; it was visible to the ends of the earth. ¹² Its leaves were beautiful, its fruit abundant, and on it was food for all. Under it the wild animals found shelter, and the birds lived in its branches; from it every creature was fed.

¹³ 'In the visions I saw while lying in bed, I looked, and there before me was a holy one, a messenger,*ᶜ* coming down from heaven. ¹⁴ He called in a loud voice: "Cut down the tree and trim off its branches; strip off its leaves and scatter its fruit. Let the animals flee from under it and the birds from its branches. ¹⁵ But let the stump and its roots, bound with iron and bronze, remain in the ground, in the grass of the field.

' "Let him be drenched with the dew of heaven, and let him live with the animals among the plants of the earth. ¹⁶ Let his mind be changed from that of a man and let him be given the mind of an animal, till seven times*ᵈ* pass by for him.

¹⁷ ' "The decision is announced by messengers, the holy ones declare the verdict, so that the living may know that the Most High is sovereign over all kingdoms on earth and gives them to anyone he wishes and sets over them the lowliest of people."

¹⁸ 'This is the dream that I, King Nebuchadnezzar, had. Now, Belteshazzar, tell me what it means, for

---

ª In Aramaic texts 4:1-3 is numbered 3:31-33, and 4:4-37 is numbered 4:1-34.
ᵇ 7 Or *Chaldeans*

ᶜ 13 Or *watchman*; also in verses 17 and 23
ᵈ 16 Or *years*; also in verses 23, 25 and 32

none of the wise men in my kingdom can interpret it for me. But you can, because the spirit of the holy gods is in you.'

Daniel interprets the dream

19 Then Daniel (also called Belteshazzar) was greatly perplexed for a time, and his thoughts terrified him. So the king said, 'Belteshazzar, do not let the dream or its meaning alarm you.'

Belteshazzar answered, 'My lord, if only the dream applied to your enemies and its meaning to your adversaries! 20 The tree you saw, which grew large and strong, with its top touching the sky, visible to the whole earth, 21 with beautiful leaves and abundant fruit, providing food for all, giving shelter to the wild animals, and having nesting places in its branches for the birds – 22 Your Majesty, you are that tree! You have become great and strong; your greatness has grown until it reaches the sky, and your dominion extends to distant parts of the earth.

23 'Your Majesty saw a holy one, a messenger, coming down from heaven and saying, "Cut down the tree and destroy it, but leave the stump, bound with iron and bronze, in the grass of the field, while its roots remain in the ground. Let him be drenched with the dew of heaven; let him live with the wild animals, until seven times pass by for him."

24 'This is the interpretation, Your Majesty, and this is the decree the Most High has issued against my lord the king: 25 you will be driven away from people and will live with the wild animals; you will eat grass like the ox and be drenched with the dew of heaven. Seven times will pass by for you until you acknowledge that the Most High is sovereign over all kingdoms on earth and gives them to anyone he wishes. 26 The command to leave the stump of the tree with its roots means that your

kingdom will be restored to you when you acknowledge that Heaven rules. 27 Therefore, Your Majesty, be pleased to accept my advice: renounce your sins by doing what is right, and your wickedness by being kind to the oppressed. It may be that then your prosperity will continue.'

The dream is fulfilled

28 All this happened to King Nebuchadnezzar. 29 Twelve months later, as the king was walking on the roof of the royal palace of Babylon, 30 he said, 'Is not this the great Babylon I have built as the royal residence, by my mighty power and for the glory of my majesty?'

31 Even as the words were on his lips, a voice came from heaven, 'This is what is decreed for you, King Nebuchadnezzar: your royal authority has been taken from you. 32 You will be driven away from people and will live with the wild animals; you will eat grass like the ox. Seven times will pass by for you until you acknowledge that the Most High is sovereign over all kingdoms on earth and gives them to anyone he wishes.'

33 Immediately what had been said about Nebuchadnezzar was fulfilled. He was driven away from people and ate grass like the ox. His body was drenched with the dew of heaven until his hair grew like the feathers of an eagle and his nails like the claws of a bird.

34 At the end of that time, I, Nebuchadnezzar, raised my eyes towards heaven, and my sanity was restored. Then I praised the Most High; I honoured and glorified him who lives for ever.

His dominion is an eternal dominion;
    his kingdom endures from
        generation to generation.
35 All the peoples of the earth
    are regarded as nothing.
He does as he pleases

with the powers of heaven
and the peoples of the earth.
No one can hold back his hand
or say to him: 'What have you done?'

36 At the same time that my sanity was restored, my honour and splendour were returned to me for the glory of my kingdom. My advisors and nobles sought me out, and I was restored to my throne and became even greater than before. 37 Now I, Nebuchadnezzar, praise and exalt and glorify the King of heaven, because everything he does is right and all his ways are just. And those who walk in pride he is able to humble.

The writing on the wall

5 King Belshazzar gave a great banquet for a thousand of his nobles and drank wine with them. 2 While Belshazzar was drinking his wine, he gave orders to bring in the gold and silver goblets that Nebuchadnezzar his father*a* had taken from the temple in Jerusalem, so that the king and his nobles, his wives and his concubines might drink from them. 3 So they brought in the gold goblets that had been taken from the temple of God in Jerusalem, and the king and his nobles, his wives and his concubines drank from them. 4 As they drank the wine, they praised the gods of gold and silver, of bronze, iron, wood and stone.

5 Suddenly the fingers of a human hand appeared and wrote on the plaster of the wall, near the lampstand in the royal palace. The king watched the hand as it wrote. 6 His face turned pale and he was so frightened that his legs became weak and his knees were knocking.

7 The king summoned the enchanters, astrologers*b* and diviners. Then he said to these wise men of Babylon, 'Whoever reads this writing and tells me what it means will be clothed in purple and have a gold chain placed round his neck, and he

will be made the third highest ruler in the kingdom.'

8 Then all the king's wise men came in, but they could not read the writing or tell the king what it meant. 9 So King Belshazzar became even more terrified and his face grew more pale. His nobles were baffled.

10 The queen,*c* hearing the voices of the king and his nobles, came into the banquet hall. 'May the king live for ever!' she said. 'Don't be alarmed! Don't look so pale! 11 There is a man in your kingdom who has the spirit of the holy gods in him. In the time of your father he was found to have insight and intelligence and wisdom like that of the gods. Your father, King Nebuchadnezzar, appointed him chief of the magicians, enchanters, astrologers and diviners. 12 He did this because Daniel, whom the king called Belteshazzar, was found to have a keen mind and knowledge and understanding, and also the ability to interpret dreams, explain riddles and solve difficult problems. Call for Daniel, and he will tell you what the writing means.'

13 So Daniel was brought before the king, and the king said to him, 'Are you Daniel, one of the exiles my father the king brought from Judah? 14 I have heard that the spirit of the gods is in you and that you have insight, intelligence and outstanding wisdom. 15 The wise men and enchanters were brought before me to read this writing and tell me what it means, but they could not explain it. 16 Now I have heard that you are able to give interpretations and to solve difficult problems. If you can read this writing and tell me what it means, you will be clothed in purple and have a gold chain placed round your neck, and you will be made the third highest ruler in the kingdom.'

17 Then Daniel answered the king, 'You may keep your gifts for yourself and give your rewards to someone else. Nevertheless, I will read the writing for the king and tell him what it means.

18 'Your Majesty, the Most High God

---

a 2 Or *ancestor*; or *predecessor*; also in verses 11, 13 and 18
b 7 Or *Chaldeans*; also in verse 11

c 10 Or *queen mother*

gave your father Nebuchadnezzar sovereignty and greatness and glory and splendour. ¹⁹ Because of the high position he gave him, all the nations and peoples of every language dreaded and feared him. Those the king wanted to put to death, he put to death; those he wanted to spare, he spared; those he wanted to promote, he promoted; and those he wanted to humble, he humbled. ²⁰ But when his heart became arrogant and hardened with pride, he was deposed from his royal throne and stripped of his glory. ²¹ He was driven away from people and given the mind of an animal; he lived with the wild donkeys and ate grass like the ox; and his body was drenched with the dew of heaven, until he acknowledged that the Most High God is sovereign over all kingdoms on earth and sets over them anyone he wishes.

²²'But you, Belshazzar, his son,*d* have not humbled yourself, though you knew all this. ²³ Instead, you have set yourself up against the Lord of heaven. You had the goblets from his temple brought to you, and you and your nobles, your wives and your concubines drank wine from them. You praised the gods of silver and gold, of bronze, iron, wood and stone, which cannot see or hear or understand. But you did not honour the God who holds in his hand your life and all your ways. ²⁴ Therefore he sent the hand that wrote the inscription.

²⁵'This is the inscription that was written:

MENE, MENE, TEKEL, PARSIN

²⁶'Here is what these words mean:

*Mene*e: God has numbered the days of your reign and brought it to an end.
²⁷ *Tekel*f: You have been weighed on the scales and found wanting.

²⁸ *Peres*ɡ: Your kingdom is divided and given to the Medes and Persians.'

²⁹ Then at Belshazzar's command, Daniel was clothed in purple, a gold chain was placed round his neck, and he was proclaimed the third highest ruler in the kingdom. ³⁰ That very night Belshazzar, king of the Babylonians,*h* was slain, ³¹ and Darius the Mede took over the kingdom, at the age of sixty-two.*i*

Daniel in the den of lions

6ᵃ It pleased Darius to appoint 120 satraps to rule throughout the kingdom, ² with three chief ministers over them, one of whom was Daniel. The satraps were made accountable to them so that the king might not suffer loss. ³ Now Daniel so distinguished himself among the chief ministers and the satraps by his exceptional qualities that the king planned to set him over the whole kingdom. ⁴ At this, the chief ministers and the satraps tried to find grounds for charges against Daniel in his conduct of government affairs, but they were unable to do so. They could find no corruption in him, because he was trustworthy and neither corrupt nor negligent. ⁵ Finally these men said, 'We will never find any basis for charges against this man Daniel unless it has something to do with the law of his God.'

⁶ So these chief ministers and satraps went as a group to the king and said: 'May King Darius live for ever! ⁷ The royal ministers, prefects, satraps, advisors and governors have all agreed that the king should issue an edict and enforce the decree that anyone who prays to any god or human being during the next thirty days, except to you, Your Majesty, shall be thrown into the lions' den. ⁸ Now,

---

d 22 Or *descendant*; or *successor*
e 26 *Mene* can mean *numbered* or *mina* (a unit of money).
f 27 *Tekel* can mean *weighed* or *shekel*.

g 28 *Peres* (the singular of *Parsin*) can mean *divided* or *Persia* or *a half mina* or *a half shekel*.
h 30 Or *Chaldeans*
i 31 In Aramaic texts this verse (5:31) is numbered 6:1.
a In Aramaic texts 6:1-28 is numbered 6:2-29.

Your Majesty, issue the decree and put it in writing so that it cannot be altered – in accordance with the law of the Medes and Persians, which cannot be repealed.' ⁹So King Darius put the decree in writing.

¹⁰ Now when Daniel learned that the decree had been published, he went home to his upstairs room where the windows opened towards Jerusalem. Three times a day he got down on his knees and prayed,

giving thanks to his God, just as he had done before. ¹¹Then these men went as a group and found Daniel praying and asking God for help. ¹²So they went to the king and spoke to him about his royal decree: 'Did you not publish a decree that during the next thirty days anyone who prays to any god or human being except to you, Your Majesty, would be thrown into the lions' den?'

PRAYER 6

A DAILY PATTERN OF PRAYER

Morning, lunchtime and evening. Those were the times when Daniel was famous for praying (Daniel 6:10).

He probably prayed more often than that, as he seems to have been someone deeply in touch with God, but he used these times to go to a private place and maintain a routine of formal times of prayer. It was so well known that he prayed in this way that his enemies were able to use it in a plot against him. They also knew that he was so committed to prayer that he wouldn't stop even if they got it made illegal!

What inspires me is that Daniel did not get arrested for praying three times a day because he made a mistake. He knew what the 'chief ministers and satraps' were up to and deliberately set out to maintain his pattern – although this time he was asking God for help (6:10–11). If he was prepared to risk death, Daniel must have believed that his routine of prayer times was essential. The source of Daniel's spiritual power was the living God, but his connection to that source was a consistent life of petition and thanksgiving. So Daniel felt safer praying as usual, being caught and then given as lunch to hungry lions than if he had changed his routine and spent a few weeks only praying in his thoughts. After all, Daniel had maintained his life of prayer while serving a series of different empires (Daniel 1 – 5), and God had come through for him in each one. The empires had fallen, but he was still standing!

I wonder what this makes you think about your own life of prayer. Do you have a regular routine of prayer? Or do you say, 'I pray when I need to. It doesn't need to be part of a routine.' Or maybe you say, 'I pray in my head. Nobody else needs to be aware.' If you were threatened with imprisonment, torture or death, would you deliberately go on praying in a way that might get you caught?

I wonder what would happen if every Christian alive today committed themselves to praying formally every morning, lunchtime and evening. It's a thought, isn't it?

Hugo Anson

 Matthew 18:18–20   Luke 17:11–19

The king answered, 'The decree stands—in accordance with the law of the Medes and Persians, which cannot be repealed.'

13 Then they said to the king, 'Daniel, who is one of the exiles from Judah, pays no attention to you, Your Majesty, or to the decree you put in writing. He still prays three times a day.' 14 When the king heard this, he was greatly distressed; he was determined to rescue Daniel and made every effort until sunset to save him.

15 Then the men went as a group to King Darius and said to him, 'Remember, Your Majesty, that according to the law of the Medes and Persians no decree or edict that the king issues can be changed.'

16 So the king gave the order, and they brought Daniel and threw him into the lions' den. The king said to Daniel, 'May your God, whom you serve continually, rescue you!'

17 A stone was brought and placed over the mouth of the den, and the king sealed it with his own signet ring and with the rings of his nobles, so that Daniel's situation might not be changed. 18 Then the king returned to his palace and spent the night without eating and without any entertainment being brought to him. And he could not sleep.

19 At the first light of dawn, the king got up and hurried to the lions' den. 20 When he came near the den, he called to Daniel in an anguished voice, 'Daniel, servant of the living God, has your God, whom you serve continually, been able to rescue you from the lions?'

21 Daniel answered, 'May the king live for ever! 22 My God sent his angel, and he shut the mouths of the lions. They have not hurt me, because I was found innocent in his sight. Nor have I ever done any wrong before you, Your Majesty.'

23 The king was overjoyed and gave orders to lift Daniel out of the den. And when Daniel was lifted from the den, no wound was found on him, because he had trusted in his God.

24 At the king's command, the men who had falsely accused Daniel were brought in and thrown into the lions' den, along with their wives and children. And before they reached the floor of the den, the lions overpowered them and crushed all their bones.

25 Then King Darius wrote to all the nations and peoples of every language in all the earth:

'May you prosper greatly!

26 'I issue a decree that in every part of my kingdom people must fear and reverence the God of Daniel.

'For he is the living God
    and he endures for ever;
his kingdom will not be destroyed,
    his dominion will never end.
27 He rescues and he saves;
    he performs signs and wonders
    in the heavens and on the earth.
He has rescued Daniel
    from the power of the lions.'

28 So Daniel prospered during the reign of Darius and the reign of Cyrus[b] the Persian.

Daniel's dream of four beasts

7 In the first year of Belshazzar king of Babylon, Daniel had a dream, and visions passed through his mind as he was lying in bed. He wrote down the substance of his dream.

2 Daniel said: 'In my vision at night I looked, and there before me were the four winds of heaven churning up the great sea. 3 Four great beasts, each different from the others, came up out of the sea.

4 'The first was like a lion, and it had the wings of an eagle. I watched until its wings were torn off and it was lifted from the ground so that it stood on two feet like a human being, and the mind of a human was given to it.

5 'And there before me was a second beast, which looked like a bear. It was raised up on one of its sides, and it had three ribs in its mouth between its teeth. It was told, "Get up and eat your fill of flesh!"

---

b 28 Or *Darius, that is, the reign of Cyrus*

6 'After that, I looked, and there before me was another beast, one that looked like a leopard. And on its back it had four wings like those of a bird. This beast had four heads, and it was given authority to rule.

7 'After that, in my vision at night I looked, and there before me was a fourth beast – terrifying and frightening and very powerful. It had large iron teeth; it crushed and devoured its victims and trampled underfoot whatever was left. It was different from all the former beasts, and it had ten horns.

8 'While I was thinking about the horns, there before me was another horn, a little one, which came up among them; and three of the first horns were uprooted before it. This horn had eyes like the eyes of a human being and a mouth that spoke boastfully.

9 'As I looked,

'thrones were set in place,
    and the Ancient of Days took his seat.
His clothing was as white as snow;
    the hair of his head was white like
        wool.
His throne was flaming with fire,
    and its wheels were all ablaze.
10 A river of fire was flowing,
    coming out from before him.
Thousands upon thousands attended
        him;
    ten thousand times ten thousand
        stood before him.
The court was seated,
    and the books were opened.

11 'Then I continued to watch because of the boastful words the horn was speaking. I kept looking until the beast was slain and its body destroyed and thrown into the blazing fire. 12 (The other beasts had been stripped of their authority, but were allowed to live for a period of time.)

13 'In my vision at night I looked, and there before me was one like a son of man,*a* coming with the clouds of heaven.

He approached the Ancient of Days and was led into his presence. 14 He was given authority, glory and sovereign power; all nations and peoples of every language worshipped him. His dominion is an everlasting dominion that will not pass away, and his kingdom is one that will never be destroyed.

The interpretation of the dream

15 'I, Daniel, was troubled in spirit, and the visions that passed through my mind disturbed me. 16 I approached one of those standing there and asked him the meaning of all this.

'So he told me and gave me the interpretation of these things: 17 "The four great beasts are four kings that will rise from the earth. 18 But the holy people of the Most High will receive the kingdom and will possess it for ever – yes, for ever and ever."

19 'Then I wanted to know the meaning of the fourth beast, which was different from all the others and most terrifying, with its iron teeth and bronze claws – the beast that crushed and devoured its victims and trampled underfoot whatever was left. 20 I also wanted to know about the ten horns on its head and about the other horn that came up, before which three of them fell – the horn that looked more imposing than the others and that had eyes and a mouth that spoke boastfully. 21 As I watched, this horn was waging war against the holy people and defeating them, 22 until the Ancient of Days came and pronounced judgment in favour of the holy people of the Most High, and the time came when they possessed the kingdom.

23 'He gave me this explanation: "The fourth beast is a fourth kingdom that will appear on earth. It will be different from all the other kingdoms and will devour the whole earth, trampling it down and crushing it. 24 The ten horns are ten kings who will come from this kingdom. After them another king will arise, different from the earlier ones; he will subdue three kings. 25 He will speak against the Most High and oppress his holy people and try to change

---

a 13 The Aramaic phrase *bar enash* means *human being*. The phrase *son of man* is retained here because of its use in the New Testament as a title of Jesus, probably based largely on this verse.

CHRIST IN ALL THE SCRIPTURES 10

The Son of Man

Jesus' favourite title for himself was 'the Son of Man'. It's an Old Testament term. It can just mean 'human' or 'mortal'. That was what God used to call the prophet Ezekiel (e.g. in Ezekiel 1). But it's much more likely that Jesus' use of the term comes from Daniel 7:9–14.

This is another Old Testament text in which we can see a prophecy about Jesus, but which also inspired and shaped his life and ministry. The setting is the throne room of heaven. The *'Ancient of Days'* (God the Father) sits in awesome majesty. It's a court scene, and the books are opened. The powers of darkness – portrayed as 'beasts' – are found guilty and stripped of their improper authority. Then *'one like a son of man'* approaches the throne. He is given authority. He establishes a kingdom that will never end, and all the nations worship him.

This is a divine figure. He is worshipped. 'Son of Man' is not a title about Jesus' humanity. It's a divine title, telling us the real identity of the one who became human. It's also a title which prepares us to understand the spiritual warfare he waged between the kingdom of God and the kingdom of darkness. The kingdom wasn't just about people accepting God's rule and living God's way. It was a conflict with the powers of evil. Jesus proclaimed the kingdom of God and drove out the demons. He came to destroy the works of darkness (1 John 3:8) and that's why there's authority when Christians pray in his name today.

But this great spiritual victory wasn't finally won as Jesus drove out demons. It was won when he hung on the cross. Once, when Jesus' disciples were competing about being the greatest, he said, *'Even the Son of Man did not come to be served, but to serve, and to give his life as a ransom for many'* (Mark 10:45). This was staggering. In Daniel everyone was to serve the Son of Man, not the other way round. One day every knee will bow to him (Philippians 2:10). But he served on the cross so that everyone could have the opportunity to serve him freely from the heart, because he had ransomed them, setting them free from sin and evil.

You have to be careful when you find Jesus in Old Testament texts. He fulfilled them all. It was the combination of them all which shaped him. The Son was the Servant. The one with all authority laid down his life. So treat each text as a thread leading you to Jesus, as he's seen in the New Testament. Each thread will tell you something about him, but you need all the threads to see him as he really is.

Graham Cray

Isaiah 52:1

the set times and the laws. The holy people will be delivered into his hands for a time, times and half a time.*b*

26 ' "But the court will sit, and his power will be taken away and completely destroyed for ever. 27 Then the sovereignty, power and greatness of all the kingdoms under heaven will be handed over to the holy people of the Most High. His kingdom will be an everlasting kingdom, and all rulers will worship and obey him."

28 'This is the end of the matter. I, Daniel, was deeply troubled by my thoughts, and my face turned pale, but I kept the matter to myself.'

Daniel's vision of a ram and a goat

8 In the third year of King Belshazzar's reign, I, Daniel, had a vision, after the one that had already appeared to me. 2 In my vision I saw myself in the citadel of Susa in the province of Elam; in the vision I was beside the Ulai Canal. 3 I looked up, and there before me was a ram with two horns, standing beside the canal, and the horns were long. One of the horns was longer than the other but grew up later. 4 I watched the ram as it charged towards the west and the north and the south. No animal could stand against it, and none could rescue from its power. It did as it pleased and became great.

5 As I was thinking about this, suddenly a goat with a prominent horn between its eyes came from the west, crossing the whole earth without touching the ground. 6 It came towards the two-horned ram I had seen standing beside the canal and charged at it in great rage. 7 I saw it attack the ram furiously, striking the ram and shattering its two horns. The ram was powerless to stand against it; the goat knocked it to the ground and trampled on it, and none could rescue the ram from its power. 8 The goat became very great, but at the height of its power the large horn was broken off, and in its place four prominent horns grew up towards the four winds of heaven.

9 Out of one of them came another horn, which started small but grew in power to the south and to the east and towards the Beautiful Land. 10 It grew until it reached the host of the heavens, and it threw some of the starry host down to the earth and trampled on them. 11 It set itself up to be as great as the commander of the army of the LORD; it took away the daily sacrifice from the LORD, and his sanctuary was thrown down. 12 Because of rebellion, the LORD's people*a* and the daily sacrifice were given over to it. It prospered in everything it did, and truth was thrown to the ground.

13 Then I heard a holy one speaking, and another holy one said to him, 'How long will it take for the vision to be fulfilled – the vision concerning the daily sacrifice, the rebellion that causes desolation, the surrender of the sanctuary and the trampling underfoot of the LORD's people?'

14 He said to me, 'It will take 2,300 evenings and mornings; then the sanctuary will be reconsecrated.'

The interpretation of the vision

15 While I, Daniel, was watching the vision and trying to understand it, there before me stood one who looked like a man. 16 And I heard a man's voice from the Ulai calling, 'Gabriel, tell this man the meaning of the vision.'

17 As he came near the place where I was standing, I was terrified and fell prostrate. 'Son of man,'*b* he said to me, 'understand that the vision concerns the time of the end.'

18 While he was speaking to me, I was in a deep sleep, with my face to the ground. Then he touched me and raised me to my feet.

19 He said: 'I am going to tell you what will happen later in the time of wrath, because the vision concerns the appointed time of the end.*c* 20 The two-horned ram that you saw represents the kings of Media

---

b 25 Or *for a year, two years and half a year*

a 12 Or *rebellion, the armies*

b 17 The Hebrew phrase *ben adam* means *human being.* The phrase *son of man* is retained as a form of address here because of its possible association with 'Son of Man' in the New Testament.

c 19 Or *because the end will be at the appointed time*

and Persia. 21 The shaggy goat is the king of Greece, and the large horn between its eyes is the first king. 22 The four horns that replaced the one that was broken off represent four kingdoms that will emerge from his nation but will not have the same power.

23 'In the latter part of their reign, when rebels have become completely wicked, a fierce-looking king, a master of intrigue, will arise. 24 He will become very strong, but not by his own power. He will cause astounding devastation and will succeed in whatever he does. He will destroy those who are mighty, the holy people. 25 He will cause deceit to prosper, and he will consider himself superior. When they feel secure, he will destroy many and take his stand against the Prince of princes. Yet he will be destroyed, but not by human power.

26 'The vision of the evenings and mornings that has been given you is true, but seal up the vision, for it concerns the distant future.'

27 I, Daniel, was worn out. I lay exhausted for several days. Then I got up and went about the king's business. I was appalled by the vision; it was beyond understanding.

Daniel's prayer

9 In the first year of Darius son of Xerxes*a* (a Mede by descent), who was made ruler over the Babylonian*b* kingdom – 2 in the first year of his reign, I, Daniel, understood from the Scriptures, according to the word of the Lord given to Jeremiah the prophet, that the desolation of Jerusalem would last seventy years. 3 So I turned to the Lord God and pleaded with him in prayer and petition, in fasting, and in sackcloth and ashes.

4 I prayed to the Lord my God and confessed:

'Lord, the great and awesome God, who keeps his covenant of love with those who love him and keep his commandments, 5 we have sinned

and done wrong. We have been wicked and have rebelled; we have turned away from your commands and laws. 6 We have not listened to your servants the prophets, who spoke in your name to our kings, our princes and our ancestors, and to all the people of the land.

7 'Lord, you are righteous, but this day we are covered with shame – the people of Judah and the inhabitants of Jerusalem and all Israel, both near and far, in all the countries where you have scattered us because of our unfaithfulness to you. 8 We and our kings, our princes and our ancestors are covered with shame, Lord, because we have sinned against you. 9 The Lord our God is merciful and forgiving, even though we have rebelled against him; 10 we have not obeyed the Lord our God or kept the laws he gave us through his servants the prophets. 11 All Israel has transgressed your law and turned away, refusing to obey you.

'Therefore the curses and sworn judgments written in the Law of Moses, the servant of God, have been poured out on us, because we have sinned against you. 12 You have fulfilled the words spoken against us and against our rulers by bringing on us great disaster. Under the whole heaven nothing has ever been done like what has been done to Jerusalem. 13 Just as it is written in the Law of Moses, all this disaster has come on us, yet we have not sought the favour of the Lord our God by turning from our sins and giving attention to your truth. 14 The Lord did not hesitate to bring the disaster on us, for the Lord our God is righteous in everything he does; yet we have not obeyed him.

15 'Now, Lord our God, who brought your people out of Egypt with a mighty hand and who made for yourself a name that endures to this day, we have sinned, we have done wrong. 16 Lord, in keeping with all your righteous acts, turn away

---

a 1 Hebrew *Ahasuerus*
b 1 Or *Chaldean*

your anger and your wrath from Jerusalem, your city, your holy hill. Our sins and the iniquities of our ancestors have made Jerusalem and your people an object of scorn to all those around us.

17 'Now, our God, hear the prayers and petitions of your servant. For your sake, Lord, look with favour on your desolate sanctuary. 18 Give ear, our God, and hear; open your eyes and see the desolation of the city that bears your Name. We do not make requests of you because we are righteous, but because of your great mercy. 19 Lord, listen! Lord, forgive! Lord, hear and act! For your sake, my God, do not delay, because your city and your people bear your Name.'

The seventy 'sevens'

20 While I was speaking and praying, confessing my sin and the sin of my people Israel and making my request to the LORD my God for his holy hill – 21 while I was still in prayer, Gabriel, the man I had seen in the earlier vision, came to me in swift flight about the time of the evening sacrifice. 22 He instructed me and said to me, 'Daniel, I have now come to give you insight and understanding. 23 As soon as you began to pray, a word went out, which I have come to tell you, for you are highly esteemed. Therefore, consider the word and understand the vision:

24 'Seventy "sevens"c are decreed for your people and your holy city to finishd transgression, to put an end to sin, to atone for wickedness, to bring in everlasting righteousness, to seal up vision and prophecy and to anoint the Most Holy Place.e

25 'Know and understand this: from the time the word goes out to restore and rebuild Jerusalem until the Anointed One,f the ruler, comes, there will be seven "sevens", and sixty-two "sevens". It will be rebuilt with streets and a trench, but in times of trouble. 26 After the sixty-two

"sevens", the Anointed One will be put to death and will have nothing.g The people of the ruler who will come will destroy the city and the sanctuary. The end will come like a flood: war will continue until the end, and desolations have been decreed. 27 He will confirm a covenant with many for one "seven".h In the middle of the "seven"h he will put an end to sacrifice and offering. And at the templei he will set up an abomination that causes desolation, until the end that is decreed is poured out on him.j k

Daniel's vision of a man

10 In the third year of Cyrus king of Persia, a revelation was given to Daniel (who was called Belteshazzar). Its message was true and it concerned a great war.a The understanding of the message came to him in a vision.

2 At that time I, Daniel, mourned for three weeks. 3 I ate no choice food; no meat or wine touched my lips; and I used no lotions at all until the three weeks were over.

4 On the twenty-fourth day of the first month, as I was standing on the bank of the great river, the Tigris, 5 I looked up and there before me was a man dressed in linen, with a belt of fine gold from Uphaz round his waist. 6 His body was like topaz, his face like lightning, his eyes like flaming torches, his arms and legs like the gleam of burnished bronze, and his voice like the sound of a multitude.

7 I, Daniel, was the only one who saw the vision; those who were with me did not see it, but such terror overwhelmed them that they fled and hid themselves. 8 So I was left alone, gazing at this great vision; I had no strength left, my face turned deathly pale and I was helpless. 9 Then I heard him speaking, and as I

---

c 24 Or "weeks"; also in verses 25 and 26
d 24 Or restrain
e 24 Or the most holy One
f 25 Or an anointed one; also in verse 26

g 26 Or death and will have no one; or death, but not for himself
h 27 Or "week"
i 27 Septuagint and Theodotion; Hebrew wing
j 27 Or it
k 27 Or And one who causes desolation will come upon the wing of the abominable temple, until the end that is decreed is poured out on the desolated city
a 1 Or true and burdensome

listened to him, I fell into a deep sleep, my face to the ground.

¹⁰A hand touched me and set me trembling on my hands and knees. ¹¹He said, 'Daniel, you who are highly esteemed, consider carefully the words I am about to speak to you, and stand up, for I have now been sent to you.' And when he said this to me, I stood up trembling.

¹²Then he continued, 'Do not be afraid, Daniel. Since the first day that you set your mind to gain understanding and to humble yourself before your God, your words were heard, and I have come in response to them. ¹³But the prince of the Persian kingdom resisted me twenty-one days. Then Michael, one of the chief princes, came to help me, because I was detained there with the king of Persia. ¹⁴Now I have come to explain to you what will happen to your people in the future, for the vision concerns a time yet to come.'

¹⁵While he was saying this to me, I bowed with my face towards the ground and was speechless. ¹⁶Then one who looked like a manᵇ touched my lips, and I opened my mouth and began to speak. I said to the one standing before me, 'I am overcome with anguish because of the vision, my lord, and I feel very weak. ¹⁷How can I, your servant, talk with you, my lord? My strength is gone and I can hardly breathe.'

¹⁸Again the one who looked like a man touched me and gave me strength. ¹⁹'Do not be afraid, you who are highly esteemed,' he said. 'Peace! Be strong now; be strong.'

When he spoke to me, I was strengthened and said, 'Speak, my lord, since you have given me strength.'

²⁰So he said, 'Do you know why I have come to you? Soon I will return to fight against the prince of Persia, and when I go, the prince of Greece will come; ²¹but first I will tell you what is written in the Book of Truth. (No one supports me

11 against them except Michael, your prince. ¹And in the first year of Darius the Mede, I took my stand to support and protect him.)

The kings of the south and the north

²'Now then, I tell you the truth: three more kings will arise in Persia, and then a fourth, who will be far richer than all the others. When he has gained power by his wealth, he will stir up everyone against the kingdom of Greece. ³Then a mighty king will arise, who will rule with great power and do as he pleases. ⁴After he has arisen, his empire will be broken up and parcelled out towards the four winds of heaven. It will not go to his descendants, nor will it have the power he exercised, because his empire will be uprooted and given to others.

⁵'The king of the South will become strong, but one of his commanders will become even stronger than he and will rule his own kingdom with great power. ⁶After some years, they will become allies. The daughter of the king of the South will go to the king of the North to make an alliance, but she will not retain her power, and he and his powerᵃ will not last. In those days she will be betrayed, together with her royal escort and her fatherᵇ and the one who supported her.

⁷'Someone from within her family will arise to take her place. He will attack the forces of the king of the North and enter his fortress; he will fight against them and be victorious. ⁸He will also seize their gods, their metal images and their valuable articles of silver and gold and carry them off to Egypt. For some years he will leave the king of the North alone. ⁹Then the king of the North will invade the realm of the king of the South but will retreat to his own country. ¹⁰His sons will prepare for war and assemble a great army, which will sweep on like an irresistible flood and carry the battle as far as his fortress.

¹¹'Then the king of the South will march out in a rage and fight against the king of

---

ᵇ 16 Most manuscripts of the Masoretic Text; one manuscript of the Masoretic Text, Dead Sea Scrolls and Septuagint *Then something that looked like a human hand*

ᵃ 6 Or *offspring*
ᵇ 6 Or *child* (see Vulgate and Syriac)

the North, who will raise a large army, but it will be defeated. 12 When the army is carried off, the king of the South will be filled with pride and will slaughter many thousands, yet he will not remain triumphant. 13 For the king of the North will muster another army, larger than the first; and after several years, he will advance with a huge army fully equipped.

14 'In those times many will rise against the king of the South. Those who are violent among your own people will rebel in fulfilment of the vision, but without success. 15 Then the king of the North will come and build up siege ramps and will capture a fortified city. The forces of the South will be powerless to resist; even their best troops will not have the strength to stand. 16 The invader will do as he pleases; no one will be able to stand against him. He will establish himself in the Beautiful Land and will have the power to destroy it. 17 He will determine to come with the might of his entire kingdom and will make an alliance with the king of the South. And he will give him a daughter in marriage in order to overthrow the kingdom, but his plansᶜ will not succeed or help him. 18 Then he will turn his attention to the coastlands and will take many of them, but a commander will put an end to his insolence and will turn his insolence back on him. 19 After this, he will turn back towards the fortresses of his own country but will stumble and fall, to be seen no more.

20 'His successor will send out a tax collector to maintain the royal splendour. In a few years, however, he will be destroyed, yet not in anger or in battle.

21 'He will be succeeded by a contemptible person who has not been given the honour of royalty. He will invade the kingdom when its people feel secure, and he will seize it through intrigue. 22 Then an overwhelming army will be swept away before him; both it and a prince of the covenant will be destroyed. 23 After coming to an agreement with him, he will act deceitfully, and with only a few people he will rise to power. 24 When the richest provinces feel secure, he will invade them and will achieve what neither his fathers nor his forefathers did. He will distribute plunder, loot and wealth among his followers. He will plot the overthrow of fortresses – but only for a time.

25 'With a large army he will stir up his strength and courage against the king of the South. The king of the South will wage war with a large and very powerful army, but he will not be able to stand because of the plots devised against him. 26 Those who eat from the king's provisions will try to destroy him; his army will be swept away, and many will fall in battle. 27 The two kings, with their hearts bent on evil, will sit at the same table and lie to each other, but to no avail, because an end will still come at the appointed time. 28 The king of the North will return to his own country with great wealth, but his heart will be set against the holy covenant. He will take action against it and then return to his own country.

29 'At the appointed time he will invade the South again, but this time the outcome will be different from what it was before. 30 Ships of the western coastlands will oppose him, and he will lose heart. Then he will turn back and vent his fury against the holy covenant. He will return and show favour to those who forsake the holy covenant.

31 'His armed forces will rise up to desecrate the temple fortress and will abolish the daily sacrifice. Then they will set up the abomination that causes desolation. 32 With flattery he will corrupt those who have violated the covenant, but the people who know their God will firmly resist him.

33 'Those who are wise will instruct many, though for a time they will fall by the sword or be burned or captured or plundered. 34 When they fall, they will receive a little help, and many who are not sincere will join them. 35 Some of the wise will stumble, so that they may be refined, purified and made spotless until the time of the end, for it will still come at the appointed time.

ᶜ 17 Or but she

The king who exalts himself

36 'The king will do as he pleases. He will exalt and magnify himself above every god and will say unheard-of things against the God of gods. He will be successful until the time of wrath is completed, for what has been determined must take place. 37 He will show no regard for the gods of his ancestors or for the one desired by women, nor will he regard any god, but will exalt himself above them all. 38 Instead of them, he will honour a god of fortresses; a god unknown to his ancestors he will honour with gold and silver, with precious stones and costly gifts. 39 He will attack the mightiest fortresses with the help of a foreign god and will greatly honour those who acknowledge him. He will make them rulers over many people and will distribute the land at a price.*d*

40 'At the time of the end the king of the South will engage him in battle, and the king of the North will storm out against him with chariots and cavalry and a great fleet of ships. He will invade many countries and sweep through them like a flood. 41 He will also invade the Beautiful Land. Many countries will fall, but Edom, Moab and the leaders of Ammon will be delivered from his hand. 42 He will extend his power over many countries; Egypt will not escape. 43 He will gain control of the treasures of gold and silver and all the riches of Egypt, with the Libyans and Cushites*e* in submission. 44 But reports from the east and the north will alarm him, and he will set out in a great rage to destroy and annihilate many. 45 He will pitch his royal tents between the seas at*f* the beautiful holy mountain. Yet he will come to his end, and no one will help him.

The end times

12 'At that time Michael, the great prince who protects your people, will arise. There will be a time of distress such as has not happened from the beginning of nations until then. But at that time your people – everyone whose name is found written in the book – will be delivered. 2 Multitudes who sleep in the dust of the earth will awake: some to everlasting life, others to shame and everlasting contempt. 3 Those who are wise*a* will shine like the brightness of the heavens, and those who lead many to righteousness, like the stars for ever and ever. 4 But you, Daniel, roll up and seal the words of the scroll until the time of the end. Many will go here and there to increase knowledge.'

5 Then I, Daniel, looked, and there before me stood two others, one on this bank of the river and one on the opposite bank. 6 One of them said to the man clothed in linen, who was above the waters of the river, 'How long will it be before these astonishing things are fulfilled?'

7 The man clothed in linen, who was above the waters of the river, lifted his right hand and his left hand towards heaven, and I heard him swear by him who lives for ever, saying, 'It will be for a time, times and half a time.*b* When the power of the holy people has been finally broken, all these things will be completed.'

8 I heard, but I did not understand. So I asked, 'My lord, what will the outcome of all this be?'

9 He replied, 'Go your way, Daniel, because the words are rolled up and sealed until the time of the end. 10 Many will be purified, made spotless and refined, but the wicked will continue to be wicked. None of the wicked will understand, but those who are wise will understand.

11 'From the time that the daily sacrifice is abolished and the abomination that causes desolation is set up, there will be 1,290 days. 12 Blessed is the one who waits for and reaches the end of the 1,335 days.

13 'As for you, go your way till the end. You will rest, and then at the end of the days you will rise to receive your allotted inheritance.'

---

d 39 Or *land for a reward*
e 43 That is, people from the upper Nile region
f 45 Or *the sea and*

a 3 Or *who impart wisdom*
b 7 Or *a year, two years and half a year*

HOSEA

DATE

Hosea prophesied from around 760 to 720 BC

AUTHOR

Hosea

WHAT'S IT ALL ABOUT?

Hosea's book is the first of the twelve Minor Prophets and his message was for the Northern tribes (the Kingdom of Israel), calling them to repentance for their actions. One of God's main complaints against Israel was that they weren't faithful to him but persisted in serving other gods. He continued to love them, regardless of their behaviour, and was desperate for their hearts to turn back to him. As a picture of this, God called Hosea to take a prostitute for a wife. Even though she was unfaithful to him, God asked Hosea to be faithful to her and to continue to love her. Having felt at first hand how painful it was to be treated like this, Hosea spoke passionately and eloquently to the people from his personal pain, imploring them to repent. Although judgement was to come when the people were conquered by the Assyrians, it's clear that God still loved his people and wasn't willing to give up on them easily. The message he sent via Hosea was full of love and grace.

WHY SHOULD WE READ IT?

- To be assured of God's great love for his people, despite their unfaithfulness to him.

- To gain insight into how God feels when his people put other gods before him.

- To see Hosea's obedience in carrying out all that God asked of him, though it cost him greatly.

Andy Croft with Liza Hoeksma

1

The word of the LORD that came to Hosea son of Beeri during the reigns of Uzziah, Jotham, Ahaz and Hezekiah, kings of Judah, and during the reign of Jeroboam son of Joash king of Israel:

Hosea's wife and children

2 When the LORD began to speak through Hosea, the LORD said to him, 'Go, marry a promiscuous woman and have children with her, for like an adulterous wife this land is guilty of unfaithfulness to the LORD.' 3 So he married Gomer daughter of Diblaim, and she conceived and bore him a son.

4 Then the LORD said to Hosea, 'Call him Jezreel, because I will soon punish the house of Jehu for the massacre at Jezreel, and I will put an end to the kingdom of Israel. 5 In that day I will break Israel's bow in the Valley of Jezreel.'

6 Gomer conceived again and gave birth to a daughter. Then the LORD said to Hosea, 'Call her Lo-Ruhamah (which means "not loved"), for I will no longer show love to Israel, that I should at all forgive them. 7 Yet I will show love to Judah; and I will save them – not by bow, sword or battle, or by horses and horsemen, but I, the LORD their God, will save them.'

8 After she had weaned Lo-Ruhamah, Gomer had another son. 9 Then the LORD said, 'Call him Lo-Ammi (which means "not my people"), for you are not my people, and I am not your God.ᵃ

10 'Yet the Israelites will be like the sand on the seashore, which cannot be measured or counted. In the place where it was said to them, "You are not my people", they will be called "children of the living God". 11 The people of Judah and the people of Israel will come together; they will appoint one leader and will come up out of the land, for great will be the day of Jezreel.ᵇ

2

ᵃ 'Say of your brothers, "My people", and of your sisters, "My loved one".

Israel punished and restored

2 'Rebuke your mother, rebuke her,
    for she is not my wife,
    and I am not her husband.
Let her remove the adulterous look
        from her face
    and the unfaithfulness from between
        her breasts.
3 Otherwise I will strip her naked
    and make her as bare as on the day
        she was born;
I will make her like a desert,
    turn her into a parched land,
    and slay her with thirst.
4 I will not show my love to her children,
    because they are the children of
        adultery.
5 Their mother has been unfaithful
    and has conceived them in disgrace.
She said, "I will go after my lovers,
    who give me my food and my water,
    my wool and my linen, my olive oil
        and my drink."
6 Therefore I will block her path with
        thornbushes;
    I will wall her in so that she cannot
        find her way.
7 She will chase after her lovers but not
        catch them;
    she will look for them but not find
        them.
Then she will say,
    "I will go back to my husband as at
        first,
    for then I was better off than now."
8 She has not acknowledged that I was
        the one
    who gave her the grain, the new wine
        and oil,
who lavished on her the silver and
        gold –
    which they used for Baal.

9 'Therefore I will take away my corn
        when it ripens,
    and my new wine when it is ready.
I will take back my wool and my linen,
    intended to cover her naked body.
10 So now I will expose her lewdness
    before the eyes of her lovers;
    no one will take her out of my hands.
11 I will stop all her celebrations:

ᵃ 9 Or your I AM
ᵇ 11 In Hebrew texts 1:10,11 is numbered 2:1,2.
ᵃ In Hebrew texts 2:1-23 is numbered 2:3-25.

her yearly festivals, her New Moons,
    her Sabbath days – all her appointed
        festivals.
12 I will ruin her vines and her fig-trees,
    which she said were her pay from her
        lovers;
    I will make them a thicket,
    and wild animals will devour them.
13 I will punish her for the days
    she burned incense to the Baals;
    she decked herself with rings and
        jewellery,
    and went after her lovers,
    but me she forgot,'
                    declares the LORD.

14 'Therefore I am now going to allure her;
    I will lead her into the wilderness
    and speak tenderly to her.
15 There I will give her back her vineyards,
    and will make the Valley of Achor*b* a
        door of hope.
    There she will respond*c* as in the days of
        her youth,
    as in the day she came up out of
        Egypt.

16 'In that day,' declares the LORD,
    'you will call me "my husband";
    you will no longer call me "my
        master".*d*
17 I will remove the names of the Baals
        from her lips;
    no longer will their names be
        invoked.
18 In that day I will make a covenant for
        them
    with the beasts of the field, the birds
        in the sky
    and the creatures that move along
        the ground.
    Bow and sword and battle
    I will abolish from the land,
    so that all may lie down in safety.
19 I will betroth you to me for ever;
    I will betroth you in*e* righteousness
        and justice,
    in*e* love and compassion.

20 I will betroth you in*f* faithfulness,
    and you will acknowledge the LORD.

21 'In that day I will respond,'
    declares the LORD –
    'I will respond to the skies,
    and they will respond to the earth;
22 and the earth will respond to the grain,
    the new wine and the olive oil,
    and they will respond to Jezreel.*g*
23 I will plant her for myself in the land;
    I will show my love to the one I called
        "Not my loved one".*h*
    I will say to those called "Not my
        people",*i* "You are my people";
    and they will say, "You are my God."'

Hosea's reconciliation with his wife

3 The LORD said to me, 'Go, show your
    love to your wife again, though she is
loved by another man and is an adulteress. Love her as the LORD loves the Israelites, though they turn to other gods and
love the sacred raisin cakes.'

2 So I bought her for fifteen shekels*a* of
silver and about a homer and a lethek*b* of
barley. 3 Then I told her, 'You are to live with
me for many days; you must not be a prostitute or be intimate with any man, and I
will behave the same way toward you.'

4 For the Israelites will live for many
days without king or prince, without sacrifice or sacred stones, without ephod or
household gods. 5 Afterwards the Israelites will return and seek the LORD their
God and David their king. They will come
trembling to the LORD and to his blessings
in the last days.

The charge against Israel

4 Hear the word of the LORD, you
    Israelites,
    because the LORD has a charge to
        bring
    against you who live in the land:

---

b 15 *Achor* means *trouble.*
c 15 Or *sing*
d 16 Hebrew *baal*
e 19 Or *with*

f 20 Or *with*
g 22 *Jezreel* means *God plants.*
h 23 Hebrew *Lo-Ruhamah* (see 1:6)
i 23 Hebrew *Lo-Ammi* (see 1:9)
a 2 That is, about 170 grams
b 2 A homer and a lethek possibly weighed about
195 kilograms.

'There is no faithfulness, no love,
  no acknowledgment of God in the
    land.
2 There is only cursing,*a* lying and
    murder,
  stealing and adultery;
  they break all bounds,
    and bloodshed follows bloodshed.
3 Because of this the land dries up,
    and all who live in it waste away;
  the beasts of the field, the birds in the
    sky
  and the fish in the sea are swept
    away.

4 'But let no one bring a charge,
    let no one accuse another,
  for your people are like those
    who bring charges against a priest.
5 You stumble day and night,
    and the prophets stumble with you.
  So I will destroy your mother –
6   my people are destroyed from lack of
      knowledge.

'Because you have rejected knowledge,
    I also reject you as my priests;
  because you have ignored the law of
      your God,
    I also will ignore your children.
7 The more priests there were,
    the more they sinned against me;
  they exchanged their glorious God*b*
      for something disgraceful.
8 They feed on the sins of my people
    and relish their wickedness.
9 And it will be: like people, like priests.
  I will punish both of them for their
      ways
    and repay them for their deeds.

10 'They will eat but not have enough;
    they will engage in prostitution but
      not flourish,
  because they have deserted the LORD
    to give themselves 11 to prostitution;
  old wine and new wine
    take away their understanding.

12 My people consult a wooden idol,
    and a diviner's rod speaks to them.
  A spirit of prostitution leads them
      astray;
    they are unfaithful to their God.
13 They sacrifice on the mountaintops
    and burn offerings on the hills,
  under oak, poplar and terebinth,
    where the shade is pleasant.
  Therefore your daughters turn to
      prostitution
    and your daughters-in-law to
      adultery.

14 'I will not punish your daughters
    when they turn to prostitution,
  nor your daughters-in-law
    when they commit adultery,
  because the men themselves consort
      with harlots
    and sacrifice with shrine-
      prostitutes –
  a people without understanding will
    come to ruin!

15 'Though you, Israel, commit adultery,
    do not let Judah become guilty.

'Do not go to Gilgal;
    do not go up to Beth Aven.*c*
  And do not swear, "As surely as the
    LORD lives!"
16 The Israelites are stubborn,
    like a stubborn heifer.
  How then can the LORD pasture them
    like lambs in a meadow?
17 Ephraim is joined to idols;
    leave him alone!
18 Even when their drinks are gone,
    they continue their prostitution;
  their rulers dearly love shameful
      ways.
19 A whirlwind will sweep them away,
    and their sacrifices will bring them
      shame.

Judgment against Israel

5 'Hear this, you priests!
    Pay attention, you Israelites!

---

a 2 That is, to pronounce a curse on
b 7 Syriac (see also an ancient Hebrew scribal
tradition); Masoretic Text *me*; / *I will exchange their glory*

c 15 *Beth Aven* means *house of wickedness* (a derogatory
name for Bethel, which means *house of God*).

Listen, royal house!
    This judgment is against you:
you have been a snare at Mizpah,
    a net spread out on Tabor.
² The rebels are knee-deep in slaughter.
    I will discipline all of them.
³ I know all about Ephraim;
    Israel is not hidden from me.
Ephraim, you have now turned to
        prostitution;
    Israel is corrupt.

⁴ 'Their deeds do not permit them
    to return to their God.
A spirit of prostitution is in their heart;
    they do not acknowledge the LORD.
⁵ Israel's arrogance testifies against
        them;
    the Israelites, even Ephraim, stumble
        in their sin;
    Judah also stumbles with them.
⁶ When they go with their flocks and
        herds
    to seek the LORD,
they will not find him;
    he has withdrawn himself from
        them.
⁷ They are unfaithful to the LORD;
    they give birth to illegitimate
        children.
When they celebrate their New Moon
        feasts,
    he will devour*a* their fields.

⁸ 'Sound the trumpet in Gibeah,
    the horn in Ramah.
Raise the battle cry in Beth Aven*b*;
    lead on, Benjamin.
⁹ Ephraim will be laid waste
    on the day of reckoning.
Among the tribes of Israel
    I proclaim what is certain.
¹⁰ Judah's leaders are like those
    who move boundary stones.
I will pour out my wrath on them
    like a flood of water.
¹¹ Ephraim is oppressed,
    trampled in judgment,

intent on pursuing idols.*c*
¹² I am like a moth to Ephraim,
    like rot to the people of Judah.

¹³ 'When Ephraim saw his sickness,
    and Judah his sores,
then Ephraim turned to Assyria,
    and sent to the great king for help.
But he is not able to cure you,
    not able to heal your sores.
¹⁴ For I will be like a lion to Ephraim,
    like a great lion to Judah.
I will tear them to pieces and go away;
    I will carry them off, with no one to
        rescue them.
¹⁵ Then I will return to my lair
    until they have borne their guilt
    and seek my face –
in their misery
    they will earnestly seek me.'

Israel unrepentant

6 'Come, let us return to the LORD.
    He has torn us to pieces
        but he will heal us;
he has injured us
        but he will bind up our wounds.
² After two days he will revive us;
    on the third day he will restore us,
    that we may live in his presence.
³ Let us acknowledge the LORD;
    let us press on to acknowledge him.
As surely as the sun rises,
    he will appear;
he will come to us like the winter rains,
    like the spring rains that water the
        earth.'

⁴ 'What can I do with you, Ephraim?
    What can I do with you, Judah?
Your love is like the morning mist,
    like the early dew that disappears.
⁵ Therefore I cut you in pieces with my
        prophets,
    I killed you with the words of my
        mouth –
    then my judgments go forth like the
        sun.*a*

---

a 7 Or *Now their New Moon feasts / will devour them and*
b 8 *Beth Aven* means *house of wickedness* (a derogatory
name for Bethel, which means *house of God*).

c 11 The meaning of the Hebrew for this word is
uncertain.
a 5 The meaning of the Hebrew for this line is
uncertain.

⁶ For I desire mercy, not sacrifice,
  and acknowledgment of God rather
    than burnt offerings.
⁷ As at Adam,ᵇ they have broken the
    covenant;
  they were unfaithful to me there.
⁸ Gilead is a city of evildoers,
  stained with footprints of blood.
⁹ As marauders lie in ambush for a
    victim,
  so do bands of priests;
  they murder on the road to Shechem,
    carrying out their wicked schemes.
¹⁰ I have seen a horrible thing in Israel:
  there Ephraim is given to
    prostitution,
  Israel is defiled.

¹¹ 'Also for you, Judah,
  a harvest is appointed.

'Whenever I would restore the fortunes
    of my people,
7 ¹ whenever I would heal Israel,
  the sins of Ephraim are exposed
  and the crimes of Samaria revealed.
They practise deceit,
  thieves break into houses,
  bandits rob in the streets;
² but they do not realise
  that I remember all their evil deeds.
  Their sins engulf them;
  they are always before me.

³ 'They delight the king with their
    wickedness,
  the princes with their lies.
⁴ They are all adulterers,
  burning like an oven
  whose fire the baker need not stir
  from the kneading of the dough till it
    rises.
⁵ On the day of the festival of our king
  the princes become inflamed with
    wine,
  and he joins hands with the
    mockers.
⁶ Their hearts are like an oven;
  they approach him with intrigue.
  Their passion smoulders all night;

in the morning it blazes like a
    flaming fire.
⁷ All of them are hot as an oven;
  they devour their rulers.
All their kings fall,
  and none of them calls on me.

⁸ 'Ephraim mixes with the nations;
  Ephraim is a flat loaf not turned over.
⁹ Foreigners sap his strength,
  but he does not realise it.
His hair is sprinkled with grey,
  but he does not notice.
¹⁰ Israel's arrogance testifies against him,
  but despite all this
  he does not return to the LORD his God
  or search for him.

¹¹ 'Ephraim is like a dove,
  easily deceived and senseless –
now calling to Egypt,
  now turning to Assyria.
¹² When they go, I will throw my net over
    them;
  I will pull them down like the birds in
    the sky.
When I hear them flocking together,
  I will catch them.
¹³ Woe to them,
  because they have strayed from me!
Destruction to them,
  because they have rebelled against
    me!
I long to redeem them
  but they speak about me falsely.
¹⁴ They do not cry out to me from their
    hearts
  but wail on their beds.
They slash themselves,ᵃ appealing to
    their gods
  for grain and new wine,
  but they turn away from me.
¹⁵ I trained them and strengthened their
    arms,
  but they plot evil against me.
¹⁶ They do not turn to the Most High;
  they are like a faulty bow.
Their leaders will fall by the sword
  because of their insolent words.

ᵇ 7 Or Like Adam; or Like human beings

ᵃ 14 Some Hebrew manuscripts and Septuagint;
most Hebrew manuscripts They gather together

For this they will be ridiculed
   in the land of Egypt.

Israel to reap the whirlwind

8 'Put the trumpet to your lips!
   An eagle is over the house of the
   LORD
because the people have broken my
   covenant
   and rebelled against my law.
2 Israel cries out to me,
   "Our God, we acknowledge you!"
3 But Israel has rejected what is good;
   an enemy will pursue him.
4 They set up kings without my consent;
   they choose princes without my
     approval.
With their silver and gold
   they make idols for themselves
   to their own destruction.
5 Throw out your calf-idol, Samaria!
   My anger burns against them.
How long will they be incapable of
   purity?
6   They are from Israel!
This calf – a metalworker has made it;
   it is not God.
It will be broken in pieces,
   that calf of Samaria.

7 'They sow the wind
   and reap the whirlwind.
The stalk has no head;
   it will produce no flour.
Were it to yield grain,
   foreigners would swallow it up.
8 Israel is swallowed up;
   now she is among the nations
   like something no one wants.
9 For they have gone up to Assyria
   like a wild donkey wandering alone.
   Ephraim has sold herself to lovers.
10 Although they have sold themselves
     among the nations,
   I will now gather them together.
They will begin to waste away
   under the oppression of the mighty
     king.

11 'Though Ephraim built many altars for
     sin offerings,
   these have become altars for sinning.
12 I wrote for them the many things of my
     law,
   but they regarded them as
     something foreign.
13 Though they offer sacrifices as gifts
     to me,
   and though they eat the meat,
   the LORD is not pleased with them.
Now he will remember their
     wickedness
   and punish their sins:
   they will return to Egypt.
14 Israel has forgotten his Maker
   and built palaces;
   Judah has fortified many towns.
But I will send fire on their cities
   that will consume their fortresses.'

Punishment for Israel

9 Do not rejoice, Israel;
   do not be jubilant like the other
   nations.
For you have been unfaithful to your
     God;
   you love the wages of a prostitute
   at every threshing-floor.
2 Threshing-floors and winepresses will
     not feed the people;
   the new wine will fail them.
3 They will not remain in the LORD's land;
   Ephraim will return to Egypt
   and eat unclean food in Assyria.
4 They will not pour out wine offerings to
     the LORD,
   nor will their sacrifices please him.
Such sacrifices will be to them like the
     bread of mourners;
   all who eat them will be unclean.
This food will be for themselves;
   it will not come into the temple of
     the LORD.

5 What will you do on the day of your
     appointed festivals,
   on the feast days of the LORD?
6 Even if they escape from destruction,
   Egypt will gather them,
   and Memphis will bury them.
Their treasures of silver will be taken
     over by briers,
   and thorns will overrun their tents.
7 The days of punishment are coming,

the days of reckoning are at hand.
Let Israel know this.
Because your sins are so many
and your hostility so great,
the prophet is considered a fool,
the inspired person a maniac.
⁸ The prophet, along with my God,
is the watchman over Ephraim,ᵃ
yet snares await him on all his paths,
and hostility in the house of his God.
⁹ They have sunk deep into corruption,
as in the days of Gibeah.
God will remember their wickedness
and punish them for their sins.

¹⁰ 'When I found Israel,
it was like finding grapes in the
desert;
when I saw your ancestors,
it was like seeing the early fruit on
the fig-tree.
But when they came to Baal Peor,
they consecrated themselves to that
shameful idol
and became as vile as the thing they
loved.
¹¹ Ephraim's glory will fly away like a
bird –
no birth, no pregnancy, no
conception.
¹² Even if they bring up children,
I will bereave them of every one.
Woe to them
when I turn away from them!
¹³ I have seen Ephraim, like Tyre,
planted in a pleasant place.
But Ephraim will bring out
their children to the slayer.'

¹⁴ Give them, Lord –
what will you give them?
Give them wombs that miscarry
and breasts that are dry.

¹⁵ 'Because of all their wickedness in
Gilgal,
I hated them there.
Because of their sinful deeds,
I will drive them out of my house.

I will no longer love them;
all their leaders are rebellious.
¹⁶ Ephraim is blighted,
their root is withered,
they yield no fruit.
Even if they bear children,
I will slay their cherished offspring.'

¹⁷ My God will reject them
because they have not obeyed him;
they will be wanderers among the
nations.

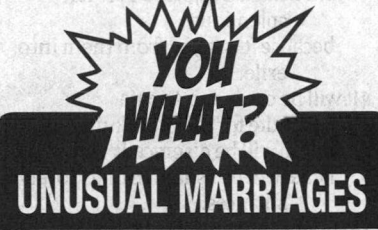

UNUSUAL MARRIAGES

THE BENJAMINITES GRAB SOME BRIDES
Judges 21:13–23
JACOB MARRIES TWO SISTERS
Genesis 29:16–30
HOSEA MARRIES A PROSTITUTE
Hosea 1:1–11
SAMSON MARRIES A PHILISTINE
Judges 14:1–19
BOAZ REDEEMS RUTH
Ruth 4:1–22
JOSEPH MARRIES MARY
Matthew 1:18–25
JERUSALEM WEARS A WEDDING GOWN
Revelation 21:1–4

10 Israel was a spreading vine;
he brought forth fruit for himself.
As his fruit increased,
he built more altars;
as his land prospered,
he adorned his sacred stones.
² Their heart is deceitful,
and now they must bear their guilt.
The Lord will demolish their altars
and destroy their sacred stones.

³ Then they will say, 'We have no king
because we did not revere the Lord.

ᵃ 8 Or *The prophet is the watchman over Ephraim, / the
people of my God*

But even if we had a king,
what could he do for us?'
4 They make many promises,
take false oaths
and make agreements;
therefore lawsuits spring up
like poisonous weeds in a ploughed
field.
5 The people who live in Samaria fear
for the calf-idol of Beth Aven.*a*
Its people will mourn over it,
and so will its idolatrous priests,
those who had rejoiced over its
splendour,
because it is taken from them into
exile.
6 It will be carried to Assyria
as tribute for the great king.
Ephraim will be disgraced;
Israel will be ashamed of its foreign
alliances.
7 Samaria's king will be destroyed,
swept away like a twig on the surface
of the waters.
8 The high places of wickedness*b* will be
destroyed –
it is the sin of Israel.
Thorns and thistles will grow up
and cover their altars.
Then they will say to the mountains,
'Cover us!'
and to the hills, 'Fall on us!'

9 'Since the days of Gibeah, you have
sinned, Israel,
and there you have remained.*c*
Will not war again overtake
the evildoers in Gibeah?
10 When I please, I will punish them;
nations will be gathered against them
to put them in bonds for their
double sin.
11 Ephraim is a trained heifer
that loves to thresh;
so I will put a yoke
on her fair neck.
I will drive Ephraim,

Judah must plough,
and Jacob must break up the ground.
12 Sow righteousness for yourselves,
reap the fruit of unfailing love,
and break up your unploughed ground;
for it is time to seek the LORD,
until he comes
and showers his righteousness on
you.
13 But you have planted wickedness,
you have reaped evil,
you have eaten the fruit of deception.
Because you have depended on your
own strength
and on your many warriors,
14 the roar of battle will rise against your
people,
so that all your fortresses will be
devastated –
as Shalman devastated Beth Arbel on
the day of battle,
when mothers were dashed to the
ground with their children.
15 So will it happen to you, Bethel,
because your wickedness is great.
When that day dawns,
the king of Israel will be completely
destroyed.

God's love for Israel

11 'When Israel was a child, I loved
him,
and out of Egypt I called my son.
2 But the more they were called,
the more they went away from me.*a*
They sacrificed to the Baals
and they burned incense to images.
3 It was I who taught Ephraim to walk,
taking them by the arms;
but they did not realise
it was I who healed them.
4 I led them with cords of human
kindness,
with ties of love.
To them I was like one who lifts
a little child to the cheek,
and I bent down to feed them.

5 'Will they not return to Egypt
and will not Assyria rule over them

---

a 5 Beth Aven means *house of wickedness* (a derogatory
name for Bethel, which means *house of God*).
b 8 Hebrew *aven*, a reference to Beth Aven (a
derogatory name for Bethel); see verse 5.
c 9 Or *there a stand was taken*

---

a 2 Septuagint; Hebrew *them*

and repay him according to his
deeds.
³ In the womb he grasped his brother's
heel;
as a man he struggled with God.
⁴ He struggled with the angel and
overcame him;
he wept and begged for his favour.
He found him at Bethel
and talked with him there –
⁵ the LORD God Almighty,
the LORD is his name!
⁶ But you must return to your God;
maintain love and justice,
and wait for your God always.

⁷ The merchant uses dishonest scales
and loves to defraud.
⁸ Ephraim boasts,
'I am very rich; I have become
wealthy.
With all my wealth they will not find in
me
any iniquity or sin.'

⁹ 'I have been the LORD your God
ever since you came out of Egypt;
I will make you live in tents again,
as in the days of your appointed
festivals.
¹⁰ I spoke to the prophets,
gave them many visions
and told parables through them.'

¹¹ Is Gilead wicked?
Its people are worthless!
Do they sacrifice bulls in Gilgal?
Their altars will be like piles of stones
on a ploughed field.
¹² Jacob fled to the country of Aramᶜ;
Israel served to get a wife,
and to pay for her he tended sheep.
¹³ The LORD used a prophet to bring Israel
up from Egypt,
by a prophet he cared for him.
¹⁴ But Ephraim has aroused his bitter
anger;
his Lord will leave on him the guilt of
his bloodshed
and will repay him for his contempt.

because they refuse to repent?
⁶ A sword will flash in their cities;
it will devour their false prophets
and put an end to their plans.
⁷ My people are determined to turn from
me.
Even though they call me God Most
High,
I will by no means exalt them.

⁸ 'How can I give you up, Ephraim?
How can I hand you over, Israel?
How can I treat you like Admah?
How can I make you like Zeboyim?
My heart is changed within me;
all my compassion is aroused.
⁹ I will not carry out my fierce anger,
nor will I devastate Ephraim again.
For I am God, and not a man –
the Holy One among you.
I will not come against their cities.
¹⁰ They will follow the LORD;
he will roar like a lion.
When he roars,
his children will come trembling
from the west.
¹¹ They will come from Egypt,
trembling like sparrows,
from Assyria, fluttering like doves.
I will settle them in their homes,'
declares the LORD.

Israel's sin
¹² Ephraim has surrounded me with lies,
Israel with deceit.
And Judah is unruly against God,
even against the faithful Holy One.ᵇ

12 ᵃ ¹ Ephraim feeds on the wind;
he pursues the east wind all day
and multiplies lies and violence.
He makes a treaty with Assyria
and sends olive oil to Egypt.
² The LORD has a charge to bring against
Judah;
he will punish Jacobᵇ according to
his ways

ℎ 12 In Hebrew texts this verse (11:12) is numbered 12:1.
ᵃ In Hebrew texts 12:1-14 is numbered 12:2-15.
ᵇ 2 *Jacob* means *he grasps the heel,* a Hebrew idiom for *he takes advantage of* or *he deceives.*
ᶜ 12 That is, North-west Mesopotamia

The Lord's anger against Israel

13 When Ephraim spoke, people
trembled;
he was exalted in Israel.
But he became guilty of Baal worship
and died.
2 Now they sin more and more;
they make idols for themselves from
their silver,
cleverly fashioned images,
all of them the work of craftsmen.
It is said of these people,
'They offer human sacrifices!
They kiss*a* calf-idols!'
3 Therefore they will be like the morning
mist,
like the early dew that disappears,
like chaff swirling from a
threshing-floor,
like smoke escaping through a
window.

4 'But I have been the Lord your God
ever since you came out of Egypt.
You shall acknowledge no God but me,
no Saviour except me.
5 I cared for you in the wilderness,
in the land of burning heat.
6 When I fed them, they were satisfied;
when they were satisfied, they
became proud;
then they forgot me.
7 So I will be like a lion to them,
like a leopard I will lurk by the path.
8 Like a bear robbed of her cubs,
I will attack them and rip them
open;
like a lion I will devour them –
a wild animal will tear them apart.

9 'You are destroyed, Israel,
because you are against me, against
your helper.
10 Where is your king, that he may save
you?
Where are your rulers in all your
towns,
of whom you said,
"Give me a king and princes"?
11 So in my anger I gave you a king,

and in my wrath I took him away.
12 The guilt of Ephraim is stored up,
his sins are kept on record.
13 Pains as of a woman in childbirth come
to him,
but he is a child without wisdom;
when the time arrives,
he doesn't have the sense to come
out of the womb.

14 'I will deliver this people from the
power of the grave;
I will redeem them from death.
Where, O death, are your plagues?
Where, O grave, is your destruction?

'I will have no compassion,
15 even though he thrives among his
brothers.
An east wind from the Lord will come,
blowing in from the desert;
his spring will fail
and his well dry up.
His storehouse will be plundered
of all its treasures.
16 The people of Samaria must bear their
guilt,
because they have rebelled against
their God.
They will fall by the sword;
their little ones will be dashed to the
ground,
their pregnant women ripped
open.'*b*

Repentance to bring blessing

14 *a* Return, Israel, to the Lord your
God.
Your sins have been your downfall!
2 Take words with you
and return to the Lord.
Say to him:
'Forgive all our sins
and receive us graciously,
that we may offer the fruit of our
lips.*b*
3 Assyria cannot save us;
we will not mount war-horses.

---

a 2 Or 'Men who sacrifice / kiss

b 16 In Hebrew texts this verse (13:16) is numbered
14:1.
a In Hebrew texts 14:1-9 is numbered 14:2-10.
b 2 Or *offer our lips as sacrifices of bulls*

We will never again say "Our gods"
   to what our own hands have made,
   for in you the fatherless find
      compassion.'

4 'I will heal their waywardness
   and love them freely,
   for my anger has turned away from
      them.
5 I will be like the dew to Israel;
   he will blossom like a lily.
Like a cedar of Lebanon
   he will send down his roots;
6   his young shoots will grow.
His splendour will be like an olive tree,
   his fragrance like a cedar of
      Lebanon.
7 People will dwell again in his shade;
   they will flourish like the corn,
they will blossom like the vine –
   Israel's fame will be like the wine of
      Lebanon.
8 Ephraim, what more have I[c] to do with
      idols?
   I will answer him and care for him.
I am like a flourishing juniper;
   your fruitfulness comes from me.'

9 Who is wise? Let them realise these
      things.
   Who is discerning? Let them
      understand.
The ways of the LORD are right;
   the righteous walk in them,
   but the rebellious stumble in them.

---

c 8   Or Hebrew; Septuagint *What more has Ephraim*

FAVOURITE VERSES
Isaiah 43:1a–2b

Do not fear, for I have redeemed you;
  I have summoned you by name;
   you are mine.
When you pass through the waters,
  I will be with you.

- -

I love this verse because it tells
me that whatever's happening in
my life, God is with me. Recently
my wife has been suffering with
cancer, I have been unemployed,
and everything has looked pretty
gloomy. But I have been reading
this Bible verse a lot –and giving it
to others – and it has really lifted
me up.

You know the best way to read
it? After the word 'you', add your
own name. Or, better, when you're
reading it to a friend, brother or
sister, add their name in. It makes it
so much cooler.

Alex, 34

JOEL

i

DATE

Just after 800 BC

AUTHOR

Joel

WHAT'S IT ALL ABOUT?

Joel was witness to a great plague of locusts that swarmed through Judah. It was a disaster for the people: crops and vineyards were destroyed, their homes were infested and they saw their land turned into a barren wasteland. Joel believed the crisis was the work of God. He described the locusts as being God's army, bringing God's judgement on his people. He called the people to repent and turn from their evil ways, speaking passionately about God's desire to be gracious to them.

WHY SHOULD WE READ IT?

- To hear about the great punishment God brought on his people for their unfaithfulness (Joel 1).

- To read an impassioned plea for God's people to show true emotion rather than go through the motions of religious practices (Joel 1).

- To see God's compassion on his people and his desire for them to repent (Joel 2).

- To hear God's promise that he would pour out the Holy Spirit on all believers (Joel 2). This is a promise we later see fulfilled in the book of Acts.

Andy Croft with Liza Hoeksma

1

The word of the LORD that came to Joel son of Pethuel.

An invasion of locusts

2 Hear this, you elders;
    listen, all who live in the land.
Has anything like this ever happened in
        your days
    or in the days of your ancestors?
3 Tell it to your children,
    and let your children tell it to their
        children,
    and their children to the next
        generation.
4 What the locust swarm has left
    the great locusts have eaten;
what the great locusts have left
    the young locusts have eaten;
what the young locusts have left
    other locusts*a* have eaten.

5 Wake up, you drunkards, and weep!
    Wail, all you drinkers of wine;
wail because of the new wine,
    for it has been snatched from your
        lips.
6 A nation has invaded my land,
    a mighty army without number;
it has the teeth of a lion,
    the fangs of a lioness.
7 It has laid waste my vines
    and ruined my fig-trees.
It has stripped off their bark
    and thrown it away,
    leaving their branches white.

8 Mourn like a virgin in sackcloth
    grieving for the betrothed of her
        youth.
9 Grain offerings and drink offerings
    are cut off from the house of the
        LORD.
The priests are in mourning,
    those who minister before the LORD.
10 The fields are ruined,
    the ground is dried up;
the grain is destroyed,
    the new wine is dried up,
    the olive oil fails.

11 Despair, you farmers,
    wail, you vine growers;
grieve for the wheat and the barley,
    because the harvest of the field is
        destroyed.
12 The vine is dried up
    and the fig-tree is withered;
the pomegranate, the palm and the
        apple*b* tree –
    all the trees of the field – are dried up.
Surely the people's joy
    is withered away.

A call to lamentation

13 Put on sackcloth, you priests, and
        mourn;
    wail, you who minister before the
        altar.
Come, spend the night in sackcloth,
    you who minister before my God;
for the grain offerings and drink
        offerings
    are withheld from the house of your
        God.
14 Declare a holy fast;
    call a sacred assembly.
Summon the elders
    and all who live in the land
to the house of the LORD your God,
    and cry out to the LORD.

15 Alas for that day!
    For the day of the LORD is near;
    it will come like destruction from the
        Almighty.*c*

16 Has not the food been cut off
    before our very eyes –
joy and gladness
    from the house of our God?
17 The seeds are shrivelled
    beneath the clods.*d*
The storehouses are in ruins,
    the granaries have been broken
        down,
    for the grain has dried up.
18 How the cattle moan!
    The herds mill about

---

a 4 The precise meaning of the four Hebrew words used here for locusts is uncertain.

b 12 Or possibly *apricot*
c 15 Hebrew *Shaddai*
d 17 The meaning of the Hebrew for this word is uncertain.

because they have no pasture;
even the flocks of sheep are suffering.

19 To you, LORD, I call,
for fire has devoured the pastures in
the wilderness

and flames have burned up all the
trees of the field.
20 Even the wild animals pant for you;
the streams of water have dried up
and fire has devoured the pastures in
the wilderness.

WAR

Imagine you're a child living in a city under military attack. Shells pummel the houses around you. A mortar explodes on the other side of the street, destroying the school you attended only yesterday. Outside the tiny house in which you're hiding you can hear the screams of people maimed and the wails of those who have lost their closest friends. This is war from the other side. It's scary, bloody and brutal.

In the first half of Joel's prophecy (1:1 – 2:11) he uses the image of an army of locusts to express the pain of a people under attack. Locusts were a common feature of Ancient Near Eastern life. They would swarm over the land, destroying everything in their path. Nothing would survive their invasion. And just like marauding locusts, an army is coming to destroy Joel's people, coming to maim, to strip bare and to kill.

Most of us will never have experienced war. And yet this terrifying reality is happening right now to countless people across the planet.

It's hard to know what to do in the face of such suffering when we feel so powerless. But prayer is a mighty weapon – one that we can wield for peace and not violence.

So let's pray.

Father, Strong Deliverer
Armies swarm and destroy without mercy
Children scream and their innocence is stolen by a starless night
Death comes and snatches away calm
Panic is raw and fear is unleashed on streets tonight

Jesus, Prince of Peace
Sneak your peace through the cracks in war-torn houses
Squash violence under the weight of love
Squeeze the forces of darkness with untamed forgiveness
Let hope and healing flow down cheeks tonight

Spirit, Life of Creation
We hear your deepest roar, your wildest growl
We feel your breath on the wind whispering change
We kneel to salute your covert mission
Behind enemy lines. Let lives be saved tonight.

Matt Valler

An army of locusts

2 Blow the trumpet in Zion;
   sound the alarm on my holy hill.

Let all who live in the land tremble,
   for the day of the LORD is coming.
It is close at hand –
2 a day of darkness and gloom,
   a day of clouds and blackness.
Like dawn spreading across the
      mountains
   a large and mighty army comes,
such as never was in ancient times
   nor ever will be in ages to come.

3 Before them fire devours,
   behind them a flame blazes.
Before them the land is like the garden
      of Eden,
   behind them, a desert waste –
   nothing escapes them.
4 They have the appearance of horses;
   they gallop along like cavalry.
5 With a noise like that of chariots
   they leap over the mountaintops,
like a crackling fire consuming stubble,
   like a mighty army drawn up for
      battle.

6 At the sight of them, nations are in
      anguish;
   every face turns pale.
7 They charge like warriors;
   they scale walls like soldiers.
They all march in line,
   not swerving from their course.
8 They do not jostle each other;
   each marches straight ahead.
They plunge through defences
   without breaking ranks.
9 They rush upon the city;
   they run along the wall.
They climb into the houses;
   like thieves they enter through the
      windows.

10 Before them the earth shakes,
   the heavens tremble,
the sun and moon are darkened,
   and the stars no longer shine.
11 The LORD thunders
   at the head of his army;

his forces are beyond number,
   and mighty is the army that obeys his
      command.
The day of the LORD is great;
   it is dreadful.
   Who can endure it?

Rend your heart

12 'Even now,' declares the LORD,
   'return to me with all your heart,
   with fasting and weeping and
      mourning.'

13 Rend your heart
   and not your garments.
Return to the LORD your God,
   for he is gracious and
      compassionate,
slow to anger and abounding in love,
   and he relents from sending
      calamity.
14 Who knows? He may turn and relent
   and leave behind a blessing –
grain offerings and drink offerings
   for the LORD your God.

15 Blow the trumpet in Zion,
   declare a holy fast,
   call a sacred assembly.
16 Gather the people,
   consecrate the assembly;
bring together the elders,
   gather the children,
   those nursing at the breast.
Let the bridegroom leave his room
   and the bride her chamber.
17 Let the priests, who minister before the
      LORD,
   weep between the portico and the
      altar.
Let them say, 'Spare your people, LORD.
   Do not make your inheritance an
      object of scorn,
   a byword among the nations.
Why should they say among the
      peoples,
   "Where is their God?" '

The LORD's answer

18 Then the LORD was jealous for his
      land
   and took pity on his people.

19 The Lord replied[a] to them:

'I am sending you grain, new wine and
　　olive oil,
　　enough to satisfy you fully;
never again will I make you
　　an object of scorn to the nations.

20 'I will drive the northern horde far from
　　you,
　　pushing it into a parched and barren
　　　land;
its eastern ranks will drown in the Dead
　　Sea
and its western ranks in the
　　Mediterranean Sea.
And its stench will go up;
　　its smell will rise.'

Surely he has done great things!
21　　Do not be afraid, land of Judah;
　　　be glad and rejoice.
Surely the Lord has done great things!
22　　Do not be afraid, you wild animals,
　　　for the pastures in the wilderness are
　　　becoming green.
The trees are bearing their fruit;
　　the fig-tree and the vine yield their
　　　riches.
23 Be glad, people of Zion,
　　rejoice in the Lord your God,
for he has given you the autumn rains
　　because he is faithful.
He sends you abundant showers,
　　both autumn and spring rains, as
　　　before.
24 The threshing-floors will be filled with
　　grain;
　　the vats will overflow with new wine
　　　and oil.

25 'I will repay you for the years the locusts
　　have eaten –
　　the great locust and the young
　　　locust,
　　the other locusts and the locust
　　　swarm[b] –
my great army that I sent among you.

26 You will have plenty to eat, until you are
　　full,
and you will praise the name of the
　　Lord your God,
who has worked wonders for you;
never again will my people be shamed.
27 Then you will know that I am in Israel,
　　that I am the Lord your God,
　　and that there is no other;
never again will my people be shamed.

The day of the Lord

28 'And afterwards,
　　I will pour out my Spirit on all
　　　people.
Your sons and daughters will prophesy,
　　your old men will dream dreams,
　　your young men will see visions.
29 Even on my servants, both men and
　　women,
　　I will pour out my Spirit in those
　　　days.
30 I will show wonders in the heavens
　　and on the earth,
　　blood and fire and billows of smoke.
31 The sun will be turned to darkness
　　and the moon to blood
　　before the coming of the great and
　　　dreadful day of the Lord.
32 And everyone who calls
　　on the name of the Lord will be
　　　saved;
for on Mount Zion and in Jerusalem
　　there will be deliverance,
　　as the Lord has said,
even among the survivors
　　whom the Lord calls.[c]

The nations judged

3[a] 'In those days and at that time,
　　when I restore the fortunes of Judah
　　　and Jerusalem,
2 I will gather all nations
　　and bring them down to the Valley of
　　　Jehoshaphat.[b]
There I will put them on trial
　　for what they did to my inheritance,
　　my people Israel,

---

a 18,19　Or *Lord will be jealous . . . / and take pity . . . /*[19]*The
Lord will reply*
b 25　The precise meaning of the four Hebrew words
used here for locusts is uncertain.

c 32　In Hebrew texts 2:28-32 is numbered 3:1-5.
a In Hebrew texts 3:1-21 is numbered 4:1-21.
b 2　*Jehoshaphat* means *the Lord judges*; also in
verse 12.

NATURALLY SUPERNATURAL 3

GIFTS OF THE HOLY SPIRIT FOR ALL BELIEVERS

One of the amazing things about the work of God's kingdom is that everyone gets to play!

There's no celebrity status where only the elite get a chance to use the gifts of the Holy Spirit. We often discount ourselves and think God couldn't use us, but that's not true. You can't be too young or too old. There's no sexism. It doesn't matter how long you have been a Christian. It doesn't matter what social class you are. You're not discounted because of anything you have ever done, or anything you will do. God pours out his Spirit on each of us without favouritism.

To emphasise this promise, we read it again in Acts 2 when the apostle Paul recalls the words from Joel 2:28 on the day of Pentecost. That was the day when these amazing promises were first fulfilled. As the Holy Spirit fell on all the disciples, everyone began speaking in tongues, unknowingly declaring the wonders of God in the native languages of the crowd of non-believers that had gathered.

Jesus had also told the disciples the Holy Spirit was going to come to them when he had ascended to heaven (John 16). He said it was better for us to have the Holy Spirit than for him to stay here on earth, because the Holy Spirit convicts the world, guides us in truth and brings us all closer to Jesus. We also read that the Holy Spirit gives gifts to his followers (see 1 Corinthians 12), which are given for the common good of the body of Christ. These gifts are wisdom, words of knowledge, faith, healing, miraculous powers, prophecy, the ability to distinguish between spirits, the ability to speak in tongues and the ability to interpret tongues. We are told that they are distributed amongst us as God determines and so we shouldn't be comparing one another's gifts or valuing one over the other. Instead we should all offer our gifts for the good of God's people.

But the Holy Spirit is also a blessing to those outside the church. When Jesus spoke the famous words of the prophet Isaiah, he said, *'The Spirit of the Lord is on me, because he has anointed me to proclaim good news to the poor. He has sent me to proclaim freedom for the prisoners and recovery of sight for the blind, to set the oppressed free, to proclaim the year of the Lord's favour'* (Luke 4:18–19; Isaiah 61). The Holy Spirit lives in us so that we might do these same things and continue Jesus' work today.

So let's make sure we don't discount ourselves for any reason, but instead believe the truth that God gives his Holy Spirit to all of us who believe in him. Let's ask him to give us dreams, visions and prophetic words for the Church and for those who don't yet believe.

Mike Pilavachi

because they scattered my people
 among the nations
 and divided up my land.
3 They cast lots for my people
 and traded boys for prostitutes;
 they sold girls for wine to drink.

4 'Now what have you against me, Tyre and Sidon and all you regions of Philistia? Are you repaying me for something I have done? If you are paying me back, I will swiftly and speedily return on your own heads what you have done. 5 For you took my silver and my gold and carried off my finest treasures to your temples. c 6 You sold the people of Judah and Jerusalem to the Greeks, that you might send them far from their homeland.

7 'See, I am going to rouse them out of the places to which you sold them, and I will return on your own heads what you have done. 8 I will sell your sons and daughters to the people of Judah, and they will sell them to the Sabeans, a nation far away.' The LORD has spoken.

9 Proclaim this among the nations:
 Prepare for war!
 Rouse the warriors!
 Let all the fighting men draw near
  and attack.
10 Beat your ploughshares into swords
 and your pruning hooks into spears.
 Let the weakling say,
  'I am strong!'
11 Come quickly, all you nations from
  every side,
 and assemble there.

 Bring down your warriors, LORD!

12 'Let the nations be roused;
 let them advance into the Valley of
  Jehoshaphat,
 for there I will sit
  to judge all the nations on every
   side.
13 Swing the sickle,
 for the harvest is ripe.

Come, trample the grapes,
 for the winepress is full
 and the vats overflow –
 so great is their wickedness!'

14 Multitudes, multitudes
 in the valley of decision!
For the day of the LORD is near
 in the valley of decision.
15 The sun and moon will be darkened,
 and the stars no longer shine.
16 The LORD will roar from Zion
 and thunder from Jerusalem;
 the earth and the heavens will
  tremble.
But the LORD will be a refuge for his
  people,
 a stronghold for the people of Israel.

Blessings for God's people

17 'Then you will know that I, the LORD
  your God,
 dwell in Zion, my holy hill.
Jerusalem will be holy;
 never again will foreigners invade
  her.

18 'In that day the mountains will drip new
  wine,
 and the hills will flow with milk;
 all the ravines of Judah will run with
  water.
A fountain will flow out of the LORD's
  house
 and will water the valley of acacias. d
19 But Egypt will be desolate,
 Edom a desert waste,
 because of violence done to the people
  of Judah,
 in whose land they shed innocent
  blood.
20 Judah will be inhabited for ever
 and Jerusalem through all
  generations.
21 Shall I leave their innocent blood
  unavenged?
 No, I will not.'

 The LORD dwells in Zion!

---

c 5 Or *palaces*   d 18 Or *Valley of Shittim*

AMOS

DATE

Amos is likely to have prophesied mainly between 760 and 750 BC

AUTHOR

Amos

WHAT'S IT ALL ABOUT?

Amos was a shepherd and no doubt used to a simple life. He saw the ways in which the people of Israel (the Northern Kingdom) were living it up, enjoying comfortable lives with fine riches, and he knew that their lifestyle was built on slavery, dishonesty and oppression of the poor. Amos's overwhelming message was that God is a God of justice. He wasn't interested in having people pay him lip service, turning up to worship events and offering sacrifices but then trampling on the poor and oppressed. Sadly, the people didn't want to listen to Amos's calls to repentance. Life was good for them and they didn't see the point in changing their ways. But as Amos predicted, judgement soon came: Israel was conquered and the kingdom ceased to exist.

WHY SHOULD WE READ IT?

- To understand God's passion for justice.

- To understand that although it was a warning for the Kingdom of Israel many years ago, it is a warning we still need to listen to today. We must not claim to worship God while we oppress the poor in order to live a more comfortable lifestyle ourselves.

- To see how God rejected his people's worship festivals and sacrifices because of the dishonesty in the rest of their lives.

- To be reminded to seek God even when things are going well in our lives.

Andy Croft with Liza Hoeksma

1 The words of Amos, one of the shepherds of Tekoa – the vision he saw concerning Israel two years before the earthquake, when Uzziah was king of Judah and Jeroboam son of Jehoash[a] was king of Israel.

² He said:

'The LORD roars from Zion
   and thunders from Jerusalem;
the pastures of the shepherds dry up,
   and the top of Carmel withers.'

Judgment on Israel's neighbours

³ This is what the LORD says:

'For three sins of Damascus,
   even for four, I will not relent.
Because she threshed Gilead
   with sledges having iron teeth,
⁴ I will send fire on the house of Hazael
   that will consume the fortresses of
   Ben-Hadad.
⁵ I will break down the gate of Damascus;
   I will destroy the king who is in[b] the
   Valley of Aven[c]
and the one who holds the sceptre in
   Beth Eden.
The people of Aram will go into exile
   to Kir,'
           says the LORD.

⁶ This is what the LORD says:

'For three sins of Gaza,
   even for four, I will not relent.
Because she took captive whole
   communities
   and sold them to Edom,
⁷ I will send fire on the walls of Gaza
   that will consume her fortresses.
⁸ I will destroy the king[d] of Ashdod
   and the one who holds the sceptre in
   Ashkelon.
I will turn my hand against Ekron,
   till the last of the Philistines are
   dead,'
      says the Sovereign LORD.

⁹ This is what the LORD says:

'For three sins of Tyre,
   even for four, I will not relent.
Because she sold whole communities
   of captives to Edom,
   disregarding a treaty of brotherhood,
¹⁰ I will send fire on the walls of Tyre
   that will consume her fortresses.'

¹¹ This is what the LORD says:

'For three sins of Edom,
   even for four, I will not relent.
Because he pursued his brother with a
   sword
   and slaughtered the women of the
   land,
because his anger raged continually
   and his fury flamed unchecked,
¹² I will send fire on Teman
   that will consume the fortresses of
   Bozrah.'

¹³ This is what the LORD says:

'For three sins of Ammon,
   even for four, I will not relent.
Because he ripped open the pregnant
   women of Gilead
   in order to extend his borders,
¹⁴ I will set fire to the walls of Rabbah
   that will consume her fortresses
amid war cries on the day of battle,
   amid violent winds on a stormy day.
¹⁵ Her king[e] will go into exile,
   he and his officials together,'
           says the LORD.

2 This is what the LORD says:

'For three sins of Moab,
   even for four, I will not relent.
Because he burned to ashes
   the bones of Edom's king,
² I will send fire on Moab
   that will consume the fortresses of
   Kerioth.[a]
Moab will go down in great tumult

---

a 1 Hebrew *Joash*, a variant of *Jehoash*
b 5 Or *the inhabitants of*
c 5 *Aven* means *wickedness.*
d 8 Or *inhabitants*

---

e 15 Or / *Molek*
a 2 Or *of her cities*

amid war cries and the blast of the
trumpet.
³ I will destroy her ruler
and kill all her officials with him,'
says the LORD.

⁴ This is what the LORD says:

'For three sins of Judah,
even for four, I will not relent.
Because they have rejected the law of
the LORD
and have not kept his decrees,
because they have been led astray by
false gods,ᵇ
the godsᶜ their ancestors followed,
⁵ I will send fire on Judah
that will consume the fortresses of
Jerusalem.'

Judgment on Israel

⁶ This is what the LORD says:

'For three sins of Israel,
even for four, I will not relent.
They sell the innocent for silver,
and the needy for a pair of sandals.
⁷ They trample on the heads of the poor
as on the dust of the ground
and deny justice to the oppressed.
Father and son use the same girl
and so profane my holy name.
⁸ They lie down beside every altar
on garments taken in pledge.
In the house of their god
they drink wine taken as fines.

⁹ 'Yet I destroyed the Amorites before
them,
though they were tall as the cedars
and strong as the oaks.
I destroyed their fruit above
and their roots below.
¹⁰ I brought you up out of Egypt
and led you for forty years in the
wilderness
to give you the land of the
Amorites.

¹¹ 'I also raised up prophets from among
your children
and Nazirites from among your
youths.
Is this not true, people of Israel?'
declares the LORD.
¹² 'But you made the Nazirites drink wine
and commanded the prophets not
to prophesy.

¹³ 'Now then, I will crush you
as a cart crushes when loaded with
grain.
¹⁴ The swift will not escape,
the strong will not muster their
strength,
and the warrior will not save his life.
¹⁵ The archer will not stand his ground,
the fleet-footed soldier will not get
away,
and the horseman will not save his
life.
¹⁶ Even the bravest warriors
will flee naked on that day,'
declares the LORD.

Witnesses summoned against Israel

3 Hear this word, people of Israel, the
word the LORD has spoken against
you – against the whole family I brought
up out of Egypt:

² 'You only have I chosen
of all the families of the earth;
therefore I will punish you
for all your sins.'

³ Do two walk together
unless they have agreed to do so?
⁴ Does a lion roar in the thicket
when it has no prey?
Does it growl in its den
when it has caught nothing?
⁵ Does a bird swoop down to a trap on
the ground
when no bait is there?
Does a trap spring up from the ground
if it has not caught anything?
⁶ When a trumpet sounds in a city,
do not the people tremble?
When disaster comes to a city,
has not the LORD caused it?

---

b 4 Or by lies
c 4 Or lies

7 Surely the Sovereign LORD does nothing
  without revealing his plan
    to his servants the prophets.

8 The lion has roared –
  who will not fear?
The Sovereign LORD has spoken –
  who can but prophesy?

9 Proclaim to the fortresses of Ashdod
  and to the fortresses of Egypt:
'Assemble yourselves on the mountains
    of Samaria;
  see the great unrest within her
  and the oppression among her
    people.'

10 'They do not know how to do right,'
    declares the LORD,
  'who store up in their fortresses
  what they have plundered and
    looted.'

11 Therefore this is what the Sovereign
LORD says:

  'An enemy will overrun your land,
    pull down your strongholds
    and plunder your fortresses.'

12 This is what the LORD says:

  'As a shepherd rescues from the lion's
    mouth
    only two leg bones or a piece of an
      ear,
  so will the Israelites living in Samaria be
    rescued,
    with only the head of a bed
    and a piece of fabric*a* from a couch.'*b*

13 'Hear this and testify against the descendants of Jacob,' declares the Lord, the
LORD God Almighty.

14 'On the day I punish Israel for her sins,
  I will destroy the altars of Bethel;
  the horns of the altar will be cut off

and fall to the ground.
15 I will tear down the winter house
  along with the summer house;
  the houses adorned with ivory will be
    destroyed
  and the mansions will be
    demolished,'
               declares the LORD.

Israel has not returned to God

4 Hear this word, you cows of Bashan
  on Mount Samaria,
  you women who oppress the poor
    and crush the needy
  and say to your husbands, 'Bring us
    some drinks!'
2 The Sovereign LORD has sworn by his
    holiness:
  'The time will surely come
  when you will be taken away with
    hooks,
  the last of you with fishhooks.*a*
3 You will each go straight out
  through breaches in the wall,
  and you will be cast out towards
    Harmon,'*b*
               declares the LORD.
4 'Go to Bethel and sin;
  go to Gilgal and sin yet more.
Bring your sacrifices every morning,
  your tithes every three years.*c*
5 Burn leavened bread as a thank-offering
  and brag about your freewill
    offerings –
boast about them, you Israelites,
  for this is what you love to do,'
        declares the Sovereign LORD.

6 'I gave you empty stomachs in every city
  and lack of bread in every town,
  yet you have not returned to me,'
            declares the LORD.

7 'I also withheld rain from you
  when the harvest was still three
    months away.
  I sent rain on one town,

---

a 12   The meaning of the Hebrew for this phrase is
uncertain.
b 12   Or *Israelites be rescued, / those who sit in Samaria / on
the edge of their beds / and in Damascus on their couches.*

a 2   Or *away in baskets, / the last of you in fish baskets*
b 3   Masoretic Text; with a different word division
of the Hebrew (see Septuagint) *out, you mountain of
oppression*
c 4   Or *days*

but withheld it from another.
One field had rain;
  another had none and dried up.
8 People staggered from town to town for
    water
  but did not get enough to drink,
  yet you have not returned to me,'
            declares the LORD.

9 'Many times I struck your gardens and
      vineyards,
  destroying them with blight and
    mildew.
Locusts devoured your fig and olive
  trees,
  yet you have not returned to me,'
            declares the LORD.

10 'I sent plagues among you
    as I did to Egypt.
  I killed your young men with the sword,
    along with your captured horses.
  I filled your nostrils with the stench of
    your camps,
  yet you have not returned to me,'
            declares the LORD.

11 'I overthrew some of you
    as I overthrew Sodom and Gomorrah.
  You were like a burning stick snatched
    from the fire,
  yet you have not returned to me,'
            declares the LORD.

12 'Therefore this is what I will do to you,
      Israel,
  and because I will do this to you,
      Israel,
  prepare to meet your God.'

13 He who forms the mountains,
    who creates the wind,
  and who reveals his thoughts to
    mankind,
  who turns dawn to darkness,
    and treads on the heights of the
      earth –
  the LORD God Almighty is his name.

A lament and call to repentance

5 Hear this word, Israel, this lament I
take up concerning you:

2 'Fallen is Virgin Israel,
    never to rise again,
  deserted in her own land,
    with no one to lift her up.'

3 This is what the Sovereign LORD says
to Israel:

'Your city that marches out a thousand
    strong
  will have only a hundred left;
your town that marches out a hundred
    strong
  will have only ten left.'

4 This is what the LORD says to Israel:

'Seek me and live;
5   do not seek Bethel,
  do not go to Gilgal,
    do not journey to Beersheba.
For Gilgal will surely go into exile,
    and Bethel will be reduced to
      nothing.' *a*
6 Seek the LORD and live,
    or he will sweep through the tribes of
      Joseph like a fire;
  it will devour them,
    and Bethel will have no one to
      quench it.

7 There are those who turn justice into
    bitterness
  and cast righteousness to the
    ground.

8 He who made the Pleiades and Orion,
    who turns midnight into dawn
    and darkens day into night,
  who calls for the waters of the sea
    and pours them out over the face of
      the land –
    the LORD is his name.
9 With a blinding flash he destroys the
    stronghold
  and brings the fortified city to ruin.

10 There are those who hate the one who
    upholds justice in court

---

a 5 Hebrew *aven*, a reference to Beth Aven (a
derogatory name for Bethel); see Hosea 4:15.

and detest the one who tells the truth.

11 You levy a straw tax on the poor
    and impose a tax on their grain.
Therefore, though you have built stone mansions,
    you will not live in them;
though you have planted lush vineyards,
    you will not drink their wine.
12 For I know how many are your offences
    and how great your sins.

There are those who oppress the innocent and take bribes
    and deprive the poor of justice in the courts.
13 Therefore the prudent keep quiet in such times,
    for the times are evil.

14 Seek good, not evil,
    that you may live.
Then the Lord God Almighty will be with you,
    just as you say he is.
15 Hate evil, love good;
    maintain justice in the courts.
Perhaps the Lord God Almighty will have mercy
    on the remnant of Joseph.

16 Therefore this is what the Lord, the Lord God Almighty, says:

'There will be wailing in all the streets
    and cries of anguish in every public square.
The farmers will be summoned to weep
    and the mourners to wail.
17 There will be wailing in all the vineyards,
    for I will pass through your midst,'
                    says the Lord.

The day of the Lord

18 Woe to you who long
    for the day of the Lord!
Why do you long for the day of the Lord?
    That day will be darkness, not light.

19 It will be as though a man fled from a lion
    only to meet a bear,
as though he entered his house
    and rested his hand on the wall
    only to have a snake bite him.
20 Will not the day of the Lord be darkness, not light –
    pitch-dark, without a ray of brightness?

21 'I hate, I despise your religious festivals;
    your assemblies are a stench to me.
22 Even though you bring me burnt offerings and grain offerings,
    I will not accept them.
Though you bring choice fellowship offerings,
    I will have no regard for them.
23 Away with the noise of your songs!
    I will not listen to the music of your harps.
24 But let justice roll on like a river,
    righteousness like a never-failing stream!

25 'Did you bring me sacrifices and offerings
    for forty years in the wilderness, people of Israel?
26 You have lifted up the shrine of your king,
    the pedestal of your idols,
    the star of your god[b] –
which you made for yourselves.
27 Therefore I will send you into exile beyond Damascus,'
    says the Lord, whose name is God Almighty.

Woe to the complacent

6 Woe to you who are complacent in Zion,
    and to you who feel secure on Mount Samaria,
you notable men of the foremost nation,
    to whom the people of Israel come!

---

b 26 Or lifted up Sakkuth your king / and Kaiwan your idols, / your star-gods; Septuagint lifted up the shrine of Molek / and the star of your god Rephan, / their idols

2 Go to Kalneh and look at it;
  go from there to great Hamath,
  and then go down to Gath in Philistia.
Are they better off than your two
      kingdoms?
  Is their land larger than yours?
3 You put off the day of disaster
  and bring near a reign of terror.
4 You lie on beds adorned with ivory
  and lounge on your couches.
You dine on choice lambs
  and fattened calves.
5 You strum away on your harps like David

and improvise on musical
  instruments.
6 You drink wine by the bowlful
  and use the finest lotions,
  but you do not grieve over the ruin of
      Joseph.
7 Therefore you will be among the first to
      go into exile;
  your feasting and lounging will end.

The Lord abhors the pride of Israel
8 The Sovereign Lord has sworn by himself – the Lord God Almighty declares:

WORSHIP 10

With integrity

We have all been let down at some point in life, and we have all let others down too. One of the big ways in which people get let down is when a promise is made and then broken, or when something is spoken but not followed through. This not only leaves us disappointed and hurt, but we can also struggle to take that person at their word after they have let us down.

Our words carry power, and so do our actions. To live with integrity is to make sure that the two match up, that we are honest before the Lord, and that he is glorified by what we say *and* by what we do.

It's easy to think that worship is just about singing songs, but it's so much more than that. Worship is a lifestyle. God's desire is that the words we sing should overflow into the way we live and go on to affect our actions. The products of our worship should be acting justly, loving mercy and walking humbly (Micah 6:8).

God makes it so clear in Amos 5 that he doesn't even want to hear our songs of worship if we're showing no regard for the poor and the oppressed. He's not interested in our praise if we aren't reaching out to love our neighbours. Whatever we do for the least, we're doing for God (Matthew 25:40), and so he has no time for our music if we're ignoring the call to live lives of holiness.

There must be consistency between what we sing on a Sunday and the way we act during the week, because worship isn't just something we do on a Sunday but involves every part of our lives, every day of the week.

Our greatest model is Jesus, who not only preached good news – he was good news. With the help of the Holy Spirit, we too can ask God to 'keep us from just singing' and 'move us into action'.

Beth Croft

Job 1:13–21

'I abhor the pride of Jacob
   and detest his fortresses;
I will deliver up the city
   and everything in it.'

⁹ If ten people are left in one house, they too will die. ¹⁰ And if the relative who comes to carry the bodies out of the house to burn them*ᵃ* asks anyone who might be hiding there, 'Is anyone else with you?' and he says, 'No,' then he will go on to say, 'Hush! We must not mention the name of the LORD.'

¹¹ For the LORD has given the command,
   and he will smash the great house
      into pieces
   and the small house into bits.

¹² Do horses run on the rocky crags?
   Does one plough the sea*ᵇ* with oxen?
But you have turned justice into poison
   and the fruit of righteousness into
      bitterness –
¹³ you who rejoice in the conquest of Lo
      Debar*ᶜ*
   and say, 'Did we not take Karnaim*ᵈ* by
      our own strength?'

¹⁴ For the LORD God Almighty declares,
   'I will stir up a nation against you,
      Israel,
   that will oppress you all the way
      from Lebo Hamath to the valley of
      the Arabah.'

Locusts, fire and a plumb-line

7 This is what the Sovereign LORD showed me: he was preparing swarms of locusts after the king's share had been harvested and just as the late crops were coming up. ² When they had stripped the land clean, I cried out, 'Sovereign LORD, forgive! How can Jacob survive? He is so small!'

³ So the LORD relented.

'This will not happen,' the LORD said.
⁴ This is what the Sovereign LORD showed me: the Sovereign LORD was calling for judgment by fire; it dried up the great deep and devoured the land. ⁵ Then I cried out, 'Sovereign LORD, I beg you, stop! How can Jacob survive? He is so small!'
⁶ So the LORD relented.

'This will not happen either,' the Sovereign LORD said.

⁷ This is what he showed me: the Lord was standing by a wall that had been built true to plumb,*ᵃ* with a plumb-line*ᵇ* in his hand. ⁸ And the LORD asked me, 'What do you see, Amos?'

'A plumb-line,' I replied.

Then the Lord said, 'Look, I am setting a plumb-line among my people Israel; I will spare them no longer.

⁹ 'The high places of Isaac will be
      destroyed
   and the sanctuaries of Israel will be
      ruined;
   with my sword I will rise against the
      house of Jeroboam.'

Amos and Amaziah

¹⁰ Then Amaziah the priest of Bethel sent a message to Jeroboam king of Israel: 'Amos is raising a conspiracy against you in the very heart of Israel. The land cannot bear all his words. ¹¹ For this is what Amos is saying:

' "Jeroboam will die by the sword,
   and Israel will surely go into exile,
      away from their native land." '

¹² Then Amaziah said to Amos, 'Get out, you seer! Go back to the land of Judah. Earn your bread there and do your prophesying there. ¹³ Don't prophesy any more at Bethel, because this is the king's sanctuary and the temple of the kingdom.'

¹⁴ Amos answered Amaziah, 'I was neither a prophet nor the son of a prophet,

---

a 10   Or *to make a funeral fire in honour of the dead*
b 12   With a different word division of the Hebrew; Masoretic Text *plough*
c 13   *Lo Debar* means *nothing.*
d 13   *Karnaim* means *horns; horn* here symbolises strength.

---

a 7   The meaning of the Hebrew for this phrase is uncertain.
b 7   The meaning of the Hebrew for this phrase is uncertain; also in verse 8.

but I was a shepherd, and I also took care of sycamore-fig trees. ¹⁵ But the LORD took me from tending the flock and said to me, "Go, prophesy to my people Israel." ¹⁶ Now then, hear the word of the LORD. You say,

' "Do not prophesy against Israel,
and stop preaching against the
descendants of Isaac."

¹⁷ 'Therefore this is what the LORD says:

' "Your wife will become a prostitute in
the city,
and your sons and daughters will fall
by the sword.
Your land will be measured and divided
up,
and you yourself will die in a pagan[c]
country.
And Israel will surely go into exile,
away from their native land." '

A basket of ripe fruit

8 This is what the Sovereign LORD showed me: a basket of ripe fruit. ² 'What do you see, Amos?' he asked.

'A basket of ripe fruit,' I answered.

Then the LORD said to me, 'The time is ripe for my people Israel; I will spare them no longer.

³ 'In that day,' declares the Sovereign LORD, 'the songs in the temple will turn to wailing.[a] Many, many bodies – flung everywhere! Silence!'

⁴ Hear this, you who trample the needy
and do away with the poor of the
land,

⁵ saying,

'When will the New Moon be over
that we may sell grain,
and the Sabbath be ended
that we may market wheat?' –
skimping on the measure,
boosting the price
and cheating with dishonest scales,

⁶ buying the poor with silver
and the needy for a pair of sandals,
selling even the sweepings with the
wheat.

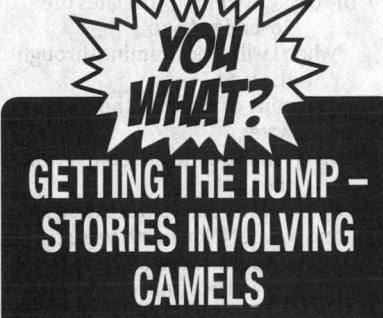

YOU WHAT?

GETTING THE HUMP – STORIES INVOLVING CAMELS

○ **REBEKAH AT THE WELL**
Genesis 24:42–50
○ **JOSEPH IS SOLD INTO SLAVERY**
Genesis 37:12–28
○ **GIDEON'S IDOLATRY**
Judges 8:18–28
○ **JOB'S CAMELS ARE STOLEN**
Job 1:13–22
○ **JOHN WEARS CAMEL'S HAIR**
Matthew 3:1–6
○ **THE CAMEL AND THE NEEDLE**
Mark 10:17–27

⁷ The LORD has sworn by himself, the Pride of Jacob: 'I will never forget anything they have done.

⁸ 'Will not the land tremble for this,
and all who live in it mourn?
The whole land will rise like the Nile;
it will be stirred up and then sink
like the river of Egypt.

⁹ 'In that day,' declares the Sovereign LORD,

'I will make the sun go down at noon
and darken the earth in broad
daylight.
¹⁰ I will turn your religious festivals into
mourning
and all your singing into weeping.
I will make all of you wear sackcloth

c 17 Hebrew *an unclean*
a 3 Or *'the temple singers will wail'*

and shave your heads.
I will make that time like mourning for
an only son
and the end of it like a bitter day.

11 'The days are coming,' declares the
Sovereign LORD,
'when I will send a famine through
the land –
not a famine of food or a thirst for
water,
but a famine of hearing the words of
the LORD.
12 People will stagger from sea to sea
and wander from north to east,
searching for the word of the LORD,
but they will not find it.

13 'In that day

'the lovely young women and strong
young men
will faint because of thirst.
14 Those who swear by the sin of
Samaria –
who say, "As surely as your god lives,
Dan",
or, "As surely as the god^b of
Beersheba lives" –
they will fall, never to rise again.'

Israel to be destroyed

9 I saw the Lord standing by the altar,
and he said:

'Strike the tops of the pillars
so that the thresholds shake.
Bring them down on the heads of all
the people;
those who are left I will kill with the
sword.
Not one will get away,
none will escape.
2 Though they dig down to the depths
below,
from there my hand will take them.
Though they climb up to the heavens
above,
from there I will bring them down.

3 Though they hide themselves on the
top of Carmel,
there I will hunt them down and
seize them.
Though they hide from my eyes at the
bottom of the sea,
there I will command the serpent to
bite them.
4 Though they are driven into exile by
their enemies,
there I will command the sword to
slay them.

'I will keep my eye on them
for harm and not for good.'

5 The Lord, the LORD Almighty –
he touches the earth and it melts,
and all who live in it mourn;
the whole land rises like the Nile,
then sinks like the river of Egypt;
6 he builds his lofty palace^a in the
heavens
and sets its foundation^b on the
earth;
he calls for the waters of the sea
and pours them out over the face of
the land –
the LORD is his name.

7 'Are not you Israelites
the same to me as the Cushites?'^c
declares the LORD.
'Did I not bring Israel up from Egypt,
the Philistines from Caphtor^d
and the Arameans from Kir?

8 'Surely the eyes of the Sovereign LORD
are on the sinful kingdom.
I will destroy it
from the face of the earth.
Yet I will not totally destroy
the descendants of Jacob,'
declares the LORD.
9 'For I will give the command,
and I will shake the people of Israel

---

a 6 The meaning of the Hebrew for this phrase is
uncertain.
b 6 The meaning of the Hebrew for this word is
uncertain.
c 7 That is, people from the upper Nile region
d 7 That is, Crete

among all the nations
as grain is shaken in a sieve,
   and not a pebble will reach the
     ground.
10 All the sinners among my people
   will die by the sword,
all those who say,
   "Disaster will not overtake or meet
     us."

Israel's restoration

11 'In that day

'I will restore David's fallen shelter –
   I will repair its broken walls
   and restore its ruins –
   and will rebuild it as it used to be,
12 so that they may possess the remnant
     of Edom
   and all the nations that bear my
     name,'e
          declares the LORD,
        who will do these things.

---

e 12 Hebrew; Septuagint *so that the remnant of people /
and all the nations that bear my name may seek me*

13 'The days are coming,' declares the
LORD,

'when the reaper will be overtaken by
     the ploughman
   and the planter by the one treading
     grapes.
New wine will drip from the mountains
   and flow from all the hills,
14   and I will bring my people Israel back
     from exile.f

'They will rebuild the ruined cities and
     live in them.
They will plant vineyards and drink
     their wine;
they will make gardens and eat their
     fruit.
15 I will plant Israel in their own land,
   never again to be uprooted
   from the land I have given them,'

        says the LORD your God.

---

f 14 Or *will restore the fortunes of my people Israel*

OBADIAH

DATE

It is likely that Obadiah prophesied around 605–586 BC

AUTHOR

Obadiah

WHAT'S IT ALL ABOUT?

Obadiah is the shortest book in the Old Testament and it speaks to Judah's enemy, the Edomites. Although they shared a distant heritage (the two tribes were descended from the brothers Jacob and Esau, about whom we read in Genesis 25 and 27), they had been enemies for many years. When Judah was attacked by the Babylonians, Edom not only didn't help, they rejoiced in the fall of the kingdom. The Edomites felt secure in their position: their land was high in the mountains and they thought no enemies could reach them to conquer or destroy. Obadiah told them that their high position meant nothing. They would be overcome and all of them would be slaughtered. The Lord promised that Judah would rise again, while Edom would be wiped out. History shows us that this is exactly what happened.

WHY SHOULD WE READ IT?

- To see that although God punished his people, he also carried out revenge on their behalf.

- To be reminded how passionately God cared about his people and their reputation, despite the judgement he brought on them.

- As a reminder that we shouldn't base our security on our circumstances, but on God alone.

Andy Croft with Liza Hoeksma

Obadiah's vision

¹ The vision of Obadiah.

This is what the Sovereign LORD says
about Edom –

We have heard a message from the
    LORD:
    an envoy was sent to the nations to
        say,
    'Rise, let us go against her for battle' –

² 'See, I will make you small among the
        nations;
    you will be utterly despised.
³ The pride of your heart has deceived
        you,
    you who live in the clefts of the
        rocks*a*
    and make your home on the heights,
    you who say to yourself,
        "Who can bring me down to the
            ground?"
⁴ Though you soar like the eagle
    and make your nest among the stars,
    from there I will bring you down,'
                    declares the LORD.
⁵ 'If thieves came to you,
    if robbers in the night –
oh, what a disaster awaits you –
    would they not steal only as much as
        they wanted?
If grape pickers came to you,
    would they not leave a few grapes?
⁶ But how Esau will be ransacked,
    his hidden treasures pillaged!
⁷ All your allies will force you to the
        border;
    your friends will deceive and
        overpower you;
those who eat your bread will set a trap
        for you,*b*
    but you will not detect it.

⁸ 'In that day,' declares the LORD,
    'will I not destroy the wise men of
        Edom,

those of understanding in the
    mountains of Esau?
⁹ Your warriors, Teman, will be terrified,
    and everyone in Esau's mountains
    will be cut down in the slaughter.
¹⁰ Because of the violence against your
        brother Jacob,
    you will be covered with shame;
    you will be destroyed for ever.
¹¹ On the day you stood aloof
    while strangers carried off his
        wealth
and foreigners entered his gates
    and cast lots for Jerusalem,
    you were like one of them.
¹² You should not gloat over your brother
    in the day of his misfortune,
nor rejoice over the people of Judah
    in the day of their destruction,
nor boast so much
    in the day of their trouble.
¹³ You should not march through the
        gates of my people
    in the day of their disaster,
nor gloat over them in their calamity
    in the day of their disaster,
nor seize their wealth
    in the day of their disaster.
¹⁴ You should not wait at the crossroads
    to cut down their fugitives,
nor hand over their survivors
    in the day of their trouble.

¹⁵ 'The day of the LORD is near
    for all nations.
As you have done, it will be done to you;
    your deeds will return upon your
        own head.
¹⁶ Just as you drank on my holy hill,
    so all the nations will drink
        continually;
    they will drink and drink
    and be as if they had never been.
¹⁷ But on Mount Zion will be deliverance;
    it will be holy,
    and Jacob will possess his
        inheritance.
¹⁸ Jacob will be a fire
    and Joseph a flame;
Esau will be stubble,
    and they will set him on fire and
        destroy him.

---

a 3 Or *of Sela*
b 7 The meaning of the Hebrew for this clause is
uncertain.

There will be no survivors
from Esau.'
            The LORD has spoken.

19 People from the Negev will occupy
   the mountains of Esau,
and people from the foothills will
       possess
   the land of the Philistines.
They will occupy the fields of Ephraim
   and Samaria,
     and Benjamin will possess Gilead.

20 This company of Israelite exiles who are
   in Canaan
   will possess the land as far as
      Zarephath;
   the exiles from Jerusalem who are in
      Sepharad
   will possess the towns of the Negev.
21 Deliverers will go up on^c Mount Zion
   to govern the mountains of Esau.
   And the kingdom will be the LORD's.

c 21 Or *from*

JONAH

DATE

Jonah ministered between 800 and 750 BC

AUTHOR

Traditionally attributed to Jonah

WHAT'S IT ALL ABOUT?

Jonah tells us one of the most famous stories from the Old Testament. Some see it as a parable, others as a literal history of events. Jonah didn't want to be a prophet, so when God asked him to go to Nineveh (the capital of Assyria, an enemy of Israel) to call the people there to repentance, Jonah not only refused, he ran away. It's not easy to outrun God, and when Jonah got on a ship, God simply created a storm that resulted in Jonah being thrown overboard and ending up inside a big fish. Thankful that God hadn't killed him for his disobedience, Jonah went to Nineveh and delivered God's message. The people repented and turned to God, and you would think this would be good news – revival had come! Not for Jonah. He was angry that God was so compassionate that he wouldn't punish the people for their sins. But in the end Jonah learned a hard lesson that it wasn't up to him to decide who was worthy of God's love and forgiveness.

WHY SHOULD WE READ IT?

- Because it highlights God's compassion, mercy and desire to forgive. He didn't want to destroy Nineveh, but was willing to forgive the people after they repented (see especially Jonah 4). In the same way, he wants to bring all people to repentance.

- Because it shows us that God uses flawed people to fulfil his plans.

- To be reminded that we can't sit in judgement on who is or isn't worthy to receive God's forgiveness.

Andy Croft with Liza Hoeksma

Jonah flees from the LORD

1 The word of the LORD came to Jonah son of Amittai: ² 'Go to the great city of Nineveh and preach against it, because its wickedness has come up before me.'

³ But Jonah ran away from the LORD and headed for Tarshish. He went down to Joppa, where he found a ship bound for that port. After paying the fare, he went aboard and sailed for Tarshish to flee from the LORD.

⁴ Then the LORD sent a great wind on the sea, and such a violent storm arose that the ship threatened to break up. ⁵ All the sailors were afraid and each cried out to his own god. And they threw the cargo into the sea to lighten the ship.

But Jonah had gone below deck, where he lay down and fell into a deep sleep. ⁶ The captain went to him and said, 'How can you sleep? Get up and call on your god! Maybe he will take notice of us so that we will not perish.'

⁷ Then the sailors said to each other, 'Come, let us cast lots to find out who is responsible for this calamity.' They cast lots and the lot fell on Jonah. ⁸ So they asked him, 'Tell us, who is responsible for making all this trouble for us? What kind of work do you do? Where do you come from? What is your country? From what people are you?'

⁹ He answered, 'I am a Hebrew and I worship the LORD, the God of heaven, who made the sea and the dry land.'

¹⁰ This terrified them and they asked, 'What have you done?' (They knew he was running away from the LORD, because he had already told them so.)

¹¹ The sea was getting rougher and rougher. So they asked him, 'What should we do to you to make the sea calm down for us?'

¹² 'Pick me up and throw me into the sea,' he replied, 'and it will become calm. I know that it is my fault that this great storm has come upon you.'

¹³ Instead, the men did their best to row back to land. But they could not, for the sea grew even wilder than before. ¹⁴ Then they cried out to the LORD, 'Please, LORD, do not let us die for taking this man's life.

Do not hold us accountable for killing an innocent man, for you, LORD, have done as you pleased.' ¹⁵ Then they took Jonah and threw him overboard, and the raging sea grew calm. ¹⁶ At this the men greatly feared the LORD, and they offered a sacrifice to the LORD and made vows to him.

Jonah's prayer

¹⁷ Now the LORD provided a huge fish to swallow Jonah, and Jonah was in the belly of the fish three days and three nights.

2^a ¹ From inside the fish Jonah prayed to the LORD his God. ² He said:

'In my distress I called to the LORD,
    and he answered me.
From deep in the realm of the dead I
        called for help,
    and you listened to my cry.
³ You hurled me into the depths,
    into the very heart of the seas,
    and the currents swirled about me;
all your waves and breakers
    swept over me.
⁴ I said, "I have been banished
    from your sight;
yet I will look again
    towards your holy temple."
⁵ The engulfing waters threatened me,^b
    the deep surrounded me;
    seaweed was wrapped around my
        head.
⁶ To the roots of the mountains I sank
        down;
    the earth beneath barred me in for
        ever.
But you, LORD my God,
    brought my life up from the pit.

⁷ 'When my life was ebbing away,
    I remembered you, LORD,
and my prayer rose to you,
    to your holy temple.

⁸ 'Those who cling to worthless idols
    turn away from God's love for them.
⁹ But I, with shouts of grateful praise,

---

a In Hebrew texts 2:1 is numbered 1:17, and 2:1-10 is numbered 2:2-11.
b 5 Or *waters were at my throat*

PEOPLE USED BY GOD 4

Jonah

Jonah is probably best known as the man who was swallowed by a fish, but there's more we can learn from looking at his story.

God spoke to Jonah and wanted him to go and warn the people of Nineveh that they were going to be destroyed. Jonah's first response was to run in the opposite direction, as he felt it would be a complete waste of time. If he went, then God would most likely change his mind and not destroy them, and if he didn't go, it didn't matter because they probably deserved it!

God took control and set it up for Jonah to be thrown into the sea, where he was swallowed by the fish. Now God had his attention! After three days Jonah and God came to an understanding and the fish spat him out on the beach near Nineveh.

Jonah went into the city with the message. The people heard it and decided to change their ways and call out to God. Even the king told the whole city to beg God for mercy. Jonah made his way up a hill where he could watch what God did. God made a plant grow up and cover him from the sun. Sure enough, God had mercy on the people and this really made Jonah mad. God added to his frustration and caused the plant to wither. By now Jonah was beside himself and didn't even want to live.

We're sometimes the same: God wants us to follow his way, but we decide there's a better way, so we go with the plan that looks good and ignore God's voice. What does it take for God to get our attention? We're running around doing our own thing and miss the direction God has for us. It's only when we find ourselves up against a wall that we decide to allow God to speak to us. We're looking out for our own plans, in our comfort zone, we want God to support us, and when we don't see the results we get frustrated.

From the very beginning, though, Jonah missed the point. God was looking to save the people; he didn't want to destroy them. Sometimes we like to believe we know what should happen and how things should be. We assume God thinks like us, but God's ways are greater than ours. His plans are for the best of all, not just what we think is best. God asks us to turn our eyes away from ourselves and learn his heart towards his people.

So while Jonah was crying over a plant because it was his little world, he forgot that God was dealing with the whole world. We need to see the big picture and know that God's plan is for the good of all. If we let him lead us, he will show his mercy to all in need. If we're going to follow him, we need to go where he leads us.

Tom Brock

◀◀ Ruth 1:17–18   Mark 16:9 ▶▶

will sacrifice to you.
What I have vowed I will make good.
I will say, "Salvation comes from the
LORD."'

¹⁰And the LORD commanded the fish,
and it vomited Jonah onto dry land.

Jonah goes to Nineveh

3 Then the word of the LORD came to
Jonah a second time: ²'Go to the
great city of Nineveh and proclaim to it
the message I give you.'

³Jonah obeyed the word of the LORD and
went to Nineveh. Now Nineveh was a very
large city; it took three days to go through
it. ⁴Jonah began by going a day's journey
into the city, proclaiming, 'Forty more
days and Nineveh will be overthrown.'
⁵The Ninevites believed God. A fast was
proclaimed, and all of them, from the
greatest to the least, put on sackcloth.

⁶When Jonah's warning reached the king
of Nineveh, he rose from his throne, took
off his royal robes, covered himself with
sackcloth and sat down in the dust. ⁷This is
the proclamation he issued in Nineveh:

'By the decree of the king and his nobles:

Do not let people or animals,
herds or flocks, taste anything; do
not let them eat or drink. ⁸But let
people and animals be covered
with sackcloth. Let everyone call urgently on God. Let them give up their
evil ways and their violence. ⁹Who
knows? God may yet relent and with
compassion turn from his fierce
anger so that we will not perish.'

¹⁰When God saw what they did and
how they turned from their evil ways, he
relented and did not bring on them the
destruction he had threatened.

Jonah's anger at the LORD's compassion

4 But to Jonah this seemed very wrong,
and he became angry. ²He prayed to
the LORD, 'Isn't this what I said, LORD,
when I was still at home? That is what I
tried to forestall by fleeing to Tarshish. I
knew that you are a gracious and compassionate God, slow to anger and abounding
in love, a God who relents from sending
calamity. ³Now, LORD, take away my life,
for it is better for me to die than to live.'

⁴But the LORD replied, 'Is it right for you
to be angry?'

⁵Jonah had gone out and sat down at a
place east of the city. There he made himself a shelter, sat in its shade and waited to
see what would happen to the city. ⁶Then
the LORD God provided a leafy plant*ᵃ* and
made it grow up over Jonah to give shade
for his head to ease his discomfort, and
Jonah was very happy about the plant.
⁷But at dawn the next day God provided a
worm, which chewed the plant so that it
withered. ⁸When the sun rose, God provided a scorching east wind, and the sun
blazed on Jonah's head so that he grew
faint. He wanted to die, and said, 'It would
be better for me to die than to live.'

⁹But God said to Jonah, 'Is it right for
you to be angry about the plant?'

'It is,' he said. 'And I'm so angry I wish
I were dead.'

¹⁰But the LORD said, 'You have been
concerned about this plant, though you
did not tend it or make it grow. It sprang
up overnight and died overnight. ¹¹And
should I not have concern for the great
city of Nineveh, in which there are more
than a hundred and twenty thousand people who cannot tell their right hand from
their left – and also many animals?'

---

a 6 The precise identification of this plant is
uncertain; also in verses 7, 9 and 10.

MICAH

DATE

Micah prophesied somewhere between 750 and 686 BC

AUTHOR

Micah

WHAT'S IT ALL ABOUT?

Micah was another of the Minor Prophets who was around at the same time as Isaiah, Amos and Hosea. While Amos was busy calling the people of the Northern Kingdom back to a life of justice, Micah was delivering a similar message to the Southern Kingdom, who had developed the same practices of oppressing the poor. Micah warned that God would bring punishment for their actions and predicted the fall of both Samaria and Judah. He told the people that their sacrifices weren't pleasing to God if they were acting unjustly and were full of pride. While much of the message is downbeat, there is some hope. Micah talked of a time when a ruler would come from Bethlehem (a prophecy fulfilled in Jesus) and declared that God would not stay angry for ever, but would be compassionate and merciful.

WHY SHOULD WE READ IT?

- To hear Micah's prophecy concerning Jesus (Micah 5).

- To read what God says he requires of his people as true worship (Micah 6).

- To understand God's passion for justice.

- To understand that although it was a warning for the Kingdom of Judah many years ago, it is a warning we still need to listen to today. We mustn't claim to worship God while we oppress the poor and are disobedient to him.

Andy Croft with Liza Hoeksma

1
The word of the LORD that came to Micah of Moresheth during the reigns of Jotham, Ahaz and Hezekiah, kings of Judah – the vision he saw concerning Samaria and Jerusalem.

² Hear, you peoples, all of you,
  listen, earth and all who live in it,
that the Sovereign LORD may bear
    witness against you,
  the Lord from his holy temple.

Judgment against Samaria and Jerusalem

³ Look! The LORD is coming from his
    dwelling-place;
  he comes down and treads on the
    heights of the earth.
⁴ The mountains melt beneath him
  and the valleys split apart,
like wax before the fire,
  like water rushing down a slope.
⁵ All this is because of Jacob's
    transgression,
  because of the sins of the people
    of Israel.
What is Jacob's transgression?
  Is it not Samaria?
What is Judah's high place?
  Is it not Jerusalem?

⁶ 'Therefore I will make Samaria a heap
    of rubble,
  a place for planting vineyards.
I will pour her stones into the valley
  and lay bare her foundations.
⁷ All her idols will be broken to pieces;
  all her temple gifts will be burned
    with fire;
  I will destroy all her images.
Since she gathered her gifts from the
    wages of prostitutes,
  as the wages of prostitutes they will
    again be used.'

Weeping and mourning
⁸ Because of this I will weep and wail;
  I will go about barefoot and naked.
I will howl like a jackal
  and moan like an owl.
⁹ For Samaria's plague is incurable;
  it has spread to Judah.

It has reached the very gate of my
    people,
  even to Jerusalem itself.
¹⁰ Tell it not in Gath;*a*
  weep not at all.
In Beth Ophrah*b*
  roll in the dust.
¹¹ Pass by naked and in shame,
  you who live in Shaphir.*c*
Those who live in Zaanan*d*
  will not come out.
Beth Ezel is in mourning;
  it no longer protects you.
¹² Those who live in Maroth*e* writhe in
    pain,
  waiting for relief,
because disaster has come from the
    LORD,
  even to the gate of Jerusalem.
¹³ You who live in Lachish,
  harness fast horses to the chariot.
You are where the sin of Daughter Zion
    began,
  for the transgressions of Israel were
    found in you.
¹⁴ Therefore you will give parting gifts
    to Moresheth Gath.
The town of Akzib*f* will prove deceptive
  to the kings of Israel.
¹⁵ I will bring a conqueror against you
  who live in Mareshah.*g*
The nobles of Israel
  will flee to Adullam.
¹⁶ Shave your head in mourning
  for the children in whom you
    delight;
make yourself as bald as the vulture,
  for they will go from you into exile.

Human plans and God's plans

2
Woe to those who plan iniquity,
  to those who plot evil on their beds!
At morning's light they carry it out
  because it is in their power to do it.
² They covet fields and seize them,

---

a 10 *Gath* sounds like the Hebrew for *tell.*
b 10 *Beth Ophrah* means *house of dust.*
c 11 *Shaphir* means *pleasant.*
d 11 *Zaanan* sounds like the Hebrew for *come out.*
e 12 *Maroth* sounds like the Hebrew for *bitter.*
f 14 *Akzib* means *deception.*
g 15 *Mareshah* sounds like the Hebrew for *conqueror.*

and houses, and take them.
They defraud people of their homes,
  they rob them of their inheritance.

3 Therefore, the LORD says:

'I am planning disaster against this
    people,
  from which you cannot save
    yourselves.
You will no longer walk proudly,
  for it will be a time of calamity.
4 In that day people will ridicule you;
  they will taunt you with this
    mournful song:
"We are utterly ruined;
  my people's possession is
    divided up.
He takes it from me!
  He assigns our fields to traitors." '

5 Therefore you will have no one in the
    assembly of the LORD
  to divide the land by lot.

False prophets

6 'Do not prophesy,' their prophets say.
  'Do not prophesy about these
    things;
  disgrace will not overtake us.'
7 You descendants of Jacob, should it be
    said,
  'Does the LORD become[a] impatient?
  Does he do such things?'

'Do not my words do good
  to the one whose ways are upright?
8 Lately my people have risen up
  like an enemy.
You strip off the rich robe
  from those who pass by without a
    care,
  like men returning from battle.
9 You drive the women of my people
  from their pleasant homes.
You take away my blessing
  from their children for ever.
10 Get up, go away!
  For this is not your resting place,
  because it is defiled,

it is ruined, beyond all remedy.
11 If a liar and deceiver comes and says,
  "I will prophesy for you plenty of
    wine and beer,"
  that would be just the prophet for
    this people!

Deliverance promised

12 'I will surely gather all of you, Jacob;
  I will surely bring together the
    remnant of Israel.
I will bring them together like sheep in
    a sheepfold,
  like a flock in its pasture;
  the place will throng with people.
13 The One who breaks open the way will
    go up before them;
  they will break through the gate and
    go out.
Their King will pass through before
    them,
  the LORD at their head.'

Leaders and prophets rebuked

3 Then I said,

'Listen, you leaders of Jacob,
  you rulers of Israel.
Should you not embrace justice,
2   you who hate good and love evil;
  who tear the skin from my people
  and the flesh from their bones;
3 who eat my people's flesh,
  strip off their skin
  and break their bones in pieces;
  who chop them up like meat for the
    pan,
  like flesh for the pot.'

4 Then they will cry out to the LORD,
  but he will not answer them.
At that time he will hide his face from
    them
  because of the evil they have done.

5 This is what the LORD says:

'As for the prophets
  who lead my people astray,
they proclaim "peace"
  if they have something to eat,
but prepare to wage war against anyone

---
a 7 Or Is the Spirit of the LORD

who refuses to feed them.
⁶ Therefore night will come over you,
    without visions,
    and darkness, without divination.
The sun will set for the prophets,
    and the day will go dark for them.
⁷ The seers will be ashamed
    and the diviners disgraced.
They will all cover their faces
    because there is no answer from
        God.'
⁸ But as for me, I am filled with power,
    with the Spirit of the LORD,
    and with justice and might,
to declare to Jacob his transgression,
    to Israel his sin.

⁹ Hear this, you leaders of Jacob,
    you rulers of Israel,
who despise justice
    and distort all that is right;
¹⁰ who build Zion with bloodshed,
    and Jerusalem with wickedness.
¹¹ Her leaders judge for a bribe,
    her priests teach for a price,
    and her prophets tell fortunes for
        money.
Yet they look for the LORD's support
        and say,
    'Is not the LORD among us?
    No disaster will come upon us.'
¹² Therefore because of you,
    Zion will be ploughed like a field,
Jerusalem will become a heap of
        rubble,
    the temple hill a mound overgrown
        with thickets.

The mountain of the LORD

4 In the last days

the mountain of the LORD's temple will
        be established
    as the highest of the mountains;
it will be exalted above the hills,
    and peoples will stream to it.

² Many nations will come and say,

'Come, let us go up to the mountain of
        the LORD,
    to the temple of the God of Jacob.

He will teach us his ways,
    so that we may walk in his paths.'
The law will go out from Zion,
    the word of the LORD from
        Jerusalem.
³ He will judge between many peoples
    and will settle disputes for strong
        nations far and wide.
They will beat their swords into
        ploughshares
    and their spears into pruning hooks.
Nation will not take up sword against
        nation,
    nor will they train for war any more.
⁴ Everyone will sit under their own vine
    and under their own fig-tree,
and no one will make them afraid,
    for the LORD Almighty has spoken.
⁵ All the nations may walk
    in the name of their gods,
but we will walk in the name of the
    LORD
    our God for ever and ever.

The LORD's plan

⁶ 'In that day,' declares the LORD,

'I will gather the lame;
    I will assemble the exiles
    and those I have brought to grief.
⁷ I will make the lame my remnant,
    those driven away a strong nation.
The LORD will rule over them in Mount
        Zion
    from that day and for ever.
⁸ As for you, watchtower of the flock,
    strongholdᵃ of Daughter Zion,
the former dominion will be restored
        to you;
    kingship will come to Daughter
        Jerusalem.'

⁹ Why do you now cry aloud –
    have you no king?ᵇ
Has your rulerᶜ perished,
    that pain seizes you like that of a
        woman in labour?
¹⁰ Writhe in agony, Daughter Zion,

ᵃ 8 Or hill
ᵇ 9 Or King
ᶜ 9 Or Ruler

like a woman in labour,
for now you must leave the city
 to camp in the open field.
You will go to Babylon;
 there you will be rescued.
There the LORD will redeem you
 out of the hand of your enemies.

11 But now many nations
 are gathered against you.
They say, 'Let her be defiled,
 let our eyes gloat over Zion!'
12 But they do not know
 the thoughts of the LORD;
they do not understand his plan,
 that he has gathered them like
  sheaves to the threshing-floor.
13 'Rise and thresh, Daughter Zion,
 for I will give you horns of iron;
I will give you hooves of bronze,
 and you will break to pieces many
  nations.'
You will devote their ill-gotten gains to
 the LORD,
 their wealth to the Lord of all the
  earth.

A promised ruler from Bethlehem

5^a Marshal your troops now, city of
 troops,
 for a siege is laid against us.
They will strike Israel's ruler
 on the cheek with a rod.

2 'But you, Bethlehem Ephrathah,
 though you are small among the
  clans^b of Judah,
out of you will come for me
 one who will be ruler over Israel,
whose origins are from of old,
 from ancient times.'

3 Therefore Israel will be abandoned
 until the time when she who is in
  labour bears a son,
and the rest of his brothers return
 to join the Israelites.

---

a In Hebrew texts 5:1 is numbered 4:14, and 5:2-15 is
numbered 5:1-14.
b 2 Or *rulers*

4 He will stand and shepherd his flock
 in the strength of the LORD,
 in the majesty of the name of the
  LORD his God.
And they will live securely, for then his
 greatness
 will reach to the ends of the earth.

FAVOURITE VERSES

1 Timothy 4:12

*Don't let anyone look down on you
because you are young, but set an
example for the believers in speech,
in conduct, in love, in faith and in
purity.*

This is my favourite verse because
it's so relevant to our lives today.
Just because you're young, it
doesn't mean you can't make a
difference, and it doesn't mean you
don't matter, because you do. Try
not to become sidetracked from
the plans God has for you, because
–trust me – if you let him take
control, and if you put all your trust
in him, you and those around you
really will see what a difference he
has made in your life, and you will
never regret it.

Jordan, 15

5 And he will be our peace
 when the Assyrians invade our land
 and march through our fortresses.
We will raise against them seven
  shepherds,
 even eight commanders,
6 who will rule^c the land of Assyria with
 the sword,

---

c 6 Or *crush*

the land of Nimrod with drawn
　　sword. *d*
He will deliver us from the Assyrians
　　when they invade our land
　　and march across our borders.

7 The remnant of Jacob will be
　　in the midst of many peoples
like dew from the LORD,
　　like showers on the grass,
which do not wait for anyone
　　or depend on man.
8 The remnant of Jacob will be among
　　the nations,
　　in the midst of many peoples,
like a lion among the beasts of the
　　forest,
　　like a young lion among flocks of
　　sheep,
which mauls and mangles as it goes,
　　and no one can rescue.
9 Your hand will be lifted up in triumph
　　over your enemies,
　　and all your foes will be destroyed.

10 'In that day,' declares the LORD,

'I will destroy your horses from among
　　you
　　and demolish your chariots.
11 I will destroy the cities of your land
　　and tear down all your strongholds.
12 I will destroy your witchcraft
　　and you will no longer cast spells.
13 I will destroy your idols
　　and your sacred stones from among
　　you;
you will no longer bow down
　　to the work of your hands.
14 I will uproot from among you your
　　Asherah poles *e*
　　when I demolish your cities.
15 I will take vengeance in anger and
　　wrath
　　on the nations that have not obeyed
　　me.'

---

d 6 Or *Nimrod in its gates*
e 14 That is, wooden symbols of the goddess
Asherah

The LORD's case against Israel

6 Listen to what the LORD says:

'Stand up, plead my case before the
　　mountains;
　　let the hills hear what you have to
　　say.

2 'Hear, you mountains, the LORD's
　　accusation;
　　listen, you everlasting foundations of
　　the earth.
For the LORD has a case against his
　　people;
　　he is lodging a charge against
　　Israel.

3 'My people, what have I done to you?
　　How have I burdened you? Answer
　　me.
4 I brought you up out of Egypt
　　and redeemed you from the land of
　　slavery.
I sent Moses to lead you,
　　also Aaron and Miriam.
5 My people, remember
　　what Balak king of Moab plotted
　　and what Balaam son of Beor
　　answered.
Remember your journey from Shittim
　　to Gilgal,
　　that you may know the righteous acts
　　of the LORD.'

6 With what shall I come before the
　　LORD
　　and bow down before the exalted
　　God?
Shall I come before him with burnt
　　offerings,
　　with calves a year old?
7 Will the LORD be pleased with
　　thousands of rams,
　　with ten thousand rivers of oil?
Shall I offer my firstborn for my
　　transgression,
　　the fruit of my body for the sin of my
　　soul?
8 He has shown you, O mortal, what is
　　good.
　　And what does the LORD require of
　　you?

To act justly and to love mercy
and to walk humbly*a* with your God.

Israel's guilt and punishment

⁹ Listen! The Lᴏʀᴅ is calling to the city –
and to fear your name is wisdom –
'Heed the rod and the One who
appointed it.*b*
¹⁰ Am I still to forget your ill-gotten
treasures, you wicked house,
and the short ephah,*c* which is
accursed?
¹¹ Shall I acquit someone with dishonest
scales,
with a bag of false weights?
¹² Your rich people are violent;
your inhabitants are liars

---

a 8 Or *prudently*
b 9 The meaning of the Hebrew for this line is
uncertain.
c 10 An ephah was a dry measure.

and their tongues speak deceitfully.
¹³ Therefore, I have begun to destroy you,
to ruin*d* you because of your sins.
¹⁴ You will eat but not be satisfied;
your stomach will still be empty.*e*
You will store up but save nothing,
because what you save*f* I will give to
the sword.
¹⁵ You will plant but not harvest;
you will press olives but not use the
oil,
you will crush grapes but not drink
the wine.
¹⁶ You have observed the statutes of Omri
and all the practices of Ahab's house;

---

d 13 Or *Therefore, I will make you ill and destroy you; / I
will ruin*
e 14 The meaning of the Hebrew for this word is
uncertain.
f 14 Or *You will press toward birth but not give birth, / and
what you bring to birth*

JUSTICE AND MERCY 5

FREEDOM

**In Micah 6, God reminds his people of how much has changed since they
were slaves in Egypt.**

He reminds them just how far he has brought them and helps them to remember
that once they were slaves in Egypt. They were an oppressed people, living
under a tyrannical regime, being treated like slaves with absolutely no rights.
God acted to set them free, and this chapter is all about what he wants in return
– and it's a surprise. They thought that God would want sacrifices: calves, burnt
offerings, or their money. But no. Instead God is seeking people who will look
out for other people the way God has looked out for them. He wants them to act
justly – to treat people as they should be treated. He wants them to love mercy –
not just to be merciful, but to be passionate about mercy. And he wants them to
walk humbly with him (Micah 6:8).

God wants the same from us. Through Jesus we have been given freedom; we
have been given life. Now we need to extend that to others. We should be doing
all we can to ensure that others get treated properly. This is the worship that God
requires. Yes, he wants the songs of our hearts and the words of our mouths, but
he also wants us to put that worship into action in the way we treat others.

David Westlake

 Isaiah 58   Matthew 14:13

you have followed their traditions.
Therefore I will give you over to ruin
    and your people to derision;
you will bear the scorn of the
    nations.'*g*

Israel's misery

7 What misery is mine!
    I am like one who gathers summer
    fruit
    at the gleaning of the vineyard;
there is no cluster of grapes to eat,
    none of the early figs that I crave.
² The faithful have been swept from the
        land;
    not one upright person remains.
Everyone lies in wait to shed blood;
    they hunt each other with nets.
³ Both hands are skilled in doing evil;
    the ruler demands gifts,
the judge accepts bribes,
    the powerful dictate what they
        desire –
    they all conspire together.
⁴ The best of them is like a brier,
    the most upright worse than a thorn
        hedge.
The day God visits you has come,
    the day your watchmen sound the
        alarm.
Now is the time of your confusion.
⁵ Do not trust a neighbour;
    put no confidence in a friend.
Even with the woman who lies in your
        embrace
    guard the words of your lips.
⁶ For a son dishonours his father,
    a daughter rises up against her
        mother,
a daughter-in-law against her
        mother-in-law –
    a man's enemies are the members of
        his own household.

⁷ But as for me, I watch in hope for the
    LORD,
    I wait for God my Saviour;
    my God will hear me.

Israel will rise

⁸ Do not gloat over me, my enemy!
    Though I have fallen, I will rise.
Though I sit in darkness,
    the LORD will be my light.
⁹ Because I have sinned against him,
    I will bear the LORD's wrath,
until he pleads my case
    and upholds my cause.
He will bring me out into the light;
    I will see his righteousness.
¹⁰ Then my enemy will see it
    and will be covered with shame,
she who said to me,
    'Where is the LORD your God?'
My eyes will see her downfall;
    even now she will be trampled
        underfoot
    like mire in the streets.

¹¹ The day for building your walls will
        come,
    the day for extending your
        boundaries.
¹² In that day people will come to you
    from Assyria and the cities of Egypt,
even from Egypt to the Euphrates
    and from sea to sea
    and from mountain to
        mountain.
¹³ The earth will become desolate because
        of its inhabitants,
    as the result of their deeds.

Prayer and praise

¹⁴ Shepherd your people with your staff,
    the flock of your inheritance,
which lives by itself in a forest,
    in fertile pasture-lands.*a*
Let them feed in Bashan and Gilead
    as in days long ago.

¹⁵ 'As in the days when you came out of
        Egypt,
    I will show them my wonders.'

¹⁶ Nations will see and be ashamed,
    deprived of all their power.
They will put their hands over their
        mouths

---

g 16 Septuagint; Hebrew *scorn due to my people*   *a* 14 Or *in the middle of Carmel*

and their ears will become deaf.
17 They will lick dust like a snake,
    like creatures that crawl on the
        ground.
They will come trembling out of their
        dens;
    they will turn in fear to the LORD our
        God
    and will be afraid of you.
18 Who is a God like you,
    who pardons sin and forgives the
        transgression

of the remnant of his inheritance?
You do not stay angry for ever
    but delight to show mercy.
19 You will again have compassion on us;
    you will tread our sins underfoot
    and hurl all our iniquities into the
        depths of the sea.
20 You will be faithful to Jacob,
    and show love to Abraham,
as you pledged on oath to our
    ancestors
    in days long ago.

NAHUM

DATE

Nahum prophesied between 663 and 612 BC

AUTHOR

Nahum

WHAT'S IT ALL ABOUT?

Like the prophet Obadiah, Nahum wasn't speaking to his own people, but to one of their enemies. His words were for Assyria, who had been attacking Israel and Judah for many years and had just conquered the Northern Kingdom of Israel (Nahum was part of the Southern Kingdom of Judah). He addressed Nineveh, the capital of Assyria and the same city that was brought to repentance by the prophet Jonah, but here Nahum prophesied the city's destruction. Considering their mighty army that had conquered many places, it would not have sounded likely at the time – but sure enough, within a hundred years Nineveh had fallen.

The name Nahum means 'to comfort', and these prophecies would have brought much comfort to God's people. They offered reassurance that God would bring vengeance on those who attacked them and would defeat their enemies, something they were powerless to do themselves.

WHY SHOULD WE READ IT?

- To see how God brought justice for his people.
- To remember that no army is a match for the strength and might of God.

Andy Croft with Liza Hoeksma

1

A prophecy concerning Nineveh. The book of the vision of Nahum the Elkoshite.

The LORD's anger against Nineveh

2 The LORD is a jealous and avenging God;
    the LORD takes vengeance and is
        filled with wrath.
The LORD takes vengeance on his foes
    and vents his wrath against his
        enemies.
3 The LORD is slow to anger but great in
        power;
    the LORD will not leave the guilty
        unpunished.
His way is in the whirlwind and the
        storm,
    and clouds are the dust of his feet.
4 He rebukes the sea and dries it up;
    he makes all the rivers run dry.
Bashan and Carmel wither
    and the blossoms of Lebanon fade.
5 The mountains quake before him
    and the hills melt away.
The earth trembles at his presence,
    the world and all who live in it.
6 Who can withstand his indignation?
    Who can endure his fierce anger?
His wrath is poured out like fire;
    the rocks are shattered before him.

7 The LORD is good,
    a refuge in times of trouble.
He cares for those who trust in him,
8   but with an overwhelming flood
he will make an end of Nineveh;
    he will pursue his foes into the realm
        of darkness.

9 Whatever they plot against the LORD
    he will bring[a] to an end;
    trouble will not come a second time.
10 They will be entangled among thorns
    and drunk from their wine;
    they will be consumed like dry
        stubble.[b]
11 From you, Nineveh, has one come forth
    who plots evil against the LORD

and devises wicked plans.

12 This is what the LORD says:

'Although they have allies and are
        numerous,
    they will be destroyed and pass away.
Although I have afflicted you, Judah,
    I will afflict you no more.
13 Now I will break their yoke from your
        neck
    and tear your shackles away.'

14 The LORD has given a command
        concerning you, Nineveh:
    'You will have no descendants to bear
        your name.
I will destroy the images and idols
    that are in the temple of your gods.
I will prepare your grave,
    for you are vile.'

15 Look, there on the mountains,
    the feet of one who brings good
        news,
    who proclaims peace!
Celebrate your festivals, Judah,
    and fulfil your vows.
No more will the wicked invade you;
    they will be completely destroyed.[c]

Nineveh to fall

2

[a] An attacker advances against you,
    Nineveh.
Guard the fortress,
    watch the road,
    brace yourselves,
    marshal all your strength!

2 The LORD will restore the splendour of
        Jacob
    like the splendour of Israel,
though destroyers have laid them waste
    and have ruined their vines.

3 The shields of the soldiers are red;
    the warriors are clad in scarlet.
The metal on the chariots flashes

---

a 9 Or *What do you foes plot against the LORD? / He will bring it*
b 10 The meaning of the Hebrew for this verse is uncertain.

c 15 In Hebrew texts this verse (1:15) is numbered 2:1.
a In Hebrew texts 2:1-13 is numbered 2:2-14.

on the day they are made ready;
the spears of juniper are
brandished.[b]
[4] The chariots storm through the streets,
rushing back and forth through the
squares.
They look like flaming torches;
they dart about like lightning.

[5] Nineveh summons her picked troops,
yet they stumble on their way.
They dash to the city wall;
the protective shield is put in place.
[6] The river gates are thrown open
and the palace collapses.
[7] It is decreed[c] that Nineveh
be exiled and carried away.
Her female slaves moan like doves
and beat on their breasts.
[8] Nineveh is like a pool
whose water is draining away.
'Stop! Stop!' they cry,
but no one turns back.
[9] Plunder the silver!
Plunder the gold!
The supply is endless,
the wealth from all its treasures!
[10] She is pillaged, plundered, stripped!
Hearts melt, knees give way,
bodies tremble, every face grows
pale.

[11] Where now is the lions' den,
the place where they fed their young,
where the lion and lioness went,
and the cubs, with nothing to fear?
[12] The lion killed enough for his cubs
and strangled the prey for his mate,
filling his lairs with the kill
and his dens with the prey.

[13] 'I am against you,'
declares the LORD Almighty.
'I will burn up your chariots in smoke,
and the sword will devour your
young lions.
I will leave you no prey on the earth.

The voices of your messengers
will no longer be heard.'

Woe to Nineveh

3 Woe to the city of blood,
full of lies,
full of plunder,
never without victims!
[2] The crack of whips,
the clatter of wheels,
galloping horses
and jolting chariots!
[3] Charging cavalry,
flashing swords
and glittering spears!
Many casualties,
piles of dead,
bodies without number,
people stumbling over the corpses –
[4] all because of the wanton lust of a
prostitute,
alluring, the mistress of sorceries,
who enslaved nations by her
prostitution
and peoples by her witchcraft.

[5] 'I am against you,' declares the LORD
Almighty.
'I will lift your skirts over your face.
I will show the nations your nakedness
and the kingdoms your shame.
[6] I will pelt you with filth,
I will treat you with contempt
and make you a spectacle.
[7] All who see you will flee from you and
say,
"Nineveh is in ruins – who will
mourn for her?"
Where can I find anyone to comfort
you?'

[8] Are you better than Thebes,
situated on the Nile,
with water around her?
The river was her defence,
the waters her wall.
[9] Cush[a] and Egypt were her boundless
strength;
Put and Libya were among her allies.
[10] Yet she was taken captive

---

b 3 Hebrew; Septuagint and Syriac *ready; / the
horsemen rush to and fro.*
c 7 The meaning of the Hebrew for this word is
uncertain.

---

a 9 That is, the upper Nile region

and went into exile.
Her infants were dashed to pieces
    at every street corner.
Lots were cast for her nobles,
    and all her great men were put in
      chains.
¹¹ You too will become drunk;
    you will go into hiding
    and seek refuge from the enemy.

¹² All your fortresses are like fig-trees
    with their first ripe fruit;
when they are shaken,
    the figs fall into the mouth of the
      eater.
¹³ Look at your troops –
    they are all weaklings.
The gates of your land
    are wide open to your enemies;
    fire has consumed the bars of your
      gates.

¹⁴ Draw water for the siege,
    strengthen your defences!
Work the clay,
    tread the mortar,
    repair the brickwork!
¹⁵ There the fire will consume you;
    the sword will cut you down –
    and it will devour you like a swarm of
      locusts.

Multiply like grasshoppers,
    multiply like locusts!
¹⁶ You have increased the number of your
    merchants
    till they are more numerous than the
      stars in the sky,
but like locusts they strip the land
    and then fly away.
¹⁷ Your guards are like locusts,
    your officials like swarms of locusts
    that settle in the walls on a cold
      day –
but when the sun appears they fly away,
    and no one knows where.

¹⁸ King of Assyria, your shepherds*b*
    slumber;
    your nobles lie down to rest.
Your people are scattered on the
    mountains
    with no one to gather them.
¹⁹ Nothing can heal you;
    your wound is fatal.
All who hear the news about you
    clap their hands at your fall,
for who has not felt
    your endless cruelty?

---

b 18 That is, rulers

HABAKKUK

DATE

Habakkuk lived around 600 BC

AUTHOR

Habakkuk

WHAT'S IT ALL ABOUT?

Habakkuk was another of the twelve Minor Prophets and he was alive at the same time as Jeremiah. His book is unique in that, unlike the other prophetic books, it doesn't bring prophecies to the people, but instead records a conversation between Habakkuk and God. Habakkuk questioned God about why the world was so unfair, and he cried out to God, asking why he would allow his chosen people (Judah) to sin. God responded by saying he was raising up the Babylonians to punish Judah, but this argument brought Habakkuk no comfort. How could God use an ungodly and even more wicked nation like Babylon to punish his people? God promised Habakkuk that, although it wouldn't happen immediately, Babylon would be brought to justice for their actions. In the third and final chapter of the book, Habakkuk sings a beautiful song of worship, praising God and promising to wait for him to act.

WHY SHOULD WE READ IT?

- To remind ourselves that we don't need to be afraid of asking God tough questions when we don't understand the things going on in our lives and in the world.

- To remind us to be patient and wait for God to make things right, even if he seems slow to act (Habakkuk 2).

- To remember that no matter how hard life is, there is always reason to worship and rejoice in God (Habakkuk 3).

Andy Croft with Liza Hoeksma

1

The prophecy that Habakkuk the prophet received.

Habakkuk's complaint

² How long, LORD, must I call for help,
   but you do not listen?
Or cry out to you, 'Violence!'
   but you do not save?
³ Why do you make me look at injustice?
   Why do you tolerate wrongdoing?
Destruction and violence are
         before me;
   there is strife, and conflict abounds.
⁴ Therefore the law is paralysed,
   and justice never prevails.
The wicked hem in the righteous,
   so that justice is perverted.

The LORD's answer

⁵ 'Look at the nations and watch –
   and be utterly amazed.
For I am going to do something in your
      days
   that you would not believe,
   even if you were told.
⁶ I am raising up the Babylonians,ᵃ
   that ruthless and impetuous
         people,
who sweep across the whole earth
   to seize dwellings not their own.
⁷ They are a feared and dreaded people;
   they are a law to themselves
   and promote their own honour.
⁸ Their horses are swifter than leopards,
   fiercer than wolves at dusk.
Their cavalry gallops headlong;
   their horsemen come from afar.
They fly like an eagle swooping to
         devour;
⁹   they all come intent on violence.
Their hordesᵇ advance like a desert
      wind
   and gather prisoners like sand.
¹⁰ They mock kings
   and scoff at rulers.
They laugh at all fortified cities;
   by building earthen ramps they
         capture them.

¹¹ Then they sweep past like the wind and
      go on –
   guilty people, whose own strength is
      their god.'

Habakkuk's second complaint

¹² LORD, are you not from everlasting?
   My God, my Holy One, youᶜ will
      never die.
You, LORD, have appointed them to
      execute judgment;
   you, my Rock, have ordained them to
      punish.
¹³ Your eyes are too pure to look on evil;
   you cannot tolerate wrongdoing.
Why then do you tolerate the
      treacherous?
   Why are you silent while the wicked
   swallow up those more righteous
      than themselves?
¹⁴ You have made people like the fish in
      the sea,
   like the sea creatures that have no
      ruler.
¹⁵ The wicked foe pulls all of them up with
      hooks,
   he catches them in his net,
he gathers them up in his drag-net;
   and so he rejoices and is glad.
¹⁶ Therefore he sacrifices to his net
   and burns incense to his drag-net,
for by his net he lives in luxury
   and enjoys the choicest food.
¹⁷ Is he to keep on emptying his net,
   destroying nations without mercy?

2

I will stand at my watch
and station myself on the ramparts;
I will look to see what he will say
      to me,
   and what answer I am to give to this
      complaint.ᵃ

The LORD's answer

² Then the LORD replied:

'Write down the revelation
   and make it plain on tablets

ᵃ 6 Or *Chaldeans*
ᵇ 9 The meaning of the Hebrew for this word is
uncertain.

ᶜ 12 An ancient Hebrew scribal tradition; Masoretic
Text *we*
ᵃ 1 Or *and what to answer when I am rebuked*

so that a herald[b] may run with it.
3 For the revelation awaits an appointed
time;
    it speaks of the end
    and will not prove false.
  Though it linger, wait for it;
    it[c] will certainly come
    and will not delay.

4 'See, the enemy is puffed up;
    his desires are not upright —
  but the righteous person will live by
    his faithfulness[d] —
5 indeed, wine betrays him;
    he is arrogant and never at rest.
Because he is as greedy as the grave
    and like death is never satisfied,
he gathers to himself all the nations
    and takes captive all the peoples.

6 'Will not all of them taunt him with
ridicule and scorn, saying,

  ' "Woe to him who piles up stolen
    goods
    and makes himself wealthy by
    extortion!
  How long must this go on?"
7 Will not your creditors suddenly arise?
    Will they not wake up and make you
    tremble?
  Then you will become their prey.
8 Because you have plundered many
    nations,
  the peoples who are left will plunder
    you.
For you have shed human blood;
  you have destroyed lands and cities
    and everyone in them.

9 'Woe to him who builds his house by
    unjust gain,
  setting his nest on high
  to escape the clutches of ruin!
10 You have plotted the ruin of many
    peoples,
  shaming your own house and
    forfeiting your life.

11 The stones of the wall will cry out,
  and the beams of the woodwork will
    echo it.

12 'Woe to him who builds a city with
    bloodshed
  and establishes a town by injustice!
13 Has not the LORD Almighty determined
  that the people's labour is only fuel
    for the fire,
  that the nations exhaust themselves
    for nothing?
14 For the earth will be filled with the
    knowledge of the glory of the
    LORD
  as the waters cover the sea.

15 'Woe to him who gives drink to his
    neighbours,
  pouring it from the wineskin till they
    are drunk,
  so that he can gaze on their naked
    bodies!
16 You will be filled with shame instead of
    glory.
  Now it is your turn! Drink and let
    your nakedness be exposed![e]
The cup from the LORD's right hand is
    coming round to you,
  and disgrace will cover your glory.
17 The violence you have done to Lebanon
    will overwhelm you,
  and your destruction of animals will
    terrify you.
For you have shed human blood;
  you have destroyed lands and cities
    and everyone in them.

18 'Of what value is an idol carved by a
    craftsman?
  Or an image that teaches lies?
For the one who makes it trusts in his
    own creation;
  he makes idols that cannot speak.
19 Woe to him who says to wood, "Come
    to life!"
  Or to lifeless stone, "Wake up!"
Can it give guidance?

---

b 2 Or *so that whoever reads it*
c 3 Or *Though he linger, wait for him;* / *he*
d 4 Or *faith*

e 16 Masoretic Text; Dead Sea Scrolls, Aquila,
Vulgate and Syriac (see also Septuagint) *and stagger*

It is covered with gold and silver;
there is no breath in it.'

20 The LORD is in his holy temple;
let all the earth be silent before him.

Habakkuk's prayer

3 A prayer of Habakkuk the prophet.
On *shigionoth.ª*

––––––

a 1 Probably a literary or musical term

PAIN AND SUFFERING 4

WORSHIP GOD IN THE MIDST OF PAIN

One of the most common questions people ask about the existence of God is this: 'How can there be a loving God when there's so much pain in the world?'

Even as Jesus' disciples, we don't always have the answers. Sometimes life is too difficult to make sense of. We suffer. We see friends and family suffer. There are wars, famines and disasters that leave thousands dead, hungry, homeless and hopeless. But this isn't a twenty-first-century problem. Habakkuk was a prophet who lived about 600 years before Jesus and this short book in the Bible shows us how he was trying to make sense of the pain he saw around him. He asks in effect, 'Why is there so much injustice in the world? Why is there so much destruction and violence? Why does God sit back and do nothing when he could change everything so easily?'

The Lord graciously replies to Habakkuk, saying that a time of justice will come. He makes it clear that he sees all the wicked things people are doing and that there will be a day when the world will be as it should. In the meantime, Habakkuk learns an important lesson. His closing words show that he has learned to trust in God's goodness no matter what the circumstances are. He says that even if he looks around and has nothing, he will rejoice in God (Habakkuk 3:17). He always has reason to rejoice because God is his Saviour (v. 18).

The same is true for us. When life is looking bleak and miserable, when we're not getting the things we want and we don't see any signs of the good things we long for, we still worship. Sometimes our worship is most meaningful when it's given through our tears. In the Old Testament they used to sacrifice animals as part of their worship. I'm thankful we don't do that any more, but we can still bring a sacrifice of praise. We can tell God he's amazing even when our lives look messy and difficult and we don't feel like praising him. King David had the same attitude as Habakkuk, worshipping God straight after his beloved son's life was taken (2 Samuel 12). Job too fell to the ground and worshipped God when all his children and his livelihood were destroyed in one day (Job 1).

No matter what is going on in our lives, let's follow the example of these godly men and worship God no matter what. In times of trouble, let's remember the truth that God is always worthy of our praise. We can always be joyful in God our Saviour.

Mike Pilavachi

 Psalm 13   John 16:33

2 Lord, I have heard of your fame;
  I stand in awe of your deeds, Lord.
Repeat them in our day,
  in our time make them known;
  in wrath remember mercy.

3 God came from Teman,
  the Holy One from Mount Paran.*b*
His glory covered the heavens
  and his praise filled the earth.
4 His splendour was like the sunrise;
  rays flashed from his hand,
  where his power was hidden.
5 Plague went before him;
  pestilence followed his steps.
6 He stood, and shook the earth;
  he looked, and made the nations
    tremble.
The ancient mountains crumbled
  and the age-old hills collapsed –
  but he marches on for ever.
7 I saw the tents of Cushan in distress,
  the dwellings of Midian in anguish.

8 Were you angry with the rivers, Lord?
  Was your wrath against the streams?
Did you rage against the sea
  when you rode your horses
  and your chariots to victory?
9 You uncovered your bow,
  you called for many arrows.
You split the earth with rivers;
10   the mountains saw you and
    writhed.
Torrents of water swept by;
  the deep roared
  and lifted its waves on high.

11 Sun and moon stood still in the
    heavens
  at the glint of your flying arrows,

at the lightning of your flashing
    spear.
12 In wrath you strode through the earth
  and in anger you threshed the
    nations.
13 You came out to deliver your people,
  to save your anointed one.
You crushed the leader of the land of
    wickedness,
  you stripped him from head to foot.
14 With his own spear you pierced his
    head
  when his warriors stormed out to
    scatter us,
gloating as though about to devour
  the wretched who were in hiding.
15 You trampled the sea with your
    horses,
  churning the great waters.

16 I heard and my heart pounded,
  my lips quivered at the sound;
decay crept into my bones,
  and my legs trembled.
Yet I will wait patiently for the day of
    calamity
  to come on the nation invading us.
17 Though the fig-tree does not bud
  and there are no grapes on the vines,
though the olive crop fails
  and the fields produce no food,
though there are no sheep in the
    sheepfold
  and no cattle in the stalls,
18 yet I will rejoice in the Lord,
  I will be joyful in God my Saviour.

19 The Sovereign Lord is my strength;
  he makes my feet like the feet of a
    deer,
  he enables me to tread on the
    heights.

---

b 3 The Hebrew has *Selah* (a word of uncertain
meaning) here and at the middle of verse 9 and at
the end of verse 13.

For the director of music. On my
  stringed instruments.

ZEPHANIAH

DATE

Zephaniah prophesied between 640 and 609 BC

AUTHOR

Zephaniah

WHAT'S IT ALL ABOUT?

Zephaniah was a Minor Prophet and a descendant of King Hezekiah who spoke to the people of Judah at around the same time as prophets like Jeremiah and Nahum. He spoke of God's judgement of the people, citing their worship of Baal and Molech, whose practices included child sacrifice. He raged against the officials, the rulers, the prophets and the priests for being treacherous, dishonest and ungodly. He called the people back to seeking God and trusting in him again, so that they might be saved from God's anger and punishment. In his final words, the prophet speaks God's tender words to those who want to be faithful and promises to restore the fortunes for a remnant of his people.

Zephaniah's words may have had an impact on the king of the time, Josiah, because part-way through his reign he introduced wide reforms, doing away with pagan practices and idol worship, and turning the nation towards God once more.

WHY SHOULD WE READ IT?

- To hear the great destruction God promised to those who turned away from him.

- To put into context the famous verse, *'The LORD your God is with you, the Mighty Warrior who saves. He will take great delight in you; in his love he will no longer rebuke you, but will rejoice over you with singing'* (Zephaniah 3:17).

Andy Croft with Liza Hoeksma

1 The word of the LORD that came to Zephaniah son of Cushi, the son of Gedaliah, the son of Amariah, the son of Hezekiah, during the reign of Josiah son of Amon king of Judah:

Judgment on the whole earth in the day of the LORD

2 'I will sweep away everything
    from the face of the earth,'
              declares the LORD.
3 'I will sweep away both man and beast;
    I will sweep away the birds in the sky
    and the fish in the sea –
    and the idols that cause the wicked to
      stumble.'ᵃ

'When I destroy all mankind
    on the face of the earth,'
              declares the LORD,
4 'I will stretch out my hand against
      Judah
    and against all who live in Jerusalem.
I will destroy every remnant of Baal
    worship in this place,
    the very names of the idolatrous
      priests –
5 those who bow down on the roofs
    to worship the starry host,
    those who bow down and swear by the
      LORD
    and who also swear by Molek,ᵇ
6 those who turn back from following
      the LORD
    and neither seek the LORD nor
      enquire of him.'

7 Be silent before the Sovereign LORD,
    for the day of the LORD is near.
The LORD has prepared a sacrifice;
    he has consecrated those he has
      invited.

8 'On the day of the LORD's sacrifice
    I will punish the officials
    and the king's sons
    and all those clad
      in foreign clothes.

9 On that day I will punish
    all who avoid stepping on the
      threshold,ᶜ
who fill the temple of their gods
    with violence and deceit.

10 'On that day,'
    declares the LORD,
   'a cry will go up from the Fish Gate,
    wailing from the New Quarter,
    and a loud crash from the hills.
11 Wail, you who live in the market
      districtᵈ;
    all your merchants will be wiped out,
    all who trade withᵉ silver will be
      destroyed.
12 At that time I will search Jerusalem with
      lamps
    and punish those who are
      complacent,
    who are like wine left on its dregs,
who think, "The LORD will do nothing,
    either good or bad."
13 Their wealth will be plundered,
    their houses demolished.
Though they build houses,
    they will not live in them;
though they plant vineyards,
    they will not drink the wine.'

14 The great day of the LORD is near –
    near and coming quickly.
The cry on the day of the LORD is bitter;
    the Mighty Warrior shouts his battle
      cry.
15 That day will be a day of wrath –
    a day of distress and anguish,
    a day of trouble and ruin,
    a day of darkness and gloom,
    a day of clouds and blackness –
16   a day of trumpet and battle cry
    against the fortified cities
    and against the corner towers.

17 'I will bring such distress on all people
    that they will grope about like those
      who are blind,

---

a 3 The meaning of the Hebrew for this line is uncertain.
b 5 Hebrew *Malkam*

c 9 See 1 Samuel 5:5.
d 11 Or *the Mortar*
e 11 Or *in*

because they have sinned against the
Lord.
Their blood will be poured out like dust
and their entrails like dung.
18 Neither their silver nor their gold
will be able to save them
on the day of the Lord's wrath.'

In the fire of his jealousy
the whole earth will be consumed,
for he will make a sudden end
of all who live on the earth.

Judah and Jerusalem judged along with the nations

Judah summoned to repent

2 Gather together, gather yourselves
together,
you shameful nation,
2 before the decree takes effect
and that day passes like windblown
chaff,
before the Lord's fierce anger
comes upon you,
before the day of the Lord's wrath
comes upon you.
3 Seek the Lord, all you humble of the
land,
you who do what he commands.
Seek righteousness, seek humility;
perhaps you will be sheltered
on the day of the Lord's anger.

Philistia

4 Gaza will be abandoned
and Ashkelon left in ruins.
At midday Ashdod will be emptied
and Ekron uprooted.
5 Woe to you who live by the sea,
you Kerethite people;
the word of the Lord is against you,
Canaan, land of the Philistines.
He says, 'I will destroy you,
and none will be left.'
6 The land by the sea will become
pastures
having wells for shepherds
and sheepfolds for flocks.
7 That land will belong
to the remnant of the people of
Judah;
there they will find pasture.

In the evening they will lie down
in the houses of Ashkelon.
The Lord their God will care for them;
he will restore their fortunes.ᵃ

Moab and Ammon

8 'I have heard the insults of Moab
and the taunts of the Ammonites,
who insulted my people
and made threats against their land.
9 Therefore, as surely as I live,'
declares the Lord Almighty,
the God of Israel,
'surely Moab will become like Sodom,
the Ammonites like Gomorrah –
a place of weeds and salt pits,
a wasteland for ever.
The remnant of my people will plunder
them;
the survivors of my nation will
inherit their land.'

10 This is what they will get in return for
their pride,
for insulting and mocking
the people of the Lord Almighty.
11 The Lord will be awesome to them
when he destroys all the gods of the
earth.
Distant nations will bow down to him,
all of them in their own lands.

Cush

12 'You Cushites,ᵇ too,
will be slain by my sword.'

Assyria

13 He will stretch out his hand against the
north
and destroy Assyria,
leaving Nineveh utterly desolate
and dry as the desert.
14 Flocks and herds will lie down there,
creatures of every kind.
The desert owl and the screech owl
will roost on her columns.
Their hooting will echo through the
windows,
rubble will fill the doorways,

ᵃ 7 Or *will bring back their captives*
ᵇ 12 That is, people from the upper Nile region

the beams of cedar will be exposed.
¹⁵ This is the city of revelry
    that lived in safety.
She said to herself,
    'I am the one! And there is none
        besides me.'
What a ruin she has become,
    a lair for wild beasts!
All who pass by her scoff
    and shake their fists.

Jerusalem

3 Woe to the city of oppressors,
    rebellious and defiled!
² She obeys no one,
    she accepts no correction.
She does not trust in the LORD,
    she does not draw near to her God.
³ Her officials within her
    are roaring lions;
her rulers are evening wolves,
    who leave nothing for the morning.
⁴ Her prophets are unprincipled;
    they are treacherous people.
Her priests profane the sanctuary
    and do violence to the law.
⁵ The LORD within her is righteous;
    he does no wrong.
Morning by morning he dispenses his
        justice,
    and every new day he does not fail,
    yet the unrighteous know no shame.

Jerusalem remains unrepentant

⁶ 'I have destroyed nations;
    their strongholds are demolished.
I have left their streets deserted,
    with no one passing through.
Their cities are laid waste;
    they are deserted and empty.
⁷ Of Jerusalem I thought,
    "Surely you will fear me
    and accept correction!"
Then her place of refuge*ᵃ* would not be
        destroyed,
    nor all my punishments come upon*ᵇ*
        her.
But they were still eager

to act corruptly in all they did.
⁸ Therefore wait for me,'
    declares the LORD,
    'for the day I will stand up to testify.*ᶜ*
I have decided to assemble the nations,
    to gather the kingdoms
and to pour out my wrath on them –
    all my fierce anger.
The whole world will be consumed
    by the fire of my jealous anger.

Restoration of Israel's remnant

⁹ 'Then I will purify the lips of the peoples,
    that all of them may call on the name
        of the LORD
    and serve him shoulder to shoulder.
¹⁰ From beyond the rivers of Cush*ᵈ*
    my worshippers, my scattered
        people,
    will bring me offerings.
¹¹ On that day you, Jerusalem, will not be
        put to shame
    for all the wrongs you have done
        to me,
because I will remove from you
    your arrogant boasters.
Never again will you be haughty
    on my holy hill.
¹² But I will leave within you
    the meek and humble.
The remnant of Israel
    will trust in the name of the LORD.
¹³ They will do no wrong;
    they will tell no lies.
A deceitful tongue
    will not be found in their mouths.
They will eat and lie down
    and no one will make them afraid.'

¹⁴ Sing, Daughter Zion;
    shout aloud, Israel!
Be glad and rejoice with all your heart,
    Daughter Jerusalem!
¹⁵ The LORD has taken away your
        punishment,
    he has turned back your enemy.
The LORD, the King of Israel, is with you;
    never again will you fear any harm.
¹⁶ On that day
    they will say to Jerusalem,

---

a 7   Or *her sanctuary*
b 7   Or *all those I appointed over*
c 8   Septuagint and Syriac; Hebrew *will rise up to plunder*

d 10   That is, the upper Nile region

'Do not fear, Zion;
  do not let your hands hang limp.
17 The LORD your God is with you,
  the Mighty Warrior who saves.
He will take great delight in you;
  in his love he will no longer rebuke
    you,
  but will rejoice over you with
    singing.'

18 'I will remove from you
  all who mourn over the loss of your
    appointed festivals,
  which is a burden and reproach for
    you.
19 At that time I will deal

with all who oppressed you.
I will rescue the lame;
  I will gather the exiles.
I will give them praise and honour
  in every land where they have
    suffered shame.
20 At that time I will gather you;
  at that time I will bring you home.
I will give you honour and praise
  among all the peoples of the earth
when I restore your fortunes*e*
  before your very eyes,'
                              says the LORD.

_____

e 20 Or I bring back your captives

HAGGAI

DATE

Haggai delivered his message in 520 BC

AUTHOR

Haggai

WHAT'S IT ALL ABOUT?

When the people of Judah returned from exile in Babylon to Jerusalem, they set about rebuilding the temple of God (we read about this in the book of Ezra). The temple was hugely important as it was a representation of God's presence among his people, yet after a short while they let their rebuilding efforts lapse. They started focusing instead on rebuilding their own homes and rebuilding their former wealth, but they found that they could never harvest as much as they needed. About twenty years after the first exiles returned to Jerusalem, Haggai prophesied and urged the people to recommit to the building of the temple. He said the problems they were experiencing were because they were being disobedient. Yet if they would refocus on the temple and be obedient to God, he would bless them. The people listened to Haggai (and his fellow prophet Zechariah, who brought a similar message) and picked up their tools again within weeks of these prophecies, managing finally to complete the rebuilding of God's temple.

WHY SHOULD WE READ IT?

- As a reminder to keep God and his priorities at the centre of our lives.
- To see the consequences for disobedience and obedience.

Andy Croft with Liza Hoeksma

A call to build the house of the LORD

1 In the second year of King Darius, on the first day of the sixth month, the word of the LORD came through the prophet Haggai to Zerubbabel son of Shealtiel, governor of Judah, and to Joshua son of Jozadak,ᵃ the high priest:

2 This is what the LORD Almighty says: 'These people say, "The time has not yet come to rebuild the LORD's house."'

3 Then the word of the LORD came through the prophet Haggai: **4** 'Is it a time for you yourselves to be living in your panelled houses, while this house remains a ruin?'

5 Now this is what the LORD Almighty says: 'Give careful thought to your ways. **6** You have planted much, but harvested little. You eat, but never have enough. You drink, but never have your fill. You put on clothes, but are not warm. You earn wages, only to put them in a purse with holes in it.'

7 This is what the LORD Almighty says: 'Give careful thought to your ways. **8** Go up into the mountains and bring down timber and build my house, so that I may take pleasure in it and be honoured,' says the LORD. **9** 'You expected much, but see, it turned out to be little. What you brought home, I blew away. Why?' declares the LORD Almighty. 'Because of my house, which remains a ruin, while each of you is busy with your own house. **10** Therefore, because of you the heavens have withheld their dew and the earth its crops. **11** I called for a drought on the fields and the mountains, on the grain, the new wine, the olive oil and everything else the ground produces, on people and livestock, and on all the labour of your hands.'

12 Then Zerubbabel son of Shealtiel, Joshua son of Jozadak, the high priest, and the whole remnant of the people obeyed the voice of the LORD their God and the message of the prophet Haggai, because the LORD their God had sent him. And the people feared the LORD.

13 Then Haggai, the LORD's messenger, gave this message of the LORD to the people: 'I am with you,' declares the LORD. **14** So the LORD stirred up the spirit of Zerubbabel son of Shealtiel, governor of Judah, and the spirit of Joshua son of Jozadak, the high priest, and the spirit of the whole remnant of the people. They came and began to work on the house of the LORD Almighty, their God, **15** on the twenty-fourth day of the sixth month.

The promised glory of the new house

2 In the second year of King Darius, **1** on the twenty-first day of the seventh month, the word of the LORD came through the prophet Haggai: **2** 'Speak to Zerubbabel son of Shealtiel, governor of Judah, to Joshua son of Jozadak,ᵃ the high priest, and to the remnant of the people. Ask them, **3** "Who of you is left who saw this house in its former glory? How does it look to you now? Does it not seem to you like nothing? **4** But now be strong, Zerubbabel," declares the LORD. "Be strong, Joshua son of Jozadak, the high priest. Be strong, all you people of the land," declares the LORD, "and work. For I am with you," declares the LORD Almighty. **5** "This is what I covenanted with you when you came out of Egypt. And my Spirit remains among you. Do not fear."

6 'This is what the LORD Almighty says: "In a little while I will once more shake the heavens and the earth, the sea and the dry land. **7** I will shake all nations, and what is desired by all nations will come, and I will fill this house with glory," says the LORD Almighty. **8** "The silver is mine and the gold is mine," declares the LORD Almighty. **9** "The glory of this present house will be greater than the glory of the former house," says the LORD Almighty. "And in this place I will grant peace," declares the LORD Almighty.'

Blessings for a defiled people

10 On the twenty-fourth day of the ninth month, in the second year of Darius, the

---

a 1 Hebrew *Jehozadak*, a variant of *Jozadak*; also in verses 12 and 14

a 2 Hebrew *Jehozadak*, a variant of *Jozadak*; also in verse 4 word of the LORD came to the prophet Haggai: 11 'This is what the LORD Almighty says: "Ask the priests what the law says: 12 if someone carries consecrated meat in the fold of their garment, and that fold touches some bread or stew, some wine, olive oil or other food, does it become consecrated?" '

The priests answered, 'No.'

13 Then Haggai said, 'If a person defiled by contact with a dead body touches one of these things, does it become defiled?'

'Yes,' the priests replied, 'it becomes defiled.'

14 Then Haggai said, ' "So it is with this people and this nation in my sight," declares the LORD. "Whatever they do and whatever they offer there is defiled.

15 ' "Now give careful thought to this from this day on[b] – consider how things were before one stone was laid on another in the LORD's temple. 16 When anyone came to a heap of twenty measures, there were only ten. When anyone went to a wine vat to draw fifty measures, there were only twenty. 17 I struck all the work of

b 15   Or *to the days past*

your hands with blight, mildew and hail, yet you did not return to me," declares the LORD. 18 "From this day on, from this twenty-fourth day of the ninth month, give careful thought to the day when the foundation of the LORD's temple was laid. Give careful thought: 19 is there yet any seed left in the barn? Until now, the vine and the fig-tree, the pomegranate and the olive tree have not borne fruit.

' "From this day on I will bless you." '

Zerubbabel the LORD's signet ring

20 The word of the LORD came to Haggai a second time on the twenty-fourth day of the month: 21 'Tell Zerubbabel governor of Judah that I am going to shake the heavens and the earth. 22 I will overturn royal thrones and shatter the power of the foreign kingdoms. I will overthrow chariots and their drivers; horses and their riders will fall, each by the sword of his brother.

23 ' "On that day," declares the LORD Almighty, "I will take you, my servant Zerubbabel son of Shealtiel," declares the LORD, "and I will make you like my signet ring, for I have chosen you," declares the LORD Almighty.'

ZECHARIAH

DATE

Zechariah delivered his message between 520 and 518 BC

AUTHOR

Traditionally attributed to Zechariah, though there may have been two authors

WHAT'S IT ALL ABOUT?

Like the prophet Haggai, Zechariah ministered at the time when the Jews were brought back to Jerusalem after their exile to Babylon. He too encouraged the people to resume their work to rebuild God's temple as the first step towards seeing God's kingdom coming on earth. While Haggai focused on the 'here and now', Zechariah pointed towards a time when there would be a 'new Jerusalem', which was key in keeping up the spirits of the people. They had returned to their land, which was a reason to rejoice, but only a few had made it back, the city was in ruins, and the temple that represented God's presence among his people was destroyed. Zechariah talked of his visions of a time of great glory for God's people, when Israel's enemies would fall and she would be restored just as God had promised.

The messages brought by Zechariah and Haggai must have struck a chord with the people, as they returned to their work of rebuilding the temple.

WHY SHOULD WE READ IT?

- To read the prophecies concerning Jesus.
- To see the importance of justice, mercy and compassion over religious rituals (Zechariah 7).
- To see that God never forgot his promises to his people, despite their disobedience and despite his punishments for their actions.

Andy Croft with Liza Hoeksma

A call to return to the LORD

1 In the eighth month of the second year of Darius, the word of the LORD came to the prophet Zechariah son of Berekiah, the son of Iddo:

2 'The LORD was very angry with your ancestors. **3** Therefore tell the people: this is what the LORD Almighty says: "Return to me," declares the LORD Almighty, "and I will return to you," says the LORD Almighty. **4** Do not be like your ancestors, to whom the earlier prophets proclaimed: this is what the LORD Almighty says: "Turn from your evil ways and your evil practices." But they would not listen or pay attention to me, declares the LORD. **5** Where are your ancestors now? And the prophets, do they live for ever? **6** But did not my words and my decrees, which I commanded my servants the prophets, overtake your ancestors?

'Then they repented and said, "The LORD Almighty has done to us what our ways and practices deserve, just as he determined to do."'

The man among the myrtle trees

7 On the twenty-fourth day of the eleventh month, the month of Shebat, in the second year of Darius, the word of the LORD came to the prophet Zechariah son of Berekiah, the son of Iddo.

8 During the night I had a vision, and there before me was a man mounted on a red horse. He was standing among the myrtle trees in a ravine. Behind him were red, brown and white horses.

9 I asked, 'What are these, my lord?'

The angel who was talking with me answered, 'I will show you what they are.'

10 Then the man standing among the myrtle trees explained, 'They are the ones the LORD has sent to go throughout the earth.'

11 And they reported to the angel of the LORD who was standing among the myrtle trees, 'We have gone throughout the earth and found the whole world at rest and in peace.'

12 Then the angel of the LORD said, 'LORD Almighty, how long will you withhold mercy from Jerusalem and from the towns of Judah, which you have been angry with these seventy years?' **13** So the LORD spoke kind and comforting words to the angel who talked with me.

14 Then the angel who was speaking to me said, 'Proclaim this word: this is what the LORD Almighty says: "I am very jealous for Jerusalem and Zion, **15** and I am very angry with the nations that feel secure. I was only a little angry, but they went too far with the punishment."

16 'Therefore this is what the LORD says: "I will return to Jerusalem with mercy, and there my house will be rebuilt. And the measuring line will be stretched out over Jerusalem," declares the LORD Almighty.

17 'Proclaim further: this is what the LORD Almighty says: "My towns will again overflow with prosperity, and the LORD will again comfort Zion and choose Jerusalem."'

Four horns and four craftsmen

18 Then I looked up, and there before me were four horns. **19** I asked the angel who was speaking to me, 'What are these?'

He answered me, 'These are the horns that scattered Judah, Israel and Jerusalem.'

20 Then the LORD showed me four craftsmen. **21** I asked, 'What are these coming to do?'

He answered, 'These are the horns that scattered Judah so that no one could raise their head, but the craftsmen have come to terrify them and throw down these horns of the nations who lifted up their horns against the land of Judah to scatter its people.'ᵃ

A man with a measuring line

2ᵃ Then I looked up, and there before me was a man with a measuring line in his hand. **2** I asked, 'Where are you going?'

He answered me, 'To measure Jerusalem, to find out how wide and how long it is.'

3 While the angel who was speaking to

---

a 21 In Hebrew texts 1:18-21 is numbered 2:1-4.
a In Hebrew texts 2:1-13 is numbered 2:5-17.

me was leaving, another angel came to meet him ⁴and said to him: 'Run, tell that young man, "Jerusalem will be a city without walls because of the great number of people and animals in it. ⁵And I myself will be a wall of fire around it," declares the LORD, "and I will be its glory within."

⁶'Come! Come! Flee from the land of the north,' declares the LORD, 'for I have scattered you to the four winds of heaven,' declares the LORD.

⁷'Come, Zion! Escape, you who live in Daughter Babylon!' ⁸For this is what the LORD Almighty says: 'After the Glorious One has sent me against the nations that have plundered you – for whoever touches you touches the apple of his eye – ⁹I will surely raise my hand against them so that their slaves will plunder them.ᵇ Then you will know that the LORD Almighty has sent me.

¹⁰'Shout and be glad, Daughter Zion. For I am coming, and I will live among you,' declares the LORD. ¹¹'Many nations will be joined with the LORD in that day and will become my people. I will live among you and you will know that the LORD Almighty has sent me to you. ¹²The LORD will inherit Judah as his portion in the holy land and will again choose Jerusalem. ¹³Be still before the LORD, all mankind, because he has roused himself from his holy dwelling.'

Clean garments for the high priest

3 Then he showed me Joshua the high priest standing before the angel of the LORD, and Satanᵃ standing at his right side to accuse him. ²The LORD said to Satan, 'The LORD rebuke you, Satan! The LORD, who has chosen Jerusalem, rebuke you! Is not this man a burning stick snatched from the fire?'

³Now Joshua was dressed in filthy clothes as he stood before the angel. ⁴The angel said to those who were standing before him, 'Take off his filthy clothes.'

Then he said to Joshua, 'See, I have taken away your sin, and I will put fine garments on you.'

⁵Then I said, 'Put a clean turban on his head.' So they put a clean turban on his head and clothed him, while the angel of the LORD stood by.

⁶The angel of the LORD gave this charge to Joshua: ⁷'This is what the LORD Almighty says: "If you will walk in obedience to me and keep my requirements, then you will govern my house and have charge of my courts, and I will give you a place among these standing here.

⁸'"Listen, High Priest Joshua, you and your associates seated before you, who are men symbolic of things to come: I am going to bring my servant, the Branch. ⁹See, the stone I have set in front of Joshua! There are seven eyesᵇ on that one stone, and I will engrave an inscription on it," says the LORD Almighty, "and I will remove the sin of this land in a single day.

¹⁰'"In that day each of you will invite your neighbour to sit under your vine and fig-tree," declares the LORD Almighty.'

The gold lampstand and the two olive trees

4 Then the angel who talked with me returned and woke me up, like someone awakened from sleep. ²He asked me, 'What do you see?'

I answered, 'I see a solid gold lampstand with a bowl at the top and seven lamps on it, with seven channels to the lamps. ³Also there are two olive trees by it, one on the right of the bowl and the other on its left.'

⁴I asked the angel who talked with me, 'What are these, my lord?'

⁵He answered, 'Do you not know what these are?'

'No, my lord,' I replied.

⁶So he said to me, 'This is the word of the LORD to Zerubbabel: "Not by might nor by power, but by my Spirit," says the LORD Almighty.

⁷'What are you, mighty mountain? Before Zerubbabel you will become level ground. Then he will bring out the

---

b 8,9 Or *says after... eye:* ⁹'I ... *plunder them.'*
a 1 Hebrew *satan* means *adversary.*

b 9 Or *facets*

capstone to shouts of "God bless it! God bless it!"'

8 Then the word of the Lord came to me: 9 'The hands of Zerubbabel have laid the foundation of this temple; his hands will also complete it. Then you will know that the Lord Almighty has sent me to you.

10 'Who dares despise the day of small things, since the seven eyes of the Lord that range throughout the earth will rejoice when they see the chosen capstone*a* in the hand of Zerubbabel?'

11 Then I asked the angel, 'What are these two olive trees on the right and the left of the lampstand?'

12 Again I asked him, 'What are these two olive branches beside the two gold pipes that pour out golden oil?'

13 He replied, 'Do you not know what these are?'

'No, my lord,' I said.

14 So he said, 'These are the two who are anointed to*b* serve the Lord of all the earth.'

The flying scroll

5 I looked again, and there before me was a flying scroll.

2 He asked me, 'What do you see?'

I answered, 'I see a flying scroll, twenty cubits long and ten cubits wide.'*a*

3 And he said to me, 'This is the curse that is going out over the whole land; for according to what it says on one side, every thief will be banished, and according to what it says on the other, everyone who swears falsely will be banished. 4 The Lord Almighty declares, "I will send it out, and it will enter the house of the thief and the house of anyone who swears falsely by my name. It will remain in that house and destroy it completely, both its timbers and its stones."'

The woman in a basket

5 Then the angel who was speaking to me came forward and said to me, 'Look up and see what is appearing.'

6 I asked, 'What is it?'

He replied, 'It is a basket.' And he added, 'This is the iniquity*b* of the people throughout the land.'

7 Then the cover of lead was raised, and there in the basket sat a woman! 8 He said, 'This is wickedness,' and he pushed her back into the basket and pushed its lead cover down on it.

9 Then I looked up – and there before me were two women, with the wind in their wings! They had wings like those of a stork, and they lifted up the basket between heaven and earth.

10 'Where are they taking the basket?' I asked the angel who was speaking to me.

11 He replied, 'To the country of Babylonia*c* to build a house for it. When the house is ready, the basket will be set there in its place.'

Four chariots

6 I looked up again, and there before me were four chariots coming out from between two mountains – mountains of bronze. 2 The first chariot had red horses, the second black, 3 the third white, and the fourth dappled – all of them powerful. 4 I asked the angel who was speaking to me, 'What are these, my lord?'

5 The angel answered me, 'These are the four spirits*a* of heaven, going out from standing in the presence of the Lord of the whole world. 6 The one with the black horses is going towards the north country, the one with the white horses towards the west,*b* and the one with the dappled horses towards the south.'

7 When the powerful horses went out, they were straining to go throughout the earth. And he said, 'Go throughout the earth!' So they went throughout the earth.

8 Then he called to me, 'Look, those going towards the north country have given my Spirit*c* rest in the land of the north.'

---

a 10 Or *the plumb-line*
b 14 Or *two who bring oil and*
a 2 That is, about 9 metres long and 4.5 metres wide

b 6 Or *appearance*
c 11 Hebrew *Shinar*
a 5 Or *winds*
b 6 Or *horses after them*
c 8 Or *spirit*

A crown for Joshua

9 The word of the LORD came to me: 10 'Take silver and gold from the exiles Heldai, Tobijah and Jedaiah, who have arrived from Babylon. Go the same day to the house of Josiah son of Zephaniah. 11 Take the silver and gold and make a crown, and set it on the head of the high priest, Joshua son of Jozadak.*d* 12 Tell him this is what the LORD Almighty says: "Here is the man whose name is the Branch, and he will branch out from his place and build the temple of the LORD. 13 It is he who will build the temple of the LORD, and he will be clothed with majesty and will sit and rule on his throne. And he*e* will be a priest on his throne. And there will be harmony between the two." 14 The crown will be given to Heldai,*f* Tobijah, Jedaiah and Hen*g* son of Zephaniah as a memorial in the temple of the LORD. 15 Those who are far away will come and help to build the temple of the LORD, and you will know that the LORD Almighty has sent me to you. This will happen if you diligently obey the LORD your God.'

Justice and mercy, not fasting

7 In the fourth year of King Darius, the word of the LORD came to Zechariah on the fourth day of the ninth month, the month of Kislev. 2 The people of Bethel had sent Sharezer and Regem-Melek, together with their men, to entreat the LORD 3 by asking the priests of the house of the LORD Almighty and the prophets, 'Should I mourn and fast in the fifth month, as I have done for so many years?'

4 Then the word of the LORD Almighty came to me: 5 'Ask all the people of the land and the priests, "When you fasted and mourned in the fifth and seventh months for the past seventy years, was it really for me that you fasted? 6 And when you were eating and drinking, were you not just feasting for yourselves? 7 Are these not the words the LORD proclaimed through the earlier prophets when Jerusalem and

its surrounding towns were at rest and prosperous, and the Negev and the western foothills were settled?" '

8 And the word of the LORD came again to Zechariah: 9 'This is what the LORD Almighty said: "Administer true justice; show mercy and compassion to one another. 10 Do not oppress the widow or the fatherless, the foreigner or the poor. Do not plot evil against each other."

11 'But they refused to pay attention; stubbornly they turned their backs and covered their ears. 12 They made their hearts as hard as flint and would not listen to the law or to the words that the LORD Almighty had sent by his Spirit through the earlier prophets. So the LORD Almighty was very angry.

13 ' "When I called, they did not listen; so when they called, I would not listen," says the LORD Almighty. 14 "I scattered them with a whirlwind among all the nations, where they were strangers. The land they left behind them was so desolate that no one travelled through it. This is how they made the pleasant land desolate." '

The LORD promises to bless Jerusalem

8 The word of the LORD Almighty came to me.

2 This is what the LORD Almighty says: 'I am very jealous for Zion; I am burning with jealousy for her.'

3 This is what the LORD says: 'I will return to Zion and dwell in Jerusalem. Then Jerusalem will be called the Faithful City, and the mountain of the LORD Almighty will be called the Holy Mountain.'

4 This is what the LORD Almighty says: 'Once again men and women of ripe old age will sit in the streets of Jerusalem, each of them with cane in hand because of their age. 5 The city streets will be filled with boys and girls playing there.'

6 This is what the LORD Almighty says: 'It may seem marvellous to the remnant of this people at that time, but will it seem marvellous to me?' declares the LORD Almighty.

7 This is what the LORD Almighty says: 'I will save my people from the countries of the east and the west. 8 I will bring them

---

d 11 Hebrew *Jehozadak*, a variant of *Jozadak*
e 13 Or *there*
f 14 Syriac; Hebrew *Helem*
g 14 Or *and the gracious one, the*

back to live in Jerusalem; they will be my people, and I will be faithful and righteous to them as their God.'

9 This is what the LORD Almighty says: 'Now hear these words, "Let your hands be strong so that the temple may be built." This is also what the prophets said who were present when the foundation was laid for the house of the LORD Almighty. 10 Before that time there were no wages for people or hire for animals. No one could go about their business safely because of their enemies, since I had turned everyone against their neighbour. 11 But now I will not deal with the remnant of this people as I did in the past,' declares the LORD Almighty.

12 'The seed will grow well, the vine will yield its fruit, the ground will produce its crops, and the heavens will drop their dew. I will give all these things as an inheritance to the remnant of this people. 13 Just as you, Judah and Israel, have been a curse*a* among the nations, so I will save you, and you will be a blessing.*b* Do not be afraid, but let your hands be strong.'

14 This is what the LORD Almighty says: 'Just as I had determined to bring disaster on you and showed no pity when your ancestors angered me,' says the LORD Almighty, 15 'so now I have determined to do good again to Jerusalem and Judah. Do not be afraid. 16 These are the things you are to do: Speak the truth to each other, and render true and sound judgment in your courts; 17 do not plot evil against each other, and do not love to swear falsely. I hate all this,' declares the LORD.

18 The word of the LORD Almighty came to me. 19 This is what the LORD Almighty says: 'The fasts of the fourth, fifth, seventh and tenth months will become joyful and glad occasions and happy festivals for Judah. Therefore love truth and peace.'

20 This is what the LORD Almighty says: 'Many peoples and the inhabitants of many cities will yet come, 21 and the inhabitants of one city will go to another and say, "Let us go at once to entreat the LORD and seek the LORD Almighty. I myself am going." 22 And many peoples and powerful nations will come to Jerusalem to seek the LORD Almighty and to entreat him.'

23 This is what the LORD Almighty says: 'In those days ten people from all languages and nations will take firm hold of one Jew by the hem of his robe and say, "Let us go with you, because we have heard that God is with you."'

Judgment on Israel's enemies

9

A prophecy:

The word of the LORD is against the land
　　of Hadrak
　　and will come to rest on Damascus –
for the eyes of all people and all the
　　tribes of Israel
　　are on the LORD – *a*
2 and on Hamath too, which borders
　　on it,
　　and on Tyre and Sidon, though they
　　are very skilful.
3 Tyre has built herself a stronghold;
　　she has heaped up silver like dust,
　　and gold like the dirt of the streets.
4 But the Lord will take away her
　　possessions
　　and destroy her power on the sea,
　　and she will be consumed by fire.
5 Ashkelon will see it and fear;
　　Gaza will writhe in agony,
　　and Ekron too, for her hope will
　　wither.
Gaza will lose her king
　　and Ashkelon will be deserted.
6 A mongrel people will occupy Ashdod,
　　and I will put an end to the pride of
　　the Philistines.
7 I will take the blood from their
　　mouths,
　　the forbidden food from between
　　their teeth.

---

a 13 That is, your name has been used in cursing (see Jer. 29:23); or, you have been regarded as under a curse.

b 13 Or *and your name will be used in blessings* (see Gen. 48:20); or *and you will be seen as blessed*

---

a 1 Or *Damascus. / For the eye of the LORD is on all people, / as well as on the tribes of Israel,*

Those who are left will belong to our
God
and become a clan in Judah,
and Ekron will be like the Jebusites.
⁸ But I will encamp at my temple
to guard it against marauding forces.
Never again will an oppressor overrun
my people,
for now I am keeping watch.

The coming of Zion's king

⁹ Rejoice greatly, Daughter Zion!
Shout, Daughter Jerusalem!
See, your king comes to you,
righteous and victorious,
lowly and riding on a donkey,
on a colt, the foal of a donkey.
¹⁰ I will take away the chariots from
Ephraim
and the war-horses from Jerusalem,
and the battle-bow will be broken.
He will proclaim peace to the nations.
His rule will extend from sea to sea
and from the River[b] to the ends of
the earth.
¹¹ As for you, because of the blood of my
covenant with you,
I will free your prisoners from the
waterless pit.
¹² Return to your fortress, you prisoners
of hope;
even now I announce that I will
restore twice as much to you.
¹³ I will bend Judah as I bend my bow
and fill it with Ephraim.
I will rouse your sons, Zion,
against your sons, Greece,
and make you like a warrior's sword.

The LORD will appear

¹⁴ Then the LORD will appear over them;
his arrow will flash like lightning.
The Sovereign LORD will sound the
trumpet;
he will march in the storms of the
south,
¹⁵ and the LORD Almighty will shield
them.
They will destroy
and overcome with slingstones.

They will drink and roar as with wine;
they will be full like a bowl
used for sprinkling[c] the corners of
the altar.
¹⁶ The LORD their God will save his people
on that day
as a shepherd saves his flock.
They will sparkle in his land
like jewels in a crown.
¹⁷ How attractive and beautiful they
will be!
Grain will make the young men
thrive,
and new wine the young women.

FACT

CHAPTER AND VERSE

The Bible wasn't written in chapters and
verses. The chapter system was introduced
around AD 1230, and the verses were only
added in 1551 by Robertus Stephanus, after
the advent of printing.

The LORD will care for Judah

10 Ask the LORD for rain in the
springtime;
it is the LORD who sends the
thunderstorms.
He gives showers of rain to all people,
and plants of the field to everyone.
² The idols speak deceitfully,
diviners see visions that lie;
they tell dreams that are false,
they give comfort in vain.
Therefore the people wander like sheep
oppressed for lack of a shepherd.

³ 'My anger burns against the shepherds,
and I will punish the leaders;
for the LORD Almighty will care
for his flock, the people of Judah,

---

b 10 That is, the Euphrates   **c** 15 Or *bowl,* / *like*

and make them like a proud horse in battle.
⁴ From Judah will come the cornerstone,
   from him the tent peg,
from him the battle-bow,
   from him every ruler.
⁵ Together theyᵃ will be like warriors in battle
   trampling their enemy into the mud of the streets.
They will fight because the LORD is with them,
   and they will put the enemy horsemen to shame.

⁶ 'I will strengthen Judah
   and save the tribes of Joseph.
I will restore them
   because I have compassion on them.
They will be as though
   I had not rejected them,
for I am the LORD their God
   and I will answer them.
⁷ The Ephraimites will become like warriors,
   and their hearts will be glad as with wine.
Their children will see it and be joyful;
   their hearts will rejoice in the LORD.
⁸ I will signal for them
   and gather them in.
Surely I will redeem them;
   they will be as numerous as before.
⁹ Though I scatter them among the peoples,
   yet in distant lands they will remember me.
They and their children will survive,
   and they will return.
¹⁰ I will bring them back from Egypt
   and gather them from Assyria.
I will bring them to Gilead and Lebanon,
   and there will not be room enough for them.
¹¹ They will pass through the sea of trouble;
   the surging sea will be subdued
   and all the depths of the Nile will dry up.

Assyria's pride will be brought down
   and Egypt's sceptre will pass away.
¹² I will strengthen them in the LORD
   and in his name they will live securely,'

                     declares the LORD.

11 Open your doors, Lebanon,
   so that fire may devour your cedars!
² Wail, you juniper, for the cedar has fallen;
   the stately trees are ruined!
Wail, oaks of Bashan;
   the dense forest has been cut down!
³ Listen to the wail of the shepherds:
   their rich pastures are destroyed!
Listen to the roar of the lions;
   the lush thicket of the Jordan is ruined!

Two shepherds

⁴ This is what the LORD my God says: 'Shepherd the flock marked for slaughter. ⁵ Their buyers slaughter them and go unpunished. Those who sell them say, "Praise the LORD, I am rich!" Their own shepherds do not spare them. ⁶ For I will no longer have pity on the people of the land,' declares the LORD. 'I will give everyone into the hands of their neighbours and their king. They will devastate the land, and I will not rescue anyone from their hands.'

⁷ So I shepherded the flock marked for slaughter, particularly the oppressed of the flock. Then I took two staffs and called one Favour and the other Union, and I shepherded the flock. ⁸ In one month I got rid of the three shepherds.

The flock detested me, and I grew weary of them ⁹ and said, 'I will not be your shepherd. Let the dying die, and the perishing perish. Let those who are left eat one another's flesh.'

¹⁰ Then I took my staff called Favour and broke it, revoking the covenant I had made with all the nations. ¹¹ It was revoked on that day, and so the oppressed of the flock who were watching me knew it was the word of the LORD.

¹² I told them, 'If you think it best, give

ᵃ 4,5 Or ruler, all of them together. / ⁵ They

me my pay; but if not, keep it.' So they paid me thirty pieces of silver.

¹³ And the Lord said to me, 'Throw it to the potter' – the handsome price at which they valued me! So I took the thirty pieces of silver and threw them to the potter at the house of the Lord.

¹⁴ Then I broke my second staff called Union, breaking the family bond between Judah and Israel.

¹⁵ Then the Lord said to me, 'Take again the equipment of a foolish shepherd. ¹⁶ For I am going to raise up a shepherd over the land who will not care for the lost, or seek the young, or heal the injured, or feed the healthy, but will eat the meat of the choice sheep, tearing off their hooves.

¹⁷ 'Woe to the worthless shepherd,
    who deserts the flock!
May the sword strike his arm and his
    right eye!
May his arm be completely withered,
    his right eye totally blinded!'

Jerusalem's enemies to be destroyed

12 A prophecy: the word of the Lord concerning Israel.

The Lord, who stretches out the heavens, who lays the foundation of the earth, and who forms the human spirit within a person, declares: ² 'I am going to make Jerusalem a cup that sends all the surrounding peoples reeling. Judah will be besieged as well as Jerusalem. ³ On that day, when all the nations of the earth are gathered against her, I will make Jerusalem an immovable rock for all the nations. All who try to move it will injure themselves. ⁴ On that day I will strike every horse with panic and its rider with madness,' declares the Lord. 'I will keep a watchful eye over Judah, but I will blind all the horses of the nations. ⁵ Then the clans of Judah will say in their hearts, "The people of Jerusalem are strong, because the Lord Almighty is their God."

⁶ 'On that day I will make the clans of Judah like a brazier in a woodpile, like a flaming torch among sheaves. They will consume all the surrounding peoples right and left, but Jerusalem will remain intact in her place.

⁷ 'The Lord will save the dwellings of Judah first, so that the honour of the house of David and of Jerusalem's inhabitants may not be greater than that of Judah. ⁸ On that day the Lord will shield those who live in Jerusalem, so that the feeblest among them will be like David, and the house of David will be like God, like the angel of the Lord going before them. ⁹ On that day I will set out to destroy all the nations that attack Jerusalem.

Mourning for the one they pierced

¹⁰ 'And I will pour out on the house of David and the inhabitants of Jerusalem a spirit*ᵃ* of grace and supplication. They will look on*ᵇ* me, the one they have pierced, and they will mourn for him as one mourns for an only child, and grieve bitterly for him as one grieves for a firstborn son. ¹¹ On that day the weeping in Jerusalem will be as great as the weeping of Hadad Rimmon in the plain of Megiddo. ¹² The land will mourn, each clan by itself, with their wives by themselves: the clan of the house of David and their wives, the clan of the house of Nathan and their wives, ¹³ the clan of the house of Levi and their wives, the clan of Shimei and their wives, ¹⁴ and all the rest of the clans and their wives.

Cleansing from sin

13 'On that day a fountain will be opened to the house of David and the inhabitants of Jerusalem, to cleanse them from sin and impurity.

² 'On that day, I will banish the names of the idols from the land, and they will be remembered no more,' declares the Lord Almighty. 'I will remove both the prophets and the spirit of impurity from the land. ³ And if anyone still prophesies, their father and mother, to whom they were born, will say to them, "You must die, because you have told lies in the

---

a 10 Or *the Spirit*
b 10 Or *to*

LORD's name." Then their own parents will stab the one who prophesies.

4 'On that day every prophet will be ashamed of their prophetic vision. They will not put on a prophet's garment of hair in order to deceive. 5 Each will say, "I am not a prophet. I am a farmer; the land has been my livelihood since my youth.*a*" 6 If someone asks, "What are these wounds on your body?"*b* they will answer, "The wounds I was given at the house of my friends."

The shepherd struck, the sheep scattered

7 'Awake, sword, against my shepherd,
   against the man who is close to me!'
   declares the LORD Almighty.
'Strike the shepherd,
   and the sheep will be scattered,
   and I will turn my hand against the
      little ones.
8 In the whole land,' declares the LORD,
   'two-thirds will be struck down and
      perish;
   yet one-third will be left in it.
9 This third I will put into the fire;
   I will refine them like silver
   and test them like gold.
They will call on my name
   and I will answer them;
I will say, "They are my people,"
   and they will say, "The LORD is our
      God."'

The LORD comes and reigns

14 A day of the LORD is coming, Jerusalem, when your possessions will be plundered and divided up within your very walls.

2 I will gather all the nations to Jerusalem to fight against it; the city will be captured, the houses ransacked, and the women raped. Half of the city will go into exile, but the rest of the people will not be taken from the city. 3 Then the LORD will go out and fight against those nations, as he fights on a day of battle. 4 On that day his feet will stand on the Mount of Olives, east of Jerusalem, and the Mount of Olives will be split in two from east to west, forming a great valley, with half of the mountain moving north and half moving south. 5 You will flee by my mountain valley, for it will extend to Azel. You will flee as you fled from the earthquake*a* in the days of Uzziah king of Judah. Then the LORD my God will come, and all the holy ones with him.

6 On that day there will be neither sunlight nor cold, frosty darkness. 7 It will be a unique day — a day known only to the LORD — with no distinction between day and night. When evening comes, there will be light.

8 On that day living water will flow out from Jerusalem, half of it east to the Dead Sea and half of it west to the Mediterranean Sea, in summer and in winter.

9 The LORD will be king over the whole earth. On that day there will be one LORD, and his name the only name.

10 The whole land, from Geba to Rimmon, south of Jerusalem, will become like the Arabah. But Jerusalem will be raised up high from the Benjamin Gate to the site of the First Gate, to the Corner Gate, and from the Tower of Hananel to the royal winepresses, and will remain in its place. 11 It will be inhabited; never again will it be destroyed. Jerusalem will be secure.

12 This is the plague with which the LORD will strike all the nations that fought against Jerusalem: their flesh will rot while they are still standing on their feet, their eyes will rot in their sockets, and their tongues will rot in their mouths. 13 On that day people will be stricken by the LORD with great panic. They will seize each other by the hand and attack one another. 14 Judah too will fight at Jerusalem. The wealth of all the surrounding nations will be collected — great quantities of gold and silver and clothing. 15 A similar plague will strike the horses and mules, the camels and donkeys, and all the animals in those camps.

---

a 5 Or *farmer; a man sold me in my youth*
b 6 Or *wounds between your hands*

a 5 Or *5My mountain valley will be blocked and will extend to Azel. It will be blocked as it was blocked because of the earthquake*

¹⁶Then the survivors from all the nations that have attacked Jerusalem will go up year after year to worship the King, the LORD Almighty, and to celebrate the Festival of Tabernacles. ¹⁷If any of the peoples of the earth do not go up to Jerusalem to worship the King, the LORD Almighty, they will have no rain. ¹⁸If the Egyptian people do not go up and take part, they will have no rain. The LORD^b will bring on them the plague he inflicts on the nations that do not go up to celebrate the Festival of Tabernacles. ¹⁹This will be the punishment of Egypt and the punishment of all the nations that do not go up to celebrate the Festival of Tabernacles.

²⁰On that day HOLY TO THE LORD will be inscribed on the bells of the horses, and the cooking pots in the LORD's house will be like the sacred bowls in front of the altar. ²¹Every pot in Jerusalem and Judah will be holy to the LORD Almighty, and all who come to sacrifice will take some of the pots and cook in them. And on that day there will no longer be a Canaanite^c in the house of the LORD Almighty.

---

b 18 Or *part, then the* LORD

c 21 Or *merchant*

MALACHI

DATE

This book is dated around 460–430 BC

AUTHOR

Malachi

WHAT'S IT ALL ABOUT?

Malachi was the last of the twelve Minor Prophets and after him there was no word from God for four hundred years (the time between the Old and New Testaments). He prophesied about eighty years after Haggai and Zechariah, who had encouraged the returned exiles to rebuild God's temple. The temple had been rebuilt, but it wasn't comparable with the original splendour of Solomon's temple. The people longed for the prosperity that God had promised them, but they hadn't yet seen it. Somewhere along the line, their hearts had become distanced from God. The people had lowered their standards and were bringing injured and diseased animals to sacrifice to God. They weren't giving God their best any more, but were going through the motions with animals which were no good to them anyway. The priests were doing their basic duties, but their hearts weren't turned towards God. In short, the people weren't giving God all that he deserved. Malachi brought God's word that they should honour God and then, during the time of judgement, they would receive their reward.

WHY SHOULD WE READ IT?

- As a reminder that we should always give God the honour that he deserves. He is worthy of our full devotion.

- To read the prophecy concerning John the Baptist (Malachi 3).

- To see how God's love for his people was unchanging despite their lukewarm hearts.

- To read God's promise to look after his people if they gave their tithes as they should (the tithes were for the upkeep of the temple and to look after the ministers who served in God's house; see Malachi 3). This is a great principle for us to remember today.

Andy Croft with Liza Hoeksma

1
A prophecy: the word of the LORD to Israel through Malachi.*a*

Israel doubts God's love

2 'I have loved you,' says the LORD.

'But you ask, "How have you loved us?" 'Was not Esau Jacob's brother?' declares the LORD. 'Yet I have loved Jacob, 3 but Esau I have hated, and I have turned his hill country into a wasteland and left his inheritance to the desert jackals.'

4 Edom may say, 'Though we have been crushed, we will rebuild the ruins.'

But this is what the LORD Almighty says: 'They may build, but I will demolish. They will be called the Wicked Land, a people always under the wrath of the LORD. 5 You will see it with your own eyes and say, "Great is the LORD – even beyond the borders of Israel!"

Breaking covenant through blemished sacrifices

6 'A son honours his father, and a slave his master. If I am a father, where is the honour due to me? If I am a master, where is the respect due to me?' says the LORD Almighty.

'It is you priests who show contempt for my name.

'But you ask, "How have we shown contempt for your name?"

7 'By offering defiled food on my altar.

'But you ask, "How have we defiled you?"

'By saying that the LORD's table is contemptible. 8 When you offer blind animals for sacrifice, is that not wrong? When you sacrifice lame or diseased animals, is that not wrong? Try offering them to your governor! Would he be pleased with you? Would he accept you?' says the LORD Almighty.

9 'Now plead with God to be gracious to us. With such offerings from your hands, will he accept you?' – says the LORD Almighty.

10 'Oh, that one of you would shut the temple doors, so that you would not light useless fires on my altar! I am not pleased

with you,' says the LORD Almighty, 'and I will accept no offering from your hands. 11 My name will be great among the nations, from where the sun rises to where it sets. In every place incense and pure offerings will be brought to me, because my name will be great among the nations,' says the LORD Almighty.

12 'But you profane it by saying, "The Lord's table is defiled," and, "Its food is contemptible." 13 And you say, "What a burden!" and you sniff at it contemptuously,' says the LORD Almighty.

'When you bring injured, lame or diseased animals and offer them as sacrifices, should I accept them from your hands?' says the LORD. 14 'Cursed is the cheat who has an acceptable male in his flock and vows to give it, but then sacrifices a blemished animal to the Lord. For I am a great king,' says the LORD Almighty, 'and my name is to be feared among the nations.

Additional warning to the priests

2
'And now, you priests, this warning is for you. 2 If you do not listen, and if you do not resolve to honour my name,' says the LORD Almighty, 'I will send a curse on you, and I will curse your blessings. Yes, I have already cursed them, because you have not resolved to honour me.

3 'Because of you I will rebuke your descendants*a*; I will smear on your faces the dung from your festival sacrifices, and you will be carried off with it. 4 And you will know that I have sent you this warning so that my covenant with Levi may continue,' says the LORD Almighty. 5 'My covenant was with him, a covenant of life and peace, and I gave them to him; this called for reverence and he revered me and stood in awe of my name. 6 True instruction was in his mouth and nothing false was found on his lips. He walked with me in peace and uprightness, and turned many from sin.

7 'For the lips of a priest ought to preserve knowledge, because he is the messenger of the LORD Almighty and people

---

a 1 Malachi means *my messenger.*   *a* 3 Or *will blight your corn* seek instruction from his mouth. ⁸But you have turned from the way and by your teaching have caused many to stumble; you have violated the covenant with Levi,' says the LORD Almighty. ⁹'So I have caused you to be despised and humiliated before all the people, because you have not followed my ways but have shown partiality in matters of the law.'

Breaking covenant through divorce

¹⁰Do we not all have one Father?ᵇ Did not one God create us? Why do we profane the covenant of our ancestors by being unfaithful to one another?

¹¹Judah has been unfaithful. A detestable thing has been committed in Israel and in Jerusalem: Judah has desecrated the sanctuary the LORD loves by marrying women who worship a foreign god. ¹²As for the man who does this, whoever he may be, may the LORD remove him from the tents of Jacobᶜ – even though he brings an offering to the LORD Almighty.

¹³Another thing you do: you flood the LORD's altar with tears. You weep and wail because he no longer looks with favour on your offerings or accepts them with pleasure from your hands. ¹⁴You ask, 'Why?' It is because the LORD is the witness between you and the wife of your youth. You have been unfaithful to her, though she is your partner, the wife of your marriage covenant.

¹⁵Has not the one God made you? You belong to him in body and spirit. And what does the one God seek? Godly offspring.ᵈ So be on your guard, and do not be unfaithful to the wife of your youth.

¹⁶'The man who hates and divorces his wife,' says the LORD, the God of Israel, 'does violence to the one he should protect,'ᵉ says the LORD Almighty.

ᵇ 10 Or *father*

ᶜ 12 Or *¹²May the LORD remove from the tents of Jacob anyone who gives testimony on behalf of the man who does this*

ᵈ 15 The meaning of the Hebrew for the first part of this verse is uncertain.

ᵉ 16 Or *'I hate divorce,' says the LORD, the God of Israel, 'because the man who divorces his wife covers his garment with violence,'*

So be on your guard, and do not be unfaithful.

Breaking covenant through injustice

¹⁷You have wearied the LORD with your words.

'How have we wearied him?' you ask.

By saying, 'All who do evil are good in the eyes of the LORD, and he is pleased with them' or 'Where is the God of justice?'

FAVOURITE VERSES

Proverbs 3:5–6

Trust in the LORD with all your heart
    and lean not on your own
        understanding;
in all your ways submit to him,
    and he will make your paths
        straight.

It's one of those verses everyone quotes quickly ... but if we check out *every* word slowly and we do all the bits we're meant to do, then God promises to do his bit and we'll stay on track.

Jayne

3 'I will send my messenger, who will prepare the way before me. Then suddenly the Lord you are seeking will come to his temple; the messenger of the covenant, whom you desire, will come,' says the LORD Almighty.

²But who can endure the day of his coming? Who can stand when he appears? For he will be like a refiner's fire or a launderer's soap. ³He will sit as a refiner and purifier of silver; he will purify the Levites and refine them like gold and silver. Then the LORD will have men who will bring offerings in righteousness, ⁴and the offerings of Judah and Jerusalem will

be acceptable to the Lord, as in days gone by, as in former years.

⁵ 'So I will come to put you on trial. I will be quick to testify against sorcerers, adulterers and perjurers, against those who defraud labourers of their wages, who oppress the widows and the fatherless, and deprive the foreigners among you of justice, but do not fear me,' says the Lord Almighty.

Breaking covenant by withholding tithes

⁶ 'I the Lord do not change. So you, the descendants of Jacob, are not destroyed. ⁷ Ever since the time of your ancestors you have turned away from my decrees and have not kept them. Return to me, and I will return to you,' says the Lord Almighty.

'But you ask, "How are we to return?"

⁸ 'Will a mere mortal rob God? Yet you rob me.

'But you ask, "How are we robbing you?"

'In tithes and offerings. ⁹ You are under a curse – your whole nation – because you are robbing me. ¹⁰ Bring the whole tithe into the storehouse, that there may be food in my house. Test me in this,' says the Lord Almighty, 'and see if I will not throw open the floodgates of heaven and pour out so much blessing that there will not be room enough to store it. ¹¹ I will prevent pests from devouring your crops, and the vines in your fields will not drop their fruit before it is ripe,' says the Lord Almighty. ¹² 'Then all the nations will call you blessed, for yours will be a delightful land,' says the Lord Almighty.

Israel speaks arrogantly against God

¹³ 'You have spoken arrogantly against me,' says the Lord.

'Yet you ask, "What have we said against you?"

¹⁴ 'You have said, "It is futile to serve God. What do we gain by carrying out his requirements and going about like

mourners before the Lord Almighty? ¹⁵ But now we call the arrogant blessed. Certainly evildoers prosper, and even when they put God to the test, they get away with it." '

The faithful remnant

¹⁶ Then those who feared the Lord talked with each other, and the Lord listened and heard. A scroll of remembrance was written in his presence concerning those who feared the Lord and honoured his name.

¹⁷ 'On the day when I act,' says the Lord Almighty, 'they will be my treasured possession. I will spare them, just as a father has compassion and spares his son who serves him. ¹⁸ And you will again see the distinction between the righteous and the wicked, between those who serve God and those who do not.

Judgment and covenant renewal

4 *ᵃ* 'Surely the day is coming; it will burn like a furnace. All the arrogant and every evildoer will be stubble, and that day that is coming will set them on fire,' says the Lord Almighty. 'Not a root or a branch will be left to them. ² But for you who revere my name, the sun of righteousness will rise with healing in its rays. And you will go out and frolic like well-fed calves. ³ Then you will trample on the wicked; they will be ashes under the soles of your feet on the day when I act,' says the Lord Almighty.

⁴ 'Remember the law of my servant Moses, the decrees and laws I gave him at Horeb for all Israel.

⁵ 'See, I will send the prophet Elijah to you before that great and dreadful day of the Lord comes. ⁶ He will turn the hearts of the parents to their children, and the hearts of the children to their parents; or else I will come and strike the land with total destruction.'

---

a In Hebrew texts 4:1-6 is numbered 3:19-24.

THE NEW TESTAMENT

THE NEW TESTAMENT

MATTHEW

DATE

Matthew focuses on events between Jesus' birth (when time begins to be measured as AD instead of BC) and his death 33 years later

AUTHOR

Traditionally attributed to Matthew, one of the twelve disciples

WHAT'S IT ALL ABOUT?

Matthew is one of the four Gospels which tell the story of the birth, life, death and resurrection of Jesus. It's similar in style and content to the Gospels of Mark and Luke and the three are known as the 'Synoptic Gospels', though each has a slightly different perspective. Matthew focuses on Jesus' teaching, with about two thirds of the book devoted to the things Jesus said. He includes five talks Jesus gave, the most famous being the Sermon on the Mount (Matthew 5 – 7). Matthew was a Jewish tax-collector, so he wrote for a Jewish audience. He takes care to show how Jesus is the Messiah prophesied about in the Old Testament (starting with his family history, to show he was born from the line of Abraham and King David), quoting more of the Old Testament than any of the other Gospel writers. Matthew is desperate for his readers to see that even though Jesus might not have behaved how they imagined their Messiah would act, he was in fact God in human form and the fulfilment of all God's promises concerning their Saviour.

WHY SHOULD WE READ THE GOSPELS?

- Because this is where we meet Jesus! By reading about his life and what he said and did, we develop our relationship with him and our understanding of who he is. Relationship is key to the Christian life. Christianity is about a person, not a set of ideas. Jesus is the central figure of the whole of history and it's through him that we make sense of life and the Bible. The whole Bible is a witness to Jesus, but the four Gospels are the books that uniquely tell us about his time on earth.

- To understand the events that led to Jesus being killed on a cross like a criminal, even though he had done nothing wrong.

- To see that Jesus was separated from his Father on the cross, taking on himself the punishment we deserve, so that we might become pure in God's eyes.

- To read how Jesus overcame death and rose from the grave, giving us eternal life.

- To read Jesus' teaching on how we should live, including how to treat our enemies, how to pray, not judging people, handling money, having humility, finding faith and dealing with worry.

- To see the miraculous things Jesus did, from the feeding of the five thousand to walking on water, and from giving blind people their sight to raising the dead.

WHY SHOULD WE READ MATTHEW'S GOSPEL?

- Because there are certain events and pieces of teaching that are only recorded in Matthew:

  o God warning Joseph in a dream to take his new-born son (Jesus) home from Bethlehem via Egypt to escape King Herod, who wanted to kill him;

  o King Herod's massacre of all boys under the age of two in order to try to kill Jesus;

  o the Magi visiting Jesus;

  o the death of Judas;

  o the parables of the pearl, the talents and the workers in the vineyard.

- To read the greatest commandment (Matthew 22) and the Great Commission (Matthew 28).

Andy Croft with Liza Hoeksma

The genealogy of Jesus the Messiah

1 This is the genealogy[a] of Jesus the Messiah[b] the son of David, the son of Abraham:

2 Abraham was the father of Isaac,
Isaac the father of Jacob,
Jacob the father of Judah and his brothers,
3 Judah the father of Perez and Zerah, whose mother was Tamar,
Perez the father of Hezron,
Hezron the father of Ram,
4 Ram the father of Amminadab,
Amminadab the father of Nahshon,
Nahshon the father of Salmon,
5 Salmon the father of Boaz, whose mother was Rahab,
Boaz the father of Obed, whose mother was Ruth,
Obed the father of Jesse,
6 and Jesse the father of King David.

David was the father of Solomon, whose mother had been Uriah's wife,
7 Solomon the father of Rehoboam,
Rehoboam the father of Abijah,
Abijah the father of Asa,
8 Asa the father of Jehoshaphat,
Jehoshaphat the father of Jehoram,
Jehoram the father of Uzziah,
9 Uzziah the father of Jotham,
Jotham the father of Ahaz,
Ahaz the father of Hezekiah,
10 Hezekiah the father of Manasseh,
Manasseh the father of Amon,
Amon the father of Josiah,
11 and Josiah the father of Jeconiah[c] and his brothers at the time of the exile to Babylon.

12 After the exile to Babylon:
Jeconiah was the father of Shealtiel,
Shealtiel the father of Zerubbabel,
13 Zerubbabel the father of Abihud,
Abihud the father of Eliakim,
Eliakim the father of Azor,
14 Azor the father of Zadok,
Zadok the father of Akim,
Akim the father of Elihud,
15 Elihud the father of Eleazar,
Eleazar the father of Matthan,
Matthan the father of Jacob,
16 and Jacob the father of Joseph, the husband of Mary, and Mary was the mother of Jesus who is called the Messiah.

17 Thus there were fourteen generations in all from Abraham to David, fourteen from David to the exile to Babylon, and fourteen from the exile to the Messiah.

Joseph accepts Jesus as his son

18 This is how the birth of Jesus the Messiah came about[d]: his mother Mary was pledged to be married to Joseph, but before they came together, she was found to be pregnant through the Holy Spirit. 19 Because Joseph her husband was faithful to the law, and yet[e] did not want to expose her to public disgrace, he had in mind to divorce her quietly.

20 But after he had considered this, an angel of the Lord appeared to him in a dream and said, 'Joseph son of David, do not be afraid to take Mary home as your wife, because what is conceived in her is from the Holy Spirit. 21 She will give birth to a son, and you are to give him the name Jesus,[f] because he will save his people from their sins.'

22 All this took place to fulfil what the Lord had said through the prophet: 23 'The virgin will conceive and give birth to a son, and they will call him Immanuel'[g] (which means 'God with us').

---

a 1 Or is an account of the origin
b 1 Or Jesus Christ. Messiah (Hebrew) and Christ (Greek) both mean Anointed One; also in verse 18.
c 11 That is, Jehoiachin; also in verse 12
d 18 Or The origin of Jesus the Messiah was like this
e 19 Or was a righteous man and
f 21 Jesus is the Greek form of Joshua, which means the LORD saves.
g 23 Isaiah 7:14

LIFE OF JESUS 1

God's greatest promise

As a young child, did you ever go with your mother and father to some crowded place and, after tearing yourself away, find yourself lost and heading into trouble?

According to the Bible, that's what the human race has done. What we could call the 'Great Separation' is a fundamental theme of Scripture and can be traced from the very first to the very last page of the Bible. As the first three chapters of Genesis point out, *'in the beginning'* we were created to be with God. We were made *'in his own image'* (Genesis 1:26–27) so that we could relate to God. Yet in the third chapter of Genesis we read that our distant ancestors disobeyed God and, as a result, the relationship between humankind and God disintegrated. Adam and Eve then hid from God and were expelled from the Garden of Eden where they had lived in fellowship with God. The vast and tragic theme of separation from God dominates human history. To be separated from God is the most serious thing in life. Because God is the source of all wisdom, power and good, if we are with him we can benefit from who he is. Not being with him, we will lack what we need.

The plot of the Old Testament can be summarised as the outworking of God's plan to restore fellowship between human beings and God. So we see God allowing himself to take up temporary residence with human beings at the heart of the sacred tent complex of the tabernacle and then the awesome building of the temple. Yet the localised presence of God was never enough. God was still distant: not everyone could get to the temple, and even there only a few high priests could actually come into his awesome presence.

Then, two thousand years ago, a child was conceived in miraculous circumstances and an old prophecy (Isaiah 7:14) was revived and its meaning made more intense. The infant would be called Immanuel, *'God with us'* (Matthew 1:22–23). It's an astonishing prophecy: God *in person* is going to come and live once more with human beings. It's a theme that's picked up at the end of Matthew's Gospel where Jesus makes the extraordinary prophecy, *'I am with you always, to the very end of the age'* (Matthew 28:20). It's a theme that will be fulfilled completely in heaven, and at the very end of the Bible (Revelation 21:3) we read, *'And I heard a loud voice from the throne saying, "Look! God's dwelling-place is now among the people, and he will dwell with them. They will be his people, and God himself will be with them and be their God."'*

Who is Jesus? He is more than a prophet, more than a man who talked about God. He is God himself come to be with us. He is the answer to our deepest needs.

J.John

Matthew 21:1–11 ▶

²⁴When Joseph woke up, he did what the angel of the Lord had commanded him and took Mary home as his wife. ²⁵But he did not consummate their marriage until she gave birth to a son. And he gave him the name Jesus.

The Magi visit the Messiah

2 After Jesus was born in Bethlehem in Judea, during the time of King Herod, Magi*a* from the east came to Jerusalem ²and asked, 'Where is the one who has been born king of the Jews? We saw his star when it rose and have come to worship him.'

³When King Herod heard this he was disturbed, and all Jerusalem with him. ⁴When he had called together all the people's chief priests and teachers of the law, he asked them where the Messiah was to be born. ⁵'In Bethlehem in Judea,' they replied, 'for this is what the prophet has written:

⁶' "But you, Bethlehem, in the land of
    Judah,
  are by no means least among the
    rulers of Judah;
for out of you will come a ruler
  who will shepherd my people
    Israel."*b*'

⁷Then Herod called the Magi secretly and found out from them the exact time the star had appeared. ⁸He sent them to Bethlehem and said, 'Go and search carefully for the child. As soon as you find him, report to me, so that I too may go and worship him.'

⁹After they had heard the king, they went on their way, and the star they had seen when it rose went ahead of them until it stopped over the place where the child was. ¹⁰When they saw the star, they were overjoyed. ¹¹On coming to the house, they saw the child with his mother Mary, and they bowed down and worshipped him. Then they opened their treasures and presented him with gifts of gold, frankincense and myrrh. ¹²And

having been warned in a dream not to go back to Herod, they returned to their country by another route.

The escape to Egypt

¹³When they had gone, an angel of the Lord appeared to Joseph in a dream. 'Get up,' he said, 'take the child and his mother and escape to Egypt. Stay there until I tell you, for Herod is going to search for the child to kill him.'

¹⁴So he got up, took the child and his mother during the night and left for Egypt, ¹⁵where he stayed until the death of Herod. And so was fulfilled what the Lord had said through the prophet: 'Out of Egypt I called my son.'*c*

THREE? KINGS?

The Bible doesn't say that three kings visited Jesus. They were *magi* – wise men – and the Bible doesn't say how many there were (Matthew 2:1).

¹⁶When Herod realised that he had been outwitted by the Magi, he was furious, and he gave orders to kill all the boys in Bethlehem and its vicinity who were two years old and under, in accordance with the time he had learned from the Magi. ¹⁷Then what was said through the prophet Jeremiah was fulfilled:

¹⁸'A voice is heard in Ramah,
  weeping and great mourning,
Rachel weeping for her children
  and refusing to be comforted,
  because they are no more.'*d*

---

a 1   Traditionally *wise men*
b 6   Micah 5:2,4

c 15   Hosea 11:1
d 18   Jer. 31:15

The return to Nazareth

¹⁹After Herod died, an angel of the Lord appeared in a dream to Joseph in Egypt ²⁰and said, 'Get up, take the child and his mother and go to the land of Israel, for those who were trying to take the child's life are dead.'

²¹So he got up, took the child and his mother and went to the land of Israel. ²²But when he heard that Archelaus was reigning in Judea in place of his father Herod, he was afraid to go there. Having been warned in a dream, he withdrew to the district of Galilee, ²³and he went and lived in a town called Nazareth. So was fulfilled what was said through the prophets, that he would be called a Nazarene.

John the Baptist prepares the way

3 In those days John the Baptist came, preaching in the wilderness of Judea ²and saying, 'Repent, for the kingdom of heaven has come near.' ³This is he who was spoken of through the prophet Isaiah:

'A voice of one calling in the
    wilderness,
"Prepare the way for the Lord,
    make straight paths for him." ' ᵃ

⁴John's clothes were made of camel's hair, and he had a leather belt round his waist. His food was locusts and wild honey. ⁵People went out to him from Jerusalem and all Judea and the whole region of the Jordan. ⁶Confessing their sins, they were baptised by him in the River Jordan.

⁷But when he saw many of the Pharisees and Sadducees coming to where he was baptising, he said to them: 'You brood of vipers! Who warned you to flee from the coming wrath? ⁸Produce fruit in keeping with repentance. ⁹And do not think you can say to yourselves, "We have Abraham as our father." I tell you that out of these stones God can raise up children for Abraham. ¹⁰The axe has been laid to the root of the trees, and every tree that does not produce good fruit will be cut down and thrown into the fire.

¹¹'I baptise you withᵇ water for repentance. But after me comes one who is more powerful than I, whose sandals I am not worthy to carry. He will baptise you withᵇ the Holy Spirit and fire. ¹²His winnowing fork is in his hand, and he will clear his threshing-floor, gathering his wheat into the barn and burning up the chaff with unquenchable fire.'

The baptism of Jesus

¹³Then Jesus came from Galilee to the Jordan to be baptised by John. ¹⁴But John tried to deter him, saying, 'I need to be baptised by you, and do you come to me?'

¹⁵Jesus replied, 'Let it be so now; it is proper for us to do this to fulfil all righteousness.' Then John consented.

¹⁶As soon as Jesus was baptised, he went up out of the water. At that moment heaven was opened, and he saw the Spirit of God descending like a dove and alighting on him. ¹⁷And a voice from heaven said, 'This is my Son, whom I love; with him I am well pleased.'

Jesus is tested in the wilderness

4 Then Jesus was led by the Spirit into the wilderness to be temptedᵃ by the devil. ²After fasting for forty days and forty nights, he was hungry. ³The tempter came to him and said, 'If you are the Son of God, tell these stones to become bread.'

⁴Jesus answered, 'It is written: "Man shall not live on bread alone, but on every word that comes from the mouth of God."ᵇ'

⁵Then the devil took him to the holy city and set him on the highest point of the temple. ⁶'If you are the Son of God,' he said, 'throw yourself down. For it is written:

" He will command his angels
        concerning you,

ᵃ3 Isaiah 40:3

b 11 Or in
a 1 The Greek for tempted can also mean tested.
b 4 Deut. 8:3

WHAT IS CHRISTIANITY? 4

Doctrine of the Trinity: the dance of God

No matter how long we follow God, there will always be more of him to discover. The Christian life is a relationship – an adventure getting to know the most incredible being in existence. You might have been following God for a while, but how well do you know him? How would you describe him?

Some of the early Christians tried to figure out this question. Who does God show himself to be? After years of pondering, the answer they arrived at was the doctrine of the Trinity, the teaching that God is one God but exists as three distinct persons.

The Bible clearly shows that there's only one God. *'The LORD our God, the LORD is one'* (Deuteronomy 6:4). *'I am the LORD, and there is no other'* (Isaiah 45:5). Yet from the beginning of the Bible (Genesis 1:26) there are also hints of plurality within God. As we continue reading, we come to realise that God is Father, Son and Holy Spirit. There is only one God, but within God there are three persons.

In passages like Matthew 3:13–17 we get a glimpse of this. God the Son comes up out of the water, God the Holy Spirit descends like a dove, and God the Father speaks from heaven. Jesus tells us we are to go and make disciples, *'baptising them in the name of the Father and of the Son and of the Holy Spirit'* (Matthew 28:19). All the way through the New Testament, the Father, Son and Spirit are hanging out with each other.

One of the things God being Trinity means is that he has always been a family. God didn't need to create humanity in order to have some friends. He wasn't lonely before we came along. For the whole of eternity God has been in relationship. And when we look at the way the persons of God are towards each another, what shines out most clearly is love. The Father loves the Son, who loves the Spirit, who loves the Father, who loves the Spirit, who loves the Son, who loves the Father! As they saw it, the early Christians gave this relationship a nickname – they called it 'the dance of God'. They saw that our God isn't static or boring; he's a dynamic, pulsating life, and the dance of the Father, Son and Spirit is a party full of joy, laughter and love.

God didn't create us because he needed our company – but he did create us to invite us into the party, the relationship. When Jesus arrives it's as if, for a moment in eternity, God the Son has come to the edge of the dance floor. He announces, *'My Father's house has many rooms ... I will come back and take you to be with me that you also may be where I am'* (John 14:2–3).

This is the relationship we become part of today, and I suspect, knowing the trinitarian God, that the party will never end.

Andy Croft

and they will lift you up in their
hands,
so that you will not strike your foot
against a stone."*c*'

7 Jesus answered him, 'It is also written:
"Do not put the Lord your God to the
test."*d*'

8 Again, the devil took him to a very
high mountain and showed him all the
kingdoms of the world and their splen-
dour. **9** 'All this I will give you,' he said, 'if
you will bow down and worship me.'

10 Jesus said to him, 'Away from me,
Satan! For it is written: "Worship the Lord
your God, and serve him only."*e*'

11 Then the devil left him, and angels
came and attended him.

Jesus begins to preach

12 When Jesus heard that John had been
put in prison, he withdrew to Galilee.
13 Leaving Nazareth, he went and lived in
Capernaum, which was by the lake in the
area of Zebulun and Naphtali – **14** to fulfil
what was said through the prophet Isaiah:

15 'Land of Zebulun and land of Naphtali,
the Way of the Sea, beyond the
Jordan,
Galilee of the Gentiles –
16 the people living in darkness
have seen a great light;
on those living in the land of the
shadow of death
a light has dawned.'*f*

17 From that time on Jesus began to
preach, 'Repent, for the kingdom of
heaven has come near.'

Jesus calls his first disciples

18 As Jesus was walking beside the Sea
of Galilee, he saw two brothers, Simon
called Peter and his brother Andrew. They
were casting a net into the lake, for they
were fishermen. **19** 'Come, follow me,'
Jesus said, 'and I will send you out to fish

for people.' **20** At once they left their nets
and followed him.

21 Going on from there, he saw two
other brothers, James son of Zebedee and
his brother John. They were in a boat with
their father Zebedee, preparing their nets.
Jesus called them, **22** and immediately they
left the boat and their father and followed
him.

Jesus heals the sick

23 Jesus went throughout Galilee, teaching in their synagogues, proclaiming the
good news of the kingdom, and healing
every disease and illness among the people. **24** News about him spread all over Syria, and people brought to him all who were
ill with various diseases, those suffering
severe pain, the demon-possessed, those
having seizures, and the paralysed; and he
healed them. **25** Large crowds from Galilee,
the Decapolis,*g* Jerusalem, Judea and the
region across the Jordan followed him.

Introduction to the Sermon on the Mount

5 Now when Jesus saw the crowds, he
went up on a mountainside and sat
down. His disciples came to him, **2** and he
began to teach them.

The Beatitudes
He said:

3 'Blessed are the poor in spirit,
for theirs is the kingdom of heaven.
4 Blessed are those who mourn,
for they will be comforted.
5 Blessed are the meek,
for they will inherit the earth.
6 Blessed are those who hunger and
thirst for righteousness,
for they will be filled.
7 Blessed are the merciful,
for they will be shown mercy.
8 Blessed are the pure in heart,
for they will see God.
9 Blessed are the peacemakers,
for they will be called children of
God.

---

*c*6 Psalm 91:11,12
*d*7 Deut. 6:16
*e*10 Deut. 6:13
*f*16 Isaiah 9:1,2

*g*25 That is, the Ten Cities

[10] Blessed are those who are persecuted
    because of righteousness,
    for theirs is the kingdom of heaven.

[11] 'Blessed are you when people insult
you, persecute you and falsely say all kinds
of evil against you because of me. [12] Rejoice and be glad, because great is your reward in heaven, for in the same way they
persecuted the prophets who were before
you.

Salt and light

[13] 'You are the salt of the earth. But if the
salt loses its saltiness, how can it be made
salty again? It is no longer good for anything, except to be thrown out and trampled underfoot.
    [14] 'You are the light of the world. A town
built on a hill cannot be hidden. [15] Neither
do people light a lamp and put it under a
bowl. Instead they put it on its stand, and
it gives light to everyone in the house. [16] In
the same way, let your light shine before
others, that they may see your good deeds
and glorify your Father in heaven.

The fulfilment of the law

[17] 'Do not think that I have come to
abolish the Law or the Prophets; I have
not come to abolish them but to fulfil
them. [18] For truly I tell you, until heaven
and earth disappear, not the smallest letter, not the least stroke of a pen, will by
any means disappear from the Law until
everything is accomplished. [19] Therefore
anyone who sets aside one of the least of
these commands and teaches others accordingly will be called least in the kingdom of heaven, but whoever practises and
teaches these commands will be called
great in the kingdom of heaven. [20] For I
tell you that unless your righteousness
surpasses that of the Pharisees and the
teachers of the law, you will certainly not
enter the kingdom of heaven.

Murder

[21] 'You have heard that it was said to the
people long ago, "You shall not murder,[a]

---

[a] 21   Exodus 20:13

and anyone who murders will be subject
to judgment." [22] But I tell you that anyone
who is angry with a brother or sister[b,c] will
be subject to judgment. Again, anyone
who says to a brother or sister, "Raca,"[d] is
answerable to the court. And anyone who
says, "You fool!" will be in danger of the
fire of hell.
    [23] 'Therefore, if you are offering your gift
at the altar and there remember that your
brother or sister has something against
you, [24] leave your gift there in front of the
altar. First go and be reconciled to them;
then come and offer your gift.
    [25] 'Settle matters quickly with your ad-
versary who is taking you to court. Do it
while you are still together on the way, or
your adversary may hand you over to the
judge, and the judge may hand you over
to the officer, and you may be thrown into
prison. [26] Truly I tell you, you will not get
out until you have paid the last penny.

Adultery

[27] 'You have heard that it was said, "You
shall not commit adultery."[e] [28] But I tell
you that anyone who looks at a woman
lustfully has already committed adultery
with her in his heart. [29] If your right eye
causes you to stumble, gouge it out and
throw it away. It is better for you to lose
one part of your body than for your whole
body to be thrown into hell. [30] And if your
right hand causes you to stumble, cut it
off and throw it away. It is better for you
to lose one part of your body than for your
whole body to go into hell.

Divorce

[31] 'It has been said, "Anyone who divorces his wife must give her a certificate
of divorce."[f] [32] But I tell you that anyone
who divorces his wife, except for sexual immorality, makes her the victim of

---

[b] 22   The Greek word for *brother or sister* (*adelphos*)
refers here to a fellow disciple, whether man or
woman; also in verse 23.
[c] 22   Some manuscripts *brother or sister without cause*
[d] 22   An Aramaic term of contempt
[e] 27   Exodus 20:14
[f] 31   Deut. 24:1

WHAT DOES GOD THINK ABOUT WAR? (PART I)

This is the first of a two-part discussion where we look at different answers to this question. As we read the Bible, we see there isn't always an obvious answer to some of the most difficult questions we have to ask about our faith. Read this, and the article near Matthew 26:52, and see what you think. Ask God to speak to you through his Word.

The Old Testament seems to be full of people fighting one another. God orders the Israelites to go to war (1 Samuel 15:3; Joshua 4:13), requires the death penalty for some offences (Exodus 21:12, 15; 22:19; Leviticus 20:11), David kills Goliath (1 Samuel 17), and all of this appears to happen with God's blessing, even after he says *'You shall not commit murder'* (Exodus 20:13).

Something changes when Jesus starts his ministry. He begins to show a different kind of life (Luke 6:30; Matthew 5:9–44), and James (who we think was Jesus' brother) wrote, *'But the wisdom that comes from heaven is first of all pure; then peace-loving, considerate, submissive, full of mercy and good fruit, impartial and sincere'* (James 3:17). God commands us to live in peace with each other throughout the New Testament (1 Corinthians 7:15; 2 Corinthians 13:11; 1 Thessalonians 5:13; 1 Timothy 2:2).

In *A Christian Manifesto*, Francis Schaeffer writes:

I am walking down the street. I see a great big, burly man who is beating a helpless little girl to death. I come up and I plead with him to stop. If he won't stop, what does love mean? Love means I stop him in any way I can including, quite frankly, hitting him. To me this is necessary Christian love in a fallen world. What about the little girl? If I desert the little girl to the bully, I have deserted the true meaning of Christian love and responsibility to my neighbour.

Schaeffer's old solution, *'eye for eye'* (Exodus 21:24), could make the situation worse. I think we know that Jesus wouldn't simply plead with the man to stop, and nor would he beat the man to a pulp. I think we can be fairly sure of what Jesus would do: he would put himself between the man and the girl, and take the beating on her behalf.

Most respected scholars agree that nearly all the early Christians were pacifists. In fact, the idea of 'just war' comes into Christian history in AD 313 when the first Roman Emperor, Constantine, converted to Christianity, but we know that his military deserters were still being brutally punished – suggesting there were areas of his life left unchanged by his conversion.

If our lives are radically changed by knowing Jesus, whether we classify ourselves as pacifists isn't the real issue – it's our relationship with God and one another. What marks us out as Christians, and shapes the course of our lives, is the action we take to express our love for God and the way we treat others.

Freddie Pimm with Jane Plackett

adultery, and anyone who marries a divorced woman commits adultery.

Oaths

33 'Again, you have heard that it was said to the people long ago, "Do not break your oath, but fulfil to the Lord the oaths you have made." **34** But I tell you, do not swear an oath at all: either by heaven, for it is God's throne; **35** or by the earth, for it is his footstool; or by Jerusalem, for it is the city of the Great King. **36** And do not swear by your head, for you cannot make even one hair white or black. **37** All you need to say is simply "Yes," or "No"; anything beyond this comes from the evil one.*g*

Eye for eye

38 'You have heard that it was said, "Eye for eye, and tooth for tooth."*h* **39** But I tell you, do not resist an evil person. If anyone slaps you on the right cheek, turn to them the other cheek also. **40** And if anyone wants to sue you and take your shirt, hand over your coat as well. **41** If anyone forces you to go one mile, go with them two miles. **42** Give to the one who asks you, and do not turn away from the one who wants to borrow from you.

Love for enemies

43 'You have heard that it was said, "Love your neighbour*i* and hate your enemy." **44** But I tell you, love your enemies and pray for those who persecute you, **45** that you may be children of your Father in heaven. He causes his sun to rise on the evil and the good, and sends rain on the righteous and the unrighteous. **46** If you love those who love you, what reward will you get? Are not even the tax collectors doing that? **47** And if you greet only your own people, what are you doing more than others? Do not even pagans do that? **48** Be perfect, therefore, as your heavenly Father is perfect.

Giving to the needy

6 'Be careful not to practise your righteousness in front of others to be seen by them. If you do, you will have no reward from your Father in heaven.

2 'So when you give to the needy, do not announce it with trumpets, as the hypocrites do in the synagogues and on the streets, to be honoured by others. Truly I tell you, they have received their reward in full. **3** But when you give to the needy, do not let your left hand know what your right hand is doing, **4** so that your giving may be in secret. Then your Father, who sees what is done in secret, will reward you.

Prayer

5 'And when you pray, do not be like the hypocrites, for they love to pray standing in the synagogues and on the street corners to be seen by others. Truly I tell you, they have received their reward in full. **6** But when you pray, go into your room, close the door and pray to your Father, who is unseen. Then your Father, who sees what is done in secret, will reward you. **7** And when you pray, do not keep on babbling like pagans, for they think they will be heard because of their many words. **8** Do not be like them, for your Father knows what you need before you ask him.

9 'This, then, is how you should pray:

' "Our Father in heaven,
hallowed be your name,
10 your kingdom come,
your will be done,
on earth as it is in heaven.
11 Give us today our daily bread.
12 And forgive us our debts,
as we also have forgiven our
debtors.
13 And lead us not into temptation,*a*
but deliver us from the evil one.*b* "

14 For if you forgive other people when they sin against you, your heavenly Father

g 37 Or *from evil*
h 38 Exodus 21:24; Lev. 24:20; Deut. 19:21
i 43 Lev. 19:18

a 13 The Greek for *temptation* can also mean *testing.*
b 13 Or *from evil*; some late manuscripts *one, / for yours is the kingdom and the power and the glory for ever. Amen.*

WHY DOES GOD NOT ANSWER MY PRAYERS?

It can be really frustrating when we pray for things and they don't happen. We read the Bible and hear about the amazing miracles that Jesus did, then sometimes we look at our own lives and wonder why we don't see those things happening all the time.

In Mark 1:15, at the start of Jesus' ministry, he declared, *'The kingdom of God has come near.'* He went on to work miracles, healings and resurrections. The New Testament is full of stories of his power, but Jesus also said that his Holy Spirit would be given to us too, so that through the Holy Spirit we would see God work amazing acts of power.

So why don't we see them every day? Well, many Christians like to call the period we live in the time of the 'now and the not yet'. That means that Jesus has come, and he brought God's kingdom with him, but he didn't bring the kingdom in its entirety. So the kingdom of God is here now in part, but it's not here fully yet.

When Jesus talked about the 'kingdom of God', he was talking about God's will. When the kingdom of God comes fully, God's perfect will (his plan for humanity since before time began) will be complete. The book of Revelation is often believed to be about the end of time, as it talks about Jesus making a new heaven and new earth free from war, disease and suffering – the completion of God's plan for humanity.

Jesus tells the disciples to pray that God's kingdom will come. In Matthew 6:10, Jesus is teaching the disciples the Lord's Prayer and in it is the line *'your kingdom come, your will be done, on earth as it is in heaven'*. We should be asking God to come and restore the world to be in line with his perfect plan.

So what does all this mean for us? Well, because God's perfect will isn't here fully yet, sometimes when we pray God does stuff and we see amazing miracles, but at other times we pray and nothing happens. It can be really frustrating and upsetting, but it doesn't mean we should stop praying!

It's also worth remembering that God sometimes answers our prayers with a response we weren't looking for. God is our Father and knows us better than we know ourselves and he loves to bless us, but sometimes we ask for stuff and God says 'no' because it isn't good for us to have it. Parents don't always give children everything they ask for, because often they want things that won't be good for them. It doesn't mean they love their children any less, it means they're looking out for their child's best interests. God does the same for us.

So why doesn't God answer our prayers? Well, sometimes he answers us by saying 'no', because God's kingdom, his perfect will, isn't complete on earth yet.

Freddie Pimm

will also forgive you. ¹⁵But if you do not forgive others their sins, your Father will not forgive your sins.

Fasting

¹⁶'When you fast, do not look sombre as the hypocrites do, for they disfigure their faces to show others they are fasting. Truly I tell you, they have received their reward in full. ¹⁷But when you fast, put oil on your head and wash your face, ¹⁸so that it will not be obvious to others that you are fasting, but only to your Father, who is unseen; and your Father, who sees what is done in secret, will reward you.

Treasures in heaven

¹⁹'Do not store up for yourselves treasures on earth, where moths and vermin destroy, and where thieves break in and steal. ²⁰But store up for yourselves treasures in heaven, where moths and vermin do not destroy, and where thieves do not break in and steal. ²¹For where your treasure is, there your heart will be also.

²²'The eye is the lamp of the body. If your eyes are healthy,ᶜ your whole body will be full of light. ²³But if your eyes are unhealthy,ᵈ your whole body will be full of darkness. If then the light within you is darkness, how great is that darkness!

²⁴'No one can serve two masters. Either you will hate the one and love the other, or you will be devoted to the one and despise the other. You cannot serve both God and Money.

Do not worry

²⁵'Therefore I tell you, do not worry about your life, what you will eat or drink; or about your body, what you will wear. Is not life more than food, and the body more than clothes? ²⁶Look at the birds of the air; they do not sow or reap or store away in barns, and yet your heavenly Father feeds them. Are you not much more valuable than they? ²⁷Can any one of you

by worrying add a single hour to your lifeᵉ?

²⁸'And why do you worry about clothes? See how the flowers of the field grow. They do not labour or spin. ²⁹Yet I tell you that not even Solomon in all his splendour was dressed like one of these. ³⁰If that is how God clothes the grass of the field, which is here today and tomorrow is thrown into the fire, will he not much more clothe you – you of little faith? ³¹So do not worry, saying, "What shall we eat?" or "What shall we drink?" or "What shall we wear?" ³²For the pagans run after all these things, and your heavenly Father knows that you need them. ³³But seek first his kingdom and his righteousness, and all these things will be given to you as well. ³⁴Therefore do not worry about tomorrow, for tomorrow will worry about itself. Each day has enough trouble of its own.

Judging others

7 'Do not judge, or you too will be judged. ²For in the same way as you judge others, you will be judged, and with the measure you use, it will be measured to you.

³'Why do you look at the speck of sawdust in your brother's eye and pay no attention to the plank in your own eye? ⁴How can you say to your brother, "Let me take the speck out of your eye," when all the time there is a plank in your own eye? ⁵You hypocrite, first take the plank out of your own eye, and then you will see clearly to remove the speck from your brother's eye.

⁶'Do not give dogs what is sacred; do not throw your pearls to pigs. If you do, they may trample them under their feet, and turn and tear you to pieces.

Ask, seek, knock

⁷'Ask and it will be given to you; seek and you will find; knock and the door will be opened to you. ⁸For everyone who asks receives; the one who seeks finds; and to the one who knocks, the door will be opened.

---

c 22 The Greek for *healthy* here implies *generous*.
d 23 The Greek for *unhealthy* here implies *stingy*.

e 27 Or *single cubit to your height*

⁹'Which of you, if your son asks for bread, will give him a stone? ¹⁰Or if he asks for a fish, will give him a snake? ¹¹If you, then, though you are evil, know how to give good gifts to your children, how much more will your Father in heaven give good gifts to those who ask him! ¹²So in everything, do to others what you would

MONEY 9

SIMPLE LIVING

Hundreds of years ago, the great philosopher René Descartes said we know we exist because we think. 'I think, therefore I am.' Today we might say, 'I shop, therefore I am.'

We live in a world that is driven by consumerism; we see hundreds of adverts every day telling us what we need to purchase to make life better. They advise us on how to make the girls/boys fling themselves at us, what will make us smarter, hotter, fitter and cooler. It's a strong force encouraging us to spend, spend, spend!

And it works.

Our culture urges us to define who we are by what we have. From fashion, to music, to technology. Are you Mac or PC? These are external symbols that tell the world where we belong, what group we're part of and who we want to be.

Matthew is suggesting an alternative symbol (Matthew 6:19–24). Instead of being identified by what we have, our identity is expressed by what we don't have. He is asking us to treasure something different, not the stuff we own but the life we live. With this perspective we have an opportunity to live differently on earth, not defined by materialism and consumerism, but in an opposite spirit of living lightly on this earth, not obsessed with the 'stuff'.

Tony Campolo says, 'Live simply so others can simply live.' As Christians we're sometimes stereotyped as being judgemental, boring, irrelevant, but here Matthew gives us an opportunity to be stereotyped by living dynamically differently on this earth – to live a simpler life, without the all-defining drive to spend, spend, spend; to choose to limit our spending, even if we could afford it. For example, by not buying the latest item every time a new version appears on the market, or by choosing to buy second-hand items, or by fixing things before we buy a new one, we would free up money that we might have spent on ourselves to put to a more productive use.

It's a liberating challenge. Money and the things money buys can be a very tempting distraction, something that we end up devoting a lot of time and energy to. It has the power to captivate our hearts and minds. We are warned at the end of this passage that we *cannot serve both God and Money* (v. 24). Choosing to live simply not only enables us to use our money productively, it's also a life-giving antidote to a culture of 'more'!

Kiera Singlehurst-Phyo

 James 5:4   Genesis 41:34 ▶▶

have them do to you, for this sums up the Law and the Prophets.

The narrow and wide gates

13 'Enter through the narrow gate. For wide is the gate and broad is the road that leads to destruction, and many enter through it. 14 But small is the gate and narrow the road that leads to life, and only a few find it.

True and false prophets

15 'Watch out for false prophets. They come to you in sheep's clothing, but inwardly they are ferocious wolves. 16 By their fruit you will recognise them. Do people pick grapes from thorn-bushes, or figs from thistles? 17 Likewise, every good tree bears good fruit, but a bad tree bears bad fruit. 18 A good tree cannot bear bad fruit, and a bad tree cannot bear good fruit. 19 Every tree that does not bear good fruit is cut down and thrown into the fire. 20 Thus, by their fruit you will recognise them.

True and false disciples

21 'Not everyone who says to me, "Lord, Lord," will enter the kingdom of heaven, but only the one who does the will of my Father who is in heaven. 22 Many will say to me on that day, "Lord, Lord, did we not prophesy in your name and in your name drive out demons and in your name perform many miracles?" 23 Then I will tell them plainly, "I never knew you. Away from me, you evildoers!"

The wise and foolish builders

24 'Therefore everyone who hears these words of mine and puts them into practice is like a wise man who built his house on the rock. 25 The rain came down, the streams rose, and the winds blew and beat against that house; yet it did not fall, because it had its foundation on the rock. 26 But everyone who hears these words of mine and does not put them into practice is like a foolish man who built his house on sand. 27 The rain came down, the streams rose, and the winds blew and beat against that house, and it fell with a great crash.'

28 When Jesus had finished saying these things, the crowds were amazed at his teaching, 29 because he taught as one who had authority, and not as their teachers of the law.

Jesus heals a man with leprosy

8 When Jesus came down from the mountainside, large crowds followed him. 2 A man with leprosy*a* came and knelt before him and said, 'Lord, if you are willing, you can make me clean.'

3 Jesus reached out his hand and touched the man. 'I am willing,' he said. 'Be clean!' Immediately he was cleansed of his leprosy. 4 Then Jesus said to him, 'See that you don't tell anyone. But go, show yourself to the priest and offer the gift Moses commanded, as a testimony to them.'

The faith of the centurion

5 When Jesus had entered Capernaum, a centurion came to him, asking for help. 6 'Lord,' he said, 'my servant lies at home paralysed, suffering terribly.'

7 Jesus said to him, 'Shall I come and heal him?'

8 The centurion replied, 'Lord, I do not deserve to have you come under my roof. But just say the word, and my servant will be healed. 9 For I myself am a man under authority, with soldiers under me. I tell this one, "Go," and he goes; and that one, "Come," and he comes. I say to my servant, "Do this," and he does it.'

10 When Jesus heard this, he was amazed and said to those following him, 'Truly I tell you, I have not found anyone in Israel with such great faith. 11 I say to you that many will come from the east and the west, and will take their places at the feast with Abraham, Isaac and Jacob in the kingdom of heaven. 12 But the subjects of the kingdom will be thrown outside, into the darkness, where there will be weeping and gnashing of teeth.'

13 Then Jesus said to the centurion, 'Go! Let it be done just as you believed it

---

a 2 The Greek word traditionally translated *leprosy* was used for various diseases affecting the skin.

would.' And his servant was healed at that moment.

Jesus heals many

¹⁴When Jesus came into Peter's house, he saw Peter's mother-in-law lying in bed with a fever. ¹⁵He touched her hand and the fever left her, and she got up and began to wait on him.

¹⁶When evening came, many who were demon-possessed were brought to him, and he drove out the spirits with a word and healed all who were ill. ¹⁷This was to fulfil what was spoken through the prophet Isaiah:

'He took up our infirmities
and bore our diseases.'ᵇ

The cost of following Jesus

¹⁸When Jesus saw the crowd around him, he gave orders to cross to the other side of the lake. ¹⁹Then a teacher of the law came to him and said, 'Teacher, I will follow you wherever you go.'

²⁰Jesus replied, 'Foxes have dens and birds have nests, but the Son of Man has nowhere to lay his head.'

_____

b 17 Isaiah 53:4 (see Septuagint)

DISEASE AND HIV

In Matthew 8:1–4, Jesus is coming down a mountain having just talked to a large crowd. The first person he meets is a man suffering from leprosy, a serious skin disease. In Jewish society a person with leprosy was 'unclean' – they couldn't be involved in worship, and often they would have to live outside the community, sometimes with a bell around their neck so that no one would come into physical contact with them and become unclean themselves. They were called the 'untouchables'.

This man falls on his knees before Jesus and says, *'Lord, if you are willing, you can make me clean'* (v. 2), and Jesus reaches out and touches the man, the 'untouchable'.

There are two miracles going on here. Jesus heals the man's leprosy, which is amazing enough, but by crossing the divide between 'clean' and 'unclean' Jesus breaks down the walls that kept this man excluded, and he heals this man at a much deeper level.

There are over thirty-three million people worldwide living with HIV today. Around sixteen million children now live in child-headed households because they have lost their parents to AIDS-related illness. This is a global crisis with a cost paid most heavily by poor communities who can't afford or access treatment or the nutrition necessary to manage their illness. Decades of successful development work risks being undone by the impact of so many deaths and so many more people unable to work or attend school.

How should we respond to this crisis? We need to act to make sure that people can access the life-saving treatment they need, but we also need to treat people differently so that disease doesn't lead to stigma. We can be Jesus to people living with HIV by reaching out and touching lives – whether in our own communities or around the world.

Matt Valler

²¹Another disciple said to him, 'Lord, first let me go and bury my father.'

²²But Jesus told him, 'Follow me, and let the dead bury their own dead.'

Jesus calms the storm

²³Then he got into the boat and his disciples followed him. ²⁴Suddenly a furious storm came up on the lake, so that the waves swept over the boat. But Jesus was sleeping. ²⁵The disciples went and woke him, saying, 'Lord, save us! We're going to drown!'

²⁶He replied, 'You of little faith, why are you so afraid?' Then he got up and rebuked the winds and the waves, and it was completely calm.

²⁷The men were amazed and asked, 'What kind of man is this? Even the winds and the waves obey him!'

Jesus restores two demon-possessed men

²⁸When he arrived at the other side in the region of the Gadarenes,ᶜ two demon-possessed men coming from the tombs met him. They were so violent that no one could pass that way. ²⁹'What do you want with us, Son of God?' they shouted. 'Have you come here to torture us before the appointed time?'

³⁰Some distance from them a large herd of pigs was feeding. ³¹The demons begged Jesus, 'If you drive us out, send us into the herd of pigs.'

³²He said to them, 'Go!' So they came out and went into the pigs, and the whole herd rushed down the steep bank into the lake and died in the water. ³³Those tending the pigs ran off, went into the town and reported all this, including what had happened to the demon-possessed men. ³⁴Then the whole town went out to meet Jesus. And when they saw him, they pleaded with him to leave their region.

Jesus forgives and heals a paralysed man

9 Jesus stepped into a boat, crossed over and came to his own town.

²Some men brought to him a paralysed man, lying on a mat. When Jesus saw their faith, he said to the man, 'Take heart, son; your sins are forgiven.'

³At this, some of the teachers of the law said to themselves, 'This fellow is blaspheming!'

⁴Knowing their thoughts, Jesus said, 'Why do you entertain evil thoughts in your hearts? ⁵Which is easier: to say, "Your sins are forgiven," or to say, "Get up and walk"? ⁶But I want you to know that the Son of Man has authority on earth to forgive sins.' So he said to the paralysed man, 'Get up, take your mat and go home.' ⁷Then the man got up and went home. ⁸When the crowd saw this, they were filled with awe; and they praised God, who had given such authority to man.

The calling of Matthew

⁹As Jesus went on from there, he saw a man named Matthew sitting at the tax collector's booth. 'Follow me,' he told him, and Matthew got up and followed him.

¹⁰While Jesus was having dinner at Matthew's house, many tax collectors and sinners came and ate with him and his disciples. ¹¹When the Pharisees saw this, they asked his disciples, 'Why does your teacher eat with tax collectors and sinners?'

¹²On hearing this, Jesus said, 'It is not the healthy who need a doctor, but those who are ill. ¹³But go and learn what this means: "I desire mercy, not sacrifice."ᵃ For I have not come to call the righteous, but sinners.'

Jesus questioned about fasting

¹⁴Then John's disciples came and asked him, 'How is it that we and the Pharisees fast often, but your disciples do not fast?'

¹⁵Jesus answered, 'How can the guests of the bridegroom mourn while he is with them? The time will come when the bridegroom will be taken from them; then they will fast.

¹⁶'No one sews a patch of unshrunk cloth on an old garment, for the patch

will pull away from the garment, making the tear worse. ¹⁷Neither do people pour new wine into old wineskins. If they do, the skins will burst; the wine will run out, and the wineskins will be ruined. No, they pour new wine into new wineskins, and both are preserved.'

Jesus raises a dead girl and heals a sick woman

¹⁸While he was saying this, a synagogue leader came and knelt before him and said, 'My daughter has just died. But come and put your hand on her, and she will live.' ¹⁹Jesus got up and went with him, and so did his disciples.

²⁰Just then a woman who had been subject to bleeding for twelve years came up behind him and touched the edge of his cloak. ²¹She said to herself, 'If I only touch his cloak, I will be healed.'

²²Jesus turned and saw her. 'Take heart, daughter,' he said, 'your faith has healed you.' And the woman was healed at that moment.

²³When Jesus entered the synagogue leader's house and saw the noisy crowd and the people playing pipes, ²⁴he said,

EVANGELISM 2

Why?

When it comes to evangelism we tend to have one of two responses. Either we race on and do lots of activity, or we shy away from it completely! Whatever your first response, it helps to know the 'why' behind it all.

Jesus clearly demonstrates the 'why': it's because of compassion (Matthew 9:36). He saw people and his heart was moved for them. When we are captured by the heart of compassion we are less likely to give up after a few failed attempts. Reaching our friends for Jesus can be tough. If you are doing it because someone at church told you to, then at the tough points you are likely to simply give up. However, if God has moved your heart for the people around you, then you have a God-given focus that can spur you on.

I remember asking God to let me see people the way he sees them. Be careful before you pray that prayer: I found that it produced a huge change in me! For the first time I saw hurting people who had been ripped off by life and needed the love of a compassionate and caring God. I became driven by something other than my own feelings.

When our hearts are broken for the lost, our motives are completely clean. We are not trying to win people for God to score points in a crazy 'how-good-am-I-at-being-a-Christian?' kind of way. Before you continue in these devotions on evangelism and burst into a flurry of activity, why not take some time with God? Ask him to open your eyes, to open your heart, maybe even to break your heart for the things that break his. Pray that your actions will come from the compassion that he gives.

Do it now – pray that prayer. I dare you!

Mark Ritchie

 Acts 1:8   Luke 10:1–4 ▶

'Go away. The girl is not dead but asleep.' But they laughed at him. 25 After the crowd had been put outside, he went in and took the girl by the hand, and she got up. 26 News of this spread through all that region.

Jesus heals the blind and the mute

27 As Jesus went on from there, two blind men followed him, calling out, 'Have mercy on us, Son of David!' 28 When he had gone indoors, the blind men came to him, and he asked them, 'Do you believe that I am able to do this?'

'Yes, Lord,' they replied.

29 Then he touched their eyes and said, 'According to your faith let it be done to you'; 30 and their sight was restored. Jesus warned them sternly, 'See that no one knows about this.' 31 But they went out and spread the news about him all over that region.

32 While they were going out, a man who was demon-possessed and could not talk was brought to Jesus. 33 And when the demon was driven out, the man who had been mute spoke. The crowd was amazed and said, 'Nothing like this has ever been seen in Israel.'

34 But the Pharisees said, 'It is by the prince of demons that he drives out demons.'

The workers are few

35 Jesus went through all the towns and villages, teaching in their synagogues, proclaiming the good news of the kingdom and healing every disease and illness. 36 When he saw the crowds, he had compassion on them, because they were harassed and helpless, like sheep without a shepherd. 37 Then he said to his disciples, 'The harvest is plentiful but the workers are few. 38 Ask the Lord of the harvest, therefore, to send out workers into his harvest field.'

Jesus sends out the Twelve

10 Jesus called his twelve disciples to him and gave them authority to drive out impure spirits and to heal every disease and illness.

2 These are the names of the twelve apostles: first, Simon (who is called Peter) and his brother Andrew; James son of Zebedee, and his brother John; 3 Philip and Bartholomew; Thomas and Matthew the tax collector; James son of Alphaeus, and Thaddaeus; 4 Simon the Zealot and Judas Iscariot, who betrayed him.

5 These twelve Jesus sent out with the following instructions: 'Do not go among the Gentiles or enter any town of the Samaritans. 6 Go rather to the lost sheep of Israel. 7 As you go, proclaim this message: "The kingdom of heaven has come near." 8 Heal those who are ill, raise the dead, cleanse those who have leprosy,ᵃ drive out demons. Freely you have received; freely give.

9 'Do not get any gold or silver or copper to take with you in your belts – 10 no bag for the journey or extra shirt or sandals or a staff, for the worker is worth his keep. 11 Whatever town or village you enter, search there for some worthy person and stay at their house until you leave. 12 As you enter the home, give it your greeting. 13 If the home is deserving, let your peace rest on it; if it is not, let your peace return to you. 14 If anyone will not welcome you or listen to your words, leave that home or town and shake the dust off your feet. 15 Truly I tell you, it will be more bearable for Sodom and Gomorrah on the day of judgment than for that town.

16 'I am sending you out like sheep among wolves. Therefore be as shrewd as snakes and as innocent as doves. 17 Be on your guard; you will be handed over to the local councils and be flogged in the synagogues. 18 On my account you will be brought before governors and kings as witnesses to them and to the Gentiles. 19 But when they arrest you, do not worry about what to say or how to say it. At that time you will be given what to say, 20 for it will not be you speaking, but the Spirit of your Father speaking through you.

21 'Brother will betray brother to death, and a father his child; children will rebel against their parents and have them put to

---

a 8 The Greek word traditionally translated *leprosy* was used for various diseases affecting the skin.

death. 22 You will be hated by everyone because of me, but the one who stands firm to the end will be saved. 23 When you are persecuted in one place, flee to another. Truly I tell you, you will not finish going through the towns of Israel before the Son of Man comes.

24 'The student is not above the teacher, nor a servant above his master. 25 It is enough for students to be like their teachers, and servants like their masters. If the head of the house has been called Beelzebul, how much more the members of his household!

26 'So do not be afraid of them, for there is nothing concealed that will not be disclosed, or hidden that will not be made known. 27 What I tell you in the dark, speak in the daylight; what is whispered in your ear, proclaim from the roofs. 28 Do not be afraid of those who kill the body but cannot kill the soul. Rather, be afraid of the One who can destroy both soul and body in hell. 29 Are not two sparrows sold for a penny? Yet not one of them will fall to the ground outside your Father's care. b 30 And even the very hairs of your head are all numbered. 31 So don't be afraid; you are worth more than many sparrows.

32 'Whoever acknowledges me before others, I will also acknowledge before my Father in heaven. 33 But whoever disowns me before others, I will disown before my Father in heaven.

34 'Do not suppose that I have come to bring peace to the earth. I did not come to bring peace, but a sword. 35 For I have come to turn

' "a man against his father,
    a daughter against her mother,
a daughter-in-law against her
        mother-in-law –
36   a man's enemies will be the
        members of his own
        household." c

37 'Anyone who loves their father or mother more than me is not worthy

of me; anyone who loves their son or daughter more than me is not worthy of me. 38 Whoever does not take up their cross and follow me is not worthy of me. 39 Whoever finds their life will lose it, and whoever loses their life for my sake will find it.

40 'Anyone who welcomes you welcomes me, and anyone who welcomes me welcomes the one who sent me. 41 Whoever welcomes a prophet as a prophet will receive a prophet's reward, and whoever welcomes a righteous person as a righteous person will receive a righteous person's reward. 42 And if anyone gives even a cup of cold water to one of these little ones who is my disciple, truly I tell you, that person will certainly not lose their reward.'

Jesus and John the Baptist

11 After Jesus had finished instructing his twelve disciples, he went on from there to teach and preach in the towns of Galilee. a

2 When John, who was in prison, heard about the deeds of the Messiah, he sent his disciples 3 to ask him, 'Are you the one who is to come, or should we expect someone else?'

4 Jesus replied, 'Go back and report to John what you hear and see: 5 the blind receive sight, the lame walk, those who have leprosy b are cleansed, the deaf hear, the dead are raised, and the good news is proclaimed to the poor. 6 Blessed is anyone who does not stumble on account of me.'

7 As John's disciples were leaving, Jesus began to speak to the crowd about John: 'What did you go out into the wilderness to see? A reed swayed by the wind? 8 If not, what did you go out to see? A man dressed in fine clothes? No, those who wear fine clothes are in kings' palaces. 9 Then what did you go out to see? A prophet? Yes, I tell you, and more than a prophet. 10 This is the one about whom it is written:

---

b 29 Or will; or knowledge
c 36 Micah 7:6

a 1 Greek in their towns
b 5 The Greek word traditionally translated leprosy was used for various diseases affecting the skin.

HELL (WHY WOULD A LOVING GOD SEND PEOPLE TO HELL?)

Welcome to a discussion that has been going on for over two thousand years! First, it's useful to look at what the Bible says about hell and about God, before directly addressing this question.

The Old Testament doesn't mention hell, although Daniel 12:2 talks about people who have died rising again to be sent *'to shame and everlasting contempt'*. Jesus is the first to use the word 'hell' in the Bible. The main Greek word used in the Gospels that we translate as 'hell' is *Gehenna*, which was a valley near Jerusalem and the place where Ahab and Manasseh sacrificed children to Molech, the god of the dead. It was a place associated with idolatry, death and judgement. Some ancient rabbis used it as a picture of where evildoers would go when they died, and Jesus uses it in a similar way.

As well as Matthew 10:28, there are many other verses mentioning hell in the Gospels, although none in the book of Acts or Paul's letters. Paul does talk about judgement beyond this life, and the wicked being *'punished with everlasting destruction'* (2 Thessalonians 1:9). The Bible seems to be clear that we will have to account for our actions in this life, and for those who reject Jesus there will be punishment in hell.

Over the centuries there have been many debates about the nature of hell. The majority in the church throughout its history have taught that hell is a place of punishment that will never end, reserved for all who reject Jesus in this life. A significant minority have drawn attention to the many verses, including Matthew 10:28, that use the language of destruction when talking about hell. These 'annihilationists' suggest that hell itself will be destroyed one day, thus ending the torment of those in hell and resulting in the destruction of all evil from creation. There is also universalism, which suggests that if hell exists, it will eventually be empty, on the day that God becomes *'all in all'* (1 Corinthians 15:28).

Whatever our view on the nature of hell, how could a loving God send people to a place of punishment and torment? The God we read about in the Bible is utterly trustworthy. He is totally faithful to his word. He is absolutely good, loving and merciful. His desire is that none should *'perish'* (2 Peter 3:9). But he also gives us free choice. We can choose to walk away from him. If we didn't have that choice, we would be like robots, incapable of true relationship. Free will means that we can choose to spend eternity away from the presence of God, separated from his love. It's less a case of God sending us there, and more that we choose to reject him.

Ultimately, we can trust that when we see God face to face, we will realise that whoever is right about the nature of hell, God will have done what is most loving, most just and most right.

Chris Lane

' "I will send my messenger ahead of you,
who will prepare your way before you." c

11 Truly I tell you, among those born of women there has not risen anyone greater than John the Baptist; yet whoever is least in the kingdom of heaven is greater than he. 12 From the days of John the Baptist until now, the kingdom of heaven has been subjected to violence, d and violent people have been raiding it. 13 For all the Prophets and the Law prophesied until John. 14 And if you are willing to accept it,

c 10 Mal. 3:1

d 12 Or been forcefully advancing

NATURALLY SUPERNATURAL 6

HEALING AS SIGNS OF THE KINGDOM

As a Messiah, Jesus wasn't what everyone was expecting. Many of the Jews who had prayed and longed for him to come for years were looking for someone who would overturn the Roman rule and set his people free. They may have imagined him as a great warrior like King David. Instead Jesus came along and taught about love and compassion.

Even John the Baptist, whose job it was to prepare the way for the Messiah, got confused: 'Are you the one?' he asked Jesus. 'Is this it? Is this what we've been waiting for?' Jesus replied by telling John about the signs of God's kingdom and how they were being fulfilled: people were being healed and set free, and good news was being delivered to the poor (Matthew 11:1–5).

When we pray the Lord's Prayer, we are asking for God's kingdom to come on earth as it is in heaven (Matthew 6:10), meaning that we want to see the same signs of the kingdom that Jesus revealed. God asks us to play our part in making that happen. We can pray for people and ask God to heal them. When someone's bad leg is healed and they can walk again, that's the kingdom come. When someone is on the outskirts of society (like people with leprosy were in New Testament times) and we can bring them into community, that's the kingdom come on earth. We don't have to sit back and accept that pain and suffering are just a part of life; we can ask God to show how much he cares and how powerful he is by bringing his healing.

Jesus said the Holy Spirit was on him so he could bring good news to the poor (Luke 4). That's why the Holy Spirit is in us too, so that we can bring good news to the poor. Being poor isn't just about not having enough money – it can be a poverty of loneliness or lack of community, a poverty of choice or a poverty of hope. When we get stuck into our communities and do something to help people living in these situations, we become God's kingdom coming *'on earth as it is in heaven'*. That's the power of the Holy Spirit living in us. That's a naturally supernatural life.

Mike Pilavachi

 Ephesians 1:13–14   1 Corinthians 2:4–5

he is the Elijah who was to come. ¹⁵ Whoever has ears, let them hear.

¹⁶ 'To what can I compare this generation? They are like children sitting in the market-places and calling out to others:

¹⁷ ' "We played the pipe for you,
     and you did not dance;
we sang a dirge,
     and you did not mourn."

¹⁸ For John came neither eating nor drinking, and they say, "He has a demon." ¹⁹ The Son of Man came eating and drinking, and they say, "Here is a glutton and a drunkard, a friend of tax collectors and sinners." But wisdom is proved right by her deeds.'

Woe on unrepentant towns

²⁰ Then Jesus began to denounce the towns in which most of his miracles had been performed, because they did not repent. ²¹ 'Woe to you, Chorazin! Woe to you, Bethsaida! For if the miracles that were performed in you had been performed in Tyre and Sidon, they would have repented long ago in sackcloth and ashes. ²² But I tell you, it will be more bearable for Tyre and Sidon on the day of judgment than for you. ²³ And you, Capernaum, will you be lifted to the heavens? No, you will go down to Hades.ᵉ For if the miracles that were performed in you had been performed in Sodom, it would have remained to this day. ²⁴ But I tell you that it will be more bearable for Sodom on the day of judgment than for you.'

The Father revealed in the Son

²⁵ At that time Jesus said, 'I praise you, Father, Lord of heaven and earth, because you have hidden these things from the wise and learned, and revealed them to little children. ²⁶ Yes, Father, for this is what you were pleased to do.

²⁷ 'All things have been committed to me by my Father. No one knows the Son except the Father, and no one knows the Father except the Son and those to whom the Son chooses to reveal him.

²⁸ 'Come to me, all you who are weary and burdened, and I will give you rest. ²⁹ Take my yoke upon you and learn from me, for I am gentle and humble in heart, and you will find rest for your souls. ³⁰ For my yoke is easy and my burden is light.'

Jesus is Lord of the Sabbath

12 At that time Jesus went through the cornfields on the Sabbath. His disciples were hungry and began to pick some ears of corn and eat them. ² When the Pharisees saw this, they said to him, 'Look! Your disciples are doing what is unlawful on the Sabbath.'

³ He answered, 'Haven't you read what David did when he and his companions were hungry? ⁴ He entered the house of God, and he and his companions ate the consecrated bread – which was not lawful for them to do, but only for the priests. ⁵ Or haven't you read in the Law that the priests on Sabbath duty in the temple desecrate the Sabbath and yet are innocent? ⁶ I tell you that something greater than the temple is here. ⁷ If you had known what these words mean, "I desire mercy, not sacrifice,"ᵃ you would not have condemned the innocent. ⁸ For the Son of Man is Lord of the Sabbath.'

⁹ Going on from that place, he went into their synagogue, ¹⁰ and a man with a shrivelled hand was there. Looking for a reason to bring charges against Jesus, they asked him, 'Is it lawful to heal on the Sabbath?'

¹¹ He said to them, 'If any of you has a sheep and it falls into a pit on the Sabbath, will you not take hold of it and lift it out? ¹² How much more valuable is a person than a sheep! Therefore it is lawful to do good on the Sabbath.'

¹³ Then he said to the man, 'Stretch out your hand.' So he stretched it out and it was completely restored, just as sound as the other. ¹⁴ But the Pharisees went out and plotted how they might kill Jesus.

God's chosen servant

¹⁵ Aware of this, Jesus withdrew from that place. A large crowd followed him,

---

ᵉ 23 That is, the realm of the dead   ᵃ 7 Hosea 6:6

and he healed all who were ill. ¹⁶He warned them not to tell others about him. ¹⁷This was to fulfil what was spoken through the prophet Isaiah:

¹⁸ 'Here is my servant whom I have
    chosen,
    the one I love, in whom I delight;
I will put my Spirit on him,
    and he will proclaim justice to the
        nations.
¹⁹ He will not quarrel or cry out;
    no one will hear his voice in the
        streets.
²⁰ A bruised reed he will not break,
    and a smouldering wick he will not
        snuff out,
    till he has brought justice through to
        victory.
²¹   In his name the nations will put
        their hope.'ᵇ

Jesus and Beelzebul

²²Then they brought him a demon-possessed man who was blind and mute, and Jesus healed him, so that he could both talk and see. ²³All the people were astonished and said, 'Could this be the Son of David?'

²⁴But when the Pharisees heard this, they said, 'It is only by Beelzebul, the prince of demons, that this fellow drives out demons.'

²⁵Jesus knew their thoughts and said to them, 'Every kingdom divided against itself will be ruined, and every city or household divided against itself will not stand. ²⁶If Satan drives out Satan, he is divided against himself. How then can his kingdom stand? ²⁷And if I drive out demons by Beelzebul, by whom do your people drive them out? So then, they will be your judges. ²⁸But if it is by the Spirit of God that I drive out demons, then the kingdom of God has come upon you.

²⁹'Or again, how can anyone enter a strong man's house and carry off his possessions unless he first ties up the strong man? Then he can plunder his house.

³⁰'Whoever is not with me is against me, and whoever does not gather with me scatters. ³¹And so I tell you, every kind of sin and slander can be forgiven, but blasphemy against the Spirit will not be forgiven. ³²Anyone who speaks a word against the Son of Man will be forgiven, but anyone who speaks against the Holy Spirit will not be forgiven, either in this age or in the age to come.

³³'Make a tree good and its fruit will be good, or make a tree bad and its fruit will be bad, for a tree is recognised by its fruit. ³⁴You brood of vipers, how can you who are evil say anything good? For the mouth speaks what the heart is full of. ³⁵A good man brings good things out of the good stored up in him, and an evil man brings evil things out of the evil stored up in him. ³⁶But I tell you that everyone will have to give account on the day of judgment for every empty word they have spoken. ³⁷For by your words you will be acquitted, and by your words you will be condemned.'

The sign of Jonah

³⁸Then some of the Pharisees and teachers of the law said to him, 'Teacher, we want to see a sign from you.'

³⁹He answered, 'A wicked and adulterous generation asks for a sign! But none will be given it except the sign of the prophet Jonah. ⁴⁰For as Jonah was three days and three nights in the belly of a huge fish, so the Son of Man will be three days and three nights in the heart of the earth. ⁴¹The men of Nineveh will stand up at the judgment with this generation and condemn it; for they repented at the preaching of Jonah, and now something greater than Jonah is here. ⁴²The Queen of the South will rise at the judgment with this generation and condemn it; for she came from the ends of the earth to listen to Solomon's wisdom, and now something greater than Solomon is here.

⁴³'When an impure spirit comes out of a person, it goes through arid places seeking rest and does not find it. ⁴⁴Then it says, "I will return to the house I left." When it arrives, it finds the house unoccupied, swept clean and put in order. ⁴⁵Then it goes and takes with it seven other

---

ᵇ 21 Isaiah 42:1-4

spirits more wicked than itself, and they go in and live there. And the final condition of that person is worse than the first. That is how it will be with this wicked generation.'

Jesus' mother and brothers

46 While Jesus was still talking to the crowd, his mother and brothers stood outside, wanting to speak to him. 47 Someone told him, 'Your mother and brothers are standing outside, wanting to speak to you.'

48 He replied to him, 'Who is my mother, and who are my brothers?' 49 Pointing to his disciples, he said, 'Here are my mother and my brothers. 50 For whoever does the will of my Father in heaven is my brother and sister and mother.'

The parable of the sower

13 That same day Jesus went out of the house and sat by the lake. 2 Such large crowds gathered round him that he got into a boat and sat in it, while all the people stood on the shore. 3 Then he told them many things in parables, saying: 'A farmer went out to sow his seed. 4 As he was scattering the seed, some fell along the path, and the birds came and ate it up. 5 Some fell on rocky places, where it did not have much soil. It sprang up quickly, because the soil was shallow. 6 But when the sun came up, the plants were scorched, and they withered because they had no root. 7 Other seed fell among thorns, which grew up and choked the plants. 8 Still other seed fell on good soil, where it produced a crop – a hundred, sixty or thirty times what was sown. 9 Whoever has ears, let them hear.'

10 The disciples came to him and asked, 'Why do you speak to the people in parables?'

11 He replied, 'Because the knowledge of the secrets of the kingdom of heaven has been given to you, but not to them. 12 Whoever has will be given more, and they will have an abundance. Whoever does not have, even what they have will be taken from them. 13 This is why I speak to them in parables:

'Though seeing, they do not see;
    though hearing, they do not hear or understand.'

14 In them is fulfilled the prophecy of Isaiah:

' "You will be ever hearing but never understanding;
    you will be ever seeing but never perceiving.
15 For this people's heart has become calloused;
    they hardly hear with their ears,
    and they have closed their eyes.
Otherwise they might see with their eyes,
    hear with their ears,
    understand with their hearts
and turn, and I would heal them." *a*

16 But blessed are your eyes because they see, and your ears because they hear. 17 For truly I tell you, many prophets and righteous people longed to see what you see but did not see it, and to hear what you hear but did not hear it.

18 'Listen then to what the parable of the sower means: 19 when anyone hears the message about the kingdom and does not understand it, the evil one comes and snatches away what was sown in their heart. This is the seed sown along the path. 20 The seed falling on rocky ground refers to someone who hears the word and at once receives it with joy. 21 But since they have no root, they last only a short time. When trouble or persecution comes because of the word, they quickly fall away. 22 The seed falling among the thorns refers to someone who hears the word, but the worries of this life and the deceitfulness of wealth choke the word, making it unfruitful. 23 But the seed falling on good soil refers to someone who hears the word and understands it. This is the one who produces a crop, yielding a hundred, sixty or thirty times what was sown.'

---

a 15 Isaiah 6:9,10 (see Septuagint)

The parable of the weeds

24 Jesus told them another parable: 'The kingdom of heaven is like a man who sowed good seed in his field. 25 But while everyone was sleeping, his enemy came and sowed weeds among the wheat, and went away. 26 When the wheat sprouted and formed ears, then the weeds also appeared.

27 'The owner's servants came to him and said, "Sir, didn't you sow good seed in your field? Where then did the weeds come from?"

28 ' "An enemy did this," he replied.

'The servants asked him, "Do you want us to go and pull them up?"

29 ' "No," he answered, "because while you are pulling up the weeds, you may uproot the wheat with them. 30 Let both grow together until the harvest. At that time I will tell the harvesters: first collect the weeds and tie them in bundles to be burned; then gather the wheat and bring it into my barn." '

The parables of the mustard seed and the yeast

31 He told them another parable: 'The kingdom of heaven is like a mustard seed, which a man took and planted in his field. 32 Though it is the smallest of all seeds, yet when it grows, it is the largest of garden plants and becomes a tree, so that the birds come and perch in its branches.'

33 He told them still another parable: 'The kingdom of heaven is like yeast that a woman took and mixed into about thirty kilograms of flour until it worked all through the dough.'

34 Jesus spoke all these things to the crowd in parables; he did not say anything to them without using a parable. 35 So was fulfilled what was spoken through the prophet:

'I will open my mouth in parables,
     I will utter things hidden since the
       creation of the world.' [b]

---

b 35 Psalm 78:2

The parable of the weeds explained

36 Then he left the crowd and went into the house. His disciples came to him and said, 'Explain to us the parable of the weeds in the field.'

37 He answered, 'The one who sowed the good seed is the Son of Man. 38 The field is the world, and the good seed stands for the people of the kingdom. The weeds are the people of the evil one, 39 and the enemy who sows them is the devil. The harvest is the end of the age, and the harvesters are angels.

YOU WHAT?

NOTORIOUS MURDERS

CAIN KILLS ABEL
Genesis 4:8–16
DAVID KILLS URIAH
2 Samuel 11:14–27
ZIMRI ASSASSINATES ELAH
1 Kings 16:8–14
NEBUCHADNEZZAR KILLS ZEDEKIAH'S SONS
2 Kings 25:1–7
HEROD KILLS JOHN THE BAPTIST
Matthew 14:1–12
THE CROWD KILL STEPHEN
Acts 7:56–60
HEROD KILLS JAMES
Acts 12:1–2

40 'As the weeds are pulled up and burned in the fire, so it will be at the end of the age. 41 The Son of Man will send out his angels, and they will weed out of his kingdom everything that causes sin and all who do evil. 42 They will throw them into the blazing furnace, where there will be weeping and gnashing of teeth. 43 Then the righteous will shine like the sun in the kingdom of their Father. Whoever has ears, let them hear.

The parables of the hidden treasure and the pearl

44 'The kingdom of heaven is like treasure hidden in a field. When a man found it, he hid it again, and then in his joy went and sold all he had and bought that field.

45 'Again, the kingdom of heaven is like a merchant looking for fine pearls. 46 When he found one of great value, he went away and sold everything he had and bought it.

The parable of the net

47 'Once again, the kingdom of heaven is like a net that was let down into the lake and caught all kinds of fish. 48 When it was full, the fishermen pulled it up on the shore. Then they sat down and collected the good fish in baskets, but threw the bad away. 49 This is how it will be at the end of the age. The angels will come and separate the wicked from the righteous 50 and throw them into the blazing furnace, where there will be weeping and gnashing of teeth.

51 'Have you understood all these things?' Jesus asked.

'Yes,' they replied.

52 He said to them, 'Therefore every teacher of the law who has become a disciple in the kingdom of heaven is like the owner of a house who brings out of his storeroom new treasures as well as old.'

A prophet without honour

53 When Jesus had finished these parables, he moved on from there. 54 Coming to his home town, he began teaching the people in their synagogue, and they were amazed. 'Where did this man get this wisdom and these miraculous powers?' they asked. 55 'Isn't this the carpenter's son? Isn't his mother's name Mary, and aren't his brothers James, Joseph, Simon and Judas? 56 Aren't all his sisters with us? Where then did this man get all these things?' 57 And they took offence at him.

But Jesus said to them, 'A prophet is not without honour except in his own town and in his own home.'

58 And he did not do many miracles there because of their lack of faith.

John the Baptist beheaded

14 At that time Herod the tetrarch heard the reports about Jesus, 2 and he said to his attendants, 'This is John the Baptist; he has risen from the dead! That is why miraculous powers are at work in him.'

3 Now Herod had arrested John and bound him and put him in prison because of Herodias, his brother Philip's wife, 4 for John had been saying to him: 'It is not lawful for you to have her.' 5 Herod wanted to kill John, but he was afraid of the people, because they considered John a prophet.

6 On Herod's birthday the daughter of Herodias danced for the guests and pleased Herod so much 7 that he promised with an oath to give her whatever she asked. 8 Prompted by her mother, she said, 'Give me here on a dish the head of John the Baptist.' 9 The king was distressed, but because of his oaths and his dinner guests, he ordered that her request be granted 10 and had John beheaded in the prison. 11 His head was brought in on a dish and given to the girl, who carried it to her mother. 12 John's disciples came and took his body and buried it. Then they went and told Jesus.

Jesus feeds the five thousand

13 When Jesus heard what had happened, he withdrew by boat privately to a solitary place. Hearing of this, the crowds followed him on foot from the towns. 14 When Jesus landed and saw a large crowd, he had compassion on them and healed those who were ill.

15 As evening approached, the disciples came to him and said, 'This is a remote place, and it's already getting late. Send the crowds away, so that they can go to the villages and buy themselves some food.'

16 Jesus replied, 'They do not need to go away. You give them something to eat.'

17 'We have here only five loaves of bread and two fish,' they answered.

18 'Bring them here to me,' he said. 19 And he told the people to sit down on the grass. Taking the five loaves and the two fish and looking up to heaven, he

gave thanks and broke the loaves. Then he gave them to the disciples, and the disciples gave them to the people. ²⁰They all ate and were satisfied, and the disciples picked up twelve basketfuls of broken pieces that were left over. ²¹The number of those who ate was about five thousand men, besides women and children.

Jesus walks on the water

²²Immediately Jesus made the disciples get into the boat and go on ahead of him to the other side, while he dismissed the crowd. ²³After he had dismissed them, he went up on a mountainside by himself to pray. Later that night, he was there alone, ²⁴and the boat was

JUSTICE AND MERCY 6

WHAT CAN YOU OFFER?

The feeding of the five thousand (Matthew 14:13–21) must be one of the most famous stories from the life of Jesus. It's dramatic, it's miraculous, and it has a small boy with a packed lunch as the hero. It's also radical and challenging, because it shows what matters to Jesus and what he wants his people to do.

Jesus has been holding a festival, teaching and healing huge crowds of people. He has been feeding their spirits and minds and healing their bodies. The problem is that there's no catering! It's now getting late and people are hungry. The disciples are worried and want to send people away. This is when Jesus unveils his first big surprise: *'You give them something to eat'* (v. 16). This is not what the disciples are expecting. They thought Jesus was about spiritual stuff and praying for healing. They didn't think he was interested in the mundane, messy stuff of people being hungry. But Jesus shows them that he cares about people's bodies as well as their spirits and minds. He also tells them that it's their job to care as well. They are not to focus exclusively on 'spiritual' stuff, but should care for people's physical needs too.

The second surprise is the miracle. They have searched around for the answer to the huge food problem, but have only found one inadequate packed lunch. They are astonished when Jesus seems to think that will be enough. They are even more astonished when it turns out to be plenty! The point that Jesus is trying to teach them is that he doesn't need them to have all the resources or answers or skills to solve the problem. He doesn't need them to be rich enough or clever enough to be the solution. He just needs everything they have. And everything we have, however inadequate, in his hands becomes plenty.

God looks at a world of hunger where 2 billion people live on less than $2 per day, and then he looks at his people and says to us, 'You feed them.' This is our mission and calling. He doesn't ask that we have enough to solve the problems, just that we give him all we have, because in his hands a boy's packed lunch feeds a multitude. What miracles could happen if we gave ourselves to Jesus?

David Westlake

 Micah 6:8   Luke 4:18–19

already a considerable distance from land, buffeted by the waves because the wind was against it.

25 Shortly before dawn Jesus went out to them, walking on the lake. 26 When the disciples saw him walking on the lake, they were terrified. 'It's a ghost,' they said, and cried out in fear.

27 But Jesus immediately said to them: 'Take courage! It is I. Don't be afraid.'

28 'Lord, if it's you,' Peter replied, 'tell me to come to you on the water.'

29 'Come,' he said.

Then Peter got down out of the boat, walked on the water and came towards Jesus. 30 But when he saw the wind, he was afraid and, beginning to sink, cried out, 'Lord, save me!'

31 Immediately Jesus reached out his hand and caught him. 'You of little faith,' he said, 'why did you doubt?'

32 And when they climbed into the boat, the wind died down. 33 Then those who were in the boat worshipped him, saying, 'Truly you are the Son of God.'

34 When they had crossed over, they landed at Gennesaret. 35 And when the men of that place recognised Jesus, they sent word to all the surrounding country. People brought all who were ill to him 36 and begged him to let those who were ill just touch the edge of his cloak, and all who touched it were healed.

That which defiles

15 Then some Pharisees and teachers of the law came to Jesus from Jerusalem and asked, 2 'Why do your disciples break the tradition of the elders? They don't wash their hands before they eat!'

3 Jesus replied, 'And why do you break the command of God for the sake of your tradition? 4 For God said, "Honour your father and mother"*a* and "Anyone who curses their father or mother is to be put to death."*b* 5 But you say that if anyone declares that what might have been used to help their father or mother is "devoted to

God," 6 they are not to "honour their father or mother" with it. Thus you nullify the word of God for the sake of your tradition. 7 You hypocrites! Isaiah was right when he prophesied about you:

8 ' "These people honour me with their lips,
but their hearts are far from me.
9 They worship me in vain;
their teachings are merely human rules."*c*

10 Jesus called the crowd to him and said, 'Listen and understand. 11 What goes into someone's mouth does not defile them, but what comes out of their mouth, that is what defiles them.'

12 Then the disciples came to him and asked, 'Do you know that the Pharisees were offended when they heard this?'

13 He replied, 'Every plant that my heavenly Father has not planted will be pulled up by the roots. 14 Leave them; they are blind guides.*d* If the blind lead the blind, both will fall into a pit.'

15 Peter said, 'Explain the parable to us.'

16 'Are you still so dull?' Jesus asked them. 17 'Don't you see that whatever enters the mouth goes into the stomach and then out of the body? 18 But the things that come out of a person's mouth come from the heart, and these defile them. 19 For out of the heart come evil thoughts – murder, adultery, sexual immorality, theft, false testimony, slander. 20 These are what defile a person; but eating with unwashed hands does not defile them.'

The faith of a Canaanite woman

21 Leaving that place, Jesus withdrew to the region of Tyre and Sidon. 22 A Canaanite woman from that vicinity came to him, crying out, 'Lord, Son of David, have mercy on me! My daughter is demon-possessed and suffering terribly.'

23 Jesus did not answer a word. So his disciples came to him and urged him,

---

a 4 Exodus 20:12; Deut. 5:16
b 4 Exodus 21:17; Lev. 20:9

c 9 Isaiah 29:13
d 14 Some manuscripts *blind guides of the blind*

'Send her away, for she keeps crying out after us.'

24 He answered, 'I was sent only to the lost sheep of Israel.'

25 The woman came and knelt before him. 'Lord, help me!' she said.

26 He replied, 'It is not right to take the children's bread and toss it to the dogs.'

HEALING & MIRACLES 1

Healing is the children's bread

When I look at all that God has given to us, I'm filled with an overwhelming feeling of gratitude for just how generous our God is. The story in Matthew 15:21–28 of the Canaanite woman who doesn't give up is an example to us of what we have as God's children.

The persistence of those in need is something to watch throughout the Gospels. When we read this story we find a woman is desperate for her daughter to get well, and she'll ask for it no matter what people think. Even the disciples are trying to pull Jesus away from this woman as they want her to leave them alone. Yet it is in her persistence that she is able to get what she needs. Sometimes we give up when we don't see healing right away, or don't get the answer to prayer we hoped for. Then it's easy to walk away feeling that Jesus isn't listening.

Jesus is *always* listening. He's fully aware of what's going on in your life and of all those areas where you want to see him move. Many times we will find that we need to make the choice to push through and ask again, because Jesus is listening and he will respond – it's just a matter of when. This lady had to push through the disciples' rejection, and she had to be willing not to care so much about what she looked like. It's often pride that keeps us from the healing we need. Like this woman, we need to know that healing is in Jesus and just a bit of what he releases will set us or our friends free.

Jesus makes it clear to whom he has been sent, and she doesn't quite fit into his target group. How can she expect to eat the children's bread if she's not part of this family? It's a harsh message, but she's not discouraged, and she doesn't doubt him or question if he's the man of compassion she's heard about. She just asks again – *'Lord, help me!'* (v. 25) – and believes that Jesus can and will help her. It's her responses that reveal her faith and it's in her humility, meekness, patience and perseverance in prayer that Jesus responds with healing.

Even if God seems to be healing other people and you're not seeing it for yourself, know that your faith in the situation matters. Jesus loves it when we persevere in faith. Some of the most amazing miracles I have seen in the last several years have been a product of persistence. It's a choice not to give up and to continue to pray until we see the results we need. It's important in our walk with the Lord that even when others around us don't believe healing will happen or think God won't answer our prayer, we know God is listening and, no matter the circumstance, understand that he loves it when we choose to push through in our faith.

Christy Wimber

1 Peter 2:24

27 'Yes it is, Lord,' she said. 'Even the dogs eat the crumbs that fall from their master's table.'

28 Then Jesus said to her, 'Woman, you have great faith! Your request is granted.' And her daughter was healed at that moment.

Jesus feeds the four thousand

29 Jesus left there and went along the Sea of Galilee. Then he went up on a mountainside and sat down. 30 Great crowds came to him, bringing the lame, the blind, the crippled, the mute and many others, and laid them at his feet; and he healed them. 31 The people were amazed when they saw the mute speaking, the crippled made well, the lame walking and the blind seeing. And they praised the God of Israel.

32 Jesus called his disciples to him and said, 'I have compassion for these people; they have already been with me three days and have nothing to eat. I do not want to send them away hungry, or they may collapse on the way.'

33 His disciples answered, 'Where could we get enough bread in this remote place to feed such a crowd?'

34 'How many loaves do you have?' Jesus asked.

'Seven,' they replied, 'and a few small fish.'

35 He told the crowd to sit down on the ground. 36 Then he took the seven loaves and the fish, and when he had given thanks, he broke them and gave them to the disciples, and they in turn to the people. 37 They all ate and were satisfied. Afterwards the disciples picked up seven basketfuls of broken pieces that were left over. 38 The number of those who ate was four thousand men, besides women and children. 39 After Jesus had sent the crowd away, he got into the boat and went to the vicinity of Magadan.

The demand for a sign

16 The Pharisees and Sadducees came to Jesus and tested him by asking him to show them a sign from heaven.

2 He replied, 'When evening comes, you say, "It will be fair weather, for the sky is red," 3 and in the morning, "Today it will be stormy, for the sky is red and overcast." You know how to interpret the appearance of the sky, but you cannot interpret the signs of the times.*a* 4 A wicked and adulterous generation looks for a sign, but none will be given it except the sign of Jonah.' Jesus then left them and went away.

The yeast of the Pharisees and Sadducees

5 When they went across the lake, the disciples forgot to take bread. 6 'Be careful,' Jesus said to them. 'Be on your guard against the yeast of the Pharisees and Sadducees.'

7 They discussed this among themselves and said, 'It is because we didn't bring any bread.'

8 Aware of their discussion, Jesus asked, 'You of little faith, why are you talking among yourselves about having no bread? 9 Do you still not understand? Don't you remember the five loaves for the five thousand, and how many basketfuls you gathered? 10 Or the seven loaves for the four thousand, and how many basketfuls you gathered? 11 How is it you don't understand that I was not talking to you about bread? But be on your guard against the yeast of the Pharisees and Sadducees.' 12 Then they understood that he was not telling them to guard against the yeast used in bread, but against the teaching of the Pharisees and Sadducees.

Peter declares that Jesus is the Messiah

13 When Jesus came to the region of Caesarea Philippi, he asked his disciples, 'Who do people say the Son of Man is?'

14 They replied, 'Some say John the Baptist; others say Elijah; and still others, Jeremiah or one of the prophets.'

15 'But what about you?' he asked. 'Who do you say I am?'

---

a 2,3 Some early manuscripts do not have When evening comes . . . of the times.

16 Simon Peter answered, 'You are the Messiah, the Son of the living God.'

17 Jesus replied, 'Blessed are you, Simon son of Jonah, for this was not revealed to you by flesh and blood, but by my Father in heaven. 18 And I tell you that you are Peter,b and on this rock I will build my church, and the gates of Hadesc will not overcome it. 19 I will give you the keys of the kingdom of heaven; whatever you bind on earth will bed bound in heaven, and whatever you loose on earth will bed loosed in heaven.' 20 Then he ordered his disciples not to tell anyone that he was the Messiah.

Jesus predicts his death

21 From that time on Jesus began to explain to his disciples that he must go to Jerusalem and suffer many things at the hands of the elders, the chief priests and the teachers of the law, and that he must be killed and on the third day be raised to life.

22 Peter took him aside and began to rebuke him. 'Never, Lord!' he said. 'This shall never happen to you!'

23 Jesus turned and said to Peter, 'Get behind me, Satan! You are a stumbling-block to me; you do not have in mind the concerns of God, but merely human concerns.'

24 Then Jesus said to his disciples, 'Whoever wants to be my disciple must deny themselves and take up their cross and follow me. 25 For whoever wants to save their lifee will lose it, but whoever loses their life for me will find it. 26 What good will it be for someone to gain the whole world, yet forfeit their soul? Or what can anyone give in exchange for their soul? 27 For the Son of Man is going to come in his Father's glory with his angels, and then he will reward each person according to what they have done.

---

b 18 The Greek word for Peter means rock.
c 18 That is, the realm of the dead
d 19 Or will have been
e 25 The Greek word means either life or soul; also in verse 26.

28 'Truly I tell you, some who are standing here will not taste death before they see the Son of Man coming in his kingdom.'

The transfiguration

17 After six days Jesus took with him Peter, James and John the brother of James, and led them up a high mountain by themselves. 2 There he was transfigured before them. His face shone like the sun, and his clothes became as white as the light. 3 Just then there appeared before them Moses and Elijah, talking with Jesus.

4 Peter said to Jesus, 'Lord, it is good for us to be here. If you wish, I will put up three shelters – one for you, one for Moses and one for Elijah.'

5 While he was still speaking, a bright cloud covered them, and a voice from the cloud said, 'This is my Son, whom I love; with him I am well pleased. Listen to him!'

6 When the disciples heard this, they fell face down to the ground, terrified. 7 But Jesus came and touched them. 'Get up,' he said. 'Don't be afraid.' 8 When they looked up, they saw no one except Jesus.

9 As they were coming down the mountain, Jesus instructed them, 'Don't tell anyone what you have seen, until the Son of Man has been raised from the dead.'

10 The disciples asked him, 'Why then do the teachers of the law say that Elijah must come first?'

11 Jesus replied, 'To be sure, Elijah comes and will restore all things. 12 But I tell you, Elijah has already come, and they did not recognise him, but have done to him everything they wished. In the same way the Son of Man is going to suffer at their hands.' 13 Then the disciples understood that he was talking to them about John the Baptist.

Jesus heals a demon-possessed boy

14 When they came to the crowd, a man approached Jesus and knelt before him. 15 'Lord, have mercy on my son,' he said. 'He has seizures and is suffering greatly. He often falls into the fire or into the

water. **16** I brought him to your disciples, but they could not heal him.'

17 'You unbelieving and perverse generation,' Jesus replied, 'how long shall I stay with you? How long shall I put up with you? Bring the boy here to me.' **18** Jesus re-

buked the demon, and it came out of the boy, and he was healed at that moment.

19 Then the disciples came to Jesus in private and asked, 'Why couldn't we drive it out?'

20 He replied, 'Because you have so

HEALING & MIRACLES 4

Empowered by faith

If you look at your life, you're choosing to believe in things all the time. We choose to have faith in the postman that he will deliver our mail; we choose to have faith in doctors when they give us a diagnosis; we choose to have faith that shops and supermarkets will be open for us to buy food; in fact, think of all the choices we make daily that mean we have to have faith.

Most of us would say that the most important faith we have is found in Christ, so why do we have so much faith in places, people and things, yet run low when it comes to having faith in what God says?

In Matthew 17:20 Jesus brings clarity to how much faith we really need, and he uses the example of the tiniest seed. If we have just the smallest amount of faith, it can move all the mountains in our life. Jesus could have chosen any seed as an example, yet he chooses the smallest of all seeds. It's not meant to overwhelm us, but to encourage us, as it should help us to realise that the power needed to deal with the unmoveable mountains in life rests with God and not with us. The faith Jesus talks about will have the power to change things that look impossible: even the smallest amount of faith contains moving power.

How many things would you like removed out of your life? If you begin to think and believe that 'whatever I believe God can move, he can move', it puts the emphasis on the power of faith and not the hugeness of the mountain.

Faith is a gift from God that can only be received (1 Corinthians 12:9). You can't earn faith, you can't strive to find it, and you can't be good enough to deserve it. While it is a gift, freely given, sometimes we do have to ask for more of it. It's not often that we're given faith and – 'ping!' – we suddenly have more of it, but by experiencing more of the goodness of God and his provision for us we gain the faith to pray, hope and ask for more. Sometimes asking for more faith simply opens our eyes to see all the ways in which God is already faithful to us.

Ask God to give you faith where you don't have it. Where you don't have faith is an area of your life that needs to experience God's kingdom. Then you can begin to see God ruling over that area of your life which needs to change. Ask, ask, and then ask God again. You can never ask God for too much faith.

Christy Wimber

 2 Kings 5:1–19   Mark 9:14–32

little faith. Truly I tell you, if you have faith as small as a mustard seed, you can say to this mountain, "Move from here to there," and it will move. Nothing will be impossible for you.' [21]*a*

Jesus predicts his death a second time

22 When they came together in Galilee, he said to them, 'The Son of Man is going to be delivered into the hands of men. 23 They will kill him, and on the third day he will be raised to life.' And the disciples were filled with grief.

The temple tax

24 After Jesus and his disciples arrived in Capernaum, the collectors of the two-drachma temple tax came to Peter and asked, 'Doesn't your teacher pay the temple tax?'

25 'Yes, he does,' he replied.

When Peter came into the house, Jesus was the first to speak. 'What do you think, Simon?' he asked. 'From whom do the kings of the earth collect duty and taxes – from their own children or from others?'

26 'From others,' Peter answered.

'Then the children are exempt,' Jesus said to him. 27 'But so that we may not cause offence, go to the lake and throw out your line. Take the first fish you catch; open its mouth and you will find a four-drachma coin. Take it and give it to them for my tax and yours.'

The greatest in the kingdom of heaven

18 At that time the disciples came to Jesus and asked, 'Who, then, is the greatest in the kingdom of heaven?'

2 He called a little child to him, and placed the child among them. 3 And he said: 'Truly I tell you, unless you change and become like little children, you will never enter the kingdom of heaven. 4 Therefore, whoever takes the lowly position of this child is the greatest in the kingdom of heaven. 5 And whoever welcomes one such child in my name welcomes me.

Causing to stumble

6 'If anyone causes one of these little ones – those who believe in me – to stumble, it would be better for them to have a large millstone hung round their neck and to be drowned in the depths of the sea. 7 Woe to the world because of the things that cause people to stumble! Such things must come, but woe to the person through whom they come! 8 If your hand or your foot causes you to stumble, cut it off and throw it away. It is better for you to enter life maimed or crippled than to have two hands or two feet and be thrown into eternal fire. 9 And if your eye causes you to stumble, gouge it out and throw it away. It is better for you to enter life with one eye than to have two eyes and be thrown into the fire of hell.

The parable of the wandering sheep

10 'See that you do not despise one of these little ones. For I tell you that their angels in heaven always see the face of my Father in heaven. [11]*a*

12 'What do you think? If a man owns a hundred sheep, and one of them wanders away, will he not leave the ninety-nine on the hills and go to look for the one that wandered off? 13 And if he finds it, truly I tell you, he is happier about that one sheep than about the ninety-nine that did not wander off. 14 In the same way your Father in heaven is not willing that any of these little ones should perish.

Dealing with sin in the church

15 'If your brother or sister*b* sins,*c* go and point out their fault, just between the two of you. If they listen to you, you have won them over. 16 But if they will not listen, take one or two others along, so that "every matter may be established by the testimony of two or three witnesses."*d* 17 If they still refuse to listen, tell it to the

---

a 11 Some manuscripts include here the words of Luke 19:10.
b 15 The Greek word for *brother or sister* (*adelphos*) refers here to a fellow disciple, whether man or woman; also in verses 21 and 35.
c 15 Some manuscripts *sins against you*
d 16 Deut. 19:15

---

a 21 Some manuscripts include here words similar to Mark 9:29.

church; and if they refuse to listen even to the church, treat them as you would a pagan or a tax collector.

18 'Truly I tell you, whatever you bind on earth will be^e bound in heaven, and whatever you loose on earth will be^e loosed in heaven.

19 'Again, truly I tell you that if two of you on earth agree about anything they ask for, it will be done for them by my Father in heaven. 20 For where two or three gather in my name, there am I with them.'

---

^e 18 Or *will have been*

The parable of the unmerciful servant

21 Then Peter came to Jesus and asked, 'Lord, how many times shall I forgive my brother or sister who sins against me? Up to seven times?'

22 Jesus answered, 'I tell you, not seven times, but seventy-seven times.*f*

23 'Therefore, the kingdom of heaven is like a king who wanted to settle accounts with his servants. 24 As he began the settlement, a man who owed him ten thousand bags of gold*g* was brought to him. 25 Since

---

f 22 Or *seventy times seven*
g 24 Greek *ten thousand talents*; a talent was worth about 20 years of a day labourer's wages.

PRAYER 5

AGREEING TO AGREE, AMEN

It's remarkable what two or more human beings can do if only they agree on something! If you have read about the Tower of Babel (Genesis 11:1–9, particularly v. 6), you will know that sometimes this can have a huge negative effect. Imagine, then, how much good can happen when two or more of us *agree with God*! It's amazing to think that he doesn't need a whole city or movement to join in. Matthew 18:18–20 tells us that just two willing people are needed. It can be more, but two will do.

There are a number of ways for us to symbolise our joint requests to God – our prayers of agreement. The traditional way is to wait until the end of a prayer that someone else has prayed and then join together in unison saying, 'Amen!' This is the way we say, 'We completely agree with that one, Lord. Let it be done!' Every time we say 'Amen' at the end of someone else's prayer, we are symbolising that we know that what is written in Matthew 18:19 is a promise from God.

In this passage the Greek word for 'agree' can be translated as 'harmonise'. Think about a piano: when the right two notes are played together, a harmony is created. The notes are already there, they just need to be struck simultaneously and the beautiful sound is created. In the same way, if we have two people working together and praying to God that his kingdom will come, then we will see God do beautiful things – although not necessarily what we expect!

So when two or more Christians meet and share what they think God has said to them, when they agree their prayers harmonise. Those are the areas where they can pray and be sure that God will work. *'It will be done'* (v. 19). What an amazing promise!

Hugo Anson

 Nehemiah 1   Daniel 6

he was not able to pay, the master ordered that he and his wife and his children and all that he had be sold to repay the debt.

26 'At this the servant fell on his knees before him. "Be patient with me," he begged, "and I will pay back everything."
27 The servant's master took pity on him, cancelled the debt and let him go.

28 'But when that servant went out, he found one of his fellow servants who owed him a hundred silver coins.*h* He grabbed him and began to choke him. "Pay back what you owe me!" he demanded.

29 'His fellow servant fell to his knees and begged him, "Be patient with me, and I will pay it back."

30 'But he refused. Instead, he went off and had the man thrown into prison until he could pay the debt. 31 When the other servants saw what had happened, they were outraged and went and told their master everything that had happened.

32 'Then the master called the servant in. "You wicked servant," he said, "I cancelled all that debt of yours because you begged me to. 33 Shouldn't you have had mercy on your fellow servant just as I had on you?" 34 In anger his master handed him over to the jailers to be tortured, until he should pay back all he owed.

35 'This is how my heavenly Father will treat each of you unless you forgive your brother or sister from your heart.'

Divorce

19 When Jesus had finished saying these things, he left Galilee and went into the region of Judea to the other side of the Jordan. 2 Large crowds followed him, and he healed them there.

3 Some Pharisees came to him to test him. They asked, 'Is it lawful for a man to divorce his wife for any and every reason?'

4 'Haven't you read,' he replied, 'that at the beginning the Creator "made them male and female,"*a* 5 and said, "For this reason a man will leave his father and mother and be united to his wife, and the two will become one flesh"*b*? 6 So they are no longer two, but one flesh. Therefore what God has joined together, let no one separate.'

7 'Why then,' they asked, 'did Moses command that a man give his wife a certificate of divorce and send her away?'

8 Jesus replied, 'Moses permitted you to divorce your wives because your hearts were hard. But it was not this way from the beginning. 9 I tell you that anyone who divorces his wife, except for sexual immorality, and marries another woman commits adultery.'

10 The disciples said to him, 'If this is the situation between a husband and wife, it is better not to marry.'

11 Jesus replied, 'Not everyone can accept this word, but only those to whom it has been given. 12 For there are eunuchs who were born that way, and there are eunuchs who have been made eunuchs by others – and there are those who choose to live like eunuchs for the sake of the kingdom of heaven. The one who can accept this should accept it.'

The little children and Jesus

13 Then people brought little children to Jesus for him to place his hands on them and pray for them. But the disciples rebuked them.

14 Jesus said, 'Let the little children come to me, and do not hinder them, for the kingdom of heaven belongs to such as these.' 15 When he had placed his hands on them, he went on from there.

The rich and the kingdom of God

16 Just then a man came up to Jesus and asked, 'Teacher, what good thing must I do to get eternal life?'

17 'Why do you ask me about what is good?' Jesus replied. 'There is only One who is good. If you want to enter life, keep the commandments.'

18 'Which ones?' he enquired.

Jesus replied, ' "You shall not murder, you shall not commit adultery, you shall not steal, you shall not give false

---

h 28 Greek *a hundred denarii*; a denarius was the usual daily wage of a day labourer (see 20:2).
a 4 Gen. 1:27

b 5 Gen. 2:24

RELATIONSHIPS 10

RELATIONSHIPS FOR MARRIAGE

It might not seem particularly relevant to be talking about marriage when you're young, but no series that talks about relationships between men and women in a Christian context would be right without looking at it.

What's so special about marriage? From Adam and Eve to Revelation, God shows he's really passionate about it. It's the only place where we're designed to enjoy the amazing gift of sex; where we flourish; where we can serve God more effectively than we could if we were single; and it's designed to be for life (Matthew 19:4–6).

In our culture we can almost forget that marriage is a unique commitment between two people for life. When divorce is prevalent in our society and the media shows that living together and having a sexual relationship before marriage is the norm, it results in us losing something of the godly idea of marriage. As a result, more and more of us grow up without knowing what a good Christian marriage or relationship should look like.

In modern dating it has become acceptable, if not normal, for us to spend lots of time alone with the person we're dating, and to share some of our most intimate thoughts with one other. Outside the church, we find that sexual relationships and living together are all 'normal'. What the Bible suggests, however, is that this level of vulnerability is meant for a marriage relationship alone.

You see, a Christian marriage is meant to be the place of ultimate vulnerability, a place of openness and exposure that's only appropriate when it comes with a commitment for a lifetime. This is another reason why sex is for marriage. Marriage is the only place where you should be completely vulnerable with one another – emotionally, financially and physically. It's only right that we're completely vulnerable with someone when they're committed to us in all those ways – this is another way that we guard our hearts (Proverbs 4:23).

I hate to break it to you, but I'm assured that the moment of having a marriage certificate in your hands isn't actually the thing that changes your life. It's doing life together, sharing dreams, money, time and hopes. It's all those things, as well as a sexual relationship, that mean two people are 'cleaved' together and become one flesh. God designed that attachment to be in marriage, but when we behave as if we're married by the level of vulnerability that we have with one another, the same effect occurs and we become 'cleaved' to one another. By treating our relationships in the same way that God would have us treat marriages, we are preparing ourselves to be a little bit more broken in all our future relationships as we effectively undergo the agony of a 'divorce' with each relationship break-up.

So guard your hearts, and ask God to help guide you in the right level of vulnerability in your relationships.

Jane Plackett & Calum Dyke

 Galatians 5:13　　　　　　　　　Ephesians 5:26

testimony, ¹⁹honour your father and mother,"ᶜ and "love your neighbour as yourself."ᵈ'

²⁰'All these I have kept,' the young man said. 'What do I still lack?'

²¹Jesus answered, 'If you want to be perfect, go, sell your possessions and give to the poor, and you will have treasure in heaven. Then come, follow me.'

²²When the young man heard this, he went away sad, because he had great wealth.

²³Then Jesus said to his disciples, 'Truly I tell you, it is hard for someone who is rich to enter the kingdom of heaven. ²⁴Again I tell you, it is easier for a camel to go through the eye of a needle than for someone who is rich to enter the kingdom of God.'

²⁵When the disciples heard this, they were greatly astonished and asked, 'Who then can be saved?'

²⁶Jesus looked at them and said, 'With man this is impossible, but with God all things are possible.'

²⁷Peter answered him, 'We have left everything to follow you! What then will there be for us?'

²⁸Jesus said to them, 'Truly I tell you, at the renewal of all things, when the Son of Man sits on his glorious throne, you who have followed me will also sit on twelve thrones, judging the twelve tribes of Israel. ²⁹And everyone who has left houses or brothers or sisters or father or mother or wifeᵉ or children or fields for my sake will receive a hundred times as much and will inherit eternal life. ³⁰But many who are first will be last, and many who are last will be first.

The parable of the workers in the vineyard

20 'For the kingdom of heaven is like a landowner who went out early in the morning to hire workers for his vineyard. ²He agreed to pay them a denariusᵃ for the day and sent them into his vineyard.

³'About nine in the morning he went out and saw others standing in the market-place doing nothing. ⁴He told them, "You also go and work in my vineyard, and I will pay you whatever is right." ⁵So they went.

'He went out again about noon and about three in the afternoon and did the same thing. ⁶About five in the afternoon he went out and found still others standing around. He asked them, "Why have you been standing here all day long doing nothing?"

⁷'"Because no one has hired us," they answered.

'He said to them, "You also go and work in my vineyard."

⁸'When evening came, the owner of the vineyard said to his foreman, "Call the workers and pay them their wages, beginning with the last ones hired and going on to the first."

⁹'The workers who were hired about five in the afternoon came and each received a denarius. ¹⁰So when those came who were hired first, they expected to receive more. But each one of them also received a denarius. ¹¹When they received it, they began to grumble against the landowner. ¹²"These who were hired last worked only one hour," they said, "and you have made them equal to us who have borne the burden of the work and the heat of the day."

¹³'But he answered one of them, "I am not being unfair to you, friend. Didn't you agree to work for a denarius? ¹⁴Take your pay and go. I want to give the one who was hired last the same as I gave you. ¹⁵Don't I have the right to do what I want with my own money? Or are you envious because I am generous?"

¹⁶'So the last will be first, and the first will be last.'

---

c 19 Exodus 20:12-16; Deut. 5:16-20
d 19 Lev. 19:18
e 29 Some manuscripts do not have *or wife*.

a 2 A denarius was the usual daily wage of a day labourer.

Jesus predicts his death a third time

17 Now Jesus was going up to Jerusalem. On the way, he took the Twelve aside and said to them, 18 'We are going up to Jerusalem, and the Son of Man will be delivered over to the chief priests and the teachers of the law. They will condemn him to death 19 and will hand him over to the Gentiles to be mocked and flogged and crucified. On the third day he will be raised to life!'

A mother's request

20 Then the mother of Zebedee's sons came to Jesus with her sons and, kneeling down, asked a favour of him.

21 'What is it you want?' he asked.

She said, 'Grant that one of these two sons of mine may sit at your right and the other at your left in your kingdom.'

22 'You don't know what you are asking,' Jesus said to them. 'Can you drink the cup I am going to drink?'

'We can,' they answered.

23 Jesus said to them, 'You will indeed drink from my cup, but to sit at my right or left is not for me to grant. These places belong to those for whom they have been prepared by my Father.'

24 When the ten heard about this, they were indignant with the two brothers. 25 Jesus called them together and said, 'You know that the rulers of the Gentiles lord it over them, and their high officials exercise authority over them. 26 Not so with you. Instead, whoever wants to become great among you must be your servant, 27 and whoever wants to be first must be your slave – 28 just as the Son of Man did not come to be served, but to serve, and to give his life as a ransom for many.'

Two blind men receive sight

29 As Jesus and his disciples were leaving Jericho, a large crowd followed him. 30 Two blind men were sitting by the roadside, and when they heard that Jesus was passing by, they shouted, 'Lord, Son of David, have mercy on us!'

31 The crowd rebuked them and told them to be quiet, but they shouted all the louder, 'Lord, Son of David, have mercy on us!'

32 Jesus stopped and called them. 'What do you want me to do for you?' he asked.

33 'Lord,' they answered, 'we want our sight.'

34 Jesus had compassion on them and touched their eyes. Immediately they received their sight and followed him.

Jesus comes to Jerusalem as king

21 As they approached Jerusalem and came to Bethphage on the Mount of Olives, Jesus sent two disciples, 2 saying to them, 'Go to the village ahead of you, and at once you will find a donkey tied there, with her colt by her. Untie them and bring them to me. 3 If anyone says anything to you, say that the Lord needs them, and he will send them right away.'

4 This took place to fulfil what was spoken through the prophet:

> 5 'Say to Daughter Zion,
>   "See, your king comes to you,
> gentle and riding on a donkey,
>   and on a colt, the foal of a donkey." ' [a]

6 The disciples went and did as Jesus had instructed them. 7 They brought the donkey and the colt and placed their cloaks on them for Jesus to sit on. 8 A very large crowd spread their cloaks on the road, while others cut branches from the trees and spread them on the road. 9 The crowds that went ahead of him and those that followed shouted,

> 'Hosanna[b] to the Son of David!'

> 'Blessed is he who comes in the name of the Lord!'[c]

> 'Hosanna[d] in the highest heaven!'

10 When Jesus entered Jerusalem, the whole city was stirred and asked, 'Who is this?'

---

a 5 Zech. 9:9
b 9 A Hebrew expression meaning 'Save!' which became an exclamation of praise; also in verse 15
c 9 Psalm 118:25,26
d 9 A Hebrew expression meaning 'Save!' which became an exclamation of praise; also in verse 15

LIFE OF JESUS 2

King of God's people

One of the great themes in tales ancient and modern is the idea of the king who will come and 'put things right', by such heroic ventures as slaying the evil dragon or killing the cave trolls, and, in some spectacular and epic way, bring about peace and justice.

In a world that is always to some extent a mess, the idea of someone who will 'put things right' with power and authority is an appealing one. It was certainly an important idea in Jewish belief. Under the kingship of David and his son Solomon, the Jews had known independence, stability and prosperity, but that was in the distant past. By the time of Jesus they had been trampled on for a thousand years by an almost continuous succession of foreigners – 'the nations' – who bullied, taxed and despised them. Yet there was hope: the Scriptures – what we call the Old Testament – talked repeatedly of a King, a Messiah (*Christ* in Greek) who would appear, defeat the enemies of God's people and begin the rule of God's kingdom.

When Jesus came, he revealed both in his teaching and through his miracles that he was indeed that long-expected King. He became widely known as the 'Son of David' and Jewish hopes ran high. Yet Jesus seems to have played things very cautiously; after all, there were many people who had a lot to lose if there really was a true king of Israel. A deeper problem was the way that the Old Testament idea of a Messiah had been twisted and distorted into the image of a nationalistic military avenger destroying Israel's enemies.

Expectations ran high as Jesus came to Jerusalem for the Passover and all the people were waiting for him to proclaim who he was (Matthew 21:1–11). In answer Jesus carries out a carefully prepared symbolic act. He rides in on a donkey and in doing so acts out a prophecy in the Old Testament book of Zechariah (9:9–10) which talks of a gentle king whose rule of peace will extend over all nations. Jesus is saying that he is King, but a king in God's way and not just the king of Israel.

The years have rolled on, but the human race's need for a king has not gone away. We all long for someone with power who will rule for us and defend us from all our enemies. But having a king is something that cuts both ways. After all, any king who rules *for* us must also rule *over* us. What we would all really like is a king – a tame monarch – whom we can order about. This was the problem Jesus faced with the Jewish leadership when he was here on earth: they wanted him to do their bidding. Sadly, the temptation to try to make Jesus our king but still give him orders has never gone away. If we accept Jesus as King, it must be on his terms, not ours.

J.John

11 The crowds answered, 'This is Jesus, the prophet from Nazareth in Galilee.'

Jesus at the temple

12 Jesus entered the temple courts and drove out all who were buying and selling there. He overturned the tables of the money-changers and the benches of those selling doves. **13** 'It is written,' he said to them, ' "My house will be called a house of prayer," *e* but you are making it "a den of robbers." *f*'

14 The blind and the lame came to him at the temple, and he healed them. **15** But when the chief priests and the teachers of the law saw the wonderful things he did and the children shouting in the temple courts, 'Hosanna to the Son of David,' they were indignant.

16 'Do you hear what these children are saying?' they asked him.

'Yes,' replied Jesus, 'have you never read,

' "From the lips of children and infants you, Lord, have called forth your praise" *g* ?'

17 And he left them and went out of the city to Bethany, where he spent the night.

Jesus curses a fig-tree

18 Early in the morning, as Jesus was on his way back to the city, he was hungry. **19** Seeing a fig-tree by the road, he went up to it but found nothing on it except leaves. Then he said to it, 'May you never bear fruit again!' Immediately the tree withered.

20 When the disciples saw this, they were amazed. 'How did the fig-tree wither so quickly?' they asked.

21 Jesus replied, 'Truly I tell you, if you have faith and do not doubt, not only can you do what was done to the fig-tree, but also you can say to this mountain, "Go, throw yourself into the sea," and it will be done. **22** If you believe, you will receive whatever you ask for in prayer.'

The authority of Jesus questioned

23 Jesus entered the temple courts, and, while he was teaching, the chief priests and the elders of the people came to him. 'By what authority are you doing these things?' they asked. 'And who gave you this authority?'

24 Jesus replied, 'I will also ask you one question. If you answer me, I will tell you by what authority I am doing these things. **25** John's baptism – where did it come from? Was it from heaven, or of human origin?'

They discussed it among themselves and said, 'If we say, "From heaven", he will ask, "Then why didn't you believe him?" **26** But if we say, "Of human origin" – we are afraid of the people, for they all hold that John was a prophet.'

27 So they answered Jesus, 'We don't know.'

Then he said, 'Neither will I tell you by what authority I am doing these things.

The parable of the two sons

28 'What do you think? There was a man who had two sons. He went to the first and said, "Son, go and work today in the vineyard."

29 ' "I will not," he answered, but later he changed his mind and went.

30 'Then the father went to the other son and said the same thing. He answered, "I will, sir," but he did not go.

31 'Which of the two did what his father wanted?'

'The first,' they answered.

Jesus said to them, 'Truly I tell you, the tax collectors and the prostitutes are entering the kingdom of God ahead of you. **32** For John came to you to show you the way of righteousness, and you did not believe him, but the tax collectors and the prostitutes did. And even after you saw this, you did not repent and believe him.

The parable of the tenants

33 'Listen to another parable: there was a landowner who planted a vineyard. He put a wall round it, dug a winepress in it and built a watchtower. Then he rented the vineyard to some farmers and moved

---

e 13   Isaiah 56:7
f 13   Jer. 7:11
g 16   Psalm 8:2 (see Septuagint)

to another place. ³⁴When the harvest time approached, he sent his servants to the tenants to collect his fruit.

³⁵'The tenants seized his servants; they beat one, killed another, and stoned a third. ³⁶Then he sent other servants to them, more than the first time, and the tenants treated them in the same way. ³⁷Last of all, he sent his son to them. "They will respect my son," he said.

³⁸'But when the tenants saw the son, they said to each other, "This is the heir. Come, let's kill him and take his inheritance." ³⁹So they took him and threw him out of the vineyard and killed him.

⁴⁰'Therefore, when the owner of the vineyard comes, what will he do to those tenants?'

⁴¹'He will bring those wretches to a wretched end,' they replied, 'and he will rent the vineyard to other tenants, who will give him his share of the crop at harvest time.'

⁴²Jesus said to them, 'Have you never read in the Scriptures:

' "The stone the builders rejected
    has become the cornerstone;
the Lord has done this,
    and it is marvellous in our eyes"ʰ?

⁴³'Therefore I tell you that the kingdom of God will be taken away from you and given to a people who will produce its fruit. ⁴⁴Anyone who falls on this stone will be broken to pieces; anyone on whom it falls will be crushed.'ⁱ

⁴⁵When the chief priests and the Pharisees heard Jesus' parables, they knew he was talking about them. ⁴⁶They looked for a way to arrest him, but they were afraid of the crowd because the people held that he was a prophet.

The parable of the wedding banquet

22 Jesus spoke to them again in parables, saying: ²'The kingdom of heaven is like a king who prepared a wedding banquet for his son. ³He sent his servants to those who had been invited to the banquet to tell them to come, but they refused to come.

⁴'Then he sent some more servants and said, "Tell those who have been invited that I have prepared my dinner: my oxen and fattened cattle have been slaughtered, and everything is ready. Come to the wedding banquet."

⁵'But they paid no attention and went off – one to his field, another to his business. ⁶The rest seized his servants, ill-treated them and killed them. ⁷The king was enraged. He sent his army and destroyed those murderers and burned their city.

⁸'Then he said to his servants, "The wedding banquet is ready, but those I invited did not deserve to come. ⁹So go to the street corners and invite to the banquet anyone you find." ¹⁰So the servants went out into the streets and gathered all the people they could find, the bad as well as the good, and the wedding hall was filled with guests.

¹¹'But when the king came in to see the guests, he noticed a man there who was not wearing wedding clothes. ¹²He asked, "How did you get in here without wedding clothes, friend?" The man was speechless.

¹³'Then the king told the attendants, "Tie him hand and foot, and throw him outside, into the darkness, where there will be weeping and gnashing of teeth."

¹⁴'For many are invited, but few are chosen.'

Paying the poll-tax to Caesar

¹⁵Then the Pharisees went out and laid plans to trap him in his words. ¹⁶They sent their disciples to him along with the Herodians. 'Teacher,' they said, 'we know that you are a man of integrity and that you teach the way of God in accordance with the truth. You aren't swayed by others, because you pay no attention to who they are. ¹⁷Tell us then, what is your opinion? Is it right to pay the poll-taxᵃ to Caesar or not?'

ʰ 42 Psalm 118:22,23
ⁱ 44 Some manuscripts do not have verse 44.

ᵃ 17 A special tax levied on subject peoples, not on Roman citizens

[18] But Jesus, knowing their evil intent, said, 'You hypocrites, why are you trying to trap me? [19] Show me the coin used for paying the tax.' They brought him a denarius, [20] and he asked them, 'Whose image is this? And whose inscription?'

[21] 'Caesar's,' they replied.

Then he said to them, 'So give back to Caesar what is Caesar's, and to God what is God's.'

[22] When they heard this, they were amazed. So they left him and went away.

Marriage at the resurrection

[23] That same day the Sadducees, who say there is no resurrection, came to him with a question. [24] 'Teacher,' they said, 'Moses told us that if a man dies without having children, his brother must marry the widow and raise up offspring for him. [25] Now there were seven brothers among us. The first one married and died, and since he had no children, he left his wife to his brother. [26] The same thing happened to the second and third brother, right on down to the seventh. [27] Finally, the woman died. [28] Now then, at the resurrection, whose wife will she be of the seven, since all of them were married to her?'

[29] Jesus replied, 'You are in error because you do not know the Scriptures or the power of God. [30] At the resurrection people will neither marry nor be given in marriage; they will be like the angels in heaven. [31] But about the resurrection of the dead – have you not read what God said to you, [32] "I am the God of Abraham, the God of Isaac, and the God of Jacob"[b]? He is not the God of the dead but of the living.'

[33] When the crowds heard this, they were astonished at his teaching.

The greatest commandment

[34] Hearing that Jesus had silenced the Sadducees, the Pharisees got together. [35] One of them, an expert in the law, tested him with this question: [36] 'Teacher, which is the greatest commandment in the Law?'

[37] Jesus replied: ' "Love the Lord your God with all your heart and with all your soul and with all your mind."[c] [38] This is the first and greatest commandment. [39] And the second is like it: "Love your neighbour as yourself."[d] [40] All the Law and the Prophets hang on these two commandments.'

Whose son is the Messiah?

[41] While the Pharisees were gathered together, Jesus asked them, [42] 'What do you think about the Messiah? Whose son is he?'

'The son of David,' they replied.

[43] He said to them, 'How is it then that David, speaking by the Spirit, calls him "Lord"? For he says,

[44] ' "The Lord said to my Lord:
    'Sit at my right hand
    until I put your enemies
      under your feet.' "[e]

[45] If then David calls him "Lord", how can he be his son?' [46] No one could say a word in reply, and from that day on no one dared to ask him any more questions.

A warning against hypocrisy

23 Then Jesus said to the crowds and to his disciples: [2] 'The teachers of the law and the Pharisees sit in Moses' seat. [3] So you must be careful to do everything they tell you. But do not do what they do, for they do not practise what they preach. [4] They tie up heavy, cumbersome loads and put them on other people's shoulders, but they themselves are not willing to lift a finger to move them.

[5] 'Everything they do is done for people to see: They make their phylacteries[a] wide and the tassels on their garments long; [6] they love the place of honour at banquets and the most important seats in the synagogues; [7] they love to be greeted with respect in the market-places and to be called "Rabbi" by others.

---

b 32 Exodus 3:6

c 37 Deut. 6:5
d 39 Lev. 19:18
e 44 Psalm 110:1
a 5 That is, boxes containing Scripture verses, worn on forehead and arm

8 'But you are not to be called "Rabbi", for you have one Teacher, and you are all brothers. 9 And do not call anyone on earth "father", for you have one Father, and he is in heaven. 10 Nor are you to be called instructors, for you have one Instructor, the Messiah. 11 The greatest among you will be your servant. 12 For those who exalt themselves will be humbled, and those who humble themselves will be exalted.

Seven woes on the teachers of the law and the Pharisees

13 'Woe to you, teachers of the law and Pharisees, you hypocrites! You shut the door of the kingdom of heaven in people's faces. You yourselves do not enter, nor will you let those enter who are trying to. [14] *b*

b 14 Some manuscripts include here words similar to Mark 12:40 and Luke 20:47.

WORSHIP 4

A command

There are some verses in the Bible that just say it how it is. There's no beating around the bush or searching for a hidden meaning. In Matthew 22:34–40, a straight-up question gets a straight-up answer: the greatest commandment is to love God. Another word for this is 'worship'.

It's as though the first thing on God's priority list is to find wholehearted worshippers. He isn't seeking worship leaders, musicians or great songwriters. God doesn't care whether we're musical or not, he's simply looking for people who will devote themselves to him in heart, soul and mind.

If the first commandment is to worship God, then what flows from this is a love for others. *'All the Law and the Prophets hang on these two commandments'* (Matthew 22:40), so they're both pretty important! Loving people is important, but we have to remember the starting place – the God of love himself. We can easily busy ourselves with good things like helping a mate in trouble, serving at church or on a project for the homeless, but if we lose sight of the first commandment, then we miss the point.

The amazing thing about worship and loving others is that one leads us to the other. Whenever we spend time gazing on the beauty of God, we find ourselves drawn to a broken and hurting world in desperate need of his love, and when we see God working through our lives as we reach out to others, we find ourselves drawn to worship! The two go together. In fact, there's a danger if we separate them: worship without mission is self-indulgent; mission without worship is self-defeating.

Have a think about your own priorities and ask God if there are any practical things you could do today to help obey the two greatest commandments.

Beth Croft

 Colossians 3:12–17   Psalm 31:9–14

15 'Woe to you, teachers of the law and Pharisees, you hypocrites! You travel over land and sea to win a single convert, and when you have succeeded, you make them twice as much a child of hell as you are.

16 'Woe to you, blind guides! You say, "If anyone swears by the temple, it means nothing; but anyone who swears by the gold of the temple is bound by that oath." 17 You blind fools! Which is greater: the gold, or the temple that makes the gold sacred? 18 You also say, "If anyone swears by the altar, it means nothing; but anyone who swears by the gift on the altar is bound by that oath." 19 You blind men! Which is greater: the gift, or the altar that makes the gift sacred? 20 Therefore, anyone who swears by the altar swears by it and by everything on it. 21 And anyone who swears by the temple swears by it and by the one who dwells in it. 22 And anyone who swears by heaven swears by God's throne and by the one who sits on it.

23 'Woe to you, teachers of the law and Pharisees, you hypocrites! You give a tenth of your spices – mint, dill and cumin. But you have neglected the more important matters of the law – justice, mercy and faithfulness. You should have practised the latter, without neglecting the former. 24 You blind guides! You strain out a gnat but swallow a camel.

25 'Woe to you, teachers of the law and Pharisees, you hypocrites! You clean the outside of the cup and dish, but inside they are full of greed and self-indulgence. 26 Blind Pharisee! First clean the inside of the cup and dish, and then the outside also will be clean.

27 'Woe to you, teachers of the law and Pharisees, you hypocrites! You are like whitewashed tombs, which look beautiful on the outside but on the inside are full of the bones of the dead and everything unclean. 28 In the same way, on the outside you appear to people as righteous but on the inside you are full of hypocrisy and wickedness.

29 'Woe to you, teachers of the law and Pharisees, you hypocrites! You build tombs for the prophets and decorate the graves of the righteous. 30 And you say, "If we had lived in the days of our ancestors, we would not have taken part with them in shedding the blood of the prophets." 31 So you testify against yourselves that you are the descendants of those who murdered the prophets. 32 Go ahead, then, and complete what your ancestors started!

33 'You snakes! You brood of vipers! How will you escape being condemned to hell? 34 Therefore I am sending you prophets and sages and teachers. Some of them you will kill and crucify; others you will flog in your synagogues and pursue from town to town. 35 And so upon you will come all the righteous blood that has been shed on earth, from the blood of righteous Abel to the blood of Zechariah son of Berekiah, whom you murdered between the temple and the altar. 36 Truly I tell you, all this will come upon this generation.

37 'Jerusalem, Jerusalem, you who kill the prophets and stone those sent to you, how often I have longed to gather your children together, as a hen gathers her chicks under her wings, and you were not willing. 38 Look, your house is left to you desolate. 39 For I tell you, you will not see me again until you say, "Blessed is he who comes in the name of the Lord." c'

The destruction of the temple and signs of the end times

24 Jesus left the temple and was walking away when his disciples came up to him to call his attention to its buildings. 2 'Do you see all these things?' he asked. 'Truly I tell you, not one stone here will be left on another; every one will be thrown down.'

3 As Jesus was sitting on the Mount of Olives, the disciples came to him privately. 'Tell us,' they said, 'when will this happen, and what will be the sign of your coming and of the end of the age?'

4 Jesus answered: 'Watch out that no one deceives you. 5 For many will come in my name, claiming, "I am the Messiah," and will deceive many. 6 You will hear of wars and rumours of wars, but see to it that you are not alarmed. Such things must

---

c 39 Psalm 118:26

happen, but the end is still to come. 7 Nation will rise against nation, and kingdom against kingdom. There will be famines and earthquakes in various places. 8 All these are the beginning of birth-pains.

9 'Then you will be handed over to be persecuted and put to death, and you will be hated by all nations because of me. 10 At that time many will turn away from the faith and will betray and hate each other, 11 and many false prophets will appear and deceive many people. 12 Because of the increase of wickedness, the love of most will grow cold, 13 but the one who stands firm to the end will be saved. 14 And this gospel of the kingdom will be preached in the whole world as a testimony to all nations, and then the end will come.

15 'So when you see standing in the holy place "the abomination that causes desolation,"*a* spoken of through the prophet Daniel – let the reader understand – 16 then let those who are in Judea flee to the mountains. 17 Let no one on the housetop go down to take anything out of the house. 18 Let no one in the field go back to get their cloak. 19 How dreadful it will be in those days for pregnant women and nursing mothers! 20 Pray that your flight will not take place in winter or on the Sabbath. 21 For then there will be great distress, unequalled from the beginning of the world until now – and never to be equalled again.

22 'If those days had not been cut short, no one would survive, but for the sake of the elect those days will be shortened. 23 At that time if anyone says to you, "Look, here is the Messiah!" or, "There he is!" do not believe it. 24 For false messiahs and false prophets will appear and perform great signs and wonders to deceive, if possible, even the elect. 25 See, I have told you in advance.

26 'So if anyone tells you, "There he is, out in the desert," do not go out; or, "Here he is, in the inner rooms," do not believe it. 27 For as lightning that comes from the east is visible even in the west, so will be the coming of the Son of Man.

28 Wherever there is a carcass, there the vultures will gather.

29 'Immediately after the distress of those days

' "the sun will be darkened,
    and the moon will not give its light;
the stars will fall from the sky,
    and the heavenly bodies will be
    shaken."*b*

30 'Then will appear the sign of the Son of Man in heaven. And then all the peoples of the earth*c* will mourn when they see the Son of Man coming on the clouds of heaven, with power and great glory.*d* 31 And he will send his angels with a loud trumpet call, and they will gather his elect from the four winds, from one end of the heavens to the other.

32 'Now learn this lesson from the fig-tree: as soon as its twigs become tender and its leaves come out, you know that summer is near. 33 Even so, when you see all these things, you know that it*e* is near, right at the door. 34 Truly I tell you, this generation will certainly not pass away until all these things have happened. 35 Heaven and earth will pass away, but my words will never pass away.

The day and hour unknown

36 'But about that day or hour no one knows, not even the angels in heaven, nor the Son,*f* but only the Father. 37 As it was in the days of Noah, so it will be at the coming of the Son of Man. 38 For in the days before the flood, people were eating and drinking, marrying and giving in marriage, up to the day Noah entered the ark; 39 and they knew nothing about what would happen until the flood came and took them all away. That is how it will be at the coming of the Son of Man. 40 Two men will be in the field; one will be taken and the other left. 41 Two women will be

---

a 15 Daniel 9:27; 11:31; 12:11

b 29 Isaiah 13:10; 34:4
c 30 Or *the tribes of the land*
d 30 See Daniel 7:13-14.
e 33 Or *he*
f 36 Some manuscripts do not have *nor the Son.*

grinding with a hand mill; one will be taken and the other left.

42 'Therefore keep watch, because you do not know on what day your Lord will come. 43 But understand this: if the owner of the house had known at what time of night the thief was coming, he would have kept watch and would not have let his house be broken into. 44 So you also must be ready, because the Son of Man will come at an hour when you do not expect him.

45 'Who then is the faithful and wise servant, whom the master has put in charge of the servants in his household to give them their food at the proper time? 46 It will be good for that servant whose master finds him doing so when he returns. 47 Truly I tell you, he will put him in charge of all his possessions. 48 But suppose that servant is wicked and says to himself, "My master is staying away a long time," 49 and he then begins to beat his fellow servants and to eat and drink with drunkards. 50 The master of that servant will come on a day when he does not expect him and at an hour he is not aware of. 51 He will cut him to pieces and assign him a place with the hypocrites, where there will be weeping and gnashing of teeth.

The parable of the ten virgins

25 'At that time the kingdom of heaven will be like ten virgins who took their lamps and went out to meet the bridegroom. 2 Five of them were foolish and five were wise. 3 The foolish ones took their lamps but did not take any oil with them. 4 The wise ones, however, took oil in jars along with their lamps. 5 The bridegroom was a long time in coming, and they all became drowsy and fell asleep.

6 'At midnight the cry rang out: "Here's the bridegroom! Come out to meet him!"

7 'Then all the virgins woke up and trimmed their lamps. 8 The foolish ones said to the wise, "Give us some of your oil; our lamps are going out."

9 ' "No," they replied, "there may not be enough for both us and you. Instead, go to those who sell oil and buy some for yourselves."

10 'But while they were on their way to buy the oil, the bridegroom arrived. The virgins who were ready went in with him to the wedding banquet. And the door was shut.

11 'Later the others also came. "Lord, Lord," they said, "open the door for us!"

12 'But he replied, "Truly I tell you, I don't know you."

13 'Therefore keep watch, because you do not know the day or the hour.

The parable of the bags of gold

14 'Again, it will be like a man going on a journey, who called his servants and entrusted his wealth to them. 15 To one he gave five bags of gold, to another two bags, and to another one bag,*a* each according to his ability. Then he went on his journey. 16 The man who had received five bags of gold went at once and put his money to work and gained five bags more. 17 So also, the one with two bags of gold gained two more. 18 But the man who had received one bag went off, dug a hole in the ground and hid his master's money.

19 'After a long time the master of those servants returned and settled accounts with them. 20 The man who had received five bags of gold brought the other five. "Master," he said, "you entrusted me with five bags of gold. See, I have gained five more."

21 'His master replied, "Well done, good and faithful servant! You have been faithful with a few things; I will put you in charge of many things. Come and share your master's happiness!"

22 'The man with two bags of gold also came. "Master," he said, "you entrusted me with two bags of gold: see, I have gained two more."

23 'His master replied, "Well done, good and faithful servant! You have been faithful with a few things; I will put you in charge of many things. Come and share your master's happiness!"

24 'Then the man who had received one

---

a 15 Greek *five talents . . . two talents . . . one talent;* also throughout this parable; a talent was worth about 20 years of a day labourer's wage.

bag of gold came. "Master," he said, "I knew that you are a hard man, harvesting where you have not sown and gathering where you have not scattered seed. 25 So I was afraid and went out and hid your gold in the ground. See, here is what belongs to you."

26 'His master replied, "You wicked, lazy servant! So you knew that I harvest where I have not sown and gather where I have not scattered seed? 27 Well then, you should have put my money on deposit with the bankers, so that when I returned I would have received it back with interest.

28 '"So take the bag of gold from him and give it to the one who has ten bags. 29 For whoever has will be given more, and they will have an abundance. Whoever does not have, even what they have will be taken from them. 30 And throw that worthless servant outside, into the darkness, where there will be weeping and gnashing of teeth."

The sheep and the goats

31 'When the Son of Man comes in his glory, and all the angels with him, he will sit on his glorious throne. 32 All the nations will be gathered before him, and he will separate the people one from another as a shepherd separates the sheep from the goats. 33 He will put the sheep on his right and the goats on his left.

34 'Then the King will say to those on his right, "Come, you who are blessed by my Father; take your inheritance, the kingdom prepared for you since the creation of the world. 35 For I was hungry and you gave me something to eat, I was thirsty and you gave me something to drink, I was a stranger and you invited me in, 36 I needed clothes and you clothed me, I was ill and you looked after me, I was in prison and you came to visit me."

37 'Then the righteous will answer him, "Lord, when did we see you hungry and feed you, or thirsty and give you something to drink? 38 When did we see you a stranger and invite you in, or needing clothes and clothe you? 39 When did we see you ill or in prison and go to visit you?"

40 'The King will reply, "Truly I tell you, whatever you did for one of the least of these brothers and sisters of mine, you did for me."

41 'Then he will say to those on his left, "Depart from me, you who are cursed, into the eternal fire prepared for the devil and his angels. 42 For I was hungry and you gave me nothing to eat, I was thirsty and you gave me nothing to drink, 43 I was a stranger and you did not invite me in, I needed clothes and you did not clothe me, I was ill and in prison and you did not look after me."

44 'They also will answer, "Lord, when did we see you hungry or thirsty or a stranger or needing clothes or ill or in prison, and did not help you?"

45 'He will reply, "Truly I tell you, whatever you did not do for one of the least of these, you did not do for me."

46 'Then they will go away to eternal punishment, but the righteous to eternal life.'

The plot against Jesus

26 When Jesus had finished saying all these things, he said to his disciples, 2 'As you know, the Passover is two days away – and the Son of Man will be handed over to be crucified.'

3 Then the chief priests and the elders of the people assembled in the palace of the high priest, whose name was Caiaphas, 4 and they schemed to arrest Jesus secretly and kill him. 5 'But not during the festival,' they said, 'or there may be a riot among the people.'

Jesus anointed at Bethany

6 While Jesus was in Bethany in the home of Simon the Leper, 7 a woman came to him with an alabaster jar of very expensive perfume, which she poured on his head as he was reclining at the table.

8 When the disciples saw this, they were indignant. 'Why this waste?' they asked. 9 'This perfume could have been sold at a high price and the money given to the poor.'

10 Aware of this, Jesus said to them, 'Why are you bothering this woman? She has done a beautiful thing to me. 11 The

FAITH IN THE WORLD 8

WHAT THE WORLD NEEDS NOW

Bono, the lead singer of the extremely successful rock band U2, once said, 'Distance does not decide who is your brother, and who is not. The church is going to have to become the conscience of the free market if it's to have any meaning in this world – and stop being its apologist.' What does he mean?

First, that as the church of Christ one of our mottos is 'Our World, Our Responsibility': if people are suffering anywhere in the world, near or far, we have a responsibility to try to stop that suffering. In Matthew 25:31–46 Jesus makes this extremely clear. Those who are his good servants – the sheep – are those who seek to clothe the naked, feed the hungry, provide shelter for strangers, visit those in prison. Think about all those situations: they're about seeing an obvious need and responding to it.

They're also about mercy: showing favour and giving help even if we think the person doesn't deserve it. Jesus doesn't say that the people we should visit in prison have been wrongly accused, does he? Thanks to the internet and TV, we now see suffering right around the globe. Bono's right – the distance doesn't matter; we have a responsibility to stop it. But how?

The quote points to the real crisis: many of the problems in the world are caused by greed. The 'free market' refers to the way in which we make money in developed countries. Our focus is on making more and more profit, for companies to get bigger and bigger until they have a monopoly. We can and must respond directly to people's needs. Families suffering from famine in drought-stricken areas need our aid now, but we must also have long-term solutions to help the needs of the world.

That's where your career comes in. We need scientists to help create drought-resistant strains of wheat; politicians to insist that this is exactly the type of research our country needs to undertake; lawyers to fight for the rights of the poor across the world. If we're going to help heal the world, if we're going to meet very visible needs, then we can't just do that as full-time church workers. God's kingdom needs people at every level of society to make a difference.

Often we pray that God will drop a sign from the sky to let us know what we should do as a career! But when we look at the Bible, God paints a clear picture of what he wants us to get on with. If you choose a career where you use your skills to help alleviate people's suffering, then you are doing the will of God. It doesn't mean that you're working full time to help people in need around the world: you could be a builder who helps build schools in developing countries during two weeks of your holidays. Whenever we respond to people's needs, we're serving God, we're doing his will. What a privilege.

Jason Gardner

 Mark 6:1–6   Acts 18:1–4

poor you will always have with you,[a] but you will not always have me. 12When she poured this perfume on my body, she did it to prepare me for burial. 13Truly I tell you, wherever this gospel is preached throughout the world, what she has done will also be told, in memory of her.'

Judas agrees to betray Jesus

14Then one of the Twelve – the one called Judas Iscariot – went to the chief priests 15and asked, 'What are you willing to give me if I deliver him over to you?' So they counted out for him thirty pieces of silver. 16From then on Judas watched for an opportunity to hand him over.

The Last Supper

17On the first day of the Festival of Unleavened Bread, the disciples came to Jesus and asked, 'Where do you want us to make preparations for you to eat the Passover?'

18He replied, 'Go into the city to a certain man and tell him, "The Teacher says: my appointed time is near. I am going to celebrate the Passover with my disciples at your house."' 19So the disciples did as Jesus had directed them and prepared the Passover.

20When evening came, Jesus was reclining at the table with the Twelve. 21And while they were eating, he said, 'Truly I tell you, one of you will betray me.'

22They were very sad and began to say to him one after the other, 'Surely you don't mean me, Lord?'

23Jesus replied, 'The one who has dipped his hand into the bowl with me will betray me. 24The Son of Man will go just as it is written about him. But woe to that man who betrays the Son of Man! It would be better for him if he had not been born.'

25Then Judas, the one who would betray him, said, 'Surely you don't mean me, Rabbi?'

Jesus answered, 'You have said so.'

26While they were eating, Jesus took bread, and when he had given thanks, he broke it and gave it to his disciples, saying, 'Take and eat; this is my body.'

27Then he took a cup, and when he had given thanks, he gave it to them, saying, 'Drink from it, all of you. 28This is my blood of the[b] covenant, which is poured out for many for the forgiveness of sins. 29I tell you, I will not drink from this fruit of the vine from now on until that day when I drink it new with you in my Father's kingdom.'

30When they had sung a hymn, they went out to the Mount of Olives.

Jesus predicts Peter's denial

31Then Jesus told them, 'This very night you will all fall away on account of me, for it is written:

' "I will strike the shepherd,
    and the sheep of the flock will be
        scattered."[c]

32But after I have risen, I will go ahead of you into Galilee.'

33Peter replied, 'Even if all fall away on account of you, I never will.'

34'Truly I tell you,' Jesus answered, 'this very night, before the cock crows, you will disown me three times.'

35But Peter declared, 'Even if I have to die with you, I will never disown you.' And all the other disciples said the same.

Gethsemane

36Then Jesus went with his disciples to a place called Gethsemane, and he said to them, 'Sit here while I go over there and pray.' 37He took Peter and the two sons of Zebedee along with him, and he began to be sorrowful and troubled. 38Then he said to them, 'My soul is overwhelmed with sorrow to the point of death. Stay here and keep watch with me.'

39Going a little farther, he fell with his face to the ground and prayed, 'My Father, if it is possible, may this cup be taken from me. Yet not as I will, but as you will.'

40Then he returned to his disciples and

---

a 11 See Deut. 15:11.

b 28 Some manuscripts *the new*
c 31 Zech. 13:7

WHAT DOES GOD THINK ABOUT WAR? PART 2

This is the second part of a two-part discussion where we look at different answers to this question. As we read the Bible, we see there isn't always an obvious answer to some of the most difficult questions we have to ask about our faith. Read this, and the article near Matthew 5:3–12, and see what you think. Ask God to speak to you through his Word.

God commands us to live in peace with each other, so surely war must be wrong? Certainly some Christians would argue that all forms of conflict are wrong. However, we know that we live in a world that is sinful, and we have also been told that we should defend the weak and protect the vulnerable – so what are we supposed to do when there seems to be no alternative to the use of force?

If an armed force were to attack a defenceless group, most people would agree that it would be wrong to stand by and allow a massacre to occur. In such situations, we can understand that the use of force is justified. However, most of us would also agree that using physical force to achieve our own ends, whether as individuals or as nation states, is wrong. This is consistent with how Jesus responds when approached by a group of soldiers in Luke 3. Jesus doesn't tell them to stop being soldiers, but he does tell them they shouldn't abuse the power they have been given.

Similarly, in Matthew 26:52, Jesus makes it clear that violent force should not be used as a way to solve disagreements. Doing so only leads to more violence.

Augustine, a Christian in the fourth and fifth centuries, wrote a theory that helps to show whether a cause for war is justifiable. This is called the 'Just War Theory'. Augustine said that in order for a war to be just:

1. The war must be declared by a just government.

2. The cause must be just – ultimately the war must occur in order to protect life.

3. Those who fight must do so with the intention of bringing about good and destroying evil.

4. War must be the last resort; all other methods for peace through diplomacy must have been tried first.

5. The good achieved because of the war must outweigh the evil which led to the war.

Ultimately, we know that war is an unfortunate – and tragic – necessity, while we live in a wicked and sinful world. However, the good news is that there will come a day when *'He will judge between the nations and will settle disputes for many peoples. They will beat their swords into ploughshares and their spears into pruning hooks. Nation will not take up sword against nation, nor will they train for war any more'* (Isaiah 2:4).

Freddie Pimm with Ben Hall

found them sleeping. 'Couldn't you men keep watch with me for one hour?' he asked Peter. ⁴¹'Watch and pray so that you will not fall into temptation. The spirit is willing, but the flesh is weak.'

⁴²He went away a second time and prayed, 'My Father, if it is not possible for this cup to be taken away unless I drink it, may your will be done.'

⁴³When he came back, he again found them sleeping, because their eyes were heavy. ⁴⁴So he left them and went away once more and prayed the third time, saying the same thing.

⁴⁵Then he returned to the disciples and said to them, 'Are you still sleeping and resting? Look, the hour has come, and the Son of Man is delivered into the hands of sinners. ⁴⁶Rise! Let us go! Here comes my betrayer!'

Jesus arrested

⁴⁷While he was still speaking, Judas, one of the Twelve, arrived. With him was a large crowd armed with swords and clubs, sent from the chief priests and the elders of the people. ⁴⁸Now the betrayer had arranged a signal with them: 'The one I kiss is the man; arrest him.' ⁴⁹Going at once to Jesus, Judas said, 'Greetings, Rabbi!' and kissed him.

⁵⁰Jesus replied, 'Do what you came for, friend.'ᵈ

Then the men stepped forward, seized Jesus and arrested him. ⁵¹With that, one of Jesus' companions reached for his sword, drew it out and struck the servant of the high priest, cutting off his ear.

⁵²'Put your sword back in its place,' Jesus said to him, 'for all who draw the sword will die by the sword. ⁵³Do you think I cannot call on my Father, and he will at once put at my disposal more than twelve legions of angels? ⁵⁴But how then would the Scriptures be fulfilled that say it must happen in this way?'

⁵⁵In that hour Jesus said to the crowd, 'Am I leading a rebellion, that you have come out with swords and clubs to capture me? Every day I sat in the temple courts teaching, and you did not arrest me. ⁵⁶But this has all taken place that the writings of the prophets might be fulfilled.' Then all the disciples deserted him and fled.

Jesus before the Sanhedrin

⁵⁷Those who had arrested Jesus took him to Caiaphas the high priest, where the teachers of the law and the elders had assembled. ⁵⁸But Peter followed him at a distance, right up to the courtyard of the high priest. He entered and sat down with the guards to see the outcome.

⁵⁹The chief priests and the whole Sanhedrin were looking for false evidence against Jesus so that they could put him to death. ⁶⁰But they did not find any, though many false witnesses came forward.

Finally two came forward ⁶¹and declared, 'This fellow said, "I am able to destroy the temple of God and rebuild it in three days."'

⁶²Then the high priest stood up and said to Jesus, 'Are you not going to answer? What is this testimony that these men are bringing against you?' ⁶³But Jesus remained silent.

The high priest said to him, 'I charge you under oath by the living God: Tell us if you are the Messiah, the Son of God.'

⁶⁴'You have said so,' Jesus replied. 'But I say to all of you: from now on you will see the Son of Man sitting at the right hand of the Mighty One and coming on the clouds of heaven.'ᵉ

⁶⁵Then the high priest tore his clothes and said, 'He has spoken blasphemy! Why do we need any more witnesses? Look, now you have heard the blasphemy. ⁶⁶What do you think?'

'He is worthy of death,' they answered.

⁶⁷Then they spat in his face and struck him with their fists. Others slapped him ⁶⁸and said, 'Prophesy to us, Messiah. Who hit you?'

Peter disowns Jesus

⁶⁹Now Peter was sitting out in the courtyard, and a servant-girl came to him. 'You also were with Jesus of Galilee,' she said.

---

d 50 Or 'Why have you come, friend?'   *e* 64 See Psalm 110:1; Daniel 7:13.

70 But he denied it before them all. 'I don't know what you're talking about,' he said.

71 Then he went out to the gateway, where another servant-girl saw him and said to the people there, 'This fellow was with Jesus of Nazareth.'

72 He denied it again, with an oath: 'I don't know the man!'

73 After a little while, those standing there went up to Peter and said, 'Surely you are one of them; your accent gives you away.'

74 Then he began to call down curses,

FRIENDSHIP 9

When friends let you down

We have all done it. We have all had that horrible moment when we realise we have hurt a friend and let them down. It's one of the worst feelings in the world when we see it all over their face: they trusted us and we wounded them. Ouch. And we have all had it happen to us too, when we have been on the receiving end, the one who has been hurt by someone we love.

Jesus knew that same pain. In the Garden of Gethsemane he asked his disciples to pray for him, but instead they fell asleep. He was about to endure the cross and they couldn't even stay awake! Then Judas sold him to his enemies for the price of a slave. Can you imagine the agony Jesus was about to endure, knowing that it was a friend who had led him into it? Soon after that, Peter, one of his very closest friends, denied ever having known him (Matthew 26:69–75). Jesus knows about the pain of being betrayed.

People let us down. They may not mean to: we're all human, which means we're flawed, and it happens. So what do we do? First, we mustn't deny that it's painful. If we try to gloss over it and pretend we haven't been hurt, it can drive a wedge into the friendship which can lead to it slowly dying. We naturally pull away from people who have hurt us, and if they don't realise what they did, they will be confused and hurt themselves.

If possible, try to speak to the person who hurt you and explain how you feel and why their actions were painful. We don't do this as an opportunity to unleash our anger on them or to say nasty things to get our own back. We speak to them as an opportunity to put things right. Jesus showed Peter amazing grace (see John 21). He didn't punish him or make him stew. He forgave Peter for denying him and graciously welcomed him back into relationship. Let's use this as our model – aiming to show the love and grace of Jesus even when someone has hurt us.

Ali Martin

 Job 2:11–13   Proverbs 13:20

and he swore to them, 'I don't know the man!'

Immediately a cock crowed. 75 Then Peter remembered the word Jesus had spoken: 'Before the cock crows, you will disown me three times.' And he went outside and wept bitterly.

JUDAS

PERFUME
John 12:1–8
MONEY
Matthew 26:1–5, 14–16
TABLE
John 13:21–30
KISS
Luke 22:47–53
REMORSE
Matthew 27:3–9

Judas hangs himself

27 Early in the morning, all the chief priests and the elders of the people made their plans how to have Jesus executed. 2 So they bound him, led him away and handed him over to Pilate the governor.

3 When Judas, who had betrayed him, saw that Jesus was condemned, he was seized with remorse and returned the thirty pieces of silver to the chief priests and the elders. 4 'I have sinned,' he said, 'for I have betrayed innocent blood.'

'What is that to us?' they replied. 'That's your responsibility.'

5 So Judas threw the money into the temple and left. Then he went away and hanged himself.

6 The chief priests picked up the coins and said, 'It is against the law to put this into the treasury, since it is blood money.' 7 So they decided to use the money to buy the potter's field as a burial place for foreigners. 8 That is why it has been called the

Field of Blood to this day. 9 Then what was spoken by Jeremiah the prophet was fulfilled: 'They took the thirty pieces of silver, the price set on him by the people of Israel, 10 and they used them to buy the potter's field, as the Lord commanded me.'*a*

Jesus before Pilate

11 Meanwhile Jesus stood before the governor, and the governor asked him, 'Are you the king of the Jews?'

'You have said so,' Jesus replied.

12 When he was accused by the chief priests and the elders, he gave no answer. 13 Then Pilate asked him, 'Don't you hear the testimony they are bringing against you?' 14 But Jesus made no reply, not even to a single charge – to the great amazement of the governor.

15 Now it was the governor's custom at the festival to release a prisoner chosen by the crowd. 16 At that time they had a well-known prisoner whose name was Jesus*b* Barabbas. 17 So when the crowd had gathered, Pilate asked them, 'Which one do you want me to release to you: Jesus Barabbas, or Jesus who is called the Messiah?' 18 For he knew it was out of self-interest that they had handed Jesus over to him.

19 While Pilate was sitting on the judge's seat, his wife sent him this message: 'Don't have anything to do with that innocent man, for I have suffered a great deal today in a dream because of him.'

20 But the chief priests and the elders persuaded the crowd to ask for Barabbas and to have Jesus executed.

21 'Which of the two do you want me to release to you?' asked the governor.

'Barabbas,' they answered.

22 'What shall I do, then, with Jesus who is called the Messiah?' Pilate asked.

They all answered, 'Crucify him!'

23 'Why? What crime has he committed?' asked Pilate.

But they shouted all the louder, 'Crucify him!'

24 When Pilate saw that he was getting

---

a 10 See Zech. 11:12,13; Jer. 19:1-13; 32:6-9.
b 16 Many manuscripts do not have *Jesus*; also in verse 17.

nowhere, but that instead an uproar was starting, he took water and washed his hands in front of the crowd. 'I am innocent of this man's blood,' he said. 'It is your responsibility!'

25 All the people answered, 'His blood is on us and on our children!'

26 Then he released Barabbas to them. But he had Jesus flogged, and handed him over to be crucified.

The soldiers mock Jesus

27 Then the governor's soldiers took Jesus into the Praetorium and gathered the whole company of soldiers round him. 28 They stripped him and put a scarlet robe on him, 29 and then twisted together a crown of thorns and set it on his head. They put a staff in his right hand. Then they knelt in front of him and mocked him. 'Hail, king of the Jews!' they said. 30 They spat on him, and took the staff and struck him on the head again and again. 31 After they had mocked him, they took off the robe and put his own clothes on him. Then they led him away to crucify him.

The crucifixion of Jesus

32 As they were going out, they met a man from Cyrene, named Simon, and they forced him to carry the cross. 33 They came to a place called Golgotha (which means 'the place of the skull'). 34 There they offered Jesus wine to drink, mixed with gall; but after tasting it, he refused to drink it. 35 When they had crucified him, they divided up his clothes by casting lots. 36 And sitting down, they kept watch over him there. 37 Above his head they placed the written charge against him: THIS IS JESUS, THE KING OF THE JEWS.

38 Two rebels were crucified with him, one on his right and one on his left. 39 Those who passed by hurled insults at him, shaking their heads 40 and saying, 'You who are going to destroy the temple and build it in three days, save yourself! Come down from the cross, if you are the Son of God!' 41 In the same way the chief priests, the teachers of the law and the elders mocked him. 42 'He saved others,' they said, 'but he can't save himself! He's

the king of Israel! Let him come down now from the cross, and we will believe in him. 43 He trusts in God. Let God rescue him now if he wants him, for he said, "I am the Son of God."' 44 In the same way the rebels who were crucified with him also heaped insults on him.

The death of Jesus

45 From noon until three in the afternoon darkness came over all the land. 46 About three in the afternoon Jesus cried out in a loud voice, 'Eli, Eli,c lema sabachthani?' (which means 'My God, my God, why have you forsaken me?').d

47 When some of those standing there heard this, they said, 'He's calling Elijah.' 48 Immediately one of them ran and got a sponge. He filled it with wine vinegar, put it on a staff, and offered it to Jesus to drink. 49 The rest said, 'Now leave him alone. Let's see if Elijah comes to save him.'

50 And when Jesus had cried out again in a loud voice, he gave up his spirit.

51 At that moment the curtain of the temple was torn in two from top to bottom. The earth shook, the rocks split 52 and the tombs broke open. The bodies of many holy people who had died were raised to life. 53 They came out of the tombs after Jesus' resurrection ande went into the holy city and appeared to many people.

54 When the centurion and those with him who were guarding Jesus saw the earthquake and all that had happened, they were terrified, and exclaimed, 'Surely he was the Son of God!'

55 Many women were there, watching from a distance. They had followed Jesus from Galilee to care for his needs. 56 Among them were Mary Magdalene, Mary the mother of James and Joseph,f and the mother of Zebedee's sons.

---

c 46 Some manuscripts Eloi, Eloi
d 46 Psalm 22:1
e 53 Or tombs, and after Jesus' resurrection they
f 56 Greek Joses, a variant of Joseph

The burial of Jesus

57 As evening approached, there came a rich man from Arimathea, named Joseph, who had himself become a disciple of Jesus. 58 Going to Pilate, he asked for Jesus' body, and Pilate ordered that it be given to him. 59 Joseph took the body, wrapped it in a clean linen cloth, 60 and placed it in his own new tomb that he had cut out of the rock. He rolled a big stone in front of the entrance to the tomb and went away. 61 Mary Magdalene and the other Mary were sitting there opposite the tomb.

The guard at the tomb

62 The next day, the one after Preparation Day, the chief priests and the Pharisees went to Pilate. 63 'Sir,' they said, 'we remember that while he was still alive that deceiver said, "After three days I will rise again." 64 So give the order for the

EVANGELISM 10

Go!

I remember watching the news and seeing a group of people who had been rescued from a burning building. They were in a huddle with those silver rescue blankets on their shoulders. I watched as one guy broke out of the huddle. He sprinted back towards the building, grabbed a rope and joined in with the rescue. As I watched, Jesus' words from Matthew 28:19–20 came to mind: 'Go and make disciples of all nations.'

Sometimes I see the church as that huddle of rescued people. They are saved and they are so grateful, yet seem blind to the others who need rescuing. The huddle is tight and often unwelcoming to those on the outside.

When I read Jesus' words, I feel that a better picture of the church is that young guy breaking out of the huddle – realising that he has been rescued to rescue others; he has been saved to see others saved. I believe that loads of people are coming to understand that true church is not about being an exclusive club, but about being a rescue team.

It starts and ends with God. By prayer we connect with what God is doing. We are relational beings and therefore have earned the right to speak into people's lives. We must not shrink back from the opportunities as they arise, but should be fully prepared to have those conversations. This journey of faith looks different for everyone. Will we stand up and do whatever it takes to see a broken world connect to God? But, as I said, it starts and ends with God. We go with the compassion that he gives and speak when he offers us the opportunity. The rest is up to him.

As you go into your schools, colleges, work and families in response to this Great Commission, be blessed, fulfilled and know his love.

Mark Ritchie

⏪ Luke 2:16–18   ⏹

tomb to be made secure until the third day. Otherwise, his disciples may come and steal the body and tell the people that he has been raised from the dead. This last deception will be worse than the first.'

65 'Take a guard,' Pilate answered. 'Go, make the tomb as secure as you know how.' 66 So they went and made the tomb secure by putting a seal on the stone and posting the guard.

Jesus has risen

28 After the Sabbath, at dawn on the first day of the week, Mary Magdalene and the other Mary went to look at the tomb.

2 There was a violent earthquake, for an angel of the Lord came down from heaven and, going to the tomb, rolled back the stone and sat on it. 3 His appearance was like lightning, and his clothes were white as snow. 4 The guards were so afraid of him that they shook and became like dead men.

5 The angel said to the women, 'Do not be afraid, for I know that you are looking for Jesus, who was crucified. 6 He is not here; he has risen, just as he said. Come and see the place where he lay. 7 Then go quickly and tell his disciples: "He has risen from the dead and is going ahead of you into Galilee. There you will see him." Now I have told you.'

8 So the women hurried away from the tomb, afraid yet filled with joy, and ran to tell his disciples. 9 Suddenly Jesus met them. 'Greetings,' he said. They came to him, clasped his feet and worshipped him. 10 Then Jesus said to them, 'Do not be afraid. Go and tell my brothers to go to Galilee; there they will see me.'

The guards' report

11 While the women were on their way, some of the guards went into the city and reported to the chief priests everything that had happened. 12 When the chief priests had met with the elders and devised a plan, they gave the soldiers a large sum of money, 13 telling them, 'You are to say, "His disciples came during the night and stole him away while we were asleep." 14 If this report gets to the governor, we will satisfy him and keep you out of trouble.' 15 So the soldiers took the money and did as they were instructed. And this story has been widely circulated among the Jews to this very day.

The great commission

16 Then the eleven disciples went to Galilee, to the mountain where Jesus had told them to go. 17 When they saw him, they worshipped him; but some doubted. 18 Then Jesus came to them and said, 'All authority in heaven and on earth has been given to me. 19 Therefore go and make disciples of all nations, baptising them in the name of the Father and of the Son and of the Holy Spirit, 20 and teaching them to obey everything I have commanded you. And surely I am with you always, to the very end of the age.'

MARK

DATE

Mark starts with John the Baptist's prophecies just before Jesus began his ministry in
AD 30 and continues until just after Jesus' death and resurrection in AD 33

AUTHOR

Traditionally attributed to John Mark, who was a friend of the disciple Peter and who
travelled with Paul

WHAT'S IT ALL ABOUT?

Mark is the second of four Gospels and one of the Synoptic Gospels, with similar
style and teaching to Matthew and Luke. It's believed that Mark was written first and
that Matthew and Luke used Mark's Gospel when writing their own, as almost all the
content in Mark is recorded in the other Gospels.

The Gospels record the events of Jesus' life, and Mark jumps straight into the story
without even pausing to tell us about Mary and Joseph, or Jesus' birth! This is typical
of Mark's writing: his is the shortest Gospel and it's packed full of action. He records
seventeen miracles in just sixteen chapters and captures something of the pace,
power and force of Jesus and his mission. He wrote his accounts for a Gentile (non-
Jewish) audience and wanted them to understand who Jesus was and what he did.
While he includes some teaching, his focus is on the things Jesus did during his time
on earth.

WHY SHOULD WE READ THE GOSPELS?

- Because this is where we meet Jesus! By reading about his life and what he
  said and did, we develop our relationship with him and our understanding
  of who he is. Relationship is key to the Christian life. Christianity is about a
  person, not a set of ideas. Jesus is the central figure of the whole of history and
  it's through him that we make sense of life and the Bible. The whole Bible is a
  witness to Jesus, but the four Gospels are the books that uniquely tell us about
  his time on earth.

- To understand the events that led to Jesus being killed on a cross like a
  criminal, even though he had done nothing wrong.

- To see that Jesus was separated from his Father on the cross, taking on himself
  the punishment we deserve, so that we might become pure in God's eyes.

- To read how Jesus overcame death and rose from the grave, giving us eternal
  life.

- To read Jesus' teaching on how we should live, including how to treat our enemies, how to pray, not judging people, handling money, having humility, finding faith and dealing with worry.

- To see the miraculous things Jesus did, from the feeding of the five thousand to walking on water, and from giving blind people their sight to raising the dead.

WHY SHOULD WE READ MARK'S GOSPEL?

- Because it's fast-paced and loaded with action.

- Because it's probably the easiest Gospel to understand if you're new to Jesus' teachings.

- To understand the events we celebrate during Easter, including Jesus' triumphal entry into Jerusalem on a donkey; the Last Supper Jesus shared with his disciples when he gave the instructions for us to take Communion; the events in the Garden of Gethsemane when Jesus prayed that he might not have to face the cross; Jesus' arrest, trial, crucifixion and death; and his resurrection from the dead (Mark 11 onwards).

- To read about some of the many miracles Jesus did, including driving out evil spirits, healing a paralytic, calming a storm, raising a dead girl to life, feeding the five thousand and walking on water.

Andy Croft with Liza Hoeksma

John the Baptist prepares the way

1 The beginning of the good news about Jesus the Messiah,*a* the Son of God,*b* 2 as it is written in Isaiah the prophet:

'I will send my messenger ahead of
     you,
who will prepare your way'*c* –
3 'a voice of one calling in the
     wilderness,
"Prepare the way for the Lord,
     make straight paths for him." '*d*

4 And so John the Baptist appeared in the wilderness, preaching a baptism of repentance for the forgiveness of sins. 5 The whole Judean countryside and all the people of Jerusalem went out to him. Confessing their sins, they were baptised by him in the River Jordan. 6 John wore clothing made of camel's hair, with a leather belt round his waist, and he ate locusts and wild honey. 7 And this was his message: 'After me comes the one more powerful than I, the straps of whose sandals I am not worthy to stoop down and untie. 8 I baptise you with*e* water, but he will baptise you with*e* the Holy Spirit.'

The baptism and testing of Jesus

9 At that time Jesus came from Nazareth in Galilee and was baptised by John in the Jordan. 10 Just as Jesus was coming up out of the water, he saw heaven being torn open and the Spirit descending on him like a dove. 11 And a voice came from heaven: 'You are my Son, whom I love; with you I am well pleased.'

12 At once the Spirit sent him out into the wilderness, 13 and he was in the wilderness for forty days, being tempted*f* by Satan. He was with the wild animals, and angels attended him.

Jesus announces the good news

14 After John was put in prison, Jesus went into Galilee, proclaiming the good news of God. 15 'The time has come,' he said. 'The kingdom of God has come near. Repent and believe the good news!'

Jesus calls his first disciples

16 As Jesus walked beside the Sea of Galilee, he saw Simon and his brother Andrew casting a net into the lake, for they were fishermen. 17 'Come, follow me,' Jesus said, 'and I will send you out to fish for people.' 18 At once they left their nets and followed him.

19 When he had gone a little farther, he saw James son of Zebedee and his brother John in a boat, preparing their nets. 20 Without delay he called them, and they left their father Zebedee in the boat with the hired men and followed him.

Jesus drives out an impure spirit

21 They went to Capernaum, and when the Sabbath came, Jesus went into the synagogue and began to teach. 22 The people were amazed at his teaching, because he taught them as one who had authority, not as the teachers of the law. 23 Just then a man in their synagogue who was possessed by an impure spirit cried out, 24 'What do you want with us, Jesus of Nazareth? Have you come to destroy us? I know who you are – the Holy One of God!'

25 'Be quiet!' said Jesus sternly. 'Come out of him!' 26 The impure spirit shook the man violently and came out of him with a shriek.

27 The people were all so amazed that they asked each other, 'What is this? A new teaching – and with authority! He even gives orders to impure spirits and they obey him.' 28 News about him spread quickly over the whole region of Galilee.

Jesus heals many

29 As soon as they left the synagogue, they went with James and John to the home of Simon and Andrew. 30 Simon's mother-in-law was in bed with a fever, and they immediately told Jesus about

---

a 1 Or *Jesus Christ. Messiah* (Hebrew) and *Christ* (Greek) both mean *Anointed One.*
b 1 Some manuscripts do not have *the Son of God.*
c 2 Mal. 3:1
d 3 Isaiah 40:3
e 8 Or *in*
f 13 The Greek for *tempted* can also mean *tested.*

LIFE OF JESUS 3

Lord over spiritual powers

The Bible acknowledges the existence of supernatural powers other than God. The first thing to say is that we must always remember that, compared to the creating, sustaining and redeeming God who is the central figure of the whole world, history and the Bible, they are minor.

There is a 'devil' or 'Satan', who has barely a dozen mentions in Scripture, although there are a larger number of references to demons, hostile spiritual powers and evil or 'unclean' spirits. Whatever the Bible says about the strength of other spiritual powers, though, one thing is unmistakeable: Jesus has ultimate supremacy and the ability to set people free. When we look at this subject, we do so standing firm in this knowledge and with our focus firmly on Jesus.

Even if it's a subject we're uncomfortable with, it's important for us to talk about it. There are two features of Jesus' dealings with those 'spirits' that should make us think.

The first is that the New Testament is clear that his ultimate victory over the powers of evil was at the cross (see, for instance, Colossians 2:14). What appeared to be an appalling defeat turned out to be a monumental victory, and one way of understanding this is to realise that as 'God in the flesh', Jesus always had the *power* to destroy evil, but by dying on the cross as an innocent, sinless man he earned the *right* to destroy evil.

The second feature is something we might overlook when we read the stories of Jesus' exorcisms (like the one described in Mark 1:23–27). The general pattern for driving out a demon then and now is for the person to appeal to God through prayer for him to use his authority over the powers of evil. Remarkably, Jesus does nothing of the sort – he simply uses his own authority and casts out demons in his own name. This is strong proof that he was far more than a man or even a prophet. He had no need to appeal to the authority of God because he was God.

The name of Jesus is powerful. *'And these signs will accompany those who believe: in my name they will drive out demons; they will speak in new tongues; they will pick up snakes with their hands; and when they drink deadly poison, it will not hurt them at all; they will place their hands on people who are ill, and they will get well'* (Mark 16:17–18).

Jesus gives us the ability to use his authority, which means we have the power to take a stand against the devil, against sickness, against demons, against evil in the world. The power of our words, spoken in Jesus' name, is effectively as powerful as if God himself had spoken them.

While we should never seek to tangle with evil supernatural powers, if we come across them we can know that God in Christ is so much more powerful than they are.

J.John

◀◀ Matthew 21:1–11   Luke 7:36–50 ▶▶

her. **31** So he went to her, took her hand and helped her up. The fever left her and she began to wait on them.

32 That evening after sunset the people brought to Jesus all who were ill and demon-possessed. **33** The whole town gathered at the door, **34** and Jesus healed many who had various diseases. He also drove out many demons, but he would not let the demons speak because they knew who he was.

Jesus prays in a solitary place

35 Very early in the morning, while it was still dark, Jesus got up, left the house and went off to a solitary place, where he prayed. **36** Simon and his companions went to look for him, **37** and when they found him, they exclaimed: 'Everyone is looking for you!'

38 Jesus replied, 'Let us go somewhere else – to the nearby villages – so that I can preach there also. That is why I have come.' **39** So he travelled throughout Galilee, preaching in their synagogues and driving out demons.

Jesus heals a man with leprosy

40 A man with leprosy*g* came to him and begged him on his knees, 'If you are willing, you can make me clean.'

41 Jesus was indignant.*h* He reached out his hand and touched the man. 'I am willing,' he said. 'Be clean!' **42** Immediately the leprosy left him and he was cleansed.

43 Jesus sent him away at once with a strong warning: **44** 'See that you don't tell this to anyone. But go, show yourself to the priest and offer the sacrifices that Moses commanded for your cleansing, as a testimony to them.' **45** Instead he went out and began to talk freely, spreading the news. As a result, Jesus could no longer enter a town openly but stayed outside in lonely places. Yet the people still came to him from everywhere.

Jesus forgives and heals a paralysed man

2 A few days later, when Jesus again entered Capernaum, the people heard that he had come home. **2** They gathered in such large numbers that there was no room left, not even outside the door, and he preached the word to them. **3** Some men came, bringing to him a paralysed man, carried by four of them. **4** Since they could not get him to Jesus because of the crowd, they made an opening in the roof above Jesus by digging through it and then lowered the mat the man was lying on. **5** When Jesus saw their faith, he said to the paralysed man, 'Son, your sins are forgiven.'

6 Now some teachers of the law were sitting there, thinking to themselves, **7** 'Why does this fellow talk like that? He's blaspheming! Who can forgive sins but God alone?'

8 Immediately Jesus knew in his spirit that this was what they were thinking in their hearts, and he said to them, 'Why are you thinking these things? **9** Which is easier: to say to this paralysed man, "Your sins are forgiven," or to say, "Get up, take your mat and walk"? **10** But I want you to know that the Son of Man has authority on earth to forgive sins.' So he said to the man, **11** 'I tell you, get up, take your mat and go home.' **12** He got up, took his mat and walked out in full view of them all. This amazed everyone and they praised God, saying, 'We have never seen anything like this!'

Jesus calls Levi and eats with sinners

13 Once again Jesus went out beside the lake. A large crowd came to him, and he began to teach them. **14** As he walked along, he saw Levi son of Alphaeus sitting at the tax collector's booth. 'Follow me,' Jesus told him, and Levi got up and followed him.

15 While Jesus was having dinner at Levi's house, many tax collectors and sinners were eating with him and his disciples, for there were many who followed him. **16** When the teachers of the law who were Pharisees saw him eating with the

g 40 The Greek word traditionally translated *leprosy* was used for various diseases affecting the skin.
h 41 Many manuscripts *Jesus was filled with compassion*

sinners and tax collectors, they asked his disciples: 'Why does he eat with tax collectors and sinners?'

17 On hearing this, Jesus said to them, 'It is not the healthy who need a doctor, but those who are ill. I have not come to call the righteous, but sinners.'

Jesus questioned about fasting

18 Now John's disciples and the Pharisees were fasting. Some people came and asked Jesus, 'How is it that John's disciples and the disciples of the Pharisees are fasting, but yours are not?'

19 Jesus answered, 'How can the guests of the bridegroom fast while he is with them? They cannot, so long as they have him with them. **20** But the time will come when the bridegroom will be taken from them, and on that day they will fast.

21 'No one sews a patch of unshrunk cloth on an old garment. Otherwise, the new piece will pull away from the old, making the tear worse. **22** And no

EVANGELISM 4

You've earned the right

I love the story told in Mark 2:1–12 of the four guys lowering their friend down to land nicely in front of Jesus. It must have been quite an uncomfortable ride for the guy on the stretcher. He had been carried who knows how far, confronted by a big crowd, manhandled up to the roof and finally lowered down to land awkwardly in front of the great teacher. At times the man must have wondered whether all this fuss was really a good idea! But the people bringing him were his friends and he trusted them – they had earned the right to take him on the roller-coaster ride of faith.

Some people find it easy to chat to a stranger on a bus about where they will spend eternity. If you are one of these people, then great, go for it! Let's be honest, though: most of us would rather walk home than have a conversation like that! However, there are people in our lives with whom we have earned the right to journey, and we must not shrink back from speaking when the opportunities arise.

It's possible that there will be a few bumps and bruises on their journey to faith. Maybe there will be some uncomfortable moments as they consider huge issues like sin and eternity. These are the moments to remember that as their friend you have their best interests at heart – you have earned the right to be there and journey with them.

Do you have friends you would shrink back from when given the opportunity to talk about God? Don't forget, you're not on your own! When the four friends had lowered the man down, they had done their part. Jesus then did what only he can do. The challenge for us is to do our part and then look on as Jesus transforms our friends from the inside out.

Mark Ritchie

 Luke 10:1–4   Acts 26:28–29

one pours new wine into old wineskins. Otherwise, the wine will burst the skins, and both the wine and the wineskins will be ruined. No, they pour new wine into new wineskins.'

Jesus is Lord of the Sabbath

23 One Sabbath Jesus was going through the cornfields, and as his disciples walked along, they began to pick some ears of corn. 24 The Pharisees said to him, 'Look, why are they doing what is unlawful on the Sabbath?'

25 He answered, 'Have you never read what David did when he and his companions were hungry and in need? 26 In the days of Abiathar the high priest, he entered the house of God and ate the consecrated bread, which is lawful only for priests to eat. And he also gave some to his companions.'

27 Then he said to them, 'The Sabbath was made for man, not man for the Sabbath. 28 So the Son of Man is Lord even of the Sabbath.'

Jesus heals on the Sabbath

3 Another time Jesus went into the synagogue, and a man with a shrivelled hand was there. 2 Some of them were looking for a reason to accuse Jesus, so they watched him closely to see if he would heal him on the Sabbath. 3 Jesus said to the man with the shrivelled hand, 'Stand up in front of everyone.'

4 Then Jesus asked them, 'Which is lawful on the Sabbath: to do good or to do evil, to save life or to kill?' But they remained silent.

5 He looked around at them in anger and, deeply distressed at their stubborn hearts, said to the man, 'Stretch out your hand.' He stretched it out, and his hand was completely restored. 6 Then the Pharisees went out and began to plot with the Herodians how they might kill Jesus.

Crowds follow Jesus

7 Jesus withdrew with his disciples to the lake, and a large crowd from Galilee followed. 8 When they heard all he was doing, many people came to him from Judea, Jerusalem, Idumea, and the regions across the Jordan and around Tyre and Sidon. 9 Because of the crowd he told his disciples to have a small boat ready for him, to keep the people from crowding him. 10 For he had healed many, so that those with diseases were pushing forward to touch him. 11 Whenever the impure spirits saw him, they fell down before him and cried out, 'You are the Son of God.' 12 But he gave them strict orders not to tell others about him.

Jesus appoints the Twelve

13 Jesus went up on a mountainside and called to him those he wanted, and they came to him. 14 He appointed twelve[a] that they might be with him and that he might send them out to preach 15 and to have authority to drive out demons. 16 These are the twelve he appointed: Simon (to whom he gave the name Peter); 17 James son of Zebedee and his brother John (to them he gave the name Boanerges, which means 'sons of thunder'), 18 Andrew, Philip, Bartholomew, Matthew, Thomas, James son of Alphaeus, Thaddaeus, Simon the Zealot 19 and Judas Iscariot, who betrayed him.

Jesus accused by his family and by teachers of the law

20 Then Jesus entered a house, and again a crowd gathered, so that he and his disciples were not even able to eat. 21 When his family[b] heard about this, they went to take charge of him, for they said, 'He is out of his mind.'

22 And the teachers of the law who came down from Jerusalem said, 'He is possessed by Beelzebul! By the prince of demons he is driving out demons.'

23 So Jesus called them over to him and began to speak to them in parables: 'How can Satan drive out Satan? 24 If a kingdom is divided against itself, that kingdom

---

a 14 Some manuscripts *twelve – designating them apostles –*
b 21 Or *his associates*

TERRORISM

Did you know that one of Jesus' disciples was a terrorist? This guy called Simon the Zealot, mentioned in Mark 3:18, was, well, a Zealot – the Zealots were freedom fighters from Galilee who challenged the Roman oppression of Israel's Promised Land. They believed it was God's will for them to liberate his people, so they engaged in guerrilla warfare against Rome, and many of their leaders were crucified as a result.

Of course, whether you celebrate freedom fighters or hate terrorists may depend which side you're on.

Terrorism is a pretty hard thing to understand. Why do ordinary people go to such extreme lengths to hurt other innocent people? There's no easy answer, but a big reason in many cases is prejudice against the person who is different from us. Prejudice hardens into fear and hatred and pretty soon we have forgotten that the other person is a person at all. Often such prejudice comes from assuming something about someone else, or another group of people, that isn't really true.

It's easy to judge terrorists for their cruel and destructive actions – but terrorism almost always arises out of situations of relative powerlessness. When governments kill innocent people it's called war or counter-terrorism; so there can be an element of language use affecting our perceptions.

But the most surprising thing about Jesus choosing Simon to be one of his followers is that Jesus directly challenged the Zealots. He said, *'Blessed are the peacemakers'* (Matthew 5:9), and *'love your enemies and pray for those who persecute you'* (Matthew 5:44). Jesus wasn't scared to welcome someone whose principles he disagreed with. That's the kind of approach that could break down the walls between us. Might we even learn to love the person who hates us?

Actions

One of the biggest things we can do to fight terrorism is to challenge our own prejudice. Find someone you know you disagree with, or whose lifestyle you find difficult to accept. Ask if you can talk with them about what motivates them. Don't argue – just listen.

This prayer might be helpful:

Lord, I'm trying to be open-minded
But I don't want my brain to fall out!
I'm trying to have open hands
But I don't want to lose my grip on you!
Help me to have the confidence of Jesus:
To have nothing to prove or defend that can't be proved or defended by you;
To love unconditionally, to listen intently and to learn sensitively.
Amen

Matt Valler

cannot stand. ²⁵If a house is divided against itself, that house cannot stand. ²⁶And if Satan opposes himself and is divided, he cannot stand; his end has come. ²⁷In fact, no one can enter a strong man's house without first tying him up. Then he can plunder the strong man's house. ²⁸Truly I tell you, people can be forgiven all their sins and every slander they utter, ²⁹but whoever blasphemes against the Holy Spirit will never be forgiven; they are guilty of an eternal sin.'

³⁰He said this because they were saying, 'He has an impure spirit.'

³¹Then Jesus' mother and brothers arrived. Standing outside, they sent someone in to call him. ³²A crowd was sitting round him, and they told him, 'Your mother and brothers are outside looking for you.'

³³'Who are my mother and my brothers?' he asked.

³⁴Then he looked at those seated in a circle round him and said, 'Here are my mother and my brothers! ³⁵Whoever does God's will is my brother and sister and mother.'

The parable of the sower

4 Again Jesus began to teach by the lake. The crowd that gathered round him was so large that he got into a boat and sat in it out on the lake, while all the people were along the shore at the water's edge. ²He taught them many things by parables, and in his teaching said: ³'Listen! A farmer went out to sow his seed. ⁴As he was scattering the seed, some fell along the path, and the birds came and ate it up. ⁵Some fell on rocky places, where it did not have much soil. It sprang up quickly, because the soil was shallow. ⁶But when the sun came up, the plants were scorched, and they withered because they had no root. ⁷Other seed fell among thorns, which grew up and choked the plants, so that they did not bear grain. ⁸Still other seed fell on good soil. It came up, grew and produced a crop, some multiplying thirty, some sixty, some a hundred times.'

⁹Then Jesus said, 'Whoever has ears to hear, let them hear.'

¹⁰When he was alone, the Twelve and the others around him asked him about the parables. ¹¹He told them, 'The secret of the kingdom of God has been given to you. But to those on the outside everything is said in parables ¹²so that,

'"they may be ever seeing but never perceiving,
and ever hearing but never understanding;
otherwise they might turn and be forgiven!"^a'

¹³Then Jesus said to them, 'Don't you understand this parable? How then will you understand any parable? ¹⁴The farmer sows the word. ¹⁵Some people are like seed along the path, where the word is sown. As soon as they hear it, Satan comes and takes away the word that was sown in them. ¹⁶Others, like seed sown on rocky places, hear the word and at once receive it with joy. ¹⁷But since they have no root, they last only a short time. When trouble or persecution comes because of the word, they quickly fall away. ¹⁸Still others, like seed sown among thorns, hear the word; ¹⁹but the worries of this life, the deceitfulness of wealth and the desires for other things come in and choke the word, making it unfruitful. ²⁰Others, like seed sown on good soil, hear the word, accept it, and produce a crop – some thirty, some sixty, some a hundred times what was sown.'

A lamp on a stand

²¹He said to them, 'Do you bring in a lamp to put it under a bowl or a bed? Instead, don't you put it on its stand? ²²For whatever is hidden is meant to be disclosed, and whatever is concealed is meant to be brought out into the open. ²³If anyone has ears to hear, let them hear.'

²⁴'Consider carefully what you hear,' he continued. 'With the measure you use, it will be measured to you – and even more. ²⁵Whoever has will be given more;

^a 12 Isaiah 6:9,10

whoever does not have, even what they have will be taken from them.'

The parable of the growing seed

26 He also said, 'This is what the kingdom of God is like. A man scatters seed on the ground. 27 Night and day, whether he sleeps or gets up, the seed sprouts and grows, though he does not know how. 28 All by itself the soil produces corn – first the stalk, then the ear, then the full grain in the ear. 29 As soon as the corn is ripe, he puts the sickle to it, because the harvest has come.'

The parable of the mustard seed

30 Again he said, 'What shall we say the kingdom of God is like, or what parable shall we use to describe it? 31 It is like a mustard seed, which is the smallest of all seeds on earth. 32 Yet when planted, it grows and becomes the largest of all garden plants, with such big branches that the birds can perch in its shade.'

33 With many similar parables Jesus spoke the word to them, as much as they could understand. 34 He did not say anything to them without using a parable. But when he was alone with his own disciples, he explained everything.

Jesus calms the storm

35 That day when evening came, he said to his disciples, 'Let us go over to the other side.' 36 Leaving the crowd behind, they took him along, just as he was, in the boat. There were also other boats with him. 37 A furious squall came up, and the waves broke over the boat, so that it was nearly swamped. 38 Jesus was in the stern, sleeping on a cushion. The disciples woke him and said to him, 'Teacher, don't you care if we drown?'

39 He got up, rebuked the wind and said to the waves, 'Quiet! Be still!' Then the wind died down and it was completely calm.

40 He said to his disciples, 'Why are you so afraid? Do you still have no faith?'

41 They were terrified and asked each other, 'Who is this? Even the wind and the waves obey him!'

Jesus restores a demon-possessed man

5 They went across the lake to the region of the Gerasenes.*a* 2 When Jesus got out of the boat, a man with an impure spirit came from the tombs to meet him. 3 This man lived in the tombs, and no one could bind him anymore, not even with a chain. 4 For he had often been chained hand and foot, but he tore the chains apart and broke the irons on his feet. No one was strong enough to subdue him. 5 Night and day among the tombs and in the hills he would cry out and cut himself with stones.

6 When he saw Jesus from a distance, he ran and fell on his knees in front of him. 7 He shouted at the top of his voice, 'What do you want with me, Jesus, Son of the Most High God? In God's name don't torture me!' 8 For Jesus had said to him, 'Come out of this man, you impure spirit!'

9 Then Jesus asked him, 'What is your name?'

'My name is Legion,' he replied, 'for we are many.' 10 And he begged Jesus again and again not to send them out of the area.

11 A large herd of pigs was feeding on the nearby hillside. 12 The demons begged Jesus, 'Send us among the pigs; allow us to go into them.' 13 He gave them permission, and the impure spirits came out and went into the pigs. The herd, about two thousand in number, rushed down the steep bank into the lake and were drowned.

14 Those tending the pigs ran off and reported this in the town and countryside, and the people went out to see what had happened. 15 When they came to Jesus, they saw the man who had been possessed by the legion of demons, sitting there, dressed and in his right mind; and they were afraid. 16 Those who had seen it told the people what had happened to the demon-possessed man – and told about

---

a 1 Some manuscripts *Gadarenes*; other manuscripts *Gergesenes* the pigs as well. ¹⁷Then the people began to plead with Jesus to leave their region.

¹⁸As Jesus was getting into the boat, the man who had been demon-possessed begged to go with him. ¹⁹Jesus did not let him, but said, 'Go home to your own people and tell them how much the Lord has done for you, and how he has had mercy on you.' ²⁰So the man went away and began to tell in the Decapolis[b] how much Jesus had done for him. And all the people were amazed.

Jesus raises a dead girl and heals a sick woman

²¹When Jesus had again crossed over by boat to the other side of the lake, a large crowd gathered round him while he was by the lake. ²²Then one of the synagogue leaders, named Jairus, came, and when he saw Jesus, he fell at his feet. ²³He pleaded earnestly with him, 'My little daughter is dying. Please come and put your hands on her so that she will be healed and live.' ²⁴So Jesus went with him.

A large crowd followed and pressed round him. ²⁵And a woman was there who had been subject to bleeding for twelve years. ²⁶She had suffered a great deal under the care of many doctors and had spent all she had, yet instead of getting better she grew worse. ²⁷When she heard about Jesus, she came up behind him in the crowd and touched his cloak, ²⁸because she thought, 'If I just touch his clothes, I will be healed.' ²⁹Immediately her bleeding stopped and she felt in her body that she was freed from her suffering.

³⁰At once Jesus realised that power had gone out from him. He turned round in the crowd and asked, 'Who touched my clothes?'

³¹'You see the people crowding against you,' his disciples answered, 'and yet you can ask, "Who touched me?"'

³²But Jesus kept looking around to see who had done it. ³³Then the woman, knowing what had happened to her, came and fell at his feet and, trembling with fear, told him the whole truth. ³⁴He said to her, 'Daughter, your faith has healed you. Go in peace and be freed from your suffering.'

³⁵While Jesus was still speaking, some people came from the house of Jairus, the synagogue leader. 'Your daughter is dead,' they said. 'Why bother the teacher anymore?'

³⁶Overhearing[c] what they said, Jesus told him, 'Don't be afraid; just believe.'

³⁷He did not let anyone follow him except Peter, James and John the brother of James. ³⁸When they came to the home of the synagogue leader, Jesus saw a commotion, with people crying and wailing loudly. ³⁹He went in and said to them, 'Why all this commotion and wailing? The child is not dead but asleep.' ⁴⁰But they laughed at him.

After he put them all out, he took the child's father and mother and the disciples who were with him, and went in where the child was. ⁴¹He took her by the hand and said to her, 'Talitha koum!' (which means 'Little girl, I say to you, get up!'). ⁴²Immediately the girl stood up and began to walk around (she was twelve years old). At this they were completely astonished. ⁴³He gave strict orders not to let anyone know about this, and told them to give her something to eat.

A prophet without honour

6 Jesus left there and went to his home town, accompanied by his disciples. ²When the Sabbath came, he began to teach in the synagogue, and many who heard him were amazed.

'Where did this man get these things?' they asked. 'What's this wisdom that has been given him? What are these remarkable miracles he is performing? ³Isn't this the carpenter? Isn't this Mary's son and the brother of James, Joseph,[a] Judas and Simon? Aren't his sisters here with us?' And they took offence at him.

⁴Jesus said to them, 'A prophet is not

---

20 That is, the Ten Cities

c 36 Or Ignoring
a 3 Greek Joses, a variant of Joseph

without honour except in his own town, among his relatives and in his own home.' ⁵He could not do any miracles there, except lay his hands on a few people who were ill and heal them. ⁶He was amazed at their lack of faith.

Jesus sends out the Twelve

Then Jesus went around teaching from village to village. ⁷Calling the Twelve to him, he began to send them out two by two and gave them authority over impure spirits.

HEALING & MIRACLES 8

Pushing through obstacles

Can you imagine having a condition or disease that kept you away from society? Can you imagine if you couldn't be with your family or you knew people didn't want to be around you? Can you imagine the rejection? Mark 5:25–34 is about a lady in that exact situation. Pause for a moment and put yourself in her place.

This woman was full of faith. She had heard about Jesus and she had faith that he could heal her. She made difficult choices to overcome her circumstances just so she could get to Jesus. Bleeding for that long was likely to result in anaemia, and it would be exhausting just to get out of bed. Also, if she was to touch anyone else, they would also become ceremonially unclean. Everyone at that time lived under strict Jewish law (see Leviticus 15:19–28), so all of her community would know about her problem and want to avoid touching her. In such a bustling environment, though, avoiding contact with anyone would have been virtually impossible.

She was desperate to get to Jesus. She squeezed through the crowd, pushing on regardless of what they thought. It's pretty amazing that she had the faith to know, *'If I just touch his clothes, I will be healed'* (v. 28). And indeed, in the act of touching Jesus, she was healed. This lady put her faith into action, she overcame her seemingly hopeless situation, her tiredness, her illness and the social stigma, and took a massive risk. As she touched Jesus he took away her uncleanness – an amazing reward for a huge step of faith.

John Wimber used to say, 'Faith is spelt R.I.S.K.' As followers of Jesus, we are called to live a life of risk-taking, even when it comes to seeking healing for ourselves and others.

Jesus tells the woman it was her faith that made her well. This woman's faith got her to the place where healing could happen – it took her close to Jesus. Whatever you may be walking through, or whatever another may be troubled with, hold onto the fact that when we act in faith we get the attention of Jesus. He may not heal you right away, or it may feel that elements of your situation are impossible to overcome, but never allow your faith to be taken from you. Choose to come close to Jesus: allow him to meet you or the person you are praying for. Know that he has the power to heal, and have the faith that he will.

Christy Wimber

 Luke 8:40–56   Proverbs 12:18

FAITH IN THE WORLD 7

JESUS WAS A WHITE VAN DRIVER

There's one question that's difficult to avoid during your teenage years, from parents and other well-meaning adults: 'What do you want to do when you leave school or university? What do you want to *do* with your life?'

Somehow we just know they're not looking for an answer like 'Play computer games 24/7', or 'Tour the world non-stop on my private jet ski'. No, they're thinking about the 'j' word – *job*. So how do you decide what you want to do? Work expert Claire Pedrick talks about three things that you need to consider in answering this question. A couple of them are mentioned earlier on in this series on work.

First, what's your passion? Not just what motivates you, but what you're good at. Working with your hands? Maths? Programming? Then ask: what does the world *really* need? Get adults around you to help you answer this one. This is a hard thing to realise, I know, but sometimes what we really want to do might not match the needs of the market place. Do we need more rock stars and professional footballers? Or do we need more aeronautical engineers? Music and entertainment are big business, but if everyone wanted to do them and nothing else, we would struggle to survive! Finally, in thinking about actually getting work, we need to match our passions and our understanding of what the world needs with the requirements of a particular organisation. Will we fit in with them? Do we have the same goals?

All of this is a lot to think about during your teen years, when you're often more focused on decisions that impact things right now rather than further down the line. That's why it's no surprise that we would love God to do the easy thing and *tell* us what we're supposed to be doing – but in the Bible God rarely tells anyone what job they're supposed to do. And often people spend a long time doing a straightforward job before God calls them into a particular role. Moses was a shepherd for a good length of time before he led the nation of Israel, and so was King David! The influential prophet Amos never stopped being a shepherd – prophecy was his sideline.

And Jesus? Jesus was a white van driver for most of his life. Well, not exactly. When Jesus is referred to as a *'carpenter'* in Mark 6:1–6, the Greek word is *tekton*. That meant that Jesus' carpentry didn't just involve putting up shelves. He could have worked with various materials, including stone – building extensions to houses, or bridges over streams. If Jesus had lived today, chances are that 'Joseph & Son' *would* be travelling around in a white van. In Jesus' day, people simply adopted the career of their parents. God won't necessarily give us direct careers advice, but he will expect us to choose our career wisely and honour him in whatever job we do.

Jason Gardner

 Isaiah 28:23–29   Matthew 25:31–46 ▶▶

8These were his instructions: 'Take nothing for the journey except a staff – no bread, no bag, no money in your belts. **9**Wear sandals but not an extra shirt. **10**Whenever you enter a house, stay there until you leave that town. **11**And if any place will not welcome you or listen to you, leave that place and shake the dust off your feet as a testimony against them.'

12They went out and preached that people should repent. **13**They drove out many demons and anointed with oil many people who were ill and healed them.

John the Baptist beheaded

14King Herod heard about this, for Jesus' name had become well known. Some were saying,*b* 'John the Baptist has been raised from the dead, and that is why miraculous powers are at work in him.'

15Others said, 'He is Elijah.'

And still others claimed, 'He is a prophet, like one of the prophets of long ago.'

16But when Herod heard this, he said, 'John, whom I beheaded, has been raised from the dead!'

17For Herod himself had given orders to have John arrested, and he had him bound and put in prison. He did this because of Herodias, his brother Philip's wife, whom he had married. **18**For John had been saying to Herod, 'It is not lawful for you to have your brother's wife.' **19**So Herodias nursed a grudge against John and wanted to kill him. But she was not able to, **20**because Herod feared John and protected him, knowing him to be a righteous and holy man. When Herod heard John, he was greatly puzzled*c*; yet he liked to listen to him.

21Finally the opportune time came. On his birthday Herod gave a banquet for his high officials and military commanders and the leading men of Galilee. **22**When the daughter of*d* Herodias came in and danced, she pleased Herod and his dinner guests.

The king said to the girl, 'Ask me for anything you want, and I'll give it to you.' **23**And he promised her with an oath, 'Whatever you ask I will give you, up to half my kingdom.'

24She went out and said to her mother, 'What shall I ask for?'

'The head of John the Baptist,' she answered.

25At once the girl hurried in to the king with the request: 'I want you to give me right now the head of John the Baptist on a dish.'

26The king was greatly distressed, but because of his oaths and his dinner guests, he did not want to refuse her. **27**So he immediately sent an executioner with orders to bring John's head. The man went, beheaded John in the prison, **28**and brought back his head on a dish. He presented it to the girl, and she gave it to her mother. **29**On hearing of this, John's disciples came and took his body and laid it in a tomb.

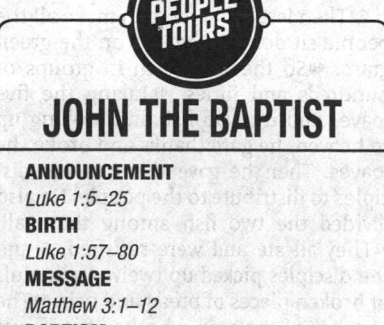

PEOPLE TOURS

JOHN THE BAPTIST

ANNOUNCEMENT
Luke 1:5–25
BIRTH
Luke 1:57–80
MESSAGE
Matthew 3:1–12
BAPTISM
Matthew 3:13–17
DEATH
Mark 6:14–29

Jesus feeds the five thousand

30The apostles gathered round Jesus and reported to him all they had done and taught. **31**Then, because so many people were coming and going that they did not even have a chance to eat, he said to them, 'Come with me by yourselves to a quiet place and get some rest.'

---

b 14 Some early manuscripts *He was saying*
c 20 Some early manuscripts *he did many things*
d 22 Some early manuscripts *When his daughter*

32 So they went away by themselves in a boat to a solitary place. 33 But many who saw them leaving recognised them and ran on foot from all the towns and got there ahead of them. 34 When Jesus landed and saw a large crowd, he had compassion on them, because they were like sheep without a shepherd. So he began teaching them many things.

35 By this time it was late in the day, so his disciples came to him. 'This is a remote place,' they said, 'and it's already very late. 36 Send the people away so that they can go to the surrounding countryside and villages and buy themselves something to eat.'

37 But he answered, 'You give them something to eat.'

They said to him, 'That would take more than half a year's wages[e]! Are we to go and spend that much on bread and give it to them to eat?'

38 'How many loaves do you have?' he asked. 'Go and see.'

When they found out, they said, 'Five – and two fish.'

39 Then Jesus told them to make all the people sit down in groups on the green grass. 40 So they sat down in groups of hundreds and fifties. 41 Taking the five loaves and the two fish and looking up to heaven, he gave thanks and broke the loaves. Then he gave them to his disciples to distribute to the people. He also divided the two fish among them all. 42 They all ate and were satisfied, 43 and the disciples picked up twelve basketfuls of broken pieces of bread and fish. 44 The number of the men who had eaten was five thousand.

Jesus walks on the water

45 Immediately Jesus made his disciples get into the boat and go on ahead of him to Bethsaida, while he dismissed the crowd. 46 After leaving them, he went up on a mountainside to pray.

47 Later that night, the boat was in the middle of the lake, and he was alone on land. 48 He saw the disciples straining at the oars, because the wind was against them. Shortly before dawn he went out to them, walking on the lake. He was about to pass by them, 49 but when they saw him walking on the lake, they thought he was a ghost. They cried out, 50 because they all saw him and were terrified.

Immediately he spoke to them and said, 'Take courage! It is I. Don't be afraid.' 51 Then he climbed into the boat with them, and the wind died down. They were completely amazed, 52 for they had not understood about the loaves; their hearts were hardened.

53 When they had crossed over, they landed at Gennesaret and anchored there. 54 As soon as they got out of the boat, people recognised Jesus. 55 They ran throughout that whole region and carried those who were ill on mats to wherever they heard he was. 56 And wherever he went – into villages, towns or countryside – they placed those who were ill in the marketplaces. They begged him to let them touch even the edge of his cloak, and all who touched it were healed.

That which defiles

7 The Pharisees and some of the teachers of the law who had come from Jerusalem gathered round Jesus 2 and saw some of his disciples eating food with hands that were defiled, that is, unwashed. 3 (The Pharisees and all the Jews do not eat unless they give their hands a ceremonial washing, holding to the tradition of the elders. 4 When they come from the market-place they do not eat unless they wash. And they observe many other traditions, such as the washing of cups, pitchers and kettles.[a])

5 So the Pharisees and teachers of the law asked Jesus, 'Why don't your disciples live according to the tradition of the elders instead of eating their food with defiled hands?'

6 He replied, 'Isaiah was right when he prophesied about you hypocrites; as it is written:

---

e 37 Greek take two hundred denarii

a 4 Some early manuscripts pitchers, kettles and dining couches

' "These people honour me with their
lips,
but their hearts are far from me.
7 They worship me in vain;
their teachings are merely human
rules."*b*

8 You have let go of the commands of God
and are holding on to human traditions.'

9 And he continued, 'You have a fine
way of setting aside the commands of God
in order to observe*c* your own traditions!
10 For Moses said, "Honour your father and
mother,"*d* and, "Anyone who curses their
father or mother is to be put to death."*e*
11 But you say that if anyone declares that
what might have been used to help their
father or mother is Corban (that is, devoted
to God) – 12 then you no longer let them
do anything for their father or mother.
13 Thus you nullify the word of God by your
tradition that you have handed down. And
you do many things like that.'

14 Again Jesus called the crowd to him
and said, 'Listen to me, everyone, and
understand this. 15 Nothing outside a person can defile them by going into them.
Rather, it is what comes out of a person
that defiles them.' [16]*f*

17 After he had left the crowd and entered the house, his disciples asked him
about this parable. 18 'Are you so dull?' he
asked. 'Don't you see that nothing that
enters a person from the outside can defile them? 19 For it doesn't go into their
heart but into their stomach, and then out
of the body.' (In saying this, Jesus declared
all foods clean.)

20 He went on: 'What comes out of a
person is what defiles them. 21 For it is
from within, out of a person's heart, that
evil thoughts come – sexual immorality,
theft, murder, 22 adultery, greed, malice,
deceit, lewdness, envy, slander, arrogance
and folly. 23 All these evils come from inside and defile a person.'

Jesus honours a Syro-Phoenician woman's faith

24 Jesus left that place and went to the vicinity of Tyre.*g* He entered a house and did
not want anyone to know it; yet he could
not keep his presence secret. 25 In fact, as
soon as she heard about him, a woman
whose little daughter was possessed by
an impure spirit came and fell at his feet.
26 The woman was a Greek, born in Syrian
Phoenicia. She begged Jesus to drive the
demon out of her daughter.

27 'First let the children eat all they
want,' he told her, 'for it is not right to
take the children's bread and toss it to the
dogs.'

28 'Lord,' she replied, 'even the dogs under the table eat the children's crumbs.'

29 Then he told her, 'For such a reply,
you may go; the demon has left your
daughter.'

30 She went home and found her child
lying on the bed, and the demon gone.

Jesus heals a deaf and mute man

31 Then Jesus left the vicinity of Tyre and
went through Sidon, down to the Sea of
Galilee and into the region of the Decapolis.*h* 32 There some people brought to him
a man who was deaf and could hardly talk,
and they begged Jesus to place his hand on
him.

33 After he took him aside, away from
the crowd, Jesus put his fingers into the
man's ears. Then he spat and touched the
man's tongue. 34 He looked up to heaven
and with a deep sigh said to him, '*Ephpha-
tha!*' (which means 'Be opened!'). 35 At
this, the man's ears were opened, his
tongue was loosed and he began to speak
plainly.

36 Jesus commanded them not to tell
anyone. But the more he did so, the more
they kept talking about it. 37 People were
overwhelmed with amazement. 'He has
done everything well,' they said. 'He even
makes the deaf hear and the mute speak.'

---

b 6,7 Isaiah 29:13
c 9 Some manuscripts *set up*
d 10 Exodus 20:12; Deut. 5:16
e 10 Exodus 21:17; Lev. 20:9
f 16 Some manuscripts include here the words of
4:23.

g 24 Many early manuscripts *Tyre and Sidon*
h 31 That is, the Ten Cities

THE BIG STORY 3

Every heart

'It wasn't my fault!' is a frequent response to being challenged about doing something wrong. We live in a culture which likes to find someone to blame, apart from ourselves. We like to see ourselves as victims of circumstances beyond our control and responsibility. There *can* be circumstances beyond our control. Things *can* happen which are not directly any one person's fault. But Jesus has uncomfortable things to say about basic human nature (Mark 7:14–23).

When he talks about 'the heart', he doesn't mean our feelings. In Jewish culture the heart was the centre of the personality from which everything else flows. Above all, it was the centre of our will. So when he says, *'from within, out of a person's heart … evil thoughts come – sexual immorality, theft, murder, adultery, greed, malice, deceit, lewdness, envy, slander, arrogance and folly. All these evils come from inside'* (vv. 21–23), he makes it clear that no one can ever say that the problems in the world and the ways we offend God 'aren't our fault'. The list includes planning evil acts and having evil attitudes. There are sexual sins – sex outside marriage, being unfaithful to your spouse; sins about possession – theft, greed, envy; sins of violence – murder; sins of evil intent against others – deceit, slander, malice, lewdness (dirty jokes to embarrass someone); and sins of pride – arrogance and folly.

The point Jesus is making is not that some people think and do such things – which we know very well – but that we are all capable of such things, because our hearts are wrong. Because these are attitudes of the heart, it's as much a sin to think and plan them as to do them. God looks at the intention of our hearts, not just (or primarily) at our actions. Sins against other people are also sins against God and he is concerned about what we are, not just about what we do.

In the Jewish religion at that time there were ceremonies about washing, which Jesus' followers did not always observe (see Mark 7:1–5). Some things made people ceremonially unclean, so that they could not go to the temple to worship before they were cleansed. Jesus is saying that the uncleanness of our hearts makes us unclean before God. We cannot approach him with 'dirty hearts'. In this teaching Jesus is saying what the Old Testament prophets used to say. *'The heart is deceitful above all things and beyond cure'* (Jeremiah 17:9). But the prophets also promised that God would give his people a new start. *'I will give you a new heart and put a new spirit in you'* (Ezekiel 36:26). What they promised, Jesus fulfilled. He not only gave the diagnosis, he is the cure. We won't seek it, though, if nothing is really 'our fault'.

Graham Cray

 Romans 5:12–14   Genesis 12:1–3

Jesus feeds the four thousand

8 During those days another large crowd gathered. Since they had nothing to eat, Jesus called his disciples to him and said, ²'I have compassion for these people; they have already been with me three days and have nothing to eat. ³If I send them home hungry, they will collapse on the way, because some of them have come a long distance.'

⁴His disciples answered, 'But where in this remote place can anyone get enough bread to feed them?'

⁵'How many loaves do you have?' Jesus asked.

'Seven,' they replied.

⁶He told the crowd to sit down on the ground. When he had taken the seven loaves and given thanks, he broke them and gave them to his disciples to distribute to the people, and they did so. ⁷They had a few small fish as well; he gave thanks for them also and told the disciples to distribute them. ⁸The people ate and were satisfied. Afterwards the disciples picked up seven basketfuls of broken pieces that were left over. ⁹About four thousand were present. After he had sent them away, ¹⁰he got into the boat with his disciples and went to the region of Dalmanutha.

¹¹The Pharisees came and began to question Jesus. To test him, they asked him for a sign from heaven. ¹²He sighed deeply and said, 'Why does this generation ask for a sign? Truly I tell you, no sign will be given to it.' ¹³Then he left them, got back into the boat and crossed to the other side.

The yeast of the Pharisees and Herod

¹⁴The disciples had forgotten to bring bread, except for one loaf they had with them in the boat. ¹⁵'Be careful,' Jesus warned them. 'Watch out for the yeast of the Pharisees and that of Herod.'

¹⁶They discussed this with one another and said, 'It is because we have no bread.'

¹⁷Aware of their discussion, Jesus asked them: 'Why are you talking about having no bread? Do you still not see or understand? Are your hearts hardened? ¹⁸Do you have eyes but fail to see, and ears but fail to hear? And don't you remember? ¹⁹When I broke the five loaves for the five thousand, how many basketfuls of pieces did you pick up?'

'Twelve,' they replied.

²⁰'And when I broke the seven loaves for the four thousand, how many basketfuls of pieces did you pick up?'

They answered, 'Seven.'

²¹He said to them, 'Do you still not understand?'

Jesus heals a blind man at Bethsaida

²²They came to Bethsaida, and some people brought a blind man and begged Jesus to touch him. ²³He took the blind man by the hand and led him outside the village. When he had spat on the man's eyes and put his hands on him, Jesus asked, 'Do you see anything?'

²⁴He looked up and said, 'I see people; they look like trees walking around.'

²⁵Once more Jesus put his hands on the man's eyes. Then his eyes were opened, his sight was restored, and he saw everything clearly. ²⁶Jesus sent him home, saying, 'Don't even go into*ᵃ* the village.'

Peter declares that Jesus is the Messiah

²⁷Jesus and his disciples went on to the villages around Caesarea Philippi. On the way he asked them, 'Who do people say I am?'

²⁸They replied, 'Some say John the Baptist; others say Elijah; and still others, one of the prophets.'

²⁹'But what about you?' he asked. 'Who do you say I am?'

Peter answered, 'You are the Messiah.'

³⁰Jesus warned them not to tell anyone about him.

Jesus predicts his death

³¹He then began to teach them that the Son of Man must suffer many things and be rejected by the elders, the chief priests and the teachers of the law, and that he must be killed and after three days rise again. ³²He spoke plainly about this, and

---

a 26 Some manuscripts *go and tell anyone in*

Peter took him aside and began to rebuke him.

33 But when Jesus turned and looked at his disciples, he rebuked Peter. 'Get behind me, Satan!' he said. 'You do not have in mind the concerns of God, but merely human concerns.'

The way of the cross

34 Then he called the crowd to him along with his disciples and said: 'Whoever wants to be my disciple must deny themselves and take up their cross and follow me. 35 For whoever wants to save their life*b* will lose it, but whoever loses their life for me and for the gospel will save it. 36 What good is it for someone to gain the whole world, yet forfeit their soul? 37 Or what can anyone give in exchange for their soul? 38 If anyone is ashamed of me and my words in this adulterous and sinful generation, the Son of Man will be ashamed of them when he comes in his Father's glory with the holy angels.'

9 And he said to them, 'Truly I tell you, some who are standing here will not taste death before they see that the kingdom of God has come with power.'

The transfiguration

2 After six days Jesus took Peter, James and John with him and led them up a high mountain, where they were all alone. There he was transfigured before them. 3 His clothes became dazzling white, whiter than anyone in the world could bleach them. 4 And there appeared before them Elijah and Moses, who were talking with Jesus.

5 Peter said to Jesus, 'Rabbi, it is good for us to be here. Let us put up three shelters – one for you, one for Moses and one for Elijah.' 6 (He did not know what to say, they were so frightened.)

7 Then a cloud appeared and covered them, and a voice came from the cloud: 'This is my Son, whom I love. Listen to him!'

8 Suddenly, when they looked around,

they no longer saw anyone with them except Jesus.

9 As they were coming down the mountain, Jesus gave them orders not to tell anyone what they had seen until the Son of Man had risen from the dead. 10 They kept the matter to themselves, discussing what 'rising from the dead' meant.

11 And they asked him, 'Why do the teachers of the law say that Elijah must come first?'

12 Jesus replied, 'To be sure, Elijah does come first, and restores all things. Why then is it written that the Son of Man must suffer much and be rejected? 13 But I tell you, Elijah has come, and they have done to him everything they wished, just as it is written about him.'

Jesus heals a boy possessed by an impure spirit

14 When they came to the other disciples, they saw a large crowd around them and the teachers of the law arguing with them. 15 As soon as all the people saw Jesus, they were overwhelmed with wonder and ran to greet him.

16 'What are you arguing with them about?' he asked.

17 A man in the crowd answered, 'Teacher, I brought you my son, who is possessed by a spirit that has robbed him of speech. 18 Whenever it seizes him, it throws him to the ground. He foams at the mouth, gnashes his teeth and becomes rigid. I asked your disciples to drive out the spirit, but they could not.'

19 'You unbelieving generation,' Jesus replied, 'how long shall I stay with you? How long shall I put up with you? Bring the boy to me.'

20 So they brought him. When the spirit saw Jesus, it immediately threw the boy into a convulsion. He fell to the ground and rolled around, foaming at the mouth.

21 Jesus asked the boy's father, 'How long has he been like this?'

'From childhood,' he answered. 22 'It has often thrown him into fire or water to kill him. But if you can do anything, take pity on us and help us.'

---

b 35 The Greek word means either *life* or *soul*; also in verses 36 and 37.

HEALING & MIRACLES 5

Trouble believing

In Mark 9:14–32, Jesus is having a conversation with a man whose son is really ill. His child has been sick *'from childhood'* (v. 21), and the father has taken him to Jesus' disciples, but they couldn't help. In desperation the father calls out to Jesus. This is a situation that so many people know today: we have friends or family who aren't well, we have tried doctors and treatments, we have tried everything, and we don't know who else to turn to.

The father is probably scared that his son will never get well, full of concern, hope and disappointment. Jesus' response is gentle, a question filled with compassion. He asks the boy's father, 'How long has he been like this?' (v. 21). Maybe Jesus knew the answer already, maybe he knew that the father needed to share some of his heartache and be healed himself. Either way, Jesus' compassion is profound for these two amongst the crowd.

The father then says to Jesus, *'If you can do anything, take pity on us and help us'* (v. 22). The hope for healing is loud in his words. 'Please, Jesus. Please help my son. Please help me. I've tried everything else. You are my only hope.' Jesus replies with the assurance of faith, a deep knowledge of the power of belief: *'"If you can"? ... Everything is possible for one who believes.'*

Faith isn't something we just pretend to have; it's an understanding deep inside us. We know without a doubt that things can and will change. Despite what circumstances tell us, faith says something different. Faith gives us hope for any situation because we know it can be changed. *We know it because we know it because we know it.* Not because it makes sense, but because we have the assurance of faith in a God of power and mercy.

Faith is often built through experience. Jesus' response to the father's plea – *'help me overcome my unbelief!'* (v. 24) – is not to give him more faith, but to heal his son. The father's faith is grown through experiencing the power of God. When we experience and see Jesus, it changes everything. Every time I see the Lord heal and feel his presence, it reminds me how powerful he is. It feeds and builds my faith in new areas of my life.

This story isn't only about a sick boy healed, but also about his desperate father who had the right response in the area he was lacking: 'Help me.' This father was ministered to, just as much as his son was. When healing takes place, it always impacts more widely than the one who is healed. It reveals Jesus to the people around them. Let's be people who ask for the faith to pray for healing, that Jesus would be revealed to everyone around us.

Christy Wimber

 Matthew 17:20–21 Luke 11 ▶▶

23 ' "If you can"?' said Jesus. 'Everything is possible for one who believes.'

24 Immediately the boy's father exclaimed, 'I do believe; help me overcome my unbelief!'

25 When Jesus saw that a crowd was running to the scene, he rebuked the impure spirit. 'You deaf and mute spirit,' he said, 'I command you, come out of him and never enter him again.'

26 The spirit shrieked, convulsed him violently and came out. The boy looked so much like a corpse that many said, 'He's dead.' **27** But Jesus took him by the hand and lifted him to his feet, and he stood up.

28 After Jesus had gone indoors, his disciples asked him privately, 'Why couldn't we drive it out?'

29 He replied, 'This kind can come out only by prayer.*a*'

Jesus predicts his death a second time

30 They left that place and passed through Galilee. Jesus did not want anyone to know where they were, **31** because he was teaching his disciples. He said to them, 'The Son of Man is going to be delivered into the hands of men. They will kill him, and after three days he will rise.' **32** But they did not understand what he meant and were afraid to ask him about it.

33 They came to Capernaum. When he was in the house, he asked them, 'What were you arguing about on the road?' **34** But they kept quiet because on the way they had argued about who was the greatest.

35 Sitting down, Jesus called the Twelve and said, 'Anyone who wants to be first must be the very last, and the servant of all.'

36 He took a little child whom he placed among them. Taking the child in his arms, he said to them, **37** 'Whoever welcomes one of these little children in my name welcomes me; and whoever welcomes me does not welcome me but the one who sent me.'

Whoever is not against us is for us

38 'Teacher,' said John, 'we saw someone driving out demons in your name and we told him to stop, because he was not one of us.'

39 'Do not stop him,' Jesus said. 'For no one who does a miracle in my name can in the next moment say anything bad about me, **40** for whoever is not against us is for us. **41** Truly I tell you, anyone who gives you a cup of water in my name because you belong to the Messiah will certainly not lose their reward.

Causing to stumble

42 'If anyone causes one of these little ones – those who believe in me – to stumble, it would be better for them if a large millstone were hung round their neck and they were thrown into the sea. **43** If your hand causes you to stumble, cut it off. It is better for you to enter life maimed than with two hands to go into hell, where the fire never goes out. [44] *b* **45** And if your foot causes you to stumble, cut it off. It is better for you to enter life crippled than to have two feet and be thrown into hell. [46] *b* **47** And if your eye causes you to stumble, pluck it out. It is better for you to enter the kingdom of God with one eye than to have two eyes and be thrown into hell, **48** where

' "the worms that eat them do not die,
    and the fire is not quenched." *c*

49 Everyone will be salted with fire.

50 'Salt is good, but if it loses its saltiness, how can you make it salty again? Have salt among yourselves, and be at peace with each other.'

Divorce

10 Jesus then left that place and went into the region of Judea and across the Jordan. Again crowds of people came to him, and as was his custom, he taught them.

---

a 29 Some manuscripts *prayer and fasting*

b 44,46 Some manuscripts include here the words of verse 48.
c 48 Isaiah 66:24

SPIRITUAL DISCIPLINES 4

SUBMISSION

'Submission' has become a very controversial word. It has been misused to justify prejudice against women, to empower abusive church leaders, even to justify slavery. Yet the spiritual discipline of submission isn't about something that is done to us, but rather about an action that we do before others. Submission isn't allowing someone to walk all over you – it's making a choice to put others first.

In Mark 9:30–35, Jesus calls the disciples together after they have been arguing over which of them is the greatest. It may seem like a nonsensical argument, or you may secretly identify with their desire to be their leader's favourite. They each want to be top, yet Jesus reveals that they are asking the wrong question. They should be aiming to be the least, not the greatest.

When Jesus tells them they should aim to be 'last', not 'first', he is talking about the way they interact with others; he's calling them to 'submit' to each other and to the community around them, to put others first. Couple this with Jesus' various calls to love our brothers, sisters and neighbours, and we start to get a picture of the spiritual discipline of submission.

In his book *Celebration of Discipline,* writer Richard Foster outlines seven ways to submit – that is, to put the needs of others before our own. This might seem like a lot to ask, but remember, Jesus calls us to make ourselves last: servants to all.

These seven 'directions of submission' remind us of the many people whose needs we should put ahead of our own. Challenging, yes – but also liberating!

- **To God.** We aren't ours any more – we belong to God, so we should be able to do, go and say whatever God asks of us.

- **To the Bible.** We want to give time to get to know the Bible as well as possible so we can really understand the character and way of God when we're making decisions.

- **To our family.** We should submit to our parents, brothers and sisters to show them we love and honour them, just as God commands Moses.

- **To our neighbours.** True community is about sharing what we have so that no one goes without or is lonely. What can you do?

- **To the church.** The church is a key part of God's rescue plan for the world, and we have to learn to give ourselves, our money and our time.

- **To the broken.** The Bible is overflowing with references to the poor, and asks us to serve them.

- **To the world.** In our global culture we need to submit to living responsibly with our spending and our choices.

Martin Saundera

²Some Pharisees came and tested him by asking, 'Is it lawful for a man to divorce his wife?'

³'What did Moses command you?' he replied.

⁴They said, 'Moses permitted a man to write a certificate of divorce and send her away.'

⁵'It was because your hearts were hard that Moses wrote you this law,' Jesus replied. ⁶'But at the beginning of creation God "made them male and female".ᵃ ⁷"For this reason a man will leave his father and mother and be united to his wife,ᵇ ⁸and the two will become one flesh."ᶜ So they are no longer two, but one flesh. ⁹Therefore what God has joined together, let no one separate.'

¹⁰When they were in the house again, the disciples asked Jesus about this. ¹¹He answered, 'Anyone who divorces his wife and marries another woman commits adultery against her. ¹²And if she divorces her husband and marries another man, she commits adultery.'

The little children and Jesus

¹³People were bringing little children to Jesus for him to place his hands on them, but the disciples rebuked them. ¹⁴When Jesus saw this, he was indignant. He said to them, 'Let the little children come to me, and do not hinder them, for the kingdom of God belongs to such as these. ¹⁵Truly I tell you, anyone who will not receive the kingdom of God like a little child will never enter it.' ¹⁶And he took the children in his arms, placed his hands on them and blessed them.

The rich and the kingdom of God

¹⁷As Jesus started on his way, a man ran up to him and fell on his knees before him. 'Good teacher,' he asked, 'what must I do to inherit eternal life?'

¹⁸'Why do you call me good?' Jesus answered. 'No one is good – except God alone. ¹⁹You know the commandments: "You shall not murder, you shall not commit adultery, you shall not steal, you shall not give false testimony, you shall not defraud, honour your father and mother."ᵈ

²⁰'Teacher,' he declared, 'all these I have kept since I was a boy.'

²¹Jesus looked at him and loved him. 'One thing you lack,' he said. 'Go, sell everything you have and give to the poor, and you will have treasure in heaven. Then come, follow me.'

²²At this the man's face fell. He went away sad, because he had great wealth.

²³Jesus looked round and said to his disciples, 'How hard it is for the rich to enter the kingdom of God!'

²⁴The disciples were amazed at his words. But Jesus said again, 'Children, how hard it isᵉ to enter the kingdom of God! ²⁵It is easier for a camel to go through the eye of a needle than for someone who is rich to enter the kingdom of God.'

²⁶The disciples were even more amazed, and said to each other, 'Who then can be saved?'

²⁷Jesus looked at them and said, 'With man this is impossible, but not with God; all things are possible with God.'

²⁸Then Peter spoke up, 'We have left everything to follow you!'

²⁹'Truly I tell you,' Jesus replied, 'no one who has left home or brothers or sisters or mother or father or children or fields for me and the gospel ³⁰will fail to receive a hundred times as much in this present age: homes, brothers, sisters, mothers, children and fields – along with persecutions – and in the age to come eternal life. ³¹But many who are first will be last, and the last first.'

Jesus predicts his death a third time

³²They were on their way up to Jerusalem, with Jesus leading the way, and the disciples were astonished, while those who followed were afraid. Again he took the Twelve aside and told them what was going to happen to him. ³³'We are going up to Jerusalem,' he said, 'and the Son

---

ᵃ 6 Gen. 1:27
ᵇ 7 Some early manuscripts do not have *and be united to his wife.*
ᶜ 8 Gen. 2:24

ᵈ 19 Exodus 20:12-16; Deut. 5:16-20
ᵉ 24 Some manuscripts *is for those who trust in riches*

of Man will be delivered over to the chief priests and the teachers of the law. They will condemn him to death and will hand him over to the Gentiles, 34who will mock him and spit on him, flog him and kill him. Three days later he will rise.'

The request of James and John

35Then James and John, the sons of Zebedee, came to him. 'Teacher,' they said, 'we want you to do for us whatever we ask.'

36'What do you want me to do for you?' he asked.

37They replied, 'Let one of us sit at your right and the other at your left in your glory.'

38'You don't know what you are asking,' Jesus said. 'Can you drink the cup I drink or be baptised with the baptism I am baptised with?'

39'We can,' they answered.

Jesus said to them, 'You will drink the cup I drink and be baptised with the baptism I am baptised with, 40but to sit at my right or left is not for me to grant. These places belong to those for whom they have been prepared.'

41When the ten heard about this, they became indignant with James and John. 42Jesus called them together and said, 'You know that those who are regarded as rulers of the Gentiles lord it over them, and their high officials exercise authority over them. 43Not so with you. Instead, whoever wants to become great among you must be your servant, 44and whoever wants to be first must be slave of all. 45For even the Son of Man did not come to be served, but to serve, and to give his life as a ransom for many.'

Blind Bartimaeus receives his sight

46Then they came to Jericho. As Jesus and his disciples, together with a large crowd, were leaving the city, a blind man, Bartimaeus (which means 'son of Timaeus'), was sitting by the roadside begging. 47When he heard that it was Jesus of Nazareth, he began to shout, 'Jesus, Son of David, have mercy on me!'

48Many rebuked him and told him to be quiet, but he shouted all the more, 'Son of David, have mercy on me!'

49Jesus stopped and said, 'Call him.'

So they called to the blind man, 'Cheer up! On your feet! He's calling you.' 50Throwing his cloak aside, he jumped to his feet and came to Jesus.

51'What do you want me to do for you?' Jesus asked him.

The blind man said, 'Rabbi, I want to see.'

52'Go,' said Jesus, 'your faith has healed you.' Immediately he received his sight and followed Jesus along the road.

FAVOURITE VERSES

Lamentations 3:57

You came near when I called you, and you said, 'Do not fear.'

This is such a positive verse in a book that's supposed to be full of misery. It proves to me that we were made to praise the Lord, and always should, even when we're not really in the mood. He tells us not to fear and so we shouldn't, because he will always come to us when we ask him to.

Anon.

Jesus comes to Jerusalem as king

11 As they approached Jerusalem and came to Bethphage and Bethany at the Mount of Olives, Jesus sent two of his disciples, 2saying to them, 'Go to the village ahead of you, and just as you enter it, you will find a colt tied there, which no one has ever ridden. Untie it and bring it here. 3If anyone asks you, "Why are you doing this?" say, "The Lord needs it and will send it back here shortly."'

4They went and found a colt outside in

the street, tied at a doorway. As they untied it, ⁵some people standing there asked, 'What are you doing, untying that colt?' ⁶They answered as Jesus had told them to, and the people let them go. ⁷When they brought the colt to Jesus and threw their cloaks over it, he sat on it. ⁸Many people spread their cloaks on the road, while others spread branches they had cut in the fields. ⁹Those who went ahead and those who followed shouted,

'Hosanna!*ᵃ*'

'Blessed is he who comes in the name of the Lord!'*ᵇ*

¹⁰'Blessed is the coming kingdom of our father David!'

'Hosanna in the highest heaven!'

¹¹Jesus entered Jerusalem and went into the temple courts. He looked around at everything, but since it was already late, he went out to Bethany with the Twelve.

Jesus curses a fig-tree and clears the temple courts

¹²The next day as they were leaving Bethany, Jesus was hungry. ¹³Seeing in the distance a fig-tree in leaf, he went to find out if it had any fruit. When he reached it, he found nothing but leaves, because it was not the season for figs. ¹⁴Then he said to the tree, 'May no one ever eat fruit from you again.' And his disciples heard him say it.

¹⁵On reaching Jerusalem, Jesus entered the temple courts and began driving out those who were buying and selling there. He overturned the tables of the money-changers and the benches of those selling doves, ¹⁶and would not allow anyone to carry merchandise through the temple courts. ¹⁷And as he taught them, he said, 'Is it not written: "My house will be called

a house of prayer for all nations"*ᶜ*? But you have made it "a den of robbers".*ᵈ*'

¹⁸The chief priests and the teachers of the law heard this and began looking for a way to kill him, for they feared him, because the whole crowd was amazed at his teaching.

¹⁹When evening came, Jesus and his disciples*ᵉ* went out of the city.

²⁰In the morning, as they went along, they saw the fig-tree withered from the roots. ²¹Peter remembered and said to Jesus, 'Rabbi, look! The fig-tree you cursed has withered!'

²²'Have faith in God,' Jesus answered. ²³'Truly*f* I tell you, if anyone says to this mountain, "Go, throw yourself into the sea," and does not doubt in their heart but believes that what they say will happen, it will be done for them. ²⁴Therefore I tell you, whatever you ask for in prayer, believe that you have received it, and it will be yours. ²⁵And when you stand praying, if you hold anything against anyone, forgive them, so that your Father in heaven may forgive you your sins.' [26]*g*

The authority of Jesus questioned

²⁷They arrived again in Jerusalem, and while Jesus was walking in the temple courts, the chief priests, the teachers of the law and the elders came to him. ²⁸'By what authority are you doing these things?' they asked. 'And who gave you authority to do this?'

²⁹Jesus replied, 'I will ask you one question. Answer me, and I will tell you by what authority I am doing these things. ³⁰John's baptism – was it from heaven, or of human origin? Tell me!'

³¹They discussed it among themselves and said, 'If we say, "From heaven," he will ask, "Then why didn't you believe him?" ³²But if we say, "Of human origin" . . .'

---

c 17 Isaiah 56:7
d 17 Jer. 7:11
e 19 Some early manuscripts *came, Jesus*
f 22,23 Some early manuscripts *'If you have faith in God,' Jesus answered,* ²³*'truly*
g 26 Some manuscripts include here words similar to Matt. 6:15.

---

a 9 A Hebrew expression meaning 'Save!' which became an exclamation of praise; also in verse 10
b 9 Psalm 118:25,26

(They feared the people, for everyone held that John really was a prophet.)

33 So they answered Jesus, 'We don't know.'

Jesus said, 'Neither will I tell you by what authority I am doing these things.'

The parable of the tenants

12 Jesus then began to speak to them in parables: 'A man planted a vineyard. He put a wall round it, dug a pit for the winepress and built a watchtower. Then he rented the vineyard to some farmers and moved to another place. 2 At harvest time he sent a servant to the tenants to collect from them some of the fruit of the vineyard. 3 But they seized him, beat him and sent him away empty-handed. 4 Then he sent another servant to them; they struck this man on the head and treated him shamefully. 5 He sent still another, and that one they killed. He sent many others; some of them they beat, others they killed.

6 'He had one left to send, a son, whom he loved. He sent him last of all, saying, "They will respect my son."

7 'But the tenants said to one another, "This is the heir. Come, let's kill him, and the inheritance will be ours." 8 So they took him and killed him, and threw him out of the vineyard.

9 'What then will the owner of the vineyard do? He will come and kill those tenants and give the vineyard to others. 10 Haven't you read this passage of Scripture:

' "The stone the builders rejected
     has become the cornerstone;
11 the Lord has done this,
     and it is marvellous in our eyes"ᵃ?'

12 Then the chief priests, the teachers of the law and the elders looked for a way to arrest him because they knew he had spoken the parable against them. But they were afraid of the crowd; so they left him and went away.

Paying the poll-tax to Caesar

13 Later they sent some of the Pharisees and Herodians to Jesus to catch him in his words. 14 They came to him and said, 'Teacher, we know that you are a man of integrity. You aren't swayed by others, because you pay no attention to who they are; but you teach the way of God in accordance with the truth. Is it right to pay the poll-taxᵇ to Caesar or not? 15 Should we pay or shouldn't we?'

But Jesus knew their hypocrisy. 'Why are you trying to trap me?' he asked. 'Bring me a denarius and let me look at it.' 16 They brought the coin, and he asked them, 'Whose image is this? And whose inscription?'

'Caesar's,' they replied.

17 Then Jesus said to them, 'Give back to Caesar what is Caesar's and to God what is God's.'

And they were amazed at him.

Marriage at the resurrection

18 Then the Sadducees, who say there is no resurrection, came to him with a question. 19 'Teacher,' they said, 'Moses wrote for us that if a man's brother dies and leaves a wife but no children, the man must marry the widow and raise up offspring for his brother. 20 Now there were seven brothers. The first one married and died without leaving any children. 21 The second one married the widow, but he also died, leaving no child. It was the same with the third. 22 In fact, none of the seven left any children. Last of all, the woman died too. 23 At the resurrectionᶜ whose wife will she be, since the seven were married to her?'

24 Jesus replied, 'Are you not in error because you do not know the Scriptures or the power of God? 25 When the dead rise, they will neither marry nor be given in marriage; they will be like the angels in heaven. 26 Now about the dead rising – have you not read in the Book of Moses, in the account of the burning bush, how God

b 14 A special tax levied on subject peoples, not on Roman citizens

c 23 Some manuscripts *resurrection, when people rise from the dead,*

a 11 Psalm 118:22,23

said to him, "I am the God of Abraham, the God of Isaac, and the God of Jacob"*d*? 27 He is not the God of the dead, but of the living. You are badly mistaken!'

The greatest commandment

28 One of the teachers of the law came and heard them debating. Noticing that Jesus had given them a good answer, he asked him, 'Of all the commandments, which is the most important?'

29 'The most important one,' answered Jesus, 'is this: "Hear, O Israel: the Lord our God, the Lord is one.*e* 30 Love the Lord your God with all your heart and with all your soul and with all your mind and with all your strength."*f* 31 The second is this: "Love your neighbour as yourself."*g* There is no commandment greater than these.'

32 'Well said, teacher,' the man replied. 'You are right in saying that God is one and there is no other but him. 33 To love him with all your heart, with all your understanding and with all your strength, and to love your neighbour as yourself is more important than all burnt offerings and sacrifices.'

34 When Jesus saw that he had answered wisely, he said to him, 'You are not far from the kingdom of God.' And from then on no one dared ask him any more questions.

Whose son is the Messiah?

35 While Jesus was teaching in the temple courts, he asked, 'Why do the teachers of the law say that the Messiah is the son of David? 36 David himself, speaking by the Holy Spirit, declared:

' "The Lord said to my Lord:
  'Sit at my right hand
  until I put your enemies
    under your feet.' "*h*

37 David himself calls him "Lord". How then can he be his son?'

_____
d 26 Exodus 3:6
e 29 Or *the Lord our God is one Lord*
f 30 Deut. 6:4,5
g 31 Lev. 19:18
h 36 Psalm 110:1

The large crowd listened to him with delight.

Warning against the teachers of the law

38 As he taught, Jesus said, 'Watch out for the teachers of the law. They like to walk around in flowing robes and be greeted with respect in the market-places, 39 and have the most important seats in the synagogues and the places of honour at banquets. 40 They devour widows' houses and for a show make lengthy prayers. These men will be punished most severely.'

The widow's offering

41 Jesus sat down opposite the place where the offerings were put and watched the crowd putting their money into the temple treasury. Many rich people threw in large amounts. 42 But a poor widow came and put in two very small copper coins, worth only a few pence.

43 Calling his disciples to him, Jesus said, 'Truly I tell you, this poor widow has put more into the treasury than all the others. 44 They all gave out of their wealth; but she, out of her poverty, put in everything – all she had to live on.'

The destruction of the temple and signs of the end times

13 As Jesus was leaving the temple, one of his disciples said to him, 'Look, Teacher! What massive stones! What magnificent buildings!'

2 'Do you see all these great buildings?' replied Jesus. 'Not one stone here will be left on another; every one will be thrown down.'

3 As Jesus was sitting on the Mount of Olives opposite the temple, Peter, James, John and Andrew asked him privately, 4 'Tell us, when will these things happen? And what will be the sign that they are all about to be fulfilled?'

5 Jesus said to them: 'Watch out that no one deceives you. 6 Many will come in my name, claiming, "I am he," and will deceive many. 7 When you hear of wars and rumours of wars, do not be alarmed. Such things must happen, but the end is still to

come. **8**Nation will rise against nation, and kingdom against kingdom. There will be earthquakes in various places, and famines. These are the beginning of birth-pains.

9'You must be on your guard. You will be handed over to the local councils and flogged in the synagogues. On account of me you will stand before governors and kings as witnesses to them. **10**And the gospel must first be preached to all nations. **11**Whenever you are arrested and brought to trial, do not worry beforehand about what to say. Just say whatever is given you at the time, for it is not you speaking, but the Holy Spirit.

12'Brother will betray brother to death, and a father his child. Children will rebel against their parents and have them put to death. **13**Everyone will hate you because of me, but the one who stands firm to the end will be saved.

14'When you see "the abomination that causes desolation"*a* standing where it*b* does not belong – let the reader understand – then let those who are in Judea flee to the mountains. **15**Let no one on the housetop go down or enter the house to take anything out. **16**Let no one in the field go back to get their cloak. **17**How dreadful it will be in those days for pregnant women and nursing mothers! **18**Pray that this will not take place in winter, **19**because those will be days of distress unequalled from the beginning, when God created the world, until now – and never to be equalled again.

20'If the Lord had not cut short those days, no one would survive. But for the sake of the elect, whom he has chosen, he has shortened them. **21**At that time if anyone says to you, "Look, here is the Messiah!" or, "Look, there he is!" do not believe it. **22**For false messiahs and false prophets will appear and perform signs and wonders to deceive, if possible, even the elect. **23**So be on your guard; I have told you everything in advance.

24'But in those days, following that distress,

' "the sun will be darkened,
    and the moon will not give its light;
25 the stars will fall from the sky,
    and the heavenly bodies will be
        shaken."*c*

26'At that time people will see the Son of Man coming in clouds with great power and glory. **27**And he will send his angels and gather his elect from the four winds, from the ends of the earth to the ends of the heavens.

28'Now learn this lesson from the fig-tree: as soon as its twigs get tender and its leaves come out, you know that summer is near. **29**Even so, when you see these things happening, you know that it*d* is near, right at the door. **30**Truly I tell you, this generation will certainly not pass away until all these things have happened. **31**Heaven and earth will pass away, but my words will never pass away.

The day and hour unknown

32'But about that day or hour no one knows, not even the angels in heaven, nor the Son, but only the Father. **33**Be on guard! Be alert*e*! You do not know when that time will come. **34**It's like a man going away: he leaves his house and puts his servants in charge, each with their assigned task, and tells the one at the door to keep watch.

35'Therefore keep watch because you do not know when the owner of the house will come back – whether in the evening, or at midnight, or when the cock crows, or at dawn. **36**If he comes suddenly, do not let him find you sleeping. **37**What I say to you, I say to everyone: "Watch!" '

Jesus anointed at Bethany

14 Now the Passover and the Festival of Unleavened Bread were only two days away, and the chief priests and the teachers of the law were scheming to arrest Jesus secretly and kill him. **2**'But not

*a*14 Daniel 9:27; 11:31; 12:11
*b*14 Or *he*

*c*25 Isaiah 13:10; 34:4
*d*29 Or *he*
*e*33 Some manuscripts *alert and pray*

LIFE OF JESUS 5

The ultimate teacher

A very common piece of advice says, 'Take nothing on trust. Prove everything for yourself.' It's a great idea in theory, but in practice it's actually utterly impossible. The world is so large and so complex that we have to trust other people.

This means that you believe South Cyprus exists although you have never been there; you trust that there's going to be a petrol station within the next three miles because that's what the map says; you believe that D-Day happened because you have read the books. It would be foolish not to rely on other people and on their authority. Relying on others can, of course, be a very serious matter. Buying a house, going to university or having a major operation are all areas where we try to seek the best possible advice. So when it comes to the most important subject of all – how we relate to God and where we're going to spend eternity – we need someone who speaks with authority.

Authority is something that people recognised in Jesus (see, for example, Matthew 7:28–29). Other religious teachers tended to justify their arguments by reference to other teachers, which gave their opinions a rather second-hand feel. Jesus was different: the authority he referred to was himself. It was quite common for him to take an argument and then say, 'You have heard this, but I say… ' In Mark 13:31, Jesus makes the stunning claim that his words will outlast the very universe itself. The cosmos is mind-blowingly vast and doesn't appear to be about to vanish any day soon. Yet what Jesus said was that his words would outlast everything.

This saying would have been as extraordinary then as it is now, yet it's clear that Jesus' followers believed what he said. He was viewed by his followers as the final and greatest teacher, a prophet above all other prophets. In John's Gospel, Jesus is described as being the Word of God (John 1:1, 14), identical with the word that God spoke which brought the universe into being. Prophets report God's word; Jesus is God's Word.

Why did his followers believe Jesus' claims about the value of his teaching? The answer is that they saw the resurrection as God's stamp of approval over all Jesus' teaching. The first Christians felt able to trust themselves to Christ's words even though it would cost them their lives. Nearly two thousand years later, we should have no hesitation in giving him the same trust. The world itself may fail, but the words of Jesus will endure.

J.John

◀◀ Luke 7:36–50　　　　　　　　　　　　　　John 4:46–54 ▶▶

during the festival,' they said, 'or the people may riot.'

3 While he was in Bethany, reclining at the table in the home of Simon the Leper, a woman came with an alabaster jar of very expensive perfume, made of pure nard. She broke the jar and poured the perfume on his head.

4 Some of those present were saying indignantly to one another, 'Why this waste of perfume? 5 It could have been sold for more than a year's wages*a* and the money given to the poor.' And they rebuked her harshly.

6 'Leave her alone,' said Jesus. 'Why are you bothering her? She has done a beautiful thing to me. 7 The poor you will always have with you,*b* and you can help them any time you want. But you will not always have me. 8 She did what she could. She poured perfume on my body beforehand to prepare for my burial. 9 Truly I tell you, wherever the gospel is preached throughout the world, what she has done will also be told, in memory of her.'

10 Then Judas Iscariot, one of the Twelve, went to the chief priests to betray Jesus to them. 11 They were delighted to hear this and promised to give him money. So he watched for an opportunity to hand him over.

The Last Supper

12 On the first day of the Festival of Unleavened Bread, when it was customary to sacrifice the Passover lamb, Jesus' disciples asked him, 'Where do you want us to go and make preparations for you to eat the Passover?'

13 So he sent two of his disciples, telling them, 'Go into the city, and a man carrying a jar of water will meet you. Follow him. 14 Say to the owner of the house he enters, "The Teacher asks: where is my guest room, where I may eat the Passover with my disciples?" 15 He will show you a large room upstairs, furnished and ready. Make preparations for us there.'

16 The disciples left, went into the city and found things just as Jesus had told them. So they prepared the Passover.

17 When evening came, Jesus arrived with the Twelve. 18 While they were reclining at the table eating, he said, 'Truly I tell you, one of you will betray me – one who is eating with me.'

19 They were saddened, and one by one they said to him, 'Surely you don't mean me?'

20 'It is one of the Twelve,' he replied, 'one who dips bread into the bowl with me. 21 The Son of Man will go just as it is written about him. But woe to that man who betrays the Son of Man! It would be better for him if he had not been born.'

22 While they were eating, Jesus took bread, and when he had given thanks, he broke it and gave it to his disciples, saying, 'Take it; this is my body.'

23 Then he took a cup, and when he had given thanks, he gave it to them, and they all drank from it.

24 'This is my blood of the*c* covenant, which is poured out for many,' he said to them. 25 'Truly I tell you, I will not drink again from the fruit of the vine until that day when I drink it new in the kingdom of God.'

26 When they had sung a hymn, they went out to the Mount of Olives.

Jesus predicts Peter's denial

27 'You will all fall away,' Jesus told them, 'for it is written:

' "I will strike the shepherd,
    and the sheep will be scattered." *d*

28 But after I have risen, I will go ahead of you into Galilee.'

29 Peter declared, 'Even if all fall away, I will not.'

30 'Truly I tell you,' Jesus answered, 'today – yes, tonight – before the cock crows twice*e* you yourself will disown me three times.'

31 But Peter insisted emphatically, 'Even

---

a 5 Greek *than three hundred denarii*
b 7 See Deut. 15:11.

c 24 Some manuscripts *the new*
d 27 Zech. 13:7
e 30 Some early manuscripts do not have *twice*.

if I have to die with you, I will never disown you.' And all the others said the same.

Gethsemane

32 They went to a place called Gethsemane, and Jesus said to his disciples, 'Sit here while I pray.' 33 He took Peter, James and John along with him, and he began to be deeply distressed and troubled. 34 'My soul is overwhelmed with sorrow to the point of death,' he said to them. 'Stay here and keep watch.'

35 Going a little farther, he fell to the ground and prayed that if possible the hour might pass from him. 36 'Abba,f Father,' he said, 'everything is possible for you. Take this cup from me. Yet not what I will, but what you will.'

37 Then he returned to his disciples and found them sleeping. 'Simon,' he said to Peter, 'are you asleep? Couldn't you keep watch for one hour? 38 Watch and pray so

f 36 Aramaic for *father*

WORSHIP 6

Extravagant

Have you ever gone totally over the top for someone you love? Have you pulled out all the stops on Mother's Day, or impressed your girlfriend with a trip to Venice on your anniversary?

As strange as it may seem, the scene described in Mark 14:1–11 is one of worship. Over-the-top, extravagant worship. A sinful woman comes and pours perfume all over Jesus. It can seem pretty weird reading about that today – in fact, the people standing around at the time were shocked. But look at Jesus' response: *'She has done a beautiful thing to me'* (v. 6).

This woman didn't just give a bit of perfume to Jesus; she soaked him in it. What's more, this perfume was worth an absolute fortune – probably about £25,000! Can you imagine wasting £25,000-worth of perfume like that? She went all out for the Lord.

Here's what we can learn from the example of this woman: it's OK to go all out for God. It's a good thing to worship him in a way that's so over the top, so full of passion, emotion and joy that people around us don't get it. Sometimes, if we are typical reserved English people, we are afraid to throw our hands in the air and dance like nutters. We can draw back from lavishing God with our time or from just deciding to give him a whole load of our money.

One time my cell group went to our church building at night. We switched off the lights, put a worship CD on and then, in the darkness, we went crazy for God – dancing, jumping, shouting and singing. Anyone who heard us might have thought we were a bit mental. I think there was something about that evening that God loved.

Why not do something just a bit mad for God today?

Beth Croft

 Psalm 31:9–14   1 Samuel 16:14–23

that you will not fall into temptation. The spirit is willing, but the flesh is weak.'

39 Once more he went away and prayed the same thing. 40 When he came back, he again found them sleeping, because their eyes were heavy. They did not know what to say to him.

41 Returning the third time, he said to them, 'Are you still sleeping and resting? Enough! The hour has come. Look, the Son of Man is delivered into the hands of sinners. 42 Rise! Let us go! Here comes my betrayer!'

Jesus arrested

43 Just as he was speaking, Judas, one of the Twelve, appeared. With him was a crowd armed with swords and clubs, sent from the chief priests, the teachers of the law, and the elders.

44 Now the betrayer had arranged a signal with them: 'The one I kiss is the man; arrest him and lead him away under guard.' 45 Going at once to Jesus, Judas said, 'Rabbi!' and kissed him. 46 The men seized Jesus and arrested him. 47 Then one of those standing near drew his sword and struck the servant of the high priest, cutting off his ear.

48 'Am I leading a rebellion,' said Jesus, 'that you have come out with swords and clubs to capture me? 49 Every day I was with you, teaching in the temple courts, and you did not arrest me. But the Scriptures must be fulfilled.' 50 Then everyone deserted him and fled.

51 A young man, wearing nothing but a linen garment, was following Jesus. When they seized him, 52 he fled naked, leaving his garment behind.

Jesus before the Sanhedrin

53 They took Jesus to the high priest, and all the chief priests, the elders and the teachers of the law came together. 54 Peter followed him at a distance, right into the courtyard of the high priest. There he sat with the guards and warmed himself at the fire.

55 The chief priests and the whole Sanhedrin were looking for evidence against Jesus so that they could put him to death,

but they did not find any. 56 Many testified falsely against him, but their statements did not agree.

57 Then some stood up and gave this false testimony against him: 58 'We heard him say, "I will destroy this temple made with human hands and in three days will build another, not made with hands."' 59 Yet even then their testimony did not agree.

60 Then the high priest stood up before them and asked Jesus, 'Are you not going to answer? What is this testimony that these men are bringing against you?' 61 But Jesus remained silent and gave no answer.

Again the high priest asked him, 'Are you the Messiah, the Son of the Blessed One?'

62 'I am,' said Jesus. 'And you will see the Son of Man sitting at the right hand of the Mighty One and coming on the clouds of heaven.'

63 The high priest tore his clothes. 'Why do we need any more witnesses?' he asked. 64 'You have heard the blasphemy. What do you think?'

They all condemned him as worthy of death. 65 Then some began to spit at him; they blindfolded him, struck him with their fists, and said, 'Prophesy!' And the guards took him and beat him.

Peter disowns Jesus

66 While Peter was below in the courtyard, one of the servant-girls of the high priest came by. 67 When she saw Peter warming himself, she looked closely at him.

'You also were with that Nazarene, Jesus,' she said.

68 But he denied it. 'I don't know or understand what you're talking about,' he said, and went out into the entrance. *g*

69 When the servant-girl saw him there, she said again to those standing round them, 'This fellow is one of them.' 70 Again he denied it.

---

g 68 Some early manuscripts *entrance and the cock crowed*

After a little while, those standing near said to Peter, 'Surely you are one of them, for you are a Galilean.'

71 He began to call down curses, and he swore to them, 'I don't know this man you're talking about.'

72 Immediately the cock crowed the second time.[h] Then Peter remembered the word Jesus had spoken to him:

h 72 Some early manuscripts do not have *the second time.*

FAILURE

Failure is one of the most difficult things we face in life. Failure hurts. When we strive for something and it doesn't come off, it can be really painful – and it can be especially hard when we start to believe that our value as a person is related to how successful we are.

Thankfully God doesn't love us because of what we have or haven't achieved. He loves us because of who he is; he can't help but love us! If God doesn't value us based on our success or failure, then we shouldn't value ourselves in that way either.

Sometimes, even in church, we can feel undervalued if we aren't talented or successful. But the truth is that Jesus didn't choose the talented and successful people to build his church. Jesus chose twelve ordinary men to be his disciples. Some of them were fishermen, one was a despised tax collector and one of them was even a political extremist (a Zealot). They weren't the successful over-achievers or popular celebrities of their time.

The Bible is littered with stories of people God used despite their failings. Some of the most influential figures in the Bible failed spectacularly. Abraham let Pharaoh sleep with his wife; Jacob was a deceiver; Joseph was arrogant; Moses killed someone; David was an adulterer; Paul was a murderer. Even Peter, one of Jesus' closest friends, failed him. We read in Mark 14:66–72 how Peter denied that he knew Jesus when he was questioned. This happened just after Jesus had been arrested and was about to be crucified. At the very moment when it seemed Jesus needed his friends to stand by him the most, Peter gave up on him.

But despite these failings, Jesus still used Peter to build his church; Abraham was still the father of the nation of Israel; Joseph still saved a nation. In fact, God still used all those people for his glory. God loves us because of who he is, and he uses us even though he knows we fail.

When we fail, the best thing to do is to learn from the experience. When Jesus rose from the grave, he forgave Peter. Peter then went on to be an early leader in the church and it's generally believed that he was martyred for his faith. Peter learned from his experience of failure and didn't give up on Jesus again, even going as far as dying for him.

Failure is a difficult part of life that we all have to face, but it's important to learn when we make mistakes and to remember that God loves us and continues to use us despite our failings.

Freddie Pimm

'Before the cock crows twice[i] you will dis-own me three times.' And he broke down and wept.

Jesus before Pilate

15 Very early in the morning, the chief priests, with the elders, the teachers of the law and the whole Sanhedrin, made their plans. So they bound Jesus, led him away and handed him over to Pilate.

2 'Are you the king of the Jews?' asked Pilate.

'You have said so,' Jesus replied.

3 The chief priests accused him of many things. 4 So again Pilate asked him, 'Aren't you going to answer? See how many things they are accusing you of.'

5 But Jesus still made no reply, and Pilate was amazed.

6 Now it was the custom at the festival to release a prisoner whom the people requested. 7 A man called Barabbas was in prison with the rebels who had committed murder in the uprising. 8 The crowd came up and asked Pilate to do for them what he usually did.

9 'Do you want me to release to you the king of the Jews?' asked Pilate, 10 knowing it was out of self-interest that the chief priests had handed Jesus over to him. 11 But the chief priests stirred up the crowd to get Pilate to release Barabbas instead.

12 'What shall I do, then, with the one you call the king of the Jews?' Pilate asked them.

13 'Crucify him!' they shouted.

14 'Why? What crime has he committed?' asked Pilate.

But they shouted all the louder, 'Crucify him!'

15 Wanting to satisfy the crowd, Pilate released Barabbas to them. He had Jesus flogged, and handed him over to be crucified.

The soldiers mock Jesus

16 The soldiers led Jesus away into the palace (that is, the Praetorium) and called together the whole company of soldiers.

17 They put a purple robe on him, then twisted together a crown of thorns and set it on him. 18 And they began to call out to him, 'Hail, king of the Jews!' 19 Again and again they struck him on the head with a staff and spat on him. Falling on their knees, they paid homage to him. 20 And when they had mocked him, they took off the purple robe and put his own clothes on him. Then they led him out to crucify him.

The crucifixion of Jesus

21 A certain man from Cyrene, Simon, the father of Alexander and Rufus, was passing by on his way in from the country, and they forced him to carry the cross. 22 They brought Jesus to the place called Golgotha (which means 'the place of the skull'). 23 Then they offered him wine mixed with myrrh, but he did not take it. 24 And they crucified him. Dividing up his clothes, they cast lots to see what each would get.

25 It was nine in the morning when they crucified him. 26 The written notice of the charge against him read: THE KING OF THE JEWS.

27 They crucified two rebels with him, one on his right and one on his left. [28][a] 29 Those who passed by hurled insults at him, shaking their heads and saying, 'So! You who are going to destroy the temple and build it in three days, 30 come down from the cross and save yourself!' 31 In the same way the chief priests and the teachers of the law mocked him among themselves. 'He saved others,' they said, 'but he can't save himself! 32 Let this Messiah, this king of Israel, come down now from the cross, that we may see and believe.' Those crucified with him also heaped insults on him.

The death of Jesus

33 At noon, darkness came over the whole land until three in the afternoon. 34 And at three in the afternoon Jesus cried out in a loud voice, 'Eloi, Eloi, lema

sabachthani?' (which means 'My God, my God, why have you forsaken me?').[b]

35 When some of those standing near heard this, they said, 'Listen, he's calling Elijah.'

36 Someone ran, filled a sponge with

wine vinegar, put it on a staff, and offered it to Jesus to drink. 'Now leave him alone. Let's see if Elijah comes to take him down,' he said.

37 With a loud cry, Jesus breathed his last.

38 The curtain of the temple was torn in two from top to bottom. 39 And when

b 34   Psalm 22:1

PEOPLE USED BY GOD 5

Mary Magdalene

Have you ever seen a movie where someone is rescued, and because of their deep gratitude they proclaim that they are now indebted to their rescuer for ever – and they fall at the feet of their hero and proclaim, 'I owe you my life. I am forever at your service'?

Well, in a way, that's exactly how it was with Mary Magdalene. Mary came from a village on the shore of the Sea of Galilee called Magdala (hence her name, Magdalene). No one really knows what exactly it was that plagued Mary Magdalene, but the Bible says she was tormented with evil spirits and diseases.

Jesus came upon Mary Magdalene and saved her from her demonic bondage and healed her. He wasn't just telling people about the good news, he was the Good News! Jesus set Mary Magdalene free, healing her once and for all. From that moment on, she followed Jesus – and in her gratitude she not only followed him, she also helped to support him and his disciples out of her own means (Luke 8:3).

This was life-changing for Mary Magdalene. Her heart was so full of thanksgiving that she gave her life to Jesus! She loved and served him not just in words, but with all that she was and all that she had. Her gratitude led her to greatness in the eyes of those of us who still read about her life today, but also in the eyes of Jesus, who honoured her in a most wonderful way. In her great love she followed Jesus to the foot of the cross where he was being crucified (John 19:25) and then to the tomb, where she was the first to find that he was not there (Mark 16:9)! She was the first to proclaim his resurrection to others, the first to see the risen Saviour, and the first person to whom Jesus spoke before he ascended to the Father. What a wonderful privilege and blessing!

Mary Magdalene's attitude of gratitude was a life choice that set the course of her destiny, leading her into a life of freedom, healing, love and acceptance.

Susie Brock

 Jonah 1:1   Luke 1 ▶▶

the centurion, who stood there in front of Jesus, saw how he died,[c] he said, 'Surely this man was the Son of God!'

⁴⁰Some women were watching from a distance. Among them were Mary Magdalene, Mary the mother of James the younger and of Joseph,[d] and Salome. ⁴¹In Galilee these women had followed him and cared for his needs. Many other women who had come up with him to Jerusalem were also there.

The burial of Jesus

⁴²It was Preparation Day (that is, the day before the Sabbath). So as evening approached, ⁴³Joseph of Arimathea, a prominent member of the Council, who was himself waiting for the kingdom of God, went boldly to Pilate and asked for Jesus' body. ⁴⁴Pilate was surprised to hear that he was already dead. Summoning the centurion, he asked him if Jesus had already died. ⁴⁵When he learned from the centurion that it was so, he gave the body to Joseph. ⁴⁶So Joseph bought some linen cloth, took down the body, wrapped it in the linen, and placed it in a tomb cut out of rock. Then he rolled a stone against the entrance of the tomb. ⁴⁷Mary Magdalene and Mary the mother of Joseph saw where he was laid.

Jesus has risen

16 When the Sabbath was over, Mary Magdalene, Mary the mother of James, and Salome bought spices so that they might go to anoint Jesus' body. ²Very early on the first day of the week, just after sunrise, they were on their way to the tomb ³and they asked each other, 'Who will roll the stone away from the entrance of the tomb?'

⁴But when they looked up, they saw that the stone, which was very large, had been rolled away. ⁵As they entered the tomb, they saw a young man dressed in a white robe sitting on the right side, and they were alarmed.

⁶'Don't be alarmed,' he said. 'You are looking for Jesus the Nazarene, who was crucified. He has risen! He is not here. See the place where they laid him. ⁷But go, tell his disciples and Peter, "He is going ahead of you into Galilee. There you will see him, just as he told you." '

⁸Trembling and bewildered, the women went out and fled from the tomb. They said nothing to anyone, because they were afraid.[a]

[The earliest manuscripts and some other ancient witnesses do not have verses 9–20.]

⁹When Jesus rose early on the first day of the week, he appeared first to Mary Magdalene, out of whom he had driven seven demons. ¹⁰She went and told those who had been with him and who were mourning and weeping. ¹¹When they heard that Jesus was alive and that she had seen him, they did not believe it.

¹²Afterwards Jesus appeared in a different form to two of them while they were walking in the country. ¹³These returned and reported it to the rest; but they did not believe them either.

¹⁴Later Jesus appeared to the Eleven as they were eating; he rebuked them for their lack of faith and their stubborn refusal to believe those who had seen him after he had risen.

¹⁵He said to them, 'Go into all the world and preach the gospel to all creation. ¹⁶Whoever believes and is baptised will be saved, but whoever does not believe will be condemned. ¹⁷And these signs will accompany those who believe: in my name they will drive out demons; they will speak in new tongues; ¹⁸they will pick up snakes with their hands; and when they drink deadly poison, it will not hurt them at all; they will place their hands on people who are ill, and they will get well.'

¹⁹After the Lord Jesus had spoken to them, he was taken up into heaven and he sat at the right hand of God. ²⁰Then the disciples went out and preached everywhere, and the Lord worked with them and confirmed his word by the signs that accompanied it.

---

c 39 Some manuscripts *saw that he died with such a cry*
d 40 Greek *Joses*, a variant of *Joseph*; also in verse 47

a 8 Some manuscripts have the following ending between verses 8 and 9, and one manuscript has it after verse 8 (omitting verses 9-20): *Then they quickly reported all these instructions to those around Peter. After this, Jesus himself also sent out through them from east to west the sacred and imperishable proclamation of eternal salvation. Amen.*

LUKE

DATE

Luke focuses on events from just before Jesus' birth (when time begins to be measured as AD instead of BC) until his death and resurrection 33 years later

AUTHOR

Luke (who also wrote the book of Acts)

WHAT'S IT ALL ABOUT?

Luke is one of the four Gospel accounts of Jesus' life and the last of the three Synoptic Gospels (meaning it's similar in style and content to the Gospels of Matthew and Mark). Luke was the only Gentile (non-Jewish) writer of a Gospel and so he emphasises Jesus as the Saviour of everyone, not just the Jewish people. He wrote to his friend Theophilus, but his words were intended for many more people and he particularly wanted to extend the good news of Jesus to those who were lonely or felt like outcasts. The way he describes events reflects this. When he writes about Jesus' birth, he shows what happened to Mary rather than Joseph (in Jewish culture women were seen as inferior to men, so this was unusual), and he describes the angels visiting the lowly shepherds rather than the wise men visiting Jesus. Luke was also keen to show how Jesus took on people's burdens and how caring he was, emphasising how often crowds were drawn to him. Luke details the many miracles Jesus did – like raising a widow's son to life, calming a storm and healing demon-possessed people – as well as recording his teaching on subjects like fasting, the Sabbath, loving our enemies and not judging other people.

WHY SHOULD WE READ THE GOSPELS?

- Because this is where we meet Jesus! By reading about his life and what he said and did, we develop our relationship with him and our understanding of who he is. This relationship is key to the Christian life. Christianity is about a person, not a set of ideas. Jesus is the central figure in our history and it's through him that we make sense of life and the Bible. The whole Bible is a witness to Jesus, but the four Gospels are the books that focus on his time on earth.

- To understand the events that led to Jesus being killed on a cross like a criminal, even though he had done nothing wrong.

- To see that Jesus was separated from his Father on the cross, taking on himself the punishment we deserve, so that we might become pure in God's eyes.

- To read how Jesus overcame death and rose from the grave, giving us eternal life.

- To read Jesus' teaching on how we should live, including how to treat our enemies and not judge people, as well as how to pray, handle money, have humility, find faith and deal with worry.

- To see the miraculous things Jesus did, including the feeding of the five thousand, walking on water, giving blind people their sight and raising the dead.

WHY SHOULD WE READ LUKE'S GOSPEL?

- Because it demonstrates God's compassion and love for people who feel like outcasts.

- To get a unique perspective on Jesus' life.

- Because some of the events and teaching of Jesus' life are only recorded in Luke:

  o the prophecy and birth of John the Baptist;

  o the angel's visit to Mary to tell her she would give birth to Jesus, and her song in response;

  o Jesus' childhood (Luke 2);

  o the parables of the Good Samaritan (Luke 10) and the Prodigal Son (Luke 15);

  o the raising from the dead of the widow's son;

  o the involvement of women in Jesus' ministry (Luke 8);

  o Jesus' encounter with Zacchaeus (Luke 19).

- Because Luke gives us the most detailed account of Jesus' birth.

Andy Croft with Liza Hoeksma

Introduction

1 Many have undertaken to draw up an account of the things that have been fulfilled[a] among us, 2 just as they were handed down to us by those who from the first were eye witnesses and servants of the word. 3 With this in mind, since I myself have carefully investigated everything from the beginning, I too decided to write an orderly account for you, most excellent Theophilus, 4 so that you may know the certainty of the things you have been taught.

The birth of John the Baptist foretold

5 In the time of Herod king of Judea there was a priest named Zechariah, who belonged to the priestly division of Abijah; his wife Elizabeth was also a descendant of Aaron. 6 Both of them were righteous in the sight of God, observing all the Lord's commands and decrees blamelessly. 7 But they were childless because Elizabeth was not able to conceive, and they were both very old.

8 Once when Zechariah's division was on duty and he was serving as priest before God, 9 he was chosen by lot, according to the custom of the priesthood, to go into the temple of the Lord and burn incense. 10 And when the time for the burning of incense came, all the assembled worshippers were praying outside.

11 Then an angel of the Lord appeared to him, standing at the right side of the altar of incense. 12 When Zechariah saw him, he was startled and was gripped with fear. 13 But the angel said to him: 'Do not be afraid, Zechariah; your prayer has been heard. Your wife Elizabeth will bear you a son, and you are to call him John. 14 He will be a joy and delight to you, and many will rejoice because of his birth, 15 for he will be great in the sight of the Lord. He is never to take wine or other fermented drink, and he will be filled with the Holy Spirit even before he is born. 16 He will bring back many of the people of Israel to the Lord their God. 17 And he will go on before the Lord, in the spirit and power of Elijah, to turn the hearts of the parents to their children and the disobedient to the wisdom of the righteous – to make ready a people prepared for the Lord.'

18 Zechariah asked the angel, 'How can I be sure of this? I am an old man and my wife is well on in years.'

19 The angel said to him, 'I am Gabriel. I stand in the presence of God, and I have been sent to speak to you and to tell you this good news. 20 And now you will be silent and not able to speak until the day this happens, because you did not believe my words, which will come true at their appointed time.'

21 Meanwhile, the people were waiting for Zechariah and wondering why he stayed so long in the temple. 22 When he came out, he could not speak to them. They realised he had seen a vision in the temple, for he kept making signs to them but remained unable to speak.

23 When his time of service was completed, he returned home. 24 After this his wife Elizabeth became pregnant and for five months remained in seclusion. 25 'The Lord has done this for me,' she said. 'In these days he has shown his favour and taken away my disgrace among the people.'

The birth of Jesus foretold

26 In the sixth month of Elizabeth's pregnancy, God sent the angel Gabriel to Nazareth, a town in Galilee, 27 to a virgin pledged to be married to a man named Joseph, a descendant of David. The virgin's name was Mary. 28 The angel went to her and said, 'Greetings, you who are highly favoured! The Lord is with you.'

29 Mary was greatly troubled at his words and wondered what kind of greeting this might be. 30 But the angel said to her, 'Do not be afraid, Mary, you have found favour with God. 31 You will conceive and give birth to a son, and you are to call him Jesus. 32 He will be great and will be called the Son of the Most High. The Lord God will give him the throne of his father David, 33 and he will reign over Jacob's descendants for ever; his kingdom will never end.'

---

a 1 Or *been surely believed*

PEOPLE USED BY GOD 6

Elizabeth

Have you ever felt like damaged goods? Well, this is probably how Elizabeth felt for most of her life (Luke 1). She was unable to have a child, which was not just an unfortunate situation back then, it was considered shameful – and even grounds for divorce! She would have endured people whispering behind her back, as well as listening to others joyfully announcing pregnancies. However, Elizabeth was blessed.

She had a husband who loved both her and God. He was pretty fortunate to have her too, as she was a good woman. In fact, the Bible says she was a *'righteous'* woman, both of them blameless before the Lord (v. 6)! The love they had for God helped them to love each other enough to deal with the pain of not having children. She was not only in love with her husband, but passionate about her walk with God, and this gave her strength. She probably never felt like damaged goods before the Father. She served him all the days of her life, right into old age.

And it was in her old age that God surprised both her and Zechariah, as she became pregnant! As if that wasn't good enough news, an angel of the Lord came to Zechariah to assure them that the child was God's gift. Elizabeth's long wait was over. It might have come later than she wanted, but it was the perfect time, as this child would make ready a people for Jesus!

The story gets even better as her cousin, a young girl named Mary, comes along to announce the good news of her own pregnancy. Elizabeth had the most amazing reaction in that moment. Rather than feeling disappointed or jealous that she had to share the spotlight with someone else, she welcomed Mary with open arms and rejoiced. Elizabeth was used to the presence of God in her life, and she wasn't caught off guard by Mary's announcement because she felt both the baby and her heart leap for joy at the news. Because her life was filled with the love of God, she was able to share that love and not feel insecure or have her joy made incomplete.

Spending time with God, reading his Word, praying and serving him is never a waste of time. He knows the plans he has for us, and they are good plans. Every moment spent with him is a preparation for the plans he's leading us into. They may not always come in our timing, but God's timing is always perfect.

You're not damaged goods, you're fearfully and wonderfully made, a person of destiny awaiting the unfolding of God's blessings before you. Spend that waiting time in his presence and prepare yourself for the surprises God has in store for you!

Susie Brock

 Mark 16:9   Luke 19:1–9 ▶▶

³⁴'How will this be,' Mary asked the angel, 'since I am a virgin?'

³⁵The angel answered, 'The Holy Spirit will come on you, and the power of the Most High will overshadow you. So the holy one to be born will be called[b] the Son of God. ³⁶Even Elizabeth your relative is going to have a child in her old age, and she who was said to be unable to conceive is in her sixth month. ³⁷For no word from God will ever fail.'

³⁸'I am the Lord's servant,' Mary answered. 'May your word to me be fulfilled.' Then the angel left her.

Mary visits Elizabeth

³⁹At that time Mary got ready and hurried to a town in the hill country of Judea, ⁴⁰where she entered Zechariah's home and greeted Elizabeth. ⁴¹When Elizabeth heard Mary's greeting, the baby leaped in her womb, and Elizabeth was filled with the Holy Spirit. ⁴²In a loud voice she exclaimed: 'Blessed are you among women, and blessed is the child you will bear! ⁴³But why am I so favoured, that the mother of my Lord should come to me? ⁴⁴As soon as the sound of your greeting reached my ears, the baby in my womb leaped for joy. ⁴⁵Blessed is she who has believed that the Lord would fulfil his promises to her!'

Mary's song

⁴⁶And Mary said:

'My soul glorifies the Lord
⁴⁷   and my spirit rejoices in God my
        Saviour,
⁴⁸for he has been mindful
        of the humble state of his servant.
    From now on all generations will call
        me blessed,
⁴⁹   for the Mighty One has done great
        things for me –
        holy is his name.
⁵⁰His mercy extends to those who fear
        him,
        from generation to generation.
⁵¹He has performed mighty deeds with
        his arm;

he has scattered those who
        are proud in their inmost
        thoughts.
⁵²He has brought down rulers from their
        thrones
    but has lifted up the humble.
⁵³He has filled the hungry with good
        things
    but has sent the rich away empty.
⁵⁴He has helped his servant Israel,
        remembering to be merciful
⁵⁵to Abraham and his descendants for
        ever,
        just as he promised our ancestors.'

⁵⁶Mary stayed with Elizabeth for about three months and then returned home.

The birth of John the Baptist

⁵⁷When it was time for Elizabeth to have her baby, she gave birth to a son. ⁵⁸Her neighbours and relatives heard that the Lord had shown her great mercy, and they shared her joy.

⁵⁹On the eighth day they came to circumcise the child, and they were going to name him after his father Zechariah, ⁶⁰but his mother spoke up and said, 'No! He is to be called John.'

⁶¹They said to her, 'There is no one among your relatives who has that name.'

⁶²Then they made signs to his father, to find out what he would like to name the child. ⁶³He asked for a writing tablet, and to everyone's astonishment he wrote, 'His name is John.' ⁶⁴Immediately his mouth was opened and his tongue set free, and he began to speak, praising God. ⁶⁵All the neighbours were filled with awe, and throughout the hill country of Judea people were talking about all these things. ⁶⁶Everyone who heard this wondered about it, asking, 'What then is this child going to be?' For the Lord's hand was with him.

Zechariah's song

⁶⁷His father Zechariah was filled with the Holy Spirit and prophesied:

⁶⁸'Praise be to the Lord, the God of
        Israel,

---

b 35 Or So the child to be born will be called holy,

THE BIG STORY 6

Jesus fulfils

The Old Testament is like a collection of unfulfilled promises and loose ends, until Jesus comes and draws them all together. He's the fulfilment of all the Old Testament hopes. The documents which show how he fulfilled them are called the New Testament. The prophecies about the Messiah said that he would be a descendant of David, Israel's greatest king.

In Luke 1:26–55, Mary is engaged to Joseph, a descendant of David, and is told that God will give the child she's to bear *'the throne of his father David'* (v. 32). This will not just be a normal monarch's reign, for *'his kingdom will never end'* (v. 33). The child is to be called Jesus (Joshua), meaning 'Deliverer'. He will also be called *'the Son of God'* (v. 35). This has a triple meaning. God called Israel his *'son'* (Hosea 11:1), so, in Jesus, Israel would be restored. The king of Israel was thought of as God's son, God's personal representative, leading the nation and demonstrating the character of God's rule (Psalm 72). Jesus was the only one to fulfil this high calling perfectly. But as he fulfilled his ministry, some began to recognise him as God's eternal Son, through whom the world was made, come to earth for us, to reign eternally. The Gospels are all written from this perspective (Mark 1:1; John 1:1–14).

Mary sang a song of praise because the angel's message meant that God was fulfilling his promises. *'He has helped his servant Israel, remembering to be merciful to Abraham and his descendants for ever, just as he promised our ancestors'* (vv. 54–55). The promise to Abraham (Genesis 12:1–3) was going to be fulfilled in Jesus. In fact, Paul says that *'no matter how many promises God has made, they are "Yes" in Christ'* (2 Corinthians 1:20).

The whole of Jesus' life and ministry fulfils God's promises, not just his death and resurrection alone. He proclaimed God's kingdom (Mark 1:14–15) and he ministered the power of that kingdom in healing and deliverance through the power of the Holy Spirit (Matthew 12:28). He embodied God's kingdom by living in perfect obedience to the Father, as fallen humans had never done. His commitment to the human race was and remains total. He was everything that God intended Adam to be, and everything God intended Israel to be. He became human (*'flesh'*, John 1:14), lived our life, died our death, rose as the firstborn of God's new creation and carried his risen humanity into the Father's presence at his ascension. Fully human and fully divine, he has opened the presence of God for us.

Graham Cray

 Exodus 19:1–6   1 John 1:5–10 ▶

because he has come to his people
and redeemed them.
69 He has raised up a horn[c] of salvation
for us
in the house of his servant David
70 (as he said through his holy prophets
of long ago),
71 salvation from our enemies
and from the hand of all who hate
us –
72 to show mercy to our ancestors
and to remember his holy covenant,
73 the oath he swore to our father
Abraham:
74 to rescue us from the hand of our
enemies,
and to enable us to serve him
without fear
75 in holiness and righteousness
before him all our days.

76 And you, my child, will be called a
prophet of the Most High;
for you will go on before the Lord to
prepare the way for him,
77 to give his people the knowledge of
salvation
through the forgiveness of their sins,
78 because of the tender mercy of our
God,
by which the rising sun will come to
us from heaven
79 to shine on those living in darkness
and in the shadow of death,
to guide our feet into the path of
peace.'

80 And the child grew and became strong
in spirit[d]; and he lived in the wilderness
until he appeared publicly to Israel.

The birth of Jesus

2 In those days Caesar Augustus issued
a decree that a census should be taken
of the entire Roman world. 2 (This was the
first census that took place while[a] Quirinius was governor of Syria.) 3 And everyone
went to their own town to register.

4 So Joseph also went up from the town
of Nazareth in Galilee to Judea, to Bethlehem the town of David, because he belonged to the house and line of David. 5 He
went there to register with Mary, who was
pledged to be married to him and was expecting a child. 6 While they were there, the
time came for the baby to be born, 7 and
she gave birth to her firstborn, a son. She
wrapped him in cloths and placed him in a
manger, because there was no guest room
available for them.

FACT

UNSTABLE

The Bible doesn't say that Jesus was born in
a stable. He was laid in an animal's feeding
trough, but that could have been inside
a peasant's house (Luke 2:7). And there
was probably no inn: the word Luke uses
normally means 'guest room'.

8 And there were shepherds living out
in the fields near by, keeping watch over
their flocks at night. 9 An angel of the Lord
appeared to them, and the glory of the
Lord shone around them, and they were
terrified. 10 But the angel said to them,
'Do not be afraid. I bring you good news
that will cause great joy for all the people.
11 Today in the town of David a Saviour has
been born to you; he is the Messiah, the
Lord. 12 This will be a sign to you: you will
find a baby wrapped in cloths and lying in
a manger.'

13 Suddenly a great company of the
heavenly host appeared with the angel,
praising God and saying,

14 'Glory to God in the highest heaven,
and on earth peace to those on
whom his favour rests.'

15 When the angels had left them and

---

c 69 *Horn* here symbolises a strong king.
d 80 Or *in the Spirit*
a 2 Or *This census took place before*

gone into heaven, the shepherds said to one another, 'Let's go to Bethlehem and see this thing that has happened, which the Lord has told us about.'

¹⁶So they hurried off and found Mary and Joseph, and the baby, who was lying in the manger. ¹⁷When they had seen him, they spread the word concerning what had been told them about this child, ¹⁸and all who heard it were amazed at what the shepherds said to them. ¹⁹But Mary treasured up all these things and pondered them in her heart. ²⁰The shepherds returned, glorifying and praising God for all the things they had heard and seen, which were just as they had been told.

²¹On the eighth day, when it was time to circumcise the child, he was named Jesus, the name the angel had given him before he was conceived.

Jesus presented in the temple

²²When the time came for the purification rites required by the Law of Moses, Joseph and Mary took him to Jerusalem to present him to the Lord ²³(as it is written in the Law of the Lord, 'Every firstborn

EVANGELISM 9

Naturally supernatural

Have you ever seen a really good film or enjoyed a gripping football match? Do you find that you naturally just tell people about it? I find that it spills out of me, I'm not reading it from a script or speaking in a weird voice (well, no more weird than usual). I'm being Mark Ritchie, and it just comes out of me. I love the shepherds' response in Luke 2:16–18. They had encountered something amazing and they shared it with everyone they met. They were inviting people to share in their experience.

The shepherds were the first ones to meet Jesus in person and then go and share their encounter. But they weren't the last. All the way through the New Testament, people encounter Jesus and can't help but go and tell others. Jesus models honesty and acceptance to the woman at the well, and her response is to tell others. Jesus heals the leper, and his response is to tell others. After Andrew had spent the day with Jesus, the first thing he did was to find his brother and tell him all about this man he had met.

The shepherds had literally just encountered Jesus. I find it's always easier to talk about things that you have just experienced. Recently a friend of mine was sharing with her friends about praying for her family. I was amazed at how the conversation opened up just because she decided to be natural about the supernatural things of God. Instead of placing these encounters in a holy bubble, she just talked about them openly and honestly. Praying is part of her life, and so she shared it!

Do I allow the supernatural encounters with God to flow out of me and impact not only me, but the people around me? Let's be natural about the supernatural.

Mark Ritchie

 2 Chronicles 7:14   Matthew 28:19–20

male is to be consecrated to the Lord'ᵇ), ²⁴and to offer a sacrifice in keeping with what is said in the Law of the Lord: 'a pair of doves or two young pigeons'.ᶜ

²⁵Now there was a man in Jerusalem called Simeon, who was righteous and devout. He was waiting for the consolation of Israel, and the Holy Spirit was on him. ²⁶It had been revealed to him by the Holy Spirit that he would not die before he had seen the Lord's Messiah. ²⁷Moved by the Spirit, he went into the temple courts. When the parents brought in the child Jesus to do for him what the custom of the Law required, ²⁸Simeon took him in his arms and praised God, saying:

²⁹'Sovereign Lord, as you have promised,
  you may now dismissᵈ your servant
  in peace.
³⁰For my eyes have seen your salvation,
³¹   which you have prepared in the
    sight of all nations:
³²a light for revelation to the Gentiles,
  and the glory of your people Israel.'

³³The child's father and mother marvelled at what was said about him. ³⁴Then Simeon blessed them and said to Mary, his mother: 'This child is destined to cause the falling and rising of many in Israel, and to be a sign that will be spoken against, ³⁵so that the thoughts of many hearts will be revealed. And a sword will pierce your own soul too.'

³⁶There was also a prophet, Anna, the daughter of Penuel, of the tribe of Asher. She was very old; she had lived with her husband seven years after her marriage, ³⁷and then was a widow until she was eighty-four.ᵉ She never left the temple but worshipped night and day, fasting and praying. ³⁸Coming up to them at that very moment, she gave thanks to God and spoke about the child to all who were looking forward to the redemption of Jerusalem.

³⁹When Joseph and Mary had done everything required by the Law of the Lord, they returned to Galilee to their own town of Nazareth. ⁴⁰And the child grew and became strong; he was filled with wisdom, and the grace of God was on him.

The boy Jesus at the temple

⁴¹Every year Jesus' parents went to Jerusalem for the Festival of the Passover. ⁴²When he was twelve years old, they went up to the festival, according to the custom. ⁴³After the festival was over, while his parents were returning home, the boy Jesus stayed behind in Jerusalem, but they were unaware of it. ⁴⁴Thinking he was in their company, they travelled on for a day. Then they began looking for him among their relatives and friends. ⁴⁵When they did not find him, they went back to Jerusalem to look for him. ⁴⁶After three days they found him in the temple courts, sitting among the teachers, listening to them and asking them questions. ⁴⁷Everyone who heard him was amazed at his understanding and his answers. ⁴⁸When his parents saw him, they were astonished. His mother said to him, 'Son, why have you treated us like this? Your father and I have been anxiously searching for you.'

⁴⁹'Why were you searching for me?' he asked. 'Didn't you know I had to be in my Father's house?'ᶠ⁵⁰But they did not understand what he was saying to them.

⁵¹Then he went down to Nazareth with them and was obedient to them. But his mother treasured all these things in her heart. ⁵²And Jesus grew in wisdom and stature, and in favour with God and man.

John the Baptist prepares the way

3 In the fifteenth year of the reign of Tiberius Caesar – when Pontius Pilate was governor of Judea, Herod tetrarch of Galilee, his brother Philip tetrarch of Iturea and Traconitis, and Lysanias tetrarch of Abilene – ²during the high-priesthood of Annas and Caiaphas, the word of God came to John son of Zechariah in the wilderness. ³He went into all the country around the Jordan, preaching a baptism

b 23 Exodus 13:2,12
c 24 Lev. 12:8
d 29 Or promised, / now dismiss
e 37 Or then had been a widow for eighty-four years.

f 49 Or be about my Father's business

of repentance for the forgiveness of sins. 4 As it is written in the book of the words of Isaiah the prophet:

'A voice of one calling in the
   wilderness,
"Prepare the way for the Lord,
   make straight paths for him.
5 Every valley shall be filled in,
   every mountain and hill made low.
The crooked roads shall become
   straight,
   the rough ways smooth.
6 And all people will see God's
   salvation." '*a*

7 John said to the crowds coming out to be baptised by him, 'You brood of vipers! Who warned you to flee from the coming wrath? 8 Produce fruit in keeping with repentance. And do not begin to say to yourselves, "We have Abraham as our father." For I tell you that out of these stones God can raise up children for Abraham. 9 The axe has been laid to the root of the trees, and every tree that does not produce good fruit will be cut down and thrown into the fire.'

10 'What should we do then?' the crowd asked.

11 John answered, 'Anyone who has two shirts should share with the one who has none, and anyone who has food should do the same.'

12 Even tax collectors came to be baptised. 'Teacher,' they asked, 'what should we do?'

13 'Don't collect any more than you are required to,' he told them.

14 Then some soldiers asked him, 'And what should we do?'

He replied, 'Don't extort money and don't accuse people falsely – be content with your pay.'

15 The people were waiting expectantly and were all wondering in their hearts if John might possibly be the Messiah. 16 John answered them all, 'I baptise you with*b* water. But one who is more powerful than I will come, the straps of whose sandals I am not worthy to untie. He will baptise you with*c* the Holy Spirit and fire. 17 His winnowing fork is in his hand to clear his threshing-floor and to gather the wheat into his barn, but he will burn up the chaff with unquenchable fire.' 18 And with many other words John exhorted the people and proclaimed the good news to them.

19 But when John rebuked Herod the tetrarch because of his marriage to Herodias, his brother's wife, and all the other evil things he had done, 20 Herod added this to them all: he locked John up in prison.

The baptism and genealogy of Jesus

21 When all the people were being baptised, Jesus was baptised too. And as he was praying, heaven was opened 22 and the Holy Spirit descended on him in bodily form like a dove. And a voice came from heaven: 'You are my Son, whom I love; with you I am well pleased.'

23 Now Jesus himself was about thirty years old when he began his ministry. He was the son, so it was thought, of Joseph,

the son of Heli, 24 the son of Matthat,
the son of Levi, the son of Melki,
the son of Jannai, the son of Joseph,
25 the son of Mattathias, the son of
   Amos,
the son of Nahum, the son of Esli,
the son of Naggai, 26 the son of
   Maath,
the son of Mattathias, the son of
   Semein,
the son of Josek, the son of Joda,
27 the son of Joanan, the son of Rhesa,
the son of Zerubbabel, the son of
   Shealtiel,
the son of Neri, 28 the son of Melki,
the son of Addi, the son of Cosam,
the son of Elmadam, the son of Er,
29 the son of Joshua, the son of Eliezer,
the son of Jorim, the son of Matthat,
the son of Levi, 30 the son of Simeon,

---

a 6 Isaiah 40:3-5
b 16 Or *in*

c 16 Or *in*

the son of Judah, the son of Joseph,
the son of Jonam, the son of Eliakim,
31 the son of Melea, the son of Menna,
the son of Mattatha, the son of Nathan,
the son of David, 32 the son of Jesse,
the son of Obed, the son of Boaz,
the son of Salmon,*d* the son of Nahshon,
33 the son of Amminadab, the son of
Ram,*e*
the son of Hezron, the son of Perez,
the son of Judah, 34 the son of Jacob,
the son of Isaac, the son of Abraham,
the son of Terah, the son of Nahor,
35 the son of Serug, the son of Reu,
the son of Peleg, the son of Eber,
the son of Shelah, 36 the son of Cainan,
the son of Arphaxad, the son of
Shem,
the son of Noah, the son of Lamech,
37 the son of Methuselah, the son of
Enoch,
the son of Jared, the son of Mahalalel,
the son of Kenan, 38 the son of
Enosh,
the son of Seth, the son of Adam,
the son of God.

Jesus is tested in the wilderness

4 Jesus, full of the Holy Spirit, left the
Jordan and was led by the Spirit into
the wilderness, 2 where for forty days he
was tempted*a* by the devil. He ate nothing
during those days, and at the end of them
he was hungry.
3 The devil said to him, 'If you are the
Son of God, tell this stone to become
bread.'
4 Jesus answered, 'It is written: "Man
shall not live on bread alone."*b*'
5 The devil led him up to a high place
and showed him in an instant all the

kingdoms of the world. 6 And he said to
him, 'I will give you all their authority and
splendour; it has been given to me, and I
can give it to anyone I want to. 7 If you worship me, it will all be yours.'
8 Jesus answered, 'It is written: "Worship
the Lord your God and serve him only."*c*'
9 The devil led him to Jerusalem and
had him stand on the highest point of
the temple. 'If you are the Son of God,'
he said, 'throw yourself down from here.
10 For it is written:

' "He will command his angels
concerning you
to guard you carefully;
11 they will lift you up in their hands,
so that you will not strike your foot
against a stone."*d*'

12 Jesus answered, 'It is said: "Do not
put the Lord your God to the test."*e*'
13 When the devil had finished all this
tempting, he left him until an opportune
time.

Jesus rejected at Nazareth

14 Jesus returned to Galilee in the power
of the Spirit, and news about him spread
through the whole countryside. 15 He was
teaching in their synagogues, and everyone praised him.
16 He went to Nazareth, where he had
been brought up, and on the Sabbath day
he went into the synagogue, as was his
custom. He stood up to read, 17 and the
scroll of the prophet Isaiah was handed
to him. Unrolling it, he found the place
where it is written:

18 'The Spirit of the Lord is on me,
because he has anointed me
to proclaim good news to the poor.
He has sent me to proclaim freedom
for the prisoners
and recovery of sight for the blind,
to set the oppressed free,

---

d 32 Some early manuscripts *Sala*
e 33 Some manuscripts *Amminadab, the son of Admin,*
the son of Arni; other manuscripts vary widely.
a 2 The Greek for *tempted* can also mean *tested.*
b 4 Deut. 8:3

c 8 Deut. 6:13
d 11 Psalm 91:11,12
e 12 Deut. 6:16

19 to proclaim the year of the Lord's favour.'f

20 Then he rolled up the scroll, gave it back to the attendant and sat down. The eyes of everyone in the synagogue were

---

f 19 Isaiah 61:1,2 (see Septuagint); Isaiah 58:6

fastened on him. 21 He began by saying to them, 'Today this scripture is fulfilled in your hearing.'

22 All spoke well of him and were amazed at the gracious words that came from his lips. 'Isn't this Joseph's son?' they asked.

23 Jesus said to them, 'Surely you will quote this proverb to me: "Physician, heal yourself!" And you will tell me, "Do here

SPIRITUAL DISCIPLINES 1

FASTING

Our culture is all about consuming things – food, clothes, media, gadgets – and the idea of intentionally going without something could be seen as a sign of madness.

What's more, Western culture is marked by a sense of entitlement: we don't just want our basic human rights, we want the right to do and be and have what we want. In the past many things were obtainable only through careful saving, and some things were simply out of reach. Now the marketing men tell us that anything can be ours – and not just that, we can buy now, pay later...

The discipline of fasting is about going without something (usually food) in order to make space in our lives for God. If we spend our days filling ourselves to bursting with more than we need of everything, we become distracted by our own constant need for self-satisfaction. Fasting is a way of refocusing ourselves on what's important.

In the Bible, fasting is a key part of the lives of those who follow God. In the snapshot of the early church found in Acts 13:1–3, for instance, prayer and fasting are twinned together, as if one 'feeds' the other. Perhaps the most important passage on fasting in the Bible, however, is here in Luke 4:1–15, as Jesus embarks on an incredible forty days without food. Before he begins his ministry, Jesus takes himself away into the wilderness for this extended period, and while Satan himself finds and tempts him there, *he* isn't the one Jesus set out to meet. Instead, Jesus fasts (much more drastically than is healthy in normal circumstances) in order to have a divine encounter with his Father, which then propels him into his future work on earth. Straight after this story, in verse 14, we read that Jesus returns *'in the power of the Spirit'*. Fasting has brought him so close to his Father that he has become radically changed and filled with power.

Just like Jesus, and just like Paul and Barnabas in Acts, this is why we fast as well. Going without the things of which we have plenty not only focuses us back on God, it opens the way for the Holy Spirit's power to move in us.

Martin Saunders

Psalm 46

JUSTICE AND MERCY 7

FILLED AND SENT OUT

Luke 4:18–19 is the closest Jesus comes to having a mission statement. He had been baptised, tested by the devil and filled with the Holy Spirit. He had done a little preaching and created a stir. On this Sabbath everyone wanted to hear from him, so they handed him the scroll. After Jesus had read, he looked round and said, 'Today this scripture is happening before your eyes.'

These words describe the life and mission of Jesus. These were the things that mattered to him, the things he was going to spend his earthly life doing – the things he asks us to do if we want to follow him. He acknowledges that he has been filled with the Holy Spirit and that he has been sent to do some things. This should be our starting point too: asking God to fill us and tell us what he wants us to do today.

Jesus talks about good news, freedom and healing. This is his mission. It's ours too: to bring good news, freedom and healing wherever we go, in every part of life.

First, the good news is about our relationship with God. We can be forgiven and reunited with our Maker. To follow the mission of Jesus means to talk about the things God has done in Christ and what he has done in us because of Christ. People who are captive to sin can be set free, but to hear this good news they need someone to speak.

Second, the good news is that we can know God's healing and help today. Today is the day of salvation and today we can know the Holy Spirit's presence and power to deliver us from our oppressions and bring healing. God is interested in our illnesses, hurts and fears, and is with us to heal and deliver. As followers of Jesus, we learn how to be filled with the Holy Spirit, pray for others and see God's power bring freedom.

Third, the good news is not just about us. Jesus came to transform society. The words Jesus read are from Isaiah, and Isaiah refers to Leviticus 25. This is where the phrase 'the year of the Lord's favour' comes from. This year, coming once a generation, was when God fixed society. Debts were cancelled, slaves set free, land redistributed, so that every family had somewhere to live and grow food. God hates the idea that the rich get richer while the poor get poorer. He doesn't want any children to have their potential defined by the wealth or poverty of their parents rather than their own ability and work. So Israel had laws to heal society and set the oppressed free.

This is what Jesus talks about here. He has come to bring us peace with God and freedom from our hurts, and to transform society so that the least, the last and the lost have a new beginning. And he asks his followers to get involved in this work.

David Westlake

 Matthew 14:13   1 Corinthians 16:14

in your home town what we have heard that you did in Capernaum." '

24 'Truly I tell you,' he continued, 'no prophet is accepted in his home town. 25 I assure you that there were many widows in Israel in Elijah's time, when the sky was shut for three and a half years and there was a severe famine throughout the land. 26 Yet Elijah was not sent to any of them, but to a widow in Zarephath in the region of Sidon. 27 And there were many in Israel with leprosy*g* in the time of Elisha the prophet, yet not one of them was cleansed – only Naaman the Syrian.'

28 All the people in the synagogue were furious when they heard this. 29 They got up, drove him out of the town, and took him to the brow of the hill on which the town was built, in order to throw him off the cliff. 30 But he walked right through the crowd and went on his way.

Jesus drives out an impure spirit

31 Then he went down to Capernaum, a town in Galilee, and on the Sabbath he taught the people. 32 They were amazed at his teaching, because his words had authority.

33 In the synagogue there was a man possessed by a demon, an impure spirit. He cried out at the top of his voice, 34 'Go away! What do you want with us, Jesus of Nazareth? Have you come to destroy us? I know who you are – the Holy One of God!'

35 'Be quiet!' Jesus said sternly. 'Come out of him!' Then the demon threw the man down before them all and came out without injuring him.

36 All the people were amazed and said to each other, 'What words these are! With authority and power he gives orders to impure spirits and they come out!' 37 And the news about him spread throughout the surrounding area.

Jesus heals many

38 Jesus left the synagogue and went to the home of Simon. Now Simon's mother-in-law was suffering from a high fever, and they asked Jesus to help her. 39 So he bent over her and rebuked the fever, and it left her. She got up at once and began to wait on them.

40 At sunset, the people brought to Jesus all who had various kinds of illness, and laying his hands on each one, he healed them. 41 Moreover, demons came out of many people, shouting, 'You are the Son of God!' But he rebuked them and would not allow them to speak, because they knew he was the Messiah.

42 At daybreak, Jesus went out to a solitary place. The people were looking for him and when they came to where he was, they tried to keep him from leaving them. 43 But he said, 'I must proclaim the good news of the kingdom of God to the other towns also, because that is why I was sent.' 44 And he kept on preaching in the synagogues of Judea.

Jesus calls his first disciples

5 One day as Jesus was standing by the Lake of Gennesaret,*a* the people were crowding round him and listening to the word of God. 2 He saw at the water's edge two boats, left there by the fishermen, who were washing their nets. 3 He got into one of the boats, the one belonging to Simon, and asked him to put out a little from the shore. Then he sat down and taught the people from the boat.

4 When he had finished speaking, he said to Simon, 'Put out into deep water, and let down the nets for a catch.'

5 Simon answered, 'Master, we've worked hard all night and haven't caught anything. But because you say so, I will let down the nets.'

6 When they had done so, they caught such a large number of fish that their nets began to break. 7 So they signalled to their partners in the other boat to come and help them, and they came and filled both boats so full that they began to sink.

8 When Simon Peter saw this, he fell at Jesus' knees and said, 'Go away from me, Lord; I am a sinful man!' 9 For he and all

---

g 27 The Greek word traditionally translated *leprosy* was used for various diseases affecting the skin.

a 1 That is, Sea of Galilee

his companions were astonished at the catch of fish they had taken, [10]and so were James and John, the sons of Zebedee, Simon's partners.

Then Jesus said to Simon, 'Don't be afraid; from now on you will fish for people.' [11]So they pulled their boats up on shore, left everything and followed him.

Jesus heals a man with leprosy

[12]While Jesus was in one of the towns, a man came along who was covered with leprosy.[b] When he saw Jesus, he fell with his face to the ground and begged him, 'Lord, if you are willing, you can make me clean.'

[13]Jesus reached out his hand and touched the man. 'I am willing,' he said. 'Be clean!' And immediately the leprosy left him.

[14]Then Jesus ordered him, 'Don't tell anyone, but go, show yourself to the priest and offer the sacrifices that Moses commanded for your cleansing, as a testimony to them.'

[15]Yet the news about him spread all the more, so that crowds of people came to hear him and to be healed of their illnesses. [16]But Jesus often withdrew to lonely places and prayed.

Jesus forgives and heals a paralysed man

[17]One day Jesus was teaching, and Pharisees and teachers of the law were sitting there. They had come from every village of Galilee and from Judea and Jerusalem. And the power of the Lord was with Jesus to heal those who were ill. [18]Some men came carrying a paralysed man on a mat and tried to take him into the house to lay him before Jesus. [19]When they could not find a way to do this because of the crowd, they went up on the roof and lowered him on his mat through the tiles into the middle of the crowd, right in front of Jesus.

[20]When Jesus saw their faith, he said, 'Friend, your sins are forgiven.'

[21]The Pharisees and the teachers of the law began thinking to themselves, 'Who is this fellow who speaks blasphemy? Who can forgive sins but God alone?'

[22]Jesus knew what they were thinking and asked, 'Why are you thinking these things in your hearts? [23]Which is easier: to say, "Your sins are forgiven," or to say, "Get up and walk"? [24]But I want you to know that the Son of Man has authority on earth to forgive sins.' So he said to the paralysed man, 'I tell you, get up, take your mat and go home.' [25]Immediately he stood up in front of them, took what he had been lying on and went home praising God. [26]Everyone was amazed and gave praise to God. They were filled with awe and said, 'We have seen remarkable things today.'

Jesus calls Levi and eats with sinners

[27]After this, Jesus went out and saw a tax collector by the name of Levi sitting at his tax booth. 'Follow me,' Jesus said to him, [28]and Levi got up, left everything and followed him.

[29]Then Levi held a great banquet for Jesus at his house, and a large crowd of tax collectors and others were eating with them. [30]But the Pharisees and the teachers of the law who belonged to their sect complained to his disciples, 'Why do you eat and drink with tax collectors and sinners?'

[31]Jesus answered them, 'It is not the healthy who need a doctor, but those who are ill. [32]I have not come to call the righteous, but sinners to repentance.'

Jesus questioned about fasting

[33]They said to him, 'John's disciples often fast and pray, and so do the disciples of the Pharisees, but yours go on eating and drinking.'

[34]Jesus answered, 'Can you make the friends of the bridegroom fast while he is with them? [35]But the time will come when the bridegroom will be taken from them; in those days they will fast.'

[36]He told them this parable: 'No one tears a piece out of a new garment to patch an old one. Otherwise, they will have torn

---

b 12 The Greek word traditionally translated *leprosy* was used for various diseases affecting the skin.

SPIRITUAL DISCIPLINES 7

SOLITUDE

Let's be honest: silence and solitude are not easy. Unless we particularly love our own space, or we're raising money for charity, being deliberately quiet is not something we relish! Yet the practice of silence has been one of the most important spiritual disciplines for Christians over thousands of years, and it's one that we should make an effort to try for ourselves.

Why? Because, quite simply, when we stay silent, God speaks.

Silence is difficult, but quite possible to master with practice. Christians have been using silence as a way of connecting with God since Jesus himself modelled it in passages like Luke 6:12–16. It might seem strange to us to read that, just as his ministry was ramping up, just as he was becoming more popular and famous, he withdrew to a lonely place to pray. Jesus thirsted for silence in the midst of his busy life – spending time alone was the way he reconnected with God and re-energised in preparation for his next miracle or sermon.

While it might seem daunting, the best way to get into the discipline of solitude is simply to begin. The exercise below is brief and straightforward, and can take just five minutes. However, it can be extended to ten minutes, fifteen and more as you become more comfortable with the practice, and as you become more familiar with how God speaks to you in times of silence. Because, like all the spiritual disciplines, solitude teaches us that when we slow down and create space for God, he rushes in to inhabit it.

Practising solitude

There is no wrong way to do this activity – provided you remain silent. You should have nothing with you, apart from perhaps a pen and paper to note down anything you feel God might be saying to you. If possible, ask someone else to time you, and let you know when the time is up.

- Find a space, and switch off any distractions. Now say a quick prayer, asking God to speak. You might want to use the words of Samuel, 'Speak, your servant is listening.'

- Relax. Quieten yourself. You may want to close your eyes: if you fall asleep, you do so in the presence of God, so that's OK too!

- Now, listen out for the 'gentle whisper' of God's voice. If you find yourself becoming distracted, you may want to use a word or short phrase which you repeat in your head to bring your focus back to him. Then, for as long as you can, simply offer your open mind to God.

- When your time is up, perhaps take a moment to note down what you think God might have been saying to you. Even if it seems like a small thing, go and tell another Christian, such as a youth leader.

- Commit to trying the activity at least three times, increasing your time of silence slightly each time if you can.

Martin Saunders

 John 13:34–35   1 John 4:7–21

the new garment, and the patch from the new will not match the old. ³⁷And no one pours new wine into old wineskins. Otherwise, the new wine will burst the skins; the wine will run out and the wineskins will be ruined. ³⁸No, new wine must be poured into new wineskins. ³⁹And no one after drinking old wine wants the new, for they say, "The old is better." '

Jesus is Lord of the Sabbath

6 One Sabbath Jesus was going through the cornfields, and his disciples began to pick some ears of corn, rub them in their hands and eat the grain. ²Some of the Pharisees asked, 'Why are you doing what is unlawful on the Sabbath?'

³Jesus answered them, 'Have you never read what David did when he and his companions were hungry? ⁴He entered the house of God, and taking the consecrated bread, he ate what is lawful only for priests to eat. And he also gave some to his companions.' ⁵Then Jesus said to them, 'The Son of Man is Lord of the Sabbath.'

⁶On another Sabbath he went into the synagogue and was teaching, and a man was there whose right hand was shrivelled. ⁷The Pharisees and the teachers of the law were looking for a reason to accuse Jesus, so they watched him closely to see if he would heal on the Sabbath. ⁸But Jesus knew what they were thinking and said to the man with the shrivelled hand, 'Get up and stand in front of everyone.' So he got up and stood there.

⁹Then Jesus said to them, 'I ask you, which is lawful on the Sabbath: to do good or to do evil, to save life or to destroy it?'

¹⁰He looked round at them all, and then said to the man, 'Stretch out your hand.' He did so, and his hand was completely restored. ¹¹But the Pharisees and the teachers of the law were furious and began to discuss with one another what they might do to Jesus.

The twelve apostles

¹²One of those days Jesus went out to a mountainside to pray, and spent the night praying to God. ¹³When morning came, he called his disciples to him and chose twelve of them, whom he also designated apostles: ¹⁴Simon (whom he named Peter), his brother Andrew, James, John, Philip, Bartholomew, ¹⁵Matthew, Thomas, James son of Alphaeus, Simon who was called the Zealot, ¹⁶Judas son of James, and Judas Iscariot, who became a traitor.

Blessings and woes

¹⁷He went down with them and stood on a level place. A large crowd of his disciples was there and a great number of people from all over Judea, from Jerusalem, and from the coastal region around Tyre and Sidon, ¹⁸who had come to hear him and to be healed of their diseases. Those troubled by impure spirits were cured, ¹⁹and the people all tried to touch him, because power was coming from him and healing them all.

²⁰Looking at his disciples, he said:

'Blessed are you who are poor,
  for yours is the kingdom of God.
²¹Blessed are you who hunger now,
  for you will be satisfied.
Blessed are you who weep now,
  for you will laugh.
²²Blessed are you when people hate
    you,
  when they exclude you and insult
    you
  and reject your name as evil,
    because of the Son of Man.

²³'Rejoice in that day and leap for joy, because great is your reward in heaven. For that is how their ancestors treated the prophets.

²⁴'But woe to you who are rich,
  for you have already received your
    comfort.
²⁵Woe to you who are well fed now,
  for you will go hungry.
Woe to you who laugh now,
  for you will mourn and weep.
²⁶Woe to you when everyone speaks well
    of you,
  for that is how their ancestors
    treated the false prophets.

Love for enemies

27 'But to you who are listening I say: love your enemies, do good to those who hate you, **28** bless those who curse you, pray for those who ill-treat you. **29** If someone slaps you on one cheek, turn to them the other also. If someone takes your coat, do not withhold your shirt from them. **30** Give to everyone who asks you, and if anyone takes what belongs to you, do not demand it back. **31** Do to others as you would have them do to you.

32 'If you love those who love you, what credit is that to you? Even sinners love those who love them. **33** And if you do good to those who are good to you, what credit is that to you? Even sinners do that. **34** And if you lend to those from whom you expect repayment, what credit is that to you? Even sinners lend to sinners, expecting to be repaid in full. **35** But love your enemies, do good to them, and lend to them without expecting to get anything back. Then your reward will be great, and you will be children of the Most High, because he is kind to the ungrateful and wicked. **36** Be merciful, just as your Father is merciful.

Judging others

37 'Do not judge, and you will not be judged. Do not condemn, and you will not be condemned. Forgive, and you will be forgiven. **38** Give, and it will be given to you. A good measure, pressed down, shaken together and running over, will be poured into your lap. For with the measure you use, it will be measured to you.'

39 He also told them this parable: 'Can the blind lead the blind? Will they not both fall into a pit? **40** The student is not above the teacher, but everyone who is fully trained will be like their teacher.

41 'Why do you look at the speck of sawdust in your brother's eye and pay no attention to the plank in your own eye? **42** How can you say to your brother, "Brother, let me take the speck out of your eye," when you yourself fail to see the plank in your own eye? You hypocrite, first take the plank out of your eye, and then you will see clearly to remove the speck from your brother's eye.

A tree and its fruit

43 'No good tree bears bad fruit, nor does a bad tree bear good fruit. **44** Each tree is recognised by its own fruit. People do not pick figs from thorn-bushes, or grapes from briers. **45** A good man brings good things out of the good stored up in his heart, and an evil man brings evil things out of the evil stored up in his heart. For the mouth speaks what the heart is full of.

The wise and foolish builders

46 'Why do you call me, "Lord, Lord," and do not do what I say? **47** As for everyone who comes to me and hears my words and puts them into practice, I will show you what they are like. **48** They are like a man building a house, who dug down deep and laid the foundation on rock. When the flood came, the torrent struck that house but could not shake it, because it was well built. **49** But the one who hears my words and does not put them into practice is like a man who built a house on the ground without a foundation. The moment the torrent struck that house, it collapsed and its destruction was complete.'

The faith of the centurion

7 When Jesus had finished saying all this to the people who were listening, he entered Capernaum. **2** There a centurion's servant, whom his master valued highly, was ill and about to die. **3** The centurion heard of Jesus and sent some elders of the Jews to him, asking him to come and heal his servant. **4** When they came to Jesus, they pleaded earnestly with him, 'This man deserves to have you do this, **5** because he loves our nation and has built our synagogue.' **6** So Jesus went with them.

He was not far from the house when the centurion sent friends to say to him: 'Lord, don't trouble yourself, for I do not deserve to have you come under my roof. **7** That is why I did not even consider myself worthy to come to you. But say the word, and my servant will be healed. **8** For I myself am a man under authority, with soldiers under me. I tell this one, "Go", and he goes; and that one, "Come", and he comes. I say to my servant, "Do this", and he does it.'

9 When Jesus heard this, he was amazed at him, and turning to the crowd following him, he said, 'I tell you, I have not found such great faith even in Israel.' 10 Then the men who had been sent returned to the house and found the servant well.

Jesus raises a widow's son

11 Soon afterwards, Jesus went to a town called Nain, and his disciples and a large crowd went along with him. 12 As he approached the town gate, a dead person

was being carried out – the only son of his mother, and she was a widow. And a large crowd from the town was with her. 13 When the Lord saw her, his heart went out to her and he said, 'Don't cry.'

14 Then he went up and touched the bier they were carrying him on, and the bearers stood still. He said, 'Young man, I say to you, get up!' 15 The dead man sat up and began to talk, and Jesus gave him back to his mother.

16 They were all filled with awe and praised God. 'A great prophet has appeared among us,' they said. 'God has

---

NATURALLY SUPERNATURAL 1

MOTIVATION FOR HEALING IS COMPASSION

Throughout the Gospels we hear of Jesus healing people. We can't even count how many people he healed, because sometimes the Bible just tells us that a crowd gathered and he healed everyone in need.

The healing described in Luke 7:11–14, where Jesus actually raises someone from the dead, shows us what his motivation was. It wasn't to get a name for himself, to show off his power, to prove a point, or to shut up anyone who doubted him. He healed people because he saw their suffering and he had compassion for them. He did it because he cares. He cares that people are living with physical and emotional pain, and he wants us to care when we come across people suffering in the same way.

Jesus showed us how to live, in his words and through his actions. He wants us to have soft hearts that are compassionate towards other people's sufferings. This way, when we're moved by someone's circumstances, we don't stop at giving them our pity. Instead we help, we act and we do everything we can to relieve their suffering. We may not be able to heal them ourselves, but we know someone who can – so let's take every opportunity to pray that sickness and injuries are healed. When we're scared or nervous, let's pray for the Holy Spirit to fill us with boldness, just as the disciples prayed in Acts 4.

We won't always see everyone we pray for get healed, but we're much more likely to see healing if we pray than if we don't! But let's always keep a check on our motivations too. Let's be soft-hearted and ask God to give us his compassion for people who are suffering. When we know how much he cares about those around us, we will be bold to ask for his presence to break into their lives and heal them.

Mike Pilavachi

Luke 9 ▶▶

come to help his people.' ¹⁷This news about Jesus spread throughout Judea and the surrounding country.

Jesus and John the Baptist

¹⁸John's disciples told him about all these things. Calling two of them, ¹⁹he sent them to the Lord to ask, 'Are you the one who is to come, or should we expect someone else?'

²⁰When the men came to Jesus, they said, 'John the Baptist sent us to you to ask, "Are you the one who is to come, or should we expect someone else?"'

²¹At that very time Jesus cured many who had diseases, illnesses and evil spirits, and gave sight to many who were blind. ²²So he replied to the messengers, 'Go back and report to John what you have seen and heard: the blind receive sight, the lame walk, those who have leprosy*a* are cleansed, the deaf hear, the dead are raised, and the good news is proclaimed to the poor. ²³Blessed is anyone who does not stumble on account of me.'

²⁴After John's messengers left, Jesus began to speak to the crowd about John: 'What did you go out into the wilderness to see? A reed swayed by the wind? ²⁵If not, what did you go out to see? A man dressed in fine clothes? No, those who wear expensive clothes and indulge in luxury are in palaces. ²⁶But what did you go out to see? A prophet? Yes, I tell you, and more than a prophet. ²⁷This is the one about whom it is written:

' "I will send my messenger ahead of
    you,
who will prepare your way before
    you."*b*

²⁸I tell you, among those born of women there is no one greater than John; yet the one who is least in the kingdom of God is greater than he.'

²⁹(All the people, even the tax collectors, when they heard Jesus' words, acknowledged that God's way was right, because they had been baptised by John. ³⁰But the Pharisees and the experts in the law rejected God's purpose for themselves, because they had not been baptised by John.)

³¹Jesus went on to say, 'To what, then, can I compare the people of this generation? What are they like? ³²They are like children sitting in the market-place and calling out to each other:

' "We played the pipe for you,
    and you did not dance;
we sang a dirge,
    and you did not cry."

³³For John the Baptist came neither eating bread nor drinking wine, and you say, "He has a demon." ³⁴The Son of Man came eating and drinking, and you say, "Here is a glutton and a drunkard, a friend of tax collectors and sinners." ³⁵But wisdom is proved right by all her children.'

Jesus anointed by a sinful woman

³⁶When one of the Pharisees invited Jesus to have dinner with him, he went to the Pharisee's house and reclined at the table. ³⁷A woman in that town who lived a sinful life learned that Jesus was eating at the Pharisee's house, so she came there with an alabaster jar of perfume. ³⁸As she stood behind him at his feet weeping, she began to wet his feet with her tears. Then she wiped them with her hair, kissed them and poured perfume on them.

³⁹When the Pharisee who had invited him saw this, he said to himself, 'If this man were a prophet, he would know who is touching him and what kind of woman she is – that she is a sinner.'

⁴⁰Jesus answered him, 'Simon, I have something to tell you.'

'Tell me, teacher,' he said.

⁴¹'Two people owed money to a certain money-lender. One owed him five hundred denarii,*c* and the other fifty. ⁴²Neither of them had the money to pay him

---

a 22 The Greek word traditionally translated *leprosy* was used for various diseases affecting the skin.
b 27 Mal. 3:1

c 41 A denarius was the usual daily wage of a day labourer (see Matt. 20:2).

back, so he forgave the debts of both. Now which of them will love him more?'

⁴³ Simon replied, 'I suppose the one who had the bigger debt forgiven.'

'You have judged correctly,' Jesus said. ⁴⁴ Then he turned towards the woman and said to Simon, 'Do you see this woman? I came into your house. You did

LIFE OF JESUS 4

The Lord who saves us from sin

Forgiveness is a serious matter. If a person has offended someone, whether another human being or God, and there has been no forgiveness, then that relationship is badly damaged. The fact that all human beings have sinned against God is the problem that lies at the core of the tragic separation that runs throughout the Bible. In Luke 7:36–50 we see Jesus – almost as an aside – declaring that someone is forgiven. This is so extraordinary that it needs careful thought.

There are two problems with offering forgiveness. The first revolves around who exactly has the authority to forgive. The fact is that forgiveness is normally a matter for two people. So, if someone does something wrong to you, we would agree that it's your business – and yours alone – to offer forgiveness to the person who offended you. It would be outrageous for someone else to come along and tell whoever had committed the offence that they were forgiven. So what was Jesus doing in offering forgiveness to this woman? The answer the Bible gives is very significant. It says that because we all belong to God, when someone does something wrong to another person it's also a sin against God (see Psalm 51:4). Think of a situation where there's a king or queen and someone attacks and injures one of their servants. The offence is not just against the royal servant, it's also against the monarch. Put like that, you can see how God – but only God – can intervene. In offering forgiveness, Jesus is claiming to be far more than a man or even a prophet: he's claiming to be God (see Luke 5:21).

The second problem with forgiveness revolves around who pays the price. In the Bible, as often today, issues of wrongdoing are considered as debts that need compensation. So you may say, 'Look, I'm sorry, let me try to make it up to you.' In the Old Testament, sins against God were dealt with by sacrificing animals, as if the sin could be paid off by shed blood. What's clear in the New Testament is that Jesus pays the price himself; he's the ultimate and final sacrifice. One of the most welcome phrases in the English language is 'Don't worry, I'll take care of the bill'. Because he's God in the flesh, Jesus is able to offer his followers forgiveness on those terms. That's what grace is all about.

J.John

 Mark 1:24–28   Mark 13:31 ▶

not give me any water for my feet, but she wet my feet with her tears and wiped them with her hair. ⁴⁵You did not give me a kiss, but this woman, from the time I entered, has not stopped kissing my feet. ⁴⁶You did not put oil on my head, but she has poured perfume on my feet. ⁴⁷Therefore, I tell you, her many sins have been forgiven – as her great love has shown. But whoever has been forgiven little loves little.'

⁴⁸Then Jesus said to her, 'Your sins are forgiven.'

⁴⁹The other guests began to say among themselves, 'Who is this who even forgives sins?'

⁵⁰Jesus said to the woman, 'Your faith has saved you; go in peace.'

The parable of the sower

8 After this, Jesus travelled about from one town and village to another, proclaiming the good news of the kingdom of God. The Twelve were with him, ²and also some women who had been cured of evil spirits and diseases: Mary (called Magdalene) from whom seven demons had come out; ³Joanna the wife of Chuza, the manager of Herod's household; Susanna; and many others. These women were helping to support them out of their own means.

⁴While a large crowd was gathering and people were coming to Jesus from town after town, he told this parable: ⁵'A farmer went out to sow his seed. As he was scattering the seed, some fell along the path; it was trampled on, and the birds ate it up. ⁶Some fell on rocky ground, and when it came up, the plants withered because they had no moisture. ⁷Other seed fell among thorns, which grew up with it and choked the plants. ⁸Still other seed fell on good soil. It came up and yielded a crop, a hundred times more than was sown.'

When he said this, he called out, 'Whoever has ears to hear, let them hear.'

⁹His disciples asked him what this parable meant. ¹⁰He said, 'The knowledge of the secrets of the kingdom of God has been given to you, but to others I speak in parables, so that,

' "though seeing, they may not see;
   though hearing, they may not
   understand." ᵃ

¹¹'This is the meaning of the parable: the seed is the word of God. ¹²Those along the path are the ones who hear, and then the devil comes and takes away the word from their hearts, so that they may not believe and be saved. ¹³Those on the rocky ground are the ones who receive the word with joy when they hear it, but they have no root. They believe for a while, but in the time of testing they fall away. ¹⁴The seed that fell among thorns stands for those who hear, but as they go on their way they are choked by life's worries, riches and pleasures, and they do not mature. ¹⁵But the seed on good soil stands for those with a noble and good heart, who hear the word, retain it, and by persevering produce a crop.

A lamp on a stand

¹⁶'No one lights a lamp and hides it in a clay jar or puts it under a bed. Instead, they put it on a stand, so that those who come in can see the light. ¹⁷For there is nothing hidden that will not be disclosed, and nothing concealed that will not be known or brought out into the open. ¹⁸Therefore consider carefully how you listen. Whoever has will be given more; whoever does not have, even what they think they have will be taken from them.'

Jesus' mother and brothers

¹⁹Now Jesus' mother and brothers came to see him, but they were not able to get near him because of the crowd. ²⁰Someone told him, 'Your mother and brothers are standing outside, wanting to see you.'

²¹He replied, 'My mother and brothers are those who hear God's word and put it into practice.'

Jesus calms the storm

²²One day Jesus said to his disciples, 'Let us go over to the other side of the lake.' So

---

a 10 Isaiah 6:9

WHAT IS CHRISTIANITY? 6

Doctrine of Christ: Jesus

'Who is this?' the disciples ask of Jesus in Luke 8:25. It's the most significant question any person can ever ask. Most of the people you will meet will have one opinion or another as to who Jesus was. The most reliable place to look for the answer, however, is in the stories of Jesus' life in the Gospels. Many people, across the world and throughout the ages, have lived and died for Jesus because of the truth they discovered about him in these books.

The Gospels show us clearly that Jesus isn't just a nice guy, or a good example to us: he's God himself. The disciples get the shock of their lives when Jesus wakes up and tells the storm to calm down (Luke 8:22–25). He can control creation. He can also cast out demons, heal sick people and raise the dead. Where Jesus walks, life follows. What's more, Jesus didn't just bring healing to people's bodies; he brought salvation to their hearts. When he meets people he's able to proclaim, *'Your sins are forgiven'* – something only God himself can do (Mark 2:5–6).

It took the disciples a while to grasp the amazing fullness of Jesus' identity. By the time we get to the end of the Gospels, it's beginning to dawn on them. Thomas, on meeting Jesus raised from the dead, declares, *'My Lord and my God!'* (John 20:28). Worship is an activity we reserve for God, and at the end of both Matthew and Luke the disciples worship Jesus before he returns to heaven (Matthew 28:17; Luke 24:52). John introduces Jesus as *'the Word'* made *'flesh'*, God himself walking among us (John 1:14), and Paul speaks of Jesus as *'the image of the invisible God'* (Colossians 1:15). Jesus is wonderfully and completely divine.

At the same time the Gospels show the full humanity of Jesus. He isn't floating six feet off the ground wearing a white dress. Jesus is a real human being. He has a human mind as well as human emotions, needs and desires. We see him express surprise, joy and determination. He eats, he jokes, he weeps at the grave of Lazarus and he washes his disciples' feet. At the start of the passage in Luke 8:22 he's asleep – what an amazing picture of the humanity and divinity of Jesus! Dozing one moment, commanding creation the next.

In the Gospels we don't meet a Jesus who is half-God, half-human. We're confronted with the reality of Jesus who is fully divine and fully human. In Jesus, God took on himself everything it meant to be human in order to redeem everything about humanity.

Jesus is compassionate and fierce; he's wild and kind; he's tender and terrifying; he receives worship and he serves. He's human and he's God. Recognising who he is must be the most significant thing we will ever do, and it's through him that we're saved, freed and transformed.

Andy Croft

◀◀ John 1   Romans 5:1–11 ▶▶

they got into a boat and set out. ²³As they sailed, he fell asleep. A squall came down on the lake, so that the boat was being swamped, and they were in great danger.

²⁴The disciples went and woke him, saying, 'Master, Master, we're going to drown!'

He got up and rebuked the wind and the raging waters; the storm subsided, and all was calm. ²⁵'Where is your faith?' he asked his disciples.

In fear and amazement they asked one another, 'Who is this? He commands even the winds and the water, and they obey him.'

Jesus restores a demon-possessed man

²⁶They sailed to the region of the Gerasenes,ᵇ which is across the lake from Galilee. ²⁷When Jesus stepped ashore, he was met by a demon-possessed man from the town. For a long time this man had not worn clothes or lived in a house, but had lived in the tombs. ²⁸When he saw Jesus, he cried out and fell at his feet, shouting at the top of his voice, 'What do you want with me, Jesus, Son of the Most High God? I beg you, don't torture me!' ²⁹For Jesus had commanded the impure spirit to come out of the man. Many times it had seized him, and though he was chained hand and foot and kept under guard, he had broken his chains and had been driven by the demon into solitary places.

³⁰Jesus asked him, 'What is your name?'

'Legion,' he replied, because many demons had gone into him. ³¹And they begged Jesus repeatedly not to order them to go into the Abyss.

³²A large herd of pigs was feeding there on the hillside. The demons begged Jesus to let them go into the pigs, and he gave them permission. ³³When the demons came out of the man, they went into the pigs, and the herd rushed down the steep bank into the lake and was drowned.

³⁴When those tending the pigs saw what had happened, they ran off and reported this in the town and countryside, ³⁵and the people went out to see what had happened. When they came to Jesus, they found the man from whom the demons had gone out, sitting at Jesus' feet, dressed and in his right mind; and they were afraid. ³⁶Those who had seen it told the people how the demon-possessed man had been cured. ³⁷Then all the people of the region of the Gerasenes asked Jesus to leave them, because they were overcome with fear. So he got into the boat and left.

³⁸The man from whom the demons had gone out begged to go with him, but Jesus sent him away, saying, ³⁹'Return home and tell how much God has done for you.' So the man went away and told all over the town how much Jesus had done for him.

Jesus raises a dead girl and heals a sick woman

⁴⁰Now when Jesus returned, a crowd welcomed him, for they were all expecting him. ⁴¹Then a man named Jairus, a synagogue leader, came and fell at Jesus' feet, pleading with him to come to his house ⁴²because his only daughter, a girl of about twelve, was dying.

As Jesus was on his way, the crowds almost crushed him. ⁴³And a woman was there who had been subject to bleeding for twelve years,ᶜ but no one could heal her. ⁴⁴She came up behind him and touched the edge of his cloak, and immediately her bleeding stopped.

⁴⁵'Who touched me?' Jesus asked.

When they all denied it, Peter said, 'Master, the people are crowding and pressing against you.'

⁴⁶But Jesus said, 'Someone touched me; I know that power has gone out from me.'

⁴⁷Then the woman, seeing that she could not go unnoticed, came trembling and fell at his feet. In the presence of all the people, she told why she had touched

ᵇ 26 Some manuscripts *Gadarenes*; other manuscripts *Gergesenes*; also in verse 37

ᶜ 43 Many manuscripts *years, and she had spent all she had on doctors* him and how she had been instantly healed. 48 Then he said to her, 'Daughter, your faith has healed you. Go in peace.'

49 While Jesus was still speaking, someone came from the house of Jairus, the synagogue leader. 'Your daughter is dead,' he said. 'Don't bother the teacher anymore.'

50 Hearing this, Jesus said to Jairus,

'Don't be afraid; just believe, and she will be healed.'

51 When he arrived at the house of Jairus, he did not let anyone go in with him except Peter, John and James, and the child's father and mother. 52 Meanwhile, all the people were wailing and mourning for her. 'Stop wailing,' Jesus said. 'She is not dead but asleep.'

HEALING & MIRACLES 7

When healing doesn't come right away

Luke 8:49–56 tells the story of Jairus and his young daughter, who was dying. Luke makes it clear that it was important that Jairus went to Jesus himself. Jairus was a wealthy man, and it would have been normal and easy for him to have sent someone to fetch Jesus. Yet in his desperation and love for his daughter, he was not too proud to go in person and beg Jesus for help.

That's not the only example of Jairus's lack of pride, though. Think of how he must have felt as Jesus stopped on the way to take care of some other things – including healing another person! Time was ticking and Jairus was scared, yet Jesus didn't rush. Jairus had a choice: was he going to get angry and demand that Jesus hurry up, or was he going to trust him?

Before they leave, Jesus turns to Jairus and says to him in effect, 'Don't stop believing.' He sees and understands the worry and concern this father is feeling, and he encourages him. So he says, 'I know what's going on with your daughter, and I know you're anxious, but don't stop believing.' Jesus understands our pain and frustration when we don't see healing the minute we want it.

We have a choice to make when we don't see things we want happening, just as Jairus had to choose to keep on believing. There will be many times in our lives when we have to choose to believe, and many times these will be in our most desperate moments. That's what faith is. Faith is choosing to believe not because we see, but because we trust. We wouldn't need faith if we saw and understood everything. We have to hold on and remember that it's always God's desire to heal. We don't know when the healing will actually take place, but this story shows that Jesus encourages us not to give up.

Even when things look bad, don't stop trusting and believing that not only does Jesus care, but his desire is to heal. Healing may come today, tomorrow, next year, or when we're with Jesus, but we will never know unless we keep believing and keep asking.

Christy Wimber

◀◀ Luke 11   Mark 5:25–34 ▶▶

53They laughed at him, knowing that she was dead. 54But he took her by the hand and said, 'My child, get up!' 55Her spirit returned, and at once she stood up. Then Jesus told them to give her something to eat. 56Her parents were astonished, but he ordered them not to tell anyone what had happened.

Jesus sends out the Twelve

9 When Jesus had called the Twelve together, he gave them power and authority to drive out all demons and to cure diseases, 2and he sent them out to proclaim the kingdom of God and to heal those who were ill. 3He told them: 'Take nothing for the journey – no staff, no bag, no bread, no money, no extra shirt. 4Whatever house you enter, stay there until you leave that town. 5If people do not welcome you, leave their town and shake the dust off your feet as a testimony against them.' 6So they set out and went from village to village, proclaiming

---

NATURALLY SUPERNATURAL 2

JESUS' MISSION FOR HIS DISCIPLES AND US

Jesus gave his disciples a mission (Luke 9:1–6): he wanted them to carry on doing the things he had been doing. He knew his time on earth was short, so he gave them instructions for how to continue his work after he was gone.

He asks us to continue this mission today: to tell people about the kingdom of God, to heal the sick and to drive out demons. We should be proclaiming good news, but hand in hand with delivering good news. The good news that God loves us enough to get involved in our life now. He's not far off, he's close, and he wants us to be healed.

We might look at ourselves and think, 'How could we possibly do any of that?' And rightly so. We don't do it in our own strength (we wouldn't get very far). Jesus gives us the *'power and authority'* (v. 1) to do these things. Most of us have no idea of the authority we walk in. We tiptoe about timidly, forgetting that we are sons and daughters of the Creator of the universe, the King of all kings, the one who can do anything. Literally anything. But if we know that he gives us his authority, we start to think about things differently. We pray knowing we can tell a broken leg to be healed and it can be healed. We know we can rely on him to give us the words to use to proclaim his kingdom. We know we can trust him to help us bring people out of darkness. Jesus told his disciples not to take anything with them on their journey. The whole mission required them to trust God to provide for all their needs. They had to lean on him wholeheartedly. We need to do the same if we want to continue the mission.

Luke goes straight on to tell the story of Jesus feeding more than five thousand people with just a few loaves and fish. What a reminder about what God can do when we offer him the little we have! Let's trust in the authority of our Saviour and be bold to live out the mission he left for us.

Mike Pilavachi

 Luke 7:11–14   Joel 2:28

the good news and healing people everywhere.

7 Now Herod the tetrarch heard about all that was going on. And he was perplexed because some were saying that John had been raised from the dead, 8 others that Elijah had appeared, and still others that one of the prophets of long ago had come back to life. 9 But Herod said, 'I beheaded John. Who, then, is this I hear such things about?' And he tried to see him.

Jesus feeds the five thousand

10 When the apostles returned, they reported to Jesus what they had done. Then he took them with him and they withdrew by themselves to a town called Bethsaida, 11 but the crowds learned about it and followed him. He welcomed them and spoke to them about the kingdom of God, and healed those who needed healing.

12 Late in the afternoon the Twelve came to him and said, 'Send the crowd away so they can go to the surrounding villages and countryside and find food and lodging, because we are in a remote place here.'

13 He replied, 'You give them something to eat.'

They answered, 'We have only five loaves of bread and two fish – unless we go and buy food for all this crowd.' 14 (About five thousand men were there.)

But he said to his disciples, 'Make them sit down in groups of about fifty each.' 15 The disciples did so, and everyone sat down. 16 Taking the five loaves and the two fish and looking up to heaven, he gave thanks and broke them. Then he gave them to the disciples to distribute to the people. 17 They all ate and were satisfied, and the disciples picked up twelve basketfuls of broken pieces that were left over.

Peter declares that Jesus is the Messiah

18 Once when Jesus was praying in private and his disciples were with him, he asked them, 'Who do the crowds say I am?'

19 They replied, 'Some say John the Baptist; others say Elijah; and still others, that one of the prophets of long ago has come back to life.'

20 'But what about you?' he asked. 'Who do you say I am?'

Peter answered, 'God's Messiah.'

Jesus predicts his death

21 Jesus strictly warned them not to tell this to anyone. 22 And he said, 'The Son of Man must suffer many things and be rejected by the elders, the chief priests and the teachers of the law, and he must be killed and on the third day be raised to life.'

23 Then he said to them all: 'Whoever wants to be my disciple must deny themselves and take up their cross daily and follow me. 24 For whoever wants to save their life will lose it, but whoever loses their life for me will save it. 25 What good is it for someone to gain the whole world, and yet lose or forfeit their very self? 26 Whoever is ashamed of me and my words, the Son of Man will be ashamed of them when he comes in his glory and in the glory of the Father and of the holy angels.

27 'Truly I tell you, some who are standing here will not taste death before they see the kingdom of God.'

The transfiguration

28 About eight days after Jesus said this, he took Peter, John and James with him and went up onto a mountain to pray. 29 As he was praying, the appearance of his face changed, and his clothes became as bright as a flash of lightning. 30 Two men, Moses and Elijah, appeared in glorious splendour, talking with Jesus. 31 They spoke about his departure,[a] which he was about to bring to fulfilment at Jerusalem. 32 Peter and his companions were very sleepy, but when they became fully awake, they saw his glory and the two men standing with him. 33 As the men were leaving Jesus, Peter said to him, 'Master, it is good for us to be here. Let us put up three shelters – one for you, one for Moses and one

---

a 31 Greek *exodos*

for Elijah.' (He did not know what he was saying.)

³⁴While he was speaking, a cloud appeared and covered them, and they were afraid as they entered the cloud. ³⁵A voice came from the cloud, saying, 'This is my Son, whom I have chosen; listen to him.' ³⁶When the voice had spoken, they found that Jesus was alone. The disciples kept this to themselves and did not tell anyone at that time what they had seen.

Jesus heals a demon-possessed boy

³⁷The next day, when they came down from the mountain, a large crowd met him. ³⁸A man in the crowd called out, 'Teacher, I beg you to look at my son, for he is my only child. ³⁹A spirit seizes him and he suddenly screams; it throws him into convulsions so that he foams at the mouth. It scarcely ever leaves him and is destroying him. ⁴⁰I begged your disciples to drive it out, but they could not.'

⁴¹'You unbelieving and perverse generation,' Jesus replied, 'how long shall I stay with you and put up with you? Bring your son here.'

⁴²Even while the boy was coming, the demon threw him to the ground in a convulsion. But Jesus rebuked the impure spirit, healed the boy and gave him back to his father. ⁴³And they were all amazed at the greatness of God.

Jesus predicts his death a second time

While everyone was marvelling at all that Jesus did, he said to his disciples, ⁴⁴'Listen carefully to what I am about to tell you: the Son of Man is going to be delivered into the hands of men.' ⁴⁵But they did not understand what this meant. It was hidden from them, so that they did not grasp it, and they were afraid to ask him about it.

⁴⁶An argument started among the disciples as to which of them would be the greatest. ⁴⁷Jesus, knowing their thoughts, took a little child and made him stand beside him. ⁴⁸Then he said to them, 'Whoever welcomes this little child in my name welcomes me; and whoever welcomes me welcomes the one who sent me. For it is the one who is least among you all who is the greatest.'

⁴⁹'Master,' said John, 'we saw someone driving out demons in your name and we tried to stop him, because he is not one of us.'

⁵⁰'Do not stop him,' Jesus said, 'for whoever is not against you is for you.'

Samaritan opposition

⁵¹As the time approached for him to be taken up to heaven, Jesus resolutely set out for Jerusalem. ⁵²And he sent messengers on ahead, who went into a Samaritan village to get things ready for him; ⁵³but the people there did not welcome him, because he was heading for Jerusalem. ⁵⁴When the disciples James and John saw this, they asked, 'Lord, do you want us to call fire down from heaven to destroy them*b*?' ⁵⁵But Jesus turned and rebuked them. ⁵⁶Then he and his disciples went to another village.

The cost of following Jesus

⁵⁷As they were walking along the road, a man said to him, 'I will follow you wherever you go.'

⁵⁸Jesus replied, 'Foxes have dens and birds have nests, but the Son of Man has nowhere to lay his head.'

⁵⁹He said to another man, 'Follow me.'

But he replied, 'Lord, first let me go and bury my father.'

⁶⁰Jesus said to him, 'Let the dead bury their own dead, but you go and proclaim the kingdom of God.'

⁶¹Still another said, 'I will follow you, Lord; but first let me go back and say goodbye to my family.'

⁶²Jesus replied, 'No one who puts a hand to the plough and looks back is fit for service in the kingdom of God.'

Jesus sends out the seventy-two

10 After this the Lord appointed seventy-two*a* others and sent them two by two ahead of him to every town and place where he was about to go. ²He

---

b 54 Some manuscripts *them, just as Elijah did*
a 1 Some manuscripts *seventy*; also in verse 17

told them, 'The harvest is plentiful, but the workers are few. Ask the Lord of the harvest, therefore, to send out workers into his harvest field. ³Go! I am sending you out like lambs among wolves. ⁴Do not take a purse or bag or sandals; and do not greet anyone on the road.

⁵'When you enter a house, first say, "Peace to this house." ⁶If someone who promotes peace is there, your peace will rest on them; if not, it will return to you. ⁷Stay there, eating and drinking whatever they give you, for the worker deserves his wages. Do not move around from house to house.

⁸'When you enter a town and are welcomed, eat what is offered to you. ⁹Heal those there who are ill and tell them, "The kingdom of God has come near to you." ¹⁰But when you enter a town and are not welcomed, go into its streets and say, ¹¹"Even the dust of your town we wipe from our feet as a warning to you. Yet be sure of this: the kingdom of God has come near." ¹²I tell you, it will be more bearable on that day for Sodom than for that town.

¹³'Woe to you, Chorazin! Woe to you, Bethsaida! For if the miracles that were performed in you had been performed in Tyre and Sidon, they would have repented long ago, sitting in sackcloth and ashes. ¹⁴But it will be more bearable for Tyre and Sidon at the judgment than for you. ¹⁵And you, Capernaum, will you be lifted to the heavens? No, you will go down to Hades.ᵇ

ᵇ 15 That is, the realm of the dead

EVANGELISM 3

Sent

The passage in Luke 10:1–4 is worth taking some time over. Just in these few sentences Jesus introduces some really thought-provoking concepts. I want to look at the fact that these people were *sent*.

Back when I was sixteen, I used to share a room with my fourteen-year-old brother. Once we got into a fight. Fists were thumping and it was all quite nasty. At that point our little sister came to the door and told us to stop. My brother and I looked at this little girl, laughed and then got stuck back into the brawl. She then said these words: 'Dad sent me.' As soon as we heard that powerful phrase, the fight was over. She may have been a little girl with no physical ability to stop the fight, but she was sent by my dad and therefore carried his authority.

When we looked at Acts 1:8, we saw that we can have the Holy Spirit in us and can carry the power of God. We also carry his authority. We may feel feeble and wonder what difference we can make. We may hear some strong anti-God arguments and feel out of our depth. We may appear to others to be weak – and that's because, on our own, we are! But in our weakness God is strong, and we also come in his strength and with his authority. In Matthew 28:18 Jesus says, *'All authority in heaven and on earth has been given to me.'* We have been sent by the one who holds supreme power. We can do more than stop a fight. We can save lives!

Mark Ritchie

 Matthew 9:16   Mark 2:1–12

16 'Whoever listens to you listens to me; whoever rejects you rejects me; but whoever rejects me rejects him who sent me.'

17 The seventy-two returned with joy and said, 'Lord, even the demons submit to us in your name.'

18 He replied, 'I saw Satan fall like lightning from heaven. **19** I have given you authority to trample on snakes and scorpions and to overcome all the power of the enemy; nothing will harm you. **20** However, do not rejoice that the spirits submit to you, but rejoice that your names are written in heaven.'

21 At that time Jesus, full of joy through the Holy Spirit, said, 'I praise you, Father, Lord of heaven and earth, because you have hidden these things from the wise and learned, and revealed them to little children. Yes, Father, for this is what you were pleased to do.

22 'All things have been committed to me by my Father. No one knows who the Son is except the Father, and no one knows who the Father is except the Son and those to whom the Son chooses to reveal him.'

23 Then he turned to his disciples and said privately, 'Blessed are the eyes that see what you see. **24** For I tell you that many prophets and kings wanted to see what you see but did not see it, and to hear what you hear but did not hear it.'

The parable of the good Samaritan

25 On one occasion an expert in the law stood up to test Jesus. 'Teacher,' he asked, 'what must I do to inherit eternal life?'

26 'What is written in the Law?' he replied. 'How do you read it?'

27 He answered, ' "Love the Lord your God with all your heart and with all your soul and with all your strength and with all your mind"*c*; and, "Love your neighbour as yourself."*d*'

28 'You have answered correctly,' Jesus replied. 'Do this and you will live.'

29 But he wanted to justify himself, so he asked Jesus, 'And who is my neighbour?'

30 In reply Jesus said: 'A man was going down from Jerusalem to Jericho, when he was attacked by robbers. They stripped him of his clothes, beat him and went away, leaving him half-dead. **31** A priest happened to be going down the same road, and when he saw the man, he passed by on the other side. **32** So too, a Levite, when he came to the place and saw him, passed by on the other side. **33** But a Samaritan, as he travelled, came where the man was; and when he saw him, he took pity on him. **34** He went to him and bandaged his wounds, pouring on oil and wine. Then he put the man on his own donkey, brought him to an inn and took care of him. **35** The next day he took out two denarii*e* and gave them to the innkeeper. "Look after him," he said, "and when I return, I will reimburse you for any extra expense you may have."

36 'Which of these three do you think was a neighbour to the man who fell into the hands of robbers?'

37 The expert in the law replied, 'The one who had mercy on him.'

Jesus told him, 'Go and do likewise.'

At the home of Martha and Mary

38 As Jesus and his disciples were on their way, he came to a village where a woman named Martha opened her home to him. **39** She had a sister called Mary, who sat at the Lord's feet listening to what he said. **40** But Martha was distracted by all the preparations that had to be made. She came to him and asked, 'Lord, don't you care that my sister has left me to do the work by myself? Tell her to help me!'

41 'Martha, Martha,' the Lord answered, 'you are worried and upset about many things, **42** but few things are needed – or indeed only one.*f* Mary has chosen what is better, and it will not be taken away from her.'

---

c 27 Deut. 6:5
d 27 Lev. 19:18

e 35 A denarius was the usual daily wage of a day labourer (see Matt. 20:2).
f 42 Some manuscripts *but only one thing is needed*

Jesus' teaching on prayer

11 One day Jesus was praying in a certain place. When he finished, one of his disciples said to him, 'Lord, teach us to pray, just as John taught his disciples.'

² He said to them, 'When you pray, say:

' "Father,*a*
hallowed be your name,
your kingdom come.*b*
³ Give us each day our daily bread.

⁴ Forgive us our sins,
for we also forgive everyone who
sins against us.*c*
And lead us not into temptation." ' *d*

⁵ Then Jesus said to them, 'Suppose you have a friend, and you go to him at midnight and say, "Friend, lend me three loaves of bread; ⁶ a friend of mine on a journey has come to me, and I have no food to offer him." ⁷ And suppose the one

---

a 2 Some manuscripts *Our Father in heaven*
b 2 Some manuscripts *come. May your will be done on earth as it is in heaven.*

c 4 Greek *everyone who is indebted to us*
d 4 Some manuscripts *temptation, but deliver us from the evil one*

EVANGELISM 6

Whatever it takes

Let's focus on the Samaritan in the parable told in Luke 10:30–37. Imagine this story as a picture of our world today, replacing the broken man with our broken generation. There are people who see the pain going on around them but, for whatever reason, choose not to get involved. They hide their eyes from the brokenness and don't want to get their hands dirty. Are we willing to be like the Samaritan and step out of our comfort zone to help bring healing to the broken?

The Samaritan seemed to have an attitude that said, 'I will do whatever it takes to see healing come to this guy. It doesn't matter how much it costs – I will pay it.' Ask yourself, 'Do I have the same attitude? If it cost me to carry the presence of God to the lost, would I turn away?' It could cost us in time and convenience, but are we willing to say that it's a cost worth paying?

I was inspired by a couple of teenagers I met last year. These two sisters were at a tough school and they were determined to tell their friends about Jesus. Lots of their fellow pupils didn't like this and put together a hate petition which many signed. I'm sure that the petition hurt the girls, as it would hurt anyone, but the fact that they had led one of their friends to Jesus meant they knew it was worth it. They decided to do whatever it takes to get our generation in front of Jesus. Wow! What a challenge! Are we willing to pay the price with our image or our street cred?

Do I have the spirit of the Good Samaritan? It's a spirit that says, 'I will do whatever it takes to see the broken healed and the lost brought back to Jesus. Father, with your help, I'm willing to pay the price.'

Mark Ritchie

 Acts 26:28–29   1 Peter 3:15 ⏩

inside answers, "Don't bother me. The door is already locked, and my children and I are in bed. I can't get up and give you anything." ⁸ I tell you, even though he will not get up and give you the bread because of friendship, yet because of your shameless audacity⁰ he will surely get up and give you as much as you need.

⁹ 'So I say to you: ask and it will be given to you; seek and you will find; knock and the door will be opened to you. ¹⁰ For everyone who asks receives; the one who seeks finds; and to the one who knocks, the door will be opened.

¹¹ 'Which of you fathers, if your son asks for⁰ a fish, will give him a snake instead? ¹² Or if he asks for an egg, will give him a scorpion? ¹³ If you then, though you are evil, know how to give good gifts to your children, how much more will your

_____
e 8   Or yet to preserve his good name

_____
f 11   Some manuscripts *for bread, will give him a stone? Or if he asks for*

ASKING FOR THE HOLY SPIRIT

'Please, Daddy. Please! Please! Please! Pleeeease!' A scene we have all witnessed at the shops or on the beach a hundred times.

Parents find it hard to resist when children ask, ask and ask again – particularly if their children are asking for something they already want to give them.

So why am I telling you this? Look at Luke 11:1–13, particularly verse 9. The words 'ask', 'seek' and 'knock' are in an interesting tense in the original language that's difficult to translate into English. It could be written as, *'Ask and ask and keep on asking, and it will be given to you.'* Then again in verse 13: *'...how much more will your Father in heaven give the Holy Spirit to those who ask and ask and keep on asking him!'*

The most basic prayer is to ask and ask Father God to give you the Holy Spirit. Our greatest need is to know God inside, upon us and overflowing us, and for his presence to set us apart from our sin and into his service. Then our hearts are his and the life and prayers that flow from us are in tune with his purpose. And the great thing is that the key to knowing God like this is not endless religious discipline, but simply trusting Father God enough to ask and ask him, because God loves you!

So let's do it now! Take a few moments to prayerfully ask your Father in Heaven to give you the Holy Spirit. Jesus clearly says that the Father always wants to answer that prayer with a resounding 'Yes!' Every morning we should ask. Every afternoon we should ask. Every evening and even every night we should ask. Ask! Ask and ask again to have more of the Holy Spirit's presence. Every time the Father will be thrilled. Every time he will move heaven and earth to fill you with his Spirit, mend you and empower you, because that's what he delights to do.

Hugo Anson

Luke 15:21

Father in heaven give the Holy Spirit to those who ask him!'

Jesus and Beelzebul

14 Jesus was driving out a demon that was mute. When the demon left, the man who had been mute spoke, and the crowd was amazed. 15 But some of them said, 'By Beelzebul, the prince of demons, he is driving out demons.' 16 Others tested him by asking for a sign from heaven.

17 Jesus knew their thoughts and said to them: 'Any kingdom divided against itself will be ruined, and a house divided against itself will fall. 18 If Satan is divided against himself, how can his kingdom stand? I say this because you claim that I drive out demons by Beelzebul. 19 Now if I drive out

HEALING & MIRACLES 6

How healing can impact many

I remember a few years ago watching our kids' church re-enact the story of how Jesus healed Lazarus (John 11). My son was in the drama and all the kids wrapped him up in toilet paper so that he looked like a mummy. It was so funny, but they all understood what Jesus had done. Lazarus was no stranger to Jesus, they had spent time together and Lazarus was a friend. Jesus gets the news: *'The one you love is ill'* (v. 3).

Fear is the emotion running through this entire story – the fear of Lazarus dying. Fear will always try to get our focus on the circumstances of what is or isn't happening, rather than on Jesus' promises to us. Jesus says to his disciples, *'This illness will not end in death'* (v. 4) – but then he stays where he is for two more days, and Lazarus dies. I'm sure the disciples had questions. Why didn't Jesus just heal Lazarus from afar? I mean, isn't this one of the ways we show someone we love them: how we respond to them in their time of need?

In this case, it's not that Jesus doesn't have the time, desire or power to heal – he loves Lazarus, and he weeps when he goes to the grave – but he knows that every healing allows God's glory to be revealed. You see, God's delays aren't signs of failure, they are an opportunity to reveal his power and glory. Nothing Lazarus's family and friends suffered was wasted, and it's the same in our lives. Often it's in the suffering, when we're waiting for God to act, that we can reflect and be the most effective witness of his love.

There's a great quotation that says, 'Never doubt in the darkness what you believed in the light.' Sometimes we have to walk through things that seem impossible, and these are the times to remember and hold onto what God has already revealed to us. God's timing is there for a reason. Don't get caught up in how healing takes place, but rather remember that God is in control. When you encounter a tough circumstance, the way you walk it out shows your faith: even in suffering where pain and hardship are present, your actions have the power to bring glory to God.

Christy Wimber

 Mark 9:14–32   Luke 8:40–56

demons by Beelzebul, by whom do your followers drive them out? So then, they will be your judges. **20** But if I drive out demons by the finger of God, then the kingdom of God has come upon you.

21 'When a strong man, fully armed, guards his own house, his possessions are safe. **22** But when someone stronger attacks and overpowers him, he takes away the armour in which the man trusted and divides up his plunder.

23 'Whoever is not with me is against me, and whoever does not gather with me scatters.

24 'When an impure spirit comes out of a person, it goes through arid places seeking rest and does not find it. Then it says, "I will return to the house I left." **25** When it arrives, it finds the house swept clean and put in order. **26** Then it goes and takes seven other spirits more wicked than itself, and they go in and live there. And the final condition of that person is worse than the first.'

27 As Jesus was saying these things, a woman in the crowd called out, 'Blessed is the mother who gave you birth and nursed you.'

28 He replied, 'Blessed rather are those who hear the word of God and obey it.'

The sign of Jonah

29 As the crowds increased, Jesus said, 'This is a wicked generation. It asks for a sign, but none will be given it except the sign of Jonah. **30** For as Jonah was a sign to the Ninevites, so also will the Son of Man be to this generation. **31** The Queen of the South will rise at the judgment with the people of this generation and condemn them, for she came from the ends of the earth to listen to Solomon's wisdom; and now something greater than Solomon is here. **32** The men of Nineveh will stand up at the judgment with this generation and condemn it, for they repented at the preaching of Jonah; and now something greater than Jonah is here.

The lamp of the body

33 'No one lights a lamp and puts it in a place where it will be hidden, or under a bowl. Instead they put it on its stand, so that those who come in may see the light. **34** Your eye is the lamp of your body. When your eyes are healthy,*g* your whole body also is full of light. But when they are unhealthy,*h* your body also is full of darkness. **35** See to it, then, that the light within you is not darkness. **36** Therefore, if your whole body is full of light, and no part of it dark, it will be just as full of light as when a lamp shines its light on you.'

Woes on the Pharisees and the experts in the law

37 When Jesus had finished speaking, a Pharisee invited him to eat with him; so he went in and reclined at the table. **38** But the Pharisee was surprised when he noticed that Jesus did not first wash before the meal.

39 Then the Lord said to him, 'Now then, you Pharisees clean the outside of the cup and dish, but inside you are full of greed and wickedness. **40** You foolish people! Did not the one who made the outside make the inside also? **41** But now as for what is inside you – be generous to the poor, and everything will be clean for you.

42 'Woe to you Pharisees, because you give God a tenth of your mint, rue and all other kinds of garden herbs, but you neglect justice and the love of God. You should have practised the latter without leaving the former undone.

43 'Woe to you Pharisees, because you love the most important seats in the synagogues and respectful greetings in the market-places.

44 'Woe to you, because you are like unmarked graves, which people walk over without knowing it.'

45 One of the experts in the law answered him, 'Teacher, when you say these things, you insult us also.'

46 Jesus replied, 'And you experts in the law, woe to you, because you load people down with burdens they can hardly carry, and you yourselves will not lift one finger to help them.

---

g 34 The Greek for *healthy* here implies *generous*.
h 34 The Greek for *unhealthy* here implies *stingy*.

47 'Woe to you, because you build tombs for the prophets, and it was your ancestors who killed them. 48 So you testify that you approve of what your ancestors did; they killed the prophets, and you build their tombs. 49 Because of this, God in his wisdom said, "I will send them prophets and apostles, some of whom they will kill and others they will persecute." 50 Therefore this generation will be held responsible for the blood of all the prophets that has been shed since the beginning of the world, 51 from the blood of Abel to the blood of Zechariah, who was killed between the altar and the sanctuary. Yes, I tell you, this generation will be held responsible for it all.

52 'Woe to you experts in the law, because you have taken away the key to knowledge. You yourselves have not entered, and you have hindered those who were entering.'

53 When Jesus went outside, the Pharisees and the teachers of the law began to oppose him fiercely and to besiege him with questions, 54 waiting to catch him in something he might say.

Warnings and encouragements

12 Meanwhile, when a crowd of many thousands had gathered, so that they were trampling on one another, Jesus began to speak first to his disciples, saying: 'Be*a* on your guard against the yeast of the Pharisees, which is hypocrisy. 2 There is nothing concealed that will not be disclosed, or hidden that will not be made known. 3 What you have said in the dark will be heard in the daylight, and what you have whispered in the ear in the inner rooms will be proclaimed from the roofs.

4 'I tell you, my friends, do not be afraid of those who kill the body and after that can do no more. 5 But I will show you whom you should fear: fear him who, after your body has been killed, has authority to throw you into hell. Yes, I tell you, fear him. 6 Are not five sparrows sold for two pennies? Yet not one of them is forgotten by God. 7 Indeed, the very hairs of your head are all numbered. Don't be afraid; you are worth more than many sparrows.

8 'I tell you, whoever publicly acknowledges me before others, the Son of Man will also acknowledge before the angels of God. 9 But whoever disowns me before others will be disowned before the angels of God. 10 And everyone who speaks a word against the Son of Man will be forgiven, but anyone who blasphemes against the Holy Spirit will not be forgiven.

11 'When you are brought before synagogues, rulers and authorities, do not worry about how you will defend yourselves or what you will say, 12 for the Holy Spirit will teach you at that time what you should say.'

FAVOURITE VERSES
Luke 4:18–19

The Spirit of the Lord is on me, because he has anointed me to proclaim good news to the poor. He has sent me to proclaim freedom for the prisoners and recovery of sight for the blind, to set the oppressed free, to proclaim the year of the Lord's favour.

This verse sums up Jesus' ministry brilliantly, reminds me of God's love for everyone and inspires me to live my life doing the same things.

Charlotte, 18

The parable of the rich fool

13 Someone in the crowd said to him, 'Teacher, tell my brother to divide the inheritance with me.'

14 Jesus replied, 'Man, who appointed me a judge or an arbiter between you?' 15 Then he said to them, 'Watch out! Be on

---

a 1 Or speak to his disciples, saying: 'First of all, be

your guard against all kinds of greed; life does not consist in an abundance of possessions.'

16 And he told them this parable: 'The ground of a certain rich man yielded an abundant harvest. 17 He thought to himself, "What shall I do? I have no place to store my crops."

18 'Then he said, "This is what I'll do. I will tear down my barns and build bigger ones, and there I will store my surplus grain. 19 And I'll say to myself, 'You have plenty of grain laid up for many years. Take life easy; eat, drink and be merry.' "

20 'But God said to him, "You fool! This very night your life will be demanded from you. Then who will get what you have prepared for yourself?"

21 'This is how it will be with whoever stores up things for themselves but is not rich towards God.'

Do not worry

22 Then Jesus said to his disciples: 'Therefore I tell you, do not worry about your life, what you will eat; or about your body, what you will wear. 23 For life is more than food, and the body more than clothes. 24 Consider the ravens: they do not sow or reap, they have no storeroom or barn; yet God feeds them. And how much more valuable you are than birds! 25 Who of you by worrying can add a single hour to your life*b*? 26 Since you cannot do this very little thing, why do you worry about the rest?

27 'Consider how the wild flowers grow. They do not labour or spin. Yet I tell you, not even Solomon in all his splendour was dressed like one of these. 28 If that is how God clothes the grass of the field, which is here today, and tomorrow is thrown into the fire, how much more will he clothe you – you of little faith! 29 And do not set your heart on what you will eat or drink; do not worry about it. 30 For the pagan world runs after all such things, and your Father knows that you need them. 31 But seek his kingdom, and these things will be given to you as well.

b 25 Or single cubit to your height

32 'Do not be afraid, little flock, for your Father has been pleased to give you the kingdom. 33 Sell your possessions and give to the poor. Provide purses for yourselves that will not wear out, a treasure in heaven that will never fail, where no thief comes near and no moth destroys. 34 For where your treasure is, there your heart will be also.

Watchfulness

35 'Be dressed ready for service and keep your lamps burning, 36 like servants waiting for their master to return from a wedding banquet, so that when he comes and knocks they can immediately open the door for him. 37 It will be good for those servants whose master finds them watching when he comes. Truly I tell you, he will dress himself to serve, will make them recline at the table and will come and wait on them. 38 It will be good for those servants whose master finds them ready, even if he comes in the middle of the night or towards daybreak. 39 But understand this: if the owner of the house had known at what hour the thief was coming, he would not have let his house be broken into. 40 You also must be ready, because the Son of Man will come at an hour when you do not expect him.'

41 Peter asked, 'Lord, are you telling this parable to us, or to everyone?'

42 The Lord answered, 'Who then is the faithful and wise manager, whom the master puts in charge of his servants to give them their food allowance at the proper time? 43 It will be good for that servant whom the master finds doing so when he returns. 44 Truly I tell you, he will put him in charge of all his possessions. 45 But suppose the servant says to himself, "My master is taking a long time in coming," and he then begins to beat the other servants, both men and women, and to eat and drink and get drunk. 46 The master of that servant will come on a day when he does not expect him and at an hour he is not aware of. He will cut him to pieces and assign him a place with the unbelievers.

47 'The servant who knows the master's

will and does not get ready or does not do what the master wants will be beaten with many blows. 48 But the one who does not know and does things deserving punishment will be beaten with few blows. From everyone who has been given much, much will be demanded; and from the one who has been entrusted with much, much more will be asked.

Not peace but division

49 'I have come to bring fire on the earth, and how I wish it were already kindled! 50 But I have a baptism to undergo, and what constraint I am under until it is completed! 51 Do you think I came to bring peace on earth? No, I tell you, but division. 52 From now on there will be five in one family divided against each other, three against two and two against three. 53 They will be divided, father against son and son against father, mother against daughter and daughter against mother, mother-in-law against daughter-in-law and daughter-in-law against mother-in-law.'

Interpreting the times

54 He said to the crowd: 'When you see a cloud rising in the west, immediately you say, "It's going to rain," and it does. 55 And when the south wind blows, you say, "It's going to be hot," and it is. 56 Hypocrites! You know how to interpret the appearance of the earth and the sky. How is it that you don't know how to interpret this present time?

57 'Why don't you judge for yourselves what is right? 58 As you are going with your adversary to the magistrate, try hard to be reconciled on the way, or your adversary may drag you off to the judge, and the judge turn you over to the officer, and the officer throw you into prison. 59 I tell you, you will not get out until you have paid the last penny.'

Repent or perish

13 Now there were some present at that time who told Jesus about the Galileans whose blood Pilate had mixed with their sacrifices. 2 Jesus answered, 'Do you think that these Galileans were worse sinners than all the other Galileans because they suffered this way? 3 I tell you, no! But unless you repent, you too will all perish. 4 Or those eighteen who died when the tower in Siloam fell on them – do you think they were more guilty than all the others living in Jerusalem? 5 I tell you, no! But unless you repent, you too will all perish.'

6 Then he told this parable: 'A man had a fig-tree growing in his vineyard, and he went to look for fruit on it but did not find any. 7 So he said to the man who took care of the vineyard, "For three years now I've been coming to look for fruit on this fig-tree and haven't found any. Cut it down! Why should it use up the soil?"

8 ' "Sir," the man replied, "leave it alone for one more year, and I'll dig round it and fertilise it. 9 If it bears fruit next year, fine! If not, then cut it down." '

Jesus heals a crippled woman on the Sabbath

10 On a Sabbath Jesus was teaching in one of the synagogues, 11 and a woman was there who had been crippled by a spirit for eighteen years. She was bent over and could not straighten up at all. 12 When Jesus saw her, he called her forward and said to her, 'Woman, you are set free from your infirmity.' 13 Then he put his hands on her, and immediately she straightened up and praised God.

14 Indignant because Jesus had healed on the Sabbath, the synagogue leader said to the people, 'There are six days for work. So come and be healed on those days, not on the Sabbath.'

15 The Lord answered him, 'You hypocrites! Doesn't each of you on the Sabbath untie your ox or donkey from the stall and lead it out to give it water? 16 Then should not this woman, a daughter of Abraham, whom Satan has kept bound for eighteen long years, be set free on the Sabbath day from what bound her?'

17 When he said this, all his opponents were humiliated, but the people were delighted with all the wonderful things he was doing.

The parables of the mustard seed and the yeast

18Then Jesus asked, 'What is the kingdom of God like? What shall I compare it to? **19**It is like a mustard seed, which a man took and planted in his garden. It grew and became a tree, and the birds perched in its branches.'

20Again he asked, 'What shall I compare the kingdom of God to? **21**It is like yeast that a woman took and mixed into about thirty kilograms of flour until it worked all through the dough.'

The narrow door

22Then Jesus went through the towns and villages, teaching as he made his way to Jerusalem. **23**Someone asked him, 'Lord, are only a few people going to be saved?'

He said to them, **24**'Make every effort to enter through the narrow door, because many, I tell you, will try to enter and will not be able to. **25**Once the owner of the house gets up and closes the door, you will stand outside knocking and pleading, "Sir, open the door for us."

'But he will answer, "I don't know you or where you come from."

26'Then you will say, "We ate and drank with you, and you taught in our streets."

27'But he will reply, "I don't know you or where you come from. Away from me, all you evildoers!"

28'There will be weeping there, and gnashing of teeth, when you see Abraham, Isaac and Jacob and all the prophets in the kingdom of God, but you yourselves thrown out. **29**People will come from east and west and north and south, and will take their places at the feast in the kingdom of God. **30**Indeed there are those who are last who will be first, and first who will be last.'

Jesus' sorrow for Jerusalem

31At that time some Pharisees came to Jesus and said to him, 'Leave this place and go somewhere else. Herod wants to kill you.'

32He replied, 'Go and tell that fox, "I will keep on driving out demons and healing people today and tomorrow, and on the third day I will reach my goal." **33**In any case, I must press on today and tomorrow and the next day – for surely no prophet can die outside Jerusalem!

34'Jerusalem, Jerusalem, you who kill the prophets and stone those sent to you, how often I have longed to gather your children together, as a hen gathers her chicks under her wings, and you were not willing. **35**Look, your house is left to you desolate. I tell you, you will not see me again until you say, "Blessed is he who comes in the name of the Lord."*a*'

Jesus at a Pharisee's house

14 One Sabbath, when Jesus went to eat in the house of a prominent Pharisee, he was being carefully watched. **2**There in front of him was a man suffering from abnormal swelling of his body. **3**Jesus asked the Pharisees and experts in the law, 'Is it lawful to heal on the Sabbath or not?' **4**But they remained silent. So taking hold of the man, he healed him and sent him on his way.

5Then he asked them, 'If one of you has a child*a* or an ox that falls into a well on the Sabbath day, will you not immediately pull it out?' **6**And they had nothing to say.

7When he noticed how the guests picked the places of honour at the table, he told them this parable: **8**'When someone invites you to a wedding feast, do not take the place of honour, for a person more distinguished than you may have been invited. **9**If so, the host who invited both of you will come and say to you, "Give this person your seat." Then, humiliated, you will have to take the least important place. **10**But when you are invited, take the lowest place, so that when your host comes, he will say to you, "Friend, move up to a better place." Then you will be honoured in the presence of all the other guests. **11**For all those who exalt themselves will be humbled, and those who humble themselves will be exalted.'

a 35 Psalm 118:26
a 5 Some manuscripts donkey

12 Then Jesus said to his host, 'When you give a luncheon or dinner, do not invite your friends, your brothers or sisters, your relatives, or your rich neighbours; if you do, they may invite you back and so you will be repaid. 13 But when you give a banquet, invite the poor, the crippled, the lame, the blind, 14 and you will be blessed. Although they cannot repay you, you will be repaid at the resurrection of the righteous.'

The parable of the great banquet

15 When one of those at the table with him heard this, he said to Jesus, 'Blessed is the one who will eat at the feast in the kingdom of God.'

16 Jesus replied: 'A certain man was preparing a great banquet and invited many guests. 17 At the time of the banquet he sent his servant to tell those who had been invited, "Come, for everything is now ready."

18 'But they all alike began to make excuses. The first said, "I have just bought a field, and I must go and see it. Please excuse me."

19 'Another said, "I have just bought five yoke of oxen, and I'm on my way to try them out. Please excuse me."

20 'Still another said, "I have just got married, so I can't come."

21 'The servant came back and reported this to his master. Then the owner of the house became angry and ordered his servant, "Go out quickly into the streets and alleys of the town and bring in the poor, the crippled, the blind and the lame."

22 ' "Sir," the servant said, "what you ordered has been done, but there is still room."

23 'Then the master told his servant, "Go out to the roads and country lanes and compel them to come in, so that my house will be full. 24 I tell you, not one of those who were invited will get a taste of my banquet." '

The cost of being a disciple

25 Large crowds were travelling with Jesus, and turning to them he said: 26 'If anyone comes to me and does not hate father and mother, wife and children, brothers and sisters – yes, even their own life – such a person cannot be my disciple. 27 And whoever does not carry their cross and follow me cannot be my disciple.

28 'Suppose one of you wants to build a tower. Won't you first sit down and estimate the cost to see if you have enough money to complete it? 29 For if you lay the foundation and are not able to finish it, everyone who sees it will ridicule you, 30 saying, "This person began to build and wasn't able to finish."

31 'Or suppose a king is about to go to war against another king. Won't he first sit down and consider whether he is able with ten thousand men to oppose the one coming against him with twenty thousand? 32 If he is not able, he will send a delegation while the other is still a long way off and will ask for terms of peace. 33 In the same way, those of you who do not give up everything you have cannot be my disciples.

34 'Salt is good, but if it loses its saltiness, how can it be made salty again? 35 It is fit neither for the soil nor for the manure heap; it is thrown out.

'Whoever has ears to hear, let them hear.'

The parable of the lost sheep

15 Now the tax collectors and sinners were all gathering round to hear Jesus. 2 But the Pharisees and the teachers of the law muttered, 'This man welcomes sinners, and eats with them.'

3 Then Jesus told them this parable: 4 'Suppose one of you has a hundred sheep and loses one of them. Doesn't he leave the ninety-nine in the open country and go after the lost sheep until he finds it? 5 And when he finds it, he joyfully puts it on his shoulders 6 and goes home. Then he calls his friends and neighbours together and says, "Rejoice with me; I have found my lost sheep." 7 I tell you that in the same way there will be more rejoicing in heaven over one sinner who repents than over ninety-nine righteous people who do not need to repent.

The parable of the lost coin

8 'Or suppose a woman has ten silver coins[a] and loses one. Doesn't she light a lamp, sweep the house and search carefully until she finds it? 9 And when she finds it, she calls her friends and neighbours together and says, "Rejoice with me; I have found my lost coin." 10 In the same way, I tell you, there is rejoicing in the presence of the angels of God over one sinner who repents.'

---

[a] 8 Greek *ten drachmas*, each worth about a day's wages

The parable of the lost son

11 Jesus continued: 'There was a man who had two sons. 12 The younger one said to his father, "Father, give me my share of the estate." So he divided his property between them.

13 'Not long after that, the younger son got together all he had, set off for a distant country and there squandered his wealth in wild living. 14 After he had spent everything, there was a severe famine in that whole country, and he began to be in need. 15 So he went and hired himself out to a citizen of that country, who sent

MONEY 2

SACRIFICE

It's much easier to be generous with people who I know will be generous back, like buying my sister a nice Christmas present and knowing she'll buy me a nice gift too. But is this generosity, or just a game of swaps? Being really generous often means sacrificing something we want for someone else – giving something away without expecting anything in return.

A friend of mine was once writing a cheque to give to a good cause, and as he started to write the numbers on the cheque he felt the Holy Spirit prompt him with a question, 'Does that number cost you something? Do you notice that number not being in your bank account?' He felt challenged to write a cheque that he knew would have an impact on his lifestyle, one that meant he had to give up something, so that someone else could have something.

Are we willing to give when we know we won't see anything in return; when it means we go without? It could be something as simple as choosing not to buy a new pair of trainers when we want them, or not buying the brand we really like, so that we have money to help someone else buy a pair of trainers they really want.

In Luke 14:12–14, Jesus' words are strong: don't just invite all your friends over for dinner, invite the people no one else invites – the awkward people at church, on your road, in your class, the people who don't have much and won't be able to invite you over for a fancy meal in return.

The challenge of this passage is twofold. First, are we willing for our generosity to cost us something, sacrificing the things we want so that someone else can have the things they need or want? Second, are we willing to give to people who can't give us something back?

Kiera Singlehurst-Phyo

 1 Chronicles 29:14

1 Timothy 6

him to his fields to feed pigs. ¹⁶He longed to fill his stomach with the pods that the pigs were eating, but no one gave him anything.

¹⁷'When he came to his senses, he said, "How many of my father's hired servants have food to spare, and here I am starving to death! ¹⁸I will set out and go back to my father and say to him: Father, I have sinned against heaven and against you. ¹⁹I am no longer worthy to be called your son; make

me like one of your hired servants." ²⁰So he got up and went to his father.

'But while he was still a long way off, his father saw him and was filled with compassion for him; he ran to his son, threw his arms round him and kissed him.

²¹'The son said to him, "Father, I have sinned against heaven and against you. I am no longer worthy to be called your son."

²²'But the father said to his servants,

PRAYER 2

FATHER I HAVE SINNED, SORRY...

My son loves to say 'sorry'. I would be pleased about that, but unfortunately he sometimes uses it as a way to get out of things when he knows he has done wrong. The moment he gets caught, he says 'sorry'. Then, if I tell him not to do it again, he'll say, 'I said "sorry". You're meant to forgive me now!'

Saying 'sorry' is not always the point. If we are really sorry for what we did, then we need to show remorse. We need to put into words or action something that shows we regret what has happened and are prepared to pay the consequences.

The younger son of the father in Luke 15:11–32 is trying to do this. At the beginning of the story he leaves home after asking for his inheritance – something he should only have received after his dad was dead. He wastes all the money and then gets into trouble. Finally, at his wits' end, he realises, 'I was better off at home.' Then he starts thinking about going home and what might happen when he gets there. He knows that he has done the wrong thing and that there is a clear barrier to being accepted again by his father. He needs to find a way to say 'sorry'.

He starts planning his 'sorry' speech while sitting in a pig pen (vv. 18–19), feeling so hungry he could happily eat the pigs' food. He plans to say, *'Father, I have sinned against heaven and against you. I am no longer worthy to be called your son; make me like one of your hired servants.'* However, when it comes to it, before he has time to get all this out, the father cuts him off after the second phrase. He never even gets to the bit about becoming a hired servant. The father has already got the message. He has seen his son walking back down the road, and he knows that he is coming to admit his sins. He knows his son is truly sorry.

Are you serious about wanting to get back with God? If you are, the first prayer you will need to find words for is one that says 'sorry'.

Hugo Anson

 Luke 11:1–13   Acts 12:1–19

"Quick! Bring the best robe and put it on him. Put a ring on his finger and sandals on his feet. 23 Bring the fattened calf and kill it. Let's have a feast and celebrate. 24 For this son of mine was dead and is alive again; he was lost and is found." So they began to celebrate.

25 'Meanwhile, the elder son was in the field. When he came near the house, he heard music and dancing. 26 So he called one of the servants and asked him what was going on. 27 "Your brother has come," he replied, "and your father has killed the fattened calf because he has him back safe and sound."

28 'The elder brother became angry and refused to go in. So his father went out and pleaded with him. 29 But he answered his father, "Look! All these years I've been slaving for you and never disobeyed your orders. Yet you never gave me even a young goat so I could celebrate with my friends. 30 But when this son of yours who has squandered your property with prostitutes comes home, you kill the fattened calf for him!"

31 ' "My son," the father said, "you are always with me, and everything I have is yours. 32 But we had to celebrate and be glad, because this brother of yours was dead and is alive again; he was lost and is found." '

The parable of the shrewd manager

16 Jesus told his disciples: 'There was a rich man whose manager was accused of wasting his possessions. 2 So he called him in and asked him, "What is this I hear about you? Give an account of your management, because you cannot be manager any longer."

3 'The manager said to himself, "What shall I do now? My master is taking away my job. I'm not strong enough to dig, and I'm ashamed to beg – 4 I know what I'll do so that, when I lose my job here, people will welcome me into their houses."

5 'So he called in each one of his master's debtors. He asked the first, "How much do you owe my master?"

6 ' "Three thousand litres of olive oil," he replied.

'The manager told him, "Take your bill, sit down quickly, and make it fifteen hundred."

7 'Then he asked the second, "And how much do you owe?"

' "Thirty tons of wheat," he replied.

'He told him, "Take your bill and make it twenty-four."

8 'The master commended the dishonest manager because he had acted shrewdly. For the people of this world are more shrewd in dealing with their own kind than are the people of the light. 9 I tell you, use worldly wealth to gain friends for yourselves, so that when it is gone, you will be welcomed into eternal dwellings.

10 'Whoever can be trusted with very little can also be trusted with much, and whoever is dishonest with very little will also be dishonest with much. 11 So if you have not been trustworthy in handling worldly wealth, who will trust you with true riches? 12 And if you have not been trustworthy with someone else's property, who will give you property of your own?

13 'No one can serve two masters. Either you will hate the one and love the other, or you will be devoted to the one and despise the other. You cannot serve both God and Money.'

14 The Pharisees, who loved money, heard all this and were sneering at Jesus. 15 He said to them, 'You are the ones who justify yourselves in the eyes of others, but God knows your hearts. What people value highly is detestable in God's sight.

Additional teachings

16 'The Law and the Prophets were proclaimed until John. Since that time, the good news of the kingdom of God is being preached, and everyone is forcing their way into it. 17 It is easier for heaven and earth to disappear than for the least stroke of a pen to drop out of the Law.

18 'Anyone who divorces his wife and marries another woman commits adultery, and the man who marries a divorced woman commits adultery.

The rich man and Lazarus

19 There was a rich man who was dressed in purple and fine linen and lived in luxury every day. 20 At his gate was laid a beggar named Lazarus, covered with sores 21 and longing to eat what fell from the rich man's table. Even the dogs came and licked his sores.

22 'The time came when the beggar died and the angels carried him to Abraham's side. The rich man also died and was buried. 23 In Hades, where he was in torment, he looked up and saw Abraham far away, with Lazarus by his side. 24 So he called to him, "Father Abraham, have pity on me and send Lazarus to dip the tip of his finger in water and cool my tongue, because I am in agony in this fire."

25 'But Abraham replied, "Son, remember that in your lifetime you received your good things, while Lazarus received bad things, but now he is comforted here and you are in agony. 26 And besides all this, between us and you a great chasm has been set in place, so that those who want to go from here to you cannot, nor can anyone cross over from there to us."

27 'He answered, "Then I beg you, father, send Lazarus to my family, 28 for I have five brothers. Let him warn them, so that they will not also come to this place of torment."

29 'Abraham replied, "They have Moses and the Prophets; let them listen to them."

30 ' "No, father Abraham," he said, "but if someone from the dead goes to them, they will repent."

31 'He said to him, "If they do not listen to Moses and the Prophets, they will not be convinced even if someone rises from the dead." '

Sin, faith, duty

17 Jesus said to his disciples: 'Things that cause people to stumble are bound to come, but woe to anyone through whom they come. 2 It would be better for them to be thrown into the sea with a millstone tied round their neck than to cause one of these little ones to stumble. 3 So watch yourselves.

'If your brother or sister*a* sins against you, rebuke them; and if they repent, forgive them. 4 Even if they sin against you seven times in a day and seven times come back to you saying "I repent," you must forgive them.'

5 The apostles said to the Lord, 'Increase our faith!'

6 He replied, 'If you have faith as small as a mustard seed, you can say to this mulberry tree, "Be uprooted and planted in the sea," and it will obey you.

7 'Suppose one of you has a servant ploughing or looking after the sheep. Will he say to the servant when he comes in from the field, "Come along now and sit down to eat"? 8 Won't he rather say, "Prepare my supper, get yourself ready and wait on me while I eat and drink; after that you may eat and drink"? 9 Will he thank the servant because he did what he was told to do? 10 So you also, when you have done everything you were told to do, should say, "We are unworthy servants; we have only done our duty." '

Jesus heals ten men with leprosy

11 Now on his way to Jerusalem, Jesus travelled along the border between Samaria and Galilee. 12 As he was going into a village, ten men who had leprosy*b* met him. They stood at a distance 13 and called out in a loud voice, 'Jesus, Master, have pity on us!'

14 When he saw them, he said, 'Go, show yourselves to the priests.' And as they went, they were cleansed.

15 One of them, when he saw he was healed, came back, praising God in a loud voice. 16 He threw himself at Jesus' feet and thanked him – and he was a Samaritan.

17 Jesus asked, 'Were not all ten cleansed? Where are the other nine? 18 Has no one returned to give praise to God except this foreigner?' 19 Then he said to him, 'Rise and go; your faith has made you well.'

---

a 3 The Greek word for *brother or sister* (*adelphos*) refers here to a fellow disciple, whether man or woman.
b 12 The Greek word traditionally translated *leprosy* was used for various diseases affecting the skin.

The coming of the kingdom of God

20 Once, on being asked by the Pharisees when the kingdom of God would come, Jesus replied, 'The coming of the kingdom of God is not something that can be observed, 21 nor will people say, "Here it is," or "There it is," because the kingdom of God is in your midst.'ᶜ

22 Then he said to his disciples, 'The time is coming when you will long to see

ᶜ 21 Or *is within you*

PRAYER 7

SAYING THANK YOU

Luke 17:11–19 tells the story of ten people who came to Jesus and asked to be healed of leprosy. When they left him, none of them were sure they had got what they had asked for. Jesus had told them to go and see the priests – whose responsibilities included checking whether people still had deadly diseases and deciding whether they could come back into society.

As the ten walked along, their bodies changed. Their leprosy disappeared: feeling returned to their fingertips; sores dried up. Miracles! Ten of them! The real deal!

They had set off to see the priests in faith, and now they knew that when they got there they would be given a clean bill of health. They would be allowed to see their families, allowed into the town, allowed into the synagogues, allowed to rejoin their community. Their lives had started again. I bet they ran down that road.

But one of these men was a Samaritan (vv. 15–16). He wasn't part of the Jewish religious system and the priests could do nothing for him. For him, the big deal was getting healed. And he was! So he stopped, turned around and went back to Jesus to say 'thank you'.

Ten got healed. Nine got back their place in society. But only one got a relationship with Jesus. Ten got a miracle. But only one got praise from Jesus. Saying 'thank you' didn't make the healing any more real, but it did change everything else. This man didn't share the religion of those around him, but he came back – and stood there talking to God. We have all been told that saying 'thank you' is polite, but saying a genuine 'thank you' to Jesus means something far greater. It means you have a relationship with God.

If you have a major need, then saying 'please' to God opens the door for him to act. So say 'please' to Jesus for all your needs and the many needs of those you know. But remember that when the miracle happens, there's another thing to say to God. Saying 'thank you' may not get you another miracle, but it will deepen your relationship with him.

Hugo Anson

 Daniel 6   James 5:13–18

one of the days of the Son of Man, but you will not see it. 23 People will tell you, "There he is!" or "Here he is!" Do not go running off after them. 24 For the Son of Man in his day[d] will be like the lightning, which flashes and lights up the sky from one end to the other. 25 But first he must suffer many things and be rejected by this generation.

26 'Just as it was in the days of Noah, so also will it be in the days of the Son of Man. 27 People were eating, drinking, marrying and being given in marriage up to the day Noah entered the ark. Then the flood came and destroyed them all.

28 'It was the same in the days of Lot. People were eating and drinking, buying and selling, planting and building. 29 But the day Lot left Sodom, fire and sulphur rained down from heaven and destroyed them all.

30 'It will be just like this on the day the Son of Man is revealed. 31 On that day no one who is on the housetop, with possessions inside, should go down to get them. Likewise, no one in the field should go back for anything. 32 Remember Lot's wife! 33 Whoever tries to keep their life will lose it, and whoever loses their life will preserve it. 34 I tell you, on that night two people will be in one bed; one will be taken and the other left. 35 Two women will be grinding corn together; one will be taken and the other left.' [36][e]

37 'Where, Lord?' they asked.

He replied, 'Where there is a dead body, there the vultures will gather.'

The parable of the persistent widow

18 Then Jesus told his disciples a parable to show them that they should always pray and not give up. 2 He said: 'In a certain town there was a judge who neither feared God nor cared what people thought. 3 And there was a widow in that town who kept coming to him with the plea, "Grant me justice against my adversary."

4 'For some time he refused. But finally he said to himself, "Even though I don't fear God or care what people think, 5 yet because this widow keeps bothering me, I will see that she gets justice, so that she won't eventually come and attack me!" '

6 And the Lord said, 'Listen to what the unjust judge says. 7 And will not God bring about justice for his chosen ones, who cry out to him day and night? Will he keep putting them off? 8 I tell you, he will see that they get justice, and quickly. However, when the Son of Man comes, will he find faith on the earth?'

The parable of the Pharisee and the tax collector

9 To some who were confident of their own righteousness and looked down on everyone else, Jesus told this parable: 10 'Two men went up to the temple to pray, one a Pharisee and the other a tax collector. 11 The Pharisee stood by himself and prayed: "God, I thank you that I am not like other people – robbers, evildoers, adulterers – or even like this tax collector. 12 I fast twice a week and give a tenth of all I get."

13 'But the tax collector stood at a distance. He would not even look up to heaven, but beat his breast and said, "God, have mercy on me, a sinner."

14 'I tell you that this man, rather than the other, went home justified before God. For all those who exalt themselves will be humbled, and those who humble themselves will be exalted.'

The little children and Jesus

15 People were also bringing babies to Jesus for him to place his hands on them. When the disciples saw this, they rebuked them. 16 But Jesus called the children to him and said, 'Let the little children come to me, and do not hinder them, for the kingdom of God belongs to such as these. 17 Truly I tell you, anyone who will not receive the kingdom of God like a little child will never enter it.'

---

d 24 Some manuscripts do not have *in his day.*
e 36 Some manuscripts include here words similar to Matt. 24:40.

The rich and the kingdom of God

18 A certain ruler asked him, 'Good teacher, what must I do to inherit eternal life?'

19 'Why do you call me good?' Jesus answered. 'No one is good – except God alone. 20 You know the commandments:

"You shall not commit adultery, you shall not murder, you shall not steal, you shall not give false testimony, honour your father and mother."*a*

a 20 Exodus 20:12-16; Deut. 5:16-20

MONEY

The subject of money can be one of the most difficult aspects of our lives as Christians. It clearly concerned Jesus, as the Gospels show him spending more time talking about money than anything else other than the kingdom of God.

In Luke 18:18–29, we read the story of a ruler who was told by Jesus that he must give away all his money in order to inherit eternal life. It would be easy to conclude from this that we can only inherit eternal life if we give all our possessions away. However, in Luke 19:1–9, we read the story of Zacchaeus's encounter with Jesus. At the end of this episode, when salvation comes to Zacchaeus, he declares that he will give away half his possessions and repay anyone he has cheated four times the amount he cheated them.

Why is it that Zacchaeus only had to give away half his possessions in order to be saved, when the ruler had to give everything away – and what does that mean for us? The answer is that Jesus is more concerned with our attitude to money than with amounts or percentages. When Zacchaeus encountered Jesus, he stopped his old money-grabbing way of life and fell in love with Jesus. The rich young ruler, however, was more in love with money than God, despite his righteous lifestyle (v. 23).

Jesus taught that we should seek God's kingdom and righteousness first. This means our aim in life should be to glorify God. He also says that we can't serve both God and money: we must choose whether we want to live our lives with Jesus at the centre, or wealth. That means we shouldn't focus on getting rich, or spend our time worrying about money, because it gets in the way of us serving God (v. 25).

This is not to say that there's anything inherently wrong with wealth or wealth creation. In fact, there are examples in the New Testament of wealthy Christians who helped finance the work of the church. But wealth should never be an end in itself: it shouldn't be our goal. It should be a tool that we use to serve the church and support those in need.

So what is a Christian attitude to money? Money shouldn't be our aim in life; we should try to glorify God instead. Also, money should not preoccupy or worry us; instead we should rely on God for provision. The Bible suggests that we tithe, or give, at least 10 per cent of our income to the church and to people who need it. So ultimately money is a tool we use to serve God, rather than a purpose for our lives.

Freddie Pimm

21 'All these I have kept since I was a boy,' he said.

22 When Jesus heard this, he said to him, 'You still lack one thing. Sell everything you have and give to the poor, and you will have treasure in heaven. Then come, follow me.'

23 When he heard this, he became very sad, because he was very wealthy. 24 Jesus looked at him and said, 'How hard it is for the rich to enter the kingdom of God! 25 Indeed, it is easier for a camel to go through the eye of a needle than for someone who is rich to enter the kingdom of God.'

26 Those who heard this asked, 'Who then can be saved?'

27 Jesus replied, 'What is impossible with man is possible with God.'

28 Peter said to him, 'We have left all we had to follow you!'

29 'Truly I tell you,' Jesus said to them, 'no one who has left home or wife or brothers or sisters or parents or children for the sake of the kingdom of God 30 will fail to receive many times as much in this age, and in the age to come eternal life.'

Jesus predicts his death a third time

31 Jesus took the Twelve aside and told them, 'We are going up to Jerusalem, and everything that is written by the prophets about the Son of Man will be fulfilled. 32 He will be handed over to the Gentiles. They will mock him, insult him and spit on him; 33 they will flog him and kill him. On the third day he will rise again.'

34 The disciples did not understand any of this. Its meaning was hidden from them, and they did not know what he was talking about.

A blind beggar receives his sight

35 As Jesus approached Jericho, a blind man was sitting by the roadside begging. 36 When he heard the crowd going by, he asked what was happening. 37 They told him, 'Jesus of Nazareth is passing by.'

38 He called out, 'Jesus, Son of David, have mercy on me!'

39 Those who led the way rebuked him and told him to be quiet, but he shouted all the more, 'Son of David, have mercy on me!'

40 Jesus stopped and ordered the man to be brought to him. When he came near, Jesus asked him, 41 'What do you want me to do for you?'

'Lord, I want to see,' he replied.

42 Jesus said to him, 'Receive your sight; your faith has healed you.' 43 Immediately he received his sight and followed Jesus, praising God. When all the people saw it, they also praised God.

Zacchaeus the tax collector

19 Jesus entered Jericho and was passing through. 2 A man was there by the name of Zacchaeus; he was a chief tax collector and was wealthy. 3 He wanted to see who Jesus was, but because he was short he could not see over the crowd. 4 So he ran ahead and climbed a sycamore-fig tree to see him, since Jesus was coming that way.

5 When Jesus reached the spot, he looked up and said to him, 'Zacchaeus, come down immediately. I must stay at your house today.' 6 So he came down at once and welcomed him gladly.

7 All the people saw this and began to mutter, 'He has gone to be the guest of a sinner.'

8 But Zacchaeus stood up and said to the Lord, 'Look, Lord! Here and now I give half of my possessions to the poor, and if I have cheated anybody out of anything, I will pay back four times the amount.'

9 Jesus said to him, 'Today salvation has come to this house, because this man, too, is a son of Abraham. 10 For the Son of Man came to seek and to save the lost.'

The parable of the ten minas

11 While they were listening to this, he went on to tell them a parable, because he was near Jerusalem and the people thought that the kingdom of God was going to appear at once. 12 He said: 'A man of noble birth went to a distant country to have himself appointed king and then to return. 13 So he called ten of his servants

PEOPLE USED BY GOD 7

Zacchaeus

In a mere ten verses in Luke 19:1–10, we see the amazing transformation of a human being as a result of the power of acceptance.

Zacchaeus, like most of us, had a few things going for him and more than a few things going against him. On the plus side, he was a rich man with a secure job as a tax collector. On the down side, he was hated for being a tax collector and his job caused him to be a social outcast. Being rich just isn't enough when you feel the whole world hates you. Maybe it was the severe rejection he felt on a daily basis that caused him to find a way to see this man Jesus, whom he had heard about.

As Jesus was scheduled to arrive in his town, Zacchaeus, being a short man, knew he wouldn't stand a chance against the clamouring crowds. Where there's a will, there's a way – and Zacchaeus found that way by climbing a sycamore fig tree, yet another social *faux pas*! Sycamore fig trees at that time were considered unclean, and the fruit was fed only to pigs. What Zacchaeus did was unacceptable for a Jew. He was risking rejection once again, but his desperate need to see a man who could bring him hope made it worth the risk, even if it was just one more reason for people to bad-mouth him.

The risk paid off. The Bible says that when we seek, we will find (Matthew 7:7). This time it was Zacchaeus doing the seeking, and Jesus doing the finding. As Jesus entered the town, he found Zacchaeus up the tree and called for him to come down. As if that wasn't enough, he then proclaimed in front of everyone that he would like to dine at the home of Zacchaeus. Acceptance! In front of everyone, without fear about what others would think of him, Jesus reached out to the unpopular Zacchaeus. People now began to bad-mouth Jesus, judging him for even speaking to such a man, much less eating with him. But Jesus saw in Zacchaeus the child of God that he was, the person he would become, someone of great worth. Jesus was not worried about his reputation. He was more interested in showing Zacchaeus the Father's love. And there it was, in that moment of acceptance: at the first drop of love, Zacchaeus was changed! He rose up, repented before Jesus in the hearing of all, and Jesus joyfully accepted him, forgave him and brought salvation to his heart.

To this day, Jesus is standing by the 'tree' of every human heart requesting an invitation to dine with us. He is not concerned with our reputations or shortcomings; his heart is to reunite us with the heart of the Father and to show us true acceptance (Revelation 3:20).

Susie Brock

and gave them ten minas. *a* "Put this money to work," he said, "until I come back."

14 'But his subjects hated him and sent a delegation after him to say, "We don't want this man to be our king."

15 'He was made king, however, and returned home. Then he sent for the servants to whom he had given the money, in order to find out what they had gained with it.

16 'The first one came and said, "Sir, your mina has earned ten more."

17 ' "Well done, my good servant!" his master replied. "Because you have been trustworthy in a very small matter, take charge of ten cities."

18 'The second came and said, "Sir, your mina has earned five more."

19 'His master answered, "You take charge of five cities."

20 'Then another servant came and said, "Sir, here is your mina; I have kept it laid away in a piece of cloth. 21 I was afraid of you, because you are a hard man. You take out what you did not put in and reap what you did not sow."

22 'His master replied, "I will judge you by your own words, you wicked servant! You knew, did you, that I am a hard man, taking out what I did not put in, and reaping what I did not sow? 23 Why then didn't you put my money on deposit, so that when I came back, I could have collected it with interest?"

24 'Then he said to those standing by, "Take his mina away from him and give it to the one who has ten minas."

25 ' "Sir," they said, "he already has ten!"

26 'He replied, "I tell you that to everyone who has, more will be given, but as for the one who has nothing, even what they have will be taken away. 27 But those enemies of mine who did not want me to be king over them – bring them here and kill them in front of me." '

Jesus comes to Jerusalem as king

28 After Jesus had said this, he went on ahead, going up to Jerusalem. 29 As he approached Bethphage and Bethany at the hill called the Mount of Olives, he sent two of his disciples, saying to them, 30 'Go to the village ahead of you, and as you enter it, you will find a colt tied there, which no one has ever ridden. Untie it and bring it here. 31 If anyone asks you, "Why are you untying it?" say, "The Lord needs it." '

32 Those who were sent ahead went and found it just as he had told them. 33 As they were untying the colt, its owners asked them, 'Why are you untying the colt?'

34 They replied, 'The Lord needs it.'

35 They brought it to Jesus, threw their cloaks on the colt and put Jesus on it. 36 As he went along, people spread their cloaks on the road.

37 When he came near the place where the road goes down the Mount of Olives, the whole crowd of disciples began joyfully to praise God in loud voices for all the miracles they had seen:

38 'Blessed is the king who comes in the name of the Lord!' *b*

'Peace in heaven and glory in the highest!'

39 Some of the Pharisees in the crowd said to Jesus, 'Teacher, rebuke your disciples!'

40 'I tell you,' he replied, 'if they keep quiet, the stones will cry out.'

41 As he approached Jerusalem and saw the city, he wept over it 42 and said, 'If you, even you, had only known on this day what would bring you peace – but now it is hidden from your eyes. 43 The days will come upon you when your enemies will build an embankment against you and encircle you and hem you in on every side. 44 They will dash you to the ground, you and the children within your walls. They will not leave one stone on another, because you did not recognise the time of God's coming to you.'

Jesus at the temple

45 When Jesus entered the temple courts, he began to drive out those who

---

a 13 A mina was about three months' wages.　　*b* 38 Psalm 118:26

were selling. **46** 'It is written,' he said to them, ' "My house will be a house of prayer" *c*; but you have made it "a den of robbers".*d*'

47 Every day he was teaching at the temple. But the chief priests, the teachers of the law and the leaders among the people were trying to kill him. **48** Yet they could not find any way to do it, because all the people hung on his words.

The authority of Jesus questioned

20 One day as Jesus was teaching the people in the temple courts and proclaiming the good news, the chief priests and the teachers of the law, together with the elders, came up to him. **2** 'Tell us by what authority you are doing these things,' they said. 'Who gave you this authority?'

3 He replied, 'I will also ask you a question. Tell me: **4** John's baptism – was it from heaven, or of human origin?'

5 They discussed it among themselves and said, 'If we say, "From heaven," he will ask, "Why didn't you believe him?" **6** But if we say, "Of human origin," all the people will stone us, because they are persuaded that John was a prophet.'

7 So they answered, 'We don't know where it was from.'

8 Jesus said, 'Neither will I tell you by what authority I am doing these things.'

The parable of the tenants

9 He went on to tell the people this parable: 'A man planted a vineyard, rented it to some farmers and went away for a long time. **10** At harvest time he sent a servant to the tenants so they would give him some of the fruit of the vineyard. But the tenants beat him and sent him away empty-handed. **11** He sent another servant, but that one also they beat and treated shamefully and sent away empty-handed. **12** He sent still a third, and they wounded him and threw him out.

13 'Then the owner of the vineyard said, "What shall I do? I will send my son, whom I love; perhaps they will respect him."

14 'But when the tenants saw him, they talked the matter over. "This is the heir," they said. "Let's kill him, and the inheritance will be ours." **15** So they threw him out of the vineyard and killed him.

'What then will the owner of the vineyard do to them? **16** He will come and kill those tenants and give the vineyard to others.'

When the people heard this, they said, 'God forbid!'

17 Jesus looked directly at them and asked, 'Then what is the meaning of that which is written:

' "The stone the builders rejected
    has become the cornerstone" *a*?

18 Everyone who falls on that stone will be broken to pieces; anyone on whom it falls will be crushed.'

19 The teachers of the law and the chief priests looked for a way to arrest him immediately, because they knew he had spoken this parable against them. But they were afraid of the people.

Paying taxes to Caesar

20 Keeping a close watch on him, they sent spies, who pretended to be sincere. They hoped to catch Jesus in something he said, so that they might hand him over to the power and authority of the governor. **21** So the spies questioned him: 'Teacher, we know that you speak and teach what is right, and that you do not show partiality but teach the way of God in accordance with the truth. **22** Is it right for us to pay taxes to Caesar or not?'

23 He saw through their duplicity and said to them, **24** 'Show me a denarius. Whose image and inscription are on it?'

'Caesar's,' they replied.

25 He said to them, 'Then give back to Caesar what is Caesar's, and to God what is God's.'

26 They were unable to trap him in what

---

c 46 Isaiah 56:7
d 46 Jer. 7:11

a 17 Psalm 118:22

he had said there in public. And astonished by his answer, they became silent.

The resurrection and marriage

27 Some of the Sadducees, who say there is no resurrection, came to Jesus with a question. 28 'Teacher,' they said, 'Moses wrote for us that if a man's brother dies and leaves a wife but no children, the man must marry the widow and raise up offspring for his brother. 29 Now there were seven brothers. The first one married a woman and died childless. 30 The second 31 and then the third married her, and in the same way the seven died, leaving no children. 32 Finally, the woman died too. 33 Now then, at the resurrection whose wife will she be, since the seven were married to her?'

34 Jesus replied, 'The people of this age marry and are given in marriage. 35 But those who are considered worthy of taking part in the age to come and in the resurrection from the dead will neither marry nor be given in marriage, 36 and they can no longer die; for they are like the angels. They are God's children, since they are children of the resurrection. 37 But in the account of the burning bush, even Moses showed that the dead rise, for he calls the Lord "the God of Abraham, and the God of Isaac, and the God of Jacob".[b] 38 He is not the God of the dead, but of the living, for to him all are alive.'

39 Some of the teachers of the law responded, 'Well said, teacher!' 40 And no one dared to ask him any more questions.

Whose son is the Messiah?

41 Then Jesus said to them, 'Why is it said that the Messiah is the son of David? 42 David himself declares in the Book of Psalms:

' "The Lord said to my Lord:
   'Sit at my right hand
43 until I make your enemies
   a footstool for your feet.' "[c]

---

b 37 Exodus 3:6
c 43 Psalm 110:1

44 David calls him "Lord." How then can he be his son?'

Warning against the teachers of the law

45 While all the people were listening, Jesus said to his disciples, 46 'Beware of the teachers of the law. They like to walk around in flowing robes and love to be greeted with respect in the market-places and have the most important seats in the synagogues and the places of honour at banquets. 47 They devour widows' houses and for a show make lengthy prayers. These men will be punished most severely.'

The widow's offering

21 As Jesus looked up, he saw the rich putting their gifts into the temple treasury. 2 He also saw a poor widow put in two very small copper coins. 3 'Truly I tell you,' he said, 'this poor widow has put in more than all the others. 4 All these people gave their gifts out of their wealth; but she out of her poverty put in all she had to live on.'

The destruction of the temple and signs of the end times

5 Some of his disciples were remarking about how the temple was adorned with beautiful stones and with gifts dedicated to God. But Jesus said, 6 'As for what you see here, the time will come when not one stone will be left on another; every one of them will be thrown down.'

7 'Teacher,' they asked, 'when will these things happen? And what will be the sign that they are about to take place?'

8 He replied: 'Watch out that you are not deceived. For many will come in my name, claiming, "I am he," and, "The time is near." Do not follow them. 9 When you hear of wars and uprisings, do not be frightened. These things must happen first, but the end will not come right away.'

10 Then he said to them: 'Nation will rise against nation, and kingdom against kingdom. 11 There will be great earthquakes, famines and pestilences in

various places, and fearful events and great signs from heaven. 12 'But before all this, they will seize you and persecute you. They will hand you over to synagogues and put you in prison, and you will be brought before kings and governors, and all on account of my name. 13 And so you will bear testimony to me. 14 But make up your mind not to worry beforehand how you will defend yourselves. 15 For I will give you words and wisdom that none of your adversaries will be able to resist or contradict. 16 You will be betrayed even by parents, brothers and sisters, relatives and friends, and they will put some of you to death. 17 Everyone will hate you because of me. 18 But not a hair of your head will perish. 19 Stand firm, and you will win life.

FACT

LUKE THE GENTILE

Luke is the only non-Jewish writer in the New Testament. All the other authors are Christian Jews.

20 'When you see Jerusalem being surrounded by armies, you will know that its desolation is near. 21 Then let those who are in Judea flee to the mountains, let those in the city get out, and let those in the country not enter the city. 22 For this is the time of punishment in fulfilment of all that has been written. 23 How dreadful it will be in those days for pregnant women and nursing mothers! There will be great distress in the land and wrath against this people. 24 They will fall by the sword and will be taken as prisoners to all the nations. Jerusalem will be trampled on by the Gentiles until the times of the Gentiles are fulfilled. 25 'There will be signs in the sun, moon and stars. On the earth, nations will be in anguish and perplexity at the roaring and tossing of the sea. 26 People will faint from terror, apprehensive of what is coming on the world, for the heavenly bodies will be shaken. 27 At that time they will see the Son of Man coming in a cloud with power and great glory. 28 When these things begin to take place, stand up and lift up your heads, because your redemption is drawing near.'

29 He told them this parable: 'Look at the fig-tree and all the trees. 30 When they sprout leaves, you can see for yourselves and know that summer is near. 31 Even so, when you see these things happening, you know that the kingdom of God is near.

32 'Truly I tell you, this generation will certainly not pass away until all these things have happened. 33 Heaven and earth will pass away, but my words will never pass away.

34 'Be careful, or your hearts will be weighed down with carousing, drunkenness and the anxieties of life, and that day will close on you suddenly like a trap. 35 For it will come on all those who live on the face of the whole earth. 36 Be always on the watch, and pray that you may be able to escape all that is about to happen, and that you may be able to stand before the Son of Man.'

37 Each day Jesus was teaching at the temple, and each evening he went out to spend the night on the hill called the Mount of Olives, 38 and all the people came early in the morning to hear him at the temple.

Judas agrees to betray Jesus

22 Now the Festival of Unleavened Bread, called the Passover, was approaching, 2 and the chief priests and the teachers of the law were looking for some way to get rid of Jesus, for they were afraid of the people. 3 Then Satan entered Judas, called Iscariot, one of the Twelve. 4 And Judas went to the chief priests and the officers of the temple guard and discussed with them how he might betray Jesus. 5 They were delighted and agreed to give him money. 6 He consented, and watched for an opportunity to hand Jesus over to them when no crowd was present.

The Last Supper

7 Then came the day of Unleavened Bread on which the Passover lamb had to be sacrificed. **8** Jesus sent Peter and John, saying, 'Go and make preparations for us to eat the Passover.'

9 'Where do you want us to prepare for it?' they asked.

10 He replied, 'As you enter the city, a man carrying a jar of water will meet you. Follow him to the house that he enters, **11** and say to the owner of the house, "The Teacher asks: where is the guest room, where I may eat the Passover with my disciples?" **12** He will show you a large room upstairs, all furnished. Make preparations there.'

13 They left and found things just as Jesus had told them. So they prepared the Passover.

14 When the hour came, Jesus and his apostles reclined at the table. **15** And he said to them, 'I have eagerly desired to eat this Passover with you before I suffer. **16** For I tell you, I will not eat it again until it finds fulfilment in the kingdom of God.'

17 After taking the cup, he gave thanks and said, 'Take this and divide it among you. **18** For I tell you I will not drink again from the fruit of the vine until the kingdom of God comes.'

19 And he took bread, gave thanks and broke it, and gave it to them, saying, 'This is my body given for you; do this in remembrance of me.'

20 In the same way, after the supper he took the cup, saying, 'This cup is the new covenant in my blood, which is poured out for you.*a* **21** But the hand of him who is going to betray me is with mine on the table. **22** The Son of Man will go as it has been decreed. But woe to that man who betrays him!' **23** They began to question among themselves which of them it might be who would do this.

24 A dispute also arose among them as to which of them was considered to be greatest. **25** Jesus said to them, 'The kings of the Gentiles lord it over them; and those who exercise authority over them call themselves Benefactors. **26** But you are not to be like that. Instead, the greatest among you should be like the youngest, and the one who rules like the one who serves. **27** For who is greater, the one who is at the table or the one who serves? Is it not the one who is at the table? But I am among you as one who serves. **28** You are those who have stood by me in my trials. **29** And I confer on you a kingdom, just as my Father conferred one on me, **30** so that you may eat and drink at my table in my kingdom and sit on thrones, judging the twelve tribes of Israel.

31 'Simon, Simon, Satan has asked to sift all of you as wheat. **32** But I have prayed for you, Simon, that your faith may not fail. And when you have turned back, strengthen your brothers.'

33 But he replied, 'Lord, I am ready to go with you to prison and to death.'

34 Jesus answered, 'I tell you, Peter, before the cock crows today, you will deny three times that you know me.'

35 Then Jesus asked them, 'When I sent you without purse, bag or sandals, did you lack anything?'

'Nothing,' they answered.

36 He said to them, 'But now if you have a purse, take it, and also a bag; and if you don't have a sword, sell your cloak and buy one. **37** It is written: "And he was numbered with the transgressors"*b*; and I tell you that this must be fulfilled in me. Yes, what is written about me is reaching its fulfilment.'

38 The disciples said, 'See, Lord, here are two swords.'

'That's enough!' he replied.

Jesus prays on the Mount of Olives

39 Jesus went out as usual to the Mount of Olives, and his disciples followed him. **40** On reaching the place, he said to them, 'Pray that you will not fall into

a 19,20 Some manuscripts do not have *given for you . . . poured out for you.*

b 37 Isaiah 53:12

temptation.' ⁴¹He withdrew about a stone's throw beyond them, knelt down and prayed, ⁴²'Father, if you are willing, take this cup from me; yet not my will, but yours be done.' ⁴³An angel from heaven appeared to him and strengthened him. ⁴⁴And being in anguish, he prayed more earnestly, and his sweat was like drops of blood falling to the ground.ᶜ

⁴⁵When he rose from prayer and went back to the disciples, he found them

_____

ᶜ 43,44 Many early manuscripts do not have verses 43 and 44.

PAIN AND SUFFERING 6

CHOOSING GOD'S WILL IN PAIN

I can't even imagine how painful it was for Jesus to pray the prayer recorded in Luke 22:42. He knew what he was letting himself in for. He sweated drops of blood because he was so acutely aware of what he was going to have to endure (v. 44).

He was about to be deserted by his friends. He was about to suffer public humiliation and have people think he had been defeated. He was about to face the most agonising physical pain a human being could know. And, worst of all, he was about to be separated from his Father when the sin of the world was placed upon him. Jesus knew all of this when he prayed. Understandably, he asked God to take away his suffering and not to put him through it. I love the honesty he displayed in asking God to save him from the cross. Yet he went on to say that what he really wanted, even more than avoiding pain, was to do God's will. He surrendered himself to God, trusting that his Father always knows what is best.

These are some of the most humbling words in the whole of the Bible. Jesus was willing to suffer anything in order to be obedient to God. The first disciples also suffered all sorts of pain in following God's commands. They were imprisoned, beaten and stoned to death for telling people about Jesus, and shipwrecked when they tried to take the gospel to other countries.

The truth is, we'll never have to face the things that Jesus did, and we're very unlikely to go through the disciples' suffering either. But if we're fully surrendered to God, there will be times when life will be hard for us. God might ask us to walk away from things we want. We might have to sacrifice things. We might have to suffer humiliation in the world's eyes for his name. Our reputations might take a beating. People might talk about us and judge us. We probably won't get to lead a comfortable life. But to be truly obedient, we need to put God before everything and everyone else in our lives. Only Jesus was perfect, so we'll never quite get it right, but let's try to follow his attitude and say that, over and above our own desires, we want to do God's will, even when it costs us dearly.

Mike Pilavachi

asleep, exhausted from sorrow. 46'Why are you sleeping?' he asked them. 'Get up and pray so that you will not fall into temptation.'

Jesus arrested

47While he was still speaking a crowd came up, and the man who was called Judas, one of the Twelve, was leading them. He approached Jesus to kiss him, 48but Jesus asked him, 'Judas, are you betraying the Son of Man with a kiss?'

49When Jesus' followers saw what was going to happen, they said, 'Lord, should we strike with our swords?' 50And one of them struck the servant of the high priest, cutting off his right ear.

51But Jesus answered, 'No more of this!' And he touched the man's ear and healed him.

52Then Jesus said to the chief priests, the officers of the temple guard, and the elders, who had come for him, 'Am I leading a rebellion, that you have come with swords and clubs? 53Every day I was with you in the temple courts, and you did not lay a hand on me. But this is your hour – when darkness reigns.'

Peter disowns Jesus

54Then seizing him, they led him away and took him into the house of the high priest. Peter followed at a distance. 55And when some there had kindled a fire in the middle of the courtyard and had sat down together, Peter sat down with them. 56A servant-girl saw him seated there in the firelight. She looked closely at him and said, 'This man was with him.'

57But he denied it. 'Woman, I don't know him,' he said.

58A little later someone else saw him and said, 'You also are one of them.'

'Man, I am not!' Peter replied.

59About an hour later another asserted, 'Certainly this fellow was with him, for he is a Galilean.'

60Peter replied, 'Man, I don't know what you're talking about!' Just as he was speaking, the cock crowed. 61The Lord turned and looked straight at Peter. Then Peter remembered the word the Lord had spoken to him: 'Before the cock crows today, you will disown me three times.' 62And he went outside and wept bitterly.

The guards mock Jesus

63The men who were guarding Jesus began mocking and beating him. 64They blindfolded him and demanded, 'Prophesy! Who hit you?' 65And they said many other insulting things to him.

Jesus before Pilate and Herod

66At daybreak the council of the elders of the people, both the chief priests and the teachers of the law, met together, and Jesus was led before them. 67'If you are the Messiah,' they said, 'tell us.'

Jesus answered, 'If I tell you, you will not believe me, 68and if I asked you, you would not answer. 69But from now on, the Son of Man will be seated at the right hand of the mighty God.'

70They all asked, 'Are you then the Son of God?'

He replied, 'You say that I am.'

71Then they said, 'Why do we need any more testimony? We have heard it from his own lips.'

23 Then the whole assembly rose and led him off to Pilate. 2And they began to accuse him, saying, 'We have found this man subverting our nation. He opposes payment of taxes to Caesar and claims to be Messiah, a king.'

3So Pilate asked Jesus, 'Are you the king of the Jews?'

'You have said so,' Jesus replied.

4Then Pilate announced to the chief priests and the crowd, 'I find no basis for a charge against this man.'

5But they insisted, 'He stirs up the people all over Judea by his teaching. He started in Galilee and has come all the way here.'

6On hearing this, Pilate asked if the man was a Galilean. 7When he learned that Jesus was under Herod's jurisdiction, he sent him to Herod, who was also in Jerusalem at that time.

8When Herod saw Jesus, he was greatly pleased, because for a long time he had been wanting to see him. From what he had heard about him, he hoped to see him perform a sign of some sort. 9 He plied him with many questions, but Jesus gave him no answer. 10 The chief priests and the teachers of the law were standing there, vehemently accusing him. 11 Then Herod and his soldiers ridiculed and mocked him. Dressing him in an elegant robe, they sent him back to Pilate. 12 That day Herod and Pilate became friends – before this they had been enemies.

13 Pilate called together the chief priests, the rulers and the people, 14 and said to them, 'You brought me this man as one who was inciting the people to rebellion. I have examined him in your presence and have found no basis for your charges against him. 15 Neither has Herod, for he sent him back to us; as you can see, he has done nothing to deserve death. 16 Therefore, I will punish him and then release him.' [17] a

18 But the whole crowd shouted, 'Away with this man! Release Barabbas to us!' 19 (Barabbas had been thrown into prison for an insurrection in the city, and for murder.)

20 Wanting to release Jesus, Pilate appealed to them again. 21 But they kept shouting, 'Crucify him! Crucify him!'

22 For the third time he spoke to them: 'Why? What crime has this man committed? I have found in him no grounds for the death penalty. Therefore I will have him punished and then release him.'

23 But with loud shouts they insistently demanded that he be crucified, and their shouts prevailed. 24 So Pilate decided to grant their demand. 25 He released the man who had been thrown into prison for insurrection and murder, the one they asked for, and surrendered Jesus to their will.

The crucifixion of Jesus

26 As the soldiers led him away, they seized Simon from Cyrene, who was on his way in from the country, and put the cross on him and made him carry it

behind Jesus. 27 A large number of people followed him, including women who mourned and wailed for him. 28 Jesus turned and said to them, 'Daughters of Jerusalem, do not weep for me; weep for yourselves and for your children. 29 For the time will come when you will say, "Blessed are the childless women, the wombs that never bore and the breasts that never nursed!" 30 Then

' "they will say to the mountains, 'Fall on us!'
and to the hills, 'Cover us!' " b

31 For if people do these things when the tree is green, what will happen when it is dry?'

32 Two other men, both criminals, were also led out with him to be executed. 33 When they came to the place called the Skull, they crucified him there, along with the criminals – one on his right, the other on his left. 34 Jesus said, 'Father, forgive them, for they do not know what they are doing.' c And they divided up his clothes by casting lots.

35 The people stood watching, and the rulers even sneered at him. They said, 'He saved others; let him save himself if he is God's Messiah, the Chosen One.'

36 The soldiers also came up and mocked him. They offered him wine vinegar 37 and said, 'If you are the king of the Jews, save yourself.'

38 There was a written notice above him, which read: THIS IS THE KING OF THE JEWS.

39 One of the criminals who hung there hurled insults at him: 'Aren't you the Messiah? Save yourself and us!'

40 But the other criminal rebuked him. 'Don't you fear God,' he said, 'since you are under the same sentence? 41 We are punished justly, for we are getting what our deeds deserve. But this man has done nothing wrong.'

42 Then he said, 'Jesus, remember me when you come into your kingdom. d '

a 17 Some manuscripts include here words similar to Matt. 27:15 and Mark 15:6.

b 30 Hosea 10:8
c 34 Some early manuscripts do not have this sentence.
d 42 Some manuscripts come with your kingly power

43 Jesus answered him, 'Truly I tell you, today you will be with me in paradise.'

The death of Jesus

44 It was now about noon, and darkness came over the whole land until three in the afternoon, **45** for the sun stopped shining. And the curtain of the temple was torn in two. **46** Jesus called out with a loud voice, 'Father, into your hands I commit my spirit.'[e] When he had said this, he breathed his last.

47 The centurion, seeing what had happened, praised God and said, 'Surely this was a righteous man.' **48** When all the people who had gathered to witness this sight saw what took place, they beat their breasts and went away. **49** But all those who knew him, including the women who had followed him from Galilee, stood at a distance, watching these things.

The burial of Jesus

50 Now there was a man named Joseph, a member of the Council, a good and upright man, **51** who had not consented to their decision and action. He came from the Judean town of Arimathea, and he himself was waiting for the kingdom of God. **52** Going to Pilate, he asked for Jesus' body. **53** Then he took it down, wrapped it in linen cloth and placed it in a tomb cut in the rock, one in which no one had yet been laid. **54** It was Preparation Day, and the Sabbath was about to begin.

55 The women who had come with Jesus from Galilee followed Joseph and saw the tomb and how his body was laid in it. **56** Then they went home and prepared spices and perfumes. But they rested on the Sabbath in obedience to the commandment.

Jesus has risen

24 On the first day of the week, very early in the morning, the women took the spices they had prepared and went to the tomb. **2** They found the stone rolled away from the tomb, **3** but when they entered, they did not find the body of the Lord Jesus. **4** While they were wondering about this, suddenly two men in clothes that gleamed like lightning stood beside them. **5** In their fright the women bowed down with their faces to the ground, but the men said to them, 'Why do you look for the living among the dead? **6** He is not here; he has risen! Remember how he told you, while he was still with you in Galilee: **7** "The Son of Man must be delivered over to the hands of sinners, be crucified and on the third day be raised again." ' **8** Then they remembered his words.

9 When they came back from the tomb, they told all these things to the Eleven and to all the others. **10** It was Mary Magdalene, Joanna, Mary the mother of James, and the others with them who told this to the apostles. **11** But they did not believe the women, because their words seemed to them like nonsense. **12** Peter, however, got up and ran to the tomb. Bending over, he saw the strips of linen lying by themselves, and he went away, wondering to himself what had happened.

On the road to Emmaus

13 Now that same day two of them were going to a village called Emmaus, about seven miles[a] from Jerusalem. **14** They were talking with each other about everything that had happened. **15** As they talked and discussed these things with each other, Jesus himself came up and walked along with them; **16** but they were kept from recognising him.

17 He asked them, 'What are you discussing together as you walk along?'

They stood still, their faces downcast. **18** One of them, named Cleopas, asked him, 'Are you the only one visiting Jerusalem who does not know the things that have happened there in these days?'

19 'What things?' he asked.

'About Jesus of Nazareth,' they replied. 'He was a prophet, powerful in word and deed before God and all the people. **20** The

CHRIST IN ALL THE SCRIPTURES 1

The key

Christ is the key to understanding the Bible. It's all about him. The New Testament shows how he fulfils the promises and prophecies in the Old Testament. In Luke 24:44–49, following his resurrection, Jesus reminds his disciples of his teaching. *'Everything must be fulfilled that is written about me.'*

The Jewish people divided their Scriptures, our Old Testament, into three parts: the Law of Moses (Genesis to Deuteronomy), the Prophets (not just the books by prophets, but the history books about the times of the prophets), and the Writings (mainly the wisdom books) which began with the Psalms. Jesus is saying that the whole Old Testament is about him and points forward to him (John 5:39–40).

If the Old Testament is about him, then we should look for him there, and that's what this thread will do. But we need to know how to look, not just where to look, as it's easy to make mistakes. Like the two disciples earlier in this chapter, we need him to *'open the Scriptures to us'* (Luke 24:25–32).

Jesus is God the Son. God the Son has always existed. So we shouldn't be surprised to find traces of his presence before he became human and was born on earth.

Jesus spoke about *'the Messiah'* (vv. 26, 46) in all the Scriptures. 'Messiah' is a title. It means the one anointed by the Holy Spirit to bring God's kingdom. That was what Jesus came to do. So we won't be looking for the name Jesus (which is the equivalent of Joshua, meaning 'Deliverer' or 'Saviour'), but for the things he would achieve.

There will be analogies or parallels where, in the light of the New Testament, we see patterns in the Old. There are many parallels between the story of Jesus and the story of Joseph, for example. But we can only see them in the light of Jesus. They could not have been seen before and are not the main point of the story of Joseph. The Old Testament events were written down for us because they were important in themselves, in preparing the way for Jesus, not primarily because we can sometimes find parallels to Jesus in them. The Bible must be taken seriously as history.

We can expect prophecies which Jesus fulfils. In the Gospels you will quite often find the phrase 'this was to fulfil', followed by a scripture quotation. Jesus' words in Luke 24:25, 46–47 tell us to expect to find prophecies and anticipations of his death, his resurrection and the new start with God that is to be preached beyond Israel to all nations. But when the Bible says that these were *'according to the Scriptures'* (1 Corinthians 15:3–4), it does not chiefly mean there were prophecies. It means that all the Old Testament threads lead to Jesus. Otherwise the Old Testament is a story without an ending.

Graham Cray

Psalm 8   ⏭

chief priests and our rulers handed him over to be sentenced to death, and they crucified him; 21 but we had hoped that he was the one who was going to redeem Israel. And what is more, it is the third day since all this took place. 22 In addition, some of our women amazed us. They went to the tomb early this morning 23 but didn't find his body. They came and told us that they had seen a vision of angels, who said he was alive. 24 Then some of our companions went to the tomb and found it just as the women had said, but they did not see Jesus.'

25 He said to them, 'How foolish you are, and how slow to believe all that the prophets have spoken! 26 Did not the Messiah have to suffer these things and then enter his glory?' 27 And beginning with Moses and all the Prophets, he explained to them what was said in all the Scriptures concerning himself.

28 As they approached the village to which they were going, Jesus continued on as if he were going further. 29 But they urged him strongly, 'Stay with us, for it is nearly evening; the day is almost over.' So he went in to stay with them.

30 When he was at the table with them, he took bread, gave thanks, broke it and began to give it to them. 31 Then their eyes were opened and they recognised him, and he disappeared from their sight. 32 They asked each other, 'Were not our hearts burning within us while he talked with us on the road and opened the Scriptures to us?'

33 They got up and returned at once to Jerusalem. There they found the Eleven and those with them, assembled together 34 and saying, 'It is true! The Lord has risen and has appeared to Simon.' 35 Then the two told what had happened on the way, and how Jesus was recognised by them when he broke the bread.

Jesus appears to the disciples

36 While they were still talking about this, Jesus himself stood among them and said to them, 'Peace be with you.'

37 They were startled and frightened, thinking they saw a ghost. 38 He said to them, 'Why are you troubled, and why do doubts rise in your minds? 39 Look at my hands and my feet. It is I myself! Touch me and see; a ghost does not have flesh and bones, as you see I have.'

40 When he had said this, he showed them his hands and feet. 41 And while they still did not believe it because of joy and amazement, he asked them, 'Do you have anything here to eat?' 42 They gave him a piece of broiled fish, 43 and he took it and ate it in their presence.

44 He said to them, 'This is what I told you while I was still with you: everything must be fulfilled that is written about me in the Law of Moses, the Prophets and the Psalms.'

45 Then he opened their minds so they could understand the Scriptures. 46 He told them, 'This is what is written: the Messiah will suffer and rise from the dead on the third day, 47 and repentance for the forgiveness of sins will be preached in his name to all nations, beginning at Jerusalem. 48 You are witnesses of these things. 49 I am going to send you what my Father has promised; but stay in the city until you have been clothed with power from on high.'

The ascension of Jesus

50 When he had led them out to the vicinity of Bethany, he lifted up his hands and blessed them. 51 While he was blessing them, he left them and was taken up into heaven. 52 Then they worshipped him and returned to Jerusalem with great joy. 53 And they stayed continually at the temple, praising God.

JOHN

DATE

John details Jesus' earthly ministry, which began in AD 30 and continued until his death and resurrection in AD 33

AUTHOR

The disciple John

WHAT'S IT ALL ABOUT?

The book of John is the last of the four Gospels, but it differs greatly from the other three. While Matthew, Mark and Luke are similar in style and content, John is in a world of his own with a huge percentage of his content not recorded in the other Gospels and his book written in a style utterly unique to him. He still tells us about the same Jesus who was born, did miracles, taught widely, died and rose again, but he tells us about events from a different perspective. He had a good vantage point to tell his version of events as he was 'the disciple whom Jesus loved', so he saw the events first hand. John's emphasis is on the fact that Jesus was not just a man who did amazing things, but God himself, in human flesh, walking the earth. He is less concerned than the other Gospel writers on the things Jesus said and did, and more concerned with the significance of God's physical presence among people. He includes far fewer parables than the other Gospel writers, but records more conversations, such as Jesus talking to Nicodemus (John 3) and the Samaritan woman at the well (John 4).

WHY SHOULD WE READ THE GOSPELS?

- Because this is where we meet Jesus! By reading about his life and what he said and did, we develop our relationship with him and our understanding of who he is. Relationship is key to the Christian life. Christianity is about a person, not a set of ideas. Jesus is the central figure of the whole of history and it's through him that we make sense of life and the Bible. The whole Bible is a witness to Jesus, but the four Gospels are the books that uniquely tell us about his time on earth.

- To understand the events that led to Jesus being killed on a cross like a criminal, even though he had done nothing wrong.

- To see that Jesus was separated from his Father on the cross, taking on himself the punishment we deserve, so that we might become pure in God's eyes.

- To read how Jesus overcame death and rose from the grave, giving us eternal life.

- To read Jesus' teaching on how we should live, including how to treat our enemies, how to pray, not judging people, handling money, having humility, finding faith and dealing with worry.

- To see the miraculous things Jesus did, from the feeding of the five thousand to walking on water, and from giving blind people their sight to raising the dead.

WHY SHOULD WE READ JOHN'S GOSPEL?

- To read John's unique perspective on Jesus' life.

- To understand the importance of Jesus being the Son of God.

- To read one of the Bible's most famous verses, *'For God so loved the world that he gave his one and only Son, that whoever believes in him shall not perish but have eternal life'* (John 3:16).

- To read the longest account of the disciples in the Upper Room with Jesus before his death (John 13 – 17).

- Because some key events and teachings are only recorded in John's Gospel:

  o Jesus turning water into wine at a wedding (John 2);

  o Jesus meeting a Samaritan woman at a well (John 4);

  o Jesus raising Lazarus from the dead (John 11);

  o Jesus' teaching on his being the true vine and his disciples the branches (John 15);

  o Jesus' prayer for himself and for all believers (including us!) to be united (John 17).

Andy Croft with Liza Hoeksma

The Word became flesh

1 In the beginning was the Word, and the Word was with God, and the Word was God. ² He was with God in the beginning. ³ Through him all things were made; without him nothing was made that has been made. ⁴ In him was life, and that life was the light of all mankind. ⁵ The light shines in the darkness, and the darkness has not overcome[a] it.

⁶ There was a man sent from God whose name was John. ⁷ He came as a witness to testify concerning that light, so that through him all might believe. ⁸ He himself was not the light; he came only as a witness to the light.

⁹ The true light that gives light to everyone was coming into the world. ¹⁰ He was in the world, and though the world was made through him, the world did not recognise him. ¹¹ He came to that which was his own, but his own did not receive him. ¹² Yet to all who did receive him, to those who believed in his name, he gave the right to become children of God – ¹³ children born not of natural descent, nor of human decision or a husband's will, but born of God.

¹⁴ The Word became flesh and made his dwelling among us. We have seen his glory, the glory of the one and only Son, who came from the Father, full of grace and truth.

¹⁵ (John testified concerning him. He cried out, saying, 'This is the one I spoke about when I said, "He who comes after me has surpassed me because he was before me."') ¹⁶ Out of his fullness we have all received grace in place of grace already given. ¹⁷ For the law was given through Moses; grace and truth came through Jesus Christ. ¹⁸ No one has ever seen God, but the one and only Son, who is himself God and[b] is in the closest relationship with the Father, has made him known.

John the Baptist denies being the Messiah

¹⁹ Now this was John's testimony when the Jewish leaders[c] in Jerusalem sent priests and Levites to ask him who he was. ²⁰ He did not fail to confess, but confessed freely, 'I am not the Messiah.'

²¹ They asked him, 'Then who are you? Are you Elijah?'

He said, 'I am not.'

'Are you the Prophet?'

He answered, 'No.'

²² Finally they said, 'Who are you? Give us an answer to take back to those who sent us. What do you say about yourself?'

²³ John replied in the words of Isaiah the prophet, 'I am the voice of one calling in the wilderness, "Make straight the way for the Lord."'[d]

²⁴ Now the Pharisees who had been sent ²⁵ questioned him, 'Why then do you baptise if you are not the Messiah, nor Elijah, nor the Prophet?'

²⁶ 'I baptise with[e] water,' John replied, 'but among you stands one you do not know. ²⁷ He is the one who comes after me, the straps of whose sandals I am not worthy to untie.'

²⁸ This all happened at Bethany on the other side of the Jordan, where John was baptising.

John testifies about Jesus

²⁹ The next day John saw Jesus coming towards him and said, 'Look, the Lamb of God, who takes away the sin of the world! ³⁰ This is the one I meant when I said, "A man who comes after me has surpassed me because he was before me." ³¹ I myself did not know him, but the reason I came baptising with water was that he might be revealed to Israel.'

³² Then John gave this testimony: 'I saw the Spirit come down from heaven as a dove and remain on him. ³³ And I myself

---

a 5 Or *understood*

b 18 Some manuscripts *but the only Son, who*

c 19 The Greek term traditionally translated *the Jews* (*hoi Ioudaioi*) refers here and elsewhere in John's Gospel to those Jewish leaders who opposed Jesus; also in 5:10, 15, 16; 7:1, 11, 13; 9:22; 18:14, 28, 36; 19:7, 12, 31, 38; 20:19.

d 23 Isaiah 40:3

e 26 Or *in*; also in verses 31 and 33 (twice)

WHAT IS CHRISTIANITY? 5

Doctrine of incarnation: God with us

Throughout the Old Testament we see moments when people glimpse the glory of God. It happens to Moses in Exodus 33 and to the whole of Israel in 2 Chronicles 7. Have you ever wondered what the glory of God might look like?

At the start of his Gospel, John is making an astonishing claim: *'We have seen his glory'* (John 1:14). But this isn't just a glimpse – John met the 'glory of God' face to face, he went for walks and ate breakfast with the 'glory of God', he went fishing with the 'glory of God'. All this happened because John met Jesus. Jesus is *'the image of the invisible God'* (Colossians 1:15); he is fully man and fully God (see Luke 8:22–25).

At the start of the Bible we read about how humanity rejected God and chose to live a life independent of him (Genesis 3). God could have stopped us walking away: he's bigger than us. He could have stopped us in the many 'walking-away' moments since then, both in the story of Israel and throughout our own lives, but he gives us a real choice. He won't force anyone to follow him.

Throughout the Bible God is revealing who he is and his plan of salvation for Israel. This moment, at the start of John's Gospel, is the pinnacle of that plan. God the Son, the Word of God, *'became flesh and made his dwelling among us'* (John 1:14). This event is the turning point of history. It's the moment all creation had been waiting for. It has significance for every human being who has ever lived and who will ever live. Creation is fallen, the world is desperate, but with the arrival of Jesus the tide turns. It's like the sun coming up in the morning: you see a single ray of light piercing the fog and darkness and you know the night is almost over. The light of the world is born.

The first three words of John, *'In the beginning'* (John 1:1), mirror the first three words of the Bible, *'In the beginning'* (Genesis 1:1). From before he created, God had known this day would come. The birth of Jesus wasn't an afterthought and it wasn't God's Plan B. From the beginning God had intended to become a part of his creation and live among us.

The incarnation, or 'enfleshment', of God the Son shows us how committed God is to us. He could have opened up a window in heaven and shouted down, 'I love you!' Instead he came himself. He came and joined us in our lostness in order to bring us home again. This is why we worship Jesus and why he is called Immanuel, *'God with us'* (Matthew 1:22).

Andy Croft

 Matthew 3:13–17   Luke 8:22–25 ▶▶

did not know him, but the one who sent me to baptise with water told me, "The man on whom you see the Spirit come down and remain is the one who will baptise with the Holy Spirit." 34 I have seen and I testify that this is God's Chosen One.'f

John's disciples follow Jesus

35 The next day John was there again with two of his disciples. 36 When he saw Jesus passing by, he said, 'Look, the Lamb of God!'

37 When the two disciples heard him say this, they followed Jesus. 38 Turning round, Jesus saw them following and asked, 'What do you want?'

They said, 'Rabbi' (which means 'Teacher'), 'where are you staying?'

39 'Come,' he replied, 'and you will see.'

So they went and saw where he was staying, and they spent that day with him. It was about four in the afternoon.

40 Andrew, Simon Peter's brother, was one of the two who heard what John had said and who had followed Jesus. 41 The first thing Andrew did was to find his brother Simon and tell him, 'We have found the Messiah' (that is, the Christ). 42 And he brought him to Jesus.

Jesus looked at him and said, 'You are Simon son of John. You will be called Cephas' (which, when translated, is Peterg).

Jesus calls Philip and Nathanael

43 The next day Jesus decided to leave for Galilee. Finding Philip, he said to him, 'Follow me.'

44 Philip, like Andrew and Peter, was from the town of Bethsaida. 45 Philip found Nathanael and told him, 'We have found the one Moses wrote about in the Law, and about whom the prophets also wrote – Jesus of Nazareth, the son of Joseph.'

46 'Nazareth! Can anything good come from there?' Nathanael asked.

'Come and see,' said Philip.

47 When Jesus saw Nathanael approaching, he said of him, 'Here truly is an Israelite in whom there is no deceit.'

48 'How do you know me?' Nathanael asked.

Jesus answered, 'I saw you while you were still under the fig-tree before Philip called you.'

49 Then Nathanael declared, 'Rabbi, you are the Son of God; you are the king of Israel.'

50 Jesus said, 'You believeh because I told you I saw you under the fig-tree. You will see greater things than that.' 51 He then added, 'Very truly I tell you,i youi will see "heaven open, and the angels of God ascending and descending on"j the Son of Man.'

Jesus changes water into wine

2 On the third day a wedding took place at Cana in Galilee. Jesus' mother was there, 2 and Jesus and his disciples had also been invited to the wedding. 3 When the wine was gone, Jesus' mother said to him, 'They have no more wine.'

4 'Woman,a why do you involve me?' Jesus replied. 'My hour has not yet come.'

5 His mother said to the servants, 'Do whatever he tells you.'

6 Nearby stood six stone water jars, the kind used by the Jews for ceremonial washing, each holding from eighty to a hundred and twenty litres.

7 Jesus said to the servants, 'Fill the jars with water'; so they filled them to the brim.

8 Then he told them, 'Now draw some out and take it to the master of the banquet.'

They did so, 9 and the master of the banquet tasted the water that had been turned into wine. He did not realise where it had come from, though the servants who had drawn the water knew. Then he called the bridegroom aside 10 and said, 'Everyone brings out the choice wine first and then

---

f 34 See Isaiah 42:1; many manuscripts is the Son of God.

g 42 Cephas (Aramaic) and Peter (Greek) both mean rock.

h 50 Or Do you believe . . . ?

i 51 The Greek is plural.

j 51 Gen. 28:12

a 4 The Greek for Woman does not denote any disrespect.

PEOPLE USED BY GOD 8

Nathanael

As soon as Jesus began to call a few people together to be his disciples, they started to gather others. The joyous impact of Jesus' life caused them to share it with others, a natural reaction when we find something good.

The good part of our nature, perhaps the 'God' part, is to share with others the wonderful things we find. When we see an awesome movie, find a great restaurant or read a book we can't put down, we want to share it with the world! The same thing happened here, only it wasn't a movie, a book or good food, it was an amazing human being.

One of these new followers, Philip, went straight out to find his friend Nathanael and told him that they had found the 'one' – the one for whom all Jews were waiting, the one about whom Moses and the prophets had written. Nathanael's immediate response was, 'You've got to be kidding: a Messiah from Nazareth?' It was prejudice, cold, fast and hard. It's not necessarily that Nathanael was against the town of Nazareth, but more that he couldn't believe the King and Saviour of the world would come from some obscure little town. Nonetheless, he had a prejudice, limited thinking, an instantaneous judgement before giving that person a chance. So many of us do.

When he laid eyes on Nathanael, Jesus saw the real man inside. He didn't see his shortcomings, he saw a seeker of God. Jesus picked out the good in Nathanael – the potential, the bit that reflected him and his Father God. Jesus proclaimed, *'Here truly is an Israelite in whom there is no deceit'* (John 1:47). Other versions of the Bible say 'a man without guile', 'a man of integrity', someone 'without a false bone in his body'. Wow. Do you ever wonder if God sees the good in you? The answer is: yes, he looks for the good, he recognises it even when others don't and even when we can't see it ourselves. What Jesus recognised in Nathanael was a quality that he himself possessed. In 1 Peter 2:22 it says of Jesus, *'He committed no sin, and no deceit was found in his mouth.'* Jesus quickly reassured Nathanael that he was no ordinary man; that he had seen Nathanael when no others had, alone under a fig tree. Perhaps that's where Nathanael had sat in deep reflection and prayer, calling out to God and wondering if he had been heard. As Jesus revealed that he had seen him, he was also revealing that he had heard the cries of Nathanael's heart, that he saw the good in him as he sought for God.

God the Father sees us, he hears our heart, he sees the good, repairs the bad, and forgives us as we repent from our prejudices and shortcomings. We have only to rise up and follow, and proclaim with Nathanael, *'Rabbi, you are the Son of God; you are the king of Israel'* (John 1:49).

Susie Brock

 Luke 19:1–9   John 19:27 ▶▶

the cheaper wine after the guests have had too much to drink; but you have saved the best till now.'

11 What Jesus did here in Cana of Galilee was the first of the signs through which he revealed his glory; and his disciples believed in him.

12 After this he went down to Capernaum with his mother and brothers and his disciples. There they stayed for a few days.

MARY

ANNOUNCEMENT
Luke 1:26–38
SONG
Luke 1:27–56
BIRTH
Luke 2:1–21
ESCAPE
Matthew 2:13–23
LOST
Luke 2:41–52
FAMILY
Mark 3:20–35
WEDDING
John 2:1–12
AT THE CRUCIFIXION
John 19:25–27

Jesus clears the temple courts

13 When it was almost time for the Jewish Passover, Jesus went up to Jerusalem. 14 In the temple courts he found people selling cattle, sheep and doves, and others sitting at tables exchanging money. 15 So he made a whip out of cords, and drove all from the temple courts, both sheep and cattle; he scattered the coins of the money-changers and overturned their tables. 16 To those who sold doves he said, 'Get these out of here! Stop turning my Father's house into a market!' 17 His

disciples remembered that it is written: 'Zeal for your house will consume me.'[b]

18 The Jews then responded to him, 'What sign can you show us to prove your authority to do all this?'

19 Jesus answered them, 'Destroy this temple, and I will raise it again in three days.'

20 They replied, 'It has taken forty-six years to build this temple, and you are going to raise it in three days?' 21 But the temple he had spoken of was his body. 22 After he was raised from the dead, his disciples recalled what he had said. Then they believed the Scripture and the words that Jesus had spoken.

23 Now while he was in Jerusalem at the Passover Festival, many people saw the signs he was performing and believed in his name.[c] 24 But Jesus would not entrust himself to them, for he knew all people. 25 He did not need any testimony about mankind, for he knew what was in each person.

Jesus teaches Nicodemus

3 Now there was a Pharisee, a man named Nicodemus who was a member of the Jewish ruling council. 2 He came to Jesus at night and said, 'Rabbi, we know that you are a teacher who has come from God. For no one could perform the signs you are doing if God were not with him.'

3 Jesus replied, 'Very truly I tell you, no one can see the kingdom of God unless they are born again.[a]'

4 'How can someone be born when they are old?' Nicodemus asked. 'Surely they cannot enter a second time into their mother's womb to be born!'

5 Jesus answered, 'Very truly I tell you, no one can enter the kingdom of God unless they are born of water and the Spirit. 6 Flesh gives birth to flesh, but the Spirit[b] gives birth to spirit. 7 You should not be surprised at my saying, "You[c] must be

---

b 17 Psalm 69:9
c 23 Or *in him*
a 3 The Greek for *again* also means *from above*; also in verse 7.
b 6 Or *but spirit*
c 7 The Greek is plural.

born again." ⁸The wind blows wherever it pleases. You hear its sound, but you cannot tell where it comes from or where it is going. So it is with everyone born of the Spirit.'ᵈ

⁹'How can this be?' Nicodemus asked.

¹⁰'You are Israel's teacher,' said Jesus, 'and do you not understand these things? ¹¹Very truly I tell you, we speak of what we know, and we testify to what we have seen, but still you people do not accept our testimony. ¹²I have spoken to you of earthly things and you do not believe; how then will you believe if I speak of heavenly things? ¹³No one has ever gone into heaven except the one who came from heaven – the Son of Man.ᵉ ¹⁴Just as Moses lifted up the snake in the wilderness, so the Son of Man must be lifted up,ᶠ ¹⁵that everyone who believes may have eternal life in him.'ᵍ

¹⁶For God so loved the world that he gave his one and only Son, that whoever believes in him shall not perish but have eternal life. ¹⁷For God did not send his Son into the world to condemn the world, but to save the world through him. ¹⁸Whoever believes in him is not condemned, but whoever does not believe stands condemned already because they have not believed in the name of God's one and only Son. ¹⁹This is the verdict: light has come into the world, but people loved darkness instead of light because their deeds were evil. ²⁰Everyone who does evil hates the light, and will not come into the light for fear that their deeds will be exposed. ²¹But whoever lives by the truth comes into the light, so that it may be seen plainly that what they have done has been done in the sight of God.

John testifies again about Jesus

²²After this, Jesus and his disciples went out into the Judean countryside, where he spent some time with them, and baptised. ²³Now John also was baptising at Aenon near Salim, because there was plenty of water, and people were coming and being baptised. ²⁴(This was before John was put in prison.) ²⁵An argument developed between some of John's disciples and a certain Jew over the matter of ceremonial washing. ²⁶They came to John and said to him, 'Rabbi, that man who was with you on the other side of the Jordan – the one you testified about – look, he is baptising, and everyone is going to him.'

²⁷To this John replied, 'A person can receive only what is given them from heaven. ²⁸You yourselves can testify that I said, "I am not the Messiah but am sent ahead of him." ²⁹The bride belongs to the bridegroom. The friend who attends the bridegroom waits and listens for him, and is full of joy when he hears the bridegroom's voice. That joy is mine, and it is now complete. ³⁰He must become greater; I must become less.'ʰ

³¹The one who comes from above is above all; the one who is from the earth belongs to the earth, and speaks as one from the earth. The one who comes from heaven is above all. ³²He testifies to what he has seen and heard, but no one accepts his testimony. ³³Whoever has accepted it has certified that God is truthful. ³⁴For the one whom God has sent speaks the words of God, for Godⁱ gives the Spirit without limit. ³⁵The Father loves the Son and has placed everything in his hands. ³⁶Whoever believes in the Son has eternal life, but whoever rejects the Son will not see life, for God's wrath remains on them.

Jesus talks with a Samaritan woman

4 Now Jesus learned that the Pharisees had heard that he was gaining and baptising more disciples than John – ²although in fact it was not Jesus who baptised, but his disciples. ³So he left Judea and went back once more to Galilee. ⁴Now he had to go through Samaria. ⁵So he came to a town in Samaria called Sychar, near the plot of ground Jacob had

---

ᵈ8 The Greek for *Spirit* is the same as that for *wind*.
ᵉ13 Some manuscripts *Man, who is in heaven*
ᶠ14 The Greek for *lifted up* also means *exalted*.
ᵍ15 Some interpreters end the quotation with verse 21.

ʰ30 Some interpreters end the quotation with verse 36.
ⁱ34 Greek *he*

LAW AND GRACE 5

The grace embrace

John 3:16 is the most well-known verse in the Bible. It sums up God's extravagant grace – his desire to do all he can to ensure we have life, and life to the full. Time and again the Bible tells us that because God treasures us as his creation, he didn't wait until we got our act together before rescuing us. His first instinct is to love us and forgive us, and nothing we can do can change this. God loves us. Full stop.

The writer Philip Yancey said, 'There is nothing we can do to make God love us more, there is nothing we can do to make God love us less.' This is the truth about law and grace. The law teaches us that we get it wrong; we go against God's standard of right and wrong; we sin. God's grace means that he forgives us when we ask, and from that point on it doesn't matter whether we sinned ten years, ten hours or ten seconds ago: God's love for us remains the same.

The Bible is clear: we can do nothing to earn God's favour. Jesus coming to earth and dying for us is proof that we *already* had it! God loved us, and because he loved us, he sent Jesus. God has done all the work for us and our response should be a heartfelt desire to serve him. We don't do (or not do!) things because we want to earn God's love. We make the right choice because we understand how amazingly loved we are, and out of gratitude we offer ourselves back to God. Nothing but offering our whole lives to God can feel like enough when we begin to understand how much Jesus loved us and what that cost him.

It's this that sets Christianity apart from other world religions. We don't have to do stuff to have a shot at eternity with God, and our relationship with God isn't dependent on us getting it right all the time. God has a right and wrong way for us to live, but failing to meet that standard doesn't exclude us from living with God for ever. God pursues relationship with us, and rescues us even when we disappoint him. We see God in a deep ongoing relationship with Adam and Eve even after they left Eden. We find God rescuing his people from Egypt, then caring for them while they're in exile in Babylon and bringing them home again, but the greatest rescue effort is God himself becoming human so we can receive eternal life.

God doesn't only love us when we get it right, when we're worshipping him, or when we're in church. No matter where we are or what we have done, God's word to us is, 'I love you.' His love is so rich, so unconditional and so full of grace that it clearly deserves to be returned. Will we love God by living lives of true, sacrificial worship for the next ten seconds, ten years or for the rest of eternity? With God's Spirit working in us, we can spend the rest of eternity in an increasingly deep and loving relationship with God.

Jason Gardner

 Romans 7:1–3

SEXISM

The Bible is an account of God's dealings with individuals, societies and nations, good and bad. Some of the stuff people do and think isn't great, but God takes people from where they are – sin, bad thinking, bad actions and the rest – and begins a process of transformation. God calls people and cultures from their wrong thinking and actions, asking them to repent and live under the values of his kingdom. So even if the heart of biblical culture comes across as sexist, the question is really, 'Is God himself sexist?'

Throughout the Bible we see God acting positively towards and about women. God creates both Adam and Eve in his image. He raises up female leaders in Israel, notably Deborah (Judges 4 – 5) and Esther (Esther 1 – 10), and women play a significant role in Israel's story (Sarah, Rebekah, Miriam, Rahab and Ruth) and in Jesus' family history (Rahab, Elizabeth and Mary). Yet it's in Jesus that we see God's heart revealed most clearly.

In the encounter between Jesus and the Samaritan woman (John 4), we start to see how Jesus breaks down the traditional values of a culture. There are two reasons why she should be a second-class citizen to Jesus: her race and her gender. Jesus breaks through these prejudices, giving value to both aspects of her identity. Jesus initiates the conversation, makes a request of the woman even though she's a Samaritan and sinful, and takes the conversation further with personal revelations. Finally he offers this woman eternal life. She is one of the first evangelists, revealing Jesus to her village, and many follow him because of her personal witness. If Jesus was sexist, he wouldn't have bothered talking to her in the first place and certainly wouldn't have used her in furthering God's kingdom. God's heart is for everyone, regardless of background, race or gender.

Jesus continues to work closely with women: Mary Magdalene, Mary and Martha and Joanna are named, but others he encounters may not be named but are still significant in his ministry and teaching (Mark 14:1–11; Luke 13:10–17; 21:1–4). Women are accepted and valued along with men, not placed above or below them.

Sometimes we make God seem sexist by using 'he', 'him' and 'his' to describe God. This is a problem of language rather than God's biology! Our language falls short and we either have to describe God as male or female, or as 'it'. God is personal, and 'it' fails even more than 'he' or 'she' in demonstrating this very important part of God's character. We have most often used male classifications because these are more dominant in the Bible, although at times God is referred to with female characteristics (Luke 13:34). However, God is not male or female. God is beyond maleness and femaleness. You might say that the cultures in the Bible are sometimes sexist, that the church is sometimes sexist, but that God is most definitely not sexist.

Ali Etheridge

given to his son Joseph. ⁶Jacob's well was there, and Jesus, tired as he was from the journey, sat down by the well. It was about noon.

⁷When a Samaritan woman came to draw water, Jesus said to her, 'Will you give me a drink?' ⁸(His disciples had gone into the town to buy food.)

⁹The Samaritan woman said to him, 'You are a Jew and I am a Samaritan woman. How can you ask me for a drink?' (For Jews do not associate with Samaritans.ᵃ)

¹⁰Jesus answered her, 'If you knew the gift of God and who it is that asks you for a drink, you would have asked him and he would have given you living water.'

¹¹'Sir,' the woman said, 'you have nothing to draw with and the well is deep. Where can you get this living water? ¹²Are you greater than our father Jacob, who gave us the well and drank from it himself, as did also his sons and his livestock?'

¹³Jesus answered, 'Everyone who drinks this water will be thirsty again, ¹⁴but whoever drinks the water I give them will never thirst. Indeed, the water I give them will become in them a spring of water welling up to eternal life.'

¹⁵The woman said to him, 'Sir, give me this water so that I won't get thirsty and have to keep coming here to draw water.'

¹⁶He told her, 'Go, call your husband and come back.'

¹⁷'I have no husband,' she replied.

Jesus said to her, 'You are right when you say you have no husband. ¹⁸The fact is, you have had five husbands, and the man you now have is not your husband. What you have just said is quite true.'

¹⁹'Sir,' the woman said, 'I can see that you are a prophet. ²⁰Our ancestors worshipped on this mountain, but you Jews claim that the place where we must worship is in Jerusalem.'

²¹'Woman,' Jesus replied, 'believe me, a time is coming when you will worship the Father neither on this mountain nor in Jerusalem. ²²You Samaritans worship what you do not know; we worship what

we do know, for salvation is from the Jews. ²³Yet a time is coming and has now come when the true worshippers will worship the Father in the Spirit and in truth, for they are the kind of worshippers the Father seeks. ²⁴God is spirit, and his worshippers must worship in the Spirit and in truth.'

²⁵The woman said, 'I know that Messiah' (called Christ) 'is coming. When he comes, he will explain everything to us.'

²⁶Then Jesus declared, 'I, the one speaking to you – I am he.'

The disciples rejoin Jesus

²⁷Just then his disciples returned and were surprised to find him talking with a woman. But no one asked, 'What do you want?' or 'Why are you talking with her?'

²⁸Then, leaving her water jar, the woman went back to the town and said to the people, ²⁹'Come, see a man who told me everything I've ever done. Could this be the Messiah?' ³⁰They came out of the town and made their way towards him.

³¹Meanwhile his disciples urged him, 'Rabbi, eat something.'

³²But he said to them, 'I have food to eat that you know nothing about.'

³³Then his disciples said to each other, 'Could someone have brought him food?'

³⁴'My food,' said Jesus, 'is to do the will of him who sent me and to finish his work. ³⁵Don't you have a saying, "It's still four months until harvest"? I tell you, open your eyes and look at the fields! They are ripe for harvest. ³⁶Even now the one who reaps draws a wage and harvests a crop for eternal life, so that the sower and the reaper may be glad together. ³⁷Thus the saying "One sows and another reaps" is true. ³⁸I sent you to reap what you have not worked for. Others have done the hard work, and you have reaped the benefits of their labour.'

Many Samaritans believe

³⁹Many of the Samaritans from that town believed in him because of the woman's testimony, 'He told me everything I've ever done.' ⁴⁰So when the Samaritans came to him, they urged him to stay with them, and he stayed two days.

ᵃ 9 Or do not use dishes Samaritans have used

⁴¹And because of his words many more became believers.

⁴²They said to the woman, 'We no longer believe just because of what you said; now we have heard for ourselves, and we know that this man really is the Saviour of the world.'

Jesus heals an official's son

⁴³After the two days he left for Galilee. ⁴⁴(Now Jesus himself had pointed out that a prophet has no honour in his own country.) ⁴⁵When he arrived in Galilee, the Galileans welcomed him. They had seen all that he had done in Jerusalem at the Passover Festival, for they also had been there.

⁴⁶Once more he visited Cana in Galilee, where he had turned the water into wine. And there was a certain royal official whose son lay ill at Capernaum. ⁴⁷When this man heard that Jesus had arrived in

LIFE OF JESUS 6

Lord over sickness

Few people question that Jesus was a healer. Even his critics didn't doubt this: they just questioned whether it was God or the devil who allowed him to do this. The Gospels indicate that Jesus was able to cure a range of ailments: epilepsy, deformed limbs, blindness, deafness, even death and – evidently – decomposition.

The miracle in John 4:46–54 is a fairly typical one. A child with an unspecified, but apparently terminal illness is healed at a distance by Jesus, who appears to do no more than simply command the healing to occur. John, however, sees this as being a sign, a symbolic action that Jesus was not just a good man, but the Messiah and God come to earth.

But why is it a sign? The answer lies in the fact that the Bible's teaching is that sickness and death are results of the great separation between human beings and God. Decay, suffering and death are the inevitable consequences of humankind rebelling against God (Genesis 3:16–19). Jesus' healing is a sign – like a first crocus in winter – that the rule of death and disease is not going to be for ever. Jesus is the man who is able to reverse the effects of sin; through him the powers that have bound the human race and made life miserable for generations are defeated. The healings therefore look forward to what the Bible calls the 'Last Day', the time when death and disease will be completely eradicated (Revelation 21:1–5).

Will Jesus answer our individual prayers for healing? I hope he will, and let's be persistent in prayer as he has instructed. In the meantime we can be sure that one day Jesus will permanently complete and remake all creation into an awesome, glorious wonder that will endure for ever beyond all death and decay.

J.John

 Mark 13:31   John 6:5–21 ▶

Galilee from Judea, he went to him and begged him to come and heal his son, who was close to death.

48'Unless you people see signs and wonders,' Jesus told him, 'you will never believe.'

49The royal official said, 'Sir, come down before my child dies.'

50'Go,' Jesus replied, 'your son will live.'

The man took Jesus at his word and departed. 51While he was still on the way, his servants met him with the news that his boy was living. 52When he enquired as to the time when his son got better, they said to him, 'Yesterday, at one in the afternoon, the fever left him.'

53Then the father realised that this was the exact time at which Jesus had said to him, 'Your son will live.' So he and his whole household believed.

54This was the second sign Jesus performed after coming from Judea to Galilee.

The healing at the pool

5 Some time later, Jesus went up to Jerusalem for one of the Jewish festivals. 2Now there is in Jerusalem near the Sheep Gate a pool, which in Aramaic is called Bethesda*a* and which is surrounded by five covered colonnades. 3Here a great number of disabled people used to lie – the blind, the lame, the paralysed. [4]*b* 5One who was there had been an invalid for thirty-eight years. 6When Jesus saw him lying there and learned that he had been in this condition for a long time, he asked him, 'Do you want to get well?'

7'Sir,' the invalid replied, 'I have no one to help me into the pool when the water is stirred. While I am trying to get in, someone else goes down ahead of me.'

8Then Jesus said to him, 'Get up! Pick up your mat and walk.' 9At once the man

---

a 2 Some manuscripts *Bethzatha*; other manuscripts *Bethsaida*

b 3,4 Some manuscripts include here, wholly or in part, *paralysed – and they waited for the moving of the waters.* *From time to time an angel of the Lord would come down and stir up the waters. The first one into the pool after each such disturbance would be cured of whatever disease they had.*

---

was cured; he picked up his mat and walked.

The day on which this took place was a Sabbath, 10and so the Jewish leaders said to the man who had been healed, 'It is the Sabbath; the law forbids you to carry your mat.'

11But he replied, 'The man who made me well said to me, "Pick up your mat and walk."'

12So they asked him, 'Who is this fellow who told you to pick it up and walk?'

13The man who was healed had no idea who it was, for Jesus had slipped away into the crowd that was there.

14Later Jesus found him at the temple and said to him, 'See, you are well again. Stop sinning or something worse may happen to you.' 15The man went away and told the Jewish leaders that it was Jesus who had made him well.

The authority of the Son

16So, because Jesus was doing these things on the Sabbath, the Jewish leaders began to persecute him. 17In his defence Jesus said to them, 'My Father is always at his work to this very day, and I too am working.' 18For this reason they tried all the more to kill him; not only was he breaking the Sabbath, but he was even calling God his own Father, making himself equal with God.

19Jesus gave them this answer: 'Very truly I tell you, the Son can do nothing by himself; he can do only what he sees his Father doing, because whatever the Father does the Son also does. 20For the Father loves the Son and shows him all he does. Yes, and he will show him even greater works than these, so that you will be amazed. 21For just as the Father raises the dead and gives them life, even so the Son gives life to whom he is pleased to give it. 22Moreover, the Father judges no one, but has entrusted all judgment to the Son, 23that all may honour the Son just as they honour the Father. Whoever does not honour the Son does not honour the Father, who sent him.

24'Very truly I tell you, whoever hears my word and believes him who sent me has eternal life and will not be judged but has crossed over from death to life. 25 Very truly I tell you, a time is coming and has now come when the dead will hear the voice of the Son of God and those who hear will live. 26 For as the Father has life in himself, so he has granted the Son also to have life in himself. 27 And he has given him authority to judge because he is the Son of Man.

28 'Do not be amazed at this, for a time is coming when all who are in their graves will hear his voice 29 and come out – those who have done what is good will rise to

HOW CAN I BE SURE I'M SAVED?

Being certain that we're saved can be a real challenge for many Christians. One of the best ways to be sure we're saved is to read the Bible. In John 5:24, Jesus says, *'Very truly I tell you, whoever hears my word and believes him who sent me has eternal life and will not be judged but has crossed over from death to life.'* Jesus is making a promise here: he's saying that if we believe in him, we're saved.

In Revelation 3:20, Jesus also says, *'Here I am! I stand at the door and knock. If anyone hears my voice and opens the door, I will come in and eat with that person, and they with me.'* Jesus is speaking figuratively here, but what he means is that if we invite him into our lives, he will 'come in and eat'. In Middle Eastern culture, eating with someone is a sign of friendship, so what Jesus is saying in these two verses is that if we believe in him and invite him into our lives, we're saved and Jesus begins a friendship with us.

When we believe in Jesus, we have faith in him; we believe that he is God, that he lived on earth and died for our sins, that he rose again, and that he is alive today and has the power to change us through our relationship with him. As part of that we repent of our sins, saying sorry for the wrong things we have done and turning away from them so that we try not to do them again. When we do this, the Bible promises us in John 5:24 that we're saved. Therefore we can know that we're saved because God says so!

Another way that we can know we're saved is by the work of the Holy Spirit. In Revelation 3:20, Jesus says he will come into our lives if we invite him, but it's not actually him who comes in, but his Holy Spirit. And as we spend time with God, studying the Bible, praying and worshipping him, the Holy Spirit starts to change us. In Galatians 5:22–23, the apostle Paul lists some of the changes that the Holy Spirit works in us; he says we grow in love, joy, peace, patience, kindness, goodness, faithfulness, gentleness and self-control. Sometimes it can seem that these changes are taking a long time, but this work of the Holy Spirit also shows us, and those around us, that we're saved.

So how can we be sure that we're saved? By the promises we read in the Bible and also by the work the Holy Spirit performs in our lives.

Freddie Pimm

live, and those who have done what is evil will rise to be condemned. **30** By myself I can do nothing; I judge only as I hear, and my judgment is just, for I seek not to please myself but him who sent me.

Testimonies about Jesus

31 'If I testify about myself, my testimony is not true. **32** There is another who testifies in my favour, and I know that his testimony about me is true.

33 'You have sent to John and he has testified to the truth. **34** Not that I accept human testimony; but I mention it that you may be saved. **35** John was a lamp that burned and gave light, and you chose for a time to enjoy his light.

36 'I have testimony weightier than that of John. For the works that the Father has given me to finish – the very works that I am doing – testify that the Father has sent me. **37** And the Father who sent me has himself testified concerning me. You have never heard his voice nor seen his form, **38** nor does his word dwell in you, for you do not believe the one he sent. **39** You study^c the Scriptures diligently because you think that in them you have eternal life. These are the very Scriptures that testify about me, **40** yet you refuse to come to me to have life.

41 'I do not accept glory from human beings, **42** but I know you. I know that you do not have the love of God in your hearts. **43** I have come in my Father's name, and you do not accept me; but if someone else comes in his own name, you will accept him. **44** How can you believe since you accept glory from one another but do not seek the glory that comes from the only God^d?

45 'But do not think I will accuse you before the Father. Your accuser is Moses, on whom your hopes are set. **46** If you believed Moses, you would believe me, for he wrote about me. **47** But since you do not believe what he wrote, how are you going to believe what I say?'

Jesus feeds the five thousand

6 Some time after this, Jesus crossed to the far shore of the Sea of Galilee (that is, the Sea of Tiberias), **2** and a great crowd of people followed him because they saw the signs he had performed by healing those who were ill. **3** Then Jesus went up on a mountainside and sat down with his disciples. **4** The Jewish Passover Festival was near.

5 When Jesus looked up and saw a great crowd coming towards him, he said to Philip, 'Where shall we buy bread for these people to eat?' **6** He asked this only to test him, for he already had in mind what he was going to do.

7 Philip answered him, 'It would take more than half a year's wages^a to buy enough bread for each one to have a bite!'

8 Another of his disciples, Andrew, Simon Peter's brother, spoke up, **9** 'Here is a boy with five small barley loaves and two small fish, but how far will they go among so many?'

10 Jesus said, 'Make the people sit down.' There was plenty of grass in that place, and they sat down (about five thousand men were there). **11** Jesus then took the loaves, gave thanks, and distributed to those who were seated as much as they wanted. He did the same with the fish.

12 When they had all had enough to eat, he said to his disciples, 'Gather the pieces that are left over. Let nothing be wasted.' **13** So they gathered them and filled twelve baskets with the pieces of the five barley loaves left over by those who had eaten.

14 After the people saw the sign Jesus performed, they began to say, 'Surely this is the Prophet who is to come into the world.' **15** Jesus, knowing that they intended to come and make him king by force, withdrew again to a mountain by himself.

Jesus walks on the water

16 When evening came, his disciples went down to the lake, **17** where they got into a boat and set off across the lake for

---

c 39 Or ³⁹Study
d 44 Some early manuscripts the Only One

a 7 Greek two hundred denarii

Capernaum. By now it was dark, and Jesus had not yet joined them. ¹⁸A strong wind was blowing and the waters grew rough. ¹⁹When they had rowed about three or four miles,ᵇ they saw Jesus approaching the boat, walking on the water; and they

ᵇ 19 Or about 5 or 6 kilometres

LIFE OF JESUS 7

Lord over nature

Often our world doesn't seem that big. We can fly around the globe in little more than a day, we think nothing of phoning Australia. Mountains and rugged coastlines no longer scare us, but instead are merely sites for photographs or adventure activities. We seem to have tamed nature. Or have we? Every year on average tens of thousands of people are killed by earthquakes, volcanoes and tsunamis. Many more die because of drought and extreme weather. There's a powerful side to nature that deserves respect.

Although in ancient times the Jewish people had no specific word for what we call 'nature', they knew what it was all about and they knew all too well that it could kill them. Consider the narrow strip of land that they lived on. To the east, across the Jordan Valley, lay the baking wilderness where starvation was inevitable. To the west lay the 'Great Sea' – the Mediterranean – the source of winter storms whose waves could devastate harbours, shatter ships and drown sailors. For the Jewish people the sea came to be the very personification of chaos. Significantly, when leaving Egypt during the exodus, the Israelites had faced both the threat of the sea and the wilderness.

In John 6:5–21, in a pair of miraculous acts reported in various ways in every Gospel, Jesus demonstrates mastery over both wilderness and water. In the wilderness, in another of what John's Gospel calls 'signs', Jesus provides food. That was something that God had done through Moses centuries earlier in the days of the exodus. Then, in another action full of significance, Jesus walks to the disciples on the threatening storm waves. To us there's an odd note in the account when the disciples are not relieved by the appearance of Jesus, but instead terrified. As sailors who knew their Old Testament, they knew that the one being who could walk on water was Yahweh, God himself (Job 9:8; Habakkuk 3:15). Who is Jesus? The lessons are obvious for those who care to think about it: he's more than Moses, he's God himself.

This pair of miracles goes further than just simply establishing the identity of Jesus. They tell us that, in Jesus, we have someone who is master of nature. There are times when we may need reminding of that fact.

J. John

 John 4:46–54   John 20:28 ▶

were frightened. ²⁰But he said to them, 'It is I; don't be afraid.' ²¹Then they were willing to take him into the boat, and immediately the boat reached the shore where they were heading.

²²The next day the crowd that had stayed on the opposite shore of the lake realised that only one boat had been there, and that Jesus had not entered it with his disciples, but that they had gone away alone. ²³Then some boats from Tiberias landed near the place where the people had eaten the bread after the Lord had given thanks. ²⁴Once the crowd realised that neither Jesus nor his disciples were there, they got into the boats and went to Capernaum in search of Jesus.

Jesus the bread of life

²⁵When they found him on the other side of the lake, they asked him, 'Rabbi, when did you get here?'

²⁶Jesus answered, 'Very truly I tell you, you are looking for me, not because you saw the signs I performed but because you ate the loaves and had your fill. ²⁷Do not work for food that spoils, but for food that endures to eternal life, which the Son of Man will give you. For on him God the Father has placed his seal of approval.'

²⁸Then they asked him, 'What must we do to do the works God requires?'

²⁹Jesus answered, 'The work of God is this: to believe in the one he has sent.'

³⁰So they asked him, 'What sign then will you give that we may see it and believe you? What will you do? ³¹Our ancestors ate the manna in the wilderness; as it is written: "He gave them bread from heaven to eat."ᶜ'

³²Jesus said to them, 'Very truly I tell you, it is not Moses who has given you the bread from heaven, but it is my Father who gives you the true bread from heaven. ³³For the bread of God is the bread that comes down from heaven and gives life to the world.'

³⁴'Sir,' they said, 'always give us this bread.'

³⁵Then Jesus declared, 'I am the bread of life. Whoever comes to me will never go hungry, and whoever believes in me will never be thirsty. ³⁶But as I told you, you have seen me and still you do not believe. ³⁷All those the Father gives me will come to me, and whoever comes to me I will never drive away. ³⁸For I have come down from heaven not to do my will but to do the will of him who sent me. ³⁹And this is the will of him who sent me, that I shall lose none of all those he has given me, but raise them up at the last day. ⁴⁰For my Father's will is that everyone who looks to the Son and believes in him shall have eternal life, and I will raise them up at the last day.'

⁴¹At this the Jews there began to grumble about him because he said, 'I am the bread that came down from heaven.' ⁴²They said, 'Is this not Jesus, the son of Joseph, whose father and mother we know? How can he now say, "I came down from heaven"?'

⁴³'Stop grumbling among yourselves,' Jesus answered. ⁴⁴'No one can come to me unless the Father who sent me draws them, and I will raise them up at the last day. ⁴⁵It is written in the Prophets: "They will all be taught by God."ᵈ Everyone who has heard the Father and learned from him comes to me. ⁴⁶No one has seen the Father except the one who is from God; only he has seen the Father. ⁴⁷Very truly I tell you, the one who believes has eternal life. ⁴⁸I am the bread of life. ⁴⁹Your ancestors ate the manna in the wilderness, yet they died. ⁵⁰But here is the bread that comes down from heaven, which anyone may eat and not die. ⁵¹I am the living bread that came down from heaven. Whoever eats this bread will live for ever. This bread is my flesh, which I will give for the life of the world.'

⁵²Then the Jews began to argue sharply among themselves, 'How can this man give us his flesh to eat?'

⁵³Jesus said to them, 'Very truly I tell you, unless you eat the flesh of the Son

---

ᶜ 31 Exodus 16:4; Neh. 9:15; Psalm 78:24,25 ᵈ 45 Isaiah 54:13

of Man and drink his blood, you have no life in you. ⁵⁴Whoever eats my flesh and drinks my blood has eternal life, and I will raise them up at the last day. ⁵⁵For my flesh is real food and my blood is real drink. ⁵⁶Whoever eats my flesh and drinks my blood remains in me, and I in them. ⁵⁷Just as the living Father sent me and I live because of the Father, so the one who feeds on me will live because of me. ⁵⁸This is the bread that came down from heaven. Your ancestors ate manna and died, but whoever feeds on this bread will live for ever.' ⁵⁹He said this while teaching in the synagogue in Capernaum.

Many disciples desert Jesus

⁶⁰On hearing it, many of his disciples said, 'This is a hard teaching. Who can accept it?'

⁶¹Aware that his disciples were grumbling about this, Jesus said to them, 'Does this offend you? ⁶²Then what if you see the Son of Man ascend to where he was before! ⁶³The Spirit gives life; the flesh counts for nothing. The words I have spoken to you – they are full of the Spirit*e* and life. ⁶⁴Yet there are some of you who do not believe.' For Jesus had known from the beginning which of them did not believe and who would betray him. ⁶⁵He went on to say, 'This is why I told you that no one can come to me unless the Father has enabled them.'

⁶⁶From this time many of his disciples turned back and no longer followed him.

⁶⁷'You do not want to leave too, do you?' Jesus asked the Twelve.

⁶⁸Simon Peter answered him, 'Lord, to whom shall we go? You have the words of eternal life. ⁶⁹We have come to believe and to know that you are the Holy One of God.'

⁷⁰Then Jesus replied, 'Have I not chosen you, the Twelve? Yet one of you is a devil!' ⁷¹(He meant Judas, the son of Simon Iscariot, who, though one of the Twelve, was later to betray him.)

Jesus goes to the Festival of Tabernacles

7 After this, Jesus went around in Galilee. He did not want*a* to go about in Judea because the Jewish leaders there were looking for a way to kill him. ²But when the Jewish Festival of Tabernacles was near, ³Jesus' brothers said to him, 'Leave Galilee and go to Judea, so that your disciples there may see the works you do. ⁴No one who wants to become a public figure acts in secret. Since you are doing these things, show yourself to the world.' ⁵For even his own brothers did not believe in him.

⁶Therefore Jesus told them, 'My time is not yet here; for you any time will do. ⁷The world cannot hate you, but it hates me because I testify that its works are evil. ⁸You go to the festival. I am not*b* going up to this festival, because my time has not yet fully come.' ⁹After he had said this, he stayed in Galilee.

¹⁰However, after his brothers had left for the festival, he went also, not publicly, but in secret. ¹¹Now at the festival the Jewish leaders were watching for Jesus and asking, 'Where is he?'

¹²Among the crowds there was widespread whispering about him. Some said, 'He is a good man.'

Others replied, 'No, he deceives the people.' ¹³But no one would say anything publicly about him for fear of the leaders.

Jesus teaches at the festival

¹⁴Not until halfway through the festival did Jesus go up to the temple courts and begin to teach. ¹⁵The Jews there were amazed and asked, 'How did this man get such learning without having been taught?'

¹⁶Jesus answered, 'My teaching is not my own. It comes from the one who sent me. ¹⁷Anyone who chooses to do the will of God will find out whether my teaching comes from God or whether I speak on my own. ¹⁸Whoever speaks on their own

---

e 63 Or *are Spirit; or are spirit*

a 1 Some manuscripts *not have authority*
b 8 Some manuscripts *not yet*

does so to gain personal glory, but he who seeks the glory of the one who sent him is a man of truth; there is nothing false about him. ¹⁹ Has not Moses given you the law? Yet not one of you keeps the law. Why are you trying to kill me?'

²⁰ 'You are demon-possessed,' the crowd answered. 'Who is trying to kill you?'

²¹ Jesus said to them, 'I did one miracle, and you are all amazed. ²² Yet, because Moses gave you circumcision (though actually it did not come from Moses, but from the patriarchs), you circumcise a boy on the Sabbath. ²³ Now if a boy can be circumcised on the Sabbath so that the law of Moses may not be broken, why are you angry with me for healing a man's whole body on the Sabbath? ²⁴ Stop judging by mere appearances, but instead judge correctly.'

Division over who Jesus is

²⁵ At that point some of the people of Jerusalem began to ask, 'Isn't this the man they are trying to kill? ²⁶ Here he is, speaking publicly, and they are not saying a word to him. Have the authorities really concluded that he is the Messiah? ²⁷ But we know where this man is from; when the Messiah comes, no one will know where he is from.'

²⁸ Then Jesus, still teaching in the temple courts, cried out, 'Yes, you know me, and you know where I am from. I am not here on my own authority, but he who sent me is true. You do not know him, ²⁹ but I know him because I am from him and he sent me.'

³⁰ At this they tried to seize him, but no one laid a hand on him, because his hour had not yet come. ³¹ Still, many in the crowd believed in him. They said, 'When the Messiah comes, will he perform more signs than this man?'

³² The Pharisees heard the crowd whispering such things about him. Then the chief priests and the Pharisees sent temple guards to arrest him.

³³ Jesus said, 'I am with you for only a short time, and then I am going to the one who sent me. ³⁴ You will look for me, but

you will not find me; and where I am, you cannot come.'

³⁵ The Jews said to one another, 'Where does this man intend to go that we cannot find him? Will he go where our people live scattered among the Greeks, and teach the Greeks? ³⁶ What did he mean when he said, "You will look for me, but you will not find me," and "Where I am, you cannot come"?'

³⁷ On the last and greatest day of the festival, Jesus stood and said in a loud voice, 'Let anyone who is thirsty come to me and drink. ³⁸ Whoever believes in me, as Scripture has said, rivers of living water will flow from within them.'ᶜ ³⁹ By this he meant the Spirit, whom those who believed in him were later to receive. Up to that time the Spirit had not been given, since Jesus had not yet been glorified.

⁴⁰ On hearing his words, some of the people said, 'Surely this man is the Prophet.'

⁴¹ Others said, 'He is the Messiah.'

Still others asked, 'How can the Messiah come from Galilee? ⁴² Does not Scripture say that the Messiah will come from David's descendants and from Bethlehem, the town where David lived?' ⁴³ Thus the people were divided because of Jesus. ⁴⁴ Some wanted to seize him, but no one laid a hand on him.

Unbelief of the Jewish leaders

⁴⁵ Finally the temple guards went back to the chief priests and the Pharisees, who asked them, 'Why didn't you bring him in?'

⁴⁶ 'No one ever spoke the way this man does,' the guards replied.

⁴⁷ 'You mean he has deceived you also?' the Pharisees retorted. ⁴⁸ 'Have any of the rulers or of the Pharisees believed in him? ⁴⁹ No! But this mob that knows nothing of the law – there is a curse on them.'

⁵⁰ Nicodemus, who had gone to Jesus earlier and who was one of their own number, asked, ⁵¹ 'Does our law condemn

---

ᶜ 37,38 Or me. And let anyone drink ³⁸who believes in me.' As Scripture has said, 'Out of him (or them) will flow rivers of living water.'

a man without first hearing him to find out what he has been doing?'

52 They replied, 'Are you from Galilee, too? Look into it, and you will find that a prophet does not come out of Galilee.'

_____

[The earliest manuscripts and many other ancient witnesses do not have John 7:53 – 8:11. A few manuscripts include these verses, wholly or in part, after John 7:36, John 21:25, Luke 21:38 or Luke 24:53.]

8 53 *Then they all went home,* 1 *but Jesus went to the Mount of Olives.*

2 *At dawn he appeared again in the temple courts, where all the people gathered round him, and he sat down to teach them.* 3 *The teachers of the law and the Pharisees brought in a woman caught in adultery. They made her stand before the group* 4 *and said to Jesus, 'Teacher, this woman was caught in the act of adultery.* 5 *In the Law Moses commanded us to stone such women. Now what do you say?'* 6 *They were using this question as a trap, in order to have a basis for accusing him.*

But Jesus bent down and started to write on the ground with his finger. 7 *When they kept on questioning him, he straightened up and said to them, 'Let anyone of you who is without sin be the first to throw a stone at her.'* 8 *Again he stooped down and wrote on the ground.*

9 *At this, those who heard began to go away one at a time, the older ones first, until only Jesus was left, with the woman still standing there.* 10 *Jesus straightened up and asked her, 'Woman, where are they? Has no one condemned you?'*

11 *'No one, sir,' she said.*

'Then neither do I condemn you,' Jesus declared. 'Go now and leave your life of sin.'

_____

Dispute over Jesus' testimony

12 When Jesus spoke again to the people, he said, 'I am the light of the world. Whoever follows me will never walk in darkness, but will have the light of life.'

13 The Pharisees challenged him, 'Here you are, appearing as your own witness; your testimony is not valid.'

14 Jesus answered, 'Even if I testify on my own behalf, my testimony is valid, for I know where I came from and where I am going. But you have no idea where I come from or where I am going. 15 You judge by human standards; I pass judgment on no one. 16 But if I do judge, my decisions are true, because I am not alone. I stand with the Father, who sent me. 17 In your own Law it is written that the testimony of two witnesses is true. 18 I am one who testifies for myself; my other witness is the Father, who sent me.'

19 Then they asked him, 'Where is your father?'

'You do not know me or my Father,' Jesus replied. 'If you knew me, you would know my Father also.' 20 He spoke these words while teaching in the temple courts near the place where the offerings were put. Yet no one seized him, because his hour had not yet come.

Dispute over who Jesus is

21 Once more Jesus said to them, 'I am going away, and you will look for me, and you will die in your sin. Where I go, you cannot come.'

22 This made the Jews ask, 'Will he kill himself? Is that why he says, "Where I go, you cannot come"?'

23 But he continued, 'You are from below; I am from above. You are of this world; I am not of this world. 24 I told you that you would die in your sins; if you do not believe that I am he, you will indeed die in your sins.'

25 'Who are you?' they asked.

'Just what I have been telling you from the beginning,' Jesus replied. 26 'I have much to say in judgment of you. But he who sent me is trustworthy, and what I have heard from him I tell the world.'

27 They did not understand that he was telling them about his Father. 28 So Jesus said, 'When you have lifted up *a* the Son of Man, then you will know that I am he and that I do nothing on my own but speak just what the Father has taught me. 29 The one who sent me is with me; he has not left me alone, for I always do what pleases him.' 30 Even as he spoke, many believed in him.

_____

a 28 The Greek for *lifted up* also means *exalted.*

Dispute over whose children Jesus' opponents are

³¹ To the Jews who had believed him, Jesus said, 'If you hold to my teaching, you are really my disciples. ³²Then you will know the truth, and the truth will set you free.'

³³ They answered him, 'We are

LAW AND GRACE 3

Finding your balance

Studying to pass an exam can be hard work, but let's say that there's an exam you really want to pass. Maybe it's a driving test, or perhaps it's because you want a particular career. Miracle of miracles, though, you don't have to take that test! A letter comes through the post to say that you have passed with flying colours. That's great, you think, I've got the qualification I want without the work!

But then the truth settles in. The reason why we study hard to pass a test is that studying 'transforms' us into the person who has the knowledge or skills *needed* to pass that test. Would you want to travel in a car with a driver who had been given a pass without having to learn anything?

This is a bit like the relationship between grace and law. The law is the exam, the law sets the standard, God's rules about right and wrong, but God's grace says that we all pass with flying colours without having to take the test! Why? One way in which we understand Jesus' death is that Jesus takes the test on our behalf. His score is so good – he lives a life of such perfect obedience to God – that the whole of humanity has an A* pass into God's good kingdom life. Amazing! The thing is, though, that we haven't got the skills and knowledge necessary to lead that good life. That's why God, in his grace, sends us his Spirit to help us live like Jesus.

It's almost as if God does things in reverse. We've all passed the test, but now we have to study. In this passage in John 8, some of Jesus' adversaries bring a woman caught in adultery to him. In their eyes she had clearly failed; she was living a life of sin and needed punishing. Jesus tells them, 'Wait, she's not the only one here who hasn't met God's standard. She's not the only one who has sinned.' And so they all leave one by one. Jesus – who has lived a sinless life – tells her that she's free to go. He doesn't 'condemn' her. She has her A* pass, but now she must study! She must seek to live a life free of sin – to live according to God's rule.

That's not easy to do, but God's grace means that he doesn't leave us to 'study' alone. His Spirit is here to help us and his forgiveness means that we'll always get a second chance.

Jason Gardner

 Exodus 20:1–17   Romans 7:1–3

Abraham's descendants and have never been slaves of anyone. How can you say that we shall be set free?'

³⁴Jesus replied, 'Very truly I tell you, everyone who sins is a slave to sin. ³⁵Now a slave has no permanent place in the family, but a son belongs to it for ever. ³⁶So if the Son sets you free, you will be free indeed. ³⁷I know you are Abraham's descendants. Yet you are looking for a way to kill me, because you have no room for my word. ³⁸I am telling you what I have seen in the Father's presence, and you are doing what you have heard from your father.*b*'

³⁹'Abraham is our father,' they answered.

'If you were Abraham's children,' said Jesus, 'then you would*c* do what Abraham did. ⁴⁰As it is, you are looking for a way to kill me, a man who has told you the truth that I heard from God. Abraham did not do such things. ⁴¹You are doing the works of your own father.'

'We are not illegitimate children,' they protested. 'The only Father we have is God himself.'

⁴²Jesus said to them, 'If God were your Father, you would love me, for I have come here from God. I have not come on my own; God sent me. ⁴³Why is my language not clear to you? Because you are unable to hear what I say. ⁴⁴You belong to your father, the devil, and you want to carry out your father's desires. He was a murderer from the beginning, not holding to the truth, for there is no truth in him. When he lies, he speaks his native language, for he is a liar and the father of lies. ⁴⁵Yet because I tell the truth, you do not believe me! ⁴⁶Can any of you prove me guilty of sin? If I am telling the truth, why don't you believe me? ⁴⁷Whoever belongs to God hears what God says. The reason you do not hear is that you do not belong to God.'

Jesus' claims about himself

⁴⁸The Jews answered him, 'Aren't we right in saying that you are a Samaritan and demon-possessed?'

⁴⁹'I am not possessed by a demon,' said Jesus, 'but I honour my Father and you dishonour me. ⁵⁰I am not seeking glory for myself; but there is one who seeks it, and he is the judge. ⁵¹Very truly I tell you, whoever obeys my word will never see death.'

⁵²At this they exclaimed, 'Now we know that you are demon-possessed! Abraham died and so did the prophets, yet you say that whoever obeys your word will never taste death. ⁵³Are you greater than our father Abraham? He died, and so did the prophets. Who do you think you are?'

⁵⁴Jesus replied, 'If I glorify myself, my glory means nothing. My Father, whom you claim as your God, is the one who glorifies me. ⁵⁵Though you do not know him, I know him. If I said I did not, I would be a liar like you, but I do know him and obey his word. ⁵⁶Your father Abraham rejoiced at the thought of seeing my day; he saw it and was glad.'

⁵⁷'You are not yet fifty years old,' they said to him, 'and you have seen Abraham!'

⁵⁸'Very truly I tell you,' Jesus answered, 'before Abraham was born, I am!' ⁵⁹At this, they picked up stones to stone him, but Jesus hid himself, slipping away from the temple grounds.

Jesus heals a man born blind

9 As he went along, he saw a man blind from birth. ²His disciples asked him, 'Rabbi, who sinned, this man or his parents, that he was born blind?'

³'Neither this man nor his parents sinned,' said Jesus, 'but this happened so that the works of God might be displayed in him. ⁴As long as it is day, we must do the works of him who sent me. Night is coming, when no one can work. ⁵While I am in the world, I am the light of the world.'

⁶After saying this, he spat on the ground, made some mud with the saliva, and put it on the man's eyes. ⁷'Go,' he told him, 'wash in the Pool of Siloam' (this

---

b 38 Or *presence. Therefore do what you have heard from the Father.*
c 39 Some early manuscripts *'If you are Abraham's children,' said Jesus, 'then*

word means 'Sent'). So the man went and washed, and came home seeing.

8 His neighbours and those who had formerly seen him begging asked, 'Isn't this the same man who used to sit and beg?' 9 Some claimed that he was.

Others said, 'No, he only looks like him.'

But he himself insisted, 'I am the man.'

10 'How then were your eyes opened?' they asked.

11 He replied, 'The man they call Jesus made some mud and put it on my eyes. He told me to go to Siloam and wash. So I went and washed, and then I could see.'

12 'Where is this man?' they asked him.

'I don't know,' he said.

The Pharisees investigate the healing

13 They brought to the Pharisees the man who had been blind. 14 Now the day on which Jesus had made the mud and opened the man's eyes was a Sabbath. 15 Therefore the Pharisees also asked him how he had received his sight. 'He put mud on my eyes,' the man replied, 'and I washed, and now I see.'

16 Some of the Pharisees said, 'This man is not from God, for he does not keep the Sabbath.'

But others asked, 'How can a sinner perform such signs?' So they were divided.

17 Then they turned again to the blind man, 'What have you to say about him? It was your eyes he opened.'

The man replied, 'He is a prophet.'

18 They still did not believe that he had been blind and had received his sight until they sent for the man's parents. 19 'Is this your son?' they asked. 'Is this the one you say was born blind? How is it that now he can see?'

20 'We know he is our son,' the parents answered, 'and we know he was born blind. 21 But how he can see now, or who opened his eyes, we don't know. Ask him. He is of age; he will speak for himself.' 22 His parents said this because they were afraid of the Jewish leaders, who already had decided that anyone who acknowledged that Jesus was the Messiah would

be put out of the synagogue. 23 That was why his parents said, 'He is of age; ask him.'

24 A second time they summoned the man who had been blind. 'Give glory to God by telling the truth,' they said. 'We know this man is a sinner.'

25 He replied, 'Whether he is a sinner or not, I don't know. One thing I do know. I was blind but now I see!'

26 Then they asked him, 'What did he do to you? How did he open your eyes?'

27 He answered, 'I have told you already and you did not listen. Why do you want to hear it again? Do you want to become his disciples too?'

28 Then they hurled insults at him and said, 'You are this fellow's disciple! We are disciples of Moses! 29 We know that God spoke to Moses, but as for this fellow, we don't even know where he comes from.'

30 The man answered, 'Now that is remarkable! You don't know where he comes from, yet he opened my eyes. 31 We know that God does not listen to sinners. He listens to the godly person who does his will. 32 Nobody has ever heard of opening the eyes of a man born blind. 33 If this man were not from God, he could do nothing.'

34 To this they replied, 'You were steeped in sin at birth; how dare you lecture us!' And they threw him out.

Spiritual blindness

35 Jesus heard that they had thrown him out, and when he found him, he said, 'Do you believe in the Son of Man?'

36 'Who is he, sir?' the man asked. 'Tell me so that I may believe in him.'

37 Jesus said, 'You have now seen him; in fact, he is the one speaking with you.'

38 Then the man said, 'Lord, I believe,' and he worshipped him.

39 Jesus said,*a* 'For judgment I have come into this world, so that the blind will see and those who see will become blind.'

40 Some Pharisees who were with him

---

a 38,39 Some early manuscripts do not have *Then the man said . . . 39 Jesus said.*

heard him say this and asked, 'What? Are we blind too?'

⁴¹ Jesus said, 'If you were blind, you would not be guilty of sin; but now that you claim you can see, your guilt remains.

The good shepherd and his sheep

10 'Very truly I tell you Pharisees, anyone who does not enter the sheepfold by the gate, but climbs in by some other way, is a thief and a robber. ² The one who enters by the gate is the shepherd of the sheep. ³ The gatekeeper opens the gate for him, and the sheep listen to his voice. He calls his own sheep by name and leads them out. ⁴ When he has brought out all his own, he goes on ahead of them, and his sheep follow him because they know his voice. ⁵ But they will never follow a stranger; in fact, they will run away from him because they do not recognise a stranger's voice.' ⁶ Jesus used this figure of speech, but the Pharisees did not understand what he was telling them.

⁷ Therefore Jesus said again, 'Very truly I tell you, I am the gate for the sheep. ⁸ All who have come before me are thieves and robbers, but the sheep have not listened to them. ⁹ I am the gate; whoever enters through me will be saved.ᵃ They will come in and go out, and find pasture. ¹⁰ The thief comes only to steal and kill and destroy; I have come that they may have life, and have it to the full.

¹¹ 'I am the good shepherd. The good shepherd lays down his life for the sheep. ¹² The hired hand is not the shepherd and does not own the sheep. So when he sees the wolf coming, he abandons the sheep and runs away. Then the wolf attacks the flock and scatters it. ¹³ The man runs away because he is a hired hand and cares nothing for the sheep.

¹⁴ 'I am the good shepherd; I know my sheep and my sheep know me – ¹⁵ just as the Father knows me and I know the Father – and I lay down my life for the sheep. ¹⁶ I have other sheep that are not of this sheepfold. I must bring them also. They too will listen to my voice, and there shall be one flock and one shepherd. ¹⁷ The reason my Father loves me is that I lay down my life – only to take it up again. ¹⁸ No one takes it from me, but I lay it down of my own accord. I have authority to lay it down and authority to take it up again. This command I received from my Father.'

¹⁹ The Jews who heard these words were again divided. ²⁰ Many of them said, 'He is demon-possessed and raving mad. Why listen to him?'

²¹ But others said, 'These are not the sayings of a man possessed by a demon. Can a demon open the eyes of the blind?'

Further conflict over Jesus' claims

²² Then came the Festival of Dedicationᵇ at Jerusalem. It was winter, ²³ and Jesus was in the temple courts walking in Solomon's Colonnade. ²⁴ The Jews who were there gathered round him, saying, 'How long will you keep us in suspense? If you are the Messiah, tell us plainly.'

²⁵ Jesus answered, 'I did tell you, but you do not believe. The works I do in my Father's name testify about me, ²⁶ but you do not believe because you are not my sheep. ²⁷ My sheep listen to my voice; I know them, and they follow me. ²⁸ I give them eternal life, and they shall never perish; no one will snatch them out of my hand. ²⁹ My Father, who has given them to me, is greater than allᶜ; no one can snatch them out of my Father's hand. ³⁰ I and the Father are one.'

³¹ Again his Jewish opponents picked up stones to stone him, ³² but Jesus said to them, 'I have shown you many good works from the Father. For which of these do you stone me?'

³³ 'We are not stoning you for any good work,' they replied, 'but for blasphemy, because you, a mere man, claim to be God.'

³⁴ Jesus answered them, 'Is it not written

ᵃ 9 Or *kept safe*

ᵇ 22 That is, Hanukkah
ᶜ 29 Many early manuscripts *What my Father has given me is greater than all*

in your Law, "I have said you are 'gods' "*d*? 35 If he called them "gods", to whom the word of God came – and Scripture cannot be set aside – 36 what about the one whom the Father set apart as his very own and sent into the world? Why then do you accuse me of blasphemy because I said, "I am God's Son"? 37 Do not believe me unless I do the works of my Father. 38 But if I do them, even though you do not believe me, believe the works, that you may know and understand that the Father is in me, and I in the Father.' 39 Again they tried to seize him, but he escaped their grasp.

40 Then Jesus went back across the Jordan to the place where John had been baptising in the early days. There he stayed, 41 and many people came to him. They said, 'Though John never performed a sign, all that John said about this man was true.' 42 And in that place many believed in Jesus.

The death of Lazarus

11 Now a man named Lazarus was ill. He was from Bethany, the village of Mary and her sister Martha. 2 (This Mary, whose brother Lazarus now lay ill, was the same one who poured perfume on the Lord and wiped his feet with her hair.) 3 So the sisters sent word to Jesus, 'Lord, the one you love is ill.'

4 When he heard this, Jesus said, 'This illness will not end in death. No, it is for God's glory so that God's Son may be glorified through it.' 5 Now Jesus loved Martha and her sister and Lazarus. 6 So when he heard that Lazarus was ill, he stayed where he was two more days, 7 and then he said to his disciples, 'Let us go back to Judea.'

8 'But Rabbi,' they said, 'a short while ago the Jews there tried to stone you, and yet you are going back?'

9 Jesus answered, 'Are there not twelve hours of daylight? Anyone who walks in the day-time will not stumble, for they see by this world's light. 10 It is when a person walks at night that they stumble, for they have no light.'

11 After he had said this, he went on to tell them, 'Our friend Lazarus has fallen asleep; but I am going there to wake him up.'

12 His disciples replied, 'Lord, if he sleeps, he will get better.' 13 Jesus had been speaking of his death, but his disciples thought he meant natural sleep.

14 So then he told them plainly, 'Lazarus is dead, 15 and for your sake I am glad I was not there, so that you may believe. But let us go to him.'

16 Then Thomas (also known as Didymus*a*) said to the rest of the disciples, 'Let us also go, that we may die with him.'

Jesus comforts the sisters of Lazarus

17 On his arrival, Jesus found that Lazarus had already been in the tomb for four days. 18 Now Bethany was less than two miles*b* from Jerusalem, 19 and many Jews had come to Martha and Mary to comfort them in the loss of their brother. 20 When Martha heard that Jesus was coming, she went out to meet him, but Mary stayed at home.

21 'Lord,' Martha said to Jesus, 'if you had been here, my brother would not have died. 22 But I know that even now God will give you whatever you ask.'

23 Jesus said to her, 'Your brother will rise again.'

24 Martha answered, 'I know he will rise again in the resurrection at the last day.'

25 Jesus said to her, 'I am the resurrection and the life. The one who believes in me will live, even though they die; 26 and whoever lives by believing in me will never die. Do you believe this?'

27 'Yes, Lord,' she replied, 'I believe that you are the Messiah, the Son of God, who is to come into the world.'

28 After she had said this, she went back and called her sister Mary aside. 'The Teacher is here,' she said, 'and is asking for you.' 29 When Mary heard this, she got up quickly and went to him. 30 Now Jesus had not yet entered the village, but was still at the place where Martha had

---

d 34 Psalm 82:6

a 16 *Thomas* (Aramaic) and *Didymus* (Greek) both mean *twin.*
b 18 Or about 3 kilometres

met him. 31 When the Jews who had been with Mary in the house, comforting her, noticed how quickly she got up and went out, they followed her, supposing she was going to the tomb to mourn there.

32 When Mary reached the place where Jesus was and saw him, she fell at his feet and said, 'Lord, if you had been here, my brother would not have died.'

33 When Jesus saw her weeping, and the Jews who had come along with her also weeping, he was deeply moved in spirit and troubled. 34 'Where have you laid him?' he asked.

'Come and see, Lord,' they replied.

35 Jesus wept.

36 Then the Jews said, 'See how he loved him!'

37 But some of them said, 'Could not he who opened the eyes of the blind man have kept this man from dying?'

FACT

SHORTEST VERSE

The shortest verse in the Bible is John 11:35, which has only two words: 'Jesus wept.' (In the original Greek, it's actually one word longer.)

Jesus raises Lazarus from the dead

38 Jesus, once more deeply moved, came to the tomb. It was a cave with a stone laid across the entrance. 39 'Take away the stone,' he said.

'But, Lord,' said Martha, the sister of the dead man, 'by this time there is a bad odour, for he has been there four days.'

40 Then Jesus said, 'Did I not tell you that if you believe, you will see the glory of God?'

41 So they took away the stone. Then Jesus looked up and said, 'Father, I thank you that you have heard me. 42 I knew that you always hear me, but I said this for the

benefit of the people standing here, that they may believe that you sent me.'

43 When he had said this, Jesus called in a loud voice, 'Lazarus, come out!' 44 The dead man came out, his hands and feet wrapped with strips of linen, and a cloth round his face.

Jesus said to them, 'Take off the grave clothes and let him go.'

The plot to kill Jesus

45 Therefore many of the Jews who had come to visit Mary, and had seen what Jesus did, believed in him. 46 But some of them went to the Pharisees and told them what Jesus had done. 47 Then the chief priests and the Pharisees called a meeting of the Sanhedrin.

'What are we accomplishing?' they asked. 'Here is this man performing many signs. 48 If we let him go on like this, everyone will believe in him, and then the Romans will come and take away both our temple and our nation.'

49 Then one of them, named Caiaphas, who was high priest that year, spoke up, 'You know nothing at all! 50 You do not realise that it is better for you that one man die for the people than that the whole nation perish.'

51 He did not say this on his own, but as high priest that year he prophesied that Jesus would die for the Jewish nation, 52 and not only for that nation but also for the scattered children of God, to bring them together and make them one. 53 So from that day on they plotted to take his life.

54 Therefore Jesus no longer moved about publicly among the people of Judea. Instead he withdrew to a region near the wilderness, to a village called Ephraim, where he stayed with his disciples.

55 When it was almost time for the Jewish Passover, many went up from the country to Jerusalem for their ceremonial cleansing before the Passover. 56 They kept looking for Jesus, and as they stood in the temple courts they asked one another, 'What do you think? Isn't he coming to the festival at all?' 57 But the chief priests and the Pharisees had given orders that

anyone who found out where Jesus was should report it so that they might arrest him.

Jesus anointed at Bethany

12 Six days before the Passover, Jesus came to Bethany, where Lazarus lived, whom Jesus had raised from the dead. ² Here a dinner was given in Jesus' honour. Martha served, while Lazarus was among those reclining at the table with him. ³ Then Mary took about half a litre of pure nard, an expensive perfume; she poured it on Jesus' feet and wiped his feet with her hair. And the house was filled with the fragrance of the perfume.

⁴ But one of his disciples, Judas Iscariot, who was later to betray him, objected, ⁵ 'Why wasn't this perfume sold and the money given to the poor? It was worth a year's wages.ᵃ' ⁶ He did not say this because he cared about the poor but because he was a thief; as keeper of the money bag, he used to help himself to what was put into it.

⁷ 'Leave her alone,' Jesus replied. 'It was intended that she should save this perfume for the day of my burial. ⁸ You will always have the poor among you,ᵇ but you will not always have me.'

⁹ Meanwhile a large crowd of Jews found out that Jesus was there and came, not only because of him but also to see Lazarus, whom he had raised from the dead. ¹⁰ So the chief priests made plans to kill Lazarus as well, ¹¹ for on account of him many of the Jews were going over to Jesus and believing in him.

Jesus comes to Jerusalem as king

¹² The next day the great crowd that had come for the festival heard that Jesus was on his way to Jerusalem. ¹³ They took palm branches and went out to meet him, shouting,

'Hosanna!ᶜ'

'Blessed is he who comes in the name of the Lord!'ᵈ

'Blessed is the king of Israel!'

¹⁴ Jesus found a young donkey and sat upon it, as it is written:

¹⁵ 'Do not be afraid, Daughter Zion;
    see, your king is coming,
    seated on a donkey's colt.'ᵉ

¹⁶ At first his disciples did not understand all this. Only after Jesus was glorified did they realise that these things had been written about him and that these things had been done to him.

¹⁷ Now the crowd that was with him when he called Lazarus from the tomb and raised him from the dead continued to spread the word. ¹⁸ Many people, because they had heard that he had performed this sign, went out to meet him. ¹⁹ So the Pharisees said to one another, 'See, this is getting us nowhere. Look how the whole world has gone after him!'

Jesus predicts his death

²⁰ Now there were some Greeks among those who went up to worship at the festival. ²¹ They came to Philip, who was from Bethsaida in Galilee, with a request. 'Sir,' they said, 'we would like to see Jesus.' ²² Philip went to tell Andrew; Andrew and Philip in turn told Jesus.

²³ Jesus replied, 'The hour has come for the Son of Man to be glorified. ²⁴ Very truly I tell you, unless a grain of wheat falls to the ground and dies, it remains only a single seed. But if it dies, it produces many seeds. ²⁵ Anyone who loves their life will lose it, while anyone who hates their life in this world will keep it for eternal life. ²⁶ Whoever serves me must follow me; and where I am, my servant also will be. My Father will honour the one who serves me.

²⁷ 'Now my soul is troubled, and what shall I say? "Father, save me from this hour"? No, it was for this very reason I

ᵃ 5 Greek *three hundred denarii*
ᵇ 8 See Deut. 15:11.
ᶜ 13 A Hebrew expression meaning 'Save!' which became an exclamation of praise

ᵈ 13 Psalm 118:25,26
ᵉ 15 Zech. 9:9

came to this hour. ²⁸Father, glorify your name!'

Then a voice came from heaven, 'I have glorified it, and will glorify it again.' ²⁹The crowd that was there and heard it said it had thundered; others said an angel had spoken to him.

³⁰Jesus said, 'This voice was for your benefit, not mine. ³¹Now is the time for judgment on this world; now the prince of this world will be driven out. ³²And I, when I am lifted up*f* from the earth, will draw all people to myself.' ³³He said this to show the kind of death he was going to die.

³⁴The crowd spoke up, 'We have heard from the Law that the Messiah will remain for ever, so how can you say, "The Son of Man must be lifted up"? Who is this "Son of Man"?'

³⁵Then Jesus told them, 'You are going to have the light just a little while longer. Walk while you have the light, before darkness overtakes you. Whoever walks in the dark does not know where they are going. ³⁶Believe in the light while you have the light, so that you may become children of light.' When he had finished speaking, Jesus left and hid himself from them.

Belief and unbelief among the Jews

³⁷Even after Jesus had performed so many signs in their presence, they still would not believe in him. ³⁸This was to fulfil the word of Isaiah the prophet:

'Lord, who has believed our message
    and to whom has the arm of the
        Lord been revealed?'*g*

³⁹For this reason they could not believe, because, as Isaiah says elsewhere:

⁴⁰'He has blinded their eyes
    and hardened their hearts,
so they can neither see with their eyes,
    nor understand with their hearts,
    nor turn – and I would heal them.'*h*

*f*32 The Greek for *lifted up* also means *exalted*.
*g*38 Isaiah 53:1
*h*40 Isaiah 6:10

⁴¹Isaiah said this because he saw Jesus' glory and spoke about him.

⁴²Yet at the same time many even among the leaders believed in him. But because of the Pharisees they would not openly acknowledge their faith for fear they would be put out of the synagogue; ⁴³for they loved human praise more than praise from God.

⁴⁴Then Jesus cried out, 'Whoever believes in me does not believe in me only, but in the one who sent me. ⁴⁵The one who looks at me is seeing the one who sent me. ⁴⁶I have come into the world as a light, so that no one who believes in me should stay in darkness.

⁴⁷'If anyone hears my words but does not keep them, I do not judge that person. For I did not come to judge the world, but to save the world. ⁴⁸There is a judge for the one who rejects me and does not accept my words; the very words I have spoken will condemn them at the last day. ⁴⁹For I did not speak on my own, but the Father who sent me commanded me to say all that I have spoken. ⁵⁰I know that his command leads to eternal life. So whatever I say is just what the Father has told me to say.'

Jesus washes his disciples' feet

13 It was just before the Passover Festival. Jesus knew that the hour had come for him to leave this world and go to the Father. Having loved his own who were in the world, he loved them to the end.

²The evening meal was in progress, and the devil had already prompted Judas, the son of Simon Iscariot, to betray Jesus. ³Jesus knew that the Father had put all things under his power, and that he had come from God and was returning to God; ⁴so he got up from the meal, took off his outer clothing, and wrapped a towel round his waist. ⁵After that, he poured water into a basin and began to wash his disciples' feet, drying them with the towel that was wrapped round him.

⁶He came to Simon Peter, who said to him, 'Lord, are you going to wash my feet?'

7 Jesus replied, 'You do not realise now what I am doing, but later you will understand.'

8 'No,' said Peter, 'you shall never wash my feet.'

Jesus answered, 'Unless I wash you, you have no part with me.'

9 'Then, Lord,' Simon Peter replied, 'not just my feet but my hands and my head as well!'

10 Jesus answered, 'Those who have had a bath need only to wash their feet; their whole body is clean. And you are clean, though not every one of you.' 11 For he knew who was going to betray him, and that was why he said not every one was clean.

12 When he had finished washing their feet, he put on his clothes and returned to his place. 'Do you understand what I have done for you?' he asked them. 13 'You call me "Teacher" and "Lord", and rightly so, for that is what I am. 14 Now that I, your Lord and Teacher, have washed your feet, you also should wash one another's feet. 15 I have set you an example that you should do as I have done for you. 16 Very truly I tell you, no servant is greater than his master, nor is a messenger greater than the one who sent him. 17 Now that you know these things, you will be blessed if you do them.

Jesus predicts his betrayal

18 'I am not referring to all of you; I know those I have chosen. But this is to fulfil this passage of Scripture: "He who shared my bread has turned*a* against me."*b*

19 'I am telling you now before it happens, so that when it does happen you will believe that I am who I am. 20 Very truly I tell you, whoever accepts anyone I send accepts me; and whoever accepts me accepts the one who sent me.'

21 After he had said this, Jesus was troubled in spirit and testified, 'Very truly I tell you, one of you is going to betray me.'

22 His disciples stared at one another, at a loss to know which of them he meant.

23 One of them, the disciple whom Jesus loved, was reclining next to him. 24 Simon Peter motioned to this disciple and said, 'Ask him which one he means.'

25 Leaning back against Jesus, he asked him, 'Lord, who is it?'

26 Jesus answered, 'It is the one to whom I will give this piece of bread when I have dipped it in the dish.' Then, dipping the piece of bread, he gave it to Judas, the son of Simon Iscariot. 27 As soon as Judas took the bread, Satan entered into him.

So Jesus told him, 'What you are about to do, do quickly.' 28 But no one at the meal understood why Jesus said this to him. 29 Since Judas had charge of the money, some thought Jesus was telling him to buy what was needed for the festival, or to give something to the poor. 30 As soon as Judas had taken the bread, he went out. And it was night.

Jesus predicts Peter's denial

31 When he was gone, Jesus said, 'Now the Son of Man is glorified and God is glorified in him. 32 If God is glorified in him,*c* God will glorify the Son in himself, and will glorify him at once.

33 'My children, I will be with you only a little longer. You will look for me, and just as I told the Jews, so I tell you now: where I am going, you cannot come.

34 'A new command I give you: love one another. As I have loved you, so you must love one another. 35 By this everyone will know that you are my disciples, if you love one another.'

36 Simon Peter asked him, 'Lord, where are you going?'

Jesus replied, 'Where I am going, you cannot follow now, but you will follow later.'

37 Peter asked, 'Lord, why can't I follow you now? I will lay down my life for you.'

38 Then Jesus answered, 'Will you really lay down your life for me? Very truly I tell you, before the cock crows, you will disown me three times!

---

a 18 Greek *has lifted up his heel*
b 18 Psalm 41:9

c 32 Many early manuscripts do not have *If God is glorified in him.*

SPIRITUAL DISCIPLINES 6

SERVICE

Jackie Pullinger believed that God had called her to one of the most dangerous parts of the world to work with people no one else wanted to touch. Trying to be obedient, she left her home in England in 1966 and moved to Hong Kong's notorious Walled City, where she worked as a missionary among the drug addicts and prostitutes. Despite being in constant danger, she would spend each day trying to build relationships with the people who lived in the slum, hoping to tell them that there was a God who loved them.

Six months into her time in Hong Kong, Jackie was in total despair. She had seen people living in unimaginably bad conditions, yet they didn't want to hear her message of hope. She had achieved almost nothing.

Jackie couldn't work out what she was doing wrong. It simply made no sense to her. After all, if anyone needed a Saviour, it was these people. Then, after much soul searching, the penny dropped. She had been great at *telling* these people about Jesus – that he loved them and wanted to forgive them – but what she hadn't done was *show* them. Her message consisted entirely of words, in a place where actions spoke far louder. She didn't need simply to tell them about Jesus; she needed to be him to them.

From that moment, Jackie radically altered her approach. She spent her time providing food and shelter for those who had none, and visiting prisons and becoming an advocate for people with no voice. Instead of words, these practical acts of service soon became the thing she was known for. Her impact is still felt in that place today.

Jackie's story is a great example of the spiritual discipline of service. She finally realised the truth of Jesus' words in John 13:34–35 – that the world would know his disciples by the way they loved. Jackie's ministry had very little success among the poor and marginalised when she just brought words, because talk is cheap. When, instead, she brought the words of the Bible to life by putting them into action, she saw hundreds of people – many of them involved in serious crime – flocking to give their lives to God.

Service is the natural progression from the discipline of submission. When we make ourselves 'the very last', putting the needs of everyone we meet before our own, then the natural response is to serve. Submission is the heart decision; service is what we do with our hands and feet as a result. Put together, they are an incredible tool to help restore God's intended order for mankind, with everyone looking out for and serving the needs of everyone else. When we live like this, we begin to make the world a little bit more like it was meant to be. And while we don't do it to trick them into the church, those we serve can't fail to be struck by the rightness of the kingdom of God.

Martin Saunders

Jesus comforts his disciples

14 'Do not let your hearts be troubled. You believe in God^a; believe also in me. ²My Father's house has many rooms; if that were not so, would I have told you that I am going there to prepare a place for you? ³And if I go and prepare a place for you, I will come back and take you to be with me that you also may be where I am. ⁴You know the way to the place where I am going.'

Jesus the way to the Father

⁵Thomas said to him, 'Lord, we don't know where you are going, so how can we know the way?'

⁶Jesus answered, 'I am the way and the truth and the life. No one comes to the Father except through me. ⁷If you really know me, you will know^b my Father as well. From now on, you do know him and have seen him.'

⁸Philip said, 'Lord, show us the Father and that will be enough for us.'

⁹Jesus answered: 'Don't you know me, Philip, even after I have been among you such a long time? Anyone who has seen me has seen the Father. How can you say, "Show us the Father"? ¹⁰Don't you believe that I am in the Father, and that the Father is in me? The words I say to you I do not speak on my own authority. Rather, it is the Father, living in me, who is doing his work. ¹¹Believe me when I say that I am in the Father and the Father is in me; or at least believe on the evidence of the works themselves. ¹²Very truly I tell you, whoever believes in me will do the works I have been doing, and they will do even greater things than these, because I am going to the Father. ¹³And I will do whatever you ask in my name, so that the Father may be glorified in the Son. ¹⁴You may ask me for anything in my name, and I will do it.

Jesus promises the Holy Spirit

¹⁵'If you love me, keep my commands. ¹⁶And I will ask the Father, and he will give you another advocate to help you and be with you for ever – ¹⁷the Spirit of truth. The world cannot accept him, because it neither sees him nor knows him. But you know him, for he lives with you and will be^c in you. ¹⁸I will not leave you as orphans; I will come to you. ¹⁹Before long, the world will not see me any more, but you will see me. Because I live, you also will live. ²⁰On that day you will realise that I am in my Father, and you are in me, and I am in you. ²¹Whoever has my commands and keeps them is the one who loves me. The one who loves me will be loved by my Father, and I too will love them and show myself to them.'

²²Then Judas (not Judas Iscariot) said, 'But, Lord, why do you intend to show yourself to us and not to the world?'

²³Jesus replied, 'Anyone who loves me will obey my teaching. My Father will love them, and we will come to them and make our home with them. ²⁴Anyone who does not love me will not obey my teaching. These words you hear are not my own; they belong to the Father who sent me.

²⁵'All this I have spoken while still with you. ²⁶But the Advocate, the Holy Spirit, whom the Father will send in my name, will teach you all things and will remind you of everything I have said to you. ²⁷Peace I leave with you; my peace I give you. I do not give to you as the world gives. Do not let your hearts be troubled and do not be afraid.

²⁸'You heard me say, "I am going away and I am coming back to you." If you loved me, you would be glad that I am going to the Father, for the Father is greater than I. ²⁹I have told you now before it happens, so that when it does happen you will believe. ³⁰I will not say much more to you, for the prince of this world is coming. He has no hold over me, ³¹but he comes so that the world may learn that I love the Father and do exactly what my Father has commanded me.

'Come now; let us leave.

---

a 1 Or *Believe in God*
b 7 Some manuscripts *If you really knew me, you would know*

c 17 Some early manuscripts *and is*

The vine and the branches

15 ¹ 'I am the true vine, and my Father is the gardener. ²He cuts off every branch in me that bears no fruit, while every branch that does bear fruit he prunes*a* so that it will be even more fruitful. ³You are already clean because of the word I have spoken to you. ⁴Remain in me, as I also remain in you. No branch can bear fruit by itself; it must remain in the vine. Neither can you bear fruit unless you remain in me.

---

a 2 The Greek for *he prunes* also means *he cleans.*

⁵ 'I am the vine; you are the branches. If you remain in me and I in you, you will bear much fruit; apart from me you can do nothing. ⁶If you do not remain in me, you are like a branch that is thrown away and withers; such branches are picked up, thrown into the fire and burned. ⁷If you remain in me and my words remain in you, ask whatever you wish, and it will be done for you. ⁸This is to my Father's glory, that you bear much fruit, showing yourselves to be my disciples.

⁹ 'As the Father has loved me, so have I loved you. Now remain in my love. ¹⁰If

FAITH IN THE WORLD 10

FINDING FULFILLING WORK

Sometimes we *really* hate doing work. Remember those times when your parents have asked you to do a chore at home? Sometimes we'll just get on and do it. Other times we'll find any excuse to wriggle out of it.

We *could* sit down and think why doing work for our family – obeying our parents – is really worthwhile. Our parents do so much work for us, so isn't it right we should help out? And doesn't the work of tidying our room bring benefits to us and others? But we shouldn't just do the right thing because we're nagged into something. We should want to help people because we love them.

In John 14:28–31, Jesus lets his disciples in on the thing that drives him the most, the thing that's behind everything he does. It's simply this: Jesus is *all* about being obedient to his Father. And Jesus makes it more than clear that, as his followers, this is exactly what we should be about as well.

If we want to know God's will for our lives, if we want to know what career we should choose, then this comes first: are we trying hard to be obedient to God? If we're honest, we know the kind of things that we could do that will please our parents: helping out before being asked to, trying our best at school. Because we *know* our parents. The more we seek to know God, the more we'll learn what pleases him. God's Word is full of ways in which we can please God, and a lot of it has to do with caring for each other, caring for the poor, fighting injustice. We might have a clear idea of what we want for our lives, and we expect God just to make it happen. That wasn't the way Jesus lived. Jesus found perfect fulfilment in knowing what God the Father wanted him to do and then doing it. The same goes for us too.

Jason Gardner

 Acts 18:1–4   ⏹

you keep my commands, you will remain in my love, just as I have kept my Father's commands and remain in his love. **11** I have told you this so that my joy may be in you and that your joy may be complete. **12** My command is this: love each other as I have loved you. **13** Greater love has no one than this: to lay down one's life for one's friends. **14** You are my friends if you do what I command. **15** I no longer call you servants, because a servant does not know his master's business. Instead, I have called you friends, for everything that I learned from my Father I have made known to you. **16** You did not choose me, but I chose you and appointed you so that you might go and bear fruit – fruit that will last – and so that whatever you ask in my name the Father will give you. **17** This is my command: love each other.

IDENTITY – WHO WE ARE IN CHRIST 8

Nothing without Christ

We might sing songs about Jesus being the oxygen of our lives and the air we breathe. We have heard that we're a new creation and alive in Christ, or that we're spiritually alive because of what Jesus did on the cross. But what does it mean to be 'alive in Christ', to know this man from the past, who died on a cross? We experience it in our lives when we become Christians, whether we're aware of it or not.

Jesus described it in terms of him being the vine and us the branches (John 15). He then said that apart from him we can do nothing. Part of our identity in Christ is that without him, not only would we not have spiritual life and freedom now, but we wouldn't be able to do anything.

That seems a bit odd: we know we can do plenty without him. In fact, we do far too much without him. However, this passage means that our very existence should be about Jesus and dependent on him. It's just as it was with Jesus himself – he often said that apart from the Father he could do nothing.

As Christians, we're dependent on Jesus for everything that's of any worth and we should live accordingly. Our problem is that we place value on all the wrong things, so when we look at our lives we think we could do pretty well without him. Without Jesus, though, we can't love people as we should, we can't serve our friends as we should, we don't notice the poor and needy, we don't worship continuously. Basically, all the things that bring about God's kingdom we can't do without him. We should be finding out what God's will is for every area of our lives, rather than just the churchy part, or the 'God bits'.

Do we let God's truth (most clearly revealed in his Word, the Bible) not only influence but transform our attitudes and thinking? Do we offer him all of ourselves – our possessions, our relationships, our time and our future? It's amazing to think what Christ could do, alive in us, if we offered him all of ourselves.

James Grier

 Philippians 3:17–21   1 Corinthians 6:18–20 ▶

The world hates the disciples

18 'If the world hates you, keep in mind that it hated me first. 19 If you belonged to the world, it would love you as its own. As it is, you do not belong to the world, but I have chosen you out of the world. That is why the world hates you. 20 Remember what I told you: "A servant is not greater than his master."*b* If they persecuted me, they will persecute you also. If they obeyed my teaching, they will obey yours also. 21 They will treat you this way because of my name, for they do not know the one who sent me. 22 If I had not come and spoken to them, they would not be guilty of sin; but now they have no excuse for their sin. 23 Whoever hates me hates my Father as well. 24 If I had not done among them the works no one else did, they would not be guilty of sin. As it is, they have seen, and yet they have hated both me and my Father. 25 But this is to fulfil what is written in their Law: "They hated me without reason."*c*

The work of the Holy Spirit

26 'When the Advocate comes, whom I will send to you from the Father – the Spirit of truth who goes out from the Father – he will testify about me. 27 And you also must testify, for you have been with me from the beginning.

16 'All this I have told you so that you will not fall away. 2 They will put you out of the synagogue; in fact, the time is coming when anyone who kills you will think they are offering a service to God. 3 They will do such things because they have not known the Father or me. 4 I have told you this, so that when their time comes you will remember that I warned you about them. I did not tell you this from the beginning because I was with you, 5 but now I am going to him who sent me. None of you asks me, "Where are you going?" 6 Rather, you are filled with grief because I have said these things. 7 But very truly I tell you, it is for your good that I am

going away. Unless I go away, the Advocate will not come to you; but if I go, I will send him to you. 8 When he comes, he will prove the world to be in the wrong about sin and righteousness and judgment: 9 about sin, because people do not believe in me; 10 about righteousness, because I am going to the Father, where you can see me no longer; 11 and about judgment, because the prince of this world now stands condemned.

12 'I have much more to say to you, more than you can now bear. 13 But when he, the Spirit of truth, comes, he will guide you into all the truth. He will not speak on his own; he will speak only what he hears, and he will tell you what is yet to come. 14 He will glorify me because it is from me that he will receive what he will make known to you. 15 All that belongs to the Father is mine. That is why I said the Spirit will receive from me what he will make known to you.'

The disciples' grief will turn to joy

16 Jesus went on to say, 'In a little while you will see me no more, and then after a little while you will see me.'

17 At this, some of his disciples said to one another, 'What does he mean by saying, "In a little while you will see me no more, and then after a little while you will see me," and "Because I am going to the Father"?' 18 They kept asking, 'What does he mean by "a little while"? We don't understand what he is saying.'

19 Jesus saw that they wanted to ask him about this, so he said to them, 'Are you asking one another what I meant when I said, "In a little while you will see me no more, and then after a little while you will see me"? 20 Very truly I tell you, you will weep and mourn while the world rejoices. You will grieve, but your grief will turn to joy. 21 A woman giving birth to a child has pain because her time has come; but when her baby is born she forgets the anguish because of her joy that a child is born into the world. 22 So with you: now is your time of grief, but I will see you again and you will rejoice, and no one will take away your joy. 23 In that day you will no longer

---

b 20 John 13:16
c 25 Psalms 35:19; 69:4

ask me anything. Very truly I tell you, my Father will give you whatever you ask in my name. 24 Until now you have not asked for anything in my name. Ask and you will receive, and your joy will be complete.

25 'Though I have been speaking figuratively, a time is coming when I will no longer use this kind of language but will tell you plainly about my Father. 26 In that day you will ask in my name. I am not saying that I will ask the Father on your behalf. 27 No, the Father himself loves you because you have loved me and have believed that I came from God. 28 I came from the Father and entered the world; now I am leaving the world and going back to the Father.'

29 Then Jesus' disciples said, 'Now you are speaking clearly and without figures of speech. 30 Now we can see that you know all things and that you do not even need to have anyone ask you questions. This makes us believe that you came from God.'

31 'Do you now believe?' Jesus replied. 32 'A time is coming and in fact has come when you will be scattered, each to your own home. You will leave me all alone. Yet I am not alone, for my Father is with me.

33 'I have told you these things, so that in me you may have peace. In this world you will have trouble. But take heart! I have overcome the world.'

PAIN AND SUFFERING 5

DON'T BE SURPRISED BY PAIN AND SUFFERING

None of us want pain. That's pretty much a given. I think one of our bigger problems with pain is that we just don't expect it. Sometimes we get the impression that if we're a Christian we'll be fast-tracked to a smooth, easy and comfortable life, but that was never the gospel. Rather than taking us out of the world, God asks us to stay living in it and he warned us it wouldn't be easy.

Life is full of problems and pains as we live in a fallen world. That means this is a world where God's kingdom isn't fully known. When we're in God's kingdom there will be no more tears, no more pain and no more death (Revelation 21). We will live for ever with God. Until that day, we have to live here – where sometimes we see amazingly wonderful things happen, but at other times we see painful stuff. We're not immune from suffering just because we know God.

At the same time, Jesus gives us this amazing promise to hold onto: he has overcome the world (John 16:33)! He has the ultimate victory and there will be a day when we are free from suffering and pain. In the meantime, he doesn't leave us alone in our troubles. He promises never to leave us, no matter what – so if we're suffering, it doesn't mean that God is angry with us and is punishing us. Jesus took all the punishment that we deserve to the cross for us. Suffering doesn't mean that God isn't working in our lives. Sometimes he does more through life's difficulties than he does in the times of blessing. So no matter what, we know that God is with us in the midst of our pain. He is our peace in times of trouble: he is all we need.

Mike Pilavachi

 Habakkuk 3:17　　　　　　　　　　　　　　　Luke 22:42 ▶▶

Jesus prays to be glorified

17 After Jesus said this, he looked towards heaven and prayed:

'Father, the hour has come. Glorify your Son, that your Son may glorify you. ²For you granted him authority over all people that he might give eternal life to all those you have given him. ³Now this is eternal life: that they know you, the only true God, and Jesus Christ, whom you have sent. ⁴I have brought you glory on earth by finishing the work you gave me to do. ⁵And now, Father, glorify me in your presence with the glory I had with you before the world began.

Jesus prays for his disciples

⁶'I have revealed you^a to those whom you gave me out of the world. They were yours; you gave them to me and they have obeyed your word. ⁷Now they know that everything you have given me comes from you. ⁸For I gave them the words you gave me and they accepted them. They knew with certainty that I came from you, and they believed that you sent me. ⁹I pray for them. I am not praying for the world, but for those you have given me, for they are yours. ¹⁰All I have is yours, and all you have is mine. And glory has come to me through them. ¹¹I will remain in the world no longer, but they are still in the world, and I am coming to you. Holy Father, protect them by the power of^b your name, the name you gave me, so that they may be one as we are one. ¹²While I was with them, I protected them and kept them safe by^c that name you gave me. None has been lost except the one doomed to destruction so that Scripture would be fulfilled.

¹³'I am coming to you now, but I say these things while I am still in the world, so that they may have the full measure of my joy within them. ¹⁴I have given them your word and the world has hated them, for they are not of the world any more than I am of the world. ¹⁵My prayer is not that you take them out of the world but that you protect them from the evil one. ¹⁶They are not of the world, even as I am not of it. ¹⁷Sanctify them by^d the truth; your word is truth. ¹⁸As you sent me into the world, I have sent them into the world. ¹⁹For them I sanctify myself, that they too may be truly sanctified.

Jesus prays for all believers

²⁰'My prayer is not for them alone. I pray also for those who will believe in me through their message, ²¹that all of them may be one, Father, just as you are in me and I am in you. May they also be in us so that the world may believe that you have sent me. ²²I have given them the glory that you gave me, that they may be one as we are one – ²³I in them and you in me – so that they may be brought to complete unity. Then the world will know that you sent me and have loved them even as you have loved me.

²⁴'Father, I want those you have given me to be with me where I am, and to see my glory, the glory you have given me because you loved me before the creation of the world. ²⁵'Righteous Father, though the world does not know you, I know you, and they know that you have sent me. ²⁶I have made you^e known to them, and will continue to make you known in order that the love you have for me may be in them and that I myself may be in them.'

Jesus arrested

18 When he had finished praying, Jesus left with his disciples and

---

a 6 Greek *your name*
b 11 Or *Father, keep them faithful to*
c 12 Or *kept them faithful to*

d 17 Or *them to live in accordance with*
e 26 Greek *your name*

crossed the Kidron Valley. On the other side there was a garden, and he and his disciples went into it.

2 Now Judas, who betrayed him, knew the place, because Jesus had often met there with his disciples. 3 So Judas came to the garden, guiding a detachment of soldiers and some officials from the chief priests and the Pharisees. They were carrying torches, lanterns and weapons.

4 Jesus, knowing all that was going to happen to him, went out and asked them, 'Who is it you want?'

5 'Jesus of Nazareth,' they replied.

'I am he,' Jesus said. (And Judas the traitor was standing there with them.) 6 When Jesus said, 'I am he,' they drew back and fell to the ground.

7 Again he asked them, 'Who is it you want?'

'Jesus of Nazareth,' they said.

8 Jesus answered, 'I told you that I am he. If you are looking for me, then let these men go.' 9 This happened so that the words he had spoken would be fulfilled: 'I have not lost one of those you gave me.' a

10 Then Simon Peter, who had a sword, drew it and struck the high priest's servant, cutting off his right ear. (The servant's name was Malchus.)

11 Jesus commanded Peter, 'Put your sword away! Shall I not drink the cup the Father has given me?'

12 Then the detachment of soldiers with its commander and the Jewish officials arrested Jesus. They bound him 13 and brought him first to Annas, who was the father-in-law of Caiaphas, the high priest that year. 14 Caiaphas was the one who had advised the Jewish leaders that it would be good if one man died for the people.

Peter's first denial

15 Simon Peter and another disciple were following Jesus. Because this disciple was known to the high priest, he went with Jesus into the high priest's courtyard, 16 but Peter had to wait outside at the door. The other disciple, who

was known to the high priest, came back, spoke to the servant-girl on duty there and brought Peter in.

17 'You aren't one of this man's disciples too, are you?' she asked Peter.

He replied, 'I am not.'

18 It was cold, and the servants and officials stood round a fire they had made to keep warm. Peter also was standing with them, warming himself.

The high priest questions Jesus

19 Meanwhile, the high priest questioned Jesus about his disciples and his teaching.

20 'I have spoken openly to the world,' Jesus replied. 'I always taught in synagogues or at the temple, where all the Jews come together. I said nothing in secret. 21 Why question me? Ask those who heard me. Surely they know what I said.'

22 When Jesus said this, one of the officials near by slapped him in the face. 'Is this the way you answer the high priest?' he demanded.

23 'If I said something wrong,' Jesus replied, 'testify as to what is wrong. But if I spoke the truth, why did you strike me?' 24 Then Annas sent him bound to Caiaphas the high priest.

Peter's second and third denials

25 Meanwhile, Simon Peter was still standing there warming himself. So they asked him, 'You aren't one of his disciples too, are you?'

He denied it, saying, 'I am not.'

26 One of the high priest's servants, a relative of the man whose ear Peter had cut off, challenged him, 'Didn't I see you with him in the garden?' 27 Again Peter denied it, and at that moment a cock began to crow.

Jesus before Pilate

28 Then the Jewish leaders took Jesus from Caiaphas to the palace of the Roman governor. By now it was early morning, and to avoid ceremonial uncleanness they did not enter the palace, because they wanted to be able to eat the Passover. 29 So Pilate came out to them and asked,

a 9 John 6:39

'What charges are you bringing against this man?'

30 'If he were not a criminal,' they replied, 'we would not have handed him over to you.'

31 Pilate said, 'Take him yourselves and judge him by your own law.'

'But we have no right to execute anyone,' they objected. 32 This took place to fulfil what Jesus had said about the kind of death he was going to die.

33 Pilate then went back inside the palace, summoned Jesus and asked him, 'Are you the king of the Jews?'

34 'Is that your own idea,' Jesus asked, 'or did others talk to you about me?'

35 'Am I a Jew?' Pilate replied. 'Your own people and chief priests handed you over to me. What is it you have done?'

36 Jesus said, 'My kingdom is not of this world. If it were, my servants would fight to prevent my arrest by the Jewish leaders. But now my kingdom is from another place.'

37 'You are a king, then!' said Pilate.

Jesus answered, 'You say that I am a king. In fact, the reason I was born and came into the world is to testify to the truth. Everyone on the side of truth listens to me.'

38 'What is truth?' retorted Pilate. With this he went out again to the Jews gathered there and said, 'I find no basis for a charge against him. 39 But it is your custom for me to release to you one prisoner at the time of the Passover. Do you want me to release "the king of the Jews"?'

40 They shouted back, 'No, not him! Give us Barabbas!' Now Barabbas had taken part in an uprising.

Jesus sentenced to be crucified

19 Then Pilate took Jesus and had him flogged. 2 The soldiers twisted together a crown of thorns and put it on his head. They clothed him in a purple robe 3 and went up to him again and again, saying, 'Hail, king of the Jews!' And they slapped him in the face.

4 Once more Pilate came out and said to the Jews gathered there, 'Look, I am bringing him out to you to let you know that I find no basis for a charge against him.' 5 When Jesus came out wearing the crown of thorns and the purple robe, Pilate said to them, 'Here is the man!'

6 As soon as the chief priests and their officials saw him, they shouted, 'Crucify! Crucify!'

But Pilate answered, 'You take him and crucify him. As for me, I find no basis for a charge against him.'

7 The Jewish leaders insisted, 'We have a law, and according to that law he must die, because he claimed to be the Son of God.'

8 When Pilate heard this, he was even more afraid, 9 and he went back inside the palace. 'Where do you come from?' he asked Jesus, but Jesus gave him no answer. 10 'Do you refuse to speak to me?' Pilate said. 'Don't you realise I have power either to free you or to crucify you?'

11 Jesus answered, 'You would have no power over me if it were not given to you from above. Therefore the one who handed me over to you is guilty of a greater sin.'

12 From then on, Pilate tried to set Jesus free, but the Jewish leaders kept shouting, 'If you let this man go, you are no friend of Caesar. Anyone who claims to be a king opposes Caesar.'

13 When Pilate heard this, he brought Jesus out and sat down on the judge's seat at a place known as the Stone Pavement (which in Aramaic is Gabbatha). 14 It was the day of Preparation of the Passover; it was about noon.

'Here is your king,' Pilate said to the Jews.

15 But they shouted, 'Take him away! Take him away! Crucify him!'

'Shall I crucify your king?' Pilate asked.

'We have no king but Caesar,' the chief priests answered.

16 Finally Pilate handed him over to them to be crucified.

The crucifixion of Jesus

So the soldiers took charge of Jesus. 17 Carrying his own cross, he went out to the place of the Skull (which in Aramaic is called Golgotha). 18 There they crucified

PEOPLE USED BY GOD 9

John

John, son of Zebedee, was one of the twelve disciples and the brother of James, and the two of them were known as 'the sons of thunder'. John lived until AD 85 and he's the only disciple to die of natural causes, aged 100 – despite (according to other historical books) being put into a cauldron of boiling oil for preaching the gospel, when he was miraculously unharmed. He's the author of a Gospel, three letters and the book of Revelation. Matthew, Mark and Luke are all 'Synoptic Gospels', which means they summarise a narrative for us, but John talks about Jesus in his Gospel in a completely different way.

John was always at the significant places when important things took place with Jesus. He was there when Jesus raised a girl from the dead, at the transfiguration when Jesus changed and appeared in radiant glory (Matthew 17:2; Mark 9:2–3; Luke 9:28–36), in the Garden of Gethsemane before Jesus was arrested, and at his death on the cross.

John had an amazing understanding of grace and love and the part they play in knowing God. He also understood the humanity of Jesus as well as his divinity and taught both these things. There was a popular belief that Jesus wasn't really God made flesh, but that the Spirit of God just came on the man Jesus and then left him when he was on the cross. They couldn't understand how God could die. John makes a point of showing that God was made flesh and was indeed God on earth. He points to Jesus' humanity – Jesus wept (John 11:35), was thirsty (John 19:28) and tired (John 4:6) – and he also points to his divinity (John 1:1–5).

He also recorded three key things for us to know about Jesus. First, he lined up with the prophetic promises in the Old Testament of what the Messiah would bring. Second, Jesus did miracles among the people. Third, there was a promise of things to come. All these things confirmed that Jesus was the promised Messiah of old, the present manifestation to meet people's needs, and the coming King everyone was looking for.

John's place in Jesus' life was special. He was part of the inner circle along with Peter and James, his brother. At his death Jesus told Mary (his mother), *'Woman, here is your son'*, and to John he said, *'Here is your mother'* (John 19:26–27). The love Jesus expressed for John is unmistakeable in this action and John always refers to himself as *'the disciple whom Jesus loved'*. I'm sure this added to John's understanding that God's gift to the world was love, shown in the giving of his Son.

John is a great example to us. He always wanted to be with Jesus, even when it could have cost him his life. There's a great value in that type of relationship. Faithfulness is a foundation on which the things of the kingdom are built.

Tom Brock

 John 1:47　　　　　　　　Acts 8:3 ▶▶

him, and with him two others – one on each side and Jesus in the middle.

19 Pilate had a notice prepared and fastened to the cross. It read: JESUS OF NAZARETH, THE KING OF THE JEWS. 20 Many of the Jews read this sign, for the place where Jesus was crucified was near the city, and the sign was written in Aramaic, Latin and Greek. 21 The chief priests of the Jews protested to Pilate, 'Do not write "The King of the Jews", but that this man claimed to be king of the Jews.'

22 Pilate answered, 'What I have written, I have written.'

23 When the soldiers crucified Jesus, they took his clothes, dividing them into four shares, one for each of them, with the undergarment remaining. This garment was seamless, woven in one piece from top to bottom.

24 'Let's not tear it,' they said to one another. 'Let's decide by lot who will get it.'

This happened that the scripture might be fulfilled that said,

'They divided my clothes among them
    and cast lots for my garment.' *a*

So this is what the soldiers did.

25 Near the cross of Jesus stood his mother, his mother's sister, Mary the wife of Clopas, and Mary Magdalene. 26 When Jesus saw his mother there, and the disciple whom he loved standing near by, he said to her, 'Woman,*b* here is your son,' 27 and to the disciple, 'Here is your mother.' From that time on, this disciple took her into his home.

The death of Jesus

28 Later, knowing that everything had now been finished, and so that Scripture would be fulfilled, Jesus said, 'I am thirsty.' 29 A jar of wine vinegar was there, so they soaked a sponge in it, put the sponge on a stalk of the hyssop plant, and lifted it to Jesus' lips. 30 When he had received the drink, Jesus said, 'It is finished.' With that, he bowed his head and gave up his spirit.

31 Now it was the day of Preparation, and the next day was to be a special Sabbath. Because the Jewish leaders did not want the bodies left on the crosses during the Sabbath, they asked Pilate to have the legs broken and the bodies taken down. 32 The soldiers therefore came and broke the legs of the first man who had been crucified with Jesus, and then those of the other. 33 But when they came to Jesus and found that he was already dead, they did not break his legs. 34 Instead, one of the soldiers pierced Jesus' side with a spear, bringing a sudden flow of blood and water. 35 The man who saw it has given testimony, and his testimony is true. He knows that he tells the truth, and he testifies so that you also may believe. 36 These things happened so that the scripture would be fulfilled: 'Not one of his bones will be broken,'*c* 37 and, as another scripture says, 'They will look on the one they have pierced.'*d*

The burial of Jesus

38 Later, Joseph of Arimathea asked Pilate for the body of Jesus. Now Joseph was a disciple of Jesus, but secretly because he feared the Jewish leaders. With Pilate's permission, he came and took the body away. 39 He was accompanied by Nicodemus, the man who earlier had visited Jesus at night. Nicodemus brought a mixture of myrrh and aloes, about thirty-five kilograms. 40 Taking Jesus' body, the two of them wrapped it, with the spices, in strips of linen. This was in accordance with Jewish burial customs. 41 At the place where Jesus was crucified, there was a garden, and in the garden a new tomb, in which no one had ever been laid. 42 Because it was the Jewish day of Preparation and since the tomb was near by, they laid Jesus there.

---

a 24 Psalm 22:18
b 26 The Greek for *Woman* does not denote any disrespect.

c 36 Exodus 12:46; Num. 9:12; Psalm 34:20
d 37 Zech. 12:10

The empty tomb

20 Early on the first day of the week, while it was still dark, Mary Magdalene went to the tomb and saw that the stone had been removed from the entrance. ²So she came running to Simon Peter and the other disciple, the one Jesus loved, and said, 'They have taken the Lord out of the tomb, and we don't know where they have put him!'

³So Peter and the other disciple started for the tomb. ⁴Both were running, but the other disciple outran Peter and reached the tomb first. ⁵He bent over and looked in at the strips of linen lying there but did not go in. ⁶Then Simon Peter came along behind him and went straight into the tomb. He saw the strips of linen lying there, ⁷as well as the cloth that had been wrapped round Jesus' head. The cloth was still lying in its place, separate from the linen. ⁸Finally the other disciple, who had reached the tomb first, also went inside. He saw and believed. ⁹(They still did not understand from Scripture that Jesus had to rise from the dead.) ¹⁰Then the disciples went back to where they were staying.

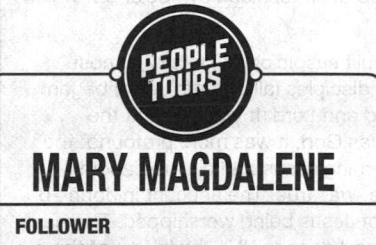

PEOPLE TOURS

MARY MAGDALENE

FOLLOWER
Luke 8:1–3
CRUCIFIXION
Mark 15:42–47
GARDENER
John 19:11–18

Jesus appears to Mary Magdalene

¹¹Now Mary stood outside the tomb crying. As she wept, she bent over to look into the tomb ¹²and saw two angels in white, seated where Jesus' body had been, one at the head and the other at the foot. ¹³They asked her, 'Woman, why are you crying?'

'They have taken my Lord away,' she said, 'and I don't know where they have put him.' ¹⁴At this, she turned round and saw Jesus standing there, but she did not realise that it was Jesus.

¹⁵He asked her, 'Woman, why are you crying? Who is it you are looking for?'

Thinking he was the gardener, she said, 'Sir, if you have carried him away, tell me where you have put him, and I will get him.'

¹⁶Jesus said to her, 'Mary.'

She turned towards him and cried out in Aramaic, 'Rabboni!' (which means 'Teacher').

¹⁷Jesus said, 'Do not hold on to me, for I have not yet ascended to the Father. Go instead to my brothers and tell them, "I am ascending to my Father and your Father, to my God and your God."'

¹⁸Mary Magdalene went to the disciples with the news: 'I have seen the Lord!' And she told them that he had said these things to her.

Jesus appears to his disciples

¹⁹On the evening of that first day of the week, when the disciples were together, with the doors locked for fear of the Jewish leaders, Jesus came and stood among them and said, 'Peace be with you!' ²⁰After he said this, he showed them his hands and side. The disciples were overjoyed when they saw the Lord.

²¹Again Jesus said, 'Peace be with you! As the Father has sent me, I am sending you.' ²²And with that he breathed on them and said, 'Receive the Holy Spirit. ²³If you forgive anyone's sins, their sins are forgiven; if you do not forgive them, they are not forgiven.'

Jesus appears to Thomas

²⁴Now Thomas (also known as Didymus*ᵃ*), one of the Twelve, was not with the disciples when Jesus came. ²⁵So the other disciples told him, 'We have seen the Lord!'

But he said to them, 'Unless I see the

---

a 24 *Thomas* (Aramaic) and *Didymus* (Greek) both mean *twin*.

nail marks in his hands and put my finger where the nails were, and put my hand into his side, I will not believe.' ²⁶A week later his disciples were in the house again, and Thomas was with them. Though the doors were locked, Jesus came and stood among them and said, 'Peace be with you!' ²⁷Then he said to Thomas,

LIFE OF JESUS 8

The one who can be worshipped

'Idol worship' is something that's always viewed negatively. Even if we use the term without any religious meaning, in purely psychological terms there's the implication that someone is wasting their time and energy in being devoted to someone or something that doesn't deserve it. Spiritually, the phrase is used in a similar sense. To be involved in idol worship is to adore something that's utterly unworthy.

By the time of Jesus, the Jewish people were particularly sensitive to idol worship and were good at detecting even the slightest hint of it. They knew that centuries of misery in defeat, exile and occupation had occurred because of their failure to keep the first two of the Ten Commandments (Exodus 20:1–17; Deuteronomy 5:7–21). They had finally learned the hard lesson that there was only one almighty God and nothing (and no one) else came even remotely close. Indeed, they were so sensitive on this issue that many of the violent confrontations with occupying powers in Jesus' day started with what the Romans thought was a trivial issue of banners, statues and symbols, but which the Jewish people saw as idolatry.

The astounding fact is that despite this inbuilt suspicion of idolatry, almost immediately after the resurrection, the first disciples (all of them Jews) began worshipping Jesus and treating him as God and Lord. It was not that the resurrection had convinced them that he was God, it was more profound: the resurrection had proved to them that everything Jesus had claimed about himself, including those claims to be divine, was true. The account in John 20 is one of the earliest and clearest records of Jesus being worshipped. Thomas's simple statement in verse 28 is expanded and deepened in the letters of the New Testament (e.g., 1 Corinthians 1:2; Colossians 1:15–17; 2:9; 1 Timothy 3:16; Titus 2:13). Indeed, the phrase 'Lord Jesus' which is widely used in the letters of the New Testament carries a great significance: to a Jew there was no Lord but Yahweh, the God of Israel. Nevertheless, Thomas's words remain a great statement of truth. We can all come to the risen Christ and say, *'My Lord and my God!'* But in doing so, let's not forget that personal little word *'my'*. We must all take Jesus to be our own personal Lord.

J.John

'Put your finger here; see my hands. Reach out your hand and put it into my side. Stop doubting and believe.'

28 Thomas said to him, 'My Lord and my God!'

29 Then Jesus told him, 'Because you have seen me, you have believed; blessed are those who have not seen and yet have believed.'

The purpose of John's gospel

30 Jesus performed many other signs in the presence of his disciples, which are not recorded in this book. 31 But these are written that you may believe[b] that Jesus is the Messiah, the Son of God, and that by believing you may have life in his name.

Jesus and the miraculous catch of fish

21 Afterwards Jesus appeared again to his disciples, by the Sea of Galilee.[a] It happened this way: 2 Simon Peter, Thomas (also known as Didymus[b]), Nathanael from Cana in Galilee, the sons of Zebedee, and two other disciples were together. 3 'I'm going out to fish,' Simon Peter told them, and they said, 'We'll go with you.' So they went out and got into the boat, but that night they caught nothing.

4 Early in the morning, Jesus stood on the shore, but the disciples did not realise that it was Jesus.

5 He called out to them, 'Friends, haven't you any fish?'

'No,' they answered.

6 He said, 'Throw your net on the right side of the boat and you will find some.' When they did, they were unable to haul the net in because of the large number of fish.

7 Then the disciple whom Jesus loved said to Peter, 'It is the Lord!' As soon as Simon Peter heard him say, 'It is the Lord,' he wrapped his outer garment round him

(for he had taken it off) and jumped into the water. 8 The other disciples followed in the boat, towing the net full of fish, for they were not far from shore, about a hundred metres. 9 When they landed, they saw a fire of burning coals there with fish on it, and some bread.

10 Jesus said to them, 'Bring some of the fish you have just caught.' 11 So Simon Peter climbed back into the boat and dragged the net ashore. It was full of large fish, 153, but even with so many the net was not torn. 12 Jesus said to them, 'Come and have breakfast.' None of the disciples dared ask him, 'Who are you?' They knew it was the Lord. 13 Jesus came, took the bread and gave it to them, and did the same with the fish. 14 This was now the third time Jesus appeared to his disciples after he was raised from the dead.

Jesus reinstates Peter

15 When they had finished eating, Jesus said to Simon Peter, 'Simon son of John, do you love me more than these?'

'Yes, Lord,' he said, 'you know that I love you.'

Jesus said, 'Feed my lambs.'

16 Again Jesus said, 'Simon son of John, do you love me?'

He answered, 'Yes, Lord, you know that I love you.'

Jesus said, 'Take care of my sheep.'

17 The third time he said to him, 'Simon son of John, do you love me?'

Peter was hurt because Jesus asked him the third time, 'Do you love me?' He said, 'Lord, you know all things; you know that I love you.'

Jesus said, 'Feed my sheep. 18 Very truly I tell you, when you were younger you dressed yourself and went where you wanted; but when you are old you will stretch out your hands, and someone else will dress you and lead you where you do not want to go.' 19 Jesus said this to indicate the kind of death by which Peter would glorify God. Then he said to him, 'Follow me!'

20 Peter turned and saw that the disciple whom Jesus loved was following them. (This was the one who had leaned

---

b 31 Or *may continue to believe*
a 1 Greek *Tiberias*
b 2 *Thomas* (Aramaic) and *Didymus* (Greek) both mean *twin.*

back against Jesus at the supper and had said, 'Lord, who is going to betray you?') ²¹When Peter saw him, he asked, 'Lord, what about him?'

²²Jesus answered, 'If I want him to remain alive until I return, what is that to you? You must follow me.' ²³Because of this, the rumour spread among the believers that this disciple would not die. But Jesus did not say that he would not die; he only said, 'If I want him to remain alive until I return, what is that to you?'

²⁴This is the disciple who testifies to these things and who wrote them down. We know that his testimony is true.

²⁵Jesus did many other things as well. If every one of them were written down, I suppose that even the whole world would not have room for the books that would be written.

FRIENDSHIP 5

True intimacy

Jesus knew he couldn't be friends with everyone. No one has that capacity! So he chose twelve people (his disciples) with whom he was going to spend the majority of his time. Amongst those twelve there were three disciples he was closer to than the others: Peter, John and James. Of those three, there was one who was his closest friend: John. Five times in the book of John he is referred to as *'the disciple whom Jesus loved'*.

We don't click with everyone, but God asks us to show love and kindness to all. Picking your closest friends isn't about forming a clique or leaving people out; church is meant to be inclusive and so should our friendships be at school and elsewhere too.

But as we can see from the example of Jesus, it's good to have a couple friends you are particularly close to. They are the ones you can tell everything to – the good, the bad and the ugly. A good friend will let you confess your sin without judging you. They won't make you feel bad, but they also won't tell you your sin doesn't matter. A good friend will correct you when you're going wrong and help you bring your sin before Jesus and receive his forgiveness. A good friend will stick around on your bad days and love you when you feel unlovable. A good friend shares in your joys, cheers you on and rejoices with you in your successes. The best way to get friends like this? Be one yourself.

Choose your friends wisely. Consider who you want as really close friends you can be committed to. Invest in those friendships; don't just expect amazing friendships to blossom overnight. Spend time together. Talk honestly. Be real. And enjoy the blessing of true, intimate friendship.

Ali Martin

 1 Samuel 18:1–3   Acts 15:36–41

ACTS

DATE

Acts details events from after Jesus' death in AD 33 up to around thirty years later

AUTHOR

Luke (who also wrote one of the Gospels)

WHAT'S IT ALL ABOUT?

This book was written by the same Luke who wrote the third Gospel and it's the second part of his writings to his friend Theophilus. While the Gospels all focus on what happened while Jesus was on earth, Acts picks up the story as Jesus was taken up to heaven and follows what happened over the next thirty years. It shows how the church got started and what it looked like, the fulfilment of Jesus' promise to send the Holy Spirit to his disciples, and what the believers got up to as they spread the gospel. The book is packed with miraculous healings as the disciples followed Jesus' example and prayed for those who were sick or demon-possessed. It details how Saul (whose name was changed to Paul) persecuted Christians, but then encountered God in a dramatic way and gave his life to Christ. He was one of the first ever missionaries, sent out to spread the gospel message around the world. During his travels he was arrested, flogged, imprisoned and even shipwrecked, but nothing deterred him from his mission.

WHY SHOULD WE READ IT?

- Because Acts shows us that the death and resurrection of Jesus were far from the end of the story. They were in fact the beginning, and Acts shows us how Jesus' first disciples lived out his teaching.

- To see how the church began (Acts 1– 2).

- To see the amazing community of believers and how they cared for one another (especially Acts 2:42–47).

- To read about Saul's dramatic conversion (Acts 9) when his name was changed to Paul.

- To read how the Holy Spirit empowered the early believers on the day of Pentecost and beyond (Acts 2 onwards).

- To be inspired about the way God wants you to live your life in his power and strength.

Andy Croft with Liza Hoeksma

Jesus taken up into heaven

1 In my former book, Theophilus, I wrote about all that Jesus began to do and to teach ²until the day he was taken up to heaven, after giving instructions through the Holy Spirit to the apostles he had chosen. ³After his suffering, he presented himself to them and gave many convincing proofs that he was alive. He appeared to them over a period of forty days and spoke about the kingdom of God. ⁴On one occasion, while he was eating with them, he gave them this command: 'Do not leave Jerusalem, but wait for the gift my Father promised, which you have heard me speak about. ⁵For John baptised with*a* water, but in a few days you will be baptised with*a* the Holy Spirit.'

⁶Then they gathered round him and asked him, 'Lord, are you at this time going to restore the kingdom to Israel?'

⁷He said to them: 'It is not for you to know the times or dates the Father has set by his own authority. ⁸But you will receive power when the Holy Spirit comes on you; and you will be my witnesses in Jerusalem, and in all Judea and Samaria, and to the ends of the earth.'

⁹After he said this, he was taken up before their very eyes, and a cloud hid him from their sight.

¹⁰They were looking intently up into the sky as he was going, when suddenly two men dressed in white stood beside them. ¹¹'Men of Galilee,' they said, 'why do you stand here looking into the sky? This same Jesus, who has been taken from you into heaven, will come back in the same way you have seen him go into heaven.'

Matthias chosen to replace Judas

¹²Then the apostles returned to Jerusalem from the hill called the Mount of Olives, a Sabbath day's walk*b* from the city. ¹³When they arrived, they went upstairs to the room where they were staying. Those present were Peter, John, James and Andrew; Philip and Thomas, Bartholomew

and Matthew; James son of Alphaeus and Simon the Zealot, and Judas son of James. ¹⁴They all joined together constantly in prayer, along with the women and Mary the mother of Jesus, and with his brothers.

¹⁵In those days Peter stood up among the believers (a group numbering about a hundred and twenty) ¹⁶and said, 'Brothers and sisters,*c* the Scripture had to be fulfilled in which the Holy Spirit spoke long ago through David concerning Judas, who served as guide for those who arrested Jesus. ¹⁷He was one of our number and shared in our ministry.'

¹⁸(With the payment he received for his wickedness, Judas bought a field; there he fell headlong, his body burst open and all his intestines spilled out. ¹⁹Everyone in Jerusalem heard about this, so they called that field in their language Akeldama, that is, Field of Blood.)

²⁰'For,' said Peter, 'it is written in the Book of Psalms:

'"May his place be deserted;
   let there be no one to dwell in it,"*d*

and,

'"May another take his place of
   leadership."*e*

²¹Therefore it is necessary to choose one of the men who have been with us the whole time the Lord Jesus was living among us, ²²beginning from John's baptism to the time when Jesus was taken up from us. For one of these must become a witness with us of his resurrection.'

²³So they nominated two men: Joseph called Barsabbas (also known as Justus) and Matthias. ²⁴Then they prayed, 'Lord, you know everyone's heart. Show us which of these two you have chosen ²⁵to take over this apostolic ministry, which

---

a 5 Or *in*
b 12 That is, about 5/8 mile or about 1 kilometre

c 16 The Greek word for *brothers and sisters (adelphoi)* refers here to believers, both men and women, as part of God's family; also in 6:3; 11:29; 12:17; 16:40; 18:18, 27; 21:7, 17; 28:14, 15.
d 20 Psalm 69:25
e 20 Psalm 109:8

Judas left to go where he belongs.' ²⁶Then they cast lots, and the lot fell to Matthias; so he was added to the eleven apostles.

The Holy Spirit comes at Pentecost

2 When the day of Pentecost came, they were all together in one place. ²Suddenly a sound like the blowing of a violent wind came from heaven and filled the whole house where they were sitting. ³They saw what seemed to be tongues of fire that separated and came to rest on each of them. ⁴All of them were filled with the Holy Spirit and began to speak

in other tongues*ᵃ* as the Spirit enabled them.

⁵Now there were staying in Jerusalem God-fearing Jews from every nation under heaven. ⁶When they heard this sound, a crowd came together in bewilderment, because each one heard their own language being spoken. ⁷Utterly amazed, they asked: 'Aren't all these who are speaking Galileans? ⁸Then how is it that each of us hears them in our native language? ⁹Parthians, Medes and Elamites;

a 4 Or *languages*; also in verse 11

EVANGELISM 1

The starting place

Evangelism can be a scary topic to look at. Let's face it: it's tough enough trying to be a Christian without adding extra bits like winning the world for God! It's easy to feel overwhelmed with the challenges of life, and then we add the monster challenge of reaching out to our friends about Jesus. But before we stress ourselves out completely, let's look at what Jesus promised his disciples before he went to heaven (Acts 1:8).

He said that they would *'receive power'* when the Holy Spirit came on them. Good news, guys: we don't have to do this thing on our own! Do you feel as if you can't do the whole evangelism thing and it all seems too big and hard for you? If so, brilliant! God isn't looking for people who think they are totally sorted and could win the world for Jesus before breakfast. It's not like having a piece of homework to do and you could do it by yourself or you could get someone to help you. When it comes to evangelism, you *have* to get help! If we don't do this with God, then we can't do it.

So how do we get filled with the Holy Spirit? Being filled with the power of the Holy Spirit is not a one-off, one-time encounter. It's an ongoing and daily thing, and we can actively ask God for it to happen. Why not take a moment now and ask God to fill you with his Holy Spirit?

God says, 'I will give you whatever you need.' If you have just asked God to fill you, you may feel different or you may not. Either way, be confident that you have now received the power that you need to be God's witness in your family, your school and wherever you find yourself today.

Mark Ritchie

Matthew 9:16

residents of Mesopotamia, Judea and Cappadocia, Pontus and Asia,*b* 10 Phrygia and Pamphylia, Egypt and the parts of Libya near Cyrene; visitors from Rome 11 (both Jews and converts to Judaism); Cretans and Arabs – we hear them declaring the wonders of God in our own tongues!' 12 Amazed and perplexed, they asked one another, 'What does this mean?'

13 Some, however, made fun of them and said, 'They have had too much wine.'

Peter addresses the crowd

14 Then Peter stood up with the Eleven, raised his voice and addressed the crowd: 'Fellow Jews and all of you who live in Jerusalem, let me explain this to you; listen carefully to what I say. 15 These people are not drunk, as you suppose. It's only nine in the morning! 16 No, this is what was spoken by the prophet Joel:

17 ' "In the last days, God says,
    I will pour out my Spirit on all
        people.
Your sons and daughters will prophesy,
    your young men will see visions,
    your old men will dream dreams.
18 Even on my servants, both men and
        women,
    I will pour out my Spirit in those days,
    and they will prophesy.
19 I will show wonders in the heavens
        above
    and signs on the earth below,
    blood and fire and billows of
        smoke.
20 The sun will be turned to darkness
    and the moon to blood
    before the coming of the great and
        glorious day of the Lord.
21 And everyone who calls
    on the name of the Lord will be
        saved." *c*

22 'Fellow Israelites, listen to this: Jesus of Nazareth was a man accredited by God to you by miracles, wonders and signs, which God did among you through him,

as you yourselves know. 23 This man was handed over to you by God's deliberate plan and foreknowledge; and you, with the help of wicked men,*d* put him to death by nailing him to the cross. 24 But God raised him from the dead, freeing him from the agony of death, because it was impossible for death to keep its hold on him. 25 David said about him:

' "I saw the Lord always before me.
    Because he is at my right hand,
    I will not be shaken.
26 Therefore my heart is glad and my
        tongue rejoices;
    my body also will rest in hope,
27 because you will not abandon me to
        the realm of the dead,
    you will not let your holy one see
        decay.
28 You have made known to me the paths
        of life;
    you will fill me with joy in your
        presence." *e*

29 'Fellow Israelites, I can tell you confidently that the patriarch David died and was buried, and his tomb is here to this day. 30 But he was a prophet and knew that God had promised him on oath that he would place one of his descendants on his throne. 31 Seeing what was to come, he spoke of the resurrection of the Messiah, that he was not abandoned to the realm of the dead, nor did his body see decay. 32 God has raised this Jesus to life, and we are all witnesses of it. 33 Exalted to the right hand of God, he has received from the Father the promised Holy Spirit and has poured out what you now see and hear. 34 For David did not ascend to heaven, and yet he said,

' "The Lord said to my Lord:
    'Sit at my right hand
35 until I make your enemies
    a footstool for your feet.' " *f*

---

b 9 That is, the Roman province by that name
c 21 Joel 2:28-32

d 23 Or *of those not having the law* (that is, Gentiles)
e 28 Psalm 16:8-11 (see Septuagint)
f 35 Psalm 110:1

36 'Therefore let all Israel be assured of this: God has made this Jesus, whom you crucified, both Lord and Messiah.'

37 When the people heard this, they were cut to the heart and said to Peter and the other apostles, 'Brothers, what shall we do?'

38 Peter replied, 'Repent and be baptised, every one of you, in the name of Jesus Christ for the forgiveness of your sins. And you will receive the gift of the Holy Spirit. **39** The promise is for you and your children and for all who are far off – for all whom the Lord our God will call.'

40 With many other words he warned them; and he pleaded with them, 'Save yourselves from this corrupt generation.' **41** Those who accepted his message were baptised, and about three thousand were added to their number that day.

The fellowship of the believers

42 They devoted themselves to the apostles' teaching and to fellowship, to the breaking of bread and to prayer. **43** Everyone was filled with awe at the many wonders and signs performed by the apostles. **44** All the believers were together and had everything in common. **45** They sold property and possessions to give to anyone who had need. **46** Every day they continued to meet together in the temple courts. They broke bread in their homes and ate together with glad and sincere hearts, **47** praising God and enjoying the favour of all the people. And the Lord added to their number daily those who were being saved.

Peter heals a lame beggar

3 One day Peter and John were going up to the temple at the time of prayer – at three in the afternoon. **2** Now a man who was lame from birth was being carried to the temple gate called Beautiful, where he was put every day to beg from those going into the temple courts. **3** When he saw Peter and John about to enter, he asked them for money. **4** Peter looked straight at him, as did John. Then Peter said, 'Look at us!' **5** So the man gave them his attention, expecting to get something from them.

6 Then Peter said, 'Silver or gold I do not have, but what I do have I give you. In the name of Jesus Christ of Nazareth, walk.' **7** Taking him by the right hand, he helped him up, and instantly the man's feet and ankles became strong. **8** He jumped to his feet and began to walk. Then he went with them into the temple courts, walking and jumping, and praising God. **9** When all the people saw him walking and praising God, **10** they recognised him as the same man who used to sit begging at the temple gate called Beautiful, and they were filled with wonder and amazement at what had happened to him.

Peter speaks to the onlookers

11 While the man held on to Peter and John, all the people were astonished and came running to them in the place called Solomon's Colonnade. **12** When Peter saw this, he said to them: 'Fellow Israelites, why does this surprise you? Why do you stare at us as if by our own power or godliness we had made this man walk? **13** The God of Abraham, Isaac and Jacob, the God of our fathers, has glorified his servant Jesus. You handed him over to be killed, and you disowned him before Pilate, though he had decided to let him go. **14** You disowned the Holy and Righteous One and asked that a murderer be released to you. **15** You killed the author of life, but God raised him from the dead. We are witnesses of this. **16** By faith in the name of Jesus, this man whom you see and know was made strong. It is Jesus' name and the faith that comes through him that has completely healed him, as you can all see.

17 'Now, fellow Israelites, I know that you acted in ignorance, as did your leaders. **18** But this is how God fulfilled what he had foretold through all the prophets, saying that his Messiah would suffer. **19** Repent, then, and turn to God, so that your sins may be wiped out, that times of refreshing may come from the Lord, **20** and that he may send the Messiah, who has been appointed for you – even Jesus. **21** Heaven must receive him until the time comes for God to restore everything, as he promised long ago through his holy prophets. 22 For Moses said, "The Lord your God will raise up for you a prophet like me from among your own people; you must listen to everything he tells you. 23 Anyone who does not

listen to him will be completely cut off from their people."*a*

24 'Indeed, beginning with Samuel, all

a 23 Deut. 18:15,18,19

NATURALLY SUPERNATURAL 9

PRAYING IN THE NAME OF JESUS

What do I have to offer people? It's a question most of us ask ourselves at one time or another. We know we're not perfect and sometimes we even feel totally inadequate. Especially when it comes to things like praying for healing. We know we can't heal someone ourselves.

Peter knew that too. He knew he didn't have the money to offer people to get them better. And he knew he didn't have any healing powers of his own. But he also knew he had something much more valuable: he had a God who cares, a God who is powerful and able to do more than we ask or imagine (Ephesians 3:20), a God who longs to heal. We have the same God!

In Acts 3:6–7, Peter doesn't offer himself or pretend he has the answers, he just prays in the powerful name of Jesus. When we pray in Jesus' name, we acknowledge we have nothing on our own. Sure, some people seem to have a gift of healing and when they pray for people stuff seems to happen. But they are just relying on Jesus in the same way that we all need to. We can all pray for healing!

There are some really simple steps you can follow if you're not sure how to. First, if it's appropriate, you might want to put your hands on the part of the body that's in pain. (If it's not appropriate, you could just put your hand on the person's shoulder or arm.) Then pray in Jesus' name. In his authority, speak to the sickness or pain and tell it to be gone. Keep your eyes open when you pray so you can watch what God is doing. Don't be worried if the person you're praying for manifests (responds physically to the presence of the Holy Spirit), or if they don't show any signs of the Holy Spirit at all. Keep praying and listen to the Holy Spirit. See if he gives you any words to pray or to offer to the person you're praying for. If you're praying for someone who doesn't yet know Jesus, you might just want to pray a simple and quick blessing over them and leave it there. If you're praying for a Christian, they might be more comfortable waiting on the Holy Spirit a bit longer.

Don't worry if you don't feel very confident: remember you're not offering people your own healing power or technique, all you're doing is asking God to heal in the ways that you have read about in the Bible. Trust in him and see what he does as you pray in the powerful name of Jesus.

Mike Pilavachi

 1 Corinthians 15:22–25   Galatians 5:22

the prophets who have spoken have foretold these days. 25 And you are heirs of the prophets and of the covenant God made with your fathers. He said to Abraham, "Through your offspring all peoples on earth will be blessed."*b* 26 When God raised up his servant, he sent him first to you to bless you by turning each of you from your wicked ways.'

Peter and John before the Sanhedrin

4 The priests and the captain of the temple guard and the Sadducees came up to Peter and John while they were speaking to the people. 2 They were greatly disturbed because the apostles were teaching the people, proclaiming in Jesus the resurrection of the dead. 3 They seized Peter and John and, because it was evening, they put them in jail until the next day. 4 But many who heard the message believed; so the number of men who believed grew to about five thousand.

5 The next day the rulers, the elders and the teachers of the law met in Jerusalem. 6 Annas the high priest was there, and so were Caiaphas, John, Alexander and others of the high priest's family. 7 They had Peter and John brought before them and began to question them: 'By what power or what name did you do this?'

8 Then Peter, filled with the Holy Spirit, said to them: 'Rulers and elders of the people! 9 If we are being called to account today for an act of kindness shown to a man who was lame and are being asked how he was healed, 10 then know this, you and all the people of Israel: it is by the name of Jesus Christ of Nazareth, whom you crucified but whom God raised from the dead, that this man stands before you healed. 11 Jesus is

' "the stone you builders rejected,
    which has become the
        cornerstone."*a*

12 Salvation is found in no one else, for there is no other name under heaven given to mankind by which we must be saved.'

13 When they saw the courage of Peter and John and realised that they were unschooled, ordinary men, they were astonished and they took note that these men had been with Jesus. 14 But since they could see the man who had been healed standing there with them, there was nothing they could say. 15 So they ordered them to withdraw from the Sanhedrin and then conferred together. 16 'What are we going to do with these men?' they asked. 'Everyone living in Jerusalem knows they have performed a notable sign, and we cannot deny it. 17 But to stop this thing from spreading any further among the people, we must warn them to speak no longer to anyone in this name.'

18 Then they called them in again and commanded them not to speak or teach at all in the name of Jesus. 19 But Peter and John replied, 'Which is right in God's eyes: to listen to you, or to him? You be the judges! 20 As for us, we cannot help speaking about what we have seen and heard.'

21 After further threats they let them go. They could not decide how to punish them, because all the people were praising God for what had happened. 22 For the man who was miraculously healed was over forty years old.

The believers pray

23 On their release, Peter and John went back to their own people and reported all that the chief priests and the elders had said to them. 24 When they heard this, they raised their voices together in prayer to God. 'Sovereign Lord,' they said, 'you made the heavens and the earth and the sea, and everything in them. 25 You spoke by the Holy Spirit through the mouth of your servant, our father David:

' "Why do the nations rage
    and the peoples plot in vain?
26 The kings of the earth rise up
    and the rulers band together

---

b 25 Gen. 22:18; 26:4
a 11 Psalm 118:22

against the Lord
    and against his anointed one.*b"c*

27 Indeed Herod and Pontius Pilate met together with the Gentiles and the people of Israel in this city to conspire against your holy servant Jesus, whom you anointed. 28 They did what your power and will had

---

b 26 That is, Messiah or Christ
c 26 Psalm 2:1,2

decided beforehand should happen. 29 Now, Lord, consider their threats and enable your servants to speak your word with great boldness. 30 Stretch out your hand to heal and perform signs and wonders through the name of your holy servant Jesus.'

31 After they prayed, the place where they were meeting was shaken. And they were all filled with the Holy Spirit and spoke the word of God boldly.

PRAYER 10

THEY RAISED THEIR VOICES TOGETHER IN PRAYER

Sometimes we need to pray together as the church. In those times listening to one person and saying 'Amen' at the end is just not good enough.

It had been a big couple of days. Peter and John had very publicly healed a beggar, and had then spoken to an enormous crowd about Jesus. This led the local religious leaders to get annoyed and have Peter and John kept overnight in jail and then brought before a religious court. Just when they were deep in discussion, the Holy Spirit got hold of Peter and he made a fantastic speech. It was so good that those sitting in judgement decided merely to threaten them and let them go.

Imagine walking out of that court, back to where the rest of the church was waiting for them, and stepping into the room to cheers and whoops. Everyone wanted to know what had happened. So the story was told. Then someone said, 'Let's give thanks to God for your release and pray!' Everyone agreed. And everyone wanted to pray. So they all *raised their voices together in prayer to God'* (Acts 4:23–31).

But how do you all pray at the same time and about the same thing? Acts shows that one of those leading set the theme. They spoke loudly, quoting a relevant passage of Scripture (vv. 25–26), while everyone else put the same ideas into their own words. It didn't matter that they couldn't hear each other. After all, the only audience that mattered was God himself. It was like a symphony orchestra: everyone made their own noises, but together it was like one big voice of praise and intercession. The noise grew louder and louder, and soon they realised that the noise was louder than all their voices together could make it. The very foundations of the room were shaking (v. 31). Very exciting! God on the move. God's Spirit all around them, in them and on them. Just like the first time the Holy Spirit came on the church at Pentecost (Acts 2). No wonder they all got 'bold' and went out to speak fearlessly about Jesus!

Hugo Anson

 Ephesians 6:10–20

The believers share their possessions

32 All the believers were one in heart and mind. No one claimed that any of their possessions was their own, but they shared everything they had. 33 With great power the apostles continued to testify to the resurrection of the Lord Jesus. And God's grace was so powerfully at work in them all 34 that there was no needy person among them. For from time to time those who owned land or houses sold them, brought the money from the sales 35 and put it at the apostles' feet, and it was distributed to anyone who had need.

36 Joseph, a Levite from Cyprus, whom the apostles called Barnabas (which means 'son of encouragement'), 37 sold a field he owned and brought the money and put it at the apostles' feet.

Ananias and Sapphira

5 Now a man named Ananias, together with his wife Sapphira, also sold a piece of property. 2 With his wife's full knowledge he kept back part of the money for himself, but brought the rest and put it at the apostles' feet.

3 Then Peter said, 'Ananias, how is it that Satan has so filled your heart that you have lied to the Holy Spirit and have kept for yourself some of the money you received for the land? 4 Didn't it belong to you before it was sold? And after it was sold, wasn't the money at your disposal? What made you think of doing such a thing? You have not lied just to human beings but to God.'

5 When Ananias heard this, he fell down and died. And great fear seized all who heard what had happened. 6 Then some young men came forward, wrapped up his body, and carried him out and buried him.

7 About three hours later his wife came in, not knowing what had happened. 8 Peter asked her, 'Tell me, is this the price you and Ananias got for the land?'

'Yes,' she said, 'that is the price.'

9 Peter said to her, 'How could you conspire to test the Spirit of the Lord? Listen! The feet of the men who buried your husband are at the door, and they will carry you out also.'

10 At that moment she fell down at his feet and died. Then the young men came in and, finding her dead, carried her out and buried her beside her husband. 11 Great fear seized the whole church and all who heard about these events.

The apostles heal many

12 The apostles performed many signs and wonders among the people. And all the believers used to meet together in Solomon's Colonnade. 13 No one else dared join them, even though they were highly regarded by the people. 14 Nevertheless, more and more men and women believed in the Lord and were added to their number. 15 As a result, people brought those who were ill into the streets and laid them on beds and mats so that at least Peter's shadow might fall on some of them as he passed by. 16 Crowds gathered also from the towns around Jerusalem, bringing those who were ill and those tormented by impure spirits, and all of them were healed.

The apostles persecuted

17 Then the high priest and all his associates, who were members of the party of the Sadducees, were filled with jealousy. 18 They arrested the apostles and put them in the public jail. 19 But during the night an angel of the Lord opened the doors of the jail and brought them out. 20 'Go, stand in the temple courts,' he said, 'and tell the people all about this new life.'

21 At daybreak they entered the temple courts, as they had been told, and began to teach the people.

When the high priest and his associates arrived, they called together the Sanhedrin – the full assembly of the elders of Israel – and sent to the jail for the apostles. 22 But on arriving at the jail, the officers did not find them there. So they went back and reported, 23 'We found the jail securely locked, with the guards standing at the doors; but when we opened them, we found no one inside.' 24 On hearing this report, the captain of the temple guard and the chief priests were at a loss, wondering what this might lead to.

25 Then someone came and said, 'Look! The men you put in jail are standing in the temple courts teaching the people.' 26 At that, the captain went with his officers and brought the apostles. They did not use force, because they feared that the people would stone them.

27 The apostles were brought in and

MONEY 6

SHARING

It's Friday night, you're going out and your outfit's sorted. But when you go to your wardrobe to get ready, your outfit is missing. You look out of the window and see someone across the street wearing your clothes!

Can you imagine sharing everything you have (Acts 2:42–47; 4:32–37)?

Admittedly, these passages in Acts are not recommending that people break into each other's houses and steal their clothes, but they do describe a different perspective on money and possessions. We read earlier in 1 Chronicles 29 that everything we have also belongs to the Lord. But what if we went a step further and said that not only is our money God's as well, but everyone else's too?

The people we read about in Acts were some of the first Christians who existed, and they decided to live differently from their surrounding culture, challenging the idea that money was about personal gain. They decided to share what they had with one another. If someone was in need they would work together to meet that need, even if it meant selling their house.

As Christians, we grapple with different aspects of following Jesus, in our relationships, families, careers, hopes and fears. We keep each other accountable and pray for one another, but being open about money is sometimes more difficult. Our culture is very private about money.

There was something powerful about the way these early Christians lived, something that was so profound it inspired those around them to become followers of Christ. They used their money and resources to create a different kind of community. It included the rich and the poor, it was about everyone, people weren't just focused on their immediate family and their best friends. Instead they were one in heart and mind: they knew each other, loved one another and worshipped Jesus together. They were church.

What impact would it make on your school, campus or town if a group of Jesus followers lived like this? Would you be up for it? Genuinely sharing life with others, getting to know people different from you and being willing to offer all your money and possessions freely.

The profoundly different way of life we see in the early Christians may challenge our mindset that money is a deeply private issue and makes us ask if we should be more open about it. How should it form part of our life-building conversations? How should it be part of the way we follow Jesus?

Kiera Singlehurst-Phyo

 2 Corinthians 8:1–15   Proverbs 31:10–31

made to appear before the Sanhedrin to be questioned by the high priest. 28 'We gave you strict orders not to teach in this name,' he said. 'Yet you have filled Jerusalem with your teaching and are determined to make us guilty of this man's blood.'

29 Peter and the other apostles replied: 'We must obey God rather than human beings! 30 The God of our ancestors raised Jesus from the dead – whom you killed by hanging him on a cross. 31 God exalted him to his own right hand as Prince and Saviour that he might bring Israel to repentance and forgive their sins. 32 We are witnesses of these things, and so is the Holy Spirit, whom God has given to those who obey him.'

33 When they heard this, they were furious and wanted to put them to death. 34 But a Pharisee named Gamaliel, a teacher of the law, who was honoured by all the people, stood up in the Sanhedrin and ordered that the men be put outside for a little while. 35 Then he addressed the Sanhedrin: 'Men of Israel, consider carefully what you intend to do to these men. 36 Some time ago Theudas appeared, claiming to be somebody, and about four hundred men rallied to him. He was killed, all his followers were dispersed, and it all came to nothing. 37 After him, Judas the Galilean appeared in the days of the census and led a band of people in revolt. He too was killed, and all his followers were scattered. 38 Therefore, in the present case I advise you: leave these men alone! Let them go! For if their purpose or activity is of human origin, it will fail. 39 But if it is from God, you will not be able to stop these men; you will only find yourselves fighting against God.'

40 His speech persuaded them. They called the apostles in and had them flogged. Then they ordered them not to speak in the name of Jesus, and let them go.

41 The apostles left the Sanhedrin, rejoicing because they had been counted worthy of suffering disgrace for the Name. 42 Day after day, in the temple courts and from house to house, they never stopped

teaching and proclaiming the good news that Jesus is the Messiah.

The choosing of the seven

6 In those days when the number of disciples was increasing, the Hellenistic Jews*a* among them complained against the Hebraic Jews because their widows were being overlooked in the daily distribution of food. 2 So the Twelve gathered all the disciples together and said, 'It would not be right for us to neglect the ministry of the word of God in order to wait on tables. 3 Brothers and sisters, choose seven men from among you who are known to be full of the Spirit and wisdom. We will turn this responsibility over to them 4 and will give our attention to prayer and the ministry of the word.'

PETER

FISHERMAN
Luke 5:1–11
WATER
Matthew 14:22–32
ROCKY
Matthew 16:13–20
DENIAL
Matthew 26:31–35; 69–75
RESTORATION
John 21:1–19
PENTECOST
Acts 2:1–42
CORNELIUS
Acts 10:1–48

5 This proposal pleased the whole group. They chose Stephen, a man full of faith and of the Holy Spirit; also Philip, Procorus, Nicanor, Timon, Parmenas, and Nicolas from Antioch, a convert to

a 1 That is, Jews who had adopted the Greek language and culture

Judaism. 6They presented these men to the apostles, who prayed and laid their hands on them.

7So the word of God spread. The number of disciples in Jerusalem increased rapidly, and a large number of priests became obedient to the faith.

Stephen seized

8Now Stephen, a man full of God's grace and power, performed great wonders and signs among the people. 9Opposition arose, however, from members of the Synagogue of the Freedmen (as it was called) – Jews of Cyrene and Alexandria as well as the provinces of Cilicia and Asia – who began to argue with Stephen. 10But they could not stand up against the wisdom the Spirit gave him as he spoke.

11Then they secretly persuaded some men to say, 'We have heard Stephen speak blasphemous words against Moses and against God.'

12So they stirred up the people and the elders and the teachers of the law. They seized Stephen and brought him before the Sanhedrin. 13They produced false witnesses, who testified, 'This fellow never stops speaking against this holy place and against the law. 14For we have heard him say that this Jesus of Nazareth will destroy this place and change the customs Moses handed down to us.'

15All who were sitting in the Sanhedrin looked intently at Stephen, and they saw that his face was like the face of an angel.

Stephen's speech to the Sanhedrin

7 Then the high priest asked Stephen, 'Are these charges true?'

2To this he replied: 'Brothers and fathers, listen to me! The God of glory appeared to our father Abraham while he was still in Mesopotamia, before he lived in Harran. 3"Leave your country and your people," God said, "and go to the land I will show you."a

4'So he left the land of the Chaldeans and settled in Harran. After the death of his father, God sent him to this land where you are now living. 5He gave him no inheritance here, not even enough ground to set his foot on. But God promised him that he and his descendants after him would possess the land, even though at that time Abraham had no child. 6God spoke to him in this way: "For four hundred years your descendants will be strangers in a country not their own, and they will be enslaved and ill-treated. 7But I will punish the nation they serve as slaves," God said, "and afterwards they will come out of that country and worship me in this place."b 8Then he gave Abraham the covenant of circumcision. And Abraham became the father of Isaac and circumcised him eight days after his birth. Later Isaac became the father of Jacob, and Jacob became the father of the twelve patriarchs.

9'Because the patriarchs were jealous of Joseph, they sold him as a slave into Egypt. But God was with him 10and rescued him from all his troubles. He gave Joseph wisdom and enabled him to gain the goodwill of Pharaoh king of Egypt. So Pharaoh made him ruler over Egypt and all his palace.

11'Then a famine struck all Egypt and Canaan, bringing great suffering, and our ancestors could not find food. 12When Jacob heard that there was grain in Egypt, he sent our forefathers on their first visit. 13On their second visit, Joseph told his brothers who he was, and Pharaoh learned about Joseph's family. 14After this, Joseph sent for his father Jacob and his whole family, seventy-five in all. 15Then Jacob went down to Egypt, where he and our ancestors died. 16Their bodies were brought back to Shechem and placed in the tomb that Abraham had bought from the sons of Hamor at Shechem for a certain sum of money.

17'As the time drew near for God to fulfil his promise to Abraham, the number of our people in Egypt had greatly increased. 18Then "a new king, to whom Joseph meant nothing, came to power in Egypt".c 19He dealt treacherously with our people

a3 Gen. 12:1

b7 Gen. 15:13,14
c18 Exodus 1:8

and oppressed our ancestors by forcing them to throw out their newborn babies so that they would die. ²⁰'At that time Moses was born, and he was no ordinary child.ᵈ For three months he was cared for by his family. ²¹When he was placed outside, Pharaoh's daughter took him and brought him up as her own son. ²²Moses was educated in all the wisdom of the Egyptians and was powerful in speech and action.

²³'When Moses was forty years old, he decided to visit his own people, the Israelites. ²⁴He saw one of them being ill-treated by an Egyptian, so he went to his defence and avenged him by killing the Egyptian. ²⁵Moses thought that his own people would realise that God was using him to rescue them, but they did not. ²⁶The next day Moses came upon two Israelites who were fighting. He tried to reconcile them by saying, "Men, you are brothers; why do you want to hurt each other?"

²⁷'But the man who was ill-treating the other pushed Moses aside and said, "Who made you ruler and judge over us? ²⁸Are you thinking of killing me as you killed the Egyptian yesterday?"ᵉ ²⁹When Moses heard this, he fled to Midian, where he settled as a foreigner and had two sons.

³⁰'After forty years had passed, an angel appeared to Moses in the flames of a burning bush in the desert near Mount Sinai. ³¹When he saw this, he was amazed at the sight. As he went over to get a closer look, he heard the Lord say: ³²"I am the God of your fathers, the God of Abraham, Isaac and Jacob."ᶠ Moses trembled with fear and did not dare to look.

³³'Then the Lord said to him, "Take off your sandals, for the place where you are standing is holy ground. ³⁴I have indeed seen the oppression of my people in Egypt. I have heard their groaning and have come down to set them free. Now come, I will send you back to Egypt."ᵍ

³⁵'This is the same Moses they had rejected with the words, "Who made you ruler and judge?" He was sent to be their ruler and deliverer by God himself, through the angel who appeared to him in the bush. ³⁶He led them out of Egypt and performed wonders and signs in Egypt, at the Red Sea and for forty years in the wilderness.

³⁷'This is the Moses who told the Israelites, "God will raise up for you a prophet like me from your own people."ʰ ³⁸He was in the assembly in the wilderness, with the angel who spoke to him on Mount Sinai, and with our ancestors; and he received living words to pass on to us.

³⁹'But our ancestors refused to obey him. Instead, they rejected him and in their hearts turned back to Egypt. ⁴⁰They told Aaron, "Make us gods who will go before us. As for this fellow Moses who led us out of Egypt – we don't know what has happened to him!"ⁱ ⁴¹That was the time they made an idol in the form of a calf. They brought sacrifices to it and revelled in what their own hands had made. ⁴²But God turned away from them and gave them over to the worship of the sun, moon and stars. This agrees with what is written in the book of the prophets:

'"Did you bring me sacrifices and offerings
    for forty years in the wilderness,
        people of Israel?
⁴³You have taken up the tabernacle of Molek
    and the star of your god Rephan,
    the idols you made to worship.
Therefore I will send you into exile"ʲ
    beyond Babylon.

⁴⁴'Our ancestors had the tabernacle of the covenant law with them in the wilderness. It had been made as God directed Moses, according to the pattern he had seen. ⁴⁵After receiving the tabernacle, our ancestors under Joshua brought it with them when they took the land from the nations God drove out before them. It

---

d 20 Or *was fair in the sight of God*
e 28 Exodus 2:14
f 32 Exodus 3:6
g 34 Exodus 3:5,7,8,10

h 37 Deut. 18:15
i 40 Exodus 32:1
j 43 Amos 5:25-27 (see Septuagint)

remained in the land until the time of David, 46 who enjoyed God's favour and asked that he might provide a dwelling-place for the God of Jacob.*k* 47 But it was Solomon who built a house for him.

48 'However, the Most High does not live in houses made by human hands. As the prophet says:

49 ' "Heaven is my throne,
    and the earth is my footstool.
What kind of house will you build
        for me?
                        says the Lord.
Or where will my resting place be?
50 Has not my hand made all these
        things?"*l*

51 'You stiff-necked people! Your hearts and ears are still uncircumcised. You are just like your ancestors: you always resist the Holy Spirit! 52 Was there ever a prophet your ancestors did not persecute? They even killed those who predicted the coming of the Righteous One. And now you have betrayed and murdered him – 53 you who have received the law that was given through angels but have not obeyed it.'

The stoning of Stephen

54 When the members of the Sanhedrin heard this, they were furious and gnashed their teeth at him. 55 But Stephen, full of the Holy Spirit, looked up to heaven and saw the glory of God, and Jesus standing at the right hand of God. 56 'Look,' he said, 'I see heaven open and the Son of Man standing at the right hand of God.'

57 At this they covered their ears and, yelling at the top of their voices, they all rushed at him, 58 dragged him out of the city and began to stone him. Meanwhile, the witnesses laid their coats at the feet of a young man named Saul.

59 While they were stoning him, Stephen prayed, 'Lord Jesus, receive my spirit.' 60 Then he fell on his knees and cried out, 'Lord, do not hold this sin

against them.' When he had said this, he fell asleep.

8 And Saul approved of their killing him.

The church persecuted and scattered

On that day a great persecution broke out against the church in Jerusalem, and all except the apostles were scattered throughout Judea and Samaria. 2 Godly men buried Stephen and mourned deeply for him. 3 But Saul began to destroy the church. Going from house to house, he dragged off both men and women and put them in prison.

Philip in Samaria

4 Those who had been scattered preached the word wherever they went. 5 Philip went down to a city in Samaria and proclaimed the Messiah there. 6 When the crowds heard Philip and saw the signs he performed, they all paid close attention to what he said. 7 For with shrieks, impure spirits came out of many, and many who were paralysed or lame were healed. 8 So there was great joy in that city.

Simon the sorcerer

9 Now for some time a man named Simon had practised sorcery in the city and amazed all the people of Samaria. He boasted that he was someone great, 10 and all the people, both high and low, gave him their attention and exclaimed, 'This man is rightly called the Great Power of God.' 11 They followed him because he had amazed them for a long time with his sorcery. 12 But when they believed Philip as he proclaimed the good news of the kingdom of God and the name of Jesus Christ, they were baptised, both men and women. 13 Simon himself believed and was baptised. And he followed Philip everywhere, astonished by the great signs and miracles he saw.

14 When the apostles in Jerusalem heard that Samaria had accepted the word of God, they sent Peter and John to Samaria. 15 When they arrived, they prayed for the new believers there that they might receive the Holy Spirit, 16 because the Holy

---

k 46 Some early manuscripts *the house of Jacob*
l 50 Isaiah 66:1,2

PEOPLE USED BY GOD 10

Paul

Sometimes we're on our own path, doing all we can to fulfil our plans. As we're on the journey, we wonder if God has something for us. Can he find us and help us find our way in him? Let's look at the life of Paul and see what God can do.

Saul, who became Paul, was born in a city called Tarsus in what's now Turkey. His parents were Jewish and were part of a group known as Pharisees. Paul's parents were well off and were in the right social scene – so they were able to buy very desirable Roman citizenship for the family.

When Saul was fourteen, he went to Jerusalem to train as a rabbi. His teacher was named Gamaliel, who was one of the best, so it was an honour to learn from him. He also learned a trade – training to be a tent-maker, which would allow him to earn a living. Everything he did was part of a plan for him to succeed in life.

While he was studying, he became a radical spokesman for the Jewish way. He became known as the person to go to if things didn't line up with the proper beliefs of the law: he would speak up and sort it out. When a new group, known as Christians, appeared he confronted them and tried to stop them any way he could. He was the one who allowed the people to stone and kill Stephen, one of the first followers and the first martyr of Jesus. Saul was committed to his cause.

Saul had a plan for his life, but God had a plan for him and turned things around. One day, when he was on the way to Damascus, he had a vision and Jesus spoke to him (Acts 9). It was dramatic. First he fell to the ground and heard a voice saying, *'Saul, Saul, why do you persecute me?'* He asked, *'Who are you?'* and the voice said, *'I am Jesus, whom you are persecuting.'* Saul was renamed Paul, and given instructions on what to do. From there, his new journey began.

This was more than just a man encountering Jesus. Everything in this man's life changed radically. This is the meaning of conversion.

Paul became one of the most outspoken Christians. He wrote almost two thirds of the New Testament. He established doctrine and practices for the running of the church that most still follow to this day. It's impossible to speak about church history without his name being in the forefront.

We all have paths that we design for our own lives. We're looking for success within our chosen fields. Paul was a man whom God redirected to his true destiny. God can and will do the same for us. God can take us and direct us, if we let him. Even with well-laid plans like those Paul had, God can touch our lives to change the world.

Tom Brock

Spirit had not yet come on any of them; they had simply been baptised in the name of the Lord Jesus. ¹⁷Then Peter and John placed their hands on them, and they received the Holy Spirit.

¹⁸When Simon saw that the Spirit was given at the laying on of the apostles' hands, he offered them money ¹⁹and said, 'Give me also this ability so that everyone on whom I lay my hands may receive the Holy Spirit.'

²⁰Peter answered: 'May your money perish with you, because you thought you could buy the gift of God with money! ²¹You have no part or share in this ministry, because your heart is not right before God. ²²Repent of this wickedness and pray to the Lord in the hope that he may forgive you for having such a thought in your heart. ²³For I see that you are full of bitterness and captive to sin.'

²⁴Then Simon answered, 'Pray to the Lord for me so that nothing you have said may happen to me.'

²⁵After they had further proclaimed the word of the Lord and testified about Jesus, Peter and John returned to Jerusalem, preaching the gospel in many Samaritan villages.

Philip and the Ethiopian

²⁶Now an angel of the Lord said to Philip, 'Go south to the road – the desert road – that goes down from Jerusalem to Gaza.' ²⁷So he started out, and on his way he met an Ethiopian*a* eunuch, an important official in charge of all the treasury of the Kandake (which means 'queen of the Ethiopians'). This man had gone to Jerusalem to worship, ²⁸and on his way home was sitting in his chariot reading the Book of Isaiah the prophet. ²⁹The Spirit told Philip, 'Go to that chariot and stay near it.'

³⁰Then Philip ran up to the chariot and heard the man reading Isaiah the prophet. 'Do you understand what you are reading?' Philip asked.

³¹'How can I,' he said, 'unless someone explains it to me?' So he invited Philip to come up and sit with him.

³²This is the passage of Scripture the eunuch was reading:

'He was led like a sheep to the slaughter,
and as a lamb before its shearer is silent,
so he did not open his mouth.
³³In his humiliation he was deprived of justice.
Who can speak of his descendants?
For his life was taken from the earth.'*b*

³⁴The eunuch asked Philip, 'Tell me, please, who is the prophet talking about, himself or someone else?' ³⁵Then Philip began with that very passage of Scripture and told him the good news about Jesus.

³⁶As they travelled along the road, they came to some water and the eunuch said, 'Look, here is water. What can stand in the way of my being baptised?' [37]*c* ³⁸And he gave orders to stop the chariot. Then both Philip and the eunuch went down into the water and Philip baptised him. ³⁹When they came up out of the water, the Spirit of the Lord suddenly took Philip away, and the eunuch did not see him again, but went on his way rejoicing. ⁴⁰Philip, however, appeared at Azotus and travelled about, preaching the gospel in all the towns until he reached Caesarea.

Saul's conversion

9 Meanwhile, Saul was still breathing out murderous threats against the Lord's disciples. He went to the high priest ²and asked him for letters to the synagogues in Damascus, so that if he found any there who belonged to the Way, whether men or women, he might take them as prisoners to Jerusalem. ³As he neared Damascus on his journey, suddenly a light from heaven flashed around him. ⁴He fell to the ground and heard a

---

*a*27 That is, from the southern Nile region
*b*33 Isaiah 53:7,8 (see Septuagint)
*c*37 Some manuscripts include here *Philip said, 'If you believe with all your heart, you may.' The eunuch answered, 'I believe that Jesus Christ is the Son of God.'*

voice say to him, 'Saul, Saul, why do you persecute me?'

5 'Who are you, Lord?' Saul asked.

'I am Jesus, whom you are persecuting,' he replied. **6** 'Now get up and go into the city, and you will be told what you must do.'

7 The men travelling with Saul stood there speechless; they heard the sound but did not see anyone. **8** Saul got up from the ground, but when he opened his eyes he could see nothing. So they led him by the hand into Damascus. **9** For three days he was blind, and did not eat or drink anything.

10 In Damascus there was a disciple named Ananias. The Lord called to him in a vision, 'Ananias!'

'Yes, Lord,' he answered.

11 The Lord told him, 'Go to the house of Judas on Straight Street and ask for a man from Tarsus named Saul, for he is praying. **12** In a vision he has seen a man named Ananias come and place his hands on him to restore his sight.'

13 'Lord,' Ananias answered, 'I have heard many reports about this man and all the harm he has done to your holy people in Jerusalem. **14** And he has come here with authority from the chief priests to arrest all who call on your name.'

15 But the Lord said to Ananias, 'Go! This man is my chosen instrument to proclaim my name to the Gentiles and their kings and to the people of Israel. **16** I will show him how much he must suffer for my name.'

17 Then Ananias went to the house and entered it. Placing his hands on Saul, he said, 'Brother Saul, the Lord – Jesus, who appeared to you on the road as you were coming here – has sent me so that you may see again and be filled with the Holy Spirit.' **18** Immediately, something like scales fell from Saul's eyes, and he could see again. He got up and was baptised, **19** and after taking some food, he regained his strength.

Saul in Damascus and Jerusalem

Saul spent several days with the disciples in Damascus. **20** At once he began to preach in the synagogues that Jesus is the Son of God. **21** All those who heard him were astonished and asked, 'Isn't he the man who caused havoc in Jerusalem among those who call on this name? And hasn't he come here to take them as prisoners to the chief priests?' **22** Yet Saul grew more and more powerful and baffled the Jews living in Damascus by proving that Jesus is the Messiah.

FACT

THE WAY

Following Jesus was not known as 'Christianity' until a long time after his death. Before that, Christianity was known as 'the Way' (Acts 9:2; 18:25–26; 19:9, 23; 24:14, 22). In Jerusalem, Jesus' disciples were known as 'the Nazarenes' (Acts 24:5).

23 After many days had gone by, there was a conspiracy among the Jews to kill him, **24** but Saul learned of their plan. Day and night they kept close watch on the city gates in order to kill him. **25** But his followers took him by night and lowered him in a basket through an opening in the wall.

26 When he came to Jerusalem, he tried to join the disciples, but they were all afraid of him, not believing that he really was a disciple. **27** But Barnabas took him and brought him to the apostles. He told them how Saul on his journey had seen the Lord and that the Lord had spoken to him, and how in Damascus he had preached fearlessly in the name of Jesus. **28** So Saul stayed with them and moved about freely in Jerusalem, speaking boldly in the name of the Lord. **29** He talked and debated with the Hellenistic Jews, *a* but they tried to kill him. **30** When the believers learned of this,

a 29 That is, Jews who had adopted the Greek language and culture they took him down to Caesarea and sent him off to Tarsus.

³¹ Then the church throughout Judea, Galilee and Samaria enjoyed a time of peace and was strengthened. Living in the fear of the Lord and encouraged by the Holy Spirit, it increased in numbers.

Aeneas and Dorcas

³² As Peter travelled about the country, he went to visit the Lord's people who lived in Lydda. ³³ There he found a man named Aeneas, who was paralysed and had been bedridden for eight years. ³⁴ 'Aeneas,' Peter said to him, 'Jesus Christ heals you. Get up and roll up your mat.' Immediately Aeneas got up. ³⁵ All those who lived in Lydda and Sharon saw him and turned to the Lord.

³⁶ In Joppa there was a disciple named Tabitha (in Greek her name is Dorcas); she was always doing good and helping the poor. ³⁷ About that time she became ill and died, and her body was washed and placed in an upstairs room. ³⁸ Lydda was near Joppa; so when the disciples heard that Peter was in Lydda, they sent two men to him and urged him, 'Please come at once!'

³⁹ Peter went with them, and when he arrived he was taken upstairs to the room. All the widows stood round him, crying and showing him the robes and other clothing that Dorcas had made while she was still with them.

⁴⁰ Peter sent them all out of the room; then he got down on his knees and prayed. Turning towards the dead woman, he said, 'Tabitha, get up.' She opened her eyes, and seeing Peter she sat up. ⁴¹ He took her by the hand and helped her to her feet. Then he called for the believers, especially the widows, and presented her to them alive. ⁴² This became known all over Joppa, and many people believed in the Lord. ⁴³ Peter stayed in Joppa for some time with a tanner named Simon.

Cornelius calls for Peter

10 At Caesarea there was a man named Cornelius, a centurion in what was known as the Italian Regiment.

² He and all his family were devout and God-fearing; he gave generously to those in need and prayed to God regularly. ³ One day at about three in the afternoon he had a vision. He distinctly saw an angel of God, who came to him and said, 'Cornelius!'

⁴ Cornelius stared at him in fear. 'What is it, Lord?' he asked.

The angel answered, 'Your prayers and gifts to the poor have come up as a memorial offering before God. ⁵ Now send men to Joppa to bring back a man named Simon who is called Peter. ⁶ He is staying with Simon the tanner, whose house is by the sea.'

⁷ When the angel who spoke to him had gone, Cornelius called two of his servants and a devout soldier who was one of his attendants. ⁸ He told them everything that had happened and sent them to Joppa.

FACT

FORBIDDEN FOODS

It's not just pork that was forbidden to Jews. According to Old Testament law, Jews were not allowed to eat camels, hyraxes, rabbits and seafood (other than fish) (Leviticus 11:1–12). Also banned were weasels, rats, various lizards, geckos, skinks and the chameleon (Leviticus 11:30).

Peter's vision

⁹ About noon the following day as they were on their journey and approaching the city, Peter went up on the roof to pray. ¹⁰ He became hungry and wanted something to eat, and while the meal was being prepared, he fell into a trance. ¹¹ He saw heaven opened and something like a large sheet being let down to earth by its four corners. ¹² It contained all kinds of four-footed animals, as well as reptiles and birds. ¹³ Then a voice told him, 'Get up, Peter. Kill and eat.'

14 'Surely not, Lord!' Peter replied. 'I have never eaten anything impure or unclean.'

15 The voice spoke to him a second time, 'Do not call anything impure that God has made clean.'

16 This happened three times, and immediately the sheet was taken back to heaven.

17 While Peter was wondering about the meaning of the vision, the men sent by Cornelius found out where Simon's house was and stopped at the gate. 18 They called out, asking if Simon who was known as Peter was staying there.

19 While Peter was still thinking about the vision, the Spirit said to him, 'Simon, three*a* men are looking for you. 20 So get up and go downstairs. Do not hesitate to go with them, for I have sent them.'

21 Peter went down and said to the men, 'I'm the one you're looking for. Why have you come?'

22 The men replied, 'We have come from Cornelius the centurion. He is a righteous and God-fearing man, who is respected by all the Jewish people. A holy angel told him to ask you to come to his house so that he could hear what you have to say.' 23 Then Peter invited the men into the house to be his guests.

Peter at Cornelius' house

The next day Peter started out with them, and some of the believers from Joppa went along. 24 The following day he arrived in Caesarea. Cornelius was expecting them and had called together his relatives and close friends. 25 As Peter entered the house, Cornelius met him and fell at his feet in reverence. 26 But Peter made him get up. 'Stand up,' he said, 'I am only a man myself.'

27 While talking with him, Peter went inside and found a large gathering of people. 28 He said to them: 'You are well aware that it is against our law for a Jew to associate with or visit a Gentile. But God has

shown me that I should not call anyone impure or unclean. 29 So when I was sent for, I came without raising any objection. May I ask why you sent for me?'

30 Cornelius answered: 'Three days ago I was in my house praying at this hour, at three in the afternoon. Suddenly a man in shining clothes stood before me 31 and said, "Cornelius, God has heard your prayer and remembered your gifts to the poor. 32 Send to Joppa for Simon who is called Peter. He is a guest in the home of Simon the tanner, who lives by the sea." 33 So I sent for you immediately, and it was good of you to come. Now we are all here in the presence of God to listen to everything the Lord has commanded you to tell us.'

34 Then Peter began to speak: 'I now realise how true it is that God does not show favouritism 35 but accepts from every nation the one who fears him and does what is right. 36 You know the message God sent to the people of Israel, announcing the good news of peace through Jesus Christ, who is Lord of all. 37 You know what has happened throughout the province of Judea, beginning in Galilee after the baptism that John preached – 38 how God anointed Jesus of Nazareth with the Holy Spirit and power, and how he went around doing good and healing all who were under the power of the devil, because God was with him.

39 'We are witnesses of everything he did in the country of the Jews and in Jerusalem. They killed him by hanging him on a cross, 40 but God raised him from the dead on the third day and caused him to be seen. 41 He was not seen by all the people, but by witnesses whom God had already chosen – by us who ate and drank with him after he rose from the dead. 42 He commanded us to preach to the people and to testify that he is the one whom God appointed as judge of the living and the dead. 43 All the prophets testify about him that everyone who believes in him receives forgiveness of sins through his name.'

44 While Peter was still speaking these words, the Holy Spirit came on all who

---

a 19 One early manuscript *two*; other manuscripts do not have the number.

heard the message. **45** The circumcised believers who had come with Peter were astonished that the gift of the Holy Spirit had been poured out even on Gentiles. **46** For

they heard them speaking in tongues[b] and praising God.

b 46 Or *other languages*

LIFE OF JESUS 9

Judge of the world

Every year, in almost every country, a scandal emerges. Although the details differ, the pattern is often the same. Someone admired and respected in their community dies at an advanced age. Shortly after the funeral – attended by sorrowful relatives and friends – the truth emerges. Years ago, the deceased person committed some terrible crime, perhaps bank fraud, adultery or brutal assault that took or ruined the lives of many others. Yet the perpetrator walked away from the deed, escaped the workings of the law and lived out their years in peace and prosperity.

'It's not fair!' people say. 'They have escaped justice.' However, running throughout the Bible is the confident assertion that one day there will be a judgement for everybody and what has been done wrong will be judged. Ultimately, justice *will* be done (Acts 10:42).

The Old Testament promises that there will be a day when Yahweh, the Lord of Israel, will judge the entire world. It is therefore utterly astonishing when, turning to the New Testament, we read how on several occasions Jesus states that he personally would be the judge of the world (see, e.g. Matthew 10:32–33, 25:31–46; John 5:22; 12:48). It's a claim that you might imagine his first followers would have dropped after Jesus had been executed by the Roman legal system – hardly a promising start to a career as 'Judge of the world'. Yet the resurrection allowed the early church to make Jesus' claim to be the universal Judge central to its message (for just a few other examples, see Acts 17:30–31; Romans 2:16; 2 Thessalonians 1:5–10; 2 Timothy 4:1; Revelation 5:12–14) – and that's what's going on here in Acts 10:42.

No one is absolutely sure how the Last Judgement is going to operate. One thing we do know is that it will be absolutely just and fair. Another is that Jesus will be in charge. That means that in the meantime we have a window of opportunity to get to know him. At the moment he is Saviour, but Scripture teaches that there will be a time when it will be too late to turn to him, for he will have become Judge, condemning those who have rejected him and defending those who know him. We don't know how long this window of opportunity will last – minutes, days, years. We must take it while we can.

J.John

◀◀ John 20:28   Hebrews 1:1–3 ▶▶

Then Peter said, 47'Surely no one can stand in the way of their being baptised with water. They have received the Holy Spirit just as we have.' 48So he ordered that they be baptised in the name of Jesus Christ. Then they asked Peter to stay with them for a few days.

Peter explains his actions

11 The apostles and the believers throughout Judea heard that the Gentiles also had received the word of God. 2So when Peter went up to Jerusalem, the circumcised believers criticised him 3and said, 'You went into the house of uncircumcised men and ate with them.'

4Starting from the beginning, Peter told them the whole story: 5'I was in the city of Joppa praying, and in a trance I saw a vision. I saw something like a large sheet being let down from heaven by its four corners, and it came down to where I was. 6I looked into it and saw four-footed animals of the earth, wild beasts, reptiles and birds. 7Then I heard a voice telling me, "Get up, Peter. Kill and eat."

8'I replied, "Surely not, Lord! Nothing impure or unclean has ever entered my mouth."

9'The voice spoke from heaven a second time, "Do not call anything impure that God has made clean." 10This happened three times, and then it was all pulled up to heaven again.

11'Right then three men who had been sent to me from Caesarea stopped at the house where I was staying. 12The Spirit told me to have no hesitation about going with them. These six brothers also went with me, and we entered the man's house. 13He told us how he had seen an angel appear in his house and say, "Send to Joppa for Simon who is called Peter. 14He will bring you a message through which you and all your household will be saved."

15'As I began to speak, the Holy Spirit came on them as he had come on us at the beginning. 16Then I remembered what the Lord had said: "John baptised with*a* water, but you will be baptised with*a* the

---

a 16 Or in

Holy Spirit." 17So if God gave them the same gift he gave us who believed in the Lord Jesus Christ, who was I to think that I could stand in God's way?'

18When they heard this, they had no further objections and praised God, saying, 'So then, even to Gentiles God has granted repentance that leads to life.'

'CHRISTIANS'

According to Acts, the followers of Jesus were not originally called 'Christians'. That name was given to them at Antioch (Acts 11:26). It's probably a piece of mockery – mixing up 'Christ' (Greek for 'Messiah') and 'Chrestus', which was a popular slave's name, meaning 'good'.

The church in Antioch

19Now those who had been scattered by the persecution that broke out when Stephen was killed travelled as far as Phoenicia, Cyprus and Antioch, spreading the word only among Jews. 20Some of them, however, men from Cyprus and Cyrene, went to Antioch and began to speak to Greeks also, telling them the good news about the Lord Jesus. 21The Lord's hand was with them, and a great number of people believed and turned to the Lord.

22News of this reached the church in Jerusalem, and they sent Barnabas to Antioch. 23When he arrived and saw what the grace of God had done, he was glad and encouraged them all to remain true to the Lord with all their hearts. 24He was a good man, full of the Holy Spirit and faith, and a great number of people were brought to the Lord.

25Then Barnabas went to Tarsus to look for Saul, 26and when he found him, he brought him to Antioch. So for a whole year Barnabas and Saul met with the church and taught great numbers of people. The disciples were called Christians first at Antioch.

27 During this time some prophets came down from Jerusalem to Antioch. 28 One of them, named Agabus, stood up and through the Spirit predicted that a severe famine would spread over the entire Roman world. (This happened during the reign of Claudius.) 29 The disciples, as each one was able, decided to provide help for the brothers and sisters living in Judea. 30 This they did, sending their gift to the elders by Barnabas and Saul.

Peter's miraculous escape from prison

12 It was about this time that King Herod arrested some who belonged to the church, intending to persecute them. 2 He had James, the brother of John, put to death with the sword. 3 When he saw that this met with approval among the Jews, he proceeded to seize Peter also. This happened during the Festival of Unleavened Bread. 4 After arresting him, he put him in prison, handing him over to be guarded by four squads of four soldiers each. Herod intended to bring him out for public trial after the Passover.

5 So Peter was kept in prison, but the church was earnestly praying to God for him.

6 The night before Herod was to bring him to trial, Peter was sleeping between two soldiers, bound with two chains, and sentries stood guard at the entrance. 7 Suddenly an angel of the Lord appeared and a light shone in the cell. He struck Peter on the side and woke him up. 'Quick, get up!' he said, and the chains fell off Peter's wrists.

8 Then the angel said to him, 'Put on your clothes and sandals.' And Peter did so. 'Wrap your cloak round you and follow me,' the angel told him. 9 Peter followed him out of the prison, but he had no idea that what the angel was doing was really happening; he thought he was seeing a vision. 10 They passed the first and second guards and came to the iron gate leading to the city. It opened for them by itself, and they went through it. When they had walked the length of one street, suddenly the angel left him.

11 Then Peter came to himself and said, 'Now I know without a doubt that the Lord has sent his angel and rescued me from Herod's clutches and from everything the Jewish people were hoping would happen.'

12 When this had dawned on him, he went to the house of Mary the mother of John, also called Mark, where many people had gathered and were praying. 13 Peter knocked at the outer entrance, and a servant named Rhoda came to answer the door. 14 When she recognised Peter's voice, she was so overjoyed she ran back without opening it and exclaimed, 'Peter is at the door!'

15 'You're out of your mind,' they told her. When she kept insisting that it was so, they said, 'It must be his angel.'

16 But Peter kept on knocking, and when they opened the door and saw him, they were astonished. 17 Peter motioned with his hand for them to be quiet and described how the Lord had brought him out of prison. 'Tell James and the other brothers and sisters about this,' he said, and then he left for another place.

18 In the morning, there was no small commotion among the soldiers as to what had become of Peter. 19 After Herod had a thorough search made for him and did not find him, he cross-examined the guards and ordered that they be executed.

Herod's death

Then Herod went from Judea to Caesarea and stayed there. 20 He had been quarrelling with the people of Tyre and Sidon; they now joined together and sought an audience with him. After securing the support of Blastus, a trusted personal servant of the king, they asked for peace, because they depended on the king's country for their food supply.

21 On the appointed day Herod, wearing his royal robes, sat on his throne and

delivered a public address to the people. ²²They shouted, 'This is the voice of a god, not of a man.' ²³Immediately, because Herod did not give praise to God, an angel of the Lord struck him down, and he was eaten by worms and died.

²⁴But the word of God continued to spread and flourish.

Barnabas and Saul sent off

²⁵When Barnabas and Saul had finished their mission, they returned from*a* Jerusalem, taking with them John, also called Mark. **13** ¹Now in the church at Antioch there were prophets and

a 25 Some manuscripts *to*

PRAYER 3

SURPRISE AT PRAYER WORKING

In Acts 12:1–19, the Christian group had gathered to pray. It was probably in the same upper room as the Last Supper, as John Mark's mum is thought to have owned that house. They had lots to pray about. They were seeing great things happening – new people becoming believers all the time, some enormous events in the temple and amazing healings happening. But they also lived in really difficult times. The new church's main leaders were being persecuted, some were dead and Peter was in prison. So I think it's safe to assume that their prayers included one asking God to get Peter released from prison.

Then there was a knock at the door. The owners of the house were not going to let a caller interrupt their prayers, so the servant girl went to look through the spy hole to see who it was. Wow! It looked like Peter – smiling back at her! She ran straight back to the prayer meeting: *'Peter is at the door!'* (v. 14).

'You're out of your mind,' they said (v. 15). 'It can't be Peter. He's in prison. You know that. When you're in prison, you can't just turn up and knock on the door. Even if people are praying for him to be released, things like that don't just happen! There must be another explanation. Maybe you did see something, but the best that could happen is that his angel has come to us.' And all the time they were talking like this, a miracle had already happened, their prayers had already been answered, and Peter was still locked outside the door!

Those Christians were just like many of us. We pray like mad for God to help us, but when he does, we're very surprised! Even though they were praying for Peter's release, they were not really expecting their prayers to be *'powerful and effective'* (James 5:16).

I'm encouraged. If God could work powerfully with these prayers, when they clearly didn't expect it to work out, then he can use our prayers too. We may be those of *'little faith'* (one of Jesus' favourite ways of describing his disciples, e.g. Matthew 6:30; 8:26; 14:31), but he still loves to do amazing and surprising things to answer our prayers.

Hugo Anson

 Luke 15:21   Nehemiah 1

teachers: Barnabas, Simeon called Niger, Lucius of Cyrene, Manaen (who had been brought up with Herod the tetrarch) and Saul. ²While they were worshipping the Lord and fasting, the Holy Spirit said, 'Set apart for me Barnabas and Saul for the work to which I have called them.' ³So after they had fasted and prayed, they placed their hands on them and sent them off.

On Cyprus

⁴The two of them, sent on their way by the Holy Spirit, went down to Seleucia and sailed from there to Cyprus. ⁵When they arrived at Salamis, they proclaimed the word of God in the Jewish synagogues. John was with them as their helper.

⁶They travelled through the whole island until they came to Paphos. There they met a Jewish sorcerer and false prophet named Bar-Jesus, ⁷who was an attendant of the proconsul, Sergius Paulus. The proconsul, an intelligent man, sent for Barnabas and Saul because he wanted to hear the word of God. ⁸But Elymas the sorcerer (for that is what his name means) opposed them and tried to turn the proconsul from the faith. ⁹Then Saul, who was also called Paul, filled with the Holy Spirit, looked straight at Elymas and said, ¹⁰'You are a child of the devil and an enemy of everything that is right! You are full of all kinds of deceit and trickery. Will you never stop perverting the right ways of the Lord? ¹¹Now the hand of the Lord is against you. You are going to be blind for a time, not even able to see the light of the sun.'

Immediately mist and darkness came over him, and he groped about, seeking someone to lead him by the hand. ¹²When the proconsul saw what had happened, he believed, for he was amazed at the teaching about the Lord.

In Pisidian Antioch

¹³From Paphos, Paul and his companions sailed to Perga in Pamphylia, where John left them to return to Jerusalem. ¹⁴From Perga they went on to Pisidian Antioch. On the Sabbath they entered

the synagogue and sat down. ¹⁵After the reading from the Law and the Prophets, the leaders of the synagogue sent word to them, saying, 'Brothers, if you have a word of exhortation for the people, please speak.'

¹⁶Standing up, Paul motioned with his hand and said: 'Fellow Israelites and you Gentiles who worship God, listen to me! ¹⁷The God of the people of Israel chose our ancestors; he made the people prosper during their stay in Egypt; with mighty power he led them out of that country; ¹⁸for about forty years he endured their conduct[a] in the wilderness; ¹⁹and he overthrew seven nations in Canaan, giving their land to his people as their inheritance. ²⁰All this took about 450 years.

'After this, God gave them judges until the time of Samuel the prophet. ²¹Then the people asked for a king, and he gave them Saul son of Kish, of the tribe of Benjamin, who ruled for forty years. ²²After removing Saul, he made David their king. God testified concerning him: "I have found David son of Jesse, a man after my own heart; he will do everything I want him to do."

²³'From this man's descendants God has brought to Israel the Saviour Jesus, as he promised. ²⁴Before the coming of Jesus, John preached repentance and baptism to all the people of Israel. ²⁵As John was completing his work, he said: "Who do you suppose I am? I am not the one you are looking for. But there is one coming after me whose sandals I am not worthy to untie."

²⁶'Fellow children of Abraham and you God-fearing Gentiles, it is to us that this message of salvation has been sent. ²⁷The people of Jerusalem and their rulers did not recognise Jesus, yet in condemning him they fulfilled the words of the prophets that are read every Sabbath. ²⁸Though they found no proper ground for a death sentence, they asked Pilate to have him executed. ²⁹When they had carried out all that was written about him, they took him down from the cross and laid him in

_____

a 18 Some manuscripts *he cared for them*

a tomb. 30But God raised him from the dead, 31and for many days he was seen by those who had travelled with him from Galilee to Jerusalem. They are now his witnesses to our people.

32'We tell you the good news: what God promised our ancestors 33he has fulfilled for us, their children, by raising up Jesus. As it is written in the second Psalm:

'"You are my son;
    today I have become your father."b

34God raised him from the dead so that he will never be subject to decay. As God has said,

'"I will give you the holy and sure
    blessings promised to David."c

35So it is also stated elsewhere:

'"You will not let your holy one see
    decay."d

36'Now when David had served God's purpose in his own generation, he fell asleep; he was buried with his ancestors and his body decayed. 37But the one whom God raised from the dead did not see decay.

38'Therefore, my friends, I want you to know that through Jesus the forgiveness of sins is proclaimed to you. 39Through him everyone who believes is set free from every sin, a justification you were not able to obtain under the law of Moses. 40Take care that what the prophets have said does not happen to you:

41'"Look, you scoffers,
    wonder and perish,
  for I am going to do something in your
      days
    that you would never believe,
    even if someone told you."e'

42As Paul and Barnabas were leaving the synagogue, the people invited them to speak further about these things on the next Sabbath. 43When the congregation was dismissed, many of the Jews and devout converts to Judaism followed Paul and Barnabas, who talked with them and urged them to continue in the grace of God.

44On the next Sabbath almost the whole city gathered to hear the word of the Lord. 45When the Jews saw the crowds, they were filled with jealousy. They began to contradict what Paul was saying and heaped abuse on him.

46Then Paul and Barnabas answered them boldly: 'We had to speak the word of God to you first. Since you reject it and do not consider yourselves worthy of eternal life, we now turn to the Gentiles. 47For this is what the Lord has commanded us:

'"I have made youf a light for the
      Gentiles,
    that youf may bring salvation to the
      ends of the earth."g'

48When the Gentiles heard this, they were glad and honoured the word of the Lord; and all who were appointed for eternal life believed.

49The word of the Lord spread through the whole region. 50But the Jewish leaders incited the God-fearing women of high standing and the leading men of the city. They stirred up persecution against Paul and Barnabas, and expelled them from their region. 51So they shook the dust off their feet as a warning to them and went to Iconium. 52And the disciples were filled with joy and with the Holy Spirit.

In Iconium

14 At Iconium Paul and Barnabas went as usual into the Jewish synagogue. There they spoke so effectively that a great number of Jews and Greeks believed. 2But the Jews who refused to believe stirred up the other Gentiles and poisoned their minds against the brothers.

---

b 33 Psalm 2.7
c 34 Isaiah 55:3
d 35 Psalm 16:10 (see Septuagint)
e 41 Hab. 1:5

f 47 The Greek is singular.
g 47 Isaiah 49:6

³So Paul and Barnabas spent considerable time there, speaking boldly for the Lord, who confirmed the message of his grace by enabling them to perform signs and wonders. ⁴The people of the city were divided; some sided with the Jews, others with the apostles. ⁵There was a plot afoot among both Gentiles and Jews, together with their leaders, to ill-treat them and stone them. ⁶But they found out about it and fled to the Lycaonian cities of Lystra and Derbe and to the surrounding country, ⁷where they continued to preach the gospel.

In Lystra and Derbe

⁸In Lystra there sat a man who was lame. He had been that way from birth and had never walked. ⁹He listened to Paul as he was speaking. Paul looked directly at him, saw that he had faith to be healed ¹⁰and called out, 'Stand up on your feet!' At that, the man jumped up and began to walk.

¹¹When the crowd saw what Paul had done, they shouted in the Lycaonian language, 'The gods have come down to us in human form!' ¹²Barnabas they called Zeus, and Paul they called Hermes because he was the chief speaker. ¹³The priest of Zeus, whose temple was just outside the city, brought bulls and wreaths to the city gates because he and the crowd wanted to offer sacrifices to them.

¹⁴But when the apostles Barnabas and Paul heard of this, they tore their clothes and rushed out into the crowd, shouting: ¹⁵'Friends, why are you doing this? We too are only human, like you. We are bringing you good news, telling you to turn from these worthless things to the living God, who made the heavens and the earth and the sea and everything in them. ¹⁶In the past, he let all nations go their own way. ¹⁷Yet he has not left himself without testimony: he has shown kindness by giving you rain from heaven and crops in their seasons; he provides you with plenty of food and fills your hearts with joy.' ¹⁸Even with these words, they had difficulty keeping the crowd from sacrificing to them.

¹⁹Then some Jews came from Antioch and Iconium and won the crowd over. They stoned Paul and dragged him outside the city, thinking he was dead. ²⁰But after the disciples had gathered round him, he got up and went back into the city. The next day he and Barnabas left for Derbe.

FAVOURITE VERSES

Psalm 18:1–3

I love you, LORD, my strength.

*The LORD is my rock, my fortress
    and my deliverer;
  my God is my rock, in whom I take
    refuge,
  my shield and the horn of my
    salvation, my stronghold.*

*I called to the LORD, who is worthy
    of praise,
  and I have been saved from my
    enemies.*

These verses mean so much to me because they are a constant reminder that God is your place of security and refuge, and he is your shield in times of trouble.

James, 18

The return to Antioch in Syria

²¹They preached the gospel in that city and won a large number of disciples. Then they returned to Lystra, Iconium and Antioch, ²²strengthening the disciples and encouraging them to remain true to the faith. 'We must go through many hardships to enter the kingdom of God,' they said. ²³Paul and Barnabas appointed elders*ᵃ* for them in each church

a 23 Or *Barnabas ordained elders;* or *Barnabas had elders elected* and, with prayer and fasting, committed them to the Lord, in whom they had put their trust. 24After going through Pisidia, they came into Pamphylia, 25and when they had preached the word in Perga, they went down to Attalia.

26From Attalia they sailed back to Antioch, where they had been committed to the grace of God for the work they had now completed. 27On arriving there, they gathered the church together and reported all that God had done through them and how he had opened a door of faith to the Gentiles. 28And they stayed there a long time with the disciples.

The council at Jerusalem

15 Certain people came down from Judea to Antioch and were teaching the believers: 'Unless you are circumcised, according to the custom taught by Moses, you cannot be saved.' 2This brought Paul and Barnabas into sharp dispute and debate with them. So Paul and Barnabas were appointed, along with some other believers, to go up to Jerusalem to see the apostles and elders about this question. 3The church sent them on their way, and as they travelled through Phoenicia and Samaria, they told how the Gentiles had been converted. This news made all the believers very glad. 4When they came to Jerusalem, they were welcomed by the church and the apostles and elders, to whom they reported everything God had done through them.

5Then some of the believers who belonged to the party of the Pharisees stood up and said, 'The Gentiles must be circumcised and required to keep the law of Moses.'

6The apostles and elders met to consider this question. 7After much discussion, Peter got up and addressed them: 'Brothers, you know that some time ago God made a choice among you that the Gentiles should hear from my lips the message of the gospel and believe. 8God, who knows the heart, showed that he accepted them by giving the Holy Spirit to them, just as he did to us. 9He did not discriminate between us and them, for he

purified their hearts by faith. 10Now then, why do you try to test God by putting on the necks of Gentiles a yoke that neither we nor our ancestors have been able to bear? 11No! We believe it is through the grace of our Lord Jesus that we are saved, just as they are.'

12The whole assembly became silent as they listened to Barnabas and Paul telling about the signs and wonders God had done among the Gentiles through them. 13When they finished, James spoke up. 'Brothers,' he said, 'listen to me. 14Simon*a* has described to us how God first intervened to choose a people for his name from the Gentiles. 15The words of the prophets are in agreement with this, as it is written:

16 ' "After this I will return
     and rebuild David's fallen tent.
   Its ruins I will rebuild,
     and I will restore it,
17 that the rest of mankind may seek the
     Lord,
     even all the Gentiles who bear my
       name,
   says the Lord, who does these
       things"*b* –
18   things known from long ago.*c*

19'It is my judgment, therefore, that we should not make it difficult for the Gentiles who are turning to God. 20Instead we should write to them, telling them to abstain from food polluted by idols, from sexual immorality, from the meat of strangled animals and from blood. 21For the law of Moses has been preached in every city from the earliest times and is read in the synagogues on every Sabbath.'

The council's letter to Gentile believers

22Then the apostles and elders, with the whole church, decided to choose some of their own men and send them to Antioch with Paul and Barnabas. They chose Judas

---

a 14 Greek *Simeon*, a variant of *Simon*; that is, Peter
b 17 Amos 9:11,12 (see Septuagint)
c 17,18 Some manuscripts *things'* – /*18the Lord's work is known to him from long ago*

(called Barsabbas) and Silas, men who were leaders among the believers. ²³With them they sent the following letter:

The apostles and elders, your brothers,

To the Gentile believers in Antioch, Syria and Cilicia:

Greetings.

²⁴We have heard that some went out from us without our authorisation and disturbed you, troubling your minds by what they said. ²⁵So we all agreed to choose some men and send them to you with our dear friends Barnabas and Paul – ²⁶men who have risked their lives for the name of our Lord Jesus Christ. ²⁷Therefore we are sending Judas and Silas to confirm by word of mouth what we are writing. ²⁸It seemed good to the Holy Spirit and to us not to burden you with anything beyond the following requirements: ²⁹You are to abstain from food sacrificed to idols, from blood, from the meat of strangled animals and from sexual immorality. You will do well to avoid these things.

Farewell.

³⁰So the men were sent off and went down to Antioch, where they gathered the church together and delivered the letter. ³¹The people read it and were glad for its encouraging message. ³²Judas and Silas, who themselves were prophets, said much to encourage and strengthen the believers. ³³After spending some time there, they were sent off by the believers with the blessing of peace to return to those who had sent them. [³⁴]^d ³⁵But Paul and Barnabas remained in Antioch, where they and many others taught and preached the word of the Lord.

---

^d 34 Some manuscripts include here *But Silas decided to remain there.*

Disagreement between Paul and Barnabas

³⁶Some time later Paul said to Barnabas, 'Let us go back and visit the believers in all the towns where we preached the word of the Lord and see how they are doing.' ³⁷Barnabas wanted to take John, also called Mark, with them, ³⁸but Paul did not think it wise to take him, because he had deserted them in Pamphylia and had not continued with them in the work. ³⁹They had such a sharp disagreement that they parted company. Barnabas took Mark and sailed for Cyprus, ⁴⁰but Paul chose Silas and left, commended by the believers to the grace of the Lord. ⁴¹He went through Syria and Cilicia, strengthening the churches.

Timothy joins Paul and Silas

16 Paul came to Derbe and then to Lystra, where a disciple named Timothy lived, whose mother was Jewish and a believer but whose father was a Greek. ²The believers at Lystra and Iconium spoke well of him. ³Paul wanted to take him along on the journey, so he circumcised him because of the Jews who lived in that area, for they all knew that his father was a Greek. ⁴As they travelled from town to town, they delivered the decisions reached by the apostles and elders in Jerusalem for the people to obey. ⁵So the churches were strengthened in the faith and grew daily in numbers.

Paul's vision of the man of Macedonia

⁶Paul and his companions travelled throughout the region of Phrygia and Galatia, having been kept by the Holy Spirit from preaching the word in the province of Asia. ⁷When they came to the border of Mysia, they tried to enter Bithynia, but the Spirit of Jesus would not allow them to. ⁸So they passed by Mysia and went down to Troas. ⁹During the night Paul had a vision of a man of Macedonia standing and begging him, 'Come over to Macedonia and help us.' ¹⁰After Paul had seen the vision, we got ready at once to leave for Macedonia, concluding that God had called us to preach the gospel to them.

FRIENDSHIP 6

When friendships go wrong

Right at the beginning of the Bible, in the book of Genesis, we see how relationships were intended to be. We were supposed to live in God's presence and be at peace with one another, able to be ourselves completely and know no shame (Genesis 2). Then Adam and Eve decided to go their own way and what's known as 'the fall' happened. It separated us from God and it drove a wedge between human relationships. Immediately Adam and Eve started fighting, blaming one another and feeling ashamed of their vulnerability for the first time (Genesis 3). Human relationships had broken down.

The Bible catalogues the whole history of chaos that this caused: from one of Adam's and Eve's sons killing the other (Cain and Abel, Genesis 4) to Paul and Barnabas falling out here in the book of Acts (Acts 15:36–41). Up until this point Paul and Barnabas had been firm friends, but suddenly they had a disagreement so strong they went their separate ways. (The Bible gives us no details about what happened, whether one was in the right and one was in the wrong, or whether the disagreement could have been resolved.)

It's always sad when friends argue, but because of the fall we're unable to live in complete agreement with each other. We have different opinions, different ways of living, different ideas about how best to spend time, money and energy. It's fine to have different opinions: they often make for interesting and good relationships! Problems occur when we can't put aside our differences or find a compromise. And we let each other down. We try not to and we may love someone to the very best of our ability, but because we're not perfect, we'll never love them perfectly. Even the best friend in the world lets people down.

If you fall out with a friend and you're in the wrong, be quick to say 'sorry'. Have the humility to admit your mistake and ask for forgiveness. If you were the one who was hurt, then ask God to help you forgive the person for what they did. It might take time, but keep praying and asking God to bring healing. Even if you were 100 per cent in the right (which we rarely are – these things usually happen because both parties were to some extent in the wrong), don't bad-mouth your friend. Be honest with them about how they have hurt you, but don't go around telling everyone else why you were right and they were wrong. That only brings more damage. While arguments can be painful, the healthiest relationships are ones where you allow each other to learn and grow. That means recognising that even best friends fall out, but it doesn't need to be the end of that friendship altogether. Good friendships are worth fighting for.

Ali Martin

 John 21:20   2 Timothy 1 ▶

Lydia's conversion in Philippi

11 From Troas we put out to sea and sailed straight for Samothrace, and the next day we went on to Neapolis. 12 From there we travelled to Philippi, a Roman colony and the leading city of that district*a* of Macedonia. And we stayed there several days.

13 On the Sabbath we went outside the city gate to the river, where we expected to find a place of prayer. We sat down and began to speak to the women who had gathered there. 14 One of those listening was a woman from the city of Thyatira named Lydia, a dealer in purple cloth. She was a worshipper of God. The Lord opened her heart to respond to Paul's message. 15 When she and the members of her household were baptised, she invited us to her home. 'If you consider me a believer in the Lord,' she said, 'come and stay at my house.' And she persuaded us.

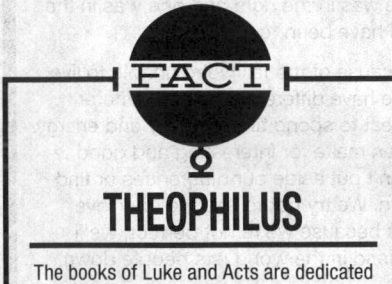

FACT

♀ THEOPHILUS

The books of Luke and Acts are dedicated to a man called Theophilus (Luke 1:3; Acts 1:1). He was probably an aristocratic Roman (Luke calls him 'most excellent'). His name means 'God lover'.

Paul and Silas in prison

16 Once when we were going to the place of prayer, we were met by a female slave who had a spirit by which she predicted the future. She earned a great deal of money for her owners by fortune-telling. 17 She followed Paul and the rest of us, shouting, 'These men are servants of the Most High God, who are telling you the way to be saved.' 18 She kept this

up for many days. Finally Paul became so annoyed that he turned round and said to the spirit, 'In the name of Jesus Christ I command you to come out of her!' At that moment the spirit left her.

19 When her owners realised that their hope of making money was gone, they seized Paul and Silas and dragged them into the market-place to face the authorities. 20 They brought them before the magistrates and said, 'These men are Jews, and are throwing our city into an uproar 21 by advocating customs unlawful for us Romans to accept or practise.'

22 The crowd joined in the attack against Paul and Silas, and the magistrates ordered them to be stripped and beaten with rods. 23 After they had been severely flogged, they were thrown into prison, and the jailer was commanded to guard them carefully. 24 When he received these orders, he put them in the inner cell and fastened their feet in the stocks.

25 About midnight Paul and Silas were praying and singing hymns to God, and the other prisoners were listening to them. 26 Suddenly there was such a violent earthquake that the foundations of the prison were shaken. At once all the prison doors flew open, and everyone's chains came loose. 27 The jailer woke up, and when he saw the prison doors open, he drew his sword and was about to kill himself because he thought the prisoners had escaped. 28 But Paul shouted, 'Don't harm yourself! We are all here!'

29 The jailer called for lights, rushed in and fell trembling before Paul and Silas. 30 He then brought them out and asked, 'Sirs, what must I do to be saved?'

31 They replied, 'Believe in the Lord Jesus, and you will be saved – you and your household.' 32 Then they spoke the word of the Lord to him and to all the others in his house. 33 At that hour of the night the jailer took them and washed their wounds; then immediately he and all his household were baptised. 34 The jailer brought them into his house and set a meal before them; he was filled with joy because he had come to believe in God – he and his whole household.

---

a 12 The text and meaning of the Greek for *the leading city of that district* are uncertain.

35 When it was daylight, the magistrates sent their officers to the jailer with the order: 'Release those men.' **36** The jailer told Paul, 'The magistrates have ordered that you and Silas be released. Now you can leave. Go in peace.'

37 But Paul said to the officers: 'They beat us publicly without a trial, even though we are Roman citizens, and threw us into prison. And now do they want to get rid of us quietly? No! Let them come themselves and escort us out.'

38 The officers reported this to the magistrates, and when they heard that Paul and Silas were Roman citizens, they were alarmed. **39** They came to appease them and escorted them from the prison, requesting them to leave the city. **40** After Paul and Silas came out of the prison, they went to Lydia's house, where they met with the brothers and sisters and encouraged them. Then they left.

In Thessalonica

17 When Paul and his companions had passed through Amphipolis and Apollonia, they came to Thessalonica, where there was a Jewish synagogue. **2** As was his custom, Paul went into the synagogue, and on three Sabbath days he reasoned with them from the Scriptures, **3** explaining and proving that the Messiah had to suffer and rise from the dead. 'This Jesus I am proclaiming to you is the Messiah,' he said. **4** Some of the Jews were persuaded and joined Paul and Silas, as did a large number of God-fearing Greeks and quite a few prominent women.

5 But other Jews were jealous; so they rounded up some bad characters from the market-place, formed a mob and started a riot in the city. They rushed to Jason's house in search of Paul and Silas in order to bring them out to the crowd.*a* **6** But when they did not find them, they dragged Jason and some other believers before the city officials, shouting: 'These men who have caused trouble all over the world have now come here, **7** and Jason has welcomed them into his house. They

are all defying Caesar's decrees, saying that there is another king, one called Jesus.' **8** When they heard this, the crowd and the city officials were thrown into turmoil. **9** Then they put Jason and the others on bail and let them go.

In Berea

10 As soon as it was night, the believers sent Paul and Silas away to Berea. On arriving there, they went to the Jewish synagogue. **11** Now the Berean Jews were of more noble character than those in Thessalonica, for they received the message with great eagerness and examined the Scriptures every day to see if what Paul said was true. **12** As a result, many of them believed, as did also a number of prominent Greek women and many Greek men.

13 But when the Jews in Thessalonica learned that Paul was preaching the word of God at Berea, some of them went there too, agitating the crowds and stirring them up. **14** The believers immediately sent Paul to the coast, but Silas and Timothy stayed at Berea. **15** Those who escorted Paul brought him to Athens and then left with instructions for Silas and Timothy to join him as soon as possible.

In Athens

16 While Paul was waiting for them in Athens, he was greatly distressed to see that the city was full of idols. **17** So he reasoned in the synagogue with both Jews and God-fearing Greeks, as well as in the market-place day by day with those who happened to be there. **18** A group of Epicurean and Stoic philosophers began to debate with him. Some of them asked, 'What is this babbler trying to say?' Others remarked, 'He seems to be advocating foreign gods.' They said this because Paul was preaching the good news about Jesus and the resurrection. **19** Then they took him and brought him to a meeting of the Areopagus, where they said to him, 'May we know what this new teaching is that you are presenting? **20** You are bringing some strange ideas to our ears, and we would like to know what they mean.' **21** (All the Athenians and the foreigners

a 5 Or the assembly of the people

who lived there spent their time doing nothing but talking about and listening to the latest ideas.)

22 Paul then stood up in the meeting of the Areopagus and said: 'People of Athens! I see that in every way you are very religious. 23 For as I walked around and looked carefully at your objects of worship, I even found an altar with this inscription: TO AN UNKNOWN GOD. So you are ignorant of the very thing you worship – and this is what I am going to proclaim to you.

24 'The God who made the world and everything in it is the Lord of heaven and earth and does not live in temples built by human hands. 25 And he is not served by human hands, as if he needed anything. Rather, he himself gives everyone life and breath and everything else. 26 From one man he made all the nations, that they should inhabit the whole earth; and he marked out their appointed times in history and the boundaries of their lands. 27 God did this so that they would seek him and perhaps reach out for him and find him, though he is not far from any one of us. 28 "For in him we live and move and have our being."b As some of your own poets have said, "We are his offspring."c

29 'Therefore since we are God's offspring, we should not think that the divine being is like gold or silver or stone – an image made by human design and skill. 30 In the past God overlooked such ignorance, but now he commands all people everywhere to repent. 31 For he has set a day when he will judge the world with justice by the man he has appointed. He has given proof of this to everyone by raising him from the dead.'

32 When they heard about the resurrection of the dead, some of them sneered, but others said, 'We want to hear you again on this subject.' 33 At that, Paul left the Council. 34 Some of the people became followers of Paul and believed. Among them was Dionysius, a member of the Areopagus, also a woman named Damaris, and a number of others.

___
b 28 From the Cretan philosopher Epimenides
c 28 From the Cilician Stoic philosopher Aratus

In Corinth

18 After this, Paul left Athens and went to Corinth. 2 There he met a Jew named Aquila, a native of Pontus, who had recently come from Italy with his wife Priscilla, because Claudius had ordered all Jews to leave Rome. Paul went to see them, 3 and because he was a tentmaker as they were, he stayed and worked with them. 4 Every Sabbath he reasoned in the synagogue, trying to persuade Jews and Greeks.

5 When Silas and Timothy came from Macedonia, Paul devoted himself exclusively to preaching, testifying to the Jews that Jesus was the Messiah. 6 But when they opposed Paul and became abusive, he shook out his clothes in protest and said to them, 'Your blood be on your own heads! I am innocent of it. From now on I will go to the Gentiles.'

7 Then Paul left the synagogue and went next door to the house of Titius Justus, a worshipper of God. 8 Crispus, the synagogue leader, and his entire household believed in the Lord; and many of the Corinthians who heard Paul believed and were baptised.

9 One night the Lord spoke to Paul in a vision: 'Do not be afraid; keep on speaking, do not be silent. 10 For I am with you, and no one is going to attack and harm you, because I have many people in this city.' 11 So Paul stayed in Corinth for a year and a half, teaching them the word of God.

12 While Gallio was proconsul of Achaia, the Jews of Corinth made a united attack on Paul and brought him to the place of judgment. 13 'This man,' they charged, 'is persuading the people to worship God in ways contrary to the law.'

14 Just as Paul was about to speak, Gallio said to them, 'If you Jews were making a complaint about some misdemeanour or serious crime, it would be reasonable for me to listen to you. 15 But since it involves questions about words and names and your own law – settle the matter yourselves. I will not be a judge of such things.' 16 So he drove them off. 17 Then the crowd there turned on Sosthenes the synagogue

leader and beat him in front of the pro-consul; and Gallio showed no concern whatever.

Priscilla, Aquila and Apollos

18 Paul stayed on in Corinth for some time. Then he left the brothers and sisters and sailed for Syria, accompanied by Priscilla and Aquila. Before he sailed, he had his hair cut off at Cenchreae because of a vow he had taken. 19 They arrived at Ephesus, where Paul left Priscilla and Aquila. He himself went into the synagogue and reasoned with the Jews. 20 When they asked him to spend more time with them, he declined. 21 But as he left, he promised, 'I will come back if it is God's will.' Then he set sail from Ephesus. 22 When he landed

FAITH IN THE WORLD 7

FOR THE LOVE OF ... POLITICS?

In Acts 18:1–4, we find the apostle Paul going back to his old day job, making tents.

Paul is still doing the work of reaching people with God's good news on Saturdays (i.e. the Sabbath), but he's happily stitching canvas together for the rest of the time. Nowhere do we read that Paul was frustrated by having to go back to tent-making for a while – he knew that God is really happy with people doing a decent day's work with their hands. That goes for doing graphic design as well as designing marquees!

Abraham Kuyper was a man who thought this way. He was the prime minister of the Netherlands from 1901 to 1905. He loved politics and he loved God, and he knew that he could love God better by excelling in his chosen profession. He famously said, 'There is not an inch of creation which Christ did not proclaim mine!' What does this mean? In Genesis we looked at how much of the work God gave us to do was in providing 'order' within his creation. Much work is about this – bringing order to the world – and it means that God is concerned with every area of work. Abraham Kuyper knew that God cared about his work as Dutch prime minister. More than that, Kuyper knew that he could make a real difference for God by doing his work to the best of his ability.

Work that brings benefit to us and others, work that helps to order society and therefore God's world, is *good* work. God cared about Paul's role, whether he was preaching the gospel or mending patches in tents. All of creation is God's, so he cares about the way *we* seek to take care of his world and each other.

Realising this can really help us as we try to find our path through education and then employment. For instance, we might struggle with school, and learning can be difficult, but we should see it as an opportunity to improve ourselves. More importantly, though, we should see that by doing our school work well, we're also serving God.

Jason Gardner

 Matthew 25:31–46

John 14:28–31

at Caesarea, he went up to Jerusalem and greeted the church and then went down to Antioch.

23 After spending some time in Antioch, Paul set out from there and travelled from place to place throughout the region of Galatia and Phrygia, strengthening all the disciples.

24 Meanwhile a Jew named Apollos, a native of Alexandria, came to Ephesus. He was a learned man, with a thorough knowledge of the Scriptures. 25 He had been instructed in the way of the Lord, and he spoke with great fervour*a* and taught about Jesus accurately, though he knew only the baptism of John. 26 He began to speak boldly in the synagogue. When Priscilla and Aquila heard him, they invited him to their home and explained to him the way of God more adequately.

27 When Apollos wanted to go to Achaia, the brothers and sisters encouraged him and wrote to the disciples there to welcome him. When he arrived, he was a great help to those who by grace had believed. 28 For he vigorously refuted his Jewish opponents in public debate, proving from the Scriptures that Jesus was the Messiah.

Paul in Ephesus

19 While Apollos was at Corinth, Paul took the road through the interior and arrived at Ephesus. There he found some disciples 2 and asked them, 'Did you receive the Holy Spirit when*a* you believed?'

They answered, 'No, we have not even heard that there is a Holy Spirit.'

3 So Paul asked, 'Then what baptism did you receive?'

'John's baptism,' they replied.

4 Paul said, 'John's baptism was a baptism of repentance. He told the people to believe in the one coming after him, that is, in Jesus.' 5 On hearing this, they were baptised in the name of the Lord Jesus. 6 When Paul placed his hands on them, the Holy Spirit came on them, and they

spoke in tongues*b* and prophesied. 7 There were about twelve men in all.

8 Paul entered the synagogue and spoke boldly there for three months, arguing persuasively about the kingdom of God. 9 But some of them became obstinate; they refused to believe and publicly maligned the Way. So Paul left them. He took the disciples with him and had discussions daily in the lecture hall of Tyrannus. 10 This went on for two years, so that all the Jews and Greeks who lived in the province of Asia heard the word of the Lord.

11 God did extraordinary miracles through Paul, 12 so that even handkerchiefs and aprons that had touched him were taken to those who were ill, and their illnesses were cured and the evil spirits left them.

13 Some Jews who went around driving out evil spirits tried to invoke the name of the Lord Jesus over those who were demon-possessed. They would say, 'In the name of the Jesus whom Paul preaches, I command you to come out.' 14 Seven sons of Sceva, a Jewish chief priest, were doing this. 15 One day the evil spirit answered them, 'Jesus I know, and Paul I know about, but who are you?' 16 Then the man who had the evil spirit jumped on them and overpowered them all. He gave them such a beating that they ran out of the house naked and bleeding.

17 When this became known to the Jews and Greeks living in Ephesus, they were all seized with fear, and the name of the Lord Jesus was held in high honour. 18 Many of those who believed now came and openly confessed what they had done. 19 A number who had practised sorcery brought their scrolls together and burned them publicly. When they calculated the value of the scrolls, the total came to fifty thousand drachmas.*c* 20 In this way the word of the Lord spread widely and grew in power.

21 After all this had happened, Paul decided*d* to go to Jerusalem, passing through Macedonia and Achaia. 'After I have been

a 25 Or *with fervour in the Spirit*
a 2 Or *after*

b 6 Or *other languages*
c 19 A drachma was a silver coin worth about a day's wages.
d 21 Or *decided in the Spirit*

there,' he said, 'I must visit Rome also.' 22 He sent two of his helpers, Timothy and Erastus, to Macedonia, while he stayed in the province of Asia a little longer.

The riot in Ephesus

23 About that time there arose a great disturbance about the Way. 24 A silversmith named Demetrius, who made silver shrines of Artemis, brought in a lot of business for the craftsmen there. 25 He called them together, along with the workers in related trades, and said: 'You know, my friends, that we receive a good income from this business. 26 And you see and hear how this fellow Paul has convinced and led astray large numbers of people here in Ephesus and in practically the whole province of Asia. He says that gods made by human hands are no gods at all. 27 There is danger not only that our trade will lose its good name, but also that the temple of the great goddess Artemis will be discredited; and the goddess herself, who is worshipped throughout the province of Asia and the world, will be robbed of her divine majesty.'

28 When they heard this, they were furious and began shouting: 'Great is Artemis of the Ephesians!' 29 Soon the whole city was in an uproar. The people seized Gaius and Aristarchus, Paul's travelling companions from Macedonia, and all of them rushed into the theatre together. 30 Paul wanted to appear before the crowd, but the disciples would not let him. 31 Even some of the officials of the province, friends of Paul, sent him a message begging him not to venture into the theatre.

32 The assembly was in confusion: some were shouting one thing, some another. Most of the people did not even know why they were there. 33 The Jews in the crowd pushed Alexander to the front, and they shouted instructions to him. He motioned for silence in order to make a defence before the people. 34 But when they realised he was a Jew, they all shouted in unison for about two hours: 'Great is Artemis of the Ephesians!'

35 The city clerk quietened the crowd and said: 'Fellow Ephesians, doesn't all the world know that the city of Ephesus is the guardian of the temple of the great Artemis and of her image, which fell from heaven? 36 Therefore, since these facts are undeniable, you ought to calm down and not do anything rash. 37 You have brought these men here, though they have neither robbed temples nor blasphemed our goddess. 38 If, then, Demetrius and his fellow craftsmen have a grievance against anybody, the courts are open and there are proconsuls. They can press charges. 39 If there is anything further you want to bring up, it must be settled in a legal assembly. 40 As it is, we are in danger of being charged with rioting because of what happened today. In that case we would not be able to account for this commotion, since there is no reason for it.' 41 After he had said this, he dismissed the assembly.

Through Macedonia and Greece

20 When the uproar had ended, Paul sent for the disciples and, after encouraging them, said goodbye and set out for Macedonia. 2 He travelled through that area, speaking many words of encouragement to the people, and finally arrived in Greece, 3 where he stayed three months. Because some Jews had plotted against him just as he was about to sail for Syria, he decided to go back through Macedonia. 4 He was accompanied by Sopater son of Pyrrhus from Berea, Aristarchus and Secundus from Thessalonica, Gaius from Derbe, Timothy also, and Tychicus and Trophimus from the province of Asia. 5 These men went on ahead and waited for us at Troas. 6 But we sailed from Philippi after the Festival of Unleavened Bread, and five days later joined the others at Troas, where we stayed seven days.

Eutychus raised from the dead at Troas

7 On the first day of the week we came together to break bread. Paul spoke to the people and, because he intended to leave the next day, kept on talking until midnight. 8 There were many lamps in the upstairs room where we were meeting. 9 Seated in a window was a young man named Eutychus, who was sinking

into a deep sleep as Paul talked on and on. When he was sound asleep, he fell to the ground from the third storey and was picked up dead. 10 Paul went down, threw himself on the young man and put his arms round him. 'Don't be alarmed,' he said. 'He's alive!' 11 Then he went upstairs again and broke bread and ate. After talking until daylight, he left. 12 The people took the young man home alive and were greatly comforted.

Paul's farewell to the Ephesian elders

13 We went on ahead to the ship and sailed for Assos, where we were going to take Paul aboard. He had made this arrangement because he was going there on foot. 14 When he met us at Assos, we took him aboard and went on to Mitylene. 15 The next day we set sail from there and arrived off Chios. The day after that we crossed over to Samos, and on the following day arrived at Miletus. 16 Paul had decided to sail past Ephesus to avoid spending time in the province of Asia, for he was in a hurry to reach Jerusalem, if possible, by the day of Pentecost.

17 From Miletus, Paul sent to Ephesus for the elders of the church. 18 When they arrived, he said to them: 'You know how I lived the whole time I was with you, from the first day I came into the province of Asia. 19 I served the Lord with great humility and with tears and in the midst of severe testing by the plots of my Jewish opponents. 20 You know that I have not hesitated to preach anything that would be helpful to you but have taught you publicly and from house to house. 21 I have declared to both Jews and Greeks that they must turn to God in repentance and have faith in our Lord Jesus.

22 'And now, compelled by the Spirit, I am going to Jerusalem, not knowing what will happen to me there. 23 I only know that in every city the Holy Spirit warns me that prison and hardships are facing me. 24 However, I consider my life worth nothing to me; my only aim is to finish the race and complete the task the Lord Jesus has given me – the task of testifying to the good news of God's grace.

25 'Now I know that none of you among whom I have gone about preaching the kingdom will ever see me again. 26 Therefore, I declare to you today that I am innocent of the blood of any of you. 27 For I have not hesitated to proclaim to you the whole will of God. 28 Keep watch over yourselves and all the flock of which the Holy Spirit has made you overseers. Be shepherds of the church of God,a which he bought with his own blood.b 29 I know that after I leave, savage wolves will come in among you and will not spare the flock. 30 Even from your own number men will arise and distort the truth in order to draw away disciples after them. 31 So be on your guard! Remember that for three years I never stopped warning each of you night and day with tears.

32 'Now I commit you to God and to the word of his grace, which can build you up and give you an inheritance among all those who are sanctified. 33 I have not coveted anyone's silver or gold or clothing. 34 You yourselves know that these hands of mine have supplied my own needs and the needs of my companions. 35 In everything I did, I showed you that by this kind of hard work we must help the weak, remembering the words the Lord Jesus himself said: "It is more blessed to give than to receive." '

36 When Paul had finished speaking, he knelt down with all of them and prayed. 37 They all wept as they embraced him and kissed him. 38 What grieved them most was his statement that they would never see his face again. Then they accompanied him to the ship.

On to Jerusalem

21 After we had torn ourselves away from them, we put out to sea and sailed straight to Kos. The next day we went to Rhodes and from there to Patara. 2 We found a ship crossing over to Phoenicia, went on board and set sail. 3 After sighting Cyprus and passing to the south of it, we sailed on to Syria.

a 28 Many manuscripts of the Lord
b 28 Or with the blood of his own Son.

We landed at Tyre, where our ship was to unload its cargo. **4** We sought out the disciples there and stayed with them seven days. Through the Spirit they urged Paul not to go on to Jerusalem. **5** When it was time to leave, we left and continued on our way. All of them, including wives and children, accompanied us out of the city, and there on the beach we knelt to pray. **6** After saying goodbye to each other, we went aboard the ship, and they returned home.

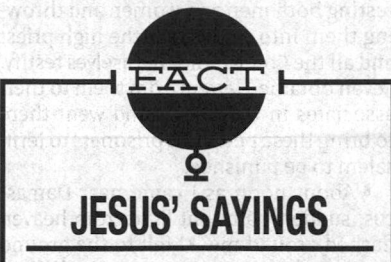

JESUS' SAYINGS

Not all the sayings of Jesus made it into the Gospels. Paul quotes Jesus in Acts 20:35: *'It is more blessed to give than to receive.'* But this doesn't appear in any Gospel, so he must have got it from another collection of Jesus' sayings.

7 We continued our voyage from Tyre and landed at Ptolemais, where we greeted the brothers and sisters and stayed with them for a day. **8** Leaving the next day, we reached Caesarea and stayed at the house of Philip the evangelist, one of the Seven. **9** He had four unmarried daughters who prophesied.

10 After we had been there a number of days, a prophet named Agabus came down from Judea. **11** Coming over to us, he took Paul's belt, tied his own hands and feet with it and said, 'The Holy Spirit says, "In this way the Jewish leaders in Jerusalem will bind the owner of this belt and will hand him over to the Gentiles."'

12 When we heard this, we and the people there pleaded with Paul not to go up to Jerusalem. **13** Then Paul answered, 'Why are you weeping and breaking my heart? I am ready not only to be bound, but also to die in Jerusalem for the name of the Lord Jesus.' **14** When he would not be dissuaded, we gave up and said, 'The Lord's will be done.'

15 After this, we started on our way up to Jerusalem. **16** Some of the disciples from Caesarea accompanied us and brought us to the home of Mnason, where we were to stay. He was a man from Cyprus and one of the early disciples.

Paul's arrival at Jerusalem

17 When we arrived at Jerusalem, the brothers and sisters received us warmly. **18** The next day Paul and the rest of us went to see James, and all the elders were present. **19** Paul greeted them and reported in detail what God had done among the Gentiles through his ministry.

20 When they heard this, they praised God. Then they said to Paul: 'You see, brother, how many thousands of Jews have believed, and all of them are zealous for the law. **21** They have been informed that you teach all the Jews who live among the Gentiles to turn away from Moses, telling them not to circumcise their children or live according to our customs. **22** What shall we do? They will certainly hear that you have come, **23** so do what we tell you. There are four men with us who have made a vow. **24** Take these men, join in their purification rites and pay their expenses, so that they can have their heads shaved. Then everyone will know there is no truth in these reports about you, but that you yourself are living in obedience to the law. **25** As for the Gentile believers, we have written to them our decision that they should abstain from food sacrificed to idols, from blood, from the meat of strangled animals and from sexual immorality.'

26 The next day Paul took the men and purified himself along with them. Then he went to the temple to give notice of the date when the days of purification would end and the offering would be made for each of them.

Paul arrested

27 When the seven days were nearly over, some Jews from the province of Asia saw Paul at the temple. They stirred up the whole crowd and seized him, **28** shouting, 'Fellow Israelites, help us! This is the man who teaches everyone everywhere against our people and our law and this place. And besides, he has brought Greeks into the temple and defiled this holy place.' **29** (They had previously seen Trophimus the Ephesian in the city with Paul and assumed that Paul had brought him into the temple.)

30 The whole city was aroused, and the people came running from all directions. Seizing Paul, they dragged him from the temple, and immediately the gates were shut. **31** While they were trying to kill him, news reached the commander of the Roman troops that the whole city of Jerusalem was in an uproar. **32** He at once took some officers and soldiers and ran down to the crowd. When the rioters saw the commander and his soldiers, they stopped beating Paul.

33 The commander came up and arrested him and ordered him to be bound with two chains. Then he asked who he was and what he had done. **34** Some in the crowd shouted one thing and some another, and since the commander could not get at the truth because of the uproar, he ordered that Paul be taken into the barracks. **35** When Paul reached the steps, the violence of the mob was so great he had to be carried by the soldiers. **36** The crowd that followed kept shouting, 'Get rid of him!'

Paul speaks to the crowd

37 As the soldiers were about to take Paul into the barracks, he asked the commander, 'May I say something to you?'

'Do you speak Greek?' he replied. **38** 'Aren't you the Egyptian who started a revolt and led four thousand terrorists out into the wilderness some time ago?'

39 Paul answered, 'I am a Jew, from Tarsus in Cilicia, a citizen of no ordinary city. Please let me speak to the people.'

40 After receiving the commander's permission, Paul stood on the steps and motioned to the crowd. When they were all

22 silent, he said to them in Aramaic*a*: **1** 'Brothers and fathers, listen now to my defence.'

2 When they heard him speak to them in Aramaic, they became very quiet.

Then Paul said: **3** 'I am a Jew, born in Tarsus of Cilicia, but brought up in this city. I studied under Gamaliel and was thoroughly trained in the law of our ancestors. I was just as zealous for God as any of you are today. **4** I persecuted the followers of this Way to their death, arresting both men and women and throwing them into prison, **5** as the high priest and all the Council can themselves testify. I even obtained letters from them to their associates in Damascus, and went there to bring these people as prisoners to Jerusalem to be punished.

6 'About noon as I came near Damascus, suddenly a bright light from heaven flashed around me. **7** I fell to the ground and heard a voice say to me, "Saul! Saul! Why do you persecute me?"

8 ' "Who are you, Lord?" I asked.

' "I am Jesus of Nazareth, whom you are persecuting," he replied. **9** My companions saw the light, but they did not understand the voice of him who was speaking to me.

10 ' "What shall I do, Lord?" I asked.

' "Get up," the Lord said, "and go into Damascus. There you will be told all that you have been assigned to do." **11** My companions led me by the hand into Damascus, because the brilliance of the light had blinded me.

12 'A man named Ananias came to see me. He was a devout observer of the law and highly respected by all the Jews living there. **13** He stood beside me and said, "Brother Saul, receive your sight!" And at that very moment I was able to see him.

14 'Then he said: "The God of our ancestors has chosen you to know his will and to see the Righteous One and to hear words from his mouth. **15** You will be his witness to all people of what you have seen and heard. **16** And now what are you

---

a 40 Or possibly *Hebrew*; also in 22:2

waiting for? Get up, be baptised and wash your sins away, calling on his name."

17 'When I returned to Jerusalem and was praying at the temple, I fell into a trance 18 and saw the Lord speaking to me. "Quick!" he said. "Leave Jerusalem immediately, because the people here will not accept your testimony about me."

19 '"Lord," I replied, "these people know that I went from one synagogue to another to imprison and beat those who believe in you. 20 And when the blood of your martyr*a* Stephen was shed, I stood there giving my approval and guarding the clothes of those who were killing him."

21 'Then the Lord said to me, "Go; I will send you far away to the Gentiles." '

Paul the Roman citizen

22 The crowd listened to Paul until he said this. Then they raised their voices and shouted, 'Rid the earth of him! He's not fit to live!'

23 As they were shouting and throwing off their cloaks and flinging dust into the air, 24 the commander ordered that Paul be taken into the barracks. He directed that he be flogged and interrogated in order to find out why the people were shouting at him like this. 25 As they stretched him out to flog him, Paul said to the centurion standing there, 'Is it legal for you to flog a Roman citizen who hasn't even been found guilty?'

26 When the centurion heard this, he went to the commander and reported it. 'What are you going to do?' he asked. 'This man is a Roman citizen.'

27 The commander went to Paul and asked, 'Tell me, are you a Roman citizen?'

'Yes, I am,' he answered.

28 Then the commander said, 'I had to pay a lot of money for my citizenship.'

'But I was born a citizen,' Paul replied.

29 Those who were about to interrogate him withdrew immediately. The commander himself was alarmed when he realised that he had put Paul, a Roman citizen, in chains.

Paul before the Sanhedrin

30 The commander wanted to find out exactly why Paul was being accused by the Jews. So the next day he released him and ordered the chief priests and all the members of the Sanhedrin to assemble. Then he brought Paul and set him before them.

23 Paul looked straight at the Sanhedrin and said, 'My brothers, I have fulfilled my duty to God in all good conscience to this day.' 2 At this the high priest Ananias ordered those standing near Paul to strike him on the mouth. 3 Then Paul said to him, 'God will strike you, you whitewashed wall! You sit there to judge me according to the law, yet you yourself violate the law by commanding that I be struck!'

4 Those who were standing near Paul said, 'How dare you insult God's high priest!'

5 Paul replied, 'Brothers, I did not realise that he was the high priest; for it is written: "Do not speak evil about the ruler of your people."*a*'

6 Then Paul, knowing that some of them were Sadducees and the others Pharisees, called out in the Sanhedrin, 'My brothers, I am a Pharisee, descended from Pharisees. I stand on trial because of the hope of the resurrection of the dead.' 7 When he said this, a dispute broke out between the Pharisees and the Sadducees, and the assembly was divided. 8 (The Sadducees say that there is no resurrection, and that there are neither angels nor spirits, but the Pharisees believe all these things.)

9 There was a great uproar, and some of the teachers of the law who were Pharisees stood up and argued vigorously. 'We find nothing wrong with this man,' they said. 'What if a spirit or an angel has spoken to him?' 10 The dispute became so violent that the commander was afraid Paul would be torn to pieces by them. He ordered the troops to go down and take him away from them by force and bring him into the barracks.

---

a 20 Or *witness*

a 5 Exodus 22:28

11 The following night the Lord stood near Paul and said, 'Take courage! As you have testified about me in Jerusalem, so you must also testify in Rome.'

The plot to kill Paul

12 The next morning some Jews formed a conspiracy and bound themselves with an oath not to eat or drink until they had killed Paul. **13** More than forty men were involved in this plot. **14** They went to the chief priests and the elders and said, 'We have taken a solemn oath not to eat anything until we have killed Paul. **15** Now then, you and the Sanhedrin petition the commander to bring him before you on the pretext of wanting more accurate information about his case. We are ready to kill him before he gets here.'

16 But when the son of Paul's sister heard of this plot, he went into the barracks and told Paul.

17 Then Paul called one of the centurions and said, 'Take this young man to the commander; he has something to tell him.' **18** So he took him to the commander.

The centurion said, 'Paul, the prisoner, sent for me and asked me to bring this young man to you because he has something to tell you.'

19 The commander took the young man by the hand, drew him aside and asked, 'What is it you want to tell me?'

20 He said: 'Some Jews have agreed to ask you to bring Paul before the Sanhedrin tomorrow on the pretext of wanting more accurate information about him. **21** Don't give in to them, because more than forty of them are waiting in ambush for him. They have taken an oath not to eat or drink until they have killed him. They are ready now, waiting for your consent to their request.'

22 The commander dismissed the young man with this warning: 'Don't tell anyone that you have reported this to me.'

Paul transferred to Caesarea

23 Then he called two of his centurions and ordered them, 'Get ready a detachment of two hundred soldiers, seventy horsemen and two hundred spearmen[b] to go to Caesarea at nine tonight. **24** Provide horses for Paul so that he may be taken safely to Governor Felix.'

25 He wrote a letter as follows:

26 Claudius Lysias,

To His Excellency, Governor Felix:

Greetings.

27 This man was seized by the Jews and they were about to kill him, but I came with my troops and rescued him, for I had learned that he is a Roman citizen. **28** I wanted to know why they were accusing him, so I brought him to their Sanhedrin. **29** I found that the accusation had to do with questions about their law, but there was no charge against him that deserved death or imprisonment. **30** When I was informed of a plot to be carried out against the man, I sent him to you at once. I also ordered his accusers to present to you their case against him.

31 So the soldiers, carrying out their orders, took Paul with them during the night and brought him as far as Antipatris. **32** The next day they let the cavalry go on with him, while they returned to the barracks. **33** When the cavalry arrived in Caesarea, they delivered the letter to the governor and handed Paul over to him. **34** The governor read the letter and asked what province he was from. Learning that he was from Cilicia, **35** he said, 'I will hear your case when your accusers get here.' Then he ordered that Paul be kept under guard in Herod's palace.

Paul's trial before Felix

24 Five days later the high priest Ananias went down to Caesarea with some of the elders and a lawyer named Tertullus, and they brought their charges

---

b 23 The meaning of the Greek for this word is uncertain.

against Paul before the governor. ²When Paul was called in, Tertullus presented his case before Felix: 'We have enjoyed a long period of peace under you, and your foresight has brought about reforms in this nation. ³Everywhere and in every way, most excellent Felix, we acknowledge this with profound gratitude. ⁴But in order not to weary you further, I would request that you be kind enough to hear us briefly.

⁵'We have found this man to be a troublemaker, stirring up riots among the Jews all over the world. He is a ringleader of the Nazarene sect ⁶and even tried to desecrate the temple; so we seized him. [7]ᵃ ⁸By examining him yourself you will be able to learn the truth about all these charges we are bringing against him.'

⁹The other Jews joined in the accusation, asserting that these things were true.

¹⁰When the governor motioned for him to speak, Paul replied: 'I know that for a number of years you have been a judge over this nation; so I gladly make my defence. ¹¹You can easily verify that no more than twelve days ago I went up to Jerusalem to worship. ¹²My accusers did not find me arguing with anyone at the temple, or stirring up a crowd in the synagogues or anywhere else in the city. ¹³And they cannot prove to you the charges they are now making against me. ¹⁴However, I admit that I worship the God of our ancestors as a follower of the Way, which they call a sect. I believe everything that is in accordance with the Law and that is written in the Prophets, ¹⁵and I have the same hope in God as these men themselves have, that there will be a resurrection of both the righteous and the wicked. ¹⁶So I strive always to keep my conscience clear before God and man.

¹⁷'After an absence of several years, I came to Jerusalem to bring my people gifts for the poor and to present offerings. ¹⁸I was ceremonially clean when they found me in the temple courts doing this. There was no crowd with me, nor was I involved in any disturbance. ¹⁹But there are some Jews from the province of Asia, who ought to be here before you and bring charges if they have anything against me. ²⁰Or these who are here should state what crime they found in me when I stood before the Sanhedrin – ²¹unless it was this one thing I shouted as I stood in their presence: "It is concerning the resurrection of the dead that I am on trial before you today." '

²²Then Felix, who was well acquainted with the Way, adjourned the proceedings. 'When Lysias the commander comes,' he said, 'I will decide your case.' ²³He ordered the centurion to keep Paul under guard but to give him some freedom and permit his friends to take care of his needs.

²⁴Several days later Felix came with his wife Drusilla, who was Jewish. He sent for Paul and listened to him as he spoke about faith in Christ Jesus. ²⁵As Paul talked about righteousness, self-control and the judgment to come, Felix was afraid and said, 'That's enough for now! You may leave. When I find it convenient, I will send for you.' ²⁶At the same time he was hoping that Paul would offer him a bribe, so he sent for him frequently and talked with him.

²⁷When two years had passed, Felix was succeeded by Porcius Festus, but because Felix wanted to grant a favour to the Jews, he left Paul in prison.

Paul's trial before Festus

25 Three days after arriving in the province, Festus went up from Caesarea to Jerusalem, ²where the chief priests and the Jewish leaders appeared before him and presented the charges against Paul. ³They requested Festus, as a favour to them, to have Paul transferred to Jerusalem, for they were preparing an ambush to kill him along the way. ⁴Festus answered, 'Paul is being held at Caesarea, and I myself am going there soon. ⁵Let some of your leaders come with me, and if the man has done anything wrong, they can press charges against him there.'

⁶After spending eight or ten days with

ᵃ 6-8 Some manuscripts include here *him, and we would have judged him in accordance with our law.* ⁷*But the commander Lysias came and took him from us with much violence,* ⁸*ordering his accusers to come before you.*

them, Festus went down to Caesarea. The next day he convened the court and ordered that Paul be brought before him. **7** When Paul came in, the Jews who had come down from Jerusalem stood round him. They brought many serious charges against him, but they could not prove them.

8 Then Paul made his defence: 'I have done nothing wrong against the Jewish law or against the temple or against Caesar.'

9 Festus, wishing to do the Jews a favour, said to Paul, 'Are you willing to go up to Jerusalem and stand trial before me there on these charges?'

10 Paul answered: 'I am now standing before Caesar's court, where I ought to be tried. I have not done any wrong to the Jews, as you yourself know very well. **11** If, however, I am guilty of doing anything deserving death, I do not refuse to die. But if the charges brought against me by these Jews are not true, no one has the right to hand me over to them. I appeal to Caesar!'

12 After Festus had conferred with his council, he declared: 'You have appealed to Caesar. To Caesar you will go!'

Festus consults King Agrippa

13 A few days later King Agrippa and Bernice arrived at Caesarea to pay their respects to Festus. **14** Since they were spending many days there, Festus discussed Paul's case with the king. He said: 'There is a man here whom Felix left as a prisoner. **15** When I went to Jerusalem, the chief priests and the elders of the Jews brought charges against him and asked that he be condemned.

16 'I told them that it is not the Roman custom to hand over anyone before they have faced their accusers and have had an opportunity to defend themselves against the charges. **17** When they came here with me, I did not delay the case, but convened the court the next day and ordered the man to be brought in. **18** When his accusers got up to speak, they did not charge him with any of the crimes I had expected. **19** Instead, they had some points

of dispute with him about their own religion and about a dead man named Jesus whom Paul claimed was alive. **20** I was at a loss how to investigate such matters; so I asked if he would be willing to go to Jerusalem and stand trial there on these charges. **21** But when Paul made his appeal to be held over for the Emperor's decision, I ordered him to be held until I could send him to Caesar.'

22 Then Agrippa said to Festus, 'I would like to hear this man myself.'

He replied, 'Tomorrow you will hear him.'

Paul before Agrippa

23 The next day Agrippa and Bernice came with great pomp and entered the audience room with the high-ranking military officers and the prominent men of the city. At the command of Festus, Paul was brought in. **24** Festus said: 'King Agrippa, and all who are present with us, you see this man! The whole Jewish community has petitioned me about him in Jerusalem and here in Caesarea, shouting that he ought not to live any longer. **25** I found he had done nothing deserving of death, but because he made his appeal to the Emperor I decided to send him to Rome. **26** But I have nothing definite to write to His Majesty about him. Therefore I have brought him before all of you, and especially before you, King Agrippa, so that as a result of this investigation I may have something to write. **27** For I think it is unreasonable to send a prisoner on to Rome without specifying the charges against him.'

26 Then Agrippa said to Paul, 'You have permission to speak for yourself.'

So Paul motioned with his hand and began his defence: **2** 'King Agrippa, I consider myself fortunate to stand before you today as I make my defence against all the accusations of the Jews, **3** and especially so because you are well acquainted with all the Jewish customs and controversies. Therefore, I beg you to listen to me patiently.

4 'The Jewish people all know the way I

have lived ever since I was a child, from the beginning of my life in my own country, and also in Jerusalem. 5 They have known me for a long time and can testify, if they are willing, that I conformed to the strictest sect of our religion, living as a Pharisee. 6 And now it is because of my hope in what God has promised our ancestors that I am on trial today. 7 This is the promise our twelve tribes are hoping to see fulfilled as they earnestly serve God day and night. King Agrippa, it is because of this hope that these Jews are accusing me. 8 Why should any of you consider it incredible that God raises the dead?

9 'I too was convinced that I ought to do all that was possible to oppose the name of Jesus of Nazareth. 10 And that is just what I did in Jerusalem. On the authority of the chief priests I put many of the Lord's people in prison, and when they were put to death, I cast my vote against them. 11 Many a time I went from one synagogue to another to have them punished, and I tried to force them to blaspheme. I was so obsessed with persecuting them that I even hunted them down in foreign cities.

12 'On one of these journeys I was going to Damascus with the authority and commission of the chief priests. 13 About noon, King Agrippa, as I was on the road, I saw a light from heaven, brighter than the sun, blazing around me and my companions. 14 We all fell to the ground, and I heard a voice saying to me in Aramaic,a "Saul, Saul, why do you persecute me? It is hard for you to kick against the goads."

15 'Then I asked, "Who are you, Lord?"

'"I am Jesus, whom you are persecuting," the Lord replied. 16 "Now get up and stand on your feet. I have appeared to you to appoint you as a servant and as a witness of what you have seen and will see of me. 17 I will rescue you from your own people and from the Gentiles. I am sending you to them 18 to open their eyes and turn them from darkness to light, and from the power of Satan to God, so that they may receive forgiveness of sins and a

place among those who are sanctified by faith in me."

19 'So then, King Agrippa, I was not disobedient to the vision from heaven. 20 First to those in Damascus, then to those in Jerusalem and in all Judea, and then to the Gentiles, I preached that they should repent and turn to God and demonstrate their repentance by their deeds. 21 That is why some Jews seized me in the temple courts and tried to kill me. 22 But God has helped me to this very day; so I stand here and testify to small and great alike. I am saying nothing beyond what the prophets and Moses said would happen – 23 that the Messiah would suffer and, as the first to rise from the dead, would bring the message of light to his own people and to the Gentiles.'

24 At this point Festus interrupted Paul's defence. 'You are out of your mind, Paul!' he shouted. 'Your great learning is driving you insane.'

25 'I am not insane, most excellent Festus,' Paul replied. 'What I am saying is true and reasonable. 26 The king is familiar with these things, and I can speak freely to him. I am convinced that none of this has escaped his notice, because it was not done in a corner. 27 King Agrippa, do you believe the prophets? I know you do.'

28 Then Agrippa said to Paul, 'Do you think that in such a short time you can persuade me to be a Christian?'

29 Paul replied, 'Short time or long – I pray to God that not only you but all who are listening to me today may become what I am, except for these chains.'

30 The king rose, and with him the governor and Bernice and those sitting with them. 31 After they left the room, they began saying to one another, 'This man is not doing anything that deserves death or imprisonment.'

32 Agrippa said to Festus, 'This man could have been set free if he had not appealed to Caesar.'

Paul sails for Rome

27 When it was decided that we would sail for Italy, Paul and some other prisoners were handed over to a

---

a 14 Or Hebrew

centurion named Julius, who belonged to the Imperial Regiment. ²We boarded a ship from Adramyttium about to sail for ports along the coast of the province of Asia, and we put out to sea. Aristarchus, a Macedonian from Thessalonica, was with us.

³The next day we landed at Sidon; and Julius, in kindness to Paul, allowed him to go to his friends so they might provide for his needs. ⁴From there we put out to sea again and passed to the lee of Cyprus because the winds were against us. ⁵When we had sailed across the open sea off the coast of Cilicia and Pamphylia, we landed at Myra in Lycia. ⁶There the centurion found an Alexandrian ship sailing for Italy and put us on board. ⁷We made slow headway for many days and had difficulty arriving off Cnidus. When the wind did not allow us to hold our course, we sailed to the lee of Crete, opposite Salmone. ⁸We moved along the coast with difficulty and came to a place called Fair Havens, near the town of Lasea.

⁹Much time had been lost, and sailing had already become dangerous because by now it was after the Day of Atonement.ᵃ

---

a 9 That is, Yom Kippur

EVANGELISM 5

Short or long

You have probably heard a story like this: Bob casually asks Tom to church and he immediately says 'yes' and becomes a Christian during the first worship song. This is great, but it can be a little discouraging if *your* friend is totally disinterested. However, all our friends are different, which means their journey to God is going to be unique.

I find Acts 26:28–29 really encouraging. Paul's words show that once we have accepted that our friend coming to faith in God is the most important thing, it actually doesn't matter if the journey is long or short. In some cases, we will invite friends to church, or talk to them about Jesus, and they will connect very quickly with God. Some of our other friends may be a long way off. That's OK. We just need to prepare ourselves for it being a longer journey.

As Paul says, we have no idea whether the journey is going to be long or short. It may be a long trek with our friend and therefore it's important to be fully equipped. I remember being involved in an outdoor activity that included quite a long trek. One young person turned up in flip-flops (in my experience, only my Australian friend Tom can climb mountains in flip-flops)! If we're going on a long journey with our friends towards God, we need to spend time with them, asking and answering questions and making sure that we actively listen to them.

Put simply, when you ask your friend to church for the first time and they don't come, remember that the journey is longer for some people. Keep travelling with them. You may find that the end point is nearer than you think! We do what we can, and trust God to do his work in them.

Mark Ritchie

 Mark 2:1–12   Luke 10:30–37 ⏩

So Paul warned them, [10]'Men, I can see that our voyage is going to be disastrous and bring great loss to ship and cargo, and to our own lives also.' [11] But the centurion, instead of listening to what Paul said, followed the advice of the pilot and of the owner of the ship. [12] Since the harbour was unsuitable to winter in, the majority decided that we should sail on, hoping to reach Phoenix and winter there. This was a harbour in Crete, facing both south-west and north-west.

The storm

[13] When a gentle south wind began to blow, they saw their opportunity; so they weighed anchor and sailed along the shore of Crete. [14] Before very long, a wind of hurricane force, called the 'North-Easter', swept down from the island. [15] The ship was caught by the storm and could not head into the wind; so we gave way to it and were driven along. [16] As we passed to the lee of a small island called Cauda, we were hardly able to make the lifeboat secure, [17] so the men hoisted it aboard. Then they passed ropes under the ship itself to hold it together. Because they were afraid they would run aground on the sand-bars of Syrtis, they lowered the sea anchor[b] and let the ship be driven along. [18] We took such a violent battering from the storm that the next day they began to throw the cargo overboard. [19] On the third day, they threw the ship's tackle overboard with their own hands. [20] When neither sun nor stars appeared for many days and the storm continued raging, we finally gave up all hope of being saved.

[21] After they had gone a long time without food, Paul stood up before them and said: 'Men, you should have taken my advice not to sail from Crete; then you would have spared yourselves this damage and loss. [22] But now I urge you to keep up your courage, because not one of you will be lost; only the ship will be destroyed. [23] Last night an angel of the God to whom I belong and whom I serve stood beside me [24] and said, "Do not be afraid, Paul.

You must stand trial before Caesar; and God has graciously given you the lives of all who sail with you." [25] So keep up your courage, men, for I have faith in God that it will happen just as he told me. [26] Nevertheless, we must run aground on some island.'

The shipwreck

[27] On the fourteenth night we were still being driven across the Adriatic[c] Sea, when about midnight the sailors sensed they were approaching land. [28] They took soundings and found that the water was forty metres deep. A short time later they took soundings again and found it was thirty metres deep. [29] Fearing that we would be dashed against the rocks, they dropped four anchors from the stern and prayed for daylight. [30] In an attempt to escape from the ship, the sailors let the lifeboat down into the sea, pretending they were going to lower some anchors from the bow. [31] Then Paul said to the centurion and the soldiers, 'Unless these men stay with the ship, you cannot be saved.' [32] So the soldiers cut the ropes that held the lifeboat and let it drift away.

[33] Just before dawn Paul urged them all to eat. 'For the last fourteen days,' he said, 'you have been in constant suspense and have gone without food – you haven't eaten anything. [34] Now I urge you to take some food. You need it to survive. Not one of you will lose a single hair from his head.' [35] After he said this, he took some bread and gave thanks to God in front of them all. Then he broke it and began to eat. [36] They were all encouraged and ate some food themselves. [37] Altogether there were 276 of us on board. [38] When they had eaten as much as they wanted, they lightened the ship by throwing the grain into the sea.

[39] When daylight came, they did not recognise the land, but they saw a bay with a sandy beach, where they decided to run the ship aground if they could. [40] Cutting

---

c 27 In ancient times the name referred to an area extending well south of Italy.

loose the anchors, they left them in the sea and at the same time untied the ropes that held the rudders. Then they hoisted the foresail to the wind and made for the beach. ⁴¹ But the ship struck a sand-bar and ran aground. The bow stuck fast and would not move, and the stern was broken to pieces by the pounding of the surf.

⁴² The soldiers planned to kill the prisoners to prevent any of them from swimming away and escaping. ⁴³ But the centurion wanted to spare Paul's life and kept them from carrying out their plan. He ordered those who could swim to jump overboard first and get to land. ⁴⁴ The rest were to get there on planks or on other pieces of the ship. In this way everyone reached land safely.

Paul ashore on Malta

28 Once safely on shore, we found out that the island was called Malta. ² The islanders showed us unusual kindness. They built a fire and welcomed us all because it was raining and cold. ³ Paul gathered a pile of brushwood and, as he put it on the fire, a viper, driven out by the heat, fastened itself on his hand. ⁴ When the islanders saw the snake hanging from his hand, they said to each other, 'This man must be a murderer; for though he escaped from the sea, the goddess Justice has not allowed him to live.' ⁵ But Paul shook the snake off into the fire and suffered no ill effects. ⁶ The people expected him to swell up or suddenly fall dead; but after waiting a long time and seeing nothing unusual happen to him, they changed their minds and said he was a god.

⁷ There was an estate near by that belonged to Publius, the chief official of the island. He welcomed us to his home and showed us generous hospitality for three days. ⁸ His father was ill in bed, suffering from fever and dysentery. Paul went in to see him and, after prayer, placed his hands on him and healed him. ⁹ When this had happened, the rest of those on the island who were ill came and were cured. ¹⁰ They honoured us in many ways; and when we were ready to sail, they furnished us with the supplies we needed.

Paul's arrival at Rome

¹¹ After three months we put out to sea in a ship that had wintered in the island – it was an Alexandrian ship with the figurehead of the twin gods Castor and Pollux. ¹² We put in at Syracuse and stayed there three days. ¹³ From there we set sail and arrived at Rhegium. The next day the south wind came up, and on the following day we reached Puteoli. ¹⁴ There we found some brothers and sisters who invited us to spend a week with them. And so we came to Rome. ¹⁵ The brothers and sisters there had heard that we were coming, and they travelled as far as the Forum of Appius and the Three Taverns to meet us. At the sight of these people Paul thanked God and was encouraged. ¹⁶ When we got to Rome, Paul was allowed to live by himself, with a soldier to guard him.

Paul preaches at Rome under guard

¹⁷ Three days later he called together the local Jewish leaders. When they had assembled, Paul said to them: 'My brothers, although I have done nothing against our people or against the customs of our ancestors, I was arrested in Jerusalem and handed over to the Romans. ¹⁸ They examined me and wanted to release me, because I was not guilty of any crime deserving death. ¹⁹ The Jews objected, so I was compelled to make an appeal to Caesar. I certainly did not intend to bring any charge against my own people. ²⁰ For this reason I have asked to see you and talk with you. It is because of the hope of Israel that I am bound with this chain.'

²¹ They replied, 'We have not received any letters from Judea concerning you, and none of our people who have come from there has reported or said anything bad about you. ²² But we want to hear what your views are, for we know that people everywhere are talking against this sect.'

²³ They arranged to meet Paul on a certain day, and came in even larger numbers to the place where he was staying. He witnessed to them from morning till evening, explaining about the kingdom of God, and from the Law of Moses and from the Prophets he tried to persuade them

about Jesus. 24Some were convinced by what he said, but others would not believe. 25They disagreed among themselves and began to leave after Paul had made this final statement: 'The Holy Spirit spoke the truth to your ancestors when he said through Isaiah the prophet:

26' "Go to this people and say,
  'You will be ever hearing but never understanding;
    you will be ever seeing but never perceiving.'
27 For this people's heart has become calloused;
    they hardly hear with their ears,
    and they have closed their eyes.
  Otherwise they might see with their eyes,

hear with their ears,
  understand with their hearts
and turn, and I would heal them.'' a

28 'Therefore I want you to know that God's salvation has been sent to the Gentiles, and they will listen!' [29] b

30 For two whole years Paul stayed there in his own rented house and welcomed all who came to see him. 31 He proclaimed the kingdom of God and taught about the Lord Jesus Christ – with all boldness and without hindrance!

---

a 27 Isaiah 6:9,10 (see Septuagint)
b 29 Some manuscripts include here *After he said this, the Jews left, arguing vigorously among themselves.*

ROMANS

DATE

This letter was written in AD 57

AUTHOR

The apostle Paul

WHAT'S IT ALL ABOUT?

Paul wrote this letter to the church in Rome, a church he desperately wanted to visit. Rome was the centre of the empire ruling the world at that time and it was important that the Christians there grasped the gospel with both hands and continued spreading its message. Unable to get to Rome himself, Paul wrote to the Christians there to lay out his teaching. He plainly set out the gospel, speaking about God's plan for salvation and how this was available to everyone, whether they were Jews or Gentiles. He emphasised that everyone is in need of God's grace and forgiveness. As Paul hadn't visited the church, this letter doesn't contain many personal details – it's more of a teaching letter, explaining the gospel and urging readers to live out their faith in the church and in the world.

WHY SHOULD WE READ IT?

- Because it provides a great background to the Christian faith.

- To read how nothing can separate us from God's love (Romans 8).

- To find reasons to rejoice in suffering (Romans 5) and to see that God is always working for our good even when life is hard (Romans 8).

- To be reminded to offer ourselves as sacrifices to God (Romans 12).

Andy Croft with Liza Hoeksma

1 Paul, a servant of Christ Jesus, called to be an apostle and set apart for the gospel of God – 2 the gospel he promised beforehand through his prophets in the Holy Scriptures 3 regarding his Son, who as to his earthly life*a* was a descendant of David, 4 and who through the Spirit of holiness was appointed the Son of God in power*b* by his resurrection from the dead: Jesus Christ our Lord. 5 Through him we received grace and apostleship to call all the Gentiles to the obedience that comes from*c* faith for his name's sake. 6 And you also are among those Gentiles who are called to belong to Jesus Christ.

7 To all in Rome who are loved by God and called to be his holy people:

Grace and peace to you from God our Father and from the Lord Jesus Christ.

Paul's longing to visit Rome

8 First, I thank my God through Jesus Christ for all of you, because your faith is being reported all over the world. 9 God, whom I serve in my spirit in preaching the gospel of his Son, is my witness how constantly I remember you 10 in my prayers at all times; and I pray that now at last by God's will the way may be opened for me to come to you.

11 I long to see you so that I may impart to you some spiritual gift to make you strong – 12 that is, that you and I may be mutually encouraged by each other's faith. 13 I do not want you to be unaware, brothers and sisters,*d* that I planned many times to come to you (but have been prevented from doing so until now) in order that I might have a harvest among you, just as I have had among the other Gentiles.

14 I am a debtor both to Greeks and non-Greeks, both to the wise and the foolish.

15 That is why I am so eager to preach the gospel also to you who are in Rome.

16 For I am not ashamed of the gospel, because it is the power of God that brings salvation to everyone who believes: first to the Jew, then to the Gentile. 17 For in the gospel the righteousness of God is revealed – a righteousness that is by faith from first to last,*e* just as it is written: 'The righteous will live by faith.'*f*

God's wrath against sinful humanity

18 The wrath of God is being revealed from heaven against all the godlessness and wickedness of people, who suppress the truth by their wickedness, 19 since what may be known about God is plain to them, because God has made it plain to them. 20 For since the creation of the world God's invisible qualities – his eternal power and divine nature – have been clearly seen, being understood from what has been made, so that people are without excuse.

21 For although they knew God, they neither glorified him as God nor gave thanks to him, but their thinking became futile and their foolish hearts were darkened. 22 Although they claimed to be wise, they became fools 23 and exchanged the glory of the immortal God for images made to look like a mortal human being and birds and animals and reptiles.

24 Therefore God gave them over in the sinful desires of their hearts to sexual impurity for the degrading of their bodies with one another. 25 They exchanged the truth about God for a lie, and worshipped and served created things rather than the Creator – who is for ever praised. Amen.

26 Because of this, God gave them over to shameful lusts. Even their women exchanged natural sexual relations for unnatural ones. 27 In the same way the men also abandoned natural relations with women and were inflamed with lust for one another. Men committed shameful acts with other men, and received in themselves the due penalty for their error.

28 Furthermore, just as they did not

---

a 3 Or *who according to the flesh*
b 4 Or *was declared with power to be the Son of God*
c 5 Or *that is*
d 13 The Greek word for *brothers and sisters (adelphoi)* refers here to believers, both men and women, as part of God's family; also in 7:1, 4; 8:12, 29; 10:1; 11:25; 12:1; 15:14, 30; 16:14, 17.

e 17 Or *is from faith to faith*
f 17 Hab. 2:4

think it worth while to retain the knowledge of God, so God gave them over to a depraved mind, so that they do what ought not to be done. ²⁹They have become filled with every kind of wickedness, evil, greed and depravity. They are full of envy, murder, strife, deceit and malice. They are gossips, ³⁰slanderers, God-haters, insolent, arrogant and boastful; they invent ways of doing evil; they disobey their parents; ³¹they have no understanding, no fidelity, no love, no mercy. ³²Although they know God's righteous decree that those who do such things deserve death, they not only continue to do these very things but also approve of those who practise them.

God's righteous judgment

2 You, therefore, have no excuse, you who pass judgment on someone else, for at whatever point you judge another, you are condemning yourself, because you who pass judgment do the same things. ²Now we know that God's judgment against those who do such things is based on truth. ³So when you, a mere human being, pass judgment on them and yet do the same things, do you think you will escape God's judgment? ⁴Or do you show contempt for the riches of his kindness, forbearance and patience, not realising that God's kindness is intended to lead you to repentance?

⁵But because of your stubbornness and your unrepentant heart, you are storing up wrath against yourself for the day of God's wrath, when his righteous judgment will be revealed. ⁶God 'will repay each person according to what they have done.'[a] ⁷To those who by persistence in doing good seek glory, honour and immortality, he will give eternal life. ⁸But for those who are self-seeking and who reject the truth and follow evil, there will be wrath and anger. ⁹There will be trouble and distress for every human being who does evil: first for the Jew, then for the Gentile; ¹⁰but glory, honour and peace for everyone who does good: first for the Jew, then for the

Gentile. ¹¹For God does not show favouritism.

¹²All who sin apart from the law will also perish apart from the law, and all who sin under the law will be judged by the law. ¹³For it is not those who hear the law who are righteous in God's sight, but it is those who obey the law who will be declared righteous. ¹⁴(Indeed, when Gentiles, who do not have the law, do by nature things required by the law, they are a law for themselves, even though they do not have the law. ¹⁵They show that the requirements of the law are written on their hearts, their consciences also bearing witness, and their thoughts sometimes accusing them and at other times even defending them.) ¹⁶This will take place on the day when God judges people's secrets through Jesus Christ, as my gospel declares.

The Jews and the law

¹⁷Now you, if you call yourself a Jew; if you rely on the law and boast in God; ¹⁸if you know his will and approve of what is superior because you are instructed by the law; ¹⁹if you are convinced that you are a guide for the blind, a light for those who are in the dark, ²⁰an instructor of the foolish, a teacher of little children, because you have in the law the embodiment of knowledge and truth – ²¹you, then, who teach others, do you not teach yourself? You who preach against stealing, do you steal? ²²You who say that people should not commit adultery, do you commit adultery? You who abhor idols, do you rob temples? ²³You who boast in the law, do you dishonour God by breaking the law? ²⁴As it is written: 'God's name is blasphemed among the Gentiles because of you.'[b]

²⁵Circumcision has value if you observe the law, but if you break the law, you have become as though you had not been circumcised. ²⁶So then, if those who are not circumcised keep the law's requirements, will they not be regarded as though they were circumcised? ²⁷The one who is not circumcised physically and yet obeys the law will condemn you who, even though

---

a 6 Psalm 62:12; Prov. 24:12   *b* 24 Isaiah 52:5 (see Septuagint); Ezek. 36:20,22 you have the^c written code and circumcision, are a law-breaker.

28 A person is not a Jew who is one only outwardly, nor is circumcision merely outward and physical. 29 No, a person is a Jew who is one inwardly; and circumcision is circumcision of the heart, by the Spirit, not by the written code. Such a person's praise is not from other people, but from God.

God's faithfulness

3 What advantage, then, is there in being a Jew, or what value is there in circumcision? 2 Much in every way! First of all, the Jews have been entrusted with the very words of God.

3 What if some were unfaithful? Will their unfaithfulness nullify God's faithfulness? 4 Not at all! Let God be true, and every human being a liar. As it is written:

'So that you may be proved right when
　　you speak
　and prevail when you judge.'^a

5 But if our unrighteousness brings out God's righteousness more clearly, what shall we say? That God is unjust in bringing his wrath on us? (I am using a human argument.) 6 Certainly not! If that were so, how could God judge the world? 7 Someone might argue, 'If my falsehood enhances God's truthfulness and so increases his glory, why am I still condemned as a sinner?' 8 Why not say – as some slanderously claim that we say – 'Let us do evil that good may result'? Their condemnation is just!

No one is righteous

9 What shall we conclude then? Do we have any advantage? Not at all! For we have already made the charge that Jews and Gentiles alike are all under the power of sin. 10 As it is written:

'There is no one righteous, not even
　　one;
11 　there is no one who understands;

there is no one who seeks God.
12 All have turned away,
　they have together become
　　worthless;
　there is no one who does good,
　　not even one.'^b
13 'Their throats are open graves;
　their tongues practise deceit.'^c
'The poison of vipers is on their lips.'^d
14 　'Their mouths are full of cursing and
　　bitterness.'^e
15 'Their feet are swift to shed blood;
16 　ruin and misery mark their ways,
17 and the way of peace they do not
　　know.'^f
18 　'There is no fear of God before their
　　eyes.'^g

FACT

CHRIST

'Christ' isn't Jesus' surname: it's his job title. The word 'Christ' comes from the Greek word *christos*, which means 'anointed'. It was the word used to translate the Hebrew word *Messiah*. So when we say 'Jesus Christ', we're saying 'Jesus the Anointed One'.

19 Now we know that whatever the law says, it says to those who are under the law, so that every mouth may be silenced and the whole world held accountable to God. 20 Therefore no one will be declared righteous in God's sight by the works of the law; rather, through the law we become conscious of our sin.

c 27 Or *who, by means of a*
a 4 Psalm 51:4

b 12 Psalms 14:1-3; 53:1-3; Eccles. 7:20
c 13 Psalm 5:9
d 13 Psalm 140:3
e 14 Psalm 10:7 (see Septuagint)
f 17 Isaiah 59:7,8
g 18 Psalm 36:1

Righteousness through faith

21 But now apart from the law the righteousness of God has been made known, to which the Law and the Prophets testify. 22 This righteousness is given through faith in[h] Jesus Christ to all who believe. There is no difference between Jew and Gentile, 23 for all have sinned and fall short of the glory of God, 24 and all are justified freely by his grace through the redemption that came by Christ Jesus. 25 God presented Christ as a sacrifice of atonement,[i] through the shedding of his blood – to be received by faith. He did this to demonstrate his righteousness, because in his forbearance he had left the sins committed beforehand unpunished 26 – he did it to demonstrate his righteousness at the present time, so as to be just and the one who justifies those who have faith in Jesus.

27 Where, then, is boasting? It is excluded. Because of what law? The law that requires works? No, because of the 'law' that requires faith. 28 For we maintain that a person is justified by faith apart from the works of the law. 29 Or is God the God of Jews only? Is he not the God of Gentiles too? Yes, of Gentiles too, 30 since there is only one God, who will justify the circumcised by faith and the uncircumcised through that same faith. 31 Do we, then, nullify the law by this faith? Not at all! Rather, we uphold the law.

Abraham justified by faith

4 What then shall we say that Abraham, our forefather according to the flesh, discovered in this matter? 2 If, in fact, Abraham was justified by works, he had something to boast about – but not before God. 3 What does Scripture say? 'Abraham believed God, and it was credited to him as righteousness.'[a]

4 Now to the one who works, wages are not credited as a gift but as an obligation. 5 However, to the one who does not work but trusts God who justifies the ungodly,

their faith is credited as righteousness. 6 David says the same thing when he speaks of the blessedness of the one to whom God credits righteousness apart from works:

7 'Blessed are those
    whose transgressions are forgiven,
    whose sins are covered.
8 Blessed is the one
    whose sin the Lord will never count
        against them.'[b]

9 Is this blessedness only for the circumcised, or also for the uncircumcised? We have been saying that Abraham's faith was credited to him as righteousness. 10 Under what circumstances was it credited? Was it after he was circumcised, or before? It was not after, but before! 11 And he received circumcision as a sign, a seal of the righteousness that he had by faith while he was still uncircumcised. So then, he is the father of all who believe but have not been circumcised, in order that righteousness might be credited to them. 12 And he is then also the father of the circumcised who not only are circumcised but who also follow in the footsteps of the faith that our father Abraham had before he was circumcised.

13 It was not through the law that Abraham and his offspring received the promise that he would be heir of the world, but through the righteousness that comes by faith. 14 For if those who depend on the law are heirs, faith means nothing and the promise is worthless, 15 because the law brings wrath. And where there is no law there is no transgression.

16 Therefore, the promise comes by faith, so that it may be by grace and may be guaranteed to all Abraham's offspring – not only to those who are of the law but also to those who have the faith of Abraham. He is the father of us all. 17 As it is written: 'I have made you a father of many nations.'[c] He is our father in the sight of God, in whom he believed – the God who gives life to the dead and calls into being things that were not.

---

h 22   Or *through the faithfulness of*
i 25   The Greek for *sacrifice of atonement* refers to the atonement cover on the ark of the covenant (see Lev. 16:15,16).
a 3   Gen. 15:6; also in verse 22

b 8   Psalm 32:1,2
c 17   Gen. 17:5

18Against all hope, Abraham in hope believed and so became the father of many nations, just as it had been said to him, 'So shall your offspring be.'*d* **19**Without weakening in his faith, he faced the fact that his body was as good as dead – since he was about a hundred years old – and that Sarah's womb was also dead. **20**Yet he did not waver through unbelief regarding the promise of God, but was strengthened in his faith and gave glory to God, **21**being fully persuaded that God had power to do what he had promised. **22**This is why 'it was credited to him as righteousness.' **23**The words 'it was credited to him' were written not for him alone, **24**but also for us, to whom God will credit righteousness – for us who believe in him who raised Jesus our Lord from the dead. **25**He was delivered over to death for our sins and was raised to life for our justification.

Peace and hope

5 Therefore, since we have been justified through faith, we*a* have peace with God through our Lord Jesus Christ, **2**through whom we have gained access by faith into this grace in which we now stand. And we*b* boast in the hope of the glory of God. **3**Not only so, but we*b* also glory in our sufferings, because we know that suffering produces perseverance; **4**perseverance, character; and character, hope. **5**And hope does not put us to shame, because God's love has been poured out into our hearts through the Holy Spirit, who has been given to us.

6You see, at just the right time, when we were still powerless, Christ died for the ungodly. **7**Very rarely will anyone die for a righteous person, though for a good person someone might possibly dare to die. **8**But God demonstrates his own love for us in this: while we were still sinners, Christ died for us.

9Since we have now been justified by his blood, how much more shall we be saved from God's wrath through him!

10For if, while we were God's enemies, we were reconciled to him through the death of his Son, how much more, having been reconciled, shall we be saved through his life! **11**Not only is this so, but we also boast in God through our Lord Jesus Christ, through whom we have now received reconciliation.

Death through Adam, life through Christ

12Therefore, just as sin entered the world through one man, and death through sin, and in this way death came to all people, because all sinned –

13To be sure, sin was in the world before the law was given, but sin is not charged against anyone's account where there is no law. **14**Nevertheless, death reigned from the time of Adam to the time of Moses, even over those who did not sin by breaking a command, as did Adam, who is a pattern of the one to come.

15But the gift is not like the trespass. For if the many died by the trespass of the one man, how much more did God's grace and the gift that came by the grace of the one man, Jesus Christ, overflow to the many! **16**Nor can the gift of God be compared with the result of one man's sin: the judgment followed one sin and brought condemnation, but the gift followed many trespasses and brought justification. **17**For if, by the trespass of the one man, death reigned through that one man, how much more will those who receive God's abundant provision of grace and of the gift of righteousness reign in life through the one man, Jesus Christ! **18**Consequently, just as one trespass resulted in condemnation for all people, so also one righteous act resulted in justification and life for all people. **19**For just as through the disobedience of the one man the many were made sinners, so also through the obedience of the one man the many will be made righteous.

20The law was brought in so that the trespass might increase. But where sin increased, grace increased all the more, **21**so that, just as sin reigned in death, so also grace might reign through righteousness

---

d 18 Gen. 15:5
a 1 Many manuscripts *let us*
b 2,3 Or *let us*

WHAT IS CHRISTIANITY? 7

Doctrine of salvation: the perfect rescue

Every doctrine of the Christian faith is wonderful, but Romans 5:1–11 is one of the most stunning. It's the Christian teaching about how we are saved.

From the moment the human race walked away from God and sinned (see Genesis 3), God has been finding a way to bring us back into relationship with himself. The whole story of the Bible is a salvation story: God rescues Israel from Egypt, and again and again throughout the Old Testament. But the story of salvation climaxes when Jesus dies on a cross, on a hill outside Jerusalem. As strange as it might seem, from this dark hour and horrific death shines the hope of the entire world. *'God demonstrates his own love for us in this: while we were still sinners, Christ died for us'* (Romans 5:8).

We only understand the cross when we understand God. He is holy, and when the human race sinned, God needed to act. A just God can never allow injustice. At the same time, God is love: he didn't want to simply wipe us out. Because of his holiness, he couldn't bear to look at us; because of his love, he couldn't bear to look away.

On the cross God's love and justice meet. Jesus bears the consequences of our sin and for a moment God the Son is cut off from God the Father. God is able to deal justly with sin. At the same time God's love is satisfied, because he takes this penalty on himself rather than pass it on to us. When Jesus dies on the cross, as incredible as it might seem, he dies for everything you and I have ever done to offend God. It's dealt with once and for all.

What this means is that salvation is a free gift from God. All we need do is receive it!

The way we receive salvation is by turning away from living for ourselves and turning towards living for God. In other words, we repent, and we have faith.

'Receiving salvation' isn't about us stopping being bad and starting being good (although our behaviour does change). It's about us accepting that Jesus has done something for us we could never do for ourselves. He has lived a perfect and righteous life before God.

Salvation is about a beautiful exchange. Jesus took the consequences of our sin and we now share with him in the consequences of his righteousness. The Bible talks of salvation as utterly dramatic. When you accepted Jesus – even if at the time you didn't feel anything different – at that moment everything changed. You were *'born again'*, you became a *'new creation'*, you were given a *'new heart'* (John 3:3; 2 Corinthians 5:17; Ezekiel 11:19).

The extent of the change salvation brings shows us that we could never save ourselves. Have you ever tried giving yourself heart surgery? It had to be done through grace. It had to be God. All we need do is receive.

Andy Croft

 Luke 8:22–25　　　　　　　　　　　　1 Corinthians 12:12–31

to bring eternal life through Jesus Christ our Lord.

Dead to sin, alive in Christ

6 What shall we say, then? Shall we go on sinning, so that grace may increase? **2** By no means! We are those who have died to sin; how can we live in it any longer? **3** Or don't you know that all of us who were baptised into Christ Jesus were baptised into his death? **4** We were therefore buried with him through baptism into death in order that, just as Christ was raised from the dead through the glory of the Father, we too may live a new life.

5 For if we have been united with him in a death like his, we will certainly also be united with him in a resurrection like his. **6** For we know that our old self was crucified with him so that the body ruled by sin might be done away with,*a* that we should no longer be slaves to sin – **7** because anyone who has died has been set free from sin.

8 Now if we died with Christ, we believe that we will also live with him. **9** For we know that since Christ was raised from the dead, he cannot die again; death no longer has mastery over him. **10** The death he died, he died to sin once for all; but the life he lives, he lives to God.

11 In the same way, count yourselves dead to sin but alive to God in Christ Jesus. **12** Therefore do not let sin reign in your mortal body so that you obey its evil desires. **13** Do not offer any part of yourself to sin as an instrument of wickedness, but rather offer yourselves to God as those who have been brought from death to life; and offer every part of yourself to him as an instrument of righteousness. **14** For sin shall no longer be your master, because you are not under the law, but under grace.

Slaves to righteousness

15 What then? Shall we sin because we are not under the law but under grace? By no means! **16** Don't you know that when you offer yourselves to someone as obedient slaves, you are slaves of the one you obey – whether you are slaves to sin, which

leads to death, or to obedience, which leads to righteousness? **17** But thanks be to God that, though you used to be slaves to sin, you have come to obey from your heart the pattern of teaching that has now claimed your allegiance. **18** You have been set free from sin and have become slaves to righteousness.

19 I am using an example from everyday life because of your human limitations. Just as you used to offer yourselves as slaves to impurity and to ever-increasing wickedness, so now offer yourselves as slaves to righteousness leading to holiness. **20** When you were slaves to sin, you were free from the control of righteousness. **21** What benefit did you reap at that time from the things you are now ashamed of? Those things result in death! **22** But now that you have been set free from sin and have become slaves of God, the benefit you reap leads to holiness, and the result is eternal life. **23** For the wages of sin is death, but the gift of God is eternal life in*b* Christ Jesus our Lord.

Released from the law, bound to Christ

7 Do you not know, brothers and sisters – for I am speaking to those who know the law – that the law has authority over someone only as long as that person lives? **2** For example, by law a married woman is bound to her husband as long as he is alive, but if her husband dies, she is released from the law that binds her to him. **3** So then, if she has sexual relations with another man while her husband is still alive, she is called an adulteress. But if her husband dies, she is released from that law and is not an adulteress if she marries another man.

4 So, my brothers and sisters, you also died to the law through the body of Christ, that you might belong to another, to him who was raised from the dead, in order that we might bear fruit for God. **5** For when we were in the realm of the flesh,*a* the sinful passions aroused by the law were at work in us, so that we bore fruit for death. **6** But

---

a 6 Or *be rendered powerless*

b 23 Or *through*

a 5 In contexts like this, the Greek word for *flesh* (*sarx*) refers to the sinful state of human beings, often presented as a power in opposition to the Spirit.

THE BIG STORY 2

The fall

It all went wrong at the beginning (Romans 5:12–14). Christians call it 'the fall'. God created the first humans, and every human since, *'in his image'* (Genesis 1:26–27). That meant being sufficiently like God to be able to have a relationship with God, to represent God, and to display what God was like on the earth. It also meant obeying God.

Adam means 'human'. This first human broke God's command (Romans 5:14; for the full story see Genesis 3). The result was that *'sin entered the world'* (v. 12). 'Sin' is to fall short of God's standards for our life, to miss the mark. It's a basic tendency to live for ourselves rather than for God our Creator. It's like an 'independence from God' gene, a mutation from the Creator's design, which we all share since that first act of rebellion and disobedience. We become more concerned with our image than with reflecting God's image. Because of 'sin', we all commit sins (*'all sinned'*, v. 12), acts of wrongdoing for which we are answerable to God. Sin is like the disease and sins are like the symptoms. The consequence of sin is death (v. 12)– not just physical death, in that one day each of us will die, but spiritual death as opposed to eternal life (see Romans 6:23). We were made to relate to God and to reflect him, but instead we are separated from God, and one day we will have to face him as our Judge. From this perspective, fallen humans really are 'the living dead'.

This 'independence from God' gene is not improved by knowing moral rules. Our problem is not ignorance. We often do what's wrong, even when we know what's right. Tell someone not to do something, and that action becomes even more tempting. The problem exists despite God having given his law, his Maker's instructions, through Moses (vv. 13–14). The law is summed up in the Ten Commandments (Exodus 20:1–17), which Jesus applied to our attitudes and motivations, not just to our actions (e.g. Matthew 5:21–28). Knowing what's right isn't the same as doing it, or even wanting to do it. The story of the fall and human sinfulness isn't a detached religious theory. The evidence for it is seen in every news bulletin and newspaper front page. Violence, war, theft and everyday selfishness are not the whole truth about human beings: we're still made in God's image and are capable of wonderful self-sacrifice. But only too often we behave appallingly. Men and women behaving badly isn't surprising news. We're used to it, even though extreme examples still shock us. But we're too often blind to the fact that each sin against another is a sin against God.

Sin is fatal, unless we get help. Mercifully, this passage points to a new human (a new Adam) who would come and do something about it (v. 14).

Graham Cray

now, by dying to what once bound us, we have been released from the law so that we serve in the new way of the Spirit, and not in the old way of the written code.

The law and sin

7 What shall we say, then? Is the law sinful? Certainly not! Nevertheless, I would not have known what sin was had it not

LAW AND GRACE 4

A marriage made in heaven

You might not have been on a stag or hen 'do', but no doubt you have heard stories from people who have! They are often described as a last night of freedom – when a man or a woman who is about to get married celebrates and lets off steam with close friends and family.

In reality, they're not giving up their freedom, but swapping one type of freedom for another: sharing intimacy with that one other special person. How does your freedom change? For example, in sharing the remote control or choosing a DVD to watch, sometimes you have to watch all sorts of strange stuff that your partner chooses! All relationships need compromise. If we lived on an island on our own, we could do what we want, but we would be lonely. That's why we recognise that the compromise is worth it.

In Romans 7, Paul uses the example of marriage (vv. 1–3) to talk about our relationship with God. Once, he says, we were 'married' to the law, and although God's law is good, we struggled to compromise: we kept wanting to do what we wanted to do. But now God has found a new way for us to live out his good rules for our life. It's as if we have been widowed and married a new spouse – the Spirit of Christ. This is a much richer relationship. It's almost like we used to be married to someone we didn't love, but we kept trying to be faithful to our wedding vows.

Now we're 'married' to Christ and we aim to be obedient out of a very real love. This isn't giving up one type of freedom for another, but understanding that the freedom we experience by being faithful to Jesus is a level of freedom we could never experience elsewhere. Knowing that someone is always there for you, always faithful, always caring, brings a level of confidence and freedom that's hard to beat. That's what God's grace offers us and why we offer our obedience in return. Sorry, guys, but it's a bit like the reverse of the Cinderella story: the ugly sister (that's us) gets to marry Prince Charming and share his inheritance of the kingdom! The ugly sister has no need to behave badly any longer, because all she has ever dreamed of comes true. The thing is, the more we seek to live up to our wedding vows, the less ugly we get and the more like Cinderella we become. That's God's grace, offering us an irresistible relationship that we didn't deserve. Does it require compromise? Does it require living up to a law? Yes, but it's a freedom so rich that we should do all we can – God being our helper – to protect it.

Jason Gardner

 John 8:1–11   John 3:16 ►►

been for the law. For I would not have known what coveting really was if the law had not said, 'You shall not covet.'*b* 8 But sin, seizing the opportunity afforded by the commandment, produced in me every kind of coveting. For apart from the law, sin was dead. 9 Once I was alive apart from the law; but when the commandment came, sin sprang to life and I died. 10 I found that the very commandment that was intended to bring life actually brought death. 11 For sin, seizing the opportunity afforded by the commandment, deceived me, and through the commandment put me to death. 12 So then, the law is holy, and the commandment is holy, righteous and good.

13 Did that which is good, then, become death to me? By no means! Nevertheless, in order that sin might be recognised as sin, it used what is good to bring about my death, so that through the commandment sin might become utterly sinful. 14 We know that the law is spiritual; but I am unspiritual, sold as a slave to sin. 15 I do not understand what I do. For what I want to do I do not do, but what I hate I do. 16 And if I do what I do not want to do, I agree that the law is good. 17 As it is, it is no longer I myself who do it, but it is sin living in me. 18 For I know that good itself does not dwell in me, that is, in my sinful nature.*c* For I have the desire to do what is good, but I cannot carry it out. 19 For I do not do the good I want to do, but the evil I do not want to do – this I keep on doing. 20 Now if I do what I do not want to do, it is no longer I who do it, but it is sin living in me that does it.

21 So I find this law at work: although I want to do good, evil is right there with me. 22 For in my inner being I delight in God's law; 23 but I see another law at work in me, waging war against the law of my mind and making me a prisoner of the law of sin at work within me. 24 What a wretched man I am! Who will rescue me from this body that is subject to death? 25 Thanks be to God, who delivers me through Jesus Christ our Lord!

So then, I myself in my mind am a slave to God's law, but in my sinful nature*d* a slave to the law of sin.

Life through the Spirit

8 Therefore, there is now no condemnation for those who are in Christ Jesus, 2 because through Christ Jesus the law of the Spirit who gives life has set you*a* free from the law of sin and death. 3 For what the law was powerless to do because it was weakened by the flesh,*b* God did by sending his own Son in the likeness of sinful flesh to be a sin offering.*c* And so he condemned sin in the flesh, 4 in order that the righteous requirement of the law might be fully met in us, who do not live according to the flesh but according to the Spirit.

5 Those who live according to the flesh have their minds set on what the flesh desires; but those who live in accordance with the Spirit have their minds set on what the Spirit desires. 6 The mind governed by the flesh is death, but the mind governed by the Spirit is life and peace. 7 The mind governed by the flesh is hostile to God; it does not submit to God's law, nor can it do so. 8 Those who are in the realm of the flesh cannot please God.

9 You, however, are not in the realm of the flesh but are in the realm of the Spirit, if indeed the Spirit of God lives in you. And if anyone does not have the Spirit of Christ, they do not belong to Christ. 10 But if Christ is in you, then even though your body is subject to death because of sin, the Spirit gives life*d* because of righteousness. 11 And if the Spirit of him who raised Jesus from the dead is living in you, he who raised Christ from the dead will also give life to your mortal bodies because of*e* his Spirit who lives in you.

12 Therefore, brothers and sisters, we

---

b 7　Exodus 20:17; Deut. 5:21
c 18　Or *my flesh*

d 25　Or *in the flesh*
a 2　The Greek is singular; some manuscripts *me*
b 3　In contexts like this, the Greek word for *flesh* (*sarx*) refers to the sinful state of human beings, often presented as a power in opposition to the Spirit; also in verses 4-13.
c 3　Or *flesh, for sin*
d 10　Or *you, your body is dead because of sin, yet your spirit is alive*
e 11　Some manuscripts *bodies through*

have an obligation – but it is not to the flesh, to live according to it. **13** For if you live according to the flesh, you will die; but if by the Spirit you put to death the misdeeds of the body, you will live.

14 For those who are led by the Spirit of God are the children of God. **15** The Spirit you received does not make you slaves, so that you live in fear again; rather, the Spirit you received brought about your adoption to sonship.*f* And by him we cry, '*Abba,g* Father.' **16** The Spirit himself testifies with our spirit that we are God's children. **17** Now if we are children, then we are heirs – heirs of God and co-heirs with Christ, if indeed

---

f 15 The Greek word for *adoption to sonship* is a term referring to the full legal standing of an adopted male heir in Roman culture; also in verse 23.

g 15 Aramaic for *father*

we share in his sufferings in order that we may also share in his glory.

Present suffering and future glory

18 I consider that our present sufferings are not worth comparing with the glory that will be revealed in us. **19** For the creation waits in eager expectation for the children of God to be revealed. **20** For the creation was subjected to frustration, not by its own choice, but by the will of the one who subjected it, in hope **21** that*h* the creation itself will be liberated from its bondage to decay and brought into the freedom and glory of the children of God.

22 We know that the whole creation has been groaning as in the pains of

---

h 20,21 Or *subjected it in hope. ²¹For*

IDENTITY – WHO WE ARE IN CHRIST 3

Indwelt by the Spirit

God has given us a fresh start and made us good at the core of our being. Yet that's not often how it feels. That's because we still have 'the flesh' – our habits, attitudes and thought patterns, developed over the course of our lives.

When we become Christians, the flesh doesn't get deleted in the system reboot of becoming a new creation. At heart, the core of who we are, we are now a new creation set free from sin, but our old fleshly ways are still alive. Yet we have a choice. Jesus broke sin's power and hold over us on the cross. As Christians, we also have God himself living in us, by his Holy Spirit (Romans 8:9–11). We don't have to try to persuade him to be there, or be good enough for him to be there. When we become Christians, the Holy Spirit comes to dwell within us, without fail! He's there within us, ready to empower us to choose to live according to our new godly nature rather than our old sinful ways.

Before we become Christians, we have no power over the flesh other than determination and willpower. Once we become Christians, however, we have God's power at work in us. We still have to keep making choices, though, as life can be a bit of a battle – but God gives us all that we need within us to choose life and the way of God.

James Grier

 2 Corinthians 5:17   Galatians 4 ▶

childbirth right up to the present time. ²³ Not only so, but we ourselves, who have the firstfruits of the Spirit, groan inwardly as we wait eagerly for our adoption to sonship, the redemption of our bodies. ²⁴ For in this hope we were saved. But hope that is seen is no hope at all. Who hopes for what they already have? ²⁵ But if we hope for what we do not yet have, we wait for it patiently.

²⁶ In the same way, the Spirit helps us in our weakness. We do not know what we ought to pray for, but the Spirit himself intercedes for us through wordless groans. ²⁷ And he who searches our hearts knows the mind of the Spirit, because the Spirit intercedes for God's people in accordance with the will of God.

²⁸ And we know that in all things God works for the good of those who love him, who[i] have been called according to his purpose. ²⁹ For those God foreknew he also predestined to be conformed to the image of his Son, that he might be the firstborn among many brothers and sisters. ³⁰ And those he predestined, he also called; those he called, he also justified; those he justified, he also glorified.

More than conquerors

³¹ What, then, shall we say in response to these things? If God is for us, who can be against us? ³² He who did not spare his own Son, but gave him up for us all – how

---

i 28 Or that all things work together for good to those who love God, who; or that in all things God works together with those who love him to bring about what is good – with those who

---

THE NAMES OF GOD 9

God Our Father (Abba)

'The Spirit you received does not make you slaves, so that you live in fear again; rather, the Spirit you received brought about your adoption to sonship. And by him we cry, "Abba, Father"' (Romans 8:15–16).

Jesus taught his disciples to pray, *'Our Father in heaven...'* His own relationship to God was one of intimate dependency and he went so far as to call his Father *Abba* – a familiar term, rather like saying 'Daddy'. In John's Gospel he encourages his disciples to have a similar relationship with God. This is why Paul so confidently tells the Christians in Rome to call out to God using the familiar term of *'Abba*, Father'.

We live in an imperfect world and few of us have been fathered in the way we would have liked. Most fathers do the best they can in the fraught world in which we live, but the protective, affirming presence of a father figure is often missing in homes today, which can leave us with a void in our hearts. Jesus came to heal the broken-hearted and points us to his Father as the answer to our needs.

All earthly relationships, even the good ones, pale in comparison to the one we are privileged to enjoy with God the Father. We are heirs, together with Jesus, of the riches of God, our Father's kingdom. We can walk in that same intimate relationship with God this very day.

David and Mary Pytches

 Isaiah 43:3   Leviticus 11:44

WHY DOES GOD ALLOW NATURAL DISASTERS TO HAPPEN?

The natural world has an incredible beauty, but also a destructive power. We're fascinated by both: marvelling at the vastness of the ocean or the colours of a sunset, and drawn to the power and chaos of events like hurricanes or earthquakes. They create a sense of awe, but also of horror – and we question why they happen.

There's something in us that knows this is not the way it's supposed to be. In Romans 8:18–25, Paul writes that creation is frustrated and awaiting liberation (vv. 20–21).

It seems that the effects of the fall in Genesis had consequences beyond our human relationships and our relationship with God. Our relationship with creation also broke down. This is a result of the freedom God gave us – allowing us to turn away from the harmony intended for humanity and creation and do life by ourselves rather than living with God. Since then, creation and humanity have not been in harmony, instead bringing suffering, pain and death to each other. Natural disasters are part of this, highlighting that humanity and creation are out of sync.

On the very few occasions the Bible records God using natural disasters as a punishment (Genesis 6:13; 19:23), we also see God making plans so that his saving work can be demonstrated. Noah is warned of the flood as part of God's rescue plan (Genesis 7:1). In the book of Job it's Satan, rather than God, who brings natural disasters upon Job and his family (Job 1:1–12), highlighting that these events are nothing to do with God. This is also Elijah's experience, as he discovers that God is not in the three natural disasters he faces (1 Kings 19:1–18), but in the gentle whisper that follows them (v. 12).

As we look at Jesus, we get a clearer sense of God's perspective on nature's destructive power. Jesus fulfils the task given to Adam and Eve to subdue the natural events that threaten humanity (Genesis 1:28). In the calming of the storm (Luke 8:22–25) Jesus rebukes the wind and waves and they become quiet. He restores the harmony between humanity and creation and shows that God is active in working against the disharmony in our world.

Jesus also describes natural disasters as a sign that something new is coming (Matthew 24:7). The process may be difficult, but the new creation will be free from these catastrophic events – a place where our relationships with each other, with God and with creation will be marked by peace and freedom. This day is more exciting and awesome than any natural disaster.

God seems to allow natural disasters because he allows us freedom. As we turned away from him, all creation became subjected to disharmony and disasters. But God is at work: Jesus came *'to reconcile to himself all things, whether things on earth or things in heaven, by making peace through his blood, shed on the cross'* (Colossians 1:20).

Ali Etheridge

will he not also, along with him, graciously give us all things? ³³Who will bring any charge against those whom God has chosen? It is God who justifies. ³⁴Who then is the one who condemns? No one. Christ Jesus who died – more than that, who was raised to life – is at the right hand of God and is also interceding for us. ³⁵Who shall separate us from the love of Christ? Shall trouble or hardship or persecution or famine or nakedness or danger or sword? ³⁶As it is written:

> 'For your sake we face death all day long;
> we are considered as sheep to be slaughtered.'*j*

³⁷No, in all these things we are more than conquerors through him who loved us. ³⁸For I am convinced that neither death nor life, neither angels nor demons,*k* neither the present nor the future, nor any powers, ³⁹neither height nor depth, nor anything else in all creation, will be able to separate us from the love of God that is in Christ Jesus our Lord.

Paul's anguish over Israel

9 I speak the truth in Christ – I am not lying, my conscience confirms it through the Holy Spirit – ²I have great sorrow and unceasing anguish in my heart. ³For I could wish that I myself were cursed and cut off from Christ for the sake of my people, those of my own race, ⁴the people of Israel. Theirs is the adoption to sonship; theirs the divine glory, the covenants, the receiving of the law, the temple worship and the promises. ⁵Theirs are the patriarchs, and from them is traced the human ancestry of the Messiah, who is God over all, for ever praised!*a* Amen.

God's sovereign choice

⁶It is not as though God's word had failed. For not all who are descended from Israel are Israel. ⁷Nor because they are his descendants are they all Abraham's children. On the contrary, 'It is through Isaac that your offspring will be reckoned.'*b* ⁸In other words, it is not the children by physical descent who are God's children, but it is the children of the promise who are regarded as Abraham's offspring. ⁹For this was how the promise was stated: 'At the appointed time I will return, and Sarah will have a son.'*c*

¹⁰Not only that, but Rebekah's children were conceived at the same time by our father Isaac. ¹¹Yet, before the twins were born or had done anything good or bad – in order that God's purpose in election might stand: ¹²not by works but by him who calls – she was told, 'The older will serve the younger.'*d* ¹³Just as it is written: 'Jacob I loved, but Esau I hated.'*e*

¹⁴What then shall we say? Is God unjust? Not at all! ¹⁵For he says to Moses,

> 'I will have mercy on whom I have mercy,
> and I will have compassion on whom I have compassion.'*f*

¹⁶It does not, therefore, depend on human desire or effort, but on God's mercy. ¹⁷For Scripture says to Pharaoh: 'I raised you up for this very purpose, that I might display my power in you and that my name might be proclaimed in all the earth.'*g* ¹⁸Therefore God has mercy on whom he wants to have mercy, and he hardens whom he wants to harden.

¹⁹One of you will say to me: 'Then why does God still blame us? For who is able to resist his will?' ²⁰But who are you, a human being, to talk back to God? 'Shall what is formed say to the one who formed it, "Why did you make me like this?"'*h* ²¹Does not the potter have the right to make out of the same lump of clay some pottery for special purposes and some for common use?

j 36 Psalm 44:22
k 38 Or *nor heavenly rulers*
a 5 Or *Messiah, who is over all. God be for ever praised!* Or *Messiah. God who is over all be for ever praised!*

b 7 Gen. 21:12
c 9 Gen. 18:10,14
d 12 Gen. 25:23
e 13 Mal. 1:2,3
f 15 Exodus 33:19
g 17 Exodus 9:16
h 20 Isaiah 29:16; 45:9

22 What if God, although choosing to show his wrath and make his power known, bore with great patience the objects of his wrath – prepared for destruction? 23 What if he did this to make the riches of his glory known to the objects of his mercy, whom he prepared in advance for glory – 24 even us, whom he also called, not only from the Jews but also from the Gentiles? 25 As he says in Hosea:

'I will call them "my people" who are
    not my people;
and I will call her "my loved one"
    who is not my loved one,'[i]

26 and,

'In the very place where it was said to
    them,
    "You are not my people,"
    there they will be called "children of
    the living God." '[j]

27 Isaiah cries out concerning Israel:

'Though the number of the Israelites
    be like the sand by the sea,
    only the remnant will be saved.
28 For the Lord will carry out
    his sentence on earth with speed
    and finality.'[k]

29 It is just as Isaiah said previously:

'Unless the Lord Almighty
    had left us descendants,
we would have become like Sodom,
    we would have been like Gomorrah.'[l]

Israel's unbelief

30 What then shall we say? That the Gentiles, who did not pursue righteousness, have obtained it, a righteousness that is by faith; 31 but the people of Israel, who pursued the law as the way of righteousness, have not attained their goal. 32 Why not? Because they pursued it not by faith but as

---

i 25   Hosea 2:23
j 26   Hosea 1:10
k 28   Isaiah 10:22,23 (see Septuagint)
l 29   Isaiah 1:9

---

if it were by works. They stumbled over the 'stumbling stone.' 33 As it is written:

'See, I lay in Zion a stone that causes
    people to stumble
and a rock that makes them fall,
    and the one who believes in him
    will never be put to shame.'[m]

FAVOURITE VERSES

Psalm 46:10

He says, 'Be still, and know that
    I am God;
I will be exalted among the nations,
    I will be exalted in the earth.'

We are so blessed that we have a God who wants us to rest in his presence and wait on him. We can pause from the busyness of life by being still; and when things are going badly or you are angry, just remember that it is all in God's hands.

Jacob, 17

10 Brothers and sisters, my heart's desire and prayer to God for the Israelites is that they may be saved. 2 For I can testify about them that they are zealous for God, but their zeal is not based on knowledge. 3 Since they did not know the righteousness of God and sought to establish their own, they did not submit to God's righteousness. 4 Christ is the culmination of the law so that there may be righteousness for everyone who believes.

5 Moses writes this about the righteousness that is by the law: 'The person who does these things will live by them.'[a] 6 But

---

m 33   Isaiah 8:14; 28:16
a 5   Lev. 18:5

the righteousness that is by faith says: 'Do not say in your heart, "Who will ascend into heaven?" '[b] (that is, to bring Christ down) [7] or "Who will descend into the deep?" '[c] (that is, to bring Christ up from the dead). [8] But what does it say? 'The word is near you; it is in your mouth and in your heart,'[d] that is, the message concerning faith that we proclaim: [9] if you declare with your mouth, 'Jesus is Lord,' and believe in your heart that God raised him from the dead, you will be saved. [10] For it is with your heart that you believe and are justified, and it is with your mouth that you profess your faith and are saved. [11] As Scripture says, 'Anyone who believes in him will never be put to shame.'[e] [12] For there is no difference between Jew and Gentile – the same Lord is Lord of all and richly blesses all who call on him, [13] for, 'Everyone who calls on the name of the Lord will be saved.'[f]

[14] How, then, can they call on the one they have not believed in? And how can they believe in the one of whom they have not heard? And how can they hear without someone preaching to them? [15] And how can anyone preach unless they are sent? As it is written: 'How beautiful are the feet of those who bring good news!'[g]

[16] But not all the Israelites accepted the good news. For Isaiah says, 'Lord, who has believed our message?'[h] [17] Consequently, faith comes from hearing the message, and the message is heard through the word about Christ. [18] But I ask: did they not hear? Of course they did:

'Their voice has gone out into all the
    earth,
    their words to the ends of the world.'[i]

[19] Again I ask: did Israel not understand? First, Moses says,

'I will make you envious by those who
    are not a nation;
I will make you angry by a nation
    that has no understanding.'[j]

[20] And Isaiah boldly says,

'I was found by those who did not seek
    me;
I revealed myself to those who did
    not ask for me.'[k]

[21] But concerning Israel he says,

'All day long I have held out my hands
    to a disobedient and obstinate
    people.'[l]

The remnant of Israel

11 I ask then: did God reject his people? By no means! I am an Israelite myself, a descendant of Abraham, from the tribe of Benjamin. [2] God did not reject his people, whom he foreknew. Don't you know what Scripture says in the passage about Elijah – how he appealed to God against Israel: [3] 'Lord, they have killed your prophets and torn down your altars; I am the only one left, and they are trying to kill me'[a]? [4] And what was God's answer to him? 'I have reserved for myself seven thousand who have not bowed the knee to Baal.'[b] [5] So too, at the present time there is a remnant chosen by grace. [6] And if by grace, then it cannot be based on works; if it were, grace would no longer be grace.

[7] What then? What the people of Israel sought so earnestly they did not obtain. The elect among them did, but the others were hardened, [8] as it is written:

'God gave them a spirit of stupor,
    eyes that could not see
    and ears that could not hear,
    to this very day.'[c]

---

b 6 Deut. 30:12
c 7 Deut. 30:13
d 8 Deut. 30:14
e 11 Isaiah 28:16 (see Septuagint)
f 13 Joel 2:32
g 15 Isaiah 52:7
h 16 Isaiah 53:1
i 18 Psalm 19:4

j 19 Deut. 32:21
k 20 Isaiah 65:1
l 21 Isaiah 65:2
a 3 1 Kings 19:10,14
b 4 1 Kings 19:18
c 8 Deut. 29:4; Isaiah 29:10

⁹ And David says:

'May their table become a snare and a trap,
   a stumbling-block and a retribution for them.
¹⁰ May their eyes be darkened so they cannot see,
   and their backs be bent for ever.'^d

Ingrafted branches

¹¹ Again I ask: did they stumble so as to fall beyond recovery? Not at all! Rather, because of their transgression, salvation has come to the Gentiles to make Israel envious. ¹² But if their transgression means riches for the world, and their loss means riches for the Gentiles, how much greater riches will their full inclusion bring!

¹³ I am talking to you Gentiles. Inasmuch as I am the apostle to the Gentiles, I take pride in my ministry ¹⁴ in the hope that I may somehow arouse my own people to envy and save some of them. ¹⁵ For if their rejection brought reconciliation to the world, what will their acceptance be but life from the dead? ¹⁶ If the part of the dough offered as firstfruits is holy, then the whole batch is holy; if the root is holy, so are the branches.

¹⁷ If some of the branches have been broken off, and you, though a wild olive shoot, have been grafted in among the others and now share in the nourishing sap from the olive root, ¹⁸ do not consider yourself to be superior to those other branches. If you do, consider this: you do not support the root, but the root supports you. ¹⁹ You will say then, 'Branches were broken off so that I could be grafted in.' ²⁰ Granted. But they were broken off because of unbelief, and you stand by faith. Do not be arrogant, but tremble. ²¹ For if God did not spare the natural branches, he will not spare you either.

²² Consider therefore the kindness and sternness of God: sternness to those who fell, but kindness to you, provided that you continue in his kindness. Otherwise,

you also will be cut off. ²³ And if they do not persist in unbelief, they will be grafted in, for God is able to graft them in again. ²⁴ After all, if you were cut out of an olive tree that is wild by nature, and contrary to nature were grafted into a cultivated olive tree, how much more readily will these, the natural branches, be grafted into their own olive tree!

All Israel will be saved

²⁵ I do not want you to be ignorant of this mystery, brothers and sisters, so that you may not be conceited: Israel has experienced a hardening in part until the full number of the Gentiles has come in, ²⁶ and in this way^e all Israel will be saved. As it is written:

'The deliverer will come from Zion;
   he will turn godlessness away from Jacob.
²⁷ And this is^f my covenant with them
   when I take away their sins.'^g

²⁸ As far as the gospel is concerned, they are enemies for your sake; but as far as election is concerned, they are loved on account of the patriarchs, ²⁹ for God's gifts and his call are irrevocable. ³⁰ Just as you who were at one time disobedient to God have now received mercy as a result of their disobedience, ³¹ so they too have now become disobedient in order that they too may now^h receive mercy as a result of God's mercy to you. ³² For God has bound everyone over to disobedience so that he may have mercy on them all.

Doxology

³³ Oh, the depth of the riches of the wisdom andⁱ knowledge of God!
   How unsearchable his judgments,
   and his paths beyond tracing out!
³⁴ 'Who has known the mind of the Lord?

---

^d 10 Psalm 69:22,23

^e 26 Or and so
^f 27 Or will be
^g 27 Isaiah 59.20,21, 27.9 (see Septuagint); Jer. 31:33,34
^h 31 Some manuscripts do not have now.
ⁱ 33 Or riches and the wisdom and the

Or who has been his counsellor?'*j*

35 'Who has ever given to God,
     that God should repay them?'*k*

36 For from him and through him and for
     him are all things.
   To him be the glory for ever! Amen.

A living sacrifice

12 Therefore, I urge you, brothers and sisters, in view of God's mercy, to offer your bodies as a living sacrifice,

j 34 Isaiah 40:13
k 35 Job 41:11

holy and pleasing to God – this is your true and proper worship. 2 Do not conform to the pattern of this world, but be transformed by the renewing of your mind. Then you will be able to test and approve what God's will is – his good, pleasing and perfect will.

Humble service in the body of Christ

3 For by the grace given me I say to every one of you: do not think of yourself more highly than you ought, but rather think of yourself with sober judgment, in accordance with the faith God has distributed

SACRIFICE 5

Worship as sacrifice

Romans 12:1-2 is my favourite scripture passage. I love it because it describes in a nutshell the reality of what worship is: how to live differently, where we find God's will – pretty much all the essentials of our life of faith in two verses! It's incredible.

The way we worship is by offering our whole lives to God as a sacrifice. It's not with singing; it's not with guitars or choirs or iPods or candles. When we willingly lay down our lives God can take them and infuse them with what they were always meant to be. Often people make a big deal of other people they know who have given their whole lives to God. "That John Smith – he's AMAZING!", and there are many people we know who ARE amazing … but no matter how incredible it may seem to you, it's likely that they are only doing what makes sense for them to do. They're giving to God what is rightfully God's. By giving their entire lives to God they come to know what God's will is.

When you know how to worship – and out of your sacrificed life comes singing that is heart-felt (not so tuneful, but definitely heavenly), dancing, abandonment, service, justice, prayer – well, you get the idea - your life becomes a LIVING sacrifice. This is what worship is. I think we tend to forget this. We'd all prefer it if worship were simply something we 'did' but God insists and is pretty clear about this sacrifice business from the start to the finish – true worship is about offering all of ourselves to God. Reckless abandon is how Oswald Chambers put it. So, sacrifice turns out to be our way to ultimate freedom. Why not worship for real today?! Give your whole life as a sacrifice.

Danielle Strickland

 1 Samuel 1:24–28   Leviticus 9:7

to each of you. 4 For just as each of us has one body with many members, and these members do not all have the same function, 5 so in Christ we, though many, form one body, and each member belongs to all the others. 6 We have different gifts, according to the grace given to each of us. If your gift is prophesying, then prophesy in accordance with your*a* faith; 7 if it is serving, then serve; if it is teaching, then teach; 8 if it is to encourage, then give encouragement; if it is giving, then give generously; if it is to lead,*b* do it diligently; if it is to show mercy, do it cheerfully.

Love in action

9 Love must be sincere. Hate what is evil; cling to what is good. 10 Be devoted to one another in love. Honour one another above yourselves. 11 Never be lacking in zeal, but keep your spiritual fervour, serving the Lord. 12 Be joyful in hope, patient in affliction, faithful in prayer. 13 Share with the Lord's people who are in need. Practise hospitality.

14 Bless those who persecute you; bless and do not curse. 15 Rejoice with those who rejoice; mourn with those who mourn. 16 Live in harmony with one another. Do not be proud, but be willing to associate with people of low position.*c* Do not be conceited.

17 Do not repay anyone evil for evil. Be careful to do what is right in the eyes of everyone. 18 If it is possible, as far as it depends on you, live at peace with everyone. 19 Do not take revenge, my dear friends, but leave room for God's wrath, for it is written: 'It is mine to avenge; I will repay,'*d* says the Lord. 20 On the contrary:

'If your enemy is hungry, feed him;
    if he is thirsty, give him something
    to drink.
In doing this, you will heap burning
    coals on his head.'*e*

21 Do not be overcome by evil, but overcome evil with good.

Submission to governing authorities

13 Let everyone be subject to the governing authorities, for there is no authority except that which God has established. The authorities that exist have been established by God. 2 Consequently, whoever rebels against the authority is rebelling against what God has instituted, and those who do so will bring judgment on themselves. 3 For rulers hold no terror for those who do right, but for those who do wrong. Do you want to be free from fear of the one in authority? Then do what is right and you will be commended. 4 For the one in authority is God's servant for your good. But if you do wrong, be afraid, for rulers do not bear the sword for no reason. They are God's servants, agents of wrath to bring punishment on the wrongdoer. 5 Therefore, it is necessary to submit to the authorities, not only because of possible punishment but also as a matter of conscience.

6 This is also why you pay taxes, for the authorities are God's servants, who give their full time to governing. 7 Give to everyone what you owe them: if you owe taxes, pay taxes; if revenue, then revenue; if respect, then respect; if honour, then honour.

Love fulfils the law

8 Let no debt remain outstanding, except the continuing debt to love one another, for whoever loves others has fulfilled the law. 9 The commandments, 'You shall not commit adultery,' 'You shall not murder,' 'You shall not steal,' 'You shall not covet,'*a* and whatever other command there may be, are summed up in this one command: 'Love your neighbour as yourself.'*b* 10 Love does no harm to a neighbour. Therefore love is the fulfilment of the law.

---

a 6 Or *the*
b 8 Or *to provide for others*
c 16 Or *willing to do menial work*
d 19 Deut. 32:35
e 20 Prov. 25:21,22

---

a 9 Exodus 20:13-15,17; Deut. 5:17-19,21
b 9 Lev. 19:18

The day is near

11 And do this, understanding the present time: the hour has already come for you to wake up from your slumber, because our salvation is nearer now than when we first believed. 12 The night is nearly over; the day is almost here. So let us put aside the deeds of darkness and put on the armour of light. 13 Let us behave decently, as in the daytime, not in carousing and drunkenness, not in sexual immorality and debauchery, not in dissension and jealousy.

POLITICAL AUTHORITY

Paul is his usual self in Romans 13:1–7 and gets straight to the point in verse 1, saying, *'Let everyone be subject to the governing authorities.'*

My immediate response is, 'Why?' But Paul's answer is simple: because *'there is no authority except that which God has established'*.

This is a very clear, but also a very difficult message for Paul to give. The people Paul was writing to lived in Rome and loved Jesus. Because of this, the Roman Empire wanted to kill them – and Paul was telling them to respect the authorities as they had been established by God! I don't know about you, but I would find this difficult to accept. People are persecuted today by their governments for following God or doing what's right – so why should they submit to the authorities? And in a democracy, surely authority comes from the people who vote, not from God?

What Paul is teaching is that there's a distinction between earthly authority and heavenly authority. God has called all leaders to a higher responsibility and authority, namely his (James 3:1–3). Even when good governments turn bad, they still have earthly authority, but when the kingdom of God comes and Jesus returns, all authority will be just. In the meantime, those in God-given authority are called to a higher purpose and a higher state of justice, and it's for the church to remind governments of this.

As people both of God and whatever country we're from, we're called not to disobey government but to challenge it. Jesus taught and lived a subversive gospel that calls the church to question and challenge, and ideally to create space and dialogue with government so that they never forget their calling as leaders under God – leaders who have a responsibility to the poor and marginalised. This calling on the church is sometimes forgotten, but is vitally important. The church is called to limit the power of government by offering the 'Way' as a challenge to the status quo and a reminder of the coming kingdom of God.

Some practical advice

You may not yet have a vote, but that doesn't mean you don't have a voice! Find out what your leaders are doing in your community. Write to your MP and question him/her on what your government is spending money on and why. Write to your local councillors and ask what they are doing to help your neighbours and friends who may be in difficult situations. Start taking responsibility for your government!

Jo Colman

14 Rather, clothe yourselves with the Lord Jesus Christ, and do not think about how to gratify the desires of the flesh.c

The weak and the strong

14 Accept the one whose faith is weak, without quarrelling over disputable matters. 2 One person's faith allows them to eat anything, but another, whose faith is weak, eats only vegetables. 3 The one who eats everything must not treat with contempt the one who does not, and the one who does not eat everything must not judge the one who does, for God has accepted them. 4 Who are you to judge someone else's servant? To their own master, servants stand or fall. And they will stand, for the Lord is able to make them stand.

5 One person considers one day more sacred than another; another considers every day alike. Each of them should be fully convinced in their own mind. 6 Whoever regards one day as special does so to the Lord. Whoever eats meat does so to the Lord, for they give thanks to God; and whoever abstains does so to the Lord and gives thanks to God. 7 For none of us lives for ourselves alone, and none of us dies for ourselves alone. 8 If we live, we live for the Lord; and if we die, we die for the Lord. So, whether we live or die, we belong to the Lord. 9 For this very reason, Christ died and returned to life so that he might be the Lord of both the dead and the living.

10 You, then, why do you judge your brother or sister?a Or why do you treat them with contempt? For we will all stand before God's judgment seat. 11 It is written:

' "As surely as I live," says the Lord,
"Every knee will bow before me;
 every tongue will acknowledge
 God." 'b

12 So then, each of us will give an account of ourselves to God.

13 Therefore let us stop passing judgment on one another. Instead, make up your mind not to put any stumbling-block or obstacle in the way of a brother or sister. 14 I am convinced, being fully persuaded in the Lord Jesus, that nothing is unclean in itself. But if anyone regards something as unclean, then for that person it is unclean. 15 If your brother or sister is distressed because of what you eat, you are no longer acting in love. Do not by your eating destroy someone for whom Christ died. 16 Therefore do not let what you know is good be spoken of as evil. 17 For the kingdom of God is not a matter of eating and drinking, but of righteousness, peace and joy in the Holy Spirit, 18 because anyone who serves Christ in this way is pleasing to God and receives human approval.

19 Let us therefore make every effort to do what leads to peace and to mutual edification. 20 Do not destroy the work of God for the sake of food. All food is clean, but it is wrong for a person to eat anything that causes someone else to stumble. 21 It is better not to eat meat or drink wine or to do anything else that will cause your brother or sister to fall.

22 So whatever you believe about these things keep between yourself and God. Blessed is the one who does not condemn himself by what he approves. 23 But whoever has doubts is condemned if they eat, because their eating is not from faith; and everything that does not come from faith is sin.c

15 We who are strong ought to bear with the failings of the weak and not to please ourselves. 2 Each of us should please our neighbours for their good, to build them up. 3 For even Christ did not please himself but, as it is written: 'The insults of those who insult you have fallen on me.'a 4 For everything that was written in the past was written to teach

c 14 In contexts like this, the Greek word for *flesh* (*sarx*) refers to the sinful state of human beings, often presented as a power in opposition to the Spirit.
a 10 The Greek word for *brother or sister* (*adelphos*) refers here to a believer, whether man or woman, as part of God's family; also in verses 13, 15 and 21.
b 11 Isaiah 45:23

c 23 Some manuscripts place 16:25-27 here; others after 15:33.
a 3 Psalm 69:9

us, so that through the endurance taught in the Scriptures and the encouragement they provide we might have hope.

5 May the God who gives endurance and encouragement give you the same attitude of mind toward each other that Christ Jesus had, 6 so that with one mind and one voice you may glorify the God and Father of our Lord Jesus Christ.

7 Accept one another, then, just as Christ accepted you, in order to bring praise to God. 8 For I tell you that Christ has

BEREAVEMENT

Woody Allen once said, 'I'm not afraid of dying, I just don't want to be there when it happens.' For many of us this is a statement that rings true. As humans, we seem to be a lot better at coping with the ecstatic highs of life rather than the crushing lows it can also bring. When things go well, all is right with the world, but when things take a turn for the worse, how do we handle that?

In the time of the early Roman church, life was as up and down as it could get. At the estimated time of Paul writing his letter to the Romans, the city and the empire were under the rule of the Emperor Nero, a chief protagonist in the persecution of Christians. Put plainly, Rome was a very frightening place to be. Paul would find this out as he suffered grave injustices at the hands of the Romans later in his ministry.

Considering the context of Paul's letter, his words must have taken on a greater sense of importance because – unlike today – death was a very real and present possibility to Christians in Rome.

The purpose of Paul's letter was to reaffirm the gospel to Christians already in Rome, to quash some of the myths about Christianity circling around the city, and to comfort and encourage Christians in their faith, while also addressing the very real issues they were facing – issues of actual life and death.

In Romans 14:8–9, Paul removes the human side of death, the emotion, the fear, the uncertainty, and focuses purely on the issue that really matters: God's supremacy.

Death is hard. Not necessarily for the person who has passed away, but more for the people left behind. Feelings of emptiness, loneliness and despair all come hand in hand with losing someone close to you. However, as hard as it may be, seeing beyond these emotions is the underlying truth that Paul reaffirmed to the Romans: that whether we live or we die, we belong to God.

This declaration of truth directed at people threatened with the increasing possibility of death or people who had recently lost someone close to them will have served as a great comfort and reassurance. My hope is that this is also a comfort and reassurance to you, so when the bad times come along – and they will – you will know that in life and in death, God is entirely in control.

Where better to spend this life and the next than firmly and safely in the hands of our Saviour?

Robbie Thomson

become a servant of the Jews[b] on behalf of God's truth, so that the promises made to the patriarchs might be confirmed 9 and, moreover, that the Gentiles might glorify God for his mercy. As it is written:

'Therefore I will praise you among the Gentiles;
   I will sing the praises of your name.'[c]

10 Again, it says,

'Rejoice, you Gentiles, with his people.'[d]

11 And again,

'Praise the Lord, all you Gentiles;
   let all the peoples extol him.'[e]

12 And again, Isaiah says,

'The Root of Jesse will spring up,
   one who will arise to rule over the nations;
in him the Gentiles will hope.'[f]

13 May the God of hope fill you with all joy and peace as you trust in him, so that you may overflow with hope by the power of the Holy Spirit.

Paul the minister to the Gentiles

14 I myself am convinced, my brothers and sisters, that you yourselves are full of goodness, filled with knowledge and competent to instruct one another. 15 Yet I have written to you quite boldly on some points to remind you of them again, because of the grace God gave me 16 to be a minister of Christ Jesus to the Gentiles. He gave me the priestly duty of proclaiming the gospel of God, so that the Gentiles might become an offering acceptable to God, sanctified by the Holy Spirit.

17 Therefore I glory in Christ Jesus in my service to God. 18 I will not venture to speak of anything except what Christ has accomplished through me in leading the Gentiles to obey God by what I have said and done – 19 by the power of signs and wonders, through the power of the Spirit of God. So from Jerusalem all the way round to Illyricum, I have fully proclaimed the gospel of Christ. 20 It has always been my ambition to preach the gospel where Christ was not known, so that I would not be building on someone else's foundation. 21 Rather, as it is written:

'Those who were not told about him will see,
   and those who have not heard will understand.'[g]

22 This is why I have often been hindered from coming to you.

Paul's plan to visit Rome

23 But now that there is no more place for me to work in these regions, and since I have been longing for many years to visit you, 24 I plan to do so when I go to Spain. I hope to see you while passing through and that you will assist me on my journey there, after I have enjoyed your company for a while. 25 Now, however, I am on my way to Jerusalem in the service of the Lord's people there. 26 For Macedonia and Achaia were pleased to make a contribution for the poor among the Lord's people in Jerusalem. 27 They were pleased to do it, and indeed they owe it to them. For if the Gentiles have shared in the Jews' spiritual blessings, they owe it to the Jews to share with them their material blessings. 28 So after I have completed this task and have made sure that they have received this contribution, I will go to Spain and visit you on the way. 29 I know that when I come to you, I will come in the full measure of the blessing of Christ.

30 I urge you, brothers and sisters, by our Lord Jesus Christ and by the love of the Spirit, to join me in my struggle by praying to God for me. 31 Pray that I may be kept safe from the unbelievers in Judea and

---

b 8   Greek *circumcision*
c 9   2 Samuel 22:50; Psalm 18:49
d 10   Deut. 32:43
e 11   Psalm 117:1
f 12   Isaiah 11:10 (see Septuagint)

g 21   Isaiah 52:15 (see Septuagint)

that the contribution I take to Jerusalem may be favourably received by the Lord's people there, ³²so that I may come to you with joy, by God's will, and in your company be refreshed. ³³The God of peace be with you all. Amen.

Personal greetings

16 I commend to you our sister Phoebe, a deacon*ᵃ,ᵇ* of the church in Cenchreae. ²I ask you to receive her in the Lord in a way worthy of his people and

ᵃ1 Or servant
ᵇ1 The word deacon refers here to a Christian designated to serve with the overseers/elders of the church in a variety of ways; similarly in Phil. 1:1 and 1 Tim. 3:8,12.

to give her any help she may need from you, for she has been the benefactor of many people, including me.

³Greet Priscillaᶜ and Aquila, my fellow workers in Christ Jesus. ⁴They risked their lives for me. Not only I but all the churches of the Gentiles are grateful to them. ⁵Greet also the church that meets at their house.

Greet my dear friend Epenetus, who was the first convert to Christ in the province of Asia.

ᶜ3 Greek Prisca, a variant of Priscilla

THE NAMES OF GOD 5

God of Peace (Yaweh Shalom)

Shalom is the Hebrew word for 'peace'. We long for it – but often we search for it in all the wrong places.

Romans 15:33

'The God of peace be with you all. Amen.'

2 Corinthians 13:11

'Be of one mind, live in peace. And the God of love and peace will be with you.'

A king once offered a prize for the best painting of peace. A number of artists entered the competition, but there were only two entries the king liked. One was a picture of a perfectly calm lake – a picture of perfect tranquillity. The other was of a rugged mountain, with a foaming waterfall crashing down its side. The sky looked angry, the rain fell and the lightning flashed. The picture did not reflect peace, but, looking closely, the king saw behind the waterfall a little bird which had made a nest in the crack of a rock. There, in the midst of the storm and raging torrents, sat the mother bird in perfect peace. That was the picture the king chose.

Only God can provide that inner peace which will carry us through the stresses and strains of life. Life is unlikely to be easy for any of us and, like that bird, we need a shelter for our hearts in the middle of the storm. The God of peace promises to be with us. He wants to be our shelter and our peace today and always.

David and Mary Pytches

 Exodus 15:26　　　　Psalm 23 ▶▶

⁶ Greet Mary, who worked very hard for you.

⁷ Greet Andronicus and Junia, my fellow Jews who have been in prison with me. They are outstanding among*d* the apostles, and they were in Christ before I was.

⁸ Greet Ampliatus, my dear friend in the Lord.

⁹ Greet Urbanus, our fellow worker in Christ, and my dear friend Stachys.

¹⁰ Greet Apelles, whose fidelity to Christ has stood the test.

Greet those who belong to the household of Aristobulus.

¹¹ Greet Herodion, my fellow Jew.

Greet those in the household of Narcissus who are in the Lord.

¹² Greet Tryphena and Tryphosa, those women who work hard in the Lord.

Greet my dear friend Persis, another woman who has worked very hard in the Lord.

¹³ Greet Rufus, chosen in the Lord, and his mother, who has been a mother to me, too.

¹⁴ Greet Asyncritus, Phlegon, Hermes, Patrobas, Hermas and the other brothers and sisters with them.

¹⁵ Greet Philologus, Julia, Nereus and his sister, and Olympas and all the Lord's people who are with them.

¹⁶ Greet one another with a holy kiss.

All the churches of Christ send greetings.

¹⁷ I urge you, brothers and sisters, to watch out for those who cause divisions and put obstacles in your way that are contrary to the teaching you have learned. Keep away from them. ¹⁸ For such people are not serving our Lord Christ, but their own appetites. By smooth talk and flattery they deceive the minds of naïve people. ¹⁹ Everyone has heard about your obedience, so I rejoice because of you; but I want you to be wise about what is good, and innocent about what is evil.

²⁰ The God of peace will soon crush Satan under your feet.

The grace of our Lord Jesus be with you.

²¹ Timothy, my co-worker, sends his greetings to you, as do Lucius, Jason and Sosipater, my fellow Jews.

²² I, Tertius, who wrote down this letter, greet you in the Lord.

²³ Gaius, whose hospitality I and the whole church here enjoy, sends you his greetings.

Erastus, who is the city's director of public works, and our brother Quartus send you their greetings. [24]*e*

²⁵ Now to him who is able to establish you in accordance with my gospel, the message I proclaim about Jesus Christ, in keeping with the revelation of the mystery hidden for long ages past, ²⁶ but now revealed and made known through the prophetic writings by the command of the eternal God, so that all the Gentiles might come to the obedience that comes from *f* faith – ²⁷ to the only wise God be glory for ever through Jesus Christ! Amen.

---

d 7 Or *are esteemed by*

e 24 Some manuscripts include here *May the grace of our Lord Jesus Christ be with all of you. Amen.*

f 26 Or *that is*

1 CORINTHIANS

DATE

This letter was written in AD 55

AUTHOR

The apostle Paul

WHAT'S IT ALL ABOUT?

Corinth was a busy commercial city in Greece where a young church was trying to establish itself. It faced difficult surroundings: Corinth was widely known for its immorality and had a large shrine to Aphrodite, the goddess of love, where temple prostitutes were widely used. Paul wrote this letter while he was in Ephesus (Asia Minor, now Turkey), having heard of the struggles in the Corinthian church. He wrote to strengthen the believers, to give them instructions on how to live, to correct their misunderstandings and misinterpretations of different teachings and to urge them to be holy. Rather than setting down a list of rules, Paul's letter contains one of the most famous passages in all literature about love (1 Corinthians 13), reminding readers how God's amazing love is to shape who we are.

WHY SHOULD WE READ IT?

- Because, although it was written to the Corinthians to correct their behaviour, much of it will strike a chord with us today, encouraging us to correct our own behaviour and move towards holiness.

- To be reminded that our bodies are the temple of the Holy Spirit (1 Corinthians 6).

- To read the warnings coming out of the things God's people learned from their sinful ways in the past (1 Corinthians 10).

- To understand how God's people are meant to work together and honour one another, because we all make up the body of Christ (1 Corinthians 12).

- To learn more about the spiritual gifts (1 Corinthians 12 and 14).

- To read Paul's famous passage about love (1 Corinthians 13).

Andy Croft with Liza Hoeksma

1
Paul, called to be an apostle of Christ Jesus by the will of God, and our brother Sosthenes,

2 To the church of God in Corinth, to those sanctified in Christ Jesus and called to be his holy people, together with all those everywhere who call on the name of our Lord Jesus Christ – their Lord and ours:

3 Grace and peace to you from God our Father and the Lord Jesus Christ.

Thanksgiving
4 I always thank my God for you because of his grace given you in Christ Jesus. 5 For in him you have been enriched in every way – with all kinds of speech and with all knowledge – 6 God thus confirming our testimony about Christ among you. 7 Therefore you do not lack any spiritual gift as you eagerly wait for our Lord Jesus Christ to be revealed. 8 He will also keep you firm to the end, so that you will be blameless on the day of our Lord Jesus Christ. 9 God is faithful, who has called you into fellowship with his Son, Jesus Christ our Lord.

A church divided over leaders
10 I appeal to you, brothers and sisters,*a* in the name of our Lord Jesus Christ, that all of you agree with one another in what you say and that there be no divisions among you, but that you be perfectly united in mind and thought. 11 My brothers and sisters, some from Chloe's household have informed me that there are quarrels among you. 12 What I mean is this: one of you says, 'I follow Paul'; another, 'I follow Apollos'; another, 'I follow Cephas*b*'; still another, 'I follow Christ.'

13 Is Christ divided? Was Paul crucified for you? Were you baptised in the name of Paul? 14 I thank God that I did not baptise any of you except Crispus and Gaius, 15 so no one can say that you were baptised in my name. 16 (Yes, I also baptised the household of Stephanas; beyond that, I don't remember if I baptised anyone else.) 17 For Christ did not send me to baptise, but to preach the gospel – not with wisdom and eloquence, lest the cross of Christ be emptied of its power.

Christ crucified is God's power and wisdom
18 For the message of the cross is foolishness to those who are perishing, but to us who are being saved it is the power of God. 19 For it is written:

'I will destroy the wisdom of the wise;
    the intelligence of the intelligent I
    will frustrate.'*c*

20 Where is the wise person? Where is the teacher of the law? Where is the philosopher of this age? Has not God made foolish the wisdom of the world? 21 For since in the wisdom of God the world through its wisdom did not know him, God was pleased through the foolishness of what was preached to save those who believe. 22 Jews demand signs and Greeks look for wisdom, 23 but we preach Christ crucified: a stumbling-block to Jews and foolishness to Gentiles, 24 but to those whom God has called, both Jews and Greeks, Christ the power of God and the wisdom of God. 25 For the foolishness of God is wiser than human wisdom, and the weakness of God is stronger than human strength.

26 Brothers and sisters, think of what you were when you were called. Not many of you were wise by human standards; not many were influential; not many were of noble birth. 27 But God chose the foolish things of the world to shame the wise; God chose the weak things of the world to shame the strong. 28 God chose the lowly things of this world and the despised things – and the things that are not – to nullify the things that are, 29 so that no

a 10 The Greek word for *brothers and sisters* (adelphoi) refers here to believers, both men and women, as part of God's family; also in verses 11 and 26; and in 2.1, 3.1; 4.6; 6.8; 7.24, 29; 10:1; 11:33; 12:1; 14:6, 20, 26, 39; 15:1, 6, 50, 58; 16:15, 20.
b 12 That is, Peter
c 19 Isaiah 29:14

one may boast before him. ³⁰It is because of him that you are in Christ Jesus, who has become for us wisdom from God – that is, our righteousness, holiness and redemption. ³¹Therefore, as it is written: 'Let the one who boasts boast in the Lord.'*d*

2 And so it was with me, brothers and sisters. When I came to you, I did not come with eloquence or human wisdom as I proclaimed to you the testimony about God.*a* ²For I resolved to know nothing while I was with you except Jesus Christ and him crucified. ³I came to you in weakness with great fear and trembling. ⁴My message and my preaching were not with wise and persuasive words, but with a demonstration of the Spirit's power, ⁵so that your faith might not rest on human wisdom, but on God's power.

God's wisdom revealed by the Spirit

⁶We do, however, speak a message of wisdom among the mature, but not the wisdom of this age or of the rulers of this age, who are coming to nothing. ⁷No, we declare God's wisdom, a mystery that has been hidden and that God destined for our glory before time began. ⁸None of the rulers of this age understood it, for if they had, they would not have crucified the Lord of glory. ⁹However, as it is written:

'What no eye has seen,
  what no ear has heard,
and what no human mind has
    conceived'*b* –
  the things God has prepared for
    those who love him –

¹⁰these are the things God has revealed to us by his Spirit.

The Spirit searches all things, even the deep things of God. ¹¹For who knows a person's thoughts except their own spirit within them? In the same way no one knows the thoughts of God except the Spirit of God. ¹²What we have received is not the spirit of the world, but the Spirit

who is from God, so that we may understand what God has freely given us. ¹³This is what we speak, not in words taught us by human wisdom but in words taught by the Spirit, explaining spiritual realities with Spirit-taught words.*c* ¹⁴The person without the Spirit does not accept the things that come from the Spirit of God but considers them foolishness, and cannot understand them because they are discerned only through the Spirit. ¹⁵The person with the Spirit makes judgments about all things, but such a person is not subject to merely human judgments, ¹⁶for,

'Who has known the mind of the Lord
  so as to instruct him?'*d*

But we have the mind of Christ.

The church and its leaders

3 Brothers and sisters, I could not address you as people who live by the Spirit but as people who are still worldly – mere infants in Christ. ²I gave you milk, not solid food, for you were not yet ready for it. Indeed, you are still not ready. ³You are still worldly. For since there is jealousy and quarrelling among you, are you not worldly? Are you not acting like mere humans? ⁴For when one says, 'I follow Paul,' and another, 'I follow Apollos,' are you not mere human beings?

⁵What, after all, is Apollos? And what is Paul? Only servants, through whom you came to believe – as the Lord has assigned to each his task. ⁶I planted the seed, Apollos watered it, but God has been making it grow. ⁷So neither the one who plants nor the one who waters is anything, but only God, who makes things grow. ⁸The one who plants and the one who waters have one purpose, and they will each be rewarded according to their own labour. ⁹For we are fellow workers in God's service; you are God's field, God's building.

¹⁰By the grace God has given me, I laid a foundation as a wise builder, and

---

d 31 Jer. 9:24
a 1 Some manuscripts *proclaimed to you God's mystery*
b 9 Isaiah 64:4

c 13 Or *Spirit, interpreting spiritual truths to those who are spiritual*
d 16 Isaiah 40:13

someone else is building on it. But each one should build with care. ¹¹ For no one can lay any foundation other than the one already laid, which is Jesus Christ. ¹² If anyone builds on this foundation using gold, silver, costly stones, wood, hay or straw, ¹³ their work will be shown for what it is, because the Day will bring it to light. It will be revealed with fire, and the fire will test the quality of each person's work. ¹⁴ If what has been built survives, the builder will receive a reward. ¹⁵ If it is burned up, the builder will suffer loss but yet will be saved – even though only as one escaping through the flames.

¹⁶ Don't you know that you yourselves are God's temple and that God's Spirit lives among you? ¹⁷ If anyone destroys God's temple, God will destroy that person; for God's temple is sacred, and you together are that temple.

¹⁸ Do not deceive yourselves. If any of you think you are wise by the standards of this age, you should become 'fools' so that you may become wise. ¹⁹ For the wisdom of this world is foolishness in God's sight. As it is written: 'He catches the wise in their craftiness'ᵃ; ²⁰ and again, 'The Lord knows that the thoughts of the wise are futile.'ᵇ ²¹ So then, no more boasting about human leaders! All things are yours, ²² whether Paul or Apollos or Cephasᶜ or

---

ᵃ 19 Job 5:13
ᵇ 20 Psalm 94:11
ᶜ 22 That is, Peter

NATURALLY SUPERNATURAL 7

THE POWER OF THE HOLY SPIRIT IN EVANGELISM

Do you feel the pressure when it comes to evangelism? Do you worry about finding the right thing to say, or wonder how to persuade people with intelligent arguments and win them over with witty stories? Well, you don't need to!

Paul says in 1 Corinthians 2:4–5 that if we're trying to bring people to Jesus through our own words, we're doing something wrong. Instead we should be relying on the power of the Holy Spirit, as he can fill us with wisdom and give us the right words to say. It's by the Holy Spirit that we hear the voice of God (what we call 'prophecy'), and that can be a powerful tool in evangelism.

Ask God to speak to you for a stranger and humbly offer them the words you hear. Or ask God to speak to you about a friend, giving you ways to open up conversations about their beliefs and your faith. When you pray for your friends, ask God to give you encouragements you can share with them. The next time someone tells you they're not feeling well or have hurt themselves, offer to pray for them and ask the Holy Spirit to heal them. If a friend tells you they're worried, ask if you can pray for them that the Holy Spirit might give them peace.

An encounter with the Holy Spirit is far more powerful than anything we can say or do. So let's not think we need to 'do evangelism' in our own power, but let's keep praying for opportunities when people might see the Holy Spirit's power through us.

Mike Pilavachi

 Matthew 11:1–5   1 Corinthians 15:22–25 ▶

the world or life or death or the present or the future – all are yours, ²³ and you are of Christ, and Christ is of God.

The nature of true apostleship

4 This, then, is how you ought to regard us: as servants of Christ and as those entrusted with the mysteries God has revealed. ² Now it is required that those who have been given a trust must prove faithful. ³ I care very little if I am judged by you or by any human court; indeed, I do not even judge myself. ⁴ My conscience is clear, but that does not make me innocent. It is the Lord who judges me. ⁵ Therefore judge nothing before the appointed time; wait until the Lord comes. He will bring to light what is hidden in darkness and will expose the motives of the heart. At that time each will receive their praise from God.

⁶ Now, brothers and sisters, I have applied these things to myself and Apollos for your benefit, so that you may learn from us the meaning of the saying, 'Do not go beyond what is written.' Then you will not be puffed up in being a follower of one of us over against the other. ⁷ For who makes you different from anyone else? What do you have that you did not receive? And if you did receive it, why do you boast as though you did not?

⁸ Already you have all you want! Already you have become rich! You have begun to reign – and that without us! How I wish that you really had begun to reign so that we also might reign with you! ⁹ For it seems to me that God has put us apostles on display at the end of the procession, like those condemned to die in the arena. We have been made a spectacle to the whole universe, to angels as well as to human beings. ¹⁰ We are fools for Christ, but you are so wise in Christ! We are weak, but you are strong! You are honoured, we are dishonoured! ¹¹ To this very hour we go hungry and thirsty, we are in rags, we are brutally treated, we are homeless. ¹² We work hard with our own hands. When we are cursed, we bless; when we are persecuted, we endure it;

¹³ when we are slandered, we answer kindly. We have become the scum of the earth, the garbage of the world – right up to this moment.

Paul's appeal and warning

¹⁴ I am writing this not to shame you but to warn you as my dear children. ¹⁵ Even if you had ten thousand guardians in Christ, you do not have many fathers, for in Christ Jesus I became your father through the gospel. ¹⁶ Therefore I urge you to imitate me. ¹⁷ For this reason I have sent to you Timothy, my son whom I love, who is faithful in the Lord. He will remind you of my way of life in Christ Jesus, which agrees with what I teach everywhere in every church.

¹⁸ Some of you have become arrogant, as if I were not coming to you. ¹⁹ But I will come to you very soon, if the Lord is willing, and then I will find out not only how these arrogant people are talking, but what power they have. ²⁰ For the kingdom of God is not a matter of talk but of power. ²¹ What do you prefer? Shall I come to you with a rod of discipline, or shall I come in love and with a gentle spirit?

Dealing with a case of incest

5 It is actually reported that there is sexual immorality among you, and of a kind that even pagans do not tolerate: a man is sleeping with his father's wife. ² And you are proud! Shouldn't you rather have gone into mourning and have put out of your fellowship the man who has been doing this? ³ For my part, even though I am not physically present, I am with you in spirit. As one who is present with you in this way, I have already passed judgment in the name of our Lord Jesus on the one who has been doing this. ⁴ So when you are assembled and I am with you in spirit, and the power of our Lord Jesus is present, ⁵ hand this man over to Satan for the destruction of the flesh,^{a,b} so that his spirit may be saved on the day of the Lord.

---

a 5 In contexts like this, the Greek word for *flesh* (*sarx*) refers to the sinful state of human beings, often presented as a power in opposition to the Spirit.
b 5 Or *of his body*

6 Your boasting is not good. Don't you know that a little yeast leavens the whole batch of dough? 7 Get rid of the old yeast, so that you may be a new unleavened batch – as you really are. For Christ, our Passover lamb, has been sacrificed. 8 Therefore let us keep the Festival, not with the old bread leavened with malice and wickedness, but with the unleavened bread of sincerity and truth.

9 I wrote to you in my letter not to associate with sexually immoral people – 10 not at all meaning the people of this world who are immoral, or the greedy and swindlers, or idolaters. In that case you would have to leave this world. 11 But now I am writing to you that you must not associate with anyone who claims to be a brother or sister*c* but is sexually immoral or greedy, an idolater or slanderer, a drunkard or swindler. Do not even eat with such people.

12 What business is it of mine to judge those outside the church? Are you not to judge those inside? 13 God will judge those outside. 'Expel the wicked person from among you.'*d*

Lawsuits among believers

6 If any of you has a dispute with another, do you dare to take it before the ungodly for judgment instead of before the Lord's people? 2 Or do you not know that the Lord's people will judge the world? And if you are to judge the world, are you not competent to judge trivial cases? 3 Do you not know that we will judge angels? How much more the things of this life! 4 Therefore, if you have disputes about such matters, do you ask for a ruling from those whose way of life is scorned in the church? 5 I say this to shame you. Is it possible that there is nobody among you wise enough to judge a dispute between believers? 6 But instead, one brother takes another to court – and this in front of unbelievers!

7 The very fact that you have lawsuits

among you means you have been completely defeated already. Why not rather be wronged? Why not rather be cheated? 8 Instead, you yourselves cheat and do wrong, and you do this to your brothers and sisters. 9 Or do you not know that wrongdoers will not inherit the kingdom of God? Do not be deceived: neither the sexually immoral nor idolaters nor adulterers nor men who have sex with men*a* 10 nor thieves nor the greedy nor drunkards nor slanderers nor swindlers will inherit the kingdom of God. 11 And that is what some of you were. But you were washed, you were sanctified, you were justified in the name of the Lord Jesus Christ and by the Spirit of our God.

Sexual immorality

12 'I have the right to do anything,' you say – but not everything is beneficial. 'I have the right to do anything' – but I will not be mastered by anything. 13 You say, 'Food for the stomach and the stomach for food, and God will destroy them both.' The body, however, is not meant for sexual immorality but for the Lord, and the Lord for the body. 14 By his power God raised the Lord from the dead, and he will raise us also. 15 Do you not know that your bodies are members of Christ himself? Shall I then take the members of Christ and unite them with a prostitute? Never! 16 Do you not know that he who unites himself with a prostitute is one with her in body? For it is said, 'The two will become one flesh.'*b* 17 But whoever is united with the Lord is one with him in spirit.*c*

18 Flee from sexual immorality. All other sins a person commits are outside the body, but whoever sins sexually, sins against their own body. 19 Do you not know that your bodies are temples of the Holy Spirit, who is in you, whom you have received from God? You are not your own; 20 you were bought at a price. Therefore honour God with your bodies.

---

c 11 The Greek word for *brother or sister (adelphos)* refers here to a believer, whether man or woman, as part of God's family; also in 8:11, 13.
d 13 Deut. 13:5; 17:7; 19:19; 21:21; 22:21,24; 24:7

a 9 The words *men who have sex with men* translate two Greek words that refer to the passive and active participants in homosexual acts.
b 16 Gen. 2:24
c 17 Or *in the Spirit*

Concerning married life

7 Now for the matters you wrote about: 'It is good for a man not to have sexual relations with a woman.' ²But since sexual immorality is occurring, each man should have sexual relations with his own wife, and each woman with her own husband. ³The husband should fulfil his marital duty to his wife, and likewise the wife to her husband. ⁴The wife does not have authority over her own body but yields it to her husband. In the same way, the husband does not have authority over his own body but yields it to his wife. ⁵Do not deprive each other except perhaps by mutual consent and for a time, so that you may devote yourselves to prayer. Then come together again so that Satan will not tempt you because of your lack of self-control. ⁶I say this as a concession, not as a command. ⁷I wish that all of you were as I am. But each of you has your own gift from God; one has this gift, another has that.

⁸Now to the unmarried*a* and the widows I say: it is good for them to stay unmarried, as I do. ⁹But if they cannot control themselves, they should marry, for it is better to marry than to burn with passion.

¹⁰To the married I give this command

a 8 Or *widowers*

IDENTITY – WHO WE ARE IN CHRIST 9

Temple of the Holy Spirit

In the Old Testament, we read a lot about the places where God's presence was found. The heart of the temple was considered to be so holy that there were incredibly strict rules about going near it and what could happen there.

The ark of the covenant was so holy that people died when they touched it. Now, God's presence is focused in us. He dwells in us by his Holy Spirit and that makes our bodies the modern-day temples of the Holy Spirit (1 Corinthians 6:18–20).

We have already seen that God the Holy Spirit lives in us, and because of that he can empower us to live his way rather than be ruled by our flesh. His Spirit in us confirms that we are God's children, but there's another dimension to his presence in our lives as well: his holiness. God's Holy Spirit is in us. It's another facet of being saints (Romans 1:7; Colossians 1:12).

Part of our identity is as bearers of God's holy presence. There's a responsibility that goes with that. We don't want to defile (that means 'taint or pollute') that holiness, so we need to live lives that are appropriate. We can't go doing whatever we like with our bodies with no regard for the fact that we take God into our every act. We don't just degrade ourselves. It's not just about what we want to do with our bodies.

Our bodies are not simply our own. They were bought at a price. God gave his body as a gift for us. He paid a great price for our bodies. We need to live not as our own, but as God's, for we belong to him.

James Grier

 John 15　　　　　　　Ephesians 4:25–32

(not I, but the Lord): a wife must not separate from her husband. **11** But if she does, she must remain unmarried or else be reconciled to her husband. And a husband must not divorce his wife.

12 To the rest I say this (I, not the Lord): If any brother has a wife who is not a believer and she is willing to live with him, he must not divorce her. **13** And if a woman has a husband who is not a believer and he is willing to live with her, she must not divorce him. **14** For the unbelieving husband has been sanctified through his wife, and the unbelieving wife has been sanctified through her believing husband. Otherwise your children would be unclean, but as it is, they are holy.

15 But if the unbeliever leaves, let it be so. The brother or the sister is not bound in such circumstances; God has called us to live in peace. **16** How do you know, wife, whether you will save your husband? Or, how do you know, husband, whether you will save your wife?

Concerning change of status

17 Nevertheless, each person should live as a believer in whatever situation the Lord has assigned to them, just as God has called them. This is the rule I lay down in all the churches. **18** Was a man already circumcised when he was called? He should not become uncircumcised. Was a man uncircumcised when he was called? He should not be circumcised. **19** Circumcision is nothing and uncircumcision is nothing. Keeping God's commands is what counts. **20** Each person should remain in the situation they were in when God called them.

21 Were you a slave when you were called? Don't let it trouble you – although if you can gain your freedom, do so. **22** For the one who was a slave when called to faith in the Lord is the Lord's freed person; similarly, the one who was free when called is Christ's slave. **23** You were bought at a price; do not become slaves of human beings. **24** Brothers and sisters, each person, as responsible to God, should remain in the situation they were in when God called them.

Concerning the unmarried

25 Now about virgins: I have no command from the Lord, but I give a judgment as one who by the Lord's mercy is trustworthy. **26** Because of the present crisis, I think that it is good for a man to remain as he is. **27** Are you pledged to a woman? Do not seek to be released. Are you free from such a commitment? Do not look for a wife. **28** But if you do marry, you have not sinned; and if a virgin marries, she has not sinned. But those who marry will face many troubles in this life, and I want to spare you this.

29 What I mean, brothers and sisters, is that the time is short. From now on those who have wives should live as if they do not; **30** those who mourn, as if they did not; those who are happy, as if they were not; those who buy something, as if it were not theirs to keep; **31** those who use the things of the world, as if not engrossed in them. For this world in its present form is passing away.

32 I would like you to be free from concern. An unmarried man is concerned about the Lord's affairs – how he can please the Lord. **33** But a married man is concerned about the affairs of this world – how he can please his wife – **34** and his interests are divided. An unmarried woman or virgin is concerned about the Lord's affairs: her aim is to be devoted to the Lord in both body and spirit. But a married woman is concerned about the affairs of this world – how she can please her husband. **35** I am saying this for your own good, not to restrict you, but that you may live in a right way in undivided devotion to the Lord.

36 If anyone is worried that he might not be acting honourably towards the virgin he is engaged to, and if his passions are too strong[b] and he feels he ought to marry, he should do as he wants. He is not sinning. They should get married. **37** But the man who has settled the matter in his own mind, who is under no compulsion but has control over his own will, and who has made up his mind not to marry

b 36 Or if she is getting beyond the usual age for marriage the virgin – this man also does the right thing. ³⁸So then, he who marries the virgin does right, but he who does not marry her does better.ᶜ

³⁹A woman is bound to her husband as long as he lives. But if her husband dies, she is free to marry anyone she wishes, but he must belong to the Lord. ⁴⁰In my judgment, she is happier if she stays as she is – and I think that I too have the Spirit of God.

Concerning food sacrificed to idols

8 Now about food sacrificed to idols: we know that 'We all possess knowledge.' But knowledge puffs up while love builds up. ²Those who think they know something do not yet know as they ought to know. ³But whoever loves God is known by God.ᵃ

⁴So then, about eating food sacrificed to idols: we know that 'An idol is nothing at all in the world' and that 'There is no God but one.' ⁵For even if there are so-called gods, whether in heaven or on earth (as indeed there are many 'gods' and many 'lords'), ⁶yet for us there is but one God, the Father, from whom all things came and for whom we live; and there is but one Lord, Jesus Christ, through whom all things came and through whom we live.

⁷But not everyone possesses this knowledge. Some people are still so accustomed to idols that when they eat sacrificial food they think of it as having been sacrificed to a god, and since their conscience is weak, it is defiled. ⁸But food does not bring us near to God; we are no worse if we do not eat, and no better if we do.

⁹Be careful, however, that the exercise of your rights does not become a stumbling-block to the weak. ¹⁰For if someone with a weak conscience sees you, with all your knowledge, eating in an idol's temple, won't that person be emboldened to eat what is sacrificed to idols? ¹¹So this weak brother or sister, for whom Christ died, is destroyed by your knowledge. ¹²When you sin against them in this way and wound their weak conscience, you sin against Christ. ¹³Therefore, if what I eat causes my brother or sister to fall into sin, I will never eat meat again, so that I will not cause them to fall.

Paul's rights as an apostle

9 Am I not free? Am I not an apostle? Have I not seen Jesus our Lord? Are you not the result of my work in the Lord? ²Even though I may not be an apostle to others, surely I am to you! For you are the seal of my apostleship in the Lord.

³This is my defence to those who sit in judgment on me. ⁴Don't we have the right to food and drink? ⁵Don't we have the right to take a believing wife along with us, as do the other apostles and the Lord's brothers and Cephasᵃ? ⁶Or is it only I and Barnabas who lack the right to not work for a living?

⁷Who serves as a soldier at his own expense? Who plants a vineyard and does not eat its grapes? Who tends a flock and does not drink the milk? ⁸Do I say this merely on human authority? Doesn't the Law say the same thing? ⁹For it is written in the Law of Moses: 'Do not muzzle an ox while it is treading out the grain.'ᵇ Is it about oxen that God is concerned? ¹⁰Surely he says this for us, doesn't he? Yes, this was written for us, because whoever ploughs and threshes should be able to do so in the hope of sharing in the harvest. ¹¹If we have sown spiritual seed among you, is it too much if we reap a material harvest from you? ¹²If others have this right of support from you, shouldn't we have it all the more?

ᶜ 36-38 Or ³⁶If anyone thinks he is not treating his daughter properly, and if she is getting along in years (or if her passions are too strong), and he feels she ought to marry, he should do as he wants. He is not sinning. He should let her get married. ³⁷But the man who has settled the matter in his own mind, who is under no compulsion but has control over his own will, and who has made up his mind to keep the virgin unmarried – this man also does the right thing. ³⁸So then, he who gives his virgin in marriage does right, but he who does not give her in marriage does better.

ᵃ 2,3 An early manuscript and another ancient witness think they have knowledge do not yet know as they ought to know. ³But whoever loves truly knows.

ᵃ 5 That is, Peter
ᵇ 9 Deut. 25:4

But we did not use this right. On the contrary, we put up with anything rather than hinder the gospel of Christ.

¹³ Don't you know that those who serve in the temple get their food from the temple, and that those who serve at the altar share in what is offered on the altar? ¹⁴ In the same way, the Lord has

RELATIONSHIPS 5

SINGLENESS

Singleness is a gift (1 Corinthians 7:32–34). It's likely that for many of you, it might not always feel like it, but your single months and years – however long or short – are a time not to be wasted! With that said, we know that being single can sometimes be really lonely, but we hope that what the Bible says about singleness will really encourage you.

When we look at our friends in relationships, we sometimes only see the 'public face' of their relationship, and while it may look like a really nice way to do life, the realities can often be different. Relationships take a lot of work to be really successful and often require a lot of compromise.

Sometimes our desires for relationships are rooted in the fact that we have been dreaming about our wedding day since we were five, or dreaming about our future careers, lifestyles, houses and family life. As we prepare for our future by doing practical things like choosing what subjects to study, we need to be inviting God to speak to us about our dreams and ambitions, and be prepared that what we dream about may change over time as we understand God's plan for our lives more and more. If you're not in a relationship at the moment, try to keep your focus on God and his will for your life. Try not to allow your interests to be divided until there's commitment to a person who deserves that (v. 34).

It's easy for us to look at ourselves through others' eyes and imagine what they see (and often we imagine stuff that isn't what they think at all). Just because you're single doesn't mean that you're not good enough; it doesn't mean that you're desperate; and it doesn't mean there's anything wrong with you. Starting a relationship is a big decision. It's not worth being with the wrong person just for the sake of being with someone.

In the meantime, you have loads of time to be serving God in so many ways. You're in the unique position where you don't specifically have to consider one other person's thoughts and feelings as you make decisions. You can spend more time serving God and your church. There's time to work through your problems and issues, and you're able to invest time to achieve your own ambitions. It's a time with great potential.

So ask God to speak to you about your future, and enjoy whatever season you're in, making the most of its unique opportunities.

Jane Plackett with Calum Dyke

 Proverbs 27:5–6   1 Samuel 16:1 ▶

commanded that those who preach the gospel should receive their living from the gospel.

15 But I have not used any of these rights. And I am not writing this in the hope that you will do such things for me, for I would rather die than allow anyone to deprive me of this boast. 16 For when I preach the gospel, I cannot boast, since I am compelled to preach. Woe to me if I do not preach the gospel! 17 If I preach voluntarily, I have a reward; if not voluntarily, I am simply discharging the trust committed to me. 18 What then is my reward? Just this: that in preaching the gospel I may offer it free of charge, and so not make full use of my rights as a preacher of the gospel.

Paul's use of his freedom

19 Though I am free and belong to no one, I have made myself a slave to everyone, to win as many as possible. 20 To the Jews I became like a Jew, to win the Jews. To those under the law I became like one under the law (though I myself am not under the law), so as to win those under the law. 21 To those not having the law I became like one not having the law (though I am not free from God's law but am under Christ's law), so as to win those not having the law. 22 To the weak I became weak, to win the weak. I have become all things to all people so that by all possible means I might save some. 23 I do all this for the sake of the gospel, that I may share in its blessings.

The need for self-discipline

24 Do you not know that in a race all the runners run, but only one gets the prize? Run in such a way as to get the prize. 25 Everyone who competes in the games goes into strict training. They do it to get a crown that will not last; but we do it to get a crown that will last for ever. 26 Therefore I do not run like someone running aimlessly; I do not fight like a boxer beating the air. 27 No, I strike a blow to my body and make it my slave so that after I have preached to others, I myself will not be disqualified for the prize.

Warnings from Israel's history

10 For I do not want you to be ignorant of the fact, brothers and sisters, that our ancestors were all under the cloud and that they all passed through the sea. 2 They were all baptised into Moses in the cloud and in the sea. 3 They all ate the same spiritual food 4 and drank the same spiritual drink; for they drank from the spiritual rock that accompanied them, and that rock was Christ. 5 Nevertheless, God was not pleased with most of them; their bodies were scattered in the wilderness.

6 Now these things occurred as examples to keep us from setting our hearts on evil things as they did. 7 Do not be idolaters, as some of them were; as it is written: 'The people sat down to eat and drink and got up to indulge in revelry.'a 8 We should not commit sexual immorality, as some of them did – and in one day twenty-three thousand of them died. 9 We should not test Christ,b as some of them did – and were killed by snakes. 10 And do not grumble, as some of them did – and were killed by the destroying angel.

FACT

LORD'S SUPPER

The earliest account of the Last Supper actually comes from Paul's first letter to the Corinthians, which was probably written a decade before the first Gospels.

11 These things happened to them as examples and were written down as warnings for us, on whom the culmination of the ages has come. 12 So, if you think you are standing firm, be careful that you

---

a 7 Exodus 32:6
b 9 Some manuscripts test the Lord

don't fall! [13] No temptation[c] has overtaken you except what is common to mankind. And God is faithful; he will not let you be tempted[c] beyond what you can bear. But when you are tempted,[c] he will also provide a way out so that you can endure it.

Idol feasts and the Lord's Supper

[14] Therefore, my dear friends, flee from idolatry. [15] I speak to sensible people; judge for yourselves what I say. [16] Is not the cup of thanksgiving for which we give thanks a participation in the blood of Christ? And is not the bread that we break a participation in the body of Christ? [17] Because there is one loaf, we, who are many, are one body, for we all share the one loaf.

[18] Consider the people of Israel: do not those who eat the sacrifices participate in the altar? [19] Do I mean then that food sacrificed to an idol is anything, or that an idol is anything? [20] No, but the sacrifices of pagans are offered to demons, not to God, and I do not want you to be participants with demons. [21] You cannot drink the cup of the Lord and the cup of demons too; you cannot have a part in both the Lord's table and the table of demons. [22] Are we trying to arouse the Lord's jealousy? Are we stronger than he?

The believer's freedom

[23] 'I have the right to do anything,' you say – but not everything is beneficial. 'I have the right to do anything' – but not everything is constructive. [24] No one should seek their own good, but the good of others.

[25] Eat anything sold in the meat market without raising questions of conscience, [26] for, 'The earth is the Lord's, and everything in it.'[d]

[27] If an unbeliever invites you to a meal and you want to go, eat whatever is put before you without raising questions of conscience. [28] But if someone says to you, 'This has been offered in sacrifice,'

then do not eat it, both for the sake of the one who told you and for the sake of conscience. [29] I am referring to the other person's conscience, not yours. For why is my freedom being judged by another's conscience? [30] If I take part in the meal with thankfulness, why am I denounced because of something I thank God for?

[31] So whether you eat or drink or whatever you do, do it all for the glory of God. [32] Do not cause anyone to stumble, whether Jews, Greeks or the church of God – [33] even as I try to please everyone in every way. For I am not seeking my own good but the good of many, so that they may be saved. **11** [1] Follow my example, as I follow the example of Christ.

On covering the head in worship

[2] I praise you for remembering me in everything and for holding to the traditions just as I passed them on to you. [3] But I want you to realise that the head of every man is Christ, and the head of the woman is man,[a] and the head of Christ is God. [4] Every man who prays or prophesies with his head covered dishonours his head. [5] But every woman who prays or prophesies with her head uncovered dishonours her head – it is the same as having her head shaved. [6] For if a woman does not cover her head, she might as well have her hair cut off; but if it is a disgrace for a woman to have her hair cut off or her head shaved, then she should cover her head.

[7] A man ought not to cover his head,[b] since he is the image and glory of God; but woman is the glory of man. [8] For man did not come from woman, but woman from man; [9] neither was man created for woman, but woman for man. [10] It is for this reason that a woman ought to have authority over her own[c] head, because

---

c 13 The Greek for *temptation* and *tempted* can also mean *testing* and *tested*.
d 26 Psalm 24:1

---

a 3 Or *of the wife is her husband*
b 4-7 Or [4]*Every man who prays or prophesies with long hair dishonours his head.* [5]*But every woman who prays or prophesies with no covering of hair dishonours her head – she is just like one of the 'shorn women'.* [6]*If a woman has no covering, let her be for now with short hair; but since it is a disgrace for a woman to have her hair shorn or shaved, she should grow it again.* [7]*A man ought not to have long hair*
c 10 Or *have a sign of authority on her*

of the angels. 11 Nevertheless, in the Lord woman is not independent of man, nor is man independent of woman. 12 For as woman came from man, so also man is born of woman. But everything comes from God.

13 Judge for yourselves: is it proper for a woman to pray to God with her head uncovered? 14 Does not the very nature of things teach you that if a man has long hair, it is a disgrace to him, 15 but that if a woman has long hair, it is her glory? For long hair is given to her as a covering. 16 If anyone wants to be contentious about this, we have no other practice – nor do the churches of God.

Correcting an abuse of the Lord's Supper

17 In the following directives I have no praise for you, for your meetings do more harm than good. 18 In the first place, I hear that when you come together as a church, there are divisions among you, and to some extent I believe it. 19 No doubt there have to be differences among you to show which of you have God's approval. 20 So then, when you come together, it is not the Lord's Supper you eat, 21 for when you are eating, some of you go ahead with your own private suppers. As a result, one person remains hungry and another gets drunk. 22 Don't you have homes to eat and drink in? Or do you despise the church of God by humiliating those who have nothing? What shall I say to you? Shall I praise you? Certainly not in this matter!

23 For I received from the Lord what I also passed on to you: the Lord Jesus, on the night he was betrayed, took bread, 24 and when he had given thanks, he broke it and said, 'This is my body, which is for you; do this in remembrance of me.' 25 In the same way, after supper he took the cup, saying, 'This cup is the new covenant in my blood; do this, whenever you drink it, in remembrance of me.' 26 For whenever you eat this bread and drink this cup, you proclaim the Lord's death until he comes.

27 So then, whoever eats the bread or drinks the cup of the Lord in an unworthy manner will be guilty of sinning against the body and blood of the Lord. 28 Everyone ought to examine themselves before they eat of the bread and drink from the cup. 29 For those who eat and drink without discerning the body of Christ eat and drink judgment on themselves. 30 That is why many among you are weak and ill, and a number of you have fallen asleep. 31 But if we were more discerning with regard to ourselves, we would not come under such judgment. 32 Nevertheless, when we are judged in this way by the Lord, we are being disciplined so that we will not be finally condemned with the world.

33 So then, my brothers and sisters, when you gather to eat, you should all eat together. 34 Anyone who is hungry should eat something at home, so that when you meet together it may not result in judgment.

And when I come I will give further instructions.

Concerning spiritual gifts

12 Now about the gifts of the Spirit, brothers and sisters, I do not want you to be uninformed. 2 You know that when you were pagans, somehow or other you were influenced and led astray to dumb idols. 3 Therefore I want you to know that no one who is speaking by the Spirit of God says, 'Jesus be cursed,' and no one can say, 'Jesus is Lord,' except by the Holy Spirit.

4 There are different kinds of gifts, but the same Spirit distributes them. 5 There are different kinds of service, but the same Lord. 6 There are different kinds of working, but in all of them and in everyone it is the same God at work.

7 Now to each one the manifestation of the Spirit is given for the common good. 8 To one there is given through the Spirit a message of wisdom, to another a message of knowledge by means of the same Spirit, 9 to another faith by the same Spirit, to another gifts of healing by that one Spirit, 10 to another miraculous powers, to another prophecy, to another distinguishing between spirits, to another speaking

WHAT IS CHRISTIANITY? 8

Doctrine of the church: our body

The church is one of the most amazing gifts God has given to us. Yet if we're honest, it might sometimes be the sort of 'gift' we would rather God had kept. What was God thinking when he designed the church?

The place to start is looking at God. God is one God, but he is also Trinity (Matthew 3:13–17). God is a community, Father, Son and Holy Spirit. Because of this, God made the human race to be part of a community – with him and with each other.

After God, the most important character in the Old Testament is Israel, a people not a person. In the New Testament, after Jesus the most important character is the church. Most of the letters in the New Testament are written to the different churches – the Corinthian church, the Philippian church, the Ephesian church and so on. When we read the Bible we're entering into the early community of believers.

God always intended that when we came to know him we would become part of his family. Today we can sometimes think that a building or service is 'the church', but Hebrews 11 lists saints, Christians who have gone all out for God. There have been many names added to the list since it was written – St Francis of Assisi, Mother Teresa, Martin Luther King, and, crazy as it seems, mine and yours.

In 1 Peter 2:4–5 we read that we're the living stones that make up the church. Church isn't about a place, it's about a people. We don't get in because we're special, good or holy – that's why our churches are often full of broken people. We get in because God has saved us and he loves us.

Sometimes it's hard, but if we want to grow as Christians, committing to the church is key (1 Corinthians 12:12–31). Can you imagine what would happen to your arm if you chopped it off? It wouldn't last long. The church, with Jesus at the head, has become our body. When we're attached, we're far stronger than when we cut ourselves off. We can be encouraged, challenged, inspired and held accountable by our brothers and sisters in the faith. *'As iron sharpens iron, so one person sharpens another'* (Proverbs 27:17). God made us for community and that's where we thrive.

The purpose of the church is to assault the darkness of the world we live in and, as the body of Christ, to bring Jesus into every situation. We're a group of people who love God, love each other and seek to share his love with the world. We're flawed, we're broken, we often get it wrong. But none of that changes the fact that we are *'the people of God'* (1 Peter 2:10).

To walk away from the church is easy. But you're a living stone, part of the building. Write your name into the glorious history of the saints. You're part of the family now.

Andy Croft

 Romans 5:1–11   2 Timothy 3:16 ▶

in different kinds of tongues,*a* and to still another the interpretation of tongues.*a* 11 All these are the work of one and the same Spirit, and he distributes them to each one, just as he determines.

Unity and diversity in the body

12 Just as a body, though one, has many parts, but all its many parts form one body, so it is with Christ. 13 For we were all baptised by*b* one Spirit so as to form one body – whether Jews or Gentiles, slave or free – and we were all given the one Spirit to drink. 14 And so the body is not made up of one part but of many.

15 Now if the foot should say, 'Because I am not a hand, I do not belong to the body,' it would not for that reason stop being part of the body. 16 And if the ear should say, 'Because I am not an eye, I do not belong to the body,' it would not for that reason stop being part of the body. 17 If the whole body were an eye, where would the sense of hearing be? If the whole body were an ear, where would the sense of smell be? 18 But in fact God has placed the parts in the body, every one of them, just as he wanted them to be. 19 If they were all one part, where would the body be? 20 As it is, there are many parts, but one body.

21 The eye cannot say to the hand, 'I don't need you!' And the head cannot say to the feet, 'I don't need you!' 22 On the contrary, those parts of the body that seem to be weaker are indispensable, 23 and the parts that we think are less honourable we treat with special honour. And the parts that are unpresentable are treated with special modesty, 24 while our presentable parts need no special treatment. But God has put the body together, giving greater honour to the parts that lacked it, 25 so that there should be no division in the body, but that its parts should have equal concern for each other. 26 If one part suffers, every part suffers with it; if one part is honoured, every part rejoices with it.

27 Now you are the body of Christ,

and each one of you is a part of it. 28 And God has placed in the church first of all apostles, second prophets, third teachers, then miracles, then gifts of healing, of helping, of guidance, and of different kinds of tongues. 29 Are all apostles? Are all prophets? Are all teachers? Do all work miracles? 30 Do all have gifts of healing? Do all speak in tongues*c*? Do all interpret? 31 Now eagerly desire the greater gifts.

Love is indispensable

And yet I will show you the most excellent way.

13 If I speak in the tongues*a* of men or of angels, but do not have love, I am only a resounding gong or a clanging cymbal. 2 If I have the gift of prophecy and can fathom all mysteries and all knowledge, and if I have a faith that can move mountains, but do not have love, I am nothing. 3 If I give all I possess to the poor and give over my body to hardship that I may boast,*b* but do not have love, I gain nothing.

4 Love is patient, love is kind. It does not envy, it does not boast, it is not proud. 5 It does not dishonour others, it is not self-seeking, it is not easily angered, it keeps no record of wrongs. 6 Love does not delight in evil but rejoices with the truth. 7 It always protects, always trusts, always hopes, always perseveres.

8 Love never fails. But where there are prophecies, they will cease; where there are tongues, they will be stilled; where there is knowledge, it will pass away. 9 For we know in part and we prophesy in part, 10 but when completeness comes, what is in part disappears. 11 When I was a child, I talked like a child, I thought like a child, I reasoned like a child. When I became a man, I put the ways of childhood behind me. 12 For now we see only a reflection as in a mirror; then we shall see face to face. Now I know in part; then I shall know fully, even as I am fully known.

13 And now these three remain: faith,

---

a 10 Or *languages*; also in verse 28
b 13 Or *with*; or *in*

c 30 Or *other languages*
a 1 Or *languages*
b 3 Some manuscripts *body to the flames*

hope and love. But the greatest of these is love.

Intelligibility in worship

14 Follow the way of love and eagerly desire gifts of the Spirit, especially prophecy. ² For anyone who speaks in a tongue*ᵃ* does not speak to people but to God. Indeed, no one understands them; they utter mysteries by the Spirit. ³ But the one who prophesies speaks to

a 2 Or *in another language*; also in verses 4, 13, 14, 19, 26 and 27

THE PERSECUTED CHURCH – ONE BODY

Paul gives us a beautiful image of the church being one body, something that goes way beyond gender, culture and time zones. One body, many parts.

'If one part suffers, every part suffers with it; if one part is honoured, every part rejoices with it' (1 Corinthians 12:26).

We're all important and we all have our part to play. The truth is that today many parts of the church body are suffering through persecution. Over two thirds of the world's population live where the gospel is restricted, and over 100 million believers face persecution for their faith in Jesus Christ. This persecution could range from being denied an education or being outcast by friends and family, to being tortured or even killed.

This is family business. When one part suffers, all the parts suffer with it. If someone in our family is going through a tough time, we care about it, and it should be so with the worldwide church. The Bible is littered with verses about identifying with those who suffer. Hebrews 13:3 says, *'Continue to remember those in prison as if you were together with them in prison.'* We shouldn't go out looking for suffering, but we're called to care, to stand with, to be a voice for the voiceless.

The Bible uses the wonderful Greek word *splanchnizomai,* which is translated into English as 'to have mercy', or 'to show pity'. But this comes from the root *splanchnon,* which literally means 'inward parts'. The English doesn't capture this real gut-wrenching feeling of being moved by injustice, by suffering.

We are all part of one body, and we all have our part to play.

Action

The number one thing that persecuted believers ask for is prayer. Could you gather your mates or youth group to pray? Pray for those who share your faith, but not your freedom.

Identify with the persecuted church by hosting your own secret service. Meet in a dark venue, confiscate Bibles, take out the seating, worship in whispers… be as creative as you can! Reflect on your experience and remember those who must always meet in secret.

Jonny Goodchild, Open Doors

RELATIONSHIPS 3

IT'S NOT ALWAYS GOING TO BE EASY...

What an incredible list we find in 1 Corinthians 13:4–8! These verses are a favourite reading at weddings, and have you ever wondered why? It's a daunting standard, and when we read this it's easy to feel pretty depressed that we don't love people adequately.

When someone impresses us with their wit or intelligence, or when they're kind and considerate, it's pretty easy to love them. Loving people when they're at their best is simple. But what about loving someone when they disappoint us, or make poor decisions, or are selfish and rude? Yes. We have to love them then too, and in exactly the same way.

There has been a trend recently for people to write their own marriage vows, and what's interesting is that most people's vows go something like this: 'I love you so much, I choose you, you are my everything. I know that all my prayers have been answered and that all of my dreams have come true. This is the moment I have waited my whole life for...'

And what's wrong with that? The problem is that this wedding vow isn't really about love in its biblical sense. Love isn't something you experience in the moment, it's not a feeling, and it's not about finding your completion in another person. Love is a verb – a word used to describe an action. This is why the traditional marriage vows don't say, 'I love you.' They say, 'I *will* love you.' One is a statement about the current situation. The other is a promise for life.

The Bible tells us that God is love. So if God is consistent and unchanging, then love is also consistent and unchanging. *'Love never fails'* (v. 8). It's a really tall order, but when we remember that we're an imperfect reflection of God, we realise that we can't be expected to do this relationship thing perfectly! There will always be some moments of friction. We read that *'Love is patient, love is kind. It does not envy...'* (v. 4), but sometimes we represent the opposite of that to the people we care about. We're not able to love people perfectly because we're not God, but it doesn't stop us from trying!

When things are difficult, the challenge God gives us is to look actively for ways to love that person more. When they disappoint you, encourage them; when they're angry, be patient; when they're selfish, be generous. Loving people is a costly thing. We're not asked just to love people when it's convenient and easy, but also when it's heartbreaking and difficult.

We're fed constant media images that say relationships are easy, and when they stop being easy we should get out and find someone else. This isn't God's plan for relationships. Imagine if he had done that with us!

Jane Plackett & Calum Dyke

 Ecclesiastes 4:7–12   Proverbs 27:5–6

people for their strengthening, encouraging and comfort. ⁴Anyone who speaks in a tongue edifies themselves, but the one who prophesies edifies the church. ⁵I would like every one of you to speak in tongues,ᵇ but even more to prophesy. The one who prophesies is greater than the one who speaks in tongues,ᵇ unless someone interprets, so that the church may be edified.

⁶Now, brothers and sisters, if I come to you and speak in tongues, what good will I be to you, unless I bring you some revelation or knowledge or prophecy or word of instruction? ⁷Even in the case of lifeless things that make sounds, such as the pipe or harp, how will anyone know what tune is being played unless there is a distinction in the notes? ⁸Again, if the trumpet does not sound a clear call, who will get ready for battle? ⁹So it is with you. Unless you speak intelligible words with your tongue, how will anyone know what you are saying? You will just be speaking into the air. ¹⁰Undoubtedly there are all sorts of languages in the world, yet none of them is without meaning. ¹¹If then I do not grasp the meaning of what someone is saying, I am a foreigner to the speaker, and the speaker is a foreigner to me. ¹²So it is with you. Since you are eager for gifts of the Spirit, try to excel in those that build up the church.

¹³For this reason the one who speaks in a tongue should pray that they may interpret what they say. ¹⁴For if I pray in a tongue, my spirit prays, but my mind is unfruitful. ¹⁵So what shall I do? I will pray with my spirit, but I will also pray with my understanding; I will sing with my spirit, but I will also sing with my understanding. ¹⁶Otherwise when you are praising God in the Spirit, how can someone else, who is now put in the position of an enquirer,ᶜ say 'Amen' to your thanksgiving, since they do not know what you are

saying? ¹⁷You are giving thanks well enough, but no one else is edified.

¹⁸I thank God that I speak in tongues more than all of you. ¹⁹But in the church I would rather speak five intelligible words to instruct others than ten thousand words in a tongue.

²⁰Brothers and sisters, stop thinking like children. In regard to evil be infants, but in your thinking be adults. ²¹In the Law it is written:

'With other tongues
    and through the lips of foreigners
I will speak to this people,
    but even then they will not listen
        to me,
                 says the Lord.'ᵈ

²²Tongues, then, are a sign, not for believers but for unbelievers; prophecy, however, is not for unbelievers but for believers. ²³So if the whole church comes together and everyone speaks in tongues, and enquirers or unbelievers come in, will they not say that you are out of your mind? ²⁴But if an unbeliever or an enquirer comes in while everyone is prophesying, they are convicted of sin and are brought under judgment by all, ²⁵as the secrets of their hearts are laid bare. So they will fall down and worship God, exclaiming, 'God is really among you!'

Good order in worship

²⁶What then shall we say, brothers and sisters? When you come together, each of you has a hymn, or a word of instruction, a revelation, a tongue or an interpretation. Everything must be done so that the church may be built up. ²⁷If anyone speaks in a tongue, two – or at the most three – should speak, one at a time, and someone must interpret. ²⁸If there is no interpreter, the speaker should keep quiet in the church and speak to himself and to God.

²⁹Two or three prophets should speak, and the others should weigh carefully what is said. ³⁰And if a revelation comes

---

ᵇ5 Or in other languages; also in verses 6, 18, 22, 23 and 39
ᶜ16 The Greek word for enquirer is a technical term for someone not fully initiated into a religion; also in verses 23 and 24.

ᵈ21 Isaiah 28:11,12

to someone who is sitting down, the first speaker should stop. 31 For you can all prophesy in turn so that everyone may be instructed and encouraged. 32 The spirits of prophets are subject to the control of prophets. 33 For God is not a God of disorder but of peace – as in all the congregations of the Lord's people.

34 Women[e] should remain silent in the churches. They are not allowed to speak, but must be in submission, as the law says. 35 If they want to enquire about something, they should ask their own husbands at home; for it is disgraceful for a woman to speak in the church.[f] 36 Or did the word of God originate with you? Or are you the only people it has reached? 37 If anyone thinks they are a prophet or otherwise gifted by the Spirit, let them acknowledge that what I am writing to you is the Lord's command. 38 But if anyone ignores this, they will themselves be ignored.[g]

39 Therefore, my brothers and sisters, be eager to prophesy, and do not forbid speaking in tongues. 40 But everything should be done in a fitting and orderly way.

The resurrection of Christ

15 Now, brothers and sisters, I want to remind you of the gospel I preached to you, which you received and on which you have taken your stand. 2 By this gospel you are saved, if you hold firmly to the word I preached to you. Otherwise, you have believed in vain.

3 For what I received I passed on to you as of first importance[a]: that Christ died for our sins according to the Scriptures, 4 that he was buried, that he was raised on the third day according to the Scriptures, 5 and that he appeared to Cephas,[b] and then to the Twelve. 6 After that, he appeared to more than five hundred of the brothers and sisters at the same time, most of whom are still living, though some have fallen asleep. 7 Then he appeared to James, then to all the apostles, 8 and last of all he appeared to me also, as to one abnormally born.

9 For I am the least of the apostles and do not even deserve to be called an apostle, because I persecuted the church of God. 10 But by the grace of God I am what I am, and his grace to me was not without effect. No, I worked harder than all of them – yet not I, but the grace of God that was with me. 11 Whether, then, it is I or they, this is what we preach, and this is what you believed.

The resurrection of the dead

12 But if it is preached that Christ has been raised from the dead, how can some of you say that there is no resurrection of the dead? 13 If there is no resurrection of the dead, then not even Christ has been raised. 14 And if Christ has not been raised, our preaching is useless and so is your faith. 15 More than that, we are then found to be false witnesses about God, for we have testified about God that he raised Christ from the dead. But he did not raise him if in fact the dead are not raised. 16 For if the dead are not raised, then Christ has not been raised either. 17 And if Christ has not been raised, your faith is futile; you are still in your sins. 18 Then those also who have fallen asleep in Christ are lost. 19 If only for this life we have hope in Christ, we are of all people most to be pitied.

20 But Christ has indeed been raised from the dead, the firstfruits of those who have fallen asleep. 21 For since death came through a man, the resurrection of the dead comes also through a man. 22 For as in Adam all die, so in Christ all will be made alive. 23 But each in turn: Christ, the firstfruits; then, when he comes, those who belong to him. 24 Then the end will come, when he hands over the kingdom to God the Father after he has destroyed all dominion, authority and power. 25 For he must reign until he has put all his enemies under his feet. 26 The last enemy to be destroyed is death. 27 For he 'has put

---

e 33,34 Or peace. As in all the congregations of the Lord's people, 34women
f 34,35 In a few manuscripts these verses come after verse 40.
g 38 Some manuscripts But anyone who is ignorant of this will be ignored
a 3 Or you at the first
b 5 That is, Peter

everything under his feet'.ᶜ Now when it says that 'everything' has been put under him, it is clear that this does not include God himself, who put everything under Christ. ²⁸When he has done this, then the Son himself will be made subject to him who put everything under him, so that God may be all in all.

²⁹Now if there is no resurrection, what will those do who are baptised for the dead? If the dead are not raised at all, why are people baptised for them? ³⁰And

as for us, why do we endanger ourselves every hour? ³¹I face death every day – yes, just as surely as I boast about you in Christ Jesus our Lord. ³²If I fought wild beasts in Ephesus with no more than human hopes, what have I gained? If the dead are not raised,

'Let us eat and drink,
    for tomorrow we die.'ᵈ

³³Do not be misled: 'Bad company

ᶜ 27 Psalm 8:6

ᵈ 32 Isaiah 22:13

NATURALLY SUPERNATURAL 8

THE KINGDOM NOW AND NOT YET

When we pray for healings and miracles, we don't always see God do the things we ask for. It can be confusing and painful as we try to work out why God didn't bring the change we desperately wanted. We can be tempted to wonder if God doesn't care. Or perhaps we doubt his power, or blame ourselves and think we did something wrong.

Some people have shied away from praying for any miracles or healings altogether because it's so painful when it doesn't work out. So why do we sometimes see God do amazing things and at other times nothing happens? The reality is that we live in the kingdom 'now and not yet'. That means that we see glimpses of God's power here on earth, but we don't see its fullness and we won't see that until Jesus comes again (1 Corinthians 15:22–25).

When Jesus rose from the grave, he had won a victory over death and sin. But for now we are living in tension: although he won the victory, he hasn't yet taken full control of the earth. When he does that, we will see the full kingdom come. That's when every tear will be wiped away, sickness and death will be gone (Revelation 21). Until that time we will sometimes pray and see bits of the kingdom come now. We will sometimes see people's sight restored, their cancer gone, their back problem miraculously healed. But we will also have times when nothing changes and we remember we're in the time when the kingdom is 'not yet'. In those times let's not lose sight of God and all that he is capable of doing. Let's remember that he is good, he is powerful, he is kind, and he loves us and all those we pray for. Let's remember that the more we pray, the more likely we are to see those healings and miracles. Let's keep our faith and keep asking our heavenly Father to bring his kingdom on earth as it is in heaven.

Mike Pilavachi

 1 Corinthians 2:4–5   Acts 3:6–7

corrupts good character.'ᵉ ³⁴Come back to your senses as you ought, and stop sinning; for there are some who are ignorant of God – I say this to your shame.

The resurrection body

³⁵But someone will ask, 'How are the dead raised? With what kind of body will they come?' ³⁶How foolish! What you sow does not come to life unless it dies. ³⁷When you sow, you do not plant the body that will be, but just a seed, perhaps of wheat or of something else. ³⁸But God gives it a body as he has determined, and to each kind of seed he gives its own body. ³⁹Not all flesh is the same: people have one kind of flesh, animals have another, birds another and fish another. ⁴⁰There are also heavenly bodies and there are earthly bodies; but the splendour of the heavenly bodies is one kind, and the splendour of the earthly bodies is another. ⁴¹The sun has one kind of splendour, the moon another and the stars another; and star differs from star in splendour.

⁴²So will it be with the resurrection of the dead. The body that is sown is perishable, it is raised imperishable; ⁴³it is sown in dishonour, it is raised in glory; it is sown in weakness, it is raised in power; ⁴⁴it is sown a natural body, it is raised a spiritual body.

If there is a natural body, there is also a spiritual body. ⁴⁵So it is written: 'The first man Adam became a living being'ᶠ; the last Adam, a life-giving spirit. ⁴⁶The spiritual did not come first, but the natural, and after that the spiritual. ⁴⁷The first man was of the dust of the earth; the second man is of heaven. ⁴⁸As was the earthly man, so are those who are of the earth; and as is the heavenly man, so also are those who are of heaven. ⁴⁹And just as we have borne the image of the earthly man, so shall weᵍ bear the image of the heavenly man.

⁵⁰I declare to you, brothers and sisters, that flesh and blood cannot inherit the kingdom of God, nor does the perishable inherit the imperishable. ⁵¹Listen, I tell you a mystery: we will not all sleep, but we will all be changed – ⁵²in a flash, in the twinkling of an eye, at the last trumpet. For the trumpet will sound, the dead will be raised imperishable, and we will be changed. ⁵³For the perishable must clothe itself with the imperishable, and the mortal with immortality. ⁵⁴When the perishable has been clothed with the imperishable, and the mortal with immortality, then the saying that is written will come true: 'Death has been swallowed up in victory.'ʰ

⁵⁵'Where, O death, is your victory?
    Where, O death, is your sting?'ⁱ

⁵⁶The sting of death is sin, and the power of sin is the law. ⁵⁷But thanks be to God! He gives us the victory through our Lord Jesus Christ.

⁵⁸Therefore, my dear brothers and sisters, stand firm. Let nothing move you. Always give yourselves fully to the work of the Lord, because you know that your labour in the Lord is not in vain.

The collection for the Lord's people

16 Now about the collection for the Lord's people: do what I told the Galatian churches to do. ²On the first day of every week, each one of you should set aside a sum of money in keeping with your income, saving it up, so that when I come no collections will have to be made. ³Then, when I arrive, I will give letters of introduction to the men you approve and send them with your gift to Jerusalem. ⁴If it seems advisable for me to go also, they will accompany me.

Personal requests

⁵After I go through Macedonia, I will come to you – for I will be going through Macedonia. ⁶Perhaps I will stay with you for a while, or even spend the winter, so that you can help me on my journey, wherever I go. ⁷For I do not want to see

---

e 33 From the Greek poet Menander
f 45 Gen. 2:7
g 49 Some early manuscripts *so let us*

h 54 Isaiah 25:8
i 55 Hosea 13:14

you now and make only a passing visit; I hope to spend some time with you, if the Lord permits. 8 But I will stay on at Ephesus until Pentecost, 9 because a great door for effective work has opened to me, and there are many who oppose me.

10 When Timothy comes, see to it that he has nothing to fear while he is with

RESURRECTION

There are many theories about what actually happened on that first Easter Day, each trying to explain why a group of Jews who had seen their teacher die on a cross would then travel round the known world telling everyone who would listen that he had risen from the dead.

Did he swoon and people assumed he was dead? Did someone else take his place on the cross? Or perhaps he did die, and his followers had some kind of hallucination brought on by grief? Or did they decide to make the story up to carry on his memory? But all these questions only bring up more questions. Why would the early Christians be willing to die for an idea they knew was a lie? Is it possible for well over 500 people (1 Corinthians 15:5–8) to have the same hallucination? And the Romans were experts at killing people, so there's no chance Jesus could have survived crucifixion. Many people died while being flogged even before being crucified.

There are other historical factors which lead many historians to conclude that the most obvious explanation for the stories is this: Jesus really did rise from the dead. But even if this is the case, why is it important? Does it matter if Jesus literally rose, or if it was just a spiritual experience the disciples had?

In 1 Corinthians 15, Paul gives us a very firm answer: *'If Christ has not been raised, our preaching is useless and so is your faith'* (v. 14). Jesus' resurrection is central to all we believe as Christians. It's not just a happy ending to the Easter story! It signals the start of a new era in history, the key moment in God's plan of redemption. The resurrection, a day the Jews looked forward to when all the righteous dead would rise and God would bring justice to the earth, has somehow arrived in the middle of history. The Jews believed it would happen on a global scale at the end of the age, but the early Christians began to realise that this future event had somehow invaded the present, and Jesus' resurrection was a guarantee, a signpost, a 'first fruit' of the great resurrection to come.

If Jesus has not been raised, his death on the cross is just a great martyr's death. But if he has been raised, this changes everything. Death has been defeated for ever. Paul teaches us a profound truth here: *'Therefore … your labour in the Lord is not in vain'* (v. 58).

Everything we do in this life matters. 'Every loving act, every right choice, every sacrificial deed is going to be there … taken up in some way into the new creation' (Michael Lloyd, *Café Theology*). In the same way that Jesus' resurrected body carried the scars of his great sacrifice, because of the resurrection every sacrifice we make for God, every selfless decision, every act of generosity echoes into our eternal future with Jesus.

Chris Lane

you, for he is carrying on the work of the Lord, just as I am. ¹¹ No one, then, should treat him with contempt. Send him on his way in peace so that he may return to me. I am expecting him along with the brothers.

¹² Now about our brother Apollos: I strongly urged him to go to you with the brothers. He was quite unwilling to go now, but he will go when he has the opportunity.

¹³ Be on your guard; stand firm in the faith; be courageous; be strong. ¹⁴ Do everything in love.

¹⁵ You know that the household of Stephanas were the first converts in Achaia, and they have devoted themselves to the service of the Lord's people. I urge

---

JUSTICE AND MERCY 8

LOVE IN ACTION

In this quick look through some important passages, we have discovered that how we relate to the last, the least and the lost is at the heart of God's mission in the world. Justice is not an add-on for the super keen, but the heartbeat of a God in love with his creation. That's where we are going to end this little tour through the Bible – with love (1 Corinthians 16:14).

God created us because he loves us and wants to be in relationship with us. He continued loving us when we blew it in the Garden of Eden and he keeps on loving us through all our selfishness, fear and sin. Jesus came to earth to demonstrate that love by showing us what love looks like in action. Paul tells the Corinthians in 1 Corinthians 13:3 that even if they give away everything they have to the poor, they have nothing unless they love. It's love that's at the heart of being Christian, that motivates and inspires, that compels action and sacrifice. God is passionate about seeking justice and serving the last, the least and the lost, but if we do those things out of duty or pride rather than love, then we have missed the point.

Love must be our motivation. First, it should be God's love for us that wakes us up to the fact that we are cherished and special. From this, we should find that love overflows from us to others. Second, it should be our love for God that drives us to look after those in need. Then we need to make sure that everything we do is motivated by love for those with whom we come into contact. We need to keep asking God to fill our hearts with love so that we don't find that, after all our good works, we end up bankrupt as Paul warns (1 Corinthians 13:1–3).

So, as we end this thread on Justice, let's resolve to act justly, to serve sacrificially and to speak up for others. And let's do these things because we have been touched by the amazing love of God, and that love simply has to overflow to others.

David Westlake

 Luke 4:18–19

you, brothers and sisters, **16** to submit to such people and to everyone who joins in the work and labours at it. **17** I was glad when Stephanas, Fortunatus and Achaicus arrived, because they have supplied what was lacking from you. **18** For they refreshed my spirit and yours also. Such men deserve recognition.

Final greetings

19 The churches in the province of Asia send you greetings. Aquila and Priscilla*a* greet you warmly in the Lord, and so does the church that meets at their house. **20** All the brothers and sisters here send you greetings. Greet one another with a holy kiss.

21 I, Paul, write this greeting in my own hand.

22 If anyone does not love the Lord, let that person be cursed! Come, Lord*b*!

23 The grace of the Lord Jesus be with you. **24** My love to all of you in Christ Jesus. Amen.*c*

---

a 19 Greek *Prisca*, a variant of *Priscilla*

b 22 The Greek for *Come, Lord* reproduces an Aramaic expression (*Marana tha*) used by early Christians.
c 24 Some manuscripts do not have *Amen*.

2 CORINTHIANS

DATE

This letter was written in AD 55

AUTHOR

The apostle Paul

WHAT'S IT ALL ABOUT?

This letter from Paul to the church in Corinth, Greece, was probably written within the same year as his first (1 Corinthians). Some people in the church had been causing trouble, saying that Paul couldn't be trusted and they shouldn't listen to his teaching, so Paul's letter highlights his integrity and reassures the church of his consistency of action and teaching. He speaks of the hardships he has overcome (such as being beaten, imprisoned, doing hard work, and suffering lack of sleep and food) for the sake of the gospel, showing his devotion to spreading God's word no matter what it costs him. He emphasises that the Corinthians have heard the true gospel and shouldn't be side-tracked by false teachers. Because he is defending himself, the letter is quite personal in nature and it's clear that at times Paul is uncomfortable with the way he has to speak about his own achievements in order to reassure them (even saying, 'I am out of my mind to talk like this'). This letter gives us insights into Paul's life, as well as some great teaching.

WHY SHOULD WE READ IT?

- Because this letter shows the difficulties Paul faced, both in personal accusations about his motives and behaviour, and in trying to keep the church on track in their relationship with God.

- To see the things Paul suffered as he tried to spread the gospel, and to be encouraged by his example that nothing should stand in our way as we try to do God's work (2 Corinthians 11 – 12).

- Because it shows us that being a leader brings its own set of problems and concerns.

- To read teaching on God's comfort (2 Corinthians 1), the glory of the new covenant (2 Corinthians 1), how we are new creations in Jesus (2 Corinthians 5) and how we can keep going when we are suffering (2 Corinthians 4 and 6).

- To be reminded of the importance of generosity (2 Corinthians 8 and 9).

Andy Croft with Liza Hoeksma

1 Paul, an apostle of Christ Jesus by the will of God, and Timothy our brother,

To the church of God in Corinth, together with all his holy people throughout Achaia:

² Grace and peace to you from God our Father and the Lord Jesus Christ.

Praise to the God of all comfort

³ Praise be to the God and Father of our Lord Jesus Christ, the Father of compassion and the God of all comfort, ⁴ who comforts us in all our troubles, so that we can comfort those in any trouble with the comfort we ourselves receive from God. ⁵ For just as we share abundantly in the sufferings of Christ, so also our comfort abounds through Christ. ⁶ If we are distressed, it is for your comfort and salvation; if we are comforted, it is for your comfort, which produces in you patient endurance of the same sufferings we suffer. ⁷ And our hope for you is firm, because we know that just as you share in our sufferings, so also you share in our comfort.

⁸ We do not want you to be uninformed, brothers and sisters,ᵃ about the troubles we experienced in the province of Asia. We were under great pressure, far beyond our ability to endure, so that we despaired of life itself. ⁹ Indeed, we felt we had received the sentence of death. But this happened that we might not rely on ourselves but on God, who raises the dead. ¹⁰ He has delivered us from such a deadly peril, and he will deliver us again. On him we have set our hope that he will continue to deliver us, ¹¹ as you help us by your prayers. Then many will give thanks on our behalf for the gracious favour granted us in answer to the prayers of many.

Paul's change of plans

¹² Now this is our boast: our conscience testifies that we have conducted ourselves in the world, and especially in our rela-

tions with you, with integrityᵇ and godly sincerity. We have done so, relying not on worldly wisdom but on God's grace. ¹³ For we do not write to you anything you cannot read or understand. And I hope that, ¹⁴ as you have understood us in part, you will come to understand fully that you can boast of us just as we will boast of you in the day of the Lord Jesus.

¹⁵ Because I was confident of this, I wanted to visit you first so that you might benefit twice. ¹⁶ I wanted to visit you on my way to Macedonia and to come back to you from Macedonia, and then to let you send me on my way to Judea. ¹⁷ Was I fickle when I intended to do this? Or do I make my plans in a worldly manner so that in the same breath I say both 'Yes, yes' and 'No, no'?

¹⁸ But as surely as God is faithful, our message to you is not 'Yes' and 'No'. ¹⁹ For the Son of God, Jesus Christ, who was preached among you by us – by me, Silasᶜ and Timothy – was not 'Yes' and 'No', but in him it has always been 'Yes'. ²⁰ For no matter how many promises God has made, they are 'Yes' in Christ. And so through him the 'Amen' is spoken by us to the glory of God. ²¹ Now it is God who makes both us and you stand firm in Christ. He anointed us, ²² set his seal of ownership on us, and put his Spirit in our hearts as a deposit, guaranteeing what is to come.

²³ I call God as my witness – and I stake my life on it – that it was in order to spare you that I did not return to Corinth. ²⁴ Not that we lord it over your faith, but we work with you for your joy, because it is by faith you stand firm. **2** ¹ So I made up my mind that I would not make another painful visit to you. ² For if I grieve you, who is left to make me glad but you whom I have grieved? ³ I wrote as I did, so that when I came I would not be distressed by those who should have made me rejoice. I had confidence in all of you, that you would all share my joy. ⁴ For I wrote to you out of great distress and anguish of heart and with many tears, not to grieve you but to let you know the depth of my love for you.

---

a 8 The Greek word for *brothers and sisters* (*adelphoi*) refers here to believers, both men and women, as part of God's family; also in 8:1; 13:11.

b 12 Many manuscripts *holiness*
c 19 Greek *Silvanus*, a variant of *Silas*

Forgiveness for the offender

⁵ If anyone has caused grief, he has not so much grieved me as he has grieved all of you to some extent – not to put it too severely. ⁶ The punishment inflicted on him by the majority is sufficient. ⁷ Now instead, you ought to forgive and comfort him, so that he will not be overwhelmed by excessive sorrow. ⁸ I urge you, therefore, to reaffirm your love for him. ⁹ Another reason I wrote to you was to see if you would stand the test and be obedient in everything. ¹⁰ Anyone you forgive, I also forgive. And what I have forgiven – if there was anything to forgive – I have forgiven in the sight of Christ for your sake, ¹¹ in order that Satan might not outwit us. For we are not unaware of his schemes.

PAIN AND SUFFERING 2

RELYING ON GOD

The Bible is amazingly honest. We don't just get to hear the good stuff about all the people who were saved and healed, we get to hear the difficult things God's people went through too.

Paul says in 2 Corinthians 1:8–11 that his suffering was so great he wasn't sure he was going to live through it. That's real suffering. Some of us have known similar pain and grief that feels like it might overwhelm us. Time and time again the Bible reminds us that we're not on our own. Paul felt pushed beyond his limits, but he found something good in the midst of such painful circumstances: he says that his suffering pushed him towards God.

Sometimes we pray, telling God we want to get closer to him, overlooking the fact that it's often in the hardest times of our life that we get the closest to God. One of the biggest problems in all human history is that we think we can do things on our own. We get tempted to live life in our own strength, but it's when suffering comes to us that we realise our weakness. It's when everything around us is crumbling that we give up and say, 'God, I need you. Please help me.' We lean on him and discover his strength in a whole new way. As Paul reminds us, God is able to raise the dead (v. 9), so when we rely on his power we're in safe hands!

Each of us has a choice when we face painful situations: will we turn to God, or will we walk away? Paul chose to turn to God and found that he brought Paul and his companions through their trials. When we turn to God in our difficulties, we will find the same. Paul also tells us another good thing that comes out of our pain: we receive comfort from God, which allows us to comfort other people (2 Corinthians 1:4). When we have been through pain ourselves and have grown closer to God as a result, we are better equipped to help others with the difficult things they face. So whatever difficulties you face today, thank God that they are an opportunity to rely more on him. Ask him to comfort you and use you to comfort others who are in need.

Mike Pilavachi

 Lamentations 3:1–24   Psalm 13

Ministers of the new covenant

12 Now when I went to Troas to preach the gospel of Christ and found that the Lord had opened a door for me, 13 I still had no peace of mind, because I did not find my brother Titus there. So I said goodbye to them and went on to Macedonia.

14 But thanks be to God, who always leads us as captives in Christ's triumphal procession and uses us to spread the aroma of the knowledge of him everywhere. 15 For we are to God the pleasing aroma of Christ among those who are being saved and those who are perishing. 16 To the one we are an aroma that brings death; to the other, an aroma that brings life. And who is equal to such a task? 17 Unlike so many, we do not peddle the word of God for profit. On the contrary, in Christ we speak before God with sincerity, as those sent from God.

3 Are we beginning to commend ourselves again? Or do we need, like some people, letters of recommendation to you or from you? 2 You yourselves are our letter, written on our hearts, known and read by everyone. 3 You show that you are a letter from Christ, the result of our ministry, written not with ink but with the Spirit of the living God, not on tablets of stone but on tablets of human hearts.

4 Such confidence we have through Christ before God. 5 Not that we are competent in ourselves to claim anything for ourselves, but our competence comes from God. 6 He has made us competent as ministers of a new covenant – not of the letter but of the Spirit; for the letter kills, but the Spirit gives life.

The greater glory of the new covenant

7 Now if the ministry that brought death, which was engraved in letters on stone, came with glory, so that the Israelites could not look steadily at the face of Moses because of its glory, transitory though it was, 8 will not the ministry of the Spirit be even more glorious? 9 If the ministry that brought condemnation was glorious, how much more glorious is the ministry that brings righteousness! 10 For what was glorious has no glory now in comparison with the surpassing glory. 11 And if what was transitory came with glory, how much greater is the glory of that which lasts!

12 Therefore, since we have such a hope, we are very bold. 13 We are not like Moses, who would put a veil over his face to prevent the Israelites from seeing the end of what was passing away. 14 But their minds were made dull, for to this day the same veil remains when the old covenant is read. It has not been removed, because only in Christ is it taken away. 15 Even to this day when Moses is read, a veil covers their hearts. 16 But whenever anyone turns to the Lord, the veil is taken away. 17 Now the Lord is the Spirit, and where the Spirit of the Lord is, there is freedom. 18 And we all, who with unveiled faces contemplate*a* the Lord's glory, are being transformed into his image with ever-increasing glory, which comes from the Lord, who is the Spirit.

Present weakness and resurrection life

4 Therefore, since through God's mercy we have this ministry, we do not lose heart. 2 Rather, we have renounced secret and shameful ways; we do not use deception, nor do we distort the word of God. On the contrary, by setting forth the truth plainly we commend ourselves to everyone's conscience in the sight of God. 3 And even if our gospel is veiled, it is veiled to those who are perishing. 4 The god of this age has blinded the minds of unbelievers, so that they cannot see the light of the gospel that displays the glory of Christ, who is the image of God. 5 For what we preach is not ourselves, but Jesus Christ as Lord, and ourselves as your servants for Jesus' sake. 6 For God, who said, 'Let light shine out of darkness,'*a* made his light shine in our hearts to give us the light of the knowledge of God's glory displayed in the face of Christ.

7 But we have this treasure in jars of clay to show that this all-surpassing power is from God and not from us. 8 We are hard pressed on every side, but not crushed;

---

a 18 Or *reflect*
a 6 Gen. 1:3

perplexed, but not in despair; 9 persecuted, but not abandoned; struck down, but not destroyed. 10 We always carry around in our body the death of Jesus, so that the life of Jesus may also be revealed in our body. 11 For we who are alive are always being given over to death for Jesus' sake, so that his life may also be revealed in our mortal body. 12 So then, death is at work in us, but life is at work in you.

13 It is written: 'I believed; therefore I have spoken.'b Since we have that same spirit ofc faith, we also believe and therefore speak, 14 because we know that the one who raised the Lord Jesus from the dead will also raise us with Jesus and present us with you to himself. 15 All this is for your benefit, so that the grace that is reaching more and more people may cause thanksgiving to overflow to the glory of God.

16 Therefore we do not lose heart. Though outwardly we are wasting away, yet inwardly we are being renewed day by day. 17 For our light and momentary troubles are achieving for us an eternal glory that far outweighs them all. 18 So we fix our eyes not on what is seen, but on what is unseen, since what is seen is temporary, but what is unseen is eternal.

Awaiting the new body

5 For we know that if the earthly tent we live in is destroyed, we have a building from God, an eternal house in heaven, not built by human hands. 2 Meanwhile we groan, longing to be clothed instead with our heavenly dwelling, 3 because when we are clothed, we will not be found naked. 4 For while we are in this tent, we groan and are burdened, because we do not wish to be unclothed but to be clothed instead with our heavenly dwelling, so that what is mortal may be swallowed up by life. 5 Now the one who has fashioned us for this very purpose is God, who has given us the Spirit as a deposit, guaranteeing what is to come.

6 Therefore we are always confident and know that as long as we are at home

in the body we are away from the Lord. 7 For we live by faith, not by sight. 8 We are confident, I say, and would prefer to be away from the body and at home with the Lord. 9 So we make it our goal to please him, whether we are at home in the body or away from it. 10 For we must all appear before the judgment seat of Christ, so that each of us may receive what is due to us for the things done while in the body, whether good or bad.

The ministry of reconciliation

11 Since, then, we know what it is to fear the Lord, we try to persuade others. What we are is plain to God, and I hope it is also plain to your conscience. 12 We are not trying to commend ourselves to you again, but are giving you an opportunity to take pride in us, so that you can answer those who take pride in what is seen rather than in what is in the heart. 13 If we are 'out of our mind,' as some say, it is for God; if we are in our right mind, it is for you. 14 For Christ's love compels us, because we are convinced that one died for all, and therefore all died. 15 And he died for all, that those who live should no longer live for themselves but for him who died for them and was raised again.

16 So from now on we regard no one from a worldly point of view. Though we once regarded Christ in this way, we do so no longer. 17 Therefore, if anyone is in Christ, the new creation has come:a the old has gone, the new is here! 18 All this is from God, who reconciled us to himself through Christ and gave us the ministry of reconciliation: 19 that God was reconciling the world to himself in Christ, not counting people's sins against them. And he has committed to us the message of reconciliation. 20 We are therefore Christ's ambassadors, as though God were making his appeal through us. We implore you on Christ's behalf: be reconciled to God. 21 God made him who had no sin to be sinb for us, so that in him we might become the righteousness of God.

---

b 13 Psalm 116:10 (see Septuagint)
c 13 Or Spirit-given

a 17 Or Christ, that person is a new creation.
b 21 Or be a sin offering

6

As God's fellow workers we urge you not to receive God's grace in vain. ²For he says,

'In the time of my favour I heard you,
and in the day of salvation I helped you.'ᵃ

I tell you, now is the time of God's favour, now is the day of salvation.

Paul's hardships
³We put no stumbling-block in anyone's path, so that our ministry will not be discredited. ⁴Rather, as servants of God we commend ourselves in every way: in great endurance; in troubles, hardships and distresses; ⁵in beatings, imprisonments and riots; in hard work, sleepless nights and hunger; ⁶in purity, understanding, patience and kindness; in the Holy Spirit and in sincere love; ⁷in truthful speech and in the power of God; with weapons of righteousness in the right hand and in the left; ⁸through glory and dishonour, bad report and good report; genuine, yet regarded as impostors; ⁹known, yet regarded as unknown; dying, and yet we live on; beaten, and yet not killed; ¹⁰sorrowful, yet always rejoicing;

a 2 Isaiah 49:8

IDENTITY – WHO WE ARE IN CHRIST 2

New creation

In 2 Corinthians 5:15–21, Paul says we are a *'new creation'*. God hasn't given us a new Christian outward appearance, which we hope other people will notice. He has changed us from the inside out. He made Jesus *'who had no sin to be sin for us, so that in him we might become the righteousness of God'* (v. 21). In other words, God has set us free from all the bad stuff inside. He has washed us clean.

The first thing that happened when Adam and Eve sinned was that they hid from God. There was now sin in the way of their relationship with God. The same is true with us. Yet God dealt with it on the cross and when we become Christians we are set free from it. God wipes the slate clean and we are given a fresh start.

This doesn't mean that sin isn't an issue any more – we will all struggle with sin until the day we die. The difference is that at heart, our core being is now good. Our struggle with sin has to do with the flesh, not with our core being. Our heart is clean and new, but that doesn't mean that all our unhealthy attitudes, beliefs and reactions have been washed away.

Most of us can easily feel that our core being is not great, but we can maybe deal with some surface stuff. What Paul says is the opposite: the root of our being is a new creation, all that remains is to get to work on the 'flesh'. When you feel like you're dirty and useless and can't stand up to temptation and the same old habits and lies, the truth is that you can. Believe it or not, in essence you're now good, you're a saint: now it's just a question of putting into practice and living like one!

James Grier

 Colossians 3:1–11   Romans 8:9–11

poor, yet making many rich; having nothing, and yet possessing everything.

11 We have spoken freely to you, Corinthians, and opened wide our hearts to you. 12 We are not withholding our affection from you, but you are withholding yours from us. 13 As a fair exchange – I speak as to my children – open wide your hearts also.

Warning against idolatry

14 Do not be yoked together with unbelievers. For what do righteousness and wickedness have in common? Or what fellowship can light have with darkness? 15 What harmony is there between Christ and Belial[b]? Or what does a believer have in common with an unbeliever? 16 What agreement is there between the temple of God and idols? For we are the temple of the living God. As God has said:

'I will live with them
　　and walk among them,
and I will be their God,
　　and they will be my people.'[c]

17 Therefore,

'Come out from them
　　and be separate,
　　　　　　　says the Lord.
Touch no unclean thing,
　　and I will receive you.'[d]

18 And,

'I will be a Father to you,
　　and you will be my sons and
　　　　daughters,
　　　　　　says the Lord Almighty.'[e]

7 Therefore, since we have these promises, dear friends, let us purify ourselves from everything that contaminates body and spirit, perfecting holiness out of reverence for God.

---

b 15 Greek *Beliar*, a variant of *Belial*
c 16 Lev. 26:12; Jer. 32:38; Ezek. 37:27
d 17 Isaiah 52:11; Ezek. 20:34,41
e 18 2 Samuel 7:14; 7:8

Paul's joy over the church's repentance

2 Make room for us in your hearts. We have wronged no one, we have corrupted no one, we have exploited no one. 3 I do not say this to condemn you; I have said before that you have such a place in our hearts that we would live or die with you. 4 I have spoken to you with great frankness; I take great pride in you. I am greatly encouraged; in all our troubles my joy knows no bounds.

5 For when we came into Macedonia, we had no rest, but we were harassed at every turn – conflicts on the outside, fears within. 6 But God, who comforts the downcast, comforted us by the coming of Titus, 7 and not only by his coming but also by the comfort you had given him. He told us about your longing for me, your deep sorrow, your ardent concern for me, so that my joy was greater than ever.

8 Even if I caused you sorrow by my letter, I do not regret it. Though I did regret it – I see that my letter hurt you, but only for a little while – 9 yet now I am happy, not because you were made sorry, but because your sorrow led you to repentance. For you became sorrowful as God intended and so were not harmed in any way by us. 10 Godly sorrow brings repentance that leads to salvation and leaves no regret, but worldly sorrow brings death. 11 See what this godly sorrow has produced in you: what earnestness, what eagerness to clear yourselves, what indignation, what alarm, what longing, what concern, what readiness to see justice done. At every point you have proved yourselves to be innocent in this matter. 12 So even though I wrote to you, it was neither on account of the one who did the wrong nor on account of the injured party, but rather that before God you could see for yourselves how devoted to us you are. 13 By all this we are encouraged.

In addition to our own encouragement, we were especially delighted to see how happy Titus was, because his spirit has been refreshed by all of you. 14 I had boasted to him about you, and you have not embarrassed me. But just as everything we said to you was true, so our boasting about you to Titus has proved to be true as well. ¹⁵And his affection for you is all the greater when he remembers that you were all obedient, receiving him with fear and trembling. ¹⁶I am glad I can have complete confidence in you.

The collection for the Lord's people

8 And now, brothers and sisters, we want you to know about the grace that God has given the Macedonian churches.

²In the midst of a very severe trial, their overflowing joy and their extreme poverty welled up in rich generosity. ³For I testify that they gave as much as they were able, and even beyond their ability. Entirely on their own, ⁴they urgently pleaded with us for the privilege of sharing in this service to the Lord's people. ⁵And they exceeded our expectations: they gave themselves first of all to the Lord, and then by the will

MONEY 5

GENEROSITY

Being generous is a principle that's much bigger than money. We can be generous in our attitude towards people, in our words, with our time, with our belongings, in our home and with our money. Chances are, if we're generous people it probably won't be in just one area, but will spill over into lots of areas of life. For now, let's think about being generous with our money, and when we think of money, let's include everything money buys us – so all our possessions and belongings too.

I have a lovely pair of shoes, they're fairly new and in a light colour, so could get dirty very easily. A friend was saying the other day how she needed a pair of shoes for an occasion and didn't have any. The inner greedy-me was saying, 'Don't offer your shoes, they'll get ruined!' and the generous-me was saying, 'I've got some shoes that would work great!' What to say? Luckily she had different-sized feet from me. Phew! Crisis avoided! You may be a much better person than me, but sometimes I find it really hard to be generous with my stuff. I would find it much easier to put cash in an offering bag than to lend my favourite jumper to a friend.

The passage in 2 Corinthians 8:1–15 encourages us to be eager to give, to be the first with our hands up saying, 'You can borrow mine!' or, 'Have this!' Being generous isn't about giving so much that you don't have anything, but about being able to share things and support one another when needed. It's about having a desire to give.

If we think, 'I'll be generous when I have more,' or, 'When I'm rich, I'll give a lot away,' we believe in a myth. The truth is that if we're generous now with what we have, we'll be generous later. I have seen people who have nothing be abundantly generous, as well as people who have everything. We need to begin practising generosity today, with the small, so that we will be generous later with the big.

Kiera Singlehurst-Phyo

 Deuteronomy 24:19 Acts 2

of God also to us. 6 So we urged Titus, just as he had earlier made a beginning, to bring also to completion this act of grace on your part. 7 But since you excel in everything – in faith, in speech, in knowledge, in complete earnestness and in the love we have kindled in you*a* – see that you also excel in this grace of giving.

8 I am not commanding you, but I want to test the sincerity of your love by comparing it with the earnestness of others. 9 For you know the grace of our Lord Jesus Christ, that though he was rich, yet for your sake he became poor, so that you through his poverty might become rich.

10 And here is my judgment about what is best for you in this matter. Last year you were the first not only to give but also to have the desire to do so. 11 Now finish the work, so that your eager willingness to do it may be matched by your completion of it, according to your means. 12 For if the willingness is there, the gift is acceptable according to what one has, not according to what one does not have.

13 Our desire is not that others might be relieved while you are hard pressed, but that there might be equality. 14 At the present time your plenty will supply what they need, so that in turn their plenty will supply what you need. The goal is equality, 15 as it is written: 'The one who gathered much did not have too much, and the one who gathered little did not have too little.'*b*

Titus sent to receive the collection

16 Thanks be to God, who put into the heart of Titus the same concern I have for you. 17 For Titus not only welcomed our appeal, but he is coming to you with much enthusiasm and on his own initiative. 18 And we are sending along with him the brother who is praised by all the churches for his service to the gospel. 19 What is more, he was chosen by the churches to accompany us as we carry the offering, which we administer in order to honour the Lord himself and to show our

eagerness to help. 20 We want to avoid any criticism of the way we administer this liberal gift. 21 For we are taking pains to do what is right, not only in the eyes of the Lord but also in the eyes of man.

22 In addition, we are sending with them our brother who has often proved to us in many ways that he is zealous, and now even more so because of his great confidence in you. 23 As for Titus, he is my partner and fellow worker among you; as for our brothers, they are representatives of the churches and an honour to Christ. 24 Therefore show these men the proof of your love and the reason for our pride in you, so that the churches can see it.

9 There is no need for me to write to you about this service to the Lord's people. 2 For I know your eagerness to help, and I have been boasting about it to the Macedonians, telling them that since last year you in Achaia were ready to give; and your enthusiasm has stirred most of them to action. 3 But I am sending the brothers in order that our boasting about you in this matter should not prove hollow, but that you may be ready, as I said you would be. 4 For if any Macedonians come with me and find you unprepared, we – not to say anything about you – would be ashamed of having been so confident. 5 So I thought it necessary to urge the brothers to visit you in advance and finish the arrangements for the generous gift you had promised. Then it will be ready as a generous gift, not as one grudgingly given.

Generosity encouraged

6 Remember this: whoever sows sparingly will also reap sparingly, and whoever sows generously will also reap generously. 7 Each of you should give what you have decided in your heart to give, not reluctantly or under compulsion, for God loves a cheerful giver. 8 And God is able to bless you abundantly, so that in all things at all times, having all that you need, you will abound in every good work. 9 As it is written:

'They have freely scattered their gifts to the poor;

---

a 7 Some manuscripts *and in your love for us*
b 15 Exodus 16:18

their righteousness endures for ever.'*a*

10 Now he who supplies seed to the sower and bread for food will also supply and increase your store of seed and will enlarge the harvest of your righteousness. 11 You will be enriched in every way so that you can be generous on every occasion, and through us your generosity will result in thanksgiving to God.

12 This service that you perform is not only supplying the needs of the Lord's people but is also overflowing in many expressions of thanks to God. 13 Because of the service by which you have proved yourselves, others will praise God for the obedience that accompanies your confession of the gospel of Christ, and for your generosity in sharing with them and with everyone else. 14 And in their prayers for you their hearts will go out to you, because of the surpassing grace God has given you. 15 Thanks be to God for his indescribable gift!

Paul's defence of his ministry

10 By the humility and gentleness of Christ, I appeal to you – I, Paul, who am 'timid' when face to face with you, but 'bold' towards you when away! 2 I beg you that when I come I may not have to be as bold as I expect to be towards some people who think that we live by the standards of this world. 3 For though we live in the world, we do not wage war as the world does. 4 The weapons we fight with are not the weapons of the world. On the contrary, they have divine power to demolish strongholds. 5 We demolish arguments and every pretension that sets itself up against the knowledge of God, and we take captive every thought to make it obedient to Christ. 6 And we will be ready to punish every act of disobedience, once your obedience is complete.

7 You are judging by appearances.*a* If anyone is confident that they belong to Christ, they should consider again that we

belong to Christ just as much as they do. 8 So even if I boast somewhat freely about the authority the Lord gave us for building you up rather than tearing you down, I will not be ashamed of it. 9 I do not want to seem to be trying to frighten you with my letters. 10 For some say, 'His letters are weighty and forceful, but in person he is unimpressive and his speaking amounts to nothing.' 11 Such people should realise that what we are in our letters when we are absent, we will be in our actions when we are present.

12 We do not dare to classify or compare ourselves with some who commend themselves. When they measure themselves by themselves and compare themselves with themselves, they are not wise. 13 We, however, will not boast beyond proper limits, but will confine our boasting to the sphere of service God himself has assigned to us, a sphere that also includes you. 14 We are not going too far in our boasting, as would be the case if we had not come to you, for we did get as far as you with the gospel of Christ. 15 Neither do we go beyond our limits by boasting of work done by others. Our hope is that, as your faith continues to grow, our sphere of activity among you will greatly expand, 16 so that we can preach the gospel in the regions beyond you. For we do not want to boast about work already done in someone else's territory. 17 But, 'Let the one who boasts boast in the Lord.'*b* 18 For it is not the one who commends himself who is approved, but the one whom the Lord commends.

Paul and the false apostles

11 I hope you will put up with me in a little foolishness. Yes, please put up with me! 2 I am jealous for you with a godly jealousy. I promised you to one husband, to Christ, so that I might present you as a pure virgin to him. 3 But I am afraid that just as Eve was deceived by the snake's cunning, your minds may somehow be led astray from your sincere and pure devotion to Christ. 4 For if someone comes to you and preaches a Jesus other than the Jesus we preached, or if you receive a different spirit from the Spirit you received, or a different gospel from the one you accepted, you put up with it easily enough.

FACT

BALD AND MONOBROWED

A story from the second century AD describes Paul as a small man with 'a bald head and crooked legs, in a good state of body, with eyebrows meeting and nose somewhat hooked, full of friendliness'. The description is so unflattering that many experts believe it to be authentic.

⁵ I do not think I am in the least inferior to those 'super-apostles'.ᵃ ⁶ I may indeed be untrained as a speaker, but I do have knowledge. We have made this perfectly clear to you in every way. ⁷ Was it a sin for me to lower myself in order to elevate you by preaching the gospel of God to you free of charge? ⁸ I robbed other churches by receiving support from them so as to serve you. ⁹ And when I was with you and needed something, I was not a burden to anyone, for the brothers who came from Macedonia supplied what I needed. I have kept myself from being a burden to you in any way, and will continue to do so. ¹⁰ As surely as the truth of Christ is in me, nobody in the regions of Achaia will stop this boasting of mine. ¹¹ Why? Because I do not love you? God knows I do!

¹² And I will keep on doing what I am doing in order to cut the ground from under those who want an opportunity to be considered equal with us in the things they boast about. ¹³ For such people are false apostles, deceitful workers, masquerading as apostles of Christ. ¹⁴ And no wonder, for Satan himself masquerades as an angel of light. ¹⁵ It is not surprising, then, if his servants also masquerade as servants of righteousness. Their end will be what their actions deserve.

Paul boasts about his sufferings

¹⁶ I repeat: let no one take me for a fool. But if you do, then tolerate me just as you would a fool, so that I may do a little boasting. ¹⁷ In this self-confident boasting I am not talking as the Lord would, but as a fool. ¹⁸ Since many are boasting in the way the world does, I too will boast. ¹⁹ You gladly put up with fools since you are so wise! ²⁰ In fact, you even put up with anyone who enslaves you or exploits you or takes advantage of you or puts on airs or slaps you in the face. ²¹ To my shame I admit that we were too weak for that!

Whatever anyone else dares to boast about – I am speaking as a fool – I also dare to boast about. ²² Are they Hebrews? So am I. Are they Israelites? So am I. Are they Abraham's descendants? So am I. ²³ Are they servants of Christ? (I am out of my mind to talk like this.) I am more. I have worked much harder, been in prison more frequently, been flogged more severely, and been exposed to death again and again. ²⁴ Five times I received from the Jews the forty lashes minus one. ²⁵ Three times I was beaten with rods, once I was pelted with stones, three times I was shipwrecked, I spent a night and a day in the open sea, ²⁶ I have been constantly on the move. I have been in danger from rivers, in danger from bandits, in danger from my fellow Jews, in danger from Gentiles; in danger in the city, in danger in the country, in danger at sea; and in danger from false believers. ²⁷ I have laboured and toiled and have often gone without sleep; I have known hunger and thirst and have often gone without food; I have been cold and naked. ²⁸ Besides everything else, I face daily the pressure of my concern for all the churches. ²⁹ Who is weak, and I do not feel weak? Who is led into sin, and I do not inwardly burn?

³⁰If I must boast, I will boast of the things that show my weakness. ³¹The God and Father of the Lord Jesus, who is to be praised for ever, knows that I am not lying. ³²In Damascus the governor under King Aretas had the city of the Damascenes guarded in order to arrest me. ³³But I was lowered in a basket from a window in the wall and slipped through his hands.

FAVOURITE VERSES

Matthew 10:22

You will be hated by everyone because of me, but the one who stands firm to the end will be saved.

This is my favourite Bible verse because it reminds me that being a Christian *isn't* easy, that people *will* hate you. But it's worth it.

Jack, 15

Paul's vision and his thorn

12 I must go on boasting. Although there is nothing to be gained, I will go on to visions and revelations from the Lord. ²I know a man in Christ who fourteen years ago was caught up to the third heaven. Whether it was in the body or out of the body I do not know – God knows. ³And I know that this man – whether in the body or apart from the body I do not know, but God knows – ⁴was caught up to paradise and heard inexpressible things, things that no one is permitted to tell. ⁵I will boast about a man like that, but I will not boast about myself, except about my weaknesses. ⁶Even if I should choose to boast, I would not be a fool, because I would be speaking the truth. But I refrain, so no one will think more of me than is warranted by what I do or say, ⁷or because of these surpassingly great revelations.

Therefore, in order to keep me from becoming conceited, I was given a thorn in my flesh, a messenger of Satan, to torment me. ⁸Three times I pleaded with the Lord to take it away from me. ⁹But he said to me, 'My grace is sufficient for you, for my power is made perfect in weakness.' Therefore I will boast all the more gladly about my weaknesses, so that Christ's power may rest on me. ¹⁰That is why, for Christ's sake, I delight in weaknesses, in insults, in hardships, in persecutions, in difficulties. For when I am weak, then I am strong.

Paul's concern for the Corinthians

¹¹I have made a fool of myself, but you drove me to it. I ought to have been commended by you, for I am not in the least inferior to the 'super-apostles',ᵃ even though I am nothing. ¹²I persevered in demonstrating among you the marks of a true apostle, including signs, wonders and miracles. ¹³How were you inferior to the other churches, except that I was never a burden to you? Forgive me this wrong!

¹⁴Now I am ready to visit you for the third time, and I will not be a burden to you, because what I want is not your possessions but you. After all, children should not have to save up for their parents, but parents for their children. ¹⁵So I will very gladly spend for you everything I have and expend myself as well. If I love you more, will you love me less? ¹⁶Be that as it may, I have not been a burden to you. Yet, crafty fellow that I am, I caught you by trickery! ¹⁷Did I exploit you through any of the men I sent to you? ¹⁸I urged Titus to go to you and I sent our brother with him. Titus did not exploit you, did he? Did we not walk in the same footsteps by the same Spirit?

¹⁹Have you been thinking all along that we have been defending ourselves to you? We have been speaking in the sight of God as those in Christ; and everything we do, dear friends, is for your strengthening. ²⁰For I am afraid that when I come I may not find you as I want you to be, and you

---

a 11 Or *the most eminent apostles*

may not find me as you want me to be. I fear that there may be discord, jealousy, fits of rage, selfish ambition, slander, gossip, arrogance and disorder. 21 I am afraid that when I come again my God will humble me before you, and I will be grieved over many who have sinned earlier and have not repented of the impurity, sexual sin and debauchery in which they have indulged.

Final warnings

13 This will be my third visit to you. 'Every matter must be established by the testimony of two or three witnesses.'*a* 2 I already gave you a warning when I was with you the second time. I now repeat it while absent: on my return I will not spare those who sinned earlier or any of the others, 3 since you are demanding proof that Christ is speaking through me. He is not weak in dealing with you, but is powerful among you. 4 For to be sure, he was crucified in weakness, yet he lives by God's power. Likewise, we are weak in him, yet by God's power we will live with him in our dealing with you.

5 Examine yourselves to see whether you are in the faith; test yourselves. Do

---

a 1 Deut. 19:15

you not realise that Christ Jesus is in you – unless, of course, you fail the test? 6 And I trust that you will discover that we have not failed the test. 7 Now we pray to God that you will not do anything wrong – not so that people will see that we have stood the test but so that you will do what is right even though we may seem to have failed. 8 For we cannot do anything against the truth, but only for the truth. 9 We are glad whenever we are weak but you are strong; and our prayer is that you may be fully restored. 10 This is why I write these things when I am absent, that when I come I may not have to be harsh in my use of authority – the authority the Lord gave me for building you up, not for tearing you down.

Final greetings

11 Finally, brothers and sisters, rejoice! Strive for full restoration, encourage one another, be of one mind, live in peace. And the God of love and peace will be with you.

12 Greet one another with a holy kiss. 13 All God's people here send their greetings.

14 May the grace of the Lord Jesus Christ, and the love of God, and the fellowship of the Holy Spirit be with you all.

GALATIANS

DATE

It is thought that this letter was written around AD 47–48

AUTHOR

The apostle Paul

WHAT'S IT ALL ABOUT?

This letter that Paul wrote to the church in Galatia deals mainly with the issue of grace. Paul angrily addresses the fact that new believers in Jesus were being taught that they should be following the Old Testament practices and laws of God's people, including being circumcised. He passionately explains that we can't earn God's love through observing laws and through 'human effort', but we come to know God through faith in Jesus and through grace. He urges the church to understand that they are no longer slaves to the law, but sons and daughters of a loving God, and they can receive freedom in Jesus' name. Paul thinks they might ask in response, 'Does this mean we can do what we want?' so he warns that God's incredible grace isn't a licence for people to do what they want, but an opportunity for them to love as generously as they have been loved by God.

WHY SHOULD WE READ IT?

- Because it offers us a valuable reminder that we can't earn God's love, but we live by faith and under grace.

- To hear how Paul summed up the entire law (Galatians 5:14).

- To learn about the qualities we will possess as we let the Holy Spirit fill us (the 'fruits of the Spirit', see Galatians 5:22–24).

- To be reminded that we are all heirs to God's promises (Galatians 3:26–29).

Andy Croft with Liza Hoeksma

1 Paul, an apostle – sent not from men nor by a man, but by Jesus Christ and God the Father, who raised him from the dead – ²and all the brothers and sisters*a* with me,

To the churches in Galatia:

³Grace and peace to you from God our Father and the Lord Jesus Christ, ⁴who gave himself for our sins to rescue us from the present evil age, according to the will of our God and Father, ⁵to whom be glory for ever and ever. Amen.

No other gospel

⁶I am astonished that you are so quickly deserting the one who called you to live in the grace of Christ and are turning to a different gospel – ⁷which is really no gospel at all. Evidently some people are throwing you into confusion and are trying to pervert the gospel of Christ. ⁸But even if we or an angel from heaven should preach a gospel other than the one we preached to you, let them be under God's curse! ⁹As we have already said, so now I say again: if anybody is preaching to you a gospel other than what you accepted, let them be under God's curse!

¹⁰Am I now trying to win the approval of human beings, or of God? Or am I trying to please people? If I were still trying to please people, I would not be a servant of Christ.

Paul called by God

¹¹I want you to know, brothers and sisters, that the gospel I preached is not of human origin. ¹²I did not receive it from any man, nor was I taught it; rather, I received it by revelation from Jesus Christ.

¹³For you have heard of my previous way of life in Judaism, how intensely I persecuted the church of God and tried to destroy it. ¹⁴I was advancing in Judaism beyond many of my own age among my people and was extremely zealous for

the traditions of my fathers. ¹⁵But when God, who set me apart from my mother's womb and called me by his grace, was pleased ¹⁶to reveal his Son in me so that I might preach him among the Gentiles, my immediate response was not to consult any human being. ¹⁷I did not go up to Jerusalem to see those who were apostles before I was, but I went into Arabia. Later I returned to Damascus.

¹⁸Then after three years, I went up to Jerusalem to get acquainted with Cephas*b* and stayed with him fifteen days. ¹⁹I saw none of the other apostles – only James, the Lord's brother. ²⁰I assure you before God that what I am writing to you is no lie. ²¹Then I went to Syria and Cilicia. ²²I was personally unknown to the churches of Judea that are in Christ. ²³They only heard the report: 'The man who formerly persecuted us is now preaching the faith he once tried to destroy.' ²⁴And they praised God because of me.

Paul accepted by the apostles

2 Then after fourteen years, I went up again to Jerusalem, this time with Barnabas. I took Titus along also. ²I went in response to a revelation and, meeting privately with those esteemed as leaders, I presented to them the gospel that I preach among the Gentiles. I wanted to be sure I was not running and had not been running my race in vain. ³Yet not even Titus, who was with me, was compelled to be circumcised, even though he was a Greek. ⁴This matter arose because some false believers had infiltrated our ranks to spy on the freedom we have in Christ Jesus and to make us slaves. ⁵We did not give in to them for a moment, so that the truth of the gospel might be preserved for you.

⁶As for those who were held in high esteem – whatever they were makes no difference to me; God does not show favouritism – they added nothing to my message. ⁷On the contrary, they recognised that I had been entrusted with the task of preaching the gospel to the

---

a 2 The Greek word for *brothers and sisters* (*adelphoi*) refers here to believers, both men and women, as part of God's family; also in verse 11; and in 3:15; 4:12, 28, 31; 5:11, 13; 6:1, 18.

b 18 That is, Peter

uncircumcised,*a* just as Peter had been to the circumcised.*b* 8 For God, who was at work in Peter as an apostle to the circumcised, was also at work in me as an apostle to the Gentiles. 9 James, Cephas*c* and John, those esteemed as pillars, gave me and Barnabas the right hand of fellowship when they recognised the grace given to me. They agreed that we should go to the Gentiles, and they to the circumcised. 10 All they asked was that we should continue to remember the poor, the very thing I had been eager to do all along.

Paul opposes Cephas

11 When Cephas came to Antioch, I opposed him to his face, because he stood condemned. 12 For before certain men came from James, he used to eat with the Gentiles. But when they arrived, he began to draw back and separate himself from the Gentiles because he was afraid of those who belonged to the circumcision group. 13 The other Jews joined him in his hypocrisy, so that by their hypocrisy even Barnabas was led astray.

14 When I saw that they were not acting in line with the truth of the gospel, I said to Cephas in front of them all, 'You are a Jew, yet you live like a Gentile and not like a Jew. How is it, then, that you force Gentiles to follow Jewish customs?

15 'We who are Jews by birth and not sinful Gentiles 16 know that a person is not justified by the works of the law, but by faith in Jesus Christ. So we, too, have put our faith in Christ Jesus that we may be justified by faith in*d* Christ and not by the works of the law, because by the works of the law no one will be justified.

17 'But if, in seeking to be justified in Christ, we Jews find ourselves also among the sinners, doesn't that mean that Christ promotes sin? Absolutely not! 18 If I rebuild what I destroyed, then I really would be a law-breaker.

19 'For through the law I died to the law so that I might live for God. 20 I have been crucified with Christ and I no longer live, but Christ lives in me. The life I now live in the body, I live by faith in the Son of God, who loved me and gave himself for me. 21 I do not set aside the grace of God, for if righteousness could be gained through the law, Christ died for nothing!'*e*

Faith or works of the law

3 You foolish Galatians! Who has bewitched you? Before your very eyes Jesus Christ was clearly portrayed as crucified. 2 I would like to learn just one thing from you: did you receive the Spirit by the works of the law, or by believing what you heard? 3 Are you so foolish? After beginning by means of the Spirit, are you now trying to finish by means of the flesh?*a* 4 Have you experienced*b* so much in vain – if it really was in vain? 5 So again I ask, does God give you his Spirit and work miracles among you by the works of the law, or by your believing what you heard? 6 So also Abraham 'believed God, and it was credited to him as righteousness.'*c*

7 Understand, then, that those who have faith are children of Abraham. 8 Scripture foresaw that God would justify the Gentiles by faith, and announced the gospel in advance to Abraham: 'All nations will be blessed through you.'*d* 9 So those who rely on faith are blessed along with Abraham, the man of faith.

10 For all who rely on the works of the law are under a curse, as it is written: 'Cursed is everyone who does not continue to do everything written in the Book of the Law.'*e* 11 Clearly no one who relies on the law is justified before God, because 'the righteous will live by faith.'*f* 12 The law is not based on faith; on the contrary, it

---

a 7　That is, Gentiles
b 7　That is, Jews; also in verses 8 and 9
c 9　That is, Peter; also in verses 11 and 14
d 16　Or *but through the faithfulness of . . . justified on the basis of the faithfulness of*

e 21　Some interpreters end the quotation after verse 14.
a 3　In contexts like this, the Greek word for *flesh* (*sarx*) refers to the sinful state of human beings, often presented as a power in opposition to the Spirit.
b 4　Or *suffered*
c 6　Gen. 15:6
d 8　Gen. 12:3; 18:18; 22:18
e 10　Deut. 27:26
f 11　Hab. 2:4

says, 'The person who does these things will live by them.'ᵍ ¹³Christ redeemed us from the curse of the law by becoming a curse for us, for it is written: 'Cursed is everyone who is hung on a pole.'ʰ ¹⁴He redeemed us in order that the blessing given to Abraham might come to the Gentiles through Christ Jesus, so that by faith we might receive the promise of the Spirit.

The law and the promise

¹⁵Brothers and sisters, let me take an example from everyday life. Just as no one can set aside or add to a human covenant that has been duly established, so it is in this case. ¹⁶The promises were spoken to Abraham and to his seed. Scripture does not say 'and to seeds', meaning many people, but 'and to your seed',ⁱ meaning one person, who is Christ. ¹⁷What I mean is this: the law, introduced 430 years later, does not set aside the covenant previously established by God and thus do away with the promise. ¹⁸For if the inheritance depends on the law, then it no longer depends on the promise; but God in his grace gave it to Abraham through a promise.

¹⁹Why, then, was the law given at all? It was added because of transgressions until the Seed to whom the promise referred had come. The law was given through angels and entrusted to a mediator. ²⁰A mediator, however, implies more than one party; but God is one.

²¹Is the law, therefore, opposed to the promises of God? Absolutely not! For if a law had been given that could impart life, then righteousness would certainly have come by the law. ²²But Scripture has locked up everything under the control of sin, so that what was promised, being given through faith in Jesus Christ, might be given to those who believe.

Children of God

²³Before the coming of this faith,ʲ we were held in custody under the law, locked up until the faith that was to come would be revealed. ²⁴So the law was our guardian until Christ came that we might be justified by faith. ²⁵Now that this faith has come, we are no longer under a guardian.

²⁶So in Christ Jesus you are all children of God through faith, ²⁷for all of you who were baptised into Christ have clothed yourselves with Christ. ²⁸There is neither Jew nor Gentile, neither slave nor free, nor is there male and female, for you are all one in Christ Jesus. ²⁹If you belong to Christ, then you are Abraham's seed, and heirs according to the promise.

4 What I am saying is that as long as an heir is under age, he is no different from a slave, although he owns the whole estate. ²The heir is subject to guardians and trustees until the time set by his father. ³So also, when we were under age, we were in slavery under the elemental spiritual forcesᵃ of the world. ⁴But when the set time had fully come, God sent his Son, born of a woman, born under the law, ⁵to redeem those under the law, that we might receive adoption to sonship.ᵇ ⁶Because you are his sons, God sent the Spirit of his Son into our hearts, the Spirit who calls out, 'Abba,ᶜ Father.' ⁷So you are no longer a slave, but God's child; and since you are his child, God has made you also an heir.

Paul's concern for the Galatians

⁸Formerly, when you did not know God, you were slaves to those who by nature are not gods. ⁹But now that you know God – or rather are known by God – how is it that you are turning back to those weak and miserable forcesᵈ? Do you wish to be enslaved by them all over again? ¹⁰You are observing special days and months and seasons and years! ¹¹I fear for you, that somehow I have wasted my efforts on you.

¹²I plead with you, brothers and sisters, become like me, for I became like you. You did me no wrong. ¹³As you know, it was

---

ᵍ 12 Lev. 18:5
ʰ 13 Deut. 21:23
ⁱ 16 Gen. 12:7; 13:15; 24:7
ʲ 22,23 Or *through the faithfulness of Jesus* ... ²³*Before faith came*

ᵃ 3 Or *under the basic principles*
ᵇ 5 The Greek word for *adoption to sonship* is a legal term referring to the full legal standing of an adopted male heir in Roman culture.
ᶜ 6 Aramaic for *Father*
ᵈ 9 Or *principles*

because of an illness that I first preached the gospel to you, ¹⁴and even though my illness was a trial to you, you did not treat me with contempt or scorn. Instead, you welcomed me as if I were an angel of God, as if I were Christ Jesus himself. ¹⁵Where, then, is your blessing of me now? I can testify that, if you could have done so, you would have torn out your eyes and given them to me. ¹⁶Have I now become your enemy by telling you the truth?

¹⁷Those people are zealous to win you over, but for no good. What they want is to alienate you from us, so that you may have zeal for them. ¹⁸It is fine to be zealous, provided the purpose is good, and to be so always, not just when I am with you. ¹⁹My dear children, for whom I am again in the pains of childbirth until Christ is formed in you, ²⁰how I wish I could be with you now and change my tone, because I am perplexed about you!

Hagar and Sarah

²¹Tell me, you who want to be under the law, are you not aware of what the law says? ²²For it is written that Abraham had two sons, one by the slave woman and the other by the free woman. ²³His son by the slave woman was born according to the flesh, but his son by the free woman was born as the result of a divine promise.

²⁴These things are being taken figuratively: the women represent two covenants. One covenant is from Mount Sinai and bears children who are to be slaves: this is Hagar. ²⁵Now Hagar stands for Mount Sinai in Arabia and corresponds to the present city of Jerusalem, because she is in slavery with her children. ²⁶But the

IDENTITY – WHO WE ARE IN CHRIST 4

Children of God

What is our identity as Christians? We're children of God (Galatians 4:6–7). That's not just an intellectual truth or a thought to contemplate. God sends his Holy Spirit to live in us to help us know it in the depths of our being.

The Bible shows us that we're not just children who are tolerated or loved from a distance. We can call God *Abba,* which is like saying 'Daddy', a term of intimacy conveying his intense affection and love for us.

This is for both genders. The only reason this Bible passage says 'sons' is because only sons inherited in the time of the New Testament. We are all children of God, who all inherit from God. In part we inherit on his death (well, Jesus' death), and so can have a relationship with God now in all its fullness. In part we inherit on our death, since as God's children we can have total confidence that he will welcome us into eternity with him.

Since our identity is as children of God, we can be completely assured that God loves us and accepts us. He will never turn his back on us or abandon us. There's nothing we need to do to make ourselves children loved by God, because we already are. Equally, there's nothing we can do that will stop God loving us as his children.

James Grier

 Romans 8:9–11   Ephesians 1:1–10

Jerusalem that is above is free, and she is our mother. 27 For it is written:

'Be glad, barren woman,
   you who never bore a child;
break forth and cry aloud,
   you who were never in labour;
because more are the children of the
   desolate woman
   than of her who has a husband.' *e*

e 27 Isaiah 54:1

HEALING & MIRACLES 10

Walking in wholeness

One of the greatest wonders of the church is the power we have been given to take people into freedom. It's one of my favourite things to watch in people's lives: they once were bound and caught by the enemy, only to come out with amazing freedom! But the message from the apostle Paul here is to remember that slavery will always fight freedom.

Although the enemy would like us to live feeling as though we're fighting something we'll never get free from, that's always a lie. Remember that freedom is yours when you're in Christ, because Christ is not bound by anything.

When there are signs of slavery, it's revealing an area where we have lost sight of who we are. One of the things I have seen about myself over the years is that any part of my heart that isn't free is an area that needs to encounter God's freedom and healing. When people realise that healing isn't just a one-stop deal, they can be frustrated and give up. But healing is a process at times and it's more than a physical encounter, it's learning to live in wholeness.

Staying free isn't about fighting all those areas where we're not experiencing freedom, but instead surrendering to what Christ has already done. We can stay busy all day long fighting this and fighting that, but when we learn to step back and realise what God has already done in our lives and rest, that's when we can experience the freedom we already have.

The enemy will always try to take us back to the old ways of thinking, old ways of behaviour and past patterns which in turn will always produce slavery. Paul's encouragement is to remember that we're in a race, and faith is the fuel that will keep us on the path. It's impossible to run in a race effectively if you're gazing at the people around you. No matter who tries to distract you or pull you off course, remember to be firm in your faith. Don't allow 'agitators' to distract you.

Knowing who we are in Christ is what empowers us to love and give to others. Free people usually love well. What keeps us safe from slavery is not being caught up in what we used to be or what others are doing around us, but instead choosing to live in love.

The freedom that we have is a gift. Don't waste your time trying to fight what was or the burden of what used to be, but instead learn to rest in who you are now. Let God define you in this place.

Christy Wimber

◀◀ Proverbs 12:18   ⬛

28 Now you, brothers and sisters, like Isaac, are children of promise. **29** At that time the son born according to the flesh persecuted the son born by the power of the Spirit. It is the same now. **30** But what does Scripture say? 'Get rid of the slave woman and her son, for the slave woman's son will never share in the inheritance with the free woman's son.'*f* **31** Therefore, brothers and sisters, we are not children of the slave woman, but of the free woman.

Freedom in Christ

5 It is for freedom that Christ has set us free. Stand firm, then, and do not let yourselves be burdened again by a yoke of slavery.

2 Mark my words! I, Paul, tell you that if you let yourselves be circumcised, Christ will be of no value to you at all. **3** Again I declare to every man who lets himself be circumcised that he is required to obey the whole law. **4** You who are trying to be justified by the law have been alienated from Christ; you have fallen away from grace. **5** For through the Spirit we eagerly await by faith the righteousness for which we hope. **6** For in Christ Jesus neither circumcision nor uncircumcision has any value. The only thing that counts is faith expressing itself through love.

7 You were running a good race. Who cut in on you to keep you from obeying the truth? **8** That kind of persuasion does not come from the one who calls you. **9** 'A little yeast works through the whole batch of dough.' **10** I am confident in the Lord that you will take no other view. The one who is throwing you into confusion, whoever that may be, will have to pay the penalty. **11** Brothers and sisters, if I am still preaching circumcision, why am I still being persecuted? In that case the offence of the cross has been abolished. **12** As for those agitators, I wish they would go the whole way and emasculate themselves!

Life by the Spirit

13 You, my brothers and sisters, were called to be free. But do not use your freedom to indulge the flesh*a*; rather, serve one another humbly in love. **14** For the entire law is fulfilled in keeping this one command: 'Love your neighbour as yourself.'*b* **15** If you bite and devour each other, watch out or you will be destroyed by each other.

16 So I say, live by the Spirit, and you will not gratify the desires of the flesh. **17** For the flesh desires what is contrary to the Spirit, and the Spirit what is contrary to the flesh. They are in conflict with each other, so that you are not to do whatever*c* you want. **18** But if you are led by the Spirit, you are not under the law.

19 The acts of the flesh are obvious: sexual immorality, impurity and debauchery; **20** idolatry and witchcraft; hatred, discord, jealousy, fits of rage, selfish ambition, dissensions, factions **21** and envy; drunkenness, orgies, and the like. I warn you, as I did before, that those who live like this will not inherit the kingdom of God.

22 But the fruit of the Spirit is love, joy, peace, forbearance, kindness, goodness, faithfulness, **23** gentleness and self-control. Against such things there is no law. **24** Those who belong to Christ Jesus have crucified the flesh with its passions and desires. **25** Since we live by the Spirit, let us keep in step with the Spirit. **26** Let us not become conceited, provoking and envying each other.

Doing good to all

6 Brothers and sisters, if someone is caught in a sin, you who live by the Spirit should restore that person gently. But watch yourselves, or you also may be tempted. **2** Carry each other's burdens, and in this way you will fulfil the law of Christ. **3** If anyone thinks they are something when they are not, they deceive themselves. **4** Each one should test their own actions. Then they can take pride in themselves alone, without comparing themselves to someone else, **5** for each one should carry their own load. **6** Nevertheless, the

f 30 Gen. 21:10

a 13 In contexts like this, the Greek word for *flesh* (*sarx*) refers to the sinful state of human beings, often presented as a power in opposition to the Spirit; also in verses 16, 17, 19 and 24; and in 6:8.
b 14 Lev. 19:18
c 17 Or *you do not do what*

RELATIONSHIPS 9

PURITY PART 3

We can set rules and try to live by them, but we have to remember that we're not called to live under laws, but in freedom.

It's tricky to understand: on the one hand, we know that God has designed both us and a way for us to live, and therefore we know that some things aren't good for us to do. Conversely, Galatians 5:13–26 says that we're meant to live lives of freedom, not weighed down by rules. How does that make sense? The vital thing to understand is that Christianity isn't about religion, it's about relationship: we have a living, active relationship with the God who made us, and it's his Spirit in us that transforms us. Rules help to guide us while we grow as Christians, until we're at the stage where we can overcome the temptations that once overwhelmed us.

Whatever difficult situation we're facing, we always have a choice. God gave us free will. When we look at the fruits of the Spirit (vv. 22–23) and compare them with the acts of the sinful nature (vv. 19–21), it seems as if it should be an easy choice, but when we're tempted, that's not always the case. Every time we choose what's right over what tempts us, we 'crucify' the 'flesh' (that is, our sinful nature) (v. 24). This verse (sadly!) doesn't mean that once we're Christians, nothing tempts us again. It's an active process, and means submitting ourselves to Jesus over and over again.

So how do we go about living in freedom?

- When you mess up, keep short accounts with God. Ask for forgiveness when you make ungodly decisions! God already knows our mistakes and still loves us unconditionally. Don't make the same mistake that Adam and Eve did and hide from God when he comes looking for you because you're ashamed.

- God's mercies are new every morning (Lamentations 3:22–23). Once you have asked for forgiveness, know that you're forgiven completely!

- *'Above all else, guard your heart, for everything you do flows from it'* (Proverbs 4:23). Freedom doesn't mean you no longer have to exercise caution; relationships require an investment of your heart, and your heart is too valuable to be invested lightly.

When we're tempted to go further than we know is good, we need to remember why God says that sex is for marriage. Sex is never just a physical transaction. There's something spiritual and emotional involved that's difficult to explain, but this is why Scripture is so prescriptive about sex. Sex is a wonderful gift from God, but only in its proper place, in marriage. Sex is like fire. It's appealing, keeps you warm on cold nights and it's a whole lot of fun, but out of a controlled environment it has the potential to be destructive and dangerous. We also don't want to let sex become another thing in which we search for fulfilment, but which distracts us from where we really find it – in Jesus.

Jane Plackett & Calum Dyke

 Song of Songs 2:7   Matthew 19:4–6

one who receives instruction in the word should share all good things with their instructor.

7 Do not be deceived: God cannot be mocked. A man reaps what he sows. 8 Whoever sows to please their flesh, from the flesh will reap destruction; whoever sows to please the Spirit, from the Spirit will reap eternal life. 9 Let us not become weary in doing good, for at the proper time we will reap a harvest if we do not give up. 10 Therefore, as we have opportunity, let us do good to all people, especially to those who belong to the family of believers.

Not circumcision but the new creation

11 See what large letters I use as I write to you with my own hand!

12 Those who want to impress people by means of the flesh are trying to compel you to be circumcised. The only reason they do this is to avoid being persecuted for the cross of Christ. 13 Not even those who are circumcised keep the law, yet they want you to be circumcised that they may

NATURALLY SUPERNATURAL 10

FRUITS OF THE SPIRIT

When we talk about being naturally supernatural, it's easy to focus on the visible and audible gifts of the Spirit, like speaking in tongues, prophecy, healings and miracles. But one of the ways we can tell if we're increasingly letting the Holy Spirit have control of us is to test whether we're bearing more of his fruit (Galatians 5:22–23).

That means we should see ourselves changing to be more like him and to have more of the character traits of Jesus.

People want to know more about who God is after seeing his signs and wonders, but they will also see his nature when they see us behaving like Jesus did. In a world that seems to be full of anxiety, we can have peace in the Holy Spirit. In a time when society suggests you look out for yourself, we can love others and be kind. In an age that urges us to give in to every craving and heart's desire, we can display self-control. We don't do any of this in our own strength, though.

Most of us would look at the list in Galatians 5 and know that we don't come anywhere close to having all those qualities. Thankfully, fruit isn't something you strain and strive for – it grows naturally in the right conditions. The more you ask the Holy Spirit to fill you, the more you wait on him and ask him to change and mould you, the more you will find yourself displaying his qualities. We should lean on the Holy Spirit, trying to turn away from our sinful nature, and depend increasingly on him, trusting that as we do this he will undertake the work that is needed in us.

Mike Pilavachi

 Acts 3:6–7

boast about your circumcision in the flesh. [14] May I never boast except in the cross of our Lord Jesus Christ, through which[a] the world has been crucified to me, and I to the world. [15] Neither circumcision nor uncircumcision means anything; what counts is the new creation. [16] Peace and

mercy to all who follow this rule – to[b] the Israel of God.

[17] From now on, let no one cause me trouble, for I bear on my body the marks of Jesus.

[18] The grace of our Lord Jesus Christ be with your spirit, brothers and sisters. Amen.

_a_ 14 Or _whom_   _b_ 16 Or _rule and to_

EPHESIANS

DATE

This letter was written around AD 60

AUTHOR

The apostle Paul

WHAT'S IT ALL ABOUT?

Many of Paul's letters to churches address particular issues or problems they were facing, but this letter offers more general teaching and thoughts. It may have been a circular letter intended to be read by a number of churches, including the church at Ephesus, and it was written while Paul was in prison. Considering he was locked up, Paul's spirits seem to be high and, as the letter starts, his joy and thankfulness bubble over into praise at God's blessings and the faith of his church. As in his letter to the Galatians, Paul talks about how Christians are saved by grace, and he stresses the importance of unity among the believers. He also talks about love, praying that the Ephesians might grasp the scope of God's amazing love for them and that they might live lives of love in all their relationships, whether between husband and wife or slave and master.

WHY SHOULD WE READ IT?

- To see that we are chosen by God and our lives are intended to bring him glory (Ephesians 1).
- To understand the importance of unity among Christians (Ephesians 2).
- To read Paul's amazing prayer that the Ephesians would know the depth of God's love for them (Ephesians 3).
- To learn about the armour of God (Ephesians 6).

Andy Croft with Liza Hoeksma

1 Paul, an apostle of Christ Jesus by the will of God,

To God's holy people in Ephesus,*a* the faithful in Christ Jesus:

2 Grace and peace to you from God our Father and the Lord Jesus Christ.

Praise for spiritual blessings in Christ

3 Praise be to the God and Father of our Lord Jesus Christ, who has blessed us in

the heavenly realms with every spiritual blessing in Christ. 4 For he chose us in him before the creation of the world to be holy and blameless in his sight. In love 5 he*b* predestined us for adoption to sonship*c* through Jesus Christ, in accordance with his pleasure and will – 6 to the praise of his glorious grace, which he has freely given us in the One he loves. 7 In him we have redemption through his blood, the

a 1 Some early manuscripts do not have *in Ephesus*.

b 4,5 Or *sight in love.* 5 He
c 5 The Greek word for *adoption to sonship* is a legal term referring to the full legal standing of an adopted male heir in Roman culture.

IDENTITY – WHO WE ARE IN CHRIST 5

Chosen saints

Everyone knows that saints are the people who hang around in church windows with holy halos. Many people know that in order to become a modern-day saint and be recognised as such by the church, you must be a Christian, lead a particularly holy and exemplary life, perform at least two miracles and, er, be dead.

Yet that's not true! According to the Bible, part of our identity as Christians is that we are all *'God's holy people'* (Philippians 1:1–6) – we are all saints! That's right, you're a saint. Probably best not to use it as your title when you fill in forms, though…

You might feel more like a sinner, but that's not how God views you. In fact, in the New Testament, only unbelievers are called 'sinners' (about 330 times) and believers are called 'holy' or 'righteous ones' or 'saints' (about 240 times). A saint is someone who is holy, and 'holy' means 'set apart'. We have been set apart by God as his children. We have been made righteous and holy by Jesus' death for our sins. That's what we are. OK, we do sin. We do make mistakes, but that's not our identity. When a baby takes his first steps, he falls over as much as he walks. Parents don't say, 'He's just a faller, who walks a bit.' They scream, 'He's walking! He can walk!'

If we believe we're just sinners, we end up expecting to fail and mess up. If we see ourselves as who we really are, as saints who in essence are good but who still make mistakes, then we raise our sights. We expect to live as God made us to live, and as he empowers us to live. *'He who began a good work in you will carry it on to completion'* (v. 6) – if only you'll let him.

James Grier

 Galatians 4:6–7

Colossians 1:9–14

forgiveness of sins, in accordance with the riches of God's grace ^{8} that he lavished on us. With all wisdom and understanding, ^{9} he^d made known to us the mystery of his will according to his good pleasure, which he purposed in Christ, ^{10} to be put into effect when the times reach their fulfilment – to bring unity to all things in heaven and on earth under Christ.

^{11} In him we were also chosen,^{e} having been predestined according to the plan of him who works out everything in conformity with the purpose of his will, ^{12} in order that we, who were the first to put our hope in Christ, might be for the praise of his glory. ^{13} And you also were included in Christ when you heard the message of truth, the gospel of your salvation. When

---

d 8,9 Or *us with all wisdom and understanding.* ^{9} *And he*

e 11 Or *were made heirs*

NATURALLY SUPERNATURAL 5

HOW DO I KNOW THE HOLY SPIRIT IS IN ME?

How do we know the Holy Spirit is living in us? Is it if we shake in a ministry time? Is it if we cry? Do we need to fall on the floor or cluck like a chicken? No! We know the Holy Spirit is in us because the Bible tells us so.

Paul says in Ephesians 1:13–14 that the Holy Spirit is in us if we believe in Jesus. If you want further proof that the Holy Spirit is in you, read 1 Corinthians 12. There Paul tells us that no one can say, *'Jesus is Lord,'* except by the Holy Spirit. (Of course you could say those words, but to actually believe it you need to have the Holy Spirit.) So if you believe in Jesus you really are filled with his Spirit. It's that simple.

The Holy Spirit is the promise of what's to come, God's down payment saying he's coming back for you. It's not about what we do in times of ministry when we're waiting on God's Spirit. The manifestations (the ways we physically react to the work of the Holy Spirit) aren't the important bit. I have seen lots of things happening in ministry times. Sometimes people cry because they're letting out pain, at other times because they're receiving God's compassion. Sometimes people scream or shake because they're letting go of things that have hurt them. Sometimes they're completely still as they receive God's peace. Sometimes people do all sorts of crazy things and I have had no idea what's going on. But it doesn't matter! We miss the point if we focus on that stuff. You might never even flutter an eyelid in ministry, but that doesn't mean you're not full of the Holy Spirit, or that he's not working in your life.

The key thing is that the more of the Holy Spirit we have, the more we change. The more we change, the more like Jesus we become. The true test of what God was doing in a time of ministry is how different someone's life looks afterwards. Let's not get distracted by the manifestations of the Holy Spirit, but ask him to keep filling us. Although he lives in us, there's always room for more. Let's ask God to fill us with his Holy Spirit every day and to help us become increasingly reliant on him.

Mike Pilavachi

 1 Kings 18　　　　　　　　　　Matthew 11:1–5 ▶▶

you believed, you were marked in him with a seal, the promised Holy Spirit, ¹⁴who is a deposit guaranteeing our inheritance until the redemption of those who are God's possession – to the praise of his glory.

Thanksgiving and prayer

¹⁵For this reason, ever since I heard about your faith in the Lord Jesus and your love for all God's people, ¹⁶I have not stopped giving thanks for you,

THE BIG STORY 8

Jesus rises to begin a new creation

The purpose of the extraordinary prayer in Ephesians 1:15–23 is to open our eyes to the hope, riches and power of what God has done for us in Jesus Christ. It centres on the resurrection. This sort of power is *'incomparable'* – there has never been anything like it, because it defeated death and all the forces of evil once and for all, and placed Jesus in the highest position in the universe, for us as we serve him on earth (see also Matthew 28:16–20).

The consequences of the resurrection are far reaching. It means that God honours his Son's way of life on earth and vindicates him against his accusers. It means that our sins have been forgiven. The Father has accepted the sacrifice of his Son for us and raised him to life (1 Corinthians 15:17). It means that we serve a living Lord, not a dead teacher. This gives us a relationship with him now, and an unshakeable hope for the future. It means that we need not fear death. To die is simply to go to be with him (Philippians 1:21–24) until we too are raised with a transformed body like his, at the climax of history (1 Corinthians 15:20–24). It means that, in his bodily resurrection, the new creation has begun right in the middle of the old one. That's what Paul is referring to by *'the hope to which he has called you, the riches of his glorious inheritance in his holy people'* (v. 18). The old creation is passing away. The universe, as it is now, will come to an end. But God's new creation will last for ever. The power which God used to raise Jesus is the same power that he will use to *'make everything new'* (Revelation 21:5). Because of the resurrection, and in the power of the resurrection, Christians live the life of the new world (v. 21, the age *'to come'*) in the midst of the old.

It's important that we don't misunderstand this idea of resurrection power. The first point I made about the resurrection was that God vindicated his Son's way of life. Jesus modelled a life lived in obedience to God and service to others. It was a life of sacrifice. Resurrection power is the power to do the same. It's the power to live a Christ-like life. It isn't the power to be 'Super-Christian'. It's the power to live our lives for others and to know God's strength in the midst of our human weakness. It's the power of the new creation in us, while we're still part of the old creation. It's the power to live as the body of Christ now (v. 23), to show people the future in advance by living like him.

Graham Cray

 1 John 1:5–10   Colossians 1:18–20 ▶

remembering you in my prayers. [17] I keep asking that the God of our Lord Jesus Christ, the glorious Father, may give you the Spirit *f* of wisdom and revelation, so that you may know him better. [18] I pray that the eyes of your heart may be enlightened in order that you may know the hope to which he has called you, the riches of his glorious inheritance in his holy people, [19] and his incomparably great power for us who believe. That power is the same as the mighty strength [20] he exerted when he raised Christ from the dead and seated him at his right hand in the heavenly realms, [21] far above all rule and authority, power and dominion, and every name that is invoked, not only in the present age but also in the one to come. [22] And God placed all things under his feet and appointed him to be head over everything for the church, [23] which is his body, the fullness of him who fills everything in every way.

Made alive in Christ

2 As for you, you were dead in your transgressions and sins, [2] in which you used to live when you followed the ways of this world and of the ruler of the kingdom of the air, the spirit who is now at work in those who are disobedient. [3] All of us also lived among them at one time, gratifying the cravings of our flesh *a* and following its desires and thoughts. Like the rest, we were by nature deserving of wrath. [4] But because of his great love for us, God, who is rich in mercy, [5] made us alive with Christ even when we were dead in transgressions – it is by grace you have been saved. [6] And God raised us up with Christ and seated us with him in the heavenly realms in Christ Jesus, [7] in order that in the coming ages he might show the incomparable riches of his grace, expressed in his kindness to us in Christ Jesus. [8] For it is by grace you have been saved, through faith – and this is not from yourselves, it is

the gift of God – [9] not by works, so that no one can boast. [10] For we are God's handiwork, created in Christ Jesus to do good works, which God prepared in advance for us to do.

Jew and Gentile reconciled through Christ

[11] Therefore, remember that formerly you who are Gentiles by birth and called 'uncircumcised' by those who call themselves 'the circumcision' (which is done in the body by human hands) – [12] remember that at that time you were separate from Christ, excluded from citizenship in Israel and foreigners to the covenants of the promise, without hope and without God in the world. [13] But now in Christ Jesus you who once were far away have been brought near by the blood of Christ.

[14] For he himself is our peace, who has made the two groups one and has destroyed the barrier, the dividing wall of hostility, [15] by setting aside in his flesh the law with its commands and regulations. His purpose was to create in himself one new humanity out of the two, thus making peace, [16] and in one body to reconcile both of them to God through the cross, by which he put to death their hostility. [17] He came and preached peace to you who were far away and peace to those who were near. [18] For through him we both have access to the Father by one Spirit.

[19] Consequently, you are no longer foreigners and strangers, but fellow citizens with God's people and also members of his household, [20] built on the foundation of the apostles and prophets, with Christ Jesus himself as the chief cornerstone. [21] In him the whole building is joined together and rises to become a holy temple in the Lord. [22] And in him you too are being built together to become a dwelling in which God lives by his Spirit.

God's marvellous plan for the Gentiles

3 For this reason I, Paul, the prisoner of Christ Jesus for the sake of you Gentiles –

[2] Surely you have heard about the administration of God's grace that was given

---

f 17 Or *a spirit*
a 3 In contexts like this, the Greek word for *flesh* (*sarx*) refers to the sinful state of human beings, often presented as a power in opposition to the Spirit.

to me for you, ³ that is, the mystery made known to me by revelation, as I have already written briefly. ⁴ In reading this, then, you will be able to understand my insight into the mystery of Christ, ⁵ which was not made known to people in other generations as it has now been revealed by the Spirit to God's holy apostles and

I'M A GOOD PERSON, ISN'T THAT ENOUGH?

The world is full of people who do good things. Many have compassion for others, are kind, moral and law abiding. They help charities and neighbours. These are all fantastic qualities. But just how good is good enough?

When we look closer at the Bible, we realise that we measure 'goodness' on a completely different scale from God. We see that our good deeds alone will never allow us to gain access to his kingdom. In Ephesians 2:1–10, Paul writes to the church about this. In verses 1–3, we're reminded that without Christ, we're all spiritually dead because of our sinful nature. This really does include everyone. Paul also writes in Romans 3:23 that *'all have sinned and fall short of the glory of God'.* We often try to fix ourselves and counterbalance our sinful nature by doing good things. The problem remains that no matter how many good things we do, we can't bridge the gap to reach perfection in God's eyes, because the wages of sin is death (Romans 6:23).

God knew that the only way for us to be made right with him would be for someone perfect to die in our place. This is where this passage in Ephesians really starts to get exciting! In verses 4–5, we read that because of God's great love for us, he sent himself as Jesus to take our place. He made a way for us to be with him, even though we didn't deserve it. When we think about it, it's a relief that we don't have to do good works to impress God: what could we do to impress a God who spoke this world into being? Ephesians tells us that we can only know forgiveness through Jesus and his incredible love for us. Another word for this is 'grace'.

'It is by grace you have been saved, through faith – and this is not from yourselves, it is the gift of God' (v. 8). What an awesome gift we have received, to be made right with God, to know absolutely that we're his children! Paul expands on this in verse 9: it isn't because of our good works, so we can't boast in ourselves. It's simply a gift that we may choose to receive by faith. When someone gives you a gift, do you say, 'Great, now how much do I owe you?' No. The appropriate response is, 'Thank you.' This is what God desires from us. Let's receive his gift of life with thanksgiving and joy!

Finally, it's really important to see that we have been *'created in Christ Jesus to do good works'* (v. 10). Out of a thankful heart for this amazing gift, God expects us to serve others, showing them the same kindness and love that he has shown us. Although our good works can't help us earn salvation, they can help us as we go out and play our part in showing God's love to those around us.

Mark Russell

prophets. 6This mystery is that through the gospel the Gentiles are heirs together with Israel, members together of one body, and sharers together in the promise in Christ Jesus.

7I became a servant of this gospel by the gift of God's grace given me through the working of his power. 8Although I am less than the least of all the Lord's people, this grace was given me: to preach to the Gentiles the boundless riches of Christ, 9and to make plain to everyone the administration of this mystery, which for ages past was kept hidden in God, who created all things. 10His intent was that now, through the church, the manifold wisdom of God should be made known to the rulers and authorities in the heavenly realms, 11according to his eternal purpose that he accomplished in Christ Jesus our Lord. 12In him and through faith in him we may approach God with freedom and confidence. 13I ask you, therefore, not to be discouraged because of my sufferings for you, which are your glory.

A prayer for the Ephesians

14For this reason I kneel before the Father, 15from whom every family*a* in heaven and on earth derives its name. 16I pray that out of his glorious riches he may strengthen you with power through his Spirit in your inner being, 17so that Christ may dwell in your hearts through faith. And I pray that you, being rooted and established in love, 18may have power, together with all the Lord's holy people, to grasp how wide and long and high and deep is the love of Christ, 19and to know this love that surpasses knowledge – that you may be filled to the measure of all the fullness of God.

20Now to him who is able to do immeasurably more than all we ask or imagine, according to his power that is at work within us, 21to him be glory in the church and in Christ Jesus throughout all generations, for ever and ever! Amen.

Unity and maturity in the body of Christ

4 As a prisoner for the Lord, then, I urge you to live a life worthy of the calling you have received. 2Be completely humble and gentle; be patient, bearing with one another in love. 3Make every effort to keep the unity of the Spirit through the bond of peace. 4There is one body and one Spirit, just as you were called to one hope when you were called; 5one Lord, one faith, one baptism; 6one God and Father of all, who is over all and through all and in all.

7But to each one of us grace has been given as Christ apportioned it. 8This is why it*a* says:

'When he ascended on high,
    he took many captives
    and gave gifts to his people.'*b*

9(What does 'he ascended' mean except that he also descended to the lower, earthly regions*c*? 10He who descended is the very one who ascended higher than all the heavens, in order to fill the whole universe.) 11So Christ himself gave the apostles, the prophets, the evangelists, the pastors and teachers, 12to equip his people for works of service, so that the body of Christ may be built up 13until we all reach unity in the faith and in the knowledge of the Son of God and become mature, attaining to the whole measure of the fullness of Christ.

14Then we will no longer be infants, tossed back and forth by the waves, and blown here and there by every wind of teaching and by the cunning and craftiness of people in their deceitful scheming. 15Instead, speaking the truth in love, we will grow to become in every respect the mature body of him who is the head, that is, Christ. 16From him the whole body, joined and held together by every supporting ligament, grows and builds itself up in love, as each part does its work.

---

a 15 The Greek for *family* (*patria*) is derived from the Greek for *father* (*pater*).

a 8 Or *God*
b 8 Psalm 68:18
c 9 Or *the depths of the earth*

Instructions for Christian living

17 So I tell you this, and insist on it in the Lord, that you must no longer live as the Gentiles do, in the futility of their thinking. 18 They are darkened in their understanding and separated from the life of God because of the ignorance that is in them due to the hardening of their hearts. 19 Having lost all sensitivity, they have given themselves over to sensuality so as to indulge in every kind of impurity, and they are full of greed.

20 That, however, is not the way of life you learned 21 when you heard about Christ and were taught in him in accordance with the truth that is in Jesus. 22 You were taught, with regard to your former way of life, to put off your old self, which is being corrupted by its deceitful desires; 23 to be made new in the attitude of your minds; 24 and to put on the new self,

created to be like God in true righteousness and holiness.

25 Therefore each of you must put off falsehood and speak truthfully to your neighbour, for we are all members of one body. 26 'In your anger do not sin'd: do not let the sun go down while you are still angry, 27 and do not give the devil a foothold. 28 Anyone who has been stealing must steal no longer, but must work, doing something useful with their own hands, that they may have something to share with those in need.

29 Do not let any unwholesome talk come out of your mouths, but only what is helpful for building others up according to their needs, that it may benefit those who listen. 30 And do not grieve the Holy Spirit of God, with whom you were sealed

_____
d 26 Psalm 4:4 (see Septuagint)

IDENTITY – WHO WE ARE IN CHRIST 10

Christ's body

Not only does our body belong to Christ, but also we are his body. As Teresa of Avila said, 'Christ has no body but yours, no hands, no feet on earth but yours.' He works through us on earth. Also when people see us, we embody something of Jesus. That's quite a responsibility. What would people think of Jesus by looking at me and my life?

Being the body of Christ is not just about individual Christians, though. A key part of our identity in Christ is that we are part of his body here on earth, a body made up of different people (Ephesians 4:25–32). This finds expression in the church. Together we form Christ's body as a group of people. In the words of J.John, 'None of us has got it all together … but together we've got it all!' We become Christians through our individual journey and choice, but Christian faith is meant to be lived out in community. It's not a solo journey.

This is a fantastic truth. We need never be alone as Christians. It can also be one of the hardest things about being a Christian. We need to look to the needs of others, rather than just our own. We can't go it alone: we need to care for others and sort out our differences. Church isn't an option, it's part of our Christian identity.

James Grier

 1 Corinthians 6:18–20   ◻

for the day of redemption. **31** Get rid of all bitterness, rage and anger, brawling and slander, along with every form of malice. **32** Be kind and compassionate to one another, forgiving each other, just as in Christ God forgave you. **1** Follow God's example, therefore, as dearly loved children **2** and live a life of love, just as Christ loved us and gave himself up for us as a fragrant offering and sacrifice to God.

3 But among you there must not be even a hint of sexual immorality, or of any kind of impurity, or of greed, because these are improper for God's holy people. **4** Nor should there be obscenity, foolish talk or coarse joking, which are out of place, but rather thanksgiving. **5** For of this you can be sure: no immoral, impure or greedy person – such a person is an idolater – has any inheritance in the kingdom of Christ and of God. *a* **6** Let no one deceive you with empty words, for because of such things God's wrath comes on those who are disobedient. **7** Therefore do not be partners with them.

8 For you were once darkness, but now you are light in the Lord. Live as children of light **9** (for the fruit of the light consists in all goodness, righteousness and truth) **10** and find out what pleases the Lord. **11** Have nothing to do with the fruitless deeds of darkness, but rather expose them. **12** It is shameful even to mention what the disobedient do in secret. **13** But everything exposed by the light becomes visible – and everything that is illuminated becomes a light. **14** This is why it is said:

'Wake up, sleeper,
    rise from the dead,
and Christ will shine on you.'

15 Be very careful, then, how you live – not as unwise but as wise, **16** making the most of every opportunity, because the days are evil. **17** Therefore do not be foolish, but understand what the Lord's will is. **18** Do not get drunk on wine, which leads to debauchery. Instead, be filled with the Spirit, **19** speaking to one another with psalms, hymns, and songs from the Spirit. Sing and make music from your heart to the Lord, **20** always giving thanks to God the Father for everything, in the name of our Lord Jesus Christ.

Instructions for Christian households

21 Submit to one another out of reverence for Christ.

22 Wives, submit yourselves to your own husbands as you do to the Lord. **23** For the husband is the head of the wife as Christ is the head of the church, his body, of which he is the Saviour. **24** Now as the church submits to Christ, so also wives should submit to their husbands in everything.

25 Husbands, love your wives, just as Christ loved the church and gave himself up for her **26** to make her holy, cleansing*b* her by the washing with water through the word, **27** and to present her to himself as a radiant church, without stain or wrinkle or any other blemish, but holy and blameless. **28** In this same way, husbands ought to love their wives as their own bodies. He who loves his wife loves himself. **29** After all, no one ever hated their own body, but they feed and care for their body, just as Christ does the church – **30** for we are members of his body. **31** 'For this reason a man will leave his father and mother and be united to his wife, and the two will become one flesh.'*c* **32** This is a profound mystery – but I am talking about Christ and the church. **33** However, each one of you also must love his wife as he loves himself, and the wife must respect her husband.

6 Children, obey your parents in the Lord, for this is right. **2** 'Honour your father and mother' – which is the first commandment with a promise – **3** 'so that it may go well with you and that you may enjoy long life on the earth.'*a*

4 Fathers,*b* do not exasperate your children; instead, bring them up in the training and instruction of the Lord.

---

b 26 Or *having cleansed*
c 31 Gen. 2:24
a 3 Deut. 5:16
b 4 Or *Parents*

⁵Slaves, obey your earthly masters with respect and fear, and with sincerity of heart, just as you would obey Christ. ⁶Obey them not only to win their favour when their eye is on you, but as slaves of Christ, doing the will of God from your heart. ⁷Serve wholeheartedly, as if you were serving the Lord, not people, ⁸because you know that the Lord will reward each one for whatever good they do, whether they are slave or free.

⁹And masters, treat your slaves in the

ALCOHOL AND DRUGS

Alcohol is a topic that regularly appears in the Bible. In the King James Version, the word 'wine' appears over 200 times. More often than not, it's attached to a warning to avoid rude and drunken behaviour. In Ephesians 5:18, Paul delivers a fairly damning attack on the act of getting drunk, saying that it *'leads to debauchery'*. These are very strong words for Paul to use. However, when we understand it contextually, it begins to make more sense.

Thousands of years ago, in the time that the Bible was written, many celebrations and festivals would have been accompanied with wine. Wine was a drink that was fairly easy to make and because of the climate, grapes were often the most available fruit. Mentions of drinking in the Bible are fairly frequent. Just one example was the wedding at Cana, where Jesus miraculously turned gallons of water into the finest wine.

However, it's excessive drinking and what that can lead to that Paul is so strongly against. One example was Noah, famous for his obedience to God. I think he must have had a massive hangover after we read in Genesis 9:21 that *'he drank some ... wine, he became drunk and lay uncovered inside his tent'*.

In Ephesians, Paul is writing to the church in Ephesus. Although Paul had passed on the teachings of Jesus, the Ephesians had a really bad problem of backsliding to the practices of the days before Christianity.

In another of Paul's letters, this time to the Galatians, he writes that a fruit of the Spirit is self-control. The church of Ephesus was in dire need of self-control. Paul knew the temptation would be there, so he issued a warning never to be drunk. He urged that instead of being drunk and out of control, they should instead be filled with the Spirit. This teaching is even more important when it comes to drugs, as the effects can be so unpredictable.

This is a message that transfers to us. Alcohol and drugs are a big temptation to many people today. People's lives can be ruined by dependency on alcohol or drugs and they can become an idol that we begin to worship. Paul's message applies just as much to us today. Never be drunk, but more importantly never be lacking in self-control. Instead we are urged to embrace the gift of self-control and use it to glorify God by living obedient and honest lives.

Robbie Thomson

RELATIONSHIPS 11

PREPARATION FOR ETERNITY

You will normally hear Ephesians 5:21–33 mentioned when people are talking about the roles of men and women in marriage, but it has a whole lot more to say about relationships than that!

This passage is about our roles in marriage, but mainly it talks about our mutual responsibility for each other's spiritual development. In this passage, the Bible talks about presenting each other to Jesus without stain or wrinkle, or any other blemish. It's our role to support one another, but also to challenge one another; to love each other when it's easy as well as when it's difficult; to treat each other with purity so that we can know at the end of our lives that we have loved authentically and helped to make each other into the best people we can be.

Our relationship with Jesus is the most important relationship we have. A relationship with him models the way we should love one another, and the way we love one another reveals Jesus to the world. It's our relationships that should challenge and transform us into a better reflection of God. The role of presenting each other without any blemish is an amazing privilege, but also an incredible responsibility. When we fall short of this godly aim for marriage and relationships (and I say 'when' because we all will), we need to know that God loves us regardless of how much we disappoint him, and that he will always forgive us.

So how do we go about putting God at the centre of our relationships? Here are some tips we found helpful:

- Pray together and for one another (but when it comes to personal or upsetting issues, this is stuff you should be talking through with your youth leader, not your boyfriend or girlfriend – this comes back to part 9, on intimacy and commitment).

- Read and study the Bible together (I have married friends who started a Bible reading plan together when they got engaged, and still read the Bible aloud to one another every night).

- Figure out what you both want to see God do in your town or city, and take action together.

- Thank God for one another regularly, and look at how you can love that other person sacrificially – never to meet your own agendas.

As well as loving one another in these ways, regularly think what it requires to love God with all your heart, mind and soul.

Jane Plackett with Calum Dyke

Matthew 19:4–6

same way. Do not threaten them, since you know that he who is both their Master and yours is in heaven, and there is no favouritism with him.

The armour of God

¹⁰ Finally, be strong in the Lord and in his mighty power. ¹¹ Put on the full armour of God, so that you can take your stand against the devil's schemes. ¹² For our struggle is not against flesh and blood, but against the rulers, against the authorities, against the powers of this dark world and against the spiritual forces of evil in the heavenly realms. ¹³ Therefore put on the full armour of God, so that

PRAYER 9

KEEP ON PRAYING

I remember when I first realised that praying was not so much a burden as a natural, everyday part of being alive, more like breathing than work. We don't think, 'Ooh, I really should breathe now.' We just do it. If we didn't do it, we would die. Prayer can become the same (Ephesians 6:10–20).

The key is the Holy Spirit. He helps us in our weakness (Romans 8:23) and gives us groans, sighs, words, or heavenly words we can't even understand (an experience that the Bible calls 'speaking in tongues', 1 Corinthians 14:18). Sometimes it's like we're talking to God; in other situations it feels like God is in us, talking through us. His wishes for the world seem to come through into our words and longings. Sometimes we use English words, but sometimes incomprehensible words, pleading words, hoping words, proclaiming words, complaining words, groans beyond words. Sometimes we feel as if we're battling with the *'forces of evil'* (Ephesians 6:12); at other times we're simply asking our heavenly Father for the needs of our loved ones or his people around the world. All put together, that's what they call praying *'in the Spirit'* (v. 18).

The day I first understood what it was to pray in the Spirit, I was playing tennis with a few friends. Some were Christians and others not yet. At one point I went looking for some balls we had lost in the bushes and was praying for my friends. As I prayed, I ran out of words. I wanted to keep praying and found myself making up words that made no sense but expressed how my spirit felt towards these people. Eventually I found the tennis balls and returned to my seat. To my surprise, one of those who was not yet a believer turned to me and said, 'Hey, I can see you really know God. How would I get to know him like you do?' I almost dropped off my chair.

God's power released by praying in this way for my friends was clearly deeper than my previous prayers. I knew something had changed in my understanding of the way God works. This kind of praying was possible *'on all occasions'* (v. 18). It was a natural flow of my heart inspired by God's Spirit – the essential everyday experience of living with and for Jesus.

Hugo Anson

 James 5:13–18   Acts 4:23–31

when the day of evil comes, you may be able to stand your ground, and after you have done everything, to stand. ¹⁴Stand firm then, with the belt of truth buckled round your waist, with the breastplate of righteousness in place, ¹⁵and with your feet fitted with the readiness that comes from the gospel of peace. ¹⁶In addition to all this, take up the shield of faith, with which you can extinguish all the flaming arrows of the evil one. ¹⁷Take the helmet of salvation and the sword of the Spirit, which is the word of God.

¹⁸And pray in the Spirit on all occasions with all kinds of prayers and requests. With this in mind, be alert and always keep on praying for all the Lord's people. ¹⁹Pray also for me, that whenever I speak, words may be given me so that I will fearlessly make known the mystery of the gospel, ²⁰for which I am an ambassador in chains. Pray that I may declare it fearlessly, as I should.

Final greetings

²¹Tychicus, the dear brother and faithful servant in the Lord, will tell you everything, so that you also may know how I am and what I am doing. ²²I am sending him to you for this very purpose, that you may know how we are, and that he may encourage you.

²³Peace to the brothers and sisters,ᶜ and love with faith from God the Father and the Lord Jesus Christ. ²⁴Grace to all who love our Lord Jesus Christ with an undying love.ᵈ

---

c 23 The Greek word for *brothers and sisters* (*adelphoi*) refers here to believers, both men and women, as part of God's family.
d 24 Or *Grace and immortality to all who love our Lord Jesus Christ.*

PHILIPPIANS

DATE

This letter was written around AD 61

AUTHOR

The apostle Paul

WHAT'S IT ALL ABOUT?

Paul wrote to the Christians in Philippi while he was under house arrest in Rome to thank them for a gift they had sent to help him in his ministry. He updated them on his circumstances, reassuring them that despite his imprisonment, God was using it for good and he was able to witness for Jesus amongst the guards. He encouraged his readers that his being locked up was actually helping the gospel advance, as others were becoming more fearless in proclaiming the gospel.

Knowing they were facing persecution themselves, he held up Jesus as an example to show what their attitude should be: humble and obedient to God no matter what the cost. He urged them to keep going, to understand that knowing Jesus was an incredible gift, and that anything else would be a loss compared to knowing him. He encouraged them to rejoice in God and bring everything before him in prayer, as this would be the way to true peace.

WHY SHOULD WE READ IT?

- To see how Paul valued Jesus above all things (Philippians 3).
- To hear Paul's advice on how to find peace (Philippians 4).
- To see how Paul had learned to be content no matter what his circumstances (Philippians 4).

Andy Croft with Liza Hoeksma

1
Paul and Timothy, servants of Christ Jesus,

To all God's holy people in Christ Jesus at Philippi, together with the overseers and deacons*a*:

2 Grace and peace to you from God our Father and the Lord Jesus Christ.

Thanksgiving and prayer

3 I thank my God every time I remember you. 4 In all my prayers for all of you, I always pray with joy 5 because of your partnership in the gospel from the first day until now, 6 being confident of this, that he who began a good work in you will carry it on to completion until the day of Christ Jesus.

7 It is right for me to feel this way about all of you, since I have you in my heart and, whether I am in chains or defending and confirming the gospel, all of you share in God's grace with me. 8 God can testify how I long for all of you with the affection of Christ Jesus.

9 And this is my prayer: that your love may abound more and more in knowledge and depth of insight, 10 so that you may be able to discern what is best and may be pure and blameless for the day of Christ, 11 filled with the fruit of righteousness that comes through Jesus Christ – to the glory and praise of God.

Paul's chains advance the gospel

12 Now I want you to know, brothers and sisters,*b* that what has happened to me has actually served to advance the gospel. 13 As a result, it has become clear throughout the whole palace guard*c* and to everyone else that I am in chains for Christ. 14 And because of my chains, most of the brothers and sisters have become

confident in the Lord and dare all the more to proclaim the gospel without fear.

15 It is true that some preach Christ out of envy and rivalry, but others out of goodwill. 16 The latter do so out of love, knowing that I am put here for the defence of the gospel. 17 The former preach Christ out of selfish ambition, not sincerely, supposing that they can stir up trouble for me while I am in chains. 18 But what does it matter? The important thing is that in every way, whether from false motives or true, Christ is preached. And because of this I rejoice.

Yes, and I will continue to rejoice, 19 for I know that through your prayers and God's provision of the Spirit of Jesus Christ what has happened to me will turn out for my deliverance.*d* 20 I eagerly expect and hope that I will in no way be ashamed, but will have sufficient courage so that now as always Christ will be exalted in my body, whether by life or by death. 21 For to me, to live is Christ and to die is gain. 22 If I am to go on living in the body, this will mean fruitful labour for me. Yet what shall I choose? I do not know! 23 I am torn between the two: I desire to depart and be with Christ, which is better by far; 24 but it is more necessary for you that I remain in the body. 25 Convinced of this, I know that I will remain, and I will continue with all of you for your progress and joy in the faith, 26 so that through my being with you again your boasting in Christ Jesus will abound on account of me.

Life worthy of the gospel

27 Whatever happens, conduct yourselves in a manner worthy of the gospel of Christ. Then, whether I come and see you or only hear about you in my absence, I will know that you stand firm in the one Spirit,*e* striving together as one for the faith of the gospel 28 without being frightened in any way by those who oppose you. This is a sign to them that they will be destroyed, but that you will be saved – and that by God. 29 For it has been granted to you on behalf of Christ not only to believe

---

a 1 The word *deacons* refers here to Christians designated to serve with the overseers/elders of the church in a variety of ways; similarly in Romans 16:1 and 1 Tim. 3:8,12.

b 12 The Greek word for *brothers and sisters (adelphoi)* refers here to believers, both men and women, as part of God's family; also in verse 14; and in 3:1, 13, 17; 4:1, 8, 21.

c 13 Or *whole palace*

---

d 19 Or *vindication;* or *salvation*

e 27 Or *in one spirit*

WHAT HAPPENS WHEN I DIE?

What happens when we die? Will we float on clouds playing harps for eternity? Will we join an everlasting U2 concert? Or will it be like church on a Sunday, but just going on and on...

There are many books containing stories of people who have had near-death experiences, describing what they saw in 'heaven' before being sent back to earth. These are very interesting, but are no substitute for studying what the Bible says on the subject.

The Bible is very clear that when Christians die, they will be with Jesus. In Philippians 1, Paul is very confident of this. In the Gospels Jesus tells the criminal on the cross next to him, *'Today you will be with me in paradise'* (Luke 23:43). In John 14:1–4, Jesus tells his disciples that he's going to his Father's house to *'prepare a place'* for them, and he will return one day to take them there. But what kind of a place is it?

The word 'place' in Greek, *mone,* literally means 'temporary lodging'. So Jesus is talking about a place where people will go when they die, where they will await a new and more glorious chapter. The Jewish concept of 'paradise' is similar. In Tom Wright's words, it's the Jewish way of referring to a 'temporary place of rest before the rising again from the dead'.

Many of us have been taught that when we die, we will say goodbye to earth, go to heaven and stay there for ever. But this isn't the full and glorious picture the Bible paints. Yes, we will go to be with Jesus, we will rest in peace, but that's not the end of the story. We will also rise in glory.

Paul uses the idea of sleep (1 Corinthians 15:6) to describe what happens. This confirms that our existence immediately after death will be a place of rest, where we will still be alive, but it also supports the idea that our life after death is only a temporary state, until we wake up to the great event the Jews called *'the resurrection'* (John 11:24).

In the same way that sleep refreshes us and prepares us for a new day, the Bible teaches us that all those who die, or 'fall asleep', will rise again on that great day, our bodies will be like Jesus' resurrected body (1 Corinthians 15), and we will reign with Jesus on the new earth (Revelation 21:1).

The Bible doesn't give us graphic descriptions of what happens to Christians when we die. Rather, it assures us that we will be with Christ, *'which is better by far'* (Philippians 1:23). So we can trust that it will be wonderful. However, it's also clear that this is only a temporary situation, and at the return of Jesus to earth we will rise again and reign with him in the new creation, where justice, peace and joy are all around, and sin, death and pain are defeated for ever.

Chris Lane

in him, but also to suffer for him, ³⁰ since you are going through the same struggle you saw I had, and now hear that I still have.

Imitating Christ's humility

2 Therefore if you have any encouragement from being united with Christ, if any comfort from his love, if any common sharing in the Spirit, if any tenderness and compassion, ² then make my joy complete by being like-minded, having the same love, being one in spirit and of one mind. ³ Do nothing out of selfish ambition or vain conceit. Rather, in humility value others above yourselves, ⁴ not looking to your own interests but each of you to the interests of the others.

⁵ In your relationships with one another, have the same mindset as Christ Jesus:

⁶ who, being in very nature*a* God,
did not consider equality with God
something to be used to his
own advantage;
⁷ rather, he made himself nothing
by taking the very nature*b* of a
servant,
being made in human likeness.
⁸ And being found in appearance as a
man,
he humbled himself
by becoming obedient to death –
even death on a cross!

⁹ Therefore God exalted him to the
highest place
and gave him the name that is above
every name,
¹⁰ that at the name of Jesus every knee
should bow,
in heaven and on earth and under
the earth,
¹¹ and every tongue acknowledge that
Jesus Christ is Lord,
to the glory of God the Father.

Do everything without grumbling

¹² Therefore, my dear friends, as you have always obeyed – not only in my presence, but now much more in my absence – continue to work out your salvation with fear and trembling, ¹³ for it is God who works in you to will and to act in order to fulfil his good purpose.

¹⁴ Do everything without grumbling or arguing, ¹⁵ so that you may become blameless and pure, 'children of God without fault in a warped and crooked generation.'*c* Then you will shine among them like stars in the sky ¹⁶ as you hold firmly to the word of life. And then I will be able to boast on the day of Christ that I did not run or labour in vain. ¹⁷ But even if I am being poured out like a drink offering on the sacrifice and service coming from your faith, I am glad and rejoice with all of you. ¹⁸ So you too should be glad and rejoice with me.

Timothy and Epaphroditus

¹⁹ I hope in the Lord Jesus to send Timothy to you soon, that I also may be cheered when I receive news about you. ²⁰ I have no one else like him, who will show genuine concern for your welfare. ²¹ For everyone looks out for their own interests, not those of Jesus Christ. ²² But you know that Timothy has proved himself, because as a son with his father he has served with me in the work of the gospel. ²³ I hope, therefore, to send him as soon as I see how things go with me. ²⁴ And I am confident in the Lord that I myself will come soon.

²⁵ But I think it is necessary to send back to you Epaphroditus, my brother, co-worker and fellow soldier, who is also your messenger, whom you sent to take care of my needs. ²⁶ For he longs for all of you and is distressed because you heard he was ill. ²⁷ Indeed he was ill, and almost died. But God had mercy on him, and not on him only but also on me, to spare me sorrow upon sorrow. ²⁸ Therefore I am all the more eager to send him, so that when you see him again you may be glad and I may have less anxiety. ²⁹ So then, welcome

---

a 6 Or *in the form of*
b 7 Or *the form*

c 15 Deut. 32:5

him in the Lord with great joy, and honour people like him, 30 because he almost died for the work of Christ. He risked his life to make up for the help you yourselves could not give me.

No confidence in the flesh

3 Further, my brothers and sisters, rejoice in the Lord! It is no trouble for me to write the same things to you again, and it is a safeguard for you. 2 Watch out for those dogs, those evildoers, those mutilators of the flesh. 3 For it is we who are

the circumcision, we who serve God by his Spirit, who boast in Christ Jesus, and who put no confidence in the flesh – 4 though I myself have reasons for such confidence.

If someone else thinks they have reasons to put confidence in the flesh, I have more: 5 circumcised on the eighth day, of the people of Israel, of the tribe of Benjamin, a Hebrew of Hebrews; in regard to the law, a Pharisee; 6 as for zeal, persecuting the church; as for righteousness based on the law, faultless.

7 But whatever were gains to me I now

PAIN AND SUFFERING 7

SHARING IN JESUS' PAIN

There are some verses from the Bible that we love to stick on our fridges or carry around with us because they give us a warm, fuzzy feeling about how much God loves us. There are others we are tempted to skim over because they send a shock through our system. Paul's words in Philippians 3:10 fall into the latter camp!

The first part of verse 10 is about knowing Jesus and the power of his resurrection. That sounds great; I'm all for that! Then he says that to know Christ we should participate in his sufferings and become like him in his death. Hmmm, that doesn't sound like much fun.

These words from Paul are incredibly powerful and important. In Philippians 3:8 he says that everything – *everything* – is a loss compared to knowing Jesus. Anything we could have in the entire world is absolute rubbish compared to knowing Christ. That tells us exactly where our priorities should be.

What does it mean, though, to become like Jesus in his death? I think it means that, like Jesus, we learn obedience to the Father's will and learn to die to ourselves and our desires in order to serve him. That's not something that happens easily. Often, when painful things come our way, we rant about them and rail against them. But then, if we keep focused on Jesus, somewhere along the line we surrender ourselves to God, realising we want his will and not our own. Day by day we learn to rely on him, to trust him even when life hurts, and we know that as we put our human nature to death, we're becoming increasingly like our Saviour. What is our reward for dying to our own desires? We receive more than we could ever deserve: an eternity where there's no pain or suffering and we're continually in the presence of our Lord. That's better than any warm and fuzzy feeling.

Mike Pilavachi

consider loss for the sake of Christ. **8** What is more, I consider everything a loss because of the surpassing worth of knowing Christ Jesus my Lord, for whose sake I have lost all things. I consider them garbage, that I may gain Christ **9** and be found in him, not having a righteousness of my own that comes from the law, but that which is through faith in *a* Christ – the righteousness that comes from God on the basis of faith. **10** I want to know Christ – yes, to know the power of his resurrection and participation in his sufferings, becoming like him in his death, **11** and so, somehow, attaining to the resurrection from the dead.

12 Not that I have already obtained all this, or have already arrived at my goal, but I press on to take hold of that for which Christ Jesus took hold of me. **13** Brothers and sisters, I do not consider myself yet to have taken hold of it. But one thing I do: forgetting what is behind and straining towards what is ahead, **14** I press on towards the goal to win the prize for which God has called me heavenwards in Christ Jesus.

Following Paul's example

15 All of us, then, who are mature should take such a view of things. And if on some point you think differently, that too God will make clear to you. **16** Only let us live up to what we have already attained.

17 Join together in following my example, brothers and sisters, and just as you have us as a model, keep your eyes on those who live as we do. **18** For, as I have often told you before and now tell you again even with tears, many live as enemies of the cross of Christ. **19** Their destiny is destruction, their god is their stomach, and their glory is in their shame. Their mind is set on earthly things. **20** But our citizenship is in heaven. And we eagerly await a Saviour from there, the Lord Jesus Christ, **21** who, by the power that enables him to bring everything under his control, will transform our lowly bodies so that they will be like his glorious body.

---

a 9 Or *through the faithfulness of*

Closing appeal for steadfastness and unity

4 Therefore, my brothers and sisters, you whom I love and long for, my joy and crown, stand firm in the Lord in this way, dear friends!

2 I plead with Euodia and I plead with Syntyche to be of the same mind in the Lord. **3** Yes, and I ask you, my true companion, help these women since they have contended at my side in the cause of the gospel, along with Clement and the rest of my co-workers, whose names are in the book of life.

Final exhortations

4 Rejoice in the Lord always. I will say it again: rejoice! **5** Let your gentleness be evident to all. The Lord is near. **6** Do not be anxious about anything, but in every situation, by prayer and petition, with thanksgiving, present your requests to God. **7** And the peace of God, which transcends all understanding, will guard your hearts and your minds in Christ Jesus.

8 Finally, brothers and sisters, whatever is true, whatever is noble, whatever is right, whatever is pure, whatever is lovely, whatever is admirable – if anything is excellent or praiseworthy – think about such things. **9** Whatever you have learned or received or heard from me, or seen in me – put it into practice. And the God of peace will be with you.

Thanks for their gifts

10 I rejoiced greatly in the Lord that at last you renewed your concern for me. Indeed, you were concerned, but you had no opportunity to show it. **11** I am not saying this because I am in need, for I have learned to be content whatever the circumstances. **12** I know what it is to be in need, and I know what it is to have plenty. I have learned the secret of being content in any and every situation, whether well fed or hungry, whether living in plenty or in want. **13** I can do all this through him who gives me strength.

14 Yet it was good of you to share in my troubles. **15** Moreover, as you Philippians know, in the early days of your acquaintance with the gospel, when I set out from Macedonia, not one church shared with me in the matter of giving and receiving, except you only; 16 for even when I was in Thessalonica, you sent me aid more than once when I was in need. 17 Not that I desire your gifts; what I desire is that more be credited to your account. 18 I have received full payment and have more than enough. I am amply supplied, now that I have received from Epaphroditus the gifts you sent. They are a fragrant offering, an acceptable sacrifice, pleasing to God. 19 And my God will meet all your needs according to the riches of his glory in Christ Jesus.

20 To our God and Father be glory for ever and ever. Amen.

Final greetings

21 Greet all God's people in Christ Jesus. The brothers and sisters who are with me send greetings. 22 All God's people here send you greetings, especially those who belong to Caesar's household.

23 The grace of the Lord Jesus Christ be with your spirit. Amen. *a*

---

a 23 Some manuscripts do not have *Amen.*

IDENTITY – WHO WE ARE IN CHRIST 7

Citizens of heaven

Christianity offers us a fullness of life that isn't possible to know in any other way. Although it can be tough to be a Christian, it's the best possible way of living. God wants us to live this life to the max, yet as Christians we need to live our lives in the awareness that 'this' isn't all there is. We don't actually belong here.

Our identity is not as citizens of earth, but as citizens of heaven (Philippians 3:17–21). This is the brief bit of our lives, before the wonder of eternity. This means that we don't need to fear death in any way – we know where we're going. It also means that those in the depths of suffering can hold onto the reassurance that this isn't all there is.

It also means that we're foreigners and ambassadors in a land to which we don't belong. Look at the Romans: Roman citizens lived all over the Roman Empire, as people who offered the influence and values of Rome to that place. They didn't conform to the culture of that place; instead they influenced it. When the Romans got into trouble, they knew they had the support of Rome behind them to help them out.

The same is true for us, so don't be surprised if you don't really fit in: be God's ambassador where you are and don't get too comfy. Life hasn't really begun yet!

James Grier

 Colossians 1:9–14   John 15

COLOSSIANS

DATE

This letter was written about AD 60

AUTHOR

The apostle Paul

WHAT'S IT ALL ABOUT?

This letter was written by Paul to the church in Colossae around the time he was first under house arrest in Rome. He hadn't visited this church before, but they heard the gospel from Paul's friend Epaphras, who had in turn reported back to Paul on their progress. It seems that while the church in Colossae had accepted Jesus and had great faith in him, they were also being influenced by other teaching. Paul mentions some of the untruths that had crept in (such as judgement about food and drink, 2:16, and the worship of angels, 2:18), but he didn't take these things on lie for lie. Instead he spoke the truth about Jesus. He talked of the fullness of Jesus and how he is strong enough to take all our sins. He urged them to live lives that would please God, serving him and letting go of their old and sinful ways. He encouraged them to pray, to read God's Word, to forgive one another, to be united and to make the most of conversations with those who were outside the church. In short, Paul set out practical and godly wisdom that would put them on the right path to *'live a life worthy of the Lord'* (1:10).

WHY SHOULD WE READ IT?

- To remember that Jesus is enough for us – we don't need to add any other bits of religion or spirituality that the world offers us. He is the way, the truth and the life.

- To receive some great, practical teaching and wisdom about how to live a godly life.

- To read Paul's urgings to put our old, earthly ways behind us in order to display God's amazing characteristics (Colossians 3).

- As a reminder of what our attitude should be in our daily lives, remembering that in everything we do we're serving God (Colossians 3:22–24).

- To see how passionately the early Christians prayed for each other.

Andy Croft with Liza Hoeksma

1 Paul, an apostle of Christ Jesus by the will of God, and Timothy our brother,

2 To God's holy people in Colossae, the faithful brothers and sisters*a* in Christ:

Grace and peace to you from God our Father.*b*

Thanksgiving and prayer

3 We always thank God, the Father of our Lord Jesus Christ, when we pray for you, 4 because we have heard of your faith in Christ Jesus and of the love you have for all God's people – 5 the faith and love that spring from the hope stored up for you in heaven and about which you have already heard in the true message of the gospel 6 that has come to you. In the same way, the gospel is bearing fruit and growing throughout the whole world – just as it has been doing among you since the day you heard it and truly understood God's grace. 7 You learned it from Epaphras, our dear fellow servant,*c* who is a faithful minister of Christ on our*d* behalf, 8 and who also told us of your love in the Spirit.

9 For this reason, since the day we heard about you, we have not stopped praying for you. We continually ask God to fill you with the knowledge of his will through all the wisdom and understanding that the Spirit gives,*e* 10 so that you may live a life worthy of the Lord and please him in every way: bearing fruit in every good work, growing in the knowledge of God, 11 being strengthened with all power according to his glorious might so that you may have great endurance and patience, 12 and giving joyful thanks to the Father, who has qualified you*f* to share in the inheritance of his holy people in the kingdom of light. 13 For he has rescued us from the dominion of darkness and brought us into the kingdom of the Son he loves, 14 in whom we have redemption, the forgiveness of sins.

The supremacy of the Son of God

15 The Son is the image of the invisible God, the firstborn over all creation. 16 For in him all things were created: things in heaven and on earth, visible and invisible, whether thrones or powers or rulers or authorities; all things have been created through him and for him. 17 He is before all things, and in him all things hold together. 18 And he is the head of the body, the church; he is the beginning and the firstborn from among the dead, so that in everything he might have the supremacy. 19 For God was pleased to have all his fullness dwell in him, 20 and through him to reconcile to himself all things, whether things on earth or things in heaven, by making peace through his blood, shed on the cross.

21 Once you were alienated from God and were enemies in your minds because of*g* your evil behaviour. 22 But now he has reconciled you by Christ's physical body through death to present you holy in his sight, without blemish and free from accusation – 23 if you continue in your faith, established and firm, and do not move from the hope held out in the gospel. This is the gospel that you heard and that has been proclaimed to every creature under heaven, and of which I, Paul, have become a servant.

Paul's labour for the church

24 Now I rejoice in what I am suffering for you, and I fill up in my flesh what is still lacking in regard to Christ's afflictions, for the sake of his body, which is the church. 25 I have become its servant by the commission God gave me to present to you the word of God in its fullness – 26 the mystery that has been kept hidden for ages and generations, but is now disclosed to the Lord's people. 27 To them God has chosen to make known among the Gentiles the glorious riches of this mystery, which is Christ in you, the hope of glory.

---

a 2 The Greek word for *brothers and sisters* (*adelphoi*) refers here to believers, both men and women, as part of God's family; also in 4:15.
b 2 Some manuscripts *Father and the Lord Jesus Christ*
c 7 Or *slave*
d 7 Some manuscripts *your*
e 9 Or *all spiritual wisdom and understanding*
f 12 Some manuscripts *us*

g 21 Or *minds, as shown by*

²⁸He is the one we proclaim, admonishing and teaching everyone with all wisdom, so that we may present everyone fully mature in Christ. ²⁹To this end I strenuously contend with all the energy Christ so powerfully works in me.

2 I want you to know how hard I am contending for you and for those at Laodicea, and for all who have not met me personally. ²My goal is that they may be encouraged in heart and united in love, so that they may have the full riches of complete understanding, in order that they may know the mystery of God, namely, Christ, ³in whom are hidden all the treasures of wisdom and knowledge. ⁴I tell

you this so that no one may deceive you by fine-sounding arguments. ⁵For though I am absent from you in body, I am present with you in spirit and delight to see how disciplined you are and how firm your faith in Christ is.

Spiritual fullness in Christ

⁶So then, just as you received Christ Jesus as Lord, continue to live your lives in him, ⁷rooted and built up in him, strengthened in the faith as you were taught, and overflowing with thankfulness.

⁸See to it that no one takes you captive through hollow and deceptive philosophy, which depends on human tradition

IDENTITY – WHO WE ARE IN CHRIST 6

Rescued from darkness

Colossians 1:9–14 declares that we are holy people, saints, who belong to God's kingdom of light.

Before we became Christians, we were part of the kingdom of darkness. That doesn't mean that we had deliberately 'gone over to the dark side', although for some of us that might feel exactly like what happened. It might just be that we lived in the darkness of the world without realising how dark it was until afterwards. For some, becoming a Christian is like the gradual lightening of dawn: it was dark, but little by little has become light. For others, it has been as dramatic as walking into a dark room and turning the light on.

It doesn't matter what our testimony is – what matters is that we have had a transfer and we're on a different team now. We can't go back. If a professional footballer changes teams and ends up playing against his old team, he can't play a bit for each team, depending on how things are going or how he feels. Sometimes, we're quite attracted to the dark. It can cover up things we would rather weren't brought into the light, and it can feel exciting. But our identity now is as people of light. We don't belong to the dark any more, and we don't need to cover things up or be ashamed because we can know God's forgiveness.

We also don't need to be afraid of the dark or dark things any more. All the darkness in the world can't extinguish the light of a single candle, as St Francis of Assisi said. However weak or afraid we feel as a Christian, we belong to the light that has defeated the darkness. We need not be intimidated or afraid.

James Grier

 Ephesians 1:1–10   Philippians 3:17–21

THE BIG STORY 9

Jesus: the key to it all

We need a very big picture of Jesus, because he's the meaning of the universe. Notice how often the words 'all' or 'everything' or 'all things' occur in Colossians 1:15–20! Jesus is the key to it all.

As God the Son, he has always existed. *'He is before all things'* (v. 17). Note that it says 'is', not 'was' (see also John 1:1–14). He's *'the firstborn over all creation'* – not meaning that he was never born: he's God the Son. But it does mean that he's the senior one, who inherits the whole creation. God the Father created the universe through him and by him. The universe is his. It was created *'for him'* (v. 16). He has the right to decide what to do with it. It would vanish in a millisecond should he stop holding it in existence (see Hebrews 1:3). He is its coherence: *'in him all things hold together'* (v. 17). The parts only make sense when related to him.

The one by whom the creation was made then became part of the creation. He became human and all that God the Father is (*'fullness'*, v. 19) took bodily form, for all to see. So he is *'the image of the invisible God'* (v. 15), the invisible made visible. That's why he said, *'Anyone who has seen me has seen the Father'* (John 14:9).

His death on the cross is God's way of putting the world back together again. It makes reconciliation possible across a fractured planet. His death, *'his blood, shed on the cross'* (v. 20), makes peace. On the cross God took upon himself the things that made a barrier between humans and God. He established a new relationship called 'peace'. Peace can break out between humans and God because Jesus has died for us. Humans are the stewards of creation. When peace is restored between them and their Creator, other fractured parts of the creation can be restored as a consequence. The cross makes possible an end to the broken relationship between God and his creatures, and the broken relationships within the creation.

Jesus is then the beginning (the genesis) of the new creation. It began when he rose. He's *'the firstborn from among the dead'* (v. 18), the first one raised, who makes possible the resurrection of all who believe in him, when the last day comes. But as the 'firstborn' he's also the senior one, the one who inherits. Jesus rose *'so that in everything he might have the supremacy'*. The universe was made through him; was honoured by him when he became a part of it; was reconciled by his death and re-created through his resurrection – and he's in charge! To apply the consequences of his work to every corner of creation he has a body, his church. It's physically present in each community, just as he was present in Galilee. Its task is to share everywhere, with everyone, the hope of reconciliation and a new start.

Graham Cray

◀◀ Ephesians 1:9–23   2 Peter 3:10–13 ▶▶

and the elemental spiritual forces*a* of this world rather than on Christ.

9 For in Christ all the fullness of the Deity lives in bodily form, 10 and in Christ you have been brought to fullness. He is the head over every power and authority. 11 In him you were also circumcised with a circumcision not performed by human hands. Your whole self ruled by the flesh*b* was put off when you were circumcised by*c* Christ, 12 having been buried with him in baptism, in which you were also raised with him through your faith in the working of God, who raised him from the dead.

13 When you were dead in your sins and in the uncircumcision of your flesh, God made you*d* alive with Christ. He forgave us all our sins, 14 having cancelled the charge of our legal indebtedness, which stood against us and condemned us; he has taken it away, nailing it to the cross. 15 And having disarmed the powers and authorities, he made a public spectacle of them, triumphing over them by the cross.*e*

Freedom from human rules

16 Therefore do not let anyone judge you by what you eat or drink, or with regard to a religious festival, a New Moon celebration or a Sabbath day. 17 These are a shadow of the things that were to come; the reality, however, is found in Christ. 18 Do not let anyone who delights in false humility and the worship of angels disqualify you. Such a person also goes into great detail about what they have seen; they are puffed up with idle notions by their unspiritual mind. 19 They have lost connection with the head, from whom the whole body, supported and held together by its ligaments and sinews, grows as God causes it to grow.

20 Since you died with Christ to the elemental spiritual forces of this world, why,

as though you still belonged to the world, do you submit to its rules: 21 'Do not handle! Do not taste! Do not touch'? 22 These rules, which have to do with things that are all destined to perish with use, are based on merely human commands and teachings. 23 Such regulations indeed have an appearance of wisdom, with their self-imposed worship, their false humility and their harsh treatment of the body, but they lack any value in restraining sensual indulgence.

Living as those made alive in Christ

3 Since, then, you have been raised with Christ, set your hearts on things above, where Christ is, seated at the right hand of God. 2 Set your minds on things above, not on earthly things. 3 For you died, and your life is now hidden with Christ in God. 4 When Christ, who is your*a* life, appears, then you also will appear with him in glory.

5 Put to death, therefore, whatever belongs to your earthly nature: sexual immorality, impurity, lust, evil desires and greed, which is idolatry. 6 Because of these, the wrath of God is coming.*b* 7 You used to walk in these ways, in the life you once lived. 8 But now you must also rid yourselves of all such things as these: anger, rage, malice, slander, and filthy language from your lips. 9 Do not lie to each other, since you have taken off your old self with its practices 10 and have put on the new self, which is being renewed in knowledge in the image of its Creator. 11 Here there is no Gentile or Jew, circumcised or uncircumcised, barbarian, Scythian, slave or free, but Christ is all, and is in all.

12 Therefore, as God's chosen people, holy and dearly loved, clothe yourselves with compassion, kindness, humility, gentleness and patience. 13 Bear with each other and forgive one another if any of you has a grievance against someone. Forgive as the Lord forgave you. 14 And over

---

a 8 Or *the basic principles*; also in verse 20
b 11 In contexts like this, the Greek word for *flesh* (*sarx*) refers to the sinful state of human beings, often presented as a power in opposition to the Spirit; also in verse 13.
c 11 Or *put off in the circumcision of*
d 13 Some manuscripts *us*
e 15 Or *them in him*

---

a 4 Some manuscripts *our*
b 6 Some early manuscripts *coming on those who are disobedient*

all these virtues put on love, which binds them all together in perfect unity.

15 Let the peace of Christ rule in your hearts, since as members of one body you were called to peace. And be thankful. 16 Let the message of Christ dwell among you richly as you teach and admonish one another with all wisdom through psalms, hymns, and songs from the Spirit, singing to God with gratitude in your hearts. 17 And whatever you do, whether in word or deed, do it all in the name of the Lord Jesus, giving thanks to God the Father through him.

Instructions for Christian households

18 Wives, submit yourselves to your husbands, as is fitting in the Lord.

19 Husbands, love your wives and do not be harsh with them.

20 Children, obey your parents in everything, for this pleases the Lord.

21 Fathers,*c* do not embitter your children, or they will become discouraged.

22 Slaves, obey your earthly masters in everything; and do it, not only when their eye is on you and to curry their favour, but with sincerity of heart and reverence for the Lord. 23 Whatever you do, work at it with all your heart, as working for the Lord, not for human masters, 24 since you know that you will receive an inheritance from the Lord as a reward. It is the Lord Christ you are serving. 25 Anyone who does wrong will be repaid for their wrongs, and there is no favouritism.

4 Masters, provide your slaves with what is right and fair, because you know that you also have a Master in heaven.

_____

c 21 Or *Parents*

IDENTITY – WHO WE ARE IN CHRIST 1

Our identity in Christ

Colossians 3:1–11 tells us that becoming a Christian isn't just about religious belief or practice. It isn't even about what we do. It's about becoming a new person.

We're given a whole new identity. Just as Jesus died and rose again for us, when someone becomes a Christian it's about dying to our old way of life and being raised into new life in Jesus. It's not like reincarnation or a personality transplant – it's about becoming the new you, the you God made you to be!

This changes how God views us. Our life is now *'hidden with Christ'* (v. 3). It's not just that God looks at us and sees the Jesus-wrapping, or looks at us with Jesus-tinted spectacles and so loves us. Instead we're transformed in Jesus, but still loved as ourselves. Since we have died to our old identity and have a new identity in Christ, we should now live differently. We should live according to our new identity and live like Jesus. Verses 5–9 give examples.

Very importantly, our primary identity is now as a Christian. Other labels no longer matter. Slave or free, student, employee or retired, straight or gay, black or white – none of the world's labels matter any more. We're first and foremost a child of God.

James Grier

2 Corinthians 5:17

Further instructions

2 Devote yourselves to prayer, being watchful and thankful. 3 And pray for us, too, that God may open a door for our message, so that we may proclaim the mystery of Christ, for which I am in chains. 4 Pray that I may proclaim it clearly, as I should. 5 Be wise in the way you act towards outsiders; make the most of every opportunity. 6 Let your conversation be always full of grace, seasoned with salt, so that you may know how to answer everyone.

Final greetings

7 Tychicus will tell you all the news about me. He is a dear brother, a faithful minister and fellow servant*a* in the Lord. 8 I am sending him to you for the express purpose that you may know about our*b* circumstances and that he may encourage your hearts. 9 He is coming with Onesimus, our faithful and dear brother, who is one of you. They will tell you everything that is happening here.

10 My fellow prisoner Aristarchus sends you his greetings, as does Mark, the cousin of Barnabas. (You have received instructions about him; if he comes to you, welcome him.) 11 Jesus, who is called

---

a 7 Or *slave*; also in verse 12
b 8 Some manuscripts *that he may know about your*

WORSHIP 3

A way of life

We all know someone who is completely obsessed by one thing. It might be football, music or the person they fancy. It's obvious that any kind of obsession affects the way a person lives. Someone who is a Chelsea fan goes to matches, buys the new strip, and even knows the name of the manager's pet poodle. We talk about people who 'live, eat and breathe' football or some other passion. How much more is this meant to be the case when it comes to passion for God!

In Colossians 3:12–17, Paul writes of how the Colossians sang 'psalms, hymns, and songs from the Spirit' (v. 16) – something we love to do today as we worship God. But notice the context in which he mentions this: it's one where he's instructing them to 'put on love' (v.14). Paul writes about the 'clothes' Christians are to wear, clothes that are made out of compassion, forgiveness and humility. This passage tells us the key to that: live, eat and breathe Jesus. As well as lifting him high in the songs that you sing, be sure to follow his example in the things that you do.

When a person causes you pain, as hard as it can be, choose to forgive and don't hold a grudge. When you're tempted to lose your temper, try to be patient that little bit longer. When you're about to show off or boast about something, bite your tongue and encourage someone else instead. We have an opportunity to love God 'in word or deed' (v.17). Our songs matter, and so do our lives.

Is there something you can do, a person you can care for, out of love for God today?

Beth Croft

 2 Samuel 24:18–25

Matthew 22:34–40

Justus, also sends greetings. These are the only Jews[c] among my fellow workers for the kingdom of God, and they have proved a comfort to me. [12] Epaphras, who is one of you and a servant of Christ Jesus, sends greetings. He is always wrestling in prayer for you, that you may stand firm in all the will of God, mature and fully assured. [13] I vouch for him that he is working hard for you and for those at Laodicea and Hierapolis. [14] Our dear friend Luke, the

doctor, and Demas send greetings. [15] Give my greetings to the brothers and sisters at Laodicea, and to Nympha and the church in her house.

[16] After this letter has been read to you, see that it is also read in the church of the Laodiceans and that you in turn read the letter from Laodicea.

[17] Tell Archippus: 'See to it that you complete the ministry you have received in the Lord.'

[18] I, Paul, write this greeting in my own hand. Remember my chains. Grace be with you.

---

c 11 Greek *only ones of the circumcision group*

1 THESSALONIANS

DATE

This letter was written around AD 50

AUTHOR

The apostle Paul

WHAT'S IT ALL ABOUT?

On his missionary travels to spread the gospel, Paul visited Thessalonica in Greece. Although many heard the gospel and became Christians, some of the Jews weren't happy with Paul's teaching and they forced him to flee, leaving the young believers without their teacher in the midst of persecution. Paul later sent Timothy to encourage the new church, and this letter was written after Timothy's report to Paul about their progress. It differs from some of Paul's other letters in that it's less concerned with theology and seems more like a pastor's letter, overflowing with thankfulness for their faith and love and calling them his *'glory and joy'* (1 Thessalonians 2:20). Paul wrote about his motives in spending time with them and reassured them of his desire to be back with them again. Clearly he cared a great deal about those he brought to faith and desperately wanted to encourage them to keep going no matter what persecution they faced.

WHY SHOULD WE READ IT?

- To be reminded to keep going, even when those around us don't understand our faith and may actively criticise it.

- To see Paul's advice on how to win the respect of those outside the church (1 Thessalonians 4:11–12).

- To read Paul's teaching about the second coming of Jesus (1 Thessalonians 4 – 5).

- To see Paul's instructions for how they should treat one another (1 Thessalonians 5:12–22).

Andy Croft with Liza Hoeksma

1

Paul, Silas*a* and Timothy,

To the church of the Thessalonians in God the Father and the Lord Jesus Christ:

Grace and peace to you.

Thanksgiving for the Thessalonians' faith

2 We always thank God for all of you and continually mention you in our prayers. **3** We remember before our God and Father your work produced by faith, your labour prompted by love, and your endurance inspired by hope in our Lord Jesus Christ.

4 For we know, brothers and sisters*b* loved by God, that he has chosen you, **5** because our gospel came to you not simply with words but also with power, with the Holy Spirit and deep conviction. You know how we lived among you for your sake. **6** You became imitators of us and of the Lord, for you welcomed the message in the midst of severe suffering with the joy given by the Holy Spirit. **7** And so you became a model to all the believers in Macedonia and Achaia. **8** The Lord's message rang out from you not only in Macedonia and Achaia – your faith in God has become known everywhere. Therefore we do not need to say anything about it, **9** for they themselves report what kind of reception you gave us. They tell how you turned to God from idols to serve the living and true God, **10** and to wait for his Son from heaven, whom he raised from the dead – Jesus, who rescues us from the coming wrath.

Paul's ministry in Thessalonica

2

You know, brothers and sisters, that our visit to you was not without results. **2** We had previously suffered and been treated outrageously in Philippi, as you know, but with the help of our God we dared to tell you his gospel in the face of strong opposition. **3** For the appeal we make does not spring from error or impure motives, nor are we trying to trick you. **4** On the contrary, we speak as those approved by God to be entrusted with the gospel. We are not trying to please people but God, who tests our hearts. **5** You know we never used flattery, nor did we put on a mask to cover up greed – God is our witness. **6** We were not looking for praise from people, not from you or anyone else, even though as apostles of Christ we could have asserted our authority. **7** Instead, we were like young children*a* among you.

Just as a nursing mother cares for her children, **8** so we cared for you. Because we loved you so much, we were delighted to share with you not only the gospel of God but our lives as well. **9** Surely you remember, brothers and sisters, our toil and hardship; we worked night and day in order not to be a burden to anyone while we preached the gospel of God to you. **10** You are witnesses, and so is God, of how holy, righteous and blameless we were among you who believed. **11** For you know that we dealt with each of you as a father deals with his own children, **12** encouraging, comforting and urging you to live lives worthy of God, who calls you into his kingdom and glory.

13 And we also thank God continually because, when you received the word of God, which you heard from us, you accepted it not as a human word, but as it actually is, the word of God, which is indeed at work in you who believe. **14** For you, brothers and sisters, became imitators of God's churches in Judea, which are in Christ Jesus: you suffered from your own people the same things those churches suffered from the Jews **15** who killed the Lord Jesus and the prophets and also drove us out. They displease God and are hostile to everyone **16** in their effort to keep us from speaking to the Gentiles so that they may be saved. In this way they always heap up their sins to the limit. The wrath of God has come upon them at last.*b*

---

a 1 Greek *Silvanus,* a variant of *Silas*
b 4 The Greek word for *brothers and sisters* (*adelphoi*) refers here to believers, both men and women, as part of God's family; also in 2:1, 9, 14, 17; 3:7; 4:1, 10, 13; 5:1, 4, 12, 14, 25, 27.

---

a 7 Some manuscripts *were gentle*
b 16 Or *them fully*

Paul's longing to see the Thessalonians

17 But, brothers and sisters, when we were orphaned by being separated from you for a short time (in person, not in thought), out of our intense longing we made every effort to see you. 18 For we wanted to come to you – certainly I, Paul, did, again and again – but Satan blocked our way. 19 For what is our hope, our joy, or the crown in which we will glory in the presence of our Lord Jesus when he comes? Is it not you? 20 Indeed, you are our glory and joy.

3 So when we could stand it no longer, we thought it best to be left by ourselves in Athens. 2 We sent Timothy, who is our brother and co-worker in God's service in spreading the gospel of Christ, to strengthen and encourage you in your faith, 3 so that no one would be unsettled by these trials. For you know quite well that we are destined for them. 4 In fact, when we were with you, we kept telling you that we would be persecuted. And it turned out that way, as you well know. 5 For this reason, when I could stand it no longer, I sent to find out about your faith. I was afraid that in some way the tempter had tempted you and that our labours might have been in vain.

Timothy's encouraging report

6 But Timothy has just now come to us from you and has brought good news about your faith and love. He has told us that you always have pleasant memories of us and that you long to see us, just as we also long to see you. 7 Therefore, brothers and sisters, in all our distress and persecution we were encouraged about you because of your faith. 8 For now we really live, since you are standing firm in the Lord. 9 How can we thank God enough for you in return for all the joy we have in the presence of our God because of you? 10 Night and day we pray most earnestly that we may see you again and supply what is lacking in your faith.

11 Now may our God and Father himself and our Lord Jesus clear the way for us to come to you. 12 May the Lord make your love increase and overflow for each other and for everyone else, just as ours does for you. 13 May he strengthen your hearts so that you will be blameless and holy in the presence of our God and Father when our Lord Jesus comes with all his holy ones.

Living to please God

4 As for other matters, brothers and sisters, we instructed you how to live in order to please God, as in fact you are living. Now we ask you and urge you in the Lord Jesus to do this more and more. 2 For you know what instructions we gave you by the authority of the Lord Jesus.

3 It is God's will that you should be sanctified: that you should avoid sexual immorality; 4 that each of you should learn to control your own body*a* in a way that is holy and honourable, 5 not in passionate lust like the pagans, who do not know God; 6 and that in this matter no one should wrong or take advantage of a brother or sister.*b* The Lord will punish all those who commit such sins, as we told you and warned you before. 7 For God did not call us to be impure, but to live a holy life. 8 Therefore, anyone who rejects this instruction does not reject a human being but God, the very God who gives you his Holy Spirit.

9 Now about your love for one another we do not need to write to you, for you yourselves have been taught by God to love each other. 10 And in fact, you do love all of God's family throughout Macedonia. Yet we urge you, brothers and sisters, to do so more and more, 11 and to make it your ambition to lead a quiet life: you should mind your own business and work with your hands, just as we told you, 12 so that your daily life may win the respect of outsiders and so that you will not be dependent on anybody.

---

a 4 Or *learn to live with your own wife*; or *learn to acquire a wife*

b 6 The Greek word for *brother or sister* (*adelphos*) refers here to a believer, whether man or woman, as part of God's family.

Believers who have died

13 Brothers and sisters, we do not want you to be uninformed about those who sleep in death, so that you do not grieve like the rest of mankind, who have no hope. 14 For we believe that Jesus died and rose again, and so we believe that God will bring with Jesus those who have fallen asleep in him. 15 According to the Lord's word, we tell you that we who are still alive, who are left until the coming of the Lord, will certainly not precede those

SEX

Some people think the Bible is against sex, but this is exactly the opposite of the truth. The Bible treats sex as a wonderful gift from God, which needs to be treated with extra-special care. Just read Song of Songs – a whole book in the Bible dedicated to celebrating this gift God has given to humanity.

The Bible doesn't hold back when discussing sex. It is a wonderful gift, but it must find expression in the right way, otherwise it can be destructive and harmful. As early as Genesis 2, this is clear: a man will leave his parents and be united to his wife, and they will become *'one flesh'*. One flesh – this is referring to the physical act of sex, but also to a deeper truth, that the sexual act is a covenant between two people that should not be broken. Consistently throughout the Bible, we're taught that God intends sexual desires to find fulfilment within lifelong heterosexual marriage.

The term *'sexual immorality'* that Paul uses in 1 Thessalonians 4 is quite a broad term that includes any kind of sex outside marriage. So whether in the Old or New Testaments, the teaching is consistent: God's design for sex is for use within marriage between one man and one woman. Anything outside this framework would be outside his will and potentially harmful to us.

This idea is seen by many as outdated, perhaps even oppressive or damaging to people. We can respond in two ways. First, this teaching is for those who want to follow Jesus. It's not something Christians are called to impose on others, or use to judge the lifestyles of people who choose not to follow Jesus. Our calling is not to try to make people obey the Bible, but to introduce them to Jesus. God alone convicts people of sin. The Christian way of life should be stunning to others in many areas – how we treat our money, how we love our enemies, how we approach death, to name but a few. Followers of Jesus should be *utterly different* from the world around them – not telling the world how to behave, but showing them another way to live.

Second, we need some perspective on sex. Being able to be 'free' sexually is considered one of the most important freedoms in our society. But in biblical terms, this is not the case. The two great figures of the New Testament, Jesus and Paul, were both single and celibate (Paul may have been married previously). Paul commends the celibate life: *'It is good for a man not to have sexual relations with a woman'* (1 Corinthians 7:1). This is not to play down the power of sexual desires, but to put them in their place as one part of human fulfilment that's dwarfed by the love of God himself and its transforming, freeing effect on our lives.

Chris Lane

who have fallen asleep. 16 For the Lord himself will come down from heaven, with a loud command, with the voice of the archangel and with the trumpet call of God, and the dead in Christ will rise first. 17 After that, we who are still alive and are left will be caught up together with them in the clouds to meet the Lord in the air. And so we will be with the Lord for ever. 18 Therefore encourage one another with these words.

The day of the Lord

5 Now, brothers and sisters, about times and dates we do not need to write to you, 2 for you know very well that the day of the Lord will come like a thief in the night. 3 While people are saying, 'Peace and safety', destruction will come on them suddenly, as labour pains on a pregnant woman, and they will not escape.

4 But you, brothers and sisters, are not in darkness so that this day should surprise you like a thief. 5 You are all children of the light and children of the day. We do not belong to the night or to the darkness. 6 So then, let us not be like others, who are asleep, but let us be awake and sober. 7 For those who sleep, sleep at night, and those who get drunk, get drunk at night. 8 But since we belong to the day, let us be sober, putting on faith and love as a breastplate, and the hope of salvation as a helmet. 9 For God did not appoint us to suffer wrath but to receive salvation through our Lord Jesus Christ. 10 He died for us so that, whether we are awake or asleep, we may live together with him. 11 Therefore encourage one another and build each other up, just as in fact you are doing.

Final instructions

12 Now we ask you, brothers and sisters, to acknowledge those who work hard among you, who care for you in the Lord and who admonish you. 13 Hold them in the highest regard in love because of their work. Live in peace with each other. 14 And we urge you, brothers and sisters, warn those who are idle and disruptive, encourage the disheartened, help the weak, be patient with everyone. 15 Make sure that nobody pays back wrong for wrong, but always strive to do what is good for each other and for everyone else.

16 Rejoice always, 17 pray continually, 18 give thanks in all circumstances; for this is God's will for you in Christ Jesus.

19 Do not quench the Spirit. 20 Do not treat prophecies with contempt 21 but test them all; hold on to what is good, 22 reject every kind of evil.

23 May God himself, the God of peace, sanctify you through and through. May your whole spirit, soul and body be kept blameless at the coming of our Lord Jesus Christ. 24 The one who calls you is faithful, and he will do it.

25 Brothers and sisters, pray for us. 26 Greet all God's people with a holy kiss. 27 I charge you before the Lord to have this letter read to all the brothers and sisters.

28 The grace of our Lord Jesus Christ be with you.

2 THESSALONIANS

DATE

This letter was written around AD 51 – possibly about six months after 1 Thessalonians

AUTHOR

The apostle Paul

WHAT'S IT ALL ABOUT?

Paul's second letter to the Thessalonians goes into more detail on a subject he mentioned in his first: Jesus' return to earth. The church in Thessalonica was still being persecuted and therefore death was a very real possibility. Understandably, they were keen to know what would happen to them. It seems that some false teaching had been spread, with letters forged in Paul's name saying that Jesus had already come back, and some people were so convinced he would return any minute that they had stopped doing any work. Paul writes this letter to correct their misunderstandings and encourage them to stand firm and keep going, not to listen to false rumours and not to sit around waiting for Jesus to come back, but to continue with their jobs. He reassures them of God's great love and comfort in their sufferings and praises them for persevering.

WHY SHOULD WE READ IT?

- To be reminded that when others turn against us, God will hold them to account for their actions.

- To read about the second coming of Jesus (when he will return to earth in glory).

- To remember that though we should be ready for Jesus' return, we shouldn't become obsessed with it and should carry on with our day-to-day responsibilities.

- To hear Paul's assurances that God loves us, he is faithful, and he will strengthen and protect us (2 Thessalonians 2:16–17; 3:3).

Andy Croft with Liza Hoeksma

1

Paul, Silas*a* and Timothy,

To the church of the Thessalonians in God our Father and the Lord Jesus Christ:

² Grace and peace to you from God the Father and the Lord Jesus Christ.

Thanksgiving and prayer

³ We ought always to thank God for you, brothers and sisters,*b* and rightly so, because your faith is growing more and more, and the love all of you have for one another is increasing. ⁴ Therefore, among God's churches we boast about your perseverance and faith in all the persecutions and trials you are enduring.

⁵ All this is evidence that God's judgment is right, and as a result you will be counted worthy of the kingdom of God, for which you are suffering. ⁶ God is just: he will pay back trouble to those who trouble you ⁷ and give relief to you who are troubled, and to us as well. This will happen when the Lord Jesus is revealed from heaven in blazing fire with his powerful angels. ⁸ He will punish those who do not know God and do not obey the gospel of our Lord Jesus. ⁹ They will be punished with everlasting destruction and shut out from the presence of the Lord and from the glory of his might ¹⁰ on the day he comes to be glorified in his holy people and to be marvelled at among all those who have believed. This includes you, because you believed our testimony to you.

¹¹ With this in mind, we constantly pray for you, that our God may make you worthy of his calling, and that by his power he may bring to fruition your every desire for goodness and your every deed prompted by faith. ¹² We pray this so that the name of our Lord Jesus may be glorified in you, and you in him, according to the grace of our God and the Lord Jesus Christ.*c*

The man of lawlessness

2

Concerning the coming of our Lord Jesus Christ and our being gathered to him, we ask you, brothers and sisters, ² not to become easily unsettled or alarmed by the teaching allegedly from us – whether by a prophecy or by word of mouth or by letter – asserting that the day of the Lord has already come. ³ Don't let anyone deceive you in any way, for that day will not come until the rebellion occurs and the man of lawlessness*a* is revealed, the man doomed to destruction. ⁴ He will oppose and will exalt himself over everything that is called God or is worshipped, so that he sets himself up in God's temple, proclaiming himself to be God.

⁵ Don't you remember that when I was with you I used to tell you these things? ⁶ And now you know what is holding him back, so that he may be revealed at the proper time. ⁷ For the secret power of lawlessness is already at work; but the one who now holds it back will continue to do so till he is taken out of the way. ⁸ And then the lawless one will be revealed, whom the Lord Jesus will overthrow with the breath of his mouth and destroy by the splendour of his coming. ⁹ The coming of the lawless one will be in accordance with how Satan works. He will use all sorts of displays of power through signs and wonders that serve the lie, ¹⁰ and all the ways that wickedness deceives those who are perishing. They perish because they refused to love the truth and so be saved. ¹¹ For this reason God sends them a powerful delusion so that they will believe the lie ¹² and so that all will be condemned who have not believed the truth but have delighted in wickedness.

Stand firm

¹³ But we ought always to thank God for you, brothers and sisters loved by the Lord, because God chose you as firstfruits*b*

---

a 1 Greek *Silvanus*, a variant of *Silas*
b 3 The Greek word for *brothers and sisters (adelphoi)* refers here to believers, both men and women, as part of God's family; also in 2:1, 13, 15; 3:1, 6, 13.
c 12 Or *God and Lord, Jesus Christ*

a 3 Some manuscripts *sin*
b 13 Some manuscripts *because from the beginning God chose you*

to be saved through the sanctifying work of the Spirit and through belief in the truth. ¹⁴He called you to this through our gospel, that you might share in the glory of our Lord Jesus Christ.

¹⁵So then, brothers and sisters, stand firm and hold fast to the teachings^c we passed on to you, whether by word of mouth or by letter.

¹⁶May our Lord Jesus Christ himself and God our Father, who loved us and by his grace gave us eternal encouragement and good hope, ¹⁷encourage your hearts and strengthen you in every good deed and word.

Request for prayer

3 As for other matters, brothers and sisters, pray for us that the message of the Lord may spread rapidly and be honoured, just as it was with you. ²And pray that we may be delivered from wicked and evil people, for not everyone has faith. ³But the Lord is faithful, and he will strengthen you and protect you from the evil one. ⁴We have confidence in the Lord that you are doing and will continue to do the things we command. ⁵May the Lord direct your hearts into God's love and Christ's perseverance.

Warning against idleness

⁶In the name of the Lord Jesus Christ, we command you, brothers and sisters, to keep away from every believer who is idle and disruptive and does not live according to the teaching^a you received from us. ⁷For you yourselves know how you ought to follow our example. We were not idle when we were with you, ⁸nor did we eat anyone's food without paying for it. On the contrary, we worked night and day, labouring and toiling so that we would not be a burden to any of you. ⁹We did this, not because we do not have the right to such help, but in order to offer ourselves as a model for you to imitate. ¹⁰For even when we were with you, we gave you this rule: 'The one who is unwilling to work shall not eat.'

¹¹We hear that some among you are idle and disruptive. They are not busy; they are busybodies. ¹²Such people we command and urge in the Lord Jesus Christ to settle down and earn the food they eat. ¹³And as for you, brothers and sisters, never tire of doing what is good.

¹⁴Take special note of anyone who does not obey our instruction in this letter. Do not associate with them, in order that they may feel ashamed. ¹⁵Yet do not regard them as an enemy, but warn them as you would a fellow believer.

Final greetings

¹⁶Now may the Lord of peace himself give you peace at all times and in every way. The Lord be with all of you.

¹⁷I, Paul, write this greeting in my own hand, which is the distinguishing mark in all my letters. This is how I write.

¹⁸The grace of our Lord Jesus Christ be with you all.

---

c 15 Or *traditions*

a 6 Or *tradition*

1 TIMOTHY

DATE

Around AD 63–65

AUTHOR

The apostle Paul

WHAT'S IT ALL ABOUT?

1 and 2 Timothy, alongside Titus, are known as the 'pastoral letters' that Paul wrote to the leaders of churches. Timothy had previously travelled and served alongside Paul, but had at this point been asked to stay and look after the church in Ephesus while Paul continued his missionary journeys. The church in Ephesus was encountering a number of problems, so Paul wrote to encourage Timothy in his role and to give him some advice. Paul gave instructions on prayer and worship, emphasising the importance of living godly lives at all times. He informed Timothy how to appoint good leaders, specifying the qualities and characteristics required, such as being self-controlled, respected, someone who doesn't get drunk and who is able to teach. He also advised on how to deal with false teachers, and how to deal with the widows and people in need while encouraging families to take care of their own and not leave relatives to the church's care. Lastly he provided Timothy with valuable teaching on how to find contentment and not be ruined by the love and pursuit of money.

WHY SHOULD WE READ IT?

- To be reminded that we are saved by grace – it doesn't matter how sinful we have been, God can save us and use us just as he did with Paul (1 Timothy 1:12–17).

- To see the qualities required of those in church leadership (1 Timothy 3).

- To read Paul's assurances that being young doesn't mean you can't be in a leadership position (1 Timothy 4:12).

- To read Paul's wisdom about money (1 Timothy 6:3–10, 17–19).

Andy Croft with Liza Hoeksma

1 Paul, an apostle of Christ Jesus by the command of God our Saviour and of Christ Jesus our hope,

² To Timothy my true son in the faith:

Grace, mercy and peace from God the Father and Christ Jesus our Lord.

Timothy charged to oppose false teachers

³ As I urged you when I went into Macedonia, stay there in Ephesus so that you may command certain people not to teach false doctrines any longer ⁴ or to devote themselves to myths and endless genealogies. Such things promote controversial speculations rather than advancing God's work – which is by faith. ⁵ The goal of this command is love, which comes from a pure heart and a good conscience and a sincere faith. ⁶ Some have departed from these and have turned to meaningless talk. ⁷ They want to be teachers of the law, but they do not know what they are talking about or what they so confidently affirm.

⁸ We know that the law is good if one uses it properly. ⁹ We also know that the law is made not for the righteous but for lawbreakers and rebels, the ungodly and sinful, the unholy and irreligious, for those who kill their fathers or mothers, for murderers, ¹⁰ for the sexually immoral, for those practising homosexuality, for slave traders and liars and perjurers – and for whatever else is contrary to the sound doctrine ¹¹ that conforms to the gospel concerning the glory of the blessed God, which he entrusted to me.

The Lord's grace to Paul

¹² I thank Christ Jesus our Lord, who has given me strength, that he considered me trustworthy, appointing me to his service. ¹³ Even though I was once a blasphemer and a persecutor and a violent man, I was shown mercy because I acted in ignorance and unbelief. ¹⁴ The grace of our Lord was poured out on me abundantly, along with the faith and love that are in Christ Jesus.

¹⁵ Here is a trustworthy saying that deserves full acceptance: Christ Jesus came into the world to save sinners – of whom I am the worst. ¹⁶ But for that very reason I was shown mercy so that in me, the worst of sinners, Christ Jesus might display his immense patience as an example for those who would believe in him and receive eternal life. ¹⁷ Now to the King eternal, immortal, invisible, the only God, be honour and glory for ever and ever. Amen.

The charge to Timothy renewed

¹⁸ Timothy, my son, I am giving you this command in keeping with the prophecies once made about you, so that by recalling them you may fight the battle well, ¹⁹ holding on to faith and a good conscience, which some have rejected and so have suffered shipwreck with regard to the faith. ²⁰ Among them are Hymenaeus and Alexander, whom I have handed over to Satan to be taught not to blaspheme.

Instructions on worship

2 I urge, then, first of all, that petitions, prayers, intercession and thanksgiving be made for all people – ² for kings and all those in authority, that we may live peaceful and quiet lives in all godliness and holiness. ³ This is good, and pleases God our Saviour, ⁴ who wants all people to be saved and to come to a knowledge of the truth. ⁵ For there is one God and one mediator between God and mankind, the man Christ Jesus, ⁶ who gave himself as a ransom for all people. This has now been witnessed to at the proper time. ⁷ And for this purpose I was appointed a herald and an apostle – I am telling the truth, I am not lying – and a true and faithful teacher of the Gentiles.

⁸ Therefore I want the men everywhere to pray, lifting up holy hands without anger or disputing. ⁹ I also want the women to dress modestly, with decency and propriety, adorning themselves, not with elaborate hairstyles or gold or pearls or expensive clothes, ¹⁰ but with good deeds, appropriate for women who profess to worship God.

¹¹ A woman*ᵃ* should learn in quietness

ᵃ 11 Or *wife*; also in verse 12

and full submission. ¹²I do not permit a woman to teach or to assume authority over a man;ᵇ she must be quiet. ¹³For Adam was formed first, then Eve. ¹⁴And Adam was not the one deceived; it was the woman who was deceived and became a sinner. ¹⁵But womenᶜ will be saved through childbearing – if they continue in faith, love and holiness with propriety.

Qualifications for overseers and deacons

3 Here is a trustworthy saying: whoever aspires to be an overseer desires a noble task. ²Now the overseer is to be above reproach, faithful to his wife, temperate, self-controlled, respectable, hospitable, able to teach, ³not given to drunkenness, not violent but gentle, not quarrelsome, not a lover of money. ⁴He must manage his own family well and see that his children obey him, and he must do so in a manner worthy of fullᵃ respect. ⁵(If anyone does not know how to manage his own family, how can he take care of God's church?) ⁶He must not be a recent convert, or he may become conceited and fall under the same judgment as the devil. ⁷He must also have a good reputation with outsiders, so that he will not fall into disgrace and into the devil's trap.

⁸In the same way, deaconsᵇ are to be worthy of respect, sincere, not indulging in much wine, and not pursuing dishonest gain. ⁹They must keep hold of the deep truths of the faith with a clear conscience. ¹⁰They must first be tested; and then if there is nothing against them, let them serve as deacons.

¹¹In the same way, the womenᶜ are to be worthy of respect, not malicious talkers but temperate and trustworthy in everything.

¹²A deacon must be faithful to his wife

ᵇ 12 Or over her husband

ᶜ 15 Greek she

ᵃ 4 Or him with proper

ᵇ 8 The word deacons refers here to Christians designated to serve with the overseers/elders of the church in a variety of ways; similarly in verse 12; and in Romans 16:1 and Phil. 1:1.

ᶜ 11 Possibly deacons' wives or women who are deacons

and must manage his children and his household well. ¹³Those who have served well gain an excellent standing and great assurance in their faith in Christ Jesus.

Reasons for Paul's instructions

¹⁴Although I hope to come to you soon, I am writing to you with these instructions so that, ¹⁵if I am delayed, you will know how people ought to conduct themselves in God's household, which is the church of the living God, the pillar and foundation of the truth. ¹⁶Beyond all question, the mystery from which true godliness springs is great:

> He appeared in the flesh,
>   was vindicated by the Spirit,ᵈ
> was seen by angels,
>   was preached among the nations,
> was believed on in the world,
>   was taken up in glory.

FAVOURITE VERSES

Philippians 4:13

I can do all this through him who gives me strength.

This is my favourite verse because it helped me a lot when I was growing up. It reminded me that Jesus was with me no matter what.

Jane, 23

4 The Spirit clearly says that in later times some will abandon the faith and follow deceiving spirits and things taught by demons. ²Such teachings come through hypocritical liars, whose consciences have been seared as with a hot iron. ³They forbid people to marry and order them to abstain from certain foods, which God created to

---

ᵈ 16 Or vindicated in spirit

be received with thanksgiving by those who believe and who know the truth. 4For everything God created is good, and nothing is to be rejected if it is received with thanksgiving, 5because it is consecrated by the word of God and prayer.

6If you point these things out to the brothers and sisters,*a* you will be a good minister of Christ Jesus, nourished on the truths of the faith and of the good teaching that you have followed. 7Have nothing to do with godless myths and old wives' tales; rather, train yourself to be godly. 8For physical training is of some value, but godliness has value for all things, holding promise for both the present life and the life to come. 9This is a trustworthy saying that deserves full acceptance. 10That is why we labour and strive, because we have put our hope in the living God, who is the Saviour of all people, and especially of those who believe.

11Command and teach these things. 12Don't let anyone look down on you because you are young, but set an example for the believers in speech, in conduct, in love, in faith and in purity. 13Until I come, devote yourself to the public reading of Scripture, to preaching and to teaching. 14Do not neglect your gift, which was given you through prophecy when the body of elders laid their hands on you.

15Be diligent in these matters; give yourself wholly to them, so that everyone may see your progress. 16Watch your life and doctrine closely. Persevere in them, because if you do, you will save both yourself and your hearers.

Widows, elders and slaves

5 Do not rebuke an older man harshly, but exhort him as if he were your father. Treat younger men as brothers, 2older women as mothers, and younger women as sisters, with absolute purity.

3Give proper recognition to those widows who are really in need. 4But if a widow has children or grandchildren, these should learn first of all to put their religion into practice by caring for their own family and so repaying their parents and grandparents, for this is pleasing to God. 5The widow who is really in need and left all alone puts her hope in God and continues night and day to pray and to ask God for help. 6But the widow who lives for pleasure is dead even while she lives. 7Give the people these instructions, so that no one may be open to blame. 8Anyone who does not provide for their relatives, and especially for their own household, has denied the faith and is worse than an unbeliever.

9No widow may be put on the list of widows unless she is over sixty, has been faithful to her husband, 10and is well known for her good deeds, such as bringing up children, showing hospitality, washing the feet of the Lord's people, helping those in trouble and devoting herself to all kinds of good deeds.

11As for younger widows, do not put them on such a list. For when their sensual desires overcome their dedication to Christ, they want to marry. 12Thus they bring judgment on themselves, because they have broken their first pledge. 13Besides, they get into the habit of being idle and going about from house to house. And not only do they become idlers, but also busybodies who talk nonsense, saying things they ought not to. 14So I counsel younger widows to marry, to have children, to manage their homes and to give the enemy no opportunity for slander. 15Some have in fact already turned away to follow Satan.

16If any woman who is a believer has widows in her care, she should continue to help them and not let the church be burdened with them, so that the church can help those widows who are really in need.

17The elders who direct the affairs of the church well are worthy of double honour, especially those whose work is preaching and teaching. 18For Scripture says, 'Do not muzzle an ox while it is treading out the grain,'*a* and 'The worker

---

a 6 The Greek word for *brothers and sisters* (*adelphoi*) refers here to believers, both men and women, as part of God's family.

a 18 Deut. 25:4

deserves his wages.'ᵇ ¹⁹Do not entertain an accusation against an elder unless it is brought by two or three witnesses. ²⁰But those elders who are sinning you are to reprove before everyone, so that the others may take warning. ²¹I charge you, in the sight of God and Christ Jesus and the elect angels, to keep these instructions without partiality, and to do nothing out of favouritism.

ᵇ 18 Luke 10:7

²²Do not be hasty in the laying on of hands, and do not share in the sins of others. Keep yourself pure.

²³Stop drinking only water, and use a little wine because of your stomach and your frequent illnesses.

²⁴The sins of some are obvious, reaching the place of judgment ahead of them; the sins of others trail behind them. ²⁵In the same way, good deeds are obvious, and even those that are not obvious cannot remain hidden for ever.

RELATIONSHIPS 7

KEEPING RELATIONSHIPS PURE (PART 1)

Hopefully you haven't started reading this earnestly anticipating that we're going to define 'how far is too far' and answer your questions once and for all. That's not to say we don't have an opinion on this, but we think asking this question is completely the wrong place to start when we're talking about how to conduct ourselves in a godly way when we're in relationships.

You see, the problem is actually with the question. What it really asks is, 'How close is it possible to get to the line without actually crossing it?' The fundamental problem with this is that when we're in relationship with Jesus, we shouldn't want to get anywhere near the line, let alone risk crossing it (1 Corinthians 6:18).

If you're thinking about setting some boundaries for your relationships, here are a few scriptures to think about. Are your boundaries:

- holy and honourable (1 Thessalonians 4:4)?
- about building your partner up spiritually (1 Corinthians 6:20)?
- about treating them with *absolute* purity (1 Timothy 5:2)?
- without a hint of sexual immorality (Ephesians 5:3–5)?
- not set merely to satisfy your lusts (1 Thessalonians 4:5)?

In 1 Timothy 5 we're asked to treat all other believers as if they're members of our family. *'Do not rebuke an older man harshly, but exhort him as if he were your father. Treat younger men as brothers, older women as mothers, and younger women as sisters, with absolute purity.'* It's not often (four times in the English translation) that the Bible talks about something being 'absolute', so it's something for us to think about carefully.

Jane Plackett & Calum Dyke

 1 Samuel 16:1

Song of Songs 2:7

6 All who are under the yoke of slavery should consider their masters worthy of full respect, so that God's name and our teaching may not be slandered. ²Those who have believing masters should not show them disrespect just because they are fellow believers. Instead, they should serve them even better because their masters are dear to them as fellow believers and are devoted to the welfare*a* of their slaves.

False teachers and the love of money

These are the things you are to teach and insist on. ³If anyone teaches

---

a 2 Or *and benefit from the service*

otherwise and does not agree to the sound instruction of our Lord Jesus Christ and to godly teaching, ⁴they are conceited and understand nothing. They have an unhealthy interest in controversies and quarrels about words that result in envy, strife, malicious talk, evil suspicions ⁵and constant friction between people of corrupt mind, who have been robbed of the truth and who think that godliness is a means to financial gain.

⁶But godliness with contentment is great gain. ⁷For we brought nothing into the world, and we can take nothing out of it. ⁸But if we have food and clothing, we will be content with that. ⁹Those who want to get rich fall into temptation and a trap and into many foolish and

---

MONEY 3

CONTENTMENT

There aren't many moments in life when I wish I had loads of money – but I almost always have that desire when I'm boarding a long-haul flight. I've bought the cheapest plane ticket I could find and am making my way to Row F in economy class, and en route I have to walk past the amazing first-class seats with their big TVs and chairs that turn into beds... Oh, I want one!

That may sound silly, but life throws a lot of messages at us that make us believe that if only we had a first-class seat on a flight, we would all be a lot happier. We're advertised at all the time.

I won't pretend that money doesn't make life easier – it may well alleviate stress in life, allowing us to live securely and provide for people we love. This is not a wrong feeling at all, it's a good, sensible feeling. It's different from searching for fulfilment and happiness in riches. A bit like my desire to sit in a plush first-class seat on the plane – it isn't really going to make me any happier, except for a fleeting moment when I feel like a rock star! It won't bring me deep contentment, nor will having the latest fashion item or fastest car or coolest bedroom.

1 Timothy 6 tells us that putting our hope in these things, believing they may fulfil us and give us deep contentment in life, is a myth. Don't spend your days chasing happiness in wealth. It will let you down. Instead pursue righteousness, love and gentleness – chase those things.

Kiera Singlehurst-Phyo

 Luke 14:12–14   Deuteronomy 24:19 ▶

SPIRITUAL DISCIPLINES 5

SIMPLICITY

You almost certainly have too much stuff. That's not a judgement on you so much as on the culture around you. In the West we're relentlessly sold to; we spend our lives being told we need to spend and accumulate more.

The average teenage bedroom contains thousands of pounds' worth of clothes, media and technology, not to mention the huge (and expensive) collection of digital content we're amassing on our computers. We're born and raised consumers.

You probably also do too much. Sometimes several things at once. Your life is complicated, because modern life is complicated. But does it need to be? Are you missing out on crucial, simple God-experiences because you have made yourself too busy?

The spiritual discipline of simplicity (1 Timothy 6:6–10) is about addressing these imbalances in our culture. It's about learning contentment in a world obsessed with accumulating more stuff and having more and greater experiences and highs. How do you start to get to a point where you don't want more to feel satisfied? The thing about material gain is that you never do have quite enough. You keep wanting more. The answer that simplicity gives us might seem strange, but it also makes a weird kind of sense: the way to stop wanting more is to have less.

When we turn from *'the foolish and harmful desires'* (v. 9), we find that something else moves into view: God. The problem with stuff is that it fills our lives and squeezes out God. When we start to reduce our stuff, we find that God rushes in to fill the space. It's the same with our time. When we start to do less, the quality of our experiences increases – often because God has inhabited them more deeply.

Not only that. The discipline of simplicity is an outward discipline. Practising it changes us for the better, but when we suddenly take 90 per cent of our DVD collection to the charity shop, or give away our secondary games console, it also has a profound effect on the people in our lives. Choosing to live simply is an amazing signpost to others – one that leads away from the culture of 'I spend therefore I am'; one that points towards God.

How can you live more simply? Which areas of your life are too complicated, too full of stuff? Where do you have so much going on that you don't have time to notice God? How do you waste time, money and other resources when you could be spending them more wisely? If we start to address these questions, then the life that others see in us becomes not only more sensible than what our culture offers, but irresistibly more attractive.

Martin Saunders

 Mark 9:30–35   John 13:34–35 ▶▶

harmful desires that plunge people into ruin and destruction. 10 For the love of money is a root of all kinds of evil. Some people, eager for money, have wandered from the faith and pierced themselves with many griefs.

Final charge to Timothy

11 But you, man of God, flee from all this, and pursue righteousness, godliness, faith, love, endurance and gentleness. 12 Fight the good fight of the faith. Take hold of the eternal life to which you were called when you made your good confession in the presence of many witnesses. 13 In the sight of God, who gives life to everything, and of Christ Jesus, who while testifying before Pontius Pilate made the good confession, I charge you 14 to keep this command without spot or blame until the appearing of our Lord Jesus Christ, 15 which God will bring about in his own time – God, the blessed and only Ruler, the King of kings and Lord of lords, 16 who alone is immortal and who lives in unapproachable light, whom no one has seen or can see. To him be honour and might for ever. Amen.

17 Command those who are rich in this present world not to be arrogant nor to put their hope in wealth, which is so uncertain, but to put their hope in God, who richly provides us with everything for our enjoyment. 18 Command them to do good, to be rich in good deeds, and to be generous and willing to share. 19 In this way they will lay up treasure for themselves as a firm foundation for the coming age, so that they may take hold of the life that is truly life.

20 Timothy, guard what has been entrusted to your care. Turn away from godless chatter and the opposing ideas of what is falsely called knowledge, 21 which some have professed and in so doing have departed from the faith.

Grace be with you all.

2 TIMOTHY

DATE

Around AD 67–68

AUTHOR

The apostle Paul

WHAT'S IT ALL ABOUT?

This is the second of the three 'pastoral letters' written by Paul to leaders of churches and, chronologically, Paul's last letter. He wrote it to Timothy in Ephesus while he was in Rome, imprisoned for the second time, and just before he was executed. Unlike previous house arrests, this time Paul was in a dungeon where he was chained up like a criminal. He urged Timothy to come to him as quickly as possible and gave him further advice for the church in the meantime. He taught that Christians should stay away from *'godless chatter'* (2 Timothy 2:16) and arguments, and not follow false teachings just because it was in line with their own ungodly desires.

Paul was suffering, both through being in prison and through the fact that he was alone (apart from Luke), and he knew he was about to die. Rather than complaining about his situation, though, he seemed content to know that he had done the things God had asked of him and would therefore receive his reward upon his death.

WHY SHOULD WE READ IT?

- To be reminded that we are not given a Spirit of timidity, but one of power, love and self-discipline (2 Timothy 1:7).

- To read Paul's encouragements that followers of Jesus shouldn't be ashamed of telling others about Christ, or about their own suffering for the gospel (2 Timothy 1:8–12).

- To read Paul's encouragements to endure hardships and suffering (2 Timothy 1:3–13).

- To hear Paul's view of the importance of God's Word (2 Timothy 3:16–17).

- To see how Paul had no fear of death. He had lived his life well since his conversion and knew he would be rewarded for his faith by receiving eternal life (2 Timothy 4).

Andy Croft with Liza Hoeksma

1

Paul, an apostle of Christ Jesus by the will of God, in keeping with the promise of life that is in Christ Jesus,

² To Timothy, my dear son:

Grace, mercy and peace from God the Father and Christ Jesus our Lord.

Thanksgiving

³ I thank God, whom I serve, as my ancestors did, with a clear conscience, as night and day I constantly remember you in my prayers. ⁴ Recalling your tears, I long to see you, so that I may be filled with joy. ⁵ I am reminded of your sincere faith, which first lived in your grandmother Lois and in your mother Eunice and, I am persuaded, now lives in you also.

Appeal for loyalty to Paul and the gospel

⁶ For this reason I remind you to fan into flame the gift of God, which is in you

FRIENDSHIP 7

Encouraging each other

We all need encouragement. Part of the reason God put us in a church family is so that we can help each other to keep going when things get tough. Paul knew the importance of encouragement and in 2 Timothy 1 he's writing to his friend Timothy to encourage him to persevere in knowing God and doing all that he was called to do.

We need to form friendships where we encourage each other in the same way. When friends are having a hard time, encourage them to hold on to God's truths, to trust in him, to believe and to do the things God has called them to do. Your encouragement may give them strength, courage, confidence, faith and hope, as well as the feeling that they are loved and supported.

Of course, encouragement isn't just for the hard times. It's also great to give specific encouragements to friends about the things they are good at. Make a decision to support your friends and to be someone who cheers them on. If they do something well, tell them – everyone loves to hear a genuine compliment!

Romans 12 describes the ability to encourage others as a gift, and some people do have a specific, God-given gift to uplift others and build them up. That said, we all have the ability to encourage. If it doesn't come naturally to you it might be something you have to work harder at, but if you try to do it regularly, you will soon find it has become a habit. Paul gives us a great example of someone who spent time encouraging others in their faith, so let's follow his example and his urging and *'encourage one another and build each other up'* (1 Thessalonians 5:11).

Ali Martin

 Acts 15:36–41   Job 2:11–13 ▶

through the laying on of my hands. **7** For the Spirit God gave us does not make us timid, but gives us power, love and self-discipline. **8** So do not be ashamed of the testimony about our Lord or of me his prisoner. Rather, join with me in suffering for the gospel, by the power of God. **9** He has saved us and called us to a holy life – not because of anything we have done but because of his own purpose and grace. This grace was given us in Christ Jesus before the beginning of time, **10** but it has now been revealed through the appearing of our Saviour, Christ Jesus, who has destroyed death and has brought life and immortality to light through the gospel. **11** And of this gospel I was appointed a herald and an apostle and a teacher. **12** That is why I am suffering as I am. Yet this is no cause for shame, because I know whom I have believed, and am convinced that he is able to guard what I have entrusted to him until that day.

13 What you heard from me, keep as the pattern of sound teaching, with faith and love in Christ Jesus. **14** Guard the good deposit that was entrusted to you – guard it with the help of the Holy Spirit who lives in us.

Examples of disloyalty and loyalty

15 You know that everyone in the province of Asia has deserted me, including Phygelus and Hermogenes.

16 May the Lord show mercy to the household of Onesiphorus, because he often refreshed me and was not ashamed of my chains. **17** On the contrary, when he was in Rome, he searched hard for me until he found me. **18** May the Lord grant that he will find mercy from the Lord on that day! You know very well in how many ways he helped me in Ephesus.

The appeal renewed

2 You then, my son, be strong in the grace that is in Christ Jesus. **2** And the things you have heard me say in the presence of many witnesses entrust to reliable people who will also be qualified to teach others. **3** Join with me in suffering, like a good soldier of Christ Jesus. **4** No one

serving as a soldier gets entangled in civilian affairs, but rather tries to please his commanding officer. **5** Similarly, anyone who competes as an athlete does not receive the victor's crown except by competing according to the rules. **6** The hardworking farmer should be the first to receive a share of the crops. **7** Reflect on what I am saying, for the Lord will give you insight into all this.

8 Remember Jesus Christ, raised from the dead, descended from David. This is my gospel, **9** for which I am suffering even to the point of being chained like a criminal. But God's word is not chained. **10** Therefore I endure everything for the sake of the elect, that they too may obtain the salvation that is in Christ Jesus, with eternal glory.

11 Here is a trustworthy saying:

If we died with him,
we will also live with him;
12 if we endure,
we will also reign with him.
If we disown him,
he will also disown us;
13 if we are faithless,
he remains faithful,
for he cannot disown himself.

Dealing with false teachers

14 Keep reminding God's people of these things. Warn them before God against quarrelling about words; it is of no value, and only ruins those who listen. **15** Do your best to present yourself to God as one approved, a worker who does not need to be ashamed and who correctly handles the word of truth. **16** Avoid godless chatter, because those who indulge in it will become more and more ungodly. **17** Their teaching will spread like gangrene. Among them are Hymenaeus and Philetus, **18** who have departed from the truth. They say that the resurrection has already taken place, and they destroy the faith of some. **19** Nevertheless, God's solid foundation stands firm, sealed with this inscription: 'The Lord knows those who are his,' and, 'Everyone who confesses the name of the Lord must turn away from wickedness.'

20 In a large house there are articles not

only of gold and silver, but also of wood and clay; some are for special purposes and some for common use. ²¹Those who cleanse themselves from the latter will be instruments for special purposes, made holy, useful to the Master and prepared to do any good work.

²²Flee the evil desires of youth and pursue righteousness, faith, love and peace, along with those who call on the Lord out of a pure heart. ²³Don't have anything to do with foolish and stupid arguments, because you know they produce quarrels. ²⁴And the Lord's servant must not be quarrelsome but must be kind to everyone, able to teach, not resentful. ²⁵Opponents must be gently instructed, in the hope that God will grant them repentance leading them to a knowledge of the truth, ²⁶and that they will come to their senses and escape from the trap of the devil, who has taken them captive to do his will.

3 But mark this: there will be terrible times in the last days. ²People will be lovers of themselves, lovers of money, boastful, proud, abusive, disobedient to their parents, ungrateful, unholy, ³without love, unforgiving, slanderous, without self-control, brutal, not lovers of the good, ⁴treacherous, rash, conceited, lovers of pleasure rather than lovers of God – ⁵having a form of godliness but denying its power. Have nothing to do with such people.

⁶They are the kind who worm their way into homes and gain control over gullible women, who are loaded down with sins and are swayed by all kinds of evil desires, ⁷always learning but never able to come to a knowledge of the truth. ⁸Just as Jannes and Jambres opposed Moses, so also these teachers oppose the truth. They are men of depraved minds, who, as far as the faith is concerned, are rejected. ⁹But they will not get very far because, as in the case of those men, their folly will be clear to everyone.

A final charge to Timothy

¹⁰You, however, know all about my teaching, my way of life, my purpose, faith, patience, love, endurance,

¹¹persecutions, sufferings – what kinds of things happened to me in Antioch, Iconium and Lystra, the persecutions I endured. Yet the Lord rescued me from all of them. ¹²In fact, everyone who wants to live a godly life in Christ Jesus will be persecuted, ¹³while evildoers and impostors will go from bad to worse, deceiving and being deceived. ¹⁴But as for you, continue in what you have learned and have become convinced of, because you know those from whom you learned it, ¹⁵and how from infancy you have known the Holy Scriptures, which are able to make you wise for salvation through faith in Christ Jesus. ¹⁶All Scripture is God-breathed and is useful for teaching, rebuking, correcting and training in righteousness, ¹⁷so that the servant of God*ᵃ* may be thoroughly equipped for every good work.

4 In the presence of God and of Christ Jesus, who will judge the living and the dead, and in view of his appearing and his kingdom, I give you this charge: ²preach the word; be prepared in season and out of season; correct, rebuke and encourage – with great patience and careful instruction. ³For the time will come when people will not put up with sound doctrine. Instead, to suit their own desires, they will gather round them a great number of teachers to say what their itching ears want to hear. ⁴They will turn their ears away from the truth and turn aside to myths. ⁵But you, keep your head in all situations, endure hardship, do the work of an evangelist, discharge all the duties of your ministry.

⁶For I am already being poured out like a drink offering, and the time for my departure is near. ⁷I have fought the good fight, I have finished the race, I have kept the faith. ⁸Now there is in store for me the crown of righteousness, which the Lord, the righteous Judge, will award to me on that day – and not only to me, but also to all who have longed for his appearing.

_____

a 17 Or that you, a man of God,

WHAT IS CHRISTIANITY? 9

Doctrine of the Word: God's book...

All of us want to hear God speak. Often we want this to be dramatic; perhaps we want him to shout down from heaven or write something in fire in the sky. God has made his words far more accessible than that: you're holding them in your hands. Any time we want, we can pick up the Bible and we're reading God's message to us. That's why we refer to Scripture as 'the Word of God'.

The story of the Bible is full of God speaking. Often in the Old Testament a prophet will declare, 'This is what the LORD says...' and give a message from God. Elsewhere God writes down the words of the Ten Commandments and gives them to Moses (Exodus 31:12–16). At the start of John's Gospel, Jesus is described as *'the Word'* (John 1:14). This is because he's the ultimate revelation of God himself. Jesus doesn't just speak the message of God, he's God made flesh.

The Bible is totally unique. It's written by human beings – writing about who God is, what he has done and how we're to live. They write with their own aims and in different historical contexts. God breathed his life and truth into the words of the Bible as they were being written. Just as he could speak through a prophet in the desert, he can speak through an author at their desk. That's why, in 2 Timothy 3:16, Paul tells us, *'All Scripture is God-breathed.'* It's not just some of the Bible, the bits we like, that are trustworthy and come from God – it's the whole thing, *all* Scripture.

The more we trust and submit to the Word of God, the better we get to know him. When God makes a promise to us in the Bible, we can trust that he will keep it. When God warns us in the Bible, we can trust that it matters. David sings in Psalm 139:17, *'How precious to me are your thoughts, God! How vast is the sum of them!'* We hold in our hands the book that contains the very thoughts of God himself. And these words point us to life: *'Your word is a lamp for my feet, a light on my path'* (Psalm 119:105).

The point of reading the Bible is never that we might get more information; it's always that we might grow in relationship with God. As such, we need to ask him to help us understand it. Just as Jesus did with his disciples – *'Were not our hearts burning within us while he talked with us on the road and opened the Scriptures to us?'* (Luke 24:32) – so too the Holy Spirit will help us as we seek God through these pages.

When it comes to the Bible, never stop with just the words. This is the Word that leads us to God himself.

Andy Croft

 1 Corinthians 12:12–31   Revelation 22

Personal remarks

9 Do your best to come to me quickly, 10 for Demas, because he loved this world, has deserted me and has gone to Thessalonica. Crescens has gone to Galatia, and Titus to Dalmatia. 11 Only Luke is with me. Get Mark and bring him with you, because he is helpful to me in my ministry. 12 I sent Tychicus to Ephesus. 13 When you come, bring the cloak that I left with Carpus at Troas, and my scrolls, especially the parchments.

14 Alexander the metalworker did me a great deal of harm. The Lord will repay him for what he has done. 15 You too should be on your guard against him, because he strongly opposed our message.

16 At my first defence, no one came to my support, but everyone deserted me. May it not be held against them. 17 But the Lord stood at my side and gave me strength, so that through me the message might be fully proclaimed and all the Gentiles might hear it. And I was delivered from the lion's mouth. 18 The Lord will rescue me from every evil attack and will bring me safely to his heavenly kingdom. To him be glory for ever and ever. Amen.

Final greetings

19 Greet Priscilla*a* and Aquila and the household of Onesiphorus. 20 Erastus stayed in Corinth, and I left Trophimus ill in Miletus. 21 Do your best to get here before winter. Eubulus greets you, and so do Pudens, Linus, Claudia and all the brothers and sisters.*b*

22 The Lord be with your spirit. Grace be with you all.

---

a 19 Greek *Prisca*, a variant of *Priscilla*
b 21 The Greek word for *brothers and sisters* (*adelphoi*) refers here to believers, both men and women, as part of God's family.

TITUS

DATE

This letter was probably written between AD 63 and 65

AUTHOR

The apostle Paul

WHAT'S IT ALL ABOUT?

Titus was a Gentile who had heard the gospel through Paul, become a believer and served alongside Paul in his missionary work. Twice Paul had sent him to Corinth to deal with the problems in the church there (see 1 and 2 Corinthians for more details on the challenges the church faced), and at the time of this letter, Titus was in Crete. The people of the area were known for their low moral standards (described by one of their own as *'liars, evil brutes, lazy gluttons'*, Titus 1:12), so Paul was at pains to point out that the church should be different and to instruct Titus to teach them how they should behave. This short letter gives instructions to men, women and slaves and encourages them to grasp the grace of God so that they might turn from their worldly passions and live a godly life. Paul instructed Titus to appoint elders of good character and to teach, encourage and rebuke the church with God's authority.

WHY SHOULD WE READ IT?

- To see the qualities required of those in church leadership (Titus 1).
- To hear Paul's instructions for how God's people should behave.
- To be reminded that it's by God's grace that we're changed from our old, earthly ways and can instead become godly people (Titus 2:11 – 3:11).

Andy Croft with Liza Hoeksma

1 Paul, a servant of God and an apostle of Jesus Christ to further the faith of God's elect and their knowledge of the truth that leads to godliness – 2 in the hope of eternal life, which God, who does not lie, promised before the beginning of time, 3 and which now at his appointed season he has brought to light through the preaching entrusted to me by the command of God our Saviour,

4 To Titus, my true son in our common faith:

Grace and peace from God the Father and Christ Jesus our Saviour.

Appointing elders who love what is good

5 The reason I left you in Crete was that you might put in order what was left unfinished and appoint*a* elders in every town, as I directed you. 6 An elder must be blameless, faithful to his wife, a man whose children believe*b* and are not open to the charge of being wild and disobedient. 7 Since an overseer manages God's household, he must be blameless – not overbearing, not quick-tempered, not given to drunkenness, not violent, not pursuing dishonest gain. 8 Rather, he must be hospitable, one who loves what is good, who is self-controlled, upright, holy and disciplined. 9 He must hold firmly to the trustworthy message as it has been taught, so that he can encourage others by sound doctrine and refute those who oppose it.

Rebuking those who fail to do good

10 For there are many rebellious people, full of meaningless talk and deception, especially those of the circumcision group. 11 They must be silenced, because they are disrupting whole households by teaching things they ought not to teach – and that for the sake of dishonest gain. 12 One of Crete's own prophets has said it: 'Cretans are always liars, evil brutes, lazy gluttons.'*c* 13 This saying is true. Therefore rebuke them sharply, so that they will be sound in the faith 14 and will pay no attention to Jewish myths or to the merely human commands of those who reject the truth. 15 To the pure, all things are pure, but to those who are corrupted and do not believe, nothing is pure. In fact, both their minds and consciences are corrupted. 16 They claim to know God, but by their actions they deny him. They are detestable, disobedient and unfit for doing anything good.

Doing good for the sake of the gospel

2 You, however, must teach what is appropriate to sound doctrine. 2 Teach the older men to be temperate, worthy of respect, self-controlled, and sound in faith, in love and in endurance.

3 Likewise, teach the older women to be reverent in the way they live, not to be slanderers or addicted to much wine, but to teach what is good. 4 Then they can urge the younger women to love their husbands and children, 5 to be self-controlled and pure, to be busy at home, to be kind, and to be subject to their husbands, so that no one will malign the word of God.

6 Similarly, encourage the young men to be self-controlled. 7 In everything set them an example by doing what is good. In your teaching show integrity, seriousness 8 and soundness of speech that cannot be condemned, so that those who oppose you may be ashamed because they have nothing bad to say about us.

9 Teach slaves to be subject to their masters in everything, to try to please them, not to talk back to them, 10 and not to steal from them, but to show that they can be fully trusted, so that in every way they will make the teaching about God our Saviour attractive.

11 For the grace of God has appeared that offers salvation to all people. 12 It teaches us to say 'No' to ungodliness and worldly passions, and to live self-controlled, upright and godly lives in this present age, 13 while we wait for the blessed hope – the

---

a 5 Or *ordain*
b 6 Or *children are trustworthy*

c 12 From the Cretan philosopher Epimenides

appearing of the glory of our great God and Saviour, Jesus Christ, **14** who gave himself for us to redeem us from all wickedness and to purify for himself a people that are his very own, eager to do what is good. **15** These, then, are the things you should teach. Encourage and rebuke with all authority. Do not let anyone despise you.

Saved in order to do good

3 Remind the people to be subject to rulers and authorities, to be obedient, to be ready to do whatever is good, **2** to slander no one, to be peaceable and considerate, and always to be gentle towards everyone.

3 At one time we too were foolish, disobedient, deceived and enslaved by all kinds of passions and pleasures. We lived in malice and envy, being hated and hating one another. **4** But when the kindness and love of God our Saviour appeared, **5** he saved us, not because of righteous things we had done, but because of his mercy. He saved us through the washing of rebirth and renewal by the Holy Spirit, **6** whom he poured out on us generously through Jesus Christ our Saviour, **7** so that, having been justified by his grace, we might become heirs having the hope of eternal life.

8 This is a trustworthy saying. And I want you to stress these things, so that those who have trusted in God may be careful to devote themselves to doing what is good. These things are excellent and profitable for everyone.

9 But avoid foolish controversies and genealogies and arguments and quarrels about the law, because these are unprofitable and useless. **10** Warn a divisive person once, and then warn them a second time. After that, have nothing to do with them. **11** You may be sure that such people are warped and sinful; they are self-condemned.

Final remarks

12 As soon as I send Artemas or Tychicus to you, do your best to come to me at Nicopolis, because I have decided to winter there. **13** Do everything you can to help Zenas the lawyer and Apollos on their way and see that they have everything they need. **14** Our people must learn to devote themselves to doing what is good, in order to provide for urgent needs and not live unproductive lives.

15 Everyone with me sends you greetings. Greet those who love us in the faith. Grace be with you all.

PHILEMON

DATE

This letter was written in about AD 60

AUTHOR

The apostle Paul

WHAT'S IT ALL ABOUT?

This short letter (only 25 verses long) is a personal plea from Paul to Philemon, a Christian slave owner in Colossae. One of Philemon's slaves, Onesimus, had apparently stolen from his master and run away, but, having encountered Paul and become a believer, Onesimus wanted to return to Philemon and make up for his actions. The situation was fraught, because under Roman law Philemon could have had Onesimus killed for his actions. So Paul wrote this letter to appeal to his fellow worker and ask him to treat his former slave as a brother in the faith. Paul cleverly laid out his request, reassuring Philemon that he was not ordering him to do anything, while stressing how much he loved Onesimus and reminding Philemon that he owed Paul a great deal. Paul even offered to pay Onesimus's debt himself, ensuring that all his bases were covered and it would be almost impossible for Philemon to say 'no'.

WHY SHOULD WE READ IT?

- To see that Paul didn't order Philemon to do what he wanted – he appealed to him in love (vv. 8–9).

- Because it demonstrates how the gospel turned ordinary customs of the day on their head. Paul asked Philemon to treat Onesimus as a brother in Christ instead of the slave he had previously been.

Andy Croft with Liza Hoeksma

1 Paul, a prisoner of Christ Jesus, and Timothy our brother,

To Philemon our dear friend and fellow worker – **2** also to Apphia our sister and Archippus our fellow soldier – and to the church that meets in your home:

3 Grace and peace to you*ᵃ* from God our Father and the Lord Jesus Christ.

Thanksgiving and prayer

4 I always thank my God as I remember you in my prayers, **5** because I hear about your love for all his holy people and your faith in the Lord Jesus. **6** I pray that your partnership with us in the faith may be effective in deepening your understanding of every good thing we share for the sake of Christ. **7** Your love has given me great joy and encouragement, because you, brother, have refreshed the hearts of the Lord's people.

Paul's plea for Onesimus

8 Therefore, although in Christ I could be bold and order you to do what you ought to do, **9** yet I prefer to appeal to you on the basis of love. It is as none other than Paul – an old man and now also a prisoner of Christ Jesus – **10** that I appeal to you for my son Onesimus,*ᵇ* who became my son while I was in chains. **11** Formerly he was useless to you, but now he has become useful both to you and to me.

12 I am sending him – who is my very heart – back to you. **13** I would have liked to keep him with me so that he could take your place in helping me while I am in chains for the gospel. **14** But I did not want to do anything without your consent, so that any favour you do would not seem forced but would be voluntary. **15** Perhaps the reason he was separated from you for a little while was that you might have him back for ever – **16** no longer as a slave, but better than a slave, as a dear brother. He is very dear to me but even dearer to you, both as a fellow man and as a brother in the Lord.

17 So if you consider me a partner, welcome him as you would welcome me. **18** If he has done you any wrong or owes you anything, charge it to me. **19** I, Paul, am writing this with my own hand. I will pay it back – not to mention that you owe me your very self. **20** I do wish, brother, that I may have some benefit from you in the Lord; refresh my heart in Christ. **21** Confident of your obedience, I write to you, knowing that you will do even more than I ask.

22 And one thing more: prepare a guest room for me, because I hope to be restored to you in answer to your prayers.

23 Epaphras, my fellow prisoner in Christ Jesus, sends you greetings. **24** And so do Mark, Aristarchus, Demas and Luke, my fellow workers.

25 The grace of the Lord Jesus Christ be with your spirit.

---

a 3 The Greek is plural; also in verses 22 and 25; elsewhere in this letter 'you' is singular.
b 10 *Onesimus* means *useful*.

HEBREWS

DATE

An exact date is not known, but it is thought Hebrews was written before AD 70

AUTHOR

Unknown. The style of the book is considered too different from Paul's known letters for him to be the author. It's suggested that either Barnabas or Apollos, who were associated with Paul, may have written it, but we just don't know.

WHAT'S IT ALL ABOUT?

This letter was written to Jews who had converted to Christianity but seemed to be tempted back towards Judaism. They were still hung up on some of the old teachings and the old ways, missing out on the amazing things that were available to them. They were distracted by thinking about things like angels and the priesthood system of the Old Testament, so the author wrote to them about how Jesus is greater than any of those. They no longer needed the old ways – they had Jesus. The people he was writing to may have been persecuted for their faith and so he urged them to keep going and not give up. He urged them to follow the example set by men and women of faith, knowing that the fulfilment of their faith – and ours – is in Jesus.

WHY SHOULD WE READ IT?

- To be reminded that Jesus is enough; we don't need any add-ons to our faith.

- To see how powerful the Word of God is (Hebrews 4:12).

- To find teaching on why we should keep going in our faith, even when things are tough (Hebrews 10 and 12), and to remember that sometimes God disciplines us for our own good (Hebrews 12).

- To read the roll call of the 'heroes of the faith' (Hebrews 11), which details some of the men and women whose stories are in the Old Testament, who faithfully served God and achieved amazing things through their perseverance and faith.

Andy Croft with Liza Hoeksma

God's final word: his Son

1 In the past God spoke to our ancestors through the prophets at many times and in various ways, **2** but in these last days he has spoken to us by his Son, whom he appointed heir of all things, and through whom also he made the universe. **3** The Son is the radiance of God's glory and the exact representation of his being, sustaining all things by his powerful word. After he had provided purification for sins, he sat down at the right hand of the Majesty in heaven. **4** So he became as much superior to the angels as the name he has inherited is superior to theirs.

The Son superior to angels

5 For to which of the angels did God ever say,

'You are my Son;
today I have become your Father'*ª*?

Or again,

'I will be his Father,
and he will be my Son'*b*?

6 And again, when God brings his firstborn into the world, he says,

'Let all God's angels worship him.'*c*

7 In speaking of the angels he says,

'He makes his angels spirits,
and his servants flames of fire.'*d*

8 But about the Son he says,

'Your throne, O God, will last for ever
and ever;
a sceptre of justice will be the
sceptre of your kingdom.
9 You have loved righteousness and
hated wickedness;

therefore God, your God, has set you
above your companions
by anointing you with the oil of joy.'*e*

10 He also says,

'In the beginning, Lord, you laid the
foundations of the earth,
and the heavens are the work of
your hands.
11 They will perish, but you remain;
they will all wear out like a garment.
12 You will roll them up like a robe;
like a garment they will be changed.
But you remain the same,
and your years will never end.'*f*

13 To which of the angels did God ever say,

'Sit at my right hand
until I make your enemies
a footstool for your feet'*g*?

14 Are not all angels ministering spirits sent to serve those who will inherit salvation?

Warning to pay attention

2 We must pay the most careful attention, therefore, to what we have heard, so that we do not drift away. **2** For since the message spoken through angels was binding, and every violation and disobedience received its just punishment, **3** how shall we escape if we ignore so great a salvation? This salvation, which was first announced by the Lord, was confirmed to us by those who heard him. **4** God also testified to it by signs, wonders and various miracles, and by gifts of the Holy Spirit distributed according to his will.

Jesus made fully human

5 It is not to angels that he has subjected the world to come, about which we are speaking. **6** But there is a place where someone has testified:

---

a 5 Psalm 2:7
b 5 2 Samuel 7:14; 1 Chron. 17:13
c 6 Deut. 32:43 (see Dead Sea Scrolls and Septuagint)
d 7 Psalm 104:4

e 9 Psalm 45:6,7
f 12 Psalm 102:25-27
g 13 Psalm 110:1

'What is mankind that you are mindful
of them,
a son of man that you care for
him?

7 You made them a little*a* lower than the
angels;

a 7 Or *them for a little while*

LIFE OF JESUS 10

Lord of the universe

When we're young, it's easy to be so enthusiastic about something that we overstate the case. Let me warn you that, when you reach middle age, you will probably realise that the football team you supported in your youth was not, in reality, 'the best in the world', that the band you raved about was actually not brilliant but rather mediocre, and (unless you marry him or her) your first love actually wasn't that amazing.

You will be able to say (perhaps rather sadly), 'I now know better.' Some people suggest that this is rather what happened with Jesus: his first followers were just a bit *too* enthusiastic. They suggest that the disciples overstated his claims and the real Jesus actually wasn't quite that great. 'We now know better' is their verdict.

We have certainly seen that Jesus claimed all sorts of astonishing things: to be the forgiver of sins, the King of Israel, the ultimate Authority, the One who delivers people from sickness, the Lord over all evil powers, the Judge of all the earth. These dramatic claims are so extraordinary, you might expect that a few decades later the church would have delivered 'a revised opinion', a toning down of some of the more dramatic claims of the disciples.

This is not at all what happened. As Hebrews 1:1–3 (and other passages such as Colossians 1:15–20 and Philippians 2:5–11) shows, the early Christians in no way retreated from what Jesus said about himself. They may have rephrased some of the concepts for a culture that was now more Greek than Jewish, but they confidently and unhesitatingly proclaimed everything that Jesus said of himself. So here, in this passage to Christians from a Jewish background, the writer points out some awesome truths in just two verses. For a start, we read that Jesus is God's Son, the heir of all things and instrumental in making the universe. Then the writer adds that Jesus reflects the full glory of God and represents completely who God is, and offers as a final thought the claim that he keeps the entire cosmos going through his word. This passage suggests that our problem may not be overstating who Jesus is, but *understating* who he is.

Who is Jesus? The simple answer is that he's bigger than we could imagine him to be. He's so big that we must use the language of God for him. He's King, Lord and Saviour. Practically, all we need to know is this: he's big and powerful enough for any problem that we may face now or in the future. He's God with us.

J.John

Acts 10:42

you crowned them with glory and honour
8 and put everything under their feet.'*b,c*

In putting everything under them,*d* God left nothing that is not subject to them.*d* Yet at present we do not see everything subject to them.*d* 9 But we do see Jesus, who was made lower than the angels for a little while, now crowned with glory and honour because he suffered death, so that by the grace of God he might taste death for everyone.

10 In bringing many sons and daughters to glory, it was fitting that God, for whom and through whom everything exists, should make the pioneer of their salvation perfect through what he suffered. 11 Both the one who makes people holy and those who are made holy are of the same family. So Jesus is not ashamed to call them brothers and sisters.*e* 12 He says,

'I will declare your name to my brothers and sisters;
in the assembly I will sing your praises.'*f*

13 And again,

'I will put my trust in him.'*g*

And again he says,

'Here am I, and the children God has given me.'*h*

14 Since the children have flesh and blood, he too shared in their humanity so that by his death he might break the power of him who holds the power of

death – that is, the devil – 15 and free those who all their lives were held in slavery by their fear of death. 16 For surely it is not angels he helps, but Abraham's descendants. 17 For this reason he had to be made like them,*i* fully human in every way, in order that he might become a merciful and faithful high priest in service to God, and that he might make atonement for the sins of the people. 18 Because he himself suffered when he was tempted, he is able to help those who are being tempted.

Jesus greater than Moses

3 Therefore, holy brothers and sisters, who share in the heavenly calling, fix your thoughts on Jesus, whom we acknowledge as our apostle and high priest. 2 He was faithful to the one who appointed him, just as Moses was faithful in all God's house. 3 Jesus has been found worthy of greater honour than Moses, just as the builder of a house has greater honour than the house itself. 4 For every house is built by someone, but God is the builder of everything. 5 'Moses was faithful as a servant in all God's house,'*a* bearing witness to what would be spoken by God in the future. 6 But Christ is faithful as the Son over God's house. And we are his house, if indeed we hold firmly to our confidence and the hope in which we glory.

Warning against unbelief

7 So, as the Holy Spirit says:

'Today, if you hear his voice,
8 do not harden your hearts
as you did in the rebellion,
during the time of testing in the wilderness,
9 where your ancestors tested and tried me,
though for forty years they saw what I did.
10 That is why I was angry with that generation;
I said, "Their hearts are always going astray,

b 6-8 Psalm 8:4-6
c 7,8 Or *'You made him a little lower than the angels;/you crowned him with glory and honour/* 8 *and put everything under his feet.'*
d 8 Or *him*
e 11 The Greek word for *brothers and sisters (adelphoi)* refers here to believers, both men and women, as part of God's family; also in verse 12; and in 3:1, 12; 10:19; 13:22.
f 12 Psalm 22:22
g 13 Isaiah 8:17
h 13 Isaiah 8:18

i 17 Or *like his brothers*
a 5 Num. 12:7

and they have not known my ways." :
11 So I declared on oath in my anger,
    "They shall never enter my rest." 'b

12 See to it, brothers and sisters, that
none of you has a sinful, unbelieving heart
that turns away from the living God. 13 But
encourage one another daily, as long as it
is called 'Today', so that none of you may
be hardened by sin's deceitfulness. 14 We
have come to share in Christ, if indeed we
hold our original conviction firmly to the
very end. 15 As has just been said:

'Today, if you hear his voice,
    do not harden your hearts
    as you did in the rebellion.' c

16 Who were they who heard and rebelled? Were they not all those Moses led
out of Egypt? 17 And with whom was he angry for forty years? Was it not with those
who sinned, whose bodies perished in the
wilderness? 18 And to whom did God swear
that they would never enter his rest if not
to those who disobeyed? 19 So we see that
they were not able to enter, because of
their unbelief.

A Sabbath-rest for the people of God

4 Therefore, since the promise of entering his rest still stands, let us be
careful that none of you be found to have
fallen short of it. 2 For we also have had the
good news proclaimed to us, just as they
did; but the message they heard was of no
value to them, because they did not share
the faith of those who obeyed. a 3 Now we
who have believed enter that rest, just as
God has said,

'So I declared on oath in my anger,
    "They shall never enter my rest." 'b

And yet his works have been finished
since the creation of the world. 4 For
somewhere he has spoken about the

seventh day in these words: 'On the seventh day God rested from all his works.' c
5 And again in the passage above he says,
'They shall never enter my rest.'

6 Therefore since it still remains for
some to enter that rest, and since those
who formerly had the good news proclaimed to them did not go in because
of their disobedience, 7 God again set a
certain day, calling it 'Today'. This he did
when a long time later he spoke through
David, as in the passage already quoted:

'Today, if you hear his voice,
    do not harden your hearts.' d

8 For if Joshua had given them rest, God
would not have spoken later about another
day. 9 There remains, then, a Sabbath-rest
for the people of God; 10 for anyone who
enters God's rest also rests from their
works, e just as God did from his. 11 Let us,
therefore, make every effort to enter that
rest, so that no one will perish by following their example of disobedience.

12 For the word of God is alive and active. Sharper than any double-edged
sword, it penetrates even to dividing soul
and spirit, joints and marrow; it judges
the thoughts and attitudes of the heart.
13 Nothing in all creation is hidden from
God's sight. Everything is uncovered and
laid bare before the eyes of him to whom
we must give account.

Jesus the great high priest

14 Therefore, since we have a great high
priest who has ascended into heaven, f
Jesus the Son of God, let us hold firmly to
the faith we profess. 15 For we do not have
a high priest who is unable to feel sympathy for our weaknesses, but we have one
who has been tempted in every way, just
as we are – yet he did not sin. 16 Let us then
approach God's throne of grace with confidence, so that we may receive mercy and
find grace to help us in our time of need.

---

b 11 Psalm 95:7-11
c 15 Psalm 95:7,8
a 2 Some manuscripts *because those who heard did not*
combine it with faith
b 3 Psalm 95:11; also in verse 5

c 4 Gen. 2:2
d 7 Psalm 95:7,8
e 10 Or *labour*
f 14 Greek *has gone through the heavens*

5 Every high priest is selected from among the people and is appointed to represent the people in matters related to God, to offer gifts and sacrifices for sins. ²He is able to deal gently with those who are ignorant and are going astray, since he himself is subject to weakness. ³This is why he has to offer sacrifices for his own sins, as well as for the sins of the people. ⁴And no one takes this honour on himself, but he receives it when called by God, just as Aaron was.

⁵In the same way, Christ did not take on himself the glory of becoming a high priest. But God said to him,

'You are my Son;
    today I have become your Father.'ᵃ

⁶And he says in another place,

'You are a priest for ever,
    in the order of Melchizedek.'ᵇ

⁷During the days of Jesus' life on earth, he offered up prayers and petitions with fervent cries and tears to the one who could save him from death, and he was heard because of his reverent submission. ⁸Son though he was, he learned obedience from what he suffered ⁹and, once made perfect, he became the source of eternal salvation for all who obey him ¹⁰and was designated by God to be high priest in the order of Melchizedek.

Warning against falling away

¹¹We have much to say about this, but it is hard to make it clear to you because you no longer try to understand. ¹²In fact, though by this time you ought to be teachers, you need someone to teach you the elementary truths of God's word all over again. You need milk, not solid food! ¹³Anyone who lives on milk, being still an infant, is not acquainted with the teaching about righteousness. ¹⁴But solid food is for the mature, who by constant use

have trained themselves to distinguish good from evil.

6 Therefore let us move beyond the elementary teachings about Christ and be taken forward to maturity, not laying again the foundation of repentance from acts that lead to death,ᵃ and of faith in God, ²instruction about cleansing rites,ᵇ the laying on of hands, the resurrection of the dead, and eternal judgment. ³And God permitting, we will do so.

⁴It is impossible for those who have once been enlightened, who have tasted the heavenly gift, who have shared in the Holy Spirit, ⁵who have tasted the goodness of the word of God and the powers of the coming age ⁶and who have fallenᶜ away, to be brought back to repentance. To their loss they are crucifying the Son of God all over again and subjecting him to public disgrace. ⁷Land that drinks in the rain often falling on it and that produces a crop useful to those for whom it is farmed receives the blessing of God. ⁸But land that produces thorns and thistles is worthless and is in danger of being cursed. In the end it will be burned.

⁹Even though we speak like this, dear friends, we are convinced of better things in your case – the things that have to do with salvation. ¹⁰God is not unjust; he will not forget your work and the love you have shown him as you have helped his people and continue to help them. ¹¹We want each of you to show this same diligence to the very end, so that what you hope for may be fully realized. ¹²We do not want you to become lazy, but to imitate those who through faith and patience inherit what has been promised.

The certainty of God's promise

¹³When God made his promise to Abraham, since there was no one greater for him to swear by, he swore by himself, ¹⁴saying, 'I will surely bless you and give you many descendants.'ᵈ ¹⁵And so after

---

ᵃ 5 Psalm 2:7
ᵇ 6 Psalm 110:4

ᵃ 1 Or from useless rituals
ᵇ 2 Or about baptisms
ᶜ 6 Or age, ⁶if they fall
ᵈ 14 Gen. 22:17

waiting patiently, Abraham received what was promised.

16 People swear by someone greater than themselves, and the oath confirms what is said and puts an end to all argument. 17 Because God wanted to make the unchanging nature of his purpose very clear to the heirs of what was promised, he confirmed it with an oath. 18 God did this so that, by two unchangeable things in which it is impossible for God to lie, we who have fled to take hold of the hope set before us may be greatly encouraged. 19 We have this hope as an anchor for the soul, firm and secure. It enters the inner sanctuary behind the curtain, 20 where our forerunner, Jesus, has entered on our behalf. He has become a high priest for ever, in the order of Melchizedek.

Melchizedek the priest

7 This Melchizedek was king of Salem and priest of God Most High. He met Abraham returning from the defeat of the kings and blessed him, 2 and Abraham gave him a tenth of everything. First, the name Melchizedek means 'king of righteousness'; then also, 'king of Salem' means 'king of peace'. 3 Without father or mother, without genealogy, without beginning of days or end of life, resembling the Son of God, he remains a priest for ever.

4 Just think how great he was: even the patriarch Abraham gave him a tenth of the plunder! 5 Now the law requires the descendants of Levi who become priests to collect a tenth from the people – that is, from their fellow Israelites – even though they also are descended from Abraham. 6 This man, however, did not trace his descent from Levi, yet he collected a tenth from Abraham and blessed him who had the promises. 7 And without doubt the lesser is blessed by the greater. 8 In the one case, the tenth is collected by people who die; but in the other case, by him who is declared to be living. 9 One might even say that Levi, who collects the tenth, paid the tenth through Abraham, 10 because when Melchizedek met Abraham, Levi was still in the body of his ancestor.

Jesus like Melchizedek

11 If perfection could have been attained through the Levitical priesthood – and indeed the law given to the people established that priesthood – why was there still need for another priest to come, one in the order of Melchizedek, not in the order of Aaron? 12 For when the priesthood is changed, the law must be changed also. 13 He of whom these things are said belonged to a different tribe, and no one from that tribe has ever served at the altar. 14 For it is clear that our Lord descended from Judah, and in regard to that tribe Moses said nothing about priests. 15 And what we have said is even more clear if another priest like Melchizedek appears, 16 one who has become a priest not on the basis of a regulation as to his ancestry but on the basis of the power of an indestructible life. 17 For it is declared:

'You are a priest for ever,
    in the order of Melchizedek.' [a]

18 The former regulation is set aside because it was weak and useless 19 (for the law made nothing perfect), and a better hope is introduced, by which we draw near to God. 20 And it was not without an oath! Others became priests without any oath, 21 but he became a priest with an oath when God said to him:

'The Lord has sworn
    and will not change his mind:
    "You are a priest for ever." ' [a]

22 Because of this oath, Jesus has become the guarantor of a better covenant.

23 Now there have been many of those priests, since death prevented them from continuing in office; 24 but because Jesus lives for ever, he has a permanent priesthood. 25 Therefore he is able to save completely [b] those who come to God through him, because he always lives to intercede for them.

26 Such a high priest truly meets our need – one who is holy, blameless, pure,

---

a 17,21 Psalm 110:4
b 25 Or for ever

set apart from sinners, exalted above the heavens. **27** Unlike the other high priests, he does not need to offer sacrifices day after day, first for his own sins, and then for the sins of the people. He sacrificed for their sins once for all when he offered himself. **28** For the law appoints as high priests men in all their weakness; but the oath, which came after the law, appointed the Son, who has been made perfect for ever.

FAVOURITE VERSES

Micah 6:8

*He has shown you, O mortal, what
   is good.
And what does the LORD require
   of you?
To act justly and to love mercy
   and to walk humbly with your God.*

I love this verse because it plainly and simply reminds you of the important things in life. I feel it sums up ideal guidelines for a Christian to live by: to be compassionate and loving to your neighbour, and not to take everything too seriously – unless it's from God, as you should be taking God seriously.

Michelle, 21

The high priest of a new covenant

8 Now the main point of what we are saying is this: we do have such a high priest, who sat down at the right hand of the throne of the Majesty in heaven, **2** and who serves in the sanctuary, the true tabernacle set up by the Lord, not by a mere human being.

3 Every high priest is appointed to offer both gifts and sacrifices, and so it was necessary for this one also to have

something to offer. **4** If he were on earth, he would not be a priest, for there are already priests who offer the gifts prescribed by the law. **5** They serve at a sanctuary that is a copy and shadow of what is in heaven. This is why Moses was warned when he was about to build the tabernacle: 'See to it that you make everything according to the pattern shown you on the mountain.'*a* **6** But in fact the ministry Jesus has received is as superior to theirs as the covenant of which he is mediator is superior to the old one, since the new covenant is established on better promises.

7 For if there had been nothing wrong with that first covenant, no place would have been sought for another. **8** But God found fault with the people and said*b*:

'The days are coming, declares the
   Lord,
when I will make a new covenant
   with the people of Israel
   and with the people of Judah.
9 It will not be like the covenant
   I made with their ancestors
when I took them by the hand
   to lead them out of Egypt,
because they did not remain faithful to
      my covenant,
   and I turned away from them,
                      declares the Lord.
10 This is the covenant I will establish
         with the people of Israel
      after that time, declares the Lord.
I will put my laws in their minds
   and write them on their hearts.
I will be their God,
   and they will be my people.
11 No longer will they teach their
         neighbours,
   or say to one another, "Know the
      Lord,"
because they will all know me,
   from the least of them to the
      greatest.
12 For I will forgive their wickedness

---

a 5 Exodus 25:40
b 8 Some manuscripts may be translated *fault and said to the people.*

and will remember their sins no more.'ᶜ

¹³ By calling this covenant 'new', he has made the first one obsolete; and what is obsolete and outdated will soon disappear.

Worship in the earthly tabernacle

9 Now the first covenant had regulations for worship and also an earthly sanctuary. ²A tabernacle was set up. In its first room were the lampstand and the table with its consecrated bread; this was called the Holy Place. ³Behind the second curtain was a room called the Most Holy Place, ⁴which had the golden altar of incense and the gold-covered ark of the covenant. This ark contained the gold jar of manna, Aaron's staff that had budded, and the stone tablets of the covenant. ⁵Above the ark were the cherubim of the Glory, overshadowing the atonement cover. But we cannot discuss these things in detail now.

⁶When everything had been arranged like this, the priests entered regularly into the outer room to carry on their ministry. ⁷But only the high priest entered the inner room, and that only once a year, and never without blood, which he offered for himself and for the sins the people had committed in ignorance. ⁸The Holy Spirit was showing by this that the way into the Most Holy Place had not yet been disclosed as long as the first tabernacle was still functioning. ⁹This is an illustration for the present time, indicating that the gifts and sacrifices being offered were not able to clear the conscience of the worshipper. ¹⁰They are only a matter of food and drink and various ceremonial washings – external regulations applying until the time of the new order.

The blood of Christ

¹¹ But when Christ came as high priest of the good things that are now already here,ᵃ he went through the greater and more perfect tabernacle that is not made with human hands, that is to say, is not a part of this creation. ¹²He did not enter by means of the blood of goats and calves; but he entered the Most Holy Place once for all by his own blood, so obtainingᵇ eternal redemption. ¹³The blood of goats and bulls and the ashes of a heifer sprinkled on those who are ceremonially unclean sanctify them so that they are outwardly clean. ¹⁴How much more, then, will the blood of Christ, who through the eternal Spirit offered himself unblemished to God, cleanse our consciences from acts that lead to death,ᶜ so that we may serve the living God!

HOLY OF HOLIES

Inside the temple was a room shaped like a perfect cube. This was the Holy of Holies. Only one man was allowed in there – the high priest – and then only on one day of the year, the Day of Atonement (Hebrews 9:25).

¹⁵For this reason Christ is the mediator of a new covenant, that those who are called may receive the promised eternal inheritance – now that he has died as a ransom to set them free from the sins committed under the first covenant.

¹⁶In the case of a will,ᵈ it is necessary to prove the death of the one who made it, ¹⁷because a will is in force only when somebody has died; it never takes effect while the one who made it is living. ¹⁸This is why even the first covenant was not put into effect without blood. ¹⁹When Moses had proclaimed every command of the law to all the people, he took the blood of

---

ᶜ 12 Jer. 31:31-34
ᵃ 11 Some early manuscripts *are to come*

ᵇ 12 Or *blood, having obtained*
ᶜ 14 Or *from useless rituals*
ᵈ 16 Same Greek word as *covenant*; also in verse 17

calves, together with water, scarlet wool and branches of hyssop, and sprinkled the scroll and all the people. ²⁰ He said, 'This is the blood of the covenant, which God has commanded you to keep.'ᵉ ²¹ In the same way, he sprinkled with the blood both the tabernacle and everything used in its ceremonies. ²² In fact, the law requires that nearly everything be cleansed with blood, and without the shedding of blood there is no forgiveness.

²³ It was necessary, then, for the copies of the heavenly things to be purified with these sacrifices, but the heavenly things themselves with better sacrifices than these. ²⁴ For Christ did not enter a sanctuary made with human hands that was only a copy of the true one; he entered heaven itself, now to appear for us in God's presence. ²⁵ Nor did he enter heaven to offer himself again and again, the way the high priest enters the Most Holy Place every year with blood that is not his own. ²⁶ Otherwise Christ would have had to suffer many times since the creation of the world. But he has appeared once for all at the culmination of the ages to do away with sin by the sacrifice of himself. ²⁷ Just as people are destined to die once, and after that to face judgment, ²⁸ so Christ was sacrificed once to take away the sins of many; and he will appear a second time, not to bear sin, but to bring salvation to those who are waiting for him.

Christ's sacrifice once for all

10 The law is only a shadow of the good things that are coming – not the realities themselves. For this reason it can never, by the same sacrifices repeated endlessly year after year, make perfect those who draw near to worship. ² Otherwise, would they not have stopped being offered? For the worshippers would have been cleansed once for all, and would no longer have felt guilty for their sins. ³ But those sacrifices are an annual reminder of sins. ⁴ It is impossible for the blood of bulls and goats to take away sins.

⁵ Therefore, when Christ came into the world, he said:

'Sacrifice and offering you did not
    desire,
    but a body you prepared for me;
⁶ with burnt offerings and sin offerings
    you were not pleased.
⁷ Then I said, "Here I am – it is written
    about me in the scroll –
    I have come to do your will, my
    God."'ᵃ

⁸ First he said, 'Sacrifices and offerings, burnt offerings and sin offerings you did not desire, nor were you pleased with them' – though they were offered in accordance with the law. ⁹ Then he said, 'Here I am, I have come to do your will.' He sets aside the first to establish the second. ¹⁰ And by that will, we have been made holy through the sacrifice of the body of Jesus Christ once for all.

¹¹ Day after day every priest stands and performs his religious duties; again and again he offers the same sacrifices, which can never take away sins. ¹² But when this priest had offered for all time one sacrifice for sins, he sat down at the right hand of God, ¹³ and since that time he waits for his enemies to be made his footstool. ¹⁴ For by one sacrifice he has made perfect for ever those who are being made holy.

¹⁵ The Holy Spirit also testifies to us about this. First he says:

¹⁶ 'This is the covenant I will make with
    them
    after that time, says the Lord.
    I will put my laws in their hearts,
    and I will write them on their
        minds.'ᵇ

¹⁷ Then he adds:

'Their sins and lawless acts
    I will remember no more.'ᶜ

ᵃ 7 Psalm 40.6-8 (see Septuagint)
ᵇ 16 Jer. 31:33
ᶜ 17 Jer. 31:34

18 And where these have been forgiven, sacrifice for sin is no longer necessary.

A call to persevere in faith

19 Therefore, brothers and sisters, since we have confidence to enter the Most Holy Place by the blood of Jesus, **20** by a new and living way opened for us through the curtain, that is, his body, **21** and since we have a great priest over the house of God, **22** let us draw near to God with a sincere heart and with the full assurance that faith brings, having our hearts sprinkled to cleanse us from a guilty conscience and having our bodies washed with pure water. **23** Let us hold unswervingly to the hope we profess, for he who promised is faithful. **24** And let us consider how we may spur one another on towards love and good deeds, **25** not giving up meeting together, as some are in the habit of doing, but encouraging one another – and all the more as you see the Day approaching.

26 If we deliberately keep on sinning after we have received the knowledge of the truth, no sacrifice for sins is left, **27** but only a fearful expectation of judgment and of raging fire that will consume the enemies of God. **28** Anyone who rejected the law of Moses died without mercy on the testimony of two or three witnesses. **29** How much more severely do you think someone deserves to be punished who has trampled the Son of God underfoot, who has treated as an unholy thing the blood of the covenant that sanctified them, and who has insulted the Spirit of grace? **30** For we know him who said, 'It is mine to avenge; I will repay,'**d** and again, 'The Lord will judge his people.'**e** **31** It is a dreadful thing to fall into the hands of the living God.

32 Remember those earlier days after you had received the light, when you endured in a great conflict full of suffering. **33** Sometimes you were publicly exposed to insult and persecution; at other times you stood side by side with those who were so treated. **34** You suffered along with those

in prison and joyfully accepted the confiscation of your property, because you knew that you yourselves had better and lasting possessions. **35** So do not throw away your confidence; it will be richly rewarded.

36 You need to persevere so that when you have done the will of God, you will receive what he has promised. **37** For,

'In just a little while,
    he who is coming will come
    and will not delay.'**f**

38 And,

'But my righteous **g** one will live by
    faith.
And I take no pleasure
    in the one who shrinks back.'**h**

39 But we do not belong to those who shrink back and are destroyed, but to those who have faith and are saved.

Faith in action

11 Now faith is confidence in what we hope for and assurance about what we do not see. **2** This is what the ancients were commended for.

3 By faith we understand that the universe was formed at God's command, so that what is seen was not made out of what was visible.

4 By faith Abel brought God a better offering than Cain did. By faith he was commended as righteous, when God spoke well of his offerings. And by faith Abel still speaks, even though he is dead.

5 By faith Enoch was taken from this life, so that he did not experience death: 'He could not be found, because God had taken him away.'**a** For before he was taken, he was commended as one who pleased God. **6** And without faith it is impossible to please God, because anyone who comes to him must believe that he exists and that he rewards those who earnestly seek him.

---

d 30 Deut. 32:35
e 30 Deut. 32:36; Psalm 135:14

---

f 37 Isaiah 26:20; Hab. 2:3
g 38 Some early manuscripts But the righteous
h 38 Hab. 2:4 (see Septuagint)
a 5 Gen. 5:24

7 By faith Noah, when warned about things not yet seen, in holy fear built an ark to save his family. By his faith he condemned the world and became heir of the righteousness that is in keeping with faith.

8 By faith Abraham, when called to go to a place he would later receive as his inheritance, obeyed and went, even though he did not know where he was going. 9 By faith he made his home in the promised land like a stranger in a foreign country; he lived in tents, as did Isaac and Jacob, who were heirs with him of the same promise. 10 For he was looking forward to the city with foundations, whose architect and builder is God. 11 And by faith even Sarah, who was past childbearing age, was enabled to bear children because she b considered him faithful who had made the promise. 12 And so from this one man, and he as good as dead, came descendants as numerous as the stars in the sky and as countless as the sand on the seashore.

13 All these people were still living by faith when they died. They did not receive the things promised; they only saw them and welcomed them from a distance, admitting that they were foreigners and strangers on earth. 14 People who say such things show that they are looking for a country of their own. 15 If they had been thinking of the country they had left, they would have had opportunity to return. 16 Instead, they were longing for a better country – a heavenly one. Therefore God is not ashamed to be called their God, for he has prepared a city for them.

17 By faith Abraham, when God tested him, offered Isaac as a sacrifice. He who had embraced the promises was about to sacrifice his one and only son, 18 even though God had said to him, 'It is through Isaac that your offspring will be reckoned.' c 19 Abraham reasoned that God could even raise the dead, and so in a manner of speaking he did receive Isaac back from death.

20 By faith Isaac blessed Jacob and Esau in regard to their future.

21 By faith Jacob, when he was dying, blessed each of Joseph's sons, and worshipped as he leaned on the top of his staff.

22 By faith Joseph, when his end was near, spoke about the exodus of the Israelites from Egypt and gave instructions concerning the burial of his bones.

23 By faith Moses' parents hid him for three months after he was born, because they saw he was no ordinary child, and they were not afraid of the king's edict.

24 By faith Moses, when he had grown up, refused to be known as the son of Pharaoh's daughter. 25 He chose to be ill-treated along with the people of God rather than to enjoy the fleeting pleasures of sin. 26 He regarded disgrace for the sake of Christ as of greater value than the treasures of Egypt, because he was looking ahead to his reward. 27 By faith he left Egypt, not fearing the king's anger; he persevered because he saw him who is invisible. 28 By faith he kept the Passover and the application of blood, so that the destroyer of the firstborn would not touch the firstborn of Israel.

29 By faith the people passed through the Red Sea as on dry land; but when the Egyptians tried to do so, they were drowned.

30 By faith the walls of Jericho fell, after the army had marched round them for seven days.

31 By faith the prostitute Rahab, because she welcomed the spies, was not killed with those who were disobedient. d

32 And what more shall I say? I do not have time to tell about Gideon, Barak, Samson and Jephthah, about David and Samuel and the prophets, 33 who through faith conquered kingdoms, administered justice, and gained what was promised; who shut the mouths of lions, 34 quenched the fury of the flames, and escaped the edge of the sword; whose weakness was turned to strength; and who became powerful in battle and routed foreign

---

b 11 Or By faith Abraham, even though he was too old to have children – and Sarah herself was not able to conceive – was enabled to become a father because he
c 18 Gen. 21:12

d 31 Or unbelieving

armies. **35**Women received back their dead, raised to life again. There were others who were tortured, refusing to be released so that they might gain an even better resurrection. **36**Some faced jeers and flogging, and even chains and imprisonment. **37**They were put to death by stoning;*e* they were sawn in two; they were killed by the sword. They went about in sheepskins and goatskins, destitute, persecuted and ill-treated – **38**the world was not worthy of them. They wandered in deserts and mountains, living in caves and in holes in the ground.

39These were all commended for their faith, yet none of them received what had been promised, **40**since God had planned something better for us so that only together with us would they be made perfect.

12 Therefore, since we are surrounded by such a great cloud of witnesses, let us throw off everything that hinders and the sin that so easily entangles. And let us run with perseverance the race marked out for us, **2**fixing our eyes on Jesus, the pioneer and perfecter of faith. For the joy that was set before him he endured the cross, scorning its shame, and sat down at the right hand of the throne of God. **3**Consider him who endured such opposition from sinners, so that you will not grow weary and lose heart.

God disciplines his children

4In your struggle against sin, you have not yet resisted to the point of shedding your blood. **5**And have you completely forgotten this word of encouragement that addresses you as a father addresses his son? It says,

'My son, do not make light of the
    Lord's discipline,
and do not lose heart when he
    rebukes you,
6because the Lord disciplines the one
    he loves,

and he chastens everyone he accepts as his son.'*a*

7Endure hardship as discipline; God is treating you as his children. For what children are not disciplined by their father? **8**If you are not disciplined – and everyone undergoes discipline – then you are not legitimate, not true sons and daughters at all. **9**Moreover, we have all had human fathers who disciplined us and we respected them for it. How much more should we submit to the Father of spirits and live! **10**They disciplined us for a little while as they thought best; but God disciplines us for our good, in order that we may share in his holiness. **11**No discipline seems pleasant at the time, but painful. Later on, however, it produces a harvest of righteousness and peace for those who have been trained by it.

12Therefore, strengthen your feeble arms and weak knees. **13**'Make level paths for your feet,'*b* so that the lame may not be disabled, but rather healed.

Warning and encouragement

14Make every effort to live in peace with everyone and to be holy; without holiness no one will see the Lord. **15**See to it that no one falls short of the grace of God and that no bitter root grows up to cause trouble and defile many. **16**See that no one is sexually immoral, or is godless like Esau, who for a single meal sold his inheritance rights as the oldest son. **17**Afterwards, as you know, when he wanted to inherit this blessing, he was rejected. Even though he sought the blessing with tears, he could not change what he had done.

The mountain of fear and the mountain of joy

18You have not come to a mountain that can be touched and that is burning with fire; to darkness, gloom and storm; **19**to a trumpet blast or to such a voice speaking words that those who heard it begged that no further word be spoken to them,

---

e 37 Some early manuscripts *stoning; they were put to the test;*

a 5,6 Prov. 3:11,12 (see Septuagint)
b 13 Prov. 4:26

20 because they could not bear what was commanded: 'If even an animal touches the mountain, it must be stoned to death.'[c] **21** The sight was so terrifying that Moses said, 'I am trembling with fear.'[d]

22 But you have come to Mount Zion, to the city of the living God, the heavenly Jerusalem. You have come to thousands upon thousands of angels in joyful assembly, **23** to the church of the firstborn, whose names are written in heaven. You have come to God, the Judge of all, to the spirits of the righteous made perfect, **24** to Jesus the mediator of a new covenant, and to the sprinkled blood that speaks a better word than the blood of Abel.

25 See to it that you do not refuse him who speaks. If they did not escape when they refused him who warned them on earth, how much less will we, if we turn away from him who warns us from

c 20 Exodus 19:12,13
d 21 See Deut. 9:19.

PAIN AND SUFFERING 10

KEEPING OUR EYES FIXED ON JESUS

Being a Christian isn't always easy. It requires perseverance. This was as true when the New Testament was written as it is for us today. Some of the circumstances and challenges may be different, but life is equally hard.

The writer of Hebrews goes to great pains to encourage us to keep going and never give up. When hard times come our way, it can sometimes be tempting to think about turning our back on our faith – maybe in an outwardly obvious way where we walk away from church and Christian friends; maybe in more subtle ways where we just don't talk to God as much as we used to, or we decide to do things our way. Hebrews 12:1–3 gives us some good advice to come back to when we feel those temptations. We're encouraged to remember our Christian brothers and sisters who have gone before us (the *'great cloud of witnesses'* listed in chapter 11). Many of them had to endure incredible pain and hardship, but they didn't give up and they achieved amazing things for God's kingdom as a result. Reading and re-reading the stories of what they went through and how God used them can encourage us to keep going and not to quit before we see God do all that he has planned.

The other piece of advice we're given is this: fix your eyes on Jesus (12:2). Pain and suffering has a way of making us look at ourselves. When we spend too much time focusing on our own problems, we get discouraged and our hope and joy dry up. When we shift our gaze and look back at Jesus, something amazing happens. We see a God who loves us. We see a God who cares. We see a God who is powerful. We remember that God gave his only Son so that we might be in relationship with him. When life gets tough, let's take our eyes off ourselves and our problems and focus instead on Jesus. Let's remember his promises, let's read about his life and his death, let's worship him with all we have, because he is *'the pioneer and perfecter of faith'* (v. 2).

Mike Pilavachi

 Job 40

heaven? ²⁶At that time his voice shook the earth, but now he has promised, 'Once more I will shake not only the earth but also the heavens.'ᵉ ²⁷The words 'once more' indicate the removing of what can be shaken – that is, created things – so that what cannot be shaken may remain.

²⁸Therefore, since we are receiving a kingdom that cannot be shaken, let us be thankful, and so worship God acceptably with reverence and awe, ²⁹for our 'God is a consuming fire.'ᶠ

e 26 Haggai 2:6
f 29 Deut. 4:24

Concluding exhortations

13 Keep on loving one another as brothers and sisters. ²Do not forget to show hospitality to strangers, for by so doing some people have shown hospitality to angels without knowing it. ³Continue to remember those in prison as if you were together with them in prison, and those who are ill-treated as if you yourselves were suffering.

⁴Marriage should be honoured by all, and the marriage bed kept pure, for God will judge the adulterer and all the sexually immoral. ⁵Keep your lives free from the love of money and be content with what you have, because God has said,

WORSHIP 8

In reverence and awe

There are things in the world around us that command a certain amount of respect. Massive predators are one – you're not going to go and poke a lion in the eye! Another thing might be a tropical storm, or a huge burning fire.

In Hebrews 12:18–29, we get a glimpse of who God is. We see that he deserves more than just our respect. The writer uses a much richer phrase: we're told to worship God with *'reverence and awe'* (v. 28). To have reverence and awe for God is to have something like respect for him, but also to mix it up with a bit of fear and a bit of wonder.

This passage describes a time when God appeared to the Israelites back in Exodus 19. No one could go near God's mountain; he was so holy that they would be consumed by his presence. Yet this same powerful God makes himself available to us through Jesus, *'the mediator of a new covenant'* (v.24). We can draw near to God any time we want, twenty-four hours a day, seven days a week. God is just as fiercely, wonderfully holy as he always has been – his voice shakes the earth and he is *'a consuming fire'* (v. 29) – but we can still be near to him!

Know this: when you sing your songs of worship to God (in your bedroom, the shower or on the walk home from school), you're joining in the song of thousands and thousands of angels. We often worship God because of his kindness and love towards us, so if you have a chance today, why not join with the angels and lift him high because he is the mighty King of the universe?

Beth Croft

 1 Samuel 16:14–23   Job 1:13–21

'Never will I leave you;
　　never will I forsake you.'*a*

6 So we say with confidence,

'The Lord is my helper; I will not be
　　afraid.
　What can mere mortals do to me?'*b*

7 Remember your leaders, who spoke the word of God to you. Consider the outcome of their way of life and imitate their faith. 8 Jesus Christ is the same yesterday and today and for ever.

9 Do not be carried away by all kinds of

a 5 Deut. 31:6
b 6 Psalm 118:6,7

strange teachings. It is good for our hearts to be strengthened by grace, not by eating ceremonial foods, which is of no benefit to those who do so. 10 We have an altar from which those who minister at the tabernacle have no right to eat.

11 The high priest carries the blood of animals into the Most Holy Place as a sin offering, but the bodies are burned outside the camp. 12 And so Jesus also suffered outside the city gate to make the people holy through his own blood. 13 Let us, then, go to him outside the camp, bearing the disgrace he bore. 14 For here we do not have an enduring city, but we are looking for the city that is to come.

15 Through Jesus, therefore, let us continually offer to God a sacrifice of praise –

THE NAMES OF GOD 7

God Who Is Here (Yaweh Shammah)

'God has said, "Never will I leave you; never will I forsake you"' (Hebrews 13:5).

With the joys of e-mail, Facebook and Twitter, perhaps we have several hundred or more friends or 'followers'. But do you find that for all the hours you spend social networking, if the truth be known, there are times when you feel alone and as if no one really knows who or where you are?

There is one who knows us through and through. In the famous Holman Hunt paintings (hung in Kebel College, Oxford, and St Paul's Cathedral, London) Jesus is depicted as standing outside a door, holding a lantern and knocking on the door. The picture illustrates Revelation 3:20, *'Here I am! I stand at the door and knock. If anyone hears my voice and opens the door, I will come in and eat with that person, and they with me.'* In the picture there is no handle on the outside of the door. Jesus will not force himself on anyone, even though he longs to come in and share with us, to get to know us, to heal our hurts, to banish our fears and to stay close for the rest of our days. He waits for each of us to open the door and invite him in. The promise is that wherever we go, he will go with us. He says he will never leave us or forsake us.

Next time we feel lonely, let's remind ourselves of this amazing promise.

David and Mary Pytches

 Psalm 23　　　　　Isaiah 43:3 ▶

the fruit of lips that openly profess his name. 16 And do not forget to do good and to share with others, for with such sacrifices God is pleased.

17 Have confidence in your leaders and submit to their authority, because they keep watch over you as those who must give an account. Do this so that their work will be a joy, not a burden, for that would be of no benefit to you. 18 Pray for us. We are sure that we have a clear conscience and desire to live honourably in every way. 19 I particularly urge you to pray so that I may be restored to you soon.

Benediction and final greetings

20 Now may the God of peace, who through the blood of the eternal covenant brought back from the dead our Lord Jesus, that great Shepherd of the sheep, 21 equip you with everything good for doing his will, and may he work in us what is pleasing to him, through Jesus Christ, to whom be glory for ever and ever. Amen.

22 Brothers and sisters, I urge you to bear with my word of exhortation, for in fact I have written to you quite briefly. 23 I want you to know that our brother Timothy has been released. If he arrives soon, I will come with him to see you. 24 Greet all your leaders and all the Lord's people. Those from Italy send you their greetings. 25 Grace be with you all.

JAMES

DATE

Dates for this letter vary between AD 40 (which would make it one of the earliest New Testament writings) and around AD 60

AUTHOR

James, who was probably Jesus' brother

WHAT'S IT ALL ABOUT?

This letter isn't aimed at a specific individual or church, but addressed to Jewish Christians in general. After a quick greeting, James jumps right into some very practical teaching and instructions on what it means to live as a Christian. James was the leader of the church in Jerusalem which, like many churches, was being persecuted, so he begins by encouraging them to keep going in their trials and even to consider suffering a joy. He then continues with lots of straightforward and practical teaching about the Christian life, which is just as important for us today as it was for his readers so many years ago. He covers topics such as not showing favouritism to the rich, submission to God, not fighting with each other, not oppressing the poor, and praying for one another.

One of the things the letter is best known for is James's emphasis on the link between faith and works. He points out that simply hearing God's word isn't enough: we have to put it into action. He says that true faith can't help but motivate us towards action. He also writes about the importance of watching what we say. Our words have an incredible power – both to hurt and to heal – and he warns that if we can't control our tongues, we don't have control of ourselves.

WHY SHOULD WE READ IT?

- Because this letter is packed full of practical and easy-to-understand wisdom for us today as we work out what it means to live as disciples of Jesus.

- To see the fruits of persevering in hard times (James 1) and read teaching on how to be patient in suffering (James 5).

- To understand how true faith prompts us to action (James 1 – 2).

- To read teaching on the importance of watching what we say (James 1 and 3).

Andy Croft with Liza Hoeksma

1 James, a servant of God and of the Lord Jesus Christ,

To the twelve tribes scattered among the nations:

Greetings.

Trials and temptations

2 Consider it pure joy, my brothers and sisters, *a* whenever you face trials of many kinds, 3 because you know that the testing of your faith produces perseverance. 4 Let perseverance finish its work so that you may be mature and complete, not lacking anything. 5 If any of you lacks wisdom, you should ask God, who gives generously to all without finding fault, and it will be given to you. 6 But when you ask, you must believe and not doubt, because the one who doubts is like a wave of the sea, blown and tossed by the wind. 7 That person should not expect to receive anything from the Lord. 8 Such a person is double-minded and unstable in all they do.

9 Believers in humble circumstances ought to take pride in their high position. 10 But the rich should take pride in their humiliation – since they will pass away like a wild flower. 11 For the sun rises with scorching heat and withers the plant; its blossom falls and its beauty is destroyed. In the same way, the rich will fade away even while they go about their business.

12 Blessed is the one who perseveres under trial because, having stood the test, that person will receive the crown of life that the Lord has promised to those who love him.

13 When tempted, no one should say, 'God is tempting me.' For God cannot be tempted by evil, nor does he tempt anyone; 14 but each person is tempted when they are dragged away by their own evil desire and enticed. 15 Then, after desire has conceived, it gives birth to sin; and sin, when it is full-grown, gives birth to death. 16 Don't be deceived, my dear brothers

and sisters. 17 Every good and perfect gift is from above, coming down from the Father of the heavenly lights, who does not change like shifting shadows. 18 He chose to give us birth through the word of truth, that we might be a kind of firstfruits of all he created.

Listening and doing

19 My dear brothers and sisters, take note of this: everyone should be quick to listen, slow to speak and slow to become angry, 20 because human anger does not produce the righteousness that God desires. 21 Therefore, get rid of all moral filth and the evil that is so prevalent, and humbly accept the word planted in you, which can save you.

22 Do not merely listen to the word, and so deceive yourselves. Do what it says. 23 Anyone who listens to the word but does not do what it says is like someone who looks at his face in a mirror 24 and, after looking at himself, goes away and immediately forgets what he looks like. 25 But whoever looks intently into the perfect law that gives freedom and continues in it – not forgetting what they have heard but doing it – they will be blessed in what they do.

26 Those who consider themselves religious and yet do not keep a tight rein on their tongues deceive themselves, and their religion is worthless. 27 Religion that God our Father accepts as pure and faultless is this: to look after orphans and widows in their distress and to keep oneself from being polluted by the world.

Favouritism forbidden

2 My brothers and sisters, believers in our glorious Lord Jesus Christ must not show favouritism. 2 Suppose a man comes into your meeting wearing a gold ring and fine clothes, and a poor man in filthy old clothes also comes in. 3 If you show special attention to the man wearing fine clothes and say, 'Here's a good seat for you,' but say to the poor man, 'You stand there' or 'Sit on the floor by my feet,' 4 have you not discriminated among yourselves and become judges with evil thoughts? 5 Listen, my dear brothers and sisters:

---

a 2 The Greek word for *brothers and sisters* (*adelphoi*) refers here to believers, both men and women, as part of God's family; also in verses 16 and 19; and in 2:1, 5, 14; 3:10, 12; 4:11; 5:7, 9, 10, 12, 19.

has not God chosen those who are poor in the eyes of the world to be rich in faith and to inherit the kingdom he promised those who love him? ⁶But you have dishonoured the poor. Is it not the rich who are exploiting you? Are they not the ones who are dragging you into court? ⁷Are they not the ones who are blaspheming the noble name of him to whom you belong?

⁸If you really keep the royal law found in Scripture, 'Love your neighbour as yourself,'ᵃ you are doing right. ⁹But if you show favouritism, you sin and are convicted by the law as law-breakers. ¹⁰For whoever keeps the whole law and yet stumbles at just one point is guilty of breaking all of it. ¹¹For he who said, 'You shall not commit adultery,'ᵇ also said, 'You shall not murder.'ᶜ If you do not commit adultery but do commit murder, you have become a law-breaker.

¹²Speak and act as those who are going to be judged by the law that gives freedom, ¹³because judgment without mercy will be shown to anyone who has not been merciful. Mercy triumphs over judgment.

Faith and deeds

¹⁴What good is it, my brothers and sisters, if someone claims to have faith but has no deeds? Can such faith save them? ¹⁵Suppose a brother or a sister is without clothes and daily food. ¹⁶If one of you says to them, 'Go in peace; keep warm and well fed,' but does nothing about their physical needs, what good is it? ¹⁷In the same way, faith by itself, if it is not accompanied by action, is dead.

¹⁸But someone will say, 'You have faith; I have deeds.'

Show me your faith without deeds, and I will show you my faith by my deeds. ¹⁹You believe that there is one God. Good! Even the demons believe that – and shudder.

²⁰You foolish person, do you want evidence that faith without deeds is useless⁴? ²¹Was not our father Abraham considered righteous for what he did when he offered his son Isaac on the altar? ²²You see that his faith and his actions were working together, and his faith was made complete by what he did. ²³And the scripture was fulfilled that says, 'Abraham believed God, and it was credited to him as righteousness,'ᵉ and he was called God's friend. ²⁴You see that a person is considered righteous by what they do and not by faith alone.

²⁵In the same way, was not even Rahab the prostitute considered righteous for what she did when she gave lodging to the spies and sent them off in a different direction? ²⁶As the body without the spirit is dead, so faith without deeds is dead.

Taming the tongue

3 Not many of you should become teachers, my fellow believers, because you know that we who teach will be judged more strictly. ²We all stumble in many ways. Anyone who is never at fault in what they say is perfect, able to keep their whole body in check.

³When we put bits into the mouths of horses to make them obey us, we can turn the whole animal. ⁴Or take ships as an example. Although they are so large and are driven by strong winds, they are steered by a very small rudder wherever the pilot wants to go. ⁵Likewise, the tongue is a small part of the body, but it makes great boasts. Consider what a great forest is set on fire by a small spark. ⁶The tongue also is a fire, a world of evil among the parts of the body. It corrupts the whole body, sets the whole course of one's life on fire, and is itself set on fire by hell.

⁷All kinds of animals, birds, reptiles and sea creatures are being tamed and have been tamed by mankind, ⁸but no human being can tame the tongue. It is a restless evil, full of deadly poison.

⁹With the tongue we praise our Lord and Father, and with it we curse human beings, who have been made in God's likeness. ¹⁰Out of the same mouth come

---

ᵃ8 Lev. 19:18
ᵇ11 Exodus 20:14; Deut. 5:18
ᶜ11 Exodus 20:13; Deut. 5:17
ᵈ20 Some early manuscripts *dead*

ᵉ23 Gen. 15:6

praise and cursing. My brothers and sisters, this should not be. ¹¹Can both fresh water and salt water flow from the same spring? ¹²My brothers and sisters, can a fig-tree bear olives, or a grapevine bear figs? Neither can a salt spring produce fresh water.

Two kinds of wisdom

¹³Who is wise and understanding among you? Let them show it by their good life, by deeds done in the humility that comes from wisdom. ¹⁴But if you harbour bitter envy and selfish ambition in your hearts, do not boast about it or deny the truth. ¹⁵Such 'wisdom' does not come down from heaven but is earthly, unspiritual, demonic. ¹⁶For where you have envy and selfish ambition, there you find disorder and every evil practice.

¹⁷But the wisdom that comes from heaven is first of all pure; then peace-loving, considerate, submissive, full of mercy and good fruit, impartial and sincere. ¹⁸Peacemakers who sow in peace reap a harvest of righteousness.

Submit yourselves to God

4 What causes fights and quarrels among you? Don't they come from your desires that battle within you? ²You desire but do not have, so you kill. You covet but you cannot get what you want, so you quarrel and fight. You do not have because you do not ask God. ³When you ask, you do not receive, because you ask with wrong motives, that you may spend what you get on your pleasures.

⁴You adulterous people,*a* don't you know that friendship with the world means enmity against God? Therefore, anyone who chooses to be a friend of the world becomes an enemy of God. ⁵Or do you think Scripture says without reason that he jealously longs for the spirit he has caused to dwell in us*b*? ⁶But he gives us more grace. That is why Scripture says:

'God opposes the proud
    but shows favour to the humble.'*c*

⁷Submit yourselves, then, to God. Resist the devil, and he will flee from you. ⁸Come near to God and he will come near to you. Wash your hands, you sinners, and purify your hearts, you double-minded. ⁹Grieve, mourn and wail. Change your laughter to mourning and your joy to gloom. ¹⁰Humble yourselves before the Lord, and he will lift you up.

¹¹Brothers and sisters, do not slander one another. Anyone who speaks against a brother or sister*d* or judges them speaks against the law and judges it. When you judge the law, you are not keeping it, but sitting in judgment on it. ¹²There is only one Lawgiver and Judge, the one who is able to save and destroy. But you – who are you to judge your neighbour?

Boasting about tomorrow

¹³Now listen, you who say, 'Today or tomorrow we will go to this or that city, spend a year there, carry on business and make money.' ¹⁴Why, you do not even know what will happen tomorrow. What is your life? You are a mist that appears for a little while and then vanishes. ¹⁵Instead, you ought to say, 'If it is the Lord's will, we will live and do this or that.' ¹⁶As it is, you boast in your arrogant schemes. All such boasting is evil. ¹⁷If anyone, then, knows the good they ought to do and doesn't do it, it is sin for them.

Warning to rich oppressors

5 Now listen, you rich people, weep and wail because of the misery that is coming on you. ²Your wealth has rotted, and moths have eaten your clothes. ³Your gold and silver are corroded. Their corrosion will testify against you and eat your flesh like fire. You have hoarded wealth in the last days. ⁴Look! The wages you failed to pay the workers who mowed your fields are crying out against you. The

---

a 4 An allusion to covenant unfaithfulness; see Hosea 3:1.
b 5 Or that the spirit he caused to dwell in us envies intensely; or that the Spirit he caused to dwell in us longs jealously

c 6 Prov. 3:34
d 11 The Greek word for *brother or sister* (adelphos) refers here to a believer, whether man or woman, as part of God's family.

WHY DOES GOD SOMETIMES FEEL DISTANT?

Feeling distant from God can be one of the most difficult experiences we face. It can seem as if we're isolated, abandoned and cut off. Thankfully, we're not alone. This is an experience shared by many in the Bible, and the Psalms are full of songs and poems written by people who felt cut off from God. Hebrews 13:8 tells us that God is always the same. This means he continues to love us and won't forsake us whether we feel close to him or distant.

James gives us two reasons why God may feel distant (James 4:8). The first of these is sin. When we continue to repeat the same sin over and over again, it can act like a barrier, keeping us from being close to God. Are there things in your life you know you're doing that are unhelpful for your relationship with God? Are there things you're doing that you know don't delight him?

James's second reason why we may feel distant from God is 'double-mindedness'. In the Gospels Jesus tells us to seek God's kingdom first in everything we do, which means having no desire or ambition greater than God. It's easy for us to be inconsistent in our desire for God; we say we have no desire greater than God, but the next moment we're forgetting God and pursuing our own interests. Be aware too that sometimes our busy schedule of church activities can be the very thing that stops us from hearing God clearly – focusing on getting through our busy schedules rather than on Jesus can also stop us from hearing God's voice.

When we're feeling separated from God and are desperate to hear his voice, we often expect him to speak loudly into our situation, but God isn't always like this. In 1 Kings 19:11–18, Elijah stands on a mountaintop to hear God's voice. He experiences a great wind, an earthquake and a mighty fire, but God isn't in any of those; God is in the quiet whisper after those things have passed. God's voice rarely booms and shouts; instead he speaks softly to us. You can only hear soft noises when you're close to them, and God wants us to be close to him.

One place where we can always hear God is through his Word. Don't give up on reading the Bible because you don't feel God speaking to you personally through it. Reading the Bible helps us identify the voice of God more easily in the rest of our lives.

So when God feels distant, the best thing we can do is to carry on praying and seeking him. Sometimes talking about it to trusted Christian friends helps too – there's something really contagious about being with people who love Jesus and are meeting with him, but the most important thing is to carry on seeking God wholeheartedly.

Freddie Pimm

cries of the harvesters have reached the ears of the Lord Almighty. **5** You have lived on earth in luxury and self-indulgence. You have fattened yourselves in the day of slaughter.*ᵃ* **6** You have condemned and

murdered the innocent one, who was not opposing you.

Patience in suffering

7 Be patient, then, brothers and sisters, until the Lord's coming. See how the farmer waits for the land to yield its

---

a 5 Or *yourselves as in a day of feasting*

CONSCIOUS CONSUMERISM

I personally don't employ harvesters, I definitely don't own any fields and I'm not even sure what a day of slaughter is, so how is James 5:1–5 related to me and my money?

When we look at where our clothes have been made, or when we think about where our daily breakfast comes from, we realise they have been made all around the world: my jeans are from China, my tea is from India and my chocolate spread is from Brazil. The people who picked the cotton for my jeans, or the leaves for my tea, or harvested the cocoa beans for my chocolate spread are harvesters who work in fields and may not receive a decent wage.

Everything we do connects us with people who employ workers and own a lot of fields. It connects us with people who work in fields and are not paid a fair wage – whose names and faces we will never know, but who made the shirt on our back and picked the orange we had for lunch.

When we spend our money, we're investing it and giving profit to the company we buy from – shoes, ice cream, bags, books, phones, etc. Although we're not directly employing the harvesters in the fields, we have a responsibility to them, because they are making something for us.

This is where we can become something very powerful: a conscious consumer – a consumer who buys what they need but does so in an intentional way. When we spend our money, we can use that moment to remember the people behind the products.

There are different ways to respond using your finances. You may stop buying from a particular brand and write to the company to tell them why. You could also purchase ethical brands wherever possible. And when you go into shops, approach them as a valued customer, letting them know your concerns, asking them about their policies and the working conditions of the people behind the products.

This is a really practical way in which we can use our money to speak up for those who are not treated fairly.

Kiera Singlehurst-Phyo

 Proverbs 31:10–31   Matthew 6:19–24 ▶

valuable crop, patiently waiting for the autumn and spring rains. **8** You too, be patient and stand firm, because the Lord's coming is near. **9** Don't grumble against one another, brothers and sisters, or you will be judged. The Judge is standing at the door!

10 Brothers and sisters, as an example of

patience in the face of suffering, take the prophets who spoke in the name of the Lord. **11** As you know, we count as blessed those who have persevered. You have heard of Job's perseverance and have seen what the Lord finally brought about. The Lord is full of compassion and mercy.

12 Above all, my brothers and sisters, do

PRAYER 8

IF ANYONE IS SICK OR IN TROUBLE ... PRAY

Today, as I write this, I have just been to a village in Kenya where they have been suffering from drought and famine. It hasn't rained there for three years. Last night a small group of Christian women gathered to pray for the village. They didn't pray to thank God for the human provision of the resources we had brought – they simply asked the Lord God to make it rain. As the rest of the team drove into the village today, the heavens opened and rain poured down. We still brought the food, but the local people spent all the time talking about the rain. They knew that only God could do that. Even today, it's true that the prayers of a group of righteous people are *'powerful and effective'* (James 5:16).

James 5:13–18 contains important advice on prayer. We should pray for ourselves – *'Is anyone among you in trouble? Let them pray'* (v. 13) – but we should also pray together for others. James asks, *'Is anyone among you ill?'* (v. 14). If so, he says, get the church to come and pray – and not in half-measures, not just a quick prayer after a long chat and a cup of tea. Make it the full deal! Ring round the leaders. Tell them all to be there. Get them to bring along a bottle of extra-virgin olive oil. As they pray together for you, get them to use the oil to symbolise the Holy Spirit's presence by pouring the oil on your head. *'And the prayer offered in faith will make the sick person well; the Lord will raise them up'* (v. 15). How cool is that!

And there's forgiveness as well (v. 15)! Something very like this happened when four people brought their friend to Jesus (Mark 2:1–12). They couldn't get through the crowd and so made a hole in the roof and lowered him on a stretcher in front of Jesus. It then says that Jesus saw the four friends' faith and told the man, *'Your sins are forgiven'* (Mark 2:5). So when we come together to pray and faithfully bring a friend before Jesus, we can expect to see miracles and we can expect to hear Jesus saying to them, 'Your sins are forgiven.'

When I read these things, it makes we want to pray with others, for others, with faith! Maybe we should all be doing more of that.

Hugo Anson

 Luke 17:11–19   Ephesians 6:10–20

not swear – not by heaven or by earth or by anything else. All you need to say is a simple 'Yes' or 'No'. Otherwise you will be condemned.

The prayer of faith

13 Is anyone among you in trouble? Let them pray. Is anyone happy? Let them sing songs of praise. 14 Is anyone among you ill? Let them call the elders of the church to pray over them and anoint them with oil in the name of the Lord. 15 And the prayer offered in faith will make the sick person well; the Lord will raise them up. If they have sinned, they will be forgiven. 16 Therefore confess your sins to each other and pray for each other so that you may be healed. The prayer of a righteous person is powerful and effective.

17 Elijah was a human being, even as we are. He prayed earnestly that it would not rain, and it did not rain on the land for three and a half years. 18 Again he prayed, and the heavens gave rain, and the earth produced its crops.

19 My brothers and sisters, if one of you should wander from the truth and someone should bring that person back, 20 remember this: whoever turns a sinner from the error of their way will save them from death and cover over a multitude of sins.

1 PETER

DATE

Early AD 60s

AUTHOR

The apostle Peter

WHAT'S IT ALL ABOUT?

Peter was one of Jesus' disciples and if you have read the Gospels, you will probably best remember him for awkward moments like when he denied ever knowing Jesus after he was arrested. You might also remember that despite that, Jesus said he would build his church through Peter, and that's exactly what he did. Peter was a strong leader in the early church and was used to the persecution that came with the territory. He didn't let it get him down: he kept going and in this letter he encourages other Christians to do the same. He reminds them that despite their sufferings, they are in fact very blessed by God. While the Jewish people had prayed and waited for years for the Messiah to come and redeem them, they are all living in that redemption. He also focuses on the positives of going through hard times, telling his readers that the process will refine them and therefore be of great benefit to them. He tells them that earthly suffering will help them let go of their own desires and instead focus on the will of God.

His letter also encourages his readers to be pure and holy, to live lives that will give no one any reason to accuse them of sin, and to follow Jesus' example not to retaliate when attacked. In addition he teaches about marriage, and submission to rulers and masters.

WHY SHOULD WE READ IT?

- To see how God can use suffering to develop your character.
- To be reminded what an amazing thing it is to live under the redemption of Jesus.
- To see that we are God's chosen people and we belong to him (1 Peter 2:9–10).
- To read Peter's thoughts on the nature of true beauty (1 Peter 3).
- To read about the human desires we should be letting go of and the godly ways we should be living (1 Peter 4).

Andy Croft with Liza Hoeksma

1 Peter, an apostle of Jesus Christ,

To God's select, exiles, scattered throughout the provinces of Pontus, Galatia, Cappadocia, Asia and Bithynia, 2 who have been chosen according to the foreknowledge of God the Father, through the sanctifying work of the Spirit, to be obedient to Jesus Christ and sprinkled with his blood:

Grace and peace be yours in abundance.

Praise to God for a living hope

3 Praise be to the God and Father of our Lord Jesus Christ! In his great mercy he has given us new birth into a living hope through the resurrection of Jesus Christ from the dead, 4 and into an inheritance that can never perish, spoil or fade. This inheritance is kept in heaven for you, 5 who through faith are shielded by God's power until the coming of the salvation that is ready to be revealed in the last time. 6 In all this you greatly rejoice, though now for a little while you may have had to suffer grief in all kinds of trials. 7 These have come so that the proven genuineness of your faith – of greater worth than gold, which perishes even though refined by fire – may result in praise, glory and honour when Jesus Christ is revealed. 8 Though you have not seen him, you love him; and even though you do not see him now, you believe in him and are filled with an inexpressible and glorious joy, 9 for you are receiving the end result of your faith, the salvation of your souls.

10 Concerning this salvation, the prophets, who spoke of the grace that was to come to you, searched intently and with the greatest care, 11 trying to find out the time and circumstances to which the Spirit of Christ in them was pointing when he predicted the sufferings of the Messiah and the glories that would follow. 12 It was revealed to them that they were not serving themselves but you, when they spoke of the things that have now been told you by those who have preached the gospel to you by the Holy Spirit sent from heaven. Even angels long to look into these things.

Be holy

13 Therefore, with minds that are alert and fully sober, set your hope on the grace to be brought to you when Jesus Christ is revealed at his coming. 14 As obedient children, do not conform to the evil desires you had when you lived in ignorance. 15 But just as he who called you is holy, so be holy in all you do; 16 for it is written: 'Be holy, because I am holy.' *a*

17 Since you call on a Father who judges each person's work impartially, live out your time as foreigners here in reverent fear. 18 For you know that it was not with perishable things such as silver or gold that you were redeemed from the empty way of life handed down to you from your ancestors, 19 but with the precious blood of Christ, a lamb without blemish or defect. 20 He was chosen before the creation of the world, but was revealed in these last times for your sake. 21 Through him you believe in God, who raised him from the dead and glorified him, and so your faith and hope are in God.

22 Now that you have purified yourselves by obeying the truth so that you have sincere love for each other, love one another deeply, from the heart. *b* 23 For you have been born again, not of perishable seed, but of imperishable, through the living and enduring word of God. 24 For,

'All people are like grass,
     and all their glory is like the flowers
          of the field;
the grass withers and the flowers fall,
25   but the word of the Lord endures for
          ever.' *c*

And this is the word that was preached to you.

2 Therefore, rid yourselves of all malice and all deceit, hypocrisy, envy, and slander of every kind. 2 Like newborn

---

a 16 Lev. 11:44,45; 19:2
b 22 Some early manuscripts *from a pure heart*
c 25 Isaiah 40:6-8 (see Septuagint)

babies, crave pure spiritual milk, so that by it you may grow up in your salvation, **3** now that you have tasted that the Lord is good.

The living Stone and a chosen people

4 As you come to him, the living Stone – rejected by humans but chosen by God and precious to him – **5** you also, like living stones, are being built into a spiritual house*a* to be a holy priesthood, offering spiritual sacrifices acceptable to God through Jesus Christ. **6** For in Scripture it says:

'See, I lay a stone in Zion,
 a chosen and precious cornerstone,
and the one who trusts in him
 will never be put to shame.'*b*

7 Now to you who believe, this stone is precious. But to those who do not believe,

'The stone the builders rejected
 has become the cornerstone,'*c*

8 and,

'A stone that causes people to stumble
and a rock that makes them fall.'*d*

They stumble because they disobey the message – which is also what they were destined for.

9 But you are a chosen people, a royal priesthood, a holy nation, God's special possession, that you may declare the praises of him who called you out of darkness into his wonderful light. **10** Once you were not a people, but now you are the people of God; once you had not received mercy, but now you have received mercy.

Living godly lives in a pagan society

11 Dear friends, I urge you, as foreigners and exiles, to abstain from sinful desires, which wage war against your soul. **12** Live such good lives among the pagans that, though they accuse you of doing wrong,

they may see your good deeds and glorify God on the day he visits us.

13 Submit yourselves for the Lord's sake to every human authority: whether to the emperor, as the supreme authority, **14** or to governors, who are sent by him to punish those who do wrong and to commend those who do right. **15** For it is God's will that by doing good you should silence the ignorant talk of foolish people. **16** Live as free people, but do not use your freedom as a cover-up for evil; live as God's slaves. **17** Show proper respect to everyone, love the family of believers, fear God, honour the emperor.

18 Slaves, in reverent fear of God submit yourselves to your masters, not only to those who are good and considerate, but also to those who are harsh. **19** For it is commendable if someone bears up under the pain of unjust suffering because they are conscious of God. **20** But how is it to your credit if you receive a beating for doing wrong and endure it? But if you suffer for doing good and you endure it, this is commendable before God. **21** To this you were called, because Christ suffered for you, leaving you an example, that you should follow in his steps.

22 'He committed no sin,
 and no deceit was found in his
 mouth.'*e*

23 When they hurled their insults at him, he did not retaliate; when he suffered, he made no threats. Instead, he entrusted himself to him who judges justly. **24** 'He himself bore our sins' in his body on the cross, so that we might die to sins and live for righteousness; 'by his wounds you have been healed.' **25** For 'you were like sheep going astray,'*f* but now you have returned to the Shepherd and Overseer of your souls.

3 Wives, in the same way submit yourselves to your own husbands so that, if any of them do not believe the word, they may be won over without words by

a5 Or *into a temple of the Spirit*
b6 Isaiah 28:16
c7 Psalm 118:22
d8 Isaiah 8:14

e22 Isaiah 53:9
f24,25 Isaiah 53:4,5,6 (see Septuagint)

HEALING & MIRACLES 2

Understanding what's ours

The words of 1 Peter 2:24 are an important foundation to our understanding of healing. 'Why does someone get healed?' 'What do I have to do for God to heal me?' 'If I don't get healed, is it because I did something wrong?' Questions like these are asked all the time by those who are searching and in need.

There are many teachings on why we deserve healing, but we need to bear in mind that anything we receive from God is not because of what we have done or deserve, but because we serve a gracious God who is full of mercy. His love for us is so great that he desires to see us become whole. He paid a price, because he wants to see you receive the full freedom he bought. It would be extremely frustrating to pay a huge price for something that no one used or saw as valuable!

The price has already been paid for our healing, yet many choose not to believe. Often our low expectations come from seeing someone we love die, or remain sick for their whole life. The Bible says God is full of compassion. Therefore, if I say I have compassion for someone and God doesn't seem to (because I want them to be healed and God doesn't heal them), I'm indirectly implying that I have more compassion than God. This isn't possible! God loved us so much that he sent his Son to die for us so we might have freedom.

The beatings Jesus took upon his body at the cross were in exchange for our healing. It's not a question of whether you're good enough to be healed, or if it's God's desire to heal you. Before you were born, that price was already paid. You're worth it because he saw you as worth it. Healing is not about our worth, but about how worthy God is. One of God's names is *Rapha,* 'Healer'.

The Bible says, *'We are healed'* (Isaiah 53:5). Our healing is a done deal. Now we just have to live in it. Healing comes in all forms, physical, emotional and spiritual: Jesus wants us completely whole. So even if your body may not be completely healed, what has God healed? Has he not given you a new mind – the mind of Christ? If it's physical healing you're waiting for, has your physical endurance brought about healing, or a fullness of life in another way?

Many times it's much easier to see the healing that hasn't taken place rather than the healing that has. Look at what God has already changed in your life. Look at the areas where maybe before you were an emotional wreck, but now you feel free. Write out the things God has healed in your life and live in that place, remembering this is part of your inheritance. It always gives the Father joy when his children walk in the inheritance he has left for them.

Christy Wimber

 Matthew 15:21–28   2 Kings 5:1–19

the behaviour of their wives, 2 when they see the purity and reverence of your lives. 3 Your beauty should not come from outward adornment, such as elaborate hairstyles and the wearing of gold jewellery or fine clothes. 4 Rather, it should be that of your inner self, the unfading beauty of a gentle and quiet spirit, which is of great worth in God's sight. 5 For this is the way the holy women of the past who put their hope in God used to adorn themselves. They submitted themselves to their own husbands, 6 like Sarah, who obeyed Abraham and called him her lord. You are her daughters if you do what is right and do not give way to fear.

7 Husbands, in the same way be considerate as you live with your wives, and treat them with respect as the weaker partner and as heirs with you of the gracious gift of life, so that nothing will hinder your prayers.

Suffering for doing good

8 Finally, all of you, be like-minded, be sympathetic, love one another, be compassionate and humble. 9 Do not repay evil with evil or insult with insult. On the contrary, repay evil with blessing, because to this you were called so that you may inherit a blessing. 10 For,

'Whoever would love life
    and see good days
must keep their tongue from evil
    and their lips from deceitful speech.
11 They must turn from evil and do good;
    they must seek peace and pursue it.
12 For the eyes of the Lord are on the
        righteous
    and his ears are attentive to their
        prayer,
but the face of the Lord is against those
    who do evil.' a

13 Who is going to harm you if you are eager to do good? 14 But even if you should suffer for what is right, you are blessed. 'Do not fear their threats b; do not be

frightened.' c 15 But in your hearts revere Christ as Lord. Always be prepared to give an answer to everyone who asks you to give the reason for the hope that you have. But do this with gentleness and respect, 16 keeping a clear conscience, so that those who speak maliciously against your good behaviour in Christ may be ashamed of their slander. 17 For it is better, if it is God's will, to suffer for doing good than for doing evil. 18 For Christ also suffered once for sins, the righteous for the unrighteous, to bring you to God. He was put to death in the body but made alive in the Spirit. 19 After being made alive, d he went and made proclamation to the imprisoned spirits – 20 to those who were disobedient long ago when God waited patiently in the days of Noah while the ark was being built. In it only a few people, eight in all, were saved through water, 21 and this water symbolises baptism that now saves you also – not the removal of dirt from the body but the pledge of a clear conscience towards God. e It saves you by the resurrection of Jesus Christ, 22 who has gone into heaven and is at God's right hand – with angels, authorities and powers in submission to him.

Living for God

4 Therefore, since Christ suffered in his body, arm yourselves also with the same attitude, because whoever suffers in the body has finished with sin. 2 As a result, they do not live the rest of their earthly lives for evil human desires, but rather for the will of God. 3 For you have spent enough time in the past doing what pagans choose to do – living in debauchery, lust, drunkenness, orgies, carousing and detestable idolatry. 4 They are surprised that you do not join them in their reckless, wild living, and they heap abuse on you. 5 But they will have to give account to him who is ready to judge the living and the dead. 6 For this is the reason the gospel was preached even to those who are now

---

a 12 Psalm 34:12-16
b 14 Or fear what they fear
c 14 Isaiah 8:12
d 18,19 Or but made alive in the spirit, 19 in which also
e 21 Or but an appeal to God for a clear conscience

dead, so that they might be judged according to human standards in regard to the body, but live according to God in regard to the spirit.

7 The end of all things is near. Therefore be alert and of sober mind so that you may pray. 8 Above all, love each other deeply, because love covers over a multitude of sins. 9 Offer hospitality to one another without grumbling. 10 Each of you should use whatever gift you have received to serve others, as faithful stewards of God's grace in its various forms. 11 If anyone speaks, they should do so as one who speaks the very words of God.

If anyone serves, they should do so with the strength God provides, so that in all things God may be praised through Jesus Christ. To him be the glory and the power for ever and ever. Amen.

Suffering for being a Christian

12 Dear friends, do not be surprised at the fiery ordeal that has come on you to test you, as though something strange were happening to you. 13 But rejoice inasmuch as you participate in the sufferings of Christ, so that you may be overjoyed when his glory is revealed. 14 If you are insulted because of the name of Christ, you

EVANGELISM 7

Be prepared

A few years ago, a group of my mates talked me into cycling the Coast to Coast route (236 miles). I was determined that I wasn't going to be caught out and that I would be prepared. Not only did my bike need preparing, but I also needed to be fit and ready. Similarly, 1 Peter 3:15 urges us to be prepared for those who have questions. Like the cycling, we need to be prepared both in ourselves and with refined and ready tools.

A great tool that we have is our own faith story. Many times we see Paul share his story to great effect. When we share our story, it's good to steer clear of religious jargon and speak in ways that those listening will understand. Keeping your story sharp is also helpful. Could you tell it in 2–5 minutes? Whatever your story is, don't belittle it. There are people whose lives are very similar to yours and they will be fascinated to hear how you found God.

Always being prepared to give an answer can seem really scary. I'll be honest: we do need to know what we believe and why we believe it! But as we mature in our walk with God, we will naturally learn and understand more of the Christian faith. When the questions get tough, don't feel pressurised to make up an answer. If you don't know the answer, tell them you don't know, but say you will find out. Remember, you're not doing this alone. Ask other Christians who can help you with some of the tougher questions.

To be prepared means that we are alert and alive to the possibilities around us. Are you prepared in your heart to grab those moments when they present themselves? Don't worry about 'getting it right' – just be yourself and be prepared with an open and honest answer.

Mark Ritchie

 Luke 10:30–37   2 Chronicles 7:14

are blessed, for the Spirit of glory and of God rests on you. ¹⁵ If you suffer, it should not be as a murderer or thief or any other kind of criminal, or even as a meddler. ¹⁶ However, if you suffer as a Christian, do not be ashamed, but praise God that you

DEPRESSION

I can't really pinpoint when my depression began – it crept in and made itself comfy while I was busy trying to deal with other things, like life. I hadn't felt particularly happy for a while, but I put that down to a series of circumstances. Then, one day, someone made me laugh. As I laughed I realised something didn't feel normal: I hadn't laughed in a long time. I realised I had been this way for months and that was when the tears started. I'm no stranger to tears, but those preceding months had been different. No tears, and no laughter either; just a real numbness.

So much happened in the following months. My healing took time, both with God and with some faithful and wonderful friends. Over the months of healing, I was forced to accept three things.

1. **It's OK to sit in God's presence and say nothing.** (1 Peter 5:7). Sometimes we can do nothing more. God is our Father and we are his children – there's a place for silence and letting his presence be your comfort. No pressure. Just you and your Dad.

2. **We live under grace and not law.** We're all supposed to know this, but knowing it is another thing entirely. Yes, in order to know God, to become like him and to live lives that please him, we need to be reading his Word and spending time with him in prayer – but we live under grace, not law; relationship, not legalism. If I couldn't pick up my Bible, God understood, and he just kept me close while I chose to let myself off the hook and simply rest in his presence.

3. **It's OK to let your friends do the work.** If it's good enough for a lame man to be dropped in front of Jesus through a hole in the roof by the strength of his mates (Luke 5:17–26), then it's good enough for you and me. We don't know if the man was desperate for healing and pleaded with his friends to take him to Jesus, or if the friends had faith when the man's own had run out. The end result was the same: the man was touched by Jesus and healed.

The prayers of my family and friends supported me and carried me to Jesus. I was crippled and couldn't walk myself. It was hard to believe that this was OK, and that the Lord finds us acceptable in that state to enter his presence, but I know now that he does.

I'm so thankful for the gift of prayer. I'm also thankful for Prozac. In my case I needed a good dose of both. It was a painful time and I wouldn't want to go there again. However, there has been something so healthy about being in that place of weakness, resting in God and allowing his presence to be my comfort and healing. I think I'll just take it a day at a time...

Ali Martin

bear that name. [17] For it is time for judgment to begin with God's household; and if it begins with us, what will the outcome be for those who do not obey the gospel of God? [18] And,

> 'If it is hard for the righteous to be saved,
>> what will become of the ungodly and the sinner?'[a]

[19] So then, those who suffer according to God's will should commit themselves to their faithful Creator and continue to do good.

To the elders and the flock

5 To the elders among you, I appeal as a fellow elder and a witness of Christ's sufferings who also will share in the glory to be revealed: [2] be shepherds of God's flock that is under your care, watching over them – not because you must, but because you are willing, as God wants you to be; not pursuing dishonest gain, but eager to serve; [3] not lording it over those entrusted to you, but being examples to the flock. [4] And when the Chief Shepherd appears, you will receive the crown of glory that will never fade away.

[5] In the same way, you who are younger, submit yourselves to your elders. All of you, clothe yourselves with humility towards one another, because,

> 'God opposes the proud
>> but shows favour to the humble.'[a]

[6] Humble yourselves, therefore, under God's mighty hand, that he may lift you up in due time. [7] Cast all your anxiety on him because he cares for you.

[8] Be alert and of sober mind. Your enemy the devil prowls around like a roaring lion looking for someone to devour. [9] Resist him, standing firm in the faith, because you know that the family of believers throughout the world is undergoing the same kind of sufferings.

[10] And the God of all grace, who called you to his eternal glory in Christ, after you have suffered a little while, will himself restore you and make you strong, firm and steadfast. [11] To him be the power for ever and ever. Amen.

Final greetings

[12] With the help of Silas,[b] whom I regard as a faithful brother, I have written to you briefly, encouraging you and testifying that this is the true grace of God. Stand fast in it.

[13] She who is in Babylon, chosen together with you, sends you her greetings, and so does my son Mark. [14] Greet one another with a kiss of love.

Peace to all of you who are in Christ.

---

a 18 Prov. 11:31 (see Septuagint)

a 5 Prov. 3:34   *b* 12 Greek *Silvanus*, a variant of *Silas*

2 PETER

DATE

This letter was probably written around AD 65–68

AUTHOR

The apostle Peter

WHAT'S IT ALL ABOUT?

While Peter's first letter was concerned with external sources of conflict in the form of the persecution the church was facing, this second one deals with internal sources – the false teachers and people intent on evil among them. Peter knew he was near the end of his own life, but he wanted to write to them so they would remember God's truths after he had died. His teaching counters the false claims being made – and Peter, of course, was in a good position to teach the truth as he was an eyewitness to Jesus' ministry. He reassures his readers that Jesus will return to bring judgement and, though it might seem slow in happening to their eyes, it will certainly be as Jesus promised. He also teaches how people should live in the meantime, urging them to be of good character and to keep growing as Christians.

WHY SHOULD WE READ IT?

- To be reminded that God has given us everything we need to live for him (2 Peter 1).

- To see the qualities Peter tells us will keep us from being ineffective and unproductive in our faith (2 Peter 1:5–11).

- To see that God can rescue the godly from their trials, but will judge those who do evil (2 Peter 2).

- To be reminded that God is patient and wants everyone to receive his forgiveness (2 Peter 3:8–9).

- To read Paul's teaching on Jesus' return (2 Peter 3:10–13).

Andy Croft with Liza Hoeksma

1
Simon Peter, a servant and apostle of Jesus Christ,

To those who through the righteousness of our God and Saviour Jesus Christ have received a faith as precious as ours:

2 Grace and peace be yours in abundance through the knowledge of God and of Jesus our Lord.

Confirming one's calling and election

3 His divine power has given us everything we need for a godly life through our knowledge of him who called us by his own glory and goodness. 4 Through these he has given us his very great and precious promises, so that through them you may participate in the divine nature, having escaped the corruption in the world caused by evil desires.

5 For this very reason, make every effort to add to your faith goodness; and to goodness, knowledge; 6 and to knowledge, self-control; and to self-control, perseverance; and to perseverance, godliness; 7 and to godliness, mutual affection; and to mutual affection, love. 8 For if you possess these qualities in increasing measure, they will keep you from being ineffective and unproductive in your knowledge of our Lord Jesus Christ. 9 But whoever does not have them is short-sighted and blind, forgetting that they have been cleansed from their past sins.

10 Therefore, my brothers and sisters,*a* make every effort to confirm your calling and election. For if you do these things, you will never stumble, 11 and you will receive a rich welcome into the eternal kingdom of our Lord and Saviour Jesus Christ.

Prophecy of Scripture

12 So I will always remind you of these things, even though you know them and are firmly established in the truth you now have. 13 I think it is right to refresh your memory as long as I live in the tent of this body, 14 because I know that I will soon put it aside, as our Lord Jesus Christ has made clear to me. 15 And I will make every effort to see that after my departure you will always be able to remember these things.

16 For we did not follow cleverly devised stories when we told you about the coming of our Lord Jesus Christ in power, but we were eye-witnesses of his majesty. 17 He received honour and glory from God the Father when the voice came to him from the Majestic Glory, saying, 'This is my Son, whom I love; with him I am well pleased.'*b* 18 We ourselves heard this voice that came from heaven when we were with him on the sacred mountain.

19 We also have the prophetic message as something completely reliable, and you will do well to pay attention to it, as to a light shining in a dark place, until the day dawns and the morning star rises in your hearts. 20 Above all, you must understand that no prophecy of Scripture came about by the prophet's own interpretation of things. 21 For prophecy never had its origin in the human will, but prophets, though human, spoke from God as they were carried along by the Holy Spirit.

False teachers and their destruction

2
But there were also false prophets among the people, just as there will be false teachers among you. They will secretly introduce destructive heresies, even denying the sovereign Lord who bought them – bringing swift destruction on themselves. 2 Many will follow their depraved conduct and will bring the way of truth into disrepute. 3 In their greed these teachers will exploit you with fabricated stories. Their condemnation has long been hanging over them, and their destruction has not been sleeping.

4 For if God did not spare angels when they sinned, but sent them to hell,*a* putting them in chains of darkness*b* to be

---

a 10 The Greek word for *brothers and sisters* (*adelphoi*) refers here to believers, both men and women, as part of God's family.

b 17 Matt. 17:5; Mark 9:7; Luke 9:35
a 4 Greek *Tartarus*
b 4 Some manuscripts *in gloomy dungeons*

held for judgment; **5**if he did not spare the ancient world when he brought the flood on its ungodly people, but protected Noah, a preacher of righteousness, and seven others; **6**if he condemned the cities of Sodom and Gomorrah by burning them to ashes, and made them an example of what is going to happen to the ungodly; **7**and if he rescued Lot, a righteous man, who was distressed by the depraved conduct of the lawless **8**(for that righteous man, living among them day after day, was tormented in his righteous soul by the lawless deeds he saw and heard) – **9**if this is so, then the Lord knows how to rescue the godly from trials and to hold the unrighteous for punishment on the day of judgment. **10**This is especially true of those who follow the corrupt desire of the flesh*c* and despise authority.

Bold and arrogant, they are not afraid to heap abuse on celestial beings; **11**yet even angels, although they are stronger and more powerful, do not heap abuse on such beings when bringing judgment on them from*d* the Lord. **12**But these people blaspheme in matters they do not understand. They are like unreasoning animals, creatures of instinct, born only to be caught and destroyed, and like animals they too will perish.

13They will be paid back with harm for the harm they have done. Their idea of pleasure is to carouse in broad daylight. They are blots and blemishes, revelling in their pleasures while they feast with you.*e* **14**With eyes full of adultery, they never stop sinning; they seduce the unstable; they are experts in greed – an accursed brood! **15**They have left the straight way and wandered off to follow the way of Balaam son of Bezer,*f* who loved the wages of wickedness. **16**But he was rebuked for his wrongdoing by a donkey – an animal without speech – who spoke with a human voice and restrained the prophet's madness.

17These people are springs without water and mists driven by a storm. Blackest darkness is reserved for them. **18**For they mouth empty, boastful words and, by appealing to the lustful desires of the flesh, they entice people who are just escaping from those who live in error. **19**They promise them freedom, while they themselves are slaves of depravity – for 'people are slaves to whatever has mastered them.' **20**If they have escaped the corruption of the world by knowing our Lord and Saviour Jesus Christ and are again entangled in it and are overcome, they are worse off at the end than they were at the beginning. **21**It would have been better for them not to have known the way of righteousness, than to have known it and then to turn their backs on the sacred command that was passed on to them. **22**Of them the proverbs are true: 'A dog returns to its vomit,'*g* and, 'A sow that is washed returns to her wallowing in the mud.'

The day of the Lord

3 Dear friends, this is now my second letter to you. I have written both of them as reminders to stimulate you to wholesome thinking. **2**I want you to recall the words spoken in the past by the holy prophets and the command given by our Lord and Saviour through your apostles.

3Above all, you must understand that in the last days scoffers will come, scoffing and following their own evil desires. **4**They will say, 'Where is this "coming" he promised? Ever since our ancestors died, everything goes on as it has since the beginning of creation.' **5**But they deliberately forget that long ago by God's word the heavens came into being and the earth was formed out of water and by water. **6**By these waters also the world of that time was deluged and destroyed. **7**By the same word the present heavens and earth are reserved for fire, being kept for the day of judgment and destruction of the ungodly.

c 10 In contexts like this, the Greek word for *flesh* (*sarx*) refers to the sinful state of human beings, often presented as a power in opposition to the Spirit; also in verse 18.
d 11 Many manuscripts *beings in the presence of*
e 13 Some manuscripts *in their love feasts*
f 15 Greek *Bosor*
g 22 Prov. 26:11

THE BIG STORY 10

Heaven and earth made new

God's Big Story has a big ending. In 2 Peter 3:10–13 it's called *'the day of the Lord'*. This is when Jesus returns, as he promised. It's also the time of the final judgement. Peter repeats Jesus' teaching that he will return *'like a thief'* (v. 10), that is, unexpectedly (see Matthew 24:42–44). We're not meant to try to work out when it will happen.

Peter uses a dramatic picture of a blazing fire, so hot that the elements melt and the heavens are dissolved. This is a metaphor, a picture to help us understand. It's not meant to be literal. (The heavens aren't physical, so literal fire wouldn't melt them!) Often in the Bible fire is a metaphor for purification. Gold is melted so that the impurities can be scooped off and what's left will be pure. When Jesus the pure and holy one returns, the whole universe – invisible to us (the heavens) and visible (the earth) – will be purified. The result will be *'a new heaven and a new earth'* (v. 13). The New Testament was written in Greek, and there are two Greek words for 'new'. The one used here means 'renewed' or 'made new'. It doesn't mean that the old will be destroyed and completely new ones created instead. God's final fire will purify all time and all history. Only the things which survive that purifying can have a place in the renewed heavens and earth. In neither the visible nor the (to us) invisible world will anything evil survive.

Note that the future God has prepared for us includes a future for the earth. We won't be disembodied spirits in a purely 'spiritual' world. We will have transformed bodies, like the one Jesus took into the presence of the Father. We will experience a transformed earth and physical universe as well as the heavens. It will be different. It's hard for us to imagine. But there will be real continuity between this life and the next, eternal one. This means that in this life we can do things which last into the next. It matters, for instance, how we treat the planet, for the planet has an eternal future!

Peter is writing to Christians (2 Peter 1:1–2). Those who have already been cleansed by Jesus need not fear this purifying fire. They can be sure of their salvation. But Peter doesn't want them to scrape into this new world. (Paul says the same, in 1 Corinthians 3:11–15.) He wants them to live the life of the future world today, to be holy and hasten the coming of the day of the Lord by actions that bring Jesus near to others and treat God's creation with proper respect. If you're awed by this picture of purifying fire, ask yourself Peter's question: *'What kind of people ought you to be?'* (v. 11). Don't try to work out when he will come. Live the life you want him to see when he does!

Graham Cray

Colossians 1:18–20

8 But do not forget this one thing, dear friends: with the Lord a day is like a thousand years, and a thousand years are like a day. **9** The Lord is not slow in keeping his promise, as some understand slowness. Instead he is patient with you, not wanting anyone to perish, but everyone to come to repentance.

10 But the day of the Lord will come like a thief. The heavens will disappear with a roar; the elements will be destroyed by fire, and the earth and everything done in it will be laid bare.*ᵃ*

11 Since everything will be destroyed in this way, what kind of people ought you to be? You ought to live holy and godly lives **12** as you look forward to the day of God and speed its coming.*ᵇ* That day will bring about the destruction of the heavens by fire, and the elements will melt in the heat. **13** But in keeping with his promise we are looking forward to a new heaven and a new earth, where righteousness dwells.

14 So then, dear friends, since you are looking forward to this, make every effort to be found spotless, blameless and at peace with him. **15** Bear in mind that our Lord's patience means salvation, just as our dear brother Paul also wrote to you with the wisdom that God gave him. **16** He writes the same way in all his letters, speaking in them of these matters. His letters contain some things that are hard to understand, which ignorant and unstable people distort, as they do the other Scriptures, to their own destruction.

17 Therefore, dear friends, since you have been forewarned, be on your guard so that you may not be carried away by the error of the lawless and fall from your secure position. **18** But grow in the grace and knowledge of our Lord and Saviour Jesus Christ. To him be glory both now and for ever! Amen.

---

a 10 Some manuscripts *be burned up*
b 12 Or *as you wait eagerly for the day of God to come*

1 JOHN

DATE

This letter was probably written between AD 85 and 95

AUTHOR

The apostle John (who also wrote one of the Gospels)

WHAT'S IT ALL ABOUT?

We don't know much about who John was writing to, and this may have been a circular letter sent to a number of churches. It seems that the readers had been influenced by incorrect teaching and John is writing to put right their misunderstandings and point people back to the truth about Jesus. The letter is also focused on one of John's favourite topics: love. In his Gospel he refers to himself as *'the disciple whom Jesus loved'* (John 13:23) and this love obviously had a profound effect on him. He overflows with talk of how God is love, how he lavishes great love upon us, how he calls us his children, how he showed his love for us by sending Jesus to die for us, and how anyone who lives in love lives in God. He encourages his readers to love God and to love each other in response to this awesome love; but he also warns that the world may well hate them for it. He also teaches them to live in God's light instead of the darkness they knew before, knowing that *'Whoever has the Son has life'* (5:12).

WHY SHOULD WE READ IT?

- To be reminded of God's amazing love for us and the importance of loving one another.

- To see that we love and serve God as a response to knowing and receiving his great love for us (1 John 4).

- To be reminded that we have all messed up, but God will forgive us if we confess our sin (1 John 1:5–10).

- To remember that God has overcome the enemy and is stronger than him (1 John 4:4).

Andy Croft with Liza Hoeksma

The incarnation of the Word of life

1 That which was from the beginning, which we have heard, which we have seen with our eyes, which we have looked at and our hands have touched – this we proclaim concerning the Word of life. ²The life appeared; we have seen it and testify to it, and we proclaim to you the eternal life, which was with the Father and has appeared to us. ³We proclaim to you what we have seen and heard, so that you also may have fellowship with us. And our fellowship is with the Father and with his Son, Jesus Christ. ⁴We write this to make our*a* joy complete.

Light and darkness, sin and forgiveness

⁵This is the message we have heard from him and declare to you: God is light; in him there is no darkness at all. ⁶If we claim to have fellowship with him and yet walk in the darkness, we lie and do not live out the truth. ⁷But if we walk in the light, as he is in the light, we have fellowship with one another, and the blood of Jesus, his Son, purifies us from all*b* sin.

⁸If we claim to be without sin, we deceive ourselves and the truth is not in us. ⁹If we confess our sins, he is faithful and just and will forgive us our sins and purify us from all unrighteousness. ¹⁰If we claim we have not sinned, we make him out to be a liar and his word is not in us.

2 My dear children, I write this to you so that you will not sin. But if anybody does sin, we have an advocate with the Father – Jesus Christ, the Righteous One. ²He is the atoning sacrifice for our sins, and not only for ours but also for the sins of the whole world.

Love and hatred for fellow believers

³We know that we have come to know him if we keep his commands. ⁴Whoever says, 'I know him,' but does not do what he commands is a liar, and the truth is not in that person. ⁵But if anyone obeys his word, love for God*a* is truly made

complete in them. This is how we know we are in him: ⁶whoever claims to live in him must live as Jesus did.

⁷Dear friends, I am not writing you a new command but an old one, which you have had since the beginning. This old command is the message you have heard. ⁸Yet I am writing you a new command; its truth is seen in him and in you, because the darkness is passing and the true light is already shining.

⁹Anyone who claims to be in the light but hates a brother or sister*b* is still in the darkness. ¹⁰Anyone who loves their brother and sister*c* lives in the light, and there is nothing in them to make them stumble. ¹¹But anyone who hates a brother or sister is in the darkness and walks around in the darkness. They do not know where they are going, because the darkness has blinded them.

Reasons for writing

¹²I am writing to you, dear children,
　　because your sins have been
　　　　forgiven on account of his
　　　　name.
¹³I am writing to you, fathers,
　　because you know him who is from
　　　　the beginning.
I am writing to you, young men,
　　because you have overcome the evil
　　　　one.

¹⁴I write to you, dear children,
　　because you know the Father.
I write to you, fathers,
　　because you know him who is from
　　　　the beginning.
I write to you, young men,
　　because you are strong,
　　and the word of God lives in you,
　　and you have overcome the evil one.

---

b 9 The Greek word for *brother or sister* (*adelphos*) refers here to a believer, whether man or woman, as part of God's family; also in verse 11; and in 3:15, 17; 4:20; 5:16.
c 10 The Greek word for *brother and sister* (*adelphos*) refers here to a believer, whether man or woman, as part of God's family; also in 3:10; 4:20, 21.

---

a 4 Some manuscripts *your*
b 7 Or *every*
a 5 Or *word, God's love*

THE BIG STORY 7

Jesus dies for our forgiveness

There are many passages explaining the meaning of Jesus' death, using different pictures to help us understand. The verses in 1 John 1:5–10 explain it very clearly.

God and sinful people are as opposite as light and darkness. God's character is righteous, morally perfect. As fallen humans, we sin and are unrighteous. To be restored to God we need to be made clean, to be purified. We can't do this for ourselves. Our only hope is for someone to do it for us. Jesus, God's Son, does for us what we can't do. He dies for us, and his blood, meaning his death, is the only thing that can make us clean. His death was for everyone, and he loves everyone equally, but forgiveness is not forced on us. We have to recognise our need and confess our sins, rather than *'claim we have not sinned'* (v. 10). But if we confess, God is utterly reliable and will forgive and cleanse us.

Verse 5 tells us that *'God is light'*. But this letter by John goes on to say that God is also love. *'This is how God showed his love among us: he sent his one and only Son into the world that we might live through him. This is love: not that we loved God, but that he loved us and sent his Son as an atoning sacrifice for our sins'* (1 John 4:9–10). The cross shows what God's love means. It means that God has taken the initiative, loving us when we didn't love him, and in Jesus, sacrificing himself for our sins. The Bible frequently uses sacrifice as an explanation for the cross. In the Old Testament there was a system of animal sacrifice in the temple. In particular the high priest offered a sacrifice for the sins of the people each year, on the Day of Atonement. Jesus, our high priest, gave himself as that atoning sacrifice (1 John 4:10) once and for all, so that it would never need to be made again (see also Hebrews 9:11–12). God's Son sacrifices himself for God's fallen human creatures. The death of Jesus provides the basis for our forgiveness and is the basis for the assurance that we have been forgiven. Assurance is not arrogance, presuming on God's mercy. It's taking God at his word, because God's actions on the cross of Jesus could not speak more clearly.

Perhaps the most amazing statement in these verses is the claim that, in forgiving us, because of the death of Jesus, God is *'just'* (v. 9). How can it be just when one person who is innocent dies for those who admit they are guilty? God is light. God takes sin with great moral seriousness. It can't be ignored. But God is also love, utterly committed to restore fallen humans to himself at whatever personal cost. The purpose of his justice is *restoration,* not just the payment of the proper penalty. The world needs justice like this.

Graham Cray

 Luke 1:26–48   Ephesians 1:19–23

On not loving the world

¹⁵ Do not love the world or anything in the world. If anyone loves the world, love for the Father[d] is not in them. ¹⁶ For everything in the world – the lust of the flesh, the lust of the eyes, and the pride of life – comes not from the Father but from the world. ¹⁷ The world and its desires pass away, but whoever does the will of God lives for ever.

Warnings against denying the Son

¹⁸ Dear children, this is the last hour; and as you have heard that the antichrist is coming, even now many antichrists have come. This is how we know it is the last hour. ¹⁹ They went out from us, but they did not really belong to us. For if they had belonged to us, they would have remained with us; but their going showed that none of them belonged to us. ²⁰ But you have an anointing from the Holy One, and all of you know the truth.[e] ²¹ I do not write to you because you do not know the truth, but because you do know it and because no lie comes from the truth. ²² Who is the liar? It is whoever denies that Jesus is the Christ. Such a person is the antichrist – denying the Father and the Son. ²³ No one who denies the Son has the Father; whoever acknowledges the Son has the Father also.

²⁴ As for you, see that what you have heard from the beginning remains in you. If it does, you also will remain in the Son and in the Father. ²⁵ And this is what he promised us – eternal life.

²⁶ I am writing these things to you about those who are trying to lead you astray. ²⁷ As for you, the anointing you received from him remains in you, and you do not need anyone to teach you. But as his anointing teaches you about all things and as that anointing is real, not counterfeit – just as it has taught you, remain in him.

God's children and sin

²⁸ And now, dear children, continue in him, so that when he appears we may be confident and unashamed before him at his coming.

²⁹ If you know that he is righteous, you know that everyone who does what is right has been born of him.

3 See what great love the Father has lavished on us, that we should be called children of God! And that is what we are! The reason the world does not know us is that it did not know him. ² Dear friends, now we are children of God, and what we will be has not yet been made known. But we know that when Christ appears,[a] we shall be like him, for we shall see him as he is. ³ All who have this hope in him purify themselves, just as he is pure.

⁴ Everyone who sins breaks the law; in fact, sin is lawlessness. ⁵ But you know that he appeared so that he might take away our sins. And in him is no sin. ⁶ No one who lives in him keeps on sinning. No one who continues to sin has either seen him or known him.

⁷ Dear children, do not let anyone lead you astray. The one who does what is right is righteous, just as he is righteous. ⁸ The one who does what is sinful is of the devil, because the devil has been sinning from the beginning. The reason the Son of God appeared was to destroy the devil's work. ⁹ No one who is born of God will continue to sin, because God's seed remains in them; they cannot go on sinning, because they have been born of God. ¹⁰ This is how we know who the children of God are and who the children of the devil are: anyone who does not do what is right is not God's child, nor is anyone who does not love their brother and sister.

More on love and hatred

¹¹ For this is the message you heard from the beginning: we should love one another. ¹² Do not be like Cain, who belonged to the evil one and murdered his brother. And why did he murder him? Because his own actions were evil and his brother's were righteous. ¹³ Do not be

---

d 15 Or world, the Father's love
e 20 Some manuscripts and you know all things

a 2 Or when it is made known

surprised, my brothers and sisters,b if the world hates you. 14We know that we have passed from death to life, because we love each other. Anyone who does not love remains in death. 15Anyone who hates a brother or sister is a murderer, and you know that no murderer has eternal life residing in him.

16This is how we know what love is: Jesus Christ laid down his life for us. And we ought to lay down our lives for our brothers and sisters. 17If anyone has material possessions and sees a brother or sister in need but has no pity on them, how can the love of God be in that person? 18Dear children, let us not love with words or speech but with actions and in truth.

19This is how we know that we belong to the truth and how we set our hearts at rest in his presence: 20if our hearts condemn us, we know that God is greater than our hearts, and he knows everything. 21Dear friends, if our hearts do not condemn us, we have confidence before God 22and receive from him anything we ask, because we keep his commands and do what pleases him. 23And this is his command: to believe in the name of his Son, Jesus Christ, and to love one another as he commanded us. 24The one who keeps God's commands lives in him, and he in them. And this is how we know that he lives in us: we know it by the Spirit he gave us.

On denying the incarnation

4 Dear friends, do not believe every spirit, but test the spirits to see whether they are from God, because many false prophets have gone out into the world. 2This is how you can recognise the Spirit of God: every spirit that acknowledges that Jesus Christ has come in the flesh is from God, 3but every spirit that does not acknowledge Jesus is not from God. This is the spirit of the antichrist, which you have heard is coming and even now is already in the world.

4You, dear children, are from God and have overcome them, because the one who is in you is greater than the one who is in the world. 5They are from the world and therefore speak from the viewpoint of the world, and the world listens to them. 6We are from God, and whoever knows God listens to us; but whoever is not from God does not listen to us. This is how we recognise the Spirita of truth and the spirit of falsehood.

God's love and ours

7Dear friends, let us love one another, for love comes from God. Everyone who loves has been born of God and knows God. 8Whoever does not love does not know God, because God is love. 9This is how God showed his love among us: he sent his one and only Son into the world that we might live through him. 10This is love: not that we loved God, but that he loved us and sent his Son as an atoning sacrifice for our sins. 11Dear friends, since God so loved us, we also ought to love one another. 12No one has ever seen God; but if we love one another, God lives in us and his love is made complete in us.

13This is how we know that we live in him and he in us: he has given us of his Spirit. 14And we have seen and testify that the Father has sent his Son to be the Saviour of the world. 15If anyone acknowledges that Jesus is the Son of God, God lives in them and they in God. 16And so we know and rely on the love God has for us.

God is love. Whoever lives in love lives in God, and God in them. 17This is how love is made complete among us so that we will have confidence on the day of judgment: in this world we are like Jesus. 18There is no fear in love. But perfect love drives out fear, because fear has to do with punishment. The one who fears is not made perfect in love.

19We love because he first loved us. 20Whoever claims to love God yet hates a brother or sister is a liar. For whoever does not love their brother and sister, whom they have seen, cannot love God, whom they have not seen. 21And he has given

b 13 The Greek word for brothers and sisters (adelphoi) refers here to believers, both men and women, as part of God's family; also in verse 16.

a 6 Or spirit

SPIRITUAL DISCIPLINES 7

GUIDANCE

The spiritual disciplines are about decisions we make as followers of God, deliberate steps we take towards him. Of course, we only make baby steps in his direction, while he strides towards us – the doting dad who gets excited that we're finally walking! One of the decisions we can make, and one of the most difficult, is to hand authority over our lives not just to God, but to other people.

In his famous novel *The Dice Man*, American author Luke Rhinehart tells the story of a man who starts making all his decisions based on the roll of a dice. Sometimes this leads him to commit acts of kindness, but at other times he's led down a darker path – even committing murder because of his obsession with obeying the results of the dice rolls. The moral of the story – although possibly not the one intended by the author – is that chaos leads to chaos. If we don't have a better way of making decisions in our lives, we won't get very far.

The discipline of guidance is about entrusting part of the responsibility for our decision-making to others. Not just anyone, but godly people who are either further on in the journey or running the race alongside us – people who know God, who can be trusted, and who can speak wisdom into our lives. That can take several forms:

- **Church:** Our leaders are not there by accident. They (should) have been through a lengthy and intensive process of selection, they're trained, and they have devoted their lives to God. Part of church membership is submitting to their authority, and following their leadership.

- **Spiritual direction:** We may seek out another (usually older) Christian to help us in our relationship with God. Their role is to usher us towards God, our real Director.

- **Accountability relationships:** We all have 'running mates' in the Christian journey. One key way of practising guidance is to agree with one or two friends to commit to a culture of total honesty and accountability. You will share your struggles and your hopes with one another; you will encourage and cheer each other on in the successes, and be brutally honest about the failures. This close relationship is vital if we're to break free from a cycle of sin such as an addiction. It goes without saying: these must be people you would trust with your life.

The passage in 1 John 4:7–21 is a beautiful blueprint for the way we're to practise guidance as Christian communities. The discipline is entirely rooted in love – it simply doesn't work if there's anything else behind it (for that reason, guidance is open to abuse and we must be wise to this). God's love for us is a template for the way we should seek to love one another, and while we'll never hit his heights, we can – through our advice, care and leadership – demonstrate that love which always seeks to put each other first.

Martin Saunders

 Luke 5:12–16   2 Samuel 12:1–20 ▶▶

RELATIONSHIPS 1

CREATED BY THE CREATOR

We're going to start and end this series with the most important thing in any relationship: *knowing* God as Jesus, Father and Holy Spirit.

If you're reading this with a big, burning question, you're unlikely to find the answer to it directly! This isn't written to give a yes/no answer to all your big relationship questions, but what it will try to do is to tour you round some important Bible passages on relationships and give you some questions to think, talk and pray through.

So let's get started! The passage in 1 John 5:6–13 might seem like a really strange one to begin with, but we have chosen it because this is one of the only places in the Bible where the Trinity (God as Father, God as the Son, and God as the Holy Spirit) is spoken about clearly (see also Matthew 28:19, and Crofty's 'Doctrine of the Trinity' in Matthew 3:13–17). God has been in existence as the Trinity since before we were created, living in a perfect relationship with himself.

So why create humans?

The short answer is 'for his pleasure' (see Revelation 4:11). Thankfully, this doesn't mean God made humans to entertain him or provide him with amusement! He wants to have a genuine relationship with people, but not because he is lonely. God is God – he doesn't need anything. Yes, he loves us, but this is not the same as needing us. If we had never been created, God would still have been God. He is unchanging (Malachi 3:6) and the '*I AM*' (Exodus 3:14) and was never dissatisfied with his own eternal existence.

God is creative, and it gives him pleasure to create things. We know from Genesis that God created us in his own image. Like any reflection, it's not a perfect imitation of the original, but it does show us a lot of the characteristics of the initial object. Humans show many of the characteristics of God, but we're only a poor reflection of our Creator. As such, we love and need relationships with one another.

Our relationships with one another are meant to reflect God's love for his people (Ephesians 5:32; John 13:35) and since the very beginning of creation, before man's relationship with God was tainted by the fall, God has known our need for companionship. In Genesis 2:18, we read, '*It is not good for the man to be alone.*' So God looks through creation to find a companion for Adam. No suitable companion is found, and so God creates woman. This is the person with whom he is to share the responsibility for the creation.

God has always known that we thrive in relationship, not only with him, but with each other too. First and foremost, though, we're created for a relationship with God, our Creator, and as such it's only a relationship with him that can completely fulfil, equip and sustain us.

Jane Plackett with Calum Dyke

Ecclesiastes 4:7–12

us this command: anyone who loves God must also love their brother and sister.

Faith in the incarnate Son of God

5 Everyone who believes that Jesus is the Christ is born of God, and everyone who loves the father loves his child as well. ²This is how we know that we love the children of God: by loving God and carrying out his commands. ³In fact, this is love for God: to keep his commands. And his commands are not burdensome, ⁴for everyone born of God overcomes the world. This is the victory that has overcome the world, even our faith. ⁵Who is it that overcomes the world? Only the one who believes that Jesus is the Son of God.

⁶This is the one who came by water and blood – Jesus Christ. He did not come by water only, but by water and blood. And it is the Spirit who testifies, because the Spirit is the truth. ⁷For there are three that testify: ⁸theᵃ Spirit, the water and the blood; and the three are in agreement. ⁹We accept human testimony, but God's testimony is greater because it is the testimony of God, which he has given about his Son. ¹⁰Whoever believes in the Son of God accepts this testimony. Whoever does not believe God has made him out to be a liar, because they have not believed the testimony God has given about his Son.

---

a 7,8 Late manuscripts of the Vulgate *testify in heaven: the Father, the Word and the Holy Spirit, and these three are one.* ⁸*And there are three that testify on earth: the* (not found in any Greek manuscript before the fourteenth century)

¹¹And this is the testimony: God has given us eternal life, and this life is in his Son. ¹²Whoever has the Son has life; whoever does not have the Son of God does not have life.

Concluding affirmations

¹³I write these things to you who believe in the name of the Son of God so that you may know that you have eternal life. ¹⁴This is the confidence we have in approaching God: that if we ask anything according to his will, he hears us. ¹⁵And if we know that he hears us – whatever we ask – we know that we have what we asked of him.

¹⁶If you see any brother or sister commit a sin that does not lead to death, you should pray and God will give them life. I refer to those whose sin does not lead to death. There is a sin that leads to death. I am not saying that you should pray about that. ¹⁷All wrongdoing is sin, and there is sin that does not lead to death.

¹⁸We know that anyone born of God does not continue to sin; the One who was born of God keeps them safe, and the evil one cannot harm them. ¹⁹We know that we are children of God, and that the whole world is under the control of the evil one. ²⁰We know also that the Son of God has come and has given us understanding, so that we may know him who is true. And we are in him who is true by being in his Son Jesus Christ. He is the true God and eternal life.

²¹Dear children, keep yourselves from idols.

2 JOHN

DATE

This letter was probably written between AD 85 and 95

AUTHOR

The apostle John (who also wrote one of the Gospels)

WHAT'S IT ALL ABOUT?

This short letter may have been written to one woman in the church, or the 'lady' referred to may be a church itself. It addresses a problem that occurred for the early church, who were used to hosting missionaries in their homes, giving them food and shelter while they preached God's Word. Some heretical teachers were also looking for the same treatment and so John warns the reader to be discerning and only look after teachers who preach the truth about Jesus. He also uses the letter as an opportunity to come back to his favourite theme: love. He highlights the importance of Christians loving one another and showing their love for God by being obedient to his commands.

WHY SHOULD WE READ IT?

- To see the link between loving God and being obedient to him (2 John 6).

- To be reminded of both God's great love for us and the importance of loving other people.

- To remind us to be discerning and wise, and not to get distracted by teaching that isn't true to Jesus.

Andy Croft with Liza Hoeksma

1 The elder,

To the lady chosen by God and to her children, whom I love in the truth – and not I only, but also all who know the truth – 2 because of the truth, which lives in us and will be with us for ever:

3 Grace, mercy and peace from God the Father and from Jesus Christ, the Father's Son, will be with us in truth and love.

4 It has given me great joy to find some of your children walking in the truth, just as the Father commanded us. 5 And now, dear lady, I am not writing you a new command but one we have had from the beginning. I ask that we love one another. 6 And this is love: that we walk in obedience to his commands. As you have heard from the beginning, his command is that you walk in love.

7 I say this because many deceivers, who do not acknowledge Jesus Christ as coming in the flesh, have gone out into the world. Any such person is the deceiver and the antichrist. 8 Watch out that you do not lose what we*a* have worked for, but that you may be rewarded fully. 9 Anyone who runs ahead and does not continue in the teaching of Christ does not have God; whoever continues in the teaching has both the Father and the Son. 10 If anyone comes to you and does not bring this teaching, do not take them into your house or welcome them. 11 Anyone who welcomes them shares in their wicked work.

12 I have much to write to you, but I do not want to use paper and ink. Instead, I hope to visit you and talk with you face to face, so that our joy may be complete.

13 The children of your sister, who is chosen by God, send their greetings.

---

a 8 Some manuscripts *you*

3 JOHN

DATE

This letter was probably written between AD 85 and 95

AUTHOR

The apostle John (who also wrote one of the Gospels)

WHAT'S IT ALL ABOUT?

This short letter was written to Gaius, a Christian who was part of a church likely to have been in Asia Minor (now Turkey). Gaius had recently welcomed and looked after missionaries sent out by John, even though they were previously strangers to him, and they had reported good things back to the apostle. In contrast, another Christian, Diotrephes, was not only refusing to accommodate the travellers but was throwing people out of the church who wanted to host them. John promises to deal with the problem himself when he's able to visit, and reminds Gaius to keep away from evil actions and to do what is good.

WHY SHOULD WE READ IT?

- To see Gaius's example of *'walking in the truth'* (3 John 4) and looking after missionaries even though they were strangers to him.

- To see that gossiping was as much a problem in the early church as it can be today.

Andy Croft with Liza Hoeksma

¹The elder,

To my dear friend Gaius, whom I love in the truth.

²Dear friend, I pray that you may enjoy good health and that all may go well with you, just as you are progressing spiritually. ³It gave me great joy when some believers came and testified about your faithfulness to the truth, telling how you continue to walk in it. ⁴I have no greater joy than to hear that my children are walking in the truth.

⁵Dear friend, you are faithful in what you are doing for the brothers and sisters,ᵃ even though they are strangers to you. ⁶They have told the church about your love. Please send them on their way in a manner that honours God. ⁷It was for the sake of the Name that they went out, receiving no help from the pagans. ⁸We ought therefore to show hospitality to such people so that we may work together for the truth.

⁹I wrote to the church, but Diotrephes, who loves to be first, will not welcome us. ¹⁰So when I come, I will call attention to what he is doing, spreading malicious nonsense about us. Not satisfied with that, he even refuses to welcome other believers. He also stops those who want to do so and puts them out of the church.

¹¹Dear friend, do not imitate what is evil but what is good. Anyone who does what is good is from God. Anyone who does what is evil has not seen God. ¹²Demetrius is well spoken of by everyone – and even by the truth itself. We also speak well of him, and you know that our testimony is true.

¹³I have much to write to you, but I do not want to do so with pen and ink. ¹⁴I hope to see you soon, and we will talk face to face.

Peace to you. The friends here send their greetings. Greet the friends there by name.

ᵃ 5 The Greek word for *brothers and sisters* (*adelphoi*) refers here to believers, both men and women, as part of God's family.

JUDE

DATE

Written around AD 80

AUTHOR

Jude – traditionally thought to be one of Jesus' brothers

WHAT'S IT ALL ABOUT?

It's not entirely clear who Jude was writing to, as it's thought the issue he was addressing may have been a problem in a large number of churches. Jude starts by saying he had wanted to write about salvation, but has been pushed to write about a more pressing matter: false teaching that is infecting the church. Some of that teaching may have been a distortion about God's grace, claiming that because of God's great mercy it was OK for people to do whatever they wanted to do. Although it may sound quite appealing, Jude is quite clear that is not the case. He draws on examples from the Old Testament about what happened to people and angels who were immoral and rebellious, reminding readers of the sexual immorality of Sodom and Gomorrah which led to their destruction, and the angels who were sent from God's presence because they wouldn't do as they had been instructed. Jude encourages the Christians to keep away from this false teaching and any ungodly desires. Instead he urges them to build up their faith, to pray, to try to help those who are falling into destructive ways, and to remember that Jesus will keep them from failing and bring them safely into God's presence and eternal life.

WHY SHOULD WE READ IT?

- As a reminder that we shouldn't use God's grace as an excuse to sin.
- To remember what happened to the angels and people who rebelled against God.

Andy Croft with Liza Hoeksma

[1] Jude, a servant of Jesus Christ and a brother of James,

To those who have been called, who are loved in God the Father and kept for*a* Jesus Christ:

[2] Mercy, peace and love be yours in abundance.

The sin and doom of ungodly people

[3] Dear friends, although I was very eager to write to you about the salvation we share, I felt compelled to write and urge you to contend for the faith that was once for all entrusted to God's holy people. [4] For certain individuals whose condemnation was written about*b* long ago have secretly slipped in among you. They are ungodly people, who pervert the grace of our God into a licence for immorality and deny Jesus Christ our only Sovereign and Lord.

[5] Though you already know all this, I want to remind you that the Lord*c* at one time delivered his people out of Egypt, but later destroyed those who did not believe. [6] And the angels who did not keep their positions of authority but abandoned their proper dwelling – these he has kept in darkness, bound with everlasting chains for judgment on the great Day. [7] In a similar way, Sodom and Gomorrah and the surrounding towns gave themselves up to sexual immorality and perversion. They serve as an example of those who suffer the punishment of eternal fire.

[8] In the very same way, on the strength of their dreams these ungodly people pollute their own bodies, reject authority and heap abuse on celestial beings. [9] But even the archangel Michael, when he was disputing with the devil about the body of Moses, did not himself dare to condemn him for slander but said, 'The Lord rebuke you!'*d* [10] Yet these people slander whatever they do not understand, and the very things they do understand by instinct – as irrational animals do – will destroy them. [11] Woe to them! They have taken the way of Cain; they have rushed for profit into Balaam's error; they have been destroyed in Korah's rebellion.

[12] These people are blemishes at your love feasts, eating with you without the slightest qualm – shepherds who feed only themselves. They are clouds without rain, blown along by the wind; autumn trees, without fruit and uprooted – twice dead. [13] They are wild waves of the sea, foaming up their shame; wandering stars, for whom blackest darkness has been reserved for ever.

[14] Enoch, the seventh from Adam, prophesied about them: 'See, the Lord is coming with thousands upon thousands of his holy ones [15] to judge everyone, and to convict all of them of all the ungodly acts they have committed in their ungodliness, and of all the defiant words ungodly sinners have spoken against him.'*e* [16] These people are grumblers and faultfinders; they follow their own evil desires; they boast about themselves and flatter others for their own advantage.

A call to persevere

[17] But, dear friends, remember what the apostles of our Lord Jesus Christ foretold. [18] They said to you, 'In the last times there will be scoffers who will follow their own ungodly desires.' [19] These are the people who divide you, who follow mere natural instincts and do not have the Spirit. [20] But you, dear friends, by building yourselves up in your most holy faith and praying in the Holy Spirit, [21] keep yourselves in God's love as you wait for the mercy of our Lord Jesus Christ to bring you to eternal life.

[22] Be merciful to those who doubt; [23] save others by snatching them from the fire; to others show mercy, mixed with fear – hating even the clothing stained by corrupted flesh.*f*

---

a 1 Or *by*; or *in*
b 4 Or *individuals who were marked out for condemnation*
c 5 Some early manuscripts *Jesus*
d 9 Jude is alluding to the Jewish *Testament of Moses* (approximately the first century A.D.).

e 14,15 From the Jewish *First Book of Enoch* (approximately the first century B.C.)
f 22,23 The Greek manuscripts of these verses vary at several points.

Doxology

²⁴To him who is able to keep you from stumbling and to present you before his glorious presence without fault and with great joy – ²⁵to the only God our Saviour be glory, majesty, power and authority, through Jesus Christ our Lord, before all ages, now and for evermore! Amen.

REVELATION

DATE

It is thought this letter was written around AD 95

AUTHOR

Traditionally thought to be the apostle John, who also wrote one of the Gospels

WHAT'S IT ALL ABOUT?

John wrote Revelation during a time of intense persecution for the church. John had been exiled to the island of Patmos and this book tells of a vision (a 'revelation') he had there while worshipping Jesus. Revelation can be a bit confusing to read, as John uses lots of symbolism, but there is still great truth that we can draw out from John's vision. He paints a new picture of Jesus: instead of the helpless baby born to Mary and Joseph, or the suffering saint who died on a cross, he shows him glorified in heaven, surrounded by never-ending praise. He focuses on encouraging the persecuted Christians to remain faithful, writing letters to seven churches in Asia Minor and offering them words of rebuke and warning as well as encouragement.

Revelation tells us what's to come – a time when God will return and create a new heaven and earth. While there are different theories about how that might happen and what that might look like, the book reminds us that we know for sure there will come a time when God will return everything to be the way that he intended it. We, like the early believers, need to hold on to our faith, be obedient to God and wait patiently until that time comes.

WHY SHOULD WE READ IT?

- To understand God's pleasure at the seven churches in Asia Minor, as well as his complaints about some of their behaviour (Revelation 2 – 3). Many of the charges could just as easily be levelled at some of our churches today.

- To hear John's amazing description of the throne room of God and the worship of heaven (Revelation 4).

- To hear John's vision for a new heaven and a new earth with no more death, mourning or pain (Revelation 21).

- To remember that while we don't know the day or time, we can be assured that one day Jesus will return to earth in all his glory.

Andy Croft with Liza Hoeksma

Prologue

1 The revelation from Jesus Christ, which God gave him to show his servants what must soon take place. He made it known by sending his angel to his servant John, ²who testifies to everything he saw – that is, the word of God and the testimony of Jesus Christ. ³Blessed is the one who reads aloud the words of this prophecy, and blessed are those who hear it and take to heart what is written in it, because the time is near.

Greetings and doxology

⁴John,

To the seven churches in the province of Asia:

Grace and peace to you from him who is, and who was, and who is to come, and from the seven spirits*ª* before his throne, ⁵and from Jesus Christ, who is the faithful witness, the firstborn from the dead, and the ruler of the kings of the earth.

To him who loves us and has freed us from our sins by his blood, ⁶and has made us to be a kingdom and priests to serve his God and Father – to him be glory and power for ever and ever! Amen.

⁷ 'Look, he is coming with the clouds,'*ᵇ*
and 'every eye will see him,
even those who pierced him';
    and all peoples on earth 'will mourn
       because of him.'*ᶜ*
          So shall it be! Amen.

⁸'I am the Alpha and the Omega,' says the Lord God, 'who is, and who was, and who is to come, the Almighty.'

John's vision of Christ

⁹I, John, your brother and companion in the suffering and kingdom and patient endurance that are ours in Jesus, was on the island of Patmos because of the word of God and the testimony of Jesus. ¹⁰On the Lord's Day I was in the Spirit, and I heard behind me a loud voice like a trumpet, ¹¹which said: 'Write on a scroll what you see and send it to the seven churches: to Ephesus, Smyrna, Pergamum, Thyatira, Sardis, Philadelphia and Laodicea.'

¹²I turned round to see the voice that was speaking to me. And when I turned I saw seven golden lampstands, ¹³and among the lampstands was someone like a son of man,*ᵈ* dressed in a robe reaching down to his feet and with a golden sash round his chest. ¹⁴The hair on his head was white like wool, as white as snow, and his eyes were like blazing fire. ¹⁵His feet were like bronze glowing in a furnace, and his voice was like the sound of rushing waters. ¹⁶In his right hand he held seven stars, and coming out of his mouth was a sharp, double-edged sword. His face was like the sun shining in all its brilliance.

¹⁷When I saw him, I fell at his feet as though dead. Then he placed his right hand on me and said: 'Do not be afraid. I am the First and the Last. ¹⁸I am the Living One; I was dead, and now look, I am alive for ever and ever! And I hold the keys of death and Hades.

¹⁹'Write, therefore, what you have seen, what is now and what will take place later. ²⁰The mystery of the seven stars that you saw in my right hand and of the seven golden lampstands is this: the seven stars are the angels*ᵉ* of the seven churches, and the seven lampstands are the seven churches.

To the church in Ephesus

2 'To the angel*ª* of the church in Ephesus write:

These are the words of him who holds the seven stars in his right hand and walks among the seven golden lampstands. ²I know your deeds, your hard work and your perseverance. I know that you cannot tolerate

---

*ª*4   That is, the sevenfold Spirit
*ᵇ*7   Daniel 7:13
*ᶜ*7   Zech. 12:10

*ᵈ*13   See Daniel 7:13.
*ᵉ*20   Or *messengers*
*ª*1   Or *messenger*; also in verses 8, 12 and 18

wicked people, that you have tested those who claim to be apostles but are not, and have found them false. 3 You have persevered and have endured hardships for my name, and have not grown weary. 4 Yet I hold this against you: you have forsaken the love you had at first. 5 Consider how far you have fallen! Repent and do the things you did at first. If you do not repent, I will come to you and remove your lampstand from its place. 6 But you have this in your favour: you hate the practices of the Nicolaitans, which I also hate.

7 Whoever has ears, let them hear what the Spirit says to the churches. To the one who is victorious, I will give the right to eat from the tree of life, which is in the paradise of God.

To the church in Smyrna

8 'To the angel of the church in Smyrna write:

These are the words of him who is the First and the Last, who died and came to life again. 9 I know your afflictions and your poverty – yet you are rich! I know about the slander of those who say they are Jews and are not, but are a synagogue of Satan. 10 Do not be afraid of what you are about to suffer. I tell you, the devil will put some of you in prison to test you, and you will suffer persecution for ten days. Be faithful, even to the point of death, and I will give you life as your victor's crown.

11 Whoever has ears, let them hear what the Spirit says to the churches. The one who is victorious will not be hurt at all by the second death.

To the church in Pergamum

12 'To the angel of the church in Pergamum write:

These are the words of him who has the sharp, double-edged sword. 13 I know where you live – where Satan has his throne. Yet you remain true to my name. You did not renounce your faith in me, not even in the days of Antipas, my faithful witness, who was put to death in your city – where Satan lives.

14 Nevertheless, I have a few things against you: there are some among you who hold to the teaching of Balaam, who taught Balak to entice the Israelites to sin so that they ate food sacrificed to idols and committed sexual immorality. 15 Likewise, you also have those who hold to the teaching of the Nicolaitans. 16 Repent therefore! Otherwise, I will soon come to you and will fight against them with the sword of my mouth.

17 Whoever has ears, let them hear what the Spirit says to the churches. To the one who is victorious, I will give some of the hidden manna. I will also give that person a white stone with a new name written on it, known only to the one who receives it.

To the church in Thyatira

18 'To the angel of the church in Thyatira write:

These are the words of the Son of God, whose eyes are like blazing fire and whose feet are like burnished bronze. 19 I know your deeds, your love and faith, your service and perseverance, and that you are now doing more than you did at first.

20 Nevertheless, I have this against you: you tolerate that woman Jezebel, who calls herself a prophet. By her teaching she misleads my servants into sexual immorality and the eating of food sacrificed to idols. 21 I have given her time to repent of her immorality, but she is unwilling. 22 So I will cast her on a bed of suffering, and I will make those who commit adultery with her suffer intensely, unless they repent of her ways. 23 I will strike her children dead. Then all the churches will know that I am he who searches hearts and minds, and

I will repay each of you according to your deeds.

24 Now I say to the rest of you in Thyatira, to you who do not hold to her teaching and have not learned Satan's so-called deep secrets, "I will not impose any other burden on you, 25 except to hold on to what you have until I come."

26 To the one who is victorious and does my will to the end, I will give authority over the nations – 27 that one "will rule them with an iron sceptre and will dash them to pieces like pottery"[b] – just as I have received authority from my Father. 28 I will also give that one the morning star. 29 Whoever has ears, let them hear what the Spirit says to the churches.

To the church in Sardis

3 'To the angel[a] of the church in Sardis write:

These are the words of him who holds the seven spirits[b] of God and the seven stars. I know your deeds; you have a reputation of being alive, but you are dead. 2 Wake up! Strengthen what remains and is about to die, for I have found your deeds unfinished in the sight of my God. 3 Remember, therefore, what you have received and heard; hold it fast, and repent. But if you do not wake up, I will come like a thief, and you will not know at what time I will come to you.

4 Yet you have a few people in Sardis who have not soiled their clothes. They will walk with me, dressed in white, for they are worthy. 5 The one who is victorious will, like them, be dressed in white. I will never blot out the name of that person from the book of life, but will acknowledge that name before my Father and his angels. 6 Whoever has ears,

let them hear what the Spirit says to the churches.

To the church in Philadelphia

7 'To the angel of the church in Philadelphia write:

These are the words of him who is holy and true, who holds the key of David. What he opens no one can shut, and what he shuts no one can open. 8 I know your deeds. See, I have placed before you an open door that no one can shut. I know that you have little strength, yet you have kept my word and have not denied my name. 9 I will make those who are of the synagogue of Satan, who claim to be Jews though they are not, but are liars – I will make them come and fall down at your feet and acknowledge that I have loved you. 10 Since you have kept my command to endure patiently, I will also keep you from the hour of trial that is going to come on the whole world to test the inhabitants of the earth.

11 I am coming soon. Hold on to what you have, so that no one will take your crown. 12 The one who is victorious I will make a pillar in the temple of my God. Never again will they leave it. I will write on them the name of my God and the name of the city of my God, the new Jerusalem, which is coming down out of heaven from my God; and I will also write on them my new name. 13 Whoever has ears, let them hear what the Spirit says to the churches.

To the church in Laodicea

14 'To the angel of the church in Laodicea write:

These are the words of the Amen, the faithful and true witness, the ruler of God's creation. 15 I know your deeds, that you are neither cold nor hot. I wish you were either one or the other! 16 So, because you are lukewarm – neither hot nor cold – I am

---

b 27 Psalm 2:9
a 1 Or *messenger*; also in verses 7 and 14
b 1 That is, the sevenfold Spirit

about to spit you out of my mouth.
¹⁷You say, "I am rich; I have acquired wealth and do not need a thing." But you do not realise that you are wretched, pitiful, poor, blind and naked. ¹⁸I counsel you to buy from me gold refined in the fire, so that you can become rich; and white clothes to wear, so that you can cover your shameful nakedness; and salve to put on your eyes, so that you can see.

¹⁹Those whom I love I rebuke and discipline. So be earnest and repent. ²⁰Here I am! I stand at the door and knock. If anyone hears my voice and opens the door, I will come in and eat with that person, and they with me.

²¹To the one who is victorious, I will give the right to sit with me on my throne, just as I was victorious and sat down with my Father on his throne. ²²Whoever has ears, let them hear what the Spirit says to the churches.'

The throne in heaven

4 After this I looked, and there before me was a door standing open in heaven. And the voice I had first heard speaking to me like a trumpet said, 'Come up here, and I will show you what must take place after this.' ²At once I was in the Spirit, and there before me was a throne in heaven with someone sitting on it. ³And the one who sat there had the appearance of jasper and ruby. A rainbow that shone like an emerald encircled the throne. ⁴Surrounding the throne were twenty-four other thrones, and seated on them were twenty-four elders. They were dressed in white and had crowns of gold on their heads. ⁵From the throne came flashes of lightning, rumblings and peals of thunder. In front of the throne, seven lamps were blazing. These are the seven spirits*a* of God. ⁶Also in front of the throne there was what looked like a sea of glass, clear as crystal.

In the centre, round the throne, were four living creatures, and they were covered with eyes, in front and behind. ⁷The first living creature was like a lion, the second was like an ox, the third had a face like a man, the fourth was like a flying eagle. ⁸Each of the four living creatures had six wings and was covered with eyes all round, even under its wings. Day and night they never stop saying:

'"Holy, holy, holy
is the Lord God Almighty,"*b*
who was, and is, and is to come.'

⁹Whenever the living creatures give glory, honour and thanks to him who sits on the throne and who lives for ever and ever, ¹⁰the twenty-four elders fall down before him who sits on the throne and worship him who lives for ever and ever. They lay their crowns before the throne and say:

¹¹ 'You are worthy, our Lord and God,
to receive glory and honour and power,
for you created all things,
and by your will they were created
and have their being.'

The scroll and the Lamb

5 Then I saw in the right hand of him who sat on the throne a scroll with writing on both sides and sealed with seven seals. ²And I saw a mighty angel proclaiming in a loud voice, 'Who is worthy to break the seals and open the scroll?' ³But no one in heaven or on earth or under the earth could open the scroll or even look inside it. ⁴I wept and wept because no one was found who was worthy to open the scroll or look inside. ⁵Then one of the elders said to me, 'Do not weep! See, the Lion of the tribe of Judah, the Root of David, has triumphed. He is able to open the scroll and its seven seals.'

⁶Then I saw a Lamb, looking as if it had been slain, standing at the centre of the throne, encircled by the four living creatures and the elders. The Lamb had seven horns and seven eyes, which are the seven

---

a 5 That is, the sevenfold Spirit   *b* 8 Isaiah 6:3

spirits*a* of God sent out into all the earth. ⁷He went and took the scroll from the right hand of him who sat on the throne. ⁸And when he had taken it, the four living creatures and the twenty-four elders fell down before the Lamb. Each one had a harp and they were holding golden bowls full of incense, which are the prayers of God's people. ⁹And they sang a new song, saying:

> 'You are worthy to take the scroll
>   and to open its seals,
> because you were slain,
>   and with your blood you purchased
>   for God
>   persons from every tribe and
>   language and people and
>   nation.
> ¹⁰You have made them to be a kingdom
>   and priests to serve our God,
>   and they will reign*b* on the earth.'

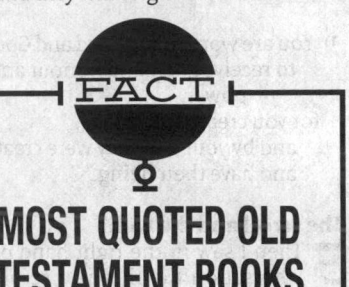

FACT

MOST QUOTED OLD TESTAMENT BOOKS

The first Christians didn't have the New Testament – that was still being written! But they did have – and use – the Old Testament or Hebrew Scriptures. The most quoted Old Testament book in the New Testament is Isaiah (419 quotes), followed by Psalms (414), Genesis (260), Exodus (250) and Deuteronomy (208).

¹¹Then I looked and heard the voice of many angels, numbering thousands upon thousands, and ten thousand times ten thousand. They encircled the throne and the living creatures and the elders. ¹²In a loud voice they were saying:

> 'Worthy is the Lamb, who was slain,
>   to receive power and wealth and
>   wisdom and strength
>   and honour and glory and praise!'

¹³Then I heard every creature in heaven and on earth and under the earth and on the sea, and all that is in them, saying:

> 'To him who sits on the throne and to
>   the Lamb
>   be praise and honour and glory and
>   power,
>   for ever and ever!'

¹⁴The four living creatures said, 'Amen', and the elders fell down and worshipped.

The seals

6 I watched as the Lamb opened the first of the seven seals. Then I heard one of the four living creatures say in a voice like thunder, 'Come!' ²I looked, and there before me was a white horse! Its rider held a bow, and he was given a crown, and he rode out as a conqueror bent on conquest.

³When the Lamb opened the second seal, I heard the second living creature say, 'Come!' ⁴Then another horse came out, a fiery red one. Its rider was given power to take peace from the earth and to make people kill each other. To him was given a large sword.

⁵When the Lamb opened the third seal, I heard the third living creature say, 'Come!' I looked, and there before me was a black horse! Its rider was holding a pair of scales in his hand. ⁶Then I heard what sounded like a voice among the four living creatures, saying, 'A kilogram of wheat for a day's wages,*a* and three kilograms of barley for a day's wages,*a* and do not damage the oil and the wine!'

⁷When the Lamb opened the fourth seal, I heard the voice of the fourth living creature say, 'Come!' ⁸I looked, and there before me was a pale horse! Its rider was named Death, and Hades was following close behind him. They were given power

---

a 6 That is, the sevenfold Spirit
b 10 Some manuscripts *they reign*

a 6 Greek *a denarius*

over a quarter of the earth to kill by sword, famine and plague, and by the wild beasts of the earth.

⁹When he opened the fifth seal, I saw under the altar the souls of those who had been slain because of the word of God and the testimony they had maintained. ¹⁰They called out in a loud voice, 'How long, Sovereign Lord, holy and true, until you judge the inhabitants of the earth and avenge our blood?' ¹¹Then each of them was given a white robe, and they were told to wait a little longer, until the full number of their fellow servants, their brothers and sisters,ᵇ were killed just as they had been.

¹²I watched as he opened the sixth seal. There was a great earthquake. The sun turned black like sackcloth made of goat hair, the whole moon turned blood red, ¹³and the stars in the sky fell to earth, as figs drop from a fig-tree when shaken by a strong wind. ¹⁴The heavens receded like a scroll being rolled up, and every mountain and island was removed from its place.

¹⁵Then the kings of the earth, the princes, the generals, the rich, the mighty, and everyone else, both slave and free, hid in caves and among the rocks of the mountains. ¹⁶They called to the mountains and the rocks, 'Fall on us and hide usᶜ from the face of him who sits on the throne and from the wrath of the Lamb! ¹⁷For the great day of theirᵈ wrath has come, and who can withstand it?'

144,000 sealed

7 After this I saw four angels standing at the four corners of the earth, holding back the four winds of the earth to prevent any wind from blowing on the land or on the sea or on any tree. ²Then I saw another angel coming up from the east, having the seal of the living God. He called out in a loud voice to the four angels who had been given power to harm the land and the sea: ³'Do not harm the land or the sea or the

trees until we put a seal on the foreheads of the servants of our God.' ⁴Then I heard the number of those who were sealed: 144,000 from all the tribes of Israel.

⁵From the tribe of Judah 12,000 were sealed,
from the tribe of Reuben 12,000,
from the tribe of Gad 12,000,
⁶from the tribe of Asher 12,000,
from the tribe of Naphtali 12,000,
from the tribe of Manasseh 12,000,
⁷from the tribe of Simeon 12,000,
from the tribe of Levi 12,000,
from the tribe of Issachar 12,000,
⁸from the tribe of Zebulun 12,000,
from the tribe of Joseph 12,000,
from the tribe of Benjamin 12,000.

The great multitude in white robes

⁹After this I looked, and there before me was a great multitude that no one could count, from every nation, tribe, people and language, standing before the throne and before the Lamb. They were wearing white robes and were holding palm branches in their hands. ¹⁰And they cried out in a loud voice:

'Salvation belongs to our God,
who sits on the throne,
and to the Lamb.'

¹¹All the angels were standing round the throne and round the elders and the four living creatures. They fell down on their faces before the throne and worshipped God, ¹²saying:

'Amen!
Praise and glory
and wisdom and thanks and honour
and power and strength
be to our God for ever and ever.
Amen!'

¹³Then one of the elders asked me, 'These in white robes – who are they, and where did they come from?'

¹⁴I answered, 'Sir, you know.'
And he said, 'These are they who have come out of the great tribulation; they

---

ᵇ 11 The Greek word for *brothers and sisters* (*adelphoi*) refers here to believers, both men and women, as part of God's family; also in 12:10; 19:10.
ᶜ 16 See Hosea 10:8.
ᵈ 17 Some manuscripts *his*

have washed their robes and made them white in the blood of the Lamb. 15 Therefore,

'they are before the throne of God
and serve him day and night in his temple;
and he who sits on the throne
will shelter them with his presence.
16 "Never again will they hunger;
never again will they thirst.
The sun will not beat down on them,"*a*
nor any scorching heat.
17 For the Lamb at the centre of the throne
will be their shepherd;
"he will lead them to springs of living water."*b*
"And God will wipe away every tear from their eyes."*c*

The seventh seal and the golden censer

8 When he opened the seventh seal, there was silence in heaven for about half an hour.

2 And I saw the seven angels who stand before God, and seven trumpets were given to them.

3 Another angel, who had a golden censer, came and stood at the altar. He was given much incense to offer, with the prayers of all God's people, on the golden altar in front of the throne. 4 The smoke of the incense, together with the prayers of God's people, went up before God from the angel's hand. 5 Then the angel took the censer, filled it with fire from the altar, and hurled it on the earth; and there came peals of thunder, rumblings, flashes of lightning and an earthquake.

The trumpets

6 Then the seven angels who had the seven trumpets prepared to sound them.

7 The first angel sounded his trumpet, and there came hail and fire mixed with blood, and it was hurled down on the earth. A third of the earth was burned up,

a third of the trees were burned up, and all the green grass was burned up.

8 The second angel sounded his trumpet, and something like a huge mountain, all ablaze, was thrown into the sea. A third of the sea turned into blood, 9 a third of the living creatures in the sea died, and a third of the ships were destroyed.

10 The third angel sounded his trumpet, and a great star, blazing like a torch, fell from the sky on a third of the rivers and on the springs of water – 11 the name of the star is Wormwood.*a* A third of the waters turned bitter, and many people died from the waters that had become bitter.

12 The fourth angel sounded his trumpet, and a third of the sun was struck, a third of the moon, and a third of the stars, so that a third of them turned dark. A third of the day was without light, and also a third of the night.

13 As I watched, I heard an eagle that was flying in mid-air call out in a loud voice: 'Woe! Woe! Woe to the inhabitants of the earth, because of the trumpet blasts about to be sounded by the other three angels!'

9 The fifth angel sounded his trumpet, and I saw a star that had fallen from the sky to the earth. The star was given the key to the shaft of the Abyss. 2 When he opened the Abyss, smoke rose from it like the smoke from a gigantic furnace. The sun and sky were darkened by the smoke from the Abyss. 3 And out of the smoke locusts came down on the earth and were given power like that of scorpions of the earth. 4 They were told not to harm the grass of the earth or any plant or tree, but only those people who did not have the seal of God on their foreheads. 5 They were not allowed to kill them but only to torture them for five months. And the agony they suffered was like that of the sting of a scorpion when it strikes. 6 During those days people will seek death but will not find it; they will long to die, but death will elude them.

7 The locusts looked like horses prepared for battle. On their heads they wore something like crowns of gold, and their

a 16 Isaiah 49:10
b 17 Isaiah 49:10
c 17 Isaiah 25:8

a 11 Wormwood is a bitter substance.

faces resembled human faces. **8**Their hair was like women's hair, and their teeth were like lions' teeth. **9**They had breastplates like breastplates of iron, and the sound of their wings was like the thundering of many horses and chariots rushing into battle. **10**They had tails with stings, like scorpions, and in their tails they had power to torment people for five months. **11**They had as king over them the angel of the Abyss, whose name in Hebrew is Abaddon and in Greek is Apollyon (that is, Destroyer).

12The first woe is past; two other woes are yet to come.

13The sixth angel sounded his trumpet, and I heard a voice coming from the four horns of the golden altar that is before God. **14**It said to the sixth angel who had the trumpet, 'Release the four angels who are bound at the great river Euphrates.' **15**And the four angels who had been kept ready for this very hour and day and month and year were released to kill a third of mankind. **16**The number of the mounted troops was twice ten thousand times ten thousand. I heard their number.

17The horses and riders I saw in my vision looked like this: their breastplates were fiery red, dark blue, and yellow as sulphur. The heads of the horses resembled the heads of lions, and out of their mouths came fire, smoke and sulphur. **18**A third of mankind was killed by the three plagues of fire, smoke and sulphur that came out of their mouths. **19**The power of the horses was in their mouths and in their tails; for their tails were like snakes, having heads with which they inflict injury.

20The rest of mankind who were not killed by these plagues still did not repent of the work of their hands; they did not stop worshipping demons, and idols of gold, silver, bronze, stone and wood – idols that cannot see or hear or walk. **21**Nor did they repent of their murders, their magic arts, their sexual immorality or their thefts.

The angel and the little scroll

10 Then I saw another mighty angel coming down from heaven. He was robed in a cloud, with a rainbow above his head; his face was like the sun, and his legs were like fiery pillars. **2**He was holding a little scroll, which lay open in his hand. He planted his right foot on the sea and his left foot on the land, **3**and he gave a loud shout like the roar of a lion. When he shouted, the voices of the seven thunders spoke. **4**And when the seven thunders spoke, I was about to write; but I heard a voice from heaven say, 'Seal up what the seven thunders have said and do not write it down.'

FAVOURITE VERSES
Mark 16:20

Then the disciples went out and preached everywhere, and the Lord worked with them and confirmed his word by the signs that accompanied it.

I love this verse because it shows in a nutshell what Jesus wants us to do within his world, and it shows how much the disciples trusted him, to just go out straight away to spread his Word. If I can have half the faith they had, I would be more than happy.

Erin, 15

5Then the angel I had seen standing on the sea and on the land raised his right hand to heaven. **6**And he swore by him who lives for ever and ever, who created the heavens and all that is in them, the earth and all that is in it, and the sea and all that is in it, and said, 'There will be no more delay! **7**But in the days when the seventh angel is about to sound his trumpet, the mystery of God will be accomplished, just as he announced to his servants the prophets.'

8 Then the voice that I had heard from heaven spoke to me once more: 'Go, take the scroll that lies open in the hand of the angel who is standing on the sea and on the land.'

9 So I went to the angel and asked him to give me the little scroll. He said to me, 'Take it and eat it. It will turn your stomach sour, but "in your mouth it will be as sweet as honey."*a* 10 I took the little scroll from the angel's hand and ate it. It tasted as sweet as honey in my mouth, but when I had eaten it, my stomach turned sour. 11 Then I was told, 'You must prophesy again about many peoples, nations, languages and kings.'

The two witnesses

11 I was given a reed like a measuring rod and was told, 'Go and measure the temple of God and the altar, with its worshippers. 2 But exclude the outer court; do not measure it, because it has been given to the Gentiles. They will trample on the holy city for 42 months. 3 And I will appoint my two witnesses, and they will prophesy for 1,260 days, clothed in sackcloth.' 4 They are 'the two olive trees' and the two lampstands, and 'they stand before the Lord of the earth.'*a* 5 If anyone tries to harm them, fire comes from their mouths and devours their enemies. This is how anyone who wants to harm them must die. 6 They have power to shut up the heavens so that it will not rain during the time they are prophesying; and they have power to turn the waters into blood and to strike the earth with every kind of plague as often as they want.

7 Now when they have finished their testimony, the beast that comes up from the Abyss will attack them, and overpower and kill them. 8 Their bodies will lie in the public square of the great city – which is figuratively called Sodom and Egypt – where also their Lord was crucified. 9 For three and a half days some from every people, tribe, language and nation will gaze on their bodies and refuse them burial. 10 The inhabitants of the earth will gloat over them

and will celebrate by sending each other gifts, because these two prophets had tormented those who live on the earth. 11 But after the three and a half days the breath*b* of life from God entered them, and they stood on their feet, and terror struck those who saw them. 12 Then they heard a loud voice from heaven saying to them, 'Come up here.' And they went up to heaven in a cloud, while their enemies looked on.

13 At that very hour there was a severe earthquake and a tenth of the city collapsed. Seven thousand people were killed in the earthquake, and the survivors were terrified and gave glory to the God of heaven.

14 The second woe has passed; the third woe is coming soon.

The seventh trumpet

15 The seventh angel sounded his trumpet, and there were loud voices in heaven, which said:

'The kingdom of the world has become
    the kingdom of our Lord and of his
    Messiah,
    and he will reign for ever and ever.'

16 And the twenty-four elders, who were seated on their thrones before God, fell on their faces and worshipped God, 17 saying:

'We give thanks to you, Lord God
    Almighty,
    the One who is and who was,
    because you have taken your great
    power
    and have begun to reign.
18 The nations were angry,
    and your wrath has come.
The time has come for judging the
    dead,
    and for rewarding your servants the
    prophets
and your people who revere your name,
    both great and small –
    and for destroying those who destroy
    the earth.'

---

a 9 Ezek. 3:3
a 4 See Zech. 4:3,11,14.

b 11 Or *Spirit* (see Ezek. 37:5,14)

¹⁹Then God's temple in heaven was opened, and within his temple was seen the ark of his covenant. And there came flashes of lightning, rumblings, peals of thunder, an earthquake and a severe hailstorm.

The woman and the dragon

12 A great sign appeared in heaven: a woman clothed with the sun, with the moon under her feet and a crown of twelve stars on her head. ²She was pregnant and cried out in pain as she was about to give birth. ³Then another sign appeared in heaven: an enormous red dragon with seven heads and ten horns and seven crowns on its heads. ⁴Its tail swept a third of the stars out of the sky and flung them to the earth. The dragon stood in front of the woman who was about to give birth, so that it might devour her child the moment he was born. ⁵She gave birth to a son, a male child, who 'will rule all the nations with an iron sceptre.'ᵘ And her child was snatched up to God and to his throne. ⁶The woman fled into the wilderness to a place prepared for her by God, where she might be taken care of for 1,260 days.

⁷Then war broke out in heaven. Michael and his angels fought against the dragon, and the dragon and his angels fought back. ⁸But he was not strong enough, and they lost their place in heaven. ⁹The great dragon was hurled down – that ancient snake called the devil, or Satan, who leads the whole world astray. He was hurled to the earth, and his angels with him.

¹⁰Then I heard a loud voice in heaven say:

'Now have come the salvation and the power
and the kingdom of our God,
and the authority of his Messiah.
For the accuser of our brothers and sisters,
who accuses them before our God day and night,
has been hurled down.

¹¹They triumphed over him
by the blood of the Lamb
and by the word of their testimony;
they did not love their lives so much
as to shrink from death.
¹²Therefore rejoice, you heavens
and you who dwell in them!
But woe to the earth and the sea,
because the devil has gone down to you!
He is filled with fury,
because he knows that his time is short.'

¹³When the dragon saw that he had been hurled to the earth, he pursued the woman who had given birth to the male child. ¹⁴The woman was given the two wings of a great eagle, so that she might fly to the place prepared for her in the wilderness, where she would be taken care of for a time, times and half a time, out of the snake's reach. ¹⁵Then from his mouth the snake spewed water like a river, to overtake the woman and sweep her away with the torrent. ¹⁶But the earth helped the woman by opening its mouth and swallowing the river that the dragon had spewed out of his mouth. ¹⁷Then the dragon was enraged at the woman and went off to wage war against the rest of her offspring – those who keep God's commands and hold fast their testimony about Jesus.

The beast out of the sea

13 The dragonᵃ stood on the shore of the sea. And I saw a beast coming out of the sea. It had ten horns and seven heads, with ten crowns on its horns, and on each head a blasphemous name. ²The beast I saw resembled a leopard, but had feet like those of a bear and a mouth like that of a lion. The dragon gave the beast his power and his throne and great authority. ³One of the heads of the beast seemed to have had a fatal wound, but the fatal wound had been healed. The whole world was filled with wonder and followed the beast. ⁴People worshipped the dragon because he had given authority to the beast, and they also worshipped the beast and asked, 'Who is like the beast? Who can wage war against it?'

5 The beast was given a mouth to utter proud words and blasphemies and to exercise its authority for forty-two months. 6 It opened its mouth to blaspheme God, and to slander his name and his dwelling-place and those who live in heaven. 7 It was given power to wage war against God's holy people and to conquer them. And it was given authority over every tribe, people, language and nation. 8 All inhabitants of the earth will worship the beast – all whose names have not been written in the Lamb's book of life, the Lamb who was slain from the creation of the world.[b]

9 Whoever has ears, let them hear.

10 'If anyone is to go into captivity,
    into captivity they will go.
If anyone is to be killed[c] with the sword,
    with the sword they will be killed.'[d]

This calls for patient endurance and faithfulness on the part of God's people.

---

b 8 Or written from the creation of the world in the book of life belonging to the Lamb who was slain
c 10 Some manuscripts anyone kills
d 10 Jer. 15:2

FAVOURITE VERSES

Philippians 3:14–21

I press on towards the goal to win the prize for which God has called me heavenwards in Christ Jesus. All of us, then, who are mature should take such a view of things. And if on some point you think differently, that too God will make clear to you. Only let us live up to what we have already attained. Join together in following my example, brothers and sisters, and just as you have us as a model, keep your eyes on those who live as we do. For, as I have often told you before and now tell you again even with tears, many live as enemies of the cross of Christ. Their destiny is destruction, their god is their stomach, and their glory is in their shame. Their mind is set on earthly things. But our citizenship is in heaven. And we eagerly await a Saviour from there, the Lord Jesus Christ, who, by the power that enables him to bring everything under his control, will transform our lowly bodies so that they will be like his glorious body.

This passage speaks of such joy and a passion for life. It takes away the feeling of guilt that many feel about 'not being good enough for God' and being 'lost and fumbling around not really knowing what or how to do things for God'. But actually, if our hearts, eyes and lives are focused God-wards, many miracles, wonders, joys and blessings will follow. It highlights that I am part of something truly amazing, I am set apart, special, and my inheritance in God is so much more than I could imagine or honestly ever wish for! God is so good to us. He loves us and wants to spoil us rotten!

Rachael, 20

The beast out of the earth

11 Then I saw a second beast, coming out of the earth. It had two horns like a lamb, but it spoke like a dragon. 12 It exercised all the authority of the first beast on its behalf, and made the earth and its inhabitants worship the first beast, whose fatal wound had been healed. 13 And it performed great signs, even causing fire to come down from heaven to the earth in full view of the people. 14 Because of the signs it was given power to perform on behalf of the first beast, it deceived the inhabitants of the earth. It ordered them to set up an image in honour of the beast who was wounded by the sword and yet lived. 15 The second beast was given power to give breath to the image of the first beast, so that the image could speak and cause all who refused to worship the image to be killed. 16 It also forced all people, great and small, rich and poor, free and slave, to receive a mark on their right hands or on their foreheads, 17 so that they could not buy or sell unless they had the mark, which is the name of the beast or the number of its name.

18 This calls for wisdom. Let the person who has insight calculate the number of the beast, for it is the number of a man.^e That number is 666.

The Lamb and the 144,000

14 Then I looked, and there before me was the Lamb, standing on Mount Zion, and with him 144,000 who had his name and his Father's name written on their foreheads. 2 And I heard a sound from heaven like the roar of rushing waters and like a loud peal of thunder. The sound I heard was like that of harpists playing their harps. 3 And they sang a new song before the throne and before the four living creatures and the elders. No one could learn the song except the 144,000 who had been redeemed from the earth. 4 These are those who did not defile themselves with women, for they remained virgins. They follow the Lamb wherever he

goes. They were purchased from among mankind and offered as firstfruits to God and the Lamb. 5 No lie was found in their mouths; they are blameless.

The three angels

6 Then I saw another angel flying in mid-air, and he had the eternal gospel to proclaim to those who live on the earth – to every nation, tribe, language and people. 7 He said in a loud voice, 'Fear God and give him glory, because the hour of his judgment has come. Worship him who made the heavens, the earth, the sea and the springs of water.'

8 A second angel followed and said, ' "Fallen! Fallen is Babylon the Great," ^a which made all the nations drink the maddening wine of her adulteries.'

9 A third angel followed them and said in a loud voice: 'If anyone worships the beast and its image and receives its mark on their forehead or on their hand, 10 they, too, will drink the wine of God's fury, which has been poured full strength into the cup of his wrath. They will be tormented with burning sulphur in the presence of the holy angels and of the Lamb. 11 And the smoke of their torment will rise for ever and ever. There will be no rest day or night for those who worship the beast and its image, or for anyone who receives the mark of its name.' 12 This calls for patient endurance on the part of the people of God who keep his commands and remain faithful to Jesus.

13 Then I heard a voice from heaven say, 'Write this: blessed are the dead who die in the Lord from now on.'

'Yes,' says the Spirit, 'they will rest from their labour, for their deeds will follow them.'

Harvesting the earth and trampling the winepress

14 I looked, and there before me was a white cloud, and seated on the cloud was one like a son of man^b with a crown

---

e 18 Or *is humanity's number*

a 8 Isaiah 21:9
b 14 See Daniel 7:13.

of gold on his head and a sharp sickle in his hand. ¹⁵Then another angel came out of the temple and called in a loud voice to him who was sitting on the cloud, 'Take your sickle and reap, because the time to reap has come, for the harvest of the earth is ripe.' ¹⁶So he who was seated on the cloud swung his sickle over the earth, and the earth was harvested.

¹⁷Another angel came out of the temple in heaven, and he too had a sharp sickle. ¹⁸Still another angel, who had charge of the fire, came from the altar and called in a loud voice to him who had the sharp sickle, 'Take your sharp sickle and gather the clusters of grapes from the earth's vine, because its grapes are ripe.' ¹⁹The angel swung his sickle on the earth, gathered its grapes and threw them into the great winepress of God's wrath. ²⁰They were trampled in the winepress outside the city, and blood flowed out of the press, rising as high as the horses' bridles for a distance of 1,600 stadia.ᶜ

Seven angels with seven plagues

15 I saw in heaven another great and marvellous sign: seven angels with the seven last plagues – last, because with them God's wrath is completed. ²And I saw what looked like a sea of glass glowing with fire and, standing beside the sea, those who had been victorious over the beast and its image and over the number of its name. They held harps given them by God ³and sang the song of God's servant Moses and of the Lamb:

'Great and marvellous are your deeds,
   Lord God Almighty.
Just and true are your ways,
   King of the nations.ᵃ
⁴Who will not fear you, Lord,
   and bring glory to your name?
For you alone are holy.
All nations will come
   and worship before you,

for your righteous acts have been
   revealed.'ᵇ

⁵After this I looked, and I saw in heaven the temple – that is, the tabernacle of the covenant law – and it was opened. ⁶Out of the temple came the seven angels with the seven plagues. They were dressed in clean, shining linen and wore golden sashes round their chests. ⁷Then one of the four living creatures gave to the seven angels seven golden bowls filled with the wrath of God, who lives for ever and ever. ⁸And the temple was filled with smoke from the glory of God and from his power, and no one could enter the temple until the seven plagues of the seven angels were completed.

The seven bowls of God's wrath

16 Then I heard a loud voice from the temple saying to the seven angels, 'Go, pour out the seven bowls of God's wrath on the earth.'

²The first angel went and poured out his bowl on the land, and ugly, festering sores broke out on the people who had the mark of the beast and worshipped its image.

³The second angel poured out his bowl on the sea, and it turned into blood like that of a dead person, and every living thing in the sea died.

⁴The third angel poured out his bowl on the rivers and springs of water, and they became blood. ⁵Then I heard the angel in charge of the waters say:

'You are just in these judgments,
   O Holy One,
you who are and who were;
⁶for they have shed the blood of your
      holy people and your prophets,
   and you have given them blood to
      drink as they deserve.'

⁷And I heard the altar respond:

ᶜ20 That is, about 180 miles or about 300 kilometres
ᵃ3 Some manuscripts *ages*

ᵇ3,4 Phrases in this song are drawn from Psalm 111:2,3; Deut. 32:4; Jer. 10:7; Psalms 86:9; 98:2.

'Yes, Lord God Almighty,
true and just are your judgments.'

8 The fourth angel poured out his bowl on the sun, and the sun was allowed to scorch people with fire. **9** They were seared by the intense heat and they cursed the name of God, who had control over these plagues, but they refused to repent and glorify him.

10 The fifth angel poured out his bowl on the throne of the beast, and its kingdom was plunged into darkness. People gnawed their tongues in agony **11** and cursed the God of heaven because of their pains and their sores, but they refused to repent of what they had done.

12 The sixth angel poured out his bowl on the great river Euphrates, and its water was dried up to prepare the way for the kings from the East. **13** Then I saw three impure spirits that looked like frogs; they came out of the mouth of the dragon, out of the mouth of the beast and out of the mouth of the false prophet. **14** They are demonic spirits that perform signs, and they go out to the kings of the whole world, to gather them for the battle on the great day of God Almighty.

15 'Look, I come like a thief! Blessed is the one who stays awake and remains clothed, so as not to go naked and be shamefully exposed.'

16 Then they gathered the kings together to the place that in Hebrew is called Armageddon.

17 The seventh angel poured out his bowl into the air, and out of the temple came a loud voice from the throne, saying, 'It is done!' **18** Then there came flashes of lightning, rumblings, peals of thunder and a severe earthquake. No earthquake like it has ever occurred since mankind has been on earth, so tremendous was the quake. **19** The great city split into three parts, and the cities of the nations collapsed. God remembered Babylon the Great and gave her the cup filled with the wine of the fury of his wrath. **20** Every island fled away and the mountains could not be found.

21 From the sky huge hailstones, each weighing about forty kilograms fell on people. And they cursed God on account of the plague of hail, because the plague was so terrible.

Babylon, the prostitute on the beast

17 One of the seven angels who had the seven bowls came and said to me, 'Come, I will show you the punishment of the great prostitute, who sits by many waters. **2** With her the kings of the earth committed adultery, and the inhabitants of the earth were intoxicated with the wine of her adulteries.'

3 Then the angel carried me away in the Spirit into a desert. There I saw a woman sitting on a scarlet beast that was covered with blasphemous names and had seven heads and ten horns. **4** The woman was dressed in purple and scarlet, and was glittering with gold, precious stones and pearls. She held a golden cup in her hand, filled with abominable things and the filth of her adulteries. **5** The name written on her forehead was a mystery:

BABYLON THE GREAT
THE MOTHER OF PROSTITUTES
AND OF THE ABOMINATIONS OF THE EARTH.

6 I saw that the woman was drunk with the blood of God's holy people, the blood of those who bore testimony to Jesus.

When I saw her, I was greatly astonished. **7** Then the angel said to me: 'Why are you astonished? I will explain to you the mystery of the woman and of the beast she rides, which has the seven heads and ten horns. **8** The beast, which you saw, once was, now is not, and yet will come up out of the Abyss and go to its destruction. The inhabitants of the earth whose names have not been written in the book of life from the creation of the world will be astonished when they see the beast, because it once was, now is not, and yet will come.

9 'This calls for a mind with wisdom. The seven heads are seven hills on which the woman sits. **10** They are also seven kings. Five have fallen, one is, the other has not yet come; but when he does come, he must remain for only a little while. ¹¹The beast who once was, and now is not, is an eighth king. He belongs to the seven and is going to his destruction.

¹²'The ten horns you saw are ten kings who have not yet received a kingdom, but who for one hour will receive authority as kings along with the beast. ¹³They have one purpose and will give their power and authority to the beast. ¹⁴They will wage war against the Lamb, but the Lamb will triumph over them because he is Lord of lords and King of kings – and with him will be his called, chosen and faithful followers.'

¹⁵Then the angel said to me, 'The waters you saw, where the prostitute sits, are peoples, multitudes, nations and languages. ¹⁶The beast and the ten horns you saw will hate the prostitute. They will bring her to ruin and leave her naked; they will eat her flesh and burn her with fire. ¹⁷For God has put it into their hearts to accomplish his purpose by agreeing to hand over to the beast their royal authority, until God's words are fulfilled. ¹⁸The woman you saw is the great city that rules over the kings of the earth.'

Lament over fallen Babylon

18 After this I saw another angel coming down from heaven. He had great authority, and the earth was illuminated by his splendour. ²With a mighty voice he shouted:

'"Fallen! Fallen is Babylon the Great!"ᵃ
  She has become a dwelling for
    demons
and a haunt for every impure spirit,
  a haunt for every unclean bird,
  a haunt for every unclean and
    detestable animal.
³For all the nations have drunk
  the maddening wine of her
    adulteries.
The kings of the earth committed
    adultery with her,
  and the merchants of the earth
    grew rich from her excessive
    luxuries.'

Warning to escape Babylon's judgment

⁴Then I heard another voice from heaven say:

'"Come out of her, my people,"ᵇ
  so that you will not share in her
    sins,
  so that you will not receive any of
    her plagues;
⁵for her sins are piled up to heaven,
  and God has remembered her
    crimes.
⁶Give back to her as she has given;
  pay her back double for what she
    has done.
  Pour her a double portion from her
    own cup.
⁷Give her as much torment and grief
  as the glory and luxury she gave
    herself.
In her heart she boasts,
  "I sit enthroned as queen.
I am not a widow;ᶜ
I will never mourn."
⁸Therefore in one day her plagues will
    overtake her:
  death, mourning and famine.
She will be consumed by fire,
  for mighty is the Lord God who
    judges her.

Threefold woe over Babylon's fall

⁹'When the kings of the earth who committed adultery with her and shared her luxury see the smoke of her burning, they will weep and mourn over her. ¹⁰Terrified at her torment, they will stand far off and cry:

'"Woe! Woe to you, great city,
  you mighty city of Babylon!
In one hour your doom has come!"

¹¹'The merchants of the earth will weep and mourn over her because no one buys their cargoes any more – ¹²cargoes of gold, silver, precious stones and pearls; fine linen, purple, silk and scarlet cloth;

ᵃ2 Isaiah 21:9

ᵇ4 Jer. 51:45
ᶜ7 See Isaiah 47:7,8.

every sort of citron wood, and articles of every kind made of ivory, costly wood, bronze, iron and marble; ¹³cargoes of cinnamon and spice, of incense, myrrh and frankincense, of wine and olive oil, of fine flour and wheat; cattle and sheep; horses and carriages; and human beings sold as slaves.

PEARLY GATES

Have you ever heard someone talking about the 'Pearly Gates', meaning heaven? The image comes from Revelation, which describes a city with twelve gates, carved out of giant pearls (Revelation 21:21).

¹⁴'They will say, "The fruit you longed for is gone from you. All your luxury and splendour have vanished, never to be recovered." ¹⁵The merchants who sold these things and gained their wealth from her will stand far off, terrified at her torment. They will weep and mourn ¹⁶and cry out:

'"Woe! Woe to you, great city,
    dressed in fine linen, purple and
        scarlet,
    and glittering with gold, precious
        stones and pearls!
¹⁷In one hour such great wealth has
        been brought to ruin!"

'Every sea captain, and all who travel by ship, the sailors, and all who earn their living from the sea, will stand far off. ¹⁸When they see the smoke of her burning, they will exclaim, "Was there ever a city like this great city?" ¹⁹They will throw dust on their heads, and with weeping and mourning cry out:

'"Woe! Woe to you, great city,
    where all who had ships on the sea

became rich through her wealth!
In one hour she has been brought to
        ruin!"

²⁰'Rejoice over her, you heavens!
    Rejoice, you people of God!
    Rejoice, apostles and prophets!
For God has judged her
    with the judgment she imposed on
        you.'

The finality of Babylon's doom
²¹Then a mighty angel picked up a boulder the size of a large millstone and threw it into the sea, and said:

'With such violence
    the great city of Babylon will be
        thrown down,
    never to be found again.
²²The music of harpists and musicians,
        pipers and trumpeters,
    will never be heard in you again.
No worker of any trade
    will ever be found in you again.
The sound of a millstone
    will never be heard in you again.
²³The light of a lamp
    will never shine in you again.
The voice of bridegroom and bride
    will never be heard in you again.
Your merchants were the world's
        important people.
By your magic spell all the nations
        were led astray.
²⁴In her was found the blood of
        prophets and of God's holy
        people,
    of all who have been slaughtered on
        the earth.'

Threefold hallelujah over Babylon's fall
19 After this I heard what sounded like the roar of a great multitude in heaven shouting:

'Hallelujah!
Salvation and glory and power belong
        to our God,
²   for true and just are his judgments.
He has condemned the great prostitute

who corrupted the earth by her
  adulteries.
He has avenged on her the blood of his
  servants.'

3 And again they shouted:

'Hallelujah!
The smoke from her goes up for ever
  and ever.'

4 The twenty-four elders and the four
living creatures fell down and worshipped
God, who was seated on the throne. And
they cried:

'Amen, Hallelujah!'

5 Then a voice came from the throne,
saying:

'Praise our God,
  all you his servants,
you who fear him,
  both great and small!'

6 Then I heard what sounded like a great
multitude, like the roar of rushing waters
and like loud peals of thunder, shouting:

'Hallelujah!
For our Lord God Almighty reigns.
7 Let us rejoice and be glad
  and give him glory!
For the wedding of the Lamb has come,
  and his bride has made herself ready.
8 Fine linen, bright and clean,
  was given her to wear.'
(Fine linen stands for the righteous acts of
God's holy people.)

9 Then the angel said to me, 'Write this:
Blessed are those who are invited to the
wedding supper of the Lamb!' And he
added, 'These are the true words of God.'

10 At this I fell at his feet to worship him.
But he said to me, 'Don't do that! I am a
fellow servant with you and with your
brothers and sisters who hold to the testimony of Jesus. Worship God! For it is the
Spirit of prophecy who bears testimony to
Jesus.'

The heavenly warrior defeats the beast

11 I saw heaven standing open and there
before me was a white horse, whose rider
is called Faithful and True. With justice he
judges and wages war. 12 His eyes are like
blazing fire, and on his head are many
crowns. He has a name written on him
that no one knows but he himself. 13 He
is dressed in a robe dipped in blood, and
his name is the Word of God. 14 The armies of heaven were following him, riding on white horses and dressed in fine
linen, white and clean. 15 Coming out of
his mouth is a sharp sword with which
to strike down the nations. 'He will rule
them with an iron sceptre.'*a* He treads the
winepress of the fury of the wrath of God
Almighty. 16 On his robe and on his thigh
he has this name written:

KING OF KINGS AND LORD OF LORDS.

17 And I saw an angel standing in the
sun, who cried in a loud voice to all the
birds flying in mid-air, 'Come, gather together for the great supper of God, 18 so
that you may eat the flesh of kings, generals, and the mighty, of horses and their
riders, and the flesh of all people, free and
slave, great and small.'

19 Then I saw the beast and the kings of
the earth and their armies gathered together to wage war against the rider on
the horse and his army. 20 But the beast
was captured, and with it the false prophet
who had performed the signs on its behalf.
With these signs he had deluded those
who had received the mark of the beast
and worshipped its image. The two of
them were thrown alive into the fiery lake
of burning sulphur. 21 The rest were killed
with the sword coming out of the mouth
of the rider on the horse, and all the birds
gorged themselves on their flesh.

The thousand years

20 And I saw an angel coming down
out of heaven, having the key
to the Abyss and holding in his hand a
great chain. 2 He seized the dragon, that

ancient snake, who is the devil, or Satan, and bound him for a thousand years. ³He threw him into the Abyss, and locked and sealed it over him, to keep him from deceiving the nations any more until the thousand years were ended. After that, he must be set free for a short time.

⁴I saw thrones on which were seated those who had been given authority to judge. And I saw the souls of those who had been beheaded because of their testimony about Jesus and because of the word of God. They*ᵃ* had not worshipped the beast or its image and had not received its mark on their foreheads or their hands. They came to life and reigned with Christ for a thousand years. ⁵(The rest of the dead did not come to life until the thousand years were ended.) This is the first resurrection. ⁶Blessed and holy are those who share in the first resurrection. The second death has no power over them, but they will be priests of God and of Christ and will reign with him for a thousand years.

The judgment of Satan

⁷When the thousand years are over, Satan will be released from his prison ⁸and will go out to deceive the nations in the four corners of the earth – Gog and Magog – and to gather them for battle. In number they are like the sand on the seashore. ⁹They marched across the breadth of the earth and surrounded the camp of God's people, the city he loves. But fire came down from heaven and devoured them. ¹⁰And the devil, who deceived them, was thrown into the lake of burning sulphur, where the beast and the false prophet had been thrown. They will be tormented day and night for ever and ever.

The judgment of the dead

¹¹Then I saw a great white throne and him who was seated on it. The earth and the heavens fled from his presence, and there was no place for them. ¹²And I saw the dead, great and small, standing before the throne, and books were opened. Another book was opened, which is the book of life. The dead were judged according to what they had done as recorded in the books. ¹³The sea gave up the dead that were in it, and death and Hades gave up the dead that were in them, and each person was judged according to what they had done. ¹⁴Then death and Hades were thrown into the lake of fire. The lake of fire is the second death. ¹⁵Anyone whose name was not found written in the book of life was thrown into the lake of fire.

A new heaven and a new earth

21 Then I saw 'a new heaven and a new earth,'*ᵃ* for the first heaven and the first earth had passed away, and there was no longer any sea. ²I saw the Holy City, the new Jerusalem, coming down out of heaven from God, prepared as a bride beautifully dressed for her husband. ³And I heard a loud voice from the throne saying, 'Look! God's dwelling-place is now among the people, and he will dwell with them. They will be his people, and God himself will be with them and be their God. ⁴"He will wipe every tear from their eyes. There will be no more death"*ᵇ* or mourning or crying or pain, for the old order of things has passed away.'

⁵He who was seated on the throne said, 'I am making everything new!' Then he said, 'Write this down, for these words are trustworthy and true.'

⁶He said to me: 'It is done. I am the Alpha and the Omega, the Beginning and the End. To the thirsty I will give water without cost from the spring of the water of life. ⁷Those who are victorious will inherit all this, and I will be their God and they will be my children. ⁸But the cowardly, the unbelieving, the vile, the murderers, the sexually immoral, those who practise magic arts, the idolaters and all liars – they will be consigned to the fiery lake of burning sulphur. This is the second death.'

---

a 4 Or *God; I also saw those who*

a 1 Isaiah 65:17
b 4 Isaiah 25:8

JESUS' RETURN

Every year or two a blockbuster film is released about an apocalyptic event that wipes out part of the world's population and threatens the earth's existence. There's also a constant stream of books claiming to have 'unlocked the mysteries of the book of Revelation', often predicting a date in the near future when Jesus will return and graphically describing the horror of events surrounding his coming.

There's a long list dating back thousands of years of people who have predicted the end of the world and been proved wrong, and our generation is no different. What does the Bible actually teach us? Some people believe Revelation gives us a chronological countdown of the last days before Jesus' return, and the symbolic language is all applicable to present-day events in the Middle East and beyond. Others see the imagery of a great cosmic battle as applicable to every generation, while others believe most of Revelation describes events in the first century AD. Certainly its primary role was to assure early Christians of the Lordship of Jesus in the midst of an intimidating empire, rather than inform them of events thousands of years in advance.

Whatever our view, it's important to note that the Bible consistently teaches us that the return of Jesus will be the culmination of God's great plan to put right the mess humans have made of the world. This plan is not to destroy the world and start again, but to cleanse and renew it, and ultimately bring heaven and earth together as one again. In 2 Peter 3 it's compared to the time of Noah, when God 'destroyed' the earth by cleansing it with water. This time the destruction of evil will come with God's holy fire.

This act of restoring the whole creation is referred to in different ways in the Bible. Revelation 21 describes *'a new heaven and a new earth'*. It's a 'new' earth in the way that Jesus' resurrected body is new – renewed, of the same essence and still recognisable, yet greater in every way. Other writers describe a time when God will *'restore everything'* (Acts 3:21), or a day when God will *'reconcile to himself all things'* (Colossians 1:20).

In this wonderful passage in Revelation 21, we read of a coming day when *'there will be no more death or mourning or crying or pain'* (v. 4). Whatever differences we have in interpreting the events leading up to Jesus' return, Christians can all agree that we have this great, transforming hope: Jesus is making everything new, and one day he will return to put everything right and even death itself will be abolished.

In our day, when we pray for God's kingdom to come on earth as in heaven, we can see glimpses of that future: when the sick are healed, when justice is done, when sins are forgiven, when the bereaved are comforted, we know God has started a good work and he will bring it to completion when he returns.

Chris Lane

The new Jerusalem, the bride of the Lamb

9 One of the seven angels who had the seven bowls full of the seven last plagues came and said to me, 'Come, I will show you the bride, the wife of the Lamb.' 10 And he carried me away in the Spirit to a mountain great and high, and showed me the Holy City, Jerusalem, coming down out of heaven from God. 11 It shone with the glory of God, and its brilliance was like that of a very precious jewel, like a jasper, clear as crystal. 12 It had a great, high wall with twelve gates, and with twelve angels at the gates. On the gates were written the names of the twelve tribes of Israel. 13 There were three gates on the east, three on the north, three on the south and three on the west. 14 The wall of the city had twelve foundations, and on them were the names of the twelve apostles of the Lamb.

15 The angel who talked with me had a measuring rod of gold to measure the city, its gates and its walls. 16 The city was laid out like a square, as long as it was wide. He measured the city with the rod and found it to be 12,000 stadia*c* in length, and as wide and high as it is long. 17 The angel measured the wall using human measurement, and it was 144 cubits*d* thick.*e* 18 The wall was made of jasper, and the city of pure gold, as pure as glass. 19 The foundations of the city walls were decorated with every kind of precious stone. The first foundation was jasper, the second sapphire, the third agate, the fourth emerald, 20 the fifth onyx, the sixth ruby, the seventh chrysolite, the eighth beryl, the ninth topaz, the tenth turquoise, the eleventh jacinth, and the twelfth amethyst.*f* 21 The twelve gates were twelve pearls, each gate made of a single pearl. The great street of the city was of gold, as pure as transparent glass.

22 I did not see a temple in the city, because the Lord God Almighty and the Lamb are its temple. 23 The city does not need the sun or the moon to shine on it, for the glory of God gives it light, and the Lamb is its lamp. 24 The nations will walk by its light, and the kings of the earth will bring their splendour into it. 25 On no day will its gates ever be shut, for there will be no night there. 26 The glory and honour of the nations will be brought into it. 27 Nothing impure will ever enter it, nor will anyone who does what is shameful or deceitful, but only those whose names are written in the Lamb's book of life.

Eden restored

22 Then the angel showed me the river of the water of life, as clear as crystal, flowing from the throne of God and of the Lamb 2 down the middle of the great street of the city. On each side of the river stood the tree of life, bearing twelve crops of fruit, yielding its fruit every month. And the leaves of the tree are for the healing of the nations. 3 No longer will there be any curse. The throne of God and of the Lamb will be in the city, and his servants will serve him. 4 They will see his face, and his name will be on their foreheads. 5 There will be no more night. They will not need the light of a lamp or the light of the sun, for the Lord God will give them light. And they will reign for ever and ever.

John and the angel

6 The angel said to me, 'These words are trustworthy and true. The Lord, the God who inspires the prophets, sent his angel to show his servants the things that must soon take place.'

7 'Look, I am coming soon! Blessed is the one who keeps the words of the prophecy written in this scroll.'

8 I, John, am the one who heard and saw these things. And when I had heard and seen them, I fell down to worship at the feet of the angel who had been showing them to me. 9 But he said to me, 'Don't do that! I am a fellow servant with

---

c 16 That is, about 1,400 miles or about 2,200 kilometres
d 17 That is, about 65 metres
e 17 Or *high*
f 20 The precise identification of some of these precious stones is uncertain.

WHAT IS CHRISTIANITY? 10

Doctrine of the future: he is coming

The Bible began in a garden with two people. It ends in a city with a multitude. The book of Revelation is sometimes confusing, but it makes one point about the future very clearly: God wins.

Many people today live lives full of anxiety. Since Adam and Eve sinned and then, in fear, hid from God, we have been afraid. Among all our other fears, we all know a fear of death and the future.

The book of Revelation is not always the most comforting book to read. It's full of crazy plagues and weird monsters. But in the midst of all this there comes the message of the Lamb of God. Jesus laid down his own life so that all who know him might receive eternal life. Paul and others longed for the return of Jesus (2 Timothy 4:8). They weren't afraid of the end of all things. When we see what this will bring, we begin to see why.

Some people are into the habit of predicting dates when the world will end. Jesus warns us that this is a bit of a waste of time: *'About that day or hour no one knows…'* (Matthew 24:36). At the same time he does tell us to be ready for his return (Matthew 25:13), and we know what we can expect.

When Jesus returns, evil will finally be judged. We look at many people suffering around us and we ask where God's justice is. There will come a day when everyone will have to give account for the life they have lived. We will stand before God, and as Christians we believe Jesus has been judged on our behalf. The cross is God's justice. But we still believe that the whole of creation will be called to account. Evil will be dealt with once and for all.

The return of Jesus will see the triumph of good. In many ways, the cross and resurrection signalled the defeat of sin and death, but we are still waiting for the great climax of this victory. It's hard to imagine at the moment (because evil and good are so intertwined in our world), but there will come a time when everything in the world is good. This is what is meant by the final victory of God. Isaiah paints a picture of this in Isaiah 11:6–9, and Revelation 21 – 22 shows a world saturated with God's goodness.

Jesus has triumphed on the cross and though he is with us now, he has yet to return finally. We live in this 'time in between', this tension, and it's sometimes very tough (2 Corinthians 4:8–9). Be assured, there will come a day when we see him face to face. Then our pains and our deep hurts will be finally healed and we will know wholeness, peace and life everlasting. God wins, and remember, *'our salvation is nearer now than when we first believed'* (Romans 13:11).

Andy Croft

 2 Timothy 3:16

you and with your fellow prophets and with all who keep the words of this scroll. Worship God!'

¹⁰Then he told me, 'Do not seal up the words of the prophecy of this scroll, because the time is near. ¹¹Let the one who does wrong continue to do wrong; let the vile person continue to be vile; let the one who does right continue to do right; and let the holy person continue to be holy.'

Epilogue: invitation and warning

¹²'Look, I am coming soon! My reward is with me, and I will give to each person according to what they have done. ¹³I am the Alpha and the Omega, the First and the Last, the Beginning and the End.

¹⁴'Blessed are those who wash their robes, that they may have the right to the tree of life and may go through the gates into the city. ¹⁵Outside are the dogs, those who practise magic arts, the sexually immoral, the murderers, the idolaters and everyone who loves and practises falsehood.

¹⁶'I, Jesus, have sent my angel to give you*ᵃ* this testimony for the churches. I am the Root and the Offspring of David, and the bright Morning Star.'

¹⁷The Spirit and the bride say, 'Come!' And let the one who hears say, 'Come!' Let the one who is thirsty come; and let the one who wishes take the free gift of the water of life.

¹⁸I warn everyone who hears the words of the prophecy of this scroll: if anyone adds anything to them, God will add to that person the plagues described in this scroll. ¹⁹And if anyone takes words away from this scroll of prophecy, God will take away from that person any share in the tree of life and in the Holy City, which are described in this scroll.

²⁰He who testifies to these things says, 'Yes, I am coming soon.'

Amen. Come, Lord Jesus.

²¹The grace of the Lord Jesus be with God's people. Amen.

---

a 16 The Greek is plural.

The Story of the Bible
A Great Big Bible Timeline

START HERE

CREATION

Adam & Eve

Cain & Abel

Noah

1. 'In the beginning God...' God creates everything: animals and plants, men and women... The first humans, Adam and Eve, choose to disobey God and are expelled from the garden in Eden... Sin enters the world... Evil spreads... God sends a huge flood to wash the world clean and start again... Only Noah and his family survive... God promises never to destroy humanity again.

Books about, or set in this time

Genesis

God makes a promise to Abraham: his descendants will be a mighty nation

Famine in Canaan. Jacob's family move to Egypt

Jacob is given the name 'Israel'

Joseph is taken to Egypt

BC

2100

2000

1900

Abraham

Ishmael

Isaac

Jacob & Esau

Joseph

PATRIARCHS

2. God begins a new plan... He tells Abraham to move to Canaan and promises that his descendants will be a mighty nation, which will bless all the people of earth... This promise, or covenant, is repeated to Abraham, to his son Isaac and his grandson Jacob... These are the Patriarchs, the 'fathers' of Israel... Jacob's son, Joseph, is taken as a slave to Egypt... Famine hits Canaan... Jacob and his family are reunited with Joseph, but end up in Egypt...

3. The descendants of Jacob's sons become the twelve tribes of Israel and each tribe takes its name from their ancestors... In Egypt the Hebrews, or Israelites as they're also known, become slaves... Moses is a Hebrew boy who is brought up in the royal palace... After murdering a slave driver he is forced to flee... In the desert he meets God in the form of a burning bush... God tells Moses that he will set his people free...

Jacob's descendants – the Hebrews – became slaves in Egypt

SLAVERY

1800

1700

1600

1500

Moses

OLD TESTAMENT MIDDLE EAST

· Haran

Nineveh ·

ASSYRIA

R. Euphrates

R. Tigris

The Promised Land

· Damascus

BABYLON

Babylon ·

PERSIA

Susa ·

Shechem
· Jericho
Jerusalem

CANAAN

· Rameses

· Ur

EGYPT

At the end of Genesis, the Israelites are here

Abraham starts here

Mt. Sinai

Exodus

RESCUE

4. Moses leads the Israelites out of Egypt... At Sinai he is given the law by God... the Israelites' lack of faith leads to them spending 40 years in the desert... Moses dies overlooking the promised land and it is Joshua who leads the people into the land... after Joshua's death there is a time of anarchy and chaos, the time of the Judges... the people want stability and peace. They want a king...

Moses dies on Mount Nebo. Joshua leads Israel into the Promised Land

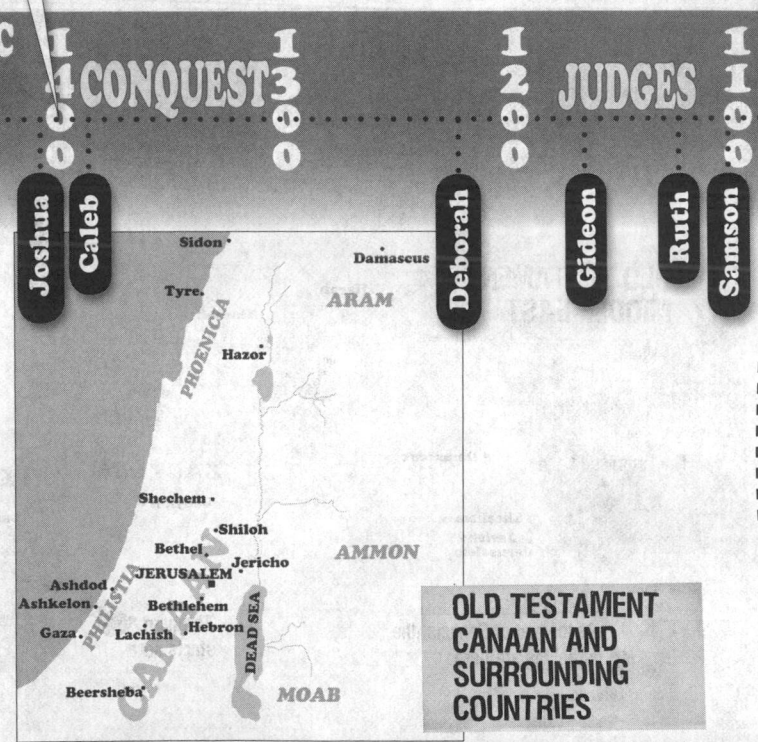

BC **1400** CONQUEST **1300** **1200** JUDGES **1100**

Joshua Caleb Deborah Gideon Ruth Samson

Sidon
Damascus
Tyre
ARAM
PHOENICIA
Hazor
Shechem
Shiloh
Bethel
Jericho
JERUSALEM
Ashdod
Ashkelon
Bethlehem
Gaza Lachish Hebron
PHILISTIA
CANAAN
DEAD SEA
AMMON
Beersheba MOAB

OLD TESTAMENT CANAAN AND SURROUNDING COUNTRIES

Exodus
Numbers
Leviticus
Deuteronomy

Joshua

Judges

Ruth

KINGS & PROPHETS

David becomes King, captures Jerusalem and brings the Ark of the Covenant into the city

After Solomon's death, the kingdom splits in two

Jonah

The Assyrians destroy Israel

Saul becomes King

Solomon builds the temple

Elijah

Elisha

Amos

Hosea

ISRAEL

JUDAH

Samuel

Saul

David

Solomon

Obadiah

Micah

Isaiah

5. Saul is first king of Israel, but he is rejected by God in favour of David... When David becomes king he captures Jerusalem and makes it his capital... David's son, Solomon, builds a magnificent temple in Jerusalem... After Solomon's death, a civil war splits the kingdom into two: Israel in the north and Judah in the south... In Israel and Judah, there are a few good kings, but most of them are evil men who worship false gods... So God sends the prophets to challenge the people... The northern kingdom of Israel is destroyed in 722 BC when the Assyrians invade and take everyone away... The southern kingdom of Judah limps on...

1&2 Samuel   1 &2 Kings   Obadiah   Joel   Jonah   Isaiah
                    1 &2 Chronicles   Habakkuk Micah Hosea
Psalms   Proverbs Ecclesiastes   Amos
                    Song of Songs

6. Judah is a weak country and in 522 BC it, too, is destroyed, this time by the Babylonians... Jerusalem is destroyed, the temple is demolished and the Judean people are led into captivity in Babylon... Is this the end for Judah? The prophets don't think so... after decades of captivity, the Jews are released when a persian called Cyrus defeats the Babylonians... Some Jews, led by people like Nehemiah and Ezra, return home to rebuild their shattered country...

The Babylonians destroy Jerusalem and take the Judean people into exile

Cyrus the Great allows the Jews to return home

Jews rebuild the temple

Alexander the Great conquers Judea

BC

6 0 0

EXILE

5 0 0

4 0 0

3 0 0

Nahum

Zephaniah

Jeremiah

Daniel

Ezekiel

Haggai

Zechariah

Ezra

Nehemiah

Malachi

EXILE & RETURN

2 Kings
2 Chronicles
Jeremiah
Nahum
Zephaniah

Lamentations
Ezekiel
Daniel

Haggai
Zechariah

Esther

Ezra   Malachi
Nehemiah

BETWEEN THE TESTAMENTS

7. A succession of empires take over... After a brief spell of independence, Judea becomes a part of the Roman empire in 63 BC... The people talk about a champion predicted by the prophets, someone anointed by God to free them and make the country great again... They call this person the Messiah... But when will he come? How long must they wait?

Judea achieves independence

The Romans conquer Judea

Herod the Great made king by the Romans. He rebuilds the Temple

300 **200** **100** **AD 0** **100**

New Testament starts here! The action in the New Testament covers from c.4 BC to c.90 AD. See next pages for more details.

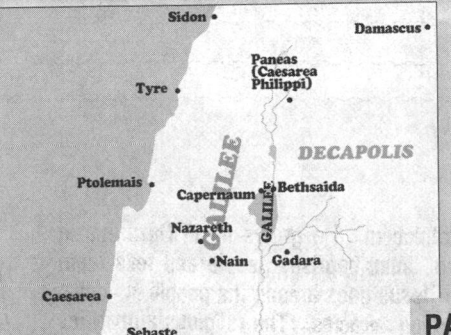

Sidon
Damascus
Paneas (Caesarea Philippi)
Tyre
GALILEE
DECAPOLIS
Ptolemais
Capernaum • Bethsaida
Nazareth
GALILEE
Nain • Gadara
Caesarea
Sebaste (Samaria)
SAMARIA
PEREA
Joppa
Arimathea
Jerusalem ■ Jericho
JUDEA • Bethlehem
Ashkelon
Gaza • Hebron
IDUMEA
DEAD SEA

PALESTINE UNDER THE ROMANS

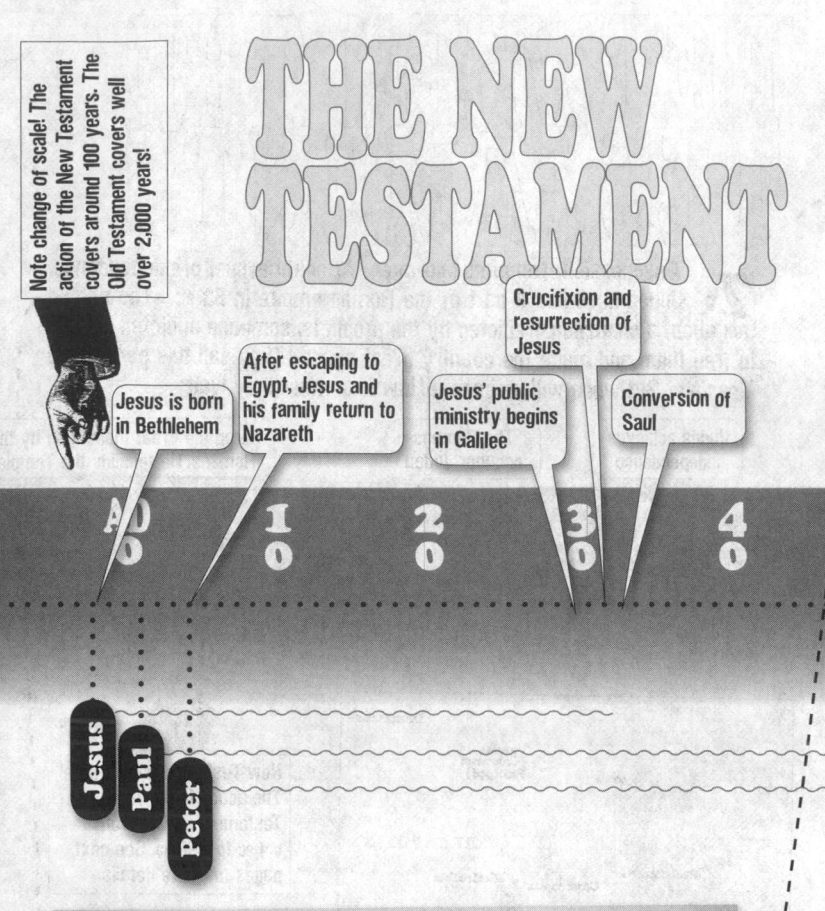

THE NEW TESTAMENT

Jesus is born in Bethlehem

After escaping to Egypt, Jesus and his family return to Nazareth

Crucifixion and resurrection of Jesus

Jesus' public ministry begins in Galilee

Conversion of Saul

A D 0   1 0   2 0   3 0   4 0

Jesus

Paul

Peter

8. Jesus is born in Bethlehem... He grows up in Nazareth, in Galilee... His relative, John, baptises people and tells them to prepare for the Messiah... Jesus goes among the people in Judea, healing, teaching and performing miracles... The religious authorities criticise him because he spends time with all the wrong sorts of people... He comes to Jerusalem where he is arrested, tried and executed... But then his followers start making amazing claims... He has risen from the dead and appeared to his followers...

Matthew
Luke

John
Mark

Acts

9. In Jerusalem the Holy Spirit descends on Jesus' followers... Empowered by the Spirit the church spreads the good news through words, actions and miracles... The new church spreads like wildfire... Saul is converted when he has a vision of Jesus... Gentiles start to follow Jesus as well as Jews... Saul, (a.k.a Paul) starts his missionary journeys... Letters fly back and forth between the churches discussing how to follow Jesus... Paul is arrested in Jerusalem and sent to Rome for trial... The church faces persecution... then, one Sunday, on a prison-island called Patmos, a man called John, has a vision...

Paul's first missionary journey. Jerusalem Council

Paul is arrested and sent to Rome

Emperor Nero persecutes Christians. Probable death of Peter and Paul in Rome

Jewish revolt against Roman rule ends in defeat. Temple is completely destroyed

On Patmos, John has a vision of the end of time

50 60 70 80 90 100

THE MEDITERRANEAN IN NEW TESTAMENT TIMES

Illyricum Thracia
Rome Macedonia Philippi
Italia Thessalonica Bithynia
Epirus Asia Cappadocia
Nicopolis Sardis Galatia
Corinth Athens Ephesus
Achaia Lycia Tarsus
Cilicia Antioch
Syria
Mediterranean Sea Sidon Damascus
Cyrene Jerusalem
Cyrene Judea
Alexandria

Galatians 1 & 2 Corinthians Titus 1 & 2 Peter 1, 2 & 3 John Revelation
James Romans Philippians Jude
1&2 Thessalonians Philemon
Ephesians 1 & 2 Timothy
Hebrews Colossians

NEW
CREATION

END
HERE

You are somewhere
in this bit!

10. John's vision shows him stuff that is happening around him, and stuff in the future that has yet to happen... Most of all it shows that Jesus will return and how god will end the big story... It ends as it began, with creation, this time the creation of a new heaven and a new earth... No one knows when this will happen... 'I've seen the future,' says John: 'God wins.'

Help and guidance

Feeling abandoned
- Psalm 37:28
- Psalm 68:5–6
- Hebrews 13:5–6

Thinking about abortion
- Deuteronomy 30:15–20
- Psalm 139:13–16
- Luke 12:6–7
- Psalm 103

Struggling with alcohol
- 1 Corinthians 10:31
- Ephesians 5:18
- 1 Thessalonians 5:6–11

Angry (with God)
- Exodus 34:5–6
- Numbers 11:18–20
- Psalm 7:6
- John 2:15–17

Angry (with others)
- Job 10:1–3
- Job 40:6–10
- Proverbs 29:11

Attacked
- Luke 23:34
- Psalm 35:1, 2
- Psalm 54:1–4

Bereaved or broken-hearted
- 1 Corinthians 15:51–57
- 1 Thessalonians 4:13–18
- Revelation 21:3–5
- Psalm 147:3

Bullied
- 2 Corinthians 12:10
- 2 Thessalonians 1:4
- Matthew 5:10
- Matthew 5:44
- Exodus 34:5–9

Choosing a career
- Jeremiah 17:7
- Isaiah 30:21

- Proverbs 3:5–6

Death
- John 3:16; 14:1–3
- Revelation 21:4
- Psalm 23:4

Desperate
- Psalm 55:16–22
- Psalm 61:1–3
- Psalm 62:1,2
- Psalm 94:18, 19, 22
- Psalm 121:1, 2, 7

Disappointed
- Philippians 4:6–7
- Romans 8:28
- Colossians 3:23–25
- Psalm 121:1–8

Doubting
- Mark 9:23, 24
- John 20:24–31
- Psalm 53:1

Envious
- Galatians 5:26
- Philippians 4:11
- James 3:16

Faith is weak
- Matthew 8:5–13
- Luke 12:22–31
- Hebrews 11

Feeling far from God
- Acts 17:22–30
- James 4:8
- Psalm 42:5–11
- Psalm 139:1–18
- Psalm 145:18

Friends
- John 15:13

Feeling inadequate
- 1 Corinthians 1:20–31
- 2 Corinthians 12:9–10
- Philippians 4:12–13

- Psalm 138:8
- Ecclesiastes 4:9–12
- Proverbs 18:24
- Hebrews 10:24–25
- Proverbs 27:17

Feeling Lost
- Luke 19:10
- Ephesians 2:12–13
- Psalm 107:4–9

Forgiveness
- Ephesians 4:32
- Mark 11:25
- Matthew 5:43–48
- 1 John 1:9
- Colossians 3:13
- Luke 6:27–37
- Matthew 5:7
- Luke 17:4
- Matthew 18:21–35

Friends let you down
- Luke 17:3–4
- 2 Timothy 4:16–18
- Psalm 27:10–14
- Psalm 41

Homework
- Colossians 3:23
- Luke 16:10
- Proverbs 1:7

In danger or threatened
- Mark 4:37–41
- 1 Peter 3:13, 14
- Psalm 27:1
- Psalm 118:6–9

Insulted
- Romans 15:3–4
- 1 Peter 2:23
- Psalm 69:9

Intimidated
- Psalm 3:1–3
- Psalm 55:20–22

Keeping fit
- 1 Timothy 4:8
- 1 Corinthians 6:19
- Proverbs 24:5

Lonely
- Revelation 3:20
- Psalm 23

Looking for a job
- Colossians 3:17, 23
- Psalm 71:3

Love
- 1 Corinthians 13:4–13
- Matthew 22:37–39
- Deuteronomy 6:5
- 1 Corinthians 16:14
- Leviticus 19:18
- 1 John 4:8
- 1 John 4:19
- 1 John 4:12
- 1 John 4:18
- Mark 12:30

Struggling with masturbation
- 1 Corinthians 6:18
- 1 Thessalonians 4:3–5
- Matthew 5:28
- James 1:14–15
- 1 John 1:9

Money
- Hebrews 13:5
- 1 Timothy 6:10
- Matthew 6:24
- Luke 16:11
- Proverbs 22:7
- Matthew 6:19–21
- Matthew 6:31–33

Needing guidance
- Romans 12:1, 2
- Psalm 32:8–10
- Proverbs 16:3

Needing peace
- John 14:27
- Colossians 3:15
- Romans 5:1–5

Parents
- Ephesians 6:1–4
- Luke 11:11–13
- Isaiah 49:15

Perseverance
- 1 Chronicles 16:11
- James 1:12
- Romans 5:3–5
- Galatians 6:9
- Revelation 3:11

Praying
- Luke 11:1–13
- John 14:12–14
- James 5:13,16
- 1 John 5:14, 15
- Psalm 66:17,20

Scared
- Isaiah 41:13
- Mark 4:35–41
- Psalm 56:3, 4, 10, 11

Sleepless
- Matthew 11:28
- 1 Peter 5:7
- Psalm 3:5
- Psalm 4:1, 6–8

Sickness
- 2 Corinthians 12:9, 10
- James 5:14–16
- Psalm 38:3–10
- Psalm 103: 1–4

Feeling sinful
- Luke 15:11–24
- 1 John 5–10
- Psalm 51
- Psalm 103:12

Tattoos and piercings
- 1 Corinthians 6:19–20
- Leviticus 19:28
- 1 Corinthians 10:31

Tempted to commit suicide
- 1 Corinthians 3:16,17
- Psalm 31:9,14,15.
- Psalm 88:1–5,13

Sex
- 1 Corinthians 6:9–13
- Galatians 5:19–23
- 1 Thessalonians 4:3–7

Skint
- Ecclesiastes 5:10–20
- Matthew 6:24–34
- 1 Timothy 6:6–10

Stressed
- Philippians 4:6
- John 14:27
- Romans 8:31
- Romans 8:28
- Luke 10:41–42

Tempted
- Psalm 1:1–6
- 1 Corinthians 10:12–13
- James 4:7

Thankful
- 2 Corinthians 2:14
- Ephesians 5:19, 20
- Psalm 92:1–5
- Psalm 100

Under pressure
- Exodus 18:17–23
- Psalm 43 1–4

Unfairly Treated
- Luke 6:27, 28
- Hebrews 12:3
- 1 Peter 2:19–24

Going to university
- Colossians 3:23
- Proverbs 1:1–33
- 1 Corinthians 10:13

Victimised
- Hebrews 13:6
- Psalm 37:8–11, 34
- Psalm 59:3–10

Tired
- Matthew 11:28–30
- 2 Corinthians 4:16–18
- Psalm 116:5–14

Needing help
- Habakkuk 3:10
- Isaiah 41:13
- 2 Corinthians 3:4–6

Telling people about Jesus
- Acts 1:8
- Acts 5:20, 21
- Acts 18:9, 10
- 1 Peter 3:15

Worried
- Matthew 6:25–34
- Philippians 4:6, 7
- Psalm 46

Following Jesus

MIKE PILAVACHI

As you have read this Bible you will have encountered a Jesus who has things to say to you today, including the biggest invitation you will ever receive.

When Jesus met people in the Gospels he didn't say, 'Come to a religious meeting,' or, 'Come and get spiritual,' or even, 'Come and change your life and the world.' The first thing he said was, 'Come and follow me.'

Christianity is a relationship with Jesus – except it isn't a relationship on our terms. He invites us into that relationship, so he sets the terms. It isn't like, 'Let's go on a few dates and see how it develops.' Neither does he say, 'Keep in touch and I'll come and hang out next time you're free.' No. When Jesus invited Peter and Andrew and the others to have a relationship with him, he told them to leave their old lives to follow him. This relationship isn't about Jesus following us around and making our lives a bit happier. Oh no. It's about us following him around and re-focusing our lives around him. It is about friendship, yes. He calls us friends. The question is, who are we friends with? The Creator and Ruler of the universe. We're invited into a friendship with the King of kings, the Prime Minister of prime ministers, the President of presidents.

So in this relationship he's our Friend and our Ruler (our head of government, if you like, though he never needs to stand for re-election). He's also our Saviour. That means he saves us – and *man* do we need saving! We have messed up and we are messed up. Even the best of us. We were made to look like him. To love like him. But we chose selfishness. We declared independence. The word is 'sin'. Sin is selfishness. 'I' is at the heart of sin.

So God had a problem. Because he's completely pure and holy and perfectly loving, he couldn't look at us with all the mess of our sin. But also because he's completely pure and holy and perfectly loving, he couldn't look away. So in Jesus, God became one of us and allowed our representatives to do the most sinful, evil, hateful things to him as they nailed him to a wooden cross to die. On the cross, our perfect selfishness and his perfect love met. And his love won! On the cross, Jesus took the punishment for our wrong doing and wrong thinking. On the cross, Jesus was separated from his Father so that we could be reconciled. On the cross, Jesus paid the price so that he could rescue us from slavery. On the cross, Jesus won the victory over death so that we could live with him for ever.

Paul says in 2 Corinthians 5:21, *'God made him who had no sin to be sin for us, so that in him we might become the righteousness of God.'*

On the cross, an exchange took place. He took our sin, pain, brokenness and shattered relationships on himself so that we might be declared 'not guilty' and set free. We have a chance at a brand-new beginning, free from our past, a chance to be 'born again'.

To follow Jesus is to swallow our pride and say, 'Jesus, you're right, I'm wrong. I come to you on your terms. I want to know you, receive your forgiveness and follow you. I give my life to you and ask that you now come and live in me. Be my King, my Friend and my Saviour. My life belongs to you now. I say I want to belong to you – for richer, for poorer, for better, for worse, in sickness and in health. And death cannot part us. Change me from the inside out and use me to change the world that you love so much. Amen.'

It's as easy and as difficult as that! You want to become a Christian? Come to Christ. You don't have to do any more, but you can't do any less. Take 'Christ' out of 'Christian', and you know what you're left with? 'Ian'. Ian can't help you. Ian isn't going to save you. Only Christ can. Come and follow him.

Now what?

If you have made the decision to follow, the first and best thing to do is to tell someone! Find someone who is already in a relationship with Jesus, and join a church where you will find a whole new family of people on the same exciting, challenging and amazing journey that you have just begun!

Life in all its fullness

MATT GREENE

So you've been reading the Bible, and you're getting to grips with understanding it more and more, but how does this change your daily life? What does it mean to follow Jesus in every aspect of life? That's a big question. Before we answer that, let's start with Jesus' death. Jesus died to save us from our sins: from our selfish way of living and from the power of evil. Jesus' death shows us not only that we're saved _from_ things. That's great. It's fantastic to get out of prison. Once you're out, though, what if you have nothing to go to? No friends or family, work or home? You're left lost in the world. Mercifully, our Father doesn't leave us like that. We're saved _for_ something...

We're saved by God so that we can have life in all its fullness! Those aren't my words – they're Jesus' words (John 10:10). What is this 'life to the full' that Jesus invites us to?

It's many things: it's being close to God; it's becoming kinder and braver as he changes us; it's somehow being at peace when we really shouldn't be able to be; it's worshipping and enjoying God; it's sharing life with the church – and more.

Sometimes it can feel like we don't have life in all its fullness – we have life in all its dividedness! It's easy for us to feel that what God really cares about is our prayer times, Bible reading, Christian camps, our youth group, our attempts to share our faith, and that he's not really interested in much else. Well, the good news is, we're wrong!

The Bible tells us in Colossians that all things were created by him and for him. Pause there for a second. If you made a cake for yourself, then you would be interested in what happens to your cake, right? (I certainly would be!) It's the same with God. If God made everything and made it for himself, then surely he would be interested in all things? He's so interested that he gave up his life _'to reconcile to himself_ [bring back into perfect relationship with himself] _all things, whether things on earth or things in heaven, by making peace through his blood, shed on the cross'_ (Colossians 1:20).

This means two wonderful things. First, God's interest in us is so great that he cares about everything in our lives, not just so-called 'spiritual things'. He's interested in absolutely everything: from the music you like to listen to and the sport you like to play, to your passion for good hairstyles and adoration of Twitter; from your cappuccino fascination to your enjoyment of all things purple ... whatever, wherever, whenever ... God is interested.

Second, it means God's interest in his world is so great that he cares about everything and wants to make the world like heaven. So he invites us to take part in his great mission of bringing his love and joy into whatever we're doing: whether that's helping friends with their exam revision or leading a Bible study; whether that's fighting for the poor or frying an egg for a mate; whether that's praying for peace or playing cards ...

So whatever you're doing – working, studying, playing, praying, resting – God invites you to do it with him, bringing his love and joy into it all.

The Bible helps us live like this because it shows us the life of the one who did it! In all Jesus did, he made earth a little more like heaven. It also points us to the Spirit who lives in us and enables us to be loving, joyful and peaceful when we can't do it by ourselves. The Bible assures us of God's mercy when we fail and promises us that in the end God will make the earth perfect again.

Through the book you're holding now, God is making you an offer you can't refuse: 'life in all its fullness'! Why settle for less?

So how do you get the most out of the Bible? You could start by looking at the articles on how to read the Bible at the front of this book, or you could choose a walk to go on with Jesus with one of the reading plans here. The more you read, the more you will encounter God and the more you will learn how to use the Bible well. Don't just try this in isolation: ask for God's help by his Holy Spirit as you read and share your experiences with others. Let's do this together!

Walks

New to the Bible? Take our guided tour!

Join us to wander through the story of the Bible, and to see the sights of the Bible. Consider this your mini tour guide, and your forays into Scripture like exploring a new city – you want to start by taking short excursions in different directions, and then as you become more familiar you can begin to delve in a little deeper!

Unlike most books, sometimes with the Bible the beginning isn't always a very good place to start. The first section will help you explore the life of Jesus, of Paul and the early church, and give you an introduction into the Old Testament too, then once you have got yourself familiar, venture into the second section for a more involved look at Scripture.

We have sectioned this up in 'steps' – for some of you this will be just the right amount of text to really get to grips with; others will want to spend a couple of sessions on each one. You don't need to rush through it, after all you want to stay excited about this for the rest of your life!

Section 1 – Getting to know the essentials

Consider this as the biblical equivalent of finding your nearest cashpoint, supermarket and Chinese takeaway – you don't want to go to long without familiarising yourself!

WALK ONE: Discovering Jesus

❑ **Step 1**   Luke 2
His birth and childhood

❑ **Step 2**   Mark 1
The start of his ministry

❑ **Step 3**   Matthew 9
A day in his life

❑ **Step 4**   Luke 6
A summary of his teaching

❑ **Step 5**   Luke 9
'Who do you say I am?'

❑ **Step 6**   Luke 15
'Lost and found' parables

❑ **Step 7**   Matthew 25
Parables about faithfulness

❑ **Step 8**   John 3
Sincerity is not enough

❑ **Step 9**   John 14
Final instructions

❑ **Step 10**   John 17
His prayer for his followers

❑ **Step 11**   Matthew 26
His last hours

❑ **Step 12**   Matthew 27
The crucifixion

❑ **Step 13**   John 20
He rises from the dead

❑ **Step 14**   Luke 24
The disciples see him again

WALK TWO: Discovering Paul

☐ **Step 1**   Acts 9
His dramatic conversion

☐ **Step 2**   Acts 13
His first missionary journey

☐ **Step 3**   Acts 14
Mission accomplished

☐ **Step 4**   Acts 16
Jailbreak in Philippi

☐ **Step 5**   Acts 26
Witnessing to a king

☐ **Step 6**   Acts 27
Shipwrecked

☐ **Step 7**   Acts 28
Mission in Rome

☐ **Step 8**   Ephesians 3
Paul's ministry and prayer

☐ **Step 9**   Romans 3
Christ makes us right with God (1)

☐ **Step 10**   Romans 5
Christ makes us right with God (2)

☐ **Step 11**   1 Corinthians 13
In praise of love

☐ **Step 12**   Philippians 2
In praise of Jesus

☐ **Step 13**   Galatians 5
Life in the Spirit

☐ **Step 14**   1 Corinthians 15
What happens after we die

WALK THREE: Discovering the Old Testament

☐ **Step 1**   Genesis 1
The beginning of everything

☐ **Step 2**   Genesis 12
God calls Abraham

☐ **Step 3**   Genesis 22
Abraham and Isaac

☐ **Step 4**   Exodus 3
Moses encounters God

☐ **Step 5**   Exodus 20
The summary of God's law

☐ **Step 6**   Joshua 6
The battle of Jericho

☐ **Step 7**   1 Samuel 17
David's victory over Goliath

☐ **Step 8**   2 Samuel 11
David's sin

☐ **Step 9**   Psalm 51
David's prayer of repentance

☐ **Step 10**   1 Kings 18
The dedication of Solomon's temple

☐ **Step 11**   1 Kings 18
Elijah and the pagan prophets

☐ **Step 12**   Amos 4
A warning against persistent sin

☐ **Step 13**   Isaiah 40
God's words of comfort

☐ **Step 14**   Daniel 6
Daniel puts God before death threats

Section 2 – Exploring further afield

So, we've found our local essentials – now it's time to find the nearest decent shopping centre, local tourist attractions, get to know our neighbours, settle in to our new school, and make ourselves at home!

WALK FOUR: Mark's story of Jesus

Step 1	Mark 2	Step 6	Mark 7	Step 11	Mark 12
Step 2	Mark 3	Step 7	Mark 8	Step 12	Mark 13
Step 3	Mark 4	Step 8	Mark 9	Step 13	Mark 14
Step 4	Mark 5	Step 9	Mark 10	Step 14	Mark 15, 16
Step 5	Mark 6	Step 10	Mark 11		

WALK FIVE: Paul's letters to Ephesus, Philippi and Galatia

Step 1	Ephesians 1	Step 6	Ephesians 6	Step 11	Galatians 2
Step 2	Ephesians 2	Step 7	Philippians 1	Step 12	Galatians 3
Step 3	Ephesians 3	Step 8	Philippians 3	Step 13	Galatians 4
Step 4	Ephesians 4	Step 9	Philippians 4	Step 14	Galatians 6
Step 5	Ephesians 5	Step 10	Galatians 1		

WALK SIX: Early experiences of God

Step 1	Genesis 2	Step 6	Genesis 15	Step 11	Genesis 32
Step 2	Genesis 3	Step 7	Genesis 18	Step 12	Genesis 37
Step 3	Genesis 4	Step 8	Genesis 19	Step 13	Genesis 41
Step 4	Genesis 7	Step 9	Genesis 24	Step 14	Genesis 45
Step 5	Genesis 8	Step 10	Genesis 27		

WALK SEVEN: God's rescue plans

Step 1	Exodus 2	Step 6	Exodus 16	Step 11	John 10
Step 2	Exodus 5	Step 7	Exodus 32	Step 12	John 11
Step 3	Exodus 10, 11	Step 8	John 1	Step 13	John 15
Step 4	Exodus 12	Step 9	John 6	Step 14	John 19
Step 5	Exodus 14	Step 10	John 8		

WALK EIGHT: Paul's letters to Rome and Corinth

Step 1	Romans 1	Step 6	Romans 13	Step 11	2 Corinthians 4
Step 2	Romans 6	Step 7	1 Corinthians 1	Step 12	2 Corinthians 5
Step 3	Romans 7	Step 8	1 Corinthians 3	Step 13	2 Corinthians 8
Step 4	Romans 8	Step 9	1 Corinthians 6	Step 14	2 Corinthians 11
Step 5	Romans 12	Step 10	1 Corinthians 12		

WALK NINE: The journey to the Promised Land

Step 1	Numbers 9	Step 6	Deuteronomy 6	Step 11	Joshua 7
Step 2	Numbers 11	Step 7	Deuteronomy 8	Step 12	Joshua 24
Step 3	Numbers 13	Step 8	Deuteronomy 31	Step 13	Psalms 1, 2
Step 4	Numbers 14	Step 9	Joshua 1	Step 14	Psalm 19
Step 5	Deuteronomy 4	Step 10	Joshua 2		

WALK TEN: The story of the first Christians

Step 1	Acts 1	Step 6	Acts 6	Step 11	Acts 18
Step 2	Acts 2	Step 7	Acts 8	Step 12	Acts 19
Step 3	Acts 3	Step 8	Acts 10	Step 13	Psalms 23, 24
Step 4	Acts 4	Step 9	Acts 12	Step 14	Psalm 27
Step 5	Acts 5	Step 10	Acts 15		

WALK ELEVEN: Paul's letters to Colossae and Thessalonica; Job

Step 1	Colossians 1	Step 6	1 Thessalonians 4	Step 11	Job 1
Step 2	Colossians 2	Step 7	1 Thessalonians 5	Step 12	Job 3
Step 3	Colossians 3	Step 8	2 Thessalonians 1	Step 13	Job 40
Step 4	Colossians 4	Step 9	2 Thessalonians 2	Step 14	Job 42
Step 5	1 Thessalonians 2	Step 10	2 Thessalonians 2		

WALK TWELVE: Israel's struggles in the Promised Land

Step 1	Judges 2	Step 6	Judges 14	Step 11	1 Samuel 8
Step 2	Judges 4	Step 7	Judges 16	Step 12	1 Samuel 9
Step 3	Judges 6	Step 8	1 Samuel 1	Step 13	1 Samuel 10
Step 4	Judges 7	Step 9	1 Samuel 3	Step 14	1 Samuel 15
Step 5	Judges 13	Step 10	1 Samuel 4		

WALK THIRTEEN: Extracts from Jesus' life and teaching

Step 1	Matthew 4	Step 6	Matthew 10	Step 11	Luke 14
Step 2	Matthew 5	Step 7	Matthew 13	Step 12	Psalm 34
Step 3	Matthew 6	Step 8	Matthew 21	Step 13	Psalm 40
Step 4	Matthew 7	Step 9	Luke 7	Step 14	Psalm 42
Step 5	Matthew 8	Step 10	Luke 10		

WALK FOURTEEN: Episodes from the times of the kings

Step 1	1 Samuel 26	Step 6	1 Kings 3	Step 11	2 Kings 17
Step 2	2 Samuel 1	Step 7	1 Kings 17	Step 12	1 Chronicles 26
Step 3	2 Samuel 5	Step 8	1 Kings 19	Step 13	1 Chronicles 34
Step 4	2 Samuel 6	Step 9	2 Kings 4	Step 14	Psalm 84
Step 5	2 Samuel 7	Step 10	2 Kings 5		

WALK FIFTEEN: Words from the prophets

Step 1	Isaiah 6	Step 6	Jeremiah 1	Step 11	Ezekiel 2, 3
Step 2	Isaiah 24	Step 7	Jeremiah 2	Step 12	Ezekiel 18
Step 3	Isaiah 52	Step 8	Jeremiah 5	Step 13	Ezekiel 34
Step 4	Isaiah 53	Step 9	Jeremiah 15	Step 14	Hosea 11
Step 5	Isaiah 55	Step 10	Jeremiah 31		

WALK SIXTEEN: Wisdom and encouragement

Step 1	1 John 1, 2	Step 6	1 Peter 4	Step 11	Psalm 139
Step 2	1 John 3	Step 7	Proverbs 3	Step 12	James 1
Step 3	1 John 4	Step 8	Proverbs 10	Step 13	Revelation 1
Step 4	1 Peter 1	Step 9	Ecclesiastes 3	Step 14	Revelation 21
Step 5	1 Peter 2	Step 10	Psalm 103		

The story of the Bible

CHRIS LANE

Creation: God speaks the universe into being. He creates a human, and he says that it is very good. But something is not good. The human needs other humans, so God creates two from the one – male and female. In the Garden of Eden there is amazing intimacy between Adam and Eve, naked and not ashamed, and between God and the humans – there is no barrier between heaven and earth.

The fall: Adam and Eve are given a wonderful garden to explore and look after, and permission to eat from all the trees – except one. They decide to disobey God. There is now a barrier between God and humankind. Genesis 3 – 11 shows us what happens when we rebel against our Creator: murder, the flood, incest, revenge and the arrogance of Babel.

The rescue plan: God calls Abram and Sarai and their descendants to show the world how to live. Galatians 3:8 tells us that they are given *'the gospel in advance'*. They are called to have faith in God and to be a blessing to all the families of the earth. Their grandson Jacob changes his name to Israel. One of Israel's twelve sons is called Joseph, and through him the whole family moves to Egypt. However, the Egyptians eventually force the twelve tribes of Israel into slavery.

The exodus: God sends Moses to rescue the people. He leads the people into the desert where the freed slaves are given the law. Moses dies on the edge of the Promised Land, and Joshua leads the people in. After Joshua dies, there is a period where God raises up twelve judges, or saviours, who lead the people back to God.

The kings and prophets: The people ask Samuel to anoint a king, and Saul is anointed. His successor David goes on to be Israel's greatest king. His son Solomon reigns over the most prosperous time in Israel's history, but his sons war against each other and eventually the kingdom divides into two – Israel and Judah. The two kingdoms are ruled over by a succession of kings who often reject God and treat the people harshly. At this time the great prophets arise to speak for justice, to call the people back to God and to speak of a coming Messiah who would deliver them from their sins. Eventually both kingdoms are overthrown and the people are taken into exile. They are allowed to return, but are no longer rulers of their own land.

Jesus: Over 400 years of hoping and praying pass before John the Baptist announces the coming of *'the Lamb of God, who takes away the sin of the world'* (John 1:29). Jesus proclaims that the kingdom of God is here and travels round healing the sick and casting out demons. He then dies on a cross, fulfilling the prophecy in Isaiah 53 as he takes the sin of the world upon himself. On the third day God raises him from the dead, defeating death and evil for ever.

Church: Jesus then commissions his disciples to take the good news about him to the ends of the earth, fulfilling Abraham's calling to bless all the families of the earth. Filled with the Holy Spirit on the Day of Pentecost, they obey his command.

The new creation: As the Church take Jesus' gospel of justice, peace and joy to the world, they anticipate the day when Jesus will return and complete this work, when *'there will be no more death or mourning or crying or pain, for the old order of things has passed away'* (Revelation 21:4) and Jesus makes everything new!

What is the Bible?

Although one book, the Bible contains sixty-six individual books. Within each of these there is often a variety of writing such as poetry, prose, biography, letters, family trees, official records, songs and prayers. It is important to recognise the type of writing when we are reading so that we read the Bible on its own terms. To read poetry, for example, as if it was an excerpt from an official record, would make it very difficult to understand.

Poetry

The main division is between prose and poetry. Several of the Old Testament books are written completely in poetry: Psalms, the Song of Songs and Lamentations for instance. Most of the book of Job is written in poetic form, and other poems are found in prose passages, for example, Exodus 15; Judges 5 and 1 Samuel 2. Modern translations show quite clearly where poetry is used and it is easy to see that most of the prophetic books are written in poetic form. In the New Testament there is some poetry, for example, Mary's Song (Luke 1:46–55), Zechariah's Song (Luke 1:68–79) and Philippians 2:6–11.

There is an important difference between Hebrew/Jewish poetry and modern poetry. Hebrew poetry uses **rhythm** and not **rhyme**. It also uses 'parallelism' which means that the idea or thought in one line is repeated in the next line in a different way and using different words. A glance at any poetic passage will illustrate this, for example:

Job 33:4 The Spirit of God has made me;
       the breath of the Almighty gives me life.

There are also many **different types of poetry**. The Song of Songs and the book of Job are each written as a play with various actors. In the Psalms there are poetic songs and prayers for many different occasions: songs of thanksgiving, songs for pilgrims, songs for the coronation of a king, prayers for the congregation and prayers for individuals. In the New Testament it is probable that Philippians 2:6–11, for example, was a hymn sung by the first Christians.

Law

Israel's laws are found in the books of Exodus through to Deuteronomy. These formed the foundation of the life of the nation and of its relationship with God. Thus the law is regarded as an expression of God's character and will; the law shows how God wants his people to behave, to worship, and to live in society.

The best-known list of laws is the Ten Commandments (Exodus 20). These are a summary of the essential points of the many laws contained in Exodus through to Deuteronomy. Three groups of laws have been drawn out: Covenant law or the **Book of the Covenant** (Exodus 21 – 23), which contains moral, civil and religious laws.

The Holiness Code (Leviticus 17 – 26) which, as its name suggests, arises from the frequent statements, 'I the LORD am holy – I who make you holy' (Leviticus 21:8). This law 'book' sets out rules for worship, especially about priests and sacrifices. **The Deuteronomic Code** (Deuteronomy 12 – 25) is set out like a sermon and includes warnings about the consequences of breaking the laws.

These laws touch on every area of life, not only religion. There are laws about family life (marriage etc.), human rights, theft, damage to property, personal and food hygiene and so on. Many of them are uncompromising, or absolute statements: 'You shall/shall not' (as in Exodus 20), but many are what we call 'case laws': 'if … then' – what to do in particular situations.

There are no new lists of commandments in the New Testament, though some regard the **Sermon on the Mount** (Matthew 5 – 7) as the new law for Christians. The standards set out there are even more difficult to achieve than in the Old Testament law. Some Christians therefore regard these as ideals to be aimed at, even if they can never fully attain them. Paul has much to say about the Law (and uses the word in different ways), but basically he teaches that while it is good, it is limited. This is because people can never earn God's love – it is given freely.

A special kind of history

There is much in the Bible which helps us to piece together the early history of the Jewish nation and, later, the early church. The history books of the Old Testament are Joshua through to 2 Kings, and 1 and 2 Chronicles record some of the same events. There are historical passages in Isaiah and Jeremiah, and parts of Genesis, Exodus and Numbers could be described as 'history'. In the New Testament there are some historical references in the Gospels and Acts.

In the Hebrew Bible Joshua – 2 Kings are grouped together and called 'The Former Prophets'. This will help us to understand that biblical history is not history told for its own sake, but history told from a particular point of view. It does not tell us everything that happened but only those events which show how God is at work in his world, developing his plan in the Jewish nation and later in the church. This does not mean that this history is unreliable, for archaeology and comparative studies of other nations show it to be trustworthy.

There are many references in the Old Testament books of history which show that the writers and editors used older writings and records. For example Joshua 10:13 and 2 Samuel 1:18 refer to 'The Book of Jashar', 1 Kings 11:41 to the 'annals of Solomon' and 1 Chronicles 29:29 to 'the records of Nathan the prophet and the records of Gad the seer'. Reference is also made to particular people writing down God's words: Exodus 24:4 (Moses); 1 Samuel 10:25 (Samuel). The many family trees (genealogies) were other sources used by the writers. In the New Testament the writer of Luke and Acts indicates that he has investigated other accounts (Luke 1:3).

Prophecy

There are many prophetic books in the Old Testament and they are grouped together from Isaiah through to Malachi. The popular idea of prophecy is that it is the prediction of future events, but biblical prophecy is much more than this. The prophets announced God's message not only, or necessarily, about the future, but very often about the present. Frequently they began with the words, 'This is what the Lord says'. They spoke God's word and that meant that they condemned social injustice and sham worship. They exposed mistaken, cosy ideas about God and his laws and warned the people that God must punish them if they did not mend their ways.

The prophets communicated what they had to say in many different ways: dialogue, narrative, poetry, picture language and drama. Many prophets have given us an account of how God called them to their work. Their conviction was that they said what God had told them to say, but how they received those words we do not know.

There are a few references to prophets writing down at least some of their message: Isaiah 30:8 (Isaiah), and Jeremiah 30:2 (Jeremiah). Jeremiah 36 also tells us that Jeremiah dictated some of his message to Baruch who must have been a follower of his.

Other prophecies have both an immediate and a long-term meaning: they were fulfilled in the prophet's lifetime or soon after, but only partly so. The New Testament writers understood this and show how many of the Old Testament promises were finally fulfilled in the life, death and resurrection of Jesus.

Apocalyptic

This is a particular type of prophetic literature found notably in Daniel (chapters 6 – 12) and Revelation, but also in Isaiah 24 – 27, Ezekiel 38 – 39, Zechariah 9 – 14 (the first part of the book is apocalyptic in thought) and Mark 13, which is known as 'the little Apocalypse'. The word comes from Greek, and means 'unveiling' or 'revealing' and the book of Revelation is often called 'The Apocalypse' since it is the unveiling or revealing of the future. Apocalyptic writing is full of strange symbols and creatures, as well as angels. The interpretation of apocalyptic writing gives rise to a variety of points of view.

Wisdom

We know that many ancient nations had 'wisdom writings'. Job, Ecclesiastes and Proverbs are the main biblical Wisdom books, but many of the Psalms belong to this type of writing (for example, 1, 34, 37, 73 etc.). Wisdom writing was interested in the problems of existence: why are we here? why are things the way they are? why do people suffer? In its simplest and earliest form wisdom was communicated in riddles (Judges 14:14; 1 Samuel 24:13 for example) and the proverbs found in the biblical book of that name. The book of Proverbs is full of statements and observations, often amusing, about life. Sometimes they are presented as if a father or teacher were talking to his son or student, teaching him how to behave in various situations.

Gospel

Although there are four Gospels the word actually applies to what they contain, for the announcement that a new age has begun with Jesus is the gospel, which means 'good news'. The Gospels are, nevertheless, a new and particular kind of biblical literature. It is important to understand that the Gospels are not biographies; they do not simply recount the life of Jesus. Rather, each Gospel presents the story of Jesus from a particular viewpoint, and each has a distinctive way of telling the story. Matthew has grouped Jesus' teaching together; Mark is a vivid, fast-moving story; Luke has beautiful pen sketches of many of the people who featured in the story of Jesus; John is a deeply religious, almost otherworldly study.

Scholars have discussed the writing of the Gospels a great deal. A very early record tells us that Mark wrote down Peter's memories of Jesus. Luke was probably written by the man who helped Paul in some of his missionary work.

Letters

The writers of the New Testament letters follow the 'rules' for letter writing of the first century AD. This began with an opening sentence giving the name of the writer and the recipient. Then followed a general greeting and enquiry into the health of the recipient. The main section of the letter was concluded with a personal greeting. However, the New Testament letters are much longer than the average 150–200 words of the letters of that period. Even Philemon, the shortest, is 470 words. Paul's letters are usually characterised by a main section which deals first with teaching and then with the way Christians should put into practice what they have learned. Although most of the New Testament letters tell us the name of the author, some do not.

There are some interesting letters in the Old Testament. The best example is in Jeremiah 29, but others are found in 1 Kings 21; 2 Chronicles 30; Ezra 4 and 5 and Nehemiah 6.

About Soul Survivor

Soul Survivor grew out of an Anglican church, St Andrew's Chorleywood, that was equipping Christians to move in the power of the Holy Spirit through the 'New Wine' family conferences. Back then the vicar of St Andrew's Chorleywood was a very nice and very wise chap called David Pytches. For some reason (which in hindsight he may regret) he unleashed a young(ish) Greek lad called Mike Pilavachi to help out with the church's youth work.

In the late 1980s, David Pytches started running New Wine – summer conferences to resource, equip and refresh the church – and it's at New Wine that the Soul Survivor story really begins. It was clear from the growth in the youth work at New Wine that something separate was needed for young people, so in 1993 Soul Survivor launched its first annual five-day conference in Shepton Mallet, Somerset.

This first event hosted just under 2,000 people and the number of delegates has grown every year. In 2011 around 30,000 people came along. This now means there are a number of events held each summer to be able to accommodate everybody. Soul Survivor events are aimed at secondary school age and we have two of these in Somerset and one further north (in Stafford). Since 2004 we have also held a separate event for students and twenty-somethings called Momentum.

We also keep ourselves busy the rest of the year with events such as Soul Sista, one-day conferences, SoulNet youth leaders' network and the Soul Action partnership that enables young people to work with Tearfund in some of the poorest areas of the world. There are also six international Soul Survivor centres across the world that share our vision and values and hold annual events for the young people of Australia, Holland, Malaysia, New Zealand, South Africa and the USA.

Most importantly, our heart is to envision young people from any church background, or none, and give them an opportunity to capture a vision of Jesus. Then we hope to equip, train and empower them, and see them released into his ministry in their everyday lives.

www.soulsurvivor.com/uk

About the NIV

The goal of the New International Version (NIV) is to enable English-speaking people from around the world to read and hear God's eternal Word in their own language. Our work as translators is motivated by our conviction that the Bible is God's Word in written form. We believe that the Bible contains the divine answer to the deepest needs of humanity, sheds unique light on our path in a dark world and sets forth the way to our eternal well-being. Out of these deep convictions, we have sought to recreate as far as possible the experience of the original audience – blending transparency to the original text with accessibility for the millions of English speakers around the world. We have prioritised accuracy, clarity and literary quality with the goal of creating a translation suitable for public and private reading, evangelism, teaching, preaching, memorizing and liturgical use. We have also sought to preserve a measure of continuity with the long tradition of translating the Scriptures into English.

The complete NIV Bible was first published in 1978. It was a completely new translation made by over a hundred scholars working directly from the best available Hebrew, Aramaic and Greek texts. The translators came from the United States, Great Britain, Canada, Australia and New Zealand, giving the translation an international scope. They were from many denominations and churches – including Anglican, Assemblies of God, Baptist, Brethren, Christian Reformed, Church of Christ, Evangelical Covenant, Evangelical Free, Lutheran, Mennonite, Methodist, Nazarene, Presbyterian, Wesleyan and others. This breadth of denominational and theological perspective helped to safeguard the translation from sectarian bias. For these reasons, and by the grace of God, the NIV has gained a wide readership in all parts of the English-speaking world.

The work of translating the Bible is never finished. As good as they are, English translations must be regularly updated so that they will continue to communicate accurately the meaning of God's Word. Updates are needed in order to reflect the latest developments in our understanding of the biblical world and its languages and to keep pace with changes in English usage. Recognising, then, that the NIV would retain its ability to communicate God's Word accurately only if it were regularly updated, the original translators established The Committee on Bible Translation (CBT). The committee is a self-perpetuating group of biblical scholars charged with keeping abreast of advances in biblical scholarship and changes in English and issuing periodic updates to the NIV. CBT is an independent, self-governing body and has sole responsibility for the NIV text. The committee mirrors the original group of translators in its diverse international and denominational makeup and in its unifying commitment to the Bible as God's inspired Word.

In obedience to its mandate, the committee has issued periodic updates to the NIV. An initial revision was released in 1984. A more thorough revision process was completed in 2005, resulting in the separately published Today's New International Version (TNIV). The updated NIV you now have in your hands builds on both the original NIV and the TNIV and represents the latest effort of the committee to articulate God's unchanging Word in the way the original authors might have said it had they been speaking in English to the global English-speaking audience today.

The first concern of the translators has continued to be the accuracy of the translation and its faithfulness to the intended meaning of the biblical writers. This has moved the translators to go beyond a formal word-for-word rendering of the original texts. Because thought patterns and syntax differ from language to language, accurate communication of the meaning of the biblical authors demands constant regard for varied contextual uses of words and idioms and for frequent modifications in sentence structures.

As an aid to the reader, sectional headings have been inserted. They are not to be regarded as part of the biblical text and are not intended for oral reading. It is the committee's hope that these headings may prove more helpful to the reader than the traditional chapter divisions, which were introduced long after the Bible was written.

For the Old Testament the standard Hebrew text, the Masoretic Text as published in the latest edition of *Biblia Hebraica*, has been used throughout. The Masoretic Text tradition contains marginal notations that offer variant readings. These have sometimes been followed instead of the text itself. Because such instances involve variants within the Masoretic tradition, they have not been indicated in the textual notes. In a few cases, words in the basic consonantal text have been divided differently than in the Masoretic Text. Such cases are usually indicated in the textual footnotes. The Dead Sea Scrolls contain biblical texts that represent an earlier stage of the transmission of the Hebrew text. They have been consulted, as have been the Samaritan Pentateuch and the ancient scribal traditions concerning deliberate textual changes. The translators also consulted the more important early versions – the Greek Septuagint, Aquila, Symmachus and Theodotion, the Latin Vulgate, the Syriac Peshitta, the Aramaic Targums and, for the Psalms, the *Juxta Hebraica* of Jerome. Readings from these versions, the Dead Sea Scrolls and the scribal traditions were occasionally followed where the Masoretic Text seemed doubtful and where accepted principles of textual criticism showed that one or more of these textual witnesses appeared to provide the correct reading. In rare cases, the committee has emended the Hebrew text where it appears to have become corrupted at an even earlier stage of its transmission. These departures from the Masoretic Text are also indicated in the textual footnotes. Sometimes the vowel indicators (which are later additions to the basic consonantal text) found in the Masoretic Text did not, in the judgment of the committee, represent the correct vowels for the original text. Accordingly, some words have been read with a different set of vowels. These instances are usually not indicated in the footnotes.

The Greek text used in translating the New Testament is an eclectic one, based on the latest editions of the Nestle-Aland/United Bible Societies' Greek New Testament. The committee has made its choices among the variant readings in accordance with widely accepted principles of New Testament textual criticism. Footnotes call attention to places where uncertainty remains.

The New Testament authors, writing in Greek, often quote the Old Testament from its ancient Greek version, the Septuagint. This is one reason why some of the Old Testament quotations in the NIV New Testament are not identical to the corresponding passages in the NIV Old Testament. Such quotations in the New Testament are indicated with the footnote '(see Septuagint)'.

Other footnotes in this version are of several kinds, most of which need no explanation. Those giving alternative translations begin with 'Or' and generally introduce the alternative with the last word preceding it in the text, except when it is a single-word alternative. When poetry is quoted in a footnote, a slash mark indicates a line division.

It should be noted that references to diseases, minerals, flora and fauna, architectural details, clothing, jewelry, musical instruments and other articles cannot always be identified with precision. Also, linear measurements and measures of capacity can only be approximated (see the Appendix). Although *Selah*, used mainly in the Psalms, is probably a musical term, its meaning is uncertain. Since it may interrupt reading and distract the reader, this word has not been kept in the English text, but every occurrence has been signalled by a footnote.

One of the main reasons the task of Bible translation is never finished is the change in our own language, English. Although a basic core of the language remains relatively stable, many diverse and complex linguistic factors continue to bring about subtle shifts in the meanings and/or connotations of even old, well established words and phrases. One of the shifts that creates particular challenges to writers and translators alike is the manner in which gender is presented. The original NIV (1978) was published in a time when 'a man' would naturally be understood, in many contexts, to be referring to a person, whether male or female. But most English speakers today tend to hear a distinctly male connotation in this word. In recognition of this change in English, this edition of the NIV, along with almost all other recent English translations, substitutes other expressions when the original text intends to refer generically to men and women equally. Thus, for instance, the NIV (1984) rendering of 1 Corinthians 8:3, 'But the man who loves God is known by God' becomes in this edition 'But whoever loves God is known by God.' On the other hand, 'man' and 'mankind', as ways of denoting the human race, are still widely used. This edition of the NIV therefore continues to use these words, along with other expressions, in this way.

A related shift in English creates a greater challenge for modern translations: the move away from using the third-person masculine singular pronouns – 'he/him/his' – to refer to men and women equally. This usage does persist at a low level in some forms of English, and this revision therefore occasionally uses these pronouns in a generic sense. But the tendency, recognized in day-to-day usage and confirmed by extensive research, is away from the generic use of 'he,' 'him', and 'his.' In recognition of this shift in language and in an effort to translate into the 'common' English that people are actually using, this revision of the NIV generally uses other constructions when the biblical text is plainly addressed to men and women equally. The reader will frequently encounter a 'they', 'them' or 'their' to express a generic singular idea. Thus, for instance, Mark 8:36 reads: 'What good is it for someone to gain the whole world, yet forfeit their soul?' This generic use of the indefinite or 'singular' 'they/them/their' has a venerable place in English idiom and has quickly become established as standard English, spoken and written, all over the world. Where an individual emphasis is deemed to be present, 'anyone' or 'everyone' or some other equivalent is generally used as the antecedent of such pronouns.

Sometimes the chapter and/or verse numbering in English translations of the Old Testament differs from that found in published Hebrew texts. This is particularly the case in the Psalms, where the traditional titles are often included in the Hebrew verse numbering. Such differences are indicated in the footnotes at the bottom of the page. In the New Testament, verse numbers that marked off portions of the traditional English text not supported by the best Greek manuscripts now appear in brackets, with a footnote indicating the text that has been omitted (see, for example, Matthew 17:[21]).

Mark 16:9–20 and John 7:53–8:11, although long accorded virtually equal status with the rest of the Gospels in which they stand, have a very questionable – and confused – standing in the textual history of the New Testament, as noted in the bracketed annotations with which they are set off. A different typeface has been chosen for these passages to indicate even more clearly their uncertain status.

Basic formatting of the text, such as lining the poetry, paragraphing (both prose and poetry), setting up of (administrative-like) lists, indenting letters and lengthy prayers within narratives and the insertion of sectional headings, has been the work of the committee. However, the choice between single-column and double-column formats has been left to the publishers. Also the issuing of 'red-letter' editions is a publisher's choice – one the committee does not endorse.

The committee has again been reminded that every human effort is flawed –

including this revision of the NIV. We trust, however, that many will find in it an improved representation of the Word of God, through which they hear his call to faith in our Lord Jesus Christ and to service in his kingdom. We offer this version of the Bible to him in whose name and for whose glory it has been made.

The Committee on Bible Translation
September 2010

Table of weights and measures

	Biblical Unit	Approximate Metric Equivalent
Weights	talent (60 minas)	34 kilograms
	mina (50 shekels)	560 grams
	shekel (2 bekas)	11.5 grams
	daric	8.4 grams
	pim ($^2/_3$ shekel)	7.8 grams
	beka (10 gerahs)	5.7 grams
	gerah	0.6 gram
Length	stadion (pl. stadia)	183 metres
	cubit	45 centimetres
	span	23 centimetres
	handbreadth	7.5 centimetres
Capacity		
Dry Measure	cor [homer] (10 ephahs)	220 litres
	lethek (5 ephahs)	110 litres
	ephah (10 omers)	22 litres
	seah ($^1/_3$ ephah)	7.5 litres
	omer ($^1/_{10}$ ephah)	2 litres
	cab ($^1/_{18}$ ephah)	1 litre
Liquid Measure	bath (1 ephah)	22 litres
	hin ($^1/_6$ bath)	3.8 litres
	log ($^1/_{72}$ bath)	0.3 litre

The figures of the table are calculated on the basis of a shekel equalling 11.5 grams, a cubit equalling 18 inches and an ephah equalling 22 litres.

This table is based upon the best available information, but it is not intended to be mathematically precise; like the measurement equivalents in the footnotes, it merely gives approximate amounts and distances. Weights and measures differed somewhat at various times and places in the ancient world. There is uncertainty particularly about the ephah and the bath; further discoveries may shed more light on these units of capacity.

Ancient Middle East
with Abraham's journey and the route of the exodus

Abraham
.... Abraham's journey from Ur to Canaan c.2000 BC

Moses
▪▪▪▪▪▪ The exodus from Egypt c.1400 BC
▬ ▬ ▬ The entry into Canaan c.1350 BC

SUSA

NINEVEH
ASSYRIA
Calah
Asshur
Nuzi

River Tigris

BABYLONIA

BABYLON
Kish
Nippur
Isin
Uruk
Lagash
Larsa
Ur

Edessa
Haran
Carchemish
Aleppo
Tadmor
Hamath

River Euphrates

DAMASCUS

Ugarit

Shechem
Megiddo
Jericho
JERUSALEM
Ashdod
Gaza
Lachish
Beer-sheba

Ezion-geber
Elath

Mt. Sinai

Kadesh-barnea

Rameses
Succoth
Heliopolis
Giza
Memphis
EGYPT

The Division of the Land
After the Israelites conquered the land, it was divided between the tribes.

Asher
Naphtali
Zebulun
Issachar
Manasseh
Gad
Reuben
Ephraim
Benjamin
Dan
Judah
Simeon

Palestine in the time of Jesus

— Roman road

km 0 10 20 30 40 50
miles 0 10 20 30

Damascus

Kenath

Bostra

DECAPOLIS

Paneas (Caesarea Philippi)

Bethsaida

Adraa

GALILEE

Rabbah

Capernaum

Gadara

Heshbon

PEREA

Medeba

Sidon

Tiberias

Nazareth

Pella

Dibon

Rabbath-moab

Nain

Scythopolis

Tyre

Sepphoris

Tirzah

Jericho

DEAD SEA

En-gedi

Ptolemais

Sebaste (Samaria)

SAMARIA

Shiloh

Bethel

JERUSALEM

Mampsis

Neapolis

Arimathea

Bethlehem

Hebron

Caesarea

Lydda

Nicopolis

JUDEA

IDUMEA

Apollonia

Jamnia

Beersheba

Elusa

Oboda

Ioppa

Ashkelon

Gaza

Nessana

Israel in the Old Testament

— — Ancient highway

km 0 10 20 30 40 50
miles 0 10 20 30

Damascus

ARAM

Dan

AMMON

Hazor

PHOENICIA

Beth-shan

ISRAEL

Tirzah

Sidon

Samaria

Shechem

Shiloh

Heshbon

Tyre

Bethel

Jericho

DEAD SEA

MOAB

Dor

Megiddo

Gezer

JERUSALEM

Bozrah

Bethlehem

Hebron

Ashdod

Ekron

Lachish

JUDAH

Petra

Ashkelon

Gerar

Beersheba

EDOM

Gaza

Kadesh-barnea

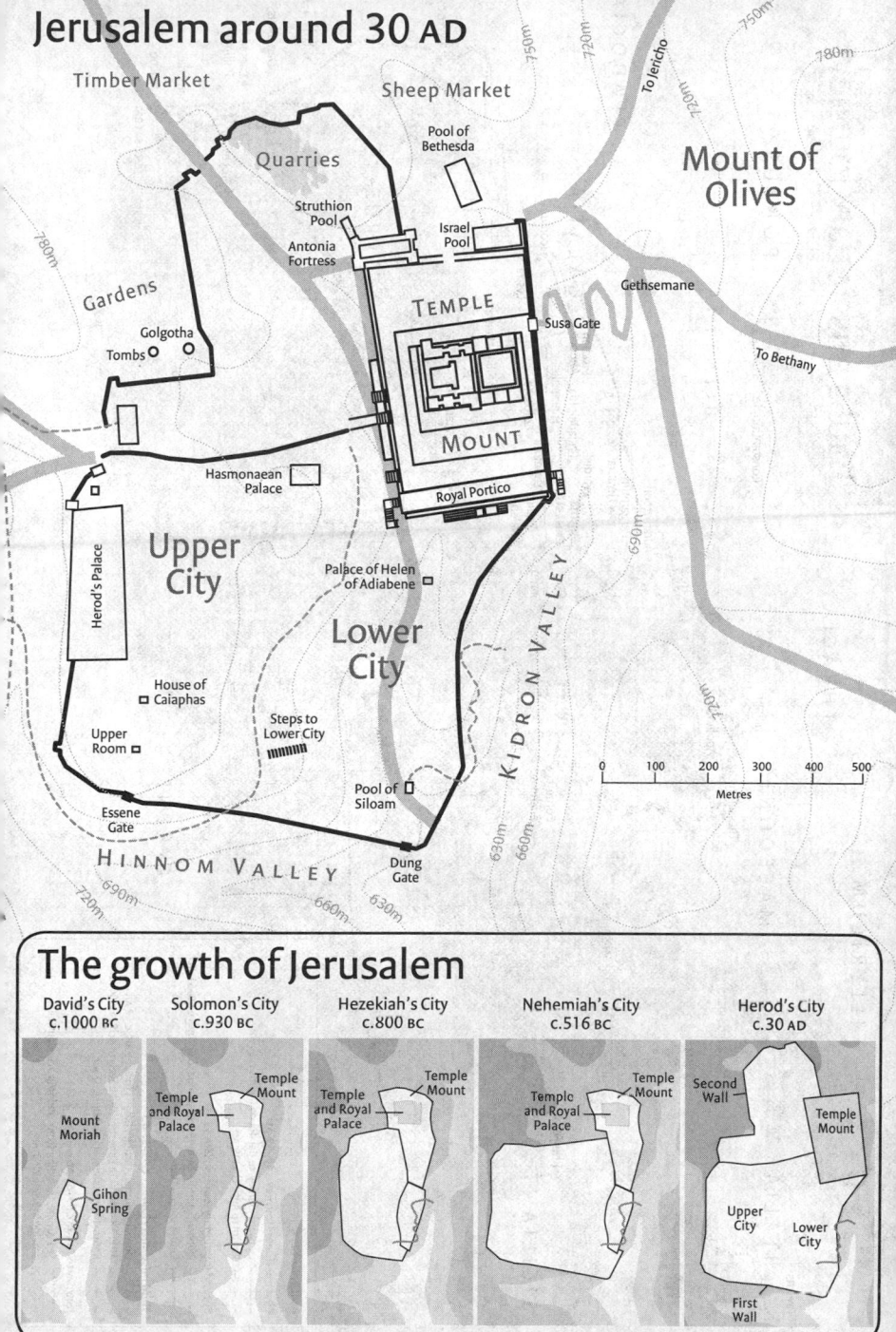

Jerusalem around 30 AD

Timber Market

Sheep Market

Quarries

Pool of Bethesda

Struthion Pool

Antonia Fortress

Israel Pool

Mount of Olives

Gardens

Golgotha

Tombs

TEMPLE

Susa Gate

Gethsemane

To Bethany

MOUNT

Hasmonaean Palace

Royal Portico

Upper City

Palace of Helen of Adiabene

Herod's Palace

Lower City

KIDRON VALLEY

House of Caiaphas

Upper Room

Steps to Lower City

Essene Gate

Pool of Siloam

Dung Gate

HINNOM VALLEY

| 0 | 100 | 200 | 300 | 400 | 500 |

Metres

The growth of Jerusalem

David's City
c.1000 BC

Mount Moriah

Gihon Spring

Solomon's City
c.930 BC

Temple and Royal Palace

Temple Mount

Hezekiah's City
c.800 BC

Temple and Royal Palace

Temple Mount

Nehemiah's City
c.516 BC

Temple and Royal Palace

Temple Mount

Herod's City
c.30 AD

Second Wall

Temple Mount

Upper City

Lower City

First Wall

To Jericho

Paul's missionary journeys

ILLYRICUM · **ITALIA** · Brundisium · Puteoli · Ill Taverns · Forum of Appius · Rhegium · SICILIA · Syracuse · MALTA

THRACIA · **MACEDONIA** · Constantinople · Neapolis · Philippi · Thessalonica · Apollonia · Berea · Samothrace · Troas · Assos · EPIRUS · Nicopolis · **ACHAIA** · ATHENS · Corinth · Cenchreae

PONTUS · **BITHYNIA** · Cyzicos · Adramyttium · Pergamum · Thyatira · Chios · Smyrna · Sardis · Philadelphia · EPHESUS · Tralles · Hierapolis · Laodicea · Colossae · Miletus · Samos · Cos · Rhodes

CAPPADOCIA · **GALATIA** · Iconium · Derbe · Lystra · Pisidian Antioch · Perga · Attalia · **LYCIA** · Myra · Patara

CILICIA · Tarsus · Seleucia · **SYRIA** · **ANTIOCH** · Damascus · Caesarea Philippi · Sidon · Tyre · Ptolemais · Caesarea · Samaria · Jericho · Joppa · **JERUSALEM**

CYPRUS · Salamis · Paphos

CRETE · Phoenix

Mediterranean Sea

CYRENE · Cyrene · **ALEXANDRIA**

Paul's Journeys

First missionary journey c.48–49 AD
········· Outward journey, to Galatia via Cyprus c.48 AD
– – – – – Return to Antioch c.49 AD

Second missionary journey c.50–53 AD
········· Outward journey, through Macedonia to Corinth c.50–51 AD
········· Return to Jerusalem c.53 AD

Third missionary journey c.53–57 AD
–··–··– Outward journey, through Galatia to Ephesus, c.53 AD
○–○–○ After 18 months in Ephesus, Paul travels to Achaia c.56 AD
●–●–● Return to Jerusalem, via Philippi c.57 AD

Journey to Rome c.59–60 AD
········· Sea voyage, including storm and shipwreck on Malta, arriving in Rome c.60 AD